Peterson's®
How to Get Money for College 2021

About Peterson's

Peterson's® has been your trusted educational publisher for over 50 years. It's a milestone we're quite proud of, as we continue to offer the most accurate, dependable, high-quality educational content in the field, providing you with everything you need to succeed. No matter where you are on your academic or professional path, you can rely on Peterson's for its books, online information, expert test-prep tools, the most up-to-date education exploration data, and the highest quality career success resources—everything you need to achieve your education goals. For our complete line of products, visit **www.petersons.com.**

For more information about Peterson's range of educational products, contact Peterson's, 4380 S. Syracuse Street, Suite 200, Denver, CO 80237, or find us online at **www.petersons.com.**

ISSN 1544-2330
ISBN: 978-0-7689-4403-7

Printed in the United States of America

10 9 8 7 6 5 4 3 2 1 21 20

Thirty-eighth Edition

Contents

A Note from the Peterson's® Editors

The news media seem to constantly remind us that a college education is expensive. It certainly appears to be beyond the means of many Americans. The sticker price for four years at state-supported colleges can be more than $45,000, and private colleges and universities can cost more than $150,000. And these numbers continue to rise.

But there is good news. The system operates to provide the needed money so that most families and students are able to afford a college education while making only a reasonable financial sacrifice. However, because the college financial aid system is complex, finding the money is often easier said than done. That is why the process demands study, planning, calculation, flexibility, filling out forms, and meeting deadlines. Fortunately, for most people, it can produce positive results. There are many ways to manage college costs and many channels through which you can receive help. Be sure to take full advantage of the opportunities that have been opened up to students and their families by the many organizations, foundations, and businesses that have organized to help you with the burden of college expenses.

For nearly forty years, Peterson's has given students and parents the most comprehensive, up-to-date information on how to get their fair share of the financial aid pie. *Peterson's How to Get Money for College* is both a quick reference and a comprehensive resource that puts valuable information about college costs and financial aid opportunities at your fingertips.

- **The ABC's of Paying for College** provides insight into federal financial aid programs that are available, offers an overview of the financial aid landscape, walks you through the process of filing for aid, and provides proven tips on how to successfully navigate the financial aid process to obtain the federal, state, and institutional aid you deserve.
- The **Quick-Reference Chart** offers a snapshot comparison of the financial aid programs available at more than 2,200 four-year institutions across the country.
- The **Profiles of College Financial Aid Programs** provide unbiased financial aid data for each of the more than 2,200 four-year institutions listed.
- The **Appendix** lists the state scholarship and grant programs offered by all fifty states and the District of Columbia.
- The six **Indexes** included in the back of the book allow you to search for specific award programs based on a variety of criteria, including merit-based awards, athletic grants, ROTC programs, and much more.

Peterson's publishes a full line of books—financial aid, education exploration, test prep, and career preparation. Peterson's publications can be found at high school guidance offices, college libraries and career centers, and your local bookstore and library. Peterson's books are also available at www.petersonsbooks.com.

We welcome any comments or suggestions you may have about this publication. Your feedback will help us make educational dreams possible for you—and others like you.

The ABC's of Paying for College

What You Need to Know About the FAFSA®

The Free Application for Federal Student Aid or FAFSA® (https://fafsa.ed.gov/FAFSA/app/fafsa) is a critical form that anyone seeking college financial aid must complete.

WHY YOU MUST FILE THE FAFSA®

The FAFSA is required in order for a student to be considered for any type of federal financial aid, including grants and loans. Even if you think your family makes too much for you to qualify for need-based aid, you should still complete the FAFSA. For one thing, many people are surprised to find that they may actually qualify for need-based aid—the eligibility for which is determined by a number of factors, in addition to household income.

Also, the FAFSA is required to apply for students loans (for which there is no need-based element such as income limits). If you don't initially think you want to apply for student loans but later change your mind, having a completed FAFSA already on file will help speed up the process.

In addition, most schools will require a student to have a completed FAFSA on file before the student can be considered for any school-based aid programs such as scholarships. A completed FAFSA is also required for federal work study jobs.

IT'S EASIER TO FILE ONLINE

While you can opt to print and complete a paper version of the FAFSA, it is much quicker and easier to complete the online version. The system walks you through the process and can alert you to sections you can skip if they don't apply to you.

If you have completed a FAFSA in the past, some of your information will be automatically entered when you start to work on your newest one, giving you a head start. You will further save a lot of time by using the IRS data retrieval tool, which will be discussed later in this article.

Filing online means your form will be processed faster, and it also eliminates the worry that your paperwork will be lost or delayed in the mail.

For those who want or need to print and submit a paper version of the FAFSA, you can print a PDF version of the FAFSA online. Students and parents can request up to three copies of the paper FAFSA (in English or Spanish) by calling the Federal Student Aid Information Center toll-free at 800-4-FED-AID.

THE NEW FEDERAL STUDENT AID ID

In order for a student to complete the online FAFSA, he or she must obtain a Federal Student Aid (FSA) ID. You can get this online at https://fsaid.ed.gov/npas/index.htm. The FSA ID replaced the PIN system that was previously used prior to May 2015. Parents of dependent students also need to obtain their own FSA ID in order to sign their child's FAFSA electronically online.

The FSA ID can be used to access several federal aid-related websites, including FAFSA.gov and StudentLoans.gov. It consists of a username and password and can be used to electronically sign Federal Student Aid documents, access your personal records, and make binding legal obligations. The FSA ID is beneficial in several ways:

- It removes your personally identifiable information (PII), such as your Social Security number, from your log-in credentials.
- It creates a more secure and efficient way to verify your information when you log in to access to your federal student aid information online.
- It gives you the ability to easily update your personal information.
- It allows you to easily retrieve your username and password by requesting a secure code be sent to your e-mail address or by answering challenge questions.

It's relatively simple to create an FSA ID and should only take a few minutes. In addition, you will have an opportunity to link your current Federal Student Aid PIN (if you already have one) to your FSA ID. The final step is to confirm your e-mail address. You will receive a secure code to the e-mail address you provided when you set up your FSA ID. Once you retrieve the code from your e-mail account and enter it—to confirm your e-mail address is valid—you will be able to use this e-mail address instead of your username to log in to any of the federal aid-related websites, making the log-in process even simpler for you and your parents.

When you initially create your FSA ID, your information will need to be verified with the Social Security Administration. This process can take anywhere from one to three days. For that reason, it's a good idea to take care of setting up your FSA ID as early as possible, so it will be all set when you are ready to begin completing your FAFSA.

IMPORTANT NOTE: Since your FSA ID provides access to your personal information and is used to sign online documents, it's imperative that you protect this ID. Don't share it with *anyone* or write it down in an insecure location—you could place yourself at great risk for identify theft.

If your FSA ID is lost or stolen, you must do one of the following:

- Contact Federal Student Aid's Customer Service center at 800-433-3243 (toll-free).
- Update your username and password by selecting "Edit My FSA ID."
- Disable your FSA ID so that no one can use it by selecting "Edit My FSA ID" and then selecting "Disable my FSA ID."

INFORMATION YOU WILL NEED

Completing your FAFSA (or updating one you have already started) will be much easier if you have some basic information and documentation handy when you prepare to complete the form. The first section of the FAFSA involves your basic personal information that you should know offhand, such as your name, address, and Social Security number. After that, you will need to provide details about your income, assets, and other financial issues. If you file taxes, much of this information will be taken from your tax return. If you haven't yet completed your taxes for that year, you can enter estimated figures and update the form with the final numbers later.

If you're a student who is married, you will also need to provide information about your spouse and their finances. If you're a dependent student, information about one or both or your parents and their finances will be required.

You will also need to provide information about the school(s) you attend or plan to attend. If you haven't made your final school choices yet, you can list the ones you know at this point and add others later.

BE MINDFUL OF DEADLINES

The new FAFSA for the upcoming school year is available online starting on October 1. It is smart to complete your FAFSA as early as possible. If you file taxes, you will need information from your tax return (and from your parents, too, if you are a dependent student). However, you can complete your FAFSA before you file your tax return by entering estimated information and then returning to the online system and making any necessary updates once you have filed your taxes.

For federal aid, the final deadline to submit your FAFSA is June 30 during the school year for which you are applying. So for the 2020–2021 school year, the final deadline to submit your FAFSA would be June 30, 2021. However, you would normally want to apply for aid before the start of a semester—and ideally, as far in advance as possible. That's because schools frequently require all of your financial aid to be processed (or at least be in process) before your registration is considered official.

It can sometimes be tricky to keep track of other financial aid deadlines because the deadlines for different types of aid can vary by state and school. Be sure to check with your school—or the schools you are considering attending—to find out their financial aid deadlines so you can get all of your forms submitted in time.

Check the website for your state's department of education to find out the deadlines to submit the FAFSA and other forms in order to be considered for any state-funded financial aid that may be available to you.

DEPENDENCY

One of the biggest misconceptions—or most misunderstood aspects of the FAFSA and financial aid—is that a student can simply declare himself or herself independent, and then their parents' information will not be considered. In the past, dependency wasn't viewed in such strict terms, and it was easier for a student who lived on their own to be considered independent.

It's important to keep in mind that dependency for financial aid purposes has nothing to do with tax status or whether a student's parents claimed the student as a dependent on their tax return. Dependency for taxes and financial aid are two completely different and separate things.

There are now strict criteria that determine a student's dependency status. To be considered independent, a student must meet one of the following conditions:

- Age 24 or older by December 31 of the school year for which the student is applying for aid
- Married
- Have children or other dependents for whom the student provides more than half of their support
- Currently serving in the military
- Having been homeless, in foster care, or a ward of the court

Even if one of these conditions applies, that doesn't necessarily grant the student automatic independent status. There may still be additional required documentation or other conditions that must be met.

IRS DATA RETRIEVAL TOOL

A common complaint about the FAFSA is that it takes too long to complete. But a fairly recent change has made the form considerably less time-consuming for many people. The IRS Data Retrieval tool now allows the tax information of students or parents to be automatically imported into the FAFSA.

Once you reach the section of the online FAFSA that deals with financial information of the student (and parent, if applicable), you will see a button that says "Link to IRS" if that option is available to you. You will then follow the steps to log into the IRS system and have your information transferred to your FAFSA. In order to access the Data Retrieval Tool, the information you enter on the IRS login screen—including your name, address, and filing status—must exactly match the information on your most recent tax return.

Those who decide to skip this step for whatever reason should know that there's a good chance they will then be required to submit copies of their tax return and possibly even an IRS transcript in order to verify their tax information. (An IRS transcript is an official document that must be obtained from the IRS. That can be a time-consuming and inconvenient process, so you are usually better off just using the IRA data retrieval tool in the first place.)

There are certain situations in which the FAFSA will not allow you to use the Data Retrieval Tool. This tool is not an option for students or parents who are married and filed as Married Filing Separately, are married and filed as Head of Household, filed a Form 1040X amended tax return, or filed a Puerto Rican or foreign tax return. If you fall into one of these categories, you will need to enter your tax information manually.

Also, if you have just filed your tax return within a few weeks prior to completing the FAFSA, your current information may not be in the IRS system yet and may not be accessible by the Data Retrieval Tool.

PARENTS' MARITAL STATUS

For dependent students, their parents' marital status can have a big impact on financial aid eligibility. If the parents are married, financial information for both parents must be reported. If the parents are separated but still living together, they are still listed as "married or remarried" on the FAFSA. Parents who are legally separated or living in separate households are classified as "divorced or separated."

If parents are divorced, the FAFSA must be completed by the parent with whom the student lived with most during the previous twelve-month period. If the student lived equally with both parents, the form would be completed by the parent who provided the most support.

LISTING SCHOOL CHOICES

When completing the FAFSA, you must specify which colleges should receive the report generated by your FAFSA application. On the paper FAFSA, you can only list four colleges. On the online version, you can list ten. If you complete the paper version and want to have your information provided to more than four schools, you can go online to the FAFSA website after your form has been processed and add more schools to your list (up to a total of ten).

From a federal aid standpoint, it doesn't matter in what order you list the colleges. However, the FAFSA instructions note that for state aid purposes, you may want to list the colleges in order of preference. Keep in mind that each school on your list will see everything on your FAFSA—including the names of the other colleges you have listed. There have been reports that schools are using students' college listings to determine how likely a specific student is to attend their particular school (based on the theory that students tend to list colleges in the order of how much they want to attend each). The speculation is that a college may reserve its best financial aid offers for students who seem most interested in attending. While most schools won't confirm that practice, it is probably in your best interest to list your colleges in order of the ones you most want to attend.

Falsifying Information on Your FAFSA® Could Bring Big Problems

With the cost of college rising each year and college graduates saddled with more than $1 trillion in debt to pay for their postsecondary studies, more and more families are desperate to secure payment-free options for higher education. Nothing illuminates this fact better than the meteoric rise in applications for financial aid through the annually Free Application for Federal Student Aid (FAFSA®). In the 2004–05 academic year, more than 11 million students sent in FAFSA applications. Less than seven years later, that number doubled to more than 22 million. With more and more students applying for federal financial aid, there is, unfortunately, an increased temptation to commit fraud. Parents try to do whatever they can to lower their Expected Family Contribution (EFC), and sometimes this can lead to falsifying information. This is a big no-no, but that doesn't stop people from trying.

A quick search on Google, and you can find parents and students asking boldly, "Do people lying on their FAFSA really get caught?" or "How do I hide the fact that I have money from FAFSA?" Cheating on the FAFSA seems as intuitive as forgetting to report that second job you have to the Internal Revenue Service.

A report released by the Government Accountability Office, the Congress-created financial watchdog, found that fifteen for-profit universities encouraged fraud and/or engaged in deceptive marketing practices. The report stated that one college admission worker encouraged an undercover applicant to not report $250,000 in savings on the student's FAFSA. Another college representative told an undercover applicant to falsify the number of dependents he had from 0 to 3.

It all seems so deceptively easy—giving thousands of dollars in savings to a student's uncle temporarily to hide that asset; writing down grandma's address to gain in-state tuition rates; forgetting to mention your true immigration status; or the extreme example of one Alaskan woman who used a false identity. In that situation, after claiming she suffered from years of child abuse, the woman used an obscure federal law to secure a new identity to hide from her accused abuser. (The abuser she named was never charged with a crime.) She received a new social security number and card. But instead of living a new life in anonymity, she used her *old* identity to apply for federal student loans—a lot of them. Arrested and convicted, the woman was sentenced to five years in prison and ordered to pay back nearly $1 million.

The prospect of going to jail for filling out false information on your FAFSA application may not have crossed your mind, but it is certainly a possibility. Falsifying information—knowingly or unknowingly—is a federal crime. It is punishable by up to $20,000 in fines and up to five years in prison. And though there are books offering tantalizing options to "game," the federal student aid system—do not be tempted.

You do not want to start your college career by committing a crime against the government. It's just not worth it. Your FAFSA is checked against your IRS documents by professionals who do not want to take the chance that they will use their precious scarce financial aid resources to support students who really do not need it. Students who falsify information to get financial aid leave deserving cash-strapped students out in the cold. Fortunately, though, fraud in the federal aid system is low—a recent government study found that about 5 percent of applications contain false information.

Even if you do not intend to defraud the government, inaccurate information on your FAFSA can get you into trouble. It is critical that you fill the application out as accurately as possible. It may look like an innocuous document, but it amounts to a partnership between you and the federal government, and it is essential that partnership is based upon trust.

Here are some tips to avoid making mistakes on your FAFSA that could cost you financial aid or even your freedom:

- Accurately report your assets, address, dependents, income, and so on. It just doesn't make sense to lie. All that information is easily verifiable. Income includes wages, tips, social security payments, child support payments, and other untaxed income. But retirement income such as those in a 401K or IRA does not have to be reported. Check with your tax advisor when filling out your FAFSA application.
- Fill out your FAFSA completely. Mistakes can cost you time as you might have to reapply, and that will literally cost you money.
- Avoid books, consultants, and websites that promise to lower your EFC by questionable means. Trying to "game," the federal aid system is just going to cause you headaches.

College is expensive, and families are smart to try to lower that expense as much as possible. But planning, saving, and focusing on academic pursuits to garner scholarships and grants is a much better way of acquiring money for college than trying to put one over on the federal government. Being honest is always the best policy—especially when applying for federal financial aid.

Tips for Financing Your Child's College Education

by Don Betterton

Given the lifelong benefit of a college degree (college graduates are projected to earn in a lifetime $1 million more than those with only a high school diploma), higher education is a worthwhile investment. However, it is also an expensive one made even more difficult to manage by cost increases that have outpaced both inflation and gains in family income. The reality of higher education economics is that paying for a child's college education is an issue that shows no sign of getting easier.

Because of the high cost involved (even the most inexpensive four-year education at a public institution costs more than $10,000 a year), good information about college budgets and strategies for reducing the "sticker price" is essential. You have made a good start by taking the time to read *Peterson's How to Get Money for College.* In the pages that follow, you will find valuable information about the four main sources of aid—federal, state, institutional, and private. Before you learn about the various programs, however, it will be helpful if you have an overview of how the college financial aid system operates and what long-range financing strategies are available.

FINANCIAL AID

Financial aid refers to money that is awarded to a student, usually in a "package" that consists of gift aid (commonly called a scholarship or grant), a student loan, and/or a campus job.

COLLEGE COSTS

The starting point for organizing a plan to pay for your child's college education is to make a good estimate of the yearly cost of attendance. You can use the **College Cost Worksheet** on the next page to do this.

To estimate your college costs for 2020-2021, refer to the tuition and fees and room and board figures shown in the **College Cost Worksheet**. If your child will commute from your home, use $2,500 instead of the college's room and board charges and $900 for transportation. We have used $800 for books and $1,500 for personal expenses. Finally, estimate the cost of two round trips if your home is more than a few hundred miles from the college. Add the items to calculate the total budget. You should now have a reasonably good estimate of college costs for 2020-2021. (To determine the costs for later years, adding 4 percent per year will probably give you a fairly accurate estimate.)

DO YOU QUALIFY FOR NEED-BASED AID?

The next step is to evaluate whether or not you are likely to qualify for financial aid based on need. This step is critical, since more than 90 percent of the yearly total of $128 billion in student aid is awarded only after a determination is made that the family lacks sufficient financial resources to pay the full cost of college on its own. To judge your chance of receiving need-based aid, it is necessary to estimate an Expected Family Contribution (EFC) according to a government formula known as the Federal Methodology (FM). The official Federal Student Aid Website provides a FAFSA4caster tool (similar to an EFC calculator) that helps you get a head start on the financial aid process, including getting an early estimate of your eligibility for federal aid. The tool will also allow you to transfer the information provided into the actual Free Application for Federal Student Aid (FAFSA®) form when you are ready to complete it. You can find the tool on the Fafsa.ed.gov website.

APPLYING FOR NEED-BASED AID

Because the federal government provides about 67 percent of all aid awarded, the application, FAFSA, and need evaluation process is controlled by the U.S. Department of Education. In addition, nearly every state that offers student assistance uses the federal government's system to award its own aid. Furthermore, in addition to arranging for the payment of federal and state aid, many colleges use the FAFSA to award their own funds to eligible students. (Note: In addition to the FAFSA, many private colleges and universities also ask the family to complete the CSS/Financial Aid PROFILE® application.)

The FAFSA is your "passport" to receiving your share of the billions of dollars awarded annually in need-based aid. If you didn't read the first article in this section about the FAFSA, go back and take a look at it now. You will find the latest information on the FAFSA, including important details on the change from the PIN to the new FSA ID.

AWARDING AID

The colleges you list on the FAFSA will receive your information in order to calculate a financial aid award in a package that

College Cost Worksheet

	College 1	College 2	College 3	Commuter College
Tuition and Fees	______	______	______	______
Room and Board	______	______	______	$2,500
Books	$ 800	$ 800	$ 800	$ 750
Personal Expenses	$1,500	$1,500	$1,500	$1,500
Travel	______	______	______	$ 900
Total Budget	______	______	______	______

typically includes aid from at least one of the major sources—federal, state, college, or private. In addition, the award will probably consist of a combination of a scholarship, grant, loan, or campus job. These last two pieces—loan and job—are called self-help aid because they require effort on your child's part (that is, the aid must be either earned through work or paid back later). Scholarships or grants are outright gifts that have no such obligation.

It is important that you understand each part of the package. You'll want to know, for example, how much aid is a gift, the interest rate and repayment terms of the student loan, or how many hours per week the campus job requires. There should be an enclosure with the award letter that answers these questions. If not, make a list of your questions and call or visit the financial aid office.

Once you understand the terms of each item in the award letter, you should turn your attention to the "bottom line"—how much you will have to pay at each college where your child is accepted. In addition to understanding the aid award, this means having a good estimate of the college budget so you can accurately calculate how much you and your child will have to contribute. (Often, an aid package does not cover the entire need.) Colleges differ in how much detail they include in their award notifications. Many colleges provide full information—types and amounts of aid, yearly costs, and the EFC for the parent and student shares. If these important items are missing or incomplete, you can do the work on your own. (See the **Comparing Financial Aid Awards and Family Contribution Worksheet** on the next page.) For example, if the award letter only shows the college's direct charges—tuition, room, and board— you need to estimate indirect costs such as books, personal expenses, and travel. Then subtract the total aid awarded from the yearly cost to get the EFC. A portion of that amount may be your child's contribution (35 percent of student assets and 50 percent of student earnings over $2,200) and the remainder is the parental share. If you can afford this amount at your child's first-choice college, the financial aid system has worked well for you, and your child's college enrollment plans can go forward.

How Need Is Calculated and Aid Is Awarded

	College 1	College 2
Total Cost of Attendance	$10,000	$ 24,000
− Expected Family Contribution	− 5,500	− 5,500
= Financial Need	$ 4,500	$ 18,500
− Grant Aid Awarded	− 675	−14,575
− Campus Job (Work-Study) Awarded	− 1,400	− 1,300
− Student Loan Awarded	− 2,425	− 2,625
= Unmet Need	0	0

Note: Sometimes an institution is unable to meet all need. The amount of unmet need is called "the gap."

Comparing Financial Aid Awards and Family Contribution Worksheet

	College 1	College 2	College 3
Cost of Attendance	________	________	________
Aid Awarded	________	________	________
Grant/Scholarship	________	________	________
Loan	________	________	________
Job	________	________	________
Total Aid	________	________	________
Expected Family Contribution	________	________	________
Student Contribution	________	________	________
Parent Contribution	________	________	________

But if you think your EFC is too high, you should contact the college's financial aid office and ask whether additional aid is available. Many private high-cost colleges are willing to work with families to help make attendance at their institutions possible. Most colleges also allow applicants to appeal their financial aid awards, the budget used for you, or any of the elements used to determine the family contribution, especially if there are extenuating circumstances or if the information has changed since the application was submitted. Some colleges may also reconsider an award based on a "competitive appeal," the submission of a more favorable award letter from another college.

If your appeal is unsuccessful and there is still a gap between the expected family contribution and what you feel you can pay from income and savings, you are left with two choices. One option is for your child to attend a college where paying your share of the bill will not be a problem. (This assumes that an affordable option was included on your child's original list of colleges, a wise admission application strategy.) The second is to look into alternate methods of financing. At this stage, parental loans and tuition payment plans are the best financing options. A parental loan can bring the yearly cost down to a manageable level by spreading payments over a number of years. This is the type of financing that families use when purchasing a home or automobile. A tuition payment plan is essentially a short-term loan and allows you to pay the costs over ten to twelve months. It is an option for families who have the resources available but need help with managing their cash flow.

NON-NEED-BASED AID

Regardless of whether you might qualify for a need-based award, it is always worthwhile to look into merit, or non-need, scholarships from sources such as foundations, agencies, religious groups, and service organizations. For a family that isn't eligible for need-based aid, merit scholarships are the only form of gift aid available. If your child later qualifies for a need-based award, a merit scholarship can be quite helpful in providing additional resources if the aid does not fully cover the costs. Even if the college meets 100 percent of need, a merit scholarship reduces the self-help (loan and job) portion of an award.

In searching for merit-based scholarships, keep in mind that there are relatively few awards (compared to those that are need-based), and most of them are highly competitive. Use the following checklist in your search.

- Take advantage of any scholarships for which your child is automatically eligible based on parents' employer benefits, military service, association or church membership, other affiliations, or student or parent attributes (ethnic background, nationality, and so on). Company or union tuition remissions are the most common examples of these awards.
- Look for other awards for which your child might be eligible based on the previous characteristics and affiliations but where there is a selection process and an application is required. Free computerized searches are available on the Internet. (You should not pay a fee for a scholarship search.) Peterson's free scholarship search can be accessed by logging on to www.petersons.com/finaid. Scholarship directories, such as *Peterson's Scholarships, Grants & Prizes*, which details more than 2,600 scholarship programs are useful resources and can be found in bookstores, high school guidance offices, or your local library. You can also find these books at **www.petersonsbooks.com.**
- See if your state has a merit scholarship program.
- Look into national scholarship competitions. High school guidance counselors usually know about these scholarships. Examples of these awards are the National Meritt Scholarship Program, the Coca-Cola Scholarship, Gates Millennium Scholars, Intel Science Talent Search, and the U.S. Senate Youth Program.

- ROTC (Reserve Officers' Training Corps) scholarships are offered by the Army, Navy, Air Force, and Marine Corps. A full ROTC scholarship covers tuition, fees, textbook costs, and, in some cases, a stipend. Acceptance of an ROTC scholarship entails a commitment to take military science courses and to serve for a specific number of years as an officer in the sponsoring branch of the service. Competition is heavy, and preference may be given to students in certain fields of study, such as engineering, languages, science, and health professions. Application procedures vary by service. Contact an armed services recruiter or high school guidance counselor for further information.
- Investigate community scholarships. High school guidance counselors usually have a list of these awards and announcements are published in local newspapers. Most common are awards given by service organizations like the American Legion, Rotary International, and the local women's club.
- If your child is strong academically or is very talented in fields such as athletics or performing/creative arts, you may want to consider colleges that offer their own merit awards to gifted students they wish to enroll. Refer to the Non-Need Scholarships for Undergraduates index in the back part of this guide.

In addition to merit scholarships, there are loan and job opportunities for students who do not qualify for need-based aid. Some of the organizations that sponsor scholarships—for example, the Air Force Aid Society—also provide loans.

Work opportunities during the academic year are another type of assistance that is not restricted to aid recipients. Many colleges will, after assigning jobs to students on aid, open campus positions to all students looking for work. In addition, there are usually off-campus employment opportunities available to everyone.

FINANCING YOUR CHILD'S COLLEGE EDUCATION

"Financing" means putting together resources to pay the balance due the college over and above payments from the primary sources of aid—grants, scholarships, student loans, and jobs. Financing strategies are important because the high cost of a college education today often requires a family, whether or not it receives aid, to think about stretching its college payment beyond the four-year period of enrollment. For high-cost colleges, it is not unreasonable to think about a 10-4-10 plan: ten years of saving; four years of paying college bills out of current income, savings, and borrowing; and ten years to repay a parental loan.

Note

A point of clarification about whether to put college savings in your name or your child's: If you are certain that your child will not be a candidate for need-based aid, there may be a tax advantage to accumulating money in his or her name. However, when it comes to maximizing aid eligibility, it is important to understand that student assets are assessed at a 20 percent rate and parental assets at about 5 percent. Therefore, if your college savings are in your child's name, it may be wise to reestablish title to these funds before applying for financial aid. You should contact your financial planner or accountant before making any modifications to your asset structure.

Savings

Although saving for college is always a good idea, many families are unclear about its advantages. Some families do not save because after normal living expenses have been covered, they do not have much money to set aside. An affordable but regular savings plan through a payroll deduction is usually the answer to the problem of spending your entire paycheck every month.

The second reason why saving for college is not a high priority is the belief that the financial aid system penalizes a family by lowering aid eligibility. The Federal Methodology of need determination is very kind to families that save. In fact, savings are ignored completely for most families that earn less than $50,000. Savings in the form of home equity, retirement plans, and most annuities are excluded from the calculation. And even when savings are counted, a maximum of 5 percent of the total is expected each year. In other words, if a family has $40,000 in savings after an asset protection allowance is considered, the contribution is no greater than $2,000. Given the impact of compound interest it is easy to see that a long-term savings plan can make paying for college much easier.

A sensible savings plan is important because of the financial advantage of saving compared to borrowing. The amount of money students borrow for college is now greater than the amount they receive in grants and scholarships. With loans becoming so widespread, savings should be carefully con-

What Is CSS/Financial Aid PROFILE

There are many complexities in the financial aid process: knowing which aid is merit-based and which aid is need-based; understanding the difference between grants, loans, and work-study; and determining whether funds are from federal, state, institutional, or private sources.

In addition, the aid application process itself can be confusing. It can involve more than the Free Application for Federal Student Aid (FAFSA®) and the Federal Methodology (FM). Many colleges feel that the federal aid system (FAFSA and FM) does not collect or evaluate information thoroughly enough for them to award their own institutional funds. These colleges have made an arrangement with the College Scholarship Service, a branch of the College Board, to establish a separate application system.

The application is called the CSS/Financial Aid PROFILE®, and the need-analysis formula is referred to as the Institutional Methodology (IM). If you apply for financial aid at one of the colleges that uses the PROFILE, the admission material will state that the PROFILE is required in addition to the FAFSA. You should read the information carefully and file the PROFILE to meet the earliest college deadline. Before you can receive the PROFILE, however, you must register, either by phone or online at https://student.collegeboard.org/css-financial-aid-profile, providing enough basic information so the PROFILE package can be designed specifically for you. The FAFSA is free, but there is a charge for the PROFILE. As with the FAFSA, the PROFILE can be submitted via the Internet.

In addition to the requirement by certain colleges that you submit both the FAFSA and PROFILE (when used, the PROFILE is always in addition to the FAFSA; it does not replace it), you should understand that each system has its own method for analyzing a family's ability to pay for college. The main differences between PROFILE's Institutional Methodology and the FAFSA's Federal Methodology are:

- PROFILE includes equity in the family home as an asset; the FAFSA doesn't.
- PROFILE takes a broader look at assets not included on the FAFSA.
- PROFILE expects a minimum student contribution, usually in the form of summer earnings; the FAFSA has no such minimum.
- PROFILE may collect information on the noncustodial parent; the FAFSA does not.
- PROFILE allows for more professional judgment than the FAFSA. Medical expenses, private secondary school costs, and a variety of special circumstances are considered under PROFILE, subject to the discretion of the aid counselor on campus.
- PROFILE includes information on assets not reported on the FAFSA, including life insurance, annuities, retirement plans, etc.

To summarize: PROFILE's Institutional Methodology tends to be both more complete in its data collection and more rigorous in its analysis than the FAFSA's Federal Methodology. When IM results are compared to FM results for thousands of applicants, IM will usually come up with a somewhat higher expected parental contribution than FM.

Creditworthiness

If you will be borrowing to pay for your child's college education, making sure you qualify for a loan is critical. For the most part, that means your credit record must be free of default or delinquency. You can check your credit history with one or more of the following three major credit bureaus and clean up any adverse information that appears. The numbers below will offer specific information on what you need to provide to obtain a report. All of the credit bureaus accept credit report requests over their Web sites. You will usually be asked to provide your full name, phone number, social security number, birth date, and addresses for the last five years. You are entitled to a free report from each bureau.

Equifax Credit Information
P.O. Box 740241
Atlanta, GA 30374
800-685-1111
http://www.equifax.com

Trans Union
800-888-4213
http://www.transunion.com

Experian
888-397-3742
http://www.experian.com

sidered as an alternative to borrowing. Your incentive for saving is that a dollar saved is a dollar not borrowed.

Borrowing

Once you've calculated your "bottom-line" parental contribution and determined that the amount is not affordable out of your current income and assets, the most likely alternative is borrowing. Beginning July 1, 2010, as a result of the Health Care and Education Reconciliation Act, federal student loans are no longer made by private lenders under the Federal Family Education Loan (FFEL) Program. Instead, all new federal student loans come directly from the U.S. Department of Education under the Direct Loan Program, which offers subsidized and unsubsidized (Stafford) loans for students, PLUS loans for parents and graduate/professional students, and consolidation loans for both students and parents. For additional information, go online to https://studentloans.gov/myDirectLoan/index.action or call 800-4-FED-AID (toll-free).

For the Direct PLUS Loan, parents must complete a Direct PLUS Loan application and promissory note, contained in a single form that can be obtained from a school's financial aid office. The yearly limit on a PLUS Loan is equal to the student's cost of attendance minus any other financial aid the student receives. For example, if your cost of attendance is $6,000, and you receive $4,500 in other financial aid, your parents can borrow up to $1,500. Loans are disbursed between July 1 and June 30 of each year and have a fixed interest rate throughout the life of the loan. The rate for undergraduate students will never exceed 8.25%. Interest is charged on a PLUS Loan from the date of the first disbursement until the loan is paid in full. A PLUS Loan made to the parent cannot be transferred to the student. The parent is responsible for repaying the PLUS Loan. For more details about PLUS Loans, visit www.direct.ed.gov/about.html.

MAKE FINANCIAL AID WORK FOR YOU

If you are like millions of families that benefit from financial aid, it is likely that your child's college plans can go forward without undue worry about the costs involved. The key is to understand the financial aid system and to follow the best path for your family. The result of good information and good planning should be that you will receive your fair share of the billions of dollars available each year and that the cost of college will not prevent your child from attending.

Don Betterton is a former Director of Undergraduate Financial Aid at Princeton University and a Certified College Planner (CCP).

Residency: Its Impact on Tuition

When it comes to college tuition at a state school, a student's *in-state* or *out-of-state* status can often make a big difference. For those students who are unable to cover a school's price tag, it can often be quite frustrating. However, there is a legitimate reason why colleges charge more to out-of-state students, even if this happens to be thousands more. And here's why.

Public universities receive public funding by way of tax dollars paid by state residents. A large chunk of money that these public universities get each year are paid by taxpayers who live in that state. It only make sense then that in-state students should catch a break in tuition costs since their families, as residents, have helped pay for the public universities' operating costs.

Another reason for in-state tuition to be less expensive is because states want to offer an incentive to keep their residents in state. Their investment for keeping their students in-state pays off when a student graduates and starts working in-state as well, essentially helping boost the economy from within, and contributing to the social and cultural climate of the state.

RECIPROCITY

In some cases, a public college or university will offer in-state tuition to out-of-state students. Typically this happens when a program of study is not available to the student in his or her home state, or the states make an agreement with one another to offer in-state or close to in-state tuition to students from each other's states. For example, the Western Undergraduate Exchange (WUE) program offers out-of-state students tuition at 1.5 times as much as in-state tuition; states included are Alaska, Arizona, California, Colorado, Hawaii, Idaho, Montana, Nevada, New Mexico, North Dakota, South Dakota, Utah, Washington, and Wyoming.

Check with your high school guidance counselor and/or the financial aid office at your school(s) of interest to see if there are any options like this in your state

IN-STATE REQUIREMENTS

In-state requirements and establishing residency varies state to state, but you can always ask your prospective school what is required to establish residency. Typically it takes at least one year of living in the state, and you will be required to perform certain tasks, such as obtaining a driver's license in the state, filing taxes in the state, and so on. You may need to demonstrate that you are in the state for years to come—not only for the duration of your undergraduate education. It is important that you research this thoroughly and contact the school to be sure you are taking the right steps to obtain residency.

Although not easy, some students may find a way to move to the state they want to go to school in a year (or two) before they even apply. If you want to attend an out-of-state institution and cannot afford the out-of-state tuition, establishing residency is crucial to lowering your tuition cost and ensuring you will be able to afford to attend until graduation. Establishing residency might also open up other financial aid opportunities as well, so be sure to ask if there are any scholarships, grants, or other sources of funding available only to in-state students. Whether or not you want to obtain residency will have to do with your specific financial situation, so you should be sure to weigh your all of your options carefully before making your decision.

Federal Financial Aid Programs

There are a number of sources of financial aid available to students: federal and state governments, private agencies, and the colleges themselves. In addition, there are three different forms of aid: grants, earnings, and loans.

The federal government is the single largest source of financial aid for students. In recent years, the U.S. Department of Education's student financial aid programs made more than $80 billion available in loans, grants, and other aid to 14 million students. At present, there are four federal grant programs—Federal Pell Grant, Federal Supplemental Educational Opportunity Grant (FSEOG), Teacher Education Assistance for College and Higher Education (TEACH) Grant, and Iraq and Afghanistan Service Grant. There are two federal loan programs: Federal Perkins Loan Program and the William D. Ford Federal Direct Loan Program. The federal government also has a job program, Federal Work-Study Program (FWS), which helps colleges provide employment for students. In addition to the student aid programs, there are also tuition tax credits and deductions. They are the American Opportunity Credit, the Lifetime Learning Credit, the Tuition and Fees Tax Deduction, and the Student Loan Interest Tax Deduction. Also, there is AmeriCorps. AmeriCorps will pay the interest that is accrued on qualified student loans for members who complete the service program.

The majority of federal higher education loans are made in the Direct Loan Program, which makes available two kinds of loans: loans to students and PLUS loans to parents or to graduate or professional students. These loans are either subsidized or unsubsidized. Subsidized loans are made on the basis of demonstrated student need, and the interest is paid by the government during the time the student is in school or deferment. For the unsubsidized (non-need-based) loans and PLUS loans, interest begins to accrue as funds are disbursed.

All new federal student loans come directly from the U.S. Department of Education under the Direct Loan Program. Students interested in receiving federal student aid should continue to complete a Free Application for Federal Student Aid (FAFSA®) for each school year that they wish to be considered for aid. For more information about applying for federal student aid, call 800-4-FED-AID (800-433-3243)(toll-free) or visit www.fafsa.ed.gov.

FEDERAL PELL GRANT

The Federal Pell Grant is the largest grant program; more than 9 million students receive Pell Grants annually. This grant is intended to be the starting point of assistance for lower-income families. Eligibility for a Pell Grant is based on the Expected Family Contribution. The amount you receive will depend on your EFC and the cost of education at the college you will attend. The highest award depends on how much funding the program receives from the government. For the 2020-2021 award year (July 1, 2020 to June 30, 2021), the maximum award is $6,345. As of July 1, 2012, a student cannot receive a Federal Pell Grant for more than 12 semesters or the equivalent. A student will receive notice when he/she is close to their limit.

FEDERAL SUPPLEMENTAL EDUCATIONAL OPPORTUNITY GRANT (FSEOG)

As its name implies, Federal Supplemental Educational Opportunity Grants provide additional need-based federal grant money to supplement the Federal Pell Grant Program. Each participating college is given funds to award to especially needy students. The maximum award is $4,000 per year, but the amount you receive depends on the college's awarding policy, the availability of FSEOG funds, the total cost of education, and the amount of other aid awarded.

FEDERAL WORK-STUDY PROGRAM (FWS)

This program provides jobs for students who demonstrate need. Salaries are paid by funds from the federal government as well as the college. Students work on an hourly basis on or off campus and must be paid at least the federal minimum wage. Students may earn only up to the amount awarded in the financial aid package.

FEDERAL PERKINS LOAN PROGRAM

This is a low-interest (5%) loan for students with exceptional financial need. Perkins Loans are made through the college's financial aid office with the college as the lender. Undergraduate students can borrow a maximum of $5,500 per year, and there is a cumulative limit of $27,500. The annual limit for graduate and professional-degree-seeking students is $8,500 with a total cumulative limit (including the $27,500) of $60,000. Borrowers may take up to ten years to repay the loan, beginning nine months after they graduate, leave school, or drop below half-time status. No interest accrues while they are in school, and, under certain conditions (e.g., they teach in low-income areas, work in law enforcement, are full-time nurses or medical technicians, serve as Peace Corps or VISTA volunteers, etc.), some or all of the loan can be cancelled. In addition, payments can be deferred under certain conditions such as unemployment.

Federal Financial Aid Programs

Name of Program	Type of Program	Maximum Award Per Year
Federal Pell Grant	need-based grant	$6,345
Federal Supplemental Educational Opportunity Grant (FSEOG)	need-based grant	$4,000
Teacher Education Assistance for College and Higher Education (TEACH) Grants	need/merit	up to $4,000 a year for undergraduates
Iraq and Afghanistan Service Grant	need/merit	$6,345 (based on strict criteria being met)
Federal Work-Study Program (FWS)	need-based part-time job	no maximum
Federal Perkins Loan Program	need-based loan	$5,500
Subsidized Federal Direct Loan	need-based grant student loan	$3,500 (first year)
Unsubsidized Federal Direct Loan	non-need based	$5,500 (first year, dependent student)

FEDERAL DIRECT LOANS

A Direct Loan is borrowed directly from the U.S. Department of Education through the college's financial aid office.

The interest rate on Direct Subsidized and Unsubsidized Loans for undergraduates with a first disbursement date between July 1, 2019, and June 30, 2020, is 4.53 percent. For those loans with a first disbursement date between July 1, 2018, and June 30, 2019, the interest rate was 4.29 percent.

The maximum amount dependent students may borrow in any one year is $5,500 for freshmen, $6,500 for sophomores, and $7,500 for juniors and seniors, with a maximum of $31,000 for the total undergraduate program (of which not more than $23,000 can be subsidized). The maximum amount independent students can borrow is $9,500 for freshmen (of which no more than $3,500 can be subsidized), $10,500 for sophomores (of which no more than $4,500 can be subsidized), and $12,500 for juniors and seniors (of which no more than $5,500 can be subsidized). Independent students can borrow up to $57,500 (of which no more than $23,000 can be subsidized) for the total undergraduate program. Borrowers may be charged a small origination fee, which is deducted from the loan proceeds. See the helpful, easy-to-read chart on the next page for maximum annual and total subsidized and unsubsidized loan limits.

To apply for a Federal Student Loan, you must first complete the FAFSA to determine eligibility for a subsidized loan and then complete a separate loan application that is submitted to the Department of Education. The Department of Education will send a master promissory for completion. The proceeds of the loan, less the origination fee, will be sent to the college to be either credited to your account or released to you directly. Direct loans are processed by the financial aid office as part of the overall financial aid package.

Once the repayment period starts, borrowers of both subsidized and unsubsidized Federal Direct Loans have to pay a combination of interest and principal monthly for up to a 25-year period. There are a number of repayment options as well as opportunities to consolidate federal loans. There are also provisions for extended repayments, deferments, and repayment forbearance, if needed. Note: If you received a Direct Subsidized Loan that was first disbursed between July 1, 2012, and July 1, 2014, you are responsible for paying any interest that accrued during your grace period (first six months after graduation). If you choose not to pay the interest that accrued during your grace period, the interest will be added to your principal balance.

Maximum Annual and Total Subsidized and Unsubsidized Loan Limits

Year	Dependent Students (except students whose parents are unable to obtain PLUS Loans)	Independent Students (and dependent undergraduate students whose parents are unable to obtain PLUS Loans)
First-Year Undergraduate	$5,500—No more than $3,500 of this amount may be in subsidized loans.	$9,500—No more than $3,500 of this amount may be in subsidized loans.
Second-Year Undergraduate	$6,500—No more than $4,500 of this amount may be in subsidized loans.	$10,500—No more than $4,500 of this amount may be in subsidized loans.
Third-Year and Beyond Undergraduate	$7,500 per year—No more than $5,500 of this amount may be in subsidized loans.	$12,500 per year—No more than $5,500 of this amount may be in subsidized loans.
Graduate or Professional Degree Students	Not Applicable	$20,500
Maximum Total Debt from Subsidized and Unsubsidized Loans	$31,000—No more than $23,000 of this amount may be in subsidized loans.	$57,500 for undergraduates—No more than $23,000 of this amount may be in subsidized loans. $138,500 for graduate or professional students—No more than $65,500 of this amount may be in subsidized loans. The graduate debt limit includes all federal loans received for undergraduate study.

Source: https://studentaid.ed.gov/sa/types/loans/subsidized-unsubsidized

DIRECT PLUS LOANS

PLUS loans are for parents of dependent students to help families with the cost of education. There is no needs test to qualify. For Direct PLUS Loans first disbursed on or after July 1, 2018, and before July 1, 2019, the interest rate is 7%. For Direct PLUS Loans first disbursed on or after July 1, 2019, and before July 1, 2020, the interest rate is 5%. There is no yearly limit; you can borrow up to the cost of your child's education, less other financial aid received. Repayment begins sixty days after the funds are disbursed. The origination fee is approximately 4 percent and may be subtracted from the proceeds. Parent borrowers must generally have a good credit record to qualify.

AMERICAN OPPORTUNITY CREDIT AND LIFETIME LEARNING CREDIT

Tuition tax credits allow families to reduce their tax bill by the out-of-pocket college tuition expense. Unlike a tax deduction, which is modified according to your tax bracket, a tax credit is a dollar-for-dollar reduction in taxes paid.

There are two programs: the American Opportunity Credit and the Lifetime Learning Credit. As is true of many federal programs, there are numerous rules and restrictions that apply. You should check with your tax preparer, financial adviser, or IRS Publication 970 for information about your own particular situation.

American Opportunity Credit

The American Opportunity Credit (formerly the Hope Credit) can be claimed for expenses for the first four years of postsecondary education. This is a change from the previous Hope Credit. The American Opportunity Credit can be claimed now through tax-year 2019 for expenses for course-related books, supplies, and equipment. It is a tax credit of up to $2,500 of the cost of qualifying tuition and expenses, and up to 40 percent of the credit is refundable (up to $1,000).

Eligibility also differs from the former Hope Credit. A taxpayer who pays qualified tuition and related expenses and whose federal income tax return has a modified adjusted gross income of $80,000 or less ($160,000 or less for joint filers) is eligible for the credit. The credit is reduced ratably if a taxpayer's modified adjusted gross income exceeds those amounts. A taxpayer whose modified adjusted gross income is greater than $90,000 ($180,000 for joint filers) cannot benefit from this credit.

For more information about the American Opportunity Tax Credit, go online to http://www.irs.gov/uac/American-Opportunity-Tax-Credit:-Questions-and-Answers.

Lifetime Learning Credit

The Lifetime Learning Credit is the counterpart of the American Opportunity Credit. The qualifying taxpayer can claim an annual tax credit of up to $2,000—20 percent of the first $10,000 of tuition. The credit is available for net tuition and fees, less grant aid. The total credit available is limited to $2,000 per year per taxpayer (or joint-filing couple). There is no limit on the number of years the lifetime learning credit can be claimed for each student. However, a taxpayer cannot claim both the American Opportunity Credit and Lifetime Learning Credit for the same student in one year. For more information, visit http://www.irs.gov/Individuals/LLC.

TUITION AND FEES TAX DEDUCTION

The Tuition and Fees Tax Deduction could reduce taxable income by as much as $4,000. This deduction is taken as an adjustment to income, which means you can claim this deduction even if you do not itemize deductions on Schedule A of Form 1040. This deduction may benefit taxpayers who do not qualify for either the American Opportunity Credit or Lifetime Learning Credit.

Up to $4,000 may be deducted for tuition and fees required for enrollment or attendance at an eligible postsecondary institution. Personal living and family expenses, including room and board, insurance, medical, and transportation, are not deductible expenses.

The exact amount of the Tuition and Fees Tax Deduction depends on the amount of qualified tuition and related expenses paid for one's self, spouse, or dependents, and your Adjusted Gross Income. Consult the IRS or your tax preparer for more information.

STUDENT LOAN INTEREST TAX DEDUCTION

If you made student loan interest payments, you may be able to reduce your taxable income by up to $2,500. You should check with your lender with regards to the amount of interest you paid if you did not receive an IRS Form 1098-E and your tax preparer or IRS Publication 970 for additional information, which can be found online at http://www.irs.gov/publications/p970/ch04.html.

AMERICORPS

AmeriCorps is a national umbrella group of service programs for students. Participants work in a public or private nonprofit agency and provide service to the community in one of four priority areas: education, human services, the environment, and public safety. For all AmeriCorps programs, members receive a modest living allowance, and some programs provide housing. Individuals may not save much money during their year of service, but most find the living allowance to be adequate to cover their needs. AmeriCorps members who complete a term of service also receive an AmeriCorps Education Award. Many student-loan lenders will postpone the repayment of student loans during service in AmeriCorps, and AmeriCorps will pay the interest that is accrued on qualified student loans for members who complete the service program. Participants can work before, during, or after college and can use the funds to either pay current educational expenses or repay federal student loans. For more information, visit http://www.nationalservice.gov/programs/americorps.

College Financial Aid: Impressing the Financial Aid Counselor

The best way to impress a financial aid counselor is to be prepared and do as much research as you can before your meeting. You want to build a positive relationship with the individuals in the financial aid office as they often are the ones who will ultimately help you receive the most financial aid possible, including scholarships and grants.

Here are some things to know and do:

- Be aware of the school's financial aid application deadline.
- Meet with the financial aid counselor as soon as possible.
- Keep copies of everything that will help complete your application.
- Check with the financial aid office to make sure your file is complete and that everything was filled out correctly.
- Speak with the financial aid officer about any scholarships you receive, whether they are from the school itself or from outside of the school.
- Never be late to an appointment, and call to cancel if you need to do so.

ACTION ITEMS

Be sure to gather and submit any documentation that will provide a truthful claim of your financial situation, and always ask for a confirmation of submission. Don't lie about anything in your financial aid application, and always be open to discussing your situation. Financial aid counselors are here to help.

Be patient. Financial aid decisions can take time. Appeals can typically take more time than usual, as well as the fact that committees usually only meet a couple of times a month to review appeal submissions. Ask your financial aid counselor about an expected date, and if you haven't heard from him/her in a couple of weeks at minimum, call them to follow up.

While you want to be assertive and make sure that your questions are answered to your satisfaction, you also want to be sure you are polite and respectful. Politeness goes a long way. Often financial aid counselors will work with you every year when applying for scholarships, grants, and loans, so you want to be sure you establish a good long-term relationship.

Keep these "DO" tips in mind:

- Do call ahead to make an appointment—otherwise you might be waiting all day to speak with the counselor.
- Do make a list of any questions or concerns you have.
- Do ask what requirements are needed in order to keep getting aid in the future, for example a minimum GPA.
- Do compare your family's expected contribution (EFC) with other schools and ask the counselor to explain the differences.
- Do ask about employment opportunities on campus.
- Do fill out and submit all applications by the deadline.
- Do ask what changes in your financial situation can affect your award.
- Do ask if outside scholarships will affect your financial aid award.
- Do thank the counselor for helping you.

Remember, financial aid counselors are there to help you. While some may seem rude or be rushed, it doesn't mean that you have to be as well. Patience goes a long way in getting the help you need.

Keep these "DON'T" tips in mind:

- Don't try to compare your award with others as each situation is different. Ask your counselor if you have any questions.
- Don't discuss consumer debt with your counselor. Consumer debt will not be taken into account.
- Don't give up; you can always apply again the following year.
- Don't take out student loans just because you can. Loans HAVE to be repaid, usually with interest. Only take out loans that you absolutely need.
- Don't be ashamed to discuss your personal finances, including bankruptcy, child-support, medical expenses, and anything else that may affect your ability to pay for tuition.

Keep these tips in mind as you are meeting with your financial aid counselor, and always remember that they are there to help you find the best financial aid package as possible.

Inside the Federal Work-Study Program

If you're like millions of other families with college-age youth you may have had that moment. It's the stomach-churching wrinkle in time when you realize that the gap between the amount of money you've saved for your child's college education and the cost of that dream university seems as insurmountable as crossing the ocean on a surfboard. Even as you fill out the Free Application for Federal Student Aid (FAFSA®) and your child gets the award letter from the college, the sticker shock can be depressing. But there is glimmer of hope, and it's called the Federal Work-Study Program (FWS).

The federally funded FWS, formerly known as the College Campus Work-Study Program, was a part of the anti-poverty legislation that swept the country in the 1960s. FWS partners with 3,400 institutions in the country to pay students to work on a college or university campus. Looking at the words "work study," may instill fear in some parent's hearts. They may think of nightmarish scenarios where their son or daughter spends so much time guarding the science building that they won't have time for their studies. This isn't necessarily true. There are several aspects to the federally supported work-study program that makes it an attractive option for students looking to lower their college bill.

WORK-STUDY CAN BE A VALUABLE EXPERIENCE

The Federal Work-Study (FWS) Program is a federal student aid program that provides part-time employment while you are enrolled in school to help pay your education expenses. The Federal Work-Study Program emphasizes, whenever possible, employment in civic education and work that is related to your course of study.

If you work on campus, you'll most likely work for your school. If you work off campus, your employer might be a private nonprofit organization or a public agency, and the work performed must be in the public interest.

Colleges and universities like that the FWS is federally subsidized, so they will offer this option as part of a financial aid package first because it saves them money. So send your FASFA as early as possible, especially if you want to beat out the millions of students who seek work-study jobs! Also, don't forget to indicate on your FASFA that you are interested in a work-study job.

In addition, it may be best to choose work-study over outside employment. You may believe that work is work, but when it comes to work-study jobs that sentiment is not true. Work-study jobs are usually better for students because the payment you receive is NOT counted against you when applying for financial aid. This could make a huge difference in how much aid you receive from your chosen institution.

WORK-STUDY JOBS—NOT ALWAYS "BORING"

Not all work-study jobs have to be through educational institutions. The program also funds jobs at a federal, state, or local public agency; a private nonprofit organization; or even aprivate for-profit organization. Check and see if your school has a partnership with an off-campus workplace. You might be able to find a work-study position in your field of study. This allows you to gain valuable experience and not just collect "man hours" while you pay down your college price tag.

Still, the type of job a student is privy to largely depends upon the intuition's work-study program. Some programs focus on interesting options such as janitorial services, cafeteria work, or even telemarketer. But with a little ingenuity, students can find a work-study assignment that fits their academic and financial need. For example, at Colorado College, a private school in Colorado Springs, work-study students can apply for jobs as diverse as stage manager for theater productions or work off campus at a nonprofit such as the Children's Literacy Center. To ensure you get a work-study position that fits your career goals, it's best to talk to officials at your institution early and often about available work-study options. For example, according to the U.S. Department of Education, a college must use 7 percent of its work-study funds to support students "working in community service jobs, including reading tutors for preschool age or elementary school children, mathematics tutors for students enrolled in elementary school through ninth grade, literacy tutors in a family literacy project performing family literacy activities, or emergency preparedness and response." When you talk to your institution's financial aid office you might mention your experience in any of these areas. This won't guarantee you a "better" work-study job, but it certainly can't hurt.

TAKE ANOTHER LOOK AT WORK-STUDY

With flexible hours, guaranteed pay and the ability to help your institution and community, the work-study option is an attractive way for students to pay for their college education. Do not overlook its benefits. Indicate work-study on your FAFSA® application and apply early. Who knows? You could end up as a tennis racquet stringer at Colorado College. For more information about FWS, go to http://www2.ed.gov/programs/fws/index.html.

Analyzing Financial Aid Award Letters

by Richard Woodland

You have just received the financial aid award letters. Now what? This is the time to do a detailed analysis of each college's offer to help you pay for your child's education. Remember, accepting financial aid is a family matter. More often than not, parents need to borrow money to send their dependent children to college. You need to clearly understand the types of aid you and your child are being offered. How much is "free" money in the form of grants and/or scholarships that does not have to be repaid? If your financial aid award package includes loans, what are the terms and conditions for these loans? A good tool to have with you is the federal government's most recent issue of *Funding Your Education* or *Do You Need Money for College? Federal Student Aid at a Glance,* available from the school's financial aid office or at **studentaid.gov/** This publication is very helpful in explaining the federal grant and loan programs that are usually a part of the aid package.

Let's take a minute to explain what is meant by "financial aid award package." A college will offer an aid applicant a combination of aid types, "packaged" in the form of grants and scholarships, loans, and a work-study job, based on the information provided on the FAFSA® and/or another application. Many schools use a priority filing date, which guarantees that all applications received by this date will be considered for the full range of institutional aid programs available. Late applicants (by even one day!) often are only awarded the basic aid programs from state and federal sources. *It is important to apply on time.*

EVALUATE EACH LETTER

As each award letter comes in, read it through carefully. The following are some critical points to consider:

- **Does the Cost of Attendance (COA) include all projected costs?** Each award letter should state the school's academic year COA. Tuition, fees, room, board, books, transportation, and personal expenses are what normally make up the COA. Does the award letter itemize all these components? Or does it omit some? This is crucial because this is what you will need to budget for. If you need additional information, be sure to contact the financial aid office. They will be glad to provide you with information or answer any questions you may have about their costs.
- **What is your Expected Family Contribution (EFC)?** Is the school's—not just the federal government's—EFC listed on the award letter? Some schools may require a higher EFC than you expected. Be aware that the EFC may increase or decrease each year depending on the information you provide on the renewal FAFSA or other financial aid application.
- **Is there unmet need?** Does the aid package cover the difference between the COA and the EFC? Not every school can cover your full need. If the aid package does not cover your full need, does the information with the award letter provide you with alternative loan options? If not, contact the financial aid office for more information.
- **Is the scholarship renewable for four years?** If your child is awarded a scholarship based on scholastic achievement or talent, you need to ask these questions: Is there a minimum grade point average he has to maintain? Can he switch majors but keep the scholarship? Does he need to participate in an "honors college" program to maintain the scholarship? If he needs to change to part-time status, will the award amount be prorated, or does he need to maintain full-time status? If it is an athletic or "special talent" scholarship, will he continue to receive the award if for some reason he cannot continue with the specific program? Renewal of scholarship funds is often the biggest misunderstanding between families and colleges. Be sure you clearly understand the terms and conditions of all grants and scholarships.
- **What will the college do to your child's award if she receives outside, noninstitutional scholarships?** Will the award be used to cover unmet need or reduce her student loans? Will the college reduce her institutional grants or scholarships? Or will they reduce her work-study award? (This is a good time to compare each school's policy on this matter.) Remember, your overall aid cannot total more than the COA, and many programs cannot exceed your financial need.
- **What are the interest rates of the loans that are offered?** Did another school offer you more than one loan and why? *Do not* sign the award letter until you understand your loan obligations. Again, *Funding Education Beyond High School: The Guide to Federal Student Aid* can be very helpful with this part of the analysis.
- **Is the school likely to cover the same expenses every year?** In particular, ask if grant or scholarship funds are normally reduced or increased after the freshman year, even if family income and EFC remain the same. Some colleges will

increase the self-help (loan, job) percentage every year but not necessarily the free money.

- **If work-study was awarded, how many hours a week will your child be expected to work?** If you feel working that many hours will have a negative impact on your child's academic performance, you may want to request that the awarded job funds be changed to a loan. You must ask immediately because funds are limited. Many schools are flexible with these funds early in the process.
- **What happens if (or more likely, when) tuition increases?** Check with the financial aid office to find out what its policy is for renewing an aid package. If, for example, tuition increases by 5 percent each of the next three years and your EFC remains the same, what will happen to your scholarships, grants, and loans?

You can always appeal your award letter if you feel that your needs are not being met, if your family situation has changed, or if you have received a better award from a competitive school. You have the right to ask for a reconsideration of your award. (Do not use the word *negotiate*.) When asking for reconsideration, be sure to provide the aid officer with all relevant information.

COMPARE LETTERS

After you have received and reviewed all the award letters from the schools your child is considering, the next step is to compare them and determine which schools are offering the best aid packages. Following are three sample award letters and a sample spreadsheet that shows you how to analyze and compare each school's awards.

(Note: These award letters are simply for discussion purposes. They should not be considered to be representative award letters with an EFC of $9,550.)

Once you have entered all the information into a spreadsheet of your own and come up with the balances, here are some things to consider for each school:

- **How much is the balance?** Ideally, your balance should be $0, but look to see which school has the lowest balance amount.
- **What part of the aid package comes in the form of grants and scholarships?** It is important to note this because these awards (gift aid) do not have to be paid back.
- **Look at the loans.** Usually, the best financial deal contains more money in scholarships and less in loan dollars. Based on expected freshman-year borrowing, determine the debt burden at each school once your child graduates. You have to multiply the amount of your loan by four or five years, depending on how long it will take for your child to graduate.

UNIVERSITY A
FINANCIAL AID AWARD LETTER
2019-2020

Date: 4/21/19
ID#: 0000000009

Dear Jane Smith,
We are pleased to inform you that you are eligible to receive the financial assistance indicate in the area labeled "Your Financial Aid." We estimated your budget based on the following assumptions:

In-state resident and living on campus.

	FALL	SPRING	TOTAL
Tuition and Fees	$3,849	$3,849	$7,698
Room & Board	3,769	3,770	7,539
Books	420	420	840
Transportation	973	974	1,947
Personal expenses	369	369	738
Estimated Coast of Attendance	**$9,380**	**$9,382**	**$18,762**

Your Financial Aid

	FALL	SPRING	TOTAL
Federal Pell Grant	$1,950	$1,950	$3,900
Federal Direct Subsidized Loan	$1,750	$1,750	$3,500
State Grant	432	432	864
Total Financial Aid	**$4,132**	**$4,132**	**$8,264**
Unmet Need	**$5,248**	**$5,250**	**$10,498**

What to Do Next:

- Verify that accurate assumptions have been used to determine your awards.
- Carefully review and follow the instructions on the Data Changes Form.
- To reduce or decline all or part of your loans, you must complete and return the Data Changes Form.
- We will assume you fully accept the awards above unless you submit changes to us immediately.
- Return corrections and required documents promptly.
- Retain this letter for your records.

UNIVERSITY B
FINANCIAL AID AWARD LETTER
2019-2020

Date: 4/21/19
ID#: 0000000009

Dear Jane Smith,
We are pleased to inform you that you are eligible to receive the financial assistance indicate in the area labeled "Your Financial Aid." We estimated your budget based on the following assumptions:

Nonresident and living on campus.

	FALL	SPRING	TOTAL
Tuition and Fees	$9,805	$9,085	$18,170
Room & Board	2,835	2,835	5,670
Books	410	410	820
Transportation	875	875	1,750
Personal Expenses	378	377	755
Estimated Coast of Attendance	**$13,583**	**$13,582**	**$27,165**

Your Financial Aid

Lorem ipsur

	FALL	SPRING	TOTAL
Federal Pell Grant	$1,950	$1,950	$3,900
Federal SEOG Grant	225	225	450
Academic Excellence Scholarship	500	500	1,000
Federal Work-Study	1,050	1,050	2,100
Federal Perkins Loan Program	1,250	1,250	2,500
Subsidized Federal Stafford Student Loan	1,750	1,750	3,500
University Student Loan	2,000	2,000	4,000
Total Financial Aid	**$8,725**	**$8,725**	**$17,450**
Unmet Need	**$4,858**	**$4,857**	**$9,715**

What to Do Next:

- Verify that accurate assumptions have been used to determine your awards.
- Carefully review and follow the instructions on the Data Changes Form.
- To reduce or decline all or part of your loans, you must complete and return the Data Changes Form.
- We will assume you fully accept the awards above unless you submit changes to us immediately.
- Return corrections and required documents promptly.
- Retain this letter for your records.

UNIVERSITY C
FINANCIAL AID AWARD LETTER
2019-2020

Date: 4/21/19
ID#: 0000000009

Dear Jane Smith,
We are pleased to inform you that you are eligible to receive the financial assistance indicate in the area labeled "Your Financial Aid." We estimated your budget based on the following assumptions:

Living on campus.

	FALL	SPRING	TOTAL
Tuition and Fees	$14,955	$14,955	$29,910
Room & Board	4,194	4,193	8,387
Books	450	450	900
Transportation	350	350	700
Personal Expenses	1,295	1,293	2,588
Estimated Coast of Attendance	**$21,244**	**$21,241**	**$42,485**

Your Financial Aid

	FALL	SPRING	TOTAL
Institutional Grant	$10,805	$10,805	$21,610
Federal Pell Grant	$1,950	$1,950	$3,900
Federal SEOG Grant	2,000	2,000	4,000
Federal Work-Study Program	1,713	1,712	3,425
Total Financial Aid	**$16,468**	**$16,467**	**$32,935**
Unmet Need	**$4,776**	**$4,774**	**$9,550**

What to Do Next:

- Verify that accurate assumptions have been used to determine your awards.
- Carefully review and follow the instructions on the Data Changes Form.
- To reduce or decline all or part of your loans, you must complete and return the Data Changes Form.
- We will assume you fully accept the awards above unless you submit changes to us immediately.
- Return corrections and required documents promptly.
- Retain this letter for your records.

Comparison Grid

	University A (State University)	University B (Nonresident State University)	University C (Private College)
Cost of Attendance	$18,762	$27,165	$42,485
Tuition and Fees	7,698	18,170	29,910
Room & Board	7,539	5,670	8,367
Books	840	820	900
Transportation	1,947	1,750	700
Personal Expenses	738	755	2,558
Grants and Scholarships	**4,764**	**5,350**	**29,510**
Loans	**3,500**	**10,000**	**0**
Work-Study	**0**	**2,00**	**3,425**
Expected Family Contribution	**9,550**	**9,550**	**9,550**
Balance	**$948**	**$165**	**$0**

Some things to notice:

- At all schools, the federal Pell Grant remains the same.
- The loan amounts varied greatly among these schools.
- Even though University C (a private college) has the highest "sticker price," the net cost is less than the state schools.
- University B is a state university, but you are classified as an out-of-state resident (or nonresident). Many Students in this situation find that the higher out-of-state costs combined with lower grant aid make this a costly decision.
- All schools assume that you will be residing in on-campus housing. But if you choose to commute to University A, you would save a substatial amount because you would not have the $7,539 room and board cost.

And remember that the loan amounts will probably increase each year. You also should take into consideration that you will have to borrow even more as the COA increases each year. To determine the best loan deal, consider:

—What are the terms of the loans?
—What are interest rates?
—Do you pay the yearly interest rate during enrollment or is the interest subsidized or paid by the government?
—Is any money due during enrollment or is it deferred until after graduation? Figuring out how much you will owe at each school at graduation will give you a clear picture of what your financial situation will be after graduation.

However, unless cost is your only concern, you shouldn't simply choose the school offering the lowest loan amounts. Many other factors need to be considered, such as academic and social environment. And you should never reject a school based solely on insufficient financial aid. Consult with an aid administrator to discuss possible alternatives.

Finally, if the college that costs the most is still the one your child wants to attend, there are a number of ways to find money to cover the gap between the aid package and your actual cost, including paying more than the EFC figure, increasing student borrowing, working more hours, and taking out a PLUS loan.

Richard Woodland is Vice President of Development for ProEd Solutions. He previously served as Director of Financial Aid at Rutgers University–Camden and as Director of Student Services and Financial Assistance at the Curtis Institute of Music.

The "Non-Offer"—Dealing With a Low Financial Aid Letter

by Ken O'Connor
Chief Impact Officer, Invite Education

When the last of college financial aid award letters are sent out, plenty of congratulations are in order to families that have their choice school lined up with their funding eligibility ready to go.

But there's a less publicized occurrence that's common as well: the disappointment of realizing that the financial aid awards cannot cover enough of the costs of a preferred college. In certain cases, I call it the "Non-Offer," when a family of modest means applies to a school with the hopes of gaining enough funding to make it affordable, and the school responds with limited awards.

GOING TO A STATE SCHOOL THAT IS OUT OF YOUR STATE

It's often discussed how affordable state schools are in comparison to private schools. But this is not the case when a person wants to attend a state school that is out of their state of residence. In an interesting twist of budgetary fate, state schools looking to boost their revenues may admit many students from out of state, charging them the full out-of-state tuition, plus requiring them to live on campus freshman year. For many state schools, pulling students from out of state is a financial win, practically doubling or even tripling the tuition costs but also leaving one less seat for an in-state student who was hoping to attend locally on discounted (in-state) tuition. Receiving an award letter with a $30,000+ shortfall in the first year adds up to a fair warning. Yes, you are invited to join this school—all you need is enough extra money over four years that could buy a 1-BR, mid-market condo.

UNDERSTANDING THE REAL COST OF STUDENT LOANS

Many 18-year-olds are excited just to get away from their parents and going away to college seems to provide the perfect venue until you take a step back and look at the real costs. I used the 1-BR condo example earlier to help illustrate in real terms *cost versus value.*[1]

Cost is an issue only in the absence of Value: What is most valuable to your child at 18?

Without real-world context, it's simply impossible for teenagers to understand the long-term implications of debt. But they do value independence—or at least the perception of it. To get around this, I use examples of property values, mortgage, and rent payments as the closest comparison to large student loan debt (!).

So, go ahead and run the numbers with a loan calculator. No fancy math required. $120k @ 6% would require payments of around $1,332 per month over ten years and cost about $40,000 in interest. Now look at the student's major. Question: Does this seem at all reasonable for an undergraduate degree from this particular institution? It's tough to justify, but once it's realized that the amount of debt used for their education would be enough to purchase real estate, then the young student at least has some context of their college costs. It's up to them to respond by evaluating this school option accordingly, while parents can more clearly see what they would be cosigning for.

RE-CHART THE COURSE

There's no time for optimism or pessimism when making the final school choice. It's time for *realism* in the decision-making process, given the short time ahead.

Here are three things to consider:

1. **Appeal for additional funding—if there is a legitimate reason to do so.** Real financial aid appeals are necessary due to specific circumstances including, but not limited to, a parent being laid-off, divorce, or a major medical issue and its ensuing expenses. In these types of appeals, documentation is required to prove that the financial need of the family has increased greatly due to such major life circumstances. If you are asking the school for more funding without one of these documentable circumstances, it will not go very far. If your student is looking at a $20,000–$30,000 gap per year without the cash to pay for it, you cannot expect a financial aid office to fund the difference.
2. **Eliminate the options that are not financially feasible.** It's time to say no and entertain the process of elimination. This is tough as some students grow quite attached to a preferred

school choice, but they are going to have to get over it when it's simply unaffordable. Financial discipline is in short supply, but it's needed now more than ever during these uneasy economic times.

3. **Focus on your next simple step forward.** Take the pragmatic approach to affordability and value in higher education. Attend a school close by, and commute from home. Community college is still the go-to option to complete a substantial amount of required college credits while preparing to transfer to a four-year degree institution elsewhere.

What Long-Term Planners Learn From This

The last thing you want is to be stuck between a rock and a hard place, but that's exactly where most middle-income families are when financial aid award letters finally arrive. Avoid this by having these key areas well understood.

- Aptitude: Planning well for college also means honestly accounting for the student's aptitude. Early testing, excellent grades, and incredible mental acuity far above the average can be spotted rather quickly, even before starting high school. There will always be winners on the high end of the intelligence spectrum who have everything to gain from the college admissions process. This is a minority of students, so if your child is not on this level, it's not anyone's fault. It's better to be honest about your child's capabilities than to dream that somehow they will magically receive a perfect on the SAT® or ACT®. In such cases, expect college to remain an expense covered mainly by income, savings, student loans, and perhaps some need-based aid. If it turns out your child is able to earn a scholarship, it's an additional blessing, but good planners know well in advance the odds of qualifying and make up the difference by locating and applying for as many opportunities as they can find.
- Savings: It's cheaper to save than to borrow.[2] Planners remember this every month they contribute to their child's 529 plan by Kindergarten—or perhaps much earlier. They already know college is expensive, and if they, as a parent are already experienced with student loan debt, they may be even more motivated to save so their child can avoid it. College savings are up this past year,[3] with increases in assets and new accounts being opened. This is a good sign, as truly the entire higher education system is dealing with a flux of funding, where state support has dwindled, and the Parent Plus loan[4] may be subject to change in credit-approval criteria in the future. Without any savings, college options are just further limited to scholarship and financial aid eligibility that may or may not be robust when the child finally graduates high school.

REFERENCES

1. *http://www.theatlantic.com/education/archive/2015/10/the-allure-of-the-out-of-state-student/410656/*
2. *https://b2b.inviteeducation.com/2016/04/05/top-5-reasons-for-529/*
3. *http://time.com/money/4259055/saving-more-for-college-529-plan/*
4. *http://www.studentloanborrowerassistance.org/new-rules-plus-loan-credit-checks/*

Ken O'Connor has served parents and students for over fifteen years with high-quality knowledge and information about the college financing process. Ken developed his expertise as a financial aid officer, working face-to-face with families creating college payment strategies. At Invite Education, he continues to help thousands of families make smart college choices through the use of educational planning technology, blending his practical wisdom with in-depth knowledge of the financial aid process. He holds a B.S. an MBA in Finance from Fairleigh Dickinson University in New Jersey.

Parents' and Students' Common Questions Answered

Q ***Are a student's chances of being admitted to a college reduced if the student applies for financial aid?***

A Generally no. Nearly all colleges have a policy of "need-blind" admissions, which means that a student's financial need is not taken into account in the admission decision. There are a few selective colleges, however, that do consider ability to pay before deciding whether or not to admit a student. Some colleges will mention this in their literature; others may not. The best advice is to apply for financial aid if the student needs assistance to attend college.

Q ***Are parents penalized for saving money for college?***

A No. As a matter of fact, families that have made a concerted effort to save money for college are in a much better position than those that have not. For example, a student from a family that has saved money may not have to borrow as much. Furthermore, the "taxing rate" on savings is quite low—only about 5 percent of the parents' assets are assessed and neither the home equity nor retirement savings are included. For example, a single 40-year-old parent who saved $40,000 for college expenses will have about $1,900 counted as part of the parental contribution. Two parents, if the older one is 40 years old (a parent's age factors into the formulation), would have about $300 counted. (Note: The "taxing rate" for student assets is much higher—20 percent—compared to 5 percent for parents.)

Q ***How does the financial aid system work in cases of divorce or separation? How are stepparents treated?***

A In cases of divorce or separation, the financial aid application(s) should be completed by the parent with whom the student lived for the longest period of time in the past twelve months (custodial parent). If the custodial parent has remarried, the stepparent is considered a family member and must complete the application along with the biological parent. If your family has any special circumstances, you should discuss these directly with the financial aid office. (Note: Colleges that award their own aid may ask the noncustodial biological parent to complete a separate aid application and a contribution will be calculated.)

Q ***When are students considered independent of parental support in applying for financial aid?***

A The student must be at least 24 years of age in order to be considered independent. If younger than 24, the student must be married, be a graduate or professional student, have legal dependents other than a spouse, be an orphan or ward of the court, or be a veteran of the armed forces or on active military duty. However, in very unusual situations, students who can clearly document estrangement from their parents can appeal to the financial aid office for additional consideration.

Q ***What can a family do if a job loss occurs?***

A Financial aid eligibility is based on the previous year's income. Currently, the family's 2018 income would be reported to determine eligibility for the 2019–20 academic year. It is possible that that income tax return may not reflect the family's current financial situation, due to a job loss or other hardship. So, families should discuss the situation directly with the financial aid office and be prepared to provide appropriate documentation.

Q ***When my daughter first went to college, we applied for financial aid and were denied because our Expected Family Contribution was too high. Now, my son is a high school senior, and we will soon have two in college. Will we get the same results?***

A The results will definitely be different. Both your son and your daughter should apply. As described earlier, need-based financial aid is based on your Expected Family Contribution, or EFC. When you have two children in college, this amount is divided in half for each child.

Q ***I've heard about the "middle-income squeeze" in regard to financial aid. What is it?***

A The so-called "middle-income squeeze" is the idea that low-income families qualify for aid, high-income families have adequate resources to pay for education, and those in the middle are not eligible for aid but do not have the ability to pay full college costs. There is no provision in the Federal Methodology that treats middle-income students differently than others (such as an income cutoff for eligibility). The Expected Family Contribution rises proportionately as income and assets increase. If a middle-income family does not qualify for aid, it is because the need analysis formula yields a contribution that exceeds college costs. But keep in mind that if a $65,000-income family does not qualify for grant aid at a public university with a $16,000 cost, the same family will likely be eligible for aid at a private college with a cost of $25,000 or more. Also, there are loan programs available to parents and students that are not based on need. Middle-income families should realize, however, that many of the grant programs funded by federal and state governments are directed at lower-income families. It is therefore likely that a larger share of an aid package for a middle-income student will consist of loans rather than grants.

Q ***Given our financial condition, my daughter will be receiving financial aid. We will help out as much as we can, and, in fact, we ourselves will be borrowing. But I am concerned that she will have to take on a lot of loans in order to go to the college of her choice. Does she have any options?***

A She does. If offered a loan, she can decline all or part of it. One option is for her to ask in the financial aid office to have some of the loan changed to a work-study job. If this is not possible, she can find her own part-time work. Often there is an employment office on campus that can help her locate a job. In most cases, the more she works, the less she has to borrow. It is important to remember that the education loans offered to students have very attractive terms and conditions, with flexible repayment options. Students should look upon these loans as a long-term investment that will reap significant rewards.

Q ***What are some easy ways to improve my chances of receiving aid?***

A When filling out your scholarship or financial aid application, it's important to remember that the smallest mistake could hurt your chances for landing free money, or even worse, it could disqualify you completely from an awards contest. Grants and scholarships are highly competitive, so it's a good idea to make a list of what's needed and make sure you have everything before submitting your application. If you are submitting an essay, have another pair of eyes look at it for any spelling and grammar errors. Keep a file on everything you're applying for so that you don't miss any elements of an application. Make sure you're using reputable sites to conduct your free scholarship searches. If you have to pay to apply for an award or look for scholarships, chances are you're being scammed. In a nutshell, the best advice is to follow all directions, and make sure that you meet all deadlines.

In addition, when filling out the FAFSA®, it's important to pay close attention to the details, since any errors may delay the application process. These days, it's preferable to fill out the FAFSA online, since mailed forms can take weeks to process. If you're confused or concerned about something on the application, contact the Federal Student Aid Information Center at 1-800-4FED-AID; questions can also be asked through the FAFSA website. Your college's financial aid office should also be able to assist you. The FAFSA is available this year starting October 1, and it's essential that you don't miss the deadline to apply. The sooner you apply, the sooner you'll know the kind of funding package you are likely to receive, and this will help you determine if you need to apply for any additional aid.

Q ***Is it possible to change your financial aid package?***

A Yes. Most colleges have an appeal process. A request to change a need-based loan to a work-study job is usually approved if funds are available. A request to consider special financial circumstances may also be granted. At most colleges, a request for more grant money is rarely approved unless it is based on a change in the information reported. Applicants should speak with the financial aid office if they have concerns about their financial package. Some colleges may even respond to a competitive appeal, that is, a request to match another college's offer.

Q ***The cost of attending college seems to be going up so much faster than the Consumer Price Index. Why is that, and how can I plan for my child's four years?***

A The cost of higher education cannot be compared to the Consumer Price Index (CPI). The CPI does not take into account most of the costs faced by colleges. For example, the dollars that universities spend on grants and scholarships have risen rapidly. Many universities have increased enrollment of students from less affluent families, further increasing the need for institutional financial aid. Colleges are expected to be on the cutting edge of technology, not only in research but also in the classroom and in the library. Many colleges have deferred needed maintenance and repairs that can now no longer be put off. In addition, there is market pressure to provide many expensive lifestyle amenities that were not expected ten years ago. In general, you can expect that college costs will rise at least 2 to 3 percent faster than inflation.

Q ***I'm struggling with the idea that all students should apply to the college of their choice, regardless of cost, because financial aid will level the playing field. I feel I will be penalized because I have saved for college. My son has been required to save half of his allowance since age six for his college education. Will that count against him when he applies for financial aid? It's difficult to explain to him that his college choices may be limited because of the responsible choices and sacrifices we have made as a family. What can we do to make the most of our situation?***

A In general, it is always better to have planned ahead for college by saving. Families that have put away sufficient funds to pay for college will quickly realize that they have made the burden easier for themselves and their children. In today's college financing world, schools assume that paying for the cost of attendance is a ten-year commitment. So by saving when your child is young, you reap significant advantages from compound interest on the assets and reduce the need to borrow as much while in school. This should reduce the number of years after college that you will be burdened with loans. Families should spend the student's assets first, since the financial aid formulas count these more heavily than parental assets. Then, after the first year, you can explain to the college how you spent these assets, and why you might now need assistance. When looking at parental information, the income of the family is by far the most important component. Contrary to popular belief, parental assets play a minor role in the calculation of need. With this strategy, you have done the right thing, and in the long run, it should prove to be a wise financial plan.

Picking the right college also involves other factors. Students should select the colleges to which they are going to apply in two ways. First, and most important, is to look at colleges that meet your son's academic and lifestyle interests. Most experts will tell him to pick a few "reach" schools (i.e., schools where he is not sure he has the grades and scores required) and at least one or two academically "safe" schools. He should also select one or two financially "safe" schools that you are sure you can afford with either moderate or little financial aid. Most students do not get into all of their first-choice schools, and not everyone can afford the schools to which they are admitted. By working closely with the guidance office in high school and the admissions and financial aid offices at the college, you can maximize your options.

Q ***My son was awarded a $2,500 scholarship. This can be split and used for two years. When filling out the FAFSA, do we have to claim the full amount, or just the $1,250 he plans to use the first year?***

A Congratulations to your son on the scholarship. Nowhere on the FAFSA® should you report this scholarship. It is not considered income or an asset. However, once you choose a school to attend, you must notify the financial aid office for its advice on how to take the funds. But remember, do NOT report it on the FAFSA.

Q ***I will be receiving a scholarship from my local high school. How will this scholarship be treated in my financial aid award?***

A Federal student aid regulations specify that all forms of aid must be included within the defined level of need. This means that additional aid, such as outside scholarships, must be combined with any need-based aid you receive; it may not be kept separate and used to reduce your family's contribution. If the college has not filled 100 percent of your need, it will usually allow outside scholarships to close the gap. Once your total need has been met, the college must reduce other aid and replace it with the outside award. Most colleges will allow you to use some, if not all, of an outside scholarship to replace self-help aid (loans and Federal Work-Study Program awards) rather than grant aid.

Q ***Is there enough aid available to make it worthwhile for me to consider colleges that are more expensive than I can afford?***

A Definitely. More than $100 billion in aid is awarded to undergraduates every year. With more than half of all enrolled students qualifying for some type of assistance, this totals more than $5,500 per student. You should view financial aid as a large, national system of tuition discounts, some given according to a student's ability and talent, others based on what a student's family can afford to pay. If you qualify for need-based financial aid, you will essentially pay only your calculated family contribution, regardless of the cost of the college. You will not pay the "sticker price" (the cost of attendance listed in the college catalog) but a lower rate that is reduced by the amount of aid you receive. No college should be ruled out until after financial aid is considered. In addition, when deciding which college to attend, consider that the short-term cost of a college education is only one criterion. If the college meets your educational needs and you are convinced it can launch you on an exciting career, a significant up-front investment may turn out to be a bargain over the long run.

Q ***If I don't qualify for need-based aid, what options are available?***

A You should try to put together your own aid package to help reduce your parents' share. There are three sources to look into. First, search for merit scholarships. Second, seek employment, during both the summer and the academic year. The student employment office should be able to help you find a campus job. Third, look into borrowing. Even if you don't qualify for the need-based loan programs, the unsubsidized Federal Direct Loan is available to all students. The terms and conditions are the same as the subsidized loan programs except that interest accrues while you are in college.

After you have contributed what you can through scholarships, employment, and loans, your parents will be faced with their share of the college bill. Many colleges have monthly payment plans that allow families to spread their payments over the academic year. If these monthly payments turn out to be more than your parents can afford, they can take out a parent loan. By borrowing from the college itself, from a commercial agency or lender, or through PLUS, your parents can extend the payments over a ten-year period or longer. Borrowing reduces the monthly obligation to its lowest level, but the total amount paid will be the highest due to principal and interest payments. Before making a decision on where to borrow parental loan funds, be sure to first check with the financial aid office to determine what is the best source of alternative funds.

Q ***After applying to college and receiving a financial award letter, am I able to back out of attending if I can't afford it?***

A Of course! This actually happens quite often. If you end up not being able to afford the college you applied to, don't worry. The first step would be to contact the financial aid office just to make sure the award is accurate and there aren't any other ways to cover the costs of attendance, for example a scholarship and/or grant. You never know what may have been missed in the initial application.

Second, if there aren't any other funds that can be awarded, send the admissions office an e-mail letting them know you won't be able to attend, thanking them for their time. They will greatly appreciate your e-mail, and it will help to stay on good terms with the school if you decide to apply again. Never burn bridges!

How to Use This Guide

QUICK-REFERENCE CHART

The amount of aid available at colleges can vary greatly. "College Costs At-a-Glance" lists the percent of freshmen who applied for and received need-based gift aid and the percent of those whose need was fully met. Also listed are the average freshman financial aid package, the average cost after aid, and the average indebtedness upon graduation.

PROFILES OF COLLEGE FINANCIAL AID PROGRAMS

After the federal government, colleges provide the largest amount of financial aid to students. In addition, they control most of the money channeled to students from the federal government. The amount and makeup of your financial aid package will depend on the institution's particular circumstances and its decisions concerning your application. The main section of this book shows you the pattern and extent of each college's current awards. The profiles present detailed factual and statistical data for each school in a uniform format to enable easy, quick references and comparisons. Items that could not be collected in time for publication for specific institutions do not appear in those institutions' profiles. Colleges that supplied no data are listed by name and address only so that you do not overlook them in your search for colleges.

There is much anecdotal evidence that students and their families fail to apply for financial aid under the misconception that student aid goes only to poor families. Financial need in the context of college expenses is not the same as being needy in the broad social context. Middle-class families typically qualify for need-based financial aid; at expensive schools, even upper-middle income families can qualify for need-based financial aid. Peterson's encourages you to apply for financial aid whether or not you think that you will qualify.

To help you understand the definition and significance of each item, the following outline of the profile format explains what is covered in each section. The term college or colleges is frequently used throughout to refer to any institution of higher education, regardless of its official definition.

The College

The name of the college is the official name as it appears on the institution's charter. The city and state listed are the official location of the school. The subhead line shows tuition and required fees, as they were charged to the majority of full-time undergraduate students in the 2018–19 academic year. Any exceptions to the 2018–19 academic year are so noted. For a public institution, the tuition and fees shown are for state residents, and this is noted. If a college's annual expenses are expressed as a comprehensive fee (including full-time tuition, mandatory fees, and college room and board), this is noted, as are any unusual definitions, such as tuition only. The average undergraduate aid package is the average total package of grant, loan, and work-study aid that was awarded to meet the officially defined financial need of full-time undergraduates enrolled in fall 2017 (or fall 2016) who applied for financial aid, were determined to have need, and then actually received financial aid. This information appears in more detail in each profile.

About the Institution

This paragraph gives the reader a brief introduction to a college. It contains the following elements:

Institutional Control

Private institutions are designated as *independent* (nonprofit), *independent/religious* (sponsored by or affiliated with a religious group or having a nondenominational or interdenominational religious orientation), or *proprietary* (profit-making). Public institutions are designated by their primary source of support, such as *federal, state, commonwealth* (Puerto Rico), *territory* (U.S. territories), *county, district* (an administrative unit of public education, often having boundaries different from those of units of local government), *state-and locally-supported* ("locally" refers to county, district, or city), *state-supported* (funded by the state), or *state-related* (funded primarily by the state but administered autonomously).

Type of Student Body

The categories are *men* (100 percent of student body), *coed-primarily men, women* (100 percent of student body), *coed-primarily women*, and *coed*. A few schools are designated as *undergraduate: women only, graduate: coed* or *undergraduate: men only, graduate: coed.*

Degrees Awarded

Associate, bachelor's (baccalaureate), *master's, doctoral* (doctorate), and *first professional* (in such fields as law and medicine). There are no institutions in this book that award the associate degree only. Many award the bachelor's as the highest degree.

Number of Undergraduate Majors

This shows the number of academic fields in which the institution offers associate and/or bachelors degrees. The purpose of this is to give you an indication of the range of subjects available.

Enrollment

These figures are based on the actual number of full-time and part-time students enrolled in degree programs as of fall 2018 (or 2017 if the 2018 figure was not available). In most instances, they are designated as *total enrollment* (for the specific college or university) and *freshmen*. If the institution is a university and its total enrollment figure includes graduate students, a separate figure for *undergraduates* may be provided. If the profiled institution is a subunit of a university, the figures may be designated *total university enrollment* for the entire university and *total unit enrollment* for the specific subunit.

Methodology Used for Determining Need

Private colleges usually have larger financial aid programs, but public colleges usually have lower sticker prices, especially for in-state or local students. At a public college, your financial need will be less, and you will receive a smaller financial aid package. This note on whether a college uses federal (FAFSA) or institutional methodology (usually CSS/Financial Aid PRO-FILE®) will let you know whether you will have to complete one or two kinds of financial aid application forms. Federal Methodology is the needs-analysis formula used by the U.S. Department of Education to determine the Expected Family Contribution (EFC), which, when subtracted from the cost of attendance at an institution, determines the financial need of a student. There is no relative advantage or disadvantage to using one methodology over the other.

Undergraduate Expenses

If provided by the institution, the one-time application fee is listed. Costs are given for the 2019-2020 academic year or for the 2018–19 academic year if 2019-2020 figures were not yet available. (Peterson's collects information for freshmen specifically.) Annual expenses may be expressed as a comprehensive fee (including full-time tuition, mandatory fees, and college room and board) or may be given as separate figures for full-time tuition, fees, room and board, or room only. For public institutions where tuition differs according to state residence, separate figures are given for area or state residents and for nonresidents. Part-time tuition is expressed in terms of a per-unit rate (per credit, per semester hour, etc.), as specified by the institution.

The tuition structure at some institutions is complex. Freshmen and sophomores may be charged a different rate from that charged juniors and seniors, a professional or vocational division may have a different fee structure from the liberal arts division of the same institution, or part-time tuition may be prorated on a sliding scale according to the number of credit hours taken. Tuition and fees may vary according to academic program, campus/location, class time (day, evening, weekend), course/credit load, course level, degree level, reciprocity agreements, and student level. If tuition and fees differ for international students, the rate charged is listed.

Room and board charges are reported as a double occupancy and nineteen meals per week plan or the equivalent and may vary according to board plan selected, campus/location, gender, type of housing facility, or student level. If no college-owned or -operated housing facilities are offered, the phrase *college housing not available* will appear.

If a college offers a *guaranteed tuition* plan, it promises that the tuition rate of an entering student will not increase for the entire term of enrollment, from entrance to graduation. Other payment plans might include *tuition prepayment*, which allows an entering student to lock in the current tuition rate for the entire term of enrollment by paying the full amount in advance rather than year by year, and *installment* and *deferred payment* plans, which allow students to delay the payment of the full tuition.

Guaranteed tuition and tuition prepayment help you to plan the total cost of education and can save you from the financial distress sometimes caused by tuition hikes. Colleges that offer such plans may also help you to arrange financing, which in the long run can cost less than the total of four years of increasing tuition rates. Deferred payment or installment payments may better fit your personal financial situation, especially if you do not qualify for financial aid and, due to other financial commitments, find that obtaining the entire amount due is burdensome. Carefully investigate these plans, however, to see what premium you may pay at the end to allow you to defer immediate payment.

Freshman Financial Aid

Usually, these are actual figures for the 2018-19 term, beginning in fall; figures may also be estimated for the 2019-2020 term. The particular term for which these data apply is indicated. The figures are for degree-seeking full-time freshman students. The first figure is the number of freshmen who applied for any kind of financial aid. The next figure is the percentage of those freshmen financial aid applicants who were determined to have financial need—that is, through the formal needs-assessment process, had a calculated expected family contribution that was less than the total college cost. The next figure is the percentage of this group of eligible freshmen who received any financial aid. The next figure is the percentage of this preceding group of eligible aid recipients whose need was fully met by financial aid. The *Average percent of need met* is the average percentage of financial need met for freshmen who received any need-based aid. The *Average financial aid package* is the average dollar amount awarded (need-based or non-need-based) to freshmen who applied for aid, were deemed eligible, and received any aid; awards used to reduce the expected family contribution are excluded from this average. The final line in most profiles is the percentage of freshmen who had no financial need but who received non-need-based aid other than athletic scholarships or special-group tuition benefits.

What do these data mean to you? If financial aid is important in your comparison of colleges, the relative percentage of students who received any aid, whose need was fully met, and the average percentage of need met have the most weight. These figures reflect the relative abundance of student aid available to the average eligible applicant. The average dollar amount of the aid package has real meaning, but only in relation to the college's expense; you will be especially interested in the difference between this figure and the costs figure, which is what the average student (in any given statistical group, there actually may be no average individual) will have to pay. Of course, if the financial aid package is largely loans rather than grants, you will have to pay this amount eventually. Relative differences in the figures of the number of students who apply for aid and who are deemed eligible can hinge on any number of factors: the relative sticker price of the college, the relative level of wealth of the students' families, the proportion of only children in college and students with siblings in college (families with two or more children in college are more likely to apply for aid and be considered eligible), or the relative sophistication in financial aid matters (or quality of college counseling they may have received) of the students and their families. While these may be interesting, they will not mean too much to most students and families. If you are among the unlucky (or, perhaps, lucky) families who do not qualify for need-based financial aid, the final sentence of this paragraph in the profile will be of interest because it reveals the relative policies that the college has in distributing merit-based aid to students who cannot demonstrate need.

Undergraduate Financial Aid

This is the parallel paragraph to the Freshman Financial Aid paragraph. The same definitions apply, except that the group being considered is degree-seeking full-time undergraduate students (including freshmen).

There are cases of students who chose a particular college because they received a really generous financial aid package in their freshman year and then had to scramble to pay the tuition bill in their later years. If a financial aid package is a key factor in the decision to attend a particular college, you want to be certain that the package offered to all undergraduates is not too far from that offered to freshmen. The key figures are those for the percentage of students who received any aid, the percentage of financial aid recipients whose need was fully met, the average percentage of need met, and the dollar figure of the average financial aid package. Generally, colleges assume that after the freshman year, students develop study habits and time-management skills that will allow them to take on part-time and summer employment without hurting their academic performance. So, the proportion of self-help aid (work-study and student loans) in the financial aid package tends to increase after the freshman year. This pattern, which is true of most colleges, can be verified in the freshman-undergraduate figures in the paragraph on Gift Aid (Need-Based).

Gift Aid (Need-Based)

Total amount is the total dollar figure in 2018-19 (estimated) or 2017–18 (actual) of need-based scholarships and grant (gift) aid awarded to degree-seeking full-time and part-time students that was used to meet financial need. The percentages of this aid from federal, state, institutional (college or university), and external (e.g., foundations, civic organizations, etc.) sources are shown. *Receiving aid* shows the percentages (and number, in parentheses) of freshmen and of all undergraduates who applied for aid, were considered eligible, and received any need-based gift aid. *Average award* is the average dollar amount of awards to freshmen and all undergraduates who applied for aid, were considered eligible, and received any need-based gift aid. *Scholarships, grants, and awards* cites major categories of need-based gift aid provided by the college; these include Federal Pell Grants, Federal Supplemental Educational Opportunity Grants (FSEOG), state scholarships, private scholarships, college/university gift aid from institutional funds, United Negro College Fund aid, Federal Nursing Scholarships, and others.

Scholarships and grants are gifts awarded to students that do not need to be repaid. These are preferable to loans, which have to be repaid, or work-study wages, which may take time away from studies and personal pursuits. The total amount of need-based gift aid has to be placed into the context of the total number of undergraduate students (shown in the About the Institution paragraph) and the relative expense of the institution. Filing the FAFSA automatically puts you in line to receive any available federal grants for which you may qualify. However, if the college being considered has a higher than usual proportion of gift aid coming from state, institutional, or external sources, be sure to check with the financial aid office to find out what these sources may be and how to apply for them. For almost all colleges, the percentage of freshmen receiving need-based gift aid will be higher than the percentage of all undergraduates receiving need-based gift aid. However, if you are dependent on need-based gift aid and the particular college under consideration shows a sharper drop from the freshman to undergraduate years than other colleges of a similar type, you might want to think about how this change will affect your ability to pay for later years at this college.

Gift Aid (Non-Need-Based)

Total amount is the total dollar figure in 2018-19 (estimated) or 2017-18 (actual) of non-need-based scholarships and grant (gift) aid awarded to degree-seeking full-time and part-time students. Non-need-based aid that was used to meet financial need is not included in this total. The percentages of this aid from federal, state, institutional (college or university), and external (e.g., National Merit Scholarships, civic, religious, fraternal organizations, etc.) sources are shown. *Receiving aid* shows the percentages (and number, in parentheses) of freshmen and of all undergraduates who were determined to have need and received non-need-based gift aid. *Average award* is the average dollar amount of awards to freshmen and all undergraduates determined to have no need but received non-need-based awards. *Scholarships, grants, and awards by category* cites the major categories in which non-need-based awards are available and the number of awards made in that category (in parentheses, the total dollar value of these awards). The categories listed are *Academic interests/achievement*, *Creative arts/performance*, *Special achievements/activities*, and *Special characteristics. Tuition waivers* indicate special categories of students (minority students, children of alumni, college employees or children of employees, adult students, and senior citizens) who may qualify for a full or partial waiver of tuition. *ROTC* indicates Army, Naval, and Air Force ROTC programs that are offered on campus; a program offered by arrangement on another campus is indicated by the word *cooperative*.

This section covers college-administered scholarships awarded to undergraduates on the basis of merit or personal attributes without regard to need. If you do not qualify for financial aid but nevertheless lack the resources to pay for college, non-need-based awards will be of special interest to you. Some personal characteristics are completely beyond an individual's control, and talents and achievements take a number of years to develop or attain. However, certain criteria for these awards, such as religious involvement, community service, and special academic interests can be attained in a relatively brief period of time. ROTC programs offer such benefits as tuition, the cost of textbooks, and living allowances. In return, you must fulfill a service obligation after graduating from college. Because they can be a significant help in paying for college, these programs have become quite competitive. Certain subject areas, such as nursing, health care, or the technical fields, are in stronger demand than others. Among the obligations to consider about ROTC are that you must spend a regular portion of your available time in military training programs and that ROTC entails a multiyear commitment after your graduation to serve as an officer in the armed services branch sponsoring the program.

Loans

The figures here represent loans that are part of the financial aid award package. *Student loans* represents the total dollar amount of loans from all sources to full-time and part-time degree-seeking undergraduates or their parents. *Average need-based loan* represents the percentage of these loans that goes to meet financial need, and the percentage that goes to pay the non-need portion (the expected family contribution) are indicated. The percentage of a past graduating class who borrowed through any loan program (except parent loans) while enrolled at the college is shown, as is the average dollar figure per-borrower of cumulative undergraduate indebtedness (this does not include loans from other institutions). *Parent loans* shows the total amount borrowed through parent loan programs as well as the percentages that were applied to the need-based and non-needbased portions of financial need. *Programs* indicates the major loan programs available to undergraduates. These include Direct Student Loans (subsidized and unsubsidized and PLUS), Perkins Loans, Federal Nursing Loans, state loans, college/university loans, and other types.

Note: As a result of the Health Care and Education Reconciliation Act, as of July 1, 2010, federal student loans are no longer made by private lenders under the Federal Family Education Loan (FFEL) Program. Instead, all new federal student loans come directly from the U.S. Department of Education under the Direct Loan Program. Any FFEL loans noted in this section of an institution's profile are no longer available.

Loans are forms of aid that must be repaid with interest. Most people will borrow money to pay college costs. The loans available through financial aid programs are offered at very favorable interest rates. In comparing colleges, the dollar amount of total indebtedness is a factor to be considered. Typically, this amount would increase proportionate to the tuition. However, if it does not, this could mean that the college provides relatively generous grant or work-study aid rather than loans in its financial aid package.

Work-Study

The total dollar amounts, number, and average dollar amount of *Federal work-study* (FWS) jobs appear first. The total dollar figure of *State or other work-study/employment*, if available, is shown, as is the percentage of those dollars that go to meet financial need. The number of part-time jobs available on campus to undergraduates, other than work-study, is shown last.

FWS is a federally funded program that enables students with demonstrated need to earn money by working on or off campus, usually in a nonprofit organization. FWS jobs are a special category of jobs that are open to students only through the financial aid office. Other kinds of part-time jobs are routinely available at most colleges and may vary widely. In comparing colleges, you may find characteristic differences in how the "self-help" amounts (loans and work-study) are apportioned.

Athletic Awards

The total dollar amount of athletic scholarships given by the college to undergraduate students, including percentages that are need-based and non-need-based, is indicated.

Applying for Financial Aid

Required financial aid forms include the FAFSA (Free Application for Federal Student Aid), the institution's own form, CSS/Financial Aid PROFILE, a state aid form, a noncustodial (divorced/separated) parent's statement, a business/farm supplement, and others. The college's financial aid application deadline is noted as the *Financial aid deadline* and is shown in one of three ways: as a specific date if it is an absolute deadline; noted as *continuous*, which means processing goes on without a deadline or until all available aid has been awarded; or as a date with the note *(priority)*, meaning that you are encouraged to apply before that date in order to have the best chance of obtaining aid. *Notification date* is listed as either a specific date or *continuous*. The date by which a reply to the college with the decision to accept or decline its financial aid package is listed as either a specific date or as a number of weeks from the date of notification.

Be prepared to check early with the colleges as to exactly which forms will be required. All colleges require the FAFSA for students applying for federal aid. In most cases, colleges have a limited amount of funds set aside to use as financial aid. It is possible that the first eligible students will get a larger share of what is available.

Contact

The name, title, address, telephone and fax numbers, and e-mail address of the person to contact for further information (student financial aid contact) are given at the end of the profile. You should feel free to write or call for any materials you need or if you have questions.

APPENDIX

This section lists nearly 300 state-specific grants and loans. Award amounts, number of awards, eligibility requirements, application requirements, and deadlines are given for all programs.

INDEXES

Six indexes in the back of the book allow you to search for particular award programs based on the following criteria:

Non-Need Scholarships for Undergraduates

This index lists the colleges that report that they offer scholarships based on academic interests, abilities, achievements, or personal characteristics other than financial need. Specific categories appear in alphabetical order under the following broad groups:

- Academic Interests/Achievements
- Creative Arts/Performance
- Special Achievements/Activities
- Special Characteristics

See the index for specific categories in each group.

Athletic Grants for Undergraduates

This index lists the colleges that report offering scholarships on the basis of athletic abilities.

Co-op Programs

This index lists colleges that report offering cooperative education programs. These are formal arrangements with off-campus employers that are designed to allow students to combine study and work, often in a position related to the student's field of study. Salaries typically are set at regular marketplace levels, and academic credit is often given.

ROTC Programs

This index lists colleges that offer Reserve Officers' Training Corps programs. The index is arranged by the branch of service that sponsors the program.

Tuition Waivers

This index lists colleges that report offering full or partial tuition waivers for certain categories of students. A majority of colleges offer tuition waivers to employees or children of employees.

Because this benefit is so common and the affected employees usually are aware of it, no separate index of schools offering this option is provided. However, this information is included in the individual college profiles.

Tuition Payment Alternatives

This index lists colleges that report offering tuition payment alternatives. These payment alternatives include deferred payment plans, guaranteed tuition plans, installment payment plans, and prepayment plans.

DATA COLLECTION PROCEDURES

The data contained in the college chart, profiles, and indexes were collected in winter and spring 2019 through *Peterson's Annual Survey of Undergraduate Financial Aid* and *Peterson's Annual Survey of Undergraduate Institutions.* Questionnaires were sent to the more than 4,100 institutions of higher education that are accredited in the United States and U.S. territories and offer full four- or five-year baccalaureate degrees via full-time on-campus programs of study. Officials at the colleges—usually financial aid or admission officers but sometimes registrars or institutional research staff members—completed and returned the forms. Peterson's has every reason to believe that the data presented in this book are accurate. However, students should always confirm costs and other facts with a specific school at the time of application, since colleges can and do change policies and fees whenever necessary.

The state aid data presented in *Peterson's How to Get Money for College* was submitted by state officials (usually the director of the state scholarship commission) to Peterson's in the spring of 2019. Because regulations for any government-sponsored program may be changed at any time, you should request written descriptive materials from the office administering a program in which you are interested.

CRITERIA FOR INCLUSION IN THIS BOOK

To be included in this guide, an institution must have full accreditation or be a candidate for accreditation (preaccreditation) status by an institutional or specialized accrediting body recognized by the U.S. Department of Education or the Council for Higher Education Accreditation (CHEA). Institutional accrediting bodies, which review each institution as a whole, include the six regional associations of schools and colleges (Middle States, New England, North Central, Northwest, Southern, and Western), each of which is responsible for a specified portion of the United States and its territories. Other institutional accrediting bodies are national in scope and accredit specific kinds of institutions (e.g., Bible colleges, independent colleges, and rabbinical and Talmudic schools). Program registration by the New York State Board of Regents is considered to be the equivalent of institutional accreditation, since the board requires that all programs offered by an institution meet its standards before recognition is granted. There are recognized specialized or professional accrediting bodies in more than forty different fields, each of which is authorized to accredit institutions or specific programs in its particular field. For specialized institutions that offer programs in one field only, we designate this to be the equivalent of institutional accreditation. A full explanation of the accrediting process and complete information on recognized, institutional (regional and national) and specialized accrediting bodies can be found online at www.chea.org or at www.ed.gov/admins/finaid/accred/index.html.

Quick-Reference Chart

College Costs At-a-Glance

by Michael Steidel

Dean of Admission, Carnegie Mellon University

To help shed some light on the typical patterns of financial aid offered by colleges, we have prepared the following chart. This chart can help you to better understand financial aid practices in general, form realistic expectations about the amounts of aid that might be provided by specific colleges or universities and prepare for meaningful discussions with the financial aid officers at colleges being considered. The data appearing in the chart have been supplied by the schools themselves and are also shown in the individual college profiles.

Tuition and fees are based on the total of full-time tuition and mandatory fees for the 2016–2017 academic year or for the 2015–2016 academic year if 2016–2017 figures are not available. More information about these costs, as well as the costs of room and board and the year for which they are current, can be found in the individual college profiles. For institutions that have two or more tuition rates for different categories of students or types of programs, the lowest rate is used in figuring the cost.

The colleges are listed alphabetically by state. An "NR" in any individual column indicates that the applicable data element was "Not Reported."

The chart is divided into eight columns of information for each college:

1. Institutional Control
Whether the school is independent (ind.), including independent, independent–religious, and proprietary, or public (pub.), including federal, state, commonwealth, territory, county, district, city, state, local, and state-related.

2. Tuition and Fees
Based on the total of full-time tuition and mandatory fees. An asterisk indicates that the school includes room and board in their mandatory fees.

3. Room and Board
If a school has room and board costs that vary according to the type of accommodation and meal plan, either the lowest figures are represented or the figures are for the most common room arrangement and a full meal plan. If a school has only housing arrangements, a dagger appears to the right of the number. An "NA" will appear in this column if no college-owned or -operated housing facilities are offered.

4. Percent of Eligible Freshmen Receiving Need-Based Gift Awards
Calculated by dividing the number of freshman students determined to have need who received need-based gift aid by the number of full-time freshmen.

5. Percent of Freshmen Whose Need Was Fully Met
Calculated by dividing the number of freshman students whose financial need was fully met by the number of freshmen with need.

6. Average Financial Aid Package for Freshmen
The average dollar amount from all sources, including *gift aid* (scholarships and grants) and *self-help* (jobs and loans), awarded to freshmen receiving aid. Note that this aid package may exceed tuition and fees if the average aid package included coverage of room and board expenses.

7. Average Net Cost After Aid
Average aid package subtracted from published costs (tuition, fees, room, and board) to produce what the average student will have to pay.

8. Average Indebtedness Upon Graduation
Average per-student indebtedness of graduating seniors.

Because personal situations vary widely, it is very important to note that an individual's aid package can be quite different from the averages. Moreover, the data shown for each school can fluctuate widely from year to year, depending on the number of applicants, the amount of need to be met, and the financial resources and policies of the college. Peterson's intent in presenting this chart is to provide you with useful facts and figures that can serve as general guidelines in the pursuit of financial aid. We caution you to use the data only as a jumping-off point for further investigation and analysis, not as a means to rank or select colleges.

After you have narrowed down the choice of colleges based on academic and personal criteria, we recommend that you carefully study this chart. From it, you can develop a list of questions for financial aid officers at the colleges under serious consideration. Here are just a few questions you might want to ask: About the Institution

- What are the specific types and sources of aid provided to freshmen at this school?
- What factors does this college consider in determining whether a financial aid applicant is qualified for its need-based aid programs?
- How does the college determine the combination of types of aid that make up an individual's package?
- How are non-need-based awards treated: as a part of the aid package or as a part of the parental/family contribution?
- Does this school "guarantee" financial aid and, if so, how is its policy implemented? Guaranteed aid means that, by policy, 100 percent of need is met for all students judged to

have need. Implementation determines *how* need is met and varies widely from school to school. For example, grade point average may determine the apportioning of scholarship, loan, and work-study aid. Rules for freshmen may be different from those for upperclass students.

- To what degree is the admission process "need-blind"? Need-blind means that admission decisions are made without regard to the student's need for financial aid.
- What are the norms and practices for upperclass students? Peterson's chart presents information on *freshmen* financial aid only; however, the financial aid office should be able and willing to provide you with comparable figures for upperclass students. A college might offer a wonderful package for the freshman year, then leave students mostly on their own to fund the remaining three years. Or the school may provide a higher proportion of scholarship money for freshmen, then rebalance its aid packages to contain more self-help aid (loans and work-study) in upperclass years. There is an assumption that, all other factors being equal, students who have settled into the pattern of college time management can handle more work-study hours than freshmen. Grade point average, tuition increases, changes in parental financial circumstances, and other factors may also affect the redistribution.

College Costs At-a-Glance

	Institutional Control ind.=independent; pub.=public	Tuition and Fees	Room and Board	Percent of Eligible Freshmen Receiving Need-Based Gift Awards	Percent of Freshmen Whose Need Was Fully Met	Average Financial Aid Package for Freshmen	Average Net Cost After Aid	Average Indebtedness Upon Graduation
Alabama								
Athens State University	pub.	$7710	NA	NR	NR	NR	NR	NR
Auburn University	pub.	$11,492	$13,600	86%	17%	$11,161	$13,931	$29,331
Auburn University at Montgomery	pub.	$8860	$7268	94%	5%	$9175	$6953	$30,138
Jacksonville State University	pub.	$11,120	$8000	50%	NR	$10,116	$9004	NR
Samford University	ind.	$32,850	$10,980	100%	26%	$21,938	$21,892	$29,676
Spring Hill College	ind.	$40,648	$13,652	82%	18%	$27,808	$26,492	NR
Talladega College	ind.	$13,846	$6655	97%	7%	$19,708	$793	$41,300
The University of Alabama	pub.	$10,780	$10,836	82%	24%	$15,518	$6098	$34,975
The University of Alabama at Birmingham	pub.	$10,710	$10,910	56%	21%	$11,168	$10,452	$29,941
University of Mobile	ind.	$23,860	$9700	61%	27%	$28,622	$4938	$22,872
University of Montevallo	pub.	$13,710	$9810	98%	22%	$13,194	$10,326	$29,968
University of North Alabama	pub.	$10,800	$7830	48%	32%	$8827	$9803	$29,021
The University of West Alabama	pub.	$10,990	$7510	71%	NR	$9596	$8904	$24,408
Alaska								
University of Alaska Fairbanks	pub.	$10,308	$10,440	94%	20%	$9321	$11,427	$26,406
University of Alaska Southeast	pub.	$7560	$8900	83%	26%	$19,272	—	$33,869
Arizona								
Arizona Christian University	ind.	$30,624	$12,000	98%	14%	$8347	$34,277	NR
Arizona State University at the Downtown Phoenix campus	pub.	$11,338	$14,924	98%	22%	$18,271	$7991	$25,136
Arizona State University at the Polytechnic campus	pub.	$10,803	$12,728	97%	19%	$14,555	$8976	$26,096
Arizona State University at the Tempe campus	pub.	$11,338	$13,164	99%	24%	$17,745	$6757	$23,711
Arizona State University at the West campus	pub.	$10,803	$11,914	99%	13%	$15,977	$6740	$25,021
Northern Arizona University	pub.	$11,896	$10,780	70%	18%	$15,061	$7615	$23,560
The University of Arizona	pub.	$12,379	$13,050	97%	20%	$16,301	$9128	$26,414
Arkansas								
John Brown University	ind.	$27,668	$9456	86%	25%	$22,238	$14,886	$25,593
Lyon College	ind.	$29,140	$9630	100%	23%	$22,473	$16,297	$5912
Ouachita Baptist University	ind.	$27,900	$8000	98%	55%	$28,780	$7120	$24,157
University of Arkansas	pub.	$9384	$11,330	83%	16%	$9715	$10,999	$27,123
University of Central Arkansas	pub.	$9188	$7198	NR	NR	NR	NR	NR
California								
Academy of Art University	ind.	$30,630	$18,386	87%	3%	$12,413	$36,603	$31,360
Biola University	ind.	$53,490	$11,514	100%	15%	$26,680	$38,324	$36,330
California Baptist University	ind.	$36,340	$12,600	100%	23%	$23,305	$25,635	$36,383
California Christian College	ind.	$10,050	$6750	100%	NR	$16,229	$571	NR
California Institute of Technology	ind.	$54,600	$16,644	100%	100%	$51,195	$20,049	$20,192
California Lutheran University	ind.	$45,982	$14,595	100%	18%	$35,900	$24,677	$31,000
California Polytechnic State University, San Luis Obispo	pub.	$9943	$14,208	95%	11%	$10,459	$13,692	$22,411
California State Polytechnic University, Pomona	pub.	$7396	$15,791	80%	2%	$9700	$13,487	$21,730
California State University, Chico	pub.	$23,418	$13,422	97%	13%	$12,422	$24,418	$5894

NA = not applicable; NR = not reported; * = includes room and board; † = room only; — = not available.

College Costs At-a-Glance

	Institutional Control ind.=independent; pub.=public	Tuition and Fees	Room and Board	Percent of Eligible Freshmen Receiving Need-Based Gift Awards	Percent of Freshmen Whose Need Was Fully Met	Average Financial Aid Package for Freshmen	Average Net Cost After Aid	Average Indebtedness Upon Graduation
California State University, Dominguez Hills	pub.	$8140	$13,984	91%	1%	$6029	$16,095	$14,585
California State University, Fullerton	pub.	$8108	NR	97%	15%	$10,480	$11,612	$7665
California State University, Long Beach	pub.	$6846	$13,070	84%	59%	$12,617	$7299	$18,686
California State University, Los Angeles	pub.	$6768	$15,992	99%	3%	$12,515	$10,245	$13,458
California State University, Monterey Bay	pub.	$7143	$13,711	84%	14%	$11,828	$9026	$19,859
California State University, Northridge	pub.	$8554	$16,188	NR	NR	$11,731	$13,011	NR
California State University, Sacramento	pub.	$7368	$15,224	95%	15%	$10,331	$12,261	$23,460
California State University, San Bernardino	pub.	$6956	$13,435	99%	9%	$10,735	$9656	$18,294
California State University, San Marcos	pub.	$25,164*	$13,150	94%	5%	$11,020	$27,294	$23,725
California State University, Stanislaus	pub.	$7584	$10,950	98%	9%	$16,819	$1715	$17,952
Chapman University	ind.	$54,924	$15,518	92%	17%	$39,214	$31,228	$27,117
Charles R. Drew University of Medicine and Science	ind.	$17,440	NA	100%	4%	$19,478	—	NR
Claremont McKenna College	ind.	$56,475	$17,300	98%	100%	$60,818	$12,957	$21,450
Dominican University of California	ind.	$47,870	$15,634	100%	10%	$34,767	$28,737	$31,978
Harvey Mudd College	ind.	$58,660	$18,679	97%	100%	$50,030	$27,309	$29,139
Hope International University	ind.	$34,450	$11,050	54%	22%	$15,570	$29,930	$35,427
Humboldt State University	pub.	$7780	$13,562	96%	8%	$14,670	$6672	$23,028
La Sierra University	ind.	$35,208	$13,245	90%	26%	$25,842	$22,611	NR
Loyola Marymount University	ind.	$50,283	$15,610	98%	23%	$30,841	$35,052	$33,742
Marymount California University	ind.	$37,158	NR	100%	23%	$28,687	$24,081	$24,143
Mount Saint Mary's University	ind.	$42,792	$12,455	99%	1%	$37,089	$18,158	$29,482
National University	ind.	$13,320	NA	71%	1%	$5787	$7533	$48,851
Occidental College	ind.	$56,576	$16,034	100%	100%	$52,303	$20,307	$29,306
Pepperdine University	ind.	$55,892	$15,670	100%	22%	$40,747	$30,815	$34,711
Pitzer College	ind.	$56,018	$17,432	98%	99%	$52,894	$20,556	$26,489
Point Loma Nazarene University	ind.	$36,950	$10,650	100%	20%	$24,555	$23,045	$35,374
Pomona College	ind.	$54,762	$17,218	100%	100%	$57,415	$14,565	$18,829
Saint Mary's College of California	ind.	$50,660	$15,706	61%	NR	$38,051	$28,315	$30,693
San Diego State University	pub.	$7510	$17,752	63%	11%	$9300	$15,962	$21,172
San Francisco Art Institute	ind.	$46,614	$14,500	86%	7%	$21,353	$39,761	$28,432
San Francisco State University	pub.	$7266	$14,384	96%	26%	$16,962	$4688	$5928
San Jose State University	pub.	$7852	$16,248	94%	71%	$19,414	$4686	$18,225
Santa Clara University	ind.	$55,629	$15,972	87%	34%	$37,952	$33,649	$26,603
Scripps College	ind.	$57,188	$17,600	98%	100%	$44,089	$30,699	$30,150
Stanford University	ind.	$56,169	$17,255	98%	93%	$58,633	$14,791	$22,897
Thomas Aquinas College - California	ind.	$25,600	$8800	91%	100%	$21,627	$12,773	$18,967
University of California, Berkeley	pub.	$14,253	$17,220	96%	30%	$28,230	$3243	$19,773
University of California, Davis	pub.	$14,492	$15,863	98%	26%	$24,494	$5861	$18,985
University of California, Los Angeles	pub.	$13,564	$16,625	97%	27%	$24,920	$5269	$21,441
University of California, Merced	pub.	$13,538	$17,046	99%	24%	$30,133	$451	$17,872
University of California, Riverside	pub.	$15,626	$17,350	98%	17%	$24,592	$8384	$20,779
University of California, San Diego	pub.	$14,480	$14,295	96%	40%	$25,062	$3713	$20,536

NA = not applicable; NR = not reported; * = includes room and board; † = room only; — = not available.

College Costs At-a-Glance

	Institutional Control ind.=independent; pub.=public	Tuition and Fees	Room and Board	Percent of Eligible Freshmen Receiving Need-Based Gift Awards	Percent of Freshmen Whose Need Was Fully Met	Average Financial Aid Package for Freshmen	Average Net Cost After Aid	Average Indebtedness Upon Graduation
University of California, Santa Barbara	pub.	$14,391	$15,389	94%	95%	$30,801	—	$18,995
University of California, Santa Cruz	pub.	$14,054	$16,916	98%	22%	$25,044	$5926	$21,375
University of Saint Katherine	ind.	$25,300	NR	100%	8%	$19,156	$23,060	$34,245
University of San Diego	ind.	$52,864	$15,156	99%	18%	$42,279	$25,741	$30,497
University of San Francisco	ind.	$52,482	$15,990	99%	9%	$36,087	$32,385	$33,752
University of Southern California	ind.	$58,195	$15,916	86%	91%	$57,520	$16,591	$28,434
University of the Pacific	ind.	$49,588	$13,740	99%	11%	$39,884	$23,444	$29,929
Vanguard University of Southern California	ind.	$36,550	$12,222	62%	100%	$16,874	$31,898	$18,769
Westmont College	ind.	$46,594	$14,646	100%	26%	$40,025	$21,215	$39,145
Whittier College	ind.	$49,314	NR	88%	14%	$40,382	$23,578	$35,328
Woodbury University	ind.	$42,596	$13,331	92%	5%	$31,334	$24,593	$35,814
Colorado								
Adams State University	pub.	$9440	$8760	96%	6%	$14,751	$3449	$426,673
The Colorado College	ind.	$60,864	$13,392	100%	100%	$57,862	$16,394	$23,579
Colorado Mesa University	pub.	$9306	$11,168	90%	24%	$10,072	$10,402	$27,269
Colorado Mountain College	pub.	$2700	$10,322	50%	NR	NR	NR	NR
Colorado School of Mines	pub.	$19,062	$14,211	59%	32%	$15,908	$17,365	$32,482
Colorado State University	pub.	$11,831	$11,964	81%	28%	$11,101	$12,694	$27,142
Colorado State University–Global Campus	pub.	$10,500	NR	NR	NR	NR	NR	NR
Fort Lewis College	pub.	$8881	$9878	90%	16%	$18,822	—	$19,429
Nazarene Bible College	ind.	$10,080	NR	NR	NR	NR	NR	$36,370
University of Colorado Boulder	pub.	$12,500	$14,778	79%	44%	$18,037	$9241	$27,568
University of Colorado Colorado Springs	pub.	$10,463	$10,798	55%	7%	$8766	$12,495	$23,805
University of Colorado Denver	pub.	$11,447	$12,620	87%	2%	$9773	$14,294	$20,859
University of Denver	ind.	$53,775	$14,178	100%	29%	$43,335	$24,618	$27,938
University of Northern Colorado	pub.	$10,188	$11,204	88%	33%	$14,842	$6550	$23,967
Western Colorado University	pub.	$10,437	$9704	96%	4%	$12,301	$7840	$26,060
Connecticut								
Central Connecticut State University	pub.	$11,068	$12,528	92%	6%	$9968	$13,628	$29,709
Charter Oak State College	pub.	$10,243	NA	NR	NR	NR	NR	NR
Connecticut College	ind.	$56,890	$15,700	96%	100%	$46,820	$25,770	$37,817
Fairfield University	ind.	$51,325	$15,610	75%	33%	$32,358	$34,577	$39,214
Paier College of Art, Inc.	ind.	$19,670	$3500	75%	8%	$7566	$15,604	$37,318
Sacred Heart University	ind.	$43,070	$15,960	100%	19%	$22,433	$36,597	$45,630
Trinity College	ind.	$59,050	$15,300	97%	100%	$50,612	$23,738	$30,893
University of New Haven	ind.	$40,440	$16,360	100%	14%	$25,679	$31,121	$47,457
Wesleyan University	ind.	$57,004	$15,724	100%	100%	$58,419	$14,309	$26,016
Western Connecticut State University	pub.	$11,781	$13,921	74%	12%	$10,133	$15,569	$38,657
Yale University	ind.	$57,700	$17,200	100%	100%	$62,879	$12,021	$15,379

NA = not applicable; NR = not reported; * = includes room and board; † = room only; — = not available.

College Costs At-a-Glance

	Institutional Control ind.=independent; pub.=public	Tuition and Fees	Room and Board	Percent of Eligible Freshmen Receiving Need-Based Gift Awards	Percent of Freshmen Whose Need Was Fully Met	Average Financial Aid Package for Freshmen	Average Net Cost After Aid	Average Indebtedness Upon Graduation
District of Columbia								
American University	ind.	$51,361	$14,980	95%	24%	$38,820	$27,521	NR
The Catholic University of America	ind.	$49,416	$15,820	98%	43%	$35,635	$29,601	$46,702
Gallaudet University	ind.	$17,038	$8000	96%	19%	$26,099	—	$20,038
Georgetown University	ind.	$55,794	$11,404	94%	100%	$49,624	$17,574	$26,759
The George Washington University	ind.	$56,935	$14,300	96%	44%	$49,366	$21,869	$34,768
Florida								
AdventHealth University	ind.	$16,350	$4200	100%	16%	$9162	$11,388	$33,823
Barry University	ind.	$29,850	$11,224	91%	5%	$27,725	$13,349	$37,228
Beacon College	ind.	$42,900	$12,570	100%	NR	$20,834	$34,636	$27,000
Bethune-Cookman University	ind.	$14,814	$9462	98%	7%	$16,217	$8059	$37,258
Eckerd College	ind.	$46,096	$13,026	99%	18%	$38,871	$20,251	$33,661
Florida Agricultural and Mechanical University	pub.	$5785	$10,986	86%	9%	$13,694	$3077	$28,284
Florida Atlantic University	pub.	$6099	$12,030	85%	10%	$15,027	$3102	$23,439
Florida Gulf Coast University	pub.	$6170	$8580	67%	8%	$10,446	$4304	$28,581
Florida Institute of Technology	ind.	$42,470	$12,880	100%	34%	$37,926	$17,424	$38,943
Florida International University	pub.	$6566	$11,136	70%	12%	$10,913	$6789	$19,705
Florida National University	ind.	$13,688	NA	98%	NR	NR	NR	$11,700
Florida State University	pub.	$6516	$10,780	95%	71%	$13,823	$3473	$25,013
Jacksonville University	ind.	$39,900	$14,810	98%	20%	$32,208	$22,502	$44,279
Johnson University Florida	ind.	$17,630	$3600	100%	10%	$11,770	$9460	NR
Keiser University	ind.	$32,868	$14,086	93%	100%	$6815	$40,139	NR
Lynn University	ind.	$39,850	$12,470	82%	100%	$26,280	$26,040	$3451
New College of Florida	pub.	$6916	NR	98%	20%	$15,282	$4104	$18,953
Palm Beach Atlantic University	ind.	$33,475	$5696	100%	14%	$26,011	$13,160	$27,530
Ringling College of Art and Design	ind.	$47,970	$15,580	100%	7%	$28,044	$35,506	$46,947
Rollins College	ind.	$53,716	$15,200	100%	37%	$41,871	$27,045	$31,992
Saint Leo University	ind.	$24,640	$13,500	100%	17%	$26,780	$11,360	$27,813
Southeastern University	ind.	$26,620	$10,030	66%	12%	$17,247	$19,403	$30,027
Stetson University	ind.	$49,500	$14,540	100%	27%	$43,440	$20,600	$32,601
Trinity College of Florida	ind.	$16,300	$7600	100%	19%	$16,715	$7185	$26,617
University of Central Florida	pub.	$6368	$9580	70%	28%	$12,655	$3293	$22,561
University of Florida	pub.	$6381	$10,220	66%	29%	$15,339	$1262	$20,388
University of Miami	ind.	$53,682	$15,470	73%	95%	$43,776	$25,376	$21,000
University of South Florida	pub.	$6410	$11,836	96%	21%	$14,742	$3504	$21,463
The University of Tampa	ind.	$30,884	$11,526	99%	16%	$18,244	$24,166	$35,034
Webber International University	ind.	$28,498	$9940	100%	9%	$18,973	$19,465	$27,083
Georgia								
Agnes Scott College	ind.	$44,250	$13,050	100%	25%	$38,877	$18,423	$31,271
Berry College	ind.	$37,246	$13,070	100%	34%	$32,015	$18,301	$31,336
Columbus State University	pub.	$7200	$9380	68%	2%	$10,568	$6012	$32,587

NA = not applicable; NR = not reported; * = includes room and board; † = room only; — = not available.

College Costs At-a-Glance

	Institutional Control ind.=independent; pub.=public	Tuition and Fees	Room and Board	Percent of Eligible Freshmen Receiving Need-Based Gift Awards	Percent of Freshmen Whose Need Was Fully Met	Average Financial Aid Package for Freshmen	Average Net Cost After Aid	Average Indebtedness Upon Graduation
Covenant College	ind.	$36,710	$10,970	99%	44%	$29,439	$18,241	$23,723
Emmanuel College	ind.	$21,220	$8062	79%	21%	$16,417	$12,865	$24,028
Emory University	ind.	$55,998	$15,572	94%	100%	$50,425	$21,145	$24,889
Georgia College & State University	pub.	$5770	NR	41%	23%	$11,603	$9739	$33,124
Georgia Gwinnett College	pub.	$5752	NR	81%	6%	$11,821	$9503	$37,357
Georgia Institute of Technology	pub.	$12,682	$14,830	94%	33%	$15,696	$11,816	$31,545
Georgia State University	pub.	$8948	$14,958	69%	8%	$12,784	$11,122	$28,864
LaGrange College	ind.	$31,540	$11,970	96%	15%	$26,777	$16,733	$37,680
Life University	ind.	$13,101	$14,400	51%	NR	$11,500	$16,001	$26,000
Oglethorpe University	ind.	$41,410	$13,800	100%	23%	$36,811	$18,399	$35,732
Piedmont College	ind.	$26,692	$10,524	100%	19%	$24,520	$12,696	$30,559
Reinhardt University	ind.	$24,300	$10,500	100%	15%	$17,875	$16,925	$32,384
Toccoa Falls College	ind.	$21,120	$8500	100%	13%	$19,857	$9763	NR
Truett McConnell University	ind.	$21,938	$8160	99%	24%	$15,826	$14,272	$29,610
University of Georgia	pub.	$12,080	$10,314	97%	34%	$14,573	$7821	$22,918
University of West Georgia	pub.	$7488	$10,340	68%	65%	$8234	$9594	$26,376
Valdosta State University	pub.	$6583	$8332	89%	10%	$16,227	—	$27,058
Wesleyan College	ind.	$25,190	$10,365	99%	12%	$24,497	$11,058	$28,882
Guam								
University of Guam	pub.	$5804	$3850	NR	NR	NR	NR	NR
Hawaii								
Chaminade University of Honolulu	ind.	$26,914	$14,610	93%	10%	$23,706	$17,818	$22,158
University of Hawaii at Manoa	pub.	$12,186	$13,366	98%	32%	$15,787	$9765	$24,223
Idaho								
Boise State University	pub.	$8068	$9760	67%	19%	$11,059	$6769	$27,052
The College of Idaho	ind.	$32,855	$10,600	79%	26%	$25,219	$18,236	$29,130
Lewis-Clark State College	pub.	$10,552	$6650	74%	18%	$8670	$8532	$25,473
Northwest Nazarene University	ind.	$32,630	$8800	100%	22%	$27,351	$14,079	$27,339
University of Idaho	pub.	$8304	$9080	58%	38%	$12,929	$4455	$23,105
Illinois								
Augustana College	ind.	$45,136	$11,216	NR	NR	NR	NR	$34,964
Aurora University	ind.	$25,960	$12,020	96%	13%	$24,485	$13,495	$27,851
Benedictine University	ind.	$32,700*	$4960	68%	NR	$25,093	$12,567	$26,447
Bradley University	ind.	$35,480	$11,280	100%	20%	$26,122	$20,638	$31,111
Columbia College Chicago	ind.	$28,318	$16,456	100%	65%	$20,086	$24,688	$34,328
Concordia University Chicago	ind.	$33,636	$10,226	100%	15%	$26,954	$16,908	$28,122
DePaul University	ind.	$41,202	$14,736	99%	12%	$28,110	$27,828	$29,621
Dominican University	ind.	$35,420	$10,865	100%	16%	$27,910	$18,375	$28,760
Eastern Illinois University	pub.	$11,989	$10,030	83%	8%	$14,985	$7034	$30,695
Governors State University	pub.	$12,616	$8102	96%	82%	$11,984	$8734	NR
Greenville University	ind.	$27,910	$9548	100%	22%	$22,057	$15,401	$28,759

NA = not applicable; NR = not reported; * = includes room and board; † = room only; — = not available.

College Costs At-a-Glance

	Institutional Control ind.=independent; pub.=public	Tuition and Fees	Room and Board	Percent of Eligible Freshmen Receiving Need-Based Gift Awards	Percent of Freshmen Whose Need Was Fully Met	Average Financial Aid Package for Freshmen	Average Net Cost After Aid	Average Indebtedness Upon Graduation
Illinois State University	pub.	$14,832	$9850	58%	9%	$12,810	$11,872	$31,687
Illinois Wesleyan University	ind.	$51,336	$11,840	100%	21%	$38,316	$24,860	$34,268
Judson University	ind.	$29,870	$10,790	72%	16%	$22,139	$18,521	$24,736
Lake Forest College	ind.	$49,822	$10,954	100%	35%	$44,475	$16,301	$34,587
Lewis University	ind.	$34,478	$11,050	100%	24%	$31,341	$14,187	$36,653
Lincoln College	ind.	$19,000	$7900	100%	NR	$13,137	$13,763	$7385
Loyola University Chicago	ind.	$46,898	$15,020	98%	18%	$36,133	$25,785	$35,030
McKendree University	ind.	$31,640	$9920	100%	20%	$23,152	$18,408	$28,754
Millikin University	ind.	$39,592	$11,450	82%	29%	$29,921	$21,121	$35,596
North Central College	ind.	$40,040	$11,456	NR	NR	NR	NR	$37,396
Northeastern Illinois University	pub.	$13,998	$8426	100%	4%	$12,077	$10,347	$11,355
Northern Illinois University	pub.	$12,261	$10,880	99%	11%	$14,875	$8266	$33,915
Northwestern University	ind.	$56,691	$17,019	98%	100%	$56,115	$17,595	$36,350
Olivet Nazarene University	ind.	$36,950	$8990	100%	20%	$32,721	$13,219	$31,640
Principia College	ind.	$30,190	$11,960	100%	52%	$33,300	$8850	$19,613
Saint Anthony College of Nursing	ind.	$26,692	NA	NR	NR	NR	NR	NR
Southern Illinois University Carbondale	pub.	$14,864	$10,622	60%	21%	$17,603	$7883	$30,292
Southern Illinois University Edwardsville	pub.	$12,219	$10,701	95%	40%	$14,111	$8809	$22,610
Trinity Christian College	ind.	$30,950	$9950	NR	NR	NR	NR	$41,752
University of Illinois at Chicago	pub.	$13,874	$12,479	92%	8%	$15,543	$10,810	$21,934
University of Illinois at Springfield	pub.	$11,813	$11,660	96%	25%	$16,980	$6493	$22,248
University of Illinois at Urbana-Champaign	pub.	$16,210	$11,672	89%	18%	$19,033	$8849	$24,655
University of St. Francis	ind.	$35,000	$10,210	100%	37%	$31,462	$13,748	$30,274
Western Illinois University	pub.	$11,666	$9800	91%	39%	$15,777	$5689	$30,522
Wheaton College	ind.	$39,100	$10,990	100%	13%	$29,035	$21,055	$29,555
Indiana								
Anderson University	ind.	$31,200	$10,040	75%	18%	$26,427	$14,813	NR
Ball State University	pub.	$10,020	$10,870	67%	42%	$14,712	$6178	$28,603
Bethel University	ind.	$29,790	$9310	NR	NR	NR	NR	$30,797
Butler University	ind.	$43,400	$14,380	98%	14%	$26,933	$30,847	$36,695
Calumet College of Saint Joseph	ind.	$20,970	$6000	83%	NR	$10,700	$16,270	$24,431
DePauw University	ind.	$52,710	$13,788	100%	34%	$43,603	$22,895	$25,904
Earlham College	ind.	$48,091	$6020	100%	62%	$39,047	$15,064	$26,103
Franklin College	ind.	$33,954	$10,546	100%	12%	$25,332	$19,168	$38,057
Goshen College	ind.	$35,230	$10,870	100%	16%	$30,986	$15,114	$28,693
Hanover College	ind.	$39,650	$12,300	100%	32%	$32,647	$19,303	$29,190
Indiana State University	pub.	$9466	$11,016	64%	12%	$10,849	$9633	$26,223
Indiana University Bloomington	pub.	$10,948	$10,830	90%	33%	$14,411	$7367	$27,555
Indiana University East	pub.	$7527	NA	96%	21%	$9768	—	$22,513
Indiana University Kokomo	pub.	$7527	NA	88%	13%	$8352	—	$23,518
Indiana University Northwest	pub.	$7527	NA	86%	16%	$8037	—	$26,940
Indiana University-Purdue University Indianapolis	pub.	$9702	$10,000	89%	23%	$12,256	$7446	$27,022

NA = not applicable; NR = not reported; * = includes room and board; † = room only; — = not available.

College Costs At-a-Glance

	Institutional Control ind.=independent; pub.=public	Tuition and Fees	Room and Board	Percent of Eligible Freshmen Receiving Need-Based Gift Awards	Percent of Freshmen Whose Need Was Fully Met	Average Financial Aid Package for Freshmen	Average Net Cost After Aid	Average Indebtedness Upon Graduation
Indiana University South Bend	pub.	$7527	$7346	94%	12%	$9145	$5728	$24,879
Indiana University Southeast	pub.	$6922	$6290	91%	8%	$8522	$4690	$21,460
Purdue University	pub.	$9992	$10,030	71%	40%	$13,511	$6511	$27,673
Purdue University Fort Wayne	pub.	$9708	$9620	84%	11%	$10,489	$8839	$22,354
Purdue University Northwest	pub.	$7942	$7821	86%	14%	$8391	$7372	$12,568
Rose-Hulman Institute of Technology	ind.	$49,527	$15,414	99%	22%	$33,978	$30,963	$47,953
Saint Mary's College	ind.	$45,720	$13,470	99%	20%	$38,513	$20,677	$34,084
Taylor University	ind.	$35,305	$9950	100%	32%	$27,031	$18,224	$26,009
Trine University	ind.	$33,490	$6700	99%	20%	$27,209	$12,981	$33,933
University of Notre Dame	ind.	$57,699	$15,984	97%	100%	$52,793	$20,890	$27,460
University of Saint Francis	ind.	$32,420	$10,490	100%	19%	$26,714	$16,196	$42,336
Valparaiso University	ind.	$43,286	$12,620	100%	50%	$33,195	$22,711	$35,968
Wabash College	ind.	$45,850	$10,900	99%	77%	$42,606	$14,144	$35,273
Iowa								
Allen College	ind.	$19,512	$7280	NR	NR	NR	NR	NR
Buena Vista University	ind.	$35,194	$9872	100%	23%	$34,025	$11,041	$35,267
Central College	ind.	$18,600	$10,280	100%	29%	$35,905	—	$37,983
Clarke University	ind.	$33,350	NR	100%	27%	$33,091	$10,539	$11,079
Coe College	ind.	$47,220	$10,134	100%	22%	$41,316	$16,038	$35,012
Cornell College	ind.	$44,096	$9760	100%	26%	$33,319	$20,537	$38,215
Drake University	ind.	$44,334	$11,152	99%	29%	$32,378	$23,108	$34,492
Graceland University	ind.	$31,320	$9440	100%	16%	$26,273	$14,487	$44,984
Grinnell College	ind.	$56,680	$13,864	100%	100%	$51,770	$18,774	$20,093
Loras College	ind.	$35,218	$8600	100%	24%	$30,438	$13,380	$28,964
St. Ambrose University	ind.	$32,758	$11,354	99%	31%	$25,603	$18,509	$38,149
University of Dubuque	ind.	$36,610	$10,500	92%	17%	$27,855	$19,255	$33,454
University of Northern Iowa	pub.	$8938	$9160	59%	17%	$8179	$9919	$23,671
Wartburg College	ind.	$45,680	$9592	100%	28%	$32,857	$22,415	$39,559
Kansas								
Baker University	ind.	$29,880	$8350	65%	NR	$24,615	$13,615	$33,046
Bethel College	ind.	$29,390	$8980	70%	25%	$29,434	$8936	$5633
Emporia State University	pub.	$6960	$9408	100%	18%	$9702	$6666	$22,692
MidAmerica Nazarene University	ind.	$32,872	$9282	99%	14%	$25,601	$16,553	$28,755
Southwestern College	ind.	$33,250	$8500	100%	13%	$24,235	$17,515	$37,490
Sterling College	ind.	$27,300	$3516	97%	21%	$21,677	$9139	$24,843
Tabor College	ind.	$29,375	$9975	46%	19%	$24,094	$15,256	$27,126
The University of Kansas	pub.	$11,166	$10,350	91%	46%	$17,896	$3620	$28,176
University of Saint Mary	ind.	$29,930	$8140	98%	16%	$21,843	$16,227	$27,409
Wichita State University	pub.	$8299	$12,620	67%	21%	$7956	$12,963	$24,839
Kentucky								
Alice Lloyd College	ind.	$2230	$7160	100%	8%	$13,598	—	$11,844

NA = not applicable; NR = not reported; * = includes room and board; † = room only; — = not available.

College Costs At-a-Glance

	Institutional Control ind.=independent; pub.=public	Tuition and Fees	Room and Board	Percent of Eligible Freshmen Receiving Need-Based Gift Awards	Percent of Freshmen Whose Need Was Fully Met	Average Financial Aid Package for Freshmen	Average Net Cost After Aid	Average Indebtedness Upon Graduation
Bellarmine University	ind.	$42,430	$9420	100%	32%	$35,461	$16,389	$30,850
Campbellsville University	ind.	$25,400	$8000	100%	13%	$23,250	$10,150	$20,439
Centre College	ind.	$43,000	$10,740	100%	36%	$38,964	$14,776	$27,418
Eastern Kentucky University	pub.	$9806	$10,173	62%	32%	$13,414	$6565	$27,465
Georgetown College	ind.	$40,800	$10,670	100%	33%	$37,826	$13,644	$34,766
Kentucky Mountain Bible College	ind.	$10,190	$5140	100%	5%	$10,762	$4568	$7370
Kentucky State University	pub.	$7796	$6690	99%	6%	$13,101	$1385	$28,394
Midway University	ind.	$24,850	$8600	80%	8%	$19,999	$13,451	NR
Morehead State University	pub.	$9290	$9490	64%	23%	$12,794	$5986	$26,576
Transylvania University	ind.	$41,610	$11,310	100%	24%	$30,248	$22,672	$30,826
Union College	ind.	$27,950	$7500	100%	10%	$23,286	$12,164	NR
University of Kentucky	pub.	$12,360	$13,210	43%	20%	$15,077	$10,493	$33,927
University of Louisville	pub.	$11,928	$9452	98%	21%	$14,805	$6575	$24,840
University of Pikeville	ind.	$22,050	$8050	100%	43%	$23,423	$6677	$24,825
Western Kentucky University	pub.	$10,802	$8432	59%	23%	$14,844	$4390	$26,803
Louisiana								
Centenary College of Louisiana	ind.	$37,310	$13,670	100%	20%	$34,293	$16,687	$25,363
Dillard University	ind.	$19,281	$6156	100%	7%	$17,656	$7781	NR
Grambling State University	pub.	$16,706	$5572	89%	NR	$10,848	$11,430	$42,963
Louisiana College	ind.	$17,500	$5646	100%	23%	$15,685	$7461	$25,656
Louisiana State University and Agricultural & Mechanical College	pub.	$11,962	$12,276	97%	15%	$16,507	$7731	$24,851
Loyola University New Orleans	ind.	$42,030	$13,606	100%	16%	$36,351	$19,285	$27,049
Nicholls State University	pub.	$7898	$9818	96%	14%	$9168	$8548	NR
Northwestern State University of Louisiana	pub.	$8768	$9244	96%	17%	$15,407	$2605	$29,793
Southeastern Louisiana University	pub.	$8329	$8600	64%	12%	NR	NR	$19,356
Tulane University	ind.	$56,800	$15,774	98%	51%	$47,132	$25,442	$31,306
University of Louisiana at Lafayette	pub.	$10,382	$10,708	54%	16%	$10,443	$10,647	NR
Xavier University of Louisiana	ind.	$25,185	$10,000	99%	49%	$10,757	$24,428	$21,820
Maine								
Bates College	ind.	$55,683	$15,705	100%	100%	$50,844	$20,544	$23,383
Bowdoin College	ind.	$56,350	$15,360	100%	100%	$53,004	$18,706	$26,775
Colby College	ind.	$57,280	$14,720	100%	100%	$55,762	$16,238	$24,380
College of the Atlantic	ind.	$43,542	$9747	100%	41%	$44,186	$9103	$29,731
Husson University	ind.	$19,772	$10,632	97%	23%	$17,918	$12,486	$35,681
University of Maine	pub.	$11,438	$10,966	100%	22%	$16,058	$6346	$34,703
University of Maine at Farmington	pub.	$9344	$9902	99%	43%	$15,617	$3629	$30,315
University of Maine at Machias	pub.	$8036	$9180	100%	33%	$13,766	$3450	$24,116
University of Maine at Presque Isle	pub.	$8574	$8738	99%	60%	$12,790	$4522	$22,205
University of Southern Maine	pub.	$9850	$9826	98%	43%	$14,477	$5199	NR
Maryland								
Bowie State University	pub.	$8445	$9916	78%	22%	$9004	$9357	$28,807

NA = not applicable; NR = not reported; * = includes room and board; † = room only; — = not available.

College Costs At-a-Glance

	Institutional Control ind.=independent; pub.=public	Tuition and Fees	Room and Board	Percent of Eligible Freshmen Receiving Need-Based Gift Awards	Percent of Freshmen Whose Need Was Fully Met	Average Financial Aid Package for Freshmen	Average Net Cost After Aid	Average Indebtedness Upon Graduation
Goucher College	ind.	$47,300	$13,882	100%	20%	$42,205	$18,977	$28,145
Johns Hopkins University	ind.	$55,350	$16,310	99%	100%	$53,723	$17,937	$24,107
Loyola University Maryland	ind.	$50,265	$14,710	93%	31%	$35,659	$29,316	$41,443
McDaniel College	ind.	$44,540	$11,772	100%	1%	$41,491	$14,821	$16,622
Mount St. Mary's University	ind.	$43,650	$6940	100%	30%	$32,577	$18,013	$38,998
St. John's College	ind.	$35,635	$13,636	100%	10%	$27,853	$21,418	$20,067
Salisbury University	pub.	$10,044	$12,360	88%	12%	$9179	$13,225	$27,355
Stevenson University	ind.	$37,142	$13,624	99%	21%	$27,894	$22,872	$37,112
Towson University	pub.	$10,198	$13,446	61%	11%	$11,875	$11,769	$27,610
University of Maryland, Baltimore County	pub.	$12,028	$12,000	83%	19%	$12,955	$11,073	$26,359
University of Maryland, College Park	pub.	$10,779	$12,935	78%	21%	$11,937	$11,777	$29,133
University of Maryland Global Campus	pub.	$7560	NA	76%	NR	$5751	$1809	NR
Washington College	ind.	$49,768	$12,722	100%	20%	$4167	$58,323	$34,903
Massachusetts								
Amherst College	ind.	$60,890	$15,910	99%	100%	$59,559	$17,241	$22,629
Assumption University	ind.	$42,316	$13,128	100%	31%	$32,020	$23,424	NR
Becker College	ind.	$40,150	$13,800	100%	1%	$22,697	$31,253	NR
Bentley University	ind.	$51,830	$16,960	98%	29%	$38,082	$30,708	$35,187
Berklee College of Music	ind.	$47,230	$18,830	48%	10%	$23,876	$42,184	$43,826
Boston Architectural College	ind.	$26,503	NA	100%	NR	$9071	$17,432	NR
Boston College	ind.	$56,780	$14,826	89%	100%	$46,504	$25,102	$23,136
Boston University	ind.	$55,892	$16,160	99%	34%	$51,652	$20,400	$40,349
Brandeis University	ind.	$57,561	$16,080	97%	122%	$47,398	$26,243	$32,158
Clark University	ind.	$47,200	$9480	100%	28%	$36,130	$20,550	$34,390
College of the Holy Cross	ind.	$56,520	$15,560	77%	100%	$44,288	$27,792	$26,258
Dean College	ind.	$41,318	$17,648	100%	16%	$31,980	$26,986	NR
Elms College	ind.	$38,391	$14,010	100%	12%	$31,285	$21,116	$49,156
Emmanuel College	ind.	$42,516	$15,846	91%	31%	$32,631	$25,731	NR
Endicott College	ind.	$35,320	$16,130	99%	13%	$21,746	$29,704	$44,178
Fisher College	ind.	$32,700	$16,569	73%	NR	$30,581	$18,688	$32,551
Fitchburg State University	pub.	$10,505	$11,261	75%	NR	$9962	$11,804	$26,543
Framingham State University	pub.	$11,100	$12,604	82%	9%	$10,987	$12,717	$31,465
Franklin W. Olin College of Engineering	ind.	$54,700	$17,460	100%	100%	$53,995	$18,165	$13,480
Gordon College	ind.	$39,230	$11,420	100%	22%	$28,874	$21,776	$35,210
Hampshire College	ind.	$52,068	$14,120	100%	11%	$45,005	$21,183	$29,499
Lasell College	ind.	$39,000	$16,000	63%	28%	$34,041	$20,959	$40,580
Lesley University	ind.	$29,450	$17,630	100%	9%	$19,036	$28,044	$22,371
Massachusetts College of Art and Design	pub.	$13,700	NR	94%	6%	$12,432	$18,898	$26,720
Massachusetts College of Liberal Arts	pub.	$10,930	$11,430	84%	77%	$17,933	$4427	$29,416
Massachusetts Institute of Technology	ind.	$53,790	$16,390	99%	100%	$51,721	$18,459	$23,517
Massachusetts Maritime Academy	pub.	$10,314	$13,352	53%	34%	$15,467	$8199	$37,414
Mount Holyoke College	ind.	$52,258	$15,320	98%	100%	$44,203	$23,375	$25,811

NA = not applicable; NR = not reported; * = includes room and board; † = room only; — = not available.

College Costs At-a-Glance

	Institutional Control ind.=independent; pub.=public	Tuition and Fees	Room and Board	Percent of Eligible Freshmen Receiving Need-Based Gift Awards	Percent of Freshmen Whose Need Was Fully Met	Average Financial Aid Package for Freshmen	Average Net Cost After Aid	Average Indebtedness Upon Graduation
New England Conservatory of Music	ind.	$50,460	$16,500	100%	26%	$27,524	$39,436	$29,479
Nichols College	ind.	$36,540	$13,950	100%	NR	$30,891	$19,599	NR
Northeastern University	ind.	$53,506	$16,930	99%	18%	$38,871	$31,565	$33,661
Simmons University	ind.	$43,330	$15,660	99%	35%	$36,295	$22,695	$37,935
Smith College	ind.	$56,114	$18,760	100%	100%	$56,078	$18,796	$21,460
Springfield College	ind.	$38,565	$12,930	100%	20%	$29,593	$21,902	$43,821
Stonehill College	ind.	$44,420	$16,620	99%	48%	$32,799	$28,241	$38,359
Suffolk University	ind.	$41,908	$18,134	91%	9%	$30,292	$29,750	$28,582
Tufts University	ind.	$58,578	$15,086	93%	100%	$48,215	$25,449	$27,006
University of Massachusetts Amherst	pub.	$16,389	$13,598	93%	13%	$17,787	$12,200	$31,755
University of Massachusetts Boston	pub.	$14,613	$16,902	94%	17%	$18,300	$13,215	$25,645
University of Massachusetts Dartmouth	pub.	$14,358	$14,064	98%	21%	$18,112	$10,310	$34,824
Wentworth Institute of Technology	ind.	$34,970	$14,190	74%	7%	$2725	$46,435	$58,867
Western New England University	ind.	$39,226	$14,244	100%	20%	$29,045	$24,425	$43,980
Wheaton College	ind.	$56,366	$14,378	100%	40%	$49,469	$21,275	$34,530
Williams College	ind.	$59,660	$15,000	100%	100%	$58,125	$16,535	$15,911
Worcester Polytechnic Institute	ind.	$54,146	$15,838	100%	65%	$39,646	$30,338	NR
Worcester State University	pub.	$10,161	$12,360	92%	33%	$16,083	$6438	$30,629
Michigan								
Albion College	ind.	$50,590	$12,380	100%	32%	$47,934	$15,036	$35,529
Alma College	ind.	$41,398	$11,384	100%	23%	$32,161	$20,621	$40,387
Andrews University	ind.	$31,008	$9540	55%	32%	$31,022	$9526	$33,335
Aquinas College	ind.	$35,086	$9876	100%	35%	$27,329	$17,633	$30,158
Calvin College	ind.	$37,806	$10,800	100%	31%	$27,581	$21,025	$25,888
Central Michigan University	pub.	$13,260	$10,328	96%	100%	$14,194	$9394	$31,683
Eastern Michigan University	pub.	$11,128	$10,248	70%	8%	$11,093	$10,283	$27,475
Ferris State University	pub.	$12,930	$10,044	84%	19%	$14,500	$8474	$34,590
Grand Valley State University	pub.	$12,860	$8820	88%	23%	$11,883	$9797	$28,131
Hillsdale College	ind.	$29,482	$11,910	59%	35%	$19,423	$21,969	$32,198
Hope College	ind.	$35,330	$10,630	92%	24%	$29,671	$16,289	$33,856
Kalamazoo College	ind.	$52,530	$10,530	98%	41%	$45,727	$17,333	$34,179
Kettering University	ind.	$44,380	$8400	100%	16%	$26,444	$26,336	$46,620
Lake Superior State University	pub.	$12,190	$10,230	96%	37%	$13,104	$9316	$28,259
Lawrence Technological University	ind.	$36,630	$10,900	99%	19%	$24,707	$22,823	$32,735
Michigan State University	pub.	$14,460	$10,522	72%	11%	$16,433	$8549	$31,393
Michigan Technological University	pub.	$15,960	$11,004	87%	28%	$18,626	$8338	$37,903
Northern Michigan University	pub.	$11,525	$10,774	70%	13%	$12,037	$10,262	$30,125
Oakland University	pub.	$13,346	$10,430	80%	13%	$12,689	$11,087	$27,095
Olivet College	ind.	$28,692	$10,100	99%	14%	$20,150	$18,642	$26,872
Rochester University	ind.	$24,720	$8840	NR	NR	NR	NR	NR
Saginaw Valley State University	pub.	$10,814	$10,440	100%	13%	$12,305	$8949	$31,353
University of Michigan	pub.	$15,558	$11,996	80%	69%	$27,596	—	$25,777

NA = not applicable; NR = not reported; * = includes room and board; † = room only; — = not available.

College Costs At-a-Glance

	Institutional Control ind.=independent; pub.=public	Tuition and Fees	Room and Board	Percent of Eligible Freshmen Receiving Need-Based Gift Awards	Percent of Freshmen Whose Need Was Fully Met	Average Financial Aid Package for Freshmen	Average Net Cost After Aid	Average Indebtedness Upon Graduation
University of Michigan–Dearborn	pub.	$14,236	$2262	90%	12%	$12,468	$4030	$25,268
University of Michigan–Flint	pub.	$12,406	$9116	75%	8%	$12,241	$9281	$29,645
Walsh College of Accountancy and Business Administration	ind.	$18,309	NA	NR	NR	NR	NR	NR
Western Michigan University	pub.	$13,017	$10,567	79%	11%	$10,699	$12,885	$35,204
Minnesota								
Academy College	ind.	$18,451	NA	67%	NR	NR	NR	NR
Augsburg University	ind.	$41,086	$10,885	100%	10%	$33,989	$17,982	$40,574
Bemidji State University	pub.	$4299	$8660	70%	7%	$8362	$4597	NR
Bethany Lutheran College	ind.	$28,380	$8150	100%	24%	$23,918	$12,612	$32,152
Bethel University	ind.	$39,030	$10,960	100%	19%	$32,032	$17,958	$38,286
Carleton College	ind.	$57,111	$14,658	100%	100%	$52,349	$19,420	$19,405
College of Saint Benedict	ind.	$48,442	$11,346	97%	41%	$40,353	$19,435	$43,615
The College of St. Scholastica	ind.	$39,410	$10,340	66%	33%	$34,112	$15,638	$41,577
Concordia College	ind.	$41,566	$8610	100%	25%	$33,419	$16,757	NR
Concordia University, St. Paul	ind.	$23,400	$9600	100%	10%	$21,420	$11,580	$32,815
Gustavus Adolphus College	ind.	$48,460	$10,430	97%	50%	$44,514	$14,376	$35,145
Hamline University	ind.	$44,230	$10,810	100%	20%	$33,954	$21,086	$36,676
Macalester College	ind.	$56,292	$12,592	99%	76%	$48,689	$20,195	$23,060
Martin Luther College	ind.	$16,420	$6480	99%	10%	$11,855	$11,045	$26,791
Minneapolis College of Art and Design	ind.	$56,124	$5980	100%	11%	$29,404	$32,700	$37,788
North Central University	ind.	$34,460*	$8180	NR	NR	NR	NR	$21,965
Saint John's University	ind.	$49,000	$11,362	99%	37%	$37,360	$23,002	$38,642
St. Olaf College	ind.	$51,450	$11,660	100%	100%	$45,655	$17,455	$28,950
University of Minnesota, Crookston	pub.	$12,116	$9020	100%	29%	$15,040	$6096	$26,107
University of Minnesota, Duluth	pub.	$13,681	$8374	94%	31%	$13,620	$8435	$30,687
University of Minnesota, Twin Cities Campus	pub.	$15,027	$10,768	89%	27%	$14,956	$10,839	$27,077
University of Northwestern–St. Paul	ind.	$33,200	$10,000	99%	12%	$23,660	$19,540	$44,561
Winona State University	pub.	$9666	$9086	79%	9%	$8183	$10,569	$33,312
Mississippi								
Alcorn State University	pub.	$7290	$10,788	93%	8%	$8011	$10,067	$33,766
Belhaven University	ind.	$27,025	$8800	100%	13%	$20,820	$15,005	NR
Delta State University	pub.	$7671	$7908	83%	NR	$10,250	$5329	NR
Mississippi State University	pub.	$8910	$10,436	97%	25%	$16,164	$3182	$31,060
University of Mississippi	pub.	$8828	$10,734	90%	23%	$14,752	$4810	$33,411
Missouri								
Central Methodist University	ind.	$25,770	$8400	97%	21%	$21,279	$12,891	$31,118
Columbia College	ind.	$23,498	$8400	65%	25%	$18,638	$13,260	$23,979
Drury University	ind.	$30,915	$9172	100%	22%	$24,205	$15,882	$37,144
Evangel University	ind.	$24,327	$8522	100%	9%	$17,342	$15,507	$31,560
Kansas City Art Institute	ind.	$39,200	$8200	100%	13%	$28,857	$18,543	$32,607
Lindenwood University	ind.	$18,600	$9300	99%	36%	$18,310	$9590	$33,365

NA = not applicable; NR = not reported; * = includes room and board; † = room only; — = not available.

College Costs At-a-Glance

	Institutional Control ind.=independent; pub.=public	Tuition and Fees	Room and Board	Percent of Eligible Freshmen Receiving Need-Based Gift Awards	Percent of Freshmen Whose Need Was Fully Met	Average Financial Aid Package for Freshmen	Average Net Cost After Aid	Average Indebtedness Upon Graduation
Maryville University of Saint Louis	ind.	$28,470	$10,300	100%	22%	$22,630	$16,140	$30,657
Missouri Baptist University	ind.	$28,220	$9070	80%	52%	$24,172	$13,118	$25,674
Missouri State University	pub.	$7588	$9128	87%	19%	$12,012	$4704	$26,446
Missouri University of Science and Technology	pub.	$10,653	$10,402	97%	53%	$16,303	$4752	$30,168
Missouri Valley College	ind.	$21,100	$9400	100%	8%	$16,713	$13,787	$37,801
Northwest Missouri State University	pub.	$10,298	$10,106	91%	58%	$11,105	$9299	$35,920
St. Louis College of Pharmacy	ind.	$29,596	$12,256	100%	18%	$22,505	$19,347	NR
Saint Louis University	ind.	$45,424	$12,600	96%	26%	$36,119	$21,905	$34,188
Southeast Missouri State University	pub.	$7800	$9279	96%	17%	$10,526	$6553	$25,380
Southwest Baptist University	ind.	$25,440	$8040	98%	25%	$24,167	$9313	$25,880
Stevens–The Institute of Business & Arts	ind.	$12,750	NA	100%	NR	$6139	$6611	NR
Truman State University	pub.	$8120	$9012	99%	43%	$12,911	$4221	$25,660
University of Central Missouri	pub.	$8043	$8962	59%	17%	$9073	$7932	$27,385
University of Missouri–St. Louis	pub.	$11,079	$9550	98%	19%	$14,891	$5738	$25,110
Washington University in St. Louis	ind.	$57,386	$17,402	98%	100%	$54,751	$20,037	$24,247
Montana								
Montana State University	pub.	$7472	$10,300	NR	NR	NR	NR	$27,764
Montana Technological University	pub.	$7397	$10,170	90%	23%	$11,570	$5997	$23,632
Rocky Mountain College	ind.	$30,586	$8596	99%	12%	$24,613	$14,569	$26,935
University of Montana	pub.	$7354	$9966	57%	12%	$12,398	$4922	$27,132
University of Providence	ind.	$26,662	$10,170	80%	1%	$20,499	$16,333	$26,200
Nebraska								
College of Saint Mary	ind.	$20,750	$7850	100%	28%	$18,878	$9722	$30,516
Creighton University	ind.	$43,018	$11,600	99%	33%	$30,787	$23,831	$38,042
Nebraska Methodist College	ind.	$16,308	$9586	98%	9%	$9557	$16,337	$30,407
Nebraska Wesleyan University	ind.	$35,564	$10,172	100%	19%	$26,475	$19,261	$31,715
University of Nebraska at Kearney	pub.	$7701	$9942	97%	22%	$12,988	$4655	$20,774
University of Nebraska–Lincoln	pub.	$9366	$11,830	92%	21%	$15,543	$5653	$22,290
Nevada								
University of Nevada, Las Vegas	pub.	$7986	$10,924	78%	11%	$8437	$10,473	$19,605
University of Nevada, Reno	pub.	$8452	$10,686	92%	13%	$9480	$9658	$22,418
New Hampshire								
Colby-Sawyer College	ind.	$44,930	$15,428	100%	25%	$39,348	$21,010	$40,767
Dartmouth College	ind.	$57,204	$16,374	92%	100%	$55,918	$17,660	$25,071
Franklin Pierce University	ind.	$38,200	$13,900	100%	20%	$27,091	$25,009	$38,237
Keene State College	pub.	$14,568	$11,560	80%	14%	$13,421	$12,707	$40,125
Saint Anselm College	ind.	$41,800	$14,750	100%	36%	$31,756	$24,794	$29,699
University of New Hampshire	pub.	$18,938	$12,242	94%	17%	$24,541	$6639	$42,246
New Jersey								
Caldwell University	ind.	$36,900	$12,760	100%	12%	$34,984	$14,676	$26,962
The College of New Jersey	pub.	$16,923	$14,048	48%	12%	$12,274	$18,697	$38,166

NA = not applicable; NR = not reported; * = includes room and board; † = room only; — = not available.

College Costs At-a-Glance

	Institutional Control ind.=independent; pub.=public	Tuition and Fees	Room and Board	Percent of Eligible Freshmen Receiving Need-Based Gift Awards	Percent of Freshmen Whose Need Was Fully Met	Average Financial Aid Package for Freshmen	Average Net Cost After Aid	Average Indebtedness Upon Graduation
College of Saint Elizabeth	ind.	$34,871	$12,744	100%	8%	$34,615	$13,000	$29,315
Drew University	ind.	$40,660	$14,672	100%	15%	$37,650	$17,682	$25,049
Felician University	ind.	$35,000	$13,140	89%	10%	$31,961	$16,179	NR
Georgian Court University	ind.	$33,768	$11,424	99%	29%	$30,573	$14,619	$38,183
Kean University	pub.	$12,595	$14,802	77%	2%	$11,364	$16,033	$34,275
Montclair State University	pub.	$13,073	$15,674	75%	1%	$10,772	$17,975	$45,354
New Jersey City University	pub.	$12,414	$14,574	87%	3%	$12,248	$14,740	$25,463
New Jersey Institute of Technology	pub.	$17,674	$13,900	100%	16%	$16,022	$15,552	$38,718
Princeton University	ind.	$50,340	$16,360	100%	100%	$59,598	$7102	$9445
Ramapo College of New Jersey	pub.	$14,678	$12,840	53%	5%	$11,339	$16,179	$35,658
Rider University	ind.	$42,860	$15,280	100%	18%	$37,576	$20,564	$35,781
Rutgers University - Newark	pub.	$14,826	$13,929	87%	1%	$15,283	$13,472	$27,343
Rutgers University - New Brunswick	pub.	$15,407	$13,075	65%	5%	$14,538	$13,944	$30,829
Stevens Institute of Technology	ind.	$55,952	$16,244	75%	17%	$35,647	$36,549	$37,900
Stockton University	pub.	$14,047	$12,496	90%	46%	$18,594	$7949	$31,470
William Paterson University of New Jersey	pub.	$13,370	$11,900	76%	22%	$12,459	$12,811	$30,272
New Mexico								
Eastern New Mexico University	pub.	$6528	$7526	98%	23%	$12,651	$1403	$20,497
New Mexico Institute of Mining and Technology	pub.	$8156	$8624	92%	28%	$12,511	$4269	$20,771
New Mexico State University	pub.	$7087	$9538	99%	19%	$15,777	$848	$21,429
St. John's College	ind.	$36,410	$12,860	100%	51%	$26,980	$22,290	$26,744
University of New Mexico	pub.	$7875	$9390	97%	14%	NR	NR	$20,532
Western New Mexico University	pub.	$8610	$11,390	78%	12%	$11,245	$8755	NR
New York								
Alfred University	ind.	$36,276	$12,924	99%	35%	$31,797	$17,403	$33,666
Barnard College	ind.	$57,668	$17,856	93%	93%	$50,365	$25,159	$20,829
Baruch College of the City University of New York	pub.	$7461	NR	NR	NR	NR	NR	NR
Binghamton University, State University of New York	pub.	$10,494	$16,549	84%	19%	$13,666	$13,377	$27,679
Canisius College	ind.	$29,428	$11,526	100%	35%	$27,579	$13,375	$35,503
Cazenovia College	ind.	$36,026	$14,743	100%	22%	$34,146	$16,623	$35,863
City College of the City University of New York	pub.	$14,500	$12,123	74%	52%	$3850	$22,773	NR
Clarkson University	ind.	$52,724	$15,786	100%	27%	$48,600	$19,910	$29,000
Colgate University	ind.	$58,045	$14,540	100%	100%	$59,503	$13,082	$25,044
The College of Saint Rose	ind.	$34,354	$13,158	83%	18%	$26,740	$20,772	$36,596
College of Staten Island of the City University of New York	pub.	$7489	$14,745	94%	6%	$8564	$13,670	NR
Columbia University	ind.	$61,850	$14,490	99%	98%	$65,056	$11,284	NR
Cornell University	ind.	$57,222	$15,296	97%	100%	$50,772	$21,746	$27,094
The Culinary Institute of America	ind.	$33,690	$11,880	NR	NR	NR	NR	$51,200
Dominican College	ind.	$29,844	$13,414	85%	12%	$25,631	$17,627	$39,347
Elmira College	ind.	$35,400	$12,500	100%	30%	$28,495	$19,405	$27,679
Farmingdale State College	pub.	$8538	$13,318	92%	8%	$8938	$12,918	$24,531
Fashion Institute of Technology	pub.	$6110	$14,556	76%	53%	$11,319	$9347	$25,832

NA = not applicable; NR = not reported; * = includes room and board; † = room only; — = not available.

College Costs At-a-Glance

	Institutional Control ind.=independent; pub.=public	Tuition and Fees	Room and Board	Percent of Eligible Freshmen Receiving Need-Based Gift Awards	Percent of Freshmen Whose Need Was Fully Met	Average Financial Aid Package for Freshmen	Average Net Cost After Aid	Average Indebtedness Upon Graduation
Fordham University	ind.	$55,788	$19,066	96%	29%	$39,608	$35,246	$37,283
Hamilton College	ind.	$56,530	$14,360	100%	100%	$54,168	$16,722	$17,292
Hobart and William Smith Colleges	ind.	$58,650	$15,090	100%	27%	$43,257	$30,483	$34,456
Hofstra University	ind.	$47,510	$16,428	99%	27%	$36,000	$27,938	NR
Iona College	ind.	$41,580	$16,208	40%	19%	$28,081	$29,707	$32,948
Ithaca College	ind.	$46,610	$15,844	97%	59%	$39,878	$22,576	$42,000
The Juilliard School	ind.	$47,470	$17,970	100%	24%	$37,820	$27,620	$26,326
Keuka College	ind.	$34,032	$12,144	79%	95%	$38,596	$7580	$44,211
The King's College	ind.	$37,690	$1440	100%	21%	$27,660	$11,470	$34,876
Le Moyne College	ind.	$35,910	$14,470	100%	28%	$28,810	$21,570	$40,522
Manhattan College	ind.	$44,564	$16,870	97%	NR	$18,553	$42,881	$11,170
Manhattanville College	ind.	$40,330	$14,810	81%	19%	$30,750	$24,390	$35,092
Marist College	ind.	$40,525	$17,920	98%	20%	$30,065	$28,380	$40,007
Mercy College	ind.	$19,594	$14,400	92%	4%	$17,029	$16,965	$23,942
Molloy College	ind.	$32,600	$15,560	99%	17%	$19,593	$28,567	$34,553
Mount Saint Mary College	ind.	$34,412	$16,658	99%	26%	$24,901	$26,169	$28,519
Nazareth College of Rochester	ind.	$35,416	$14,230	100%	45%	$29,222	$20,424	$49,827
New York Institute of Technology	ind.	$39,760	$14,290	75%	NR	$31,242	$22,808	NR
New York University	ind.	$53,308	$18,684	100%	12%	$41,475	$30,517	$29,242
Niagara University	ind.	$35,240	$11,850	98%	48%	$30,608	$16,482	$34,046
Nyack College	ind.	$25,500	$10,000	NR	NR	NR	NR	$28,926
Pratt Institute	ind.	$55,630	$13,988	36%	17%	$31,889	$37,729	$41,305
Purchase College, State University of New York	pub.	$8953	$14,548	96%	5%	$10,606	$12,895	$23,987
Rensselaer Polytechnic Institute	ind.	$55,375	$15,580	100%	24%	$43,770	$27,185	$34,595
St. Bonaventure University	ind.	$36,515	$13,620	100%	24%	$29,428	$20,707	$34,877
St. John Fisher College	ind.	$35,150	$12,650	100%	21%	$24,491	$23,309	$37,064
St. Joseph's College, Long Island Campus	ind.	$29,200	NA	100%	32%	$18,552	$10,648	$31,518
St. Joseph's College, New York	ind.	$29,190	$14,800	100%	16%	$20,869	$23,121	$27,278
St. Lawrence University	ind.	$56,766	$14,628	99%	31%	$52,542	$18,852	$32,390
St. Thomas Aquinas College	ind.	$33,050	$13,650	94%	24%	$17,250	$29,450	$31,000
Sarah Lawrence College	ind.	$57,520	$15,820	100%	18%	$41,552	$31,788	$26,808
School of Visual Arts	ind.	$43,400	$18,800	91%	7%	$22,164	$40,036	$45,588
Siena College	ind.	$39,500	$15,915	100%	34%	$33,696	$21,719	$35,057
Skidmore College	ind.	$56,172	$15,000	100%	100%	$51,600	$19,572	$31,381
State University of New York at Fredonia	pub.	$8717	$12,830	87%	28%	$13,876	$7671	$26,722
State University of New York at New Paltz	pub.	$8502	$13,928	56%	12%	$12,626	$9804	$26,771
State University of New York at Oswego	pub.	$8717	$14,603	88%	28%	$13,241	$10,079	NR
State University of New York at Plattsburgh	pub.	$8872	$13,630	91%	21%	$14,298	$8204	$30,919
State University of New York College at Cortland	pub.	$8806	$13,100	75%	12%	$15,349	$6557	$31,176
State University of New York College at Geneseo	pub.	$8927	$14,018	77%	15%	$10,664	$12,281	$23,666
State University of New York College at Oneonta	pub.	$8922	NR	82%	8%	$15,916	$7024	$26,092
State University of New York College at Potsdam	pub.	$8711	$13,900	79%	16%	$15,715	$6896	$30,057

NA = not applicable; NR = not reported; * = includes room and board; † = room only; — = not available.

College Costs At-a-Glance

	Institutional Control ind.=independent; pub.=public	Tuition and Fees	Room and Board	Percent of Eligible Freshmen Receiving Need-Based Gift Awards	Percent of Freshmen Whose Need Was Fully Met	Average Financial Aid Package for Freshmen	Average Net Cost After Aid	Average Indebtedness Upon Graduation
State University of New York College of Environmental Science and Forestry	pub.	$9115	$16,270	99%	22%	$10,604	$14,781	$21,885
State University of New York College of Technology at Canton	pub.	$8660	$13,200	88%	17%	$11,436	$10,424	$31,214
State University of New York College of Technology at Delhi	pub.	$8920	$12,900	92%	6%	$11,269	$10,551	$27,915
State University of New York Empire State College	pub.	$7605	NA	NR	NR	NR	NR	NR
Stony Brook University, State University of New York	pub.	$10,175	$14,278	92%	13%	$13,657	$10,796	$25,678
SUNY Brockport	pub.	$8926	$14,160	84%	14%	$10,889	$12,197	$31,695
Syracuse University	ind.	$53,849	$15,910	97%	71%	$45,190	$24,569	$37,563
Union College	ind.	$59,427	$14,583	100%	100%	$46,760	$27,250	$36,921
University at Albany, State University of New York	pub.	$9956	$13,864	90%	8%	$11,214	$12,606	$27,555
University at Buffalo, the State University of New York	pub.	$10,524	$14,631	88%	8%	$11,375	$13,780	$25,157
Utica College	ind.	$22,110	$11,670	99%	8%	$16,783	$16,997	$30,402
Vassar College	ind.	$58,770	$14,220	100%	100%	$56,675	$16,315	$19,474
Yeshiva University	ind.	$44,900	$12,500	99%	34%	$42,629	$14,771	$22,388
North Carolina								
Appalachian State University	pub.	$7410	$8568	81%	20%	$10,465	$5513	$23,105
Barton College	ind.	$31,732	$10,422	100%	15%	$26,498	$15,656	$27,227
Belmont Abbey College	ind.	$18,500	$10,390	100%	15%	$14,014	$14,876	NR
Carolina Christian College	ind.	$8890	$1750	100%	93%	$9590	$1050	NR
Catawba College	ind.	$78,510	$10,804	90%	27%	$29,432	$59,882	$27,806
Davidson College	ind.	$55,060	$15,225	100%	100%	$51,899	$18,386	$23,535
Duke University	ind.	$57,931	$15,588	96%	100%	$54,990	$18,529	$22,369
East Carolina University	pub.	$7239	$9712	70%	7%	$9468	$7483	$23,709
Elon University	ind.	$37,921	$13,131	88%	14%	$19,972	$31,080	$32,028
Fayetteville State University	pub.	$4975	$8616	98%	11%	$12,818	$773	NR
Guilford College	ind.	$40,120	$12,200	99%	67%	$29,257	$23,063	$35,392
High Point University	ind.	$36,268	$14,702	100%	15%	$19,915	$31,055	$34,079
Lees-McRae College	ind.	$27,521	$10,870	100%	1%	$25,136	$13,255	NR
Mid-Atlantic Christian University	ind.	$14,415	$8600	64%	4%	$8506	$14,509	$26,414
North Carolina Central University	pub.	$6534	$10,227	92%	1%	$14,832	$1929	$44,228
North Carolina State University	pub.	$9101	$11,359	96%	23%	$13,766	$6694	$25,893
University of North Carolina Asheville	pub.	$7230	$9660	95%	22%	$12,982	$3908	$24,476
The University of North Carolina at Chapel Hill	pub.	$9232	$11,740	93%	81%	$17,732	$3240	$22,466
The University of North Carolina at Charlotte	pub.	$7096	$11,060	59%	11%	$9540	$8616	$28,316
The University of North Carolina at Greensboro	pub.	$7403	$9264	87%	13%	$12,134	$4533	$23,317
The University of North Carolina at Pembroke	pub.	$3490	$8924	86%	7%	$8807	$3607	$27,193
The University of North Carolina Wilmington	pub.	$7181	$10,897	97%	12%	$8680	$9398	$26,568
Wake Forest University	ind.	$57,760	$9848	95%	100%	$53,585	$14,023	$34,053
Western Carolina University	pub.	$1000	NR	95%	12%	$10,880	—	$20,123
William Peace University	ind.	$32,450	$11,800	93%	10%	$26,013	$18,237	$26,929
Wingate University	ind.	$38,896	$9910	100%	27%	$31,028	$17,778	$29,823

NA = not applicable; NR = not reported; * = includes room and board; † = room only; — = not available.

College Costs At-a-Glance

	Institutional Control ind.=independent; pub.=public	Tuition and Fees	Room and Board	Percent of Eligible Freshmen Receiving Need-Based Gift Awards	Percent of Freshmen Whose Need Was Fully Met	Average Financial Aid Package for Freshmen	Average Net Cost After Aid	Average Indebtedness Upon Graduation
North Dakota								
Minot State University	pub.	$7590	$7315	97%	28%	$9560	$5345	$25,324
North Dakota State University	pub.	$9619	$8878	84%	42%	$13,398	$5099	$33,639
University of Jamestown	ind.	$23,498	$8316	100%	28%	$17,346	$14,468	$28,889
University of North Dakota	pub.	$9737	$9544	89%	45%	$15,120	$4161	NR
Valley City State University	pub.	$7707	$6610	100%	52%	$13,920	$397	NR
Ohio								
Ashland University	ind.	$21,980	$10,190	98%	23%	$19,439	$12,731	NR
Baldwin Wallace University	ind.	$33,530	$10,110	100%	43%	$28,614	$15,026	$33,919
Bluffton University	ind.	$49,848*	$11,346	100%	15%	$31,745	$29,449	$35,601
Bowling Green State University	pub.	$11,317	$10,396	92%	16%	$14,297	$7416	$30,603
Capital University	ind.	$38,298	$11,602	98%	22%	$32,506	$17,394	$33,461
Case Western Reserve University	ind.	$50,924	$15,614	98%	96%	$48,693	$17,845	$33,946
Cedarville University	ind.	$32,564	$7922	67%	51%	$24,220	$16,266	$24,027
Cleveland Institute of Art	ind.	$44,385	$11,590	100%	8%	$26,970	$29,005	$41,326
Cleveland State University	pub.	$9874	$14,348	88%	7%	$10,221	$14,001	$25,895
The College of Wooster	ind.	$50,250	$11,850	97%	48%	$48,431	$13,669	$32,194
Hiram College	ind.	$37,710	$10,290	100%	7%	$31,055	$16,945	$36,500
John Carroll University	ind.	$44,405	$12,560	98%	28%	$34,460	$22,505	$32,956
Kenyon College	ind.	$61,100	$12,830	100%	78%	$47,815	$26,115	$26,865
Malone University	ind.	$32,416	$9900	100%	19%	$27,862	$14,454	$32,495
Marietta College	ind.	$36,764	$12,740	98%	36%	$36,438	$13,066	NR
Miami University	pub.	$15,232	$13,397	90%	22%	$16,409	$12,220	$29,652
Mount Carmel College of Nursing	ind.	$14,372	$5000	88%	4%	$9985	$9387	$35,781
Mount Vernon Nazarene University	ind.	$31,610	$8890	100%	71%	$27,335	$13,165	$22,778
Muskingum University	ind.	$29,740	$12,032	100%	21%	$26,072	$15,700	$33,026
Oberlin College	ind.	$56,868	$16,826	100%	100%	$46,673	$27,021	$26,175
Ohio Christian University	ind.	$20,790	$8320	88%	NR	$9373	$19,737	$30,000
The Ohio State University	pub.	$11,084	$12,708	92%	29%	$16,288	$7504	$27,242
Ohio University	pub.	$12,612	$12,172	93%	12%	$9777	$15,007	$28,856
Ohio University–Chillicothe	pub.	$5674	NA	89%	99%	$5389	$285	$28,856
Ohio University–Eastern	pub.	$5674	NA	94%	100%	$5468	$206	NR
Ohio University–Lancaster	pub.	$5674	NA	85%	97%	$4825	$849	NR
Ohio University–Southern Campus	pub.	$5674	NA	96%	97%	$4729	$945	NR
Ohio University–Zanesville	pub.	$5674	NA	86%	100%	$5469	$205	NR
Ohio Wesleyan University	ind.	$47,130	$13,330	100%	19%	$37,739	$22,721	$36,680
Otterbein University	ind.	$32,474	$11,484	98%	21%	$22,413	$21,545	NR
Tiffin University	ind.	$27,610	$11,700	100%	14%	$20,530	$18,780	$31,788
University of Cincinnati	pub.	$11,010	$11,530	41%	15%	$6477	$16,063	$30,350
University of Dayton	ind.	$44,100	$14,050	99%	98%	$32,131	$26,019	$37,533
The University of Findlay	ind.	$35,410	$10,200	100%	27%	$28,576	$17,034	$37,424
University of Mount Union	ind.	$31,700	$10,500	100%	19%	$23,639	$18,561	$40,112

NA = not applicable; NR = not reported; * = includes room and board; † = room only; — = not available.

College Costs At-a-Glance

	Institutional Control ind.=independent; pub.=public	Tuition and Fees	Room and Board	Percent of Eligible Freshmen Receiving Need-Based Gift Awards	Percent of Freshmen Whose Need Was Fully Met	Average Financial Aid Package for Freshmen	Average Net Cost After Aid	Average Indebtedness Upon Graduation
The University of Toledo	pub.	$10,539	$12,285	99%	15%	$12,242	$10,582	$27,145
Ursuline College	ind.	$34,630	$11,514	100%	11%	$31,712	$14,432	$29,220
Wittenberg University	ind.	$41,476	$10,830	39%	39%	$37,465	$14,841	NR
Wright State University	pub.	$9578	$12,084	91%	20%	$11,335	$10,327	$28,607
Wright State University–Lake Campus	pub.	$6410	$5030	84%	25%	$8670	$2770	$25,975
Xavier University	ind.	$42,460	$13,310	60%	10%	$24,281	$31,489	$10,348
Youngstown State University	pub.	$9279	$9700	78%	12%	$9566	$9413	$29,360
Oklahoma								
Cameron University	pub.	$6450	$5452	92%	7%	$9557	$2345	$13,890
East Central University	pub.	$7052	$7072	75%	28%	$5726	$8398	$21,665
Northeastern State University	pub.	$6915	$7340	92%	83%	$13,190	$1065	$20,707
Oklahoma Baptist University	ind.	$31,352	$7720	82%	5%	$20,421	$18,651	$25,673
Oklahoma City University	ind.	$32,594	$9236	100%	77%	$22,672	$19,158	$26,696
Oklahoma State University	pub.	$9018	$9106	79%	15%	$16,237	$1887	$25,185
Oral Roberts University	ind.	$39,580*	$8650	100%	35%	$28,303	$19,927	$35,230
Rogers State University	pub.	$7470	$8975	93%	8%	$9062	$7383	$13,052
Southwestern Oklahoma State University	pub.	$7695	$6030	89%	27%	$6892	$6833	$23,292
University of Oklahoma	pub.	$9062	$10,994	51%	84%	$14,673	$5383	$30,258
The University of Tulsa	ind.	$43,500	$12,062	98%	34%	$37,646	$17,916	$36,176
Oregon								
George Fox University	ind.	$37,130	$11,650	99%	45%	$27,128	$21,652	$31,299
Lewis & Clark College	ind.	$52,780	$13,008	99%	37%	$44,236	$21,552	$30,460
Linfield College	ind.	$45,062	$12,930	78%	33%	$40,200	$17,792	$36,082
Northwest Christian University	ind.	$32,320	$10,050	100%	17%	$27,003	$15,367	$25,058
Oregon Institute of Technology	pub.	$10,485	$9133	57%	13%	$11,847	$7771	$27,007
Pacific University	ind.	$48,260	$13,420	97%	19%	$37,575	$24,105	$34,429
Portland State University	pub.	$9578	$11,172	82%	8%	$12,268	$8482	$26,426
Reed College	ind.	$58,440	$14,620	100%	100%	$45,748	$27,312	$25,657
University of Oregon	pub.	$10,755	$12,783	80%	8%	$11,921	$11,617	$26,548
University of Portland	ind.	$47,818	$13,968	70%	10%	$32,227	$29,559	$32,027
Warner Pacific University	ind.	$18,660	$10,020	84%	18%	$18,544	$10,136	$30,774
Willamette University	ind.	$53,624	$13,328	99%	13%	$38,006	$28,946	$26,973
Pennsylvania								
Allegheny College	ind.	$50,980	$13,080	100%	42%	$45,059	$19,001	NR
Bloomsburg University of Pennsylvania	pub.	$10,958	$9686	64%	17%	$104,088	—	$38,013
Bryn Mawr College	ind.	$54,440	$17,100	99%	100%	$50,941	$20,599	$28,772
Bucknell University	ind.	$58,202	$14,670	86%	NR	$39,500	$33,372	$31,000
California University of Pennsylvania	pub.	$10,902	$10,186	91%	13%	$11,416	$9672	$42,029
Carlow University	ind.	$30,528	$11,902	100%	21%	$24,053	$18,377	$40,958
Carnegie Mellon University	ind.	$58,924	$15,550	96%	93%	$47,549	$26,925	$31,342
Cedar Crest College	ind.	$41,567	$12,322	100%	18%	$32,826	$21,063	$39,866

NA = not applicable; NR = not reported; * = includes room and board; † = room only; — = not available.

College Costs At-a-Glance

	Institutional Control ind.=independent; pub.=public	Tuition and Fees	Room and Board	Percent of Eligible Freshmen Receiving Need-Based Gift Awards	Percent of Freshmen Whose Need Was Fully Met	Average Financial Aid Package for Freshmen	Average Net Cost After Aid	Average Indebtedness Upon Graduation
Chatham University	ind.	$39,902	$12,853	94%	18%	$30,638	$22,117	$35,199
Chestnut Hill College	ind.	$37,200	$11,000	84%	23%	$35,637	$12,563	$47,542
Clarion University of Pennsylvania	pub.	$7716	NR	69%	9%	$12,391	$6325	$35,054
Delaware Valley University	ind.	$40,620	$14,620	99%	18%	$32,720	$22,520	$48,278
DeSales University	ind.	$38,700	$13,000	100%	28%	$29,648	$22,052	$40,776
Dickinson College	ind.	$58,680	$14,672	97%	93%	$47,914	$25,438	$27,030
Drexel University	ind.	$54,516	$14,241	100%	30%	$43,051	$25,706	$72,883
Duquesne University	ind.	$39,992	$13,088	100%	22%	$27,833	$25,247	$44,243
Eastern University	ind.	$34,706	$11,824	91%	23%	$26,796	$19,734	$40,488
East Stroudsburg University of Pennsylvania	pub.	$10,688	$11,760	95%	46%	$8677	$13,771	$12,070
Edinboro University of Pennsylvania	pub.	$10,543	$9800	76%	3%	$9009	$11,334	$42,694
Franklin & Marshall College	ind.	$58,800	$14,450	100%	100%	$55,102	$18,148	$27,928
Gettysburg College	ind.	$56,390	$13,460	98%	90%	$46,063	$23,787	$34,630
Grove City College	ind.	$18,470	$10,060	99%	11%	$8385	$20,145	$40,600
Gwynedd Mercy University	ind.	$35,600	$12,680	100%	13%	$26,417	$21,863	$35,827
Haverford College	ind.	$56,698	$16,770	100%	100%	$53,527	$19,941	$11,500
Immaculata University	ind.	$27,750	$12,620	64%	15%	$18,228	$22,142	$55,126
Indiana University of Pennsylvania	pub.	$13,354	$12,744	68%	4%	$10,773	$15,325	$41,222
Keystone College	ind.	$17,000	$11,900	NR	NR	NR	NR	NR
King's College	ind.	$40,080	$14,008	100%	15%	$29,083	$25,005	$40,818
Kutztown University of Pennsylvania	pub.	$10,950	$10,434	63%	7%	$9089	$12,295	$40,592
Lafayette College	ind.	$57,052	$16,874	98%	100%	$51,259	$22,667	$30,181
Lancaster Bible College	ind.	$26,070	$9000	100%	30%	$24,047	$11,023	$32,751
La Roche University	ind.	$30,320	$12,270	54%	35%	$34,141	$8449	$33,433
Lebanon Valley College	ind.	$44,910	$12,200	99%	26%	$36,250	$20,860	$42,880
Lehigh University	ind.	$57,450	$14,740	99%	88%	$53,876	$18,314	$39,609
Lincoln University	pub.	$11,266	$9828	80%	4%	$10,705	$10,389	$36,567
Lock Haven University of Pennsylvania	pub.	$10,878	$10,368	70%	5%	$8776	$12,470	$23,490
Lycoming College	ind.	$41,626	$13,008	100%	21%	$49,803	$4831	NR
Mansfield University of Pennsylvania	pub.	$10,596	$10,147	78%	65%	$1710	$19,033	$42,457
Marywood University	ind.	$36,928	$14,338	100%	22%	$31,924	$19,342	$41,925
Messiah College	ind.	$37,180	$10,900	100%	19%	$27,916	$20,164	$41,859
Millersville University of Pennsylvania	pub.	$12,250	$12,980	76%	4%	$8885	$16,345	$32,815
Misericordia University	ind.	$34,560	$14,220	100%	23%	$25,954	$22,826	$46,756
Moravian College	ind.	$47,367	$14,471	100%	18%	$33,774	$28,064	$38,514
Penn State Abington	pub.	$15,524	$8420	69%	10%	$10,487	$13,457	$32,957
Penn State Altoona	pub.	$15,206	$11,884	46%	32%	$10,020	$17,070	$43,294
Penn State Beaver	pub.	$13,710	$11,510	59%	24%	$10,458	$14,762	$38,026
Penn State Berks	pub.	$15,206	$13,080	51%	23%	$9527	$18,759	$41,278
Penn State Brandywine	pub.	$14,476	$12,586	59%	24%	$9752	$17,310	$33,019
Penn State Erie, The Behrend College	pub.	$15,206	$11,884	48%	27%	$10,522	$16,568	$41,841
Penn State Greater Allegheny	pub.	$13,710	$11,510	70%	21%	$12,620	$12,600	$36,645

NA = not applicable; NR = not reported; * = includes room and board; † = room only; — = not available.

College Costs At-a-Glance

	Institutional Control ind.=independent; pub.=public	Tuition and Fees	Room and Board	Percent of Eligible Freshmen Receiving Need-Based Gift Awards	Percent of Freshmen Whose Need Was Fully Met	Average Financial Aid Package for Freshmen	Average Net Cost After Aid	Average Indebtedness Upon Graduation
Penn State Harrisburg	pub.	$15,206	$13,750	49%	27%	$10,555	$18,401	$39,036
Penn State Hazleton	pub.	$14,476	$11,510	67%	26%	$12,110	$13,876	$38,737
Penn State Lehigh Valley	pub.	$14,476	NA	61%	14%	$9423	$5053	$35,834
Penn State New Kensington	pub.	$13,710	NA	65%	20%	$9034	$4676	$34,304
Penn State Schuylkill	pub.	$14,476	$6766	67%	25%	$12,222	$9020	$41,749
Penn State Shenango	pub.	$13,350	NA	74%	16%	$12,925	$425	$40,515
Penn State University Park	pub.	$18,450	$11,884	38%	34%	$10,346	$19,988	$40,128
Penn State Wilkes-Barre	pub.	$13,594	NA	70%	19%	$10,673	$2921	$34,928
Penn State Worthington Scranton	pub.	$14,476	NA	68%	17%	$10,409	$4067	$39,015
Penn State York	pub.	$14,476	NA	56%	19%	$9417	$5059	$37,420
Pennsylvania Academy of the Fine Arts	ind.	$40,376	$12,010	NR	NR	NR	NR	NR
Pennsylvania College of Technology	pub.	$17,160	$11,715	78%	NR	$13,904	$14,971	NR
Saint Francis University	ind.	$39,378	$12,472	100%	25%	$26,924	$24,926	$40,676
Saint Joseph's University	ind.	$47,940	$14,840	99%	24%	$33,687	$29,093	NR
Saint Vincent College	ind.	$36,904	$12,161	67%	29%	$34,531	$14,534	$36,745
Slippery Rock University of Pennsylvania	pub.	$10,517	$10,446	71%	13%	$9433	$11,530	$37,450
Susquehanna University	ind.	$51,140	$13,680	100%	27%	$40,504	$24,316	$40,455
Swarthmore College	ind.	$54,656	$16,088	100%	100%	$56,923	$13,821	$24,099
Temple University	pub.	$19,748	$12,188	96%	5%	$12,848	$19,088	$38,634
University of Pennsylvania	ind.	$60,042	$16,784	99%	100%	$55,680	$21,146	$23,009
University of Pittsburgh	pub.	$19,718	$11,250	81%	21%	$13,674	$17,294	$39,417
University of Pittsburgh at Bradford	pub.	$14,158	$10,532	92%	11%	$12,652	$12,038	$38,322
University of Pittsburgh at Greensburg	pub.	$14,148	$10,870	92%	15%	$11,743	$13,275	$33,844
University of Pittsburgh at Johnstown	pub.	$14,156	$10,060	92%	15%	$11,743	$12,473	$39,603
The University of Scranton	ind.	$45,790	$15,310	81%	18%	$31,889	$29,211	$41,570
Villanova University	ind.	$55,280	$14,444	94%	15%	$41,496	$28,228	$36,716
Washington & Jefferson College	ind.	$49,338	$13,044	100%	22%	$42,656	$19,726	$48,582
Waynesburg University	ind.	$26,640	$10,890	100%	19%	$21,912	$15,618	$23,316
West Chester University of Pennsylvania	pub.	$10,421	$9326	71%	8%	$8858	$10,889	$36,469
Widener University	ind.	$48,740	$14,812	98%	22%	$38,316	$25,236	NR
Wilkes University	ind.	$37,622	$15,108	100%	18%	$28,957	$23,773	NR
Wilson College	ind.	$25,300	$11,594	100%	18%	$19,747	$17,147	$39,090
York College of Pennsylvania	ind.	$21,790	$11,890	73%	19%	$14,890	$18,790	$44,077
Puerto Rico								
Bayamón Central University	ind.	$6260	$5724	NR	NR	NR	NR	NR
Inter American University of Puerto Rico, Aguadilla Campus	ind.	$5254	NA	100%	NR	NR	NR	NR
Inter American University of Puerto Rico, Metropolitan Campus	ind.	$8796	NA	100%	NR	NR	NR	NR
Rhode Island								
Brown University	ind.	$60,596	$15,908	100%	100%	$55,758	$20,746	$24,304
Bryant University	ind.	$46,863	$16,204	61%	22%	$25,023	$38,044	$53,350
New England Institute of Technology	ind.	$31,545	$14,505	NR	NR	NR	NR	NR

NA = not applicable; NR = not reported; * = includes room and board; † = room only; — = not available.

College Costs At-a-Glance

	Institutional Control ind.=independent; pub.=public	Tuition and Fees	Room and Board	Percent of Eligible Freshmen Receiving Need-Based Gift Awards	Percent of Freshmen Whose Need Was Fully Met	Average Financial Aid Package for Freshmen	Average Net Cost After Aid	Average Indebtedness Upon Graduation
Providence College	ind.	$52,438	$15,140	99%	25%	$38,107	$29,471	$44,529
Roger Williams University	ind.	$32,789	$15,390	73%	9%	$26,407	$21,772	$44,753
Salve Regina University	ind.	$42,920	$15,400	100%	20%	$29,491	$28,829	$40,958
University of Rhode Island	pub.	$14,566	$8010	97%	65%	$19,311	$3265	$35,883
South Carolina								
Anderson University	ind.	$29 980	$10,640	100%	36%	$22,571	$18,049	$32,609
The Citadel, The Military College of South Carolina	pub.	$14,483	$7957	89%	23%	$17,935	$4505	$28,159
Clemson University	pub.	$14,970	$6812	92%	15%	$12,592	$9190	$32,510
Coastal Carolina University	pub.	$11,640	$9290	50%	12%	$11,241	$9689	$37,717
Columbia College	ind.	$19,890	$8295	100%	4%	$14,988	$13,197	$25,241
Columbia International University	ind.	$8950*	$8950	100%	17%	$20,131	—	$23,695
Limestone College	ind.	$26,300	$9900	99%	13%	$19,363	$16,837	$33,427
North Greenville University	ind.	$22,050	$10,450	100%	NR	$19,065	$13,435	NR
Presbyterian College	ind.	$39,460	$10,680	100%	31%	$36,648	$13,492	$33,956
University of South Carolina	pub.	$12,688	$10,670	35%	30%	$9402	$13,956	$30,449
University of South Carolina Aiken	pub.	$10,760	$7946	96%	16%	$12,210	$6496	$28,176
Wofford College	ind.	$61,440*	$13,790	100%	40%	$40,736	$34,494	$31,107
South Dakota								
Augustana University	ind.	$35,884	$8616	100%	18%	$28,812	$15,688	$37,647
Black Hills State University	pub.	$9009	$7142	NR	NR	NR	NR	NR
Dakota State University	pub.	$9536	$7033	54%	11%	$7882	$8687	$27,928
Mount Marty College	ind.	$28,126	$8146	99%	54%	$33,203	$3069	NR
Northern State University	pub.	$8750	$8925	92%	34%	$11,179	$6496	$29,635
University of South Dakota	pub.	$9332	$8409	47%	16%	$8225	$9516	$28,363
Tennessee								
Austin Peay State University	pub.	$8303	$11,114	70%	NR	$5991	$13,426	$25,938
Belmont University	ind.	$35,650	$12,520	98%	15%	$28,487	$19,683	$29,702
Bryan College	ind.	$16,900	$7800	100%	47%	$25,887	—	$24,630
Carson-Newman University	ind.	$29,500	$8150	100%	14%	$24,928	$12,722	$28,014
Freed-Hardeman University	ind.	$22,950	$7950	100%	27%	$20,952	$9948	$29,103
Johnson University	ind.	$18,290	$3500	NR	NR	NR	NR	NR
King University	ind.	$31,840	$9386	99%	18%	$23,666	$17,560	$29,417
Lee University	ind.	$19,540	$8260	97%	25%	$15,360	$12,440	$30,846
Lincoln Memorial University	ind.	$25,038	$10,638	99%	1%	$24,048	$11,628	$22,290
Lipscomb University	ind.	$34,744	$13,804	100%	30%	$27,488	$21,060	$31,116
Maryville College	ind.	$35,578	$11,710	100%	20%	$31,451	$15,837	$29,844
Middle Tennessee State University	pub.	$11,176	$8976	62%	13%	$11,158	$8994	$24,936
Mid-South Christian College	ind.	$7490	$3400	NR	NR	NR	NR	NR
Milligan University	ind.	$35,600	$7400	100%	30%	$26,563	$16,437	$28,864
Tennessee Wesleyan University	ind.	$25,150	$8050	55%	30%	$22,799	$10,401	$24,338
Trevecca Nazarene University	ind.	$26,898	$9100	NR	NR	NR	NR	$24,895

NA = not applicable; NR = not reported; * = includes room and board; † = room only; — = not available.

College Costs At-a-Glance

	Institutional Control ind.=independent; pub.=public	Tuition and Fees	Room and Board	Percent of Eligible Freshmen Receiving Need-Based Gift Awards	Percent of Freshmen Whose Need Was Fully Met	Average Financial Aid Package for Freshmen	Average Net Cost After Aid	Average Indebtedness Upon Graduation
Union University	ind.	$34,780	$10,880	76%	16%	$25,655	$20,005	NR
University of Memphis	pub.	$9912	$10,175	68%	9%	$13,314	$6773	$30,931
The University of Tennessee	pub.	$13,264	$11,482	92%	16%	$14,918	$9828	$27,060
The University of Tennessee at Chattanooga	pub.	$9656	$10,159	97%	17%	$12,207	$7608	$23,059
The University of Tennessee at Martin	pub.	$9748	$6396	70%	24%	$13,216	$2928	$24,096
The University of the South	ind.	$47,980	$13,700	98%	31%	$35,079	$26,601	$31,737
Vanderbilt University	ind.	$55,032	$17,670	98%	100%	$56,739	$15,963	$22,727
Texas								
Abilene Christian University	ind.	$37,800	$11,350	100%	34%	$26,260	$22,890	NR
Angelo State University	pub.	$9011	$9630	91%	15%	$11,490	$7151	$24,496
Austin College	ind.	$41,155	$12,752	100%	25%	$40,581	$13,326	NR
Baylor University	ind.	$49,246	$13,274	109%	22%	$31,871	$30,649	$49,610
Dallas Baptist University	ind.	$31,940	$8568	64%	41%	$21,845	$18,663	$27,248
East Texas Baptist University	ind.	$27,210	$9328	72%	17%	$18,826	$17,712	$30,351
Hardin-Simmons University	ind.	$31,366	$9740	79%	30%	$32,163	$8943	$36,707
Houston Baptist University	ind.	$34,500	$9130	100%	15%	$30,589	$13,041	$32,538
LeTourneau University	ind.	$32,490	$10,070	100%	23%	$25,542	$17,018	$36,103
Messenger College	ind.	$11,070	$6470	50%	NR	$2375	$15,165	$32,313
Prairie View A&M University	pub.	$10,786	$9076	84%	6%	$16,001	$3861	$32,960
Rice University	ind.	$49,112	$14,140	98%	100%	$51,891	$11,361	$24,292
St. Mary's University	ind.	$34,740	$10,980	99%	15%	$28,580	$17,140	$34,187
Schreiner University	ind.	$31,938	$10,579	82%	9%	$21,261	$21,256	$47,330
Southern Methodist University	ind.	$58,540	$17,110	63%	44%	$45,742	$29,908	$30,697
Southwestern University	ind.	$45,120	$12,450	100%	26%	$37,308	$20,262	$34,551
Stephen F. Austin State University	pub.	$7620	$9012	77%	14%	$12,711	$3921	$26,477
Sul Ross State University	pub.	$8980	NR	87%	75%	$11,456	$6536	$13,073
Tarleton State University	pub.	$9138	$10,712	88%	5%	$10,373	$9477	$23,820
Texas A&M International University	pub.	$9254	$8809	89%	NR	NR	NR	$3477
Texas A&M University	pub.	$11,232	$10,400	95%	23%	$18,575	$3057	$24,590
Texas A&M University–Central Texas	pub.	$8696	$9136	NR	NR	NR	NR	NR
Texas A&M University–Commerce	pub.	$8958	$8868	97%	14%	$11,962	$5864	$25,546
Texas A&M University–Corpus Christi	pub.	$4992	$10,220	77%	21%	$11,611	$3601	$17,748
Texas A&M University–Kingsville	pub.	$9136	$8848	83%	19%	$11,703	$6281	$30,726
Texas Christian University	ind.	$51,660	$14,040	95%	36%	$32,932	$32,768	$47,931
Texas Lutheran University	ind.	$30,860	$10,440	100%	20%	$26,997	$14,303	$29,735
Texas State University	pub.	$11,550	$7646	85%	23%	$12,082	$7114	$24,950
Texas Tech University	pub.	$11,320	$9772	89%	26%	$10,479	$10,613	$32,829
Texas Woman's University	pub.	$9748	$9050	98%	36%	$16,016	$2782	$22,206
Trinity University	ind.	$46,456	$13,740	100%	67%	$43,257	$16,939	$43,005
University of Dallas	ind.	$44,810	$13,080	97%	20%	$36,448	$21,442	$34,205
University of Houston	pub.	$11,276	$9368	92%	14%	$13,468	$7176	$22,858
University of Houston–Clear Lake	pub.	$7961	$5109	72%	10%	$11,943	$1127	$18,992

NA = not applicable; NR = not reported; * = includes room and board; † = room only; — = not available.

College Costs At-a-Glance

	Institutional Control ind.=independent; pub.=public	Tuition and Fees	Room and Board	Percent of Eligible Freshmen Receiving Need-Based Gift Awards	Percent of Freshmen Whose Need Was Fully Met	Average Financial Aid Package for Freshmen	Average Net Cost After Aid	Average Indebtedness Upon Graduation
University of Houston - Downtown	pub.	$8664	NA	98%	5%	$8911	—	$4902
University of Mary Hardin-Baylor	ind.	$29,800	$8782	100%	8%	$19,823	$18,759	$34,104
University of St. Thomas	ind.	$31,560	$9470	99%	15%	$26,860	$14,170	$25,969
The University of Texas at Austin	pub.	$10,824	$11,812	77%	27%	$12,693	$9943	$24,263
The University of Texas at Dallas	pub.	$13,442	$11,532	88%	22%	$15,950	$9024	$23,176
The University of Texas at El Paso	pub.	$8961	$9496	74%	15%	$11,631	$6826	$23,632
The University of Texas at San Antonio	pub.	$9723	$7590	90%	5%	$10,815	$6498	$24,214
The University of Texas at Tyler	pub.	$8742	$9502	90%	16%	$11,486	$6758	$19,691
The University of Texas Rio Grande Valley	pub.	$8916	$8342	97%	3%	$10,375	$6883	$16,662
University of the Incarnate Word	ind.	$32,286	$13,014	100%	11%	$24,843	$20,457	$36,178
Wayland Baptist University	ind.	$23,298	$7722	99%	7%	$13,681	$17,339	$29,555
West Texas A&M University	pub.	$8688	$7196	83%	8%	$10,900	$4984	$28,132
Utah								
Brigham Young University	ind.	$5970	$7808	57%	2%	$7146	$6632	$14,672
Neumont College of Computer Science	ind.	$24,750	$6300	NR	NR	NR	NR	$39,623
Southern Utah University	pub.	$6770	$7349	49%	21%	$9404	$4715	$16,958
University of Utah	pub.	$9498	$10,201	92%	15%	$25,969	—	$19,656
Utah State University	pub.	$7859	$5960	48%	19%	$10,938	$2881	$21,171
Weber State University	pub.	$5967	$8400	74%	108%	$2530	$11,837	$21,690
Westminster College	ind.	$37,960	$11,097	100%	20%	$30,624	$18,433	$25,219
Vermont								
Bennington College	ind.	$58,124	$16,840	100%	27%	$47,458	$27,506	$29,443
Champlain College	ind.	$41,828	$15,766	99%	25%	$33,229	$24,365	$36,976
Middlebury College	ind.	$56,216	$16,032	98%	100%	$52,823	$19,425	$19,838
Vermont Technical College	pub.	$16,471	$11,694	73%	6%	$12,000	$16,165	$24,410
Virginia								
Averett University	ind.	$35,600	$6570	100%	9%	$26,458	$15,712	$33,711
Bridgewater College	ind.	$37,720	$13,360	100%	28%	$34,825	$16,255	$31,871
Christopher Newport University	pub.	$14,924	$11,760	78%	23%	$10,257	$16,427	$32,878
Eastern Mennonite University	ind.	$39,220	$11,730	98%	18%	$37,852	$13,098	$43,893
ECPI University	ind.	$16,584	NA	NR	NR	NR	NR	NR
Emory & Henry College	ind.	$35,300	$13,125	99%	17%	$39,198	$9227	$30,360
George Mason University	pub.	$12,564	$11,705	88%	4%	$16,141	$8128	$33,362
Hampden-Sydney College	ind.	$48,110	$13,876	100%	22%	$34,796	$27,190	$41,316
Hampton University	ind.	$29,412	$12,986	99%	39%	$6436	$35,962	$33,680
Hollins University	ind.	$40,010	$13,930	100%	26%	$38,985	$14,955	$33,691
James Madison University	pub.	$11,576	$10,582	70%	87%	$10,649	$11,509	$28,554
Liberty University	ind.	$24,910	$10,462	99%	11%	$16,157	$19,215	$20,876
Longwood University	pub.	$13,520	$11,668	70%	12%	$11,263	$13,925	$30,133
Marymount University	ind.	$33,950	$14,400	85%	24%	$29,914	$18,436	$33,682
Old Dominion University	pub.	$11,020	$12,836	78%	18%	$11,508	$12,348	$31,142

NA = not applicable; NR = not reported; * = includes room and board; † = room only; — = not available.

College Costs At-a-Glance

	Institutional Control ind.=independent; pub.=public	Tuition and Fees	Room and Board	Percent of Eligible Freshmen Receiving Need-Based Gift Awards	Percent of Freshmen Whose Need Was Fully Met	Average Financial Aid Package for Freshmen	Average Net Cost After Aid	Average Indebtedness Upon Graduation
Patrick Henry College	ind.	$28,400	$11,020	65%	20%	$15,075	$24,345	$50,668
Radford University	pub.	$11,350	$9637	89%	14%	$11,788	$9199	$32,261
Randolph College	ind.	$25,610	$11,000	100%	24%	$37,381	—	$42,569
Randolph-Macon College	ind.	$43,940	$12,680	100%	37%	$32,631	$23,989	$22,206
Regent University	ind.	$20,120	$7220	98%	22%	$8224	$19,116	$32,982
Roanoke College	ind.	$46,870	$14,580	97%	19%	$38,997	$22,453	$37,335
Shenandoah University	ind.	$33,830	$10,810	64%	21%	$21,911	$22,729	$36,370
University of Mary Washington	pub.	$13,270	$11,500	62%	13%	$10,199	$14,571	$31,157
University of Richmond	ind.	$56,860	$13,430	99%	89%	$52,557	$17,733	$28,341
University of Virginia	pub.	$18,878	$12,350	89%	100%	$31,105	$123	$26,023
Virginia Wesleyan University	ind.	$10,338*	$10,338	100%	11%	$26,515	—	$32,515
William & Mary	pub.	$23,628	$12,926	90%	19%	$23,686	$12,868	$28,895
Washington								
Central Washington University	pub.	$7562	$12,637	68%	13%	$10,546	$9653	$24,498
Eastern Washington University	pub.	$7461	$12,708	85%	7%	$12,419	$7750	$23,301
Gonzaga University	ind.	$46,920	$12,951	94%	21%	$30,533	$29,338	$29,685
Northwest University	ind.	$33,980	$9420	95%	19%	$20,248	$23,152	$24,825
Pacific Lutheran University	ind.	$43,674	$10,876	72%	29%	$34,951	$19,599	$25,449
Saint Martin's University	ind.	$38,560	$12,000	100%	22%	$30,919	$19,641	$30,672
Seattle Pacific University	ind.	$45,078	$12,285	100%	8%	$40,870	$16,493	$29,782
Seattle University	ind.	$48,390	$12,780	83%	29%	$38,555	$22,615	$28,053
University of Puget Sound	ind.	$53,800	$13,480	99%	16%	$40,565	$26,715	$36,290
University of Washington	pub.	$11,465	$13,296	91%	23%	$16,916	$7845	$19,198
University of Washington, Bothell	pub.	$11,390	$12,636	89%	11%	$14,357	$9669	$18,449
University of Washington, Tacoma	pub.	$11,639	$12,636	96%	13%	$14,257	$10,018	$16,716
Walla Walla University	ind.	$29,931	$8376	74%	38%	$25,676	$12,631	$35,777
Washington State University	pub.	$11,841	$11,648	95%	15%	$13,160	$10,329	$25,899
Western Washington University	pub.	$8341	$12,037	91%	20%	$18,180	$2198	$22,466
Whitman College	ind.	$53,820	$13,512	100%	31%	$47,524	$19,808	$18,328
Whitworth University	ind.	$46,250	$12,150	99%	27%	$44,590	$13,810	$32,607
West Virginia								
Concord University	pub.	$8385	$9762	80%	38%	$8929	$9218	$20,004
Marshall University	pub.	$8532	$10,644	81%	46%	$13,317	$5859	$27,472
Shepherd University	pub.	$7784	$10,654	67%	32%	$12,429	$6009	$28,371
Wisconsin								
Alverno College	ind.	$29,456	$8800	100%	NR	$24,506	$13,750	$38,959
Beloit College	ind.	$53,348	$9688	99%	32%	$49,825	$13,211	$23,534
Cardinal Stritch University	ind.	$31,798	$8946	100%	24%	$28,565	$12,179	$33,553
Carthage College	ind.	$63,000	$12,400	NR	NR	NR	NR	$54,496
Concordia University Wisconsin	ind.	$31,182	$11,470	98%	34%	$28,774	$13,878	$36,651
Edgewood College	ind.	$31,700	$11,700	100%	11%	$25,066	$18,334	$37,332

NA = not applicable; NR = not reported; * = includes room and board; † = room only; — = not available.

College Costs At-a-Glance

	Institutional Control ind.=independent; pub.=public	Tuition and Fees	Room and Board	Percent of Eligible Freshmen Receiving Need-Based Gift Awards	Percent of Freshmen Whose Need Was Fully Met	Average Financial Aid Package for Freshmen	Average Net Cost After Aid	Average Indebtedness Upon Graduation
Lawrence University	ind.	$49,122	$10,719	100%	49%	$45,058	$14,783	$28,828
Marquette University	ind.	$45,666	$13,656	99%	23%	$34,469	$24,853	$38,173
Milwaukee School of Engineering	ind.	$43,575	$6339	100%	20%	$30,567	$19,347	$36,150
St. Norbert College	ind.	$40,885	$10,885	97%	32%	$28,147	$23,623	$40,265
University of Wisconsin–Eau Claire	pub.	$8840	$8216	84%	20%	$9101	$7955	$27,129
University of Wisconsin–Green Bay	pub.	$7878	$6790	86%	24%	$10,252	$4416	$24,668
University of Wisconsin–La Crosse	pub.	$8953	$6465	67%	24%	$7598	$7820	$25,926
University of Wisconsin–Madison	pub.	$10,725	$11,558	82%	51%	$19,067	$3216	$27,973
University of Wisconsin–Milwaukee	pub.	$9588	$10,792	61%	6%	$8042	$12,338	$37,261
University of Wisconsin–Parkside	pub.	$7422	$8200	77%	11%	$8854	$6768	$29,551
University of Wisconsin–Platteville	pub.	$7846	$7770	54%	9%	$5386	$10,230	$29,707
University of Wisconsin–Stevens Point	pub.	$8290	$7428	91%	73%	$9106	$6612	$31,669
University of Wisconsin–Stout	pub.	$9463	$6944	53%	15%	$10,561	$5846	$31,372
University of Wisconsin–Superior	pub.	$8132	$7280	69%	30%	$10,305	$5107	$31,490
University of Wisconsin–Whitewater	pub.	$7694	$6878	60%	38%	$7747	$6825	$28,008
Wyoming								
University of Wyoming	pub.	$5791	$10,615	60%	26%	$11,472	$4934	$23,444

NA = not applicable; NR = not reported; * = includes room and board; † = room only; — = not available.

Profiles of College Financial Aid Programs

ABILENE CHRISTIAN UNIVERSITY

Abilene, TX

Tuition & fees: $37,800 | **Average undergraduate aid package: $25,017**

ABOUT THE INSTITUTION Independent Church of Christ, coed. ***Awards:*** certificates, associate, bachelor's, master's, and doctoral degrees. 65 undergraduate majors. ***Total enrollment:*** 5,292. Undergraduates: 3,525. Freshmen: 932. Federal methodology is used as a basis for awarding need-based institutional aid.

UNDERGRADUATE EXPENSES for 2020–2021 ***Application fee:*** $50. ***Comprehensive fee:*** $49,150 includes full-time tuition ($37,750), mandatory fees ($50), and room and board ($11,350). ***College room only:*** $5850. Full-time tuition and fees vary according to course load. Room and board charges vary according to board plan and housing facility. Part-time tuition and fees vary according to course load. ***Payment plan:*** Tuition prepayment.

FRESHMAN FINANCIAL AID (Fall 2019, est.) 837 applied for aid; of those 82% were deemed to have need. 100% of freshmen with need received aid; of those 34% had need fully met. ***Average percent of need met:*** 71% (excluding resources awarded to replace EFC). ***Average financial aid package:*** $26,260 (excluding resources awarded to replace EFC). 27% of all full-time freshmen had no need and received non-need-based gift aid.

UNDERGRADUATE FINANCIAL AID (Fall 2019, est.) 2,583 applied for aid; of those 87% were deemed to have need. 100% of undergraduates with need received aid; of those 31% had need fully met. ***Average percent of need met:*** 67% (excluding resources awarded to replace EFC). ***Average financial aid package:*** $25,017 (excluding resources awarded to replace EFC). 34% of all full-time undergraduates had no need and received non-need-based gift aid.

GIFT AID (NEED-BASED) ***Receiving aid:*** Freshmen: 76% (688); all full-time undergraduates: 67% (2,230). ***Average award:*** Freshmen: $24,266; Undergraduates: $22,497. ***Scholarships, grants, and awards:*** Federal Pell, FSEOG, state, private, college/university gift aid from institutional funds.

GIFT AID (NON-NEED-BASED) ***Receiving aid:*** Freshmen: 75% (677). Undergraduates: 66% (2,193). ***Average award:*** Freshmen: $17,104. Undergraduates: $14,877. ***Scholarships, grants, and awards by category:*** *Academic interests/achievement:* agriculture, biological sciences, business, communication, education, engineering/technologies, English, foreign languages, general academic interests/achievements, mathematics, physical sciences, religion/biblical studies, social sciences. *Creative arts/performance:* applied art and design, debating, journalism/publications, music, theater/drama. *Special achievements/activities:* cheerleading/drum major, leadership. *Special characteristics:* children of faculty/staff, ethnic background, first-generation college students, local/state students, members of minority groups, out-of-state students, previous college experience, relatives of clergy, religious affiliation. ***Tuition waivers:*** Full or partial for employees or children of employees.

LOANS ***Average need-based loan:*** Freshmen: $3250. Undergraduates: $4100. ***Programs:*** Federal Direct (Subsidized and Unsubsidized Stafford, PLUS), Perkins, state, private loans.

WORK-STUDY Federal work-study jobs available. ***State or other work-study/employment:*** Part-time jobs available.

APPLYING FOR FINANCIAL AID ***Required financial aid form:*** FAFSA. ***Notification date:*** Continuous. Students must reply within 3 weeks of notification.

CONTACT Student Financial Services, Abilene Christian University, 212 Zellner Hall, ACU Box 29007, Abilene, TX 79699, 888-588-6083 or toll-free 800-460-6228. *Fax:* 325-674-2963. *E-mail:* wildcatcentral@acu.edu.
Website: http://www.acu.edu/.

ABRAHAM BALDWIN AGRICULTURAL COLLEGE

Tifton, GA

CONTACT Michael Wright, Director of Student Financial Services, Abraham Baldwin Agricultural College, 2802 Moore Highway, ABAC 23, Tifton, GA 31793-2601, 229-391-4910 or toll-free 800-733-3653. *Fax:* 229-391-4871. *E-mail:* sfs@abac.edu.
Website: http://www.abac.edu/.

ABRAHAM LINCOLN UNIVERSITY

Los Angeles, CA

CONTACT Financial Aid Office, Abraham Lincoln University, 3530 Wilshire Boulevard, Suite 1430, Los Angeles, CA 90010, 213-252-5100.
Website: http://www.alu.edu/.

ACADEMY COLLEGE

Bloomington, MN

Tuition & fees: $18,451 | **Average undergraduate aid package: N/A**

ABOUT THE INSTITUTION Proprietary, coed. ***Awards:*** diplomas, associate, and bachelor's degrees. 7 undergraduate majors. Federal methodology is used as a basis for awarding need-based institutional aid.

UNDERGRADUATE EXPENSES for 2019–2020 ***Tuition:*** full-time $18,051; part-time $455 per credit hour. ***Required fees:*** full-time $400; $40 per term. Full-time tuition and fees vary according to course load and program. Part-time tuition and fees vary according to course load and program.

FRESHMAN FINANCIAL AID (Fall 2018) 9 applied for aid; of those 100% were deemed to have need. 100% of freshmen with need received aid.

UNDERGRADUATE FINANCIAL AID (Fall 2018) 64 applied for aid; of those 100% were deemed to have need. 100% of undergraduates with need received aid.

GIFT AID (NEED-BASED) ***Total amount:*** $437,040 (60% federal, 40% state). ***Receiving aid:*** Freshmen: 67% (6); all full-time undergraduates: 57% (46). ***Scholarships, grants, and awards:*** Federal Pell, FSEOG, state, private, college/university gift aid from institutional funds.

GIFT AID (NON-NEED-BASED) ***Total amount:*** $4979 (100% external sources). ***Receiving aid:*** Freshmen: 44% (4). Undergraduates: 31% (25). ***Tuition waivers:*** Full or partial for employees or children of employees.

LOANS ***Student loans:*** $1,299,439 (17% need-based, 83% non-need-based). ***Parent loans:*** $837,726 (100% non-need-based). ***Programs:*** Federal Direct (Subsidized and Unsubsidized Stafford, PLUS), state, alternative loans.

WORK-STUDY Federal work-study jobs available. ***State or other work-study/employment:*** Part-time jobs available.

APPLYING FOR FINANCIAL AID ***Required financial aid forms:*** FAFSA, institution's own form, state aid form. ***Financial aid deadline:*** Continuous. ***Notification date:*** Continuous.

CONTACT Kellye MacLeod, Director of Financial Aid, Academy College, 1101 East 78th Street, Bloomington, MN 55420, 952-851-0066 or toll-free 800-292-9149. *Fax:* 952-851-0093. *E-mail:* finaid@academycollege.edu.
Website: http://www.academycollege.edu/.

ACADEMY OF ART UNIVERSITY

San Francisco, CA

Tuition & fees: $30,630 | **Average undergraduate aid package: $13,401**

ABOUT THE INSTITUTION Proprietary, coed. ***Awards:*** certificates, associate, bachelor's, and master's degrees. 43 undergraduate majors. ***Total enrollment:*** 9,826. Undergraduates: 6,694. Freshmen: 803. Federal methodology is used as a basis for awarding need-based institutional aid.

UNDERGRADUATE EXPENSES for 2020–2021 ***Application fee:*** $50. ***Comprehensive fee:*** $49,016 includes full-time tuition ($30,330), mandatory fees ($300), and room and board ($18,386). ***College room only:*** $12,328. Full-time tuition and fees vary according to course load. Room and board charges vary according to board plan and housing facility. ***Part-time tuition:*** $1011 per credit hour. ***Part-time fees:*** $1011 per credit hour. Part-time tuition and fees vary according to course load.

FRESHMAN FINANCIAL AID (Fall 2018) 193 applied for aid; of those 85% were deemed to have need. 96% of freshmen with need received aid; of those 3% had need fully met. ***Average percent of need met:*** 31% (excluding resources awarded to replace EFC). ***Average financial aid package:*** $12,413 (excluding resources awarded to replace EFC). 6% of all full-time freshmen had no need and received non-need-based gift aid.

UNDERGRADUATE FINANCIAL AID (Fall 2018) 1,872 applied for aid; of those 93% were deemed to have need. 98% of undergraduates with need received aid; of those 3% had need fully met. ***Average percent of need met:*** 35% (excluding resources awarded to replace EFC). ***Average financial aid package:*** $13,401 (excluding resources awarded to replace EFC). 4% of all full-time undergraduates had no need and received non-need-based gift aid.

GIFT AID (NEED-BASED) ***Total amount:*** $22,808,316 (46% federal, 10% state, 10% institutional, 34% external sources). ***Receiving aid:*** Freshmen: 41% (137); all full-time undergraduates: 35% (1,434). ***Average award:*** Freshmen: $11,428; Undergraduates: $12,104. ***Scholarships, grants, and awards:*** Federal Pell, FSEOG, state, private, college/university gift aid from institutional funds.

GIFT AID (NON-NEED-BASED) ***Total amount:*** $6,139,758 (17% institutional, 83% external sources). ***Receiving aid:*** Freshmen: 4% (13). Undergraduates: 4% (168). ***Average award:*** Freshmen: $3270. Undergraduates: $4486. ***ROTC:*** Army cooperative.

LOANS ***Student loans:*** $27,628,342 (89% need-based, 11% non-need-based). 57% of past graduating class borrowed through all loan programs. *Average indebtedness per student:* $31,360. ***Average need-based loan:*** Freshmen: $3088. Undergraduates: $3853. ***Parent loans:*** $21,307,776 (74% need-based, 26% non-need-based). ***Programs:*** Federal Direct (Subsidized and Unsubsidized Stafford, PLUS).

WORK-STUDY ***Federal work-study:*** Total amount: $525,730; jobs available.

ATHLETIC AWARDS Total amount: $4,045,591 (37% need-based, 63% non-need-based).

APPLYING FOR FINANCIAL AID ***Required financial aid forms:*** FAFSA, institution's own form. ***Financial aid deadline (priority):*** 3/1. ***Notification date:*** Continuous beginning 3/15. Students must reply within 2 weeks of notification.

CONTACT Mr. Joe Vollaro, Executive Vice President of Financial Aid and Compliance, Academy of Art University, 79 New Montgomery Street, San Francisco, CA 94105-3410, 415-618-6528 or toll-free 800-544-ARTS. *Fax:* 415-618-6273. *E-mail:* jvollaro@academyart.edu.
Website: http://www.academyart.edu/.

ADAMS STATE UNIVERSITY

Alamosa, CO

Tuition & fees (area res): $9440	Average undergraduate aid package: $14,804

ABOUT THE INSTITUTION State-supported, coed. ***Awards:*** associate, bachelor's, master's, and doctoral degrees. 78 undergraduate majors. ***Total enrollment:*** 3,101. Undergraduates: 1,959. Freshmen: 398. Federal methodology is used as a basis for awarding need-based institutional aid.

UNDERGRADUATE EXPENSES for 2020–2021 ***Application fee:*** $30. ***Tuition, area resident:*** full-time $5736; part-time $333 per credit hour. ***Tuition, state resident:*** full-time $5736; part-time $333 per credit hour. ***Tuition, nonresident:*** full-time $17,160; part-time $715 per credit hour. ***Required fees:*** full-time $3704. Full-time tuition and fees vary according to course load, location, program, and reciprocity agreements. Part-time tuition and fees vary according to course load, location, program, and reciprocity agreements. ***College room and board:*** $8760; ***Room only:*** $4200. Room and board charges vary according to board plan and housing facility. ***Payment plan:*** Guaranteed tuition.

FRESHMAN FINANCIAL AID (Fall 2019, est.) 343 applied for aid; of those 81% were deemed to have need. 100% of freshmen with need received aid; of those 6% had need fully met. ***Average percent of need met:*** 64% (excluding resources awarded to replace EFC). ***Average financial aid package:*** $14,751 (excluding resources awarded to replace EFC).

UNDERGRADUATE FINANCIAL AID (Fall 2019, est.) 1,353 applied for aid; of those 78% were deemed to have need. 99% of undergraduates with need received aid; of those 6% had need fully met. ***Average percent of need met:*** 62% (excluding resources awarded to replace EFC). ***Average financial aid package:*** $14,804 (excluding resources awarded to replace EFC).

GIFT AID (NEED-BASED) ***Total amount:*** $10,428,817 (39% federal, 18% state, 30% institutional, 13% external sources). ***Receiving aid:*** Freshmen: 78% (268); all full-time undergraduates: 73% (994). ***Average award:*** Freshmen: $10,762; Undergraduates: $10,079. ***Scholarships, grants, and awards:*** Federal Pell, FSEOG, state, private, college/university gift aid from institutional funds.

GIFT AID (NON-NEED-BASED) ***Total amount:*** $1,170,789 (1% federal, 1% state, 75% institutional, 23% external sources). ***Receiving aid:*** Freshmen: 47% (162). Undergraduates: 30% (408). ***Tuition waivers:*** Full or partial for employees or children of employees, senior citizens.

LOANS ***Student loans:*** $5,863,385 (92% need-based, 8% non-need-based). 66% of past graduating class borrowed through all loan programs. *Average indebtedness per student:* $426,673. ***Average need-based loan:*** Freshmen: $3245. Undergraduates: $4018. ***Parent loans:*** $1,986,144 (77% need-based, 23% non-need-based). ***Programs:*** Federal Direct (Subsidized and Unsubsidized Stafford, PLUS), Perkins.

WORK-STUDY ***Federal work-study:*** Total amount: $687,283; jobs available. ***State or other work-study/employment:*** Total amount: $1,439,670 (87% need-based, 13% non-need-based). Part-time jobs available.

ATHLETIC AWARDS Total amount: $1,880,874 (71% need-based, 29% non-need-based).

APPLYING FOR FINANCIAL AID ***Required financial aid form:*** FAFSA. ***Financial aid deadline:*** Continuous. ***Notification date:*** Continuous beginning 1/1.

CONTACT Philip Schroeder, Director of Financial Aid, Adams State University, 208 Edgemont Boulevard, Alamosa, CO 81101, 719-587-7306 or toll-free 800-824-6494. *Fax:* 719-587-7366. *E-mail:* financialaid@adams.edu.
Website: http://www.adams.edu/.

ADELPHI UNIVERSITY

Garden City, NY

ABOUT THE INSTITUTION Independent, coed. ***Awards:*** certificates, associate, bachelor's, master's, and doctoral degrees. 50 undergraduate majors. ***Total enrollment:*** 8,149. Undergraduates: 5,391. Freshmen: 1,245.

GIFT AID (NEED-BASED) ***Scholarships, grants, and awards:*** Federal Pell, FSEOG, state, private, college/university gift aid from institutional funds, United Negro College Fund, endowed and restricted scholarships and grants.

GIFT AID (NON-NEED-BASED) ***Scholarships, grants, and awards by category:*** *Academic interests/achievement:* business, communication, computer science, foreign languages, general academic interests/achievements, mathematics, physical sciences. *Creative arts/performance:* applied art and design, cinema/film/broadcasting, dance, music, performing arts, theater/drama. *Special achievements/activities:* community service, general special achievements/activities, leadership, memberships. *Special characteristics:* adult students, children and siblings of alumni, children of faculty/staff, veterans.

LOANS ***Programs:*** Federal Direct (Subsidized and Unsubsidized Stafford, PLUS), Federal Nursing.

WORK-STUDY ***Federal work-study:*** Total amount: $1,584,136; 317 jobs averaging $1873. ***State or other work-study/employment:*** Total amount: $4,544,815 (100% non-need-based). 1,165 part-time jobs averaging $2181.

APPLYING FOR FINANCIAL AID ***Required financial aid forms:*** FAFSA, state aid form.

CONTACT Ms. Debra Evans, Senior Associate Director of Student Financial Services, Adelphi University, 1 South Avenue, PO Box 701, Garden City, NY 11530, 516-877-3394 or toll-free 800-ADELPHI. *Fax:* 516-877-3380. *E-mail:* evans@adelphi.edu.
Website: http://www.adelphi.edu/.

ADRIAN COLLEGE

Adrian, MI

CONTACT Mr. Matthew Rheinecker, Director of Financial Aid, Adrian College, 110 South Madison Street, Adrian, MI 49221-2575, 517-264-3109 or toll-free 800-877-2246. *Fax:* 517-264-3394. *E-mail:* mrheinecker@adrian.edu.
Website: http://www.adrian.edu/.

ADVENTHEALTH UNIVERSITY

Orlando, FL

Tuition & fees: $16,350	Average undergraduate aid package: $8883

ABOUT THE INSTITUTION Independent, coed. ***Awards:*** certificates, associate, bachelor's, master's, and doctoral degrees. 9 undergraduate majors. ***Total***

enrollment: 1,688. Undergraduates: 1,234. Freshmen: 64. Federal methodology is used as a basis for awarding need-based institutional aid.

UNDERGRADUATE EXPENSES for 2020–2021 ***Application fee:*** $20. ***Tuition:*** full-time $15,750; part-time $525 per credit hour. ***Required fees:*** full-time $600; $300 per term. ***College room only:*** $4200.

FRESHMAN FINANCIAL AID (Fall 2019, est.) 45 applied for aid; of those 78% were deemed to have need. 91% of freshmen with need received aid; of those 16% had need fully met. ***Average percent of need met:*** 29% (excluding resources awarded to replace EFC). ***Average financial aid package:*** $9162 (excluding resources awarded to replace EFC). 8% of all full-time freshmen had no need and received non-need-based gift aid.

UNDERGRADUATE FINANCIAL AID (Fall 2019, est.) 456 applied for aid; of those 80% were deemed to have need. 92% of undergraduates with need received aid; of those 5% had need fully met. ***Average percent of need met:*** 28% (excluding resources awarded to replace EFC). ***Average financial aid package:*** $8883 (excluding resources awarded to replace EFC). 4% of all full-time undergraduates had no need and received non-need-based gift aid.

GIFT AID (NEED-BASED) ***Total amount:*** $1,681,747 (72% federal, 17% state, 11% institutional). ***Receiving aid:*** Freshmen: 67% (32); all full-time undergraduates: 68% (318). ***Average award:*** Freshmen: $7430; Undergraduates: $6715. ***Scholarships, grants, and awards:*** Federal Pell, FSEOG, state, private, college/university gift aid from institutional funds.

GIFT AID (NON-NEED-BASED) ***Total amount:*** $1,381,271 (66% state, 6% institutional, 28% external sources). ***Receiving aid:*** Freshmen: 8% (4). Undergraduates: 3% (16). ***Average award:*** Freshmen: $2695. Undergraduates: $3158. ***Scholarships, grants, and awards by category:*** *Academic interests/achievement:* 26 awards ($96,474 total): home economics. *Special achievements/activities:* 4 awards ($8400 total): leadership. *Special characteristics:* 7 awards ($30,857 total): veterans, veterans' children. ***Tuition waivers:*** Full or partial for employees or children of employees.

LOANS ***Student loans:*** $12,450,070 (14% need-based, 86% non-need-based). 66% of past graduating class borrowed through all loan programs. *Average indebtedness per student:* $33,823. ***Average need-based loan:*** Freshmen: $3079. Undergraduates: $3668. ***Parent loans:*** $411,431 (100% non-need-based). ***Programs:*** Federal Direct (Subsidized and Unsubsidized Stafford, PLUS), college/university.

APPLYING FOR FINANCIAL AID ***Required financial aid forms:*** FAFSA, institution's own form. ***Financial aid deadline (priority):*** 10/1. ***Notification date:*** Continuous beginning 10/9. Students must reply within 2 weeks of notification.

CONTACT Mrs. Daisy Tabachow, Director of Financial Aid, AdventHealth University, 671 Winyah Drive, Orlando, FL 32803, 407-303-6963 or toll-free 800-500-7747. *Fax:* 407-303-7680. *E-mail:* www.finaid@ahu.edu.
Website: http://www.ahu.edu/.

AGNES SCOTT COLLEGE

Decatur, GA

Tuition & fees: $44,250	Average undergraduate aid package: $38,618

ABOUT THE INSTITUTION Independent Presbyterian Church (U.S.A.), women only. ***Awards:*** certificates, bachelor's, and master's degrees. 36 undergraduate majors. ***Total enrollment:*** 1,067. Undergraduates: 1,005. Freshmen: 299. Both federal and institutional methodology are used as a basis for awarding need-based institutional aid.

UNDERGRADUATE EXPENSES for 2020–2021 ***One-time required fee:*** $200. ***Comprehensive fee:*** $57,300 includes full-time tuition ($43,920), mandatory fees ($330), and room and board ($13,050). Room and board charges vary according to board plan and housing facility. ***Part-time tuition:*** $1830 per credit hour.

FRESHMAN FINANCIAL AID (Fall 2019, est.) 277 applied for aid; of those 88% were deemed to have need. 100% of freshmen with need received aid; of those 25% had need fully met. ***Average percent of need met:*** 86% (excluding resources awarded to replace EFC). ***Average financial aid package:*** $38,877 (excluding resources awarded to replace EFC). 18% of all full-time freshmen had no need and received non-need-based gift aid.

UNDERGRADUATE FINANCIAL AID (Fall 2019, est.) 829 applied for aid; of those 90% were deemed to have need. 100% of undergraduates with need received aid; of those 22% had need fully met. ***Average percent of need met:*** 85% (excluding resources awarded to replace EFC). ***Average financial aid package:*** $38,618 (excluding resources awarded to replace EFC). 22% of all full-time undergraduates had no need and received non-need-based gift aid.

GIFT AID (NEED-BASED) ***Receiving aid:*** Freshmen: 81% (243); all full-time undergraduates: 78% (748). ***Average award:*** Freshmen: $32,382; Undergraduates: $31,975. ***Scholarships, grants, and awards:*** Federal Pell, FSEOG, state, private, college/university gift aid from institutional funds.

GIFT AID (NON-NEED-BASED) ***Receiving aid:*** Freshmen: 20% (61). Undergraduates: 16% (158). ***Average award:*** Freshmen: $31,077. Undergraduates: $30,458. ***Scholarships, grants, and awards by category:*** *Academic interests/achievement:* general academic interests/achievements. *Creative arts/performance:* music. *Special achievements/activities:* community service, leadership. *Special characteristics:* adult students, children of educators, children of faculty/staff, international students, local/state students, religious affiliation, veterans. ***Tuition waivers:*** Full or partial for employees or children of employees. ***ROTC:*** Army cooperative, Air Force cooperative.

LOANS ***Student loans:*** 64% of past graduating class borrowed through all loan programs. *Average indebtedness per student:* $31,271. ***Average need-based loan:*** Freshmen: $3471. Undergraduates: $4433. ***Programs:*** Federal Direct (Subsidized and Unsubsidized Stafford, PLUS).

WORK-STUDY Federal work-study jobs available. ***State or other work-study/employment:*** Part-time jobs available.

APPLYING FOR FINANCIAL AID ***Required financial aid form:*** FAFSA. ***Notification date:*** Continuous.

CONTACT Patrick Bonones, Director of Financial Aid, Agnes Scott College, 141 East College Avenue, Decatur, GA 30030-3797, 404-471-6395 or toll-free 800-868-8602. *Fax:* 404-471-6159. *E-mail:* finaid@agnesscott.edu.
Website: http://www.agnesscott.edu/.

ALABAMA AGRICULTURAL AND MECHANICAL UNIVERSITY

Huntsville, AL

CONTACT Ms. Deborah Gordon, Financial Aid Officer, Alabama Agricultural and Mechanical University, PO Box 907, Huntsville, AL 35762, 256-372-4853 or toll-free 800-553-0816. *Fax:* 256-372-5407. *E-mail:* deborah.gordon@aamu.edu.
Website: http://www.aamu.edu/.

ALABAMA STATE UNIVERSITY

Montgomery, AL

Tuition & fees: N/R	Average undergraduate aid package: $16,730

ABOUT THE INSTITUTION State-supported, coed. ***Awards:*** certificates, bachelor's, master's, and doctoral degrees. 36 undergraduate majors. ***Total enrollment:*** 4,413. Undergraduates: 3,903. Freshmen: 1,042. Federal methodology is used as a basis for awarding need-based institutional aid.

FRESHMAN FINANCIAL AID (Fall 2019, est.) 766 applied for aid; of those 99% were deemed to have need. 98% of freshmen with need received aid; of those 28% had need fully met. ***Average percent of need met:*** 68% (excluding resources awarded to replace EFC). ***Average financial aid package:*** $17,083 (excluding resources awarded to replace EFC). 1% of all full-time freshmen had no need and received non-need-based gift aid.

UNDERGRADUATE FINANCIAL AID (Fall 2019, est.) 3,350 applied for aid; of those 98% were deemed to have need. 100% of undergraduates with need received aid; of those 39% had need fully met. ***Average percent of need met:*** 71% (excluding resources awarded to replace EFC). ***Average financial aid package:*** $16,730 (excluding resources awarded to replace EFC). 2% of all full-time undergraduates had no need and received non-need-based gift aid.

GIFT AID (NEED-BASED) ***Total amount:*** $22,065,841 (99% federal, 1% state). ***Receiving aid:*** Freshmen: 65% (647); all full-time undergraduates: 83% (2,845). ***Average award:*** Freshmen: $5661; Undergraduates: $5472. ***Scholarships, grants, and awards:*** Federal Pell, FSEOG, state, private, college/university gift aid from institutional funds, United Negro College Fund.

GIFT AID (NON-NEED-BASED) ***Total amount:*** $12,179,849 (18% state, 63% institutional, 19% external sources). ***Receiving aid:*** Freshmen: 32% (319). Undergraduates: 51% (1,771). ***Average award:*** Freshmen: $7847. Undergraduates: $9822. ***Scholarships, grants, and awards by category:*** *Academic interests/achievement:* general academic interests/achievements. *Creative arts/performance:* art/fine arts, dance, general creative arts/performance, music, theater/drama. *Special achievements/activities:* leadership. *Special characteristics:* general special characteristics, members of minority groups. ***ROTC:*** Army cooperative, Air Force.

LOANS ***Student loans:*** $10,884,538 (100% non-need-based). 91% of past graduating class borrowed through all loan programs. *Average indebtedness per student:* $3486. ***Average need-based loan:*** Freshmen: $3427. Undergraduates: $4104. ***Parent loans:*** $4,697,267 (44% need-based, 56% non-need-based). ***Programs:*** Federal Direct (Subsidized and Unsubsidized Stafford, PLUS), Perkins, state, college/university.

WORK-STUDY ***Federal work-study:*** Total amount: $104,000; jobs available. ***State or other work-study/employment:*** Total amount: $303,012 (100% non-need-based). Part-time jobs available.

ATHLETIC AWARDS Total amount: $11,197,277 (64% need-based, 36% non-need-based).

APPLYING FOR FINANCIAL AID ***Required financial aid form:*** FAFSA. ***Financial aid deadline (priority):*** 4/1. ***Notification date:*** Continuous beginning 5/1. Students must reply by 7/31 or within 2 weeks of notification.

CONTACT Ms. Robyn Siddell, Assistant Director of Financial Aid, Alabama State University, PO Box 271, Montgomery, AL 36101-0271, 334-229-4862 or toll-free 800-253-5037. *Fax:* 334-299-4924. *E-mail:* treaux@alasu.edu.
Website: http://www.alasu.edu/.

ALASKA BIBLE COLLEGE

Palmer, AK

Tuition & fees: N/R — **Average undergraduate aid package: N/A**

ABOUT THE INSTITUTION Independent nondenominational, coed. ***Awards:*** certificates, associate, and bachelor's degrees. 1 undergraduate major. ***Total enrollment:*** 50. Undergraduates: 50. Freshmen: 6. Institutional methodology is used as a basis for awarding need-based institutional aid.

GIFT AID (NEED-BASED) ***Scholarships, grants, and awards:*** Federal Pell, FSEOG, state, private, college/university gift aid from institutional funds.

GIFT AID (NON-NEED-BASED) ***Scholarships, grants, and awards by category:*** *Academic interests/achievement:* general academic interests/achievements, religion/biblical studies. *Special achievements/activities:* general special achievements/activities, religious involvement. *Special characteristics:* children of faculty/staff, married students, spouses of current students.

LOANS ***Programs:*** Federal Direct (Subsidized and Unsubsidized Stafford, PLUS), state.

WORK-STUDY ***Federal work-study:*** 4 jobs averaging $1250.

APPLYING FOR FINANCIAL AID ***Required financial aid form:*** FAFSA. ***Financial aid deadline:*** Continuous. ***Notification date:*** Students must reply within 2 weeks of notification.

CONTACT Christy Coté, Financial Aid Administrator, Alaska Bible College, 248 East Elmwood Avenue, Palmer, AK 99645, 907-745-3201 or toll-free 800-478-7884. *E-mail:* financialaid@akbible.edu.
Website: http://www.akbible.edu/.

ALASKA PACIFIC UNIVERSITY

Anchorage, AK

CONTACT Financial Aid Office, Alaska Pacific University, 4101 University Drive, Carr-Gottstein Room 106, Anchorage, AK 99508-4672, 907-564-8341 or toll-free 800-252-7528. *Fax:* 907-564-8317. *E-mail:* finaid@alaskapacific.edu.
Website: http://www.alaskapacific.edu/.

ALBANY COLLEGE OF PHARMACY AND HEALTH SCIENCES

Albany, NY

Tuition & fees: N/R — **Average undergraduate aid package: $18,096**

ABOUT THE INSTITUTION Independent, coed. ***Awards:*** bachelor's, master's, and doctoral degrees. 6 undergraduate majors. Federal methodology is used as a basis for awarding need-based institutional aid.

FRESHMAN FINANCIAL AID (Fall 2018) 175 applied for aid; of those 86% were deemed to have need. 100% of freshmen with need received aid; of those 19% had need fully met. ***Average percent of need met:*** 63% (excluding resources awarded to replace EFC). ***Average financial aid package:*** $20,449 (excluding resources awarded to replace EFC). 21% of all full-time freshmen had no need and received non-need-based gift aid.

UNDERGRADUATE FINANCIAL AID (Fall 2018) 772 applied for aid; of those 90% were deemed to have need. 100% of undergraduates with need received aid; of those 11% had need fully met. ***Average percent of need met:*** 46% (excluding resources awarded to replace EFC). ***Average financial aid package:*** $18,096 (excluding resources awarded to replace EFC). 17% of all full-time undergraduates had no need and received non-need-based gift aid.

GIFT AID (NEED-BASED) ***Total amount:*** $4,083,651 (37% federal, 14% state, 49% institutional). ***Receiving aid:*** Freshmen: 79% (150); all full-time undergraduates: 79% (676). ***Average award:*** Freshmen: $17,887; Undergraduates: $14,391. ***Scholarships, grants, and awards:*** Federal Pell, FSEOG, state, private, college/university gift aid from institutional funds.

GIFT AID (NON-NEED-BASED) ***Total amount:*** $7,995,649 (1% state, 95% institutional, 4% external sources). ***Receiving aid:*** Freshmen: 13% (24). Undergraduates: 6% (53). ***Average award:*** Freshmen: $13,397. Undergraduates: $11,767. ***Scholarships, grants, and awards by category:*** *Special characteristics:* children and siblings of alumni, children of faculty/staff, siblings of current students.

LOANS ***Student loans:*** $13,549,898 (74% need-based, 26% non-need-based). ***Average need-based loan:*** Freshmen: $3122. Undergraduates: $4417. ***Parent loans:*** $2,271,120 (100% non-need-based). ***Programs:*** Federal Direct (Subsidized and Unsubsidized Stafford, PLUS), Health Professions Student Loans (HPSL).

WORK-STUDY ***Federal work-study:*** Total amount: $187,725; 181 jobs averaging $1037.

ATHLETIC AWARDS Total amount: $4300 (100% non-need-based).

APPLYING FOR FINANCIAL AID ***Required financial aid form:*** FAFSA. ***Financial aid deadline:*** 5/1 (priority: 2/1). ***Notification date:*** 2/15. Students must reply within 2 weeks of notification.

CONTACT Kathleen Montague, Director of Financial Aid, Albany College of Pharmacy and Health Sciences, 106 New Scotland Avenue, Albany, NY 12208-3425, 518-694-7256 or toll-free 888-203-8010. *Fax:* 518-694-7322. *E-mail:* financial_aid@acphs.edu.
Website: http://www.acphs.edu/.

ALBANY STATE UNIVERSITY

Albany, GA

CONTACT Mr. Thomas A. Harris, Director of Financial Aid, Albany State University, 504 College Drive, Albany, GA 31705-2717, 229-430-4650 or toll-free 800-822-7267. *Fax:* 229-430-3936.
Website: http://www.asurams.edu/.

ALBERTUS MAGNUS COLLEGE

New Haven, CT

Tuition & fees: N/R — **Average undergraduate aid package: $19,337**

ABOUT THE INSTITUTION Independent Roman Catholic, coed. ***Awards:*** certificates, diplomas, associate, bachelor's, and master's degrees. 45 undergraduate majors. ***Total enrollment:*** 1,456. Undergraduates: 2,226. Freshmen: 169. Federal methodology is used as a basis for awarding need-based institutional aid.

FRESHMAN FINANCIAL AID (Fall 2019, est.) 220 applied for aid; of those 98% were deemed to have need. 100% of freshmen with need received aid; of those 10% had need fully met. ***Average percent of need met:*** 57% (excluding resources awarded to replace EFC). ***Average financial aid package:*** $26,534 (excluding resources awarded to replace EFC). 13% of all full-time freshmen had no need and received non-need-based gift aid.

UNDERGRADUATE FINANCIAL AID (Fall 2019, est.) 890 applied for aid; of those 97% were deemed to have need. 99% of undergraduates with need received aid; of those 6% had need fully met. ***Average percent of need met:*** 50% (excluding resources awarded to replace EFC). ***Average financial aid package:*** $19,337 (excluding resources awarded to replace EFC). 6% of all full-time undergraduates had no need and received non-need-based gift aid.

GIFT AID (NEED-BASED) ***Total amount:*** $5,994,991 (48% federal, 7% state, 45% institutional). ***Receiving aid:*** Freshmen: 58% (143); all full-time undergraduates: 66% (649). ***Average award:*** Freshmen: $7004; Undergraduates: $9059. ***Scholarships, grants, and awards:*** Federal Pell, FSEOG, state, college/university gift aid from institutional funds.

GIFT AID (NON-NEED-BASED) ***Total amount:*** $8,189,748 (1% state, 96% institutional, 3% external sources). ***Receiving aid:*** Freshmen: 81% (200). Undergraduates: 45% (441). ***Average award:*** Freshmen: $22,000. Undergraduates: $19,435. ***Scholarships, grants, and awards by category:*** *Special achievements/activities:* 91 awards ($144,000 total): community service, general special achievements/activities, leadership. *Special characteristics:* 86 awards ($201,105 total): religious affiliation, siblings of current students.

LOANS ***Student loans:*** $8,119,756 (42% need-based, 58% non-need-based). 92% of past graduating class borrowed through all loan programs. *Average indebtedness per student:* $34,935. ***Average need-based loan:*** Freshmen: $2774. Undergraduates: $3685. ***Parent loans:*** $1,438,327 (100% non-need-based). ***Programs:*** Federal Direct (Subsidized and Unsubsidized Stafford, PLUS).

WORK-STUDY ***Federal work-study:*** Total amount: $160,513; 64 jobs averaging $2508. ***State or other work-study/employment:*** Total amount: $194,303 (100% non-need-based).

APPLYING FOR FINANCIAL AID ***Required financial aid form:*** FAFSA. ***Financial aid deadline (priority):*** 3/15. ***Notification date:*** Continuous beginning 3/15. Students must reply within 2 weeks of notification.

CONTACT Michelle Cochran, Director of Financial Aid, Albertus Magnus College, 700 Prospect Street, New Haven, CT 06511-1189, 203-773-8508 or toll-free 800-578-9160. *Fax:* 203-773-8972. *E-mail:* financial_aid@albertus.edu.
Website: http://www.albertus.edu/.

ALBION COLLEGE

Albion, MI

Tuition & fees: $50,590	Average undergraduate aid package: $45,275

ABOUT THE INSTITUTION Independent Methodist, coed. ***Awards:*** bachelor's degrees. 61 undergraduate majors. ***Total enrollment:*** 1,475. Undergraduates: 1,475. Freshmen: 401. Federal methodology is used as a basis for awarding need-based institutional aid.

UNDERGRADUATE EXPENSES for 2020–2021 ***One-time required fee:*** $185. ***Comprehensive fee:*** $62,970 includes full-time tuition ($50,070), mandatory fees ($520), and room and board ($12,380). ***College room only:*** $6080. Room and board charges vary according to board plan and housing facility. ***Part-time tuition:*** $2080 per semester hour. ***Part-time fees:*** $520 per year. Part-time tuition and fees vary according to course load.

FRESHMAN FINANCIAL AID (Fall 2019, est.) 381 applied for aid; of those 91% were deemed to have need. 100% of freshmen with need received aid; of those 32% had need fully met. ***Average percent of need met:*** 94% (excluding resources awarded to replace EFC). ***Average financial aid package:*** $47,934 (excluding resources awarded to replace EFC). 17% of all full-time freshmen had no need and received non-need-based gift aid.

UNDERGRADUATE FINANCIAL AID (Fall 2019, est.) 1,251 applied for aid; of those 93% were deemed to have need. 100% of undergraduates with need received aid; of those 22% had need fully met. ***Average percent of need met:*** 89% (excluding resources awarded to replace EFC). ***Average financial aid package:*** $45,275 (excluding resources awarded to replace EFC). 20% of all full-time undergraduates had no need and received non-need-based gift aid.

GIFT AID (NEED-BASED) ***Receiving aid:*** Freshmen: 83% (345); all full-time undergraduates: 80% (1,158). ***Average award:*** Freshmen: $44,083; Undergraduates: $40,700. ***Scholarships, grants, and awards:*** Federal Pell, FSEOG, state, private, college/university gift aid from institutional funds.

GIFT AID (NON-NEED-BASED) ***Receiving aid:*** Freshmen: 82% (340). Undergraduates: 78% (1,136). ***Average award:*** Freshmen: $32,818. Undergraduates: $29,727. ***Scholarships, grants, and awards by category:*** *Academic interests/achievement:* 1,398 awards ($31,280,884 total): communication, general academic interests/achievements. *Creative arts/performance:* 47 awards ($118,150 total): art/fine arts, music, performing arts, theater/drama. *Special characteristics:* 509 awards ($2,125,905 total): children and siblings of alumni, international students, out-of-state students, relatives of clergy. ***Tuition waivers:*** Full or partial for employees or children of employees. ***ROTC:*** Army cooperative.

LOANS ***Student loans:*** 69% of past graduating class borrowed through all loan programs. *Average indebtedness per student:* $35,529. ***Average need-based loan:*** Freshmen: $3334. Undergraduates: $4524. ***Programs:*** Federal Direct (Subsidized and Unsubsidized Stafford, PLUS).

WORK-STUDY ***Federal work-study:*** 424 jobs averaging $1724. ***State or other work-study/employment:*** 103 part-time jobs averaging $1343.

APPLYING FOR FINANCIAL AID ***Required financial aid form:*** FAFSA. ***Financial aid deadline:*** Continuous. ***Notification date:*** Continuous.

CONTACT Mr. Trevor Markovich, Director of Financial Aid, Albion College, Kellogg Center Box 4670, Albion, MI 49224-1831, 517-629-0440 or toll-free 800-858-6770. *Fax:* 517-629-0581. *E-mail:* financialaid@albion.edu.
Website: http://www.albion.edu/.

ALBIZU UNIVERSITY - MIAMI

Miami, FL

CONTACT Violeta Velasquez, Financial Aid Officer, Albizu University - Miami, 2173 Northwest 99th Avenue, Miami, FL 33172, 305-593-1223 Ext. 3179 or toll-free 888-GO-TO-CAU (in-state), 800-GO-TO-CAU (out-of-state). *Fax:* 305-593-8902. *E-mail:* vvelasquez@albizu.edu.
Website: http://www.albizu.edu/.

ALBIZU UNIVERSITY - SAN JUAN

San Juan, PR

ABOUT THE INSTITUTION Independent, coed. ***Awards:*** bachelor's, master's, and doctoral degrees. 3 undergraduate majors.

GIFT AID (NEED-BASED) ***Scholarships, grants, and awards:*** Federal Pell, FSEOG, state, college/university gift aid from institutional funds.

GIFT AID (NON-NEED-BASED) ***Scholarships, grants, and awards by category:*** *Academic interests/achievement:* social sciences.

LOANS ***Programs:*** Federal Direct (Subsidized and Unsubsidized Stafford, PLUS).

WORK-STUDY ***Federal work-study:*** Total amount: $47,421; jobs available (averaging $1980).

APPLYING FOR FINANCIAL AID ***Required financial aid form:*** FAFSA.

CONTACT Mrs. Doris J. Quero, Director of Financial Aid, Albizu University - San Juan, PO Box 9023711, San Juan, PR 00901, 787-725-6500 Ext. 1529. *Fax:* 787-721-4008. *E-mail:* dquero@albizu.edu.
Website: http://www.albizu.edu/.

ALBRIGHT COLLEGE

Reading, PA

ABOUT THE INSTITUTION Independent United Methodist Church, coed. ***Awards:*** certificates, bachelor's, and master's degrees. 61 undergraduate majors. ***Total enrollment:*** 1,934. Undergraduates: 1,912. Freshmen: 575.

GIFT AID (NEED-BASED) ***Scholarships, grants, and awards:*** Federal Pell, FSEOG, state, private, college/university gift aid from institutional funds, United Negro College Fund.

GIFT AID (NON-NEED-BASED) ***Scholarships, grants, and awards by category:*** *Academic interests/achievement:* general academic interests/achievements. *Creative arts/performance:* applied art and design, journalism/publications, music, theater/drama. *Special achievements/activities:* memberships, religious involvement. *Special characteristics:* children and siblings of alumni, ethnic background, local/state students, religious affiliation, siblings of current students.

LOANS ***Programs:*** Federal Direct (Subsidized and Unsubsidized Stafford, PLUS).

WORK-STUDY ***Federal work-study:*** Total amount: $211,000; jobs available. ***State or other work-study/employment:*** Part-time jobs available.

APPLYING FOR FINANCIAL AID ***Required financial aid form:*** FAFSA.

CONTACT Chris Hanlon, Director of Financial Aid, Albright College, PO Box 15234, Reading, PA 19612-5234, 610-921-7515 or toll-free 800-252-1856. *Fax:* 610-921-7729. *E-mail:* chanlon@albright.edu.
Website: http://www.albright.edu/.

ALCORN STATE UNIVERSITY

Lorman, MS

Tuition & fees (MS res): $7290	Average undergraduate aid package: $8015

ABOUT THE INSTITUTION State-supported, coed. ***Awards:*** certificates, associate, bachelor's, and master's degrees. 29 undergraduate majors. Both federal and institutional methodology are used as a basis for awarding need-based institutional aid.

UNDERGRADUATE EXPENSES for 2019–2020 ***Tuition, state resident:*** full-time $7290; part-time $608 per credit hour. ***Tuition, nonresident:*** full-time $7290; part-time $608 per credit hour. Full-time tuition and fees vary according to course load. Part-time tuition and fees vary according to course load. ***College room and board:*** $10,788; ***Room only:*** $7360. Room and board charges vary according to board plan and housing facility.

FRESHMAN FINANCIAL AID (Fall 2019, est.) 567 applied for aid; of those 95% were deemed to have need. 100% of freshmen with need received aid; of those 8% had need fully met. ***Average percent of need met:*** 59% (excluding resources awarded to replace EFC). ***Average financial aid package:*** $8011 (excluding resources awarded to replace EFC). 13% of all full-time freshmen had no need and received non-need-based gift aid.

UNDERGRADUATE FINANCIAL AID (Fall 2019, est.) 1,095 applied for aid; of those 97% were deemed to have need. 100% of undergraduates with need received aid; of those 9% had need fully met. ***Average percent of need met:*** 34% (excluding resources awarded to replace EFC). ***Average financial aid package:*** $8015 (excluding resources awarded to replace EFC). 31% of all full-time undergraduates had no need and received non-need-based gift aid.

GIFT AID (NEED-BASED) ***Total amount:*** $13,270,499 (88% federal, 12% state). ***Receiving aid:*** Freshmen: 57% (500); all full-time undergraduates: 32% (919). ***Average award:*** Freshmen: $1776; Undergraduates: $3118. ***Scholarships, grants, and awards:*** Federal Pell, FSEOG, state, private, college/university gift aid from institutional funds.

GIFT AID (NON-NEED-BASED) ***Total amount:*** $8,168,170 (100% institutional). ***Receiving aid:*** Freshmen: 13% (111). Undergraduates: 8% (229). ***Average award:*** Freshmen: $2894. Undergraduates: $4889. ***Scholarships, grants, and awards by category:*** *Academic interests/achievement:* 557 awards ($7,366,412 total): general academic interests/achievements. *Creative arts/performance:* 220 awards ($986,667 total): music. *Special achievements/activities:* 1 award ($5000 total): leadership. *Special characteristics:* 52 awards ($184,077 total): children of faculty/staff. ***Tuition waivers:*** Full or partial for employees or children of employees. ***ROTC:*** Army.

LOANS ***Student loans:*** $15,338,585 (52% need-based, 48% non-need-based). 87% of past graduating class borrowed through all loan programs. *Average indebtedness per student:* $33,766. ***Average need-based loan:*** Freshmen: $1735. Undergraduates: $1953. ***Parent loans:*** $4,778,951 (87% need-based, 13% non-need-based). ***Programs:*** Federal Direct (Subsidized and Unsubsidized Stafford, PLUS).

WORK-STUDY ***Federal work-study:*** Total amount: $417,065.50; 216 jobs averaging $1931. ***State or other work-study/employment:*** Part-time jobs available.

ATHLETIC AWARDS Total amount: $184,077 (100% non-need-based).

APPLYING FOR FINANCIAL AID ***Required financial aid form:*** FAFSA. ***Financial aid deadline (priority):*** 3/15. ***Notification date:*** Continuous beginning 4/1. Students must reply within 4 weeks of notification.

CONTACT Ms. Juanita McKenzie Edwards, Director of Financial Aid, Alcorn State University, 1000 ASU Drive #28, Lorman, MS 39096-7500, 601-877-6112 or toll-free 800-222-6790. *Fax:* 601-877-6110. *E-mail:* juanita@alcorn.edu.
Website: http://www.alcorn.edu/.

ALDERSON BROADDUS UNIVERSITY

Philippi, WV

CONTACT Amy L. King, Director of Financial Aid, Alderson Broaddus University, College Hill Road, Philippi, WV 26416, 304-457-6354 or toll-free 800-263-1549. *Fax:* 304-457-6391.
Website: http://www.ab.edu/.

ALFRED UNIVERSITY

Alfred, NY

Tuition & fees: $36,276	Average undergraduate aid package: $28,774

ABOUT THE INSTITUTION Independent, coed. ***Awards:*** certificates, bachelor's, master's, and doctoral degrees. 44 undergraduate majors. ***Total enrollment:*** 2,382. Undergraduates: 1,715. Freshmen: 458. Both federal and institutional methodology are used as a basis for awarding need-based institutional aid.

UNDERGRADUATE EXPENSES for 2020–2021 ***Application fee:*** $50. ***Comprehensive fee:*** $49,200 includes full-time tuition ($35,076), mandatory fees ($1200), and room and board ($12,924). ***College room only:*** $6498. Full-time tuition and fees vary according to program. Room and board charges vary according to board plan. ***Part-time tuition:*** $1076 per credit hour. ***Part-time fees:*** $86 per term.

FRESHMAN FINANCIAL AID (Fall 2019, est.) 441 applied for aid; of those 92% were deemed to have need. 100% of freshmen with need received aid; of those 35% had need fully met. ***Average percent of need met:*** 89% (excluding resources awarded to replace EFC). ***Average financial aid package:*** $31,797 (excluding resources awarded to replace EFC). 2% of all full-time freshmen had no need and received non-need-based gift aid.

UNDERGRADUATE FINANCIAL AID (Fall 2019, est.) 1,529 applied for aid; of those 91% were deemed to have need. 99% of undergraduates with need received aid; of those 26% had need fully met. ***Average percent of need met:*** 82% (excluding resources awarded to replace EFC). ***Average financial aid package:*** $28,774 (excluding resources awarded to replace EFC). 1% of all full-time undergraduates had no need and received non-need-based gift aid.

GIFT AID (NEED-BASED) ***Total amount:*** $31,791,727 (14% federal, 8% state, 78% institutional). ***Receiving aid:*** Freshmen: 88% (402); all full-time undergraduates: 87% (1,358). ***Average award:*** Freshmen: $27,729; Undergraduates: $24,438. ***Scholarships, grants, and awards:*** Federal Pell, FSEOG, state, private, college/university gift aid from institutional funds.

GIFT AID (NON-NEED-BASED) ***Total amount:*** $4,099,552 (1% federal, 91% institutional, 8% external sources). ***Receiving aid:*** Freshmen: 48% (222). Undergraduates: 52% (812). ***Average award:*** Freshmen: $15,182. Undergraduates: $14,824. ***Scholarships, grants, and awards by category:*** *Academic interests/achievement:* 812 awards ($3,727,386 total): biological sciences, business, communication, education, engineering/technologies, English, foreign languages, general academic interests/achievements, humanities, international studies, mathematics, physical sciences, premedicine, social sciences. *Creative arts/performance:* applied art and design. *Special characteristics:* children of educators, children of faculty/staff. ***Tuition waivers:*** Full or partial for employees or children of employees. ***ROTC:*** Army cooperative.

LOANS ***Student loans:*** $12,778,915 (50% need-based, 50% non-need-based). 83% of past graduating class borrowed through all loan programs. *Average indebtedness per student:* $33,666. ***Average need-based loan:*** Freshmen: $4877. Undergraduates: $5454. ***Parent loans:*** $3,644,890 (100% non-need-based). ***Programs:*** Federal Direct (Subsidized and Unsubsidized Stafford, PLUS), Perkins, college/university, alternative loans.

WORK-STUDY ***Federal work-study:*** Total amount: $1,837,116; jobs available.

APPLYING FOR FINANCIAL AID ***Required financial aid forms:*** FAFSA, state aid form. ***Financial aid deadline:*** 3/15. ***Notification date:*** Continuous beginning 1/15. Students must reply by 5/1 or within 2 weeks of notification.

CONTACT Ms. Jane Gilliland, Executive Director of Student Financial Services, Alfred University, Alumni Hall, One Saxon Drive, Alfred, NY 14802-1205, 607-871-2159 or toll-free 800-541-9229. *Fax:* 607-871-2252. *E-mail:* gilliland@alfred.edu.
Website: http://www.alfred.edu/.

ALICE LLOYD COLLEGE

Pippa Passes, KY

Tuition & fees: $2230 | **Average undergraduate aid package: $14,247**

ABOUT THE INSTITUTION Independent, coed. ***Awards:*** bachelor's degrees. 15 undergraduate majors. Federal methodology is used as a basis for awarding need-based institutional aid.

UNDERGRADUATE EXPENSES for 2019–2020 ***College room only:*** $3430. Full-time tuition and fees vary according to course load. ***Part-time fees:*** $225 per credit hour. Part-time tuition and fees vary according to course load. The cost of tuition is covered by a combination of scholarships and other financial aid.

FRESHMAN FINANCIAL AID (Fall 2019, est.) 198 applied for aid; of those 94% were deemed to have need. 97% of freshmen with need received aid; of those 8% had need fully met. ***Average percent of need met:*** 62% (excluding resources awarded to replace EFC). ***Average financial aid package:*** $13,598 (excluding resources awarded to replace EFC). 6% of all full-time freshmen had no need and received non-need-based gift aid.

UNDERGRADUATE FINANCIAL AID (Fall 2019, est.) 548 applied for aid; of those 91% were deemed to have need. 98% of undergraduates with need received aid; of those 12% had need fully met. ***Average percent of need met:*** 67% (excluding resources awarded to replace EFC). ***Average financial aid package:*** $14,247 (excluding resources awarded to replace EFC). 10% of all full-time undergraduates had no need and received non-need-based gift aid.

GIFT AID (NEED-BASED) ***Total amount:*** $5,043,559 (31% federal, 37% state, 29% institutional, 3% external sources). ***Receiving aid:*** Freshmen: 90% (180); all full-time undergraduates: 88% (486). ***Average award:*** Freshmen: $13,598; Undergraduates: $14,247. ***Scholarships, grants, and awards:*** Federal Pell, FSEOG, state, private, college/university gift aid from institutional funds.

GIFT AID (NON-NEED-BASED) ***Total amount:*** $790,635 (23% state, 73% institutional, 4% external sources). ***Receiving aid:*** Freshmen: 7% (14). Undergraduates: 9% (50). ***Average award:*** Freshmen: $7557. Undergraduates: $7967. ***Scholarships, grants, and awards by category:*** *Special achievements/activities:* community service, general special achievements/activities, leadership. *Special characteristics:* members of minority groups.

LOANS ***Student loans:*** $129,894 (100% need-based). 68% of past graduating class borrowed through all loan programs. *Average indebtedness per student:* $11,844. ***Average need-based loan:*** Freshmen: $1665. Undergraduates: $2099. ***Parent loans:*** $77,760 (62% need-based, 38% non-need-based). ***Programs:*** Federal Direct (Subsidized and Unsubsidized Stafford, PLUS), college/university.

WORK-STUDY ***Federal work-study:*** Total amount: $949,071; 300 jobs averaging $2893. ***State or other work-study/employment:*** Total amount: $490,920 (14% need-based, 86% non-need-based). 230 part-time jobs averaging $2710.

APPLYING FOR FINANCIAL AID ***Required financial aid form:*** FAFSA. ***Financial aid deadline:*** 7/1 (priority: 11/1). ***Notification date:*** 10/14. Students must reply by 7/1 or within 6 weeks of notification.

CONTACT Ms. Tori Nairn, Director of Financial Aid, Alice Lloyd College, 100 Purpose Road, Pippa Passes, KY 41844, 606-368-6058 or toll-free 888-280-4252. *Fax:* 606-368-6002. *E-mail:* torinairn@alc.edu.
Website: http://www.alc.edu/.

ALLEGHENY COLLEGE

Meadville, PA

Tuition & fees: $50,980 | **Average undergraduate aid package: $45,117**

ABOUT THE INSTITUTION Independent, coed. ***Awards:*** bachelor's degrees. 31 undergraduate majors. ***Total enrollment:*** 1,775. Undergraduates: 1,775. Freshmen: 500. Federal methodology is used as a basis for awarding need-based institutional aid.

UNDERGRADUATE EXPENSES for 2020–2021 ***Comprehensive fee:*** $64,060 includes full-time tuition ($50,480), mandatory fees ($500), and room and board ($13,080). ***College room only:*** $6900. Room and board charges vary according to board plan and housing facility. ***Part-time tuition:*** $2103 per credit hour. ***Part-time fees:*** $250 per term.

FRESHMAN FINANCIAL AID (Fall 2019, est.) 451 applied for aid; of those 86% were deemed to have need. 100% of freshmen with need received aid; of those 42% had need fully met. ***Average percent of need met:*** 92% (excluding resources awarded to replace EFC). ***Average financial aid package:*** $45,059 (excluding resources awarded to replace EFC). 22% of all full-time freshmen had no need and received non-need-based gift aid.

UNDERGRADUATE FINANCIAL AID (Fall 2019, est.) 1,460 applied for aid; of those 90% were deemed to have need. 100% of undergraduates with need received aid; of those 31% had need fully met. ***Average percent of need met:*** 90% (excluding resources awarded to replace EFC). ***Average financial aid package:*** $45,117 (excluding resources awarded to replace EFC). 22% of all full-time undergraduates had no need and received non-need-based gift aid.

GIFT AID (NEED-BASED) ***Receiving aid:*** Freshmen: 78% (387); all full-time undergraduates: 77% (1,311). ***Average award:*** Freshmen: $36,765; Undergraduates: $37,471. ***Scholarships, grants, and awards:*** Federal Pell, FSEOG, state, private, college/university gift aid from institutional funds, Veterans Educational Benefits (GI Bill), Yellow Ribbon Program.

GIFT AID (NON-NEED-BASED) ***Receiving aid:*** Freshmen: 25% (123). Undergraduates: 15% (249). ***Average award:*** Freshmen: $33,300. Undergraduates: $27,761. ***Scholarships, grants, and awards by category:*** *Academic interests/achievement:* 1,646 awards ($44,161,854 total): general academic interests/achievements. *Creative arts/performance:* 49 awards ($79,200 total): art/fine arts, dance, music, performing arts, theater/drama. *Special achievements/activities:* general special achievements/activities. *Special characteristics:* 764 awards ($4,914,700 total): adult students, children of educators, children of faculty/staff, international students, local/state students. ***Tuition waivers:*** Full or partial for employees or children of employees. ***ROTC:*** Army cooperative.

LOANS ***Average need-based loan:*** Freshmen: $3382. Undergraduates: $4465. ***Programs:*** Federal Direct (Subsidized and Unsubsidized Stafford, PLUS), college/university, private loans.

WORK-STUDY ***Federal work-study:*** 768 jobs averaging $2470. ***State or other work-study/employment:*** 123 part-time jobs averaging $5117.

APPLYING FOR FINANCIAL AID ***Required financial aid form:*** FAFSA. ***Financial aid deadline:*** Continuous. ***Notification date:*** Continuous. Students must reply within 4 weeks of notification.

CONTACT Ms. Natasha Eckart, Associate Director of Financial Aid, Allegheny College, Box 43, 520 North Main Street, Meadville, PA 16335, 800-835-7780 or toll-free 800-521-5293. *Fax:* 814-332-2349. *E-mail:* fao@allegheny.edu.
Website: http://www.allegheny.edu/.

ALLEGHENY WESLEYAN COLLEGE

Salem, OH

Tuition & fees: N/R | **Average undergraduate aid package: N/A**

ABOUT THE INSTITUTION Independent Wesleyan, coed. ***Awards:*** bachelor's degrees. 2 undergraduate majors. Both federal and institutional methodology are used as a basis for awarding need-based institutional aid.

FRESHMAN FINANCIAL AID (Fall 2018) 12 applied for aid; of those 83% were deemed to have need. 100% of freshmen with need received aid; of those 20% had need fully met. 15% of all full-time freshmen had no need and received non-need-based gift aid.

UNDERGRADUATE FINANCIAL AID (Fall 2018) 45 applied for aid; of those 100% were deemed to have need. 93% of undergraduates with need received aid; of those 29% had need fully met. 5% of all full-time undergraduates had no need and received non-need-based gift aid.

GIFT AID (NEED-BASED) ***Total amount:*** $284,142 (84% federal, 14% institutional, 2% external sources). ***Receiving aid:*** Freshmen: 77% (10); all full-time undergraduates: 64% (42). ***Scholarships, grants, and awards:*** Federal Pell, FSEOG, state, private, college/university gift aid from institutional funds.

GIFT AID (NON-NEED-BASED) ***Total amount:*** $51,244 (100% institutional). ***Receiving aid:*** Freshmen: 8% (1). Undergraduates: 61% (40). ***Scholarships, grants, and awards by category:*** *Academic interests/achievement:* religion/biblical studies.

LOANS ***Student loans:*** $5500 (100% need-based). 20% of past graduating class borrowed through all loan programs. *Average indebtedness per student:* $9500. ***Programs:*** Federal Direct (Subsidized and Unsubsidized Stafford, PLUS).

WORK-STUDY ***State or other work-study/employment:*** Total amount: $44,488 (100% need-based). 20 part-time jobs averaging $2200.

APPLYING FOR FINANCIAL AID ***Required financial aid forms:*** FAFSA, institution's own form. ***Financial aid deadline (priority):*** 7/31. ***Notification date:*** 8/15. Students must reply within 3 weeks of notification.

CONTACT Mrs. Esther Phelps, Financial Aid Director, Allegheny Wesleyan College, 2161 Woodsdale Road, Salem, OH 44460, 330-337-6403 Ext. 111 or toll-free 800-292-3153. *Fax:* 424-228-3006. *E-mail:* ephelps@awc.edu.
Website: http://www.awc.edu/.

ALLEN COLLEGE

Waterloo, IA

Tuition & fees: $19,512 | **Average undergraduate aid package: N/A**

ABOUT THE INSTITUTION Independent, coed, primarily women. ***Awards:*** certificates, associate, bachelor's, master's, and doctoral degrees (liberal arts and general education courses offered at either University of North Iowa or Wartburg College). 6 undergraduate majors. ***Total enrollment:*** 655. Undergraduates: 338. Federal methodology is used as a basis for awarding need-based institutional aid.

UNDERGRADUATE EXPENSES for 2020–2021 ***Application fee:*** $50. ***Comprehensive fee:*** $26,792 includes full-time tuition ($17,864), mandatory fees ($1648), and room and board ($7280). ***College room only:*** $3640. ***Part-time tuition:*** $638 per credit hour. ***Part-time fees:*** $87 per credit hour.

UNDERGRADUATE FINANCIAL AID (Fall 2018) 275 applied for aid; of those 84% were deemed to have need. 100% of undergraduates with need received aid; of those 7% had need fully met. 13% of all full-time undergraduates had no need and received non-need-based gift aid.

GIFT AID (NEED-BASED) ***Total amount:*** $2,504,329 (23% federal, 37% state, 31% institutional, 9% external sources). ***Receiving aid:*** All full-time undergraduates: 68% (205). ***Average award:*** Undergraduates: $8238. ***Scholarships, grants, and awards:*** Federal Pell, FSEOG, state, private, college/university gift aid from institutional funds, Federal Nursing.

GIFT AID (NON-NEED-BASED) ***Average award:*** Undergraduates: $1576. ***Scholarships, grants, and awards by category:*** *Academic interests/achievement:* home economics. *Special achievements/activities:* community service, general special achievements/activities, leadership. *Special characteristics:* children and siblings of alumni, general special characteristics, local/state students, members of minority groups. ***ROTC:*** Army cooperative.

LOANS ***Student loans:*** $3,392,317 (33% need-based, 67% non-need-based). ***Average need-based loan:*** Undergraduates: $4245. ***Parent loans:*** $418,175 (100% non-need-based). ***Programs:*** Federal Direct (Subsidized and Unsubsidized Stafford, PLUS), Federal Nursing, college/university.

WORK-STUDY ***Federal work-study:*** Total amount: $52,423; 14 jobs averaging $3744.

APPLYING FOR FINANCIAL AID ***Required financial aid form:*** FAFSA. ***Financial aid deadline:*** Continuous. ***Notification date:*** Continuous beginning 4/1. Students must reply within 2 weeks of notification.

CONTACT Renae S Carrillo, Director of Financial Aid, Allen College, Barrett Forum, 1825 Logan Avenue, Waterloo, IA 50703-1990, 319-226-2515. *Fax:* 319-226-2051. *E-mail:* renae.carrillo@allencollege.edu.
Website: http://www.allencollege.edu/.

ALLEN UNIVERSITY

Columbia, SC

Tuition & fees: N/R | **Average undergraduate aid package: $8081**

ABOUT THE INSTITUTION Independent African Methodist Episcopal, coed. ***Awards:*** bachelor's degrees. 8 undergraduate majors. Federal methodology is used as a basis for awarding need-based institutional aid.

FRESHMAN FINANCIAL AID (Fall 2019, est.) 167 applied for aid; of those 72% were deemed to have need. 100% of freshmen with need received aid. ***Average percent of need met:*** 70% (excluding resources awarded to replace EFC). ***Average financial aid package:*** $7025 (excluding resources awarded to replace EFC).

UNDERGRADUATE FINANCIAL AID (Fall 2019, est.) 552 applied for aid; of those 80% were deemed to have need. 100% of undergraduates with need received aid; of those 12% had need fully met. ***Average percent of need met:*** 74% (excluding resources awarded to replace EFC). ***Average financial aid package:*** $8081 (excluding resources awarded to replace EFC). 1% of all full-time undergraduates had no need and received non-need-based gift aid.

GIFT AID (NEED-BASED) ***Total amount:*** $2,258,966 (70% federal, 26% state, 2% institutional, 2% external sources). ***Receiving aid:*** Freshmen: 72% (121); all full-time undergraduates: 80% (442). ***Average award:*** Freshmen: $2213; Undergraduates: $2213. ***Scholarships, grants, and awards:*** Federal Pell, FSEOG, state, private.

GIFT AID (NON-NEED-BASED) ***Receiving aid:*** Freshmen: 9% (15). Undergraduates: 11% (58). ***Average award:*** Undergraduates: $3609. ***Scholarships, grants, and awards by category:*** *Academic interests/achievement:* 10 awards ($45,646 total): general academic interests/achievements. ***ROTC:*** Army cooperative.

LOANS ***Student loans:*** $2,859,791 (100% need-based). 78% of past graduating class borrowed through all loan programs. *Average indebtedness per student:* $13,037. ***Average need-based loan:*** Freshmen: $2625. Undergraduates: $4833. ***Parent loans:*** $33,368 (100% need-based).

WORK-STUDY ***Federal work-study:*** Total amount: $189,180; 160 jobs averaging $1000.

ATHLETIC AWARDS Total amount: $90,950 (100% need-based).

APPLYING FOR FINANCIAL AID ***Required financial aid form:*** FAFSA. ***Financial aid deadline (priority):*** 6/30.

CONTACT Ms. 'Lola L. Kennedy, Director of Financial Aid, Allen University, 1530 Harden Street, Columbia, SC 29204-1085, 803-376-5791 or toll-free 877-625-5368. *Fax:* 803-799-3042. *E-mail:* lkennedy@allenuniversity.edu.
Website: http://www.allenuniversity.edu/.

ALLIANT INTERNATIONAL UNIVERSITY - SAN DIEGO

San Diego, CA

Tuition & fees: N/R | **Average undergraduate aid package: $14,625**

ABOUT THE INSTITUTION Independent, coed. ***Awards:*** certificates, bachelor's, master's, and doctoral degrees. 2 undergraduate majors. Federal methodology is used as a basis for awarding need-based institutional aid.

UNDERGRADUATE FINANCIAL AID (Fall 2018) 40 applied for aid; of those 100% were deemed to have need. 100% of undergraduates with need received aid; of those 5% had need fully met. ***Average percent of need met:*** 63% (excluding resources awarded to replace EFC). ***Average financial aid package:*** $14,625 (excluding resources awarded to replace EFC).

GIFT AID (NEED-BASED) ***Total amount:*** $368,153 (82% federal, 18% state). ***Receiving aid:*** All full-time undergraduates: 6% (39). ***Average award:*** Undergraduates: $10,125. ***Scholarships, grants, and awards:*** Federal Pell, FSEOG, state, private, college/university gift aid from institutional funds.

GIFT AID (NON-NEED-BASED) ***Total amount:*** $192,966 (9% institutional, 91% external sources). ***Receiving aid:*** Undergraduates: 1% (4). ***Scholarships, grants, and awards by category:*** *Academic interests/achievement:* business, education, general academic interests/achievements, humanities, social sciences. *Special achievements/activities:* community service, general special achievements/activities, leadership. *Special characteristics:* children and siblings of alumni, children of faculty/staff, general special characteristics, international students, local/state students, public servants, siblings of current students, spouses of current students, veterans.

LOANS *Student loans:* $178,813 (50% need-based, 50% non-need-based). ***Average need-based loan:*** Undergraduates: $5350. ***Parent loans:*** $21,750 (100% non-need-based). ***Programs:*** Federal Direct (Subsidized and Unsubsidized Stafford, PLUS), alternative loans.

WORK-STUDY *Federal work-study:* Total amount: $52,000; 8 jobs averaging $6500. ***State or other work-study/employment:*** Part-time jobs available.

APPLYING FOR FINANCIAL AID *Required financial aid form:* FAFSA. ***Financial aid deadline (priority):*** 3/2. ***Notification date:*** Continuous beginning 3/15. Students must reply within 3 weeks of notification.

CONTACT Ms. Deborah Spindler, University Director of Financial Aid, Alliant International University - San Diego, 10455 Pomerado Road, San Diego, CA 92131-1799, 858-635-4700 Ext. 4700 or toll-free 866-825-5426. *Fax:* 858-635-4848. *E-mail:* dspindler@alliant.edu.
Website: http://www.alliant.edu/.

ALMA COLLEGE

Alma, MI

Tuition & fees: $41,398	Average undergraduate aid package: $30,408

ABOUT THE INSTITUTION Independent Presbyterian, coed. ***Awards:*** bachelor's degrees. 39 undergraduate majors. ***Total enrollment:*** 1,426. Undergraduates: 1,426. Freshmen: 408. Federal methodology is used as a basis for awarding need-based institutional aid.

UNDERGRADUATE EXPENSES for 2019–2020 *Application fee:* $25. ***Comprehensive fee:*** $52,782 includes full-time tuition ($41,138), mandatory fees ($260), and room and board ($11,384). Room and board charges vary according to board plan and housing facility. ***Part-time tuition:*** $1285 per credit hour. Part-time tuition and fees vary according to course load.

FRESHMAN FINANCIAL AID (Fall 2019, est.) 368 applied for aid; of those 90% were deemed to have need. 99% of freshmen with need received aid; of those 23% had need fully met. ***Average percent of need met:*** 76% (excluding resources awarded to replace EFC). ***Average financial aid package:*** $32,161 (excluding resources awarded to replace EFC). 12% of all full-time freshmen had no need and received non-need-based gift aid.

UNDERGRADUATE FINANCIAL AID (Fall 2019, est.) 1,277 applied for aid; of those 91% were deemed to have need. 100% of undergraduates with need received aid; of those 16% had need fully met. ***Average percent of need met:*** 72% (excluding resources awarded to replace EFC). ***Average financial aid package:*** $30,408 (excluding resources awarded to replace EFC). 15% of all full-time undergraduates had no need and received non-need-based gift aid.

GIFT AID (NEED-BASED) *Receiving aid:* Freshmen: 87% (328); all full-time undergraduates: 85% (1,157). ***Average award:*** Freshmen: $30,353; Undergraduates: $29,259. ***Scholarships, grants, and awards:*** Federal Pell, FSEOG, state, private, college/university gift aid from institutional funds.

GIFT AID (NON-NEED-BASED) *Receiving aid:* Freshmen: 20% (76). Undergraduates: 14% (189). ***Average award:*** Freshmen: $28,680. Undergraduates: $25,269. ***Scholarships, grants, and awards by category:*** *Academic interests/achievement:* 1,297 awards ($26,737,616 total): general academic interests/achievements. *Creative arts/performance:* 307 awards ($852,931 total): applied art and design, dance, music, performing arts, theater/drama. *Special achievements/activities:* 14 awards ($21,000 total): religious involvement. *Special characteristics:* 465 awards ($751,150 total): children and siblings of alumni, members of minority groups, out-of-state students, siblings of current students. ***Tuition waivers:*** Full or partial for employees or children of employees. ***ROTC:*** Army cooperative, Naval cooperative.

LOANS *Student loans:* 77% of past graduating class borrowed through all loan programs. *Average indebtedness per student:* $40,387. ***Average need-based loan:*** Freshmen: $3527. Undergraduates: $4634. ***Programs:*** Federal Direct (Subsidized and Unsubsidized Stafford, PLUS), college/university, alternative loans.

WORK-STUDY *Federal work-study:* 600 jobs averaging $1200.

APPLYING FOR FINANCIAL AID *Required financial aid form:* FAFSA. ***Financial aid deadline:*** Continuous. ***Notification date:*** Continuous.

CONTACT Mrs. Michelle L. McNier, Director of Financial Aid, Alma College, 614 West Superior Street, Alma, MI 48801-1599, 989-463-7347 or toll-free 800-321-ALMA. *Fax:* 989-463-7993. *E-mail:* mcnierml@alma.edu.
Website: http://www.alma.edu/.

ALVERNIA UNIVERSITY

Reading, PA

CONTACT Ms. Christine Saadi, Director of Student Financial Planning, Alvernia University, 400 Saint Bernardine Street, Reading, PA 19607-1799, 610-796-8213 or toll-free 888-ALVERNIA (in-state). *Fax:* 610-796-8336. *E-mail:* christine.saadi@alvernia.edu.
Website: http://www.alvernia.edu/.

ALVERNO COLLEGE

Milwaukee, WI

Tuition & fees: $29,456	Average undergraduate aid package: $21,594

ABOUT THE INSTITUTION Independent Roman Catholic, undergraduate: women only; graduate: coed. ***Awards:*** certificates, associate, bachelor's, master's, and doctoral degrees (also offers weekend program with significant enrollment not reflected in profile). 54 undergraduate majors. ***Total enrollment:*** 1,743. Undergraduates: 1,104. Freshmen: 170. Federal methodology is used as a basis for awarding need-based institutional aid.

UNDERGRADUATE EXPENSES for 2019–2020 *Comprehensive fee:* $38,256 includes full-time tuition ($28,656), mandatory fees ($800), and room and board ($8800). Full-time tuition and fees vary according to program. Room and board charges vary according to board plan and housing facility. ***Part-time tuition:*** $1194 per credit hour. Part-time tuition and fees vary according to program.

FRESHMAN FINANCIAL AID (Fall 2019, est.) 168 applied for aid; of those 96% were deemed to have need. 100% of freshmen with need received aid. ***Average financial aid package:*** $24,506 (excluding resources awarded to replace EFC). 4% of all full-time freshmen had no need and received non-need-based gift aid.

UNDERGRADUATE FINANCIAL AID (Fall 2019, est.) 849 applied for aid; of those 96% were deemed to have need. 99% of undergraduates with need received aid. ***Average financial aid package:*** $21,594 (excluding resources awarded to replace EFC). 9% of all full-time undergraduates had no need and received non-need-based gift aid.

GIFT AID (NEED-BASED) *Total amount:* $15,300,517 (19% federal, 13% state, 67% institutional, 1% external sources). ***Receiving aid:*** Freshmen: 96% (162); all full-time undergraduates: 88% (795). ***Average award:*** Freshmen: $21,386; Undergraduates: $17,715. ***Scholarships, grants, and awards:*** Federal Pell, FSEOG, state, private, college/university gift aid from institutional funds.

GIFT AID (NON-NEED-BASED) *Total amount:* $1,234,482 (97% institutional, 3% external sources). ***Receiving aid:*** Freshmen: 79% (133). Undergraduates: 78% (704). ***Average award:*** Freshmen: $16,416. Undergraduates: $12,533. ***Scholarships, grants, and awards by category:*** *Academic interests/achievement:* 1,285 awards ($8,445,293 total): education, general academic interests/achievements, library science. *Creative arts/performance:* 40 awards ($43,490 total): applied art and design, music. *Special achievements/activities:* 10 awards ($84,636 total): community service, memberships. *Special characteristics:* 217 awards ($328,492 total): children and siblings of alumni, children of faculty/staff, ethnic background, international students, out-of-state students, religious affiliation. ***Tuition waivers:*** Full or partial for employees or children of employees. ***ROTC:*** Army cooperative, Air Force cooperative.

LOANS *Student loans:* $7,467,644 (89% need-based, 11% non-need-based). 85% of past graduating class borrowed through all loan programs. *Average indebtedness per student:* $38,959. ***Average need-based loan:*** Freshmen: $2590. Undergraduates: $3986. ***Parent loans:*** $1,529,624 (57% need-based, 43% non-need-based). ***Programs:*** Federal Direct (Subsidized and Unsubsidized Stafford, PLUS), Perkins, state.

WORK-STUDY *Federal work-study:* Total amount: $442,437; 267 jobs averaging $1148. ***State or other work-study/employment:*** Part-time jobs available.

APPLYING FOR FINANCIAL AID ***Required financial aid form:*** FAFSA. ***Financial aid deadline:*** Continuous. ***Notification date:*** Continuous beginning 11/1. Students must reply within 2 weeks of notification.

CONTACT Ms. Amy Christen, Director of Financial Aid, Alverno College, 3400 South 43rd Street, PO Box 343922, Milwaukee, WI 53234-3922, 414-382-6040 or toll-free 800-933-3401. *Fax:* 414-382-6354. *E-mail:* amy.christen@alverno.edu.
Website: http://www.alverno.edu/.

AMDA COLLEGE AND CONSERVATORY OF THE PERFORMING ARTS, LOS ANGELES CAMPUS

Los Angeles, CA

CONTACT Financial Aid Office, AMDA College and Conservatory of the Performing Arts, Los Angeles Campus, 6305 Yucca Street, Los Angeles, CA 90028, 323-469-3300 or toll-free 888-474-9444.
Website: http://www.amda.edu/.

AMERICA EVANGELICAL UNIVERSITY

Los Angeles, CA

CONTACT Financial Aid Office, America Evangelical University, 1818 South Western Avenue, Los Angeles, CA 90006.
Website: http://www.aeu.edu/.

AMERICAN ACADEMY OF ART

Chicago, IL

CONTACT Ms. Ione Fitzgerald, Director of Financial Aid, American Academy of Art, 332 South Michigan Avenue, Suite 300, Chicago, IL 60604, 312-461-0600 or toll-free 888-461-0600. *Fax:* 312-294-9570.
Website: http://www.aaart.edu/.

AMERICAN BAPTIST COLLEGE

Nashville, TN

CONTACT Miss Sharonda Campbell, Financial Aid Administrator, American Baptist College, 1800 Baptist World Center Drive, Nashville, TN 37207, 615-687-6903. *Fax:* 615-226-7855. *E-mail:* scampbell@abcnash.edu.
Website: http://www.abcnash.edu/.

AMERICAN BUSINESS & TECHNOLOGY UNIVERSITY

Saint Joseph, MO

CONTACT Financial Aid Office, American Business & Technology University, 1018 West St.Maartens Drive, Saint Joseph, MO 64506, 816-279-7000 or toll-free 800-804-1388.
Website: http://www.abtu.edu/.

AMERICAN COLLEGE FOR MEDICAL CAREERS

Orlando, FL

CONTACT Financial Aid Office, American College for Medical Careers, 5959 Lake Ellenor Drive, Orlando, FL 32809, 407-738-4488 or toll-free 888-599-7887.
Website: http://www.acmc.edu/.

AMERICAN COLLEGE OF HEALTHCARE SCIENCES

Portland, OR

CONTACT Financial Aid Office, American College of Healthcare Sciences, 5005 SW Macadam Avenue, Portland, OR 97239-3719, 503-244-0726 or toll-free 800-487-8839.
Website: http://www.achs.edu/.

AMERICAN INTERCONTINENTAL UNIVERSITY ATLANTA

Atlanta, GA

CONTACT Financial Aid Office, American InterContinental University Atlanta, 6600 Peachtree-Dunwoody Road, 500 Embassy Row, Atlanta, GA 30328, 404-965-6500 or toll-free 800-353-1744.
Website: http://www.aiuniv.edu/.

AMERICAN INTERCONTINENTAL UNIVERSITY HOUSTON

Houston, TX

CONTACT Financial Aid Office, American InterContinental University Houston, 9999 Richmond Avenue, Houston, TX 77042, 832-201-3600 or toll-free 888-607-9888.
Website: http://www.aiuniv.edu/.

AMERICAN INTERCONTINENTAL UNIVERSITY ONLINE

Schaumburg, IL

CONTACT Financial Aid Office, American InterContinental University Online, 231 N. Martingale Road, 6th Floor, Schaumburg, IL 60173, 847-851-5000 or toll-free 877-701-3800.
Website: http://www.aiuniv.edu/.

AMERICAN INTERNATIONAL COLLEGE

Springfield, MA

CONTACT Ms. Sage Stachowiak, Director of Financial Aid, American International College, 1000 State Street, Springfield, MA 01109-3189, 413-205-3521 or toll-free 800-242-3142. *Fax:* 413-205-3912. *E-mail:* sage.stachowiak@aic.edu.
Website: http://www.aic.edu/.

AMERICAN NATIONAL UNIVERSITY - ROANOKE VALLEY

Salem, VA

CONTACT Financial Aid Office, American National University - Roanoke Valley, 1813 East Main Street, Salem, VA 24153, 540-986-1800 or toll-free 888-9-JOBREADY. *Website:* http://www.an.edu/.

AMERICAN SENTINEL UNIVERSITY

Aurora, CO

CONTACT Financial Aid Office, American Sentinel University, 2260 South Xanadu Way, Suite 310, Aurora, CO 80014, toll-free 800-729-2427.
Website: http://www.americansentinel.edu/.

AMERICAN UNIVERSITY

Washington, DC

Tuition & fees: $51,361	Average undergraduate aid package: $35,880

ABOUT THE INSTITUTION Independent Methodist, coed. ***Awards:*** certificates, bachelor's, master's, and doctoral degrees. 73 undergraduate majors. ***Total enrollment:*** 14,318. Undergraduates: 8,527. Freshmen: 1,754. Institutional methodology is used as a basis for awarding need-based institutional aid.

UNDERGRADUATE EXPENSES for 2020–2021 ***Application fee:*** $70. ***Comprehensive fee:*** $66,341 includes full-time tuition ($50,542), mandatory fees ($819), and room and board ($14,980). ***College room only:*** $10,096. Full-time tuition and fees vary according to course load. Room and board charges vary according to board plan, housing facility, and location. ***Part-time tuition:*** $1684 per credit hour. Part-time tuition and fees vary according to course load. ***Payment plan:*** Tuition prepayment.

FRESHMAN FINANCIAL AID (Fall 2019, est.) 1237 applied for aid; of those 59% were deemed to have need. 98% of freshmen with need received aid; of those 24% had need fully met. ***Average percent of need met:*** 87% (excluding resources awarded to replace EFC). ***Average financial aid package:*** $38,820 (excluding resources awarded to replace EFC). 12% of all full-time freshmen had no need and received non-need-based gift aid.

UNDERGRADUATE FINANCIAL AID (Fall 2019, est.) 4,458 applied for aid; of those 77% were deemed to have need. 98% of undergraduates with need received aid; of those 16% had need fully met. ***Average percent of need met:*** 74% (excluding resources awarded to replace EFC). ***Average financial aid package:*** $35,880 (excluding resources awarded to replace EFC). 5% of all full-time undergraduates had no need and received non-need-based gift aid.

GIFT AID (NEED-BASED) ***Total amount:*** $88,424,306 (6% federal, 94% institutional). ***Receiving aid:*** Freshmen: 39% (676); all full-time undergraduates: 41% (3,046). ***Average award:*** Freshmen: $28,681; Undergraduates: $29,427. ***Scholarships, grants, and awards:*** Federal Pell, FSEOG, private, college/university gift aid from institutional funds.

GIFT AID (NON-NEED-BASED) ***Total amount:*** $19,289,332 (100% institutional). ***Receiving aid:*** Freshmen: 13% (234). Undergraduates: 12% (873). ***Average award:*** Freshmen: $12,899. Undergraduates: $12,939. ***Scholarships, grants, and awards by category:*** *Academic interests/achievement:* general academic interests/achievements. *Creative arts/performance:* general creative arts/performance. *Special achievements/activities:* general special achievements/activities, leadership, memberships. *Special characteristics:* ethnic background, members of minority groups, relatives of clergy. ***Tuition waivers:*** Full or partial for employees or children of employees. ***ROTC:*** Army cooperative, Air Force cooperative.

LOANS ***Student loans:*** $19,767,831 (60% need-based, 40% non-need-based). ***Average need-based loan:*** Freshmen: $3369. Undergraduates: $4358. ***Parent loans:*** $21,779,707 (100% non-need-based). ***Programs:*** Federal Direct (Subsidized and Unsubsidized Stafford, PLUS), Perkins, college/university.

WORK-STUDY ***Federal work-study:*** Total amount: $3,031,094; 1,608 jobs averaging $1885.

ATHLETIC AWARDS Total amount: $5,954,349 (100% non-need-based).

APPLYING FOR FINANCIAL AID ***Required financial aid forms:*** FAFSA, CSS Financial Aid PROFILE. ***Financial aid deadline:*** 1/15 (priority: 11/15). ***Notification date:*** 4/1. Students must reply within 4 weeks of notification.

CONTACT Mr. Brian Lee Sang, Assistant Vice Provost of Financial Aid, American University, 4400 Massachusetts Avenue, NW, Washington, DC 20016-8001, 202-885-6500. *Fax:* 202-885-1129. *E-mail:* facounselor@american.edu.
Website: http://www.american.edu/.

AMERICAN UNIVERSITY OF HEALTH SCIENCES

Signal Hill, CA

CONTACT Financial Aid Office, American University of Health Sciences, 1600 East Hill Street, Building #1, Signal Hill, CA 90755, 562-988-2278.
Website: http://www.auhs.edu/.

AMERICAN UNIVERSITY OF PUERTO RICO - BAYAMON

Bayamon, PR

CONTACT Mr. Yahaira Melendez, Financial Aid Director, American University of Puerto Rico - Bayamon, PO Box 2037, Bayamón, PR 00960-2037, 787-620-2040 Ext. 2031. *Fax:* 787-785-7377. *E-mail:* melendezy@aupr.edu.
Website: http://www.aupr.edu/.

AMERICAN UNIVERSITY OF PUERTO RICO - MANATI

Manati, PR

CONTACT Financial Aid Office, American University of Puerto Rico - Manati, Carretera Estatal #2 Km. 48.7, PO Box 1082, Manati, PR 00674-1082, 787-621-2835.
Website: http://www.aupr.edu/.

AMHERST COLLEGE

Amherst, MA

Tuition & fees: $60,890	Average undergraduate aid package: $58,806

ABOUT THE INSTITUTION Independent, coed. ***Awards:*** bachelor's degrees. 42 undergraduate majors. ***Total enrollment:*** 1,839. Undergraduates: 1,839. Freshmen: 470. Both federal and institutional methodology are used as a basis for awarding need-based institutional aid.

UNDERGRADUATE EXPENSES for 2020–2021 ***Application fee:*** $65. ***Comprehensive fee:*** $76,800 includes full-time tuition ($59,890), mandatory fees ($1000), and room and board ($15,910). ***College room only:*** $8630.

FRESHMAN FINANCIAL AID (Fall 2019, est.) 328 applied for aid; of those 82% were deemed to have need. 100% of freshmen with need received aid; of those 100% had need fully met. ***Average percent of need met:*** 100% (excluding resources awarded to replace EFC). ***Average financial aid package:*** $59,559 (excluding resources awarded to replace EFC).

UNDERGRADUATE FINANCIAL AID (Fall 2019, est.) 1,234 applied for aid; of those 89% were deemed to have need. 100% of undergraduates with need received aid; of those 100% had need fully met. ***Average percent of need met:*** 100% (excluding resources awarded to replace EFC). ***Average financial aid package:*** $58,806 (excluding resources awarded to replace EFC).

GIFT AID (NEED-BASED) ***Total amount:*** $63,198,474 (4% federal, 95% institutional, 1% external sources). ***Receiving aid:*** Freshmen: 57% (266); all full-time undergraduates: 57% (1,086). ***Average award:*** Freshmen: $58,697; Undergraduates: $57,760. ***Scholarships, grants, and awards:*** Federal Pell, FSEOG, state, private, college/university gift aid from institutional funds.

GIFT AID (NON-NEED-BASED) ***Total amount:*** $713,490 (100% external sources). ***ROTC:*** Army cooperative, Air Force cooperative.

LOANS ***Student loans:*** $2,368,457 (36% need-based, 64% non-need-based). 28% of past graduating class borrowed through all loan programs. *Average indebtedness per student:* $22,629. ***Average need-based loan:*** Freshmen: $332. Undergraduates: $389. ***Parent loans:*** $3,356,242 (100% non-need-based). ***Programs:*** Federal Direct (Subsidized and Unsubsidized Stafford, PLUS), college/university.

WORK-STUDY ***Federal work-study:*** Total amount: $1,253,543; 866 jobs averaging $1564. ***State or other work-study/employment:*** Total amount: $418,666 (100% need-based). 223 part-time jobs averaging $1724.

APPLYING FOR FINANCIAL AID ***Required financial aid forms:*** FAFSA, CSS Financial Aid PROFILE, noncustodial (divorced/separated) parent's statement, business/farm supplement, federal income tax form(s), W-2 forms. ***Financial aid deadline (priority):*** 1/1. ***Notification date:*** 4/1. Students must reply by 5/1.

CONTACT Gail W. Holt, Dean of Financial Aid, Amherst College, B-5 Converse Hall, PO Box 5000, Amherst, MA 01002-5000, 413-542-2296. *Fax:* 413-542-2628. *E-mail:* finaid@amherst.edu.
Website: http://www.amherst.edu/.

AMRIDGE UNIVERSITY

Montgomery, AL

ABOUT THE INSTITUTION Independent Church of Christ, coed. ***Awards:*** associate, bachelor's, master's, and doctoral degrees. 9 undergraduate majors. ***Total enrollment:*** 758. Undergraduates: 356. Freshmen: 3.

GIFT AID (NEED-BASED) ***Scholarships, grants, and awards:*** Federal Pell, FSEOG, state, private, college/university gift aid from institutional funds.

GIFT AID (NON-NEED-BASED) ***Scholarships, grants, and awards by category:*** *Special achievements/activities:* religious involvement. *Special characteristics:* children of educators, children of faculty/staff, public servants, veterans.

LOANS ***Programs:*** Federal Direct (Subsidized and Unsubsidized Stafford, PLUS).

APPLYING FOR FINANCIAL AID ***Required financial aid forms:*** FAFSA, institution's own form, state aid form.

CONTACT Starr Fain, Director of Financial Aid, Amridge University, 1200 Taylor Road, Montgomery, AL 36117, 334-387-3877 Ext. 7523 or toll-free 888-790-8080. *Fax:* 334-387-3878. *E-mail:* starrfain@amridgeuniversity.edu.
Website: http://www.amridgeuniversity.edu/.

ANDERSON UNIVERSITY

Anderson, IN

Tuition & fees: $31,200	Average undergraduate aid package: $25,964

ABOUT THE INSTITUTION Independent Church of God, coed. ***Awards:*** associate, bachelor's, master's, and doctoral degrees. 65 undergraduate majors. ***Total enrollment:*** 1,567. Undergraduates: 1,311. Freshmen: 330. Federal methodology is used as a basis for awarding need-based institutional aid.

UNDERGRADUATE EXPENSES for 2019–2020 ***Comprehensive fee:*** $41,240 includes full-time tuition ($30,700), mandatory fees ($500), and room and board ($10,040). ***College room only:*** $6240. ***Part-time tuition:*** $1280 per semester hour.

FRESHMAN FINANCIAL AID (Fall 2019, est.) 392 applied for aid; of those 72% were deemed to have need. 100% of freshmen with need received aid; of those 18% had need fully met. ***Average percent of need met:*** 73% (excluding resources awarded to replace EFC). ***Average financial aid package:*** $26,427 (excluding resources awarded to replace EFC). 8% of all full-time freshmen had no need and received non-need-based gift aid.

UNDERGRADUATE FINANCIAL AID (Fall 2019, est.) 1,146 applied for aid; of those 87% were deemed to have need. 100% of undergraduates with need received aid; of those 15% had need fully met. ***Average percent of need met:*** 75% (excluding resources awarded to replace EFC). ***Average financial aid package:*** $25,964 (excluding resources awarded to replace EFC). 10% of all full-time undergraduates had no need and received non-need-based gift aid.

GIFT AID (NEED-BASED) ***Total amount:*** $6,586,929 (37% federal, 32% state, 31% institutional). ***Receiving aid:*** Freshmen: 52% (212); all full-time undergraduates: 62% (748). ***Average award:*** Freshmen: $8406; Undergraduates: $8492. ***Scholarships, grants, and awards:*** Federal Pell, FSEOG, state, private, college/university gift aid from institutional funds.

GIFT AID (NON-NEED-BASED) ***Total amount:*** $17,779,587 (5% state, 89% institutional, 6% external sources). ***Receiving aid:*** Freshmen: 70% (284). Undergraduates: 79% (964). ***Average award:*** Freshmen: $15,210. Undergraduates: $13,523. ***Scholarships, grants, and awards by category:*** *Academic interests/achievement:* biological sciences, business, computer science, education, engineering/technologies, English, foreign languages, general academic interests/achievements, home economics, mathematics, physical sciences, premedicine, religion/biblical studies, social sciences. *Creative arts/performance:* applied art and design, dance, music, theater/drama. *Special achievements/activities:* general special achievements/activities, leadership, religious involvement. *Special characteristics:* adult students, children and siblings of alumni, children of faculty/staff, ethnic background, international students, local/state students, members of minority groups, out-of-state students, relatives of clergy, religious affiliation.

LOANS ***Student loans:*** $8,487,122 (39% need-based, 61% non-need-based). ***Average need-based loan:*** Freshmen: $2970. Undergraduates: $3781. ***Parent loans:*** $11,059,648 (100% non-need-based). ***Programs:*** Federal Direct (Subsidized and Unsubsidized Stafford, PLUS).

WORK-STUDY ***Federal work-study:*** Total amount: $2,159,905; jobs available. ***State or other work-study/employment:*** Total amount: $4000 (100% non-need-based). Part-time jobs available.

APPLYING FOR FINANCIAL AID ***Financial aid deadline:*** Continuous. ***Notification date:*** Continuous.

CONTACT Mrs. Christina Maggart, Director of Financial Aid, Anderson University, 1100 East Fifth Street, Anderson, IN 46012-3495, 765-641-4180 or toll-free 800-428-6414. *Fax:* 765-641-3831. *E-mail:* clmaggart@anderson.edu.
Website: http://www.anderson.edu/.

ANDERSON UNIVERSITY

Anderson, SC

Tuition & fees: $29,980	Average undergraduate aid package: $21,124

ABOUT THE INSTITUTION Independent Baptist, coed. ***Awards:*** bachelor's, master's, and doctoral degrees. 65 undergraduate majors. ***Total enrollment:*** 3,497. Undergraduates: 2,983. Freshmen: 681. Federal methodology is used as a basis for awarding need-based institutional aid.

UNDERGRADUATE EXPENSES for 2020–2021 ***Application fee:*** $25. ***Comprehensive fee:*** $40,620 includes full-time tuition ($26,820), mandatory fees ($3160), and room and board ($10,640). ***College room only:*** $5430. ***Part-time tuition:*** $665 per credit hour.

FRESHMAN FINANCIAL AID (Fall 2019, est.) 568 applied for aid; of those 79% were deemed to have need. 100% of freshmen with need received aid; of those 36% had need fully met. ***Average percent of need met:*** 76% (excluding resources awarded to replace EFC). ***Average financial aid package:*** $22,571 (excluding resources awarded to replace EFC). 23% of all full-time freshmen had no need and received non-need-based gift aid.

UNDERGRADUATE FINANCIAL AID (Fall 2019, est.) 2,366 applied for aid; of those 83% were deemed to have need. 99% of undergraduates with need received aid; of those 31% had need fully met. ***Average percent of need met:*** 73% (excluding resources awarded to replace EFC). ***Average financial aid package:*** $21,124 (excluding resources awarded to replace EFC). 21% of all full-time undergraduates had no need and received non-need-based gift aid.

GIFT AID (NEED-BASED) ***Receiving aid:*** Freshmen: 72% (451); all full-time undergraduates: 74% (1,906). ***Average award:*** Freshmen: $20,892; Undergraduates: $18,752. ***Scholarships, grants, and awards:*** Federal Pell, FSEOG, state, private, college/university gift aid from institutional funds.

GIFT AID (NON-NEED-BASED) ***Receiving aid:*** Freshmen: 25% (154). Undergraduates: 21% (533). ***Average award:*** Freshmen: $13,080. Undergraduates: $12,794. ***Scholarships, grants, and awards by category:*** *Academic interests/achievement:* 2,862 awards ($20,553,078 total): business, education, general academic interests/achievements, religion/biblical studies. *Creative arts/performance:* 351 awards ($985,523 total): applied art and design, art/fine arts, music, performing arts, theater/drama. *Special achievements/activities:* 398 awards ($557,830 total): cheerleading/drum major, leadership, memberships, religious involvement. *Special characteristics:* 2,144 awards ($5,584,472 total): children of faculty/staff, general special characteristics, international students, out-of-state students, previous college experience, religious affiliation, veterans, veterans' children. ***ROTC:*** Army cooperative, Air Force cooperative.

LOANS *Student loans:* 69% of past graduating class borrowed through all loan programs. *Average indebtedness per student:* $32,609. ***Average need-based loan:*** Freshmen: $3087. Undergraduates: $3896. ***Programs:*** Federal Direct (Subsidized and Unsubsidized Stafford, PLUS), state.

WORK-STUDY *Federal work-study:* 201 jobs averaging $4000. ***State or other work-study/employment:*** 282 part-time jobs averaging $850.

APPLYING FOR FINANCIAL AID *Required financial aid form:* FAFSA. ***Notification date:*** Continuous. Students must reply within 2 weeks of notification.

CONTACT Nancy Tate, Director of Financial Aid Services, Anderson University, 316 Boulevard, Anderson, SC 29621-4035, 864-231-2181 or toll-free 800-542-3594. *Fax:* 864-231-2008. *E-mail:* ntate@andersonuniversity.edu.
Website: http://www.andersonuniversity.edu/.

ANDREWS UNIVERSITY

Berrien Springs, MI

Tuition & fees: $31,008	Average undergraduate aid package: $32,665

ABOUT THE INSTITUTION Independent Seventh-day Adventist, coed. ***Awards:*** certificates, associate, bachelor's, master's, and doctoral degrees. 71 undergraduate majors. ***Total enrollment:*** 3,412. Undergraduates: 1,708. Freshmen: 283. Federal methodology is used as a basis for awarding need-based institutional aid.

UNDERGRADUATE EXPENSES for 2020–2021 *Application fee:* $30. ***Comprehensive fee:*** $40,548 includes full-time tuition ($29,808), mandatory fees ($1200), and room and board ($9540). ***College room only:*** $5040. Full-time tuition and fees vary according to course load. Room and board charges vary according to board plan. ***Part-time tuition:*** $1242 per credit hour. ***Part-time fees:*** $140. Part-time tuition and fees vary according to course load.

FRESHMAN FINANCIAL AID (Fall 2019, est.) 207 applied for aid; of those 82% were deemed to have need. 100% of freshmen with need received aid; of those 32% had need fully met. ***Average percent of need met:*** 86% (excluding resources awarded to replace EFC). ***Average financial aid package:*** $31,022 (excluding resources awarded to replace EFC). 38% of all full-time freshmen had no need and received non-need-based gift aid.

UNDERGRADUATE FINANCIAL AID (Fall 2019, est.) 834 applied for aid; of those 90% were deemed to have need. 100% of undergraduates with need received aid; of those 22% had need fully met. ***Average percent of need met:*** 88% (excluding resources awarded to replace EFC). ***Average financial aid package:*** $32,665 (excluding resources awarded to replace EFC). 40% of all full-time undergraduates had no need and received non-need-based gift aid.

GIFT AID (NEED-BASED) *Receiving aid:* Freshmen: 34% (94); all full-time undergraduates: 35% (470). ***Average award:*** Freshmen: $6038; Undergraduates: $7072. ***Scholarships, grants, and awards:*** Federal Pell, FSEOG, state, private, college/university gift aid from institutional funds.

GIFT AID (NON-NEED-BASED) *Receiving aid:* Freshmen: 61% (170). Undergraduates: 54% (737). ***Average award:*** Freshmen: $14,798. Undergraduates: $14,359. ***Scholarships, grants, and awards by category:*** *Academic interests/achievement:* 1,112 awards ($9,893,265 total): general academic interests/achievements. *Creative arts/performance:* 25 awards ($33,000 total): music. *Special achievements/activities:* 205 awards ($342,869 total): leadership, religious involvement. *Special characteristics:* 122 awards ($1,634,539 total): children of faculty/staff, general special characteristics, international students, spouses of current students. ***Tuition waivers:*** Full or partial for employees or children of employees, senior citizens.

LOANS *Student loans:* 61% of past graduating class borrowed through all loan programs. *Average indebtedness per student:* $33,335. ***Average need-based loan:*** Freshmen: $3160. Undergraduates: $4196. ***Programs:*** Federal Direct (Subsidized and Unsubsidized Stafford, PLUS), Perkins.

WORK-STUDY *Federal work-study:* 478 jobs averaging $932. ***State or other work-study/employment:*** Part-time jobs available.

APPLYING FOR FINANCIAL AID *Required financial aid forms:* FAFSA, institution's own form, CSS Financial Aid PROFILE. ***Financial aid deadline:*** Continuous.

CONTACT Cynthia Gammon, Assistant Director of Student Financial Services, Andrews University, Student Financial Services Administration Building, Berrien Springs, MI 49104, 800-253-2874. *Fax:* 269-471-3228. *E-mail:* sfs@andrews.edu.
Website: http://www.andrews.edu/.

ANGELES COLLEGE

Los Angeles, CA

CONTACT Financial Aid Office, Angeles College, 3440 Wilshire Boulevard, Suite 310, Los Angeles, CA 90010, 213-487-2211.
Website: http://www.angelescollege.edu/.

ANGELO STATE UNIVERSITY

San Angelo, TX

Tuition & fees (area res): $9011	Average undergraduate aid package: $10,572

ABOUT THE INSTITUTION State-supported, coed. ***Awards:*** certificates, bachelor's, master's, and doctoral degrees. 40 undergraduate majors. ***Total enrollment:*** 10,568. Undergraduates: 9,046. Freshmen: 1,260. Federal methodology is used as a basis for awarding need-based institutional aid.

UNDERGRADUATE EXPENSES for 2020–2021 *Application fee:* $40. ***One-time required fee:*** $100. ***Tuition, area resident:*** full-time $5516; part-time $184 per credit hour. ***Tuition, state resident:*** full-time $5516; part-time $184 per credit hour. ***Tuition, nonresident:*** full-time $17,786; part-time $593 per credit hour. ***Required fees:*** full-time $3495. Full-time tuition and fees vary according to course level, course load, degree level, location, and program. Part-time tuition and fees vary according to course level, course load, degree level, location, and program. ***College room and board:*** $9630. Room and board charges vary according to board plan and housing facility. ***Payment plan:*** Guaranteed tuition.

FRESHMAN FINANCIAL AID (Fall 2018) 1404 applied for aid; of those 82% were deemed to have need. 99% of freshmen with need received aid; of those 15% had need fully met. ***Average percent of need met:*** 71% (excluding resources awarded to replace EFC). ***Average financial aid package:*** $11,490 (excluding resources awarded to replace EFC). 16% of all full-time freshmen had no need and received non-need-based gift aid.

UNDERGRADUATE FINANCIAL AID (Fall 2018) 4,696 applied for aid; of those 85% were deemed to have need. 99% of undergraduates with need received aid; of those 14% had need fully met. ***Average percent of need met:*** 64% (excluding resources awarded to replace EFC). ***Average financial aid package:*** $10,572 (excluding resources awarded to replace EFC). 18% of all full-time undergraduates had no need and received non-need-based gift aid.

GIFT AID (NEED-BASED) *Total amount:* $37,474,797 (52% federal, 48% state). ***Receiving aid:*** Freshmen: 66% (1,036); all full-time undergraduates: 61% (3,552). ***Average award:*** Freshmen: $3982; Undergraduates: $3607. ***Scholarships, grants, and awards:*** Federal Pell, FSEOG, state, private, college/university gift aid from institutional funds, Federal Nursing.

GIFT AID (NON-NEED-BASED) *Total amount:* $18,609,972 (96% institutional, 4% external sources). ***Receiving aid:*** Freshmen: 43% (674). Undergraduates: 37% (2,161). ***Average award:*** Freshmen: $3380. Undergraduates: $3246. ***Scholarships, grants, and awards by category:*** *Academic interests/achievement:* agriculture, biological sciences, business, communication, computer science, education, engineering/technologies, English, foreign languages, general academic interests/achievements, home economics, humanities, international studies, mathematics, military science, physical sciences, premedicine, social sciences. *Creative arts/performance:* applied art and design, art/fine arts, cinema/film/broadcasting, music, performing arts, theater/drama. *Special achievements/activities:* cheerleading/drum major, general special achievements/activities, memberships. *Special characteristics:* children of faculty/staff, local/state students, veterans, veterans' children. ***Tuition***

waivers: Full or partial for employees or children of employees, senior citizens. ***ROTC:*** Air Force.

LOANS ***Student loans:*** $67,869,980 (34% need-based, 66% non-need-based). 55% of past graduating class borrowed through all loan programs. *Average indebtedness per student:* $24,496. ***Average need-based loan:*** Freshmen: $3243. Undergraduates: $3843. ***Parent loans:*** $38,635,212 (100% non-need-based). ***Programs:*** Federal Direct (Subsidized and Unsubsidized Stafford, PLUS), Perkins, Federal Nursing, state, college/university.

WORK-STUDY ***Federal work-study:*** Total amount: $3,325,849; 125 jobs averaging $2100. ***State or other work-study/employment:*** Total amount: $65,334 (100% need-based). 16 part-time jobs averaging $1827.

ATHLETIC AWARDS Total amount: $2,447,339 (100% non-need-based).

APPLYING FOR FINANCIAL AID ***Required financial aid form:*** FAFSA. ***Financial aid deadline (priority):*** 4/1. ***Notification date:*** Continuous beginning 4/1. Students must reply within 4 weeks of notification.

CONTACT Mr. Ed Kerestly, Director of Financial Aid, Angelo State University, ASU Station #11015, San Angelo, TX 76909-1015, 325-942-2246 or toll-free 800-946-8627. *Fax:* 325-942-2082. *E-mail:* financial.aid@angelo.edu.
Website: http://www.angelo.edu/.

ANNA MARIA COLLEGE

Paxton, MA

CONTACT Sandra J. Pereira, Director of Financial Aid, Anna Maria College, 50 Sunset Lane, Paxton, MA 01612-1198, 508-849-3363. *Fax:* 508-849-3735. *E-mail:* spereira@annamaria.edu.
Website: http://www.annamaria.edu/.

ANTIOCH COLLEGE

Yellow Springs, OH

CONTACT Financial Aid Office, Antioch College, 1 Morgan Place, Yellow Springs, OH 45387, 937-767-1286.
Website: http://www.antiochcollege.edu/.

ANTIOCH UNIVERSITY LOS ANGELES

Culver City, CA

CONTACT Financial Aid Office, Antioch University Los Angeles, 400 Corporate Pointe, Culver City, CA 90230, 310-578-1080 or toll-free 800-726-8462.
Website: http://www.antioch.edu/los-angeles/.

ANTIOCH UNIVERSITY SANTA BARBARA

Santa Barbara, CA

CONTACT Heather Nguyen, Assistant Director of Financial Aid, Antioch University Santa Barbara, 602 Anacapa Street, Santa Barbara, CA 93101, 805-962-8179 Ext. 5219 or toll-free 866-526-8462. *Fax:* 805-879-7062. *E-mail:* financialaid.ausb@antioch.edu.
Website: http://www.antioch.edu/santa-barbara/.

ANTIOCH UNIVERSITY SEATTLE

Seattle, WA

CONTACT Katy Stahl, Director of Financial Aid, Antioch University Seattle, 2326 Sixth Avenue, Seattle, WA 98121-1814, 206-268-4004 or toll-free 888-268-4477. *Fax:* 206-268-4242. *E-mail:* kstahl@antiochseattle.edu.
Website: http://www.antioch.edu/seattle/.

APEX SCHOOL OF THEOLOGY

Durham, NC

CONTACT Financial Aid Office, Apex School of Theology, 1701 T.W. Alexander Drive, Durham, NC 27703, 919-572-1625.
Website: http://www.apexsot.edu/.

APPALACHIAN BIBLE COLLEGE

Mount Hope, WV

Tuition & fees: N/R	Average undergraduate aid package: $15,319

ABOUT THE INSTITUTION Independent nondenominational, coed. ***Awards:*** certificates, diplomas, associate, bachelor's, and master's degrees. 2 undergraduate majors. Federal methodology is used as a basis for awarding need-based institutional aid.

FRESHMAN FINANCIAL AID (Fall 2019, est.) 34 applied for aid; of those 71% were deemed to have need. 100% of freshmen with need received aid; of those 8% had need fully met. ***Average percent of need met:*** 64% (excluding resources awarded to replace EFC). ***Average financial aid package:*** $15,254 (excluding resources awarded to replace EFC). 11% of all full-time freshmen had no need and received non-need-based gift aid.

UNDERGRADUATE FINANCIAL AID (Fall 2019, est.) 134 applied for aid; of those 69% were deemed to have need. 100% of undergraduates with need received aid; of those 2% had need fully met. ***Average percent of need met:*** 65% (excluding resources awarded to replace EFC). ***Average financial aid package:*** $15,319 (excluding resources awarded to replace EFC). 6% of all full-time undergraduates had no need and received non-need-based gift aid.

GIFT AID (NEED-BASED) ***Total amount:*** $1,895,219 (24% federal, 6% state, 58% institutional, 12% external sources). ***Receiving aid:*** Freshmen: 65% (24); all full-time undergraduates: 54% (93). ***Average award:*** Freshmen: $13,749; Undergraduates: $13,287. ***Scholarships, grants, and awards:*** Federal Pell, FSEOG, state, private, college/university gift aid from institutional funds.

GIFT AID (NON-NEED-BASED) ***Average award:*** Freshmen: $7919. Undergraduates: $7416.

LOANS ***Student loans:*** $374,018 (83% need-based, 17% non-need-based). 41% of past graduating class borrowed through all loan programs. *Average indebtedness per student:* $14,616. ***Average need-based loan:*** Freshmen: $3500. Undergraduates: $3759. ***Parent loans:*** $19,200 (100% need-based). ***Programs:*** Federal Direct (Subsidized and Unsubsidized Stafford, PLUS).

WORK-STUDY ***Federal work-study:*** Total amount: $12,441; 16 jobs averaging $778.

APPLYING FOR FINANCIAL AID ***Required financial aid forms:*** FAFSA, institution's own form, state aid form. ***Financial aid deadline (priority):*** 6/15. ***Notification date:*** Continuous.

CONTACT Laura Martin, Director of Financial Aid, Appalachian Bible College, 161 College Drive, Mount Hope, WV 25880, 304-877-6428 Ext. 321 or toll-free 800-678-9ABC. *Fax:* 304-877-5082. *E-mail:* financialaid@abc.edu.
Website: http://www.abc.edu/.

APPALACHIAN STATE UNIVERSITY

Boone, NC

Tuition & fees (area res): $7410	Average undergraduate aid package: $10,279

ABOUT THE INSTITUTION State-supported, coed. ***Awards:*** certificates, bachelor's, master's, and doctoral degrees. 74 undergraduate majors. ***Total enrollment:*** 19,280. Undergraduates: 17,518. Freshmen: 3,501. Federal methodology is used as a basis for awarding need-based institutional aid.

UNDERGRADUATE EXPENSES for 2019–2020 ***Application fee:*** $65. ***Tuition, area resident:*** full-time $4242. ***Tuition, state resident:*** full-time $4242; part-time $143 per credit hour. ***Tuition, nonresident:*** full-time $19,049; part-time $644 per credit hour. ***Required fees:*** full-time $3168; $104 per credit hour. Part-time tuition and fees vary according to course load. ***College room and board:***

$8568; ***Room only:*** $4620. Room and board charges vary according to board plan and housing facility. ***Payment plan:*** Guaranteed tuition.

FRESHMAN FINANCIAL AID (Fall 2019, est.) 3040 applied for aid; of those 61% were deemed to have need. 91% of freshmen with need received aid; of those 20% had need fully met. ***Average percent of need met:*** 65% (excluding resources awarded to replace EFC). ***Average financial aid package:*** $10,465 (excluding resources awarded to replace EFC). 3% of all full-time freshmen had no need and received non-need-based gift aid.

UNDERGRADUATE FINANCIAL AID (Fall 2019, est.) 11,842 applied for aid; of those 73% were deemed to have need. 93% of undergraduates with need received aid; of those 15% had need fully met. ***Average percent of need met:*** 61% (excluding resources awarded to replace EFC). ***Average financial aid package:*** $10,279 (excluding resources awarded to replace EFC). 4% of all full-time undergraduates had no need and received non-need-based gift aid.

GIFT AID (NEED-BASED) ***Total amount:*** $55,705,310 (41% federal, 27% state, 25% institutional, 7% external sources). ***Receiving aid:*** Freshmen: 39% (1,372); all full-time undergraduates: 39% (6,402). ***Average award:*** Freshmen: $9688; Undergraduates: $8916. ***Scholarships, grants, and awards:*** Federal Pell, FSEOG, state, private, college/university gift aid from institutional funds.

GIFT AID (NON-NEED-BASED) ***Total amount:*** $5,037,918 (12% state, 46% institutional, 42% external sources). ***Receiving aid:*** Freshmen: 4% (137). Undergraduates: 2% (332). ***Average award:*** Freshmen: $4775. Undergraduates: $3074. ***Scholarships, grants, and awards by category:*** *Academic interests/achievement:* general academic interests/achievements. *Creative arts/performance:* general creative arts/performance. *Special achievements/activities:* general special achievements/activities. *Special characteristics:* general special characteristics. ***Tuition waivers:*** Full or partial for employees or children of employees. ***ROTC:*** Army.

LOANS ***Student loans:*** $59,285,310 (74% need-based, 26% non-need-based). 57% of past graduating class borrowed through all loan programs. *Average indebtedness per student:* $23,105. ***Average need-based loan:*** Freshmen: $3428. Undergraduates: $4201. ***Parent loans:*** $18,241,868 (70% need-based, 30% non-need-based). ***Programs:*** Federal Direct (Subsidized and Unsubsidized Stafford, PLUS), Perkins.

WORK-STUDY ***Federal work-study:*** Total amount: $1,066,459; jobs available. ***State or other work-study/employment:*** Total amount: $52,000 (100% need-based).

ATHLETIC AWARDS Total amount: $5,981,145 (42% need-based, 58% non-need-based).

APPLYING FOR FINANCIAL AID ***Required financial aid form:*** FAFSA. ***Financial aid deadline:*** Continuous. ***Notification date:*** Continuous beginning 3/15.

CONTACT Wes Armstrong, Director of Financial Aid, Appalachian State University, 287 Rivers St, John E. Thomas Hall, Boone, NC 28608-2059, 828-262-2190. *Fax:* 828-262-2585. *E-mail:* financialaid@appstate.edu.
Website: http://www.appstate.edu/.

AQUINAS COLLEGE

Grand Rapids, MI

Tuition & fees: $35,086	Average undergraduate aid package: $26,667

ABOUT THE INSTITUTION Independent Roman Catholic, coed. ***Awards:*** associate, bachelor's, and master's degrees. 74 undergraduate majors. ***Total enrollment:*** 1,600. Undergraduates: 1,456. Freshmen: 262. Federal methodology is used as a basis for awarding need-based institutional aid.

UNDERGRADUATE EXPENSES for 2020–2021 ***Comprehensive fee:*** $44,962 includes full-time tuition ($34,386), mandatory fees ($700), and room and board ($9876). ***College room only:*** $4630. Full-time tuition and fees vary according to course load. Room and board charges vary according to board plan and housing facility. ***Part-time tuition:*** $536 per credit hour. Part-time tuition and fees vary according to course load.

FRESHMAN FINANCIAL AID (Fall 2019, est.) 234 applied for aid; of those 87% were deemed to have need. 100% of freshmen with need received aid; of those 35% had need fully met. ***Average percent of need met:*** 81% (excluding resources awarded to replace EFC). ***Average financial aid package:*** $27,329 (excluding resources awarded to replace EFC). 9% of all full-time freshmen had no need and received non-need-based gift aid.

UNDERGRADUATE FINANCIAL AID (Fall 2019, est.) 998 applied for aid; of those 88% were deemed to have need. 100% of undergraduates with need received aid; of those 28% had need fully met. ***Average percent of need met:*** 79% (excluding resources awarded to replace EFC). ***Average financial aid package:*** $26,667 (excluding resources awarded to replace EFC). 14% of all full-time undergraduates had no need and received non-need-based gift aid.

GIFT AID (NEED-BASED) ***Total amount:*** $18,780,814 (11% federal, 9% state, 80% institutional). ***Receiving aid:*** Freshmen: 79% (203); all full-time undergraduates: 74% (879). ***Average award:*** Freshmen: $25,854; Undergraduates: $24,317. ***Scholarships, grants, and awards:*** Federal Pell, FSEOG, state, private, college/university gift aid from institutional funds, United Negro College Fund.

GIFT AID (NON-NEED-BASED) ***Total amount:*** $5,029,597 (100% institutional). ***Receiving aid:*** Freshmen: 48% (123). Undergraduates: 35% (420). ***Average award:*** Freshmen: $18,102. Undergraduates: $17,280. ***Scholarships, grants, and awards by category:*** *Academic interests/achievement:* general academic interests/achievements. *Creative arts/performance:* general creative arts/performance. *Special achievements/activities:* general special achievements/activities, leadership. *Special characteristics:* children of faculty/staff. ***Tuition waivers:*** Full or partial for employees or children of employees.

LOANS ***Student loans:*** $6,028,825 (91% need-based, 9% non-need-based). 74% of past graduating class borrowed through all loan programs. *Average indebtedness per student:* $30,158. ***Average need-based loan:*** Freshmen: $1475. Undergraduates: $2350. ***Parent loans:*** $1,142,209 (94% need-based, 6% non-need-based). ***Programs:*** Federal Direct (Subsidized and Unsubsidized Stafford, PLUS).

WORK-STUDY ***Federal work-study:*** Total amount: $122,090; 92 jobs averaging $1327.

ATHLETIC AWARDS Total amount: $4,267,118 (71% need-based, 29% non-need-based).

APPLYING FOR FINANCIAL AID ***Required financial aid form:*** FAFSA. ***Financial aid deadline (priority):*** 3/1. ***Notification date:*** Continuous beginning 12/13.

CONTACT Darcy Kampfschulte, Director of Financial Aid, Aquinas College, 1700 Fulton Street E, Grand Rapids, MI 49506-1801, 616-632-2894 or toll-free 800-678-9593. *Fax:* 616-732-4547. *E-mail:* kampfdar@aquinas.edu.
Website: http://www.aquinas.edu/.

AQUINAS COLLEGE

Nashville, TN

CONTACT Mrs. Kylie Pruitt, Director of Financial Aid, Aquinas College, 4210 Harding Road, Nashville, TN 37205-2005, 615-297-7545 Ext. 431 or toll-free 800-649-9956. *Fax:* 615-279-3891. *E-mail:* pruittk@aquinascollege.edu.
Website: http://www.aquinascollege.edu/.

ARCADIA UNIVERSITY

Glenside, PA

CONTACT Alison Venditti, Assistant Director of Financial Aid, Arcadia University, 450 South Easton Road, Glenside, PA 19038, 215-572-2837 or toll-free 877-ARCADIA. *Fax:* 215-572-4049. *E-mail:* venditta@arcadia.edu.
Website: http://www.arcadia.edu/.

ARGOSY UNIVERSITY, ATLANTA

Atlanta, GA

CONTACT Financial Aid Office, Argosy University, Atlanta, 980 Hammond Drive, Suite 100, Atlanta, GA 30328, 770-671-1200 or toll-free 888-671-4777.

ARGOSY UNIVERSITY, CHICAGO

Chicago, IL

CONTACT Financial Aid Office, Argosy University, Chicago, 225 North Michigan Avenue, Suite 1300, Chicago, IL 60601, 312-777-7600 or toll-free 800-626-4123.

ARGOSY UNIVERSITY, HAWAI`I

Honolulu, HI

CONTACT Financial Aid Office, Argosy University, Hawai`i, 1001 Bishop Street, Suite 400, Honolulu, HI 96813, 808-536-5555 or toll-free 888-323-2777.

ARGOSY UNIVERSITY, LOS ANGELES

Los Angeles, CA

CONTACT Financial Aid Office, Argosy University, Los Angeles, 5230 Pacific Concourse, Suite 200, Los Angeles, CA 90045, 310-531-9700 or toll-free 866-505-0332.

ARGOSY UNIVERSITY, NORTHERN VIRGINIA

Arlington, VA

CONTACT Financial Aid Office, Argosy University, Northern Virginia, 1550 Wilson Boulevard, Suite 600, Arlington, VA 22209, 703-526-5800 or toll-free 866-703-2777.

ARGOSY UNIVERSITY, ORANGE COUNTY

Orange, CA

CONTACT Financial Aid Office, Argosy University, Orange County, 601 South Lewis Street, Orange, CA 92868, 714-620-3700 or toll-free 800-716-9598.

ARGOSY UNIVERSITY, PHOENIX

Phoenix, AZ

CONTACT Financial Aid Office, Argosy University, Phoenix, 2233 West Dunlap Avenue, Phoenix, AZ 85021, 602-216-2600 or toll-free 866-216-2777.

ARGOSY UNIVERSITY, SEATTLE

Seattle, WA

CONTACT Financial Aid Office, Argosy University, Seattle, 2601-A Elliott Avenue, Seattle, WA 98121, 206-283-4500 or toll-free 866-283-2777.

ARGOSY UNIVERSITY, TAMPA

Tampa, FL

CONTACT Financial Aid Office, Argosy University, Tampa, 1403 North Howard Avenue, Tampa, FL 33607, 813-393-5290 or toll-free 800-850-6488.

ARGOSY UNIVERSITY, TWIN CITIES

Eagan, MN

CONTACT Financial Aid Office, Argosy University, Twin Cities, 1515 Central Parkway, Eagan, MN 55121, 651-846-2882 or toll-free 888-844-2004.

ARIZONA CHRISTIAN UNIVERSITY

Glendale, AZ

Tuition & fees: $30,624	**Average undergraduate aid package: $9070**

ABOUT THE INSTITUTION Independent Conservative Baptist, coed. ***Awards:*** certificates, associate, and bachelor's degrees. 22 undergraduate majors. ***Total enrollment:*** 870. Undergraduates: 870. Freshmen: 222. Both federal and institutional methodology are used as a basis for awarding need-based institutional aid.

UNDERGRADUATE EXPENSES for 2020–2021 ***Comprehensive fee:*** $42,624 includes full-time tuition ($28,874), mandatory fees ($1750), and room and board ($12,000). ***Part-time tuition:*** $1203 per credit hour.

FRESHMAN FINANCIAL AID (Fall 2018) 172 applied for aid; of those 80% were deemed to have need. 77% of freshmen with need received aid; of those 14% had need fully met. ***Average percent of need met:*** 32% (excluding resources awarded to replace EFC). ***Average financial aid package:*** $8347 (excluding resources awarded to replace EFC). 64% of all full-time freshmen had no need and received non-need-based gift aid.

UNDERGRADUATE FINANCIAL AID (Fall 2018) 601 applied for aid; of those 82% were deemed to have need. 70% of undergraduates with need received aid; of those 14% had need fully met. ***Average percent of need met:*** 32% (excluding resources awarded to replace EFC). ***Average financial aid package:*** $9070 (excluding resources awarded to replace EFC). 23% of all full-time undergraduates had no need and received non-need-based gift aid.

GIFT AID (NEED-BASED) ***Total amount:*** $12,829,046 (54% federal, 44% institutional, 2% external sources). ***Receiving aid:*** Freshmen: 47% (104); all full-time undergraduates: 48% (336). ***Average award:*** Freshmen: $7691; Undergraduates: $8275. ***Scholarships, grants, and awards:*** Federal Pell, FSEOG, state, private, college/university gift aid from institutional funds.

GIFT AID (NON-NEED-BASED) ***Total amount:*** $3,258,218 (6% federal, 93% institutional, 1% external sources). ***Receiving aid:*** Freshmen: 7% (15). Undergraduates: 6% (41). ***Average award:*** Freshmen: $15,512. Undergraduates: $15,167. ***Scholarships, grants, and awards by category:*** *Academic interests/achievement:* general academic interests/achievements. *Creative arts/performance:* music. *Special achievements/activities:* community service, general special achievements/activities, leadership. ***ROTC:*** Air Force cooperative.

LOANS ***Student loans:*** $3,897,656 (72% need-based, 28% non-need-based). ***Average need-based loan:*** Freshmen: $3357. Undergraduates: $3581. ***Parent loans:*** $1,367,310 (42% need-based, 58% non-need-based). ***Programs:*** Federal Direct (Subsidized and Unsubsidized Stafford, PLUS).

WORK-STUDY ***Federal work-study:*** Total amount: $32,651; jobs available.

APPLYING FOR FINANCIAL AID ***Required financial aid form:*** FAFSA. ***Financial aid deadline:*** Continuous. ***Notification date:*** Continuous.

CONTACT Mr. Steven Young, Director of Financial Aid, Arizona Christian University, 2625 East Cactus Road, Phoenix, AZ 85032-7042, 602-386-4115 or toll-free 800-247-2697. *Fax:* 602-404-2159. *E-mail:* steven.young@arizonachristian.edu.
Website: http://arizonachristian.edu/.

ARIZONA COLLEGE–LAS VEGAS

Las Vegas, NV

CONTACT Financial Aid Office, Arizona College–Las Vegas, 2320 South Rancho Drive, Las Vegas, NV 89102.
Website: http://www.arizonacollege.edu/.

ARIZONA COLLEGE–MESA

Mesa, AZ

CONTACT Financial Aid Office, Arizona College–Mesa, 163 N Dobson Road, Mesa, AZ 85201.
Website: http://www.arizonacollege.edu/.

ARIZONA STATE UNIVERSITY AT THE DOWNTOWN PHOENIX CAMPUS

Phoenix, AZ

Tuition & fees (AZ res): $11,338	Average undergraduate aid package: $15,792

ABOUT THE INSTITUTION State-supported, coed. ***Awards:*** certificates, bachelor's, master's, and doctoral degrees. 27 undergraduate majors. ***Total enrollment:*** 11,420. Undergraduates: 8,513. Freshmen: 1,676. Federal methodology is used as a basis for awarding need-based institutional aid.

UNDERGRADUATE EXPENSES for 2019–2020 ***Application fee:*** $50. ***Tuition, state resident:*** full-time $10,710; part-time $765 per credit hour. ***Tuition, nonresident:*** full-time $28,800; part-time $1200 per credit hour. ***Required fees:*** full-time $628; $157 per term. Full-time tuition and fees vary according to program. Part-time tuition and fees vary according to program. ***College room and board:*** $14,924; ***Room only:*** $9750. Room and board charges vary according to board plan.

FRESHMAN FINANCIAL AID (Fall 2018) 1322 applied for aid; of those 78% were deemed to have need. 100% of freshmen with need received aid; of those 22% had need fully met. ***Average percent of need met:*** 69% (excluding resources awarded to replace EFC). ***Average financial aid package:*** $18,271 (excluding resources awarded to replace EFC). 24% of all full-time freshmen had no need and received non-need-based gift aid.

UNDERGRADUATE FINANCIAL AID (Fall 2018) 6,394 applied for aid; of those 85% were deemed to have need. 100% of undergraduates with need received aid; of those 18% had need fully met. ***Average percent of need met:*** 60% (excluding resources awarded to replace EFC). ***Average financial aid package:*** $15,792 (excluding resources awarded to replace EFC). 17% of all full-time undergraduates had no need and received non-need-based gift aid.

GIFT AID (NEED-BASED) ***Total amount:*** $59,400,113 (35% federal, 58% institutional, 7% external sources). ***Receiving aid:*** Freshmen: 72% (1,008); all full-time undergraduates: 65% (5,035). ***Average award:*** Freshmen: $14,362; Undergraduates: $11,434. ***Scholarships, grants, and awards:*** Federal Pell, FSEOG, state, private, college/university gift aid from institutional funds, United Negro College Fund, Federal Nursing.

GIFT AID (NON-NEED-BASED) ***Total amount:*** $17,479,415 (6% federal, 77% institutional, 17% external sources). ***Receiving aid:*** Freshmen: 10% (145). Undergraduates: 6% (447). ***Average award:*** Freshmen: $9754. Undergraduates: $8827. ***Scholarships, grants, and awards by category:*** *Academic interests/achievement:* general academic interests/achievements. *Special achievements/activities:* leadership. *Special characteristics:* children of faculty/staff, international students, local/state students, out-of-state students. ***Tuition waivers:*** Full or partial for employees or children of employees. ***ROTC:*** Army cooperative, Naval cooperative, Air Force cooperative.

LOANS ***Student loans:*** $33,859,931 (74% need-based, 26% non-need-based). 61% of past graduating class borrowed through all loan programs. *Average indebtedness per student:* $25,136. ***Average need-based loan:*** Freshmen: $2948. Undergraduates: $3923. ***Parent loans:*** $19,562,894 (46% need-based, 54% non-need-based). ***Programs:*** Federal Direct (Subsidized and Unsubsidized Stafford, PLUS), Perkins, Federal Nursing, state, college/university, private loans from endowment funds.

WORK-STUDY ***Federal work-study:*** Total amount: $1,305,125; 443 jobs averaging $2952. ***State or other work-study/employment:*** Total amount: $3,769,769 (33% need-based, 67% non-need-based). 1,208 part-time jobs averaging $3118.

ATHLETIC AWARDS Total amount: $1,992,137 (30% need-based, 70% non-need-based).

APPLYING FOR FINANCIAL AID ***Required financial aid form:*** FAFSA. ***Financial aid deadline (priority):*** 1/15. ***Notification date:*** Continuous beginning 12/1.

CONTACT Financial Aid and Scholarship Services, Arizona State University at the Downtown Phoenix campus, PO Box 870412, Tempe, AZ 85287-0412, 855-278-5080. *Fax:* 480-965-9484.
Website: http://campus.asu.edu/downtown/.

ARIZONA STATE UNIVERSITY AT THE POLYTECHNIC CAMPUS

Mesa, AZ

Tuition & fees (AZ res): $10,803	Average undergraduate aid package: $14,674

ABOUT THE INSTITUTION State-supported, coed. ***Awards:*** certificates, bachelor's, master's, and doctoral degrees. 33 undergraduate majors. ***Total enrollment:*** 5,243. Undergraduates: 4,611. Freshmen: 659. Federal methodology is used as a basis for awarding need-based institutional aid.

UNDERGRADUATE EXPENSES for 2019–2020 ***Application fee:*** $50. ***Tuition, state resident:*** full-time $10,175; part-time $727 per credit hour. ***Tuition, nonresident:*** full-time $27,360; part-time $1140 per credit hour. ***Required fees:*** full-time $628; $157 per term. Full-time tuition and fees vary according to program. Part-time tuition and fees vary according to program. ***College room and board:*** $12,728; ***Room only:*** $7554. Room and board charges vary according to board plan and housing facility.

FRESHMAN FINANCIAL AID (Fall 2018) 553 applied for aid; of those 73% were deemed to have need. 100% of freshmen with need received aid; of those 19% had need fully met. ***Average percent of need met:*** 65% (excluding resources awarded to replace EFC). ***Average financial aid package:*** $14,555 (excluding resources awarded to replace EFC). 30% of all full-time freshmen had no need and received non-need-based gift aid.

UNDERGRADUATE FINANCIAL AID (Fall 2018) 2,924 applied for aid; of those 82% were deemed to have need. 100% of undergraduates with need received aid; of those 18% had need fully met. ***Average percent of need met:*** 59% (excluding resources awarded to replace EFC). ***Average financial aid package:*** $14,674 (excluding resources awarded to replace EFC). 16% of all full-time undergraduates had no need and received non-need-based gift aid.

GIFT AID (NEED-BASED) ***Total amount:*** $23,339,356 (45% federal, 49% institutional, 6% external sources). ***Receiving aid:*** Freshmen: 61% (392); all full-time undergraduates: 56% (2,201). ***Average award:*** Freshmen: $11,904; Undergraduates: $9993. ***Scholarships, grants, and awards:*** Federal Pell, FSEOG, state, private, college/university gift aid from institutional funds, United Negro College Fund.

GIFT AID (NON-NEED-BASED) ***Total amount:*** $9,451,420 (8% federal, 54% institutional, 38% external sources). ***Receiving aid:*** Freshmen: 8% (51). Undergraduates: 5% (188). ***Average award:*** Freshmen: $7651. Undergraduates: $7428. ***Scholarships, grants, and awards by category:*** *Academic interests/achievement:* general academic interests/achievements. *Special achievements/activities:* leadership. *Special characteristics:* children of faculty/staff, international students, local/state students, out-of-state students. ***Tuition waivers:*** Full or partial for employees or children of employees. ***ROTC:*** Army cooperative, Naval cooperative, Air Force cooperative.

LOANS ***Student loans:*** $16,688,637 (74% need-based, 26% non-need-based). 56% of past graduating class borrowed through all loan programs. *Average indebtedness per student:* $26,096. ***Average need-based loan:*** Freshmen: $3012. Undergraduates: $4127. ***Parent loans:*** $7,889,122 (45% need-based, 55% non-need-based). ***Programs:*** Federal Direct (Subsidized and Unsubsidized Stafford, PLUS), Perkins, state, college/university, private loans from endowment funds.

WORK-STUDY ***Federal work-study:*** Total amount: $559,596; 186 jobs averaging $3026. ***State or other work-study/employment:*** Total amount: $3,081,986 (36% need-based, 64% non-need-based). 808 part-time jobs averaging $3810.

ATHLETIC AWARDS Total amount: $1,395,624 (51% need-based, 49% non-need-based).

APPLYING FOR FINANCIAL AID ***Required financial aid form:*** FAFSA. ***Financial aid deadline (priority):*** 1/15. ***Notification date:*** Continuous beginning 12/1.

CONTACT Financial Aid and Scholarship Services, Arizona State University at the Polytechnic campus, PO Box 870412, Tempe, AZ 85287-0412, 855-278-5080. *Fax:* 480-965-9484.
Website: http://campus.asu.edu/polytechnic.

ARIZONA STATE UNIVERSITY AT THE TEMPE CAMPUS

Tempe, AZ

Tuition & fees (AZ res): $11,338 **Average undergraduate aid package: $15,878**

ABOUT THE INSTITUTION State-supported, coed. ***Awards:*** certificates, bachelor's, master's, and doctoral degrees (profile includes data for the West, Polytechnic and Downtown Phoenix campuses). 100 undergraduate majors. ***Total enrollment:*** 53,286. Undergraduates: 44,461. Freshmen: 10,044. Federal methodology is used as a basis for awarding need-based institutional aid.

UNDERGRADUATE EXPENSES for 2019–2020 ***Application fee:*** $50. ***Tuition, state resident:*** full-time $10,710; part-time $765 per credit hour. ***Tuition, nonresident:*** full-time $28,800; part-time $1200 per credit hour. ***Required fees:*** full-time $628; $157 per term. Full-time tuition and fees vary according to program. Part-time tuition and fees vary according to program. ***College room and board:*** $13,164; ***Room only:*** $7990. Room and board charges vary according to board plan and housing facility.

FRESHMAN FINANCIAL AID (Fall 2018) 7475 applied for aid; of those 69% were deemed to have need. 100% of freshmen with need received aid; of those 24% had need fully met. ***Average percent of need met:*** 71% (excluding resources awarded to replace EFC). ***Average financial aid package:*** $17,745 (excluding resources awarded to replace EFC). 37% of all full-time freshmen had no need and received non-need-based gift aid.

UNDERGRADUATE FINANCIAL AID (Fall 2018) 26,961 applied for aid; of those 78% were deemed to have need. 100% of undergraduates with need received aid; of those 20% had need fully met. ***Average percent of need met:*** 63% (excluding resources awarded to replace EFC). ***Average financial aid package:*** $15,878 (excluding resources awarded to replace EFC). 27% of all full-time undergraduates had no need and received non-need-based gift aid.

GIFT AID (NEED-BASED) ***Total amount:*** $239,108,595 (30% federal, 64% institutional, 6% external sources). ***Receiving aid:*** Freshmen: 58% (5,105); all full-time undergraduates: 51% (19,959). ***Average award:*** Freshmen: $13,988; Undergraduates: $11,690. ***Scholarships, grants, and awards:*** Federal Pell, FSEOG, state, private, college/university gift aid from institutional funds, United Negro College Fund.

GIFT AID (NON-NEED-BASED) ***Total amount:*** $152,755,702 (2% federal, 69% institutional, 29% external sources). ***Receiving aid:*** Freshmen: 9% (827). Undergraduates: 5% (2,141). ***Average award:*** Freshmen: $10,158. Undergraduates: $8977. ***Scholarships, grants, and awards by category:*** *Academic interests/achievement:* general academic interests/achievements. *Creative arts/performance:* art/fine arts, dance, music, theater/drama. *Special achievements/activities:* leadership. *Special characteristics:* children of faculty/staff, international students, local/state students, out-of-state students. ***Tuition waivers:*** Full or partial for employees or children of employees. ***ROTC:*** Army, Naval, Air Force.

LOANS ***Student loans:*** $122,109,694 (68% need-based, 32% non-need-based). 45% of past graduating class borrowed through all loan programs. *Average indebtedness per student:* $23,711. ***Average need-based loan:*** Freshmen: $3027. Undergraduates: $3959. ***Parent loans:*** $47,498,934 (6% need-based, 94% non-need-based). ***Programs:*** Federal Direct (Subsidized and Unsubsidized Stafford, PLUS), Perkins, state, college/university, private loans from endowment funds.

WORK-STUDY ***Federal work-study:*** Total amount: $3,425,266; 1,214 jobs averaging $2844. ***State or other work-study/employment:*** Total amount: $21,641,637 (30% need-based, 70% non-need-based). 6,324 part-time jobs averaging $3418.

ATHLETIC AWARDS Total amount: $8,481,058 (27% need-based, 73% non-need-based).

APPLYING FOR FINANCIAL AID ***Required financial aid form:*** FAFSA. ***Financial aid deadline (priority):*** 1/15. ***Notification date:*** Continuous beginning 12/1.

CONTACT Financial Aid and Scholarship Services, Arizona State University at the Tempe campus, PO Box 870412, Tempe, AZ 85287-0412, 855-278-5080. *Fax:* 480-965-9484.

Website: http://www.asu.edu/.

ARIZONA STATE UNIVERSITY AT THE WEST CAMPUS

Glendale, AZ

Tuition & fees (AZ res): $10,803 **Average undergraduate aid package: $13,747**

ABOUT THE INSTITUTION State-supported, coed. ***Awards:*** certificates, bachelor's, master's, and doctoral degrees. 44 undergraduate majors. ***Total enrollment:*** 4,929. Undergraduates: 4,601. Freshmen: 789. Federal methodology is used as a basis for awarding need-based institutional aid.

UNDERGRADUATE EXPENSES for 2019–2020 ***Application fee:*** $50. ***Tuition, state resident:*** full-time $10,175; part-time $727 per credit hour. ***Tuition, nonresident:*** full-time $27,360; part-time $1140 per credit hour. ***Required fees:*** full-time $628; $157 per term. Full-time tuition and fees vary according to program. Part-time tuition and fees vary according to program. ***College room and board:*** $11,914; ***Room only:*** $6740. Room and board charges vary according to board plan.

FRESHMAN FINANCIAL AID (Fall 2018) 602 applied for aid; of those 82% were deemed to have need. 100% of freshmen with need received aid; of those 13% had need fully met. ***Average percent of need met:*** 68% (excluding resources awarded to replace EFC). ***Average financial aid package:*** $15,977 (excluding resources awarded to replace EFC). 22% of all full-time freshmen had no need and received non-need-based gift aid.

UNDERGRADUATE FINANCIAL AID (Fall 2018) 2,944 applied for aid; of those 88% were deemed to have need. 100% of undergraduates with need received aid; of those 14% had need fully met. ***Average percent of need met:*** 60% (excluding resources awarded to replace EFC). ***Average financial aid package:*** $13,747 (excluding resources awarded to replace EFC). 11% of all full-time undergraduates had no need and received non-need-based gift aid.

GIFT AID (NEED-BASED) ***Total amount:*** $26,977,589 (44% federal, 50% institutional, 6% external sources). ***Receiving aid:*** Freshmen: 75% (492); all full-time undergraduates: 70% (2,459). ***Average award:*** Freshmen: $13,539; Undergraduates: $10,523. ***Scholarships, grants, and awards:*** Federal Pell, FSEOG, state, private, college/university gift aid from institutional funds, United Negro College Fund.

GIFT AID (NON-NEED-BASED) ***Total amount:*** $4,879,145 (10% federal, 63% institutional, 27% external sources). ***Receiving aid:*** Freshmen: 5% (34). Undergraduates: 4% (154). ***Average award:*** Freshmen: $6991. Undergraduates: $6974. ***Scholarships, grants, and awards by category:*** *Academic interests/achievement:* general academic interests/achievements. *Special achievements/activities:* leadership. *Special characteristics:* children of faculty/staff, international students, local/state students, out-of-state students. ***Tuition waivers:*** Full or partial for employees or children of employees. ***ROTC:*** Army cooperative, Naval cooperative, Air Force cooperative.

LOANS ***Student loans:*** $14,058,051 (79% need-based, 21% non-need-based). 56% of past graduating class borrowed through all loan programs. *Average indebtedness per student:* $25,021. ***Average need-based loan:*** Freshmen: $3022. Undergraduates: $4152. ***Parent loans:*** $4,507,642 (47% need-based, 53% non-need-based). ***Programs:*** Federal Direct (Subsidized and Unsubsidized Stafford, PLUS), Perkins, state, college/university, private loans from endowment funds.

WORK-STUDY ***Federal work-study:*** Total amount: $506,334; 188 jobs averaging $2730. ***State or other work-study/employment:*** Total amount: $1,593,719 (32% need-based, 68% non-need-based). 543 part-time jobs averaging $2922.

ATHLETIC AWARDS Total amount: $11,676 (54% need-based, 46% non-need-based).

APPLYING FOR FINANCIAL AID ***Required financial aid form:*** FAFSA. ***Financial aid deadline (priority):*** 1/15. ***Notification date:*** Continuous beginning 12/1.

CONTACT Financial Aid and Scholarship Services, Arizona State University at the West campus, PO Box 870412, Tempe, AZ 85287-0412, 855-278-5080. *Fax:* 480-965-9484.

Website: http://campus.asu.edu/west.

ARKANSAS BAPTIST COLLEGE

Little Rock, AR

CONTACT Office of Financial Aid, Arkansas Baptist College, 1600 Bishop Street, Little Rock, AR 72202-6067, 501-374-7856.
Website: http://www.arkansasbaptist.edu/.

ARKANSAS STATE UNIVERSITY

Jonesboro, AR

CONTACT Mr. Terry Finney, Director of Financial Aid, Arkansas State University, PO Box 1620, State University, AR 72467, 870-972-2310 or toll-free 800-382-3030. *Fax:* 870-972-2794. *E-mail:* finaid@astate.edu.
Website: http://www.astate.edu/.

ARKANSAS TECH UNIVERSITY

Russellville, AR

Tuition & fees: N/R	Average undergraduate aid package: $10,702

ABOUT THE INSTITUTION State-supported, coed. ***Awards:*** certificates, associate, bachelor's, master's, and doctoral degrees. 90 undergraduate majors. ***Total enrollment:*** 11,829. Undergraduates: 11,015. Freshmen: 2,091. Federal methodology is used as a basis for awarding need-based institutional aid.

UNDERGRADUATE EXPENSES for 2020–2021 *Tuition, state resident:* part-time $232 per credit hour. ***Tuition, nonresident:*** part-time $464 per credit hour. ***Required fees:*** $87.50 per credit hour. Full-time tuition and fees vary according to course load and location. Part-time tuition and fees vary according to course load and location. Room and board charges vary according to board plan, housing facility, and location.

FRESHMAN FINANCIAL AID (Fall 2018) 1585 applied for aid; of those 74% were deemed to have need. 97% of freshmen with need received aid; of those 9% had need fully met. ***Average percent of need met:*** 62% (excluding resources awarded to replace EFC). ***Average financial aid package:*** $10,570 (excluding resources awarded to replace EFC). 25% of all full-time freshmen had no need and received non-need-based gift aid.

UNDERGRADUATE FINANCIAL AID (Fall 2018) 5,812 applied for aid; of those 76% were deemed to have need. 97% of undergraduates with need received aid; of those 12% had need fully met. ***Average percent of need met:*** 62% (excluding resources awarded to replace EFC). ***Average financial aid package:*** $10,702 (excluding resources awarded to replace EFC). 17% of all full-time undergraduates had no need and received non-need-based gift aid.

GIFT AID (NEED-BASED) *Total amount:* $20,195,381 (99% federal, 1% state). ***Receiving aid:*** Freshmen: 55% (900); all full-time undergraduates: 52% (3,307). ***Average award:*** Freshmen: $4946; Undergraduates: $5002. ***Scholarships, grants, and awards:*** Federal Pell, FSEOG, state, private.

GIFT AID (NON-NEED-BASED) *Total amount:* $30,257,659 (37% state, 57% institutional, 6% external sources). ***Receiving aid:*** Freshmen: 57% (934). Undergraduates: 42% (2,649). ***Average award:*** Freshmen: $6319. Undergraduates: $6915. ***Scholarships, grants, and awards by category:*** *Academic interests/achievement:* agriculture, biological sciences, business, communication, computer science, education, engineering/technologies, English, foreign languages, general academic interests/achievements, home economics, humanities, international studies, mathematics, military science, physical sciences, premedicine, social sciences. *Creative arts/performance:* applied art and design, cinema/film/broadcasting, creative writing, journalism/publications, music, theater/drama. *Special achievements/activities:* cheerleading/drum major, general special achievements/activities, junior miss. *Special characteristics:* children of faculty/staff, general special characteristics, international students, out-of-state students, parents of current students, previous college experience, public servants, veterans. ***Tuition waivers:*** Full or partial for employees or children of employees, senior citizens. ***ROTC:*** Army cooperative.

LOANS *Student loans:* $34,581,807 (37% need-based, 63% non-need-based). 61% of past graduating class borrowed through all loan programs. *Average indebtedness per student:* $24,142. ***Average need-based loan:*** Freshmen: $2953. Undergraduates: $3622. ***Parent loans:*** $2,571,233 (100% non-need-based). ***Programs:*** Federal Direct (Subsidized and Unsubsidized Stafford, PLUS).

WORK-STUDY *Federal work-study:* Total amount: $534,974; jobs available. ***State or other work-study/employment:*** Total amount: $579,159 (21% need-based, 79% non-need-based). Part-time jobs available.

ATHLETIC AWARDS Total amount: $1,861,167 (100% non-need-based).

APPLYING FOR FINANCIAL AID *Required financial aid forms:* FAFSA, institution's own form. ***Financial aid deadline (priority):*** 11/15. ***Notification date:*** Continuous beginning 12/1. Students must reply within 2 weeks of notification.

CONTACT Niki Schwartz, Director of Student Aid, Arkansas Tech University, Brown Hall Suite 206, 105 West O Street, Russellville, AR 72801, 479-968-0399 or toll-free 800-582-6953. *Fax:* 479-964-0857. *E-mail:* fa.help@atu.edu.
Website: http://www.atu.edu/.

ARLINGTON BAPTIST UNIVERSITY

Arlington, TX

CONTACT Mr. David B. Clogston Jr., Business Manager, Arlington Baptist University, 3001 West Division Street, Arlington, TX 76012-3425, 817-461-8741 Ext. 110. *Fax:* 817-274-1138.
Website: http://www.abu.edu/.

ART ACADEMY OF CINCINNATI

Cincinnati, OH

CONTACT Ms. Dawn Reck, Director of Financial Aid, Art Academy of Cincinnati, 1212 Jackson Street, Cincinnati, OH 45202, 513-562-8773 or toll-free 800-323-5692. *Fax:* 513-562-8778. *E-mail:* financialaid@artacademy.edu.
Website: http://www.artacademy.edu/.

ARTCENTER COLLEGE OF DESIGN

Pasadena, CA

CONTACT Clema McKenzie, Director of Financial Aid, ArtCenter College of Design, 1700 Lida Street, Pasadena, CA 91103-1999, 626-396-2215. *Fax:* 626-683-8684.
Website: http://www.artcenter.edu/.

THE ART INSTITUTE OF ATLANTA

Atlanta, GA

CONTACT Financial Aid Office, The Art Institute of Atlanta, 6600 Peachtree Dunwoody Road, NE, 100 Embassy Row, Atlanta, GA 30328, 770-394-8300 or toll-free 800-275-4242.

THE ART INSTITUTE OF AUSTIN, A BRANCH OF THE ART INSTITUTE OF HOUSTON

Austin, TX

CONTACT Financial Aid Office, The Art Institute of Austin, a branch of The Art Institute of Houston, 101 W. Louis Henna Boulevard, Suite 100, Austin, TX 78728, 512-691-1707 or toll-free 866-583-7952.

THE ART INSTITUTE OF CALIFORNIA–HOLLYWOOD, A CAMPUS OF ARGOSY UNIVERSITY

North Hollywood, CA

CONTACT Financial Aid Office, The Art Institute of California–Hollywood, a campus of Argosy University, 5250 Lankershim Boulevard, North Hollywood, CA 91601, 818-299-5100 or toll-free 877-468-6232.

THE ART INSTITUTE OF DALLAS, A BRANCH OF MIAMI INTERNATIONAL UNIVERSITY OF ART & DESIGN

Dallas, TX

CONTACT Financial Aid Office, The Art Institute of Dallas, a branch of Miami International University of Art & Design, 8080 Park Lane, Suite 100, Dallas, TX 75231-5993, 214-692-8080 or toll-free 800-275-4243.

THE ART INSTITUTE OF HOUSTON

Houston, TX

CONTACT Financial Aid Office, The Art Institute of Houston, 4140 Southwest Freeway, Houston, TX 77027, 713-623-2040 or toll-free 800-275-4244.

THE ART INSTITUTE OF LAS VEGAS

Henderson, NV

CONTACT Financial Aid Office, The Art Institute of Las Vegas, 2350 Corporate Circle Drive, Henderson, NV 89074, 702-369-9944 or toll-free 800-833-2678.

THE ART INSTITUTE OF PITTSBURGH

Pittsburgh, PA

CONTACT Financial Aid Office, The Art Institute of Pittsburgh, 420 Boulevard of the Allies, Pittsburgh, PA 15219, 412-263-6600 or toll-free 800-275-2470.

THE ART INSTITUTE OF SAN ANTONIO, A BRANCH OF THE ART INSTITUTE OF HOUSTON

San Antonio, TX

CONTACT Financial Aid Office, The Art Institute of San Antonio, a branch of The Art Institute of Houston, 1000 IH-10 West, Suite 200, San Antonio, TX 78230, 210-338-7320 or toll-free 888-222-0040.

THE ART INSTITUTE OF SEATTLE

Seattle, WA

CONTACT Financial Aid Office, The Art Institute of Seattle, 2323 Elliott Avenue, Seattle, WA 98121-1642, 206-448-6600 or toll-free 800-275-2471.

THE ART INSTITUTE OF TAMPA, A BRANCH OF MIAMI INTERNATIONAL UNIVERSITY OF ART & DESIGN

Tampa, FL

CONTACT Financial Aid Office, The Art Institute of Tampa, a branch of Miami International University of Art & Design, Parkside at Tampa Bay Park, 4401 North Himes Avenue, Suite 150, Tampa, FL 33614, 813-873-2112 or toll-free 866-703-3277.

THE ART INSTITUTE OF VIRGINIA BEACH, A BRANCH OF THE ART INSTITUTE OF ATLANTA

Virginia Beach, VA

CONTACT Financial Aid Office, The Art Institute of Virginia Beach, a branch of The Art Institute of Atlanta, Two Columbus Center, 4500 Main Street, Suite 100, Virginia Beach, VA 23462, 757-493-6700 or toll-free 877-437-4428.

ASBURY UNIVERSITY

Wilmore, KY

Tuition & fees: N/R	Average undergraduate aid package: $22,279

ABOUT THE INSTITUTION Independent nondenominational, coed. ***Awards:*** associate, bachelor's, and master's degrees. 47 undergraduate majors. Both federal and institutional methodology are used as a basis for awarding need-based institutional aid.

UNDERGRADUATE EXPENSES for 2019–2020 ***Tuition:*** part-time $1179 per credit hour. Full-time tuition and fees vary according to course load and program. Part-time tuition and fees vary according to course load and program. Room and board charges vary according to board plan and housing facility.

FRESHMAN FINANCIAL AID (Fall 2019, est.) 263 applied for aid; of those 82% were deemed to have need. 100% of freshmen with need received aid; of those 21% had need fully met. ***Average percent of need met:*** 76% (excluding resources awarded to replace EFC). ***Average financial aid package:*** $25,023 (excluding resources awarded to replace EFC). 16% of all full-time freshmen had no need and received non-need-based gift aid.

UNDERGRADUATE FINANCIAL AID (Fall 2019, est.) 1,165 applied for aid; of those 89% were deemed to have need. 100% of undergraduates with need received aid; of those 16% had need fully met. ***Average percent of need met:*** 69% (excluding resources awarded to replace EFC). ***Average financial aid package:*** $22,279 (excluding resources awarded to replace EFC). 9% of all full-time undergraduates had no need and received non-need-based gift aid.

GIFT AID (NEED-BASED) ***Total amount:*** $18,644,814 (13% federal, 16% state, 66% institutional, 5% external sources). ***Receiving aid:*** Freshmen: 74% (216); all full-time undergraduates: 76% (1,038). ***Average award:*** Freshmen: $17,499; Undergraduates: $15,244. ***Scholarships, grants, and awards:*** Federal Pell, FSEOG, state, private, college/university gift aid from institutional funds.

GIFT AID (NON-NEED-BASED) ***Total amount:*** $2,214,647 (1% federal, 4% state, 85% institutional, 10% external sources). ***Receiving aid:*** Freshmen: 9% (27). Undergraduates: 6% (86). ***Average award:*** Freshmen: $11,511. Undergraduates: $11,317. ***Scholarships, grants, and awards by category:*** *Academic interests/achievement:* biological sciences, business, communication, education, foreign languages, general academic interests/achievements. *Creative arts/performance:* applied art and design, art/fine arts, music, theater/drama. *Special achievements/activities:* cheerleading/drum major, leadership, religious involvement. *Special characteristics:* children and siblings of alumni, children of faculty/staff, ethnic background, international students, married students, members of minority groups, out-of-state students, relatives of clergy, religious affiliation, siblings of current students, veterans, veterans' children. ***Tuition waivers:*** Full or partial for employees or children of employees, senior citizens. ***ROTC:*** Army cooperative, Air Force cooperative.

LOANS ***Student loans:*** $7,548,079 (77% need-based, 23% non-need-based). 72% of past graduating class borrowed through all loan programs. *Average indebtedness per student:* $33,795. ***Average need-based loan:*** Freshmen: $3430. Undergrad-

uates: $4338. ***Parent loans:*** $1,654,931 (52% need-based, 48% non-need-based). ***Programs:*** Federal Direct (Subsidized and Unsubsidized Stafford, PLUS), college/university, alternative loans.

WORK-STUDY *Federal work-study:* Total amount: $884,457; 530 jobs averaging $1669.

ATHLETIC AWARDS Total amount: $2,200,336 (66% need-based, 34% non-need-based).

APPLYING FOR FINANCIAL AID *Financial aid deadline:* Continuous. ***Notification date:*** Continuous beginning 10/15. Students must reply by 5/1 or within 2 weeks of notification.

CONTACT Mr. Ronald Anderson, AVP for Enrollment, Asbury University, One Macklem Drive, Wilmore, KY 40390-1152, 859-858-3511 Ext. 2195 or toll-free 800-888-1818. *Fax:* 859-858-9149. *E-mail:* ron.anderson@asbury.edu.
Website: http://www.asbury.edu/.

ASHFORD UNIVERSITY

San Diego, CA

CONTACT Lisa Kramer, Director of Financial Aid, Ashford University, 400 North Bluff Boulevard, PO Box 2967, Clinton, IA 52733-2967, 563-242-4023 Ext. 1243 or toll-free 866-711-1700. *Fax:* 563-242-8684.
Website: http://www.ashford.edu/.

ASHLAND UNIVERSITY

Ashland, OH

Tuition & fees: $21,980	Average undergraduate aid package: $14,785

ABOUT THE INSTITUTION Independent Brethren Church, coed. ***Awards:*** certificates, diplomas, associate, bachelor's, master's, and doctoral degrees. 81 undergraduate majors. ***Total enrollment:*** 6,579. Undergraduates: 4,536. Freshmen: 623. Federal methodology is used as a basis for awarding need-based institutional aid.

UNDERGRADUATE EXPENSES for 2019–2020 *Comprehensive fee:* $32,170 includes full-time tuition ($20,950), mandatory fees ($1030), and room and board ($10,190). ***College room only:*** $5460. Full-time tuition and fees vary according to class time, course level, course load, degree level, location, program, reciprocity agreements, and student level. Room and board charges vary according to board plan, housing facility, and location. ***Part-time tuition:*** $940 per credit hour. Part-time tuition and fees vary according to class time, course level, course load, degree level, location, program, reciprocity agreements, and student level.

FRESHMAN FINANCIAL AID (Fall 2019, est.) 503 applied for aid; of those 83% were deemed to have need. 100% of freshmen with need received aid; of those 23% had need fully met. ***Average percent of need met:*** 79% (excluding resources awarded to replace EFC). ***Average financial aid package:*** $19,439 (excluding resources awarded to replace EFC). 15% of all full-time freshmen had no need and received non-need-based gift aid.

UNDERGRADUATE FINANCIAL AID (Fall 2019, est.) 3,033 applied for aid; of those 90% were deemed to have need. 99% of undergraduates with need received aid; of those 46% had need fully met. ***Average percent of need met:*** 82% (excluding resources awarded to replace EFC). ***Average financial aid package:*** $14,785 (excluding resources awarded to replace EFC). 11% of all full-time undergraduates had no need and received non-need-based gift aid.

GIFT AID (NEED-BASED) *Total amount:* $38,529,465 (45% federal, 5% state, 49% institutional, 1% external sources). ***Receiving aid:*** Freshmen: 76% (407); all full-time undergraduates: 77% (2,595). ***Average award:*** Freshmen: $14,881; Undergraduates: $11,678. ***Scholarships, grants, and awards:*** Federal Pell, FSEOG, state, private, college/university gift aid from institutional funds.

GIFT AID (NON-NEED-BASED) *Total amount:* $4,118,062 (99% institutional, 1% external sources). ***Average award:*** Freshmen: $9011. Undergraduates: $8805. ***Scholarships, grants, and awards by category:*** *Academic interests/achievement:* general academic interests/achievements, mathematics, physical sciences, social sciences. *Creative arts/performance:* art/fine arts, music, theater/drama. *Special achievements/activities:* cheerleading/drum major, leadership, religious involvement. *Special characteristics:* children and siblings of alumni, children of faculty/staff, ethnic background, international students, members of minority groups, out-of-state students, relatives of clergy, religious affiliation, siblings of current students, veterans. ***Tuition waivers:*** Full or partial for children of alumni, employees or children of employees, senior citizens.

LOANS *Student loans:* $18,306,776 (87% need-based, 13% non-need-based). ***Average need-based loan:*** Freshmen: $3483. Undergraduates: $4542. ***Parent loans:*** $3,944,024 (89% need-based, 11% non-need-based). ***Programs:*** Federal Direct (Subsidized and Unsubsidized Stafford, PLUS), Federal Nursing, college/university.

WORK-STUDY *Federal work-study:* Total amount: $3,097,817; jobs available. ***State or other work-study/employment:*** Part-time jobs available.

ATHLETIC AWARDS Total amount: $3,345,152 (66% need-based, 34% non-need-based).

APPLYING FOR FINANCIAL AID *Required financial aid form:* FAFSA. ***Financial aid deadline (priority):*** 3/15. ***Notification date:*** Continuous beginning 11/1. Students must reply by 5/1.

CONTACT Mr. Stephen C. Howell, Director of Financial Aid, Ashland University, 401 College Avenue, Ashland, OH 44805-3702, 419-289-5944 or toll-free 800-882-1548. *Fax:* 419-289-5976. *E-mail:* showell@ashland.edu.
Website: http://www.ashland.edu/.

ASHWORTH COLLEGE

Norcross, GA

CONTACT Financial Aid Office, Ashworth College, 6625 The Corners Parkway, Suite 500, Norcross, GA 30092, 770-729-8400 or toll-free 800-957-5412.
Website: http://www.ashworthcollege.edu/.

ASPEN UNIVERSITY

Denver, CO

CONTACT Jennifer Quinn, Director of Financial Aid, Aspen University, 720 South Colorado Bouleavrd #1150N, Denver, CO 80246, 800-441-4746. *Fax:* 303-336-1144. *E-mail:* jquinn@aspen.edu.
Website: http://www.aspen.edu/.

ASSUMPTION UNIVERSITY

Worcester, MA

Tuition & fees: $42,316	Average undergraduate aid package: $30,845

ABOUT THE INSTITUTION Independent Roman Catholic, coed. ***Awards:*** certificates, bachelor's, and master's degrees. 33 undergraduate majors. ***Total enrollment:*** 2,376. Undergraduates: 1,982. Freshmen: 563. Federal methodology is used as a basis for awarding need-based institutional aid.

UNDERGRADUATE EXPENSES for 2019–2020 *Application fee:* $50. ***Comprehensive fee:*** $55,444 includes full-time tuition ($41,516), mandatory fees ($800), and room and board ($13,128). ***College room only:*** $8310. Full-time tuition and fees vary according to course load, reciprocity agreements, and student level. Room and board charges vary according to board plan and housing facility. ***Part-time tuition:*** $1384 per credit hour. Part-time tuition and fees vary according to course load.

FRESHMAN FINANCIAL AID (Fall 2019, est.) 530 applied for aid; of those 87% were deemed to have need. 100% of freshmen with need received aid; of those 31% had need fully met. ***Average percent of need met:*** 79% (excluding resources awarded to replace EFC). ***Average financial aid package:*** $32,020 (excluding resources awarded to replace EFC). 17% of all full-time freshmen had no need and received non-need-based gift aid.

UNDERGRADUATE FINANCIAL AID (Fall 2019, est.) 1,669 applied for aid; of those 88% were deemed to have need. 100% of undergraduates with need received aid; of those 30% had need fully met. ***Average percent of need met:*** 79% (excluding resources awarded to replace EFC). ***Average financial aid package:*** $30,845 (excluding resources awarded to replace EFC). 22% of all full-time undergraduates had no need and received non-need-based gift aid.

GIFT AID (NEED-BASED) ***Total amount:*** $34,578,129 (6% federal, 2% state, 91% institutional, 1% external sources). ***Receiving aid:*** Freshmen: 82% (462); all full-time undergraduates: 75% (1,466). ***Average award:*** Freshmen: $26,390; Undergraduates: $25,250. ***Scholarships, grants, and awards:*** Federal Pell, FSEOG, state, private, college/university gift aid from institutional funds.

GIFT AID (NON-NEED-BASED) ***Total amount:*** $10,244,502 (99% institutional, 1% external sources). ***Receiving aid:*** Freshmen: 20% (112). Undergraduates: 15% (288). ***Average award:*** Freshmen: $22,502. Undergraduates: $18,304. ***Scholarships, grants, and awards by category:*** *Academic interests/achievement:* 1,724 awards ($30,638,450 total): general academic interests/achievements. *Creative arts/performance:* 33 awards ($214,016 total): music. *Special characteristics:* members of minority groups. ***Tuition waivers:*** Full or partial for employees or children of employees. ***ROTC:*** Army cooperative, Air Force cooperative.

LOANS ***Student loans:*** $15,707,796 (54% need-based, 46% non-need-based). ***Average need-based loan:*** Freshmen: $3374. Undergraduates: $4370. ***Parent loans:*** $6,961,558 (43% need-based, 57% non-need-based). ***Programs:*** Federal Direct (Subsidized and Unsubsidized Stafford, PLUS), Perkins, state.

WORK-STUDY ***Federal work-study:*** Total amount: $679,180; 439 jobs averaging $1547.

ATHLETIC AWARDS Total amount: $2,726,057 (46% need-based, 54% non-need-based).

APPLYING FOR FINANCIAL AID ***Required financial aid form:*** FAFSA. ***Financial aid deadline:*** 2/15 (priority: 1/15). ***Notification date:*** Continuous beginning 2/16. Students must reply by 5/1.

CONTACT Monica Blondin, Director of Financial Aid, Assumption University, 500 Salisbury Street, Worcester, MA 01609-1296, 508-767-7158 or toll-free 866-477-7776. *Fax:* 508-767-7376. *E-mail:* fa@assumption.edu.
Website: http://www.assumption.edu/.

ATENAS COLLEGE

Manati, PR

CONTACT Financial Aid Office, Atenas College, Paseo de La Atenas #101 Altos, Manati, PR 00674, 787-884-3838.
Website: http://www.atenascollege.edu/.

ATHENS STATE UNIVERSITY

Athens, AL

Tuition & fees (AL res): $7710	Average undergraduate aid package: $10,504

ABOUT THE INSTITUTION State-supported, coed. ***Awards:*** certificates, bachelor's, and master's degrees. 35 undergraduate majors. ***Total enrollment:*** 2,945. Undergraduates: 2,778. Federal methodology is used as a basis for awarding need-based institutional aid.

UNDERGRADUATE EXPENSES for 2019–2020 ***Application fee:*** $30. ***Tuition, state resident:*** full-time $6180. ***Tuition, nonresident:*** full-time $12,360. ***Required fees:*** full-time $1530.

UNDERGRADUATE FINANCIAL AID (Fall 2018) 990 applied for aid; of those 89% were deemed to have need. 100% of undergraduates with need received aid; of those 5% had need fully met. ***Average percent of need met:*** 44% (excluding resources awarded to replace EFC). ***Average financial aid package:*** $10,504 (excluding resources awarded to replace EFC). 1% of all full-time undergraduates had no need and received non-need-based gift aid.

GIFT AID (NEED-BASED) ***Receiving aid:*** All full-time undergraduates: 45% (551). ***Average award:*** Undergraduates: $4543. ***Scholarships, grants, and awards:*** Federal Pell, FSEOG, state, private, college/university gift aid from institutional funds.

GIFT AID (NON-NEED-BASED) ***Receiving aid:*** Undergraduates: 11% (140). ***Average award:*** Undergraduates: $1256. ***Tuition waivers:*** Full or partial for employees or children of employees, senior citizens.

LOANS ***Average need-based loan:*** Undergraduates: $3312. ***Programs:*** Federal Direct (Subsidized and Unsubsidized Stafford, PLUS), college/university.

WORK-STUDY Federal work-study jobs available.

APPLYING FOR FINANCIAL AID ***Required financial aid form:*** FAFSA. ***Financial aid deadline:*** Continuous. ***Notification date:*** Continuous. Students must reply within 2 weeks of notification.

CONTACT Mitchell Bazzel, Financial Aid Director, Athens State University, 300 North Beaty Street, Athens, AL 35611, 256-233-8161 or toll-free 800-522-0272. *Fax:* 256-233-8161. *E-mail:* mitchell.bazzel@athens.edu.
Website: http://www.athens.edu/.

ATLANTIC UNIVERSITY COLLEGE

Guaynabo, PR

CONTACT Mrs. Velma Aponte, Financial Aid Coordinator, Atlantic University College, Calle Colton #9, Guaynabo, PR 00970, 787-720-1092. *E-mail:* atlaneco@coqui.net.
Website: http://www.atlanticu.edu/.

ATLANTIS UNIVERSITY

Miami, FL

CONTACT Financial Aid Office, Atlantis University, 1442 Biscayne Boulevard, Miami, FL 33132.
Website: http://www.atlantisuniversity.edu/.

AUBURN UNIVERSITY

Auburn University, AL

Tuition & fees (area res): $11,492	Average undergraduate aid package: $10,961

ABOUT THE INSTITUTION State-supported, coed. ***Awards:*** certificates, bachelor's, master's, and doctoral degrees. 154 undergraduate majors. ***Total enrollment:*** 30,460. Undergraduates: 24,594. Freshmen: 4,808. Federal methodology is used as a basis for awarding need-based institutional aid.

UNDERGRADUATE EXPENSES for 2020–2021 ***Application fee:*** $50. ***Tuition, area resident:*** full-time $9816; part-time $409 per credit hour. ***Tuition, state resident:*** full-time $9816; part-time $409 per credit hour. ***Tuition, nonresident:*** full-time $29,448; part-time $1227 per credit hour. ***Required fees:*** full-time $1676. Full-time tuition and fees vary according to program and reciprocity agreements. Part-time tuition and fees vary according to course load, program, and reciprocity agreements. ***College room and board:*** $13,600; ***Room only:*** $8014. Room and board charges vary according to board plan and housing facility.

FRESHMAN FINANCIAL AID (Fall 2018) 3402 applied for aid; of those 55% were deemed to have need. 100% of freshmen with need received aid; of those 17% had need fully met. ***Average percent of need met:*** 51% (excluding resources awarded to replace EFC). ***Average financial aid package:*** $11,161 (excluding resources awarded to replace EFC). 27% of all full-time freshmen had no need and received non-need-based gift aid.

UNDERGRADUATE FINANCIAL AID (Fall 2018) 14,813 applied for aid; of those 53% were deemed to have need. 100% of undergraduates with need received aid; of those 13% had need fully met. ***Average percent of need met:*** 45% (excluding resources awarded to replace EFC). ***Average financial aid package:*** $10,961 (excluding resources awarded to replace EFC). 21% of all full-time undergraduates had no need and received non-need-based gift aid.

GIFT AID (NEED-BASED) ***Receiving aid:*** Freshmen: 33% (1,594); all full-time undergraduates: 26% (5,836). ***Average award:*** Freshmen: $9040; Undergraduates: $8343. ***Scholarships, grants, and awards:*** Federal Pell, FSEOG, state, private, college/university gift aid from institutional funds.

GIFT AID (NON-NEED-BASED) ***Receiving aid:*** Freshmen: 5% (242). Undergraduates: 3% (674). ***Average award:*** Freshmen: $7562. Undergraduates: $7706. ***Scholarships, grants, and awards by category:*** *Academic interests/achievement:* agriculture, architecture, biological sciences, business, communication, computer science, education, engineering/technologies, English, foreign languages, general academic interests/achievements, health fields, home economics, humanities, mathematics, physical sciences, premedicine, social sciences. *Creative arts/perfor-*

mance: applied art and design, art/fine arts, cinema/film/broadcasting, creative writing, journalism/publications, music, performing arts, theater/drama. *Special achievements/activities:* cheerleading/drum major, leadership, memberships. *Special characteristics:* children and siblings of alumni, children of faculty/staff, children of union members/company employees, ethnic background, local/state students, married students, out-of-state students. ***Tuition waivers:*** Full or partial for employees or children of employees. ***ROTC:*** Army, Naval, Air Force.

LOANS *Student loans:* 39% of past graduating class borrowed through all loan programs. *Average indebtedness per student:* $29,331. ***Average need-based loan:*** Freshmen: $3316. Undergraduates: $4224. ***Programs:*** Federal Direct (Subsidized and Unsubsidized Stafford, PLUS), Perkins, Federal Nursing, college/university.

WORK-STUDY *Federal work-study:* 142 jobs averaging $4539.

APPLYING FOR FINANCIAL AID *Required financial aid form:* FAFSA. ***Notification date:*** Continuous.

CONTACT Mr. Mike Reynolds, Director of Student Financial Services, Auburn University, 203 Mary Martin Hall, Auburn University, AL 36849, 334-844-4634 or toll-free 800-AUBURN9. *Fax:* 334-844-6085. *E-mail:* finaid7@auburn.edu. *Website:* http://www.auburn.edu/.

AUBURN UNIVERSITY AT MONTGOMERY

Montgomery, AL

Tuition & fees (AL res): $8860	Average undergraduate aid package: $9176

ABOUT THE INSTITUTION State-supported, coed. ***Awards:*** certificates, bachelor's, master's, and doctoral degrees. 35 undergraduate majors. ***Total enrollment:*** 5,188. Undergraduates: 4,523. Freshmen: 626. Federal methodology is used as a basis for awarding need-based institutional aid.

UNDERGRADUATE EXPENSES for 2020–2021 *One-time required fee:* $125. ***Tuition, state resident:*** full-time $7992; part-time $333 per credit hour. ***Tuition, nonresident:*** full-time $17,952; part-time $748 per credit hour. ***Required fees:*** full-time $868. Full-time tuition and fees vary according to course load and degree level. Part-time tuition and fees vary according to course load and degree level. ***College room and board:*** $7268; ***Room only:*** $4580. Room and board charges vary according to board plan and housing facility.

FRESHMAN FINANCIAL AID (Fall 2018) 629 applied for aid; of those 87% were deemed to have need. 99% of freshmen with need received aid; of those 5% had need fully met. ***Average percent of need met:*** 54% (excluding resources awarded to replace EFC). ***Average financial aid package:*** $9175 (excluding resources awarded to replace EFC). 17% of all full-time freshmen had no need and received non-need-based gift aid.

UNDERGRADUATE FINANCIAL AID (Fall 2018) 2,786 applied for aid; of those 88% were deemed to have need. 98% of undergraduates with need received aid; of those 7% had need fully met. ***Average percent of need met:*** 56% (excluding resources awarded to replace EFC). ***Average financial aid package:*** $9176 (excluding resources awarded to replace EFC). 11% of all full-time undergraduates had no need and received non-need-based gift aid.

GIFT AID (NEED-BASED) *Total amount:* $14,500,803 (78% federal, 1% state, 17% institutional, 4% external sources). ***Receiving aid:*** Freshmen: 70% (513); all full-time undergraduates: 59% (2,081). ***Average award:*** Freshmen: $4248; Undergraduates: $4815. ***Scholarships, grants, and awards:*** Federal Pell, FSEOG, state, private, college/university gift aid from institutional funds.

GIFT AID (NON-NEED-BASED) *Total amount:* $2,091,082 (86% institutional, 14% external sources). ***Receiving aid:*** Freshmen: 72% (525). Undergraduates: 35% (1,239). ***Average award:*** Freshmen: $2562. Undergraduates: $2927. ***Scholarships, grants, and awards by category:*** *Academic interests/achievement:* business, education, general academic interests/achievements, military science. *Special achievements/activities:* leadership. *Special characteristics:* international students. ***Tuition waivers:*** Full or partial for employees or children of employees. ***ROTC:*** Army, Air Force cooperative.

LOANS *Student loans:* $17,196,755 (92% need-based, 8% non-need-based). 68% of past graduating class borrowed through all loan programs. *Average indebtedness per student:* $30,138. ***Average need-based loan:*** Freshmen: $2475. Undergraduates: $3329. ***Parent loans:*** $2,500,966 (72% need-based, 28% non-need-based). ***Programs:*** Federal Direct (Subsidized and Unsubsidized Stafford, PLUS), Perkins.

WORK-STUDY *Federal work-study:* Total amount: $221,318; 64 jobs averaging $3458.

ATHLETIC AWARDS Total amount: $652,733 (100% need-based).

APPLYING FOR FINANCIAL AID *Required financial aid form:* FAFSA. ***Financial aid deadline (priority):*** 3/1. ***Notification date:*** Continuous beginning 4/15.

CONTACT Mr. Anthony Richey, Senior Director of Financial Aid, Auburn University at Montgomery, PO Box 244023, Montgomery, AL 36124-4023, 334-244-3571 or toll-free 800-227-2649. *Fax:* 334-244-3913. *E-mail:* aumfinancialaidoffice@aum.edu. *Website:* http://www.aum.edu/.

AUGSBURG UNIVERSITY

Minneapolis, MN

Tuition & fees: $41,086	Average undergraduate aid package: $32,507

ABOUT THE INSTITUTION Independent Lutheran, coed. ***Awards:*** certificates, bachelor's, master's, and doctoral degrees. 70 undergraduate majors. ***Total enrollment:*** 3,425. Undergraduates: 2,512. Freshmen: 636. Federal methodology is used as a basis for awarding need-based institutional aid.

UNDERGRADUATE EXPENSES for 2020–2021 *Comprehensive fee:* $51,971 includes full-time tuition ($40,376), mandatory fees ($710), and room and board ($10,885). ***College room only:*** $5740. Full-time tuition and fees vary according to class time and location. Room and board charges vary according to board plan and housing facility. ***Part-time tuition:*** $1228 per credit hour. Part-time tuition and fees vary according to class time and location.

FRESHMAN FINANCIAL AID (Fall 2018) 386 applied for aid; of those 93% were deemed to have need. 99% of freshmen with need received aid; of those 10% had need fully met. ***Average percent of need met:*** 78% (excluding resources awarded to replace EFC). ***Average financial aid package:*** $33,989 (excluding resources awarded to replace EFC). 13% of all full-time freshmen had no need and received non-need-based gift aid.

UNDERGRADUATE FINANCIAL AID (Fall 2018) 1,719 applied for aid; of those 94% were deemed to have need. 99% of undergraduates with need received aid; of those 11% had need fully met. ***Average percent of need met:*** 74% (excluding resources awarded to replace EFC). ***Average financial aid package:*** $32,507 (excluding resources awarded to replace EFC). 17% of all full-time undergraduates had no need and received non-need-based gift aid.

GIFT AID (NEED-BASED) *Total amount:* $43,737,867 (14% federal, 14% state, 66% institutional, 6% external sources). ***Receiving aid:*** Freshmen: 85% (357); all full-time undergraduates: 81% (1,606). ***Average award:*** Freshmen: $29,083; Undergraduates: $26,902. ***Scholarships, grants, and awards:*** Federal Pell, FSEOG, state, private, college/university gift aid from institutional funds.

GIFT AID (NON-NEED-BASED) *Total amount:* $8,243,615 (5% state, 84% institutional, 11% external sources). ***Receiving aid:*** Freshmen: 5% (21). Undergraduates: 6% (115). ***Average award:*** Freshmen: $19,574. Undergraduates: $17,864. ***Scholarships, grants, and awards by category:*** *Academic interests/achievement:* biological sciences, business, communication, computer science, education, English, foreign languages, general academic interests/achievements, home economics, international studies, mathematics, physical sciences, religion/biblical studies, social sciences. *Creative arts/performance:* applied art and design, music, performing arts, theater/drama. *Special achievements/activities:* community service, general special achievements/activities, junior miss, leadership, religious involvement. *Special characteristics:* children and siblings of alumni, international students, members of minority groups, relatives of clergy, siblings of current students. ***Tuition waivers:*** Full or partial for employees or children of employees. ***ROTC:*** Army cooperative, Air Force cooperative.

LOANS *Student loans:* $15,729,427 (79% need-based, 21% non-need-based). 85% of past graduating class borrowed through all loan programs. *Average indebtedness per student:* $40,574. ***Average need-based loan:*** Freshmen: $3365. Undergraduates: $4154. ***Parent loans:*** $3,480,143 (56% need-based, 44% non-need-based). ***Programs:*** Federal Direct (Subsidized and Unsubsidized Stafford, PLUS).

WORK-STUDY *Federal work-study:* Total amount: $431,525; jobs available. ***State or other work-study/employment:*** Total amount: $2,756,780 (95% need-based, 5% non-need-based). Part-time jobs available.

APPLYING FOR FINANCIAL AID ***Required financial aid form:*** FAFSA. ***Financial aid deadline (priority):*** 5/1. ***Notification date:*** Continuous beginning 12/15.

CONTACT Gina Jones, Assistant Vice President of Enrollment and Director of Financial Aid, Augsburg University, 2211 Riverside Avenue, Minneapolis, MN 55454-1351, 612-330-1051 or toll-free 800-788-5678. *Fax:* 612-330-1308. *E-mail:* jonesg@augsburg.edu.
Website: http://www.augsburg.edu/.

AUGUSTANA COLLEGE

Rock Island, IL

Tuition & fees: $45,136 — **Average undergraduate aid package: N/A**

ABOUT THE INSTITUTION Independent Evangelical Lutheran Church in America, coed. ***Awards:*** bachelor's degrees. 61 undergraduate majors. ***Total enrollment:*** 2,546. Undergraduates: 2,546. Freshmen: 678. Federal methodology is used as a basis for awarding need-based institutional aid.

UNDERGRADUATE EXPENSES for 2020–2021 ***Comprehensive fee:*** $56,352 includes full-time tuition ($45,136) and room and board ($11,216). ***College room only:*** $5538. ***Part-time tuition:*** $1882 per credit hour.

GIFT AID (NEED-BASED) ***Scholarships, grants, and awards:*** Federal Pell, FSEOG, state, private, college/university gift aid from institutional funds.

GIFT AID (NON-NEED-BASED) ***Scholarships, grants, and awards by category:*** *Academic interests/achievement:* 2,095 awards ($44,051,905 total): area/ethnic studies, biological sciences, business, communication, computer science, education, English, foreign languages, general academic interests/achievements, humanities, mathematics, physical sciences, religion/biblical studies, social sciences. *Creative arts/performance:* 385 awards ($1,114,308 total): art/fine arts, creative writing, music, theater/drama. *Special achievements/activities:* 32 awards ($66,990 total): leadership, religious involvement. *Special characteristics:* 394 awards ($1,210,149 total): children and siblings of alumni, children of faculty/staff, ethnic background, first-generation college students, international students, members of minority groups, out-of-state students, religious affiliation, siblings of current students.

LOANS ***Student loans:*** 73% of past graduating class borrowed through all loan programs. *Average indebtedness per student:* $34,964. ***Programs:*** Federal Direct (Subsidized and Unsubsidized Stafford, PLUS), Perkins.

WORK-STUDY Federal work-study jobs available.

APPLYING FOR FINANCIAL AID ***Required financial aid forms:*** FAFSA, institution's own form. ***Financial aid deadline (priority):*** 11/1. ***Notification date:*** Continuous beginning 12/15. Students must reply by 5/1.

CONTACT Ms. Sue Standley, Director of Financial Aid, Augustana College, 639 38th Street, Rock Island, IL 61201-2296, 309-794-7207 Ext. 7447 or toll-free 800-798-8100. *Fax:* 309-794-7174. *E-mail:* suestandley@augustana.edu.
Website: http://www.augustana.edu/.

AUGUSTANA UNIVERSITY

Sioux Falls, SD

Tuition & fees: $35,884 — **Average undergraduate aid package: $27,245**

ABOUT THE INSTITUTION Independent Evangelical Lutheran Church in America, coed. ***Awards:*** bachelor's and master's degrees. 64 undergraduate majors. ***Total enrollment:*** 2,113. Undergraduates: 1,818. Freshmen: 432. Federal methodology is used as a basis for awarding need-based institutional aid.

UNDERGRADUATE EXPENSES for 2020–2021 ***Comprehensive fee:*** $44,500 includes full-time tuition ($34,934), mandatory fees ($950), and room and board ($8616). ***College room only:*** $3854. Full-time tuition and fees vary according to course load and degree level. Room and board charges vary according to board plan and housing facility. Part-time tuition and fees vary according to course load and degree level.

FRESHMAN FINANCIAL AID (Fall 2019, est.) 362 applied for aid; of those 78% were deemed to have need. 100% of freshmen with need received aid; of those 18% had need fully met. ***Average percent of need met:*** 86% (excluding resources awarded to replace EFC). ***Average financial aid package:*** $28,812 (excluding resources awarded to replace EFC). 34% of all full-time freshmen had no need and received non-need-based gift aid.

UNDERGRADUATE FINANCIAL AID (Fall 2019, est.) 1,262 applied for aid; of those 84% were deemed to have need. 99% of undergraduates with need received aid; of those 15% had need fully met. ***Average percent of need met:*** 83% (excluding resources awarded to replace EFC). ***Average financial aid package:*** $27,245 (excluding resources awarded to replace EFC). 38% of all full-time undergraduates had no need and received non-need-based gift aid.

GIFT AID (NEED-BASED) ***Receiving aid:*** Freshmen: 66% (283); all full-time undergraduates: 59% (1,027). ***Average award:*** Freshmen: $26,073; Undergraduates: $24,114. ***Scholarships, grants, and awards:*** Federal Pell, FSEOG, state, private, college/university gift aid from institutional funds, need-linked special talent scholarships, minority scholarships.

GIFT AID (NON-NEED-BASED) ***Receiving aid:*** Freshmen: 65% (280). Undergraduates: 59% (1,017). ***Average award:*** Freshmen: $19,756. Undergraduates: $17,674. ***Scholarships, grants, and awards by category:*** *Academic interests/achievement:* biological sciences, business, communication, computer science, education, English, foreign languages, general academic interests/achievements, health fields, home economics, humanities, international studies, mathematics, physical sciences, premedicine, religion/biblical studies, social sciences. *Creative arts/performance:* applied art and design, creative writing, dance, journalism/publications, music, performing arts, theater/drama. *Special achievements/activities:* cheerleading/drum major, community service, general special achievements/activities, leadership, religious involvement. *Special characteristics:* adult students, children and siblings of alumni, children of current students, children of faculty/staff, ethnic background, international students, local/state students, members of minority groups, religious affiliation, siblings of current students, spouses of current students, veterans. ***Tuition waivers:*** Full or partial for employees or children of employees. ***ROTC:*** Army cooperative, Air Force cooperative.

LOANS ***Student loans:*** 69% of past graduating class borrowed through all loan programs. *Average indebtedness per student:* $37,647. ***Average need-based loan:*** Freshmen: $3425. Undergraduates: $4630. ***Programs:*** Federal Direct (Subsidized and Unsubsidized Stafford, PLUS), Perkins, Federal Nursing, college/university, private loans.

WORK-STUDY ***Federal work-study:*** 324 jobs averaging $1788. ***State or other work-study/employment:*** 152 part-time jobs averaging $879.

APPLYING FOR FINANCIAL AID ***Required financial aid form:*** FAFSA. ***Notification date:*** Continuous. Students must reply within 4 weeks of notification.

CONTACT Ms. Tresse J. Evenson, Director of Financial Aid, Augustana University, 2001 South Summit Avenue, Sioux Falls, SD 57197, 605-274-5216 or toll-free 800-727-2844. *Fax:* 605-274-5295. *E-mail:* tresse.evenson@augie.edu.
Website: http://www.augie.edu/.

AUGUSTA UNIVERSITY

Augusta, GA

CONTACT Victoria Saraceno, Interim Director of Financial Aid, Augusta University, 1120 Fifteenth Street, Fanning Hall, Augusta, GA 30912-7320, 706-667-4199 or toll-free 800-519-3388. *Fax:* 706-737-1777. *E-mail:* vsaraceno@augusta.edu.
Website: http://www.augusta.edu/.

AULTMAN COLLEGE OF NURSING AND HEALTH SCIENCES

Canton, OH

CONTACT Financial Aid Office, Aultman College of Nursing and Health Sciences, 2600 6th Street, SW, Canton, OH 44710, 330-363-6347.
Website: http://www.aultmancollege.edu/.

AURORA UNIVERSITY

Aurora, IL

Tuition & fees: $25,960 **Average undergraduate aid package: $21,920**

ABOUT THE INSTITUTION Independent, coed. ***Awards:*** certificates, bachelor's, master's, and doctoral degrees. 41 undergraduate majors. ***Total enrollment:*** 6,246. Undergraduates: 4,104. Freshmen: 814. Federal methodology is used as a basis for awarding need-based institutional aid.

UNDERGRADUATE EXPENSES for 2020–2021 ***Comprehensive fee:*** $37,980 includes full-time tuition ($25,600), mandatory fees ($360), and room and board ($12,020). ***College room only:*** $6690. Full-time tuition and fees vary according to course load, location, and program. Room and board charges vary according to board plan, housing facility, and location. ***Part-time tuition:*** $735 per semester hour. Part-time tuition and fees vary according to course load, location, and program.

FRESHMAN FINANCIAL AID (Fall 2019, est.) 761 applied for aid; of those 89% were deemed to have need. 100% of freshmen with need received aid; of those 13% had need fully met. ***Average percent of need met:*** 82% (excluding resources awarded to replace EFC). ***Average financial aid package:*** $24,485 (excluding resources awarded to replace EFC). 16% of all full-time freshmen had no need and received non-need-based gift aid.

UNDERGRADUATE FINANCIAL AID (Fall 2019, est.) 3,230 applied for aid; of those 91% were deemed to have need. 100% of undergraduates with need received aid; of those 11% had need fully met. ***Average percent of need met:*** 80% (excluding resources awarded to replace EFC). ***Average financial aid package:*** $21,920 (excluding resources awarded to replace EFC). 17% of all full-time undergraduates had no need and received non-need-based gift aid.

GIFT AID (NEED-BASED) ***Total amount:*** $45,514,397 (19% federal, 20% state, 60% institutional, 1% external sources). ***Receiving aid:*** Freshmen: 81% (653); all full-time undergraduates: 73% (2,747). ***Average award:*** Freshmen: $18,860; Undergraduates: $16,342. ***Scholarships, grants, and awards:*** Federal Pell, FSEOG, state, private, college/university gift aid from institutional funds.

GIFT AID (NON-NEED-BASED) ***Total amount:*** $11,132,002 (2% federal, 96% institutional, 2% external sources). ***Receiving aid:*** Freshmen: 16% (133). Undergraduates: 13% (497). ***Average award:*** Freshmen: $14,332. Undergraduates: $11,200. ***Scholarships, grants, and awards by category:*** *Academic interests/achievement:* business, education, general academic interests/achievements. *Creative arts/performance:* applied art and design, music, theater/drama. *Special achievements/activities:* leadership. *Special characteristics:* children and siblings of alumni, children of current students, children of faculty/staff, general special characteristics, local/state students, out-of-state students, parents of current students, religious affiliation, siblings of current students, spouses of current students, veterans. ***Tuition waivers:*** Full or partial for employees or children of employees. ***ROTC:*** Army cooperative.

LOANS ***Student loans:*** $20,217,365 (71% need-based, 29% non-need-based). 72% of past graduating class borrowed through all loan programs. *Average indebtedness per student:* $27,851. ***Average need-based loan:*** Freshmen: $2251. Undergraduates: $3222. ***Parent loans:*** $3,734,254 (25% need-based, 75% non-need-based). ***Programs:*** Federal Direct (Subsidized and Unsubsidized Stafford, PLUS), private loans.

WORK-STUDY ***Federal work-study:*** Total amount: $4,187,528; jobs available. ***State or other work-study/employment:*** Total amount: $352,450 (54% need-based, 46% non-need-based). Part-time jobs available.

APPLYING FOR FINANCIAL AID ***Required financial aid form:*** FAFSA. ***Financial aid deadline:*** Continuous. ***Notification date:*** Continuous beginning 11/15. Students must reply by 5/1.

CONTACT Ms. Heather Granart, Executive Dean of Student Financial Services, Aurora University, 347 South Gladstone Avenue, Aurora, IL 60506-4892, 630-844-6190 or toll-free 800-742-5281. *Fax:* 630-844-6191. *E-mail:* finaid@aurora.edu. *Website:* http://www.aurora.edu/.

AUSTIN COLLEGE

Sherman, TX

Tuition & fees: $41,155 **Average undergraduate aid package: $39,081**

ABOUT THE INSTITUTION Independent Presbyterian, coed. ***Awards:*** bachelor's and master's degrees. 54 undergraduate majors. ***Total enrollment:*** 1,314. Undergraduates: 1,293. Freshmen: 378. Federal methodology is used as a basis for awarding need-based institutional aid.

UNDERGRADUATE EXPENSES for 2019–2020 ***One-time required fee:*** $25. ***Comprehensive fee:*** $53,907 includes full-time tuition ($40,970), mandatory fees ($185), and room and board ($12,752). ***College room only:*** $5900. ***Part-time tuition:*** $5850 per course. ***Part-time fees:*** $90 per term.

FRESHMAN FINANCIAL AID (Fall 2019, est.) 335 applied for aid; of those 81% were deemed to have need. 100% of freshmen with need received aid; of those 25% had need fully met. ***Average percent of need met:*** 88% (excluding resources awarded to replace EFC). ***Average financial aid package:*** $40,581 (excluding resources awarded to replace EFC). 28% of all full-time freshmen had no need and received non-need-based gift aid.

UNDERGRADUATE FINANCIAL AID (Fall 2019, est.) 1,016 applied for aid; of those 85% were deemed to have need. 100% of undergraduates with need received aid; of those 27% had need fully met. ***Average percent of need met:*** 89% (excluding resources awarded to replace EFC). ***Average financial aid package:*** $39,081 (excluding resources awarded to replace EFC). 32% of all full-time undergraduates had no need and received non-need-based gift aid.

GIFT AID (NEED-BASED) ***Total amount:*** $28,706,410 (9% federal, 6% state, 84% institutional, 1% external sources). ***Receiving aid:*** Freshmen: 72% (271); all full-time undergraduates: 67% (861). ***Average award:*** Freshmen: $35,872; Undergraduates: $34,058. ***Scholarships, grants, and awards:*** Federal Pell, FSEOG, state, private, college/university gift aid from institutional funds.

GIFT AID (NON-NEED-BASED) ***Total amount:*** $11,725,917 (99% institutional, 1% external sources). ***Receiving aid:*** Freshmen: 13% (50). Undergraduates: 12% (158). ***Average award:*** Freshmen: $24,885. Undergraduates: $24,825. ***Scholarships, grants, and awards by category:*** *Academic interests/achievement:* biological sciences, business, communication, computer science, education, engineering/technologies, English, foreign languages, general academic interests/achievements, health fields, humanities, international studies, mathematics, physical sciences, premedicine, religion/biblical studies, social sciences. *Creative arts/performance:* applied art and design, music, theater/drama. *Special achievements/activities:* community service, general special achievements/activities, leadership, religious involvement. *Special characteristics:* children of faculty/staff, first-generation college students, general special characteristics, international students, local/state students, out-of-state students, previous college experience, relatives of clergy, religious affiliation, veterans. ***Tuition waivers:*** Full or partial for employees or children of employees.

LOANS ***Student loans:*** $6,755,335 (58% need-based, 42% non-need-based). ***Average need-based loan:*** Freshmen: $3883. Undergraduates: $4197. ***Parent loans:*** $2,384,951 (30% need-based, 70% non-need-based). ***Programs:*** Federal Direct (Subsidized and Unsubsidized Stafford, PLUS), state.

WORK-STUDY ***Federal work-study:*** Total amount: $652,104; jobs available. ***State or other work-study/employment:*** Total amount: $155,950 (5% need-based, 95% non-need-based). Part-time jobs available.

APPLYING FOR FINANCIAL AID ***Required financial aid form:*** FAFSA. ***Financial aid deadline (priority):*** 3/1. ***Notification date:*** Continuous beginning 12/1. Students must reply by 5/1.

CONTACT Mrs. Laurie Coulter, Executive Director of Financial Aid, Austin College, 900 North Grand Avenue, Sherman, TX 75090, 903-813-2900 or toll-free 800-596-4276 (in-state), 800-526-4276 (out-of-state). *Fax:* 903-813-3198. *E-mail:* finaid@austincollege.edu. *Website:* http://www.austincollege.edu/.

AUSTIN GRADUATE SCHOOL OF THEOLOGY

Austin, TX

Tuition & fees: N/R **Average undergraduate aid package: N/A**

ABOUT THE INSTITUTION Independent Church of Christ, coed. ***Awards:*** bachelor's and master's degrees. 1 undergraduate major. Both federal and institutional methodology are used as a basis for awarding need-based institutional aid.

GIFT AID (NEED-BASED) ***Total amount:*** $79,207 (50% federal, 50% institutional). ***Scholarships, grants, and awards:*** Federal Pell, FSEOG, college/university gift aid from institutional funds.

GIFT AID (NON-NEED-BASED) ***Scholarships, grants, and awards by category:*** *Academic interests/achievement:* religion/biblical studies. *Special achievements/activities:* religious involvement.

LOANS ***Student loans:*** $81,850 (56% need-based, 44% non-need-based). ***Programs:*** Federal Direct (Subsidized and Unsubsidized Stafford, PLUS).

WORK-STUDY ***Federal work-study:*** Total amount: $7008; jobs available.

APPLYING FOR FINANCIAL AID ***Required financial aid forms:*** FAFSA, institution's own form. ***Financial aid deadline:*** Continuous.

CONTACT David Arthur, Director of Financial Aid, Austin Graduate School of Theology, 7640 Guadalupe Street, Austin, TX 78752, 512-476-2772 Ext. 105 or toll-free 866-AUS-GRAD. *Fax:* 512-476-3919. *E-mail:* darthur@austingrad.edu.
Website: http://www.austingrad.edu/.

AUSTIN PEAY STATE UNIVERSITY

Clarksville, TN

Tuition & fees (TN res): $8303 **Average undergraduate aid package: $5776**

ABOUT THE INSTITUTION State-supported, coed. ***Awards:*** certificates, associate, bachelor's, master's, and doctoral degrees. 38 undergraduate majors. ***Total enrollment:*** 11,048. Undergraduates: 9,971. Freshmen: 1,716. Federal methodology is used as a basis for awarding need-based institutional aid.

UNDERGRADUATE EXPENSES for 2019–2020 ***Application fee:*** $25. ***One-time required fee:*** $75. ***Tuition, state resident:*** full-time $6720; part-time $280 per credit hour. ***Tuition, nonresident:*** full-time $12,264; part-time $511 per credit hour. ***Required fees:*** full-time $1583. Full-time tuition and fees vary according to location and program. Part-time tuition and fees vary according to location and program. ***College room and board:*** $11,114; ***Room only:*** $7200. Room and board charges vary according to board plan and housing facility.

FRESHMAN FINANCIAL AID (Fall 2018) 1781 applied for aid; of those 88% were deemed to have need. 99% of freshmen with need received aid. ***Average financial aid package:*** $5991 (excluding resources awarded to replace EFC). 11% of all full-time freshmen had no need and received non-need-based gift aid.

UNDERGRADUATE FINANCIAL AID (Fall 2018) 6,460 applied for aid; of those 89% were deemed to have need. 98% of undergraduates with need received aid. ***Average financial aid package:*** $5776 (excluding resources awarded to replace EFC). 8% of all full-time undergraduates had no need and received non-need-based gift aid.

GIFT AID (NEED-BASED) ***Receiving aid:*** Freshmen: 60% (1,099); all full-time undergraduates: 56% (3,921). ***Average award:*** Freshmen: $3500; Undergraduates: $3241. ***Scholarships, grants, and awards:*** Federal Pell, FSEOG, state, private, college/university gift aid from institutional funds.

GIFT AID (NON-NEED-BASED) ***Receiving aid:*** Freshmen: 74% (1,341). Undergraduates: 53% (3,711). ***Average award:*** Freshmen: $2640. Undergraduates: $2648. ***Scholarships, grants, and awards by category:*** *Academic interests/achievement:* 1,268 awards ($3,796,253 total): agriculture, biological sciences, business, communication, computer science, education, engineering/technologies, English, foreign languages, general academic interests/achievements, home economics, humanities, international studies, mathematics, military science, physical sciences, social sciences. *Creative arts/performance:* 402 awards ($511,758 total): applied art and design, creative writing, debating, journalism/publications, music, performing arts, theater/drama. *Special achievements/activities:* 144 awards ($191,193 total): general special achievements/activities, leadership, memberships. *Special characteristics:* 93 awards ($185,926 total): children of educators, children of faculty/staff, ethnic background, general special characteristics, members of minority groups, veterans. ***Tuition waivers:*** Full or partial for employees or children of employees, senior citizens. ***ROTC:*** Army, Air Force cooperative.

LOANS ***Student loans:*** 68% of past graduating class borrowed through all loan programs. *Average indebtedness per student:* $25,938. ***Average need-based loan:*** Freshmen: $1704. Undergraduates: $2070. ***Programs:*** Federal Direct (Subsidized and Unsubsidized Stafford, PLUS).

WORK-STUDY ***Federal work-study:*** 127 jobs averaging $3189. ***State or other work-study/employment:*** 579 part-time jobs averaging $1747.

APPLYING FOR FINANCIAL AID ***Required financial aid form:*** FAFSA. ***Financial aid deadline:*** Continuous. ***Notification date:*** Continuous.

CONTACT Ms. Donna Price, Director of Student Financial Aid, Austin Peay State University, PO Box 4546, Clarksville, TN 37044, 931-221-7907 or toll-free 800-844-2778. *Fax:* 931-221-6329. *E-mail:* priced@apsu.edu.
Website: http://www.apsu.edu/.

AVE MARIA UNIVERSITY

Ave Maria, FL

Tuition & fees: N/R **Average undergraduate aid package: $22,513**

ABOUT THE INSTITUTION Independent Roman Catholic, coed. ***Awards:*** bachelor's, master's, and doctoral degrees. 30 undergraduate majors. Federal methodology is used as a basis for awarding need-based institutional aid.

FRESHMAN FINANCIAL AID (Fall 2019, est.) 274 applied for aid; of those 76% were deemed to have need. 100% of freshmen with need received aid; of those 25% had need fully met. ***Average percent of need met:*** 79% (excluding resources awarded to replace EFC). ***Average financial aid package:*** $21,984 (excluding resources awarded to replace EFC). 29% of all full-time freshmen had no need and received non-need-based gift aid.

UNDERGRADUATE FINANCIAL AID (Fall 2019, est.) 793 applied for aid; of those 81% were deemed to have need. 100% of undergraduates with need received aid; of those 23% had need fully met. ***Average percent of need met:*** 80% (excluding resources awarded to replace EFC). ***Average financial aid package:*** $22,513 (excluding resources awarded to replace EFC). 37% of all full-time undergraduates had no need and received non-need-based gift aid.

GIFT AID (NEED-BASED) ***Total amount:*** $9,626,326 (15% federal, 10% state, 74% institutional, 1% external sources). ***Receiving aid:*** Freshmen: 66% (206); all full-time undergraduates: 60% (643). ***Average award:*** Freshmen: $15,721; Undergraduates: $15,902. ***Scholarships, grants, and awards:*** Federal Pell, FSEOG, state, private, college/university gift aid from institutional funds.

GIFT AID (NON-NEED-BASED) ***Total amount:*** $5,873,887 (13% state, 85% institutional, 2% external sources). ***Receiving aid:*** Freshmen: 16% (51). Undergraduates: 13% (138). ***Average award:*** Freshmen: $8981. Undergraduates: $10,912. ***Scholarships, grants, and awards by category:*** *Academic interests/achievement:* 856 awards ($4,023,111 total): business, education, general academic interests/achievements. *Creative arts/performance:* 27 awards ($57,452 total): music. *Special achievements/activities:* 596 awards ($2,946,293 total): leadership, religious involvement. *Special characteristics:* 369 awards ($1,025,972 total): children of faculty/staff, religious affiliation, siblings of current students.

LOANS ***Student loans:*** $4,668,773 (59% need-based, 41% non-need-based). 63% of past graduating class borrowed through all loan programs. *Average indebtedness per student:* $24,620. ***Average need-based loan:*** Freshmen: $3295. Undergraduates: $4072. ***Parent loans:*** $1,318,486 (40% need-based, 60% non-need-based). ***Programs:*** Federal Direct (Subsidized and Unsubsidized Stafford, PLUS).

WORK-STUDY ***Federal work-study:*** Total amount: $95,720; 64 jobs averaging $1496. ***State or other work-study/employment:*** Total amount: $7422 (100% need-based). 8 part-time jobs averaging $928.

ATHLETIC AWARDS Total amount: $3,715,783 (53% need-based, 47% non-need-based).

APPLYING FOR FINANCIAL AID ***Required financial aid forms:*** FAFSA, state aid form. ***Financial aid deadline:*** Continuous. ***Notification date:*** Continuous beginning 11/1.

CONTACT Sandy Shimp, Director of Financial Aid, Ave Maria University, 5050 Ave Maria Boulevard, Ave Maria, FL 34142, 239-280-1669 or toll-free 877-283-8648. *Fax:* 239-280-2566. *E-mail:* amufinancialaid@avemaria.edu.
Website: http://www.avemaria.edu/.

AVERETT UNIVERSITY
Danville, VA

Tuition & fees: $35,600	Average undergraduate aid package: $27,096

ABOUT THE INSTITUTION Independent Baptist General Association of Virginia, coed. ***Awards:*** associate and bachelor's degrees. 57 undergraduate majors. ***Total enrollment:*** 903. Undergraduates: 903. Freshmen: 232. Federal methodology is used as a basis for awarding need-based institutional aid.

UNDERGRADUATE EXPENSES for 2019–2020 ***Comprehensive fee:*** $42,170 includes full-time tuition ($35,450), mandatory fees ($150), and room and board ($6570). ***College room only:*** $3990. Full-time tuition and fees vary according to class time, course load, degree level, location, and program. Room and board charges vary according to board plan and housing facility. ***Part-time tuition:*** $1105 per credit hour. ***Part-time fees:*** $40 per term. Part-time tuition and fees vary according to class time, course load, degree level, location, and program.

FRESHMAN FINANCIAL AID (Fall 2019, est.) 213 applied for aid; of those 93% were deemed to have need. 100% of freshmen with need received aid; of those 9% had need fully met. ***Average percent of need met:*** 70% (excluding resources awarded to replace EFC). ***Average financial aid package:*** $26,458 (excluding resources awarded to replace EFC). 13% of all full-time freshmen had no need and received non-need-based gift aid.

UNDERGRADUATE FINANCIAL AID (Fall 2019, est.) 798 applied for aid; of those 93% were deemed to have need. 100% of undergraduates with need received aid; of those 12% had need fully met. ***Average percent of need met:*** 73% (excluding resources awarded to replace EFC). ***Average financial aid package:*** $27,096 (excluding resources awarded to replace EFC). 15% of all full-time undergraduates had no need and received non-need-based gift aid.

GIFT AID (NEED-BASED) ***Total amount:*** $17,789,727 (12% federal, 7% state, 73% institutional, 8% external sources). ***Receiving aid:*** Freshmen: 87% (198); all full-time undergraduates: 85% (746). ***Average award:*** Freshmen: $23,568; Undergraduates: $23,713. ***Scholarships, grants, and awards:*** Federal Pell, FSEOG, state, private, college/university gift aid from institutional funds.

GIFT AID (NON-NEED-BASED) ***Total amount:*** $2,884,082 (7% state, 84% institutional, 9% external sources). ***Receiving aid:*** Freshmen: 7% (17). Undergraduates: 7% (64). ***Average award:*** Freshmen: $16,616. Undergraduates: $16,235. ***Scholarships, grants, and awards by category:*** *Academic interests/achievement:* biological sciences, business, education, engineering/technologies, English, foreign languages, general academic interests/achievements, health fields, home economics, humanities, mathematics, physical sciences, premedicine, religion/biblical studies. *Creative arts/performance:* applied art and design, journalism/publications, music, theater/drama. *Special achievements/activities:* general special achievements/activities, leadership, memberships, religious involvement. *Special characteristics:* adult students, children and siblings of alumni, children of union members/company employees, first-generation college students, general special characteristics, international students, local/state students, out-of-state students, relatives of clergy, religious affiliation. ***Tuition waivers:*** Full or partial for employees or children of employees, senior citizens.

LOANS ***Student loans:*** $5,715,801 (82% need-based, 18% non-need-based). 75% of past graduating class borrowed through all loan programs. *Average indebtedness per student:* $33,711. ***Average need-based loan:*** Freshmen: $3117. Undergraduates: $3754. ***Parent loans:*** $4,792,733 (53% need-based, 47% non-need-based). ***Programs:*** Federal Direct (Subsidized and Unsubsidized Stafford, PLUS), state.

WORK-STUDY ***Federal work-study:*** Total amount: $165,540; jobs available. ***State or other work-study/employment:*** Part-time jobs available.

APPLYING FOR FINANCIAL AID ***Required financial aid forms:*** FAFSA, state aid form. ***Notification date:*** Continuous. Students must reply within 2 weeks of notification.

CONTACT Mr. Carl Bradsher, Director of Student Financial Services, Averett University, 420 West Main Street, Danville, VA 24541-3692, 434-791-5646 or toll-free 800-AVERETT. *Fax:* 434-791-5647. *E-mail:* cbradsher@averett.edu.
Website: http://www.averett.edu/.

AVILA UNIVERSITY
Kansas City, MO

CONTACT Nancy Merz, Director of Financial Aid, Avila University, 11901 Wornall Road, Kansas City, MO 64145, 816-501-3782 or toll-free 800-GO-AVILA. *Fax:* 816-501-2462. *E-mail:* nancy.merz@avila.edu.
Website: http://www.avila.edu/.

AZUSA PACIFIC UNIVERSITY
Azusa, CA

ABOUT THE INSTITUTION Independent nondenominational, coed. ***Awards:*** certificates, bachelor's, master's, and doctoral degrees. 50 undergraduate majors. ***Total enrollment:*** 10,095. Undergraduates: 5,657. Freshmen: 1,005.

GIFT AID (NEED-BASED) ***Scholarships, grants, and awards:*** Federal Pell, FSEOG, state, private, college/university gift aid from institutional funds.

WORK-STUDY ***Federal work-study:*** Total amount: $1,576,085; jobs available. ***State or other work-study/employment:*** Part-time jobs available.

CONTACT Todd Ross, Associate Vice-President for Undergraduate Academic and Financial Services, Azusa Pacific University, 901 East Alosta Avenue, PO Box 7000, Azusa, CA 91702-7000, 626-812-3009 or toll-free 800-TALK-APU. *E-mail:* tross@apu.edu.
Website: http://www.apu.edu/.

BABSON COLLEGE
Wellesley, MA

ABOUT THE INSTITUTION Independent, coed. ***Awards:*** certificates, bachelor's, and master's degrees. 24 undergraduate majors. ***Total enrollment:*** 3,325. Undergraduates: 2,334. Freshmen: 600.

GIFT AID (NEED-BASED) ***Scholarships, grants, and awards:*** Federal Pell, FSEOG, state, private, college/university gift aid from institutional funds.

GIFT AID (NON-NEED-BASED) ***Scholarships, grants, and awards by category:*** *Academic interests/achievement:* business, general academic interests/achievements. *Special achievements/activities:* leadership. *Special characteristics:* veterans.

LOANS ***Programs:*** Federal Direct (Subsidized and Unsubsidized Stafford, PLUS), state.

WORK-STUDY ***Federal work-study:*** Total amount: $1,336,000; jobs available. ***State or other work-study/employment:*** Total amount: $198,000 (100% non-need-based). Part-time jobs available.

APPLYING FOR FINANCIAL AID ***Required financial aid forms:*** FAFSA, CSS Financial Aid PROFILE, noncustodial (divorced/separated) parent's statement.

CONTACT Ms. Meredith Stover, Director of Financial Aid, Babson College, Hollister Hall, Third Floor, Babson Park, MA 02457-0310, 781-239-4219 or toll-free 800-488-3696. *Fax:* 781-239-5510. *E-mail:* stoverm@babson.edu.
Website: http://www.babson.edu/.

BACONE COLLEGE
Muskogee, OK

CONTACT Mrs. Misty Oleson, Assistant Director of Financial Aid, Bacone College, 2299 Old Bacone Road, Muskogee, OK 74403-1597, 918-781-7225 or toll-free 888-682-5514 Ext.7340. *Fax:* 866-498-1487. *E-mail:* finaid@bacone.edu.
Website: http://www.bacone.edu/.

BAIS BINYOMIN ACADEMY
Stamford, CT

CONTACT Financial Aid Office, Bais Binyomin Academy, 132 Prospect Street, Stamford, CT 06901-1202, 203-325-4351.

BAIS HAMEDRASH AND MESIVTA OF BALTIMORE

Baltimore, MD

CONTACT Financial Aid Office, Bais HaMedrash and Mesivta of Baltimore, 6823 Old Pimlico Road, Baltimore, MD 21209, 410-486-0006.
Website: http://www.bhmb.edu/.

BAIS MEDRASH MAYAN HATORAH

Lakewood, NJ

CONTACT Financial Aid Office, Bais Medrash Mayan Hatorah, 101 Milton Street, Lakewood, NJ 08701.
Website: http://www.baismedrashmayanhatorah.com/.

BAIS MEDRASH TORAS CHESED

Lakewood, NJ

CONTACT Financial Aid Office, Bais Medrash Toras Chesed, 910 Monmouth Avenue, Lakewood, NJ 08701.
Website: http://www.bmtc.edu/.

BAKER COLLEGE

Flint, MI

CONTACT Financial Aid Office, Baker College, Baker College System Headquarters, 1050 West Bristol Road, Flint, MI 48507, 810-766-4000 or toll-free 800-964-4299.
Website: http://www.baker.edu/.

BAKER UNIVERSITY

Baldwin City, KS

Tuition & fees: $29,880	Average undergraduate aid package: $24,639

ABOUT THE INSTITUTION Independent United Methodist, coed. ***Awards:*** bachelor's, master's, and doctoral degrees (profile includes information primarily for undergraduate residential campus in Baldwin City, KS). 38 undergraduate majors. ***Total enrollment:*** 1,214. Undergraduates: 1,214. Freshmen: 244. Federal methodology is used as a basis for awarding need-based institutional aid.

UNDERGRADUATE EXPENSES for 2019–2020 ***One-time required fee:*** $100. ***Comprehensive fee:*** $38,230 includes full-time tuition ($29,300), mandatory fees ($580), and room and board ($8350). ***College room only:*** $3950. Room and board charges vary according to board plan and housing facility. ***Part-time tuition:*** $945 per credit hour. ***Part-time fees:*** $200 per year.

FRESHMAN FINANCIAL AID (Fall 2018) 232 applied for aid; of those 84% were deemed to have need. 100% of freshmen with need received aid. ***Average percent of need met:*** 80% (excluding resources awarded to replace EFC). ***Average financial aid package:*** $24,615 (excluding resources awarded to replace EFC). 8% of all full-time freshmen had no need and received non-need-based gift aid.

UNDERGRADUATE FINANCIAL AID (Fall 2018) 780 applied for aid; of those 86% were deemed to have need. 99% of undergraduates with need received aid. ***Average percent of need met:*** 85% (excluding resources awarded to replace EFC). ***Average financial aid package:*** $24,639 (excluding resources awarded to replace EFC). 17% of all full-time undergraduates had no need and received non-need-based gift aid.

GIFT AID (NEED-BASED) ***Receiving aid:*** Freshmen: 52% (126); all full-time undergraduates: 56% (477). ***Average award:*** Freshmen: $6808; Undergraduates: $6453. ***Scholarships, grants, and awards:*** Federal Pell, FSEOG, state, private, college/university gift aid from institutional funds.

GIFT AID (NON-NEED-BASED) ***Receiving aid:*** Freshmen: 80% (195). Undergraduates: 78% (660). ***Average award:*** Freshmen: $9212. Undergraduates: $9332. ***Scholarships, grants, and awards by category:*** *Academic interests/achievement:* general academic interests/achievements. *Creative arts/performance:* applied art and design, cinema/film/broadcasting, dance, debating, journalism/publications, music, theater/drama. *Special achievements/activities:* cheerleading/drum major, leadership, religious involvement. *Special characteristics:* children and siblings of alumni, children of faculty/staff, ethnic background, international students, members of minority groups, out-of-state students, relatives of clergy, religious affiliation. ***Tuition waivers:*** Full or partial for employees or children of employees, senior citizens. ***ROTC:*** Army cooperative, Air Force cooperative.

LOANS ***Student loans:*** 65% of past graduating class borrowed through all loan programs. *Average indebtedness per student:* $33,046. ***Average need-based loan:*** Freshmen: $3372. Undergraduates: $4095. ***Programs:*** Federal Direct (Subsidized and Unsubsidized Stafford, PLUS), Perkins, alternative loans.

WORK-STUDY Federal work-study jobs available. ***State or other work-study/employment:*** Part-time jobs available.

APPLYING FOR FINANCIAL AID ***Required financial aid forms:*** FAFSA, institution's own form. ***Notification date:*** Continuous. Students must reply within 6 weeks of notification.

CONTACT Jana Parks, Financial Aid Director, Baker University, Box 65, Baldwin City, KS 66006-0065, 785-594-4595 or toll-free 800-873-4282. *Fax:* 785-594-8358.
Website: http://www.bakeru.edu/.

BALDWIN WALLACE UNIVERSITY

Berea, OH

Tuition & fees: $33,530	Average undergraduate aid package: $26,293

ABOUT THE INSTITUTION Independent Methodist, coed. ***Awards:*** certificates, bachelor's, and master's degrees. 78 undergraduate majors. ***Total enrollment:*** 3,741. Undergraduates: 3,136. Freshmen: 677. Federal methodology is used as a basis for awarding need-based institutional aid.

UNDERGRADUATE EXPENSES for 2019–2020 ***Application fee:*** $25. ***Comprehensive fee:*** $43,640 includes full-time tuition ($33,530) and room and board ($10,110). ***College room only:*** $5678. Full-time tuition and fees vary according to class time, course level, course load, degree level, program, and reciprocity agreements. Room and board charges vary according to housing facility. ***Part-time tuition:*** $1042 per credit hour. Part-time tuition and fees vary according to class time, course level, course load, degree level, program, and reciprocity agreements.

FRESHMAN FINANCIAL AID (Fall 2019, est.) 633 applied for aid; of those 82% were deemed to have need. 100% of freshmen with need received aid; of those 43% had need fully met. ***Average percent of need met:*** 92% (excluding resources awarded to replace EFC). ***Average financial aid package:*** $28,614 (excluding resources awarded to replace EFC). 17% of all full-time freshmen had no need and received non-need-based gift aid.

UNDERGRADUATE FINANCIAL AID (Fall 2019, est.) 2,428 applied for aid; of those 85% were deemed to have need. 100% of undergraduates with need received aid; of those 42% had need fully met. ***Average percent of need met:*** 90% (excluding resources awarded to replace EFC). ***Average financial aid package:*** $26,293 (excluding resources awarded to replace EFC). 24% of all full-time undergraduates had no need and received non-need-based gift aid.

GIFT AID (NEED-BASED) ***Receiving aid:*** Freshmen: 79% (522); all full-time undergraduates: 73% (2,025). ***Average award:*** Freshmen: $23,588; Undergraduates: $21,130. ***Scholarships, grants, and awards:*** Federal Pell, FSEOG, state, private, college/university gift aid from institutional funds.

GIFT AID (NON-NEED-BASED) ***Receiving aid:*** Freshmen: 17% (111). Undergraduates: 16% (436). ***Average award:*** Freshmen: $17,650. Undergraduates: $16,759. ***Scholarships, grants, and awards by category:*** *Academic interests/achievement:* 2,856 awards ($28,822,000 total): general academic interests/achievements. *Creative arts/performance:* 191 awards ($763,000 total): music. *Special characteristics:* 1,654 awards ($8,504,000 total): children and siblings of alumni, children of educators, children of faculty/staff, ethnic background, international students, members of minority groups, out-of-state students, relatives of clergy, religious affiliation, siblings of current students, veterans. ***Tuition waivers:*** Full or partial for children of alumni, employees or children of employees. ***ROTC:*** Army cooperative, Air Force cooperative.

LOANS ***Student loans:*** 76% of past graduating class borrowed through all loan programs. *Average indebtedness per student:* $33,919. ***Average need-based loan:*** Freshmen: $2851. Undergraduates: $4166. ***Programs:*** Federal Direct (Subsidized and Unsubsidized Stafford, PLUS).

WORK-STUDY ***Federal work-study:*** 881 jobs averaging $1382. ***State or other work-study/employment:*** 500 part-time jobs averaging $1350.

APPLYING FOR FINANCIAL AID ***Required financial aid form:*** FAFSA. ***Financial aid deadline:*** Continuous. ***Notification date:*** Continuous.

CONTACT Dr. George L. Rolleston, Director of Financial Aid, Baldwin Wallace University, 275 Eastland Road, Berea, OH 44017-2088, 440-826-2108 or toll-free 877-BW-APPLY. *Fax:* 440-826-8048. *E-mail:* grollest@bw.edu.
Website: http://www.bw.edu/.

BALL STATE UNIVERSITY

Muncie, IN

Tuition & fees (area res): $10,020	Average undergraduate aid package: $14,335

ABOUT THE INSTITUTION State-supported, coed. ***Awards:*** certificates, bachelor's, master's, and doctoral degrees. 124 undergraduate majors. ***Total enrollment:*** 22,510. Undergraduates: 16,645. Freshmen: 4,003. Federal methodology is used as a basis for awarding need-based institutional aid.

UNDERGRADUATE EXPENSES for 2020–2021 ***Application fee:*** $60. ***Tuition, area resident:*** full-time $9358. ***Tuition, state resident:*** full-time $9358. ***Tuition, nonresident:*** full-time $26,138. ***Required fees:*** full-time $662. Full-time tuition and fees vary according to program and reciprocity agreements. Part-time tuition and fees vary according to course load, program, and reciprocity agreements. ***College room and board:*** $10,870; ***Room only:*** $4742. Room and board charges vary according to board plan and housing facility.

FRESHMAN FINANCIAL AID (Fall 2019, est.) 3840 applied for aid; of those 78% were deemed to have need. 100% of freshmen with need received aid; of those 42% had need fully met. ***Average percent of need met:*** 75% (excluding resources awarded to replace EFC). ***Average financial aid package:*** $14,712 (excluding resources awarded to replace EFC). 14% of all full-time freshmen had no need and received non-need-based gift aid.

UNDERGRADUATE FINANCIAL AID (Fall 2019, est.) 12,684 applied for aid; of those 78% were deemed to have need. 100% of undergraduates with need received aid; of those 48% had need fully met. ***Average percent of need met:*** 74% (excluding resources awarded to replace EFC). ***Average financial aid package:*** $14,335 (excluding resources awarded to replace EFC). 14% of all full-time undergraduates had no need and received non-need-based gift aid.

GIFT AID (NEED-BASED) ***Total amount:*** $42,866,136 (61% federal, 18% state, 21% institutional). ***Receiving aid:*** Freshmen: 50% (2,017); all full-time undergraduates: 41% (6,357). ***Average award:*** Freshmen: $7239; Undergraduates: $6715. ***Scholarships, grants, and awards:*** Federal Pell, FSEOG, state, private, college/university gift aid from institutional funds.

GIFT AID (NON-NEED-BASED) ***Total amount:*** $74,784,539 (2% federal, 35% state, 53% institutional, 10% external sources). ***Receiving aid:*** Freshmen: 51% (2,086). Undergraduates: 38% (5,891). ***Average award:*** Freshmen: $7280. Undergraduates: $8040. ***Scholarships, grants, and awards by category:*** *Academic interests/achievement:* architecture, biological sciences, business, communication, education, engineering/technologies, English, foreign languages, general academic interests/achievements, home economics, humanities, international studies, mathematics, military science, physical sciences, social sciences. *Creative arts/performance:* cinema/film/broadcasting, dance, debating, general creative arts/performance, journalism/publications, music, performing arts, theater/drama. *Special achievements/activities:* community service, general special achievements/activities, leadership. *Special characteristics:* adult students, children of faculty/staff, ethnic background, general special characteristics, international students, local/state students, members of minority groups, out-of-state students, veterans. ***Tuition waivers:*** Full or partial for employees or children of employees, senior citizens. ***ROTC:*** Army.

LOANS ***Student loans:*** $99,565,581 (37% need-based, 63% non-need-based). 70% of past graduating class borrowed through all loan programs. *Average indebtedness per student:* $28,603. ***Average need-based loan:*** Freshmen: $3204. Undergraduates: $4121. ***Parent loans:*** $23,509,513 (100% non-need-based). ***Programs:*** Federal Direct (Subsidized and Unsubsidized Stafford, PLUS), college/university.

WORK-STUDY ***Federal work-study:*** Total amount: $8,242,722; jobs available. ***State or other work-study/employment:*** Total amount: $4,491,842 (100% non-need-based). Part-time jobs available.

ATHLETIC AWARDS Total amount: $7,525,554 (100% non-need-based).

APPLYING FOR FINANCIAL AID ***Required financial aid form:*** FAFSA. ***Financial aid deadline (priority):*** 4/15. ***Notification date:*** Continuous beginning 1/15.

CONTACT Dr. John McPherson, Assistant Vice President of Enrollment Services and Executive Director of Financial Aid and Scholarships, Ball State University, Lucina Hall, Room 245, Muncie, IN 47306, 765-285-8894 or toll-free 800-482-4BSU. *Fax:* 765-285-4247. *E-mail:* finaid@bsu.edu.
Website: http://www.bsu.edu/.

BAPTIST BIBLE COLLEGE

Springfield, MO

CONTACT Bob Kotulski, Director of Financial Aid, Baptist Bible College, 628 East Kearney, Springfield, MO 65803-3498, 417-268-6036 or toll-free 800-228-5754. *Fax:* 417-268-6694.
Website: http://www.gobbc.edu/.

THE BAPTIST COLLEGE OF FLORIDA

Graceville, FL

Tuition & fees: N/R	Average undergraduate aid package: $9263

ABOUT THE INSTITUTION Independent Southern Baptist, coed. ***Awards:*** associate, bachelor's, and master's degrees. 17 undergraduate majors. ***Total enrollment:*** 452. Undergraduates: 427. Freshmen: 25. Federal methodology is used as a basis for awarding need-based institutional aid.

UNDERGRADUATE EXPENSES for 2019–2020 ***Application fee:*** $25. ***Comprehensive fee:*** $16,312 includes full-time tuition ($10,800), mandatory fees ($900), and room and board ($4612). Room and board charges vary according to board plan and housing facility. ***Part-time tuition:*** $360 per credit hour. ***Part-time fees:*** $30 per credit hour.

FRESHMAN FINANCIAL AID (Fall 2019, est.) 51 applied for aid; of those 80% were deemed to have need. 27% of freshmen with need received aid; of those 9% had need fully met. ***Average percent of need met:*** 16% (excluding resources awarded to replace EFC). ***Average financial aid package:*** $8842 (excluding resources awarded to replace EFC). 6% of all full-time freshmen had no need and received non-need-based gift aid.

UNDERGRADUATE FINANCIAL AID (Fall 2019, est.) 294 applied for aid; of those 87% were deemed to have need. 65% of undergraduates with need received aid; of those 4% had need fully met. ***Average percent of need met:*** 32% (excluding resources awarded to replace EFC). ***Average financial aid package:*** $9263 (excluding resources awarded to replace EFC). 6% of all full-time undergraduates had no need and received non-need-based gift aid.

GIFT AID (NEED-BASED) ***Total amount:*** $1,289,485 (54% federal, 27% state, 17% institutional, 2% external sources). ***Receiving aid:*** Freshmen: 21% (11); all full-time undergraduates: 48% (165). ***Average award:*** Freshmen: $6981; Undergraduates: $7190. ***Scholarships, grants, and awards:*** Federal Pell, FSEOG, state, private, college/university gift aid from institutional funds.

GIFT AID (NON-NEED-BASED) ***Total amount:*** $123,262 (62% state, 35% institutional, 3% external sources). ***Receiving aid:*** Freshmen: 2% (1). Undergraduates: 1% (4). ***Average award:*** Freshmen: $1523. Undergraduates: $1939. ***Scholarships, grants, and awards by category:*** *Academic interests/achievement:* 174 awards ($296,280 total): education, general academic interests/achievements, religion/biblical studies. ***Tuition waivers:*** Full or partial for employees or children of employees.

LOANS ***Student loans:*** $719,623 (85% need-based, 15% non-need-based). 62% of past graduating class borrowed through all loan programs. *Average indebtedness per student:* $18,945. ***Average need-based loan:*** Freshmen: $3930. Undergraduates: $3241. ***Parent loans:*** $45,290 (28% need-based, 72% non-need-based). ***Programs:*** Federal Direct (Subsidized and Unsubsidized Stafford, PLUS).

WORK-STUDY ***Federal work-study:*** Total amount: $52,018; 26 jobs averaging $2000.

APPLYING FOR FINANCIAL AID ***Required financial aid forms:*** FAFSA, institution's own form. ***Financial aid deadline:*** Continuous. ***Notification date:*** Continuous beginning 6/1. Students must reply within 6 weeks of notification.

CONTACT Stephanie E. Powell, Director of Financial Aid, The Baptist College of Florida, 5400 College Drive, Graceville, FL 32440-3306, 850-263-3261 Ext. 461 or toll-free 800-328-2660 Ext.460. *Fax:* 850-263-2141. *E-mail:* finaid@baptistcollege.edu.
Website: http://www.baptistcollege.edu/.

BAPTIST COLLEGE OF HEALTH SCIENCES

Memphis, TN

CONTACT Joanna Darden, Director of Financial Aid, Baptist College of Health Sciences, 1003 Monroe Avenue, Memphis, TN 38104, 901-227-4330 or toll-free 866-575-2247. *E-mail:* joanna.darden@bchs.edu.
Website: http://www.bchs.edu/.

BAPTIST HEALTH SYSTEM SCHOOL OF HEALTH PROFESSIONS

San Antonio, TX

CONTACT Financial Aid Office, Baptist Health System School of Health Professions, 8400 Datapoint Drive, San Antonio, TX 78229, 210-297-9636.
Website: http://www.bshp.edu/.

BAPTIST MISSIONARY ASSOCIATION THEOLOGICAL SEMINARY

Jacksonville, TX

CONTACT Dr. Philip Attebery, Dean/Registrar, Baptist Missionary Association Theological Seminary, 1530 East Pine Street, PO Box 670, Jacksonville, TX 75766-5407, 903-586-2501 or toll-free 800-259-5673. *Fax:* 903-586-0378. *E-mail:* bmatsem@bmats.edu.
Website: http://www.bmats.edu/.

BAPTIST UNIVERSITY OF THE AMERICAS

San Antonio, TX

Tuition & fees: N/R — **Average undergraduate aid package: N/A**

ABOUT THE INSTITUTION Independent Baptist, coed. ***Awards:*** certificates, diplomas, associate, and bachelor's degrees (associate degree in Cross-Cultural Studies). 7 undergraduate majors. Both federal and institutional methodology are used as a basis for awarding need-based institutional aid.

GIFT AID (NEED-BASED) ***Total amount:*** $466,563 (21% institutional, 79% external sources). ***Scholarships, grants, and awards:*** Federal Pell, FSEOG, private, college/university gift aid from institutional funds.

LOANS ***Student loans:*** $75,925 (100% need-based). ***Programs:*** Federal Direct (Subsidized and Unsubsidized Stafford).

WORK-STUDY ***Federal work-study:*** Total amount: $5060; 3 jobs averaging $1687. ***State or other work-study/employment:*** 52 part-time jobs averaging $1602.

APPLYING FOR FINANCIAL AID ***Required financial aid forms:*** FAFSA, institution's own form. ***Financial aid deadline:*** Continuous.

CONTACT Mrs. Araceli G. Acosta, Financial Aid Director, Baptist University of the Americas, 7838 Barlite Boulevard, San Antonio, TX 78224, 210-924-4338 Ext. 214 or toll-free 800-721-1396. *Fax:* 210-924-2701. *E-mail:* araceli.acosta@bua.edu.
Website: http://www.bua.edu/.

BARCLAY COLLEGE

Haviland, KS

CONTACT Ryan Haase, Financial Aid Coordinator, Barclay College, 607 North Kingman, Haviland, KS 67059, 800-862-0226. *Fax:* 620-862-5403. *E-mail:* financialaid@barclaycollege.edu.
Website: http://www.barclaycollege.edu/.

BARD COLLEGE

Annandale-on-Hudson, NY

ABOUT THE INSTITUTION Independent, coed. ***Awards:*** bachelor's, master's, and doctoral degrees. 57 undergraduate majors. ***Total enrollment:*** 2,207. Undergraduates: 1,930. Freshmen: 470.

GIFT AID (NEED-BASED) ***Scholarships, grants, and awards:*** Federal Pell, FSEOG, state, private, college/university gift aid from institutional funds.

GIFT AID (NON-NEED-BASED) ***Scholarships, grants, and awards by category:*** *Special characteristics:* children of educators, children of faculty/staff.

LOANS ***Programs:*** Federal Direct (Subsidized and Unsubsidized Stafford, PLUS).

WORK-STUDY ***Federal work-study:*** Total amount: $1,496,622; 825 jobs averaging $1694.

APPLYING FOR FINANCIAL AID ***Required financial aid forms:*** FAFSA, CSS Financial Aid PROFILE, state aid form, noncustodial (divorced/separated) parent's statement.

CONTACT Denise Ann Ackerman, Director of Financial Aid, Bard College, Annandale Road, Annandale-on-Hudson, NY 12504, 845-758-7525. *Fax:* 845-758-7336. *E-mail:* finaid@bard.edu.
Website: http://www.bard.edu/.

BARD COLLEGE AT SIMON'S ROCK

Great Barrington, MA

ABOUT THE INSTITUTION Independent, coed. ***Awards:*** associate and bachelor's degrees. 39 undergraduate majors. ***Total enrollment:*** 396. Undergraduates: 329. Freshmen: 116.

GIFT AID (NEED-BASED) ***Scholarships, grants, and awards:*** Federal Pell, FSEOG, state, private, college/university gift aid from institutional funds.

GIFT AID (NON-NEED-BASED) ***Scholarships, grants, and awards by category:*** *Academic interests/achievement:* general academic interests/achievements. *Special characteristics:* children and siblings of alumni, children of faculty/staff, local/state students, members of minority groups.

LOANS ***Programs:*** Federal Direct (Subsidized and Unsubsidized Stafford, PLUS).

WORK-STUDY ***Federal work-study:*** Total amount: $188,982; jobs available.

APPLYING FOR FINANCIAL AID ***Required financial aid forms:*** FAFSA, CSS Financial Aid PROFILE, noncustodial (divorced/separated) parent's statement.

CONTACT Ms. Moira Buhr, Associate Director of Financial Aid, Bard College at Simon's Rock, 84 Alford Road, Great Barrington, MA 01230-9702, 413-528-7297 or toll-free 800-235-7186. *Fax:* 413-528-7339. *E-mail:* moira@simons-rock.edu.
Website: http://www.simons-rock.edu/.

BARNARD COLLEGE
New York, NY

Tuition & fees: $57,668 | **Average undergraduate aid package: $50,557**

ABOUT THE INSTITUTION Independent, women only. ***Awards:*** bachelor's degrees. 54 undergraduate majors. ***Total enrollment:*** 2,631. Undergraduates: 2,631. Freshmen: 632. Institutional methodology is used as a basis for awarding need-based institutional aid.

UNDERGRADUATE EXPENSES for 2019–2020 ***Application fee:*** $75. ***Comprehensive fee:*** $75,524 includes full-time tuition ($55,781), mandatory fees ($1887), and room and board ($17,856). ***College room only:*** $10,826. Room and board charges vary according to board plan and housing facility. ***Payment plan:*** Tuition prepayment.

FRESHMAN FINANCIAL AID (Fall 2019, est.) 363 applied for aid; of those 76% were deemed to have need. 97% of freshmen with need received aid; of those 93% had need fully met. ***Average percent of need met:*** 100% (excluding resources awarded to replace EFC). ***Average financial aid package:*** $50,365 (excluding resources awarded to replace EFC).

UNDERGRADUATE FINANCIAL AID (Fall 2019, est.) 1,197 applied for aid; of those 84% were deemed to have need. 99% of undergraduates with need received aid; of those 93% had need fully met. ***Average percent of need met:*** 100% (excluding resources awarded to replace EFC). ***Average financial aid package:*** $50,557 (excluding resources awarded to replace EFC).

GIFT AID (NEED-BASED) ***Total amount:*** $45,865,265 (5% federal, 3% state, 89% institutional, 3% external sources). ***Receiving aid:*** Freshmen: 40% (248); all full-time undergraduates: 35% (927). ***Average award:*** Freshmen: $50,835; Undergraduates: $49,096. ***Scholarships, grants, and awards:*** Federal Pell, FSEOG, state, private, college/university gift aid from institutional funds.

GIFT AID (NON-NEED-BASED) ***Total amount:*** $4,841,969 (27% institutional, 73% external sources). ***Tuition waivers:*** Full or partial for employees or children of employees. ***ROTC:*** Army cooperative, Naval cooperative, Air Force cooperative.

LOANS ***Student loans:*** $5,647,893 (59% need-based, 41% non-need-based). 43% of past graduating class borrowed through all loan programs. *Average indebtedness per student:* $20,829. ***Average need-based loan:*** Freshmen: $2204. Undergraduates: $3195. ***Parent loans:*** $5,673,881 (13% need-based, 87% non-need-based). ***Programs:*** Federal Direct (Subsidized and Unsubsidized Stafford, PLUS), college/university.

WORK-STUDY ***Federal work-study:*** Total amount: $447,281; 216 jobs averaging $2655. ***State or other work-study/employment:*** Total amount: $2,089,977 (65% need-based, 35% non-need-based). 252 part-time jobs averaging $2940.

APPLYING FOR FINANCIAL AID ***Required financial aid forms:*** FAFSA, CSS Financial Aid PROFILE, noncustodial (divorced/separated) parent's statement, Federal Tax Returns & W-2 Forms. ***Financial aid deadline (priority):*** 2/1. ***Notification date:*** 3/31. Students must reply by 5/1.

CONTACT Nanette DiLauro, Director of Financial Aid, Barnard College, 3009 Broadway, New York, NY 10027-6598, 212-854-2154. *Fax:* 212-280-8794. *E-mail:* finaid@barnard.edu.
Website: http://www.barnard.edu/.

BARRY UNIVERSITY
Miami Shores, FL

Tuition & fees: $29,850 | **Average undergraduate aid package: $24,378**

ABOUT THE INSTITUTION Independent Roman Catholic, coed. ***Awards:*** certificates, bachelor's, master's, and doctoral degrees. 58 undergraduate majors. ***Total enrollment:*** 7,401. Undergraduates: 3,747. Freshmen: 717. Federal methodology is used as a basis for awarding need-based institutional aid.

UNDERGRADUATE EXPENSES for 2019–2020 ***Comprehensive fee:*** $41,074 includes full-time tuition ($29,700), mandatory fees ($150), and room and board ($11,224). ***Part-time tuition:*** $925 per credit hour.

FRESHMAN FINANCIAL AID (Fall 2019, est.) 664 applied for aid; of those 96% were deemed to have need. 100% of freshmen with need received aid; of those 5% had need fully met. ***Average percent of need met:*** 65% (excluding resources awarded to replace EFC). ***Average financial aid package:*** $27,725 (excluding resources awarded to replace EFC). 7% of all full-time freshmen had no need and received non-need-based gift aid.

UNDERGRADUATE FINANCIAL AID (Fall 2019, est.) 2,462 applied for aid; of those 95% were deemed to have need. 99% of undergraduates with need received aid; of those 5% had need fully met. ***Average percent of need met:*** 59% (excluding resources awarded to replace EFC). ***Average financial aid package:*** $24,378 (excluding resources awarded to replace EFC). 10% of all full-time undergraduates had no need and received non-need-based gift aid.

GIFT AID (NEED-BASED) ***Total amount:*** $19,276,542 (49% federal, 7% state, 44% institutional). ***Receiving aid:*** Freshmen: 82% (581); all full-time undergraduates: 67% (2,018). ***Average award:*** Freshmen: $9839; Undergraduates: $9277.

GIFT AID (NON-NEED-BASED) ***Total amount:*** $34,086,493 (13% state, 84% institutional, 3% external sources). ***Receiving aid:*** Freshmen: 90% (640). Undergraduates: 74% (2,234). ***Average award:*** Freshmen: $13,318. Undergraduates: $10,416. ***ROTC:*** Army cooperative, Air Force cooperative.

LOANS ***Student loans:*** $16,729,127 (45% need-based, 55% non-need-based). 69% of past graduating class borrowed through all loan programs. *Average indebtedness per student:* $37,228. ***Average need-based loan:*** Freshmen: $3094. Undergraduates: $4154. ***Parent loans:*** $2,875,133 (100% non-need-based).

WORK-STUDY ***Federal work-study:*** Total amount: $2,717,748; jobs available. ***State or other work-study/employment:*** Total amount: $424,104 (100% non-need-based). Part-time jobs available.

ATHLETIC AWARDS Total amount: $3,768,414 (100% non-need-based).

APPLYING FOR FINANCIAL AID ***Required financial aid form:*** FAFSA. ***Financial aid deadline:*** Continuous. ***Notification date:*** 10/15. Students must reply within 1 week of notification.

CONTACT Mr. Dart Humeston, Director of Financial Aid, Barry University, 11300 Northeast Second Avenue, Miami Shores, FL 33161-6695, 305-899-3673 or toll-free 800-695-2279. *E-mail:* finaid@mail.barry.edu.
Website: http://www.barry.edu/.

BARTON COLLEGE
Wilson, NC

Tuition & fees: $31,732 | **Average undergraduate aid package: $25,681**

ABOUT THE INSTITUTION Independent Christian Church (Disciples of Christ), coed. ***Awards:*** bachelor's and master's degrees. 32 undergraduate majors. ***Total enrollment:*** 1,059. Undergraduates: 976. Freshmen: 277. Both federal and institutional methodology are used as a basis for awarding need-based institutional aid.

UNDERGRADUATE EXPENSES for 2019–2020 ***Comprehensive fee:*** $42,154 includes full-time tuition ($31,732) and room and board ($10,422). ***College room only:*** $4500. Room and board charges vary according to housing facility. ***Part-time tuition:*** $450 per credit hour.

FRESHMAN FINANCIAL AID (Fall 2019, est.) 297 applied for aid; of those 91% were deemed to have need. 100% of freshmen with need received aid; of those 15% had need fully met. ***Average percent of need met:*** 70% (excluding resources awarded to replace EFC). ***Average financial aid package:*** $26,498 (excluding resources awarded to replace EFC). 15% of all full-time freshmen had no need and received non-need-based gift aid.

UNDERGRADUATE FINANCIAL AID (Fall 2019, est.) 889 applied for aid; of those 93% were deemed to have need. 100% of undergraduates with need received aid; of those 14% had need fully met. ***Average percent of need met:*** 69% (excluding resources awarded to replace EFC). ***Average financial aid package:*** $25,681 (excluding resources awarded to replace EFC). 15% of all full-time undergraduates had no need and received non-need-based gift aid.

GIFT AID (NEED-BASED) ***Receiving aid:*** Freshmen: 84% (269); all full-time undergraduates: 83% (821). ***Average award:*** Freshmen: $22,773; Undergraduates: $21,277. ***Scholarships, grants, and awards:*** Federal Pell, FSEOG, state, private, college/university gift aid from institutional funds.

GIFT AID (NON-NEED-BASED) ***Receiving aid:*** Freshmen: 12% (37). Undergraduates: 10% (97). ***Average award:*** Freshmen: $11,989. Undergraduates: $12,163. ***Scholarships, grants, and awards by category:*** *Academic interests/achievement:* biological sciences, business, communication, education, English, general academic interests/achievements, home economics, humanities, mathematics, physical sciences, religion/biblical studies, social sciences. *Creative arts/performance:* applied art and design, music, theater/drama. *Special achievements/activities:* cheerleading/drum major, general special achievements/activities, leadership, religious involvement. *Special characteristics:* adult students, children and siblings of alumni, children of faculty/staff, international students, local/state students, relatives of clergy, religious affiliation, siblings of current students, veterans. ***Tuition waivers:*** Full or partial for employees or children of employees.

LOANS *Student loans:* 78% of past graduating class borrowed through all loan programs. *Average indebtedness per student:* $27,227. ***Average need-based loan:*** Freshmen: $2986. Undergraduates: $3867. ***Programs:*** Federal Direct (Subsidized and Unsubsidized Stafford, PLUS), Perkins, Private loans.

WORK-STUDY *Federal work-study:* 122 jobs averaging $1287. ***State or other work-study/employment:*** Part-time jobs available.

APPLYING FOR FINANCIAL AID *Required financial aid forms:* FAFSA, NC State Residency Form (RDS), if applicable. ***Financial aid deadline:*** Continuous. ***Notification date:*** Continuous.

CONTACT Mr. Thomas Welch, Director of Financial Aid, Barton College, Box 5000, Wilson, NC 27893, 252-399-6371 or toll-free 800-345-4973. *Fax:* 252-399-6572. *E-mail:* twelch@barton.edu.
Website: http://www.barton.edu/.

BARUCH COLLEGE OF THE CITY UNIVERSITY OF NEW YORK

New York, NY

Tuition & fees (NY res): $7461 **Average undergraduate aid package: N/A**

ABOUT THE INSTITUTION State and locally supported, coed. ***Awards:*** certificates, bachelor's, and master's degrees. 32 undergraduate majors. ***Total enrollment:*** 18,679. Undergraduates: 15,482. Freshmen: 2,268. Federal methodology is used as a basis for awarding need-based institutional aid.

UNDERGRADUATE EXPENSES for 2019–2020 *Application fee:* $65. ***Tuition, state resident:*** full-time $6930; part-time $305 per credit hour. ***Tuition, nonresident:*** full-time $18,600; part-time $620 per credit hour. ***Required fees:*** full-time $531. Full-time tuition and fees vary according to course load. Part-time tuition and fees vary according to course load. Room and board charges vary according to housing facility.

GIFT AID (NEED-BASED) *Scholarships, grants, and awards:* Federal Pell, FSEOG, state, private, college/university gift aid from institutional funds.

GIFT AID (NON-NEED-BASED) *Scholarships, grants, and awards by category:* *Academic interests/achievement:* general academic interests/achievements. ***Tuition waivers:*** Full or partial for employees or children of employees, senior citizens. ***ROTC:*** Army cooperative.

LOANS *Programs:* Federal Direct (Subsidized and Unsubsidized Stafford, PLUS), Perkins.

WORK-STUDY Federal work-study jobs available. ***State or other work-study/employment:*** Part-time jobs available.

APPLYING FOR FINANCIAL AID *Notification date:* Continuous.

CONTACT Ms. Elizabeth Riquez, Financial Aid Services, Baruch College of the City University of New York, One Bernard Baruch Way, Box H-880, New York, NY 10010-5585, 646-312-1399. *Fax:* 646-312-1361. *E-mail:* elizabeth.riquez@baruch.cuny.edu.
Website: http://www.baruch.cuny.edu/.

BASTYR UNIVERSITY

Kenmore, WA

CONTACT Katy Chapin, Financial Aid Advisor, Bastyr University, 14500 Juanita Drive NE, Kenmore, WA 98028-4966, 425-602-3085. *Fax:* 425-602-3094. *E-mail:* finaid@bastyr.edu.
Website: http://www.bastyr.edu/.

BATES COLLEGE

Lewiston, ME

Tuition & fees: $55,683 **Average undergraduate aid package: $51,099**

ABOUT THE INSTITUTION Independent, coed. ***Awards:*** bachelor's degrees. 36 undergraduate majors. ***Total enrollment:*** 1,820. Undergraduates: 1,820. Freshmen: 499. Institutional methodology is used as a basis for awarding need-based institutional aid.

UNDERGRADUATE EXPENSES for 2019–2020 *Application fee:* $60. ***Comprehensive fee:*** $71,388 includes full-time tuition ($55,683) and room and board ($15,705). ***Payment plan:*** Tuition prepayment.

FRESHMAN FINANCIAL AID (Fall 2019, est.) 235 applied for aid; of those 87% were deemed to have need. 100% of freshmen with need received aid; of those 100% had need fully met. ***Average percent of need met:*** 100% (excluding resources awarded to replace EFC). ***Average financial aid package:*** $50,844 (excluding resources awarded to replace EFC).

UNDERGRADUATE FINANCIAL AID (Fall 2019, est.) 806 applied for aid; of those 97% were deemed to have need. 100% of undergraduates with need received aid; of those 100% had need fully met. ***Average percent of need met:*** 100% (excluding resources awarded to replace EFC). ***Average financial aid package:*** $51,099 (excluding resources awarded to replace EFC).

GIFT AID (NEED-BASED) *Total amount:* $36,949,765 (4% federal, 96% institutional). ***Receiving aid:*** Freshmen: 41% (205); all full-time undergraduates: 43% (785). ***Average award:*** Freshmen: $47,569; Undergraduates: $47,069. ***Scholarships, grants, and awards:*** Federal Pell, FSEOG, state, private, college/university gift aid from institutional funds.

GIFT AID (NON-NEED-BASED) *Total amount:* $631,117 (100% external sources). ***Tuition waivers:*** Full or partial for employees or children of employees.

LOANS *Student loans:* $4,363,322 (40% need-based, 60% non-need-based). 33% of past graduating class borrowed through all loan programs. *Average indebtedness per student:* $23,383. ***Average need-based loan:*** Freshmen: $2169. Undergraduates: $2935. ***Parent loans:*** $1,999,851 (100% non-need-based). ***Programs:*** Federal Direct (Subsidized and Unsubsidized Stafford, PLUS).

WORK-STUDY *Federal work-study:* Total amount: $778,879; jobs available. ***State or other work-study/employment:*** Total amount: $625,573 (100% need-based). Part-time jobs available.

APPLYING FOR FINANCIAL AID *Required financial aid forms:* FAFSA, CSS Financial Aid PROFILE, noncustodial (divorced/separated) parent's statement. ***Financial aid deadline:*** 1/1. ***Notification date:*** 4/1. Students must reply by 5/1.

CONTACT Ms. Wendy G. Glass, Director of Student Financial Services, Bates College, 44 Mountain Avenue, Lewiston, ME 04240, 207-786-6096 or toll-free 855-228-3755. *Fax:* 207-786-8350. *E-mail:* wglass@bates.edu.
Website: http://www.bates.edu/.

BAYAMÓN CENTRAL UNIVERSITY

Bayamón, PR

Tuition & fees: $6260 **Average undergraduate aid package: N/A**

ABOUT THE INSTITUTION Independent Roman Catholic, coed. ***Awards:*** certificates, associate, bachelor's, and master's degrees. 38 undergraduate majors. ***Total enrollment:*** 1,286. Undergraduates: 1,077. Freshmen: 166. Federal methodology is used as a basis for awarding need-based institutional aid.

UNDERGRADUATE EXPENSES for 2020–2021 *Application fee:* $25. ***Comprehensive fee:*** $11,984 includes full-time tuition ($5290), mandatory fees ($970), and room and board ($5724). ***College room only:*** $4500.

GIFT AID (NEED-BASED) *Scholarships, grants, and awards:* Federal Pell, FSEOG, state, college/university gift aid from institutional funds.

GIFT AID (NON-NEED-BASED) *ROTC:* Army cooperative, Air Force cooperative.

LOANS *Programs:* Federal Direct (Subsidized and Unsubsidized Stafford).

WORK-STUDY Federal work-study jobs available.

APPLYING FOR FINANCIAL AID *Required financial aid forms:* FAFSA, institution's own form. ***Financial aid deadline (priority):*** 4/15. ***Notification date:*** 7/15. Students must reply by 8/15.

CONTACT Edna Ortiz, Financial Aid Director, Bayamón Central University, PO Box 1725, Bayamon, PR 00960-1725, 787-786-3030 Ext. 2115. *Fax:* 787-785-4365. *Website:* http://www.ucb.edu.pr/.

BAYLOR UNIVERSITY

Waco, TX

Tuition & fees: $49,246 | **Average undergraduate aid package: $32,093**

ABOUT THE INSTITUTION Independent Baptist, coed. ***Awards:*** certificates, bachelor's, master's, and doctoral degrees. 125 undergraduate majors. ***Total enrollment:*** 18,033. Undergraduates: 14,108. Freshmen: 3,307. Federal methodology is used as a basis for awarding need-based institutional aid.

UNDERGRADUATE EXPENSES for 2020–2021 ***Comprehensive fee:*** $62,520 includes full-time tuition ($44,544), mandatory fees ($4702), and room and board ($13,274). ***College room only:*** $7200. Room and board charges vary according to board plan, housing facility, and location. ***Part-time tuition:*** $1856 per semester hour. ***Part-time fees:*** $196 per semester hour.

FRESHMAN FINANCIAL AID (Fall 2019, est.) 2540 applied for aid; of those 71% were deemed to have need. 100% of freshmen with need received aid; of those 22% had need fully met. ***Average percent of need met:*** 68% (excluding resources awarded to replace EFC). ***Average financial aid package:*** $31,871 (excluding resources awarded to replace EFC). 39% of all full-time freshmen had no need and received non-need-based gift aid.

UNDERGRADUATE FINANCIAL AID (Fall 2019, est.) 8,772 applied for aid; of those 82% were deemed to have need. 100% of undergraduates with need received aid; of those 16% had need fully met. ***Average percent of need met:*** 66% (excluding resources awarded to replace EFC). ***Average financial aid package:*** $32,093 (excluding resources awarded to replace EFC). 38% of all full-time undergraduates had no need and received non-need-based gift aid.

GIFT AID (NEED-BASED) ***Receiving aid:*** Freshmen: 59% (1,954); all full-time undergraduates: 50% (6,943). ***Average award:*** Freshmen: $26,522; Undergraduates: $26,384. ***Scholarships, grants, and awards:*** Federal Pell, FSEOG, state, college/university gift aid from institutional funds.

GIFT AID (NON-NEED-BASED) ***Receiving aid:*** Freshmen: 52% (1,730). Undergraduates: 49% (6,706). ***Average award:*** Freshmen: $18,255. Undergraduates: $16,890. ***Scholarships, grants, and awards by category:*** *Academic interests/achievement:* 13,223 awards ($169,802,828 total): business, communication, computer science, education, engineering/technologies, English, foreign languages, general academic interests/achievements, health fields, home economics, humanities, international studies, mathematics, military science, physical sciences, premedicine, religion/biblical studies, social sciences. *Creative arts/performance:* 389 awards ($2,490,241 total): applied art and design, cinema/film/broadcasting, debating, journalism/publications, music, theater/drama. *Special achievements/activities:* 516 awards ($3,070,787 total): community service, leadership, religious involvement. *Special characteristics:* 246 awards ($7,820,868 total): children of faculty/staff, veterans. ***Tuition waivers:*** Full or partial for employees or children of employees. ***ROTC:*** Army, Air Force.

LOANS ***Student loans:*** 51% of past graduating class borrowed through all loan programs. *Average indebtedness per student:* $49,610. ***Average need-based loan:*** Freshmen: $2435. Undergraduates: $3300. ***Programs:*** Federal Direct (Subsidized and Unsubsidized Stafford, PLUS), Perkins, Federal Nursing, state, private loans.

WORK-STUDY ***Federal work-study:*** 4,740 jobs averaging $2928. ***State or other work-study/employment:*** Part-time jobs available.

APPLYING FOR FINANCIAL AID ***Required financial aid forms:*** FAFSA, State Residency Affirmation (TX residents only). ***Notification date:*** Continuous. Students must reply within 2 weeks of notification.

CONTACT Mrs. Lisa Martin, Student Financial Aid, Baylor University, PO Box 97028, Waco, TX 76798-7028, 254-710-2611 or toll-free 800-BAYLORU. *Fax:* 254-710-2695. *E-mail:* finaidtech@baylor.edu. *Website:* http://www.baylor.edu/.

BAY PATH UNIVERSITY

Longmeadow, MA

Tuition & fees: N/R | **Average undergraduate aid package: $30,111**

ABOUT THE INSTITUTION Independent, undergraduate: women only; graduate: coed. ***Awards:*** certificates, associate, bachelor's, master's, and doctoral degrees. 30 undergraduate majors. Both federal and institutional methodology are used as a basis for awarding need-based institutional aid.

FRESHMAN FINANCIAL AID (Fall 2019, est.) 129 applied for aid; of those 95% were deemed to have need. 98% of freshmen with need received aid; of those 7% had need fully met. ***Average percent of need met:*** 77% (excluding resources awarded to replace EFC). ***Average financial aid package:*** $33,942 (excluding resources awarded to replace EFC). 7% of all full-time freshmen had no need and received non-need-based gift aid.

UNDERGRADUATE FINANCIAL AID (Fall 2019, est.) 559 applied for aid; of those 95% were deemed to have need. 100% of undergraduates with need received aid; of those 8% had need fully met. ***Average percent of need met:*** 75% (excluding resources awarded to replace EFC). ***Average financial aid package:*** $30,111 (excluding resources awarded to replace EFC). 8% of all full-time undergraduates had no need and received non-need-based gift aid.

GIFT AID (NEED-BASED) ***Total amount:*** $13,251,127 (15% federal, 3% state, 80% institutional, 2% external sources). ***Receiving aid:*** Freshmen: 92% (120); all full-time undergraduates: 91% (530). ***Average award:*** Freshmen: $29,313; Undergraduates: $25,006. ***Scholarships, grants, and awards:*** Federal Pell, FSEOG, state, private, college/university gift aid from institutional funds.

GIFT AID (NON-NEED-BASED) ***Total amount:*** $950,096 (99% institutional, 1% external sources). ***Receiving aid:*** Freshmen: 6% (8). Undergraduates: 5% (32). ***Average award:*** Freshmen: $18,052. Undergraduates: $14,626. ***Scholarships, grants, and awards by category:*** *Academic interests/achievement:* general academic interests/achievements. *Special characteristics:* adult students, children of faculty/staff, children with a deceased or disabled parent, general special characteristics, international students, siblings of current students. ***ROTC:*** Army cooperative, Air Force cooperative.

LOANS ***Student loans:*** $5,186,455 (79% need-based, 21% non-need-based). 88% of past graduating class borrowed through all loan programs. *Average indebtedness per student:* $40,384. ***Average need-based loan:*** Freshmen: $3277. Undergraduates: $4390. ***Parent loans:*** $1,790,309 (62% need-based, 38% non-need-based). ***Programs:*** Federal Direct (Subsidized and Unsubsidized Stafford, PLUS).

WORK-STUDY ***Federal work-study:*** Total amount: $477,525; jobs available. ***State or other work-study/employment:*** Total amount: $200,000 (100% non-need-based). Part-time jobs available.

APPLYING FOR FINANCIAL AID ***Required financial aid form:*** FAFSA. ***Financial aid deadline (priority):*** 10/1. ***Notification date:*** 1/15. Students must reply within 2 weeks of notification.

CONTACT Stephanie King, Director of Student Financial Services, Bay Path University, 588 Longmeadow Street, Longmeadow, MA 01106-2292, 413-565-1345 or toll-free 800-782-7284 Ext.1331. *Fax:* 413-565-1101. *E-mail:* sking@baypath.edu. *Website:* http://www.baypath.edu/.

BEACON COLLEGE

Leesburg, FL

Tuition & fees: $42,900 | **Average undergraduate aid package: $15,496**

ABOUT THE INSTITUTION Independent, coed. ***Awards:*** bachelor's degrees. 8 undergraduate majors. ***Total enrollment:*** 416. Undergraduates: 416. Freshmen: 98. Both federal and institutional methodology are used as a basis for awarding need-based institutional aid.

UNDERGRADUATE EXPENSES for 2020–2021 ***Application fee:*** $50. ***Comprehensive fee:*** $55,470 includes full-time tuition ($42,600), mandatory fees ($300), and room and board ($12,570). ***College room only:*** $7590. Full-time tuition and fees vary according to course load. Room and board charges vary according to board plan and housing facility. ***Part-time tuition:*** $1420 per credit hour. ***Part-time fees:*** $300 per year. Part-time tuition and fees vary according to course load.

FRESHMAN FINANCIAL AID (Fall 2018) 75 applied for aid; of those 76% were deemed to have need. 100% of freshmen with need received aid. ***Average financial aid package:*** $20,834 (excluding resources awarded to replace EFC). 8% of all full-time freshmen had no need and received non-need-based gift aid.

UNDERGRADUATE FINANCIAL AID (Fall 2018) 359 applied for aid; of those 90% were deemed to have need. 100% of undergraduates with need received aid. ***Average financial aid package:*** $15,496 (excluding resources awarded to replace EFC). 3% of all full-time undergraduates had no need and received non-need-based gift aid.

GIFT AID (NEED-BASED) ***Total amount:*** $1,189,946 (45% federal, 4% state, 50% institutional, 1% external sources). ***Receiving aid:*** Freshmen: 64% (57); all full-time undergraduates: 72% (289). ***Average award:*** Freshmen: $8500; Undergraduates: $5000. ***Scholarships, grants, and awards:*** Federal Pell, FSEOG, state, private, college/university gift aid from institutional funds.

GIFT AID (NON-NEED-BASED) ***Total amount:*** $590,817 (9% state, 91% institutional). ***Receiving aid:*** Freshmen: 15% (13). Undergraduates: 22% (87). ***Average award:*** Freshmen: $8000. Undergraduates: $6000. ***Tuition waivers:*** Full or partial for employees or children of employees.

LOANS ***Student loans:*** $459,023 (100% need-based). 60% of past graduating class borrowed through all loan programs. *Average indebtedness per student:* $27,000. ***Average need-based loan:*** Freshmen: $6500. Undergraduates: $3783. ***Parent loans:*** $2,498,094 (100% non-need-based). ***Programs:*** Federal Direct (Subsidized and Unsubsidized Stafford, PLUS).

WORK-STUDY ***Federal work-study:*** Total amount: $53,000; 53,000 jobs averaging $53,000. ***State or other work-study/employment:*** Total amount: $10,000 (100% need-based). 10,000 part-time jobs averaging $9000.

APPLYING FOR FINANCIAL AID ***Required financial aid forms:*** FAFSA, state aid form. ***Financial aid deadline (priority):*** 5/1. ***Notification date:*** 5/1. Students must reply within 2 weeks of notification.

CONTACT Mrs. Stephanie Knight, Director of Financial Aid, Beacon College, 105 East Main Street, Leesburg, FL 34788, 352-638-9733. *Fax:* 800-360-1974. *E-mail:* financialaid@beaconcollege.edu.
Website: http://www.beaconcollege.edu/.

BECKER COLLEGE
Worcester, MA

Tuition & fees: $40,150	Average undergraduate aid package: $21,586

ABOUT THE INSTITUTION Independent, coed. ***Awards:*** certificates, associate, bachelor's, and master's degrees (also includes Leicester, MA small town campus). 27 undergraduate majors. ***Total enrollment:*** 1,698. Undergraduates: 1,672. Freshmen: 259. Federal methodology is used as a basis for awarding need-based institutional aid.

UNDERGRADUATE EXPENSES for 2020–2021 ***Comprehensive fee:*** $53,950 includes full-time tuition ($36,300), mandatory fees ($3850), and room and board ($13,800). Full-time tuition and fees vary according to class time, course load, and program. Room and board charges vary according to housing facility. ***Part-time tuition:*** $1515 per credit hour. Part-time tuition and fees vary according to class time, course load, and program.

FRESHMAN FINANCIAL AID (Fall 2018) 278 applied for aid; of those 76% were deemed to have need. 100% of freshmen with need received aid; of those 1% had need fully met. ***Average percent of need met:*** 58% (excluding resources awarded to replace EFC). ***Average financial aid package:*** $22,697 (excluding resources awarded to replace EFC). 31% of all full-time freshmen had no need and received non-need-based gift aid.

UNDERGRADUATE FINANCIAL AID (Fall 2018) 1,297 applied for aid; of those 77% were deemed to have need. 100% of undergraduates with need received aid; of those 20% had need fully met. ***Average percent of need met:*** 55% (excluding resources awarded to replace EFC). ***Average financial aid package:*** $21,586 (excluding resources awarded to replace EFC). 11% of all full-time undergraduates had no need and received non-need-based gift aid.

GIFT AID (NEED-BASED) ***Total amount:*** $26,689,775 (12% federal, 3% state, 84% institutional, 1% external sources). ***Receiving aid:*** Freshmen: 69% (211); all full-time undergraduates: 66% (974). ***Average award:*** Freshmen: $19,517; Undergraduates: $17,856. ***Scholarships, grants, and awards:*** Federal Pell, FSEOG, state, private, college/university gift aid from institutional funds.

GIFT AID (NON-NEED-BASED) ***Total amount:*** $3,584,381 (99% institutional, 1% external sources). ***Receiving aid:*** Undergraduates: 6% (94). ***Average award:*** Freshmen: $17,534. Undergraduates: $14,481. ***Scholarships, grants, and awards by category:*** *Academic interests/achievement:* general academic interests/achievements. *Special characteristics:* children of faculty/staff, siblings of current students. ***Tuition waivers:*** Full or partial for employees or children of employees. ***ROTC:*** Army cooperative, Naval cooperative, Air Force cooperative.

LOANS ***Student loans:*** $16,940,404 (94% need-based, 6% non-need-based). ***Average need-based loan:*** Freshmen: $3346. Undergraduates: $4135. ***Parent loans:*** $9,491,467 (96% need-based, 4% non-need-based). ***Programs:*** Federal Direct (Subsidized and Unsubsidized Stafford, PLUS), state.

WORK-STUDY ***Federal work-study:*** Total amount: $227,257; jobs available.

APPLYING FOR FINANCIAL AID ***Required financial aid form:*** FAFSA. ***Financial aid deadline (priority):*** 1/15. ***Notification date:*** Continuous beginning 12/15.

CONTACT Mr. Allen Cowett, Director of Financial Aid, Becker College, 61 Sever Street, Worcester, MA 01615-0071, 508-373-9430 or toll-free 877-5BECKER. *Fax:* 508-890-1511. *E-mail:* financialaid@becker.edu.
Website: http://www.becker.edu/.

BE'ER YAAKOV TALMUDIC SEMINARY
Spring Valley, NY

CONTACT Financial Aid Office, Be'er Yaakov Talmudic Seminary, 12 Jefferson Avenue, Spring Valley, NY 10977, 845-406-9699.

BEIS MEDRASH HEICHAL DOVID
Far Rockaway, NY

CONTACT Financial Aid Office, Beis Medrash Heichal Dovid, 257 Beach 17th Street, Far Rockaway, NY 11691, 718-868-2300.

BELHAVEN UNIVERSITY
Jackson, MS

Tuition & fees: $27,025	Average undergraduate aid package: $18,628

ABOUT THE INSTITUTION Independent Presbyterian, coed. ***Awards:*** certificates, associate, bachelor's, master's, and doctoral degrees. 38 undergraduate majors. ***Total enrollment:*** 4,600. Undergraduates: 2,370. Freshmen: 198. Federal methodology is used as a basis for awarding need-based institutional aid.

UNDERGRADUATE EXPENSES for 2020–2021 ***Application fee:*** $25. ***Comprehensive fee:*** $35,825 includes full-time tuition ($26,650), mandatory fees ($375), and room and board ($8800). Full-time tuition and fees vary according to location and program. Room and board charges vary according to housing facility. ***Part-time tuition:*** $485 per credit hour. ***Part-time fees:*** $25 per credit hour. Part-time tuition and fees vary according to course load, location, and program.

FRESHMAN FINANCIAL AID (Fall 2018) 165 applied for aid; of those 79% were deemed to have need. 100% of freshmen with need received aid; of those 13% had need fully met. ***Average percent of need met:*** 69% (excluding resources awarded to replace EFC). ***Average financial aid package:*** $20,820 (excluding resources awarded to replace EFC). 25% of all full-time freshmen had no need and received non-need-based gift aid.

UNDERGRADUATE FINANCIAL AID (Fall 2018) 893 applied for aid; of those 87% were deemed to have need. 100% of undergraduates with need received aid; of those 11% had need fully met. ***Average percent of need met:*** 65% (excluding resources awarded to replace EFC). ***Average financial aid package:*** $18,628 (excluding resources awarded to replace EFC). 20% of all full-time undergraduates had no need and received non-need-based gift aid.

GIFT AID (NEED-BASED) ***Receiving aid:*** Freshmen: 75% (130); all full-time undergraduates: 73% (743). ***Average award:*** Freshmen: $16,730; Undergraduates: $13,913. ***Scholarships, grants, and awards:*** Federal Pell, FSEOG, state, private, college/university gift aid from institutional funds.

GIFT AID (NON-NEED-BASED) ***Receiving aid:*** Freshmen: 75% (130). Undergraduates: 63% (645). ***Average award:*** Freshmen: $14,038. Undergraduates:

$12,541. ***Scholarships, grants, and awards by category:*** *Academic interests/achievement:* biological sciences, business, communication, education, English, foreign languages, general academic interests/achievements, humanities, international studies, mathematics, premedicine, religion/biblical studies, social sciences. *Creative arts/performance:* applied art and design, art/fine arts, cinema/film/broadcasting, creative writing, dance, general creative arts/performance, journalism/publications, music, performing arts, theater/drama. *Special achievements/activities:* cheerleading/drum major, general special achievements/activities, junior miss, leadership. *Special characteristics:* children and siblings of alumni, children of faculty/staff, general special characteristics, international students, local/state students, religious affiliation, siblings of current students, veterans. ***Tuition waivers:*** Full or partial for employees or children of employees. ***ROTC:*** Army cooperative, Air Force cooperative.

LOANS *Average need-based loan:* Freshmen: $3209. Undergraduates: $4317. ***Programs:*** Federal Direct (Subsidized and Unsubsidized Stafford, PLUS), Perkins, state.

WORK-STUDY Federal work-study jobs available. ***State or other work-study/employment:*** Part-time jobs available.

APPLYING FOR FINANCIAL AID *Required financial aid form:* FAFSA. ***Financial aid deadline:*** Continuous. ***Notification date:*** Continuous.

CONTACT Mrs. Debbi Braswell, Director of Financial Services, Belhaven University, 1500 Peachtree Street, Box 159, Jackson, MS 39202-1789, 601-968-5933 or toll-free 800-960-5940. *E-mail:* dbraswell@belhaven.edu.
Website: http://www.belhaven.edu/.

BELLARMINE UNIVERSITY

Louisville, KY

Tuition & fees: $42,430	Average undergraduate aid package: $34,671

ABOUT THE INSTITUTION Independent Roman Catholic, coed. ***Awards:*** certificates, bachelor's, master's, and doctoral degrees. 46 undergraduate majors. ***Total enrollment:*** 3,369. Undergraduates: 2,552. Freshmen: 618. Both federal and institutional methodology are used as a basis for awarding need-based institutional aid.

UNDERGRADUATE EXPENSES for 2019–2020 *Application fee:* $25. ***One-time required fee:*** $400. ***Comprehensive fee:*** $51,850 includes full-time tuition ($40,880), mandatory fees ($1550), and room and board ($9420). ***College room only:*** $4800. ***Part-time tuition:*** $950 per credit hour.

FRESHMAN FINANCIAL AID (Fall 2019, est.) 601 applied for aid; of those 86% were deemed to have need. 100% of freshmen with need received aid; of those 32% had need fully met. ***Average percent of need met:*** 82% (excluding resources awarded to replace EFC). ***Average financial aid package:*** $35,461 (excluding resources awarded to replace EFC). 16% of all full-time freshmen had no need and received non-need-based gift aid.

UNDERGRADUATE FINANCIAL AID (Fall 2019, est.) 2,162 applied for aid; of those 87% were deemed to have need. 96% of undergraduates with need received aid; of those 29% had need fully met. ***Average percent of need met:*** 80% (excluding resources awarded to replace EFC). ***Average financial aid package:*** $34,671 (excluding resources awarded to replace EFC). 19% of all full-time undergraduates had no need and received non-need-based gift aid.

GIFT AID (NEED-BASED) *Total amount:* $52,369,675 (6% federal, 11% state, 81% institutional, 2% external sources). ***Receiving aid:*** Freshmen: 84% (518); all full-time undergraduates: 76% (1,817). ***Average award:*** Freshmen: $27,400; Undergraduates: $26,705. ***Scholarships, grants, and awards:*** Federal Pell, FSEOG, state, private, college/university gift aid from institutional funds.

GIFT AID (NON-NEED-BASED) *Total amount:* $15,766,325 (6% state, 91% institutional, 3% external sources). ***Receiving aid:*** Freshmen: 35% (213). Undergraduates: 28% (676). ***Average award:*** Freshmen: $28,408. Undergraduates: $25,373. ***Scholarships, grants, and awards by category:*** *Academic interests/achievement:* biological sciences, business, education, general academic interests/achievements, physical sciences. *Creative arts/performance:* applied art and design, music. *Special achievements/activities:* cheerleading/drum major, community service, general special achievements/activities, leadership, religious involvement. *Special characteristics:* adult students, children and siblings of alumni, children of faculty/staff, ethnic background, international students, local/state students, members of minority groups, out-of-state students, previous college experience, religious affiliation. ***Tuition waivers:*** Full or partial for employees or children of employees. ***ROTC:*** Army cooperative, Air Force cooperative.

LOANS *Student loans:* $13,978,785 (71% need-based, 29% non-need-based). 69% of past graduating class borrowed through all loan programs. *Average indebtedness per student:* $30,850. ***Average need-based loan:*** Freshmen: $3202. Undergraduates: $4165. ***Parent loans:*** $2,884,577 (51% need-based, 49% non-need-based). ***Programs:*** Federal Direct (Subsidized and Unsubsidized Stafford, PLUS), college/university.

WORK-STUDY *Federal work-study:* Total amount: $587,207; jobs available. ***State or other work-study/employment:*** Total amount: $158,541 (53% need-based, 47% non-need-based). Part-time jobs available.

ATHLETIC AWARDS Total amount: $2,992,352 (44% need-based, 56% non-need-based).

APPLYING FOR FINANCIAL AID *Required financial aid form:* FAFSA. ***Financial aid deadline (priority):*** 11/1. ***Notification date:*** 1/31. Students must reply by 5/1.

CONTACT Ms. Heather Boutell, Director of Financial Aid, Bellarmine University, 2001 Newburg Road, Louisville, KY 40205-0671, 502-272-7300 or toll-free 800-274-4723 Ext.8131. *Fax:* 502-272-8486. *E-mail:* hboutell@bellarmine.edu.
Website: http://www.bellarmine.edu/.

BELLEVUE UNIVERSITY

Bellevue, NE

CONTACT Ms. Janet Yale, Director of Financial Aid, Bellevue University, 1000 Galvin Road South, Bellevue, NE 68005, 402-293-2000 or toll-free 800-756-7920. *Fax:* 402-557-5425.
Website: http://www.bellevue.edu/.

BELLIN COLLEGE

Green Bay, WI

CONTACT Mrs. Lena C. Goodman, Director of Financial Aid, Bellin College, 3201 Eaton Road, Green Bay, WI 54311, 920-433-6638 or toll-free 800-236-8707. *Fax:* 920-433-1922. *E-mail:* lena.goodman@bellincollege.edu.
Website: http://www.bellincollege.edu/.

BELMONT ABBEY COLLEGE

Belmont, NC

Tuition & fees: $18,500	Average undergraduate aid package: $13,565

ABOUT THE INSTITUTION Independent Roman Catholic, coed. ***Awards:*** bachelor's degrees. 21 undergraduate majors. ***Total enrollment:*** 1,507. Undergraduates: 1,507. Freshmen: 368. Federal methodology is used as a basis for awarding need-based institutional aid.

UNDERGRADUATE EXPENSES for 2020–2021 *Comprehensive fee:* $28,890 includes full-time tuition ($18,500) and room and board ($10,390). ***College room only:*** $5826. Full-time tuition and fees vary according to course load. Room and board charges vary according to board plan and housing facility. ***Part-time tuition:*** $617 per credit hour. Part-time tuition and fees vary according to course load. ***Payment plan:*** Guaranteed tuition.

FRESHMAN FINANCIAL AID (Fall 2019, est.) 314 applied for aid; of those 76% were deemed to have need. 100% of freshmen with need received aid; of those 15% had need fully met. ***Average percent of need met:*** 58% (excluding resources awarded to replace EFC). ***Average financial aid package:*** $14,014 (excluding resources awarded to replace EFC). 34% of all full-time freshmen had no need and received non-need-based gift aid.

UNDERGRADUATE FINANCIAL AID (Fall 2019, est.) 1,105 applied for aid; of those 81% were deemed to have need. 99% of undergraduates with need received aid; of those 12% had need fully met. ***Average percent of need met:*** 56% (excluding resources awarded to replace EFC). ***Average financial aid package:*** $13,565

(excluding resources awarded to replace EFC). 32% of all full-time undergraduates had no need and received non-need-based gift aid.

GIFT AID (NEED-BASED) ***Total amount:*** $7,905,142 (29% federal, 23% state, 37% institutional, 11% external sources). ***Receiving aid:*** Freshmen: 65% (238); all full-time undergraduates: 62% (864). ***Average award:*** Freshmen: $11,012; Undergraduates: $10,261. ***Scholarships, grants, and awards:*** Federal Pell, FSEOG, state, private, college/university gift aid from institutional funds.

GIFT AID (NON-NEED-BASED) ***Total amount:*** $2,738,440 (89% institutional, 11% external sources). ***Receiving aid:*** Freshmen: 5% (20). Undergraduates: 4% (57). ***Average award:*** Freshmen: $4819. Undergraduates: $5252. ***Scholarships, grants, and awards by category:*** *Academic interests/achievement:* business, education, general academic interests/achievements, humanities. *Creative arts/performance:* theater/drama. *Special achievements/activities:* cheerleading/drum major, religious involvement. *Special characteristics:* children of faculty/staff. ***Tuition waivers:*** Full or partial for employees or children of employees. ***ROTC:*** Army cooperative, Air Force cooperative.

LOANS ***Student loans:*** $6,787,276 (70% need-based, 30% non-need-based). ***Average need-based loan:*** Freshmen: $3767. Undergraduates: $4349. ***Parent loans:*** $4,222,851 (33% need-based, 67% non-need-based). ***Programs:*** Federal Direct (Subsidized and Unsubsidized Stafford, PLUS).

WORK-STUDY ***Federal work-study:*** Total amount: $140,942; jobs available.

ATHLETIC AWARDS Total amount: $2,226,699 (42% need-based, 58% non-need-based).

APPLYING FOR FINANCIAL AID ***Required financial aid forms:*** FAFSA, state aid form. ***Financial aid deadline (priority):*** 4/1. ***Notification date:*** Continuous beginning 3/15. Students must reply within 2 weeks of notification.

CONTACT Ms. Julie Hodge, Associate Director of Financial Aid, Belmont Abbey College, 100 Belmont Mt. Holly Road, Belmont, NC 28012-1802, 704-461-7000 or toll-free 888-BAC-0110. *Fax:* 704-461-6727. *E-mail:* juliehodge@bac.edu.
Website: http://www.belmontabbeycollege.edu/.

BELMONT UNIVERSITY

Nashville, TN

Tuition & fees: $35,650	Average undergraduate aid package: $22,526

ABOUT THE INSTITUTION Independent Christian, coed. ***Awards:*** certificates, bachelor's, master's, and doctoral degrees. 89 undergraduate majors. ***Total enrollment:*** 8,428. Undergraduates: 6,808. Freshmen: 1,684. Federal methodology is used as a basis for awarding need-based institutional aid.

UNDERGRADUATE EXPENSES for 2019–2020 ***Application fee:*** $50. ***Comprehensive fee:*** $48,170 includes full-time tuition ($34,000), mandatory fees ($1650), and room and board ($12,520). ***College room only:*** $6860. Full-time tuition and fees vary according to course load and location. Room and board charges vary according to board plan and housing facility. ***Part-time tuition:*** $1280 per credit hour. Part-time tuition and fees vary according to course load and location.

FRESHMAN FINANCIAL AID (Fall 2019, est.) 1410 applied for aid; of those 70% were deemed to have need. 99% of freshmen with need received aid; of those 15% had need fully met. ***Average percent of need met:*** 76% (excluding resources awarded to replace EFC). ***Average financial aid package:*** $28,487 (excluding resources awarded to replace EFC). 30% of all full-time freshmen had no need and received non-need-based gift aid.

UNDERGRADUATE FINANCIAL AID (Fall 2019, est.) 4,605 applied for aid; of those 75% were deemed to have need. 99% of undergraduates with need received aid; of those 11% had need fully met. ***Average percent of need met:*** 60% (excluding resources awarded to replace EFC). ***Average financial aid package:*** $22,526 (excluding resources awarded to replace EFC). 28% of all full-time undergraduates had no need and received non-need-based gift aid.

GIFT AID (NEED-BASED) ***Total amount:*** $61,076,669 (10% federal, 7% state, 83% institutional). ***Receiving aid:*** Freshmen: 57% (957); all full-time undergraduates: 48% (3,149). ***Average award:*** Freshmen: $25,585; Undergraduates: $18,960. ***Scholarships, grants, and awards:*** Federal Pell, FSEOG, state, private, college/university gift aid from institutional funds.

GIFT AID (NON-NEED-BASED) ***Total amount:*** $18,242,175 (7% state, 93% institutional). ***Receiving aid:*** Freshmen: 9% (148). Undergraduates: 5% (358). ***Average award:*** Freshmen: $9027. Undergraduates: $9793. ***Scholarships, grants, and awards by category:*** *Academic interests/achievement:* biological sciences, business, general academic interests/achievements, home economics, religion/biblical studies, social sciences. *Creative arts/performance:* applied art and design, art/fine arts, cinema/film/broadcasting, creative writing, dance, general creative arts/performance, journalism/publications, music, performing arts, theater/drama. *Special achievements/activities:* cheerleading/drum major, community service, general special achievements/activities, leadership, religious involvement. *Special characteristics:* children and siblings of alumni, children of faculty/staff, local/state students, members of minority groups, siblings of current students, veterans. ***Tuition waivers:*** Full or partial for employees or children of employees, senior citizens. ***ROTC:*** Army cooperative, Naval cooperative, Air Force cooperative.

LOANS ***Student loans:*** $29,215,161 (82% need-based, 18% non-need-based). 50% of past graduating class borrowed through all loan programs. *Average indebtedness per student:* $29,702. ***Average need-based loan:*** Freshmen: $2486. Undergraduates: $3708. ***Parent loans:*** $36,666,438 (81% need-based, 19% non-need-based). ***Programs:*** Federal Direct (Subsidized and Unsubsidized Stafford, PLUS), Perkins.

WORK-STUDY ***Federal work-study:*** Total amount: $2,871,588; jobs available.

ATHLETIC AWARDS Total amount: $5,697,954 (33% need-based, 67% non-need-based).

APPLYING FOR FINANCIAL AID ***Required financial aid form:*** FAFSA. ***Financial aid deadline (priority):*** 3/1. ***Notification date:*** Continuous beginning 3/15. Students must reply by 5/1 or within 2 weeks of notification.

CONTACT Mrs. Pat Smedley, Director of Student Financial Services, Belmont University, 1900 Belmont Boulevard, Nashville, TN 37212-3757, 615-460-6403. *E-mail:* pat.smedley@belmont.edu.
Website: http://www.belmont.edu/.

BELOIT COLLEGE

Beloit, WI

Tuition & fees: $53,348	Average undergraduate aid package: $48,229

ABOUT THE INSTITUTION Independent, coed. ***Awards:*** bachelor's degrees. 50 undergraduate majors. ***Total enrollment:*** 1,143. Undergraduates: 1,143. Freshmen: 259. Both federal and institutional methodology are used as a basis for awarding need-based institutional aid.

UNDERGRADUATE EXPENSES for 2020–2021 ***Comprehensive fee:*** $63,036 includes full-time tuition ($52,858), mandatory fees ($490), and room and board ($9688). ***College room only:*** $5518. ***Part-time tuition:*** $1652 per credit hour.

FRESHMAN FINANCIAL AID (Fall 2019, est.) 205 applied for aid; of those 91% were deemed to have need. 100% of freshmen with need received aid; of those 32% had need fully met. ***Average percent of need met:*** 96% (excluding resources awarded to replace EFC). ***Average financial aid package:*** $49,825 (excluding resources awarded to replace EFC). 27% of all full-time freshmen had no need and received non-need-based gift aid.

UNDERGRADUATE FINANCIAL AID (Fall 2019, est.) 725 applied for aid; of those 92% were deemed to have need. 100% of undergraduates with need received aid; of those 31% had need fully met. ***Average percent of need met:*** 95% (excluding resources awarded to replace EFC). ***Average financial aid package:*** $48,229 (excluding resources awarded to replace EFC). 36% of all full-time undergraduates had no need and received non-need-based gift aid.

GIFT AID (NEED-BASED) ***Total amount:*** $24,696,537 (6% federal, 1% state, 92% institutional, 1% external sources). ***Receiving aid:*** Freshmen: 71% (184); all full-time undergraduates: 62% (654). ***Average award:*** Freshmen: $39,493; Undergraduates: $37,603. ***Scholarships, grants, and awards:*** Federal Pell, FSEOG, state, private, college/university gift aid from institutional funds.

GIFT AID (NON-NEED-BASED) ***Total amount:*** $13,364,570 (99% institutional, 1% external sources). ***Receiving aid:*** Freshmen: 34% (87). Undergraduates: 31% (331). ***Average award:*** Freshmen: $36,511. Undergraduates: $31,593. ***Scholarships, grants, and awards by category:*** *Academic interests/achievement:* general academic interests/achievements. *Creative arts/performance:* music. *Special achievements/activities:* community service, general special achievements/activities, leadership.

LOANS ***Student loans:*** $6,933,494 (68% need-based, 32% non-need-based). 61% of past graduating class borrowed through all loan programs. *Average indebtedness per student:* $23,534. ***Average need-based loan:*** Freshmen: $6412. Undergraduates: $7320. ***Parent loans:*** $976,246 (23% need-based, 77% non-need-based). ***Pro-***

grams: Federal Direct (Subsidized and Unsubsidized Stafford, PLUS), Perkins, college/university.

WORK-STUDY *Federal work-study:* Total amount: $835,075; jobs available. ***State or other work-study/employment:*** Total amount: $1,046,285 (7% need-based, 93% non-need-based). Part-time jobs available.

APPLYING FOR FINANCIAL AID *Required financial aid form:* FAFSA. ***Financial aid deadline:*** 3/1. ***Notification date:*** Continuous. Students must reply by 5/1.

CONTACT Ms. Deb Dew, Director of Financial Aid, Beloit College, 700 College Street, Beloit, WI 53511-5596, 608-363-2618 or toll-free 800-9-BELOIT. *Fax:* 608-363-7139. *E-mail:* dewd@beloit.edu.
Website: http://www.beloit.edu/.

BEMIDJI STATE UNIVERSITY

Bemidji, MN

Tuition & fees (area res): $4299	Average undergraduate aid package: $9725

ABOUT THE INSTITUTION State-supported, coed. ***Awards:*** certificates, associate, bachelor's, and master's degrees. 64 undergraduate majors. ***Total enrollment:*** 4,868. Undergraduates: 4,476. Freshmen: 631. Federal methodology is used as a basis for awarding need-based institutional aid.

UNDERGRADUATE EXPENSES for 2020–2021 *Application fee:* $20. ***Tuition, area resident:*** full-time $3929; part-time $274 per credit. ***Tuition, state resident:*** full-time $3929; part-time $274 per credit. ***Tuition, nonresident:*** full-time $3929; part-time $274 per credit. ***Required fees:*** full-time $370. ***College room and board:*** $8660.

FRESHMAN FINANCIAL AID (Fall 2018) 667 applied for aid; of those 68% were deemed to have need. 98% of freshmen with need received aid; of those 7% had need fully met. ***Average percent of need met:*** 56% (excluding resources awarded to replace EFC). ***Average financial aid package:*** $8362 (excluding resources awarded to replace EFC). 13% of all full-time freshmen had no need and received non-need-based gift aid.

UNDERGRADUATE FINANCIAL AID (Fall 2018) 2,684 applied for aid; of those 76% were deemed to have need. 98% of undergraduates with need received aid; of those 17% had need fully met. ***Average percent of need met:*** 60% (excluding resources awarded to replace EFC). ***Average financial aid package:*** $9725 (excluding resources awarded to replace EFC). 18% of all full-time undergraduates had no need and received non-need-based gift aid.

GIFT AID (NEED-BASED) *Total amount:* $11,752,618 (62% federal, 36% state, 2% institutional). ***Receiving aid:*** Freshmen: 42% (310); all full-time undergraduates: 46% (1,508). ***Average award:*** Freshmen: $6033; Undergraduates: $6082. ***Scholarships, grants, and awards:*** Federal Pell, FSEOG, state, private, college/university gift aid from institutional funds.

GIFT AID (NON-NEED-BASED) *Total amount:* $6,592,098 (11% federal, 9% state, 61% institutional, 19% external sources). ***Receiving aid:*** Freshmen: 44% (324). Undergraduates: 41% (1,344). ***Average award:*** Freshmen: $9524. Undergraduates: $10,333. ***Scholarships, grants, and awards by category:*** *Academic interests/achievement:* 965 awards ($1,362,357 total): biological sciences, business, communication, computer science, education, engineering/technologies, English, foreign languages, general academic interests/achievements, home economics, humanities, international studies, mathematics, physical sciences, premedicine, social sciences. *Creative arts/performance:* 77 awards ($157,571 total): applied art and design, art/fine arts, cinema/film/broadcasting, creative writing, general creative arts/performance, journalism/publications, music, performing arts. *Special achievements/activities:* 8 awards ($16,800 total): general special achievements/activities, leadership. *Special characteristics:* 111 awards ($95,950 total): children and siblings of alumni, handicapped students, international students, members of minority groups, out-of-state students, previous college experience.

LOANS *Student loans:* $21,673,393 (36% need-based, 64% non-need-based). ***Average need-based loan:*** Freshmen: $3002. Undergraduates: $3779. ***Parent loans:*** $1,159,034 (100% non-need-based). ***Programs:*** Federal Direct (Subsidized and Unsubsidized Stafford, PLUS), state, Private Loans.

WORK-STUDY *Federal work-study:* Total amount: $391,400; 233 jobs averaging $1680. ***State or other work-study/employment:*** Total amount: $424,593 (100% need-based). 249 part-time jobs averaging $1705.

ATHLETIC AWARDS Total amount: $1,545,687 (100% non-need-based).

APPLYING FOR FINANCIAL AID *Required financial aid form:* FAFSA. ***Financial aid deadline:*** Continuous. ***Notification date:*** Continuous beginning 6/15.

CONTACT Financial Aid Office, Bemidji State University, 1500 Birchmont Drive NE, #14, Bemidji, MN 56601, 218-755-2034 or toll-free 800-475-2001. *Fax:* 218-755-4361. *E-mail:* financialaid@bemidjistate.edu.
Website: http://www.bemidjistate.edu/.

BENEDICT COLLEGE

Columbia, SC

CONTACT Mrs. Bichevia Green, Associate Director of Financial Aid, Benedict College, 1600 Harden Street, Columbia, SC 29204, 803-705-4418 or toll-free 800-868-6598. *Fax:* 803-705-6629. *E-mail:* greenb@benedict.edu.
Website: http://www.benedict.edu/.

BENEDICTINE COLLEGE

Atchison, KS

CONTACT Mr. Tony Tanking, Director of Financial Aid, Benedictine College, 1020 North Second Street, Atchison, KS 66002-1499, 913-360-7484 or toll-free 800-467-5340. *Fax:* 913-367-5462. *E-mail:* ttanking@benedictine.edu.
Website: http://www.benedictine.edu/.

BENEDICTINE UNIVERSITY

Lisle, IL

Comprehensive fee: $32,700	Average undergraduate aid package: $25,511

ABOUT THE INSTITUTION Independent Roman Catholic, coed. ***Awards:*** certificates, bachelor's, master's, and doctoral degrees. 51 undergraduate majors. ***Total enrollment:*** 4,401. Undergraduates: 2,493. Freshmen: 347. Federal methodology is used as a basis for awarding need-based institutional aid.

UNDERGRADUATE EXPENSES for 2020–2021 *Application fee:* $40. ***Comprehensive fee:*** $32,700 includes mandatory fees ($1590) and room and board ($4960). ***College room only:*** $3250. Room and board charges vary according to board plan, housing facility, and location. ***Part-time tuition:*** $1090 per credit hour.

FRESHMAN FINANCIAL AID (Fall 2019, est.) 300 applied for aid; of those 89% were deemed to have need. 100% of freshmen with need received aid. ***Average financial aid package:*** $25,093 (excluding resources awarded to replace EFC). 15% of all full-time freshmen had no need and received non-need-based gift aid.

UNDERGRADUATE FINANCIAL AID (Fall 2019, est.) 1,764 applied for aid; of those 93% were deemed to have need. 99% of undergraduates with need received aid. ***Average financial aid package:*** $25,511 (excluding resources awarded to replace EFC). 19% of all full-time undergraduates had no need and received non-need-based gift aid.

GIFT AID (NEED-BASED) *Total amount:* $11,163,513 (43% federal, 32% state, 25% institutional). ***Receiving aid:*** Freshmen: 53% (182); all full-time undergraduates: 52% (1,111). ***Average award:*** Freshmen: $11,039; Undergraduates: $9674. ***Scholarships, grants, and awards:*** Federal Pell, FSEOG, state, college/university gift aid from institutional funds.

GIFT AID (NON-NEED-BASED) *Total amount:* $26,434,750 (99% institutional, 1% external sources). ***Receiving aid:*** Freshmen: 77% (264). Undergraduates: 71% (1,508). ***Average award:*** Freshmen: $14,325. Undergraduates: $14,352. ***Scholarships, grants, and awards by category:*** *Academic interests/achievement:* general academic interests/achievements. *Creative arts/performance:* music. *Special achievements/activities:* community service, general special achievements/activities, leadership, memberships. *Special characteristics:* children and siblings of alumni, children of faculty/staff, general special characteristics, international students, local/state students, out-of-state students, relatives of clergy, siblings of current students, veterans. ***ROTC:*** Army cooperative.

LOANS ***Student loans:*** $11,586,792 (42% need-based, 58% non-need-based), 73% of past graduating class borrowed through all loan programs. *Average indebtedness per student:* $26,447. ***Average need-based loan:*** Freshmen: $3421. Undergraduates: $4285. ***Parent loans:*** $4,210,482 (100% non-need-based). ***Programs:*** Federal Direct (Subsidized and Unsubsidized Stafford, PLUS).
WORK-STUDY ***Federal work-study:*** Total amount: $456,263; jobs available. ***State or other work-study/employment:*** Part-time jobs available.
ATHLETIC AWARDS Total amount: $2,205,980 (100% non-need-based).
APPLYING FOR FINANCIAL AID ***Required financial aid form:*** FAFSA. ***Financial aid deadline (priority):*** 2/1. ***Notification date:*** Continuous beginning 10/28. Students must reply within 2 weeks of notification.
CONTACT Adrian Gonzalez, Director of Financial Aid, Benedictine University, 5700 College Road, Lisle, IL 60532, 630-829-6415 or toll-free 888-829-6363 (out-of-state). *E-mail:* agonzalez11@ben.edu.
Website: http://www.ben.edu/.

BENNETT COLLEGE

Greensboro, NC

CONTACT Ms. Keisha Ragsdale, Director of Financial Aid, Bennett College, 900 East Washington Street, Greensboro, NC 27401, 336-370-8678 or toll-free 800-413-5323. *Fax:* 336-517-2204. *E-mail:* kragsdale@bennett.edu.
Website: http://www.bennett.edu/.

BENNINGTON COLLEGE

Bennington, VT

Tuition & fees: $58,124	Average undergraduate aid package: $45,551

ABOUT THE INSTITUTION Independent, coed. ***Awards:*** bachelor's and master's degrees. 103 undergraduate majors. ***Total enrollment:*** 830. Undergraduates: 733. Freshmen: 179. Both federal and institutional methodology are used as a basis for awarding need-based institutional aid.
UNDERGRADUATE EXPENSES for 2020–2021 ***One-time required fee:*** $660. ***Comprehensive fee:*** $74,964 includes full-time tuition ($57,350), mandatory fees ($774), and room and board ($16,840). ***College room only:*** $9140. Full-time tuition and fees vary according to degree level. Room and board charges vary according to board plan. ***Part-time tuition:*** $2390 per credit hour.
FRESHMAN FINANCIAL AID (Fall 2018) 191 applied for aid; of those 81% were deemed to have need. 93% of freshmen with need received aid; of those 27% had need fully met. ***Average percent of need met:*** 86% (excluding resources awarded to replace EFC). ***Average financial aid package:*** $47,458 (excluding resources awarded to replace EFC). 21% of all full-time freshmen had no need and received non-need-based gift aid.
UNDERGRADUATE FINANCIAL AID (Fall 2018) 672 applied for aid; of those 71% were deemed to have need. 92% of undergraduates with need received aid; of those 16% had need fully met. ***Average percent of need met:*** 83% (excluding resources awarded to replace EFC). ***Average financial aid package:*** $45,551 (excluding resources awarded to replace EFC). 32% of all full-time undergraduates had no need and received non-need-based gift aid.
GIFT AID (NEED-BASED) ***Total amount:*** $17,736,315 (6% federal, 90% institutional, 4% external sources). ***Receiving aid:*** Freshmen: 72% (143); all full-time undergraduates: 63% (436). ***Average award:*** Freshmen: $44,614; Undergraduates: $41,440. ***Scholarships, grants, and awards:*** Federal Pell, FSEOG, state, private, college/university gift aid from institutional funds.
GIFT AID (NON-NEED-BASED) ***Total amount:*** $7,827,443 (83% institutional, 17% external sources). ***Receiving aid:*** Freshmen: 8% (15). Undergraduates: 6% (40). ***Average award:*** Freshmen: $26,211. Undergraduates: $27,277. ***Scholarships, grants, and awards by category:*** *Academic interests/achievement:* 138 awards ($1,736,780 total): general academic interests/achievements. ***Tuition waivers:*** Full or partial for employees or children of employees.
LOANS ***Student loans:*** $2,769,238 (77% need-based, 23% non-need-based). 61% of past graduating class borrowed through all loan programs. *Average indebtedness per student:* $29,443. ***Average need-based loan:*** Freshmen: $2224. Undergraduates: $3440. ***Parent loans:*** $811,662 (57% need-based, 43% non-need-based). ***Programs:*** Federal Direct (Subsidized and Unsubsidized Stafford, PLUS).
WORK-STUDY ***Federal work-study:*** Total amount: $594,307; 349 jobs averaging $2136. ***State or other work-study/employment:*** Total amount: $227,700 (22% need-based, 78% non-need-based). 122 part-time jobs averaging $2097.
APPLYING FOR FINANCIAL AID ***Required financial aid forms:*** FAFSA, institution's own form, CSS Financial Aid PROFILE, noncustodial (divorced/separated) parent's statement, Noncustodial (Divorced/Separated) Parent's Statement, CSS PROFILE required of early decision app. ***Financial aid deadline:*** 1/3. ***Notification date:*** 3/27. Students must reply by 5/1 or within 4 weeks of notification.
CONTACT Heather Clifford, Director of Financial Aid, Bennington College, One College Drive, Bennington, VT 05201, 802-440-4325 or toll-free 800-833-6845. *Fax:* 802-440-4880. *E-mail:* finaid@bennington.edu.
Website: http://www.bennington.edu/.

BENTLEY UNIVERSITY

Waltham, MA

Tuition & fees: $51,830	Average undergraduate aid package: $39,159

ABOUT THE INSTITUTION Independent, coed. ***Awards:*** certificates, bachelor's, master's, and doctoral degrees. 27 undergraduate majors. ***Total enrollment:*** 5,314. Undergraduates: 4,228. Freshmen: 944. Both federal and institutional methodology are used as a basis for awarding need-based institutional aid.
UNDERGRADUATE EXPENSES for 2019–2020 ***Application fee:*** $75. ***Comprehensive fee:*** $68,790 includes full-time tuition ($50,060), mandatory fees ($1770), and room and board ($16,960). ***College room only:*** $10,290. Room and board charges vary according to board plan and housing facility. Part-time tuition and fees vary according to course load.
FRESHMAN FINANCIAL AID (Fall 2018) 682 applied for aid; of those 67% were deemed to have need. 99% of freshmen with need received aid; of those 29% had need fully met. ***Average percent of need met:*** 89% (excluding resources awarded to replace EFC). ***Average financial aid package:*** $38,082 (excluding resources awarded to replace EFC). 30% of all full-time freshmen had no need and received non-need-based gift aid.
UNDERGRADUATE FINANCIAL AID (Fall 2018) 2,456 applied for aid; of those 73% were deemed to have need. 100% of undergraduates with need received aid; of those 36% had need fully met. ***Average percent of need met:*** 92% (excluding resources awarded to replace EFC). ***Average financial aid package:*** $39,159 (excluding resources awarded to replace EFC). 25% of all full-time undergraduates had no need and received non-need-based gift aid.
GIFT AID (NEED-BASED) ***Receiving aid:*** Freshmen: 44% (447); all full-time undergraduates: 43% (1,764). ***Average award:*** Freshmen: $34,669; Undergraduates: $34,395. ***Scholarships, grants, and awards:*** Federal Pell, FSEOG, state, private, college/university gift aid from institutional funds.
GIFT AID (NON-NEED-BASED) ***Receiving aid:*** Freshmen: 7% (76). Undergraduates: 6% (253). ***Average award:*** Freshmen: $18,366. Undergraduates: $19,768. ***Scholarships, grants, and awards by category:*** *Academic interests/achievement:* 1,922 awards ($38,033,681 total): general academic interests/achievements. *Special achievements/activities:* 160 awards ($1,588,000 total): community service, leadership. *Special characteristics:* 72 awards ($1,488,590 total): international students, members of minority groups. ***Tuition waivers:*** Full or partial for employees or children of employees. ***ROTC:*** Army cooperative, Air Force cooperative.
LOANS ***Student loans:*** 55% of past graduating class borrowed through all loan programs. *Average indebtedness per student:* $35,187. ***Average need-based loan:*** Freshmen: $3503. Undergraduates: $4631. ***Programs:*** Federal Direct (Subsidized and Unsubsidized Stafford, PLUS), state.
WORK-STUDY ***Federal work-study:*** 813 jobs averaging $2181. ***State or other work-study/employment:*** 829 part-time jobs averaging $1807.
APPLYING FOR FINANCIAL AID ***Required financial aid forms:*** FAFSA, CSS Financial Aid PROFILE, noncustodial (divorced/separated) parent's statement, business/farm supplement, Parents and student tax returns (including W-2 and all schedules filed). ***Financial aid deadline:*** 1/7. ***Notification date:*** 4/1.
CONTACT Lauren Sullivan, Director of Financial Assistance, Bentley University, 175 Forest Street, Waltham, MA 02452-4705, 781-891-3441 or toll-free 800-523-2354. *Fax:* 781-891-2448. *E-mail:* finaid@bentley.edu.
Website: http://www.bentley.edu/.

BEREA COLLEGE

Berea, KY

Tuition & fees: N/R	Average undergraduate aid package: $46,997

ABOUT THE INSTITUTION Independent, coed. ***Awards:*** bachelor's degrees. 34 undergraduate majors. ***Total enrollment:*** 1,688. Undergraduates: 1,688. Freshmen: 413. Federal methodology is used as a basis for awarding need-based institutional aid.

UNDERGRADUATE EXPENSES for 2020–2021 Financial aid is provided to all students for tuition costs.

FRESHMAN FINANCIAL AID (Fall 2018) 438 applied for aid; of those 100% were deemed to have need. 100% of freshmen with need received aid; of those 2% had need fully met. ***Average percent of need met:*** 94% (excluding resources awarded to replace EFC). ***Average financial aid package:*** $47,094 (excluding resources awarded to replace EFC).

UNDERGRADUATE FINANCIAL AID (Fall 2018) 1,626 applied for aid; of those 100% were deemed to have need. 100% of undergraduates with need received aid; of those 1% had need fully met. ***Average percent of need met:*** 94% (excluding resources awarded to replace EFC). ***Average financial aid package:*** $46,997 (excluding resources awarded to replace EFC).

GIFT AID (NEED-BASED) ***Total amount:*** $79,707,734 (10% federal, 5% state, 85% institutional). ***Receiving aid:*** Freshmen: 100% (438); all full-time undergraduates: 100% (1,626). ***Average award:*** Freshmen: $45,271; Undergraduates: $44,650. ***Scholarships, grants, and awards:*** Federal Pell, FSEOG, state, private, college/university gift aid from institutional funds.

LOANS ***Student loans:*** $1,032,497 (55% need-based, 45% non-need-based). 51% of past graduating class borrowed through all loan programs. *Average indebtedness per student:* $5517. ***Average need-based loan:*** Freshmen: $638. Undergraduates: $1349. ***Parent loans:*** $700 (100% need-based). ***Programs:*** Federal Direct (Subsidized and Unsubsidized Stafford, PLUS), college/university.

WORK-STUDY ***Federal work-study:*** Total amount: $3,900,718; jobs available. ***State or other work-study/employment:*** Total amount: $935,336 (100% need-based). Part-time jobs available.

APPLYING FOR FINANCIAL AID ***Required financial aid form:*** FAFSA. ***Financial aid deadline:*** 5/1 (priority: 10/31). ***Notification date:*** Continuous beginning 11/15. Students must reply by 5/1.

CONTACT Theresa Lowder, Director of Student Financial Aid Services, Berea College, CPO 2172, Berea, KY 40404, 859-985-3313 or toll-free 800-326-5948. *Fax:* 859-985-3914. *E-mail:* lowdert@berea.edu.
Website: http://www.berea.edu/.

BERGIN UNIVERSITY OF CANINE STUDIES

Rohnert Park, CA

CONTACT Financial Aid Office, Bergin University of Canine Studies, 5860 Labath Avenue, Rohnert Park, CA 94928, 707-545-3647.
Website: http://www.berginu.edu/.

BERKELEY COLLEGE–NEW YORK CITY CAMPUS

New York, NY

CONTACT Office of Financial Aid, Berkeley College–New York City Campus, 3 East 43rd Street, New York, NY 10017, 800-446-5400. *E-mail:* info@berkeleycollege.edu.
Website: http://www.berkeleycollege.edu/.

BERKELEY COLLEGE–WHITE PLAINS CAMPUS

White Plains, NY

CONTACT Office of Financial Aid, Berkeley College–White Plains Campus, 99 Church Street, White Plains, NY 10601, 800-446-5400. *E-mail:* financialaid@berkeleycollege.edu.
Website: http://www.berkeleycollege.edu/.

BERKELEY COLLEGE–WOODLAND PARK CAMPUS

Woodland Park, NJ

CONTACT Office of Financial Aid, Berkeley College–Woodland Park Campus, 44 Rifle Camp Road, Woodland Park, NJ 07424, 800-446-5400. *E-mail:* financialaid@berkeleycollege.edu.
Website: http://www.berkeleycollege.edu/.

BERKLEE COLLEGE OF MUSIC

Boston, MA

Tuition & fees: $47,230	Average undergraduate aid package: $24,330

ABOUT THE INSTITUTION Independent, coed. ***Awards:*** certificates, diplomas, bachelor's, and master's degrees. 13 undergraduate majors. ***Total enrollment:*** 6,999. Undergraduates: 6,439. Freshmen: 1,311. Both federal and institutional methodology are used as a basis for awarding need-based institutional aid.

UNDERGRADUATE EXPENSES for 2020–2021 ***Application fee:*** $150. ***Comprehensive fee:*** $66,060 includes full-time tuition ($45,890), mandatory fees ($1340), and room and board ($18,830). ***Part-time tuition:*** $1670 per credit hour.

FRESHMAN FINANCIAL AID (Fall 2019, est.) 718 applied for aid; of those 80% were deemed to have need. 95% of freshmen with need received aid; of those 10% had need fully met. ***Average percent of need met:*** 64% (excluding resources awarded to replace EFC). ***Average financial aid package:*** $23,876 (excluding resources awarded to replace EFC). 24% of all full-time freshmen had no need and received non-need-based gift aid.

UNDERGRADUATE FINANCIAL AID (Fall 2019, est.) 2,351 applied for aid; of those 84% were deemed to have need. 97% of undergraduates with need received aid; of those 10% had need fully met. ***Average percent of need met:*** 65% (excluding resources awarded to replace EFC). ***Average financial aid package:*** $24,330 (excluding resources awarded to replace EFC). 28% of all full-time undergraduates had no need and received non-need-based gift aid.

GIFT AID (NEED-BASED) ***Receiving aid:*** Freshmen: 21% (261); all full-time undergraduates: 19% (909). ***Average award:*** Freshmen: $8319; Undergraduates: $7229. ***Scholarships, grants, and awards:*** Federal Pell, FSEOG, state, private, college/university gift aid from institutional funds.

GIFT AID (NON-NEED-BASED) ***Receiving aid:*** Freshmen: 27% (328). Undergraduates: 28% (1,340). ***Average award:*** Freshmen: $19,046. Undergraduates: $20,521. ***Scholarships, grants, and awards by category:*** *Academic interests/achievement:* education, engineering/technologies, general academic interests/achievements. *Creative arts/performance:* dance, music, performing arts, theater/drama. ***ROTC:*** Army cooperative.

LOANS ***Student loans:*** 21% of past graduating class borrowed through all loan programs. *Average indebtedness per student:* $43,826. ***Average need-based loan:*** Freshmen: $2574. Undergraduates: $3424. ***Programs:*** Federal Direct (Subsidized and Unsubsidized Stafford, PLUS), Perkins, college/university.

WORK-STUDY Federal work-study jobs available.

APPLYING FOR FINANCIAL AID ***Required financial aid forms:*** FAFSA, CSS Financial Aid PROFILE. ***Financial aid deadline:*** Continuous. ***Notification date:*** Continuous.

CONTACT Office of Student Financial Services, Berklee College of Music, 921 Boylston Street, Boston, MA 02215, 617-747-2274 or toll-free 800-BERKLEE. *Fax:* 617-747-2073. *E-mail:* financialaid@berklee.edu.
Website: http://www.berklee.edu/.

BERRY COLLEGE

Mount Berry, GA

Tuition & fees: $37,246	Average undergraduate aid package: $31,911

ABOUT THE INSTITUTION Independent interdenominational, coed. ***Awards:*** bachelor's and master's degrees. 47 undergraduate majors. ***Total enrollment:*** 2,034. Undergraduates: 1,943. Freshmen: 577. Federal methodology is used as a basis for awarding need-based institutional aid.

UNDERGRADUATE EXPENSES for 2019–2020 ***Comprehensive fee:*** $50,316 includes full-time tuition ($37,020), mandatory fees ($226), and room and board ($13,070). ***College room only:*** $7360. Room and board charges vary according to board plan and housing facility. ***Part-time tuition:*** $1234 per credit hour.

FRESHMAN FINANCIAL AID (Fall 2019, est.) 545 applied for aid; of those 76% were deemed to have need. 100% of freshmen with need received aid; of those 34% had need fully met. ***Average percent of need met:*** 86% (excluding resources awarded to replace EFC). ***Average financial aid package:*** $32,015 (excluding resources awarded to replace EFC). 28% of all full-time freshmen had no need and received non-need-based gift aid.

UNDERGRADUATE FINANCIAL AID (Fall 2019, est.) 1,663 applied for aid; of those 80% were deemed to have need. 100% of undergraduates with need received aid; of those 30% had need fully met. ***Average percent of need met:*** 85% (excluding resources awarded to replace EFC). ***Average financial aid package:*** $31,911 (excluding resources awarded to replace EFC). 30% of all full-time undergraduates had no need and received non-need-based gift aid.

GIFT AID (NEED-BASED) ***Total amount:*** $56,214,259 (39% federal, 6% state, 54% institutional, 1% external sources). ***Receiving aid:*** Freshmen: 71% (412); all full-time undergraduates: 69% (1,324). ***Average award:*** Freshmen: $28,711; Undergraduates: $27,857. ***Scholarships, grants, and awards:*** Federal Pell, FSEOG, state, private, college/university gift aid from institutional funds, Loans from private/outside lenders.

GIFT AID (NON-NEED-BASED) ***Total amount:*** $15,056,618 (16% state, 80% institutional, 4% external sources). ***Receiving aid:*** Freshmen: 19% (110). Undergraduates: 16% (305). ***Average award:*** Freshmen: $19,555. Undergraduates: $18,274. ***Scholarships, grants, and awards by category:*** *Academic interests/achievement:* agriculture, business, communication, education, English, general academic interests/achievements, humanities, religion/biblical studies. *Creative arts/performance:* applied art and design, debating, journalism/publications, music, theater/drama. *Special achievements/activities:* community service, leadership, religious involvement. *Special characteristics:* adult students, children of faculty/staff, ethnic background, first-generation college students, international students, local/state students, members of minority groups, out-of-state students, veterans, veterans' children. ***Tuition waivers:*** Full or partial for employees or children of employees, senior citizens.

LOANS ***Student loans:*** $9,016,338 (62% need-based, 38% non-need-based). 61% of past graduating class borrowed through all loan programs. *Average indebtedness per student:* $31,336. ***Average need-based loan:*** Freshmen: $4458. Undergraduates: $4665. ***Parent loans:*** $3,033,294 (31% need-based, 69% non-need-based). ***Programs:*** Federal Direct (Subsidized and Unsubsidized Stafford, PLUS), state, college/university.

WORK-STUDY ***Federal work-study:*** Total amount: $888,816; jobs available. ***State or other work-study/employment:*** Total amount: $721,106 (55% need-based, 45% non-need-based). Part-time jobs available.

APPLYING FOR FINANCIAL AID ***Required financial aid forms:*** FAFSA, CSS Financial Aid PROFILE, state aid form, CSS Profile not required for domestic applicants. ***Financial aid deadline (priority):*** 1/15. ***Notification date:*** Continuous beginning 11/1. Students must reply by 5/1.

CONTACT Ms. Noemi Sarrion-Cortes, Director of Financial Aid, Berry College, 2277 Martha Berry Highway, NW, Mount Berry, GA 30149-5007, 706-236-1714 or toll-free 800-237-7942. *Fax:* 706-290-2160. *E-mail:* financialaid@berry.edu.
Website: http://www.berry.edu/.

BETHANY COLLEGE

Lindsborg, KS

CONTACT Ms. Amber Maneth, Office of Financial Aid, Bethany College, 335 East Swensson, Lindsborg, KS 67456-1897, 785-227-3311 Ext. 8248 or toll-free 800-826-2281. *Fax:* 785-227-2004. *E-mail:* manetha@bethanylb.edu.
Website: http://www.bethanylb.edu/.

BETHANY COLLEGE

Bethany, WV

Tuition & fees: N/R	Average undergraduate aid package: $33,200

ABOUT THE INSTITUTION Independent Christian Church (Disciples of Christ), coed. ***Awards:*** bachelor's and master's degrees. 59 undergraduate majors. Both federal and institutional methodology are used as a basis for awarding need-based institutional aid.

FRESHMAN FINANCIAL AID (Fall 2018) 174 applied for aid; of those 95% were deemed to have need. 100% of freshmen with need received aid; of those 48% had need fully met. ***Average percent of need met:*** 86% (excluding resources awarded to replace EFC). ***Average financial aid package:*** $34,100 (excluding resources awarded to replace EFC). 6% of all full-time freshmen had no need and received non-need-based gift aid.

UNDERGRADUATE FINANCIAL AID (Fall 2018) 552 applied for aid; of those 95% were deemed to have need. 100% of undergraduates with need received aid; of those 47% had need fully met. ***Average percent of need met:*** 90% (excluding resources awarded to replace EFC). ***Average financial aid package:*** $33,200 (excluding resources awarded to replace EFC). 5% of all full-time undergraduates had no need and received non-need-based gift aid.

GIFT AID (NEED-BASED) ***Total amount:*** $5,949,543 (30% federal, 4% state, 61% institutional, 5% external sources). ***Receiving aid:*** Freshmen: 94% (165); all full-time undergraduates: 94% (523). ***Average award:*** Freshmen: $28,600; Undergraduates: $27,700. ***Scholarships, grants, and awards:*** Federal Pell, FSEOG, state, private, college/university gift aid from institutional funds.

GIFT AID (NON-NEED-BASED) ***Total amount:*** $1,551,232 (100% institutional). ***Receiving aid:*** Freshmen: 6% (10). Undergraduates: 5% (30). ***Average award:*** Freshmen: $25,000. Undergraduates: $25,000. ***Scholarships, grants, and awards by category:*** *Academic interests/achievement:* general academic interests/achievements. *Creative arts/performance:* music. *Special achievements/activities:* community service, hobbies/interests, leadership, religious involvement. *Special characteristics:* children and siblings of alumni, children of faculty/staff, international students, local/state students, out-of-state students, relatives of clergy, religious affiliation.

LOANS ***Student loans:*** $3,268,172 (100% need-based). 95% of past graduating class borrowed through all loan programs. *Average indebtedness per student:* $27,057. ***Average need-based loan:*** Freshmen: $5500. Undergraduates: $5500. ***Parent loans:*** $2,364,753 (100% need-based). ***Programs:*** Federal Direct (Subsidized and Unsubsidized Stafford, PLUS), Perkins, alternative loans.

WORK-STUDY ***Federal work-study:*** Total amount: $178,027; 148 jobs averaging $1202. ***State or other work-study/employment:*** 62 part-time jobs averaging $2349.

APPLYING FOR FINANCIAL AID ***Required financial aid form:*** FAFSA. ***Financial aid deadline:*** Continuous. ***Notification date:*** Continuous beginning 2/15. Students must reply within 2 weeks of notification.

CONTACT Jill Fernandes, Assistant Vice President of Financial Aid, Bethany College, Bethany Colleg, 31 East Campus Drive, Bethany, WV 26032, 304-829-7611 or toll-free 800-922-7611. *Fax:* 304-829-7142. *E-mail:* financialaid@bethanywv.edu.
Website: http://www.bethanywv.edu/.

BETHANY GLOBAL UNIVERSITY

Bloomington, MN

CONTACT Financial Aid Office, Bethany Global University, 6820 Auto Club Road, Suite C, Bloomington, MN 55438, 952-944-2121 or toll-free 800-323-3417.
Website: http://www.bethanygu.edu/.

BETHANY LUTHERAN COLLEGE

Mankato, MN

Tuition & fees: $28,380 | **Average undergraduate aid package: $23,183**

ABOUT THE INSTITUTION Independent Lutheran, coed. ***Awards:*** certificates and bachelor's degrees. 31 undergraduate majors. ***Total enrollment:*** 741. Undergraduates: 741. Freshmen: 179. Federal methodology is used as a basis for awarding need-based institutional aid.

UNDERGRADUATE EXPENSES for 2020–2021 *One-time required fee:* $130. ***Comprehensive fee:*** $36,530 includes full-time tuition ($27,700), mandatory fees ($680), and room and board ($8150). Full-time tuition and fees vary according to course load. Room and board charges vary according to board plan and housing facility. ***Part-time tuition:*** $1170 per credit hour. ***Part-time fees:*** $340 per term. Part-time tuition and fees vary according to course load.

FRESHMAN FINANCIAL AID (Fall 2018) 148 applied for aid; of those 90% were deemed to have need. 100% of freshmen with need received aid; of those 24% had need fully met. ***Average percent of need met:*** 87% (excluding resources awarded to replace EFC). ***Average financial aid package:*** $23,918 (excluding resources awarded to replace EFC). 10% of all full-time freshmen had no need and received non-need-based gift aid.

UNDERGRADUATE FINANCIAL AID (Fall 2018) 485 applied for aid; of those 92% were deemed to have need. 100% of undergraduates with need received aid; of those 22% had need fully met. ***Average percent of need met:*** 85% (excluding resources awarded to replace EFC). ***Average financial aid package:*** $23,183 (excluding resources awarded to replace EFC). 13% of all full-time undergraduates had no need and received non-need-based gift aid.

GIFT AID (NEED-BASED) *Receiving aid:* Freshmen: 76% (133); all full-time undergraduates: 76% (445). ***Average award:*** Freshmen: $20,924; Undergraduates: $19,208. ***Scholarships, grants, and awards:*** Federal Pell, FSEOG, state, private, college/university gift aid from institutional funds.

GIFT AID (NON-NEED-BASED) *Receiving aid:* Freshmen: 11% (20). Undergraduates: 11% (63). ***Average award:*** Freshmen: $13,468. Undergraduates: $10,584. ***Scholarships, grants, and awards by category:*** *Creative arts/performance:* 57 awards ($107,000 total): applied art and design, debating, journalism/publications, music, theater/drama. *Special characteristics:* 31 awards ($589,731 total): children of faculty/staff. ***Tuition waivers:*** Full or partial for employees or children of employees, senior citizens. ***ROTC:*** Army cooperative.

LOANS *Student loans:* 82% of past graduating class borrowed through all loan programs. *Average indebtedness per student:* $32,152. ***Average need-based loan:*** Freshmen: $3599. Undergraduates: $4522. ***Programs:*** Federal Direct (Subsidized and Unsubsidized Stafford, PLUS), state, alternative loans.

WORK-STUDY *Federal work-study:* 29 jobs averaging $1632. ***State or other work-study/employment:*** 299 part-time jobs averaging $1162.

APPLYING FOR FINANCIAL AID *Required financial aid forms:* FAFSA, institution's own form. ***Notification date:*** Continuous. Students must reply within 4 weeks of notification.

CONTACT Financial Aid Office, Bethany Lutheran College, 700 Luther Drive, Mankato, MN 56001-6163, 507-344-7000 or toll-free 800-944-3066.
Website: http://www.blc.edu/.

BETHEL COLLEGE

North Newton, KS

Tuition & fees: $29,390 | **Average undergraduate aid package: $28,735**

ABOUT THE INSTITUTION Independent Mennonite Church USA, coed. ***Awards:*** certificates and bachelor's degrees. 20 undergraduate majors. ***Total enrollment:*** 444. Undergraduates: 444. Freshmen: 107. Federal methodology is used as a basis for awarding need-based institutional aid.

UNDERGRADUATE EXPENSES for 2019–2020 *Comprehensive fee:* $38,370 includes full-time tuition ($29,150), mandatory fees ($240), and room and board ($8980). ***College room only:*** $4340.

FRESHMAN FINANCIAL AID (Fall 2019, est.) 151 applied for aid; of those 93% were deemed to have need. 100% of freshmen with need received aid; of those 25% had need fully met. ***Average percent of need met:*** 88% (excluding resources awarded to replace EFC). ***Average financial aid package:*** $29,434 (excluding resources awarded to replace EFC). 7% of all full-time freshmen had no need and received non-need-based gift aid.

UNDERGRADUATE FINANCIAL AID (Fall 2019, est.) 446 applied for aid; of those 92% were deemed to have need. 100% of undergraduates with need received aid; of those 26% had need fully met. ***Average percent of need met:*** 84% (excluding resources awarded to replace EFC). ***Average financial aid package:*** $28,735 (excluding resources awarded to replace EFC). 8% of all full-time undergraduates had no need and received non-need-based gift aid.

GIFT AID (NEED-BASED) *Total amount:* $1,411,131 (70% federal, 28% state, 2% institutional). ***Receiving aid:*** Freshmen: 64% (98); all full-time undergraduates: 64% (290). ***Average award:*** Freshmen: $6324; Undergraduates: $5782. ***Scholarships, grants, and awards:*** Federal Pell, FSEOG, state, private, college/university gift aid from institutional funds.

GIFT AID (NON-NEED-BASED) *Total amount:* $5,759,531 (94% institutional, 6% external sources). ***Receiving aid:*** Freshmen: 93% (141). Undergraduates: 90% (410). ***Average award:*** Freshmen: $8075. Undergraduates: $13,648. ***Scholarships, grants, and awards by category:*** *Academic interests/achievement:* 29 awards ($37,600 total): biological sciences, business, communication, general academic interests/achievements, health fields, humanities, mathematics, premedicine, social sciences. *Creative arts/performance:* 82 awards ($461,000 total): applied art and design, art/fine arts, debating, music, theater/drama. *Special achievements/activities:* 34 awards ($139,064 total): cheerleading/drum major, community service. *Special characteristics:* children and siblings of alumni, children of current students, children of faculty/staff, ethnic background, general special characteristics, international students, local/state students, previous college experience, relatives of clergy, religious affiliation, siblings of current students, spouses of current students.

LOANS *Student loans:* $2,991,262 (100% need-based). 72% of past graduating class borrowed through all loan programs. *Average indebtedness per student:* $5633. ***Average need-based loan:*** Freshmen: $7243. Undergraduates: $8326. ***Parent loans:*** $1,032,101 (100% non-need-based). ***Programs:*** Federal Direct (Subsidized and Unsubsidized Stafford, PLUS).

WORK-STUDY *Federal work-study:* 272 jobs averaging $1741. ***State or other work-study/employment:*** Part-time jobs available.

ATHLETIC AWARDS Total amount: $2,011,028 (100% non-need-based).

APPLYING FOR FINANCIAL AID *Required financial aid form:* FAFSA. ***Financial aid deadline (priority):*** 4/1. ***Notification date:*** Continuous beginning 2/1. Students must reply by 5/1 or within 2 weeks of notification.

CONTACT Mr. Clark Oswald, Director of Financial Aid, Bethel College, 300 East 27th Street, North Newton, KS 67117, 316-284-5232 or toll-free 800-522-1887 Ext.230. *Fax:* 316-284-5845. *E-mail:* coswald@bethelks.edu.
Website: http://www.bethelks.edu/.

BETHEL COLLEGE

Hampton, VA

CONTACT Financial Aid Office, Bethel College, 1705 Todds Lane, Hampton, VA 23666, 757-826-1426.
Website: http://www.bcva.edu/.

BETHEL UNIVERSITY

Mishawaka, IN

Tuition & fees: $29,790 | **Average undergraduate aid package: N/A**

ABOUT THE INSTITUTION Independent Missionary Church, coed. ***Awards:*** associate, bachelor's, and master's degrees. 61 undergraduate majors. ***Total enrollment:*** 1,450. Undergraduates: 1,220. Freshmen: 307. Federal methodology is used as a basis for awarding need-based institutional aid.

UNDERGRADUATE EXPENSES for 2020–2021 *Comprehensive fee:* $39,100 includes full-time tuition ($29,250), mandatory fees ($540), and room and board ($9310). ***College room only:*** $4430. Full-time tuition and fees vary according to program. Room and board charges vary according to board plan and housing facility. ***Part-time tuition:*** $930 per credit hour. ***Part-time fees:*** $310 per year. Part-time tuition and fees vary according to course load and program.

FRESHMAN FINANCIAL AID (Fall 2019, est.) 15% of all full-time freshmen had no need and received non-need-based gift aid.
UNDERGRADUATE FINANCIAL AID (Fall 2019, est.) 15% of all full-time undergraduates had no need and received non-need-based gift aid.
GIFT AID (NEED-BASED) ***Scholarships, grants, and awards:*** Federal Pell, FSEOG, state, private, college/university gift aid from institutional funds, Federal Nursing.
GIFT AID (NON-NEED-BASED) ***Average award:*** Freshmen: $17,930. Undergraduates: $17,110. ***Scholarships, grants, and awards by category:*** *Academic interests/achievement:* 887 awards ($9,366,000 total): general academic interests/achievements. *Creative arts/performance:* 53 awards ($141,400 total): applied art and design, music, theater/drama. *Special achievements/activities:* 29 awards ($59,000 total): cheerleading/drum major, leadership. *Special characteristics:* 161 awards ($636,400 total): children of faculty/staff, international students, members of minority groups, religious affiliation. ***Tuition waivers:*** Full or partial for employees or children of employees. ***ROTC:*** Army cooperative, Air Force cooperative.
LOANS ***Student loans:*** 70% of past graduating class borrowed through all loan programs. *Average indebtedness per student:* $30,797. ***Programs:*** Federal Direct (Subsidized and Unsubsidized Stafford, PLUS), Federal Nursing.
WORK-STUDY ***Federal work-study:*** 84 jobs averaging $721.
APPLYING FOR FINANCIAL AID ***Required financial aid form:*** FAFSA. ***Notification date:*** Continuous.
CONTACT Mrs. Cindi Pedersen, Director of Financial Aid, Bethel University, 1001 Bethel Circle, Mishawaka, IN 46545-5591, 574-807-7239 or toll-free 800-422-4101. *Fax:* 574-807-7122. *E-mail:* cindi.pedersen@betheluniversity.edu.
Website: betheluniversity.edu.

BETHEL UNIVERSITY

St. Paul, MN

Tuition & fees: $39,030	Average undergraduate aid package: $31,730

ABOUT THE INSTITUTION Independent Baptist General Conference, coed. ***Awards:*** certificates, associate, bachelor's, master's, and doctoral degrees. 65 undergraduate majors. ***Total enrollment:*** 4,339. Undergraduates: 2,799. Freshmen: 590. Federal methodology is used as a basis for awarding need-based institutional aid.
UNDERGRADUATE EXPENSES for 2020–2021 ***Comprehensive fee:*** $49,990 includes full-time tuition ($38,870), mandatory fees ($160), and room and board ($10,960). ***College room only:*** $5900. Room and board charges vary according to board plan. ***Part-time tuition:*** $1620 per credit. ***Payment plan:*** Tuition prepayment.
FRESHMAN FINANCIAL AID (Fall 2019, est.) 553 applied for aid; of those 82% were deemed to have need. 100% of freshmen with need received aid; of those 19% had need fully met. ***Average percent of need met:*** 84% (excluding resources awarded to replace EFC). ***Average financial aid package:*** $32,032 (excluding resources awarded to replace EFC). 22% of all full-time freshmen had no need and received non-need-based gift aid.
UNDERGRADUATE FINANCIAL AID (Fall 2019, est.) 1,953 applied for aid; of those 84% were deemed to have need. 100% of undergraduates with need received aid; of those 23% had need fully met. ***Average percent of need met:*** 84% (excluding resources awarded to replace EFC). ***Average financial aid package:*** $31,730 (excluding resources awarded to replace EFC). 24% of all full-time undergraduates had no need and received non-need-based gift aid.
GIFT AID (NEED-BASED) ***Total amount:*** $41,552,982 (7% federal, 11% state, 80% institutional, 2% external sources). ***Receiving aid:*** Freshmen: 78% (453); all full-time undergraduates: 74% (1,634). ***Average award:*** Freshmen: $25,969; Undergraduates: $24,922. ***Scholarships, grants, and awards:*** Federal Pell, FSEOG, state, private, college/university gift aid from institutional funds.
GIFT AID (NON-NEED-BASED) ***Total amount:*** $11,620,308 (1% federal, 1% state, 93% institutional, 5% external sources). ***Receiving aid:*** Freshmen: 10% (58). Undergraduates: 12% (263). ***Average award:*** Freshmen: $17,296. Undergraduates: $16,678. ***Scholarships, grants, and awards by category:*** *Academic interests/achievement:* general academic interests/achievements. *Creative arts/performance:* applied art and design, debating, music, theater/drama. *Special characteristics:* general special characteristics. ***Tuition waivers:*** Full or partial for employees or children of employees. ***ROTC:*** Army cooperative, Air Force cooperative.
LOANS ***Student loans:*** $15,425,923 (63% need-based, 37% non-need-based). 73% of past graduating class borrowed through all loan programs. *Average indebtedness per student:* $38,286. ***Average need-based loan:*** Freshmen: $2901. Undergraduates: $3827. ***Parent loans:*** $3,178,826 (38% need-based, 62% non-need-based). ***Programs:*** Federal Direct (Subsidized and Unsubsidized Stafford, PLUS), state, alternative loans.
WORK-STUDY ***Federal work-study:*** Total amount: $600,000; jobs available. ***State or other work-study/employment:*** Total amount: $2,716,136 (70% need-based, 30% non-need-based). Part-time jobs available.
APPLYING FOR FINANCIAL AID ***Required financial aid form:*** FAFSA. ***Financial aid deadline (priority):*** 4/15. ***Notification date:*** Continuous beginning 1/15. Students must reply by 7/1.
CONTACT Mr. Jeffrey D. Olson, Director of Financial Aid, Bethel University, 3900 Bethel Drive, St. Paul, MN 55112-6999, 651-638-6241 or toll-free 800-255-8706 Ext.6242. *Fax:* 651-635-1491. *E-mail:* finaid@bethel.edu.
Website: http://www.bethel.edu/.

BETHEL UNIVERSITY

McKenzie, TN

CONTACT Laura Bateman, Office of Financial Aid, Bethel University, 325 Cherry Avenue, McKenzie, TN 38201, 901-352-4007. *Fax:* 901-352-4069.
Website: http://www.bethelu.edu/.

BETHESDA UNIVERSITY

Anaheim, CA

CONTACT Ms. Grace Choi, Financial Aid Administrator, Bethesda University, 730 North Euclid Street, Anaheim, CA 92801, 714-683-1413. *Fax:* 714-517-1948. *E-mail:* financialaid@bcu.edu.
Website: http://www.buc.edu/.

BETH HAMEDRASH SHAAREI YOSHER INSTITUTE

Brooklyn, NY

CONTACT Financial Aid Office, Beth HaMedrash Shaarei Yosher Institute, 4102-10 16th Avenue, Brooklyn, NY 11204, 718-854-2290.
Website: http://www.bethhamedrashshaareiyosher.com/.

BETH HATALMUD RABBINICAL COLLEGE

Brooklyn, NY

CONTACT Financial Aid Office, Beth Hatalmud Rabbinical College, 2127 82nd Street, Brooklyn, NY 11204, 718-259-2525.

BETHLEHEM COLLEGE & SEMINARY

Minneapolis, MN

CONTACT Financial Aid Office, Bethlehem College & Seminary, 720 13th Avenue South, Minneapolis, MN 55415.
Website: http://www.bcsmn.edu/.

BETH MEDRASH GOVOHA

Lakewood, NJ

CONTACT Financial Aid Office, Beth Medrash Govoha, 617 Sixth Street, Lakewood, NJ 08701-2797, 732-367-1060.

BETH MEDRASH MEOR YITZCHOK

Monsey, NY

CONTACT Financial Aid Office, Beth Medrash Meor Yitzchok, 85 Dykstras Way East, Monsey, NY 10952.
Website: http://www.bethmedrashmeoryitzchok.com/.

BETHUNE-COOKMAN UNIVERSITY

Daytona Beach, FL

Tuition & fees: $14,814	Average undergraduate aid package: $15,144

ABOUT THE INSTITUTION Independent Methodist, coed. ***Awards:*** bachelor's and master's degrees. 36 undergraduate majors. Federal methodology is used as a basis for awarding need-based institutional aid.

UNDERGRADUATE EXPENSES for 2019–2020 *One-time required fee:* $300. ***Comprehensive fee:*** $24,276 includes full-time tuition ($13,844), mandatory fees ($970), and room and board ($9462). Full-time tuition and fees vary according to degree level. Room and board charges vary according to board plan and housing facility. ***Part-time tuition:*** $577 per credit hour. ***Part-time fees:*** $50 per credit hour. Part-time tuition and fees vary according to course load and degree level.

FRESHMAN FINANCIAL AID (Fall 2019, est.) 569 applied for aid; of those 97% were deemed to have need. 100% of freshmen with need received aid; of those 7% had need fully met. ***Average percent of need met:*** 58% (excluding resources awarded to replace EFC). ***Average financial aid package:*** $16,217 (excluding resources awarded to replace EFC). 3% of all full-time freshmen had no need and received non-need-based gift aid.

UNDERGRADUATE FINANCIAL AID (Fall 2019, est.) 2,551 applied for aid; of those 97% were deemed to have need. 100% of undergraduates with need received aid; of those 6% had need fully met. ***Average percent of need met:*** 53% (excluding resources awarded to replace EFC). ***Average financial aid package:*** $15,144 (excluding resources awarded to replace EFC). 1% of all full-time undergraduates had no need and received non-need-based gift aid.

GIFT AID (NEED-BASED) *Receiving aid:* Freshmen: 92% (540); all full-time undergraduates: 91% (2,367). ***Average award:*** Freshmen: $13,482; Undergraduates: $11,521. ***Scholarships, grants, and awards:*** Federal Pell, FSEOG, state, private, college/university gift aid from institutional funds, United Negro College Fund.

GIFT AID (NON-NEED-BASED) *Receiving aid:* Freshmen: 4% (25). Undergraduates: 4% (98). ***Average award:*** Freshmen: $7743. Undergraduates: $10,662. ***Scholarships, grants, and awards by category:*** *Academic interests/achievement:* 150 awards ($1,373,169 total): general academic interests/achievements. ***Tuition waivers:*** Full or partial for employees or children of employees. ***ROTC:*** Army cooperative, Air Force cooperative.

LOANS *Student loans:* 94% of past graduating class borrowed through all loan programs. *Average indebtedness per student:* $37,258. ***Average need-based loan:*** Freshmen: $3519. Undergraduates: $4356. ***Programs:*** Federal Direct (Subsidized and Unsubsidized Stafford, PLUS), Alternative Private Loans.

WORK-STUDY *Federal work-study:* 200 jobs averaging $2500. ***State or other work-study/employment:*** 100 part-time jobs averaging $2000.

APPLYING FOR FINANCIAL AID *Required financial aid form:* FAFSA. ***Notification date:*** Continuous. Students must reply within 3 weeks of notification.

CONTACT Ms. Veronica Evans, Director of Financial Aid, Bethune-Cookman University, 640 Dr. Mary McLeod Bethune Boulevard, Daytona Beach, FL 32114-3099, 386-481-2024 or toll-free 800-448-0228. *Fax:* 386-481-2621. *E-mail:* evansv@cookman.edu.
Website: http://www.cookman.edu/.

BET MEDRASH GADOL ATERET TORAH

Brooklyn, NY

CONTACT Financial Aid Office, Bet Medrash Gadol Ateret Torah, 1750 East Fourth Street, Brooklyn, NY 11223.
Website: http://www.betmedrashgadolaterettorah.com/.

BEULAH HEIGHTS UNIVERSITY

Atlanta, GA

CONTACT Ms. Patricia Banks, Director of Financial Aid, Beulah Heights University, 892 Berne Street, SE, Atlanta, GA 30316, 404-627-2681 or toll-free 888-777-BHBC. *Fax:* 404-627-0702. *E-mail:* pat.banks@beulah.org.
Website: http://www.beulah.edu/.

BINGHAMTON UNIVERSITY, STATE UNIVERSITY OF NEW YORK

Binghamton, NY

Tuition & fees (area res): $10,494	Average undergraduate aid package: $14,458

ABOUT THE INSTITUTION State-supported, coed. ***Awards:*** certificates, bachelor's, master's, and doctoral degrees. 75 undergraduate majors. ***Total enrollment:*** 18,124. Undergraduates: 14,165. Freshmen: 2,912. Institutional methodology is used as a basis for awarding need-based institutional aid.

UNDERGRADUATE EXPENSES for 2020–2021 *Application fee:* $50. ***Tuition, area resident:*** full-time $7270; part-time $303 per credit hour. ***Tuition, state resident:*** full-time $7270; part-time $303 per credit hour. ***Tuition, nonresident:*** full-time $27,043; part-time $1028 per credit hour. ***Required fees:*** full-time $3224. Full-time tuition and fees vary according to program. Part-time tuition and fees vary according to course load and program. ***College room and board:*** $16,549. Room and board charges vary according to board plan and housing facility.

FRESHMAN FINANCIAL AID (Fall 2019, est.) 2556 applied for aid; of those 59% were deemed to have need. 100% of freshmen with need received aid; of those 19% had need fully met. ***Average percent of need met:*** 70% (excluding resources awarded to replace EFC). ***Average financial aid package:*** $13,666 (excluding resources awarded to replace EFC). 6% of all full-time freshmen had no need and received non-need-based gift aid.

UNDERGRADUATE FINANCIAL AID (Fall 2019, est.) 10,107 applied for aid; of those 70% were deemed to have need. 100% of undergraduates with need received aid; of those 19% had need fully met. ***Average percent of need met:*** 69% (excluding resources awarded to replace EFC). ***Average financial aid package:*** $14,458 (excluding resources awarded to replace EFC). 4% of all full-time undergraduates had no need and received non-need-based gift aid.

GIFT AID (NEED-BASED) *Total amount:* $59,897,193 (34% federal, 56% state, 8% institutional, 2% external sources). ***Receiving aid:*** Freshmen: 43% (1,259); all full-time undergraduates: 43% (5,944). ***Average award:*** Freshmen: $9918; Undergraduates: $9765. ***Scholarships, grants, and awards:*** Federal Pell, FSEOG, private, college/university gift aid from institutional funds.

GIFT AID (NON-NEED-BASED) *Total amount:* $9,316,203 (55% state, 37% institutional, 8% external sources). ***Receiving aid:*** Freshmen: 10% (292). Undergraduates: 4% (604). ***Average award:*** Freshmen: $8331. Undergraduates: $7883. ***Scholarships, grants, and awards by category:*** *Academic interests/achievement:* 810 awards ($4,910,376 total): area/ethnic studies, biological sciences, business, computer science, education, engineering/technologies, English, foreign languages, general academic interests/achievements, home economics, humanities, international studies, mathematics, physical sciences, premedicine, social sciences. *Creative arts/performance:* 32 awards ($38,900 total): applied art and design, cinema/film/broadcasting, creative writing, dance, general creative arts/performance, journalism/publications, music, performing arts, theater/drama. *Special achievements/activities:* 60 awards ($181,845 total): community service, general special achievements/activities, leadership. *Special characteristics:* 417 awards ($671,918 total): adult students, children and siblings of alumni, children of faculty/staff, children with a deceased or disabled parent, ethnic background, first-generation college students, general special characteristics, handicapped students, international students, local/state students, married students, members of minority groups, out-of-state students, previous college experience, religious affiliation, veterans, veterans' children. ***Tuition waivers:*** Full or partial for employees or children of employees. ***ROTC:*** Army cooperative, Air Force cooperative.

LOANS ***Student loans:*** $86,615,735 (72% need-based, 28% non-need-based). 49% of past graduating class borrowed through all loan programs. *Average indebtedness per student:* $27,679. ***Average need-based loan:*** Freshmen: $3524. Undergraduates: $4768. ***Parent loans:*** $16,124,516 (71% need-based, 29% non-need-based). ***Programs:*** Federal Direct (Subsidized and Unsubsidized Stafford, PLUS), Perkins, college/university.

WORK-STUDY ***Federal work-study:*** Total amount: $571,881; 289 jobs averaging $1953.

ATHLETIC AWARDS Total amount: $5,003,010 (100% non-need-based).

APPLYING FOR FINANCIAL AID ***Required financial aid forms:*** FAFSA, state aid form. ***Financial aid deadline:*** 5/1 (priority: 1/1). ***Notification date:*** Continuous beginning 1/31. Students must reply within 2 weeks of notification.

CONTACT Ms. Patricia Donahue, Director, Financial Aid Operations, Binghamton University, State University of New York, PO Box 6000, Binghamton, NY 13902-6000, 607-777-2428. *Fax:* 607-777-6897. *E-mail:* finaid@binghamton.edu.
Website: http://www.binghamton.edu/.

BIOLA UNIVERSITY

La Mirada, CA

Tuition & fees: $53,490	Average undergraduate aid package: $25,339

ABOUT THE INSTITUTION Independent interdenominational, coed. ***Awards:*** certificates, diplomas, bachelor's, master's, and doctoral degrees. 98 undergraduate majors. ***Total enrollment:*** 6,103. Undergraduates: 4,043. Freshmen: 841. Federal methodology is used as a basis for awarding need-based institutional aid.

UNDERGRADUATE EXPENSES for 2020–2021 ***Application fee:*** $45. ***Comprehensive fee:*** $65,004 includes full-time tuition ($41,976), mandatory fees ($11,514), and room and board ($11,514). Full-time tuition and fees vary according to course load and degree level. Room and board charges vary according to board plan and housing facility. ***Part-time tuition:*** $1749 per credit hour. Part-time tuition and fees vary according to course load and degree level.

FRESHMAN FINANCIAL AID (Fall 2018) 723 applied for aid; of those 86% were deemed to have need. 100% of freshmen with need received aid; of those 15% had need fully met. ***Average percent of need met:*** 61% (excluding resources awarded to replace EFC). ***Average financial aid package:*** $26,680 (excluding resources awarded to replace EFC). 25% of all full-time freshmen had no need and received non-need-based gift aid.

UNDERGRADUATE FINANCIAL AID (Fall 2018) 2,794 applied for aid; of those 90% were deemed to have need. 100% of undergraduates with need received aid; of those 9% had need fully met. ***Average percent of need met:*** 55% (excluding resources awarded to replace EFC). ***Average financial aid package:*** $25,339 (excluding resources awarded to replace EFC). 31% of all full-time undergraduates had no need and received non-need-based gift aid.

GIFT AID (NEED-BASED) ***Total amount:*** $48,799,441 (12% federal, 15% state, 73% institutional). ***Receiving aid:*** Freshmen: 73% (618); all full-time undergraduates: 67% (2,490). ***Average award:*** Freshmen: $21,767; Undergraduates: $19,347. ***Scholarships, grants, and awards:*** Federal Pell, FSEOG, state, private, college/university gift aid from institutional funds, United Negro College Fund.

GIFT AID (NON-NEED-BASED) ***Total amount:*** $14,986,112 (100% institutional). ***Receiving aid:*** Freshmen: 9% (73). Undergraduates: 4% (162). ***Average award:*** Freshmen: $15,705. Undergraduates: $11,917. ***Scholarships, grants, and awards by category:*** *Academic interests/achievement:* biological sciences, communication, general academic interests/achievements. *Creative arts/performance:* cinema/film/broadcasting, journalism/publications, music, theater/drama. *Special achievements/activities:* community service, leadership. *Special characteristics:* children of faculty/staff, ethnic background, international students, members of minority groups, relatives of clergy. ***Tuition waivers:*** Full or partial for employees or children of employees. ***ROTC:*** Army cooperative, Air Force cooperative.

LOANS ***Student loans:*** $23,795,051 (76% need-based, 24% non-need-based). 65% of past graduating class borrowed through all loan programs. *Average indebtedness per student:* $36,330. ***Average need-based loan:*** Freshmen: $2107. Undergraduates: $3129. ***Parent loans:*** $12,786,540 (62% need-based, 38% non-need-based). ***Programs:*** Federal Direct (Subsidized and Unsubsidized Stafford, PLUS), Federal Nursing, college/university.

WORK-STUDY ***Federal work-study:*** Total amount: $905,111; jobs available.

ATHLETIC AWARDS Total amount: $3,207,832 (48% need-based, 52% non-need-based).

APPLYING FOR FINANCIAL AID ***Required financial aid form:*** FAFSA. ***Financial aid deadline (priority):*** 2/1. ***Notification date:*** 12/1.

CONTACT Financial Aid Office, Biola University, 13800 Biola Avenue, La Mirada, CA 90639-0001, 562-903-6000 or toll-free 800-652-4652.
Website: http://www.biola.edu/.

BIRMINGHAM-SOUTHERN COLLEGE

Birmingham, AL

Tuition & fees: N/R	Average undergraduate aid package: $16,057

ABOUT THE INSTITUTION Independent Methodist, coed. ***Awards:*** bachelor's degrees. 42 undergraduate majors. ***Total enrollment:*** 1,209. Undergraduates: 1,209. Freshmen: 332. Federal methodology is used as a basis for awarding need-based institutional aid.

FRESHMAN FINANCIAL AID (Fall 2018) 285 applied for aid; of those 74% were deemed to have need. 100% of freshmen with need received aid; of those 19% had need fully met. ***Average percent of need met:*** 58% (excluding resources awarded to replace EFC). ***Average financial aid package:*** $15,153 (excluding resources awarded to replace EFC). 32% of all full-time freshmen had no need and received non-need-based gift aid.

UNDERGRADUATE FINANCIAL AID (Fall 2018) 872 applied for aid; of those 80% were deemed to have need. 100% of undergraduates with need received aid; of those 22% had need fully met. ***Average percent of need met:*** 56% (excluding resources awarded to replace EFC). ***Average financial aid package:*** $16,057 (excluding resources awarded to replace EFC). 38% of all full-time undergraduates had no need and received non-need-based gift aid.

GIFT AID (NEED-BASED) ***Total amount:*** $2,395,807 (64% federal, 2% state, 33% institutional, 1% external sources). ***Receiving aid:*** Freshmen: 53% (174); all full-time undergraduates: 40% (501). ***Average award:*** Freshmen: $6651; Undergraduates: $6401. ***Scholarships, grants, and awards:*** Federal Pell, FSEOG, state, private, college/university gift aid from institutional funds.

GIFT AID (NON-NEED-BASED) ***Total amount:*** $9,800,376 (5% state, 86% institutional, 9% external sources). ***Receiving aid:*** Freshmen: 59% (194). Undergraduates: 54% (681). ***Average award:*** Freshmen: $6618. Undergraduates: $7946. ***Scholarships, grants, and awards by category:*** *Academic interests/achievement:* area/ethnic studies, biological sciences, business, communication, computer science, education, engineering/technologies, English, foreign languages, general academic interests/achievements, health fields, home economics, humanities, international studies, mathematics, physical sciences, premedicine, religion/biblical studies, social sciences. *Creative arts/performance:* applied art and design, dance, music, performing arts, theater/drama. *Special achievements/activities:* junior miss, leadership, memberships, religious involvement. *Special characteristics:* adult students, children and siblings of alumni, children of faculty/staff, ethnic background, first-generation college students, general special characteristics, international students, local/state students, previous college experience, relatives of clergy, religious affiliation, veterans. ***ROTC:*** Army cooperative, Air Force cooperative.

LOANS ***Student loans:*** $7,214,416 (35% need-based, 65% non-need-based). 48% of past graduating class borrowed through all loan programs. *Average indebtedness per student:* $28,007. ***Average need-based loan:*** Freshmen: $3227. Undergraduates: $4230. ***Parent loans:*** $3,429,175 (100% non-need-based). ***Programs:*** Federal Direct (Subsidized and Unsubsidized Stafford, PLUS), Perkins, college/university.

WORK-STUDY ***Federal work-study:*** Total amount: $373,988; jobs available. ***State or other work-study/employment:*** Total amount: $225,650 (100% non-need-based). Part-time jobs available.

APPLYING FOR FINANCIAL AID ***Required financial aid forms:*** FAFSA, state aid form. ***Financial aid deadline (priority):*** 3/1. ***Notification date:*** 3/1. Students must reply by 5/1.

CONTACT Melissa S Burgett, Director of Financial Aid, Birmingham-Southern College, 900 Arkadelphia Road, Birmingham, AL 35254, 205-226-4688 or toll-free 800-523-5793. *Fax:* 205-226-3082. *E-mail:* finaid@bsc.edu.
Website: http://www.bsc.edu/.

BIRTHINGWAY COLLEGE OF MIDWIFERY

Portland, OR

CONTACT Financial Aid Office, Birthingway College of Midwifery, 12113 SE Foster Road, Portland, OR 97299, 503-760-3131.
Website: http://www.birthingway.edu/.

BLACKBURN COLLEGE

Carlinville, IL

ABOUT THE INSTITUTION Independent Presbyterian, coed. ***Awards:*** bachelor's degrees. 50 undergraduate majors. ***Total enrollment:*** 566. Undergraduates: 566. Freshmen: 168.

GIFT AID (NEED-BASED) ***Scholarships, grants, and awards:*** Federal Pell, FSEOG, state, private, college/university gift aid from institutional funds.

GIFT AID (NON-NEED-BASED) ***Scholarships, grants, and awards by category:*** *Academic interests/achievement:* general academic interests/achievements. *Special achievements/activities:* general special achievements/activities. *Special characteristics:* siblings of current students.

LOANS ***Programs:*** Federal Direct (Subsidized and Unsubsidized Stafford, PLUS).

WORK-STUDY ***Federal work-study:*** Total amount: $2,227,277; jobs available. ***State or other work-study/employment:*** Total amount: $212,667 (100% non-need-based). Part-time jobs available.

APPLYING FOR FINANCIAL AID ***Required financial aid form:*** FAFSA.

CONTACT Mrs. Alisha Kapp, Director of Financial Aid, Blackburn College, 700 College Avenue, Carlinville, IL 62626-1498, 217-854-5773 Ext. 5773 or toll-free 800-233-3550. *Fax:* 217-854-3731.
Website: http://www.blackburn.edu/.

BLACK HILLS STATE UNIVERSITY

Spearfish, SD

Tuition & fees (SD res): $9009	Average undergraduate aid package: N/A

ABOUT THE INSTITUTION State-supported, coed. ***Awards:*** certificates, associate, bachelor's, and master's degrees. 47 undergraduate majors. ***Total enrollment:*** 3,858. Undergraduates: 3,682. Freshmen: 520. Federal methodology is used as a basis for awarding need-based institutional aid.

UNDERGRADUATE EXPENSES for 2019–2020 ***Application fee:*** $20. ***Tuition, state resident:*** full-time $9009; part-time $300 per credit hour. ***Tuition, nonresident:*** full-time $12,155; part-time $405 per credit hour. Full-time tuition and fees vary according to course load, location, and reciprocity agreements. Part-time tuition and fees vary according to course load, location, and reciprocity agreements. ***College room and board:*** $7142; ***Room only:*** $3608. Room and board charges vary according to board plan, housing facility, and location.

GIFT AID (NEED-BASED) ***Scholarships, grants, and awards:*** Federal Pell, FSEOG, state, private, college/university gift aid from institutional funds, Academic Competitiveness Grants, National SMART Grants, TEACH Grants.

GIFT AID (NON-NEED-BASED) ***Scholarships, grants, and awards by category:*** *Academic interests/achievement:* biological sciences, business, communication, computer science, education, English, foreign languages, general academic interests/achievements, home economics, humanities, mathematics, military science, physical sciences, social sciences. *Creative arts/performance:* applied art and design, music, theater/drama. ***Tuition waivers:*** Full or partial for employees or children of employees, senior citizens. ***ROTC:*** Army.

LOANS ***Programs:*** Federal Direct (Subsidized and Unsubsidized Stafford, PLUS), Perkins.

WORK-STUDY Federal work-study jobs available. ***State or other work-study/employment:*** Part-time jobs available.

APPLYING FOR FINANCIAL AID ***Required financial aid form:*** FAFSA. ***Financial aid deadline (priority):*** 2/15. ***Notification date:*** Continuous beginning 5/15. Students must reply within 3 weeks of notification.

CONTACT Ms. Kim Nida, Director of Financial Aid, Black Hills State University, 1200 University Street, Spearfish, SD 57799-9670, 605-642-6113 or toll-free 800-255-2478. *Fax:* 605-642-6913. *E-mail:* Kim.Nida@bhsu.edu.
Website: http://www.bhsu.edu/.

BLESSING-RIEMAN COLLEGE OF NURSING & HEALTH SCIENCES

Quincy, IL

ABOUT THE INSTITUTION Independent, coed, primarily women. ***Awards:*** bachelor's and master's degrees. 1 undergraduate major.

GIFT AID (NEED-BASED) ***Scholarships, grants, and awards:*** Federal Pell, FSEOG, state, private, college/university gift aid from institutional funds.

GIFT AID (NON-NEED-BASED) ***Scholarships, grants, and awards by category:*** *Academic interests/achievement:* general academic interests/achievements.

LOANS ***Programs:*** Federal Direct (Subsidized and Unsubsidized Stafford, PLUS), Federal Nursing, college/university.

CONTACT Mrs. Erin McHargue, Financial Aid Coordinator, Blessing-Rieman College of Nursing & Health Sciences, Broadway at 11th Street, PO Box 7005, Quincy, IL 62301, 217-223-8400 Ext. 6993 or toll-free 800-877-9140. *Fax:* 217-223-1781. *E-mail:* mcharguee@brcn.edu.
Website: http://www.brcn.edu/.

BLOOMFIELD COLLEGE

Bloomfield, NJ

CONTACT Office of Financial Aid, Bloomfield College, 467 Franklin Street, Bloomfield, NJ 07003-9981, 973-748-9000 Ext. 1213 or toll-free 800-848-4555 Ext.230. *Fax:* 973-748-9735.
Website: http://www.bloomfield.edu/.

BLOOMSBURG UNIVERSITY OF PENNSYLVANIA

Bloomsburg, PA

Tuition & fees (PA res): $10,958	Average undergraduate aid package: $10,181

ABOUT THE INSTITUTION State-supported, coed. ***Awards:*** certificates, bachelor's, master's, and doctoral degrees. 43 undergraduate majors. ***Total enrollment:*** 8,924. Undergraduates: 8,253. Freshmen: 1,848. Federal methodology is used as a basis for awarding need-based institutional aid.

UNDERGRADUATE EXPENSES for 2019–2020 ***Application fee:*** $35. ***Tuition, state resident:*** full-time $7716; part-time $322 per credit hour. ***Tuition, nonresident:*** full-time $19,290; part-time $805 per credit hour. ***Required fees:*** full-time $3242. ***College room and board:*** $9686; ***Room only:*** $6308.

FRESHMAN FINANCIAL AID (Fall 2019, est.) 1907 applied for aid; of those 70% were deemed to have need. 100% of freshmen with need received aid; of those 17% had need fully met. ***Average percent of need met:*** 63% (excluding resources awarded to replace EFC). ***Average financial aid package:*** $104,088 (excluding resources awarded to replace EFC). 8% of all full-time freshmen had no need and received non-need-based gift aid.

UNDERGRADUATE FINANCIAL AID (Fall 2019, est.) 6,547 applied for aid; of those 71% were deemed to have need. 99% of undergraduates with need received aid; of those 16% had need fully met. ***Average percent of need met:*** 59% (excluding resources awarded to replace EFC). ***Average financial aid package:*** $10,181 (excluding resources awarded to replace EFC). 6% of all full-time undergraduates had no need and received non-need-based gift aid.

GIFT AID (NEED-BASED) ***Receiving aid:*** Freshmen: 43% (858); all full-time undergraduates: 41% (2,888). ***Average award:*** Freshmen: $6119; Undergraduates: $5956. ***Scholarships, grants, and awards:*** Federal Pell, FSEOG, state, private, college/university gift aid from institutional funds.

GIFT AID (NON-NEED-BASED) ***Receiving aid:*** Freshmen: 27% (537). Undergraduates: 19% (1,350). ***Average award:*** Freshmen: $3097. Undergraduates: $3030. ***Scholarships, grants, and awards by category:*** *Academic interests/achievement:* 1,525 awards ($3,669,658 total): biological sciences, business, communication, computer science, education, English, foreign languages, general academic interests/achievements, home economics, humanities, international studies, mathematics, physical sciences, religion/biblical studies, social sciences. *Special characteristics:* 311 awards ($1,357,215 total): children of faculty/staff, international students. ***ROTC:*** Army, Air Force cooperative.

LOANS ***Student loans:*** 83% of past graduating class borrowed through all loan programs. *Average indebtedness per student:* $38,013. ***Average need-based loan:*** Freshmen: $3185. Undergraduates: $4049. ***Programs:*** Federal Direct (Subsidized and Unsubsidized Stafford, PLUS), state, alternative loans.

WORK-STUDY ***Federal work-study:*** 1,181 jobs averaging $3847. ***State or other work-study/employment:*** 1,181 part-time jobs averaging $3847.

APPLYING FOR FINANCIAL AID ***Required financial aid form:*** FAFSA. ***Financial aid deadline:*** Continuous. ***Notification date:*** Continuous.

CONTACT Mrs. Amanda L. Kishbaugh, Director of Financial Aid, Bloomsburg University of Pennsylvania, 119 Warren Student Services Center, 400 East 2nd Street, Bloomsburg, PA 17815-1301, 570-389-4279. *Fax:* 570-389-4795. *E-mail:* akishba2@bloomu.edu.
Website: http://www.bloomu.edu/.

BLUEFIELD COLLEGE

Bluefield, VA

Tuition & fees: N/R	Average undergraduate aid package: $17,600

ABOUT THE INSTITUTION Independent Southern Baptist, coed. ***Awards:*** bachelor's and master's degrees. 43 undergraduate majors. Federal methodology is used as a basis for awarding need-based institutional aid.

FRESHMAN FINANCIAL AID (Fall 2019, est.) 186 applied for aid; of those 97% were deemed to have need. 100% of freshmen with need received aid; of those 15% had need fully met. ***Average percent of need met:*** 71% (excluding resources awarded to replace EFC). ***Average financial aid package:*** $19,787 (excluding resources awarded to replace EFC). 3% of all full-time freshmen had no need and received non-need-based gift aid.

UNDERGRADUATE FINANCIAL AID (Fall 2019, est.) 716 applied for aid; of those 95% were deemed to have need. 100% of undergraduates with need received aid; of those 12% had need fully met. ***Average percent of need met:*** 63% (excluding resources awarded to replace EFC). ***Average financial aid package:*** $17,600 (excluding resources awarded to replace EFC). 7% of all full-time undergraduates had no need and received non-need-based gift aid.

GIFT AID (NEED-BASED) ***Total amount:*** $7,501,165 (31% federal, 16% state, 45% institutional, 8% external sources). ***Receiving aid:*** Freshmen: 96% (181); all full-time undergraduates: 90% (670). ***Average award:*** Freshmen: $16,909; Undergraduates: $14,410. ***Scholarships, grants, and awards:*** Federal Pell, FSEOG, state, private, college/university gift aid from institutional funds.

GIFT AID (NON-NEED-BASED) ***Total amount:*** $883,749 (20% state, 67% institutional, 13% external sources). ***Receiving aid:*** Freshmen: 14% (26). Undergraduates: 8% (63). ***Average award:*** Freshmen: $9613. Undergraduates: $8162. ***Scholarships, grants, and awards by category:*** *Academic interests/achievement:* 511 awards ($2,939,434 total): general academic interests/achievements. *Creative arts/performance:* 51 awards ($208,948 total): applied art and design, music, performing arts, theater/drama. *Special achievements/activities:* 347 awards ($2,957,823 total): cheerleading/drum major, general special achievements/activities. *Special characteristics:* 159 awards ($446,961 total): adult students, international students, religious affiliation.

LOANS ***Student loans:*** $5,201,278 (82% need-based, 18% non-need-based). 75% of past graduating class borrowed through all loan programs. *Average indebtedness per student:* $34,618. ***Average need-based loan:*** Freshmen: $3599. Undergraduates: $4153. ***Parent loans:*** $1,143,424 (54% need-based, 46% non-need-based). ***Programs:*** Federal Direct (Subsidized and Unsubsidized Stafford, PLUS), private loans.

WORK-STUDY ***Federal work-study:*** Total amount: $100,654; 86 jobs averaging $1190. ***State or other work-study/employment:*** Total amount: $4830 (55% need-based, 45% non-need-based). 18 part-time jobs averaging $268.

ATHLETIC AWARDS Total amount: $2,875,323 (79% need-based, 21% non-need-based).

APPLYING FOR FINANCIAL AID ***Required financial aid forms:*** FAFSA, state aid form. ***Financial aid deadline (priority):*** 6/1. ***Notification date:*** Continuous.

CONTACT Mrs. Cary Grace Wright, Director of Financial Aid, Bluefield College, 3000 College Avenue, Bluefield, VA 24605, 276-326-4215 or toll-free 800-872-0175. *Fax:* 276-326-4356. *E-mail:* cwright@bluefield.edu.
Website: http://www.bluefield.edu/.

BLUEFIELD STATE COLLEGE

Bluefield, WV

Tuition & fees: N/R	Average undergraduate aid package: $3101

ABOUT THE INSTITUTION State-supported, coed. ***Awards:*** associate and bachelor's degrees. 18 undergraduate majors. ***Total enrollment:*** 1,379. Undergraduates: 2,758. Freshmen: 222. Federal methodology is used as a basis for awarding need-based institutional aid.

FRESHMAN FINANCIAL AID (Fall 2018) 192 applied for aid; of those 88% were deemed to have need. 99% of freshmen with need received aid; of those 6% had need fully met. ***Average percent of need met:*** 49% (excluding resources awarded to replace EFC). ***Average financial aid package:*** $2581 (excluding resources awarded to replace EFC). 8% of all full-time freshmen had no need and received non-need-based gift aid.

UNDERGRADUATE FINANCIAL AID (Fall 2018) 908 applied for aid; of those 92% were deemed to have need. 99% of undergraduates with need received aid; of those 4% had need fully met. ***Average percent of need met:*** 49% (excluding resources awarded to replace EFC). ***Average financial aid package:*** $3101 (excluding resources awarded to replace EFC). 7% of all full-time undergraduates had no need and received non-need-based gift aid.

GIFT AID (NEED-BASED) ***Total amount:*** $4,747,377 (78% federal, 22% state). ***Receiving aid:*** Freshmen: 80% (161); all full-time undergraduates: 77% (757). ***Average award:*** Freshmen: $2861; Undergraduates: $3331. ***Scholarships, grants, and awards:*** Federal Pell, FSEOG, state, college/university gift aid from institutional funds.

GIFT AID (NON-NEED-BASED) ***Total amount:*** $1,419,712 (32% state, 23% institutional, 45% external sources). ***Receiving aid:*** Freshmen: 35% (70). Undergraduates: 24% (241). ***Average award:*** Freshmen: $1326. Undergraduates: $898. ***Scholarships, grants, and awards by category:*** *Academic interests/achievement:* business, computer science, education, engineering/technologies, home economics. *Special achievements/activities:* community service, general special achievements/activities, religious involvement.

LOANS ***Student loans:*** $4,847,214 (47% need-based, 53% non-need-based). 70% of past graduating class borrowed through all loan programs. *Average indebtedness per student:* $25,812. ***Average need-based loan:*** Freshmen: $2978. Undergraduates: $3929. ***Parent loans:*** $153,333 (100% non-need-based). ***Programs:*** Federal Direct (Subsidized and Unsubsidized Stafford, PLUS).

WORK-STUDY ***Federal work-study:*** Total amount: $257,200; jobs available. ***State or other work-study/employment:*** Total amount: $220,000 (100% non-need-based).

ATHLETIC AWARDS Total amount: $307,422 (100% non-need-based).

APPLYING FOR FINANCIAL AID ***Required financial aid forms:*** FAFSA, institution's own form. ***Financial aid deadline (priority):*** 3/1. ***Notification date:*** Students must reply by 6/30 or within 2 weeks of notification.

CONTACT Dr. Anthony Underwood, Chief Financial Aid Officer, Bluefield State College, 219 Rock Street, Bluefield, WV 24701, 304-3274022 or toll-free 800-344-8892 Ext.4065 (in-state), 800-654-7798 Ext.4065 (out-of-state). *Fax:* 304-325-7747. *Website:* http://www.bluefieldstate.edu/.

BLUE MOUNTAIN COLLEGE

Blue Mountain, MS

CONTACT Mrs. Beverly K. Hickey, Director of Financial Aid, Blue Mountain College, PO Box 160, Blue Mountain, MS 38610-0160, 662-685-4771 Ext. 141 or toll-free 800-235-0136. *Fax:* 662-685-4776. *E-mail:* bhickey@bmc.edu.
Website: http://www.bmc.edu/.

BLUFFTON UNIVERSITY

Bluffton, OH

Comprehensive fee: $49,848	Average undergraduate aid package: $30,037

ABOUT THE INSTITUTION Independent Mennonite, coed. ***Awards:*** certificates, bachelor's, and master's degrees. 46 undergraduate majors. ***Total enrollment:*** 768. Undergraduates: 710. Freshmen: 231.

UNDERGRADUATE EXPENSES for 2020–2021 ***Comprehensive fee:*** $49,848 includes mandatory fees ($550) and room and board ($11,346). ***College room only:*** $5586. Full-time tuition and fees vary according to course load, degree level, and program. Room and board charges vary according to board plan and housing facility. ***Part-time tuition:*** $1415 per credit hour. Part-time tuition and fees vary according to course load, degree level, and program.

FRESHMAN FINANCIAL AID (Fall 2019, est.) 223 applied for aid; of those 96% were deemed to have need. 100% of freshmen with need received aid; of those 15% had need fully met. ***Average percent of need met:*** 81% (excluding resources awarded to replace EFC). ***Average financial aid package:*** $31,745 (excluding resources awarded to replace EFC). 7% of all full-time freshmen had no need and received non-need-based gift aid.

UNDERGRADUATE FINANCIAL AID (Fall 2019, est.) 546 applied for aid; of those 94% were deemed to have need. 100% of undergraduates with need received aid; of those 16% had need fully met. ***Average percent of need met:*** 78% (excluding resources awarded to replace EFC). ***Average financial aid package:*** $30,037 (excluding resources awarded to replace EFC). 17% of all full-time undergraduates had no need and received non-need-based gift aid.

GIFT AID (NEED-BASED) ***Receiving aid:*** Freshmen: 93% (214); all full-time undergraduates: 83% (512). ***Average award:*** Freshmen: $27,257; Undergraduates: $25,017. ***Scholarships, grants, and awards:*** Federal Pell, FSEOG, state, private, college/university gift aid from institutional funds.

GIFT AID (NON-NEED-BASED) ***Receiving aid:*** Freshmen: 8% (19). Undergraduates: 8% (51). ***Average award:*** Freshmen: $21,369. Undergraduates: $19,669. ***Scholarships, grants, and awards by category:*** *Academic interests/achievement:* biological sciences, general academic interests/achievements, mathematics, physical sciences, premedicine. *Creative arts/performance:* art/fine arts, music, performing arts. *Special achievements/activities:* leadership. *Special characteristics:* children and siblings of alumni, children of faculty/staff, international students, members of minority groups, out-of-state students, religious affiliation. ***Tuition waivers:*** Full or partial for employees or children of employees.

LOANS ***Student loans:*** 81% of past graduating class borrowed through all loan programs. *Average indebtedness per student:* $35,601. ***Average need-based loan:*** Freshmen: $3790. Undergraduates: $4342. ***Programs:*** Federal Direct (Subsidized and Unsubsidized Stafford).

WORK-STUDY Federal work-study jobs available. ***State or other work-study/employment:*** Part-time jobs available.

APPLYING FOR FINANCIAL AID ***Required financial aid form:*** FAFSA. ***Notification date:*** Continuous.

CONTACT Lawrence Matthews, Director of Financial Aid, Bluffton University, 1 University Drive, Bluffton, OH 45817-2104, 419-358-3266 or toll-free 800-488-3257. *Fax:* 419-358-3073. *E-mail:* finaid@bluffton.edu.
Website: http://www.bluffton.edu/.

BOB JONES UNIVERSITY

Greenville, SC

CONTACT Office of Financial Aid, Bob Jones University, 1700 Wade Hampton Boulevard, Greenville, SC 29614, 864-242-5100 Ext. 3040 or toll-free 800-252-6363.
E-mail: finaid@bju.edu.
Website: http://www.bju.edu/.

BOISE BIBLE COLLEGE

Boise, ID

Tuition & fees: N/R	Average undergraduate aid package: $14,791

ABOUT THE INSTITUTION Independent nondenominational, coed. ***Awards:*** certificates, associate, and bachelor's degrees. 14 undergraduate majors. ***Total enrollment:*** 12. Undergraduates: 121. Institutional methodology is used as a basis for awarding need-based institutional aid.

UNDERGRADUATE EXPENSES for 2020–2021 ***Application fee:*** $25. ***Tuition:*** part-time $415 per credit hour. ***Required fees:*** full-time $650. Room and board charges vary according to board plan and housing facility.

FRESHMAN FINANCIAL AID (Fall 2018) 16 applied for aid; of those 63% were deemed to have need. 100% of freshmen with need received aid. ***Average percent of need met:*** 68% (excluding resources awarded to replace EFC). ***Average financial aid package:*** $11,336 (excluding resources awarded to replace EFC). 28% of all full-time freshmen had no need and received non-need-based gift aid.

UNDERGRADUATE FINANCIAL AID (Fall 2018) 82 applied for aid; of those 71% were deemed to have need. 100% of undergraduates with need received aid. ***Average percent of need met:*** 63% (excluding resources awarded to replace EFC). ***Average financial aid package:*** $14,791 (excluding resources awarded to replace EFC). 16% of all full-time undergraduates had no need and received non-need-based gift aid.

GIFT AID (NEED-BASED) ***Total amount:*** $430,650 (100% federal). ***Receiving aid:*** Freshmen: 39% (7); all full-time undergraduates: 54% (50). ***Average award:*** Freshmen: $8361; Undergraduates: $7909. ***Scholarships, grants, and awards:*** Federal Pell, FSEOG, private, college/university gift aid from institutional funds.

GIFT AID (NON-NEED-BASED) ***Total amount:*** $162,519 (22% institutional, 78% external sources). ***Receiving aid:*** Freshmen: 56% (10). Undergraduates: 49% (46). ***Average award:*** Freshmen: $5984. Undergraduates: $6259. ***Scholarships, grants, and awards by category:*** *Academic interests/achievement:* 99 awards ($245,031 total): religion/biblical studies. *Creative arts/performance:* 12 awards ($52,575 total): music. *Special achievements/activities:* 4 awards ($8000 total): leadership. *Special characteristics:* 22 awards ($49,905 total): children of faculty/staff, general special characteristics, international students, relatives of clergy, spouses of current students. ***Tuition waivers:*** Full or partial for employees or children of employees.

LOANS ***Student loans:*** $317,767 (51% need-based, 49% non-need-based). 41% of past graduating class borrowed through all loan programs. *Average indebtedness per student:* $13,828. ***Average need-based loan:*** Freshmen: $3369. Undergraduates: $3211. ***Parent loans:*** $32,425 (100% non-need-based). ***Programs:*** Federal Direct (Subsidized and Unsubsidized Stafford, PLUS), alternative loans.

APPLYING FOR FINANCIAL AID ***Required financial aid forms:*** FAFSA, institution's own form. ***Financial aid deadline:*** Continuous. ***Notification date:*** Continuous beginning 11/1.

CONTACT Mr. Ben Bishop, Director of Financial Aid, Boise Bible College, 8695 West Marigold Street, Boise, ID 83714-1220, 208-376-7731 or toll-free 800-893-7755.
E-mail: bbishop@boisebible.edu.
Website: http://www.boisebible.edu/.

BOISE STATE UNIVERSITY

Boise, ID

Tuition & fees (ID res): $8068 | **Average undergraduate aid package: $10,384**

ABOUT THE INSTITUTION State-supported, coed. ***Awards:*** certificates, associate, bachelor's, master's, and doctoral degrees. 78 undergraduate majors. ***Total enrollment:*** 26,727. Undergraduates: 22,939. Freshmen: 3,023. Federal methodology is used as a basis for awarding need-based institutional aid.

UNDERGRADUATE EXPENSES for 2019–2020 ***Application fee:*** $50. ***Tuition, state resident:*** full-time $5532; part-time $252 per credit hour. ***Tuition, nonresident:*** full-time $22,452; part-time $609 per credit hour. ***Required fees:*** full-time $2536; $115 per term. Full-time tuition and fees vary according to course load, location, and reciprocity agreements. Part-time tuition and fees vary according to course load and location. ***College room and board:*** $9760; ***Room only:*** $6652. Room and board charges vary according to board plan, housing facility, and student level.

FRESHMAN FINANCIAL AID (Fall 2018) 1635 applied for aid; of those 99% were deemed to have need. 95% of freshmen with need received aid; of those 19% had need fully met. ***Average percent of need met:*** 60% (excluding resources awarded to replace EFC). ***Average financial aid package:*** $11,059 (excluding resources awarded to replace EFC). 4% of all full-time freshmen had no need and received non-need-based gift aid.

UNDERGRADUATE FINANCIAL AID (Fall 2018) 7,540 applied for aid; of those 99% were deemed to have need. 96% of undergraduates with need received aid; of those 14% had need fully met. ***Average percent of need met:*** 58% (excluding resources awarded to replace EFC). ***Average financial aid package:*** $10,384 (excluding resources awarded to replace EFC). 2% of all full-time undergraduates had no need and received non-need-based gift aid.

GIFT AID (NEED-BASED) ***Total amount:*** $36,399,182 (62% federal, 14% state, 18% institutional, 6% external sources). ***Receiving aid:*** Freshmen: 35% (1,029); all full-time undergraduates: 39% (5,051). ***Average award:*** Freshmen: $6510; Undergraduates: $6166. ***Scholarships, grants, and awards:*** Federal Pell, FSEOG, state, private, college/university gift aid from institutional funds, Federal Nursing.

GIFT AID (NON-NEED-BASED) ***Total amount:*** $2,377,324 (3% federal, 5% state, 56% institutional, 36% external sources). ***Receiving aid:*** Freshmen: 4% (114). Undergraduates: 2% (281). ***Average award:*** Freshmen: $2820. Undergraduates: $2739. ***Scholarships, grants, and awards by category:*** *Academic interests/achievement:* architecture, area/ethnic studies, biological sciences, business, communication, computer science, education, engineering/technologies, English, foreign languages, general academic interests/achievements, health fields, home economics, humanities, international studies, mathematics, military science, physical sciences, premedicine, religion/biblical studies, social sciences. *Creative arts/performance:* applied art and design, dance, debating, general creative arts/performance, journalism/publications, music, performing arts, theater/drama. *Special achievements/activities:* cheerleading/drum major, community service, leadership, rodeo. *Special characteristics:* ethnic background, first-generation college students, general special characteristics, handicapped students, international students, local/state students, members of minority groups, out-of-state students, previous college experience, spouses of current students, veterans. ***Tuition waivers:*** Full or partial for employees or children of employees, senior citizens. ***ROTC:*** Army.

LOANS ***Student loans:*** $55,642,604 (73% need-based, 27% non-need-based). 60% of past graduating class borrowed through all loan programs. *Average indebtedness per student:* $27,052. ***Average need-based loan:*** Freshmen: $3348. Undergraduates: $4106. ***Parent loans:*** $11,858,609 (35% need-based, 65% non-need-based). ***Programs:*** Federal Direct (Subsidized and Unsubsidized Stafford, PLUS), Perkins, Federal Nursing, college/university.

WORK-STUDY ***Federal work-study:*** Total amount: $680,341; jobs available. ***State or other work-study/employment:*** Total amount: $368,670 (100% need-based). Part-time jobs available.

ATHLETIC AWARDS Total amount: $8,258,434 (87% need-based, 13% non-need-based).

APPLYING FOR FINANCIAL AID ***Required financial aid form:*** FAFSA. ***Financial aid deadline (priority):*** 2/15. ***Notification date:*** Continuous beginning 3/15. Students must reply by 4/12 or within 4 weeks of notification.

CONTACT Financial Aid Office, Boise State University, 1910 University Drive, Boise, ID 83725-0399, 208-426-1011 or toll-free 800-824-7017.
Website: http://www.boisestate.edu/.

BON SECOURS MEMORIAL COLLEGE OF NURSING

Richmond, VA

CONTACT Financial Aid Office, Bon Secours Memorial College of Nursing, 8550 Magellan Parkway, Suite 1100, Richmond, VA 23227-1149, 804-627-5300 or toll-free 866-238-7414.
Website: http://www.bsmcon.edu/.

BORICUA COLLEGE

New York, NY

CONTACT Ms. Rosalia Cruz, Financial Aid Administrator, Boricua College, 3755 Broadway, New York, NY 10032-1560, 212-694-1000 Ext. 611. *Fax:* 212-694-1015. *E-mail:* rcruz@boricuacollege.edu.
Website: http://www.boricuacollege.edu/.

BOSTON ARCHITECTURAL COLLEGE

Boston, MA

Tuition & fees: $26,503 | **Average undergraduate aid package: $12,871**

ABOUT THE INSTITUTION Independent, coed. ***Awards:*** certificates, bachelor's, and master's degrees. 4 undergraduate majors. ***Total enrollment:*** 878. Undergraduates: 472. Freshmen: 24. Federal methodology is used as a basis for awarding need-based institutional aid.

UNDERGRADUATE EXPENSES for 2020–2021 ***One-time required fee:*** $150. ***Tuition:*** full-time $25,753; part-time $1762 per credit hour. ***Required fees:*** full-time $750; $150 per term.

FRESHMAN FINANCIAL AID (Fall 2019, est.) 5 applied for aid; of those 100% were deemed to have need. 100% of freshmen with need received aid. ***Average percent of need met:*** 27% (excluding resources awarded to replace EFC). ***Average financial aid package:*** $9071 (excluding resources awarded to replace EFC).

UNDERGRADUATE FINANCIAL AID (Fall 2019, est.) 86 applied for aid; of those 99% were deemed to have need. 98% of undergraduates with need received aid; of those 2% had need fully met. ***Average percent of need met:*** 36% (excluding resources awarded to replace EFC). ***Average financial aid package:*** $12,871 (excluding resources awarded to replace EFC). 1% of all full-time undergraduates had no need and received non-need-based gift aid.

GIFT AID (NEED-BASED) ***Total amount:*** $613,332 (66% federal, 9% state, 4% institutional, 21% external sources). ***Receiving aid:*** Freshmen: 42% (5); all full-time undergraduates: 66% (69). ***Average award:*** Freshmen: $7321; Undergraduates: $8807. ***Scholarships, grants, and awards:*** Federal Pell, FSEOG, state, private, college/university gift aid from institutional funds.

GIFT AID (NON-NEED-BASED) ***Total amount:*** $47,448 (19% institutional, 81% external sources). ***Receiving aid:*** Undergraduates: 1% (1). ***Average award:*** Undergraduates: $1012. ***Scholarships, grants, and awards by category:*** *Academic interests/achievement:* architecture, general academic interests/achievements. ***Tuition waivers:*** Full or partial for employees or children of employees.

LOANS ***Student loans:*** $1,319,327 (88% need-based, 12% non-need-based). ***Average need-based loan:*** Freshmen: $2187. Undergraduates: $5975. ***Parent loans:*** $531,781 (72% need-based, 28% non-need-based). ***Programs:*** Federal Direct (Subsidized and Unsubsidized Stafford, PLUS), private loans.

WORK-STUDY ***Federal work-study:*** Total amount: $48,238; 17 jobs averaging $2935.

APPLYING FOR FINANCIAL AID ***Required financial aid form:*** FAFSA. ***Financial aid deadline (priority):*** 4/15. ***Notification date:*** Continuous beginning 5/1. Students must reply within 2 weeks of notification.

CONTACT Ms. Janice Wilkos-Greenberg, Director of Financial Aid, Boston Architectural College, 320 Newbury Street, Boston, MA 02115, 617-585-0183. *Fax:* 617-585-0131. *E-mail:* janice.greenberg@the-bac.edu.
Website: http://www.the-bac.edu/.

BOSTON BAPTIST COLLEGE

Boston, MA

Tuition & fees: N/R **Average undergraduate aid package: N/A**

ABOUT THE INSTITUTION Independent Baptist, coed. ***Awards:*** certificates, diplomas, associate, and bachelor's degrees. 1 undergraduate major. Both federal and institutional methodology are used as a basis for awarding need-based institutional aid.

FRESHMAN FINANCIAL AID (Fall 2018) 11 applied for aid; of those 100% were deemed to have need. 100% of freshmen with need received aid.

UNDERGRADUATE FINANCIAL AID (Fall 2018) 12% of all full-time undergraduates had no need and received non-need-based gift aid.

GIFT AID (NEED-BASED) ***Scholarships, grants, and awards:*** Federal Pell, FSEOG, state, private, college/university gift aid from institutional funds.

GIFT AID (NON-NEED-BASED) ***Average award:*** Undergraduates: $5767. ***Scholarships, grants, and awards by category:*** *Academic interests/achievement:* 65 awards ($574,585 total): religion/biblical studies. *Special characteristics:* 9 awards ($55,000 total): children and siblings of alumni, children of faculty/staff.

LOANS ***Student loans:*** 71% of past graduating class borrowed through all loan programs. *Average indebtedness per student:* $6384. ***Programs:*** Federal Direct (Subsidized and Unsubsidized Stafford, PLUS), state, private loans.

WORK-STUDY ***Federal work-study:*** 5 jobs available.

APPLYING FOR FINANCIAL AID ***Required financial aid form:*** FAFSA. ***Financial aid deadline:*** Continuous.

CONTACT Mrs. Carolina Woundy, Financial Aid Officer, Boston Baptist College, 950 Metropolitan Ave, Hyde Park, MA 02136, 617-364-3510 Ext. 245 or toll-free 888-235-2014. *Fax:* 857-241-3040. *E-mail:* cwoundy@boston.edu.
Website: http://www.boston.edu/.

BOSTON COLLEGE

Chestnut Hill, MA

Tuition & fees: $56,780 **Average undergraduate aid package: $47,647**

ABOUT THE INSTITUTION Independent Roman Catholic (Jesuit), coed. ***Awards:*** certificates, bachelor's, master's, and doctoral degrees (also offers continuing education program with significant enrollment not reflected in profile). 53 undergraduate majors. ***Total enrollment:*** 14,171. Undergraduates: 9,370. Freshmen: 2,297. Institutional methodology is used as a basis for awarding need-based institutional aid.

UNDERGRADUATE EXPENSES for 2019–2020 ***Application fee:*** $80. ***Comprehensive fee:*** $71,606 includes full-time tuition ($56,780) and room and board ($14,826). ***College room only:*** $9300. Room and board charges vary according to board plan and housing facility.

FRESHMAN FINANCIAL AID (Fall 2019, est.) 1258 applied for aid; of those 82% were deemed to have need. 100% of freshmen with need received aid; of those 100% had need fully met. ***Average percent of need met:*** 100% (excluding resources awarded to replace EFC). ***Average financial aid package:*** $46,504 (excluding resources awarded to replace EFC). 1% of all full-time freshmen had no need and received non-need-based gift aid.

UNDERGRADUATE FINANCIAL AID (Fall 2019, est.) 4,459 applied for aid; of those 89% were deemed to have need. 100% of undergraduates with need received aid; of those 100% had need fully met. ***Average percent of need met:*** 100% (excluding resources awarded to replace EFC). ***Average financial aid package:*** $47,647 (excluding resources awarded to replace EFC). 2% of all full-time undergraduates had no need and received non-need-based gift aid.

GIFT AID (NEED-BASED) ***Total amount:*** $157,401,823 (6% federal, 1% state, 91% institutional, 2% external sources). ***Receiving aid:*** Freshmen: 40% (911); all full-time undergraduates: 38% (3,544). ***Average award:*** Freshmen: $43,953; Undergraduates: $44,424. ***Scholarships, grants, and awards:*** Federal Pell, FSEOG, state, private, college/university gift aid from institutional funds.

GIFT AID (NON-NEED-BASED) ***Total amount:*** $10,190,591 (25% federal, 53% institutional, 22% external sources). ***Receiving aid:*** Freshmen: 1% (16). Undergraduates: 1% (66). ***Average award:*** Freshmen: $24,843. Undergraduates: $23,898. ***Scholarships, grants, and awards by category:*** *Academic interests/achievement:* general academic interests/achievements, military science. *Special achievements/activities:* leadership. *Special characteristics:* children of faculty/staff. ***Tuition waivers:*** Full or partial for employees or children of employees. ***ROTC:*** Army cooperative, Naval cooperative, Air Force cooperative.

LOANS ***Student loans:*** $17,084,413 (75% need-based, 25% non-need-based). 48% of past graduating class borrowed through all loan programs. *Average indebtedness per student:* $23,136. ***Average need-based loan:*** Freshmen: $3327. Undergraduates: $4010. ***Parent loans:*** $39,676,087 (100% non-need-based). ***Programs:*** Federal Direct (Subsidized and Unsubsidized Stafford, PLUS), Perkins, Federal Nursing, state.

WORK-STUDY ***Federal work-study:*** Total amount: $8,563,950; jobs available.

ATHLETIC AWARDS Total amount: $20,087,383 (14% need-based, 86% non-need-based).

APPLYING FOR FINANCIAL AID ***Required financial aid forms:*** FAFSA, CSS Financial Aid PROFILE, business/farm supplement, federal income tax form(s), W-2 forms. ***Financial aid deadline (priority):*** 2/1. ***Notification date:*** 4/1. Students must reply by 5/1.

CONTACT Office of Student Services, Boston College, 140 Commonwealth Avenue, Lyons Hall, Chestnut Hill, MA 02467, 617-552-3300 or toll-free 800-360-2522. *Fax:* 617-552-4889. *E-mail:* studentservices@bc.edu.
Website: http://www.bc.edu/.

BOSTON UNIVERSITY

Boston, MA

Tuition & fees: $55,892 **Average undergraduate aid package: $46,252**

ABOUT THE INSTITUTION Independent, coed. ***Awards:*** certificates, bachelor's, master's, and doctoral degrees. 125 undergraduate majors. ***Total enrollment:*** 34,657. Undergraduates: 18,515. Freshmen: 3,612. Institutional methodology is used as a basis for awarding need-based institutional aid.

UNDERGRADUATE EXPENSES for 2019–2020 ***Application fee:*** $80. ***Comprehensive fee:*** $72,052 includes full-time tuition ($54,720), mandatory fees ($1172), and room and board ($16,160). ***College room only:*** $10,680. Full-time tuition and fees vary according to class time and course load. Room and board charges vary according to board plan, housing facility, and location. ***Part-time tuition:*** $1710 per credit. ***Part-time fees:*** $60 per term. Part-time tuition and fees vary according to class time, course level, and course load. ***Payment plan:*** Tuition prepayment.

FRESHMAN FINANCIAL AID (Fall 2019, est.) 1474 applied for aid; of those 85% were deemed to have need. 100% of freshmen with need received aid; of those 34% had need fully met. ***Average percent of need met:*** 93% (excluding resources awarded to replace EFC). ***Average financial aid package:*** $51,652 (excluding resources awarded to replace EFC). 5% of all full-time freshmen had no need and received non-need-based gift aid.

UNDERGRADUATE FINANCIAL AID (Fall 2019, est.) 8,138 applied for aid; of those 85% were deemed to have need. 100% of undergraduates with need received aid; of those 25% had need fully met. ***Average percent of need met:*** 85% (excluding resources awarded to replace EFC). ***Average financial aid package:*** $46,252 (excluding resources awarded to replace EFC). 5% of all full-time undergraduates had no need and received non-need-based gift aid.

GIFT AID (NEED-BASED) ***Total amount:*** $275,754,748 (7% federal, 1% state, 91% institutional, 1% external sources). ***Receiving aid:*** Freshmen: 39% (1,237); all full-time undergraduates: 41% (6,778). ***Average award:*** Freshmen: $47,141; Undergraduates: $40,969. ***Scholarships, grants, and awards:*** Federal Pell, FSEOG, state, private, college/university gift aid from institutional funds.

GIFT AID (NON-NEED-BASED) ***Total amount:*** $28,697,813 (3% federal, 77% institutional, 20% external sources). ***Receiving aid:*** Freshmen: 9% (293). Undergraduates: 7% (1,178). ***Average award:*** Freshmen: $26,153. Undergraduates: $23,596. ***Scholarships, grants, and awards by category:*** *Academic interests/achievement:* 1,028 awards ($16,032,206 total): engineering/technologies, general academic interests/achievements, military science. *Creative arts/performance:* 333 awards ($9,039,825 total): applied art and design, music, theater/drama. *Special achievements/activities:* 68 awards ($3,619,174 total): general special achievements/activities, memberships. *Special characteristics:* 559 awards ($11,897,647 total): children and siblings of alumni, children of faculty/staff, general special characteristics, local/state students, members of minority groups, relatives of clergy, religious affiliation, veterans. ***Tuition waivers:*** Full or partial for employees or children of employees. ***ROTC:*** Army, Naval, Air Force.

LOANS ***Student loans:*** $70,996,846 (37% need-based, 63% non-need-based). 46% of past graduating class borrowed through all loan programs. *Average indebtedness per student:* $40,349. ***Average need-based loan:*** Freshmen: $1700. Undergraduates: $3294. ***Parent loans:*** $11,094,949 (85% need-based, 15% non-need-based). ***Programs:*** Federal Direct (Subsidized and Unsubsidized Stafford, PLUS), state.

WORK-STUDY ***Federal work-study:*** Total amount: $6,488,107; 2,847 jobs averaging $2279. ***State or other work-study/employment:*** Part-time jobs available.

ATHLETIC AWARDS Total amount: $16,110,354 (15% need-based, 85% non-need-based).

APPLYING FOR FINANCIAL AID ***Required financial aid forms:*** FAFSA, CSS Financial Aid PROFILE, noncustodial (divorced/separated) parent's statement. ***Financial aid deadline:*** 1/6. ***Notification date:*** 3/25. Students must reply by 5/1 or within 2 weeks of notification.

CONTACT Julie Wickstrom, Executive Director of Financial Assistance, Boston University, 881 Commonwealth Avenue, Boston, MA 02215, 617-353-4176. *Fax:* 617-353-8200. *E-mail:* finaid@bu.edu.
Website: http://www.bu.edu/.

BOWDOIN COLLEGE

Brunswick, ME

Tuition & fees: $56,350	Average undergraduate aid package: $51,107

ABOUT THE INSTITUTION Independent, coed. ***Awards:*** bachelor's degrees. 47 undergraduate majors. ***Total enrollment:*** 1,835. Undergraduates: 1,835. Freshmen: 498. Institutional methodology is used as a basis for awarding need-based institutional aid.

UNDERGRADUATE EXPENSES for 2019–2020 ***Application fee:*** $65. ***Comprehensive fee:*** $71,710 includes full-time tuition ($55,822), mandatory fees ($528), and room and board ($15,360). ***College room only:*** $7372. Room and board charges vary according to board plan. ***Part-time tuition:*** $1090 per credit hour.

FRESHMAN FINANCIAL AID (Fall 2019, est.) 304 applied for aid; of those 81% were deemed to have need. 100% of freshmen with need received aid; of those 100% had need fully met. ***Average percent of need met:*** 100% (excluding resources awarded to replace EFC). ***Average financial aid package:*** $53,004 (excluding resources awarded to replace EFC). 2% of all full-time freshmen had no need and received non-need-based gift aid.

UNDERGRADUATE FINANCIAL AID (Fall 2019, est.) 998 applied for aid; of those 89% were deemed to have need. 100% of undergraduates with need received aid; of those 100% had need fully met. ***Average percent of need met:*** 100% (excluding resources awarded to replace EFC). ***Average financial aid package:*** $51,107 (excluding resources awarded to replace EFC). 2% of all full-time undergraduates had no need and received non-need-based gift aid.

GIFT AID (NEED-BASED) ***Total amount:*** $43,816,951 (4% federal, 95% institutional, 1% external sources). ***Receiving aid:*** Freshmen: 49% (246); all full-time undergraduates: 49% (891). ***Average award:*** Freshmen: $51,131; Undergraduates: $49,124. ***Scholarships, grants, and awards:*** Federal Pell, FSEOG, state, private, college/university gift aid from institutional funds.

GIFT AID (NON-NEED-BASED) ***Total amount:*** $1,964,920 (10% institutional, 90% external sources). ***Average award:*** Freshmen: $1000. Undergraduates: $1000. ***Scholarships, grants, and awards by category:*** *Academic interests/achievement:* 36 awards ($36,000 total): general academic interests/achievements. *Special achievements/activities:* leadership. *Special characteristics:* children of faculty/staff. ***Tuition waivers:*** Full or partial for employees or children of employees.

LOANS ***Student loans:*** 28% of past graduating class borrowed through all loan programs. *Average indebtedness per student:* $26,775. ***Programs:*** Federal Direct (Subsidized and Unsubsidized Stafford), Perkins, state.

WORK-STUDY ***Federal work-study:*** Total amount: $1,122,580; 570 jobs averaging $1969. ***State or other work-study/employment:*** Total amount: $623,655 (100% need-based). 314 part-time jobs averaging $1986.

APPLYING FOR FINANCIAL AID ***Required financial aid forms:*** FAFSA, CSS Financial Aid PROFILE, noncustodial (divorced/separated) parent's statement, business/farm supplement. ***Financial aid deadline:*** 2/1. ***Notification date:*** 4/1. Students must reply by 5/1 or within 1 week of notification.

CONTACT Mr. Michael D. Bartini, Director of Student Aid, Bowdoin College, 5300 College Station, Brunswick, ME 04011-8444, 207-725-3146. *Fax:* 207-725-3864. *E-mail:* mbartini@bowdoin.edu.
Website: http://www.bowdoin.edu/.

BOWIE STATE UNIVERSITY

Bowie, MD

Tuition & fees (MD res): $8445	Average undergraduate aid package: $8916

ABOUT THE INSTITUTION State-supported, coed. ***Awards:*** certificates, bachelor's, master's, and doctoral degrees. 29 undergraduate majors. ***Total enrollment:*** 6,436. Undergraduates: 5,306. Freshmen: 909. Federal methodology is used as a basis for awarding need-based institutional aid.

UNDERGRADUATE EXPENSES for 2019–2020 ***Application fee:*** $40. ***Tuition, state resident:*** full-time $5647; part-time $248 per credit hour. ***Tuition, nonresident:*** full-time $16,338; part-time $687 per credit hour. ***Required fees:*** full-time $2798; $124 per credit hour. ***College room and board:*** $9916. Room and board charges vary according to board plan and housing facility.

FRESHMAN FINANCIAL AID (Fall 2018) 693 applied for aid; of those 100% were deemed to have need. 100% of freshmen with need received aid; of those 22% had need fully met. ***Average percent of need met:*** 42% (excluding resources awarded to replace EFC). ***Average financial aid package:*** $9004 (excluding resources awarded to replace EFC). 2% of all full-time freshmen had no need and received non-need-based gift aid.

UNDERGRADUATE FINANCIAL AID (Fall 2018) 3,183 applied for aid; of those 100% were deemed to have need. 100% of undergraduates with need received aid; of those 18% had need fully met. ***Average percent of need met:*** 41% (excluding resources awarded to replace EFC). ***Average financial aid package:*** $8916 (excluding resources awarded to replace EFC). 2% of all full-time undergraduates had no need and received non-need-based gift aid.

GIFT AID (NEED-BASED) ***Total amount:*** $23,689,725 (54% federal, 25% state, 21% institutional). ***Receiving aid:*** Freshmen: 66% (540); all full-time undergraduates: 66% (2,461). ***Average award:*** Freshmen: $8020; Undergraduates: $7535. ***Scholarships, grants, and awards:*** Federal Pell, FSEOG, state, private, college/university gift aid from institutional funds.

GIFT AID (NON-NEED-BASED) ***Total amount:*** $647,136 (24% state, 76% institutional). ***Receiving aid:*** Freshmen: 69% (564). Undergraduates: 68% (2,526). ***Average award:*** Freshmen: $108. Undergraduates: $112. ***Scholarships, grants, and awards by category:*** *Academic interests/achievement:* biological sciences, business, communication, computer science, engineering/technologies, mathematics, military science. *Creative arts/performance:* applied art and design, art/fine arts, general creative arts/performance, music. *Special achievements/activities:* general special achievements/activities. *Special characteristics:* first-generation college students, general special characteristics. ***Tuition waivers:*** Full or partial for employees or children of employees, senior citizens. ***ROTC:*** Army, Naval cooperative.

LOANS ***Student loans:*** $23,034,184 (86% need-based, 14% non-need-based). 84% of past graduating class borrowed through all loan programs. *Average indebtedness per student:* $28,807. ***Average need-based loan:*** Freshmen: $3298. Undergraduates: $3892. ***Parent loans:*** $10,212,582 (54% need-based, 46% non-need-based). ***Programs:*** Federal Direct (Subsidized and Unsubsidized Stafford, PLUS), Perkins, Federal Nursing.

WORK-STUDY ***Federal work-study:*** Total amount: $114,508; jobs available.

APPLYING FOR FINANCIAL AID ***Required financial aid form:*** FAFSA. ***Financial aid deadline (priority):*** 3/1. ***Notification date:*** 4/1.

CONTACT Ms. Deborah Stanley, Director of Financial Aid, Bowie State University, 14000 Jericho Park Road, Bowie, MD 20715, 301-860-3543 or toll-free 877-772-6943. *Fax:* 301-860-3549. *E-mail:* dstanley@bowiestate.edu.
Website: http://www.bowiestate.edu/.

BOWLING GREEN STATE UNIVERSITY

Bowling Green, OH

Tuition & fees (OH res): $11,317 | **Average undergraduate aid package: $14,376**

ABOUT THE INSTITUTION State-supported, coed. ***Awards:*** certificates, bachelor's, master's, and doctoral degrees. 223 undergraduate majors. ***Total enrollment:*** 17,733. Undergraduates: 15,103. Freshmen: 3,389. Federal methodology is used as a basis for awarding need-based institutional aid.

UNDERGRADUATE EXPENSES for 2019–2020 ***Application fee:*** $45. ***Tuition, state resident:*** full-time $9278; part-time $387 per credit hour. ***Tuition, nonresident:*** full-time $17,267; part-time $719 per credit hour. ***Required fees:*** full-time $2039; $84.27 per credit hour. Full-time tuition and fees vary according to course load, degree level, location, program, reciprocity agreements, and student level. Part-time tuition and fees vary according to course load, degree level, location, program, reciprocity agreements, and student level. ***College room and board:*** $10,396. Room and board charges vary according to board plan and housing facility. ***Payment plan:*** Guaranteed tuition.

FRESHMAN FINANCIAL AID (Fall 2019, est.) 3155 applied for aid; of those 70% were deemed to have need. 98% of freshmen with need received aid; of those 16% had need fully met. ***Average percent of need met:*** 79% (excluding resources awarded to replace EFC). ***Average financial aid package:*** $14,297 (excluding resources awarded to replace EFC). 26% of all full-time freshmen had no need and received non-need-based gift aid.

UNDERGRADUATE FINANCIAL AID (Fall 2019, est.) 10,728 applied for aid; of those 75% were deemed to have need. 98% of undergraduates with need received aid; of those 16% had need fully met. ***Average percent of need met:*** 80% (excluding resources awarded to replace EFC). ***Average financial aid package:*** $14,376 (excluding resources awarded to replace EFC). 22% of all full-time undergraduates had no need and received non-need-based gift aid.

GIFT AID (NEED-BASED) ***Total amount:*** $50,510,819 (36% federal, 11% state, 47% institutional, 6% external sources). ***Receiving aid:*** Freshmen: 59% (1,976); all full-time undergraduates: 51% (6,595). ***Average award:*** Freshmen: $7833; Undergraduates: $7952. ***Scholarships, grants, and awards:*** Federal Pell, FSEOG, state, private, college/university gift aid from institutional funds.

GIFT AID (NON-NEED-BASED) ***Total amount:*** $21,368,236 (1% federal, 5% state, 81% institutional, 13% external sources). ***Receiving aid:*** Freshmen: 8% (277). Undergraduates: 6% (793). ***Average award:*** Freshmen: $5130. Undergraduates: $5334. ***Scholarships, grants, and awards by category:*** *Academic interests/achievement:* biological sciences, business, communication, computer science, education, engineering/technologies, English, foreign languages, general academic interests/achievements, health fields, home economics, humanities, international studies, mathematics, military science, physical sciences, social sciences. *Creative arts/performance:* applied art and design, cinema/film/broadcasting, creative writing, dance, debating, journalism/publications, music, performing arts, theater/drama. *Special achievements/activities:* general special achievements/activities, leadership. *Special characteristics:* children and siblings of alumni, children of faculty/staff, general special characteristics, international students, members of minority groups. ***Tuition waivers:*** Full or partial for employees or children of employees, senior citizens. ***ROTC:*** Army, Air Force.

LOANS ***Student loans:*** $73,735,885 (63% need-based, 37% non-need-based). 74% of past graduating class borrowed through all loan programs. *Average indebtedness per student:* $30,603. ***Average need-based loan:*** Freshmen: $3231. Undergraduates: $4085. ***Parent loans:*** $30,843,454 (41% need-based, 59% non-need-based). ***Programs:*** Federal Direct (Subsidized and Unsubsidized Stafford, PLUS), Perkins, Federal Nursing, state, college/university, alternative loans.

WORK-STUDY ***Federal work-study:*** Total amount: $369,253; 324 jobs averaging $1140.

ATHLETIC AWARDS Total amount: $6,456,996 (32% need-based, 68% non-need-based).

APPLYING FOR FINANCIAL AID ***Required financial aid form:*** FAFSA. ***Financial aid deadline:*** Continuous. ***Notification date:*** Continuous beginning 4/15. Students must reply within 3 weeks of notification.

CONTACT Betsy Johnson, Director of Student Financial Aid and Scholarships, Bowling Green State University, 319 Administration Building, Bowling Green, OH 43403, 419-372-2651. *E-mail:* betsyj@bgsu.edu.
Website: http://www.bgsu.edu/.

BRADLEY UNIVERSITY

Peoria, IL

Tuition & fees: $35,480 | **Average undergraduate aid package: $25,827**

ABOUT THE INSTITUTION Independent, coed. ***Awards:*** certificates, bachelor's, master's, and doctoral degrees. 117 undergraduate majors. ***Total enrollment:*** 5,882. Undergraduates: 4,606. Freshmen: 1,090. Federal methodology is used as a basis for awarding need-based institutional aid.

UNDERGRADUATE EXPENSES for 2020–2021 ***One-time required fee:*** $200. ***Comprehensive fee:*** $46,760 includes full-time tuition ($35,060), mandatory fees ($420), and room and board ($11,280). ***College room only:*** $6520. Full-time tuition and fees vary according to course load and program. Room and board charges vary according to board plan and housing facility. ***Part-time tuition:*** $930 per credit hour. ***Part-time fees:*** $420 per year. Part-time tuition and fees vary according to course load and program.

FRESHMAN FINANCIAL AID (Fall 2019, est.) 975 applied for aid; of those 83% were deemed to have need. 100% of freshmen with need received aid; of those 20% had need fully met. ***Average percent of need met:*** 77% (excluding resources awarded to replace EFC). ***Average financial aid package:*** $26,122 (excluding resources awarded to replace EFC). 22% of all full-time freshmen had no need and received non-need-based gift aid.

UNDERGRADUATE FINANCIAL AID (Fall 2019, est.) 3,837 applied for aid; of those 85% were deemed to have need. 99% of undergraduates with need received aid; of those 17% had need fully met. ***Average percent of need met:*** 75% (excluding resources awarded to replace EFC). ***Average financial aid package:*** $25,827 (excluding resources awarded to replace EFC). 26% of all full-time undergraduates had no need and received non-need-based gift aid.

GIFT AID (NEED-BASED) ***Total amount:*** $64,270,839 (10% federal, 11% state, 77% institutional, 2% external sources). ***Receiving aid:*** Freshmen: 78% (814); all full-time undergraduates: 71% (3,210). ***Average award:*** Freshmen: $22,430; Undergraduates: $20,854. ***Scholarships, grants, and awards:*** Federal Pell, FSEOG, state, private, college/university gift aid from institutional funds, United Negro College Fund.

GIFT AID (NON-NEED-BASED) ***Total amount:*** $18,302,057 (95% institutional, 5% external sources). ***Receiving aid:*** Freshmen: 12% (127). Undergraduates: 9% (396). ***Average award:*** Freshmen: $15,307. Undergraduates: $12,925. ***Scholarships, grants, and awards by category:*** *Academic interests/achievement:* general academic interests/achievements. *Creative arts/performance:* applied art and design, music, theater/drama. *Special achievements/activities:* community service, leadership. *Special characteristics:* children and siblings of alumni, children of faculty/staff, out-of-state students. ***Tuition waivers:*** Full or partial for employees or children of employees, senior citizens. ***ROTC:*** Army.

LOANS ***Student loans:*** $30,724,343 (67% need-based, 33% non-need-based). 71% of past graduating class borrowed through all loan programs. *Average indebtedness per student:* $31,111. ***Average need-based loan:*** Freshmen: $4204. Undergraduates: $6072. ***Parent loans:*** $13,939,261 (43% need-based, 57% non-need-based). ***Programs:*** Federal Direct (Subsidized and Unsubsidized Stafford, PLUS), Federal Nursing.

WORK-STUDY ***Federal work-study:*** Total amount: $414,047; 345 jobs averaging $1200.

ATHLETIC AWARDS Total amount: $3,923,227 (32% need-based, 68% non-need-based).

APPLYING FOR FINANCIAL AID ***Required financial aid form:*** FAFSA. ***Financial aid deadline (priority):*** 12/1. ***Notification date:*** Continuous beginning 11/15. Students must reply by 5/1 or within 2 weeks of notification.

CONTACT Debra Jackson, Director of Financial Assistance, Bradley University, 1501 West Bradley Avenue, Peoria, IL 61625, 309-677-3089 or toll-free 800-447-6460. *Fax:* 309-677-2798. *E-mail:* bufinaid@bradley.edu.
Website: http://www.bradley.edu/.

BRANDEIS UNIVERSITY

Waltham, MA

Tuition & fees: $57,561	Average undergraduate aid package: $46,990

ABOUT THE INSTITUTION Independent, coed. ***Awards:*** certificates, bachelor's, master's, and doctoral degrees. 43 undergraduate majors. ***Total enrollment:*** 5,825. Undergraduates: 3,688. Freshmen: 863. Institutional methodology is used as a basis for awarding need-based institutional aid.

UNDERGRADUATE EXPENSES for 2019–2020 ***Application fee:*** $80. ***Comprehensive fee:*** $73,641 includes full-time tuition ($55,340), mandatory fees ($2221), and room and board ($16,080). ***College room only:*** $9060. ***Part-time tuition:*** $1729 per credit hour. ***Part-time fees:*** $2221 per year.

FRESHMAN FINANCIAL AID (Fall 2018) 564 applied for aid; of those 80% were deemed to have need. 99% of freshmen with need received aid; of those 122% had need fully met. ***Average percent of need met:*** 97% (excluding resources awarded to replace EFC). ***Average financial aid package:*** $47,398 (excluding resources awarded to replace EFC). 17% of all full-time freshmen had no need and received non-need-based gift aid.

UNDERGRADUATE FINANCIAL AID (Fall 2018) 1,946 applied for aid; of those 87% were deemed to have need. 100% of undergraduates with need received aid; of those 94% had need fully met. ***Average percent of need met:*** 97% (excluding resources awarded to replace EFC). ***Average financial aid package:*** $46,990 (excluding resources awarded to replace EFC). 14% of all full-time undergraduates had no need and received non-need-based gift aid.

GIFT AID (NEED-BASED) ***Total amount:*** $68,868,343 (5% federal, 1% state, 91% institutional, 3% external sources). ***Receiving aid:*** Freshmen: 49% (435); all full-time undergraduates: 45% (1,603). ***Average award:*** Freshmen: $44,006; Undergraduates: $42,876. ***Scholarships, grants, and awards:*** Federal Pell, FSEOG, state, private, college/university gift aid from institutional funds.

GIFT AID (NON-NEED-BASED) ***Total amount:*** $10,211,242 (77% institutional, 23% external sources). ***Receiving aid:*** Freshmen: 5% (45). Undergraduates: 3% (103). ***Average award:*** Freshmen: $14,542. Undergraduates: $14,481. ***ROTC:*** Army cooperative, Air Force cooperative.

LOANS ***Student loans:*** $12,617,711 (71% need-based, 29% non-need-based). 46% of past graduating class borrowed through all loan programs. *Average indebtedness per student:* $32,158. ***Average need-based loan:*** Freshmen: $3065. Undergraduates: $4606. ***Parent loans:*** $5,255,476 (32% need-based, 68% non-need-based). ***Programs:*** Federal Direct (Subsidized and Unsubsidized Stafford, PLUS), state, college/university.

WORK-STUDY ***Federal work-study:*** Total amount: $2,788,570; 1,395 jobs averaging $2470. ***State or other work-study/employment:*** Total amount: $947,755 (64% need-based, 36% non-need-based). 69 part-time jobs averaging $2810.

APPLYING FOR FINANCIAL AID ***Required financial aid forms:*** FAFSA, CSS Financial Aid PROFILE, noncustodial (divorced/separated) parent's statement, Supplemental documents as requested. ***Financial aid deadline:*** 1/1. ***Notification date:*** 4/1. Students must reply by 5/1.

CONTACT Keone Peterson, Assistant Director for Student Services, Brandeis University, Usdan Student Center 120, 415 South Street, Waltham, MA 02453, 781-736-3700 or toll-free 800-622-0622 (out-of-state). *Fax:* 781-736-3719. *E-mail:* sfs@brandeis.edu.
Website: http://www.brandeis.edu/.

BRANDMAN UNIVERSITY

Irvine, CA

CONTACT Financial Aid Office, Brandman University, 16355 Laguna Canyon Road, Irvine, CA 92618, 949-753-4774 or toll-free 800-746-0082.
Website: http://www.brandman.edu/.

BRENAU UNIVERSITY

Gainesville, GA

ABOUT THE INSTITUTION Independent, coed, primarily women. ***Awards:*** certificates, associate, bachelor's, master's, and doctoral degrees (also offers coed evening and weekend programs with significant enrollment not reflected in profile). 37 undergraduate majors. ***Total enrollment:*** 2,817. Undergraduates: 1,756. Freshmen: 156.

GIFT AID (NEED-BASED) ***Scholarships, grants, and awards:*** Federal Pell, FSEOG, state, private, college/university gift aid from institutional funds.

GIFT AID (NON-NEED-BASED) ***Scholarships, grants, and awards by category:*** *Academic interests/achievement:* biological sciences, business, education, English, general academic interests/achievements, home economics, humanities. *Creative arts/performance:* applied art and design, art/fine arts, creative writing, dance, journalism/publications, music, performing arts, theater/drama. *Special achievements/activities:* cheerleading/drum major, community service, general special achievements/activities, leadership. *Special characteristics:* adult students, children and siblings of alumni, children of faculty/staff, first-generation college students, general special characteristics, international students, members of minority groups, siblings of current students.

LOANS ***Programs:*** Federal Direct (Subsidized and Unsubsidized Stafford, PLUS), state, private loans.

CONTACT Mrs. Pam Barrett, Associate Vice President and Director of Financial Aid, Brenau University, 500 Washington Street, SE, Gainesville, GA 30501-3697, 770-534-6176 or toll-free 800-252-5119. *Fax:* 770-538-4306. *E-mail:* pbarrett@brenau.edu.
Website: http://www.brenau.edu/.

BRESCIA UNIVERSITY

Owensboro, KY

CONTACT Ms. Kristi Eidson, Director of Financial Aid, Brescia University, 717 Frederica Street, Owensboro, KY 42301-3023, 270-686-4356 or toll-free 877-273-7242. *Fax:* 270-689-9563. *E-mail:* financial.aid@brescia.edu.
Website: http://www.brescia.edu/.

BREVARD COLLEGE

Brevard, NC

CONTACT Ms. Caron Surrett, Director of Financial Aid, Brevard College, 1 Brevard College Drive, Brevard, NC 28712, 828-884-8261 or toll-free 800-527-9090. *Fax:* 828-884-3790. *E-mail:* finaid@brevard.edu.
Website: http://www.brevard.edu/.

BREWTON-PARKER COLLEGE

Mt. Vernon, GA

CONTACT Mrs. Shannon Mullins, Executive Director of Financial Aid, Brewton-Parker College, PO Box 197, Mt. Vernon, GA 30445-0197, 800-342-1087 Ext. 213 or toll-free 800-342-1087. *Fax:* 912-583-3598. *E-mail:* smullins@bpc.edu.
Website: http://www.bpc.edu/.

BRIAR CLIFF UNIVERSITY

Sioux City, IA

CONTACT Brian K. Eben, Office of Student Financial Aid, Briar Cliff University, 3303 Rebecca Street, PO Box 2100, Sioux City, IA 51104-2100, 712-279-5239 or toll-free 800-662-3303. *Fax:* 712-279-1632.
Website: http://www.briarcliff.edu/.

BRIDGEWATER COLLEGE

Bridgewater, VA

Tuition & fees: $37,720 | **Average undergraduate aid package: $36,959**

ABOUT THE INSTITUTION Independent Church of the Brethren, coed. ***Awards:*** bachelor's and master's degrees. 32 undergraduate majors. ***Total enrollment:*** 1,754. Undergraduates: 1,713. Freshmen: 487. Federal methodology is used as a basis for awarding need-based institutional aid.

UNDERGRADUATE EXPENSES for 2020–2021 ***Comprehensive fee:*** $51,080 includes full-time tuition ($36,800), mandatory fees ($920), and room and board ($13,360). Room and board charges vary according to housing facility.

FRESHMAN FINANCIAL AID (Fall 2019, est.) 469 applied for aid; of those 92% were deemed to have need. 100% of freshmen with need received aid; of those 28% had need fully met. ***Average percent of need met:*** 85% (excluding resources awarded to replace EFC). ***Average financial aid package:*** $34,825 (excluding resources awarded to replace EFC). 11% of all full-time freshmen had no need and received non-need-based gift aid.

UNDERGRADUATE FINANCIAL AID (Fall 2019, est.) 1,533 applied for aid; of those 93% were deemed to have need. 100% of undergraduates with need received aid; of those 27% had need fully met. ***Average percent of need met:*** 85% (excluding resources awarded to replace EFC). ***Average financial aid package:*** $36,959 (excluding resources awarded to replace EFC). 16% of all full-time undergraduates had no need and received non-need-based gift aid.

GIFT AID (NEED-BASED) ***Receiving aid:*** Freshmen: 89% (431); all full-time undergraduates: 84% (1,429). ***Average award:*** Freshmen: $32,197; Undergraduates: $33,808. ***Scholarships, grants, and awards:*** Federal Pell, FSEOG, state, private, college/university gift aid from institutional funds.

GIFT AID (NON-NEED-BASED) ***Receiving aid:*** Freshmen: 88% (429). Undergraduates: 84% (1,425). ***Average award:*** Freshmen: $25,914. Undergraduates: $24,033. ***Scholarships, grants, and awards by category:*** *Academic interests/achievement:* 1,610 awards ($34,457,650 total): general academic interests/achievements. *Creative arts/performance:* 47 awards ($142,593 total): music. *Special characteristics:* 869 awards ($4,150,975 total): children of educators, children of faculty/staff, international students, out-of-state students, previous college experience, religious affiliation. ***Tuition waivers:*** Full or partial for employees or children of employees.

LOANS ***Student loans:*** 80% of past graduating class borrowed through all loan programs. *Average indebtedness per student:* $31,871. ***Average need-based loan:*** Freshmen: $3392. Undergraduates: $4174. ***Programs:*** Federal Direct (Subsidized and Unsubsidized Stafford, PLUS).

WORK-STUDY ***Federal work-study:*** 396 jobs averaging $1482. ***State or other work-study/employment:*** 91 part-time jobs averaging $1162.

APPLYING FOR FINANCIAL AID ***Required financial aid forms:*** FAFSA, state aid form. ***Financial aid deadline:*** Continuous. ***Notification date:*** Continuous. Students must reply within 2 weeks of notification.

CONTACT Mr. Scott Morrison, Director of Financial Aid, Bridgewater College, 402 East College Street, Bridgewater, VA 22812-1599, 540-828-5377 or toll-free 800-759-8328. *Fax:* 540-828-5671. *E-mail:* finaid@bridgewater.edu.
Website: http://www.bridgewater.edu/.

BRIDGEWATER STATE UNIVERSITY

Bridgewater, MA

Tuition & fees: N/R | **Average undergraduate aid package: $8521**

ABOUT THE INSTITUTION State-supported, coed. ***Awards:*** certificates, bachelor's, and master's degrees. 81 undergraduate majors. ***Total enrollment:*** 10,881. Undergraduates: 9,463. Freshmen: 1,611. Federal methodology is used as a basis for awarding need-based institutional aid.

UNDERGRADUATE EXPENSES for 2020–2021 ***Application fee:*** $50. ***Tuition, state resident:*** part-time $38 per credit hour. ***Tuition, nonresident:*** part-time $294 per credit hour. Room and board charges vary according to board plan and housing facility.

FRESHMAN FINANCIAL AID (Fall 2018) 1417 applied for aid; of those 79% were deemed to have need. 98% of freshmen with need received aid; of those 19% had need fully met. ***Average percent of need met:*** 67% (excluding resources awarded to replace EFC). ***Average financial aid package:*** $8475 (excluding resources awarded to replace EFC). 2% of all full-time freshmen had no need and received non-need-based gift aid.

UNDERGRADUATE FINANCIAL AID (Fall 2018) 7,098 applied for aid; of those 79% were deemed to have need. 99% of undergraduates with need received aid; of those 13% had need fully met. ***Average percent of need met:*** 69% (excluding resources awarded to replace EFC). ***Average financial aid package:*** $8521 (excluding resources awarded to replace EFC). 1% of all full-time undergraduates had no need and received non-need-based gift aid.

GIFT AID (NEED-BASED) ***Total amount:*** $26,401,258 (60% federal, 19% state, 21% institutional). ***Receiving aid:*** Freshmen: 62% (917); all full-time undergraduates: 54% (4,256). ***Average award:*** Freshmen: $6335; Undergraduates: $6010. ***Scholarships, grants, and awards:*** Federal Pell, FSEOG, state, private, college/university gift aid from institutional funds.

GIFT AID (NON-NEED-BASED) ***Total amount:*** $3,793,355 (1% federal, 37% state, 21% institutional, 41% external sources). ***Receiving aid:*** Freshmen: 16% (232). Undergraduates: 12% (952). ***Average award:*** Freshmen: $3298. Undergraduates: $3666. ***Scholarships, grants, and awards by category:*** *Academic interests/achievement:* general academic interests/achievements. *Special characteristics:* local/state students, members of minority groups. ***Tuition waivers:*** Full or partial for minority students, employees or children of employees. ***ROTC:*** Army cooperative, Air Force cooperative.

LOANS ***Student loans:*** $56,552,417 (38% need-based, 62% non-need-based). 78% of past graduating class borrowed through all loan programs. *Average indebtedness per student:* $33,367. ***Average need-based loan:*** Freshmen: $2975. Undergraduates: $3721. ***Parent loans:*** $11,599,100 (100% non-need-based). ***Programs:*** Federal Direct (Subsidized and Unsubsidized Stafford, PLUS), state.

WORK-STUDY ***Federal work-study:*** Total amount: $527,266; jobs available.

APPLYING FOR FINANCIAL AID ***Required financial aid form:*** FAFSA. ***Financial aid deadline (priority):*** 3/1. ***Notification date:*** 12/15. Students must reply within 3 weeks of notification.

CONTACT Laura Biechler, Office of Financial Aid, Bridgewater State University, Tillinghast Hall, Room 100, 45 School Street, Bridgewater, MA 02325-0001, 508-531-1341. *Fax:* 508-531-1728. *E-mail:* finaid@bridgew.edu.
Website: http://www.bridgew.edu/.

BRIGHAM YOUNG UNIVERSITY

Provo, UT

Tuition & fees: $5970 | **Average undergraduate aid package: $8257**

ABOUT THE INSTITUTION Independent The Church of Jesus Christ of Latter-day Saints, coed. ***Awards:*** certificates, bachelor's, master's, and doctoral degrees. 102 undergraduate majors. ***Total enrollment:*** 34,395. Undergraduates: 31,292. Freshmen: 5,731. Both federal and institutional methodology are used as a basis for awarding need-based institutional aid.

UNDERGRADUATE EXPENSES for 2020–2021 ***Application fee:*** $35. ***Comprehensive fee:*** $13,778 includes full-time tuition ($5970) and room and board ($7808). ***Part-time tuition:*** $304 per credit hour.

FRESHMAN FINANCIAL AID (Fall 2018) 3329 applied for aid; of those 55% were deemed to have need. 91% of freshmen with need received aid; of those 2% had need fully met. ***Average percent of need met:*** 32% (excluding resources awarded to replace EFC). ***Average financial aid package:*** $7146 (excluding resources awarded to replace EFC). 37% of all full-time freshmen had no need and received non-need-based gift aid.

UNDERGRADUATE FINANCIAL AID (Fall 2018) 17,104 applied for aid; of those 81% were deemed to have need. 95% of undergraduates with need received aid; of those 4% had need fully met. ***Average percent of need met:*** 35% (excluding resources awarded to replace EFC). ***Average financial aid package:*** $8257 (excluding resources awarded to replace EFC). 27% of all full-time undergraduates had no need and received non-need-based gift aid.

GIFT AID (NEED-BASED) ***Total amount:*** $67,308,909 (88% federal, 12% institutional). ***Receiving aid:*** Freshmen: 17% (941); all full-time undergraduates: 39% (11,006). ***Average award:*** Freshmen: $5545; Undergraduates: $5712. ***Scholarships, grants, and awards:*** Federal Pell, state, private, college/university gift aid from institutional funds.

GIFT AID (NON-NEED-BASED) ***Total amount:*** $79,552,587 (84% institutional, 16% external sources). ***Receiving aid:*** Freshmen: 21% (1,159). Undergraduates: 26% (7,316). ***Average award:*** Freshmen: $4310. Undergraduates: $4579. ***Scholarships, grants, and awards by category:*** *Academic interests/achievement:* general academic interests/achievements. *Creative arts/performance:* applied art and design, music, theater/drama. *Special achievements/activities:* leadership, religious involvement. *Special characteristics:* local/state students, members of minority groups, religious affiliation. ***ROTC:*** Army, Air Force.

LOANS ***Student loans:*** $25,287,224 (54% need-based, 46% non-need-based). 24% of past graduating class borrowed through all loan programs. *Average indebtedness per student:* $14,672. ***Average need-based loan:*** Freshmen: $3153. Undergraduates: $4034. ***Parent loans:*** $1,145,612 (100% non-need-based). ***Programs:*** Federal Direct (Subsidized and Unsubsidized Stafford, PLUS), college/university.

ATHLETIC AWARDS Total amount: $6,850,848 (100% non-need-based).

APPLYING FOR FINANCIAL AID ***Required financial aid form:*** FAFSA. ***Financial aid deadline (priority):*** 2/1. ***Notification date:*** Continuous.

CONTACT Noelle Pitcher, OneStop Coordinator, Brigham Young University, C-148 ASB, Provo, UT 84602, 801-422-6708.
Website: http://www.byu.edu/.

BRIGHAM YOUNG UNIVERSITY–HAWAII

Laie, HI

CONTACT Mr. Wes Duke, Director of Financial Aid, Brigham Young University–Hawaii, BYUH #1980, 55-220 Kulanui Street, Laie, HI 96762, 808-293-3530. *Fax:* 808-293-3349. *E-mail:* duekw@byuh.edu.
Website: http://www.byuh.edu/.

BRIGHAM YOUNG UNIVERSITY–IDAHO

Rexburg, ID

CONTACT Financial Aid Office, Brigham Young University–Idaho, 525 South Center Street, Rexburg, ID 83460, 208-496-2011.
Website: http://www.byui.edu/.

BROADVIEW UNIVERSITY–WEST JORDAN

West Jordan, UT

CONTACT Office of Financial Aid, Broadview University–West Jordan, 1902 West 7800 South, West Jordan, UT 84088, 801-304-4224 or toll-free 866-304-4224. *Fax:* 801-304-4229.
Website: http://www.broadviewuniversity.edu/.

BROOKLINE COLLEGE - PHOENIX CAMPUS

Phoenix, AZ

CONTACT Financial Aid Office, Brookline College - Phoenix Campus, 2445 West Dunlap Avenue, Suite 100, Phoenix, AZ 85021, 602-242-6265 or toll-free 800-793-2428.
Website: http://brooklinecollege.edu/.

BROOKLINE COLLEGE - TEMPE CAMPUS

Tempe, AZ

CONTACT Financial Aid Office, Brookline College - Tempe Campus, 1140 South Priest Drive, Tempe, AZ 85281, 480-545-8755 or toll-free 888-886-2428.
Website: http://brooklinecollege.edu/.

BROOKLYN COLLEGE OF THE CITY UNIVERSITY OF NEW YORK

Brooklyn, NY

CONTACT Mr. Ahad Farhang, Director of Financial Aid, Brooklyn College of the City University of New York, 2900 Bedford Avenue, Brooklyn, NY 11210-2889, 718-951-5669. *Fax:* 718-951-4778. *E-mail:* afarhang@brooklyn.cuny.edu.
Website: http://www.brooklyn.cuny.edu/.

BROWN UNIVERSITY

Providence, RI

Tuition & fees: $60,596	Average undergraduate aid package: $55,513

ABOUT THE INSTITUTION Independent, coed. ***Awards:*** certificates, bachelor's, master's, and doctoral degrees. 69 undergraduate majors. ***Total enrollment:*** 10,333. Undergraduates: 7,160. Freshmen: 1,660. Both federal and institutional methodology are used as a basis for awarding need-based institutional aid.

UNDERGRADUATE EXPENSES for 2020–2021 ***Application fee:*** $75. ***Comprehensive fee:*** $76,504 includes full-time tuition ($59,254), mandatory fees ($1342), and room and board ($15,908). ***College room only:*** $9774. ***Part-time tuition:*** $7407 per course.

FRESHMAN FINANCIAL AID (Fall 2019, est.) 822 applied for aid; of those 88% were deemed to have need. 100% of freshmen with need received aid; of those 100% had need fully met. ***Average percent of need met:*** 100% (excluding resources awarded to replace EFC). ***Average financial aid package:*** $55,758 (excluding resources awarded to replace EFC). 1% of all full-time freshmen had no need and received non-need-based gift aid.

UNDERGRADUATE FINANCIAL AID (Fall 2019, est.) 3,105 applied for aid; of those 91% were deemed to have need. 100% of undergraduates with need received aid; of those 100% had need fully met. ***Average percent of need met:*** 100% (excluding resources awarded to replace EFC). ***Average financial aid package:*** $55,513 (excluding resources awarded to replace EFC). 1% of all full-time undergraduates had no need and received non-need-based gift aid.

GIFT AID (NEED-BASED) ***Total amount:*** $148,381,354 (4% federal, 93% institutional, 3% external sources). ***Receiving aid:*** Freshmen: 44% (725); all full-time undergraduates: 42% (2,820). ***Average award:*** Freshmen: $52,881; Undergraduates: $52,057. ***Scholarships, grants, and awards:*** Federal Pell, FSEOG, state, private, college/university gift aid from institutional funds.

GIFT AID (NON-NEED-BASED) ***Total amount:*** $5,626,064 (2% institutional, 98% external sources). ***Average award:*** Freshmen: $10,000. Undergraduates: $8880. ***Scholarships, grants, and awards by category:*** *Special characteristics:* 9 awards ($82,160 total): veterans. ***ROTC:*** Army cooperative, Naval cooperative, Air Force cooperative.

LOANS ***Student loans:*** $9,403,791 (33% need-based, 67% non-need-based). 31% of past graduating class borrowed through all loan programs. *Average indebtedness per student:* $24,304. ***Average need-based loan:*** Freshmen: $726. Undergraduates: $738. ***Parent loans:*** $9,141,984 (1% need-based, 99% non-need-based). ***Programs:*** Federal Direct (Subsidized and Unsubsidized Stafford, PLUS).

WORK-STUDY ***Federal work-study:*** Total amount: $4,967,811; 1,911 jobs averaging $2587. ***State or other work-study/employment:*** Total amount: $1,100,335 (100% need-based). 420 part-time jobs averaging $2610.

APPLYING FOR FINANCIAL AID ***Required financial aid forms:*** FAFSA, CSS Financial Aid PROFILE, noncustodial (divorced/separated) parent's statement. ***Financial aid deadline:*** 2/1. ***Notification date:*** 4/1. Students must reply by 5/1.

CONTACT Financial Aid Office, Brown University, One Prospect Street, Providence, RI 02912, 401-863-1000.
Website: http://www.brown.edu/.

BRYAN COLLEGE

Dayton, TN

Tuition & fees: $16,900	Average undergraduate aid package: $24,217

ABOUT THE INSTITUTION Independent interdenominational, coed. ***Awards:*** certificates, diplomas, associate, bachelor's, and master's degrees. 30 undergraduate majors. ***Total enrollment:*** 1,489. Undergraduates: 1,266. Freshmen: 191. Federal methodology is used as a basis for awarding need-based institutional aid.

UNDERGRADUATE EXPENSES for 2020–2021 ***Application fee:*** $35. ***Comprehensive fee:*** $24,700 includes full-time tuition ($16,900) and room and board ($7800). Full-time tuition and fees vary according to program. Room and board charges vary according to housing facility. Part-time tuition and fees vary according to program.

FRESHMAN FINANCIAL AID (Fall 2019, est.) 180 applied for aid; of those 91% were deemed to have need. 100% of freshmen with need received aid; of those 47% had need fully met. ***Average financial aid package:*** $25,887 (excluding resources awarded to replace EFC).

UNDERGRADUATE FINANCIAL AID (Fall 2019, est.) 568 applied for aid; of those 90% were deemed to have need. 100% of undergraduates with need received aid; of those 44% had need fully met. ***Average financial aid package:*** $24,217 (excluding resources awarded to replace EFC).

GIFT AID (NEED-BASED) ***Total amount:*** $10,484,390 (18% federal, 20% state, 60% institutional, 2% external sources). ***Receiving aid:*** Freshmen: 87% (163); all full-time undergraduates: 79% (505). ***Average award:*** Freshmen: $15,115; Undergraduates: $14,140. ***Scholarships, grants, and awards:*** Federal Pell, FSEOG, state, private, college/university gift aid from institutional funds.

GIFT AID (NON-NEED-BASED) ***Total amount:*** $885,508 (17% state, 81% institutional, 2% external sources). ***Receiving aid:*** Freshmen: 86% (162). Undergraduates: 78% (495). ***Scholarships, grants, and awards by category:*** *Academic interests/achievement:* biological sciences, business, communication, computer science, education, English, foreign languages, general academic interests/achievements, humanities, mathematics, physical sciences, premedicine, religion/biblical studies, social sciences. *Creative arts/performance:* journalism/publications, music, performing arts, theater/drama. *Special achievements/activities:* community service, general special achievements/activities, leadership, religious involvement. *Special characteristics:* children and siblings of alumni, children of current students, children of educators, children of faculty/staff, general special characteristics, handicapped students, international students, local/state students, members of minority groups, relatives of clergy, spouses of current students. ***Tuition waivers:*** Full or partial for employees or children of employees.

LOANS ***Student loans:*** $4,752,897 (95% need-based, 5% non-need-based). 72% of past graduating class borrowed through all loan programs. *Average indebtedness per student:* $24,630. ***Average need-based loan:*** Freshmen: $3058. Undergraduates: $3609. ***Parent loans:*** $844,595 (94% need-based, 6% non-need-based). ***Programs:*** Federal Direct (Subsidized and Unsubsidized Stafford, PLUS).

WORK-STUDY ***Federal work-study:*** Total amount: $200,000; 150 jobs averaging $2000.

ATHLETIC AWARDS Total amount: $2,045,928 (88% need-based, 12% non-need-based).

APPLYING FOR FINANCIAL AID ***Required financial aid form:*** FAFSA. ***Financial aid deadline (priority):*** 1/31. ***Notification date:*** Continuous beginning 11/1.

CONTACT David Haggard, Director of Financial Aid, Bryan College, 721 Bryan Drive, Dayton, TN 37321, 423-775-7339 or toll-free 800-277-9522. *Fax:* 423-775-7300. *E-mail:* finaid@bryan.edu.
Website: http://www.bryan.edu/.

BRYAN COLLEGE OF HEALTH SCIENCES

Lincoln, NE

CONTACT Financial Aid Office, Bryan College of Health Sciences, 1535 South 52nd Street, Lincoln, NE 68506, 402-481 3801.
Website: http://www.bryanhealthcollege.edu/.

BRYANT & STRATTON COLLEGE–AKRON CAMPUS

Akron, OH

CONTACT Financial Aid Office, Bryant & Stratton College–Akron Campus, 190 Montrose West Avenue, Akron, OH 44321, 330-598-2500.
Website: http://www.bryantstratton.edu/.

BRYANT & STRATTON COLLEGE–CLEVELAND CAMPUS

Cleveland, OH

CONTACT Bill Davenport, Financial Aid Supervisor, Bryant & Stratton College–Cleveland Campus, 1700 East 13th Street, Cleveland, OH 44114-3203, 216-771-1700. *Fax:* 216-771-7787.
Website: http://www.bryantstratton.edu/.

BRYANT & STRATTON COLLEGE–HAMPTON CAMPUS

Hampton, VA

CONTACT Financial Aid Office, Bryant & Stratton College–Hampton Campus, 4410 East Claiborne Square, Suite 233, Hampton, VA 23666, 757-896-6001.
Website: http://www.bryantstratton.edu/.

BRYANT & STRATTON COLLEGE–WAUWATOSA CAMPUS

Wauwatosa, WI

CONTACT Financial Aid Office, Bryant & Stratton College–Wauwatosa Campus, 10950 West Potter Road, Wauwatosa, WI 53226, 414-302-7000.
Website: http://www.bryantstratton.edu/.

BRYANT UNIVERSITY

Smithfield, RI

Tuition & fees: $46,863	Average undergraduate aid package: $25,940

ABOUT THE INSTITUTION Independent, coed. ***Awards:*** certificates, bachelor's, and master's degrees. 27 undergraduate majors. ***Total enrollment:*** 3,640. Undergraduates: 3,259. Freshmen: 854. Federal methodology is used as a basis for awarding need-based institutional aid.

UNDERGRADUATE EXPENSES for 2020–2021 ***Application fee:*** $50. ***Comprehensive fee:*** $63,067 includes full-time tuition ($45,966), mandatory fees ($897), and room and board ($16,204). ***College room only:*** $9589. Full-time tuition and fees vary according to program. Room and board charges vary according to board plan. ***Part-time tuition:*** $1139 per credit hour. Part-time tuition and fees vary according to program.

FRESHMAN FINANCIAL AID (Fall 2019, est.) 553 applied for aid; of those 87% were deemed to have need. 99% of freshmen with need received aid; of those 22% had need fully met. ***Average percent of need met:*** 47% (excluding resources awarded to replace EFC). ***Average financial aid package:*** $25,023 (excluding resources awarded to replace EFC). 7% of all full-time freshmen had no need and received non-need-based gift aid.

UNDERGRADUATE FINANCIAL AID (Fall 2019, est.) 2,291 applied for aid; of those 85% were deemed to have need. 100% of undergraduates with need received aid; of those 47% had need fully met. ***Average percent of need met:*** 48% (excluding resources awarded to replace EFC). ***Average financial aid package:*** $25,940 (excluding resources awarded to replace EFC). 9% of all full-time undergraduates had no need and received non-need-based gift aid.

GIFT AID (NEED-BASED) ***Total amount:*** $35,335,890 (5% federal, 1% state, 91% institutional, 3% external sources). ***Receiving aid:*** Freshmen: 34% (293); all full-time undergraduates: 38% (1,284). ***Average award:*** Freshmen: $9941; Undergraduates: $9760. ***Scholarships, grants, and awards:*** Federal Pell, FSEOG, state, private, college/university gift aid from institutional funds.

GIFT AID (NON-NEED-BASED) ***Total amount:*** $23,982,757 (97% institutional, 3% external sources). ***Receiving aid:*** Freshmen: 41% (351). Undergraduates: 44% (1,469). ***Average award:*** Freshmen: $16,424. Undergraduates: $17,182. ***Scholarships, grants, and awards by category:*** *Academic interests/achievement:* 2,534 awards ($43,272,986 total): general academic interests/achievements. *Special characteristics:* 111 awards ($1,541,355 total): international students, members of minority groups, siblings of current students, veterans. ***Tuition waivers:*** Full or partial for employees or children of employees. ***ROTC:*** Army cooperative.

LOANS ***Student loans:*** $31,970,672 (38% need-based, 62% non-need-based). 65% of past graduating class borrowed through all loan programs. *Average indebtedness per student:* $53,350. ***Average need-based loan:*** Freshmen: $5021. Undergraduates: $4435. ***Parent loans:*** $7,519,466 (32% need-based, 68% non-need-based). ***Programs:*** Federal Direct (Subsidized and Unsubsidized Stafford, PLUS).

WORK-STUDY ***Federal work-study:*** Total amount: $436,540; jobs available. ***State or other work-study/employment:*** Total amount: $1,340,493 (31% need-based, 69% non-need-based). Part-time jobs available.

ATHLETIC AWARDS Total amount: $8,553,203 (42% need-based, 58% non-need-based).

APPLYING FOR FINANCIAL AID ***Required financial aid form:*** FAFSA. ***Financial aid deadline:*** 2/15 (priority: 2/15). ***Notification date:*** 3/24. Students must reply by 5/1.

CONTACT Mr. John B. Canning, Director of Financial Aid, Bryant University, 1150 Douglas Pike, Smithfield, RI 02917-1284, 401-232-6020 or toll-free 800-622-7001. *Fax:* 401-232-6293. *E-mail:* jcanning@bryant.edu.
Website: http://www.bryant.edu/.

BRYAN UNIVERSITY

Springfield, MO

CONTACT Financial Aid Office, Bryan University, 4255 South Nature Center Way, Springfield, MO 65804, 417-862-5700 or toll-free 855-566-0650.
Website: http://www.bryanu.edu/.

BRYN ATHYN COLLEGE OF THE NEW CHURCH

Bryn Athyn, PA

Tuition & fees: N/R	Average undergraduate aid package: $26,235

ABOUT THE INSTITUTION Independent Church of the New Jerusalem, coed. ***Awards:*** associate, bachelor's, and master's degrees. 16 undergraduate majors. ***Total enrollment:*** 307. Undergraduates: 288. Freshmen: 81. Both federal and institutional methodology are used as a basis for awarding need-based institutional aid.

UNDERGRADUATE EXPENSES for 2020–2021 ***Tuition:*** part-time $973 per credit hour. ***Required fees:*** $60 per credit hour.

FRESHMAN FINANCIAL AID (Fall 2018) 54 applied for aid; of those 54% were deemed to have need. 100% of freshmen with need received aid; of those 45% had need fully met. ***Average percent of need met:*** 45% (excluding resources awarded to replace EFC). ***Average financial aid package:*** $27,026 (excluding resources awarded to replace EFC). 33% of all full-time freshmen had no need and received non-need-based gift aid.

UNDERGRADUATE FINANCIAL AID (Fall 2018) 222 applied for aid; of those 52% were deemed to have need. 97% of undergraduates with need received aid; of those 29% had need fully met. ***Average percent of need met:*** 29% (excluding resources awarded to replace EFC). ***Average financial aid package:*** $26,235 (excluding resources awarded to replace EFC). 37% of all full-time undergraduates had no need and received non-need-based gift aid.

GIFT AID (NEED-BASED) ***Total amount:*** $1,986,458 (28% federal, 12% state, 59% institutional, 1% external sources). ***Receiving aid:*** Freshmen: 44% (29); all full-time undergraduates: 38% (112). ***Average award:*** Freshmen: $12,393; Undergraduates: $10,257. ***Scholarships, grants, and awards:*** Federal Pell, FSEOG, state, private, college/university gift aid from institutional funds.

GIFT AID (NON-NEED-BASED) ***Total amount:*** $1,266,864 (3% state, 95% institutional, 2% external sources). ***Receiving aid:*** Freshmen: 33% (22). Undergraduates: 32% (93). ***Average award:*** Freshmen: $8594. Undergraduates: $6457. ***Scholarships, grants, and awards by category:*** *Academic interests/achievement:* general academic interests/achievements. *Special achievements/activities:* community service, religious involvement. *Special characteristics:* general special characteristics, religious affiliation. ***Tuition waivers:*** Full or partial for employees or children of employees, senior citizens. ***ROTC:*** Army cooperative, Air Force cooperative.

LOANS ***Student loans:*** $2,136,391 (46% need-based, 54% non-need-based). 33% of past graduating class borrowed through all loan programs. *Average indebtedness per student:* $2825. ***Average need-based loan:*** Freshmen: $3365. Undergraduates: $4346. ***Programs:*** Federal Direct (Subsidized and Unsubsidized Stafford, PLUS).

WORK-STUDY ***Federal work-study:*** Total amount: $15,818; 15,000 jobs available. ***State or other work-study/employment:*** Total amount: $5272 (100% need-based). Part-time jobs available.

APPLYING FOR FINANCIAL AID ***Required financial aid forms:*** FAFSA, state aid form. ***Financial aid deadline (priority):*** 2/15. ***Notification date:*** 1/31. Students must reply within 3 weeks of notification.

CONTACT Ashley McCarrie, Associate Director of Financial Aid, Bryn Athyn College of the New Church, Box 717, Bryn Athyn, PA 19009, 267-502-2630 or toll-free 800-767-9552. *Fax:* 267-502-4866. *E-mail:* financialaid@brynathyn.edu.
Website: http://www.brynathyn.edu/.

BRYN MAWR COLLEGE

Bryn Mawr, PA

Tuition & fees: $54,440	Average undergraduate aid package: $53,763

ABOUT THE INSTITUTION Independent, undergraduate: women only; graduate: coed. ***Awards:*** certificates, bachelor's, master's, and doctoral degrees. 37 undergraduate majors. ***Total enrollment:*** 1,690. Undergraduates: 1,360. Freshmen: 391. Both federal and institutional methodology are used as a basis for awarding need-based institutional aid.

UNDERGRADUATE EXPENSES for 2019–2020 ***Application fee:*** $50. ***Comprehensive fee:*** $71,540 includes full-time tuition ($53,180), mandatory fees ($1260), and room and board ($17,100). ***College room only:*** $9760. ***Part-time tuition:*** $6650 per course.

FRESHMAN FINANCIAL AID (Fall 2019, est.) 250 applied for aid; of those 72% were deemed to have need. 100% of freshmen with need received aid; of those 100% had need fully met. ***Average percent of need met:*** 100% (excluding resources awarded to replace EFC). ***Average financial aid package:*** $50,941 (excluding resources awarded to replace EFC). 21% of all full-time freshmen had no need and received non-need-based gift aid.

UNDERGRADUATE FINANCIAL AID (Fall 2019, est.) 813 applied for aid; of those 87% were deemed to have need. 100% of undergraduates with need received aid; of those 100% had need fully met. ***Average percent of need met:*** 100% (excluding resources awarded to replace EFC). ***Average financial aid package:*** $53,763 (excluding resources awarded to replace EFC). 19% of all full-time undergraduates had no need and received non-need-based gift aid.

GIFT AID (NEED-BASED) ***Total amount:*** $32,830,049 (4% federal, 95% institutional, 1% external sources). ***Receiving aid:*** Freshmen: 48% (180); all full-time undergraduates: 52% (706). ***Average award:*** Freshmen: $43,829; Undergraduates: $46,447. ***Scholarships, grants, and awards:*** Federal Pell, FSEOG, state, private, college/university gift aid from institutional funds.

GIFT AID (NON-NEED-BASED) ***Total amount:*** $6,578,758 (5% federal, 84% institutional, 11% external sources). ***Receiving aid:*** Freshmen: 7% (28). Undergraduates: 6% (80). ***Average award:*** Freshmen: $19,046. Undergraduates: $18,972. ***Scholarships, grants, and awards by category:*** *Academic interests/achievement:* general academic interests/achievements. *Special achievements/activities:* leadership. ***ROTC:*** Air Force cooperative.

LOANS ***Student loans:*** $4,210,082 (66% need-based, 34% non-need-based). 52% of past graduating class borrowed through all loan programs. *Average indebtedness per student:* $28,772. ***Average need-based loan:*** Freshmen: $4884. Undergraduates: $5280. ***Parent loans:*** $1,649,072 (100% non-need-based). ***Programs:*** Federal Direct (Subsidized and Unsubsidized Stafford, PLUS), college/university.

WORK-STUDY ***Federal work-study:*** Total amount: $820,715; jobs available. ***State or other work-study/employment:*** Total amount: $446,036 (93% need-based, 7% non-need-based). Part-time jobs available.

APPLYING FOR FINANCIAL AID ***Required financial aid forms:*** FAFSA, CSS Financial Aid PROFILE, noncustodial (divorced/separated) parent's statement, parent and student tax returns or non-filer statements. ***Financial aid deadline:*** 1/15. ***Notification date:*** Students must reply by 5/1.

CONTACT Susan A Chadwick, Director of Financial Aid, Bryn Mawr College, 101 North Merion Avenue, Bryn Mawr, PA 19010-2899, 610-526-7922 or toll-free 800-BMC-1885. *E-mail:* schadwick@brynmawr.edu.
Website: http://www.brynmawr.edu/.

BUCKNELL UNIVERSITY

Lewisburg, PA

Tuition & fees: $58,202	Average undergraduate aid package: $37,000

ABOUT THE INSTITUTION Independent, coed. ***Awards:*** bachelor's and master's degrees. 68 undergraduate majors. ***Total enrollment:*** 3,697. Undergraduates: 3,627. Freshmen: 964. Both federal and institutional methodology are used as a basis for awarding need-based institutional aid.

UNDERGRADUATE EXPENSES for 2020–2021 ***Application fee:*** $40. ***Comprehensive fee:*** $72,872 includes full-time tuition ($57,882), mandatory fees ($320), and room and board ($14,670). ***College room only:*** $8946. Room and board charges vary according to board plan and housing facility. ***Part-time tuition:*** $6352 per course. ***Payment plan:*** Tuition prepayment.

FRESHMAN FINANCIAL AID (Fall 2019, est.) 577 applied for aid; of those 72% were deemed to have need. 100% of freshmen with need received aid. ***Average percent of need met:*** 92% (excluding resources awarded to replace EFC). ***Average financial aid package:*** $39,500 (excluding resources awarded to replace EFC). 6% of all full-time freshmen had no need and received non-need-based gift aid.

UNDERGRADUATE FINANCIAL AID (Fall 2019, est.) 1,715 applied for aid; of those 80% were deemed to have need. 100% of undergraduates with need received aid. ***Average percent of need met:*** 92% (excluding resources awarded to replace EFC). ***Average financial aid package:*** $37,000 (excluding resources awarded to replace EFC). 9% of all full-time undergraduates had no need and received non-need-based gift aid.

GIFT AID (NEED-BASED) ***Receiving aid:*** Freshmen: 37% (357); all full-time undergraduates: 33% (1,195). ***Average award:*** Freshmen: $33,700; Undergraduates: $32,300. ***Scholarships, grants, and awards:*** Federal Pell, FSEOG, state, private, college/university gift aid from institutional funds.

GIFT AID (NON-NEED-BASED) ***Receiving aid:*** Freshmen: 14% (136). Undergraduates: 11% (394). ***Average award:*** Freshmen: $14,024. Undergraduates: $12,978. ***Scholarships, grants, and awards by category:*** *Academic interests/achievement:* 268 awards ($4,380,744 total): business, engineering/technologies, general academic interests/achievements, mathematics, physical sciences. *Creative arts/performance:* 83 awards ($557,200 total): applied art and design, creative writing, dance, music, performing arts, theater/drama. *Special achievements/activities:* 116 awards ($6,702,478 total): general special achievements/activities, leadership. ***Tuition waivers:*** Full or partial for employees or children of employees. ***ROTC:*** Army.

LOANS ***Student loans:*** 46% of past graduating class borrowed through all loan programs. *Average indebtedness per student:* $31,000. ***Average need-based loan:*** Freshmen: $3500. Undergraduates: $5500. ***Programs:*** Federal Direct (Subsidized and Unsubsidized Stafford, PLUS).

WORK-STUDY ***Federal work-study:*** 600 jobs averaging $1500. ***State or other work-study/employment:*** 50 part-time jobs averaging $1500.

APPLYING FOR FINANCIAL AID ***Required financial aid forms:*** FAFSA, CSS Financial Aid PROFILE, institution's own non-custodial form.

CONTACT Andrea Leithner Stauffer, Director of Financial Aid, Bucknell University, 1 Dent Drive, Lewisburg, PA 17837, 570-577-1331. *Fax:* 570-577-1481. *E-mail:* finaid@bucknell.edu.
Website: http://www.bucknell.edu/.

BUENA VISTA UNIVERSITY

Storm Lake, IA

Tuition & fees: $35,194	Average undergraduate aid package: $32,002

ABOUT THE INSTITUTION Independent Presbyterian Church (U.S.A.), coed. ***Awards:*** bachelor's and master's degrees. 64 undergraduate majors. ***Total enrollment:*** 820. Undergraduates: 732. Freshmen: 201. Federal methodology is used as a basis for awarding need-based institutional aid.

UNDERGRADUATE EXPENSES for 2019–2020 ***Comprehensive fee:*** $45,066 includes full-time tuition ($35,194) and room and board ($9872). ***College room only:*** $4941. Room and board charges vary according to housing facility. ***Part-time tuition:*** $1184 per credit hour.

FRESHMAN FINANCIAL AID (Fall 2019, est.) 226 applied for aid; of those 93% were deemed to have need. 100% of freshmen with need received aid; of those 23% had need fully met. ***Average percent of need met:*** 89% (excluding resources awarded to replace EFC). ***Average financial aid package:*** $34,025 (excluding resources awarded to replace EFC). 8% of all full-time freshmen had no need and received non-need-based gift aid.

UNDERGRADUATE FINANCIAL AID (Fall 2019, est.) 670 applied for aid; of those 93% were deemed to have need. 100% of undergraduates with need received aid; of those 21% had need fully met. ***Average percent of need met:*** 84% (excluding resources awarded to replace EFC). ***Average financial aid package:*** $32,002 (excluding resources awarded to replace EFC). 12% of all full-time undergraduates had no need and received non-need-based gift aid.

GIFT AID (NEED-BASED) ***Total amount:*** $16,760,364 (12% federal, 12% state, 75% institutional, 1% external sources). ***Receiving aid:*** Freshmen: 92% (211); all full-time undergraduates: 88% (623). ***Average award:*** Freshmen: $29,967; Undergraduates: $27,197. ***Scholarships, grants, and awards:*** Federal Pell, FSEOG, state, private, college/university gift aid from institutional funds.

GIFT AID (NON-NEED-BASED) ***Total amount:*** $2,459,311 (8% federal, 1% state, 88% institutional, 3% external sources). ***Receiving aid:*** Freshmen: 11% (26). Undergraduates: 10% (71). ***Average award:*** Freshmen: $21,177. Undergraduates: $19,215. ***Scholarships, grants, and awards by category:*** *Academic interests/achievement:* biological sciences, business, computer science, general academic interests/achievements, mathematics, physical sciences. *Creative arts/performance:* applied art and design, music, theater/drama. *Special achievements/activities:* general special achievements/activities, leadership. *Special characteristics:* children of faculty/staff, ethnic background, international students, siblings of current students. ***Tuition waivers:*** Full or partial for employees or children of employees. ***ROTC:*** Army.

LOANS ***Student loans:*** $5,338,852 (43% need-based, 57% non-need-based). 85% of past graduating class borrowed through all loan programs. *Average indebtedness per student:* $35,267. ***Average need-based loan:*** Freshmen: $3814. Undergraduates: $4575. ***Parent loans:*** $1,149,483 (100% non-need-based). ***Programs:*** Federal Direct (Subsidized and Unsubsidized Stafford, PLUS), Perkins, college/university.

WORK-STUDY ***Federal work-study:*** Total amount: $505,450; jobs available. ***State or other work-study/employment:*** Total amount: $370,167 (80% need-based, 20% non-need-based). Part-time jobs available.

APPLYING FOR FINANCIAL AID ***Required financial aid form:*** FAFSA. ***Financial aid deadline (priority):*** 6/1. ***Notification date:*** Continuous beginning 2/1.

CONTACT Leanne Valentine, Executive Director of Financial Assistance, Buena Vista University, 610 West Fourth Street, Storm Lake, IA 50588, 712-749-2164 or toll-free 800-383-9600. *E-mail:* valentinel@bvu.edu.
Website: http://www.bvu.edu/.

BUFFALO STATE COLLEGE, STATE UNIVERSITY OF NEW YORK

Buffalo, NY

ABOUT THE INSTITUTION State-supported, coed. ***Awards:*** certificates, bachelor's, and master's degrees. 79 undergraduate majors. ***Total enrollment:*** 1,036. Undergraduates: 8,087. Freshmen: 1,626.

GIFT AID (NEED-BASED) ***Scholarships, grants, and awards:*** Federal Pell, FSEOG, state, private, college/university gift aid from institutional funds.

GIFT AID (NON-NEED-BASED) ***Scholarships, grants, and awards by category:*** *Academic interests/achievement:* biological sciences, business, communication, computer science, education, engineering/technologies, foreign languages, general academic interests/achievements, health fields, home economics, mathematics, physical sciences, social sciences. *Creative arts/performance:* art/fine arts, general creative arts/performance, music, performing arts, theater/drama. *Special achievements/activities:* general special achievements/activities. *Special characteristics:* general special characteristics, international students, members of minority groups, veterans.

LOANS ***Programs:*** Federal Direct (Subsidized and Unsubsidized Stafford, PLUS), Perkins.

CONTACT Connie F. Cooke, Director of Financial Aid, Buffalo State College, State University of New York, 1300 Elmwood Avenue, Buffalo, NY 14222-1095, 716-878-4902. *Fax:* 716-878-4903. *E-mail:* finaid@buffalostate.edu.
Website: http://www.buffalostate.edu/.

BUTLER UNIVERSITY

Indianapolis, IN

Tuition & fees: $43,400	Average undergraduate aid package: $25,549

ABOUT THE INSTITUTION Independent, coed. ***Awards:*** certificates, associate, bachelor's, master's, and doctoral degrees. 77 undergraduate majors. ***Total enrollment:*** 5,515. Undergraduates: 4,685. Freshmen: 1,116. Federal methodology is used as a basis for awarding need-based institutional aid.

UNDERGRADUATE EXPENSES for 2020–2021 ***Comprehensive fee:*** $57,780 includes full-time tuition ($42,410), mandatory fees ($990), and room and board ($14,380). ***College room only:*** $6950. Room and board charges vary according to board plan and housing facility. ***Part-time tuition:*** $1760 per credit hour.

FRESHMAN FINANCIAL AID (Fall 2019, est.) 1081 applied for aid; of those 57% were deemed to have need. 100% of freshmen with need received aid; of those 14% had need fully met. ***Average percent of need met:*** 64% (excluding resources awarded to replace EFC). ***Average financial aid package:*** $26,933 (excluding resources awarded to replace EFC). 41% of all full-time freshmen had no need and received non-need-based gift aid.

UNDERGRADUATE FINANCIAL AID (Fall 2019, est.) 4,509 applied for aid; of those 56% were deemed to have need. 100% of undergraduates with need received aid; of those 12% had need fully met. ***Average percent of need met:*** 65% (excluding resources awarded to replace EFC). ***Average financial aid package:*** $25,549 (excluding resources awarded to replace EFC). 42% of all full-time undergraduates had no need and received non-need-based gift aid.

GIFT AID (NEED-BASED) ***Total amount:*** $50,409,126 (6% federal, 7% state, 78% institutional, 9% external sources). ***Receiving aid:*** Freshmen: 54% (606); all full-time undergraduates: 51% (2,402). ***Average award:*** Freshmen: $22,413; Undergraduates: $21,703. ***Scholarships, grants, and awards:*** Federal Pell, FSEOG, state, private, college/university gift aid from institutional funds.

GIFT AID (NON-NEED-BASED) ***Total amount:*** $36,087,385 (92% institutional, 8% external sources). ***Receiving aid:*** Freshmen: 13% (145). Undergraduates: 9% (403). ***Average award:*** Freshmen: $17,451. Undergraduates: $16,546. ***Scholarships, grants, and awards by category:*** *Academic interests/achievement:* biological sciences, business, communication, computer science, education, engineering/technologies, English, foreign languages, general academic interests/achievements, home economics, humanities, international studies, mathematics, physical sciences, premedicine, religion/biblical studies, social sciences. *Creative arts/performance:* applied art and design, art/fine arts, cinema/film/broadcasting, dance, journalism/publications, music, performing arts, theater/drama. *Special characteristics:* veterans, veterans' children. ***Tuition waivers:*** Full or partial for employees or children of employees. ***ROTC:*** Army cooperative, Air Force cooperative.

LOANS ***Student loans:*** $31,950,617 (68% need-based, 32% non-need-based). 59% of past graduating class borrowed through all loan programs. ***Average indebtedness per student:*** $36,695. ***Average need-based loan:*** Freshmen: $3432. Undergraduates: $4497. ***Parent loans:*** $12,579,647 (45% need-based, 55% non-need-based). ***Programs:*** Federal Direct (Subsidized and Unsubsidized Stafford, PLUS).

WORK-STUDY ***Federal work-study:*** Total amount: $507,500; 276 jobs averaging $960.

ATHLETIC AWARDS Total amount: $5,548,766 (34% need-based, 66% non-need-based).

APPLYING FOR FINANCIAL AID ***Required financial aid form:*** FAFSA. ***Financial aid deadline (priority):*** 12/1. ***Notification date:*** 1/20. Students must reply within 3 weeks of notification.

CONTACT Mrs. Leslie Middleton, Associate Director of Financial Aid, Butler University, 4600 Sunset Avenue, Indianapolis, IN 46208-3485, 317-940-8200 or toll-free 888-940-8100. *Fax:* 317-940-8250. *E-mail:* lmmiddle@butler.edu.
Website: http://www.butler.edu/.

CABARRUS COLLEGE OF HEALTH SCIENCES

Concord, NC

CONTACT Valerie Richard, Director of Financial Aid, Cabarrus College of Health Sciences, 401 Medical Park Drive, Concord, NC 28025, 704-403-3507. *Fax:* 704-403-2077. *E-mail:* valerie.richard@carolinashealthcare.org.
Website: http://www.cabarruscollege.edu/.

CABRINI UNIVERSITY

Radnor, PA

CONTACT Ms. Elizabeth Gingerich, Director of Financial Aid, Cabrini University, 610 King of Prussia Road, Grace Hall, First Floor, Radnor, PA 19087-3698, 610-902-8424 or toll-free 800-848-1003. *Fax:* 610-902-8426. *E-mail:* egs34@cabrini.edu.
Website: http://www.cabrini.edu/.

CAIRN UNIVERSITY

Langhorne, PA

CONTACT Mr. Stephen Cassel, Director of Financial Aid, Cairn University, 200 Manor Avenue, Langhorne, PA 19047-2990, 215-702-4243 or toll-free 800-366-0049. *Fax:* 215-702-4248. *E-mail:* scassel@cairn.edu.
Website: http://cairn.edu/.

CALDWELL UNIVERSITY

Caldwell, NJ

Tuition & fees: $36,900	Average undergraduate aid package: $32,209

ABOUT THE INSTITUTION Independent Roman Catholic, coed. ***Awards:*** certificates, bachelor's, master's, and doctoral degrees. 33 undergraduate majors. ***Total enrollment:*** 2,200. Undergraduates: 1,704. Freshmen: 445. Federal methodology is used as a basis for awarding need-based institutional aid.

UNDERGRADUATE EXPENSES for 2020–2021 ***Application fee:*** $50. ***Comprehensive fee:*** $49,660 includes full-time tuition ($34,900), mandatory fees ($2000), and room and board ($12,760). ***College room only:*** $6690. Full-time tuition and fees vary according to course load, location, and program. Room and board charges vary according to board plan and housing facility. ***Part-time tuition:*** $950 per credit hour. ***Part-time fees:*** $235 per term. Part-time tuition and fees vary according to course load, location, and program.

FRESHMAN FINANCIAL AID (Fall 2019, est.) 412 applied for aid; of those 96% were deemed to have need. 100% of freshmen with need received aid; of those 12%

had need fully met. ***Average percent of need met:*** 82% (excluding resources awarded to replace EFC). ***Average financial aid package:*** $34,984 (excluding resources awarded to replace EFC). 10% of all full-time freshmen had no need and received non-need-based gift aid.

UNDERGRADUATE FINANCIAL AID (Fall 2019, est.) 1,335 applied for aid; of those 95% were deemed to have need. 99% of undergraduates with need received aid; of those 13% had need fully met. ***Average percent of need met:*** 78% (excluding resources awarded to replace EFC). ***Average financial aid package:*** $32,209 (excluding resources awarded to replace EFC). 18% of all full-time undergraduates had no need and received non-need-based gift aid.

GIFT AID (NEED-BASED) ***Receiving aid:*** Freshmen: 89% (394); all full-time undergraduates: 77% (1,245). ***Average award:*** Freshmen: $31,598; Undergraduates: $28,747. ***Scholarships, grants, and awards:*** Federal Pell, FSEOG, state, private, college/university gift aid from institutional funds.

GIFT AID (NON-NEED-BASED) ***Receiving aid:*** Freshmen: 10% (46). Undergraduates: 9% (138). ***Average award:*** Freshmen: $21,968. Undergraduates: $22,254. ***Scholarships, grants, and awards by category:*** *Academic interests/achievement:* general academic interests/achievements, home economics. *Creative arts/performance:* applied art and design, music. *Special achievements/activities:* community service, general special achievements/activities, leadership, memberships, religious involvement. *Special characteristics:* adult students, children and siblings of alumni, children of current students, children of educators, children of faculty/staff, general special characteristics, local/state students, parents of current students, previous college experience, public servants, relatives of clergy, religious affiliation, siblings of current students, spouses of current students, twins, veterans. ***Tuition waivers:*** Full or partial for children of alumni, employees or children of employees, adult students, senior citizens. ***ROTC:*** Army cooperative.

LOANS ***Student loans:*** 69% of past graduating class borrowed through all loan programs. *Average indebtedness per student:* $26,962. ***Average need-based loan:*** Freshmen: $3168. Undergraduates: $3980. ***Programs:*** Federal Direct (Subsidized and Unsubsidized Stafford, PLUS), state.

WORK-STUDY Federal work-study jobs available. ***State or other work-study/employment:*** Part-time jobs available.

APPLYING FOR FINANCIAL AID ***Required financial aid form:*** FAFSA. ***Notification date:*** Continuous.

CONTACT Ms. Eileen T. Felske, Director of Financial Aid, Caldwell University, 120 Bloomfield Avenue, Caldwell, NJ 07006, 973-618-3419. *Fax:* 973-618-3650. *E-mail:* efelske@caldwell.edu.
Website: http://www.caldwell.edu/.

CALIFORNIA BAPTIST UNIVERSITY

Riverside, CA

Tuition & fees: $36,340	Average undergraduate aid package: $21,442

ABOUT THE INSTITUTION Independent Southern Baptist, coed. ***Awards:*** associate, bachelor's, master's, and doctoral degrees. 75 undergraduate majors. ***Total enrollment:*** 11,045. Undergraduates: 8,190. Freshmen: 1,523. Federal methodology is used as a basis for awarding need-based institutional aid.

UNDERGRADUATE EXPENSES for 2020–2021 ***Application fee:*** $45. ***One-time required fee:*** $310. ***Comprehensive fee:*** $48,940 includes full-time tuition ($33,930), mandatory fees ($2410), and room and board ($12,600). ***College room only:*** $6710. Full-time tuition and fees vary according to course load, location, and program. Room and board charges vary according to board plan and housing facility. ***Part-time tuition:*** $1305 per unit. ***Part-time fees:*** $180 per term. Part-time tuition and fees vary according to course load, location, and program.

FRESHMAN FINANCIAL AID (Fall 2019, est.) 1506 applied for aid; of those 95% were deemed to have need. 87% of freshmen with need received aid; of those 23% had need fully met. ***Average percent of need met:*** 36% (excluding resources awarded to replace EFC). ***Average financial aid package:*** $23,305 (excluding resources awarded to replace EFC). 12% of all full-time freshmen had no need and received non-need-based gift aid.

UNDERGRADUATE FINANCIAL AID (Fall 2019, est.) 7,010 applied for aid; of those 94% were deemed to have need. 90% of undergraduates with need received aid; of those 18% had need fully met. ***Average percent of need met:*** 33% (excluding resources awarded to replace EFC). ***Average financial aid package:*** $21,442 (excluding resources awarded to replace EFC). 7% of all full-time undergraduates had no need and received non-need-based gift aid.

GIFT AID (NEED-BASED) ***Total amount:*** $109,417,069 (17% federal, 20% state, 62% institutional, 1% external sources). ***Receiving aid:*** Freshmen: 82% (1,237); all full-time undergraduates: 81% (5,946). ***Average award:*** Freshmen: $13,789; Undergraduates: $11,198. ***Scholarships, grants, and awards:*** Federal Pell, FSEOG, state, private, college/university gift aid from institutional funds, Federal Nursing.

GIFT AID (NON-NEED-BASED) ***Total amount:*** $10,440,689 (97% institutional, 3% external sources). ***Receiving aid:*** Freshmen: 69% (1,043). Undergraduates: 64% (4,659). ***Average award:*** Freshmen: $12,887. Undergraduates: $12,096. ***Scholarships, grants, and awards by category:*** *Academic interests/achievement:* architecture, engineering/technologies, general academic interests/achievements, health fields, religion/biblical studies. *Creative arts/performance:* applied art and design, art/fine arts, cinema/film/broadcasting, debating, journalism/publications, music, theater/drama. *Special achievements/activities:* cheerleading/drum major. *Special characteristics:* adult students, children of faculty/staff, international students, relatives of clergy, religious affiliation, siblings of current students, veterans. ***Tuition waivers:*** Full or partial for employees or children of employees. ***ROTC:*** Army, Air Force cooperative.

LOANS ***Student loans:*** $61,095,752 (38% need-based, 62% non-need-based). 78% of past graduating class borrowed through all loan programs. *Average indebtedness per student:* $36,383. ***Average need-based loan:*** Freshmen: $3391. Undergraduates: $4501. ***Parent loans:*** $24,600,339 (100% non-need-based). ***Programs:*** Federal Direct (Subsidized and Unsubsidized Stafford, PLUS), Perkins, alternative loans.

WORK-STUDY ***Federal work-study:*** Total amount: $949,845; 366 jobs averaging $2588.

ATHLETIC AWARDS Total amount: $8,074,454 (43% need-based, 57% non-need-based).

APPLYING FOR FINANCIAL AID ***Required financial aid forms:*** FAFSA, state aid form. ***Financial aid deadline (priority):*** 3/2. ***Notification date:*** Continuous beginning 3/2. Students must reply by 6/1.

CONTACT Mr. Joshua Morey, Director of Financial Aid, California Baptist University, 8432 Magnolia Avenue, Riverside, CA 92504-3297, 951-343-4235 or toll-free 877-228-8866. *E-mail:* finaid@calbaptist.edu.
Website: http://www.calbaptist.edu/.

CALIFORNIA CHRISTIAN COLLEGE

Fresno, CA

Tuition & fees: $10,050	Average undergraduate aid package: $11,433

ABOUT THE INSTITUTION Independent Free Will Baptist, coed. ***Awards:*** associate and bachelor's degrees. 2 undergraduate majors. ***Total enrollment:*** 11. Undergraduates: 12. Freshmen: 1. Federal methodology is used as a basis for awarding need-based institutional aid.

UNDERGRADUATE EXPENSES for 2020–2021 ***Application fee:*** $40. ***Comprehensive fee:*** $16,800 includes full-time tuition ($9360), mandatory fees ($690), and room and board ($6750). ***College room only:*** $4950. ***Part-time tuition:*** $390 per credit.

FRESHMAN FINANCIAL AID (Fall 2018) 1 applied for aid; of those 100% were deemed to have need. 100% of freshmen with need received aid. ***Average percent of need met:*** 75% (excluding resources awarded to replace EFC). ***Average financial aid package:*** $16,229 (excluding resources awarded to replace EFC).

UNDERGRADUATE FINANCIAL AID (Fall 2018) 7 applied for aid; of those 100% were deemed to have need. 100% of undergraduates with need received aid. ***Average percent of need met:*** 58% (excluding resources awarded to replace EFC). ***Average financial aid package:*** $11,433 (excluding resources awarded to replace EFC).

GIFT AID (NEED-BASED) ***Receiving aid:*** Freshmen: 100% (1); all full-time undergraduates: 86% (6). ***Average award:*** Freshmen: $16,229; Undergraduates: $8610. ***Scholarships, grants, and awards:*** Federal Pell, FSEOG, state, private, college/university gift aid from institutional funds.

GIFT AID (NON-NEED-BASED) ***Scholarships, grants, and awards by category:*** *Academic interests/achievement:* 1 award ($3028 total): general academic interests/achievements, religion/biblical studies.

LOANS ***Average need-based loan:*** Undergraduates: $7395. ***Programs:*** Federal Direct (Subsidized and Unsubsidized Stafford, PLUS).

WORK-STUDY ***Federal work-study:*** 3 jobs averaging $1658.

APPLYING FOR FINANCIAL AID ***Required financial aid forms:*** FAFSA, institution's own form. ***Financial aid deadline:*** Continuous. ***Notification date:*** Continuous.

CONTACT Mindy Scroggins, Student Finance Manager, California Christian College, 5364 East Belmont Avenue, Fresno, CA 93727, 559-251-4215 Ext. 1006. *Fax:* 559-385-2329. *E-mail:* financialaid@calchristiancollege.edu.
Website: http://www.calchristiancollege.edu/.

CALIFORNIA COAST UNIVERSITY

Santa Ana, CA

CONTACT Financial Aid Office, California Coast University, 925 North Spurgeon Street, Santa Ana, CA 92701, 714-547-9625 or toll-free 888-CCU-UNIV.
Website: http://www.calcoast.edu/.

CALIFORNIA COLLEGE OF THE ARTS

San Francisco, CA

ABOUT THE INSTITUTION Independent, coed. ***Awards:*** bachelor's and master's degrees. 22 undergraduate majors.

GIFT AID (NEED-BASED) ***Scholarships, grants, and awards:*** Federal Pell, FSEOG, state, private, college/university gift aid from institutional funds.

GIFT AID (NON-NEED-BASED) ***Scholarships, grants, and awards by category:*** *Academic interests/achievement:* general academic interests/achievements. *Creative arts/performance:* general creative arts/performance.

LOANS ***Programs:*** Federal Direct (Subsidized and Unsubsidized Stafford, PLUS), private loans.

WORK-STUDY ***Federal work-study:*** Total amount: $429,252; jobs available. ***State or other work-study/employment:*** Total amount: $1,094,745 (100% non-need-based). Part-time jobs available.

APPLYING FOR FINANCIAL AID ***Required financial aid form:*** FAFSA.

CONTACT Mr. Dewayne J. Barnes, Director of Financial Aid, California College of the Arts, 1111 Eighth Street, San Francisco, CA 94107, 415-703-9528 or toll-free 800-447-1ART. *Fax:* 415-551-9261. *E-mail:* finaid@cca.edu.
Website: http://www.cca.edu/.

CALIFORNIA COLLEGE SAN DIEGO

National City, CA

CONTACT Financial Aid Office, California College San Diego, 700 Bay Marina Drive, Suite 100, National City, CA 91950, 619-680-4421 or toll-free 800-622-3188.
Website: http://www.cc-sd.edu/.

CALIFORNIA COLLEGE SAN DIEGO

San Diego, CA

CONTACT Raul Rivera, Senior Financial Aid Officer, California College San Diego, 6602 Convoy Court, #100, San Diego, CA 92111, 619-680-4430 Ext. 1507 or toll-free 800-622-3188. *Fax:* 619-695-5793. *E-mail:* raul.rivera@cc-sd.edu.
Website: http://www.cc-sd.edu/.

CALIFORNIA COLLEGE SAN DIEGO

San Marcos, CA

CONTACT Financial Aid Office, California College San Diego, 277 Rancheros Drive, Suite 200, San Marcos, CA 92069, 760- 621-4333 or toll-free 800-622-3188.
Website: http://www.cc-sd.edu/.

CALIFORNIA INSTITUTE OF INTEGRAL STUDIES

San Francisco, CA

CONTACT Financial Aid Office, California Institute of Integral Studies, 1453 Mission Street, San Francisco, CA 94103, 415-575-6122. *Fax:* 415-575-1268. *E-mail:* finaid@ciis.edu.
Website: http://www.ciis.edu/.

CALIFORNIA INSTITUTE OF TECHNOLOGY

Pasadena, CA

Tuition & fees: $54,600	Average undergraduate aid package: $53,090

ABOUT THE INSTITUTION Independent, coed. ***Awards:*** certificates, bachelor's, master's, and doctoral degrees. 29 undergraduate majors. ***Total enrollment:*** 2,233. Undergraduates: 948. Freshmen: 231. Both federal and institutional methodology are used as a basis for awarding need-based institutional aid.

UNDERGRADUATE EXPENSES for 2019–2020 ***Application fee:*** $75. ***One-time required fee:*** $500. ***Comprehensive fee:*** $71,244 includes full-time tuition ($52,506), mandatory fees ($2094), and room and board ($16,644). ***College room only:*** $9615.

FRESHMAN FINANCIAL AID (Fall 2019, est.) 181 applied for aid; of those 74% were deemed to have need. 100% of freshmen with need received aid; of those 100% had need fully met. ***Average percent of need met:*** 100% (excluding resources awarded to replace EFC). ***Average financial aid package:*** $51,195 (excluding resources awarded to replace EFC). 1% of all full-time freshmen had no need and received non-need-based gift aid.

UNDERGRADUATE FINANCIAL AID (Fall 2019, est.) 562 applied for aid; of those 83% were deemed to have need. 100% of undergraduates with need received aid; of those 100% had need fully met. ***Average percent of need met:*** 100% (excluding resources awarded to replace EFC). ***Average financial aid package:*** $53,090 (excluding resources awarded to replace EFC). 1% of all full-time undergraduates had no need and received non-need-based gift aid.

GIFT AID (NEED-BASED) ***Receiving aid:*** Freshmen: 57% (134); all full-time undergraduates: 50% (469). ***Average award:*** Freshmen: $49,618; Undergraduates: $50,058. ***Scholarships, grants, and awards:*** Federal Pell, FSEOG, state, private, college/university gift aid from institutional funds.

GIFT AID (NON-NEED-BASED) ***Average award:*** Freshmen: $5000. Undergraduates: $5000. ***ROTC:*** Army cooperative, Air Force cooperative.

LOANS ***Student loans:*** 30% of past graduating class borrowed through all loan programs. *Average indebtedness per student:* $20,192. ***Average need-based loan:*** Freshmen: $2555. Undergraduates: $2874. ***Programs:*** Federal Direct (Subsidized and Unsubsidized Stafford, PLUS), college/university.

WORK-STUDY ***Federal work-study:*** 215 jobs averaging $2985. ***State or other work-study/employment:*** 34 part-time jobs averaging $2448.

APPLYING FOR FINANCIAL AID ***Required financial aid forms:*** FAFSA, institution's own form, CSS Financial Aid PROFILE, state aid form, noncustodial (divorced/separated) parent's statement, business/farm supplement. ***Notification date:*** Continuous. Students must reply within 2 weeks of notification.

CONTACT Mrs. Malina Chang, Acting Director of Financial Aid, California Institute of Technology, 1200 East California Boulevard, MC 20-90, Pasadena, CA 91125-3405, 626-395-3309. *Fax:* 626-564-8136. *E-mail:* machang@caltech.edu.
Website: http://www.caltech.edu/.

CALIFORNIA INSTITUTE OF THE ARTS

Valencia, CA

CONTACT Dr. Robin Bailey-Chen, Director of Financial Aid, California Institute of the Arts, 24700 McBean Parkway, Valencia, CA 91355-2340, 661-253-7869 or toll-free 800-545-2787. *Fax:* 661-287-3816. *E-mail:* rbaileychen@calarts.edu.
Website: http://www.calarts.edu/.

CALIFORNIA INTERCONTINENTAL UNIVERSITY

Irvine, CA

CONTACT Financial Aid Office, California Intercontinental University, 17310 Red Hill Avenue, #200, Irvine, CA 92614, 909-396-6090 or toll-free 866-687-2258.
Website: http://caluniversity.edu/.

CALIFORNIA JAZZ CONSERVATORY

Berkeley, CA

Tuition & fees: N/R	Average undergraduate aid package: $11,195

ABOUT THE INSTITUTION Independent, coed. Federal methodology is used as a basis for awarding need-based institutional aid.
FRESHMAN FINANCIAL AID (Fall 2019, est.) 1 applied for aid; of those 100% were deemed to have need. 100% of freshmen with need received aid. ***Average percent of need met:*** 47% (excluding resources awarded to replace EFC). ***Average financial aid package:*** $15,700 (excluding resources awarded to replace EFC).
UNDERGRADUATE FINANCIAL AID (Fall 2019, est.) 19 applied for aid; of those 95% were deemed to have need. ***Average percent of need met:*** 47% (excluding resources awarded to replace EFC). ***Average financial aid package:*** $11,195 (excluding resources awarded to replace EFC). 26% of all full-time undergraduates had no need and received non-need-based gift aid.
GIFT AID (NEED-BASED) ***Total amount:*** $133,661 (59% federal, 41% institutional). ***Receiving aid:*** Freshmen: 100% (1); all full-time undergraduates: 56% (15). ***Average award:*** Freshmen: $2400; Undergraduates: $8000. ***Scholarships, grants, and awards:*** Federal Pell, FSEOG, college/university gift aid from institutional funds.
GIFT AID (NON-NEED-BASED) ***Total amount:*** $72,400 (100% institutional). ***Receiving aid:*** Freshmen: 100% (1). Undergraduates: 48% (13). ***Average award:*** Undergraduates: $10,343. ***Scholarships, grants, and awards by category:*** *Creative arts/performance:* 7 awards ($72,400 total): music.
LOANS ***Student loans:*** $108,405 (69% need-based, 31% non-need-based). ***Average need-based loan:*** Freshmen: $5445. Undergraduates: $3428. ***Parent loans:*** $29,016 (100% non-need-based). ***Programs:*** Federal Direct (Subsidized and Unsubsidized Stafford, PLUS).
WORK-STUDY ***Federal work-study:*** Total amount: $5000; 2 jobs averaging $2500.
APPLYING FOR FINANCIAL AID ***Required financial aid form:*** FAFSA. ***Financial aid deadline:*** 4/1 (priority: 3/2). ***Notification date:*** 4/1. Students must reply within 2 weeks of notification.
CONTACT Karen Shepherd, Director of Financial Aid, California Jazz Conservatory, 2087 Addison Street, BERKELEY, CA 94704, 510-845-5373 Ext. 17. *Fax:* 510-841-5373. *E-mail:* karen@cjc.edu.
Website: http://www.cjc.edu/.

CALIFORNIA LUTHERAN UNIVERSITY

Thousand Oaks, CA

Tuition & fees: $45,982	Average undergraduate aid package: $33,112

ABOUT THE INSTITUTION Independent Lutheran, coed. ***Awards:*** certificates, bachelor's, master's, and doctoral degrees. 56 undergraduate majors. ***Total enrollment:*** 4,303. Undergraduates: 3,078. Freshmen: 647. Both federal and institutional methodology are used as a basis for awarding need-based institutional aid.
UNDERGRADUATE EXPENSES for 2020–2021 ***Application fee:*** $25. ***Comprehensive fee:*** $60,577 includes full-time tuition ($45,500), mandatory fees ($482), and room and board ($14,595). ***College room only:*** $7890. ***Part-time tuition:*** $1470 per credit.
FRESHMAN FINANCIAL AID (Fall 2019, est.) 640 applied for aid; of those 81% were deemed to have need. 100% of freshmen with need received aid; of those 18% had need fully met. ***Average percent of need met:*** 75% (excluding resources awarded to replace EFC). ***Average financial aid package:*** $35,900 (excluding resources awarded to replace EFC). 20% of all full-time freshmen had no need and received non-need-based gift aid.
UNDERGRADUATE FINANCIAL AID (Fall 2019, est.) 2,849 applied for aid; of those 74% were deemed to have need. 100% of undergraduates with need received aid; of those 11% had need fully met. ***Average percent of need met:*** 69% (excluding resources awarded to replace EFC). ***Average financial aid package:*** $33,112 (excluding resources awarded to replace EFC). 28% of all full-time undergraduates had no need and received non-need-based gift aid.
GIFT AID (NEED-BASED) ***Total amount:*** $61,595,142 (8% federal, 13% state, 78% institutional, 1% external sources). ***Receiving aid:*** Freshmen: 80% (517); all full-time undergraduates: 70% (2,084). ***Average award:*** Freshmen: $33,160; Undergraduates: $29,206. ***Scholarships, grants, and awards:*** Federal Pell, FSEOG, state, private, college/university gift aid from institutional funds.
GIFT AID (NON-NEED-BASED) ***Total amount:*** $15,709,556 (99% institutional, 1% external sources). ***Receiving aid:*** Freshmen: 11% (71). Undergraduates: 8% (230). ***Average award:*** Freshmen: $22,313. Undergraduates: $21,265. ***Scholarships, grants, and awards by category:*** *Academic interests/achievement:* biological sciences, business, communication, computer science, education, English, foreign languages, general academic interests/achievements, humanities, international studies, mathematics, physical sciences, religion/biblical studies, social sciences. *Creative arts/performance:* art/fine arts, creative writing, journalism/publications, music, performing arts, theater/drama. *Special achievements/activities:* community service, general special achievements/activities, leadership, religious involvement. *Special characteristics:* adult students, children and siblings of alumni, children of faculty/staff, international students, relatives of clergy, religious affiliation, veterans, veterans' children. ***ROTC:*** Army cooperative, Air Force cooperative.
LOANS ***Student loans:*** $15,031,494 (92% need-based, 8% non-need-based). 65% of past graduating class borrowed through all loan programs. *Average indebtedness per student:* $31,000. ***Average need-based loan:*** Freshmen: $3450. Undergraduates: $4580. ***Parent loans:*** $11,285,824 (90% need-based, 10% non-need-based). ***Programs:*** Federal Direct (Subsidized and Unsubsidized Stafford, PLUS).
WORK-STUDY ***Federal work-study:*** Total amount: $432,750; 250 jobs averaging $2500. ***State or other work-study/employment:*** Part-time jobs available.
APPLYING FOR FINANCIAL AID ***Required financial aid forms:*** FAFSA, Cal Grant forms, GPA verification form (CA residents only). ***Financial aid deadline (priority):*** 3/1. ***Notification date:*** Continuous beginning 3/15. Students must reply by 5/1 or within 2 weeks of notification.
CONTACT Jerry McKeen, Director of Financial Aid, California Lutheran University, 60 West Olsen Road, Thousand Oaks, CA 91360-2787, 805-493-3115 or toll-free 877-258-3678. *Fax:* 805-493-3114. *E-mail:* jmckeen@callutheran.edu.
Website: http://www.callutheran.edu/.

CALIFORNIA MIRAMAR UNIVERSITY

San Diego, CA

CONTACT Financial Aid Office, California Miramar University, 3550 Camino Del Rio North, Suite 208, San Diego, CA 92108, 858-653-3000 or toll-free 877-570-5678.
Website: http://www.calmu.edu/.

CALIFORNIA POLYTECHNIC STATE UNIVERSITY, SAN LUIS OBISPO

San Luis Obispo, CA

Tuition & fees (CA res): $9943	Average undergraduate aid package: $10,774

ABOUT THE INSTITUTION State-supported, coed. ***Awards:*** certificates, bachelor's, and master's degrees. 64 undergraduate majors. ***Total enrollment:*** 21,242. Undergraduates: 20,154. Freshmen: 4,613. Federal methodology is used as a basis for awarding need-based institutional aid.

UNDERGRADUATE EXPENSES for 2019–2020 ***Application fee:*** $55. ***Tuition, state resident:*** full-time $5742; part-time $3330 per year. ***Tuition, nonresident:*** full-time $19,632; part-time $8082 per year. ***Required fees:*** full-time $4201; $3185 per year. Full-time tuition and fees vary according to course load, degree level, and program. Part-time tuition and fees vary according to course load, degree level, and program. ***College room and board:*** $14,208; ***Room only:*** $8719. Room and board charges vary according to board plan and housing facility.

FRESHMAN FINANCIAL AID (Fall 2019, est.) 3456 applied for aid; of those 48% were deemed to have need. 93% of freshmen with need received aid; of those 11% had need fully met. ***Average percent of need met:*** 56% (excluding resources awarded to replace EFC). ***Average financial aid package:*** $10,459 (excluding resources awarded to replace EFC). 13% of all full-time freshmen had no need and received non-need-based gift aid.

UNDERGRADUATE FINANCIAL AID (Fall 2019, est.) 12,356 applied for aid; of those 67% were deemed to have need. 94% of undergraduates with need received aid; of those 9% had need fully met. ***Average percent of need met:*** 55% (excluding resources awarded to replace EFC). ***Average financial aid package:*** $10,774 (excluding resources awarded to replace EFC). 12% of all full-time undergraduates had no need and received non-need-based gift aid.

GIFT AID (NEED-BASED) ***Total amount:*** $61,887,442 (28% federal, 34% state, 29% institutional, 9% external sources). ***Receiving aid:*** Freshmen: 34% (1,483); all full-time undergraduates: 36% (7,264). ***Average award:*** Freshmen: $2451; Undergraduates: $3159. ***Scholarships, grants, and awards:*** Federal Pell, FSEOG, state, private, college/university gift aid from institutional funds, Federal TEACH Grant; California Dream Grant.

GIFT AID (NON-NEED-BASED) ***Total amount:*** $11,128,527 (7% state, 52% institutional, 41% external sources). ***Receiving aid:*** Freshmen: 15% (659). Undergraduates: 14% (2,853). ***Average award:*** Freshmen: $1505. Undergraduates: $1943. ***Scholarships, grants, and awards by category:*** *Academic interests/achievement:* agriculture, architecture, biological sciences, business, communication, computer science, education, engineering/technologies, English, foreign languages, general academic interests/achievements, health fields, home economics, humanities, international studies, library science, mathematics, military science, physical sciences, social sciences. *Creative arts/performance:* applied art and design, art/fine arts, cinema/film/broadcasting, creative writing, dance, debating, general creative arts/performance, journalism/publications, music, performing arts, theater/drama. *Special achievements/activities:* community service, leadership, rodeo. *Special characteristics:* children and siblings of alumni, general special characteristics, local/state students. ***Tuition waivers:*** Full or partial for employees or children of employees. ***ROTC:*** Army.

LOANS ***Student loans:*** $41,793,904 (68% need-based, 32% non-need-based). 41% of past graduating class borrowed through all loan programs. *Average indebtedness per student:* $22,411. ***Average need-based loan:*** Freshmen: $3349. Undergraduates: $4133. ***Parent loans:*** $38,991,928 (29% need-based, 71% non-need-based). ***Programs:*** Federal Direct (Subsidized and Unsubsidized Stafford, PLUS), Perkins, college/university, Alternative loans; California Dream Loan.

WORK-STUDY ***Federal work-study:*** Total amount: $1,200,262; jobs available.

ATHLETIC AWARDS Total amount: $5,434,167 (31% need-based, 69% non-need-based).

APPLYING FOR FINANCIAL AID ***Required financial aid form:*** FAFSA. ***Financial aid deadline (priority):*** 3/2. ***Notification date:*** Continuous beginning 3/15.

CONTACT Gerrie Hatten, Interim Director of Financial Aid, California Polytechnic State University, San Luis Obispo, Administration Building, Room 212, San Luis Obispo, CA 93407, 805-756-5878. *Fax:* 805-756-7243. *E-mail:* tmellick@calpoly.edu.
Website: http://www.calpoly.edu/.

CALIFORNIA STATE POLYTECHNIC UNIVERSITY, POMONA

Pomona, CA

Tuition & fees (area res): $7396	Average undergraduate aid package: $10,629

ABOUT THE INSTITUTION State-supported, coed. ***Awards:*** bachelor's, master's, and doctoral degrees. 56 undergraduate majors. ***Total enrollment:*** 27,915. Undergraduates: 26,455. Freshmen: 3,696. Federal methodology is used as a basis for awarding need-based institutional aid.

UNDERGRADUATE EXPENSES for 2020–2021 ***Application fee:*** $70. ***Tuition, area resident:*** full-time $5742. ***Tuition, state resident:*** full-time $5472. ***Tuition, nonresident:*** full-time $17,622; part-time $396 per credit hour. ***Required fees:*** full-time $1654. ***College room and board:*** $15,791; ***Room only:*** $10,363. Room and board charges vary according to board plan and housing facility.

FRESHMAN FINANCIAL AID (Fall 2019, est.) 3245 applied for aid; of those 79% were deemed to have need. 95% of freshmen with need received aid; of those 2% had need fully met. ***Average percent of need met:*** 52% (excluding resources awarded to replace EFC). ***Average financial aid package:*** $9700 (excluding resources awarded to replace EFC). 1% of all full-time freshmen had no need and received non-need-based gift aid.

UNDERGRADUATE FINANCIAL AID (Fall 2019, est.) 17,142 applied for aid; of those 88% were deemed to have need. 95% of undergraduates with need received aid; of those 4% had need fully met. ***Average percent of need met:*** 52% (excluding resources awarded to replace EFC). ***Average financial aid package:*** $10,629 (excluding resources awarded to replace EFC). 1% of all full-time undergraduates had no need and received non-need-based gift aid.

GIFT AID (NEED-BASED) ***Total amount:*** $157,489,900 (48% federal, 28% state, 24% institutional). ***Receiving aid:*** Freshmen: 52% (1,953); all full-time undergraduates: 54% (11,820). ***Average award:*** Freshmen: $9333; Undergraduates: $9847. ***Scholarships, grants, and awards:*** Federal Pell, FSEOG, state, private, college/university gift aid from institutional funds.

GIFT AID (NON-NEED-BASED) ***Total amount:*** $7,887,803 (71% state, 3% institutional, 26% external sources). ***Receiving aid:*** Freshmen: 15% (577). Undergraduates: 13% (2,753). ***Average award:*** Freshmen: $3000. Undergraduates: $2197. ***Scholarships, grants, and awards by category:*** *Academic interests/achievement:* agriculture, architecture, area/ethnic studies, biological sciences, business, communication, computer science, education, engineering/technologies, English, foreign languages, general academic interests/achievements, humanities, international studies, mathematics, physical sciences, social sciences. *Special achievements/activities:* hobbies/interests, leadership. *Special characteristics:* children and siblings of alumni, children of current students, first-generation college students, members of minority groups. ***Tuition waivers:*** Full or partial for employees or children of employees. ***ROTC:*** Army.

LOANS ***Student loans:*** $60,394,817 (51% need-based, 49% non-need-based). 52% of past graduating class borrowed through all loan programs. *Average indebtedness per student:* $21,730. ***Average need-based loan:*** Freshmen: $3455. Undergraduates: $4483. ***Parent loans:*** $5,695,940 (100% non-need-based). ***Programs:*** Federal Direct (Subsidized and Unsubsidized Stafford, PLUS), Perkins, college/university.

WORK-STUDY ***Federal work-study:*** Total amount: $975,024; jobs available.

ATHLETIC AWARDS Total amount: $9500 (100% non-need-based).

APPLYING FOR FINANCIAL AID ***Required financial aid form:*** FAFSA. ***Notification date:*** Continuous.

CONTACT Dr. Diana Minor, Director of Financial Aid and Scholarships, California State Polytechnic University, Pomona, 3801 West Temple Avenue, Pomona, CA 91768-2557, 909-869-3704. *Fax:* 909-869-4757. *E-mail:* dyminor@cpp.edu.
Website: http://www.cpp.edu/.

CALIFORNIA STATE UNIVERSITY, BAKERSFIELD

Bakersfield, CA

Tuition & fees: N/R **Average undergraduate aid package: $11,343**

ABOUT THE INSTITUTION State-supported, coed. ***Awards:*** bachelor's, master's, and doctoral degrees. 30 undergraduate majors. ***Total enrollment:*** 10,999. Undergraduates: 9,796. Freshmen: 1,434. Federal methodology is used as a basis for awarding need-based institutional aid.

FRESHMAN FINANCIAL AID (Fall 2019, est.) 1368 applied for aid; of those 92% were deemed to have need. 98% of freshmen with need received aid; of those 1% had need fully met. ***Average percent of need met:*** 66% (excluding resources awarded to replace EFC). ***Average financial aid package:*** $11,917 (excluding resources awarded to replace EFC). 1% of all full-time freshmen had no need and received non-need-based gift aid.

UNDERGRADUATE FINANCIAL AID (Fall 2019, est.) 6,989 applied for aid; of those 95% were deemed to have need. 98% of undergraduates with need received aid; of those 1% had need fully met. ***Average percent of need met:*** 58% (excluding resources awarded to replace EFC). ***Average financial aid package:*** $11,343 (excluding resources awarded to replace EFC). 1% of all full-time undergraduates had no need and received non-need-based gift aid.

GIFT AID (NEED-BASED) ***Receiving aid:*** Freshmen: 79% (1,156); all full-time undergraduates: 78% (6,075). ***Average award:*** Freshmen: $11,273; Undergraduates: $9977. ***Scholarships, grants, and awards:*** Federal Pell, FSEOG, state, private, college/university gift aid from institutional funds.

GIFT AID (NON-NEED-BASED) ***Receiving aid:*** Freshmen: 15% (221). Undergraduates: 11% (879). ***Average award:*** Freshmen: $2187. Undergraduates: $1817. ***Scholarships, grants, and awards by category:*** *Academic interests/achievement:* biological sciences, business, communication, education, foreign languages, general academic interests/achievements, home economics, humanities, mathematics, physical sciences, premedicine, religion/biblical studies, social sciences. *Creative arts/performance:* applied art and design, music, theater/drama. *Special achievements/activities:* community service, general special achievements/activities, leadership. *Special characteristics:* children of faculty/staff, children of union members/company employees, ethnic background, first-generation college students, local/state students, veterans.

LOANS ***Student loans:*** 45% of past graduating class borrowed through all loan programs. *Average indebtedness per student:* $18,941. ***Average need-based loan:*** Freshmen: $3158. Undergraduates: $4036. ***Programs:*** Federal Direct (Subsidized and Unsubsidized Stafford, PLUS), Federal Nursing, state, college/university.

WORK-STUDY Federal work-study jobs available.

APPLYING FOR FINANCIAL AID ***Required financial aid forms:*** FAFSA, state aid form. ***Financial aid deadline:*** Continuous. ***Notification date:*** Continuous. Students must reply within 3 weeks of notification.

CONTACT Mr. Chad Morris, Associate Director of Financial Aid and Scholarships, California State University, Bakersfield, 9001 Stockdale Highway, Bakersfield, CA 93311-1022, 661-654-3267 or toll-free 800-788-2782. *Fax:* 661-654-6800. *E-mail:* cmorris@csub.edu.
Website: http://www.csub.edu/.

CALIFORNIA STATE UNIVERSITY CHANNEL ISLANDS

Camarillo, CA

CONTACT Financial Aid Office, California State University Channel Islands, One University Drive, Camarillo, CA 93012, 805-437-8400.
Website: http://www.csuci.edu/.

CALIFORNIA STATE UNIVERSITY, CHICO

Chico, CA

Tuition & fees (area res): $23,418 **Average undergraduate aid package: $12,607**

ABOUT THE INSTITUTION State-supported, coed. ***Awards:*** certificates, bachelor's, and master's degrees. 46 undergraduate majors. ***Total enrollment:*** 18,073. Undergraduates: 16,420. Freshmen: 2,725. Federal methodology is used as a basis for awarding need-based institutional aid.

UNDERGRADUATE EXPENSES for 2019–2020 ***Application fee:*** $55. ***Tuition, area resident:*** full-time $7806; part-time $5394 per term. ***Tuition, state resident:*** full-time $7806; part-time $5394 per term. ***Tuition, nonresident:*** full-time $17,310; part-time $10,146 per year. ***Required fees:*** full-time $15,612. Full-time tuition and fees vary according to degree level and program. Part-time tuition and fees vary according to course load, degree level, and program. ***College room and board:*** $13,422. Room and board charges vary according to board plan and housing facility.

FRESHMAN FINANCIAL AID (Fall 2018) 2364 applied for aid; of those 75% were deemed to have need. 96% of freshmen with need received aid; of those 13% had need fully met. ***Average percent of need met:*** 65% (excluding resources awarded to replace EFC). ***Average financial aid package:*** $12,422 (excluding resources awarded to replace EFC). 7% of all full-time freshmen had no need and received non-need-based gift aid.

UNDERGRADUATE FINANCIAL AID (Fall 2018) 11,931 applied for aid; of those 85% were deemed to have need. 96% of undergraduates with need received aid; of those 8% had need fully met. ***Average percent of need met:*** 66% (excluding resources awarded to replace EFC). ***Average financial aid package:*** $12,607 (excluding resources awarded to replace EFC). 3% of all full-time undergraduates had no need and received non-need-based gift aid.

GIFT AID (NEED-BASED) ***Total amount:*** $90,715,549 (41% federal, 30% state, 29% institutional). ***Receiving aid:*** Freshmen: 61% (1,641); all full-time undergraduates: 60% (9,217). ***Average award:*** Freshmen: $9523; Undergraduates: $9116. ***Scholarships, grants, and awards:*** Federal Pell, FSEOG, state, private, college/university gift aid from institutional funds.

GIFT AID (NON-NEED-BASED) ***Total amount:*** $911,720 (3% federal, 70% state, 27% institutional). ***Receiving aid:*** Freshmen: 7% (177). Undergraduates: 3% (512). ***Average award:*** Freshmen: $2353. Undergraduates: $2124. ***Scholarships, grants, and awards by category:*** *Academic interests/achievement:* agriculture, area/ethnic studies, biological sciences, business, communication, computer science, education, engineering/technologies, English, foreign languages, general academic interests/achievements, health fields, humanities, international studies, mathematics, physical sciences, social sciences. *Creative arts/performance:* applied art and design, art/fine arts, cinema/film/broadcasting, creative writing, dance, debating, general creative arts/performance, journalism/publications, music, performing arts, theater/drama. *Special achievements/activities:* community service, general special achievements/activities, hobbies/interests, leadership, memberships. *Special characteristics:* adult students, children of faculty/staff, ethnic background, first-generation college students, handicapped students, international students, local/state students, married students, members of minority groups, out-of-state students. ***Tuition waivers:*** Full or partial for employees or children of employees, senior citizens.

LOANS ***Student loans:*** $51,193,942 (88% need-based, 12% non-need-based). 40% of past graduating class borrowed through all loan programs. *Average indebtedness per student:* $5894. ***Average need-based loan:*** Freshmen: $2749. Undergraduates: $3392. ***Parent loans:*** $4,987,327 (62% need-based, 38% non-need-based). ***Programs:*** Federal Direct (Subsidized and Unsubsidized Stafford, PLUS), college/university.

WORK-STUDY ***Federal work-study:*** Total amount: $2,157,712; 746 jobs averaging $2747. ***State or other work-study/employment:*** 746 part-time jobs averaging $2747.

ATHLETIC AWARDS Total amount: $566,758 (85% need-based, 15% non-need-based).

APPLYING FOR FINANCIAL AID ***Required financial aid forms:*** FAFSA, Scholarship Application Form. ***Financial aid deadline (priority):*** 3/2. ***Notification date:*** Continuous beginning 4/3.

CONTACT Dan Reed, Director of Financial Aid and Scholarships, California State University, Chico, 400 West First Street, Student Services Center, Room 250, Chico, CA 95929-0705, 530-898-6451 or toll-free 800-542-4426 (out-of-state). *Fax:* 530-898-6883. *E-mail:* finaid@csuchico.edu.
Website: http://www.csuchico.edu/.

CALIFORNIA STATE UNIVERSITY, DOMINGUEZ HILLS

Carson, CA

Tuition & fees (CA res): $8140	Average undergraduate aid package: $6204

ABOUT THE INSTITUTION State-supported, coed. ***Awards:*** certificates, bachelor's, master's, and doctoral degrees. 66 undergraduate majors. ***Total enrollment:*** 17,977. Undergraduates: 15,315. Freshmen: 2,533. Federal methodology is used as a basis for awarding need-based institutional aid.

UNDERGRADUATE EXPENSES for 2020–2021 ***Application fee:*** $55. ***Tuition, state resident:*** full-time $6941; part-time $4529 per term. ***Tuition, nonresident:*** full-time $16,445. ***Required fees:*** full-time $1199; $1199 per term. ***College room and board:*** $13,984.

FRESHMAN FINANCIAL AID (Fall 2018) 1697 applied for aid; of those 95% were deemed to have need. 97% of freshmen with need received aid; of those 1% had need fully met. ***Average percent of need met:*** 33% (excluding resources awarded to replace EFC). ***Average financial aid package:*** $6029 (excluding resources awarded to replace EFC). 2% of all full-time freshmen had no need and received non-need-based gift aid.

UNDERGRADUATE FINANCIAL AID (Fall 2018) 7,418 applied for aid; of those 97% were deemed to have need. 97% of undergraduates with need received aid; of those 1% had need fully met. ***Average percent of need met:*** 31% (excluding resources awarded to replace EFC). ***Average financial aid package:*** $6204 (excluding resources awarded to replace EFC). 1% of all full-time undergraduates had no need and received non-need-based gift aid.

GIFT AID (NEED-BASED) ***Total amount:*** $50,029,776 (44% federal, 55% state, 1% external sources). ***Receiving aid:*** Freshmen: 72% (1,419); all full-time undergraduates: 57% (6,115). ***Average award:*** Freshmen: $5789; Undergraduates: $5277. ***Scholarships, grants, and awards:*** Federal Pell, FSEOG, state, private, college/university gift aid from institutional funds.

GIFT AID (NON-NEED-BASED) ***Total amount:*** $42,745 (76% institutional, 24% external sources). ***Receiving aid:*** Freshmen: 14% (285). Undergraduates: 15% (1,635). ***Average award:*** Freshmen: $4367. Undergraduates: $3772. ***Tuition waivers:*** Full or partial for senior citizens. ***ROTC:*** Army, Air Force cooperative.

LOANS ***Student loans:*** $15,159,961 (95% need-based, 5% non-need-based). 38% of past graduating class borrowed through all loan programs. *Average indebtedness per student:* $14,585. ***Average need-based loan:*** Freshmen: $1660. Undergraduates: $2357. ***Parent loans:*** $380,165 (76% need-based, 24% non-need-based). ***Programs:*** Federal Direct (Subsidized and Unsubsidized Stafford, PLUS).

WORK-STUDY ***Federal work-study:*** Total amount: $397,943; jobs available.

ATHLETIC AWARDS Total amount: $366,504 (86% need-based, 14% non-need-based).

APPLYING FOR FINANCIAL AID ***Required financial aid form:*** FAFSA. ***Financial aid deadline (priority):*** 3/2. ***Notification date:*** Continuous beginning 1/31.

CONTACT Mrs. Delores S. Lee, Director of Financial Aid, California State University, Dominguez Hills, 1000 East Victoria Street, Carson, CA 90747-0001, 310-243-3189. *Fax:* 310-516-4498. *E-mail:* dslee@csudh.edu.
Website: http://www.csudh.edu/.

CALIFORNIA STATE UNIVERSITY, EAST BAY

Hayward, CA

CONTACT Office of Financial Aid, California State University, East Bay, 25800 Carlos Bee Boulevard, Hayward, CA 94542-3028, 510-885-2784. *Fax:* 510-885-2161. *E-mail:* finaid@csueastbay.edu.
Website: http://www.csueastbay.edu/.

CALIFORNIA STATE UNIVERSITY, FRESNO

Fresno, CA

Tuition & fees: N/R	Average undergraduate aid package: N/A

ABOUT THE INSTITUTION State-supported, coed. ***Awards:*** certificates, bachelor's, master's, and doctoral degrees. 87 undergraduate majors. ***Total enrollment:*** 24,139. Undergraduates: 21,462. Freshmen: 3,060. Federal methodology is used as a basis for awarding need-based institutional aid.

GIFT AID (NEED-BASED) ***Scholarships, grants, and awards:*** Federal Pell, FSEOG, state, private, college/university gift aid from institutional funds.

GIFT AID (NON-NEED-BASED) ***Scholarships, grants, and awards by category:*** *Academic interests/achievement:* agriculture, area/ethnic studies, biological sciences, business, communication, education, engineering/technologies, English, foreign languages, general academic interests/achievements, health fields, home economics, humanities, mathematics, physical sciences, social sciences. *Creative arts/performance:* applied art and design, journalism/publications, music, theater/drama. *Special achievements/activities:* community service, leadership. *Special characteristics:* handicapped students, local/state students. ***ROTC:*** Army, Air Force.

LOANS ***Student loans:*** 41% of past graduating class borrowed through all loan programs. *Average indebtedness per student:* $15,772. ***Programs:*** Federal Direct (Subsidized and Unsubsidized Stafford, PLUS), Federal Nursing, college/university, alternative loans.

WORK-STUDY Federal work-study jobs available.

APPLYING FOR FINANCIAL AID ***Required financial aid form:*** FAFSA. ***Financial aid deadline (priority):*** 3/2. ***Notification date:*** Continuous beginning 4/1. Students must reply within 3 weeks of notification.

CONTACT Kelly Russell, Director of Financial Aid and Scholarships, California State University, Fresno, 5150 North Maple Avenue, JA64, Fresno, CA 93740, 559-278-2182. *Fax:* 559-278-4833. *E-mail:* kellyr@csufresno.edu.
Website: http://www.csufresno.edu/.

CALIFORNIA STATE UNIVERSITY, FULLERTON

Fullerton, CA

Tuition & fees (area res): $8108	Average undergraduate aid package: $10,485

ABOUT THE INSTITUTION State-supported, coed. ***Awards:*** certificates, bachelor's, master's, and doctoral degrees. 66 undergraduate majors. ***Total enrollment:*** 40,445. Undergraduates: 35,169. Freshmen: 4,778. Federal methodology is used as a basis for awarding need-based institutional aid.

UNDERGRADUATE EXPENSES for 2020–2021 ***Application fee:*** $70. ***Tuition, area resident:*** full-time $6927. ***Tuition, state resident:*** full-time $6927. ***Tuition, nonresident:*** full-time $16,431; part-time $396 per credit hour. ***Required fees:*** full-time $1181.

FRESHMAN FINANCIAL AID (Fall 2018) 3593 applied for aid; of those 74% were deemed to have need. 96% of freshmen with need received aid; of those 15% had need fully met. ***Average percent of need met:*** 63% (excluding resources awarded to replace EFC). ***Average financial aid package:*** $10,480 (excluding resources awarded to replace EFC). 5% of all full-time freshmen had no need and received non-need-based gift aid.

UNDERGRADUATE FINANCIAL AID (Fall 2018) 21,570 applied for aid; of those 90% were deemed to have need. 96% of undergraduates with need received aid; of those 13% had need fully met. ***Average percent of need met:*** 65% (excluding resources awarded to replace EFC). ***Average financial aid package:*** $10,485 (excluding resources awarded to replace EFC). 3% of all full-time undergraduates had no need and received non-need-based gift aid.

GIFT AID (NEED-BASED) ***Receiving aid:*** Freshmen: 58% (2,495); all full-time undergraduates: 65% (18,042). ***Average award:*** Freshmen: $9710; Undergraduates: $9299. ***Scholarships, grants, and awards:*** Federal Pell, FSEOG, state, private, college/university gift aid from institutional funds.

GIFT AID (NON-NEED-BASED) ***Receiving aid:*** Freshmen: 12% (527). Undergraduates: 12% (3,251). ***Average award:*** Freshmen: $1512. Undergraduates: $1562. ***Scholarships, grants, and awards by category:*** *Academic interests/achievement:* area/ethnic studies, biological sciences, business, communication, computer science, education, engineering/technologies, English, foreign languages, general academic interests/achievements, health fields, home economics, humanities, international studies, mathematics, military science, physical sciences, religion/biblical studies, social sciences. *Creative arts/performance:* applied art and design, cinema/film/broadcasting, dance, journalism/publications, music, performing arts, theater/drama. *Special achievements/activities:* general special achievements/activities, leadership. *Special characteristics:* general special characteristics. ***ROTC:*** Army.

LOANS ***Student loans:*** 42% of past graduating class borrowed through all loan programs. *Average indebtedness per student:* $7665. ***Average need-based loan:*** Freshmen: $2863. Undergraduates: $4057. ***Programs:*** Federal Direct (Subsidized and Unsubsidized Stafford, PLUS), college/university.

WORK-STUDY Federal work-study jobs available.

APPLYING FOR FINANCIAL AID ***Notification date:*** Continuous. Students must reply by 4/27 or within 4 weeks of notification.

CONTACT Ms. Jessica Barco, Director of Financial Aid, California State University, Fullerton, 800 North State College Boulevard, Fullerton, CA 92831-3599, 657-278-3128. *Fax:* 657-278-7090. *E-mail:* jbarco@fullerton.edu.
Website: http://www.fullerton.edu/.

CALIFORNIA STATE UNIVERSITY, LONG BEACH

Long Beach, CA

Tuition & fees (area res): $6846	Average undergraduate aid package: $14,185

ABOUT THE INSTITUTION State-supported, coed. ***Awards:*** certificates, bachelor's, master's, and doctoral degrees. 148 undergraduate majors. ***Total enrollment:*** 38,075. Undergraduates: 32,784. Freshmen: 5,161. Federal methodology is used as a basis for awarding need-based institutional aid.

UNDERGRADUATE EXPENSES for 2020–2021 ***Application fee:*** $55. ***Tuition, area resident:*** full-time $5742. ***Tuition, state resident:*** full-time $5742. ***Tuition, nonresident:*** full-time $16,038. ***Required fees:*** full-time $1104. Full-time tuition and fees vary according to course level, course load, degree level, and program. Part-time tuition and fees vary according to course level, course load, degree level, and program. ***College room and board:*** $13,070; ***Room only:*** $8360. Room and board charges vary according to board plan.

FRESHMAN FINANCIAL AID (Fall 2019, est.) 4496 applied for aid; of those 79% were deemed to have need. 98% of freshmen with need received aid; of those 59% had need fully met. ***Average percent of need met:*** 80% (excluding resources awarded to replace EFC). ***Average financial aid package:*** $12,617 (excluding resources awarded to replace EFC).

UNDERGRADUATE FINANCIAL AID (Fall 2019, est.) 24,796 applied for aid; of those 90% were deemed to have need. 96% of undergraduates with need received aid; of those 46% had need fully met. ***Average percent of need met:*** 76% (excluding resources awarded to replace EFC). ***Average financial aid package:*** $14,185 (excluding resources awarded to replace EFC).

GIFT AID (NEED-BASED) ***Total amount:*** $199,638,501 (41% federal, 32% state, 26% institutional, 1% external sources). ***Receiving aid:*** Freshmen: 58% (2,946); all full-time undergraduates: 62% (17,826). ***Average award:*** Freshmen: $8417; Undergraduates: $8641. ***Scholarships, grants, and awards:*** Federal Pell, FSEOG, state, private, college/university gift aid from institutional funds, United Negro College Fund.

GIFT AID (NON-NEED-BASED) ***Total amount:*** $1,710,182 (5% federal, 95% institutional). ***Receiving aid:*** Freshmen: 15% (782). Undergraduates: 22% (6,429). ***Tuition waivers:*** Full or partial for employees or children of employees, senior citizens.

LOANS ***Student loans:*** $131,880,929 (67% need-based, 33% non-need-based). 47% of past graduating class borrowed through all loan programs. *Average indebtedness per student:* $18,686. ***Average need-based loan:*** Freshmen: $3375. Undergraduates: $4106. ***Parent loans:*** $4,168,588 (100% non-need-based). ***Programs:*** Federal Direct (Subsidized and Unsubsidized Stafford, PLUS), state.

WORK-STUDY ***Federal work-study:*** Total amount: $4,651,607; jobs available.

ATHLETIC AWARDS Total amount: $2,480,482 (100% non-need-based).

APPLYING FOR FINANCIAL AID ***Required financial aid form:*** FAFSA. ***Financial aid deadline (priority):*** 3/2. ***Notification date:*** Continuous beginning 3/28.

CONTACT Nicolas Valdivia, Office of Financial Aid, California State University, Long Beach, 1250 Bellflower Boulevard, Long Beach, CA 90840, 562-985-8403.
Website: http://www.csulb.edu/.

CALIFORNIA STATE UNIVERSITY, LOS ANGELES

Los Angeles, CA

Tuition & fees (area res): $6768	Average undergraduate aid package: $12,384

ABOUT THE INSTITUTION State-supported, coed. ***Awards:*** certificates, bachelor's, master's, and doctoral degrees. 57 undergraduate majors. ***Total enrollment:*** 26,360. Undergraduates: 22,626. Freshmen: 3,292. Federal methodology is used as a basis for awarding need-based institutional aid.

UNDERGRADUATE EXPENSES for 2020–2021 ***Application fee:*** $55. ***Tuition, area resident:*** full-time $5742. ***Tuition, state resident:*** full-time $5742. ***Tuition, nonresident:*** full-time $17,622; part-time $396 per unit. ***Required fees:*** full-time $1026; $1026 per year. Full-time tuition and fees vary according to course load, degree level, and program. Part-time tuition and fees vary according to course load, degree level, and program. ***College room and board:*** $15,992; ***Room only:*** $11,859. Room and board charges vary according to board plan, housing facility, and location.

FRESHMAN FINANCIAL AID (Fall 2019, est.) 3062 applied for aid; of those 95% were deemed to have need. 99% of freshmen with need received aid; of those 3% had need fully met. ***Average percent of need met:*** 67% (excluding resources awarded to replace EFC). ***Average financial aid package:*** $12,515 (excluding resources awarded to replace EFC). 1% of all full-time freshmen had no need and received non-need-based gift aid.

UNDERGRADUATE FINANCIAL AID (Fall 2019, est.) 18,084 applied for aid; of those 97% were deemed to have need. 99% of undergraduates with need received aid; of those 4% had need fully met. ***Average percent of need met:*** 64% (excluding resources awarded to replace EFC). ***Average financial aid package:*** $12,384 (excluding resources awarded to replace EFC). 1% of all full-time undergraduates had no need and received non-need-based gift aid.

GIFT AID (NEED-BASED) ***Receiving aid:*** Freshmen: 89% (2,873); all full-time undergraduates: 87% (17,016). ***Average award:*** Freshmen: $11,722; Undergraduates: $10,875. ***Scholarships, grants, and awards:*** Federal Pell, FSEOG, state, private, college/university gift aid from institutional funds.

GIFT AID (NON-NEED-BASED) ***Receiving aid:*** Undergraduates: 1. ***Average award:*** Freshmen: $7767. Undergraduates: $6661. ***Scholarships, grants, and awards by category:*** *Academic interests/achievement:* biological sciences, business, communication, computer science, education, engineering/technologies, English, foreign languages, general academic interests/achievements, home economics, mathematics, physical sciences, social sciences. *Creative arts/performance:* applied art and design, general creative arts/performance, journalism/publications, music, theater/drama. *Special achievements/activities:* community service, general special achievements/activities. *Special characteristics:* general special characteristics. ***Tuition waivers:*** Full or partial for employees or children of employees. ***ROTC:*** Army cooperative, Air Force cooperative.

LOANS ***Student loans:*** 78% of past graduating class borrowed through all loan programs. *Average indebtedness per student:* $13,458. ***Average need-based loan:***

Freshmen: $3315. Undergraduates: $4390. ***Programs:*** Federal Direct (Subsidized and Unsubsidized Stafford, PLUS), Perkins, Federal Nursing, college/university.

WORK-STUDY Federal work-study jobs available.

APPLYING FOR FINANCIAL AID ***Required financial aid form:*** FAFSA. ***Notification date:*** Continuous.

CONTACT Tamie L. Nguyen, Director of Financial Aid, California State University, Los Angeles, 5151 State University Drive, Los Angeles, CA 90032, 323-343-6260. *Fax:* 323-343-3166. *E-mail:* tnguyen10@cslanet.calstatela.edu.
Website: http://www.calstatela.edu/.

CALIFORNIA STATE UNIVERSITY MARITIME ACADEMY

Vallejo, CA

Tuition & fees: N/R | **Average undergraduate aid package: $12,576**

ABOUT THE INSTITUTION State-supported, coed. ***Awards:*** bachelor's and master's degrees. 4 undergraduate majors. ***Total enrollment:*** 1,046. Undergraduates: 1,017. Freshmen: 216. Federal methodology is used as a basis for awarding need-based institutional aid.

FRESHMAN FINANCIAL AID (Fall 2019, est.) 133 applied for aid; of those 66% were deemed to have need. 100% of freshmen with need received aid; of those 10% had need fully met. ***Average financial aid package:*** $10,624 (excluding resources awarded to replace EFC). 3% of all full-time freshmen had no need and received non-need-based gift aid.

UNDERGRADUATE FINANCIAL AID (Fall 2019, est.) 652 applied for aid; of those 70% were deemed to have need. 100% of undergraduates with need received aid; of those 4% had need fully met. ***Average financial aid package:*** $12,576 (excluding resources awarded to replace EFC). 3% of all full-time undergraduates had no need and received non-need-based gift aid.

GIFT AID (NEED-BASED) ***Total amount:*** $4,314,562 (29% federal, 52% state, 12% institutional, 7% external sources). ***Receiving aid:*** Freshmen: 36% (72); all full-time undergraduates: 43% (384). ***Average award:*** Freshmen: $8072; Undergraduates: $9592. ***Scholarships, grants, and awards:*** Federal Pell, FSEOG, state, private, college/university gift aid from institutional funds.

GIFT AID (NON-NEED-BASED) ***Receiving aid:*** Freshmen: 13% (26). Undergraduates: 10% (93). ***Average award:*** Freshmen: $707. Undergraduates: $1169. ***Scholarships, grants, and awards by category:*** *Academic interests/achievement:* business, engineering/technologies, general academic interests/achievements. ***ROTC:*** Naval cooperative, Air Force cooperative.

LOANS ***Student loans:*** $3,537,044 (41% need-based, 59% non-need-based). 62% of past graduating class borrowed through all loan programs. *Average indebtedness per student:* $30,292. ***Average need-based loan:*** Freshmen: $3324. Undergraduates: $4155. ***Parent loans:*** $2,553,966 (100% non-need-based). ***Programs:*** Federal Direct (Subsidized and Unsubsidized Stafford, PLUS).

WORK-STUDY ***Federal work-study:*** Total amount: $65,000; jobs available.

ATHLETIC AWARDS Total amount: $72,000 (100% non-need-based).

APPLYING FOR FINANCIAL AID ***Required financial aid forms:*** FAFSA, state aid form. ***Financial aid deadline (priority):*** 3/2. ***Notification date:*** Continuous beginning 3/15. Students must reply by 5/1 or within 6 weeks of notification.

CONTACT Priscilla Muha, Director of Financial Aid, California State University Maritime Academy, 200 Maritime Academy Drive, Vallejo, CA 94590-0644, 707-654-1275 or toll-free 800-561-1945. *Fax:* 707-654-1007. *E-mail:* pmuha@csum.edu.
Website: http://www.csum.edu/.

CALIFORNIA STATE UNIVERSITY, MONTEREY BAY

Seaside, CA

Tuition & fees (area res): $7143 | **Average undergraduate aid package: $11,365**

ABOUT THE INSTITUTION State-supported, coed. ***Awards:*** certificates, bachelor's, and master's degrees. 23 undergraduate majors. ***Total enrollment:*** 7,616. Undergraduates: 6,794. Freshmen: 1,045. Federal methodology is used as a basis for awarding need-based institutional aid.

UNDERGRADUATE EXPENSES for 2020–2021 ***Application fee:*** $70. ***Tuition, area resident:*** full-time $5742. ***Tuition, state resident:*** full-time $5742. ***Tuition, nonresident:*** full-time $17,622; part-time $396 per credit hour. ***Required fees:*** full-time $1401. ***College room and board:*** $13,711.

FRESHMAN FINANCIAL AID (Fall 2019, est.) 923 applied for aid; of those 80% were deemed to have need. 92% of freshmen with need received aid; of those 14% had need fully met. ***Average percent of need met:*** 52% (excluding resources awarded to replace EFC). ***Average financial aid package:*** $11,828 (excluding resources awarded to replace EFC). 2% of all full-time freshmen had no need and received non-need-based gift aid.

UNDERGRADUATE FINANCIAL AID (Fall 2019, est.) 4,754 applied for aid; of those 88% were deemed to have need. 92% of undergraduates with need received aid; of those 14% had need fully met. ***Average percent of need met:*** 66% (excluding resources awarded to replace EFC). ***Average financial aid package:*** $11,365 (excluding resources awarded to replace EFC). 2% of all full-time undergraduates had no need and received non-need-based gift aid.

GIFT AID (NEED-BASED) ***Total amount:*** $34,977,830 (42% federal, 32% state, 26% institutional). ***Receiving aid:*** Freshmen: 54% (564); all full-time undergraduates: 53% (3,222). ***Average award:*** Freshmen: $11,140; Undergraduates: $10,124. ***Scholarships, grants, and awards:*** Federal Pell, FSEOG, state, private, college/university gift aid from institutional funds.

GIFT AID (NON-NEED-BASED) ***Total amount:*** $1,731,789 (1% federal, 40% state, 17% institutional, 42% external sources). ***Receiving aid:*** Freshmen: 14% (142). Undergraduates: 11% (637). ***Average award:*** Freshmen: $1815. Undergraduates: $1952. ***Scholarships, grants, and awards by category:*** *Academic interests/achievement:* business, general academic interests/achievements. *Special achievements/activities:* leadership. *Special characteristics:* children and siblings of alumni, general special characteristics, local/state students. ***ROTC:*** Air Force cooperative.

LOANS ***Student loans:*** $15,059,035 (64% need-based, 36% non-need-based). 65% of past graduating class borrowed through all loan programs. *Average indebtedness per student:* $19,859. ***Average need-based loan:*** Freshmen: $3391. Undergraduates: $4382. ***Parent loans:*** $3,339,041 (100% non-need-based). ***Programs:*** Federal Direct (Subsidized and Unsubsidized Stafford, PLUS), state, Private, Grad Plus Loans, California Dream Loans.

WORK-STUDY ***Federal work-study:*** Total amount: $194,422; jobs available. ***State or other work-study/employment:*** Part-time jobs available.

ATHLETIC AWARDS Total amount: $673,250 (100% non-need-based).

APPLYING FOR FINANCIAL AID ***Required financial aid forms:*** FAFSA, state aid form. ***Financial aid deadline (priority):*** 5/1. ***Notification date:*** 3/31.

CONTACT Financial Aid Office, California State University, Monterey Bay, 100 Campus Center, Seaside, CA 93955-8001, 831-582-3000.
Website: http://www.csumb.edu/.

CALIFORNIA STATE UNIVERSITY, NORTHRIDGE

Northridge, CA

Tuition & fees (CA res): $8554 | **Average undergraduate aid package: $19,235**

ABOUT THE INSTITUTION State-supported, coed. ***Awards:*** bachelor's, master's, and doctoral degrees. 59 undergraduate majors. ***Total enrollment:*** 38,391. Undergraduates: 34,633. Freshmen: 4,792. Federal methodology is used as a basis for awarding need-based institutional aid.

UNDERGRADUATE EXPENSES for 2019–2020 ***Application fee:*** $55. ***Tuition, state resident:*** full-time $6972. ***Tuition, nonresident:*** full-time $12,516; part-time $396 per unit. ***Required fees:*** full-time $1582. ***College room and board:*** $16,188. Room and board charges vary according to board plan and housing facility.

FRESHMAN FINANCIAL AID (Fall 2018) 4334 applied for aid; of those 25% were deemed to have need. 100% of freshmen with need received aid. ***Average financial aid package:*** $11,731 (excluding resources awarded to replace EFC). 14% of all full-time freshmen had no need and received non-need-based gift aid.

UNDERGRADUATE FINANCIAL AID (Fall 2018) 24,428 applied for aid; of those 97% were deemed to have need. 100% of undergraduates with need received aid. ***Average financial aid package:*** $19,235 (excluding resources awarded to replace EFC). 18% of all full-time undergraduates had no need and received non-need-based gift aid.

GIFT AID (NEED-BASED) ***Total amount:*** $226,928,570 (44% federal, 55% state, 1% institutional). ***Receiving aid:*** All full-time undergraduates: 70% (20,392). ***Average award:*** Freshmen: $11,387; Undergraduates: $17,316. ***Scholarships, grants, and awards:*** Federal Pell, FSEOG, state, private, college/university gift aid from institutional funds.

GIFT AID (NON-NEED-BASED) ***Total amount:*** $10,689,918 (89% institutional, 11% external sources). ***Receiving aid:*** Freshmen: 14% (661). Undergraduates: 18% (5,219). ***Average award:*** Freshmen: $2004. Undergraduates: $2570. ***Scholarships, grants, and awards by category:*** *Academic interests/achievement:* business, communication, computer science, education, engineering/technologies, English, general academic interests/achievements, mathematics, social sciences. *Creative arts/performance:* journalism/publications, music. *Special achievements/activities:* leadership. ***Tuition waivers:*** Full or partial for employees or children of employees, senior citizens. ***ROTC:*** Army cooperative, Air Force cooperative.

LOANS ***Student loans:*** $67,554,591 (55% need-based, 45% non-need-based). ***Average need-based loan:*** Freshmen: $5052. Undergraduates: $6033. ***Parent loans:*** $2,247,507 (100% non-need-based). ***Programs:*** Perkins.

WORK-STUDY ***Federal work-study:*** Total amount: $1,652,715; jobs available.

ATHLETIC AWARDS Total amount: $3,249,725 (100% non-need-based).

APPLYING FOR FINANCIAL AID ***Required financial aid form:*** FAFSA. ***Financial aid deadline (priority):*** 3/2. ***Notification date:*** Continuous beginning 4/1.

CONTACT Linda Brignoni, Director of Financial Aid and Scholarships, California State University, Northridge, 18111 Nordhoff Street, Northridge, CA 91330-8307, 818-677-4085. *Fax:* 818-677-6787. *E-mail:* financial.aid@csun.edu.
Website: http://www.csun.edu/.

CALIFORNIA STATE UNIVERSITY, SACRAMENTO

Sacramento, CA

Tuition & fees (area res): $7368	Average undergraduate aid package: $10,010

ABOUT THE INSTITUTION State-supported, coed. ***Awards:*** bachelor's, master's, and doctoral degrees. 55 undergraduate majors. ***Total enrollment:*** 31,156. Undergraduates: 28,251. Freshmen: 4,160. Federal methodology is used as a basis for awarding need-based institutional aid.

UNDERGRADUATE EXPENSES for 2020–2021 ***Application fee:*** $55. ***Tuition, area resident:*** full-time $5742. ***Tuition, state resident:*** full-time $5742. ***Tuition, nonresident:*** full-time $17,622. ***Required fees:*** full-time $1626. ***College room and board:*** $15,224; ***Room only:*** $7744.

FRESHMAN FINANCIAL AID (Fall 2018) 2093 applied for aid; of those 90% were deemed to have need. 90% of freshmen with need received aid; of those 15% had need fully met. ***Average percent of need met:*** 61% (excluding resources awarded to replace EFC). ***Average financial aid package:*** $10,331 (excluding resources awarded to replace EFC). 1% of all full-time freshmen had no need and received non-need-based gift aid.

UNDERGRADUATE FINANCIAL AID (Fall 2018) 4,784 applied for aid; of those 92% were deemed to have need. 87% of undergraduates with need received aid; of those 11% had need fully met. ***Average percent of need met:*** 55% (excluding resources awarded to replace EFC). ***Average financial aid package:*** $10,010 (excluding resources awarded to replace EFC). 1% of all full-time undergraduates had no need and received non-need-based gift aid.

GIFT AID (NEED-BASED) ***Total amount:*** $175,212,523 (42% federal, 32% state, 26% institutional). ***Receiving aid:*** Freshmen: 44% (1,602); all full-time undergraduates: 16% (3,581). ***Average award:*** Freshmen: $8782; Undergraduates: $7939. ***Scholarships, grants, and awards:*** Federal Pell, FSEOG, state, private, college/university gift aid from institutional funds, Federal Nursing.

GIFT AID (NON-NEED-BASED) ***Total amount:*** $8,417,619 (55% institutional, 45% external sources). ***Receiving aid:*** Freshmen: 4% (130). Undergraduates: 1% (214). ***Average award:*** Freshmen: $1942. Undergraduates: $1525. ***ROTC:*** Army, Air Force.

LOANS ***Student loans:*** $83,548,373 (44% need-based, 56% non-need-based). 53% of past graduating class borrowed through all loan programs. *Average indebtedness per student:* $23,460. ***Average need-based loan:*** Freshmen: $3842. Undergraduates: $4158. ***Parent loans:*** $13,037,551 (100% non-need-based). ***Programs:*** Federal Direct (Subsidized and Unsubsidized Stafford, PLUS), Perkins, Federal Nursing, college/university.

WORK-STUDY ***Federal work-study:*** Total amount: $1,366,765; jobs available. ***State or other work-study/employment:*** Part-time jobs available.

ATHLETIC AWARDS Total amount: $5,210,358 (100% need-based).

APPLYING FOR FINANCIAL AID ***Required financial aid form:*** FAFSA. ***Financial aid deadline:*** 5/1 (priority: 3/2). ***Notification date:*** Continuous beginning 4/3. Students must reply within 4 weeks of notification.

CONTACT Anita Kermes, Director of Financial Aid and Scholarships Office, California State University, Sacramento, 6000 J Street, Sacramento, CA 95819-6044, 916-278-6980. *Fax:* 916-278-6082. *E-mail:* anita.kermes@csus.edu.
Website: http://www.csus.edu/.

CALIFORNIA STATE UNIVERSITY, SAN BERNARDINO

San Bernardino, CA

Tuition & fees (area res): $6956	Average undergraduate aid package: $9640

ABOUT THE INSTITUTION State-supported, coed. ***Awards:*** certificates, bachelor's, master's, and doctoral degrees. 42 undergraduate majors. ***Total enrollment:*** 20,311. Undergraduates: 18,114. Freshmen: 2,885.

UNDERGRADUATE EXPENSES for 2020–2021 ***Application fee:*** $55. ***Tuition, area resident:*** full-time $5742. ***Required fees:*** full-time $1214. ***College room and board:*** $13,435; ***Room only:*** $11,965. Room and board charges vary according to board plan and housing facility.

FRESHMAN FINANCIAL AID (Fall 2019, est.) 2575 applied for aid; of those 92% were deemed to have need. 98% of freshmen with need received aid; of those 9% had need fully met. ***Average percent of need met:*** 62% (excluding resources awarded to replace EFC). ***Average financial aid package:*** $10,735 (excluding resources awarded to replace EFC). 1% of all full-time freshmen had no need and received non-need-based gift aid.

UNDERGRADUATE FINANCIAL AID (Fall 2019, est.) 14,918 applied for aid; of those 94% were deemed to have need. 98% of undergraduates with need received aid; of those 10% had need fully met. ***Average percent of need met:*** 61% (excluding resources awarded to replace EFC). ***Average financial aid package:*** $9640 (excluding resources awarded to replace EFC). 1% of all full-time undergraduates had no need and received non-need-based gift aid.

GIFT AID (NEED-BASED) ***Receiving aid:*** Freshmen: 85% (2,292); all full-time undergraduates: 80% (13,307). ***Average award:*** Freshmen: $10,594; Undergraduates: $9723. ***Scholarships, grants, and awards:*** Federal Pell, FSEOG, state, private, college/university gift aid from institutional funds.

GIFT AID (NON-NEED-BASED) ***Receiving aid:*** Freshmen: 69% (1,868). Undergraduates: 40% (6,583). ***Average award:*** Freshmen: $1625. Undergraduates: $4251. ***Scholarships, grants, and awards by category:*** *Academic interests/achievement:* biological sciences, business, computer science, education, foreign languages, general academic interests/achievements, home economics, international studies, mathematics, physical sciences, social sciences. *Creative arts/performance:* applied art and design, general creative arts/performance, journalism/publications, music, theater/drama. *Special achievements/activities:* community service, general special achievements/activities, hobbies/interests, memberships. *Special characteristics:* children of public servants, children with a deceased or disabled parent, first-generation college students, handicapped students, veterans. ***Tuition waivers:*** Full or partial for employees or children of employees, senior citizens. ***ROTC:*** Army, Air Force.

LOANS ***Student loans:*** 56% of past graduating class borrowed through all loan programs. *Average indebtedness per student:* $18,294. ***Average need-based loan:*** Freshmen: $3304. Undergraduates: $4320. ***Programs:*** Federal Direct (Subsidized and Unsubsidized Stafford, PLUS), state.

WORK-STUDY Federal work-study jobs available.

APPLYING FOR FINANCIAL AID ***Required financial aid form:*** FAFSA. ***Notification date:*** Continuous.

CONTACT Ms. LaKeisha Rivers, Interim Director of Financial Aid, California State University, San Bernardino, 5500 University Parkway, San Bernardino, CA 92407-2397, 909-537-5227. *Fax:* 909-537-4024. *E-mail:* LRivers@csusb.edu.
Website: http://www.csusb.edu/.

CALIFORNIA STATE UNIVERSITY, SAN MARCOS

San Marcos, CA

Comprehensive fee: $25,164 | **Average undergraduate aid package: $10,808**

ABOUT THE INSTITUTION State-supported, coed. ***Awards:*** bachelor's and master's degrees. 49 undergraduate majors. ***Total enrollment:*** 14,519. Undergraduates: 13,879. Freshmen: 2,245. Federal methodology is used as a basis for awarding need-based institutional aid.

UNDERGRADUATE EXPENSES for 2020–2021 ***Application fee:*** $70. ***Comprehensive fee:*** $25,164 includes mandatory fees ($7712) and room and board ($13,150). ***Part-time fees:*** $2433 per term.

FRESHMAN FINANCIAL AID (Fall 2018) 2146 applied for aid; of those 80% were deemed to have need. 92% of freshmen with need received aid; of those 5% had need fully met. ***Average percent of need met:*** 59% (excluding resources awarded to replace EFC). ***Average financial aid package:*** $11,020 (excluding resources awarded to replace EFC). 1% of all full-time freshmen had no need and received non-need-based gift aid.

UNDERGRADUATE FINANCIAL AID (Fall 2018) 9,392 applied for aid; of those 88% were deemed to have need. 96% of undergraduates with need received aid; of those 5% had need fully met. ***Average percent of need met:*** 45% (excluding resources awarded to replace EFC). ***Average financial aid package:*** $10,808 (excluding resources awarded to replace EFC). 1% of all full-time undergraduates had no need and received non-need-based gift aid.

GIFT AID (NEED-BASED) ***Total amount:*** $78,492,081 (42% federal, 34% state, 22% institutional, 2% external sources). ***Receiving aid:*** Freshmen: 64% (1,488); all full-time undergraduates: 65% (7,436). ***Average award:*** Freshmen: $9925; Undergraduates: $9317. ***Scholarships, grants, and awards:*** Federal Pell, FSEOG, state, private, college/university gift aid from institutional funds.

GIFT AID (NON-NEED-BASED) ***Total amount:*** $701,766 (4% federal, 71% state, 6% institutional, 19% external sources). ***Receiving aid:*** Freshmen: 1% (20). Undergraduates: 1% (63). ***Average award:*** Freshmen: $750. Undergraduates: $2157. ***Scholarships, grants, and awards by category:*** *Academic interests/achievement:* general academic interests/achievements, mathematics. *Creative arts/performance:* applied art and design. *Special achievements/activities:* leadership. *Special characteristics:* local/state students. ***ROTC:*** Army cooperative, Naval cooperative, Air Force cooperative.

LOANS ***Student loans:*** $34,810,387 (86% need-based, 14% non-need-based). 53% of past graduating class borrowed through all loan programs. *Average indebtedness per student:* $23,725. ***Average need-based loan:*** Freshmen: $3179. Undergraduates: $4131. ***Parent loans:*** $4,206,157 (69% need-based, 31% non-need-based). ***Programs:*** Federal Direct (Subsidized and Unsubsidized Stafford, PLUS), Perkins, college/university.

WORK-STUDY ***Federal work-study:*** Total amount: $431,295; jobs available. ***State or other work-study/employment:*** Part-time jobs available.

ATHLETIC AWARDS Total amount: $785,208 (85% need-based, 15% non-need-based).

APPLYING FOR FINANCIAL AID ***Required financial aid form:*** FAFSA. ***Financial aid deadline (priority):*** 3/2. ***Notification date:*** Continuous beginning 3/2. Students must reply by 3/2 or within 4 weeks of notification.

CONTACT Financial Aid Office, California State University, San Marcos, 333 S. Twin Oaks Valley Road, San Marcos, CA 92096-0001, 760-750-4850. *E-mail:* finaid@csusm.edu.
Website: http://www.csusm.edu/.

CALIFORNIA STATE UNIVERSITY, STANISLAUS

Turlock, CA

Tuition & fees (area res): $7584 | **Average undergraduate aid package: $17,184**

ABOUT THE INSTITUTION State-supported, coed. ***Awards:*** bachelor's, master's, and doctoral degrees. 50 undergraduate majors. ***Total enrollment:*** 10,974. Undergraduates: 11,277. Freshmen: 1,568. Federal methodology is used as a basis for awarding need-based institutional aid.

UNDERGRADUATE EXPENSES for 2020–2021 ***Application fee:*** $55. ***Tuition, area resident:*** full-time $5742. ***Tuition, state resident:*** full-time $5742. ***Tuition, nonresident:*** part-time $396 per credit hour. ***Required fees:*** full-time $1842. Full-time tuition and fees vary according to course load. Part-time tuition and fees vary according to course load. ***College room and board:*** $10,950; ***Room only:*** $7150. Room and board charges vary according to board plan, housing facility, and student level.

FRESHMAN FINANCIAL AID (Fall 2019, est.) 1406 applied for aid; of those 91% were deemed to have need. 100% of freshmen with need received aid; of those 9% had need fully met. ***Average percent of need met:*** 80% (excluding resources awarded to replace EFC). ***Average financial aid package:*** $16,819 (excluding resources awarded to replace EFC). 2% of all full-time freshmen had no need and received non-need-based gift aid.

UNDERGRADUATE FINANCIAL AID (Fall 2019, est.) 7,344 applied for aid; of those 93% were deemed to have need. 100% of undergraduates with need received aid; of those 16% had need fully met. ***Average percent of need met:*** 78% (excluding resources awarded to replace EFC). ***Average financial aid package:*** $17,184 (excluding resources awarded to replace EFC). 1% of all full-time undergraduates had no need and received non-need-based gift aid.

GIFT AID (NEED-BASED) ***Total amount:*** $69,435,222 (40% federal, 36% state, 21% institutional, 3% external sources). ***Receiving aid:*** Freshmen: 84% (1,257); all full-time undergraduates: 80% (6,564). ***Average award:*** Freshmen: $10,798; Undergraduates: $9822. ***Scholarships, grants, and awards:*** Federal Pell, FSEOG, state, private, college/university gift aid from institutional funds.

GIFT AID (NON-NEED-BASED) ***Total amount:*** $815,739 (3% federal, 59% state, 38% external sources). ***Receiving aid:*** Freshmen: 6% (94). Undergraduates: 5% (400). ***Average award:*** Freshmen: $1648. Undergraduates: $2345. ***Scholarships, grants, and awards by category:*** *Academic interests/achievement:* agriculture, area/ethnic studies, biological sciences, business, communication, computer science, education, English, foreign languages, general academic interests/achievements, home economics, humanities, international studies, mathematics, physical sciences, premedicine, social sciences. *Creative arts/performance:* applied art and design, music. *Special achievements/activities:* community service, general special achievements/activities, leadership, memberships. *Special characteristics:* children of faculty/staff, first-generation college students, general special characteristics, local/state students. ***Tuition waivers:*** Full or partial for employees or children of employees.

LOANS ***Student loans:*** $45,887,955 (91% need-based, 9% non-need-based). 49% of past graduating class borrowed through all loan programs. *Average indebtedness per student:* $17,952. ***Average need-based loan:*** Freshmen: $3297. Undergraduates: $4327. ***Parent loans:*** $20,174,718 (75% need-based, 25% non-need-based). ***Programs:*** Federal Direct (Subsidized and Unsubsidized Stafford, PLUS), Federal Nursing, private loans.

WORK-STUDY ***Federal work-study:*** Total amount: $2,667,574; jobs available (averaging $4000). ***State or other work-study/employment:*** Part-time jobs available.

ATHLETIC AWARDS Total amount: $818,203 (70% need-based, 30% non-need-based).

APPLYING FOR FINANCIAL AID ***Required financial aid forms:*** FAFSA, institution's own form, state aid form. ***Financial aid deadline (priority):*** 3/2. ***Notification date:*** Continuous beginning 4/1. Students must reply within 3 weeks of notification.

CONTACT Noelia Gonzalez, Office of Financial Aid and Scholarships, California State University, Stanislaus, One University Circle, Turlock, CA 95382, 209-667-3336 or toll-free 800-300-7420. *Fax:* 209-664-7064. *E-mail:* financial_aid@csustan.edu.
Website: http://www.csustan.edu/.

CALIFORNIA UNIVERSITY OF MANAGEMENT AND SCIENCES

Anaheim, CA

CONTACT Financial Aid Office, California University of Management and Sciences, 721 North Euclid Street, Anaheim, CA 92801, 714-533-3946.
Website: http://www.calums.edu/.

CALIFORNIA UNIVERSITY OF PENNSYLVANIA

California, PA

Tuition & fees (PA res): $10,902	Average undergraduate aid package: $10,525

ABOUT THE INSTITUTION State-supported, coed. ***Awards:*** certificates, associate, bachelor's, master's, and doctoral degrees. 51 undergraduate majors. ***Total enrollment:*** 7,312. Undergraduates: 5,174. Freshmen: 1,017. Federal methodology is used as a basis for awarding need-based institutional aid.

UNDERGRADUATE EXPENSES for 2019–2020 ***Application fee:*** $35. ***Tuition, state resident:*** full-time $7716; part-time $322 per credit hour. ***Tuition, nonresident:*** full-time $11,574; part-time $482 per credit hour. ***Required fees:*** full-time $3186. ***College room and board:*** $10,186; ***Room only:*** $6592. Room and board charges vary according to board plan and housing facility.

FRESHMAN FINANCIAL AID (Fall 2018) 935 applied for aid; of those 86% were deemed to have need. 99% of freshmen with need received aid; of those 13% had need fully met. ***Average percent of need met:*** 71% (excluding resources awarded to replace EFC). ***Average financial aid package:*** $11,416 (excluding resources awarded to replace EFC). 11% of all full-time freshmen had no need and received non-need-based gift aid.

UNDERGRADUATE FINANCIAL AID (Fall 2018) 3,849 applied for aid; of those 88% were deemed to have need. 98% of undergraduates with need received aid; of those 14% had need fully met. ***Average percent of need met:*** 67% (excluding resources awarded to replace EFC). ***Average financial aid package:*** $10,525 (excluding resources awarded to replace EFC). 5% of all full-time undergraduates had no need and received non-need-based gift aid.

GIFT AID (NEED-BASED) ***Total amount:*** $19,253,771 (56% federal, 27% state, 17% institutional). ***Receiving aid:*** Freshmen: 75% (730); all full-time undergraduates: 67% (2,805). ***Average award:*** Freshmen: $7100; Undergraduates: $6260. ***Scholarships, grants, and awards:*** Federal Pell, FSEOG, state, private, college/university gift aid from institutional funds.

GIFT AID (NON-NEED-BASED) ***Total amount:*** $3,039,003 (1% federal, 2% state, 66% institutional, 31% external sources). ***Receiving aid:*** Freshmen: 54% (523). Undergraduates: 23% (980). ***Average award:*** Freshmen: $1553. Undergraduates: $1713. ***Scholarships, grants, and awards by category:*** *Academic interests/achievement:* general academic interests/achievements. *Special achievements/activities:* general special achievements/activities. *Special characteristics:* ethnic background, members of minority groups. ***Tuition waivers:*** Full or partial for employees or children of employees, senior citizens. ***ROTC:*** Army.

LOANS ***Student loans:*** $34,018,366 (39% need-based, 61% non-need-based). 87% of past graduating class borrowed through all loan programs. *Average indebtedness per student:* $42,029. ***Average need-based loan:*** Freshmen: $3290. Undergraduates: $4163. ***Parent loans:*** $6,524,428 (100% non-need-based). ***Programs:*** Federal Direct (Subsidized and Unsubsidized Stafford, PLUS).

WORK-STUDY ***Federal work-study:*** Total amount: $535,542; jobs available. ***State or other work-study/employment:*** Total amount: $1,297,378 (16% need-based, 84% non-need-based).

ATHLETIC AWARDS Total amount: $1,200,763 (100% non-need-based).

APPLYING FOR FINANCIAL AID ***Required financial aid forms:*** FAFSA, state aid form. ***Financial aid deadline:*** Continuous. ***Notification date:*** Continuous beginning 12/1. Students must reply within 2 weeks of notification.

CONTACT Jeffrey Derubbo, Director of Financial Aid, California University of Pennsylvania, 250 University Avenue, California, PA 15419-1394, 724-938-4415 or toll-free 888-412-0479. *E-mail:* derubbo@calu.edu.
Website: http://www.calu.edu/.

CALUMET COLLEGE OF SAINT JOSEPH

Whiting, IN

Tuition & fees: $20,970	Average undergraduate aid package: $10,920

ABOUT THE INSTITUTION Independent Roman Catholic, coed. ***Awards:*** certificates, associate, bachelor's, and master's degrees. 11 undergraduate majors. ***Total enrollment:*** 718. Undergraduates: 549. Freshmen: 135. Both federal and institutional methodology are used as a basis for awarding need-based institutional aid.

UNDERGRADUATE EXPENSES for 2020–2021 ***Tuition:*** full-time $19,900; part-time $635 per credit hour. ***Required fees:*** full-time $1070; $135 per term. ***College room only:*** $6000.

FRESHMAN FINANCIAL AID (Fall 2018) 104 applied for aid; of those 66% were deemed to have need. 100% of freshmen with need received aid. ***Average percent of need met:*** 35% (excluding resources awarded to replace EFC). ***Average financial aid package:*** $10,700 (excluding resources awarded to replace EFC). 1% of all full-time freshmen had no need and received non-need-based gift aid.

UNDERGRADUATE FINANCIAL AID (Fall 2018) 323 applied for aid; of those 93% were deemed to have need. 98% of undergraduates with need received aid. ***Average percent of need met:*** 36% (excluding resources awarded to replace EFC). ***Average financial aid package:*** $10,920 (excluding resources awarded to replace EFC). 1% of all full-time undergraduates had no need and received non-need-based gift aid.

GIFT AID (NEED-BASED) ***Total amount:*** $2,472,732 (47% federal, 30% state, 18% institutional, 5% external sources). ***Receiving aid:*** Freshmen: 55% (57); all full-time undergraduates: 39% (205). ***Average award:*** Freshmen: $9514; Undergraduates: $7219. ***Scholarships, grants, and awards:*** Federal Pell, FSEOG, state, private, college/university gift aid from institutional funds, United Negro College Fund.

GIFT AID (NON-NEED-BASED) ***Total amount:*** $116,890 (100% state). ***Receiving aid:*** Freshmen: 43% (45). Undergraduates: 23% (118). ***Average award:*** Freshmen: $1950. Undergraduates: $4807. ***Scholarships, grants, and awards by category:*** *Academic interests/achievement:* general academic interests/achievements. *Creative arts/performance:* art/fine arts, creative writing, general creative arts/performance, theater/drama. *Special achievements/activities:* general special achievements/activities, leadership. *Special characteristics:* children and siblings of alumni, children of faculty/staff, general special characteristics, previous college experience, religious affiliation. ***Tuition waivers:*** Full or partial for employees or children of employees.

LOANS ***Student loans:*** $1,031,820 (50% need-based, 50% non-need-based). 80% of past graduating class borrowed through all loan programs. *Average indebtedness per student:* $24,431. ***Average need-based loan:*** Freshmen: $2400. Undergraduates: $3700. ***Parent loans:*** $234,043 (100% non-need-based). ***Programs:*** Federal Direct (Subsidized and Unsubsidized Stafford, PLUS).

WORK-STUDY ***Federal work-study:*** Total amount: $40,209; 32 jobs averaging $1256. ***State or other work-study/employment:*** Part-time jobs available.

ATHLETIC AWARDS Total amount: $1,578,262 (100% need-based).

APPLYING FOR FINANCIAL AID ***Required financial aid form:*** FAFSA. ***Financial aid deadline (priority):*** 4/15. ***Notification date:*** Continuous beginning 4/1.

CONTACT Michael Schmaltz, Calumet College of Saint Joseph, Financial Aid, 2400 New York Avenue, Whiting, IN 46394, 219-473-4379 or toll-free 877-700-9100. *E-mail:* mschmaltz@ccsj.edu.
Website: http://www.ccsj.edu/.

CALVARY UNIVERSITY

Kansas City, MO

CONTACT Mr. Charles Kurtz, Assistant Director of Financial Aid, Calvary University, 15800 Calvary Road, Kansas City, MO 64147-1341, 816-425-6136 or toll-free 800-326-3960. *Fax:* 816-425-6134. *E-mail:* finaid@calvary.edu.
Website: http://www.calvary.edu/.

CALVIN COLLEGE

Grand Rapids, MI

Tuition & fees: $37,806 **Average undergraduate aid package: $25,974**

ABOUT THE INSTITUTION Independent Christian Reformed, coed. ***Awards:*** certificates, associate, bachelor's, and master's degrees. 101 undergraduate majors. ***Total enrollment:*** 3,570. Undergraduates: 3,467. Freshmen: 779. Federal methodology is used as a basis for awarding need-based institutional aid.

UNDERGRADUATE EXPENSES for 2020–2021 ***Application fee:*** $35. ***Comprehensive fee:*** $48,606 includes full-time tuition ($37,600), mandatory fees ($206), and room and board ($10,800). Full-time tuition and fees vary according to course load, program, and student level. Room and board charges vary according to board plan and housing facility. ***Part-time tuition:*** $904 per credit hour.

FRESHMAN FINANCIAL AID (Fall 2019, est.) 712 applied for aid; of those 68% were deemed to have need. 100% of freshmen with need received aid; of those 31% had need fully met. ***Average percent of need met:*** 80% (excluding resources awarded to replace EFC). ***Average financial aid package:*** $27,581 (excluding resources awarded to replace EFC). 36% of all full-time freshmen had no need and received non-need-based gift aid.

UNDERGRADUATE FINANCIAL AID (Fall 2019, est.) 2,563 applied for aid; of those 72% were deemed to have need. 100% of undergraduates with need received aid; of those 23% had need fully met. ***Average percent of need met:*** 75% (excluding resources awarded to replace EFC). ***Average financial aid package:*** $25,974 (excluding resources awarded to replace EFC). 41% of all full-time undergraduates had no need and received non-need-based gift aid.

GIFT AID (NEED-BASED) ***Total amount:*** $37,578,395 (8% federal, 6% state, 84% institutional, 2% external sources). ***Receiving aid:*** Freshmen: 62% (482); all full-time undergraduates: 57% (1,832). ***Average award:*** Freshmen: $22,316; Undergraduates: $20,082. ***Scholarships, grants, and awards:*** Federal Pell, FSEOG, state, private.

GIFT AID (NON-NEED-BASED) ***Total amount:*** $26,502,245 (97% institutional, 3% external sources). ***Receiving aid:*** Freshmen: 13% (102). Undergraduates: 8% (257). ***Average award:*** Freshmen: $18,215. Undergraduates: $14,747. ***Scholarships, grants, and awards by category:*** *Academic interests/achievement:* 2,634 awards ($32,460,000 total): general academic interests/achievements. *Special characteristics:* 3,011 awards ($13,662,000 total): children and siblings of alumni, children of faculty/staff, ethnic background, first-generation college students, international students, members of minority groups, religious affiliation. ***Tuition waivers:*** Full or partial for employees or children of employees. ***ROTC:*** Army cooperative.

LOANS ***Student loans:*** $18,536,880 (64% need-based, 36% non-need-based). 55% of past graduating class borrowed through all loan programs. *Average indebtedness per student:* $25,888. ***Average need-based loan:*** Freshmen: $3283. Undergraduates: $5753. ***Parent loans:*** $2,444,549 (53% need-based, 47% non-need-based). ***Programs:*** Federal Direct (Subsidized and Unsubsidized Stafford, PLUS), Perkins, state, college/university, alternative loans.

WORK-STUDY ***Federal work-study:*** Total amount: $1,085,900; 1,401 jobs averaging $6130. ***State or other work-study/employment:*** Part-time jobs available.

APPLYING FOR FINANCIAL AID ***Required financial aid form:*** FAFSA. ***Financial aid deadline (priority):*** 11/15. ***Notification date:*** Continuous beginning 12/15.

CONTACT Ms. Emily Aungst, Financial Aid Coordinator, Calvin College, Spoelhof Center, Grand Rapids, MI 49546, 800-688-0122. *Fax:* 616-526-6883. *E-mail:* finaid@calvin.edu.
Website: http://www.calvin.edu/.

CAMBRIDGE COLLEGE

Boston, MA

Tuition & fees: N/R **Average undergraduate aid package: N/A**

ABOUT THE INSTITUTION Independent, coed. ***Awards:*** certificates, bachelor's, master's, and doctoral degrees. 4 undergraduate majors. ***Total enrollment:*** 2,214. Undergraduates: 750. Freshmen: 22. Federal methodology is used as a basis for awarding need-based institutional aid.

GIFT AID (NEED-BASED) ***Scholarships, grants, and awards:*** Federal Pell, FSEOG, state, private, college/university gift aid from institutional funds.

LOANS ***Programs:*** Federal Direct (Subsidized and Unsubsidized Stafford, PLUS).

WORK-STUDY Federal work-study jobs available.

APPLYING FOR FINANCIAL AID ***Required financial aid form:*** FAFSA. ***Financial aid deadline:*** 10/1 (priority: 7/15). ***Notification date:*** Continuous beginning 7/1.

CONTACT Mr. Frank Lauder, Director of Financial Aid, Cambridge College, 500 Rutherford Avenue, Boston, MA 02129, 617-868-0137 or toll-free 800-877-4723. *E-mail:* francis.lauder@cambridgecollege.edu.
Website: http://www.cambridgecollege.edu/.

CAMERON UNIVERSITY

Lawton, OK

Tuition & fees (OK res): $6450 **Average undergraduate aid package: $9780**

ABOUT THE INSTITUTION State-supported, coed. ***Awards:*** associate, bachelor's, and master's degrees. 34 undergraduate majors. ***Total enrollment:*** 4,142. Undergraduates: 3,815. Freshmen: 615. Federal methodology is used as a basis for awarding need-based institutional aid.

UNDERGRADUATE EXPENSES for 2019–2020 ***Application fee:*** $20. ***Tuition, state resident:*** full-time $4740; part-time $158 per credit hour. ***Tuition, nonresident:*** full-time $14,160; part-time $472 per credit hour. ***Required fees:*** full-time $1710; $57 per credit hour. Full-time tuition and fees vary according to course level, course load, location, and program. Part-time tuition and fees vary according to course level, course load, location, and program. ***College room and board:*** $5452; ***Room only:*** $2222. Room and board charges vary according to board plan and housing facility.

FRESHMAN FINANCIAL AID (Fall 2018) 2710 applied for aid; of those 19% were deemed to have need. 96% of freshmen with need received aid; of those 7% had need fully met. ***Average percent of need met:*** 57% (excluding resources awarded to replace EFC). ***Average financial aid package:*** $9557 (excluding resources awarded to replace EFC). 10% of all full-time freshmen had no need and received non-need-based gift aid.

UNDERGRADUATE FINANCIAL AID (Fall 2018) 2,140 applied for aid; of those 89% were deemed to have need. 97% of undergraduates with need received aid; of those 6% had need fully met. ***Average percent of need met:*** 57% (excluding resources awarded to replace EFC). ***Average financial aid package:*** $9780 (excluding resources awarded to replace EFC). 9% of all full-time undergraduates had no need and received non-need-based gift aid.

GIFT AID (NEED-BASED) ***Total amount:*** $13,812,910 (77% federal, 16% state, 4% institutional, 3% external sources). ***Receiving aid:*** Freshmen: 67% (443); all full-time undergraduates: 62% (1,669). ***Average award:*** Freshmen: $7100; Undergraduates: $7181. ***Scholarships, grants, and awards:*** Federal Pell, FSEOG, state, private, college/university gift aid from institutional funds.

GIFT AID (NON-NEED-BASED) ***Total amount:*** $928,096 (33% federal, 10% state, 27% institutional, 30% external sources). ***Receiving aid:*** Freshmen: 2% (16). Undergraduates: 2% (51). ***Average award:*** Freshmen: $2005. Undergraduates: $2746. ***Scholarships, grants, and awards by category:*** *Academic interests/achievement:* agriculture, biological sciences, business, communication, computer science, education, engineering/technologies, English, foreign languages, general academic interests/achievements, home economics, humanities, mathematics, military science, physical sciences, premedicine, social sciences. *Creative arts/performance:* applied art and design, cinema/film/broadcasting, creative writing, debating, journalism/publications, music, performing arts, theater/drama. *Special achievements/activities:* cheerleading/drum major, community service, general special achievements/activities, leadership. *Special characteristics:* children and siblings of alumni, children of faculty/staff, ethnic background, international students, members of minority groups, out-of-state students, veterans. ***Tuition waivers:*** Full or partial for children of alumni, employees or children of employees, senior citizens. ***ROTC:*** Army.

LOANS ***Student loans:*** $10,474,992 (84% need-based, 16% non-need-based). 53% of past graduating class borrowed through all loan programs. *Average indebtedness*

per student: $13,890. ***Average need-based loan:*** Freshmen: $2946. Undergraduates: $3728. ***Parent loans:*** $195,690 (27% need-based, 73% non-need-based). ***Programs:*** Federal Direct (Subsidized and Unsubsidized Stafford, PLUS).

WORK-STUDY ***Federal work-study:*** Total amount: $152,330; 53 jobs averaging $2450. ***State or other work-study/employment:*** Total amount: $52,969 (77% need-based, 23% non-need-based). 234 part-time jobs averaging $2353.

ATHLETIC AWARDS Total amount: $1,020,122 (36% need-based, 64% non-need-based).

APPLYING FOR FINANCIAL AID ***Required financial aid form:*** FAFSA. ***Financial aid deadline:*** Continuous. ***Notification date:*** Continuous beginning 4/1. Students must reply by 8/1 or within 2 weeks of notification.

CONTACT Mr. Justin Streater, Director of Financial Assistance Services, Cameron University, 2800 West Gore Boulevard, Lawton, OK 73505-6377, 580-581-2293 or toll-free 888-454-7600. *Fax:* 580-581-2556. *E-mail:* jstreate@cameron.edu.
Website: http://www.cameron.edu/.

CAMPBELLSVILLE UNIVERSITY

Campbellsville, KY

Tuition & fees: $25,400 | **Average undergraduate aid package: $20,458**

ABOUT THE INSTITUTION Independent Kentucky Baptist Convention, coed. ***Awards:*** certificates, associate, bachelor's, master's, and doctoral degrees. 50 undergraduate majors. ***Total enrollment:*** 13,744. Undergraduates: 6,083. Freshmen: 662. Federal methodology is used as a basis for awarding need-based institutional aid.

UNDERGRADUATE EXPENSES for 2020–2021 ***Comprehensive fee:*** $33,400 includes full-time tuition ($24,900), mandatory fees ($500), and room and board ($8000). Full-time tuition and fees vary according to location. Room and board charges vary according to board plan, housing facility, and location. ***Part-time tuition:*** $1038 per credit hour. ***Part-time fees:*** $250 per year. Part-time tuition and fees vary according to course load and location.

FRESHMAN FINANCIAL AID (Fall 2018) 562 applied for aid; of those 96% were deemed to have need. 100% of freshmen with need received aid; of those 13% had need fully met. ***Average percent of need met:*** 72% (excluding resources awarded to replace EFC). ***Average financial aid package:*** $23,250 (excluding resources awarded to replace EFC). 5% of all full-time freshmen had no need and received non-need-based gift aid.

UNDERGRADUATE FINANCIAL AID (Fall 2018) 1,929 applied for aid; of those 94% were deemed to have need. 99% of undergraduates with need received aid; of those 13% had need fully met. ***Average percent of need met:*** 70% (excluding resources awarded to replace EFC). ***Average financial aid package:*** $20,458 (excluding resources awarded to replace EFC). 7% of all full-time undergraduates had no need and received non-need-based gift aid.

GIFT AID (NEED-BASED) ***Receiving aid:*** Freshmen: 84% (535); all full-time undergraduates: 80% (1,784). ***Average award:*** Freshmen: $20,954; Undergraduates: $18,022. ***Scholarships, grants, and awards:*** Federal Pell, FSEOG, state, private, college/university gift aid from institutional funds.

GIFT AID (NON-NEED-BASED) ***Receiving aid:*** Freshmen: 8% (51). Undergraduates: 8% (174). ***Average award:*** Freshmen: $13,701. Undergraduates: $11,408. ***Scholarships, grants, and awards by category:*** *Academic interests/achievement:* biological sciences, business, communication, computer science, education, English, general academic interests/achievements, home economics, humanities, mathematics, physical sciences, premedicine, religion/biblical studies, social sciences. *Creative arts/performance:* applied art and design, art/fine arts, journalism/publications, music, theater/drama. *Special achievements/activities:* cheerleading/drum major, junior miss, leadership, religious involvement. *Special characteristics:* adult students, children of educators, children of faculty/staff, international students, relatives of clergy, religious affiliation, veterans. ***Tuition waivers:*** Full or partial for employees or children of employees, senior citizens. ***ROTC:*** Army cooperative.

LOANS ***Student loans:*** *Average indebtedness per student:* $20,439. ***Average need-based loan:*** Freshmen: $2990. Undergraduates: $3636. ***Programs:*** Federal Direct (Subsidized and Unsubsidized Stafford, PLUS).

WORK-STUDY Federal work-study jobs available. ***State or other work-study/employment:*** Part-time jobs available.

APPLYING FOR FINANCIAL AID ***Required financial aid form:*** FAFSA. ***Financial aid deadline:*** Continuous. ***Notification date:*** Continuous. Students must reply within 2 weeks of notification.

CONTACT Mrs. Robyn Sollberger, Director of Financial Aid, Campbellsville University, 1 University Drive, Campbellsville, KY 42718, 270-789-5013 or toll-free 800-264-6014. *Fax:* 270-789-5079. *E-mail:* finaid@campbellsville.edu.
Website: http://www.campbellsville.edu/.

CAMPBELL UNIVERSITY

Buies Creek, NC

Tuition & fees: N/R | **Average undergraduate aid package: $26,472**

ABOUT THE INSTITUTION Independent North Carolina Baptist State Convention, coed. ***Awards:*** associate, bachelor's, master's, and doctoral degrees. 85 undergraduate majors. Federal methodology is used as a basis for awarding need-based institutional aid.

FRESHMAN FINANCIAL AID (Fall 2018) 806 applied for aid; of those 84% were deemed to have need. 100% of freshmen with need received aid; of those 24% had need fully met. ***Average percent of need met:*** 68% (excluding resources awarded to replace EFC). ***Average financial aid package:*** $28,409 (excluding resources awarded to replace EFC). 15% of all full-time freshmen had no need and received non-need-based gift aid.

UNDERGRADUATE FINANCIAL AID (Fall 2018) 3,307 applied for aid; of those 79% were deemed to have need. 100% of undergraduates with need received aid; of those 20% had need fully met. ***Average percent of need met:*** 64% (excluding resources awarded to replace EFC). ***Average financial aid package:*** $26,472 (excluding resources awarded to replace EFC). 19% of all full-time undergraduates had no need and received non-need-based gift aid.

GIFT AID (NEED-BASED) ***Total amount:*** $14,788,792 (51% federal, 49% state). ***Receiving aid:*** Freshmen: 47% (379); all full-time undergraduates: 49% (1,716). ***Average award:*** Freshmen: $7805; Undergraduates: $7595. ***Scholarships, grants, and awards:*** Federal Pell, FSEOG, state, private, college/university gift aid from institutional funds.

GIFT AID (NON-NEED-BASED) ***Total amount:*** $52,796,195 (93% institutional, 7% external sources). ***Receiving aid:*** Freshmen: 83% (671). Undergraduates: 66% (2,283). ***Average award:*** Freshmen: $18,532. Undergraduates: $16,386. ***Scholarships, grants, and awards by category:*** *Academic interests/achievement:* general academic interests/achievements. ***ROTC:*** Army.

LOANS ***Student loans:*** $29,880,989 (37% need-based, 63% non-need-based). 68% of past graduating class borrowed through all loan programs. *Average indebtedness per student:* $32,590. ***Average need-based loan:*** Freshmen: $3425. Undergraduates: $4406. ***Parent loans:*** $36,681,594 (100% non-need-based). ***Programs:*** Federal Direct (Subsidized and Unsubsidized Stafford, PLUS), state.

WORK-STUDY ***Federal work-study:*** Total amount: $320,743; 113 jobs averaging $2173.

ATHLETIC AWARDS Total amount: $9,825,565 (100% non-need-based).

APPLYING FOR FINANCIAL AID ***Required financial aid form:*** FAFSA. ***Notification date:*** Continuous beginning 2/1.

CONTACT Financial Aid Office, Campbell University, PO Box 36, Buies Creek, NC 27506, 910-893-1310 or toll-free 800-334-4111. *Fax:* 910-814-5788. *E-mail:* financialaid@campbell.edu.
Website: http://www.campbell.edu/.

CANISIUS COLLEGE

Buffalo, NY

Tuition & fees: $29,428 | **Average undergraduate aid package: $24,265**

ABOUT THE INSTITUTION Independent Roman Catholic (Jesuit), coed. ***Awards:*** certificates, associate, bachelor's, and master's degrees. 93 undergraduate majors. ***Total enrollment:*** 3,464. Undergraduates: 2,256. Freshmen: 485. Federal methodology is used as a basis for awarding need-based institutional aid.

UNDERGRADUATE EXPENSES for 2019–2020 ***Comprehensive fee:*** $40,954 includes full-time tuition ($27,940), mandatory fees ($1488), and room and board ($11,526). ***College room only:*** $5880. Room and board charges vary according to board plan and housing facility. ***Part-time tuition:*** $900 per credit hour. ***Part-time fees:*** $85 per term. Part-time tuition and fees vary according to course load.

FRESHMAN FINANCIAL AID (Fall 2019, est.) 503 applied for aid; of those 84% were deemed to have need. 100% of freshmen with need received aid; of those 35% had need fully met. ***Average percent of need met:*** 84% (excluding resources awarded to replace EFC). ***Average financial aid package:*** $27,579 (excluding resources awarded to replace EFC). 22% of all full-time freshmen had no need and received non-need-based gift aid.

UNDERGRADUATE FINANCIAL AID (Fall 2019, est.) 1,708 applied for aid; of those 86% were deemed to have need. 100% of undergraduates with need received aid; of those 30% had need fully met. ***Average percent of need met:*** 78% (excluding resources awarded to replace EFC). ***Average financial aid package:*** $24,265 (excluding resources awarded to replace EFC). 26% of all full-time undergraduates had no need and received non-need-based gift aid.

GIFT AID (NEED-BASED) ***Total amount:*** $25,303,404 (15% federal, 11% state, 73% institutional, 1% external sources). ***Receiving aid:*** Freshmen: 76% (423); all full-time undergraduates: 69% (1,448). ***Average award:*** Freshmen: $20,787; Undergraduates: $18,355. ***Scholarships, grants, and awards:*** Federal Pell, FSEOG, state, private, college/university gift aid from institutional funds, United Negro College Fund.

GIFT AID (NON-NEED-BASED) ***Total amount:*** $4,134,312 (2% state, 97% institutional, 1% external sources). ***Receiving aid:*** Freshmen: 30% (167). Undergraduates: 23% (475). ***Average award:*** Freshmen: $13,218. Undergraduates: $11,982. ***Scholarships, grants, and awards by category:*** *Academic interests/achievement:* 1,532 awards ($13,284,637 total): general academic interests/achievements. *Creative arts/performance:* 47 awards ($70,500 total): art/fine arts, music. *Special achievements/activities:* 48 awards ($44,750 total): community service, religious involvement. *Special characteristics:* 419 awards ($2,042,954 total): children and siblings of alumni, children of educators, children of faculty/staff, international students, out-of-state students, religious affiliation, veterans, veterans' children. ***Tuition waivers:*** Full or partial for employees or children of employees. ***ROTC:*** Army.

LOANS ***Student loans:*** $12,111,684 (63% need-based, 37% non-need-based). 72% of past graduating class borrowed through all loan programs. *Average indebtedness per student:* $35,503. ***Average need-based loan:*** Freshmen: $3326. Undergraduates: $4355. ***Parent loans:*** $2,095,721 (44% need-based, 56% non-need-based). ***Programs:*** Federal Direct (Subsidized and Unsubsidized Stafford, PLUS).

WORK-STUDY ***Federal work-study:*** Total amount: $990,110; 296 jobs averaging $1698. ***State or other work-study/employment:*** Total amount: $45,278 (83% need-based, 17% non-need-based).

ATHLETIC AWARDS Total amount: $1,799,958 (49% need-based, 51% non-need-based).

APPLYING FOR FINANCIAL AID ***Required financial aid forms:*** FAFSA, state aid form. ***Financial aid deadline:*** 5/1 (priority: 12/15). ***Notification date:*** Continuous beginning 12/15. Students must reply by 5/1.

CONTACT Ms. Mary Koehneke, Associate Director of Student Records and Financial Services, Canisius College, 2001 Main Street, Buffalo, NY 14208-1098, 716-888-2600 or toll-free 800-843-1517. *Fax:* 716-888-2377. *E-mail:* mkoehnek@canisius.edu.
Website: http://www.canisius.edu/.

CAPELLA UNIVERSITY

Minneapolis, MN

CONTACT University Services, Capella University, 222 South Ninth Street, Minneapolis, MN 55402, 888-227-3552 or toll-free 866-283-7921.
Website: http://www.capella.edu/.

CAPITAL UNIVERSITY

Columbus, OH

Tuition & fees: $38,298	**Average undergraduate aid package: $30,202**

ABOUT THE INSTITUTION Independent Evangelical Lutheran Church in America, coed. ***Awards:*** certificates, bachelor's, master's, and doctoral degrees. 60 undergraduate majors. ***Total enrollment:*** 3,226. Undergraduates: 2,504. Freshmen: 723. Federal methodology is used as a basis for awarding need-based institutional aid.

UNDERGRADUATE EXPENSES for 2020–2021 ***Application fee:*** $25. ***Comprehensive fee:*** $49,900 includes full-time tuition ($37,978), mandatory fees ($320), and room and board ($11,602). ***College room only:*** $5710. Room and board charges vary according to board plan and housing facility. ***Part-time tuition:*** $1266 per credit hour.

FRESHMAN FINANCIAL AID (Fall 2018) 562 applied for aid; of those 91% were deemed to have need. 100% of freshmen with need received aid; of those 22% had need fully met. ***Average percent of need met:*** 86% (excluding resources awarded to replace EFC). ***Average financial aid package:*** $32,506 (excluding resources awarded to replace EFC). 13% of all full-time freshmen had no need and received non-need-based gift aid.

UNDERGRADUATE FINANCIAL AID (Fall 2018) 1,990 applied for aid; of those 92% were deemed to have need. 100% of undergraduates with need received aid; of those 23% had need fully met. ***Average percent of need met:*** 80% (excluding resources awarded to replace EFC). ***Average financial aid package:*** $30,202 (excluding resources awarded to replace EFC). 2% of all full-time undergraduates had no need and received non-need-based gift aid.

GIFT AID (NEED-BASED) ***Total amount:*** $10,006,194 (36% federal, 13% state, 51% institutional). ***Receiving aid:*** Freshmen: 85% (503); all full-time undergraduates: 77% (1,748). ***Average award:*** Freshmen: $26,892; Undergraduates: $24,587. ***Scholarships, grants, and awards:*** Federal Pell, FSEOG, state, private, college/university gift aid from institutional funds, Federal Nursing.

GIFT AID (NON-NEED-BASED) ***Total amount:*** $42,541,132 (96% institutional, 4% external sources). ***Receiving aid:*** Freshmen: 87% (514). Undergraduates: 77% (1,745). ***Average award:*** Freshmen: $22,476. Undergraduates: $21,134. ***Scholarships, grants, and awards by category:*** *Academic interests/achievement:* general academic interests/achievements. *Creative arts/performance:* music, performing arts. *Special achievements/activities:* hobbies/interests, leadership, religious involvement. *Special characteristics:* children and siblings of alumni, children of faculty/staff, children of public servants, ethnic background, international students, members of minority groups, out-of-state students, relatives of clergy, religious affiliation, siblings of current students. ***Tuition waivers:*** Full or partial for employees or children of employees. ***ROTC:*** Army, Air Force cooperative.

LOANS ***Student loans:*** $14,156,417 (48% need-based, 52% non-need-based). 80% of past graduating class borrowed through all loan programs. *Average indebtedness per student:* $33,461. ***Average need-based loan:*** Freshmen: $3463. Undergraduates: $4448. ***Parent loans:*** $6,299,334 (100% non-need-based). ***Programs:*** Federal Direct (Subsidized and Unsubsidized Stafford, PLUS), Federal Nursing, college/university.

WORK-STUDY ***Federal work-study:*** Total amount: $2,623,962; jobs available. ***State or other work-study/employment:*** Part-time jobs available.

APPLYING FOR FINANCIAL AID ***Required financial aid form:*** FAFSA. ***Financial aid deadline (priority):*** 3/1. ***Notification date:*** Continuous beginning 2/1. Students must reply by 5/1.

CONTACT Mr. John Brown, Director of Financial Aid, Capital University, 1 College and Main Street, Columbus, OH 43209-2394, 614-236-6511 or toll-free 866-544-6175. *Fax:* 614-236-6926. *E-mail:* finaid@capital.edu.
Website: http://www.capital.edu/.

CAPITOL TECHNOLOGY UNIVERSITY

Laurel, MD

CONTACT Suzanne Thompson, Director of Financial Aid, Capitol Technology University, 11301 Springfield Road, Laurel, MD 20708-9759, 301-369-2800 Ext. 3037 or toll-free 800-950-1992. *Fax:* 301-369-2328. *E-mail:* sthompson@capitol-college.edu.
Website: http://www.captechu.edu/.

CARDINAL STRITCH UNIVERSITY

Milwaukee, WI

Tuition & fees: $31,798	**Average undergraduate aid package: $24,461**

ABOUT THE INSTITUTION Independent Roman Catholic, coed. ***Awards:*** certificates, associate, bachelor's, master's, and doctoral degrees. 40 undergraduate majors. ***Total enrollment:*** 2,355. Undergraduates: 1,543. Freshmen: 141. Both federal and institutional methodology are used as a basis for awarding need-based institutional aid.

UNDERGRADUATE EXPENSES for 2019–2020 ***Comprehensive fee:*** $40,744 includes full-time tuition ($31,798) and room and board ($8946). Full-time tuition and fees vary according to degree level, program, and reciprocity agreements. Room and board charges vary according to board plan and housing facility. ***Part-time tuition:*** $992 per credit hour. Part-time tuition and fees vary according to course load, degree level, program, and reciprocity agreements.

FRESHMAN FINANCIAL AID (Fall 2019, est.) 94 applied for aid; of those 97% were deemed to have need. 100% of freshmen with need received aid; of those 24% had need fully met. ***Average percent of need met:*** 82% (excluding resources awarded to replace EFC). ***Average financial aid package:*** $28,565 (excluding resources awarded to replace EFC). 33% of all full-time freshmen had no need and received non-need-based gift aid.

UNDERGRADUATE FINANCIAL AID (Fall 2019, est.) 514 applied for aid; of those 94% were deemed to have need. 100% of undergraduates with need received aid; of those 12% had need fully met. ***Average percent of need met:*** 72% (excluding resources awarded to replace EFC). ***Average financial aid package:*** $24,461 (excluding resources awarded to replace EFC). 29% of all full-time undergraduates had no need and received non-need-based gift aid.

GIFT AID (NEED-BASED) ***Receiving aid:*** Freshmen: 66% (91); all full-time undergraduates: 65% (473). ***Average award:*** Freshmen: $24,841; Undergraduates: $20,657. ***Scholarships, grants, and awards:*** Federal Pell, FSEOG, state, private, college/university gift aid from institutional funds, United Negro College Fund.

GIFT AID (NON-NEED-BASED) ***Receiving aid:*** Freshmen: 10% (14). Undergraduates: 5% (38). ***Average award:*** Freshmen: $23,850. Undergraduates: $19,124. ***Scholarships, grants, and awards by category:*** *Academic interests/achievement:* 670 awards ($7,521,295 total): general academic interests/achievements. *Creative arts/performance:* 27 awards ($50,875 total): applied art and design, music, theater/drama. *Special characteristics:* 335 awards ($993,808 total): children and siblings of alumni, children of current students, children of faculty/staff, international students, religious affiliation, siblings of current students, spouses of current students, veterans. ***Tuition waivers:*** Full or partial for employees or children of employees.

LOANS ***Student loans:*** 63% of past graduating class borrowed through all loan programs. *Average indebtedness per student:* $33,553. ***Average need-based loan:*** Freshmen: $2962. Undergraduates: $3701. ***Programs:*** Federal Direct (Subsidized and Unsubsidized Stafford, PLUS), Perkins, state.

WORK-STUDY Federal work-study jobs available. ***State or other work-study/employment:*** Part-time jobs available.

APPLYING FOR FINANCIAL AID ***Required financial aid forms:*** FAFSA, institution's own form. ***Financial aid deadline:*** Continuous. ***Notification date:*** Continuous. Students must reply within 2 weeks of notification.

CONTACT Mark Quistorf, Director of Financial Aid, Cardinal Stritch University, 6801 N Yates Road, Milwaukee, WI 53211, 414-410-4048 or toll-free 800-347-8822 Ext.4040. *E-mail:* finaid@stritch.edu.
Website: http://www.stritch.edu/.

CAREERS UNLIMITED

Orem, UT

CONTACT Financial Aid Office, Careers Unlimited, 1176 South 1480 West, Orem, UT 84058, 801-426-8234.
Website: http://www.ucdh.edu/.

CARIBBEAN UNIVERSITY

Bayamón, PR

CONTACT Financial Aid Office, Caribbean University, Box 493, Bayamón, PR 00960-0493, 787-780-0070.
Website: http://www.caribbean.edu/.

CARIBBEAN UNIVERSITY–CAROLINA

Carolina, PR

CONTACT Financial Aid Office, Caribbean University–Carolina, Calle Ignacio Arzuaga #208, Carolina, PR 00985, 787-769-0007.
Website: http://www.caribbean.edu/.

CARIBBEAN UNIVERSITY–PONCE

Ponce, PR

CONTACT Financial Aid Office, Caribbean University–Ponce, Ave. Ednita Nazario #1015, Ponce, PR 00716-7733, 787-840-2955.
Website: http://www.caribbean.edu/.

CARIBBEAN UNIVERSITY–VEGA BAJA

Vega Baja, PR

CONTACT Financial Aid Office, Caribbean University–Vega Baja, Carr 671 K.M. 5, Sector El Criollo, Bo. Algarrobo, Vega Baja, PR 00964, 787-858-3668.
Website: http://www.caribbean.edu/.

CARLETON COLLEGE

Northfield, MN

Tuition & fees: $57,111	Average undergraduate aid package: $51,761

ABOUT THE INSTITUTION Independent, coed. ***Awards:*** bachelor's degrees. 44 undergraduate majors. ***Total enrollment:*** 2,097. Undergraduates: 2,097. Freshmen: 529. Both federal and institutional methodology are used as a basis for awarding need-based institutional aid.

UNDERGRADUATE EXPENSES for 2019–2020 ***Application fee:*** $30. ***Comprehensive fee:*** $71,769 includes full-time tuition ($56,778), mandatory fees ($333), and room and board ($14,658). ***College room only:*** $7704.

FRESHMAN FINANCIAL AID (Fall 2018) 363 applied for aid; of those 82% were deemed to have need. 100% of freshmen with need received aid; of those 100% had need fully met. ***Average percent of need met:*** 100% (excluding resources awarded to replace EFC). ***Average financial aid package:*** $52,349 (excluding resources awarded to replace EFC). 2% of all full-time freshmen had no need and received non-need-based gift aid.

UNDERGRADUATE FINANCIAL AID (Fall 2018) 1,266 applied for aid; of those 91% were deemed to have need. 100% of undergraduates with need received aid; of those 100% had need fully met. ***Average percent of need met:*** 100% (excluding resources awarded to replace EFC). ***Average financial aid package:*** $51,761 (excluding resources awarded to replace EFC). 4% of all full-time undergraduates had no need and received non-need-based gift aid.

GIFT AID (NEED-BASED) ***Receiving aid:*** Freshmen: 56% (296); all full-time undergraduates: 56% (1,152). ***Average award:*** Freshmen: $47,243; Undergraduates: $44,774. ***Scholarships, grants, and awards:*** Federal Pell, FSEOG, state, private, college/university gift aid from institutional funds.

GIFT AID (NON-NEED-BASED) ***Receiving aid:*** Freshmen: 9% (45). Undergraduates: 8% (164). ***Average award:*** Freshmen: $2042. Undergraduates: $3104. ***Scholarships, grants, and awards by category:*** *Academic interests/achievement:* 89 awards ($443,846 total): general academic interests/achievements. *Creative arts/performance:* 8 awards ($11,016 total): music.

LOANS ***Student loans:*** 40% of past graduating class borrowed through all loan programs. *Average indebtedness per student:* $19,405. ***Average need-based loan:*** Freshmen: $4072. Undergraduates: $5257. ***Programs:*** Federal Direct (Subsidized and Unsubsidized Stafford, PLUS), Perkins, state, college/university.

WORK-STUDY ***Federal work-study:*** 418 jobs averaging $2697. ***State or other work-study/employment:*** 1,308 part-time jobs averaging $2723.

APPLYING FOR FINANCIAL AID ***Required financial aid forms:*** FAFSA, CSS Financial Aid PROFILE, noncustodial (divorced/separated) parent's statement. ***Notification date:*** Students must reply within 2 weeks of notification.

CONTACT Mr. Rodney M. Oto, Director of Student Financial Services, Carleton College, One North College Street, Northfield, MN 55057-4001, 507-222-4138 or toll-free 800-995-2275. *Fax:* 507-222-4269.
Website: http://www.carleton.edu/.

CARLOW UNIVERSITY

Pittsburgh, PA

Tuition & fees: $30,528 **Average undergraduate aid package: $20,076**

ABOUT THE INSTITUTION Independent Roman Catholic, coed, primarily women. ***Awards:*** certificates, bachelor's, master's, and doctoral degrees. 28 undergraduate majors. ***Total enrollment:*** 2,022. Undergraduates: 1,298. Freshmen: 163. Both federal and institutional methodology are used as a basis for awarding need-based institutional aid.

UNDERGRADUATE EXPENSES for 2019–2020 ***Comprehensive fee:*** $42,430 includes full-time tuition ($29,652), mandatory fees ($876), and room and board ($11,902). ***College room only:*** $6142. Full-time tuition and fees vary according to course load and program. Room and board charges vary according to board plan. ***Part-time tuition:*** $716 per credit hour. ***Part-time fees:*** $15 per credit hour. Part-time tuition and fees vary according to course load and program.

FRESHMAN FINANCIAL AID (Fall 2018) 242 applied for aid; of those 93% were deemed to have need. 100% of freshmen with need received aid; of those 21% had need fully met. ***Average percent of need met:*** 70% (excluding resources awarded to replace EFC). ***Average financial aid package:*** $24,053 (excluding resources awarded to replace EFC). 9% of all full-time freshmen had no need and received non-need-based gift aid.

UNDERGRADUATE FINANCIAL AID (Fall 2018) 1,051 applied for aid; of those 95% were deemed to have need. 100% of undergraduates with need received aid; of those 23% had need fully met. ***Average percent of need met:*** 61% (excluding resources awarded to replace EFC). ***Average financial aid package:*** $20,076 (excluding resources awarded to replace EFC). 8% of all full-time undergraduates had no need and received non-need-based gift aid.

GIFT AID (NEED-BASED) ***Receiving aid:*** Freshmen: 91% (226); all full-time undergraduates: 89% (997). ***Average award:*** Freshmen: $4959; Undergraduates: $4613. ***Scholarships, grants, and awards:*** Federal Pell, FSEOG, state, private, college/university gift aid from institutional funds, Federal Nursing.

GIFT AID (NON-NEED-BASED) ***Receiving aid:*** Freshmen: 33% (81). Undergraduates: 29% (327). ***Average award:*** Freshmen: $12,047. Undergraduates: $9876. ***Scholarships, grants, and awards by category:*** *Academic interests/achievement:* biological sciences, business, communication, computer science, education, English, general academic interests/achievements, humanities, mathematics, social sciences. *Special achievements/activities:* leadership, religious involvement. *Special characteristics:* children and siblings of alumni, children of educators, children of faculty/staff, international students, religious affiliation, siblings of current students. ***Tuition waivers:*** Full or partial for children of alumni, employees or children of employees, adult students. ***ROTC:*** Army cooperative, Naval cooperative, Air Force cooperative.

LOANS ***Student loans:*** 86% of past graduating class borrowed through all loan programs. *Average indebtedness per student:* $40,958. ***Average need-based loan:*** Freshmen: $3159. Undergraduates: $3788. ***Programs:*** Federal Direct (Subsidized and Unsubsidized Stafford, PLUS), Federal Nursing.

WORK-STUDY Federal work-study jobs available.

APPLYING FOR FINANCIAL AID ***Required financial aid forms:*** FAFSA, state aid form. ***Notification date:*** Continuous.

CONTACT Financial Aid Office, Carlow University, 3333 Fifth Avenue, Pittsburgh, PA 15213-3165, 412-578-6000 or toll-free 800-333-CARLOW.
Website: http://www.carlow.edu/.

CARNEGIE MELLON UNIVERSITY

Pittsburgh, PA

Tuition & fees: $58,924 **Average undergraduate aid package: $48,843**

ABOUT THE INSTITUTION Independent, coed. ***Awards:*** certificates, bachelor's, master's, and doctoral degrees. 81 undergraduate majors. ***Total enrollment:*** 14,799. Undergraduates: 7,022. Freshmen: 1,585. Both federal and institutional methodology are used as a basis for awarding need-based institutional aid.

UNDERGRADUATE EXPENSES for 2020–2021 ***Application fee:*** $75. ***Comprehensive fee:*** $74,474 includes full-time tuition ($57,560), mandatory fees ($1364), and room and board ($15,550). ***College room only:*** $9210. ***Part-time tuition:*** $800 per unit.

FRESHMAN FINANCIAL AID (Fall 2019, est.) 1004 applied for aid; of those 68% were deemed to have need. 100% of freshmen with need received aid; of those 93% had need fully met. ***Average percent of need met:*** 99% (excluding resources awarded to replace EFC). ***Average financial aid package:*** $47,549 (excluding resources awarded to replace EFC). 2% of all full-time freshmen had no need and received non-need-based gift aid.

UNDERGRADUATE FINANCIAL AID (Fall 2019, est.) 3,208 applied for aid; of those 83% were deemed to have need. 100% of undergraduates with need received aid; of those 77% had need fully met. ***Average percent of need met:*** 97% (excluding resources awarded to replace EFC). ***Average financial aid package:*** $48,843 (excluding resources awarded to replace EFC). 5% of all full-time undergraduates had no need and received non-need-based gift aid.

GIFT AID (NEED-BASED) ***Total amount:*** $112,827,754 (6% federal, 93% institutional, 1% external sources). ***Receiving aid:*** Freshmen: 42% (658); all full-time undergraduates: 38% (2,600). ***Average award:*** Freshmen: $43,599; Undergraduates: $43,475. ***Scholarships, grants, and awards:*** Federal Pell, FSEOG, state, private, college/university gift aid from institutional funds.

GIFT AID (NON-NEED-BASED) ***Total amount:*** $15,192,990 (83% institutional, 17% external sources). ***Receiving aid:*** Freshmen: 14% (224). Undergraduates: 10% (709). ***Average award:*** Freshmen: $12,151. Undergraduates: $30,380. ***Scholarships, grants, and awards by category:*** *Academic interests/achievement:* general academic interests/achievements. *Creative arts/performance:* general creative arts/performance. *Special achievements/activities:* general special achievements/activities. *Special characteristics:* children of faculty/staff, general special characteristics. ***ROTC:*** Army cooperative, Naval, Air Force cooperative.

LOANS ***Student loans:*** $21,875,304 (56% need-based, 44% non-need-based). 52% of past graduating class borrowed through all loan programs. *Average indebtedness per student:* $31,342. ***Average need-based loan:*** Freshmen: $3359. Undergraduates: $4517. ***Parent loans:*** $6,745,211 (2% need-based, 98% non-need-based). ***Programs:*** Federal Direct (Subsidized and Unsubsidized Stafford, PLUS), college/university.

WORK-STUDY ***Federal work-study:*** Total amount: $6,969,306; jobs available. ***State or other work-study/employment:*** Part-time jobs available.

APPLYING FOR FINANCIAL AID ***Required financial aid forms:*** FAFSA, CSS Financial Aid PROFILE, noncustodial (divorced/separated) parent's statement, federal income tax form(s). ***Financial aid deadline:*** 2/15. ***Notification date:*** 4/1.

CONTACT Brian Hill, Director of Student Financial Services, Carnegie Mellon University, 5000 Forbes Avenue, Pittsburgh, PA 15213-3890, 412-268-8186. *Fax:* 412-268-8084. *E-mail:* thehub@andrew.cmu.edu.
Website: http://www.cmu.edu/.

CAROLINA CHRISTIAN COLLEGE

Winston-Salem, NC

Tuition & fees: $8890 **Average undergraduate aid package: $10,590**

ABOUT THE INSTITUTION Independent nondenominational, coed. ***Awards:*** associate, bachelor's, master's, and doctoral degrees. 1 undergraduate major. ***Total enrollment:*** 53. Undergraduates: 47. Freshmen: 9. Federal methodology is used as a basis for awarding need-based institutional aid.

UNDERGRADUATE EXPENSES for 2020–2021 ***Application fee:*** $50. ***One-time required fee:*** $75. ***Comprehensive fee:*** $10,640 includes full-time tuition

($7600), mandatory fees ($1290), and room and board ($1750). ***College room only:*** $1600. ***Part-time tuition:*** $7600 per year. ***Part-time fees:*** $1290 per year.

FRESHMAN FINANCIAL AID (Fall 2019, est.) 14 applied for aid; of those 100% were deemed to have need. 100% of freshmen with need received aid; of those 93% had need fully met. ***Average percent of need met:*** 98% (excluding resources awarded to replace EFC). ***Average financial aid package:*** $9590 (excluding resources awarded to replace EFC).

UNDERGRADUATE FINANCIAL AID (Fall 2019, est.) 70 applied for aid; of those 100% were deemed to have need. 100% of undergraduates with need received aid; of those 80% had need fully met. ***Average percent of need met:*** 89% (excluding resources awarded to replace EFC). ***Average financial aid package:*** $10,590 (excluding resources awarded to replace EFC).

GIFT AID (NEED-BASED) ***Receiving aid:*** Freshmen: 100% (14); all full-time undergraduates: 84% (63). ***Average award:*** Freshmen: $5300; Undergraduates: $5300. ***Scholarships, grants, and awards:*** Federal Pell, FSEOG.

GIFT AID (NON-NEED-BASED) ***Scholarships, grants, and awards by category:*** *Academic interests/achievement:* religion/biblical studies. ***Tuition waivers:*** Full or partial for employees or children of employees.

LOANS ***Programs:*** Federal Direct (Subsidized and Unsubsidized Stafford).

APPLYING FOR FINANCIAL AID ***Required financial aid forms:*** FAFSA, institution's own form. ***Financial aid deadline:*** Continuous.

CONTACT Mrs. LaJada Crews, Financial Aid Officer, Carolina Christian College, 4209 Indiana Avenue, Winston-Salem, NC 27105, 336-744-0900 Ext. 201. *Fax:* 336-744-0901. *E-mail:* financialaid@carolina.edu.
Website: http://www.carolina.edu/.

CAROLINA COLLEGE OF BIBLICAL STUDIES

Fayetteville, NC

CONTACT Financial Aid Office, Carolina College of Biblical Studies, 817 South McPherson Church Road, Fayetteville, NC 28303, 910-323-5614.
Website: http://carolinabiblecollege.org/.

CARROLL COLLEGE

Helena, MT

Tuition & fees: N/R	Average undergraduate aid package: $29,418

ABOUT THE INSTITUTION Independent Roman Catholic, coed. ***Awards:*** certificates, associate, and bachelor's degrees. 50 undergraduate majors. ***Total enrollment:*** 1,330. Undergraduates: 1,322. Freshmen: 254. Institutional methodology is used as a basis for awarding need-based institutional aid.

FRESHMAN FINANCIAL AID (Fall 2019, est.) 277 applied for aid; of those 75% were deemed to have need. 100% of freshmen with need received aid; of those 33% had need fully met. ***Average percent of need met:*** 86% (excluding resources awarded to replace EFC). ***Average financial aid package:*** $30,621 (excluding resources awarded to replace EFC). 32% of all full-time freshmen had no need and received non-need-based gift aid.

UNDERGRADUATE FINANCIAL AID (Fall 2019, est.) 883 applied for aid; of those 82% were deemed to have need. 100% of undergraduates with need received aid; of those 28% had need fully met. ***Average percent of need met:*** 80% (excluding resources awarded to replace EFC). ***Average financial aid package:*** $29,418 (excluding resources awarded to replace EFC). 34% of all full-time undergraduates had no need and received non-need-based gift aid.

GIFT AID (NEED-BASED) ***Total amount:*** $15,929,104 (13% federal, 83% institutional, 4% external sources). ***Receiving aid:*** Freshmen: 66% (206); all full-time undergraduates: 62% (710). ***Average award:*** Freshmen: $25,416; Undergraduates: $23,494. ***Scholarships, grants, and awards:*** Federal Pell, FSEOG, private, college/university gift aid from institutional funds.

GIFT AID (NON-NEED-BASED) ***Total amount:*** $8,967,304 (10% federal, 84% institutional, 6% external sources). ***Receiving aid:*** Freshmen: 18% (56). Undergraduates: 13% (152). ***Average award:*** Freshmen: $21,109. Undergraduates: $17,783. ***Scholarships, grants, and awards by category:*** *Academic interests/achievement:* general academic interests/achievements. *Creative arts/performance:* applied art and design, creative writing, debating, music, performing arts, theater/drama. *Special achievements/activities:* cheerleading/drum major, general special achievements/activities, leadership, religious involvement. *Special characteristics:* children of faculty/staff, children of union members/company employees, international students, religious affiliation, siblings of current students, spouses of current students, veterans. ***ROTC:*** Army.

LOANS ***Student loans:*** $5,269,740 (45% need-based, 55% non-need-based). 67% of past graduating class borrowed through all loan programs. *Average indebtedness per student:* $28,667. ***Average need-based loan:*** Freshmen: $3114. Undergraduates: $4090. ***Parent loans:*** $2,576,727 (37% need-based, 63% non-need-based). ***Programs:*** Federal Direct (Subsidized and Unsubsidized Stafford, PLUS).

WORK-STUDY ***Federal work-study:*** Total amount: $779,980; jobs available. ***State or other work-study/employment:*** Part-time jobs available.

ATHLETIC AWARDS Total amount: $2,937,652 (42% need-based, 58% non-need-based).

APPLYING FOR FINANCIAL AID ***Financial aid deadline (priority):*** 12/1. ***Notification date:*** Continuous beginning 1/1. Students must reply by 5/1 or within 2 weeks of notification.

CONTACT Ms. Janet Riis, Director of Financial Aid, Carroll College, 1601 North Benton Avenue, Helena, MT 59625-0002, 406-447-5423 or toll-free 800-992-3648. *Fax:* 406-447-4533. *E-mail:* jriis@carroll.edu.
Website: http://www.carroll.edu/.

CARROLL UNIVERSITY

Waukesha, WI

Tuition & fees: N/R	Average undergraduate aid package: $26,245

ABOUT THE INSTITUTION Independent Presbyterian, coed. ***Awards:*** certificates, bachelor's, master's, and doctoral degrees. 77 undergraduate majors. Federal methodology is used as a basis for awarding need-based institutional aid.

FRESHMAN FINANCIAL AID (Fall 2019, est.) 757 applied for aid; of those 83% were deemed to have need. 100% of freshmen with need received aid; of those 49% had need fully met. ***Average percent of need met:*** 87% (excluding resources awarded to replace EFC). ***Average financial aid package:*** $27,513 (excluding resources awarded to replace EFC). 21% of all full-time freshmen had no need and received non-need-based gift aid.

UNDERGRADUATE FINANCIAL AID (Fall 2019, est.) 2,506 applied for aid; of those 84% were deemed to have need. 100% of undergraduates with need received aid; of those 43% had need fully met. ***Average percent of need met:*** 87% (excluding resources awarded to replace EFC). ***Average financial aid package:*** $26,245 (excluding resources awarded to replace EFC). 24% of all full-time undergraduates had no need and received non-need-based gift aid.

GIFT AID (NEED-BASED) ***Receiving aid:*** Freshmen: 79% (627); all full-time undergraduates: 76% (2,100). ***Average award:*** Freshmen: $23,224; Undergraduates: $21,100. ***Scholarships, grants, and awards:*** Federal Pell, FSEOG, state, private, college/university gift aid from institutional funds.

GIFT AID (NON-NEED-BASED) ***Receiving aid:*** Freshmen: 16% (130). Undergraduates: 15% (406). ***Average award:*** Freshmen: $19,533. Undergraduates: $17,727. ***Scholarships, grants, and awards by category:*** *Academic interests/achievement:* 2,547 awards ($40,328,474 total): biological sciences, business, communication, computer science, education, engineering/technologies, general academic interests/achievements, home economics, humanities, international studies, mathematics, physical sciences, premedicine, social sciences. *Creative arts/performance:* 80 awards ($65,475 total): applied art and design, art/fine arts, journalism/publications, music, performing arts, theater/drama. *Special achievements/activities:* 55 awards ($67,501 total): general special achievements/activities, junior miss, leadership, memberships, religious involvement. *Special characteristics:* 542 awards ($1,697,503 total): adult students, children and siblings of alumni, children of current students, children of faculty/staff, general special characteristics, international students, siblings of current students, spouses of current students. ***ROTC:*** Army cooperative, Air Force cooperative.

LOANS ***Student loans:*** 77% of past graduating class borrowed through all loan programs. *Average indebtedness per student:* $37,361. ***Average need-based loan:*** Freshmen: $2106. Undergraduates: $2987. ***Programs:*** Federal Direct (Subsidized and Unsubsidized Stafford, PLUS), Perkins, state, college/university.

WORK-STUDY ***Federal work-study:*** 560 jobs averaging $2302. ***State or other work-study/employment:*** 1,499 part-time jobs averaging $2234.
APPLYING FOR FINANCIAL AID ***Required financial aid form:*** FAFSA. ***Financial aid deadline:*** Continuous. ***Notification date:*** Continuous. Students must reply within 2 weeks of notification.
CONTACT Dawn Scott, AVP of Enrollment/Director of Financial Aid, Carroll University, 100 North East Avenue, Waukesha, WI 53186-5593, 262-524-7297 or toll-free 800-CARROLL. *Fax:* 262-951-3037. *E-mail:* dscott@carrollu.edu.
Website: http://www.carrollu.edu/.

CARSON-NEWMAN UNIVERSITY

Jefferson City, TN

Tuition & fees: $29,500 | **Average undergraduate aid package: $24,530**

ABOUT THE INSTITUTION Independent Southern Baptist, coed. ***Awards:*** certificates, associate, bachelor's, master's, and doctoral degrees. 77 undergraduate majors. ***Total enrollment:*** 2,560. Undergraduates: 1,774. Freshmen: 483. Federal methodology is used as a basis for awarding need-based institutional aid.
UNDERGRADUATE EXPENSES for 2019–2020 ***Comprehensive fee:*** $37,650 includes full-time tuition ($28,200), mandatory fees ($1300), and room and board ($8150). ***College room only:*** $2990. Room and board charges vary according to board plan and housing facility. ***Part-time tuition:*** $1175 per credit hour. ***Part-time fees:*** $385 per term.
FRESHMAN FINANCIAL AID (Fall 2018) 427 applied for aid; of those 100% were deemed to have need. 100% of freshmen with need received aid; of those 14% had need fully met. ***Average percent of need met:*** 74% (excluding resources awarded to replace EFC). ***Average financial aid package:*** $24,928 (excluding resources awarded to replace EFC). 6% of all full-time freshmen had no need and received non-need-based gift aid.
UNDERGRADUATE FINANCIAL AID (Fall 2018) 1,398 applied for aid; of those 100% were deemed to have need. 100% of undergraduates with need received aid; of those 19% had need fully met. ***Average percent of need met:*** 76% (excluding resources awarded to replace EFC). ***Average financial aid package:*** $24,530 (excluding resources awarded to replace EFC). 7% of all full-time undergraduates had no need and received non-need-based gift aid.
GIFT AID (NEED-BASED) ***Total amount:*** $26,207,772 (16% federal, 19% state, 62% institutional, 3% external sources). ***Receiving aid:*** Freshmen: 89% (425); all full-time undergraduates: 83% (1,369). ***Average award:*** Freshmen: $20,764; Undergraduates: $19,098. ***Scholarships, grants, and awards:*** Federal Pell, FSEOG, state, private, college/university gift aid from institutional funds, Federal Nursing.
GIFT AID (NON-NEED-BASED) ***Total amount:*** $2,518,359 (15% state, 83% institutional, 2% external sources). ***Receiving aid:*** Freshmen: 10% (50). Undergraduates: 13% (213). ***Average award:*** Freshmen: $10,997. Undergraduates: $10,791. ***Scholarships, grants, and awards by category:*** *Academic interests/achievement:* biological sciences, business, education, general academic interests/achievements, health fields, mathematics, military science, religion/biblical studies. *Creative arts/performance:* applied art and design, debating, journalism/publications, music. *Special achievements/activities:* leadership, memberships. *Special characteristics:* children and siblings of alumni, members of minority groups, relatives of clergy, siblings of current students. ***Tuition waivers:*** Full or partial for employees or children of employees. ***ROTC:*** Army.
LOANS ***Student loans:*** $8,314,413 (94% need-based, 6% non-need-based). 76% of past graduating class borrowed through all loan programs. *Average indebtedness per student:* $28,014. ***Average need-based loan:*** Freshmen: $2162. Undergraduates: $2715. ***Parent loans:*** $2,422,890 (95% need-based, 5% non-need-based). ***Programs:*** Federal Direct (Subsidized and Unsubsidized Stafford, PLUS), state.
WORK-STUDY ***Federal work-study:*** Total amount: $475,559; jobs available. ***State or other work-study/employment:*** Part-time jobs available.
ATHLETIC AWARDS Total amount: $4,959,433 (62% need-based, 38% non-need-based).
APPLYING FOR FINANCIAL AID ***Required financial aid form:*** FAFSA. ***Financial aid deadline (priority):*** 1/16. ***Notification date:*** Continuous beginning 3/1. Students must reply by 5/1.
CONTACT Mrs. Danette Seale, Director of Financial Aid, Carson-Newman University, 1646 Russell Avenue, Jefferson City, TN 37760, 865-471-3247 or toll-free 800-678-9061. *Fax:* 865-471-3502. *E-mail:* dseale@cn.edu.
Website: http://www.cn.edu/.

CARTHAGE COLLEGE

Kenosha, WI

Tuition & fees: $63,000 | **Average undergraduate aid package: N/A**

ABOUT THE INSTITUTION Independent Evangelical Lutheran Church in America, coed. ***Awards:*** bachelor's and master's degrees. 59 undergraduate majors. ***Total enrollment:*** 2,758. Undergraduates: 2,654. Freshmen: 687. Federal methodology is used as a basis for awarding need-based institutional aid.
UNDERGRADUATE EXPENSES for 2020–2021 ***Application fee:*** $35. ***Comprehensive fee:*** $75,400 includes full-time tuition ($31,500), mandatory fees ($31,500), and room and board ($12,400). Room and board charges vary according to housing facility.
GIFT AID (NEED-BASED) ***Scholarships, grants, and awards:*** Federal Pell, FSEOG, state, private, college/university gift aid from institutional funds.
GIFT AID (NON-NEED-BASED) ***Scholarships, grants, and awards by category:*** *Academic interests/achievement:* biological sciences, business, computer science, engineering/technologies, foreign languages, general academic interests/achievements, home economics, mathematics, physical sciences, premedicine, religion/biblical studies. *Creative arts/performance:* applied art and design, art/fine arts, music, theater/drama. *Special achievements/activities:* general special achievements/activities, junior miss, leadership, religious involvement. *Special characteristics:* adult students, children and siblings of alumni, children of educators, children of faculty/staff, children of public servants, first-generation college students, international students, local/state students, members of minority groups, out-of-state students, parents of current students, previous college experience, relatives of clergy, religious affiliation, siblings of current students, twins, veterans. ***Tuition waivers:*** Full or partial for children of alumni, employees or children of employees, adult students. ***ROTC:*** Army cooperative, Air Force cooperative.
LOANS ***Student loans:*** 78% of past graduating class borrowed through all loan programs. *Average indebtedness per student:* $54,496. ***Programs:*** Federal Direct (Subsidized and Unsubsidized Stafford, PLUS), Perkins, state, college/university.
WORK-STUDY Federal work-study jobs available. ***State or other work-study/employment:*** Part-time jobs available.
APPLYING FOR FINANCIAL AID ***Required financial aid form:*** FAFSA. ***Notification date:*** Continuous.
CONTACT Vatistas Vatistas, Director of Financial Aid, Carthage College, 2001 Alford Park Drive, Kenosha, WI 53140, 262-551-6001 or toll-free 800-351-4058. *Fax:* 262-551-5762. *E-mail:* vvatistas@carthage.edu.
Website: http://www.carthage.edu/.

CARVER COLLEGE

Atlanta, GA

CONTACT Financial Aid Office, Carver College, 3870 Cascade Road SW, Atlanta, GA 30331, 404-527-4520.
Website: http://www.carver.edu/.

CASE WESTERN RESERVE UNIVERSITY

Cleveland, OH

Tuition & fees: $50,924 | **Average undergraduate aid package: $47,883**

ABOUT THE INSTITUTION Independent, coed. ***Awards:*** certificates, bachelor's, master's, and doctoral degrees. 72 undergraduate majors. Both federal and institutional methodology are used as a basis for awarding need-based institutional aid.

UNDERGRADUATE EXPENSES for 2019–2020 ***One-time required fee:*** $575. ***Comprehensive fee:*** $66,538 includes full-time tuition ($50,450), mandatory fees ($474), and room and board ($15,614). ***College room only:*** $9080. Room and board charges vary according to board plan, housing facility, and student level. ***Part-time tuition:*** $2103 per credit hour. Part-time tuition and fees vary according to course load.

FRESHMAN FINANCIAL AID (Fall 2018) 1028 applied for aid; of those 75% were deemed to have need. 100% of freshmen with need received aid; of those 96% had need fully met. ***Average percent of need met:*** 100% (excluding resources awarded to replace EFC). ***Average financial aid package:*** $48,693 (excluding resources awarded to replace EFC). 36% of all full-time freshmen had no need and received non-need-based gift aid.

UNDERGRADUATE FINANCIAL AID (Fall 2018) 2,989 applied for aid; of those 82% were deemed to have need. 100% of undergraduates with need received aid; of those 81% had need fully met. ***Average percent of need met:*** 95% (excluding resources awarded to replace EFC). ***Average financial aid package:*** $47,883 (excluding resources awarded to replace EFC). 33% of all full-time undergraduates had no need and received non-need-based gift aid.

GIFT AID (NEED-BASED) ***Receiving aid:*** Freshmen: 55% (750); all full-time undergraduates: 45% (2,377). ***Average award:*** Freshmen: $37,456; Undergraduates: $35,164. ***Scholarships, grants, and awards:*** Federal Pell, FSEOG, state, private, college/university gift aid from institutional funds.

GIFT AID (NON-NEED-BASED) ***Receiving aid:*** Freshmen: 18% (243). Undergraduates: 9% (466). ***Average award:*** Freshmen: $23,188. Undergraduates: $24,214. ***Scholarships, grants, and awards by category:*** *Academic interests/achievement:* 3,840 awards ($82,666,087 total): biological sciences, business, communication, computer science, engineering/technologies, English, foreign languages, general academic interests/achievements, home economics, humanities, international studies, mathematics, physical sciences, premedicine, religion/biblical studies, social sciences. *Creative arts/performance:* 51 awards ($1,981,925 total): applied art and design, dance, music, performing arts, theater/drama. *Special achievements/activities:* 56 awards ($214,166 total): leadership. *Special characteristics:* 113 awards ($5,331,017 total): children of faculty/staff. ***Tuition waivers:*** Full or partial for employees or children of employees. ***ROTC:*** Army, Air Force cooperative.

LOANS ***Student loans:*** 44% of past graduating class borrowed through all loan programs. *Average indebtedness per student:* $33,946. ***Average need-based loan:*** Freshmen: $5021. Undergraduates: $6139. ***Programs:*** Federal Direct (Subsidized and Unsubsidized Stafford, PLUS), college/university, alternative loans.

WORK-STUDY ***Federal work-study:*** 1,418 jobs averaging $2777. ***State or other work-study/employment:*** 237 part-time jobs averaging $2548.

APPLYING FOR FINANCIAL AID ***Required financial aid forms:*** FAFSA, CSS Financial Aid PROFILE, noncustodial (divorced/separated) parent's statement. ***Notification date:*** Continuous. Students must reply within 2 weeks of notification.

CONTACT Mrs. Venus M. Puliafico, Director of University Financial Aid, Case Western Reserve University, 10900 Euclid Avenue, Cleveland, OH 44106-7049, 216-368-4530. *Fax:* 216-368-5054. *E-mail:* vxp4@case.edu.
Website: http://www.case.edu/.

CASTLETON UNIVERSITY

Castleton, VT

CONTACT Kathleen O'Meara, Director of Financial Aid, Castleton University, Castleton, VT 05735, 802-468-1292 or toll-free 800-639-8521. *Fax:* 802-468-5237. *E-mail:* kathy.omeara@castleton.edu.
Website: http://www.castleton.edu/.

CATAWBA COLLEGE

Salisbury, NC

Tuition & fees: $78,510	Average undergraduate aid package: $27,292

ABOUT THE INSTITUTION Independent United Church of Christ, coed. ***Awards:*** bachelor's and master's degrees. 42 undergraduate majors. ***Total enrollment:*** 1,331. Undergraduates: 1,331. Freshmen: 347. Federal methodology is used as a basis for awarding need-based institutional aid.

UNDERGRADUATE EXPENSES for 2020–2021 ***Comprehensive fee:*** $89,314 includes full-time tuition ($31,436), mandatory fees ($47,074), and room and board ($10,804). ***College room only:*** $6374. Full-time tuition and fees vary according to class time and course load. Room and board charges vary according to housing facility. ***Part-time tuition:*** $898 per credit hour. Part-time tuition and fees vary according to class time and course load.

FRESHMAN FINANCIAL AID (Fall 2019, est.) 316 applied for aid; of those 94% were deemed to have need. 99% of freshmen with need received aid; of those 27% had need fully met. ***Average percent of need met:*** 80% (excluding resources awarded to replace EFC). ***Average financial aid package:*** $29,432 (excluding resources awarded to replace EFC). 11% of all full-time freshmen had no need and received non-need-based gift aid.

UNDERGRADUATE FINANCIAL AID (Fall 2019, est.) 1,075 applied for aid; of those 93% were deemed to have need. 99% of undergraduates with need received aid; of those 28% had need fully met. ***Average percent of need met:*** 81% (excluding resources awarded to replace EFC). ***Average financial aid package:*** $27,292 (excluding resources awarded to replace EFC). 15% of all full-time undergraduates had no need and received non-need-based gift aid.

GIFT AID (NEED-BASED) ***Receiving aid:*** Freshmen: 76% (265); all full-time undergraduates: 58% (775). ***Average award:*** Freshmen: $9957; Undergraduates: $8222. ***Scholarships, grants, and awards:*** Federal Pell, FSEOG, state, private, college/university gift aid from institutional funds.

GIFT AID (NON-NEED-BASED) ***Receiving aid:*** Freshmen: 85% (296). Undergraduates: 69% (924). ***Average award:*** Freshmen: $15,551. Undergraduates: $17,051. ***Scholarships, grants, and awards by category:*** *Academic interests/achievement:* 244 awards ($2,114,042 total): biological sciences, business, education, general academic interests/achievements, home economics, physical sciences, premedicine. *Creative arts/performance:* 132 awards ($401,996 total): music, performing arts, theater/drama. *Special achievements/activities:* 139 awards ($271,164 total): cheerleading/drum major, community service, general special achievements/activities, leadership, religious involvement. *Special characteristics:* 15 awards ($193,655 total): children of educators, children of faculty/staff. ***Tuition waivers:*** Full or partial for employees or children of employees. ***ROTC:*** Army cooperative, Air Force cooperative.

LOANS ***Student loans:*** 81% of past graduating class borrowed through all loan programs. *Average indebtedness per student:* $27,806. ***Average need-based loan:*** Freshmen: $3217. Undergraduates: $3982. ***Programs:*** Federal Direct (Subsidized and Unsubsidized Stafford, PLUS), state, college/university, alternative loans.

WORK-STUDY ***Federal work-study:*** 154 jobs averaging $1452. ***State or other work-study/employment:*** 75 part-time jobs averaging $1332.

APPLYING FOR FINANCIAL AID ***Required financial aid forms:*** FAFSA, state aid form. ***Notification date:*** Continuous.

CONTACT Financial Aid Office, Catawba College, 2300 West Innes Street, Salisbury, NC 28144-2488, 704-637-4111 or toll-free 800-CATAWBA.
Website: http://www.catawba.edu/.

THE CATHOLIC UNIVERSITY OF AMERICA

Washington, DC

Tuition & fees: $49,416	Average undergraduate aid package: $33,655

ABOUT THE INSTITUTION Independent Roman Catholic Church, coed. ***Awards:*** certificates, bachelor's, master's, and doctoral degrees. 64 undergraduate majors. ***Total enrollment:*** 5,771. Undergraduates: 3,279. Freshmen: 818. Federal methodology is used as a basis for awarding need-based institutional aid.

UNDERGRADUATE EXPENSES for 2020–2021 ***Comprehensive fee:*** $65,236 includes full-time tuition ($48,600), mandatory fees ($816), and room and board ($15,820). Full-time tuition and fees vary according to degree level and program. Room and board charges vary according to board plan and housing facility. ***Part-time fees:*** $1925 per credit hour. Part-time tuition and fees vary according to degree level, program, and reciprocity agreements.

FRESHMAN FINANCIAL AID (Fall 2019, est.) 686 applied for aid; of those 79% were deemed to have need. 100% of freshmen with need received aid; of those 43% had need fully met. ***Average percent of need met:*** 82% (excluding resources

awarded to replace EFC). ***Average financial aid package:*** $35,635 (excluding resources awarded to replace EFC). 30% of all full-time freshmen had no need and received non-need-based gift aid.

UNDERGRADUATE FINANCIAL AID (Fall 2019, est.) 2,065 applied for aid; of those 85% were deemed to have need. 100% of undergraduates with need received aid; of those 42% had need fully met. ***Average percent of need met:*** 80% (excluding resources awarded to replace EFC). ***Average financial aid package:*** $33,655 (excluding resources awarded to replace EFC). 35% of all full-time undergraduates had no need and received non-need-based gift aid.

GIFT AID (NEED-BASED) ***Receiving aid:*** Freshmen: 65% (534); all full-time undergraduates: 54% (1,722). ***Average award:*** Freshmen: $32,780; Undergraduates: $30,418. ***Scholarships, grants, and awards:*** Federal Pell, FSEOG, state, private, college/university gift aid from institutional funds.

GIFT AID (NON-NEED-BASED) ***Average award:*** Freshmen: $24,152. Undergraduates: $22,783. ***Scholarships, grants, and awards by category:*** *Academic interests/achievement:* general academic interests/achievements. *Creative arts/performance:* cinema/film/broadcasting, music, theater/drama. *Special achievements/activities:* leadership, memberships, religious involvement. *Special characteristics:* children and siblings of alumni, children of faculty/staff, first-generation college students, religious affiliation, siblings of current students, twins, veterans. ***Tuition waivers:*** Full or partial for employees or children of employees. ***ROTC:*** Army cooperative, Naval cooperative, Air Force cooperative.

LOANS ***Student loans:*** 63% of past graduating class borrowed through all loan programs. *Average indebtedness per student:* $46,702. ***Average need-based loan:*** Freshmen: $3445. Undergraduates: $4413. ***Programs:*** Federal Direct (Subsidized and Unsubsidized Stafford, PLUS), district, alternative loans.

WORK-STUDY ***Federal work-study:*** 313 jobs averaging $1948.

APPLYING FOR FINANCIAL AID ***Required financial aid forms:*** FAFSA, CSS Financial Aid PROFILE, noncustodial (divorced/separated) parent's statement. ***Notification date:*** Continuous. Students must reply within 2 weeks of notification.

CONTACT Ms. Mindy Schaffer, Director of Financial Aid, The Catholic University of America, 620 Michigan Avenue, NE, Washington, DC 20064, 202-319-6552 or toll-free 800-673-2772. *Fax:* 202-319-5573. *E-mail:* cua-finaid@cua.edu.
Website: http://www.catholic.edu/.

CAZENOVIA COLLEGE

Cazenovia, NY

Tuition & fees: $36,026	Average undergraduate aid package: $32,093

ABOUT THE INSTITUTION Independent, coed. ***Awards:*** certificates, associate, bachelor's, and master's degrees. 24 undergraduate majors. ***Total enrollment:*** 865. Undergraduates: 854. Freshmen: 218. Federal methodology is used as a basis for awarding need-based institutional aid.

UNDERGRADUATE EXPENSES for 2020–2021 ***One-time required fee:*** $642. ***Comprehensive fee:*** $50,769 includes full-time tuition ($36,026) and room and board ($14,743). ***College room only:*** $8206. ***Part-time tuition:*** $720 per credit hour.

FRESHMAN FINANCIAL AID (Fall 2018) 197 applied for aid; of those 94% were deemed to have need. 100% of freshmen with need received aid; of those 22% had need fully met. ***Average percent of need met:*** 87% (excluding resources awarded to replace EFC). ***Average financial aid package:*** $34,146 (excluding resources awarded to replace EFC). 7% of all full-time freshmen had no need and received non-need-based gift aid.

UNDERGRADUATE FINANCIAL AID (Fall 2018) 645 applied for aid; of those 92% were deemed to have need. 100% of undergraduates with need received aid; of those 24% had need fully met. ***Average percent of need met:*** 84% (excluding resources awarded to replace EFC). ***Average financial aid package:*** $32,093 (excluding resources awarded to replace EFC). 4% of all full-time undergraduates had no need and received non-need-based gift aid.

GIFT AID (NEED-BASED) ***Receiving aid:*** Freshmen: 91% (185); all full-time undergraduates: 84% (596). ***Average award:*** Freshmen: $32,230; Undergraduates: $30,089. ***Scholarships, grants, and awards:*** Federal Pell, FSEOG, state, private, college/university gift aid from institutional funds.

GIFT AID (NON-NEED-BASED) ***Receiving aid:*** Freshmen: 13% (27). Undergraduates: 16% (116). ***Average award:*** Freshmen: $20,607. Undergraduates: $21,213. ***Scholarships, grants, and awards by category:*** *Academic interests/achievement:* general academic interests/achievements. ***Tuition waivers:*** Full or partial for employees or children of employees. ***ROTC:*** Army cooperative, Air Force cooperative.

LOANS ***Student loans:*** 88% of past graduating class borrowed through all loan programs. *Average indebtedness per student:* $35,863. ***Average need-based loan:*** Freshmen: $2616. Undergraduates: $5325. ***Programs:*** Federal Direct (Subsidized and Unsubsidized Stafford, PLUS).

WORK-STUDY Federal work-study jobs available.

APPLYING FOR FINANCIAL AID ***Required financial aid forms:*** FAFSA, noncustodial (divorced/separated) parent's statement. ***Financial aid deadline:*** Continuous. ***Notification date:*** Continuous. Students must reply within 2 weeks of notification.

CONTACT Melissa Rose, Office of Financial Aid, Cazenovia College, 3 Sullivan Street, Cazenovia, NY 13035, 315-655-7250 or toll-free 800-654-3210. *Fax:* 315-655-7219. *E-mail:* finaid@cazenovia.edu.
Website: http://www.cazenovia.edu/.

CEDAR CREST COLLEGE

Allentown, PA

Tuition & fees: $41,567	Average undergraduate aid package: $30,972

ABOUT THE INSTITUTION Independent United Church of Christ, coed, primarily women. ***Awards:*** certificates, bachelor's, master's, and doctoral degrees. 41 undergraduate majors. ***Total enrollment:*** 1,526. Undergraduates: 1,216. Freshmen: 205. Federal methodology is used as a basis for awarding need-based institutional aid.

UNDERGRADUATE EXPENSES for 2020–2021 ***Comprehensive fee:*** $53,889 includes full-time tuition ($40,967), mandatory fees ($600), and room and board ($12,322). ***College room only:*** $5750. Full-time tuition and fees vary according to class time, course load, and program. Room and board charges vary according to board plan and housing facility. ***Part-time tuition:*** $1366 per credit hour. Part-time tuition and fees vary according to class time, course load, and program.

FRESHMAN FINANCIAL AID (Fall 2019, est.) 198 applied for aid; of those 94% were deemed to have need. 100% of freshmen with need received aid; of those 18% had need fully met. ***Average percent of need met:*** 81% (excluding resources awarded to replace EFC). ***Average financial aid package:*** $32,826 (excluding resources awarded to replace EFC). 6% of all full-time freshmen had no need and received non-need-based gift aid.

UNDERGRADUATE FINANCIAL AID (Fall 2019, est.) 704 applied for aid; of those 93% were deemed to have need. 100% of undergraduates with need received aid; of those 16% had need fully met. ***Average percent of need met:*** 77% (excluding resources awarded to replace EFC). ***Average financial aid package:*** $30,972 (excluding resources awarded to replace EFC). 8% of all full-time undergraduates had no need and received non-need-based gift aid.

GIFT AID (NEED-BASED) ***Total amount:*** $17,472,385 (9% federal, 6% state, 83% institutional, 2% external sources). ***Receiving aid:*** Freshmen: 91% (187); all full-time undergraduates: 90% (650). ***Average award:*** Freshmen: $29,936; Undergraduates: $27,214. ***Scholarships, grants, and awards:*** Federal Pell, FSEOG, state, private, college/university gift aid from institutional funds.

GIFT AID (NON-NEED-BASED) ***Total amount:*** $2,219,523 (98% institutional, 2% external sources). ***Receiving aid:*** Freshmen: 14% (29). Undergraduates: 12% (88). ***Average award:*** Freshmen: $25,614. Undergraduates: $22,147. ***Scholarships, grants, and awards by category:*** *Academic interests/achievement:* biological sciences, business, communication, education, English, general academic interests/achievements, home economics, humanities, mathematics, physical sciences, social sciences. *Creative arts/performance:* applied art and design, creative writing, dance, performing arts, theater/drama. *Special achievements/activities:* junior miss, religious involvement. *Special characteristics:* children and siblings of alumni, siblings of current students. ***Tuition waivers:*** Full or partial for employees or children of employees.

LOANS ***Student loans:*** $6,955,509 (69% need-based, 31% non-need-based). 91% of past graduating class borrowed through all loan programs. *Average indebtedness per student:* $39,866. ***Average need-based loan:*** Freshmen: $3306. Undergraduates: $4411. ***Parent loans:*** $2,362,360 (58% need-based, 42% non-need-based). ***Programs:*** Federal Direct (Subsidized and Unsubsidized Stafford, PLUS), Federal Nursing.

WORK-STUDY ***Federal work-study:*** Total amount: $102,527; jobs available. ***State or other work-study/employment:*** Total amount: $21,433 (41% need-based, 59% non-need-based). Part-time jobs available.

APPLYING FOR FINANCIAL AID ***Required financial aid form:*** FAFSA. ***Financial aid deadline:*** Continuous. ***Notification date:*** Continuous beginning 9/15.

CONTACT Ms. Valerie D. Kreiser, Director of Student Financial Services, Cedar Crest College, Room 212 Blaney Hall, 100 College Drive, Allentown, PA 18104-6196, 610-606-4666 Ext. 3314 or toll-free 800-360-1222. *Fax:* 610-606-4653. *E-mail:* financialservices@cedarcrest.edu.
Website: http://www.cedarcrest.edu/.

CEDARVILLE UNIVERSITY

Cedarville, OH

Tuition & fees: $32,564	**Average undergraduate aid package: $23,708**

ABOUT THE INSTITUTION Independent Baptist, coed. ***Awards:*** certificates, bachelor's, master's, and doctoral degrees. 71 undergraduate majors. ***Total enrollment:*** 4,302. Undergraduates: 3,879. Freshmen: 995. Federal methodology is used as a basis for awarding need-based institutional aid.

UNDERGRADUATE EXPENSES for 2020–2021 ***Application fee:*** $30. ***Comprehensive fee:*** $40,486 includes full-time tuition ($32,364), mandatory fees ($200), and room and board ($7922). ***College room only:*** $4490. Full-time tuition and fees vary according to course load. Room and board charges vary according to board plan and housing facility. ***Part-time tuition:*** $1225 per credit. ***Part-time fees:*** $50 per term. Part-time tuition and fees vary according to course load.

FRESHMAN FINANCIAL AID (Fall 2019, est.) 925 applied for aid; of those 80% were deemed to have need. 100% of freshmen with need received aid; of those 51% had need fully met. ***Average percent of need met:*** 20% (excluding resources awarded to replace EFC). ***Average financial aid package:*** $24,220 (excluding resources awarded to replace EFC). 23% of all full-time freshmen had no need and received non-need-based gift aid.

UNDERGRADUATE FINANCIAL AID (Fall 2019, est.) 2,854 applied for aid; of those 83% were deemed to have need. 100% of undergraduates with need received aid; of those 47% had need fully met. ***Average percent of need met:*** 29% (excluding resources awarded to replace EFC). ***Average financial aid package:*** $23,708 (excluding resources awarded to replace EFC). 26% of all full-time undergraduates had no need and received non-need-based gift aid.

GIFT AID (NEED-BASED) ***Total amount:*** $11,191,631 (30% federal, 7% state, 63% institutional). ***Receiving aid:*** Freshmen: 50% (500); all full-time undergraduates: 50% (1,735). ***Average award:*** Freshmen: $5835; Undergraduates: $5973. ***Scholarships, grants, and awards:*** Federal Pell, FSEOG, state, private, college/university gift aid from institutional funds, Federal Nursing.

GIFT AID (NON-NEED-BASED) ***Total amount:*** $43,959,251 (100% institutional). ***Receiving aid:*** Freshmen: 75% (744). Undergraduates: 68% (2,322). ***Average award:*** Freshmen: $23,488. Undergraduates: $21,293. ***Scholarships, grants, and awards by category:*** *Academic interests/achievement:* 3,210 awards ($34,949,376 total): general academic interests/achievements. *Creative arts/performance:* 123 awards ($431,596 total): debating, music. *Special achievements/activities:* 574 awards ($1,447,224 total): leadership. *Special characteristics:* 1,088 awards ($6,859,933 total): children of faculty/staff, ethnic background, general special characteristics, religious affiliation, veterans. ***Tuition waivers:*** Full or partial for employees or children of employees, adult students, senior citizens. ***ROTC:*** Army cooperative, Air Force cooperative.

LOANS ***Student loans:*** $27,855,900 (28% need-based, 72% non-need-based). 63% of past graduating class borrowed through all loan programs. *Average indebtedness per student:* $24,027. ***Average need-based loan:*** Freshmen: $5331. Undergraduates: $6581. ***Parent loans:*** $24,277,736 (100% non-need-based). ***Programs:*** Federal Direct (Subsidized and Unsubsidized Stafford, PLUS), Perkins, Federal Nursing, college/university.

WORK-STUDY ***Federal work-study:*** Total amount: $460,265; 211 jobs averaging $2381. ***State or other work-study/employment:*** Total amount: $1,860,124 (100% non-need-based). 1,533 part-time jobs averaging $1208.

ATHLETIC AWARDS Total amount: $1,832,160 (100% non-need-based).

APPLYING FOR FINANCIAL AID ***Required financial aid form:*** FAFSA. ***Financial aid deadline (priority):*** 3/1. ***Notification date:*** Continuous beginning 3/1. Students must reply within 3 weeks of notification.

CONTACT Mr. Kim Jenerette, Executive Director of Financial Aid, Cedarville University, 251 North Main Street, Cedarville, OH 45314-0601, 937-766-7866 or toll-free 800-233-2784. *Fax:* 937-766-7639. *E-mail:* kimjenerette@cedarville.edu.
Website: http://www.cedarville.edu/.

CENTENARY COLLEGE OF LOUISIANA

Shreveport, LA

Tuition & fees: $37,310	**Average undergraduate aid package: $32,543**

ABOUT THE INSTITUTION Independent United Methodist, coed. ***Awards:*** bachelor's and master's degrees. 26 undergraduate majors. ***Total enrollment:*** 585. Undergraduates: 552. Freshmen: 169. Federal methodology is used as a basis for awarding need-based institutional aid.

UNDERGRADUATE EXPENSES for 2019–2020 ***One-time required fee:*** $250. ***Comprehensive fee:*** $50,980 includes full-time tuition ($37,310) and room and board ($13,670). ***Part-time tuition:*** $1554 per credit hour.

FRESHMAN FINANCIAL AID (Fall 2019, est.) 170 applied for aid; of those 88% were deemed to have need. 100% of freshmen with need received aid; of those 20% had need fully met. ***Average percent of need met:*** 76% (excluding resources awarded to replace EFC). ***Average financial aid package:*** $34,293 (excluding resources awarded to replace EFC). 13% of all full-time freshmen had no need and received non-need-based gift aid.

UNDERGRADUATE FINANCIAL AID (Fall 2019, est.) 470 applied for aid; of those 90% were deemed to have need. 100% of undergraduates with need received aid; of those 25% had need fully met. ***Average percent of need met:*** 75% (excluding resources awarded to replace EFC). ***Average financial aid package:*** $32,543 (excluding resources awarded to replace EFC). 19% of all full-time undergraduates had no need and received non-need-based gift aid.

GIFT AID (NEED-BASED) ***Total amount:*** $12,324,934 (8% federal, 11% state, 80% institutional, 1% external sources). ***Receiving aid:*** Freshmen: 87% (150); all full-time undergraduates: 78% (425). ***Average award:*** Freshmen: $30,242; Undergraduates: $28,770. ***Scholarships, grants, and awards:*** Federal Pell, FSEOG, state, private, college/university gift aid from institutional funds.

GIFT AID (NON-NEED-BASED) ***Total amount:*** $4,241,631 (7% state, 92% institutional, 1% external sources). ***Receiving aid:*** Freshmen: 16% (28). Undergraduates: 20% (106). ***Average award:*** Freshmen: $23,091. Undergraduates: $24,820. ***Scholarships, grants, and awards by category:*** *Academic interests/achievement:* 643 awards ($8,516,015 total): biological sciences, business, communication, computer science, education, English, foreign languages, general academic interests/achievements, home economics, humanities, international studies, mathematics, physical sciences, premedicine, religion/biblical studies, social sciences. *Creative arts/performance:* 92 awards ($422,428 total): applied art and design, art/fine arts, dance, general creative arts/performance, journalism/publications, music, performing arts, theater/drama. *Special achievements/activities:* 62 awards ($128,347 total): general special achievements/activities, memberships, religious involvement. *Special characteristics:* 749 awards ($2,839,233 total): children and siblings of alumni, children of faculty/staff, first-generation college students, general special characteristics, international students, local/state students, out-of-state students, relatives of clergy, religious affiliation, siblings of current students, spouses of current students, veterans.

LOANS ***Student loans:*** $2,398,457 (48% need-based, 52% non-need-based). 67% of past graduating class borrowed through all loan programs. *Average indebtedness per student:* $25,363. ***Average need-based loan:*** Freshmen: $3368. Undergraduates: $4070. ***Parent loans:*** $1,801,754 (99% need-based, 1% non-need-based). ***Programs:*** Federal Direct (Subsidized and Unsubsidized Stafford, PLUS).

WORK-STUDY ***Federal work-study:*** Total amount: $477,717; 203 jobs averaging $2346. ***State or other work-study/employment:*** Total amount: $90,300 (100% non-need-based). 47 part-time jobs averaging $1921.

APPLYING FOR FINANCIAL AID ***Required financial aid form:*** FAFSA. ***Financial aid deadline (priority):*** 11/1. ***Notification date:*** Continuous beginning 12/15. Students must reply by 5/1.

CONTACT Mrs. Lynette Viskozki, Director of Financial Aid, Centenary College of Louisiana, PO Box 41188, Shreveport, LA 71134-1188, 318-869-5137 or toll-free 800-234-4448. *Fax:* 318-841-7266. *E-mail:* lviskozk@centenary.edu.
Website: http://www.centenary.edu/.

CENTENARY UNIVERSITY

Hackettstown, NJ

CONTACT Michelle Burwell, Associate Director of Financial Aid, Centenary University, 400 Jefferson Street, Hackettstown, NJ 07840-2100, 908-852-1400 Ext. 2240 or toll-free 800-236-8679. *Fax:* 908-813-2632. *E-mail:* burwellm@centenarycollege.edu.
Website: http://www.centenaryuniversity.edu/.

CENTRAL BAPTIST COLLEGE

Conway, AR

CONTACT Christi Bell, Financial Aid Director, Central Baptist College, 1501 College Avenue, Conway, AR 72032-6470, 800-205-6872 Ext. 185 or toll-free 800-205-6872. *Fax:* 501-329-2941. *E-mail:* financialaid@cbc.edu.
Website: http://www.cbc.edu/.

CENTRAL CHRISTIAN COLLEGE OF KANSAS

McPherson, KS

CONTACT Mike Reimer, Financial Aid Director, Central Christian College of Kansas, 1200 South Main, PO Box 1403, McPherson, KS 67460, 620-241-0723 Ext. 333 or toll-free 800-835-0078. *Fax:* 620-241-6032. *E-mail:* miker@centralchristian.edu.
Website: http://www.centralchristian.edu/.

CENTRAL CHRISTIAN COLLEGE OF THE BIBLE

Moberly, MO

CONTACT Ms. Rhonda Dunham, Financial Aid Director, Central Christian College of the Bible, 911 East Urbandale Drive, Moberly, MO 65270-1997, 660-263-3900 Ext. 121 or toll-free 888-263-3900. *Fax:* 660-263-3936. *E-mail:* rdunham@cccb.edu.
Website: http://www.cccb.edu/.

CENTRAL COLLEGE

Pella, IA

Tuition & fees: $18,600	Average undergraduate aid package: $33,653

ABOUT THE INSTITUTION Independent Reformed Church in America, coed. ***Awards:*** bachelor's degrees. 38 undergraduate majors. ***Total enrollment:*** 1,274. Undergraduates: 1,274. Freshmen: 317. Federal methodology is used as a basis for awarding need-based institutional aid.

UNDERGRADUATE EXPENSES for 2020–2021 ***Application fee:*** $25. ***Comprehensive fee:*** $28,880 includes full-time tuition ($18,600) and room and board ($10,280). ***College room only:*** $4892. Room and board charges vary according to board plan. ***Part-time tuition:*** $775 per credit hour. ***Part-time fees:*** $775 per credit hour. Part-time tuition and fees vary according to course load.

FRESHMAN FINANCIAL AID (Fall 2019, est.) 331 applied for aid; of those 88% were deemed to have need. 100% of freshmen with need received aid; of those 29% had need fully met. ***Average percent of need met:*** 88% (excluding resources awarded to replace EFC). ***Average financial aid package:*** $35,905 (excluding resources awarded to replace EFC). 12% of all full-time freshmen had no need and received non-need-based gift aid.

UNDERGRADUATE FINANCIAL AID (Fall 2019, est.) 1,002 applied for aid; of those 90% were deemed to have need. 100% of undergraduates with need received aid; of those 23% had need fully met. ***Average percent of need met:*** 84% (excluding resources awarded to replace EFC). ***Average financial aid package:*** $33,653 (excluding resources awarded to replace EFC). 18% of all full-time undergraduates had no need and received non-need-based gift aid.

GIFT AID (NEED-BASED) ***Total amount:*** $25,146,078 (7% federal, 9% state, 83% institutional, 1% external sources). ***Receiving aid:*** Freshmen: 86% (290); all full-time undergraduates: 81% (904). ***Average award:*** Freshmen: $32,969; Undergraduates: $26,453. ***Scholarships, grants, and awards:*** Federal Pell, FSEOG, state, private, college/university gift aid from institutional funds.

GIFT AID (NON-NEED-BASED) ***Total amount:*** $6,928,268 (4% federal, 93% institutional, 3% external sources). ***Receiving aid:*** Freshmen: 6% (20). Undergraduates: 7% (75). ***Average award:*** Freshmen: $27,873. Undergraduates: $23,884. ***Scholarships, grants, and awards by category:*** *Academic interests/achievement:* biological sciences, business, computer science, education, engineering/technologies, foreign languages, general academic interests/achievements, home economics, humanities, international studies, mathematics, physical sciences, premedicine, religion/biblical studies, social sciences. *Creative arts/performance:* applied art and design, creative writing, music, theater/drama. *Special achievements/activities:* community service, religious involvement. *Special characteristics:* children and siblings of alumni, children of current students, children of faculty/staff, general special characteristics, handicapped students, international students, local/state students, members of minority groups, out-of-state students, previous college experience, religious affiliation, siblings of current students, twins, veterans. ***Tuition waivers:*** Full or partial for employees or children of employees.

LOANS ***Student loans:*** $7,942,216 (65% need-based, 35% non-need-based). 79% of past graduating class borrowed through all loan programs. *Average indebtedness per student:* $37,983. ***Average need-based loan:*** Freshmen: $2174. Undergraduates: $3191. ***Parent loans:*** $2,092,653 (38% need-based, 62% non-need-based). ***Programs:*** Federal Direct (Subsidized and Unsubsidized Stafford, PLUS), college/university.

WORK-STUDY ***Federal work-study:*** Total amount: $630,660; jobs available. ***State or other work-study/employment:*** Total amount: $626,994 (100% non-need-based). Part-time jobs available.

APPLYING FOR FINANCIAL AID ***Required financial aid form:*** FAFSA. ***Financial aid deadline:*** Continuous. ***Notification date:*** Continuous beginning 12/9. Students must reply by 5/1 or within 2 weeks of notification.

CONTACT Wayne Dille, Director of Financial Aid, Central College, 812 University Street, Campus Box 5800, Pella, IA 50219-1999, 641-628-5336 or toll-free 877-462-3687. *Fax:* 641-628-7199. *E-mail:* dillew@central.edu.
Website: http://www.central.edu/.

CENTRAL CONNECTICUT STATE UNIVERSITY

New Britain, CT

Tuition & fees (area res): $11,068	Average undergraduate aid package: $9868

ABOUT THE INSTITUTION State-supported, coed. ***Awards:*** certificates, bachelor's, master's, and doctoral degrees. 63 undergraduate majors. ***Total enrollment:*** 11,154. Undergraduates: 17,634. Freshmen: 1,377. Federal methodology is used as a basis for awarding need-based institutional aid.

UNDERGRADUATE EXPENSES for 2019–2020 ***Application fee:*** $50. ***Tuition, area resident:*** full-time $5924; part-time $247 per credit. ***Tuition, state resident:*** full-time $5924; part-time $247 per credit. ***Tuition, nonresident:*** full-time $17,726; part-time $247 per credit. ***Required fees:*** full-time $5144; $78 per term. Part-time tuition and fees vary according to course load. ***College room and board:*** $12,528; ***Room only:*** $7130. Room and board charges vary according to board plan and housing facility.

FRESHMAN FINANCIAL AID (Fall 2019, est.) 1221 applied for aid; of those 81% were deemed to have need. 97% of freshmen with need received aid; of those 6% had need fully met. ***Average percent of need met:*** 49% (excluding resources awarded to replace EFC). ***Average financial aid package:*** $9968 (excluding resources awarded to replace EFC). 10% of all full-time freshmen had no need and received non-need-based gift aid.

UNDERGRADUATE FINANCIAL AID (Fall 2019, est.) 5,768 applied for aid; of those 86% were deemed to have need. 96% of undergraduates with need received aid; of those 4% had need fully met. ***Average percent of need met:*** 46% (excluding resources awarded to replace EFC). ***Average financial aid package:*** $9868

(excluding resources awarded to replace EFC). 4% of all full-time undergraduates had no need and received non-need-based gift aid.
GIFT AID (NEED-BASED) ***Total amount:*** $27,710,973 (54% federal, 13% state, 32% institutional, 1% external sources). ***Receiving aid:*** Freshmen: 65% (881); all full-time undergraduates: 55% (4,004). ***Average award:*** Freshmen: $3137; Undergraduates: $3686. ***Scholarships, grants, and awards:*** Federal Pell, FSEOG, state, private, college/university gift aid from institutional funds.
GIFT AID (NON-NEED-BASED) ***Total amount:*** $4,013,129 (64% institutional, 36% external sources). ***Receiving aid:*** Freshmen: 38% (522). Undergraduates: 19% (1,341). ***Average award:*** Freshmen: $1809. Undergraduates: $2856. ***Scholarships, grants, and awards by category:*** *Academic interests/achievement:* general academic interests/achievements. *Special characteristics:* members of minority groups. ***Tuition waivers:*** Full or partial for employees or children of employees, senior citizens. ***ROTC:*** Army cooperative, Air Force cooperative.
LOANS ***Student loans:*** $41,397,536 (81% need-based, 19% non-need-based). 67% of past graduating class borrowed through all loan programs. *Average indebtedness per student:* $29,709. ***Average need-based loan:*** Freshmen: $3344. Undergraduates: $4469. ***Parent loans:*** $8,386,585 (100% non-need-based). ***Programs:*** Federal Direct (Subsidized and Unsubsidized Stafford, PLUS).
WORK-STUDY ***Federal work-study:*** Total amount: $756,919; 325 jobs averaging $2198.
ATHLETIC AWARDS Total amount: $4,423,602 (100% non-need-based).
APPLYING FOR FINANCIAL AID ***Required financial aid form:*** FAFSA. ***Financial aid deadline (priority):*** 3/1. ***Notification date:*** Continuous beginning 10/31. Students must reply by 5/1 or within 2 weeks of notification.
CONTACT Ms. Keri Lupachino, Director of Financial Aid, Central Connecticut State University, Willare-DiLoreto Hall W 20801, New Britain, CT 06050-4010, 860-832-2200 or toll-free 888-733-2278 (in-state). *Fax:* 860-832-3330. *E-mail:* finaid@ccsu.edu. *Website:* http://www.ccsu.edu/.

CENTRAL METHODIST UNIVERSITY

Fayette, MO

Tuition & fees: $25,770	Average undergraduate aid package: $22,115

ABOUT THE INSTITUTION Independent Methodist, coed. ***Awards:*** associate, bachelor's, and master's degrees. 41 undergraduate majors. ***Total enrollment:*** 1,145. Undergraduates: 1,145. Freshmen: 321. Federal methodology is used as a basis for awarding need-based institutional aid.
UNDERGRADUATE EXPENSES for 2020–2021 ***Comprehensive fee:*** $34,170 includes full-time tuition ($25,000), mandatory fees ($770), and room and board ($8400). ***College room only:*** $4110. ***Part-time tuition:*** $220 per credit hour.
FRESHMAN FINANCIAL AID (Fall 2019, est.) 299 applied for aid; of those 92% were deemed to have need. 100% of freshmen with need received aid; of those 21% had need fully met. ***Average percent of need met:*** 69% (excluding resources awarded to replace EFC). ***Average financial aid package:*** $21,279 (excluding resources awarded to replace EFC). 3% of all full-time freshmen had no need and received non-need-based gift aid.
UNDERGRADUATE FINANCIAL AID (Fall 2019, est.) 967 applied for aid; of those 93% were deemed to have need. 100% of undergraduates with need received aid; of those 20% had need fully met. ***Average percent of need met:*** 72% (excluding resources awarded to replace EFC). ***Average financial aid package:*** $22,115 (excluding resources awarded to replace EFC). 7% of all full-time undergraduates had no need and received non-need-based gift aid.
GIFT AID (NEED-BASED) ***Total amount:*** $3,989,340 (64% federal, 19% state, 17% institutional). ***Receiving aid:*** Freshmen: 83% (267); all full-time undergraduates: 83% (930). ***Average award:*** Freshmen: $5168; Undergraduates: $4673. ***Scholarships, grants, and awards:*** Federal Pell, FSEOG, state, private, college/university gift aid from institutional funds.
GIFT AID (NON-NEED-BASED) ***Total amount:*** $10,626,618 (1% state, 93% institutional, 6% external sources). ***Receiving aid:*** Freshmen: 72% (230). Undergraduates: 80% (902). ***Average award:*** Freshmen: $14,290. Undergraduates: $14,123. ***Scholarships, grants, and awards by category:*** *Academic interests/achievement:* biological sciences, business, communication, computer science, education, English, foreign languages, general academic interests/achievements, home economics, humanities, mathematics, physical sciences, premedicine, religion/biblical studies, social sciences. *Creative arts/performance:* music, theater/drama. *Special achievements/activities:* cheerleading/drum major, leadership, religious involvement. *Special characteristics:* children and siblings of alumni, children of faculty/staff, general special characteristics, international students, relatives of clergy, religious affiliation, siblings of current students, spouses of current students. ***ROTC:*** Army cooperative, Air Force cooperative.
LOANS ***Student loans:*** $6,945,665 (41% need-based, 59% non-need-based). 76% of past graduating class borrowed through all loan programs. *Average indebtedness per student:* $31,118. ***Average need-based loan:*** Freshmen: $2655. Undergraduates: $3483. ***Parent loans:*** $1,694,129 (100% non-need-based). ***Programs:*** Federal Direct (Subsidized and Unsubsidized Stafford, PLUS).
WORK-STUDY ***Federal work-study:*** Total amount: $195,817; jobs available. ***State or other work-study/employment:*** Total amount: $102,662 (100% non-need-based). Part-time jobs available.
ATHLETIC AWARDS Total amount: $6,221,440 (100% non-need-based).
APPLYING FOR FINANCIAL AID ***Required financial aid forms:*** FAFSA, Scholarship Contract Letter. ***Notification date:*** Continuous beginning 11/1. Students must reply by 8/5.
CONTACT Mrs. Kristen M. Gibbs, Director of Financial Assistance, Central Methodist University, 411 Central Methodist Square, Fayette, MO 65248-1198, 660-248-6244 or toll-free 888-CMU-1854 (in-state), 877-CMU-1854 (out-of-state). *Fax:* 660-248-6288. *E-mail:* kgibbs@centralmethodist.edu. *Website:* http://www.centralmethodist.edu/.

CENTRAL MICHIGAN UNIVERSITY

Mount Pleasant, MI

Tuition & fees (MI res): $13,260	Average undergraduate aid package: $14,640

ABOUT THE INSTITUTION State-supported, coed. ***Awards:*** certificates, bachelor's, master's, and doctoral degrees. 112 undergraduate majors. ***Total enrollment:*** 19,431. Undergraduates: 14,672. Freshmen: 2,473. Federal methodology is used as a basis for awarding need-based institutional aid.
UNDERGRADUATE EXPENSES for 2019–2020 ***Application fee:*** $40. ***Tuition, state resident:*** full-time $12,810; part-time $427 per credit hour. ***Tuition, nonresident:*** full-time $12,810; part-time $427 per credit hour. ***Required fees:*** full-time $450; $225 per term. Full-time tuition and fees vary according to student level. Part-time tuition and fees vary according to student level. ***College room and board:*** $10,328; ***Room only:*** $5164. Room and board charges vary according to board plan and housing facility.
FRESHMAN FINANCIAL AID (Fall 2018) 2445 applied for aid; of those 77% were deemed to have need. 99% of freshmen with need received aid; of those 100% had need fully met. ***Average percent of need met:*** 82% (excluding resources awarded to replace EFC). ***Average financial aid package:*** $14,194 (excluding resources awarded to replace EFC). 23% of all full-time freshmen had no need and received non-need-based gift aid.
UNDERGRADUATE FINANCIAL AID (Fall 2018) 11,028 applied for aid; of those 79% were deemed to have need. 98% of undergraduates with need received aid; of those 100% had need fully met. ***Average percent of need met:*** 80% (excluding resources awarded to replace EFC). ***Average financial aid package:*** $14,640 (excluding resources awarded to replace EFC). 16% of all full-time undergraduates had no need and received non-need-based gift aid.
GIFT AID (NEED-BASED) ***Receiving aid:*** Freshmen: 66% (1,783); all full-time undergraduates: 51% (7,278). ***Average award:*** Freshmen: $9411; Undergraduates: $10,146. ***Scholarships, grants, and awards:*** Federal Pell, FSEOG, state, college/university gift aid from institutional funds.
GIFT AID (NON-NEED-BASED) ***Receiving aid:*** Freshmen: 9% (252). Undergraduates: 5% (714). ***Average award:*** Freshmen: $6497. Undergraduates: $6299. ***Scholarships, grants, and awards by category:*** *Academic interests/achievement:* 934 awards ($1,341,265 total): biological sciences, business, communication, computer science, education, engineering/technologies, English, foreign languages, general academic interests/achievements, health fields, home economics, humanities, international studies, mathematics, military science, physical sciences, premedicine, religion/biblical studies, social sciences. *Creative arts/performance:* 134 awards ($331,303 total): applied art and design, art/fine arts, cinema/film/broadcasting, creative writing, dance, general creative arts/performance, journalism/publications, music, performing arts, theater/drama. *Special achievements/activities:* 749 awards

($6,847,823 total): general special achievements/activities, leadership. *Special characteristics:* 228 awards ($171,717 total): children and siblings of alumni, children of faculty/staff, ethnic background, international students, local/state students, out-of-state students. **Tuition waivers:** Full or partial for children of alumni, employees or children of employees, senior citizens. **ROTC:** Army, Air Force cooperative.

LOANS *Student loans:* 74% of past graduating class borrowed through all loan programs. *Average indebtedness per student:* $31,683. ***Average need-based loan:*** Freshmen: $7292. Undergraduates: $5952. ***Programs:*** Federal Direct (Subsidized and Unsubsidized Stafford, PLUS), state, college/university.

WORK-STUDY *Federal work-study:* 573 jobs averaging $2262. ***State or other work-study/employment:*** 342 part-time jobs averaging $2014.

APPLYING FOR FINANCIAL AID *Required financial aid form:* FAFSA. ***Financial aid deadline:*** Continuous. ***Notification date:*** Continuous.

CONTACT Mr. Kirk M. Yats, Director of Scholarships and Financial Aid, Central Michigan University, 1200 South Franklin Street, Mount Pleasant, MI 48859, 989-774-3674 or toll-free 888-292-5366. *Fax:* 989-774-3634. *E-mail:* cmuosfa@cmich.edu.
Website: http://www.cmich.edu/.

CENTRAL PENN COLLEGE

Summerdale, PA

CONTACT Kathy Shepard, Financial Aid Director, Central Penn College, College Hill and Valley Roads, Summerdale, PA 17093, 717-728-2261 or toll-free 800-759-2727. *Fax:* 717-728-2350. *E-mail:* financial-aid@centralpenn.edu.
Website: http://www.centralpenn.edu/.

CENTRAL STATE UNIVERSITY

Wilberforce, OH

CONTACT Sonia Slomba, Director of Student Financial Aid, Central State University, PO Box 1004, Wilberforce, OH 45384, 937-376-6579 or toll-free 800-388-CSU1 (in-state), 800-388-2781 (out-of-state). *Fax:* 937-376-6519. *E-mail:* sslomba@centralstate.edu.
Website: http://www.centralstate.edu/.

CENTRAL WASHINGTON UNIVERSITY

Ellensburg, WA

Tuition & fees (area res): $7562	Average undergraduate aid package: $10,892

ABOUT THE INSTITUTION State-supported, coed. ***Awards:*** certificates, bachelor's, and master's degrees. 138 undergraduate majors. ***Total enrollment:*** 11,768. Undergraduates: 10,884. Freshmen: 2,294. Federal methodology is used as a basis for awarding need-based institutional aid.

UNDERGRADUATE EXPENSES for 2020–2021 *Application fee:* $50. ***Tuition, area resident:*** full-time $6318; part-time $1895 per term. ***Tuition, state resident:*** full-time $6318; part-time $1895 per term. ***Tuition, nonresident:*** full-time $21,999; part-time $6600 per term. ***Required fees:*** full-time $1244; $612 per quarter hour. Full-time tuition and fees vary according to course load, degree level, location, and program. Part-time tuition and fees vary according to course load, degree level, location, and program. ***College room and board:*** $12,637; ***Room only:*** $6188. Room and board charges vary according to board plan, housing facility, and location.

FRESHMAN FINANCIAL AID (Fall 2018) 1964 applied for aid; of those 77% were deemed to have need. 100% of freshmen with need received aid; of those 13% had need fully met. ***Average percent of need met:*** 62% (excluding resources awarded to replace EFC). ***Average financial aid package:*** $10,546 (excluding resources awarded to replace EFC). 1% of all full-time freshmen had no need and received non-need-based gift aid.

UNDERGRADUATE FINANCIAL AID (Fall 2018) 7,606 applied for aid; of those 80% were deemed to have need. 100% of undergraduates with need received aid; of those 7% had need fully met. ***Average percent of need met:*** 59% (excluding resources awarded to replace EFC). ***Average financial aid package:*** $10,892 (excluding resources awarded to replace EFC). 1% of all full-time undergraduates had no need and received non-need-based gift aid.

GIFT AID (NEED-BASED) *Total amount:* $76,945,721 (48% federal, 44% state, 3% institutional, 5% external sources). ***Receiving aid:*** Freshmen: 46% (1,029); all full-time undergraduates: 46% (4,401). ***Average award:*** Freshmen: $9015; Undergraduates: $8878. ***Scholarships, grants, and awards:*** Federal Pell, FSEOG, state, private, college/university gift aid from institutional funds.

GIFT AID (NON-NEED-BASED) *Total amount:* $1,679,871 (1% federal, 4% state, 4% institutional, 91% external sources). ***Receiving aid:*** Freshmen: 4% (80). Undergraduates: 2% (179). ***Average award:*** Freshmen: $1738. Undergraduates: $1587. ***Scholarships, grants, and awards by category:*** *Academic interests/achievement:* general academic interests/achievements. *Creative arts/performance:* applied art and design, general creative arts/performance, music, theater/drama. *Special achievements/activities:* leadership. *Special characteristics:* children and siblings of alumni, children of faculty/staff, children of public servants, local/state students, members of minority groups, out-of-state students, public servants, veterans. ***Tuition waivers:*** Full or partial for children of alumni, employees or children of employees, senior citizens. ***ROTC:*** Army, Air Force.

LOANS *Student loans:* $40,612,875 (75% need-based, 25% non-need-based). 64% of past graduating class borrowed through all loan programs. *Average indebtedness per student:* $24,498. ***Average need-based loan:*** Freshmen: $3057. Undergraduates: $4092. ***Parent loans:*** $20,398,788 (33% need-based, 67% non-need-based). ***Programs:*** Perkins.

WORK-STUDY *Federal work-study:* Total amount: $243,731; 151 jobs averaging $2138. ***State or other work-study/employment:*** Total amount: $161,962 (100% need-based). 162 part-time jobs averaging $2240.

ATHLETIC AWARDS Total amount: $41,752 (80% need-based, 20% non-need-based).

APPLYING FOR FINANCIAL AID *Required financial aid forms:* FAFSA, institution's own scholarship application. ***Financial aid deadline (priority):*** 2/1. ***Notification date:*** Continuous beginning 3/15. Students must reply by 6/8.

CONTACT Mr. Adrian Naranjo, Director of Student Financial Services, Central Washington University, 400 East University Way, Ellensburg, WA 98926-7495, 509-963-2091. *Fax:* 509-963-1788. *E-mail:* finaid@cwu.edu.
Website: http://www.cwu.edu/.

CENTRAL YESHIVA BETH JOSEPH

Brooklyn, NY

CONTACT Financial Aid Office, Central Yeshiva Beth Joseph, 1502 Avenue N, Brooklyn, NY 11230.
Website: http://www.centralyeshivabethjoseph.com.

CENTRAL YESHIVA TOMCHEI TMIMIM-LUBAVITCH

Brooklyn, NY

CONTACT Rabbi Moshe M. Gluckowsky, Director of Financial Aid , Central Yeshiva Tomchei Tmimim-Lubavitch, 841-853 Ocean Parkway, Brooklyn, NY 11230, 718-859-2277.

CENTRE COLLEGE

Danville, KY

Tuition & fees: $43,000	Average undergraduate aid package: $36,841

ABOUT THE INSTITUTION Independent Presbyterian Church (U.S.A.), coed. ***Awards:*** bachelor's degrees. 28 undergraduate majors. ***Total enrollment:*** 1,411. Undergraduates: 1,411. Freshmen: 355. Federal methodology is used as a basis for awarding need-based institutional aid.

UNDERGRADUATE EXPENSES for 2020–2021 ***Comprehensive fee:*** $53,740 includes full-time tuition ($43,000) and room and board ($10,740). ***College room only:*** $5370. ***Part-time tuition:*** $1536 per credit hour.

FRESHMAN FINANCIAL AID (Fall 2019, est.) 309 applied for aid; of those 80% were deemed to have need. 100% of freshmen with need received aid; of those 36% had need fully met. ***Average percent of need met:*** 90% (excluding resources awarded to replace EFC). ***Average financial aid package:*** $38,964 (excluding resources awarded to replace EFC). 29% of all full-time freshmen had no need and received non-need-based gift aid.

UNDERGRADUATE FINANCIAL AID (Fall 2019, est.) 1,010 applied for aid; of those 81% were deemed to have need. 100% of undergraduates with need received aid; of those 32% had need fully met. ***Average percent of need met:*** 87% (excluding resources awarded to replace EFC). ***Average financial aid package:*** $36,841 (excluding resources awarded to replace EFC). 39% of all full-time undergraduates had no need and received non-need-based gift aid.

GIFT AID (NEED-BASED) ***Total amount:*** $27,471,008 (5% federal, 9% state, 84% institutional, 2% external sources). ***Receiving aid:*** Freshmen: 70% (247); all full-time undergraduates: 58% (814). ***Average award:*** Freshmen: $36,467; Undergraduates: $33,652. ***Scholarships, grants, and awards:*** Federal Pell, FSEOG, state, private, college/university gift aid from institutional funds.

GIFT AID (NON-NEED-BASED) ***Total amount:*** $14,863,667 (4% state, 95% institutional, 1% external sources). ***Average award:*** Freshmen: $28,358. Undergraduates: $26,542. ***Scholarships, grants, and awards by category:*** *Academic interests/achievement:* foreign languages. *Creative arts/performance:* music, theater/drama. *Special achievements/activities:* community service. *Special characteristics:* children and siblings of alumni, children of faculty/staff, ethnic background, first-generation college students. ***ROTC:*** Army, Air Force cooperative.

LOANS ***Student loans:*** $5,745,255 (57% need-based, 43% non-need-based). 51% of past graduating class borrowed through all loan programs. *Average indebtedness per student:* $27,418. ***Average need-based loan:*** Freshmen: $3368. Undergraduates: $4495. ***Parent loans:*** $1,774,920 (100% non-need-based). ***Programs:*** Federal Direct (Subsidized and Unsubsidized Stafford, PLUS), college/university.

WORK-STUDY ***Federal work-study:*** Total amount: $592,308; jobs available. ***State or other work-study/employment:*** Total amount: $24,300 (100% non-need-based). Part-time jobs available.

APPLYING FOR FINANCIAL AID ***Required financial aid forms:*** FAFSA, institution's own form. ***Financial aid deadline:*** 1/31. ***Notification date:*** 12/23. Students must reply by 5/1.

CONTACT Mr. Kevin Lamb, Associate Dean of Admission and Financial Aid, Centre College, 600 West Walnut St, Danville, KY 40422, 859-2385365 or toll-free 800-423-6236. *Fax:* 859-238-8719. *E-mail:* kevin.lamb@centre.edu.
Website: http://www.centre.edu/.

CENTRO DE ESTUDIOS MULTIDISCIPLINARIOS - BAYAMÓN

Bayamon, PR

CONTACT Financial Aid Office, Centro de Estudios Multidisciplinarios - Bayamón, Calle Degetau #25, Bayamon, PR 00961, 787-780-8900.
Website: http://www.cemcollege.edu/.

CENTRO DE ESTUDIOS MULTIDISCIPLINARIOS - HUMACAO

Humacao, PR

CONTACT Financial Aid Office, Centro de Estudios Multidisciplinarios - Humacao, Calle Dr. Vidal #8 y #53, Humacao, PR 00791, 809-852-5505.
Website: http://www.cemcollege.edu/.

CHADRON STATE COLLEGE

Chadron, NE

CONTACT Ms. Sherry Douglas, Director of Financial Aid, Chadron State College, 1000 Main Street, Chadron, NE 69337, 308-432-6230 or toll-free 800-242-3766. *Fax:* 308-432-6229. *E-mail:* finaid@csc.edu.
Website: http://www.csc.edu/.

CHAMBERLAIN COLLEGE OF NURSING - ADDISON

Addison, IL

CONTACT Financial Aid Office, Chamberlain College of Nursing - Addison, 1221 North Swift Road, Addison, IL 60101, 630-953-3660 or toll-free 877-751-5783.
Website: http://www.chamberlain.edu/.

CHAMBERLAIN COLLEGE OF NURSING - ATLANTA

Atlanta, GA

CONTACT Financial Aid Office, Chamberlain College of Nursing - Atlanta, 5775 Peachtree Dunwoody Road NE, Suite A-100, Atlanta, GA 30342, 404-250-8500 or toll-free 877-751-5783.
Website: http://www.chamberlain.edu/.

CHAMBERLAIN COLLEGE OF NURSING - CHARLOTTE

Charlotte, NC

CONTACT Financial Aid Office, Chamberlain College of Nursing - Charlotte, 2015 Ayrsley Town Boulevard, Charlotte, NC 28273.
Website: http://www.chamberlain.edu/.

CHAMBERLAIN COLLEGE OF NURSING - CHICAGO

Chicago, IL

CONTACT Financial Aid Office, Chamberlain College of Nursing - Chicago, 3300 North Campbell Avenue, Chicago, IL 60618, 773-961-3000 or toll-free 877-751-5783.
Website: http://www.chamberlain.edu/.

CHAMBERLAIN COLLEGE OF NURSING - CLEVELAND

Cleveland, OH

CONTACT Financial Aid Office, Chamberlain College of Nursing - Cleveland, 6700 Euclid Avenue, Cleveland, OH 44103, 216-361-6005 or toll-free 877-751-5783.
Website: http://www.chamberlain.edu/.

CHAMBERLAIN COLLEGE OF NURSING - COLUMBUS

Columbus, OH

CONTACT Financial Aid Office, Chamberlain College of Nursing - Columbus, 1350 Alum Creek Drive, Columbus, OH 43209, 614-252-8890 or toll-free 877-751-5783.
Website: http://www.chamberlain.edu/.

CHAMBERLAIN COLLEGE OF NURSING - HOUSTON

Houston, TX

CONTACT Financial Aid Office, Chamberlain College of Nursing - Houston, 11025 Equity Drive, Houston, TX 77041, 713-277-9800 or toll-free 877-751-5783.
Website: http://www.chamberlain.edu/.

CHAMBERLAIN COLLEGE OF NURSING - INDIANAPOLIS

Indianapolis, IN

CONTACT Financial Aid Office, Chamberlain College of Nursing - Indianapolis, 9100 Keystone Crossing, Indianapolis, IN 46240, 317-816-7335 or toll-free 877-751-5783.
Website: http://www.chamberlain.edu/.

CHAMBERLAIN COLLEGE OF NURSING - IRVING

Irving, TX

CONTACT Financial Aid Office, Chamberlain College of Nursing - Irving, 4800 Regent Boulevard, Irving, TX 75063, 469-706-6705 or toll-free 866-593-8669.
Website: http://www.chamberlain.edu/.

CHAMBERLAIN COLLEGE OF NURSING - JACKSONVILLE

Jacksonville, FL

CONTACT Financial Aid Office, Chamberlain College of Nursing - Jacksonville, 5200 Belfort Road, Jacksonville, FL 32256, 904-251-8110 or toll-free 877-751-5783.
Website: http://www.chamberlain.edu/.

CHAMBERLAIN COLLEGE OF NURSING - LAS VEGAS

Las Vegas, NV

CONTACT Financial Aid Office, Chamberlain College of Nursing - Las Vegas, 9901 Covington Cross Drive, Las Vegas, NV 89144, 702-786-1660 or toll-free 877-751-5783.
Website: http://www.chamberlain.edu/.

CHAMBERLAIN COLLEGE OF NURSING - MIRAMAR

Miramar, FL

CONTACT Financial Aid Office, Chamberlain College of Nursing - Miramar, 2300 SW 145th Avenue, Miramar, FL 33027, 954-885-3510 or toll-free 877-751-5783.
Website: http://www.chamberlain.edu/.

CHAMBERLAIN COLLEGE OF NURSING - NORTH BRUNSWICK

North Brunswick, NJ

CONTACT Financial Aid Office, Chamberlain College of Nursing - North Brunswick, 630 U.S. Highway 1, North Brunswick, NJ 08902, 732-875-1300 or toll-free 877-751-5783.
Website: http://www.chamberlain.edu/.

CHAMBERLAIN COLLEGE OF NURSING - PEARLAND

Pearland, TX

CONTACT Financial Aid Office, Chamberlain College of Nursing - Pearland, 12000 Shadow Creek Parkway, Pearland, TX 77584, 832-664-7000 or toll-free 877-751-5783.
Website: http://www.chamberlain.edu/.

CHAMBERLAIN COLLEGE OF NURSING - PHOENIX

Phoenix, AZ

CONTACT Financial Aid Office, Chamberlain College of Nursing - Phoenix, 2149 West Dunlap Avenue, Phoenix, AZ 85021, 602-331-2720 or toll-free 877-751-5783.
Website: http://www.chamberlain.edu/.

CHAMBERLAIN COLLEGE OF NURSING - SACRAMENTO

Rancho Cordova, CA

CONTACT Financial Aid Office, Chamberlain College of Nursing - Sacramento, 10971 Sun Center Drive, Rancho Cordova, CA 95670.
Website: http://www.chamberlain.edu/.

CHAMBERLAIN COLLEGE OF NURSING - ST. LOUIS

St. Louis, MO

CONTACT Financial Aid Counselor, Chamberlain College of Nursing - St. Louis, 11830 Westline Industrial Drive, Suite 106, St. Louis, MO 63146, 314-991-6200 or toll-free 877-751-5783.
Website: http://www.chamberlain.edu/.

CHAMBERLAIN COLLEGE OF NURSING - TINLEY PARK

Tinley Park, IL

CONTACT Financial Aid Office, Chamberlain College of Nursing - Tinley Park, 18624 West Creek Drive, Tinley Park, IL 60477, 708-560-2000 or toll-free 877-751-5783.
Website: http://www.chamberlain.edu/.

CHAMBERLAIN COLLEGE OF NURSING - TROY

Troy, MI

CONTACT Financial Aid Office, Chamberlain College of Nursing - Troy, 200 Kirts Boulevard, Troy, MI 48084, 248-817-4140 or toll-free 877-751-5783.
Website: http://www.chamberlain.edu/.

CHAMBERLAIN COLLEGE OF NURSING - TYSONS CORNER

Vienna, VA

CONTACT Financial Aid Office, Chamberlain College of Nursing - Tysons Corner, 1951 Kidwell Drive, Vienna, VA 22182, 703-416-7300 or toll-free 877-751-5783.
Website: http://www.chamberlain.edu/.

CHAMINADE UNIVERSITY OF HONOLULU

Honolulu, HI

Tuition & fees: $26,914	Average undergraduate aid package: $22,052

ABOUT THE INSTITUTION Independent Roman Catholic, coed. ***Awards:*** certificates, associate, bachelor's, master's, and doctoral degrees. 26 undergraduate majors. ***Total enrollment:*** 1,675. Undergraduates: 1,099. Freshmen: 196. Federal methodology is used as a basis for awarding need-based institutional aid.

UNDERGRADUATE EXPENSES for 2020–2021 ***Application fee:*** $50. ***One-time required fee:*** $180. ***Comprehensive fee:*** $41,524 includes full-time tuition ($26,800), mandatory fees ($114), and room and board ($14,610). Full-time tuition and fees vary according to course load, location, and program. Room and board charges vary according to board plan and housing facility. ***Part-time tuition:*** $893 per credit. Part-time tuition and fees vary according to course load, location, and program.

FRESHMAN FINANCIAL AID (Fall 2018) 168 applied for aid; of those 72% were deemed to have need. 100% of freshmen with need received aid; of those 10% had need fully met. ***Average percent of need met:*** 72% (excluding resources awarded to replace EFC). ***Average financial aid package:*** $23,706 (excluding resources awarded to replace EFC). 33% of all full-time freshmen had no need and received non-need-based gift aid.

UNDERGRADUATE FINANCIAL AID (Fall 2018) 846 applied for aid; of those 81% were deemed to have need. 99% of undergraduates with need received aid; of those 11% had need fully met. ***Average percent of need met:*** 66% (excluding resources awarded to replace EFC). ***Average financial aid package:*** $22,052 (excluding resources awarded to replace EFC). 32% of all full-time undergraduates had no need and received non-need-based gift aid.

GIFT AID (NEED-BASED) ***Receiving aid:*** Freshmen: 60% (113); all full-time undergraduates: 58% (617). ***Average award:*** Freshmen: $4252; Undergraduates: $4624. ***Scholarships, grants, and awards:*** Federal Pell, FSEOG, private, college/university gift aid from institutional funds, TEACH Grants.

GIFT AID (NON-NEED-BASED) ***Receiving aid:*** Freshmen: 64% (119). Undergraduates: 63% (661). ***Average award:*** Freshmen: $16,290. Undergraduates: $13,182. ***Scholarships, grants, and awards by category:*** *Academic interests/achievement:* 831 awards ($7,727,890 total): biological sciences, education, general academic interests/achievements, health fields, home economics, premedicine. *Special achievements/activities:* 52 awards ($761,835 total): community service, memberships, religious involvement. *Special characteristics:* 145 awards ($1,807,590 total): children of faculty/staff, ethnic background, local/state students, out-of-state students, religious affiliation, siblings of current students. ***Tuition waivers:*** Full or partial for employees or children of employees. ***ROTC:*** Army cooperative, Air Force cooperative.

LOANS ***Student loans:*** 60% of past graduating class borrowed through all loan programs. *Average indebtedness per student:* $22,158. ***Average need-based loan:*** Freshmen: $3239. Undergraduates: $4280. ***Programs:*** Federal Direct (Subsidized and Unsubsidized Stafford, PLUS), alternative loans.

WORK-STUDY Federal work-study jobs available.

APPLYING FOR FINANCIAL AID ***Required financial aid form:*** FAFSA. ***Financial aid deadline:*** Continuous.

CONTACT Amy Takiguchi, Director of Financial Aid, Chaminade University of Honolulu, 3140 Waialae Avenue, Honolulu, HI 96816-1578, 808-735-4780 or toll-free 800-735-3733. *Fax:* 808-739-8362. *E-mail:* finaid@chaminade.edu.
Website: http://www.chaminade.edu/.

CHAMPLAIN COLLEGE

Burlington, VT

Tuition & fees: $41,828	Average undergraduate aid package: $31,913

ABOUT THE INSTITUTION Independent, coed. ***Awards:*** certificates, associate, bachelor's, and master's degrees. 38 undergraduate majors. ***Total enrollment:*** 2,715. Undergraduates: 2,078. Freshmen: 524. Federal methodology is used as a basis for awarding need-based institutional aid.

UNDERGRADUATE EXPENSES for 2019–2020 ***Comprehensive fee:*** $57,594 includes full-time tuition ($41,728), mandatory fees ($100), and room and board ($15,766). ***Part-time tuition:*** $1762 per credit hour. ***Payment plan:*** Tuition prepayment.

FRESHMAN FINANCIAL AID (Fall 2019, est.) 464 applied for aid; of those 83% were deemed to have need. 100% of freshmen with need received aid; of those 25% had need fully met. ***Average percent of need met:*** 79% (excluding resources awarded to replace EFC). ***Average financial aid package:*** $33,229 (excluding resources awarded to replace EFC). 15% of all full-time freshmen had no need and received non-need-based gift aid.

UNDERGRADUATE FINANCIAL AID (Fall 2019, est.) 1,530 applied for aid; of those 86% were deemed to have need. 100% of undergraduates with need received aid; of those 18% had need fully met. ***Average percent of need met:*** 75% (excluding resources awarded to replace EFC). ***Average financial aid package:*** $31,913 (excluding resources awarded to replace EFC). 10% of all full-time undergraduates had no need and received non-need-based gift aid.

GIFT AID (NEED-BASED) ***Receiving aid:*** Freshmen: 73% (379); all full-time undergraduates: 66% (1,305). ***Average award:*** Freshmen: $26,311; Undergraduates: $25,089. ***Scholarships, grants, and awards:*** Federal Pell, FSEOG, state, private, college/university gift aid from institutional funds.

GIFT AID (NON-NEED-BASED) ***Receiving aid:*** Freshmen: 15% (76). Undergraduates: 10% (190). ***Average award:*** Freshmen: $17,901. Undergraduates: $16,137. ***Scholarships, grants, and awards by category:*** *Academic interests/achievement:* business, communication, computer science, education, general academic interests/achievements, social sciences. *Special achievements/activities:* leadership. *Special characteristics:* first-generation college students, general special characteristics, international students, members of minority groups. ***ROTC:*** Army cooperative.

LOANS ***Student loans:*** 76% of past graduating class borrowed through all loan programs. *Average indebtedness per student:* $36,976. ***Average need-based loan:*** Freshmen: $2829. Undergraduates: $3850. ***Programs:*** Federal Direct (Subsidized and Unsubsidized Stafford, PLUS), Perkins, state.

WORK-STUDY Federal work-study jobs available.

APPLYING FOR FINANCIAL AID ***Required financial aid form:*** FAFSA. ***Notification date:*** Students must reply within 2 weeks of notification.

CONTACT Greg Davis, Director of Financial Aid, Champlain College, 163 South Willard Street, Burlington, VT 05401, 802-860-2777 or toll-free 800-570-5858. *Fax:* 802-860-2775. *E-mail:* gdavis@champlain.edu.
Website: http://www.champlain.edu/.

CHAPMAN UNIVERSITY

Orange, CA

Tuition & fees: $54,924 **Average undergraduate aid package: $35,854**

ABOUT THE INSTITUTION Independent Christian Church (Disciples of Christ), coed. ***Awards:*** bachelor's, master's, and doctoral degrees. 50 undergraduate majors. ***Total enrollment:*** 7,659. Undergraduates: 23,366. Freshmen: 12,525. Federal methodology is used as a basis for awarding need-based institutional aid.

UNDERGRADUATE EXPENSES for 2019–2020 ***Application fee:*** $70. ***Comprehensive fee:*** $70,442 includes full-time tuition ($54,540), mandatory fees ($384), and room and board ($15,518). ***College room only:*** $10,400. Room and board charges vary according to board plan and housing facility. ***Part-time tuition:*** $1695 per credit hour. ***Part-time fees:*** $147 per term. Part-time tuition and fees vary according to course load. ***Payment plan:*** Tuition prepayment.

FRESHMAN FINANCIAL AID (Fall 2018) 1221 applied for aid; of those 79% were deemed to have need. 100% of freshmen with need received aid; of those 17% had need fully met. ***Average percent of need met:*** 76% (excluding resources awarded to replace EFC). ***Average financial aid package:*** $39,214 (excluding resources awarded to replace EFC). 14% of all full-time freshmen had no need and received non-need-based gift aid.

UNDERGRADUATE FINANCIAL AID (Fall 2018) 4,337 applied for aid; of those 87% were deemed to have need. 100% of undergraduates with need received aid; of those 13% had need fully met. ***Average percent of need met:*** 70% (excluding resources awarded to replace EFC). ***Average financial aid package:*** $35,854 (excluding resources awarded to replace EFC). 7% of all full-time undergraduates had no need and received non-need-based gift aid.

GIFT AID (NEED-BASED) ***Total amount:*** $135,507,039 (4% federal, 6% state, 87% institutional, 3% external sources). ***Receiving aid:*** Freshmen: 54% (889); all full-time undergraduates: 51% (3,432). ***Average award:*** Freshmen: $20,910; Undergraduates: $19,239. ***Scholarships, grants, and awards:*** Federal Pell, FSEOG, state, private, college/university gift aid from institutional funds.

GIFT AID (NON-NEED-BASED) ***Total amount:*** $8,792,254 (98% institutional, 2% external sources). ***Receiving aid:*** Freshmen: 45% (749). Undergraduates: 39% (2,632). ***Average award:*** Freshmen: $18,981. Undergraduates: $18,152. ***Scholarships, grants, and awards by category:*** *Academic interests/achievement:* 4,195 awards ($71,454,636 total): biological sciences, general academic interests/achievements. *Creative arts/performance:* 298 awards ($1,203,422 total): art/fine arts, cinema/film/broadcasting, creative writing, dance, music, performing arts, theater/drama. *Special characteristics:* 189 awards ($359,130 total): children and siblings of alumni, international students, relatives of clergy. ***Tuition waivers:*** Full or partial for employees or children of employees. ***ROTC:*** Army cooperative, Air Force cooperative.

LOANS ***Student loans:*** $31,651,562 (91% need-based, 9% non-need-based). 50% of past graduating class borrowed through all loan programs. *Average indebtedness per student:* $27,117. ***Average need-based loan:*** Freshmen: $3401. Undergraduates: $4475. ***Parent loans:*** $37,302,737 (87% need-based, 13% non-need-based). ***Programs:*** Federal Direct (Subsidized and Unsubsidized Stafford, PLUS).

WORK-STUDY ***Federal work-study:*** Total amount: $9,347,884; 3,245 jobs averaging $2881.

APPLYING FOR FINANCIAL AID ***Required financial aid forms:*** FAFSA, state aid form. ***Financial aid deadline (priority):*** 3/2. ***Notification date:*** Continuous beginning 3/15. Students must reply within 3 weeks of notification.

CONTACT Mr. David Carnevale, Director of Financial Aid, Chapman University, One University Drive, Orange, CA 92866, 714-532-6049 or toll-free 888-CUAPPLY. *Fax:* 714-997-6743. *E-mail:* carneva@chapman.edu.
Website: http://www.chapman.edu/.

CHARLES R. DREW UNIVERSITY OF MEDICINE AND SCIENCE

Los Angeles, CA

Tuition & fees: $17,440 **Average undergraduate aid package: $14,566**

ABOUT THE INSTITUTION Independent, coed. ***Awards:*** certificates, associate, bachelor's, master's, and doctoral degrees. 4 undergraduate majors. ***Total enrollment:*** 749. Undergraduates: 199. Freshmen: 13. Federal methodology is used as a basis for awarding need-based institutional aid.

UNDERGRADUATE EXPENSES for 2020–2021 ***Application fee:*** $50. ***Tuition:*** full-time $17,340; part-time $578 per credit hour. ***Required fees:*** full-time $100. Full-time tuition and fees vary according to course load, degree level, and program. Part-time tuition and fees vary according to course load, degree level, and program.

FRESHMAN FINANCIAL AID (Fall 2018) 25 applied for aid; of those 100% were deemed to have need. 96% of freshmen with need received aid; of those 4% had need fully met. ***Average percent of need met:*** 50% (excluding resources awarded to replace EFC). ***Average financial aid package:*** $19,478 (excluding resources awarded to replace EFC).

UNDERGRADUATE FINANCIAL AID (Fall 2018) 110 applied for aid; of those 96% were deemed to have need. 98% of undergraduates with need received aid; of those 1% had need fully met. ***Average percent of need met:*** 41% (excluding resources awarded to replace EFC). ***Average financial aid package:*** $14,566 (excluding resources awarded to replace EFC). 4% of all full-time undergraduates had no need and received non-need-based gift aid.

GIFT AID (NEED-BASED) ***Total amount:*** $1,058,452 (47% federal, 27% state, 20% institutional, 6% external sources). ***Receiving aid:*** Freshmen: 89% (24); all full-time undergraduates: 72% (91). ***Average award:*** Freshmen: $15,798; Undergraduates: $11,177. ***Scholarships, grants, and awards:*** Federal Pell, FSEOG, state, private, college/university gift aid from institutional funds.

GIFT AID (NON-NEED-BASED) ***Total amount:*** $54,989 (42% state, 47% institutional, 11% external sources). ***Receiving aid:*** Freshmen: 4% (1). Undergraduates: 1% (1). ***Average award:*** Undergraduates: $4218.

LOANS ***Student loans:*** $1,278,915 (98% need-based, 2% non-need-based). ***Average need-based loan:*** Freshmen: $3694. Undergraduates: $4804. ***Parent loans:*** $283,146 (93% need-based, 7% non-need-based). ***Programs:*** Federal Direct (Subsidized and Unsubsidized Stafford, PLUS).

WORK-STUDY ***Federal work-study:*** Total amount: $61,316; jobs available.

APPLYING FOR FINANCIAL AID ***Required financial aid forms:*** FAFSA, state aid form. ***Financial aid deadline (priority):*** 3/1. ***Notification date:*** Continuous beginning 3/1. Students must reply by 5/1 or within 2 weeks of notification.

CONTACT Financial Aid Office, Charles R. Drew University of Medicine and Science, 1731 East 120th Street, Los Angeles, CA 90059, 323-563-4824. *Fax:* 323-569-0597.
Website: http://www.cdrewu.edu/.

CHARLESTON SOUTHERN UNIVERSITY

Charleston, SC

CONTACT Mr. Jim Rhoden, Director of Admissions, Charleston Southern University, PO Box 118087, 9200 University Boulevard, Charleston, SC 29423-8087, 843-863-7050 or toll-free 800-947-7474. *Fax:* 843-863-7070.
Website: http://www.charlestonsouthern.edu/.

CHARLOTTE CHRISTIAN COLLEGE AND THEOLOGICAL SEMINARY

Charlotte, NC

ABOUT THE INSTITUTION Independent Christian, coed. ***Awards:*** associate, bachelor's, master's, and doctoral degrees. 4 undergraduate majors.

GIFT AID (NEED-BASED) ***Scholarships, grants, and awards:*** Federal Pell, FSEOG, private, college/university gift aid from institutional funds, Veterans Education Benefits (GI Bill).

GIFT AID (NON-NEED-BASED) ***Scholarships, grants, and awards by category:*** *Academic interests/achievement:* education, foreign languages, general academic interests/achievements, religion/biblical studies. *Special achievements/activities:* memberships, religious involvement. *Special characteristics:* religious affiliation.

LOANS ***Programs:*** Federal Direct (Subsidized and Unsubsidized Stafford, PLUS).

CONTACT Mr. Kenneth Neal Roach, Financial Aid Officer, Charlotte Christian College and Theological Seminary, 3117 Whiting Avenue, PO Box 790106, Charlotte, NC 28206-7901, 704-334-6882 Ext. 114. *Fax:* 704-334-6885. *E-mail:* kroach@charlottechristian.edu.
Website: http://www.charlottechristian.edu/.

CHARTER COLLEGE

Vancouver, WA

CONTACT Financial Aid Office, Charter College, 17720 SE Mill Plain Boulevard, Suite 170, Vancouver, WA 98683.
Website: http://www.chartercollege.edu/.

CHARTER OAK STATE COLLEGE

New Britain, CT

Tuition & fees (CT res): $10,243 **Average undergraduate aid package: N/A**

ABOUT THE INSTITUTION State-supported, coed. ***Awards:*** certificates, associate, bachelor's, and master's degrees (offers only external degree programs). 12 undergraduate majors. ***Total enrollment:*** 1,611. Undergraduates: 1,547. Federal methodology is used as a basis for awarding need-based institutional aid.

UNDERGRADUATE EXPENSES for 2020–2021 ***Application fee:*** $50. ***Tuition, state resident:*** full-time $9570; part-time $319 per credit. ***Tuition, nonresident:*** full-time $12,570; part-time $419 per credit. ***Required fees:*** full-time $673; $299 per term. Full-time tuition and fees vary according to course load. Part-time tuition and fees vary according to course load.

GIFT AID (NEED-BASED) ***Scholarships, grants, and awards:*** Federal Pell, FSEOG, state, private, college/university gift aid from institutional funds, Charter Oak Foundation grants.

GIFT AID (NON-NEED-BASED) ***Scholarships, grants, and awards by category:*** *Academic interests/achievement:* general academic interests/achievements.

LOANS ***Programs:*** Federal Direct (Subsidized and Unsubsidized Stafford, PLUS), state, Alternative private loans.

APPLYING FOR FINANCIAL AID ***Required financial aid form:*** FAFSA. ***Financial aid deadline (priority):*** 7/1. ***Notification date:*** Continuous beginning 8/1.

CONTACT Ralph Brasure, Director of Financial Aid, Charter Oak State College, 55 Paul Manafort Drive, New Britain, CT 06053, 860-515-3703. *Fax:* 860-760-6540. *E-mail:* sfa@charteroak.edu.
Website: http://www.charteroak.edu/.

CHATHAM UNIVERSITY

Pittsburgh, PA

Tuition & fees: $39,902 **Average undergraduate aid package: $31,286**

ABOUT THE INSTITUTION Independent, coed, primarily women. ***Awards:*** certificates, bachelor's, master's, and doctoral degrees. 45 undergraduate majors. ***Total enrollment:*** 2,437. Undergraduates: 1,408. Freshmen: 315. Both federal and institutional methodology are used as a basis for awarding need-based institutional aid.

UNDERGRADUATE EXPENSES for 2020–2021 ***Application fee:*** $35. ***Comprehensive fee:*** $52,755 includes full-time tuition ($38,482), mandatory fees ($1420), and room and board ($12,853). ***College room only:*** $6645. Room and board charges vary according to board plan and housing facility. ***Part-time tuition:*** $934 per credit hour.

FRESHMAN FINANCIAL AID (Fall 2019, est.) 291 applied for aid; of those 87% were deemed to have need. 100% of freshmen with need received aid; of those 18% had need fully met. ***Average percent of need met:*** 68% (excluding resources awarded to replace EFC). ***Average financial aid package:*** $30,638 (excluding resources awarded to replace EFC). 12% of all full-time freshmen had no need and received non-need-based gift aid.

UNDERGRADUATE FINANCIAL AID (Fall 2019, est.) 974 applied for aid; of those 88% were deemed to have need. 100% of undergraduates with need received aid; of those 17% had need fully met. ***Average percent of need met:*** 65% (excluding resources awarded to replace EFC). ***Average financial aid package:*** $31,286 (excluding resources awarded to replace EFC). 8% of all full-time undergraduates had no need and received non-need-based gift aid.

GIFT AID (NEED-BASED) ***Total amount:*** $23,245,860 (8% federal, 6% state, 83% institutional, 3% external sources). ***Receiving aid:*** Freshmen: 77% (240); all full-time undergraduates: 66% (728). ***Average award:*** Freshmen: $8440; Undergraduates: $8926. ***Scholarships, grants, and awards:*** Federal Pell, FSEOG, state, private, college/university gift aid from institutional funds.

GIFT AID (NON-NEED-BASED) ***Total amount:*** $3,003,313 (97% institutional, 3% external sources). ***Receiving aid:*** Freshmen: 81% (254). Undergraduates: 78% (857). ***Average award:*** Freshmen: $20,383. Undergraduates: $20,436. ***Scholarships, grants, and awards by category:*** *Academic interests/achievement:* general academic interests/achievements. *Creative arts/performance:* applied art and design, art/fine arts, music. *Special achievements/activities:* leadership. *Special characteristics:* children and siblings of alumni, children of faculty/staff, siblings of current students. *ROTC:* Army cooperative, Naval cooperative, Air Force cooperative.

LOANS ***Student loans:*** $5,781,889 (54% need-based, 46% non-need-based). 76% of past graduating class borrowed through all loan programs. *Average indebtedness per student:* $35,199. ***Average need-based loan:*** Freshmen: $2949. Undergraduates: $4089. ***Parent loans:*** $3,163,879 (85% need-based, 15% non-need-based). ***Programs:*** Federal Direct (Subsidized and Unsubsidized Stafford, PLUS).

WORK-STUDY ***Federal work-study:*** Total amount: $1,087,227; jobs available. ***State or other work-study/employment:*** Total amount: $200,000 (100% non-need-based). Part-time jobs available.

APPLYING FOR FINANCIAL AID ***Required financial aid form:*** FAFSA. ***Financial aid deadline (priority):*** 3/1. ***Notification date:*** 12/1. Students must reply within 4 weeks of notification.

CONTACT Dr. Jennifer Burns, Director of Financial Aid, Chatham University, Woodland Road, Pittsburgh, PA 15232, 412-3651168 or toll-free 800-837-1290. *Fax:* 412-365-1643. *E-mail:* jburns@chatham.edu.
Website: http://www.chatham.edu/.

CHESTNUT HILL COLLEGE

Philadelphia, PA

Tuition & fees: $37,200 **Average undergraduate aid package: $28,602**

ABOUT THE INSTITUTION Independent Roman Catholic, coed. ***Awards:*** certificates, associate, bachelor's, master's, and doctoral degrees (profile includes figures from both traditional and accelerated (part-time) programs). 45 undergraduate majors. ***Total enrollment:*** 1,846. Undergraduates: 1,364. Freshmen: 207. Federal methodology is used as a basis for awarding need-based institutional aid.

UNDERGRADUATE EXPENSES for 2019–2020 ***Application fee:*** $35. ***One-time required fee:*** $480. ***Comprehensive fee:*** $48,200 includes full-time tuition ($36,950), mandatory fees ($250), and room and board ($11,000). Room and board charges vary according to housing facility. ***Part-time tuition:*** $775 per credit hour. ***Part-time fees:*** $250 per year.

FRESHMAN FINANCIAL AID (Fall 2019, est.) 192 applied for aid; of those 100% were deemed to have need. 100% of freshmen with need received aid; of those 23% had need fully met. ***Average percent of need met:*** 71% (excluding resources awarded to replace EFC). ***Average financial aid package:*** $35,637 (excluding resources awarded to replace EFC). 10% of all full-time freshmen had no need and received non-need-based gift aid.

UNDERGRADUATE FINANCIAL AID (Fall 2019, est.) 833 applied for aid; of those 100% were deemed to have need. 100% of undergraduates with need received aid; of those 25% had need fully met. ***Average percent of need met:*** 63%

(excluding resources awarded to replace EFC). ***Average financial aid package:*** $28,602 (excluding resources awarded to replace EFC). 11% of all full-time undergraduates had no need and received non-need-based gift aid.
GIFT AID (NEED-BASED) ***Total amount:*** $4,848,901 (62% federal, 24% state, 2% institutional, 12% external sources). ***Receiving aid:*** Freshmen: 76% (161); all full-time undergraduates: 67% (668). ***Average award:*** Freshmen: $14,010; Undergraduates: $9788. ***Scholarships, grants, and awards:*** Federal Pell, FSEOG, state, private, college/university gift aid from institutional funds.
GIFT AID (NON-NEED-BASED) ***Total amount:*** $40,720 (14% state, 49% institutional, 37% external sources). ***Receiving aid:*** Freshmen: 89% (189). Undergraduates: 68% (675). ***Average award:*** Freshmen: $17,404. Undergraduates: $16,730. ***Tuition waivers:*** Full or partial for employees or children of employees, senior citizens.
LOANS ***Student loans:*** $10,196,440 (90% need-based, 10% non-need-based). 88% of past graduating class borrowed through all loan programs. *Average indebtedness per student:* $47,542. ***Average need-based loan:*** Freshmen: $3508. Undergraduates: $4485. ***Parent loans:*** $2,743,130 (93% need-based, 7% non-need-based). ***Programs:*** Federal Direct (Subsidized and Unsubsidized Stafford, PLUS).
WORK-STUDY ***Federal work-study:*** Total amount: $466,148; jobs available. ***State or other work-study/employment:*** Part-time jobs available.
ATHLETIC AWARDS Total amount: $1,418,724 (53% need-based, 47% non-need-based).
APPLYING FOR FINANCIAL AID ***Required financial aid forms:*** FAFSA, state aid form, business/farm supplement. ***Financial aid deadline:*** Continuous. ***Notification date:*** Continuous beginning 9/15.
CONTACT Ms. Yalanda Cole, Assistant Director of Financial Aid, Chestnut Hill College, 9601 Germantown Avenue, Philadelphia, PA 19118-2693, 215-248-7182 or toll-free 800-248-0052. *Fax:* 215-242-7705. *E-mail:* finaid@chc.edu.
Website: http://www.chc.edu/.

CHEYNEY UNIVERSITY OF PENNSYLVANIA

Cheyney, PA

CONTACT Mr. James Brown, Director of Financial Aid, Cheyney University of Pennsylvania, 1837 University Circle, Cheyney, PA 19319, 610-399-2302 or toll-free 800-CHEYNEY. *Fax:* 610-399-2411. *E-mail:* jbrown@cheyney.edu.
Website: http://www.cheyney.edu/.

CHICAGO STATE UNIVERSITY

Chicago, IL

CONTACT Ms. Cathy Davis, Director of Student Financial Aid, Chicago State University, 9501 South Martin Luther King Drive, Chicago, IL 60628, 773-995-2304. *E-mail:* cdavis58@csu.edu.
Website: http://www.csu.edu/.

CHOWAN UNIVERSITY

Murfreesboro, NC

Tuition & fees: N/R	Average undergraduate aid package: $22,457

ABOUT THE INSTITUTION Independent Baptist, coed. ***Awards:*** associate, bachelor's, and master's degrees. 39 undergraduate majors. Federal methodology is used as a basis for awarding need-based institutional aid.
FRESHMAN FINANCIAL AID (Fall 2019, est.) 394 applied for aid; of those 95% were deemed to have need. 100% of freshmen with need received aid; of those 7% had need fully met. ***Average percent of need met:*** 73% (excluding resources awarded to replace EFC). ***Average financial aid package:*** $23,462 (excluding resources awarded to replace EFC). 4% of all full-time freshmen had no need and received non-need-based gift aid.
UNDERGRADUATE FINANCIAL AID (Fall 2019, est.) 1,261 applied for aid; of those 96% were deemed to have need. 100% of undergraduates with need received aid; of those 14% had need fully met. ***Average percent of need met:*** 81% (excluding resources awarded to replace EFC). ***Average financial aid package:*** $22,457 (excluding resources awarded to replace EFC). 4% of all full-time undergraduates had no need and received non-need-based gift aid.
GIFT AID (NEED-BASED) ***Total amount:*** $22,247,189 (22% federal, 14% state, 62% institutional, 2% external sources). ***Receiving aid:*** Freshmen: 88% (376); all full-time undergraduates: 93% (1,212). ***Average award:*** Freshmen: $19,880; Undergraduates: $17,362. ***Scholarships, grants, and awards:*** Federal Pell, FSEOG, state, private, college/university gift aid from institutional funds.
GIFT AID (NON-NEED-BASED) ***Total amount:*** $112,149 (10% federal, 90% state). ***Receiving aid:*** Undergraduates: 1% (9). ***Average award:*** Freshmen: $8988. Undergraduates: $9725. ***Scholarships, grants, and awards by category:*** *Academic interests/achievement:* 1,304 awards ($6,431,746 total): general academic interests/achievements. *Creative arts/performance:* 36 awards ($88,024 total): music. *Special achievements/activities:* 574 awards ($1,628,750 total): leadership. *Special characteristics:* 29 awards ($228,230 total): children of educators, children of faculty/staff, children of public servants, children of union members/company employees, first-generation college students, general special characteristics, handicapped students, international students, local/state students, out-of-state students, public servants, relatives of clergy, religious affiliation, veterans, veterans' children.
LOANS ***Student loans:*** $8,863,969 (46% need-based, 54% non-need-based). 85% of past graduating class borrowed through all loan programs. *Average indebtedness per student:* $37,579. ***Average need-based loan:*** Freshmen: $3008. Undergraduates: $4033. ***Parent loans:*** $3,768,879 (100% non-need-based). ***Programs:*** Federal Direct (Subsidized and Unsubsidized Stafford, PLUS), state, alternative loans.
WORK-STUDY ***Federal work-study:*** Total amount: $320,593; 260 jobs averaging $1233. ***State or other work-study/employment:*** 260 part-time jobs averaging $1640.
ATHLETIC AWARDS Total amount: $2,738,501 (100% need-based).
APPLYING FOR FINANCIAL AID ***Required financial aid form:*** FAFSA. ***Financial aid deadline (priority):*** 5/1. ***Notification date:*** Continuous beginning 12/1. Students must reply within 2 weeks of notification.
CONTACT Mrs. Ruth W. Casper, Director of Financial Aid, Chowan University, One University Place, Murfreesboro, NC 27855, 252-398-6535 Ext. 6269 or toll-free 888-4-CHOWAN. *Fax:* 252-398-6513. *E-mail:* wommar@chowan.edu.
Website: http://www.chowan.edu/.

CHRISTENDOM COLLEGE

Front Royal, VA

ABOUT THE INSTITUTION Independent Roman Catholic, coed. ***Awards:*** associate, bachelor's, and master's degrees. 8 undergraduate majors.
GIFT AID (NEED-BASED) ***Scholarships, grants, and awards:*** state, private, college/university gift aid from institutional funds.
GIFT AID (NON-NEED-BASED) ***Scholarships, grants, and awards by category:*** *Academic interests/achievement:* general academic interests/achievements. *Special characteristics:* siblings of current students.
LOANS ***Programs:*** college/university.
WORK-STUDY ***State or other work-study/employment:*** Total amount: $577,484 (100% non-need-based). 201 part-time jobs averaging $2873.
APPLYING FOR FINANCIAL AID ***Required financial aid form:*** institution's own form.
CONTACT Ms. Alisa Polk, Financial Aid Officer, Christendom College, 134 Christendom Drive, Front Royal, VA 22630-5103, 800-877-5456 Ext. 1214 or toll-free 800-877-5456. *Fax:* 540-631-0297. *E-mail:* apolk@christendom.edu.
Website: http://www.christendom.edu/.

CHRISTIAN BROTHERS UNIVERSITY

Memphis, TN

Tuition & fees: N/R | **Average undergraduate aid package: $26,172**

ABOUT THE INSTITUTION Independent Roman Catholic, coed. ***Awards:*** associate, bachelor's, and master's degrees. 43 undergraduate majors. ***Total enrollment:*** 1,888. Undergraduates: 1,674. Freshmen: 395. Federal methodology is used as a basis for awarding need-based institutional aid.

FRESHMAN FINANCIAL AID (Fall 2019, est.) 339 applied for aid; of those 75% were deemed to have need. 100% of freshmen with need received aid; of those 93% had need fully met. ***Average percent of need met:*** 98% (excluding resources awarded to replace EFC). ***Average financial aid package:*** $30,439 (excluding resources awarded to replace EFC). 25% of all full-time freshmen had no need and received non-need-based gift aid.

UNDERGRADUATE FINANCIAL AID (Fall 2019, est.) 1,353 applied for aid; of those 67% were deemed to have need. 100% of undergraduates with need received aid; of those 83% had need fully met. ***Average percent of need met:*** 92% (excluding resources awarded to replace EFC). ***Average financial aid package:*** $26,172 (excluding resources awarded to replace EFC). 26% of all full-time undergraduates had no need and received non-need-based gift aid.

GIFT AID (NEED-BASED) ***Total amount:*** $19,896,188 (16% federal, 16% state, 66% institutional, 2% external sources). ***Receiving aid:*** Freshmen: 75% (253); all full-time undergraduates: 66% (888). ***Average award:*** Freshmen: $26,105; Undergraduates: $21,458. ***Scholarships, grants, and awards:*** Federal Pell, FSEOG, state, private, college/university gift aid from institutional funds.

GIFT AID (NON-NEED-BASED) ***Total amount:*** $13,261,140 (2% state, 73% institutional, 25% external sources). ***Receiving aid:*** Freshmen: 10% (34). Undergraduates: 8% (110). ***Average award:*** Freshmen: $20,155. Undergraduates: $19,879. ***Scholarships, grants, and awards by category:*** *Academic interests/achievement:* 1,139 awards ($11,107,186 total): computer science, education, engineering/technologies, general academic interests/achievements, mathematics. *Creative arts/performance:* 4 awards ($11,500 total): performing arts. *Special achievements/activities:* 477 awards ($858,913 total): cheerleading/drum major, community service, general special achievements/activities, leadership, memberships. *Special characteristics:* 645 awards ($8,337,276 total): children and siblings of alumni, children of public servants, ethnic background, general special characteristics, international students, members of minority groups, out-of-state students, veterans, veterans' children. ***ROTC:*** Army cooperative, Naval cooperative, Air Force cooperative.

LOANS ***Student loans:*** $5,098,146 (79% need-based, 21% non-need-based). 69% of past graduating class borrowed through all loan programs. *Average indebtedness per student:* $33,649. ***Average need-based loan:*** Freshmen: $1875. Undergraduates: $2844. ***Parent loans:*** $1,297,378 (62% need-based, 38% non-need-based). ***Programs:*** Federal Direct (Subsidized and Unsubsidized Stafford, PLUS), Perkins, college/university, alternative loans.

WORK-STUDY ***Federal work-study:*** Total amount: $129,786; 118 jobs averaging $1100. ***State or other work-study/employment:*** Total amount: $112,742 (13% need-based, 87% non-need-based). 111 part-time jobs averaging $1016.

ATHLETIC AWARDS Total amount: $2,798,219 (38% need-based, 62% non-need-based).

APPLYING FOR FINANCIAL AID ***Required financial aid form:*** FAFSA. ***Financial aid deadline:*** Continuous. ***Notification date:*** Continuous beginning 2/1. Students must reply within 2 weeks of notification.

CONTACT Elizabeth Romagni, Director of Financial Aid, Christian Brothers University, 650 East Parkway South, Memphis, TN 38104, 901-321-3305 or toll-free 877-321-4CBU. *Fax:* 901-321-3327. *E-mail:* Elizabeth.Romagni@cbu.edu.
Website: http://www.cbu.edu/.

CHRISTOPHER NEWPORT UNIVERSITY

Newport News, VA

Tuition & fees (VA res): $14,924 | **Average undergraduate aid package: $10,790**

ABOUT THE INSTITUTION State-supported, coed. ***Awards:*** bachelor's and master's degrees. 39 undergraduate majors. ***Total enrollment:*** 4,957. Undergraduates: 4,857. Freshmen: 1,228. Federal methodology is used as a basis for awarding need-based institutional aid.

UNDERGRADUATE EXPENSES for 2019–2020 ***Application fee:*** $65. ***Tuition, state resident:*** full-time $9100; part-time $378 per credit hour. ***Tuition, nonresident:*** full-time $21,566; part-time $897 per credit hour. ***Required fees:*** full-time $5824; $244 per credit hour. Full-time tuition and fees vary according to course load. Part-time tuition and fees vary according to course load. ***College room and board:*** $11,760; ***Room only:*** $7238. Room and board charges vary according to board plan and housing facility.

FRESHMAN FINANCIAL AID (Fall 2019, est.) 1037 applied for aid; of those 56% were deemed to have need. 92% of freshmen with need received aid; of those 23% had need fully met. ***Average percent of need met:*** 67% (excluding resources awarded to replace EFC). ***Average financial aid package:*** $10,257 (excluding resources awarded to replace EFC). 20% of all full-time freshmen had no need and received non-need-based gift aid.

UNDERGRADUATE FINANCIAL AID (Fall 2019, est.) 3,128 applied for aid; of those 65% were deemed to have need. 93% of undergraduates with need received aid; of those 23% had need fully met. ***Average percent of need met:*** 69% (excluding resources awarded to replace EFC). ***Average financial aid package:*** $10,790 (excluding resources awarded to replace EFC). 16% of all full-time undergraduates had no need and received non-need-based gift aid.

GIFT AID (NEED-BASED) ***Total amount:*** $11,108,773 (26% federal, 50% state, 24% institutional). ***Receiving aid:*** Freshmen: 34% (417); all full-time undergraduates: 30% (1,400). ***Average award:*** Freshmen: $7361; Undergraduates: $7839. ***Scholarships, grants, and awards:*** Federal Pell, FSEOG, state, private, college/university gift aid from institutional funds.

GIFT AID (NON-NEED-BASED) ***Total amount:*** $6,597,583 (8% federal, 3% state, 73% institutional, 16% external sources). ***Receiving aid:*** Freshmen: 19% (235). Undergraduates: 15% (693). ***Average award:*** Freshmen: $3435. Undergraduates: $3674. ***Scholarships, grants, and awards by category:*** *Academic interests/achievement:* 98 awards ($287,859 total): biological sciences, business, communication, computer science, education, engineering/technologies, English, foreign languages, general academic interests/achievements, humanities, mathematics, military science, physical sciences, premedicine, social sciences. *Creative arts/performance:* 97 awards ($196,131 total): art/fine arts, music, performing arts, theater/drama. *Special achievements/activities:* 1,148 awards ($4,070,600 total): community service, general special achievements/activities, leadership. *Special characteristics:* 57 awards ($148,300 total): adult students, first-generation college students, general special characteristics, local/state students, members of minority groups. ***Tuition waivers:*** Full or partial for employees or children of employees, senior citizens. ***ROTC:*** Army.

LOANS ***Student loans:*** $23,446,342 (28% need-based, 72% non-need-based). 61% of past graduating class borrowed through all loan programs. *Average indebtedness per student:* $32,878. ***Average need-based loan:*** Freshmen: $3399. Undergraduates: $5410. ***Parent loans:*** $8,942,459 (100% non-need-based). ***Programs:*** Federal Direct (Subsidized and Unsubsidized Stafford, PLUS).

WORK-STUDY ***Federal work-study:*** Total amount: $198,700; 131 jobs averaging $1517. ***State or other work-study/employment:*** Total amount: $3,140,250 (100% non-need-based). 1,401 part-time jobs averaging $2184.

APPLYING FOR FINANCIAL AID ***Required financial aid form:*** FAFSA. ***Financial aid deadline (priority):*** 3/1. ***Notification date:*** Continuous beginning 3/1. Students must reply by 5/1.

CONTACT Christina Russell, Director of Financial Aid, Christopher Newport University, 1 Avenue of the Arts, Newport News, VA 23606, 757-594-7170 or toll-free 800-333-4268. *Fax:* 757-594-7113. *E-mail:* christina.russell@cnu.edu.
Website: http://www.cnu.edu/.

CINCINNATI COLLEGE OF MORTUARY SCIENCE

Cincinnati, OH

CONTACT Ms. Pat Leon, Financial Aid Officer , Cincinnati College of Mortuary Science, 645 West North Bend Road, Cincinnati, OH 45224-1428, 513-761-2020 or toll-free 888-377-8433.
Website: http://www.ccms.edu/.

THE CITADEL, THE MILITARY COLLEGE OF SOUTH CAROLINA

Charleston, SC

Tuition & fees (area res): $14,483	Average undergraduate aid package: $19,584

ABOUT THE INSTITUTION State-supported, coed, primarily men. ***Awards:*** certificates, bachelor's, and master's degrees. 23 undergraduate majors. ***Total enrollment:*** 3,767. Undergraduates: 2,920. Freshmen: 643. Federal methodology is used as a basis for awarding need-based institutional aid.

UNDERGRADUATE EXPENSES for 2020–2021 ***Application fee:*** $40. ***Tuition, area resident:*** full-time $14,483. ***Tuition, state resident:*** full-time $14,483. ***Tuition, nonresident:*** full-time $38,368. ***College room and board:*** $7957.

FRESHMAN FINANCIAL AID (Fall 2019, est.) 546 applied for aid; of those 72% were deemed to have need. 96% of freshmen with need received aid; of those 23% had need fully met. ***Average percent of need met:*** 58% (excluding resources awarded to replace EFC). ***Average financial aid package:*** $17,935 (excluding resources awarded to replace EFC). 28% of all full-time freshmen had no need and received non-need-based gift aid.

UNDERGRADUATE FINANCIAL AID (Fall 2019, est.) 1,985 applied for aid; of those 75% were deemed to have need. 97% of undergraduates with need received aid; of those 31% had need fully met. ***Average percent of need met:*** 67% (excluding resources awarded to replace EFC). ***Average financial aid package:*** $19,584 (excluding resources awarded to replace EFC). 25% of all full-time undergraduates had no need and received non-need-based gift aid.

GIFT AID (NEED-BASED) ***Total amount:*** $20,900,260 (15% federal, 14% state, 29% institutional, 42% external sources). ***Receiving aid:*** Freshmen: 52% (337); all full-time undergraduates: 46% (1,247). ***Average award:*** Freshmen: $17,319; Undergraduates: $19,036. ***Scholarships, grants, and awards:*** Federal Pell, FSEOG, state, private, college/university gift aid from institutional funds.

GIFT AID (NON-NEED-BASED) ***Total amount:*** $11,034,363 (1% federal, 19% state, 22% institutional, 58% external sources). ***Receiving aid:*** Freshmen: 11% (70). Undergraduates: 12% (335). ***Average award:*** Freshmen: $9343. Undergraduates: $16,160. ***Scholarships, grants, and awards by category:*** *Academic interests/achievement:* biological sciences, business, computer science, education, engineering/technologies, general academic interests/achievements, home economics, humanities, mathematics, military science, physical sciences, religion/biblical studies. *Creative arts/performance:* journalism/publications, music. *Special achievements/activities:* community service, leadership, religious involvement. *Special characteristics:* children and siblings of alumni, children with a deceased or disabled parent, ethnic background, local/state students, out-of-state students, veterans, veterans' children. ***Tuition waivers:*** Full or partial for employees or children of employees, senior citizens. ***ROTC:*** Army, Naval, Air Force.

LOANS ***Student loans:*** $16,778,150 (75% need-based, 25% non-need-based). 60% of past graduating class borrowed through all loan programs. *Average indebtedness per student:* $28,159. ***Average need-based loan:*** Freshmen: $3443. Undergraduates: $4331. ***Parent loans:*** $7,295,100 (85% need-based, 15% non-need-based). ***Programs:*** Federal Direct (Subsidized and Unsubsidized Stafford, PLUS), Perkins, SC Teacher's Loan.

WORK-STUDY ***Federal work-study:*** Total amount: $165,398; jobs available.

ATHLETIC AWARDS Total amount: $5,964,168 (49% need-based, 51% non-need-based).

APPLYING FOR FINANCIAL AID ***Required financial aid form:*** FAFSA. ***Financial aid deadline (priority):*** 3/1. ***Notification date:*** Continuous beginning 12/15. Students must reply within 2 weeks of notification.

CONTACT Hank M. Fuller, Director of Financial Aid and Scholarships, The Citadel, The Military College of South Carolina, 171 Moultrie Street, Charleston, SC 29409, 843-953-5187 or toll-free 800-868-1842. *Fax:* 843-953-6759. *E-mail:* fullerh@citadel.edu.
Website: http://www.citadel.edu/.

CITY COLLEGE OF THE CITY UNIVERSITY OF NEW YORK

New York, NY

Tuition & fees (area res): $14,500	Average undergraduate aid package: $7273

ABOUT THE INSTITUTION State and locally supported, coed. ***Awards:*** certificates, bachelor's, master's, and doctoral degrees. 66 undergraduate majors. ***Total enrollment:*** 15,682. Undergraduates: 13,224. Freshmen: 2,095. Both federal and institutional methodology are used as a basis for awarding need-based institutional aid.

UNDERGRADUATE EXPENSES for 2020–2021 ***Application fee:*** $65. ***Tuition, area resident:*** full-time $13,860; part-time $13,860 per credit hour. ***Tuition, state resident:*** full-time $13,860; part-time $13,860 per credit hour. ***Tuition, nonresident:*** full-time $18,600; part-time $18,600 per credit hour. ***Required fees:*** full-time $640. ***Room only:*** $12,123.

FRESHMAN FINANCIAL AID (Fall 2018) 4653 applied for aid; of those 99% were deemed to have need. 99% of freshmen with need received aid; of those 52% had need fully met. ***Average percent of need met:*** 84% (excluding resources awarded to replace EFC). ***Average financial aid package:*** $3850 (excluding resources awarded to replace EFC). 116% of all full-time freshmen had no need and received non-need-based gift aid.

UNDERGRADUATE FINANCIAL AID (Fall 2018) 9,040 applied for aid; of those 98% were deemed to have need. 100% of undergraduates with need received aid; of those 14% had need fully met. ***Average percent of need met:*** 82% (excluding resources awarded to replace EFC). ***Average financial aid package:*** $7273 (excluding resources awarded to replace EFC). 9% of all full-time undergraduates had no need and received non-need-based gift aid.

GIFT AID (NEED-BASED) ***Total amount:*** $94,926,358 (59% federal, 33% state, 7% institutional, 1% external sources). ***Receiving aid:*** Freshmen: 163% (3,344); all full-time undergraduates: 57% (7,855). ***Average award:*** Freshmen: $2809; Undergraduates: $6441. ***Scholarships, grants, and awards:*** Federal Pell, state, private, college/university gift aid from institutional funds.

GIFT AID (NON-NEED-BASED) ***Total amount:*** $96,182,853 (59% federal, 33% state, 7% institutional, 1% external sources). ***Receiving aid:*** Freshmen: 116% (2,385). Undergraduates: 9% (1,220). ***Average award:*** Freshmen: $329. Undergraduates: $195. ***Scholarships, grants, and awards by category:*** *Academic interests/achievement:* architecture, area/ethnic studies, biological sciences, communication, computer science, education, engineering/technologies, English, foreign languages, general academic interests/achievements, humanities, international studies, mathematics, premedicine, social sciences. *Creative arts/performance:* applied art and design, art/fine arts, cinema/film/broadcasting, creative writing, general creative arts/performance, music, performing arts. *Special achievements/activities:* community service, general special achievements/activities, leadership. *Special characteristics:* children and siblings of alumni, local/state students. ***ROTC:*** Army.

LOANS ***Student loans:*** $18,733,197 (95% need-based, 5% non-need-based). ***Average need-based loan:*** Freshmen: $3986. Undergraduates: $7354. ***Parent loans:*** $1,737,801 (50% need-based, 50% non-need-based). ***Programs:*** Federal Direct (Subsidized and Unsubsidized Stafford), Perkins, Federal Nursing, state, college/university.

WORK-STUDY ***Federal work-study:*** Total amount: $1,283,648; jobs available. ***State or other work-study/employment:*** Total amount: $76,650,571 (50% need-based, 50% non-need-based). Part-time jobs available.

APPLYING FOR FINANCIAL AID ***Required financial aid form:*** FAFSA. ***Financial aid deadline:*** Continuous. ***Notification date:*** Continuous.

CONTACT Ms. Arshaw Ramkaran, Director of Financial Aid, City College of the City University of New York, 160 Convent Avenue, Wille Administration Building, Room 104, New York, NY 10031, 212-650-5824. *Fax:* 212-650-5829. *E-mail:* aramkaran@ccny.cuny.edu.
Website: http://www.ccny.cuny.edu/.

CITY VISION UNIVERSITY

Kansas City, MO

CONTACT Mrs. Ann Marie Cameron-Thompson, Director of Financial Aid, City Vision University, City Vision Financial Aid, 48 Pleasant Street, Dorchester, MA 02125, 617-282-9798 Ext. 108. *Fax:* 816-256-8471. *E-mail:* financialaid@cityvision.edu . *Website:* http://www.cityvision.edu/.

CLAFLIN UNIVERSITY

Orangeburg, SC

CONTACT Ms. Terria C. Williams, Director of Financial Aid, Claflin University, Corson Hall, 400 Magnolia Street, Orangeburg, SC 29115, 803-535-5720 or toll-free 800-922-1276. *Fax:* 803-535-5383. *E-mail:* twilliams@claflin.edu. *Website:* http://www.claflin.edu/.

CLAREMONT MCKENNA COLLEGE

Claremont, CA

Tuition & fees: $56,475	Average undergraduate aid package: $57,151

ABOUT THE INSTITUTION Independent, coed. ***Awards:*** bachelor's and master's degrees. 34 undergraduate majors. ***Total enrollment:*** 1,346. Undergraduates: 1,343. Freshmen: 328. Both federal and institutional methodology are used as a basis for awarding need-based institutional aid.

UNDERGRADUATE EXPENSES for 2019–2020 *Application fee:* $70. ***Comprehensive fee:*** $73,775 includes full-time tuition ($56,190), mandatory fees ($285), and room and board ($17,300). ***College room only:*** $9300. Room and board charges vary according to board plan and housing facility. ***Part-time tuition:*** $9365 per course. Part-time tuition and fees vary according to course load.

FRESHMAN FINANCIAL AID (Fall 2019, est.) 152 applied for aid; of those 93% were deemed to have need. 100% of freshmen with need received aid; of those 100% had need fully met. ***Average percent of need met:*** 100% (excluding resources awarded to replace EFC). ***Average financial aid package:*** $60,818 (excluding resources awarded to replace EFC). 2% of all full-time freshmen had no need and received non-need-based gift aid.

UNDERGRADUATE FINANCIAL AID (Fall 2019, est.) 636 applied for aid; of those 89% were deemed to have need. 100% of undergraduates with need received aid; of those 100% had need fully met. ***Average percent of need met:*** 100% (excluding resources awarded to replace EFC). ***Average financial aid package:*** $57,151 (excluding resources awarded to replace EFC). 5% of all full-time undergraduates had no need and received non-need-based gift aid.

GIFT AID (NEED-BASED) *Total amount:* $29,008,084 (4% federal, 4% state, 90% institutional, 2% external sources). ***Receiving aid:*** Freshmen: 42% (138); all full-time undergraduates: 41% (550). ***Average award:*** Freshmen: $56,137; Undergraduates: $51,838. ***Scholarships, grants, and awards:*** Federal Pell, FSEOG, state, private, college/university gift aid from institutional funds.

GIFT AID (NON-NEED-BASED) *Total amount:* $1,371,569 (84% institutional, 16% external sources). ***Receiving aid:*** Freshmen: 17% (55). Undergraduates: 19% (248). ***Average award:*** Freshmen: $24,447. Undergraduates: $19,215. ***Scholarships, grants, and awards by category:*** *Academic interests/achievement:* general academic interests/achievements, military science. *Special achievements/activities:* leadership. *Special characteristics:* veterans. ***Tuition waivers:*** Full or partial for employees or children of employees. ***ROTC:*** Army, Air Force cooperative.

LOANS *Student loans:* $2,282,864 (63% need-based, 37% non-need-based). 36% of past graduating class borrowed through all loan programs. *Average indebtedness per student:* $21,450. ***Average need-based loan:*** Freshmen: $3667. Undergraduates: $4090. ***Parent loans:*** $1,432,488 (100% non-need-based). ***Programs:*** Federal Direct (Subsidized and Unsubsidized Stafford, PLUS), Perkins, college/university.

WORK-STUDY *Federal work-study:* Total amount: $987,911; jobs available. ***State or other work-study/employment:*** Total amount: $386,991 (100% need-based). Part-time jobs available.

APPLYING FOR FINANCIAL AID *Required financial aid forms:* FAFSA, CSS Financial Aid PROFILE, state aid form, noncustodial (divorced/separated) parent's statement, business/farm supplement. ***Financial aid deadline:*** 2/1 (priority: 1/5). ***Notification date:*** 4/1. Students must reply by 5/1.

CONTACT Ms. Jennifer Sandoval-Dancs, Associate Vice President and Dean of Admissions and Financial Aid, Claremont McKenna College, 888 Columbia Avenue, Claremont, CA 91711, 909-621-8356. *Fax:* 909-607-0661. *E-mail:* finaid@cmc.edu. *Website:* http://www.cmc.edu/.

CLARION UNIVERSITY OF PENNSYLVANIA

Clarion, PA

Tuition & fees (PA res): $7716	Average undergraduate aid package: $11,687

ABOUT THE INSTITUTION State-supported, coed. ***Awards:*** certificates, bachelor's, master's, and doctoral degrees. 49 undergraduate majors. ***Total enrollment:*** 4,703. Undergraduates: 3,776. Freshmen: 755. Federal methodology is used as a basis for awarding need-based institutional aid.

UNDERGRADUATE EXPENSES for 2020–2021 *Application fee:* $40. ***One-time required fee:*** $50. ***Tuition, state resident:*** full-time $7716; part-time $322 per credit hour. ***Tuition, nonresident:*** full-time $11,574; part-time $482 per credit hour. Full-time tuition and fees vary according to course load and location. Part-time tuition and fees vary according to course load and location. Room and board charges vary according to board plan and housing facility.

FRESHMAN FINANCIAL AID (Fall 2019, est.) 726 applied for aid; of those 86% were deemed to have need. 99% of freshmen with need received aid; of those 9% had need fully met. ***Average percent of need met:*** 41% (excluding resources awarded to replace EFC). ***Average financial aid package:*** $12,391 (excluding resources awarded to replace EFC). 12% of all full-time freshmen had no need and received non-need-based gift aid.

UNDERGRADUATE FINANCIAL AID (Fall 2019, est.) 2,785 applied for aid; of those 86% were deemed to have need. 99% of undergraduates with need received aid; of those 6% had need fully met. ***Average percent of need met:*** 47% (excluding resources awarded to replace EFC). ***Average financial aid package:*** $11,687 (excluding resources awarded to replace EFC). 9% of all full-time undergraduates had no need and received non-need-based gift aid.

GIFT AID (NEED-BASED) *Total amount:* $16,352,183 (41% federal, 25% state, 26% institutional, 8% external sources). ***Receiving aid:*** Freshmen: 58% (427); all full-time undergraduates: 55% (1,634). ***Average award:*** Freshmen: $6097; Undergraduates: $6100. ***Scholarships, grants, and awards:*** Federal Pell, FSEOG, state, private, college/university gift aid from institutional funds.

GIFT AID (NON-NEED-BASED) *Total amount:* $1,109,781 (7% state, 82% institutional, 11% external sources). ***Receiving aid:*** Freshmen: 66% (488). Undergraduates: 45% (1,344). ***Average award:*** Freshmen: $2633. Undergraduates: $2401. ***Scholarships, grants, and awards by category:*** *Academic interests/achievement:* biological sciences, business, communication, computer science, education, English, foreign languages, general academic interests/achievements, home economics, humanities, international studies, library science, mathematics, military science, physical sciences, premedicine, social sciences. *Creative arts/performance:* applied art and design, debating, general creative arts/performance, music, theater/drama. *Special achievements/activities:* community service, leadership. *Special characteristics:* children of faculty/staff, children of union members/company employees, children with a deceased or disabled parent, first-generation college students, local/state students, members of minority groups, previous college experience, spouses of current students, veterans. ***Tuition waivers:*** Full or partial for employees or children of employees, senior citizens. ***ROTC:*** Army.

LOANS *Student loans:* $27,408,330 (87% need-based, 13% non-need-based). 76% of past graduating class borrowed through all loan programs. *Average indebtedness per student:* $35,054. ***Average need-based loan:*** Freshmen: $3118. Undergraduates: $4047. ***Parent loans:*** $6,329,517 (89% need-based, 11% non-need-based). ***Programs:*** Federal Direct (Subsidized and Unsubsidized Stafford, PLUS), alternative loans.

WORK-STUDY Federal work-study jobs available. ***State or other work-study/employment:*** Total amount: $745,700 (100% non-need-based). 414 part-time jobs averaging $1801.

ATHLETIC AWARDS Total amount: $949,765 (78% need-based, 22% non-need-based).

APPLYING FOR FINANCIAL AID ***Required financial aid forms:*** FAFSA, state aid form. ***Financial aid deadline (priority):*** 5/1. ***Notification date:*** Continuous beginning 12/23.

CONTACT Ms. Sue A. Bloom, Director, Student Financial Services, Clarion University of Pennsylvania, 122 Becht Hall, Clarion, PA 16214, 814-393-2315 or toll-free 800-672-7171. *Fax:* 814-393-2520. *E-mail:* stfinservice@clarion.edu.
Website: http://www.clarion.edu/.

CLARK ATLANTA UNIVERSITY

Atlanta, GA

CONTACT Office of Financial Aid, Clark Atlanta University, 223 James P. Brawley Drive, Atlanta, GA 30314, 404-880-8992 or toll-free 800-688-3228. *Fax:* 404-880-8070. *E-mail:* studentfinancialaid@cau.edu.
Website: http://www.cau.edu/.

CLARKE UNIVERSITY

Dubuque, IA

Tuition & fees: $33,350	Average undergraduate aid package: $30,781

ABOUT THE INSTITUTION Independent Roman Catholic, coed. ***Awards:*** associate, bachelor's, master's, and doctoral degrees. 31 undergraduate majors. ***Total enrollment:*** 1,004. Undergraduates: 761. Freshmen: 162. Both federal and institutional methodology are used as a basis for awarding need-based institutional aid.

UNDERGRADUATE EXPENSES for 2019–2020 ***Application fee:*** $25. ***Tuition:*** full-time $33,350.

FRESHMAN FINANCIAL AID (Fall 2018) 139 applied for aid; of those 94% were deemed to have need. 100% of freshmen with need received aid; of those 27% had need fully met. ***Average percent of need met:*** 85% (excluding resources awarded to replace EFC). ***Average financial aid package:*** $33,091 (excluding resources awarded to replace EFC). 19% of all full-time freshmen had no need and received non-need-based gift aid.

UNDERGRADUATE FINANCIAL AID (Fall 2018) 417 applied for aid; of those 93% were deemed to have need. 100% of undergraduates with need received aid; of those 26% had need fully met. ***Average percent of need met:*** 81% (excluding resources awarded to replace EFC). ***Average financial aid package:*** $30,781 (excluding resources awarded to replace EFC). 18% of all full-time undergraduates had no need and received non-need-based gift aid.

GIFT AID (NEED-BASED) ***Total amount:*** $9,786,336 (12% federal, 9% state, 76% institutional, 3% external sources). ***Receiving aid:*** Freshmen: 70% (130); all full-time undergraduates: 58% (386). ***Average award:*** Freshmen: $39,030; Undergraduates: $25,738. ***Scholarships, grants, and awards:*** Federal Pell, FSEOG, state, private, college/university gift aid from institutional funds.

GIFT AID (NON-NEED-BASED) ***Total amount:*** $1,287,230 (99% institutional, 1% external sources). ***Receiving aid:*** Freshmen: 70% (130). Undergraduates: 58% (385). ***Average award:*** Freshmen: $29,323. Undergraduates: $28,892. ***Scholarships, grants, and awards by category:*** *Academic interests/achievement:* general academic interests/achievements. *Creative arts/performance:* applied art and design, music, theater/drama. *Special achievements/activities:* community service, general special achievements/activities, leadership, religious involvement. *Special characteristics:* children and siblings of alumni, children of faculty/staff, relatives of clergy, siblings of current students. ***ROTC:*** Army cooperative.

LOANS ***Student loans:*** $7,221,018 (30% need-based, 70% non-need-based). 46% of past graduating class borrowed through all loan programs. *Average indebtedness per student:* $11,079. ***Average need-based loan:*** Freshmen: $3045. Undergraduates: $4055. ***Parent loans:*** $2,067,633 (93% need-based, 7% non-need-based). ***Programs:*** Federal Direct (Subsidized and Unsubsidized Stafford, PLUS), Federal Nursing, college/university.

WORK-STUDY ***Federal work-study:*** Total amount: $898,000; jobs available.

ATHLETIC AWARDS Total amount: $2,789,194 (100% need-based).

APPLYING FOR FINANCIAL AID ***Required financial aid forms:*** FAFSA, institution's own form. ***Notification date:*** Continuous.

CONTACT Robert Hoover, Director of Financial Aid, Clarke University, 1550 Clarke Drive, Dubuque, IA 52001-3198, 563-588-6338 or toll-free 800-383-2345. *Fax:* 563-584-8605. *E-mail:* robert.hoover@clarke.edu.
Website: http://www.clarke.edu/.

CLARKSON COLLEGE

Omaha, NE

CONTACT Pam Shelton, Director of Financial Aid, Clarkson College, 101 South 42nd Street, Omaha, NE 68131-2739, 402-552-2749 or toll-free 800-647-5500. *Fax:* 402-552-6165. *E-mail:* shelton@clarksoncollege.edu.
Website: http://www.clarksoncollege.edu/.

CLARKSON UNIVERSITY

Potsdam, NY

Tuition & fees: $52,724	Average undergraduate aid package: $46,636

ABOUT THE INSTITUTION Independent, coed. ***Awards:*** certificates, bachelor's, master's, and doctoral degrees. 36 undergraduate majors. ***Total enrollment:*** 4,301. Undergraduates: 3,081. Freshmen: 790. Federal methodology is used as a basis for awarding need-based institutional aid.

UNDERGRADUATE EXPENSES for 2020–2021 ***Application fee:*** $50. ***Comprehensive fee:*** $68,510 includes full-time tuition ($51,454), mandatory fees ($1270), and room and board ($15,786). ***College room only:*** $8480. Full-time tuition and fees vary according to course load. Room and board charges vary according to board plan and housing facility. ***Part-time tuition:*** $1715 per credit hour. Part-time tuition and fees vary according to course load.

FRESHMAN FINANCIAL AID (Fall 2019, est.) 724 applied for aid; of those 89% were deemed to have need. 100% of freshmen with need received aid; of those 27% had need fully met. ***Average percent of need met:*** 90% (excluding resources awarded to replace EFC). ***Average financial aid package:*** $48,600 (excluding resources awarded to replace EFC). 16% of all full-time freshmen had no need and received non-need-based gift aid.

UNDERGRADUATE FINANCIAL AID (Fall 2019, est.) 2,620 applied for aid; of those 92% were deemed to have need. 100% of undergraduates with need received aid; of those 24% had need fully met. ***Average percent of need met:*** 90% (excluding resources awarded to replace EFC). ***Average financial aid package:*** $46,636 (excluding resources awarded to replace EFC). 16% of all full-time undergraduates had no need and received non-need-based gift aid.

GIFT AID (NEED-BASED) ***Total amount:*** $83,328,698 (6% federal, 3% state, 90% institutional, 1% external sources). ***Receiving aid:*** Freshmen: 81% (639); all full-time undergraduates: 80% (2,384). ***Average award:*** Freshmen: $38,195; Undergraduates: $34,953. ***Scholarships, grants, and awards:*** Federal Pell, FSEOG, state, private, college/university gift aid from institutional funds, HEOP.

GIFT AID (NON-NEED-BASED) ***Total amount:*** $21,349,346 (10% federal, 87% institutional, 3% external sources). ***Receiving aid:*** Freshmen: 16% (126). Undergraduates: 14% (405). ***Average award:*** Freshmen: $32,143. Undergraduates: $27,576. ***Scholarships, grants, and awards by category:*** *Academic interests/achievement:* 3,011 awards ($57,735,139 total): biological sciences, business, communication, computer science, engineering/technologies, general academic interests/achievements, humanities, mathematics, military science, physical sciences, social sciences. *Special achievements/activities:* 1,123 awards ($8,366,945 total): general special achievements/activities, leadership. *Special characteristics:* 1,621 awards ($6,318,824 total): children and siblings of alumni, children of faculty/staff, general special characteristics, international students, local/state students, members of minority groups, veterans. ***Tuition waivers:*** Full or partial for employees or children of employees. ***ROTC:*** Army, Air Force.

LOANS ***Student loans:*** $24,553,340 (69% need-based, 31% non-need-based). 100% of past graduating class borrowed through all loan programs. *Average indebtedness per student:* $29,000. ***Average need-based loan:*** Freshmen: $3498. Undergraduates: $4643. ***Parent loans:*** $7,226,659 (51% need-based, 49% non-need-based). ***Programs:*** Federal Direct (Subsidized and Unsubsidized Stafford, PLUS), Perkins, college/university, private/alternative loans.

WORK-STUDY ***Federal work-study:*** Total amount: $629,539; 1,403 jobs averaging $1800. ***State or other work-study/employment:*** Total amount: $606,592 (59% need-based, 41% non-need-based). 65 part-time jobs averaging $12,030.
ATHLETIC AWARDS Total amount: $2,288,811 (100% non-need-based).
APPLYING FOR FINANCIAL AID ***Required financial aid forms:*** FAFSA, state aid form. ***Financial aid deadline:*** 3/1 (priority: 2/1). ***Notification date:*** Continuous beginning 2/15. Students must reply by 5/1 or within 2 weeks of notification.
CONTACT Pamela Nichols, Director of Financial Aid, Clarkson University, 8 Clarkson Ave, Box 5615, Potsdam, NY 13699, 315-268-6413 or toll-free 800-527-6577. *Fax:* 315-268-3899. *E-mail:* pnichols@clarkson.edu.
Website: http://www.clarkson.edu/.

CLARKS SUMMIT UNIVERSITY

South Abington Township, PA

CONTACT Mrs. Deborah Cragle, Director of Financial Aid, Clarks Summit University, 538 Venard Road, South Abington Township, PA 18411, 570-586-2400 Ext. 9272 or toll-free 800-451-7664. *Fax:* 570-585-9470. *E-mail:* dcragle@clarkssummitu.edu.
Website: http://www.clarkssummitu.edu/.

CLARK UNIVERSITY

Worcester, MA

Tuition & fees: $47,200 **Average undergraduate aid package: $34,421**

ABOUT THE INSTITUTION Independent, coed. ***Awards:*** certificates, bachelor's, master's, and doctoral degrees. 48 undergraduate majors. ***Total enrollment:*** 3,122. Undergraduates: 2,304. Freshmen: 582. Both federal and institutional methodology are used as a basis for awarding need-based institutional aid.
UNDERGRADUATE EXPENSES for 2019–2020 ***Application fee:*** $60. ***Comprehensive fee:*** $56,680 includes full-time tuition ($46,850), mandatory fees ($350), and room and board ($9480). Room and board charges vary according to board plan and housing facility. ***Part-time tuition:*** $1464 per unit. ***Payment plan:*** Tuition prepayment.
FRESHMAN FINANCIAL AID (Fall 2019, est.) 555 applied for aid; of those 76% were deemed to have need. 99% of freshmen with need received aid; of those 28% had need fully met. ***Average percent of need met:*** 92% (excluding resources awarded to replace EFC). ***Average financial aid package:*** $36,130 (excluding resources awarded to replace EFC). 33% of all full-time freshmen had no need and received non-need-based gift aid.
UNDERGRADUATE FINANCIAL AID (Fall 2019, est.) 1,885 applied for aid; of those 77% were deemed to have need. 98% of undergraduates with need received aid; of those 29% had need fully met. ***Average percent of need met:*** 90% (excluding resources awarded to replace EFC). ***Average financial aid package:*** $34,421 (excluding resources awarded to replace EFC). 29% of all full-time undergraduates had no need and received non-need-based gift aid.
GIFT AID (NEED-BASED) ***Total amount:*** $40,503,262 (8% federal, 1% state, 91% institutional). ***Receiving aid:*** Freshmen: 62% (413); all full-time undergraduates: 63% (1,416). ***Average award:*** Freshmen: $28,463; Undergraduates: $30,669. ***Scholarships, grants, and awards:*** Federal Pell, FSEOG, state, college/university gift aid from institutional funds.
GIFT AID (NON-NEED-BASED) ***Total amount:*** $14,241,586 (100% institutional). ***Receiving aid:*** Freshmen: 14% (95). Undergraduates: 14% (321). ***Average award:*** Freshmen: $18,034. Undergraduates: $17,319. ***Scholarships, grants, and awards by category:*** *Academic interests/achievement:* general academic interests/achievements. *Special achievements/activities:* general special achievements/activities. ***Tuition waivers:*** Full or partial for employees or children of employees. ***ROTC:*** Army cooperative, Air Force cooperative.
LOANS ***Student loans:*** $13,125,453 (34% need-based, 66% non-need-based). 61% of past graduating class borrowed through all loan programs. *Average indebtedness per student:* $34,390. ***Average need-based loan:*** Freshmen: $3409. Undergraduates: $4336. ***Parent loans:*** $2,439,076 (24% need-based, 76% non-need-based). ***Programs:*** Federal Direct (Subsidized and Unsubsidized Stafford, PLUS), Perkins, state.
WORK-STUDY ***Federal work-study:*** Total amount: $1,208,874; jobs available.
APPLYING FOR FINANCIAL AID ***Required financial aid forms:*** FAFSA, CSS Financial Aid PROFILE, noncustodial (divorced/separated) parent's statement. ***Financial aid deadline:*** 2/1. ***Notification date:*** 3/31. Students must reply by 5/1 or within 2 weeks of notification.
CONTACT Ms. Mary Ellen Severance, Director of Financial Assistance, Clark University, 950 Main Street, Worcester, MA 01610-1477, 508-793-7478 or toll-free 800-GO-CLARK. *Fax:* 508-793-8802. *E-mail:* finaid@clarku.edu.
Website: http://www.clarku.edu/.

CLAYTON STATE UNIVERSITY

Morrow, GA

CONTACT Lakisha Sanders, Director of Financial Aid, Clayton State University, 2000 Clayton State Boulevard, Morrow, GA 30260, 678-466-4185. *Fax:* 678-466-4189. *E-mail:* financialaid@mail.clayton.edu.
Website: http://www.clayton.edu/.

CLEAR CREEK BAPTIST BIBLE COLLEGE

Pineville, KY

Tuition & fees: N/R **Average undergraduate aid package: $6709**

ABOUT THE INSTITUTION Independent Southern Baptist, coed, primarily men. ***Awards:*** certificates, diplomas, associate, and bachelor's degrees. 2 undergraduate majors. Both federal and institutional methodology are used as a basis for awarding need-based institutional aid.
FRESHMAN FINANCIAL AID (Fall 2019, est.) 17 applied for aid; of those 94% were deemed to have need. 100% of freshmen with need received aid. ***Average percent of need met:*** 81% (excluding resources awarded to replace EFC). ***Average financial aid package:*** $5811 (excluding resources awarded to replace EFC). 24% of all full-time freshmen had no need and received non-need-based gift aid.
UNDERGRADUATE FINANCIAL AID (Fall 2019, est.) 68 applied for aid; of those 96% were deemed to have need. 100% of undergraduates with need received aid. ***Average percent of need met:*** 53% (excluding resources awarded to replace EFC). ***Average financial aid package:*** $6709 (excluding resources awarded to replace EFC).
GIFT AID (NEED-BASED) ***Total amount:*** $651,146 (48% federal, 41% institutional, 11% external sources). ***Receiving aid:*** Freshmen: 94% (16); all full-time undergraduates: 96% (65). ***Average award:*** Freshmen: $5811; Undergraduates: $6709. ***Scholarships, grants, and awards:*** Federal Pell, FSEOG, state, private, college/university gift aid from institutional funds.
GIFT AID (NON-NEED-BASED) ***Total amount:*** $88,010 (11% federal, 89% institutional). ***Receiving aid:*** Freshmen: 71% (12). Undergraduates: 43% (29). ***Average award:*** Freshmen: $1322. ***Scholarships, grants, and awards by category:*** *Academic interests/achievement:* 4 awards ($2760 total): general academic interests/achievements. *Creative arts/performance:* 9 awards ($2250 total): music. *Special characteristics:* 2 awards ($1476 total): handicapped students, international students.
WORK-STUDY ***Federal work-study:*** Total amount: $38,081; 38 jobs averaging $1002.
APPLYING FOR FINANCIAL AID ***Required financial aid forms:*** FAFSA, institution's own form. ***Financial aid deadline:*** Continuous. ***Notification date:*** Continuous beginning 6/1.
CONTACT Mr. Edward Barker, Director of Financial Aid, Clear Creek Baptist Bible College, 300 Clear Creek Road, Pineville, KY 40977-9754, 606-337-3196 Ext. 142. *Fax:* 606-337-1631. *E-mail:* Edward.Barker@ccbbc.edu.
Website: http://www.ccbbc.edu/.

CLEARY UNIVERSITY

Howell, MI

CONTACT Vesta Smith-Campbell, Director of Financial Aid, Cleary University, 3750 Cleary Drive, Howell, MI 48843, 517-338-3042 or toll-free 800-686-1883. *Fax:* 517-552-8022. *E-mail:* vscampbell@cleary.edu.
Website: http://www.cleary.edu/.

CLEMSON UNIVERSITY

Clemson, SC

Tuition & fees (SC res): $14,970	Average undergraduate aid package: $11,679

ABOUT THE INSTITUTION State-supported, coed. ***Awards:*** certificates, bachelor's, master's, and doctoral degrees. 71 undergraduate majors. ***Total enrollment:*** 25,822. Undergraduates: 20,195. Freshmen: 3,932. Federal methodology is used as a basis for awarding need-based institutional aid.

UNDERGRADUATE EXPENSES for 2019–2020 ***Application fee:*** $70. ***Tuition, area resident:*** part-time $641 per credit hour. ***Tuition, state resident:*** full-time $13,702; part-time $641 per credit hour. ***Tuition, nonresident:*** full-time $35,056; part-time $1586 per credit hour. ***Required fees:*** full-time $1268. ***Room only:*** $6812.

FRESHMAN FINANCIAL AID (Fall 2019, est.) 3291 applied for aid; of those 57% were deemed to have need. 95% of freshmen with need received aid; of those 15% had need fully met. ***Average percent of need met:*** 52% (excluding resources awarded to replace EFC). ***Average financial aid package:*** $12,592 (excluding resources awarded to replace EFC). 27% of all full-time freshmen had no need and received non-need-based gift aid.

UNDERGRADUATE FINANCIAL AID (Fall 2019, est.) 13,367 applied for aid; of those 69% were deemed to have need. 96% of undergraduates with need received aid; of those 14% had need fully met. ***Average percent of need met:*** 50% (excluding resources awarded to replace EFC). ***Average financial aid package:*** $11,679 (excluding resources awarded to replace EFC). 24% of all full-time undergraduates had no need and received non-need-based gift aid.

GIFT AID (NEED-BASED) ***Total amount:*** $76,899,115 (21% federal, 42% state, 31% institutional, 6% external sources). ***Receiving aid:*** Freshmen: 42% (1,654); all full-time undergraduates: 37% (7,377). ***Average award:*** Freshmen: $10,838; Undergraduates: $9711. ***Scholarships, grants, and awards:*** Federal Pell, FSEOG, state, private, college/university gift aid from institutional funds.

GIFT AID (NON-NEED-BASED) ***Total amount:*** $56,271,955 (47% state, 47% institutional, 6% external sources). ***Receiving aid:*** Freshmen: 42% (1,654). Undergraduates: 37% (7,377). ***Average award:*** Freshmen: $5126. Undergraduates: $5421. ***Scholarships, grants, and awards by category:*** *Academic interests/achievement:* agriculture, architecture, biological sciences, business, communication, computer science, education, engineering/technologies, English, foreign languages, general academic interests/achievements, home economics, humanities, international studies, mathematics, military science, physical sciences, premedicine, social sciences. *Creative arts/performance:* applied art and design, art/fine arts, performing arts, theater/drama. *Special achievements/activities:* community service, general special achievements/activities, leadership. *Special characteristics:* children of faculty/staff, ethnic background, local/state students, members of minority groups, veterans. ***ROTC:*** Army, Air Force.

LOANS ***Student loans:*** $90,724,510 (76% need-based, 24% non-need-based). 47% of past graduating class borrowed through all loan programs. *Average indebtedness per student:* $32,510. ***Average need-based loan:*** Freshmen: $3398. Undergraduates: $4351. ***Parent loans:*** $43,649,887 (81% need-based, 19% non-need-based). ***Programs:*** Federal Direct (Subsidized and Unsubsidized Stafford, PLUS), college/university.

WORK-STUDY ***Federal work-study:*** Total amount: $3,575,554; jobs available. ***State or other work-study/employment:*** Part-time jobs available.

ATHLETIC AWARDS Total amount: $8,352,614 (38% need-based, 62% non-need-based).

APPLYING FOR FINANCIAL AID ***Required financial aid form:*** FAFSA. ***Financial aid deadline (priority):*** 1/2. ***Notification date:*** Continuous beginning 3/1.

CONTACT Ms. Elizabeth Milam, Director of Financial Aid, Clemson University, G-01 Sikes Hall, Box 345123, Clemson, SC 29634-5123, 864-656-2280. *Fax:* 864-656-1831. *E-mail:* finaid@clemson.edu.
Website: http://www.clemson.edu/.

CLEVELAND INSTITUTE OF ART

Cleveland, OH

Tuition & fees: $44,385	Average undergraduate aid package: $27,398

ABOUT THE INSTITUTION Independent, coed. ***Awards:*** bachelor's degrees. 15 undergraduate majors. ***Total enrollment:*** 632. Undergraduates: 632. Freshmen: 156. Federal methodology is used as a basis for awarding need-based institutional aid.

UNDERGRADUATE EXPENSES for 2020–2021 ***Application fee:*** $40. ***Comprehensive fee:*** $55,975 includes full-time tuition ($41,490), mandatory fees ($2895), and room and board ($11,590). ***College room only:*** $8940. ***Part-time fees:*** $75 per credit hour.

FRESHMAN FINANCIAL AID (Fall 2019, est.) 148 applied for aid; of those 96% were deemed to have need. 100% of freshmen with need received aid; of those 8% had need fully met. ***Average percent of need met:*** 58% (excluding resources awarded to replace EFC). ***Average financial aid package:*** $26,970 (excluding resources awarded to replace EFC). 12% of all full-time freshmen had no need and received non-need-based gift aid.

UNDERGRADUATE FINANCIAL AID (Fall 2019, est.) 583 applied for aid; of those 87% were deemed to have need. 100% of undergraduates with need received aid; of those 10% had need fully met. ***Average percent of need met:*** 60% (excluding resources awarded to replace EFC). ***Average financial aid package:*** $27,398 (excluding resources awarded to replace EFC). 13% of all full-time undergraduates had no need and received non-need-based gift aid.

GIFT AID (NEED-BASED) ***Total amount:*** $11,586,211 (13% federal, 4% state, 81% institutional, 2% external sources). ***Receiving aid:*** Freshmen: 92% (142); all full-time undergraduates: 81% (510). ***Average award:*** Freshmen: $23,176; Undergraduates: $23,073. ***Scholarships, grants, and awards:*** Federal Pell, FSEOG, state, private, college/university gift aid from institutional funds.

GIFT AID (NON-NEED-BASED) ***Total amount:*** $1,483,389 (99% institutional, 1% external sources). ***Receiving aid:*** Freshmen: 6% (10). Undergraduates: 6% (39). ***Average award:*** Freshmen: $17,472. Undergraduates: $14,168. ***Scholarships, grants, and awards by category:*** *Creative arts/performance:* applied art and design, art/fine arts. *Special achievements/activities:* 6 awards ($60,005 total): leadership. ***ROTC:*** Army cooperative, Air Force cooperative.

LOANS ***Student loans:*** $5,352,264 (85% need-based, 15% non-need-based). 96% of past graduating class borrowed through all loan programs. *Average indebtedness per student:* $41,326. ***Average need-based loan:*** Freshmen: $4312. Undergraduates: $4697. ***Parent loans:*** $2,706,049 (79% need-based, 21% non-need-based). ***Programs:*** Federal Direct (Subsidized and Unsubsidized Stafford, PLUS).

WORK-STUDY ***Federal work-study:*** Total amount: $143,389; 137 jobs averaging $1158.

APPLYING FOR FINANCIAL AID ***Required financial aid form:*** FAFSA. ***Financial aid deadline (priority):*** 3/15. ***Notification date:*** Continuous beginning 12/15. Students must reply by 5/1 or within 3 weeks of notification.

CONTACT Mr. Martin Joseph Carney Jr., Director of Financial Aid, Cleveland Institute of Art, 11610 Euclid Avenue, Cleveland, OH 44106-4387, 216-421-7425 or toll-free 800-223-4700. *Fax:* 216-754-3634. *E-mail:* financialaid@cia.edu.
Website: http://www.cia.edu/.

CLEVELAND INSTITUTE OF MUSIC

Cleveland, OH

Tuition & fees: N/R	Average undergraduate aid package: $32,532

ABOUT THE INSTITUTION Independent, coed. ***Awards:*** certificates, bachelor's, and master's degrees. 3 undergraduate majors. ***Total enrollment:*** 439. Undergraduates: 238. Both federal and institutional methodology are used as a basis for awarding need-based institutional aid.

FRESHMAN FINANCIAL AID (Fall 2019, est.) 48 applied for aid; of those 67% were deemed to have need. 100% of freshmen with need received aid; of those 9% had need fully met. ***Average percent of need met:*** 70% (excluding resources awarded to replace EFC). ***Average financial aid package:*** $31,758 (excluding resources awarded to replace EFC). 41% of all full-time freshmen had no need and received non-need-based gift aid.

UNDERGRADUATE FINANCIAL AID (Fall 2019, est.) 150 applied for aid; of those 77% were deemed to have need. 100% of undergraduates with need received aid; of those 26% had need fully met. ***Average percent of need met:*** 76% (excluding resources awarded to replace EFC). ***Average financial aid package:*** $32,532 (excluding resources awarded to replace EFC). 48% of all full-time undergraduates had no need and received non-need-based gift aid.

GIFT AID (NEED-BASED) ***Total amount:*** $3,336,878 (5% federal, 94% institutional, 1% external sources). ***Receiving aid:*** Freshmen: 59% (32); all full-time undergraduates: 51% (116). ***Average award:*** Freshmen: $28,204; Undergraduates: $28,766. ***Scholarships, grants, and awards:*** Federal Pell, FSEOG, state, private, college/university gift aid from institutional funds.

GIFT AID (NON-NEED-BASED) ***Total amount:*** $2,772,160 (96% institutional, 4% external sources). ***Receiving aid:*** Freshmen: 4% (2). Undergraduates: 11% (25). ***Average award:*** Freshmen: $16,204. Undergraduates: $21,885. ***Scholarships, grants, and awards by category:*** *Creative arts/performance:* music. *Special characteristics:* children of faculty/staff. ***ROTC:*** Army cooperative, Air Force cooperative.

LOANS ***Student loans:*** $744,034 (59% need-based, 41% non-need-based). 52% of past graduating class borrowed through all loan programs. *Average indebtedness per student:* $22,156. ***Average need-based loan:*** Freshmen: $3000. Undergraduates: $3474. ***Parent loans:*** $518,740 (31% need-based, 69% non-need-based). ***Programs:*** Federal Direct (Subsidized and Unsubsidized Stafford, PLUS), private loans.

WORK-STUDY ***Federal work-study:*** Total amount: $95,000; 76 jobs averaging $2415. ***State or other work-study/employment:*** Total amount: $30,500 (100% non-need-based).

APPLYING FOR FINANCIAL AID ***Required financial aid forms:*** FAFSA, institution's own form, CSS Financial Aid PROFILE. ***Financial aid deadline (priority):*** 2/1. ***Notification date:*** 4/1. Students must reply by 5/1.

CONTACT Ms. Kristie Gripp, Director of Financial Aid, Cleveland Institute of Music, 11021 East Boulevard, Cleveland, OH 44106-1776, 216-795-3192. *Fax:* 216-707-4519. *E-mail:* kristine.gripp@cim.edu.
Website: http://www.cim.edu/.

CLEVELAND STATE UNIVERSITY

Cleveland, OH

Tuition & fees (area res): $9874	Average undergraduate aid package: $9686

ABOUT THE INSTITUTION State-supported, coed. ***Awards:*** certificates, bachelor's, master's, and doctoral degrees. 77 undergraduate majors. ***Total enrollment:*** 16,949. Undergraduates: 12,430. Freshmen: 1,917. Federal methodology is used as a basis for awarding need-based institutional aid.

UNDERGRADUATE EXPENSES for 2019–2020 ***Application fee:*** $40. ***Tuition, area resident:*** full-time $9636. ***Tuition, state resident:*** full-time $9636; part-time $433 per credit hour. ***Tuition, nonresident:*** full-time $13,711; part-time $615 per credit hour. ***Required fees:*** full-time $238. Full-time tuition and fees vary according to course load, degree level, location, and program. Part-time tuition and fees vary according to course load, degree level, location, and program. ***College room and board:*** $14,348; ***Room only:*** $9388. Room and board charges vary according to board plan and housing facility.

FRESHMAN FINANCIAL AID (Fall 2019, est.) 1724 applied for aid; of those 83% were deemed to have need. 99% of freshmen with need received aid; of those 7% had need fully met. ***Average percent of need met:*** 47% (excluding resources awarded to replace EFC). ***Average financial aid package:*** $10,221 (excluding resources awarded to replace EFC). 13% of all full-time freshmen had no need and received non-need-based gift aid.

UNDERGRADUATE FINANCIAL AID (Fall 2019, est.) 7,404 applied for aid; of those 87% were deemed to have need. 98% of undergraduates with need received aid; of those 7% had need fully met. ***Average percent of need met:*** 32% (excluding resources awarded to replace EFC). ***Average financial aid package:*** $9686 (excluding resources awarded to replace EFC). 10% of all full-time undergraduates had no need and received non-need-based gift aid.

GIFT AID (NEED-BASED) ***Total amount:*** $42,617,670 (52% federal, 19% state, 23% institutional, 6% external sources). ***Receiving aid:*** Freshmen: 64% (1,250); all full-time undergraduates: 56% (5,135). ***Average award:*** Freshmen: $8634; Undergraduates: $7790. ***Scholarships, grants, and awards:*** Federal Pell, FSEOG, state, private, college/university gift aid from institutional funds.

GIFT AID (NON-NEED-BASED) ***Total amount:*** $6,106,830 (5% state, 87% institutional, 8% external sources). ***Receiving aid:*** Freshmen: 3% (67). Undergraduates: 3% (247). ***Average award:*** Freshmen: $4562. Undergraduates: $5229. ***Scholarships, grants, and awards by category:*** *Academic interests/achievement:* biological sciences, business, communication, computer science, education, engineering/technologies, English, general academic interests/achievements, health fields, humanities, mathematics, physical sciences, premedicine, social sciences. *Creative arts/performance:* applied art and design, creative writing, dance, journalism/publications, music, performing arts, theater/drama. *Special achievements/activities:* cheerleading/drum major. *Special characteristics:* children of faculty/staff, general special characteristics, out-of-state students. ***Tuition waivers:*** Full or partial for employees or children of employees, senior citizens. ***ROTC:*** Army cooperative, Air Force cooperative.

LOANS ***Student loans:*** $52,890,398 (81% need-based, 19% non-need-based). 62% of past graduating class borrowed through all loan programs. *Average indebtedness per student:* $25,895. ***Average need-based loan:*** Freshmen: $3290. Undergraduates: $4072. ***Parent loans:*** $8,312,657 (50% need-based, 50% non-need-based). ***Programs:*** Federal Direct (Subsidized and Unsubsidized Stafford, PLUS), state, alternative loans.

WORK-STUDY ***Federal work-study:*** Total amount: $1,269,287; 348 jobs averaging $3550. ***State or other work-study/employment:*** Part-time jobs available.

ATHLETIC AWARDS Total amount: $3,295,592 (32% need-based, 68% non-need-based).

APPLYING FOR FINANCIAL AID ***Required financial aid form:*** FAFSA. ***Financial aid deadline (priority):*** 2/15. ***Notification date:*** Continuous beginning 1/31. Students must reply within 4 weeks of notification.

CONTACT Financial Aid Office, Cleveland State University, 2121 Euclid Avenue, Cleveland, OH 44115, 216-687-2000 or toll-free 888-CSU-OHIO.
Website: http://www.csuohio.edu/.

CLEVELAND UNIVERSITY–KANSAS CITY

Overland Park, KS

CONTACT Financial Aid Office, Cleveland University–Kansas City, 10850 Lowell Avenue, Overland Park, KS 66210, 913-234-0600 or toll-free 800-467-2252.
Website: http://www.cleveland.edu/.

COASTAL CAROLINA UNIVERSITY

Conway, SC

Tuition & fees (SC res): $11,640	Average undergraduate aid package: $11,168

ABOUT THE INSTITUTION State-supported, coed. ***Awards:*** certificates, bachelor's, master's, and doctoral degrees. 45 undergraduate majors. ***Total enrollment:*** 10,484. Undergraduates: 9,760. Freshmen: 2,304. Federal methodology is used as a basis for awarding need-based institutional aid.

UNDERGRADUATE EXPENSES for 2019–2020 ***Application fee:*** $45. ***Tuition, state resident:*** full-time $11,460; part-time $487 per credit hour. ***Tuition, nonresident:*** full-time $27,214; part-time $1138 per credit hour. ***Required fees:*** full-time $180; $5 per credit hour. Full-time tuition and fees vary according to course load, degree level, and reciprocity agreements. Part-time tuition and fees vary according to course load, degree level, and reciprocity agreements. ***College room and board:*** $9290; ***Room only:*** $5440. Room and board charges vary according to board plan and housing facility.

FRESHMAN FINANCIAL AID (Fall 2018) 2119 applied for aid; of those 81% were deemed to have need. 100% of freshmen with need received aid; of those 12% had need fully met. ***Average percent of need met:*** 46% (excluding resources awarded to replace EFC). ***Average financial aid package:*** $11,241 (excluding

resources awarded to replace EFC). 21% of all full-time freshmen had no need and received non-need-based gift aid.

UNDERGRADUATE FINANCIAL AID (Fall 2018) 7,439 applied for aid; of those 82% were deemed to have need. 100% of undergraduates with need received aid; of those 11% had need fully met. ***Average percent of need met:*** 48% (excluding resources awarded to replace EFC). ***Average financial aid package:*** $11,168 (excluding resources awarded to replace EFC). 21% of all full-time undergraduates had no need and received non-need-based gift aid.

GIFT AID (NEED-BASED) ***Receiving aid:*** Freshmen: 37% (855); all full-time undergraduates: 37% (3,273). ***Average award:*** Freshmen: $5214; Undergraduates: $5337. ***Scholarships, grants, and awards:*** Federal Pell, FSEOG, state, private, college/university gift aid from institutional funds.

GIFT AID (NON-NEED-BASED) ***Receiving aid:*** Freshmen: 33% (772). Undergraduates: 24% (2,126). ***Average award:*** Freshmen: $13,304. Undergraduates: $14,254. ***Scholarships, grants, and awards by category:*** *Academic interests/achievement:* 4,008 awards ($13,003,132 total): biological sciences, business, communication, computer science, education, English, foreign languages, general academic interests/achievements, humanities, international studies, mathematics, physical sciences, social sciences. *Creative arts/performance:* 75 awards ($141,734 total): applied art and design, music, performing arts, theater/drama. *Special achievements/activities:* 15 awards ($25,000 total): cheerleading/drum major. *Special characteristics:* 3,241 awards ($13,337,064 total): children of faculty/staff, general special characteristics, international students, local/state students, out-of-state students. ***Tuition waivers:*** Full or partial for employees or children of employees, senior citizens. ***ROTC:*** Army.

LOANS ***Student loans:*** 76% of past graduating class borrowed through all loan programs. *Average indebtedness per student:* $37,717. ***Average need-based loan:*** Freshmen: $9030. Undergraduates: $9620. ***Programs:*** Federal Direct (Subsidized and Unsubsidized Stafford, PLUS), state.

WORK-STUDY ***Federal work-study:*** 315 jobs averaging $1790. ***State or other work-study/employment:*** 1,568 part-time jobs averaging $1775.

APPLYING FOR FINANCIAL AID ***Required financial aid form:*** FAFSA. ***Notification date:*** Continuous.

CONTACT Ms. Sarah K. Weaver, Associate Director of Operations, Technology & Communication, Coastal Carolina University, PO Box 261954, Conway, SC 29528-6054, 843-349-2474 or toll-free 800-277-7000. *Fax:* 843-349-2347. *E-mail:* sweaver@coastal.edu.
Website: http://www.coastal.edu/.

COE COLLEGE
Cedar Rapids, IA

Tuition & fees: $47,220	Average undergraduate aid package: $39,070

ABOUT THE INSTITUTION Independent Presbyterian Church, coed. ***Awards:*** bachelor's degrees. 64 undergraduate majors. ***Total enrollment:*** 1,428. Undergraduates: 1,428. Freshmen: 379. Federal methodology is used as a basis for awarding need-based institutional aid.

UNDERGRADUATE EXPENSES for 2020–2021 ***Application fee:*** $30. ***Comprehensive fee:*** $57,354 includes full-time tuition ($46,870), mandatory fees ($350), and room and board ($10,134). Room and board charges vary according to board plan and housing facility. ***Part-time tuition:*** $1465 per semester hour. Part-time tuition and fees vary according to course load.

FRESHMAN FINANCIAL AID (Fall 2019, est.) 371 applied for aid; of those 91% were deemed to have need. 100% of freshmen with need received aid; of those 22% had need fully met. ***Average percent of need met:*** 88% (excluding resources awarded to replace EFC). ***Average financial aid package:*** $41,316 (excluding resources awarded to replace EFC). 11% of all full-time freshmen had no need and received non-need-based gift aid.

UNDERGRADUATE FINANCIAL AID (Fall 2019, est.) 1,224 applied for aid; of those 93% were deemed to have need. 100% of undergraduates with need received aid; of those 20% had need fully met. ***Average percent of need met:*** 84% (excluding resources awarded to replace EFC). ***Average financial aid package:*** $39,070 (excluding resources awarded to replace EFC). 16% of all full-time undergraduates had no need and received non-need-based gift aid.

GIFT AID (NEED-BASED) ***Total amount:*** $38,737,962 (6% federal, 5% state, 87% institutional, 2% external sources). ***Receiving aid:*** Freshmen: 89% (339); all full-time undergraduates: 83% (1,144). ***Average award:*** Freshmen: $37,679; Undergraduates: $34,609. ***Scholarships, grants, and awards:*** Federal Pell, FSEOG, state, private, college/university gift aid from institutional funds, Federal Nursing, ROTC Scholarships.

GIFT AID (NON-NEED-BASED) ***Total amount:*** $8,122,169 (1% federal, 96% institutional, 3% external sources). ***Receiving aid:*** Freshmen: 15% (58). Undergraduates: 13% (172). ***Average award:*** Freshmen: $28,636. Undergraduates: $27,713. ***Scholarships, grants, and awards by category:*** *Academic interests/achievement:* general academic interests/achievements. *Creative arts/performance:* applied art and design, creative writing, music, performing arts, theater/drama. *Special characteristics:* adult students, children and siblings of alumni, children of educators, children of faculty/staff, ethnic background, general special characteristics, international students, members of minority groups, religious affiliation, siblings of current students, veterans. ***Tuition waivers:*** Full or partial for employees or children of employees. ***ROTC:*** Army, Air Force cooperative.

LOANS ***Student loans:*** $8,980,193 (71% need-based, 29% non-need-based). 80% of past graduating class borrowed through all loan programs. *Average indebtedness per student:* $35,012. ***Average need-based loan:*** Freshmen: $3478. Undergraduates: $4213. ***Programs:*** Federal Direct (Subsidized and Unsubsidized Stafford, PLUS), college/university.

WORK-STUDY ***Federal work-study:*** Total amount: $926,764; 668 jobs averaging $1743. ***State or other work-study/employment:*** Total amount: $538,950 (18% need-based, 82% non-need-based). 327 part-time jobs averaging $1629.

APPLYING FOR FINANCIAL AID ***Required financial aid form:*** FAFSA. ***Financial aid deadline:*** Continuous. ***Notification date:*** Continuous beginning 12/1. Students must reply by 5/1 or within 2 weeks of notification.

CONTACT Ms. Barbara Hoffman, Director of Financial Aid, Coe College, 1220 First Avenue, NE, Cedar Rapids, IA 52402-5070, 319-399-8540 or toll-free 877-225-5263. *Fax:* 319-399-8886.
Website: http://www.coe.edu/.

COGSWELL POLYTECHNICAL COLLEGE
San Jose, CA

CONTACT Yariela Perez, Director of Financial Aid, Cogswell Polytechnical College, 191 Baypointe Parkway, San Jose, CA 95134, 408-498-5100 or toll-free 800-264-7955. *E-mail:* yperez@cogswell.edu.
Website: http://www.cogswell.edu/.

COKER COLLEGE
Hartsville, SC

ABOUT THE INSTITUTION Independent, coed. ***Awards:*** bachelor's and master's degrees (also offers evening program with significant enrollment not reflected in profile). 39 undergraduate majors.

GIFT AID (NEED-BASED) ***Scholarships, grants, and awards:*** Federal Pell, FSEOG, state, private, college/university gift aid from institutional funds.

GIFT AID (NON-NEED-BASED) ***Scholarships, grants, and awards by category:*** *Academic interests/achievement:* biological sciences, business, communication, English, foreign languages, general academic interests/achievements, physical sciences. *Creative arts/performance:* applied art and design, creative writing, dance, general creative arts/performance, music, theater/drama. *Special achievements/activities:* cheerleading/drum major, leadership. *Special characteristics:* adult students, children and siblings of alumni, children of faculty/staff, international students, local/state students, out-of-state students, previous college experience, veterans.

LOANS ***Programs:*** Federal Direct (Subsidized and Unsubsidized Stafford, PLUS), Perkins, state, private loans.

CONTACT Mrs. Betty Williams, Director of Student Financial Planning, Coker College, 300 East College Avenue, Hartsville, SC 29550, 843-383-8055 or toll-free 800-950-1908. *Fax:* 843-383-8056. *E-mail:* bwilliams@coker.edu.
Website: http://www.coker.edu/.

THE COLBURN SCHOOL CONSERVATORY OF MUSIC

Los Angeles, CA

CONTACT Ms. Misha Starks, Registrar, The Colburn School Conservatory of Music, 200 South Grand Avenue, Los Angeles, CA 90012, 213-621-4788. *Fax:* 213-625-0371. *E-mail:* mstarks@colburnschool.edu.
Website: http://www.colburnschool.edu/.

COLBY COLLEGE

Waterville, ME

Tuition & fees: $57,280	Average undergraduate aid package: $50,475

ABOUT THE INSTITUTION Independent, coed. ***Awards:*** bachelor's degrees. 46 undergraduate majors. ***Total enrollment:*** 2,003. Undergraduates: 2,003. Freshmen: 522. Both federal and institutional methodology are used as a basis for awarding need-based institutional aid.

UNDERGRADUATE EXPENSES for 2019–2020 *Comprehensive fee:* $72,000 includes full-time tuition ($54,870), mandatory fees ($2410), and room and board ($14,720). ***Part-time tuition:*** $2100 per credit hour. Part-time tuition and fees vary according to course load.

FRESHMAN FINANCIAL AID (Fall 2019, est.) 273 applied for aid; of those 76% were deemed to have need. 100% of freshmen with need received aid; of those 100% had need fully met. ***Average percent of need met:*** 100% (excluding resources awarded to replace EFC). ***Average financial aid package:*** $55,762 (excluding resources awarded to replace EFC).

UNDERGRADUATE FINANCIAL AID (Fall 2019, est.) 1,051 applied for aid; of those 79% were deemed to have need. 100% of undergraduates with need received aid; of those 100% had need fully met. ***Average percent of need met:*** 100% (excluding resources awarded to replace EFC). ***Average financial aid package:*** $50,475 (excluding resources awarded to replace EFC).

GIFT AID (NEED-BASED) *Total amount:* $46,204,547 (4% federal, 95% institutional, 1% external sources). ***Receiving aid:*** Freshmen: 40% (207); all full-time undergraduates: 41% (830). ***Average award:*** Freshmen: $55,650; Undergraduates: $51,617. ***Scholarships, grants, and awards:*** Federal Pell, FSEOG, state, college/university gift aid from institutional funds.

GIFT AID (NON-NEED-BASED) *Total amount:* $61,548 (100% external sources). ***Receiving aid:*** Undergraduates: 1% (19). ***Scholarships, grants, and awards by category:*** *Academic interests/achievement:* general academic interests/achievements. *Special characteristics:* general special characteristics. ***Tuition waivers:*** Full or partial for employees or children of employees. ***ROTC:*** Army cooperative.

LOANS *Student loans:* $2,712,224 (21% need-based, 79% non-need-based). 30% of past graduating class borrowed through all loan programs. *Average indebtedness per student:* $24,380. ***Parent loans:*** $1,856,631 (100% non-need-based). ***Programs:*** Federal Direct (Subsidized and Unsubsidized Stafford, PLUS), Perkins.

WORK-STUDY *Federal work-study:* Total amount: $722,501; jobs available. ***State or other work-study/employment:*** Total amount: $598,238 (100% need-based). Part-time jobs available.

APPLYING FOR FINANCIAL AID *Required financial aid forms:* FAFSA, CSS Financial Aid PROFILE, business/farm supplement, Federal Tax Forms. ***Financial aid deadline:*** 2/1. ***Notification date:*** 4/1.

CONTACT Cindy Wells, Director of Financial Aid, Colby College, 4850 Mayflower Hill, Waterville, ME 04901-8848, 207-859-4132 or toll-free 800-723-3032. *Fax:* 207-859-4828. *E-mail:* finaid@colby.edu.
Website: http://www.colby.edu/.

COLBY-SAWYER COLLEGE

New London, NH

Tuition & fees: $44,930	Average undergraduate aid package: $37,574

ABOUT THE INSTITUTION Independent, coed. ***Awards:*** certificates, associate, and bachelor's degrees. 22 undergraduate majors. ***Total enrollment:*** 855. Undergraduates: 851. Freshmen: 264. Federal methodology is used as a basis for awarding need-based institutional aid.

UNDERGRADUATE EXPENSES for 2020–2021 *Application fee:* $45. ***Comprehensive fee:*** $60,358 includes full-time tuition ($44,130), mandatory fees ($800), and room and board ($15,428). ***Part-time tuition:*** $1471 per credit hour. ***Part-time fees:*** $10 per credit.

FRESHMAN FINANCIAL AID (Fall 2019, est.) 212 applied for aid; of those 89% were deemed to have need. 100% of freshmen with need received aid; of those 25% had need fully met. ***Average percent of need met:*** 86% (excluding resources awarded to replace EFC). ***Average financial aid package:*** $39,348 (excluding resources awarded to replace EFC). 17% of all full-time freshmen had no need and received non-need-based gift aid.

UNDERGRADUATE FINANCIAL AID (Fall 2019, est.) 646 applied for aid; of those 93% were deemed to have need. 100% of undergraduates with need received aid; of those 25% had need fully met. ***Average percent of need met:*** 84% (excluding resources awarded to replace EFC). ***Average financial aid package:*** $37,574 (excluding resources awarded to replace EFC). 18% of all full-time undergraduates had no need and received non-need-based gift aid.

GIFT AID (NEED-BASED) *Total amount:* $19,004,501 (6% federal, 1% state, 93% institutional). ***Receiving aid:*** Freshmen: 82% (188); all full-time undergraduates: 81% (597). ***Average award:*** Freshmen: $35,825; Undergraduates: $33,305. ***Scholarships, grants, and awards:*** Federal Pell, FSEOG, state, private, college/university gift aid from institutional funds.

GIFT AID (NON-NEED-BASED) *Total amount:* $4,688,458 (100% institutional). ***Receiving aid:*** Freshmen: 15% (34). Undergraduates: 14% (100). ***Average award:*** Freshmen: $29,595. Undergraduates: $28,330. ***Scholarships, grants, and awards by category:*** *Academic interests/achievement:* general academic interests/achievements. *Special characteristics:* children of faculty/staff. ***Tuition waivers:*** Full or partial for employees or children of employees. ***ROTC:*** Army cooperative, Air Force cooperative.

LOANS *Student loans:* $6,745,676 (56% need-based, 44% non-need-based). 78% of past graduating class borrowed through all loan programs. *Average indebtedness per student:* $40,767. ***Average need-based loan:*** Freshmen: $3040. Undergraduates: $3763. ***Parent loans:*** $2,082,779 (41% need-based, 59% non-need-based). ***Programs:*** Federal Direct (Subsidized and Unsubsidized Stafford, PLUS).

WORK-STUDY *Federal work-study:* Total amount: $106,254; jobs available.

APPLYING FOR FINANCIAL AID *Required financial aid form:* FAFSA. ***Financial aid deadline:*** 3/1 (priority: 3/1). ***Notification date:*** 2/15. Students must reply by 5/1.

CONTACT Ms. Beth Renzulli, Director of Financial Aid, Colby-Sawyer College, 541 Main Street, New London, NH 03257-7835, 603-526-3717 or toll-free 800-272-1015. *Fax:* 603-526-3737. *E-mail:* cscfinaid@colby-sawyer.edu.
Website: http://www.colby-sawyer.edu/.

COLEGIO UNIVERSITARIO DE SAN JUAN

San Juan, PR

CONTACT Ken Lira, Director of Financial Aid, Colegio Universitario de San Juan, 43-500 Monterey Avenue, Palm Desert, AB 92260, 760-776-7428. *Fax:* 760-776-7338. *E-mail:* klira@collegeofthedesert.edu.
Website: http://www.cunisanjuan.edu/.

COLGATE UNIVERSITY
Hamilton, NY

Tuition & fees: $58,045 | **Average undergraduate aid package: $57,355**

ABOUT THE INSTITUTION Independent, coed. ***Awards:*** bachelor's and master's degrees. 54 undergraduate majors. ***Total enrollment:*** 2,992. Undergraduates: 2,980. Freshmen: 786. Both federal and institutional methodology are used as a basis for awarding need-based institutional aid.

UNDERGRADUATE EXPENSES for 2019–2020 ***Application fee:*** $60. ***One-time required fee:*** $50. ***Comprehensive fee:*** $72,585 includes full-time tuition ($57,695), mandatory fees ($350), and room and board ($14,540). ***College room only:*** $7020. Room and board charges vary according to board plan. ***Payment plan:*** Tuition prepayment.

FRESHMAN FINANCIAL AID (Fall 2019, est.) 273 applied for aid; of those 84% were deemed to have need. 100% of freshmen with need received aid; of those 100% had need fully met. ***Average percent of need met:*** 100% (excluding resources awarded to replace EFC). ***Average financial aid package:*** $59,503 (excluding resources awarded to replace EFC).

UNDERGRADUATE FINANCIAL AID (Fall 2019, est.) 1,086 applied for aid; of those 89% were deemed to have need. 99% of undergraduates with need received aid; of those 100% had need fully met. ***Average percent of need met:*** 100% (excluding resources awarded to replace EFC). ***Average financial aid package:*** $57,355 (excluding resources awarded to replace EFC).

GIFT AID (NEED-BASED) ***Total amount:*** $51,132,406 (3% federal, 1% state, 94% institutional, 2% external sources). ***Receiving aid:*** Freshmen: 29% (228); all full-time undergraduates: 32% (956). ***Average award:*** Freshmen: $55,553; Undergraduates: $53,556. ***Scholarships, grants, and awards:*** Federal Pell, FSEOG, college/university gift aid from institutional funds.

GIFT AID (NON-NEED-BASED) ***Total amount:*** $1,662,201 (14% state, 10% institutional, 76% external sources). ***Scholarships, grants, and awards by category:*** *Special characteristics:* veterans. ***ROTC:*** Army cooperative.

LOANS ***Student loans:*** $2,759,956 (62% need-based, 38% non-need-based). 37% of past graduating class borrowed through all loan programs. *Average indebtedness per student:* $25,044. ***Average need-based loan:*** Freshmen: $1295. Undergraduates: $3400. ***Parent loans:*** $4,266,247 (100% non-need-based). ***Programs:*** Federal Direct (Subsidized and Unsubsidized Stafford, PLUS), college/university.

WORK-STUDY ***Federal work-study:*** Total amount: $1,120,585; jobs available. ***State or other work-study/employment:*** Total amount: $665,932 (100% need-based). Part-time jobs available.

ATHLETIC AWARDS Total amount: $14,172,487 (100% non-need-based).

APPLYING FOR FINANCIAL AID ***Required financial aid forms:*** FAFSA, CSS Financial Aid PROFILE, noncustodial (divorced/separated) parent's statement, business/farm supplement. ***Financial aid deadline:*** 1/15 (priority: 1/15). ***Notification date:*** 3/21. Students must reply by 5/1.

CONTACT Financial Aid Office, Colgate University, 13 Oak Drive, Hamilton, NY 13346-1386, 315-228-1000.
Website: http://www.colgate.edu/.

COLLEGE FOR CREATIVE STUDIES
Detroit, MI

CONTACT Office of Financial Aid, College for Creative Studies, 201 East Kirby, Detroit, MI 48202-4034, 313-664-7495 or toll-free 800-952-ARTS. *Fax:* 313-872-1521. *E-mail:* finaid@collegeforcreativestudies.edu.
Website: http://www.collegeforcreativestudies.edu/.

COLLEGE OF BIBLICAL STUDIES–HOUSTON
Houston, TX

CONTACT Roshanna Hardison, Director of Student Financial Services, College of Biblical Studies–Houston, 7000 Regency Square Boulevard, Houston, TX 77036, 832-252-0728 or toll-free 844-227-9673. *E-mail:* roshanna.hardison@cbshouston.edu.
Website: http://www.cbshouston.edu/.

COLLEGE OF CHARLESTON
Charleston, SC

ABOUT THE INSTITUTION State-supported, coed. ***Awards:*** certificates, bachelor's, and master's degrees (also offers graduate degree programs through University of Charleston, South Carolina). 61 undergraduate majors. ***Total enrollment:*** 10,545. Undergraduates: 9,600. Freshmen: 2,051.

GIFT AID (NEED-BASED) ***Scholarships, grants, and awards:*** Federal Pell, FSEOG, state, private, college/university gift aid from institutional funds.

GIFT AID (NON-NEED-BASED) ***Scholarships, grants, and awards by category:*** *Academic interests/achievement:* biological sciences, business, communication, computer science, education, engineering/technologies, English, foreign languages, general academic interests/achievements, home economics, humanities, mathematics, physical sciences, premedicine, social sciences. *Creative arts/performance:* applied art and design, music, performing arts, theater/drama. *Special characteristics:* general special characteristics.

LOANS ***Programs:*** Federal Direct (Subsidized and Unsubsidized Stafford, PLUS), Perkins.

WORK-STUDY ***Federal work-study:*** Total amount: $408,111; jobs available. ***State or other work-study/employment:*** Part-time jobs available.

APPLYING FOR FINANCIAL AID ***Required financial aid form:*** FAFSA.

CONTACT Derwin Simpson, Director of Student Services and Programs, College of Charleston, 66 George Street, Charleston, SC 29424, 843-953-5540. *Fax:* 843-953-7192. *E-mail:* financialaid@cofc.edu.
Website: http://www.cofc.edu/.

COLLEGE OF COASTAL GEORGIA
Brunswick, GA

ABOUT THE INSTITUTION State-supported, coed. ***Awards:*** associate and bachelor's degrees. 21 undergraduate majors. ***Total enrollment:*** 3,546. Undergraduates: 3,546. Freshmen: 795.

GIFT AID (NEED-BASED) ***Scholarships, grants, and awards:*** Federal Pell, FSEOG, state, private, college/university gift aid from institutional funds.

GIFT AID (NON-NEED-BASED) ***Scholarships, grants, and awards by category:*** *Academic interests/achievement:* biological sciences, business, education, health fields, mathematics, premedicine, social sciences. *Creative arts/performance:* applied art and design. *Special achievements/activities:* community service, leadership. *Special characteristics:* children and siblings of alumni, first-generation college students, international students, local/state students, members of minority groups.

LOANS ***Programs:*** Federal Direct (Subsidized and Unsubsidized Stafford, PLUS), state, college/university.

CONTACT Ms. Terral L. Harris, Financial Aid Office, College of Coastal Georgia, One College Drive, Brunswick, GA 31520, 912-279-5722 or toll-free 800-675-7235. *Fax:* 912-264-7320. *E-mail:* finaid@ccga.edu.
Website: http://www.ccga.edu/.

THE COLLEGE OF IDAHO

Caldwell, ID

Tuition & fees: $32,855 **Average undergraduate aid package: $23,045**

ABOUT THE INSTITUTION Independent, coed. ***Awards:*** bachelor's and master's degrees. 36 undergraduate majors. ***Total enrollment:*** 1,091. Undergraduates: 1,077. Freshmen: 361. Federal methodology is used as a basis for awarding need-based institutional aid.

UNDERGRADUATE EXPENSES for 2020–2021 ***Comprehensive fee:*** $43,455 includes full-time tuition ($32,100), mandatory fees ($755), and room and board ($10,600). ***Part-time tuition:*** $1330 per credit.

FRESHMAN FINANCIAL AID (Fall 2019, est.) 266 applied for aid; of those 84% were deemed to have need. 100% of freshmen with need received aid; of those 26% had need fully met. ***Average percent of need met:*** 26% (excluding resources awarded to replace EFC). ***Average financial aid package:*** $25,219 (excluding resources awarded to replace EFC). 38% of all full-time freshmen had no need and received non-need-based gift aid.

UNDERGRADUATE FINANCIAL AID (Fall 2019, est.) 727 applied for aid; of those 86% were deemed to have need. 100% of undergraduates with need received aid; of those 28% had need fully met. ***Average percent of need met:*** 28% (excluding resources awarded to replace EFC). ***Average financial aid package:*** $23,045 (excluding resources awarded to replace EFC). 40% of all full-time undergraduates had no need and received non-need-based gift aid.

GIFT AID (NEED-BASED) ***Total amount:*** $11,166,999 (13% federal, 1% state, 55% institutional, 31% external sources). ***Receiving aid:*** Freshmen: 49% (176); all full-time undergraduates: 41% (431). ***Average award:*** Freshmen: $7239; Undergraduates: $6156. ***Scholarships, grants, and awards:*** Federal Pell, FSEOG, state, private, college/university gift aid from institutional funds.

GIFT AID (NON-NEED-BASED) ***Total amount:*** $17,674,230 (97% institutional, 3% external sources). ***Receiving aid:*** Freshmen: 62% (224). Undergraduates: 59% (625). ***Average award:*** Freshmen: $25,521. Undergraduates: $24,348. ***Scholarships, grants, and awards by category:*** *Academic interests/achievement:* biological sciences, business, education, English, foreign languages, general academic interests/achievements, humanities, mathematics, physical sciences, premedicine, religion/biblical studies, social sciences. *Creative arts/performance:* applied art and design, debating, music, performing arts, theater/drama. *Special achievements/activities:* leadership. *Special characteristics:* children and siblings of alumni, children of educators, children of faculty/staff, first-generation college students, international students, local/state students, married students, members of minority groups, out-of-state students, siblings of current students. ***ROTC:*** Army cooperative.

LOANS ***Student loans:*** $3,664,372 (60% need-based, 40% non-need-based). 95% of past graduating class borrowed through all loan programs. *Average indebtedness per student:* $29,130. ***Average need-based loan:*** Freshmen: $3383. Undergraduates: $4205. ***Parent loans:*** $2,632,127 (100% non-need-based). ***Programs:*** Federal Direct (Subsidized and Unsubsidized Stafford, PLUS).

WORK-STUDY ***Federal work-study:*** Total amount: $134,061; jobs available. ***State or other work-study/employment:*** Total amount: $316,000 (6% need-based, 94% non-need-based). Part-time jobs available.

ATHLETIC AWARDS Total amount: $2,738,969 (100% non-need-based).

APPLYING FOR FINANCIAL AID ***Required financial aid form:*** FAFSA. ***Financial aid deadline:*** Continuous. ***Notification date:*** 12/11.

CONTACT Jennifer Worden, Director of Financial Aid Services, The College of Idaho, 2112 Cleveland Boulevard, Caldwell, ID 83605, 208-459-5307 or toll-free 800-244-3246. *Fax:* 208-459-5844. *E-mail:* jworden@collegeofidaho.edu.
Website: http://www.collegeofidaho.edu/.

THE COLLEGE OF NEW JERSEY

Ewing, NJ

Tuition & fees (NJ res): $16,923 **Average undergraduate aid package: $11,920**

ABOUT THE INSTITUTION State-supported, coed. ***Awards:*** certificates, bachelor's, and master's degrees. 53 undergraduate majors. ***Total enrollment:*** 7,686. Undergraduates: 7,048. Freshmen: 1,551. Federal methodology is used as a basis for awarding need-based institutional aid.

UNDERGRADUATE EXPENSES for 2019–2020 ***Application fee:*** $75. ***Tuition, state resident:*** full-time $13,239; part-time $470 per credit hour. ***Tuition, nonresident:*** full-time $25,217; part-time $893 per credit hour. ***Required fees:*** full-time $3684; $153.04 per credit hour. Full-time tuition and fees vary according to course load. Part-time tuition and fees vary according to course load. ***College room and board:*** $14,048; ***Room only:*** $4532. Room and board charges vary according to board plan.

FRESHMAN FINANCIAL AID (Fall 2019, est.) 1424 applied for aid; of those 65% were deemed to have need. 94% of freshmen with need received aid; of those 12% had need fully met. ***Average percent of need met:*** 40% (excluding resources awarded to replace EFC). ***Average financial aid package:*** $12,274 (excluding resources awarded to replace EFC). 14% of all full-time freshmen had no need and received non-need-based gift aid.

UNDERGRADUATE FINANCIAL AID (Fall 2019, est.) 5,010 applied for aid; of those 71% were deemed to have need. 96% of undergraduates with need received aid; of those 12% had need fully met. ***Average percent of need met:*** 42% (excluding resources awarded to replace EFC). ***Average financial aid package:*** $11,920 (excluding resources awarded to replace EFC). 9% of all full-time undergraduates had no need and received non-need-based gift aid.

GIFT AID (NEED-BASED) ***Total amount:*** $27,039,607 (24% federal, 29% state, 38% institutional, 9% external sources). ***Receiving aid:*** Freshmen: 26% (418); all full-time undergraduates: 23% (1,612). ***Average award:*** Freshmen: $13,254; Undergraduates: $11,794. ***Scholarships, grants, and awards:*** Federal Pell, FSEOG, state, private, college/university gift aid from institutional funds, Federal Nursing.

GIFT AID (NON-NEED-BASED) ***Total amount:*** $6,712,628 (1% state, 82% institutional, 17% external sources). ***Receiving aid:*** Freshmen: 24% (383). Undergraduates: 16% (1,115). ***Average award:*** Freshmen: $5873. Undergraduates: $5357. ***Scholarships, grants, and awards by category:*** *Academic interests/achievement:* general academic interests/achievements. *Creative arts/performance:* applied art and design, music. *Special characteristics:* children with a deceased or disabled parent, members of minority groups. ***Tuition waivers:*** Full or partial for employees or children of employees, senior citizens. ***ROTC:*** Army cooperative, Air Force cooperative.

LOANS ***Student loans:*** $37,145,211 (75% need-based, 25% non-need-based). 63% of past graduating class borrowed through all loan programs. *Average indebtedness per student:* $38,166. ***Average need-based loan:*** Freshmen: $3264. Undergraduates: $4283. ***Parent loans:*** $7,624,951 (73% need-based, 27% non-need-based). ***Programs:*** Federal Direct (Subsidized and Unsubsidized Stafford, PLUS), Perkins, Federal Nursing, private loans.

WORK-STUDY ***Federal work-study:*** Total amount: $210,170; jobs available.

APPLYING FOR FINANCIAL AID ***Required financial aid form:*** FAFSA. ***Financial aid deadline:*** 10/1 (priority: 3/1). ***Notification date:*** Continuous beginning 6/1. Students must reply within 2 weeks of notification.

CONTACT Mr. Wilbert Casaine, Executive Director of Financial Aid and Student Success, The College of New Jersey, PO Box 7718, Ewing, NJ 08628, 609-771-2602. *Fax:* 609-637-5154. *E-mail:* casainew@tcnj.edu.
Website: http://www.tcnj.edu/.

COLLEGE OF MOUNT SAINT VINCENT

Riverdale, NY

CONTACT Mr. Emmett Cooper, Director of Financial Aid, College of Mount Saint Vincent, 6301 Riverdale Avenue, Riverdale, NY 10471, 718-405-3309 or toll-free 800-665-CMSV. *Fax:* 718-405-3490. *E-mail:* emmett.cooper@mountsaintvincent.edu.
Website: http://www.mountsaintvincent.edu/.

THE COLLEGE OF NEW ROCHELLE

New Rochelle, NY

CONTACT Vincent Tunstall, Director of Financial Aid, The College of New Rochelle, 29 Castle Place, New Rochelle, NY 10805-2339, 914-654-5466 or toll-free 800-933-5923. *Fax:* 914-654-5420. *E-mail:* vtunstall@cnr.edu.
Website: http://www.cnr.edu/.

COLLEGE OF SAINT BENEDICT

Saint Joseph, MN

Tuition & fees: $48,442 | **Average undergraduate aid package: $38,360**

ABOUT THE INSTITUTION Independent Roman Catholic, women only. ***Awards:*** bachelor's degrees (coordinate with Saint John's University for men). 36 undergraduate majors. ***Total enrollment:*** 1,748. Undergraduates: 1,748. Freshmen: 439. Federal methodology is used as a basis for awarding need-based institutional aid.

UNDERGRADUATE EXPENSES for 2020–2021 ***Comprehensive fee:*** $59,788 includes full-time tuition ($47,330), mandatory fees ($1112), and room and board ($11,346). ***College room only:*** $5630. Room and board charges vary according to board plan and housing facility. ***Part-time tuition:*** $1905 per credit hour. Part-time tuition and fees vary according to course load. ***Payment plan:*** Tuition prepayment.

FRESHMAN FINANCIAL AID (Fall 2019, est.) 396 applied for aid; of those 85% were deemed to have need. 100% of freshmen with need received aid; of those 41% had need fully met. ***Average percent of need met:*** 89% (excluding resources awarded to replace EFC). ***Average financial aid package:*** $40,353 (excluding resources awarded to replace EFC). 19% of all full-time freshmen had no need and received non-need-based gift aid.

UNDERGRADUATE FINANCIAL AID (Fall 2019, est.) 1,441 applied for aid; of those 87% were deemed to have need. 100% of undergraduates with need received aid; of those 34% had need fully met. ***Average percent of need met:*** 89% (excluding resources awarded to replace EFC). ***Average financial aid package:*** $38,360 (excluding resources awarded to replace EFC). 26% of all full-time undergraduates had no need and received non-need-based gift aid.

GIFT AID (NEED-BASED) ***Total amount:*** $41,168,541 (5% federal, 8% state, 84% institutional, 3% external sources). ***Receiving aid:*** Freshmen: 71% (326); all full-time undergraduates: 70% (1,209). ***Average award:*** Freshmen: $34,813; Undergraduates: $32,636. ***Scholarships, grants, and awards:*** Federal Pell, FSEOG, state, private, college/university gift aid from institutional funds.

GIFT AID (NON-NEED-BASED) ***Total amount:*** $10,739,930 (93% institutional, 7% external sources). ***Receiving aid:*** Freshmen: 69% (320). Undergraduates: 68% (1,173). ***Average award:*** Freshmen: $25,030. Undergraduates: $21,784. ***Scholarships, grants, and awards by category:*** *Academic interests/achievement:* 1,603 awards ($30,201,795 total): computer science, engineering/technologies, general academic interests/achievements, mathematics, military science, physical sciences. *Creative arts/performance:* 219 awards ($632,083 total): applied art and design, music, theater/drama. *Special characteristics:* 656 awards ($2,807,707 total): children and siblings of alumni, international students, out-of-state students. ***Tuition waivers:*** Full or partial for employees or children of employees. ***ROTC:*** Army cooperative.

LOANS ***Student loans:*** $15,315,116 (90% need-based, 10% non-need-based). 71% of past graduating class borrowed through all loan programs. *Average indebtedness per student:* $43,615. ***Average need-based loan:*** Freshmen: $3290. Undergraduates: $4446. ***Parent loans:*** $890,576 (93% need-based, 7% non-need-based). ***Programs:*** Federal Direct (Subsidized and Unsubsidized Stafford, PLUS), state, private loans.

WORK-STUDY ***Federal work-study:*** Total amount: $706,895; 273 jobs averaging $2827. ***State or other work-study/employment:*** Total amount: $3,205,274 (74% need-based, 26% non-need-based). 1,023 part-time jobs averaging $2959.

APPLYING FOR FINANCIAL AID ***Required financial aid form:*** FAFSA. ***Financial aid deadline (priority):*** 3/15. ***Notification date:*** Continuous beginning 1/15. Students must reply by 5/1.

CONTACT Mr. Stuart Perry, Executive Director of Financial Aid, College of Saint Benedict, 37 South College Avenue, Saint Joseph, MN 56374-2099, 320-363-5388 or toll-free 800-544-1489. *Fax:* 320-363-6090. *E-mail:* sperry@csbsju.edu.
Website: http://www.csbsju.edu/.

COLLEGE OF SAINT ELIZABETH

Morristown, NJ

Tuition & fees: $34,871 | **Average undergraduate aid package: $30,405**

ABOUT THE INSTITUTION Independent Roman Catholic, coed. ***Awards:*** certificates, bachelor's, master's, and doctoral degrees (also offers coed adult undergraduate degree program and coed graduate programs). 24 undergraduate majors. ***Total enrollment:*** 1,281. Undergraduates: 828. Freshmen: 169. Federal methodology is used as a basis for awarding need-based institutional aid.

UNDERGRADUATE EXPENSES for 2020–2021 ***One-time required fee:*** $175. ***Comprehensive fee:*** $47,615 includes full-time tuition ($32,895), mandatory fees ($1976), and room and board ($12,744). Full-time tuition and fees vary according to course load. Room and board charges vary according to housing facility. ***Part-time tuition:*** $914 per credit hour. Part-time tuition and fees vary according to course load.

FRESHMAN FINANCIAL AID (Fall 2018) 171 applied for aid; of those 97% were deemed to have need. 100% of freshmen with need received aid; of those 8% had need fully met. ***Average percent of need met:*** 79% (excluding resources awarded to replace EFC). ***Average financial aid package:*** $34,615 (excluding resources awarded to replace EFC). 5% of all full-time freshmen had no need and received non-need-based gift aid.

UNDERGRADUATE FINANCIAL AID (Fall 2018) 566 applied for aid; of those 96% were deemed to have need. 100% of undergraduates with need received aid; of those 7% had need fully met. ***Average percent of need met:*** 75% (excluding resources awarded to replace EFC). ***Average financial aid package:*** $30,405 (excluding resources awarded to replace EFC). 5% of all full-time undergraduates had no need and received non-need-based gift aid.

GIFT AID (NEED-BASED) ***Total amount:*** $14,391,697 (16% federal, 28% state, 56% institutional). ***Receiving aid:*** Freshmen: 91% (166); all full-time undergraduates: 82% (516). ***Average award:*** Freshmen: $30,593; Undergraduates: $27,408. ***Scholarships, grants, and awards:*** Federal Pell, FSEOG, state, private, college/university gift aid from institutional funds.

GIFT AID (NON-NEED-BASED) ***Total amount:*** $911,913 (92% institutional, 8% external sources). ***Receiving aid:*** Freshmen: 62% (113). Undergraduates: 48% (302). ***Average award:*** Freshmen: $21,397. Undergraduates: $14,486. ***Scholarships, grants, and awards by category:*** *Academic interests/achievement:* general academic interests/achievements. *Creative arts/performance:* music. *Special achievements/activities:* community service. *Special characteristics:* adult students, children and siblings of alumni, first-generation college students, handicapped students, local/state students, members of minority groups, out-of-state students. ***Tuition waivers:*** Full or partial for employees or children of employees, senior citizens.

LOANS ***Student loans:*** $4,030,652 (87% need-based, 13% non-need-based). 88% of past graduating class borrowed through all loan programs. *Average indebtedness per student:* $29,315. ***Average need-based loan:*** Freshmen: $6467. Undergraduates: $7130. ***Parent loans:*** $940,635 (67% need-based, 33% non-need-based). ***Programs:*** Federal Direct (Subsidized and Unsubsidized Stafford, PLUS), state.

WORK-STUDY ***Federal work-study:*** Total amount: $100,000; jobs available. ***State or other work-study/employment:*** Total amount: $189,772 (53% need-based, 47% non-need-based).

APPLYING FOR FINANCIAL AID ***Required financial aid form:*** FAFSA. ***Financial aid deadline:*** Continuous. ***Notification date:*** Continuous beginning 12/1.

CONTACT James Kulhawy, Assistant Director of Financial Aid, College of Saint Elizabeth, 2 Convent Road, Morristown, NJ 07960-6989, 973-290-4432 or toll-free 800-210-7900. *E-mail:* jkulhawy@cse.edu.
Website: http://www.cse.edu/.

COLLEGE OF ST. JOSEPH

Rutland, VT

CONTACT Julie Rosmus, Director of Financial Aid, College of St. Joseph, 71 Clement Road, Rutland, VT 05701-3899, 802-773-5900 Ext. 3274 or toll-free 877-270-9998. *Fax:* 802-776-5275. *E-mail:* jrosmus@csj.edu.
Website: http://www.csj.edu/.

COLLEGE OF SAINT MARY

Omaha, NE

Tuition & fees: $20,750 | **Average undergraduate aid package: $16,679**

ABOUT THE INSTITUTION Independent Roman Catholic, women only. ***Awards:*** certificates, associate, bachelor's, master's, and doctoral degrees. 30 undergraduate majors. ***Total enrollment:*** 1,168. Undergraduates: 861. Freshmen: 119. Federal methodology is used as a basis for awarding need-based institutional aid.

UNDERGRADUATE EXPENSES for 2019–2020 ***Application fee:*** $30. ***Comprehensive fee:*** $28,600 includes full-time tuition ($20,750) and room and board ($7850). ***Part-time tuition:*** $765 per credit.

FRESHMAN FINANCIAL AID (Fall 2019, est.) 88 applied for aid; of those 84% were deemed to have need. 100% of freshmen with need received aid; of those 28% had need fully met. ***Average percent of need met:*** 82% (excluding resources awarded to replace EFC). ***Average financial aid package:*** $18,878 (excluding resources awarded to replace EFC). 26% of all full-time freshmen had no need and received non-need-based gift aid.

UNDERGRADUATE FINANCIAL AID (Fall 2019, est.) 636 applied for aid; of those 89% were deemed to have need. 100% of undergraduates with need received aid; of those 13% had need fully met. ***Average percent of need met:*** 62% (excluding resources awarded to replace EFC). ***Average financial aid package:*** $16,679 (excluding resources awarded to replace EFC). 19% of all full-time undergraduates had no need and received non-need-based gift aid.

GIFT AID (NEED-BASED) ***Total amount:*** $6,105,508 (26% federal, 5% state, 65% institutional, 4% external sources). ***Receiving aid:*** Freshmen: 74% (74); all full-time undergraduates: 78% (555). ***Average award:*** Freshmen: $15,851; Undergraduates: $12,017. ***Scholarships, grants, and awards:*** Federal Pell, FSEOG, state, private, college/university gift aid from institutional funds.

GIFT AID (NON-NEED-BASED) ***Total amount:*** $1,610,296 (94% institutional, 6% external sources). ***Receiving aid:*** Freshmen: 15% (15). Undergraduates: 5% (39). ***Average award:*** Freshmen: $11,637. Undergraduates: $10,341. ***Scholarships, grants, and awards by category:*** *Academic interests/achievement:* 705 awards ($2,910,100 total): biological sciences, education, general academic interests/achievements, mathematics. *Special achievements/activities:* 23 awards ($16,750 total): general special achievements/activities, leadership. *Special characteristics:* 10 awards ($184,550 total): children of faculty/staff, international students. ***Tuition waivers:*** Full or partial for employees or children of employees. ***ROTC:*** Army cooperative, Air Force cooperative.

LOANS ***Student loans:*** $4,552,738 (85% need-based, 15% non-need-based). 74% of past graduating class borrowed through all loan programs. *Average indebtedness per student:* $30,516. ***Average need-based loan:*** Freshmen: $2963. Undergraduates: $4408. ***Parent loans:*** $937,363 (36% need-based, 64% non-need-based). ***Programs:*** Federal Direct (Subsidized and Unsubsidized Stafford, PLUS), Federal Nursing.

WORK-STUDY ***Federal work-study:*** Total amount: $586,507; 130 jobs averaging $2576. ***State or other work-study/employment:*** Total amount: $86,350 (42% need-based, 58% non-need-based). 13 part-time jobs averaging $6642.

ATHLETIC AWARDS Total amount: $925,063 (60% need-based, 40% non-need-based).

APPLYING FOR FINANCIAL AID ***Required financial aid form:*** FAFSA. ***Financial aid deadline (priority):*** 3/15. ***Notification date:*** Continuous beginning 12/15. Students must reply within 2 weeks of notification.

CONTACT Beth Sisk, Chief Financial Aid Officer and Express Center Director, College of Saint Mary, 7000 Mercy Road, Omaha, NE 68106, 402-399-2362 or toll-free 800-926-5534. *Fax:* 402-399-2480. *E-mail:* finaid@csm.edu.
Website: http://www.csm.edu/.

THE COLLEGE OF SAINT ROSE

Albany, NY

Tuition & fees: $34,354 | **Average undergraduate aid package: $24,919**

ABOUT THE INSTITUTION Independent, coed. ***Awards:*** certificates, bachelor's, and master's degrees. 43 undergraduate majors. ***Total enrollment:*** 4,004. Undergraduates: 2,433. Freshmen: 640. Federal methodology is used as a basis for awarding need-based institutional aid.

UNDERGRADUATE EXPENSES for 2020–2021 ***One-time required fee:*** $455. ***Comprehensive fee:*** $47,512 includes full-time tuition ($33,152), mandatory fees ($1202), and room and board ($13,158). ***College room only:*** $6712. Full-time tuition and fees vary according to course load. Room and board charges vary according to board plan and housing facility. ***Part-time tuition:*** $1098 per credit hour. ***Part-time fees:*** $145 per term. Part-time tuition and fees vary according to course load.

FRESHMAN FINANCIAL AID (Fall 2018) 586 applied for aid; of those 94% were deemed to have need. 100% of freshmen with need received aid; of those 18% had need fully met. ***Average percent of need met:*** 83% (excluding resources awarded to replace EFC). ***Average financial aid package:*** $26,740 (excluding resources awarded to replace EFC). 8% of all full-time freshmen had no need and received non-need-based gift aid.

UNDERGRADUATE FINANCIAL AID (Fall 2018) 2,152 applied for aid; of those 94% were deemed to have need. 100% of undergraduates with need received aid; of those 17% had need fully met. ***Average percent of need met:*** 79% (excluding resources awarded to replace EFC). ***Average financial aid package:*** $24,919 (excluding resources awarded to replace EFC). 10% of all full-time undergraduates had no need and received non-need-based gift aid.

GIFT AID (NEED-BASED) ***Total amount:*** $13,453,972 (44% federal, 29% state, 22% institutional, 5% external sources). ***Receiving aid:*** Freshmen: 74% (455); all full-time undergraduates: 64% (1,542). ***Average award:*** Freshmen: $7273; Undergraduates: $7503. ***Scholarships, grants, and awards:*** Federal Pell, FSEOG, state, private, college/university gift aid from institutional funds.

GIFT AID (NON-NEED-BASED) ***Total amount:*** $38,104,551 (97% institutional, 3% external sources). ***Receiving aid:*** Freshmen: 89% (545). Undergraduates: 73% (1,753). ***Average award:*** Freshmen: $18,689. Undergraduates: $15,670. ***Scholarships, grants, and awards by category:*** *Academic interests/achievement:* general academic interests/achievements. *Creative arts/performance:* applied art and design, music. *Special achievements/activities:* community service. *Special characteristics:* children and siblings of alumni, children of faculty/staff, children of union members/company employees, ethnic background, general special characteristics, members of minority groups, out-of-state students, siblings of current students, twins. ***Tuition waivers:*** Full or partial for employees or children of employees. ***ROTC:*** Army, Air Force cooperative.

LOANS ***Student loans:*** $12,051,201 (55% need-based, 45% non-need-based). 86% of past graduating class borrowed through all loan programs. *Average indebtedness per student:* $36,596. ***Average need-based loan:*** Freshmen: $7273. Undergraduates: $7503. ***Parent loans:*** $7,822,429 (61% need-based, 39% non-need-based). ***Programs:*** Federal Direct (Subsidized and Unsubsidized Stafford, PLUS).

WORK-STUDY ***Federal work-study:*** Total amount: $331,955; jobs available. ***State or other work-study/employment:*** Total amount: $11,052 (100% non-need-based). Part-time jobs available.

ATHLETIC AWARDS Total amount: $2,371,860 (25% need-based, 75% non-need-based).

APPLYING FOR FINANCIAL AID ***Required financial aid forms:*** FAFSA, state aid form. ***Financial aid deadline:*** 5/1 (priority: 2/1). ***Notification date:*** 2/1. Students must reply by 5/1 or within 2 weeks of notification.

CONTACT Steven Dwire, Assistant Vice President of Financial Aid and Enrollment Management, The College of Saint Rose, 432 Western Avenue, Albertus Hall, Room 206, Albany, NY 12203-1419, 518-458-4915 or toll-free 800-637-8556. *Fax:* 518-454-2802. *E-mail:* finaid@strose.edu.
Website: http://www.strose.edu/.

THE COLLEGE OF ST. SCHOLASTICA

Duluth, MN

Tuition & fees: $39,410 | **Average undergraduate aid package: $27,478**

ABOUT THE INSTITUTION Independent Roman Catholic Church, coed. ***Awards:*** certificates, bachelor's, master's, and doctoral degrees. 40 undergraduate majors. ***Total enrollment:*** 3,906. Undergraduates: 2,482. Freshmen: 450. Federal methodology is used as a basis for awarding need-based institutional aid.

UNDERGRADUATE EXPENSES for 2020–2021 ***Comprehensive fee:*** $49,750 includes full-time tuition ($38,750), mandatory fees ($660), and room and board ($10,340). ***College room only:*** $5742. Room and board charges vary according to housing facility. ***Part-time tuition:*** $1215 per credit.

FRESHMAN FINANCIAL AID (Fall 2019, est.) 424 applied for aid; of those 85% were deemed to have need. 100% of freshmen with need received aid; of those 33% had need fully met. ***Average percent of need met:*** 87% (excluding resources awarded to replace EFC). ***Average financial aid package:*** $34,112 (excluding resources awarded to replace EFC). 19% of all full-time freshmen had no need and received non-need-based gift aid.

UNDERGRADUATE FINANCIAL AID (Fall 2019, est.) 1,822 applied for aid; of those 90% were deemed to have need. 99% of undergraduates with need received aid; of those 24% had need fully met. ***Average percent of need met:*** 73% (excluding resources awarded to replace EFC). ***Average financial aid package:*** $27,478 (excluding resources awarded to replace EFC). 18% of all full-time undergraduates had no need and received non-need-based gift aid.

GIFT AID (NEED-BASED) ***Total amount:*** $9,563,229 (33% federal, 48% state, 19% institutional). ***Receiving aid:*** Freshmen: 53% (236); all full-time undergraduates: 55% (1,137). ***Average award:*** Freshmen: $7278; Undergraduates: $7826. ***Scholarships, grants, and awards:*** Federal Pell, FSEOG, state, private, college/university gift aid from institutional funds.

GIFT AID (NON-NEED-BASED) ***Total amount:*** $34,701,898 (97% institutional, 3% external sources). ***Receiving aid:*** Freshmen: 80% (359). Undergraduates: 64% (1,314). ***Average award:*** Freshmen: $23,761. Undergraduates: $20,311. ***Scholarships, grants, and awards by category:*** *Academic interests/achievement:* general academic interests/achievements. *Creative arts/performance:* music. *Special characteristics:* children and siblings of alumni, children of faculty/staff, handicapped students, international students, local/state students, previous college experience, religious affiliation, siblings of current students, spouses of current students. ***ROTC:*** Air Force cooperative.

LOANS ***Student loans:*** $18,783,647 (28% need-based, 72% non-need-based). 74% of past graduating class borrowed through all loan programs. *Average indebtedness per student:* $41,577. ***Average need-based loan:*** Freshmen: $3365. Undergraduates: $4452. ***Parent loans:*** $1,491,101 (100% non-need-based). ***Programs:*** Federal Direct (Subsidized and Unsubsidized Stafford, PLUS), Federal Nursing, state, Private Educational Loans.

WORK-STUDY ***Federal work-study:*** Total amount: $376,988; jobs available. ***State or other work-study/employment:*** Total amount: $1,883,704 (20% need-based, 80% non-need-based). Part-time jobs available.

APPLYING FOR FINANCIAL AID ***Required financial aid form:*** FAFSA. ***Financial aid deadline (priority):*** 3/1. ***Notification date:*** Continuous beginning 3/1. Students must reply by 5/1 or within 2 weeks of notification.

CONTACT Tricia Johnson, Director of Financial Aid, The College of St. Scholastica, 1200 Kenwood Avenue, Duluth, MN 55811-4199, 218-723-7027 or toll-free 800-249-6412. *Fax:* 218-733-2229. *E-mail:* tjohnson@css.edu.
Website: http://www.css.edu/.

COLLEGE OF STATEN ISLAND OF THE CITY UNIVERSITY OF NEW YORK

Staten Island, NY

Tuition & fees (NY res): $7489	Average undergraduate aid package: $8645

ABOUT THE INSTITUTION State and locally supported, coed. ***Awards:*** certificates, associate, bachelor's, master's, and doctoral degrees. 45 undergraduate majors. ***Total enrollment:*** 12,782. Undergraduates: 11,700. Freshmen: 2,361. Federal methodology is used as a basis for awarding need-based institutional aid.

UNDERGRADUATE EXPENSES for 2019–2020 ***Application fee:*** $65. ***Tuition, area resident:*** part-time $305 per credit hour. ***Tuition, state resident:*** full-time $6930; part-time $305 per credit hour. ***Tuition, nonresident:*** full-time $18,600; part-time $620 per credit hour. ***Required fees:*** full-time $559; $181 per term. ***Room only:*** $14,745. Room and board charges vary according to housing facility.

FRESHMAN FINANCIAL AID (Fall 2018) 2312 applied for aid; of those 88% were deemed to have need. 93% of freshmen with need received aid; of those 6% had need fully met. ***Average percent of need met:*** 34% (excluding resources awarded to replace EFC). ***Average financial aid package:*** $8564 (excluding resources awarded to replace EFC). 3% of all full-time freshmen had no need and received non-need-based gift aid.

UNDERGRADUATE FINANCIAL AID (Fall 2018) 7,895 applied for aid; of those 90% were deemed to have need. 94% of undergraduates with need received aid; of those 7% had need fully met. ***Average percent of need met:*** 47% (excluding resources awarded to replace EFC). ***Average financial aid package:*** $8645 (excluding resources awarded to replace EFC). 3% of all full-time undergraduates had no need and received non-need-based gift aid.

GIFT AID (NEED-BASED) ***Total amount:*** $52,543,493 (57% federal, 43% state). ***Receiving aid:*** Freshmen: 70% (1,782); all full-time undergraduates: 66% (6,206). ***Average award:*** Freshmen: $8221; Undergraduates: $8087. ***Scholarships, grants, and awards:*** Federal Pell, FSEOG, state, private, college/university gift aid from institutional funds.

GIFT AID (NON-NEED-BASED) ***Total amount:*** $5,426,159 (45% state, 17% institutional, 38% external sources). ***Receiving aid:*** Freshmen: 29% (744). Undergraduates: 19% (1,799). ***Average award:*** Freshmen: $3304. Undergraduates: $4194. ***Scholarships, grants, and awards by category:*** *Academic interests/achievement:* area/ethnic studies, biological sciences, business, communication, computer science, education, engineering/technologies, English, foreign languages, general academic interests/achievements, home economics, humanities, international studies, mathematics, physical sciences, premedicine, social sciences. *Creative arts/performance:* applied art and design, art/fine arts, cinema/film/broadcasting, creative writing, general creative arts/performance, journalism/publications, music, performing arts, theater/drama. *Special achievements/activities:* community service, general special achievements/activities, hobbies/interests, leadership, memberships. *Special characteristics:* adult students, children and siblings of alumni, ethnic background, general special characteristics, handicapped students, international students, local/state students, members of minority groups, out-of-state students, previous college experience, public servants, veterans, veterans' children. ***Tuition waivers:*** Full or partial for employees or children of employees, senior citizens.

LOANS ***Student loans:*** $12,260,467 (43% need-based, 57% non-need-based). ***Average need-based loan:*** Freshmen: $9770. Undergraduates: $9494. ***Parent loans:*** $866,177 (100% non-need-based). ***Programs:*** Federal Direct (Subsidized and Unsubsidized Stafford, PLUS).

WORK-STUDY ***Federal work-study:*** Total amount: $1,095,272; jobs available.

APPLYING FOR FINANCIAL AID ***Required financial aid forms:*** FAFSA, state aid form. ***Financial aid deadline (priority):*** 1/31. ***Notification date:*** Continuous beginning 2/15.

CONTACT Ms. Terri Sangiorgio, Director of Student Financial Aid, College of Staten Island of the City University of New York, 2800 Victory Boulevard, 2A-401A, Staten Island, NY 10314-6600, 718-982-2030. *Fax:* 718-982-2037. *E-mail:* financialaid@csi.cuny.edu.
Website: http://www.csi.cuny.edu/.

COLLEGE OF THE ATLANTIC

Bar Harbor, ME

Tuition & fees: $43,542	Average undergraduate aid package: $41,235

ABOUT THE INSTITUTION Independent, coed. ***Awards:*** bachelor's and master's degrees. 42 undergraduate majors. ***Total enrollment:*** 354. Undergraduates: 349. Freshmen: 91. Both federal and institutional methodology are used as a basis for awarding need-based institutional aid.

UNDERGRADUATE EXPENSES for 2019–2020 ***Application fee:*** $50. ***Comprehensive fee:*** $53,289 includes full-time tuition ($42,993), mandatory fees ($549), and room and board ($9747). ***College room only:*** $6210. Full-time tuition and fees vary according to course load and degree level. Room and board charges vary according to board plan. ***Part-time tuition:*** $4777 per credit. ***Part-time fees:*** $183 per term. Part-time tuition and fees vary according to course load and degree level.

FRESHMAN FINANCIAL AID (Fall 2019, est.) 99 applied for aid; of those 92% were deemed to have need. 100% of freshmen with need received aid; of those 41% had need fully met. ***Average percent of need met:*** 96% (excluding resources awarded to replace EFC). ***Average financial aid package:*** $44,186 (excluding resources awarded to replace EFC). 12% of all full-time freshmen had no need and received non-need-based gift aid.

UNDERGRADUATE FINANCIAL AID (Fall 2019, est.) 320 applied for aid; of those 92% were deemed to have need. 100% of undergraduates with need received aid; of those 44% had need fully met. ***Average percent of need met:*** 95% (excluding resources awarded to replace EFC). ***Average financial aid package:***

$41,235 (excluding resources awarded to replace EFC). 12% of all full-time undergraduates had no need and received non-need-based gift aid.

GIFT AID (NEED-BASED) ***Total amount:*** $10,643,751 (3% federal, 1% state, 95% institutional, 1% external sources). ***Receiving aid:*** Freshmen: 87% (91); all full-time undergraduates: 85% (293). ***Average award:*** Freshmen: $39,441; Undergraduates: $35,910. ***Scholarships, grants, and awards:*** Federal Pell, FSEOG, state, private, college/university gift aid from institutional funds.

GIFT AID (NON-NEED-BASED) ***Total amount:*** $802,639 (100% institutional). ***Receiving aid:*** Undergraduates: 2% (7). ***Average award:*** Freshmen: $18,769. Undergraduates: $16,305. ***Scholarships, grants, and awards by category:*** *Academic interests/achievement:* 41 awards ($696,150 total): general academic interests/achievements. ***Tuition waivers:*** Full or partial for employees or children of employees.

LOANS ***Student loans:*** $1,273,356 (61% need-based, 39% non-need-based). 69% of past graduating class borrowed through all loan programs. *Average indebtedness per student:* $29,731. ***Average need-based loan:*** Freshmen: $3368. Undergraduates: $4389. ***Parent loans:*** $179,011 (100% non-need-based). ***Programs:*** Federal Direct (Subsidized and Unsubsidized Stafford, PLUS).

WORK-STUDY ***Federal work-study:*** Total amount: $485,603; 171 jobs averaging $2840. ***State or other work-study/employment:*** Total amount: $418,000 (71% need-based, 29% non-need-based). 141 part-time jobs averaging $2965.

APPLYING FOR FINANCIAL AID ***Required financial aid forms:*** FAFSA, institution's own form, noncustodial (divorced/separated) parent's statement. ***Financial aid deadline:*** 2/1. ***Notification date:*** 4/1. Students must reply by 5/1 or within 2 weeks of notification.

CONTACT Linda Black, Director of Financial Aid, College of the Atlantic, 105 Eden Street, Bar Harbor, ME 04609-1198, 207-801-5645 or toll-free 800-528-0025. *Fax:* 207-288-4126. *E-mail:* lblack@coa.edu.
Website: http://www.coa.edu/.

COLLEGE OF THE HOLY CROSS

Worcester, MA

Tuition & fees: $56,520	Average undergraduate aid package: $41,584

ABOUT THE INSTITUTION Independent Roman Catholic (Jesuit), coed. ***Awards:*** bachelor's degrees. 40 undergraduate majors. ***Total enrollment:*** 3,174. Undergraduates: 3,174. Freshmen: 829. Both federal and institutional methodology are used as a basis for awarding need-based institutional aid.

UNDERGRADUATE EXPENSES for 2020–2021 ***Application fee:*** $60. ***Comprehensive fee:*** $72,080 includes full-time tuition ($55,800), mandatory fees ($720), and room and board ($15,560). ***College room only:*** $8520.

FRESHMAN FINANCIAL AID (Fall 2019, est.) 629 applied for aid; of those 75% were deemed to have need. 100% of freshmen with need received aid; of those 100% had need fully met. ***Average percent of need met:*** 100% (excluding resources awarded to replace EFC). ***Average financial aid package:*** $44,288 (excluding resources awarded to replace EFC). 7% of all full-time freshmen had no need and received non-need-based gift aid.

UNDERGRADUATE FINANCIAL AID (Fall 2019, est.) 2,083 applied for aid; of those 81% were deemed to have need. 100% of undergraduates with need received aid; of those 100% had need fully met. ***Average percent of need met:*** 100% (excluding resources awarded to replace EFC). ***Average financial aid package:*** $41,584 (excluding resources awarded to replace EFC). 5% of all full-time undergraduates had no need and received non-need-based gift aid.

GIFT AID (NEED-BASED) ***Receiving aid:*** Freshmen: 44% (367); all full-time undergraduates: 43% (1,355). ***Average award:*** Freshmen: $42,069; Undergraduates: $40,064. ***Scholarships, grants, and awards:*** Federal Pell, FSEOG, state, private, college/university gift aid from institutional funds.

GIFT AID (NON-NEED-BASED) ***Receiving aid:*** Freshmen: 15% (122). Undergraduates: 9% (277). ***Average award:*** Freshmen: $16,357. Undergraduates: $20,393. ***Scholarships, grants, and awards by category:*** *Academic interests/achievement:* general academic interests/achievements. *Creative arts/performance:* music. *Special characteristics:* children of faculty/staff. ***ROTC:*** Army cooperative, Naval, Air Force cooperative.

LOANS ***Student loans:*** 52% of past graduating class borrowed through all loan programs. *Average indebtedness per student:* $26,258. ***Average need-based loan:*** Freshmen: $3428. Undergraduates: $4484. ***Programs:*** Federal Direct (Subsidized and Unsubsidized Stafford, PLUS), college/university.

WORK-STUDY Federal work-study jobs available.

APPLYING FOR FINANCIAL AID ***Required financial aid forms:*** FAFSA, CSS Financial Aid PROFILE, noncustodial (divorced/separated) parent's statement, business/farm supplement, federal income tax form(s).

CONTACT Ms. Nicole Cunningham, Director of Financial Aid, College of the Holy Cross, One College Street, Hogan 314, Worcester, MA 01610-2395, 508-793-2265 or toll-free 800-442-2421. *Fax:* 508-793-2527.
Website: http://www.holycross.edu/.

COLLEGE OF THE OZARKS

Point Lookout, MO

Tuition & fees: N/R	Average undergraduate aid package: $19,200

ABOUT THE INSTITUTION Independent Presbyterian, coed. ***Awards:*** bachelor's degrees. 67 undergraduate majors. ***Total enrollment:*** 1,546. Undergraduates: 1,546. Freshmen: 255. Federal methodology is used as a basis for awarding need-based institutional aid.

UNDERGRADUATE EXPENSES for 2020–2021 ***Tuition:*** part-time $310 per credit hour. ***Required fees:*** full-time $460; $230 per term.

FRESHMAN FINANCIAL AID (Fall 2018) 255 applied for aid; of those 91% were deemed to have need. 100% of freshmen with need received aid; of those 34% had need fully met. ***Average percent of need met:*** 84% (excluding resources awarded to replace EFC). ***Average financial aid package:*** $19,200 (excluding resources awarded to replace EFC). 9% of all full-time freshmen had no need and received non-need-based gift aid.

UNDERGRADUATE FINANCIAL AID (Fall 2018) 1,504 applied for aid; of those 91% were deemed to have need. 100% of undergraduates with need received aid; of those 44% had need fully met. ***Average percent of need met:*** 84% (excluding resources awarded to replace EFC). ***Average financial aid package:*** $19,200 (excluding resources awarded to replace EFC). 10% of all full-time undergraduates had no need and received non-need-based gift aid.

GIFT AID (NEED-BASED) ***Total amount:*** $21,999,955 (18% federal, 5% state, 77% institutional). ***Receiving aid:*** Freshmen: 91% (231); all full-time undergraduates: 91% (1,369). ***Average award:*** Freshmen: $13,908; Undergraduates: $13,908. ***Scholarships, grants, and awards:*** Federal Pell, FSEOG, state, private, college/university gift aid from institutional funds.

GIFT AID (NON-NEED-BASED) ***Total amount:*** $109,500 (100% state). ***Average award:*** Freshmen: $19,200. Undergraduates: $19,200.

LOANS ***Average need-based loan:*** Freshmen: $5292. Undergraduates: $5292.

WORK-STUDY ***Federal work-study:*** Total amount: $3,101,020.

ATHLETIC AWARDS Total amount: $336,380 (100% need-based).

APPLYING FOR FINANCIAL AID ***Required financial aid form:*** FAFSA. ***Financial aid deadline (priority):*** 11/15. ***Notification date:*** 7/1.

CONTACT Office of Financial Aid, College of the Ozarks, PO Box 17, Point Lookout, MO 65726, 417-690-3290 or toll-free 800-222-0525. *Fax:* 417-690-3286.
Website: http://www.cofo.edu/.

THE COLLEGE OF WOOSTER

Wooster, OH

Tuition & fees: $50,250	Average undergraduate aid package: $47,142

ABOUT THE INSTITUTION Independent Presbyterian Church (U.S.A.), coed. ***Awards:*** bachelor's degrees. 46 undergraduate majors. ***Total enrollment:*** 1,947. Undergraduates: 1,947. Freshmen: 542. Both federal and institutional methodology are used as a basis for awarding need-based institutional aid.

UNDERGRADUATE EXPENSES for 2020–2021 ***Comprehensive fee:*** $62,100 includes full-time tuition ($49,810), mandatory fees ($440), and room and board ($11,850). ***College room only:*** $5750. Full-time tuition and fees vary according to course load. Room and board charges vary according to board plan and housing facility. ***Part-time tuition:*** $1545 per credit hour. Part-time tuition and fees vary according to course load.

FRESHMAN FINANCIAL AID (Fall 2019, est.) 475 applied for aid; of those 85% were deemed to have need. 100% of freshmen with need received aid; of those 48% had need fully met. ***Average percent of need met:*** 94% (excluding resources awarded to replace EFC). ***Average financial aid package:*** $48,431 (excluding resources awarded to replace EFC). 25% of all full-time freshmen had no need and received non-need-based gift aid.

UNDERGRADUATE FINANCIAL AID (Fall 2019, est.) 1,439 applied for aid; of those 89% were deemed to have need. 100% of undergraduates with need received aid; of those 45% had need fully met. ***Average percent of need met:*** 93% (excluding resources awarded to replace EFC). ***Average financial aid package:*** $47,142 (excluding resources awarded to replace EFC). 31% of all full-time undergraduates had no need and received non-need-based gift aid.

GIFT AID (NEED-BASED) ***Receiving aid:*** Freshmen: 71% (388); all full-time undergraduates: 64% (1,244). ***Average award:*** Freshmen: $37,249; Undergraduates: $35,524. ***Scholarships, grants, and awards:*** Federal Pell, FSEOG, state, private, college/university gift aid from institutional funds.

GIFT AID (NON-NEED-BASED) ***Receiving aid:*** Freshmen: 25% (137). Undergraduates: 21% (399). ***Average award:*** Freshmen: $28,971. Undergraduates: $26,400. ***Scholarships, grants, and awards by category:*** *Academic interests/achievement:* 1,343 awards ($34,640,146 total): general academic interests/achievements. *Creative arts/performance:* 145 awards ($632,000 total): dance, music, theater/drama. *Special achievements/activities:* 267 awards ($1,979,595 total): community service, religious involvement. *Special characteristics:* 453 awards ($14,889,445 total): children of educators, children of faculty/staff, international students, members of minority groups. ***Tuition waivers:*** Full or partial for employees or children of employees.

LOANS ***Student loans:*** 53% of past graduating class borrowed through all loan programs. *Average indebtedness per student:* $32,194. ***Average need-based loan:*** Freshmen: $6154. Undergraduates: $7084. ***Programs:*** Federal Direct (Subsidized and Unsubsidized Stafford, PLUS), Perkins.

WORK-STUDY ***Federal work-study:*** 719 jobs averaging $2201. ***State or other work-study/employment:*** 242 part-time jobs averaging $3585.

APPLYING FOR FINANCIAL AID ***Required financial aid forms:*** FAFSA, institution's own form. ***Notification date:*** Continuous. Students must reply within 2 weeks of notification.

CONTACT Dana Kennedy, Director of Financial Aid, The College of Wooster, Pearl House, 804 Beall Avenue, Wooster, OH 44691, 800-877-3688 or toll-free 800-877-9905. *Fax:* 330-263-2634. *E-mail:* financialaid@wooster.edu.
Website: http://www.wooster.edu/.

COLORADO CHRISTIAN UNIVERSITY

Lakewood, CO

CONTACT Mr. Steve Woodburn, Director of Financial Aid, Colorado Christian University, 180 South Garrison Street, Lakewood, CO 80226-7499, 303-963-3230 or toll-free 800-44-FAITH. *Fax:* 303-963-3231. *E-mail:* sfs@ccu.edu.
Website: http://www.ccu.edu/.

THE COLORADO COLLEGE

Colorado Springs, CO

Tuition & fees: $60,864	Average undergraduate aid package: $47,954

ABOUT THE INSTITUTION Independent, coed. ***Awards:*** bachelor's and master's degrees (master's degree in education only). 49 undergraduate majors. ***Total enrollment:*** 2,124. Undergraduates: 2,099. Freshmen: 535. Institutional methodology is used as a basis for awarding need-based institutional aid.

UNDERGRADUATE EXPENSES for 2020–2021 ***One-time required fee:*** $250. ***Comprehensive fee:*** $74,256 includes full-time tuition ($60,390), mandatory fees ($474), and room and board ($13,392). ***College room only:*** $7992. Full-time tuition and fees vary according to course load. Room and board charges vary according to board plan and housing facility. ***Part-time tuition:*** $10,144 per course. Part-time tuition and fees vary according to course load.

FRESHMAN FINANCIAL AID (Fall 2019, est.) 280 applied for aid; of those 74% were deemed to have need. 100% of freshmen with need received aid; of those 100% had need fully met. ***Average percent of need met:*** 100% (excluding resources awarded to replace EFC). ***Average financial aid package:*** $57,862 (excluding resources awarded to replace EFC). 6% of all full-time freshmen had no need and received non-need-based gift aid.

UNDERGRADUATE FINANCIAL AID (Fall 2019, est.) 897 applied for aid; of those 93% were deemed to have need. 100% of undergraduates with need received aid; of those 100% had need fully met. ***Average percent of need met:*** 100% (excluding resources awarded to replace EFC). ***Average financial aid package:*** $47,954 (excluding resources awarded to replace EFC). 5% of all full-time undergraduates had no need and received non-need-based gift aid.

GIFT AID (NEED-BASED) ***Total amount:*** $35,329,491 (4% federal, 96% institutional). ***Receiving aid:*** Freshmen: 39% (206); all full-time undergraduates: 36% (752). ***Average award:*** Freshmen: $53,720; Undergraduates: $48,600. ***Scholarships, grants, and awards:*** Federal Pell, FSEOG, state, private, college/university gift aid from institutional funds.

GIFT AID (NON-NEED-BASED) ***Total amount:*** $3,293,389 (30% institutional, 70% external sources). ***Receiving aid:*** Freshmen: 2% (10). Undergraduates: 4% (76). ***Average award:*** Freshmen: $8718. Undergraduates: $9763. ***Scholarships, grants, and awards by category:*** *Academic interests/achievement:* biological sciences, general academic interests/achievements, mathematics, physical sciences. *Special characteristics:* children of faculty/staff. ***Tuition waivers:*** Full or partial for employees or children of employees. ***ROTC:*** Army cooperative.

LOANS ***Student loans:*** $3,779,758 (36% need-based, 64% non-need-based). 33% of past graduating class borrowed through all loan programs. *Average indebtedness per student:* $23,579. ***Average need-based loan:*** Freshmen: $3146. Undergraduates: $3968. ***Parent loans:*** $1,218,526 (100% non-need-based). ***Programs:*** Federal Direct (Subsidized and Unsubsidized Stafford, PLUS).

WORK-STUDY ***Federal work-study:*** Total amount: $657,176; jobs available. ***State or other work-study/employment:*** Total amount: $332,661 (99% need-based, 1% non-need-based). Part-time jobs available.

ATHLETIC AWARDS Total amount: $2,081,263 (10% need-based, 90% non-need-based).

APPLYING FOR FINANCIAL AID ***Required financial aid forms:*** FAFSA, CSS Financial Aid PROFILE, state aid form, noncustodial (divorced/separated) parent's statement. ***Financial aid deadline:*** 1/15 (priority: 11/1). ***Notification date:*** 3/15. Students must reply by 5/1.

CONTACT Ms. Shannon L. Amundson, Director of Financial Aid, The Colorado College, 14 East Cache La Poudre Street, Colorado Springs, CO 80903-3294, 719-389-6651 or toll-free 800-542-7214. *Fax:* 719-389-6173. *E-mail:* financialaid@coloradocollege.edu.
Website: http://www.coloradocollege.edu/.

COLORADO MESA UNIVERSITY

Grand Junction, CO

Tuition & fees (area res): $9306	Average undergraduate aid package: $10,393

ABOUT THE INSTITUTION State-supported, coed. ***Awards:*** certificates, associate, bachelor's, master's, and doctoral degrees. 63 undergraduate majors. ***Total enrollment:*** 9,492. Undergraduates: 9,365. Freshmen: 2,065. Federal methodology is used as a basis for awarding need-based institutional aid.

UNDERGRADUATE EXPENSES for 2019–2020 ***Application fee:*** $30. ***Tuition, area resident:*** full-time $8343; part-time $278 per credit hour. ***Tuition, state resident:*** full-time $8343; part-time $278 per credit hour. ***Tuition, nonresident:*** full-time $22,200; part-time $740 per credit hour. ***Required fees:*** full-time $963. ***College room and board:*** $11,168; ***Room only:*** $6100.

FRESHMAN FINANCIAL AID (Fall 2018) 1745 applied for aid; of those 73% were deemed to have need. 99% of freshmen with need received aid; of those 24% had need fully met. ***Average percent of need met:*** 65% (excluding resources awarded to replace EFC). ***Average financial aid package:*** $10,072 (excluding resources awarded to replace EFC). 13% of all full-time freshmen had no need and received non-need-based gift aid.

UNDERGRADUATE FINANCIAL AID (Fall 2018) 5,696 applied for aid; of those 78% were deemed to have need. 99% of undergraduates with need received aid; of those 20% had need fully met. ***Average percent of need met:*** 64% (excluding resources awarded to replace EFC). ***Average financial aid package:*** $10,393

(excluding resources awarded to replace EFC). 8% of all full-time undergraduates had no need and received non-need-based gift aid.
GIFT AID (NEED-BASED) ***Total amount:*** $32,635,889 (48% federal, 25% state, 16% institutional, 11% external sources). ***Receiving aid:*** Freshmen: 58% (1,130); all full-time undergraduates: 54% (3,824). ***Average award:*** Freshmen: $8267; Undergraduates: $8047. ***Scholarships, grants, and awards:*** Federal Pell, FSEOG, state, private, college/university gift aid from institutional funds.
GIFT AID (NON-NEED-BASED) ***Total amount:*** $7,085,337 (8% federal, 4% state, 75% institutional, 13% external sources). ***Receiving aid:*** Freshmen: 10% (190). Undergraduates: 6% (452). ***Average award:*** Freshmen: $3510. Undergraduates: $3639. ***Scholarships, grants, and awards by category:*** *Academic interests/achievement:* biological sciences, business, communication, computer science, education, engineering/technologies, English, foreign languages, general academic interests/achievements, home economics, humanities, mathematics, physical sciences, social sciences. *Creative arts/performance:* applied art and design, dance, music, performing arts, theater/drama. *Special achievements/activities:* cheerleading/drum major, general special achievements/activities, hobbies/interests, leadership, rodeo. *Special characteristics:* adult students, children and siblings of alumni, ethnic background, first-generation college students, international students, local/state students, members of minority groups, out-of-state students, previous college experience, veterans.
LOANS ***Student loans:*** $35,300,078 (79% need-based, 21% non-need-based). 64% of past graduating class borrowed through all loan programs. *Average indebtedness per student:* $27,269. ***Average need-based loan:*** Freshmen: $3086. Undergraduates: $3705. ***Parent loans:*** $23,361,914 (62% need-based, 38% non-need-based). ***Programs:*** Federal Direct (Subsidized and Unsubsidized Stafford, PLUS), Perkins.
WORK-STUDY ***Federal work-study:*** Total amount: $508,641; jobs available. ***State or other work-study/employment:*** Total amount: $6,188,904 (35% need-based, 65% non-need-based). Part-time jobs available.
ATHLETIC AWARDS Total amount: $2,651,660 (44% need-based, 56% non-need-based).
APPLYING FOR FINANCIAL AID ***Required financial aid form:*** FAFSA. ***Financial aid deadline:*** Continuous.
CONTACT Mr. Curt Martin, Director of Financial Aid, Colorado Mesa University, 1100 North Avenue, Grand Junction, CO 81501-3122, 970-248-1065 or toll-free 800-982-MESA. *Fax:* 970-248-1191. *E-mail:* cumartin@coloradomesa.edu.
Website: http://www.coloradomesa.edu/.

COLORADO MOUNTAIN COLLEGE
Glenwood Springs, CO

Tuition & fees (area res): $2700	Average undergraduate aid package: N/A

ABOUT THE INSTITUTION District-supported, coed. ***Awards:*** certificates, associate, and bachelor's degrees. 26 undergraduate majors. ***Total enrollment:*** 5,796. Undergraduates: 5,796. Freshmen: 503. Both federal and institutional methodology are used as a basis for awarding need-based institutional aid.
UNDERGRADUATE EXPENSES for 2019–2020 ***Tuition, area resident:*** full-time $2400; part-time $80 per credit hour. ***Tuition, state resident:*** full-time $5400; part-time $180 per credit hour. ***Tuition, nonresident:*** full-time $13,590; part-time $453 per credit hour. ***Required fees:*** full-time $300. ***College room and board:*** $10,322; ***Room only:*** $6000.
FRESHMAN FINANCIAL AID (Fall 2018) 170 applied for aid. 15% of all full-time freshmen had no need and received non-need-based gift aid.
UNDERGRADUATE FINANCIAL AID (Fall 2018) 826 applied for aid. 21% of all full-time undergraduates had no need and received non-need-based gift aid.
GIFT AID (NEED-BASED) ***Total amount:*** $4,284,966 (66% federal, 34% state). ***Receiving aid:*** Freshmen: 36% (85); all full-time undergraduates: 40% (484). ***Average award:*** Freshmen: $1695; Undergraduates: $1711. ***Scholarships, grants, and awards:*** Federal Pell, FSEOG, state, private, college/university gift aid from institutional funds.
GIFT AID (NON-NEED-BASED) ***Total amount:*** $1,450,684 (62% institutional, 38% external sources). ***Receiving aid:*** Freshmen: 24% (57). Undergraduates: 30% (357). ***Average award:*** Freshmen: $1406. Undergraduates: $1273. ***Scholarships, grants, and awards by category:*** *Special characteristics:* local/state students.
LOANS ***Student loans:*** $2,611,419 (46% need-based, 54% non-need-based). ***Parent loans:*** $478,858 (100% non-need-based). ***Programs:*** Federal Direct (Subsidized and Unsubsidized Stafford, PLUS), Perkins, Federal Nursing, state, college/university.
WORK-STUDY ***Federal work-study:*** Total amount: $100,156; jobs available. ***State or other work-study/employment:*** Total amount: $403,991 (42% need-based, 58% non-need-based). Part-time jobs available.
APPLYING FOR FINANCIAL AID ***Notification date:*** Continuous.
CONTACT Mr. Thomas S. Valles, Director of Financial Aid, Colorado Mountain College, 802 Grand Avenue, Glenwood Springs, CO 81601, 970-947-8338 or toll-free 800-621-8559. *E-mail:* tvalles@coloradomtn.edu.
Website: http://www.coloradomtn.edu/.

COLORADO MOUNTAIN COLLEGE
Leadville, CO

CONTACT Financial Aid Office, Colorado Mountain College, 901 South Highway 24, Leadville, CO 80461, 719-486-2015 or toll-free 800-621-8559.
Website: http://www.coloradomtn.edu/.

COLORADO MOUNTAIN COLLEGE
Steamboat Springs, CO

CONTACT Mr. Thomas S. Valles, Director of Financial Aid, Colorado Mountain College, 802 Grand Avenue, Glenwood Springs, CO 81601, 800-621-8559 Ext. 8338 or toll-free 800-621-8559. *Fax:* 970-947-8318. *E-mail:* finaid@coloradomtn.edu.
Website: http://www.coloradomtn.edu/.

COLORADO SCHOOL OF MINES
Golden, CO

Tuition & fees (CO res): $19,062	Average undergraduate aid package: $15,006

ABOUT THE INSTITUTION State-supported, coed. ***Awards:*** certificates, bachelor's, master's, and doctoral degrees. 17 undergraduate majors. ***Total enrollment:*** 6,605. Undergraduates: 5,154. Freshmen: 1,282. Federal methodology is used as a basis for awarding need-based institutional aid.
UNDERGRADUATE EXPENSES for 2019–2020 ***Application fee:*** $45. ***Tuition, state resident:*** full-time $16,650; part-time $555 per credit hour. ***Tuition, nonresident:*** full-time $37,350; part-time $1245 per credit hour. ***Required fees:*** full-time $2412. ***College room and board:*** $14,211. Room and board charges vary according to board plan and housing facility.
FRESHMAN FINANCIAL AID (Fall 2018) 998 applied for aid; of those 60% were deemed to have need. 100% of freshmen with need received aid; of those 32% had need fully met. ***Average percent of need met:*** 61% (excluding resources awarded to replace EFC). ***Average financial aid package:*** $15,908 (excluding resources awarded to replace EFC). 36% of all full-time freshmen had no need and received non-need-based gift aid.
UNDERGRADUATE FINANCIAL AID (Fall 2018) 3,168 applied for aid; of those 68% were deemed to have need. 100% of undergraduates with need received aid; of those 23% had need fully met. ***Average percent of need met:*** 58% (excluding resources awarded to replace EFC). ***Average financial aid package:*** $15,006 (excluding resources awarded to replace EFC). 33% of all full-time undergraduates had no need and received non-need-based gift aid.
GIFT AID (NEED-BASED) ***Total amount:*** $23,090,578 (15% federal, 7% state, 69% institutional, 9% external sources). ***Receiving aid:*** Freshmen: 30% (353); all full-time undergraduates: 26% (1,214). ***Average award:*** Freshmen: $6126; Undergraduates: $6653. ***Scholarships, grants, and awards:*** Federal Pell, FSEOG, state, private, college/university gift aid from institutional funds.
GIFT AID (NON-NEED-BASED) ***Total amount:*** $15,027,411 (92% institutional, 8% external sources). ***Receiving aid:*** Freshmen: 42% (504). Undergraduates: 34% (1,590). ***Average award:*** Freshmen: $8896. Undergraduates: $8904. ***Scholarships, grants, and awards by category:*** *Academic interests/achievement:* business, computer science, engineering/technologies, general academic interests/

achievements, mathematics, military science, physical sciences. ***Tuition waivers:*** Full or partial for employees or children of employees. ***ROTC:*** Army, Air Force.

LOANS ***Student loans:*** $30,263,424 (47% need-based, 53% non-need-based). 49% of past graduating class borrowed through all loan programs. *Average indebtedness per student:* $32,482. ***Average need-based loan:*** Freshmen: $3386. Undergraduates: $4363. ***Parent loans:*** $15,427,776 (61% need-based, 39% non-need-based). ***Programs:*** Federal Direct (Subsidized and Unsubsidized Stafford, PLUS), Perkins, college/university.

WORK-STUDY ***Federal work-study:*** Total amount: $845,280; 340 jobs averaging $1666. ***State or other work-study/employment:*** Total amount: $4,600,650 (16% need-based, 84% non-need-based). 430 part-time jobs averaging $1551.

ATHLETIC AWARDS Total amount: $4,118,802 (26% need-based, 74% non-need-based).

APPLYING FOR FINANCIAL AID ***Required financial aid form:*** FAFSA. ***Financial aid deadline (priority):*** 3/1. ***Notification date:*** Continuous beginning 1/1. Students must reply by 4/1.

CONTACT Jill Robertson, Director of Financial Aid, Colorado School of Mines, 1200 16th St, Golden, CO 80401-1887, 303-273-3301 or toll-free 800-446-9488 Ext.3220. *Fax:* 303-384-2252. *E-mail:* finaid@mines.edu.
Website: http://www.mines.edu/.

COLORADO STATE UNIVERSITY

Fort Collins, CO

Tuition & fees (CO res): $11,831	Average undergraduate aid package: $11,515

ABOUT THE INSTITUTION State-supported, coed. ***Awards:*** certificates, bachelor's, master's, and doctoral degrees. 76 undergraduate majors. ***Total enrollment:*** 33,996. Undergraduates: 26,559. Freshmen: 5,137. Both federal and institutional methodology are used as a basis for awarding need-based institutional aid.

UNDERGRADUATE EXPENSES for 2019–2020 ***Application fee:*** $50. ***Tuition, state resident:*** full-time $9426; part-time $428 per credit hour. ***Tuition, nonresident:*** full-time $27,327; part-time $1366 per credit hour. ***Required fees:*** full-time $2405; $296 per term. ***College room and board:*** $11,964; ***Room only:*** $5746.

FRESHMAN FINANCIAL AID (Fall 2018) 4277 applied for aid; of those 63% were deemed to have need. 91% of freshmen with need received aid; of those 28% had need fully met. ***Average percent of need met:*** 66% (excluding resources awarded to replace EFC). ***Average financial aid package:*** $11,101 (excluding resources awarded to replace EFC). 21% of all full-time freshmen had no need and received non-need-based gift aid.

UNDERGRADUATE FINANCIAL AID (Fall 2018) 16,332 applied for aid; of those 72% were deemed to have need. 91% of undergraduates with need received aid; of those 20% had need fully met. ***Average percent of need met:*** 65% (excluding resources awarded to replace EFC). ***Average financial aid package:*** $11,515 (excluding resources awarded to replace EFC). 17% of all full-time undergraduates had no need and received non-need-based gift aid.

GIFT AID (NEED-BASED) ***Total amount:*** $94,817,086 (28% federal, 13% state, 51% institutional, 8% external sources). ***Receiving aid:*** Freshmen: 41% (1,970); all full-time undergraduates: 33% (7,938). ***Average award:*** Freshmen: $9289; Undergraduates: $8892. ***Scholarships, grants, and awards:*** Federal Pell, FSEOG, state, private, college/university gift aid from institutional funds.

GIFT AID (NON-NEED-BASED) ***Total amount:*** $29,190,777 (1% federal, 2% state, 82% institutional, 15% external sources). ***Receiving aid:*** Freshmen: 24% (1,163). Undergraduates: 14% (3,334). ***Average award:*** Freshmen: $6462. Undergraduates: $6127. ***Scholarships, grants, and awards by category:*** *Academic interests/achievement:* general academic interests/achievements. *Creative arts/performance:* applied art and design, creative writing, dance, music, performing arts, theater/drama. *Special achievements/activities:* general special achievements/activities. *Special characteristics:* children of faculty/staff, first-generation college students, international students, members of minority groups, veterans. ***ROTC:*** Army, Air Force.

LOANS ***Student loans:*** $94,059,067 (67% need-based, 33% non-need-based). 53% of past graduating class borrowed through all loan programs. *Average indebtedness per student:* $27,142. ***Average need-based loan:*** Freshmen: $5005. Undergraduates: $6250. ***Parent loans:*** $65,440,602 (43% need-based, 57% non-need-based). ***Programs:*** Federal Direct (Subsidized and Unsubsidized Stafford, PLUS), Perkins.

WORK-STUDY ***Federal work-study:*** Total amount: $1,010,218; jobs available. ***State or other work-study/employment:*** Total amount: $2,770,436 (59% need-based, 41% non-need-based). Part-time jobs available.

ATHLETIC AWARDS Total amount: $9,084,747 (30% need-based, 70% non-need-based).

APPLYING FOR FINANCIAL AID ***Required financial aid forms:*** FAFSA, institution's own form. ***Financial aid deadline (priority):*** 3/1. ***Notification date:*** Continuous beginning 3/1.

CONTACT Financial Aid Office, Colorado State University, Fort Collins, CO 80523, 970-491-1101.
Website: http://www.colostate.edu/.

COLORADO STATE UNIVERSITY–GLOBAL CAMPUS

Greenwood Village, CO

Tuition & fees (area res): $10,500	Average undergraduate aid package: N/A

ABOUT THE INSTITUTION State-supported, coed. ***Awards:*** certificates, bachelor's, and master's degrees. ***Total enrollment:*** 12,670. Undergraduates: 8,114.

UNDERGRADUATE EXPENSES for 2020–2021 ***Application fee:*** $25. ***Tuition, area resident:*** full-time $10,500; part-time $350 per credit hour. ***Tuition, state resident:*** full-time $10,500; part-time $350 per credit hour. ***Tuition, nonresident:*** full-time $10,500; part-time $350 per credit hour. ***Required fees:*** $350 per credit hour. Full-time tuition and fees vary according to course load. Part-time tuition and fees vary according to course load. ***Payment plan:*** Guaranteed tuition.

GIFT AID (NON-NEED-BASED) ***Tuition waivers:*** Full or partial for employees or children of employees.

CONTACT Financial Aid Office, Colorado State University–Global Campus, 8000 E. Maplewood Avenue, Greenwood Village, CO 80111, 720-279-0159 or toll-free 800-920-6723.
Website: http://csuglobal.edu/.

COLORADO STATE UNIVERSITY-PUEBLO

Pueblo, CO

CONTACT Justin Streater, Associate Director of Financial Aid, Colorado State University-Pueblo, 2200 Bonforte Boulevard, Pueblo, CO 81001-4901, 719-549-2967. *Fax:* 719-549-2088. *E-mail:* justin.streater@csupueblo.edu.
Website: http://www.csupueblo.edu/.

COLORADO TECHNICAL UNIVERSITY AURORA

Aurora, CO

CONTACT Ms. Natalie Dietsch, Financial Aid Manager, Colorado Technical University Aurora, 5775 Denver Tech Center Boulevard, Suite 100, Greenwood Village, CO 80111, 303-694-6600 or toll-free 888-309-6555. *Fax:* 303-694-6673.
Website: http://www.coloradotech.edu/.

COLORADO TECHNICAL UNIVERSITY COLORADO SPRINGS

Colorado Springs, CO

CONTACT Jacqueline Harris, Senior Director of Student Finance Services, Colorado Technical University Colorado Springs, 4435 North Chestnut Street, Colorado Springs, CO 80907-3896, 719-598-0200 or toll-free 866-942-6555. *Fax:* 719-598-3740.
Website: http://www.coloradotech.edu/.

COLUMBIA CENTRAL UNIVERSITY

Caguas, PR

CONTACT Financial Aid Officer, Columbia Central University, Carr 183, Km 1.7, PO Box 8517, Caguas, PR 00726, 787-743-4041 Ext. 244. *Fax:* 787-744-7031. *Website:* http://www.columbiacentral.edu/.

COLUMBIA CENTRAL UNIVERSITY

Yauco, PR

CONTACT Financial Aid Office, Columbia Central University, Calle Betances #3, Box 3062, Yauco, PR 00698, 787-856-0945. *Website:* http://www.columbiacentral.edu/.

COLUMBIA COLLEGE

Columbia, MO

Tuition & fees: $23,498	Average undergraduate aid package: $16,846

ABOUT THE INSTITUTION Independent Christian Church (Disciples of Christ), coed. ***Awards:*** certificates, associate, bachelor's, and master's degrees (offers continuing education program with significant enrollment not reflected in profile). 46 undergraduate majors. ***Total enrollment:*** 1,152. Undergraduates: 1,023. Freshmen: 146. Federal methodology is used as a basis for awarding need-based institutional aid.

UNDERGRADUATE EXPENSES for 2019–2020 ***Comprehensive fee:*** $31,898 includes full-time tuition ($23,498) and room and board ($8400). ***College room only:*** $4900. Full-time tuition and fees vary according to class time, course load, program, reciprocity agreements, and student level. Room and board charges vary according to board plan and housing facility. ***Part-time tuition:*** $504 per credit hour. Part-time tuition and fees vary according to class time, course load, location, and reciprocity agreements. ***Payment plan:*** Guaranteed tuition.

FRESHMAN FINANCIAL AID (Fall 2018) 131 applied for aid; of those 90% were deemed to have need. 100% of freshmen with need received aid; of those 25% had need fully met. ***Average percent of need met:*** 70% (excluding resources awarded to replace EFC). ***Average financial aid package:*** $18,638 (excluding resources awarded to replace EFC). 9% of all full-time freshmen had no need and received non-need-based gift aid.

UNDERGRADUATE FINANCIAL AID (Fall 2018) 692 applied for aid; of those 91% were deemed to have need. 99% of undergraduates with need received aid; of those 17% had need fully met. ***Average percent of need met:*** 62% (excluding resources awarded to replace EFC). ***Average financial aid package:*** $16,846 (excluding resources awarded to replace EFC). 11% of all full-time undergraduates had no need and received non-need-based gift aid.

GIFT AID (NEED-BASED) ***Total amount:*** $2,799,829 (67% federal, 14% state, 19% institutional). ***Receiving aid:*** Freshmen: 53% (77); all full-time undergraduates: 52% (457). ***Average award:*** Freshmen: $5907; Undergraduates: $5600. ***Scholarships, grants, and awards:*** Federal Pell, FSEOG, state, private, college/university gift aid from institutional funds.

GIFT AID (NON-NEED-BASED) ***Total amount:*** $4,871,556 (1% state, 95% institutional, 4% external sources). ***Receiving aid:*** Freshmen: 78% (114). Undergraduates: 61% (537). ***Average award:*** Freshmen: $57. Undergraduates: $252. ***Scholarships, grants, and awards by category:*** *Academic interests/achievement:* 107 awards ($476,683 total): biological sciences, business, communication, computer science, education, English, general academic interests/achievements, humanities, mathematics, physical sciences, religion/biblical studies, social sciences. *Creative arts/performance:* 23 awards ($27,350 total): applied art and design, creative writing, journalism/publications, music. *Special achievements/activities:* 139 awards ($1,014,441 total): community service, general special achievements/activities, leadership, religious involvement. *Special characteristics:* 194 awards ($509,288 total): adult students, children and siblings of alumni, children of current students, children of educators, children of faculty/staff, children of union members/company employees, ethnic background, first-generation college students, general special characteristics, international students, local/state students, members of minority groups, parents of current students, previous college experience, religious affiliation, siblings of current students, spouses of current students, veterans. ***Tuition waivers:*** Full or partial for children of alumni, employees or children of employees, senior citizens. ***ROTC:*** Army cooperative, Naval cooperative, Air Force cooperative.

LOANS ***Student loans:*** $4,784,104 (36% need-based, 64% non-need-based). 59% of past graduating class borrowed through all loan programs. *Average indebtedness per student:* $23,979. ***Average need-based loan:*** Freshmen: $2624. Undergraduates: $3576. ***Parent loans:*** $1,204,134 (100% non-need-based). ***Programs:*** Federal Direct (Subsidized and Unsubsidized Stafford, PLUS).

WORK-STUDY ***Federal work-study:*** Total amount: $465,365; jobs available. ***State or other work-study/employment:*** Total amount: $217,257 (100% need-based). Part-time jobs available.

ATHLETIC AWARDS Total amount: $3,365,934 (100% non-need-based).

APPLYING FOR FINANCIAL AID ***Required financial aid form:*** FAFSA. ***Financial aid deadline (priority):*** 3/1. ***Notification date:*** Continuous.

CONTACT Colleen Brown, Director of Financial Aid, Columbia College, 1001 Rogers Street, Columbia, MO 65216-0002, 573-875-7362 or toll-free 800-231-2391. *Fax:* 573-875-7452. *E-mail:* ctbrown@ccis.edu. *Website:* http://www.ccis.edu/.

COLUMBIA COLLEGE

Columbia, SC

Tuition & fees: $19,890	Average undergraduate aid package: $14,022

ABOUT THE INSTITUTION Independent United Methodist, coed, primarily women. ***Awards:*** bachelor's and master's degrees. 41 undergraduate majors. ***Total enrollment:*** 1,243. Undergraduates: 1,102. Freshmen: 178. Both federal and institutional methodology are used as a basis for awarding need-based institutional aid.

UNDERGRADUATE EXPENSES for 2020–2021 ***One-time required fee:*** $150. ***Comprehensive fee:*** $28,185 includes full-time tuition ($19,890) and room and board ($8295). Full-time tuition and fees vary according to class time and location. Room and board charges vary according to board plan and housing facility. ***Part-time tuition:*** $650 per semester hour. Part-time tuition and fees vary according to class time and location. ***Payment plan:*** Guaranteed tuition.

FRESHMAN FINANCIAL AID (Fall 2019, est.) 162 applied for aid; of those 94% were deemed to have need. 99% of freshmen with need received aid; of those 4% had need fully met. ***Average percent of need met:*** 53% (excluding resources awarded to replace EFC). ***Average financial aid package:*** $14,988 (excluding resources awarded to replace EFC). 5% of all full-time freshmen had no need and received non-need-based gift aid.

UNDERGRADUATE FINANCIAL AID (Fall 2019, est.) 722 applied for aid; of those 92% were deemed to have need. 99% of undergraduates with need received aid; of those 7% had need fully met. ***Average percent of need met:*** 57% (excluding resources awarded to replace EFC). ***Average financial aid package:*** $14,022 (excluding resources awarded to replace EFC). 7% of all full-time undergraduates had no need and received non-need-based gift aid.

GIFT AID (NEED-BASED) ***Total amount:*** $7,144,411 (35% federal, 34% state, 30% institutional, 1% external sources). ***Receiving aid:*** Freshmen: 91% (151); all full-time undergraduates: 84% (642). ***Average award:*** Freshmen: $12,221; Undergraduates: $10,732. ***Scholarships, grants, and awards:*** Federal Pell, FSEOG, state, private, college/university gift aid from institutional funds.

GIFT AID (NON-NEED-BASED) ***Total amount:*** $827,529 (25% state, 73% institutional, 2% external sources). ***Receiving aid:*** Freshmen: 5% (9). Undergraduates: 8% (63). ***Average award:*** Freshmen: $2957. Undergraduates: $5541. ***Scholarships, grants, and awards by category:*** *Academic interests/achievement:* 652 awards ($1,279,156 total): biological sciences, business, communication, education, English, foreign languages, general academic interests/achievements, humanities, mathematics, religion/biblical studies. *Creative arts/performance:* 38 awards ($114,559 total): art/fine arts, dance, music. *Special achievements/activities:* 127 awards ($112,763 total): community service, leadership, memberships. *Special characteristics:* 20 awards ($78,845 total): children of faculty/staff, international students, previous college experience, relatives of clergy, religious affiliation. ***Tuition waivers:*** Full or partial for employees or children of employees. ***ROTC:*** Army cooperative.

LOANS ***Student loans:*** $4,923,008 (83% need-based, 17% non-need-based). 70% of past graduating class borrowed through all loan programs. *Average indebtedness per student:* $25,241. ***Average need-based loan:*** Freshmen: $3063. Undergraduates: $3800. ***Parent loans:*** $1,513,541 (70% need-based, 30% non-need-based).

Programs: Federal Direct (Subsidized and Unsubsidized Stafford, PLUS), Perkins, state, South Carolina Teacher Loans, United Methodist Student Loans.

WORK-STUDY Federal work-study jobs available. ***State or other work-study/ employment:*** Part-time jobs available.

ATHLETIC AWARDS Total amount: $735,723 (81% need-based, 19% non-need-based).

APPLYING FOR FINANCIAL AID ***Required financial aid form:*** FAFSA. ***Financial aid deadline (priority):*** 3/15. ***Notification date:*** Continuous beginning 4/1. Students must reply within 4 weeks of notification.

CONTACT Mr. Justin Pichey, Director of Financial Aid, Columbia College, 1301 Columbia College Drive, Columbia, SC 29203-5998, 803-786-3883 or toll-free 800-277-1301. *E-mail:* fa@columbiasc.edu.
Website: http://www.columbiasc.edu/.

COLUMBIA COLLEGE CHICAGO

Chicago, IL

Tuition & fees: $28,318 | **Average undergraduate aid package: $14,717**

ABOUT THE INSTITUTION Independent, coed. ***Awards:*** certificates, bachelor's, and master's degrees. 48 undergraduate majors. ***Total enrollment:*** 6,947. Undergraduates: 6,708. Freshmen: 1,748. Federal methodology is used as a basis for awarding need-based institutional aid.

UNDERGRADUATE EXPENSES for 2020–2021 ***Application fee:*** $25. ***Comprehensive fee:*** $44,774 includes full-time tuition ($27,142), mandatory fees ($1176), and room and board ($16,456). Room and board charges vary according to housing facility. ***Part-time tuition:*** $937 per credit hour.

FRESHMAN FINANCIAL AID (Fall 2019, est.) 1617 applied for aid; of those 76% were deemed to have need. 100% of freshmen with need received aid; of those 65% had need fully met. ***Average percent of need met:*** 62% (excluding resources awarded to replace EFC). ***Average financial aid package:*** $20,086 (excluding resources awarded to replace EFC). 1% of all full-time freshmen had no need and received non-need-based gift aid.

UNDERGRADUATE FINANCIAL AID (Fall 2019, est.) 5,169 applied for aid; of those 77% were deemed to have need. 100% of undergraduates with need received aid; of those 38% had need fully met. ***Average percent of need met:*** 47% (excluding resources awarded to replace EFC). ***Average financial aid package:*** $14,717 (excluding resources awarded to replace EFC). 1% of all full-time undergraduates had no need and received non-need-based gift aid.

GIFT AID (NEED-BASED) ***Total amount:*** $119,846,865 (15% federal, 9% state, 75% institutional, 1% external sources). ***Receiving aid:*** Freshmen: 71% (1,233); all full-time undergraduates: 61% (3,758). ***Average award:*** Freshmen: $19,848; Undergraduates: $14,998. ***Scholarships, grants, and awards:*** Federal Pell, FSEOG, state, private, college/university gift aid from institutional funds.

GIFT AID (NON-NEED-BASED) ***Total amount:*** $2,552,794 (100% institutional). ***Receiving aid:*** Freshmen: 1% (9). Undergraduates: 2% (130). ***Average award:*** Freshmen: $14,538. Undergraduates: $18,959. ***Scholarships, grants, and awards by category:*** *Academic interests/achievement:* business, communication, English, general academic interests/achievements. *Creative arts/performance:* applied art and design, art/fine arts, cinema/film/broadcasting, creative writing, dance, general creative arts/performance, journalism/publications, music, performing arts, theater/ drama. *Special achievements/activities:* community service. *Special characteristics:* children of faculty/staff. ***Tuition waivers:*** Full or partial for employees or children of employees. ***ROTC:*** Army cooperative, Naval cooperative, Air Force cooperative.

LOANS ***Student loans:*** $64,993,894 (100% need-based). 71% of past graduating class borrowed through all loan programs. *Average indebtedness per student:* $34,328. ***Average need-based loan:*** Freshmen: $3030. Undergraduates: $4070. ***Parent loans:*** $34,530,841 (100% need-based). ***Programs:*** Federal Direct (Subsidized and Unsubsidized Stafford, PLUS).

WORK-STUDY ***Federal work-study:*** Total amount: $1,329,889; 139 jobs averaging $4609.

APPLYING FOR FINANCIAL AID ***Required financial aid form:*** FAFSA. ***Financial aid deadline:*** 6/30 (priority: 12/1). ***Notification date:*** Continuous beginning 12/1.

CONTACT Financial Aid Office, Columbia College Chicago, 600 S. Michigan Ave., Suite 300, Chicago, IL 60605, 312-369-7140. *E-mail:* columbiacentral@colum.edu.
Website: http://www.colum.edu/.

COLUMBIA COLLEGE HOLLYWOOD

Tarzana, CA

CONTACT Ms. Maricela Guzman, Financial Aid Administrator, Columbia College Hollywood, 18618 Oxnard Street, Tarzana, CA 91356, 818-401-1030 or toll-free 800-785-0585. *Fax:* 818-345-8660. *E-mail:* mguzman@columbiacollege.edu.
Website: http://www.columbiacollege.edu/.

COLUMBIA COLLEGE OF NURSING

Glendale, WI

CONTACT Wendy Hilvo, Financial Aid Director, Columbia College of Nursing, 4425 North Port Washington Road, Suite 302, Glendale, WI 53212, 414-326-2337. *Fax:* 414-326-2362. *E-mail:* financialaid@ccon.edu.
Website: http://www.ccon.edu/.

COLUMBIA INTERNATIONAL UNIVERSITY

Columbia, SC

Comprehensive fee: $8950 | **Average undergraduate aid package: $19,354**

ABOUT THE INSTITUTION Independent nondenominational, coed. ***Awards:*** certificates, associate, bachelor's, master's, and doctoral degrees. 18 undergraduate majors. ***Total enrollment:*** 1,460. Undergraduates: 621. Freshmen: 146. Federal methodology is used as a basis for awarding need-based institutional aid.

UNDERGRADUATE EXPENSES for 2020–2021 ***Application fee:*** $25. ***Comprehensive fee:*** $8950 includes mandatory fees ($1100) and room and board ($8950). Full-time tuition and fees vary according to course load, program, and reciprocity agreements. Room and board charges vary according to board plan and housing facility. ***Part-time tuition:*** $980 per credit hour. Part-time tuition and fees vary according to course load, program, and reciprocity agreements.

FRESHMAN FINANCIAL AID (Fall 2018) 130 applied for aid; of those 90% were deemed to have need. 100% of freshmen with need received aid; of those 17% had need fully met. ***Average percent of need met:*** 74% (excluding resources awarded to replace EFC). ***Average financial aid package:*** $20,131 (excluding resources awarded to replace EFC). 17% of all full-time freshmen had no need and received non-need-based gift aid.

UNDERGRADUATE FINANCIAL AID (Fall 2018) 447 applied for aid; of those 91% were deemed to have need. 100% of undergraduates with need received aid; of those 13% had need fully met. ***Average percent of need met:*** 69% (excluding resources awarded to replace EFC). ***Average financial aid package:*** $19,354 (excluding resources awarded to replace EFC). 16% of all full-time undergraduates had no need and received non-need-based gift aid.

GIFT AID (NEED-BASED) ***Receiving aid:*** Freshmen: 82% (117); all full-time undergraduates: 83% (404). ***Average award:*** Freshmen: $17,868; Undergraduates: $16,305. ***Scholarships, grants, and awards:*** Federal Pell, FSEOG, state, private, college/university gift aid from institutional funds.

GIFT AID (NON-NEED-BASED) ***Receiving aid:*** Freshmen: 10% (15). Undergraduates: 8% (37). ***Average award:*** Freshmen: $10,162. Undergraduates: $9852. ***Scholarships, grants, and awards by category:*** *Academic interests/ achievement:* general academic interests/achievements. *Special achievements/activities:* general special achievements/activities, leadership, religious involvement. *Special characteristics:* children and siblings of alumni, children of faculty/staff, ethnic background, international students, local/state students, members of minority groups, spouses of current students, veterans, veterans' children. ***Tuition waivers:*** Full or partial for employees or children of employees.

LOANS ***Student loans:*** 63% of past graduating class borrowed through all loan programs. *Average indebtedness per student:* $23,695. ***Average need-based loan:*** Freshmen: $3129. Undergraduates: $3891. ***Programs:*** Federal Direct (Subsidized and Unsubsidized Stafford, PLUS).

WORK-STUDY Federal work-study jobs available. ***State or other work-study/ employment:*** Part-time jobs available.

APPLYING FOR FINANCIAL AID ***Required financial aid forms:*** FAFSA, institution's own form, state aid form. ***Financial aid deadline:*** Continuous. ***Notification date:*** Continuous.

CONTACT Mrs. Patty Jean Hix, Director of Financial Aid, Columbia International University, 7435 Monticello Road, Columbia, SC 29203, 800-777-2227 Ext. 5037 or toll-free 800-777-2227 Ext.5024. *Fax:* 803-223-2505. *E-mail:* phix@ciu.edu.
Website: http://www.ciu.edu/.

COLUMBIA UNIVERSITY

New York, NY

Tuition & fees: $61,850	Average undergraduate aid package: $63,897

ABOUT THE INSTITUTION Independent, coed. ***Awards:*** bachelor's, master's, and doctoral degrees. 88 undergraduate majors. ***Total enrollment:*** 6,270. Undergraduates: 6,270. Freshmen: 1,423. Institutional methodology is used as a basis for awarding need-based institutional aid.

UNDERGRADUATE EXPENSES for 2019–2020 ***Application fee:*** $85. ***Comprehensive fee:*** $76,340 includes full-time tuition ($58,920), mandatory fees ($2930), and room and board ($14,490). Room and board charges vary according to board plan. ***Payment plan:*** Tuition prepayment.

FRESHMAN FINANCIAL AID (Fall 2019, est.) 785 applied for aid; of those 94% were deemed to have need. 100% of freshmen with need received aid; of those 98% had need fully met. ***Average percent of need met:*** 100% (excluding resources awarded to replace EFC). ***Average financial aid package:*** $65,056 (excluding resources awarded to replace EFC).

UNDERGRADUATE FINANCIAL AID (Fall 2019, est.) 3,302 applied for aid; of those 95% were deemed to have need. 100% of undergraduates with need received aid; of those 95% had need fully met. ***Average percent of need met:*** 100% (excluding resources awarded to replace EFC). ***Average financial aid package:*** $63,897 (excluding resources awarded to replace EFC).

GIFT AID (NEED-BASED) ***Total amount:*** $185,126,692 (3% federal, 1% state, 94% institutional, 2% external sources). ***Receiving aid:*** Freshmen: 52% (725); all full-time undergraduates: 50% (3,118). ***Average award:*** Freshmen: $61,365; Undergraduates: $59,239. ***Scholarships, grants, and awards:*** Federal Pell, FSEOG, state, private, college/university gift aid from institutional funds.

GIFT AID (NON-NEED-BASED) ***Total amount:*** $980,209 (18% federal, 5% state, 77% external sources). ***Receiving aid:*** Freshmen: 4% (54). Undergraduates: 2% (144). ***Tuition waivers:*** Full or partial for employees or children of employees. ***ROTC:*** Army cooperative, Naval, Air Force cooperative.

LOANS ***Student loans:*** $8,603,057 (41% need-based, 59% non-need-based). ***Average need-based loan:*** Freshmen: $2764. Undergraduates: $3661. ***Parent loans:*** $7,090,789 (16% need-based, 84% non-need-based). ***Programs:*** Federal Direct (Subsidized and Unsubsidized Stafford, PLUS), college/university, alternative loans.

WORK-STUDY ***Federal work-study:*** Total amount: $3,886,384; jobs available. ***State or other work-study/employment:*** Total amount: $2,742,846 (82% need-based, 18% non-need-based). Part-time jobs available.

APPLYING FOR FINANCIAL AID ***Required financial aid forms:*** FAFSA, CSS Financial Aid PROFILE, noncustodial (divorced/separated) parent's statement, parent and student income tax forms. ***Financial aid deadline (priority):*** 2/15. ***Notification date:*** 4/1. Students must reply by 5/1 or within 1 week of notification.

CONTACT Financial Aid Office, Columbia University, 116th Street and Broadway, New York, NY 10027, 212-854-1754.
Website: http://www.columbia.edu/.

COLUMBIA UNIVERSITY SCHOOL OF GENERAL STUDIES

New York, NY

CONTACT Mr. William Skip Bailey, Director of Educational Financing, Columbia University School of General Studies, 408 Lewisohn Hall, 2970 Broadway, New York, NY 10027, 212-854-5410 or toll-free 800-895-1169. *Fax:* 212-854-6316. *E-mail:* gs_financial_aid@columbia.edu.
Website: http://www.gs.columbia.edu/.

COLUMBUS COLLEGE OF ART & DESIGN

Columbus, OH

CONTACT Mrs. Anna Marie Schofield, Director of Financial Aid, Columbus College of Art & Design, 60 Cleveland Avenue, Columbus, OH 43215-1758, 614-224-9101 Ext. 3274 or toll-free 877-997-2223. *Fax:* 614-222-4034. *E-mail:* aschofield@ccad.edu.
Website: http://www.ccad.edu/.

COLUMBUS STATE UNIVERSITY

Columbus, GA

Tuition & fees (area res): $7200	Average undergraduate aid package: $10,142

ABOUT THE INSTITUTION State-supported, coed. ***Awards:*** certificates, associate, bachelor's, master's, and doctoral degrees. 41 undergraduate majors. ***Total enrollment:*** 8,076. Undergraduates: 6,640. Freshmen: 1,076. Federal methodology is used as a basis for awarding need-based institutional aid.

UNDERGRADUATE EXPENSES for 2019–2020 ***Application fee:*** $40. ***Tuition, area resident:*** full-time $5330; part-time $178 per credit hour. ***Tuition, state resident:*** full-time $5330; part-time $178 per credit hour. ***Tuition, nonresident:*** full-time $18,812; part-time $627 per credit hour. ***Required fees:*** full-time $1870. ***College room and board:*** $9380; ***Room only:*** $5830.

FRESHMAN FINANCIAL AID (Fall 2019, est.) 892 applied for aid; of those 80% were deemed to have need. 100% of freshmen with need received aid; of those 2% had need fully met. ***Average percent of need met:*** 60% (excluding resources awarded to replace EFC). ***Average financial aid package:*** $10,568 (excluding resources awarded to replace EFC). 5% of all full-time freshmen had no need and received non-need-based gift aid.

UNDERGRADUATE FINANCIAL AID (Fall 2019, est.) 3,965 applied for aid; of those 80% were deemed to have need. 99% of undergraduates with need received aid; of those 3% had need fully met. ***Average percent of need met:*** 62% (excluding resources awarded to replace EFC). ***Average financial aid package:*** $10,142 (excluding resources awarded to replace EFC). 5% of all full-time undergraduates had no need and received non-need-based gift aid.

GIFT AID (NEED-BASED) ***Total amount:*** $14,095,573 (100% federal). ***Receiving aid:*** Freshmen: 51% (485); all full-time undergraduates: 50% (2,209). ***Average award:*** Freshmen: $5320; Undergraduates: $5165. ***Scholarships, grants, and awards:*** Federal Pell, FSEOG, state, private, college/university gift aid from institutional funds, Federal Nursing.

GIFT AID (NON-NEED-BASED) ***Total amount:*** $12,154,972 (88% state, 6% institutional, 6% external sources). ***Receiving aid:*** Freshmen: 51% (484). Undergraduates: 34% (1,518). ***Average award:*** Freshmen: $2016. Undergraduates: $1880. ***Scholarships, grants, and awards by category:*** *Academic interests/achievement:* biological sciences, business, communication, computer science, education, English, general academic interests/achievements, home economics, humanities, international studies, mathematics, military science, physical sciences. *Creative arts/performance:* applied art and design, dance, music, performing arts, theater/drama. *Special achievements/activities:* cheerleading/drum major, community service, general special achievements/activities, leadership. ***ROTC:*** Army.

LOANS ***Student loans:*** $30,401,499 (44% need-based, 56% non-need-based). 71% of past graduating class borrowed through all loan programs. *Average indebtedness*

per student: $32,587. ***Average need-based loan:*** Freshmen: $3600. Undergraduates: $4318. ***Parent loans:*** $3,425,187 (100% non-need-based). ***Programs:*** Federal Direct (Subsidized and Unsubsidized Stafford, PLUS), Perkins, Federal Nursing, state, college/university.

WORK-STUDY ***Federal work-study:*** Total amount: $417,810; jobs available.

ATHLETIC AWARDS Total amount: $1,147,398 (100% non-need-based).

APPLYING FOR FINANCIAL AID ***Financial aid deadline (priority):*** 5/1. ***Notification date:*** Continuous beginning 5/15.

CONTACT Ms. Patricia Garrett, Associate Director of Financial Aid, Columbus State University, 4225 University Avenue, Columbus, GA 31907-5645, 706-507-8800 or toll-free 866-264-2035. *Fax:* 706-568-2230. *E-mail:* garrett_patricia2@columbusstate.edu.
Website: http://www.columbusstate.edu/.

COMPASS COLLEGE OF CINEMATIC ARTS

Grand Rapids, MI

CONTACT Financial Aid Office, Compass College of Cinematic Arts, 41 Sheldon Boulevard SE, Grand Rapids, MI 49503, 616-988-1000.
Website: http://www.compass.edu/.

CONCEPTION SEMINARY COLLEGE

Conception, MO

CONTACT Br. Justin Hernandez, Financial Aid Director, Conception Seminary College, 37174 State Highway VV, Conception, MO 64433-0502, 660-944-2851. *Fax:* 660-944-2829. *E-mail:* financialaid@conception.edu.
Website: http://www.conception.edu/.

CONCORDIA COLLEGE

Moorhead, MN

Tuition & fees: $41,566	Average undergraduate aid package: $32,140

ABOUT THE INSTITUTION Independent Evangelical Lutheran Church in America, coed. ***Awards:*** bachelor's and master's degrees. 53 undergraduate majors. ***Total enrollment:*** 2,042. Undergraduates: 2,010. Freshmen: 517. Federal methodology is used as a basis for awarding need-based institutional aid.

UNDERGRADUATE EXPENSES for 2020–2021 ***Comprehensive fee:*** $50,176 includes full-time tuition ($41,150), mandatory fees ($416), and room and board ($8610). ***College room only:*** $3740. Full-time tuition and fees vary according to course load. Room and board charges vary according to board plan and housing facility. ***Part-time tuition:*** $1545 per credit hour.

FRESHMAN FINANCIAL AID (Fall 2018) 531 applied for aid; of those 88% were deemed to have need. 100% of freshmen with need received aid; of those 25% had need fully met. ***Average percent of need met:*** 90% (excluding resources awarded to replace EFC). ***Average financial aid package:*** $33,419 (excluding resources awarded to replace EFC). 21% of all full-time freshmen had no need and received non-need-based gift aid.

UNDERGRADUATE FINANCIAL AID (Fall 2018) 1,707 applied for aid; of those 88% were deemed to have need. 100% of undergraduates with need received aid; of those 23% had need fully met. ***Average percent of need met:*** 89% (excluding resources awarded to replace EFC). ***Average financial aid package:*** $32,140 (excluding resources awarded to replace EFC). 24% of all full-time undergraduates had no need and received non-need-based gift aid.

GIFT AID (NEED-BASED) ***Receiving aid:*** Freshmen: 78% (464); all full-time undergraduates: 73% (1,489). ***Average award:*** Freshmen: $27,429; Undergraduates: $25,284. ***Scholarships, grants, and awards:*** Federal Pell, FSEOG, state, private, college/university gift aid from institutional funds.

GIFT AID (NON-NEED-BASED) ***Receiving aid:*** Freshmen: 15% (92). Undergraduates: 13% (273). ***Average award:*** Freshmen: $21,731. Undergraduates: $18,683. ***Scholarships, grants, and awards by category:*** *Academic interests/achievement:* biological sciences, business, general academic interests/achievements, home economics, physical sciences, premedicine. *Creative arts/performance:* applied art and design, music, theater/drama. *Special characteristics:* international students. ***Tuition waivers:*** Full or partial for employees or children of employees. ***ROTC:*** Army cooperative, Air Force cooperative.

LOANS ***Student loans:*** 75% of past graduating class borrowed through all loan programs. ***Average need-based loan:*** Freshmen: $3222. Undergraduates: $4239. ***Programs:*** Federal Direct (Subsidized and Unsubsidized Stafford, PLUS), state, college/university, private loans.

WORK-STUDY Federal work-study jobs available. ***State or other work-study/employment:*** Part-time jobs available.

APPLYING FOR FINANCIAL AID ***Required financial aid form:*** FAFSA. ***Financial aid deadline:*** Continuous. ***Notification date:*** Continuous. Students must reply within 6 weeks of notification.

CONTACT Mr. Eric Addington, Associate Vice President for Enrollment and Financial Aid, Concordia College, 901 South 8th Street, Moorhead, MN 56562, 218-299-3010 or toll-free 800-699-9897. *Fax:* 218-299-3025. *E-mail:* eaddingt@cord.edu.
Website: http://www.concordiacollege.edu/.

CONCORDIA COLLEGE–NEW YORK

Bronxville, NY

CONTACT Janice Spikereit, Director of Financial Aid, Concordia College–New York, 171 White Plains Road, Bronxville, NY 10708, 914-337-9300 Ext. 2146 or toll-free 800-YES-COLLEGE. *Fax:* 914-395-4500. *E-mail:* financialaid@concordia-ny.edu.
Website: http://www.concordia-ny.edu/.

CONCORDIA UNIVERSITY ANN ARBOR

Ann Arbor, MI

CONTACT Vicki Waschow, Financial Aid Office, Concordia University Ann Arbor, 4090 Geddes Road, Ann Arbor, MI 48105-2797, 734-995-7408 or toll-free 877-995-7520 (in-state), 877-955-7520 (out-of-state). *Fax:* 734-995-4610. *E-mail:* vicki.waschow@cuaa.edu.
Website: http://www.cuaa.edu/.

CONCORDIA UNIVERSITY CHICAGO

River Forest, IL

Tuition & fees: $33,636	Average undergraduate aid package: $24,637

ABOUT THE INSTITUTION Independent Lutheran Church–Missouri Synod, coed. ***Awards:*** certificates, associate, bachelor's, master's, and doctoral degrees. 70 undergraduate majors. ***Total enrollment:*** 6,132. Undergraduates: 1,515. Freshmen: 351. Federal methodology is used as a basis for awarding need-based institutional aid.

UNDERGRADUATE EXPENSES for 2020–2021 ***Comprehensive fee:*** $43,862 includes full-time tuition ($32,660), mandatory fees ($976), and room and board ($10,226). ***College room only:*** $6424. Room and board charges vary according to board plan and housing facility. ***Part-time tuition:*** $978 per credit hour.

FRESHMAN FINANCIAL AID (Fall 2018) 377 applied for aid; of those 95% were deemed to have need. 100% of freshmen with need received aid; of those 15% had need fully met. ***Average percent of need met:*** 80% (excluding resources awarded to replace EFC). ***Average financial aid package:*** $26,954 (excluding resources awarded to replace EFC). 6% of all full-time freshmen had no need and received non-need-based gift aid.

UNDERGRADUATE FINANCIAL AID (Fall 2018) 1,232 applied for aid; of those 94% were deemed to have need. 99% of undergraduates with need received aid; of those 18% had need fully met. ***Average percent of need met:*** 79% (excluding resources awarded to replace EFC). ***Average financial aid package:*** $24,637 (excluding resources awarded to replace EFC). 13% of all full-time undergraduates had no need and received non-need-based gift aid.

GIFT AID (NEED-BASED) ***Total amount:*** $23,596,905 (14% federal, 10% state, 76% institutional). ***Receiving aid:*** Freshmen: 94% (357); all full-time undergraduates: 83% (1,133). ***Average award:*** Freshmen: $23,577; Undergraduates: $20,666. ***Scholarships, grants, and awards:*** Federal Pell, FSEOG, state, private, college/university gift aid from institutional funds.

GIFT AID (NON-NEED-BASED) ***Total amount:*** $4,335,444 (86% institutional, 14% external sources). ***Receiving aid:*** Freshmen: 9% (35). Undergraduates: 9% (121). ***Average award:*** Freshmen: $18,584. Undergraduates: $15,698. ***Scholarships, grants, and awards by category:*** *Academic interests/achievement:* biological sciences, business, communication, computer science, education, English, foreign languages, general academic interests/achievements, mathematics, religion/biblical studies. *Creative arts/performance:* music. *Special characteristics:* children and siblings of alumni, children of faculty/staff, international students, religious affiliation. ***Tuition waivers:*** Full or partial for children of alumni, employees or children of employees.

LOANS ***Student loans:*** $7,640,168 (45% need-based, 55% non-need-based). 82% of past graduating class borrowed through all loan programs. *Average indebtedness per student:* $28,122. ***Average need-based loan:*** Freshmen: $3154. Undergraduates: $3962. ***Parent loans:*** $1,869,275 (100% non-need-based). ***Programs:*** Federal Direct (Subsidized and Unsubsidized Stafford, PLUS).

WORK-STUDY ***Federal work-study:*** Total amount: $486,006; jobs available. ***State or other work-study/employment:*** Part-time jobs available.

APPLYING FOR FINANCIAL AID ***Required financial aid form:*** FAFSA. ***Financial aid deadline:*** 6/1 (priority: 12/1). ***Notification date:*** Continuous beginning 12/15.

CONTACT Aida Asencio-Pinto, Director of Financial Aid, Concordia University Chicago, 7400 Augusta Street, River Forest, IL 60305-1499, 708-209-3113 or toll-free 800-285-2668. *Fax:* 708-488-4102. *E-mail:* aida.asenciopinto@cuchicago.edu.
Website: http://www.cuchicago.edu/.

CONCORDIA UNIVERSITY IRVINE

Irvine, CA

ABOUT THE INSTITUTION Independent Lutheran Church–Missouri Synod, coed. ***Awards:*** certificates, associate, bachelor's, master's, and doctoral degrees (associate's degree for international students only). 29 undergraduate majors. ***Total enrollment:*** 4,182. Undergraduates: 1,801. Freshmen: 319.

GIFT AID (NEED-BASED) ***Scholarships, grants, and awards:*** Federal Pell, FSEOG, state, private, college/university gift aid from institutional funds.

GIFT AID (NON-NEED-BASED) ***Scholarships, grants, and awards by category:*** *Academic interests/achievement:* general academic interests/achievements. *Creative arts/performance:* debating, music, theater/drama. *Special characteristics:* children of faculty/staff, first-generation college students, religious affiliation.

LOANS ***Programs:*** Federal Direct (Subsidized and Unsubsidized Stafford, PLUS), private loans.

WORK-STUDY ***Federal work-study:*** Total amount: $186,988; 76 jobs averaging $2582. ***State or other work-study/employment:*** Part-time jobs available.

APPLYING FOR FINANCIAL AID ***Required financial aid forms:*** FAFSA, state aid form, department scholarship application form.

CONTACT Lori McDonald, Director of Financial Aid, Concordia University Irvine, 1530 Concordia West, Irvine, CA 92612-3299, 949-214-3074 or toll-free 800-229-1200. *Fax:* 949-214-3500. *E-mail:* lori.mcdonald@cui.edu.
Website: http://www.cui.edu/.

CONCORDIA UNIVERSITY, NEBRASKA

Seward, NE

CONTACT Mr. Aaron W. Roberts, Director of Undergraduate Admissions, Concordia University, Nebraska, 800 North Columbia Avenue, Seward, NE 68434-1556, 800-535-5494. *Fax:* 402-643-4073. *E-mail:* admiss@cune.edu.
Website: http://www.cune.edu/.

CONCORDIA UNIVERSITY, ST. PAUL

St. Paul, MN

Tuition & fees: $23,400	Average undergraduate aid package: $16,836

ABOUT THE INSTITUTION Independent Lutheran Church–Missouri Synod, coed. ***Awards:*** certificates, associate, bachelor's, master's, and doctoral degrees. 61 undergraduate majors. ***Total enrollment:*** 5,139. Undergraduates: 3,127. Freshmen: 351. Federal methodology is used as a basis for awarding need-based institutional aid.

UNDERGRADUATE EXPENSES for 2020–2021 ***Comprehensive fee:*** $33,000 includes full-time tuition ($23,400) and room and board ($9600). Full-time tuition and fees vary according to degree level and program. Room and board charges vary according to board plan and housing facility. ***Part-time tuition:*** $420 per credit. Part-time tuition and fees vary according to course load, degree level, and program.

FRESHMAN FINANCIAL AID (Fall 2019, est.) 332 applied for aid; of those 88% were deemed to have need. 100% of freshmen with need received aid; of those 10% had need fully met. ***Average percent of need met:*** 73% (excluding resources awarded to replace EFC). ***Average financial aid package:*** $21,420 (excluding resources awarded to replace EFC). 9% of all full-time freshmen had no need and received non-need-based gift aid.

UNDERGRADUATE FINANCIAL AID (Fall 2019, est.) 1,431 applied for aid; of those 86% were deemed to have need. 99% of undergraduates with need received aid; of those 11% had need fully met. ***Average percent of need met:*** 62% (excluding resources awarded to replace EFC). ***Average financial aid package:*** $16,836 (excluding resources awarded to replace EFC). 10% of all full-time undergraduates had no need and received non-need-based gift aid.

GIFT AID (NEED-BASED) ***Total amount:*** $16,381,044 (39% federal, 25% state, 35% institutional, 1% external sources). ***Receiving aid:*** Freshmen: 83% (292); all full-time undergraduates: 71% (1,156). ***Average award:*** Freshmen: $16,514; Undergraduates: $12,501. ***Scholarships, grants, and awards:*** Federal Pell, FSEOG, state, private, college/university gift aid from institutional funds.

GIFT AID (NON-NEED-BASED) ***Total amount:*** $1,868,341 (1% state, 99% institutional). ***Receiving aid:*** Freshmen: 6% (20). Undergraduates: 5% (79). ***Average award:*** Freshmen: $5693. Undergraduates: $5128. ***Scholarships, grants, and awards by category:*** *Academic interests/achievement:* 1,110 awards ($5,227,417 total): general academic interests/achievements, religion/biblical studies. *Creative arts/performance:* 198 awards ($187,945 total): music, theater/drama. *Special characteristics:* 222 awards ($560,841 total): children of faculty/staff, religious affiliation, veterans. ***Tuition waivers:*** Full or partial for employees or children of employees. ***ROTC:*** Army cooperative, Air Force cooperative.

LOANS ***Student loans:*** $17,155,976 (38% need-based, 62% non-need-based). 75% of past graduating class borrowed through all loan programs. *Average indebtedness per student:* $32,815. ***Average need-based loan:*** Freshmen: $3426. Undergraduates: $4369. ***Parent loans:*** $1,065,566 (100% non-need-based). ***Programs:*** Federal Direct (Subsidized and Unsubsidized Stafford, PLUS), Perkins, state, private loans.

WORK-STUDY ***Federal work-study:*** Total amount: $203,775; 148 jobs averaging $2384. ***State or other work-study/employment:*** Total amount: $1,224,225 (100% need-based). 520 part-time jobs averaging $2464.

ATHLETIC AWARDS Total amount: $2,627,549 (63% need-based, 37% non-need-based).

APPLYING FOR FINANCIAL AID ***Required financial aid forms:*** FAFSA, state aid form. ***Financial aid deadline (priority):*** 5/1. ***Notification date:*** Continuous beginning 5/10.

CONTACT Ms. Jeanie Peck, Financial Aid Director, Concordia University, St. Paul, 1282 Concordia Avenue, St. Paul, MN 55104-5494, 651-603-6300 or toll-free 800-333-4705. *Fax:* 651-603-6298. *E-mail:* finaid@csp.edu.
Website: http://www.csp.edu/.

CONCORDIA UNIVERSITY TEXAS

Austin, TX

Tuition & fees: N/R | **Average undergraduate aid package: $22,350**

ABOUT THE INSTITUTION Independent Lutheran Church–Missouri Synod, coed. ***Awards:*** associate, bachelor's, and master's degrees. 24 undergraduate majors. Federal methodology is used as a basis for awarding need-based institutional aid.

FRESHMAN FINANCIAL AID (Fall 2019, est.) 150 applied for aid; of those 91% were deemed to have need. 85% of freshmen with need received aid; of those 15% had need fully met. ***Average percent of need met:*** 72% (excluding resources awarded to replace EFC). ***Average financial aid package:*** $24,992 (excluding resources awarded to replace EFC). 15% of all full-time freshmen had no need and received non-need-based gift aid.

UNDERGRADUATE FINANCIAL AID (Fall 2019, est.) 735 applied for aid; of those 93% were deemed to have need. 91% of undergraduates with need received aid; of those 15% had need fully met. ***Average percent of need met:*** 67% (excluding resources awarded to replace EFC). ***Average financial aid package:*** $22,350 (excluding resources awarded to replace EFC). 10% of all full-time undergraduates had no need and received non-need-based gift aid.

GIFT AID (NEED-BASED) ***Receiving aid:*** Freshmen: 54% (115); all full-time undergraduates: 42% (561). ***Average award:*** Freshmen: $18,832; Undergraduates: $17,404. ***Scholarships, grants, and awards:*** Federal Pell, FSEOG, state, private, college/university gift aid from institutional funds.

GIFT AID (NON-NEED-BASED) ***Receiving aid:*** Freshmen: 8% (16). Undergraduates: 6% (74). ***Average award:*** Freshmen: $15,677. Undergraduates: $14,604. ***Scholarships, grants, and awards by category:*** *Academic interests/achievement:* biological sciences, business, communication, computer science, education, English, foreign languages, general academic interests/achievements, home economics, international studies, mathematics, physical sciences, religion/biblical studies, social sciences. *Creative arts/performance:* music. *Special achievements/activities:* religious involvement. *Special characteristics:* children and siblings of alumni, children of faculty/staff, international students, religious affiliation, siblings of current students, veterans. ***ROTC:*** Army cooperative, Air Force cooperative.

LOANS ***Student loans:*** 71% of past graduating class borrowed through all loan programs. *Average indebtedness per student:* $30,999. ***Average need-based loan:*** Freshmen: $6238. Undergraduates: $7523. ***Programs:*** Federal Direct (Subsidized and Unsubsidized Stafford, PLUS), state.

WORK-STUDY ***Federal work-study:*** 78 jobs averaging $2622.

APPLYING FOR FINANCIAL AID ***Required financial aid forms:*** FAFSA, state aid form. ***Financial aid deadline:*** Continuous. ***Notification date:*** Continuous. Students must reply within 2 weeks of notification.

CONTACT Mr. Russell Jeffrey, Director of Student Financial Services, Concordia University Texas, 11400 Concordia University Drive, Austin, TX 78726, 512-313-4672 or toll-free 800-865-4282. *Fax:* 512-313-1670. *E-mail:* russell.jeffrey@concordia.edu. *Website:* http://www.concordia.edu/.

CONCORDIA UNIVERSITY WISCONSIN

Mequon, WI

Tuition & fees: $31,182 | **Average undergraduate aid package: $25,017**

ABOUT THE INSTITUTION Independent Lutheran Church–Missouri Synod, coed. ***Awards:*** certificates, associate, bachelor's, master's, and doctoral degrees. 73 undergraduate majors. ***Total enrollment:*** 5,776. Undergraduates: 3,308. Freshmen: 578.

UNDERGRADUATE EXPENSES for 2020–2021 ***Comprehensive fee:*** $42,652 includes full-time tuition ($30,890), mandatory fees ($292), and room and board ($11,470). ***College room only:*** $8600. Full-time tuition and fees vary according to program. Room and board charges vary according to board plan. ***Part-time tuition:*** $1287 per credit hour. Part-time tuition and fees vary according to program.

FRESHMAN FINANCIAL AID (Fall 2019, est.) 553 applied for aid; of those 85% were deemed to have need. 100% of freshmen with need received aid; of those 34% had need fully met. ***Average percent of need met:*** 83% (excluding resources awarded to replace EFC). ***Average financial aid package:*** $28,774 (excluding resources awarded to replace EFC). 17% of all full-time freshmen had no need and received non-need-based gift aid.

UNDERGRADUATE FINANCIAL AID (Fall 2019, est.) 2,125 applied for aid; of those 84% were deemed to have need. 100% of undergraduates with need received aid; of those 30% had need fully met. ***Average percent of need met:*** 75% (excluding resources awarded to replace EFC). ***Average financial aid package:*** $25,017 (excluding resources awarded to replace EFC). 18% of all full-time undergraduates had no need and received non-need-based gift aid.

GIFT AID (NEED-BASED) ***Total amount:*** $29,217,224 (12% federal, 6% state, 78% institutional, 4% external sources). ***Receiving aid:*** Freshmen: 80% (461); all full-time undergraduates: 73% (1,682). ***Average award:*** Freshmen: $20,119; Undergraduates: $16,758. ***Scholarships, grants, and awards:*** Federal Pell, FSEOG, state, private, college/university gift aid from institutional funds.

GIFT AID (NON-NEED-BASED) ***Total amount:*** $10,745,885 (100% institutional). ***Receiving aid:*** Freshmen: 24% (139). Undergraduates: 20% (455). ***Average award:*** Freshmen: $17,085. Undergraduates: $15,333. ***Scholarships, grants, and awards by category:*** *Academic interests/achievement:* religion/biblical studies. *Creative arts/performance:* music. *Special characteristics:* out-of-state students.

LOANS ***Student loans:*** $19,100,125 (64% need-based, 36% non-need-based). 80% of past graduating class borrowed through all loan programs. *Average indebtedness per student:* $36,651. ***Average need-based loan:*** Freshmen: $6950. Undergraduates: $7893. ***Parent loans:*** $3,403,702 (100% non-need-based). ***Programs:*** Federal Direct (Subsidized and Unsubsidized Stafford, PLUS), state.

WORK-STUDY ***Federal work-study:*** Total amount: $1,236,400; jobs available.

APPLYING FOR FINANCIAL AID ***Required financial aid form:*** FAFSA. ***Financial aid deadline (priority):*** 11/1. ***Notification date:*** Continuous beginning 11/15.

CONTACT Mr. Steven P. Taylor, Director of Financial Aid, Concordia University Wisconsin, 12800 North Lake Shore Drive, Mequon, WI 53097-2402, 262-243-4392 or toll-free 888-628-9472. *Fax:* 262-243-2992. *E-mail:* steve.taylor@cuw.edu. *Website:* http://www.cuw.edu/.

CONCORD UNIVERSITY

Athens, WV

Tuition & fees (WV res): $8385 | **Average undergraduate aid package: $8849**

ABOUT THE INSTITUTION State-supported, coed. ***Awards:*** certificates, bachelor's, and master's degrees. 31 undergraduate majors. ***Total enrollment:*** 2,194. Undergraduates: 1,853. Freshmen: 434. Federal methodology is used as a basis for awarding need-based institutional aid.

UNDERGRADUATE EXPENSES for 2019–2020 ***Tuition, state resident:*** full-time $8050; part-time $336 per credit hour. ***Tuition, nonresident:*** full-time $17,702; part-time $738 per credit hour. ***Required fees:*** full-time $335. Full-time tuition and fees vary according to course load and program. Part-time tuition and fees vary according to course load and program. ***College room and board:*** $9762; ***Room only:*** $5118. Room and board charges vary according to board plan.

FRESHMAN FINANCIAL AID (Fall 2019, est.) 343 applied for aid; of those 83% were deemed to have need. 100% of freshmen with need received aid; of those 38% had need fully met. ***Average percent of need met:*** 85% (excluding resources awarded to replace EFC). ***Average financial aid package:*** $8929 (excluding resources awarded to replace EFC). 15% of all full-time freshmen had no need and received non-need-based gift aid.

UNDERGRADUATE FINANCIAL AID (Fall 2019, est.) 1,272 applied for aid; of those 84% were deemed to have need. 99% of undergraduates with need received aid; of those 35% had need fully met. ***Average percent of need met:*** 86% (excluding resources awarded to replace EFC). ***Average financial aid package:*** $8849 (excluding resources awarded to replace EFC). 16% of all full-time undergraduates had no need and received non-need-based gift aid.

GIFT AID (NEED-BASED) ***Total amount:*** $5,553,174 (67% federal, 26% state, 2% institutional, 5% external sources). ***Receiving aid:*** Freshmen: 62% (226); all full-time undergraduates: 60% (852). ***Average award:*** Freshmen: $6050; Undergraduates: $6122. ***Scholarships, grants, and awards:*** Federal Pell, FSEOG, state, private, college/university gift aid from institutional funds.

GIFT AID (NON-NEED-BASED) ***Total amount:*** $4,783,249 (33% state, 49% institutional, 18% external sources). ***Receiving aid:*** Freshmen: 54% (196). Under-

graduates: 50% (715). ***Average award:*** Freshmen: $3980. Undergraduates: $3991. ***Scholarships, grants, and awards by category:*** *Academic interests/achievement:* 742 awards ($1,024,342 total): biological sciences, business, communication, education, English, general academic interests/achievements, mathematics, physical sciences, premedicine, social sciences. *Creative arts/performance:* 112 awards ($197,426 total): applied art and design, journalism/publications, music, theater/drama. *Special achievements/activities:* 2 awards ($1000 total): community service, general special achievements/activities, leadership. *Special characteristics:* 44 awards ($306,219 total): children of faculty/staff, veterans. ***Tuition waivers:*** Full or partial for employees or children of employees.

LOANS *Student loans:* $6,203,979 (37% need-based, 63% non-need-based). 97% of past graduating class borrowed through all loan programs. *Average indebtedness per student:* $20,004. ***Average need-based loan:*** Freshmen: $2646. Undergraduates: $3318. ***Parent loans:*** $834,269 (100% non-need-based). ***Programs:*** Federal Direct (Subsidized and Unsubsidized Stafford, PLUS), Perkins.

WORK-STUDY *Federal work-study:* Total amount: $314,785; 152 jobs averaging $2078.

ATHLETIC AWARDS Total amount: $1,471,323 (100% non-need-based).

APPLYING FOR FINANCIAL AID *Required financial aid forms:* FAFSA, institution's own form, state aid form, verification worksheet. ***Financial aid deadline:*** 4/15. ***Notification date:*** Continuous beginning 11/1. Students must reply within 3 weeks of notification.

CONTACT Tammy Brown, Director of Financial Aid, Concord University, PO Box 1000, Athens, WV 24712-1000, 304-384-5358 or toll-free 888-384-5249. *Fax:* 304-384-3084. *E-mail:* tbrown@concord.edu.
Website: http://www.concord.edu/.

CONNECTICUT COLLEGE

New London, CT

Tuition & fees: $56,890	Average undergraduate aid package: $46,607

ABOUT THE INSTITUTION Independent, coed. ***Awards:*** bachelor's degrees. 43 undergraduate majors. ***Total enrollment:*** 1,844. Undergraduates: 1,844. Freshmen: 508. Both federal and institutional methodology are used as a basis for awarding need-based institutional aid.

UNDERGRADUATE EXPENSES for 2019–2020 *Comprehensive fee:* $72,590 includes full-time tuition ($56,540), mandatory fees ($350), and room and board ($15,700). ***College room only:*** $9070. ***Part-time tuition:*** $1683 per credit hour.

FRESHMAN FINANCIAL AID (Fall 2019, est.) 363 applied for aid; of those 86% were deemed to have need. 100% of freshmen with need received aid; of those 100% had need fully met. ***Average percent of need met:*** 100% (excluding resources awarded to replace EFC). ***Average financial aid package:*** $46,820 (excluding resources awarded to replace EFC). 36% of all full-time freshmen had no need and received non-need-based gift aid.

UNDERGRADUATE FINANCIAL AID (Fall 2019, est.) 1,198 applied for aid; of those 89% were deemed to have need. 100% of undergraduates with need received aid; of those 100% had need fully met. ***Average percent of need met:*** 100% (excluding resources awarded to replace EFC). ***Average financial aid package:*** $46,607 (excluding resources awarded to replace EFC). 24% of all full-time undergraduates had no need and received non-need-based gift aid.

GIFT AID (NEED-BASED) *Receiving aid:* Freshmen: 59% (301); all full-time undergraduates: 57% (1,033). ***Average award:*** Freshmen: $44,953; Undergraduates: $43,639. ***Scholarships, grants, and awards:*** Federal Pell, FSEOG, state, college/university gift aid from institutional funds.

GIFT AID (NON-NEED-BASED) *Receiving aid:* Freshmen: 10% (51). Undergraduates: 7% (136). ***Average award:*** Freshmen: $15,662. Undergraduates: $14,798. ***Tuition waivers:*** Full or partial for employees or children of employees.

LOANS *Student loans:* 54% of past graduating class borrowed through all loan programs. *Average indebtedness per student:* $37,817. ***Average need-based loan:*** Freshmen: $3342. Undergraduates: $4487. ***Programs:*** Federal Direct (Subsidized and Unsubsidized Stafford, PLUS), college/university.

WORK-STUDY Federal work-study jobs available.

APPLYING FOR FINANCIAL AID *Required financial aid forms:* FAFSA, CSS Financial Aid PROFILE, noncustodial (divorced/separated) parent's statement.

CONTACT Sean Martin, Director of Financial Aid Services, Connecticut College, 270 Mohegan Avenue, Larrabee Annex, New London, CT 06320, 860-439-2058. *Fax:* 860-439-5357. *E-mail:* finaid@conncoll.edu.
Website: http://www.conncoll.edu/.

CONSERVATORIO DE MUSICA DE PUERTO RICO

San Juan, PR

CONTACT Mr. Michael Rajaballey, Director of Financial Aid, Conservatorio de Musica de Puerto Rico, 951 Ave. Ponce de Leon, Miramar, San Juan, PR 00907, 787-751-0160 Ext. 231. *Fax:* 787-763-3886. *E-mail:* mrajaballey@cmpr.gobierno.pr.
Website: http://www.cmpr.edu/.

CONVERSE COLLEGE

Spartanburg, SC

Tuition & fees: N/R	Average undergraduate aid package: N/A

ABOUT THE INSTITUTION Independent, undergraduate: women only; graduate: coed. ***Awards:*** certificates, bachelor's, and master's degrees. 49 undergraduate majors. Federal methodology is used as a basis for awarding need-based institutional aid.

GIFT AID (NEED-BASED) *Scholarships, grants, and awards:* Federal Pell, FSEOG, state, private, college/university gift aid from institutional funds.

GIFT AID (NON-NEED-BASED) *Scholarships, grants, and awards by category:* *Academic interests/achievement:* general academic interests/achievements. *Creative arts/performance:* art/fine arts, general creative arts/performance, music, theater/drama. *Special characteristics:* children and siblings of alumni, children of faculty/staff. ***ROTC:*** Army cooperative.

LOANS *Student loans:* 85% of past graduating class borrowed through all loan programs. *Average indebtedness per student:* $29,580. ***Programs:*** Federal Direct (Subsidized and Unsubsidized Stafford, PLUS), state, Alternative Student Loans through private lenders.

WORK-STUDY Federal work-study jobs available. ***State or other work-study/employment:*** Part-time jobs available.

APPLYING FOR FINANCIAL AID *Required financial aid form:* FAFSA. ***Financial aid deadline:*** Continuous. ***Notification date:*** Continuous. Students must reply within 2 weeks of notification.

CONTACT Mr. James W. Kellam, Director of Financial Planning, Converse College, 580 East Main Street, Spartanburg, SC 29302-0006, 864-596-9019 or toll-free 800-766-1125. *Fax:* 864-596-9749. *E-mail:* james.kellam@converse.edu.
Website: http://www.converse.edu/.

COOPER UNION FOR THE ADVANCEMENT OF SCIENCE AND ART

New York, NY

CONTACT Mr. Charlie Xu, Director of Financial Aid, Cooper Union for the Advancement of Science and Art, 30 Cooper Square, New York, NY 10003-7120, 212-353-4043. *Fax:* 212-353-4343. *E-mail:* cxu@cooper.edu.
Website: http://www.cooper.edu/.

COPPIN STATE UNIVERSITY

Baltimore, MD

CONTACT Ms. Thelma Ross, Director of Financial Aid, Coppin State University, 2500 West North Avenue, Baltimore, MD 21216-3698, 410-951-3633 or toll-free 800-635-3674. *Fax:* 410-951-3637. *E-mail:* thross@coppin.edu.
Website: http://www.coppin.edu/.

CORBAN UNIVERSITY

Salem, OR

ABOUT THE INSTITUTION Independent Christian, coed. ***Awards:*** associate, bachelor's, master's, and doctoral degrees. 44 undergraduate majors.
GIFT AID (NEED-BASED) ***Scholarships, grants, and awards:*** Federal Pell, FSEOG, state, private, college/university gift aid from institutional funds.
GIFT AID (NON-NEED-BASED) ***Scholarships, grants, and awards by category:*** *Academic interests/achievement:* agriculture, biological sciences, business, communication, education, foreign languages, general academic interests/achievements, home economics, premedicine, social sciences. *Creative arts/performance:* debating, journalism/publications, music, performing arts, theater/drama. *Special achievements/activities:* general special achievements/activities, leadership, memberships. *Special characteristics:* children and siblings of alumni, children of faculty/staff, international students, relatives of clergy, siblings of current students, veterans.
LOANS ***Programs:*** Federal Direct (Subsidized and Unsubsidized Stafford, PLUS), Private Outside Student Loans.
CONTACT Ellen Zarfas, Director of Financial Aid, Corban University, 5000 Deer Park Drive, SE, Salem, OR 97317, 503-375-7106 or toll-free 800-845-3005. *Fax:* 503-585-4316. *E-mail:* financialaid@corban.edu.
Website: http://www.corban.edu/.

CORNELL COLLEGE

Mount Vernon, IA

Tuition & fees: $44,096	Average undergraduate aid package: $33,307

ABOUT THE INSTITUTION Independent Methodist, coed. 52 undergraduate majors. Federal methodology is used as a basis for awarding need-based institutional aid.
UNDERGRADUATE EXPENSES for 2019–2020 ***Comprehensive fee:*** $53,856 includes full-time tuition ($43,550), mandatory fees ($546), and room and board ($9760). ***College room only:*** $4500. ***Part-time tuition:*** $3266 per course. ***Part-time fees:*** $160 per year.
FRESHMAN FINANCIAL AID (Fall 2019, est.) 250 applied for aid; of those 86% were deemed to have need. 100% of freshmen with need received aid; of those 26% had need fully met. ***Average percent of need met:*** 84% (excluding resources awarded to replace EFC). ***Average financial aid package:*** $33,319 (excluding resources awarded to replace EFC). 17% of all full-time freshmen had no need and received non-need-based gift aid.
UNDERGRADUATE FINANCIAL AID (Fall 2019, est.) 795 applied for aid; of those 88% were deemed to have need. 100% of undergraduates with need received aid; of those 24% had need fully met. ***Average percent of need met:*** 82% (excluding resources awarded to replace EFC). ***Average financial aid package:*** $33,307 (excluding resources awarded to replace EFC). 29% of all full-time undergraduates had no need and received non-need-based gift aid.
GIFT AID (NEED-BASED) ***Total amount:*** $20,038,498 (5% federal, 4% state, 89% institutional, 2% external sources). ***Receiving aid:*** Freshmen: 79% (214); all full-time undergraduates: 69% (699). ***Average award:*** Freshmen: $32,207; Undergraduates: $30,116. ***Scholarships, grants, and awards:*** Federal Pell, FSEOG, state, college/university gift aid from institutional funds.
GIFT AID (NON-NEED-BASED) ***Total amount:*** $8,619,741 (98% institutional, 2% external sources). ***Receiving aid:*** Freshmen: 20% (54). Undergraduates: 14% (137). ***Average award:*** Freshmen: $28,293. Undergraduates: $23,751. ***Scholarships, grants, and awards by category:*** *Academic interests/achievement:* general academic interests/achievements. *Creative arts/performance:* applied art and design, dance, music, performing arts, theater/drama. *Special characteristics:* children and siblings of alumni, children of faculty/staff.
LOANS ***Student loans:*** $5,884,866 (64% need-based, 36% non-need-based). 79% of past graduating class borrowed through all loan programs. *Average indebtedness per student:* $38,215. ***Average need-based loan:*** Freshmen: $3315. Undergraduates: $4446. ***Parent loans:*** $1,245,339 (46% need-based, 54% non-need-based). ***Programs:*** Federal Direct (Subsidized and Unsubsidized Stafford, PLUS), college/university, McElroy, Sherman, and United Methodist Loans.
WORK-STUDY ***Federal work-study:*** Total amount: $468,860; jobs available. ***State or other work-study/employment:*** Total amount: $155,270 (100% non-need-based). Part-time jobs available.
APPLYING FOR FINANCIAL AID ***Required financial aid form:*** FAFSA. ***Financial aid deadline (priority):*** 3/1. ***Notification date:*** Continuous beginning 1/15. Students must reply by 5/1 or within 2 weeks of notification.
CONTACT Ms. Pam Perry, Director of Financial Assistance, Cornell College, 600 First Street South West, Mount Vernon, IA 52314-1098, 319-895-4216 or toll-free 800-747-1112. *Fax:* 319-895-4106. *E-mail:* pperry@cornellcollege.edu.
Website: http://www.cornellcollege.edu/.

CORNELL UNIVERSITY

Ithaca, NY

Tuition & fees: $57,222	Average undergraduate aid package: $50,492

ABOUT THE INSTITUTION Independent, coed. ***Awards:*** bachelor's, master's, and doctoral degrees. 75 undergraduate majors. ***Total enrollment:*** 24,027. Undergraduates: 15,043. Freshmen: 3,189. Institutional methodology is used as a basis for awarding need-based institutional aid.
UNDERGRADUATE EXPENSES for 2019–2020 ***Application fee:*** $80. ***Comprehensive fee:*** $72,518 includes full-time tuition ($56,550), mandatory fees ($672), and room and board ($15,296). ***College room only:*** $9152. Room and board charges vary according to board plan and housing facility.
FRESHMAN FINANCIAL AID (Fall 2019, est.) 1716 applied for aid; of those 87% were deemed to have need. 100% of freshmen with need received aid; of those 100% had need fully met. ***Average percent of need met:*** 100% (excluding resources awarded to replace EFC). ***Average financial aid package:*** $50,772 (excluding resources awarded to replace EFC).
UNDERGRADUATE FINANCIAL AID (Fall 2019, est.) 7,665 applied for aid; of those 92% were deemed to have need. 100% of undergraduates with need received aid; of those 100% had need fully met. ***Average percent of need met:*** 100% (excluding resources awarded to replace EFC). ***Average financial aid package:*** $50,492 (excluding resources awarded to replace EFC).
GIFT AID (NEED-BASED) ***Total amount:*** $309,896,418 (5% federal, 2% state, 87% institutional, 6% external sources). ***Receiving aid:*** Freshmen: 46% (1,456); all full-time undergraduates: 46% (6,822). ***Average award:*** Freshmen: $44,767; Undergraduates: $44,026. ***Scholarships, grants, and awards:*** Federal Pell, FSEOG, state, private, college/university gift aid from institutional funds.
GIFT AID (NON-NEED-BASED) ***Total amount:*** $3,531,450 (100% external sources). ***Tuition waivers:*** Full or partial for employees or children of employees. ***ROTC:*** Army, Naval, Air Force.
LOANS ***Student loans:*** $40,267,201 (91% need-based, 9% non-need-based). 40% of past graduating class borrowed through all loan programs. *Average indebtedness per student:* $27,094. ***Average need-based loan:*** Freshmen: $4770. Undergraduates: $5092. ***Parent loans:*** $11,628,695 (92% need-based, 8% non-need-based). ***Programs:*** Federal Direct (Subsidized and Unsubsidized Stafford, PLUS), college/university.
WORK-STUDY ***Federal work-study:*** Total amount: $12,843,865; jobs available. ***State or other work-study/employment:*** Total amount: $2,020,911 (100% need-based). Part-time jobs available.
APPLYING FOR FINANCIAL AID ***Required financial aid forms:*** FAFSA, CSS Financial Aid PROFILE, noncustodial (divorced/separated) parent's statement. ***Financial aid deadline:*** 2/15. ***Notification date:*** 4/1. Students must reply by 5/1.
CONTACT Ms. Diane Corbett, Director of Financial Aid and Student Employment, Cornell University, 203 Day Hall, Ithaca, NY 14853-2488, 607-255-5145.
Website: http://www.cornell.edu/.

CORNERSTONE UNIVERSITY

Grand Rapids, MI

Tuition & fees: N/R | **Average undergraduate aid package:** $19,549

ABOUT THE INSTITUTION Independent nondenominational, coed. ***Awards:*** diplomas, associate, bachelor's, master's, and doctoral degrees. 59 undergraduate majors. Federal methodology is used as a basis for awarding need-based institutional aid.

FRESHMAN FINANCIAL AID (Fall 2019, est.) 265 applied for aid; of those 86% were deemed to have need. 100% of freshmen with need received aid; of those 20% had need fully met. ***Average percent of need met:*** 68% (excluding resources awarded to replace EFC). ***Average financial aid package:*** $19,372 (excluding resources awarded to replace EFC). 21% of all full-time freshmen had no need and received non-need-based gift aid.

UNDERGRADUATE FINANCIAL AID (Fall 2019, est.) 870 applied for aid; of those 89% were deemed to have need. 100% of undergraduates with need received aid; of those 17% had need fully met. ***Average percent of need met:*** 67% (excluding resources awarded to replace EFC). ***Average financial aid package:*** $19,549 (excluding resources awarded to replace EFC). 24% of all full-time undergraduates had no need and received non-need-based gift aid.

GIFT AID (NEED-BASED) ***Total amount:*** $10,921,464 (14% federal, 13% state, 70% institutional, 3% external sources). ***Receiving aid:*** Freshmen: 79% (229); all full-time undergraduates: 75% (769). ***Average award:*** Freshmen: $15,832; Undergraduates: $15,172. ***Scholarships, grants, and awards:*** Federal Pell, FSEOG, state, private, college/university gift aid from institutional funds.

GIFT AID (NON-NEED-BASED) ***Total amount:*** $2,596,571 (96% institutional, 4% external sources). ***Receiving aid:*** Freshmen: 11% (32). Undergraduates: 9% (94). ***Average award:*** Freshmen: $10,727. Undergraduates: $9036. ***Scholarships, grants, and awards by category:*** *Academic interests/achievement:* business, communication, education, English, general academic interests/achievements, home economics, humanities, mathematics, physical sciences, religion/biblical studies, social sciences. *Creative arts/performance:* music. *Special characteristics:* children of faculty/staff, ethnic background, international students, members of minority groups, relatives of clergy. ***ROTC:*** Army cooperative.

LOANS ***Student loans:*** $6,208,992 (41% need-based, 59% non-need-based). 73% of past graduating class borrowed through all loan programs. *Average indebtedness per student:* $31,611. ***Average need-based loan:*** Freshmen: $3500. Undergraduates: $4699. ***Parent loans:*** $1,398,089 (100% non-need-based). ***Programs:*** Federal Direct (Subsidized and Unsubsidized Stafford, PLUS).

WORK-STUDY ***Federal work-study:*** Total amount: $168,102; jobs available.

ATHLETIC AWARDS Total amount: $1,547,678 (64% need-based, 36% non-need-based).

APPLYING FOR FINANCIAL AID ***Required financial aid form:*** FAFSA. ***Financial aid deadline:*** Continuous. ***Notification date:*** Continuous beginning 12/1. Students must reply within 4 weeks of notification.

CONTACT Mrs. Carol S. Carpenter, Director of Student Financial Services, Cornerstone University, 1001 East Beltline Avenue, NE, Grand Rapids, MI 49525-5897, 616-222-1424 or toll-free 800-787-9778. *Fax:* 616-222-1400. *E-mail:* carol.carpenter@cornerstone.edu.
Website: http://www.cornerstone.edu/.

CORNISH COLLEGE OF THE ARTS

Seattle, WA

CONTACT Monique Theriault, Office of Financial Aid, Cornish College of the Arts, 1000 Lenora Street, Seattle, WA 98121, 206-726-5013 or toll-free 800-726-ARTS. *Fax:* 206-720-1011. *E-mail:* mtheriault@cornish.edu.
Website: http://www.cornish.edu/.

COVENANT COLLEGE

Lookout Mountain, GA

Tuition & fees: $36,710 | **Average undergraduate aid package:** $29,745

ABOUT THE INSTITUTION Independent Presbyterian Church in America, coed. ***Awards:*** bachelor's and master's degrees (master's degree in education only). 27 undergraduate majors. ***Total enrollment:*** 989. Undergraduates: 946. Freshmen: 219. Federal methodology is used as a basis for awarding need-based institutional aid.

UNDERGRADUATE EXPENSES for 2020–2021 ***Application fee:*** $35. ***Comprehensive fee:*** $47,680 includes full-time tuition ($35,670), mandatory fees ($1040), and room and board ($10,970). ***Part-time tuition:*** $1530 per credit hour.

FRESHMAN FINANCIAL AID (Fall 2018) 223 applied for aid; of those 81% were deemed to have need. 100% of freshmen with need received aid; of those 44% had need fully met. ***Average percent of need met:*** 82% (excluding resources awarded to replace EFC). ***Average financial aid package:*** $29,439 (excluding resources awarded to replace EFC). 27% of all full-time freshmen had no need and received non-need-based gift aid.

UNDERGRADUATE FINANCIAL AID (Fall 2018) 770 applied for aid; of those 85% were deemed to have need. 100% of undergraduates with need received aid; of those 36% had need fully met. ***Average percent of need met:*** 80% (excluding resources awarded to replace EFC). ***Average financial aid package:*** $29,745 (excluding resources awarded to replace EFC). 31% of all full-time undergraduates had no need and received non-need-based gift aid.

GIFT AID (NEED-BASED) ***Total amount:*** $15,701,146 (8% federal, 5% state, 84% institutional, 3% external sources). ***Receiving aid:*** Freshmen: 72% (180); all full-time undergraduates: 67% (650). ***Average award:*** Freshmen: $24,708; Undergraduates: $24,148. ***Scholarships, grants, and awards:*** Federal Pell, FSEOG, state, private, college/university gift aid from institutional funds.

GIFT AID (NON-NEED-BASED) ***Total amount:*** $5,869,856 (4% state, 90% institutional, 6% external sources). ***Receiving aid:*** Freshmen: 21% (53). Undergraduates: 14% (134). ***Average award:*** Freshmen: $19,270. Undergraduates: $17,545. ***Scholarships, grants, and awards by category:*** *Academic interests/achievement:* general academic interests/achievements. *Creative arts/performance:* music. *Special achievements/activities:* leadership. *Special characteristics:* children of faculty/staff, international students, members of minority groups, religious affiliation. ***ROTC:*** Army cooperative.

LOANS ***Student loans:*** $3,671,513 (89% need-based, 11% non-need-based). 58% of past graduating class borrowed through all loan programs. *Average indebtedness per student:* $23,723. ***Average need-based loan:*** Freshmen: $5367. Undergraduates: $6273. ***Parent loans:*** $1,072,136 (85% need-based, 15% non-need-based). ***Programs:*** Perkins, state.

WORK-STUDY ***Federal work-study:*** Total amount: $317,678; jobs available. ***State or other work-study/employment:*** Total amount: $837,406 (73% need-based, 27% non-need-based). Part-time jobs available.

APPLYING FOR FINANCIAL AID ***Required financial aid forms:*** FAFSA, state aid form. ***Financial aid deadline (priority):*** 2/1. ***Notification date:*** 3/15. Students must reply by 5/1 or within 3 weeks of notification.

CONTACT Mrs. Margaret Stewart, Assistant Director of Financial Aid, Covenant College, 14049 Scenic Highway, Lookout Mountain, GA 30750, 706-419-1152 or toll-free 888-451-2683. *Fax:* 706-820-2820. *E-mail:* margaret.stewart@covenant.edu.
Website: http://www.covenant.edu/.

COX COLLEGE

Springfield, MO

ABOUT THE INSTITUTION Independent, coed, primarily women. ***Awards:*** certificates, associate, bachelor's, and master's degrees. 5 undergraduate majors.

GIFT AID (NEED-BASED) ***Scholarships, grants, and awards:*** Federal Pell, FSEOG, state, private, college/university gift aid from institutional funds, United Negro College Fund, Federal Nursing.

LOANS ***Programs:*** Federal Direct (Subsidized and Unsubsidized Stafford, PLUS).

CONTACT Leesa Taylor, Financial Aid Counselor, Cox College, 1423 North Jefferson Avenue, Springfield, MO 65802, 417-269-3160 or toll-free 866-898-5355 (in-state). *Fax:* 417-269-3586. *E-mail:* leesa.taylor@coxcollege.edu.
Website: http://www.coxcollege.edu/.

CREATIVE CENTER

Omaha, NE

CONTACT Financial Aid Office, Creative Center, 10850 Emmet Street, Omaha, NE 68164, 402-898-1000 or toll-free 888-898-1789.
Website: http://www.creativecenter.edu/.

CREIGHTON UNIVERSITY

Omaha, NE

Tuition & fees: $43,018	Average undergraduate aid package: $29,120

ABOUT THE INSTITUTION Independent Roman Catholic (Jesuit), coed. ***Awards:*** certificates, associate, bachelor's, master's, and doctoral degrees. 53 undergraduate majors. ***Total enrollment:*** 8,821. Undergraduates: 4,472. Freshmen: 1,076. Federal methodology is used as a basis for awarding need-based institutional aid.

UNDERGRADUATE EXPENSES for 2020–2021 ***Application fee:*** $40. ***One-time required fee:*** $160. ***Comprehensive fee:*** $54,618 includes full-time tuition ($41,176), mandatory fees ($1842), and room and board ($11,600). Room and board charges vary according to board plan, housing facility, and location. ***Part-time tuition:*** $1288 per credit hour. ***Part-time fees:*** $182 per term.

FRESHMAN FINANCIAL AID (Fall 2019, est.) 932 applied for aid; of those 66% were deemed to have need. 100% of freshmen with need received aid; of those 33% had need fully met. ***Average percent of need met:*** 84% (excluding resources awarded to replace EFC). ***Average financial aid package:*** $30,787 (excluding resources awarded to replace EFC). 40% of all full-time freshmen had no need and received non-need-based gift aid.

UNDERGRADUATE FINANCIAL AID (Fall 2019, est.) 2,906 applied for aid; of those 75% were deemed to have need. 100% of undergraduates with need received aid; of those 25% had need fully met. ***Average percent of need met:*** 78% (excluding resources awarded to replace EFC). ***Average financial aid package:*** $29,120 (excluding resources awarded to replace EFC). 42% of all full-time undergraduates had no need and received non-need-based gift aid.

GIFT AID (NEED-BASED) ***Total amount:*** $42,889,913 (7% federal, 1% state, 90% institutional, 2% external sources). ***Receiving aid:*** Freshmen: 57% (612); all full-time undergraduates: 47% (2,038). ***Average award:*** Freshmen: $22,856; Undergraduates: $22,255. ***Scholarships, grants, and awards:*** Federal Pell, FSEOG, state, private, college/university gift aid from institutional funds.

GIFT AID (NON-NEED-BASED) ***Total amount:*** $38,670,187 (97% institutional, 3% external sources). ***Receiving aid:*** Freshmen: 17% (183). Undergraduates: 11% (476). ***Average award:*** Freshmen: $19,839. Undergraduates: $18,558. ***Scholarships, grants, and awards by category:*** *Academic interests/achievement:* 3,526 awards ($61,069,609 total): business, education, general academic interests/achievements, military science. *Creative arts/performance:* 21 awards ($82,000 total): applied art and design, art/fine arts, dance, music, performing arts, theater/drama. *Special characteristics:* 33 awards ($968,189 total): members of minority groups, religious affiliation. ***Tuition waivers:*** Full or partial for employees or children of employees. ***ROTC:*** Army, Air Force cooperative.

LOANS ***Student loans:*** $35,569,444 (54% need-based, 46% non-need-based). 59% of past graduating class borrowed through all loan programs. *Average indebtedness per student:* $38,042. ***Average need-based loan:*** Freshmen: $4967. Undergraduates: $5981. ***Parent loans:*** $6,823,318 (35% need-based, 65% non-need-based). ***Programs:*** Federal Direct (Subsidized and Unsubsidized Stafford, PLUS), Federal Nursing, college/university.

WORK-STUDY ***Federal work-study:*** Total amount: $1,881,175; 829 jobs averaging $2259.

ATHLETIC AWARDS Total amount: $5,392,705 (15% need-based, 85% non-need-based).

APPLYING FOR FINANCIAL AID ***Required financial aid forms:*** FAFSA, institution's own form. ***Financial aid deadline (priority):*** 1/15. ***Notification date:*** Continuous beginning 2/15. Students must reply within 4 weeks of notification.

CONTACT Ms. Paula S. Kohles, Director of Financial Aid, Creighton University, 2500 California Plaza, Omaha, NE 68178, 402-280-2731 or toll-free 800-282-5835. *Fax:* 402-280-2895. *E-mail:* paulakohles@creighton.edu.
Website: http://www.creighton.edu/.

CRISWELL COLLEGE

Dallas, TX

ABOUT THE INSTITUTION Independent Southern Baptist Convention, coed. ***Awards:*** associate, bachelor's, and master's degrees. 6 undergraduate majors.

GIFT AID (NEED-BASED) ***Scholarships, grants, and awards:*** Federal Pell, private, college/university gift aid from institutional funds.

GIFT AID (NON-NEED-BASED) ***Scholarships, grants, and awards by category:*** *Academic interests/achievement:* general academic interests/achievements, religion/biblical studies. *Special achievements/activities:* religious involvement.

LOANS ***Programs:*** Federal Direct (Subsidized and Unsubsidized Stafford, PLUS).

CONTACT Jimmy Criswell, Director of Financial Aid, Criswell College, 4010 Gaston Avenue, Dallas, TX 75246, 214-818-1393 or toll-free 800-899-0012. *Fax:* 214-370-0497. *E-mail:* jcriswell@criswell.edu.
Website: http://www.criswell.edu/.

CROSSROADS BIBLE COLLEGE

Indianapolis, IN

CONTACT Mrs. Phyllis Dodson, Senior Director of Financial Aid, Crossroads Bible College, 601 North Shortridge Road, Indianapolis, IN 46219, 317-789-8250 or toll-free 800-822-3119. *Fax:* 317-789-8253. *E-mail:* pdodson@crossroads.edu.
Website: http://www.crossroads.edu/.

CROWLEY'S RIDGE COLLEGE

Paragould, AR

CONTACT Financial Aid Office, Crowley's Ridge College, 100 College Drive, Paragould, AR 72450-9731, 870-236-6901 or toll-free 800-264-1096.
Website: http://www.crc.edu/.

CROWN COLLEGE

St. Bonifacius, MN

CONTACT Mr. Jon Erickson, Interim Director of Financial Aid, Crown College, 8700 College View Drive, St. Bonifacius, MN 55375-9001, 952-446-4177 or toll-free 800-68-CROWN. *Fax:* 952-446-4178. *E-mail:* finaid@crown.edu.
Website: http://www.crown.edu/.

THE CULINARY INSTITUTE OF AMERICA

Hyde Park, NY

Tuition & fees: $33,690	Average undergraduate aid package: N/A

ABOUT THE INSTITUTION Independent, coed. ***Awards:*** certificates, associate, bachelor's, and master's degrees. 5 undergraduate majors. ***Total enrollment:*** 3,094. Undergraduates: 3,007. Freshmen: 610. Federal methodology is used as a basis for awarding need-based institutional aid.

UNDERGRADUATE EXPENSES for 2019–2020 ***Application fee:*** $50. ***Comprehensive fee:*** $45,570 includes full-time tuition ($31,080), mandatory fees ($2610), and room and board ($11,880). ***College room only:*** $8080. Full-time tuition and fees vary according to location. Room and board charges vary according to board plan, housing facility, and location. Part-time tuition and fees vary according to course load.

GIFT AID (NEED-BASED) ***Scholarships, grants, and awards:*** Federal Pell, FSEOG, state, private, college/university gift aid from institutional funds.

GIFT AID (NON-NEED-BASED) ***Scholarships, grants, and awards by category:*** *Academic interests/achievement:* general academic interests/achievements.

Creative arts/performance: general creative arts/performance. *Special achievements/activities:* general special achievements/activities.
LOANS *Student loans:* 63% of past graduating class borrowed through all loan programs. *Average indebtedness per student:* $51,200. ***Programs:*** Federal Direct (Subsidized and Unsubsidized Stafford, PLUS), alternative loans.
WORK-STUDY Federal work-study jobs available. ***State or other work-study/employment:*** Part-time jobs available.
APPLYING FOR FINANCIAL AID *Required financial aid forms:* FAFSA, state aid form. ***Financial aid deadline:*** Continuous. ***Notification date:*** Continuous beginning 12/15. Students must reply within 2 weeks of notification.
CONTACT Kathleen Gailor, Director of Student Financial Planning, The Culinary Institute of America, 1946 Campus Drive, Hyde Park, NY 12538-1499, 845-451-1500 or toll-free 800-CULINARY. *Fax:* 845-905-4030. *E-mail:* sfrs@culinary.edu.
Website: http://www.ciachef.edu/.

CULINARY INSTITUTE OF VIRGINIA

Norfolk, VA

CONTACT Ms. Lynn Robinson, Director of Financial Aid, Culinary Institute of Virginia, 8 Abbott Park Place, Providence, RI 02903, 401-598-4648 or toll-free 866-619-CHEF. *Fax:* 401-598-1040. *E-mail:* fp@jwu.edu.
Website: http://www.chefva.com/.

CULVER-STOCKTON COLLEGE

Canton, MO

CONTACT Ms. Tina M. Wiseman, Director of Financial Aid, Culver-Stockton College, One College Hill, Canton, MO 63435, 573-288-6307 or toll-free 800-537-1883. *Fax:* 573-288-6308. *E-mail:* twiseman@culver.edu.
Website: http://www.culver.edu/.

CUMBERLAND UNIVERSITY

Lebanon, TN

CONTACT Ms. Beatrice LaChance, Executive Director of Enrollment Services, Cumberland University, 1 Cumberland Square, Lebanon, TN 37087-3554, 615-444-2562 Ext. 1244 or toll-free 800-467-0562. *Fax:* 615-443-8424. *E-mail:* lvaughan@cumberland.edu.
Website: http://www.cumberland.edu/.

CURRY COLLEGE

Milton, MA

CONTACT Linda Brennan, Director of Financial Aid, Curry College, 1071 Blue Hill Avenue, Milton, MA 02186-2395, 617-333-2354 or toll-free 800-669-0686. *Fax:* 617-333-2915. *E-mail:* fin-aid@curry.edu.
Website: http://www.curry.edu/.

CURTIS INSTITUTE OF MUSIC

Philadelphia, PA

CONTACT Veronica McAuley, Director of Student Financial Assistance, Curtis Institute of Music, 1726 Locust Street, Philadelphia, PA 19103-6107, 215-717-3188. *E-mail:* veronica.mcauley@curtis.edu.
Website: http://www.curtis.edu/.

DAEMEN COLLEGE

Amherst, NY

CONTACT Mr. Jeffrey Pagano, Director of Financial Aid, Daemen College, 4380 Main Street, Amherst, NY 14226-3592, 716-839-8254 or toll-free 800-462-7652. *Fax:* 716-839-8378. *E-mail:* jpagano@daemen.edu.
Website: http://www.daemen.edu/.

DAKOTA STATE UNIVERSITY

Madison, SD

Tuition & fees (SD res): $9536	Average undergraduate aid package: $8362

ABOUT THE INSTITUTION State-supported, coed. ***Awards:*** certificates, associate, bachelor's, master's, and doctoral degrees. 28 undergraduate majors. ***Total enrollment:*** 3,268. Undergraduates: 2,818. Freshmen: 425. Federal methodology is used as a basis for awarding need-based institutional aid.
UNDERGRADUATE EXPENSES for 2019–2020 *Application fee:* $20. ***Tuition, state resident:*** full-time $7541; part-time $251 per credit hour. ***Tuition, nonresident:*** full-time $10,611; part-time $354 per credit hour. ***Required fees:*** full-time $1995; $40.05 per credit hour. Full-time tuition and fees vary according to location and reciprocity agreements. Part-time tuition and fees vary according to location and reciprocity agreements. ***College room and board:*** $7033; ***Room only:*** $3805. Room and board charges vary according to board plan and housing facility.
FRESHMAN FINANCIAL AID (Fall 2018) 343 applied for aid; of those 76% were deemed to have need. 100% of freshmen with need received aid; of those 11% had need fully met. ***Average percent of need met:*** 53% (excluding resources awarded to replace EFC). ***Average financial aid package:*** $7882 (excluding resources awarded to replace EFC). 15% of all full-time freshmen had no need and received non-need-based gift aid.
UNDERGRADUATE FINANCIAL AID (Fall 2018) 1,198 applied for aid; of those 80% were deemed to have need. 100% of undergraduates with need received aid; of those 10% had need fully met. ***Average percent of need met:*** 53% (excluding resources awarded to replace EFC). ***Average financial aid package:*** $8362 (excluding resources awarded to replace EFC). 10% of all full-time undergraduates had no need and received non-need-based gift aid.
GIFT AID (NEED-BASED) *Receiving aid:* Freshmen: 36% (141); all full-time undergraduates: 38% (547). ***Average award:*** Freshmen: $4494; Undergraduates: $4754. ***Scholarships, grants, and awards:*** Federal Pell, FSEOG, state, private, college/university gift aid from institutional funds, Veterans Education Benefits (GI Bill).
GIFT AID (NON-NEED-BASED) *Receiving aid:* Freshmen: 50% (193). Undergraduates: 35% (499). ***Average award:*** Freshmen: $4513. Undergraduates: $5209. ***Scholarships, grants, and awards by category:*** *Academic interests/achievement:* 507 awards ($696,000 total): biological sciences, business, communication, computer science, education, English, general academic interests/achievements, health fields, mathematics, physical sciences. *Creative arts/performance:* 11 awards ($3450 total): music. *Special characteristics:* 1 award ($750 total): veterans. ***Tuition waivers:*** Full or partial for employees or children of employees, senior citizens. ***ROTC:*** Army cooperative, Air Force cooperative.
LOANS *Student loans:* 77% of past graduating class borrowed through all loan programs. *Average indebtedness per student:* $27,928. ***Average need-based loan:*** Freshmen: $3081. Undergraduates: $4024. ***Programs:*** Federal Direct (Subsidized and Unsubsidized Stafford, PLUS), alternative loans.
WORK-STUDY *Federal work-study:* 117 jobs averaging $2339. ***State or other work-study/employment:*** 27 part-time jobs averaging $6895.
APPLYING FOR FINANCIAL AID *Required financial aid forms:* FAFSA, institutional scholarship application form. ***Financial aid deadline:*** Continuous. ***Notification date:*** Continuous. Students must reply within 2 weeks of notification.
CONTACT Denise Grayson, Financial Aid Director, Dakota State University, 103 Heston Hall, 820 North Washington Avenue, Madison, SD 57042-1799, 605-256-5158 or toll-free 888-DSU-9988. *Fax:* 605-256-5020. *E-mail:* fa@dsu.edu.
Website: http://www.dsu.edu/.

DAKOTA WESLEYAN UNIVERSITY

Mitchell, SD

CONTACT Mary Alexander, Director of Financial Aid, Dakota Wesleyan University, 1200 West University Avenue, Mitchell, SD 57301, 605-995-2663 or toll-free 800-333-8506. *Fax:* 605-995-2122. *E-mail:* maalexan@dwu.edu.
Website: http://www.dwu.edu/.

DALLAS BAPTIST UNIVERSITY

Dallas, TX

Tuition & fees: $31,940	Average undergraduate aid package: $19,713

ABOUT THE INSTITUTION Independent Baptist General Convention of Texas, coed. ***Awards:*** certificates, associate, bachelor's, master's, and doctoral degrees. 49 undergraduate majors. ***Total enrollment:*** 4,487. Undergraduates: 2,883. Freshmen: 572. Federal methodology is used as a basis for awarding need-based institutional aid.

UNDERGRADUATE EXPENSES for 2020–2021 *Comprehensive fee:* $40,508 includes full-time tuition ($30,690), mandatory fees ($1250), and room and board ($8568). ***College room only:*** $4156. Full-time tuition and fees vary according to course load. Room and board charges vary according to board plan and housing facility. ***Part-time tuition:*** $1023 per credit hour. ***Part-time fees:*** $625 per term. Part-time tuition and fees vary according to course load.

FRESHMAN FINANCIAL AID (Fall 2019, est.) 562 applied for aid; of those 72% were deemed to have need. 100% of freshmen with need received aid; of those 41% had need fully met. ***Average percent of need met:*** 74% (excluding resources awarded to replace EFC). ***Average financial aid package:*** $21,845 (excluding resources awarded to replace EFC). 25% of all full-time freshmen had no need and received non-need-based gift aid.

UNDERGRADUATE FINANCIAL AID (Fall 2019, est.) 1,972 applied for aid; of those 75% were deemed to have need. 98% of undergraduates with need received aid; of those 38% had need fully met. ***Average percent of need met:*** 66% (excluding resources awarded to replace EFC). ***Average financial aid package:*** $19,713 (excluding resources awarded to replace EFC). 23% of all full-time undergraduates had no need and received non-need-based gift aid.

GIFT AID (NEED-BASED) *Receiving aid:* Freshmen: 45% (260); all full-time undergraduates: 38% (873). ***Average award:*** Freshmen: $4386; Undergraduates: $4517. ***Scholarships, grants, and awards:*** Federal Pell, FSEOG, state, private, college/university gift aid from institutional funds.

GIFT AID (NON-NEED-BASED) *Receiving aid:* Freshmen: 69% (394). Undergraduates: 59% (1,364). ***Average award:*** Freshmen: $13,671. Undergraduates: $11,289. ***Scholarships, grants, and awards by category:*** *Academic interests/achievement:* 1,205 awards ($6,813,505 total): biological sciences, business, communication, computer science, education, English, general academic interests/achievements, humanities, mathematics, physical sciences, premedicine, religion/biblical studies, social sciences. *Creative arts/performance:* 114 awards ($493,910 total): art/fine arts, music. *Special achievements/activities:* 1,690 awards ($7,564,931 total): community service, general special achievements/activities, leadership, memberships, religious involvement. *Special characteristics:* 273 awards ($986,261 total): children of faculty/staff, general special characteristics, relatives of clergy, religious affiliation, veterans. ***Tuition waivers:*** Full or partial for employees or children of employees. ***ROTC:*** Army cooperative, Air Force cooperative.

LOANS *Student loans:* 78% of past graduating class borrowed through all loan programs. *Average indebtedness per student:* $27,248. ***Average need-based loan:*** Freshmen: $3367. Undergraduates: $4186. ***Programs:*** Federal Direct (Subsidized and Unsubsidized Stafford, PLUS), state.

WORK-STUDY *Federal work-study:* 80 jobs averaging $2897. ***State or other work-study/employment:*** 21 part-time jobs averaging $3448.

APPLYING FOR FINANCIAL AID *Required financial aid forms:* FAFSA, institution's own form. ***Financial aid deadline:*** Continuous. ***Notification date:*** Continuous.

CONTACT Mrs. Shermain Reed, Director of Financial Aid, Dallas Baptist University, 3000 Mountain Creek Parkway, Dallas, TX 75211-9299, 214-333-5363 or toll-free 800-460-1328. *Fax:* 214-333-5586. *E-mail:* shermain@dbu.edu.
Website: http://www.dbu.edu/.

DALLAS CHRISTIAN COLLEGE

Dallas, TX

CONTACT Robin L. Walker, Director of Student Financial Aid, Dallas Christian College, 2700 Christian Parkway, Dallas, TX 75234-7299, 972-241-3371 Ext. 105 or toll-free 800-688-1029. *Fax:* 972-241-8021. *E-mail:* finaid@dallas.edu.
Website: http://www.dallas.edu/.

DALLAS INTERNATIONAL UNIVERSITY

Dallas, TX

CONTACT Financial Aid Office, Dallas International University, 7500 West Camp Wisdom Road, Dallas, TX 75236, 972-708-7340.
Website: http://www.diu.edu/.

DALTON STATE COLLEGE

Dalton, GA

CONTACT Holly Woods, Assistant Director of Financial Aid, Dalton State College, 650 College Drive, Dalton, GA 30720, 706-272-4545 or toll-free 800-829-4436. *Fax:* 706-272-2458. *E-mail:* finaid@daltonstate.edu.
Website: http://www.daltonstate.edu/.

DARTMOUTH COLLEGE

Hanover, NH

Tuition & fees: $57,204	Average undergraduate aid package: $54,535

ABOUT THE INSTITUTION Independent, coed. ***Awards:*** bachelor's, master's, and doctoral degrees. 55 undergraduate majors. ***Total enrollment:*** 6,608. Undergraduates: 4,459. Freshmen: 1,190. Both federal and institutional methodology are used as a basis for awarding need-based institutional aid.

UNDERGRADUATE EXPENSES for 2019–2020 *Application fee:* $80. ***One-time required fee:*** $418. ***Comprehensive fee:*** $73,578 includes full-time tuition ($55,605), mandatory fees ($1599), and room and board ($16,374). ***College room only:*** $9879. Room and board charges vary according to board plan. ***Payment plan:*** Tuition prepayment.

FRESHMAN FINANCIAL AID (Fall 2019, est.) 688 applied for aid; of those 85% were deemed to have need. 100% of freshmen with need received aid; of those 100% had need fully met. ***Average percent of need met:*** 100% (excluding resources awarded to replace EFC). ***Average financial aid package:*** $55,918 (excluding resources awarded to replace EFC).

UNDERGRADUATE FINANCIAL AID (Fall 2019, est.) 2,486 applied for aid; of those 90% were deemed to have need. 100% of undergraduates with need received aid; of those 100% had need fully met. ***Average percent of need met:*** 100% (excluding resources awarded to replace EFC). ***Average financial aid package:*** $54,535 (excluding resources awarded to replace EFC).

GIFT AID (NEED-BASED) *Total amount:* $114,101,005 (5% federal, 93% institutional, 2% external sources). ***Receiving aid:*** Freshmen: 45% (538); all full-time undergraduates: 48% (2,113). ***Average award:*** Freshmen: $57,562; Undergraduates: $53,952. ***Scholarships, grants, and awards:*** Federal Pell, FSEOG, state, private, college/university gift aid from institutional funds.

GIFT AID (NON-NEED-BASED) *Total amount:* $719,579 (8% federal, 92% external sources). ***ROTC:*** Army cooperative.

LOANS *Student loans:* $7,969,303 (42% need-based, 58% non-need-based). 40% of past graduating class borrowed through all loan programs. *Average indebtedness per student:* $25,071. ***Average need-based loan:*** Freshmen: $3257. Undergraduates: $3953. ***Parent loans:*** $4,327,012 (100% non-need-based). ***Programs:*** Federal Direct (Subsidized and Unsubsidized Stafford, PLUS), Perkins, state, college/university.

WORK-STUDY ***Federal work-study:*** Total amount: $2,710,423; 1,211 jobs averaging $2640. ***State or other work-study/employment:*** Total amount: $1,736,009 (100% need-based). 726 part-time jobs averaging $1827.

APPLYING FOR FINANCIAL AID ***Required financial aid forms:*** FAFSA, CSS Financial Aid PROFILE, noncustodial (divorced/separated) parent's statement, business/farm supplement, current W-2 or federal tax returns. ***Financial aid deadline:*** 2/1. ***Notification date:*** 4/2. Students must reply by 5/1.

CONTACT Mr. Gordon D. Koff, Director of Financial Aid, Dartmouth College, 6024 McNutt Hall, Hanover, NH 03755, 603-646-2451. *Fax:* 603-646-1414. *E-mail:* gordon.d.koff@dartmouth.edu.
Website: http://www.dartmouth.edu/.

DAVENPORT UNIVERSITY

Grand Rapids, MI

CONTACT David DeBoer, Executive Director of Financial Aid, Davenport University, 6191 Kraft Avenue SE, Grand Rapids, MI 49512, 616-732-1132 or toll-free 800-686-1600 (in-state), 866-686-1600 (out-of-state). *Fax:* 616-732-1167. *E-mail:* david.debore@davenport.edu.
Website: http://www.davenport.edu/.

DAVIDSON COLLEGE

Davidson, NC

Tuition & fees: $55,060	Average undergraduate aid package: $51,275

ABOUT THE INSTITUTION Independent Presbyterian, coed. ***Awards:*** bachelor's degrees. 27 undergraduate majors. ***Total enrollment:*** 1,837. Undergraduates: 1,837. Freshmen: 527. Both federal and institutional methodology are used as a basis for awarding need-based institutional aid.

UNDERGRADUATE EXPENSES for 2020–2021 ***Application fee:*** $50. ***Comprehensive fee:*** $70,285 includes full-time tuition ($54,520), mandatory fees ($540), and room and board ($15,225). ***College room only:*** $7700. Room and board charges vary according to board plan and housing facility.

FRESHMAN FINANCIAL AID (Fall 2019, est.) 365 applied for aid; of those 76% were deemed to have need. 100% of freshmen with need received aid; of those 100% had need fully met. ***Average percent of need met:*** 100% (excluding resources awarded to replace EFC). ***Average financial aid package:*** $51,899 (excluding resources awarded to replace EFC). 3% of all full-time freshmen had no need and received non-need-based gift aid.

UNDERGRADUATE FINANCIAL AID (Fall 2019, est.) 1,108 applied for aid; of those 83% were deemed to have need. 100% of undergraduates with need received aid; of those 100% had need fully met. ***Average percent of need met:*** 100% (excluding resources awarded to replace EFC). ***Average financial aid package:*** $51,275 (excluding resources awarded to replace EFC). 6% of all full-time undergraduates had no need and received non-need-based gift aid.

GIFT AID (NEED-BASED) ***Total amount:*** $44,290,261 (3% federal, 1% state, 94% institutional, 2% external sources). ***Receiving aid:*** Freshmen: 53% (278); all full-time undergraduates: 50% (918). ***Average award:*** Freshmen: $47,531; Undergraduates: $47,233. ***Scholarships, grants, and awards:*** Federal Pell, FSEOG, state, private, college/university gift aid from institutional funds.

GIFT AID (NON-NEED-BASED) ***Total amount:*** $5,601,220 (12% federal, 54% institutional, 34% external sources). ***Receiving aid:*** Freshmen: 23% (122). Undergraduates: 15% (271). ***Average award:*** Freshmen: $17,526. Undergraduates: $24,493. ***Scholarships, grants, and awards by category:*** *Academic interests/achievement:* biological sciences, business, education, foreign languages, general academic interests/achievements, international studies, mathematics, physical sciences, premedicine, social sciences. *Creative arts/performance:* applied art and design, creative writing, music, performing arts, theater/drama. *Special achievements/activities:* community service, general special achievements/activities, leadership, religious involvement. *Special characteristics:* general special characteristics, out-of-state students, relatives of clergy, religious affiliation. ***ROTC:*** Army.

LOANS ***Student loans:*** $2,886,115 (100% non-need-based). 30% of past graduating class borrowed through all loan programs. *Average indebtedness per student:* $23,535. ***Average need-based loan:*** Freshmen: $2641. Undergraduates: $3551. ***Parent loans:*** $2,443,567 (100% non-need-based). ***Programs:*** Federal Direct (Subsidized and Unsubsidized Stafford, PLUS).

WORK-STUDY ***Federal work-study:*** Total amount: $806,064; jobs available. ***State or other work-study/employment:*** Total amount: $351,550 (100% need-based). Part-time jobs available.

ATHLETIC AWARDS Total amount: $4,588,392 (11% need-based, 89% non-need-based).

APPLYING FOR FINANCIAL AID ***Required financial aid forms:*** FAFSA, CSS Financial Aid PROFILE, noncustodial (divorced/separated) parent's statement, business/farm supplement, Noncustodial (Divorced/Separated) Parent's Statement;corporate tax return and/or noncustodial parent. ***Financial aid deadline:*** 2/15 (priority: 2/15). ***Notification date:*** 4/1. Students must reply by 5/1.

CONTACT Mr. Chad A Spencer, Senior Associate Dean of Admission and Financial Aid, Davidson College, 413 North Main Street, PO Box 7157, Davidson, NC 28035-7157, 704-894-2232 or toll-free 800-768-0380. *Fax:* 704-894-2845. *E-mail:* chspencer@davidson.edu.
Website: http://www.davidson.edu/.

DAVIS & ELKINS COLLEGE

Elkins, WV

CONTACT Susan M. George, Director of Financial Planning, Davis & Elkins College, 100 Campus Drive, Elkins, WV 26241-3996, 304-637-1373 or toll-free 800-624-3157. *Fax:* 304-637-1986. *E-mail:* ssw@davisandelkins.edu.
Website: http://www.dewv.edu/.

DAVIS COLLEGE

Johnson City, NY

CONTACT Sandra Conklin, Financial Aid Director, Davis College, 400 Riverside Drive, Johnson City, NY 13790, 607-729-1581 Ext. 331 or toll-free 877-949-3248. *Fax:* 607-798-7754. *E-mail:* financialaid@davisny.edu.
Website: http://www.davisny.edu/.

DEAN COLLEGE

Franklin, MA

Tuition & fees: $41,318	Average undergraduate aid package: $31,567

ABOUT THE INSTITUTION Independent, coed. ***Awards:*** certificates, associate, and bachelor's degrees. 29 undergraduate majors. ***Total enrollment:*** 1,320. Undergraduates: 1,320. Freshmen: 442. Federal methodology is used as a basis for awarding need-based institutional aid.

UNDERGRADUATE EXPENSES for 2020–2021 ***One-time required fee:*** $300. ***Comprehensive fee:*** $58,966 includes full-time tuition ($41,118), mandatory fees ($200), and room and board ($17,648). Full-time tuition and fees vary according to class time and course load. Room and board charges vary according to housing facility. ***Part-time tuition:*** $365 per credit hour. ***Part-time fees:*** $25 per term. Part-time tuition and fees vary according to class time and course load.

FRESHMAN FINANCIAL AID (Fall 2019, est.) 384 applied for aid; of those 94% were deemed to have need. 100% of freshmen with need received aid; of those 16% had need fully met. ***Average percent of need met:*** 68% (excluding resources awarded to replace EFC). ***Average financial aid package:*** $31,980 (excluding resources awarded to replace EFC). 17% of all full-time freshmen had no need and received non-need-based gift aid.

UNDERGRADUATE FINANCIAL AID (Fall 2019, est.) 993 applied for aid; of those 93% were deemed to have need. 100% of undergraduates with need received aid; of those 15% had need fully met. ***Average percent of need met:*** 69% (excluding resources awarded to replace EFC). ***Average financial aid package:*** $31,567 (excluding resources awarded to replace EFC). 22% of all full-time undergraduates had no need and received non-need-based gift aid.

GIFT AID (NEED-BASED) ***Total amount:*** $24,155,914 (9% federal, 2% state, 88% institutional, 1% external sources). ***Receiving aid:*** Freshmen: 83% (361); all full-

time undergraduates: 78% (921). ***Average award:*** Freshmen: $28,938; Undergraduates: $27,872. ***Scholarships, grants, and awards:*** Federal Pell, FSEOG, state, private, college/university gift aid from institutional funds.

GIFT AID (NON-NEED-BASED) ***Receiving aid:*** Freshmen: 83% (361). Undergraduates: 77% (914). ***Average award:*** Freshmen: $20,072. Undergraduates: $19,314. ***Tuition waivers:*** Full or partial for employees or children of employees.

LOANS ***Student loans:*** $8,391,727 (100% need-based). 78% of past graduating class borrowed through all loan programs. ***Average need-based loan:*** Freshmen: $2654. Undergraduates: $3393. ***Parent loans:*** $4,454,438 (100% need-based). ***Programs:*** Federal Direct (Subsidized and Unsubsidized Stafford, PLUS), state.

WORK-STUDY ***Federal work-study:*** Total amount: $160,110; jobs available.

APPLYING FOR FINANCIAL AID ***Required financial aid form:*** FAFSA. ***Financial aid deadline (priority):*** 3/15. ***Notification date:*** Continuous beginning 3/15. Students must reply by 5/1 or within 2 weeks of notification.

CONTACT Mr. Frank Dunning Mullen, Dean of Student Financial Planning and Services, Dean College, 99 Main Street, Franklin, MA 02038, 508-541-1518 or toll-free 877-TRY-DEAN. *Fax:* 508-541-1941. *E-mail:* fmullen@dean.edu.
Website: http://www.dean.edu/.

DEFIANCE COLLEGE

Defiance, OH

ABOUT THE INSTITUTION Independent United Church of Christ, coed. ***Awards:*** associate, bachelor's, and master's degrees. 33 undergraduate majors.

GIFT AID (NEED-BASED) ***Scholarships, grants, and awards:*** Federal Pell, FSEOG, state, private, college/university gift aid from institutional funds.

GIFT AID (NON-NEED-BASED) ***Scholarships, grants, and awards by category:*** *Academic interests/achievement:* biological sciences, business, communication, education, English, general academic interests/achievements, humanities, international studies, mathematics, physical sciences, premedicine, religion/biblical studies, social sciences. *Creative arts/performance:* art/fine arts, music. *Special achievements/activities:* community service, general special achievements/activities, leadership, religious involvement. *Special characteristics:* children and siblings of alumni, children of faculty/staff, international students, religious affiliation, veterans.

LOANS ***Programs:*** Federal Direct (Subsidized and Unsubsidized Stafford, PLUS), alternative loans.

WORK-STUDY ***Federal work-study:*** Total amount: $525,109; jobs available. ***State or other work-study/employment:*** Part-time jobs available.

APPLYING FOR FINANCIAL AID ***Required financial aid form:*** FAFSA.

CONTACT Amy Francis, Director of Financial Aid, Defiance College, 701 North Clinton Street, Defiance, OH 43512-1610, 419-783-2376 or toll-free 800-520-4632. *Fax:* 419-783-2579. *E-mail:* afrancis@defiance.edu.
Website: http://www.defiance.edu/.

DELAWARE STATE UNIVERSITY

Dover, DE

CONTACT Office of Student Financial Aid Services, Delaware State University, 1200 North DuPont Highway, Dover, DE 19901-2277, 302-857-6250 or toll-free 800-845-2544. *E-mail:* faid@desu.edu.
Website: http://www.desu.edu/.

DELAWARE TECHNICAL COMMUNITY COLLEGE

Dover, DE

CONTACT Financial Aid Office, Delaware Technical Community College, 100 Campus Drive, Dover, DE 19904.
Website: https://www.dtcc.edu/.

DELAWARE VALLEY UNIVERSITY

Doylestown, PA

Tuition & fees: $40,620	Average undergraduate aid package: $31,252

ABOUT THE INSTITUTION Independent, coed. ***Awards:*** certificates, bachelor's, master's, and doctoral degrees. 30 undergraduate majors. ***Total enrollment:*** 2,369. Undergraduates: 1,924. Freshmen: 377. Federal methodology is used as a basis for awarding need-based institutional aid.

UNDERGRADUATE EXPENSES for 2020–2021 ***Application fee:*** $50. ***Comprehensive fee:*** $55,240 includes full-time tuition ($38,070), mandatory fees ($2550), and room and board ($14,620). ***College room only:*** $6950. Full-time tuition and fees vary according to location and program. Room and board charges vary according to board plan and housing facility. ***Part-time tuition:*** $1049 per credit hour. Part-time tuition and fees vary according to course load, location, and program.

FRESHMAN FINANCIAL AID (Fall 2019, est.) 367 applied for aid; of those 91% were deemed to have need. 100% of freshmen with need received aid; of those 18% had need fully met. ***Average percent of need met:*** 73% (excluding resources awarded to replace EFC). ***Average financial aid package:*** $32,720 (excluding resources awarded to replace EFC). 11% of all full-time freshmen had no need and received non-need-based gift aid.

UNDERGRADUATE FINANCIAL AID (Fall 2019, est.) 1,465 applied for aid; of those 91% were deemed to have need. 100% of undergraduates with need received aid; of those 16% had need fully met. ***Average percent of need met:*** 71% (excluding resources awarded to replace EFC). ***Average financial aid package:*** $31,252 (excluding resources awarded to replace EFC). 18% of all full-time undergraduates had no need and received non-need-based gift aid.

GIFT AID (NEED-BASED) ***Total amount:*** $34,422,716 (10% federal, 4% state, 85% institutional, 1% external sources). ***Receiving aid:*** Freshmen: 88% (330); all full-time undergraduates: 81% (1,330). ***Average award:*** Freshmen: $32,075; Undergraduates: $27,031. ***Scholarships, grants, and awards:*** Federal Pell, FSEOG, state, private, college/university gift aid from institutional funds.

GIFT AID (NON-NEED-BASED) ***Total amount:*** $6,967,031 (99% institutional, 1% external sources). ***Receiving aid:*** Freshmen: 87% (328). Undergraduates: 80% (1,317). ***Average award:*** Freshmen: $21,247. Undergraduates: $19,443. ***Scholarships, grants, and awards by category:*** *Creative arts/performance:* music. *Special achievements/activities:* general special achievements/activities. *Special characteristics:* ethnic background, members of minority groups, siblings of current students, veterans. ***Tuition waivers:*** Full or partial for employees or children of employees.

LOANS ***Student loans:*** $17,039,496 (68% need-based, 32% non-need-based). 79% of past graduating class borrowed through all loan programs. *Average indebtedness per student:* $48,278. ***Average need-based loan:*** Freshmen: $3331. Undergraduates: $4272. ***Parent loans:*** $8,155,335 (59% need-based, 41% non-need-based). ***Programs:*** Federal Direct (Subsidized and Unsubsidized Stafford, PLUS), state.

WORK-STUDY ***Federal work-study:*** Total amount: $393,201; jobs available.

APPLYING FOR FINANCIAL AID ***Required financial aid forms:*** FAFSA, state aid form. ***Financial aid deadline (priority):*** 4/1. ***Notification date:*** Continuous beginning 12/7. Students must reply by 5/1 or within 2 weeks of notification.

CONTACT Ms. Joan Hock, Director of Financial Aid, Delaware Valley University, 700 East Butler Avenue, Doylestown, PA 18901, 215-4892975 or toll-free 800-2DELVAL. *E-mail:* Joan.Hock@delval.edu.
Website: http://www.delval.edu/.

DELTA STATE UNIVERSITY

Cleveland, MS

Tuition & fees (area res): $7671	Average undergraduate aid package: $10,887

ABOUT THE INSTITUTION State-supported, coed. ***Awards:*** certificates, bachelor's, master's, and doctoral degrees. 35 undergraduate majors. Federal methodology is used as a basis for awarding need-based institutional aid.

UNDERGRADUATE EXPENSES for 2019–2020 ***Tuition, area resident:*** full-time $7501; part-time $313 per credit hour. ***Tuition, state resident:*** full-time $7501; part-time $313 per credit hour. ***Tuition, nonresident:*** full-time $7501; part-time $313 per credit hour. ***Required fees:*** full-time $170; $7.08 per credit hour. Full-time tuition and fees vary according to course load. Part-time tuition and fees vary according to course load. ***College room and board:*** $7908; ***Room only:*** $4530. Room and board charges vary according to board plan and housing facility.

FRESHMAN FINANCIAL AID (Fall 2018) 259 applied for aid; of those 65% were deemed to have need. 100% of freshmen with need received aid. ***Average financial aid package:*** $10,250 (excluding resources awarded to replace EFC). 18% of all full-time freshmen had no need and received non-need-based gift aid.

UNDERGRADUATE FINANCIAL AID (Fall 2018) 1,629 applied for aid; of those 71% were deemed to have need. 100% of undergraduates with need received aid. ***Average financial aid package:*** $10,887 (excluding resources awarded to replace EFC). 17% of all full-time undergraduates had no need and received non-need-based gift aid.

GIFT AID (NEED-BASED) ***Total amount:*** $5,945,879 (86% federal, 9% state, 5% institutional). ***Receiving aid:*** Freshmen: 49% (139); all full-time undergraduates: 49% (971). ***Average award:*** Freshmen: $5844; Undergraduates: $5622. ***Scholarships, grants, and awards:*** Federal Pell, FSEOG, state, private, college/university gift aid from institutional funds, Federal Nursing.

GIFT AID (NON-NEED-BASED) ***Total amount:*** $5,042,332 (5% federal, 9% state, 79% institutional, 7% external sources). ***Receiving aid:*** Freshmen: 40% (114). Undergraduates: 37% (724). ***Average award:*** Freshmen: $5948. Undergraduates: $4801. ***Scholarships, grants, and awards by category:*** *Academic interests/achievement:* 444 awards ($242,571 total): biological sciences, business, education, English, general academic interests/achievements, home economics, mathematics, physical sciences, premedicine, social sciences. *Creative arts/performance:* 81 awards ($162,854 total): art/fine arts, creative writing, journalism/publications, music. *Special achievements/activities:* 752 awards ($3,309,731 total): cheerleading/drum major, general special achievements/activities, leadership, memberships. ***Tuition waivers:*** Full or partial for employees or children of employees, senior citizens.

LOANS ***Student loans:*** $9,527,206 (100% need-based). ***Average need-based loan:*** Freshmen: $3001. Undergraduates: $4155. ***Parent loans:*** $1,983,769 (100% need-based). ***Programs:*** Federal Direct (Subsidized and Unsubsidized Stafford, PLUS).

WORK-STUDY ***Federal work-study:*** Total amount: $477,231; 244 jobs averaging $1956.

ATHLETIC AWARDS Total amount: $1,365,290 (100% non-need-based).

APPLYING FOR FINANCIAL AID ***Required financial aid forms:*** FAFSA, institution's own form, state aid form. ***Financial aid deadline (priority):*** 3/1. ***Notification date:*** Continuous beginning 5/1.

CONTACT Mrs. Megan Smith, Director of Student Financial Assistance, Delta State University, Kent Wyatt Hall 144, Highway 8 West, Cleveland, MS 38733-0001, 662-846-4670 or toll-free 800-468-6378. *Fax:* 662-846-4683. *E-mail:* finaid@deltastate.edu. *Website:* http://www.deltastate.edu/.

DENISON UNIVERSITY

Granville, OH

Tuition & fees: N/R	Average undergraduate aid package: $44,087

ABOUT THE INSTITUTION Independent, coed. ***Awards:*** bachelor's degrees. 39 undergraduate majors. ***Total enrollment:*** 2,341. Undergraduates: 2,341. Freshmen: 617. Both federal and institutional methodology are used as a basis for awarding need-based institutional aid.

FRESHMAN FINANCIAL AID (Fall 2019, est.) 467 applied for aid; of those 73% were deemed to have need. 100% of freshmen with need received aid; of those 100% had need fully met. ***Average percent of need met:*** 100% (excluding resources awarded to replace EFC). ***Average financial aid package:*** $40,207 (excluding resources awarded to replace EFC). 44% of all full-time freshmen had no need and received non-need-based gift aid.

UNDERGRADUATE FINANCIAL AID (Fall 2019, est.) 1,646 applied for aid; of those 82% were deemed to have need. 100% of undergraduates with need received aid; of those 100% had need fully met. ***Average percent of need met:*** 99% (excluding resources awarded to replace EFC). ***Average financial aid package:*** $44,087 (excluding resources awarded to replace EFC). 37% of all full-time undergraduates had no need and received non-need-based gift aid.

GIFT AID (NEED-BASED) ***Receiving aid:*** Freshmen: 55% (341); all full-time undergraduates: 60% (1,353). ***Average award:*** Freshmen: $32,405; Undergraduates: $35,428. ***Scholarships, grants, and awards:*** Federal Pell, FSEOG, state, private, college/university gift aid from institutional funds.

GIFT AID (NON-NEED-BASED) ***Receiving aid:*** Freshmen: 10% (65). Undergraduates: 8% (184). ***Average award:*** Freshmen: $22,528. Undergraduates: $21,786. ***Scholarships, grants, and awards by category:*** *Academic interests/achievement:* general academic interests/achievements. *Creative arts/performance:* creative writing, general creative arts/performance, music. ***ROTC:*** Army cooperative.

LOANS ***Student loans:*** 48% of past graduating class borrowed through all loan programs. *Average indebtedness per student:* $33,548. ***Average need-based loan:*** Freshmen: $3285. Undergraduates: $4442. ***Programs:*** Federal Direct (Subsidized and Unsubsidized Stafford, PLUS), college/university.

WORK-STUDY Federal work-study jobs available. ***State or other work-study/employment:*** Part-time jobs available.

APPLYING FOR FINANCIAL AID ***Required financial aid forms:*** FAFSA, CSS Financial Aid PROFILE, noncustodial (divorced/separated) parent's statement. ***Notification date:*** Continuous.

CONTACT Ms. Laura Meek, Director of Financial Aid, Denison University, 100 West College Street, Granville, OH 43023, 740-587-6276 or toll-free 800-DENISON. *E-mail:* finaid@denison.edu. *Website:* http://www.denison.edu/.

DENVER COLLEGE OF NURSING

Denver, CO

CONTACT Financial Aid Office, Denver College of Nursing, 1401 19th Street, Denver, CO 80202, 303-292-0015 or toll-free 888-479-5550. *Website:* http://www.denvercollegeofnursing.edu/.

DEPAUL UNIVERSITY

Chicago, IL

Tuition & fees: $41,202	Average undergraduate aid package: $25,548

ABOUT THE INSTITUTION Independent Roman Catholic, coed. ***Awards:*** certificates, bachelor's, master's, and doctoral degrees. 102 undergraduate majors. ***Total enrollment:*** 22,064. Undergraduates: 14,214. Freshmen: 2,627. Federal methodology is used as a basis for awarding need-based institutional aid.

UNDERGRADUATE EXPENSES for 2019–2020 ***Comprehensive fee:*** $55,938 includes full-time tuition ($40,551), mandatory fees ($651), and room and board ($14,736). ***College room only:*** $10,428. Full-time tuition and fees vary according to course load, program, and student level. Room and board charges vary according to board plan, housing facility, and location. ***Part-time tuition:*** $655 per credit hour. Part-time tuition and fees vary according to course load, program, and student level.

FRESHMAN FINANCIAL AID (Fall 2018) 2305 applied for aid; of those 84% were deemed to have need. 100% of freshmen with need received aid; of those 12% had need fully met. ***Average percent of need met:*** 70% (excluding resources awarded to replace EFC). ***Average financial aid package:*** $28,110 (excluding resources awarded to replace EFC). 21% of all full-time freshmen had no need and received non-need-based gift aid.

UNDERGRADUATE FINANCIAL AID (Fall 2018) 10,371 applied for aid; of those 88% were deemed to have need. 99% of undergraduates with need received aid; of those 9% had need fully met. ***Average percent of need met:*** 65% (excluding resources awarded to replace EFC). ***Average financial aid package:*** $25,548 (excluding resources awarded to replace EFC). 19% of all full-time undergraduates had no need and received non-need-based gift aid.

GIFT AID (NEED-BASED) ***Total amount:*** $200,326,000 (13% federal, 9% state, 77% institutional, 1% external sources). ***Receiving aid:*** Freshmen: 74% (1,910); all full-time undergraduates: 68% (8,745). ***Average award:*** Freshmen: $24,581; Undergraduates: $21,739. ***Scholarships, grants, and awards:*** Federal Pell, FSEOG, state, private, college/university gift aid from institutional funds, TEACH grants, Veteran Awards.

GIFT AID (NON-NEED-BASED) ***Total amount:*** $42,337,000 (7% federal, 92% institutional, 1% external sources). ***Receiving aid:*** Freshmen: 8% (210). Undergraduates: 5% (645). ***Average award:*** Freshmen: $17,820. Undergraduates: $14,886.

Scholarships, grants, and awards by category: *Academic interests/achievement:* general academic interests/achievements. *Creative arts/performance:* art/fine arts, music, theater/drama. *Special achievements/activities:* community service, leadership. *Special characteristics:* children of faculty/staff, local/state students, veterans. ***Tuition waivers:*** Full or partial for employees or children of employees. ***ROTC:*** Army.

LOANS ***Student loans:*** $76,698,000 (82% need-based, 18% non-need-based). 64% of past graduating class borrowed through all loan programs. *Average indebtedness per student:* $29,621. ***Average need-based loan:*** Freshmen: $3208. Undergraduates: $4116. ***Parent loans:*** $58,986,000 (57% need-based, 43% non-need-based). ***Programs:*** Federal Direct (Subsidized and Unsubsidized Stafford, PLUS), Perkins, Private Loans.

WORK-STUDY ***Federal work-study:*** Total amount: $2,364,000; 679 jobs averaging $4308. ***State or other work-study/employment:*** Part-time jobs available.

ATHLETIC AWARDS Total amount: $6,277,000 (35% need-based, 65% non-need-based).

APPLYING FOR FINANCIAL AID ***Required financial aid form:*** FAFSA. ***Financial aid deadline (priority):*** 12/1. ***Notification date:*** Continuous beginning 12/15. Students must reply by 5/1 or within 4 weeks of notification.

CONTACT DePaul Central, Office of Financial Aid, DePaul University, 1 East Jackson Boulevard, Chicago, IL 60604-2287, 312-362-8610 or toll-free 800-4DE-PAUL (out-of-state). *Fax:* 312-362-5748.
Website: http://www.depaul.edu/.

DEPAUW UNIVERSITY

Greencastle, IN

Tuition & fees: $52,710	Average undergraduate aid package: $44,766

ABOUT THE INSTITUTION Independent United Methodist Church, coed. ***Awards:*** bachelor's degrees. 44 undergraduate majors. ***Total enrollment:*** 1,972. Undergraduates: 1,972. Freshmen: 423. Federal methodology is used as a basis for awarding need-based institutional aid.

UNDERGRADUATE EXPENSES for 2020–2021 ***Comprehensive fee:*** $66,498 includes full-time tuition ($52,710) and room and board ($13,788). Room and board charges vary according to board plan. ***Part-time tuition:*** $1617 per credit hour.

FRESHMAN FINANCIAL AID (Fall 2019, est.) 355 applied for aid; of those 83% were deemed to have need. 100% of freshmen with need received aid; of those 34% had need fully met. ***Average percent of need met:*** 88% (excluding resources awarded to replace EFC). ***Average financial aid package:*** $43,603 (excluding resources awarded to replace EFC). 30% of all full-time freshmen had no need and received non-need-based gift aid.

UNDERGRADUATE FINANCIAL AID (Fall 2019, est.) 1,325 applied for aid; of those 87% were deemed to have need. 100% of undergraduates with need received aid; of those 28% had need fully met. ***Average percent of need met:*** 89% (excluding resources awarded to replace EFC). ***Average financial aid package:*** $44,766 (excluding resources awarded to replace EFC). 38% of all full-time undergraduates had no need and received non-need-based gift aid.

GIFT AID (NEED-BASED) ***Total amount:*** $46,334,465 (4% federal, 2% state, 85% institutional, 9% external sources). ***Receiving aid:*** Freshmen: 70% (296); all full-time undergraduates: 59% (1,152). ***Average award:*** Freshmen: $40,708; Undergraduates: $40,242. ***Scholarships, grants, and awards:*** Federal Pell, FSEOG, state, private, college/university gift aid from institutional funds.

GIFT AID (NON-NEED-BASED) ***Total amount:*** $23,166,047 (87% institutional, 13% external sources). ***Receiving aid:*** Freshmen: 15% (64). Undergraduates: 11% (206). ***Average award:*** Freshmen: $27,293. Undergraduates: $25,101. ***Scholarships, grants, and awards by category:*** *Academic interests/achievement:* general academic interests/achievements. *Special achievements/activities:* community service. *Special characteristics:* children and siblings of alumni, children of faculty/staff. ***Tuition waivers:*** Full or partial for employees or children of employees. ***ROTC:*** Army cooperative, Air Force cooperative.

LOANS ***Student loans:*** $10,080,450 (60% need-based, 40% non-need-based). 72% of past graduating class borrowed through all loan programs. *Average indebtedness per student:* $25,904. ***Average need-based loan:*** Freshmen: $2888. Undergraduates: $4439. ***Parent loans:*** $4,525,080 (25% need-based, 75% non-need-based). ***Programs:*** Federal Direct (Subsidized and Unsubsidized Stafford, PLUS), college/university.

WORK-STUDY ***Federal work-study:*** Total amount: $873,580; jobs available. ***State or other work-study/employment:*** Total amount: $1,236,068 (31% need-based, 69% non-need-based). Part-time jobs available.

APPLYING FOR FINANCIAL AID ***Required financial aid form:*** FAFSA. ***Financial aid deadline:*** 2/1 (priority: 12/15). ***Notification date:*** Students must reply by 5/1.

CONTACT Office of Financial Aid, DePauw University, 200 East Seminary, Greencastle, IN 46135-0037, 765-658-4030 or toll-free 800-447-2495. *Fax:* 765-658-4137. *E-mail:* financialaid@depauw.edu.
Website: http://www.depauw.edu/.

DESALES UNIVERSITY

Center Valley, PA

Tuition & fees: $38,700	Average undergraduate aid package: $26,908

ABOUT THE INSTITUTION Independent Roman Catholic, coed. ***Awards:*** certificates, bachelor's, master's, and doctoral degrees. 48 undergraduate majors. ***Total enrollment:*** 3,460. Undergraduates: 2,492. Freshmen: 500. Federal methodology is used as a basis for awarding need-based institutional aid.

UNDERGRADUATE EXPENSES for 2019–2020 ***One-time required fee:*** $200. ***Comprehensive fee:*** $51,700 includes full-time tuition ($37,200), mandatory fees ($1500), and room and board ($13,000). Full-time tuition and fees vary according to class time and course load. Room and board charges vary according to board plan and housing facility. ***Part-time tuition:*** $1550 per credit hour. Part-time tuition and fees vary according to class time and course load.

FRESHMAN FINANCIAL AID (Fall 2019, est.) 456 applied for aid; of those 84% were deemed to have need. 100% of freshmen with need received aid; of those 28% had need fully met. ***Average percent of need met:*** 73% (excluding resources awarded to replace EFC). ***Average financial aid package:*** $29,648 (excluding resources awarded to replace EFC). 19% of all full-time freshmen had no need and received non-need-based gift aid.

UNDERGRADUATE FINANCIAL AID (Fall 2019, est.) 1,721 applied for aid; of those 88% were deemed to have need. 99% of undergraduates with need received aid; of those 25% had need fully met. ***Average percent of need met:*** 69% (excluding resources awarded to replace EFC). ***Average financial aid package:*** $26,908 (excluding resources awarded to replace EFC). 18% of all full-time undergraduates had no need and received non-need-based gift aid.

GIFT AID (NEED-BASED) ***Total amount:*** $29,958,000 (12% federal, 6% state, 81% institutional, 1% external sources). ***Receiving aid:*** Freshmen: 81% (383); all full-time undergraduates: 74% (1,444). ***Average award:*** Freshmen: $23,694; Undergraduates: $21,264. ***Scholarships, grants, and awards:*** Federal Pell, FSEOG, state, private, college/university gift aid from institutional funds.

GIFT AID (NON-NEED-BASED) ***Total amount:*** $10,030,076 (4% federal, 95% institutional, 1% external sources). ***Receiving aid:*** Freshmen: 77% (367). Undergraduates: 64% (1,263). ***Average award:*** Freshmen: $20,925. Undergraduates: $18,583. ***Scholarships, grants, and awards by category:*** *Academic interests/achievement:* 1,818 awards ($17,348,780 total): biological sciences, business, communication, computer science, education, English, foreign languages, general academic interests/achievements, health fields, home economics, humanities, mathematics, physical sciences, premedicine, religion/biblical studies, social sciences. *Creative arts/performance:* 189 awards ($486,873 total): cinema/film/broadcasting, dance, performing arts, theater/drama. *Special achievements/activities:* 547 awards ($2,017,784 total): leadership. *Special characteristics:* 58 awards ($217,423 total): ethnic background, international students, siblings of current students, veterans' children. ***Tuition waivers:*** Full or partial for employees or children of employees, adult students, senior citizens. ***ROTC:*** Army cooperative.

LOANS ***Student loans:*** $20,411,798 (60% need-based, 40% non-need-based). 76% of past graduating class borrowed through all loan programs. *Average indebtedness per student:* $40,776. ***Average need-based loan:*** Freshmen: $3376. Undergraduates: $4472. ***Parent loans:*** $5,122,542 (32% need-based, 68% non-need-based). ***Programs:*** Federal Direct (Subsidized and Unsubsidized Stafford, PLUS), Perkins, Federal Nursing, state.

WORK-STUDY ***Federal work-study:*** Total amount: $639,550; 366 jobs averaging $1966. ***State or other work-study/employment:*** Total amount: $584,703 (9% need-based, 91% non-need-based). 335 part-time jobs averaging $1990.

APPLYING FOR FINANCIAL AID ***Required financial aid forms:*** FAFSA, institution's own form, state aid form, PHEAA form (PA residents only). ***Financial aid deadline (priority):*** 12/1. ***Notification date:*** Continuous beginning 12/1. Students must reply by 5/1 or within 2 weeks of notification.

CONTACT Mrs. Joyce Farmer, Director of Financial Aid, DeSales University, 2755 Station Avenue, Center Valley, PA 18034-9568, 610-282-1100 Ext. 1208. *Fax:* 610-282-0131. *E-mail:* joyce.farmer@desales.edu.
Website: http://www.desales.edu/.

DESIGN INSTITUTE OF SAN DIEGO

San Diego, CA

CONTACT Financial Aid Office, Design Institute of San Diego, 8555 Commerce Avenue, San Diego, CA 92121, 858-566-1200 or toll-free 800-619-4337.
Website: http://www.disd.edu/.

DEVRY COLLEGE OF NEW YORK–MIDTOWN MANHATTAN CAMPUS

New York, NY

CONTACT Elvira Senese, Dean of Student Finance, DeVry College of New York–Midtown Manhattan Campus, 30-20 Thomson Avenue, Long Island City, NY 11101, 718-472-2728 or toll-free 866-338-7934. *Fax:* 718-269-4284.
Website: http://www.devry.edu/.

DEVRY UNIVERSITY–ADDISON CAMPUS

Addison, IL

CONTACT Sejal Amin, Director of Student Finance, DeVry University–Addison Campus, 1221 North Swift Road, Addison, IL 60101-6106, 630-953-1300 or toll-free 866-338-7934.
Website: http://www.devry.edu/.

DEVRY UNIVERSITY–ALPHARETTA CAMPUS

Alpharetta, GA

CONTACT David Pickett, Assistant Director of Financial Aid, DeVry University–Alpharetta Campus, 2555 Northwinds Parkway, Alpharetta, GA 30004, 770-521-4900 or toll-free 866-338-7934. *Fax:* 770-664-8024.
Website: http://www.devry.edu/.

DEVRY UNIVERSITY–ARLINGTON CAMPUS

Arlington, VA

CONTACT Roberta McDevitt, Director of Student Finance, DeVry University–Arlington Campus, 2341 Jefferson Davis Highway, Arlington, VA 22202, 866-338-7932 or toll-free 866-338-7934. *Fax:* 703-414-4040.
Website: http://www.devry.edu/.

DEVRY UNIVERSITY–CHARLOTTE CAMPUS

Charlotte, NC

CONTACT Financial Aid Office, DeVry University–Charlotte Campus, 2015 Ayrsley Town Boulevard, Suite 109, Charlotte, NC 28273, 704-697-1020 or toll-free 866-338-7934.
Website: http://www.devry.edu/.

DEVRY UNIVERSITY–CHESAPEAKE CAMPUS

Chesapeake, VA

CONTACT Financial Aid Office, DeVry University–Chesapeake Campus, 1317 Executive Boulevard, Suite 100, Chesapeake, VA 23320, 757-382-5680 or toll-free 866-338-7934.
Website: http://www.devry.edu/.

DEVRY UNIVERSITY–CHICAGO CAMPUS

Chicago, IL

CONTACT Milena Dobrina, Director of Financial Aid, DeVry University–Chicago Campus, 3300 North Campbell Avenue, Chicago, IL 60618-5994, 773-929-8500 or toll-free 866-338-7934. *Fax:* 773-348-1780.
Website: http://www.devry.edu/.

DEVRY UNIVERSITY–CHICAGO LOOP CAMPUS

Chicago, IL

CONTACT Financial Aid Office, DeVry University–Chicago Loop Campus, 225 West Washington Street, Suite 100, Chicago, IL 60606, 312-372-4900 or toll-free 866-338-7934.
Website: http://www.devry.edu/.

DEVRY UNIVERSITY–CINCINNATI CAMPUS

Cincinnati, OH

CONTACT Financial Aid Office, DeVry University–Cincinnati Campus, 8800 Governors Hill Drive, Suite 100, Cincinnati, OH 45249, 513-583-5000 or toll-free 866-338-7934.
Website: http://www.devry.edu/.

DEVRY UNIVERSITY–COLUMBUS CAMPUS

Columbus, OH

CONTACT Student Finance Office, DeVry University–Columbus Campus, 1350 Alum Creek Drive, Columbus, OH 43209-2705, 614-253-7291 or toll-free 866-338-7934. *Fax:* 614-252-4108.
Website: http://www.devry.edu/.

DEVRY UNIVERSITY–DECATUR CAMPUS

Decatur, GA

CONTACT Student Finance Office, DeVry University–Decatur Campus, 1 West Court Square, Suite 100, Decatur, GA 30030-2556, 404-270-2702 or toll-free 866-338-7934.
Website: http://www.devry.edu/.

DEVRY UNIVERSITY–FOLSOM CAMPUS

Folsom, CA

CONTACT Financial Aid Office, DeVry University–Folsom Campus, 950 Iron Point Road, Folsom, CA 95630, 916-351-3700 or toll-free 866-338-7934.
Website: http://www.devry.edu/.

DEVRY UNIVERSITY–FREMONT CAMPUS

Fremont, CA

CONTACT Kim Kane, Director of Student Finance, DeVry University–Fremont Campus, 6600 Dumbarton Circle, Fremont, CA 94555, 510-574-1100 or toll-free 866-338-7934. *Fax:* 510-742-0868.
Website: http://www.devry.edu/.

DEVRY UNIVERSITY–FRESNO CAMPUS

Fresno, CA

CONTACT Financial Aid Office, DeVry University–Fresno Campus, 7575 North Fresno Street, Fresno, CA 93720, 559-439-8595 or toll-free 866-338-7934.
Website: http://www.devry.edu/.

DEVRY UNIVERSITY–FT. WASHINGTON CAMPUS

Fort Washington, PA

CONTACT Financial Aid Office, DeVry University–Ft. Washington Campus, 1140 Virginia Drive, Fort Washington, PA 19034, 215-591-5700 or toll-free 866-338-7934.
Website: http://www.devry.edu/.

DEVRY UNIVERSITY–HENDERSON CAMPUS

Henderson, NV

CONTACT Financial Aid Office, DeVry University–Henderson Campus, 2490 Paseo Verde Parkway, Suite 150, Henderson, NV 89074, 702-933-9700 or toll-free 866-338-7934.
Website: http://www.devry.edu/.

DEVRY UNIVERSITY–IRVING CAMPUS

Irving, TX

CONTACT Student Finance Office, DeVry University–Irving Campus, 4800 Regent Boulevard, Irving, TX 75063-2440, 972-929-9310 or toll-free 866-338-7934.
Website: http://www.devry.edu/.

DEVRY UNIVERSITY–JACKSONVILLE CAMPUS

Jacksonville, FL

CONTACT Financial Aid Office, DeVry University–Jacksonville Campus, 5200 Belfort Road, Suite 175, Jacksonville, FL 32256, 904-367-4942 or toll-free 866-338-7934.
Website: http://www.devry.edu/.

DEVRY UNIVERSITY–KANSAS CITY CAMPUS

Kansas City, MO

CONTACT Maureen Kelly, Senior Associate Director of Financial Aid, DeVry University–Kansas City Campus, 11224 Holmes Street, Kansas City, MO 64131-3698, 816-941-0430 or toll-free 866-338-7934.
Website: http://www.devry.edu/.

DEVRY UNIVERSITY–LONG BEACH CAMPUS

Long Beach, CA

CONTACT Kathy Odom, Director of Financial Aid, DeVry University–Long Beach Campus, 3880 Kilroy Airport Way, Long Beach, CA 90806, 562-427-0861 or toll-free 866-338-7934. *Fax:* 562-989-1578.
Website: http://www.devry.edu/.

DEVRY UNIVERSITY–MIRAMAR CAMPUS

Miramar, FL

CONTACT Office of Financial Aid, DeVry University–Miramar Campus, 2300 Southwest 145th Avenue, Miramar, FL 33027, 954-499-9700 or toll-free 866-338-7934.
Website: http://www.devry.edu/.

DEVRY UNIVERSITY–MORRISVILLE CAMPUS

Morrisville, NC

CONTACT Financial Aid Office, DeVry University–Morrisville Campus, 1600 Perimeter Park Drive, Suite 100, Morrisville, NC 27560, 919-463-1380 or toll-free 866-338-7934.
Website: http://www.devry.edu/.

DEVRY UNIVERSITY–NASHVILLE CAMPUS

Nashville, TN

CONTACT Financial Aid Office, DeVry University–Nashville Campus, 3343 Perimeter Hill Drive, Suite 200, Nashville, TN 37211, 615-445-3456 or toll-free 866-338-7934.
Website: http://www.devry.edu/.

DEVRY UNIVERSITY–NORTH BRUNSWICK CAMPUS

North Brunswick, NJ

CONTACT Student Finance Office, DeVry University–North Brunswick Campus, 630 U.S. Highway 1, North Brunswick, NJ 08902, 732-729-3777 or toll-free 866-338-7934.
Website: http://www.devry.edu/.

DEVRY UNIVERSITY ONLINE

Addison, IL

CONTACT Financial Aid Office, DeVry University Online, 1221 North Swift Road, Addison, IL 60101, toll-free 866-338-7934.
Website: http://www.devry.edu/.

DEVRY UNIVERSITY–ORLANDO CAMPUS

Orlando, FL

CONTACT Estrella Velazquez-Domenech, Director of Student Finance, DeVry University–Orlando Campus, 4000 Millenia Boulevard, Orlando, FL 32839, 407-345-2816 or toll-free 866-338-7934. *Fax:* 407-355-4855.
Website: http://www.devry.edu/.

DEVRY UNIVERSITY–PHOENIX CAMPUS

Phoenix, AZ

CONTACT Student Finance Office, DeVry University–Phoenix Campus, 2149 West Dunlap Avenue, Phoenix, AZ 85021-2995, 602-749-4545 or toll-free 866-338-7934.
Website: http://www.devry.edu/.

DEVRY UNIVERSITY–POMONA CAMPUS

Pomona, CA

CONTACT Student Finance Office, DeVry University–Pomona Campus, 901 Corporate Center Drive, Pomona, CA 91768-2642, 909-622-8866 or toll-free 866-338-7934.
Website: http://www.devry.edu/.

DEVRY UNIVERSITY–SAN ANTONIO CAMPUS

San Antonio, TX

CONTACT Financial Aid Office, DeVry University–San Antonio Campus, 618 NW Loop 410, Suite 202, San Antonio, TX 78216, 210-524-5400 or toll-free 866-338-7934.
Website: http://www.devry.edu/.

DEVRY UNIVERSITY–SAN DIEGO CAMPUS

San Diego, CA

CONTACT Financial Aid Office, DeVry University–San Diego Campus, 2655 Camino Del Rio North, Suite 360, San Diego, CA 92108, 619-683-2446 or toll-free 866-338-7934.
Website: http://www.devry.edu/.

DEVRY UNIVERSITY–SEVEN HILLS CAMPUS

Seven Hills, OH

CONTACT Financial Aid Office, DeVry University–Seven Hills Campus, 4141 Rockside Road, Suite 110, Seven Hills, OH 44131, 216-328-8754 or toll-free 866-338-7934.
Website: http://www.devry.edu/.

DEVRY UNIVERSITY–SHERMAN OAKS CAMPUS

Sherman Oaks, CA

CONTACT Financial Aid Office, DeVry University–Sherman Oaks Campus, 15301 Ventura Boulevard, Building D-100, Sherman Oaks, CA 91403, 818-713-8111 or toll-free 866-338-7934.
Website: http://www.devry.edu/.

DEVRY UNIVERSITY–TINLEY PARK CAMPUS

Tinley Park, IL

CONTACT Director of Student Finance, DeVry University–Tinley Park Campus, 18624 West Creek Drive, Tinley Park, IL 60477, 708-342-3300 or toll-free 866-338-7934. *Fax:* 708-342-3120.
Website: http://www.devry.edu/.

DEVRY UNIVERSITY–WESTMINSTER CAMPUS

Westminster, CO

CONTACT Office of Financial Aid, DeVry University–Westminster Campus, 1870 West 122nd Avenue, Westminster, CO 80234-2010, 303-280-7400 or toll-free 866-338-7934.
Website: http://www.devry.edu/.

DICKINSON COLLEGE

Carlisle, PA

Tuition & fees: $58,680	Average undergraduate aid package: $49,622

ABOUT THE INSTITUTION Independent, coed. ***Awards:*** bachelor's degrees. 45 undergraduate majors. ***Total enrollment:*** 2,133. Undergraduates: 2,133. Freshmen: 453. Both federal and institutional methodology are used as a basis for awarding need-based institutional aid.

UNDERGRADUATE EXPENSES for 2020–2021 ***Application fee:*** $65. ***One-time required fee:*** $25. ***Comprehensive fee:*** $73,352 includes full-time tuition ($58,130), mandatory fees ($550), and room and board ($14,672). ***College room only:*** $7566. Room and board charges vary according to board plan and housing facility. ***Part-time tuition:*** $7265 per course. ***Part-time fees:*** $70 per course.

FRESHMAN FINANCIAL AID (Fall 2019, est.) 330 applied for aid; of those 90% were deemed to have need. 100% of freshmen with need received aid; of those 93% had need fully met. ***Average percent of need met:*** 99% (excluding resources awarded to replace EFC). ***Average financial aid package:*** $47,914 (excluding resources awarded to replace EFC). 15% of all full-time freshmen had no need and received non-need-based gift aid.

UNDERGRADUATE FINANCIAL AID (Fall 2019, est.) 1,422 applied for aid; of those 94% were deemed to have need. 99% of undergraduates with need received aid; of those 74% had need fully met. ***Average percent of need met:*** 98% (excluding resources awarded to replace EFC). ***Average financial aid package:*** $49,622 (excluding resources awarded to replace EFC). 14% of all full-time undergraduates had no need and received non-need-based gift aid.

GIFT AID (NEED-BASED) ***Total amount:*** $56,739,645 (3% federal, 1% state, 95% institutional, 1% external sources). ***Receiving aid:*** Freshmen: 64% (288); all full-time undergraduates: 63% (1,307). ***Average award:*** Freshmen: $41,571; Undergraduates: $43,188. ***Scholarships, grants, and awards:*** Federal Pell, FSEOG, state, private, college/university gift aid from institutional funds.

GIFT AID (NON-NEED-BASED) ***Total amount:*** $5,753,008 (23% federal, 67% institutional, 10% external sources). ***Receiving aid:*** Freshmen: 4% (20). Undergraduates: 4% (94). ***Average award:*** Freshmen: $12,798. Undergraduates: $12,027. ***Scholarships, grants, and awards by category:*** *Academic interests/achievement:* general academic interests/achievements, military science. *Special characteristics:* children and siblings of alumni, children of faculty/staff, veterans. ***Tuition waivers:*** Full or partial for employees or children of employees, senior citizens. ***ROTC:*** Army.

LOANS ***Student loans:*** $10,431,678 (66% need-based, 34% non-need-based). 55% of past graduating class borrowed through all loan programs. *Average indebtedness per student:* $27,030. ***Average need-based loan:*** Freshmen: $4082. Undergraduates: $4958. ***Parent loans:*** $3,213,129 (25% need-based, 75% non-need-based). ***Programs:*** Federal Direct (Subsidized and Unsubsidized Stafford, PLUS), state, college/university.

WORK-STUDY ***Federal work-study:*** Total amount: $2,048,278; jobs available. ***State or other work-study/employment:*** Total amount: $909,815 (74% need-based, 26% non-need-based). Part-time jobs available.

APPLYING FOR FINANCIAL AID ***Required financial aid forms:*** FAFSA, CSS Financial Aid PROFILE, state aid form, noncustodial (divorced/separated) parent's statement. ***Financial aid deadline:*** 1/15 (priority: 11/15). ***Notification date:*** Students must reply by 5/1 or within 2 weeks of notification.

CONTACT Leah Young, Director of Financial Aid, Dickinson College, PO Box 1773, Carlisle, PA 17013-2896, 717-245-1308 or toll-free 800-644-1773. *Fax:* 717-245-1972. *E-mail:* finaid@dickinson.edu. *Website:* http://www.dickinson.edu/.

DICKINSON STATE UNIVERSITY

Dickinson, ND

ABOUT THE INSTITUTION State-supported, coed. ***Awards:*** certificates, associate, bachelor's, and master's degrees. 46 undergraduate majors. ***Total enrollment:*** 1,350. Undergraduates: 1,321. Freshmen: 202.

GIFT AID (NEED-BASED) ***Scholarships, grants, and awards:*** Federal Pell, FSEOG, state, private, college/university gift aid from institutional funds, Federal Nursing.

GIFT AID (NON-NEED-BASED) ***Scholarships, grants, and awards by category:*** *Academic interests/achievement:* agriculture, biological sciences, business, communication, computer science, education, English, foreign languages, general academic interests/achievements, home economics, humanities, mathematics, physical sciences, premedicine, social sciences. *Creative arts/performance:* applied art and design, creative writing, journalism/publications, music, theater/drama. *Special achievements/activities:* cheerleading/drum major, leadership, rodeo. *Special characteristics:* children of faculty/staff, children with a deceased or disabled parent, ethnic background, general special characteristics, international students, members of minority groups, veterans.

LOANS ***Programs:*** Federal Direct (Subsidized and Unsubsidized Stafford, PLUS), Perkins, Federal Nursing.

CONTACT Mr. Chris Meek, Director of Financial Aid, Dickinson State University, 291 Campus Drive, Dickinson, ND 58601-4896, 701-483-2565 or toll-free 800-279-4295. *Fax:* 701-483-2720. *E-mail:* christopher.meek@dickinsonstate.edu. *Website:* http://www.dickinsonstate.edu/.

DIGIPEN INSTITUTE OF TECHNOLOGY

Redmond, WA

ABOUT THE INSTITUTION Proprietary, coed. ***Awards:*** bachelor's and master's degrees. 8 undergraduate majors. ***Total enrollment:*** 1,166. Undergraduates: 1,064. Freshmen: 218.

GIFT AID (NEED-BASED) ***Scholarships, grants, and awards:*** Federal Pell, FSEOG, state, private, college/university gift aid from institutional funds.

GIFT AID (NON-NEED-BASED) ***Scholarships, grants, and awards by category:*** *Academic interests/achievement:* computer science, engineering/technologies, mathematics. *Creative arts/performance:* applied art and design. *Special achievements/activities:* general special achievements/activities, leadership.

LOANS ***Programs:*** Federal Direct (Subsidized and Unsubsidized Stafford, PLUS), private loans.

WORK-STUDY ***Federal work-study:*** Total amount: $133,146; 22 jobs averaging $2000.

APPLYING FOR FINANCIAL AID ***Required financial aid form:*** FAFSA.

CONTACT Mrs. Robin Reid, Director of Financial Aid and Scholarships, DigiPen Institute of Technology, 9931 Willows Road, Redmond, WA 98052, 425-629-5096 or toll-free 866-478-5236. *Fax:* 425-558-0378. *E-mail:* r.reid@digipen.edu. *Website:* http://www.digipen.edu/.

DILLARD UNIVERSITY

New Orleans, LA

Tuition & fees: $19,281	Average undergraduate aid package: $17,207

ABOUT THE INSTITUTION Independent interdenominational, coed. ***Awards:*** bachelor's degrees. 23 undergraduate majors. ***Total enrollment:*** 1,235. Undergraduates: 1,225. Freshmen: 319.

UNDERGRADUATE EXPENSES for 2020–2021 ***Application fee:*** $36. ***Tuition:*** full-time $17,410; part-time $726 per credit hour. ***Required fees:*** full-time $1871. ***College room only:*** $6156.

FRESHMAN FINANCIAL AID (Fall 2018) 376 applied for aid; of those 95% were deemed to have need. 100% of freshmen with need received aid; of those 7% had need fully met. ***Average percent of need met:*** 60% (excluding resources awarded to replace EFC). ***Average financial aid package:*** $17,656 (excluding resources awarded to replace EFC). 6% of all full-time freshmen had no need and received non-need-based gift aid.

UNDERGRADUATE FINANCIAL AID (Fall 2018) 1,223 applied for aid; of those 97% were deemed to have need. 99% of undergraduates with need received aid; of those 7% had need fully met. ***Average percent of need met:*** 58% (excluding resources awarded to replace EFC). ***Average financial aid package:*** $17,207 (excluding resources awarded to replace EFC). 3% of all full-time undergraduates had no need and received non-need-based gift aid.

GIFT AID (NEED-BASED) ***Total amount:*** $15,049,805 (34% federal, 9% state, 46% institutional, 11% external sources). ***Receiving aid:*** Freshmen: 93% (356); all full-time undergraduates: 93% (1,150). ***Average award:*** Freshmen: $14,914; Undergraduates: $13,644.

GIFT AID (NON-NEED-BASED) ***Total amount:*** $968,126 (16% state, 58% institutional, 26% external sources). ***Receiving aid:*** Freshmen: 6% (24). Undergraduates: 6% (78). ***Average award:*** Freshmen: $8245. Undergraduates: $8283. ***Scholarships, grants, and awards by category:*** *Academic interests/achievement:* general academic interests/achievements. *Creative arts/performance:* art/fine arts, music, theater/drama. *Special characteristics:* children of faculty/staff, relatives of clergy, religious affiliation. ***ROTC:*** Army cooperative, Naval cooperative, Air Force cooperative.

LOANS ***Student loans:*** $9,191,540 (93% need-based, 7% non-need-based). ***Average need-based loan:*** Freshmen: $3122. Undergraduates: $4044. ***Parent loans:*** $4,608,293 (75% need-based, 25% non-need-based).

WORK-STUDY ***Federal work-study:*** Total amount: $253,464; jobs available.

ATHLETIC AWARDS Total amount: $938,839 (82% need-based, 18% non-need-based).

APPLYING FOR FINANCIAL AID ***Notification date:*** Continuous.

CONTACT Mr. Theodis Wright, Director of Financial Aid and Scholarships, Dillard University, 2601 Gentilly Boulevard, New Orleans, LA 70122-3097, 504-816-4677 or toll-free 800-216-8094. *Fax:* 504-816-5456. *E-mail:* twright@dillard.edu.
Website: http://www.dillard.edu/.

DIXIE STATE UNIVERSITY

St. George, UT

ABOUT THE INSTITUTION State-supported, coed. ***Awards:*** certificates, diplomas, associate, and bachelor's degrees. 60 undergraduate majors. ***Total enrollment:*** 9,673. Undergraduates: 9,673. Freshmen: 2,320.

GIFT AID (NEED-BASED) ***Scholarships, grants, and awards:*** Federal Pell, FSEOG, state, private, college/university gift aid from institutional funds.

GIFT AID (NON-NEED-BASED) ***Scholarships, grants, and awards by category:*** *Academic interests/achievement:* general academic interests/achievements.

LOANS ***Programs:*** Federal Direct (Subsidized and Unsubsidized Stafford, PLUS), Perkins.

CONTACT J. D. Robertson, Director of Financial Aid, Dixie State University, 225 South 700 East, St. George, UT 84770, 435-652-7575. *Fax:* 435-656-4087. *E-mail:* finaid@dixie.edu.
Website: http://www.dixie.edu/.

DOANE UNIVERSITY

Crete, NE

Tuition & fees: N/R	Average undergraduate aid package: $27,876

ABOUT THE INSTITUTION Independent United Church of Christ, coed. ***Awards:*** certificates, bachelor's, master's, and doctoral degrees (non-traditional undergraduate programs and graduate programs offered at Lincoln campus). 47 undergraduate majors. ***Total enrollment:*** 1,002. Undergraduates: 1,002. Freshmen: 314. Both federal and institutional methodology are used as a basis for awarding need-based institutional aid.

UNDERGRADUATE EXPENSES for 2020–2021 ***Tuition:*** part-time $1150 per credit hour. Full-time tuition and fees vary according to location. Part-time tuition and fees vary according to course load and location. Room and board charges vary according to board plan, housing facility, and location.

FRESHMAN FINANCIAL AID (Fall 2019, est.) 293 applied for aid; of those 88% were deemed to have need. 100% of freshmen with need received aid; of those 39% had need fully met. ***Average percent of need met:*** 93% (excluding resources awarded to replace EFC). ***Average financial aid package:*** $30,107 (excluding resources awarded to replace EFC). 5% of all full-time freshmen had no need and received non-need-based gift aid.

UNDERGRADUATE FINANCIAL AID (Fall 2019, est.) 829 applied for aid; of those 89% were deemed to have need. 100% of undergraduates with need received aid; of those 35% had need fully met. ***Average percent of need met:*** 89% (excluding resources awarded to replace EFC). ***Average financial aid package:*** $27,876 (excluding resources awarded to replace EFC). 7% of all full-time undergraduates had no need and received non-need-based gift aid.

GIFT AID (NEED-BASED) ***Receiving aid:*** Freshmen: 82% (259); all full-time undergraduates: 74% (734). ***Average award:*** Freshmen: $28,605; Undergraduates: $24,668. ***Scholarships, grants, and awards:*** Federal Pell, FSEOG, state, private, college/university gift aid from institutional funds.

GIFT AID (NON-NEED-BASED) ***Receiving aid:*** Freshmen: 18% (57). Undergraduates: 26% (255). ***Average award:*** Freshmen: $18,941. Undergraduates: $20,742. ***Scholarships, grants, and awards by category:*** *Academic interests/achievement:* general academic interests/achievements. *Creative arts/performance:* applied art and design, debating, music, performing arts, theater/drama. *Special characteristics:* children and siblings of alumni, children of faculty/staff, religious affiliation, siblings of current students. ***Tuition waivers:*** Full or partial for employees or children of employees, senior citizens. ***ROTC:*** Army cooperative, Air Force cooperative.

LOANS ***Student loans:*** 84% of past graduating class borrowed through all loan programs. *Average indebtedness per student:* $28,490. ***Average need-based loan:*** Freshmen: $3276. Undergraduates: $4278. ***Programs:*** Federal Direct (Subsidized and Unsubsidized Stafford, PLUS), Perkins.

WORK-STUDY Federal work-study jobs available. ***State or other work-study/employment:*** Part-time jobs available.

APPLYING FOR FINANCIAL AID ***Required financial aid form:*** FAFSA. ***Financial aid deadline:*** Continuous. ***Notification date:*** Continuous. Students must reply within 4 weeks of notification.

CONTACT Ms. Peggy Tvrdy, Director of Financial Aid, Doane University, 1014 Boswell Avenue, Crete, NE 68333-2430, 402-826-8260 or toll-free 800-333-6263. *Fax:* 402-826-8600. *E-mail:* peggy.tvrdy@doane.edu.
Website: http://www.doane.edu/.

DOMINICAN COLLEGE

Orangeburg, NY

Tuition & fees: $29,844	Average undergraduate aid package: $23,609

ABOUT THE INSTITUTION Independent, coed. ***Awards:*** certificates, diplomas, associate, bachelor's, master's, and doctoral degrees. 32 undergraduate majors. ***Total enrollment:*** 1,868. Undergraduates: 2,754. Freshmen: 293. Federal methodology is used as a basis for awarding need-based institutional aid.

UNDERGRADUATE EXPENSES for 2020–2021 ***Application fee:*** $35. ***Comprehensive fee:*** $43,258 includes full-time tuition ($28,984), mandatory fees ($860), and room and board ($13,414). Room and board charges vary according to housing facility. ***Part-time tuition:*** $877 per credit hour. ***Part-time fees:*** $877 per credit hour.

FRESHMAN FINANCIAL AID (Fall 2019, est.) 279 applied for aid; of those 90% were deemed to have need. 117% of freshmen with need received aid; of those 12% had need fully met. ***Average percent of need met:*** 71% (excluding resources awarded to replace EFC). ***Average financial aid package:*** $25,631 (excluding resources awarded to replace EFC). 13% of all full-time freshmen had no need and received non-need-based gift aid.

UNDERGRADUATE FINANCIAL AID (Fall 2019, est.) 1,158 applied for aid; of those 90% were deemed to have need. 99% of undergraduates with need received aid; of those 13% had need fully met. ***Average percent of need met:*** 66% (excluding resources awarded to replace EFC). ***Average financial aid package:*** $23,609 (excluding resources awarded to replace EFC). 13% of all full-time undergraduates had no need and received non-need-based gift aid.

GIFT AID (NEED-BASED) ***Total amount:*** $20,294,343 (15% federal, 7% state, 76% institutional, 2% external sources). ***Receiving aid:*** Freshmen: 85% (250); all full-time undergraduates: 79% (998). ***Average award:*** Freshmen: $21,834; Undergraduates: $19,298. ***Scholarships, grants, and awards:*** Federal Pell, FSEOG, state, private, college/university gift aid from institutional funds.

GIFT AID (NON-NEED-BASED) ***Total amount:*** $3,147,632 (24% state, 73% institutional, 3% external sources). ***Receiving aid:*** Freshmen: 10% (28). Undergraduates: 8% (104). ***Average award:*** Freshmen: $13,614. Undergraduates: $11,115. ***Scholarships, grants, and awards by category:*** *Academic interests/achievement:* education, general academic interests/achievements. *Special characteristics:* children of faculty/staff, general special characteristics, relatives of clergy.

LOANS ***Student loans:*** $8,489,441 (74% need-based, 26% non-need-based). 52% of past graduating class borrowed through all loan programs. *Average indebtedness per student:* $39,347. ***Average need-based loan:*** Freshmen: $3613. Undergraduates: $5259. ***Parent loans:*** $2,194,354 (64% need-based, 36% non-need-based). ***Programs:*** Federal Direct (Subsidized and Unsubsidized Stafford, PLUS), Perkins, Federal Nursing.

WORK-STUDY ***Federal work-study:*** Total amount: $240,099; 211 jobs averaging $2000. ***State or other work-study/employment:*** Total amount: $289,455 (56% need-based, 44% non-need-based).

ATHLETIC AWARDS Total amount: $2,444,518 (54% need-based, 46% non-need-based).

APPLYING FOR FINANCIAL AID ***Required financial aid forms:*** FAFSA, CSS Financial Aid PROFILE, state aid form. ***Financial aid deadline (priority):*** 3/15. ***Notification date:*** Continuous beginning 11/1. Students must reply within 4 weeks of notification.

CONTACT Ms. Stacy Salinas, Director of Financial Aid, Dominican College, 470 Western Highway, Orangeburg, NY 10962-1210, 845-848-7818 or toll-free 866-432-4636. *Fax:* 845-359-4317. *E-mail:* stacy.salinas@dc.edu.
Website: http://www.dc.edu/.

DOMINICAN UNIVERSITY

River Forest, IL

Tuition & fees: $35,420 | **Average undergraduate aid package: $26,039**

ABOUT THE INSTITUTION Independent Roman Catholic, coed. ***Awards:*** certificates, bachelor's, master's, and doctoral degrees. 67 undergraduate majors. ***Total enrollment:*** 3,029. Undergraduates: 2,151. Freshmen: 419. Federal methodology is used as a basis for awarding need-based institutional aid.

UNDERGRADUATE EXPENSES for 2020–2021 ***Application fee:*** $25. ***One-time required fee:*** $150. ***Comprehensive fee:*** $46,285 includes full-time tuition ($34,950), mandatory fees ($470), and room and board ($10,865). Full-time tuition and fees vary according to program. Room and board charges vary according to housing facility. ***Part-time tuition:*** $1167 per credit hour. ***Part-time fees:*** $90 per term. Part-time tuition and fees vary according to program.

FRESHMAN FINANCIAL AID (Fall 2019, est.) 375 applied for aid; of those 93% were deemed to have need. 100% of freshmen with need received aid; of those 16% had need fully met. ***Average percent of need met:*** 80% (excluding resources awarded to replace EFC). ***Average financial aid package:*** $27,910 (excluding resources awarded to replace EFC). 17% of all full-time freshmen had no need and received non-need-based gift aid.

UNDERGRADUATE FINANCIAL AID (Fall 2019, est.) 1,704 applied for aid; of those 94% were deemed to have need. 99% of undergraduates with need received aid; of those 11% had need fully met. ***Average percent of need met:*** 72% (excluding resources awarded to replace EFC). ***Average financial aid package:*** $26,039 (excluding resources awarded to replace EFC). 17% of all full-time undergraduates had no need and received non-need-based gift aid.

GIFT AID (NEED-BASED) ***Total amount:*** $1437 (100% federal). ***Receiving aid:*** Freshmen: 83% (348); all full-time undergraduates: 81% (1,569). ***Average award:*** Freshmen: $24,836; Undergraduates: $22,672. ***Scholarships, grants, and awards:*** Federal Pell, FSEOG, state, private, college/university gift aid from institutional funds.

GIFT AID (NON-NEED-BASED) ***Receiving aid:*** Freshmen: 10% (40). Undergraduates: 6% (116). ***Average award:*** Freshmen: $23,928. Undergraduates: $20,253. ***Scholarships, grants, and awards by category:*** *Academic interests/achievement:* general academic interests/achievements, home economics. *Creative arts/performance:* applied art and design, art/fine arts. *Special characteristics:* children and siblings of alumni, children of faculty/staff, siblings of current students, spouses of current students. ***Tuition waivers:*** Full or partial for employees or children of employees.

LOANS ***Student loans:*** 81% of past graduating class borrowed through all loan programs. *Average indebtedness per student:* $28,760. ***Average need-based loan:*** Freshmen: $3061. Undergraduates: $4257. ***Programs:*** Federal Direct (Subsidized and Unsubsidized Stafford, PLUS).

WORK-STUDY Federal work-study jobs available (averaging $2500). ***State or other work-study/employment:*** Part-time jobs available.

APPLYING FOR FINANCIAL AID ***Required financial aid form:*** FAFSA. ***Financial aid deadline (priority):*** 2/15. ***Notification date:*** Continuous beginning 12/1. Students must reply within 2 weeks of notification.

CONTACT Victoria Spivak, Director of Financial Aid, Dominican University, 7900 West Division Street, Lewis Room 120, River Forest, IL 60305-1099, 708-524-6950 or toll-free 800-828-8475. *Fax:* 708-366-6478. *E-mail:* vlamick@dom.edu.
Website: http://www.dom.edu/.

DOMINICAN UNIVERSITY OF CALIFORNIA

San Rafael, CA

Tuition & fees: $47,870 | **Average undergraduate aid package: $32,288**

ABOUT THE INSTITUTION Independent Roman Catholic Church, coed. ***Awards:*** bachelor's and master's degrees. 24 undergraduate majors. ***Total enrollment:*** 1,879. Undergraduates: 1,461. Freshmen: 322. Federal methodology is used as a basis for awarding need-based institutional aid.

UNDERGRADUATE EXPENSES for 2020–2021 ***Comprehensive fee:*** $63,504 includes full-time tuition ($47,190), mandatory fees ($680), and room and board ($15,634). ***College room only:*** $8702. Room and board charges vary according to board plan and housing facility. ***Part-time tuition:*** $1970 per credit hour.

FRESHMAN FINANCIAL AID (Fall 2018) 283 applied for aid; of those 82% were deemed to have need. 100% of freshmen with need received aid; of those 10% had need fully met. ***Average percent of need met:*** 71% (excluding resources awarded to replace EFC). ***Average financial aid package:*** $34,767 (excluding resources awarded to replace EFC). 19% of all full-time freshmen had no need and received non-need-based gift aid.

UNDERGRADUATE FINANCIAL AID (Fall 2018) 1,113 applied for aid; of those 81% were deemed to have need. 100% of undergraduates with need received aid; of those 11% had need fully met. ***Average percent of need met:*** 67% (excluding resources awarded to replace EFC). ***Average financial aid package:*** $32,288 (excluding resources awarded to replace EFC). 17% of all full-time undergraduates had no need and received non-need-based gift aid.

GIFT AID (NEED-BASED) ***Total amount:*** $24,186,989 (8% federal, 11% state, 79% institutional, 2% external sources). ***Receiving aid:*** Freshmen: 81% (233); all full-time undergraduates: 80% (905). ***Average award:*** Freshmen: $32,189; Undergraduates: $28,149. ***Scholarships, grants, and awards:*** Federal Pell, FSEOG, state, private, college/university gift aid from institutional funds, Scholarships for Disadvantaged Students .

GIFT AID (NON-NEED-BASED) ***Total amount:*** $4,840,465 (94% institutional, 6% external sources). ***Receiving aid:*** Freshmen: 8% (22). Undergraduates: 3% (33). ***Average award:*** Freshmen: $19,776. Undergraduates: $18,529. ***Scholarships, grants, and awards by category:*** *Academic interests/achievement:* general academic interests/achievements, home economics, humanities. *Creative arts/performance:* dance, music. *Special achievements/activities:* community service, leadership. *Special characteristics:* adult students, children and siblings of alumni, children of faculty/staff, international students, members of minority groups, veterans. ***Tuition waivers:*** Full or partial for employees or children of employees.

LOANS ***Student loans:*** $8,374,745 (78% need-based, 22% non-need-based). 78% of past graduating class borrowed through all loan programs. *Average indebtedness per student:* $31,978. ***Average need-based loan:*** Freshmen: $3344. Undergraduates: $4610. ***Parent loans:*** $6,956,498 (54% need-based, 46% non-need-based). ***Programs:*** Federal Direct (Subsidized and Unsubsidized Stafford, PLUS), Perkins, Private Loans.

WORK-STUDY ***Federal work-study:*** Total amount: $401,594; jobs available. ***State or other work-study/employment:*** Total amount: $191,835 (100% need-based). Part-time jobs available.

ATHLETIC AWARDS Total amount: $938,332 (64% need-based, 36% non-need-based).

APPLYING FOR FINANCIAL AID ***Required financial aid forms:*** FAFSA, institution's own form. ***Financial aid deadline (priority):*** 3/1. ***Notification date:*** Continuous beginning 3/15.

CONTACT Ms. Lauren Coburn, Associate Director of Financial Aid, Dominican University of California, 50 Acacia Avenue, San Rafael, CA 94901-2298, 415-257-1348 or toll-free 888-323-6763. *Fax:* 415-485-3294. *E-mail:* lauren.coburn@dominican.edu. *Website:* http://www.dominican.edu/.

DORDT UNIVERSITY

Sioux Center, IA

Tuition & fees: N/R **Average undergraduate aid package: $25,970**

ABOUT THE INSTITUTION Independent Christian Reformed, coed. ***Awards:*** associate, bachelor's, and master's degrees. 86 undergraduate majors. Federal methodology is used as a basis for awarding need-based institutional aid.

FRESHMAN FINANCIAL AID (Fall 2019, est.) 348 applied for aid; of those 82% were deemed to have need. 100% of freshmen with need received aid; of those 46% had need fully met. ***Average percent of need met:*** 80% (excluding resources awarded to replace EFC). ***Average financial aid package:*** $26,442 (excluding resources awarded to replace EFC). 20% of all full-time freshmen had no need and received non-need-based gift aid.

UNDERGRADUATE FINANCIAL AID (Fall 2019, est.) 1,063 applied for aid; of those 84% were deemed to have need. 100% of undergraduates with need received aid; of those 42% had need fully met. ***Average percent of need met:*** 78% (excluding resources awarded to replace EFC). ***Average financial aid package:*** $25,970 (excluding resources awarded to replace EFC). 24% of all full-time undergraduates had no need and received non-need-based gift aid.

GIFT AID (NEED-BASED) ***Total amount:*** $18,085,257 (8% federal, 9% state, 80% institutional, 3% external sources). ***Receiving aid:*** Freshmen: 72% (281); all full-time undergraduates: 68% (885). ***Average award:*** Freshmen: $20,220; Undergraduates: $18,834. ***Scholarships, grants, and awards:*** Federal Pell, FSEOG, state, private, college/university gift aid from institutional funds.

GIFT AID (NON-NEED-BASED) ***Total amount:*** $4,312,359 (98% institutional, 2% external sources). ***Receiving aid:*** Freshmen: 16% (62). Undergraduates: 13% (170). ***Average award:*** Freshmen: $22,188. Undergraduates: $22,750. ***Scholarships, grants, and awards by category:*** *Academic interests/achievement:* 1,036 awards ($10,135,813 total): agriculture, biological sciences, business, communication, computer science, education, engineering/technologies, English, foreign languages, general academic interests/achievements, home economics, humanities, mathematics, physical sciences, premedicine, religion/biblical studies, social sciences. *Creative arts/performance:* 328 awards ($116,258 total): art/fine arts, dance, debating, journalism/publications, music, theater/drama. *Special achievements/activities:* 62 awards ($84,400 total): community service, general special achievements/activities, leadership. *Special characteristics:* 1,108 awards ($1,822,359 total): children and siblings of alumni, children of faculty/staff, general special characteristics, handicapped students, international students, local/state students, members of minority groups, out-of-state students, religious affiliation.

LOANS ***Student loans:*** $9,858,567 (87% need-based, 13% non-need-based). 75% of past graduating class borrowed through all loan programs. *Average indebtedness per student:* $30,327. ***Average need-based loan:*** Freshmen: $4145. Undergraduates: $4463. ***Parent loans:*** $3,330,137 (86% need-based, 14% non-need-based). ***Programs:*** Federal Direct (Subsidized and Unsubsidized Stafford, PLUS), college/university, alternative loans.

WORK-STUDY ***Federal work-study:*** Total amount: $1,127,906; 340 jobs averaging $2855. ***State or other work-study/employment:*** Total amount: $1,800,658 (80% need-based, 20% non-need-based). 503 part-time jobs averaging $3181.

ATHLETIC AWARDS Total amount: $3,773,941 (73% need-based, 27% non-need-based).

APPLYING FOR FINANCIAL AID ***Required financial aid forms:*** FAFSA, institution's own form. ***Financial aid deadline:*** Continuous. ***Notification date:*** Continuous beginning 1/15. Students must reply within 3 weeks of notification.

CONTACT Mr. Harlan Harmelink, Director of Financial Aid, Dordt University, 700 7th Street NE, Sioux Center, IA 51250-1697, 712-722-6082 or toll-free 800-343-6738. *Fax:* 712-722-6035. *E-mail:* harlan.harmelink@dordt.edu. *Website:* http://www.dordt.edu/.

DRAKE UNIVERSITY

Des Moines, IA

Tuition & fees: $44,334 **Average undergraduate aid package: $30,942**

ABOUT THE INSTITUTION Independent, coed. ***Awards:*** certificates, bachelor's, master's, and doctoral degrees. 67 undergraduate majors. ***Total enrollment:*** 4,884. Undergraduates: 2,954. Freshmen: 782. Federal methodology is used as a basis for awarding need-based institutional aid.

UNDERGRADUATE EXPENSES for 2020–2021 ***Comprehensive fee:*** $55,486 includes full-time tuition ($44,188), mandatory fees ($146), and room and board ($11,152). ***College room only:*** $6084. Full-time tuition and fees vary according to course load, degree level, program, and student level. Room and board charges vary according to board plan and housing facility. ***Part-time tuition:*** $1133 per credit hour. Part-time tuition and fees vary according to class time, degree level, and program. ***Payment plan:*** Guaranteed tuition.

FRESHMAN FINANCIAL AID (Fall 2019, est.) 700 applied for aid; of those 80% were deemed to have need. 100% of freshmen with need received aid; of those 29% had need fully met. ***Average percent of need met:*** 77% (excluding resources awarded to replace EFC). ***Average financial aid package:*** $32,378 (excluding resources awarded to replace EFC). 24% of all full-time freshmen had no need and received non-need-based gift aid.

UNDERGRADUATE FINANCIAL AID (Fall 2019, est.) 2,127 applied for aid; of those 84% were deemed to have need. 100% of undergraduates with need received aid; of those 28% had need fully met. ***Average percent of need met:*** 77% (excluding resources awarded to replace EFC). ***Average financial aid package:*** $30,942 (excluding resources awarded to replace EFC). 30% of all full-time undergraduates had no need and received non-need-based gift aid.

GIFT AID (NEED-BASED) ***Receiving aid:*** Freshmen: 71% (553); all full-time undergraduates: 62% (1,740). ***Average award:*** Freshmen: $25,850; Undergraduates: $24,256. ***Scholarships, grants, and awards:*** Federal Pell, FSEOG, state, private, college/university gift aid from institutional funds.

GIFT AID (NON-NEED-BASED) ***Receiving aid:*** Freshmen: 17% (130). Undergraduates: 13% (358). ***Average award:*** Freshmen: $22,868. Undergraduates: $20,058. ***Scholarships, grants, and awards by category:*** *Academic interests/achievement:* 2,379 awards ($42,171,435 total): general academic interests/achievements. *Creative arts/performance:* 313 awards ($2,526,444 total): applied art and design, music, theater/drama. *Special characteristics:* 223 awards ($330,750 total): children and siblings of alumni, international students. ***Tuition waivers:*** Full or partial for children of alumni, employees or children of employees, senior citizens. ***ROTC:*** Army cooperative, Air Force cooperative.

LOANS ***Student loans:*** 60% of past graduating class borrowed through all loan programs. *Average indebtedness per student:* $34,492. ***Average need-based loan:*** Freshmen: $3173. Undergraduates: $3976. ***Programs:*** Federal Direct (Subsidized and Unsubsidized Stafford, PLUS), college/university, Health Professions Student Loans (HPSL).

WORK-STUDY ***Federal work-study:*** 1,354 jobs averaging $1900.

APPLYING FOR FINANCIAL AID ***Required financial aid form:*** FAFSA. ***Financial aid deadline:*** Continuous. ***Notification date:*** Continuous. Students must reply within 3 weeks of notification.

CONTACT Financial Aid Office, Drake University, 2507 University Avenue, Des Moines, IA 50311-4516, 515-271-2011 or toll-free 800-44-DRAKE Ext.3181. *Website:* http://www.drake.edu/.

DREW UNIVERSITY

Madison, NJ

Tuition & fees: $40,660 **Average undergraduate aid package: $37,235**

ABOUT THE INSTITUTION Independent United Methodist Church, coed. ***Awards:*** certificates, bachelor's, master's, and doctoral degrees. 35 undergraduate majors. ***Total enrollment:*** 2,319. Undergraduates: 1,712. Freshmen: 400. Federal methodology is used as a basis for awarding need-based institutional aid.

UNDERGRADUATE EXPENSES for 2019–2020 ***Application fee:*** $40. ***Comprehensive fee:*** $55,332 includes full-time tuition ($39,828), mandatory fees ($832), and room and board ($14,672). ***College room only:*** $9264. Room and board charges vary according to board plan and housing facility. ***Part-time tuition:*** $1660 per credit. Part-time tuition and fees vary according to course load. ***Payment plan:*** Tuition prepayment.

FRESHMAN FINANCIAL AID (Fall 2019, est.) 343 applied for aid; of those 87% were deemed to have need. 100% of freshmen with need received aid; of those 15% had need fully met. ***Average percent of need met:*** 83% (excluding resources awarded to replace EFC). ***Average financial aid package:*** $37,650 (excluding resources awarded to replace EFC). 21% of all full-time freshmen had no need and received non-need-based gift aid.

UNDERGRADUATE FINANCIAL AID (Fall 2019, est.) 1,161 applied for aid; of those 91% were deemed to have need. 100% of undergraduates with need received aid; of those 15% had need fully met. ***Average percent of need met:*** 83% (excluding resources awarded to replace EFC). ***Average financial aid package:*** $37,235 (excluding resources awarded to replace EFC). 27% of all full-time undergraduates had no need and received non-need-based gift aid.

GIFT AID (NEED-BASED) ***Total amount:*** $32,872,564 (8% federal, 11% state, 79% institutional, 2% external sources). ***Receiving aid:*** Freshmen: 75% (299); all full-time undergraduates: 67% (1,059). ***Average award:*** Freshmen: $32,964; Undergraduates: $31,510. ***Scholarships, grants, and awards:*** Federal Pell, FSEOG, state, private, college/university gift aid from institutional funds.

GIFT AID (NON-NEED-BASED) ***Total amount:*** $7,373,597 (97% institutional, 3% external sources). ***Receiving aid:*** Freshmen: 7% (27). Undergraduates: 5% (86). ***Average award:*** Freshmen: $18,493. Undergraduates: $15,394. ***Scholarships, grants, and awards by category:*** *Academic interests/achievement:* general academic interests/achievements. *Creative arts/performance:* applied art and design, music, performing arts, theater/drama. *Special achievements/activities:* community service. ***Tuition waivers:*** Full or partial for employees or children of employees. ***ROTC:*** Army cooperative.

LOANS ***Student loans:*** $6,012,441 (57% need-based, 43% non-need-based). 62% of past graduating class borrowed through all loan programs. *Average indebtedness per student:* $25,049. ***Average need-based loan:*** Freshmen: $3381. Undergraduates: $4418. ***Parent loans:*** $4,908,452 (42% need-based, 58% non-need-based). ***Programs:*** Federal Direct (Subsidized and Unsubsidized Stafford, PLUS), Perkins, state.

WORK-STUDY ***Federal work-study:*** Total amount: $1,486,915; 752 jobs averaging $2000. ***State or other work-study/employment:*** Total amount: $432,905 (84% need-based, 16% non-need-based). Part-time jobs available.

APPLYING FOR FINANCIAL AID ***Required financial aid form:*** FAFSA. ***Financial aid deadline (priority):*** 1/1. ***Notification date:*** 3/25. Students must reply by 5/1.

CONTACT Colby McCarthy, Associate Vice President for Scholarships and Financial Aid, Drew University, 36 Madison Avenue, Madison, NJ 07940-1493, 973-408-3112. *Fax:* 973-408-3188. *E-mail:* finaid@drew.edu.
Website: http://www.drew.edu/.

DREXEL UNIVERSITY

Philadelphia, PA

Tuition & fees: $54,516	Average undergraduate aid package: $38,995

ABOUT THE INSTITUTION Independent, coed. ***Awards:*** certificates, bachelor's, master's, and doctoral degrees. 81 undergraduate majors. ***Total enrollment:*** 24,205. Undergraduates: 15,346. Freshmen: 3,178. Federal methodology is used as a basis for awarding need-based institutional aid.

UNDERGRADUATE EXPENSES for 2019–2020 ***Application fee:*** $50. ***Comprehensive fee:*** $68,757 includes full-time tuition ($52,146), mandatory fees ($2370), and room and board ($14,241). ***College room only:*** $8400. Room and board charges vary according to board plan and housing facility. ***Part-time tuition:*** $1173 per credit hour. ***Part-time fees:*** $150 per term. Part-time tuition and fees vary according to program.

FRESHMAN FINANCIAL AID (Fall 2019, est.) 2884 applied for aid; of those 83% were deemed to have need. 100% of freshmen with need received aid; of those 30% had need fully met. ***Average percent of need met:*** 80% (excluding resources awarded to replace EFC). ***Average financial aid package:*** $43,051 (excluding resources awarded to replace EFC). 24% of all full-time freshmen had no need and received non-need-based gift aid.

UNDERGRADUATE FINANCIAL AID (Fall 2019, est.) 10,053 applied for aid; of those 88% were deemed to have need. 100% of undergraduates with need received aid; of those 24% had need fully met. ***Average percent of need met:*** 74% (excluding resources awarded to replace EFC). ***Average financial aid package:*** $38,995 (excluding resources awarded to replace EFC). 32% of all full-time undergraduates had no need and received non-need-based gift aid.

GIFT AID (NEED-BASED) ***Total amount:*** $251,894,971 (7% federal, 3% state, 88% institutional, 2% external sources). ***Receiving aid:*** Freshmen: 76% (2,402); all full-time undergraduates: 62% (8,646). ***Average award:*** Freshmen: $33,379; Undergraduates: $29,367. ***Scholarships, grants, and awards:*** Federal Pell, FSEOG, state, private, college/university gift aid from institutional funds.

GIFT AID (NON-NEED-BASED) ***Total amount:*** $85,529,344 (97% institutional, 3% external sources). ***Receiving aid:*** Freshmen: 12% (369). Undergraduates: 7% (1,015). ***Average award:*** Freshmen: $16,014. Undergraduates: $16,986. ***Scholarships, grants, and awards by category:*** *Academic interests/achievement:* general academic interests/achievements. *Creative arts/performance:* dance, music, performing arts, theater/drama. *Special achievements/activities:* cheerleading/drum major. *Special characteristics:* children and siblings of alumni, siblings of current students, twins. ***Tuition waivers:*** Full or partial for employees or children of employees. ***ROTC:*** Army, Naval cooperative, Air Force cooperative.

LOANS ***Student loans:*** $92,285,263 (72% need-based, 28% non-need-based). 67% of past graduating class borrowed through all loan programs. *Average indebtedness per student:* $72,883. ***Average need-based loan:*** Freshmen: $8658. Undergraduates: $10,122. ***Parent loans:*** $44,781,179 (100% non-need-based). ***Programs:*** Federal Direct (Subsidized and Unsubsidized Stafford, PLUS), Perkins, state.

WORK-STUDY ***Federal work-study:*** Total amount: $4,462,408; jobs available.

ATHLETIC AWARDS Total amount: $9,524,274 (20% need-based, 80% non-need-based).

APPLYING FOR FINANCIAL AID ***Required financial aid forms:*** FAFSA, CSS Financial Aid PROFILE. ***Financial aid deadline:*** 2/15. ***Notification date:*** Continuous beginning 4/1. Students must reply by 5/1.

CONTACT Helen Gourousis, Director of Financial Aid, Drexel University, 3141 Chestnut Street, Philadelphia, PA 19104-2875, 215-895-5928 or toll-free 800-2-DREXEL. *Fax:* 215-895-6903. *E-mail:* gouroush@drexel.edu.
Website: http://www.drexel.edu/.

DRURY UNIVERSITY

Springfield, MO

Tuition & fees: $30,915	Average undergraduate aid package: $23,426

ABOUT THE INSTITUTION Independent, coed. ***Awards:*** certificates, bachelor's, and master's degrees (also offers evening program with significant enrollment not reflected in profile). 31 undergraduate majors. ***Total enrollment:*** 1,743. Undergraduates: 1,478. Freshmen: 343. Federal methodology is used as a basis for awarding need-based institutional aid.

UNDERGRADUATE EXPENSES for 2020–2021 ***Comprehensive fee:*** $40,087 includes full-time tuition ($29,900), mandatory fees ($1015), and room and board ($9172). ***College room only:*** $5860. Full-time tuition and fees vary according to degree level. Room and board charges vary according to board plan and housing facility. ***Part-time tuition:*** $959 per credit hour. Part-time tuition and fees vary according to degree level.

FRESHMAN FINANCIAL AID (Fall 2019, est.) 310 applied for aid; of those 82% were deemed to have need. 100% of freshmen with need received aid; of those 22% had need fully met. ***Average percent of need met:*** 78% (excluding resources awarded to replace EFC). ***Average financial aid package:*** $24,205 (excluding resources awarded to replace EFC). 25% of all full-time freshmen had no need and received non-need-based gift aid.

UNDERGRADUATE FINANCIAL AID (Fall 2019, est.) 1,134 applied for aid; of those 86% were deemed to have need. 100% of undergraduates with need received aid; of those 25% had need fully met. ***Average percent of need met:*** 76% (excluding resources awarded to replace EFC). ***Average financial aid package:*** $23,426 (excluding resources awarded to replace EFC). 31% of all full-time undergraduates had no need and received non-need-based gift aid.

GIFT AID (NEED-BASED) ***Total amount:*** $18,384,244 (13% federal, 5% state, 79% institutional, 3% external sources). ***Receiving aid:*** Freshmen: 74% (255); all full-time undergraduates: 67% (972). ***Average award:*** Freshmen: $21,735; Undergrad-

uates: $20,513. ***Scholarships, grants, and awards:*** Federal Pell, FSEOG, state, private, college/university gift aid from institutional funds.

GIFT AID (NON-NEED-BASED) ***Total amount:*** $6,904,895 (2% state, 94% institutional, 4% external sources). ***Receiving aid:*** Freshmen: 13% (45). Undergraduates: 13% (191). ***Average award:*** Freshmen: $14,039. Undergraduates: $12,543. ***Scholarships, grants, and awards by category:*** *Academic interests/achievement:* architecture, biological sciences, business, communication, computer science, education, English, foreign languages, general academic interests/achievements, home economics, humanities, international studies, mathematics, physical sciences, premedicine, social sciences. *Creative arts/performance:* applied art and design, creative writing, debating, music, theater/drama. *Special achievements/activities:* cheerleading/drum major, leadership, religious involvement. *Special characteristics:* children and siblings of alumni, children of faculty/staff, ethnic background, international students, members of minority groups, relatives of clergy, religious affiliation, siblings of current students, veterans. ***Tuition waivers:*** Full or partial for employees or children of employees.

LOANS ***Student loans:*** $7,169,239 (65% need-based, 35% non-need-based). 62% of past graduating class borrowed through all loan programs. *Average indebtedness per student:* $37,144. ***Average need-based loan:*** Freshmen: $3238. Undergraduates: $4015. ***Parent loans:*** $1,860,511 (40% need-based, 60% non-need-based). ***Programs:*** Federal Direct (Subsidized and Unsubsidized Stafford, PLUS).

WORK-STUDY ***Federal work-study:*** Total amount: $284,680; jobs available. ***State or other work-study/employment:*** Part-time jobs available.

ATHLETIC AWARDS Total amount: $4,099,906 (29% need-based, 71% non-need-based).

APPLYING FOR FINANCIAL AID ***Financial aid deadline:*** Continuous. ***Notification date:*** Continuous beginning 1/15. Students must reply by 5/1.

CONTACT Ms. Becky Ahrens, Director of Financial Aid, Drury University, 900 North Benton Avenue, Springfield, MO 65802-3791, 417-873-7312 or toll-free 800-922-2274. *Fax:* 417-873-6906. *E-mail:* bahrens@drury.edu.
Website: http://www.drury.edu/.

DUKE UNIVERSITY

Durham, NC

Tuition & fees: $57,931	Average undergraduate aid package: $57,235

ABOUT THE INSTITUTION Independent United Methodist Church, coed. ***Awards:*** certificates, bachelor's, master's, and doctoral degrees. 45 undergraduate majors. ***Total enrollment:*** 16,606. Undergraduates: 6,682. Freshmen: 1,745. Both federal and institutional methodology are used as a basis for awarding need-based institutional aid.

UNDERGRADUATE EXPENSES for 2019–2020 ***Application fee:*** $85. ***Comprehensive fee:*** $73,519 includes full-time tuition ($55,880), mandatory fees ($2051), and room and board ($15,588). ***College room only:*** $8924. Room and board charges vary according to board plan and housing facility. ***Part-time tuition:*** $1746 per credit hour. ***Payment plan:*** Tuition prepayment.

FRESHMAN FINANCIAL AID (Fall 2019, est.) 1105 applied for aid; of those 71% were deemed to have need. 100% of freshmen with need received aid; of those 100% had need fully met. ***Average percent of need met:*** 100% (excluding resources awarded to replace EFC). ***Average financial aid package:*** $54,990 (excluding resources awarded to replace EFC). 1% of all full-time freshmen had no need and received non-need-based gift aid.

UNDERGRADUATE FINANCIAL AID (Fall 2019, est.) 3,631 applied for aid; of those 82% were deemed to have need. 100% of undergraduates with need received aid; of those 100% had need fully met. ***Average percent of need met:*** 100% (excluding resources awarded to replace EFC). ***Average financial aid package:*** $57,235 (excluding resources awarded to replace EFC). 2% of all full-time undergraduates had no need and received non-need-based gift aid.

GIFT AID (NEED-BASED) ***Total amount:*** $150,585,101 (3% federal, 1% state, 92% institutional, 4% external sources). ***Receiving aid:*** Freshmen: 44% (755); all full-time undergraduates: 44% (2,858). ***Average award:*** Freshmen: $53,400; Undergraduates: $55,374. ***Scholarships, grants, and awards:*** Federal Pell, FSEOG, state, private, college/university gift aid from institutional funds, ROTC and veteran's benefits.

GIFT AID (NON-NEED-BASED) ***Total amount:*** $18,264,076 (60% institutional, 40% external sources). ***Receiving aid:*** Freshmen: 8% (146). Undergraduates: 5% (341). ***Average award:*** Freshmen: $76,181. Undergraduates: $74,761. ***Scholarships, grants, and awards by category:*** *Academic interests/achievement:* 98 awards ($7,079,053 total): general academic interests/achievements, mathematics. *Special achievements/activities:* 82 awards ($5,757,019 total): general special achievements/activities, leadership. *Special characteristics:* 75 awards ($5,812,162 total): children and siblings of alumni, ethnic background, first-generation college students, international students, local/state students, members of minority groups. ***ROTC:*** Army, Naval, Air Force.

LOANS ***Student loans:*** $18,711,292 (71% need-based, 29% non-need-based). 32% of past graduating class borrowed through all loan programs. *Average indebtedness per student:* $22,369. ***Average need-based loan:*** Freshmen: $3039. Undergraduates: $3207. ***Parent loans:*** $7,047,939 (77% need-based, 23% non-need-based). ***Programs:*** Federal Direct (Subsidized and Unsubsidized Stafford, PLUS), Perkins, college/university, alternative loans.

WORK-STUDY ***Federal work-study:*** Total amount: $3,862,044; 1,746 jobs averaging $2217. ***State or other work-study/employment:*** Total amount: $2,726,481 (54% need-based, 46% non-need-based). 1,226 part-time jobs averaging $2024.

ATHLETIC AWARDS Total amount: $22,582,587 (34% need-based, 66% non-need-based).

APPLYING FOR FINANCIAL AID ***Required financial aid forms:*** FAFSA, CSS Financial Aid PROFILE, noncustodial (divorced/separated) parent's statement, business/farm supplement, federal income tax form(s), W-2 forms. ***Financial aid deadline (priority):*** 2/1. ***Notification date:*** 4/1. Students must reply by 5/1.

CONTACT Alison Rabil, Director of Financial Aid, Duke University, 2127 Campus Drive Addition, Box 90397, Durham, NC 27708-0397, 919-684-6225. *Fax:* 919-660-9811. *E-mail:* finaid@duke.edu.
Website: http://www.duke.edu/.

DUNLAP-STONE UNIVERSITY

Phoenix, AZ

CONTACT Office of the Bursar, Dunlap-Stone University, 19820 North 7th Street, Suite #100, Phoenix, AZ 85024, 800-474-8013. *E-mail:* info@expandglobal.com.
Website: http://www.dunlap-stone.edu/.

DUQUESNE UNIVERSITY

Pittsburgh, PA

Tuition & fees: $39,992	Average undergraduate aid package: $26,543

ABOUT THE INSTITUTION Independent Roman Catholic, coed. ***Awards:*** certificates, bachelor's, master's, and doctoral degrees. 73 undergraduate majors. ***Total enrollment:*** 9,274. Undergraduates: 6,013. Freshmen: 1,512. Federal methodology is used as a basis for awarding need-based institutional aid.

UNDERGRADUATE EXPENSES for 2019–2020 ***Application fee:*** $50. ***Comprehensive fee:*** $53,080 includes full-time tuition ($39,992) and room and board ($13,088). ***College room only:*** $7194. Full-time tuition and fees vary according to course load and program. Room and board charges vary according to board plan and housing facility. ***Part-time tuition:*** $1325 per credit. Part-time tuition and fees vary according to course load and program.

FRESHMAN FINANCIAL AID (Fall 2018) 1356 applied for aid; of those 83% were deemed to have need. 100% of freshmen with need received aid; of those 22% had need fully met. ***Average percent of need met:*** 75% (excluding resources awarded to replace EFC). ***Average financial aid package:*** $27,833 (excluding resources awarded to replace EFC). 25% of all full-time freshmen had no need and received non-need-based gift aid.

UNDERGRADUATE FINANCIAL AID (Fall 2018) 4,645 applied for aid; of those 86% were deemed to have need. 100% of undergraduates with need received aid; of those 19% had need fully met. ***Average percent of need met:*** 71% (excluding resources awarded to replace EFC). ***Average financial aid package:*** $26,543 (excluding resources awarded to replace EFC). 29% of all full-time undergraduates had no need and received non-need-based gift aid.

GIFT AID (NEED-BASED) ***Total amount:*** $83,097,177 (7% federal, 6% state, 83% institutional, 4% external sources). ***Receiving aid:*** Freshmen: 75% (1,128); all full-time undergraduates: 66% (3,888). ***Average award:*** Freshmen: $25,353; Undergraduates: $23,681. ***Scholarships, grants, and awards:*** Federal Pell, FSEOG, state, private, college/university gift aid from institutional funds, United Negro College Fund.

GIFT AID (NON-NEED-BASED) ***Total amount:*** $27,300,548 (97% institutional, 3% external sources). ***Receiving aid:*** Freshmen: 75% (1,128). Undergraduates: 65% (3,843). ***Average award:*** Freshmen: $16,524. Undergraduates: $15,309. ***Scholarships, grants, and awards by category:*** *Academic interests/achievement:* education, general academic interests/achievements. *Creative arts/performance:* dance, music. *Special characteristics:* children and siblings of alumni, children of faculty/staff, ethnic background, general special characteristics, international students, members of minority groups, relatives of clergy, religious affiliation, veterans. ***Tuition waivers:*** Full or partial for employees or children of employees. ***ROTC:*** Army, Naval cooperative, Air Force cooperative.

LOANS ***Student loans:*** $49,065,241 (89% need-based, 11% non-need-based). 58% of past graduating class borrowed through all loan programs. *Average indebtedness per student:* $44,243. ***Average need-based loan:*** Freshmen: $3344. Undergraduates: $4251. ***Parent loans:*** $25,223,027 (93% need-based, 7% non-need-based). ***Programs:*** Federal Direct (Subsidized and Unsubsidized Stafford, PLUS), Federal Nursing, private loans.

WORK-STUDY ***Federal work-study:*** Total amount: $1,107,359; jobs available.

ATHLETIC AWARDS Total amount: $7,702,890 (46% need-based, 54% non-need-based).

APPLYING FOR FINANCIAL AID ***Required financial aid forms:*** FAFSA, institution's own form. ***Financial aid deadline:*** 5/1. ***Notification date:*** Continuous beginning 1/31. Students must reply by 5/1 or within 3 weeks of notification.

CONTACT Mr. Richard C. Esposito, Director of Financial Aid, Duquesne University, 600 Forbes Avenue, Pittsburgh, PA 15282-0299, 412-396-6607 or toll-free 800-456-0590. *Fax:* 412-396-5284. *E-mail:* esposito@duq.edu.
Website: http://www.duq.edu/.

D'YOUVILLE COLLEGE

Buffalo, NY

CONTACT Mr. Matthew R. Metz, Director of Financial Aid, D'Youville College, 320 Porter Avenue, Buffalo, NY 14201-1084, 716-829-7500 or toll-free 800-777-3921. *Fax:* 716-829-7779. *E-mail:* metzm@dyc.edu.
Website: http://www.dyc.edu/.

EAGLE GATE COLLEGE

Layton, UT

CONTACT Financial Aid Office, Eagle Gate College, 915 North 400 West, Layton, UT 84041, 801-546-7500 or toll-free 866-29-EAGLE.
Website: http://eaglegatecollege.edu/.

EAGLE GATE COLLEGE

Murray, UT

CONTACT Financial Aid Office, Eagle Gate College, 5588 South Green Street, Murray, UT 84123, 801-333-8100 or toll-free 866-29-EAGLE.
Website: http://eaglegatecollege.edu/.

EARLHAM COLLEGE

Richmond, IN

Tuition & fees: $48,091	Average undergraduate aid package: $40,435

ABOUT THE INSTITUTION Independent Society of Friends, coed. ***Awards:*** certificates, bachelor's, and master's degrees. 38 undergraduate majors. ***Total enrollment:*** 1,005. Undergraduates: 957. Freshmen: 172.

UNDERGRADUATE EXPENSES for 2020–2021 ***Tuition:*** full-time $47,106. ***Required fees:*** full-time $985. ***College room only:*** $6020. Room and board charges vary according to board plan.

FRESHMAN FINANCIAL AID (Fall 2018) 265 applied for aid; of those 93% were deemed to have need. 100% of freshmen with need received aid; of those 62% had need fully met. ***Average percent of need met:*** 92% (excluding resources awarded to replace EFC). ***Average financial aid package:*** $39,047 (excluding resources awarded to replace EFC). 9% of all full-time freshmen had no need and received non-need-based gift aid.

UNDERGRADUATE FINANCIAL AID (Fall 2018) 941 applied for aid; of those 95% were deemed to have need. 100% of undergraduates with need received aid; of those 52% had need fully met. ***Average percent of need met:*** 93% (excluding resources awarded to replace EFC). ***Average financial aid package:*** $40,435 (excluding resources awarded to replace EFC). 12% of all full-time undergraduates had no need and received non-need-based gift aid.

GIFT AID (NEED-BASED) ***Receiving aid:*** Freshmen: 91% (247); all full-time undergraduates: 88% (896). ***Average award:*** Freshmen: $34,196; Undergraduates: $34,312. ***Scholarships, grants, and awards:*** Federal Pell, FSEOG, state, private, college/university gift aid from institutional funds.

GIFT AID (NON-NEED-BASED) ***Receiving aid:*** Freshmen: 16% (44). Undergraduates: 18% (186). ***Average award:*** Freshmen: $26,285. Undergraduates: $24,726. ***Scholarships, grants, and awards by category:*** *Academic interests/achievement:* area/ethnic studies, biological sciences, business, computer science, engineering/technologies, English, foreign languages, general academic interests/achievements, humanities, mathematics, physical sciences, religion/biblical studies, social sciences. *Creative arts/performance:* applied art and design, music, theater/drama. *Special achievements/activities:* general special achievements/activities, leadership. *Special characteristics:* general special characteristics. ***Tuition waivers:*** Full or partial for employees or children of employees.

LOANS ***Student loans:*** 44% of past graduating class borrowed through all loan programs. *Average indebtedness per student:* $26,103. ***Average need-based loan:*** Freshmen: $3098. Undergraduates: $4275. ***Programs:*** Federal Direct (Subsidized and Unsubsidized Stafford, PLUS).

WORK-STUDY Federal work-study jobs available. ***State or other work-study/employment:*** Part-time jobs available.

APPLYING FOR FINANCIAL AID ***Required financial aid form:*** FAFSA. ***Notification date:*** Continuous.

CONTACT Kathy Gottschalk, Director of Financial Aid, Earlham College, National Road West, Richmond, IN 47374-4095, 765-983-1217 or toll-free 800-327-5426. *Fax:* 765-983-1299. *E-mail:* gottska@earlham.edu.
Website: http://www.earlham.edu/.

EAST CAROLINA UNIVERSITY

Greenville, NC

Tuition & fees (NC res): $7239	Average undergraduate aid package: $10,758

ABOUT THE INSTITUTION State-supported, coed. ***Awards:*** certificates, bachelor's, master's, and doctoral degrees. 74 undergraduate majors. ***Total enrollment:*** 28,651. Undergraduates: 23,081. Freshmen: 4,364. Federal methodology is used as a basis for awarding need-based institutional aid.

UNDERGRADUATE EXPENSES for 2019–2020 ***Application fee:*** $75. ***Tuition, state resident:*** full-time $4452; part-time $150 per credit hour. ***Tuition, nonresident:*** full-time $20,729; part-time $700 per credit hour. ***Required fees:*** full-time $2787; $16 per term. Full-time tuition and fees vary according to location and program. Part-time tuition and fees vary according to course load, location, and program. ***College room and board:*** $9712; ***Room only:*** $5520. Room and board charges vary according to board plan and housing facility. ***Payment plan:*** Guaranteed tuition.

FRESHMAN FINANCIAL AID (Fall 2019, est.) 3015 applied for aid; of those 70% were deemed to have need. 98% of freshmen with need received aid; of those 7% had need fully met. ***Average percent of need met:*** 56% (excluding resources awarded to replace EFC). ***Average financial aid package:*** $9468 (excluding resources awarded to replace EFC). 6% of all full-time freshmen had no need and received non-need-based gift aid.

UNDERGRADUATE FINANCIAL AID (Fall 2019, est.) 13,620 applied for aid; of those 78% were deemed to have need. 98% of undergraduates with need received aid; of those 9% had need fully met. ***Average percent of need met:*** 62% (excluding resources awarded to replace EFC). ***Average financial aid package:*** $10,758 (excluding resources awarded to replace EFC). 3% of all full-time undergraduates had no need and received non-need-based gift aid.

GIFT AID (NEED-BASED) ***Total amount:*** $79,789,564 (47% federal, 23% state, 27% institutional, 3% external sources). ***Receiving aid:*** Freshmen: 41% (1,437); all full-time undergraduates: 43% (7,759). ***Average award:*** Freshmen: $7873; Undergraduates: $7918. ***Scholarships, grants, and awards:*** Federal Pell, FSEOG, state, private, college/university gift aid from institutional funds, Federal Nursing.

GIFT AID (NON-NEED-BASED) ***Total amount:*** $945,098 (2% state, 43% institutional, 55% external sources). ***Receiving aid:*** Freshmen: 17% (602). Undergraduates: 12% (2,235). ***Average award:*** Freshmen: $1637. Undergraduates: $2770. ***Scholarships, grants, and awards by category:*** *Academic interests/achievement:* biological sciences, business, communication, computer science, education, engineering/technologies, English, foreign languages, general academic interests/achievements, health fields, home economics, humanities, international studies, library science, mathematics, military science, physical sciences, social sciences. *Creative arts/performance:* applied art and design, art/fine arts, dance, music, performing arts. *Special characteristics:* adult students, children and siblings of alumni, children of faculty/staff, ethnic background, general special characteristics, handicapped students. ***Tuition waivers:*** Full or partial for employees or children of employees. ***ROTC:*** Army, Air Force.

LOANS ***Student loans:*** $115,065,910 (96% need-based, 4% non-need-based). 68% of past graduating class borrowed through all loan programs. *Average indebtedness per student:* $23,709. ***Average need-based loan:*** Freshmen: $5651. Undergraduates: $6877. ***Parent loans:*** $25,459,617 (100% need-based). ***Programs:*** Federal Direct (Subsidized and Unsubsidized Stafford, PLUS), Federal Nursing, state.

WORK-STUDY ***Federal work-study:*** Total amount: $1,745,039; jobs available. ***State or other work-study/employment:*** Part-time jobs available.

ATHLETIC AWARDS Total amount: $7,858,771 (92% need-based, 8% non-need-based).

APPLYING FOR FINANCIAL AID ***Required financial aid form:*** FAFSA. ***Financial aid deadline (priority):*** 3/1. ***Notification date:*** 5/1. Students must reply within 3 weeks of notification.

CONTACT Ms. Julie Poorman, Director of Financial Aid, East Carolina University, East 5th Street, Greenville, NC 27858-4353, 252-328-6610. *Fax:* 252-328-4347. *E-mail:* poormanj@ecu.edu.
Website: http://www.ecu.edu/.

EAST CENTRAL UNIVERSITY

Ada, OK

Tuition & fees (area res): $7052	Average undergraduate aid package: $6222

ABOUT THE INSTITUTION State-supported, coed. ***Awards:*** certificates, bachelor's, and master's degrees. 83 undergraduate majors. ***Total enrollment:*** 3,613. Undergraduates: 2,981. Freshmen: 494. Federal methodology is used as a basis for awarding need-based institutional aid.

UNDERGRADUATE EXPENSES for 2019–2020 ***Application fee:*** $25. ***Tuition, area resident:*** full-time $5648; part-time $276 per credit hour. ***Tuition, state resident:*** full-time $5648; part-time $276 per credit hour. ***Tuition, nonresident:*** full-time $15,008; part-time $633 per credit hour. ***Required fees:*** full-time $1404; $46.80 per semester hour. ***College room and board:*** $7072; ***Room only:*** $3662. Room and board charges vary according to board plan. ***Payment plan:*** Guaranteed tuition.

FRESHMAN FINANCIAL AID (Fall 2018) 401 applied for aid; of those 83% were deemed to have need. 100% of freshmen with need received aid; of those 28% had need fully met. ***Average financial aid package:*** $5726 (excluding resources awarded to replace EFC). 8% of all full-time freshmen had no need and received non-need-based gift aid.

UNDERGRADUATE FINANCIAL AID (Fall 2018) 1,958 applied for aid; of those 85% were deemed to have need. 100% of undergraduates with need received aid. ***Average financial aid package:*** $6222 (excluding resources awarded to replace EFC). 5% of all full-time undergraduates had no need and received non-need-based gift aid.

GIFT AID (NEED-BASED) ***Total amount:*** $11,213,089 (57% federal, 27% state, 16% external sources). ***Receiving aid:*** Freshmen: 58% (251); all full-time undergraduates: 49% (1,199). ***Average award:*** Freshmen: $4824; Undergraduates: $4508. ***Scholarships, grants, and awards:*** Federal Pell, FSEOG, state, private, college/university gift aid from institutional funds.

GIFT AID (NON-NEED-BASED) ***Total amount:*** $1,660,645 (9% state, 72% institutional, 19% external sources). ***Receiving aid:*** Freshmen: 22% (93). Undergraduates: 17% (413). ***Average award:*** Freshmen: $2267. Undergraduates: $3029. ***Scholarships, grants, and awards by category:*** *Creative arts/performance:* music, performing arts, theater/drama. *Special characteristics:* children of faculty/staff, general special characteristics, international students, members of minority groups, out-of-state students, veterans. ***Tuition waivers:*** Full or partial for employees or children of employees.

LOANS ***Student loans:*** $6,328,425 (100% need-based). 17% of past graduating class borrowed through all loan programs. *Average indebtedness per student:* $21,665. ***Average need-based loan:*** Freshmen: $2945. Undergraduates: $4049. ***Parent loans:*** $2,583,750 (100% need-based). ***Programs:*** Federal Direct (Subsidized and Unsubsidized Stafford, PLUS).

WORK-STUDY ***Federal work-study:*** Total amount: $386,888; jobs available. ***State or other work-study/employment:*** Part-time jobs available.

ATHLETIC AWARDS Total amount: $1,229,783 (100% non-need-based).

APPLYING FOR FINANCIAL AID ***Required financial aid form:*** FAFSA. ***Financial aid deadline (priority):*** 3/1. ***Notification date:*** Continuous beginning 4/15. Students must reply within 6 weeks of notification.

CONTACT Becky Isaacs, Director of Financial Aid, East Central University, 1100 East 14th Street, Ada, OK 74820-6999, 580-332-8000 Ext. 242. *E-mail:* bisaacs@ecok.edu.
Website: http://www.ecok.edu/.

EASTERN CONNECTICUT STATE UNIVERSITY

Willimantic, CT

CONTACT Jennifer Horner, Director of Financial Aid, Eastern Connecticut State University, 83 Windham Street, Wood SSC, Willimantic, CT 06226-2295, 860-465-5775. *E-mail:* hornerje@easternct.edu.
Website: http://www.easternct.edu/.

EASTERN ILLINOIS UNIVERSITY

Charleston, IL

Tuition & fees (IL res): $11,989	Average undergraduate aid package: $14,088

ABOUT THE INSTITUTION State-supported, coed. ***Awards:*** certificates, bachelor's, and master's degrees. 58 undergraduate majors. ***Total enrollment:*** 7,806. Undergraduates: 6,229. Freshmen: 925. Federal methodology is used as a basis for awarding need-based institutional aid.

UNDERGRADUATE EXPENSES for 2019–2020 ***Application fee:*** $30. ***Tuition, state resident:*** full-time $9060; part-time $302 per credit hour. ***Tuition, nonresident:*** full-time $11,340; part-time $378 per credit hour. ***Required fees:*** full-time $2929; $115.50 per credit hour. Full-time tuition and fees vary according to course load and program. Part-time tuition and fees vary according to course load and program. ***College room and board:*** $10,030. Room and board charges vary according to board plan and housing facility. ***Payment plan:*** Guaranteed tuition.

FRESHMAN FINANCIAL AID (Fall 2019, est.) 837 applied for aid; of those 84% were deemed to have need. 100% of freshmen with need received aid; of those 8% had need fully met. ***Average percent of need met:*** 59% (excluding resources awarded to replace EFC). ***Average financial aid package:*** $14,985 (excluding resources awarded to replace EFC). 12% of all full-time freshmen had no need and received non-need-based gift aid.

UNDERGRADUATE FINANCIAL AID (Fall 2019, est.) 3,485 applied for aid; of those 83% were deemed to have need. 100% of undergraduates with need received aid; of those 9% had need fully met. ***Average percent of need met:*** 58% (excluding resources awarded to replace EFC). ***Average financial aid package:*** $14,088 (excluding resources awarded to replace EFC). 12% of all full-time undergraduates had no need and received non-need-based gift aid.

GIFT AID (NEED-BASED) ***Total amount:*** $27,189,267 (38% federal, 37% state, 19% institutional, 6% external sources). ***Receiving aid:*** Freshmen: 66% (578); all full-

time undergraduates: 57% (2,275). ***Average award:*** Freshmen: $10,633; Undergraduates: $9705. ***Scholarships, grants, and awards:*** Federal Pell, FSEOG, state, private, college/university gift aid from institutional funds.

GIFT AID (NON-NEED-BASED) ***Total amount:*** $2,595,483 (4% federal, 8% state, 66% institutional, 22% external sources). ***Receiving aid:*** Freshmen: 51% (445). Undergraduates: 40% (1,607). ***Average award:*** Freshmen: $4787. Undergraduates: $4211. ***Scholarships, grants, and awards by category:*** *Academic interests/achievement:* biological sciences, business, communication, computer science, education, engineering/technologies, English, foreign languages, general academic interests/achievements, health fields, home economics, humanities, international studies, mathematics, physical sciences, premedicine, social sciences. *Creative arts/performance:* applied art and design, art/fine arts, cinema/film/broadcasting, creative writing, debating, general creative arts/performance, journalism/publications, music, performing arts, theater/drama. *Special achievements/activities:* general special achievements/activities, leadership. ***Tuition waivers:*** Full or partial for employees or children of employees, senior citizens. ***ROTC:*** Army.

LOANS ***Student loans:*** $21,090,493 (85% need-based, 15% non-need-based). 77% of past graduating class borrowed through all loan programs. *Average indebtedness per student:* $30,695. ***Average need-based loan:*** Freshmen: $3335. Undergraduates: $4233. ***Parent loans:*** $3,250,180 (76% need-based, 24% non-need-based). ***Programs:*** Federal Direct (Subsidized and Unsubsidized Stafford, PLUS).

WORK-STUDY ***Federal work-study:*** Total amount: $332,347; 157 jobs averaging $786. ***State or other work-study/employment:*** 1,106 part-time jobs averaging $1249.

ATHLETIC AWARDS Total amount: $2,617,626 (57% need-based, 43% non-need-based).

APPLYING FOR FINANCIAL AID ***Required financial aid form:*** FAFSA. ***Financial aid deadline (priority):*** 3/1. ***Notification date:*** Continuous beginning 3/1. Students must reply within 2 weeks of notification.

CONTACT Mandi Starwalt, Director of Financial Aid and Scholarships, Eastern Illinois University, 600 Lincoln Avenue, Charleston, IL 61920, 217-581-7812 or toll-free 877-581-2348. *Fax:* 217-581-6422. *E-mail:* finaid@eiu.edu.
Website: http://www.eiu.edu/.

EASTERN KENTUCKY UNIVERSITY

Richmond, KY

Tuition & fees (area res): $9806	Average undergraduate aid package: $12,422

ABOUT THE INSTITUTION State-supported, coed. ***Awards:*** certificates, associate, bachelor's, master's, and doctoral degrees. 112 undergraduate majors. ***Total enrollment:*** 14,980. Undergraduates: 12,662. Freshmen: 2,345. Federal methodology is used as a basis for awarding need-based institutional aid.

UNDERGRADUATE EXPENSES for 2020–2021 ***Application fee:*** $35. ***Tuition, area resident:*** full-time $9266; part-time $386 per credit hour. ***Tuition, state resident:*** full-time $9266. ***Tuition, nonresident:*** full-time $10,173; part-time $806 per credit hour. ***Required fees:*** full-time $540. ***College room and board:*** $10,173.

FRESHMAN FINANCIAL AID (Fall 2019, est.) 2162 applied for aid; of those 82% were deemed to have need. 100% of freshmen with need received aid; of those 32% had need fully met. ***Average percent of need met:*** 77% (excluding resources awarded to replace EFC). ***Average financial aid package:*** $13,414 (excluding resources awarded to replace EFC). 15% of all full-time freshmen had no need and received non-need-based gift aid.

UNDERGRADUATE FINANCIAL AID (Fall 2019, est.) 8,314 applied for aid; of those 85% were deemed to have need. 98% of undergraduates with need received aid; of those 28% had need fully met. ***Average percent of need met:*** 76% (excluding resources awarded to replace EFC). ***Average financial aid package:*** $12,422 (excluding resources awarded to replace EFC). 15% of all full-time undergraduates had no need and received non-need-based gift aid.

GIFT AID (NEED-BASED) ***Total amount:*** $58,938,934 (40% federal, 25% state, 33% institutional, 2% external sources). ***Receiving aid:*** Freshmen: 48% (1,094); all full-time undergraduates: 45% (4,409). ***Average award:*** Freshmen: $6667; Undergraduates: $6427. ***Scholarships, grants, and awards:*** Federal Pell, FSEOG, state, private, college/university gift aid from institutional funds, Federal Nursing.

GIFT AID (NON-NEED-BASED) ***Total amount:*** $12,982,793 (25% state, 71% institutional, 4% external sources). ***Receiving aid:*** Freshmen: 74% (1,706). Undergraduates: 51% (5,007). ***Average award:*** Freshmen: $6348. Undergraduates: $5968. ***Scholarships, grants, and awards by category:*** *Academic interests/achievement:* general academic interests/achievements. *Creative arts/performance:* music. *Special achievements/activities:* cheerleading/drum major. *Special characteristics:* children and siblings of alumni, children of faculty/staff, members of minority groups. ***ROTC:*** Army, Air Force cooperative.

LOANS ***Student loans:*** $51,919,954 (87% need-based, 13% non-need-based). 67% of past graduating class borrowed through all loan programs. *Average indebtedness per student:* $27,465. ***Average need-based loan:*** Freshmen: $3031. Undergraduates: $3974. ***Parent loans:*** $7,925,807 (84% need-based, 16% non-need-based). ***Programs:*** Federal Direct (Subsidized and Unsubsidized Stafford, PLUS).

WORK-STUDY ***Federal work-study:*** Total amount: $4,419,259; jobs available. ***State or other work-study/employment:*** Total amount: $3,218,437 (100% non-need-based). Part-time jobs available.

ATHLETIC AWARDS Total amount: $4,906,158 (49% need-based, 51% non-need-based).

APPLYING FOR FINANCIAL AID ***Required financial aid form:*** FAFSA. ***Financial aid deadline (priority):*** 11/1. ***Notification date:*** Continuous beginning 2/1.

CONTACT Financial Aid Office, Eastern Kentucky University, 521 Lancaster Avenue, Richmond, KY 40475-3102, 859-622-1000 or toll-free 800-465-9191.
Website: http://www.eku.edu/.

EASTERN MENNONITE UNIVERSITY

Harrisonburg, VA

Tuition & fees: $39,220	Average undergraduate aid package: $33,326

ABOUT THE INSTITUTION Independent Mennonite, coed. ***Awards:*** certificates, associate, bachelor's, master's, and doctoral degrees. 41 undergraduate majors. ***Total enrollment:*** 1,360. Undergraduates: 980. Freshmen: 204. Federal methodology is used as a basis for awarding need-based institutional aid.

UNDERGRADUATE EXPENSES for 2020–2021 ***Application fee:*** $25. ***Comprehensive fee:*** $50,950 includes full-time tuition ($38,850), mandatory fees ($370), and room and board ($11,730). ***College room only:*** $6760. Room and board charges vary according to board plan and housing facility. ***Part-time tuition:*** $1430 per credit hour. ***Part-time fees:*** $18 per credit hour. Part-time tuition and fees vary according to course load.

FRESHMAN FINANCIAL AID (Fall 2019, est.) 190 applied for aid; of those 95% were deemed to have need. 100% of freshmen with need received aid; of those 18% had need fully met. ***Average percent of need met:*** 79% (excluding resources awarded to replace EFC). ***Average financial aid package:*** $37,852 (excluding resources awarded to replace EFC). 10% of all full-time freshmen had no need and received non-need-based gift aid.

UNDERGRADUATE FINANCIAL AID (Fall 2019, est.) 775 applied for aid; of those 93% were deemed to have need. 100% of undergraduates with need received aid; of those 18% had need fully met. ***Average percent of need met:*** 69% (excluding resources awarded to replace EFC). ***Average financial aid package:*** $33,326 (excluding resources awarded to replace EFC). 19% of all full-time undergraduates had no need and received non-need-based gift aid.

GIFT AID (NEED-BASED) ***Total amount:*** $15,608,276 (12% federal, 8% state, 75% institutional, 5% external sources). ***Receiving aid:*** Freshmen: 87% (177); all full-time undergraduates: 73% (691). ***Average award:*** Freshmen: $28,350; Undergraduates: $21,552. ***Scholarships, grants, and awards:*** Federal Pell, FSEOG, state, private, college/university gift aid from institutional funds, Federal Nursing.

GIFT AID (NON-NEED-BASED) ***Total amount:*** $4,534,942 (7% state, 83% institutional, 10% external sources). ***Receiving aid:*** Freshmen: 12% (25). Undergraduates: 9% (83). ***Average award:*** Freshmen: $21,552. Undergraduates: $17,264. ***Scholarships, grants, and awards by category:*** *Academic interests/achievement:* biological sciences, business, education, engineering/technologies, English, foreign languages, general academic interests/achievements, humanities, mathematics, physical sciences, premedicine, religion/biblical studies, social sciences. *Creative arts/performance:* art/fine arts, music. *Special achievements/activities:* general special achievements/activities, religious involvement. *Special characteristics:* children and siblings of alumni, children of faculty/staff, ethnic background, general special characteristics, international students, religious affiliation. ***Tuition waivers:*** Full or partial for employees or children of employees.

LOANS ***Student loans:*** $7,534,097 (82% need-based, 18% non-need-based). 73% of past graduating class borrowed through all loan programs. *Average indebtedness per student:* $43,893. ***Average need-based loan:*** Freshmen: $5349. Undergraduates: $8217. ***Parent loans:*** $1,860,099 (75% need-based, 25% non-need-based). ***Programs:*** Federal Direct (Subsidized and Unsubsidized Stafford, PLUS), Perkins, Federal Nursing.

WORK-STUDY ***Federal work-study:*** Total amount: $238,626; 243 jobs averaging $1043. ***State or other work-study/employment:*** Total amount: $50,279 (100% need-based). 45 part-time jobs averaging $1196.

APPLYING FOR FINANCIAL AID ***Required financial aid forms:*** FAFSA, state aid form. ***Financial aid deadline (priority):*** 4/15. ***Notification date:*** Continuous beginning 2/1. Students must reply within 5 weeks of notification.

CONTACT Ms. Michele Hensley, Director of Financial Assistance, Eastern Mennonite University, 1200 Park Road, Harrisonburg, VA 22802-2462, 540-432-4138 or toll-free 800-368-2665. *Fax:* 540-432-4081. *E-mail:* michele.hensley@emu.edu.
Website: http://www.emu.edu/.

EASTERN MICHIGAN UNIVERSITY

Ypsilanti, MI

Tuition & fees (area res): $11,128	Average undergraduate aid package: $10,477

ABOUT THE INSTITUTION State-supported, coed. ***Awards:*** certificates, bachelor's, master's, and doctoral degrees. 131 undergraduate majors. ***Total enrollment:*** 18,833. Undergraduates: 15,725. Freshmen: 2,404. Federal methodology is used as a basis for awarding need-based institutional aid.

UNDERGRADUATE EXPENSES for 2019–2020 ***Application fee:*** $35. ***Tuition, area resident:*** full-time $11,128; part-time $414 per credit hour. ***Tuition, state resident:*** full-time $11,128; part-time $414 per credit hour. ***Tuition, nonresident:*** full-time $27,170; part-time $414 per credit hour. ***College room and board:*** $10,248; ***Room only:*** $4434.

FRESHMAN FINANCIAL AID (Fall 2018) 2157 applied for aid; of those 81% were deemed to have need. 99% of freshmen with need received aid; of those 8% had need fully met. ***Average percent of need met:*** 41% (excluding resources awarded to replace EFC). ***Average financial aid package:*** $11,093 (excluding resources awarded to replace EFC). 23% of all full-time freshmen had no need and received non-need-based gift aid.

UNDERGRADUATE FINANCIAL AID (Fall 2018) 9,206 applied for aid; of those 85% were deemed to have need. 98% of undergraduates with need received aid; of those 5% had need fully met. ***Average percent of need met:*** 42% (excluding resources awarded to replace EFC). ***Average financial aid package:*** $10,477 (excluding resources awarded to replace EFC). 19% of all full-time undergraduates had no need and received non-need-based gift aid.

GIFT AID (NEED-BASED) ***Receiving aid:*** Freshmen: 51% (1,202); all full-time undergraduates: 47% (5,373). ***Average award:*** Freshmen: $6705; Undergraduates: $6191. ***Scholarships, grants, and awards:*** Federal Pell, FSEOG, state, private, college/university gift aid from institutional funds, Federal Nursing.

GIFT AID (NON-NEED-BASED) ***Receiving aid:*** Freshmen: 56% (1,336). Undergraduates: 36% (4,067). ***Average award:*** Freshmen: $5320. Undergraduates: $5399. ***Scholarships, grants, and awards by category:*** *Academic interests/achievement:* 6,033 awards ($26,404,267 total): agriculture, architecture, biological sciences, business, communication, computer science, education, engineering/technologies, English, foreign languages, general academic interests/achievements, health fields, home economics, humanities, mathematics, physical sciences, religion/biblical studies, social sciences. *Creative arts/performance:* 136 awards ($128,767 total): applied art and design, art/fine arts, cinema/film/broadcasting, creative writing, dance, debating, general creative arts/performance, music, performing arts, theater/drama. *Special achievements/activities:* 93 awards ($114,984 total): general special achievements/activities, leadership, memberships, religious involvement. *Special characteristics:* 151 awards ($1,906,710 total): children and siblings of alumni, ethnic background, international students, members of minority groups, out-of-state students, previous college experience, religious affiliation. ***ROTC:*** Army, Naval cooperative, Air Force cooperative.

LOANS ***Student loans:*** 67% of past graduating class borrowed through all loan programs. *Average indebtedness per student:* $27,475. ***Average need-based loan:*** Freshmen: $3130. Undergraduates: $4066. ***Programs:*** Federal Direct (Subsidized and Unsubsidized Stafford, PLUS), Perkins, private loans.

WORK-STUDY ***Federal work-study:*** 505 jobs averaging $2289.

APPLYING FOR FINANCIAL AID ***Required financial aid form:*** FAFSA. ***Financial aid deadline:*** Continuous. ***Notification date:*** Continuous.

CONTACT Donna Holubik, Director of Financial Aid, Eastern Michigan University, 403 Pierce Hall, Ypsilanti, MI 48197, 734-487-1048 or toll-free 800-GO TO EMU. *Fax:* 734-487-4281. *E-mail:* dholubik@emich.edu.
Website: http://www.emich.edu/.

EASTERN NAZARENE COLLEGE

Quincy, MA

CONTACT Lisa Seals, Interim Director of Financial Aid, Eastern Nazarene College, 23 East Elm Avenue, Quincy, MA 02170, 617-745-3869 or toll-free 800-88-ENC88. *Fax:* 617-745-3992. *E-mail:* lisa.seals@enc .edu.
Website: http://www.enc.edu/.

EASTERN NEW MEXICO UNIVERSITY

Portales, NM

Tuition & fees (NM res): $6528	Average undergraduate aid package: $12,830

ABOUT THE INSTITUTION State-supported, coed. ***Awards:*** certificates, associate, bachelor's, and master's degrees. 52 undergraduate majors. ***Total enrollment:*** 1,221. Undergraduates: 4,473. Freshmen: 558. Federal methodology is used as a basis for awarding need-based institutional aid.

UNDERGRADUATE EXPENSES for 2020–2021 ***One-time required fee:*** $95. ***Tuition, state resident:*** full-time $4074; part-time $272 per credit hour. ***Tuition, nonresident:*** full-time $6114; part-time $357 per credit hour. ***Required fees:*** full-time $2454; $102.25 per credit hour. ***College room and board:*** $7526; ***Room only:*** $3672.

FRESHMAN FINANCIAL AID (Fall 2018) 532 applied for aid; of those 77% were deemed to have need. 99% of freshmen with need received aid; of those 23% had need fully met. ***Average percent of need met:*** 81% (excluding resources awarded to replace EFC). ***Average financial aid package:*** $12,651 (excluding resources awarded to replace EFC). 6% of all full-time freshmen had no need and received non-need-based gift aid.

UNDERGRADUATE FINANCIAL AID (Fall 2018) 2,079 applied for aid; of those 79% were deemed to have need. 98% of undergraduates with need received aid; of those 21% had need fully met. ***Average percent of need met:*** 80% (excluding resources awarded to replace EFC). ***Average financial aid package:*** $12,830 (excluding resources awarded to replace EFC). 5% of all full-time undergraduates had no need and received non-need-based gift aid.

GIFT AID (NEED-BASED) ***Total amount:*** $12,195,540 (54% federal, 40% state, 6% institutional). ***Receiving aid:*** Freshmen: 72% (398); all full-time undergraduates: 63% (1,509). ***Average award:*** Freshmen: $7423; Undergraduates: $6418. ***Scholarships, grants, and awards:*** Federal Pell, FSEOG, state, private, college/university gift aid from institutional funds.

GIFT AID (NON-NEED-BASED) ***Total amount:*** $1,068,244 (100% external sources). ***Receiving aid:*** Freshmen: 23% (128). Undergraduates: 15% (349). ***Average award:*** Freshmen: $2310. Undergraduates: $2379. ***Scholarships, grants, and awards by category:*** *Academic interests/achievement:* agriculture, biological sciences, business, communication, computer science, education, engineering/technologies, English, foreign languages, general academic interests/achievements, health fields, home economics, humanities, mathematics, military science, physical sciences, premedicine, religion/biblical studies, social sciences. *Creative arts/performance:* applied art and design, art/fine arts, cinema/film/broadcasting, creative writing, dance, debating, general creative arts/performance, journalism/publications, music, performing arts, theater/drama. *Special achievements/activities:* community service, general special achievements/activities, hobbies/interests, leadership, memberships, rodeo. *Special characteristics:* children and siblings of alumni, ethnic background, first-generation college students, general special characteristics, international students, members of minority groups, out-of-state students, veterans.

LOANS ***Student loans:*** $7,762,057 (44% need-based, 56% non-need-based). 48% of past graduating class borrowed through all loan programs. *Average indebtedness per student:* $20,497. ***Average need-based loan:*** Freshmen: $2779. Undergrad-

uates: $3592. ***Parent loans:*** $246,776 (100% non-need-based). ***Programs:*** Federal Direct (Subsidized and Unsubsidized Stafford, PLUS), Perkins, state, college/university.
WORK-STUDY ***Federal work-study:*** Total amount: $445,753; jobs available. ***State or other work-study/employment:*** Total amount: $125,457 (67% need-based, 33% non-need-based). Part-time jobs available.
ATHLETIC AWARDS Total amount: $1,501,242 (100% non-need-based).
APPLYING FOR FINANCIAL AID ***Required financial aid form:*** FAFSA. ***Financial aid deadline:*** Continuous. ***Notification date:*** Continuous beginning 3/1.
CONTACT Mr. Brent Small, Director of Financial Aid, Eastern New Mexico University, Station 20, 1500 South Avenue K, Portales, NM 88130, 575-562-2194 or toll-free 800-367-3668. *Fax:* 575-562-2198. *E-mail:* brent.small@enmu.edu.
Website: http://www.enmu.edu/.

EASTERN OREGON UNIVERSITY

La Grande, OR

Tuition & fees: N/R | **Average undergraduate aid package: $10,357**

ABOUT THE INSTITUTION State-supported, coed. ***Awards:*** certificates, associate, bachelor's, and master's degrees. 23 undergraduate majors. ***Total enrollment:*** 3,067. Undergraduates: 2,867. Freshmen: 330. Federal methodology is used as a basis for awarding need-based institutional aid.
FRESHMAN FINANCIAL AID (Fall 2018) 292 applied for aid; of those 77% were deemed to have need. 99% of freshmen with need received aid; of those 19% had need fully met. ***Average percent of need met:*** 61% (excluding resources awarded to replace EFC). ***Average financial aid package:*** $10,967 (excluding resources awarded to replace EFC). 20% of all full-time freshmen had no need and received non-need-based gift aid.
UNDERGRADUATE FINANCIAL AID (Fall 2018) 1,544 applied for aid; of those 90% were deemed to have need. 92% of undergraduates with need received aid; of those 14% had need fully met. ***Average percent of need met:*** 57% (excluding resources awarded to replace EFC). ***Average financial aid package:*** $10,357 (excluding resources awarded to replace EFC). 9% of all full-time undergraduates had no need and received non-need-based gift aid.
GIFT AID (NEED-BASED) ***Receiving aid:*** Freshmen: 70% (212); all full-time undergraduates: 70% (1,240). ***Average award:*** Freshmen: $7746; Undergraduates: $8368. ***Scholarships, grants, and awards:*** Federal Pell, FSEOG, state, private, college/university gift aid from institutional funds.
GIFT AID (NON-NEED-BASED) ***Receiving aid:*** Freshmen: 61% (184). Undergraduates: 39% (691). ***Average award:*** Freshmen: $2528. Undergraduates: $2390. ***Scholarships, grants, and awards by category:*** *Academic interests/achievement:* computer science, education, engineering/technologies, general academic interests/achievements, mathematics. *Creative arts/performance:* applied art and design, art/fine arts, general creative arts/performance, music, theater/drama. *Special achievements/activities:* general special achievements/activities, leadership. *Special characteristics:* ethnic background, local/state students, members of minority groups. ***ROTC:*** Army.
LOANS ***Student loans:*** 68% of past graduating class borrowed through all loan programs. *Average indebtedness per student:* $25,756. ***Average need-based loan:*** Freshmen: $3139. Undergraduates: $4170. ***Programs:*** Federal Direct (Subsidized and Unsubsidized Stafford, PLUS), Perkins.
WORK-STUDY ***Federal work-study:*** 165 jobs averaging $2138.
APPLYING FOR FINANCIAL AID ***Required financial aid form:*** FAFSA. ***Financial aid deadline:*** Continuous. ***Notification date:*** Continuous. Students must reply within 4 weeks of notification.
CONTACT Financial Aid Office, Eastern Oregon University, One University Boulevard, Inlow Hall, Suite 104, La Grande, OR 97850, 800-4528639 or toll-free 800-452-8639. *Fax:* 541-9623661. *E-mail:* fao@eou.edu.
Website: http://www.eou.edu/.

EASTERN UNIVERSITY

St. Davids, PA

Tuition & fees: $34,706 | **Average undergraduate aid package: $24,846**

ABOUT THE INSTITUTION Independent Christian, coed. ***Awards:*** certificates, diplomas, associate, bachelor's, master's, and doctoral degrees. 40 undergraduate majors. ***Total enrollment:*** 3,100. Undergraduates: 1,752. Freshmen: 357. Both federal and institutional methodology are used as a basis for awarding need-based institutional aid.
UNDERGRADUATE EXPENSES for 2020–2021 ***Application fee:*** $35. ***One-time required fee:*** $75. ***Comprehensive fee:*** $46,530 includes full-time tuition ($34,136), mandatory fees ($570), and room and board ($11,824). ***College room only:*** $6290. Full-time tuition and fees vary according to course load, degree level, and program. Room and board charges vary according to housing facility. ***Part-time tuition:*** $748 per credit. ***Part-time fees:*** $285 per term. Part-time tuition and fees vary according to course load, degree level, and program.
FRESHMAN FINANCIAL AID (Fall 2018) 341 applied for aid; of those 90% were deemed to have need. 100% of freshmen with need received aid; of those 23% had need fully met. ***Average percent of need met:*** 83% (excluding resources awarded to replace EFC). ***Average financial aid package:*** $26,796 (excluding resources awarded to replace EFC). 9% of all full-time freshmen had no need and received non-need-based gift aid.
UNDERGRADUATE FINANCIAL AID (Fall 2018) 1,299 applied for aid; of those 92% were deemed to have need. 100% of undergraduates with need received aid; of those 23% had need fully met. ***Average percent of need met:*** 81% (excluding resources awarded to replace EFC). ***Average financial aid package:*** $24,846 (excluding resources awarded to replace EFC). 6% of all full-time undergraduates had no need and received non-need-based gift aid.
GIFT AID (NEED-BASED) ***Receiving aid:*** Freshmen: 77% (279); all full-time undergraduates: 71% (1,032). ***Average award:*** Freshmen: $9121; Undergraduates: $8460. ***Scholarships, grants, and awards:*** Federal Pell, FSEOG, state, private, college/university gift aid from institutional funds.
GIFT AID (NON-NEED-BASED) ***Receiving aid:*** Freshmen: 83% (301). Undergraduates: 75% (1,093). ***Average award:*** Freshmen: $12,548. Undergraduates: $13,282. ***Scholarships, grants, and awards by category:*** *Academic interests/achievement:* 84 awards ($158,000 total): engineering/technologies. *Creative arts/performance:* 35 awards ($342,891 total): music. *Special achievements/activities:* 453 awards ($910,516 total): leadership. *Special characteristics:* 291 awards ($570,717 total): children and siblings of alumni, children of faculty/staff, international students, out-of-state students, previous college experience, relatives of clergy, siblings of current students, veterans, veterans' children. ***Tuition waivers:*** Full or partial for children of alumni, employees or children of employees. ***ROTC:*** Army cooperative, Air Force cooperative.
LOANS ***Student loans:*** 80% of past graduating class borrowed through all loan programs. *Average indebtedness per student:* $40,488. ***Average need-based loan:*** Freshmen: $3465. Undergraduates: $4172. ***Programs:*** Federal Direct (Subsidized and Unsubsidized Stafford, PLUS).
WORK-STUDY ***Federal work-study:*** 318 jobs averaging $1059. ***State or other work-study/employment:*** Part-time jobs available.
APPLYING FOR FINANCIAL AID ***Required financial aid form:*** FAFSA. ***Financial aid deadline:*** Continuous. ***Notification date:*** Continuous.
CONTACT Mrs. Andrea L. Ruth, Director of Financial Aid, Eastern University, 1300 Eagle Road, St. Davids, PA 19087-3696, 610-225-5102 or toll-free 800-452-0996. *Fax:* 610-225-5651. *E-mail:* finaid@eastern.edu.
Website: http://www.eastern.edu/.

EASTERN WASHINGTON UNIVERSITY

Cheney, WA

Tuition & fees (area res): $7461 | **Average undergraduate aid package: $13,326**

ABOUT THE INSTITUTION State-supported, coed. ***Awards:*** certificates, bachelor's, master's, and doctoral degrees. 93 undergraduate majors. ***Total enrollment:*** 12,325. Undergraduates: 10,671. Freshmen: 1,810. Federal methodology is used as a basis for awarding need-based institutional aid.

UNDERGRADUATE EXPENSES for 2019–2020 ***Application fee:*** $60. ***Tuition, area resident:*** full-time $6522. ***Tuition, state resident:*** full-time $6522; part-time $218 per credit hour. ***Tuition, nonresident:*** full-time $24,018; part-time $801 per credit hour. ***Required fees:*** full-time $939. ***College room and board:*** $12,708; ***Room only:*** $7260.

FRESHMAN FINANCIAL AID (Fall 2018) 1574 applied for aid; of those 61% were deemed to have need. 100% of freshmen with need received aid; of those 7% had need fully met. ***Average percent of need met:*** 83% (excluding resources awarded to replace EFC). ***Average financial aid package:*** $12,419 (excluding resources awarded to replace EFC). 18% of all full-time freshmen had no need and received non-need-based gift aid.

UNDERGRADUATE FINANCIAL AID (Fall 2018) 7,445 applied for aid; of those 69% were deemed to have need. 100% of undergraduates with need received aid; of those 7% had need fully met. ***Average percent of need met:*** 61% (excluding resources awarded to replace EFC). ***Average financial aid package:*** $13,326 (excluding resources awarded to replace EFC). 6% of all full-time undergraduates had no need and received non-need-based gift aid.

GIFT AID (NEED-BASED) ***Receiving aid:*** Freshmen: 47% (817); all full-time undergraduates: 41% (4,358). ***Average award:*** Freshmen: $8284; Undergraduates: $8616. ***Scholarships, grants, and awards:*** Federal Pell, FSEOG, state, private, college/university gift aid from institutional funds.

GIFT AID (NON-NEED-BASED) ***Receiving aid:*** Freshmen: 33% (569). Undergraduates: 12% (1,327). ***Average award:*** Freshmen: $2654. Undergraduates: $3641. ***Scholarships, grants, and awards by category:*** *Academic interests/achievement:* 697 awards ($1,305,789 total): area/ethnic studies, biological sciences, business, communication, computer science, education, engineering/technologies, English, foreign languages, general academic interests/achievements, home economics, humanities, international studies, mathematics, military science, physical sciences, premedicine, social sciences. *Creative arts/performance:* applied art and design, cinema/film/broadcasting, creative writing, journalism/publications, music, theater/drama. *Special characteristics:* adult students, children and siblings of alumni, children of union members/company employees, ethnic background, first-generation college students, handicapped students, local/state students, married students, out-of-state students, spouses of deceased or disabled public servants, veterans. ***ROTC:*** Army.

LOANS ***Student loans:*** 50% of past graduating class borrowed through all loan programs. *Average indebtedness per student:* $23,301. ***Average need-based loan:*** Freshmen: $3013. Undergraduates: $3952. ***Programs:*** Federal Direct (Subsidized and Unsubsidized Stafford, PLUS), credit-based education loans from commercial lenders.

WORK-STUDY ***Federal work-study:*** 199 jobs averaging $2857. ***State or other work-study/employment:*** 151 part-time jobs averaging $2977.

APPLYING FOR FINANCIAL AID ***Required financial aid forms:*** FAFSA, Washington Application for Student Financial Aid (WASFA) for undocumented state residents and DACA students only. ***Notification date:*** Continuous. Students must reply within 4 weeks of notification.

CONTACT Ms. Samantha Hennessey, Customer Service Supervisor - Financial Aid and Scholarships, Eastern Washington University, 102 Sutton Hall, Cheney, WA 99004-2447, 509-359-2314. *Fax:* 509-359-4330. *E-mail:* shennessey@ewu.edu.
Website: http://www.ewu.edu/.

EAST STROUDSBURG UNIVERSITY OF PENNSYLVANIA

East Stroudsburg, PA

Tuition & fees (PA res): $10,688	Average undergraduate aid package: $9194

ABOUT THE INSTITUTION State-supported, coed. ***Awards:*** certificates, bachelor's, master's, and doctoral degrees. 44 undergraduate majors. ***Total enrollment:*** 6,425. Undergraduates: 5,713. Freshmen: 1,135.

UNDERGRADUATE EXPENSES for 2019–2020 ***Application fee:*** $25. ***Tuition, state resident:*** full-time $7716; part-time $322 per credit hour. ***Tuition, nonresident:*** full-time $19,290; part-time $805 per credit hour. ***Required fees:*** full-time $2972; $155 per credit hour. Full-time tuition and fees vary according to course load, location, and program. Part-time tuition and fees vary according to location and program. ***College room and board:*** $11,760; ***Room only:*** $8700. Room and board charges vary according to board plan and housing facility. ***Payment plan:*** Guaranteed tuition.

FRESHMAN FINANCIAL AID (Fall 2018) 1221 applied for aid; of those 83% were deemed to have need. 97% of freshmen with need received aid; of those 46% had need fully met. ***Average percent of need met:*** 51% (excluding resources awarded to replace EFC). ***Average financial aid package:*** $8677 (excluding resources awarded to replace EFC).

UNDERGRADUATE FINANCIAL AID (Fall 2018) 3,824 applied for aid; of those 85% were deemed to have need. 97% of undergraduates with need received aid; of those 46% had need fully met. ***Average percent of need met:*** 63% (excluding resources awarded to replace EFC). ***Average financial aid package:*** $9194 (excluding resources awarded to replace EFC).

GIFT AID (NEED-BASED) ***Total amount:*** $37,296,795 (71% federal, 14% state, 15% institutional). ***Receiving aid:*** Freshmen: 73% (929); all full-time undergraduates: 52% (2,998). ***Average award:*** Freshmen: $7803; Undergraduates: $8634. ***Scholarships, grants, and awards:*** Federal Pell, FSEOG, state, private, college/university gift aid from institutional funds.

GIFT AID (NON-NEED-BASED) ***Total amount:*** $1,182,620 (100% external sources). ***Tuition waivers:*** Full or partial for employees or children of employees, senior citizens. ***ROTC:*** Army, Air Force cooperative.

LOANS ***Student loans:*** $51,432,932 (27% need-based, 73% non-need-based). 36% of past graduating class borrowed through all loan programs. *Average indebtedness per student:* $12,070. ***Average need-based loan:*** Freshmen: $3103. Undergraduates: $4220. ***Parent loans:*** $10,347,449 (100% non-need-based). ***Programs:*** Federal Direct (Subsidized and Unsubsidized Stafford, PLUS), Perkins.

WORK-STUDY ***Federal work-study:*** Total amount: $375,316; jobs available. ***State or other work-study/employment:*** Part-time jobs available.

ATHLETIC AWARDS Total amount: $1,252,341 (100% need-based).

APPLYING FOR FINANCIAL AID ***Required financial aid form:*** FAFSA. ***Financial aid deadline (priority):*** 2/19. ***Notification date:*** 3/19. Students must reply by 5/1.

CONTACT Ms. Tiffany Wilson, Office of Financial Aid, East Stroudsburg University of Pennsylvania, 200 Prospect Street, East Stroudsburg, PA 18301-2999, 570-422-2800 or toll-free 877-230-5547. *Fax:* 570-422-2849. *E-mail:* finaid@esu.edu.
Website: http://www.esu.edu/.

EAST TENNESSEE STATE UNIVERSITY

Johnson City, TN

CONTACT Financial Aid Office, East Tennessee State University, PO Box 70722, 105 Burgin Dossett, Johnson City, TN 37614-1710, 423-439-4300 or toll-free 800-462-3878. *Fax:* 423-439-5855. *E-mail:* finaid@etsu.edu.
Website: http://www.etsu.edu/.

EAST TEXAS BAPTIST UNIVERSITY

Marshall, TX

Tuition & fees: $27,210	Average undergraduate aid package: $19,534

ABOUT THE INSTITUTION Independent Baptist, coed. ***Awards:*** certificates, bachelor's, and master's degrees. 43 undergraduate majors. ***Total enrollment:*** 1,593. Undergraduates: 1,471. Freshmen: 345. Federal methodology is used as a basis for awarding need-based institutional aid.

UNDERGRADUATE EXPENSES for 2019–2020 ***Application fee:*** $25. ***Comprehensive fee:*** $36,538 includes full-time tuition ($26,100), mandatory fees ($1110), and room and board ($9328). ***College room only:*** $4576. Full-time tuition and fees vary according to program. Room and board charges vary according to board plan and housing facility. ***Part-time tuition:*** $870 per credit hour. ***Part-time fees:*** $46 per credit hour. Part-time tuition and fees vary according to program.

FRESHMAN FINANCIAL AID (Fall 2018) 387 applied for aid; of those 90% were deemed to have need. 100% of freshmen with need received aid; of those 17% had need fully met. ***Average percent of need met:*** 26% (excluding resources awarded to replace EFC). ***Average financial aid package:*** $18,826 (excluding resources awarded to replace EFC). 13% of all full-time freshmen had no need and received non-need-based gift aid.

UNDERGRADUATE FINANCIAL AID (Fall 2018) 1,208 applied for aid; of those 90% were deemed to have need. 100% of undergraduates with need received aid; of those 14% had need fully met. ***Average percent of need met:*** 29% (excluding resources awarded to replace EFC). ***Average financial aid package:*** $19,534 (excluding resources awarded to replace EFC). 16% of all full-time undergraduates had no need and received non-need-based gift aid.

GIFT AID (NEED-BASED) ***Receiving aid:*** Freshmen: 63% (252); all full-time undergraduates: 61% (788). ***Average award:*** Freshmen: $5749; Undergraduates: $5834. ***Scholarships, grants, and awards:*** Federal Pell, FSEOG, state, private, college/university gift aid from institutional funds.

GIFT AID (NON-NEED-BASED) ***Receiving aid:*** Freshmen: 86% (344). Undergraduates: 82% (1,058). ***Average award:*** Freshmen: $11,985. Undergraduates: $12,013. ***Scholarships, grants, and awards by category:*** *Academic interests/achievement:* 1,087 awards ($7,780,421 total): biological sciences, business, communication, education, English, general academic interests/achievements, home economics, humanities, mathematics, physical sciences, religion/biblical studies, social sciences. *Creative arts/performance:* 148 awards ($443,707 total): music, theater/drama. *Special achievements/activities:* 1,139 awards ($3,617,164 total): general special achievements/activities, leadership, religious involvement. *Special characteristics:* 110 awards ($751,485 total): adult students, children and siblings of alumni, children of faculty/staff, general special characteristics, international students, married students, previous college experience, public servants, religious affiliation. ***Tuition waivers:*** Full or partial for employees or children of employees, adult students.

LOANS ***Student loans:*** 77% of past graduating class borrowed through all loan programs. *Average indebtedness per student:* $30,351. ***Average need-based loan:*** Freshmen: $3041. Undergraduates: $3875. ***Programs:*** Federal Direct (Subsidized and Unsubsidized Stafford, PLUS), Perkins, state.

WORK-STUDY ***Federal work-study:*** 230 jobs averaging $1777. ***State or other work-study/employment:*** 9 part-time jobs averaging $1857.

APPLYING FOR FINANCIAL AID ***Required financial aid forms:*** FAFSA, institution's own form. ***Notification date:*** Continuous.

CONTACT Mr. Nathan Flory, Director of Financial Aid, East Texas Baptist University, One Tiger Drive, Marshall, TX 75670-1498, 903-923-2137 or toll-free 800-804-ETBU. *Fax:* 903-934-8120. *E-mail:* nflory@etbu.edu.
Website: http://www.etbu.edu/.

EAST-WEST UNIVERSITY

Chicago, IL

CONTACT Cesar Campos, Director of Financial Aid, East-West University, 816 South Michigan Avenue, Chicago, IL 60605-2103, 312-939-0111 Ext. 1806. *Fax:* 312-939-0083. *E-mail:* cesar@eastwest.edu.
Website: http://www.eastwest.edu/.

ECCLESIA COLLEGE

Springdale, AR

CONTACT Financial Aid Office, Ecclesia College, 9653 Nations Drive, Springdale, AR 72762, 479-248-7236.
Website: http://www.ecollege.edu/.

ECKERD COLLEGE

St. Petersburg, FL

Tuition & fees: $46,096	Average undergraduate aid package: $38,819

ABOUT THE INSTITUTION Independent Presbyterian, coed. ***Awards:*** bachelor's degrees. 38 undergraduate majors. ***Total enrollment:*** 1,999. Undergraduates: 2,000. Freshmen: 581. Federal methodology is used as a basis for awarding need-based institutional aid.

UNDERGRADUATE EXPENSES for 2019–2020 ***Application fee:*** $40. ***Comprehensive fee:*** $59,122 includes full-time tuition ($45,452), mandatory fees ($644), and room and board ($13,026). ***College room only:*** $6814. Room and board charges vary according to board plan and housing facility.

FRESHMAN FINANCIAL AID (Fall 2019, est.) 449 applied for aid; of those 80% were deemed to have need. 100% of freshmen with need received aid; of those 18% had need fully met. ***Average percent of need met:*** 84% (excluding resources awarded to replace EFC). ***Average financial aid package:*** $38,871 (excluding resources awarded to replace EFC). 32% of all full-time freshmen had no need and received non-need-based gift aid.

UNDERGRADUATE FINANCIAL AID (Fall 2019, est.) 1,425 applied for aid; of those 81% were deemed to have need. 100% of undergraduates with need received aid; of those 21% had need fully met. ***Average percent of need met:*** 85% (excluding resources awarded to replace EFC). ***Average financial aid package:*** $38,819 (excluding resources awarded to replace EFC). 38% of all full-time undergraduates had no need and received non-need-based gift aid.

GIFT AID (NEED-BASED) ***Total amount:*** $31,551,245 (7% federal, 4% state, 87% institutional, 2% external sources). ***Receiving aid:*** Freshmen: 66% (355); all full-time undergraduates: 60% (1,161). ***Average award:*** Freshmen: $27,507; Undergraduates: $27,705. ***Scholarships, grants, and awards:*** Federal Pell, FSEOG, state, college/university gift aid from institutional funds.

GIFT AID (NON-NEED-BASED) ***Total amount:*** $15,473,169 (5% state, 94% institutional, 1% external sources). ***Average award:*** Freshmen: $17,966. Undergraduates: $18,120. ***Scholarships, grants, and awards by category:*** *Academic interests/achievement:* general academic interests/achievements. *Creative arts/performance:* applied art and design, creative writing, music, theater/drama. *Special characteristics:* children of faculty/staff, international students, local/state students, religious affiliation. ***Tuition waivers:*** Full or partial for employees or children of employees. ***ROTC:*** Army cooperative, Air Force cooperative.

LOANS ***Student loans:*** $13,280,121 (62% need-based, 38% non-need-based). 58% of past graduating class borrowed through all loan programs. *Average indebtedness per student:* $33,661. ***Average need-based loan:*** Freshmen: $5508. Undergraduates: $6473. ***Parent loans:*** $8,089,848 (40% need-based, 60% non-need-based). ***Programs:*** Federal Direct (Subsidized and Unsubsidized Stafford, PLUS), college/university.

WORK-STUDY ***Federal work-study:*** Total amount: $1,896,400; jobs available. ***State or other work-study/employment:*** Total amount: $14,000 (100% non-need-based). Part-time jobs available.

ATHLETIC AWARDS Total amount: $2,855,401 (32% need-based, 68% non-need-based).

APPLYING FOR FINANCIAL AID ***Required financial aid form:*** FAFSA. ***Financial aid deadline (priority):*** 2/1. ***Notification date:*** Continuous.

CONTACT Dr. Pat Garrett Watkins, Director of Financial Aid, Eckerd College, 4200 54th Avenue, South, St. Petersburg, FL 33711, 727-864-8334 or toll-free 800-456-9009. *Fax:* 727-866-2304. *E-mail:* watkinpe@eckerd.edu.
Website: http://www.eckerd.edu/.

ECPI UNIVERSITY

Virginia Beach, VA

Tuition & fees: $16,584	Average undergraduate aid package: N/A

ABOUT THE INSTITUTION Proprietary, coed. ***Awards:*** certificates, diplomas, associate, bachelor's, and master's degrees. 28 undergraduate majors. ***Total enrollment:*** 13,487. Undergraduates: 13,142. Freshmen: 1,385. Federal methodology is used as a basis for awarding need-based institutional aid.

UNDERGRADUATE EXPENSES for 2020–2021 ***Application fee:*** $45. ***Tuition:*** full-time $16,584. Full-time tuition and fees vary according to course load, degree level, location, program, and reciprocity agreements. ***Payment plans:*** Guaranteed tuition, tuition prepayment.

GIFT AID (NEED-BASED) ***Scholarships, grants, and awards:*** Federal Pell, FSEOG, state, private, college/university gift aid from institutional funds.

GIFT AID (NON-NEED-BASED) ***Scholarships, grants, and awards by category:*** *Academic interests/achievement:* business, computer science, engineering/technologies, health fields, home economics. *Special achievements/activities:* community service, general special achievements/activities, hobbies/interests, leadership, memberships. *Special characteristics:* adult students, children and siblings of alumni, children of current students, children of faculty/staff, general special characteristics, parents of current students, veterans, veterans' children. ***Tuition waivers:*** Full or partial for employees or children of employees.

LOANS ***Programs:*** Federal Direct (Subsidized and Unsubsidized Stafford, PLUS), Perkins, college/university, private loans.

WORK-STUDY Federal work-study jobs available. ***State or other work-study/employment:*** Part-time jobs available.

APPLYING FOR FINANCIAL AID *Required financial aid forms:* FAFSA, institution's own form. ***Financial aid deadline:*** Continuous. ***Notification date:*** Continuous beginning 1/1. Students must reply within 12 weeks of notification.

CONTACT Mrs. Kathi Turner, Director of Financial Aid, ECPI University, 5555 Greenwich Road, Suite 300, Virginia Beach, VA 23462, 757-490-9090 or toll-free 844-611-0766. *Fax:* 757-671-8661. *E-mail:* kturner@ecpi.edu.
Website: http://www.ecpi.edu/.

EDGEWOOD COLLEGE

Madison, WI

Tuition & fees: $31,700	Average undergraduate aid package: $22,736

ABOUT THE INSTITUTION Independent Roman Catholic, coed. ***Awards:*** certificates, bachelor's, master's, and doctoral degrees. 45 undergraduate majors. ***Total enrollment:*** 2,038. Undergraduates: 1,407. Freshmen: 239. Federal methodology is used as a basis for awarding need-based institutional aid.

UNDERGRADUATE EXPENSES for 2020–2021 *Application fee:* $30. ***Comprehensive fee:*** $43,400 includes full-time tuition ($31,700) and room and board ($11,700). Full-time tuition and fees vary according to degree level. Room and board charges vary according to housing facility. ***Part-time tuition:*** $994 per credit. Part-time tuition and fees vary according to course load and degree level.

FRESHMAN FINANCIAL AID (Fall 2018) 240 applied for aid; of those 87% were deemed to have need. 100% of freshmen with need received aid; of those 11% had need fully met. ***Average percent of need met:*** 79% (excluding resources awarded to replace EFC). ***Average financial aid package:*** $25,066 (excluding resources awarded to replace EFC). 17% of all full-time freshmen had no need and received non-need-based gift aid.

UNDERGRADUATE FINANCIAL AID (Fall 2018) 1,056 applied for aid; of those 88% were deemed to have need. 99% of undergraduates with need received aid; of those 14% had need fully met. ***Average percent of need met:*** 75% (excluding resources awarded to replace EFC). ***Average financial aid package:*** $22,736 (excluding resources awarded to replace EFC). 19% of all full-time undergraduates had no need and received non-need-based gift aid.

GIFT AID (NEED-BASED) *Total amount:* $15,672,304 (15% federal, 10% state, 60% institutional, 15% external sources). ***Receiving aid:*** Freshmen: 81% (208); all full-time undergraduates: 74% (909). ***Average award:*** Freshmen: $19,943; Undergraduates: $16,946. ***Scholarships, grants, and awards:*** Federal Pell, FSEOG, state, private, college/university gift aid from institutional funds.

GIFT AID (NON-NEED-BASED) *Total amount:* $3,286,227 (8% federal, 64% institutional, 28% external sources). ***Receiving aid:*** Freshmen: 6% (15). Undergraduates: 6% (73). ***Average award:*** Freshmen: $10,109. Undergraduates: $7856. ***Scholarships, grants, and awards by category:*** *Academic interests/achievement:* 1,004 awards ($7,089,250 total): area/ethnic studies, foreign languages, general academic interests/achievements. *Creative arts/performance:* 97 awards ($130,000 total): art/fine arts, creative writing, music, performing arts, theater/drama. *Special achievements/activities:* 73 awards ($451,833 total): community service, religious involvement. *Special characteristics:* 85 awards ($739,310 total): children and siblings of alumni, children of faculty/staff. ***Tuition waivers:*** Full or partial for employees or children of employees. ***ROTC:*** Army cooperative, Naval cooperative, Air Force cooperative.

LOANS *Student loans:* $9,071,305 (68% need-based, 32% non-need-based). 77% of past graduating class borrowed through all loan programs. *Average indebtedness per student:* $37,332. ***Average need-based loan:*** Freshmen: $4235. Undergraduates: $5424. ***Parent loans:*** $947,292 (8% need-based, 92% non-need-based). ***Programs:*** Federal Direct (Subsidized and Unsubsidized Stafford, PLUS), Perkins, state.

WORK-STUDY *Federal work-study:* Total amount: $906,889; 504 jobs averaging $1971. ***State or other work-study/employment:*** Total amount: $1,030,112 (33% need-based, 67% non-need-based). 416 part-time jobs averaging $1976.

APPLYING FOR FINANCIAL AID *Required financial aid form:* FAFSA. ***Financial aid deadline (priority):*** 12/1. ***Notification date:*** Continuous beginning 12/15. Students must reply by 5/1 or within 2 weeks of notification.

CONTACT Ms. Kari J. Gribble, Assistant Vice President for Enrollment Management, Edgewood College, 1000 Edgewood College Drive, Madison, WI 53711-1997, 608-663-4300 or toll-free 800-444-4861 Ext.2294. *E-mail:* ecentral@edgewood.edu.
Website: http://www.edgewood.edu/.

EDINBORO UNIVERSITY OF PENNSYLVANIA

Edinboro, PA

Tuition & fees (PA res): $10,543	Average undergraduate aid package: $9914

ABOUT THE INSTITUTION State-supported, coed. ***Awards:*** certificates, bachelor's, master's, and doctoral degrees. 81 undergraduate majors. ***Total enrollment:*** 4,646. Undergraduates: 3,399. Freshmen: 706. Both federal and institutional methodology are used as a basis for awarding need-based institutional aid.

UNDERGRADUATE EXPENSES for 2019–2020 *Application fee:* $30. ***Tuition, state resident:*** full-time $7716; part-time $322 per credit hour. ***Tuition, nonresident:*** full-time $11,574; part-time $482 per credit hour. ***Required fees:*** full-time $2827; $182.20 per credit hour. Full-time tuition and fees vary according to location and program. Part-time tuition and fees vary according to course load, location, and program. ***College room and board:*** $9800; ***Room only:*** $6660. Room and board charges vary according to board plan and housing facility.

FRESHMAN FINANCIAL AID (Fall 2018) 557 applied for aid; of those 88% were deemed to have need. 97% of freshmen with need received aid; of those 3% had need fully met. ***Average percent of need met:*** 43% (excluding resources awarded to replace EFC). ***Average financial aid package:*** $9009 (excluding resources awarded to replace EFC). 1% of all full-time freshmen had no need and received non-need-based gift aid.

UNDERGRADUATE FINANCIAL AID (Fall 2018) 3,066 applied for aid; of those 83% were deemed to have need. 97% of undergraduates with need received aid; of those 3% had need fully met. ***Average percent of need met:*** 48% (excluding resources awarded to replace EFC). ***Average financial aid package:*** $9914 (excluding resources awarded to replace EFC). 1% of all full-time undergraduates had no need and received non-need-based gift aid.

GIFT AID (NEED-BASED) *Receiving aid:* Freshmen: 63% (361); all full-time undergraduates: 57% (1,806). ***Average award:*** Freshmen: $5787; Undergraduates: $5909. ***Scholarships, grants, and awards:*** Federal Pell, FSEOG, state, private, college/university gift aid from institutional funds.

GIFT AID (NON-NEED-BASED) *Receiving aid:* Freshmen: 14% (81). Undergraduates: 20% (645). ***Average award:*** Freshmen: $1529. Undergraduates: $3183. ***Scholarships, grants, and awards by category:*** *Academic interests/achievement:* biological sciences, business, communication, computer science, education, engineering/technologies, English, foreign languages, general academic interests/achievements, home economics, humanities, mathematics, physical sciences, premedicine, social sciences. *Creative arts/performance:* applied art and design, art/fine arts, cinema/film/broadcasting, creative writing, journalism/publications. *Special achievements/activities:* community service, leadership. *Special characteristics:* adult students, children of faculty/staff, first-generation college students, handicapped students, local/state students, members of minority groups, out-of-state students, public servants, veterans, veterans' children. ***Tuition waivers:*** Full or partial for employees or children of employees, senior citizens. ***ROTC:*** Army.

LOANS *Student loans:* 84% of past graduating class borrowed through all loan programs. *Average indebtedness per student:* $42,694. ***Average need-based loan:*** Freshmen: $2236. Undergraduates: $2702. ***Programs:*** Federal Direct (Subsidized and Unsubsidized Stafford, PLUS), Federal Nursing.

WORK-STUDY Federal work-study jobs available. ***State or other work-study/employment:*** Part-time jobs available.

APPLYING FOR FINANCIAL AID *Required financial aid forms:* FAFSA, state aid form. ***Notification date:*** Continuous.

CONTACT Ms. Kelly Vitelli, Director of Financial Aid, Edinboro University of Pennsylvania, Hamilton Hall, Edinboro, PA 16444, 814-732-3500 or toll-free 888-846-2676. *Fax:* 814-732-2129. *E-mail:* finaid@edinboro.edu.
Website: http://www.edinboro.edu/.

EDP UNIVERSITY OF PUERTO RICO

Hato Rey, PR

CONTACT Yaitzaenid Gonzalez, Financial Aid Administrator, EDP University of Puerto Rico, PO Box 192303, San Juan, PR 00919-2303, 787-765-3560 Ext. 253. *Fax:* 787-777-0025. *E-mail:* ygonzalez@edpcollege.edu.
Website: http://www.edpuniversity.edu/.

EDP UNIVERSITY OF PUERTO RICO–SAN SEBASTIAN

San Sebastian, PR

CONTACT Mrs. Yaitzaenid Gonzalez, Financial Aid Administrator, EDP University of Puerto Rico–San Sebastian, PO Box 192303, San Juan , PR 00919, 787-765-3560 Ext. 253. *Fax:* 787-777-0025. *E-mail:* ygonzalez@edpcollege.edu.
Website: http://www.edpuniversity.edu/.

EDWARD WATERS COLLEGE

Jacksonville, FL

CONTACT Gabriel Mbomeh, Director of Financial Aid, Edward Waters College, 1658 Kings Road, Jacksonville, FL 32209-6199, 904-366-2528 or toll-free 888-898-3191.
Website: http://www.ewc.edu/.

ELIZABETH CITY STATE UNIVERSITY

Elizabeth City, NC

ABOUT THE INSTITUTION State-supported, coed. ***Awards:*** bachelor's and master's degrees. 25 undergraduate majors. ***Total enrollment:*** 1,677. Undergraduates: 1,636. Freshmen: 418.

GIFT AID (NEED-BASED) ***Scholarships, grants, and awards:*** Federal Pell, FSEOG, state, college/university gift aid from institutional funds, Thurgood Marshall College Fund.

GIFT AID (NON-NEED-BASED) ***Scholarships, grants, and awards by category:*** *Academic interests/achievement:* computer science, education, general academic interests/achievements, mathematics, military science. *Creative arts/performance:* music, performing arts. *Special characteristics:* ethnic background, handicapped students, international students, members of minority groups, veterans.

LOANS ***Programs:*** Federal Direct (Subsidized and Unsubsidized Stafford, PLUS), Perkins, state, college/university.

CONTACT Jeremi Watkins, Director of Financial Aid, Elizabeth City State University, 1704 Weeksville Road, Campus Box 914, Elizabeth City, NC 27909-7806, 252-335-3283 or toll-free 800-347-3278. *Fax:* 252-335-3716. *E-mail:* jwwatkins@ecsu.edu.
Website: http://www.ecsu.edu/.

ELIZABETHTOWN COLLEGE

Elizabethtown, PA

Tuition & fees: N/R	Average undergraduate aid package: $22,695

ABOUT THE INSTITUTION Independent Church of the Brethren, coed. ***Awards:*** bachelor's and master's degrees. 40 undergraduate majors. Institutional methodology is used as a basis for awarding need-based institutional aid.

FRESHMAN FINANCIAL AID (Fall 2019, est.) 349 applied for aid; of those 81% were deemed to have need. 100% of freshmen with need received aid; of those 24% had need fully met. ***Average percent of need met:*** 80% (excluding resources awarded to replace EFC). ***Average financial aid package:*** $23,872 (excluding resources awarded to replace EFC). 22% of all full-time freshmen had no need and received non-need-based gift aid.

UNDERGRADUATE FINANCIAL AID (Fall 2019, est.) 1,291 applied for aid; of those 83% were deemed to have need. 100% of undergraduates with need received aid; of those 22% had need fully met. ***Average percent of need met:*** 76% (excluding resources awarded to replace EFC). ***Average financial aid package:*** $22,695 (excluding resources awarded to replace EFC). 27% of all full-time undergraduates had no need and received non-need-based gift aid.

GIFT AID (NEED-BASED) ***Total amount:*** $20,273,879 (9% federal, 7% state, 74% institutional, 10% external sources). ***Receiving aid:*** Freshmen: 76% (281); all full-time undergraduates: 71% (1,064). ***Average award:*** Freshmen: $20,802; Undergraduates: $18,625. ***Scholarships, grants, and awards:*** Federal Pell, FSEOG, state, private, college/university gift aid from institutional funds.

GIFT AID (NON-NEED-BASED) ***Total amount:*** $6,797,751 (70% institutional, 30% external sources). ***Receiving aid:*** Freshmen: 12% (46). Undergraduates: 9% (141). ***Average award:*** Freshmen: $13,694. Undergraduates: $10,673. ***Scholarships, grants, and awards by category:*** *Academic interests/achievement:* biological sciences, business, communication, computer science, education, engineering/technologies, English, foreign languages, general academic interests/achievements, home economics, humanities, international studies, mathematics, physical sciences, premedicine, religion/biblical studies, social sciences. *Creative arts/performance:* applied art and design, music, performing arts, theater/drama. *Special achievements/activities:* religious involvement. *Special characteristics:* children of faculty/staff, international students, local/state students, members of minority groups, religious affiliation, siblings of current students.

LOANS ***Student loans:*** $13,146,052 (55% need-based, 45% non-need-based). 79% of past graduating class borrowed through all loan programs. *Average indebtedness per student:* $42,548. ***Average need-based loan:*** Freshmen: $3038. Undergraduates: $4191. ***Parent loans:*** $4,027,797 (34% need-based, 66% non-need-based). ***Programs:*** Federal Direct (Subsidized and Unsubsidized Stafford, PLUS), Perkins.

WORK-STUDY ***Federal work-study:*** Total amount: $688,586; jobs available.

APPLYING FOR FINANCIAL AID ***Required financial aid form:*** FAFSA. ***Financial aid deadline (priority):*** 3/15. ***Notification date:*** Continuous beginning 12/2. Students must reply by 5/1 or within 2 weeks of notification.

CONTACT Ms. Melodie R. Jackson, Director of Financial Aid, Elizabethtown College, 1 Alpha Drive, Elizabethtown, PA 17022, 717-361-1404. *Fax:* 717-361-1514. *E-mail:* jacksonmr@etown.edu.
Website: http://www.etown.edu/.

ELMHURST COLLEGE

Elmhurst, IL

ABOUT THE INSTITUTION Independent United Church of Christ, coed. ***Awards:*** bachelor's and master's degrees. 70 undergraduate majors.

GIFT AID (NEED-BASED) ***Scholarships, grants, and awards:*** Federal Pell, FSEOG, state, private, college/university gift aid from institutional funds.

GIFT AID (NON-NEED-BASED) ***Scholarships, grants, and awards by category:*** *Academic interests/achievement:* biological sciences, business, communication, computer science, education, English, foreign languages, general academic interests/achievements, humanities, international studies, mathematics, physical sciences, premedicine, religion/biblical studies, social sciences. *Creative arts/performance:* applied art and design, music, theater/drama. *Special characteristics:* children and siblings of alumni, children of current students, children with a deceased or disabled parent, ethnic background, members of minority groups, religious affiliation, siblings of current students, spouses of current students, veterans.

LOANS ***Programs:*** Federal Direct (Subsidized and Unsubsidized Stafford, PLUS).

WORK-STUDY ***Federal work-study:*** Total amount: $462,264; jobs available. ***State or other work-study/employment:*** Part-time jobs available.

APPLYING FOR FINANCIAL AID ***Required financial aid form:*** FAFSA.

CONTACT Julia Jenkins, Director of Student Financial Services, Elmhurst College, Goebel Hall 106A, 190 Prospect Avenue, Elmhurst, IL 60126-3296, 630-617-3015 or toll-free 800-697-1871. *Fax:* 630-617-3487. *E-mail:* julia.jenkins@elmhurst.edu.
Website: http://www.elmhurst.edu/.

ELMIRA COLLEGE

Elmira, NY

Tuition & fees: $35,400	Average undergraduate aid package: $27,799

ABOUT THE INSTITUTION Independent, coed. ***Awards:*** certificates, associate, bachelor's, and master's degrees. 48 undergraduate majors. Federal methodology is used as a basis for awarding need-based institutional aid.

UNDERGRADUATE EXPENSES for 2019–2020 ***Comprehensive fee:*** $47,900 includes full-time tuition ($33,900), mandatory fees ($1500), and room and board ($12,500). Full-time tuition and fees vary according to course load. Room and board charges vary according to housing facility. ***Part-time tuition:*** $983 per credit hour. Part-time tuition and fees vary according to course load. ***Payment plan:*** Tuition prepayment.

FRESHMAN FINANCIAL AID (Fall 2019, est.) 201 applied for aid; of those 93% were deemed to have need. 100% of freshmen with need received aid; of those 30% had need fully met. ***Average percent of need met:*** 80% (excluding resources awarded to replace EFC). ***Average financial aid package:*** $28,495 (excluding resources awarded to replace EFC). 14% of all full-time freshmen had no need and received non-need-based gift aid.

UNDERGRADUATE FINANCIAL AID (Fall 2019, est.) 672 applied for aid; of those 89% were deemed to have need. 100% of undergraduates with need received aid; of those 25% had need fully met. ***Average percent of need met:*** 78% (excluding resources awarded to replace EFC). ***Average financial aid package:*** $27,799 (excluding resources awarded to replace EFC). 17% of all full-time undergraduates had no need and received non-need-based gift aid.

GIFT AID (NEED-BASED) ***Total amount:*** $14,357,945 (10% federal, 5% state, 83% institutional, 2% external sources). ***Receiving aid:*** Freshmen: 86% (187); all full-time undergraduates: 82% (599). ***Average award:*** Freshmen: $25,951; Undergraduates: $24,574. ***Scholarships, grants, and awards:*** Federal Pell, FSEOG, state, private, college/university gift aid from institutional funds.

GIFT AID (NON-NEED-BASED) ***Total amount:*** $3,631,065 (95% institutional, 5% external sources). ***Receiving aid:*** Freshmen: 22% (47). Undergraduates: 17% (121). ***Average award:*** Freshmen: $23,878. Undergraduates: $20,871. ***Scholarships, grants, and awards by category:*** *Academic interests/achievement:* 670 awards ($10,139,670 total): general academic interests/achievements. *Special characteristics:* 1,744 awards ($4,443,611 total): children and siblings of alumni, children of faculty/staff, general special characteristics, international students, previous college experience, siblings of current students, twins, veterans, veterans' children. ***Tuition waivers:*** Full or partial for employees or children of employees, adult students. ***ROTC:*** Army, Air Force cooperative.

LOANS ***Student loans:*** $5,959,254 (59% need-based, 41% non-need-based). 87% of past graduating class borrowed through all loan programs. *Average indebtedness per student:* $27,679. ***Average need-based loan:*** Freshmen: $2982. Undergraduates: $3766. ***Parent loans:*** $2,625,957 (44% need-based, 56% non-need-based). ***Programs:*** Federal Direct (Subsidized and Unsubsidized Stafford, PLUS).

WORK-STUDY ***Federal work-study:*** Total amount: $217,056; 103 jobs averaging $900. ***State or other work-study/employment:*** Total amount: $151,453 (33% need-based, 67% non-need-based). 93 part-time jobs averaging $850.

APPLYING FOR FINANCIAL AID ***Required financial aid forms:*** FAFSA, state aid form. ***Financial aid deadline:*** Continuous. ***Notification date:*** Continuous beginning 11/15. Students must reply by 5/1 or within 3 weeks of notification.

CONTACT Mrs. Lorraine Marie Mothershed, Director of Financial Aid, Elmira College, One Park Place, Elmira, NY 14901-2099, 607-735-1728 or toll-free 800-935-6472. *Fax:* 607-378-2030. *E-mail:* lmothershed@elmira.edu.
Website: http://www.elmira.edu/.

ELMS COLLEGE

Chicopee, MA

Tuition & fees: $38,391	Average undergraduate aid package: $22,908

ABOUT THE INSTITUTION Independent Roman Catholic, coed. ***Awards:*** certificates, associate, bachelor's, master's, and doctoral degrees. 31 undergraduate majors. ***Total enrollment:*** 1,495. Undergraduates: 1,123. Freshmen: 180. Federal methodology is used as a basis for awarding need-based institutional aid.

UNDERGRADUATE EXPENSES for 2020–2021 ***Comprehensive fee:*** $52,401 includes full-time tuition ($36,596), mandatory fees ($1795), and room and board ($14,010). Room and board charges vary according to board plan. ***Part-time tuition:*** $742 per credit hour. Part-time tuition and fees vary according to location and program.

FRESHMAN FINANCIAL AID (Fall 2019, est.) 177 applied for aid; of those 92% were deemed to have need. 100% of freshmen with need received aid; of those 12% had need fully met. ***Average percent of need met:*** 76% (excluding resources awarded to replace EFC). ***Average financial aid package:*** $31,285 (excluding resources awarded to replace EFC). 8% of all full-time freshmen had no need and received non-need-based gift aid.

UNDERGRADUATE FINANCIAL AID (Fall 2019, est.) 926 applied for aid; of those 94% were deemed to have need. 100% of undergraduates with need received aid; of those 7% had need fully met. ***Average percent of need met:*** 61% (excluding resources awarded to replace EFC). ***Average financial aid package:*** $22,908 (excluding resources awarded to replace EFC). 5% of all full-time undergraduates had no need and received non-need-based gift aid.

GIFT AID (NEED-BASED) ***Receiving aid:*** Freshmen: 92% (163); all full-time undergraduates: 82% (816). ***Average award:*** Freshmen: $28,729; Undergraduates: $19,543. ***Scholarships, grants, and awards:*** Federal Pell, FSEOG, state, private, college/university gift aid from institutional funds.

GIFT AID (NON-NEED-BASED) ***Receiving aid:*** Freshmen: 16% (28). Undergraduates: 4% (36). ***Average award:*** Freshmen: $17,679. Undergraduates: $16,182. ***Scholarships, grants, and awards by category:*** *Academic interests/achievement:* 608 awards ($7,854,595 total): general academic interests/achievements. *Special characteristics:* 66 awards ($439,464 total): children of faculty/staff, general special characteristics, religious affiliation, siblings of current students. ***Tuition waivers:*** Full or partial for employees or children of employees, senior citizens. ***ROTC:*** Army cooperative, Air Force cooperative.

LOANS ***Student loans:*** 85% of past graduating class borrowed through all loan programs. *Average indebtedness per student:* $49,156. ***Average need-based loan:*** Freshmen: $3250. Undergraduates: $4580. ***Programs:*** Federal Direct (Subsidized and Unsubsidized Stafford, PLUS).

WORK-STUDY ***Federal work-study:*** 121 jobs averaging $1123. ***State or other work-study/employment:*** Part-time jobs available.

APPLYING FOR FINANCIAL AID ***Required financial aid form:*** FAFSA. ***Financial aid deadline:*** Continuous. ***Notification date:*** Continuous. Students must reply within 2 weeks of notification.

CONTACT Richard O'Connor, Director of Financial Aid, Elms College, 291 Springfield Street, Chicopee, MA 01013-2839, 413-265-2249 or toll-free 800-255-ELMS. *E-mail:* finaid@elms.edu.
Website: http://www.elms.edu/.

ELON UNIVERSITY

Elon, NC

Tuition & fees: $37,921	Average undergraduate aid package: $21,162

ABOUT THE INSTITUTION Independent United Church of Christ, coed. ***Awards:*** bachelor's, master's, and doctoral degrees. 65 undergraduate majors. ***Total enrollment:*** 7,088. Undergraduates: 6,475. Freshmen: 1,659. Institutional methodology is used as a basis for awarding need-based institutional aid.

UNDERGRADUATE EXPENSES for 2020–2021 ***Application fee:*** $60. ***Comprehensive fee:*** $51,052 includes full-time tuition ($37,414), mandatory fees ($507), and room and board ($13,131). ***College room only:*** $6445. ***Part-time tuition:*** $1191 per credit hour. ***Part-time fees:*** $181 per term.

FRESHMAN FINANCIAL AID (Fall 2019, est.) 1059 applied for aid; of those 58% were deemed to have need. 100% of freshmen with need received aid; of those 14% had need fully met. ***Average percent of need met:*** 58% (excluding resources awarded to replace EFC). ***Average financial aid package:*** $19,972 (excluding resources awarded to replace EFC). 30% of all full-time freshmen had no need and received non-need-based gift aid.

UNDERGRADUATE FINANCIAL AID (Fall 2019, est.) 2,945 applied for aid; of those 70% were deemed to have need. 100% of undergraduates with need received aid; of those 17% had need fully met. ***Average percent of need met:*** 61%

(excluding resources awarded to replace EFC). ***Average financial aid package:*** $21,162 (excluding resources awarded to replace EFC). 26% of all full-time undergraduates had no need and received non-need-based gift aid.

GIFT AID (NEED-BASED) ***Receiving aid:*** Freshmen: 33% (543); all full-time undergraduates: 31% (1,849). ***Average award:*** Freshmen: $15,187; Undergraduates: $16,206. ***Scholarships, grants, and awards:*** Federal Pell, FSEOG, state, private, college/university gift aid from institutional funds.

GIFT AID (NON-NEED-BASED) ***Receiving aid:*** Freshmen: 24% (391). Undergraduates: 19% (1,143). ***Average award:*** Freshmen: $6603. Undergraduates: $7819. ***Scholarships, grants, and awards by category:*** *Academic interests/achievement:* 3,495 awards ($18,180,187 total): biological sciences, business, communication, computer science, education, engineering/technologies, general academic interests/achievements, mathematics, military science, physical sciences, premedicine, religion/biblical studies, social sciences. *Creative arts/performance:* 188 awards ($646,017 total): applied art and design, journalism/publications, music, performing arts, theater/drama. *Special achievements/activities:* 153 awards ($457,453 total): community service, general special achievements/activities, leadership, religious involvement. *Special characteristics:* 178 awards ($3,124,194 total): adult students, children of faculty/staff, ethnic background, first-generation college students, international students, members of minority groups, relatives of clergy, veterans. ***ROTC:*** Army, Air Force cooperative.

LOANS ***Student loans:*** 34% of past graduating class borrowed through all loan programs. *Average indebtedness per student:* $32,028. ***Average need-based loan:*** Freshmen: $3426. Undergraduates: $4331. ***Programs:*** Federal Direct (Subsidized and Unsubsidized Stafford, PLUS), state, college/university, private loans.

WORK-STUDY ***Federal work-study:*** 1,460 jobs averaging $2374.

APPLYING FOR FINANCIAL AID ***Required financial aid forms:*** FAFSA, CSS Financial Aid PROFILE. ***Notification date:*** Continuous.

CONTACT Dr. Patrick Murphy, Director of Financial Planning, Elon University, 2725 Campus Box, Elon, NC 27244, 336-278-7640 or toll-free 800-334-8448. *Fax:* 336-278-7639. *E-mail:* finaid@elon.edu.
Website: http://www.elon.edu/.

EMBRY-RIDDLE AERONAUTICAL UNIVERSITY–DAYTONA

Daytona Beach, FL

ABOUT THE INSTITUTION Independent, coed. ***Awards:*** certificates, associate, bachelor's, master's, and doctoral degrees. 24 undergraduate majors. ***Total enrollment:*** 6,338. Undergraduates: 5,729. Freshmen: 1,357.

GIFT AID (NEED-BASED) ***Scholarships, grants, and awards:*** Federal Pell, FSEOG, state, private, college/university gift aid from institutional funds.

GIFT AID (NON-NEED-BASED) ***Scholarships, grants, and awards by category:*** *Special achievements/activities:* leadership.

LOANS ***Programs:*** Federal Direct (Subsidized and Unsubsidized Stafford, PLUS), college/university.

WORK-STUDY ***Federal work-study:*** Total amount: $402,272; jobs available. ***State or other work-study/employment:*** Total amount: $3,581,476 (100% need-based). Part-time jobs available.

APPLYING FOR FINANCIAL AID ***Required financial aid form:*** FAFSA.

CONTACT Financial Aid Office, Embry-Riddle Aeronautical University–Daytona, 600 South Clyde Morris Boulevard, Daytona Beach, FL 32114-3900, 386-226-6000 or toll-free 800-862-2416.
Website: http://www.daytonabeach.erau.edu/.

EMBRY-RIDDLE AERONAUTICAL UNIVERSITY–PRESCOTT

Prescott, AZ

ABOUT THE INSTITUTION Independent, coed. ***Awards:*** bachelor's and master's degrees. 22 undergraduate majors. ***Total enrollment:*** 2,776. Undergraduates: 2,726. Freshmen: 609.

GIFT AID (NEED-BASED) ***Scholarships, grants, and awards:*** Federal Pell, FSEOG, state, private, college/university gift aid from institutional funds.

LOANS ***Programs:*** Federal Direct (Subsidized and Unsubsidized Stafford, PLUS), college/university.

WORK-STUDY ***Federal work-study:*** Total amount: $96,454; jobs available. ***State or other work-study/employment:*** Total amount: $1,706,757 (100% need-based).

APPLYING FOR FINANCIAL AID ***Required financial aid form:*** FAFSA.

CONTACT Mr. John Hanson, Director of Financial Aid, Prescott Campus, Embry-Riddle Aeronautical University–Prescott, 3700 Willow Creek Road, Prescott, AZ 86301-3720, 928-777-3765 or toll-free 800-888-3728. *Fax:* 928-777-3893. *E-mail:* prfinaid@erau.edu.
Website: http://www.prescott.erau.edu/.

EMBRY-RIDDLE AERONAUTICAL UNIVERSITY–WORLDWIDE

Daytona Beach, FL

CONTACT Ms. Dagmar Bowen, Director of Financial Aid, Worldwide, Embry-Riddle Aeronautical University–Worldwide, 600 South Clyde Morris Boulevard, Daytona Beach, FL 32114-3900, 800-522-6787. *Fax:* 386-226-6915. *E-mail:* wwfinaid@erau.edu.
Website: http://www.worldwide.erau.edu/.

EMERSON COLLEGE

Boston, MA

ABOUT THE INSTITUTION Independent, coed. ***Awards:*** certificates, bachelor's, master's, and doctoral degrees. 30 undergraduate majors. ***Total enrollment:*** 4,582. Undergraduates: 3,855. Freshmen: 923.

GIFT AID (NEED-BASED) ***Scholarships, grants, and awards:*** Federal Pell, FSEOG, state, private, college/university gift aid from institutional funds.

GIFT AID (NON-NEED-BASED) ***Scholarships, grants, and awards by category:*** *Academic interests/achievement:* general academic interests/achievements. *Creative arts/performance:* performing arts. *Special characteristics:* parents of current students.

LOANS ***Programs:*** Federal Direct (Subsidized and Unsubsidized Stafford, PLUS), Perkins, state.

WORK-STUDY ***Federal work-study:*** Total amount: $1,016,784; jobs available. ***State or other work-study/employment:*** Total amount: $1,154,161 (60% need-based, 40% non-need-based). Part-time jobs available.

APPLYING FOR FINANCIAL AID ***Required financial aid forms:*** FAFSA, CSS Financial Aid PROFILE, noncustodial (divorced/separated) parent's statement, business/farm supplement.

CONTACT Ms. Angela Grant, Director of Financial Aid, Emerson College, 120 Boylston Street, Boston, MA 02116-4624, 617-824-8655. *Fax:* 617-824-8655. *E-mail:* finaid@emerson.edu.
Website: http://www.emerson.edu/.

EMMANUEL COLLEGE

Franklin Springs, GA

Tuition & fees: $21,220	Average undergraduate aid package: $16,881

ABOUT THE INSTITUTION Independent Pentecostal Holiness Church, coed. ***Awards:*** associate and bachelor's degrees. 27 undergraduate majors. ***Total enrollment:*** 958. Undergraduates: 958. Freshmen: 248. Federal methodology is used as a basis for awarding need-based institutional aid.

UNDERGRADUATE EXPENSES for 2020–2021 ***Application fee:*** $25. ***Comprehensive fee:*** $29,282 includes full-time tuition ($20,760), mandatory fees ($460), and room and board ($8062). Full-time tuition and fees vary according to location. Room and board charges vary according to housing facility. ***Part-time tuition:*** $873 per credit hour. ***Part-time fees:*** $115 per term.

FRESHMAN FINANCIAL AID (Fall 2019, est.) 216 applied for aid; of those 86% were deemed to have need. 100% of freshmen with need received aid; of those 21% had need fully met. ***Average percent of need met:*** 71% (excluding resources

awarded to replace EFC). ***Average financial aid package:*** $16,417 (excluding resources awarded to replace EFC). 14% of all full-time freshmen had no need and received non-need-based gift aid.

UNDERGRADUATE FINANCIAL AID (Fall 2019, est.) 681 applied for aid; of those 88% were deemed to have need. 100% of undergraduates with need received aid; of those 21% had need fully met. ***Average percent of need met:*** 71% (excluding resources awarded to replace EFC). ***Average financial aid package:*** $16,881 (excluding resources awarded to replace EFC). 17% of all full-time undergraduates had no need and received non-need-based gift aid.

GIFT AID (NEED-BASED) ***Total amount:*** $5,079,171 (35% federal, 21% state, 39% institutional, 5% external sources). ***Receiving aid:*** Freshmen: 62% (147); all full-time undergraduates: 58% (465). ***Average award:*** Freshmen: $12,952; Undergraduates: $13,074. ***Scholarships, grants, and awards:*** Federal Pell, FSEOG, state, college/university gift aid from institutional funds.

GIFT AID (NON-NEED-BASED) ***Total amount:*** $1,343,998 (42% state, 53% institutional, 5% external sources). ***Receiving aid:*** Freshmen: 12% (29). Undergraduates: 12% (92). ***Average award:*** Freshmen: $3703. Undergraduates: $4764. ***Scholarships, grants, and awards by category:*** *Academic interests/achievement:* 390 awards ($1,537,457 total): agriculture, business, communication, education, English, general academic interests/achievements, home economics, religion/biblical studies. *Creative arts/performance:* 18 awards ($32,900 total): applied art and design, art/fine arts, creative writing, dance, general creative arts/performance, journalism/publications, music, performing arts, theater/drama. *Special achievements/activities:* 13 awards ($89,109 total): cheerleading/drum major, general special achievements/activities, hobbies/interests, leadership, memberships, religious involvement. *Special characteristics:* 220 awards ($481,099 total): adult students, children of current students, children of educators, children of faculty/staff, first-generation college students, general special characteristics, international students, local/state students, married students, parents of current students, relatives of clergy, religious affiliation, siblings of current students, spouses of current students, twins. ***Tuition waivers:*** Full or partial for employees or children of employees, senior citizens.

LOANS ***Student loans:*** $3,708,223 (81% need-based, 19% non-need-based). 56% of past graduating class borrowed through all loan programs. *Average indebtedness per student:* $24,028. ***Average need-based loan:*** Freshmen: $3220. Undergraduates: $3842. ***Parent loans:*** $2,341,611 (54% need-based, 46% non-need-based). ***Programs:*** Federal Direct (Subsidized and Unsubsidized Stafford, PLUS), state.

WORK-STUDY ***Federal work-study:*** Total amount: $502,900; 100 jobs averaging $1038. ***State or other work-study/employment:*** 91 part-time jobs averaging $1281.

ATHLETIC AWARDS Total amount: $4,764,224 (55% need-based, 45% non-need-based).

APPLYING FOR FINANCIAL AID ***Required financial aid forms:*** FAFSA, institution's own form, state aid form. ***Financial aid deadline:*** 6/15 (priority: 5/1). ***Notification date:*** Continuous beginning 3/1. Students must reply within 2 weeks of notification.

CONTACT Mrs. Niki Stinson, Director of Financial Aid, Emmanuel College, PO Box 129, Franklin Springs, GA 30639-0129, 706-245-2871 or toll-free 800-860-8800. *Fax:* 706-245-2846. *E-mail:* nstinson@ec.edu.
Website: http://www.ec.edu/.

EMMANUEL COLLEGE

Boston, MA

Tuition & fees: $42,516	Average undergraduate aid package: $30,737

ABOUT THE INSTITUTION Independent Roman Catholic, coed. ***Awards:*** certificates, bachelor's, and master's degrees. 44 undergraduate majors. ***Total enrollment:*** 2,222. Undergraduates: 2,112. Freshmen: 582. Federal methodology is used as a basis for awarding need-based institutional aid.

UNDERGRADUATE EXPENSES for 2020–2021 ***Application fee:*** $60. ***One-time required fee:*** $350. ***Comprehensive fee:*** $58,362 includes full-time tuition ($42,096), mandatory fees ($420), and room and board ($15,846). Full-time tuition and fees vary according to course load. Room and board charges vary according to board plan and housing facility. ***Part-time tuition:*** $1316 per credit hour. Part-time tuition and fees vary according to course load.

FRESHMAN FINANCIAL AID (Fall 2018) 535 applied for aid; of those 91% were deemed to have need. 100% of freshmen with need received aid; of those 31% had need fully met. ***Average percent of need met:*** 78% (excluding resources awarded to replace EFC). ***Average financial aid package:*** $32,631 (excluding resources awarded to replace EFC). 15% of all full-time freshmen had no need and received non-need-based gift aid.

UNDERGRADUATE FINANCIAL AID (Fall 2018) 1,695 applied for aid; of those 92% were deemed to have need. 100% of undergraduates with need received aid; of those 40% had need fully met. ***Average percent of need met:*** 74% (excluding resources awarded to replace EFC). ***Average financial aid package:*** $30,737 (excluding resources awarded to replace EFC). 20% of all full-time undergraduates had no need and received non-need-based gift aid.

GIFT AID (NEED-BASED) ***Receiving aid:*** Freshmen: 76% (440); all full-time undergraduates: 72% (1,401). ***Average award:*** Freshmen: $29,106; Undergraduates: $26,831. ***Scholarships, grants, and awards:*** Federal Pell, FSEOG, state, private, college/university gift aid from institutional funds.

GIFT AID (NON-NEED-BASED) ***Receiving aid:*** Freshmen: 84% (486). Undergraduates: 80% (1,561). ***Average award:*** Freshmen: $20,680. Undergraduates: $23,488. ***Scholarships, grants, and awards by category:*** *Academic interests/achievement:* general academic interests/achievements. *Creative arts/performance:* general creative arts/performance. *Special achievements/activities:* general special achievements/activities. *Special characteristics:* children of faculty/staff, general special characteristics, siblings of current students, spouses of current students, veterans. ***Tuition waivers:*** Full or partial for employees or children of employees. ***ROTC:*** Army cooperative.

LOANS ***Average need-based loan:*** Freshmen: $3408. Undergraduates: $4438. ***Programs:*** Federal Direct (Subsidized and Unsubsidized Stafford, PLUS), Perkins, state.

WORK-STUDY ***Federal work-study:*** 456 jobs averaging $2005. ***State or other work-study/employment:*** Part-time jobs available.

APPLYING FOR FINANCIAL AID ***Required financial aid form:*** FAFSA. ***Notification date:*** Continuous.

CONTACT Jennifer Porter, Associate Vice President for Student Financial Services, Emmanuel College, 400 The Fenway, Boston, MA 02115, 617-735-9938. *Fax:* 617-735-9939. *E-mail:* financialservices@emmanuel.edu.
Website: http://www.emmanuel.edu/.

EMMAUS BIBLE COLLEGE

Dubuque, IA

CONTACT Steve Seeman, Financial Aid Director, Emmaus Bible College, 2570 Asbury Road, Dubuque, IA 52001-3097, 800-397-2425 Ext. 1309 or toll-free 800-397-2425. *Fax:* 563-588-1216. *E-mail:* financialaid@emmaus.edu.
Website: http://www.emmaus.edu/.

EMORY & HENRY COLLEGE

Emory, VA

Tuition & fees: $35,300	Average undergraduate aid package: $37,101

ABOUT THE INSTITUTION Independent United Methodist, coed. ***Awards:*** bachelor's, master's, and doctoral degrees. 71 undergraduate majors. ***Total enrollment:*** 1,292. Undergraduates: 1,019. Freshmen: 271. Federal methodology is used as a basis for awarding need-based institutional aid.

UNDERGRADUATE EXPENSES for 2020–2021 ***Comprehensive fee:*** $48,425 includes full-time tuition ($34,500), mandatory fees ($800), and room and board ($13,125). ***College room only:*** $6900. ***Part-time tuition:*** $1350 per credit hour. ***Part-time fees:*** $50 per term.

FRESHMAN FINANCIAL AID (Fall 2019, est.) 270 applied for aid; of those 94% were deemed to have need. 100% of freshmen with need received aid; of those 17% had need fully met. ***Average percent of need met:*** 93% (excluding resources awarded to replace EFC). ***Average financial aid package:*** $39,198 (excluding resources awarded to replace EFC). 6% of all full-time freshmen had no need and received non-need-based gift aid.

UNDERGRADUATE FINANCIAL AID (Fall 2019, est.) 941 applied for aid; of those 93% were deemed to have need. 100% of undergraduates with need received aid; of those 23% had need fully met. ***Average percent of need met:*** 84%

(excluding resources awarded to replace EFC). ***Average financial aid package:*** $37,101 (excluding resources awarded to replace EFC). 11% of all full-time undergraduates had no need and received non-need-based gift aid.

GIFT AID (NEED-BASED) ***Receiving aid:*** Freshmen: 93% (251); all full-time undergraduates: 87% (872). ***Average award:*** Freshmen: $32,824; Undergraduates: $29,846. ***Scholarships, grants, and awards:*** Federal Pell, FSEOG, state, private, college/university gift aid from institutional funds.

GIFT AID (NON-NEED-BASED) ***Receiving aid:*** Freshmen: 7% (19). Undergraduates: 7% (65). ***Average award:*** Freshmen: $16,456. Undergraduates: $20,368. ***Scholarships, grants, and awards by category:*** *Academic interests/achievement:* 932 awards ($15,391,255 total): general academic interests/achievements, premedicine. *Creative arts/performance:* 150 awards ($285,325 total): applied art and design, journalism/publications, music, performing arts, theater/drama. *Special achievements/activities:* 80 awards ($291,225 total): cheerleading/drum major, community service. *Special characteristics:* 473 awards ($1,648,964 total): children and siblings of alumni, children of educators, children of faculty/staff, out-of-state students, religious affiliation, siblings of current students. ***Tuition waivers:*** Full or partial for employees or children of employees. ***ROTC:*** Army cooperative.

LOANS ***Student loans:*** 79% of past graduating class borrowed through all loan programs. *Average indebtedness per student:* $30,360. ***Average need-based loan:*** Freshmen: $3066. Undergraduates: $3955. ***Programs:*** Federal Direct (Subsidized and Unsubsidized Stafford, PLUS).

WORK-STUDY ***Federal work-study:*** 400 jobs averaging $1925.

APPLYING FOR FINANCIAL AID ***Required financial aid forms:*** FAFSA, state aid form. ***Financial aid deadline:*** Continuous. ***Notification date:*** Continuous. Students must reply within 2 weeks of notification.

CONTACT Ms. Scarlett C. Blevins, Director of Financial Aid, Emory & Henry College, PO Box 947, Emory, VA 24327-0010, 276-944-6940 or toll-free 800-848-5493. *Fax:* 276-944-6884. *E-mail:* scblevins@ehc.edu.
Website: http://www.ehc.edu/.

EMORY UNIVERSITY

Atlanta, GA

Tuition & fees: $55,998	Average undergraduate aid package: $47,223

ABOUT THE INSTITUTION Independent Methodist, coed. ***Awards:*** certificates, bachelor's, master's, and doctoral degrees (enrollment figures include Emory University, Oxford College; application data for main campus only). 67 undergraduate majors. ***Total enrollment:*** 14,417. Undergraduates: 7,118. Freshmen: 1,374. Both federal and institutional methodology are used as a basis for awarding need-based institutional aid.

UNDERGRADUATE EXPENSES for 2020–2021 ***Application fee:*** $75. ***Comprehensive fee:*** $71,570 includes full-time tuition ($55,200), mandatory fees ($798), and room and board ($15,572). ***College room only:*** $8984. Room and board charges vary according to board plan and housing facility. ***Part-time tuition:*** $2300 per credit hour.

FRESHMAN FINANCIAL AID (Fall 2019, est.) 803 applied for aid; of those 80% were deemed to have need. 100% of freshmen with need received aid; of those 100% had need fully met. ***Average percent of need met:*** 100% (excluding resources awarded to replace EFC). ***Average financial aid package:*** $50,425 (excluding resources awarded to replace EFC). 4% of all full-time freshmen had no need and received non-need-based gift aid.

UNDERGRADUATE FINANCIAL AID (Fall 2019, est.) 3,743 applied for aid; of those 88% were deemed to have need. 100% of undergraduates with need received aid; of those 98% had need fully met. ***Average percent of need met:*** 100% (excluding resources awarded to replace EFC). ***Average financial aid package:*** $47,223 (excluding resources awarded to replace EFC). 5% of all full-time undergraduates had no need and received non-need-based gift aid.

GIFT AID (NEED-BASED) ***Total amount:*** $143,924,900 (6% federal, 2% state, 91% institutional, 1% external sources). ***Receiving aid:*** Freshmen: 44% (607); all full-time undergraduates: 46% (3,133). ***Average award:*** Freshmen: $48,738; Undergraduates: $43,659. ***Scholarships, grants, and awards:*** Federal Pell, state, private, college/university gift aid from institutional funds.

GIFT AID (NON-NEED-BASED) ***Total amount:*** $16,046,506 (10% state, 72% institutional, 18% external sources). ***Receiving aid:*** Freshmen: 16% (218). Undergraduates: 10% (712). ***Average award:*** Freshmen: $19,225. Undergraduates: $28,668. ***Scholarships, grants, and awards by category:*** *Academic interests/achievement:* business, general academic interests/achievements, humanities. *Creative arts/performance:* applied art and design, cinema/film/broadcasting, creative writing, debating, journalism/publications, music, performing arts, theater/drama. *Special achievements/activities:* community service, general special achievements/activities, leadership. *Special characteristics:* children of faculty/staff, international students, local/state students, parents of current students, religious affiliation, veterans. ***Tuition waivers:*** Full or partial for employees or children of employees. ***ROTC:*** Army cooperative, Naval cooperative, Air Force cooperative.

LOANS ***Student loans:*** $27,566,171 (61% need-based, 39% non-need-based). 35% of past graduating class borrowed through all loan programs. *Average indebtedness per student:* $24,889. ***Average need-based loan:*** Freshmen: $3412. Undergraduates: $6151. ***Parent loans:*** $4,911,622 (14% need-based, 86% non-need-based). ***Programs:*** Federal Direct (Subsidized and Unsubsidized Stafford, PLUS), Federal Nursing, state, college/university, alternative loans.

WORK-STUDY ***Federal work-study:*** Total amount: $6,717,723; jobs available. ***State or other work-study/employment:*** Total amount: $872,438 (19% need-based, 81% non-need-based). Part-time jobs available.

APPLYING FOR FINANCIAL AID ***Required financial aid forms:*** FAFSA, CSS Financial Aid PROFILE, noncustodial (divorced/separated) parent's statement. ***Financial aid deadline:*** 3/1 (priority: 2/15). ***Notification date:*** 4/1. Students must reply by 5/1.

CONTACT Financial Aid Office, Emory University, 200 Dowman Drive, Atlanta, GA 30322-1960, 404-727-6039 or toll-free 800-727-6036. *Fax:* 404-727-6709. *E-mail:* finaid@emory.edu.
Website: http://www.emory.edu/.

EMPORIA STATE UNIVERSITY

Emporia, KS

Tuition & fees (KS res): $6960	Average undergraduate aid package: $9587

ABOUT THE INSTITUTION State-supported, coed. ***Awards:*** certificates, bachelor's, master's, and doctoral degrees. 34 undergraduate majors. ***Total enrollment:*** 5,877. Undergraduates: 3,405. Freshmen: 680. Federal methodology is used as a basis for awarding need-based institutional aid.

UNDERGRADUATE EXPENSES for 2019–2020 ***Application fee:*** $30. ***Tuition, state resident:*** full-time $5154; part-time $172 per credit hour. ***Tuition, nonresident:*** full-time $19,071; part-time $636 per credit hour. ***Required fees:*** full-time $1806; $90.95 per credit hour. Full-time tuition and fees vary according to course load, degree level, and location. Part-time tuition and fees vary according to course load, degree level, and location. ***College room and board:*** $9408; ***Room only:*** $6120. Room and board charges vary according to board plan, housing facility, and location.

FRESHMAN FINANCIAL AID (Fall 2019, est.) 608 applied for aid; of those 74% were deemed to have need. 100% of freshmen with need received aid; of those 18% had need fully met. ***Average percent of need met:*** 60% (excluding resources awarded to replace EFC). ***Average financial aid package:*** $9702 (excluding resources awarded to replace EFC). 18% of all full-time freshmen had no need and received non-need-based gift aid.

UNDERGRADUATE FINANCIAL AID (Fall 2019, est.) 2,418 applied for aid; of those 79% were deemed to have need. 100% of undergraduates with need received aid; of those 17% had need fully met. ***Average percent of need met:*** 60% (excluding resources awarded to replace EFC). ***Average financial aid package:*** $9587 (excluding resources awarded to replace EFC). 16% of all full-time undergraduates had no need and received non-need-based gift aid.

GIFT AID (NEED-BASED) ***Receiving aid:*** Freshmen: 67% (450); all full-time undergraduates: 61% (1,898). ***Average award:*** Freshmen: $6430; Undergraduates: $6173. ***Scholarships, grants, and awards:*** Federal Pell, FSEOG, state, private, college/university gift aid from institutional funds, Jones Foundation Grants.

GIFT AID (NON-NEED-BASED) ***Receiving aid:*** Freshmen: 6% (43). Undergraduates: 4% (131). ***Average award:*** Freshmen: $2637. Undergraduates: $2886. ***Scholarships, grants, and awards by category:*** *Academic interests/achievement:* 1,483 awards ($3,663,111 total): biological sciences, business, communication, computer science, education, engineering/technologies, English, foreign languages, general academic interests/achievements, home economics, humanities, mathematics, physical sciences, premedicine, social sciences. *Creative arts/perfor-*

mance: 175 awards ($124,660 total): applied art and design, creative writing, debating, music, theater/drama. *Special achievements/activities:* 47 awards ($38,775 total): general special achievements/activities, leadership. *Special characteristics:* 147 awards ($114,183 total): children and siblings of alumni, children of faculty/staff, children of union members/company employees, first-generation college students, general special characteristics, handicapped students, international students, members of minority groups, religious affiliation, veterans. ***Tuition waivers:*** Full or partial for employees or children of employees, senior citizens.

LOANS *Student loans:* 65% of past graduating class borrowed through all loan programs. *Average indebtedness per student:* $22,692. ***Average need-based loan:*** Freshmen: $5206. Undergraduates: $6164. ***Programs:*** Federal Direct (Subsidized and Unsubsidized Stafford, PLUS), Perkins, alternative loans, Alaska Loans.

WORK-STUDY *Federal work-study:* 162 jobs averaging $2224. ***State or other work-study/employment:*** 13 part-time jobs averaging $2200.

APPLYING FOR FINANCIAL AID *Required financial aid forms:* FAFSA, state aid form. ***Notification date:*** Continuous. Students must reply within 2 weeks of notification.

CONTACT Jaime Morris, Director of Financial Aid, Emporia State University, 1 Kellogg Circle, Emporia, KS 66801-5087, 620-341-5457 or toll-free 877-GOTOESU (in-state), 877-468-6378 (out-of-state). *Fax:* 620-341-6088. *E-mail:* jmorri12@emporia.edu.
Website: http://www.emporia.edu/.

ENDICOTT COLLEGE

Beverly, MA

Tuition & fees: $35,320	Average undergraduate aid package: $22,560

ABOUT THE INSTITUTION Independent, coed. ***Awards:*** certificates, associate, bachelor's, master's, and doctoral degrees. 38 undergraduate majors. ***Total enrollment:*** 5,082. Undergraduates: 3,322. Freshmen: 842. Federal methodology is used as a basis for awarding need-based institutional aid.

UNDERGRADUATE EXPENSES for 2020–2021 *Application fee:* $50. ***Comprehensive fee:*** $51,450 includes full-time tuition ($34,470), mandatory fees ($850), and room and board ($16,130). ***College room only:*** $11,118. Full-time tuition and fees vary according to location. Room and board charges vary according to board plan and housing facility. ***Part-time tuition:*** $1060 per credit hour. Part-time tuition and fees vary according to location. ***Payment plan:*** Tuition prepayment.

FRESHMAN FINANCIAL AID (Fall 2019, est.) 728 applied for aid; of those 77% were deemed to have need. 100% of freshmen with need received aid; of those 13% had need fully met. ***Average percent of need met:*** 62% (excluding resources awarded to replace EFC). ***Average financial aid package:*** $21,746 (excluding resources awarded to replace EFC). 30% of all full-time freshmen had no need and received non-need-based gift aid.

UNDERGRADUATE FINANCIAL AID (Fall 2019, est.) 2,296 applied for aid; of those 81% were deemed to have need. 100% of undergraduates with need received aid; of those 11% had need fully met. ***Average percent of need met:*** 65% (excluding resources awarded to replace EFC). ***Average financial aid package:*** $22,560 (excluding resources awarded to replace EFC). 28% of all full-time undergraduates had no need and received non-need-based gift aid.

GIFT AID (NEED-BASED) *Total amount:* $31,371,107 (8% federal, 2% state, 90% institutional). ***Receiving aid:*** Freshmen: 66% (556); all full-time undergraduates: 60% (1,816). ***Average award:*** Freshmen: $17,272; Undergraduates: $17,391. ***Scholarships, grants, and awards:*** Federal Pell, FSEOG, state, private, college/university gift aid from institutional funds.

GIFT AID (NON-NEED-BASED) *Total amount:* $10,804,820 (93% institutional, 7% external sources). ***Receiving aid:*** Freshmen: 65% (549). Undergraduates: 58% (1,753). ***Average award:*** Freshmen: $10,911. Undergraduates: $10,823. ***Scholarships, grants, and awards by category:*** *Academic interests/achievement:* business, education, general academic interests/achievements, home economics. *Creative arts/performance:* applied art and design, music, performing arts. *Special achievements/activities:* community service, general special achievements/activities, leadership, religious involvement. *Special characteristics:* children and siblings of alumni, children of educators, general special characteristics, international students, local/state students, religious affiliation. ***Tuition waivers:*** Full or partial for employees or children of employees. ***ROTC:*** Army cooperative.

LOANS *Student loans:* $26,893,765 (26% need-based, 74% non-need-based). 77% of past graduating class borrowed through all loan programs. *Average indebtedness per student:* $44,178. ***Average need-based loan:*** Freshmen: $3402. Undergraduates: $4459. ***Parent loans:*** $6,535,257 (100% non-need-based). ***Programs:*** Federal Direct (Subsidized and Unsubsidized Stafford, PLUS), Perkins.

WORK-STUDY *Federal work-study:* Total amount: $1,549,710; jobs available. ***State or other work-study/employment:*** 796 part-time jobs averaging $2000.

APPLYING FOR FINANCIAL AID *Required financial aid form:* FAFSA. ***Financial aid deadline (priority):*** 3/15. ***Notification date:*** Continuous beginning 1/15. Students must reply within 2 weeks of notification.

CONTACT Ms. Marcia Toomey, Dean of Financial Aid, Endicott College, 376 Hale Street, Beverly, MA 01915-2096, 978-232-2060 or toll-free 800-325-1114. *Fax:* 978-232-2085. *E-mail:* mtoomey@endicott.edu.
Website: http://www.endicott.edu/.

EPIC BIBLE COLLEGE

Sacramento, CA

CONTACT Financial Aid Office, Epic Bible College, 4330 Auburn Boulevard, Sacramento, CA 95841, 916-348-4689.
Website: http://epic.edu/.

ERSKINE COLLEGE

Due West, SC

CONTACT Mrs. Becky Pressley, Director of Financial Aid, Erskine College, PO Box 337, Due West, SC 29639, 864-379-8832 or toll-free 800-241-8721. *Fax:* 864-379-2172. *E-mail:* pressley@erskine.edu.
Website: http://www.erskine.edu/.

ESCUELA DE ARTES PLASTICAS Y DISEÑO DE PUERTO RICO

San Juan, PR

CONTACT Mr. Alfred Diaz Melendez, Financial Aid Administrator, Escuela de Artes Plasticas y Diseño de Puerto Rico, PO Box 9021112, San Juan, PR 00902-1112, 787-725-8120 Ext. 317. *Fax:* 787-725-3798. *E-mail:* adiaz@eap.edu.
Website: http://www.eap.edu/.

EUGENE LANG COLLEGE OF LIBERAL ARTS

New York, NY

Tuition & fees: N/R	Average undergraduate aid package: $27,199

ABOUT THE INSTITUTION Independent, coed. ***Awards:*** bachelor's degrees. 30 undergraduate majors. ***Total enrollment:*** 1,885. Undergraduates: 1,885. Freshmen: 432. Federal methodology is used as a basis for awarding need-based institutional aid.

FRESHMAN FINANCIAL AID (Fall 2018) 366 applied for aid; of those 88% were deemed to have need. 100% of freshmen with need received aid; of those 7% had need fully met. ***Average percent of need met:*** 56% (excluding resources awarded to replace EFC). ***Average financial aid package:*** $26,770 (excluding resources awarded to replace EFC). 36% of all full-time freshmen had no need and received non-need-based gift aid.

UNDERGRADUATE FINANCIAL AID (Fall 2018) 1,093 applied for aid; of those 93% were deemed to have need. 100% of undergraduates with need received aid; of those 6% had need fully met. ***Average percent of need met:*** 62% (excluding resources awarded to replace EFC). ***Average financial aid package:*** $27,199

(excluding resources awarded to replace EFC). 36% of all full-time undergraduates had no need and received non-need-based gift aid.

GIFT AID (NEED-BASED) ***Total amount:*** $13,467,514 (17% federal, 3% state, 75% institutional, 5% external sources). ***Receiving aid:*** Freshmen: 46% (238); all full-time undergraduates: 45% (818). ***Average award:*** Freshmen: $12,295; Undergraduates: $14,803. ***Scholarships, grants, and awards:*** Federal Pell, FSEOG, state, private, college/university gift aid from institutional funds, United Negro College Fund.

GIFT AID (NON-NEED-BASED) ***Total amount:*** $22,665,457 (97% institutional, 3% external sources). ***Receiving aid:*** Freshmen: 49% (256). Undergraduates: 43% (779). ***Average award:*** Freshmen: $17,574. Undergraduates: $14,743. ***Scholarships, grants, and awards by category:*** *Special achievements/activities:* general special achievements/activities, leadership. *Special characteristics:* local/state students, members of minority groups.

LOANS ***Student loans:*** $8,018,874 (68% need-based, 32% non-need-based). 61% of past graduating class borrowed through all loan programs. *Average indebtedness per student:* $32,153. ***Average need-based loan:*** Freshmen: $2580. Undergraduates: $3377. ***Parent loans:*** $8,082,384 (100% non-need-based). ***Programs:*** Federal Direct (Subsidized and Unsubsidized Stafford, PLUS).

WORK-STUDY ***Federal work-study:*** Total amount: $464,942; jobs available.

APPLYING FOR FINANCIAL AID ***Required financial aid form:*** FAFSA. ***Financial aid deadline (priority):*** 2/1. ***Notification date:*** Continuous beginning 4/1. Students must reply within 4 weeks of notification.

CONTACT LaVerne Walker, Office of Student Financial Services, Eugene Lang College of Liberal Arts, 72 Fifth Avenue, 2nd Floor, New York, NY 10003, 212-229-8930 or toll-free 800-292-3040. *E-mail:* sfs@newschool.edu.
Website: http://www.newschool.edu/lang.

EUREKA COLLEGE

Eureka, IL

ABOUT THE INSTITUTION Independent Christian Church (Disciples of Christ), coed. ***Awards:*** bachelor's degrees. 23 undergraduate majors.

GIFT AID (NEED-BASED) ***Scholarships, grants, and awards:*** Federal Pell, FSEOG, state, private, college/university gift aid from institutional funds.

GIFT AID (NON-NEED-BASED) ***Scholarships, grants, and awards by category:*** *Academic interests/achievement:* general academic interests/achievements. *Creative arts/performance:* applied art and design, music, performing arts, theater/drama. *Special achievements/activities:* community service, leadership, religious involvement. *Special characteristics:* children and siblings of alumni, children of faculty/staff, relatives of clergy, religious affiliation, siblings of current students.

LOANS ***Programs:*** Federal Direct (Subsidized and Unsubsidized Stafford, PLUS), alternative loans.

WORK-STUDY ***Federal work-study:*** Total amount: $73,907; 205 jobs averaging $1916. ***State or other work-study/employment:*** Total amount: $975,146 (100% need-based). Part-time jobs available.

APPLYING FOR FINANCIAL AID ***Required financial aid form:*** FAFSA.

CONTACT Mrs. Tammy Crothers, Director of Financial Aid, Eureka College, 300 East College Avenue, Eureka, IL 61530, 309-467-6311 or toll-free 888-4-EUREKA. *Fax:* 309-467-6897. *E-mail:* tcrothers@eureka.edu.
Website: http://www.eureka.edu/.

EVANGEL UNIVERSITY

Springfield, MO

Tuition & fees: $24,327	Average undergraduate aid package: $18,783

ABOUT THE INSTITUTION Independent Assemblies of God, coed. ***Awards:*** associate, bachelor's, master's, and doctoral degrees. 48 undergraduate majors. ***Total enrollment:*** 2,300. Undergraduates: 1,793. Freshmen: 443. Federal methodology is used as a basis for awarding need-based institutional aid.

UNDERGRADUATE EXPENSES for 2019–2020 ***Comprehensive fee:*** $32,849 includes full-time tuition ($23,032), mandatory fees ($1295), and room and board ($8522). ***College room only:*** $4304. Full-time tuition and fees vary according to course load. Room and board charges vary according to board plan. ***Part-time tuition:*** $960 per credit hour. Part-time tuition and fees vary according to course load.

FRESHMAN FINANCIAL AID (Fall 2018) 112 applied for aid; of those 90% were deemed to have need. 100% of freshmen with need received aid; of those 9% had need fully met. ***Average percent of need met:*** 64% (excluding resources awarded to replace EFC). ***Average financial aid package:*** $17,342 (excluding resources awarded to replace EFC). 14% of all full-time freshmen had no need and received non-need-based gift aid.

UNDERGRADUATE FINANCIAL AID (Fall 2018) 1,379 applied for aid; of those 87% were deemed to have need. 100% of undergraduates with need received aid; of those 13% had need fully met. ***Average percent of need met:*** 70% (excluding resources awarded to replace EFC). ***Average financial aid package:*** $18,783 (excluding resources awarded to replace EFC). 14% of all full-time undergraduates had no need and received non-need-based gift aid.

GIFT AID (NEED-BASED) ***Receiving aid:*** Freshmen: 80% (101); all full-time undergraduates: 83% (1,198). ***Average award:*** Freshmen: $13,869; Undergraduates: $14,846. ***Scholarships, grants, and awards:*** Federal Pell, FSEOG, state, private, college/university gift aid from institutional funds.

GIFT AID (NON-NEED-BASED) ***Receiving aid:*** Freshmen: 6% (7). Undergraduates: 10% (138). ***Average award:*** Freshmen: $8625. Undergraduates: $9479. ***Scholarships, grants, and awards by category:*** *Academic interests/achievement:* 1,302 awards ($15,898,801 total): biological sciences, business, communication, computer science, education, engineering/technologies, English, foreign languages, general academic interests/achievements, health fields, humanities, international studies, mathematics, physical sciences, premedicine, religion/biblical studies, social sciences. *Creative arts/performance:* 130 awards ($86,932 total): applied art and design, debating, music, theater/drama. *Special achievements/activities:* 264 awards ($133,226 total): cheerleading/drum major, general special achievements/activities, leadership, religious involvement. *Special characteristics:* 322 awards ($1,300,297 total): adult students, children and siblings of alumni, children of educators, children of faculty/staff, general special characteristics, out-of-state students, relatives of clergy, religious affiliation. ***Tuition waivers:*** Full or partial for employees or children of employees. ***ROTC:*** Army cooperative.

LOANS ***Student loans:*** 77% of past graduating class borrowed through all loan programs. *Average indebtedness per student:* $31,560. ***Average need-based loan:*** Freshmen: $3123. Undergraduates: $3667. ***Programs:*** Federal Direct (Subsidized and Unsubsidized Stafford, PLUS), college/university.

WORK-STUDY ***Federal work-study:*** 965 jobs averaging $1821.

APPLYING FOR FINANCIAL AID ***Required financial aid form:*** FAFSA. ***Financial aid deadline:*** Continuous. ***Notification date:*** Continuous.

CONTACT Mrs. Valerie Sharp, Director of Financial Aid, Evangel University, 1111 North Glenstone Avenue, Springfield, MO 65802-2191, 417-865-2811 Ext. 7302 or toll-free 800-382-6435. *Fax:* 417-575-5478. *E-mail:* sharpv@evangel.edu.
Website: http://www.evangel.edu/.

EVERGLADES UNIVERSITY

Boca Raton, FL

CONTACT Miss Seeta Singh Moonilall, Regional Director of Financial Aid, Everglades University, 5002 T-Rex Avenue, Suite 100, Boca Raton, FL 33431, 561-912-1211 or toll-free 888-772-6077. *Fax:* 516-912-1191. *E-mail:* smoonilall@evergladesuniversity.edu.
Website: http://www.evergladesuniversity.edu/.

THE EVERGREEN STATE COLLEGE

Olympia, WA

Tuition & fees: N/R	Average undergraduate aid package: $13,549

ABOUT THE INSTITUTION State-supported, coed. ***Awards:*** bachelor's and master's degrees. 45 undergraduate majors. ***Total enrollment:*** 3,327. Undergraduates: 3,018. Freshmen: 309. Federal methodology is used as a basis for awarding need-based institutional aid.

FRESHMAN FINANCIAL AID (Fall 2018) 264 applied for aid; of those 79% were deemed to have need. 98% of freshmen with need received aid; of those 5% had need fully met. ***Average percent of need met:*** 56% (excluding resources awarded to

replace EFC). ***Average financial aid package:*** $12,608 (excluding resources awarded to replace EFC). 1% of all full-time freshmen had no need and received non-need-based gift aid.

UNDERGRADUATE FINANCIAL AID (Fall 2018) 2,174 applied for aid; of those 89% were deemed to have need. 95% of undergraduates with need received aid; of those 5% had need fully met. ***Average percent of need met:*** 63% (excluding resources awarded to replace EFC). ***Average financial aid package:*** $13,549 (excluding resources awarded to replace EFC). 1% of all full-time undergraduates had no need and received non-need-based gift aid.

GIFT AID (NEED-BASED) ***Total amount:*** $15,931,192 (45% federal, 45% state, 9% institutional, 1% external sources). ***Receiving aid:*** Freshmen: 64% (192); all full-time undergraduates: 61% (1,684). ***Average award:*** Freshmen: $10,756; Undergraduates: $10,923. ***Scholarships, grants, and awards:*** Federal Pell, FSEOG, state, private, college/university gift aid from institutional funds.

GIFT AID (NON-NEED-BASED) ***Total amount:*** $226,951 (24% state, 54% institutional, 22% external sources). ***Receiving aid:*** Freshmen: 2% (7). Undergraduates: 1% (19). ***Average award:*** Freshmen: $3500. Undergraduates: $3225. ***Scholarships, grants, and awards by category:*** *Academic interests/achievement:* general academic interests/achievements. *Creative arts/performance:* general creative arts/performance. *Special achievements/activities:* general special achievements/activities. *Special characteristics:* adult students, ethnic background, first-generation college students, general special characteristics, local/state students, out-of-state students, veterans.

LOANS ***Student loans:*** $11,860,171 (90% need-based, 10% non-need-based). 58% of past graduating class borrowed through all loan programs. *Average indebtedness per student:* $20,488. ***Average need-based loan:*** Freshmen: $3210. Undergraduates: $4210. ***Parent loans:*** $3,105,481 (82% need-based, 18% non-need-based). ***Programs:*** Federal Direct (Subsidized and Unsubsidized Stafford, PLUS), college/university.

WORK-STUDY Federal work-study jobs available. ***State or other work-study/employment:*** Total amount: $612,390 (100% need-based). Part-time jobs available.

ATHLETIC AWARDS Total amount: $217,372 (62% need-based, 38% non-need-based).

APPLYING FOR FINANCIAL AID ***Required financial aid form:*** FAFSA. ***Financial aid deadline (priority):*** 2/1. ***Notification date:*** Continuous beginning 4/1. Students must reply within 6 weeks of notification.

CONTACT Tracy Hall, Director of Financial Aid, The Evergreen State College, 2700 Evergreen Parkway NW, Olympia, WA 98505, 360-867-6205. *Fax:* 360-866-6576. *E-mail:* finaid@evergreen.edu.
Website: http://www.evergreen.edu/.

EXCELSIOR COLLEGE

Albany, NY

Tuition & fees: N/R | **Average undergraduate aid package: N/A**

ABOUT THE INSTITUTION Independent, coed. ***Awards:*** certificates, associate, bachelor's, and master's degrees (offers only external degree programs). 32 undergraduate majors. ***Total enrollment:*** 23,501. Undergraduates: 21,056. Federal methodology is used as a basis for awarding need-based institutional aid.

UNDERGRADUATE EXPENSES for 2020–2021 ***Application fee:*** $50. ***Tuition:*** part-time $510 per credit. ***Required fees:*** $20 per credit. Part-time tuition and fees vary according to reciprocity agreements.

GIFT AID (NEED-BASED) ***Total amount:*** $15,650,694 (80% federal, 4% state, 2% institutional, 14% external sources). ***Scholarships, grants, and awards:*** Federal Pell, FSEOG, state, private, college/university gift aid from institutional funds, Veterans Education Benefits (GI Bill).

GIFT AID (NON-NEED-BASED) ***Tuition waivers:*** Full or partial for employees or children of employees.

LOANS ***Student loans:*** $26,340,807 (96% need-based, 4% non-need-based). ***Parent loans:*** $25,336 (100% need-based). ***Programs:*** Federal Direct (Subsidized and Unsubsidized Stafford, PLUS).

APPLYING FOR FINANCIAL AID ***Financial aid deadline:*** Continuous. ***Notification date:*** Continuous.

CONTACT Financial Aid Office, Excelsior College, 7 Columbia Circle, Albany, NY 12203-5159, 518-464-8500 or toll-free 888-647-2388.
Website: http://www.excelsior.edu/.

FAIRFIELD UNIVERSITY

Fairfield, CT

Tuition & fees: $51,325 | **Average undergraduate aid package: $33,292**

ABOUT THE INSTITUTION Independent Roman Catholic (Jesuit), coed. ***Awards:*** certificates, bachelor's, master's, and doctoral degrees. 45 undergraduate majors. ***Total enrollment:*** 5,349. Undergraduates: 4,303. Freshmen: 1,176. Both federal and institutional methodology are used as a basis for awarding need-based institutional aid.

UNDERGRADUATE EXPENSES for 2020–2021 ***Application fee:*** $60. ***One-time required fee:*** $400. ***Comprehensive fee:*** $66,935 includes full-time tuition ($50,550), mandatory fees ($775), and room and board ($15,610). ***College room only:*** $9560. Full-time tuition and fees vary according to course load. Room and board charges vary according to board plan and housing facility. ***Part-time tuition:*** $775 per credit hour. ***Part-time fees:*** $50 per term. Part-time tuition and fees vary according to course load.

FRESHMAN FINANCIAL AID (Fall 2019, est.) 795 applied for aid; of those 64% were deemed to have need. 100% of freshmen with need received aid; of those 33% had need fully met. ***Average percent of need met:*** 89% (excluding resources awarded to replace EFC). ***Average financial aid package:*** $32,358 (excluding resources awarded to replace EFC). 50% of all full-time freshmen had no need and received non-need-based gift aid.

UNDERGRADUATE FINANCIAL AID (Fall 2019, est.) 2,231 applied for aid; of those 75% were deemed to have need. 100% of undergraduates with need received aid; of those 31% had need fully met. ***Average percent of need met:*** 87% (excluding resources awarded to replace EFC). ***Average financial aid package:*** $33,292 (excluding resources awarded to replace EFC). 46% of all full-time undergraduates had no need and received non-need-based gift aid.

GIFT AID (NEED-BASED) ***Total amount:*** $50,349,520 (5% federal, 1% state, 94% institutional). ***Receiving aid:*** Freshmen: 33% (385); all full-time undergraduates: 33% (1,354). ***Average award:*** Freshmen: $32,441; Undergraduates: $31,834. ***Scholarships, grants, and awards:*** Federal Pell, FSEOG, state, private, college/university gift aid from institutional funds.

GIFT AID (NON-NEED-BASED) ***Total amount:*** $35,385,990 (95% institutional, 5% external sources). ***Receiving aid:*** Freshmen: 41% (477). Undergraduates: 36% (1,504). ***Average award:*** Freshmen: $17,066. Undergraduates: $16,552. ***Scholarships, grants, and awards by category:*** *Academic interests/achievement:* 289 awards ($31,384,050 total): general academic interests/achievements. *Creative arts/performance:* 40 awards ($36,027 total): general creative arts/performance. *Special achievements/activities:* 23 awards ($114,329 total): general special achievements/activities. *Special characteristics:* 184 awards ($3,060,483 total): children and siblings of alumni, children of faculty/staff, children with a deceased or disabled parent, ethnic background, first-generation college students, general special characteristics, members of minority groups, veterans. ***Tuition waivers:*** Full or partial for employees or children of employees. ***ROTC:*** Army cooperative, Air Force cooperative.

LOANS ***Student loans:*** $25,668,282 (26% need-based, 74% non-need-based). 61% of past graduating class borrowed through all loan programs. *Average indebtedness per student:* $39,214. ***Average need-based loan:*** Freshmen: $3225. Undergraduates: $4300. ***Parent loans:*** $7,967,241 (100% non-need-based). ***Programs:*** Federal Direct (Subsidized and Unsubsidized Stafford, PLUS).

WORK-STUDY ***Federal work-study:*** Total amount: $991,138; 608 jobs averaging $1633.

ATHLETIC AWARDS Total amount: $6,952,754 (100% non-need-based).

APPLYING FOR FINANCIAL AID ***Required financial aid forms:*** FAFSA, CSS Financial Aid PROFILE, noncustodial (divorced/separated) parent's statement, business/farm supplement. ***Financial aid deadline:*** 1/15 (priority: 12/1). ***Notification date:*** Students must reply by 5/1.

CONTACT Diana Draper, Director of Financial Aid, Fairfield University, 1073 North Benson Road, Fairfield, CT 06824, 203-254-4125. *Fax:* 203-254-4008. *E-mail:* finaid@fairfield.edu.
Website: http://www.fairfield.edu/.

FAIRLEIGH DICKINSON UNIVERSITY

Teaneck, NJ

CONTACT Ms. Renee Volak, University Director of Financial Aid, Fairleigh Dickinson University, 1000 River Road T-KB1-04, Teaneck, NJ 07666-1914, 201-692-2363. *Fax:* 201-692-2363. *E-mail:* finaid@fdu.edu.
Website: http://www.fdu.edu/.

FAIRLEIGH DICKINSON UNIVERSITY, FLORHAM CAMPUS

Madison, NJ

CONTACT Renee Volak, Financial Aid Office, Fairleigh Dickinson University, Florham Campus, 285 Madison Avenue, M-MSO-02, Madison, NJ 07940-1099, 973-443-8700 or toll-free 800-338-8803. *Fax:* 973-443-8534. *E-mail:* finaid@fdu.edu.
Website: http://www.fdu.edu/.

FAIRLEIGH DICKINSON UNIVERSITY, METROPOLITAN CAMPUS

Teaneck, NJ

CONTACT Ms. Renee Volak, University Director of Financial Aid, Fairleigh Dickinson University, Metropolitan Campus, 1000 River Road T-KB1-04, Teaneck, NJ 07666-1914, 201-692-2363 or toll-free 800-338-8803. *Fax:* 201-692-2364. *E-mail:* finaid@fdu.edu.
Website: http://www.fdu.edu/.

FAIRMONT STATE UNIVERSITY

Fairmont, WV

CONTACT Patricia Wiemer, Director of Financial Aid and Scholarships, Fairmont State University, 1201 Locust Avenue, Fairmont, WV 26554, 304-367-4892 or toll-free 800-641-5678. *Fax:* 304-367-4789. *E-mail:* patricia.weimer@fairmontstate.edu.
Website: http://www.fairmontstate.edu/.

FAITH BAPTIST BIBLE COLLEGE AND THEOLOGICAL SEMINARY

Ankeny, IA

CONTACT Mr. Breck Appell, Director of Financial Assistance, Faith Baptist Bible College and Theological Seminary, 1900 Northwest 4th Street, Ankeny, IA 50021-2152, 515-964-0601 or toll-free 888-FAITH 4U. *Fax:* 515-964-1638.
Website: http://www.faith.edu/.

FAITH INTERNATIONAL UNIVERSITY

Tacoma, WA

CONTACT Financial Aid Office, Faith International University, 3504 North Pearl Street, Tacoma, WA 98407, 253-752-2020 or toll-free 888-777-7675 (out-of-state).
Website: http://www.faithseminary.edu/.

FAITH THEOLOGICAL SEMINARY

Baltimore, MD

CONTACT Financial Aid Office, Faith Theological Seminary, 529 Walker Avenue, Baltimore, MD 21212, 410-323-6211.
Website: http://www.fts.edu/.

FAMILY OF FAITH CHRISTIAN UNIVERSITY

Shawnee, OK

CONTACT Financial Aid Office, Family of Faith Christian University, 30 Kinville, Shawnee, OK 74802, 405-273-5331.
Website: http://www.familyoffaith.edu/.

FARMINGDALE STATE COLLEGE

Farmingdale, NY

Tuition & fees (NY res): $8538	Average undergraduate aid package: $8170

ABOUT THE INSTITUTION State-supported, coed. ***Awards:*** certificates, associate, bachelor's, and master's degrees. 37 undergraduate majors. ***Total enrollment:*** 9,996. Undergraduates: 9,939. Freshmen: 1,482. Federal methodology is used as a basis for awarding need-based institutional aid.

UNDERGRADUATE EXPENSES for 2019–2020 ***Application fee:*** $50. ***Tuition, state resident:*** full-time $7070; part-time $295 per credit. ***Tuition, nonresident:*** full-time $16,980; part-time $708 per credit. ***Required fees:*** full-time $1468; $10 per term. Full-time tuition and fees vary according to program. Part-time tuition and fees vary according to course load and program. ***College room and board:*** $13,318; ***Room only:*** $8088. Room and board charges vary according to board plan and housing facility.

FRESHMAN FINANCIAL AID (Fall 2018) 1111 applied for aid; of those 70% were deemed to have need. 91% of freshmen with need received aid; of those 8% had need fully met. ***Average percent of need met:*** 65% (excluding resources awarded to replace EFC). ***Average financial aid package:*** $8938 (excluding resources awarded to replace EFC). 1% of all full-time freshmen had no need and received non-need-based gift aid.

UNDERGRADUATE FINANCIAL AID (Fall 2018) 5,707 applied for aid; of those 76% were deemed to have need. 93% of undergraduates with need received aid; of those 5% had need fully met. ***Average percent of need met:*** 58% (excluding resources awarded to replace EFC). ***Average financial aid package:*** $8170 (excluding resources awarded to replace EFC). 1% of all full-time undergraduates had no need and received non-need-based gift aid.

GIFT AID (NEED-BASED) ***Total amount:*** $27,955,733 (50% federal, 48% state, 1% institutional, 1% external sources). ***Receiving aid:*** Freshmen: 50% (652); all full-time undergraduates: 47% (3,559). ***Average award:*** Freshmen: $8725; Undergraduates: $7313. ***Scholarships, grants, and awards:*** Federal Pell, FSEOG, state, private, college/university gift aid from institutional funds.

GIFT AID (NON-NEED-BASED) ***Total amount:*** $862,656 (31% state, 12% institutional, 57% external sources). ***Receiving aid:*** Freshmen: 6. Undergraduates: 31. ***Average award:*** Freshmen: $929. Undergraduates: $1363. ***Tuition waivers:*** Full or partial for employees or children of employees. ***ROTC:*** Army cooperative, Air Force cooperative.

LOANS ***Student loans:*** $19,392,356 (60% need-based, 40% non-need-based). 49% of past graduating class borrowed through all loan programs. *Average indebtedness per student:* $24,531. ***Average need-based loan:*** Freshmen: $2870. Undergraduates: $3721. ***Parent loans:*** $1,324,583 (35% need-based, 65% non-need-based). ***Programs:*** Federal Direct (Subsidized and Unsubsidized Stafford, PLUS), Perkins.

WORK-STUDY ***Federal work-study:*** Total amount: $588,655; jobs available. ***State or other work-study/employment:*** Total amount: $441,486 (29% need-based, 71% non-need-based). Part-time jobs available.

APPLYING FOR FINANCIAL AID ***Required financial aid form:*** FAFSA. ***Financial aid deadline (priority):*** 4/1. ***Notification date:*** Continuous beginning 3/1.

CONTACT Financial Aid Office, Farmingdale State College, 2350 Broadhollow Road, Farmingdale, NY 11735, 631-420-2000.
Website: http://www.farmingdale.edu/.

FASHION INSTITUTE OF TECHNOLOGY

New York, NY

Tuition & fees (NY res): $6110	Average undergraduate aid package: $11,874

ABOUT THE INSTITUTION State and locally supported, coed, primarily women. ***Awards:*** certificates, associate, bachelor's, and master's degrees. 23 undergraduate majors. ***Total enrollment:*** 8,726. Undergraduates: 8,508. Freshmen: 1,403. Federal methodology is used as a basis for awarding need-based institutional aid.
UNDERGRADUATE EXPENSES for 2019–2020 ***Application fee:*** $50. ***Tuition, state resident:*** full-time $5190; part-time $216 per credit. ***Tuition, nonresident:*** full-time $15,570; part-time $649 per credit. ***Required fees:*** full-time $920; $103 per year. Full-time tuition and fees vary according to degree level. Part-time tuition and fees vary according to degree level. ***College room and board:*** $14,556; ***Room only:*** $9762. Room and board charges vary according to board plan and housing facility.
FRESHMAN FINANCIAL AID (Fall 2018) 960 applied for aid; of those 77% were deemed to have need. 100% of freshmen with need received aid; of those 53% had need fully met. ***Average percent of need met:*** 70% (excluding resources awarded to replace EFC). ***Average financial aid package:*** $11,319 (excluding resources awarded to replace EFC). 8% of all full-time freshmen had no need and received non-need-based gift aid.
UNDERGRADUATE FINANCIAL AID (Fall 2018) 4,674 applied for aid; of those 81% were deemed to have need. 100% of undergraduates with need received aid; of those 51% had need fully met. ***Average percent of need met:*** 66% (excluding resources awarded to replace EFC). ***Average financial aid package:*** $11,874 (excluding resources awarded to replace EFC). 4% of all full-time undergraduates had no need and received non-need-based gift aid.
GIFT AID (NEED-BASED) ***Total amount:*** $21,564,828 (59% federal, 33% state, 7% institutional, 1% external sources). ***Receiving aid:*** Freshmen: 42% (562); all full-time undergraduates: 41% (2,978). ***Average award:*** Freshmen: $7438; Undergraduates: $6757. ***Scholarships, grants, and awards:*** Federal Pell, FSEOG, state, private, college/university gift aid from institutional funds.
GIFT AID (NON-NEED-BASED) ***Total amount:*** $678,150 (1% state, 24% institutional, 75% external sources). ***Receiving aid:*** Freshmen: 13% (173). Undergraduates: 7% (488). ***Average award:*** Freshmen: $840. Undergraduates: $858. ***Tuition waivers:*** Full or partial for employees or children of employees.
LOANS ***Student loans:*** $28,115,056 (34% need-based, 66% non-need-based). 51% of past graduating class borrowed through all loan programs. *Average indebtedness per student:* $25,832. ***Average need-based loan:*** Freshmen: $2591. Undergraduates: $3101. ***Parent loans:*** $10,533,477 (100% non-need-based). ***Programs:*** Federal Direct (Subsidized and Unsubsidized Stafford, PLUS).
WORK-STUDY ***Federal work-study:*** Total amount: $446,124; jobs available.
APPLYING FOR FINANCIAL AID ***Required financial aid forms:*** FAFSA, state aid form. ***Financial aid deadline (priority):*** 2/15. ***Notification date:*** Continuous beginning 4/1. Students must reply within 2 weeks of notification.
CONTACT Financial Aid Office, Fashion Institute of Technology, Seventh Avenue at 27th Street, New York, NY 10001-5992, 212-217-7999.
Website: http://www.fitnyc.edu/.

FAULKNER UNIVERSITY

Montgomery, AL

CONTACT Mr. William G. Jackson II, Director of Financial Aid, Faulkner University, 5345 Atlanta Highway, Montgomery, AL 36109-3398, 334-386-7195 or toll-free 800-879-9816. *Fax:* 334-386-7201. *E-mail:* faid@faulkner.edu.
Website: http://www.faulkner.edu/.

FAYETTEVILLE STATE UNIVERSITY

Fayetteville, NC

Tuition & fees (NC res): $4975	Average undergraduate aid package: $11,162

ABOUT THE INSTITUTION State-supported, coed. ***Awards:*** certificates, bachelor's, master's, and doctoral degrees. 37 undergraduate majors. ***Total enrollment:*** 6,551. Undergraduates: 5,644. Freshmen: 678. Federal methodology is used as a basis for awarding need-based institutional aid.
UNDERGRADUATE EXPENSES for 2019–2020 ***Application fee:*** $50. ***Tuition, state resident:*** full-time $2982. ***Tuition, nonresident:*** full-time $14,590. ***Required fees:*** full-time $1993. Full-time tuition and fees vary according to course level, course load, degree level, location, and program. Part-time tuition and fees vary according to course level, course load, degree level, location, and program. ***College room and board:*** $8616; ***Room only:*** $4513. Room and board charges vary according to board plan and housing facility.
FRESHMAN FINANCIAL AID (Fall 2018) 578 applied for aid; of those 94% were deemed to have need. 98% of freshmen with need received aid; of those 11% had need fully met. ***Average percent of need met:*** 75% (excluding resources awarded to replace EFC). ***Average financial aid package:*** $12,818 (excluding resources awarded to replace EFC).
UNDERGRADUATE FINANCIAL AID (Fall 2018) 3,572 applied for aid; of those 93% were deemed to have need. 97% of undergraduates with need received aid; of those 9% had need fully met. ***Average percent of need met:*** 68% (excluding resources awarded to replace EFC). ***Average financial aid package:*** $11,162 (excluding resources awarded to replace EFC). 1% of all full-time undergraduates had no need and received non-need-based gift aid.
GIFT AID (NEED-BASED) ***Total amount:*** $25,834,614 (62% federal, 18% state, 16% institutional, 4% external sources). ***Receiving aid:*** Freshmen: 88% (527); all full-time undergraduates: 77% (2,983). ***Average award:*** Freshmen: $10,064; Undergraduates: $8105. ***Scholarships, grants, and awards:*** Federal Pell, FSEOG, state, private, college/university gift aid from institutional funds, United Negro College Fund.
GIFT AID (NON-NEED-BASED) ***Total amount:*** $4506 (63% federal, 37% institutional). ***Receiving aid:*** Freshmen: 4% (25). Undergraduates: 6% (238). ***Average award:*** Undergraduates: $2189. ***Scholarships, grants, and awards by category:*** *Academic interests/achievement:* general academic interests/achievements. *Creative arts/performance:* music. *Special characteristics:* local/state students. ***Tuition waivers:*** Full or partial for employees or children of employees, senior citizens. ***ROTC:*** Army cooperative, Air Force.
LOANS ***Student loans:*** $23,973,007 (97% need-based, 3% non-need-based). ***Average need-based loan:*** Freshmen: $3429. Undergraduates: $4220. ***Parent loans:*** $1,272,914 (67% need-based, 33% non-need-based). ***Programs:*** Federal Direct (Subsidized and Unsubsidized Stafford, PLUS), Perkins.
WORK-STUDY ***Federal work-study:*** Total amount: $388,876; jobs available. ***State or other work-study/employment:*** Part-time jobs available.
ATHLETIC AWARDS Total amount: $797,788 (100% need-based).
APPLYING FOR FINANCIAL AID ***Required financial aid form:*** FAFSA. ***Financial aid deadline (priority):*** 1/15. ***Notification date:*** Continuous beginning 2/28. Students must reply within 4 weeks of notification.
CONTACT Mr. Keith Townsend, Administrative Assistant, Fayetteville State University, 1200 Murchison Road, Fayetteville, NC 28301-4298, 910-672-1327 or toll-free 800-222-2594. *Fax:* 910-672-1423. *E-mail:* ktownse7@uncfsu.edu.
Website: http://www.uncfsu.edu/.

FELICIAN UNIVERSITY

Lodi, NJ

Tuition & fees: $35,000	Average undergraduate aid package: $29,168

ABOUT THE INSTITUTION Independent Roman Catholic, coed. ***Awards:*** certificates, associate, bachelor's, master's, and doctoral degrees. 30 undergraduate majors. ***Total enrollment:*** 2,262. Undergraduates: 1,852. Freshmen: 382. Federal methodology is used as a basis for awarding need-based institutional aid.
UNDERGRADUATE EXPENSES for 2020–2021 ***Application fee:*** $30. ***Comprehensive fee:*** $48,140 includes full-time tuition ($32,550), mandatory fees

($2450), and room and board ($13,140). Full-time tuition and fees vary according to program. Room and board charges vary according to housing facility. ***Part-time tuition:*** $1075 per credit hour. ***Part-time fees:*** $485 per term. Part-time tuition and fees vary according to course load and program.

FRESHMAN FINANCIAL AID (Fall 2018) 279 applied for aid; of those 96% were deemed to have need. 100% of freshmen with need received aid; of those 10% had need fully met. ***Average percent of need met:*** 74% (excluding resources awarded to replace EFC). ***Average financial aid package:*** $31,961 (excluding resources awarded to replace EFC). 4% of all full-time freshmen had no need and received non-need-based gift aid.

UNDERGRADUATE FINANCIAL AID (Fall 2018) 1,370 applied for aid; of those 97% were deemed to have need. 99% of undergraduates with need received aid; of those 8% had need fully met. ***Average percent of need met:*** 68% (excluding resources awarded to replace EFC). ***Average financial aid package:*** $29,168 (excluding resources awarded to replace EFC). 3% of all full-time undergraduates had no need and received non-need-based gift aid.

GIFT AID (NEED-BASED) ***Receiving aid:*** Freshmen: 83% (238); all full-time undergraduates: 79% (1,146). ***Average award:*** Freshmen: $14,380; Undergraduates: $14,534. ***Scholarships, grants, and awards:*** Federal Pell, FSEOG, state, private, college/university gift aid from institutional funds.

GIFT AID (NON-NEED-BASED) ***Receiving aid:*** Freshmen: 93% (267). Undergraduates: 83% (1,203). ***Average award:*** Freshmen: $20,408. Undergraduates: $17,998. ***Scholarships, grants, and awards by category:*** *Academic interests/achievement:* business, education, English, general academic interests/achievements, health fields, religion/biblical studies. *Special characteristics:* children of faculty/staff, siblings of current students. ***Tuition waivers:*** Full or partial for employees or children of employees. ***ROTC:*** Army cooperative, Air Force cooperative.

LOANS ***Average need-based loan:*** Freshmen: $3313. Undergraduates: $4263. ***Programs:*** Federal Direct (Subsidized and Unsubsidized Stafford, PLUS), state.

WORK-STUDY ***Federal work-study:*** 71 jobs averaging $2355. ***State or other work-study/employment:*** Part-time jobs available.

APPLYING FOR FINANCIAL AID ***Required financial aid forms:*** FAFSA, state aid form. ***Financial aid deadline:*** Continuous. ***Notification date:*** Continuous.

CONTACT Ms. Cynthia Montalvo, Executive Director of Student Financial Services, Felician University, 262 South Main Street, Lodi, NJ 07644, 201-559-6036. *Fax:* 201-559-6025. *E-mail:* montalvoc@felician.edu.
Website: http://www.felician.edu/.

FERRIS STATE UNIVERSITY

Big Rapids, MI

Tuition & fees (MI res): $12,930	Average undergraduate aid package: $12,300

ABOUT THE INSTITUTION State-supported, coed. ***Awards:*** certificates, associate, bachelor's, master's, and doctoral degrees. 110 undergraduate majors. ***Total enrollment:*** 12,472. Undergraduates: 11,184. Freshmen: 1,892. Federal methodology is used as a basis for awarding need-based institutional aid.

UNDERGRADUATE EXPENSES for 2019–2020 ***Tuition, area resident:*** part-time $431 per credit hour. ***Tuition, state resident:*** full-time $12,930; part-time $431 per credit hour. ***Tuition, nonresident:*** full-time $12,930; part-time $431 per credit hour. Full-time tuition and fees vary according to location, program, and student level. Part-time tuition and fees vary according to location and student level. ***College room and board:*** $10,044. Room and board charges vary according to board plan and housing facility.

FRESHMAN FINANCIAL AID (Fall 2019, est.) 1773 applied for aid; of those 79% were deemed to have need. 99% of freshmen with need received aid; of those 19% had need fully met. ***Average percent of need met:*** 75% (excluding resources awarded to replace EFC). ***Average financial aid package:*** $14,500 (excluding resources awarded to replace EFC). 15% of all full-time freshmen had no need and received non-need-based gift aid.

UNDERGRADUATE FINANCIAL AID (Fall 2019, est.) 7,500 applied for aid; of those 75% were deemed to have need. 99% of undergraduates with need received aid; of those 18% had need fully met. ***Average percent of need met:*** 68% (excluding resources awarded to replace EFC). ***Average financial aid package:*** $12,300 (excluding resources awarded to replace EFC). 15% of all full-time undergraduates had no need and received non-need-based gift aid.

GIFT AID (NEED-BASED) ***Total amount:*** $28,229,700 (71% federal, 3% state, 26% institutional). ***Receiving aid:*** Freshmen: 62% (1,165); all full-time undergraduates: 56% (4,575). ***Average award:*** Freshmen: $5760; Undergraduates: $5440. ***Scholarships, grants, and awards:*** Federal Pell, FSEOG, state, private, college/university gift aid from institutional funds.

GIFT AID (NON-NEED-BASED) ***Total amount:*** $34,544,000 (1% federal, 38% state, 47% institutional, 14% external sources). ***Receiving aid:*** Freshmen: 62% (1,152). Undergraduates: 47% (3,788). ***Average award:*** Freshmen: $4700. Undergraduates: $4460. ***Scholarships, grants, and awards by category:*** *Academic interests/achievement:* 4,247 awards ($14,050,343 total): agriculture, architecture, biological sciences, business, communication, computer science, education, engineering/technologies, general academic interests/achievements, home economics, mathematics, physical sciences. *Creative arts/performance:* 542 awards ($1,600,358 total): applied art and design, art/fine arts, debating, general creative arts/performance, journalism/publications, music, theater/drama. *Special achievements/activities:* 112 awards ($43,206 total): general special achievements/activities, leadership, memberships. *Special characteristics:* 150 awards ($142,223 total): adult students, children and siblings of alumni, ethnic background, general special characteristics, international students, local/state students, members of minority groups, previous college experience, veterans. ***Tuition waivers:*** Full or partial for employees or children of employees. ***ROTC:*** Army cooperative.

LOANS ***Student loans:*** $50,589,240 (36% need-based, 64% non-need-based). 74% of past graduating class borrowed through all loan programs. *Average indebtedness per student:* $34,590. ***Average need-based loan:*** Freshmen: $3260. Undergraduates: $4110. ***Parent loans:*** $6,767,910 (100% non-need-based). ***Programs:*** Federal Direct (Subsidized and Unsubsidized Stafford, PLUS), Federal Nursing, college/university, alternative loans.

WORK-STUDY ***Federal work-study:*** Total amount: $967,090; 394 jobs averaging $2580. ***State or other work-study/employment:*** Total amount: $1,082,940 (100% non-need-based). 173 part-time jobs averaging $1950.

ATHLETIC AWARDS Total amount: $2,504,040 (100% non-need-based).

APPLYING FOR FINANCIAL AID ***Required financial aid form:*** FAFSA. ***Financial aid deadline (priority):*** 2/15. ***Notification date:*** Continuous beginning 12/15.

CONTACT Rebecca Vokes, Assistant Director of Financial Aid, Ferris State University, 1201 South State Street, Big Rapids, MI 49307-2020, 231-591-2100 or toll-free 800-433-7747. *Fax:* 231-591-2950. *E-mail:* rebeccavokes@ferris.edu.
Website: http://www.ferris.edu/.

FERRUM COLLEGE

Ferrum, VA

CONTACT Heather Hollandsworth, Director of Financial Aid, Ferrum College, PO Box 1000, Ferrum, VA 24088, 540-365-4282 or toll-free 800-868-9797. *Fax:* 540-365-4266. *E-mail:* hhollandsworth@ferrum.edu.
Website: http://www.ferrum.edu/.

FIDM/FASHION INSTITUTE OF DESIGN & MERCHANDISING, LOS ANGELES CAMPUS

Los Angeles, CA

CONTACT Mr. Chris Jennings, Director of Student Financial Services, FIDM/Fashion Institute of Design & Merchandising, Los Angeles Campus, 919 South Grand Avenue, Los Angeles, CA 90015, 213-624-1200 or toll-free 800-624-1200.
Website: http://www.fidm.edu/.

FIDM/FASHION INSTITUTE OF DESIGN & MERCHANDISING, SAN FRANCISCO CAMPUS

San Francisco, CA

CONTACT Financial Aid Office, FIDM/Fashion Institute of Design & Merchandising, San Francisco Campus, 55 Stockton Street, San Francisco, CA 94108-5829, 415-675-5200 or toll-free 800-422-3436.
Website: http://www.fidm.edu/.

FINLANDIA UNIVERSITY

Hancock, MI

CONTACT Sandra Turnquist, Director of Financial Aid, Finlandia University, 601 Quincy Street, Hancock, MI 49930, 906-487-7240 or toll-free 877-202-5491. *Fax:* 906-487-7383. *E-mail:* sandra.turnquist@finlandia.edu.
Website: http://www.finlandia.edu/.

FISHER COLLEGE

Boston, MA

Tuition & fees: $32,700	Average undergraduate aid package: $27,992

ABOUT THE INSTITUTION Independent, coed. ***Awards:*** certificates, associate, bachelor's, and master's degrees. 31 undergraduate majors. ***Total enrollment:*** 1,628. Undergraduates: 1,551. Freshmen: 157. Federal methodology is used as a basis for awarding need-based institutional aid.

UNDERGRADUATE EXPENSES for 2020–2021 ***Application fee:*** $50. ***Comprehensive fee:*** $49,269 includes full-time tuition ($31,700), mandatory fees ($1000), and room and board ($16,569). Room and board charges vary according to housing facility. ***Part-time tuition:*** $1057 per course. Part-time tuition and fees vary according to class time and course load.

FRESHMAN FINANCIAL AID (Fall 2019, est.) 132 applied for aid; of those 91% were deemed to have need. 122% of freshmen with need received aid. ***Average financial aid package:*** $30,581 (excluding resources awarded to replace EFC). 17% of all full-time freshmen had no need and received non-need-based gift aid.

UNDERGRADUATE FINANCIAL AID (Fall 2019, est.) 518 applied for aid; of those 91% were deemed to have need. 123% of undergraduates with need received aid. ***Average financial aid package:*** $27,992 (excluding resources awarded to replace EFC). 20% of all full-time undergraduates had no need and received non-need-based gift aid.

GIFT AID (NEED-BASED) ***Total amount:*** $6,474,373 (44% federal, 7% state, 49% institutional). ***Receiving aid:*** Freshmen: 68% (107); all full-time undergraduates: 69% (444). ***Average award:*** Freshmen: $12,240; Undergraduates: $11,621. ***Scholarships, grants, and awards:*** Federal Pell, FSEOG, state, private, college/university gift aid from institutional funds.

GIFT AID (NON-NEED-BASED) ***Total amount:*** $8,511,185 (99% institutional, 1% external sources). ***Receiving aid:*** Freshmen: 93% (146). Undergraduates: 89% (578). ***Average award:*** Freshmen: $11,911. Undergraduates: $11,451. ***Scholarships, grants, and awards by category:*** *Academic interests/achievement:* general academic interests/achievements. ***Tuition waivers:*** Full or partial for employees or children of employees. ***ROTC:*** Army cooperative.

LOANS ***Student loans:*** $5,837,683 (48% need-based, 52% non-need-based). 85% of past graduating class borrowed through all loan programs. *Average indebtedness per student:* $32,551. ***Average need-based loan:*** Freshmen: $3314. Undergraduates: $3964. ***Parent loans:*** $2,135,770 (100% non-need-based). ***Programs:*** Federal Direct (Subsidized and Unsubsidized Stafford, PLUS).

WORK-STUDY ***Federal work-study:*** Total amount: $81,090; jobs available.

APPLYING FOR FINANCIAL AID ***Required financial aid form:*** FAFSA. ***Financial aid deadline:*** 3/15 (priority: 3/15). ***Notification date:*** Continuous beginning 1/6.

CONTACT Jennifer Wilhelm, Director of Financial Aid, Fisher College, 118 Beacon Street, Boston, MA 02116, 617-236-5470. *E-mail:* jwilhelm@fisher.edu.
Website: http://www.fisher.edu/.

FISK UNIVERSITY

Nashville, TN

CONTACT Mary Chambliss, Director of Financial Aid, Fisk University, 1000 17th Avenue North, Nashville, TN 37208-3051, 615-329-8735 or toll-free 888-702-0022. *E-mail:* mchambliss@fisk.edu.
Website: http://www.fisk.edu/.

FITCHBURG STATE UNIVERSITY

Fitchburg, MA

Tuition & fees (MA res): $10,505	Average undergraduate aid package: $10,072

ABOUT THE INSTITUTION State-supported, coed. ***Awards:*** certificates, bachelor's, and master's degrees. 62 undergraduate majors. ***Total enrollment:*** 7,252. Undergraduates: 4,044. Freshmen: 674. Federal methodology is used as a basis for awarding need-based institutional aid.

UNDERGRADUATE EXPENSES for 2019–2020 ***Application fee:*** $50. ***One-time required fee:*** $50. ***Tuition, state resident:*** full-time $970; part-time $40 per credit. ***Tuition, nonresident:*** full-time $7050; part-time $294 per credit. ***Required fees:*** full-time $9535; $397.30 per credit. Full-time tuition and fees vary according to class time and reciprocity agreements. Part-time tuition and fees vary according to class time and reciprocity agreements. ***College room and board:*** $11,261; ***Room only:*** $7731. Room and board charges vary according to board plan and housing facility.

FRESHMAN FINANCIAL AID (Fall 2018) 683 applied for aid; of those 79% were deemed to have need. 94% of freshmen with need received aid. ***Average percent of need met:*** 75% (excluding resources awarded to replace EFC). ***Average financial aid package:*** $9962 (excluding resources awarded to replace EFC). 8% of all full-time freshmen had no need and received non-need-based gift aid.

UNDERGRADUATE FINANCIAL AID (Fall 2018) 2,879 applied for aid; of those 80% were deemed to have need. 95% of undergraduates with need received aid. ***Average percent of need met:*** 75% (excluding resources awarded to replace EFC). ***Average financial aid package:*** $10,072 (excluding resources awarded to replace EFC). 5% of all full-time undergraduates had no need and received non-need-based gift aid.

GIFT AID (NEED-BASED) ***Total amount:*** $11,623,938 (63% federal, 19% state, 18% institutional). ***Receiving aid:*** Freshmen: 54% (385); all full-time undergraduates: 48% (1,574). ***Average award:*** Freshmen: $7528; Undergraduates: $7110. ***Scholarships, grants, and awards:*** Federal Pell, FSEOG, state, private, college/university gift aid from institutional funds.

GIFT AID (NON-NEED-BASED) ***Total amount:*** $2,286,720 (18% state, 44% institutional, 38% external sources). ***Receiving aid:*** Freshmen: 35% (251). Undergraduates: 24% (778). ***Average award:*** Freshmen: $1607. Undergraduates: $1427. ***Tuition waivers:*** Full or partial for employees or children of employees, senior citizens. ***ROTC:*** Army.

LOANS ***Student loans:*** $24,568,637 (38% need-based, 62% non-need-based). 81% of past graduating class borrowed through all loan programs. *Average indebtedness per student:* $26,543. ***Average need-based loan:*** Freshmen: $3551. Undergraduates: $4550. ***Parent loans:*** $3,991,537 (100% non-need-based). ***Programs:*** Federal Direct (Subsidized and Unsubsidized Stafford, PLUS), Federal Nursing, state.

WORK-STUDY ***Federal work-study:*** Total amount: $298,243; 182 jobs averaging $1639.

APPLYING FOR FINANCIAL AID ***Required financial aid form:*** FAFSA. ***Financial aid deadline (priority):*** 3/1. ***Notification date:*** Continuous beginning 1/30.

CONTACT Office of Financial Aid, Fitchburg State University, 160 Pearl Street, Fitchburg, MA 01420-2697, 978-665-3156 or toll-free 800-705-9692. *E-mail:* finaid@fitchburgstate.edu.
Website: http://www.fitchburgstate.edu/.

FIVE TOWNS COLLEGE
Dix Hills, NY

Tuition & fees: N/R **Average undergraduate aid package: $14,194**

ABOUT THE INSTITUTION Independent, coed. ***Awards:*** associate, bachelor's, master's, and doctoral degrees. 19 undergraduate majors. Federal methodology is used as a basis for awarding need-based institutional aid.

FRESHMAN FINANCIAL AID (Fall 2018) 129 applied for aid; of those 90% were deemed to have need. 94% of freshmen with need received aid; of those 1% had need fully met. ***Average percent of need met:*** 48% (excluding resources awarded to replace EFC). ***Average financial aid package:*** $14,377 (excluding resources awarded to replace EFC). 9% of all full-time freshmen had no need and received non-need-based gift aid.

UNDERGRADUATE FINANCIAL AID (Fall 2018) 512 applied for aid; of those 91% were deemed to have need. 97% of undergraduates with need received aid; of those 3% had need fully met. ***Average percent of need met:*** 50% (excluding resources awarded to replace EFC). ***Average financial aid package:*** $14,194 (excluding resources awarded to replace EFC). 5% of all full-time undergraduates had no need and received non-need-based gift aid.

GIFT AID (NEED-BASED) ***Receiving aid:*** Freshmen: 77% (109); all full-time undergraduates: 77% (442). ***Average award:*** Freshmen: $12,700; Undergraduates: $11,282. ***Scholarships, grants, and awards:*** Federal Pell, FSEOG, state, private, college/university gift aid from institutional funds.

GIFT AID (NON-NEED-BASED) ***Receiving aid:*** Freshmen: 1% (1). Undergraduates: 2% (12). ***Average award:*** Freshmen: $5866. Undergraduates: $5297. ***Scholarships, grants, and awards by category:*** *Academic interests/achievement:* business, education, general academic interests/achievements. *Creative arts/performance:* cinema/film/broadcasting, music, theater/drama.

LOANS ***Student loans:*** 80% of past graduating class borrowed through all loan programs. *Average indebtedness per student:* $26,858. ***Average need-based loan:*** Freshmen: $3469. Undergraduates: $5405. ***Programs:*** Federal Direct (Subsidized and Unsubsidized Stafford, PLUS), Private parent loans.

WORK-STUDY ***Federal work-study:*** 63 jobs averaging $66,113. ***State or other work-study/employment:*** Part-time jobs available.

APPLYING FOR FINANCIAL AID ***Required financial aid forms:*** FAFSA, state aid form. ***Financial aid deadline:*** Continuous. ***Notification date:*** Continuous.

CONTACT Mr. Jason LaBonte, Financial Aid Director, Five Towns College, 305 North Service Road, Dix Hills, NY 11746-5871, 631-656-2113. *Fax:* 631-656-2191. *E-mail:* jason.labonte@ftc.edu.
Website: http://www.ftc.edu/.

FLAGLER COLLEGE
St. Augustine, FL

ABOUT THE INSTITUTION Independent, coed. ***Awards:*** bachelor's and master's degrees. 35 undergraduate majors. ***Total enrollment:*** 2,902. Undergraduates: 2,889. Freshmen: 641.

GIFT AID (NEED-BASED) ***Scholarships, grants, and awards:*** Federal Pell, FSEOG, state, private, college/university gift aid from institutional funds.

GIFT AID (NON-NEED-BASED) ***Scholarships, grants, and awards by category:*** *Academic interests/achievement:* biological sciences, business, communication, education, English, foreign languages, general academic interests/achievements, humanities, international studies, physical sciences, religion/biblical studies, social sciences. *Creative arts/performance:* applied art and design, art/fine arts, cinema/film/broadcasting, creative writing, journalism/publications, performing arts, theater/drama. *Special achievements/activities:* community service, general special achievements/activities, leadership, memberships, religious involvement. *Special characteristics:* children of educators, children of faculty/staff, ethnic background, first-generation college students, general special characteristics, international students, local/state students, members of minority groups, out-of-state students.

LOANS ***Programs:*** Federal Direct (Subsidized and Unsubsidized Stafford, PLUS), state.

CONTACT Sheia Pleasant-Doine, Office of Financial Aid, Flagler College, 74 King Street, St. Augustine, FL 32084, 904-819-6225 or toll-free 800-304-4208. *Fax:* 904-819-6453. *E-mail:* financialaid@flagler.edu.
Website: http://www.flagler.edu/.

FLAGLER COLLEGE–TALLAHASSEE
Tallahassee, FL

CONTACT Financial Aid Office, Flagler College–Tallahassee, 444 Appleyard Drive, Tallahassee, FL 32304, 850-201-8070.
Website: http://www.flagler.edu/.

FLORIDA AGRICULTURAL AND MECHANICAL UNIVERSITY
Tallahassee, FL

Tuition & fees (area res): $5785 **Average undergraduate aid package: $13,284**

ABOUT THE INSTITUTION State-supported, coed. ***Awards:*** certificates, bachelor's, master's, and doctoral degrees. 58 undergraduate majors. ***Total enrollment:*** 9,626. Undergraduates: 7,818. Freshmen: 1,340. Federal methodology is used as a basis for awarding need-based institutional aid.

UNDERGRADUATE EXPENSES for 2020–2021 ***Application fee:*** $35. ***Tuition, area resident:*** full-time $5645; part-time $188 per credit hour. ***Tuition, state resident:*** full-time $5645; part-time $188 per credit hour. ***Tuition, nonresident:*** full-time $17,585; part-time $586 per credit hour. ***Required fees:*** full-time $140. ***College room and board:*** $10,986; ***Room only:*** $6012. ***Payment plan:*** Tuition prepayment.

FRESHMAN FINANCIAL AID (Fall 2018) 1363 applied for aid; of those 90% were deemed to have need. 100% of freshmen with need received aid; of those 9% had need fully met. ***Average percent of need met:*** 60% (excluding resources awarded to replace EFC). ***Average financial aid package:*** $13,694 (excluding resources awarded to replace EFC). 2% of all full-time freshmen had no need and received non-need-based gift aid.

UNDERGRADUATE FINANCIAL AID (Fall 2018) 6,602 applied for aid; of those 93% were deemed to have need. 97% of undergraduates with need received aid; of those 10% had need fully met. ***Average percent of need met:*** 60% (excluding resources awarded to replace EFC). ***Average financial aid package:*** $13,284 (excluding resources awarded to replace EFC). 2% of all full-time undergraduates had no need and received non-need-based gift aid.

GIFT AID (NEED-BASED) ***Total amount:*** $34,106,295 (81% federal, 9% state, 10% institutional). ***Receiving aid:*** Freshmen: 76% (1,050); all full-time undergraduates: 71% (4,912). ***Average award:*** Freshmen: $7082; Undergraduates: $6660. ***Scholarships, grants, and awards:*** Federal Pell, FSEOG, state, private, college/university gift aid from institutional funds, United Negro College Fund.

GIFT AID (NON-NEED-BASED) ***Total amount:*** $12,009,370 (48% state, 23% institutional, 29% external sources). ***Receiving aid:*** Freshmen: 48% (660). Undergraduates: 32% (2,229). ***Average award:*** Freshmen: $3763. Undergraduates: $9223. ***Scholarships, grants, and awards by category:*** *Academic interests/achievement:* agriculture, architecture, area/ethnic studies, biological sciences, business, communication, computer science, education, engineering/technologies, English, foreign languages, general academic interests/achievements, health fields, humanities, mathematics, military science, physical sciences, premedicine, social sciences. *Creative arts/performance:* applied art and design, art/fine arts, cinema/film/broadcasting, creative writing, dance, journalism/publications, music, performing arts, theater/drama. *Special achievements/activities:* cheerleading/drum major, community service, general special achievements/activities, leadership. *Special characteristics:* ethnic background, first-generation college students, general special characteristics, local/state students. ***ROTC:*** Army, Naval, Air Force cooperative.

LOANS ***Student loans:*** $34,157,356 (53% need-based, 47% non-need-based). 81% of past graduating class borrowed through all loan programs. *Average indebtedness per student:* $28,284. ***Average need-based loan:*** Freshmen: $3314. Undergraduates: $4045. ***Parent loans:*** $14,042,201 (100% non-need-based). ***Programs:*** Federal Direct (Subsidized and Unsubsidized Stafford, PLUS), Perkins, private loans.

WORK-STUDY ***Federal work-study:*** Total amount: $572,554; jobs available.

ATHLETIC AWARDS Total amount: $2,882,990 (100% non-need-based).
APPLYING FOR FINANCIAL AID ***Required financial aid form:*** FAFSA. ***Financial aid deadline (priority):*** 3/1. ***Notification date:*** Continuous beginning 4/15.
CONTACT Ms. Lisa A. Stewart, Director of Financial Aid, Florida Agricultural and Mechanical University, 101 Foote-Hilyer Administration Center, Tallahassee, FL 32307, 850-599-3730 or toll-free 866-642-1198.
Website: http://www.famu.edu/.

FLORIDA ATLANTIC UNIVERSITY
Boca Raton, FL

Tuition & fees (FL res): $6099	Average undergraduate aid package: $14,639

ABOUT THE INSTITUTION State-supported, coed. ***Awards:*** certificates, associate, bachelor's, master's, and doctoral degrees. 62 undergraduate majors. ***Total enrollment:*** 30,061. Undergraduates: 24,842. Freshmen: 3,247. Federal methodology is used as a basis for awarding need-based institutional aid.
UNDERGRADUATE EXPENSES for 2020–2021 ***Application fee:*** $30. ***Tuition, state resident:*** full-time $6099; part-time $105 per credit hour. ***Tuition, nonresident:*** full-time $21,655; part-time $599 per credit hour. ***Required fees:*** $98.22. Full-time tuition and fees vary according to course load and location. Part-time tuition and fees vary according to course load and location. ***College room and board:*** $12,030; ***Room only:*** $8320. Room and board charges vary according to board plan and housing facility.
FRESHMAN FINANCIAL AID (Fall 2018) 2649 applied for aid; of those 74% were deemed to have need. 99% of freshmen with need received aid; of those 10% had need fully met. ***Average percent of need met:*** 61% (excluding resources awarded to replace EFC). ***Average financial aid package:*** $15,027 (excluding resources awarded to replace EFC). 3% of all full-time freshmen had no need and received non-need-based gift aid.
UNDERGRADUATE FINANCIAL AID (Fall 2018) 11,785 applied for aid; of those 84% were deemed to have need. 98% of undergraduates with need received aid; of those 6% had need fully met. ***Average percent of need met:*** 56% (excluding resources awarded to replace EFC). ***Average financial aid package:*** $14,639 (excluding resources awarded to replace EFC). 1% of all full-time undergraduates had no need and received non-need-based gift aid.
GIFT AID (NEED-BASED) ***Total amount:*** $80,457,518 (57% federal, 25% state, 13% institutional, 5% external sources). ***Receiving aid:*** Freshmen: 52% (1,641); all full-time undergraduates: 49% (7,919). ***Average award:*** Freshmen: $9816; Undergraduates: $8103. ***Scholarships, grants, and awards:*** Federal Pell, FSEOG, state, private, college/university gift aid from institutional funds, Federal Nursing.
GIFT AID (NON-NEED-BASED) ***Total amount:*** $12,592,820 (58% state, 11% institutional, 31% external sources). ***Receiving aid:*** Freshmen: 10% (314). Undergraduates: 5% (819). ***Average award:*** Freshmen: $3653. Undergraduates: $3609. ***Scholarships, grants, and awards by category:*** *Academic interests/achievement:* business, engineering/technologies, general academic interests/achievements, physical sciences, social sciences. *Creative arts/performance:* music, performing arts. ***Tuition waivers:*** Full or partial for employees or children of employees, senior citizens. ***ROTC:*** Army, Air Force cooperative.
LOANS ***Student loans:*** $127,154,384 (79% need-based, 21% non-need-based). 51% of past graduating class borrowed through all loan programs. *Average indebtedness per student:* $23,439. ***Average need-based loan:*** Freshmen: $5520. Undergraduates: $7131. ***Programs:*** Federal Direct (Subsidized and Unsubsidized Stafford, PLUS), Perkins, Federal Nursing, college/university.
WORK-STUDY ***Federal work-study:*** Total amount: $1,764,862; 334 jobs averaging $2376. ***State or other work-study/employment:*** Total amount: $31,158 (100% need-based). 9 part-time jobs averaging $2066.
APPLYING FOR FINANCIAL AID ***Required financial aid form:*** FAFSA. ***Notification date:*** Continuous. Students must reply by 8/23.
CONTACT Tracy Boulukos, Assistant Vice President for Financial Aid & New Student Services Initiatives, Florida Atlantic University, 777 Glades Road, Boca Raton, FL 33431-0991, 561-297-3531. *E-mail:* tbouluko@fau.edu.
Website: http://www.fau.edu/.

FLORIDA COLLEGE
Temple Terrace, FL

CONTACT Stephen Blaylock, Director of Financial Aid, Florida College, 119 North Glen Arven Avenue, Temple Terrace, FL 33617, 813-988-5131 Ext. 130. *Fax:* 813-899-6772. *E-mail:* blaylocks@floridacollege.edu.
Website: http://www.floridacollege.edu/.

FLORIDA GULF COAST UNIVERSITY
Fort Myers, FL

Tuition & fees (area res): $6170	Average undergraduate aid package: $10,750

ABOUT THE INSTITUTION State-supported, coed. ***Awards:*** certificates, associate, bachelor's, master's, and doctoral degrees. 55 undergraduate majors. ***Total enrollment:*** 15,026. Undergraduates: 13,699. Freshmen: 2,779. Federal methodology is used as a basis for awarding need-based institutional aid.
UNDERGRADUATE EXPENSES for 2019–2020 ***Application fee:*** $30. ***Tuition, area resident:*** full-time $4191. ***Tuition, state resident:*** full-time $4191. ***Tuition, nonresident:*** full-time $22,328. ***Required fees:*** full-time $1979. Full-time tuition and fees vary according to course load. Part-time tuition and fees vary according to course load. ***College room and board:*** $8580; ***Room only:*** $4820. Room and board charges vary according to board plan.
FRESHMAN FINANCIAL AID (Fall 2018) 2181 applied for aid; of those 70% were deemed to have need. 99% of freshmen with need received aid; of those 8% had need fully met. ***Average percent of need met:*** 51% (excluding resources awarded to replace EFC). ***Average financial aid package:*** $10,446 (excluding resources awarded to replace EFC). 2% of all full-time freshmen had no need and received non-need-based gift aid.
UNDERGRADUATE FINANCIAL AID (Fall 2018) 7,727 applied for aid; of those 67% were deemed to have need. 100% of undergraduates with need received aid; of those 9% had need fully met. ***Average percent of need met:*** 62% (excluding resources awarded to replace EFC). ***Average financial aid package:*** $10,750 (excluding resources awarded to replace EFC). 4% of all full-time undergraduates had no need and received non-need-based gift aid.
GIFT AID (NEED-BASED) ***Total amount:*** $32,893,106 (60% federal, 31% state, 5% institutional, 4% external sources). ***Receiving aid:*** Freshmen: 38% (1,027); all full-time undergraduates: 36% (3,967). ***Average award:*** Freshmen: $6366; Undergraduates: $6557. ***Scholarships, grants, and awards:*** Federal Pell, FSEOG, state, private, college/university gift aid from institutional funds.
GIFT AID (NON-NEED-BASED) ***Total amount:*** $14,243,125 (38% state, 57% institutional, 5% external sources). ***Receiving aid:*** Freshmen: 27% (742). Undergraduates: 14% (1,557). ***Average award:*** Freshmen: $2740. Undergraduates: $3244. ***Scholarships, grants, and awards by category:*** *Academic interests/achievement:* biological sciences, business, education, engineering/technologies, general academic interests/achievements, home economics, humanities, mathematics, physical sciences, religion/biblical studies, social sciences. *Creative arts/performance:* applied art and design, music. *Special achievements/activities:* community service, leadership. *Special characteristics:* adult students, ethnic background, handicapped students, international students, local/state students, members of minority groups, out-of-state students.
LOANS ***Student loans:*** $39,553,163 (70% need-based, 30% non-need-based). 50% of past graduating class borrowed through all loan programs. *Average indebtedness per student:* $28,581. ***Average need-based loan:*** Freshmen: $7110. Undergraduates: $7064. ***Programs:*** Federal Direct (Subsidized and Unsubsidized Stafford, PLUS).
WORK-STUDY ***Federal work-study:*** Total amount: $474,162; 242 jobs averaging $1878. ***State or other work-study/employment:*** Total amount: $20,684 (100% need-based). Part-time jobs available.
ATHLETIC AWARDS Total amount: $995,278 (100% non-need-based).
APPLYING FOR FINANCIAL AID ***Required financial aid forms:*** FAFSA, institution's own form, state aid form. ***Financial aid deadline:*** 6/30 (priority: 1/1). ***Notification date:*** Continuous beginning 3/15.

CONTACT Jorge Lopez-Rosado, Director of Student Financial Services, Florida Gulf Coast University, 10501 FGCU Boulevard South, Fort Myers, FL 33965, 239-590-1210 or toll-free 888-889-1095. *Fax:* 239-590-7923.
Website: http://www.fgcu.edu/.

FLORIDA INSTITUTE OF TECHNOLOGY

Melbourne, FL

Tuition & fees: $42,470 | **Average undergraduate aid package: $36,489**

ABOUT THE INSTITUTION Independent, coed. ***Awards:*** certificates, associate, bachelor's, master's, and doctoral degrees. 66 undergraduate majors. ***Total enrollment:*** 6,078. Undergraduates: 3,565. Freshmen: 668. Federal methodology is used as a basis for awarding need-based institutional aid.

UNDERGRADUATE EXPENSES for 2019–2020 ***Comprehensive fee:*** $55,350 includes full-time tuition ($41,720), mandatory fees ($750), and room and board ($12,880). ***College room only:*** $7000. Full-time tuition and fees vary according to course load and program. Room and board charges vary according to board plan and housing facility. ***Part-time tuition:*** $1170 per credit hour.

FRESHMAN FINANCIAL AID (Fall 2019, est.) 553 applied for aid; of those 83% were deemed to have need. 100% of freshmen with need received aid; of those 34% had need fully met. ***Average percent of need met:*** 85% (excluding resources awarded to replace EFC). ***Average financial aid package:*** $37,926 (excluding resources awarded to replace EFC). 25% of all full-time freshmen had no need and received non-need-based gift aid.

UNDERGRADUATE FINANCIAL AID (Fall 2019, est.) 2,062 applied for aid; of those 88% were deemed to have need. 100% of undergraduates with need received aid; of those 34% had need fully met. ***Average percent of need met:*** 83% (excluding resources awarded to replace EFC). ***Average financial aid package:*** $36,489 (excluding resources awarded to replace EFC). 27% of all full-time undergraduates had no need and received non-need-based gift aid.

GIFT AID (NEED-BASED) ***Receiving aid:*** Freshmen: 69% (460); all full-time undergraduates: 57% (1,799). ***Average award:*** Freshmen: $28,406; Undergraduates: $27,213. ***Scholarships, grants, and awards:*** Federal Pell, FSEOG, state, private, college/university gift aid from institutional funds.

GIFT AID (NON-NEED-BASED) ***Receiving aid:*** Freshmen: 67% (450). Undergraduates: 53% (1,671). ***Average award:*** Freshmen: $16,158. Undergraduates: $15,620. ***Scholarships, grants, and awards by category:*** *Academic interests/achievement:* biological sciences, business, communication, computer science, general academic interests/achievements, home economics, humanities, mathematics, military science, physical sciences, premedicine. *Creative arts/performance:* music. *Special achievements/activities:* cheerleading/drum major, general special achievements/activities, hobbies/interests, leadership, memberships. *Special characteristics:* children and siblings of alumni, children of faculty/staff, general special characteristics, international students, previous college experience, siblings of current students. ***Tuition waivers:*** Full or partial for employees or children of employees, senior citizens. ***ROTC:*** Army.

LOANS ***Student loans:*** 50% of past graduating class borrowed through all loan programs. *Average indebtedness per student:* $38,943. ***Average need-based loan:*** Freshmen: $3386. Undergraduates: $4379. ***Programs:*** Federal Direct (Subsidized and Unsubsidized Stafford, PLUS).

WORK-STUDY ***Federal work-study:*** 390 jobs averaging $2000. ***State or other work-study/employment:*** 522 part-time jobs averaging $2361.

APPLYING FOR FINANCIAL AID ***Required financial aid forms:*** FAFSA, state aid form. ***Financial aid deadline:*** Continuous. ***Notification date:*** Continuous. Students must reply within 4 weeks of notification.

CONTACT Mr. Jay Lally, Office of Financial Aid, Florida Institute of Technology, 150 West University Boulevard, Melbourne, FL 32901-6975, 321-674-8070 or toll-free 800-888-4348. *Fax:* 321-724-2778. *E-mail:* finaid@fit.edu.
Website: http://www.fit.edu/.

FLORIDA INTERNATIONAL UNIVERSITY

Miami, FL

Tuition & fees (area res): $6566 | **Average undergraduate aid package: $9847**

ABOUT THE INSTITUTION State-supported, coed. ***Awards:*** certificates, bachelor's, master's, and doctoral degrees. 65 undergraduate majors. ***Total enrollment:*** 58,064. Undergraduates: 48,439. Freshmen: 4,441. Federal methodology is used as a basis for awarding need-based institutional aid.

UNDERGRADUATE EXPENSES for 2019–2020 ***Application fee:*** $30. ***Tuition, area resident:*** full-time $6168; part-time $206 per credit hour. ***Tuition, state resident:*** full-time $6168; part-time $206 per credit hour. ***Tuition, nonresident:*** full-time $18,566; part-time $619 per credit hour. ***Required fees:*** full-time $398. ***College room and board:*** $11,136; ***Room only:*** $7536.

FRESHMAN FINANCIAL AID (Fall 2018) 3013 applied for aid; of those 110% were deemed to have need. 87% of freshmen with need received aid; of those 12% had need fully met. ***Average percent of need met:*** 55% (excluding resources awarded to replace EFC). ***Average financial aid package:*** $10,913 (excluding resources awarded to replace EFC). 34% of all full-time freshmen had no need and received non-need-based gift aid.

UNDERGRADUATE FINANCIAL AID (Fall 2018) 19,110 applied for aid; of those 99% were deemed to have need. 98% of undergraduates with need received aid; of those 10% had need fully met. ***Average percent of need met:*** 39% (excluding resources awarded to replace EFC). ***Average financial aid package:*** $9847 (excluding resources awarded to replace EFC). 5% of all full-time undergraduates had no need and received non-need-based gift aid.

GIFT AID (NEED-BASED) ***Total amount:*** $170,936,610 (66% federal, 15% state, 19% institutional). ***Receiving aid:*** Freshmen: 61% (2,030); all full-time undergraduates: 57% (15,683). ***Average award:*** Freshmen: $8236; Undergraduates: $7256. ***Scholarships, grants, and awards:*** Federal Pell, FSEOG, state, private, college/university gift aid from institutional funds.

GIFT AID (NON-NEED-BASED) ***Total amount:*** $69,776,550 (5% federal, 46% state, 42% institutional, 7% external sources). ***Receiving aid:*** Freshmen: 66% (2,167). Undergraduates: 24% (6,622). ***Average award:*** Freshmen: $2043. Undergraduates: $2163. ***Scholarships, grants, and awards by category:*** *Academic interests/achievement:* architecture, biological sciences, business, communication, computer science, education, engineering/technologies, English, foreign languages, general academic interests/achievements, home economics, humanities, mathematics, physical sciences, social sciences. *Creative arts/performance:* applied art and design, dance, journalism/publications, music, performing arts, theater/drama. *Special characteristics:* first-generation college students, veterans. ***ROTC:*** Army, Air Force.

LOANS ***Student loans:*** $257,015,164 (22% need-based, 78% non-need-based). 45% of past graduating class borrowed through all loan programs. *Average indebtedness per student:* $19,705. ***Average need-based loan:*** Freshmen: $3123. Undergraduates: $4485. ***Parent loans:*** $5,108,569 (100% non-need-based). ***Programs:*** Federal Direct (Subsidized and Unsubsidized Stafford, PLUS), college/university.

WORK-STUDY ***Federal work-study:*** Total amount: $2,369,629; jobs available. ***State or other work-study/employment:*** Total amount: $182,647 (100% need-based). Part-time jobs available.

ATHLETIC AWARDS Total amount: $5,233,653 (100% non-need-based).

APPLYING FOR FINANCIAL AID ***Required financial aid form:*** FAFSA. ***Financial aid deadline:*** 5/15 (priority: 3/1). ***Notification date:*** Continuous beginning 2/1. Students must reply by 5/1.

CONTACT Francisco Valines, Director of Financial Aid, Florida International University, 11200 SW 8th Street, PC 125, Miami, FL 33199, 305-348-7272. *Fax:* 305-348-2346. *E-mail:* francisco.valines@fiu.edu.
Website: http://www.fiu.edu/.

FLORIDA MEMORIAL UNIVERSITY

Miami-Dade, FL

CONTACT Brian Phillip, Director of Financial Aid, Florida Memorial University, 15800 Northwest 42nd Avenue, Miami, FL 33054, 305-626-3745 or toll-free 800-822-1362. *Fax:* 305-626-3106.
Website: http://www.fmuniv.edu/.

FLORIDA NATIONAL UNIVERSITY
Hialeah, FL

Tuition & fees: $13,688 **Average undergraduate aid package: N/A**

ABOUT THE INSTITUTION Proprietary, coed. ***Awards:*** certificates, diplomas, associate, bachelor's, and master's degrees. 31 undergraduate majors. ***Total enrollment:*** 3,981. Undergraduates: 3,708. Freshmen: 937. Institutional methodology is used as a basis for awarding need-based institutional aid.

UNDERGRADUATE EXPENSES for 2020–2021 ***Tuition:*** full-time $13,200; part-time $550 per credit hour. ***Required fees:*** full-time $488. ***Payment plans:*** Guaranteed tuition, tuition prepayment.

FRESHMAN FINANCIAL AID (Fall 2018) 374 applied for aid; of those 91% were deemed to have need. 98% of freshmen with need received aid.

UNDERGRADUATE FINANCIAL AID (Fall 2018) 2,490 applied for aid; of those 95% were deemed to have need. 100% of undergraduates with need received aid.

GIFT AID (NEED-BASED) ***Receiving aid:*** Freshmen: 79% (326); all full-time undergraduates: 87% (2,294). ***Scholarships, grants, and awards:*** Federal Pell, FSEOG, state, private, college/university gift aid from institutional funds.

GIFT AID (NON-NEED-BASED) ***Scholarships, grants, and awards by category:*** *Special achievements/activities:* 5 awards ($7500 total): community service. *Special characteristics:* 78 awards ($413,868 total): children of faculty/staff, international students. ***Tuition waivers:*** Full or partial for employees or children of employees.

LOANS ***Student loans:*** 92% of past graduating class borrowed through all loan programs. *Average indebtedness per student:* $11,700. ***Programs:*** Federal Direct (Subsidized and Unsubsidized Stafford, PLUS), Perkins.

WORK-STUDY ***Federal work-study:*** 39 jobs averaging $3962. ***State or other work-study/employment:*** Part-time jobs available.

APPLYING FOR FINANCIAL AID ***Required financial aid form:*** FAFSA. ***Financial aid deadline:*** Continuous.

CONTACT Mr. Omar Sanchez, Director of Financial Aid, Florida National University, 4425 West Jose Regueiro (20th) Avenue, Hialeah, FL 33012, 305-821-3333 Ext. 1003. *Fax:* 305-362-0595. *E-mail:* omarsnc@fnu.edu.
Website: http://www.fnu.edu/.

FLORIDA POLYTECHNIC UNIVERSITY
Lakeland, FL

ABOUT THE INSTITUTION State-supported, coed. ***Awards:*** bachelor's and master's degrees. 10 undergraduate majors. ***Total enrollment:*** 1,336. Undergraduates: 1,294. Freshmen: 277.

CONTACT eric callueng, director of financial aid, Florida Polytechnic University, 4700 research way, LAKELAND, FL 33805, 863-8748751. *E-mail:* ecallueng@floridapoly.edu.
Website: http://www.floridapoly.edu/.

FLORIDA SOUTHERN COLLEGE
Lakeland, FL

ABOUT THE INSTITUTION Independent United Methodist Church, coed. ***Awards:*** bachelor's, master's, and doctoral degrees. 60 undergraduate majors. ***Total enrollment:*** 3,305. Undergraduates: 2,755. Freshmen: 685.

GIFT AID (NEED-BASED) ***Scholarships, grants, and awards:*** Federal Pell, FSEOG, state, private, college/university gift aid from institutional funds, Federal Nursing.

GIFT AID (NON-NEED-BASED) ***Scholarships, grants, and awards by category:*** *Academic interests/achievement:* agriculture, biological sciences, business, communication, education, general academic interests/achievements, home economics, physical sciences, religion/biblical studies, social sciences. *Creative arts/performance:* applied art and design, music, theater/drama. *Special achievements/activities:* community service, general special achievements/activities, leadership. *Special characteristics:* children and siblings of alumni, children of faculty/staff, general special characteristics, local/state students, out-of-state students, relatives of clergy, religious affiliation, siblings of current students.

LOANS ***Programs:*** Federal Direct (Subsidized and Unsubsidized Stafford, PLUS), Perkins.

WORK-STUDY ***Federal work-study:*** Total amount: $388,810; 172 jobs averaging $2260. ***State or other work-study/employment:*** Part-time jobs available.

APPLYING FOR FINANCIAL AID ***Required financial aid forms:*** FAFSA, institution's own form.

CONTACT Mr. William L. Healy, Director of Financial Aid, Florida Southern College, 111 Lake Hollingsworth Drive, Lakeland, FL 33801-5698, 863-680-4140 or toll-free 800-274-4131. *Fax:* 863-680-4567. *E-mail:* whealy@flsouthern.edu.
Website: http://www.flsouthern.edu/.

FLORIDA STATE UNIVERSITY
Tallahassee, FL

Tuition & fees (area res): $6517 **Average undergraduate aid package: $13,691**

ABOUT THE INSTITUTION State-supported, coed. ***Awards:*** certificates, associate, bachelor's, master's, and doctoral degrees. 112 undergraduate majors. ***Total enrollment:*** 42,218. Undergraduates: 33,038. Freshmen: 6,874. Federal methodology is used as a basis for awarding need-based institutional aid.

UNDERGRADUATE EXPENSES for 2019–2020 ***Application fee:*** $30. ***Tuition, area resident:*** full-time $4640; part-time $216 per credit hour. ***Tuition, state resident:*** full-time $4640; part-time $216 per credit hour. ***Tuition, nonresident:*** full-time $19,806; part-time $721 per credit hour. ***Required fees:*** full-time $1877. Full-time tuition and fees vary according to course load, degree level, and location. Part-time tuition and fees vary according to course load, degree level, and location. ***College room and board:*** $10,780; ***Room only:*** $6540. Room and board charges vary according to board plan and housing facility. ***Payment plan:*** Tuition prepayment.

FRESHMAN FINANCIAL AID (Fall 2018) 5208 applied for aid; of those 100% were deemed to have need. 98% of freshmen with need received aid; of those 71% had need fully met. ***Average percent of need met:*** 95% (excluding resources awarded to replace EFC). ***Average financial aid package:*** $13,823 (excluding resources awarded to replace EFC). 10% of all full-time freshmen had no need and received non-need-based gift aid.

UNDERGRADUATE FINANCIAL AID (Fall 2018) 19,730 applied for aid; of those 96% were deemed to have need. 97% of undergraduates with need received aid; of those 67% had need fully met. ***Average percent of need met:*** 93% (excluding resources awarded to replace EFC). ***Average financial aid package:*** $13,691 (excluding resources awarded to replace EFC). 17% of all full-time undergraduates had no need and received non-need-based gift aid.

GIFT AID (NEED-BASED) ***Total amount:*** $143,637,475 (33% federal, 42% state, 22% institutional, 3% external sources). ***Receiving aid:*** Freshmen: 81% (4,839); all full-time undergraduates: 57% (16,508). ***Average award:*** Freshmen: $13,401; Undergraduates: $13,033. ***Scholarships, grants, and awards:*** Federal Pell, FSEOG, state, private, college/university gift aid from institutional funds, United Negro College Fund.

GIFT AID (NON-NEED-BASED) ***Total amount:*** $48,915,901 (2% federal, 85% state, 10% institutional, 3% external sources). ***Receiving aid:*** Freshmen: 74% (4,436). Undergraduates: 41% (11,909). ***Average award:*** Freshmen: $7875. Undergraduates: $8412. ***Scholarships, grants, and awards by category:*** *Academic interests/achievement:* general academic interests/achievements. *Creative arts/performance:* cinema/film/broadcasting, dance, music, theater/drama. *Special characteristics:* local/state students. ***Tuition waivers:*** Full or partial for employees or children of employees, senior citizens. ***ROTC:*** Army, Naval cooperative, Air Force.

LOANS ***Student loans:*** $64,830,813 (78% need-based, 22% non-need-based). 42% of past graduating class borrowed through all loan programs. *Average indebtedness per student:* $25,013. ***Average need-based loan:*** Freshmen: $3660. Undergraduates: $4890. ***Parent loans:*** $10,337,065 (48% need-based, 52% non-need-based). ***Programs:*** Federal Direct (Subsidized and Unsubsidized Stafford, PLUS).

WORK-STUDY ***Federal work-study:*** Total amount: $1,634,857; 938 jobs averaging $2400. ***State or other work-study/employment:*** Total amount: $41,641 (100% need-based). 23 part-time jobs averaging $2400.

ATHLETIC AWARDS Total amount: $8,838,282 (40% need-based, 60% non-need-based).

APPLYING FOR FINANCIAL AID *Required financial aid forms:* FAFSA, state aid form. ***Financial aid deadline:*** Continuous. ***Notification date:*** Continuous beginning 4/5.

CONTACT Somnath Chatterjee, Director of Financial Aid, Florida State University, University Center A4400, Tallahassee, FL 32306-2430, 850-644-5716. *Fax:* 850-644-6404. *E-mail:* ofacs@admin.fsu.edu.
Website: http://www.fsu.edu/.

FONTBONNE UNIVERSITY

St. Louis, MO

CONTACT Dr. Matthew Kearney, Financial Aid Office, Fontbonne University, 6800 Wydown Boulevard, St. Louis, MO 63105-3098, 314-889-1414 or toll-free 800-205-5862. *Fax:* 314-889-1457. *E-mail:* fbufinaid@fontbonne.edu.
Website: http://www.fontbonne.edu/.

FORDHAM UNIVERSITY

New York, NY

Tuition & fees: $55,788	Average undergraduate aid package: $38,157

ABOUT THE INSTITUTION Independent Roman Catholic (Jesuit), coed. ***Awards:*** certificates, bachelor's, master's, and doctoral degrees (branch locations at Rose Hill and Lincoln Center). 64 undergraduate majors. ***Total enrollment:*** 16,972. Undergraduates: 9,767. Freshmen: 2,270.

UNDERGRADUATE EXPENSES for 2020–2021 *Application fee:* $70. ***Comprehensive fee:*** $74,854 includes full-time tuition ($54,730), mandatory fees ($1058), and room and board ($19,066). Room and board charges vary according to board plan, housing facility, and location. ***Part-time tuition:*** $1824 per credit hour. Part-time tuition and fees vary according to class time and course load.

FRESHMAN FINANCIAL AID (Fall 2019, est.) 1972 applied for aid; of those 68% were deemed to have need. 100% of freshmen with need received aid; of those 29% had need fully met. ***Average percent of need met:*** 79% (excluding resources awarded to replace EFC). ***Average financial aid package:*** $39,608 (excluding resources awarded to replace EFC). 27% of all full-time freshmen had no need and received non-need-based gift aid.

UNDERGRADUATE FINANCIAL AID (Fall 2019, est.) 7,547 applied for aid; of those 71% were deemed to have need. 100% of undergraduates with need received aid; of those 27% had need fully met. ***Average percent of need met:*** 76% (excluding resources awarded to replace EFC). ***Average financial aid package:*** $38,157 (excluding resources awarded to replace EFC). 22% of all full-time undergraduates had no need and received non-need-based gift aid.

GIFT AID (NEED-BASED) *Total amount:* $148,615,312 (6% federal, 5% state, 86% institutional, 3% external sources). ***Receiving aid:*** Freshmen: 57% (1,292); all full-time undergraduates: 56% (5,153). ***Average award:*** Freshmen: $31,873; Undergraduates: $30,205. ***Scholarships, grants, and awards:*** Federal Pell, FSEOG, state, private, college/university gift aid from institutional funds.

GIFT AID (NON-NEED-BASED) *Total amount:* $60,575,079 (1% state, 94% institutional, 5% external sources). ***Receiving aid:*** Freshmen: 14% (319). Undergraduates: 13% (1,165). ***Average award:*** Freshmen: $20,363. Undergraduates: $20,142. ***Scholarships, grants, and awards by category:*** *Academic interests/achievement:* biological sciences, business, communication, foreign languages, general academic interests/achievements. *Creative arts/performance:* dance, music. *Special achievements/activities:* general special achievements/activities. *Special characteristics:* adult students, children and siblings of alumni, children of faculty/staff, children with a deceased or disabled parent, handicapped students. ***Tuition waivers:*** Full or partial for employees or children of employees. ***ROTC:*** Army, Naval cooperative, Air Force cooperative.

LOANS *Student loans:* $47,316,821 (56% need-based, 44% non-need-based). 57% of past graduating class borrowed through all loan programs. *Average indebtedness per student:* $37,283. ***Average need-based loan:*** Freshmen: $4946. Undergraduates: $6016. ***Parent loans:*** $26,678,108 (48% need-based, 52% non-need-based). ***Programs:*** Federal Direct (Subsidized and Unsubsidized Stafford, PLUS).

WORK-STUDY *Federal work-study:* Total amount: $3,713,481; jobs available. ***State or other work-study/employment:*** Part-time jobs available.

ATHLETIC AWARDS Total amount: $13,928,805 (57% need-based, 43% non-need-based).

APPLYING FOR FINANCIAL AID *Required financial aid forms:* FAFSA, CSS Financial Aid PROFILE, state aid form, noncustodial (divorced/separated) parent's statement, business/farm supplement. ***Financial aid deadline:*** 2/1 (priority: 11/15). ***Notification date:*** 2/1. Students must reply by 5/1 or within 2 weeks of notification.

CONTACT Mr. Brian Ghanoo, Assistant Vice President of Student Financial Services, Fordham University, 441 East Fordham Road, Thebaud Hall, Room 208, New York, NY 10458, 718-817-3804 or toll-free 800-FORDHAM. *Fax:* 718-817-3817. *E-mail:* ghanoo@fordham.edu.
Website: http://www.fordham.edu/.

FORT HAYS STATE UNIVERSITY

Hays, KS

Tuition & fees: N/R	Average undergraduate aid package: $7880

ABOUT THE INSTITUTION State-supported, coed. ***Awards:*** certificates, associate, bachelor's, and master's degrees. 66 undergraduate majors. ***Total enrollment:*** 15,523. Undergraduates: 12,780. Freshmen: 996. Federal methodology is used as a basis for awarding need-based institutional aid.

FRESHMAN FINANCIAL AID (Fall 2018) 368 applied for aid; of those 84% were deemed to have need. 96% of freshmen with need received aid; of those 7% had need fully met. ***Average percent of need met:*** 43% (excluding resources awarded to replace EFC). ***Average financial aid package:*** $6783 (excluding resources awarded to replace EFC). 19% of all full-time freshmen had no need and received non-need-based gift aid.

UNDERGRADUATE FINANCIAL AID (Fall 2018) 4,758 applied for aid; of those 84% were deemed to have need. 96% of undergraduates with need received aid; of those 11% had need fully met. ***Average percent of need met:*** 50% (excluding resources awarded to replace EFC). ***Average financial aid package:*** $7880 (excluding resources awarded to replace EFC). 11% of all full-time undergraduates had no need and received non-need-based gift aid.

GIFT AID (NEED-BASED) *Total amount:* $20,376,180 (71% federal, 5% state, 10% institutional, 14% external sources). ***Receiving aid:*** Freshmen: 35% (254); all full-time undergraduates: 56% (3,216). ***Average award:*** Freshmen: $5322; Undergraduates: $5755. ***Scholarships, grants, and awards:*** Federal Pell, FSEOG, state, private, college/university gift aid from institutional funds.

GIFT AID (NON-NEED-BASED) *Total amount:* $4,366,466 (1% state, 38% institutional, 61% external sources). ***Receiving aid:*** Freshmen: 1% (10). Undergraduates: 4% (207). ***Average award:*** Freshmen: $1847. Undergraduates: $2387. ***Scholarships, grants, and awards by category:*** *Academic interests/achievement:* agriculture, area/ethnic studies, biological sciences, business, communication, computer science, education, engineering/technologies, English, foreign languages, general academic interests/achievements, home economics, humanities, international studies, mathematics, physical sciences, premedicine, social sciences. *Creative arts/performance:* applied art and design, art/fine arts, cinema/film/broadcasting, creative writing, dance, general creative arts/performance, journalism/publications, music, performing arts, theater/drama. *Special achievements/activities:* cheerleading/drum major, leadership, rodeo. *Special characteristics:* adult students, children and siblings of alumni, children of faculty/staff, first-generation college students, general special characteristics, international students, local/state students, veterans.

LOANS *Student loans:* $31,736,874 (78% need-based, 22% non-need-based). 66% of past graduating class borrowed through all loan programs. *Average indebtedness per student:* $26,240. ***Average need-based loan:*** Freshmen: $2736. Undergraduates: $3754. ***Parent loans:*** $3,445,528 (28% need-based, 72% non-need-based). ***Programs:*** Federal Direct (Subsidized and Unsubsidized Stafford, PLUS), college/university.

WORK-STUDY *Federal work-study:* Total amount: $798,703; jobs available. ***State or other work-study/employment:*** Total amount: $118,083 (40% need-based, 60% non-need-based). Part-time jobs available.

ATHLETIC AWARDS Total amount: $2,190,355 (50% need-based, 50% non-need-based).

APPLYING FOR FINANCIAL AID *Required financial aid forms:* FAFSA, institution's own form. ***Financial aid deadline (priority):*** 12/1. ***Notification date:*** Continuous beginning 12/1. Students must reply within 2 weeks of notification.

CONTACT Vanessa Flipse, Director of Financial Assistance, Fort Hays State University, Picken Hall, Room 202, 600 Park Street, Hays, KS 67601, 785-6284494 or toll-free 800-628-FHSU. *Fax:* 785-628-4014. *E-mail:* vmflipse@fhsu.edu. *Website:* http://www.fhsu.edu/.

FORT LEWIS COLLEGE

Durango, CO

Tuition & fees (CO res): $8881	Average undergraduate aid package: $18,607

ABOUT THE INSTITUTION State-supported, coed. ***Awards:*** certificates, bachelor's, and master's degrees. 50 undergraduate majors. ***Total enrollment:*** 3,308. Undergraduates: 3,229. Freshmen: 761. Federal methodology is used as a basis for awarding need-based institutional aid.

UNDERGRADUATE EXPENSES for 2019–2020 *Application fee:* $40. ***Tuition, state resident:*** full-time $7065; part-time $294 per credit hour. ***Tuition, nonresident:*** full-time $17,712; part-time $738 per contact hour. ***Required fees:*** full-time $1816; $60.50 per credit hour. Full-time tuition and fees vary according to course load and reciprocity agreements. Part-time tuition and fees vary according to course load and reciprocity agreements. ***College room and board:*** $9878; ***Room only:*** $7496. Room and board charges vary according to board plan and housing facility.

FRESHMAN FINANCIAL AID (Fall 2018) 569 applied for aid; of those 80% were deemed to have need. 100% of freshmen with need received aid; of those 16% had need fully met. ***Average percent of need met:*** 91% (excluding resources awarded to replace EFC). ***Average financial aid package:*** $18,822 (excluding resources awarded to replace EFC). 12% of all full-time freshmen had no need and received non-need-based gift aid.

UNDERGRADUATE FINANCIAL AID (Fall 2018) 1,999 applied for aid; of those 83% were deemed to have need. 99% of undergraduates with need received aid; of those 20% had need fully met. ***Average percent of need met:*** 91% (excluding resources awarded to replace EFC). ***Average financial aid package:*** $18,607 (excluding resources awarded to replace EFC). 14% of all full-time undergraduates had no need and received non-need-based gift aid.

GIFT AID (NEED-BASED) *Receiving aid:* Freshmen: 55% (409); all full-time undergraduates: 51% (1,471). ***Average award:*** Freshmen: $6619; Undergraduates: $5525. ***Scholarships, grants, and awards:*** Federal Pell, FSEOG, state, private, college/university gift aid from institutional funds.

GIFT AID (NON-NEED-BASED) *Receiving aid:* Freshmen: 5% (34). Undergraduates: 4% (118). ***Average award:*** Freshmen: $12,164. Undergraduates: $5353. ***Scholarships, grants, and awards by category:*** *Academic interests/achievement:* area/ethnic studies, biological sciences, business, communication, education, English, general academic interests/achievements, humanities, mathematics, physical sciences, social sciences. *Creative arts/performance:* applied art and design, journalism/publications, music, performing arts, theater/drama. *Special achievements/activities:* general special achievements/activities, leadership. *Special characteristics:* adult students, children and siblings of alumni, children of faculty/staff, ethnic background, first-generation college students, general special characteristics, handicapped students, international students, local/state students, out-of-state students. ***Tuition waivers:*** Full or partial for minority students, employees or children of employees, senior citizens.

LOANS *Student loans:* 58% of past graduating class borrowed through all loan programs. *Average indebtedness per student:* $19,429. ***Average need-based loan:*** Freshmen: $6619. Undergraduates: $3816. ***Programs:*** Federal Direct (Subsidized and Unsubsidized Stafford, PLUS).

WORK-STUDY Federal work-study jobs available. ***State or other work-study/employment:*** Part-time jobs available.

APPLYING FOR FINANCIAL AID *Required financial aid form:* FAFSA. ***Financial aid deadline:*** Continuous. ***Notification date:*** Continuous.

CONTACT Ms. Tracey Piccoli, Director of Financial Aid, Fort Lewis College, 1000 Rim Drive, 101 Miller Student Services Building, Durango, CO 81301, 800-352-7512 or toll-free 877-FLC-COLO. *Fax:* 970-247-7108. *E-mail:* finaid_off@fortlewis.edu. *Website:* http://www.fortlewis.edu/.

FORT VALLEY STATE UNIVERSITY

Fort Valley, GA

CONTACT Mr. James Stotts, Office of Financial Aid, Fort Valley State University, 1005 State University Drive, Fort Valley, GA 31030, 478-825-6182 or toll-free 877-462-3878. *Fax:* 478-825-6976. *E-mail:* parksc@tvsu.edu. *Website:* http://www.fvsu.edu/.

FRAMINGHAM STATE UNIVERSITY

Framingham, MA

Tuition & fees (MA res): $11,100	Average undergraduate aid package: $10,051

ABOUT THE INSTITUTION State-supported, coed. ***Awards:*** certificates, bachelor's, and master's degrees. 41 undergraduate majors. ***Total enrollment:*** 5,456. Undergraduates: 3,857. Freshmen: 776. Federal methodology is used as a basis for awarding need-based institutional aid.

UNDERGRADUATE EXPENSES for 2020–2021 *Application fee:* $50. ***Tuition, state resident:*** full-time $970; part-time $162 per course. ***Tuition, nonresident:*** full-time $7050; part-time $1175 per course. ***Required fees:*** full-time $10,130; $1561 per course. ***College room and board:*** $12,604. ***Payment plan:*** Tuition prepayment.

FRESHMAN FINANCIAL AID (Fall 2018) 704 applied for aid; of those 83% were deemed to have need. 100% of freshmen with need received aid; of those 9% had need fully met. ***Average percent of need met:*** 56% (excluding resources awarded to replace EFC). ***Average financial aid package:*** $10,987 (excluding resources awarded to replace EFC). 8% of all full-time freshmen had no need and received non-need-based gift aid.

UNDERGRADUATE FINANCIAL AID (Fall 2018) 2,872 applied for aid; of those 82% were deemed to have need. 100% of undergraduates with need received aid; of those 7% had need fully met. ***Average percent of need met:*** 55% (excluding resources awarded to replace EFC). ***Average financial aid package:*** $10,051 (excluding resources awarded to replace EFC). 6% of all full-time undergraduates had no need and received non-need-based gift aid.

GIFT AID (NEED-BASED) *Total amount:* $13,127,476 (51% federal, 23% state, 22% institutional, 4% external sources). ***Receiving aid:*** Freshmen: 63% (480); all full-time undergraduates: 57% (1,947). ***Average award:*** Freshmen: $6808; Undergraduates: $6317. ***Scholarships, grants, and awards:*** Federal Pell, FSEOG, state, private, college/university gift aid from institutional funds.

GIFT AID (NON-NEED-BASED) *Total amount:* $1,176,250 (63% state, 24% institutional, 13% external sources). ***Receiving aid:*** Freshmen: 5% (37). Undergraduates: 3% (98). ***Average award:*** Freshmen: $1148. Undergraduates: $1218. ***Scholarships, grants, and awards by category:*** *Academic interests/achievement:* biological sciences, education, engineering/technologies, English, general academic interests/achievements, home economics, mathematics, physical sciences. *Special characteristics:* children of faculty/staff, children of public servants, children of union members/company employees, veterans.

LOANS *Student loans:* $23,144,170 (78% need-based, 22% non-need-based). 89% of past graduating class borrowed through all loan programs. *Average indebtedness per student:* $31,465. ***Average need-based loan:*** Freshmen: $4672. Undergraduates: $5117. ***Parent loans:*** $5,302,220 (53% need-based, 47% non-need-based). ***Programs:*** Federal Direct (Subsidized and Unsubsidized Stafford, PLUS), state.

WORK-STUDY *Federal work-study:* Total amount: $123,903; jobs available. ***State or other work-study/employment:*** Total amount: $56,243 (100% need-based). Part-time jobs available.

APPLYING FOR FINANCIAL AID *Required financial aid form:* FAFSA. ***Financial aid deadline (priority):*** 3/1. ***Notification date:*** Continuous beginning 3/15. Students must reply by 5/1 or within 2 weeks of notification.

CONTACT Office of Financial Aid, Framingham State University, 100 State Street, PO Box 9101, Framingham, MA 01701-9101, 508-626-4534. *Fax:* 508-626-4598. *Website:* http://www.framingham.edu/.

FRANCISCAN MISSIONARIES OF OUR LADY UNIVERSITY

Baton Rouge, LA

CONTACT Tiffany D. Magee, Director of Financial Aid, Franciscan Missionaries of Our Lady University, 7434 Perkins Road, Baton Rouge, LA 70808, 225-768-1701. *Fax:* 225-490-1632. *E-mail:* tiffany.magee@ololcollege.edu.
Website: http://www.franu.edu/.

FRANCISCAN UNIVERSITY OF STEUBENVILLE

Steubenville, OH

CONTACT Jody Peeler, Director of Financial Aid, Franciscan University of Steubenville, 1235 University Boulevard, Steubenville, OH 43952-1763, 740-284-5216 or toll-free 800-783-6220. *Fax:* 740-284-5469. *E-mail:* jpeeler@franciscan.edu.
Website: http://www.franciscan.edu/.

FRANCIS MARION UNIVERSITY

Florence, SC

Tuition & fees: N/R	Average undergraduate aid package: $11,180

ABOUT THE INSTITUTION State-supported, coed. ***Awards:*** certificates, bachelor's, master's, and doctoral degrees. 35 undergraduate majors. ***Total enrollment:*** 4,240. Undergraduates: 3,800. Freshmen: 716. Federal methodology is used as a basis for awarding need-based institutional aid.

FRESHMAN FINANCIAL AID (Fall 2018) 564 applied for aid; of those 99% were deemed to have need. 100% of freshmen with need received aid; of those 75% had need fully met. ***Average percent of need met:*** 68% (excluding resources awarded to replace EFC). ***Average financial aid package:*** $11,942 (excluding resources awarded to replace EFC). 4% of all full-time freshmen had no need and received non-need-based gift aid.

UNDERGRADUATE FINANCIAL AID (Fall 2018) 2,594 applied for aid; of those 90% were deemed to have need. 100% of undergraduates with need received aid; of those 93% had need fully met. ***Average percent of need met:*** 74% (excluding resources awarded to replace EFC). ***Average financial aid package:*** $11,180 (excluding resources awarded to replace EFC). 3% of all full-time undergraduates had no need and received non-need-based gift aid.

GIFT AID (NEED-BASED) ***Total amount:*** $17,570,294 (56% federal, 35% state, 5% institutional, 4% external sources). ***Receiving aid:*** Freshmen: 76% (555); all full-time undergraduates: 75% (2,159). ***Average award:*** Freshmen: $9693; Undergraduates: $8164. ***Scholarships, grants, and awards:*** Federal Pell, FSEOG, state, private, college/university gift aid from institutional funds, Federal Nursing.

GIFT AID (NON-NEED-BASED) ***Total amount:*** $2,934,337 (56% state, 21% institutional, 23% external sources). ***Receiving aid:*** Freshmen: 6% (43). Undergraduates: 5% (152). ***Average award:*** Freshmen: $3868. Undergraduates: $4027. ***Scholarships, grants, and awards by category:*** *Creative arts/performance:* 35 awards ($1950 total): art/fine arts. ***ROTC:*** Army.

LOANS ***Student loans:*** $15,973,868 (85% need-based, 15% non-need-based). 95% of past graduating class borrowed through all loan programs. *Average indebtedness per student:* $32,193. ***Average need-based loan:*** Freshmen: $3132. Undergraduates: $3915. ***Parent loans:*** $3,648,358 (70% need-based, 30% non-need-based). ***Programs:*** Federal Direct (Subsidized and Unsubsidized Stafford, PLUS), Federal Nursing, state.

WORK-STUDY ***Federal work-study:*** Total amount: $217,964; jobs available. ***State or other work-study/employment:*** Total amount: $361,685 (53% need-based, 47% non-need-based). Part-time jobs available.

ATHLETIC AWARDS Total amount: $857,746 (46% need-based, 54% non-need-based).

APPLYING FOR FINANCIAL AID ***Required financial aid form:*** FAFSA. ***Financial aid deadline:*** Continuous. ***Notification date:*** Continuous beginning 11/1.

CONTACT Kim Ellisor, Director of Financial Assistance, Francis Marion University, PO Box 100547, Florence, SC 29502-0547, 843-661-1190 or toll-free 800-368-7551. *Fax:* 843-661-1195. *E-mail:* kellisor@fmarion.edu.
Website: http://www.fmarion.edu/.

FRANKLIN & MARSHALL COLLEGE

Lancaster, PA

Tuition & fees: $58,800	Average undergraduate aid package: $54,166

ABOUT THE INSTITUTION Independent, coed. ***Awards:*** bachelor's degrees. 41 undergraduate majors. ***Total enrollment:*** 2,283. Undergraduates: 2,283. Freshmen: 645. Institutional methodology is used as a basis for awarding need-based institutional aid.

UNDERGRADUATE EXPENSES for 2019–2020 ***Application fee:*** $60. ***One-time required fee:*** $200. ***Comprehensive fee:*** $73,250 includes full-time tuition ($58,615), mandatory fees ($185), and room and board ($14,450). ***College room only:*** $8550. Room and board charges vary according to board plan and housing facility. ***Part-time tuition:*** $7325 per course. Part-time tuition and fees vary according to course load.

FRESHMAN FINANCIAL AID (Fall 2019, est.) 399 applied for aid; of those 85% were deemed to have need. 100% of freshmen with need received aid; of those 100% had need fully met. ***Average percent of need met:*** 100% (excluding resources awarded to replace EFC). ***Average financial aid package:*** $55,102 (excluding resources awarded to replace EFC).

UNDERGRADUATE FINANCIAL AID (Fall 2019, est.) 1,429 applied for aid; of those 89% were deemed to have need. 100% of undergraduates with need received aid; of those 59% had need fully met. ***Average percent of need met:*** 100% (excluding resources awarded to replace EFC). ***Average financial aid package:*** $54,166 (excluding resources awarded to replace EFC). 1% of all full-time undergraduates had no need and received non-need-based gift aid.

GIFT AID (NEED-BASED) ***Receiving aid:*** Freshmen: 54% (337); all full-time undergraduates: 55% (1,265). ***Average award:*** Freshmen: $51,407; Undergraduates: $49,637. ***Scholarships, grants, and awards:*** Federal Pell, FSEOG, state, private, college/university gift aid from institutional funds.

GIFT AID (NON-NEED-BASED) ***Receiving aid:*** Freshmen: 11% (70). Undergraduates: 12% (281). ***Average award:*** Undergraduates: $22,222. ***Scholarships, grants, and awards by category:*** *Creative arts/performance:* music. ***Tuition waivers:*** Full or partial for employees or children of employees.

LOANS ***Student loans:*** 54% of past graduating class borrowed through all loan programs. *Average indebtedness per student:* $27,928. ***Average need-based loan:*** Freshmen: $2681. Undergraduates: $3639. ***Programs:*** Federal Direct (Subsidized and Unsubsidized Stafford, PLUS), college/university.

WORK-STUDY Federal work-study jobs available. ***State or other work-study/employment:*** Part-time jobs available.

APPLYING FOR FINANCIAL AID ***Required financial aid forms:*** FAFSA, CSS Financial Aid PROFILE, noncustodial (divorced/separated) parent's statement.

CONTACT Mr. Clarke Paine, Director of Financial Aid, Franklin & Marshall College, PO Box 3003, Lancaster, PA 17604-3003, 717-358-3991 or toll-free 877-678-9111. *Fax:* 717-358-4462. *E-mail:* clarke.paine@fandm.edu.
Website: http://www.fandm.edu/.

FRANKLIN COLLEGE

Franklin, IN

Tuition & fees: $33,954	Average undergraduate aid package: $24,966

ABOUT THE INSTITUTION Independent American Baptist Churches in the U.S.A., coed. ***Awards:*** bachelor's and master's degrees. 35 undergraduate majors. ***Total enrollment:*** 910. Undergraduates: 1,016. Freshmen: 267. Federal methodology is used as a basis for awarding need-based institutional aid.

UNDERGRADUATE EXPENSES for 2020–2021 ***Application fee:*** $40. ***Comprehensive fee:*** $44,500 includes full-time tuition ($33,754), mandatory fees ($200), and room and board ($10,546). ***College room only:*** $6026. Full-time tuition and fees vary according to course load and degree level. Room and board charges vary according to board plan. ***Part-time tuition:*** $485 per credit hour. ***Part-time fees:*** $7 per credit hour. Part-time tuition and fees vary according to course load and degree level.

FRESHMAN FINANCIAL AID (Fall 2018) 262 applied for aid; of those 92% were deemed to have need. 100% of freshmen with need received aid; of those 12% had need fully met. ***Average percent of need met:*** 73% (excluding resources awarded to replace EFC). ***Average financial aid package:*** $25,332 (excluding resources awarded to replace EFC). 10% of all full-time freshmen had no need and received non-need-based gift aid.

UNDERGRADUATE FINANCIAL AID (Fall 2018) 859 applied for aid; of those 89% were deemed to have need. 100% of undergraduates with need received aid; of those 14% had need fully met. ***Average percent of need met:*** 73% (excluding resources awarded to replace EFC). ***Average financial aid package:*** $24,966 (excluding resources awarded to replace EFC). 15% of all full-time undergraduates had no need and received non-need-based gift aid.

GIFT AID (NEED-BASED) ***Total amount:*** $16,589,455 (11% federal, 17% state, 70% institutional, 2% external sources). ***Receiving aid:*** Freshmen: 89% (242); all full-time undergraduates: 83% (759). ***Average award:*** Freshmen: $22,904; Undergraduates: $22,097. ***Scholarships, grants, and awards:*** Federal Pell, FSEOG, state, private, college/university gift aid from institutional funds.

GIFT AID (NON-NEED-BASED) ***Total amount:*** $3,124,491 (1% state, 91% institutional, 8% external sources). ***Receiving aid:*** Freshmen: 10% (28). Undergraduates: 12% (108). ***Average award:*** Freshmen: $17,532. Undergraduates: $15,277. ***Scholarships, grants, and awards by category:*** *Academic interests/achievement:* general academic interests/achievements. *Creative arts/performance:* applied art and design, art/fine arts, journalism/publications, music, performing arts, theater/drama. *Special achievements/activities:* community service, general special achievements/activities, leadership, memberships, religious involvement. *Special characteristics:* children and siblings of alumni, children of current students, children of faculty/staff, ethnic background, first-generation college students, handicapped students, local/state students, members of minority groups, out-of-state students, relatives of clergy, religious affiliation, siblings of current students, spouses of current students, veterans. ***Tuition waivers:*** Full or partial for employees or children of employees, senior citizens. ***ROTC:*** Army cooperative.

LOANS ***Student loans:*** $6,004,535 (68% need-based, 32% non-need-based). 80% of past graduating class borrowed through all loan programs. *Average indebtedness per student:* $38,057. ***Average need-based loan:*** Freshmen: $2950. Undergraduates: $3797. ***Parent loans:*** $2,795,101 (41% need-based, 59% non-need-based). ***Programs:*** Federal Direct (Subsidized and Unsubsidized Stafford, PLUS), college/university.

WORK-STUDY ***Federal work-study:*** Total amount: $108,432; jobs available. ***State or other work-study/employment:*** Total amount: $4000 (32% need-based, 68% non-need-based). Part-time jobs available.

APPLYING FOR FINANCIAL AID ***Required financial aid form:*** FAFSA. ***Financial aid deadline (priority):*** 12/1. ***Notification date:*** Continuous beginning 12/15. Students must reply by 5/1 or within 2 weeks of notification.

CONTACT Mr. James Vincent-Dunn, Director of Financial Aid, Franklin College, 101 Branigin Boulevard, Franklin, IN 46131-2598, 317-738-8073 or toll-free 800-852-0232. *Fax:* 317-738-8072. *E-mail:* jvincent-dunn@franklincollege.edu.

Website: http://www.franklincollege.edu/.

FRANKLIN PIERCE UNIVERSITY

Rindge, NH

Tuition & fees: $38,200	Average undergraduate aid package: $28,204

ABOUT THE INSTITUTION Independent, coed. ***Awards:*** certificates, associate, bachelor's, master's, and doctoral degrees (profile does not reflect significant enrollment at 6 continuing education sites; master's degree is only offered at these sites). 33 undergraduate majors. ***Total enrollment:*** 2,189. Undergraduates: 1,629. Freshmen: 462. Federal methodology is used as a basis for awarding need-based institutional aid.

UNDERGRADUATE EXPENSES for 2019–2020 ***Application fee:*** $40. ***Comprehensive fee:*** $52,100 includes full-time tuition ($34,900), mandatory fees ($3300), and room and board ($13,900). ***College room only:*** $8100. ***Part-time tuition:*** $1197 per credit hour.

FRESHMAN FINANCIAL AID (Fall 2019, est.) 433 applied for aid; of those 93% were deemed to have need. 100% of freshmen with need received aid; of those 20% had need fully met. ***Average percent of need met:*** 72% (excluding resources awarded to replace EFC). ***Average financial aid package:*** $27,091 (excluding resources awarded to replace EFC). 11% of all full-time freshmen had no need and received non-need-based gift aid.

UNDERGRADUATE FINANCIAL AID (Fall 2019, est.) 1,176 applied for aid; of those 93% were deemed to have need. 100% of undergraduates with need received aid; of those 21% had need fully met. ***Average percent of need met:*** 73% (excluding resources awarded to replace EFC). ***Average financial aid package:*** $28,204 (excluding resources awarded to replace EFC). 14% of all full-time undergraduates had no need and received non-need-based gift aid.

GIFT AID (NEED-BASED) ***Total amount:*** $33,913,524 (7% federal, 1% state, 92% institutional). ***Receiving aid:*** Freshmen: 89% (402); all full-time undergraduates: 84% (1,090). ***Average award:*** Freshmen: $24,731; Undergraduates: $24,724.

GIFT AID (NON-NEED-BASED) ***Total amount:*** $5,503,211 (100% institutional). ***Receiving aid:*** Freshmen: 17% (76). Undergraduates: 16% (210). ***Average award:*** Freshmen: $20,784. Undergraduates: $20,288. ***Scholarships, grants, and awards by category:*** *Academic interests/achievement:* communication, general academic interests/achievements. *Creative arts/performance:* performing arts, theater/drama. *Special achievements/activities:* general special achievements/activities, leadership. *Special characteristics:* adult students, children and siblings of alumni, children of current students, children of educators, children of faculty/staff, general special characteristics, international students, local/state students, married students, parents of current students, siblings of current students, spouses of current students. ***ROTC:*** Army cooperative.

LOANS ***Student loans:*** $21,559,422 (58% need-based, 42% non-need-based). 82% of past graduating class borrowed through all loan programs. *Average indebtedness per student:* $38,237. ***Average need-based loan:*** Freshmen: $3068. Undergraduates: $4245. ***Parent loans:*** $5,779,656 (100% need-based).

WORK-STUDY ***Federal work-study:*** Total amount: $300,161; jobs available. ***State or other work-study/employment:*** Part-time jobs available.

ATHLETIC AWARDS Total amount: $4,089,607 (100% need-based).

APPLYING FOR FINANCIAL AID ***Notification date:*** Continuous.

CONTACT Kenneth Ferreira, Associate Vice President for Student Financial Services, Franklin Pierce University, 40 University Drive, Rindge, NH 03461-0060, 603-899-4180 or toll-free 800-437-0048. *Fax:* 603-899-4372. *E-mail:* ferreirak@franklinpierce.edu.

Website: http://www.franklinpierce.edu/.

FRANKLIN UNIVERSITY

Columbus, OH

CONTACT Ms. Marlowe Collier, Financial Aid Assistant, Franklin University, 201 South Grant Avenue, Columbus, OH 43215-5399, 614-797-4700 or toll-free 877-341-6300. *Fax:* 614-220-8931. *E-mail:* finaid@franklin.edu.

Website: http://www.franklin.edu/.

FRANKLIN W. OLIN COLLEGE OF ENGINEERING

Needham, MA

Tuition & fees: $54,700	Average undergraduate aid package: $50,583

ABOUT THE INSTITUTION Independent, coed. ***Awards:*** bachelor's degrees. 3 undergraduate majors. ***Total enrollment:*** 386. Undergraduates: 386. Freshmen: 85. Federal methodology is used as a basis for awarding need-based institutional aid.

UNDERGRADUATE EXPENSES for 2020–2021 ***Application fee:*** $85. ***One-time required fee:*** $2656. ***Comprehensive fee:*** $72,160 includes full-time tuition ($53,990), mandatory fees ($710), and room and board ($17,460). ***Part-time tuition:*** $1688 per credit.

FRESHMAN FINANCIAL AID (Fall 2019, est.) 57 applied for aid; of those 81% were deemed to have need. 100% of freshmen with need received aid; of those 100% had need fully met. ***Average percent of need met:*** 99% (excluding resources

awarded to replace EFC). ***Average financial aid package:*** $53,995 (excluding resources awarded to replace EFC). 46% of all full-time freshmen had no need and received non-need-based gift aid.

UNDERGRADUATE FINANCIAL AID (Fall 2019, est.) 196 applied for aid; of those 85% were deemed to have need. 100% of undergraduates with need received aid; of those 99% had need fully met. ***Average percent of need met:*** 99% (excluding resources awarded to replace EFC). ***Average financial aid package:*** $50,583 (excluding resources awarded to replace EFC). 53% of all full-time undergraduates had no need and received non-need-based gift aid.

GIFT AID (NEED-BASED) ***Total amount:*** $7,804,087 (4% federal, 95% institutional, 1% external sources). ***Receiving aid:*** Freshmen: 54% (46); all full-time undergraduates: 43% (153). ***Average award:*** Freshmen: $52,376; Undergraduates: $48,901. ***Scholarships, grants, and awards:*** Federal Pell, FSEOG, college/university gift aid from institutional funds.

GIFT AID (NON-NEED-BASED) ***Total amount:*** $5,240,852 (95% institutional, 5% external sources). ***Receiving aid:*** Freshmen: 54% (46). Undergraduates: 47% (165). ***Average award:*** Freshmen: $26,159. Undergraduates: $25,480. ***Scholarships, grants, and awards by category:*** *Academic interests/achievement:* 186 awards ($4,688,277 total): general academic interests/achievements.

LOANS ***Student loans:*** $742,500 (38% need-based, 62% non-need-based). 28% of past graduating class borrowed through all loan programs. *Average indebtedness per student:* $13,480. ***Average need-based loan:*** Freshmen: $3239. Undergraduates: $3174. ***Parent loans:*** $211,958 (100% non-need-based). ***Programs:*** Federal Direct (Subsidized and Unsubsidized Stafford, PLUS).

APPLYING FOR FINANCIAL AID ***Required financial aid form:*** FAFSA. ***Financial aid deadline (priority):*** 2/15. ***Notification date:*** 4/1. Students must reply by 5/1 or within 2 weeks of notification.

CONTACT Ms. Jean Ricker, Director of Financial Aid, Franklin W. Olin College of Engineering, 1000 Olin Way, Needham, MA 02492-1200, 781-292-2215. *E-mail:* finaid@olin.edu.
Website: http://www.olin.edu/.

FREED-HARDEMAN UNIVERSITY

Henderson, TN

Tuition & fees: $22,950	Average undergraduate aid package: $19,696

ABOUT THE INSTITUTION Independent Church of Christ, coed. ***Awards:*** certificates, diplomas, associate, bachelor's, master's, and doctoral degrees. 42 undergraduate majors. ***Total enrollment:*** 2,117. Undergraduates: 1,648. Freshmen: 327. Federal methodology is used as a basis for awarding need-based institutional aid.

UNDERGRADUATE EXPENSES for 2020–2021 ***Comprehensive fee:*** $30,900 includes full-time tuition ($22,950) and room and board ($7950). ***College room only:*** $4320. ***Part-time tuition:*** $750 per credit hour.

FRESHMAN FINANCIAL AID (Fall 2019, est.) 321 applied for aid; of those 75% were deemed to have need. 100% of freshmen with need received aid; of those 27% had need fully met. ***Average percent of need met:*** 73% (excluding resources awarded to replace EFC). ***Average financial aid package:*** $20,952 (excluding resources awarded to replace EFC). 28% of all full-time freshmen had no need and received non-need-based gift aid.

UNDERGRADUATE FINANCIAL AID (Fall 2019, est.) 1,224 applied for aid; of those 78% were deemed to have need. 100% of undergraduates with need received aid; of those 24% had need fully met. ***Average percent of need met:*** 71% (excluding resources awarded to replace EFC). ***Average financial aid package:*** $19,696 (excluding resources awarded to replace EFC). 26% of all full-time undergraduates had no need and received non-need-based gift aid.

GIFT AID (NEED-BASED) ***Total amount:*** $12,817,195 (15% federal, 16% state, 62% institutional, 7% external sources). ***Receiving aid:*** Freshmen: 73% (240); all full-time undergraduates: 72% (938). ***Average award:*** Freshmen: $16,747; Undergraduates: $15,341. ***Scholarships, grants, and awards:*** Federal Pell, FSEOG, state, private, college/university gift aid from institutional funds.

GIFT AID (NON-NEED-BASED) ***Total amount:*** $5,024,854 (19% state, 70% institutional, 11% external sources). ***Receiving aid:*** Freshmen: 20% (64). Undergraduates: 17% (220). ***Average award:*** Freshmen: $9612. Undergraduates: $10,338. ***ROTC:*** Army.

LOANS ***Student loans:*** $6,002,668 (64% need-based, 36% non-need-based). 71% of past graduating class borrowed through all loan programs. *Average indebtedness per student:* $29,103. ***Average need-based loan:*** Freshmen: $3006. Undergraduates: $3885. ***Parent loans:*** $2,732,588 (43% need-based, 57% non-need-based). ***Programs:*** Federal Direct (Subsidized and Unsubsidized Stafford, PLUS), Perkins.

WORK-STUDY ***Federal work-study:*** Total amount: $232,710; jobs available. ***State or other work-study/employment:*** Part-time jobs available.

ATHLETIC AWARDS Total amount: $4,090,260 (41% need-based, 59% non-need-based).

APPLYING FOR FINANCIAL AID ***Required financial aid forms:*** FAFSA, institution's own form. ***Financial aid deadline:*** Continuous. ***Notification date:*** Continuous.

CONTACT Mrs. Summer Judd, Director of Financial Aid, Freed-Hardeman University, 158 East Main Street, Henderson, TN 38340-2399, 731-989-6662 or toll-free 800-FHU-FHU-1. *Fax:* 731-989-6775. *E-mail:* sjudd@fhu.edu.
Website: http://www.fhu.edu/.

FRESNO PACIFIC UNIVERSITY

Fresno, CA

CONTACT April Powell, Director of Financial Aid, Fresno Pacific University, 1717 South Chestnut Avenue, #2004, Fresno, CA 93702, 559-453-2041 or toll-free 800-660-6089. *Fax:* 559-453-5595. *E-mail:* sfs@fresno.edu.
Website: http://www.fresno.edu/.

FRIENDS UNIVERSITY

Wichita, KS

CONTACT Tony Lubbers, Director of Financial Aid, Friends University, 2100 University Street, Wichita, KS 67213, 316-295-5599 or toll-free 800-794-6945. *Fax:* 316-295-5703. *E-mail:* lubberst@friends.edu.
Website: http://www.friends.edu/.

FROSTBURG STATE UNIVERSITY

Frostburg, MD

CONTACT Mrs. Angela Hovatter, Director of Financial Aid, Frostburg State University, 114 Pullen Hall, 101 Braddock Road, Frostburg, MD 21532-1099, 301-687-4301. *Fax:* 301-687-7074. *E-mail:* ahovatter@frostburg.edu.
Website: http://www.frostburg.edu/.

FULL SAIL UNIVERSITY

Winter Park, FL

CONTACT Financial Aid Office, Full Sail University, 3300 University Boulevard, Winter Park, FL 32792, 800-575-1142 or toll-free 800-226-7625.
Website: http://www.fullsail.edu/.

FURMAN UNIVERSITY

Greenville, SC

ABOUT THE INSTITUTION Independent, coed. ***Awards:*** certificates, bachelor's, and master's degrees. 44 undergraduate majors. ***Total enrollment:*** 2,827. Undergraduates: 2,687. Freshmen: 648.

GIFT AID (NEED-BASED) ***Scholarships, grants, and awards:*** Federal Pell, FSEOG, state, private, college/university gift aid from institutional funds.

GIFT AID (NON-NEED-BASED) ***Scholarships, grants, and awards by category:*** *Academic interests/achievement:* area/ethnic studies, biological sciences, business, communication, computer science, education, engineering/technologies, English, foreign languages, general academic interests/achievements, home economics, humanities, international studies, mathematics, military science, physical sciences, premedicine, religion/biblical studies, social sciences. *Creative arts/performance:* applied art and design, creative writing, music, theater/drama. *Special achievements/activities:* community service, leadership, religious involvement. *Special characteristics:* children of faculty/staff, ethnic background, international students, local/state students, relatives of clergy, religious affiliation, veterans.

LOANS *Programs:* Federal Direct (Subsidized and Unsubsidized Stafford, PLUS).

WORK-STUDY *Federal work-study:* Total amount: $815,122; jobs available.

APPLYING FOR FINANCIAL AID *Required financial aid forms:* FAFSA, CSS Financial Aid PROFILE, state aid form, noncustodial (divorced/separated) parent's statement.

CONTACT Ms. Andrea Byrd, Director of Financial Aid, Furman University, 3300 Poinsett Highway, Greenville, SC 29613, 864-294-2204. *Fax:* 864-294-3127. *E-mail:* andrea.byrd@furman.edu.
Website: http://www.furman.edu/.

GALEN COLLEGE OF NURSING

Cincinnati, OH

Tuition & fees: N/R | **Average undergraduate aid package: N/A**

ABOUT THE INSTITUTION Proprietary, coed. ***Awards:*** associate and bachelor's degrees. Federal methodology is used as a basis for awarding need-based institutional aid.

GIFT AID (NEED-BASED) *Scholarships, grants, and awards:* Federal Pell, FSEOG, state, private.

GIFT AID (NON-NEED-BASED) *Scholarships, grants, and awards by category:* *Academic interests/achievement:* general academic interests/achievements.

LOANS *Programs:* Federal Direct (Subsidized and Unsubsidized Stafford, PLUS), NEALP.

APPLYING FOR FINANCIAL AID *Required financial aid forms:* FAFSA, institution's own form. ***Financial aid deadline:*** Continuous.

CONTACT Darian Cappel, Financial Aid Manager, Galen College of Nursing, 100 E Business Way, Suite 200, Cincinnati, OH 45241, 513-4753600 or toll-free 877-223-7040. *E-mail:* dcappel@galencollege.edu.
Website: http://www.galencollege.edu/.

GALLAUDET UNIVERSITY

Washington, DC

Tuition & fees: $17,038 | **Average undergraduate aid package: $25,111**

ABOUT THE INSTITUTION Independent, coed. ***Awards:*** certificates, bachelor's, master's, and doctoral degrees (Undergraduate programs are open primarily to the students with hearing-impairments). 22 undergraduate majors. ***Total enrollment:*** 1,485. Undergraduates: 1,075. Freshmen: 183. Federal methodology is used as a basis for awarding need-based institutional aid.

UNDERGRADUATE EXPENSES for 2020–2021 *Application fee:* $50. ***Tuition:*** full-time $16,512; part-time $688 per credit hour. ***Required fees:*** full-time $526. Full-time tuition and fees vary according to course load. Part-time tuition and fees vary according to course load. ***College room only:*** $8000. Room and board charges vary according to board plan and housing facility.

FRESHMAN FINANCIAL AID (Fall 2018) 193 applied for aid; of those 77% were deemed to have need. 100% of freshmen with need received aid; of those 19% had need fully met. ***Average percent of need met:*** 79% (excluding resources awarded to replace EFC). ***Average financial aid package:*** $26,099 (excluding resources awarded to replace EFC). 5% of all full-time freshmen had no need and received non-need-based gift aid.

UNDERGRADUATE FINANCIAL AID (Fall 2018) 1,020 applied for aid; of those 99% were deemed to have need. 100% of undergraduates with need received aid; of those 25% had need fully met. ***Average percent of need met:*** 75% (excluding resources awarded to replace EFC). ***Average financial aid package:*** $25,111 (excluding resources awarded to replace EFC). 5% of all full-time undergraduates had no need and received non-need-based gift aid.

GIFT AID (NEED-BASED) *Total amount:* $19,556,492 (17% federal, 42% state, 40% institutional, 1% external sources). ***Receiving aid:*** Freshmen: 71% (143); all full-time undergraduates: 89% (945). ***Average award:*** Freshmen: $10,086; Undergraduates: $29,145. ***Scholarships, grants, and awards:*** Federal Pell, FSEOG, state, private, college/university gift aid from institutional funds.

GIFT AID (NON-NEED-BASED) *Total amount:* $2,437,288 (82% state, 17% institutional, 1% external sources). ***Receiving aid:*** Freshmen: 4% (8). Undergraduates: 6% (63). ***Average award:*** Freshmen: $6914. Undergraduates: $5143. ***Scholarships, grants, and awards by category:*** *Academic interests/achievement:* general academic interests/achievements. *Special achievements/activities:* leadership. *Special characteristics:* members of minority groups. ***Tuition waivers:*** Full or partial for employees or children of employees.

LOANS *Student loans:* $3,918,317 (46% need-based, 54% non-need-based). 100% of past graduating class borrowed through all loan programs. *Average indebtedness per student:* $20,038. ***Average need-based loan:*** Freshmen: $3798. Undergraduates: $3922. ***Parent loans:*** $587,632 (100% non-need-based). ***Programs:*** Federal Direct (Subsidized and Unsubsidized Stafford, PLUS), Perkins.

WORK-STUDY *Federal work-study:* Total amount: $210,377; jobs available.

APPLYING FOR FINANCIAL AID *Required financial aid form:* FAFSA. ***Notification date:*** Continuous beginning 2/1.

CONTACT Shondra Dickson, Director of Financial Aid, Gallaudet University, Chapel Hall, Room G-02, 800 Florida Avenue, NE, Washington, DC 20002, 202-651-5290 or toll-free 800-995-0550. *Fax:* 202-651-5740. *E-mail:* financial.aid@gallaudet.edu.
Website: http://www.gallaudet.edu/.

GANNON UNIVERSITY

Erie, PA

Tuition & fees: N/R | **Average undergraduate aid package: $27,213**

ABOUT THE INSTITUTION Independent Roman Catholic, coed. ***Awards:*** certificates, associate, bachelor's, master's, and doctoral degrees. 66 undergraduate majors. ***Total enrollment:*** 4,444. Undergraduates: 3,432. Freshmen: 734. Federal methodology is used as a basis for awarding need-based institutional aid.

FRESHMAN FINANCIAL AID (Fall 2019, est.) 661 applied for aid; of those 90% were deemed to have need. 99% of freshmen with need received aid; of those 27% had need fully met. ***Average percent of need met:*** 77% (excluding resources awarded to replace EFC). ***Average financial aid package:*** $27,715 (excluding resources awarded to replace EFC). 13% of all full-time freshmen had no need and received non-need-based gift aid.

UNDERGRADUATE FINANCIAL AID (Fall 2019, est.) 2,340 applied for aid; of those 90% were deemed to have need. 99% of undergraduates with need received aid; of those 23% had need fully met. ***Average percent of need met:*** 74% (excluding resources awarded to replace EFC). ***Average financial aid package:*** $27,213 (excluding resources awarded to replace EFC). 16% of all full-time undergraduates had no need and received non-need-based gift aid.

GIFT AID (NEED-BASED) *Total amount:* $45,768,404 (10% federal, 6% state, 80% institutional, 4% external sources). ***Receiving aid:*** Freshmen: 82% (587); all full-time undergraduates: 75% (2,084). ***Average award:*** Freshmen: $25,275; Undergraduates: $23,422. ***Scholarships, grants, and awards:*** Federal Pell, FSEOG, state, private, college/university gift aid from institutional funds, Federal Nursing.

GIFT AID (NON-NEED-BASED) *Total amount:* $11,426,180 (68% institutional, 32% external sources). ***Receiving aid:*** Freshmen: 14% (104). Undergraduates: 11% (300). ***Average award:*** Freshmen: $19,792. Undergraduates: $17,388. ***Scholarships, grants, and awards by category:*** *Academic interests/achievement:* biological sciences, business, education, engineering/technologies, English, foreign languages, general academic interests/achievements, humanities, international studies, mathematics, premedicine, religion/biblical studies, social sciences. *Creative arts/performance:* music, performing arts, theater/drama. *Special achievements/activities:* community service, leadership. *Special characteristics:* adult students, ethnic background, international students, members of minority groups, religious affiliation, veterans. ***ROTC:*** Army.

LOANS *Student loans:* $13,091,868 (94% need-based, 6% non-need-based). ***Average need-based loan:*** Freshmen: $3306. Undergraduates: $21,932. ***Parent loans:*** $5,945,811 (93% need-based, 7% non-need-based). ***Programs:*** Federal Direct (Subsidized and Unsubsidized Stafford, PLUS), Federal Nursing.

WORK-STUDY *Federal work-study:* Total amount: $744,598; jobs available. ***State or other work-study/employment:*** Total amount: $248,400 (100% non-need-based). Part-time jobs available.

ATHLETIC AWARDS Total amount: $4,850,328 (64% need-based, 36% non-need-based).

APPLYING FOR FINANCIAL AID ***Required financial aid form:*** FAFSA. ***Financial aid deadline (priority):*** 3/15. ***Notification date:*** Continuous beginning 11/1.

CONTACT Andrew Teets, Director of Financial Aid, Gannon University, 109 University Square, Erie, PA 16541, 814-871-7670 or toll-free 800-GANNONU. *Fax:* 814-871-5826. *E-mail:* teets001@gannon.edu.
Website: http://www.gannon.edu/.

GARDNER-WEBB UNIVERSITY

Boiling Springs, NC

ABOUT THE INSTITUTION Independent Baptist, coed. ***Awards:*** certificates, associate, bachelor's, master's, and doctoral degrees. 65 undergraduate majors. ***Total enrollment:*** 3,818. Undergraduates: 2,343. Freshmen: 444.

GIFT AID (NEED-BASED) ***Scholarships, grants, and awards:*** Federal Pell, FSEOG, state, private, college/university gift aid from institutional funds.

GIFT AID (NON-NEED-BASED) ***Scholarships, grants, and awards by category:*** *Academic interests/achievement:* biological sciences, business, communication, computer science, education, English, foreign languages, general academic interests/achievements, home economics, humanities, mathematics, physical sciences, premedicine, religion/biblical studies, social sciences. *Creative arts/performance:* applied art and design, music, theater/drama. *Special achievements/activities:* cheerleading/drum major, religious involvement. *Special characteristics:* children of faculty/staff, handicapped students, local/state students, members of minority groups, out-of-state students, previous college experience, relatives of clergy.

LOANS ***Programs:*** Federal Direct (Subsidized and Unsubsidized Stafford, PLUS), Perkins, state, alternative loans.

WORK-STUDY ***Federal work-study:*** Total amount: $553,308; 293 jobs averaging $1340. ***State or other work-study/employment:*** Total amount: $31,962 (50% need-based, 50% non-need-based). 23 part-time jobs averaging $1018.

APPLYING FOR FINANCIAL AID ***Required financial aid forms:*** FAFSA, state aid form.

CONTACT Anita Elliott, Director of Financial Planning, Gardner-Webb University, PO Box 955, Boiling Springs, NC 28017, 704-406-4243 or toll-free 800-253-6472. *Fax:* 704-406-4102.
Website: http://www.gardner-webb.edu/.

GEMINI SCHOOL OF VISUAL ARTS & COMMUNICATION

Cedar Park, TX

CONTACT Financial Aid Office, Gemini School of Visual Arts & Communication, 501 Prize Oaks Drive, Cedar Park, TX 78613.
Website: http://www.geminischool.com/.

GENEVA COLLEGE

Beaver Falls, PA

ABOUT THE INSTITUTION Independent Reformed Presbyterian Church of North America, coed. ***Awards:*** associate, bachelor's, and master's degrees (also offers non-traditional programs in Philadelphia and western Pennsylvania with significant enrollment not reflected in profile). 41 undergraduate majors. ***Total enrollment:*** 1,432. Undergraduates: 1,290. Freshmen: 314.

GIFT AID (NEED-BASED) ***Scholarships, grants, and awards:*** Federal Pell, FSEOG, state, private, college/university gift aid from institutional funds.

GIFT AID (NON-NEED-BASED) ***Scholarships, grants, and awards by category:*** *Academic interests/achievement:* general academic interests/achievements. *Creative arts/performance:* music. *Special achievements/activities:* leadership, memberships, religious involvement. *Special characteristics:* children of faculty/staff, religious affiliation.

LOANS ***Programs:*** Federal Direct (Subsidized and Unsubsidized Stafford, PLUS), Perkins.

CONTACT Mrs. Allyson Grubb, Director of Student Financial Services, Geneva College, 3200 College Avenue, Beaver Falls, PA 15010-3599, 724-847-6530 or toll-free 800-847-8255. *Fax:* 724-847-6776. *E-mail:* sfs@geneva.edu.
Website: http://www.geneva.edu/.

GEORGE FOX UNIVERSITY

Newberg, OR

Tuition & fees: $37,130	Average undergraduate aid package: $24,325

ABOUT THE INSTITUTION Independent Friends, coed. ***Awards:*** certificates, bachelor's, master's, and doctoral degrees. 46 undergraduate majors. ***Total enrollment:*** 3,899. Undergraduates: 2,569. Freshmen: 634. Federal methodology is used as a basis for awarding need-based institutional aid.

UNDERGRADUATE EXPENSES for 2019–2020 ***Application fee:*** $40. ***Comprehensive fee:*** $48,780 includes full-time tuition ($36,750), mandatory fees ($380), and room and board ($11,650). Full-time tuition and fees vary according to reciprocity agreements. Room and board charges vary according to board plan. Part-time tuition and fees vary according to course load.

FRESHMAN FINANCIAL AID (Fall 2019, est.) 558 applied for aid; of those 84% were deemed to have need. 100% of freshmen with need received aid; of those 45% had need fully met. ***Average percent of need met:*** 91% (excluding resources awarded to replace EFC). ***Average financial aid package:*** $27,128 (excluding resources awarded to replace EFC). 21% of all full-time freshmen had no need and received non-need-based gift aid.

UNDERGRADUATE FINANCIAL AID (Fall 2019, est.) 2,033 applied for aid; of those 87% were deemed to have need. 100% of undergraduates with need received aid; of those 42% had need fully met. ***Average percent of need met:*** 87% (excluding resources awarded to replace EFC). ***Average financial aid package:*** $24,325 (excluding resources awarded to replace EFC). 25% of all full-time undergraduates had no need and received non-need-based gift aid.

GIFT AID (NEED-BASED) ***Receiving aid:*** Freshmen: 77% (465); all full-time undergraduates: 70% (1,704). ***Average award:*** Freshmen: $24,121; Undergraduates: $20,962. ***Scholarships, grants, and awards:*** Federal Pell, FSEOG, state, private, college/university gift aid from institutional funds, TEACH Grants.

GIFT AID (NON-NEED-BASED) ***Receiving aid:*** Freshmen: 8% (49). Undergraduates: 6% (148). ***Average award:*** Freshmen: $15,385. Undergraduates: $15,013. ***Scholarships, grants, and awards by category:*** *Academic interests/achievement:* biological sciences, business, communication, computer science, education, engineering/technologies, English, foreign languages, general academic interests/achievements, health fields, home economics, humanities, international studies, mathematics, physical sciences, religion/biblical studies, social sciences. *Creative arts/performance:* applied art and design, cinema/film/broadcasting, debating, music, theater/drama. *Special achievements/activities:* leadership, religious involvement. *Special characteristics:* children and siblings of alumni, children of faculty/staff, ethnic background, international students, members of minority groups, out-of-state students, relatives of clergy, religious affiliation. ***Tuition waivers:*** Full or partial for employees or children of employees, senior citizens. ***ROTC:*** Air Force cooperative.

LOANS ***Student loans:*** 67% of past graduating class borrowed through all loan programs. *Average indebtedness per student:* $31,299. ***Average need-based loan:*** Freshmen: $3001. Undergraduates: $4022. ***Programs:*** Federal Direct (Subsidized and Unsubsidized Stafford, PLUS), alternative loans.

WORK-STUDY ***Federal work-study:*** 1,255 jobs averaging $2267. ***State or other work-study/employment:*** Part-time jobs available.

APPLYING FOR FINANCIAL AID ***Required financial aid forms:*** FAFSA, state aid form. ***Financial aid deadline:*** Continuous. ***Notification date:*** Continuous.

CONTACT Johanna Kaye, Director of Financial Aid, George Fox University, 414 North Meridian Street, Newberg, OR 97132-2697, 503-554-2235 or toll-free 800-765-4369. *Fax:* 503-554-3110. *E-mail:* kayej@georgefox.edu.
Website: http://www.georgefox.edu/.

GEORGE MASON UNIVERSITY

Fairfax, VA

Tuition & fees (VA res): $12,564 **Average undergraduate aid package: $14,111**

ABOUT THE INSTITUTION State-supported, coed. ***Awards:*** certificates, bachelor's, master's, and doctoral degrees. 65 undergraduate majors. ***Total enrollment:*** 37,863. Undergraduates: 26,662. Freshmen: 3,763. Federal methodology is used as a basis for awarding need-based institutional aid.

UNDERGRADUATE EXPENSES for 2019–2020 ***Application fee:*** $70. ***Tuition, state resident:*** full-time $9060; part-time $378 per credit hour. ***Tuition, nonresident:*** full-time $32,520; part-time $1355 per credit hour. ***Required fees:*** full-time $3504; $146 per credit hour. Full-time tuition and fees vary according to course load. Part-time tuition and fees vary according to course load. ***College room and board:*** $11,705. Room and board charges vary according to board plan and housing facility.

FRESHMAN FINANCIAL AID (Fall 2018) 3086 applied for aid; of those 73% were deemed to have need. 96% of freshmen with need received aid; of those 4% had need fully met. ***Average percent of need met:*** 61% (excluding resources awarded to replace EFC). ***Average financial aid package:*** $16,141 (excluding resources awarded to replace EFC). 16% of all full-time freshmen had no need and received non-need-based gift aid.

UNDERGRADUATE FINANCIAL AID (Fall 2018) 14,606 applied for aid; of those 82% were deemed to have need. 97% of undergraduates with need received aid; of those 2% had need fully met. ***Average percent of need met:*** 53% (excluding resources awarded to replace EFC). ***Average financial aid package:*** $14,111 (excluding resources awarded to replace EFC). 9% of all full-time undergraduates had no need and received non-need-based gift aid.

GIFT AID (NEED-BASED) ***Total amount:*** $77,107,997 (48% federal, 32% state, 20% institutional). ***Receiving aid:*** Freshmen: 52% (1,889); all full-time undergraduates: 49% (10,226). ***Average award:*** Freshmen: $7507; Undergraduates: $6932. ***Scholarships, grants, and awards:*** Federal Pell, FSEOG, state, private, college/university gift aid from institutional funds.

GIFT AID (NON-NEED-BASED) ***Total amount:*** $22,265,912 (4% state, 77% institutional, 19% external sources). ***Receiving aid:*** Freshmen: 24% (883). Undergraduates: 12% (2,558). ***Average award:*** Freshmen: $7565. Undergraduates: $5770. ***Scholarships, grants, and awards by category:*** *Academic interests/achievement:* 4,365 awards ($16,744,535 total): general academic interests/achievements. *Creative arts/performance:* general creative arts/performance. *Special characteristics:* general special characteristics. ***Tuition waivers:*** Full or partial for employees or children of employees, senior citizens. ***ROTC:*** Army, Air Force cooperative.

LOANS ***Student loans:*** $106,240,729 (77% need-based, 23% non-need-based). 58% of past graduating class borrowed through all loan programs. *Average indebtedness per student:* $33,362. ***Average need-based loan:*** Freshmen: $3341. Undergraduates: $4348. ***Parent loans:*** $31,677,756 (61% need-based, 39% non-need-based). ***Programs:*** Federal Direct (Subsidized and Unsubsidized Stafford, PLUS), Perkins, Federal Nursing.

WORK-STUDY ***Federal work-study:*** Total amount: $1,295,272; 654 jobs averaging $1910.

ATHLETIC AWARDS Total amount: $6,047,755 (100% non-need-based).

APPLYING FOR FINANCIAL AID ***Required financial aid form:*** FAFSA. ***Financial aid deadline (priority):*** 1/15. ***Notification date:*** 4/1. Students must reply by 5/1 or within 5 weeks of notification.

CONTACT Office of Student Financial Aid, George Mason University, 1111 Student Union Building I, Mail Stop 3B5, Fairfax, VA 22030-4444, 703-993-2353 or toll-free 888-627-6612. *Fax:* 703-993-2350. *E-mail:* finaid@gmu.edu.
Website: http://www.gmu.edu/.

GEORGETOWN COLLEGE

Georgetown, KY

Tuition & fees: $40,800 **Average undergraduate aid package: $36,964**

ABOUT THE INSTITUTION Independent Baptist Church, coed. ***Awards:*** bachelor's and master's degrees. 35 undergraduate majors. ***Total enrollment:*** 1,484. Undergraduates: 983. Freshmen: 314. Federal methodology is used as a basis for awarding need-based institutional aid.

UNDERGRADUATE EXPENSES for 2020–2021 ***Comprehensive fee:*** $51,470 includes full-time tuition ($39,810), mandatory fees ($990), and room and board ($10,670). ***College room only:*** $5145. Full-time tuition and fees vary according to course load and reciprocity agreements. Room and board charges vary according to board plan and housing facility. ***Part-time tuition:*** $1230 per credit hour. Part-time tuition and fees vary according to course load and reciprocity agreements.

FRESHMAN FINANCIAL AID (Fall 2019, est.) 303 applied for aid; of those 93% were deemed to have need. 100% of freshmen with need received aid; of those 33% had need fully met. ***Average percent of need met:*** 86% (excluding resources awarded to replace EFC). ***Average financial aid package:*** $37,826 (excluding resources awarded to replace EFC). 7% of all full-time freshmen had no need and received non-need-based gift aid.

UNDERGRADUATE FINANCIAL AID (Fall 2019, est.) 850 applied for aid; of those 94% were deemed to have need. 100% of undergraduates with need received aid; of those 33% had need fully met. ***Average percent of need met:*** 86% (excluding resources awarded to replace EFC). ***Average financial aid package:*** $36,964 (excluding resources awarded to replace EFC). 5% of all full-time undergraduates had no need and received non-need-based gift aid.

GIFT AID (NEED-BASED) ***Total amount:*** $21,266,208 (9% federal, 12% state, 78% institutional, 1% external sources). ***Receiving aid:*** Freshmen: 90% (282); all full-time undergraduates: 86% (800). ***Average award:*** Freshmen: $24,271; Undergraduates: $22,557. ***Scholarships, grants, and awards:*** Federal Pell, FSEOG, state, private, college/university gift aid from institutional funds.

GIFT AID (NON-NEED-BASED) ***Total amount:*** $2,225,854 (4% federal, 14% state, 78% institutional, 4% external sources). ***Receiving aid:*** Freshmen: 23% (71). Undergraduates: 19% (179). ***Average award:*** Freshmen: $21,810. Undergraduates: $18,431. ***Scholarships, grants, and awards by category:*** *Academic interests/achievement:* general academic interests/achievements, international studies. *Creative arts/performance:* general creative arts/performance. *Special achievements/activities:* general special achievements/activities. *Special characteristics:* general special characteristics. ***Tuition waivers:*** Full or partial for employees or children of employees. ***ROTC:*** Army cooperative, Air Force cooperative.

LOANS ***Student loans:*** $5,204,242 (61% need-based, 39% non-need-based). 73% of past graduating class borrowed through all loan programs. *Average indebtedness per student:* $34,766. ***Average need-based loan:*** Freshmen: $2003. Undergraduates: $2734. ***Parent loans:*** $2,219,984 (34% need-based, 66% non-need-based). ***Programs:*** Federal Direct (Subsidized and Unsubsidized Stafford, PLUS), college/university.

WORK-STUDY ***Federal work-study:*** Total amount: $884,257; jobs available.

ATHLETIC AWARDS Total amount: $6,949,220 (80% need-based, 20% non-need-based).

APPLYING FOR FINANCIAL AID ***Required financial aid form:*** FAFSA. ***Financial aid deadline:*** Continuous. ***Notification date:*** Continuous beginning 11/15. Students must reply by 8/17.

CONTACT Mr. Bob Fultz, Director of Student Financial Planning, Georgetown College, 400 East College Street, Georgetown, KY 40324-1696, 502-863-8029 or toll-free 800-788-9985. *E-mail:* financialaid@georgetowncollege.edu.
Website: http://www.georgetowncollege.edu/.

GEORGETOWN UNIVERSITY
Washington, DC

Tuition & fees: $55,794 | **Average undergraduate aid package: $50,261**

ABOUT THE INSTITUTION Independent Roman Catholic (Jesuit), coed. ***Awards:*** certificates, bachelor's, master's, and doctoral degrees. 48 undergraduate majors. ***Total enrollment:*** 19,204. Undergraduates: 7,459. Freshmen: 1,621. Both federal and institutional methodology are used as a basis for awarding need-based institutional aid.

UNDERGRADUATE EXPENSES for 2019–2020 *Application fee:* $75. ***Tuition:*** full-time $55,440; part-time $2310 per credit hour. ***Required fees:*** full-time $354. ***College room only:*** $11,404.

FRESHMAN FINANCIAL AID (Fall 2019, est.) 1022 applied for aid; of those 69% were deemed to have need. 100% of freshmen with need received aid; of those 100% had need fully met. ***Average percent of need met:*** 100% (excluding resources awarded to replace EFC). ***Average financial aid package:*** $49,624 (excluding resources awarded to replace EFC).

UNDERGRADUATE FINANCIAL AID (Fall 2019, est.) 3,294 applied for aid; of those 80% were deemed to have need. 100% of undergraduates with need received aid; of those 100% had need fully met. ***Average percent of need met:*** 100% (excluding resources awarded to replace EFC). ***Average financial aid package:*** $50,261 (excluding resources awarded to replace EFC).

GIFT AID (NEED-BASED) *Total amount:* $127,206,000 (6% federal, 91% institutional, 3% external sources). ***Receiving aid:*** Freshmen: 43% (669); all full-time undergraduates: 36% (2,514). ***Average award:*** Freshmen: $45,509; Undergraduates: $46,304. ***Scholarships, grants, and awards:*** Federal Pell, FSEOG, state, private, college/university gift aid from institutional funds.

GIFT AID (NON-NEED-BASED) *Total amount:* $2,200,000 (91% federal, 9% institutional). ***Receiving aid:*** Freshmen: 16% (250). Undergraduates: 11% (800). ***Scholarships, grants, and awards by category:*** *Special characteristics:* 118 awards ($4,364,580 total): children of faculty/staff. ***ROTC:*** Army, Naval cooperative, Air Force cooperative.

LOANS *Student loans:* $16,800,000 (42% need-based, 58% non-need-based). 36% of past graduating class borrowed through all loan programs. *Average indebtedness per student:* $26,759. ***Average need-based loan:*** Freshmen: $3056. Undergraduates: $4370. ***Parent loans:*** $10,000,000 (100% non-need-based). ***Programs:*** Federal Direct (Subsidized and Unsubsidized Stafford, PLUS), Perkins, Federal Nursing, college/university, alternative loans.

WORK-STUDY *Federal work-study:* Total amount: $7,400,000; 2,545 jobs averaging $2924.

ATHLETIC AWARDS Total amount: $9,800,000 (24% need-based, 76% non-need-based).

APPLYING FOR FINANCIAL AID *Required financial aid forms:* FAFSA, CSS Financial Aid PROFILE, federal income tax form(s). ***Financial aid deadline:*** 2/1. ***Notification date:*** 4/1. Students must reply by 5/1 or within 2 weeks of notification.

CONTACT Ms. Patricia A. McWade, Dean of Student Financial Services, Georgetown University, 37th and O Street, NW, Box 1252, Washington, DC 20057, 202-687-4547. *Fax:* 202-687-6542. *E-mail:* mcwadep@georgetown.edu.
Website: http://www.georgetown.edu/.

THE GEORGE WASHINGTON UNIVERSITY
Washington, DC

Tuition & fees: $56,935 | **Average undergraduate aid package: $47,368**

ABOUT THE INSTITUTION Independent, coed. ***Awards:*** certificates, associate, bachelor's, master's, and doctoral degrees. 81 undergraduate majors. ***Total enrollment:*** 27,814. Undergraduates: 12,484. Freshmen: 2,619. Both federal and institutional methodology are used as a basis for awarding need-based institutional aid.

UNDERGRADUATE EXPENSES for 2019–2020 *Application fee:* $80. ***Comprehensive fee:*** $71,235 includes full-time tuition ($56,845), mandatory fees ($90), and room and board ($14,300). Full-time tuition and fees vary according to student level. Room and board charges vary according to housing facility. ***Part-time tuition:*** $1625 per credit hour. ***Part-time fees:*** $3 per credit hour. Part-time tuition and fees vary according to course load. ***Payment plan:*** Guaranteed tuition.

FRESHMAN FINANCIAL AID (Fall 2018) 1994 applied for aid; of those 71% were deemed to have need. 98% of freshmen with need received aid; of those 44% had need fully met. ***Average percent of need met:*** 88% (excluding resources awarded to replace EFC). ***Average financial aid package:*** $49,366 (excluding resources awarded to replace EFC). 27% of all full-time freshmen had no need and received non-need-based gift aid.

UNDERGRADUATE FINANCIAL AID (Fall 2018) 6,476 applied for aid; of those 83% were deemed to have need. 98% of undergraduates with need received aid; of those 39% had need fully met. ***Average percent of need met:*** 84% (excluding resources awarded to replace EFC). ***Average financial aid package:*** $47,368 (excluding resources awarded to replace EFC). 28% of all full-time undergraduates had no need and received non-need-based gift aid.

GIFT AID (NEED-BASED) *Total amount:* $174,995,531 (6% federal, 94% institutional). ***Receiving aid:*** Freshmen: 47% (1,330); all full-time undergraduates: 43% (4,808). ***Average award:*** Freshmen: $35,061; Undergraduates: $32,089. ***Scholarships, grants, and awards:*** Federal Pell, FSEOG, state, college/university gift aid from institutional funds.

GIFT AID (NON-NEED-BASED) *Total amount:* $59,368,313 (100% institutional). ***Receiving aid:*** Freshmen: 33% (926). Undergraduates: 28% (3,184). ***Average award:*** Freshmen: $22,777. Undergraduates: $20,455. ***Scholarships, grants, and awards by category:*** *Academic interests/achievement:* general academic interests/achievements. *Creative arts/performance:* general creative arts/performance. ***Tuition waivers:*** Full or partial for employees or children of employees. ***ROTC:*** Army cooperative, Naval, Air Force cooperative.

LOANS *Student loans:* $50,270,252 (89% need-based, 11% non-need-based). 45% of past graduating class borrowed through all loan programs. *Average indebtedness per student:* $34,768. ***Average need-based loan:*** Freshmen: $5642. Undergraduates: $7098. ***Parent loans:*** $22,155,016 (30% need-based, 70% non-need-based). ***Programs:*** Federal Direct (Subsidized and Unsubsidized Stafford, PLUS), Perkins.

WORK-STUDY *Federal work-study:* Total amount: $8,882,099; jobs available.

ATHLETIC AWARDS Total amount: $11,156,826 (43% need-based, 57% non-need-based).

APPLYING FOR FINANCIAL AID *Required financial aid forms:* FAFSA, CSS Financial Aid PROFILE, noncustodial (divorced/separated) parent's statement. ***Financial aid deadline:*** 2/1 (priority: 2/1). ***Notification date:*** Continuous beginning 3/24. Students must reply by 5/1.

CONTACT Michelle Carmela Arcieri, Senior Associate Director of Student Financial Assistance, The George Washington University, 2121 I Street, NW, Rice Hall, Suite 301B, Washington, DC 21044, 202-994-5729. *Fax:* 202-994-0906. *E-mail:* finaid@gwu.edu.
Website: http://www.gwu.edu/.

GEORGIA COLLEGE & STATE UNIVERSITY
Milledgeville, GA

Tuition & fees (GA res): $5770 | **Average undergraduate aid package: $11,322**

ABOUT THE INSTITUTION State-supported, coed. ***Awards:*** certificates, bachelor's, master's, and doctoral degrees. 36 undergraduate majors. ***Total enrollment:*** 7,031. Undergraduates: 5,844. Freshmen: 1,481. Federal methodology is used as a basis for awarding need-based institutional aid.

UNDERGRADUATE EXPENSES for 2020–2021 *Application fee:* $40. ***Tuition, state resident:*** full-time $3754. ***Tuition, nonresident:*** full-time $13,344. ***Required fees:*** full-time $2016. Full-time tuition and fees vary according to course load and program. Part-time tuition and fees vary according to course load and program. Room and board charges vary according to board plan, housing facility, and location.

FRESHMAN FINANCIAL AID (Fall 2019, est.) 1305 applied for aid; of those 56% were deemed to have need. 99% of freshmen with need received aid; of those 23% had need fully met. ***Average percent of need met:*** 63% (excluding resources awarded to replace EFC). ***Average financial aid package:*** $11,603 (excluding resources awarded to replace EFC). 3% of all full-time freshmen had no need and received non-need-based gift aid.

UNDERGRADUATE FINANCIAL AID (Fall 2019, est.) 4,151 applied for aid; of those 62% were deemed to have need. 98% of undergraduates with need received aid; of those 21% had need fully met. ***Average percent of need met:*** 59% (excluding resources awarded to replace EFC). ***Average financial aid package:*** $11,322 (excluding resources awarded to replace EFC). 4% of all full-time undergraduates had no need and received non-need-based gift aid.

GIFT AID (NEED-BASED) ***Total amount:*** $4,933,269 (99% federal, 1% institutional). ***Receiving aid:*** Freshmen: 20% (292); all full-time undergraduates: 20% (1,069). ***Average award:*** Freshmen: $4673; Undergraduates: $4650. ***Scholarships, grants, and awards:*** Federal Pell, FSEOG, state, college/university gift aid from institutional funds.

GIFT AID (NON-NEED-BASED) ***Total amount:*** $29,134,135 (92% state, 5% institutional, 3% external sources). ***Receiving aid:*** Freshmen: 47% (692). Undergraduates: 41% (2,165). ***Average award:*** Freshmen: $2435. Undergraduates: $2064. ***Scholarships, grants, and awards by category:*** *Academic interests/achievement:* business, education, physical sciences, social sciences. *Creative arts/performance:* applied art and design, music. *Special achievements/activities:* general special achievements/activities. *Special characteristics:* adult students, children of faculty/staff, general special characteristics, local/state students, out-of-state students, public servants. ***Tuition waivers:*** Full or partial for employees or children of employees. ***ROTC:*** Army cooperative.

LOANS ***Student loans:*** $27,947,196 (28% need-based, 72% non-need-based). 53% of past graduating class borrowed through all loan programs. *Average indebtedness per student:* $33,124. ***Average need-based loan:*** Freshmen: $3847. Undergraduates: $4627. ***Parent loans:*** $4,825,288 (100% non-need-based). ***Programs:*** Federal Direct (Subsidized and Unsubsidized Stafford, PLUS).

WORK-STUDY ***Federal work-study:*** Total amount: $99,187; jobs available. ***State or other work-study/employment:*** Total amount: $166,029 (100% need-based). Part-time jobs available.

ATHLETIC AWARDS Total amount: $658,870 (100% non-need-based).

APPLYING FOR FINANCIAL AID ***Required financial aid form:*** FAFSA. ***Financial aid deadline:*** Continuous. ***Notification date:*** Continuous beginning 11/30.

CONTACT Ms. Shannon Simmons, Director of Financial Aid, Georgia College & State University, Campus Box 30, Milledgeville, GA 31061, 478-445-5149 or toll-free 800-342-0471. *Fax:* 478-445-0729. *E-mail:* shannon.simmons@gcsu.edu. *Website:* http://www.gcsu.edu/.

GEORGIA GWINNETT COLLEGE

Lawrenceville, GA

Tuition & fees (area res): $5752	Average undergraduate aid package: $12,331

ABOUT THE INSTITUTION State-supported, coed. ***Awards:*** associate and bachelor's degrees. 18 undergraduate majors. ***Total enrollment:*** 12,831. Undergraduates: 12,831. Freshmen: 2,800. Federal methodology is used as a basis for awarding need-based institutional aid.

UNDERGRADUATE EXPENSES for 2020–2021 ***Application fee:*** $20. ***Tuition, area resident:*** full-time $4018; part-time $134 per credit hour. ***Tuition, state resident:*** full-time $4018; part-time $134 per credit hour. ***Tuition, nonresident:*** full-time $15,000; part-time $500 per credit hour. ***Required fees:*** full-time $1734; $495 per term. Full-time tuition and fees vary according to course load. Part-time tuition and fees vary according to course load. Room and board charges vary according to board plan and housing facility.

FRESHMAN FINANCIAL AID (Fall 2019, est.) 2185 applied for aid; of those 85% were deemed to have need. 100% of freshmen with need received aid; of those 6% had need fully met. ***Average percent of need met:*** 50% (excluding resources awarded to replace EFC). ***Average financial aid package:*** $11,821 (excluding resources awarded to replace EFC). 1% of all full-time freshmen had no need and received non-need-based gift aid.

UNDERGRADUATE FINANCIAL AID (Fall 2019, est.) 7,067 applied for aid; of those 87% were deemed to have need. 100% of undergraduates with need received aid; of those 5% had need fully met. ***Average percent of need met:*** 50% (excluding resources awarded to replace EFC). ***Average financial aid package:*** $12,331 (excluding resources awarded to replace EFC). 1% of all full-time undergraduates had no need and received non-need-based gift aid.

GIFT AID (NEED-BASED) ***Total amount:*** $36,254,021 (99% federal, 1% external sources). ***Receiving aid:*** Freshmen: 63% (1,505); all full-time undergraduates: 59% (4,881). ***Average award:*** Freshmen: $5713; Undergraduates: $5898. ***Scholarships, grants, and awards:*** Federal Pell, FSEOG, state, private, college/university gift aid from institutional funds.

GIFT AID (NON-NEED-BASED) ***Total amount:*** $14,538,615 (100% state). ***Receiving aid:*** Freshmen: 27% (641). Undergraduates: 26% (2,168). ***Average award:*** Freshmen: $575. Undergraduates: $472. ***Scholarships, grants, and awards by category:*** *Academic interests/achievement:* general academic interests/achievements. *Special characteristics:* veterans. ***Tuition waivers:*** Full or partial for employees or children of employees, senior citizens. ***ROTC:*** Army.

LOANS ***Student loans:*** $27,122,166 (55% need-based, 45% non-need-based). 55% of past graduating class borrowed through all loan programs. *Average indebtedness per student:* $37,357. ***Average need-based loan:*** Freshmen: $3016. Undergraduates: $3562. ***Parent loans:*** $4,114,874 (100% non-need-based). ***Programs:*** Federal Direct (Subsidized and Unsubsidized Stafford, PLUS), state.

WORK-STUDY ***Federal work-study:*** Total amount: $374,908; jobs available. ***State or other work-study/employment:*** Total amount: $11,549 (73% need-based, 27% non-need-based).

ATHLETIC AWARDS Total amount: $716,476 (100% non-need-based).

APPLYING FOR FINANCIAL AID ***Required financial aid forms:*** FAFSA, institution's own form. ***Financial aid deadline:*** 7/6 (priority: 7/6).

CONTACT Financial Aid Office, Georgia Gwinnett College, 1000 University Center Lane, Lawrenceville, GA 30043, 678-407-5000 or toll-free 877-704-4422. *Website:* http://www.ggc.edu/.

GEORGIA INSTITUTE OF TECHNOLOGY

Atlanta, GA

Tuition & fees (area res): $12,682	Average undergraduate aid package: $14,292

ABOUT THE INSTITUTION State-supported, coed. ***Awards:*** bachelor's, master's, and doctoral degrees. 33 undergraduate majors. ***Total enrollment:*** 36,490. Undergraduates: 16,159. Freshmen: 3,076. Institutional methodology is used as a basis for awarding need-based institutional aid.

UNDERGRADUATE EXPENSES for 2020–2021 ***Application fee:*** $75. ***Tuition, area resident:*** full-time $10,258; part-time $3048 per credit hour. ***Tuition, state resident:*** full-time $10,258; part-time $3048 per credit hour. ***Tuition, nonresident:*** full-time $31,370; part-time $9308 per credit hour. ***Required fees:*** full-time $2424. Part-time tuition and fees vary according to course load. ***College room and board:*** $14,830; ***Room only:*** $9658. Room and board charges vary according to board plan, housing facility, and student level.

FRESHMAN FINANCIAL AID (Fall 2018) 2448 applied for aid; of those 50% were deemed to have need. 92% of freshmen with need received aid; of those 33% had need fully met. ***Average percent of need met:*** 65% (excluding resources awarded to replace EFC). ***Average financial aid package:*** $15,696 (excluding resources awarded to replace EFC). 31% of all full-time freshmen had no need and received non-need-based gift aid.

UNDERGRADUATE FINANCIAL AID (Fall 2018) 6,961 applied for aid; of those 64% were deemed to have need. 97% of undergraduates with need received aid; of those 26% had need fully met. ***Average percent of need met:*** 57% (excluding resources awarded to replace EFC). ***Average financial aid package:*** $14,292 (excluding resources awarded to replace EFC). 22% of all full-time undergraduates had no need and received non-need-based gift aid.

GIFT AID (NEED-BASED) ***Total amount:*** $49,543,274 (20% federal, 50% state, 30% institutional). ***Receiving aid:*** Freshmen: 34% (1,059); all full-time undergraduates: 28% (4,003). ***Average award:*** Freshmen: $14,533; Undergraduates: $12,474. ***Scholarships, grants, and awards:*** Federal Pell, FSEOG, state, private, college/university gift aid from institutional funds.

GIFT AID (NON-NEED-BASED) ***Total amount:*** $32,188,955 (85% state, 15% institutional). ***Receiving aid:*** Freshmen: 27% (831). Undergraduates: 21% (3,015). ***Average award:*** Freshmen: $11,867. Undergraduates: $9794. ***Scholarships, grants, and awards by category:*** *Academic interests/achievement:* architecture, biological sciences, computer science, engineering/technologies, general academic interests/achievements, international studies, physical sciences. *Special achievements/*

activities: cheerleading/drum major, general special achievements/activities, leadership. *Special characteristics:* children with a deceased or disabled parent, local/state students, members of minority groups, out-of-state students, veterans. ***Tuition waivers:*** Full or partial for employees or children of employees, senior citizens. ***ROTC:*** Army, Naval, Air Force.

LOANS ***Student loans:*** $2,032,324 (52% need-based, 48% non-need-based). 40% of past graduating class borrowed through all loan programs. *Average indebtedness per student:* $31,545. ***Average need-based loan:*** Freshmen: $7238. Undergraduates: $10,553. ***Parent loans:*** $18,509,904 (73% need-based, 27% non-need-based). ***Programs:*** Federal Direct (Subsidized and Unsubsidized Stafford, PLUS), Perkins, college/university.

WORK-STUDY ***Federal work-study:*** Total amount: $715,183; jobs available.

ATHLETIC AWARDS Total amount: $5,807,373 (45% need-based, 55% non-need-based).

APPLYING FOR FINANCIAL AID ***Required financial aid forms:*** FAFSA, institution's own form, CSS Financial Aid PROFILE. ***Financial aid deadline:*** 7/1 (priority: 1/31). ***Notification date:*** 4/15. Students must reply by 5/1.

CONTACT Ms. Marie Mons, Director of Student Financial Planning and Services, Georgia Institute of Technology, 225 North Avenue, NW, Atlanta, GA 30332-0460, 404-894-4160. *Fax:* 404-894-7412. *E-mail:* marie.mons@finaid.gatech.edu.
Website: http://www.gatech.edu/.

GEORGIAN COURT UNIVERSITY

Lakewood, NJ

Tuition & fees: $33,768	Average undergraduate aid package: $29,570

ABOUT THE INSTITUTION Independent Roman Catholic, coed. ***Awards:*** certificates, bachelor's, master's, and doctoral degrees. 33 undergraduate majors. ***Total enrollment:*** 2,411. Undergraduates: 1,793. Freshmen: 197. Federal methodology is used as a basis for awarding need-based institutional aid.

UNDERGRADUATE EXPENSES for 2020–2021 ***Application fee:*** $40. ***Comprehensive fee:*** $45,192 includes full-time tuition ($32,050), mandatory fees ($1718), and room and board ($11,424). Full-time tuition and fees vary according to location, program, and reciprocity agreements. ***Part-time tuition:*** $747 per credit hour. ***Part-time fees:*** $372 per term. Part-time tuition and fees vary according to location, program, and reciprocity agreements.

FRESHMAN FINANCIAL AID (Fall 2019, est.) 164 applied for aid; of those 90% were deemed to have need. 100% of freshmen with need received aid; of those 29% had need fully met. ***Average percent of need met:*** 78% (excluding resources awarded to replace EFC). ***Average financial aid package:*** $30,573 (excluding resources awarded to replace EFC). 20% of all full-time freshmen had no need and received non-need-based gift aid.

UNDERGRADUATE FINANCIAL AID (Fall 2019, est.) 1,252 applied for aid; of those 93% were deemed to have need. 100% of undergraduates with need received aid; of those 33% had need fully met. ***Average percent of need met:*** 77% (excluding resources awarded to replace EFC). ***Average financial aid package:*** $29,570 (excluding resources awarded to replace EFC). 17% of all full-time undergraduates had no need and received non-need-based gift aid.

GIFT AID (NEED-BASED) ***Total amount:*** $24,390,418 (14% federal, 18% state, 67% institutional, 1% external sources). ***Receiving aid:*** Freshmen: 78% (146); all full-time undergraduates: 82% (1,160). ***Average award:*** Freshmen: $21,715; Undergraduates: $20,606. ***Scholarships, grants, and awards:*** Federal Pell, FSEOG, state, private, college/university gift aid from institutional funds.

GIFT AID (NON-NEED-BASED) ***Total amount:*** $4,520,105 (1% federal, 5% state, 93% institutional, 1% external sources). ***Receiving aid:*** Freshmen: 9% (16). Undergraduates: 9% (128). ***Average award:*** Freshmen: $16,567. Undergraduates: $14,883. ***Scholarships, grants, and awards by category:*** *Academic interests/achievement:* biological sciences, business, communication, computer science, education, English, foreign languages, general academic interests/achievements, home economics, humanities, international studies, mathematics, physical sciences, premedicine, religion/biblical studies, social sciences. *Creative arts/performance:* applied art and design, art/fine arts, dance. *Special achievements/activities:* community service, general special achievements/activities, leadership, memberships, religious involvement. *Special characteristics:* adult students, children and siblings of alumni, children of faculty/staff, ethnic background, first-generation college students, local/state students, married students, members of minority groups, out-of-state students, previous college experience, religious affiliation, siblings of current students, veterans. ***Tuition waivers:*** Full or partial for employees or children of employees, senior citizens.

LOANS ***Student loans:*** $10,490,915 (75% need-based, 25% non-need-based). 83% of past graduating class borrowed through all loan programs. *Average indebtedness per student:* $38,183. ***Average need-based loan:*** Freshmen: $5147. Undergraduates: $6414. ***Parent loans:*** $1,794,147 (65% need-based, 35% non-need-based). ***Programs:*** Federal Direct (Subsidized and Unsubsidized Stafford, PLUS), state.

WORK-STUDY ***Federal work-study:*** Total amount: $156,160; jobs available. ***State or other work-study/employment:*** Total amount: $20,000 (10% need-based, 90% non-need-based). Part-time jobs available.

ATHLETIC AWARDS Total amount: $2,493,638 (57% need-based, 43% non-need-based).

APPLYING FOR FINANCIAL AID ***Required financial aid form:*** FAFSA. ***Financial aid deadline:*** 7/1 (priority: 1/15). ***Notification date:*** Continuous beginning 12/1.

CONTACT Ms. Cynthia McCarthy, Director of Financial Aid, Georgian Court University, 900 Lakewood Avenue, Lakewood, NJ 08701-2697, 732-987-2258 or toll-free 800-458-8422. *Fax:* 732-987-2023. *E-mail:* cmccarthy@georgian.edu.
Website: http://www.georgian.edu/.

GEORGIA SOUTHERN UNIVERSITY

Statesboro, GA

ABOUT THE INSTITUTION State-supported, coed. ***Awards:*** certificates, bachelor's, master's, and doctoral degrees. 63 undergraduate majors. ***Total enrollment:*** 3,339. Undergraduates: 22,715. Freshmen: 4,260.

GIFT AID (NEED-BASED) ***Scholarships, grants, and awards:*** Federal Pell, FSEOG, state, private, college/university gift aid from institutional funds, Hope Scholarships, Federal Work Study, TEACH Grants, Zell Miller Scholarships.

GIFT AID (NON-NEED-BASED) ***Scholarships, grants, and awards by category:*** *Academic interests/achievement:* biological sciences, business, communication, computer science, education, engineering/technologies, English, foreign languages, general academic interests/achievements, health fields, home economics, humanities, international studies, mathematics, military science, social sciences. *Creative arts/performance:* applied art and design, cinema/film/broadcasting, creative writing, general creative arts/performance, music, theater/drama. *Special achievements/activities:* cheerleading/drum major, community service, junior miss, leadership, memberships, religious involvement. *Special characteristics:* adult students, children and siblings of alumni, children of faculty/staff, children of public servants, first-generation college students, general special characteristics, handicapped students, married students, members of minority groups, religious affiliation, veterans.

LOANS ***Programs:*** Federal Direct (Subsidized and Unsubsidized Stafford, PLUS), Perkins, state, Student Access Loans (SAL) and external alternative loans.

CONTACT Mrs. Tracey Mingo, Director of Financial Aid, Georgia Southern University, PO Box 8065, Statesboro, GA 30460-8065, 912-478-5413. *Fax:* 912-478-0573. *E-mail:* tmingo@georgiasouthern.edu.
Website: http://www.georgiasouthern.edu/.

GEORGIA SOUTHERN UNIVERSITY–ARMSTRONG CAMPUS

Savannah, GA

ABOUT THE INSTITUTION State-supported, coed. ***Awards:*** certificates, associate, bachelor's, master's, and doctoral degrees. 42 undergraduate majors.

GIFT AID (NEED-BASED) ***Scholarships, grants, and awards:*** Federal Pell, FSEOG, state, private, college/university gift aid from institutional funds, Hope Scholarship, Federal Work Study, TEACH Grant, and Zell Miller Scholarships.

GIFT AID (NON-NEED-BASED) ***Scholarships, grants, and awards by category:*** *Academic interests/achievement:* biological sciences, computer science, education, engineering/technologies, English, foreign languages, general academic interests/achievements, home economics, humanities, international studies, mathematics, military science, physical sciences. *Creative arts/performance:* applied art and design, general creative arts/performance, music. *Special achievements/activities:* community service. *Special characteristics:* ethnic background, international students, religious affiliation.

LOANS ***Programs:*** Federal Direct (Subsidized and Unsubsidized Stafford, PLUS), Perkins, state, Student Access Loans (SAL) and External Alternative Loans.

CONTACT Financial Aid Office, Georgia Southern University–Armstrong Campus, 11935 Abercorn Street, Savannah, GA 31419-1997, 912-344-2576 or toll-free 800-633-2349.
Website: http://www.georgiasouthern.edu/.

GEORGIA SOUTHWESTERN STATE UNIVERSITY

Americus, GA

CONTACT Angela Bryant, Director of Financial Aid, Georgia Southwestern State University, 800 Georgia Southwestern State University Drive, Americus, GA 31709-4693, 229-928-1378 or toll-free 800-338-0082. *Fax:* 229-931-2061. *E-mail:* finaid@gsw.edu.
Website: http://www.gsw.edu/.

GEORGIA STATE UNIVERSITY

Atlanta, GA

Tuition & fees (area res): $8948	Average undergraduate aid package: $10,976

ABOUT THE INSTITUTION State-supported, coed. ***Awards:*** certificates, associate, bachelor's, master's, and doctoral degrees. 54 undergraduate majors. ***Total enrollment:*** 35,059. Undergraduates: 27,969. Freshmen: 5,018. Both federal and institutional methodology are used as a basis for awarding need-based institutional aid.

UNDERGRADUATE EXPENSES for 2020–2021 ***Application fee:*** $60. ***Tuition, area resident:*** full-time $8948; part-time $298 per credit hour. ***Tuition, state resident:*** full-time $8948; part-time $298 per credit hour. ***Tuition, nonresident:*** full-time $27,986; part-time $933 per credit hour. ***Required fees:*** $1064 per term. Part-time tuition and fees vary according to course load. ***College room and board:*** $14,958; ***Room only:*** $11,090. Room and board charges vary according to board plan and housing facility.

FRESHMAN FINANCIAL AID (Fall 2018) 4678 applied for aid; of those 84% were deemed to have need. 97% of freshmen with need received aid; of those 8% had need fully met. ***Average percent of need met:*** 59% (excluding resources awarded to replace EFC). ***Average financial aid package:*** $12,784 (excluding resources awarded to replace EFC).

UNDERGRADUATE FINANCIAL AID (Fall 2018) 24,784 applied for aid; of those 85% were deemed to have need. 98% of undergraduates with need received aid; of those 5% had need fully met. ***Average percent of need met:*** 55% (excluding resources awarded to replace EFC). ***Average financial aid package:*** $10,976 (excluding resources awarded to replace EFC).

GIFT AID (NEED-BASED) ***Receiving aid:*** Freshmen: 54% (2,619); all full-time undergraduates: 57% (15,719). ***Average award:*** Freshmen: $5535; Undergraduates: $5607. ***Scholarships, grants, and awards:*** Federal Pell, FSEOG, state, private, college/university gift aid from institutional funds, United Negro College Fund.

GIFT AID (NON-NEED-BASED) ***Receiving aid:*** Freshmen: 70% (3,431). Undergraduates: 70% (19,519). ***Tuition waivers:*** Full or partial for employees or children of employees, senior citizens. ***ROTC:*** Army, Naval cooperative, Air Force cooperative.

LOANS ***Student loans:*** 67% of past graduating class borrowed through all loan programs. *Average indebtedness per student:* $28,864. ***Programs:*** Federal Direct (Subsidized and Unsubsidized Stafford, PLUS), Perkins, Federal Nursing, state.

WORK-STUDY Federal work-study jobs available. ***State or other work-study/employment:*** Part-time jobs available.

APPLYING FOR FINANCIAL AID ***Required financial aid form:*** FAFSA. ***Notification date:*** Continuous.

CONTACT Financial Aid Office, Georgia State University, 33 Gilmer Street, Atlanta, GA 30302-3083, 404-651-2000.
Website: http://www.gsu.edu/.

GETTYSBURG COLLEGE

Gettysburg, PA

Tuition & fees: $56,390	Average undergraduate aid package: $44,448

ABOUT THE INSTITUTION Independent Evangelical Lutheran Church in America, coed. ***Awards:*** bachelor's degrees. 82 undergraduate majors. ***Total enrollment:*** 2,433. Undergraduates: 2,434. Freshmen: 748. Both federal and institutional methodology are used as a basis for awarding need-based institutional aid.

UNDERGRADUATE EXPENSES for 2019–2020 ***Application fee:*** $60. ***Comprehensive fee:*** $69,850 includes full-time tuition ($56,390) and room and board ($13,460). ***College room only:*** $7220. Room and board charges vary according to board plan and housing facility.

FRESHMAN FINANCIAL AID (Fall 2019, est.) 542 applied for aid; of those 84% were deemed to have need. 100% of freshmen with need received aid; of those 90% had need fully met. ***Average percent of need met:*** 90% (excluding resources awarded to replace EFC). ***Average financial aid package:*** $46,063 (excluding resources awarded to replace EFC). 21% of all full-time freshmen had no need and received non-need-based gift aid.

UNDERGRADUATE FINANCIAL AID (Fall 2019, est.) 1,849 applied for aid; of those 87% were deemed to have need. 99% of undergraduates with need received aid; of those 90% had need fully met. ***Average percent of need met:*** 90% (excluding resources awarded to replace EFC). ***Average financial aid package:*** $44,448 (excluding resources awarded to replace EFC). 21% of all full-time undergraduates had no need and received non-need-based gift aid.

GIFT AID (NEED-BASED) ***Total amount:*** $74,712,100 (3% federal, 1% state, 94% institutional, 2% external sources). ***Receiving aid:*** Freshmen: 65% (443); all full-time undergraduates: 60% (1,588). ***Average award:*** Freshmen: $43,235; Undergraduates: $40,404. ***Scholarships, grants, and awards:*** Federal Pell, FSEOG, state, private, college/university gift aid from institutional funds.

GIFT AID (NON-NEED-BASED) ***Total amount:*** $6,052,420 (25% federal, 66% institutional, 9% external sources). ***Receiving aid:*** Freshmen: 42% (283). Undergraduates: 35% (932). ***Average award:*** Freshmen: $18,140. Undergraduates: $16,637. ***Scholarships, grants, and awards by category:*** *Academic interests/achievement:* 1,502 awards ($26,131,875 total): general academic interests/achievements. *Creative arts/performance:* 23 awards ($226,000 total): music. ***Tuition waivers:*** Full or partial for employees or children of employees. ***ROTC:*** Army cooperative.

LOANS ***Student loans:*** $15,267,283 (63% need-based, 37% non-need-based). 60% of past graduating class borrowed through all loan programs. *Average indebtedness per student:* $34,630. ***Average need-based loan:*** Freshmen: $4029. Undergraduates: $4809. ***Parent loans:*** $6,089,411 (100% non-need-based). ***Programs:*** Federal Direct (Subsidized and Unsubsidized Stafford, PLUS), college/university.

WORK-STUDY ***Federal work-study:*** Total amount: $359,016; 381 jobs averaging $690. ***State or other work-study/employment:*** Total amount: $944,474 (100% non-need-based). 1,145 part-time jobs averaging $825.

APPLYING FOR FINANCIAL AID ***Required financial aid forms:*** FAFSA, CSS Financial Aid PROFILE. ***Financial aid deadline (priority):*** 1/15. ***Notification date:*** 3/18. Students must reply by 5/1.

CONTACT Kathryn Adams, Senior Associate Director of Financial Aid, Gettysburg College, 300 North Washington Street, Gettysburg, PA 17325, 717-337-6611 or toll-free 800-431-0803. *Fax:* 717-337-8555. *E-mail:* finaid@gettysburg.edu.
Website: http://www.gettysburg.edu/.

GLENVILLE STATE COLLEGE

Glenville, WV

Tuition & fees: N/R	Average undergraduate aid package: $14,529

ABOUT THE INSTITUTION State-supported, coed. ***Awards:*** associate and bachelor's degrees. 32 undergraduate majors. ***Total enrollment:*** 1,577. Undergraduates: 1,577. Freshmen: 352. Federal methodology is used as a basis for awarding need-based institutional aid.

FRESHMAN FINANCIAL AID (Fall 2018) 288 applied for aid; of those 96% were deemed to have need. 100% of freshmen with need received aid; of those 2% had need fully met. ***Average percent of need met:*** 60% (excluding resources awarded to replace EFC). ***Average financial aid package:*** $14,219 (excluding resources awarded to replace EFC).

UNDERGRADUATE FINANCIAL AID (Fall 2018) 979 applied for aid; of those 96% were deemed to have need. 100% of undergraduates with need received aid; of those 4% had need fully met. ***Average percent of need met:*** 63% (excluding resources awarded to replace EFC). ***Average financial aid package:*** $14,529 (excluding resources awarded to replace EFC). 1% of all full-time undergraduates had no need and received non-need-based gift aid.

GIFT AID (NEED-BASED) ***Total amount:*** $4,586,698 (76% federal, 24% state). ***Receiving aid:*** Freshmen: 68% (198); all full-time undergraduates: 63% (642). ***Average award:*** Freshmen: $5423; Undergraduates: $5464. ***Scholarships, grants, and awards:*** Federal Pell, FSEOG, state, private, college/university gift aid from institutional funds.

GIFT AID (NON-NEED-BASED) ***Total amount:*** $1,393,925 (48% state, 29% institutional, 23% external sources). ***Receiving aid:*** Freshmen: 40% (116). Undergraduates: 32% (329). ***Average award:*** Undergraduates: $958. ***Scholarships, grants, and awards by category:*** *Academic interests/achievement:* biological sciences, business, education, English, general academic interests/achievements, international studies, mathematics, social sciences. *Creative arts/performance:* applied art and design, journalism/publications, music. *Special achievements/activities:* general special achievements/activities. *Special characteristics:* children of faculty/staff, first-generation college students, out-of-state students, veterans.

LOANS ***Student loans:*** $5,177,808 (43% need-based, 57% non-need-based). 64% of past graduating class borrowed through all loan programs. *Average indebtedness per student:* $7917. ***Average need-based loan:*** Freshmen: $3322. Undergraduates: $3999. ***Parent loans:*** $773,623 (100% non-need-based). ***Programs:*** Federal Direct (Subsidized and Unsubsidized Stafford, PLUS), Perkins, state.

WORK-STUDY ***Federal work-study:*** Total amount: $140,398; jobs available. ***State or other work-study/employment:*** Total amount: $493,291 (100% non-need-based). Part-time jobs available.

ATHLETIC AWARDS Total amount: $1,398,642 (100% non-need-based).

APPLYING FOR FINANCIAL AID ***Required financial aid form:*** FAFSA. ***Financial aid deadline:*** 4/15. ***Notification date:*** Continuous.

CONTACT Ms. Stephany Harper, Financial Aid Manager, Glenville State College, 200 High Street, Glenville, WV 26351-1200, 304-462-6171 or toll-free 800-924-2010. *Fax:* 304-462-4407. *E-mail:* stephany.harper@glenville.edu.
Website: http://www.glenville.edu/.

GNOMON SCHOOL OF VISUAL EFFECTS

Hollywood, CA

CONTACT Financial Aid Office, Gnomon School of Visual Effects, 1015 N. Cahuenga Boulevard, Suite 54301, Hollywood, CA 90038, 323-466-6663.
Website: http://www.gnomon.edu/.

GODDARD COLLEGE

Plainfield, VT

Tuition & fees: N/R	Average undergraduate aid package: $9733

ABOUT THE INSTITUTION Independent, coed. ***Awards:*** bachelor's and master's degrees. 53 undergraduate majors. Federal methodology is used as a basis for awarding need-based institutional aid.

FRESHMAN FINANCIAL AID (Fall 2019, est.) 3 applied for aid; of those 100% were deemed to have need. 100% of freshmen with need received aid. ***Average percent of need met:*** 27% (excluding resources awarded to replace EFC). ***Average financial aid package:*** $9543 (excluding resources awarded to replace EFC). 40% of all full-time freshmen had no need and received non-need-based gift aid.

UNDERGRADUATE FINANCIAL AID (Fall 2019, est.) 107 applied for aid; of those 96% were deemed to have need. 97% of undergraduates with need received aid; of those 3% had need fully met. ***Average percent of need met:*** 34% (excluding resources awarded to replace EFC). ***Average financial aid package:*** $9733 (excluding resources awarded to replace EFC). 12% of all full-time undergraduates had no need and received non-need-based gift aid.

GIFT AID (NEED-BASED) ***Total amount:*** $694,189 (67% federal, 21% state, 11% institutional, 1% external sources). ***Receiving aid:*** Freshmen: 60% (3); all full-time undergraduates: 61% (93). ***Average award:*** Freshmen: $8376; Undergraduates: $7137. ***Scholarships, grants, and awards:*** Federal Pell, FSEOG, state, private, college/university gift aid from institutional funds.

GIFT AID (NON-NEED-BASED) ***Total amount:*** $219,162 (58% state, 5% institutional, 37% external sources). ***Receiving aid:*** Undergraduates: 1% (2). ***Average award:*** Freshmen: $750. Undergraduates: $586. ***Scholarships, grants, and awards by category:*** *Academic interests/achievement:* education. *Creative arts/performance:* art/fine arts, creative writing.

LOANS ***Student loans:*** $862,036 (96% need-based, 4% non-need-based). 64% of past graduating class borrowed through all loan programs. *Average indebtedness per student:* $29,135. ***Average need-based loan:*** Freshmen: $1750. Undergraduates: $3821. ***Parent loans:*** $7750 (100% non-need-based). ***Programs:*** Federal Direct (Subsidized and Unsubsidized Stafford, PLUS).

APPLYING FOR FINANCIAL AID ***Required financial aid form:*** FAFSA. ***Financial aid deadline:*** Continuous. ***Notification date:*** Continuous beginning 5/10. Students must reply within 8 weeks of notification.

CONTACT Shannon Trainor, Associate Director of Financial Aid, Goddard College, 123 Pitkin Road, Plainfield, VT 05667, 802-454-8311 Ext. 303 or toll-free 800-906-8312. *Fax:* 802-322-1000. *E-mail:* shannon.trainor@goddard.edu.
Website: http://www.goddard.edu/.

GOD'S BIBLE SCHOOL AND COLLEGE

Cincinnati, OH

CONTACT Mrs. Lori Waggoner, Financial Aid Director, God's Bible School and College, 1810 Young Street, Cincinnati, OH 45202-6899, 513-721-7944 Ext. 205 or toll-free 800-486-4637. *Fax:* 513-721-1357. *E-mail:* lwaggoner@gbs.edu.
Website: http://www.gbs.edu/.

GOLDEN GATE UNIVERSITY

San Francisco, CA

CONTACT Kathleen Kelly, Interim Director of Financial Services, Golden Gate University, 536 Mission Street, San Francisco, CA 94105-2968, 415-442-7297 or toll-free 800-448-3381. *Fax:* 415-442-7819. *E-mail:* kkelly@ggu.edu.
Website: http://www.ggu.edu/.

GOLDEY-BEACOM COLLEGE

Wilmington, DE

CONTACT Jane H. Lysle, Dean of Enrollment Management, Goldey-Beacom College, 4701 Limestone Road, Wilmington, DE 19808-1999, 302-225-6274 or toll-free 800-833-4877. *Fax:* 302-998-8631. *E-mail:* lyslej@gbc.edu.
Website: http://www.gbc.edu/.

GOLDFARB SCHOOL OF NURSING AT BARNES-JEWISH COLLEGE

St. Louis, MO

ABOUT THE INSTITUTION Independent, coed, primarily women. ***Awards:*** certificates, bachelor's, master's, and doctoral degrees. 1 undergraduate major.

GIFT AID (NEED-BASED) ***Scholarships, grants, and awards:*** Federal Pell, FSEOG, state, private.

GIFT AID (NON-NEED-BASED) ***Scholarships, grants, and awards by category:*** *Academic interests/achievement:* general academic interests/achievements.

LOANS ***Programs:*** Federal Direct (Subsidized and Unsubsidized Stafford, PLUS).

WORK-STUDY ***Federal work-study:*** Total amount: $31,557; 19 jobs averaging $31,557.

APPLYING FOR FINANCIAL AID ***Required financial aid forms:*** FAFSA, institution's own form.

CONTACT Ms. Stacy Bogier, Director, Enrollment Management, Goldfarb School of Nursing at Barnes-Jewish College, 4483 Duncan, St. Louis, MO 63110-1091, 314-454-7770 or toll-free 800-832-9009. *Fax:* 314-362-9250. *E-mail:* stacy.bogier@bjc.org. *Website:* http://www.barnesjewishcollege.edu/.

GONZAGA UNIVERSITY

Spokane, WA

Tuition & fees: $46,920 | **Average undergraduate aid package: $30,766**

ABOUT THE INSTITUTION Independent Roman Catholic, coed. ***Awards:*** bachelor's, master's, and doctoral degrees. 43 undergraduate majors. ***Total enrollment:*** 7,548. Undergraduates: 5,238. Freshmen: 1,248. Federal methodology is used as a basis for awarding need-based institutional aid.

UNDERGRADUATE EXPENSES for 2020–2021 ***Application fee:*** $50. ***Comprehensive fee:*** $59,871 includes full-time tuition ($46,060), mandatory fees ($860), and room and board ($12,951). ***College room only:*** $6670. Full-time tuition and fees vary according to course load, location, program, and reciprocity agreements. Room and board charges vary according to board plan, housing facility, and location. ***Part-time tuition:*** $1255 per credit. ***Part-time fees:*** $165 per term. Part-time tuition and fees vary according to course load, location, program, and reciprocity agreements.

FRESHMAN FINANCIAL AID (Fall 2018) 1022 applied for aid; of those 73% were deemed to have need. 100% of freshmen with need received aid; of those 21% had need fully met. ***Average percent of need met:*** 78% (excluding resources awarded to replace EFC). ***Average financial aid package:*** $30,533 (excluding resources awarded to replace EFC). 37% of all full-time freshmen had no need and received non-need-based gift aid.

UNDERGRADUATE FINANCIAL AID (Fall 2018) 3,465 applied for aid; of those 79% were deemed to have need. 100% of undergraduates with need received aid; of those 23% had need fully met. ***Average percent of need met:*** 78% (excluding resources awarded to replace EFC). ***Average financial aid package:*** $30,766 (excluding resources awarded to replace EFC). 54% of all full-time undergraduates had no need and received non-need-based gift aid.

GIFT AID (NEED-BASED) ***Total amount:*** $67,911,993 (6% federal, 4% state, 86% institutional, 4% external sources). ***Receiving aid:*** Freshmen: 58% (697); all full-time undergraduates: 48% (2,522). ***Average award:*** Freshmen: $8432; Undergraduates: $7435. ***Scholarships, grants, and awards:*** Federal Pell, FSEOG, state, private, college/university gift aid from institutional funds.

GIFT AID (NON-NEED-BASED) ***Total amount:*** $40,552,304 (96% institutional, 4% external sources). ***Receiving aid:*** Freshmen: 61% (735). Undergraduates: 51% (2,665). ***Average award:*** Freshmen: $16,782. Undergraduates: $16,064. ***Scholarships, grants, and awards by category:*** *Academic interests/achievement:* 283 awards ($1,049,944 total): business, engineering/technologies, military science. *Creative arts/performance:* 104 awards ($189,825 total): debating, music, performing arts. *Special achievements/activities:* 206 awards ($672,000 total): community service, general special achievements/activities, leadership, memberships. *Special characteristics:* 567 awards ($6,597,016 total): children and siblings of alumni, children of faculty/staff, international students, members of minority groups, siblings of current students. ***Tuition waivers:*** Full or partial for employees or children of employees. ***ROTC:*** Army.

LOANS ***Student loans:*** $19,931,702 (85% need-based, 15% non-need-based). 54% of past graduating class borrowed through all loan programs. *Average indebtedness per student:* $29,685. ***Average need-based loan:*** Freshmen: $3492. Undergraduates: $4744. ***Parent loans:*** $11,134,730 (86% need-based, 14% non-need-based). ***Programs:*** Federal Direct (Subsidized and Unsubsidized Stafford, PLUS), Federal Nursing, college/university.

WORK-STUDY ***Federal work-study:*** Total amount: $1,267,682; 452 jobs averaging $2012. ***State or other work-study/employment:*** Total amount: $617,638 (100% need-based). 140 part-time jobs averaging $2328.

ATHLETIC AWARDS Total amount: $4,832,309 (31% need-based, 69% non-need-based).

APPLYING FOR FINANCIAL AID ***Required financial aid form:*** FAFSA. ***Financial aid deadline:*** Continuous. ***Notification date:*** Continuous beginning 3/1.

CONTACT James White, Dean of Student Financial Services, Gonzaga University, 502 East Boone Avenue, Spokane, WA 99258-0072, 509-313-6568 or toll-free 800-322-2584 Ext.6572. *Fax:* 509-313-5816. *E-mail:* whitej@gonzaga.edu. *Website:* http://www.gonzaga.edu/.

GORDON COLLEGE

Wenham, MA

Tuition & fees: $39,230 | **Average undergraduate aid package: $27,240**

ABOUT THE INSTITUTION Independent nondenominational, coed. ***Awards:*** bachelor's and master's degrees. 27 undergraduate majors. ***Total enrollment:*** 1,857. Undergraduates: 1,507. Freshmen: 358. Federal methodology is used as a basis for awarding need-based institutional aid.

UNDERGRADUATE EXPENSES for 2020–2021 ***Application fee:*** $50. ***Comprehensive fee:*** $50,650 includes full-time tuition ($37,560), mandatory fees ($1670), and room and board ($11,420). ***College room only:*** $7210. Full-time tuition and fees vary according to course load and program. Room and board charges vary according to board plan and housing facility. ***Part-time tuition:*** $939 per credit hour. Part-time tuition and fees vary according to course load and program.

FRESHMAN FINANCIAL AID (Fall 2019, est.) 297 applied for aid; of those 84% were deemed to have need. 100% of freshmen with need received aid; of those 22% had need fully met. ***Average percent of need met:*** 77% (excluding resources awarded to replace EFC). ***Average financial aid package:*** $28,874 (excluding resources awarded to replace EFC). 29% of all full-time freshmen had no need and received non-need-based gift aid.

UNDERGRADUATE FINANCIAL AID (Fall 2019, est.) 1,147 applied for aid; of those 85% were deemed to have need. 100% of undergraduates with need received aid; of those 19% had need fully met. ***Average percent of need met:*** 73% (excluding resources awarded to replace EFC). ***Average financial aid package:*** $27,240 (excluding resources awarded to replace EFC). 31% of all full-time undergraduates had no need and received non-need-based gift aid.

GIFT AID (NEED-BASED) ***Total amount:*** $22,768,487 (7% federal, 1% state, 83% institutional, 9% external sources). ***Receiving aid:*** Freshmen: 70% (249); all full-time undergraduates: 67% (977). ***Average award:*** Freshmen: $25,568; Undergraduates: $23,073. ***Scholarships, grants, and awards:*** Federal Pell, FSEOG, state, private, college/university gift aid from institutional funds.

GIFT AID (NON-NEED-BASED) ***Total amount:*** $10,323,159 (89% institutional, 11% external sources). ***Receiving aid:*** Freshmen: 13% (46). Undergraduates: 10% (151). ***Average award:*** Freshmen: $19,228. Undergraduates: $17,771. ***Scholarships, grants, and awards by category:*** *Academic interests/achievement:* 1,366 awards ($16,441,625 total): general academic interests/achievements. *Creative arts/performance:* 130 awards ($397,586 total): applied art and design, music, theater/drama. *Special achievements/activities:* 165 awards ($2,415,379 total): leadership. *Special characteristics:* 496 awards ($3,405,064 total): children and siblings of alumni, children of faculty/staff, international students, relatives of clergy, veterans. ***Tuition waivers:*** Full or partial for employees or children of employees. ***ROTC:*** Army cooperative, Air Force cooperative.

LOANS ***Student loans:*** $9,680,706 (66% need-based, 34% non-need-based). 66% of past graduating class borrowed through all loan programs. *Average indebtedness per student:* $35,210. ***Average need-based loan:*** Freshmen: $3106. Undergraduates: $4149. ***Parent loans:*** $3,104,304 (46% need-based, 54% non-need-based). ***Programs:*** Federal Direct (Subsidized and Unsubsidized Stafford, PLUS), Perkins, state.

WORK-STUDY ***Federal work-study:*** Total amount: $250,000; 592 jobs averaging $422.

APPLYING FOR FINANCIAL AID ***Required financial aid form:*** FAFSA. ***Financial aid deadline (priority):*** 3/1. ***Notification date:*** Continuous beginning 1/15. Students must reply by 5/1 or within 2 weeks of notification.

CONTACT Daniel O'Connell, Senior Director of Student Financial Services, Gordon College, 255 Grapevine Road, Wenham, MA 01984-1899, 978-867-4246 or toll-free 866-464-6736. *Fax:* 978-867-4657. *E-mail:* daniel.oconnell@gordon.edu. *Website:* http://www.gordon.edu/.

GOSHEN COLLEGE

Goshen, IN

Tuition & fees: $35,230 | **Average undergraduate aid package: $29,993**

ABOUT THE INSTITUTION Independent Mennonite, coed. ***Awards:*** bachelor's, master's, and doctoral degrees. 55 undergraduate majors. ***Total enrollment:*** 907. Undergraduates: 826. Freshmen: 160. Federal methodology is used as a basis for awarding need-based institutional aid.

UNDERGRADUATE EXPENSES for 2020–2021 ***Comprehensive fee:*** $46,100 includes full-time tuition ($35,230) and room and board ($10,870). ***College room only:*** $5870. Room and board charges vary according to board plan and housing facility. ***Part-time tuition:*** $1425 per credit hour.

FRESHMAN FINANCIAL AID (Fall 2019, est.) 147 applied for aid; of those 95% were deemed to have need. 100% of freshmen with need received aid; of those 16% had need fully met. ***Average percent of need met:*** 83% (excluding resources awarded to replace EFC). ***Average financial aid package:*** $30,986 (excluding resources awarded to replace EFC). 12% of all full-time freshmen had no need and received non-need-based gift aid.

UNDERGRADUATE FINANCIAL AID (Fall 2019, est.) 624 applied for aid; of those 92% were deemed to have need. 99% of undergraduates with need received aid; of those 20% had need fully met. ***Average percent of need met:*** 82% (excluding resources awarded to replace EFC). ***Average financial aid package:*** $29,993 (excluding resources awarded to replace EFC). 23% of all full-time undergraduates had no need and received non-need-based gift aid.

GIFT AID (NEED-BASED) ***Total amount:*** $13,055,623 (12% federal, 11% state, 67% institutional, 10% external sources). ***Receiving aid:*** Freshmen: 88% (140); all full-time undergraduates: 76% (569). ***Average award:*** Freshmen: $27,637; Undergraduates: $25,573. ***Scholarships, grants, and awards:*** Federal Pell, FSEOG, state, private, college/university gift aid from institutional funds.

GIFT AID (NON-NEED-BASED) ***Total amount:*** $3,984,191 (1% state, 81% institutional, 18% external sources). ***Receiving aid:*** Freshmen: 12% (20). Undergraduates: 11% (86). ***Average award:*** Freshmen: $19,703. Undergraduates: $16,789. ***Scholarships, grants, and awards by category:*** *Academic interests/achievement:* 75 awards ($512,684 total): biological sciences, business, communication, computer science, education, engineering/technologies, English, general academic interests/achievements, home economics, humanities, mathematics, physical sciences, religion/biblical studies, social sciences. *Creative arts/performance:* 5 awards ($10,250 total): music, theater/drama. *Special achievements/activities:* 5 awards ($15,000 total): community service, leadership, religious involvement. *Special characteristics:* 121 awards ($780,676 total): children of educators, children of faculty/staff, ethnic background, international students, members of minority groups. ***Tuition waivers:*** Full or partial for employees or children of employees.

LOANS ***Student loans:*** $4,348,192 (77% need-based, 23% non-need-based). 63% of past graduating class borrowed through all loan programs. *Average indebtedness per student:* $28,693. ***Average need-based loan:*** Freshmen: $3339. Undergraduates: $4915. ***Parent loans:*** $845,250 (53% need-based, 47% non-need-based). ***Programs:*** Federal Direct (Subsidized and Unsubsidized Stafford, PLUS), Federal Nursing.

WORK-STUDY ***Federal work-study:*** Total amount: $156,412; 351 jobs averaging $1124. ***State or other work-study/employment:*** Total amount: $86,400 (100% non-need-based). 52 part-time jobs averaging $1725.

ATHLETIC AWARDS Total amount: $1,912,280 (52% need-based, 48% non-need-based).

APPLYING FOR FINANCIAL AID ***Required financial aid form:*** FAFSA. ***Financial aid deadline (priority):*** 3/1. ***Notification date:*** Continuous beginning 12/5.

CONTACT Mr. Joel D. Short, Director of Student Financial Aid, Goshen College, 1700 South Main Street, Goshen, IN 46526-4794, 574-535-7525 or toll-free 800-348-7422. *Fax:* 574-535-7654. *E-mail:* joelds@goshen.edu.
Website: http://www.goshen.edu/.

GOUCHER COLLEGE

Baltimore, MD

Tuition & fees: $47,300 | **Average undergraduate aid package: $40,413**

ABOUT THE INSTITUTION Independent, coed. ***Awards:*** certificates, bachelor's, and master's degrees. 34 undergraduate majors. ***Total enrollment:*** 2,168. Undergraduates: 1,449. Freshmen: 340. Federal methodology is used as a basis for awarding need-based institutional aid.

UNDERGRADUATE EXPENSES for 2020–2021 ***Comprehensive fee:*** $61,182 includes full-time tuition ($47,100), mandatory fees ($200), and room and board ($13,882). ***College room only:*** $7688. Room and board charges vary according to board plan and housing facility. ***Part-time tuition:*** $1570 per credit hour.

FRESHMAN FINANCIAL AID (Fall 2019, est.) 297 applied for aid; of those 85% were deemed to have need. 100% of freshmen with need received aid; of those 20% had need fully met. ***Average percent of need met:*** 85% (excluding resources awarded to replace EFC). ***Average financial aid package:*** $42,205 (excluding resources awarded to replace EFC). 25% of all full-time freshmen had no need and received non-need-based gift aid.

UNDERGRADUATE FINANCIAL AID (Fall 2019, est.) 1,077 applied for aid; of those 89% were deemed to have need. 100% of undergraduates with need received aid; of those 21% had need fully met. ***Average percent of need met:*** 82% (excluding resources awarded to replace EFC). ***Average financial aid package:*** $40,413 (excluding resources awarded to replace EFC). 26% of all full-time undergraduates had no need and received non-need-based gift aid.

GIFT AID (NEED-BASED) ***Total amount:*** $35,099,085 (7% federal, 5% state, 85% institutional, 3% external sources). ***Receiving aid:*** Freshmen: 74% (251); all full-time undergraduates: 73% (955). ***Average award:*** Freshmen: $38,848; Undergraduates: $36,594. ***Scholarships, grants, and awards:*** Federal Pell, FSEOG, state, private, college/university gift aid from institutional funds.

GIFT AID (NON-NEED-BASED) ***Total amount:*** $8,937,884 (90% institutional, 10% external sources). ***Receiving aid:*** Freshmen: 9% (31). Undergraduates: 9% (115). ***Average award:*** Freshmen: $21,456. Undergraduates: $21,434. ***Scholarships, grants, and awards by category:*** *Creative arts/performance:* applied art and design, dance, music, performing arts, theater/drama. *Special achievements/activities:* leadership. ***Tuition waivers:*** Full or partial for minority students, employees or children of employees. ***ROTC:*** Army cooperative, Air Force cooperative.

LOANS ***Student loans:*** $6,638,668 (71% need-based, 29% non-need-based). 60% of past graduating class borrowed through all loan programs. *Average indebtedness per student:* $28,145. ***Average need-based loan:*** Freshmen: $3021. Undergraduates: $3862. ***Parent loans:*** $3,121,302 (40% need-based, 60% non-need-based). ***Programs:*** Federal Direct (Subsidized and Unsubsidized Stafford, PLUS).

WORK-STUDY ***Federal work-study:*** Total amount: $850,432; jobs available. ***State or other work-study/employment:*** Part-time jobs available.

APPLYING FOR FINANCIAL AID ***Required financial aid form:*** FAFSA. ***Financial aid deadline:*** Continuous. ***Notification date:*** Continuous beginning 12/15. Students must reply by 5/1.

CONTACT Mrs. Stephanie Alford, Director of Student Financial Aid, Goucher College, 1021 Dulaney Valley Road, Baltimore, MD 21204-2794, 410-337-6141 or toll-free 800-468-2437. *Fax:* 410-337-6504. *E-mail:* stephanie.alford@goucher.edu.
Website: http://www.goucher.edu/.

GOVERNORS STATE UNIVERSITY

University Park, IL

Tuition & fees (IL res): $12,616 | **Average undergraduate aid package: $12,133**

ABOUT THE INSTITUTION State-supported, coed. ***Awards:*** certificates, bachelor's, master's, and doctoral degrees. 30 undergraduate majors. ***Total enrollment:*** 4,854. Undergraduates: 3,232. Freshmen: 240. Both federal and institutional methodology are used as a basis for awarding need-based institutional aid.

UNDERGRADUATE EXPENSES for 2020–2021 ***Application fee:*** $25. ***Tuition, state resident:*** full-time $9390; part-time $313 per credit hour. ***Tuition, nonresident:*** full-time $18,780; part-time $626 per credit hour. ***Required fees:*** full-time $3226; $38 per term. Full-time tuition and fees vary according to course load, program, and reciprocity agreements. Part-time tuition and fees vary according to course level, course load, program, and reciprocity agreements. ***College room and board:*** $8102; ***Room only:*** $6102. Room and board charges vary according to board plan and housing facility. ***Payment plan:*** Guaranteed tuition.

FRESHMAN FINANCIAL AID (Fall 2018) 178 applied for aid; of those 95% were deemed to have need. 100% of freshmen with need received aid; of those 82% had need fully met. ***Average percent of need met:*** 82% (excluding resources awarded to replace EFC). ***Average financial aid package:*** $11,984 (excluding resources awarded to replace EFC). 1% of all full-time freshmen had no need and received non-need-based gift aid.

UNDERGRADUATE FINANCIAL AID (Fall 2018) 1,576 applied for aid; of those 93% were deemed to have need. 100% of undergraduates with need received aid; of those 70% had need fully met. ***Average percent of need met:*** 70% (excluding resources awarded to replace EFC). ***Average financial aid package:*** $12,133 (excluding resources awarded to replace EFC). 1% of all full-time undergraduates had no need and received non-need-based gift aid.

GIFT AID (NEED-BASED) ***Total amount:*** $17,894,742 (62% federal, 38% state). ***Receiving aid:*** Freshmen: 80% (163); all full-time undergraduates: 70% (1,308). ***Average award:*** Freshmen: $9450; Undergraduates: $9763. ***Scholarships, grants, and awards:*** Federal Pell, FSEOG, state, private, college/university gift aid from institutional funds.

GIFT AID (NON-NEED-BASED) ***Total amount:*** $1,375,524 (44% state, 30% institutional, 26% external sources). ***Receiving aid:*** Freshmen: 41% (83). Undergraduates: 18% (340). ***Average award:*** Freshmen: $200. Undergraduates: $6819. ***Scholarships, grants, and awards by category:*** *Academic interests/achievement:* biological sciences, business, communication, education, English, general academic interests/achievements, home economics, humanities, mathematics, physical sciences, social sciences. *Special characteristics:* children of faculty/staff, veterans. ***Tuition waivers:*** Full or partial for employees or children of employees, senior citizens. ***ROTC:*** Army cooperative, Air Force cooperative.

LOANS ***Student loans:*** $14,319,599 (100% need-based). ***Average need-based loan:*** Freshmen: $3410. Undergraduates: $4377. ***Parent loans:*** $1,158,113 (100% non-need-based). ***Programs:*** Federal Direct (Subsidized and Unsubsidized Stafford, PLUS), Perkins.

WORK-STUDY ***Federal work-study:*** Total amount: $944,315; 134 jobs averaging $2455. ***State or other work-study/employment:*** Total amount: $616,189 (100% non-need-based).

ATHLETIC AWARDS Total amount: $340,770 (100% non-need-based).

APPLYING FOR FINANCIAL AID ***Required financial aid form:*** FAFSA. ***Financial aid deadline:*** 10/1 (priority: 5/1). ***Notification date:*** Continuous beginning 3/1. Students must reply within 2 weeks of notification.

CONTACT Dr. John Perry, Interim Executive Director of Financial Aid, Governors State University, 1 University Parkway, University Park, IL 60484, 708-534-5000 Ext. 4480 or toll-free 800-478-8478. *E-mail:* faid@govst.edu.
Website: http://www.govst.edu/.

GRACE BIBLE COLLEGE

Grand Rapids, MI

CONTACT Mr. Kurt Postma, Director of Financial Aid, Grace Bible College, 1011 Aldon Street, SW, Grand Rapids, MI 49509-1921, 616-538-2330 or toll-free 800-968-1887. *Fax:* 616-538-0599. *E-mail:* kpostma@gbcol.edu.
Website: http://www.gbcol.edu/.

GRACE COLLEGE

Winona Lake, IN

CONTACT Charlette Sauders, Director of Financial Aid, Grace College, 200 Seminary Drive, Winona Lake, IN 46590-1294, 574-372-5100 Ext. 6161 or toll-free 800-54-GRACE. *Fax:* 574-372-5144. *E-mail:* charlette.sauders@grace.edu.
Website: http://www.grace.edu/.

GRACE COLLEGE OF DIVINITY

Fayetteville, NC

CONTACT Financial Aid Office, Grace College of Divinity, 5117 Cliffdale Road, Fayetteville, NC 28314, 910-221-2224.
Website: http://www.gcd.edu/.

GRACELAND UNIVERSITY

Lamoni, IA

Tuition & fees: $31,320	Average undergraduate aid package: $22,852

ABOUT THE INSTITUTION Independent Community of Christ, coed. ***Awards:*** certificates, bachelor's, master's, and doctoral degrees. 33 undergraduate majors. ***Total enrollment:*** 1,739. Undergraduates: 1,038. Freshmen: 193. Federal methodology is used as a basis for awarding need-based institutional aid.

UNDERGRADUATE EXPENSES for 2020–2021 ***Comprehensive fee:*** $40,760 includes full-time tuition ($30,650), mandatory fees ($670), and room and board ($9440). ***College room only:*** $3630. Full-time tuition and fees vary according to course load, degree level, location, and program. Room and board charges vary according to housing facility and location. ***Part-time tuition:*** $950 per semester hour. Part-time tuition and fees vary according to course load, degree level, location, and program.

FRESHMAN FINANCIAL AID (Fall 2019, est.) 182 applied for aid; of those 93% were deemed to have need. 100% of freshmen with need received aid; of those 16% had need fully met. ***Average percent of need met:*** 73% (excluding resources awarded to replace EFC). ***Average financial aid package:*** $26,273 (excluding resources awarded to replace EFC). 5% of all full-time freshmen had no need and received non-need-based gift aid.

UNDERGRADUATE FINANCIAL AID (Fall 2019, est.) 805 applied for aid; of those 93% were deemed to have need. 100% of undergraduates with need received aid; of those 12% had need fully met. ***Average percent of need met:*** 65% (excluding resources awarded to replace EFC). ***Average financial aid package:*** $22,852 (excluding resources awarded to replace EFC). 6% of all full-time undergraduates had no need and received non-need-based gift aid.

GIFT AID (NEED-BASED) ***Total amount:*** $14,612,187 (16% federal, 5% state, 77% institutional, 2% external sources). ***Receiving aid:*** Freshmen: 88% (170); all full-time undergraduates: 82% (735). ***Average award:*** Freshmen: $25,143; Undergraduates: $21,904. ***Scholarships, grants, and awards:*** Federal Pell, FSEOG, state, private, college/university gift aid from institutional funds.

GIFT AID (NON-NEED-BASED) ***Total amount:*** $1,729,958 (2% federal, 94% institutional, 4% external sources). ***Receiving aid:*** Freshmen: 33% (64). Undergraduates: 26% (233). ***Average award:*** Freshmen: $21,361. Undergraduates: $16,502. ***Scholarships, grants, and awards by category:*** *Academic interests/achievement:* computer science, engineering/technologies, English, general academic interests/achievements, physical sciences. *Creative arts/performance:* applied art and design, art/fine arts, creative writing, dance, music, theater/drama. *Special achievements/activities:* cheerleading/drum major, general special achievements/activities, leadership, religious involvement, rodeo. *Special characteristics:* children and siblings of alumni, children of faculty/staff, first-generation college students, general special characteristics, international students, local/state students, members of minority groups, out-of-state students, religious affiliation. ***Tuition waivers:*** Full or partial for employees or children of employees, senior citizens.

LOANS ***Student loans:*** $5,840,928 (81% need-based, 19% non-need-based). 89% of past graduating class borrowed through all loan programs. *Average indebtedness per student:* $44,984. ***Parent loans:*** $1,718,384 (52% need-based, 48% non-need-based). ***Programs:*** Federal Direct (Subsidized and Unsubsidized Stafford, PLUS), college/university.

WORK-STUDY ***Federal work-study:*** Total amount: $198,255; jobs available. ***State or other work-study/employment:*** Total amount: $661,874 (45% need-based, 55% non-need-based). Part-time jobs available.

ATHLETIC AWARDS Total amount: $2,586,218 (72% need-based, 28% non-need-based).

APPLYING FOR FINANCIAL AID ***Required financial aid form:*** FAFSA. ***Financial aid deadline:*** Continuous. ***Notification date:*** Continuous beginning 2/1. Students must reply within 2 weeks of notification.

CONTACT Sherri Brenizer, Director of Student Financial Services, Graceland University, 1 University Place, Lamoni, IA 50140, 641-784-5051 or toll-free 866-GRACELAND. *E-mail:* brenizer@graceland.edu.
Website: http://www.graceland.edu/.

GRACE MISSION UNIVERSITY

Fullerton, CA

CONTACT Financial Aid Office, Grace Mission University, 1645 West Valencia Drive, Fullerton, CA 92833, 714-525-0088.
Website: http://www.gm.edu/.

GRACE SCHOOL OF THEOLOGY

Conroe, TX

CONTACT Financial Aid Office, Grace School of Theology, 3705 College Park Drive Suite 140, Conroe, TX 77384-4894.
Website: http://www.gsot.edu/.

GRAMBLING STATE UNIVERSITY

Grambling, LA

Tuition & fees (area res): $16,706	Average undergraduate aid package: $10,595

ABOUT THE INSTITUTION State-supported, coed. ***Awards:*** certificates, bachelor's, master's, and doctoral degrees. 27 undergraduate majors. ***Total enrollment:*** 5,232. Undergraduates: 4,153. Freshmen: 857. Federal methodology is used as a basis for awarding need-based institutional aid.
UNDERGRADUATE EXPENSES for 2020–2021 ***Application fee:*** $20. ***Tuition, area resident:*** full-time $5140; part-time $215 per credit hour. ***Tuition, state resident:*** full-time $5140. ***Tuition, nonresident:*** full-time $5140; part-time $215 per credit hour. ***Required fees:*** full-time $11,566. ***Room only:*** $5572.
FRESHMAN FINANCIAL AID (Fall 2019, est.) 831 applied for aid; of those 84% were deemed to have need. 119% of freshmen with need received aid. ***Average financial aid package:*** $10,848 (excluding resources awarded to replace EFC). 6% of all full-time freshmen had no need and received non-need-based gift aid.
UNDERGRADUATE FINANCIAL AID (Fall 2019, est.) 3,577 applied for aid; of those 84% were deemed to have need. 118% of undergraduates with need received aid. ***Average financial aid package:*** $10,595 (excluding resources awarded to replace EFC). 7% of all full-time undergraduates had no need and received non-need-based gift aid.
GIFT AID (NEED-BASED) ***Total amount:*** $17,813,560 (91% federal, 6% state, 2% institutional, 1% external sources). ***Receiving aid:*** Freshmen: 87% (733); all full-time undergraduates: 80% (3,069). ***Average award:*** Freshmen: $6602; Undergraduates: $5841. ***Scholarships, grants, and awards:*** Federal Pell, FSEOG, state, private, college/university gift aid from institutional funds.
GIFT AID (NON-NEED-BASED) ***Total amount:*** $2,504,808 (2% federal, 56% state, 42% institutional). ***Receiving aid:*** Freshmen: 27% (230). Undergraduates: 85% (3,248). ***Average award:*** Freshmen: $3252. Undergraduates: $2658. ***Scholarships, grants, and awards by category:*** *Academic interests/achievement:* biological sciences, business, communication, computer science, education, engineering/technologies, English, foreign languages, general academic interests/achievements, health fields, home economics, humanities, mathematics, military science, physical sciences, premedicine, social sciences. *Creative arts/performance:* dance, general creative arts/performance, music, performing arts, theater/drama. *Special achievements/activities:* cheerleading/drum major, junior miss, leadership. *Special characteristics:* children and siblings of alumni, children of faculty/staff, children of public servants, ethnic background, international students, local/state students, members of minority groups, out-of-state students, public servants, veterans. ***ROTC:*** Army, Air Force cooperative.
LOANS ***Student loans:*** $41,114,948 (30% need-based, 70% non-need-based). 30% of past graduating class borrowed through all loan programs. *Average indebtedness per student:* $42,963. ***Average need-based loan:*** Freshmen: $3405. Undergraduates: $4055. ***Parent loans:*** $13,952,192 (100% non-need-based). ***Programs:*** Federal Direct (Subsidized and Unsubsidized Stafford, PLUS).
WORK-STUDY ***Federal work-study:*** Total amount: $1,000,000; jobs available.
ATHLETIC AWARDS Total amount: $2,663,312 (100% non-need-based).
APPLYING FOR FINANCIAL AID ***Required financial aid form:*** FAFSA. ***Financial aid deadline:*** 6/1 (priority: 4/1). ***Notification date:*** Continuous beginning 3/1.
CONTACT Mr. Gavin Hamms, Director of Student Financial Aid and Scholarships, Grambling State University, PO Box 629, Grambling, LA 71245, 318-274-6328 or toll-free 800-569-4714. *Fax:* 318-274-3358. *E-mail:* hammsg@gram.edu.
Website: http://www.gram.edu/.

GRAND CANYON UNIVERSITY

Phoenix, AZ

CONTACT Director of Financial Aid, Grand Canyon University, 3300 West Camelback Road, PO Box 11097, Phoenix, AZ 85017-3030, 800-800-9776 Ext. 2885 or toll-free 800-800-9776. *Fax:* 602-589-2044.
Website: http://www.gcu.edu/.

GRAND VALLEY STATE UNIVERSITY

Allendale, MI

Tuition & fees (MI res): $12,860	Average undergraduate aid package: $10,716

ABOUT THE INSTITUTION State-supported, coed. ***Awards:*** certificates, bachelor's, master's, and doctoral degrees. 114 undergraduate majors. ***Total enrollment:*** 24,033. Undergraduates: 21,112. Freshmen: 3,863. Federal methodology is used as a basis for awarding need-based institutional aid.
UNDERGRADUATE EXPENSES for 2019–2020 ***Application fee:*** $30. ***Tuition, state resident:*** full-time $12,860; part-time $540 per credit hour. ***Tuition, nonresident:*** full-time $18,296; part-time $768 per credit hour. Full-time tuition and fees vary according to course level, course load, program, and student level. Part-time tuition and fees vary according to course level, course load, program, and student level. ***College room and board:*** $8820; ***Room only:*** $5570. Room and board charges vary according to board plan and housing facility.
FRESHMAN FINANCIAL AID (Fall 2019, est.) 3788 applied for aid; of those 65% were deemed to have need. 99% of freshmen with need received aid; of those 23% had need fully met. ***Average percent of need met:*** 71% (excluding resources awarded to replace EFC). ***Average financial aid package:*** $11,883 (excluding resources awarded to replace EFC). 24% of all full-time freshmen had no need and received non-need-based gift aid.
UNDERGRADUATE FINANCIAL AID (Fall 2019, est.) 15,320 applied for aid; of those 69% were deemed to have need. 99% of undergraduates with need received aid; of those 20% had need fully met. ***Average percent of need met:*** 67% (excluding resources awarded to replace EFC). ***Average financial aid package:*** $10,716 (excluding resources awarded to replace EFC). 21% of all full-time undergraduates had no need and received non-need-based gift aid.
GIFT AID (NEED-BASED) ***Total amount:*** $70,054,966 (38% federal, 4% state, 54% institutional, 4% external sources). ***Receiving aid:*** Freshmen: 51% (2,138); all full-time undergraduates: 46% (8,740). ***Average award:*** Freshmen: $10,077; Undergraduates: $8221. ***Scholarships, grants, and awards:*** Federal Pell, FSEOG, state, private, college/university gift aid from institutional funds.
GIFT AID (NON-NEED-BASED) ***Total amount:*** $19,469,490 (88% institutional, 12% external sources). ***Receiving aid:*** Freshmen: 6% (260). Undergraduates: 4% (714). ***Average award:*** Freshmen: $5135. Undergraduates: $4425. ***Scholarships, grants, and awards by category:*** *Academic interests/achievement:* business, communication, computer science, education, engineering/technologies, English, foreign languages, general academic interests/achievements, home economics, humanities, international studies, mathematics, physical sciences, premedicine, social sciences. *Creative arts/performance:* applied art and design, art/fine arts, cinema/film/broadcasting, dance, journalism/publications, music, theater/drama. *Special characteristics:* adult students, children and siblings of alumni, children of faculty/staff, children of union members/company employees, children of workers in trades, general special characteristics, handicapped students, international students, local/state students, out-of-state students, public servants, spouses of deceased or disabled public servants, vet-

erans. ***Tuition waivers:*** Full or partial for employees or children of employees. ***ROTC:*** Army cooperative, Air Force cooperative.

LOANS ***Student loans:*** $113,858,864 (35% need-based, 65% non-need-based). 72% of past graduating class borrowed through all loan programs. *Average indebtedness per student:* $28,131. ***Average need-based loan:*** Freshmen: $3245. Undergraduates: $4204. ***Parent loans:*** $2,643,178 (100% non-need-based). ***Programs:*** Federal Direct (Subsidized and Unsubsidized Stafford, PLUS), Federal Nursing.

WORK-STUDY ***Federal work-study:*** Total amount: $3,183,392; jobs available. ***State or other work-study/employment:*** Part-time jobs available.

ATHLETIC AWARDS Total amount: $4,048,944 (35% need-based, 65% non-need-based).

APPLYING FOR FINANCIAL AID ***Required financial aid form:*** FAFSA. ***Financial aid deadline (priority):*** 3/1. ***Notification date:*** Continuous beginning 1/15. Students must reply by 5/1 or within 4 weeks of notification.

CONTACT Michelle Rhodes, Office of Financial Aid, Grand Valley State University, 100 Student Services Building, Allendale, MI 49401, 616-331-3234 or toll-free 800-748-0246. *Fax:* 616-331-3180. *E-mail:* rhodesmi@gvsu.edu.
Website: http://www.gvsu.edu/.

GRAND VIEW UNIVERSITY
Des Moines, IA

Tuition & fees: N/R	Average undergraduate aid package: $22,957

ABOUT THE INSTITUTION Independent Evangelical Lutheran Church in America, coed. ***Awards:*** certificates, bachelor's, and master's degrees. 44 undergraduate majors. Federal methodology is used as a basis for awarding need-based institutional aid.

FRESHMAN FINANCIAL AID (Fall 2019, est.) 317 applied for aid; of those 89% were deemed to have need. 100% of freshmen with need received aid; of those 27% had need fully met. ***Average percent of need met:*** 80% (excluding resources awarded to replace EFC). ***Average financial aid package:*** $25,225 (excluding resources awarded to replace EFC). 15% of all full-time freshmen had no need and received non-need-based gift aid.

UNDERGRADUATE FINANCIAL AID (Fall 2019, est.) 1,418 applied for aid; of those 89% were deemed to have need. 100% of undergraduates with need received aid; of those 27% had need fully met. ***Average percent of need met:*** 79% (excluding resources awarded to replace EFC). ***Average financial aid package:*** $22,957 (excluding resources awarded to replace EFC). 18% of all full-time undergraduates had no need and received non-need-based gift aid.

GIFT AID (NEED-BASED) ***Receiving aid:*** Freshmen: 80% (264); all full-time undergraduates: 73% (1,149). ***Average award:*** Freshmen: $23,014; Undergraduates: $20,643. ***Scholarships, grants, and awards:*** Federal Pell, FSEOG, state, private, college/university gift aid from institutional funds.

GIFT AID (NON-NEED-BASED) ***Receiving aid:*** Freshmen: 16% (54). Undergraduates: 13% (206). ***Average award:*** Freshmen: $11,537. Undergraduates: $10,735. ***Scholarships, grants, and awards by category:*** *Academic interests/achievement:* biological sciences, business, communication, computer science, education, English, foreign languages, general academic interests/achievements, home economics, humanities, international studies, mathematics, physical sciences, premedicine, religion/biblical studies, social sciences. *Creative arts/performance:* applied art and design, art/fine arts, dance, music, theater/drama. *Special achievements/activities:* cheerleading/drum major, community service, junior miss, memberships, religious involvement. *Special characteristics:* adult students, children and siblings of alumni, children of educators, children of faculty/staff, ethnic background, first-generation college students, general special characteristics, international students, out-of-state students, religious affiliation, veterans. ***ROTC:*** Army cooperative, Air Force cooperative.

LOANS ***Student loans:*** 82% of past graduating class borrowed through all loan programs. *Average indebtedness per student:* $35,126. ***Average need-based loan:*** Freshmen: $3264. Undergraduates: $4156. ***Programs:*** Federal Direct (Subsidized and Unsubsidized Stafford, PLUS), college/university, private loans.

WORK-STUDY Federal work-study jobs available. ***State or other work-study/employment:*** Part-time jobs available.

APPLYING FOR FINANCIAL AID ***Required financial aid form:*** FAFSA. ***Notification date:*** Continuous. Students must reply within 3 weeks of notification.

CONTACT Ms. Sarah Freestone, Director of Financial Aid, Grand View University, 1200 Grandview Avenue, Des Moines, IA 50316-1599, 515-263-2853 or toll-free 800-444-6083. *E-mail:* sfreestone@grandview.edu.
Website: http://www.grandview.edu/.

GRANTHAM UNIVERSITY
Lenexa, KS

CONTACT Financial Aid Office, Grantham University, 16025 West 113th Street, Lenexa, KS 66219, toll-free 800-955-2527.
Website: http://www.grantham.edu/.

GREAT LAKES CHRISTIAN COLLEGE
Lansing, MI

CONTACT Financial Aid Officer, Great Lakes Christian College, 6211 West Willow Highway, Lansing, MI 48917-1299, 517-321-0242 or toll-free 800-YES-GLCC.
Website: http://www.glcc.edu/.

GREENSBORO COLLEGE
Greensboro, NC

CONTACT Lindsay Latham, Director of Financial Aid, Greensboro College, 815 West Market Street, Greensboro, NC 27401-1875, 336-272-7102 Ext. 217 or toll-free 800-346-8226. *Fax:* 336-230-9622. *E-mail:* dvanarsdale@greensborocollege.edu.
Website: http://www.greensboro.edu/.

GREENVILLE UNIVERSITY
Greenville, IL

Tuition & fees: $27,910	Average undergraduate aid package: $22,943

ABOUT THE INSTITUTION Independent Free Methodist, coed. ***Awards:*** bachelor's and master's degrees. 52 undergraduate majors. ***Total enrollment:*** 1,132. Undergraduates: 964. Freshmen: 221. Federal methodology is used as a basis for awarding need-based institutional aid.

UNDERGRADUATE EXPENSES for 2019–2020 ***Comprehensive fee:*** $37,458 includes full-time tuition ($27,580), mandatory fees ($330), and room and board ($9548). ***College room only:*** $4698. ***Part-time tuition:*** $434 per credit hour.

FRESHMAN FINANCIAL AID (Fall 2019, est.) 202 applied for aid; of those 92% were deemed to have need. 100% of freshmen with need received aid; of those 22% had need fully met. ***Average percent of need met:*** 77% (excluding resources awarded to replace EFC). ***Average financial aid package:*** $22,057 (excluding resources awarded to replace EFC). 8% of all full-time freshmen had no need and received non-need-based gift aid.

UNDERGRADUATE FINANCIAL AID (Fall 2019, est.) 690 applied for aid; of those 92% were deemed to have need. 100% of undergraduates with need received aid; of those 14% had need fully met. ***Average percent of need met:*** 74% (excluding resources awarded to replace EFC). ***Average financial aid package:*** $22,943 (excluding resources awarded to replace EFC). 14% of all full-time undergraduates had no need and received non-need-based gift aid.

GIFT AID (NEED-BASED) ***Total amount:*** $12,216,184 (16% federal, 11% state, 61% institutional, 12% external sources). ***Receiving aid:*** Freshmen: 76% (185); all full-time undergraduates: 80% (628). ***Average award:*** Freshmen: $19,434; Undergraduates: $19,123. ***Scholarships, grants, and awards:*** Federal Pell, FSEOG, state, private, college/university gift aid from institutional funds.

GIFT AID (NON-NEED-BASED) ***Total amount:*** $2,042,880 (92% institutional, 8% external sources). ***Receiving aid:*** Freshmen: 14% (35). Undergraduates: 9% (72). ***Average award:*** Freshmen: $18,223. Undergraduates: $13,738. ***Scholarships, grants, and awards by category:*** *Academic interests/achievement:* biological sciences, engineering/technologies, mathematics, physical sciences. *Creative arts/performance:* applied art and design, art/fine arts, music, performing arts. *Special achievements/activities:* cheerleading/drum major, leadership, memberships, religious involvement. *Special characteristics:* children and siblings of alumni, children of faculty/staff, international students, local/state students, out-of-state students, religious affiliation, siblings of current students. ***Tuition waivers:*** Full or partial for employees or children of employees, senior citizens.

LOANS *Student loans:* $5,364,894 (81% need-based, 19% non-need-based). 77% of past graduating class borrowed through all loan programs. *Average indebtedness per student:* $28,759. ***Average need-based loan:*** Freshmen: $3076. Undergraduates: $4061. ***Parent loans:*** $1,797,747 (42% need-based, 58% non-need-based). ***Programs:*** Federal Direct (Subsidized and Unsubsidized Stafford, PLUS), Perkins, college/university.

WORK-STUDY *Federal work-study:* Total amount: $141,954; 117 jobs averaging $1213. ***State or other work-study/employment:*** Part-time jobs available.

APPLYING FOR FINANCIAL AID *Required financial aid form:* FAFSA. ***Financial aid deadline (priority):*** 11/1. ***Notification date:*** Continuous beginning 11/1. Students must reply within 3 weeks of notification.

CONTACT David Kessinger, Director of Financial Aid, Greenville University, 315 East College Avenue, Greenville, IL 62246-0159, 618-664-7108 or toll-free 800-345-4440. *Fax:* 618-664-7198. *E-mail:* david.kessinger@greenville.edu. *Website:* http://www.greenville.edu/.

GRINNELL COLLEGE

Grinnell, IA

Tuition & fees: $56,680	Average undergraduate aid package: $51,571

ABOUT THE INSTITUTION Independent, coed. ***Awards:*** bachelor's degrees. 32 undergraduate majors. ***Total enrollment:*** 1,733. Undergraduates: 1,733. Freshmen: 459. Institutional methodology is used as a basis for awarding need-based institutional aid.

UNDERGRADUATE EXPENSES for 2020–2021 *Comprehensive fee:* $70,544 includes full-time tuition ($56,188), mandatory fees ($492), and room and board ($13,864). ***College room only:*** $6548. Room and board charges vary according to board plan and housing facility. ***Part-time tuition:*** $1684 per credit hour. ***Part-time fees:*** $1684 per credit hour.

FRESHMAN FINANCIAL AID (Fall 2019, est.) 360 applied for aid; of those 83% were deemed to have need. 100% of freshmen with need received aid; of those 100% had need fully met. ***Average percent of need met:*** 100% (excluding resources awarded to replace EFC). ***Average financial aid package:*** $51,770 (excluding resources awarded to replace EFC). 21% of all full-time freshmen had no need and received non-need-based gift aid.

UNDERGRADUATE FINANCIAL AID (Fall 2019, est.) 1,218 applied for aid; of those 91% were deemed to have need. 100% of undergraduates with need received aid; of those 100% had need fully met. ***Average percent of need met:*** 100% (excluding resources awarded to replace EFC). ***Average financial aid package:*** $51,571 (excluding resources awarded to replace EFC). 21% of all full-time undergraduates had no need and received non-need-based gift aid.

GIFT AID (NEED-BASED) *Total amount:* $49,920,584 (3% federal, 1% state, 93% institutional, 3% external sources). ***Receiving aid:*** Freshmen: 65% (299); all full-time undergraduates: 65% (1,108). ***Average award:*** Freshmen: $46,609; Undergraduates: $45,482. ***Scholarships, grants, and awards:*** Federal Pell, FSEOG, state, private, college/university gift aid from institutional funds, National Merit Scholarships, Dollars for Scholars Matching Funds.

GIFT AID (NON-NEED-BASED) *Total amount:* $7,479,945 (92% institutional, 8% external sources). ***Receiving aid:*** Freshmen: 11% (51). Undergraduates: 9% (154). ***Average award:*** Freshmen: $20,984. Undergraduates: $19,505. ***Scholarships, grants, and awards by category:*** *Academic interests/achievement:* general academic interests/achievements. *Special achievements/activities:* leadership. *Special characteristics:* local/state students, veterans, veterans' children. ***Tuition waivers:*** Full or partial for employees or children of employees.

LOANS *Student loans:* $4,630,000 (91% need-based, 9% non-need-based). 61% of past graduating class borrowed through all loan programs. *Average indebtedness per student:* $20,093. ***Average need-based loan:*** Freshmen: $2806. Undergraduates: $3866. ***Programs:*** Federal Direct (Subsidized and Unsubsidized Stafford, PLUS), state, college/university.

WORK-STUDY *Federal work-study:* Total amount: $257,343; jobs available. ***State or other work-study/employment:*** Total amount: $2,490,857 (91% need-based, 9% non-need-based). Part-time jobs available.

APPLYING FOR FINANCIAL AID *Required financial aid forms:* FAFSA, CSS Financial Aid PROFILE, noncustodial (divorced/separated) parent's statement. ***Financial aid deadline:*** 1/15 (priority: 1/15). ***Notification date:*** 4/1. Students must reply by 5/1.

CONTACT Ms. Pam Sittig, Director of Financial Aid, Grinnell College, 2nd Floor, 1227 Park Street, Grinnell, IA 50112-1670, 641-269-3250 or toll-free 800-247-0113. *Fax:* 641-269-4077. *E-mail:* sittig@grinnell.edu. *Website:* http://www.grinnell.edu/.

GROVE CITY COLLEGE

Grove City, PA

Tuition & fees: $18,470	Average undergraduate aid package: $7999

ABOUT THE INSTITUTION Independent Presbyterian, coed. ***Awards:*** bachelor's degrees. 51 undergraduate majors. ***Total enrollment:*** 2,338. Undergraduates: 2,338. Freshmen: 608. Institutional methodology is used as a basis for awarding need-based institutional aid.

UNDERGRADUATE EXPENSES for 2019–2020 *Application fee:* $50. ***Comprehensive fee:*** $28,530 includes full-time tuition ($18,470) and room and board ($10,060). ***College room only:*** $6160. Room and board charges vary according to housing facility. ***Part-time tuition:*** $595 per credit hour.

FRESHMAN FINANCIAL AID (Fall 2019, est.) 457 applied for aid; of those 72% were deemed to have need. 99% of freshmen with need received aid; of those 11% had need fully met. ***Average percent of need met:*** 52% (excluding resources awarded to replace EFC). ***Average financial aid package:*** $8385 (excluding resources awarded to replace EFC). 12% of all full-time freshmen had no need and received non-need-based gift aid.

UNDERGRADUATE FINANCIAL AID (Fall 2019, est.) 1,313 applied for aid; of those 82% were deemed to have need. 99% of undergraduates with need received aid; of those 8% had need fully met. ***Average percent of need met:*** 49% (excluding resources awarded to replace EFC). ***Average financial aid package:*** $7999 (excluding resources awarded to replace EFC). 19% of all full-time undergraduates had no need and received non-need-based gift aid.

GIFT AID (NEED-BASED) *Total amount:* $8,162,739 (10% state, 80% institutional, 10% external sources). ***Receiving aid:*** Freshmen: 66% (323); all full-time undergraduates: 49% (1,057). ***Average award:*** Freshmen: $8385; Undergraduates: $7999. ***Scholarships, grants, and awards:*** state, private, college/university gift aid from institutional funds.

GIFT AID (NON-NEED-BASED) *Total amount:* $2,916,392 (2% state, 59% institutional, 39% external sources). ***Receiving aid:*** Freshmen: 8% (37). Undergraduates: 3% (76). ***Average award:*** Freshmen: $7160. Undergraduates: $3420. ***Scholarships, grants, and awards by category:*** *Academic interests/achievement:* 788 awards ($2,209,838 total): biological sciences, business, communication, education, engineering/technologies, English, foreign languages, general academic interests/achievements, humanities, international studies, mathematics, physical sciences, religion/biblical studies, social sciences. *Creative arts/performance:* 7 awards ($9600 total): creative writing, music. *Special achievements/activities:* 49 awards ($132,667 total): community service, general special achievements/activities, leadership, memberships, religious involvement. *Special characteristics:* 18 awards ($94,379 total): ethnic background, first-generation college students, general special characteristics, handicapped students, members of minority groups. ***Tuition waivers:*** Full or partial for employees or children of employees.

LOANS *Student loans:* $11,871,140 (43% need-based, 57% non-need-based). 56% of past graduating class borrowed through all loan programs. *Average indebtedness per student:* $40,600. ***Average need-based loan:*** Undergraduates: $18. ***Parent loans:*** $87,025 (1% need-based, 99% non-need-based). ***Programs:*** state, private loans.

WORK-STUDY *State or other work-study/employment:* Total amount: $301,490 (34% need-based, 66% non-need-based).

APPLYING FOR FINANCIAL AID *Required financial aid form:* institution's own form. ***Financial aid deadline:*** 4/15. ***Notification date:*** Continuous beginning 2/25. Students must reply by 5/1.

CONTACT Mr. Thomas G. Ball, Director of Financial Aid, Grove City College, 100 Campus Drive, Grove City, PA 16127-2104, 724-458-3300. *Fax:* 724-450-4040. *E-mail:* financialaid@gcc.edu.
Website: http://www.gcc.edu/.

GUILFORD COLLEGE

Greensboro, NC

Tuition & fees: $40,120	Average undergraduate aid package: $25,481

ABOUT THE INSTITUTION Independent Society of Friends, coed. ***Awards:*** certificates, bachelor's, and master's degrees. 48 undergraduate majors. ***Total enrollment:*** 1,541. Undergraduates: 1,525. Freshmen: 380. Federal methodology is used as a basis for awarding need-based institutional aid.

UNDERGRADUATE EXPENSES for 2020–2021 ***One-time required fee:*** $170. ***Comprehensive fee:*** $52,320 includes full-time tuition ($39,400), mandatory fees ($720), and room and board ($12,200). ***College room only:*** $6000. Full-time tuition and fees vary according to student level. Room and board charges vary according to board plan and housing facility. ***Part-time tuition:*** $1085 per credit hour. ***Part-time fees:*** $120 per year. Part-time tuition and fees vary according to student level. ***Payment plan:*** Guaranteed tuition.

FRESHMAN FINANCIAL AID (Fall 2018) 396 applied for aid; of those 85% were deemed to have need. 100% of freshmen with need received aid; of those 67% had need fully met. ***Average percent of need met:*** 90% (excluding resources awarded to replace EFC). ***Average financial aid package:*** $29,257 (excluding resources awarded to replace EFC). 14% of all full-time freshmen had no need and received non-need-based gift aid.

UNDERGRADUATE FINANCIAL AID (Fall 2018) 1,206 applied for aid; of those 89% were deemed to have need. 100% of undergraduates with need received aid; of those 56% had need fully met. ***Average percent of need met:*** 74% (excluding resources awarded to replace EFC). ***Average financial aid package:*** $25,481 (excluding resources awarded to replace EFC). 9% of all full-time undergraduates had no need and received non-need-based gift aid.

GIFT AID (NEED-BASED) ***Total amount:*** $22,817,910 (14% federal, 10% state, 72% institutional, 4% external sources). ***Receiving aid:*** Freshmen: 79% (333); all full-time undergraduates: 71% (1,028). ***Average award:*** Freshmen: $4565; Undergraduates: $4418. ***Scholarships, grants, and awards:*** Federal Pell, FSEOG, state, private, college/university gift aid from institutional funds.

GIFT AID (NON-NEED-BASED) ***Total amount:*** $5,828,887 (93% institutional, 7% external sources). ***Receiving aid:*** Freshmen: 80% (335). Undergraduates: 59% (863). ***Average award:*** Freshmen: $11,543. Undergraduates: $9961. ***Scholarships, grants, and awards by category:*** *Academic interests/achievement:* general academic interests/achievements. ***Tuition waivers:*** Full or partial for employees or children of employees. ***ROTC:*** Army cooperative, Air Force cooperative.

LOANS ***Student loans:*** $9,056,853 (93% need-based, 7% non-need-based). 65% of past graduating class borrowed through all loan programs. *Average indebtedness per student:* $35,392. ***Average need-based loan:*** Freshmen: $3135. Undergraduates: $3773. ***Parent loans:*** $3,054,328 (92% need-based, 8% non-need-based). ***Programs:*** Federal Direct (Subsidized and Unsubsidized Stafford, PLUS), Perkins.

WORK-STUDY ***Federal work-study:*** Total amount: $569,389; jobs available. ***State or other work-study/employment:*** Total amount: $425,447 (52% need-based, 48% non-need-based). Part-time jobs available.

APPLYING FOR FINANCIAL AID ***Required financial aid form:*** FAFSA. ***Financial aid deadline (priority):*** 2/15. ***Notification date:*** Continuous beginning 3/1. Students must reply within 2 weeks of notification.

CONTACT Ms. Dorothy Davidson, Interim Director of Financial Aid, Guilford College, 5800 West Friendly Avenue, Greensboro, NC 27410, 336-316-2410 or toll-free 800-992-7759. *Fax:* 336-316-2942. *E-mail:* davidsonde@guilford.edu.
Website: http://www.guilford.edu/.

GUSTAVUS ADOLPHUS COLLEGE

St. Peter, MN

Tuition & fees: $48,460	Average undergraduate aid package: $44,800

ABOUT THE INSTITUTION Independent Evangelical Lutheran Church in America, coed. ***Awards:*** bachelor's degrees. 67 undergraduate majors. ***Total enrollment:*** 2,235. Undergraduates: 2,235. Freshmen: 642. Both federal and institutional methodology are used as a basis for awarding need-based institutional aid.

UNDERGRADUATE EXPENSES for 2020–2021 ***Comprehensive fee:*** $58,890 includes full-time tuition ($48,250), mandatory fees ($210), and room and board ($10,430). ***College room only:*** $6600. Room and board charges vary according to housing facility. ***Part-time tuition:*** $8300 per credit hour.

FRESHMAN FINANCIAL AID (Fall 2019, est.) 595 applied for aid; of those 85% were deemed to have need. 100% of freshmen with need received aid; of those 50% had need fully met. ***Average percent of need met:*** 96% (excluding resources awarded to replace EFC). ***Average financial aid package:*** $44,514 (excluding resources awarded to replace EFC). 20% of all full-time freshmen had no need and received non-need-based gift aid.

UNDERGRADUATE FINANCIAL AID (Fall 2019, est.) 1,817 applied for aid; of those 89% were deemed to have need. 96% of undergraduates with need received aid; of those 38% had need fully met. ***Average percent of need met:*** 92% (excluding resources awarded to replace EFC). ***Average financial aid package:*** $44,800 (excluding resources awarded to replace EFC). 25% of all full-time undergraduates had no need and received non-need-based gift aid.

GIFT AID (NEED-BASED) ***Total amount:*** $54,702,012 (5% federal, 9% state, 84% institutional, 2% external sources). ***Receiving aid:*** Freshmen: 76% (490); all full-time undergraduates: 62% (1,369). ***Average award:*** Freshmen: $37,771; Undergraduates: $37,560. ***Scholarships, grants, and awards:*** Federal Pell, FSEOG, state, private, college/university gift aid from institutional funds.

GIFT AID (NON-NEED-BASED) ***Total amount:*** $18,436,028 (95% institutional, 5% external sources). ***Receiving aid:*** Freshmen: 16% (104). Undergraduates: 13% (277). ***Average award:*** Freshmen: $26,120. Undergraduates: $26,171. ***Scholarships, grants, and awards by category:*** *Academic interests/achievement:* general academic interests/achievements. *Creative arts/performance:* applied art and design, dance, debating, music, theater/drama. *Special achievements/activities:* junior miss. *Special characteristics:* children and siblings of alumni, ethnic background, first-generation college students, international students, members of minority groups, out-of-state students, siblings of current students. ***ROTC:*** Army cooperative.

LOANS ***Student loans:*** $14,409,630 (35% need-based, 65% non-need-based). 83% of past graduating class borrowed through all loan programs. *Average indebtedness per student:* $35,145. ***Average need-based loan:*** Freshmen: $3327. Undergraduates: $4480. ***Parent loans:*** $2,465,376 (100% non-need-based). ***Programs:*** Federal Direct (Subsidized and Unsubsidized Stafford, PLUS), state.

WORK-STUDY ***Federal work-study:*** Total amount: $1,127,165; jobs available. ***State or other work-study/employment:*** Total amount: $1,952,155 (13% need-based, 87% non-need-based). Part-time jobs available.

APPLYING FOR FINANCIAL AID ***Required financial aid form:*** FAFSA. ***Financial aid deadline:*** 4/15 (priority: 2/15). ***Notification date:*** Continuous beginning 12/1. Students must reply by 5/1.

CONTACT Mr. Doug Minter, Dean of Financial Aid, Gustavus Adolphus College, 800 West College Avenue, St. Peter, MN 56082-1498, 507-933-7527 or toll-free 800-GUSTAVU(S). *Fax:* 507-933-7727. *E-mail:* finaid@gustavus.edu.
Website: http://www.gustavus.edu/.

GUTENBERG COLLEGE

Eugene, OR

CONTACT Financial Aid Office, Gutenberg College, 1883 University Street, Eugene, OR 97403, 541-683-5141.
Website: http://www.gutenberg.edu/.

GWYNEDD MERCY UNIVERSITY

Gwynedd Valley, PA

Tuition & fees: $35,600 | **Average undergraduate aid package: $22,614**

ABOUT THE INSTITUTION Independent Roman Catholic, coed. ***Awards:*** certificates, associate, bachelor's, master's, and doctoral degrees. 37 undergraduate majors. ***Total enrollment:*** 2,990. Undergraduates: 2,157. Freshmen: 239. Federal methodology is used as a basis for awarding need-based institutional aid.

UNDERGRADUATE EXPENSES for 2020–2021 ***Comprehensive fee:*** $48,280 includes full-time tuition ($34,650), mandatory fees ($950), and room and board ($12,680). ***College room only:*** $5520. Full-time tuition and fees vary according to program. Room and board charges vary according to board plan. Part-time tuition and fees vary according to program.

FRESHMAN FINANCIAL AID (Fall 2019, est.) 231 applied for aid; of those 88% were deemed to have need. 100% of freshmen with need received aid; of those 13% had need fully met. ***Average percent of need met:*** 73% (excluding resources awarded to replace EFC). ***Average financial aid package:*** $26,417 (excluding resources awarded to replace EFC). 12% of all full-time freshmen had no need and received non-need-based gift aid.

UNDERGRADUATE FINANCIAL AID (Fall 2019, est.) 1,521 applied for aid; of those 90% were deemed to have need. 99% of undergraduates with need received aid; of those 12% had need fully met. ***Average percent of need met:*** 60% (excluding resources awarded to replace EFC). ***Average financial aid package:*** $22,614 (excluding resources awarded to replace EFC). 11% of all full-time undergraduates had no need and received non-need-based gift aid.

GIFT AID (NEED-BASED) ***Total amount:*** $24,564,008 (13% federal, 9% state, 72% institutional, 6% external sources). ***Receiving aid:*** Freshmen: 88% (204); all full-time undergraduates: 73% (1,207). ***Average award:*** Freshmen: $22,473; Undergraduates: $20,455. ***Scholarships, grants, and awards:*** Federal Pell, FSEOG, state, private, college/university gift aid from institutional funds.

GIFT AID (NON-NEED-BASED) ***Total amount:*** $4,036,823 (91% institutional, 9% external sources). ***Receiving aid:*** Freshmen: 9% (20). Undergraduates: 7% (119). ***Average award:*** Freshmen: $19,062. Undergraduates: $15,892. ***Scholarships, grants, and awards by category:*** *Academic interests/achievement:* general academic interests/achievements. *Special achievements/activities:* general special achievements/activities. *Special characteristics:* children and siblings of alumni, children of faculty/staff, siblings of current students, veterans.

LOANS ***Student loans:*** $20,271,745 (76% need-based, 24% non-need-based). 88% of past graduating class borrowed through all loan programs. *Average indebtedness per student:* $35,827. ***Average need-based loan:*** Freshmen: $3063. Undergraduates: $4282. ***Parent loans:*** $3,683,155 (52% need-based, 48% non-need-based). ***Programs:*** Federal Direct (Subsidized and Unsubsidized Stafford, PLUS), Federal Nursing, private student loans.

WORK-STUDY ***Federal work-study:*** Total amount: $1,072,524; jobs available. ***State or other work-study/employment:*** Part-time jobs available.

APPLYING FOR FINANCIAL AID ***Required financial aid form:*** FAFSA. ***Financial aid deadline:*** 5/1 (priority: 1/15). ***Notification date:*** Continuous beginning 11/15. Students must reply by 5/1 or within 2 weeks of notification.

CONTACT Mrs. Elizabeth R. Howard, Director of Student Financial Aid, Gwynedd Mercy University, PO Box 901, Gwynedd Valley, PA 19437-0901, 215-646-7300 Ext. 483 or toll-free 800-342-5462. *Fax:* 215-641-5556. *E-mail:* howard.e@gmercyu.edu. *Website:* http://www.gmercyu.edu/.

HALLMARK UNIVERSITY

San Antonio, TX

CONTACT Financial Aid Office, Hallmark University, 10401 IH 10 West, San Antonio, TX 78230, 210-690-9000 or toll-free 800-880-6600. *Website:* http://www.hallmarkuniversity.edu/.

HAMILTON COLLEGE

Clinton, NY

Tuition & fees: $56,530 | **Average undergraduate aid package: $51,770**

ABOUT THE INSTITUTION Independent, coed. ***Awards:*** bachelor's degrees. 42 undergraduate majors. ***Total enrollment:*** 1,915. Undergraduates: 1,915. Freshmen: 481. Both federal and institutional methodology are used as a basis for awarding need-based institutional aid.

UNDERGRADUATE EXPENSES for 2019–2020 ***Application fee:*** $60. ***Comprehensive fee:*** $70,890 includes full-time tuition ($55,970), mandatory fees ($560), and room and board ($14,360). ***College room only:*** $7850. ***Part-time tuition:*** $6996 per course.

FRESHMAN FINANCIAL AID (Fall 2019, est.) 280 applied for aid; of those 92% were deemed to have need. 100% of freshmen with need received aid; of those 100% had need fully met. ***Average percent of need met:*** 100% (excluding resources awarded to replace EFC). ***Average financial aid package:*** $54,168 (excluding resources awarded to replace EFC).

UNDERGRADUATE FINANCIAL AID (Fall 2019, est.) 1,024 applied for aid; of those 97% were deemed to have need. 100% of undergraduates with need received aid; of those 100% had need fully met. ***Average percent of need met:*** 100% (excluding resources awarded to replace EFC). ***Average financial aid package:*** $51,770 (excluding resources awarded to replace EFC).

GIFT AID (NEED-BASED) ***Total amount:*** $46,646,974 (4% federal, 1% state, 93% institutional, 2% external sources). ***Receiving aid:*** Freshmen: 55% (258); all full-time undergraduates: 52% (989). ***Average award:*** Freshmen: $50,238; Undergraduates: $47,345. ***Scholarships, grants, and awards:*** Federal Pell, FSEOG, state, private, college/university gift aid from institutional funds.

GIFT AID (NON-NEED-BASED) ***Total amount:*** $614,444 (5% state, 22% institutional, 73% external sources). ***ROTC:*** Army cooperative, Air Force cooperative.

LOANS ***Student loans:*** $3,136,470 (99% need-based, 1% non-need-based). 44% of past graduating class borrowed through all loan programs. *Average indebtedness per student:* $17,292. ***Average need-based loan:*** Freshmen: $3300. Undergraduates: $4362. ***Programs:*** Federal Direct (Subsidized and Unsubsidized Stafford, PLUS), state, college/university.

WORK-STUDY ***Federal work-study:*** Total amount: $1,185,240; jobs available. ***State or other work-study/employment:*** Total amount: $85,280 (100% need-based). Part-time jobs available.

APPLYING FOR FINANCIAL AID ***Required financial aid forms:*** FAFSA, institution's own form, CSS Financial Aid PROFILE, noncustodial (divorced/separated) parent's statement, business/farm supplement. ***Financial aid deadline:*** 1/15 (priority: 1/15). ***Notification date:*** 4/1. Students must reply by 5/1.

CONTACT Financial Aid Office, Hamilton College, 198 College Hill Road, Clinton, NY 13323-1296, 315-859-4011 or toll-free 800-843-2655. *Website:* http://www.hamilton.edu/.

HAMILTON TECHNICAL COLLEGE

Davenport, IA

CONTACT Ms. Lisa Boyd, Executive Vice President/Director of Financial Aid, Hamilton Technical College, 1011 East 53rd Street, Davenport, IA 52807-2653, 563-386-3570 Ext. 33 or toll-free 866-966-4825. *Fax:* 563-386-6756. *Website:* http://www.hamiltontechcollege.edu/.

HAMLINE UNIVERSITY

St. Paul, MN

Tuition & fees: $44,230 | **Average undergraduate aid package: $31,667**

ABOUT THE INSTITUTION Independent United Methodist Church, coed. ***Awards:*** certificates, bachelor's, master's, and doctoral degrees. 51 undergraduate majors. ***Total enrollment:*** 3,404. Undergraduates: 2,088. Freshmen: 547. Federal methodology is used as a basis for awarding need-based institutional aid.

UNDERGRADUATE EXPENSES for 2020–2021 ***Comprehensive fee:*** $55,040 includes full-time tuition ($43,154), mandatory fees ($1076), and room and board ($10,810). ***College room only:*** $5150. Room and board charges vary according to housing facility. ***Part-time tuition:*** $1349 per credit hour. ***Part-time fees:*** $827 per year. Part-time tuition and fees vary according to course load.

FRESHMAN FINANCIAL AID (Fall 2018) 518 applied for aid; of those 94% were deemed to have need. 100% of freshmen with need received aid; of those 20% had need fully met. ***Average percent of need met:*** 83% (excluding resources awarded to replace EFC). ***Average financial aid package:*** $33,954 (excluding resources awarded to replace EFC). 9% of all full-time freshmen had no need and received non-need-based gift aid.

UNDERGRADUATE FINANCIAL AID (Fall 2018) 1,845 applied for aid; of those 93% were deemed to have need. 100% of undergraduates with need received aid; of those 17% had need fully met. ***Average percent of need met:*** 79% (excluding resources awarded to replace EFC). ***Average financial aid package:*** $31,667 (excluding resources awarded to replace EFC). 14% of all full-time undergraduates had no need and received non-need-based gift aid.

GIFT AID (NEED-BASED) ***Total amount:*** $44,218,538 (9% federal, 12% state, 77% institutional, 2% external sources). ***Receiving aid:*** Freshmen: 90% (486); all full-time undergraduates: 85% (1,714). ***Average award:*** Freshmen: $27,978; Undergraduates: $25,922. ***Scholarships, grants, and awards:*** Federal Pell, FSEOG, state, private, college/university gift aid from institutional funds, Academic Competitiveness Grants, National SMART Grants, TEACH Grants, United Methodist Scholarships.

GIFT AID (NON-NEED-BASED) ***Total amount:*** $7,397,695 (98% institutional, 2% external sources). ***Receiving aid:*** Freshmen: 13% (70). Undergraduates: 10% (194). ***Average award:*** Freshmen: $21,827. Undergraduates: $18,781. ***Scholarships, grants, and awards by category:*** *Academic interests/achievement:* biological sciences, business, engineering/technologies, English, general academic interests/achievements, home economics, mathematics, physical sciences. *Creative arts/performance:* applied art and design, art/fine arts, creative writing, general creative arts/performance, journalism/publications, music, theater/drama. *Special achievements/activities:* community service, general special achievements/activities, leadership, memberships. *Special characteristics:* children and siblings of alumni, children of faculty/staff, children of union members/company employees, first-generation college students, general special characteristics, international students, local/state students, members of minority groups, out-of-state students, previous college experience, relatives of clergy, religious affiliation, siblings of current students, veterans. ***Tuition waivers:*** Full or partial for employees or children of employees. ***ROTC:*** Army cooperative, Air Force cooperative.

LOANS ***Student loans:*** $14,917,349 (70% need-based, 30% non-need-based). 81% of past graduating class borrowed through all loan programs. *Average indebtedness per student:* $36,676. ***Average need-based loan:*** Freshmen: $3329. Undergraduates: $4344. ***Parent loans:*** $5,157,762 (46% need-based, 54% non-need-based). ***Programs:*** Federal Direct (Subsidized and Unsubsidized Stafford, PLUS), state, Alternative loans, United Methodist Student loans.

WORK-STUDY ***Federal work-study:*** Total amount: $595,609; jobs available. ***State or other work-study/employment:*** Total amount: $2,360,005 (67% need-based, 33% non-need-based). Part-time jobs available.

APPLYING FOR FINANCIAL AID ***Required financial aid form:*** FAFSA. ***Financial aid deadline (priority):*** 2/1. ***Notification date:*** Continuous beginning 1/1. Students must reply by 5/1 or within 2 weeks of notification.

CONTACT Ms. Lynette Wahl, Office of Financial Aid, Hamline University, 1536 Hewitt Avenue, MS C1915, St. Paul, MN 55104, 651-523-3000 or toll-free 800-753-9753. *Fax:* 651-523-2585. *E-mail:* finaid@hamline.edu.
Website: http://www.hamline.edu/.

HAMPDEN-SYDNEY COLLEGE

Hampden-Sydney, VA

Tuition & fees: $48,110	Average undergraduate aid package: $34,703

ABOUT THE INSTITUTION Independent Presbyterian Church (U.S.A.), men only. ***Awards:*** bachelor's degrees. 26 undergraduate majors. ***Total enrollment:*** 993. Undergraduates: 993. Freshmen: 228. Federal methodology is used as a basis for awarding need-based institutional aid.

UNDERGRADUATE EXPENSES for 2020–2021 ***Application fee:*** $30. ***Comprehensive fee:*** $61,986 includes full-time tuition ($45,690), mandatory fees ($2420), and room and board ($13,876). Room and board charges vary according to board plan. ***Part-time tuition:*** $1430 per credit hour.

FRESHMAN FINANCIAL AID (Fall 2019, est.) 204 applied for aid; of those 82% were deemed to have need. 100% of freshmen with need received aid; of those 22% had need fully met. ***Average percent of need met:*** 76% (excluding resources awarded to replace EFC). ***Average financial aid package:*** $34,796 (excluding resources awarded to replace EFC). 26% of all full-time freshmen had no need and received non-need-based gift aid.

UNDERGRADUATE FINANCIAL AID (Fall 2019, est.) 770 applied for aid; of those 86% were deemed to have need. 100% of undergraduates with need received aid; of those 26% had need fully met. ***Average percent of need met:*** 80% (excluding resources awarded to replace EFC). ***Average financial aid package:*** $34,703 (excluding resources awarded to replace EFC). 32% of all full-time undergraduates had no need and received non-need-based gift aid.

GIFT AID (NEED-BASED) ***Receiving aid:*** Freshmen: 73% (167); all full-time undergraduates: 67% (660). ***Average award:*** Freshmen: $32,315; Undergraduates: $31,288. ***Scholarships, grants, and awards:*** Federal Pell, FSEOG, state, private, college/university gift aid from institutional funds.

GIFT AID (NON-NEED-BASED) ***Receiving aid:*** Freshmen: 14% (32). Undergraduates: 14% (139). ***Average award:*** Freshmen: $22,764. Undergraduates: $18,814. ***Scholarships, grants, and awards by category:*** *Academic interests/achievement:* 836 awards ($12,163,136 total): business, general academic interests/achievements. *Special achievements/activities:* 359 awards ($1,804,987 total): general special achievements/activities, leadership. *Special characteristics:* 320 awards ($1,990,887 total): children of faculty/staff, international students, members of minority groups, out-of-state students, veterans' children. ***ROTC:*** Army cooperative.

LOANS ***Student loans:*** 63% of past graduating class borrowed through all loan programs. *Average indebtedness per student:* $41,316. ***Average need-based loan:*** Freshmen: $2841. Undergraduates: $4014. ***Programs:*** Federal Direct (Subsidized and Unsubsidized Stafford, PLUS), college/university.

WORK-STUDY ***Federal work-study:*** 140 jobs averaging $1404.

APPLYING FOR FINANCIAL AID ***Required financial aid forms:*** FAFSA, state aid form. ***Notification date:*** Students must reply within 2 weeks of notification.

CONTACT Ms. Zita Marie Barree, Director of Financial Aid, Hampden-Sydney College, PO Box 726, Hampden-Sydney, VA 23943-0726, 434-223-6119 or toll-free 800-755-0733. *Fax:* 434-223-6075. *E-mail:* hsfinaid@hsc.edu.
Website: http://www.hsc.edu/.

HAMPSHIRE COLLEGE

Amherst, MA

Tuition & fees: $52,068	Average undergraduate aid package: $41,778

ABOUT THE INSTITUTION Independent, coed. ***Awards:*** bachelor's degrees. 57 undergraduate majors. ***Total enrollment:*** 745. Undergraduates: 745. Freshmen: 19. Both federal and institutional methodology are used as a basis for awarding need-based institutional aid.

UNDERGRADUATE EXPENSES for 2020–2021 ***Comprehensive fee:*** $66,188 includes full-time tuition ($50,030), mandatory fees ($2038), and room and board ($14,120). ***College room only:*** $8520.

FRESHMAN FINANCIAL AID (Fall 2019, est.) 10 applied for aid; of those 90% were deemed to have need. 100% of freshmen with need received aid; of those 11% had need fully met. ***Average percent of need met:*** 84% (excluding resources awarded to replace EFC). ***Average financial aid package:*** $45,005 (excluding resources awarded to replace EFC). 29% of all full-time freshmen had no need and received non-need-based gift aid.

UNDERGRADUATE FINANCIAL AID (Fall 2019, est.) 577 applied for aid; of those 90% were deemed to have need. 100% of undergraduates with need received aid; of those 7% had need fully met. ***Average percent of need met:*** 82% (excluding resources awarded to replace EFC). ***Average financial aid package:*** $41,778 (excluding resources awarded to replace EFC). 26% of all full-time undergraduates had no need and received non-need-based gift aid.

GIFT AID (NEED-BASED) ***Total amount:*** $18,706,895 (9% federal, 1% state, 87% institutional, 3% external sources). ***Receiving aid:*** Freshmen: 64% (9); all full-time undergraduates: 70% (519). ***Average award:*** Freshmen: $39,576; Undergrad-

uates: $36,044. ***Scholarships, grants, and awards:*** Federal Pell, FSEOG, state, private, college/university gift aid from institutional funds.

GIFT AID (NON-NEED-BASED) ***Total amount:*** $3,244,884 (1% federal, 82% institutional, 17% external sources). ***Receiving aid:*** Undergraduates: 3% (26). ***Average award:*** Freshmen: $19,000. Undergraduates: $12,995. ***Scholarships, grants, and awards by category:*** *Academic interests/achievement:* biological sciences, English, general academic interests/achievements, humanities, international studies, mathematics, physical sciences, social sciences. *Creative arts/performance:* creative writing. *Special achievements/activities:* community service, leadership. *Special characteristics:* children of faculty/staff. ***ROTC:*** Army cooperative.

LOANS ***Student loans:*** $4,119,869 (81% need-based, 19% non-need-based). 70% of past graduating class borrowed through all loan programs. *Average indebtedness per student:* $29,499. ***Average need-based loan:*** Freshmen: $3197. Undergraduates: $4114. ***Parent loans:*** $1,575,307 (40% need-based, 60% non-need-based). ***Programs:*** Federal Direct (Subsidized and Unsubsidized Stafford, PLUS).

WORK-STUDY ***Federal work-study:*** Total amount: $959,196; jobs available. ***State or other work-study/employment:*** Total amount: $361,864 (14% need-based, 86% non-need-based). Part-time jobs available.

APPLYING FOR FINANCIAL AID ***Required financial aid forms:*** FAFSA, CSS Financial Aid PROFILE, noncustodial (divorced/separated) parent's statement. ***Financial aid deadline:*** 1/15 (priority: 1/15). ***Notification date:*** 4/1. Students must reply by 5/1.

CONTACT Ms. Jennifer Garratt Lawton, Director of Financial Aid, Hampshire College, 893 West Street, Amherst, MA 01002, 413-559-5484 or toll-free 877-937-4267. *Fax:* 413-559-5585. *E-mail:* financialaid@hampshire.edu.
Website: http://www.hampshire.edu/.

HAMPTON UNIVERSITY

Hampton, VA

Tuition & fees: $29,412	Average undergraduate aid package: $5952

ABOUT THE INSTITUTION Independent, coed. ***Awards:*** certificates, associate, bachelor's, master's, and doctoral degrees. 73 undergraduate majors. ***Total enrollment:*** 4,619. Undergraduates: 3,485. Freshmen: 704. Federal methodology is used as a basis for awarding need-based institutional aid.

UNDERGRADUATE EXPENSES for 2020–2021 ***Application fee:*** $35. ***Comprehensive fee:*** $42,398 includes full-time tuition ($26,198), mandatory fees ($3214), and room and board ($12,986). ***College room only:*** $6754. Full-time tuition and fees vary according to course load, degree level, location, program, and reciprocity agreements. Room and board charges vary according to board plan, housing facility, and location. ***Part-time fees:*** $665 per credit hour. Part-time tuition and fees vary according to class time, course load, location, and reciprocity agreements.

FRESHMAN FINANCIAL AID (Fall 2018) 692 applied for aid; of those 82% were deemed to have need. 97% of freshmen with need received aid; of those 39% had need fully met. ***Average percent of need met:*** 39% (excluding resources awarded to replace EFC). ***Average financial aid package:*** $6436 (excluding resources awarded to replace EFC). 7% of all full-time freshmen had no need and received non-need-based gift aid.

UNDERGRADUATE FINANCIAL AID (Fall 2018) 2,356 applied for aid; of those 79% were deemed to have need. 96% of undergraduates with need received aid; of those 43% had need fully met. ***Average percent of need met:*** 43% (excluding resources awarded to replace EFC). ***Average financial aid package:*** $5952 (excluding resources awarded to replace EFC). 2% of all full-time undergraduates had no need and received non-need-based gift aid.

GIFT AID (NEED-BASED) ***Total amount:*** $12,787,207 (60% federal, 10% state, 5% institutional, 25% external sources). ***Receiving aid:*** Freshmen: 69% (547); all full-time undergraduates: 54% (1,760). ***Average award:*** Freshmen: $7336; Undergraduates: $7115. ***Scholarships, grants, and awards:*** Federal Pell, FSEOG, state, private, college/university gift aid from institutional funds, Federal Nursing, Nurse Faculty Loan Program.

GIFT AID (NON-NEED-BASED) ***Total amount:*** $20,170,663 (4% federal, 4% state, 90% institutional, 2% external sources). ***Receiving aid:*** Freshmen: 52% (413). Undergraduates: 34% (1,094). ***Average award:*** Freshmen: $7018. Undergraduates: $6932. ***Scholarships, grants, and awards by category:*** *Academic interests/achievement:* 111 awards ($1,518,827 total): architecture, biological sciences, business, communication, computer science, education, engineering/technologies, general academic interests/achievements, home economics, physical sciences. *Creative arts/performance:* 6 awards ($22,000 total): music. *Special achievements/activities:* 13 awards ($31,250 total): leadership. *Special characteristics:* 613 awards ($2,730,622 total): adult students, children of faculty/staff, international students, members of minority groups, veterans. ***Tuition waivers:*** Full or partial for employees or children of employees. ***ROTC:*** Army, Naval.

LOANS ***Student loans:*** $19,722,024 (92% need-based, 8% non-need-based). 84% of past graduating class borrowed through all loan programs. *Average indebtedness per student:* $33,680. ***Average need-based loan:*** Freshmen: $5588. Undergraduates: $5885. ***Parent loans:*** $37,861,944 (89% need-based, 11% non-need-based). ***Programs:*** Federal Direct (Subsidized and Unsubsidized Stafford, PLUS), Federal Nursing, Private education (credit based).

WORK-STUDY ***Federal work-study:*** Total amount: $324,801; 215 jobs averaging $1376. ***State or other work-study/employment:*** Total amount: $4750 (100% need-based). Part-time jobs available.

ATHLETIC AWARDS Total amount: $6,672,553 (100% non-need-based).

APPLYING FOR FINANCIAL AID ***Required financial aid forms:*** FAFSA, Virginia Domiciled Residents - Virginia Tuition Assistance Grant. ***Financial aid deadline:*** 4/15 (priority: 2/15). ***Notification date:*** Continuous beginning 2/16. Students must reply within 2 weeks of notification.

CONTACT Mr. Martin Miles, Director of Financial Aid, Hampton University, Whipple Barn, 2nd Floor, Hampton, VA 23668, 757-727-5332 or toll-free 800-624-3328. *Fax:* 757-728-6567. *E-mail:* martin.miles@hamptonu.edu.
Website: http://www.hamptonu.edu/.

HANNIBAL-LAGRANGE UNIVERSITY

Hannibal, MO

CONTACT Brice Baumgardner, Director of Financial Aid, Hannibal-LaGrange University, 2800 Palmyra Road, Hannibal, MO 63401-1940, 573-629-3279 Ext. 3279 or toll-free 800-HLG-1119. *Fax:* 573-248-0954. *E-mail:* bbaumgardner@hlg.edu.
Website: http://www.hlg.edu/.

HANOVER COLLEGE

Hanover, IN

Tuition & fees: $39,650	Average undergraduate aid package: $32,942

ABOUT THE INSTITUTION Independent Presbyterian, coed. ***Awards:*** bachelor's degrees. 32 undergraduate majors. ***Total enrollment:*** 1,070. Undergraduates: 1,070. Freshmen: 290. Federal methodology is used as a basis for awarding need-based institutional aid.

UNDERGRADUATE EXPENSES for 2020–2021 ***One-time required fee:*** $350. ***Comprehensive fee:*** $51,950 includes full-time tuition ($38,880), mandatory fees ($770), and room and board ($12,300). ***College room only:*** $6125. ***Part-time tuition:*** $1080 per credit hour.

FRESHMAN FINANCIAL AID (Fall 2018) 327 applied for aid; of those 90% were deemed to have need. 100% of freshmen with need received aid; of those 32% had need fully met. ***Average percent of need met:*** 82% (excluding resources awarded to replace EFC). ***Average financial aid package:*** $32,647 (excluding resources awarded to replace EFC). 17% of all full-time freshmen had no need and received non-need-based gift aid.

UNDERGRADUATE FINANCIAL AID (Fall 2018) 943 applied for aid; of those 90% were deemed to have need. 100% of undergraduates with need received aid; of those 30% had need fully met. ***Average percent of need met:*** 83% (excluding resources awarded to replace EFC). ***Average financial aid package:*** $32,942 (excluding resources awarded to replace EFC). 22% of all full-time undergraduates had no need and received non-need-based gift aid.

GIFT AID (NEED-BASED) ***Receiving aid:*** Freshmen: 82% (293); all full-time undergraduates: 77% (852). ***Average award:*** Freshmen: $29,154; Undergraduates: $28,617. ***Scholarships, grants, and awards:*** Federal Pell, FSEOG, state, private, college/university gift aid from institutional funds.

GIFT AID (NON-NEED-BASED) ***Receiving aid:*** Freshmen: 17% (60). Undergraduates: 14% (153). ***Average award:*** Freshmen: $24,763. Undergraduates:

$23,696. ***Scholarships, grants, and awards by category:*** *Academic interests/achievement:* general academic interests/achievements. *Special characteristics:* children and siblings of alumni, children of faculty/staff, international students, members of minority groups, out-of-state students, religious affiliation, siblings of current students. ***Tuition waivers:*** Full or partial for employees or children of employees, senior citizens.

LOANS ***Student loans:*** 71% of past graduating class borrowed through all loan programs. *Average indebtedness per student:* $29,190. ***Average need-based loan:*** Freshmen: $3337. Undergraduates: $4270. ***Programs:*** Federal Direct (Subsidized and Unsubsidized Stafford, PLUS), college/university.

WORK-STUDY ***Federal work-study:*** 378 jobs averaging $1914.

APPLYING FOR FINANCIAL AID ***Required financial aid form:*** FAFSA. ***Financial aid deadline:*** Continuous. ***Notification date:*** Continuous.

CONTACT Mr. Richard A. Nash, Director of Financial Aid, Hanover College, 517 Ball Drive, Hanover, IN 47243-0108, 800-213-2178 Ext. 7029 or toll-free 800-213-2178. *Fax:* 812-866-7284. *E-mail:* finaid@hanover.edu.
Website: http://www.hanover.edu/.

HARDING UNIVERSITY

Searcy, AR

ABOUT THE INSTITUTION Independent Church of Christ, coed. ***Awards:*** certificates, bachelor's, master's, and doctoral degrees. 85 undergraduate majors. ***Total enrollment:*** 5,121. Undergraduates: 3,974. Freshmen: 857.

GIFT AID (NEED-BASED) ***Scholarships, grants, and awards:*** Federal Pell, FSEOG, state, private, college/university gift aid from institutional funds.

GIFT AID (NON-NEED-BASED) ***Scholarships, grants, and awards by category:*** *Academic interests/achievement:* communication, computer science, engineering/technologies, English, general academic interests/achievements, home economics, religion/biblical studies. *Creative arts/performance:* applied art and design, cinema/film/broadcasting, debating, general creative arts/performance, journalism/publications, music. *Special achievements/activities:* cheerleading/drum major, general special achievements/activities, leadership, religious involvement. *Special characteristics:* children of faculty/staff, children with a deceased or disabled parent, general special characteristics, international students, relatives of clergy, siblings of current students.

LOANS ***Programs:*** Federal Direct (Subsidized and Unsubsidized Stafford, PLUS), Perkins, Federal Nursing, state, college/university.

CONTACT Dr. Jonathan C. Roberts, Director of Student Financial Services, Harding University, PO Box 12282, Searcy, AR 72149-2282, 501-279-4257 or toll-free 800-477-4407. *Fax:* 501-279-4129. *E-mail:* jroberts@harding.edu.
Website: http://www.harding.edu/.

HARDIN-SIMMONS UNIVERSITY

Abilene, TX

Tuition & fees: $31,366	Average undergraduate aid package: $31,417

ABOUT THE INSTITUTION Independent Baptist, coed. ***Awards:*** certificates, bachelor's, master's, and doctoral degrees. 49 undergraduate majors. ***Total enrollment:*** 2,324. Undergraduates: 1,742. Freshmen: 479. Federal methodology is used as a basis for awarding need-based institutional aid.

UNDERGRADUATE EXPENSES for 2020–2021 ***Comprehensive fee:*** $41,106 includes full-time tuition ($29,526), mandatory fees ($1840), and room and board ($9740). ***College room only:*** $4840. Room and board charges vary according to board plan and housing facility. ***Part-time tuition:*** $935 per credit hour. ***Part-time fees:*** $500 per term. Part-time tuition and fees vary according to course load.

FRESHMAN FINANCIAL AID (Fall 2019, est.) 452 applied for aid; of those 90% were deemed to have need. 100% of freshmen with need received aid; of those 30% had need fully met. ***Average percent of need met:*** 83% (excluding resources awarded to replace EFC). ***Average financial aid package:*** $32,163 (excluding resources awarded to replace EFC). 15% of all full-time freshmen had no need and received non-need-based gift aid.

UNDERGRADUATE FINANCIAL AID (Fall 2019, est.) 1,380 applied for aid; of those 91% were deemed to have need. 100% of undergraduates with need received aid; of those 25% had need fully met. ***Average percent of need met:*** 79% (excluding resources awarded to replace EFC). ***Average financial aid package:*** $31,417 (excluding resources awarded to replace EFC). 22% of all full-time undergraduates had no need and received non-need-based gift aid.

GIFT AID (NEED-BASED) ***Total amount:*** $7,049,853 (46% federal, 28% state, 26% institutional). ***Receiving aid:*** Freshmen: 67% (319); all full-time undergraduates: 60% (966). ***Average award:*** Freshmen: $9422; Undergraduates: $7133. ***Scholarships, grants, and awards:*** Federal Pell, FSEOG, state, private, college/university gift aid from institutional funds.

GIFT AID (NON-NEED-BASED) ***Total amount:*** $24,745,474 (96% institutional, 4% external sources). ***Receiving aid:*** Freshmen: 85% (405). Undergraduates: 76% (1,224). ***Average award:*** Freshmen: $20,940. Undergraduates: $20,460. ***Scholarships, grants, and awards by category:*** *Academic interests/achievement:* biological sciences, business, communication, computer science, education, English, foreign languages, general academic interests/achievements, home economics, humanities, mathematics, physical sciences, premedicine, religion/biblical studies, social sciences. *Creative arts/performance:* applied art and design, art/fine arts, creative writing, journalism/publications, music, performing arts, theater/drama. *Special achievements/activities:* general special achievements/activities. *Special characteristics:* children and siblings of alumni, children of educators, children of faculty/staff, ethnic background, general special characteristics, handicapped students, out-of-state students, public servants, relatives of clergy, religious affiliation, siblings of current students, veterans. ***Tuition waivers:*** Full or partial for employees or children of employees.

LOANS ***Student loans:*** $12,357,046 (37% need-based, 63% non-need-based). 60% of past graduating class borrowed through all loan programs. *Average indebtedness per student:* $36,707. ***Average need-based loan:*** Freshmen: $3170. Undergraduates: $4046. ***Parent loans:*** $3,559,778 (100% non-need-based). ***Programs:*** Federal Direct (Subsidized and Unsubsidized Stafford, PLUS), Federal Nursing, state, college/university.

WORK-STUDY ***Federal work-study:*** Total amount: $173,339; jobs available. ***State or other work-study/employment:*** Total amount: $1,553,934 (1% need-based, 99% non-need-based). Part-time jobs available.

APPLYING FOR FINANCIAL AID ***Required financial aid form:*** FAFSA. ***Notification date:*** Continuous beginning 12/1.

CONTACT Mrs. Landri Ognowski, Director of Financial Aid, Hardin-Simmons University, Box 16050, Abilene, TX 79698, 325-670-1010 or toll-free 877-464-7889. *Fax:* 325-670-5822. *E-mail:* landri.ognowski@hsutx.edu.
Website: http://www.hsutx.edu/.

HARRISBURG UNIVERSITY OF SCIENCE AND TECHNOLOGY

Harrisburg, PA

ABOUT THE INSTITUTION Independent, coed. ***Awards:*** bachelor's, master's, and doctoral degrees. 8 undergraduate majors.

GIFT AID (NEED-BASED) ***Scholarships, grants, and awards:*** Federal Pell, FSEOG, state, private, college/university gift aid from institutional funds.

GIFT AID (NON-NEED-BASED) ***Scholarships, grants, and awards by category:*** *Academic interests/achievement:* biological sciences, business, computer science, physical sciences.

LOANS ***Programs:*** Federal Direct (Subsidized and Unsubsidized Stafford, PLUS).

WORK-STUDY Federal work-study jobs available. ***State or other work-study/employment:*** Total amount: $5275 (100% need-based).

APPLYING FOR FINANCIAL AID ***Required financial aid form:*** FAFSA.

CONTACT Mr. Vince P. Frank, Director of Financial Aid Services, Harrisburg University of Science and Technology, 326 Market Street, Harrisburg, PA 17101-2208, 717-901-5115 or toll-free 866-HBG-UNIV. *Fax:* 717-901-3115. *E-mail:* vfrank@harrisburgu.edu.
Website: http://www.HarrisburgU.edu/.

HARRIS-STOWE STATE UNIVERSITY

St. Louis, MO

ABOUT THE INSTITUTION State-supported, coed. ***Awards:*** certificates and bachelor's degrees. 22 undergraduate majors. ***Total enrollment:*** 1,630. Undergraduates: 1,630. Freshmen: 381.

GIFT AID (NEED-BASED) ***Scholarships, grants, and awards:*** Federal Pell, FSEOG, state, private, college/university gift aid from institutional funds, United Negro College Fund.

GIFT AID (NON-NEED-BASED) ***Scholarships, grants, and awards by category:*** *Academic interests/achievement:* general academic interests/achievements. *Creative arts/performance:* music, theater/drama.

LOANS ***Programs:*** Federal Direct (Subsidized and Unsubsidized Stafford, PLUS).

CONTACT James Green, Director of Financial Aid, Harris-Stowe State University, 3026 Laclede Avenue, St. Louis, MO 63103-2136, 314-340-3502. *Fax:* 314-340-3503. *Website:* http://www.hssu.edu/.

HARTWICK COLLEGE

Oneonta, NY

ABOUT THE INSTITUTION Independent, coed. ***Awards:*** bachelor's degrees. 37 undergraduate majors. ***Total enrollment:*** 1,176. Undergraduates: 1,176. Freshmen: 407.

GIFT AID (NEED-BASED) ***Scholarships, grants, and awards:*** Federal Pell, FSEOG, state, private, college/university gift aid from institutional funds.

GIFT AID (NON-NEED-BASED) ***Scholarships, grants, and awards by category:*** *Academic interests/achievement:* general academic interests/achievements. *Creative arts/performance:* applied art and design, music. *Special characteristics:* children and siblings of alumni, children of faculty/staff, international students, siblings of current students, veterans.

LOANS ***Programs:*** Federal Direct (Subsidized and Unsubsidized Stafford, PLUS), Perkins, Federal Nursing, college/university, alternative loans.

WORK-STUDY ***Federal work-study:*** Total amount: $1,400,876; 746 jobs averaging $1869.

APPLYING FOR FINANCIAL AID ***Required financial aid form:*** FAFSA.

CONTACT Mrs. Melissa Allen, Director of Financial Aid, Hartwick College, One Hartwick Drive, Oneonta, NY 13820, 607-431-4130 or toll-free 888-HARTWICK. *Fax:* 607-431-4006. *E-mail:* finaid@hartwick.edu. *Website:* http://www.hartwick.edu/.

HARVARD UNIVERSITY

Cambridge, MA

ABOUT THE INSTITUTION Independent, coed. ***Awards:*** bachelor's, master's, and doctoral degrees. 47 undergraduate majors. ***Total enrollment:*** 11,453. Undergraduates: 6,755. Freshmen: 1,644.

GIFT AID (NEED-BASED) ***Scholarships, grants, and awards:*** Federal Pell, FSEOG, state, private, college/university gift aid from institutional funds.

LOANS ***Programs:*** Federal Direct (Subsidized and Unsubsidized Stafford, PLUS), state, college/university.

CONTACT Financial Aid Office, Harvard University, Cambridge, MA 02138, 617-495-1000. *Website:* http://www.harvard.edu/.

HARVEY MUDD COLLEGE

Claremont, CA

Tuition & fees: $58,660	Average undergraduate aid package: $47,348

ABOUT THE INSTITUTION Independent, coed. ***Awards:*** bachelor's degrees. 7 undergraduate majors. ***Total enrollment:*** 889. Undergraduates: 889. Freshmen: 234. Both federal and institutional methodology are used as a basis for awarding need-based institutional aid.

UNDERGRADUATE EXPENSES for 2019–2020 ***Application fee:*** $70. ***One-time required fee:*** $250. ***Comprehensive fee:*** $77,339 includes full-time tuition ($58,359), mandatory fees ($301), and room and board ($18,679). ***College room only:*** $10,234. Room and board charges vary according to board plan. ***Part-time tuition:*** $1824 per unit. Part-time tuition and fees vary according to course load.

FRESHMAN FINANCIAL AID (Fall 2018) 167 applied for aid; of those 76% were deemed to have need. 100% of freshmen with need received aid; of those 100% had need fully met. ***Average percent of need met:*** 100% (excluding resources awarded to replace EFC). ***Average financial aid package:*** $50,030 (excluding resources awarded to replace EFC). 17% of all full-time freshmen had no need and received non-need-based gift aid.

UNDERGRADUATE FINANCIAL AID (Fall 2018) 513 applied for aid; of those 84% were deemed to have need. 100% of undergraduates with need received aid; of those 100% had need fully met. ***Average percent of need met:*** 100% (excluding resources awarded to replace EFC). ***Average financial aid package:*** $47,348 (excluding resources awarded to replace EFC). 19% of all full-time undergraduates had no need and received non-need-based gift aid.

GIFT AID (NEED-BASED) ***Total amount:*** $19,355,498 (4% federal, 4% state, 89% institutional, 3% external sources). ***Receiving aid:*** Freshmen: 52% (123); all full-time undergraduates: 46% (416). ***Average award:*** Freshmen: $48,474; Undergraduates: $45,010. ***Scholarships, grants, and awards:*** Federal Pell, FSEOG, state, private, college/university gift aid from institutional funds.

GIFT AID (NON-NEED-BASED) ***Total amount:*** $3,036,884 (82% institutional, 18% external sources). ***Receiving aid:*** Freshmen: 20% (47). Undergraduates: 21% (187). ***Average award:*** Freshmen: $8164. Undergraduates: $14,735. ***Scholarships, grants, and awards by category:*** *Academic interests/achievement:* 274 awards ($4,170,262 total): general academic interests/achievements. *Special characteristics:* 4 awards ($200,000 total): international students. ***Tuition waivers:*** Full or partial for employees or children of employees. ***ROTC:*** Army cooperative, Air Force cooperative.

LOANS ***Student loans:*** $2,663,479 (82% need-based, 18% non-need-based). 47% of past graduating class borrowed through all loan programs. *Average indebtedness per student:* $29,139. ***Average need-based loan:*** Freshmen: $3066. Undergraduates: $4113. ***Parent loans:*** $1,660,213 (78% need-based, 22% non-need-based). ***Programs:*** Federal Direct (Subsidized and Unsubsidized Stafford, PLUS), college/university, Private Alternative Loans.

WORK-STUDY ***Federal work-study:*** Total amount: $136,575; 129 jobs averaging $1059. ***State or other work-study/employment:*** Total amount: $212,381 (64% need-based, 36% non-need-based). 24 part-time jobs averaging $8849.

APPLYING FOR FINANCIAL AID ***Required financial aid forms:*** FAFSA, CSS Financial Aid PROFILE, state aid form, noncustodial (divorced/separated) parent's statement, business/farm supplement. ***Financial aid deadline:*** 2/1 (priority: 2/1). ***Notification date:*** 4/1. Students must reply by 5/1.

CONTACT Mrs. Gilma Lopez, Director of Financial Aid, Harvey Mudd College, 301 Platt Boulevard, Claremont, CA 91711-5994, 909-621-8055. *Fax:* 909-607-4494. *E-mail:* financial_aid@hmc.edu. *Website:* http://www.hmc.edu/.

HASKELL INDIAN NATIONS UNIVERSITY

Lawrence, KS

CONTACT Reta Brewer, Director of Financial Aid, Haskell Indian Nations University, 155 Indian Avenue, Box 5027, Lawrence, KS 66046-4800, 785-749-8468. *Fax:* 785-832-6617. *Website:* http://www.haskell.edu/.

HASTINGS COLLEGE

Hastings, NE

CONTACT Mrs. Traci Noelle Boeve, Director of Student Financial Aid, Hastings College, 710 North Turner Avenue, Hastings, NE 68901, 402-461-7431 or toll-free 800-532-7642. *Fax:* 402-461-7714. *E-mail:* tboeve@hastings.edu. *Website:* http://www.hastings.edu/.

HAVERFORD COLLEGE
Haverford, PA

Tuition & fees: $56,698 **Average undergraduate aid package: $54,803**

ABOUT THE INSTITUTION Independent, coed. ***Awards:*** bachelor's degrees. 38 undergraduate majors. ***Total enrollment:*** 1,310. Undergraduates: 1,310. Freshmen: 357. Institutional methodology is used as a basis for awarding need-based institutional aid.

UNDERGRADUATE EXPENSES for 2019–2020 ***Application fee:*** $65. ***One-time required fee:*** $254. ***Comprehensive fee:*** $73,468 includes full-time tuition ($56,200), mandatory fees ($498), and room and board ($16,770). ***College room only:*** $9790.

FRESHMAN FINANCIAL AID (Fall 2019, est.) 196 applied for aid; of those 79% were deemed to have need. 100% of freshmen with need received aid; of those 100% had need fully met. ***Average percent of need met:*** 100% (excluding resources awarded to replace EFC). ***Average financial aid package:*** $53,527 (excluding resources awarded to replace EFC).

UNDERGRADUATE FINANCIAL AID (Fall 2019, est.) 653 applied for aid; of those 90% were deemed to have need. 100% of undergraduates with need received aid; of those 100% had need fully met. ***Average percent of need met:*** 100% (excluding resources awarded to replace EFC). ***Average financial aid package:*** $54,803 (excluding resources awarded to replace EFC).

GIFT AID (NEED-BASED) ***Total amount:*** $30,546,633 (4% federal, 95% institutional, 1% external sources). ***Receiving aid:*** Freshmen: 42% (154); all full-time undergraduates: 45% (588). ***Average award:*** Freshmen: $51,262; Undergraduates: $52,045. ***Scholarships, grants, and awards:*** Federal Pell, FSEOG, state, private, college/university gift aid from institutional funds.

GIFT AID (NON-NEED-BASED) ***Receiving aid:*** Freshmen: 8% (29). Undergraduates: 5% (70). ***Tuition waivers:*** Full or partial for employees or children of employees. ***ROTC:*** Air Force cooperative.

LOANS ***Student loans:*** $1,531,059 (33% need-based, 67% non-need-based). 27% of past graduating class borrowed through all loan programs. *Average indebtedness per student:* $11,500. ***Average need-based loan:*** Freshmen: $2830. Undergraduates: $3607. ***Parent loans:*** $965,730 (100% non-need-based). ***Programs:*** Federal Direct (Subsidized and Unsubsidized Stafford, PLUS), state, college/university.

WORK-STUDY ***Federal work-study:*** Total amount: $301,605; jobs available. ***State or other work-study/employment:*** Part-time jobs available.

APPLYING FOR FINANCIAL AID ***Required financial aid forms:*** FAFSA, CSS Financial Aid PROFILE, noncustodial (divorced/separated) parent's statement, business/farm supplement. ***Financial aid deadline (priority):*** 2/1. ***Notification date:*** 3/25. Students must reply by 5/1.

CONTACT Mr. Michael Colahan, Director of Financial Aid, Haverford College, 370 Lancaster Avenue, Haverford, PA 19041-1392, 610-896-1350. *Fax:* 610-896-1338. *E-mail:* finaid@haverford.edu.
Website: http://www.haverford.edu/.

HAWAI'I PACIFIC UNIVERSITY
Honolulu, HI

CONTACT James M. Oshiro, Executive Director of Financial Aid, Hawai'i Pacific University, 1164 Bishop Street, Suite 201, Honolulu, HI 96813-2785, 808-544-0253 or toll-free 866-225-5478. *Fax:* 808-544-0884. *E-mail:* financialaid@hpu.edu.
Website: http://www.hpu.edu/.

HEBREW THEOLOGICAL COLLEGE
Skokie, IL

CONTACT Ms. Rhoda Morris, Financial Aid Administrator , Hebrew Theological College, 7135 Carpenter Road, Skokie, IL 60077-3263, 847-982-2500. *Fax:* 847-674-6381.
Website: http://www.htc.edu/.

HEIDELBERG UNIVERSITY
Tiffin, OH

Tuition & fees: N/R **Average undergraduate aid package: $27,506**

ABOUT THE INSTITUTION Independent United Church of Christ, coed. ***Awards:*** bachelor's and master's degrees. 44 undergraduate majors. Federal methodology is used as a basis for awarding need-based institutional aid.

FRESHMAN FINANCIAL AID (Fall 2019, est.) 325 applied for aid; of those 92% were deemed to have need. 100% of freshmen with need received aid; of those 31% had need fully met. ***Average percent of need met:*** 85% (excluding resources awarded to replace EFC). ***Average financial aid package:*** $28,160 (excluding resources awarded to replace EFC). 8% of all full-time freshmen had no need and received non-need-based gift aid.

UNDERGRADUATE FINANCIAL AID (Fall 2019, est.) 984 applied for aid; of those 92% were deemed to have need. 100% of undergraduates with need received aid; of those 29% had need fully met. ***Average percent of need met:*** 84% (excluding resources awarded to replace EFC). ***Average financial aid package:*** $27,506 (excluding resources awarded to replace EFC). 7% of all full-time undergraduates had no need and received non-need-based gift aid.

GIFT AID (NEED-BASED) ***Receiving aid:*** Freshmen: 90% (299); all full-time undergraduates: 87% (909). ***Average award:*** Freshmen: $24,214; Undergraduates: $22,705. ***Scholarships, grants, and awards:*** Federal Pell, FSEOG, state, private, college/university gift aid from institutional funds.

GIFT AID (NON-NEED-BASED) ***Receiving aid:*** Freshmen: 86% (286). Undergraduates: 76% (790). ***Average award:*** Freshmen: $19,018. Undergraduates: $25,448. ***Scholarships, grants, and awards by category:*** *Academic interests/achievement:* general academic interests/achievements. *Creative arts/performance:* music, performing arts, theater/drama. *Special characteristics:* children and siblings of alumni, children of faculty/staff, out-of-state students, relatives of clergy, religious affiliation. ***ROTC:*** Army cooperative, Air Force cooperative.

LOANS ***Student loans:*** 82% of past graduating class borrowed through all loan programs. *Average indebtedness per student:* $40,089. ***Average need-based loan:*** Freshmen: $3500. Undergraduates: $4294. ***Programs:*** Federal Direct (Subsidized and Unsubsidized Stafford, PLUS).

WORK-STUDY ***Federal work-study:*** 650 jobs averaging $2000. ***State or other work-study/employment:*** 100 part-time jobs averaging $1000.

APPLYING FOR FINANCIAL AID ***Required financial aid form:*** FAFSA. ***Financial aid deadline:*** Continuous. ***Notification date:*** Continuous.

CONTACT Ms. Beth A. Kagy, Director of Financial Aid, Heidelberg University, 310 East Market Street, Tiffin, OH 44883-2462, 419-448-2293 or toll-free 800-434-3352. *Fax:* 419-448-2296.
Website: http://www.heidelberg.edu/.

HELLENIC AMERICAN UNIVERSITY
Nashua, NH

CONTACT Financial Aid Office, Hellenic American University, 505 Amherst Street, Nashua, NH 03063, 603-577-8700.
Website: http://www.hauniv.edu/.

HELLENIC COLLEGE
Brookline, MA

ABOUT THE INSTITUTION Independent Greek Orthodox, coed. ***Awards:*** bachelor's and master's degrees (also offers graduate degree programs through Holy Cross Greek Orthodox School of Theology). 6 undergraduate majors.

GIFT AID (NEED-BASED) ***Scholarships, grants, and awards:*** Federal Pell, FSEOG, state, private, college/university gift aid from institutional funds.

GIFT AID (NON-NEED-BASED) ***Scholarships, grants, and awards by category:*** *Academic interests/achievement:* religion/biblical studies. *Special achievements/activities:* religious involvement.

LOANS ***Programs:*** Federal Direct (Subsidized and Unsubsidized Stafford, PLUS), state.

WORK-STUDY *Federal work-study:* Total amount: $31,500; jobs available. ***State or other work-study/employment:*** Total amount: $51,200 (72% need-based, 28% non-need-based). Part-time jobs available.

APPLYING FOR FINANCIAL AID *Required financial aid forms:* FAFSA, institution's own form.

CONTACT Michael Kirchmaier, Director of Financial Aid, Hellenic College, 50 Goddard Avenue, Brookline, MA 02146-7496, 617-850-1239 or toll-free 866-424-2338. *Fax:* 617-850-1240. *E-mail:* mkirchmaier@hchc.edu.
Website: http://www.hchc.edu/.

HENDERSON STATE UNIVERSITY

Arkadelphia, AR

CONTACT Ms. Christina Jones, Director of Financial Aid, Henderson State University, 1100 Henderson Street, HSU Box 7812, Arkadelphia, AR 71999-0001, 870-230-5138 or toll-free 800-228-7333. *Fax:* 870-230-5481. *E-mail:* jonesc@hsu.edu.
Website: http://www.hsu.edu/.

HENDRIX COLLEGE

Conway, AR

Tuition & fees: N/R	Average undergraduate aid package: $42,816

ABOUT THE INSTITUTION Independent United Methodist, coed. ***Awards:*** bachelor's and master's degrees. 30 undergraduate majors. Federal methodology is used as a basis for awarding need-based institutional aid.

FRESHMAN FINANCIAL AID (Fall 2019, est.) 271 applied for aid; of those 83% were deemed to have need. 100% of freshmen with need received aid; of those 45% had need fully met. ***Average percent of need met:*** 93% (excluding resources awarded to replace EFC). ***Average financial aid package:*** $43,933 (excluding resources awarded to replace EFC). 21% of all full-time freshmen had no need and received non-need-based gift aid.

UNDERGRADUATE FINANCIAL AID (Fall 2019, est.) 1,007 applied for aid; of those 84% were deemed to have need. 100% of undergraduates with need received aid; of those 42% had need fully met. ***Average percent of need met:*** 90% (excluding resources awarded to replace EFC). ***Average financial aid package:*** $42,816 (excluding resources awarded to replace EFC). 23% of all full-time undergraduates had no need and received non-need-based gift aid.

GIFT AID (NEED-BASED) *Total amount:* $32,175,543 (6% federal, 5% state, 88% institutional, 1% external sources). ***Receiving aid:*** Freshmen: 79% (225); all full-time undergraduates: 77% (847). ***Average award:*** Freshmen: $41,133; Undergraduates: $39,294. ***Scholarships, grants, and awards:*** Federal Pell, FSEOG, state, private, college/university gift aid from institutional funds.

GIFT AID (NON-NEED-BASED) *Total amount:* $11,723,275 (12% state, 86% institutional, 2% external sources). ***Receiving aid:*** Freshmen: 28% (80). Undergraduates: 25% (272). ***Average award:*** Freshmen: $34,937. Undergraduates: $31,405. ***Scholarships, grants, and awards by category:*** *Academic interests/achievement:* general academic interests/achievements. *Creative arts/performance:* applied art and design, dance, music, theater/drama. *Special achievements/activities:* community service, general special achievements/activities, leadership, religious involvement. *Special characteristics:* children of faculty/staff, international students, previous college experience, relatives of clergy. ***ROTC:*** Army cooperative.

LOANS *Student loans:* $4,241,910 (60% need-based, 40% non-need-based). 53% of past graduating class borrowed through all loan programs. *Average indebtedness per student:* $28,849. ***Average need-based loan:*** Freshmen: $2559. Undergraduates: $3366. ***Parent loans:*** $1,754,272 (26% need-based, 74% non-need-based). ***Programs:*** Federal Direct (Subsidized and Unsubsidized Stafford, PLUS).

WORK-STUDY *Federal work-study:* Total amount: $1,008,639; jobs available. ***State or other work-study/employment:*** Total amount: $308,596 (23% need-based, 77% non-need-based). Part-time jobs available.

APPLYING FOR FINANCIAL AID *Required financial aid form:* FAFSA. ***Financial aid deadline (priority):*** 3/1. ***Notification date:*** Continuous beginning 12/15. Students must reply by 5/1.

CONTACT Ms. Kristina Burford, Associate Vice President for Enrollment and Director of Financial Aid, Hendrix College, 1600 Washington Avenue, Conway, AR 72032, 501-450-1368 or toll-free 800-277-9017. *Fax:* 501-450-3871. *E-mail:* burford@hendrix.edu.
Website: http://www.hendrix.edu/.

HERITAGE BIBLE COLLEGE

Dunn, NC

CONTACT Ms. Kayla Bullard, Director of Financial Aid, Heritage Bible College, PO Box 1628, Dunn, NC 28335, 910-892-3178 Ext. 232 or toll-free 800-297-6351. *Fax:* 910-891-1660. *E-mail:* ksutton@heritagebiblecollege.edu.
Website: http://www.heritagebiblecollege.edu/.

HERITAGE CHRISTIAN UNIVERSITY

Florence, AL

CONTACT Mechelle R. Thompson, Associate Director of Financial Aid, Heritage Christian University, PO Box HCU, Florence, AL 35630, 800-367-3565 Ext. 303 or toll-free 800-367-3565. *Fax:* 256-716-8021. *E-mail:* mthompson@hcu.edu.
Website: http://www.hcu.edu/.

HERITAGE UNIVERSITY

Toppenish, WA

CONTACT Mr. Norberto Espindola, Director of Enrollment Management Services, Heritage University, 3240 Fort Road, Toppenish, WA 98948-9599, 509-865-8500 or toll-free 888-272-6190. *Fax:* 509-865-8659. *E-mail:* financial_aid@heritage.edu.
Website: http://www.heritage.edu/.

HERZING UNIVERSITY

Birmingham, AL

CONTACT Financial Aid Office, Herzing University, 280 West Valley Avenue, Birmingham, AL 35209, 205-916-2800 or toll-free 800-596-0724.
Website: http://www.herzing.edu/birmingham/.

HERZING UNIVERSITY

Winter Park, FL

CONTACT Financial Aid Office, Herzing University, 1865 SR 436, Winter Park, FL 32792, 407-641-5227 or toll-free 800-596-0724.
Website: http://www.herzing.edu/orlando.

HERZING UNIVERSITY

Atlanta, GA

CONTACT Financial Aid Office, Herzing University, 3393 Peachtree Road, Suite 1003, Atlanta, GA 30326, 404-816-4533 or toll-free 800-596-0724.
Website: http://www.herzing.edu/atlanta/.

HERZING UNIVERSITY

Kenner, LA

CONTACT Financial Aid Office, Herzing University, 2500 Williams Boulevard, Kenner, LA 70062, 504-733-0074 or toll-free 800-596-0724.
Website: http://www.herzing.edu/new-orleans.

HERZING UNIVERSITY

Brookfield, WI

CONTACT Financial Aid Office, Herzing University, 555 South Executive Drive, Brookfield, WI 53005, 262-649-1710 or toll-free 800-596-0724.
Website: http://www.herzing.edu/brookfield.

HERZING UNIVERSITY

Kenosha, WI

CONTACT Financial Aid Office, Herzing University, 4006 Washington Road, Kenosha, WI 53144, 262-671-0675 or toll-free 800-596-0724.
Website: http://www.herzing.edu/kenosha.

HERZING UNIVERSITY

Madison, WI

CONTACT Financial Aid Office, Herzing University, 5218 East Terrace Drive, Madison, WI 53718, 608-249-6611 or toll-free 800-596-0724.
Website: http://www.herzing.edu/madison/.

HERZING UNIVERSITY ONLINE

Menomonee Falls, WI

CONTACT Financial Aid Office, Herzing University Online, W140N8917 Lilly Road, Menomonee Falls, WI 53051, 866-508-0748.
Website: http://www.herzingonline.edu/.

HIGH POINT UNIVERSITY

High Point, NC

Tuition & fees: $36,268	Average undergraduate aid package: $18,285

ABOUT THE INSTITUTION Independent United Methodist, coed. ***Awards:*** certificates, bachelor's, master's, and doctoral degrees. 56 undergraduate majors. ***Total enrollment:*** 5,330. Undergraduates: 4,590. Freshmen: 1,400. Both federal and institutional methodology are used as a basis for awarding need-based institutional aid.

UNDERGRADUATE EXPENSES for 2019–2020 ***Application fee:*** $50. ***Comprehensive fee:*** $50,970 includes full-time tuition ($31,768), mandatory fees ($4500), and room and board ($14,702). Full-time tuition and fees vary according to course load and reciprocity agreements. Room and board charges vary according to board plan and housing facility. ***Part-time tuition:*** $1026 per credit hour. ***Part-time fees:*** $4500 per term. Part-time tuition and fees vary according to course load and reciprocity agreements.

FRESHMAN FINANCIAL AID (Fall 2018) 994 applied for aid; of those 69% were deemed to have need. 100% of freshmen with need received aid; of those 15% had need fully met. ***Average percent of need met:*** 62% (excluding resources awarded to replace EFC). ***Average financial aid package:*** $19,915 (excluding resources awarded to replace EFC). 36% of all full-time freshmen had no need and received non-need-based gift aid.

UNDERGRADUATE FINANCIAL AID (Fall 2018) 2,506 applied for aid; of those 76% were deemed to have need. 100% of undergraduates with need received aid; of those 12% had need fully met. ***Average percent of need met:*** 55% (excluding resources awarded to replace EFC). ***Average financial aid package:*** $18,285 (excluding resources awarded to replace EFC). 34% of all full-time undergraduates had no need and received non-need-based gift aid.

GIFT AID (NEED-BASED) ***Receiving aid:*** Freshmen: 48% (683); all full-time undergraduates: 42% (1,877). ***Average award:*** Freshmen: $16,662; Undergraduates: $14,388. ***Scholarships, grants, and awards:*** Federal Pell, FSEOG, state, private, college/university gift aid from institutional funds.

GIFT AID (NON-NEED-BASED) ***Receiving aid:*** Freshmen: 43% (615). Undergraduates: 36% (1,607). ***Average award:*** Freshmen: $9559. Undergraduates: $8440. ***Scholarships, grants, and awards by category:*** *Academic interests/achievement:* biological sciences, business, communication, education, English, foreign languages, general academic interests/achievements, humanities, international studies, mathematics, physical sciences, premedicine, religion/biblical studies. *Creative arts/performance:* applied art and design, music, theater/drama. *Special achievements/activities:* general special achievements/activities, leadership, religious involvement. *Special characteristics:* children of faculty/staff, first-generation college students, relatives of clergy, veterans. ***Tuition waivers:*** Full or partial for employees or children of employees. ***ROTC:*** Army cooperative, Air Force cooperative.

LOANS ***Student loans:*** 47% of past graduating class borrowed through all loan programs. *Average indebtedness per student:* $34,079. ***Average need-based loan:*** Freshmen: $3304. Undergraduates: $4236. ***Programs:*** Federal Direct (Subsidized and Unsubsidized Stafford, PLUS), Perkins.

WORK-STUDY ***Federal work-study:*** 252 jobs averaging $1823. ***State or other work-study/employment:*** Part-time jobs available.

APPLYING FOR FINANCIAL AID ***Required financial aid forms:*** FAFSA, state aid form. ***Notification date:*** Continuous. Students must reply within 3 weeks of notification.

CONTACT Sandra Norris, Senior Associate Director, High Point University, One University Parkway, High Point, NC 27268, 336-841-9032 or toll-free 800-345-6993. *E-mail:* finplan@highpoint.edu.
Website: http://www.highpoint.edu/.

HILBERT COLLEGE

Hamburg, NY

CONTACT Laura Worley, Director of Financial Aid, Hilbert College, 5200 South Park Avenue, Hamburg, NY 14075-1597, 716-649-7900 Ext. 414 or toll-free 800-649-8003. *Fax:* 716-649-1152. *E-mail:* lworley@hilbert.edu.
Website: http://www.hilbert.edu/.

HILLSDALE COLLEGE

Hillsdale, MI

Tuition & fees: $29,482	Average undergraduate aid package: $20,665

ABOUT THE INSTITUTION Independent, coed. ***Awards:*** bachelor's, master's, and doctoral degrees. 38 undergraduate majors. ***Total enrollment:*** 1,526. Undergraduates: 1,468. Freshmen: 343. Both federal and institutional methodology are used as a basis for awarding need-based institutional aid.

UNDERGRADUATE EXPENSES for 2020–2021 ***Application fee:*** $35. ***One-time required fee:*** $300. ***Comprehensive fee:*** $41,392 includes full-time tuition ($28,170), mandatory fees ($1312), and room and board ($11,910). ***College room only:*** $5900. Full-time tuition and fees vary according to degree level. Room and board charges vary according to board plan and housing facility. ***Part-time tuition:*** $1120 per credit hour. ***Part-time fees:*** $1312 per year. Part-time tuition and fees vary according to degree level.

FRESHMAN FINANCIAL AID (Fall 2019, est.) 198 applied for aid; of those 91% were deemed to have need. 100% of freshmen with need received aid; of those 35% had need fully met. ***Average percent of need met:*** 67% (excluding resources awarded to replace EFC). ***Average financial aid package:*** $19,423 (excluding

resources awarded to replace EFC). 42% of all full-time freshmen had no need and received non-need-based gift aid.

UNDERGRADUATE FINANCIAL AID (Fall 2019, est.) 748 applied for aid; of those 97% were deemed to have need. 99% of undergraduates with need received aid; of those 41% had need fully met. ***Average percent of need met:*** 60% (excluding resources awarded to replace EFC). ***Average financial aid package:*** $20,665 (excluding resources awarded to replace EFC). 44% of all full-time undergraduates had no need and received non-need-based gift aid.

GIFT AID (NEED-BASED) ***Total amount:*** $3,418,184 (100% institutional). ***Receiving aid:*** Freshmen: 31% (107); all full-time undergraduates: 33% (475). ***Average award:*** Freshmen: $8388; Undergraduates: $8184. ***Scholarships, grants, and awards:*** private, college/university gift aid from institutional funds.

GIFT AID (NON-NEED-BASED) ***Total amount:*** $21,620,440 (98% institutional, 2% external sources). ***Receiving aid:*** Freshmen: 46% (156). Undergraduates: 42% (605). ***Average award:*** Freshmen: $17,928. Undergraduates: $19,427. ***Scholarships, grants, and awards by category:*** *Academic interests/achievement:* 1,179 awards ($19,511,983 total): biological sciences, business, communication, education, engineering/technologies, English, foreign languages, general academic interests/achievements, humanities, mathematics, physical sciences, premedicine, religion/biblical studies, social sciences. *Creative arts/performance:* 231 awards ($806,392 total): applied art and design, debating, journalism/publications, music, theater/drama. *Special achievements/activities:* 80 awards ($286,935 total): community service, general special achievements/activities, hobbies/interests, leadership. *Special characteristics:* 187 awards ($2,409,769 total): children and siblings of alumni, children of educators, children of faculty/staff, first-generation college students, international students, veterans, veterans' children. ***Tuition waivers:*** Full or partial for children of alumni, employees or children of employees.

LOANS ***Student loans:*** $4,432,923 (29% need-based, 71% non-need-based). 45% of past graduating class borrowed through all loan programs. *Average indebtedness per student:* $32,198. ***Average need-based loan:*** Freshmen: $5873. Undergraduates: $5778. ***Programs:*** college/university, private loans.

ATHLETIC AWARDS Total amount: $3,574,849 (100% non-need-based).

APPLYING FOR FINANCIAL AID ***Required financial aid form:*** institution's own form. ***Financial aid deadline (priority):*** 5/1. ***Notification date:*** Continuous beginning 12/1. Students must reply within 4 weeks of notification.

CONTACT Mr. Rich Moeggengberg, Director of Student Financial Aid, Hillsdale College, 33 East College Street, Hillsdale, MI 49242-1298, 517-607-2350. *Fax:* 517-607-2298. *E-mail:* financialaid@hillsdale.edu.
Website: http://www.hillsdale.edu/.

HIRAM COLLEGE

Hiram, OH

Tuition & fees: $37,710	Average undergraduate aid package: $29,456

ABOUT THE INSTITUTION Independent, coed. ***Awards:*** bachelor's and master's degrees. 31 undergraduate majors. ***Total enrollment:*** 1,255. Undergraduates: 1,244. Freshmen: 233. Both federal and institutional methodology are used as a basis for awarding need-based institutional aid.

UNDERGRADUATE EXPENSES for 2019–2020 ***Application fee:*** $25. ***Comprehensive fee:*** $48,000 includes full-time tuition ($35,360), mandatory fees ($2350), and room and board ($10,290). ***College room only:*** $5150. Full-time tuition and fees vary according to degree level and location. Room and board charges vary according to board plan and housing facility. ***Part-time tuition:*** $1179 per credit hour. Part-time tuition and fees vary according to degree level and location. ***Payment plan:*** Guaranteed tuition.

FRESHMAN FINANCIAL AID (Fall 2019, est.) 225 applied for aid; of those 97% were deemed to have need. 100% of freshmen with need received aid; of those 7% had need fully met. ***Average percent of need met:*** 73% (excluding resources awarded to replace EFC). ***Average financial aid package:*** $31,055 (excluding resources awarded to replace EFC). 3% of all full-time freshmen had no need and received non-need-based gift aid.

UNDERGRADUATE FINANCIAL AID (Fall 2019, est.) 765 applied for aid; of those 96% were deemed to have need. 100% of undergraduates with need received aid; of those 9% had need fully met. ***Average percent of need met:*** 75% (excluding resources awarded to replace EFC). ***Average financial aid package:*** $29,456 (excluding resources awarded to replace EFC). 4% of all full-time undergraduates had no need and received non-need-based gift aid.

GIFT AID (NEED-BASED) ***Total amount:*** $17,869,275 (14% federal, 5% state, 79% institutional, 2% external sources). ***Receiving aid:*** Freshmen: 96% (219); all full-time undergraduates: 90% (717). ***Average award:*** Freshmen: $17,122; Undergraduates: $17,496. ***Scholarships, grants, and awards:*** Federal Pell, FSEOG, state, private, college/university gift aid from institutional funds.

GIFT AID (NON-NEED-BASED) ***Total amount:*** $1,093,921 (22% state, 75% institutional, 3% external sources). ***Receiving aid:*** Freshmen: 6% (13). Undergraduates: 3% (28). ***Average award:*** Freshmen: $17,833. Undergraduates: $13,997. ***Scholarships, grants, and awards by category:*** *Academic interests/achievement:* 726 awards ($8,506,001 total): English, general academic interests/achievements, humanities, physical sciences, religion/biblical studies, social sciences. *Creative arts/performance:* 19 awards ($18,500 total): art/fine arts, music, theater/drama. *Special achievements/activities:* 26 awards ($21,225 total): leadership, memberships. *Special characteristics:* 302 awards ($925,025 total): children and siblings of alumni, children of faculty/staff, general special characteristics, international students, relatives of clergy, religious affiliation, siblings of current students. ***Tuition waivers:*** Full or partial for employees or children of employees. ***ROTC:*** Army cooperative, Air Force cooperative.

LOANS ***Student loans:*** $6,897,684 (39% need-based, 61% non-need-based). 86% of past graduating class borrowed through all loan programs. *Average indebtedness per student:* $36,500. ***Average need-based loan:*** Freshmen: $3195. Undergraduates: $4176. ***Parent loans:*** $2,029,373 (88% need-based, 12% non-need-based). ***Programs:*** Federal Direct (Subsidized and Unsubsidized Stafford, PLUS), state, college/university.

WORK-STUDY ***Federal work-study:*** Total amount: $1,073,077; 562 jobs averaging $2128. ***State or other work-study/employment:*** Total amount: $264,912 (29% need-based, 71% non-need-based). Part-time jobs available.

APPLYING FOR FINANCIAL AID ***Required financial aid form:*** FAFSA. ***Financial aid deadline:*** Continuous. ***Notification date:*** Continuous beginning 11/1.

CONTACT Andrea Caputo, Director of Financial Aid, Hiram College, Box 67, Hiram, OH 44234-0067, 330-569-5441 or toll-free 800-362-5280. *Fax:* 330-569-5499. *E-mail:* financialaid@hiram.edu.
Website: http://www.hiram.edu/.

HOBART AND WILLIAM SMITH COLLEGES

Geneva, NY

Tuition & fees: $58,650	Average undergraduate aid package: $43,044

ABOUT THE INSTITUTION Independent, coed. ***Awards:*** bachelor's and master's degrees. 47 undergraduate majors. ***Total enrollment:*** 2,070. Undergraduates: 2,061. Freshmen: 458. Both federal and institutional methodology are used as a basis for awarding need-based institutional aid.

UNDERGRADUATE EXPENSES for 2020–2021 ***Comprehensive fee:*** $73,740 includes full-time tuition ($57,400), mandatory fees ($1250), and room and board ($15,090). Room and board charges vary according to board plan. ***Payment plan:*** Tuition prepayment.

FRESHMAN FINANCIAL AID (Fall 2019, est.) 388 applied for aid; of those 79% were deemed to have need. 100% of freshmen with need received aid; of those 27% had need fully met. ***Average percent of need met:*** 82% (excluding resources awarded to replace EFC). ***Average financial aid package:*** $43,257 (excluding resources awarded to replace EFC). 25% of all full-time freshmen had no need and received non-need-based gift aid.

UNDERGRADUATE FINANCIAL AID (Fall 2019, est.) 1,520 applied for aid; of those 85% were deemed to have need. 100% of undergraduates with need received aid; of those 24% had need fully met. ***Average percent of need met:*** 81% (excluding resources awarded to replace EFC). ***Average financial aid package:*** $43,044 (excluding resources awarded to replace EFC). 31% of all full-time undergraduates had no need and received non-need-based gift aid.

GIFT AID (NEED-BASED) ***Total amount:*** $49,818,799 (5% federal, 2% state, 87% institutional, 6% external sources). ***Receiving aid:*** Freshmen: 66% (307); all full-time undergraduates: 65% (1,280). ***Average award:*** Freshmen: $40,151; Undergraduates: $38,920. ***Scholarships, grants, and awards:*** Federal Pell, FSEOG, state, private, college/university gift aid from institutional funds.

GIFT AID (NON-NEED-BASED) ***Total amount:*** $17,586,075 (87% institutional, 13% external sources). ***Receiving aid:*** Freshmen: 12% (56). Undergraduates: 12% (238). ***Average award:*** Freshmen: $22,623. Undergraduates: $21,558. ***Scholarships, grants, and awards by category:*** *Academic interests/achievement:* 626 awards ($14,278,484 total): general academic interests/achievements, premedicine. *Creative arts/performance:* 108 awards ($1,152,301 total): applied art and design, creative writing, dance, music, performing arts. *Special achievements/activities:* 123 awards ($2,541,553 total): community service, general special achievements/activities, leadership. *Special characteristics:* 160 awards ($798,384 total): children and siblings of alumni, relatives of clergy. ***Tuition waivers:*** Full or partial for employees or children of employees. ***ROTC:*** Army cooperative, Air Force cooperative.

LOANS ***Student loans:*** $12,180,356 (60% need-based, 40% non-need-based). 70% of past graduating class borrowed through all loan programs. *Average indebtedness per student:* $34,456. ***Average need-based loan:*** Freshmen: $2783. Undergraduates: $3786. ***Parent loans:*** $5,341,463 (39% need-based, 61% non-need-based). ***Programs:*** Federal Direct (Subsidized and Unsubsidized Stafford, PLUS).

WORK-STUDY ***Federal work-study:*** Total amount: $1,316,852; 816 jobs averaging $2055. ***State or other work-study/employment:*** Total amount: $1,377,989 (17% need-based, 83% non-need-based). 542 part-time jobs averaging $1944.

APPLYING FOR FINANCIAL AID ***Required financial aid forms:*** FAFSA, CSS Financial Aid PROFILE, state aid form, noncustodial (divorced/separated) parent's statement. ***Financial aid deadline:*** 2/1. ***Notification date:*** 4/1. Students must reply by 5/1.

CONTACT Beth Nepa, Director of Financial Aid, Hobart and William Smith Colleges, Demarest Hall, 300 Pulteney Street, Geneva, NY 14456-3397, 315-781-3315 or toll-free 800-852-2256. *Fax:* 315-781-4048. *E-mail:* nepa@hws.edu.
Website: http://www.hws.edu/.

HOBE SOUND BIBLE COLLEGE

Hobe Sound, FL

CONTACT Director of Financial Aid, Hobe Sound Bible College, PO Box 1065, Hobe Sound, FL 33475-1065, 561-546-5534. *Fax:* 561-545-1422.
Website: http://www.hsbc.edu/.

HODGES UNIVERSITY

Naples, FL

CONTACT Mr. Joe Gilchrist, Vice President of Financial Aid, Hodges University, 2655 Northbrooke Drive, Naples, FL 34119, 239-598-6116 or toll-free 800-466-8017. *Fax:* 239-598-6257. *E-mail:* jgilchrist@hodges.edu.
Website: http://www.hodges.edu/.

HOFSTRA UNIVERSITY

Hempstead, NY

Tuition & fees: $47,510	Average undergraduate aid package: $34,000

ABOUT THE INSTITUTION Independent, coed. ***Awards:*** certificates, bachelor's, master's, and doctoral degrees. 137 undergraduate majors. ***Total enrollment:*** 10,804. Undergraduates: 6,498. Freshmen: 1,523. Federal methodology is used as a basis for awarding need-based institutional aid.

UNDERGRADUATE EXPENSES for 2019–2020 ***Application fee:*** $70. ***Comprehensive fee:*** $63,938 includes full-time tuition ($46,450), mandatory fees ($1060), and room and board ($16,428). ***College room only:*** $10,960. Full-time tuition and fees vary according to course load. Room and board charges vary according to board plan and housing facility. ***Part-time tuition:*** $1560 per credit hour. ***Part-time fees:*** $155 per term. Part-time tuition and fees vary according to course load. ***Payment plan:*** Guaranteed tuition.

FRESHMAN FINANCIAL AID (Fall 2019, est.) 1342 applied for aid; of those 80% were deemed to have need. 100% of freshmen with need received aid; of those 27% had need fully met. ***Average percent of need met:*** 72% (excluding resources awarded to replace EFC). ***Average financial aid package:*** $36,000 (excluding resources awarded to replace EFC). 24% of all full-time freshmen had no need and received non-need-based gift aid.

UNDERGRADUATE FINANCIAL AID (Fall 2019, est.) 4,691 applied for aid; of those 83% were deemed to have need. 100% of undergraduates with need received aid; of those 26% had need fully met. ***Average percent of need met:*** 69% (excluding resources awarded to replace EFC). ***Average financial aid package:*** $34,000 (excluding resources awarded to replace EFC). 27% of all full-time undergraduates had no need and received non-need-based gift aid.

GIFT AID (NEED-BASED) ***Total amount:*** $86,000,000 (10% federal, 4% state, 85% institutional, 1% external sources). ***Receiving aid:*** Freshmen: 70% (1,065); all full-time undergraduates: 62% (3,767). ***Average award:*** Freshmen: $26,000; Undergraduates: $23,000. ***Scholarships, grants, and awards:*** Federal Pell, FSEOG, state, private, college/university gift aid from institutional funds, United Negro College Fund.

GIFT AID (NON-NEED-BASED) ***Total amount:*** $45,300,000 (1% federal, 96% institutional, 3% external sources). ***Receiving aid:*** Freshmen: 17% (262). Undergraduates: 13% (777). ***Average award:*** Freshmen: $24,000. Undergraduates: $21,000. ***Scholarships, grants, and awards by category:*** *Academic interests/achievement:* 6,313 awards ($101,190,000 total): communication, engineering/technologies, general academic interests/achievements. *Creative arts/performance:* 240 awards ($804,000 total): applied art and design, art/fine arts, cinema/film/broadcasting, dance, journalism/publications, music, performing arts, theater/drama. *Special achievements/activities:* 266 awards ($6,943,000 total): cheerleading/drum major, general special achievements/activities, leadership. *Special characteristics:* 387 awards ($9,600,000 total): children and siblings of alumni, children of faculty/staff, children of union members/company employees, general special characteristics, handicapped students, local/state students, members of minority groups, public servants, veterans, veterans' children. ***Tuition waivers:*** Full or partial for employees or children of employees. ***ROTC:*** Army.

LOANS ***Student loans:*** $42,500,000 (65% need-based, 35% non-need-based). 60% of past graduating class borrowed through all loan programs. ***Average need-based loan:*** Freshmen: $3000. Undergraduates: $4000. ***Parent loans:*** $35,800,000 (58% need-based, 42% non-need-based). ***Programs:*** Federal Direct (Subsidized and Unsubsidized Stafford, PLUS), state, college/university.

WORK-STUDY ***Federal work-study:*** Total amount: $9,200,000; 3,043 jobs averaging $3000. ***State or other work-study/employment:*** Total amount: $3,600,000 (22% need-based, 78% non-need-based). 1,367 part-time jobs averaging $2600.

ATHLETIC AWARDS Total amount: $6,900,000 (38% need-based, 62% non-need-based).

APPLYING FOR FINANCIAL AID ***Required financial aid forms:*** FAFSA, state aid form. ***Financial aid deadline (priority):*** 11/15. ***Notification date:*** Continuous beginning 1/15. Students must reply by 5/1 or within 2 weeks of notification.

CONTACT Sandra Filbry-Mervius, Director of Financial Aid, Hofstra University, 126 Hofstra University, Hempstead, NY 11549, 516-463-4335 or toll-free 800-HOFSTRA. *Fax:* 516-463-4936. *E-mail:* sandra.a.filbry@hofstra.edu.
Website: http://www.hofstra.edu/.

HOLLINS UNIVERSITY

Roanoke, VA

Tuition & fees: $40,010	Average undergraduate aid package: $38,450

ABOUT THE INSTITUTION Independent, undergraduate: women only; graduate: coed. ***Awards:*** certificates, bachelor's, and master's degrees. 28 undergraduate majors. ***Total enrollment:*** 798. Undergraduates: 668. Freshmen: 185. Federal methodology is used as a basis for awarding need-based institutional aid.

UNDERGRADUATE EXPENSES for 2019–2020 ***Comprehensive fee:*** $53,940 includes full-time tuition ($39,360), mandatory fees ($650), and room and board ($13,930). Room and board charges vary according to board plan. ***Part-time tuition:*** $1233 per credit hour. ***Part-time fees:*** $325 per year. ***Payment plan:*** Tuition prepayment.

FRESHMAN FINANCIAL AID (Fall 2019, est.) 149 applied for aid; of those 94% were deemed to have need. 100% of freshmen with need received aid; of those 26% had need fully met. ***Average percent of need met:*** 86% (excluding resources awarded to replace EFC). ***Average financial aid package:*** $38,985 (excluding

resources awarded to replace EFC). 24% of all full-time freshmen had no need and received non-need-based gift aid.

UNDERGRADUATE FINANCIAL AID (Fall 2019, est.) 536 applied for aid; of those 92% were deemed to have need. 100% of undergraduates with need received aid; of those 24% had need fully met. ***Average percent of need met:*** 85% (excluding resources awarded to replace EFC). ***Average financial aid package:*** $38,450 (excluding resources awarded to replace EFC). 25% of all full-time undergraduates had no need and received non-need-based gift aid.

GIFT AID (NEED-BASED) ***Receiving aid:*** Freshmen: 76% (140); all full-time undergraduates: 75% (494). ***Average award:*** Freshmen: $32,963; Undergraduates: $32,163. ***Scholarships, grants, and awards:*** Federal Pell, FSEOG, state, private, college/university gift aid from institutional funds.

GIFT AID (NON-NEED-BASED) ***Receiving aid:*** Freshmen: 76% (140). Undergraduates: 75% (494). ***Average award:*** Freshmen: $40,131. Undergraduates: $34,877. ***Scholarships, grants, and awards by category:*** *Academic interests/achievement:* general academic interests/achievements. *Creative arts/performance:* applied art and design, creative writing, dance, music, theater/drama. *Special achievements/activities:* community service, general special achievements/activities, hobbies/interests, leadership. *Special characteristics:* adult students, children and siblings of alumni, children of faculty/staff, international students, local/state students, out-of-state students, previous college experience, veterans. ***Tuition waivers:*** Full or partial for employees or children of employees.

LOANS ***Student loans:*** 74% of past graduating class borrowed through all loan programs. *Average indebtedness per student:* $33,691. ***Average need-based loan:*** Freshmen: $3378. Undergraduates: $4473. ***Programs:*** Federal Direct (Subsidized and Unsubsidized Stafford, PLUS), college/university.

WORK-STUDY ***Federal work-study:*** 135 jobs averaging $1500. ***State or other work-study/employment:*** 165 part-time jobs averaging $1500.

APPLYING FOR FINANCIAL AID ***Required financial aid forms:*** FAFSA, state aid form. ***Financial aid deadline:*** Continuous. ***Notification date:*** Continuous.

CONTACT Mrs. MaryJean Sullivan, Director of Scholarships and Financial Assistance, Hollins University, 7916 Williamson Road, Box 9718, Roanoke, VA 24020, 540-362-6332 or toll-free 800-456-9595. *Fax:* 540-362-6093. *E-mail:* sfa@hollins.edu.
Website: http://www.hollins.edu/.

HOLY CROSS COLLEGE

Notre Dame, IN

CONTACT Robert Benjamin, Director of Financial Aid, Holy Cross College, PO Box 308, Notre Dame, IN 46556, 574-239-8362. *E-mail:* rbenjamin@hcc-nd.edu.
Website: http://www.hcc-nd.edu/.

HOLY FAMILY UNIVERSITY

Philadelphia, PA

CONTACT Ms. Janice Hetrick, Director of Financial Aid, Holy Family University, 9801 Frankford Avenue, Philadelphia, PA 19114-2094, 215-637-7700 Ext. 3233. *Fax:* 215-599-1694. *E-mail:* finaid@holyfamily.edu.
Website: http://www.holyfamily.edu/.

HOLY NAMES UNIVERSITY

Oakland, CA

CONTACT Christina Miller, Director of Financial Aid, Holy Names University, 3500 Mountain Boulevard, Oakland, CA 94619-1699, 510-436-1327 or toll-free 800-430-1321. *Fax:* 510-436-1199. *E-mail:* miller@hnu.edu.
Website: http://www.hnu.edu/.

HOOD COLLEGE

Frederick, MD

ABOUT THE INSTITUTION Independent, coed. ***Awards:*** certificates, bachelor's, master's, and doctoral degrees (also offers adult program with significant enrollment not reflected in profile). 33 undergraduate majors. ***Total enrollment:*** 2,052. Undergraduates: 1,092. Freshmen: 239.

GIFT AID (NEED-BASED) ***Scholarships, grants, and awards:*** Federal Pell, FSEOG, state, private, college/university gift aid from institutional funds.

GIFT AID (NON-NEED-BASED) ***Scholarships, grants, and awards by category:*** *Academic interests/achievement:* biological sciences, business, communication, computer science, education, English, foreign languages, general academic interests/achievements, humanities, mathematics, physical sciences, religion/biblical studies, social sciences. *Creative arts/performance:* applied art and design, creative writing, journalism/publications, music. *Special achievements/activities:* community service, leadership, memberships. *Special characteristics:* children and siblings of alumni, children of current students, children of faculty/staff, ethnic background, first-generation college students, international students, local/state students, out-of-state students, previous college experience, religious affiliation, siblings of current students, twins, veterans, veterans' children.

LOANS ***Programs:*** Federal Direct (Subsidized and Unsubsidized Stafford, PLUS).

WORK-STUDY ***Federal work-study:*** Total amount: $264,420; jobs available. ***State or other work-study/employment:*** Total amount: $214,726 (51% need-based, 49% non-need-based). Part-time jobs available.

APPLYING FOR FINANCIAL AID ***Required financial aid form:*** FAFSA.

CONTACT Financial Aid Office, Hood College, 401 Rosemont Avenue, Frederick, MD 21701-8575, 301-663-3131 or toll-free 800-922-1599.
Website: http://www.hood.edu/.

HOPE COLLEGE

Holland, MI

Tuition & fees: $35,330	Average undergraduate aid package: $28,350

ABOUT THE INSTITUTION Independent Reformed Church in America, coed. ***Awards:*** bachelor's degrees. 63 undergraduate majors. ***Total enrollment:*** 3,056. Undergraduates: 3,056. Freshmen: 686. Federal methodology is used as a basis for awarding need-based institutional aid.

UNDERGRADUATE EXPENSES for 2019–2020 ***Application fee:*** $35. ***Comprehensive fee:*** $45,960 includes full-time tuition ($34,990), mandatory fees ($340), and room and board ($10,630). ***College room only:*** $4880. Room and board charges vary according to board plan. Part-time tuition and fees vary according to course load and program.

FRESHMAN FINANCIAL AID (Fall 2019, est.) 616 applied for aid; of those 74% were deemed to have need. 100% of freshmen with need received aid; of those 24% had need fully met. ***Average percent of need met:*** 82% (excluding resources awarded to replace EFC). ***Average financial aid package:*** $29,671 (excluding resources awarded to replace EFC). 32% of all full-time freshmen had no need and received non-need-based gift aid.

UNDERGRADUATE FINANCIAL AID (Fall 2019, est.) 2,087 applied for aid; of those 79% were deemed to have need. 100% of undergraduates with need received aid; of those 28% had need fully met. ***Average percent of need met:*** 80% (excluding resources awarded to replace EFC). ***Average financial aid package:*** $28,350 (excluding resources awarded to replace EFC). 31% of all full-time undergraduates had no need and received non-need-based gift aid.

GIFT AID (NEED-BASED) ***Receiving aid:*** Freshmen: 61% (416); all full-time undergraduates: 50% (1,444). ***Average award:*** Freshmen: $24,683; Undergraduates: $22,335. ***Scholarships, grants, and awards:*** Federal Pell, FSEOG, state, private, college/university gift aid from institutional funds.

GIFT AID (NON-NEED-BASED) ***Receiving aid:*** Freshmen: 61% (417). Undergraduates: 48% (1,387). ***Average award:*** Freshmen: $11,619. Undergraduates: $9993. ***Scholarships, grants, and awards by category:*** *Academic interests/achievement:* 2,037 awards ($16,649,195 total): general academic interests/achievements. *Creative arts/performance:* 142 awards ($455,250 total): applied art and design, creative writing, dance, music, theater/drama. *Special characteristics:* 1,053 awards ($3,576,208 total): children and siblings of alumni, ethnic background, out-of-state students, religious affiliation, siblings of current students. ***Tuition waivers:*** Full or partial for employees or children of employees. ***ROTC:*** Army cooperative.

LOANS ***Student loans:*** 59% of past graduating class borrowed through all loan programs. *Average indebtedness per student:* $33,856. ***Average need-based loan:*** Freshmen: $3369. Undergraduates: $4422. ***Programs:*** Federal Direct (Subsidized and Unsubsidized Stafford, PLUS).

WORK-STUDY ***Federal work-study:*** 148 jobs averaging $2521. ***State or other work-study/employment:*** 486 part-time jobs averaging $1178.

APPLYING FOR FINANCIAL AID ***Required financial aid form:*** FAFSA. ***Notification date:*** Continuous.

CONTACT Ms. Jill Nutt, Director of Financial Aid, Hope College, 100 East 8th St., Holland, MI 49422-9000, 616-395-7765 or toll-free 800-968-7850. *Fax:* 616-395-7160. *E-mail:* nutt@hope.edu.
Website: http://www.hope.edu/.

HOPE INTERNATIONAL UNIVERSITY

Fullerton, CA

Tuition & fees: $34,450	Average undergraduate aid package: $14,962

ABOUT THE INSTITUTION Independent Christian Churches and Churches of Christ, coed. ***Awards:*** certificates, associate, bachelor's, and master's degrees. 21 undergraduate majors. ***Total enrollment:*** 1,152. Undergraduates: 651. Freshmen: 111. Federal methodology is used as a basis for awarding need-based institutional aid.

UNDERGRADUATE EXPENSES for 2020–2021 ***Application fee:*** $40. ***Comprehensive fee:*** $45,500 includes full-time tuition ($33,250), mandatory fees ($1200), and room and board ($11,050). ***College room only:*** $5150. Full-time tuition and fees vary according to course level, course load, degree level, location, program, and reciprocity agreements. Room and board charges vary according to board plan. ***Part-time tuition:*** $1500 per credit hour. ***Part-time fees:*** $1200 per year. Part-time tuition and fees vary according to course level, course load, degree level, location, program, and reciprocity agreements.

FRESHMAN FINANCIAL AID (Fall 2018) 86 applied for aid; of those 95% were deemed to have need. 100% of freshmen with need received aid; of those 22% had need fully met. ***Average percent of need met:*** 30% (excluding resources awarded to replace EFC). ***Average financial aid package:*** $15,570 (excluding resources awarded to replace EFC). 2% of all full-time freshmen had no need and received non-need-based gift aid.

UNDERGRADUATE FINANCIAL AID (Fall 2018) 412 applied for aid; of those 93% were deemed to have need. 100% of undergraduates with need received aid; of those 3% had need fully met. ***Average percent of need met:*** 33% (excluding resources awarded to replace EFC). ***Average financial aid package:*** $14,962 (excluding resources awarded to replace EFC). 4% of all full-time undergraduates had no need and received non-need-based gift aid.

GIFT AID (NEED-BASED) ***Receiving aid:*** Freshmen: 49% (44); all full-time undergraduates: 59% (270). ***Average award:*** Freshmen: $12,145; Undergraduates: $12,842. ***Scholarships, grants, and awards:*** Federal Pell, FSEOG, state, private, college/university gift aid from institutional funds.

GIFT AID (NON-NEED-BASED) ***Receiving aid:*** Freshmen: 74% (67). Undergraduates: 62% (284). ***Average award:*** Freshmen: $14,000. Undergraduates: $12,937. ***Scholarships, grants, and awards by category:*** *Academic interests/achievement:* general academic interests/achievements. *Creative arts/performance:* music. *Special achievements/activities:* leadership. *Special characteristics:* children of faculty/staff, veterans. ***Tuition waivers:*** Full or partial for employees or children of employees. ***ROTC:*** Army cooperative.

LOANS ***Student loans:*** 71% of past graduating class borrowed through all loan programs. *Average indebtedness per student:* $35,427. ***Average need-based loan:*** Freshmen: $2494. Undergraduates: $3141. ***Programs:*** Federal Direct (Subsidized and Unsubsidized Stafford, PLUS).

WORK-STUDY Federal work-study jobs available. ***State or other work-study/employment:*** Part-time jobs available.

APPLYING FOR FINANCIAL AID ***Required financial aid form:*** institution's own form. ***Financial aid deadline:*** Continuous. ***Notification date:*** Continuous. Students must reply within 2 weeks of notification.

CONTACT Ms. Shannon O'Shields, Director of Student Financial Services, Hope International University, 2500 East Nutwood Avenue, Fullerton, CA 92831, 714-879-3901 Ext. 2207 or toll-free 866-722-HOPE. *Fax:* 714-681-7421. *E-mail:* soshields@hiu.edu.
Website: http://www.hiu.edu/.

HORIZON UNIVERSITY

Indianapolis, IN

CONTACT Financial Aid Office, Horizon University, 7700 Indian Lake Road, Indianapolis, IN 46236, 858-695-8587 or toll-free 800-553-HORIZON.
Website: http://www.horizonuniversity.edu/.

HOUGHTON COLLEGE

Houghton, NY

Tuition & fees: N/R	Average undergraduate aid package: $25,049

ABOUT THE INSTITUTION Independent Wesleyan, coed. ***Awards:*** associate, bachelor's, and master's degrees. 66 undergraduate majors. Federal methodology is used as a basis for awarding need-based institutional aid.

FRESHMAN FINANCIAL AID (Fall 2019, est.) 259 applied for aid; of those 92% were deemed to have need. 98% of freshmen with need received aid; of those 23% had need fully met. ***Average percent of need met:*** 60% (excluding resources awarded to replace EFC). ***Average financial aid package:*** $24,619 (excluding resources awarded to replace EFC). 7% of all full-time freshmen had no need and received non-need-based gift aid.

UNDERGRADUATE FINANCIAL AID (Fall 2019, est.) 840 applied for aid; of those 93% were deemed to have need. 99% of undergraduates with need received aid; of those 25% had need fully met. ***Average percent of need met:*** 59% (excluding resources awarded to replace EFC). ***Average financial aid package:*** $25,049 (excluding resources awarded to replace EFC). 6% of all full-time undergraduates had no need and received non-need-based gift aid.

GIFT AID (NEED-BASED) ***Total amount:*** $7,225,506 (25% federal, 14% state, 61% institutional). ***Receiving aid:*** Freshmen: 83% (230); all full-time undergraduates: 82% (746). ***Average award:*** Freshmen: $21,175; Undergraduates: $20,986. ***Scholarships, grants, and awards:*** Federal Pell, FSEOG, state, private, college/university gift aid from institutional funds.

GIFT AID (NON-NEED-BASED) ***Total amount:*** $11,786,359 (1% state, 93% institutional, 6% external sources). ***Receiving aid:*** Freshmen: 72% (199). Undergraduates: 73% (671). ***Average award:*** Freshmen: $13,112. Undergraduates: $13,518. ***Scholarships, grants, and awards by category:*** *Academic interests/achievement:* biological sciences, business, communication, computer science, education, English, general academic interests/achievements, international studies, mathematics, physical sciences, premedicine, religion/biblical studies. *Creative arts/performance:* applied art and design, creative writing, music, performing arts. *Special achievements/activities:* community service, general special achievements/activities, leadership, religious involvement. *Special characteristics:* adult students, children and siblings of alumni, children of faculty/staff, first-generation college students, general special characteristics, handicapped students, international students, local/state students, relatives of clergy, religious affiliation, siblings of current students, veterans, veterans' children. ***ROTC:*** Army cooperative.

LOANS ***Student loans:*** $5,726,786 (40% need-based, 60% non-need-based). 75% of past graduating class borrowed through all loan programs. *Average indebtedness per student:* $47,183. ***Average need-based loan:*** Freshmen: $3351. Undergraduates: $4330. ***Parent loans:*** $1,657,957 (100% non-need-based). ***Programs:*** Federal Direct (Subsidized and Unsubsidized Stafford, PLUS).

WORK-STUDY ***Federal work-study:*** Total amount: $850,979; 452 jobs averaging $1205. ***State or other work-study/employment:*** Total amount: $190,050 (100% non-need-based). Part-time jobs available.

APPLYING FOR FINANCIAL AID ***Required financial aid form:*** FAFSA. ***Financial aid deadline (priority):*** 3/1. ***Notification date:*** Continuous beginning 12/1.

CONTACT Mrs. Marianne Loper, Director of Financial Aid, Houghton College, One Willard Avenue, Houghton, NY 14744, 585-567-9328 or toll-free 800-777-2556. *Fax:* 585-567-9610. *E-mail:* sfso@houghton.edu.
Website: http://www.houghton.edu/.

HOUSTON BAPTIST UNIVERSITY

Houston, TX

Tuition & fees: $34,500	Average undergraduate aid package: $29,796

ABOUT THE INSTITUTION Independent Baptist, coed. ***Awards:*** bachelor's, master's, and doctoral degrees. 60 undergraduate majors. ***Total enrollment:*** 3,741. Undergraduates: 2,632. Freshmen: 727. Federal methodology is used as a basis for awarding need-based institutional aid.

UNDERGRADUATE EXPENSES for 2020–2021 ***Comprehensive fee:*** $43,630 includes full-time tuition ($32,350), mandatory fees ($2150), and room and board ($9130). ***College room only:*** $4850. Room and board charges vary according to board plan and housing facility. ***Part-time tuition:*** $1350 per semester hour. ***Part-time fees:*** $1075 per term.

FRESHMAN FINANCIAL AID (Fall 2019, est.) 647 applied for aid; of those 94% were deemed to have need. 100% of freshmen with need received aid; of those 15% had need fully met. ***Average percent of need met:*** 74% (excluding resources awarded to replace EFC). ***Average financial aid package:*** $30,589 (excluding resources awarded to replace EFC). 13% of all full-time freshmen had no need and received non-need-based gift aid.

UNDERGRADUATE FINANCIAL AID (Fall 2019, est.) 1,683 applied for aid; of those 95% were deemed to have need. 100% of undergraduates with need received aid; of those 15% had need fully met. ***Average percent of need met:*** 70% (excluding resources awarded to replace EFC). ***Average financial aid package:*** $29,796 (excluding resources awarded to replace EFC). 21% of all full-time undergraduates had no need and received non-need-based gift aid.

GIFT AID (NEED-BASED) ***Receiving aid:*** Freshmen: 87% (606); all full-time undergraduates: 76% (1,581). ***Average award:*** Freshmen: $24,836; Undergraduates: $23,561. ***Scholarships, grants, and awards:*** Federal Pell, FSEOG, state, private, college/university gift aid from institutional funds.

GIFT AID (NON-NEED-BASED) ***Receiving aid:*** Freshmen: 87% (605). Undergraduates: 74% (1,537). ***Average award:*** Freshmen: $17,457. Undergraduates: $15,528. ***Scholarships, grants, and awards by category:*** *Academic interests/achievement:* 2,428 awards ($30,981,609 total): engineering/technologies, general academic interests/achievements, home economics, religion/biblical studies. *Creative arts/performance:* 102 awards ($311,000 total): art/fine arts, cinema/film/broadcasting, music, theater/drama. *Special achievements/activities:* 177 awards ($329,307 total): religious involvement. *Special characteristics:* 102 awards ($696,063 total): children of faculty/staff, local/state students, religious affiliation. ***Tuition waivers:*** Full or partial for employees or children of employees. ***ROTC:*** Army cooperative, Air Force cooperative.

LOANS ***Student loans:*** 68% of past graduating class borrowed through all loan programs. *Average indebtedness per student:* $32,538. ***Average need-based loan:*** Freshmen: $3737. Undergraduates: $4001. ***Programs:*** Federal Direct (Subsidized and Unsubsidized Stafford, PLUS), state.

WORK-STUDY ***Federal work-study:*** 1,022 jobs averaging $990.

APPLYING FOR FINANCIAL AID ***Required financial aid form:*** FAFSA. ***Financial aid deadline:*** Continuous. ***Notification date:*** Continuous. Students must reply within 4 weeks of notification.

CONTACT LeChelle Davenport, Interim Director, Houston Baptist University, 7502 Fondren Road, Houston, TX 77074-3298, 281-649-3749 or toll-free 800-696-3210. *Fax:* 281-649-3298. *E-mail:* financialaid@hbu.edu.
Website: http://www.hbu.edu/.

HOWARD PAYNE UNIVERSITY

Brownwood, TX

ABOUT THE INSTITUTION Independent Baptist General Convention of Texas, coed. ***Awards:*** certificates, bachelor's, and master's degrees. 69 undergraduate majors.

GIFT AID (NEED-BASED) ***Scholarships, grants, and awards:*** Federal Pell, FSEOG, state, private, college/university gift aid from institutional funds.

GIFT AID (NON-NEED-BASED) ***Scholarships, grants, and awards by category:*** *Academic interests/achievement:* biological sciences, business, communication, education, English, general academic interests/achievements, mathematics, physical sciences, premedicine, religion/biblical studies, social sciences. *Creative arts/performance:* applied art and design, music, theater/drama. *Special achievements/activities:* community service, leadership, religious involvement. *Special characteristics:* children and siblings of alumni, children of faculty/staff, local/state students, relatives of clergy, religious affiliation, siblings of current students.

LOANS ***Programs:*** Federal Direct (Subsidized and Unsubsidized Stafford, PLUS), Perkins, state.

WORK-STUDY ***Federal work-study:*** Total amount: $142,036; jobs available. ***State or other work-study/employment:*** Total amount: $8464 (100% need-based). Part-time jobs available.

APPLYING FOR FINANCIAL AID ***Required financial aid forms:*** FAFSA, institution's own form, Core Residency Form.

CONTACT Mrs. Glenda Huff, Director of Financial Aid, Howard Payne University, 1000 Fisk Avenue, Brownwood, TX 76801, 325-649-8014 or toll-free 800-880-4478. *Fax:* 325-649-8973. *E-mail:* ghuff@hputx.edu.
Website: http://www.hputx.edu/.

HOWARD UNIVERSITY

Washington, DC

CONTACT Office of Financial Aid, Howard University, 2400 Sixth Street, NW, Washington, DC 20059, 202-806-2864 or toll-free 800-822-6363. *Fax:* 202-806-2818. *Website:* http://www.howard.edu/.

HULT INTERNATIONAL BUSINESS SCHOOL

Cambridge, MA

ABOUT THE INSTITUTION Independent, coed. ***Awards:*** bachelor's and master's degrees. 1 undergraduate major.

GIFT AID (NEED-BASED) ***Scholarships, grants, and awards:*** college/university gift aid from institutional funds.

GIFT AID (NON-NEED-BASED) ***Scholarships, grants, and awards by category:*** *Academic interests/achievement:* business.

APPLYING FOR FINANCIAL AID ***Required financial aid form:*** institution's own form.

CONTACT Financial Aid Office, Hult International Business School, 1 Education Street, Cambridge, MA 02141, 617-746-1990.
Website: http://www.hult.edu/.

HUMBOLDT STATE UNIVERSITY

Arcata, CA

Tuition & fees (CA res): $7780	Average undergraduate aid package: $15,980

ABOUT THE INSTITUTION State-supported, coed. ***Awards:*** certificates, bachelor's, and master's degrees. 67 undergraduate majors. ***Total enrollment:*** 7,774. Undergraduates: 7,195. Freshmen: 1,051. Federal methodology is used as a basis for awarding need-based institutional aid.

UNDERGRADUATE EXPENSES for 2019–2020 ***Application fee:*** $55. ***Tuition, state resident:*** full-time $5742; part-time $3330 per term. ***Tuition, nonresident:*** full-time $17,622; part-time $396 per credit. ***Required fees:*** full-time $2038; $1674. ***College room and board:*** $13,562; ***Room only:*** $6216. Room and board charges vary according to board plan and location.

FRESHMAN FINANCIAL AID (Fall 2019, est.) 724 applied for aid; of those 81% were deemed to have need. 100% of freshmen with need received aid; of those 8% had need fully met. ***Average percent of need met:*** 71% (excluding resources awarded to replace EFC). ***Average financial aid package:*** $14,670 (excluding resources

awarded to replace EFC). 7% of all full-time freshmen had no need and received non-need-based gift aid.

UNDERGRADUATE FINANCIAL AID (Fall 2019, est.) 5,330 applied for aid; of those 88% were deemed to have need. 99% of undergraduates with need received aid; of those 10% had need fully met. ***Average percent of need met:*** 76% (excluding resources awarded to replace EFC). ***Average financial aid package:*** $15,980 (excluding resources awarded to replace EFC). 8% of all full-time undergraduates had no need and received non-need-based gift aid.

GIFT AID (NEED-BASED) ***Total amount:*** $44,175,005 (41% federal, 29% state, 26% institutional, 4% external sources). ***Receiving aid:*** Freshmen: 68% (558); all full-time undergraduates: 74% (4,463). ***Average award:*** Freshmen: $10,222; Undergraduates: $9422. ***Scholarships, grants, and awards:*** Federal Pell, FSEOG, state, private, college/university gift aid from institutional funds.

GIFT AID (NON-NEED-BASED) ***Total amount:*** $910,640 (8% federal, 28% state, 17% institutional, 47% external sources). ***Receiving aid:*** Freshmen: 2% (19). Undergraduates: 2% (91). ***Average award:*** Freshmen: $560. Undergraduates: $917. ***Scholarships, grants, and awards by category:*** *Academic interests/achievement:* general academic interests/achievements. ***Tuition waivers:*** Full or partial for employees or children of employees.

LOANS ***Student loans:*** $33,774,067 (82% need-based, 18% non-need-based). 74% of past graduating class borrowed through all loan programs. *Average indebtedness per student:* $23,028. ***Average need-based loan:*** Freshmen: $5727. Undergraduates: $7623. ***Parent loans:*** $2,540,673 (32% need-based, 68% non-need-based). ***Programs:*** Federal Direct (Subsidized and Unsubsidized Stafford, PLUS), Perkins, college/university.

WORK-STUDY ***Federal work-study:*** Total amount: $692,147; jobs available.

ATHLETIC AWARDS Total amount: $551,291 (54% need-based, 46% non-need-based).

APPLYING FOR FINANCIAL AID ***Required financial aid form:*** FAFSA. ***Financial aid deadline (priority):*** 3/2. ***Notification date:*** Continuous beginning 4/15. Students must reply within 4 weeks of notification.

CONTACT Peggy Metzger, Director of Financial Aid, Humboldt State University, 1 Harpst Street, Arcata, CA 95521-8299, 707-826-4321 or toll-free 866-850-9556. *E-mail:* pmetzger@humboldt.edu.
Website: http://www.humboldt.edu/.

HUMPHREYS UNIVERSITY

Stockton, CA

CONTACT Rita Franco, Director of Financial Aid, Humphreys University, 6650 Inglewood Avenue, Stockton, CA 95207-3896, 209-478-0800. *Fax:* 209-235-2983.
Website: http://www.humphreys.edu/.

HUNTER COLLEGE OF THE CITY UNIVERSITY OF NEW YORK

New York, NY

ABOUT THE INSTITUTION State and locally supported, coed. ***Awards:*** certificates, bachelor's, master's, and doctoral degrees. 63 undergraduate majors. ***Total enrollment:*** 23,202. Undergraduates: 17,212. Freshmen: 2,598.

GIFT AID (NEED-BASED) ***Scholarships, grants, and awards:*** Federal Pell, FSEOG, state, private, college/university gift aid from institutional funds.

GIFT AID (NON-NEED-BASED) ***Scholarships, grants, and awards by category:*** *Academic interests/achievement:* general academic interests/achievements.

LOANS ***Programs:*** Federal Direct (Subsidized and Unsubsidized Stafford, PLUS), Perkins.

WORK-STUDY ***Federal work-study:*** Total amount: $585,087; 254 jobs averaging $2303. ***State or other work-study/employment:*** Total amount: $1,226,891 (100% non-need-based). Part-time jobs available.

APPLYING FOR FINANCIAL AID ***Required financial aid forms:*** FAFSA, state aid form.

CONTACT Nigel Thompson, Director of Financial Aid, Hunter College of the City University of New York, 695 Park Avenue, New York, NY 10065-5085, 212-772-4820. *Fax:* 212-650-3666. *E-mail:* nt1109@hunter.cuny.edu.
Website: http://www.hunter.cuny.edu/.

HUNTINGDON COLLEGE

Montgomery, AL

CONTACT Ms. Brittany Davis, Director of Financial Aid, Huntingdon College, 1500 East Fairview Avenue, Montgomery, AL 36106-2148, 334-833-4428 or toll-free 800-763-0313. *Fax:* 334-833-4235. *E-mail:* finaid@hawks.huntingdon.edu.
Website: http://www.huntingdon.edu/.

HUNTINGTON UNIVERSITY

Huntington, IN

Tuition & fees: N/R	Average undergraduate aid package: $19,829

ABOUT THE INSTITUTION Independent Church of the United Brethren in Christ, coed. ***Awards:*** associate, bachelor's, master's, and doctoral degrees. 87 undergraduate majors. Both federal and institutional methodology are used as a basis for awarding need-based institutional aid.

FRESHMAN FINANCIAL AID (Fall 2019, est.) 209 applied for aid; of those 71% were deemed to have need. 100% of freshmen with need received aid; of those 4% had need fully met. ***Average percent of need met:*** 73% (excluding resources awarded to replace EFC). ***Average financial aid package:*** $20,475 (excluding resources awarded to replace EFC). 17% of all full-time freshmen had no need and received non-need-based gift aid.

UNDERGRADUATE FINANCIAL AID (Fall 2019, est.) 644 applied for aid; of those 90% were deemed to have need. 100% of undergraduates with need received aid; of those 8% had need fully met. ***Average percent of need met:*** 88% (excluding resources awarded to replace EFC). ***Average financial aid package:*** $19,829 (excluding resources awarded to replace EFC). 30% of all full-time undergraduates had no need and received non-need-based gift aid.

GIFT AID (NEED-BASED) ***Total amount:*** $10,536,964 (18% federal, 18% state, 59% institutional, 5% external sources). ***Receiving aid:*** Freshmen: 69% (149); all full-time undergraduates: 63% (571). ***Average award:*** Freshmen: $16,522; Undergraduates: $14,901. ***Scholarships, grants, and awards:*** Federal Pell, FSEOG, state, private, college/university gift aid from institutional funds.

GIFT AID (NON-NEED-BASED) ***Total amount:*** $1,615,989 (97% institutional, 3% external sources). ***Receiving aid:*** Freshmen: 16% (35). Undergraduates: 16% (147). ***Average award:*** Freshmen: $9810. Undergraduates: $9654. ***Scholarships, grants, and awards by category:*** *Academic interests/achievement:* agriculture, business, communication, general academic interests/achievements. *Creative arts/performance:* applied art and design, art/fine arts, cinema/film/broadcasting, creative writing, journalism/publications, music, performing arts, theater/drama. *Special achievements/activities:* cheerleading/drum major, leadership, memberships, religious involvement. *Special characteristics:* children and siblings of alumni, children of faculty/staff, ethnic background, international students, local/state students, relatives of clergy, religious affiliation.

LOANS ***Student loans:*** $5,829,993 (80% need-based, 20% non-need-based). 72% of past graduating class borrowed through all loan programs. *Average indebtedness per student:* $32,491. ***Average need-based loan:*** Freshmen: $3715. Undergraduates: $4571. ***Parent loans:*** $1,401,822 (79% need-based, 21% non-need-based). ***Programs:*** Federal Direct (Subsidized and Unsubsidized Stafford, PLUS).

WORK-STUDY ***Federal work-study:*** Total amount: $100,000; jobs available.

ATHLETIC AWARDS Total amount: $1,537,386 (60% need-based, 40% non-need-based).

APPLYING FOR FINANCIAL AID ***Financial aid deadline:*** Continuous. ***Notification date:*** Continuous beginning 1/1.

CONTACT Lisa Montany, Director of Financial Aid, Huntington University, 2303 College Avenue, Huntington, IN 46750, 260-359-4014 or toll-free 800-642-6493. *Fax:* 260-358-3699. *E-mail:* finaid@huntington.edu.
Website: http://www.huntington.edu/.

HUNTSVILLE BIBLE COLLEGE

Huntsville, AL

CONTACT Financial Aid Office, Huntsville Bible College, 904 Oakwood Avenue, Huntsville, AL 35811-1632, 256-539-0834.
Website: http://www.huntsvillebiblecollege.org/.

HUSSIAN COLLEGE, SCHOOL OF ART

Philadelphia, PA

CONTACT Financial Aid Office, Hussian College, School of Art, 1500 Spring Garden Street, Suite 101, Philadelphia, PA 19130, 215-981-0900.
Website: http://www.hussiancollege.edu/.

HUSSON UNIVERSITY

Bangor, ME

Tuition & fees: $19,772	Average undergraduate aid package: $15,034

ABOUT THE INSTITUTION Independent, coed. ***Awards:*** certificates, associate, bachelor's, master's, and doctoral degrees. 46 undergraduate majors. ***Total enrollment:*** 863. Undergraduates: 2,864. Freshmen: 568. Federal methodology is used as a basis for awarding need-based institutional aid.

UNDERGRADUATE EXPENSES for 2020–2021 ***Application fee:*** $40. ***Comprehensive fee:*** $30,404 includes full-time tuition ($18,972), mandatory fees ($800), and room and board ($10,632). ***College room only:*** $5354. Room and board charges vary according to housing facility. ***Part-time tuition:*** $612 per credit hour. ***Part-time fees:*** $96.

FRESHMAN FINANCIAL AID (Fall 2018) 628 applied for aid; of those 89% were deemed to have need. 100% of freshmen with need received aid; of those 23% had need fully met. ***Average percent of need met:*** 76% (excluding resources awarded to replace EFC). ***Average financial aid package:*** $17,918 (excluding resources awarded to replace EFC). 13% of all full-time freshmen had no need and received non-need-based gift aid.

UNDERGRADUATE FINANCIAL AID (Fall 2018) 2,466 applied for aid; of those 85% were deemed to have need. 100% of undergraduates with need received aid; of those 10% had need fully met. ***Average percent of need met:*** 69% (excluding resources awarded to replace EFC). ***Average financial aid package:*** $15,034 (excluding resources awarded to replace EFC). 8% of all full-time undergraduates had no need and received non-need-based gift aid.

GIFT AID (NEED-BASED) ***Total amount:*** $26,212,249 (36% federal, 5% state, 53% institutional, 6% external sources). ***Receiving aid:*** Freshmen: 83% (540); all full-time undergraduates: 80% (1,994). ***Average award:*** Freshmen: $11,966; Undergraduates: $9582. ***Scholarships, grants, and awards:*** Federal Pell, FSEOG, state, private, college/university gift aid from institutional funds.

GIFT AID (NON-NEED-BASED) ***Total amount:*** $2,108,254 (79% institutional, 21% external sources). ***Receiving aid:*** Freshmen: 77% (499). Undergraduates: 66% (1,643). ***Average award:*** Freshmen: $4757. Undergraduates: $3652. ***Scholarships, grants, and awards by category:*** *Academic interests/achievement:* general academic interests/achievements. *Special achievements/activities:* leadership. *Special characteristics:* children and siblings of alumni, children of faculty/staff, children of union members/company employees, ethnic background, international students, members of minority groups, out-of-state students. ***ROTC:*** Army, Naval cooperative.

LOANS ***Student loans:*** $19,206,250 (74% need-based, 26% non-need-based). 89% of past graduating class borrowed through all loan programs. *Average indebtedness per student:* $35,681. ***Average need-based loan:*** Freshmen: $3362. Undergraduates: $4259. ***Parent loans:*** $3,531,217 (45% need-based, 55% non-need-based). ***Programs:*** Federal Direct (Subsidized and Unsubsidized Stafford, PLUS), Perkins, state, alternative loans.

WORK-STUDY ***Federal work-study:*** Total amount: $1,140,689; 1,266 jobs averaging $1885.

APPLYING FOR FINANCIAL AID ***Required financial aid form:*** FAFSA. ***Financial aid deadline:*** 4/15. ***Notification date:*** Continuous beginning 12/1. Students must reply by 5/1 or within 2 weeks of notification.

CONTACT Anne Tabor, Director of Financial Aid, Husson University, 1 College Circle, Bangor, ME 04401, 207-941-7156 or toll-free 800-4-HUSSON. *Fax:* 207-941-7932. *E-mail:* tabora@husson.edu.
Website: http://www.husson.edu/.

HUSTON-TILLOTSON UNIVERSITY

Austin, TX

CONTACT Office of Financial Aid, Huston-Tillotson University, 900 Chicon Street, Austin, TX 78702, 512-505-3031. *Fax:* 512-505-3192.
Website: http://www.htu.edu/.

IDAHO STATE UNIVERSITY

Pocatello, ID

Tuition & fees: N/R	Average undergraduate aid package: $9154

ABOUT THE INSTITUTION State-supported, coed. ***Awards:*** certificates, bachelor's, master's, and doctoral degrees. 97 undergraduate majors. ***Total enrollment:*** 12,387. Undergraduates: 10,416. Freshmen: 1,297. Federal methodology is used as a basis for awarding need-based institutional aid.

FRESHMAN FINANCIAL AID (Fall 2018) 1069 applied for aid; of those 79% were deemed to have need. 99% of freshmen with need received aid; of those 9% had need fully met. ***Average percent of need met:*** 50% (excluding resources awarded to replace EFC). ***Average financial aid package:*** $8833 (excluding resources awarded to replace EFC). 13% of all full-time freshmen had no need and received non-need-based gift aid.

UNDERGRADUATE FINANCIAL AID (Fall 2018) 4,917 applied for aid; of those 85% were deemed to have need. 99% of undergraduates with need received aid; of those 6% had need fully met. ***Average percent of need met:*** 48% (excluding resources awarded to replace EFC). ***Average financial aid package:*** $9154 (excluding resources awarded to replace EFC). 10% of all full-time undergraduates had no need and received non-need-based gift aid.

GIFT AID (NEED-BASED) ***Total amount:*** $22,016,772 (69% federal, 10% state, 17% institutional, 4% external sources). ***Receiving aid:*** Freshmen: 53% (636); all full-time undergraduates: 52% (3,167). ***Average award:*** Freshmen: $5537; Undergraduates: $5339. ***Scholarships, grants, and awards:*** Federal Pell, FSEOG, state, private, college/university gift aid from institutional funds, Federal Nursing.

GIFT AID (NON-NEED-BASED) ***Total amount:*** $3,141,250 (11% state, 72% institutional, 17% external sources). ***Receiving aid:*** Freshmen: 44% (526). Undergraduates: 29% (1,776). ***Average award:*** Freshmen: $2787. Undergraduates: $2438. ***Scholarships, grants, and awards by category:*** *Academic interests/achievement:* architecture, biological sciences, business, communication, computer science, education, engineering/technologies, English, foreign languages, general academic interests/achievements, health fields, humanities, international studies, mathematics, military science, physical sciences, premedicine, social sciences. *Creative arts/performance:* applied art and design, dance, debating, journalism/publications, music, performing arts, theater/drama. *Special achievements/activities:* cheerleading/drum major, general special achievements/activities. *Special characteristics:* children of faculty/staff, children with a deceased or disabled parent, ethnic background, first-generation college students, general special characteristics, handicapped students, international students, local/state students, members of minority groups, out-of-state students. ***ROTC:*** Army.

LOANS ***Student loans:*** $26,258,650 (93% need-based, 7% non-need-based). 53% of past graduating class borrowed through all loan programs. *Average indebtedness per student:* $27,056. ***Average need-based loan:*** Freshmen: $2960. Undergraduates: $3775. ***Parent loans:*** $1,266,697 (78% need-based, 22% non-need-based). ***Programs:*** Federal Direct (Subsidized and Unsubsidized Stafford, PLUS), Perkins, Federal Nursing.

WORK-STUDY ***Federal work-study:*** Total amount: $712,194; jobs available. ***State or other work-study/employment:*** Total amount: $282,311 (100% need-based). Part-time jobs available.

ATHLETIC AWARDS Total amount: $2,435,375 (35% need-based, 65% non-need-based).

APPLYING FOR FINANCIAL AID ***Required financial aid form:*** FAFSA. ***Financial aid deadline (priority):*** 3/1. ***Notification date:*** Continuous beginning 4/1.

CONTACT Mr. James R. Martin, Director of Financial Aid, Idaho State University, 921 South 8th Avenue, Museum Building 337, Stop 8077, Pocatello, ID 83209-8077, 208-282-2756. *Fax:* 208-282-4755. *E-mail:* finaidem@isu.edu.
Website: http://www.isu.edu/.

IGLOBAL UNIVERSITY

Vienna, VA

CONTACT Financial Aid Office, IGlobal University, 8133 Leesburg Pike, #230, Vienna, VA 22182, 703-941-2020.
Website: http://www.igu.edu/.

ILLINOIS COLLEGE

Jacksonville, IL

Tuition & fees: N/R	Average undergraduate aid package: $29,989

ABOUT THE INSTITUTION Independent interdenominational, coed. ***Awards:*** bachelor's and master's degrees. 44 undergraduate majors. ***Total enrollment:*** 1,057. Undergraduates: 1,057. Freshmen: 323. Federal methodology is used as a basis for awarding need-based institutional aid.

FRESHMAN FINANCIAL AID (Fall 2018) 277 applied for aid; of those 94% were deemed to have need. 100% of freshmen with need received aid; of those 23% had need fully met. ***Average percent of need met:*** 87% (excluding resources awarded to replace EFC). ***Average financial aid package:*** $30,713 (excluding resources awarded to replace EFC). 6% of all full-time freshmen had no need and received non-need-based gift aid.

UNDERGRADUATE FINANCIAL AID (Fall 2018) 869 applied for aid; of those 94% were deemed to have need. 100% of undergraduates with need received aid; of those 23% had need fully met. ***Average percent of need met:*** 86% (excluding resources awarded to replace EFC). ***Average financial aid package:*** $29,989 (excluding resources awarded to replace EFC). 5% of all full-time undergraduates had no need and received non-need-based gift aid.

GIFT AID (NEED-BASED) ***Total amount:*** $19,973,171 (11% federal, 11% state, 77% institutional, 1% external sources). ***Receiving aid:*** Freshmen: 88% (260); all full-time undergraduates: 85% (819). ***Average award:*** Freshmen: $27,120; Undergraduates: $25,593. ***Scholarships, grants, and awards:*** Federal Pell, FSEOG, state, private, college/university gift aid from institutional funds.

GIFT AID (NON-NEED-BASED) ***Total amount:*** $4,013,338 (96% institutional, 4% external sources). ***Receiving aid:*** Freshmen: 14% (41). Undergraduates: 12% (112). ***Average award:*** Freshmen: $18,397. Undergraduates: $18,669. ***Scholarships, grants, and awards by category:*** *Academic interests/achievement:* general academic interests/achievements. *Creative arts/performance:* applied art and design, music, theater/drama. *Special characteristics:* children and siblings of alumni, children of faculty/staff, international students, previous college experience, siblings of current students.

LOANS ***Student loans:*** $6,068,382 (71% need-based, 29% non-need-based). 79% of past graduating class borrowed through all loan programs. *Average indebtedness per student:* $30,990. ***Average need-based loan:*** Freshmen: $3336. Undergraduates: $4080. ***Parent loans:*** $1,553,818 (32% need-based, 68% non-need-based). ***Programs:*** Federal Direct (Subsidized and Unsubsidized Stafford, PLUS).

WORK-STUDY ***Federal work-study:*** Total amount: $870,658; jobs available.

APPLYING FOR FINANCIAL AID ***Required financial aid form:*** FAFSA. ***Financial aid deadline (priority):*** 10/31. ***Notification date:*** Continuous beginning 12/15. Students must reply within 2 weeks of notification.

CONTACT Financial Aid Office, Illinois College, 1101 West College Avenue, Jacksonville, IL 62650-2299, 217-245-3000 or toll-free 866-464-5265.
Website: http://www.ic.edu/.

ILLINOIS INSTITUTE OF TECHNOLOGY

Chicago, IL

Tuition & fees: N/R	Average undergraduate aid package: $41,568

ABOUT THE INSTITUTION Independent, coed. ***Awards:*** bachelor's, master's, and doctoral degrees. 38 undergraduate majors. ***Total enrollment:*** 6,515. Undergraduates: 3,144. Freshmen: 583. Federal methodology is used as a basis for awarding need-based institutional aid.

FRESHMAN FINANCIAL AID (Fall 2018) 496 applied for aid; of those 92% were deemed to have need. 100% of freshmen with need received aid; of those 16% had need fully met. ***Average percent of need met:*** 85% (excluding resources awarded to replace EFC). ***Average financial aid package:*** $43,714 (excluding resources awarded to replace EFC). 25% of all full-time freshmen had no need and received non-need-based gift aid.

UNDERGRADUATE FINANCIAL AID (Fall 2018) 1,915 applied for aid; of those 95% were deemed to have need. 99% of undergraduates with need received aid; of those 12% had need fully met. ***Average percent of need met:*** 79% (excluding resources awarded to replace EFC). ***Average financial aid package:*** $41,568 (excluding resources awarded to replace EFC). 33% of all full-time undergraduates had no need and received non-need-based gift aid.

GIFT AID (NEED-BASED) ***Total amount:*** $66,065,441 (9% federal, 5% state, 85% institutional, 1% external sources). ***Receiving aid:*** Freshmen: 75% (455); all full-time undergraduates: 66% (1,801). ***Average award:*** Freshmen: $38,466; Undergraduates: $36,218. ***Scholarships, grants, and awards:*** Federal Pell, FSEOG, state, private, college/university gift aid from institutional funds.

GIFT AID (NON-NEED-BASED) ***Total amount:*** $26,638,526 (1% federal, 98% institutional, 1% external sources). ***Receiving aid:*** Freshmen: 11% (69). Undergraduates: 7% (206). ***Average award:*** Freshmen: $27,314. Undergraduates: $26,201. ***Scholarships, grants, and awards by category:*** *Academic interests/achievement:* architecture, biological sciences, business, communication, computer science, engineering/technologies, general academic interests/achievements, humanities, mathematics, premedicine, social sciences. *Creative arts/performance:* art/fine arts. *Special achievements/activities:* community service, general special achievements/activities, hobbies/interests, leadership, memberships. *Special characteristics:* children and siblings of alumni, children of faculty/staff, children of public servants, general special characteristics, international students, local/state students, previous college experience, veterans. ***ROTC:*** Army, Naval, Air Force.

LOANS ***Student loans:*** $12,425,436 (77% need-based, 23% non-need-based). 51% of past graduating class borrowed through all loan programs. *Average indebtedness per student:* $29,594. ***Average need-based loan:*** Freshmen: $3405. Undergraduates: $4570. ***Parent loans:*** $6,510,374 (47% need-based, 53% non-need-based). ***Programs:*** Federal Direct (Subsidized and Unsubsidized Stafford, PLUS), college/university.

WORK-STUDY ***Federal work-study:*** Total amount: $2,200,573; jobs available. ***State or other work-study/employment:*** Part-time jobs available.

APPLYING FOR FINANCIAL AID ***Required financial aid form:*** FAFSA. ***Financial aid deadline (priority):*** 10/1. ***Notification date:*** Continuous beginning 2/15.

CONTACT Abby McGrath, Director of Financial Aid, Illinois Institute of Technology, 3300 South Federal Street, Chicago, IL 60616, 312-567-5730 or toll-free 800-448-2329. *Fax:* 312-567-3982. *E-mail:* finaid@iit.edu.
Website: http://www.iit.edu/.

ILLINOIS STATE UNIVERSITY

Normal, IL

Tuition & fees (IL res): $14,832	Average undergraduate aid package: $12,087

ABOUT THE INSTITUTION State-supported, coed. ***Awards:*** certificates, bachelor's, master's, and doctoral degrees. 73 undergraduate majors. ***Total enrollment:*** 20,878. Undergraduates: 18,250. Freshmen: 3,860. Federal methodology is used as a basis for awarding need-based institutional aid.

UNDERGRADUATE EXPENSES for 2020–2021 ***Application fee:*** $50. ***Tuition, state resident:*** full-time $11,524; part-time $384 per credit hour. ***Tuition, nonresident:*** full-time $23,524; part-time $768 per credit hour. ***Required fees:*** full-time $3308; $92.28 per credit hour. Full-time tuition and fees vary according to degree level. Part-time tuition and fees vary according to degree level. ***College room and board:*** $9850; ***Room only:*** $5334. Room and board charges vary according to board plan and housing facility. ***Payment plan:*** Guaranteed tuition.
FRESHMAN FINANCIAL AID (Fall 2018) 3346 applied for aid; of those 76% were deemed to have need. 96% of freshmen with need received aid; of those 9% had need fully met. ***Average percent of need met:*** 58% (excluding resources awarded to replace EFC). ***Average financial aid package:*** $12,810 (excluding resources awarded to replace EFC). 17% of all full-time freshmen had no need and received non-need-based gift aid.
UNDERGRADUATE FINANCIAL AID (Fall 2018) 13,626 applied for aid; of those 78% were deemed to have need. 96% of undergraduates with need received aid; of those 9% had need fully met. ***Average percent of need met:*** 56% (excluding resources awarded to replace EFC). ***Average financial aid package:*** $12,087 (excluding resources awarded to replace EFC). 11% of all full-time undergraduates had no need and received non-need-based gift aid.
GIFT AID (NEED-BASED) ***Total amount:*** $78,266,141 (37% federal, 32% state, 29% institutional, 2% external sources). ***Receiving aid:*** Freshmen: 39% (1,434); all full-time undergraduates: 35% (5,943). ***Average award:*** Freshmen: $11,360; Undergraduates: $9984. ***Scholarships, grants, and awards:*** Federal Pell, FSEOG, state, private, college/university gift aid from institutional funds, Federal Nursing.
GIFT AID (NON-NEED-BASED) ***Total amount:*** $11,024,760 (8% federal, 15% state, 66% institutional, 11% external sources). ***Receiving aid:*** Freshmen: 38% (1,388). Undergraduates: 25% (4,188). ***Average award:*** Freshmen: $3575. Undergraduates: $3514. ***Scholarships, grants, and awards by category:*** *Academic interests/achievement:* agriculture, biological sciences, business, communication, computer science, education, engineering/technologies, English, foreign languages, general academic interests/achievements, health fields, home economics, humanities, international studies, library science, mathematics, military science, physical sciences, premedicine, social sciences. *Creative arts/performance:* applied art and design, art/fine arts, cinema/film/broadcasting, creative writing, debating, general creative arts/performance, music, performing arts, theater/drama. *Special achievements/activities:* community service, leadership. *Special characteristics:* children and siblings of alumni, children of faculty/staff, children of union members/company employees, children with a deceased or disabled parent, first-generation college students, general special characteristics, local/state students, members of minority groups, previous college experience, religious affiliation. ***Tuition waivers:*** Full or partial for minority students, employees or children of employees, senior citizens. ***ROTC:*** Army.
LOANS ***Student loans:*** $92,604,157 (66% need-based, 34% non-need-based). 68% of past graduating class borrowed through all loan programs. *Average indebtedness per student:* $31,687. ***Average need-based loan:*** Freshmen: $3264. Undergraduates: $4190. ***Parent loans:*** $29,654,873 (40% need-based, 60% non-need-based). ***Programs:*** Federal Direct (Subsidized and Unsubsidized Stafford, PLUS), Federal Nursing.
WORK-STUDY ***Federal work-study:*** Total amount: $1,013,864; 592 jobs averaging $1713.
ATHLETIC AWARDS Total amount: $6,466,558 (33% need-based, 67% non-need-based).
APPLYING FOR FINANCIAL AID ***Required financial aid form:*** FAFSA. ***Financial aid deadline (priority):*** 11/15. ***Notification date:*** Continuous beginning 4/1.
CONTACT Mr. David Krueger, Associate Director of Financial Aid, Illinois State University, Campus Box 2320, Normal, IL 61790-2320, 309-438-2231 or toll-free 800-366-2478. *Fax:* 309-438-3755. *E-mail:* financialaid@illinoisstate.edu.
Website: http://www.illinoisstate.edu/.

ILLINOIS WESLEYAN UNIVERSITY

Bloomington, IL

Tuition & fees: $51,336	Average undergraduate aid package: $37,608

ABOUT THE INSTITUTION Independent, coed. ***Awards:*** bachelor's degrees. 50 undergraduate majors. ***Total enrollment:*** 1,629. Undergraduates: 1,629. Freshmen: 409. Both federal and institutional methodology are used as a basis for awarding need-based institutional aid.
UNDERGRADUATE EXPENSES for 2020–2021 ***Comprehensive fee:*** $63,176 includes full-time tuition ($51,132), mandatory fees ($204), and room and board ($11,840). ***College room only:*** $7414. Room and board charges vary according to housing facility. ***Part-time tuition:*** $1598 per credit hour.
FRESHMAN FINANCIAL AID (Fall 2019, est.) 376 applied for aid; of those 83% were deemed to have need. 100% of freshmen with need received aid; of those 21% had need fully met. ***Average percent of need met:*** 83% (excluding resources awarded to replace EFC). ***Average financial aid package:*** $38,316 (excluding resources awarded to replace EFC). 23% of all full-time freshmen had no need and received non-need-based gift aid.
UNDERGRADUATE FINANCIAL AID (Fall 2019, est.) 1,350 applied for aid; of those 87% were deemed to have need. 100% of undergraduates with need received aid; of those 19% had need fully met. ***Average percent of need met:*** 83% (excluding resources awarded to replace EFC). ***Average financial aid package:*** $37,608 (excluding resources awarded to replace EFC). 26% of all full-time undergraduates had no need and received non-need-based gift aid.
GIFT AID (NEED-BASED) ***Total amount:*** $35,830,272 (5% federal, 6% state, 88% institutional, 1% external sources). ***Receiving aid:*** Freshmen: 75% (312); all full-time undergraduates: 72% (1,171). ***Average award:*** Freshmen: $33,042; Undergraduates: $31,078. ***Scholarships, grants, and awards:*** Federal Pell, FSEOG, state, private, college/university gift aid from institutional funds.
GIFT AID (NON-NEED-BASED) ***Total amount:*** $11,527,972 (100% institutional). ***Receiving aid:*** Freshmen: 28% (115). Undergraduates: 20% (321). ***Average award:*** Freshmen: $26,549. Undergraduates: $23,610. ***Scholarships, grants, and awards by category:*** *Academic interests/achievement:* general academic interests/achievements. *Creative arts/performance:* applied art and design, general creative arts/performance, music, theater/drama. *Special characteristics:* children of faculty/staff, general special characteristics, international students. ***Tuition waivers:*** Full or partial for employees or children of employees. ***ROTC:*** Army cooperative.
LOANS ***Student loans:*** $11,637,226 (42% need-based, 58% non-need-based). 68% of past graduating class borrowed through all loan programs. *Average indebtedness per student:* $34,268. ***Average need-based loan:*** Freshmen: $4394. Undergraduates: $5587. ***Parent loans:*** $4,833,214 (100% non-need-based). ***Programs:*** Federal Direct (Subsidized and Unsubsidized Stafford, PLUS), Perkins, Federal Nursing, college/university.
WORK-STUDY ***Federal work-study:*** Total amount: $332,770; jobs available. ***State or other work-study/employment:*** Total amount: $803,895 (79% need-based, 21% non-need-based). Part-time jobs available.
APPLYING FOR FINANCIAL AID ***Required financial aid forms:*** FAFSA, institution's own form. ***Financial aid deadline (priority):*** 3/1. ***Notification date:*** Continuous beginning 3/1. Students must reply by 5/1.
CONTACT Mr. Scott Seibring, Director of Financial Aid, Illinois Wesleyan University, 1312 North Park Street, PO Box 2900, Bloomington, IL 61702-2900, 309-556-3393 or toll-free 800-332-2498. *Fax:* 309-556-3833. *E-mail:* seibring@iwu.edu.
Website: http://www.iwu.edu/.

IMMACULATA UNIVERSITY

Immaculata, PA

Tuition & fees: $27,750	Average undergraduate aid package: $17,757

ABOUT THE INSTITUTION Independent Roman Catholic, coed. ***Awards:*** certificates, associate, bachelor's, master's, and doctoral degrees. 43 undergraduate majors. ***Total enrollment:*** 2,497. Undergraduates: 1,503. Freshmen: 259. Federal methodology is used as a basis for awarding need-based institutional aid.
UNDERGRADUATE EXPENSES for 2020–2021 ***Application fee:*** $35. ***Comprehensive fee:*** $40,370 includes full-time tuition ($26,900), mandatory fees ($850), and room and board ($12,620). ***College room only:*** $6390. Full-time tuition and fees vary according to degree level. Room and board charges vary according to board plan. ***Part-time tuition:*** $540 per credit hour. Part-time tuition and fees vary according to degree level.
FRESHMAN FINANCIAL AID (Fall 2018) 172 applied for aid; of those 88% were deemed to have need. 100% of freshmen with need received aid; of those 15% had need fully met. ***Average percent of need met:*** 64% (excluding resources awarded to replace EFC). ***Average financial aid package:*** $18,228 (excluding resources awarded to replace EFC). 17% of all full-time freshmen had no need and received non-need-based gift aid.

UNDERGRADUATE FINANCIAL AID (Fall 2018) 728 applied for aid; of those 88% were deemed to have need. 100% of undergraduates with need received aid; of those 14% had need fully met. ***Average percent of need met:*** 55% (excluding resources awarded to replace EFC). ***Average financial aid package:*** $17,757 (excluding resources awarded to replace EFC). 19% of all full-time undergraduates had no need and received non-need-based gift aid.

GIFT AID (NEED-BASED) ***Total amount:*** $4,074,102 (46% federal, 24% state, 30% institutional). ***Receiving aid:*** Freshmen: 53% (97); all full-time undergraduates: 54% (442). ***Average award:*** Freshmen: $6331; Undergraduates: $7522. ***Scholarships, grants, and awards:*** Federal Pell, FSEOG, state, private, college/university gift aid from institutional funds, United Negro College Fund.

GIFT AID (NON-NEED-BASED) ***Total amount:*** $6,682,095 (1% state, 96% institutional, 3% external sources). ***Receiving aid:*** Freshmen: 80% (146). Undergraduates: 70% (573). ***Average award:*** Freshmen: $10,686. Undergraduates: $9665. ***Scholarships, grants, and awards by category:*** *Academic interests/achievement:* general academic interests/achievements, military science. *Creative arts/performance:* general creative arts/performance, music, theater/drama. *Special achievements/activities:* leadership, religious involvement. *Special characteristics:* children and siblings of alumni, local/state students, religious affiliation. ***Tuition waivers:*** Full or partial for employees or children of employees. ***ROTC:*** Army cooperative.

LOANS ***Student loans:*** $9,740,788 (30% need-based, 70% non-need-based). 85% of past graduating class borrowed through all loan programs. *Average indebtedness per student:* $55,126. ***Average need-based loan:*** Freshmen: $3278. Undergraduates: $4289. ***Parent loans:*** $3,016,494 (99% need-based, 1% non-need-based). ***Programs:*** Federal Direct (Subsidized and Unsubsidized Stafford, PLUS), Perkins.

WORK-STUDY ***Federal work-study:*** Total amount: $261,747. ***State or other work-study/employment:*** Total amount: $50,220 (53% need-based, 47% non-need-based).

APPLYING FOR FINANCIAL AID ***Required financial aid forms:*** FAFSA, state aid form. ***Financial aid deadline (priority):*** 2/15. ***Notification date:*** Continuous beginning 10/15. Students must reply by 5/1 or within 2 weeks of notification.

CONTACT Mr. Robert Forest, Director of Student Financial Aid, Immaculata University, 1145 King Road, Box 500, Immaculata, PA 19345, 610-647-4400 Ext. 3026 or toll-free 877-428-6329. *Fax:* 610-640-0836. *E-mail:* rforest@immaculata.edu.
Website: http://www.immaculata.edu/.

INDEPENDENCE UNIVERSITY

Salt Lake City, UT

CONTACT Financial Aid Director, Independence University, 2423 Hoover Avenue, National City, CA 91950-6605, 619-477-4800 or toll-free 800-917-6391. *Fax:* 619-477-5202.
Website: http://www.independence.edu/.

INDIANA STATE UNIVERSITY

Terre Haute, IN

Tuition & fees (area res): $9466 | **Average undergraduate aid package: $11,089**

ABOUT THE INSTITUTION State-supported, coed. ***Awards:*** certificates, bachelor's, master's, and doctoral degrees. 78 undergraduate majors. ***Total enrollment:*** 12,146. Undergraduates: 10,216. Freshmen: 1,893. Federal methodology is used as a basis for awarding need-based institutional aid.

UNDERGRADUATE EXPENSES for 2020–2021 ***Application fee:*** $25. ***Tuition, area resident:*** full-time $9186; part-time $332 per credit hour. ***Tuition, state resident:*** full-time $9186; part-time $332 per credit hour. ***Tuition, nonresident:*** full-time $20,290; part-time $717 per credit hour. ***Required fees:*** full-time $280; $140 per term. Full-time tuition and fees vary according to reciprocity agreements. Part-time tuition and fees vary according to course load and reciprocity agreements. ***College room and board:*** $11,016; ***Room only:*** $7237. Room and board charges vary according to board plan, housing facility, and student level.

FRESHMAN FINANCIAL AID (Fall 2018) 2291 applied for aid; of those 84% were deemed to have need. 96% of freshmen with need received aid; of those 12% had need fully met. ***Average percent of need met:*** 84% (excluding resources awarded to replace EFC). ***Average financial aid package:*** $10,849 (excluding resources awarded to replace EFC). 11% of all full-time freshmen had no need and received non-need-based gift aid.

UNDERGRADUATE FINANCIAL AID (Fall 2018) 7,836 applied for aid; of those 86% were deemed to have need. 95% of undergraduates with need received aid; of those 10% had need fully met. ***Average percent of need met:*** 80% (excluding resources awarded to replace EFC). ***Average financial aid package:*** $11,089 (excluding resources awarded to replace EFC). 9% of all full-time undergraduates had no need and received non-need-based gift aid.

GIFT AID (NEED-BASED) ***Total amount:*** $28,224,595 (75% federal, 19% state, 6% institutional). ***Receiving aid:*** Freshmen: 50% (1,188); all full-time undergraduates: 46% (4,094). ***Average award:*** Freshmen: $6494; Undergraduates: $6554. ***Scholarships, grants, and awards:*** Federal Pell, FSEOG, state, private, college/university gift aid from institutional funds.

GIFT AID (NON-NEED-BASED) ***Total amount:*** $29,334,285 (52% state, 37% institutional, 11% external sources). ***Receiving aid:*** Freshmen: 50% (1,194). Undergraduates: 38% (3,407). ***Average award:*** Freshmen: $4190. Undergraduates: $5205. ***Scholarships, grants, and awards by category:*** *Academic interests/achievement:* 3,727 awards ($9,395,157 total): area/ethnic studies, biological sciences, business, communication, computer science, education, engineering/technologies, English, foreign languages, general academic interests/achievements, home economics, humanities, mathematics, physical sciences, premedicine, social sciences. *Creative arts/performance:* 80 awards ($319,500 total): applied art and design, art/fine arts, music, performing arts, theater/drama. *Special characteristics:* 287 awards ($2,135,637 total): children and siblings of alumni, children of faculty/staff, members of minority groups, out-of-state students, previous college experience, veterans. ***Tuition waivers:*** Full or partial for employees or children of employees, senior citizens. ***ROTC:*** Army, Air Force.

LOANS ***Student loans:*** $47,994,465 (40% need-based, 60% non-need-based). 69% of past graduating class borrowed through all loan programs. *Average indebtedness per student:* $26,223. ***Average need-based loan:*** Freshmen: $3025. Undergraduates: $3797. ***Parent loans:*** $12,900,481 (100% non-need-based). ***Programs:*** Federal Direct (Subsidized and Unsubsidized Stafford, PLUS), Perkins.

WORK-STUDY ***Federal work-study:*** Total amount: $495,174; 1,086 jobs averaging $2110.

ATHLETIC AWARDS Total amount: $4,910,463 (100% non-need-based).

APPLYING FOR FINANCIAL AID ***Required financial aid form:*** FAFSA. ***Financial aid deadline (priority):*** 4/15. ***Notification date:*** Continuous beginning 1/15.

CONTACT Donna Simmonds, Director of Student Financial Aid, Indiana State University, 150 Tirey Hall, Terre Haute, IN 47809-1401, 800-841-4744 or toll-free 800-468-6478. *Fax:* 812-237-4330. *E-mail:* isu-finaid@mail.indstate.edu.
Website: http://www.indstate.edu/.

INDIANA TECH

Fort Wayne, IN

Tuition & fees: N/R | **Average undergraduate aid package: $29,084**

ABOUT THE INSTITUTION Independent, coed. ***Awards:*** associate, bachelor's, master's, and doctoral degrees. 31 undergraduate majors. Federal methodology is used as a basis for awarding need-based institutional aid.

FRESHMAN FINANCIAL AID (Fall 2018) 379 applied for aid; of those 90% were deemed to have need. 100% of freshmen with need received aid; of those 18% had need fully met. ***Average percent of need met:*** 67% (excluding resources awarded to replace EFC). ***Average financial aid package:*** $29,538 (excluding resources awarded to replace EFC). 4% of all full-time freshmen had no need and received non-need-based gift aid.

UNDERGRADUATE FINANCIAL AID (Fall 2018) 1,182 applied for aid; of those 92% were deemed to have need. 100% of undergraduates with need received aid; of those 25% had need fully met. ***Average percent of need met:*** 87% (excluding resources awarded to replace EFC). ***Average financial aid package:*** $29,084 (excluding resources awarded to replace EFC). 3% of all full-time undergraduates had no need and received non-need-based gift aid.

GIFT AID (NEED-BASED) ***Total amount:*** $19,259,736 (16% federal, 13% state, 70% institutional, 1% external sources). ***Receiving aid:*** Freshmen: 72% (311); all full-time undergraduates: 65% (986). ***Average award:*** Freshmen: $9024; Undergraduates: $7406. ***Scholarships, grants, and awards:*** Federal Pell, FSEOG, state, private, college/university gift aid from institutional funds.

GIFT AID (NON-NEED-BASED) ***Receiving aid:*** Freshmen: 74% (317). Undergraduates: 63% (958). ***Average award:*** Freshmen: $11,000. Undergraduates: $10,106. ***Scholarships, grants, and awards by category:*** *Academic interests/achievement:* 1,140 awards ($10,540,207 total): computer science, engineering/technologies, general academic interests/achievements. *Special characteristics:* 259 awards ($851,827 total): children of current students, children of faculty/staff, local/state students, married students, siblings of current students, spouses of current students, veterans. ***ROTC:*** Army cooperative.

LOANS ***Student loans:*** $7,342,826 (41% need-based, 59% non-need-based). 80% of past graduating class borrowed through all loan programs. *Average indebtedness per student:* $20,689. ***Average need-based loan:*** Freshmen: $2760. Undergraduates: $3924. ***Parent loans:*** $2,582,467 (100% non-need-based). ***Programs:*** Federal Direct (Subsidized and Unsubsidized Stafford, PLUS).

WORK-STUDY ***Federal work-study:*** Total amount: $88,964; 73 jobs averaging $1218.

ATHLETIC AWARDS Total amount: $6,458,715 (100% non-need-based).

APPLYING FOR FINANCIAL AID ***Required financial aid form:*** FAFSA. ***Financial aid deadline:*** Continuous. ***Notification date:*** Continuous beginning 11/15. Students must reply within 2 weeks of notification.

CONTACT Mrs. Lisa Claudette Green, Assistant Director, Indiana Tech, 1600 East Washington Boulevard, Fort Wayne, IN 46803-1297, 800-937-2448 Ext. 2334 or toll-free 800-937-2448. *Fax:* 260-422-1578. *E-mail:* financialaid@indianatech.edu.
Website: http://www.indianatech.edu/.

INDIANA UNIVERSITY BLOOMINGTON

Bloomington, IN

Tuition & fees (area res): $10,947	Average undergraduate aid package: $14,196

ABOUT THE INSTITUTION State-supported, coed. ***Awards:*** certificates, diplomas, associate, bachelor's, master's, and doctoral degrees. 115 undergraduate majors. ***Total enrollment:*** 43,260. Undergraduates: 33,084. Freshmen: 8,291. Federal methodology is used as a basis for awarding need-based institutional aid.

UNDERGRADUATE EXPENSES for 2020–2021 ***Application fee:*** $65. ***Tuition, area resident:*** full-time $9575; part-time $299 per credit hour. ***Tuition, state resident:*** full-time $9575; part-time $299 per credit hour. ***Tuition, nonresident:*** full-time $35,140; part-time $1098 per credit hour. ***Required fees:*** full-time $1372. Full-time tuition and fees vary according to program. Part-time tuition and fees vary according to course load and program. ***College room and board:*** $10,830. Room and board charges vary according to board plan and housing facility.

FRESHMAN FINANCIAL AID (Fall 2018) 6066 applied for aid; of those 61% were deemed to have need. 96% of freshmen with need received aid; of those 33% had need fully met. ***Average percent of need met:*** 71% (excluding resources awarded to replace EFC). ***Average financial aid package:*** $14,411 (excluding resources awarded to replace EFC). 35% of all full-time freshmen had no need and received non-need-based gift aid.

UNDERGRADUATE FINANCIAL AID (Fall 2018) 19,207 applied for aid; of those 68% were deemed to have need. 96% of undergraduates with need received aid; of those 30% had need fully met. ***Average percent of need met:*** 71% (excluding resources awarded to replace EFC). ***Average financial aid package:*** $14,196 (excluding resources awarded to replace EFC). 28% of all full-time undergraduates had no need and received non-need-based gift aid.

GIFT AID (NEED-BASED) ***Receiving aid:*** Freshmen: 40% (3,185); all full-time undergraduates: 33% (10,621). ***Average award:*** Freshmen: $12,490; Undergraduates: $12,679. ***Scholarships, grants, and awards:*** Federal Pell, FSEOG, state, private, college/university gift aid from institutional funds.

GIFT AID (NON-NEED-BASED) ***Receiving aid:*** Freshmen: 11% (881). Undergraduates: 8% (2,432). ***Average award:*** Freshmen: $7338. Undergraduates: $7761. ***Tuition waivers:*** Full or partial for employees or children of employees, senior citizens. ***ROTC:*** Army, Air Force.

LOANS ***Student loans:*** 44% of past graduating class borrowed through all loan programs. *Average indebtedness per student:* $27,555. ***Average need-based loan:*** Freshmen: $3118. Undergraduates: $3934. ***Programs:*** Federal Direct (Subsidized and Unsubsidized Stafford, PLUS), Perkins, Federal Nursing, college/university.

WORK-STUDY ***Federal work-study:*** 633 jobs averaging $1863. ***State or other work-study/employment:*** Part-time jobs available.

APPLYING FOR FINANCIAL AID ***Required financial aid form:*** FAFSA. ***Financial aid deadline:*** Continuous. ***Notification date:*** Continuous.

CONTACT Jackie Kennedy-Fletcher, Director, Office of Student Financial Assistance, Indiana University Bloomington, 408 North Union Street, Bloomington, IN 47405, 812-855-6500. *Fax:* 812-855-7615. *E-mail:* scu@indiana.edu.
Website: http://www.iub.edu/.

INDIANA UNIVERSITY EAST

Richmond, IN

Tuition & fees (IN res): $7527	Average undergraduate aid package: $9366

ABOUT THE INSTITUTION State-supported, coed. ***Awards:*** certificates, bachelor's, and master's degrees. 29 undergraduate majors. ***Total enrollment:*** 3,766. Undergraduates: 3,500. Freshmen: 451. Federal methodology is used as a basis for awarding need-based institutional aid.

UNDERGRADUATE EXPENSES for 2020–2021 ***Application fee:*** $35. ***Tuition, state resident:*** full-time $6895; part-time $230 per credit hour. ***Tuition, nonresident:*** full-time $19,346; part-time $645 per credit hour. ***Required fees:*** full-time $632. Full-time tuition and fees vary according to program and reciprocity agreements. Part-time tuition and fees vary according to course load, program, and reciprocity agreements.

FRESHMAN FINANCIAL AID (Fall 2018) 402 applied for aid; of those 85% were deemed to have need. 98% of freshmen with need received aid; of those 21% had need fully met. ***Average percent of need met:*** 70% (excluding resources awarded to replace EFC). ***Average financial aid package:*** $9768 (excluding resources awarded to replace EFC). 7% of all full-time freshmen had no need and received non-need-based gift aid.

UNDERGRADUATE FINANCIAL AID (Fall 2018) 1,730 applied for aid; of those 85% were deemed to have need. 95% of undergraduates with need received aid; of those 19% had need fully met. ***Average percent of need met:*** 69% (excluding resources awarded to replace EFC). ***Average financial aid package:*** $9366 (excluding resources awarded to replace EFC). 7% of all full-time undergraduates had no need and received non-need-based gift aid.

GIFT AID (NEED-BASED) ***Receiving aid:*** Freshmen: 74% (320); all full-time undergraduates: 62% (1,223). ***Average award:*** Freshmen: $8401; Undergraduates: $7837. ***Scholarships, grants, and awards:*** Federal Pell, FSEOG, state, private, college/university gift aid from institutional funds.

GIFT AID (NON-NEED-BASED) ***Receiving aid:*** Freshmen: 10% (45). Undergraduates: 7% (147). ***Average award:*** Freshmen: $2802. Undergraduates: $2485. ***Tuition waivers:*** Full or partial for employees or children of employees, senior citizens.

LOANS ***Student loans:*** 71% of past graduating class borrowed through all loan programs. *Average indebtedness per student:* $22,513. ***Average need-based loan:*** Freshmen: $2896. Undergraduates: $3660. ***Programs:*** Federal Direct (Subsidized and Unsubsidized Stafford, PLUS), college/university.

WORK-STUDY ***Federal work-study:*** 52 jobs averaging $2059.

APPLYING FOR FINANCIAL AID ***Required financial aid forms:*** FAFSA, institution's own form. ***Financial aid deadline:*** Continuous. ***Notification date:*** Continuous. Students must reply within 2 weeks of notification.

CONTACT Sarah Soper, Executive Director, Financial Aid & Scholarships, Indiana University East, Whitewater Hall 112, 2325 Chester Boulevard, Richmond, IN 47374-1289, 765-973-8206 or toll-free 800-959-EAST. *Fax:* 765-973-8288. *E-mail:* eaosfa@iue.edu.
Website: http://www.iue.edu/.

INDIANA UNIVERSITY KOKOMO

Kokomo, IN

Tuition & fees (IN res): $7527	Average undergraduate aid package: $8934

ABOUT THE INSTITUTION State-supported, coed. ***Awards:*** certificates, associate, bachelor's, and master's degrees. 37 undergraduate majors. ***Total enrollment:*** 3,123. Undergraduates: 2,912. Freshmen: 639. Federal methodology is used as a basis for awarding need-based institutional aid.

UNDERGRADUATE EXPENSES for 2020–2021 ***Application fee:*** $35. ***Tuition, state resident:*** full-time $6895; part-time $230 per credit hour. ***Tuition, nonresident:*** full-time $19,346; part-time $645 per credit hour. ***Required fees:*** full-time $632. Full-time tuition and fees vary according to program and reciprocity agreements. Part-time tuition and fees vary according to course load, program, and reciprocity agreements.

FRESHMAN FINANCIAL AID (Fall 2018) 580 applied for aid; of those 77% were deemed to have need. 95% of freshmen with need received aid; of those 13% had need fully met. ***Average percent of need met:*** 64% (excluding resources awarded to replace EFC). ***Average financial aid package:*** $8352 (excluding resources awarded to replace EFC). 9% of all full-time freshmen had no need and received non-need-based gift aid.

UNDERGRADUATE FINANCIAL AID (Fall 2018) 1,958 applied for aid; of those 79% were deemed to have need. 95% of undergraduates with need received aid; of those 16% had need fully met. ***Average percent of need met:*** 67% (excluding resources awarded to replace EFC). ***Average financial aid package:*** $8934 (excluding resources awarded to replace EFC). 7% of all full-time undergraduates had no need and received non-need-based gift aid.

GIFT AID (NEED-BASED) ***Receiving aid:*** Freshmen: 59% (371); all full-time undergraduates: 55% (1,251). ***Average award:*** Freshmen: $7927; Undergraduates: $8061. ***Scholarships, grants, and awards:*** Federal Pell, FSEOG, state, private, college/university gift aid from institutional funds.

GIFT AID (NON-NEED-BASED) ***Receiving aid:*** Freshmen: 6% (40). Undergraduates: 6% (125). ***Average award:*** Freshmen: $2108. Undergraduates: $2336. ***Tuition waivers:*** Full or partial for employees or children of employees, senior citizens.

LOANS ***Student loans:*** 63% of past graduating class borrowed through all loan programs. *Average indebtedness per student:* $23,518. ***Average need-based loan:*** Freshmen: $2775. Undergraduates: $3519. ***Programs:*** Federal Direct (Subsidized and Unsubsidized Stafford, PLUS), Federal Nursing, college/university.

WORK-STUDY ***Federal work-study:*** 69 jobs averaging $1563.

APPLYING FOR FINANCIAL AID ***Required financial aid form:*** FAFSA. ***Financial aid deadline:*** Continuous. ***Notification date:*** Continuous.

CONTACT Dara Johnson, Director of Financial Aid, Indiana University Kokomo, Kelley Student Center, Room 230, 2300 South Washington Street, Kokomo, IN 46904-9003, 765-455-9216 or toll-free 888-875-4485. *Fax:* 765-455-9537. *E-mail:* finaidko@iuk.edu.
Website: http://www.iuk.edu/.

INDIANA UNIVERSITY NORTHWEST

Gary, IN

Tuition & fees (IN res): $7527	Average undergraduate aid package: $8847

ABOUT THE INSTITUTION State-supported, coed. ***Awards:*** certificates, associate, bachelor's, and master's degrees. 47 undergraduate majors. ***Total enrollment:*** 3,959. Undergraduates: 3,534. Freshmen: 674. Federal methodology is used as a basis for awarding need-based institutional aid.

UNDERGRADUATE EXPENSES for 2020–2021 ***Application fee:*** $35. ***Tuition, state resident:*** full-time $6895; part-time $230 per credit hour. ***Tuition, nonresident:*** full-time $19,346; part-time $645 per credit hour. ***Required fees:*** full-time $632. Full-time tuition and fees vary according to program and reciprocity agreements. Part-time tuition and fees vary according to course load, program, and reciprocity agreements.

FRESHMAN FINANCIAL AID (Fall 2018) 555 applied for aid; of those 76% were deemed to have need. 95% of freshmen with need received aid; of those 16% had need fully met. ***Average percent of need met:*** 65% (excluding resources awarded to replace EFC). ***Average financial aid package:*** $8037 (excluding resources awarded to replace EFC). 6% of all full-time freshmen had no need and received non-need-based gift aid.

UNDERGRADUATE FINANCIAL AID (Fall 2018) 2,150 applied for aid; of those 81% were deemed to have need. 94% of undergraduates with need received aid; of those 17% had need fully met. ***Average percent of need met:*** 68% (excluding resources awarded to replace EFC). ***Average financial aid package:*** $8847 (excluding resources awarded to replace EFC). 7% of all full-time undergraduates had no need and received non-need-based gift aid.

GIFT AID (NEED-BASED) ***Receiving aid:*** Freshmen: 56% (340); all full-time undergraduates: 56% (1,399). ***Average award:*** Freshmen: $7951; Undergraduates: $7850. ***Scholarships, grants, and awards:*** Federal Pell, FSEOG, state, private, college/university gift aid from institutional funds, United Negro College Fund, Federal Nursing, Illiana Scholarship, Transfer Scholarship.

GIFT AID (NON-NEED-BASED) ***Receiving aid:*** Freshmen: 5% (32). Undergraduates: 5% (132). ***Average award:*** Freshmen: $3271. Undergraduates: $4053. ***Tuition waivers:*** Full or partial for employees or children of employees, senior citizens. ***ROTC:*** Army.

LOANS ***Student loans:*** 66% of past graduating class borrowed through all loan programs. *Average indebtedness per student:* $26,940. ***Average need-based loan:*** Freshmen: $2611. Undergraduates: $3589. ***Programs:*** Federal Direct (Subsidized and Unsubsidized Stafford, PLUS), college/university.

WORK-STUDY ***Federal work-study:*** 72 jobs averaging $1562.

APPLYING FOR FINANCIAL AID ***Required financial aid form:*** FAFSA. ***Financial aid deadline:*** Continuous. ***Notification date:*** Continuous.

CONTACT Gina A Pirtle, Director, Financial Aid and Scholarships, Indiana University Northwest, 3400 Broadway, Hawthorn Hall, Room 111, Gary, IN 46408, 219-980-6778 or toll-free 800-968-7486. *Fax:* 219-981-5622. *E-mail:* finaidnw@iun.edu.
Website: http://www.iun.edu/.

INDIANA UNIVERSITY OF PENNSYLVANIA

Indiana, PA

Tuition & fees (PA res): $13,354	Average undergraduate aid package: $10,462

ABOUT THE INSTITUTION State-supported, coed. ***Awards:*** certificates, associate, bachelor's, master's, and doctoral degrees. 64 undergraduate majors. ***Total enrollment:*** 10,302. Undergraduates: 14,234. Freshmen: 7,779. Federal methodology is used as a basis for awarding need-based institutional aid.

UNDERGRADUATE EXPENSES for 2019–2020 ***Tuition, state resident:*** full-time $9570; part-time $319 per credit hour. ***Tuition, nonresident:*** full-time $13,890; part-time $463 per credit hour. ***Required fees:*** full-time $3784; $50 per term. Full-time tuition and fees vary according to course load. Part-time tuition and fees vary according to course load. ***College room and board:*** $12,744; ***Room only:*** $8950. Room and board charges vary according to board plan, housing facility, and location.

FRESHMAN FINANCIAL AID (Fall 2018) 1861 applied for aid; of those 85% were deemed to have need. 100% of freshmen with need received aid; of those 4% had need fully met. ***Average percent of need met:*** 52% (excluding resources awarded to replace EFC). ***Average financial aid package:*** $10,773 (excluding resources awarded to replace EFC). 6% of all full-time freshmen had no need and received non-need-based gift aid.

UNDERGRADUATE FINANCIAL AID (Fall 2018) 7,276 applied for aid; of those 85% were deemed to have need. 99% of undergraduates with need received aid; of those 5% had need fully met. ***Average percent of need met:*** 53% (excluding resources awarded to replace EFC). ***Average financial aid package:*** $10,462 (excluding resources awarded to replace EFC). 4% of all full-time undergraduates had no need and received non-need-based gift aid.

GIFT AID (NEED-BASED) ***Total amount:*** $35,431,770 (48% federal, 27% state, 17% institutional, 8% external sources). ***Receiving aid:*** Freshmen: 55% (1,076); all full-time undergraduates: 49% (4,084). ***Average award:*** Freshmen: $6904; Undergraduates: $6341. ***Scholarships, grants, and awards:*** Federal Pell, FSEOG, state, private, college/university gift aid from institutional funds, United Negro College Fund.

GIFT AID (NON-NEED-BASED) ***Total amount:*** $2,052,104 (11% state, 59% institutional, 30% external sources). ***Receiving aid:*** Freshmen: 46% (903). Under-

graduates: 45% (3,744). ***Average award:*** Freshmen: $2289. Undergraduates: $1960. ***Scholarships, grants, and awards by category:*** *Academic interests/achievement:* 5,022 awards ($9,045,915 total): area/ethnic studies, biological sciences, business, communication, computer science, education, engineering/technologies, English, foreign languages, general academic interests/achievements, health fields, home economics, humanities, international studies, mathematics, military science, physical sciences, premedicine, religion/biblical studies, social sciences. *Creative arts/performance:* applied art and design, art/fine arts, dance, general creative arts/performance, journalism/publications, music, performing arts, theater/drama. *Special achievements/activities:* community service, general special achievements/activities, hobbies/interests, leadership. *Special characteristics:* adult students, children of faculty/staff, ethnic background, first-generation college students, international students, local/state students, married students. ***Tuition waivers:*** Full or partial for employees or children of employees, senior citizens. ***ROTC:*** Army.

LOANS *Student loans:* $71,626,401 (68% need-based, 32% non-need-based). 84% of past graduating class borrowed through all loan programs. *Average indebtedness per student:* $41,222. ***Average need-based loan:*** Freshmen: $3150. Undergraduates: $4051. ***Parent loans:*** $20,533,682 (60% need-based, 40% non-need-based). ***Programs:*** Federal Direct (Subsidized and Unsubsidized Stafford, PLUS), Perkins.

WORK-STUDY *Federal work-study:* Total amount: $3,313,193; 902 jobs averaging $1797. ***State or other work-study/employment:*** Total amount: $966,358 (100% non-need-based). 830 part-time jobs averaging $1627.

ATHLETIC AWARDS Total amount: $1,738,108 (56% need-based, 44% non-need-based).

APPLYING FOR FINANCIAL AID *Required financial aid forms:* FAFSA, state aid form. ***Financial aid deadline (priority):*** 5/1. ***Notification date:*** Continuous beginning 12/20.

CONTACT Ms. Ragan Griffin, Director of Financial Aid, Indiana University of Pennsylvania, 1090 South Drive, 200 Clark Hall, Indiana, PA 15705, 724-357-2218 or toll-free 800-442-6830. *Fax:* 724-357-2094. *E-mail:* financial-aid@iup.edu.
Website: http://www.iup.edu/.

INDIANA UNIVERSITY-PURDUE UNIVERSITY INDIANAPOLIS

Indianapolis, IN

Tuition & fees (IN res): $9701	Average undergraduate aid package: $11,849

ABOUT THE INSTITUTION State-supported, coed. ***Awards:*** certificates, associate, bachelor's, master's, and doctoral degrees. 94 undergraduate majors. ***Total enrollment:*** 29,579. Undergraduates: 21,246. Freshmen: 4,103. Federal methodology is used as a basis for awarding need-based institutional aid.

UNDERGRADUATE EXPENSES for 2020–2021 *Application fee:* $65. ***Tuition, state resident:*** full-time $8580; part-time $286 per credit hour. ***Tuition, nonresident:*** full-time $29,589; part-time $986 per credit hour. ***Required fees:*** full-time $1121. Full-time tuition and fees vary according to location, program, and reciprocity agreements. Part-time tuition and fees vary according to course load, location, program, and reciprocity agreements. ***College room and board:*** $10,000. Room and board charges vary according to board plan and housing facility.

FRESHMAN FINANCIAL AID (Fall 2018) 3628 applied for aid; of those 76% were deemed to have need. 96% of freshmen with need received aid; of those 23% had need fully met. ***Average percent of need met:*** 71% (excluding resources awarded to replace EFC). ***Average financial aid package:*** $12,256 (excluding resources awarded to replace EFC). 12% of all full-time freshmen had no need and received non-need-based gift aid.

UNDERGRADUATE FINANCIAL AID (Fall 2018) 14,346 applied for aid; of those 81% were deemed to have need. 96% of undergraduates with need received aid; of those 22% had need fully met. ***Average percent of need met:*** 69% (excluding resources awarded to replace EFC). ***Average financial aid package:*** $11,849 (excluding resources awarded to replace EFC). 11% of all full-time undergraduates had no need and received non-need-based gift aid.

GIFT AID (NEED-BASED) *Receiving aid:* Freshmen: 60% (2,363); all full-time undergraduates: 54% (9,418). ***Average award:*** Freshmen: $11,262; Undergraduates: $10,573. ***Scholarships, grants, and awards:*** Federal Pell, FSEOG, state, private, college/university gift aid from institutional funds.

GIFT AID (NON-NEED-BASED) *Receiving aid:* Freshmen: 10% (385). Undergraduates: 8% (1,318). ***Average award:*** Freshmen: $7615. Undergraduates: $6878. ***Tuition waivers:*** Full or partial for employees or children of employees, senior citizens. ***ROTC:*** Army, Air Force cooperative.

LOANS *Student loans:* 65% of past graduating class borrowed through all loan programs. *Average indebtedness per student:* $27,022. ***Average need-based loan:*** Freshmen: $2874. Undergraduates: $3860. ***Programs:*** Federal Direct (Subsidized and Unsubsidized Stafford, PLUS), Federal Nursing, college/university.

WORK-STUDY *Federal work-study:* 801 jobs averaging $2340. ***State or other work-study/employment:*** Part-time jobs available.

APPLYING FOR FINANCIAL AID *Required financial aid form:* FAFSA. ***Financial aid deadline:*** Continuous. ***Notification date:*** Continuous.

CONTACT Mr. Marvin Smith, Executive Director, Student Financial Services, Indiana University-Purdue University Indianapolis, 420 University Boulevard, Campus Center 250, Indianapolis, IN 46202-5145, 317-274-4162. *Fax:* 317-274-3664. *E-mail:* finaid@iupui.edu.
Website: http://www.iupui.edu/.

INDIANA UNIVERSITY SOUTH BEND

South Bend, IN

Tuition & fees (IN res): $7527	Average undergraduate aid package: $9343

ABOUT THE INSTITUTION State-supported, coed. ***Awards:*** certificates, diplomas, associate, bachelor's, and master's degrees. 65 undergraduate majors. ***Total enrollment:*** 5,214. Undergraduates: 4,707. Freshmen: 929. Federal methodology is used as a basis for awarding need-based institutional aid.

UNDERGRADUATE EXPENSES for 2020–2021 *Application fee:* $35. ***Tuition, state resident:*** full-time $6895; part-time $230 per credit hour. ***Tuition, nonresident:*** full-time $19,346; part-time $645 per credit hour. ***Required fees:*** full-time $632. Full-time tuition and fees vary according to program and reciprocity agreements. Part-time tuition and fees vary according to course load, program, and reciprocity agreements. ***Room only:*** $7346. Room and board charges vary according to housing facility.

FRESHMAN FINANCIAL AID (Fall 2018) 803 applied for aid; of those 83% were deemed to have need. 96% of freshmen with need received aid; of those 12% had need fully met. ***Average percent of need met:*** 65% (excluding resources awarded to replace EFC). ***Average financial aid package:*** $9145 (excluding resources awarded to replace EFC). 13% of all full-time freshmen had no need and received non-need-based gift aid.

UNDERGRADUATE FINANCIAL AID (Fall 2018) 3,104 applied for aid; of those 84% were deemed to have need. 95% of undergraduates with need received aid; of those 13% had need fully met. ***Average percent of need met:*** 66% (excluding resources awarded to replace EFC). ***Average financial aid package:*** $9343 (excluding resources awarded to replace EFC). 9% of all full-time undergraduates had no need and received non-need-based gift aid.

GIFT AID (NEED-BASED) *Receiving aid:* Freshmen: 68% (594); all full-time undergraduates: 61% (2,198). ***Average award:*** Freshmen: $8087; Undergraduates: $7990. ***Scholarships, grants, and awards:*** Federal Pell, FSEOG, state, private, college/university gift aid from institutional funds.

GIFT AID (NON-NEED-BASED) *Receiving aid:* Freshmen: 8% (69). Undergraduates: 5% (186). ***Average award:*** Freshmen: $1614. Undergraduates: $2520. ***Tuition waivers:*** Full or partial for employees or children of employees, senior citizens. ***ROTC:*** Army cooperative, Air Force cooperative.

LOANS *Student loans:* 68% of past graduating class borrowed through all loan programs. *Average indebtedness per student:* $24,879. ***Average need-based loan:*** Freshmen: $2976. Undergraduates: $3540. ***Programs:*** Federal Direct (Subsidized and Unsubsidized Stafford, PLUS), state, college/university.

WORK-STUDY *Federal work-study:* 243 jobs averaging $1950. ***State or other work-study/employment:*** Part-time jobs available.

APPLYING FOR FINANCIAL AID *Required financial aid forms:* FAFSA, institution's own form. ***Financial aid deadline:*** Continuous. ***Notification date:*** Continuous.

CONTACT Lorie Williams, Director, Indiana University South Bend, Administration Building 116, 1700 Mishawaka Avenue, PO Box 7111, South Bend, IN 46634-7111, 574-520-4357 or toll-free 877-GO-2-IUSB. *Fax:* 574-520-5561. *E-mail:* sbfinaid@iusb.edu.
Website: http://www.iusb.edu/.

INDIANA UNIVERSITY SOUTHEAST

New Albany, IN

Tuition & fees (IN res): $6922	Average undergraduate aid package: $8724

ABOUT THE INSTITUTION State-supported, coed. ***Awards:*** certificates, bachelor's, and master's degrees. 46 undergraduate majors. ***Total enrollment:*** 4,946. Undergraduates: 4,461. Freshmen: 1,012. Federal methodology is used as a basis for awarding need-based institutional aid.

UNDERGRADUATE EXPENSES for 2020–2021 ***Application fee:*** $35. ***Tuition, state resident:*** full-time $6290; part-time $230 per credit hour. ***Tuition, nonresident:*** full-time $19,346; part-time $645 per credit hour. ***Required fees:*** full-time $632. Full-time tuition and fees vary according to program and reciprocity agreements. Part-time tuition and fees vary according to course load, program, and reciprocity agreements. ***Room only:*** $6290. Room and board charges vary according to board plan and housing facility.

FRESHMAN FINANCIAL AID (Fall 2018) 860 applied for aid; of those 79% were deemed to have need. 92% of freshmen with need received aid; of those 8% had need fully met. ***Average percent of need met:*** 59% (excluding resources awarded to replace EFC). ***Average financial aid package:*** $8522 (excluding resources awarded to replace EFC). 6% of all full-time freshmen had no need and received non-need-based gift aid.

UNDERGRADUATE FINANCIAL AID (Fall 2018) 2,678 applied for aid; of those 79% were deemed to have need. 93% of undergraduates with need received aid; of those 11% had need fully met. ***Average percent of need met:*** 63% (excluding resources awarded to replace EFC). ***Average financial aid package:*** $8724 (excluding resources awarded to replace EFC). 7% of all full-time undergraduates had no need and received non-need-based gift aid.

GIFT AID (NEED-BASED) ***Receiving aid:*** Freshmen: 60% (567); all full-time undergraduates: 54% (1,727). ***Average award:*** Freshmen: $7298; Undergraduates: $7297. ***Scholarships, grants, and awards:*** Federal Pell, FSEOG, state, private, college/university gift aid from institutional funds.

GIFT AID (NON-NEED-BASED) ***Receiving aid:*** Freshmen: 4% (42). Undergraduates: 4% (125). ***Average award:*** Freshmen: $3033. Undergraduates: $2571. ***Tuition waivers:*** Full or partial for employees or children of employees, senior citizens. ***ROTC:*** Army cooperative, Air Force cooperative.

LOANS ***Student loans:*** 60% of past graduating class borrowed through all loan programs. *Average indebtedness per student:* $21,460. ***Average need-based loan:*** Freshmen: $2955. Undergraduates: $3650. ***Programs:*** Federal Direct (Subsidized and Unsubsidized Stafford, PLUS), college/university.

WORK-STUDY ***Federal work-study:*** 119 jobs averaging $1682. ***State or other work-study/employment:*** Part-time jobs available.

APPLYING FOR FINANCIAL AID ***Required financial aid form:*** FAFSA. ***Financial aid deadline:*** Continuous. ***Notification date:*** Continuous. Students must reply within 2 weeks of notification.

CONTACT Lauren A Greider, Director of Financial Aid, Indiana University Southeast, University Center, South Room 105, New Albany, IN 47150, 812-941-2246 or toll-free 800-852-8835. *Fax:* 812-941-2546. *E-mail:* financialaid@ius.edu.
Website: http://www.ius.edu/.

INDIANA WESLEYAN UNIVERSITY

Marion, IN

CONTACT Emily Mattison, Financial Aid Office, Indiana Wesleyan University, 4201 South Washington Street, Marion, IN 46953-4999, 765-677-2839 or toll-free 866-468-6498. *Fax:* 765-677-2809. *E-mail:* finaid@indwes.edu.
Website: http://www.indwes.edu/.

INDIAN RIVER STATE COLLEGE

Fort Pierce, FL

CONTACT Mary Lewis, Director of Financial Aid, Indian River State College, W Building, Main Campus, Fort Pierce, FL 34981, 772-462-7450 or toll-free 866-792-4772. *E-mail:* financialaid-info@irsc.edu.
Website: http://www.irsc.edu/.

INSTE BIBLE COLLEGE

Ankeny, IA

CONTACT Financial Aid Office, INSTE Bible College, 2302 SW 3rd Street, Ankeny, IA 50023, 515-289-9200.
Website: http://www.inste.edu/.

INSTITUTE OF AMERICAN INDIAN ARTS

Santa Fe, NM

CONTACT Lala M. Gallegos, Director of Financial Aid, Institute of American Indian Arts, 83 Avan Nu Po Road, Santa Fe, NM 87508, 505-424-5724. *Fax:* 505-424-0909. *E-mail:* lgallegos@iaia.edu.
Website: http://www.iaia.edu/.

INTER AMERICAN UNIVERSITY OF PUERTO RICO, AGUADILLA CAMPUS

Aguadilla, PR

Tuition & fees: $5254	Average undergraduate aid package: N/A

ABOUT THE INSTITUTION Independent, coed. ***Awards:*** certificates, diplomas, bachelor's, and master's degrees. 39 undergraduate majors. ***Total enrollment:*** 3,903. Undergraduates: 3,667. Freshmen: 797. Both federal and institutional methodology are used as a basis for awarding need-based institutional aid.

UNDERGRADUATE EXPENSES for 2019–2020 ***Tuition:*** full-time $4560; part-time $190 per credit. ***Required fees:*** full-time $694; $283 per semester hour. Full-time tuition and fees vary according to course load. Part-time tuition and fees vary according to course load.

FRESHMAN FINANCIAL AID (Fall 2018) 1196 applied for aid; of those 99% were deemed to have need. 96% of freshmen with need received aid. ***Average percent of need met:*** 2% (excluding resources awarded to replace EFC).

UNDERGRADUATE FINANCIAL AID (Fall 2018) 3,180 applied for aid; of those 99% were deemed to have need. 94% of undergraduates with need received aid. ***Average percent of need met:*** 13% (excluding resources awarded to replace EFC).

GIFT AID (NEED-BASED) ***Total amount:*** $19,096,475 (93% federal, 7% institutional). ***Receiving aid:*** Freshmen: 94% (1,139); all full-time undergraduates: 92% (2,981). ***Average award:*** Freshmen: $1059; Undergraduates: $2933. ***Scholarships, grants, and awards:*** Federal Pell, FSEOG, state, college/university gift aid from institutional funds.

GIFT AID (NON-NEED-BASED) ***Receiving aid:*** Freshmen: 4. Undergraduates: 10. ***Scholarships, grants, and awards by category:*** *Academic interests/achievement:* general academic interests/achievements. *Special characteristics:* children of faculty/staff. ***Tuition waivers:*** Full or partial for employees or children of employees. ***ROTC:*** Army, Air Force.

LOANS ***Student loans:*** $3,035,458 (93% need-based, 7% non-need-based). ***Parent loans:*** $45,250 (100% need-based). ***Programs:*** Federal Direct (PLUS).

WORK-STUDY ***Federal work-study:*** Total amount: $299,505.95; jobs available. ***State or other work-study/employment:*** Total amount: $11,045.37 (100% need-based). Part-time jobs available.

APPLYING FOR FINANCIAL AID ***Required financial aid forms:*** FAFSA, institution's own form. ***Notification date:*** 6/30.

CONTACT Mrs. Gloria Cortés, Director of Financial Aid, Inter American University of Puerto Rico, Aguadilla Campus, PO Box 20000, Aguadilla, PR 00605, 787-891-0925 Ext. 2747. *Fax:* 787-882-3020. *E-mail:* gcortes@aguadilla.inter.edu.
Website: http://www.aguadilla.inter.edu/.

INTER AMERICAN UNIVERSITY OF PUERTO RICO, ARECIBO CAMPUS

Arecibo, PR

CONTACT Ramón O. de Jesús, Financial Aid Director, Inter American University of Puerto Rico, Arecibo Campus, PO Box 4050, Arecibo, PR 00614-4050, 787-878-5475 Ext. 2275. *Fax:* 787-880-1624.
Website: http://www.arecibo.inter.edu/.

INTER AMERICAN UNIVERSITY OF PUERTO RICO, BARRANQUITAS CAMPUS

Barranquitas, PR

CONTACT Mr. Eduardo Fontanez Colon, Financial Aid Officer, Inter American University of Puerto Rico, Barranquitas Campus, Box 517, Barranquitas, PR 00794, 787-857-3600 Ext. 2049. *Fax:* 787-857-2244.
Website: http://www.br.inter.edu/.

INTER AMERICAN UNIVERSITY OF PUERTO RICO, BAYAMÓN CAMPUS

Bayamón, PR

ABOUT THE INSTITUTION Independent, coed. ***Awards:*** certificates, associate, bachelor's, and master's degrees. 42 undergraduate majors. ***Total enrollment:*** 4,500. Undergraduates: 4,336. Freshmen: 876.

GIFT AID (NEED-BASED) ***Scholarships, grants, and awards:*** Federal Pell, state, college/university gift aid from institutional funds.

LOANS ***Programs:*** Perkins.

WORK-STUDY ***Federal work-study:*** Total amount: $212,102; jobs available.

APPLYING FOR FINANCIAL AID ***Required financial aid form:*** FAFSA.

CONTACT Mrs. Aurelis Baez, Director of Student Services, Inter American University of Puerto Rico, Bayamón Campus, 500 Dr. John Will Harris Road, Bayamon, PR 00957, 787-279-1912 Ext. 2017. *E-mail:* abaez@bayamon.inter.edu.
Website: http://bayamon.inter.edu/.

INTER AMERICAN UNIVERSITY OF PUERTO RICO, FAJARDO CAMPUS

Fajardo, PR

CONTACT Financial Aid Director, Inter American University of Puerto Rico, Fajardo Campus, Call Box 700003, Fajardo, PR 00738-7003, 787-863-2390 Ext. 2208.
Website: http://www.fajardo.inter.edu/.

INTER AMERICAN UNIVERSITY OF PUERTO RICO, GUAYAMA CAMPUS

Guayama, PR

CONTACT Mr. Jose A. Vechini, Director of Financial Aid, Inter American University of Puerto Rico, Guayama Campus, Call Box 10004, Guayama, PR 00785, 787-864-2222 Ext. 2206. *Fax:* 787-864-8232. *E-mail:* jose.vechini@guayama.inter.edu.
Website: http://www.guayama.inter.edu/.

INTER AMERICAN UNIVERSITY OF PUERTO RICO, METROPOLITAN CAMPUS

San Juan, PR

Tuition & fees: $8796 — **Average undergraduate aid package: N/A**

ABOUT THE INSTITUTION Independent, coed. ***Awards:*** certificates, associate, bachelor's, master's, and doctoral degrees. 57 undergraduate majors. ***Total enrollment:*** 7,791. Undergraduates: 5,508. Freshmen: 668. Both federal and institutional methodology are used as a basis for awarding need-based institutional aid.

UNDERGRADUATE EXPENSES for 2019–2020 ***Tuition:*** full-time $6840; part-time $190 per credit. ***Required fees:*** full-time $1956; $248 per term.

FRESHMAN FINANCIAL AID (Fall 2019, est.) 197 applied for aid; of those 98% were deemed to have need. 87% of freshmen with need received aid.

UNDERGRADUATE FINANCIAL AID (Fall 2019, est.) 2,172 applied for aid; of those 99% were deemed to have need. 89% of undergraduates with need received aid. ***Average percent of need met:*** 39% (excluding resources awarded to replace EFC).

GIFT AID (NEED-BASED) ***Total amount:*** $12,856,874 (87% federal, 13% institutional). ***Receiving aid:*** Freshmen: 79% (169); all full-time undergraduates: 82% (1,918). ***Average award:*** Freshmen: $89; Undergraduates: $1538. ***Scholarships, grants, and awards:*** Federal Pell, FSEOG, state, college/university gift aid from institutional funds, Federal Nursing.

GIFT AID (NON-NEED-BASED) ***Tuition waivers:*** Full or partial for employees or children of employees. ***ROTC:*** Army cooperative, Naval cooperative, Air Force cooperative.

LOANS ***Student loans:*** $5,312,667 (100% need-based). ***Parent loans:*** $488,491 (100% need-based). ***Programs:*** Federal Direct (Subsidized and Unsubsidized Stafford, PLUS), Perkins.

WORK-STUDY ***Federal work-study:*** Total amount: $132,157.93; jobs available.

APPLYING FOR FINANCIAL AID ***Required financial aid forms:*** FAFSA, institution's own form. ***Financial aid deadline:*** 4/30. ***Notification date:*** 5/1.

CONTACT Mrs. Lillian Concepcion, Director of Financial Aid, Inter American University of Puerto Rico, Metropolitan Campus, PO Box 191293, San Juan, PR 00919-1293, 787-250-1912. *Fax:* 787-250-0782 Ext.2208. *E-mail:* lconcepcion@metro.inter.edu.
Website: http://metro.inter.edu/.

INTER AMERICAN UNIVERSITY OF PUERTO RICO, PONCE CAMPUS

Mercedita, PR

ABOUT THE INSTITUTION Independent, coed. ***Awards:*** certificates, associate, bachelor's, master's, and doctoral degrees. 44 undergraduate majors.

GIFT AID (NEED-BASED) ***Scholarships, grants, and awards:*** Federal Pell, FSEOG, state, college/university gift aid from institutional funds, Federal Nursing.

LOANS ***Programs:*** Federal Direct (Subsidized and Unsubsidized Stafford, PLUS), Perkins.

CONTACT Karen Caquias, Financial Aid Officer, Inter American University of Puerto Rico, Ponce Campus, 104 Turpeaux Industrial Park, Mercedita, PR 00715-2201, 787-284-1912 Ext. 2161. *Fax:* 787-841-0103. *E-mail:* kcaquias@ponce.inter.edu.
Website: http://www.ponce.inter.edu/.

INTER AMERICAN UNIVERSITY OF PUERTO RICO, SAN GERMÁN CAMPUS

San Germán, PR

CONTACT Ms. Maria I. Lugo, Financial Aid Director, Inter American University of Puerto Rico, San Germán Campus, PO Box 5100, San German, PR 00683-5008, 787-264-1912 Ext. 7252 or toll-free 800-981-8075 (in-state). *Fax:* 787-892-6350. *Website:* http://www.sg.inter.edu/.

INTERIOR DESIGNERS INSTITUTE

Newport Beach, CA

CONTACT Office of Financial Aid, Interior Designers Institute, 1061 Camelback Road, Newport Beach, CA 92660, 949-675-4451. *Website:* http://www.idi.edu/.

INTERNATIONAL BAPTIST COLLEGE AND SEMINARY

Chandler, AZ

CONTACT Financial Aid Office, International Baptist College and Seminary, 2211 West Germann Road, Chandler, AZ 85286, 480-838-7070 Ext. 268 or toll-free 800-422-4858. *Fax:* 480-838-5432. *E-mail:* financialaid@ibconline.edu. *Website:* http://www.ibcs.edu/.

INTERNATIONAL BUSINESS COLLEGE

Fort Wayne, IN

CONTACT Financial Aid Office, International Business College, 5699 Coventry Lane, Fort Wayne, IN 46804, 260-459-4500 or toll-free 800-589-6363. *Website:* http://www.ibcfortwayne.edu/.

IONA COLLEGE

New Rochelle, NY

Tuition & fees: $41,580	Average undergraduate aid package: $27,937

ABOUT THE INSTITUTION Independent Roman Catholic Church, coed. ***Awards:*** certificates, bachelor's, and master's degrees. 52 undergraduate majors. ***Total enrollment:*** 3,613. Undergraduates: 2,981. Freshmen: 641. Federal methodology is used as a basis for awarding need-based institutional aid.

UNDERGRADUATE EXPENSES for 2020–2021 *Comprehensive fee:* $57,788 includes full-time tuition ($39,380), mandatory fees ($2200), and room and board ($16,208).

FRESHMAN FINANCIAL AID (Fall 2019, est.) 641 applied for aid; of those 89% were deemed to have need. 100% of freshmen with need received aid; of those 19% had need fully met. ***Average percent of need met:*** 13% (excluding resources awarded to replace EFC). ***Average financial aid package:*** $28,081 (excluding resources awarded to replace EFC). 11% of all full-time freshmen had no need and received non-need-based gift aid.

UNDERGRADUATE FINANCIAL AID (Fall 2019, est.) 2,673 applied for aid; of those 87% were deemed to have need. 99% of undergraduates with need received aid; of those 20% had need fully met. ***Average percent of need met:*** 16% (excluding resources awarded to replace EFC). ***Average financial aid package:*** $27,937 (excluding resources awarded to replace EFC). 12% of all full-time undergraduates had no need and received non-need-based gift aid.

GIFT AID (NEED-BASED) *Total amount:* $50,121,742 (10% federal, 5% state, 82% institutional, 3% external sources). ***Receiving aid:*** Freshmen: 36% (229); all full-time undergraduates: 35% (947). ***Average award:*** Freshmen: $6264; Undergraduates: $6322. ***Scholarships, grants, and awards:*** Federal Pell, FSEOG, state, private, college/university gift aid from institutional funds.

GIFT AID (NON-NEED-BASED) *Total amount:* $10,147,798 (1% state, 97% institutional, 2% external sources). ***Receiving aid:*** Freshmen: 89% (573). Undergraduates: 85% (2,302). ***Average award:*** Freshmen: $22,974. Undergraduates: $22,391. ***Scholarships, grants, and awards by category:*** *Academic interests/achievement:* general academic interests/achievements. *Creative arts/performance:* music. *Special achievements/activities:* community service. *Special characteristics:* children and siblings of alumni, religious affiliation, siblings of current students, veterans. ***Tuition waivers:*** Full or partial for employees or children of employees. ***ROTC:*** Army cooperative, Air Force cooperative.

LOANS *Student loans:* $15,442,954 (72% need-based, 28% non-need-based). 74% of past graduating class borrowed through all loan programs. *Average indebtedness per student:* $32,948. ***Average need-based loan:*** Freshmen: $2579. Undergraduates: $3558. ***Parent loans:*** $11,861,308 (54% need-based, 46% non-need-based). ***Programs:*** Federal Direct (Subsidized and Unsubsidized Stafford, PLUS), Perkins.

WORK-STUDY *Federal work-study:* Total amount: $662,143; jobs available. ***State or other work-study/employment:*** Total amount: $684,851 (60% need-based, 40% non-need-based). Part-time jobs available.

ATHLETIC AWARDS Total amount: $4,669,786 (62% need-based, 38% non-need-based).

APPLYING FOR FINANCIAL AID *Required financial aid forms:* FAFSA, state aid form. ***Financial aid deadline:*** 4/15 (priority: 2/15). ***Notification date:*** Continuous beginning 2/1. Students must reply by 5/1 or within 2 weeks of notification.

CONTACT Mary Grant, Director of Financial Aid, Iona College, 715 North Avenue, New Rochelle, NY 10801-1890, 914-633-2676 or toll-free 800-231-IONA. *Fax:* 914-633-2486. *E-mail:* mgrant@iona.edu. *Website:* http://www.iona.edu/.

IOWA STATE UNIVERSITY OF SCIENCE AND TECHNOLOGY

Ames, IA

ABOUT THE INSTITUTION State-supported, coed. ***Awards:*** certificates, bachelor's, master's, and doctoral degrees. 96 undergraduate majors. ***Total enrollment:*** 34,992. Undergraduates: 29,621. Freshmen: 6,047.

GIFT AID (NEED-BASED) *Scholarships, grants, and awards:* Federal Pell, FSEOG, state, college/university gift aid from institutional funds.

GIFT AID (NON-NEED-BASED) *Scholarships, grants, and awards by category:* *Academic interests/achievement:* agriculture, architecture, area/ethnic studies, biological sciences, business, communication, computer science, education, engineering/technologies, English, foreign languages, general academic interests/achievements, health fields, home economics, humanities, international studies, library science, mathematics, military science, physical sciences, premedicine, social sciences. *Creative arts/performance:* applied art and design, art/fine arts, journalism/publications, music, theater/drama. *Special achievements/activities:* community service, general special achievements/activities, leadership. *Special characteristics:* adult students, children and siblings of alumni, ethnic background, first-generation college students, general special characteristics, international students, local/state students, members of minority groups, out-of-state students, veterans, veterans' children.

LOANS *Programs:* Federal Direct (Subsidized and Unsubsidized Stafford, PLUS), Perkins, state, college/university, private loans.

CONTACT Ms. Roberta Johnson, Director of Financial Aid, Iowa State University of Science and Technology, 0210 Beardshear Hall, 515 Morrill Road, Ames, IA 50011-2103, 515-294-2223 or toll-free 800-262-3810. *Fax:* 515-294-0851. *E-mail:* rljohns@iastate.edu. *Website:* http://www.iastate.edu/.

IOWA WESLEYAN UNIVERSITY

Mount Pleasant, IA

Tuition & fees: N/R | **Average undergraduate aid package: $22,490**

ABOUT THE INSTITUTION Independent United Methodist, coed. ***Awards:*** bachelor's degrees. 25 undergraduate majors. Federal methodology is used as a basis for awarding need-based institutional aid.

FRESHMAN FINANCIAL AID (Fall 2019, est.) 139 applied for aid; of those 100% were deemed to have need. 100% of freshmen with need received aid; of those 8% had need fully met. ***Average percent of need met:*** 78% (excluding resources awarded to replace EFC). ***Average financial aid package:*** $26,969 (excluding resources awarded to replace EFC). 1% of all full-time freshmen had no need and received non-need-based gift aid.

UNDERGRADUATE FINANCIAL AID (Fall 2019, est.) 477 applied for aid; of those 100% were deemed to have need. 100% of undergraduates with need received aid; of those 11% had need fully met. ***Average percent of need met:*** 74% (excluding resources awarded to replace EFC). ***Average financial aid package:*** $22,490 (excluding resources awarded to replace EFC). 1% of all full-time undergraduates had no need and received non-need-based gift aid.

GIFT AID (NEED-BASED) ***Total amount:*** $10,609,725 (14% federal, 7% state, 78% institutional, 1% external sources). ***Receiving aid:*** Freshmen: 73% (102); all full-time undergraduates: 66% (313). ***Average award:*** Freshmen: $14,677; Undergraduates: $14,537. ***Scholarships, grants, and awards:*** Federal Pell, FSEOG, state, private, college/university gift aid from institutional funds.

GIFT AID (NON-NEED-BASED) ***Receiving aid:*** Freshmen: 73% (102). Undergraduates: 66% (313). ***Average award:*** Freshmen: $15,744. Undergraduates: $16,283. ***Scholarships, grants, and awards by category:*** *Academic interests/achievement:* business, education, English, general academic interests/achievements, home economics, social sciences. *Creative arts/performance:* applied art and design, music. *Special characteristics:* children and siblings of alumni, children of faculty/staff, international students, out-of-state students, siblings of current students.

LOANS ***Student loans:*** $2,704,892 (42% need-based, 58% non-need-based). 75% of past graduating class borrowed through all loan programs. *Average indebtedness per student:* $33,152. ***Average need-based loan:*** Freshmen: $3397. Undergraduates: $4801. ***Parent loans:*** $647,792 (100% need-based). ***Programs:*** Federal Direct (Subsidized and Unsubsidized Stafford, PLUS), alternative loans.

WORK-STUDY ***Federal work-study:*** Total amount: $62,500; 109 jobs averaging $1224. ***State or other work-study/employment:*** Total amount: $30,000 (100% need-based). 29 part-time jobs averaging $1637.

APPLYING FOR FINANCIAL AID ***Required financial aid form:*** FAFSA. ***Financial aid deadline (priority):*** 4/1. ***Notification date:*** Continuous beginning 3/15.

CONTACT Financial Aid Office, Iowa Wesleyan University, 601 North Main Street, Mount Pleasant, IA 52641-1398, 319-385-8021 or toll-free 800-582-2383. *Website:* http://www.iw.edu/.

ITHACA COLLEGE

Ithaca, NY

Tuition & fees: $46,610 | **Average undergraduate aid package: $40,304**

ABOUT THE INSTITUTION Independent, coed. ***Awards:*** certificates, bachelor's, master's, and doctoral degrees. 79 undergraduate majors. ***Total enrollment:*** 6,266. Undergraduates: 5,852. Freshmen: 1,509. Institutional methodology is used as a basis for awarding need-based institutional aid.

UNDERGRADUATE EXPENSES for 2020–2021 ***Application fee:*** $60. ***Comprehensive fee:*** $62,454 includes full-time tuition ($46,610) and room and board ($15,844). ***College room only:*** $8976. Room and board charges vary according to board plan and housing facility. ***Part-time tuition:*** $1554 per credit hour.

FRESHMAN FINANCIAL AID (Fall 2019, est.) 1392 applied for aid; of those 79% were deemed to have need. 100% of freshmen with need received aid; of those 59% had need fully met. ***Average percent of need met:*** 92% (excluding resources awarded to replace EFC). ***Average financial aid package:*** $39,878 (excluding resources awarded to replace EFC). 24% of all full-time freshmen had no need and received non-need-based gift aid.

UNDERGRADUATE FINANCIAL AID (Fall 2019, est.) 4,626 applied for aid; of those 85% were deemed to have need. 100% of undergraduates with need received aid; of those 46% had need fully met. ***Average percent of need met:*** 88% (excluding resources awarded to replace EFC). ***Average financial aid package:*** $40,304 (excluding resources awarded to replace EFC). 26% of all full-time undergraduates had no need and received non-need-based gift aid.

GIFT AID (NEED-BASED) ***Total amount:*** $117,102,995 (5% federal, 3% state, 90% institutional, 2% external sources). ***Receiving aid:*** Freshmen: 71% (1,062); all full-time undergraduates: 68% (3,886). ***Average award:*** Freshmen: $29,394; Undergraduates: $29,930. ***Scholarships, grants, and awards:*** Federal Pell, FSEOG, state, private, college/university gift aid from institutional funds.

GIFT AID (NON-NEED-BASED) ***Total amount:*** $34,242,623 (4% federal, 91% institutional, 5% external sources). ***Receiving aid:*** Freshmen: 29% (436). Undergraduates: 13% (742). ***Average award:*** Freshmen: $17,019. Undergraduates: $17,179. ***Scholarships, grants, and awards by category:*** *Academic interests/achievement:* communication, general academic interests/achievements. *Creative arts/performance:* cinema/film/broadcasting, dance, journalism/publications, music, performing arts, theater/drama. *Special achievements/activities:* leadership. *Special characteristics:* children and siblings of alumni, children of faculty/staff, general special characteristics, members of minority groups, siblings of current students. ***Tuition waivers:*** Full or partial for children of alumni, employees or children of employees. ***ROTC:*** Army cooperative, Air Force cooperative.

LOANS ***Student loans:*** $29,000,973 (69% need-based, 31% non-need-based). 69% of past graduating class borrowed through all loan programs. *Average indebtedness per student:* $42,000. ***Average need-based loan:*** Freshmen: $4665. Undergraduates: $5866. ***Parent loans:*** $27,603,531 (35% need-based, 65% non-need-based). ***Programs:*** Federal Direct (Subsidized and Unsubsidized Stafford, PLUS), Perkins, alternative loans.

WORK-STUDY ***Federal work-study:*** Total amount: $1,500,000; jobs available. ***State or other work-study/employment:*** Total amount: $10,940,300 (65% need-based, 35% non-need-based). Part-time jobs available.

APPLYING FOR FINANCIAL AID ***Required financial aid forms:*** FAFSA, CSS Financial Aid PROFILE. ***Financial aid deadline (priority):*** 2/1. ***Notification date:*** Continuous beginning 2/15. Students must reply by 5/1.

CONTACT Ms. Lisa Hoskey, Director of Student Financial Services, Ithaca College, 953 Danby Road, Ithaca, NY 14850-7002, 800-429-4275 or toll-free 800-429-4274. *Fax:* 607-274-1895. *E-mail:* finaid@ithaca.edu. *Website:* http://www.ithaca.edu/.

JACKSON STATE UNIVERSITY

Jackson, MS

Tuition & fees: N/R | **Average undergraduate aid package: $12,199**

ABOUT THE INSTITUTION State-supported, coed. ***Awards:*** certificates, bachelor's, master's, and doctoral degrees. 43 undergraduate majors. ***Total enrollment:*** 7,250. Undergraduates: 5,331. Freshmen: 831. Federal methodology is used as a basis for awarding need-based institutional aid.

FRESHMAN FINANCIAL AID (Fall 2019, est.) 770 applied for aid; of those 93% were deemed to have need. 100% of freshmen with need received aid; of those 15% had need fully met. ***Average percent of need met:*** 55% (excluding resources awarded to replace EFC). ***Average financial aid package:*** $12,719 (excluding resources awarded to replace EFC). 4% of all full-time freshmen had no need and received non-need-based gift aid.

UNDERGRADUATE FINANCIAL AID (Fall 2019, est.) 3,954 applied for aid; of those 94% were deemed to have need. 100% of undergraduates with need received aid; of those 13% had need fully met. ***Average percent of need met:*** 53% (excluding resources awarded to replace EFC). ***Average financial aid package:*** $12,199 (excluding resources awarded to replace EFC). 3% of all full-time undergraduates had no need and received non-need-based gift aid.

GIFT AID (NEED-BASED) ***Total amount:*** $20,515,118 (95% federal, 5% state). ***Receiving aid:*** Freshmen: 77% (606); all full-time undergraduates: 74% (3,049). ***Average award:*** Freshmen: $6307; Undergraduates: $5802. ***Scholarships, grants, and awards:*** Federal Pell, FSEOG, state, college/university gift aid from institutional funds.

GIFT AID (NON-NEED-BASED) ***Total amount:*** $15,704,880 (5% state, 85% institutional, 10% external sources). ***Receiving aid:*** Freshmen: 50% (394). Under-

graduates: 37% (1,525). ***Average award:*** Freshmen: $11,450. Undergraduates: $10,529. ***Scholarships, grants, and awards by category:*** *Academic interests/achievement:* 788 awards ($8,620,408 total): general academic interests/achievements. *Creative arts/performance:* 12 awards ($33,171 total): music. *Special achievements/activities:* 1 award ($1000 total): leadership. *Special characteristics:* children and siblings of alumni, children of faculty/staff. ***ROTC:*** Army, Air Force.

LOANS *Student loans:* $34,570,406 (45% need-based, 55% non-need-based). 80% of past graduating class borrowed through all loan programs. *Average indebtedness per student:* $28,260. ***Average need-based loan:*** Freshmen: $3390. Undergraduates: $4143. ***Parent loans:*** $13,645,569 (100% non-need-based). ***Programs:*** Federal Direct (Subsidized and Unsubsidized Stafford, PLUS), Perkins.

WORK-STUDY *Federal work-study:* Total amount: $2,436,742; 1,121 jobs averaging $2133.

ATHLETIC AWARDS Total amount: $3,641,922 (100% non-need-based).

APPLYING FOR FINANCIAL AID *Required financial aid form:* FAFSA. ***Financial aid deadline (priority):*** 4/15. ***Notification date:*** Continuous beginning 5/1.

CONTACT Mrs. Glenda Lattimore, Director of Financial Aid, Jackson State University, 1400 J.R. Lynch Street, PO Box 17065, Jackson, MS 39217, 601-979-2227 or toll-free 800-848-6817. *Fax:* 601-979-2237. *E-mail:* glenda.s.lattimore@jsums.edu. *Website:* http://www.jsums.edu/.

JACKSONVILLE STATE UNIVERSITY

Jacksonville, AL

Tuition & fees (area res): $11,120	Average undergraduate aid package: $10,971

ABOUT THE INSTITUTION State-supported, coed. ***Awards:*** certificates, bachelor's, master's, and doctoral degrees. 63 undergraduate majors. ***Total enrollment:*** 9,021. Undergraduates: 7,749. Freshmen: 1,493. Federal methodology is used as a basis for awarding need-based institutional aid.

UNDERGRADUATE EXPENSES for 2020–2021 *Application fee:* $35. ***Tuition, area resident:*** full-time $9720; part-time $3 per credit hour. ***Tuition, state resident:*** full-time $9720; part-time $324 per credit hour. ***Tuition, nonresident:*** full-time $19,440; part-time $648 per credit hour. ***Required fees:*** full-time $1400. ***College room and board:*** $8000.

FRESHMAN FINANCIAL AID (Fall 2018) 1027 applied for aid; of those 98% were deemed to have need. 100% of freshmen with need received aid. ***Average financial aid package:*** $10,116 (excluding resources awarded to replace EFC).

UNDERGRADUATE FINANCIAL AID (Fall 2018) 4,853 applied for aid; of those 99% were deemed to have need. 100% of undergraduates with need received aid. ***Average financial aid package:*** $10,971 (excluding resources awarded to replace EFC).

GIFT AID (NEED-BASED) *Total amount:* $46,368,830 (34% federal, 1% state, 63% institutional, 2% external sources). ***Receiving aid:*** Freshmen: 47% (499); all full-time undergraduates: 45% (2,437). ***Average award:*** Freshmen: $5524; Undergraduates: $5680.

GIFT AID (NON-NEED-BASED) *Receiving aid:* Freshmen: 66% (701). Undergraduates: 52% (2,850). ***Scholarships, grants, and awards by category:*** *Academic interests/achievement:* biological sciences, business, communication, computer science, education, English, general academic interests/achievements, health fields, home economics, humanities, mathematics, military science, physical sciences, social sciences. *Creative arts/performance:* applied art and design, journalism/publications, music, theater/drama. *Special achievements/activities:* general special achievements/activities, leadership. *Special characteristics:* children and siblings of alumni, local/state students. ***ROTC:*** Army.

LOANS *Student loans:* $35,760,585 (35% need-based, 65% non-need-based). ***Average need-based loan:*** Freshmen: $3130. Undergraduates: $3061. ***Parent loans:*** $3,826,590 (100% non-need-based). ***Programs:*** Federal Direct (Subsidized and Unsubsidized Stafford, PLUS), state, college/university.

WORK-STUDY *Federal work-study:* Total amount: $310,590; jobs available. ***State or other work-study/employment:*** Total amount: $3,918,133 (100% non-need-based). Part-time jobs available.

ATHLETIC AWARDS Total amount: $5,741,596 (100% non-need-based).

APPLYING FOR FINANCIAL AID *Required financial aid form:* FAFSA. ***Notification date:*** Continuous beginning 4/16. Students must reply within 2 weeks of notification.

CONTACT Ms. Vickie Adams, Director of Financial Aid, Jacksonville State University, 700 Pelham Road North, Jacksonville, AL 36265-9982, 256-782-5006 Ext. 8399 or toll-free 800-231-5291. *Fax:* 256-782-5476. *E-mail:* finaid@jsu.edu. *Website:* http://www.jsu.edu/.

JACKSONVILLE UNIVERSITY

Jacksonville, FL

Tuition & fees: $39,900	Average undergraduate aid package: $29,666

ABOUT THE INSTITUTION Independent, coed. ***Awards:*** certificates, bachelor's, master's, and doctoral degrees. 65 undergraduate majors. ***Total enrollment:*** 4,164. Undergraduates: 2,928. Freshmen: 657. Federal methodology is used as a basis for awarding need-based institutional aid.

UNDERGRADUATE EXPENSES for 2020–2021 *Application fee:* $30. ***Comprehensive fee:*** $54,710 includes full-time tuition ($39,900) and room and board ($14,810). ***College room only:*** $9500. Full-time tuition and fees vary according to degree level and program. Room and board charges vary according to board plan. ***Part-time tuition:*** $1335 per credit hour. ***Part-time fees:*** $28 per credit hour. Part-time tuition and fees vary according to degree level and program.

FRESHMAN FINANCIAL AID (Fall 2019, est.) 562 applied for aid; of those 88% were deemed to have need. 100% of freshmen with need received aid; of those 20% had need fully met. ***Average percent of need met:*** 73% (excluding resources awarded to replace EFC). ***Average financial aid package:*** $32,208 (excluding resources awarded to replace EFC). 22% of all full-time freshmen had no need and received non-need-based gift aid.

UNDERGRADUATE FINANCIAL AID (Fall 2019, est.) 1,900 applied for aid; of those 90% were deemed to have need. 100% of undergraduates with need received aid; of those 17% had need fully met. ***Average percent of need met:*** 67% (excluding resources awarded to replace EFC). ***Average financial aid package:*** $29,666 (excluding resources awarded to replace EFC). 21% of all full-time undergraduates had no need and received non-need-based gift aid.

GIFT AID (NEED-BASED) *Total amount:* $39,037,612 (11% federal, 10% state, 78% institutional, 1% external sources). ***Receiving aid:*** Freshmen: 74% (487); all full-time undergraduates: 66% (1,665). ***Average award:*** Freshmen: $25,024; Undergraduates: $21,262. ***Scholarships, grants, and awards:*** Federal Pell, FSEOG, state, private, college/university gift aid from institutional funds.

GIFT AID (NON-NEED-BASED) *Total amount:* $13,124,709 (9% state, 90% institutional, 1% external sources). ***Receiving aid:*** Freshmen: 13% (88). Undergraduates: 10% (241). ***Average award:*** Freshmen: $20,630. Undergraduates: $18,450. ***Scholarships, grants, and awards by category:*** *Academic interests/achievement:* general academic interests/achievements. *Creative arts/performance:* applied art and design, general creative arts/performance, music, theater/drama. *Special achievements/activities:* general special achievements/activities, leadership. *Special characteristics:* children of educators, children of faculty/staff, international students. ***Tuition waivers:*** Full or partial for employees or children of employees. ***ROTC:*** Army, Naval.

LOANS *Student loans:* $13,935,770 (74% need-based, 26% non-need-based). 60% of past graduating class borrowed through all loan programs. *Average indebtedness per student:* $44,279. ***Average need-based loan:*** Freshmen: $3215. Undergraduates: $4095. ***Parent loans:*** $6,711,749 (63% need-based, 37% non-need-based). ***Programs:*** Federal Direct (Subsidized and Unsubsidized Stafford, PLUS), Perkins.

WORK-STUDY *Federal work-study:* Total amount: $237,456; 293 jobs averaging $856. ***State or other work-study/employment:*** Total amount: $205,792 (48% need-based, 52% non-need-based). 254 part-time jobs averaging $1031.

ATHLETIC AWARDS Total amount: $5,990,462 (41% need-based, 59% non-need-based).

APPLYING FOR FINANCIAL AID *Required financial aid forms:* FAFSA, institution's own form, proof of medical insurance coverage and waiver form. ***Financial aid deadline (priority):*** 3/31. ***Notification date:*** Continuous beginning 2/20.

CONTACT Mr. Chip Moore, Director of Financial Aid, Jacksonville University, 2800 University Boulevard North, Jacksonville, FL 32211, 904-256-7062 or toll-free 800-225-2027. *Fax:* 904-256-7148. *E-mail:* cmoore@ju.edu.
Website: http://www.ju.edu/.

JAMES MADISON UNIVERSITY

Harrisonburg, VA

Tuition & fees (VA res): $11,576	Average undergraduate aid package: $9333

ABOUT THE INSTITUTION State-supported, coed. ***Awards:*** bachelor's, master's, and doctoral degrees (also offers specialist in education degree). 47 undergraduate majors. ***Total enrollment:*** 21,820. Undergraduates: 19,894. Freshmen: 4,455. Federal methodology is used as a basis for awarding need-based institutional aid.

UNDERGRADUATE EXPENSES for 2019–2020 ***Application fee:*** $70. ***Tuition, state resident:*** full-time $6620; part-time $220 per credit hour. ***Tuition, nonresident:*** full-time $23,834; part-time $777 per credit hour. ***Required fees:*** full-time $4956. ***College room and board:*** $10,582; ***Room only:*** $5510. Room and board charges vary according to board plan.

FRESHMAN FINANCIAL AID (Fall 2019, est.) 3972 applied for aid; of those 50% were deemed to have need. 87% of freshmen with need received aid; of those 87% had need fully met. ***Average percent of need met:*** 35% (excluding resources awarded to replace EFC). ***Average financial aid package:*** $10,649 (excluding resources awarded to replace EFC). 2% of all full-time freshmen had no need and received non-need-based gift aid.

UNDERGRADUATE FINANCIAL AID (Fall 2019, est.) 11,213 applied for aid; of those 67% were deemed to have need. 91% of undergraduates with need received aid; of those 73% had need fully met. ***Average percent of need met:*** 37% (excluding resources awarded to replace EFC). ***Average financial aid package:*** $9333 (excluding resources awarded to replace EFC). 1% of all full-time undergraduates had no need and received non-need-based gift aid.

GIFT AID (NEED-BASED) ***Total amount:*** $40,439,836 (34% federal, 26% state, 32% institutional, 8% external sources). ***Receiving aid:*** Freshmen: 28% (1,203); all full-time undergraduates: 23% (4,231). ***Average award:*** Freshmen: $8341; Undergraduates: $7604. ***Scholarships, grants, and awards:*** Federal Pell, FSEOG, state, private.

GIFT AID (NON-NEED-BASED) ***Total amount:*** $6,741,240 (2% state, 93% institutional, 5% external sources). ***Receiving aid:*** Freshmen: 4% (157). Undergraduates: 3% (613). ***Average award:*** Freshmen: $7105. Undergraduates: $5954. ***Scholarships, grants, and awards by category:*** *Academic interests/achievement:* architecture, biological sciences, business, computer science, education, engineering/technologies, English, general academic interests/achievements, home economics, humanities, international studies, mathematics, military science, physical sciences, premedicine, religion/biblical studies, social sciences. *Creative arts/performance:* applied art and design, cinema/film/broadcasting, dance, journalism/publications, music, theater/drama. *Special achievements/activities:* cheerleading/drum major, general special achievements/activities, leadership. *Special characteristics:* children and siblings of alumni, children of faculty/staff, handicapped students, international students, local/state students, members of minority groups, out-of-state students, siblings of current students. ***Tuition waivers:*** Full or partial for employees or children of employees. ***ROTC:*** Army, Air Force cooperative.

LOANS ***Student loans:*** $71,386,575 (30% need-based, 70% non-need-based). 51% of past graduating class borrowed through all loan programs. *Average indebtedness per student:* $28,554. ***Average need-based loan:*** Freshmen: $3462. Undergraduates: $4219. ***Parent loans:*** $49,290,613 (100% non-need-based). ***Programs:*** Federal Direct (Subsidized and Unsubsidized Stafford, PLUS), Perkins.

WORK-STUDY ***Federal work-study:*** Total amount: $895,798; jobs available. ***State or other work-study/employment:*** Total amount: $14,826,067 (100% non-need-based). Part-time jobs available.

ATHLETIC AWARDS Total amount: $7,569,069 (100% non-need-based).

APPLYING FOR FINANCIAL AID ***Required financial aid form:*** FAFSA. ***Financial aid deadline (priority):*** 3/1. ***Notification date:*** Continuous beginning 4/1. Students must reply within 4 weeks of notification.

CONTACT Lisa L. Tumer, Director of Financial Aid and Scholarships, James Madison University, 800 South Main Street, MSC 3519, Harrisonburg, VA 22807, 540-568-7820. *Fax:* 540-568-7994. *E-mail:* fin_aid@jmu.edu.
Website: http://www.jmu.edu/.

JARVIS CHRISTIAN COLLEGE

Hawkins, TX

CONTACT Alice Copeland, Director of Financial Aid, Jarvis Christian College, PO Box 1470, Hawkins, TX 75765, 903-730-4890 Ext. 2402. *Fax:* 903-730-4891. *E-mail:* alice.copeland@jarvis.edu.
Website: http://www.jarvis.edu/.

JEFFERSON COLLEGE OF HEALTH SCIENCES

Roanoke, VA

CONTACT Debra A. Johnson, Director of Financial Aid, Jefferson College of Health Sciences, 101 Elm Avenue SE, Roanoke, VA 24013-2222, 540-985-8492 or toll-free 888-985-8483. *Fax:* 540-224-6916. *E-mail:* djjohnson@jchs.edu.
Website: http://www.jchs.edu/.

THE JEWISH THEOLOGICAL SEMINARY

New York, NY

CONTACT Linda Levine, Registrar/Director of Financial Aid, The Jewish Theological Seminary, 3080 Broadway, New York, NY 10027-4649, 212-678-8007. *Fax:* 212-678-8947. *E-mail:* financialaid@jtsa.edu.
Website: http://www.jtsa.edu/.

JOHN BROWN UNIVERSITY

Siloam Springs, AR

Tuition & fees: $27,668	Average undergraduate aid package: $20,410

ABOUT THE INSTITUTION Independent interdenominational, coed. ***Awards:*** certificates, associate, bachelor's, and master's degrees. 35 undergraduate majors. ***Total enrollment:*** 2,150. Undergraduates: 1,608. Freshmen: 319. Federal methodology is used as a basis for awarding need-based institutional aid.

UNDERGRADUATE EXPENSES for 2019–2020 ***Application fee:*** $25. ***Comprehensive fee:*** $37,124 includes full-time tuition ($26,458), mandatory fees ($1210), and room and board ($9456). ***College room only:*** $4536. Full-time tuition and fees vary according to course load and degree level. Room and board charges vary according to board plan and housing facility. ***Part-time tuition:*** $882 per credit hour. ***Part-time fees:*** $303 per term. Part-time tuition and fees vary according to course load and degree level.

FRESHMAN FINANCIAL AID (Fall 2018) 276 applied for aid; of those 82% were deemed to have need. 100% of freshmen with need received aid; of those 25% had need fully met. ***Average percent of need met:*** 80% (excluding resources awarded to replace EFC). ***Average financial aid package:*** $22,238 (excluding resources awarded to replace EFC). 38% of all full-time freshmen had no need and received non-need-based gift aid.

UNDERGRADUATE FINANCIAL AID (Fall 2018) 1,150 applied for aid; of those 87% were deemed to have need. 100% of undergraduates with need received aid; of those 18% had need fully met. ***Average percent of need met:*** 70% (excluding resources awarded to replace EFC). ***Average financial aid package:*** $20,410 (excluding resources awarded to replace EFC). 32% of all full-time undergraduates had no need and received non-need-based gift aid.

GIFT AID (NEED-BASED) ***Total amount:*** $14,323,770 (17% federal, 8% state, 71% institutional, 4% external sources). ***Receiving aid:*** Freshmen: 61% (194); all full-time undergraduates: 62% (885). ***Average award:*** Freshmen: $15,371; Undergraduates: $14,144. ***Scholarships, grants, and awards:*** Federal Pell, FSEOG, state, private, college/university gift aid from institutional funds.

GIFT AID (NON-NEED-BASED) ***Total amount:*** $7,705,383 (4% state, 67% institutional, 29% external sources). ***Receiving aid:*** Freshmen: 63% (200). Under-

graduates: 54% (779). ***Average award:*** Freshmen: $12,182. Undergraduates: $11,260. ***Scholarships, grants, and awards by category:*** *Academic interests/achievement:* general academic interests/achievements. *Creative arts/performance:* applied art and design, journalism/publications, music, theater/drama. ***Tuition waivers:*** Full or partial for employees or children of employees. ***ROTC:*** Army cooperative, Air Force cooperative.

LOANS *Student loans:* $6,420,388 (66% need-based, 34% non-need-based). 60% of past graduating class borrowed through all loan programs. *Average indebtedness per student:* $25,593. ***Average need-based loan:*** Freshmen: $1965. Undergraduates: $3021. ***Parent loans:*** $1,791,023 (21% need-based, 79% non-need-based). ***Programs:*** Federal Direct (Subsidized and Unsubsidized Stafford, PLUS), Perkins, college/university.

WORK-STUDY *Federal work-study:* Total amount: $263,269; jobs available. ***State or other work-study/employment:*** Total amount: $649,165 (85% need-based, 15% non-need-based). Part-time jobs available.

ATHLETIC AWARDS Total amount: $1,782,607 (19% need-based, 81% non-need-based).

APPLYING FOR FINANCIAL AID *Required financial aid forms:* FAFSA, institution's own form, state aid form. ***Notification date:*** Continuous beginning 3/1. Students must reply by 5/1.

CONTACT Mr. David Burney, Director of Financial Aid, John Brown University, 2000 West University Street, Siloam Springs, AR 72761-2121, 479-524-7427 or toll-free 877-JBU-INFO. *E-mail:* dburney@jbu.edu.
Website: http://www.jbu.edu/.

JOHN CARROLL UNIVERSITY

University Heights, OH

Tuition & fees: $44,405	Average undergraduate aid package: $33,327

ABOUT THE INSTITUTION Independent Roman Catholic (Jesuit), coed. ***Awards:*** certificates, bachelor's, and master's degrees. 39 undergraduate majors. ***Total enrollment:*** 3,506. Undergraduates: 3,017. Freshmen: 725. Federal methodology is used as a basis for awarding need-based institutional aid.

UNDERGRADUATE EXPENSES for 2020–2021 *One-time required fee:* $325. ***Comprehensive fee:*** $56,965 includes full-time tuition ($42,675), mandatory fees ($1730), and room and board ($12,560). ***College room only:*** $6940. Full-time tuition and fees vary according to course load. Room and board charges vary according to board plan and housing facility. ***Part-time tuition:*** $1415 per credit hour. Part-time tuition and fees vary according to course load.

FRESHMAN FINANCIAL AID (Fall 2018) 788 applied for aid; of those 83% were deemed to have need. 100% of freshmen with need received aid; of those 28% had need fully met. ***Average percent of need met:*** 83% (excluding resources awarded to replace EFC). ***Average financial aid package:*** $34,460 (excluding resources awarded to replace EFC). 22% of all full-time freshmen had no need and received non-need-based gift aid.

UNDERGRADUATE FINANCIAL AID (Fall 2018) 2,556 applied for aid; of those 84% were deemed to have need. 100% of undergraduates with need received aid; of those 26% had need fully met. ***Average percent of need met:*** 81% (excluding resources awarded to replace EFC). ***Average financial aid package:*** $33,327 (excluding resources awarded to replace EFC). 26% of all full-time undergraduates had no need and received non-need-based gift aid.

GIFT AID (NEED-BASED) *Receiving aid:* Freshmen: 76% (637); all full-time undergraduates: 70% (2,104). ***Average award:*** Freshmen: $29,033; Undergraduates: $27,317. ***Scholarships, grants, and awards:*** Federal Pell, FSEOG, state, private, college/university gift aid from institutional funds.

GIFT AID (NON-NEED-BASED) *Receiving aid:* Freshmen: 76% (637). Undergraduates: 70% (2,104). ***Average award:*** Freshmen: $22,470. Undergraduates: $21,743. ***Scholarships, grants, and awards by category:*** *Academic interests/achievement:* biological sciences, business, communication, computer science, education, English, foreign languages, general academic interests/achievements, home economics, humanities, international studies, mathematics, military science, physical sciences, premedicine, religion/biblical studies, social sciences. *Creative arts/performance:* creative writing, debating, journalism/publications. *Special achievements/activities:* community service, leadership. *Special characteristics:* children of faculty/staff, general special characteristics, international students, local/state students, spouses of deceased or disabled public servants, veterans. ***Tuition waivers:*** Full or partial for employees or children of employees. ***ROTC:*** Army.

LOANS *Student loans:* 68% of past graduating class borrowed through all loan programs. *Average indebtedness per student:* $32,956. ***Average need-based loan:*** Freshmen: $3246. Undergraduates: $3976. ***Programs:*** Federal Direct (Subsidized and Unsubsidized Stafford, PLUS).

WORK-STUDY Federal work-study jobs available.

APPLYING FOR FINANCIAL AID *Required financial aid form:* FAFSA. ***Financial aid deadline:*** Continuous. ***Notification date:*** Continuous. Students must reply within 4 weeks of notification.

CONTACT Student Enrollment and Financial Services, John Carroll University, 1 John Carroll Boulevard, University Heights, OH 44118, 216-3973098 or toll-free 888-335-6800. *Fax:* 216-3974248. *E-mail:* enrollment@jcu.edu.
Website: http://www.jcu.edu/.

JOHN F. KENNEDY UNIVERSITY

Pleasant Hill, CA

CONTACT Mindy Bergeron, Director of Financial Aid, John F. Kennedy University, 100 Ellinwood Way, Pleasant Hill, CA 94523, 925-969-3385 or toll-free 800-696-JFKU. *Fax:* 925-969-3390. *E-mail:* bergeron@jfku.edu.
Website: http://www.jfku.edu/.

JOHN JAY COLLEGE OF CRIMINAL JUSTICE OF THE CITY UNIVERSITY OF NEW YORK

New York, NY

Tuition & fees: N/R	Average undergraduate aid package: $8776

ABOUT THE INSTITUTION State and locally supported, coed. ***Awards:*** certificates, bachelor's, and master's degrees. 30 undergraduate majors. ***Total enrollment:*** 15,880. Undergraduates: 13,746. Freshmen: 2,056. Federal methodology is used as a basis for awarding need-based institutional aid.

FRESHMAN FINANCIAL AID (Fall 2018) 3192 applied for aid; of those 92% were deemed to have need. 92% of freshmen with need received aid. ***Average percent of need met:*** 85% (excluding resources awarded to replace EFC). ***Average financial aid package:*** $8776 (excluding resources awarded to replace EFC).

UNDERGRADUATE FINANCIAL AID (Fall 2018) 10,713 applied for aid; of those 96% were deemed to have need. 85% of undergraduates with need received aid. ***Average percent of need met:*** 85% (excluding resources awarded to replace EFC). ***Average financial aid package:*** $8776 (excluding resources awarded to replace EFC).

GIFT AID (NEED-BASED) *Receiving aid:* Freshmen: 60% (2,496); all full-time undergraduates: 61% (8,067). ***Average award:*** Freshmen: $2745; Undergraduates: $2745. ***Scholarships, grants, and awards:*** Federal Pell, FSEOG, state, private, college/university gift aid from institutional funds.

GIFT AID (NON-NEED-BASED) *Receiving aid:* Freshmen: 5% (225). Undergraduates: 2% (236). ***Scholarships, grants, and awards by category:*** *Academic interests/achievement:* general academic interests/achievements.

LOANS *Average need-based loan:* Freshmen: $3979. Undergraduates: $3979. ***Programs:*** Federal Direct (Subsidized and Unsubsidized Stafford, PLUS), Perkins, college/university.

WORK-STUDY Federal work-study jobs available. ***State or other work-study/employment:*** Part-time jobs available.

APPLYING FOR FINANCIAL AID *Required financial aid forms:* FAFSA, state aid form. ***Financial aid deadline:*** Continuous. ***Notification date:*** Continuous. Students must reply within 2 weeks of notification.

CONTACT Mrs. Sylvia C. Lopez-Crespo, Director of Financial Aid, John Jay College of Criminal Justice of the City University of New York, 524 West 59th Street, New York, NY 10019-1093, 212-237-8897 or toll-free 877-JOHNJAY. *Fax:* 212-237-8936. *E-mail:* sylopez@jjay.cuny.edu.
Website: http://www.jjay.cuny.edu/.

JOHN PATRICK UNIVERSITY OF HEALTH AND APPLIED SCIENCES

South Bend, IN

CONTACT Financial Aid Office, John Patrick University of Health and Applied Sciences, 100 East Wayne Street, Suite 140, South Bend, IN 46601.
Website: https://jpu.edu/.

JOHN PAUL THE GREAT CATHOLIC UNIVERSITY

Escondido, CA

ABOUT THE INSTITUTION Independent Roman Catholic Church, coed. ***Awards:*** bachelor's and master's degrees. 3 undergraduate majors. ***Total enrollment:*** 308. Undergraduates: 286. Freshmen: 85.

GIFT AID (NEED-BASED) ***Scholarships, grants, and awards:*** Federal Pell, FSEOG, state, private, college/university gift aid from institutional funds.

GIFT AID (NON-NEED-BASED) ***Scholarships, grants, and awards by category:*** *Academic interests/achievement:* general academic interests/achievements. *Creative arts/performance:* general creative arts/performance. *Special achievements/activities:* leadership.

LOANS ***Programs:*** Federal Direct (Subsidized and Unsubsidized Stafford, PLUS), Alternative education loans from private lenders.

CONTACT Lisa Williams, Director of Financial Aid, John Paul the Great Catholic University, 220 West Grand Avenue, Escondido, CA 92025, 858-653-6740 Ext. 1303. *Fax:* 858-653-3791. *E-mail:* lwilliams@jpcatholic.com.
Website: http://www.jpcatholic.edu/.

JOHNS HOPKINS UNIVERSITY

Baltimore, MD

Tuition & fees: $55,350	Average undergraduate aid package: $49,032

ABOUT THE INSTITUTION Independent, coed. ***Awards:*** certificates, diplomas, bachelor's, master's, and doctoral degrees. 58 undergraduate majors. ***Total enrollment:*** 8,176. Undergraduates: 5,534. Freshmen: 1,355. Institutional methodology is used as a basis for awarding need-based institutional aid.

UNDERGRADUATE EXPENSES for 2019–2020 ***Application fee:*** $70. ***One-time required fee:*** $500. ***Comprehensive fee:*** $71,660 includes full-time tuition ($55,350) and room and board ($16,310). ***College room only:*** $9452. Room and board charges vary according to board plan and housing facility. ***Part-time tuition:*** $1845 per credit hour. Part-time tuition and fees vary according to course load.

FRESHMAN FINANCIAL AID (Fall 2019, est.) 991 applied for aid; of those 75% were deemed to have need. 97% of freshmen with need received aid; of those 100% had need fully met. ***Average percent of need met:*** 100% (excluding resources awarded to replace EFC). ***Average financial aid package:*** $53,723 (excluding resources awarded to replace EFC). 1% of all full-time freshmen had no need and received non-need-based gift aid.

UNDERGRADUATE FINANCIAL AID (Fall 2019, est.) 3,417 applied for aid; of those 82% were deemed to have need. 98% of undergraduates with need received aid; of those 100% had need fully met. ***Average percent of need met:*** 100% (excluding resources awarded to replace EFC). ***Average financial aid package:*** $49,032 (excluding resources awarded to replace EFC). 2% of all full-time undergraduates had no need and received non-need-based gift aid.

GIFT AID (NEED-BASED) ***Total amount:*** $130,244,782 (5% federal, 94% institutional, 1% external sources). ***Receiving aid:*** Freshmen: 53% (718); all full-time undergraduates: 51% (2,735). ***Average award:*** Freshmen: $52,523; Undergraduates: $47,843. ***Scholarships, grants, and awards:*** Federal Pell, FSEOG, state, private, college/university gift aid from institutional funds.

GIFT AID (NON-NEED-BASED) ***Total amount:*** $5,477,526 (10% federal, 60% institutional, 30% external sources). ***Receiving aid:*** Freshmen: 4% (53). Undergraduates: 3% (183). ***Average award:*** Freshmen: $14,093. Undergraduates: $27,380. ***Scholarships, grants, and awards by category:*** *Academic interests/achievement:* engineering/technologies, general academic interests/achievements. *Special characteristics:* children of faculty/staff, international students, local/state students, veterans. ***Tuition waivers:*** Full or partial for employees or children of employees. ***ROTC:*** Army, Air Force cooperative.

LOANS ***Student loans:*** $7,534,421 (14% need-based, 86% non-need-based). 41% of past graduating class borrowed through all loan programs. *Average indebtedness per student:* $24,107. ***Average need-based loan:*** Freshmen: $311. Undergraduates: $335. ***Parent loans:*** $8,631,806 (11% need-based, 89% non-need-based). ***Programs:*** Federal Direct (Subsidized and Unsubsidized Stafford, PLUS).

WORK-STUDY ***Federal work-study:*** Total amount: $2,669,522; jobs available. ***State or other work-study/employment:*** Total amount: $1,805,436 (100% need-based). Part-time jobs available.

ATHLETIC AWARDS Total amount: $1,446,107 (12% need-based, 88% non-need-based).

APPLYING FOR FINANCIAL AID ***Required financial aid forms:*** FAFSA, CSS Financial Aid PROFILE, noncustodial (divorced/separated) parent's statement, Prior year student and parent tax returns. ***Financial aid deadline:*** 1/15 (priority: 1/15). ***Notification date:*** 3/15. Students must reply by 5/1.

CONTACT Mr. Tom McDermott, Assistant Vice Provost for Financial Aid, Johns Hopkins University, 146 Garland Hall, Baltimore, MD 21218, 410-516-8028. *Fax:* 410-516-6015. *E-mail:* tmcderm1@jhu.edu.
Website: http://www.jhu.edu/.

JOHNSON & WALES UNIVERSITY

Denver, CO

CONTACT Ms. Lynn Robinson, Executive Director of Student Financial Services, Johnson & Wales University, 8 Abbott Park Place, Providence, RI 02903, 401-598-4648 or toll-free 877-598-3368. *Fax:* 401-598-1040. *E-mail:* fp@jwu.edu.
Website: http://www.jwu.edu/denver/.

JOHNSON & WALES UNIVERSITY

North Miami, FL

CONTACT Ms. Lynn Robinson, Executive Director of Student Financial Services, Johnson & Wales University, 8 Abbott Park Place, Providence, RI 02903, 401-598-4648 or toll-free 866-598-3567. *Fax:* 401-598-1040. *E-mail:* fp@jwu.edu.
Website: http://www.jwu.edu/northmiami/.

JOHNSON & WALES UNIVERSITY

Charlotte, NC

CONTACT Ms. Lynn Robinson, Executive Director of Student Financial Services, Johnson & Wales University, 8 Abbott Park Place, Providence, RI 02903, 401-598-1648 or toll-free 866-598-2427. *Fax:* 401-598-4751. *E-mail:* fp@jwu.edu.
Website: http://www.jwu.edu/charlotte/.

JOHNSON & WALES UNIVERSITY

Providence, RI

CONTACT Ms. Lynn Robinson, Executive Director of Student Financial Services, Johnson & Wales University, 8 Abbott Park Place, Providence, RI 02903, 401-598-4648 or toll-free 800-342-5598. *Fax:* 401-598-1040. *E-mail:* fp@jwu.edu.
Website: http://www.jwu.edu/providence/.

JOHNSON C. SMITH UNIVERSITY

Charlotte, NC

ABOUT THE INSTITUTION Independent, coed. ***Awards:*** bachelor's and master's degrees. 23 undergraduate majors. ***Total enrollment:*** 1,565. Undergraduates: 1,480. Freshmen: 350.

GIFT AID (NEED-BASED) ***Scholarships, grants, and awards:*** Federal Pell, FSEOG, state, private, college/university gift aid from institutional funds, United Negro College Fund.

GIFT AID (NON-NEED-BASED) ***Scholarships, grants, and awards by category:*** *Academic interests/achievement:* biological sciences, computer science, engineering/technologies, general academic interests/achievements, mathematics. *Creative arts/performance:* music. *Special achievements/activities:* general special achievements/activities. *Special characteristics:* children of faculty/staff, ethnic background, general special characteristics, international students, out-of-state students, siblings of current students.

LOANS ***Programs:*** Federal Direct (Subsidized and Unsubsidized Stafford, PLUS).

WORK-STUDY ***Federal work-study:*** Total amount: $589,429; 192 jobs averaging $3000. ***State or other work-study/employment:*** Part-time jobs available.

APPLYING FOR FINANCIAL AID ***Required financial aid forms:*** FAFSA, state aid form.

CONTACT Mr. Eric Sutton, Assistant Director of Financial Aid, Johnson C. Smith University, 100 Beatties Ford Road, Charlotte, NC 28216, 704-378-1291 or toll-free 800-782-7303. *Fax:* 704-378-1292.
Website: http://www.jcsu.edu/.

JOHNSON UNIVERSITY

Knoxville, TN

Tuition & fees: $18,290	Average undergraduate aid package: N/A

ABOUT THE INSTITUTION Independent Christian Churches and Churches of Christ, coed. ***Awards:*** certificates, associate, bachelor's, master's, and doctoral degrees. 12 undergraduate majors. ***Total enrollment:*** 1,086. Undergraduates: 774. Freshmen: 145. Federal methodology is used as a basis for awarding need-based institutional aid.

UNDERGRADUATE EXPENSES for 2020–2021 ***Application fee:*** $35. ***Tuition:*** full-time $16,400. ***Required fees:*** full-time $1890. Full-time tuition and fees vary according to class time, course load, degree level, location, and program. Part-time tuition and fees vary according to class time, course load, degree level, location, and program. ***College room only:*** $3500. Room and board charges vary according to board plan, housing facility, and location.

GIFT AID (NEED-BASED) ***Scholarships, grants, and awards:*** Federal Pell, FSEOG, state, private, college/university gift aid from institutional funds.

GIFT AID (NON-NEED-BASED) ***Scholarships, grants, and awards by category:*** *Academic interests/achievement:* business, communication, education, general academic interests/achievements, religion/biblical studies. *Creative arts/performance:* art/fine arts, general creative arts/performance, music. *Special achievements/activities:* community service, general special achievements/activities, leadership, religious involvement. *Special characteristics:* children of current students, children of educators, children of faculty/staff, ethnic background, general special characteristics, international students, married students, members of minority groups, parents of current students, relatives of clergy, religious affiliation, siblings of current students, spouses of current students. ***Tuition waivers:*** Full or partial for employees or children of employees.

LOANS ***Programs:*** Federal Direct (Subsidized and Unsubsidized Stafford, PLUS).

WORK-STUDY Federal work-study jobs available. ***State or other work-study/employment:*** Part-time jobs available.

APPLYING FOR FINANCIAL AID ***Required financial aid forms:*** FAFSA, institution's own form. ***Financial aid deadline:*** Continuous. ***Notification date:*** Continuous beginning 12/1. Students must reply within 4 weeks of notification.

CONTACT Office of Student Financial Aid, Johnson University, 7900 Johnson Drive, Knoxville, TN 37998, 865-251-2303 or toll-free 800-827-2122. *Fax:* 865-251-2337. *E-mail:* financialaid@johnsonu.edu.
Website: http://www.johnsonu.edu/.

JOHNSON UNIVERSITY FLORIDA

Kissimmee, FL

Tuition & fees: $17,630	Average undergraduate aid package: $12,538

ABOUT THE INSTITUTION Independent Christian Churches and Churches of Christ, coed. ***Awards:*** certificates, associate, bachelor's, and master's degrees. 18 undergraduate majors. ***Total enrollment:*** 182. Undergraduates: 182. Freshmen: 56. Federal methodology is used as a basis for awarding need-based institutional aid.

UNDERGRADUATE EXPENSES for 2020–2021 ***Application fee:*** $35. ***Tuition:*** full-time $16,400. ***Required fees:*** full-time $1230. ***College room only:*** $3600. Room and board charges vary according to board plan.

FRESHMAN FINANCIAL AID (Fall 2018) 76 applied for aid; of those 95% were deemed to have need. 100% of freshmen with need received aid; of those 10% had need fully met. ***Average percent of need met:*** 55% (excluding resources awarded to replace EFC). ***Average financial aid package:*** $11,770 (excluding resources awarded to replace EFC). 14% of all full-time freshmen had no need and received non-need-based gift aid.

UNDERGRADUATE FINANCIAL AID (Fall 2018) 177 applied for aid; of those 94% were deemed to have need. 100% of undergraduates with need received aid; of those 11% had need fully met. ***Average percent of need met:*** 58% (excluding resources awarded to replace EFC). ***Average financial aid package:*** $12,538 (excluding resources awarded to replace EFC). 10% of all full-time undergraduates had no need and received non-need-based gift aid.

GIFT AID (NEED-BASED) ***Total amount:*** $1,613,633 (37% federal, 36% state, 23% institutional, 4% external sources). ***Receiving aid:*** Freshmen: 86% (72); all full-time undergraduates: 89% (166). ***Average award:*** Freshmen: $9371; Undergraduates: $9615. ***Scholarships, grants, and awards:*** Federal Pell, FSEOG, state, private, college/university gift aid from institutional funds.

GIFT AID (NON-NEED-BASED) ***Total amount:*** $225,703 (2% federal, 34% state, 51% institutional, 13% external sources). ***Receiving aid:*** Freshmen: 6% (5). Undergraduates: 6% (12). ***Average award:*** Freshmen: $4901. Undergraduates: $5132. ***Scholarships, grants, and awards by category:*** *Academic interests/achievement:* education, religion/biblical studies. *Creative arts/performance:* music. *Special characteristics:* children and siblings of alumni, children of faculty/staff, relatives of clergy, religious affiliation, spouses of current students. ***Tuition waivers:*** Full or partial for employees or children of employees.

LOANS ***Student loans:*** $862,287 (90% need-based, 10% non-need-based). ***Average need-based loan:*** Freshmen: $2930. Undergraduates: $3458. ***Parent loans:*** $310,699 (53% need-based, 47% non-need-based). ***Programs:*** Federal Direct (Subsidized and Unsubsidized Stafford, PLUS).

WORK-STUDY ***Federal work-study:*** Total amount: $41,100; jobs available. ***State or other work-study/employment:*** Total amount: $9282 (97% need-based, 3% non-need-based). Part-time jobs available.

APPLYING FOR FINANCIAL AID ***Required financial aid forms:*** FAFSA, institution's own form. ***Financial aid deadline:*** Continuous. ***Notification date:*** Continuous beginning 12/1. Students must reply within 4 weeks of notification.

CONTACT Financial Aid Office, Johnson University Florida, 1011 Bill Beck Boulevard, Kissimmee, FL 34744-5301, 407-847-8966 or toll-free 888-468-6322.
Website: http://www.johnsonu.edu/.

JOSE MARIA VARGAS UNIVERSITY

Pembroke Pines, FL

CONTACT Financial Aid Office, Jose Maria Vargas University, 10131 Pines Boulevard, Pembroke Pines, FL 33026, 954-322-4446.
Website: http://www.jmvu.edu/.

JUDSON COLLEGE

Marion, AL

CONTACT Mrs. Melena Verity, Acting Director of Financial Aid, Judson College, 302 Bibb Street, Marion, AL 36756, 334-683-5170 or toll-free 800-447-9472. *Fax:* 334-683-5282. *E-mail:* mverity@judson.edu.
Website: http://www.judson.edu/.

JUDSON UNIVERSITY

Elgin, IL

Tuition & fees: $29,870 **Average undergraduate aid package: $20,982**

ABOUT THE INSTITUTION Independent Baptist, coed. ***Awards:*** certificates, associate, bachelor's, master's, and doctoral degrees. 42 undergraduate majors. ***Total enrollment:*** 1,256. Undergraduates: 1,034. Freshmen: 168. Federal methodology is used as a basis for awarding need-based institutional aid.

UNDERGRADUATE EXPENSES for 2019–2020 ***Application fee:*** $50. ***One-time required fee:*** $100. ***Comprehensive fee:*** $40,660 includes full-time tuition ($28,840), mandatory fees ($1030), and room and board ($10,790). Full-time tuition and fees vary according to degree level, program, and reciprocity agreements. Room and board charges vary according to board plan. ***Part-time tuition:*** $1185 per credit hour. Part-time tuition and fees vary according to course load, degree level, program, and reciprocity agreements.

FRESHMAN FINANCIAL AID (Fall 2019, est.) 160 applied for aid; of those 92% were deemed to have need. 100% of freshmen with need received aid; of those 16% had need fully met. ***Average percent of need met:*** 63% (excluding resources awarded to replace EFC). ***Average financial aid package:*** $22,139 (excluding resources awarded to replace EFC). 11% of all full-time freshmen had no need and received non-need-based gift aid.

UNDERGRADUATE FINANCIAL AID (Fall 2019, est.) 771 applied for aid; of those 67% were deemed to have need. 100% of undergraduates with need received aid; of those 26% had need fully met. ***Average percent of need met:*** 60% (excluding resources awarded to replace EFC). ***Average financial aid package:*** $20,982 (excluding resources awarded to replace EFC). 17% of all full-time undergraduates had no need and received non-need-based gift aid.

GIFT AID (NEED-BASED) ***Total amount:*** $8,880,198 (24% federal, 18% state, 8% institutional, 50% external sources). ***Receiving aid:*** Freshmen: 59% (106); all full-time undergraduates: 55% (518). ***Average award:*** Freshmen: $7980; Undergraduates: $8328. ***Scholarships, grants, and awards:*** Federal Pell, FSEOG, state, private, college/university gift aid from institutional funds.

GIFT AID (NON-NEED-BASED) ***Total amount:*** $20,918,936 (49% institutional, 51% external sources). ***Receiving aid:*** Freshmen: 82% (147). Undergraduates: 45% (421). ***Average award:*** Freshmen: $17,943. Undergraduates: $17,564. ***Scholarships, grants, and awards by category:*** *Academic interests/achievement:* general academic interests/achievements. *Creative arts/performance:* applied art and design, music, theater/drama. *Special achievements/activities:* 12 awards ($133,040 total): leadership. *Special characteristics:* 2 awards ($5000 total): members of minority groups. ***Tuition waivers:*** Full or partial for children of alumni, employees or children of employees. ***ROTC:*** Army cooperative.

LOANS ***Student loans:*** $4,189,623 (46% need-based, 54% non-need-based). 94% of past graduating class borrowed through all loan programs. *Average indebtedness per student:* $24,736. ***Average need-based loan:*** Freshmen: $3005. Undergraduates: $4153. ***Parent loans:*** $939,460 (100% non-need-based). ***Programs:*** Federal Direct (Subsidized and Unsubsidized Stafford, PLUS), Perkins.

WORK-STUDY ***Federal work-study:*** Total amount: $250,563; 162 jobs averaging $1547. ***State or other work-study/employment:*** Total amount: $528,386 (50% need-based, 50% non-need-based). Part-time jobs available.

ATHLETIC AWARDS Total amount: $3,657,059 (100% non-need-based).

APPLYING FOR FINANCIAL AID ***Required financial aid form:*** FAFSA. ***Financial aid deadline:*** 5/1 (priority: 2/15). ***Notification date:*** Continuous beginning 3/1. Students must reply by 5/1 or within 4 weeks of notification.

CONTACT Diana Winton, Director of Financial Aid, Judson University, 1151 North State Street, Elgin, IL 60123-1498, 847-628-2531 or toll-free 800-879-5376. *Fax:* 847-628-2533. *E-mail:* diana.winton@judsonu.edu.
Website: http://www.judsonu.edu/.

THE JUILLIARD SCHOOL

New York, NY

Tuition & fees: $47,470 **Average undergraduate aid package: $38,146**

ABOUT THE INSTITUTION Independent, coed. ***Awards:*** certificates, diplomas, bachelor's, master's, and doctoral degrees. 4 undergraduate majors. ***Total enrollment:*** 942. Undergraduates: 585. Freshmen: 120. Federal methodology is used as a basis for awarding need-based institutional aid.

UNDERGRADUATE EXPENSES for 2019–2020 ***Application fee:*** $110. ***Comprehensive fee:*** $65,440 includes full-time tuition ($47,370), mandatory fees ($100), and room and board ($17,970).

FRESHMAN FINANCIAL AID (Fall 2019, est.) 112 applied for aid; of those 79% were deemed to have need. 100% of freshmen with need received aid; of those 24% had need fully met. ***Average percent of need met:*** 72% (excluding resources awarded to replace EFC). ***Average financial aid package:*** $37,820 (excluding resources awarded to replace EFC). 17% of all full-time freshmen had no need and received non-need-based gift aid.

UNDERGRADUATE FINANCIAL AID (Fall 2019, est.) 424 applied for aid; of those 83% were deemed to have need. 100% of undergraduates with need received aid; of those 20% had need fully met. ***Average percent of need met:*** 71% (excluding resources awarded to replace EFC). ***Average financial aid package:*** $38,146 (excluding resources awarded to replace EFC). 13% of all full-time undergraduates had no need and received non-need-based gift aid.

GIFT AID (NEED-BASED) ***Total amount:*** $11,873,439 (5% federal, 92% institutional, 3% external sources). ***Receiving aid:*** Freshmen: 77% (89); all full-time undergraduates: 71% (347). ***Average award:*** Freshmen: $34,259; Undergraduates: $33,483. ***Scholarships, grants, and awards:*** Federal Pell, FSEOG, state, private, college/university gift aid from institutional funds, Veteran's Benefits.

GIFT AID (NON-NEED-BASED) ***Total amount:*** $3,138,385 (99% institutional, 1% external sources). ***Receiving aid:*** Freshmen: 1% (1). Undergraduates: 2. ***Average award:*** Freshmen: $27,271. Undergraduates: $23,411. ***Scholarships, grants, and awards by category:*** *Creative arts/performance:* dance, music, performing arts, theater/drama. *Special characteristics:* children of faculty/staff.

LOANS ***Student loans:*** $2,464,957 (81% need-based, 19% non-need-based). 37% of past graduating class borrowed through all loan programs. *Average indebtedness per student:* $26,326. ***Average need-based loan:*** Freshmen: $3451. Undergraduates: $4690. ***Parent loans:*** $1,550,369 (70% need-based, 30% non-need-based). ***Programs:*** Federal Direct (Subsidized and Unsubsidized Stafford, PLUS).

WORK-STUDY ***Federal work-study:*** Total amount: $368,315; jobs available. ***State or other work-study/employment:*** Total amount: $596,000 (56% need-based, 44% non-need-based). Part-time jobs available.

APPLYING FOR FINANCIAL AID ***Required financial aid forms:*** FAFSA, CSS Financial Aid PROFILE, Student and Parent Federal Tax Form. ***Financial aid deadline:*** 3/1. ***Notification date:*** 4/1. Students must reply by 5/1.

CONTACT Ms. Tina Gonzalez, Director of Financial Aid, The Juilliard School, 60 Lincoln Center Plaza, New York, NY 10023, 212-799-5000 Ext. 211. *Fax:* 212-358-2594. *E-mail:* financialaid@juilliard.edu.
Website: http://www.juilliard.edu/.

JUNIATA COLLEGE

Huntingdon, PA

ABOUT THE INSTITUTION Independent Church of the Brethren, coed. ***Awards:*** certificates, bachelor's, and master's degrees. 67 undergraduate majors. ***Total enrollment:*** 1,433. Undergraduates: 1,423. Freshmen: 350.

GIFT AID (NEED-BASED) ***Scholarships, grants, and awards:*** Federal Pell, FSEOG, state, private, college/university gift aid from institutional funds.

GIFT AID (NON-NEED-BASED) ***Scholarships, grants, and awards by category:*** *Academic interests/achievement:* biological sciences, business, communication, computer science, education, foreign languages, general academic interests/achievements, health fields, humanities, international studies, mathematics, physical sciences, premedicine, social sciences. *Creative arts/performance:* applied art and design, music, performing arts, theater/drama. *Special achievements/activities:* community service, general special achievements/activities, leadership. *Special characteristics:* children and siblings of alumni, children of faculty/staff, ethnic background, first-generation college students, international students, local/state students, siblings of current students.

LOANS ***Programs:*** Federal Direct (Subsidized and Unsubsidized Stafford, PLUS), college/university.

WORK-STUDY ***Federal work-study:*** Total amount: $1,034,675; jobs available. ***State or other work-study/employment:*** Total amount: $694,701 (11% need-based, 89% non-need-based). Part-time jobs available.

APPLYING FOR FINANCIAL AID ***Required financial aid form:*** FAFSA.

CONTACT Ms. Tracie Patrick, Director of Student Financial Planning, Juniata College, 1700 Moore Street, Huntingdon, PA 16652-2119, 814-641-3140 or toll-free 877-JUNIATA. *Fax:* 814-641-5311. *E-mail:* patrict@juniata.edu.
Website: http://www.juniata.edu/.

KALAMAZOO COLLEGE

Kalamazoo, MI

Tuition & fees: $52,530	Average undergraduate aid package: $44,311

ABOUT THE INSTITUTION Independent American Baptist Churches in the U.S.A., coed. ***Awards:*** bachelor's degrees. 26 undergraduate majors. ***Total enrollment:*** 1,286. Undergraduates: 1,286. Freshmen: 395. Both federal and institutional methodology are used as a basis for awarding need-based institutional aid.

UNDERGRADUATE EXPENSES for 2020–2021 ***Comprehensive fee:*** $63,060 includes full-time tuition ($51,999), mandatory fees ($531), and room and board ($10,530). ***College room only:*** $5121.

FRESHMAN FINANCIAL AID (Fall 2019, est.) 367 applied for aid; of those 84% were deemed to have need. 100% of freshmen with need received aid; of those 41% had need fully met. ***Average percent of need met:*** 94% (excluding resources awarded to replace EFC). ***Average financial aid package:*** $45,727 (excluding resources awarded to replace EFC). 21% of all full-time freshmen had no need and received non-need-based gift aid.

UNDERGRADUATE FINANCIAL AID (Fall 2019, est.) 1,198 applied for aid; of those 88% were deemed to have need. 100% of undergraduates with need received aid; of those 37% had need fully met. ***Average percent of need met:*** 92% (excluding resources awarded to replace EFC). ***Average financial aid package:*** $44,311 (excluding resources awarded to replace EFC). 25% of all full-time undergraduates had no need and received non-need-based gift aid.

GIFT AID (NEED-BASED) ***Total amount:*** $38,926,806 (6% federal, 2% state, 89% institutional, 3% external sources). ***Receiving aid:*** Freshmen: 77% (305); all full-time undergraduates: 71% (1,046). ***Average award:*** Freshmen: $37,879; Undergraduates: $36,997. ***Scholarships, grants, and awards:*** Federal Pell, FSEOG, state, private, college/university gift aid from institutional funds.

GIFT AID (NON-NEED-BASED) ***Total amount:*** $14,407,222 (85% institutional, 15% external sources). ***Receiving aid:*** Freshmen: 20% (79). Undergraduates: 14% (201). ***Average award:*** Freshmen: $30,345. Undergraduates: $27,315. ***Scholarships, grants, and awards by category:*** *Academic interests/achievement:* general academic interests/achievements. *Creative arts/performance:* applied art and design, music, performing arts. *Special achievements/activities:* leadership. *Special characteristics:* children and siblings of alumni. ***ROTC:*** Army cooperative.

LOANS ***Student loans:*** $8,385,205 (61% need-based, 39% non-need-based). 56% of past graduating class borrowed through all loan programs. *Average indebtedness per student:* $34,179. ***Average need-based loan:*** Freshmen: $3323. Undergraduates: $4373. ***Parent loans:*** $1,786,136 (100% non-need-based). ***Programs:*** Federal Direct (Subsidized and Unsubsidized Stafford, PLUS).

WORK-STUDY ***Federal work-study:*** Total amount: $1,470,590; jobs available. ***State or other work-study/employment:*** Total amount: $229,000 (100% need-based). Part-time jobs available.

APPLYING FOR FINANCIAL AID ***Required financial aid form:*** FAFSA. ***Financial aid deadline:*** 3/1 (priority: 11/15). ***Notification date:*** 12/20. Students must reply by 5/1.

CONTACT Financial Aid Office, Kalamazoo College, 1200 Academy Street, Kalamazoo, MI 49006-3295, 269-337-7000 or toll-free 800-253-3602.
Website: http://www.kzoo.edu/.

KANSAS CITY ART INSTITUTE

Kansas City, MO

Tuition & fees: $39,200	Average undergraduate aid package: $27,588

ABOUT THE INSTITUTION Independent, coed. ***Awards:*** certificates and bachelor's degrees. 12 undergraduate majors. ***Total enrollment:*** 672. Undergraduates: 663. Freshmen: 171. Federal methodology is used as a basis for awarding need-based institutional aid.

UNDERGRADUATE EXPENSES for 2019–2020 ***Application fee:*** $45. ***Tuition:*** full-time $38,700; part-time $1510 per credit hour. ***Required fees:*** full-time $500. Full-time tuition and fees vary according to reciprocity agreements. Part-time tuition and fees vary according to reciprocity agreements. ***College room only:*** $8200. Room and board charges vary according to board plan.

FRESHMAN FINANCIAL AID (Fall 2019, est.) 175 applied for aid; of those 90% were deemed to have need. 99% of freshmen with need received aid; of those 13% had need fully met. ***Average percent of need met:*** 69% (excluding resources awarded to replace EFC). ***Average financial aid package:*** $28,857 (excluding resources awarded to replace EFC). 14% of all full-time freshmen had no need and received non-need-based gift aid.

UNDERGRADUATE FINANCIAL AID (Fall 2019, est.) 632 applied for aid; of those 91% were deemed to have need. 100% of undergraduates with need received aid; of those 16% had need fully met. ***Average percent of need met:*** 68% (excluding resources awarded to replace EFC). ***Average financial aid package:*** $27,588 (excluding resources awarded to replace EFC). 17% of all full-time undergraduates had no need and received non-need-based gift aid.

GIFT AID (NEED-BASED) ***Total amount:*** $13,694,179 (12% federal, 2% state, 83% institutional, 3% external sources). ***Receiving aid:*** Freshmen: 86% (157); all full-time undergraduates: 83% (574). ***Average award:*** Freshmen: $26,436; Undergraduates: $23,834. ***Scholarships, grants, and awards:*** Federal Pell, FSEOG, state, private, college/university gift aid from institutional funds.

GIFT AID (NON-NEED-BASED) ***Total amount:*** $2,937,807 (1% state, 92% institutional, 7% external sources). ***Receiving aid:*** Freshmen: 10% (18). Undergraduates: 11% (73). ***Average award:*** Freshmen: $21,060. Undergraduates: $18,649. ***Scholarships, grants, and awards by category:*** *Creative arts/performance:* applied art and design. ***Tuition waivers:*** Full or partial for employees or children of employees.

LOANS ***Student loans:*** $5,190,756 (73% need-based, 27% non-need-based). 85% of past graduating class borrowed through all loan programs. *Average indebtedness per student:* $32,607. ***Average need-based loan:*** Freshmen: $3280. Undergraduates: $4216. ***Parent loans:*** $2,017,086 (64% need-based, 36% non-need-based). ***Programs:*** Federal Direct (Subsidized and Unsubsidized Stafford, PLUS).

WORK-STUDY ***Federal work-study:*** Total amount: $123,246; jobs available. ***State or other work-study/employment:*** Total amount: $207,313 (43% need-based, 57% non-need-based). Part-time jobs available.

APPLYING FOR FINANCIAL AID ***Required financial aid form:*** FAFSA. ***Financial aid deadline (priority):*** 2/1. ***Notification date:*** Continuous beginning 12/15. Students must reply within 2 weeks of notification.

CONTACT Mrs. Lori Lynn Baer, Financial Aid Director, Kansas City Art Institute, 4415 Warwick Boulevard, Kansas City, MO 64111-1874, 816-802-3337 or toll-free 800-522-5224. *Fax:* 816-802-3453. *E-mail:* financialaid@kcai.edu.
Website: http://www.kcai.edu/.

KANSAS STATE UNIVERSITY

Manhattan, KS

CONTACT Mr. Larry Moeder, Executive Director of Undergraduate Admissions and Student Financial Assistance, Kansas State University, 104 Fairchild Hall, Manhattan, KS 66506, 785-532-6420 or toll-free 800-432-8270. *E-mail:* larrym@ksu.edu.
Website: http://www.k-state.edu/.

KANSAS WESLEYAN UNIVERSITY

Salina, KS

CONTACT Mrs. Lois Elizabeth Madsen, Director of Student Financial Planning, Kansas Wesleyan University, 100 East Claflin, Hall of the Pioneers, Room 285, Salina, KS 67401-6196, 785-833-4315 or toll-free 800-874-1154 Ext.1285. *Fax:* 785-827-0927. *E-mail:* lois.madsen@kwu.edu.
Website: http://www.kwu.edu/.

KEAN UNIVERSITY

Union, NJ

Tuition & fees (NJ res): $12,595	Average undergraduate aid package: $11,242

ABOUT THE INSTITUTION State-supported, coed. ***Awards:*** certificates, bachelor's, master's, and doctoral degrees. 48 undergraduate majors. ***Total enrollment:*** 14,309. Undergraduates: 12,120. Freshmen: 1,770. Federal methodology is used as a basis for awarding need-based institutional aid.

UNDERGRADUATE EXPENSES for 2019–2020 ***Application fee:*** $75. ***Tuition, state resident:*** full-time $9935; part-time $389 per credit. ***Tuition, nonresident:*** full-time $17,111; part-time $613 per credit. ***Required fees:*** full-time $2660; $91.25 per credit. Part-time tuition and fees vary according to course load. ***College room and board:*** $14,802. Room and board charges vary according to board plan, housing facility, location, and student level.

FRESHMAN FINANCIAL AID (Fall 2019, est.) 1614 applied for aid; of those 85% were deemed to have need. 98% of freshmen with need received aid; of those 2% had need fully met. ***Average percent of need met:*** 82% (excluding resources awarded to replace EFC). ***Average financial aid package:*** $11,364 (excluding resources awarded to replace EFC). 6% of all full-time freshmen had no need and received non-need-based gift aid.

UNDERGRADUATE FINANCIAL AID (Fall 2019, est.) 8,036 applied for aid; of those 87% were deemed to have need. 98% of undergraduates with need received aid; of those 1% had need fully met. ***Average percent of need met:*** 84% (excluding resources awarded to replace EFC). ***Average financial aid package:*** $11,242 (excluding resources awarded to replace EFC). 3% of all full-time undergraduates had no need and received non-need-based gift aid.

GIFT AID (NEED-BASED) ***Receiving aid:*** Freshmen: 60% (1,030); all full-time undergraduates: 53% (5,141). ***Average award:*** Freshmen: $10,109; Undergraduates: $8928. ***Scholarships, grants, and awards:*** Federal Pell, FSEOG, state, private, college/university gift aid from institutional funds.

GIFT AID (NON-NEED-BASED) ***Receiving aid:*** Freshmen: 24% (420). Undergraduates: 16% (1,531). ***Average award:*** Freshmen: $3153. Undergraduates: $2867. ***Scholarships, grants, and awards by category:*** *Academic interests/achievement:* architecture, area/ethnic studies, biological sciences, business, communication, computer science, education, engineering/technologies, English, foreign languages, general academic interests/achievements, home economics, humanities, international studies, mathematics, physical sciences, premedicine, social sciences. *Creative arts/performance:* applied art and design, art/fine arts, cinema/film/broadcasting, dance, general creative arts/performance, music, performing arts, theater/drama. *Special achievements/activities:* community service, general special achievements/activities, leadership, memberships. *Special characteristics:* adult students, first-generation college students, general special characteristics, local/state students, out-of-state students, previous college experience, veterans. ***Tuition waivers:*** Full or partial for employees or children of employees, senior citizens. ***ROTC:*** Army cooperative, Air Force cooperative.

LOANS ***Student loans:*** 77% of past graduating class borrowed through all loan programs. *Average indebtedness per student:* $34,275. ***Average need-based loan:*** Freshmen: $3373. Undergraduates: $4359. ***Programs:*** Federal Direct (Subsidized and Unsubsidized Stafford, PLUS).

WORK-STUDY ***Federal work-study:*** 256 jobs averaging $3271.

APPLYING FOR FINANCIAL AID ***Required financial aid forms:*** FAFSA, state aid form. ***Notification date:*** Continuous.

CONTACT Ms. Sherrell Watson-Hall, Director of Financial Aid, Kean University, 1000 Morris Avenue, Union, NJ 07083, 908-737-3190. *Fax:* 908-737-3200. *E-mail:* finaid@kean.edu.
Website: http://www.kean.edu/.

KEENE STATE COLLEGE

Keene, NH

Tuition & fees (NH res): $14,568	Average undergraduate aid package: $13,647

ABOUT THE INSTITUTION State-supported, coed. ***Awards:*** certificates, bachelor's, and master's degrees. 64 undergraduate majors. ***Total enrollment:*** 3,569. Undergraduates: 4,750. Freshmen: 950. Federal methodology is used as a basis for awarding need-based institutional aid.

UNDERGRADUATE EXPENSES for 2019–2020 ***Application fee:*** $50. ***Tuition, state resident:*** full-time $11,754; part-time $490 per credit. ***Tuition, nonresident:*** full-time $20,942; part-time $874 per credit. ***Required fees:*** full-time $2814; $114 per credit. Part-time tuition and fees vary according to course load. ***College room and board:*** $11,560. Room and board charges vary according to board plan and housing facility.

FRESHMAN FINANCIAL AID (Fall 2018) 890 applied for aid; of those 79% were deemed to have need. 100% of freshmen with need received aid; of those 14% had need fully met. ***Average percent of need met:*** 67% (excluding resources awarded to replace EFC). ***Average financial aid package:*** $13,421 (excluding resources awarded to replace EFC). 22% of all full-time freshmen had no need and received non-need-based gift aid.

UNDERGRADUATE FINANCIAL AID (Fall 2018) 2,893 applied for aid; of those 80% were deemed to have need. 100% of undergraduates with need received aid; of those 15% had need fully met. ***Average percent of need met:*** 68% (excluding resources awarded to replace EFC). ***Average financial aid package:*** $13,647 (excluding resources awarded to replace EFC). 20% of all full-time undergraduates had no need and received non-need-based gift aid.

GIFT AID (NEED-BASED) ***Receiving aid:*** Freshmen: 59% (558); all full-time undergraduates: 52% (1,758). ***Average award:*** Freshmen: $6062; Undergraduates: $6803. ***Scholarships, grants, and awards:*** Federal Pell, FSEOG, state, private, college/university gift aid from institutional funds.

GIFT AID (NON-NEED-BASED) ***Receiving aid:*** Freshmen: 61% (575). Undergraduates: 48% (1,624). ***Average award:*** Freshmen: $6045. Undergraduates: $5774. ***Scholarships, grants, and awards by category:*** *Academic interests/achievement:* 1,956 awards ($10,929,152 total): general academic interests/achievements. *Creative arts/performance:* 26 awards ($103,500 total): applied art and design, art/fine arts, cinema/film/broadcasting, dance, general creative arts/performance, music, theater/drama. *Special achievements/activities:* 29 awards ($52,500 total): general special achievements/activities, leadership. *Special characteristics:* children and siblings of alumni. ***Tuition waivers:*** Full or partial for employees or children of employees, senior citizens. ***ROTC:*** Army cooperative, Air Force cooperative.

LOANS ***Student loans:*** 84% of past graduating class borrowed through all loan programs. *Average indebtedness per student:* $40,125. ***Average need-based loan:*** Freshmen: $3268. Undergraduates: $4158. ***Programs:*** Federal Direct (Subsidized and Unsubsidized Stafford, PLUS), college/university.

WORK-STUDY ***Federal work-study:*** 985 jobs averaging $2326. ***State or other work-study/employment:*** 466 part-time jobs averaging $1303.

APPLYING FOR FINANCIAL AID ***Required financial aid form:*** FAFSA. ***Notification date:*** Continuous. Students must reply within 4 weeks of notification.

CONTACT Ms. Catherine Mullins, Director of Financial Aid and Scholarships, Keene State College, 229 Main Street, Keene, NH 03435-2606, 603-358-2280 or toll-free 800-KSC-1909. *Fax:* 603-358-2794. *E-mail:* financialaid@keene.edu.
Website: http://www.keene.edu/.

KEHILATH YAKOV RABBINICAL SEMINARY

Ossining, NY

CONTACT Financial Aid Office, Kehilath Yakov Rabbinical Seminary, 206 Wilson Street, Brooklyn, NY 11211-7207, 718-963-1212.
Website: http://kehilathyakov.com/.

KEISER UNIVERSITY

Fort Lauderdale, FL

Tuition & fees: $32,868 **Average undergraduate aid package: $6254**

ABOUT THE INSTITUTION Independent, coed. ***Awards:*** certificates, associate, bachelor's, master's, and doctoral degrees (profile includes data from campuses located in Daytona Beach, Fort Lauderdale, Fort Myers, Jacksonville, Lakeland, Melbourne, Miami, Orlando, Pembroke Pines, Port St. Lucie, Sarasota, Tallahassee, Tampa, and West Palm Beach; not all programs offered at all locations, but many classes offered 100% online). 59 undergraduate majors. ***Total enrollment:*** 19,605. Undergraduates: 17,420. Freshmen: 6,267. Federal methodology is used as a basis for awarding need-based institutional aid.

UNDERGRADUATE EXPENSES for 2020–2021 ***Application fee:*** $55. ***Comprehensive fee:*** $46,954 includes full-time tuition ($30,768), mandatory fees ($2100), and room and board ($14,086). Full-time tuition and fees vary according to location and program. ***Part-time tuition:*** $1282 per credit hour. Part-time tuition and fees vary according to location and program.

FRESHMAN FINANCIAL AID (Fall 2018) 3007 applied for aid; of those 100% were deemed to have need. 100% of freshmen with need received aid; of those 100% had need fully met. ***Average percent of need met:*** 89% (excluding resources awarded to replace EFC). ***Average financial aid package:*** $6815 (excluding resources awarded to replace EFC). 86% of all full-time freshmen had no need and received non-need-based gift aid.

UNDERGRADUATE FINANCIAL AID (Fall 2018) 9,488 applied for aid; of those 100% were deemed to have need. 100% of undergraduates with need received aid; of those 100% had need fully met. ***Average percent of need met:*** 88% (excluding resources awarded to replace EFC). ***Average financial aid package:*** $6254 (excluding resources awarded to replace EFC). 74% of all full-time undergraduates had no need and received non-need-based gift aid.

GIFT AID (NEED-BASED) ***Receiving aid:*** Freshmen: 84% (2,808); all full-time undergraduates: 88% (9,488). ***Average award:*** Freshmen: $6815; Undergraduates: $6254. ***Scholarships, grants, and awards:*** Federal Pell, FSEOG, state, private, college/university gift aid from institutional funds.

GIFT AID (NON-NEED-BASED) ***Receiving aid:*** Freshmen: 86% (2,878). Undergraduates: 74% (7,911). ***Average award:*** Freshmen: $3224. Undergraduates: $3329. ***Tuition waivers:*** Full or partial for employees or children of employees.

LOANS ***Average need-based loan:*** Freshmen: $11,366. Undergraduates: $14,105. ***Programs:*** Federal Direct (Subsidized and Unsubsidized Stafford, PLUS), Perkins.

WORK-STUDY ***Federal work-study:*** 28 jobs averaging $3856.

APPLYING FOR FINANCIAL AID ***Required financial aid form:*** FAFSA. ***Financial aid deadline:*** Continuous. ***Notification date:*** Continuous. Students must reply within 2 weeks of notification.

CONTACT Mr. Fred Pfeffer, Associate Vice Chancellor for Student Financial Services, Keiser University, 1500 West Commercial Boulevard, Fort Lauderdale, FL 33309, 954-776-4456 or toll-free 888-534-7379. *Fax:* 954-749-4456. *E-mail:* fredp@keiseruniversity.edu.
Website: http://www.keiseruniversity.edu/.

KENDALL COLLEGE AT NATIONAL LOUIS UNIVERSITY

Chicago, IL

CONTACT Lauren Walker, Director of Financial Aid, Kendall College at National Louis University, 900 N. North Branch Street, Chicago, IL 60642, 312-752-2267 or toll-free 888-90-KENDALL. *E-mail:* financial_aid@kendall.edu.
Website: http://www.kendall.edu/.

KENNESAW STATE UNIVERSITY

Kennesaw, GA

Tuition & fees: N/R **Average undergraduate aid package: $11,585**

ABOUT THE INSTITUTION State-supported, coed. ***Awards:*** certificates, bachelor's, master's, and doctoral degrees. 82 undergraduate majors. ***Total enrollment:*** 37,807. Undergraduates: 34,499. Freshmen: 6,533. Federal methodology is used as a basis for awarding need-based institutional aid.

FRESHMAN FINANCIAL AID (Fall 2019, est.) 5761 applied for aid; of those 80% were deemed to have need. 99% of freshmen with need received aid; of those 6% had need fully met. ***Average percent of need met:*** 42% (excluding resources awarded to replace EFC). ***Average financial aid package:*** $13,299 (excluding resources awarded to replace EFC). 1% of all full-time freshmen had no need and received non-need-based gift aid.

UNDERGRADUATE FINANCIAL AID (Fall 2019, est.) 21,393 applied for aid; of those 84% were deemed to have need. 98% of undergraduates with need received aid; of those 5% had need fully met. ***Average percent of need met:*** 42% (excluding resources awarded to replace EFC). ***Average financial aid package:*** $11,585 (excluding resources awarded to replace EFC). 1% of all full-time undergraduates had no need and received non-need-based gift aid.

GIFT AID (NEED-BASED) ***Total amount:*** $213,373,903 (100% federal). ***Receiving aid:*** Freshmen: 34% (2,068); all full-time undergraduates: 36% (9,165). ***Average award:*** Freshmen: $7725; Undergraduates: $7250. ***Scholarships, grants, and awards:*** Federal Pell, FSEOG, state, private, college/university gift aid from institutional funds, United Negro College Fund.

GIFT AID (NON-NEED-BASED) ***Total amount:*** $384,944,099 (60% federal, 39% state, 1% institutional). ***Receiving aid:*** Freshmen: 60% (3,700). Undergraduates: 44% (11,306). ***Average award:*** Freshmen: $1309. Undergraduates: $1608. ***Scholarships, grants, and awards by category:*** *Academic interests/achievement:* biological sciences, business, communication, computer science, education, engineering/technologies, English, foreign languages, general academic interests/achievements, home economics, humanities, international studies, mathematics, physical sciences, premedicine, social sciences. *Creative arts/performance:* applied art and design, dance, music, performing arts, theater/drama. *Special achievements/activities:* community service, leadership, memberships. *Special characteristics:* ethnic background, general special characteristics, handicapped students, international students, local/state students, members of minority groups, religious affiliation, veterans. ***ROTC:*** Army cooperative, Naval cooperative, Air Force cooperative.

LOANS ***Student loans:*** $343,031,612 (35% need-based, 65% non-need-based). 60% of past graduating class borrowed through all loan programs. *Average indebtedness per student:* $26,009. ***Average need-based loan:*** Freshmen: $4174. Undergraduates: $4050. ***Parent loans:*** $21,385,839 (100% non-need-based). ***Programs:*** Federal Direct (Subsidized and Unsubsidized Stafford, PLUS), Perkins, college/university.

WORK-STUDY ***Federal work-study:*** Total amount: $1,269,596; jobs available.

ATHLETIC AWARDS Total amount: $5,431,235 (100% non-need-based).

APPLYING FOR FINANCIAL AID ***Required financial aid form:*** FAFSA. ***Financial aid deadline:*** 6/1 (priority: 3/1). ***Notification date:*** Continuous beginning 12/1.

CONTACT Mr. Ron H. Day, Director of Student Financial Aid, Kennesaw State University, 585 Cobb Avenue, NW, Mail Drop #0119, Kennesaw, GA 30144-5591, 770-423-6074. *Fax:* 470-578-9096. *E-mail:* finaid@kennesaw.edu.
Website: http://www.kennesaw.edu/.

KENT STATE UNIVERSITY

Kent, OH

Tuition & fees: N/R **Average undergraduate aid package: $11,224**

ABOUT THE INSTITUTION State-supported, coed. ***Awards:*** certificates, bachelor's, master's, and doctoral degrees. 101 undergraduate majors. Federal methodology is used as a basis for awarding need-based institutional aid.

FRESHMAN FINANCIAL AID (Fall 2019, est.) 3875 applied for aid; of those 72% were deemed to have need. 100% of freshmen with need received aid; of those 18% had need fully met. ***Average percent of need met:*** 63% (excluding resources

awarded to replace EFC). ***Average financial aid package:*** $11,797 (excluding resources awarded to replace EFC). 28% of all full-time freshmen had no need and received non-need-based gift aid.

UNDERGRADUATE FINANCIAL AID (Fall 2019, est.) 15,041 applied for aid; of those 78% were deemed to have need. 99% of undergraduates with need received aid; of those 14% had need fully met. ***Average percent of need met:*** 60% (excluding resources awarded to replace EFC). ***Average financial aid package:*** $11,224 (excluding resources awarded to replace EFC). 24% of all full-time undergraduates had no need and received non-need-based gift aid.

GIFT AID (NEED-BASED) ***Total amount:*** $81,358,182 (38% federal, 11% state, 48% institutional, 3% external sources). ***Receiving aid:*** Freshmen: 63% (2,674); all full-time undergraduates: 56% (10,543). ***Average award:*** Freshmen: $8364; Undergraduates: $7477. ***Scholarships, grants, and awards:*** Federal Pell, FSEOG, state, private, college/university gift aid from institutional funds.

GIFT AID (NON-NEED-BASED) ***Total amount:*** $29,828,734 (2% federal, 5% state, 89% institutional, 4% external sources). ***Receiving aid:*** Freshmen: 8% (348). Undergraduates: 5% (1,002). ***Average award:*** Freshmen: $5575. Undergraduates: $5096. ***Scholarships, grants, and awards by category:*** *Academic interests/achievement:* agriculture, architecture, area/ethnic studies, biological sciences, business, communication, computer science, education, engineering/technologies, English, foreign languages, general academic interests/achievements, health fields, home economics, humanities, international studies, library science, mathematics, military science, physical sciences, premedicine, religion/biblical studies, social sciences. *Creative arts/performance:* applied art and design, art/fine arts, cinema/film/broadcasting, creative writing, dance, general creative arts/performance, journalism/publications, music, performing arts, theater/drama. *Special achievements/activities:* community service, general special achievements/activities, leadership. *Special characteristics:* adult students, children and siblings of alumni, children of faculty/staff, children of union members/company employees, ethnic background, first-generation college students, handicapped students, international students, local/state students, members of minority groups, out-of-state students, previous college experience, veterans. ***ROTC:*** Army, Air Force.

LOANS ***Student loans:*** $112,810,759 (55% need-based, 45% non-need-based). 72% of past graduating class borrowed through all loan programs. *Average indebtedness per student:* $31,113. ***Average need-based loan:*** Freshmen: $3333. Undergraduates: $4170. ***Parent loans:*** $32,400,056 (45% need-based, 55% non-need-based). ***Programs:*** Federal Direct (Subsidized and Unsubsidized Stafford, PLUS), Perkins, Federal Nursing, state, college/university, alternative loans.

WORK-STUDY ***Federal work-study:*** Total amount: $1,541,900; jobs available.

ATHLETIC AWARDS Total amount: $7,174,680 (36% need-based, 64% non-need-based).

APPLYING FOR FINANCIAL AID ***Required financial aid form:*** FAFSA. ***Financial aid deadline (priority):*** 2/1. ***Notification date:*** Continuous beginning 2/1. Students must reply within 2 weeks of notification.

CONTACT Mark A. Evans, Executive Director of Student Financial Aid, Kent State University, 103 Schwartz Center, Kent, OH 44242-0001, 330-672-0507 or toll-free 800-988-KENT. *Fax:* 330-672-4036. *E-mail:* mevans@kent.edu.

Website: http://www.kent.edu/.

KENT STATE UNIVERSITY AT GEAUGA

Burton, OH

Tuition & fees: N/R	Average undergraduate aid package: $7814

ABOUT THE INSTITUTION State-supported, coed. ***Awards:*** certificates, associate, bachelor's, and master's degrees. 10 undergraduate majors. ***Total enrollment:*** 2,179. Undergraduates: 2,179. Freshmen: 277. Federal methodology is used as a basis for awarding need-based institutional aid.

FRESHMAN FINANCIAL AID (Fall 2019, est.) 168 applied for aid; of those 73% were deemed to have need. 100% of freshmen with need received aid; of those 6% had need fully met. ***Average percent of need met:*** 62% (excluding resources awarded to replace EFC). ***Average financial aid package:*** $7713 (excluding resources awarded to replace EFC). 8% of all full-time freshmen had no need and received non-need-based gift aid.

UNDERGRADUATE FINANCIAL AID (Fall 2019, est.) 462 applied for aid; of those 76% were deemed to have need. 100% of undergraduates with need received aid; of those 6% had need fully met. ***Average percent of need met:*** 60% (excluding resources awarded to replace EFC). ***Average financial aid package:*** $7814 (excluding resources awarded to replace EFC). 4% of all full-time undergraduates had no need and received non-need-based gift aid.

GIFT AID (NEED-BASED) ***Total amount:*** $2,177,220 (92% federal, 1% state, 6% institutional, 1% external sources). ***Receiving aid:*** Freshmen: 60% (115); all full-time undergraduates: 51% (297). ***Average award:*** Freshmen: $5221; Undergraduates: $5273. ***Scholarships, grants, and awards:*** Federal Pell, FSEOG, state, private, college/university gift aid from institutional funds.

GIFT AID (NON-NEED-BASED) ***Total amount:*** $65,790 (7% federal, 18% state, 61% institutional, 14% external sources). ***Receiving aid:*** Freshmen: 1% (1). Undergraduates: 1% (3). ***Average award:*** Freshmen: $950. Undergraduates: $1096. ***Scholarships, grants, and awards by category:*** *Academic interests/achievement:* agriculture, architecture, area/ethnic studies, biological sciences, business, communication, computer science, education, engineering/technologies, English, foreign languages, general academic interests/achievements, home economics, humanities, international studies, library science, mathematics, military science, physical sciences, premedicine, religion/biblical studies, social sciences. *Creative arts/performance:* applied art and design, art/fine arts, cinema/film/broadcasting, creative writing, dance, general creative arts/performance, journalism/publications, music, performing arts, theater/drama. *Special achievements/activities:* community service, general special achievements/activities, leadership. *Special characteristics:* adult students, children of faculty/staff, handicapped students, international students, local/state students, out-of-state students.

LOANS ***Student loans:*** $4,342,630 (66% need-based, 34% non-need-based). ***Average need-based loan:*** Freshmen: $3276. Undergraduates: $3638. ***Parent loans:*** $35,228 (16% need-based, 84% non-need-based). ***Programs:*** Federal Direct (Subsidized and Unsubsidized Stafford, PLUS), Federal Nursing, state, college/university, alternative loans.

WORK-STUDY ***Federal work-study:*** Total amount: $27,420; 10 jobs averaging $2443.

APPLYING FOR FINANCIAL AID ***Required financial aid form:*** FAFSA. ***Financial aid deadline (priority):*** 2/1. ***Notification date:*** Continuous beginning 2/1. Students must reply within 2 weeks of notification.

CONTACT Justin Cornelius, Financial Aid Coordinator, Kent State University at Geauga, 14111 Claridon-Troy Road, Burton, OH 44021, 330-888-6387. *Fax:* 330-888-6301. *E-mail:* jcorne17@kent.edu.

Website: http://www.geauga.kent.edu/.

KENT STATE UNIVERSITY AT STARK

Canton, OH

Tuition & fees: N/R	Average undergraduate aid package: $7321

ABOUT THE INSTITUTION State-supported, coed. ***Awards:*** associate, bachelor's, and master's degrees. 17 undergraduate majors. ***Total enrollment:*** 4,771. Undergraduates: 4,763. Freshmen: 577. Federal methodology is used as a basis for awarding need-based institutional aid.

FRESHMAN FINANCIAL AID (Fall 2019, est.) 412 applied for aid; of those 70% were deemed to have need. 100% of freshmen with need received aid; of those 15% had need fully met. ***Average percent of need met:*** 62% (excluding resources awarded to replace EFC). ***Average financial aid package:*** $6447 (excluding resources awarded to replace EFC). 5% of all full-time freshmen had no need and received non-need-based gift aid.

UNDERGRADUATE FINANCIAL AID (Fall 2019, est.) 1,506 applied for aid; of those 76% were deemed to have need. 99% of undergraduates with need received aid; of those 11% had need fully met. ***Average percent of need met:*** 62% (excluding resources awarded to replace EFC). ***Average financial aid package:*** $7321 (excluding resources awarded to replace EFC). 4% of all full-time undergraduates had no need and received non-need-based gift aid.

GIFT AID (NEED-BASED) ***Total amount:*** $5,594,254 (87% federal, 3% state, 8% institutional, 2% external sources). ***Receiving aid:*** Freshmen: 54% (248); all full-time undergraduates: 53% (973). ***Average award:*** Freshmen: $4371; Undergraduates: $4729. ***Scholarships, grants, and awards:*** Federal Pell, FSEOG, state, private, college/university gift aid from institutional funds.

GIFT AID (NON-NEED-BASED) ***Total amount:*** $430,878 (2% federal, 34% state, 44% institutional, 20% external sources). ***Receiving aid:*** Freshmen: 2% (9). Undergraduates: 1% (19). ***Average award:*** Freshmen: $2354. Undergraduates:

$2298. ***Scholarships, grants, and awards by category:*** *Academic interests/achievement:* agriculture, architecture, area/ethnic studies, biological sciences, business, communication, computer science, education, English, foreign languages, general academic interests/achievements, home economics, humanities, international studies, library science, mathematics, military science, physical sciences, premedicine, religion/biblical studies, social sciences. *Creative arts/performance:* applied art and design, art/fine arts, cinema/film/broadcasting, creative writing, dance, general creative arts/performance, journalism/publications, music, performing arts, theater/drama. *Special achievements/activities:* community service, general special achievements/activities, leadership. *Special characteristics:* adult students, children and siblings of alumni, children of faculty/staff, ethnic background, first-generation college students, general special characteristics, handicapped students, international students, local/state students, members of minority groups, out-of-state students, previous college experience, veterans. ***ROTC:*** Army cooperative, Air Force cooperative.

LOANS ***Student loans:*** $10,444,197 (62% need-based, 38% non-need-based). ***Average need-based loan:*** Freshmen: $3125. Undergraduates: $3840. ***Parent loans:*** $255,596 (34% need-based, 66% non-need-based). ***Programs:*** Federal Direct (Subsidized and Unsubsidized Stafford, PLUS), Federal Nursing, state, college/university, alternative loans.

WORK-STUDY ***Federal work-study:*** Total amount: $90,303; 51 jobs averaging $2317.

APPLYING FOR FINANCIAL AID ***Required financial aid form:*** FAFSA. ***Financial aid deadline (priority):*** 2/1. ***Notification date:*** Continuous beginning 2/1.

CONTACT Katie Schalmo, Assistant Director of Enrollment Management and Student Services, Kent State University at Stark, 132 Main Hall, North Canton, OH 44720, 330-244-3257. *Fax:* 330-499-0301. *E-mail:* pschalmo@kent.edu. *Website:* http://www.stark.kent.edu/.

KENTUCKY CHRISTIAN UNIVERSITY

Grayson, KY

ABOUT THE INSTITUTION Independent Christian Churches and Churches of Christ, coed. ***Awards:*** bachelor's and master's degrees. 20 undergraduate majors.

GIFT AID (NEED-BASED) ***Scholarships, grants, and awards:*** Federal Pell, FSEOG, state, private, college/university gift aid from institutional funds.

GIFT AID (NON-NEED-BASED) ***Scholarships, grants, and awards by category:*** *Academic interests/achievement:* business, education, general academic interests/achievements, home economics, humanities, international studies, premedicine, religion/biblical studies. *Creative arts/performance:* debating, music, performing arts, theater/drama. *Special achievements/activities:* cheerleading/drum major, community service, general special achievements/activities, leadership, religious involvement. *Special characteristics:* children and siblings of alumni, children of faculty/staff, ethnic background, general special characteristics, international students, local/state students, members of minority groups, previous college experience, religious affiliation, spouses of current students.

LOANS ***Programs:*** Federal Direct (Subsidized and Unsubsidized Stafford, PLUS), Perkins.

CONTACT Mrs. Jennie M. Bender, Director of Financial Aid, Kentucky Christian University, 100 Academic Parkway, Grayson, KY 41143-2205, 606-474-3226 or toll-free 800-522-3181. *Fax:* 606-474-3268. *E-mail:* jbender@kcu.edu. *Website:* http://www.kcu.edu/.

KENTUCKY MOUNTAIN BIBLE COLLEGE

Jackson, KY

Tuition & fees: $10,190	Average undergraduate aid package: $13,059

ABOUT THE INSTITUTION Independent interdenominational, coed. ***Awards:*** associate and bachelor's degrees. 9 undergraduate majors. ***Total enrollment:*** 72. Undergraduates: 72. Freshmen: 15. Both federal and institutional methodology are used as a basis for awarding need-based institutional aid.

UNDERGRADUATE EXPENSES for **2019–2020** ***Application fee:*** $25. ***Comprehensive fee:*** $15,330 includes full-time tuition ($9280), mandatory fees ($910), and room and board ($5140). ***College room only:*** $1940. Full-time tuition and fees vary according to program. Room and board charges vary according to housing facility. ***Part-time tuition:*** $290 per credit hour. ***Part-time fees:*** $290 per term. Part-time tuition and fees vary according to program.

FRESHMAN FINANCIAL AID (Fall 2019, est.) 21 applied for aid; of those 100% were deemed to have need. 100% of freshmen with need received aid; of those 5% had need fully met. ***Average percent of need met:*** 77% (excluding resources awarded to replace EFC). ***Average financial aid package:*** $10,762 (excluding resources awarded to replace EFC). 5% of all full-time freshmen had no need and received non-need-based gift aid.

UNDERGRADUATE FINANCIAL AID (Fall 2019, est.) 46 applied for aid; of those 100% were deemed to have need. 100% of undergraduates with need received aid. ***Average percent of need met:*** 71% (excluding resources awarded to replace EFC). ***Average financial aid package:*** $13,059 (excluding resources awarded to replace EFC). 15% of all full-time undergraduates had no need and received non-need-based gift aid.

GIFT AID (NEED-BASED) ***Total amount:*** $3,040,820 (94% federal, 5% institutional, 1% external sources). ***Receiving aid:*** Freshmen: 100% (21); all full-time undergraduates: 85% (46). ***Average award:*** Freshmen: $3780; Undergraduates: $4328. ***Scholarships, grants, and awards:*** Federal Pell, FSEOG, state, private, college/university gift aid from institutional funds.

GIFT AID (NON-NEED-BASED) ***Total amount:*** $68,791 (97% institutional, 3% external sources). ***Receiving aid:*** Freshmen: 57% (12). Undergraduates: 35% (19). ***Average award:*** Freshmen: $2808. Undergraduates: $3656. ***Scholarships, grants, and awards by category:*** *Academic interests/achievement:* 15 awards ($15,730 total): general academic interests/achievements. *Creative arts/performance:* 8 awards ($6980 total): music, theater/drama. *Special achievements/activities:* 4 awards ($3745 total): religious involvement. *Special characteristics:* 1 award ($2560 total): children of faculty/staff. ***Tuition waivers:*** Full or partial for employees or children of employees.

LOANS ***Student loans:*** $154,248 (59% need-based, 41% non-need-based). 75% of past graduating class borrowed through all loan programs. *Average indebtedness per student:* $7370. ***Average need-based loan:*** Freshmen: $4110. Undergraduates: $4960. ***Parent loans:*** $4550 (100% non-need-based). ***Programs:*** Federal Direct (Subsidized and Unsubsidized Stafford, PLUS), Private education loans.

WORK-STUDY ***Federal work-study:*** Total amount: $25,616; 25,616 jobs averaging $500. ***State or other work-study/employment:*** Total amount: $38,438 (100% non-need-based). 52,438 part-time jobs averaging $650.

APPLYING FOR FINANCIAL AID ***Required financial aid forms:*** FAFSA, institution's own form. ***Financial aid deadline (priority):*** 4/1. ***Notification date:*** 5/15.

CONTACT Mr. Joseph Ritter, Director of Financial Aid, Kentucky Mountain Bible College, 855 Highway 541, Jackson, KY 41339, 800-879-KMBC Ext. 175 or toll-free 800-879-KMBC. *Fax:* 800-659-4324. *E-mail:* finaid@kmbc.edu. *Website:* http://www.kmbc.edu/.

KENTUCKY STATE UNIVERSITY

Frankfort, KY

Tuition & fees (KY res): $7796	Average undergraduate aid package: $13,132

ABOUT THE INSTITUTION State-related, coed. ***Awards:*** certificates, associate, bachelor's, master's, and doctoral degrees. 28 undergraduate majors. ***Total enrollment:*** 1,925. Undergraduates: 44,981. Freshmen: 318. Federal methodology is used as a basis for awarding need-based institutional aid.

UNDERGRADUATE EXPENSES for 2019–2020 ***Application fee:*** $30. ***Tuition, state resident:*** full-time $7406; part-time $325 per credit hour. ***Tuition, nonresident:*** full-time $18,314; part-time $802 per credit hour. ***Required fees:*** full-time $390. Full-time tuition and fees vary according to course load. Part-time tuition and fees vary according to course load. ***College room and board:*** $6690. Room and board charges vary according to board plan and housing facility.

FRESHMAN FINANCIAL AID (Fall 2019, est.) 376 applied for aid; of those 99% were deemed to have need. 100% of freshmen with need received aid; of those 6% had need fully met. ***Average percent of need met:*** 66% (excluding resources awarded to replace EFC). ***Average financial aid package:*** $13,101 (excluding resources

awarded to replace EFC). 7% of all full-time freshmen had no need and received non-need-based gift aid.

UNDERGRADUATE FINANCIAL AID (Fall 2019, est.) 1,007 applied for aid; of those 99% were deemed to have need. 100% of undergraduates with need received aid; of those 11% had need fully met. ***Average percent of need met:*** 70% (excluding resources awarded to replace EFC). ***Average financial aid package:*** $13,132 (excluding resources awarded to replace EFC). 7% of all full-time undergraduates had no need and received non-need-based gift aid.

GIFT AID (NEED-BASED) ***Total amount:*** $8,953,014 (59% federal, 11% state, 27% institutional, 3% external sources). ***Receiving aid:*** Freshmen: 87% (368); all full-time undergraduates: 85% (964). ***Average award:*** Freshmen: $14,848; Undergraduates: $15,022. ***Scholarships, grants, and awards:*** Federal Pell, FSEOG, state, private, college/university gift aid from institutional funds.

GIFT AID (NON-NEED-BASED) ***Total amount:*** $862,953 (1% federal, 9% state, 77% institutional, 13% external sources). ***Receiving aid:*** Freshmen: 3% (12). Undergraduates: 5% (52). ***Average award:*** Freshmen: $6524. Undergraduates: $5877. ***Scholarships, grants, and awards by category:*** *Academic interests/achievement:* 13 awards ($2,166,107 total): general academic interests/achievements. *Creative arts/performance:* 3 awards ($65,000 total): music, performing arts. *Special achievements/activities:* 5 awards ($690,114 total): cheerleading/drum major, leadership. *Special characteristics:* 15 awards ($719,752 total): adult students, children of faculty/staff, children with a deceased or disabled parent, ethnic background, international students, local/state students, previous college experience, public servants, veterans. ***Tuition waivers:*** Full or partial for employees or children of employees, senior citizens. ***ROTC:*** Army, Air Force cooperative.

LOANS ***Student loans:*** $6,951,461 (90% need-based, 10% non-need-based). 76% of past graduating class borrowed through all loan programs. *Average indebtedness per student:* $28,394. ***Average need-based loan:*** Freshmen: $3462. Undergraduates: $4000. ***Parent loans:*** $2,370,509 (84% need-based, 16% non-need-based). ***Programs:*** Federal Direct (Subsidized and Unsubsidized Stafford, PLUS), private loans.

WORK-STUDY ***Federal work-study:*** Total amount: $331,653; 169 jobs averaging $1962. ***State or other work-study/employment:*** Total amount: $260,045 (50% need-based, 50% non-need-based). 43 part-time jobs averaging $6048.

ATHLETIC AWARDS Total amount: $1,357,319 (79% need-based, 21% non-need-based).

APPLYING FOR FINANCIAL AID ***Required financial aid form:*** FAFSA. ***Financial aid deadline (priority):*** 4/15. ***Notification date:*** Continuous beginning 3/15. Students must reply within 4 weeks of notification.

CONTACT Ms. Russelle Keese, Director of Financial Aid, Kentucky State University, 400 East Main Street, Academic Services Building Room 353, Frankfort, KY 40601, 502-597-5759 or toll-free 877-367-5978. *Fax:* 502-597-5950. *E-mail:* russelle.keese@kysu.edu.
Website: http://www.kysu.edu/.

KENTUCKY WESLEYAN COLLEGE

Owensboro, KY

CONTACT Mrs. Crystal Hamilton, Director of Financial Aid, Kentucky Wesleyan College, 3000 Frederica Street, Owensboro, KY 42301, 270-852-3130 or toll-free 800-999-0592 (in-state), 800-990-0592 (out-of-state). *Fax:* 270-852-3133. *E-mail:* cLhamilton@kwc.edu.
Website: http://www.kwc.edu/.

KENYON COLLEGE

Gambier, OH

Tuition & fees: $61,100	Average undergraduate aid package: $46,639

ABOUT THE INSTITUTION Independent, coed. ***Awards:*** bachelor's degrees. 36 undergraduate majors. ***Total enrollment:*** 1,734. Undergraduates: 1,734. Freshmen: 539. Institutional methodology is used as a basis for awarding need-based institutional aid.

UNDERGRADUATE EXPENSES for 2020–2021 ***Comprehensive fee:*** $73,930 includes full-time tuition ($60,800), mandatory fees ($300), and room and board ($12,830). ***College room only:*** $5420. Full-time tuition and fees vary according to reciprocity agreements. Room and board charges vary according to housing facility and student level. Part-time tuition and fees vary according to reciprocity agreements.

FRESHMAN FINANCIAL AID (Fall 2019, est.) 301 applied for aid; of those 71% were deemed to have need. 100% of freshmen with need received aid; of those 78% had need fully met. ***Average percent of need met:*** 100% (excluding resources awarded to replace EFC). ***Average financial aid package:*** $47,815 (excluding resources awarded to replace EFC). 26% of all full-time freshmen had no need and received non-need-based gift aid.

UNDERGRADUATE FINANCIAL AID (Fall 2019, est.) 994 applied for aid; of those 81% were deemed to have need. 100% of undergraduates with need received aid; of those 100% had need fully met. ***Average percent of need met:*** 100% (excluding resources awarded to replace EFC). ***Average financial aid package:*** $46,639 (excluding resources awarded to replace EFC). 22% of all full-time undergraduates had no need and received non-need-based gift aid.

GIFT AID (NEED-BASED) ***Total amount:*** $35,266,402 (3% federal, 93% institutional, 4% external sources). ***Receiving aid:*** Freshmen: 44% (215); all full-time undergraduates: 46% (805). ***Average award:*** Freshmen: $45,078; Undergraduates: $43,767. ***Scholarships, grants, and awards:*** Federal Pell, FSEOG, state, private, college/university gift aid from institutional funds.

GIFT AID (NON-NEED-BASED) ***Total amount:*** $8276 (86% institutional, 14% external sources). ***Receiving aid:*** Freshmen: 18% (88). Undergraduates: 16% (278). ***Average award:*** Freshmen: $13,843. Undergraduates: $14,632. ***Scholarships, grants, and awards by category:*** *Academic interests/achievement:* biological sciences, computer science, English, foreign languages, general academic interests/achievements, humanities, mathematics, social sciences. *Creative arts/performance:* applied art and design, creative writing, music. ***Tuition waivers:*** Full or partial for employees or children of employees.

LOANS ***Student loans:*** $4,367,108 (54% need-based, 46% non-need-based). 39% of past graduating class borrowed through all loan programs. *Average indebtedness per student:* $26,865. ***Average need-based loan:*** Freshmen: $2666. Undergraduates: $3160. ***Parent loans:*** $2,815,716 (100% non-need-based). ***Programs:*** Federal Direct (Subsidized and Unsubsidized Stafford, PLUS), college/university.

WORK-STUDY ***Federal work-study:*** Total amount: $360,681; jobs available. ***State or other work-study/employment:*** Total amount: $529,733 (95% need-based, 5% non-need-based). Part-time jobs available.

APPLYING FOR FINANCIAL AID ***Required financial aid forms:*** FAFSA, CSS Financial Aid PROFILE, noncustodial (divorced/separated) parent's statement. ***Financial aid deadline:*** 1/15 (priority: 1/15). ***Notification date:*** 3/25. Students must reply by 5/1.

CONTACT Mr. Craig Alan Slaughter, Director of Financial Aid, Kenyon College, 105 College-Park Street, Gambier, OH 43022-9623, 740-427-5430 or toll-free 800-848-2468. *Fax:* 740-427-5240. *E-mail:* finaid@kenyon.edu.
Website: http://www.kenyon.edu/.

KETTERING COLLEGE

Kettering, OH

CONTACT Financial Aid Office, Kettering College, 3737 Southern Boulevard, Kettering, OH 45429-1299, 937-395-8601 or toll-free 800-433-5262.
Website: http://www.kc.edu/.

KETTERING UNIVERSITY

Flint, MI

Tuition & fees: $44,380	Average undergraduate aid package: $23,747

ABOUT THE INSTITUTION Independent, coed. ***Awards:*** bachelor's and master's degrees. 13 undergraduate majors. ***Total enrollment:*** 2,221. Undergraduates: 1,799. Freshmen: 346. Federal methodology is used as a basis for awarding need-based institutional aid.

UNDERGRADUATE EXPENSES for 2019–2020 ***Comprehensive fee:*** $52,780 includes full-time tuition ($44,380) and room and board ($8400). ***College room only:*** $5100. ***Payment plan:*** Guaranteed tuition.

FRESHMAN FINANCIAL AID (Fall 2019, est.) 320 applied for aid; of those 85% were deemed to have need. 100% of freshmen with need received aid; of those 16% had need fully met. ***Average percent of need met:*** 69% (excluding resources awarded to replace EFC). ***Average financial aid package:*** $26,444 (excluding resources awarded to replace EFC). 22% of all full-time freshmen had no need and received non-need-based gift aid.

UNDERGRADUATE FINANCIAL AID (Fall 2019, est.) 1,387 applied for aid; of those 88% were deemed to have need. 100% of undergraduates with need received aid; of those 14% had need fully met. ***Average percent of need met:*** 66% (excluding resources awarded to replace EFC). ***Average financial aid package:*** $23,747 (excluding resources awarded to replace EFC). 27% of all full-time undergraduates had no need and received non-need-based gift aid.

GIFT AID (NEED-BASED) ***Total amount:*** $24,852,505 (8% federal, 7% state, 83% institutional, 2% external sources). ***Receiving aid:*** Freshmen: 78% (271); all full-time undergraduates: 71% (1,224). ***Average award:*** Freshmen: $24,281; Undergraduates: $20,840. ***Scholarships, grants, and awards:*** Federal Pell, FSEOG, state, private, college/university gift aid from institutional funds.

GIFT AID (NON-NEED-BASED) ***Total amount:*** $9,144,595 (95% institutional, 5% external sources). ***Receiving aid:*** Freshmen: 10% (35). Undergraduates: 8% (141). ***Average award:*** Freshmen: $18,489. Undergraduates: $16,152. ***Scholarships, grants, and awards by category:*** *Academic interests/achievement:* business, computer science, engineering/technologies, general academic interests/achievements, mathematics, physical sciences. *Special achievements/activities:* general special achievements/activities, leadership, memberships. *Special characteristics:* children of faculty/staff, siblings of current students. ***Tuition waivers:*** Full or partial for employees or children of employees.

LOANS ***Student loans:*** $10,794,737 (68% need-based, 32% non-need-based). 74% of past graduating class borrowed through all loan programs. *Average indebtedness per student:* $46,620. ***Average need-based loan:*** Freshmen: $5080. Undergraduates: $6052. ***Parent loans:*** $3,730,053 (58% need-based, 42% non-need-based). ***Programs:*** Federal Direct (Subsidized and Unsubsidized Stafford, PLUS).

WORK-STUDY ***Federal work-study:*** Total amount: $150,000; jobs available.

APPLYING FOR FINANCIAL AID ***Required financial aid form:*** FAFSA. ***Notification date:*** Continuous.

CONTACT Diane Bice, Director of Financial Aid, Kettering University, 1700 University Avenue, Flint, MI 48504, 800-955-4464 Ext. 7859 or toll-free 800-955-4464 Ext.7865 (in-state), 800-955-4464 (out-of-state). *Fax:* 810-762-9807. *E-mail:* finaid@kettering.edu.
Website: http://www.kettering.edu/.

KEUKA COLLEGE

Keuka Park, NY

Tuition & fees: $34,032 | **Average undergraduate aid package: $33,134**

ABOUT THE INSTITUTION Independent American Baptist Churches in the U.S.A., coed. ***Awards:*** certificates, bachelor's, and master's degrees. 38 undergraduate majors. ***Total enrollment:*** 1,777. Undergraduates: 1,529. Freshmen: 260. Federal methodology is used as a basis for awarding need-based institutional aid.

UNDERGRADUATE EXPENSES for 2020–2021 ***Comprehensive fee:*** $46,176 includes full-time tuition ($32,700), mandatory fees ($1332), and room and board ($12,144). Full-time tuition and fees vary according to course load, degree level, location, program, and reciprocity agreements. Room and board charges vary according to board plan and housing facility. ***Part-time tuition:*** $1092 per credit hour. Part-time tuition and fees vary according to course load, degree level, location, program, and reciprocity agreements.

FRESHMAN FINANCIAL AID (Fall 2018) 326 applied for aid; of those 94% were deemed to have need. 100% of freshmen with need received aid; of those 95% had need fully met. ***Average percent of need met:*** 72% (excluding resources awarded to replace EFC). ***Average financial aid package:*** $38,596 (excluding resources awarded to replace EFC). 6% of all full-time freshmen had no need and received non-need-based gift aid.

UNDERGRADUATE FINANCIAL AID (Fall 2018) 1,303 applied for aid; of those 95% were deemed to have need. 99% of undergraduates with need received aid; of those 79% had need fully met. ***Average percent of need met:*** 65% (excluding resources awarded to replace EFC). ***Average financial aid package:*** $33,134 (excluding resources awarded to replace EFC). 4% of all full-time undergraduates had no need and received non-need-based gift aid.

GIFT AID (NEED-BASED) ***Total amount:*** $8,407,663 (39% federal, 21% state, 40% institutional). ***Receiving aid:*** Freshmen: 74% (243); all full-time undergraduates: 70% (964). ***Average award:*** Freshmen: $9195; Undergraduates: $8114. ***Scholarships, grants, and awards:*** Federal Pell, FSEOG, state, private, college/university gift aid from institutional funds.

GIFT AID (NON-NEED-BASED) ***Total amount:*** $15,906,933 (3% federal, 2% state, 93% institutional, 2% external sources). ***Receiving aid:*** Freshmen: 88% (290). Undergraduates: 70% (966). ***Average award:*** Freshmen: $17,263. Undergraduates: $14,860. ***Tuition waivers:*** Full or partial for employees or children of employees.

LOANS ***Student loans:*** $15,401,563 (34% need-based, 66% non-need-based). 88% of past graduating class borrowed through all loan programs. *Average indebtedness per student:* $44,211. ***Average need-based loan:*** Freshmen: $3304. Undergraduates: $4369. ***Parent loans:*** $3,369,107 (100% non-need-based). ***Programs:*** Federal Direct (Subsidized and Unsubsidized Stafford, PLUS), Perkins.

WORK-STUDY ***Federal work-study:*** Total amount: $813,233. ***State or other work-study/employment:*** Total amount: $1,223,117 (100% non-need-based).

APPLYING FOR FINANCIAL AID ***Required financial aid form:*** FAFSA. ***Financial aid deadline:*** 11/1 (priority: 11/1). ***Notification date:*** Continuous beginning 11/10.

CONTACT Catherine Buzanski, Director of Financial Aid, Keuka College, 141 Central Avenue, Keuka Park, NY 14478-0098, 315-279-5232 or toll-free 800-33-KEUKA. *Fax:* 315-536-5327. *E-mail:* cbuzanski@keuka.edu.
Website: http://www.keuka.edu/.

KEYSTONE COLLEGE

La Plume, PA

Tuition & fees: $17,000 | **Average undergraduate aid package: N/A**

ABOUT THE INSTITUTION Independent, coed. ***Awards:*** certificates, associate, bachelor's, and master's degrees. ***Total enrollment:*** 1,364. Undergraduates: 1,288. Freshmen: 343.

UNDERGRADUATE EXPENSES for 2020–2021 ***Comprehensive fee:*** $28,900 includes full-time tuition ($14,500), mandatory fees ($2500), and room and board ($11,900). ***College room only:*** $6000. ***Part-time tuition:*** $575 per credit hour.

GIFT AID (NEED-BASED) ***Scholarships, grants, and awards:*** Federal Pell, FSEOG, state, private, college/university gift aid from institutional funds.

GIFT AID (NON-NEED-BASED) ***Scholarships, grants, and awards by category:*** *Academic interests/achievement:* agriculture, computer science, health fields. *Special characteristics:* children and siblings of alumni, international students, siblings of current students.

LOANS ***Programs:*** Federal Direct (Subsidized and Unsubsidized Stafford, PLUS).

WORK-STUDY Federal work-study jobs available. ***State or other work-study/employment:*** Part-time jobs available.

APPLYING FOR FINANCIAL AID ***Required financial aid forms:*** FAFSA, state aid form. ***Financial aid deadline:*** Continuous. ***Notification date:*** Continuous.

CONTACT Director of Financial Assistance and Planning, Keystone College, One College Green, La Plume, PA 18440, 570-945-8134 or toll-free 877-4-COLLEGE. *Fax:* 570-945-8134. *E-mail:* financialaid@keystone.edu.
Website: http://www.keystone.edu/.

THE KING'S COLLEGE

New York, NY

Tuition & fees: $37,690 | **Average undergraduate aid package: $28,575**

ABOUT THE INSTITUTION Independent nondenominational, coed. ***Awards:*** bachelor's degrees. 6 undergraduate majors. ***Total enrollment:*** 544. Undergraduates: 544. Freshmen: 125. Both federal and institutional methodology are used as a basis for awarding need-based institutional aid.

UNDERGRADUATE EXPENSES for 2020–2021 ***Application fee:*** $30. ***Tuition:*** full-time $37,000; part-time $1590 per credit hour. ***Required fees:*** full-time $690; $250 per term. Part-time tuition and fees vary according to course load. ***College room only:*** $1440. Room and board charges vary according to location.
FRESHMAN FINANCIAL AID (Fall 2018) 123 applied for aid; of those 84% were deemed to have need. 100% of freshmen with need received aid; of those 21% had need fully met. ***Average percent of need met:*** 71% (excluding resources awarded to replace EFC). ***Average financial aid package:*** $27,660 (excluding resources awarded to replace EFC). 29% of all full-time freshmen had no need and received non-need-based gift aid.
UNDERGRADUATE FINANCIAL AID (Fall 2018) 403 applied for aid; of those 88% were deemed to have need. 100% of undergraduates with need received aid; of those 20% had need fully met. ***Average percent of need met:*** 73% (excluding resources awarded to replace EFC). ***Average financial aid package:*** $28,575 (excluding resources awarded to replace EFC). 32% of all full-time undergraduates had no need and received non-need-based gift aid.
GIFT AID (NEED-BASED) ***Total amount:*** $8,332,467 (8% federal, 1% state, 88% institutional, 3% external sources). ***Receiving aid:*** Freshmen: 72% (103); all full-time undergraduates: 68% (352). ***Average award:*** Freshmen: $22,509; Undergraduates: $22,920. ***Scholarships, grants, and awards:*** Federal Pell, FSEOG, state, private, college/university gift aid from institutional funds.
GIFT AID (NON-NEED-BASED) ***Total amount:*** $3,010,067 (99% institutional, 1% external sources). ***Receiving aid:*** Freshmen: 13% (18). Undergraduates: 10% (51). ***Average award:*** Freshmen: $18,726. Undergraduates: $17,725. ***Scholarships, grants, and awards by category:*** *Academic interests/achievement:* 112 awards ($1,274,125 total): general academic interests/achievements. *Creative arts/performance:* 10 awards ($18,750 total): journalism/publications. *Special achievements/activities:* 343 awards ($901,725 total): general special achievements/activities, leadership. *Special characteristics:* 44 awards ($66,812 total): children and siblings of alumni, international students. ***Tuition waivers:*** Full or partial for employees or children of employees. ***ROTC:*** Army cooperative.
LOANS ***Student loans:*** $3,798,770 (88% need-based, 12% non-need-based). 59% of past graduating class borrowed through all loan programs. *Average indebtedness per student:* $34,876. ***Average need-based loan:*** Freshmen: $2755. Undergraduates: $3632. ***Parent loans:*** $2,426,171 (87% need-based, 13% non-need-based). ***Programs:*** Federal Direct (Subsidized and Unsubsidized Stafford, PLUS), private loans.
APPLYING FOR FINANCIAL AID ***Required financial aid form:*** FAFSA. ***Financial aid deadline:*** Continuous. ***Notification date:*** Continuous beginning 12/15.
CONTACT Anna Peters, Senior Director of Financial Aid, The King's College, 56 Broadway, New York, NY 10004, 646-930-0648 or toll-free 888-969-7200 Ext.3610. *E-mail:* financialservices@tkc.edu.
Website: http://www.tkc.edu/.

KING'S COLLEGE
Wilkes-Barre, PA

Tuition & fees: $40,080	Average undergraduate aid package: $28,268

ABOUT THE INSTITUTION Independent Roman Catholic, coed. ***Awards:*** certificates, bachelor's, and master's degrees. 42 undergraduate majors. ***Total enrollment:*** 2,519. Undergraduates: 2,231. Freshmen: 560. Federal methodology is used as a basis for awarding need-based institutional aid.
UNDERGRADUATE EXPENSES for 2020–2021 ***Application fee:*** $30. ***Comprehensive fee:*** $54,088 includes full-time tuition ($38,062), mandatory fees ($2018), and room and board ($14,008). ***College room only:*** $7364. ***Part-time tuition:*** $621 per credit hour. ***Part-time fees:*** $88.
FRESHMAN FINANCIAL AID (Fall 2019, est.) 539 applied for aid; of those 91% were deemed to have need. 100% of freshmen with need received aid; of those 15% had need fully met. ***Average percent of need met:*** 75% (excluding resources awarded to replace EFC). ***Average financial aid package:*** $29,083 (excluding resources awarded to replace EFC). 12% of all full-time freshmen had no need and received non-need-based gift aid.
UNDERGRADUATE FINANCIAL AID (Fall 2019, est.) 1,733 applied for aid; of those 91% were deemed to have need. 100% of undergraduates with need received aid; of those 18% had need fully met. ***Average percent of need met:*** 75% (excluding resources awarded to replace EFC). ***Average financial aid package:*** $28,268 (excluding resources awarded to replace EFC). 15% of all full-time undergraduates had no need and received non-need-based gift aid.
GIFT AID (NEED-BASED) ***Total amount:*** $34,963,616 (10% federal, 6% state, 83% institutional, 1% external sources). ***Receiving aid:*** Freshmen: 88% (488); all full-time undergraduates: 77% (1,569). ***Average award:*** Freshmen: $23,002; Undergraduates: $19,749. ***Scholarships, grants, and awards:*** Federal Pell, FSEOG, state, private, college/university gift aid from institutional funds.
GIFT AID (NON-NEED-BASED) ***Total amount:*** $7,247,896 (5% federal, 93% institutional, 2% external sources). ***Receiving aid:*** Freshmen: 10% (56). Undergraduates: 9% (179). ***Average award:*** Freshmen: $18,816. Undergraduates: $17,612. ***Scholarships, grants, and awards by category:*** *Academic interests/achievement:* 1,627 awards ($22,765,454 total): biological sciences, business, communication, computer science, education, engineering/technologies, English, foreign languages, general academic interests/achievements, humanities, international studies, mathematics, physical sciences, premedicine, religion/biblical studies, social sciences. *Special achievements/activities:* 1,250 awards ($7,272,812 total): community service, general special achievements/activities, leadership, religious involvement. *Special characteristics:* 328 awards ($3,125,484 total): children and siblings of alumni, children of educators, children of faculty/staff, general special characteristics, international students, relatives of clergy, siblings of current students, veterans. ***Tuition waivers:*** Full or partial for children of alumni, employees or children of employees. ***ROTC:*** Army, Air Force cooperative.
LOANS ***Student loans:*** $18,897,155 (65% need-based, 35% non-need-based). 83% of past graduating class borrowed through all loan programs. *Average indebtedness per student:* $40,818. ***Average need-based loan:*** Freshmen: $3406. Undergraduates: $4353. ***Parent loans:*** $4,780,918 (55% need-based, 45% non-need-based). ***Programs:*** Federal Direct (Subsidized and Unsubsidized Stafford, PLUS), private loans.
WORK-STUDY ***Federal work-study:*** Total amount: $346,415; 273 jobs averaging $1958. ***State or other work-study/employment:*** Total amount: $290,232 (100% non-need-based). 292 part-time jobs averaging $991.
APPLYING FOR FINANCIAL AID ***Required financial aid form:*** FAFSA. ***Financial aid deadline (priority):*** 2/15. ***Notification date:*** Continuous beginning 3/1. Students must reply by 5/1 or within 2 weeks of notification.
CONTACT Mr. Jared Menghini, Director of Financial Aid, King's College, 133 North River Street, Wilkes-Barre, PA 18711-0801, 570-208-5868 or toll-free 888-KINGSPA. *Fax:* 570-208-6015. *E-mail:* finaid@kings.edu.
Website: http://www.kings.edu/.

THE KING'S UNIVERSITY
Southlake, TX

CONTACT Mr. Travis Termin, Financial Aid Officer, The King's University, 2121 East Southlake Boulevard, Southlake, TX 76092, 817-722-1730 or toll-free 888-779-8040. *Fax:* 817-722-1766. *E-mail:* financialaid@tku.edu.
Website: http://www.tku.edu/.

KING UNIVERSITY
Bristol, TN

Tuition & fees: $31,840	Average undergraduate aid package: $16,246

ABOUT THE INSTITUTION Independent Presbyterian Church (U.S.A.), coed. ***Awards:*** certificates, associate, bachelor's, master's, and doctoral degrees. 35 undergraduate majors. ***Total enrollment:*** 1,974. Undergraduates: 1,617. Freshmen: 205. Federal methodology is used as a basis for awarding need-based institutional aid.
UNDERGRADUATE EXPENSES for 2020–2021 ***One-time required fee:*** $125. ***Comprehensive fee:*** $41,226 includes full-time tuition ($30,106), mandatory fees ($1734), and room and board ($9386). ***College room only:*** $4714. Full-time tuition and fees vary according to degree level, program, and reciprocity agreements. Room and board charges vary according to housing facility. ***Part-time tuition:*** $600 per semester hour. ***Part-time fees:*** $100 per course. Part-time tuition and fees vary according to degree level, program, and reciprocity agreements.

FRESHMAN FINANCIAL AID (Fall 2019, est.) 163 applied for aid; of those 93% were deemed to have need. 100% of freshmen with need received aid; of those 18% had need fully met. ***Average percent of need met:*** 77% (excluding resources awarded to replace EFC). ***Average financial aid package:*** $23,666 (excluding resources awarded to replace EFC). 11% of all full-time freshmen had no need and received non-need-based gift aid.

UNDERGRADUATE FINANCIAL AID (Fall 2019, est.) 1,319 applied for aid; of those 92% were deemed to have need. 98% of undergraduates with need received aid; of those 11% had need fully met. ***Average percent of need met:*** 63% (excluding resources awarded to replace EFC). ***Average financial aid package:*** $16,246 (excluding resources awarded to replace EFC). 8% of all full-time undergraduates had no need and received non-need-based gift aid.

GIFT AID (NEED-BASED) ***Total amount:*** $12,535,961 (31% federal, 16% state, 50% institutional, 3% external sources). ***Receiving aid:*** Freshmen: 88% (149); all full-time undergraduates: 71% (1,031). ***Average award:*** Freshmen: $20,782; Undergraduates: $14,183. ***Scholarships, grants, and awards:*** Federal Pell, FSEOG, state, private, college/university gift aid from institutional funds.

GIFT AID (NON-NEED-BASED) ***Total amount:*** $1,739,673 (11% state, 70% institutional, 19% external sources). ***Receiving aid:*** Freshmen: 12% (21). Undergraduates: 6% (91). ***Average award:*** Freshmen: $11,921. Undergraduates: $10,001. ***Scholarships, grants, and awards by category:*** *Academic interests/achievement:* general academic interests/achievements. *Creative arts/performance:* applied art and design, music, performing arts, theater/drama. *Special achievements/activities:* general special achievements/activities. *Special characteristics:* children of faculty/staff, out-of-state students, veterans. ***Tuition waivers:*** Full or partial for employees or children of employees. ***ROTC:*** Army cooperative.

LOANS ***Student loans:*** $10,144,600 (84% need-based, 16% non-need-based). 68% of past graduating class borrowed through all loan programs. *Average indebtedness per student:* $29,417. ***Average need-based loan:*** Freshmen: $2960. Undergraduates: $4403. ***Parent loans:*** $927,648 (46% need-based, 54% non-need-based). ***Programs:*** Federal Direct (Subsidized and Unsubsidized Stafford, PLUS).

WORK-STUDY ***Federal work-study:*** Total amount: $162,934; jobs available. ***State or other work-study/employment:*** Part-time jobs available.

ATHLETIC AWARDS Total amount: $3,536,635 (55% need-based, 45% non-need-based).

APPLYING FOR FINANCIAL AID ***Required financial aid form:*** FAFSA. ***Financial aid deadline:*** Continuous. ***Notification date:*** Continuous beginning 12/15. Students must reply within 4 weeks of notification.

CONTACT Mr. Richard J. Brand, Director of Financial Aid, King University, 1350 King College Road, Bristol, TN 37620-2699, 423-652-4728 or toll-free 800-362-0014. *Fax:* 423-652-6039. *E-mail:* rjbrand@king.edu.
Website: http://www.king.edu/.

KNOX COLLEGE

Galesburg, IL

ABOUT THE INSTITUTION Independent, coed. ***Awards:*** bachelor's degrees. 40 undergraduate majors. ***Total enrollment:*** 1,258. Undergraduates: 1,258. Freshmen: 320.

GIFT AID (NEED-BASED) ***Scholarships, grants, and awards:*** Federal Pell, FSEOG, state, private, college/university gift aid from institutional funds.

GIFT AID (NON-NEED-BASED) ***Scholarships, grants, and awards by category:*** *Academic interests/achievement:* general academic interests/achievements, mathematics. *Creative arts/performance:* applied art and design, creative writing, dance, music, theater/drama. *Special achievements/activities:* community service. *Special characteristics:* children of faculty/staff, veterans.

LOANS ***Programs:*** Federal Direct (Subsidized and Unsubsidized Stafford, PLUS), college/university, private loans.

WORK-STUDY ***Federal work-study:*** Total amount: $1,428,487; 648 jobs averaging $2200. ***State or other work-study/employment:*** Total amount: $394,725 (100% need-based). Part-time jobs available.

APPLYING FOR FINANCIAL AID ***Required financial aid forms:*** FAFSA, institution's own form.

CONTACT Ms. Leigh T. Brinson, Director of Financial Aid, Knox College, 2 East South Street, Galesburg, IL 61401, 309-341-7149 or toll-free 800-678-KNOX. *Fax:* 309-341-7453. *E-mail:* ltbrinson@knox.edu.
Website: http://www.knox.edu/.

KUTZTOWN UNIVERSITY OF PENNSYLVANIA

Kutztown, PA

Tuition & fees (PA res): $10,950	Average undergraduate aid package: $9403

ABOUT THE INSTITUTION State-supported, coed. ***Awards:*** certificates, bachelor's, master's, and doctoral degrees. 46 undergraduate majors. ***Total enrollment:*** 8,199. Undergraduates: 9,108. Freshmen: 1,399. Federal methodology is used as a basis for awarding need-based institutional aid.

UNDERGRADUATE EXPENSES for 2019–2020 ***Application fee:*** $35. ***One-time required fee:*** $313. ***Tuition, state resident:*** full-time $7716; part-time $322 per credit. ***Tuition, nonresident:*** full-time $11,574; part-time $805 per credit. ***Required fees:*** full-time $3234; $104 per credit. Full-time tuition and fees vary according to course load. Part-time tuition and fees vary according to course load. ***College room and board:*** $10,434; ***Room only:*** $6484. Room and board charges vary according to board plan and housing facility.

FRESHMAN FINANCIAL AID (Fall 2018) 1547 applied for aid; of those 82% were deemed to have need. 98% of freshmen with need received aid; of those 7% had need fully met. ***Average percent of need met:*** 37% (excluding resources awarded to replace EFC). ***Average financial aid package:*** $9089 (excluding resources awarded to replace EFC). 11% of all full-time freshmen had no need and received non-need-based gift aid.

UNDERGRADUATE FINANCIAL AID (Fall 2018) 6,069 applied for aid; of those 85% were deemed to have need. 98% of undergraduates with need received aid; of those 8% had need fully met. ***Average percent of need met:*** 43% (excluding resources awarded to replace EFC). ***Average financial aid package:*** $9403 (excluding resources awarded to replace EFC). 4% of all full-time undergraduates had no need and received non-need-based gift aid.

GIFT AID (NEED-BASED) ***Receiving aid:*** Freshmen: 48% (786); all full-time undergraduates: 46% (3,211). ***Average award:*** Freshmen: $6264; Undergraduates: $5939. ***Scholarships, grants, and awards:*** Federal Pell, FSEOG, state, private, college/university gift aid from institutional funds.

GIFT AID (NON-NEED-BASED) ***Receiving aid:*** Freshmen: 56% (915). Undergraduates: 34% (2,354). ***Average award:*** Freshmen: $1072. Undergraduates: $1506. ***Scholarships, grants, and awards by category:*** *Academic interests/achievement:* 402 awards ($1,474,283 total): biological sciences, business, communication, computer science, education, English, foreign languages, general academic interests/achievements, humanities, international studies, library science, mathematics, physical sciences. *Creative arts/performance:* 41 awards ($55,110 total): applied art and design, art/fine arts, dance, music. *Special achievements/activities:* 257 awards ($668,567 total): community service, general special achievements/activities, leadership, religious involvement. *Special characteristics:* 149 awards ($1,134,760 total): children of faculty/staff, children of union members/company employees, first-generation college students, handicapped students, local/state students. ***Tuition waivers:*** Full or partial for employees or children of employees, senior citizens. ***ROTC:*** Army cooperative.

LOANS ***Student loans:*** 84% of past graduating class borrowed through all loan programs. *Average indebtedness per student:* $40,592. ***Average need-based loan:*** Freshmen: $3245. Undergraduates: $4218. ***Programs:*** Federal Direct (Subsidized and Unsubsidized Stafford, PLUS), Perkins.

WORK-STUDY ***Federal work-study:*** 520 jobs averaging $3030.

APPLYING FOR FINANCIAL AID ***Required financial aid form:*** FAFSA. ***Notification date:*** Continuous. Students must reply within 4 weeks of notification.

CONTACT Mr. Bernard McCree, Director of Financial Aid, Kutztown University of Pennsylvania, 209 Stratton Administration Center, Kutztown, PA 19530-0730, 610-683-4032 or toll-free 877-628-1915. *Fax:* 610-683-1380. *E-mail:* mccree@kutztown.edu.
Website: http://www.kutztown.edu/.

KUYPER COLLEGE

Grand Rapids, MI

Tuition & fees: N/R | **Average undergraduate aid package: $17,289**

ABOUT THE INSTITUTION Independent Christian, coed. ***Awards:*** certificates, associate, bachelor's, and master's degrees. 20 undergraduate majors. ***Total enrollment:*** 160. Undergraduates: 160. Freshmen: 30. Federal methodology is used as a basis for awarding need-based institutional aid.

FRESHMAN FINANCIAL AID (Fall 2019, est.) 11 applied for aid; of those 100% were deemed to have need. 100% of freshmen with need received aid; of those 9% had need fully met. ***Average percent of need met:*** 65% (excluding resources awarded to replace EFC). ***Average financial aid package:*** $17,897 (excluding resources awarded to replace EFC).

UNDERGRADUATE FINANCIAL AID (Fall 2019, est.) 97 applied for aid; of those 94% were deemed to have need. 100% of undergraduates with need received aid; of those 11% had need fully met. ***Average percent of need met:*** 67% (excluding resources awarded to replace EFC). ***Average financial aid package:*** $17,289 (excluding resources awarded to replace EFC). 6% of all full-time undergraduates had no need and received non-need-based gift aid.

GIFT AID (NEED-BASED) ***Receiving aid:*** Freshmen: 100% (11); all full-time undergraduates: 88% (85). ***Average award:*** Freshmen: $15,529; Undergraduates: $14,597. ***Scholarships, grants, and awards:*** Federal Pell, FSEOG, state, private, college/university gift aid from institutional funds.

GIFT AID (NON-NEED-BASED) ***Receiving aid:*** Undergraduates: 73% (71). ***Average award:*** Undergraduates: $2000. ***Scholarships, grants, and awards by category:*** *Academic interests/achievement:* business, communication, religion/biblical studies, social sciences. *Creative arts/performance:* music. *Special achievements/activities:* leadership. *Special characteristics:* children and siblings of alumni, children of faculty/staff, handicapped students, international students, relatives of clergy, siblings of current students. ***ROTC:*** Army cooperative.

LOANS ***Student loans:*** 87% of past graduating class borrowed through all loan programs. *Average indebtedness per student:* $22,674. ***Average need-based loan:*** Freshmen: $2894. Undergraduates: $3940. ***Programs:*** Federal Direct (Subsidized and Unsubsidized Stafford, PLUS), Private Loans.

WORK-STUDY ***Federal work-study:*** 16 jobs averaging $2498. ***State or other work-study/employment:*** Part-time jobs available.

APPLYING FOR FINANCIAL AID ***Required financial aid form:*** FAFSA. ***Notification date:*** Continuous. Students must reply within 2 weeks of notification.

CONTACT Ms. Agnes M Russell, Director of Financial Aid, Kuyper College, 3333 East Beltline NE, Grand Rapids, MI 49525-9749, 616-222-3000 Ext. 656. *Fax:* 616-222-3045. *E-mail:* arussell@kuyper.edu.
Website: http://www.kuyper.edu/.

LAFAYETTE COLLEGE

Easton, PA

Tuition & fees: $57,052 | **Average undergraduate aid package: $51,240**

ABOUT THE INSTITUTION Independent Presbyterian Church (U.S.A.), coed. ***Awards:*** bachelor's degrees. 33 undergraduate majors. ***Total enrollment:*** 2,662. Undergraduates: 2,662. Freshmen: 698. Both federal and institutional methodology are used as a basis for awarding need-based institutional aid.

UNDERGRADUATE EXPENSES for 2020–2021 ***Application fee:*** $65. ***One-time required fee:*** $750. ***Comprehensive fee:*** $73,926 includes full-time tuition ($56,556), mandatory fees ($496), and room and board ($16,874). ***College room only:*** $10,434. ***Part-time tuition:*** $613 per credit hour.

FRESHMAN FINANCIAL AID (Fall 2019, est.) 446 applied for aid; of those 55% were deemed to have need. 100% of freshmen with need received aid; of those 100% had need fully met. ***Average percent of need met:*** 100% (excluding resources awarded to replace EFC). ***Average financial aid package:*** $51,259 (excluding resources awarded to replace EFC). 5% of all full-time freshmen had no need and received non-need-based gift aid.

UNDERGRADUATE FINANCIAL AID (Fall 2019, est.) 1,451 applied for aid; of those 63% were deemed to have need. 100% of undergraduates with need received aid; of those 100% had need fully met. ***Average percent of need met:*** 100% (excluding resources awarded to replace EFC). ***Average financial aid package:*** $51,240 (excluding resources awarded to replace EFC). 6% of all full-time undergraduates had no need and received non-need-based gift aid.

GIFT AID (NEED-BASED) ***Receiving aid:*** Freshmen: 35% (243); all full-time undergraduates: 34% (903). ***Average award:*** Freshmen: $47,148; Undergraduates: $46,031. ***Scholarships, grants, and awards:*** Federal Pell, FSEOG, state, private, college/university gift aid from institutional funds.

GIFT AID (NON-NEED-BASED) ***Receiving aid:*** Freshmen: 6% (44). Undergraduates: 5% (120). ***Average award:*** Freshmen: $27,765. Undergraduates: $31,469. ***Scholarships, grants, and awards by category:*** *Academic interests/achievement:* general academic interests/achievements. *Creative arts/performance:* applied art and design, art/fine arts, cinema/film/broadcasting, creative writing, dance, general creative arts/performance, music, performing arts, theater/drama. ***ROTC:*** Army cooperative.

LOANS ***Student loans:*** 38% of past graduating class borrowed through all loan programs. *Average indebtedness per student:* $30,181. ***Average need-based loan:*** Freshmen: $3360. Undergraduates: $3752. ***Programs:*** Federal Direct (Subsidized and Unsubsidized Stafford, PLUS), Perkins, college/university.

WORK-STUDY ***Federal work-study:*** 510 jobs averaging $1230. ***State or other work-study/employment:*** Part-time jobs available.

APPLYING FOR FINANCIAL AID ***Required financial aid forms:*** FAFSA, CSS Financial Aid PROFILE, noncustodial (divorced/separated) parent's statement, federal income tax form(s).

CONTACT Mr. Forrest Stuart, Assistant Vice President for Financial Aid, Lafayette College, 730 High Street, 107 Markle Hall, Easton, PA 18042-1777, 610-330-5055. *Fax:* 610-330-5758. *E-mail:* stuartf@lafayette.edu.
Website: http://www.lafayette.edu/.

LAGRANGE COLLEGE

LaGrange, GA

Tuition & fees: $31,540 | **Average undergraduate aid package: $27,550**

ABOUT THE INSTITUTION Independent United Methodist, coed. ***Awards:*** bachelor's and master's degrees. 28 undergraduate majors. ***Total enrollment:*** 995. Undergraduates: 822. Freshmen: 200. Federal methodology is used as a basis for awarding need-based institutional aid.

UNDERGRADUATE EXPENSES for 2019–2020 ***One-time required fee:*** $150. ***Comprehensive fee:*** $43,510 includes full-time tuition ($31,200), mandatory fees ($340), and room and board ($11,970). ***College room only:*** $6430. Full-time tuition and fees vary according to class time, course load, degree level, and program. Room and board charges vary according to board plan and housing facility. ***Part-time tuition:*** $1285 per semester hour. Part-time tuition and fees vary according to class time, course load, degree level, and program.

FRESHMAN FINANCIAL AID (Fall 2019, est.) 248 applied for aid; of those 92% were deemed to have need. 100% of freshmen with need received aid; of those 15% had need fully met. ***Average percent of need met:*** 82% (excluding resources awarded to replace EFC). ***Average financial aid package:*** $26,777 (excluding resources awarded to replace EFC). 8% of all full-time freshmen had no need and received non-need-based gift aid.

UNDERGRADUATE FINANCIAL AID (Fall 2019, est.) 819 applied for aid; of those 92% were deemed to have need. 100% of undergraduates with need received aid; of those 16% had need fully met. ***Average percent of need met:*** 81% (excluding resources awarded to replace EFC). ***Average financial aid package:*** $27,550 (excluding resources awarded to replace EFC). 9% of all full-time undergraduates had no need and received non-need-based gift aid.

GIFT AID (NEED-BASED) ***Receiving aid:*** Freshmen: 87% (217); all full-time undergraduates: 87% (731). ***Average award:*** Freshmen: $5520; Undergraduates: $5785. ***Scholarships, grants, and awards:*** Federal Pell, FSEOG, private, college/university gift aid from institutional funds.

GIFT AID (NON-NEED-BASED) ***Receiving aid:*** Freshmen: 87% (217). Undergraduates: 86% (730). ***Average award:*** Freshmen: $14,199. Undergraduates: $12,870. ***Scholarships, grants, and awards by category:*** *Academic interests/achievement:* education, general academic interests/achievements, religion/biblical studies. *Creative arts/performance:* applied art and design, music, theater/drama. *Special achievements/activities:* leadership. *Special characteristics:* children of faculty/staff, ethnic background, first-generation college students, relatives of clergy, religious affiliation. ***Tuition waivers:*** Full or partial for employees or children of employees, senior citizens.

LOANS *Student loans:* 85% of past graduating class borrowed through all loan programs. *Average indebtedness per student:* $37,680. ***Average need-based loan:*** Freshmen: $3079. Undergraduates: $4136. ***Programs:*** Federal Direct (Subsidized and Unsubsidized Stafford, PLUS).

WORK-STUDY Federal work-study jobs available. ***State or other work-study/employment:*** Part-time jobs available.

APPLYING FOR FINANCIAL AID *Required financial aid forms:* FAFSA, state aid form. ***Financial aid deadline:*** 5/1 (priority: 3/1). ***Notification date:*** Continuous beginning 12/15. Students must reply within 4 weeks of notification.

CONTACT Michelle Reeves, Assistant Director, LaGrange College, 601 Broad Street, LaGrange, GA 30240-2999, 888-253-9918 or toll-free 800-593-2885. *Fax:* 706-880-8348. *E-mail:* mreeves@lagrange.edu.
Website: http://www.lagrange.edu/.

LAGUNA COLLEGE OF ART & DESIGN

Laguna Beach, CA

ABOUT THE INSTITUTION Independent, coed. ***Awards:*** certificates, bachelor's, and master's degrees. 14 undergraduate majors.

GIFT AID (NEED-BASED) *Scholarships, grants, and awards:* Federal Pell, FSEOG, state, private, college/university gift aid from institutional funds.

GIFT AID (NON-NEED-BASED) *Scholarships, grants, and awards by category:* *Academic interests/achievement:* general academic interests/achievements. *Creative arts/performance:* applied art and design, art/fine arts.

LOANS *Programs:* Federal Direct (Subsidized and Unsubsidized Stafford, PLUS).

WORK-STUDY *Federal work-study:* Total amount: $50,000; 30 jobs averaging $1666.

APPLYING FOR FINANCIAL AID *Required financial aid form:* FAFSA.

CONTACT Christopher Brown, Director of Admissions and Financial Aid, Laguna College of Art & Design, 2825 Laguna Canyon Road, Laguna Beach, CA 92651-1136, 949-376-6000 or toll-free 800-255-0762. *Fax:* 949-715-4084. *E-mail:* cbrown@lcad.edu.
Website: http://www.lcad.edu/.

LAKE ERIE COLLEGE

Painesville, OH

Tuition & fees: N/R	Average undergraduate aid package: $25,916

ABOUT THE INSTITUTION Independent, coed. ***Awards:*** certificates, bachelor's, and master's degrees. 35 undergraduate majors. Federal methodology is used as a basis for awarding need-based institutional aid.

FRESHMAN FINANCIAL AID (Fall 2019, est.) 195 applied for aid; of those 92% were deemed to have need. 100% of freshmen with need received aid; of those 16% had need fully met. ***Average percent of need met:*** 75% (excluding resources awarded to replace EFC). ***Average financial aid package:*** $26,405 (excluding resources awarded to replace EFC). 13% of all full-time freshmen had no need and received non-need-based gift aid.

UNDERGRADUATE FINANCIAL AID (Fall 2019, est.) 602 applied for aid; of those 92% were deemed to have need. 100% of undergraduates with need received aid; of those 18% had need fully met. ***Average percent of need met:*** 73% (excluding resources awarded to replace EFC). ***Average financial aid package:*** $25,916 (excluding resources awarded to replace EFC). 18% of all full-time undergraduates had no need and received non-need-based gift aid.

GIFT AID (NEED-BASED) *Total amount:* $10,718,159 (14% federal, 4% state, 79% institutional, 3% external sources). ***Receiving aid:*** Freshmen: 86% (179); all full-time undergraduates: 79% (543). ***Average award:*** Freshmen: $24,018; Undergraduates: $23,156.

GIFT AID (NON-NEED-BASED) *Total amount:* $2,220,352 (94% institutional, 6% external sources). ***Receiving aid:*** Freshmen: 11% (23). Undergraduates: 11% (76). ***Average award:*** Freshmen: $14,077. Undergraduates: $14,354. ***Scholarships, grants, and awards by category:*** *Academic interests/achievement:* biological sciences, business, communication, education, English, foreign languages, general academic interests/achievements, humanities, international studies, mathematics, physical sciences, social sciences. *Creative arts/performance:* art/fine arts, dance, general creative arts/performance, music, performing arts, theater/drama. *Special achievements/activities:* community service, general special achievements/activities, hobbies/interests. *Special characteristics:* children of faculty/staff, twins, veterans, veterans' children.

LOANS *Student loans:* $4,745,660 (73% need-based, 27% non-need-based). 79% of past graduating class borrowed through all loan programs. *Average indebtedness per student:* $28,748. ***Average need-based loan:*** Freshmen: $2910. Undergraduates: $3746. ***Parent loans:*** $1,734,041 (50% need-based, 50% non-need-based).

WORK-STUDY *Federal work-study:* Total amount: $92,577; jobs available.

ATHLETIC AWARDS Total amount: $3,116,603 (59% need-based, 41% non-need-based).

APPLYING FOR FINANCIAL AID *Notification date:* Continuous.

CONTACT Tricia Pangonis, Director of Financial Aid, Lake Erie College, 391 West Washington Street, Painesville, OH 44077-3389, 440-375-7102 or toll-free 800-916-0904. *Fax:* 440-375-7103. *E-mail:* finaid@lec.edu.
Website: http://www.lec.edu/.

LAKE FOREST COLLEGE

Lake Forest, IL

Tuition & fees: $49,822	Average undergraduate aid package: $43,010

ABOUT THE INSTITUTION Independent, coed. ***Awards:*** certificates, bachelor's, and master's degrees. 33 undergraduate majors. ***Total enrollment:*** 1,512. Undergraduates: 1,492. Freshmen: 392. Both federal and institutional methodology are used as a basis for awarding need-based institutional aid.

UNDERGRADUATE EXPENSES for 2020–2021 *Comprehensive fee:* $60,776 includes full-time tuition ($48,920), mandatory fees ($902), and room and board ($10,954). ***College room only:*** $5274. ***Part-time tuition:*** $5960 per course.

FRESHMAN FINANCIAL AID (Fall 2019, est.) 357 applied for aid; of those 87% were deemed to have need. 100% of freshmen with need received aid; of those 35% had need fully met. ***Average percent of need met:*** 88% (excluding resources awarded to replace EFC). ***Average financial aid package:*** $44,475 (excluding resources awarded to replace EFC). 20% of all full-time freshmen had no need and received non-need-based gift aid.

UNDERGRADUATE FINANCIAL AID (Fall 2019, est.) 1,288 applied for aid; of those 85% were deemed to have need. 100% of undergraduates with need received aid; of those 30% had need fully met. ***Average percent of need met:*** 86% (excluding resources awarded to replace EFC). ***Average financial aid package:*** $43,010 (excluding resources awarded to replace EFC). 27% of all full-time undergraduates had no need and received non-need-based gift aid.

GIFT AID (NEED-BASED) *Total amount:* $42,798,352 (7% federal, 5% state, 84% institutional, 4% external sources). ***Receiving aid:*** Freshmen: 82% (311); all full-time undergraduates: 73% (1,100). ***Average award:*** Freshmen: $40,935; Undergraduates: $38,560. ***Scholarships, grants, and awards:*** Federal Pell, FSEOG, state, private, college/university gift aid from institutional funds.

GIFT AID (NON-NEED-BASED) *Total amount:* $10,049,855 (95% institutional, 5% external sources). ***Average award:*** Freshmen: $24,320. Undergraduates: $24,740. ***Scholarships, grants, and awards by category:*** *Academic interests/achievement:* biological sciences, computer science, English, foreign languages, general academic interests/achievements, mathematics, physical sciences, social sciences. *Creative arts/performance:* art/fine arts, creative writing, music, theater/drama. *Special achievements/activities:* leadership. *Special characteristics:* children and siblings of alumni, local/state students, previous college experience.

LOANS *Student loans:* $7,896,541 (90% need-based, 10% non-need-based). 70% of past graduating class borrowed through all loan programs. *Average indebtedness per student:* $34,587. ***Average need-based loan:*** Freshmen: $3470. Undergraduates: $4500. ***Parent loans:*** $1,988,545 (94% need-based, 6% non-need-based). ***Programs:*** Federal Direct (Subsidized and Unsubsidized Stafford, PLUS).

WORK-STUDY *Federal work-study:* Total amount: $965,855; jobs available. ***State or other work-study/employment:*** Part-time jobs available.

APPLYING FOR FINANCIAL AID *Required financial aid form:* FAFSA. ***Financial aid deadline:*** 5/1 (priority: 2/15). ***Notification date:*** Continuous beginning 12/1. Students must reply by 5/1.

CONTACT Mr. Jerry Cebrzynski, Associate Vice-President for Financial Aid, Lake Forest College, 555 North Sheridan Road, Lake Forest, IL 60045, 847-735-5104 or toll-free 800-828-4751. *Fax:* 847-735-6271. *E-mail:* cebrzynski@lakeforest.edu. *Website:* http://www.lakeforest.edu/.

LAKELAND UNIVERSITY

Plymouth, WI

CONTACT Ms. Patty Taylor, Director of Financial Aid, Lakeland University, PO Box 359, Sheboygan, WI 53082-0359, 920-565-1214 or toll-free 800-569-2166. *Fax:* 920-565-1470.
Website: http://www.lakeland.edu/.

LAKE SUPERIOR STATE UNIVERSITY

Sault Sainte Marie, MI

Tuition & fees (MI res): $12,190	Average undergraduate aid package: $11,732

ABOUT THE INSTITUTION State-supported, coed. ***Awards:*** certificates, associate, bachelor's, and master's degrees. 70 undergraduate majors. ***Total enrollment:*** 2,007. Undergraduates: 1,991. Freshmen: 387. Both federal and institutional methodology are used as a basis for awarding need-based institutional aid.

UNDERGRADUATE EXPENSES for 2019–2020 ***Application fee:*** $25. ***Tuition, state resident:*** full-time $12,000; part-time $500 per credit hour. ***Tuition, nonresident:*** full-time $12,000. ***Required fees:*** full-time $190. ***College room and board:*** $10,230.

FRESHMAN FINANCIAL AID (Fall 2018) 356 applied for aid; of those 78% were deemed to have need. 99% of freshmen with need received aid; of those 37% had need fully met. ***Average percent of need met:*** 57% (excluding resources awarded to replace EFC). ***Average financial aid package:*** $13,104 (excluding resources awarded to replace EFC). 21% of all full-time freshmen had no need and received non-need-based gift aid.

UNDERGRADUATE FINANCIAL AID (Fall 2018) 1,402 applied for aid; of those 82% were deemed to have need. 99% of undergraduates with need received aid; of those 30% had need fully met. ***Average percent of need met:*** 48% (excluding resources awarded to replace EFC). ***Average financial aid package:*** $11,732 (excluding resources awarded to replace EFC). 14% of all full-time undergraduates had no need and received non-need-based gift aid.

GIFT AID (NEED-BASED) ***Total amount:*** $11,299,813 (31% federal, 23% state, 41% institutional, 5% external sources). ***Receiving aid:*** Freshmen: 69% (264); all full-time undergraduates: 62% (1,027). ***Average award:*** Freshmen: $11,105; Undergraduates: $8974. ***Scholarships, grants, and awards:*** Federal Pell, FSEOG, state, private, college/university gift aid from institutional funds, Federal Nursing, Academic Competitiveness Grants, National SMART Grants.

GIFT AID (NON-NEED-BASED) ***Average award:*** Freshmen: $5017. Undergraduates: $4848.

LOANS ***Student loans:*** $8,745,384 (40% need-based, 60% non-need-based). 71% of past graduating class borrowed through all loan programs. *Average indebtedness per student:* $28,259. ***Average need-based loan:*** Freshmen: $2815. Undergraduates: $3963. ***Parent loans:*** $1,977,763 (100% non-need-based). ***Programs:*** Federal Direct (Subsidized and Unsubsidized Stafford, PLUS), Perkins, Federal Nursing, alternative loans.

WORK-STUDY ***Federal work-study:*** Total amount: $343,912; jobs available. ***State or other work-study/employment:*** Total amount: $928,761 (28% need-based, 72% non-need-based). Part-time jobs available.

ATHLETIC AWARDS Total amount: $1,393,282 (100% need-based).

APPLYING FOR FINANCIAL AID ***Required financial aid form:*** FAFSA. ***Financial aid deadline (priority):*** 3/1. ***Notification date:*** Continuous beginning 10/1. Students must reply by 5/1 or within 3 weeks of notification.

CONTACT Katelynn Coon, Director of Financial Aid, Lake Superior State University, 650 West Easterday Avenue, Sault Sainte Marie, MI 49783, 906-635-2650 or toll-free 888-800-LSSU Ext.2231. *Fax:* 906-635-6669. *E-mail:* kcoon2@lssu.edu.
Website: http://www.lssu.edu/.

LAKEVIEW COLLEGE OF NURSING

Danville, IL

Tuition & fees: N/R	Average undergraduate aid package: $22,420

ABOUT THE INSTITUTION Independent, coed, primarily women. ***Awards:*** bachelor's degrees. 1 undergraduate major. ***Total enrollment:*** 148. Undergraduates: 148. Federal methodology is used as a basis for awarding need-based institutional aid.

UNDERGRADUATE EXPENSES for 2020–2021 ***Application fee:*** $30. ***Tuition:*** part-time $450 per credit hour. ***Required fees:*** $65 per credit hour.

UNDERGRADUATE FINANCIAL AID (Fall 2019, est.) 367 applied for aid; of those 96% were deemed to have need. 99% of undergraduates with need received aid. ***Average financial aid package:*** $22,420 (excluding resources awarded to replace EFC).

GIFT AID (NEED-BASED) ***Total amount:*** $961,480 (76% federal, 24% state). ***Receiving aid:*** All full-time undergraduates: 37% (147). ***Average award:*** Undergraduates: $5800. ***Scholarships, grants, and awards:*** Federal Pell, state, private, college/university gift aid from institutional funds.

GIFT AID (NON-NEED-BASED) ***Total amount:*** $170,000 (53% institutional, 47% external sources). ***Receiving aid:*** Undergraduates: 11% (42). ***ROTC:*** Army cooperative, Air Force cooperative.

LOANS ***Student loans:*** $8,000,000 (31% need-based, 69% non-need-based). 52% of past graduating class borrowed through all loan programs. ***Average need-based loan:*** Undergraduates: $5500. ***Parent loans:*** $450,000 (100% non-need-based). ***Programs:*** Federal Direct (Subsidized and Unsubsidized Stafford, PLUS).

APPLYING FOR FINANCIAL AID ***Required financial aid forms:*** FAFSA, institution's own form. ***Financial aid deadline:*** 10/1 (priority: 3/1). ***Notification date:*** Continuous beginning 3/1. Students must reply by 10/1.

CONTACT Ms. Tammy Garza, Assistant Director of Financial Aid, Lakeview College of Nursing, 903 North Logan Avenue, Danville, IL 61832, 217-709-0928. *Fax:* 217-709-0956. *E-mail:* tgarza@lakeviewcol.edu.
Website: http://www.lakeviewcol.edu/.

LAMAR UNIVERSITY

Beaumont, TX

ABOUT THE INSTITUTION State-supported, coed. ***Awards:*** certificates, bachelor's, master's, and doctoral degrees. 52 undergraduate majors. ***Total enrollment:*** 15,460. Undergraduates: 8,697. Freshmen: 1,297.

GIFT AID (NEED-BASED) ***Scholarships, grants, and awards:*** Federal Pell, FSEOG, state, private, college/university gift aid from institutional funds, United Negro College Fund.

GIFT AID (NON-NEED-BASED) ***Scholarships, grants, and awards by category:*** *Academic interests/achievement:* general academic interests/achievements. *Creative arts/performance:* general creative arts/performance. *Special achievements/activities:* general special achievements/activities.

LOANS ***Programs:*** Federal Direct (Subsidized and Unsubsidized Stafford, PLUS), Perkins, Federal Nursing, state.

CONTACT Financial Aid Office, Lamar University, 4400 Martin Luther King Parkway, Beaumont, TX 77710, 409-880-7011.
Website: http://www.lamar.edu/.

LANCASTER BIBLE COLLEGE

Lancaster, PA

Tuition & fees: $26,070	Average undergraduate aid package: $21,306

ABOUT THE INSTITUTION Independent nondenominational, coed. ***Awards:*** certificates, associate, bachelor's, master's, and doctoral degrees. 16 undergraduate majors. ***Total enrollment:*** 2,122. Undergraduates: 1,688. Freshmen: 190. Federal methodology is used as a basis for awarding need-based institutional aid.

UNDERGRADUATE EXPENSES for 2019–2020 ***Application fee:*** $25. ***One-time required fee:*** $300. ***Comprehensive fee:*** $35,070 includes full-time tuition

($25,390), mandatory fees ($680), and room and board ($9000). Full-time tuition and fees vary according to degree level and student level. Room and board charges vary according to board plan. ***Part-time tuition:*** $840 per credit hour. ***Part-time fees:*** $35 per credit hour. Part-time tuition and fees vary according to course load and degree level.

FRESHMAN FINANCIAL AID (Fall 2019, est.) 157 applied for aid; of those 87% were deemed to have need. 100% of freshmen with need received aid; of those 30% had need fully met. ***Average percent of need met:*** 85% (excluding resources awarded to replace EFC). ***Average financial aid package:*** $24,047 (excluding resources awarded to replace EFC). 18% of all full-time freshmen had no need and received non-need-based gift aid.

UNDERGRADUATE FINANCIAL AID (Fall 2019, est.) 717 applied for aid; of those 88% were deemed to have need. 100% of undergraduates with need received aid; of those 33% had need fully met. ***Average percent of need met:*** 79% (excluding resources awarded to replace EFC). ***Average financial aid package:*** $21,306 (excluding resources awarded to replace EFC). 20% of all full-time undergraduates had no need and received non-need-based gift aid.

GIFT AID (NEED-BASED) ***Total amount:*** $8,292,409 (21% federal, 1% state, 74% institutional, 4% external sources). ***Receiving aid:*** Freshmen: 82% (137); all full-time undergraduates: 79% (627). ***Average award:*** Freshmen: $21,393; Undergraduates: $18,463. ***Scholarships, grants, and awards:*** Federal Pell, FSEOG, state, private, college/university gift aid from institutional funds, Office of Vocational Rehabilitation Awards, Blindness and Visual Services Awards.

GIFT AID (NON-NEED-BASED) ***Total amount:*** $2,026,353 (97% institutional, 3% external sources). ***Receiving aid:*** Freshmen: 81% (135). Undergraduates: 77% (613). ***Average award:*** Freshmen: $10,587. Undergraduates: $10,623. ***Scholarships, grants, and awards by category:*** *Academic interests/achievement:* 536 awards ($2,200,312 total): general academic interests/achievements. *Creative arts/performance:* 73 awards ($209,900 total): general creative arts/performance, music. *Special achievements/activities:* 61 awards ($74,350 total): general special achievements/activities, leadership, religious involvement. *Special characteristics:* 234 awards ($1,266,083 total): children and siblings of alumni, children of current students, children of faculty/staff, international students, relatives of clergy, siblings of current students. ***Tuition waivers:*** Full or partial for children of alumni, employees or children of employees, senior citizens.

LOANS ***Student loans:*** $6,048,515 (72% need-based, 28% non-need-based). 79% of past graduating class borrowed through all loan programs. *Average indebtedness per student:* $32,751. ***Average need-based loan:*** Freshmen: $3236. Undergraduates: $4239. ***Parent loans:*** $1,187,774 (61% need-based, 39% non-need-based). ***Programs:*** Federal Direct (Subsidized and Unsubsidized Stafford, PLUS), state, alternative loans.

WORK-STUDY ***Federal work-study:*** Total amount: $100,000; 96 jobs averaging $1500.

APPLYING FOR FINANCIAL AID ***Required financial aid forms:*** FAFSA, state aid form. ***Financial aid deadline (priority):*** 5/1. ***Notification date:*** Continuous beginning 11/1. Students must reply within 3 weeks of notification.

CONTACT Mrs. Karen Fox, Director of Financial Aid, Lancaster Bible College, 901 Eden Road, Lancaster, PA 17601, 717-560-8254 Ext. 5352 or toll-free 800-544-7335. *Fax:* 717-560-8216. *E-mail:* kfox@lbc.edu.
Website: http://www.lbc.edu/.

LANDER UNIVERSITY

Greenwood, SC

CONTACT Director of Financial Aid, Lander University, 320 Stanley Avenue, Greenwood, SC 29649, 864-388-8340 or toll-free 888-452-6337. *Fax:* 864-388-8811. *E-mail:* fhardin@lander.edu.
Website: http://www.lander.edu/.

LANE COLLEGE

Jackson, TN

CONTACT Mr. Tony Calhoun, Director of Financial Aid, Lane College, 545 Lane Avenue, Jackson, TN 38301, 731-426-7558 or toll-free 800-960-7533. *Fax:* 731-426-7652. *E-mail:* tcalhoun@lanecollege.edu.
Website: http://www.lanecollege.edu/.

LANGSTON UNIVERSITY

Langston, OK

CONTACT Sheila Mcgill, Director of Financial Aid, Langston University, Success Center, Langston, OK 73050, 405-466-3287. *Fax:* 405-466-2986. *E-mail:* smcgill@langston.edu.
Website: http://www.langston.edu/.

LA ROCHE UNIVERSITY

Pittsburgh, PA

Tuition & fees: $30,320	Average undergraduate aid package: $31,428

ABOUT THE INSTITUTION Independent Roman Catholic Church, coed. ***Awards:*** certificates, associate, bachelor's, master's, and doctoral degrees. 34 undergraduate majors. ***Total enrollment:*** 1,401. Undergraduates: 1,241. Freshmen: 205. Federal methodology is used as a basis for awarding need-based institutional aid.

UNDERGRADUATE EXPENSES for 2020–2021 ***Application fee:*** $50. ***Comprehensive fee:*** $42,590 includes full-time tuition ($29,470), mandatory fees ($850), and room and board ($12,270). ***College room only:*** $7770. Room and board charges vary according to board plan and housing facility. ***Part-time tuition:*** $747 per credit hour. ***Part-time fees:*** $40 per term.

FRESHMAN FINANCIAL AID (Fall 2019, est.) 171 applied for aid; of those 91% were deemed to have need. 100% of freshmen with need received aid; of those 35% had need fully met. ***Average percent of need met:*** 91% (excluding resources awarded to replace EFC). ***Average financial aid package:*** $34,141 (excluding resources awarded to replace EFC). 5% of all full-time freshmen had no need and received non-need-based gift aid.

UNDERGRADUATE FINANCIAL AID (Fall 2019, est.) 808 applied for aid; of those 93% were deemed to have need. 100% of undergraduates with need received aid; of those 43% had need fully met. ***Average percent of need met:*** 92% (excluding resources awarded to replace EFC). ***Average financial aid package:*** $31,428 (excluding resources awarded to replace EFC). 5% of all full-time undergraduates had no need and received non-need-based gift aid.

GIFT AID (NEED-BASED) ***Total amount:*** $5,677,751 (39% federal, 26% state, 35% institutional). ***Receiving aid:*** Freshmen: 41% (85); all full-time undergraduates: 50% (536). ***Average award:*** Freshmen: $6760; Undergraduates: $6374. ***Scholarships, grants, and awards:*** Federal Pell, FSEOG, state, private, college/university gift aid from institutional funds.

GIFT AID (NON-NEED-BASED) ***Total amount:*** $14,686,476 (96% institutional, 4% external sources). ***Receiving aid:*** Freshmen: 60% (123). Undergraduates: 70% (754). ***Average award:*** Freshmen: $20,368. Undergraduates: $20,928. ***Scholarships, grants, and awards by category:*** *Academic interests/achievement:* 846 awards ($11,170,625 total): general academic interests/achievements. *Creative arts/performance:* 18 awards ($315,000 total): dance. *Special characteristics:* 125 awards ($1,695,000 total): international students. ***Tuition waivers:*** Full or partial for employees or children of employees, senior citizens. ***ROTC:*** Army, Air Force.

LOANS ***Student loans:*** $8,756,882 (34% need-based, 66% non-need-based). 68% of past graduating class borrowed through all loan programs. *Average indebtedness per student:* $33,433. ***Average need-based loan:*** Freshmen: $2181. Undergraduates: $3368. ***Parent loans:*** $2,271,881 (100% non-need-based). ***Programs:*** Federal Direct (Subsidized and Unsubsidized Stafford, PLUS).

WORK-STUDY ***Federal work-study:*** Total amount: $209,178; 127 jobs averaging $1647.

APPLYING FOR FINANCIAL AID ***Required financial aid form:*** FAFSA. ***Financial aid deadline (priority):*** 5/1. ***Notification date:*** Continuous beginning 11/1. Students must reply within 2 weeks of notification.

CONTACT Mrs. Sharon E. Platt, Director of Financial Aid, La Roche University, 9000 Babcock Boulevard, Pittsburgh, PA 15237-5898, 412-536-1125 or toll-free 800-838-4LRC. *Fax:* 412-536-1072. *E-mail:* sharon.platt@laroche.edu.
Website: http://www.laroche.edu/.

LA SALLE UNIVERSITY

Philadelphia, PA

CONTACT Joseph Alaimo, Financial Aid Director, La Salle University, 1900 West Olney Avenue, Philadelphia, PA 19141-1199, 215-951-1070 or toll-free 800-328-1910. *Fax:* 215-951-5098.

Website: http://www.lasalle.edu/.

LASELL COLLEGE

Newton, MA

Tuition & fees: $39,000	Average undergraduate aid package: $23,383

ABOUT THE INSTITUTION Independent, coed. ***Awards:*** bachelor's and master's degrees. 38 undergraduate majors. ***Total enrollment:*** 2,090. Undergraduates: 1,639. Freshmen: 454. Federal methodology is used as a basis for awarding need-based institutional aid.

UNDERGRADUATE EXPENSES for 2020–2021 ***Comprehensive fee:*** $55,000 includes full-time tuition ($37,500), mandatory fees ($1500), and room and board ($16,000). Room and board charges vary according to housing facility. ***Part-time tuition:*** $1250 per credit hour. ***Part-time fees:*** $325 per term. Part-time tuition and fees vary according to course load.

FRESHMAN FINANCIAL AID (Fall 2019, est.) 401 applied for aid; of those 92% were deemed to have need. 100% of freshmen with need received aid; of those 28% had need fully met. ***Average percent of need met:*** 72% (excluding resources awarded to replace EFC). ***Average financial aid package:*** $34,041 (excluding resources awarded to replace EFC). 14% of all full-time freshmen had no need and received non-need-based gift aid.

UNDERGRADUATE FINANCIAL AID (Fall 2019, est.) 1,394 applied for aid; of those 92% were deemed to have need. 100% of undergraduates with need received aid; of those 24% had need fully met. ***Average percent of need met:*** 67% (excluding resources awarded to replace EFC). ***Average financial aid package:*** $23,383 (excluding resources awarded to replace EFC). 17% of all full-time undergraduates had no need and received non-need-based gift aid.

GIFT AID (NEED-BASED) ***Total amount:*** $28,577,050 (10% federal, 2% state, 87% institutional, 1% external sources). ***Receiving aid:*** Freshmen: 51% (232); all full-time undergraduates: 64% (1,028). ***Average award:*** Freshmen: $29,428; Undergraduates: $24,911. ***Scholarships, grants, and awards:*** Federal Pell, FSEOG, state, private, college/university gift aid from institutional funds.

GIFT AID (NON-NEED-BASED) ***Total amount:*** $20,555,744 (13% federal, 3% state, 81% institutional, 3% external sources). ***Receiving aid:*** Freshmen: 14% (62). Undergraduates: 17% (269). ***Average award:*** Freshmen: $25,031. Undergraduates: $16,992. ***Scholarships, grants, and awards by category:*** *Academic interests/achievement:* general academic interests/achievements. *Special achievements/activities:* general special achievements/activities. *Special characteristics:* children and siblings of alumni, children of faculty/staff, siblings of current students, veterans. ***Tuition waivers:*** Full or partial for children of alumni, employees or children of employees.

LOANS ***Student loans:*** $28,165,279 (49% need-based, 51% non-need-based). 94% of past graduating class borrowed through all loan programs. *Average indebtedness per student:* $40,580. ***Average need-based loan:*** Freshmen: $3367. Undergraduates: $4389. ***Parent loans:*** $4,769,345 (73% need-based, 27% non-need-based). ***Programs:*** Federal Direct (Subsidized and Unsubsidized Stafford, PLUS).

WORK-STUDY ***Federal work-study:*** Total amount: $1,700,800; jobs available.

APPLYING FOR FINANCIAL AID ***Required financial aid form:*** FAFSA. ***Financial aid deadline:*** Continuous. ***Notification date:*** Continuous beginning 12/1. Students must reply by 5/1.

CONTACT Thomas E. Hunt, Director of Student Financial Planning, Lasell College, 1844 Commonwealth Avenue, Newton, MA 02466-2709, 617-243-2227 or toll-free 888-LASELL-4. *Fax:* 617-243-2326. *E-mail:* finaid@lasell.edu.

Website: http://www.lasell.edu/.

LA SIERRA UNIVERSITY

Riverside, CA

Tuition & fees: $35,208	Average undergraduate aid package: $23,332

ABOUT THE INSTITUTION Independent Seventh-day Adventist, coed. ***Awards:*** certificates, bachelor's, master's, and doctoral degrees. 59 undergraduate majors. ***Total enrollment:*** 2,356. Undergraduates: 1,842. Freshmen: 399. Federal methodology is used as a basis for awarding need-based institutional aid.

UNDERGRADUATE EXPENSES for 2020–2021 ***Comprehensive fee:*** $48,453 includes full-time tuition ($34,218), mandatory fees ($990), and room and board ($13,245). ***College room only:*** $12,282. Full-time tuition and fees vary according to course load, location, and program. Room and board charges vary according to board plan. ***Part-time tuition:*** $951 per unit. Part-time tuition and fees vary according to course load, location, and program.

FRESHMAN FINANCIAL AID (Fall 2018) 334 applied for aid; of those 84% were deemed to have need. 100% of freshmen with need received aid; of those 26% had need fully met. ***Average percent of need met:*** 60% (excluding resources awarded to replace EFC). ***Average financial aid package:*** $25,842 (excluding resources awarded to replace EFC). 17% of all full-time freshmen had no need and received non-need-based gift aid.

UNDERGRADUATE FINANCIAL AID (Fall 2018) 1,509 applied for aid; of those 81% were deemed to have need. 100% of undergraduates with need received aid; of those 29% had need fully met. ***Average percent of need met:*** 63% (excluding resources awarded to replace EFC). ***Average financial aid package:*** $23,332 (excluding resources awarded to replace EFC). 19% of all full-time undergraduates had no need and received non-need-based gift aid.

GIFT AID (NEED-BASED) ***Total amount:*** $25,707,977 (18% federal, 21% state, 59% institutional, 2% external sources). ***Receiving aid:*** Freshmen: 75% (252); all full-time undergraduates: 79% (1,214). ***Average award:*** Freshmen: $20,028; Undergraduates: $16,768. ***Scholarships, grants, and awards:*** Federal Pell, FSEOG, state, private, college/university gift aid from institutional funds.

GIFT AID (NON-NEED-BASED) ***Total amount:*** $7,390,045 (99% institutional, 1% external sources). ***Receiving aid:*** Freshmen: 8% (28). Undergraduates: 6% (93). ***Average award:*** Freshmen: $13,549. Undergraduates: $10,741. ***Scholarships, grants, and awards by category:*** *Academic interests/achievement:* biological sciences, business, education, English, foreign languages, general academic interests/achievements, religion/biblical studies. *Creative arts/performance:* applied art and design, art/fine arts, music, theater/drama. *Special achievements/activities:* leadership. *Special characteristics:* adult students, children of faculty/staff, public servants, relatives of clergy, religious affiliation, siblings of current students. ***Tuition waivers:*** Full or partial for employees or children of employees, adult students.

LOANS ***Student loans:*** $8,117,686 (54% need-based, 46% non-need-based). ***Average need-based loan:*** Freshmen: $2682. Undergraduates: $3561. ***Parent loans:*** $4,767,945 (100% non-need-based). ***Programs:*** Federal Direct (Subsidized and Unsubsidized Stafford, PLUS), Perkins, state.

WORK-STUDY ***Federal work-study:*** Total amount: $1,560,713; 587 jobs averaging $2659.

ATHLETIC AWARDS Total amount: $300,975 (100% non-need-based).

APPLYING FOR FINANCIAL AID ***Required financial aid forms:*** FAFSA, state aid form. ***Financial aid deadline:*** 8/30 (priority: 3/2). ***Notification date:*** Continuous beginning 11/1. Students must reply by 9/1 or within 2 weeks of notification.

CONTACT Mrs. Elina Bascomb, Director of Financial Aid, La Sierra University, 4500 Riverwalk Parkway, Riverside, CA 92505, 951-785-2359 or toll-free 800-874-5587. *Fax:* 951-785-2942. *E-mail:* sfs@lasierra.edu.

Website: http://www.lasierra.edu/.

LAWRENCE TECHNOLOGICAL UNIVERSITY

Southfield, MI

Tuition & fees: $36,630 **Average undergraduate aid package: $25,476**

ABOUT THE INSTITUTION Independent, coed. ***Awards:*** certificates, associate, bachelor's, master's, and doctoral degrees. 41 undergraduate majors. ***Total enrollment:*** 2,848. Undergraduates: 2,136. Freshmen: 361. Federal methodology is used as a basis for awarding need-based institutional aid.

UNDERGRADUATE EXPENSES for 2020–2021 ***Application fee:*** $30. ***Comprehensive fee:*** $47,530 includes full-time tuition ($35,430), mandatory fees ($1200), and room and board ($10,900). ***College room only:*** $7300. Full-time tuition and fees vary according to course level, degree level, location, program, and student level. Room and board charges vary according to board plan and housing facility. ***Part-time tuition:*** $1181 per credit hour. Part-time tuition and fees vary according to course level, degree level, location, program, and student level.

FRESHMAN FINANCIAL AID (Fall 2018) 352 applied for aid; of those 77% were deemed to have need. 100% of freshmen with need received aid; of those 19% had need fully met. ***Average percent of need met:*** 71% (excluding resources awarded to replace EFC). ***Average financial aid package:*** $24,707 (excluding resources awarded to replace EFC). 21% of all full-time freshmen had no need and received non-need-based gift aid.

UNDERGRADUATE FINANCIAL AID (Fall 2018) 1,418 applied for aid; of those 74% were deemed to have need. 100% of undergraduates with need received aid; of those 16% had need fully met. ***Average percent of need met:*** 70% (excluding resources awarded to replace EFC). ***Average financial aid package:*** $25,476 (excluding resources awarded to replace EFC). 19% of all full-time undergraduates had no need and received non-need-based gift aid.

GIFT AID (NEED-BASED) ***Receiving aid:*** Freshmen: 74% (266); all full-time undergraduates: 62% (1,021). ***Average award:*** Freshmen: $16,176; Undergraduates: $15,285. ***Scholarships, grants, and awards:*** Federal Pell, FSEOG, state, private, college/university gift aid from institutional funds.

GIFT AID (NON-NEED-BASED) ***Receiving aid:*** Freshmen: 68% (242). Undergraduates: 52% (857). ***Average award:*** Freshmen: $14,846. Undergraduates: $15,496. ***Tuition waivers:*** Full or partial for employees or children of employees. ***ROTC:*** Army cooperative, Air Force cooperative.

LOANS ***Student loans:*** 69% of past graduating class borrowed through all loan programs. *Average indebtedness per student:* $32,735. ***Average need-based loan:*** Freshmen: $5603. Undergraduates: $6940. ***Programs:*** Federal Direct (Subsidized and Unsubsidized Stafford, PLUS), state, Private Alternative Loans.

WORK-STUDY Federal work-study jobs available. ***State or other work-study/employment:*** Part-time jobs available.

APPLYING FOR FINANCIAL AID ***Required financial aid form:*** FAFSA. ***Financial aid deadline:*** Continuous. ***Notification date:*** Continuous.

CONTACT Susie Poli Smith, Director of Financial Aid, Lawrence Technological University, 21000 West Ten Mile Road, Southfield, MI 48075-1058, 248-204-2126 or toll-free 800-225-5588. *Fax:* 248-204-2228. *E-mail:* spolismit@ltu.edu.
Website: http://www.ltu.edu/.

LAWRENCE UNIVERSITY

Appleton, WI

Tuition & fees: $49,122 **Average undergraduate aid package: $43,652**

ABOUT THE INSTITUTION Independent, coed. ***Awards:*** bachelor's degrees. 37 undergraduate majors. ***Total enrollment:*** 1,445. Undergraduates: 2,850. Freshmen: 386. Institutional methodology is used as a basis for awarding need-based institutional aid.

UNDERGRADUATE EXPENSES for 2019–2020 ***Comprehensive fee:*** $59,841 includes full-time tuition ($48,822), mandatory fees ($300), and room and board ($10,719). ***College room only:*** $5448.

FRESHMAN FINANCIAL AID (Fall 2019, est.) 302 applied for aid; of those 82% were deemed to have need. 100% of freshmen with need received aid; of those 49% had need fully met. ***Average percent of need met:*** 94% (excluding resources awarded to replace EFC). ***Average financial aid package:*** $45,058 (excluding resources awarded to replace EFC). 35% of all full-time freshmen had no need and received non-need-based gift aid.

UNDERGRADUATE FINANCIAL AID (Fall 2019, est.) 1,032 applied for aid; of those 84% were deemed to have need. 100% of undergraduates with need received aid; of those 50% had need fully met. ***Average percent of need met:*** 94% (excluding resources awarded to replace EFC). ***Average financial aid package:*** $43,652 (excluding resources awarded to replace EFC). 36% of all full-time undergraduates had no need and received non-need-based gift aid.

GIFT AID (NEED-BASED) ***Total amount:*** $32,096,542 (6% federal, 2% state, 89% institutional, 3% external sources). ***Receiving aid:*** Freshmen: 65% (247); all full-time undergraduates: 62% (867). ***Average award:*** Freshmen: $38,805; Undergraduates: $37,000. ***Scholarships, grants, and awards:*** Federal Pell, FSEOG, state, private, college/university gift aid from institutional funds.

GIFT AID (NON-NEED-BASED) ***Total amount:*** $14,916,494 (97% institutional, 3% external sources). ***Receiving aid:*** Freshmen: 14% (53). Undergraduates: 13% (183). ***Average award:*** Freshmen: $27,671. Undergraduates: $25,449. ***Scholarships, grants, and awards by category:*** *Academic interests/achievement:* general academic interests/achievements. *Creative arts/performance:* music, performing arts, theater/drama. *Special achievements/activities:* community service, general special achievements/activities, leadership. *Special characteristics:* children and siblings of alumni, general special characteristics, international students, siblings of current students, veterans. ***Tuition waivers:*** Full or partial for employees or children of employees.

LOANS ***Student loans:*** $5,613,301 (45% need-based, 55% non-need-based). 53% of past graduating class borrowed through all loan programs. *Average indebtedness per student:* $28,828. ***Average need-based loan:*** Freshmen: $3181. Undergraduates: $4135. ***Parent loans:*** $1,350,870 (100% non-need-based). ***Programs:*** Federal Direct (Subsidized and Unsubsidized Stafford, PLUS), Private Education Loans.

WORK-STUDY ***Federal work-study:*** Total amount: $1,229,784; jobs available. ***State or other work-study/employment:*** Total amount: $513,950 (100% non-need-based). Part-time jobs available.

APPLYING FOR FINANCIAL AID ***Required financial aid forms:*** FAFSA, CSS Financial Aid PROFILE, noncustodial (divorced/separated) parent's statement, Parent Federal Tax Return and Parent W-2 Form(s). ***Financial aid deadline (priority):*** 12/1. ***Notification date:*** Continuous beginning 12/1. Students must reply by 5/1.

CONTACT Mrs. Sara Beth Holman, Director of Financial Aid, Lawrence University, 711 East Boldt Way, SPC 32, Appleton, WI 54911, 920-832-6583 or toll-free 800-227-0982. *Fax:* 920-832-6582. *E-mail:* sara.b.holman@lawrence.edu.
Website: http://www.lawrence.edu/.

LEBANON VALLEY COLLEGE

Annville, PA

Tuition & fees: $44,910 **Average undergraduate aid package: $35,421**

ABOUT THE INSTITUTION Independent United Methodist, coed. ***Awards:*** certificates, bachelor's, master's, and doctoral degrees. 43 undergraduate majors. ***Total enrollment:*** 1,916. Undergraduates: 1,744. Freshmen: 473. Federal methodology is used as a basis for awarding need-based institutional aid.

UNDERGRADUATE EXPENSES for 2019–2020 ***Comprehensive fee:*** $57,110 includes full-time tuition ($43,650), mandatory fees ($1260), and room and board ($12,200). ***College room only:*** $5890.

FRESHMAN FINANCIAL AID (Fall 2019, est.) 469 applied for aid; of those 88% were deemed to have need. 100% of freshmen with need received aid; of those 26% had need fully met. ***Average percent of need met:*** 82% (excluding resources awarded to replace EFC). ***Average financial aid package:*** $36,250 (excluding resources awarded to replace EFC). 12% of all full-time freshmen had no need and received non-need-based gift aid.

UNDERGRADUATE FINANCIAL AID (Fall 2019, est.) 1,555 applied for aid; of those 88% were deemed to have need. 100% of undergraduates with need received aid; of those 26% had need fully met. ***Average percent of need met:*** 82% (excluding resources awarded to replace EFC). ***Average financial aid package:*** $35,421 (excluding resources awarded to replace EFC). 14% of all full-time undergraduates had no need and received non-need-based gift aid.

GIFT AID (NEED-BASED) ***Total amount:*** $38,907,436 (5% federal, 5% state, 90% institutional). ***Receiving aid:*** Freshmen: 85% (409); all full-time undergraduates: 83% (1,358). ***Average award:*** Freshmen: $30,737; Undergraduates: $29,436. ***Scholarships, grants, and awards:*** Federal Pell, FSEOG, state, private, college/university gift aid from institutional funds.

GIFT AID (NON-NEED-BASED) ***Total amount:*** $7,960,696 (89% institutional, 11% external sources). ***Receiving aid:*** Freshmen: 10% (46). Undergraduates: 11% (176). ***Average award:*** Freshmen: $24,333. Undergraduates: $22,627. ***Scholarships, grants, and awards by category:*** *Academic interests/achievement:* biological sciences, English, general academic interests/achievements, mathematics, physical sciences, religion/biblical studies, social sciences. *Creative arts/performance:* creative writing, music. *Special achievements/activities:* general special achievements/activities. *Special characteristics:* children and siblings of alumni, children of faculty/staff, general special characteristics, international students, veterans.

LOANS ***Student loans:*** $15,579,411 (30% need-based, 70% non-need-based). 81% of past graduating class borrowed through all loan programs. *Average indebtedness per student:* $42,880. ***Average need-based loan:*** Freshmen: $2831. Undergraduates: $4032. ***Parent loans:*** $5,584,051 (100% non-need-based). ***Programs:*** Federal Direct (Subsidized and Unsubsidized Stafford, PLUS).

WORK-STUDY ***Federal work-study:*** Total amount: $1,539,102; jobs available.

APPLYING FOR FINANCIAL AID ***Required financial aid form:*** FAFSA. ***Financial aid deadline (priority):*** 2/15. ***Notification date:*** Continuous beginning 12/10. Students must reply by 5/1 or within 2 weeks of notification.

CONTACT Mrs. Kendra M. Feigert, Director of Financial Aid, Lebanon Valley College, 101 North College Avenue, Annville, PA 17003, 717-867-6126 or toll-free 866-LVC-4ADM. *Fax:* 717-867-6027. *E-mail:* feigert@lvc.edu.
Website: http://www.lvc.edu/.

LEES-MCRAE COLLEGE

Banner Elk, NC

Tuition & fees: $27,521 | **Average undergraduate aid package: $23,399**

ABOUT THE INSTITUTION Independent Presbyterian Church (U.S.A.), coed. ***Awards:*** bachelor's degrees. 23 undergraduate majors. ***Total enrollment:*** 966. Undergraduates: 964. Freshmen: 212. Both federal and institutional methodology are used as a basis for awarding need-based institutional aid.

UNDERGRADUATE EXPENSES for 2019–2020 ***Application fee:*** $35. ***Comprehensive fee:*** $38,391 includes full-time tuition ($25,625), mandatory fees ($1896), and room and board ($10,870). ***College room only:*** $5320. ***Part-time tuition:*** $710 per credit hour. **Payment plan:** Guaranteed tuition.

FRESHMAN FINANCIAL AID (Fall 2018) 202 applied for aid; of those 89% were deemed to have need. 100% of freshmen with need received aid; of those 1% had need fully met. ***Average percent of need met:*** 72% (excluding resources awarded to replace EFC). ***Average financial aid package:*** $25,136 (excluding resources awarded to replace EFC). 9% of all full-time freshmen had no need and received non-need-based gift aid.

UNDERGRADUATE FINANCIAL AID (Fall 2018) 760 applied for aid; of those 94% were deemed to have need. 100% of undergraduates with need received aid; of those 1% had need fully met. ***Average percent of need met:*** 72% (excluding resources awarded to replace EFC). ***Average financial aid package:*** $23,399 (excluding resources awarded to replace EFC). 7% of all full-time undergraduates had no need and received non-need-based gift aid.

GIFT AID (NEED-BASED) ***Total amount:*** $12,319,996 (18% federal, 14% state, 66% institutional, 2% external sources). ***Receiving aid:*** Freshmen: 81% (179); all full-time undergraduates: 78% (711). ***Average award:*** Freshmen: $7991; Undergraduates: $6473. ***Scholarships, grants, and awards:*** Federal Pell, FSEOG, state, private, college/university gift aid from institutional funds.

GIFT AID (NON-NEED-BASED) ***Receiving aid:*** Freshmen: 81% (179). Undergraduates: 53% (485). ***Average award:*** Freshmen: $10,650. Undergraduates: $9688. ***Scholarships, grants, and awards by category:*** *Academic interests/achievement:* general academic interests/achievements. *Creative arts/performance:* performing arts, theater/drama. *Special achievements/activities:* general special achievements/activities. *Special characteristics:* children and siblings of alumni, children of faculty/staff, children with a deceased or disabled parent, local/state students, religious affiliation, siblings of current students, veterans.

LOANS ***Student loans:*** $4,674,167 (100% need-based). ***Average need-based loan:*** Freshmen: $3500. Undergraduates: $3694. ***Parent loans:*** $1,780,539 (100% need-based). ***Programs:*** Federal Direct (Subsidized and Unsubsidized Stafford, PLUS), state.

WORK-STUDY ***Federal work-study:*** Total amount: $130,000; jobs available. ***State or other work-study/employment:*** Total amount: $8000 (100% need-based). Part-time jobs available.

ATHLETIC AWARDS Total amount: $2,091,161 (100% need-based).

APPLYING FOR FINANCIAL AID ***Required financial aid forms:*** FAFSA, state aid form. ***Financial aid deadline (priority):*** 3/31. ***Notification date:*** Continuous beginning 12/15. Students must reply within 2 weeks of notification.

CONTACT Cathy Shell, Director of Financial Aid, Lees-McRae College, PO Box 128, Banner Elk, NC 28604-0128, 828-898-8740 or toll-free 800-280-4562. *Fax:* 828-898-8746. *E-mail:* shell@lmc.edu.
Website: http://www.lmc.edu/.

LEE UNIVERSITY

Cleveland, TN

Tuition & fees: $19,540 | **Average undergraduate aid package: $13,991**

ABOUT THE INSTITUTION Independent Church of God, coed. ***Awards:*** certificates, bachelor's, master's, and doctoral degrees. 80 undergraduate majors. ***Total enrollment:*** 5,189. Undergraduates: 4,686. Freshmen: 792. Federal methodology is used as a basis for awarding need-based institutional aid.

UNDERGRADUATE EXPENSES for 2020–2021 ***Application fee:*** $25. ***Comprehensive fee:*** $27,800 includes full-time tuition ($18,840), mandatory fees ($700), and room and board ($8260). ***College room only:*** $4270. Room and board charges vary according to board plan and housing facility. ***Part-time tuition:*** $785 per credit hour. ***Part-time fees:*** $60 per term.

FRESHMAN FINANCIAL AID (Fall 2019, est.) 732 applied for aid; of those 78% were deemed to have need. 99% of freshmen with need received aid; of those 25% had need fully met. ***Average percent of need met:*** 67% (excluding resources awarded to replace EFC). ***Average financial aid package:*** $15,360 (excluding resources awarded to replace EFC). 20% of all full-time freshmen had no need and received non-need-based gift aid.

UNDERGRADUATE FINANCIAL AID (Fall 2019, est.) 3,278 applied for aid; of those 80% were deemed to have need. 99% of undergraduates with need received aid; of those 17% had need fully met. ***Average percent of need met:*** 49% (excluding resources awarded to replace EFC). ***Average financial aid package:*** $13,991 (excluding resources awarded to replace EFC). 17% of all full-time undergraduates had no need and received non-need-based gift aid.

GIFT AID (NEED-BASED) ***Total amount:*** $26,221,407 (29% federal, 18% state, 49% institutional, 4% external sources). ***Receiving aid:*** Freshmen: 70% (547); all full-time undergraduates: 66% (2,417). ***Average award:*** Freshmen: $13,854; Undergraduates: $11,684. ***Scholarships, grants, and awards:*** Federal Pell, FSEOG, state, private, college/university gift aid from institutional funds.

GIFT AID (NON-NEED-BASED) ***Total amount:*** $8,663,093 (24% state, 71% institutional, 5% external sources). ***Receiving aid:*** Freshmen: 15% (121). Undergraduates: 9% (345). ***Average award:*** Freshmen: $10,293. Undergraduates: $8073. ***Scholarships, grants, and awards by category:*** *Academic interests/achievement:* biological sciences, business, communication, education, general academic interests/achievements, religion/biblical studies. *Creative arts/performance:* music, theater/drama. *Special achievements/activities:* cheerleading/drum major, leadership, religious involvement. *Special characteristics:* children of faculty/staff, local/state students, siblings of current students, spouses of current students. ***Tuition waivers:*** Full or partial for employees or children of employees.

LOANS ***Student loans:*** $21,685,163 (71% need-based, 29% non-need-based). 61% of past graduating class borrowed through all loan programs. *Average indebtedness per student:* $30,846. ***Average need-based loan:*** Freshmen: $3279. Undergraduates: $4215. ***Parent loans:*** $5,648,174 (58% need-based, 42% non-need-based). ***Programs:*** Federal Direct (Subsidized and Unsubsidized Stafford, PLUS), Perkins, Federal Nursing.

WORK-STUDY ***Federal work-study:*** Total amount: $446,165; 312 jobs averaging $1377. ***State or other work-study/employment:*** Total amount: $6615 (40% need-based, 60% non-need-based). 774 part-time jobs averaging $1757.

ATHLETIC AWARDS Total amount: $2,866,516 (44% need-based, 56% non-need-based).

APPLYING FOR FINANCIAL AID ***Required financial aid form:*** FAFSA. ***Financial aid deadline (priority):*** 2/1. ***Notification date:*** Continuous beginning 2/1.

CONTACT Mrs. Marian Dill, Director of Student Financial Aid, Lee University, 1120 North Ocoee St, Cleveland, TN 37311, 423-614-8300 or toll-free 800-533-9930. *Fax:* 423-614-8308. *E-mail:* finaid@leeuniversity.edu.

Website: http://www.leeuniversity.edu/.

LEHIGH UNIVERSITY

Bethlehem, PA

Tuition & fees: $57,450	Average undergraduate aid package: $53,951

ABOUT THE INSTITUTION Independent, coed. ***Awards:*** certificates, bachelor's, master's, and doctoral degrees. 67 undergraduate majors. ***Total enrollment:*** 6,953. Undergraduates: 5,178. Freshmen: 1,406. Both federal and institutional methodology are used as a basis for awarding need-based institutional aid.

UNDERGRADUATE EXPENSES for 2020–2021 ***Application fee:*** $70. ***Comprehensive fee:*** $72,190 includes full-time tuition ($56,980), mandatory fees ($470), and room and board ($14,740). ***College room only:*** $8660. Room and board charges vary according to board plan and housing facility. ***Part-time tuition:*** $2375 per credit hour. ***Payment plan:*** Tuition prepayment.

FRESHMAN FINANCIAL AID (Fall 2019, est.) 938 applied for aid; of those 65% were deemed to have need. 100% of freshmen with need received aid; of those 88% had need fully met. ***Average percent of need met:*** 98% (excluding resources awarded to replace EFC). ***Average financial aid package:*** $53,876 (excluding resources awarded to replace EFC). 4% of all full-time freshmen had no need and received non-need-based gift aid.

UNDERGRADUATE FINANCIAL AID (Fall 2019, est.) 2,860 applied for aid; of those 73% were deemed to have need. 100% of undergraduates with need received aid; of those 90% had need fully met. ***Average percent of need met:*** 99% (excluding resources awarded to replace EFC). ***Average financial aid package:*** $53,951 (excluding resources awarded to replace EFC). 5% of all full-time undergraduates had no need and received non-need-based gift aid.

GIFT AID (NEED-BASED) ***Receiving aid:*** Freshmen: 43% (600); all full-time undergraduates: 41% (2,066). ***Average award:*** Freshmen: $48,666; Undergraduates: $47,745. ***Scholarships, grants, and awards:*** Federal Pell, state, private, college/university gift aid from institutional funds.

GIFT AID (NON-NEED-BASED) ***Receiving aid:*** Freshmen: 7% (92). Undergraduates: 7% (374). ***Average award:*** Freshmen: $9909. Undergraduates: $11,202. ***Scholarships, grants, and awards by category:*** *Academic interests/achievement:* 129 awards ($1,033,670 total): business, communication, engineering/technologies, general academic interests/achievements, international studies, military science. *Creative arts/performance:* 66 awards ($69,120 total): general creative arts/performance, journalism/publications, music, performing arts, theater/drama. *Special achievements/activities:* 15 awards ($31,500 total): general special achievements/activities. *Special characteristics:* 95 awards ($5,060,136 total): children of faculty/staff, members of minority groups. ***Tuition waivers:*** Full or partial for employees or children of employees. ***ROTC:*** Army.

LOANS ***Student loans:*** 50% of past graduating class borrowed through all loan programs. *Average indebtedness per student:* $39,609. ***Average need-based loan:*** Freshmen: $3431. Undergraduates: $4017. ***Programs:*** Federal Direct (Subsidized and Unsubsidized Stafford, PLUS), college/university.

WORK-STUDY ***Federal work-study:*** 1,356 jobs averaging $1943. ***State or other work-study/employment:*** 91 part-time jobs averaging $1761.

APPLYING FOR FINANCIAL AID ***Required financial aid forms:*** FAFSA, CSS Financial Aid PROFILE, noncustodial (divorced/separated) parent's statement. ***Notification date:*** Students must reply within 3 weeks of notification.

CONTACT Jennifer Mertz, Director of Financial Aid, Lehigh University, 27 Memorial Drive West, Bethlehem, PA 18015-3094, 610-758-3181. *Fax:* 610-758-6211. *E-mail:* jlm207@lehigh.edu.

Website: http://www.lehigh.edu/.

LEHMAN COLLEGE OF THE CITY UNIVERSITY OF NEW YORK

Bronx, NY

CONTACT Financial Aid Office, Lehman College of the City University of New York, 250 Bedford Park Boulevard West, Bronx, NY 10468-1589, 718-960-8000 or toll-free 877-LEHMAN1.

Website: http://www.lehman.cuny.edu/.

LE MOYNE COLLEGE

Syracuse, NY

Tuition & fees: $35,910	Average undergraduate aid package: $27,819

ABOUT THE INSTITUTION Independent Roman Catholic (Jesuit), coed. ***Awards:*** certificates, bachelor's, master's, and doctoral degrees. 54 undergraduate majors. ***Total enrollment:*** 3,326. Undergraduates: 2,765. Freshmen: 654. Both federal and institutional methodology are used as a basis for awarding need-based institutional aid.

UNDERGRADUATE EXPENSES for 2020–2021 ***Comprehensive fee:*** $50,380 includes full-time tuition ($34,910), mandatory fees ($1000), and room and board ($14,470). ***College room only:*** $9020. Room and board charges vary according to board plan and housing facility. ***Part-time tuition:*** $732 per credit hour. ***Part-time fees:*** $70 per year. Part-time tuition and fees vary according to class time and course load.

FRESHMAN FINANCIAL AID (Fall 2018) 625 applied for aid; of those 89% were deemed to have need. 100% of freshmen with need received aid; of those 28% had need fully met. ***Average percent of need met:*** 81% (excluding resources awarded to replace EFC). ***Average financial aid package:*** $28,810 (excluding resources awarded to replace EFC). 13% of all full-time freshmen had no need and received non-need-based gift aid.

UNDERGRADUATE FINANCIAL AID (Fall 2018) 2,143 applied for aid; of those 91% were deemed to have need. 100% of undergraduates with need received aid; of those 28% had need fully met. ***Average percent of need met:*** 79% (excluding resources awarded to replace EFC). ***Average financial aid package:*** $27,819 (excluding resources awarded to replace EFC). 13% of all full-time undergraduates had no need and received non-need-based gift aid.

GIFT AID (NEED-BASED) ***Receiving aid:*** Freshmen: 85% (555); all full-time undergraduates: 83% (1,943). ***Average award:*** Freshmen: $24,374; Undergraduates: $22,964. ***Scholarships, grants, and awards:*** Federal Pell, FSEOG, state, private, college/university gift aid from institutional funds.

GIFT AID (NON-NEED-BASED) ***Receiving aid:*** Freshmen: 18% (117). Undergraduates: 16% (372). ***Average award:*** Freshmen: $19,643. Undergraduates: $16,775. ***Scholarships, grants, and awards by category:*** *Academic interests/achievement:* 1,013 awards ($18,383,822 total): general academic interests/achievements. *Creative arts/performance:* 24 awards ($9360 total): music. *Special achievements/activities:* 199 awards ($2,379,250 total): leadership. *Special characteristics:* 435 awards ($2,058,201 total): children and siblings of alumni, members of minority groups, veterans. ***Tuition waivers:*** Full or partial for employees or children of employees. ***ROTC:*** Army cooperative, Air Force cooperative.

LOANS ***Student loans:*** 88% of past graduating class borrowed through all loan programs. *Average indebtedness per student:* $40,522. ***Average need-based loan:*** Freshmen: $3295. Undergraduates: $4229. ***Programs:*** Federal Direct (Subsidized and Unsubsidized Stafford, PLUS).

WORK-STUDY ***Federal work-study:*** 399 jobs averaging $1450. ***State or other work-study/employment:*** 368 part-time jobs averaging $1650.

APPLYING FOR FINANCIAL AID ***Required financial aid forms:*** FAFSA, state aid form. ***Notification date:*** Students must reply within 2 weeks of notification.

CONTACT Mrs. Sharon J. Halpin, Director of Financial Aid, Le Moyne College, 1419 Salt Springs Road, Syracuse, NY 13214-1301, 315-445-4400 or toll-free 800-333-4733. *Fax:* 315-445-4182. *E-mail:* halpins@lemoyne.edu.

Website: http://www.lemoyne.edu/.

LEMOYNE-OWEN COLLEGE

Memphis, TN

ABOUT THE INSTITUTION Independent United Church of Christ, coed. ***Awards:*** certificates and bachelor's degrees. 25 undergraduate majors.

GIFT AID (NEED-BASED) ***Scholarships, grants, and awards:*** Federal Pell, FSEOG, state, private, college/university gift aid from institutional funds, United Negro College Fund.

GIFT AID (NON-NEED-BASED) ***Scholarships, grants, and awards by category:*** *Academic interests/achievement:* general academic interests/achievements. *Creative arts/performance:* journalism/publications, music. *Special characteristics:* children of faculty/staff.

LOANS ***Programs:*** Federal Direct (Subsidized and Unsubsidized Stafford, PLUS).

CONTACT Financial Aid Office, LeMoyne-Owen College, 807 Walker Avenue, Memphis, TN 38126-6595, 901-435-1000 or toll-free 800-737-7778.
Website: http://www.loc.edu/.

LENOIR-RHYNE UNIVERSITY

Hickory, NC

Tuition & fees: N/R	Average undergraduate aid package: $31,268

ABOUT THE INSTITUTION Independent Lutheran, coed. ***Awards:*** bachelor's, master's, and doctoral degrees. 50 undergraduate majors. ***Total enrollment:*** 2,742. Undergraduates: 1,846. Freshmen: 481. Federal methodology is used as a basis for awarding need-based institutional aid.

UNDERGRADUATE EXPENSES for 2020–2021 ***Application fee:*** $35. ***Tuition:*** part-time $1600 per credit hour.

FRESHMAN FINANCIAL AID (Fall 2018) 483 applied for aid; of those 93% were deemed to have need. 100% of freshmen with need received aid; of those 19% had need fully met. ***Average percent of need met:*** 78% (excluding resources awarded to replace EFC). ***Average financial aid package:*** $31,796 (excluding resources awarded to replace EFC). 12% of all full-time freshmen had no need and received non-need-based gift aid.

UNDERGRADUATE FINANCIAL AID (Fall 2018) 1,398 applied for aid; of those 95% were deemed to have need. 100% of undergraduates with need received aid; of those 17% had need fully met. ***Average percent of need met:*** 75% (excluding resources awarded to replace EFC). ***Average financial aid package:*** $31,268 (excluding resources awarded to replace EFC). 14% of all full-time undergraduates had no need and received non-need-based gift aid.

GIFT AID (NEED-BASED) ***Total amount:*** $32,261,864 (11% federal, 13% state, 74% institutional, 2% external sources). ***Receiving aid:*** Freshmen: 88% (451); all full-time undergraduates: 85% (1,310). ***Average award:*** Freshmen: $28,436; Undergraduates: $27,022. ***Scholarships, grants, and awards:*** Federal Pell, FSEOG, state, private, college/university gift aid from institutional funds.

GIFT AID (NON-NEED-BASED) ***Total amount:*** $5,932,501 (96% institutional, 4% external sources). ***Receiving aid:*** Freshmen: 15% (76). Undergraduates: 12% (180). ***Average award:*** Freshmen: $22,584. Undergraduates: $20,654. ***Scholarships, grants, and awards by category:*** *Academic interests/achievement:* general academic interests/achievements. *Creative arts/performance:* music. *Special achievements/activities:* cheerleading/drum major, leadership. *Special characteristics:* children and siblings of alumni, children of faculty/staff, ethnic background, local/state students, members of minority groups, relatives of clergy, religious affiliation, siblings of current students. ***Tuition waivers:*** Full or partial for employees or children of employees, senior citizens.

LOANS ***Student loans:*** $8,733,281 (84% need-based, 16% non-need-based). 87% of past graduating class borrowed through all loan programs. *Average indebtedness per student:* $32,622. ***Average need-based loan:*** Freshmen: $3079. Undergraduates: $4207. ***Parent loans:*** $4,982,304 (65% need-based, 35% non-need-based). ***Programs:*** Federal Direct (Subsidized and Unsubsidized Stafford, PLUS), Perkins, state.

WORK-STUDY ***Federal work-study:*** Total amount: $1,289,806; jobs available. ***State or other work-study/employment:*** Part-time jobs available.

ATHLETIC AWARDS Total amount: $5,640,612 (58% need-based, 42% non-need-based).

APPLYING FOR FINANCIAL AID ***Required financial aid form:*** FAFSA. ***Financial aid deadline:*** Continuous. ***Notification date:*** Continuous. Students must reply by 5/1 or within 3 weeks of notification.

CONTACT Financial Aid Office, Lenoir-Rhyne University, 625 7th Avenue NE, Hickory, NC 28601, 828-328-1741 or toll-free 800-277-5721.
Website: http://www.lr.edu/.

LESLEY UNIVERSITY

Cambridge, MA

Tuition & fees: $29,450	Average undergraduate aid package: $17,787

ABOUT THE INSTITUTION Independent, coed, primarily women. ***Awards:*** certificates, associate, bachelor's, master's, and doctoral degrees. 22 undergraduate majors. ***Total enrollment:*** 4,510. Undergraduates: 2,127. Freshmen: 320. Federal methodology is used as a basis for awarding need-based institutional aid.

UNDERGRADUATE EXPENSES for 2020–2021 ***Comprehensive fee:*** $47,080 includes full-time tuition ($29,200), mandatory fees ($250), and room and board ($17,630). ***College room only:*** $10,060. ***Part-time tuition:*** $973 per credit hour.

FRESHMAN FINANCIAL AID (Fall 2018) 213 applied for aid; of those 115% were deemed to have need. 100% of freshmen with need received aid; of those 9% had need fully met. ***Average percent of need met:*** 60% (excluding resources awarded to replace EFC). ***Average financial aid package:*** $19,036 (excluding resources awarded to replace EFC). 23% of all full-time freshmen had no need and received non-need-based gift aid.

UNDERGRADUATE FINANCIAL AID (Fall 2018) 1,243 applied for aid; of those 86% were deemed to have need. 100% of undergraduates with need received aid; of those 6% had need fully met. ***Average percent of need met:*** 60% (excluding resources awarded to replace EFC). ***Average financial aid package:*** $17,787 (excluding resources awarded to replace EFC). 31% of all full-time undergraduates had no need and received non-need-based gift aid.

GIFT AID (NEED-BASED) ***Total amount:*** $15,699,359 (21% federal, 3% state, 73% institutional, 3% external sources). ***Receiving aid:*** Freshmen: 77% (246); all full-time undergraduates: 64% (1,023). ***Average award:*** Freshmen: $14,786; Undergraduates: $13,789. ***Scholarships, grants, and awards:*** Federal Pell, FSEOG, state, private, college/university gift aid from institutional funds.

GIFT AID (NON-NEED-BASED) ***Total amount:*** $5,897,694 (100% institutional). ***Receiving aid:*** Freshmen: 29% (93). Undergraduates: 4% (64). ***Average award:*** Freshmen: $10,731. Undergraduates: $10,716. ***Scholarships, grants, and awards by category:*** *Special achievements/activities:* general special achievements/activities. *Special characteristics:* ethnic background.

LOANS ***Student loans:*** $11,310,970 (49% need-based, 51% non-need-based). 87% of past graduating class borrowed through all loan programs. *Average indebtedness per student:* $22,371. ***Average need-based loan:*** Freshmen: $3568. Undergraduates: $3668. ***Parent loans:*** $4,736,270 (100% need-based). ***Programs:*** Federal Direct (Subsidized and Unsubsidized Stafford, PLUS).

WORK-STUDY ***Federal work-study:*** Total amount: $500,000; jobs available. ***State or other work-study/employment:*** Part-time jobs available.

APPLYING FOR FINANCIAL AID ***Required financial aid form:*** FAFSA. ***Financial aid deadline (priority):*** 2/15. ***Notification date:*** Continuous.

CONTACT Scott A. Jewell, Director of Student Financial Services, Lesley University, 29 Everett Street, Cambridge, MA 02138-2790, 617-349-8714 or toll-free 800-999-1959 Ext.8800. *Fax:* 617-349-8667. *E-mail:* sjewell@lesley.edu.
Website: http://www.lesley.edu/.

LETOURNEAU UNIVERSITY

Longview, TX

Tuition & fees: $32,490	Average undergraduate aid package: $23,645

ABOUT THE INSTITUTION Independent nondenominational, coed. ***Awards:*** certificates, associate, bachelor's, and master's degrees. 66 undergraduate majors.

Total enrollment: 3,150. Undergraduates: 2,862. Freshmen: 362. Both federal and institutional methodology are used as a basis for awarding need-based institutional aid.

UNDERGRADUATE EXPENSES for 2020–2021 *Comprehensive fee:* $42,560 includes full-time tuition ($31,740), mandatory fees ($750), and room and board ($10,070).

FRESHMAN FINANCIAL AID (Fall 2019, est.) 291 applied for aid; of those 84% were deemed to have need. 100% of freshmen with need received aid; of those 23% had need fully met. ***Average percent of need met:*** 78% (excluding resources awarded to replace EFC). ***Average financial aid package:*** $25,542 (excluding resources awarded to replace EFC). 28% of all full-time freshmen had no need and received non-need-based gift aid.

UNDERGRADUATE FINANCIAL AID (Fall 2019, est.) 999 applied for aid; of those 89% were deemed to have need. 100% of undergraduates with need received aid; of those 15% had need fully met. ***Average percent of need met:*** 70% (excluding resources awarded to replace EFC). ***Average financial aid package:*** $23,645 (excluding resources awarded to replace EFC). 28% of all full-time undergraduates had no need and received non-need-based gift aid.

GIFT AID (NEED-BASED) *Total amount:* $18,597,787 (17% federal, 10% state, 70% institutional, 3% external sources). ***Receiving aid:*** Freshmen: 72% (244); all full-time undergraduates: 67% (869). ***Average award:*** Freshmen: $20,971; Undergraduates: $18,618. ***Scholarships, grants, and awards:*** Federal Pell, FSEOG, state, private, college/university gift aid from institutional funds.

GIFT AID (NON-NEED-BASED) *Total amount:* $4,363,959 (2% federal, 94% institutional, 4% external sources). ***Receiving aid:*** Freshmen: 12% (40). Undergraduates: 7% (87). ***Average award:*** Freshmen: $15,490. Undergraduates: $15,056.

LOANS *Student loans:* $13,451,879 (77% need-based, 23% non-need-based). 70% of past graduating class borrowed through all loan programs. *Average indebtedness per student:* $36,103. ***Average need-based loan:*** Freshmen: $3391. Undergraduates: $4376. ***Parent loans:*** $2,152,519 (51% need-based, 49% non-need-based). ***Programs:*** Federal Direct (Subsidized and Unsubsidized Stafford, PLUS), state, private loans.

WORK-STUDY *Federal work-study:* Total amount: $329,292; jobs available. ***State or other work-study/employment:*** Total amount: $13,272 (100% need-based). Part-time jobs available.

APPLYING FOR FINANCIAL AID *Required financial aid form:* FAFSA. ***Financial aid deadline:*** 8/1 (priority: 11/1). ***Notification date:*** Continuous beginning 11/30. Students must reply within 2 weeks of notification.

CONTACT Financial Aid Office, LeTourneau University, PO Box 7001, Longview, TX 75607-7001, 903-233-3000 or toll-free 800-759-8811.
Website: http://www.letu.edu/.

LEWIS & CLARK COLLEGE

Portland, OR

Tuition & fees: $52,780	Average undergraduate aid package: $44,874

ABOUT THE INSTITUTION Independent, coed. ***Awards:*** certificates, bachelor's, master's, and doctoral degrees. 30 undergraduate majors. ***Total enrollment:*** 3,250. Undergraduates: 1,965. Freshmen: 507. Both federal and institutional methodology are used as a basis for awarding need-based institutional aid.

UNDERGRADUATE EXPENSES for 2019–2020 *Comprehensive fee:* $65,788 includes full-time tuition ($52,346), mandatory fees ($434), and room and board ($13,008). ***College room only:*** $7418. Room and board charges vary according to board plan and housing facility. ***Part-time tuition:*** $2617 per credit hour. ***Part-time fees:*** $18 per credit hour. Part-time tuition and fees vary according to course load.

FRESHMAN FINANCIAL AID (Fall 2019, est.) 441 applied for aid; of those 68% were deemed to have need. 100% of freshmen with need received aid; of those 37% had need fully met. ***Average percent of need met:*** 88% (excluding resources awarded to replace EFC). ***Average financial aid package:*** $44,236 (excluding resources awarded to replace EFC). 27% of all full-time freshmen had no need and received non-need-based gift aid.

UNDERGRADUATE FINANCIAL AID (Fall 2019, est.) 1,355 applied for aid; of those 80% were deemed to have need. 100% of undergraduates with need received aid; of those 41% had need fully met. ***Average percent of need met:*** 87% (excluding resources awarded to replace EFC). ***Average financial aid package:*** $44,874 (excluding resources awarded to replace EFC). 14% of all full-time undergraduates had no need and received non-need-based gift aid.

GIFT AID (NEED-BASED) *Total amount:* $40,302,628 (5% federal, 1% state, 89% institutional, 5% external sources). ***Receiving aid:*** Freshmen: 59% (299); all full-time undergraduates: 57% (1,074). ***Average award:*** Freshmen: $36,807; Undergraduates: $37,401. ***Scholarships, grants, and awards:*** Federal Pell, FSEOG, state, private, college/university gift aid from institutional funds.

GIFT AID (NON-NEED-BASED) *Total amount:* $15,734,421 (98% institutional, 2% external sources). ***Receiving aid:*** Freshmen: 12% (61). Undergraduates: 7% (128). ***Average award:*** Freshmen: $23,525. Undergraduates: $22,156. ***Scholarships, grants, and awards by category:*** *Academic interests/achievement:* general academic interests/achievements. *Creative arts/performance:* debating, music. *Special achievements/activities:* community service, leadership. *Special characteristics:* children of faculty/staff, first-generation college students. ***Tuition waivers:*** Full or partial for employees or children of employees. ***ROTC:*** Army cooperative.

LOANS *Student loans:* $9,907,787 (59% need-based, 41% non-need-based). 49% of past graduating class borrowed through all loan programs. *Average indebtedness per student:* $30,460. ***Average need-based loan:*** Freshmen: $5679. Undergraduates: $6605. ***Parent loans:*** $3,076,720 (31% need-based, 69% non-need-based). ***Programs:*** Federal Direct (Subsidized and Unsubsidized Stafford, PLUS).

WORK-STUDY *Federal work-study:* Total amount: $2,408,522; 855 jobs averaging $2817. ***State or other work-study/employment:*** Total amount: $934,812 (57% need-based, 43% non-need-based). 136 part-time jobs averaging $2196.

APPLYING FOR FINANCIAL AID *Required financial aid forms:* FAFSA, CSS Financial Aid PROFILE. ***Financial aid deadline (priority):*** 1/15. ***Notification date:*** Continuous beginning 1/2. Students must reply by 7/1 or within 2 weeks of notification.

CONTACT Financial Aid Office, Office of Financial Aid, Lewis & Clark College, Templeton Campus Center, MSC 56, Portland, OR 97219-7899, 503-768-7090 or toll-free 800-444-4111. *Fax:* 503-768-7074. *E-mail:* fao@lclark.edu.
Website: http://www.lclark.edu/.

LEWIS-CLARK STATE COLLEGE

Lewiston, ID

Tuition & fees (area res): $10,552	Average undergraduate aid package: $8632

ABOUT THE INSTITUTION State-supported, coed. ***Awards:*** certificates, associate, and bachelor's degrees. 50 undergraduate majors. ***Total enrollment:*** 3,684. Undergraduates: 3,684. Freshmen: 509. Federal methodology is used as a basis for awarding need-based institutional aid.

UNDERGRADUATE EXPENSES for 2020–2021 *Tuition, area resident:* full-time $10,552; part-time $338 per credit hour. ***Tuition, state resident:*** full-time $6618; part-time $338 per credit hour. ***Tuition, nonresident:*** full-time $19,236; part-time $338 per credit hour. ***College room and board:*** $6650; ***Room only:*** $3200.

FRESHMAN FINANCIAL AID (Fall 2018) 557 applied for aid; of those 86% were deemed to have need. 87% of freshmen with need received aid; of those 18% had need fully met. ***Average percent of need met:*** 76% (excluding resources awarded to replace EFC). ***Average financial aid package:*** $8670 (excluding resources awarded to replace EFC). 18% of all full-time freshmen had no need and received non-need-based gift aid.

UNDERGRADUATE FINANCIAL AID (Fall 2018) 2,319 applied for aid; of those 55% were deemed to have need. 98% of undergraduates with need received aid; of those 10% had need fully met. ***Average percent of need met:*** 71% (excluding resources awarded to replace EFC). ***Average financial aid package:*** $8632 (excluding resources awarded to replace EFC). 9% of all full-time undergraduates had no need and received non-need-based gift aid.

GIFT AID (NEED-BASED) *Total amount:* $7,234,727 (85% federal, 14% state, 1% institutional). ***Receiving aid:*** Freshmen: 55% (312); all full-time undergraduates: 38% (954). ***Average award:*** Freshmen: $4938; Undergraduates: $4729. ***Scholarships, grants, and awards:*** Federal Pell, FSEOG, state, private, college/university gift aid from institutional funds.

GIFT AID (NON-NEED-BASED) *Total amount:* $2,550,011 (3% federal, 10% state, 64% institutional, 23% external sources). ***Receiving aid:*** Freshmen: 45% (259). Undergraduates: 16% (409). ***Average award:*** Freshmen: $3194. Undergraduates:

$2898. ***Scholarships, grants, and awards by category:*** *Academic interests/achievement:* biological sciences, business, communication, education, engineering/technologies, English, general academic interests/achievements, health fields, home economics, humanities, mathematics, physical sciences, social sciences. *Creative arts/performance:* applied art and design, creative writing, debating, music, theater/drama. *Special achievements/activities:* community service, general special achievements/activities, junior miss, leadership, memberships, rodeo. *Special characteristics:* adult students, children and siblings of alumni, children of faculty/staff, ethnic background, first-generation college students, general special characteristics, members of minority groups, out-of-state students, previous college experience. ***ROTC:*** Army cooperative, Naval cooperative, Air Force cooperative.

LOANS *Student loans:* $11,870,652 (47% need-based, 53% non-need-based). 64% of past graduating class borrowed through all loan programs. *Average indebtedness per student:* $25,473. ***Average need-based loan:*** Freshmen: $2809. Undergraduates: $3816. ***Parent loans:*** $443,046 (100% non-need-based). ***Programs:*** Federal Direct (Subsidized and Unsubsidized Stafford, PLUS), Federal Nursing.

WORK-STUDY *Federal work-study:* Total amount: $99,283; jobs available. ***State or other work-study/employment:*** Total amount: $115,185 (69% need-based, 31% non-need-based). Part-time jobs available.

ATHLETIC AWARDS Total amount: $2,038,119 (100% non-need-based).

APPLYING FOR FINANCIAL AID *Financial aid deadline (priority):* 3/1. ***Notification date:*** Continuous beginning 3/15. Students must reply within 2 weeks of notification.

CONTACT Ms. Laura Hughes, Director of Financial Aid, Lewis-Clark State College, 500 8th Avenue, Lewiston, ID 83501-2698, 208-792-2224 or toll-free 800-933-5272. *Fax:* 208-792-2063. *E-mail:* lhughes@lcsc.edu. *Website:* http://www.lcsc.edu/.

LEWIS UNIVERSITY

Romeoville, IL

Tuition & fees: $34,478 | **Average undergraduate aid package: $28,523**

ABOUT THE INSTITUTION Independent Roman Catholic Church, coed. ***Awards:*** certificates, associate, bachelor's, master's, and doctoral degrees. 76 undergraduate majors. ***Total enrollment:*** 6,359. Undergraduates: 4,274. Freshmen: 639. Federal methodology is used as a basis for awarding need-based institutional aid.

UNDERGRADUATE EXPENSES for 2020–2021 *Application fee:* $40. ***Comprehensive fee:*** $45,528 includes full-time tuition ($34,268), mandatory fees ($210), and room and board ($11,050). Full-time tuition and fees vary according to course load, location, and program. Room and board charges vary according to board plan and housing facility. ***Part-time tuition:*** $996 per credit hour. ***Part-time fees:*** $100 per term. Part-time tuition and fees vary according to course load, location, and program.

FRESHMAN FINANCIAL AID (Fall 2019, est.) 597 applied for aid; of those 88% were deemed to have need. 100% of freshmen with need received aid; of those 24% had need fully met. ***Average percent of need met:*** 91% (excluding resources awarded to replace EFC). ***Average financial aid package:*** $31,341 (excluding resources awarded to replace EFC). 17% of all full-time freshmen had no need and received non-need-based gift aid.

UNDERGRADUATE FINANCIAL AID (Fall 2019, est.) 2,954 applied for aid; of those 90% were deemed to have need. 100% of undergraduates with need received aid; of those 24% had need fully met. ***Average percent of need met:*** 91% (excluding resources awarded to replace EFC). ***Average financial aid package:*** $28,523 (excluding resources awarded to replace EFC). 19% of all full-time undergraduates had no need and received non-need-based gift aid.

GIFT AID (NEED-BASED) *Total amount:* $48,101,016 (14% federal, 14% state, 71% institutional, 1% external sources). ***Receiving aid:*** Freshmen: 82% (524); all full-time undergraduates: 72% (2,548). ***Average award:*** Freshmen: $22,416; Undergraduates: $18,996. ***Scholarships, grants, and awards:*** Federal Pell, FSEOG, state, private, college/university gift aid from institutional funds, Federal Nursing.

GIFT AID (NON-NEED-BASED) *Total amount:* $11,353,229 (1% federal, 97% institutional, 2% external sources). ***Receiving aid:*** Freshmen: 17% (109). Undergraduates: 13% (465). ***Average award:*** Freshmen: $16,067. Undergraduates: $13,503. ***Scholarships, grants, and awards by category:*** *Academic interests/achievement:* general academic interests/achievements. *Creative arts/performance:* applied art and design, art/fine arts, music, theater/drama. *Special achievements/activities:* cheerleading/drum major, community service, general special achievements/activities, leadership, memberships, religious involvement. *Special characteristics:* children and siblings of alumni, children of faculty/staff, international students, previous college experience, religious affiliation, veterans, veterans' children. ***Tuition waivers:*** Full or partial for children of alumni, employees or children of employees. ***ROTC:*** Army cooperative, Air Force cooperative.

LOANS *Student loans:* $33,314,565 (66% need-based, 34% non-need-based). 81% of past graduating class borrowed through all loan programs. *Average indebtedness per student:* $36,653. ***Average need-based loan:*** Freshmen: $3423. Undergraduates: $4456. ***Parent loans:*** $8,054,108 (41% need-based, 59% non-need-based). ***Programs:*** Federal Direct (Subsidized and Unsubsidized Stafford, PLUS), Perkins.

WORK-STUDY *Federal work-study:* Total amount: $3,660,108; jobs available. ***State or other work-study/employment:*** Total amount: $1,401,751 (26% need-based, 74% non-need-based). Part-time jobs available.

ATHLETIC AWARDS Total amount: $4,543,543 (34% need-based, 66% non-need-based).

APPLYING FOR FINANCIAL AID *Required financial aid form:* FAFSA. ***Financial aid deadline:*** 5/1 (priority: 10/31). ***Notification date:*** Continuous beginning 11/1. Students must reply by 5/1 or within 2 weeks of notification.

CONTACT Ms. Janeen Decharinte, Director of Financial Aid Services, Lewis University, 1 University Parkway, Romeoville, IL 60446, 815-836-5263 or toll-free 800-897-9000. *Fax:* 815-836-5135. *E-mail:* decharja@lewisu.edu. *Website:* http://www.lewisu.edu/.

LIBERTY UNIVERSITY

Lynchburg, VA

Tuition & fees: $24,910 | **Average undergraduate aid package: $15,336**

ABOUT THE INSTITUTION Independent nondenominational, coed. ***Awards:*** certificates, associate, bachelor's, master's, and doctoral degrees (also offers external degree program with significant enrollment not reflected in profile). 99 undergraduate majors. ***Total enrollment:*** 14,929. Undergraduates: 13,117. Freshmen: 3,256. Federal methodology is used as a basis for awarding need-based institutional aid.

UNDERGRADUATE EXPENSES for 2020–2021 *Application fee:* $50. ***Comprehensive fee:*** $35,372 includes full-time tuition ($23,800), mandatory fees ($1110), and room and board ($10,462). ***College room only:*** $6760. ***Part-time tuition:*** $815 per credit hour.

FRESHMAN FINANCIAL AID (Fall 2018) 3096 applied for aid; of those 77% were deemed to have need. 100% of freshmen with need received aid; of those 11% had need fully met. ***Average percent of need met:*** 57% (excluding resources awarded to replace EFC). ***Average financial aid package:*** $16,157 (excluding resources awarded to replace EFC). 21% of all full-time freshmen had no need and received non-need-based gift aid.

UNDERGRADUATE FINANCIAL AID (Fall 2018) 11,310 applied for aid; of those 78% were deemed to have need. 100% of undergraduates with need received aid; of those 11% had need fully met. ***Average percent of need met:*** 56% (excluding resources awarded to replace EFC). ***Average financial aid package:*** $15,336 (excluding resources awarded to replace EFC). 19% of all full-time undergraduates had no need and received non-need-based gift aid.

GIFT AID (NEED-BASED) *Receiving aid:* Freshmen: 74% (2,385); all full-time undergraduates: 70% (8,748). ***Average award:*** Freshmen: $12,662; Undergraduates: $11,262. ***Scholarships, grants, and awards:*** Federal Pell, FSEOG, state, private, college/university gift aid from institutional funds.

GIFT AID (NON-NEED-BASED) *Receiving aid:* Freshmen: 13% (435). Undergraduates: 14% (1,709). ***Average award:*** Freshmen: $7273. Undergraduates: $7440. ***Scholarships, grants, and awards by category:*** *Academic interests/achievement:* biological sciences, business, communication, computer science, education, engineering/technologies, English, general academic interests/achievements, mathematics, premedicine, religion/biblical studies. *Creative arts/performance:* cinema/film/broadcasting, debating, journalism/publications, music, performing arts. *Special achievements/activities:* cheerleading/drum major, leadership. *Special characteristics:* children of faculty/staff, international students, local/state students, religious affiliation, veterans. ***ROTC:*** Army, Air Force cooperative.

LOANS *Student loans:* 58% of past graduating class borrowed through all loan programs. *Average indebtedness per student:* $20,876. ***Average need-based loan:*** Freshmen: $3508. Undergraduates: $4244. ***Programs:*** Federal Direct (Subsidized and Unsubsidized Stafford, PLUS), state, college/university, Canadian federal and provincial loans.

WORK-STUDY Federal work-study jobs available. ***State or other work-study/employment:*** Part-time jobs available.

APPLYING FOR FINANCIAL AID ***Required financial aid forms:*** FAFSA, state aid form. ***Financial aid deadline:*** 3/1. ***Notification date:*** Continuous beginning 3/15. Students must reply within 3 weeks of notification.

CONTACT Robert Ritz, Office of Financial Aid, Liberty University, 1971 University Boulevard, Lynchburg, VA 24515, 434-582-2270 or toll-free 800-543-5317. *Fax:* 434-582-2053. *E-mail:* financialaid@liberty.edu.
Website: http://www.liberty.edu/.

LIFE PACIFIC COLLEGE

San Dimas, CA

CONTACT Mrs. Luci Perez, Director of Financial Aid, Life Pacific College, 1100 Covina Boulevard, San Dimas, CA 91773-3298, 909-599-5433 Ext. 322 or toll-free 877-886-5433 Ext.314. *Fax:* 909-706-3031. *E-mail:* lperez@lifepacific.edu.
Website: http://www.lifepacific.edu/.

LIFE UNIVERSITY

Marietta, GA

Tuition & fees: $13,101	Average undergraduate aid package: $12,500

ABOUT THE INSTITUTION Independent, coed. ***Awards:*** certificates, associate, bachelor's, master's, and doctoral degrees. 11 undergraduate majors. ***Total enrollment:*** 2,728. Undergraduates: 880. Freshmen: 136. Federal methodology is used as a basis for awarding need-based institutional aid.

UNDERGRADUATE EXPENSES for 2019–2020 ***Application fee:*** $50. ***Comprehensive fee:*** $27,501 includes full-time tuition ($11,610), mandatory fees ($1491), and room and board ($14,400). Full-time tuition and fees vary according to course load. Room and board charges vary according to housing facility. ***Part-time tuition:*** $295 per credit hour.

FRESHMAN FINANCIAL AID (Fall 2019, est.) 86 applied for aid; of those 93% were deemed to have need. 100% of freshmen with need received aid. ***Average percent of need met:*** 34% (excluding resources awarded to replace EFC). ***Average financial aid package:*** $11,500 (excluding resources awarded to replace EFC).

UNDERGRADUATE FINANCIAL AID (Fall 2019, est.) 569 applied for aid; of those 92% were deemed to have need. 100% of undergraduates with need received aid; of those 1% had need fully met. ***Average percent of need met:*** 36% (excluding resources awarded to replace EFC). ***Average financial aid package:*** $12,500 (excluding resources awarded to replace EFC). 1% of all full-time undergraduates had no need and received non-need-based gift aid.

GIFT AID (NEED-BASED) ***Total amount:*** $975,000 (100% federal). ***Receiving aid:*** Freshmen: 24% (41); all full-time undergraduates: 43% (324). ***Average award:*** Freshmen: $5600; Undergraduates: $5800. ***Scholarships, grants, and awards:*** Federal Pell, FSEOG, state, private.

GIFT AID (NON-NEED-BASED) ***Total amount:*** $682,000 (36% state, 60% institutional, 4% external sources). ***Average award:*** Freshmen: $4500. Undergraduates: $3750. ***Scholarships, grants, and awards by category:*** *Academic interests/achievement:* general academic interests/achievements. *Special achievements/activities:* cheerleading/drum major, general special achievements/activities, leadership. *Special characteristics:* children and siblings of alumni, children of faculty/staff, general special characteristics, international students, local/state students, members of minority groups. ***Tuition waivers:*** Full or partial for employees or children of employees.

LOANS ***Student loans:*** $1,810,000 (50% need-based, 50% non-need-based). 58% of past graduating class borrowed through all loan programs. *Average indebtedness per student:* $26,000. ***Average need-based loan:*** Freshmen: $3700. Undergraduates: $4250. ***Parent loans:*** $737,000 (100% need-based). ***Programs:*** Federal Direct (Subsidized and Unsubsidized Stafford), state, private/alternative.

WORK-STUDY ***Federal work-study:*** Total amount: $254,000; jobs available. ***State or other work-study/employment:*** Part-time jobs available.

ATHLETIC AWARDS Total amount: $1,374,000 (100% non-need-based).

APPLYING FOR FINANCIAL AID ***Required financial aid forms:*** FAFSA, institution's own form. ***Financial aid deadline:*** Continuous. ***Notification date:*** Continuous.

CONTACT Jessica Magazu, Director of Financial Aid, Life University, 1269 Barclay Circle, Marietta, GA 30060, 770-426-2901 or toll-free 800-543-3202. *Fax:* 770-426-2926. *E-mail:* Jessica.Magazu@LIFE.edu.
Website: http://www.life.edu/.

LIM COLLEGE

New York, NY

ABOUT THE INSTITUTION Proprietary, coed, primarily women. ***Awards:*** certificates, bachelor's, and master's degrees. 5 undergraduate majors. ***Total enrollment:*** 1,781. Undergraduates: 1,503. Freshmen: 298.

GIFT AID (NEED-BASED) ***Scholarships, grants, and awards:*** Federal Pell, FSEOG, state, private, college/university gift aid from institutional funds.

GIFT AID (NON-NEED-BASED) ***Scholarships, grants, and awards by category:*** *Academic interests/achievement:* general academic interests/achievements. *Special achievements/activities:* leadership, memberships. *Special characteristics:* children of faculty/staff, local/state students, siblings of current students.

LOANS ***Programs:*** Federal Direct (Subsidized and Unsubsidized Stafford, PLUS).

CONTACT Financial Aid Office, LIM College, 12 East 53rd Street, New York, NY 10022-5268, 212-752-1530 or toll-free 800-677-1323.
Website: http://www.limcollege.edu/.

LIMESTONE COLLEGE

Gaffney, SC

Tuition & fees: $26,300	Average undergraduate aid package: $13,019

ABOUT THE INSTITUTION Independent, coed. ***Awards:*** associate, bachelor's, and master's degrees. 62 undergraduate majors. ***Total enrollment:*** 2,219. Undergraduates: 2,129. Freshmen: 332. Federal methodology is used as a basis for awarding need-based institutional aid.

UNDERGRADUATE EXPENSES for 2020–2021 ***Application fee:*** $25. ***Comprehensive fee:*** $36,200 includes full-time tuition ($25,200), mandatory fees ($1100), and room and board ($9900). Full-time tuition and fees vary according to course load and location. Room and board charges vary according to board plan and housing facility. ***Part-time tuition:*** $1050 per credit hour. ***Part-time fees:*** $60 per credit hour. Part-time tuition and fees vary according to course load and location.

FRESHMAN FINANCIAL AID (Fall 2018) 378 applied for aid; of those 95% were deemed to have need. 99% of freshmen with need received aid; of those 13% had need fully met. ***Average percent of need met:*** 57% (excluding resources awarded to replace EFC). ***Average financial aid package:*** $19,363 (excluding resources awarded to replace EFC). 5% of all full-time freshmen had no need and received non-need-based gift aid.

UNDERGRADUATE FINANCIAL AID (Fall 2018) 1,895 applied for aid; of those 96% were deemed to have need. 99% of undergraduates with need received aid; of those 7% had need fully met. ***Average percent of need met:*** 45% (excluding resources awarded to replace EFC). ***Average financial aid package:*** $13,019 (excluding resources awarded to replace EFC). 3% of all full-time undergraduates had no need and received non-need-based gift aid.

GIFT AID (NEED-BASED) ***Total amount:*** $14,218,273 (33% federal, 20% state, 42% institutional, 5% external sources). ***Receiving aid:*** Freshmen: 92% (349); all full-time undergraduates: 86% (1,635). ***Average award:*** Freshmen: $16,990; Undergraduates: $10,773. ***Scholarships, grants, and awards:*** Federal Pell, FSEOG, state, private, college/university gift aid from institutional funds.

GIFT AID (NON-NEED-BASED) ***Total amount:*** $932,334 (18% state, 67% institutional, 15% external sources). ***Receiving aid:*** Freshmen: 12% (44). Undergraduates: 5% (97). ***Average award:*** Freshmen: $9123. Undergraduates: $6966. ***Scholarships, grants, and awards by category:*** *Academic interests/achievement:* biological sciences, business, communication, computer science, education, English, general academic interests/achievements, home economics, humanities, mathematics, physical sciences, premedicine, religion/biblical studies, social sciences. *Creative arts/performance:* applied art and design, music, performing arts, theater/drama. *Special* *achievements/activities:* cheerleading/drum major, general special achievements/activities, leadership, religious involvement. *Special characteristics:* children of faculty/staff, local/state students, out-of-state students, previous college experience, siblings of current students. ***Tuition waivers:*** Full or partial for employees or children of employees.

LOANS *Student loans:* $14,917,965 (88% need-based, 12% non-need-based). 94% of past graduating class borrowed through all loan programs. *Average indebtedness per student:* $33,427. ***Average need-based loan:*** Freshmen: $3107. Undergraduates: $3716. ***Parent loans:*** $4,223,896 (70% need-based, 30% non-need-based). ***Programs:*** Federal Direct (Subsidized and Unsubsidized Stafford, PLUS).

WORK-STUDY *Federal work-study:* Total amount: $105,377; 91 jobs averaging $2253. ***State or other work-study/employment:*** Part-time jobs available.

ATHLETIC AWARDS Total amount: $3,849,283 (84% need-based, 16% non-need-based).

APPLYING FOR FINANCIAL AID *Required financial aid form:* FAFSA. ***Financial aid deadline (priority):*** 2/1. ***Notification date:*** Continuous beginning 1/15. Students must reply within 3 weeks of notification.

CONTACT Mrs. Summer Nance, Director of Financial Aid, Limestone College, 1115 College Drive, Gaffney, SC 29340-3799, 864-488-4567 or toll-free 800-795-7151. *Fax:* 864-487-8706. *E-mail:* snance@limestone.edu.
Website: http://www.limestone.edu/.

LINCOLN CHRISTIAN UNIVERSITY

Lincoln, IL

CONTACT Nancy Siddens, Director of Financial Aid, Lincoln Christian University, 100 Campus View Drive, Lincoln, IL 62656, 217-732-3168 Ext. 2250 or toll-free 888-522-5228. *Fax:* 217-732-4199. *E-mail:* finaid@lincolnchristian.edu.
Website: http://www.lincolnchristian.edu/.

LINCOLN COLLEGE

Lincoln, IL

Tuition & fees: $19,000	Average undergraduate aid package: $13,083

ABOUT THE INSTITUTION Independent, coed. ***Awards:*** associate and bachelor's degrees. 19 undergraduate majors. Federal methodology is used as a basis for awarding need-based institutional aid.

UNDERGRADUATE EXPENSES for 2019–2020 *One-time required fee:* $50. ***Comprehensive fee:*** $26,900 includes full-time tuition ($17,900), mandatory fees ($1100), and room and board ($7900). ***College room only:*** $3100. Room and board charges vary according to housing facility. ***Part-time tuition:*** $330 per credit hour. ***Payment plans:*** Guaranteed tuition, tuition prepayment.

FRESHMAN FINANCIAL AID (Fall 2018) 272 applied for aid; of those 100% were deemed to have need. 100% of freshmen with need received aid. ***Average percent of need met:*** 99% (excluding resources awarded to replace EFC). ***Average financial aid package:*** $13,137 (excluding resources awarded to replace EFC).

UNDERGRADUATE FINANCIAL AID (Fall 2018) 846 applied for aid; of those 100% were deemed to have need. 100% of undergraduates with need received aid. ***Average percent of need met:*** 87% (excluding resources awarded to replace EFC). ***Average financial aid package:*** $13,083 (excluding resources awarded to replace EFC).

GIFT AID (NEED-BASED) *Total amount:* $8,529,525 (36% federal, 25% state, 39% institutional). ***Receiving aid:*** Freshmen: 99% (272); all full-time undergraduates: 87% (846). ***Average award:*** Freshmen: $13,137; Undergraduates: $13,083. ***Scholarships, grants, and awards:*** Federal Pell, FSEOG, state, private, college/university gift aid from institutional funds.

GIFT AID (NON-NEED-BASED) *Total amount:* $90,526 (100% external sources). ***Receiving aid:*** Freshmen: 3% (9). Undergraduates: 2% (17). ***Scholarships, grants, and awards by category:*** *Creative arts/performance:* 17 awards ($33,550 total): cinema/film/broadcasting, dance, music, theater/drama. *Special achievements/activities:* 19 awards ($23,750 total): cheerleading/drum major. *Special characteristics:* 50 awards ($105,057 total): children of faculty/staff, siblings of current students, spouses of current students. ***Tuition waivers:*** Full or partial for employees or children of employees.

LOANS *Student loans:* $5,182,194 (100% need-based). 71% of past graduating class borrowed through all loan programs. *Average indebtedness per student:* $7385. ***Average need-based loan:*** Freshmen: $2852. Undergraduates: $3643. ***Parent loans:*** $816,572 (100% need-based). ***Programs:*** Federal Direct (Subsidized and Unsubsidized Stafford, PLUS).

WORK-STUDY *Federal work-study:* Total amount: $187,579; 156 jobs averaging $187,579.

ATHLETIC AWARDS Total amount: $1,768,835 (100% need-based).

APPLYING FOR FINANCIAL AID *Required financial aid form:* FAFSA. ***Financial aid deadline (priority):*** 5/1. ***Notification date:*** Continuous beginning 6/1. Students must reply within 3 weeks of notification.

CONTACT Stephanie Claudio, Financial Aid Couselor, Lincoln College, 300 Keokuk Street, Lincoln, IL 62656, 217-735-7231 Ext. 7231 or toll-free 800-569-0558. *Fax:* 217-735-9016. *E-mail:* LCLFinancialAid@lincolncollege.edu.
Website: http://www.lincolncollege.edu/.

LINCOLN MEMORIAL UNIVERSITY

Harrogate, TN

Tuition & fees: $25,038	Average undergraduate aid package: $23,472

ABOUT THE INSTITUTION Independent, coed. ***Awards:*** certificates, associate, bachelor's, master's, and doctoral degrees. 43 undergraduate majors. ***Total enrollment:*** 4,867. Undergraduates: 1,975. Freshmen: 267. Federal methodology is used as a basis for awarding need-based institutional aid.

UNDERGRADUATE EXPENSES for 2020–2021 *Comprehensive fee:* $35,676 includes full-time tuition ($23,040), mandatory fees ($1998), and room and board ($10,638). ***Part-time tuition:*** $960 per credit hour.

FRESHMAN FINANCIAL AID (Fall 2018) 285 applied for aid; of those 82% were deemed to have need. 100% of freshmen with need received aid; of those 1% had need fully met. ***Average percent of need met:*** 63% (excluding resources awarded to replace EFC). ***Average financial aid package:*** $24,048 (excluding resources awarded to replace EFC). 7% of all full-time freshmen had no need and received non-need-based gift aid.

UNDERGRADUATE FINANCIAL AID (Fall 2018) 1,358 applied for aid; of those 85% were deemed to have need. 92% of undergraduates with need received aid; of those 4% had need fully met. ***Average percent of need met:*** 54% (excluding resources awarded to replace EFC). ***Average financial aid package:*** $23,472 (excluding resources awarded to replace EFC). 6% of all full-time undergraduates had no need and received non-need-based gift aid.

GIFT AID (NEED-BASED) *Receiving aid:* Freshmen: 82% (233); all full-time undergraduates: 67% (913). ***Average award:*** Freshmen: $15,895; Undergraduates: $14,411. ***Scholarships, grants, and awards:*** Federal Pell, FSEOG, state, private, college/university gift aid from institutional funds.

GIFT AID (NON-NEED-BASED) *Receiving aid:* Freshmen: 26% (73). Undergraduates: 18% (246). ***Average award:*** Freshmen: $6017. Undergraduates: $6316. ***Scholarships, grants, and awards by category:*** *Academic interests/achievement:* $10,590,606 total: general academic interests/achievements. *Special characteristics:* children and siblings of alumni, children of faculty/staff, local/state students. ***ROTC:*** Army.

LOANS *Student loans:* 72% of past graduating class borrowed through all loan programs. *Average indebtedness per student:* $22,290. ***Average need-based loan:*** Freshmen: $6921. Undergraduates: $8838. ***Programs:*** Federal Direct (Subsidized and Unsubsidized Stafford, PLUS), Perkins.

WORK-STUDY Federal work-study jobs available.

APPLYING FOR FINANCIAL AID *Required financial aid form:* FAFSA. ***Financial aid deadline:*** Continuous. ***Notification date:*** Continuous. Students must reply within 3 weeks of notification.

CONTACT Tammy Tomfohrde, Executive Director of Financial Aid, Lincoln Memorial University, 6965 Cumberland Gap Parkway, Harrogate, TN 37752-1901, 423-869-6465 or toll-free 800-325-0900. *Fax:* 423-869-6347. *E-mail:* tammy.tomfohrde@lmunet.edu.
Website: http://www.lmunet.edu/.

LINCOLN UNIVERSITY

Oakland, CA

CONTACT Financial Aid Office, Lincoln University, 401 15th Street, Oakland, CA 94612, 510-628-8010 or toll-free 888-810-9998.
Website: http://www.lincolnuca.edu/.

LINCOLN UNIVERSITY

Jefferson City, MO

ABOUT THE INSTITUTION State-supported, coed. ***Awards:*** certificates, associate, bachelor's, and master's degrees. 39 undergraduate majors. ***Total enrollment:*** 2,436. Undergraduates: 2,323. Freshmen: 397.

GIFT AID (NEED-BASED) ***Scholarships, grants, and awards:*** Federal Pell, FSEOG, state, private, college/university gift aid from institutional funds.

GIFT AID (NON-NEED-BASED) ***Scholarships, grants, and awards by category:*** *Academic interests/achievement:* agriculture, general academic interests/achievements, military science. *Creative arts/performance:* applied art and design, journalism/publications, music, performing arts, theater/drama. *Special achievements/activities:* cheerleading/drum major. *Special characteristics:* adult students, children of faculty/staff, international students, out-of-state students.

LOANS ***Programs:*** Federal Direct (Subsidized and Unsubsidized Stafford, PLUS), private loans.

WORK-STUDY ***Federal work-study:*** Total amount: $266,102; 207 jobs averaging $1006. ***State or other work-study/employment:*** Total amount: $34,930 (100% non-need-based). 47 part-time jobs averaging $2581.

APPLYING FOR FINANCIAL AID ***Required financial aid form:*** FAFSA.

CONTACT Mr. Alfred Robinson, Director of Student Financial Aid, Lincoln University, 820 Chestnut Street, Jefferson City, MO 65102-0029, 573-681-6156. *Fax:* 573-681-5871. *E-mail:* robinsona@lincolnu.edu.
Website: http://www.lincolnu.edu/.

LINCOLN UNIVERSITY

Lincoln University, PA

Tuition & fees (PA res): $11,266	Average undergraduate aid package: $12,732

ABOUT THE INSTITUTION State-related, coed. ***Awards:*** bachelor's and master's degrees. 31 undergraduate majors. ***Total enrollment:*** 2,241. Undergraduates: 2,040. Freshmen: 445. Federal methodology is used as a basis for awarding need-based institutional aid.

UNDERGRADUATE EXPENSES for 2019–2020 ***Tuition, state resident:*** full-time $8026; part-time $335 per credit hour. ***Tuition, nonresident:*** full-time $13,396; part-time $562 per credit hour. ***Required fees:*** full-time $3240; $145 per credit hour. Full-time tuition and fees vary according to course load, degree level, location, program, and student level. Part-time tuition and fees vary according to course load, degree level, program, and student level. ***College room and board:*** $9828; ***Room only:*** $5242. Room and board charges vary according to board plan and housing facility. ***Payment plan:*** Guaranteed tuition.

FRESHMAN FINANCIAL AID (Fall 2018) 526 applied for aid; of those 96% were deemed to have need. 99% of freshmen with need received aid; of those 4% had need fully met. ***Average percent of need met:*** 41% (excluding resources awarded to replace EFC). ***Average financial aid package:*** $10,705 (excluding resources awarded to replace EFC). 1% of all full-time freshmen had no need and received non-need-based gift aid.

UNDERGRADUATE FINANCIAL AID (Fall 2018) 1,892 applied for aid; of those 94% were deemed to have need. 99% of undergraduates with need received aid; of those 9% had need fully met. ***Average percent of need met:*** 50% (excluding resources awarded to replace EFC). ***Average financial aid package:*** $12,732 (excluding resources awarded to replace EFC). 2% of all full-time undergraduates had no need and received non-need-based gift aid.

GIFT AID (NEED-BASED) ***Total amount:*** $16,358,138 (44% federal, 13% state, 35% institutional, 8% external sources). ***Receiving aid:*** Freshmen: 75% (401); all full-time undergraduates: 72% (1,423). ***Average award:*** Freshmen: $6889; Undergraduates: $7372. ***Scholarships, grants, and awards:*** Federal Pell, FSEOG, state, private, college/university gift aid from institutional funds, United Negro College Fund.

GIFT AID (NON-NEED-BASED) ***Total amount:*** $534,645 (91% institutional, 9% external sources). ***Receiving aid:*** Freshmen: 38% (206). Undergraduates: 46% (903). ***Average award:*** Freshmen: $10,661. Undergraduates: $10,795. ***Scholarships, grants, and awards by category:*** *Academic interests/achievement:* 401 awards ($4,482,621 total): general academic interests/achievements. *Creative arts/performance:* 123 awards ($207,975 total): music. *Special achievements/activities:* cheerleading/drum major. *Special characteristics:* 104 awards ($349,768 total): children of faculty/staff. ***Tuition waivers:*** Full or partial for children of alumni, employees or children of employees. ***ROTC:*** Army cooperative.

LOANS ***Student loans:*** $14,505,118 (96% need-based, 4% non-need-based). 91% of past graduating class borrowed through all loan programs. *Average indebtedness per student:* $36,567. ***Average need-based loan:*** Freshmen: $3328. Undergraduates: $3995. ***Parent loans:*** $11,247,935 (94% need-based, 6% non-need-based). ***Programs:*** Federal Direct (Subsidized and Unsubsidized Stafford, PLUS), private loans.

WORK-STUDY ***Federal work-study:*** Total amount: $208,301; 122 jobs averaging $1716. ***State or other work-study/employment:*** Total amount: $22,102 (100% need-based). 25 part-time jobs averaging $884.

ATHLETIC AWARDS Total amount: $918,205 (97% need-based, 3% non-need-based).

APPLYING FOR FINANCIAL AID ***Required financial aid form:*** FAFSA. ***Financial aid deadline (priority):*** 4/1. ***Notification date:*** 2/20. Students must reply within 2 weeks of notification.

CONTACT Ms. Kim Anderson, Director of Financial Aid, Lincoln University, 1570 Baltimore Pike, Lincoln University, PA 19352, 800-561-2606 Ext. 57716 or toll-free 800-790-0191. *Fax:* 484-365-8198. *E-mail:* financialaid@lincoln.edu.
Website: http://www.lincoln.edu/.

LINDENWOOD UNIVERSITY

St. Charles, MO

Tuition & fees: $18,600	Average undergraduate aid package: $14,875

ABOUT THE INSTITUTION Independent Presbyterian, coed. ***Awards:*** certificates, bachelor's, master's, and doctoral degrees. 67 undergraduate majors. ***Total enrollment:*** 8,406. Undergraduates: 5,668. Freshmen: 798. Federal methodology is used as a basis for awarding need-based institutional aid.

UNDERGRADUATE EXPENSES for 2020–2021 ***Comprehensive fee:*** $27,900 includes full-time tuition ($18,500), mandatory fees ($100), and room and board ($9300). Full-time tuition and fees vary according to class time. Room and board charges vary according to board plan. ***Part-time tuition:*** $450 per credit hour. ***Part-time fees:*** $75 per term. Part-time tuition and fees vary according to class time.

FRESHMAN FINANCIAL AID (Fall 2019, est.) 681 applied for aid; of those 77% were deemed to have need. 99% of freshmen with need received aid; of those 36% had need fully met. ***Average percent of need met:*** 83% (excluding resources awarded to replace EFC). ***Average financial aid package:*** $18,310 (excluding resources awarded to replace EFC). 20% of all full-time freshmen had no need and received non-need-based gift aid.

UNDERGRADUATE FINANCIAL AID (Fall 2019, est.) 4,080 applied for aid; of those 84% were deemed to have need. 100% of undergraduates with need received aid; of those 23% had need fully met. ***Average percent of need met:*** 57% (excluding resources awarded to replace EFC). ***Average financial aid package:*** $14,875 (excluding resources awarded to replace EFC). 12% of all full-time undergraduates had no need and received non-need-based gift aid.

GIFT AID (NEED-BASED) ***Receiving aid:*** Freshmen: 65% (515); all full-time undergraduates: 58% (3,175). ***Average award:*** Freshmen: $13,232; Undergraduates: $9940. ***Scholarships, grants, and awards:*** Federal Pell, FSEOG, state, private, college/university gift aid from institutional funds.

GIFT AID (NON-NEED-BASED) ***Receiving aid:*** Freshmen: 20% (158). Undergraduates: 11% (600). ***Average award:*** Freshmen: $6915. Undergraduates: $8439. ***Scholarships, grants, and awards by category:*** *Academic interests/achievement:* 3,159 awards ($18,177,496 total): general academic interests/achievements. ***ROTC:*** Army cooperative, Air Force cooperative.

LOANS ***Student loans:*** 63% of past graduating class borrowed through all loan programs. *Average indebtedness per student:* $33,365. ***Average need-based loan:*** Freshmen: $3356. Undergraduates: $4220. ***Programs:*** Federal Direct (Subsidized and Unsubsidized Stafford, PLUS).

WORK-STUDY ***Federal work-study:*** 189 jobs averaging $2850.

APPLYING FOR FINANCIAL AID ***Required financial aid form:*** FAFSA. ***Financial aid deadline:*** Continuous. ***Notification date:*** Continuous. Students must reply within 2 weeks of notification.

CONTACT Ms. Jamie Shahin, Director, Student Financial Services, Lindenwood University, 209 South Kingshighway, St. Charles, MO 63301-1695, 636-949-4106. *Fax:* 636-949-4924. *E-mail:* JShahin@lindenwood.edu.
Website: http://www.lindenwood.edu/.

LINDSEY WILSON COLLEGE

Columbia, KY

CONTACT Ms. Marilyn D. Radford, Director of Student Financial Services, Lindsey Wilson College, 210 Lindsey Wilson Street, Columbia, KY 42728, 270-384-8022 or toll-free 800-264-0138. *Fax:* 270-384-8591. *E-mail:* radfordm@lindsey.edu.
Website: http://www.lindsey.edu/.

LINFIELD COLLEGE

McMinnville, OR

Tuition & fees: $45,062	Average undergraduate aid package: $38,507

ABOUT THE INSTITUTION Independent American Baptist Churches in the USA, coed. ***Awards:*** certificates, bachelor's, and master's degrees (Linfield College includes the Linfield College McMinnville Campus in McMinnville, Oregon; the Linfield-Good Samaritan School of Nursing in Portland, Oregon(Portland Campus) and the Linfield College Adult Degree Program online). 56 undergraduate majors. ***Total enrollment:*** 1,414. Undergraduates: 1,414. Freshmen: 459. Federal methodology is used as a basis for awarding need-based institutional aid.

UNDERGRADUATE EXPENSES for 2020–2021 ***Comprehensive fee:*** $57,992 includes full-time tuition ($44,450), mandatory fees ($612), and room and board ($12,930). ***College room only:*** $7110. Full-time tuition and fees vary according to course load, program, and reciprocity agreements. Room and board charges vary according to board plan, housing facility, and location. ***Part-time tuition:*** $1390 per semester hour. ***Part-time fees:*** $284 per year. Part-time tuition and fees vary according to course load, program, and reciprocity agreements.

FRESHMAN FINANCIAL AID (Fall 2019, est.) 430 applied for aid; of those 87% were deemed to have need. 100% of freshmen with need received aid; of those 33% had need fully met. ***Average percent of need met:*** 86% (excluding resources awarded to replace EFC). ***Average financial aid package:*** $40,200 (excluding resources awarded to replace EFC). 18% of all full-time freshmen had no need and received non-need-based gift aid.

UNDERGRADUATE FINANCIAL AID (Fall 2019, est.) 1,214 applied for aid; of those 86% were deemed to have need. 100% of undergraduates with need received aid; of those 35% had need fully met. ***Average percent of need met:*** 85% (excluding resources awarded to replace EFC). ***Average financial aid package:*** $38,507 (excluding resources awarded to replace EFC). 21% of all full-time undergraduates had no need and received non-need-based gift aid.

GIFT AID (NEED-BASED) ***Total amount:*** $31,388,446 (7% federal, 2% state, 88% institutional, 3% external sources). ***Receiving aid:*** Freshmen: 63% (290); all full-time undergraduates: 61% (831). ***Average award:*** Freshmen: $32,875; Undergraduates: $31,162. ***Scholarships, grants, and awards:*** Federal Pell, FSEOG, state, private, college/university gift aid from institutional funds.

GIFT AID (NON-NEED-BASED) ***Total amount:*** $6,755,959 (96% institutional, 4% external sources). ***Receiving aid:*** Freshmen: 79% (363). Undergraduates: 73% (996). ***Average award:*** Freshmen: $21,211. Undergraduates: $21,126. ***Scholarships, grants, and awards by category:*** *Academic interests/achievement:* 1,187 awards ($23,002,403 total): biological sciences, business, communication, computer science, education, English, foreign languages, general academic interests/achievements, humanities, international studies, mathematics, physical sciences, religion/biblical studies, social sciences. *Creative arts/performance:* 69 awards ($189,916 total): debating, music, theater/drama. *Special achievements/activities:* 3 awards ($5500 total): community service, leadership. *Special characteristics:* 564 awards ($6,431,756 total): children and siblings of alumni, children of faculty/staff, first-generation college students, international students, members of minority groups, previous college experience, siblings of current students, veterans. ***Tuition waivers:*** Full or partial for employees or children of employees, adult students, senior citizens. ***ROTC:*** Air Force cooperative.

LOANS ***Student loans:*** $10,647,723 (56% need-based, 44% non-need-based). 74% of past graduating class borrowed through all loan programs. *Average indebtedness per student:* $36,082. ***Average need-based loan:*** Freshmen: $3400. Undergraduates: $4220. ***Parent loans:*** $3,365,653 (35% need-based, 65% non-need-based). ***Programs:*** Federal Direct (Subsidized and Unsubsidized Stafford, PLUS), Federal Nursing, private loans.

WORK-STUDY ***Federal work-study:*** Total amount: $2,093,448; 460 jobs averaging $1480. ***State or other work-study/employment:*** Total amount: $2,078,699 (6% need-based, 94% non-need-based). 634 part-time jobs averaging $2544.

APPLYING FOR FINANCIAL AID ***Required financial aid form:*** FAFSA. ***Financial aid deadline (priority):*** 2/1. ***Notification date:*** 4/1. Students must reply by 5/1 or within 2 weeks of notification.

CONTACT Ms. Keri Burke, Director of Financial Aid, Linfield College, 900 Southeast Baker Street, A484, McMinnville, OR 97128-6894, 503-883-2269 or toll-free 800-640-2287. *Fax:* 503-883-2486. *E-mail:* finaid@linfield.edu.
Website: http://www.linfield.edu/.

LIPSCOMB UNIVERSITY

Nashville, TN

Tuition & fees: $34,744	Average undergraduate aid package: $30,420

ABOUT THE INSTITUTION Independent Church of Christ, coed. ***Awards:*** certificates, bachelor's, master's, and doctoral degrees. 103 undergraduate majors. ***Total enrollment:*** 4,595. Undergraduates: 2,859. Freshmen: 613. Federal methodology is used as a basis for awarding need-based institutional aid.

UNDERGRADUATE EXPENSES for 2020–2021 ***Application fee:*** $50. ***Comprehensive fee:*** $48,548 includes full-time tuition ($32,080), mandatory fees ($2664), and room and board ($13,804).

FRESHMAN FINANCIAL AID (Fall 2019, est.) 604 applied for aid; of those 69% were deemed to have need. 100% of freshmen with need received aid; of those 30% had need fully met. ***Average percent of need met:*** 67% (excluding resources awarded to replace EFC). ***Average financial aid package:*** $27,488 (excluding resources awarded to replace EFC). 31% of all full-time freshmen had no need and received non-need-based gift aid.

UNDERGRADUATE FINANCIAL AID (Fall 2019, est.) 2,605 applied for aid; of those 65% were deemed to have need. 100% of undergraduates with need received aid; of those 36% had need fully met. ***Average percent of need met:*** 61% (excluding resources awarded to replace EFC). ***Average financial aid package:*** $30,420 (excluding resources awarded to replace EFC). 30% of all full-time undergraduates had no need and received non-need-based gift aid.

GIFT AID (NEED-BASED) ***Total amount:*** $32,267,325 (10% federal, 14% state, 76% institutional). ***Receiving aid:*** Freshmen: 68% (415); all full-time undergraduates: 62% (1,658). ***Average award:*** Freshmen: $25,643; Undergraduates: $26,557. ***Scholarships, grants, and awards:*** Federal Pell, FSEOG, state, private, college/university gift aid from institutional funds.

GIFT AID (NON-NEED-BASED) ***Total amount:*** $14,022,237 (10% state, 90% institutional). ***Receiving aid:*** Freshmen: 68% (415). Undergraduates: 53% (1,413). ***Average award:*** Freshmen: $15,638. Undergraduates: $18,668. ***Scholarships, grants, and awards by category:*** *Academic interests/achievement:* biological sciences, business, communication, education, engineering/technologies, English, general academic interests/achievements, health fields, mathematics, premedicine, religion/biblical studies. *Creative arts/performance:* applied art and design, journalism/publications, music, theater/drama. *Special achievements/activities:* cheerleading/drum major, community service, general special achievements/activities, leadership, religious involvement. *Special characteristics:* adult students, children of educators, children of faculty/staff, children with a deceased or disabled parent, international students, local/state students, members of minority groups, out-of-state students, relatives of clergy, religious affiliation. ***ROTC:*** Army cooperative, Air Force cooperative.

LOANS ***Student loans:*** $11,675,190 (88% need-based, 12% non-need-based). 52% of past graduating class borrowed through all loan programs. *Average indebtedness per student:* $31,116. ***Average need-based loan:*** Freshmen: $3340. Undergrad-

uates: $5345. ***Parent loans:*** $5,969,271 (88% need-based, 12% non-need-based). ***Programs:*** Federal Direct (Subsidized and Unsubsidized Stafford, PLUS), Perkins.
WORK-STUDY ***Federal work-study:*** Total amount: $532,400; jobs available.
ATHLETIC AWARDS Total amount: $5,222,123 (55% need-based, 45% non-need-based).
APPLYING FOR FINANCIAL AID ***Required financial aid form:*** FAFSA. ***Financial aid deadline (priority):*** 3/1. ***Notification date:*** Continuous beginning 3/1.
CONTACT Ms. Tiffany Summers, Director of Financial Aid, Lipscomb University, One University Park Drive, Nashville, TN 37204-3951, 615-966-1791 or toll-free 877-582-4766. *Fax:* 615-966-7640. *E-mail:* tiffany.summers@lipscomb.edu.
Website: http://www.lipscomb.edu/.

LIVING ARTS COLLEGE

Raleigh, NC

CONTACT Financial Aid Office, Living Arts College, 3000 Wakefield Crossing Drive, Raleigh, NC 27614, 919-488-8500 or toll-free 800-288-7442.
Website: http://www.living-arts-college.edu/.

LIVINGSTONE COLLEGE

Salisbury, NC

Tuition & fees: N/R	Average undergraduate aid package: $14,477

ABOUT THE INSTITUTION Independent African Methodist Episcopal Zion Church, coed. ***Awards:*** bachelor's degrees. 22 undergraduate majors. Federal methodology is used as a basis for awarding need-based institutional aid.
FRESHMAN FINANCIAL AID (Fall 2019, est.) 336 applied for aid; of those 98% were deemed to have need. 99% of freshmen with need received aid; of those 2% had need fully met. ***Average percent of need met:*** 49% (excluding resources awarded to replace EFC). ***Average financial aid package:*** $13,837 (excluding resources awarded to replace EFC). 5% of all full-time freshmen had no need and received non-need-based gift aid.
UNDERGRADUATE FINANCIAL AID (Fall 2019, est.) 1,081 applied for aid; of those 98% were deemed to have need. 99% of undergraduates with need received aid; of those 3% had need fully met. ***Average percent of need met:*** 51% (excluding resources awarded to replace EFC). ***Average financial aid package:*** $14,477 (excluding resources awarded to replace EFC). 3% of all full-time undergraduates had no need and received non-need-based gift aid.
GIFT AID (NEED-BASED) ***Total amount:*** $11,164,957 (46% federal, 28% state, 22% institutional, 4% external sources). ***Receiving aid:*** Freshmen: 91% (322); all full-time undergraduates: 93% (1,027). ***Average award:*** Freshmen: $11,005; Undergraduates: $10,965. ***Scholarships, grants, and awards:*** Federal Pell, FSEOG, state, private, college/university gift aid from institutional funds, United Negro College Fund.
GIFT AID (NON-NEED-BASED) ***Total amount:*** $664,066 (1% state, 90% institutional, 9% external sources). ***Receiving aid:*** Freshmen: 2% (7). Undergraduates: 2% (21). ***Average award:*** Freshmen: $13,468. Undergraduates: $14,033. ***Scholarships, grants, and awards by category:*** *Academic interests/achievement:* education. *Creative arts/performance:* music. *Special characteristics:* members of minority groups. ***ROTC:*** Army cooperative.
LOANS ***Student loans:*** $8,235,869 (97% need-based, 3% non-need-based). 98% of past graduating class borrowed through all loan programs. *Average indebtedness per student:* $34,710. ***Average need-based loan:*** Freshmen: $3158. Undergraduates: $3893. ***Parent loans:*** $3,990,120 (84% need-based, 16% non-need-based). ***Programs:*** Federal Direct (Subsidized and Unsubsidized Stafford, PLUS).
WORK-STUDY ***Federal work-study:*** Total amount: $100,940; 124 jobs averaging $1600.
ATHLETIC AWARDS Total amount: $29,550 (100% need-based).
APPLYING FOR FINANCIAL AID ***Required financial aid forms:*** FAFSA, institution's own form, state aid form. ***Financial aid deadline (priority):*** 5/15. ***Notification date:*** Continuous. Students must reply within 2 weeks of notification.
CONTACT Mrs. Stephanie McNeil, Director of Financial Aid, Livingstone College, 701 West Monroe Street, Price Building, Salisbury, NC 28144-5298, 704-216-6069 or toll-free 800-835-3435. *Fax:* 704-216-6319. *E-mail:* smcneil@livingstone.edu.
Website: http://www.livingstone.edu/.

LOCK HAVEN UNIVERSITY OF PENNSYLVANIA

Lock Haven, PA

Tuition & fees (PA res): $10,878	Average undergraduate aid package: $9379

ABOUT THE INSTITUTION State-supported, coed. ***Awards:*** associate, bachelor's, and master's degrees. 36 undergraduate majors. ***Total enrollment:*** 3,158. Undergraduates: 2,748. Freshmen: 598. Federal methodology is used as a basis for awarding need-based institutional aid.
UNDERGRADUATE EXPENSES for 2019–2020 ***Application fee:*** $25. ***Tuition, state resident:*** full-time $7716; part-time $322 per credit hour. ***Tuition, nonresident:*** full-time $17,290; part-time $720 per credit hour. ***Required fees:*** full-time $3162; $167.55 per credit hour. Full-time tuition and fees vary according to course load, location, and program. Part-time tuition and fees vary according to course load, location, and program. ***College room and board:*** $10,368; ***Room only:*** $6540. Room and board charges vary according to board plan and housing facility.
FRESHMAN FINANCIAL AID (Fall 2018) 656 applied for aid; of those 90% were deemed to have need. 100% of freshmen with need received aid; of those 5% had need fully met. ***Average percent of need met:*** 55% (excluding resources awarded to replace EFC). ***Average financial aid package:*** $8776 (excluding resources awarded to replace EFC). 2% of all full-time freshmen had no need and received non-need-based gift aid.
UNDERGRADUATE FINANCIAL AID (Fall 2018) 2,480 applied for aid; of those 88% were deemed to have need. 99% of undergraduates with need received aid; of those 6% had need fully met. ***Average percent of need met:*** 58% (excluding resources awarded to replace EFC). ***Average financial aid package:*** $9379 (excluding resources awarded to replace EFC). 2% of all full-time undergraduates had no need and received non-need-based gift aid.
GIFT AID (NEED-BASED) ***Receiving aid:*** Freshmen: 60% (409); all full-time undergraduates: 54% (1,499). ***Average award:*** Freshmen: $5676; Undergraduates: $5793. ***Scholarships, grants, and awards:*** Federal Pell, FSEOG, state, private, college/university gift aid from institutional funds.
GIFT AID (NON-NEED-BASED) ***Receiving aid:*** Freshmen: 13% (92). Undergraduates: 7% (203). ***Average award:*** Freshmen: $2545. Undergraduates: $2848. ***Scholarships, grants, and awards by category:*** *Academic interests/achievement:* biological sciences, business, communication, computer science, education, English, foreign languages, general academic interests/achievements, home economics, international studies, library science, mathematics, physical sciences, premedicine, social sciences. *Creative arts/performance:* applied art and design, journalism/publications, music, performing arts. *Special achievements/activities:* community service, general special achievements/activities, leadership, memberships. *Special characteristics:* adult students, ethnic background, handicapped students, international students, local/state students, married students, members of minority groups, previous college experience. ***Tuition waivers:*** Full or partial for minority students, employees or children of employees, senior citizens. ***ROTC:*** Army.
LOANS ***Student loans:*** 79% of past graduating class borrowed through all loan programs. *Average indebtedness per student:* $23,490. ***Average need-based loan:*** Freshmen: $2805. Undergraduates: $3853. ***Programs:*** Federal Direct (Subsidized and Unsubsidized Stafford, PLUS), Perkins, college/university, alternative loans.
WORK-STUDY Federal work-study jobs available. ***State or other work-study/employment:*** Part-time jobs available.
APPLYING FOR FINANCIAL AID ***Required financial aid forms:*** FAFSA, state aid form. ***Notification date:*** Continuous. Students must reply within 2 weeks of notification.
CONTACT Financial Aid Office, Lock Haven University of Pennsylvania, 401 North Fairview Street, Lock Haven, PA 17745-2390, 570-893-2011 or toll-free 800-332-8900 (in-state), 800-233-8978 (out-of-state).
Website: http://www.lockhaven.edu/.

LOGAN UNIVERSITY

Chesterfield, MO

CONTACT Kerry R. Hallahan, Director of Financial Aid, Logan University, 1851 Schoettler Road, Chesterfield, MO 63017, 636-230-1741 or toll-free 800-533-9210. *E-mail:* kerry.hallahan@logan.edu.
Website: http://www.logan.edu/.

LOMA LINDA UNIVERSITY

Loma Linda, CA

CONTACT Verdell Schaefer, Director of Financial Aid, Loma Linda University, 11139 Anderson Street, Loma Linda, CA 92350, 909-558-4509 or toll-free 800-422-4558. *Fax:* 909-558-4879. *E-mail:* finaid@univ.llu.edu.
Website: http://www.llu.edu/.

LONG ISLAND UNIVERSITY

New York, NY

Tuition & fees: N/R	Average undergraduate aid package: $26,799

ABOUT THE INSTITUTION Independent, coed. Federal methodology is used as a basis for awarding need-based institutional aid.

UNDERGRADUATE FINANCIAL AID (Fall 2019, est.) 4,958 applied for aid; of those 87% were deemed to have need. 99% of undergraduates with need received aid; of those 10% had need fully met. ***Average percent of need met:*** 62% (excluding resources awarded to replace EFC). ***Average financial aid package:*** $26,799 (excluding resources awarded to replace EFC). 10% of all full-time undergraduates had no need and received non-need-based gift aid.

GIFT AID (NEED-BASED) ***Total amount:*** $40,719,195 (36% federal, 21% state, 43% institutional). ***Receiving aid:*** Entering class: 46% (582); all full-time undergraduates: 50% (2,760). ***Average award:*** Freshmen: $5029; Undergraduates: $6562. ***Scholarships, grants, and awards:*** Federal Pell, FSEOG, state, private, college/university gift aid from institutional funds, United Negro College Fund, Federal Nursing, Scholarships for Disadvantaged Students (SDS).

GIFT AID (NON-NEED-BASED) ***Total amount:*** $59,691,454 (98% institutional, 2% external sources). ***Receiving aid:*** Freshmen: 71% (901). Undergraduates: 54% (2,982). ***Average award:*** Freshmen: $23,363. Undergraduates: $19,445. ***Scholarships, grants, and awards by category:*** *Academic interests/achievement:* general academic interests/achievements, home economics, international studies. *Creative arts/performance:* art/fine arts, cinema/film/broadcasting, creative writing, dance, journalism/publications, music, performing arts, theater/drama. *Special achievements/activities:* cheerleading/drum major, general special achievements/activities. *Special characteristics:* children and siblings of alumni, children of current students, children of faculty/staff, general special characteristics, handicapped students, international students, siblings of current students, twins, veterans, veterans' children.

LOANS ***Student loans:*** $46,675,154 (35% need-based, 65% non-need-based). 71% of past graduating class borrowed through all loan programs. *Average indebtedness per student:* $45,218. ***Average need-based loan:*** Freshmen: $1847. Undergraduates: $3302. ***Parent loans:*** $25,189,629 (100% non-need-based). ***Programs:*** Federal Direct (Subsidized and Unsubsidized Stafford, PLUS), Perkins, Health Professions Student Loans (HPSL).

WORK-STUDY ***Federal work-study:*** Total amount: $6,402,555; 1,465 jobs averaging $4294.

ATHLETIC AWARDS Total amount: $11,295,110 (100% non-need-based).

APPLYING FOR FINANCIAL AID ***Required financial aid forms:*** FAFSA, state aid form. ***Financial aid deadline:*** Continuous. ***Notification date:*** Students must reply by 5/1 or within 2 weeks of notification.

CONTACT Mr. David Mainenti, AVP Student Finance, Long Island University, 700 Northern Blvd, Brookville, NY 11548, 516-299-2553. *E-mail:* LIU-SFS@LIU.EDU.
Website: http://www.liu.edu/.

LONGWOOD UNIVERSITY

Farmville, VA

Tuition & fees (VA res): $13,520	Average undergraduate aid package: $11,422

ABOUT THE INSTITUTION State-supported, coed. ***Awards:*** certificates, bachelor's, and master's degrees. 25 undergraduate majors. ***Total enrollment:*** 4,468. Undergraduates: 3,859. Freshmen: 799.

UNDERGRADUATE EXPENSES for 2019–2020 ***Application fee:*** $50. ***Tuition, state resident:*** full-time $7940; part-time $273 per credit hour. ***Tuition, nonresident:*** full-time $23,900; part-time $805 per credit hour. ***Required fees:*** full-time $5580; $186 per credit hour. Full-time tuition and fees vary according to course load and program. Part-time tuition and fees vary according to course load and program. ***College room and board:*** $11,668; ***Room only:*** $7762. Room and board charges vary according to board plan, housing facility, and location.

FRESHMAN FINANCIAL AID (Fall 2018) 887 applied for aid; of those 76% were deemed to have need. 99% of freshmen with need received aid; of those 12% had need fully met. ***Average percent of need met:*** 75% (excluding resources awarded to replace EFC). ***Average financial aid package:*** $11,263 (excluding resources awarded to replace EFC). 19% of all full-time freshmen had no need and received non-need-based gift aid.

UNDERGRADUATE FINANCIAL AID (Fall 2018) 2,945 applied for aid; of those 80% were deemed to have need. 99% of undergraduates with need received aid; of those 10% had need fully met. ***Average percent of need met:*** 74% (excluding resources awarded to replace EFC). ***Average financial aid package:*** $11,422 (excluding resources awarded to replace EFC). 12% of all full-time undergraduates had no need and received non-need-based gift aid.

GIFT AID (NEED-BASED) ***Total amount:*** $14,529,701 (36% federal, 35% state, 21% institutional, 8% external sources). ***Receiving aid:*** Freshmen: 46% (464); all full-time undergraduates: 43% (1,626). ***Average award:*** Freshmen: $6864; Undergraduates: $6476. ***Scholarships, grants, and awards:*** Federal Pell, FSEOG, state, private, college/university gift aid from institutional funds.

GIFT AID (NON-NEED-BASED) ***Total amount:*** $2,561,993 (1% state, 83% institutional, 16% external sources). ***Receiving aid:*** Freshmen: 38% (386). Undergraduates: 26% (1,000). ***Average award:*** Freshmen: $2795. Undergraduates: $4242. ***Scholarships, grants, and awards by category:*** *Academic interests/achievement:* biological sciences, business, computer science, education, English, general academic interests/achievements, humanities, international studies, mathematics, military science, social sciences. *Creative arts/performance:* applied art and design, music, theater/drama. *Special achievements/activities:* community service, leadership, memberships. *Special characteristics:* children and siblings of alumni, general special characteristics, local/state students. ***Tuition waivers:*** Full or partial for employees or children of employees, senior citizens. ***ROTC:*** Army.

LOANS ***Student loans:*** $21,082,280 (37% need-based, 63% non-need-based). 67% of past graduating class borrowed through all loan programs. *Average indebtedness per student:* $30,133. ***Average need-based loan:*** Freshmen: $3142. Undergraduates: $4203. ***Parent loans:*** $15,822,287 (100% non-need-based). ***Programs:*** Federal Direct (Subsidized and Unsubsidized Stafford, PLUS).

WORK-STUDY ***Federal work-study:*** Total amount: $572,161; jobs available. ***State or other work-study/employment:*** Part-time jobs available.

ATHLETIC AWARDS Total amount: $3,050,653 (30% need-based, 70% non-need-based).

APPLYING FOR FINANCIAL AID ***Required financial aid form:*** FAFSA. ***Financial aid deadline (priority):*** 3/1. ***Notification date:*** Continuous.

CONTACT Ms. Sarah Dohney, Director of Financial Aid, Longwood University, 201 High Street, Farmville, VA 23909, 434-395-2077 or toll-free 800-281-4677. *Fax:* 434-395-2829. *E-mail:* dohenysc@longwood.edu.
Website: http://www.longwood.edu/.

LORAS COLLEGE

Dubuque, IA

Tuition & fees: $35,218	Average undergraduate aid package: $29,160

ABOUT THE INSTITUTION Independent Roman Catholic, coed. ***Awards:*** bachelor's and master's degrees. 35 undergraduate majors. ***Total enrollment:*** 1,400.

Undergraduates: 1,317. Freshmen: 326. Federal methodology is used as a basis for awarding need-based institutional aid.

UNDERGRADUATE EXPENSES for 2020–2021 ***Comprehensive fee:*** $43,818 includes full-time tuition ($33,500), mandatory fees ($1718), and room and board ($8600). ***College room only:*** $4000. Full-time tuition and fees vary according to course load and degree level. Room and board charges vary according to board plan and housing facility. ***Part-time tuition:*** $750 per credit hour. ***Part-time fees:*** $55 per credit hour.

FRESHMAN FINANCIAL AID (Fall 2019, est.) 320 applied for aid; of those 86% were deemed to have need. 100% of freshmen with need received aid; of those 24% had need fully met. ***Average percent of need met:*** 87% (excluding resources awarded to replace EFC). ***Average financial aid package:*** $30,438 (excluding resources awarded to replace EFC). 16% of all full-time freshmen had no need and received non-need-based gift aid.

UNDERGRADUATE FINANCIAL AID (Fall 2019, est.) 1,160 applied for aid; of those 88% were deemed to have need. 100% of undergraduates with need received aid; of those 30% had need fully met. ***Average percent of need met:*** 87% (excluding resources awarded to replace EFC). ***Average financial aid package:*** $29,160 (excluding resources awarded to replace EFC). 19% of all full-time undergraduates had no need and received non-need-based gift aid.

GIFT AID (NEED-BASED) ***Total amount:*** $23,559,977 (8% federal, 7% state, 84% institutional, 1% external sources). ***Receiving aid:*** Freshmen: 84% (274); all full-time undergraduates: 81% (1,018). ***Average award:*** Freshmen: $24,675; Undergraduates: $23,110. ***Scholarships, grants, and awards:*** Federal Pell, FSEOG, state, private, college/university gift aid from institutional funds.

GIFT AID (NON-NEED-BASED) ***Total amount:*** $5,971,075 (98% institutional, 2% external sources). ***Receiving aid:*** Freshmen: 13% (44). Undergraduates: 14% (179). ***Average award:*** Freshmen: $19,150. Undergraduates: $18,643. ***Scholarships, grants, and awards by category:*** *Academic interests/achievement:* 1,225 awards ($19,906,845 total): biological sciences, business, communication, computer science, education, engineering/technologies, English, general academic interests/achievements, health fields, mathematics, physical sciences, premedicine, religion/biblical studies. *Creative arts/performance:* 50 awards ($69,200 total): music. *Special achievements/activities:* 404 awards ($1,147,713 total): leadership, religious involvement. *Special characteristics:* 692 awards ($1,225,235 total): first-generation college students, local/state students, out-of-state students, religious affiliation. ***Tuition waivers:*** Full or partial for employees or children of employees. ***ROTC:*** Army cooperative.

LOANS ***Student loans:*** $7,848,108 (42% need-based, 58% non-need-based). 75% of past graduating class borrowed through all loan programs. *Average indebtedness per student:* $28,964. ***Average need-based loan:*** Freshmen: $3531. Undergraduates: $4292. ***Parent loans:*** $1,502,994 (100% non-need-based). ***Programs:*** Federal Direct (Subsidized and Unsubsidized Stafford, PLUS), Perkins, college/university.

WORK-STUDY ***Federal work-study:*** Total amount: $1,467,054; 525 jobs averaging $2794. ***State or other work-study/employment:*** Total amount: $6000 (50% need-based, 50% non-need-based). 4 part-time jobs averaging $1500.

APPLYING FOR FINANCIAL AID ***Required financial aid form:*** FAFSA. ***Financial aid deadline (priority):*** 3/1. ***Notification date:*** Continuous beginning 3/1. Students must reply within 3 weeks of notification.

CONTACT Mr. Zach Gries, Assistant Director of Financial Planning, Loras College, 1450 Alta Vista Street, Dubuque, IA 52001-4327, 563-588-7278 or toll-free 800-245-6727. *Fax:* 563-588-7119. *E-mail:* zachery.gries@loras.edu.
Website: http://www.loras.edu/.

LOS ANGELES ACADEMY OF FIGURATIVE ART

Van Nuys, CA

CONTACT Financial Aid Office, Los Angeles Academy of Figurative Art, 16926 Saticoy Street, Van Nuys, CA 91406.
Website: http://www.laafa.edu/.

LOS ANGELES FILM SCHOOL

Hollywood, CA

CONTACT Financial Aid Office, Los Angeles Film School, 6363 Sunset Boulevard, Hollywood, CA 90028, 323-860-0789 or toll-free 877-952-3456.
Website: http://www.lafilm.edu/.

LOUISIANA COLLEGE

Pineville, LA

Tuition & fees: $17,500	Average undergraduate aid package: $14,410

ABOUT THE INSTITUTION Independent Southern Baptist, coed. ***Awards:*** certificates, associate, bachelor's, and master's degrees. 60 undergraduate majors. ***Total enrollment:*** 1,245. Undergraduates: 1,004. Freshmen: 261. Federal methodology is used as a basis for awarding need-based institutional aid.

UNDERGRADUATE EXPENSES for 2019–2020 ***Application fee:*** $25. ***Comprehensive fee:*** $23,146 includes full-time tuition ($17,500) and room and board ($5646). ***College room only:*** $2282. Full-time tuition and fees vary according to course load. Room and board charges vary according to board plan and housing facility. ***Part-time tuition:*** $547 per credit hour. Part-time tuition and fees vary according to course load.

FRESHMAN FINANCIAL AID (Fall 2018) 240 applied for aid; of those 82% were deemed to have need. 99% of freshmen with need received aid; of those 23% had need fully met. ***Average percent of need met:*** 71% (excluding resources awarded to replace EFC). ***Average financial aid package:*** $15,685 (excluding resources awarded to replace EFC). 19% of all full-time freshmen had no need and received non-need-based gift aid.

UNDERGRADUATE FINANCIAL AID (Fall 2018) 841 applied for aid; of those 85% were deemed to have need. 99% of undergraduates with need received aid; of those 21% had need fully met. ***Average percent of need met:*** 64% (excluding resources awarded to replace EFC). ***Average financial aid package:*** $14,410 (excluding resources awarded to replace EFC). 16% of all full-time undergraduates had no need and received non-need-based gift aid.

GIFT AID (NEED-BASED) ***Total amount:*** $8,461,128 (28% federal, 19% state, 48% institutional, 5% external sources). ***Receiving aid:*** Freshmen: 79% (196); all full-time undergraduates: 79% (692). ***Average award:*** Freshmen: $13,547; Undergraduates: $12,065. ***Scholarships, grants, and awards:*** Federal Pell, FSEOG, state, private, college/university gift aid from institutional funds.

GIFT AID (NON-NEED-BASED) ***Total amount:*** $2,540,398 (1% federal, 35% state, 56% institutional, 8% external sources). ***Receiving aid:*** Freshmen: 18% (45). Undergraduates: 17% (145). ***Average award:*** Freshmen: $8639. Undergraduates: $7728. ***Scholarships, grants, and awards by category:*** *Academic interests/achievement:* business, communication, English, general academic interests/achievements, health fields, home economics, humanities, mathematics, religion/biblical studies, social sciences. *Creative arts/performance:* applied art and design, debating, journalism/publications, music, performing arts, theater/drama. *Special achievements/activities:* cheerleading/drum major, leadership. *Special characteristics:* children of faculty/staff. ***Tuition waivers:*** Full or partial for employees or children of employees, adult students, senior citizens.

LOANS ***Student loans:*** $4,193,163 (79% need-based, 21% non-need-based). 77% of past graduating class borrowed through all loan programs. *Average indebtedness per student:* $25,656. ***Average need-based loan:*** Freshmen: $2820. Undergraduates: $3428. ***Parent loans:*** $877,166 (71% need-based, 29% non-need-based). ***Programs:*** Federal Direct (Subsidized and Unsubsidized Stafford, PLUS).

WORK-STUDY ***Federal work-study:*** Total amount: $117,882; jobs available.

APPLYING FOR FINANCIAL AID ***Required financial aid forms:*** FAFSA, institution's own form. ***Financial aid deadline (priority):*** 5/1. ***Notification date:*** Continuous beginning 2/1. Students must reply by 8/1 or within 2 weeks of notification.

CONTACT Mr. Jeremy N. Treme, Director of Financial Aid, Louisiana College, 1140 College Drive, Pineville, LA 71359-0001, 318-487-7387 or toll-free 800-487-1906. *Fax:* 318-487-7449. *E-mail:* jeremy.treme@lacollege.edu.
Website: http://www.lacollege.edu/.

LOUISIANA STATE UNIVERSITY AND AGRICULTURAL & MECHANICAL COLLEGE

Baton Rouge, LA

Tuition & fees (LA res): $11,962 **Average undergraduate aid package: $15,620**

ABOUT THE INSTITUTION State-supported, coed. ***Awards:*** certificates, bachelor's, master's, and doctoral degrees. 67 undergraduate majors. ***Total enrollment:*** 30,985. Undergraduates: 25,361. Freshmen: 5,812. Federal methodology is used as a basis for awarding need-based institutional aid.

UNDERGRADUATE EXPENSES for 2019–2020 ***Application fee:*** $50. ***Tuition, state resident:*** full-time $8038. ***Tuition, nonresident:*** full-time $24,715. ***Required fees:*** full-time $3924. Full-time tuition and fees vary according to course load. Part-time tuition and fees vary according to course load. ***College room and board:*** $12,276; ***Room only:*** $8030. Room and board charges vary according to board plan and housing facility.

FRESHMAN FINANCIAL AID (Fall 2018) 4745 applied for aid; of those 73% were deemed to have need. 100% of freshmen with need received aid; of those 15% had need fully met. ***Average percent of need met:*** 65% (excluding resources awarded to replace EFC). ***Average financial aid package:*** $16,507 (excluding resources awarded to replace EFC). 22% of all full-time freshmen had no need and received non-need-based gift aid.

UNDERGRADUATE FINANCIAL AID (Fall 2018) 14,349 applied for aid; of those 78% were deemed to have need. 100% of undergraduates with need received aid; of those 14% had need fully met. ***Average percent of need met:*** 61% (excluding resources awarded to replace EFC). ***Average financial aid package:*** $15,620 (excluding resources awarded to replace EFC). 17% of all full-time undergraduates had no need and received non-need-based gift aid.

GIFT AID (NEED-BASED) ***Total amount:*** $134,156,609 (23% federal, 40% state, 36% institutional, 1% external sources). ***Receiving aid:*** Freshmen: 58% (3,381); all full-time undergraduates: 47% (10,391). ***Average award:*** Freshmen: $14,106; Undergraduates: $12,782. ***Scholarships, grants, and awards:*** Federal Pell, FSEOG, state, private, college/university gift aid from institutional funds.

GIFT AID (NON-NEED-BASED) ***Total amount:*** $81,427,767 (2% federal, 60% state, 31% institutional, 7% external sources). ***Receiving aid:*** Freshmen: 3% (166). Undergraduates: 2% (362). ***Average award:*** Freshmen: $5414. Undergraduates: $5912. ***Scholarships, grants, and awards by category:*** *Academic interests/achievement:* agriculture, architecture, biological sciences, business, computer science, education, engineering/technologies, English, foreign languages, general academic interests/achievements, health fields, humanities, mathematics, military science, physical sciences, religion/biblical studies. *Creative arts/performance:* applied art and design, art/fine arts, journalism/publications, music, theater/drama. *Special characteristics:* children with a deceased or disabled parent, general special characteristics, out-of-state students, veterans. ***Tuition waivers:*** Full or partial for employees or children of employees. ***ROTC:*** Army, Naval cooperative, Air Force.

LOANS ***Student loans:*** $67,527,010 (73% need-based, 27% non-need-based). 44% of past graduating class borrowed through all loan programs. *Average indebtedness per student:* $24,851. ***Average need-based loan:*** Freshmen: $3314. Undergraduates: $4198. ***Parent loans:*** $45,296,474 (52% need-based, 48% non-need-based). ***Programs:*** Federal Direct (Subsidized and Unsubsidized Stafford, PLUS), college/university.

WORK-STUDY ***Federal work-study:*** Total amount: $3,069,927; jobs available. ***State or other work-study/employment:*** Total amount: $9,901,964 (40% need-based, 60% non-need-based). Part-time jobs available.

ATHLETIC AWARDS Total amount: $14,300,629 (34% need-based, 66% non-need-based).

APPLYING FOR FINANCIAL AID ***Required financial aid forms:*** FAFSA, institution's own form. ***Financial aid deadline (priority):*** 4/1. ***Notification date:*** Continuous beginning 11/15. Students must reply by 5/1.

CONTACT Ms. Amy Marix, Director of Financial Aid and Scholarships, Louisiana State University and Agricultural & Mechanical College, 1146 Pleasant Hall, Baton Rouge, LA 70803, 225-578-3103. *Fax:* 225-578-6300. *E-mail:* financialaid@lsu.edu.
Website: http://www.lsu.edu/.

LOUISIANA STATE UNIVERSITY AT ALEXANDRIA

Alexandria, LA

CONTACT Financial Aid Office, Louisiana State University at Alexandria, 8100 Highway 71 South, Alexandria, LA 71302-9121, 318-445-3672 or toll-free 888-473-6417.
Website: http://www.lsua.edu/.

LOUISIANA STATE UNIVERSITY HEALTH SCIENCES CENTER

New Orleans, LA

CONTACT Mr. Patrick Gorman, Director of Financial Aid, Louisiana State University Health Sciences Center, 433 Bolivar Street, New Orleans, LA 70112, 504-568-4821. *Fax:* 504-599-1390.
Website: http://www.lsuhsc.edu/.

LOUISIANA STATE UNIVERSITY IN SHREVEPORT

Shreveport, LA

Tuition & fees: N/R **Average undergraduate aid package: N/A**

ABOUT THE INSTITUTION State-supported, coed. ***Awards:*** certificates, bachelor's, master's, and doctoral degrees. 20 undergraduate majors. ***Total enrollment:*** 6,002. Undergraduates: 2,577. Freshmen: 338. Federal methodology is used as a basis for awarding need-based institutional aid.

GIFT AID (NEED-BASED) ***Scholarships, grants, and awards:*** Federal Pell, FSEOG, state, private, college/university gift aid from institutional funds.

GIFT AID (NON-NEED-BASED) ***Scholarships, grants, and awards by category:*** *Academic interests/achievement:* biological sciences, business, communication, computer science, education, English, general academic interests/achievements, home economics, humanities, mathematics, physical sciences, premedicine, social sciences. ***ROTC:*** Army cooperative.

LOANS ***Programs:*** Federal Direct (Subsidized and Unsubsidized Stafford, PLUS).

WORK-STUDY Federal work-study jobs available.

APPLYING FOR FINANCIAL AID ***Required financial aid form:*** FAFSA. ***Financial aid deadline:*** Continuous. ***Notification date:*** Continuous.

CONTACT Office of Student Financial Aid, Louisiana State University in Shreveport, One University Place, Shreveport, LA 71115-2399, 318-797-5363 or toll-free 800-229-5957. *Fax:* 318-797-5366. *E-mail:* finaid@lsus.edu.
Website: http://www.lsus.edu/.

LOUISIANA TECH UNIVERSITY

Ruston, LA

ABOUT THE INSTITUTION State-supported, coed. ***Awards:*** certificates, associate, bachelor's, master's, and doctoral degrees. 79 undergraduate majors. ***Total enrollment:*** 12,467. Undergraduates: 11,185. Freshmen: 2,186.

GIFT AID (NEED-BASED) ***Scholarships, grants, and awards:*** Federal Pell, FSEOG, state, private, college/university gift aid from institutional funds.

GIFT AID (NON-NEED-BASED) ***Scholarships, grants, and awards by category:*** *Academic interests/achievement:* agriculture, architecture, biological sciences, business, computer science, education, engineering/technologies, English, foreign languages, general academic interests/achievements, health fields, home economics, international studies, mathematics, military science, physical sciences, social sciences. *Creative arts/performance:* applied art and design, art/fine arts, creative writing, debating, general creative arts/performance, journalism/publications, music, performing arts, theater/drama. *Special achievements/activities:* cheerleading/drum major, junior miss. *Special characteristics:* children and siblings of alumni, children of faculty/staff, children of public servants, handicapped students, international students, members of minority groups, out-of-state students, spouses of deceased or disabled public servants, veterans.

LOANS ***Programs:*** Federal Direct (Subsidized and Unsubsidized Stafford, PLUS), Perkins, private loans.

CONTACT Mrs. Aimee D. Baxter, Office of Financial Aid, Louisiana Tech University, PO Box 7925, Ruston, LA 71272, 318-257-2641 or toll-free 800-528-3241. *Fax:* 318-257-2628. *E-mail:* techaid@latech.edu.
Website: http://www.latech.edu/.

LOURDES UNIVERSITY

Sylvania, OH

CONTACT Deb LaJeunesse, Director of Financial Aid, Lourdes University, 6832 Convent Boulevard, Sylvania, OH 43560-2898, 419-824-3732 or toll-free 800-878-3210. *Fax:* 419-517-8866. *E-mail:* finaid@lourdes.edu.
Website: http://www.lourdes.edu/.

LOYOLA MARYMOUNT UNIVERSITY

Los Angeles, CA

Tuition & fees: $50,283	Average undergraduate aid package: $31,458

ABOUT THE INSTITUTION Independent Roman Catholic, coed. ***Awards:*** certificates, bachelor's, master's, and doctoral degrees. 53 undergraduate majors. ***Total enrollment:*** 9,822. Undergraduates: 6,778. Freshmen: 1,467. Federal methodology is used as a basis for awarding need-based institutional aid.

UNDERGRADUATE EXPENSES for 2019–2020 ***Application fee:*** $60. ***One-time required fee:*** $400. ***Comprehensive fee:*** $65,893 includes full-time tuition ($49,550), mandatory fees ($733), and room and board ($15,610). ***College room only:*** $11,110. Full-time tuition and fees vary according to reciprocity agreements. Room and board charges vary according to board plan and housing facility. ***Part-time tuition:*** $2068 per credit hour. ***Part-time fees:*** $65 per term. Part-time tuition and fees vary according to course load.

FRESHMAN FINANCIAL AID (Fall 2018) 1110 applied for aid; of those 68% were deemed to have need. 99% of freshmen with need received aid; of those 23% had need fully met. ***Average percent of need met:*** 68% (excluding resources awarded to replace EFC). ***Average financial aid package:*** $30,841 (excluding resources awarded to replace EFC). 40% of all full-time freshmen had no need and received non-need-based gift aid.

UNDERGRADUATE FINANCIAL AID (Fall 2018) 4,461 applied for aid; of those 75% were deemed to have need. 99% of undergraduates with need received aid; of those 24% had need fully met. ***Average percent of need met:*** 66% (excluding resources awarded to replace EFC). ***Average financial aid package:*** $31,458 (excluding resources awarded to replace EFC). 30% of all full-time undergraduates had no need and received non-need-based gift aid.

GIFT AID (NEED-BASED) ***Total amount:*** $74,134,478 (8% federal, 10% state, 80% institutional, 2% external sources). ***Receiving aid:*** Freshmen: 49% (737); all full-time undergraduates: 50% (3,189). ***Average award:*** Freshmen: $23,161; Undergraduates: $23,162. ***Scholarships, grants, and awards:*** Federal Pell, FSEOG, state, private, college/university gift aid from institutional funds.

GIFT AID (NON-NEED-BASED) ***Total amount:*** $27,257,615 (90% institutional, 10% external sources). ***Receiving aid:*** Freshmen: 10% (147). Undergraduates: 9% (555). ***Average award:*** Freshmen: $11,045. Undergraduates: $10,616. ***Scholarships, grants, and awards by category:*** *Academic interests/achievement:* area/ethnic studies, biological sciences, business, communication, computer science, education, engineering/technologies, English, foreign languages, general academic interests/achievements, health fields, home economics, humanities, international studies, mathematics, physical sciences, religion/biblical studies, social sciences. *Creative arts/performance:* applied art and design, art/fine arts, cinema/film/broadcasting, creative writing, dance, debating, general creative arts/performance, journalism/publications, music, performing arts, theater/drama. *Special achievements/activities:* community service, general special achievements/activities, leadership, memberships, religious involvement. *Special characteristics:* adult students, children and siblings of alumni, children of faculty/staff, ethnic background, first-generation college students, general special characteristics, handicapped students, international students, local/state students, members of minority groups, out-of-state students, previous college experience, religious affiliation, veterans, veterans' children. ***Tuition waivers:*** Full or partial for employees or children of employees. ***ROTC:*** Army cooperative, Air Force.

LOANS ***Student loans:*** $26,353,788 (72% need-based, 28% non-need-based). 49% of past graduating class borrowed through all loan programs. *Average indebtedness per student:* $33,742. ***Average need-based loan:*** Freshmen: $5138. Undergraduates: $5743. ***Parent loans:*** $26,691,376 (51% need-based, 49% non-need-based). ***Programs:*** Federal Direct (Subsidized and Unsubsidized Stafford, PLUS), college/university.

WORK-STUDY ***Federal work-study:*** Total amount: $2,580,629; 1,279 jobs averaging $2018. ***State or other work-study/employment:*** Total amount: $4,609,705 (23% need-based, 77% non-need-based). 2,174 part-time jobs averaging $2120.

ATHLETIC AWARDS Total amount: $8,682,690 (37% need-based, 63% non-need-based).

APPLYING FOR FINANCIAL AID ***Required financial aid form:*** FAFSA. ***Financial aid deadline (priority):*** 2/1. ***Notification date:*** Continuous beginning 12/23. Students must reply by 5/1.

CONTACT Lindsay McCarthy, Assistant Vice Provost for Financial Aid, Loyola Marymount University, 1 LMU Drive, Los Angeles, CA 90045, 310-338-2753 or toll-free 800-LMU-INFO. *Fax:* 310-338-2793. *E-mail:* finaid@lmu.edu.
Website: http://www.lmu.edu/.

LOYOLA UNIVERSITY CHICAGO

Chicago, IL

Tuition & fees: $46,898	Average undergraduate aid package: $35,786

ABOUT THE INSTITUTION Independent Roman Catholic (Jesuit), coed. ***Awards:*** certificates, associate, bachelor's, master's, and doctoral degrees (also offers adult part-time program with significant enrollment not reflected in profile). 108 undergraduate majors. ***Total enrollment:*** 17,159. Undergraduates: 12,240. Freshmen: 2,630. Federal methodology is used as a basis for awarding need-based institutional aid.

UNDERGRADUATE EXPENSES for 2020–2021 ***Comprehensive fee:*** $61,918 includes full-time tuition ($45,500), mandatory fees ($1398), and room and board ($15,020). ***College room only:*** $9400. Full-time tuition and fees vary according to degree level. ***Part-time tuition:*** $840 per credit hour. Part-time tuition and fees vary according to degree level.

FRESHMAN FINANCIAL AID (Fall 2019, est.) 2261 applied for aid; of those 76% were deemed to have need. 100% of freshmen with need received aid; of those 18% had need fully met. ***Average percent of need met:*** 84% (excluding resources awarded to replace EFC). ***Average financial aid package:*** $36,133 (excluding resources awarded to replace EFC). 34% of all full-time freshmen had no need and received non-need-based gift aid.

UNDERGRADUATE FINANCIAL AID (Fall 2019, est.) 8,535 applied for aid; of those 85% were deemed to have need. 100% of undergraduates with need received aid; of those 16% had need fully met. ***Average percent of need met:*** 84% (excluding resources awarded to replace EFC). ***Average financial aid package:*** $35,786 (excluding resources awarded to replace EFC). 33% of all full-time undergraduates had no need and received non-need-based gift aid.

GIFT AID (NEED-BASED) ***Total amount:*** $155,280,888 (11% federal, 7% state, 80% institutional, 2% external sources). ***Receiving aid:*** Freshmen: 64% (1,689); all full-time undergraduates: 59% (6,774). ***Average award:*** Freshmen: $23,764; Undergraduates: $22,915. ***Scholarships, grants, and awards:*** Federal Pell, FSEOG, state, private, college/university gift aid from institutional funds.

GIFT AID (NON-NEED-BASED) ***Total amount:*** $78,793,425 (3% federal, 95% institutional, 2% external sources). ***Receiving aid:*** Freshmen: 9% (245). Undergraduates: 7% (816). ***Average award:*** Freshmen: $18,633. Undergraduates: $18,001. ***Scholarships, grants, and awards by category:*** *Academic interests/achievement:* 8,686 awards ($162,727,111 total): general academic interests/achievements. *Creative arts/performance:* 53 awards ($119,600 total): applied art and design, debating, journalism/publications, music, theater/drama. *Special achievements/activities:* 914 awards ($6,896,094 total): community service, general special achievements/activities, leadership, memberships. *Special characteristics:* 1,460 awards ($4,287,110 total): adult students, general special characteristics, religious affiliation. ***Tuition waivers:*** Full or partial for employees or children of employees. ***ROTC:*** Army, Naval cooperative, Air Force cooperative.

LOANS ***Student loans:*** $76,377,054 (68% need-based, 32% non-need-based). 61% of past graduating class borrowed through all loan programs. *Average indebtedness per student:* $35,030. ***Average need-based loan:*** Freshmen: $3377. Undergraduates: $4349. ***Parent loans:*** $51,165,847 (52% need-based, 48% non-need-based). ***Programs:*** Federal Direct (Subsidized and Unsubsidized Stafford, PLUS), Perkins, Federal Nursing.

WORK-STUDY ***Federal work-study:*** Total amount: $14,484,263; 5,111 jobs averaging $2764.

ATHLETIC AWARDS Total amount: $5,203,607 (23% need-based, 77% non-need-based).

APPLYING FOR FINANCIAL AID ***Required financial aid form:*** FAFSA. ***Financial aid deadline:*** Continuous. ***Notification date:*** Continuous beginning 2/15. Students must reply within 3 weeks of notification.

CONTACT Mr. Tobyn Friar, Director of Financial Aid, Loyola University Chicago, 6525 North Sheridan Road, Chicago, IL 60660, 773-508-7704 or toll-free 800-262-2373. *Fax:* 773-508-3397. *E-mail:* nmerz@luc.edu.
Website: http://www.luc.edu/.

LOYOLA UNIVERSITY MARYLAND

Baltimore, MD

Tuition & fees: $50,265	Average undergraduate aid package: $31,909

ABOUT THE INSTITUTION Independent Roman Catholic (Jesuit), coed. ***Awards:*** certificates, bachelor's, master's, and doctoral degrees. 35 undergraduate majors. ***Total enrollment:*** 5,645. Undergraduates: 3,879. Freshmen: 1,069. Institutional methodology is used as a basis for awarding need-based institutional aid.

UNDERGRADUATE EXPENSES for 2019–2020 ***Application fee:*** $60. ***Comprehensive fee:*** $64,975 includes full-time tuition ($48,700), mandatory fees ($1565), and room and board ($14,710). Full-time tuition and fees vary according to course load. Room and board charges vary according to board plan and housing facility. ***Part-time tuition:*** $785 per credit. Part-time tuition and fees vary according to course load.

FRESHMAN FINANCIAL AID (Fall 2018) 881 applied for aid; of those 66% were deemed to have need. 100% of freshmen with need received aid; of those 31% had need fully met. ***Average percent of need met:*** 85% (excluding resources awarded to replace EFC). ***Average financial aid package:*** $35,659 (excluding resources awarded to replace EFC). 33% of all full-time freshmen had no need and received non-need-based gift aid.

UNDERGRADUATE FINANCIAL AID (Fall 2018) 2,604 applied for aid; of those 79% were deemed to have need. 100% of undergraduates with need received aid; of those 7% had need fully met. ***Average percent of need met:*** 88% (excluding resources awarded to replace EFC). ***Average financial aid package:*** $31,909 (excluding resources awarded to replace EFC). 33% of all full-time undergraduates had no need and received non-need-based gift aid.

GIFT AID (NEED-BASED) ***Total amount:*** $57,159,593 (6% federal, 2% state, 90% institutional, 2% external sources). ***Receiving aid:*** Freshmen: 51% (542); all full-time undergraduates: 40% (1,518). ***Average award:*** Freshmen: $17,382; Undergraduates: $19,256. ***Scholarships, grants, and awards:*** Federal Pell, FSEOG, state, private, college/university gift aid from institutional funds.

GIFT AID (NON-NEED-BASED) ***Total amount:*** $26,126,561 (8% federal, 91% institutional, 1% external sources). ***Receiving aid:*** Freshmen: 40% (423). Undergraduates: 38% (1,438). ***Average award:*** Freshmen: $20,008. Undergraduates: $19,753. ***Scholarships, grants, and awards by category:*** *Academic interests/achievement:* general academic interests/achievements. *Special characteristics:* children of faculty/staff. ***Tuition waivers:*** Full or partial for employees or children of employees. ***ROTC:*** Army, Air Force cooperative.

LOANS ***Student loans:*** $24,738,880 (80% need-based, 20% non-need-based). 63% of past graduating class borrowed through all loan programs. *Average indebtedness per student:* $41,443. ***Average need-based loan:*** Freshmen: $3680. Undergraduates: $4640. ***Parent loans:*** $17,850,150 (100% non-need-based). ***Programs:*** Federal Direct (Subsidized and Unsubsidized Stafford, PLUS), college/university.

WORK-STUDY ***Federal work-study:*** Total amount: $1,008,779; 458 jobs averaging $3595. ***State or other work-study/employment:*** Total amount: $1,115,364 (81% need-based, 19% non-need-based). 206 part-time jobs averaging $5791.

ATHLETIC AWARDS Total amount: $6,118,297 (28% need-based, 72% non-need-based).

APPLYING FOR FINANCIAL AID ***Required financial aid forms:*** FAFSA, CSS Financial Aid PROFILE, noncustodial (divorced/separated) parent's statement. ***Financial aid deadline:*** 1/15 (priority: 1/15). ***Notification date:*** 3/15. Students must reply by 5/1.

CONTACT Office of Financial Aid, Loyola University Maryland, Knott Humanities Center, 211A, Baltimore, MD 21210, 410-617-2000 or toll-free 800-221-9107. *E-mail:* financialaid@loyola.edu.
Website: http://www.loyola.edu/.

LOYOLA UNIVERSITY NEW ORLEANS

New Orleans, LA

Tuition & fees: $42,030	Average undergraduate aid package: $33,885

ABOUT THE INSTITUTION Independent Roman Catholic (Jesuit), coed. ***Awards:*** certificates, bachelor's, master's, and doctoral degrees. 69 undergraduate majors. ***Total enrollment:*** 4,384. Undergraduates: 3,188. Freshmen: 826. Federal methodology is used as a basis for awarding need-based institutional aid.

UNDERGRADUATE EXPENSES for 2020–2021 ***One-time required fee:*** $250. ***Comprehensive fee:*** $55,636 includes full-time tuition ($40,288), mandatory fees ($1742), and room and board ($13,606). ***College room only:*** $7688. Room and board charges vary according to board plan. ***Part-time tuition:*** $1094 per credit hour. ***Part-time fees:*** $426.

FRESHMAN FINANCIAL AID (Fall 2019, est.) 767 applied for aid; of those 89% were deemed to have need. 100% of freshmen with need received aid; of those 16% had need fully met. ***Average percent of need met:*** 80% (excluding resources awarded to replace EFC). ***Average financial aid package:*** $36,351 (excluding resources awarded to replace EFC). 16% of all full-time freshmen had no need and received non-need-based gift aid.

UNDERGRADUATE FINANCIAL AID (Fall 2019, est.) 2,330 applied for aid; of those 89% were deemed to have need. 99% of undergraduates with need received aid; of those 17% had need fully met. ***Average percent of need met:*** 76% (excluding resources awarded to replace EFC). ***Average financial aid package:*** $33,885 (excluding resources awarded to replace EFC). 22% of all full-time undergraduates had no need and received non-need-based gift aid.

GIFT AID (NEED-BASED) ***Total amount:*** $60,396,933 (9% federal, 7% state, 82% institutional, 2% external sources). ***Receiving aid:*** Freshmen: 80% (680); all full-time undergraduates: 73% (2,051). ***Average award:*** Freshmen: $33,447; Undergraduates: $30,629. ***Scholarships, grants, and awards:*** Federal Pell, FSEOG, state, private, college/university gift aid from institutional funds, United Negro College Fund.

GIFT AID (NON-NEED-BASED) ***Total amount:*** $15,336,894 (7% state, 92% institutional, 1% external sources). ***Receiving aid:*** Freshmen: 12% (100). Undergraduates: 10% (270). ***Average award:*** Freshmen: $20,564. Undergraduates: $19,707. ***Scholarships, grants, and awards by category:*** *Academic interests/achievement:* general academic interests/achievements. *Creative arts/performance:* applied art and design, general creative arts/performance. *Special achievements/activities:* leadership. *Special characteristics:* children and siblings of alumni, children of faculty/staff. ***Tuition waivers:*** Full or partial for employees or children of employees, senior citizens. ***ROTC:*** Army cooperative, Naval cooperative, Air Force cooperative.

LOANS ***Student loans:*** $15,491,115 (76% need-based, 24% non-need-based). 71% of past graduating class borrowed through all loan programs. *Average indebtedness per student:* $27,049. ***Average need-based loan:*** Freshmen: $3121. Undergraduates: $4009. ***Parent loans:*** $6,373,483 (49% need-based, 51% non-need-based). ***Programs:*** Federal Direct (Subsidized and Unsubsidized Stafford, PLUS).

WORK-STUDY ***Federal work-study:*** Total amount: $849,617; jobs available.

ATHLETIC AWARDS Total amount: $3,832,033 (47% need-based, 53% non-need-based).

APPLYING FOR FINANCIAL AID ***Required financial aid form:*** FAFSA. ***Financial aid deadline (priority):*** 2/15. ***Notification date:*** Continuous beginning 3/1. Students must reply within 2 weeks of notification.

CONTACT Ms. Anna P Daigle, Director of Scholarships and Financial Aid, Loyola University New Orleans, 6363 St. Charles Avenue, New Orleans, LA 70118-6195, 504-865-3231 or toll-free 800-4-LOYOLA. *Fax:* 504-865-3233. *E-mail:* finaid@loyno.edu.
Website: http://www.loyno.edu/.

LUBBOCK CHRISTIAN UNIVERSITY

Lubbock, TX

ABOUT THE INSTITUTION Independent Church of Christ, coed. ***Awards:*** bachelor's and master's degrees. 58 undergraduate majors. ***Total enrollment:*** 1,805. Undergraduates: 6,439. Freshmen: 294.

GIFT AID (NEED-BASED) ***Scholarships, grants, and awards:*** Federal Pell, FSEOG, state, college/university gift aid from institutional funds.

GIFT AID (NON-NEED-BASED) ***Scholarships, grants, and awards by category:*** *Academic interests/achievement:* agriculture, business, communication, computer science, education, English, foreign languages, general academic interests/achievements, humanities, physical sciences, religion/biblical studies, social sciences. *Creative arts/performance:* applied art and design, journalism/publications, music, performing arts, theater/drama. *Special achievements/activities:* leadership. *Special characteristics:* children and siblings of alumni, children of faculty/staff, siblings of current students, spouses of current students.

LOANS ***Programs:*** Federal Direct (Subsidized and Unsubsidized Stafford, PLUS), state.

WORK-STUDY ***Federal work-study:*** Total amount: $913,093; 632 jobs averaging $1733. ***State or other work-study/employment:*** 14 part-time jobs averaging $735.

APPLYING FOR FINANCIAL AID ***Required financial aid forms:*** FAFSA, institution's own form.

CONTACT Mrs. Amy Hardesty, Director of Financial Aid, Lubbock Christian University, 5601 19th Street, Lubbock, TX 79407, 806-720-7176 or toll-free 800-933-7601. *Fax:* 806-720-7185. *E-mail:* amy.hardesty@lcu.edu.
Website: http://www.lcu.edu/.

LUTHER COLLEGE

Decorah, IA

ABOUT THE INSTITUTION Independent Evangelical Lutheran Church in America, coed. ***Awards:*** bachelor's degrees. 41 undergraduate majors. ***Total enrollment:*** 2,005. Undergraduates: 2,005. Freshmen: 554.

GIFT AID (NEED-BASED) ***Scholarships, grants, and awards:*** Federal Pell, FSEOG, state, private, college/university gift aid from institutional funds.

GIFT AID (NON-NEED-BASED) ***Scholarships, grants, and awards by category:*** *Academic interests/achievement:* general academic interests/achievements. *Creative arts/performance:* music, theater/drama. *Special characteristics:* children and siblings of alumni, members of minority groups, religious affiliation.

LOANS ***Programs:*** Federal Direct (Subsidized and Unsubsidized Stafford, PLUS), Perkins, college/university.

WORK-STUDY ***Federal work-study:*** Total amount: $1,571,780; 749 jobs averaging $2099. ***State or other work-study/employment:*** Total amount: $1,964,140 (10% need-based, 90% non-need-based). 71 part-time jobs averaging $4713.

APPLYING FOR FINANCIAL AID ***Required financial aid forms:*** FAFSA, institution's own form.

CONTACT Ms. Janice Cordell, Director of Financial Aid, Luther College, 700 College Drive, Decorah, IA 52101-1045, 563-387-1018 or toll-free 800-458-8437. *Fax:* 563-387-2241. *E-mail:* cordellj@luther.edu.
Website: http://www.luther.edu/.

LUTHER RICE COLLEGE & SEMINARY

Lithonia, GA

CONTACT Mr. Casey Kuffrey, Financial Aid Director, Luther Rice College & Seminary, 3038 Evans Mill Road, Lithonia, GA 30038-2418, 770-484-1204 Ext. 5284 or toll-free 800-442-1577. *Fax:* 678-990-5388. *E-mail:* casey.kuffrey@lutherrice.edu.
Website: http://www.lutherrice.edu/.

LYCOMING COLLEGE

Williamsport, PA

Tuition & fees: $41,626	Average undergraduate aid package: $43,039

ABOUT THE INSTITUTION Independent United Methodist, coed. ***Awards:*** bachelor's degrees. 48 undergraduate majors. ***Total enrollment:*** 1,142. Undergraduates: 1,142. Freshmen: 323. Federal methodology is used as a basis for awarding need-based institutional aid.

UNDERGRADUATE EXPENSES for 2019–2020 ***One-time required fee:*** $225. ***Comprehensive fee:*** $54,634 includes full-time tuition ($40,896), mandatory fees ($730), and room and board ($13,008). Room and board charges vary according to board plan. ***Part-time tuition:*** $1278 per credit hour.

FRESHMAN FINANCIAL AID (Fall 2019, est.) 323 applied for aid; of those 97% were deemed to have need. 100% of freshmen with need received aid; of those 21% had need fully met. ***Average percent of need met:*** 88% (excluding resources awarded to replace EFC). ***Average financial aid package:*** $49,803 (excluding resources awarded to replace EFC). 8% of all full-time freshmen had no need and received non-need-based gift aid.

UNDERGRADUATE FINANCIAL AID (Fall 2019, est.) 1,010 applied for aid; of those 96% were deemed to have need. 100% of undergraduates with need received aid; of those 26% had need fully met. ***Average percent of need met:*** 85% (excluding resources awarded to replace EFC). ***Average financial aid package:*** $43,039 (excluding resources awarded to replace EFC). 13% of all full-time undergraduates had no need and received non-need-based gift aid.

GIFT AID (NEED-BASED) ***Total amount:*** $35,452,590 (8% federal, 3% state, 87% institutional, 2% external sources). ***Receiving aid:*** Freshmen: 92% (314); all full-time undergraduates: 86% (967). ***Average award:*** Freshmen: $38,367; Undergraduates: $35,342. ***Scholarships, grants, and awards:*** Federal Pell, FSEOG, state, private, college/university gift aid from institutional funds.

GIFT AID (NON-NEED-BASED) ***Total amount:*** $3,010,829 (95% institutional, 5% external sources). ***Receiving aid:*** Freshmen: 8% (28). Undergraduates: 9% (97). ***Average award:*** Freshmen: $27,122. Undergraduates: $27,854. ***Scholarships, grants, and awards by category:*** *Creative arts/performance:* applied art and design, art/fine arts, creative writing, music, theater/drama. *Special characteristics:* children of faculty/staff. ***Tuition waivers:*** Full or partial for employees or children of employees. ***ROTC:*** Army cooperative.

LOANS ***Student loans:*** $8,886,237 (69% need-based, 31% non-need-based). ***Average need-based loan:*** Freshmen: $3300. Undergraduates: $4914. ***Parent loans:*** $2,997,640 (46% need-based, 54% non-need-based). ***Programs:*** Federal Direct (Subsidized and Unsubsidized Stafford, PLUS), Perkins, college/university.

WORK-STUDY ***Federal work-study:*** Total amount: $257,159; jobs available.

APPLYING FOR FINANCIAL AID ***Required financial aid form:*** FAFSA. ***Financial aid deadline (priority):*** 5/1. ***Notification date:*** Continuous beginning 11/15.

CONTACT Mr. James S. Lakis, Director of Financial Aid, Lycoming College, 700 College Place, Williamsport, PA 17701-5192, 570-321-4040 or toll-free 800-345-3920 Ext.4026. *Fax:* 570-321-4993. *E-mail:* lakis@lycoming.edu.
Website: http://www.lycoming.edu/.

LYNN UNIVERSITY

Boca Raton, FL

Tuition & fees: $39,850	Average undergraduate aid package: $24,022

ABOUT THE INSTITUTION Independent, coed. ***Awards:*** certificates, associate, bachelor's, master's, and doctoral degrees. 37 undergraduate majors. ***Total enrollment:*** 3,427. Undergraduates: 2,422. Freshmen: 739. Federal methodology is used as a basis for awarding need-based institutional aid.

UNDERGRADUATE EXPENSES for 2020–2021 ***One-time required fee:*** $1000. ***Comprehensive fee:*** $52,320 includes full-time tuition ($37,600), mandatory fees ($2250), and room and board ($12,470). Full-time tuition and fees vary according to program. Room and board charges vary according to board plan and housing facility. ***Part-time tuition:*** $1080 per credit hour. Part-time tuition and fees vary according to course load and program.

FRESHMAN FINANCIAL AID (Fall 2019, est.) 721 applied for aid; of those 55% were deemed to have need. 100% of freshmen with need received aid; of those 100% had need fully met. ***Average percent of need met:*** 61% (excluding resources awarded to replace EFC). ***Average financial aid package:*** $26,280 (excluding resources awarded to replace EFC). 42% of all full-time freshmen had no need and received non-need-based gift aid.

UNDERGRADUATE FINANCIAL AID (Fall 2019, est.) 2,102 applied for aid; of those 50% were deemed to have need. 100% of undergraduates with need received aid; of those 100% had need fully met. ***Average percent of need met:*** 55% (excluding resources awarded to replace EFC). ***Average financial aid package:*** $24,022 (excluding resources awarded to replace EFC). 37% of all full-time undergraduates had no need and received non-need-based gift aid.

GIFT AID (NEED-BASED) ***Total amount:*** $17,621,598 (18% federal, 10% state, 69% institutional, 3% external sources). ***Receiving aid:*** Freshmen: 45% (324); all full-time undergraduates: 41% (903). ***Average award:*** Freshmen: $9238; Undergraduates: $9593. ***Scholarships, grants, and awards:*** Federal Pell, FSEOG, state, private, college/university gift aid from institutional funds.

GIFT AID (NON-NEED-BASED) ***Total amount:*** $12,136,132 (5% state, 88% institutional, 7% external sources). ***Receiving aid:*** Freshmen: 53% (387). Undergraduates: 43% (954). ***Average award:*** Freshmen: $13,554. Undergraduates: $12,395. ***Scholarships, grants, and awards by category:*** *Academic interests/achievement:* 1,774 awards ($19,406,628 total): biological sciences, business, communication, general academic interests/achievements, international studies. *Creative arts/performance:* 49 awards ($1,445,338 total): music. *Special achievements/activities:* 1 award ($5000 total): leadership. *Special characteristics:* 217 awards ($1,845,584 total): children and siblings of alumni, children of educators, children of faculty/staff, out-of-state students, siblings of current students, veterans. ***Tuition waivers:*** Full or partial for children of alumni, employees or children of employees. ***ROTC:*** Air Force cooperative.

LOANS ***Student loans:*** $7,606,744 (93% need-based, 7% non-need-based). 42% of past graduating class borrowed through all loan programs. *Average indebtedness per student:* $3451. ***Average need-based loan:*** Freshmen: $4072. Undergraduates: $4597. ***Parent loans:*** $10,618,213 (93% need-based, 7% non-need-based). ***Programs:*** Federal Direct (Subsidized and Unsubsidized Stafford, PLUS).

WORK-STUDY ***Federal work-study:*** Total amount: $753,175; 157 jobs averaging $1630. ***State or other work-study/employment:*** Total amount: $344,577 (51% need-based, 49% non-need-based). 6 part-time jobs averaging $1229.

ATHLETIC AWARDS Total amount: $3,517,181 (36% need-based, 64% non-need-based).

APPLYING FOR FINANCIAL AID ***Required financial aid form:*** FAFSA. ***Financial aid deadline (priority):*** 3/1. ***Notification date:*** Continuous beginning 11/1. Students must reply within 2 weeks of notification.

CONTACT Mr. John Chambers, Director of Student Financial Assistance, Lynn University, 3601 North Military Trail, Boca Raton, FL 33431-5598, 561-237-7973 or toll-free 800-888-5966. *Fax:* 561-237-7189. *E-mail:* jchambers@lynn.edu.
Website: http://www.lynn.edu/.

LYON COLLEGE

Batesville, AR

Tuition & fees: $29,140	Average undergraduate aid package: $23,670

ABOUT THE INSTITUTION Independent Presbyterian, coed. ***Awards:*** bachelor's degrees. 14 undergraduate majors. Both federal and institutional methodology are used as a basis for awarding need-based institutional aid.

UNDERGRADUATE EXPENSES for 2019–2020 ***Comprehensive fee:*** $38,770 includes full-time tuition ($28,550), mandatory fees ($590), and room and board ($9630). ***College room only:*** $5410. Full-time tuition and fees vary according to course load. Room and board charges vary according to board plan and housing facility. ***Part-time tuition:*** $950 per credit hour. ***Part-time fees:*** $590 per year. Part-time tuition and fees vary according to course load.

FRESHMAN FINANCIAL AID (Fall 2018) 212 applied for aid; of those 90% were deemed to have need. 100% of freshmen with need received aid; of those 23% had need fully met. ***Average percent of need met:*** 12% (excluding resources awarded to replace EFC). ***Average financial aid package:*** $22,473 (excluding resources awarded to replace EFC). 8% of all full-time freshmen had no need and received non-need-based gift aid.

UNDERGRADUATE FINANCIAL AID (Fall 2018) 552 applied for aid; of those 90% were deemed to have need. 100% of undergraduates with need received aid; of those 22% had need fully met. ***Average percent of need met:*** 22% (excluding resources awarded to replace EFC). ***Average financial aid package:*** $23,670 (excluding resources awarded to replace EFC). 14% of all full-time undergraduates had no need and received non-need-based gift aid.

GIFT AID (NEED-BASED) ***Total amount:*** $11,209,095 (18% federal, 6% state, 76% institutional). ***Receiving aid:*** Freshmen: 89% (191); all full-time undergraduates: 76% (496). ***Average award:*** Freshmen: $20,419; Undergraduates: $21,168. ***Scholarships, grants, and awards:*** Federal Pell, FSEOG, state, private, college/university gift aid from institutional funds.

GIFT AID (NON-NEED-BASED) ***Total amount:*** $6,582,640 (13% state, 86% institutional, 1% external sources). ***Receiving aid:*** Freshmen: 18% (39). Undergraduates: 15% (95). ***Average award:*** Freshmen: $15,523. Undergraduates: $16,191. ***Scholarships, grants, and awards by category:*** *Academic interests/achievement:* business, general academic interests/achievements. *Creative arts/performance:* applied art and design, music, theater/drama. *Special achievements/activities:* cheerleading/drum major, general special achievements/activities. *Special characteristics:* children and siblings of alumni, children of faculty/staff, ethnic background, first-generation college students, local/state students, members of minority groups, religious affiliation. ***Tuition waivers:*** Full or partial for employees or children of employees.

LOANS ***Student loans:*** $3,761,903 (69% need-based, 31% non-need-based). 46% of past graduating class borrowed through all loan programs. *Average indebtedness per student:* $5912. ***Average need-based loan:*** Freshmen: $2993. Undergraduates: $3715. ***Parent loans:*** $61,000 (43% need-based, 57% non-need-based). ***Programs:*** Federal Direct (Subsidized and Unsubsidized Stafford, PLUS), Perkins.

WORK-STUDY Federal work-study jobs available. ***State or other work-study/employment:*** Part-time jobs available.

ATHLETIC AWARDS Total amount: $4,568,103 (42% need-based, 58% non-need-based).

APPLYING FOR FINANCIAL AID ***Required financial aid forms:*** FAFSA, state aid form. ***Financial aid deadline:*** Continuous. ***Notification date:*** Continuous beginning 12/1. Students must reply by 12/1.

CONTACT Mr. Thomas Tucker, Director of Financial Aid, Lyon College, 2300 Highland Road, Batesville, AR 72501, 870-307-7257 or toll-free 800-423-2542. *Fax:* 870-307-7542. *E-mail:* financialaid@lyon.edu.
Website: http://www.lyon.edu/.

MACALESTER COLLEGE

St. Paul, MN

Tuition & fees: $56,292	Average undergraduate aid package: $49,693

ABOUT THE INSTITUTION Independent, coed. ***Awards:*** bachelor's degrees. 37 undergraduate majors. ***Total enrollment:*** 2,174. Undergraduates: 2,174. Freshmen: 621. Both federal and institutional methodology are used as a basis for awarding need-based institutional aid.

UNDERGRADUATE EXPENSES for 2019–2020 ***Application fee:*** $40. ***Comprehensive fee:*** $68,884 includes full-time tuition ($56,062), mandatory fees ($230), and room and board ($12,592). ***College room only:*** $6762. Full-time tuition and fees vary according to course load. Room and board charges vary according to housing facility. ***Part-time tuition:*** $1751 per credit. ***Part-time fees:*** $1751 per credit. Part-time tuition and fees vary according to course load.

FRESHMAN FINANCIAL AID (Fall 2019, est.) 378 applied for aid; of those 86% were deemed to have need. 100% of freshmen with need received aid; of those 76% had need fully met. ***Average percent of need met:*** 100% (excluding resources awarded to replace EFC). ***Average financial aid package:*** $48,689 (excluding resources awarded to replace EFC). 20% of all full-time freshmen had no need and received non-need-based gift aid.

UNDERGRADUATE FINANCIAL AID (Fall 2019, est.) 1,500 applied for aid; of those 91% were deemed to have need. 100% of undergraduates with need received aid; of those 64% had need fully met. ***Average percent of need met:*** 100% (excluding resources awarded to replace EFC). ***Average financial aid package:*** $49,693 (excluding resources awarded to replace EFC). 16% of all full-time undergraduates had no need and received non-need-based gift aid.

GIFT AID (NEED-BASED) ***Total amount:*** $58,171,474 (4% federal, 1% state, 93% institutional, 2% external sources). ***Receiving aid:*** Freshmen: 64% (322); all full-

time undergraduates: 66% (1,355). ***Average award:*** Freshmen: $43,693; Undergraduates: $42,774. ***Scholarships, grants, and awards:*** Federal Pell, FSEOG, state, private, college/university gift aid from institutional funds.

GIFT AID (NON-NEED-BASED) ***Total amount:*** $5,391,815 (93% institutional, 7% external sources). ***Receiving aid:*** Freshmen: 7% (35). Undergraduates: 4% (86). ***Average award:*** Freshmen: $14,436. Undergraduates: $15,182. ***Scholarships, grants, and awards by category:*** *Academic interests/achievement:* general academic interests/achievements. *Special characteristics:* ethnic background. ***Tuition waivers:*** Full or partial for employees or children of employees. ***ROTC:*** Army cooperative, Naval cooperative, Air Force cooperative.

LOANS ***Student loans:*** $7,088,840 (93% need-based, 7% non-need-based). 59% of past graduating class borrowed through all loan programs. *Average indebtedness per student:* $23,060. ***Average need-based loan:*** Freshmen: $3654. Undergraduates: $5071. ***Parent loans:*** $1,217,655 (100% non-need-based). ***Programs:*** Federal Direct (Subsidized and Unsubsidized Stafford, PLUS), state, college/university.

WORK-STUDY ***Federal work-study:*** Total amount: $500,972; jobs available. ***State or other work-study/employment:*** Total amount: $3,101,261 (97% need-based, 3% non-need-based). Part-time jobs available.

APPLYING FOR FINANCIAL AID ***Required financial aid forms:*** FAFSA, CSS Financial Aid PROFILE, noncustodial (divorced/separated) parent's statement, federal income tax form(s). ***Financial aid deadline (priority):*** 1/22. ***Notification date:*** 4/1. Students must reply by 5/1.

CONTACT Jenae Schmidt, Director of Financial Aid, Macalester College, 1600 Grand Avenue, St. Paul, MN 55105, 651-696-6214 or toll-free 800-231-7974. *E-mail:* financialaid@macalester.edu.
Website: http://www.macalester.edu/.

MACHZIKEI HADATH RABBINICAL COLLEGE

Brooklyn, NY

CONTACT Rabbi Baruch Rozmarin, Director of Financial Aid, Machzikei Hadath Rabbinical College, 5407 16th Avenue, Brooklyn, NY 11204-1805, 718-854-8777.

MADONNA UNIVERSITY

Livonia, MI

CONTACT Cathy Durham, Financial Aid Secretary, Madonna University, 36600 Schoolcraft Road, Livonia, MI 48150-1173, 734-432-5663 or toll-free 800-852-4951. *Fax:* 734-432-5344. *E-mail:* finaid@madonna.edu.
Website: http://www.madonna.edu/.

MAGDALEN COLLEGE OF THE LIBERAL ARTS

Warner, NH

CONTACT Marie A. Lasher, Financial Aid Director, Magdalen College of the Liberal Arts, 511 Kearsarge Mountain Road, Warner, NH 03278, 603-456-4136 or toll-free 877-498-1723. *Fax:* 603-456-2660. *E-mail:* mlasher@northeastcatholic.edu.
Website: http://www.magdalen.edu/.

MAHARISHI INTERNATIONAL UNIVERSITY

Fairfield, IA

CONTACT Mr. Bill Christensen, Director of Financial Aid, Maharishi International University, 1000 North 4th Street, DB 1127, Fairfield, IA 52557-1127, 641-472-1156 or toll-free 800-369-6480. *Fax:* 641-472-1133. *E-mail:* bchrist@mum.edu.
Website: http://www.mum.edu/.

MAINE COLLEGE OF ART

Portland, ME

CONTACT Adrienne J. Amari, Director of Financial Aid, Maine College of Art, 522 Congress Street, Portland, ME 04101-3987, 207-775-3052 Ext. 5073 or toll-free 800-699-1509. *Fax:* 207-772-5069. *E-mail:* aamari@meca.edu.
Website: http://www.meca.edu/.

MAINE MARITIME ACADEMY

Castine, ME

CONTACT Mrs. Kathy S. Heath, Director of Financial Aid, Maine Maritime Academy, Pleasant Street, Castine, ME 04420, 207-326-2205 or toll-free 800-464-6565 (in-state), 800-227-8465 (out-of-state). *Fax:* 207-326-2515. *E-mail:* bbayle@mma.edu.
Website: http://www.mainemaritime.edu/.

MALONE UNIVERSITY

Canton, OH

Tuition & fees: $32,416	Average undergraduate aid package: $26,785

ABOUT THE INSTITUTION Independent Evangelical Friends Church–Eastern Region, coed. ***Awards:*** certificates, bachelor's, and master's degrees. 43 undergraduate majors. ***Total enrollment:*** 1,561. Undergraduates: 1,177. Freshmen: 244. Federal methodology is used as a basis for awarding need-based institutional aid.

UNDERGRADUATE EXPENSES for 2020–2021 ***Application fee:*** $20. ***Comprehensive fee:*** $42,316 includes full-time tuition ($31,416), mandatory fees ($1000), and room and board ($9900). ***College room only:*** $4840. Room and board charges vary according to board plan. ***Part-time tuition:*** $520 per credit hour. ***Part-time fees:*** $250 per term. Part-time tuition and fees vary according to course load.

FRESHMAN FINANCIAL AID (Fall 2018) 295 applied for aid; of those 94% were deemed to have need. 100% of freshmen with need received aid; of those 19% had need fully met. ***Average percent of need met:*** 82% (excluding resources awarded to replace EFC). ***Average financial aid package:*** $27,862 (excluding resources awarded to replace EFC). 10% of all full-time freshmen had no need and received non-need-based gift aid.

UNDERGRADUATE FINANCIAL AID (Fall 2018) 939 applied for aid; of those 94% were deemed to have need. 100% of undergraduates with need received aid; of those 16% had need fully met. ***Average percent of need met:*** 79% (excluding resources awarded to replace EFC). ***Average financial aid package:*** $26,785 (excluding resources awarded to replace EFC). 14% of all full-time undergraduates had no need and received non-need-based gift aid.

GIFT AID (NEED-BASED) ***Total amount:*** $17,168,636 (15% federal, 5% state, 77% institutional, 3% external sources). ***Receiving aid:*** Freshmen: 90% (277); all full-time undergraduates: 84% (871). ***Average award:*** Freshmen: $24,380; Undergraduates: $23,026. ***Scholarships, grants, and awards:*** Federal Pell, FSEOG, state, private, college/university gift aid from institutional funds.

GIFT AID (NON-NEED-BASED) ***Total amount:*** $2,436,710 (1% federal, 94% institutional, 5% external sources). ***Receiving aid:*** Freshmen: 14% (43). Undergraduates: 10% (105). ***Average award:*** Freshmen: $14,867. Undergraduates: $12,874. ***Scholarships, grants, and awards by category:*** *Academic interests/achievement:* 997 awards ($8,997,898 total): biological sciences, general academic interests/achievements, premedicine, social sciences. *Creative arts/performance:* 78 awards ($12,625 total): creative writing, debating, journalism/publications, music, theater/drama. *Special achievements/activities:* 108 awards ($113,875 total): cheerleading/drum major, general special achievements/activities, leadership, religious involvement. *Special characteristics:* 209 awards ($981,738 total): children and siblings of alumni, children of faculty/staff, international students, relatives of clergy, religious affiliation, veterans. ***Tuition waivers:*** Full or partial for employees or children of employees, senior citizens.

LOANS ***Student loans:*** $1,969,082 (6% need-based, 94% non-need-based). 79% of past graduating class borrowed through all loan programs. *Average indebtedness per student:* $32,495. ***Average need-based loan:*** Freshmen: $3373. Undergraduates:

$4217. ***Parent loans:*** $2,872,008 (46% need-based, 54% non-need-based). ***Programs:*** Federal Direct (Subsidized and Unsubsidized Stafford, PLUS), Federal Nursing, state, college/university, private loans.

WORK-STUDY *Federal work-study:* Total amount: $444,159; 361 jobs averaging $1866. ***State or other work-study/employment:*** 109 part-time jobs averaging $1797.

ATHLETIC AWARDS Total amount: $3,624,990 (67% need-based, 33% non-need-based).

APPLYING FOR FINANCIAL AID *Required financial aid forms:* FAFSA, CSS Financial Aid PROFILE. ***Financial aid deadline:*** 7/31 (priority: 3/1). ***Notification date:*** Continuous beginning 10/15. Students must reply within 2 weeks of notification.

CONTACT Ms. Pamela S. Pustay, Director of Financial Aid, Malone University, 2600 Cleveland Avenue NW, Canton, OH 44709, 330-471-8161 or toll-free 800-521-1146. *Fax:* 330-471-8652. *E-mail:* ppustay@malone.edu.
Website: http://www.malone.edu/.

MANCHESTER UNIVERSITY

North Manchester, IN

ABOUT THE INSTITUTION Independent Church of the Brethren, coed. ***Awards:*** associate, bachelor's, master's, and doctoral degrees. 90 undergraduate majors. ***Total enrollment:*** 1,530. Undergraduates: 1,191. Freshmen: 408.

GIFT AID (NEED-BASED) *Scholarships, grants, and awards:* Federal Pell, FSEOG, state, private, college/university gift aid from institutional funds.

GIFT AID (NON-NEED-BASED) *Scholarships, grants, and awards by category:* *Academic interests/achievement:* general academic interests/achievements. *Creative arts/performance:* music. *Special characteristics:* children and siblings of alumni, children of faculty/staff, international students, members of minority groups, out-of-state students, parents of current students, religious affiliation, siblings of current students, spouses of current students.

LOANS *Programs:* Federal Direct (Subsidized and Unsubsidized Stafford, PLUS).

WORK-STUDY *Federal work-study:* Total amount: $998,929; jobs available.

APPLYING FOR FINANCIAL AID *Required financial aid form:* FAFSA.

CONTACT Mrs. Sherri Shockey, Director of Student Financial Services, Manchester University, 604 East College Avenue, North Manchester, IN 46962-1225, 260-982-5066 or toll-free 800-852-3648. *Fax:* 260-982-5043. *E-mail:* slshockey@manchester.edu.
Website: http://www.manchester.edu/.

MANHATTAN CHRISTIAN COLLEGE

Manhattan, KS

CONTACT Mrs. Margaret Carlisle, Director of Financial Aid, Manhattan Christian College, 1415 Anderson Avenue, Manhattan, KS 66502-4081, 785-539-3571 or toll-free 877-246-4622. *E-mail:* carlisle@mccks.edu.
Website: http://www.mccks.edu/.

MANHATTAN COLLEGE

Riverdale, NY

Tuition & fees: $44,564	Average undergraduate aid package: $19,889

ABOUT THE INSTITUTION Independent Roman Catholic Church, coed. ***Awards:*** certificates, bachelor's, and master's degrees. 44 undergraduate majors. ***Total enrollment:*** 4,058. Undergraduates: 3,485. Freshmen: 853. Both federal and institutional methodology are used as a basis for awarding need-based institutional aid.

UNDERGRADUATE EXPENSES for 2019–2020 *Application fee:* $75. ***Comprehensive fee:*** $61,434 includes full-time tuition ($40,400), mandatory fees ($4164), and room and board ($16,870). Full-time tuition and fees vary according to course load, program, and student level. Room and board charges vary according to board plan. ***Part-time tuition:*** $1040 per credit. ***Part-time fees:*** $982 per term. Part-time tuition and fees vary according to course load.

FRESHMAN FINANCIAL AID (Fall 2018) 701 applied for aid; of those 97% were deemed to have need. 95% of freshmen with need received aid. ***Average percent of need met:*** 37% (excluding resources awarded to replace EFC). ***Average financial aid package:*** $18,553 (excluding resources awarded to replace EFC). 23% of all full-time freshmen had no need and received non-need-based gift aid.

UNDERGRADUATE FINANCIAL AID (Fall 2018) 3,001 applied for aid; of those 92% were deemed to have need. 77% of undergraduates with need received aid. ***Average percent of need met:*** 41% (excluding resources awarded to replace EFC). ***Average financial aid package:*** $19,889 (excluding resources awarded to replace EFC). 25% of all full-time undergraduates had no need and received non-need-based gift aid.

GIFT AID (NEED-BASED) *Total amount:* $69,570,379 (8% federal, 4% state, 86% institutional, 2% external sources). ***Receiving aid:*** Freshmen: 79% (624); all full-time undergraduates: 57% (2,006). ***Average award:*** Freshmen: $13,585; Undergraduates: $15,550. ***Scholarships, grants, and awards:*** Federal Pell, FSEOG, state, private, college/university gift aid from institutional funds.

GIFT AID (NON-NEED-BASED) *Total amount:* $3,212,963 (19% state, 81% institutional). ***Receiving aid:*** Freshmen: 77% (610). Undergraduates: 55% (1,954). ***Average award:*** Freshmen: $10,523. Undergraduates: $12,583. ***Scholarships, grants, and awards by category:*** *Academic interests/achievement:* biological sciences, business, computer science, engineering/technologies, foreign languages, general academic interests/achievements, mathematics, military science. *Creative arts/performance:* music. *Special achievements/activities:* community service, leadership. *Special characteristics:* children of faculty/staff. ***Tuition waivers:*** Full or partial for employees or children of employees. ***ROTC:*** Army cooperative, Air Force.

LOANS *Student loans:* $20,833,319 (96% need-based, 4% non-need-based). 67% of past graduating class borrowed through all loan programs. *Average indebtedness per student:* $11,170. ***Parent loans:*** $16,655,215 (96% need-based, 4% non-need-based). ***Programs:*** Federal Direct (Subsidized and Unsubsidized Stafford, PLUS).

WORK-STUDY *Federal work-study:* Total amount: $117,468; jobs available. ***State or other work-study/employment:*** Part-time jobs available.

ATHLETIC AWARDS Total amount: $7,032,926 (76% need-based, 24% non-need-based).

APPLYING FOR FINANCIAL AID *Required financial aid forms:* FAFSA, institution's own form, state aid form. ***Financial aid deadline:*** 4/15 (priority: 2/15). ***Notification date:*** 4/1. Students must reply by 5/1.

CONTACT Mrs. Denise Scalzo, Director of Financial Aid, Manhattan College, 4513 Manhattan College Parkway, Riverdale, NY 10471, 718-862-7100 or toll-free 800-622-9235. *Fax:* 718-862-8027. *E-mail:* dcsalzo01@manhattan.edu.
Website: http://www.manhattan.edu/.

MANHATTAN SCHOOL OF MUSIC

New York, NY

CONTACT Mr. Thomas Zarkos, Director of Financial Aid, Manhattan School of Music, 120 Claremont Avenue, New York, NY 10027-4698, 917-493-4462. *Fax:* 212-749-3025. *E-mail:* tzarkos@msmnyc.edu.
Website: http://www.msmnyc.edu/.

MANHATTANVILLE COLLEGE

Purchase, NY

Tuition & fees: $40,330	Average undergraduate aid package: $29,753

ABOUT THE INSTITUTION Independent, coed. ***Awards:*** certificates, bachelor's, master's, and doctoral degrees. 48 undergraduate majors. ***Total enrollment:*** 2,535. Undergraduates: 1,541. Freshmen: 401. Federal methodology is used as a basis for awarding need-based institutional aid.

UNDERGRADUATE EXPENSES for 2020–2021 *Application fee:* $50. ***Comprehensive fee:*** $55,140 includes full-time tuition ($38,880), mandatory fees ($1450), and room and board ($14,810). ***College room only:*** $8970. Room and board charges vary according to board plan. ***Part-time tuition:*** $900 per credit. ***Part-time fees:*** $60 per term. Part-time tuition and fees vary according to course load and program.

FRESHMAN FINANCIAL AID (Fall 2019, est.) 359 applied for aid; of those 87% were deemed to have need. 100% of freshmen with need received aid; of those 19% had need fully met. ***Average percent of need met:*** 70% (excluding resources awarded to replace EFC). ***Average financial aid package:*** $30,750 (excluding resources awarded to replace EFC). 29% of all full-time freshmen had no need and received non-need-based gift aid.

UNDERGRADUATE FINANCIAL AID (Fall 2019, est.) 1,136 applied for aid; of those 89% were deemed to have need. 100% of undergraduates with need received aid; of those 16% had need fully met. ***Average percent of need met:*** 73% (excluding resources awarded to replace EFC). ***Average financial aid package:*** $29,753 (excluding resources awarded to replace EFC). 30% of all full-time undergraduates had no need and received non-need-based gift aid.

GIFT AID (NEED-BASED) ***Total amount:*** $28,273,922 (10% federal, 5% state, 85% institutional). ***Receiving aid:*** Freshmen: 63% (252); all full-time undergraduates: 58% (854). ***Average award:*** Freshmen: $7941; Undergraduates: $6116. ***Scholarships, grants, and awards:*** Federal Pell, FSEOG, state, private, college/university gift aid from institutional funds, United Negro College Fund, The United Negro College Fund is the administrator of the Gates Millennium Scholar Program.

GIFT AID (NON-NEED-BASED) ***Total amount:*** $4,857,587 (2% state, 91% institutional, 7% external sources). ***Receiving aid:*** Freshmen: 78% (310). Undergraduates: 66% (966). ***Average award:*** Freshmen: $20,863. Undergraduates: $20,551. ***Scholarships, grants, and awards by category:*** *Academic interests/achievement:* 1,518 awards ($28,850,128 total): general academic interests/achievements. *Creative arts/performance:* 137 awards ($218,000 total): creative writing, dance, music, performing arts, theater/drama. *Special achievements/activities:* 460 awards ($838,475 total): community service. *Special characteristics:* 7 awards ($143,002 total): children and siblings of alumni, children of faculty/staff, veterans. ***Tuition waivers:*** Full or partial for children of alumni, employees or children of employees.

LOANS ***Student loans:*** $7,395,684 (39% need-based, 61% non-need-based). 68% of past graduating class borrowed through all loan programs. *Average indebtedness per student:* $35,092. ***Average need-based loan:*** Freshmen: $3315. Undergraduates: $4340. ***Parent loans:*** $4,095,124 (100% non-need-based). ***Programs:*** Federal Direct (Subsidized and Unsubsidized Stafford, PLUS).

WORK-STUDY ***Federal work-study:*** Total amount: $548,406; 679 jobs averaging $1810.

APPLYING FOR FINANCIAL AID ***Required financial aid forms:*** FAFSA, state aid form. ***Financial aid deadline (priority):*** 3/1. ***Notification date:*** Continuous beginning 11/15. Students must reply by 5/1 or within 2 weeks of notification.

CONTACT Mr. Robert Gilmore, Director of Financial Aid, Manhattanville College, 2900 Purchase Street, Purchase, NY 10577-2132, 914-323-5357 or toll-free 800-328-4553. *Fax:* 914-323-5382. *E-mail:* Robert.Gilmore@mville.edu.
Website: http://www.mville.edu/.

MANSFIELD UNIVERSITY OF PENNSYLVANIA

Mansfield, PA

Tuition & fees (area res): $10,596	Average undergraduate aid package: $1858

ABOUT THE INSTITUTION State-supported, coed. ***Awards:*** certificates, associate, bachelor's, and master's degrees. 51 undergraduate majors. ***Total enrollment:*** 1,663. Undergraduates: 1,640. Freshmen: 450.

UNDERGRADUATE EXPENSES for 2020–2021 ***Tuition, area resident:*** full-time $7716. ***Tuition, state resident:*** full-time $7716. ***Tuition, nonresident:*** full-time $10,032. ***Required fees:*** full-time $2880. ***College room and board:*** $10,147; ***Room only:*** $6600.

FRESHMAN FINANCIAL AID (Fall 2018) 318 applied for aid; of those 89% were deemed to have need. 100% of freshmen with need received aid; of those 65% had need fully met. ***Average percent of need met:*** 87% (excluding resources awarded to replace EFC). ***Average financial aid package:*** $1710 (excluding resources awarded to replace EFC). 5% of all full-time freshmen had no need and received non-need-based gift aid.

UNDERGRADUATE FINANCIAL AID (Fall 2018) 1,294 applied for aid; of those 90% were deemed to have need. 100% of undergraduates with need received aid; of those 65% had need fully met. ***Average percent of need met:*** 87% (excluding resources awarded to replace EFC). ***Average financial aid package:*** $1858 (excluding resources awarded to replace EFC). 13% of all full-time undergraduates had no need and received non-need-based gift aid.

GIFT AID (NEED-BASED) ***Total amount:*** $6,757,856 (54% federal, 25% state, 21% institutional). ***Receiving aid:*** Freshmen: 68% (222); all full-time undergraduates: 66% (902). ***Average award:*** Freshmen: $1389; Undergraduates: $1422. ***Scholarships, grants, and awards:*** Federal Pell, FSEOG, state, private, college/university gift aid from institutional funds, United Negro College Fund.

GIFT AID (NON-NEED-BASED) ***Total amount:*** $3,369,436 (2% federal, 18% state, 61% institutional, 19% external sources). ***Receiving aid:*** Freshmen: 65% (212). Undergraduates: 46% (631). ***Average award:*** Freshmen: $1541. Undergraduates: $1440. ***Scholarships, grants, and awards by category:*** *Academic interests/achievement:* biological sciences, communication, education, general academic interests/achievements, home economics, mathematics, physical sciences. *Creative arts/performance:* applied art and design, journalism/publications, music. *Special achievements/activities:* leadership. *Special characteristics:* children and siblings of alumni, local/state students, members of minority groups, religious affiliation. ***ROTC:*** Army cooperative.

LOANS ***Student loans:*** $8,635,677 (51% need-based, 49% non-need-based). 87% of past graduating class borrowed through all loan programs. *Average indebtedness per student:* $42,457. ***Average need-based loan:*** Freshmen: $1689. Undergraduates: $2100. ***Parent loans:*** $3,590,793 (100% non-need-based). ***Programs:*** Federal Direct (Subsidized and Unsubsidized Stafford, PLUS).

WORK-STUDY ***Federal work-study:*** Total amount: $640,966; jobs available. ***State or other work-study/employment:*** Total amount: $4,113,489 (100% non-need-based). Part-time jobs available.

ATHLETIC AWARDS Total amount: $172,383 (6% need-based, 94% non-need-based).

APPLYING FOR FINANCIAL AID ***Required financial aid form:*** FAFSA. ***Financial aid deadline (priority):*** 2/15. ***Notification date:*** Continuous beginning 2/1.

CONTACT Ms. Pamela Kathcart, Director of Financial Aid, Mansfield University of Pennsylvania, 224 South Hall, 71 South Academy Street, Mansfield, PA 16933, 570-662-4129 or toll-free 800-577-6826. *Fax:* 570-662-4136.
Website: http://www.mansfield.edu/.

MAPLE SPRINGS BAPTIST BIBLE COLLEGE AND SEMINARY

Capitol Heights, MD

CONTACT Ms. Fannie G. Thompson, Director of Business Affairs, Maple Springs Baptist Bible College and Seminary, 4130 Belt Road, Capitol Heights, MD 20743, 301-736-3631. *Fax:* 301-735-6507.
Website: http://www.msbbcs.edu/.

MARANATHA BAPTIST UNIVERSITY

Watertown, WI

Tuition & fees: N/R	Average undergraduate aid package: $10,223

ABOUT THE INSTITUTION Independent Baptist, coed. ***Awards:*** certificates, associate, bachelor's, master's, and doctoral degrees. 31 undergraduate majors. Federal methodology is used as a basis for awarding need-based institutional aid.

FRESHMAN FINANCIAL AID (Fall 2018) 150 applied for aid; of those 88% were deemed to have need. 100% of freshmen with need received aid; of those 8% had need fully met. ***Average percent of need met:*** 55% (excluding resources awarded to replace EFC). ***Average financial aid package:*** $10,523 (excluding resources awarded to replace EFC). 12% of all full-time freshmen had no need and received non-need-based gift aid.

UNDERGRADUATE FINANCIAL AID (Fall 2018) 563 applied for aid; of those 91% were deemed to have need. 100% of undergraduates with need received aid; of those 10% had need fully met. ***Average percent of need met:*** 54% (excluding resources awarded to replace EFC). ***Average financial aid package:*** $10,223

(excluding resources awarded to replace EFC). 9% of all full-time undergraduates had no need and received non-need-based gift aid.

GIFT AID (NEED-BASED) ***Total amount:*** $2,835,567 (47% federal, 9% state, 44% institutional). ***Receiving aid:*** Freshmen: 83% (131); all full-time undergraduates: 79% (471). ***Average award:*** Freshmen: $7389; Undergraduates: $6805. ***Scholarships, grants, and awards:*** Federal Pell, FSEOG, state, private, college/university gift aid from institutional funds.

GIFT AID (NON-NEED-BASED) ***Total amount:*** $213,254 (100% institutional). ***Receiving aid:*** Freshmen: 1% (2). Undergraduates: 3% (18). ***Average award:*** Freshmen: $3461. Undergraduates: $3420. ***Scholarships, grants, and awards by category:*** *Academic interests/achievement:* business, general academic interests/achievements, religion/biblical studies. *Creative arts/performance:* music. *Special characteristics:* children and siblings of alumni, children of educators, children of faculty/staff, relatives of clergy, spouses of current students. ***ROTC:*** Army, Air Force cooperative.

LOANS ***Student loans:*** $4,508,678 (82% need-based, 18% non-need-based). ***Average need-based loan:*** Freshmen: $3266. Undergraduates: $4157. ***Parent loans:*** $113,190 (39% need-based, 61% non-need-based). ***Programs:*** Federal Direct (Subsidized and Unsubsidized Stafford, PLUS), state.

WORK-STUDY ***State or other work-study/employment:*** Part-time jobs available.

APPLYING FOR FINANCIAL AID ***Required financial aid form:*** FAFSA. ***Financial aid deadline:*** Continuous. ***Notification date:*** Continuous.

CONTACT Mr. Bruce Roth, Director of Financial Aid, Maranatha Baptist University, 745 West Main Street, Watertown, WI 53094, 920-206-2318 or toll-free 800-622-2947. *Fax:* 920-261-9109. *E-mail:* financialaid@mbu.edu.
Website: http://www.mbu.edu/.

MARCONI INTERNATIONAL UNIVERSITY

Miami, FL

CONTACT Financial Aid Office, Marconi International University, 141 NE 3rd Avenue 7th Floor, Miami, FL 33132, 305-266-7678.
Website: http://www.miuniversity.edu/.

MARIA COLLEGE

Albany, NY

ABOUT THE INSTITUTION Independent, coed. ***Awards:*** certificates, associate, and bachelor's degrees. 8 undergraduate majors. ***Total enrollment:*** 912. Undergraduates: 912. Freshmen: 95.

GIFT AID (NEED-BASED) ***Scholarships, grants, and awards:*** Federal Pell, FSEOG, state, private, college/university gift aid from institutional funds.

GIFT AID (NON-NEED-BASED) ***Scholarships, grants, and awards by category:*** *Academic interests/achievement:* communication, general academic interests/achievements, health fields.

LOANS ***Programs:*** Federal Direct (Subsidized and Unsubsidized Stafford, PLUS), Perkins.

WORK-STUDY ***Federal work-study:*** Total amount: $49,732; jobs available.

APPLYING FOR FINANCIAL AID ***Required financial aid forms:*** FAFSA, state aid form.

CONTACT Ms. Karen Conrad, Director of Financial Aid, Maria College, 700 New Scotland, Albany, NY 12208, 518-861-2586. *E-mail:* kconrad@mariacollege.edu.
Website: http://www.mariacollege.edu/.

MARIAN UNIVERSITY

Indianapolis, IN

ABOUT THE INSTITUTION Independent Roman Catholic, coed. ***Awards:*** associate, bachelor's, master's, and doctoral degrees. 42 undergraduate majors. ***Total enrollment:*** 3,519. Undergraduates: 2,342. Freshmen: 385.

GIFT AID (NEED-BASED) ***Scholarships, grants, and awards:*** Federal Pell, FSEOG, state, private, college/university gift aid from institutional funds.

GIFT AID (NON-NEED-BASED) ***Scholarships, grants, and awards by category:*** *Academic interests/achievement:* area/ethnic studies, education, general academic interests/achievements, religion/biblical studies. *Creative arts/performance:* applied art and design, art/fine arts, debating, music, performing arts, theater/drama. *Special characteristics:* children and siblings of alumni, children of faculty/staff, children of workers in trades, religious affiliation.

LOANS ***Programs:*** Federal Direct (Subsidized and Unsubsidized Stafford, PLUS), Perkins, college/university.

CONTACT Ms. Monique Ware, Director of Financial Aid, Marian University, 3200 Cold Spring Road, Indianapolis, IN 46222-1997, 317-955-6040 or toll-free 800-772-7264 (in-state). *Fax:* 317-955-6424. *E-mail:* finaid@marian.edu.
Website: http://www.marian.edu/.

MARIAN UNIVERSITY

Fond du Lac, WI

CONTACT Mr. John Smith, Interim Director of Financial Aid, Marian University, 45 South National Avenue, Fond du Lac, WI 54935-4699, 920-923-7614 or toll-free 800-2-MARIAN. *Fax:* 920-923-8767. *E-mail:* jrsmith49@marianuniversity.edu.
Website: http://www.marianuniversity.edu/.

MARIETTA COLLEGE

Marietta, OH

Tuition & fees: $36,764	Average undergraduate aid package: $36,440

ABOUT THE INSTITUTION Independent, coed. ***Awards:*** certificates, associate, bachelor's, and master's degrees. 43 undergraduate majors. ***Total enrollment:*** 1,145. Undergraduates: 1,065. Freshmen: 272. Federal methodology is used as a basis for awarding need-based institutional aid.

UNDERGRADUATE EXPENSES for 2020–2021 ***One-time required fee:*** $400. ***Comprehensive fee:*** $49,504 includes full-time tuition ($35,732), mandatory fees ($1032), and room and board ($12,740). Full-time tuition and fees vary according to course load. Room and board charges vary according to board plan and housing facility. ***Part-time tuition:*** $1190 per credit hour. Part-time tuition and fees vary according to course load.

FRESHMAN FINANCIAL AID (Fall 2019, est.) 345 applied for aid; of those 94% were deemed to have need. 100% of freshmen with need received aid; of those 36% had need fully met. ***Average percent of need met:*** 100% (excluding resources awarded to replace EFC). ***Average financial aid package:*** $36,438 (excluding resources awarded to replace EFC). 8% of all full-time freshmen had no need and received non-need-based gift aid.

UNDERGRADUATE FINANCIAL AID (Fall 2019, est.) 928 applied for aid; of those 91% were deemed to have need. 100% of undergraduates with need received aid; of those 42% had need fully met. ***Average percent of need met:*** 100% (excluding resources awarded to replace EFC). ***Average financial aid package:*** $36,440 (excluding resources awarded to replace EFC). 11% of all full-time undergraduates had no need and received non-need-based gift aid.

GIFT AID (NEED-BASED) ***Receiving aid:*** Freshmen: 91% (316); all full-time undergraduates: 63% (670). ***Average award:*** Freshmen: $32,534; Undergraduates: $30,097. ***Scholarships, grants, and awards:*** Federal Pell, FSEOG, state, private, college/university gift aid from institutional funds.

GIFT AID (NON-NEED-BASED) ***Receiving aid:*** Freshmen: 85% (296). Undergraduates: 73% (775). ***Average award:*** Freshmen: $23,009. Undergraduates: $19,660. ***Scholarships, grants, and awards by category:*** *Academic interests/achievement:* general academic interests/achievements. *Creative arts/performance:* applied art and design, music, performing arts, theater/drama. *Special characteristics:* children and siblings of alumni, members of minority groups. ***Tuition waivers:*** Full or partial for employees or children of employees.

LOANS ***Average need-based loan:*** Freshmen: $3027. Undergraduates: $3520. ***Programs:*** Federal Direct (Subsidized and Unsubsidized Stafford, PLUS), Perkins.

WORK-STUDY Federal work-study jobs available.

APPLYING FOR FINANCIAL AID ***Required financial aid form:*** FAFSA. ***Notification date:*** Students must reply within 2 weeks of notification.

CONTACT Mrs. Emily Schuck, Assistant Vice President for Enrollment Management, Marietta College, 215 Fifth Street, Marietta, OH 45750-4000, 740-376-4712 or toll-free 800-331-7896. *Fax:* 740-376-4990. *E-mail:* finaid@marietta.edu. *Website:* http://www.marietta.edu/.

MARIST COLLEGE

Poughkeepsie, NY

Tuition & fees: $40,525	Average undergraduate aid package: $25,803

ABOUT THE INSTITUTION Independent, coed. ***Awards:*** certificates, bachelor's, and master's degrees. 47 undergraduate majors. ***Total enrollment:*** 6,624. Undergraduates: 5,670. Freshmen: 1,299. Federal methodology is used as a basis for awarding need-based institutional aid.

UNDERGRADUATE EXPENSES for 2019–2020 ***Application fee:*** $50. ***One-time required fee:*** $100. ***Comprehensive fee:*** $58,445 includes full-time tuition ($39,925), mandatory fees ($600), and room and board ($17,920). ***College room only:*** $12,000. Full-time tuition and fees vary according to location, program, and student level. Room and board charges vary according to board plan, housing facility, location, and student level. ***Part-time tuition:*** $730 per credit hour. ***Part-time fees:*** $40 per term. Part-time tuition and fees vary according to course load, location, and program.

FRESHMAN FINANCIAL AID (Fall 2019, est.) 1106 applied for aid; of those 74% were deemed to have need. 100% of freshmen with need received aid; of those 20% had need fully met. ***Average percent of need met:*** 75% (excluding resources awarded to replace EFC). ***Average financial aid package:*** $30,065 (excluding resources awarded to replace EFC). 33% of all full-time freshmen had no need and received non-need-based gift aid.

UNDERGRADUATE FINANCIAL AID (Fall 2019, est.) 3,618 applied for aid; of those 80% were deemed to have need. 100% of undergraduates with need received aid; of those 19% had need fully met. ***Average percent of need met:*** 69% (excluding resources awarded to replace EFC). ***Average financial aid package:*** $25,803 (excluding resources awarded to replace EFC). 32% of all full-time undergraduates had no need and received non-need-based gift aid.

GIFT AID (NEED-BASED) ***Receiving aid:*** Freshmen: 59% (801); all full-time undergraduates: 55% (2,790). ***Average award:*** Freshmen: $24,087; Undergraduates: $20,112. ***Scholarships, grants, and awards:*** Federal Pell, FSEOG, state, private, college/university gift aid from institutional funds.

GIFT AID (NON-NEED-BASED) ***Receiving aid:*** Freshmen: 8% (114). Undergraduates: 6% (318). ***Average award:*** Freshmen: $12,677. Undergraduates: $11,108. ***Scholarships, grants, and awards by category:*** *Academic interests/achievement:* 3,868 awards ($44,221,032 total): general academic interests/achievements. *Creative arts/performance:* 122 awards ($244,000 total): music, theater/drama. *Special characteristics:* 178 awards ($874,175 total): local/state students. ***Tuition waivers:*** Full or partial for employees or children of employees. ***ROTC:*** Army.

LOANS ***Student loans:*** 65% of past graduating class borrowed through all loan programs. *Average indebtedness per student:* $40,007. ***Average need-based loan:*** Freshmen: $2782. Undergraduates: $3878. ***Programs:*** Federal Direct (Subsidized and Unsubsidized Stafford, PLUS).

WORK-STUDY ***Federal work-study:*** 1,436 jobs averaging $2675. ***State or other work-study/employment:*** 566 part-time jobs averaging $2006.

APPLYING FOR FINANCIAL AID ***Required financial aid form:*** FAFSA. ***Notification date:*** Continuous. Students must reply within 2 weeks of notification.

CONTACT Joseph R. Weglarz, Executive Director of Student Financial Services, Marist College, 3399 North Road, Poughkeepsie, NY 12601, 845-575-3230 or toll-free 800-436-5483. *Fax:* 845-575-3099. *E-mail:* joseph.weglarz@marist.edu. *Website:* http://www.marist.edu/.

MARLBORO COLLEGE

Marlboro, VT

ABOUT THE INSTITUTION Independent, coed. ***Awards:*** bachelor's and master's degrees. 138 undergraduate majors.

GIFT AID (NEED-BASED) ***Scholarships, grants, and awards:*** Federal Pell, FSEOG, state, private, college/university gift aid from institutional funds.

GIFT AID (NON-NEED-BASED) ***Scholarships, grants, and awards by category:*** *Academic interests/achievement:* general academic interests/achievements. *Creative arts/performance:* applied art and design, general creative arts/performance. *Special achievements/activities:* leadership.

LOANS ***Programs:*** Federal Direct (Subsidized and Unsubsidized Stafford, PLUS).

WORK-STUDY ***Federal work-study:*** Total amount: $151,913; jobs available. ***State or other work-study/employment:*** Total amount: $67,849 (46% need-based, 54% non-need-based). Part-time jobs available.

APPLYING FOR FINANCIAL AID ***Required financial aid form:*** FAFSA.

CONTACT Cathy Fuller, Financial Aid Office, Marlboro College, PO Box A, 2582 South Road, Marlboro, VT 05344-0300, 802-258-9237 or toll-free 800-343-0049. *Fax:* 802-258-9300. *E-mail:* finaid@marlboro.edu. *Website:* http://www.marlboro.edu/.

MARQUETTE UNIVERSITY

Milwaukee, WI

Tuition & fees: $45,666	Average undergraduate aid package: $32,164

ABOUT THE INSTITUTION Independent Roman Catholic (Jesuit), coed. ***Awards:*** certificates, bachelor's, master's, and doctoral degrees. 78 undergraduate majors. ***Total enrollment:*** 11,819. Undergraduates: 8,515. Freshmen: 1,977. Federal methodology is used as a basis for awarding need-based institutional aid.

UNDERGRADUATE EXPENSES for 2020–2021 ***Comprehensive fee:*** $59,322 includes full-time tuition ($44,970), mandatory fees ($696), and room and board ($13,656). ***College room only:*** $8956. Full-time tuition and fees vary according to course load and program. Room and board charges vary according to housing facility. ***Part-time tuition:*** $1115 per credit hour. Part-time tuition and fees vary according to program.

FRESHMAN FINANCIAL AID (Fall 2019, est.) 1646 applied for aid; of those 78% were deemed to have need. 100% of freshmen with need received aid; of those 23% had need fully met. ***Average percent of need met:*** 80% (excluding resources awarded to replace EFC). ***Average financial aid package:*** $34,469 (excluding resources awarded to replace EFC). 34% of all full-time freshmen had no need and received non-need-based gift aid.

UNDERGRADUATE FINANCIAL AID (Fall 2019, est.) 5,884 applied for aid; of those 82% were deemed to have need. 100% of undergraduates with need received aid; of those 25% had need fully met. ***Average percent of need met:*** 78% (excluding resources awarded to replace EFC). ***Average financial aid package:*** $32,164 (excluding resources awarded to replace EFC). 38% of all full-time undergraduates had no need and received non-need-based gift aid.

GIFT AID (NEED-BASED) ***Total amount:*** $121,674,818 (8% federal, 3% state, 85% institutional, 4% external sources). ***Receiving aid:*** Freshmen: 65% (1,274); all full-time undergraduates: 58% (4,744). ***Average award:*** Freshmen: $29,527; Undergraduates: $25,967. ***Scholarships, grants, and awards:*** Federal Pell, FSEOG, state, private, college/university gift aid from institutional funds.

GIFT AID (NON-NEED-BASED) ***Total amount:*** $52,980,262 (93% institutional, 7% external sources). ***Receiving aid:*** Freshmen: 7% (129). Undergraduates: 6% (476). ***Average award:*** Freshmen: $15,342. Undergraduates: $14,936. ***Scholarships, grants, and awards by category:*** *Academic interests/achievement:* biological sciences, business, communication, education, engineering/technologies, English, foreign languages, general academic interests/achievements, health fields, mathematics, physical sciences. *Creative arts/performance:* theater/drama. *Special characteristics:* children of faculty/staff. ***Tuition waivers:*** Full or partial for employees or children of employees, senior citizens. ***ROTC:*** Army, Naval, Air Force.

LOANS ***Student loans:*** $47,995,506 (59% need-based, 41% non-need-based). 59% of past graduating class borrowed through all loan programs. *Average indebtedness per student:* $38,173. ***Average need-based loan:*** Freshmen: $3667. Undergraduates: $5924. ***Parent loans:*** $20,994,704 (39% need-based, 61% non-need-based). ***Programs:*** Federal Direct (Subsidized and Unsubsidized Stafford, PLUS), Federal Nursing, state, college/university.

WORK-STUDY ***Federal work-study:*** Total amount: $4,782,735; jobs available. ***State or other work-study/employment:*** Part-time jobs available.

ATHLETIC AWARDS Total amount: $6,370,476 (28% need-based, 72% non-need-based).

APPLYING FOR FINANCIAL AID ***Required financial aid form:*** FAFSA. ***Financial aid deadline:*** Continuous. ***Notification date:*** Continuous beginning 11/8.

CONTACT Susan Teerink, Director of Financial Aid, Marquette University, Zilber Hall, 1250 West Wisconsin Avenue, Milwaukee, WI 53201-1881, 414-288-4000 or toll-free 800-222-6544. *Fax:* 414-288-1718. *E-mail:* financialaid@marquette.edu. *Website:* http://www.marquette.edu/.

MARSHALL UNIVERSITY

Huntington, WV

Tuition & fees (area res): $8532	Average undergraduate aid package: $11,618

ABOUT THE INSTITUTION State-supported, coed. ***Awards:*** certificates, bachelor's, master's, and doctoral degrees. 55 undergraduate majors. ***Total enrollment:*** 12,852. Undergraduates: 9,415. Freshmen: 1,769. Federal methodology is used as a basis for awarding need-based institutional aid.

UNDERGRADUATE EXPENSES for 2020–2021 ***Application fee:*** $40. ***Tuition, area resident:*** full-time $7190; part-time $300 per credit hour. ***Tuition, state resident:*** full-time $7190; part-time $300 per credit hour. ***Tuition, nonresident:*** full-time $18,044; part-time $752 per credit hour. ***Required fees:*** full-time $1342. Full-time tuition and fees vary according to degree level, location, program, and reciprocity agreements. Part-time tuition and fees vary according to course load, degree level, location, program, and reciprocity agreements. ***College room and board:*** $10,644; ***Room only:*** $6648. Room and board charges vary according to board plan and housing facility.

FRESHMAN FINANCIAL AID (Fall 2019, est.) 1690 applied for aid; of those 77% were deemed to have need. 99% of freshmen with need received aid; of those 46% had need fully met. ***Average percent of need met:*** 50% (excluding resources awarded to replace EFC). ***Average financial aid package:*** $13,317 (excluding resources awarded to replace EFC). 15% of all full-time freshmen had no need and received non-need-based gift aid.

UNDERGRADUATE FINANCIAL AID (Fall 2019, est.) 6,291 applied for aid; of those 80% were deemed to have need. 98% of undergraduates with need received aid; of those 31% had need fully met. ***Average percent of need met:*** 46% (excluding resources awarded to replace EFC). ***Average financial aid package:*** $11,618 (excluding resources awarded to replace EFC). 13% of all full-time undergraduates had no need and received non-need-based gift aid.

GIFT AID (NEED-BASED) ***Receiving aid:*** Freshmen: 60% (1,054); all full-time undergraduates: 55% (3,894). ***Average award:*** Freshmen: $7811; Undergraduates: $6774. ***Scholarships, grants, and awards:*** Federal Pell, FSEOG, state, private, college/university gift aid from institutional funds, Federal Nursing.

GIFT AID (NON-NEED-BASED) ***Receiving aid:*** Freshmen: 51% (897). Undergraduates: 37% (2,630). ***Average award:*** Freshmen: $3636. Undergraduates: $3193. ***Scholarships, grants, and awards by category:*** *Academic interests/achievement:* general academic interests/achievements. *Creative arts/performance:* applied art and design, general creative arts/performance. *Special characteristics:* children and siblings of alumni, children of faculty/staff, local/state students, members of minority groups. ***Tuition waivers:*** Full or partial for children of alumni, employees or children of employees, senior citizens. ***ROTC:*** Army.

LOANS ***Student loans:*** 68% of past graduating class borrowed through all loan programs. *Average indebtedness per student:* $27,472. ***Average need-based loan:*** Freshmen: $5206. Undergraduates: $6554. ***Programs:*** Federal Direct (Subsidized and Unsubsidized Stafford, PLUS), Perkins, Federal Nursing.

WORK-STUDY Federal work-study jobs available. ***State or other work-study/employment:*** Part-time jobs available.

APPLYING FOR FINANCIAL AID ***Required financial aid forms:*** FAFSA, state aid form.

CONTACT Ms. Pamela Palermo, Director of Student Financial Aid, Marshall University, One John Marshall Drive, Huntington, WV 25755, 304-696-2280 or toll-free 800-642-3499. *Fax:* 304-696-3242. *E-mail:* palermo@marshall.edu. *Website:* http://www.marshall.edu/.

MARS HILL UNIVERSITY

Mars Hill, NC

CONTACT Amanda Randolph, Director of Financial Aid, Mars Hill University, PO Box 370, Mars Hill, NC 28754, 828-689-1123 or toll-free 866-648-4968. *Fax:* 828-689-1300. *E-mail:* arandolph@mhc.edu. *Website:* http://www.mhu.edu/.

MARTIN LUTHER COLLEGE

New Ulm, MN

Tuition & fees: $16,420	Average undergraduate aid package: $12,243

ABOUT THE INSTITUTION Independent Wisconsin Evangelical Lutheran Synod, coed. ***Awards:*** certificates, diplomas, bachelor's, and master's degrees. 14 undergraduate majors. ***Total enrollment:*** 993. Undergraduates: 910. Freshmen: 168. Federal methodology is used as a basis for awarding need-based institutional aid.

UNDERGRADUATE EXPENSES for 2020–2021 ***Comprehensive fee:*** $22,900 includes full-time tuition ($16,420) and room and board ($6480).

FRESHMAN FINANCIAL AID (Fall 2018) 174 applied for aid; of those 91% were deemed to have need. 99% of freshmen with need received aid; of those 10% had need fully met. ***Average percent of need met:*** 64% (excluding resources awarded to replace EFC). ***Average financial aid package:*** $11,855 (excluding resources awarded to replace EFC). 6% of all full-time freshmen had no need and received non-need-based gift aid.

UNDERGRADUATE FINANCIAL AID (Fall 2018) 631 applied for aid; of those 91% were deemed to have need. 100% of undergraduates with need received aid; of those 12% had need fully met. ***Average percent of need met:*** 66% (excluding resources awarded to replace EFC). ***Average financial aid package:*** $12,243 (excluding resources awarded to replace EFC). 12% of all full-time undergraduates had no need and received non-need-based gift aid.

GIFT AID (NEED-BASED) ***Total amount:*** $5,353,247 (18% federal, 7% state, 47% institutional, 28% external sources). ***Receiving aid:*** Freshmen: 87% (157); all full-time undergraduates: 84% (574). ***Average award:*** Freshmen: $9843; Undergraduates: $9268. ***Scholarships, grants, and awards:*** Federal Pell, FSEOG, state, private, college/university gift aid from institutional funds.

GIFT AID (NON-NEED-BASED) ***Total amount:*** $707,187 (41% institutional, 59% external sources). ***Receiving aid:*** Freshmen: 7% (12). Undergraduates: 5% (35). ***Average award:*** Freshmen: $2261. Undergraduates: $3224. ***Scholarships, grants, and awards by category:*** *Academic interests/achievement:* general academic interests/achievements. *Creative arts/performance:* music.

LOANS ***Student loans:*** $3,264,094 (72% need-based, 28% non-need-based). 75% of past graduating class borrowed through all loan programs. *Average indebtedness per student:* $26,791. ***Average need-based loan:*** Freshmen: $3318. Undergraduates: $3973. ***Parent loans:*** $154,806 (34% need-based, 66% non-need-based). ***Programs:*** Federal Direct (Subsidized and Unsubsidized Stafford, PLUS), state, college/university.

WORK-STUDY ***Federal work-study:*** Total amount: $40,541; jobs available. ***State or other work-study/employment:*** Total amount: $106,391 (85% need-based, 15% non-need-based). Part-time jobs available.

APPLYING FOR FINANCIAL AID ***Required financial aid forms:*** FAFSA, institution's own form. ***Financial aid deadline:*** 4/15 (priority: 4/15). ***Notification date:*** Continuous beginning 1/15.

CONTACT Mr. Mark Bauer, Director of Financial Aid, Martin Luther College, 1995 Luther Court, New Ulm, MN 56073, 507-233-9152 or toll-free 877-MLC-1995. *Fax:* 507-354-8225. *E-mail:* bauermd@mlc-wels.edu. *Website:* http://www.mlc-wels.edu/.

MARTIN METHODIST COLLEGE

Pulaski, TN

CONTACT Ms. Anita Beecham, Financial Aid Assistant, Martin Methodist College, 433 West Madison Street, Pulaski, TN 38478-2716, 931-363-9808 or toll-free 800-467-1273. *Fax:* 931-363-9818. *E-mail:* abeecham@martinmethodist.edu.
Website: http://www.martinmethodist.edu/.

MARTIN UNIVERSITY

Indianapolis, IN

CONTACT Berdia Marshall, Director of Financial Aid, Martin University, 2171 Avondale Place, Indianapolis, IN 46218-3867, 317-543-3670. *Fax:* 317-543-4790. *E-mail:* bmarshall@martin.edu.
Website: http://www.martin.edu/.

MARY BALDWIN UNIVERSITY

Staunton, VA

ABOUT THE INSTITUTION Independent, coed, primarily women. ***Awards:*** certificates, bachelor's, master's, and doctoral degrees. 26 undergraduate majors. ***Total enrollment:*** 1,902. Undergraduates: 1,137. Freshmen: 109.

GIFT AID (NEED-BASED) ***Scholarships, grants, and awards:*** Federal Pell, FSEOG, state, private, college/university gift aid from institutional funds.

GIFT AID (NON-NEED-BASED) ***Scholarships, grants, and awards by category:*** *Academic interests/achievement:* general academic interests/achievements. *Special characteristics:* children of educators, children of faculty/staff.

LOANS ***Programs:*** Federal Direct (Subsidized and Unsubsidized Stafford, PLUS), alternative loans.

WORK-STUDY ***Federal work-study:*** Total amount: $293,825; 226 jobs averaging $1300. ***State or other work-study/employment:*** Total amount: $116,639 (91% need-based, 9% non-need-based). 84 part-time jobs averaging $1389.

APPLYING FOR FINANCIAL AID ***Required financial aid forms:*** FAFSA, state aid form.

CONTACT Mrs. Robin Dietrich, Director of Financial Aid, Mary Baldwin University, 101 E Frederick Street, Staunton, VA 24401, 540-887-7025 or toll-free 800-468-2262. *Fax:* 540-887-7229. *E-mail:* rdietric@marybaldwin.edu.
Website: http://www.marybaldwin.edu/.

MARYLAND INSTITUTE COLLEGE OF ART

Baltimore, MD

CONTACT Ms. Diane Prengaman, Associate Vice President for Financial Aid, Maryland Institute College of Art, 1300 Mount Royal Avenue, Baltimore, MD 21217, 410-225-2285. *Fax:* 410-225-2337. *E-mail:* dprengam@mica.edu.
Website: http://www.mica.edu/.

MARYMOUNT CALIFORNIA UNIVERSITY

Rancho Palos Verdes, CA

Tuition & fees: $37,158	Average undergraduate aid package: $30,159

ABOUT THE INSTITUTION Independent Roman Catholic, coed. ***Awards:*** associate, bachelor's, and master's degrees. 9 undergraduate majors. ***Total enrollment:*** 647. Undergraduates: 601. Freshmen: 117. Federal methodology is used as a basis for awarding need-based institutional aid.

UNDERGRADUATE EXPENSES for 2020–2021 ***Application fee:*** $50. ***Tuition:*** full-time $35,158; part-time $1475 per credit hour. ***Required fees:*** full-time $2000. Room and board charges vary according to board plan and housing facility.

FRESHMAN FINANCIAL AID (Fall 2019, est.) 85 applied for aid; of those 99% were deemed to have need. 100% of freshmen with need received aid; of those 23% had need fully met. ***Average percent of need met:*** 73% (excluding resources awarded to replace EFC). ***Average financial aid package:*** $28,687 (excluding resources awarded to replace EFC). 9% of all full-time freshmen had no need and received non-need-based gift aid.

UNDERGRADUATE FINANCIAL AID (Fall 2019, est.) 409 applied for aid; of those 93% were deemed to have need. 100% of undergraduates with need received aid; of those 18% had need fully met. ***Average percent of need met:*** 73% (excluding resources awarded to replace EFC). ***Average financial aid package:*** $30,159 (excluding resources awarded to replace EFC). 16% of all full-time undergraduates had no need and received non-need-based gift aid.

GIFT AID (NEED-BASED) ***Total amount:*** $5,454,698 (23% federal, 25% state, 52% institutional). ***Receiving aid:*** Freshmen: 72% (84); all full-time undergraduates: 65% (381). ***Average award:*** Freshmen: $16,242; Undergraduates: $17,744. ***Scholarships, grants, and awards:*** Federal Pell, FSEOG, state, private, college/university gift aid from institutional funds.

GIFT AID (NON-NEED-BASED) ***Total amount:*** $3,711,722 (96% institutional, 4% external sources). ***Receiving aid:*** Freshmen: 71% (83). Undergraduates: 64% (377). ***Average award:*** Freshmen: $15,400. Undergraduates: $13,811. ***Scholarships, grants, and awards by category:*** *Creative arts/performance:* art/fine arts. ***Tuition waivers:*** Full or partial for employees or children of employees, senior citizens.

LOANS ***Student loans:*** $2,645,710 (52% need-based, 48% non-need-based). 76% of past graduating class borrowed through all loan programs. *Average indebtedness per student:* $24,143. ***Average need-based loan:*** Freshmen: $3483. Undergraduates: $4683. ***Parent loans:*** $1,864,115 (100% non-need-based). ***Programs:*** Federal Direct (Subsidized and Unsubsidized Stafford, PLUS), college/university.

WORK-STUDY Federal work-study jobs available. ***State or other work-study/employment:*** Part-time jobs available.

ATHLETIC AWARDS Total amount: $1,728,466 (100% non-need-based).

APPLYING FOR FINANCIAL AID ***Required financial aid form:*** FAFSA. ***Financial aid deadline:*** 2/15 (priority: 3/2). ***Notification date:*** 3/1.

CONTACT Ms. Eunice Cho, Director of Financial Aid, Marymount California University, 30800 Palos Verdes Drive East, Rancho Palos Verdes, CA 90275, 310-377-5501 Ext. 7285. *Fax:* 310-303-7270. *E-mail:* echo@marymountcalifornia.edu.
Website: http://www.marymountcalifornia.edu/.

MARYMOUNT MANHATTAN COLLEGE

New York, NY

ABOUT THE INSTITUTION Independent, coed. ***Awards:*** bachelor's degrees. 52 undergraduate majors. ***Total enrollment:*** 1,892. Undergraduates: 1,891. Freshmen: 437.

GIFT AID (NEED-BASED) ***Scholarships, grants, and awards:*** Federal Pell, FSEOG, state, private, college/university gift aid from institutional funds.

GIFT AID (NON-NEED-BASED) ***Scholarships, grants, and awards by category:*** *Academic interests/achievement:* biological sciences, general academic interests/achievements. *Creative arts/performance:* applied art and design, dance, performing arts, theater/drama. *Special achievements/activities:* general special achievements/activities, leadership. *Special characteristics:* general special characteristics, international students, local/state students, out-of-state students, veterans.

LOANS ***Programs:*** Federal Direct (Subsidized and Unsubsidized Stafford, PLUS).

CONTACT Ms. Christina Bennett, Director of Financial Aid, Marymount Manhattan College, 221 East 71st Street, New York, NY 10021, 212-517-0556 or toll-free 800-627-9668. *E-mail:* cbennett@mmm.edu.
Website: http://www.mmm.edu/.

MARYMOUNT UNIVERSITY

Arlington, VA

Tuition & fees: $33,950 **Average undergraduate aid package: $25,938**

ABOUT THE INSTITUTION Independent Roman Catholic Church, coed. ***Awards:*** certificates, bachelor's, master's, and doctoral degrees. 26 undergraduate majors. ***Total enrollment:*** 3,363. Undergraduates: 2,158. Freshmen: 392. Both federal and institutional methodology are used as a basis for awarding need-based institutional aid.

UNDERGRADUATE EXPENSES for 2020–2021 ***Application fee:*** $40. ***One-time required fee:*** $490. ***Comprehensive fee:*** $48,350 includes full-time tuition ($33,200), mandatory fees ($750), and room and board ($14,400). Room and board charges vary according to board plan and housing facility. ***Part-time tuition:*** $1090 per credit hour. ***Part-time fees:*** $22 per credit hour.

FRESHMAN FINANCIAL AID (Fall 2019, est.) 320 applied for aid; of those 88% were deemed to have need. 100% of freshmen with need received aid; of those 24% had need fully met. ***Average percent of need met:*** 75% (excluding resources awarded to replace EFC). ***Average financial aid package:*** $29,914 (excluding resources awarded to replace EFC). 25% of all full-time freshmen had no need and received non-need-based gift aid.

UNDERGRADUATE FINANCIAL AID (Fall 2019, est.) 1,342 applied for aid; of those 91% were deemed to have need. 100% of undergraduates with need received aid; of those 16% had need fully met. ***Average percent of need met:*** 64% (excluding resources awarded to replace EFC). ***Average financial aid package:*** $25,938 (excluding resources awarded to replace EFC). 24% of all full-time undergraduates had no need and received non-need-based gift aid.

GIFT AID (NEED-BASED) ***Total amount:*** $6,702,538 (47% federal, 2% state, 51% institutional). ***Receiving aid:*** Freshmen: 61% (238); all full-time undergraduates: 44% (859). ***Average award:*** Freshmen: $6747; Undergraduates: $7382. ***Scholarships, grants, and awards:*** Federal Pell, FSEOG, state, private, college/university gift aid from institutional funds.

GIFT AID (NON-NEED-BASED) ***Total amount:*** $23,326,423 (12% state, 87% institutional, 1% external sources). ***Receiving aid:*** Freshmen: 72% (280). Undergraduates: 55% (1,070). ***Average award:*** Freshmen: $17,665. Undergraduates: $14,687. ***Scholarships, grants, and awards by category:*** *Academic interests/achievement:* 1,629 awards ($17,175,093 total): biological sciences, business, computer science, general academic interests/achievements, humanities, mathematics, social sciences. *Special achievements/activities:* 209 awards ($1,083,143 total): community service, general special achievements/activities, leadership, memberships, religious involvement. *Special characteristics:* 1,299 awards ($2,135,154 total): children and siblings of alumni, general special characteristics, international students, local/state students, members of minority groups, out-of-state students, religious affiliation, veterans. ***Tuition waivers:*** Full or partial for employees or children of employees, senior citizens. ***ROTC:*** Army cooperative, Air Force cooperative.

LOANS ***Student loans:*** $12,591,701 (31% need-based, 69% non-need-based). 66% of past graduating class borrowed through all loan programs. *Average indebtedness per student:* $33,682. ***Average need-based loan:*** Freshmen: $3247. Undergraduates: $4374. ***Parent loans:*** $7,695,847 (100% non-need-based). ***Programs:*** Federal Direct (Subsidized and Unsubsidized Stafford, PLUS).

WORK-STUDY ***Federal work-study:*** Total amount: $1,712,425; 872 jobs averaging $1934.

APPLYING FOR FINANCIAL AID ***Required financial aid form:*** FAFSA. ***Financial aid deadline (priority):*** 3/1. ***Notification date:*** Continuous beginning 1/15. Students must reply within 3 weeks of notification.

CONTACT Mrs. Debbie A. Raines, Director of Financial Aid, Marymount University, 2807 North Glebe Road, Arlington, VA 22207-4224, 703-284-1530 or toll-free 800-548-7638. *Fax:* 703-516-4771. *E-mail:* financial.aid@marymount.edu. *Website:* http://www.marymount.edu/.

MARYVILLE COLLEGE

Maryville, TN

Tuition & fees: $35,578 **Average undergraduate aid package: $31,151**

ABOUT THE INSTITUTION Independent Presbyterian, coed. ***Awards:*** bachelor's degrees. 55 undergraduate majors. Federal methodology is used as a basis for awarding need-based institutional aid.

UNDERGRADUATE EXPENSES for 2019–2020 ***Comprehensive fee:*** $47,288 includes full-time tuition ($34,752), mandatory fees ($826), and room and board ($11,710). ***College room only:*** $5788. Room and board charges vary according to board plan and housing facility. ***Part-time tuition:*** $894 per credit hour. ***Part-time fees:*** $199 per term. Part-time tuition and fees vary according to course load.

FRESHMAN FINANCIAL AID (Fall 2018) 267 applied for aid; of those 88% were deemed to have need. 100% of freshmen with need received aid; of those 20% had need fully met. ***Average percent of need met:*** 87% (excluding resources awarded to replace EFC). ***Average financial aid package:*** $31,451 (excluding resources awarded to replace EFC). 17% of all full-time freshmen had no need and received non-need-based gift aid.

UNDERGRADUATE FINANCIAL AID (Fall 2018) 1,034 applied for aid; of those 88% were deemed to have need. 100% of undergraduates with need received aid; of those 21% had need fully met. ***Average percent of need met:*** 86% (excluding resources awarded to replace EFC). ***Average financial aid package:*** $31,151 (excluding resources awarded to replace EFC). 17% of all full-time undergraduates had no need and received non-need-based gift aid.

GIFT AID (NEED-BASED) ***Total amount:*** $23,064,357 (13% federal, 10% state, 76% institutional, 1% external sources). ***Receiving aid:*** Freshmen: 83% (234); all full-time undergraduates: 82% (906). ***Average award:*** Freshmen: $26,819; Undergraduates: $25,549. ***Scholarships, grants, and awards:*** Federal Pell, FSEOG, state, private, college/university gift aid from institutional funds.

GIFT AID (NON-NEED-BASED) ***Total amount:*** $6,280,408 (5% federal, 10% state, 82% institutional, 3% external sources). ***Receiving aid:*** Freshmen: 36% (101). Undergraduates: 34% (379). ***Average award:*** Freshmen: $29,682. Undergraduates: $26,870. ***Scholarships, grants, and awards by category:*** *Academic interests/achievement:* general academic interests/achievements. *Creative arts/performance:* applied art and design, music, theater/drama. *Special achievements/activities:* community service, leadership. *Special characteristics:* children and siblings of alumni, children of faculty/staff, members of minority groups, religious affiliation, veterans. ***Tuition waivers:*** Full or partial for employees or children of employees.

LOANS ***Student loans:*** $7,050,436 (70% need-based, 30% non-need-based). 66% of past graduating class borrowed through all loan programs. *Average indebtedness per student:* $29,844. ***Average need-based loan:*** Freshmen: $3181. Undergraduates: $4137. ***Parent loans:*** $2,623,578 (49% need-based, 51% non-need-based). ***Programs:*** Federal Direct (Subsidized and Unsubsidized Stafford, PLUS).

WORK-STUDY ***Federal work-study:*** Total amount: $195,273; jobs available. ***State or other work-study/employment:*** Total amount: $245,938 (100% non-need-based). Part-time jobs available.

APPLYING FOR FINANCIAL AID ***Required financial aid form:*** FAFSA. ***Financial aid deadline (priority):*** 5/1. ***Notification date:*** Continuous beginning 12/15. Students must reply by 5/1.

CONTACT Ms. Erin Johnson, Director of Financial Aid, Maryville College, 502 East Lamar Alexander Parkway, Maryville, TN 37804-5907, 865-981-8011 or toll-free 800-597-2687. *Fax:* 865-981-8084. *E-mail:* erin.johnson@maryvillecollege.edu. *Website:* http://www.maryvillecollege.edu/.

MARYVILLE UNIVERSITY OF SAINT LOUIS

St. Louis, MO

Tuition & fees: $28,470 **Average undergraduate aid package: $20,367**

ABOUT THE INSTITUTION Independent, coed. ***Awards:*** certificates, bachelor's, master's, and doctoral degrees. 62 undergraduate majors. ***Total***

enrollment: 10,013. Undergraduates: 4,454. Freshmen: 683. Both federal and institutional methodology are used as a basis for awarding need-based institutional aid.
UNDERGRADUATE EXPENSES for 2020–2021 ***Comprehensive fee:*** $38,770 includes full-time tuition ($26,070), mandatory fees ($2400), and room and board ($10,300). Full-time tuition and fees vary according to course load and program. Room and board charges vary according to board plan and housing facility. ***Part-time tuition:*** $781 per credit hour. ***Part-time fees:*** $375 per year. Part-time tuition and fees vary according to class time, course load, and program.
FRESHMAN FINANCIAL AID (Fall 2019, est.) 577 applied for aid; of those 85% were deemed to have need. 100% of freshmen with need received aid; of those 22% had need fully met. ***Average percent of need met:*** 66% (excluding resources awarded to replace EFC). ***Average financial aid package:*** $22,630 (excluding resources awarded to replace EFC). 27% of all full-time freshmen had no need and received non-need-based gift aid.
UNDERGRADUATE FINANCIAL AID (Fall 2019, est.) 2,275 applied for aid; of those 89% were deemed to have need. 100% of undergraduates with need received aid; of those 11% had need fully met. ***Average percent of need met:*** 60% (excluding resources awarded to replace EFC). ***Average financial aid package:*** $20,367 (excluding resources awarded to replace EFC). 27% of all full-time undergraduates had no need and received non-need-based gift aid.
GIFT AID (NEED-BASED) ***Receiving aid:*** Freshmen: 72% (492); all full-time undergraduates: 67% (2,010). ***Average award:*** Freshmen: $18,474; Undergraduates: $15,586. ***Scholarships, grants, and awards:*** Federal Pell, FSEOG, state, private, college/university gift aid from institutional funds, United Negro College Fund, Academic Competitiveness Grants, National SMART Grants, TEACH Grants.
GIFT AID (NON-NEED-BASED) ***Receiving aid:*** Freshmen: 12% (82). Undergraduates: 9% (261). ***Average award:*** Freshmen: $14,745. Undergraduates: $13,960. ***Scholarships, grants, and awards by category:*** *Academic interests/achievement:* biological sciences, business, education, English, general academic interests/achievements, health fields, home economics, international studies, mathematics, social sciences. *Creative arts/performance:* applied art and design, art/fine arts, music. *Special achievements/activities:* cheerleading/drum major, community service, general special achievements/activities, leadership, religious involvement. *Special characteristics:* adult students, children and siblings of alumni, ethnic background, first-generation college students, general special characteristics, international students, members of minority groups, out-of-state students, parents of current students. ***Tuition waivers:*** Full or partial for employees or children of employees, senior citizens. ***ROTC:*** Army cooperative.
LOANS ***Student loans:*** 70% of past graduating class borrowed through all loan programs. *Average indebtedness per student:* $30,657. ***Average need-based loan:*** Freshmen: $3402. Undergraduates: $4323. ***Programs:*** Federal Direct (Subsidized and Unsubsidized Stafford, PLUS), private loans.
WORK-STUDY ***Federal work-study:*** 525 jobs averaging $949. ***State or other work-study/employment:*** 118 part-time jobs averaging $3855.
APPLYING FOR FINANCIAL AID ***Required financial aid form:*** FAFSA. ***Financial aid deadline:*** Continuous. ***Notification date:*** Continuous. Students must reply within 2 weeks of notification.
CONTACT Liesl Flanagan, Senior Director of Financial Services and Student Accounts, Maryville University of Saint Louis, 650 Maryville University Drive, St. Louis, MO 63141-7299, 314-529 Ext. 2827 or toll-free 800-627-9855. *Fax:* 314-529-9199. *E-mail:* lflanagan1@maryville.edu.
Website: http://www.maryville.edu/.

MARYWOOD UNIVERSITY

Scranton, PA

Tuition & fees: $36,928	Average undergraduate aid package: $28,358

ABOUT THE INSTITUTION Independent Roman Catholic, coed. ***Awards:*** certificates, bachelor's, master's, and doctoral degrees. 72 undergraduate majors. ***Total enrollment:*** 2,679. Undergraduates: 1,809. Freshmen: 361. Federal methodology is used as a basis for awarding need-based institutional aid.
UNDERGRADUATE EXPENSES for 2020–2021 ***Application fee:*** $35. ***Comprehensive fee:*** $51,266 includes full-time tuition ($35,178), mandatory fees ($1750), and room and board ($14,338). ***College room only:*** $8138. Room and board charges vary according to board plan and housing facility. ***Part-time tuition:*** $670 per credit.
FRESHMAN FINANCIAL AID (Fall 2019, est.) 348 applied for aid; of those 89% were deemed to have need. 100% of freshmen with need received aid; of those 22% had need fully met. ***Average percent of need met:*** 81% (excluding resources awarded to replace EFC). ***Average financial aid package:*** $31,924 (excluding resources awarded to replace EFC). 14% of all full-time freshmen had no need and received non-need-based gift aid.
UNDERGRADUATE FINANCIAL AID (Fall 2019, est.) 1,471 applied for aid; of those 91% were deemed to have need. 99% of undergraduates with need received aid; of those 19% had need fully met. ***Average percent of need met:*** 75% (excluding resources awarded to replace EFC). ***Average financial aid package:*** $28,358 (excluding resources awarded to replace EFC). 17% of all full-time undergraduates had no need and received non-need-based gift aid.
GIFT AID (NEED-BASED) ***Receiving aid:*** Freshmen: 86% (309); all full-time undergraduates: 81% (1,330). ***Average award:*** Freshmen: $26,522; Undergraduates: $24,537. ***Scholarships, grants, and awards:*** Federal Pell, FSEOG, state, college/university gift aid from institutional funds.
GIFT AID (NON-NEED-BASED) ***Receiving aid:*** Freshmen: 16% (56). Undergraduates: 12% (205). ***Average award:*** Freshmen: $19,408. Undergraduates: $17,539. ***Scholarships, grants, and awards by category:*** *Academic interests/achievement:* architecture, biological sciences, business, communication, computer science, education, English, foreign languages, general academic interests/achievements, health fields, home economics, mathematics, premedicine, religion/biblical studies, social sciences. *Creative arts/performance:* applied art and design, music. *Special achievements/activities:* community service, general special achievements/activities, leadership. ***Tuition waivers:*** Full or partial for employees or children of employees, senior citizens. ***ROTC:*** Army cooperative, Air Force cooperative.
LOANS ***Student loans:*** 79% of past graduating class borrowed through all loan programs. *Average indebtedness per student:* $41,925. ***Average need-based loan:*** Freshmen: $3347. Undergraduates: $4191. ***Programs:*** Federal Direct (Subsidized and Unsubsidized Stafford, PLUS).
WORK-STUDY ***Federal work-study:*** 950 jobs averaging $1982.
APPLYING FOR FINANCIAL AID ***Required financial aid forms:*** FAFSA, state aid form. ***Notification date:*** Continuous. Students must reply within 3 weeks of notification.
CONTACT Barbara Schmitt, Director of Financial Aid, Marywood University, 2300 Adams Avenue, Scranton, PA 18509-1598, 570-348-6225 or toll-free 866-279-9663. *Fax:* 570-961-4739. *E-mail:* schmitt@marywood.edu.
Website: http://www.marywood.edu/.

MASSACHUSETTS COLLEGE OF ART AND DESIGN

Boston, MA

Tuition & fees (MA res): $13,700	Average undergraduate aid package: $12,403

ABOUT THE INSTITUTION State-supported, coed. ***Awards:*** certificates, bachelor's, and master's degrees. 18 undergraduate majors. ***Total enrollment:*** 2,065. Undergraduates: 1,931. Freshmen: 424. Federal methodology is used as a basis for awarding need-based institutional aid.
UNDERGRADUATE EXPENSES for 2019–2020 ***Application fee:*** $70. ***Tuition, area resident:*** part-time $340 per credit. ***Tuition, state resident:*** full-time $13,700; part-time $340 per credit. ***Tuition, nonresident:*** full-time $38,400; part-time $340 per credit. Room and board charges vary according to board plan and housing facility.
FRESHMAN FINANCIAL AID (Fall 2019, est.) 325 applied for aid; of those 78% were deemed to have need. 94% of freshmen with need received aid; of those 6% had need fully met. ***Average percent of need met:*** 51% (excluding resources awarded to replace EFC). ***Average financial aid package:*** $12,432 (excluding resources awarded to replace EFC). 11% of all full-time freshmen had no need and received non-need-based gift aid.
UNDERGRADUATE FINANCIAL AID (Fall 2019, est.) 1,321 applied for aid; of those 80% were deemed to have need. 96% of undergraduates with need received aid; of those 9% had need fully met. ***Average percent of need met:*** 59% (excluding resources awarded to replace EFC). ***Average financial aid package:*** $12,403 (excluding resources awarded to replace EFC). 11% of all full-time undergraduates had no need and received non-need-based gift aid.

GIFT AID (NEED-BASED) ***Total amount:*** $6,049,528 (42% federal, 12% state, 46% institutional). ***Receiving aid:*** Freshmen: 59% (224); all full-time undergraduates: 48% (814). ***Average award:*** Freshmen: $7891; Undergraduates: $7181. ***Scholarships, grants, and awards:*** Federal Pell, FSEOG, state, private, college/university gift aid from institutional funds.

GIFT AID (NON-NEED-BASED) ***Total amount:*** $4,187,491 (91% institutional, 9% external sources). ***Receiving aid:*** Freshmen: 34% (127). Undergraduates: 43% (731). ***Average award:*** Freshmen: $2270. Undergraduates: $2757. ***Scholarships, grants, and awards by category:*** *Special characteristics:* children of faculty/staff, children of union members/company employees, veterans.

LOANS ***Student loans:*** $12,208,286 (31% need-based, 69% non-need-based). 72% of past graduating class borrowed through all loan programs. *Average indebtedness per student:* $26,720. ***Average need-based loan:*** Freshmen: $3435. Undergraduates: $4454. ***Parent loans:*** $3,459,121 (100% non-need-based). ***Programs:*** Federal Direct (Subsidized and Unsubsidized Stafford, PLUS), Perkins, state, alternative loans.

WORK-STUDY ***Federal work-study:*** Total amount: $247,159; jobs available. ***State or other work-study/employment:*** Part-time jobs available.

APPLYING FOR FINANCIAL AID ***Required financial aid form:*** FAFSA. ***Financial aid deadline (priority):*** 3/1. ***Notification date:*** Continuous beginning 3/15. Students must reply within 3 weeks of notification.

CONTACT Auelio Ramirez, Director of Student Financial Assistance, Massachusetts College of Art and Design, 621 Huntington Avenue, Boston, MA 02115-5882, 617-879-7850. *Fax:* 617-879-7880. *E-mail:* aurelio.ramirez@massart.edu.
Website: http://www.massart.edu/.

MASSACHUSETTS COLLEGE OF LIBERAL ARTS

North Adams, MA

Tuition & fees (MA res): $10,930	Average undergraduate aid package: $16,911

ABOUT THE INSTITUTION State-supported, coed. ***Awards:*** certificates, bachelor's, and master's degrees. 43 undergraduate majors. ***Total enrollment:*** 1,452. Undergraduates: 1,277. Freshmen: 262. Federal methodology is used as a basis for awarding need-based institutional aid.

UNDERGRADUATE EXPENSES for 2019–2020 ***Tuition, state resident:*** full-time $1030; part-time $43 per credit. ***Tuition, nonresident:*** full-time $9975; part-time $416 per credit. ***Required fees:*** full-time $9900; $417.09 per credit. Full-time tuition and fees vary according to reciprocity agreements. Part-time tuition and fees vary according to course load and reciprocity agreements. ***College room and board:*** $11,430. Room and board charges vary according to board plan and housing facility.

FRESHMAN FINANCIAL AID (Fall 2019, est.) 283 applied for aid; of those 81% were deemed to have need. 100% of freshmen with need received aid; of those 77% had need fully met. ***Average percent of need met:*** 81% (excluding resources awarded to replace EFC). ***Average financial aid package:*** $17,933 (excluding resources awarded to replace EFC). 18% of all full-time freshmen had no need and received non-need-based gift aid.

UNDERGRADUATE FINANCIAL AID (Fall 2019, est.) 1,095 applied for aid; of those 80% were deemed to have need. 100% of undergraduates with need received aid; of those 77% had need fully met. ***Average percent of need met:*** 80% (excluding resources awarded to replace EFC). ***Average financial aid package:*** $16,911 (excluding resources awarded to replace EFC). 14% of all full-time undergraduates had no need and received non-need-based gift aid.

GIFT AID (NEED-BASED) ***Receiving aid:*** Freshmen: 67% (192); all full-time undergraduates: 61% (704). ***Average award:*** Freshmen: $7681; Undergraduates: $7894. ***Scholarships, grants, and awards:*** Federal Pell, FSEOG, state, private, college/university gift aid from institutional funds.

GIFT AID (NON-NEED-BASED) ***Receiving aid:*** Freshmen: 79% (225). Undergraduates: 48% (544). ***Average award:*** Freshmen: $4124. Undergraduates: $3295. ***Scholarships, grants, and awards by category:*** *Academic interests/achievement:* biological sciences, business, communication, computer science, education, English, general academic interests/achievements, home economics, humanities, mathematics, physical sciences, social sciences. *Creative arts/performance:* applied art and design, art/fine arts, cinema/film/broadcasting, journalism/publications, music, performing arts, theater/drama. *Special achievements/activities:* general special achievements/activities, leadership, memberships. ***Tuition waivers:*** Full or partial for employees or children of employees, senior citizens.

LOANS ***Student loans:*** 82% of past graduating class borrowed through all loan programs. *Average indebtedness per student:* $29,416. ***Average need-based loan:*** Freshmen: $2713. Undergraduates: $3719. ***Programs:*** Federal Direct (Subsidized and Unsubsidized Stafford, PLUS), Perkins, state.

WORK-STUDY Federal work-study jobs available. ***State or other work-study/employment:*** Part-time jobs available.

APPLYING FOR FINANCIAL AID ***Required financial aid form:*** FAFSA. ***Notification date:*** Continuous. Students must reply within 2 weeks of notification.

CONTACT Mrs. Bonnie J. Howland, Director of Student Financial Services, Massachusetts College of Liberal Arts, 375 Church Street, North Adams, MA 01247, 413-662-5219 or toll-free 800-989-MCLA. *Fax:* 413-662-5105. *E-mail:* bonnie.howland@mcla.edu.
Website: http://www.mcla.edu/.

MASSACHUSETTS INSTITUTE OF TECHNOLOGY

Cambridge, MA

Tuition & fees: $53,790	Average undergraduate aid package: $52,205

ABOUT THE INSTITUTION Independent, coed. ***Awards:*** bachelor's, master's, and doctoral degrees. 39 undergraduate majors. ***Total enrollment:*** 11,574. Undergraduates: 4,602. Freshmen: 1,114. Institutional methodology is used as a basis for awarding need-based institutional aid.

UNDERGRADUATE EXPENSES for 2019–2020 ***Application fee:*** $75. ***Comprehensive fee:*** $70,180 includes full-time tuition ($53,450), mandatory fees ($340), and room and board ($16,390). ***College room only:*** $10,430. Room and board charges vary according to housing facility. ***Part-time fees:*** $830 per credit hour. Part-time tuition and fees vary according to course load.

FRESHMAN FINANCIAL AID (Fall 2018) 909 applied for aid; of those 78% were deemed to have need. 100% of freshmen with need received aid; of those 100% had need fully met. ***Average percent of need met:*** 100% (excluding resources awarded to replace EFC). ***Average financial aid package:*** $51,721 (excluding resources awarded to replace EFC).

UNDERGRADUATE FINANCIAL AID (Fall 2018) 3,018 applied for aid; of those 89% were deemed to have need. 100% of undergraduates with need received aid; of those 100% had need fully met. ***Average percent of need met:*** 100% (excluding resources awarded to replace EFC). ***Average financial aid package:*** $52,205 (excluding resources awarded to replace EFC).

GIFT AID (NEED-BASED) ***Total amount:*** $138,824,564 (5% federal, 92% institutional, 3% external sources). ***Receiving aid:*** Freshmen: 62% (695); all full-time undergraduates: 58% (2,623). ***Average award:*** Freshmen: $50,044; Undergraduates: $50,665. ***Scholarships, grants, and awards:*** Federal Pell, FSEOG, state, private, college/university gift aid from institutional funds, United Negro College Fund.

GIFT AID (NON-NEED-BASED) ***Total amount:*** $4,174,143 (34% federal, 66% external sources). ***Receiving aid:*** Freshmen: 3% (33). Undergraduates: 2% (76). ***Tuition waivers:*** Full or partial for employees or children of employees. ***ROTC:*** Army, Naval, Air Force.

LOANS ***Student loans:*** $4,799,412 (27% need-based, 73% non-need-based). 23% of past graduating class borrowed through all loan programs. *Average indebtedness per student:* $23,517. ***Average need-based loan:*** Freshmen: $1968. Undergraduates: $2348. ***Parent loans:*** $3,695,580 (10% need-based, 90% non-need-based). ***Programs:*** Federal Direct (Subsidized and Unsubsidized Stafford, PLUS), college/university.

WORK-STUDY ***Federal work-study:*** Total amount: $1,355,276; 451 jobs averaging $3005. ***State or other work-study/employment:*** Total amount: $4,407,066 (80% need-based, 20% non-need-based). 1,512 part-time jobs averaging $2915.

APPLYING FOR FINANCIAL AID ***Required financial aid forms:*** FAFSA, CSS Financial Aid PROFILE, noncustodial (divorced/separated) parent's statement, parent's complete federal income tax form(s) and W-2s from 2 years ago. ***Financial aid deadline:*** 2/15 (priority: 2/15). ***Notification date:*** 3/17.

CONTACT Stuart Schmill, Dean of Admissions and Student Financial Services, Massachusetts Institute of Technology, 77 Massachusetts Avenue, Room 11-120, Cambridge, MA 02139-4307, 617-258-5529. *Fax:* 617-648-9968. *E-mail:* sfs@mit.edu. *Website:* http://www.mit.edu/.

MASSACHUSETTS MARITIME ACADEMY

Buzzards Bay, MA

Tuition & fees (MA res): $10,314	Average undergraduate aid package: $14,285

ABOUT THE INSTITUTION State-supported, coed. ***Awards:*** bachelor's and master's degrees. 7 undergraduate majors. ***Total enrollment:*** 1,792. Undergraduates: 1,695. Freshmen: 404. Federal methodology is used as a basis for awarding need-based institutional aid.

UNDERGRADUATE EXPENSES for 2020–2021 ***Application fee:*** $50. ***Tuition, state resident:*** full-time $1890; part-time $79 per credit hour. ***Tuition, nonresident:*** full-time $17,010; part-time $709 per credit hour. ***Required fees:*** full-time $8424; $264 per year. Full-time tuition and fees vary according to reciprocity agreements. Part-time tuition and fees vary according to course load and reciprocity agreements. ***College room and board:*** $13,352; ***Room only:*** $8004.

FRESHMAN FINANCIAL AID (Fall 2019, est.) 385 applied for aid; of those 74% were deemed to have need. 100% of freshmen with need received aid; of those 34% had need fully met. ***Average percent of need met:*** 64% (excluding resources awarded to replace EFC). ***Average financial aid package:*** $15,467 (excluding resources awarded to replace EFC). 16% of all full-time freshmen had no need and received non-need-based gift aid.

UNDERGRADUATE FINANCIAL AID (Fall 2019, est.) 931 applied for aid; of those 100% were deemed to have need. 100% of undergraduates with need received aid; of those 38% had need fully met. ***Average percent of need met:*** 68% (excluding resources awarded to replace EFC). ***Average financial aid package:*** $14,285 (excluding resources awarded to replace EFC). 9% of all full-time undergraduates had no need and received non-need-based gift aid.

GIFT AID (NEED-BASED) ***Total amount:*** $6,076,046 (22% federal, 9% state, 69% institutional). ***Receiving aid:*** Freshmen: 38% (152); all full-time undergraduates: 32% (514). ***Average award:*** Freshmen: $15,208; Undergraduates: $12,774. ***Scholarships, grants, and awards:*** Federal Pell, FSEOG, state, private, college/university gift aid from institutional funds.

GIFT AID (NON-NEED-BASED) ***Total amount:*** $3,234,000 (17% state, 77% institutional, 6% external sources). ***Receiving aid:*** Freshmen: 19% (76). Undergraduates: 11% (177). ***Average award:*** Freshmen: $6651. Undergraduates: $5236. ***Scholarships, grants, and awards by category:*** *Academic interests/achievement:* general academic interests/achievements. *Special achievements/activities:* leadership. *Special characteristics:* ethnic background. ***Tuition waivers:*** Full or partial for employees or children of employees. ***ROTC:*** Army cooperative.

LOANS ***Student loans:*** $5,982,000 (54% need-based, 46% non-need-based). 79% of past graduating class borrowed through all loan programs. *Average indebtedness per student:* $37,414. ***Average need-based loan:*** Freshmen: $3416. Undergraduates: $4300. ***Parent loans:*** $2,720,000 (100% non-need-based). ***Programs:*** Federal Direct (Subsidized and Unsubsidized Stafford, PLUS).

WORK-STUDY ***Federal work-study:*** Total amount: $200,000; 410 jobs averaging $1500.

APPLYING FOR FINANCIAL AID ***Required financial aid form:*** FAFSA. ***Financial aid deadline (priority):*** 3/1. ***Notification date:*** Continuous beginning 2/15.

CONTACT Ms. Catherine Kedski, Director of Student Financial Services, Massachusetts Maritime Academy, 101 Academy Drive, Buzzards Bay, MA 02532, 508-830-5042 or toll-free 800-544-3411. *Fax:* 508-830-5077. *E-mail:* ckedski@maritime.edu. *Website:* http://www.maritime.edu/.

THE MASTER'S UNIVERSITY

Santa Clarita, CA

CONTACT Mr. Gary Edwards, Director of Financial Aid, The Master's University, 21726 Placerita Canyon Road, Santa Clarita, CA 91321-1200, 661-362-2291 or toll-free 800-568-6248. *Fax:* 661-362-2693. *E-mail:* gedwards@masters.edu. *Website:* http://www.masters.edu/.

MAYVILLE STATE UNIVERSITY

Mayville, ND

Tuition & fees: N/R	Average undergraduate aid package: $11,685

ABOUT THE INSTITUTION State-supported, coed. ***Awards:*** certificates, associate, bachelor's, and master's degrees. 36 undergraduate majors. ***Total enrollment:*** 1,212. Undergraduates: 1,187. Freshmen: 109. Federal methodology is used as a basis for awarding need-based institutional aid.

FRESHMAN FINANCIAL AID (Fall 2019, est.) 93 applied for aid; of those 66% were deemed to have need. 98% of freshmen with need received aid; of those 43% had need fully met. ***Average percent of need met:*** 78% (excluding resources awarded to replace EFC). ***Average financial aid package:*** $12,696 (excluding resources awarded to replace EFC). 23% of all full-time freshmen had no need and received non-need-based gift aid.

UNDERGRADUATE FINANCIAL AID (Fall 2019, est.) 480 applied for aid; of those 76% were deemed to have need. 98% of undergraduates with need received aid; of those 33% had need fully met. ***Average percent of need met:*** 72% (excluding resources awarded to replace EFC). ***Average financial aid package:*** $11,685 (excluding resources awarded to replace EFC). 12% of all full-time undergraduates had no need and received non-need-based gift aid.

GIFT AID (NEED-BASED) ***Total amount:*** $2,732,718 (46% federal, 13% state, 6% institutional, 35% external sources). ***Receiving aid:*** Freshmen: 53% (56); all full-time undergraduates: 53% (311). ***Average award:*** Freshmen: $6318; Undergraduates: $5585. ***Scholarships, grants, and awards:*** Federal Pell, FSEOG, state, private, college/university gift aid from institutional funds, TEACH Grant.

GIFT AID (NON-NEED-BASED) ***Total amount:*** $308,684 (7% federal, 32% state, 35% institutional, 26% external sources). ***Receiving aid:*** Freshmen: 8% (8). Undergraduates: 3% (17). ***Average award:*** Freshmen: $1997. Undergraduates: $1388. ***Scholarships, grants, and awards by category:*** *Academic interests/achievement:* general academic interests/achievements, religion/biblical studies. *Creative arts/performance:* art/fine arts, music, theater/drama. *Special achievements/activities:* leadership, religious involvement. *Special characteristics:* children and siblings of alumni, children of faculty/staff, international students, local/state students, members of minority groups, out-of-state students. ***ROTC:*** Army cooperative, Air Force cooperative.

LOANS ***Student loans:*** $3,977,924 (60% need-based, 40% non-need-based). 100% of past graduating class borrowed through all loan programs. *Average indebtedness per student:* $31,839. ***Average need-based loan:*** Freshmen: $5319. Undergraduates: $6556. ***Parent loans:*** $165,496 (39% need-based, 61% non-need-based). ***Programs:*** Federal Direct (Subsidized and Unsubsidized Stafford, PLUS), Other private education loans.

WORK-STUDY ***Federal work-study:*** Total amount: $51,800; 36 jobs averaging $39,218.

ATHLETIC AWARDS Total amount: $293,566 (48% need-based, 52% non-need-based).

APPLYING FOR FINANCIAL AID ***Required financial aid form:*** FAFSA. ***Financial aid deadline:*** Continuous. ***Notification date:*** Continuous beginning 6/1. Students must reply within 2 weeks of notification.

CONTACT Ms. Shirley Hanson, Director of Financial Aid, Mayville State University, 330 3rd Street NE, Mayville, ND 58257-1299, 701-788-4767 or toll-free 800-437-4104. *Fax:* 701-788-4818. *E-mail:* shirley.m.hanson@mayvillestate.edu. *Website:* http://www.mayvillestate.edu/.

MCDANIEL COLLEGE
Westminster, MD

Tuition & fees: $44,540 | **Average undergraduate aid package: $39,063**

ABOUT THE INSTITUTION Independent, coed. ***Awards:*** certificates, bachelor's, and master's degrees. 32 undergraduate majors. ***Total enrollment:*** 2,888. Undergraduates: 1,680. Freshmen: 575. Federal methodology is used as a basis for awarding need-based institutional aid.

UNDERGRADUATE EXPENSES for 2019–2020 ***Comprehensive fee:*** $56,312 includes full-time tuition ($44,540) and room and board ($11,772). ***College room only:*** $5408. Full-time tuition and fees vary according to course load. Room and board charges vary according to board plan and housing facility. ***Part-time tuition:*** $1392 per credit hour. Part-time tuition and fees vary according to course load.

FRESHMAN FINANCIAL AID (Fall 2019, est.) 550 applied for aid; of those 93% were deemed to have need. 100% of freshmen with need received aid; of those 1% had need fully met. ***Average percent of need met:*** 85% (excluding resources awarded to replace EFC). ***Average financial aid package:*** $41,491 (excluding resources awarded to replace EFC). 12% of all full-time freshmen had no need and received non-need-based gift aid.

UNDERGRADUATE FINANCIAL AID (Fall 2019, est.) 1,448 applied for aid; of those 93% were deemed to have need. 100% of undergraduates with need received aid; of those 21% had need fully met. ***Average percent of need met:*** 84% (excluding resources awarded to replace EFC). ***Average financial aid package:*** $39,063 (excluding resources awarded to replace EFC). 18% of all full-time undergraduates had no need and received non-need-based gift aid.

GIFT AID (NEED-BASED) ***Receiving aid:*** Freshmen: 88% (510); all full-time undergraduates: 76% (1,345). ***Average award:*** Freshmen: $38,636; Undergraduates: $36,238. ***Scholarships, grants, and awards:*** Federal Pell, FSEOG, state, private, college/university gift aid from institutional funds, TEACH Grants.

GIFT AID (NON-NEED-BASED) ***Receiving aid:*** Freshmen: 11% (66). Undergraduates: 17% (296). ***Average award:*** Freshmen: $27,358. Undergraduates: $22,609. ***Scholarships, grants, and awards by category:*** *Academic interests/achievement:* general academic interests/achievements. *Special achievements/activities:* leadership. *Special characteristics:* children of educators, general special characteristics, local/state students, previous college experience, siblings of current students, veterans, veterans' children. ***Tuition waivers:*** Full or partial for children of alumni, employees or children of employees. ***ROTC:*** Army, Air Force cooperative.

LOANS ***Student loans:*** 67% of past graduating class borrowed through all loan programs. *Average indebtedness per student:* $16,622. ***Average need-based loan:*** Freshmen: $3300. Undergraduates: $2825. ***Programs:*** Federal Direct (Subsidized and Unsubsidized Stafford, PLUS).

WORK-STUDY Federal work-study jobs available. ***State or other work-study/employment:*** Part-time jobs available.

APPLYING FOR FINANCIAL AID ***Required financial aid form:*** FAFSA. ***Notification date:*** Continuous. Students must reply within 2 weeks of notification.

CONTACT Dr. Kemia Himon, Financial Aid Office, McDaniel College, 2 College Hill, Westminster, MD 21157-4390, 410-857-2233 or toll-free 800-638-5005. *Fax:* 410-857-2729. *E-mail:* finaid@mcdaniel.edu.
Website: http://www.mcdaniel.edu/.

MCKENDREE UNIVERSITY
Lebanon, IL

Tuition & fees: $31,640 | **Average undergraduate aid package: $22,125**

ABOUT THE INSTITUTION Independent United Methodist Church, coed. ***Awards:*** certificates, associate, bachelor's, master's, and doctoral degrees. 44 undergraduate majors. ***Total enrollment:*** 2,292. Undergraduates: 1,788. Freshmen: 332. Federal methodology is used as a basis for awarding need-based institutional aid.

UNDERGRADUATE EXPENSES for 2019–2020 ***One-time required fee:*** $400. ***Comprehensive fee:*** $41,560 includes full-time tuition ($30,540), mandatory fees ($1100), and room and board ($9920). ***College room only:*** $5370. Full-time tuition and fees vary according to course load, degree level, and location. Room and board charges vary according to board plan and housing facility. ***Part-time tuition:*** $990 per credit hour. Part-time tuition and fees vary according to course load, degree level, and location.

FRESHMAN FINANCIAL AID (Fall 2018) 323 applied for aid; of those 90% were deemed to have need. 100% of freshmen with need received aid; of those 20% had need fully met. ***Average percent of need met:*** 74% (excluding resources awarded to replace EFC). ***Average financial aid package:*** $23,152 (excluding resources awarded to replace EFC). 20% of all full-time freshmen had no need and received non-need-based gift aid.

UNDERGRADUATE FINANCIAL AID (Fall 2018) 1,312 applied for aid; of those 92% were deemed to have need. 99% of undergraduates with need received aid; of those 19% had need fully met. ***Average percent of need met:*** 72% (excluding resources awarded to replace EFC). ***Average financial aid package:*** $22,125 (excluding resources awarded to replace EFC). 18% of all full-time undergraduates had no need and received non-need-based gift aid.

GIFT AID (NEED-BASED) ***Total amount:*** $20,018,618 (16% federal, 11% state, 66% institutional, 7% external sources). ***Receiving aid:*** Freshmen: 78% (290); all full-time undergraduates: 76% (1,168). ***Average award:*** Freshmen: $20,689; Undergraduates: $19,062. ***Scholarships, grants, and awards:*** Federal Pell, FSEOG, state, private, college/university gift aid from institutional funds.

GIFT AID (NON-NEED-BASED) ***Total amount:*** $4,731,437 (89% institutional, 11% external sources). ***Receiving aid:*** Freshmen: 13% (48). Undergraduates: 11% (172). ***Average award:*** Freshmen: $12,357. Undergraduates: $13,412. ***Scholarships, grants, and awards by category:*** *Academic interests/achievement:* 1,130 awards ($9,966,486 total): biological sciences, business, general academic interests/achievements, religion/biblical studies. *Creative arts/performance:* 198 awards ($526,320 total): dance, debating, music. *Special achievements/activities:* 492 awards ($2,045,500 total): cheerleading/drum major, community service, leadership. *Special characteristics:* 219 awards ($785,280 total): children and siblings of alumni, children of faculty/staff, general special characteristics, international students, religious affiliation, veterans. ***Tuition waivers:*** Full or partial for children of alumni, employees or children of employees. ***ROTC:*** Army cooperative, Air Force cooperative.

LOANS ***Student loans:*** $9,074,766 (70% need-based, 30% non-need-based). 70% of past graduating class borrowed through all loan programs. *Average indebtedness per student:* $28,754. ***Average need-based loan:*** Freshmen: $3497. Undergraduates: $4550. ***Parent loans:*** $4,345,308 (43% need-based, 57% non-need-based). ***Programs:*** Federal Direct (Subsidized and Unsubsidized Stafford, PLUS).

WORK-STUDY ***Federal work-study:*** Total amount: $230,821; 265 jobs averaging $871. ***State or other work-study/employment:*** Total amount: $88,380 (100% non-need-based). 75 part-time jobs averaging $1178.

ATHLETIC AWARDS Total amount: $5,283,544 (49% need-based, 51% non-need-based).

APPLYING FOR FINANCIAL AID ***Required financial aid form:*** FAFSA. ***Financial aid deadline (priority):*** 5/31. ***Notification date:*** Continuous beginning 3/1.

CONTACT Ashley A. Byers, Director of Financial Aid, McKendree University, 701 College Road, Lebanon, IL 62254-1299, 618-537-6532 or toll-free 800-232-7228. *Fax:* 618-537-6530. *E-mail:* aabyers@mckendree.edu.
Website: http://www.mckendree.edu/.

MCMURRY UNIVERSITY
Abilene, TX

CONTACT Mr. Tim Sechrist, Director of Student Financial Services, McMurry University, #1 McMurry University Box 908, Abilene, TX 79697, 325-793-4978 or toll-free 800-460-2392. *Fax:* 325-793-4718. *E-mail:* financialaid@mcm.edu.
Website: http://www.mcm.edu/.

MCNEESE STATE UNIVERSITY
Lake Charles, LA

CONTACT Ms. Taina J. Savoit, Director of Financial Aid, McNeese State University, PO Box 93260, Lake Charles, LA 70609-3260, 337-475-5065 or toll-free 800-622-3352. *Fax:* 337-475-5068. *E-mail:* financialaid@mcneese.edu.
Website: http://www.mcneese.edu/.

MCPHERSON COLLEGE

McPherson, KS

Tuition & fees: N/R	Average undergraduate aid package: $27,170

ABOUT THE INSTITUTION Independent Church of the Brethren, coed. ***Awards:*** bachelor's and master's degrees. 41 undergraduate majors. ***Total enrollment:*** 733. Undergraduates: 725. Freshmen: 202. Federal methodology is used as a basis for awarding need-based institutional aid.

FRESHMAN FINANCIAL AID (Fall 2019, est.) 212 applied for aid; of those 90% were deemed to have need. 100% of freshmen with need received aid; of those 27% had need fully met. ***Average percent of need met:*** 90% (excluding resources awarded to replace EFC). ***Average financial aid package:*** $28,622 (excluding resources awarded to replace EFC). 10% of all full-time freshmen had no need and received non-need-based gift aid.

UNDERGRADUATE FINANCIAL AID (Fall 2019, est.) 690 applied for aid; of those 92% were deemed to have need. 100% of undergraduates with need received aid; of those 22% had need fully met. ***Average percent of need met:*** 86% (excluding resources awarded to replace EFC). ***Average financial aid package:*** $27,170 (excluding resources awarded to replace EFC). 7% of all full-time undergraduates had no need and received non-need-based gift aid.

GIFT AID (NEED-BASED) ***Total amount:*** $1,555,517 (80% federal, 18% state, 2% institutional). ***Receiving aid:*** Freshmen: 52% (117); all full-time undergraduates: 45% (336). ***Average award:*** Freshmen: $5817; Undergraduates: $5792. ***Scholarships, grants, and awards:*** Federal Pell, FSEOG, state, private, college/university gift aid from institutional funds.

GIFT AID (NON-NEED-BASED) ***Total amount:*** $12,376,108 (99% institutional, 1% external sources). ***Receiving aid:*** Freshmen: 85% (191). Undergraduates: 84% (636). ***Average award:*** Freshmen: $16,056. Undergraduates: $15,980. ***Scholarships, grants, and awards by category:*** *Academic interests/achievement:* general academic interests/achievements. *Creative arts/performance:* art/fine arts, music, performing arts, theater/drama. *Special achievements/activities:* cheerleading/drum major. *Special characteristics:* children and siblings of alumni, children of faculty/staff, international students, religious affiliation.

LOANS ***Student loans:*** $4,012,714 (100% need-based). 82% of past graduating class borrowed through all loan programs. *Average indebtedness per student:* $22,872. ***Average need-based loan:*** Freshmen: $8024. Undergraduates: $8513. ***Parent loans:*** $2,106,215 (100% non-need-based). ***Programs:*** Federal Direct (Subsidized and Unsubsidized Stafford, PLUS), Perkins.

WORK-STUDY ***Federal work-study:*** Total amount: $312,260; jobs available. ***State or other work-study/employment:*** Part-time jobs available.

ATHLETIC AWARDS Total amount: $2,872,563 (100% non-need-based).

APPLYING FOR FINANCIAL AID ***Required financial aid form:*** FAFSA. ***Notification date:*** Continuous beginning 12/1. Students must reply within 3 weeks of notification.

CONTACT Ms. Sara Brubaker, Director of Financial Aid and Admissions Operations, McPherson College, 1600 East Euclid, McPherson, KS 67460-1402, 620-242-0400 or toll-free 800-365-7402. *Fax:* 620-241-8443. *E-mail:* krehbieb2@mcpherson.edu.
Website: http://www.mcpherson.edu/.

MCPHS UNIVERSITY

Boston, MA

CONTACT Elizabeth Goreham, Director of Student Financial Services, MCPHS University, 179 Longwood Avenue, Boston, MA 02115-5896, 617-879-5986. *E-mail:* elizabeth.goreham@mcphs.edu.
Website: http://www.mcphs.edu/.

MECHON L'HOYROA

Monsey, NY

CONTACT Financial Aid Office, Mechon L'Hoyroa, 168 Maple Avenue, Monsey, NY 10952.
Website: http://www.mechonlhoyroa.com/.

MEDAILLE COLLEGE

Buffalo, NY

CONTACT Ms. Catherine Buzanski, Director of Financial Aid, Medaille College, 18 Agassiz Circle, Buffalo, NY 14214-2695, 716-880-2179 or toll-free 800-292-1582. *Fax:* 716-884-0291. *E-mail:* cbuzanski@medaille.edu.
Website: http://www.medaille.edu/.

MEDGAR EVERS COLLEGE OF THE CITY UNIVERSITY OF NEW YORK

Brooklyn, NY

ABOUT THE INSTITUTION State and locally supported, coed. ***Awards:*** certificates, associate, and bachelor's degrees. 15 undergraduate majors.

GIFT AID (NEED-BASED) ***Scholarships, grants, and awards:*** Federal Pell, FSEOG, state, private, college/university gift aid from institutional funds.

GIFT AID (NON-NEED-BASED) ***Scholarships, grants, and awards by category:*** *Academic interests/achievement:* general academic interests/achievements.

LOANS ***Programs:*** Federal Direct (Subsidized and Unsubsidized Stafford, PLUS), Perkins.

WORK-STUDY ***Federal work-study:*** Total amount: $305,708; jobs available. ***State or other work-study/employment:*** Part-time jobs available.

APPLYING FOR FINANCIAL AID ***Required financial aid forms:*** FAFSA, state aid form.

CONTACT Nigel Thompson, Director of Financial Aid, Medgar Evers College of the City University of New York, 1650 Bedford Avenue, Brooklyn, NY 11225, 718-270-6038. *Fax:* 718-270-6194. *E-mail:* nigel.thompson@mec.cuny.edu.
Website: http://www.mec.cuny.edu/.

MEDICAL UNIVERSITY OF SOUTH CAROLINA

Charleston, SC

Tuition & fees: N/R	Average undergraduate aid package: $10,051

ABOUT THE INSTITUTION State-supported, coed. ***Awards:*** certificates, bachelor's, master's, and doctoral degrees. 2 undergraduate majors. Federal methodology is used as a basis for awarding need-based institutional aid.

UNDERGRADUATE FINANCIAL AID (Fall 2018) 264 applied for aid; of those 92% were deemed to have need. 93% of undergraduates with need received aid; of those 1% had need fully met. ***Average percent of need met:*** 25% (excluding resources awarded to replace EFC). ***Average financial aid package:*** $10,051 (excluding resources awarded to replace EFC). 2% of all full-time undergraduates had no need and received non-need-based gift aid.

GIFT AID (NEED-BASED) ***Total amount:*** $539,029 (44% federal, 7% state, 49% institutional). ***Receiving aid:*** All full-time undergraduates: 24% (76). ***Average award:*** Undergraduates: $6843. ***Scholarships, grants, and awards:*** Federal Pell, FSEOG, state, private, college/university gift aid from institutional funds, Federal Nursing, Scholarships for Disadvantaged Students (SDS).

GIFT AID (NON-NEED-BASED) ***Total amount:*** $576,034 (6% federal, 21% state, 62% institutional, 11% external sources). ***Receiving aid:*** Undergraduates: 15% (49). ***Average award:*** Undergraduates: $14,242. ***Scholarships, grants, and awards by category:*** *Academic interests/achievement:* general academic interests/achievements, home economics. *Special characteristics:* ethnic background, general special characteristics, local/state students, members of minority groups. ***ROTC:*** Air Force cooperative.

LOANS ***Student loans:*** $4,153,744 (24% need-based, 76% non-need-based). ***Average need-based loan:*** Undergraduates: $5888. ***Parent loans:*** $191,585 (100% non-need-based). ***Programs:*** Federal Direct (Subsidized and Unsubsidized Stafford, PLUS), Perkins, Federal Nursing, state, alternative loans, Health Professions Student Loans (HPSL), Loans for Disadvantaged Students, Primary Care Loans.

WORK-STUDY ***Federal work-study:*** Total amount: $2100; jobs available.

APPLYING FOR FINANCIAL AID ***Required financial aid form:*** FAFSA.

CONTACT Mr. Joseph M. DuRant, Director for Student Financial Aid Services, Medical University of South Carolina, 45 Courtenay Drive, MSC 203, Charleston, SC 29425, 843-792-2252. *Fax:* 843-792-6356. *E-mail:* durantjm@musc.edu. *Website:* http://www.musc.edu/.

MENLO COLLEGE

Atherton, CA

CONTACT Jessica Ayers, Director of Financial Aid, Menlo College, 1000 El Camino Real, Atherton, CA 94027-4301, 650-543-3880 or toll-free 800-556-3656. *Fax:* 650-543-4103. *E-mail:* financialaid@menlo.edu. *Website:* http://www.menlo.edu/.

MERCER UNIVERSITY

Macon, GA

Tuition & fees: N/R	Average undergraduate aid package: $37,583

ABOUT THE INSTITUTION Independent Baptist, coed. ***Awards:*** certificates, bachelor's, master's, and doctoral degrees. 65 undergraduate majors. ***Total enrollment:*** 7,276. Undergraduates: 3,949. Freshmen: 900. Both federal and institutional methodology are used as a basis for awarding need-based institutional aid.

FRESHMAN FINANCIAL AID (Fall 2019, est.) 832 applied for aid; of those 77% were deemed to have need. 100% of freshmen with need received aid; of those 43% had need fully met. ***Average percent of need met:*** 89% (excluding resources awarded to replace EFC). ***Average financial aid package:*** $38,824 (excluding resources awarded to replace EFC). 28% of all full-time freshmen had no need and received non-need-based gift aid.

UNDERGRADUATE FINANCIAL AID (Fall 2019, est.) 2,783 applied for aid; of those 81% were deemed to have need. 100% of undergraduates with need received aid; of those 41% had need fully met. ***Average percent of need met:*** 85% (excluding resources awarded to replace EFC). ***Average financial aid package:*** $37,583 (excluding resources awarded to replace EFC). 31% of all full-time undergraduates had no need and received non-need-based gift aid.

GIFT AID (NEED-BASED) ***Total amount:*** $56,284,311 (9% federal, 14% state, 75% institutional, 2% external sources). ***Receiving aid:*** Freshmen: 71% (641); all full-time undergraduates: 67% (2,241). ***Average award:*** Freshmen: $29,043; Undergraduates: $26,745. ***Scholarships, grants, and awards:*** Federal Pell, FSEOG, state, private, college/university gift aid from institutional funds.

GIFT AID (NON-NEED-BASED) ***Total amount:*** $30,878,208 (20% state, 77% institutional, 3% external sources). ***Receiving aid:*** Freshmen: 19% (174). Undergraduates: 18% (586). ***Average award:*** Freshmen: $20,303. Undergraduates: $20,027. ***Scholarships, grants, and awards by category:*** *Academic interests/achievement:* biological sciences, business, education, English, general academic interests/achievements, home economics, military science. *Creative arts/performance:* applied art and design, debating, journalism/publications, music, theater/drama. *Special achievements/activities:* cheerleading/drum major, community service, general special achievements/activities, leadership, religious involvement. *Special characteristics:* adult students, children of faculty/staff, international students, religious affiliation, veterans, veterans' children. ***ROTC:*** Army.

LOANS ***Student loans:*** $16,080,154 (69% need-based, 31% non-need-based). 59% of past graduating class borrowed through all loan programs. *Average indebtedness per student:* $27,949. ***Average need-based loan:*** Freshmen: $9619. Undergraduates: $10,951. ***Parent loans:*** $5,554,582 (46% need-based, 54% non-need-based). ***Programs:*** Federal Direct (Subsidized and Unsubsidized Stafford, PLUS), Perkins, Federal Nursing, state, college/university.

WORK-STUDY ***Federal work-study:*** Total amount: $1,511,159; jobs available.

ATHLETIC AWARDS Total amount: $8,654,879 (40% need-based, 60% non-need-based).

APPLYING FOR FINANCIAL AID ***Required financial aid form:*** FAFSA. ***Financial aid deadline (priority):*** 2/1. ***Notification date:*** Continuous beginning 2/1. Students must reply within 2 weeks of notification.

CONTACT Ms. Maria Hammett, Associate Vice President, Mercer University, Office of Financial Planning, Macon, GA 31207-0003, 478-301-2226 or toll-free 800-MERCER-U. *Fax:* 478-301-2671. *E-mail:* hammett_ma@mercer.edu. *Website:* http://www.mercer.edu/.

MERCY COLLEGE

Dobbs Ferry, NY

Tuition & fees: $19,594	Average undergraduate aid package: $15,402

ABOUT THE INSTITUTION Independent Roman Catholic Church, coed. ***Awards:*** certificates, associate, bachelor's, master's, and doctoral degrees. 48 undergraduate majors. ***Total enrollment:*** 10,557. Undergraduates: 7,993. Freshmen: 999. Federal methodology is used as a basis for awarding need-based institutional aid.

UNDERGRADUATE EXPENSES for 2019–2020 ***Application fee:*** $40. ***Comprehensive fee:*** $33,994 includes full-time tuition ($18,934), mandatory fees ($660), and room and board ($14,400). ***College room only:*** $9750. Full-time tuition and fees vary according to course load. Room and board charges vary according to board plan and housing facility. ***Part-time tuition:*** $796 per credit. ***Part-time fees:*** $166 per term. Part-time tuition and fees vary according to course load.

FRESHMAN FINANCIAL AID (Fall 2018) 861 applied for aid; of those 92% were deemed to have need. 98% of freshmen with need received aid; of those 4% had need fully met. ***Average percent of need met:*** 59% (excluding resources awarded to replace EFC). ***Average financial aid package:*** $17,029 (excluding resources awarded to replace EFC). 7% of all full-time freshmen had no need and received non-need-based gift aid.

UNDERGRADUATE FINANCIAL AID (Fall 2018) 4,668 applied for aid; of those 94% were deemed to have need. 97% of undergraduates with need received aid; of those 3% had need fully met. ***Average percent of need met:*** 53% (excluding resources awarded to replace EFC). ***Average financial aid package:*** $15,402 (excluding resources awarded to replace EFC). 4% of all full-time undergraduates had no need and received non-need-based gift aid.

GIFT AID (NEED-BASED) ***Total amount:*** $44,097,776 (40% federal, 20% state, 40% institutional). ***Receiving aid:*** Freshmen: 81% (718); all full-time undergraduates: 78% (3,900). ***Average award:*** Freshmen: $13,034; Undergraduates: $11,053. ***Scholarships, grants, and awards:*** Federal Pell, FSEOG, state, private, college/university gift aid from institutional funds.

GIFT AID (NON-NEED-BASED) ***Total amount:*** $9,689,822 (11% state, 87% institutional, 2% external sources). ***Receiving aid:*** Freshmen: 73% (650). Undergraduates: 45% (2,273). ***Average award:*** Freshmen: $5558. Undergraduates: $5053. ***Scholarships, grants, and awards by category:*** *Academic interests/achievement:* 2,327 awards ($8,396,300 total): business, general academic interests/achievements. *Special characteristics:* 55 awards ($614,587 total): children of faculty/staff. ***Tuition waivers:*** Full or partial for employees or children of employees, senior citizens. ***ROTC:*** Army cooperative, Air Force cooperative.

LOANS ***Student loans:*** $30,373,774 (43% need-based, 57% non-need-based). 78% of past graduating class borrowed through all loan programs. *Average indebtedness per student:* $23,942. ***Average need-based loan:*** Freshmen: $3141. Undergraduates: $4110. ***Parent loans:*** $5,629,850 (100% non-need-based). ***Programs:*** Federal Direct (Subsidized and Unsubsidized Stafford, PLUS), Federal Nursing, state.

WORK-STUDY ***Federal work-study:*** Total amount: $700,625; 297 jobs available.

ATHLETIC AWARDS Total amount: $1,437,339 (100% non-need-based).

APPLYING FOR FINANCIAL AID ***Required financial aid forms:*** FAFSA, state aid form. ***Financial aid deadline (priority):*** 2/15. ***Notification date:*** Continuous beginning 1/1. Students must reply by 5/1 or within 2 weeks of notification.

CONTACT Margaret M. McGrail, Vice President of Enrollment Services, Mercy College, 555 Broadway, Dobbs Ferry, NY 10522, 877-637-2946 or toll-free 877-MERCY-GO (out-of-state). *Fax:* 914-674-7382. *E-mail:* admissions@mercy.edu. *Website:* http://www.mercy.edu/.

MERCY COLLEGE OF HEALTH SCIENCES

Des Moines, IA

CONTACT Lisa Croat, Financial Aid Director, Mercy College of Health Sciences, 921 Sixth Avenue, Des Moines, IA 50309, 515-643-6636 or toll-free 800-637-2994. *Fax:* 515-643-6747. *E-mail:* financialaid@mchs.edu.
Website: http://www.mchs.edu/.

MERCY COLLEGE OF OHIO

Toledo, OH

CONTACT Julie Leslie, Director of Financial Aid, Mercy College of Ohio, 2221 Madison Avenue, Toledo, OH 43604, 419-251-1598 or toll-free 888-80-MERCY. *Fax:* 419-251-0969. *E-mail:* julie.leslie@mercycollege.edu.
Website: http://www.mercycollege.edu/.

MERCYHURST UNIVERSITY

Erie, PA

CONTACT Carrie Newman, Director of Student Financial Services, Mercyhurst University, 501 East 38th Street, Erie, PA 16546, 814-824-2288 or toll-free 800-825-1926. *Fax:* 814-824-2300. *E-mail:* sfs@mercyhurst.edu.
Website: http://www.mercyhurst.edu/.

MEREDITH COLLEGE

Raleigh, NC

CONTACT Mr. Kevin Michaelsen, Director of Financial Assistance, Meredith College, 3800 Hillsborough Street, Raleigh, NC 27607-5298, 919-760-8565 or toll-free 800-MEREDITH. *Fax:* 919-760-2375. *E-mail:* michaelsen@meredith.edu.
Website: http://www.meredith.edu/.

MERRIMACK COLLEGE

North Andover, MA

Tuition & fees: N/R	Average undergraduate aid package: $26,574

ABOUT THE INSTITUTION Independent Roman Catholic, coed. ***Awards:*** certificates, bachelor's, and master's degrees. 71 undergraduate majors. ***Total enrollment:*** 4,971. Undergraduates: 4,015. Freshmen: 1,179. Federal methodology is used as a basis for awarding need-based institutional aid.

FRESHMAN FINANCIAL AID (Fall 2019, est.) 1016 applied for aid; of those 86% were deemed to have need. 100% of freshmen with need received aid; of those 18% had need fully met. ***Average percent of need met:*** 69% (excluding resources awarded to replace EFC). ***Average financial aid package:*** $27,205 (excluding resources awarded to replace EFC). 21% of all full-time freshmen had no need and received non-need-based gift aid.

UNDERGRADUATE FINANCIAL AID (Fall 2019, est.) 3,175 applied for aid; of those 87% were deemed to have need. 100% of undergraduates with need received aid; of those 15% had need fully met. ***Average percent of need met:*** 67% (excluding resources awarded to replace EFC). ***Average financial aid package:*** $26,574 (excluding resources awarded to replace EFC). 23% of all full-time undergraduates had no need and received non-need-based gift aid.

GIFT AID (NEED-BASED) ***Receiving aid:*** Freshmen: 74% (870); all full-time undergraduates: 71% (2,756). ***Average award:*** Freshmen: $24,631; Undergraduates: $23,021. ***Scholarships, grants, and awards:*** Federal Pell, FSEOG, state, private, college/university gift aid from institutional funds.

GIFT AID (NON-NEED-BASED) ***Receiving aid:*** Freshmen: 13% (148). Undergraduates: 9% (367). ***Average award:*** Freshmen: $17,578. Undergraduates: $15,918. ***Scholarships, grants, and awards by category:*** *Academic interests/achievement:* general academic interests/achievements. *Special achievements/activities:* leadership. *Special characteristics:* children of faculty/staff, international students, relatives of clergy, religious affiliation, siblings of current students, veterans. ***ROTC:*** Air Force cooperative.

LOANS ***Average need-based loan:*** Freshmen: $3368. Undergraduates: $4341. ***Programs:*** Federal Direct (Subsidized and Unsubsidized Stafford, PLUS), state, college/university.

WORK-STUDY Federal work-study jobs available. ***State or other work-study/employment:*** Part-time jobs available.

APPLYING FOR FINANCIAL AID ***Required financial aid form:*** FAFSA. ***Notification date:*** Continuous.

CONTACT Adrienne Montgomery, Director of Financial Aid, Merrimack College, 315 Turnpike Street, North Andover, MA 01845, 978-837-5186. *Fax:* 978-837-5067. *E-mail:* montgomerya@merrimack.edu.
Website: http://www.merrimack.edu/.

MESIVTA OF EASTERN PARKWAY–YESHIVA ZICHRON MEILECH

Brooklyn, NY

CONTACT Rabbi Joseph Halberstadt, Dean, Mesivta of Eastern Parkway–Yeshiva Zichron Meilech, 510 Dahill Road, Brooklyn, NY 11218-5559, 718-438-1002.

MESIVTA TORAH VODAATH RABBINICAL SEMINARY

Brooklyn, NY

CONTACT Mrs. Kayla Goldring, Director of Financial Aid, Mesivta Torah Vodaath Rabbinical Seminary, 425 East Ninth Street, Brooklyn, NY 11218-5209, 718-941-8000.
Website: http://www.torahvodaath.org/.

MESIVTHA TIFERETH JERUSALEM OF AMERICA

New York, NY

CONTACT Rabbi Dickstein, Director of Financial Aid, Mesivtha Tifereth Jerusalem of America, 141 East Broadway, New York, NY 10002-6301, 212-964-2830.

MESSENGER COLLEGE

Euless, TX

Tuition & fees: $11,070	Average undergraduate aid package: $4264

ABOUT THE INSTITUTION Independent Pentecostal, coed. ***Awards:*** associate and bachelor's degrees. 4 undergraduate majors. ***Total enrollment:*** 46. Undergraduates: 46. Freshmen: 3. Both federal and institutional methodology are used as a basis for awarding need-based institutional aid.

UNDERGRADUATE EXPENSES for 2020–2021 ***Application fee:*** $35. ***One-time required fee:*** $100. ***Comprehensive fee:*** $17,540 includes full-time tuition ($9750), mandatory fees ($1320), and room and board ($6470). ***College room only:*** $3350. ***Part-time tuition:*** $325 per credit hour. ***Part-time fees:*** $660 per term.

FRESHMAN FINANCIAL AID (Fall 2018) 2 applied for aid; of those 100% were deemed to have need. 100% of freshmen with need received aid. ***Average percent of need met:*** 30% (excluding resources awarded to replace EFC). ***Average financial aid package:*** $2375 (excluding resources awarded to replace EFC).

UNDERGRADUATE FINANCIAL AID (Fall 2018) 40 applied for aid; of those 100% were deemed to have need. 95% of undergraduates with need received aid; of those 8% had need fully met. ***Average percent of need met:*** 59% (excluding resources awarded to replace EFC). ***Average financial aid package:*** $4264 (excluding resources awarded to replace EFC).

GIFT AID (NEED-BASED) ***Total amount:*** $200,895 (76% federal, 22% institutional, 2% external sources). ***Receiving aid:*** Freshmen: 33% (1); all full-time undergraduates: 64% (27). ***Average award:*** Freshmen: $1220; Undergraduates: $2457. ***Scholarships, grants, and awards:*** Federal Pell, FSEOG, private, college/university gift aid from institutional funds.

GIFT AID (NON-NEED-BASED) ***Receiving aid:*** Freshmen: 33% (1). Undergraduates: 43% (18). ***Scholarships, grants, and awards by category:*** *Academic interests/achievement:* 6 awards ($10,818 total): general academic interests/achievements, religion/biblical studies. *Creative arts/performance:* 1 award ($1000 total): music. *Special achievements/activities:* 7 awards ($14,282 total): religious involvement. *Special characteristics:* 7 awards ($11,438 total): religious affiliation. ***Tuition waivers:*** Full or partial for employees or children of employees.

LOANS ***Student loans:*** $396,341 (100% need-based). 50% of past graduating class borrowed through all loan programs. *Average indebtedness per student:* $32,313. ***Average need-based loan:*** Freshmen: $1155. Undergraduates: $1875. ***Parent loans:*** $21,500 (100% need-based). ***Programs:*** Federal Direct (Subsidized and Unsubsidized Stafford, PLUS).

WORK-STUDY ***Federal work-study:*** Total amount: $5554.59; 3 jobs averaging $1852.

APPLYING FOR FINANCIAL AID ***Required financial aid form:*** FAFSA. ***Financial aid deadline:*** Continuous. ***Notification date:*** Continuous.

CONTACT Ms. Carolyn R. Dowd, Director of Financial Aid, Messenger College, P.O. Box 1207, Euless, TX 76039-1207, 817-554-5950 Ext. 104 or toll-free 800-385-8940. *Fax:* 817-391-4003. *E-mail:* cdowd@messengercollege.edu.
Website: http://www.messengercollege.edu/.

MESSIAH COLLEGE

Mechanicsburg, PA

Tuition & fees: $37,180	Average undergraduate aid package: $26,020

ABOUT THE INSTITUTION Independent interdenominational, coed. ***Awards:*** certificates, bachelor's, master's, and doctoral degrees. 85 undergraduate majors. ***Total enrollment:*** 3,374. Undergraduates: 2,709. Freshmen: 606. Federal methodology is used as a basis for awarding need-based institutional aid.

UNDERGRADUATE EXPENSES for 2020–2021 ***Application fee:*** $50. ***Comprehensive fee:*** $48,080 includes full-time tuition ($36,340), mandatory fees ($840), and room and board ($10,900). ***College room only:*** $5800. Room and board charges vary according to board plan and housing facility. ***Part-time tuition:*** $1515 per credit hour.

FRESHMAN FINANCIAL AID (Fall 2019, est.) 560 applied for aid; of those 86% were deemed to have need. 100% of freshmen with need received aid; of those 19% had need fully met. ***Average percent of need met:*** 76% (excluding resources awarded to replace EFC). ***Average financial aid package:*** $27,916 (excluding resources awarded to replace EFC). 20% of all full-time freshmen had no need and received non-need-based gift aid.

UNDERGRADUATE FINANCIAL AID (Fall 2019, est.) 2,148 applied for aid; of those 87% were deemed to have need. 100% of undergraduates with need received aid; of those 19% had need fully met. ***Average percent of need met:*** 73% (excluding resources awarded to replace EFC). ***Average financial aid package:*** $26,020 (excluding resources awarded to replace EFC). 27% of all full-time undergraduates had no need and received non-need-based gift aid.

GIFT AID (NEED-BASED) ***Receiving aid:*** Freshmen: 79% (477); all full-time undergraduates: 73% (1,844). ***Average award:*** Freshmen: $22,047; Undergraduates: $19,830. ***Scholarships, grants, and awards:*** Federal Pell, FSEOG, state, private, college/university gift aid from institutional funds, Federal Nursing.

GIFT AID (NON-NEED-BASED) ***Receiving aid:*** Freshmen: 11% (65). Undergraduates: 9% (234). ***Average award:*** Freshmen: $15,472. Undergraduates: $14,921. ***Scholarships, grants, and awards by category:*** *Academic interests/achievement:* 2,263 awards ($27,757,962 total): general academic interests/achievements, humanities. *Creative arts/performance:* 116 awards ($458,686 total): applied art and design, dance, music, theater/drama. *Special achievements/activities:* 599 awards ($4,441,449 total): leadership. *Special characteristics:* 183 awards ($2,603,221 total): adult students, children of faculty/staff, local/state students, religious affiliation. ***Tuition waivers:*** Full or partial for employees or children of employees, adult students, senior citizens.

LOANS ***Student loans:*** 73% of past graduating class borrowed through all loan programs. *Average indebtedness per student:* $41,859. ***Average need-based loan:*** Freshmen: $3792. Undergraduates: $4828. ***Programs:*** Federal Direct (Subsidized and Unsubsidized Stafford, PLUS), Federal Nursing.

WORK-STUDY ***Federal work-study:*** 670 jobs averaging $2141. ***State or other work-study/employment:*** 1,018 part-time jobs averaging $1871.

APPLYING FOR FINANCIAL AID ***Required financial aid form:*** FAFSA. ***Financial aid deadline:*** Continuous. ***Notification date:*** Continuous. Students must reply within 4 weeks of notification.

CONTACT Mr. Michael Strite, Associate Director of Financial Aid, Messiah College, One College Avenue, Suite 3006, Mechanicsburg, PA 17055, 717-691-6007 or toll-free 800-233-4220. *Fax:* 717-796-4791. *E-mail:* mstrite@messiah.edu.
Website: http://www.messiah.edu/.

METHODIST COLLEGE

Peoria, IL

CONTACT Financial Aid Office, Methodist College, 415 St. Mark Court, Peoria, IL 61603, 309-672-5513.
Website: http://www.methodistcol.edu/.

METHODIST UNIVERSITY

Fayetteville, NC

Tuition & fees: N/R	Average undergraduate aid package: $23,452

ABOUT THE INSTITUTION Independent United Methodist, coed. ***Awards:*** associate, bachelor's, and master's degrees. 57 undergraduate majors. ***Total enrollment:*** 2,416. Undergraduates: 2,217. Freshmen: 551. Federal methodology is used as a basis for awarding need-based institutional aid.

FRESHMAN FINANCIAL AID (Fall 2018) 337 applied for aid; of those 93% were deemed to have need. 100% of freshmen with need received aid; of those 14% had need fully met. ***Average percent of need met:*** 72% (excluding resources awarded to replace EFC). ***Average financial aid package:*** $26,032 (excluding resources awarded to replace EFC). 14% of all full-time freshmen had no need and received non-need-based gift aid.

UNDERGRADUATE FINANCIAL AID (Fall 2018) 1,274 applied for aid; of those 94% were deemed to have need. 99% of undergraduates with need received aid; of those 12% had need fully met. ***Average percent of need met:*** 65% (excluding resources awarded to replace EFC). ***Average financial aid package:*** $23,452 (excluding resources awarded to replace EFC). 18% of all full-time undergraduates had no need and received non-need-based gift aid.

GIFT AID (NEED-BASED) ***Receiving aid:*** Freshmen: 85% (315); all full-time undergraduates: 74% (1,177). ***Average award:*** Freshmen: $22,251; Undergraduates: $19,353. ***Scholarships, grants, and awards:*** Federal Pell, FSEOG, state, private, college/university gift aid from institutional funds.

GIFT AID (NON-NEED-BASED) ***Receiving aid:*** Freshmen: 8% (28). Undergraduates: 5% (83). ***Average award:*** Freshmen: $23,168. Undergraduates: $20,717. ***Scholarships, grants, and awards by category:*** *Academic interests/achievement:* 930 awards ($10,291,250 total): education, general academic interests/achievements, military science. *Creative arts/performance:* 48 awards ($549,950 total): dance, debating, music. *Special achievements/activities:* 26 awards ($28,525 total): cheerleading/drum major, leadership. *Special characteristics:* 668 awards ($4,706,411 total): children and siblings of alumni, children of faculty/staff, international students, local/state students, relatives of clergy, religious affiliation, siblings of current students. ***ROTC:*** Army, Air Force cooperative.

LOANS ***Student loans:*** 64% of past graduating class borrowed through all loan programs. *Average indebtedness per student:* $33,211. ***Average need-based loan:*** Freshmen: $3992. Undergraduates: $5408. ***Programs:*** Federal Direct (Subsidized and Unsubsidized Stafford, PLUS), state, college/university.

WORK-STUDY ***Federal work-study:*** 370 jobs averaging $697. ***State or other work-study/employment:*** 134 part-time jobs averaging $1550.
APPLYING FOR FINANCIAL AID ***Required financial aid form:*** FAFSA. ***Notification date:*** Continuous. Students must reply within 2 weeks of notification.

CONTACT Bonnie Adamson, Financial Aid Office, Methodist University, 5400 Ramsey Street, Fayetteville, NC 28311-1420, 910-630-7192 or toll-free 800-488-7110 Ext.7027. *Fax:* 910-630-7285. *E-mail:* financialaid@methodist.edu.
Website: http://www.methodist.edu/.

METROPOLITAN COLLEGE OF NEW YORK

New York, NY

CONTACT Mr. Douane Campbell, Director of Financial Aid, Metropolitan College of New York, 60 West Street, New York, NY 10006, 212-343-1234 Ext. 5004 or toll-free 800-33-THINK Ext.5001. *Fax:* 212-343-7399. *E-mail:* fa@mcny.edu.
Website: http://www.mcny.edu/.

METROPOLITAN STATE UNIVERSITY

St. Paul, MN

CONTACT Dr. Lois J. Larson, Director of Financial Aid, Metropolitan State University, 700 East 7th Street, St. Paul, MN 55106-5000, 651-793-1411. *Fax:* 651-642-0636. *E-mail:* financial.aid@metrostate.edu.
Website: http://www.metrostate.edu/.

METROPOLITAN STATE UNIVERSITY OF DENVER

Denver, CO

CONTACT Office of Financial Aid, Metropolitan State University of Denver, PO Box 173362, Denver, CO 80217-3362, 303-556-8593. *Fax:* 303-556-4927.
Website: http://www.msudenver.edu/.

MIAMI INTERNATIONAL UNIVERSITY OF ART & DESIGN

Miami, FL

CONTACT Financial Aid Office, Miami International University of Art & Design, 1737 Bayshore Drive, Miami, FL 33132, 800-225-9023 Ext. 125 or toll-free 800-225-9023. *Fax:* 305-374-7946.

MIAMI REGIONAL UNIVERSITY

Miami Springs, FL

CONTACT Financial Aid Office, Miami Regional University, 700 South Royal Poinciana Boulevard, Miami Springs, FL 33166, 305-442-9223.
Website: http://www.mru.edu/.

MIAMI UNIVERSITY

Oxford, OH

Tuition & fees (area res): $15,232	Average undergraduate aid package: $15,916

ABOUT THE INSTITUTION State-related, coed. ***Awards:*** certificates, associate, bachelor's, master's, and doctoral degrees. 112 undergraduate majors. ***Total enrollment:*** 19,716. Undergraduates: 17,246. Freshmen: 4,309. Federal methodology is used as a basis for awarding need-based institutional aid.
UNDERGRADUATE EXPENSES for 2019–2020 ***Application fee:*** $50. ***Tuition, area resident:*** full-time $14,294. ***Tuition, state resident:*** full-time $14,294. ***Tuition, nonresident:*** full-time $33,369. ***Required fees:*** full-time $938. Full-time tuition and fees vary according to location, program, and student level. Part-time tuition and fees vary according to course load, location, program, and student level. ***College room and board:*** $13,397; ***Room only:*** $8313. Room and board charges vary according to board plan, housing facility, and student level. ***Payment plan:*** Guaranteed tuition.
FRESHMAN FINANCIAL AID (Fall 2019, est.) 3257 applied for aid; of those 55% were deemed to have need. 98% of freshmen with need received aid; of those 22% had need fully met. ***Average percent of need met:*** 59% (excluding resources awarded to replace EFC). ***Average financial aid package:*** $16,409 (excluding resources awarded to replace EFC). 40% of all full-time freshmen had no need and received non-need-based gift aid.
UNDERGRADUATE FINANCIAL AID (Fall 2019, est.) 8,935 applied for aid; of those 63% were deemed to have need. 98% of undergraduates with need received aid; of those 21% had need fully met. ***Average percent of need met:*** 62% (excluding resources awarded to replace EFC). ***Average financial aid package:*** $15,916 (excluding resources awarded to replace EFC). 34% of all full-time undergraduates had no need and received non-need-based gift aid.
GIFT AID (NEED-BASED) ***Total amount:*** $56,522,757 (18% federal, 4% state, 78% institutional). ***Receiving aid:*** Freshmen: 37% (1,585); all full-time undergraduates: 30% (4,926). ***Average award:*** Freshmen: $13,182; Undergraduates: $12,484. ***Scholarships, grants, and awards:*** Federal Pell, FSEOG, state, private, college/university gift aid from institutional funds.
GIFT AID (NON-NEED-BASED) ***Total amount:*** $73,601,960 (95% institutional, 5% external sources). ***Receiving aid:*** Freshmen: 8% (341). Undergraduates: 6% (920). ***Average award:*** Freshmen: $12,770. Undergraduates: $10,859. ***Scholarships, grants, and awards by category:*** *Academic interests/achievement:* architecture, education, engineering/technologies, general academic interests/achievements. *Creative arts/performance:* applied art and design, music, theater/drama. *Special achievements/activities:* general special achievements/activities, leadership. *Special characteristics:* children of faculty/staff, local/state students, members of minority groups, out-of-state students. ***Tuition waivers:*** Full or partial for employees or children of employees. ***ROTC:*** Army cooperative, Naval, Air Force.
LOANS ***Student loans:*** $62,783,379 (26% need-based, 74% non-need-based). 45% of past graduating class borrowed through all loan programs. *Average indebtedness per student:* $29,652. ***Average need-based loan:*** Freshmen: $3700. Undergraduates: $4508. ***Parent loans:*** $25,978,653 (100% non-need-based). ***Programs:*** Federal Direct (Subsidized and Unsubsidized Stafford, PLUS), Perkins, college/university, private loans.
WORK-STUDY ***Federal work-study:*** Total amount: $1,859,282; 2,805 jobs averaging $902.
ATHLETIC AWARDS Total amount: $10,218,647 (100% non-need-based).
APPLYING FOR FINANCIAL AID ***Required financial aid form:*** FAFSA. ***Financial aid deadline (priority):*** 2/15. ***Notification date:*** Continuous beginning 3/20. Students must reply by 5/1 or within 3 weeks of notification.

CONTACT Mr. Brent Shock, Office of Student Financial Aid, Miami University, Campus Avenue Building, Oxford, OH 45056-3427, 513-529-0001. *Fax:* 513-529-8713. *E-mail:* financialaid@miamioh.edu.
Website: http://miamioh.edu/.

MIAMI UNIVERSITY HAMILTON

Hamilton, OH

CONTACT Financial Aid Office, Miami University Hamilton, 1601 Peck Boulevard, Hamilton, OH 45011-3399, 513-785-3000.
Website: http://regionals.miamioh.edu/.

MIAMI UNIVERSITY MIDDLETOWN

Middletown, OH

CONTACT Financial Aid Office, Miami University Middletown, 4200 East University Boulevard, Middletown, OH 45042-3497, 513-727-3200 or toll-free 866-426-4643.
Website: http://regionals.miamioh.edu/.

MICHIGAN STATE UNIVERSITY

East Lansing, MI

Tuition & fees (MI res): $14,460	Average undergraduate aid package: $16,389

ABOUT THE INSTITUTION State-supported, coed. ***Awards:*** certificates, bachelor's, master's, and doctoral degrees. 159 undergraduate majors. ***Total enrollment:*** 49,809. Undergraduates: 39,176. Freshmen: 8,801. Federal methodology is used as a basis for awarding need-based institutional aid.

UNDERGRADUATE EXPENSES for 2019–2020 ***Application fee:*** $65. ***Tuition, state resident:*** full-time $14,460; part-time $482 per credit. ***Tuition, nonresident:*** full-time $39,766; part-time $1326 per credit. Full-time tuition and fees vary according to course load, program, and student level. Part-time tuition and fees vary according to course load, program, and student level. ***College room and board:*** $10,522; ***Room only:*** $4374. Room and board charges vary according to board plan and housing facility.

FRESHMAN FINANCIAL AID (Fall 2019, est.) 6592 applied for aid; of those 64% were deemed to have need. 100% of freshmen with need received aid; of those 11% had need fully met. ***Average percent of need met:*** 53% (excluding resources awarded to replace EFC). ***Average financial aid package:*** $16,433 (excluding resources awarded to replace EFC). 11% of all full-time freshmen had no need and received non-need-based gift aid.

UNDERGRADUATE FINANCIAL AID (Fall 2019, est.) 22,597 applied for aid; of those 74% were deemed to have need. 99% of undergraduates with need received aid; of those 11% had need fully met. ***Average percent of need met:*** 53% (excluding resources awarded to replace EFC). ***Average financial aid package:*** $16,389 (excluding resources awarded to replace EFC). 11% of all full-time undergraduates had no need and received non-need-based gift aid.

GIFT AID (NEED-BASED) ***Total amount:*** $147,834,604 (29% federal, 4% state, 67% institutional). ***Receiving aid:*** Freshmen: 35% (3,009); all full-time undergraduates: 35% (12,275). ***Average award:*** Freshmen: $12,069; Undergraduates: $11,628. ***Scholarships, grants, and awards:*** Federal Pell, FSEOG, state, private, college/university gift aid from institutional funds, United Negro College Fund.

GIFT AID (NON-NEED-BASED) ***Total amount:*** $90,398,670 (3% federal, 76% institutional, 21% external sources). ***Receiving aid:*** Freshmen: 23% (2,017). Undergraduates: 17% (6,085). ***Average award:*** Freshmen: $9780. Undergraduates: $8977. ***Scholarships, grants, and awards by category:*** *Academic interests/achievement:* agriculture, biological sciences, business, communication, computer science, education, engineering/technologies, English, foreign languages, general academic interests/achievements, health fields, home economics, international studies, mathematics, military science, physical sciences, social sciences. *Creative arts/performance:* applied art and design, creative writing, debating, journalism/publications, music, performing arts, theater/drama. *Special achievements/activities:* community service, general special achievements/activities, hobbies/interests, leadership, memberships, rodeo. *Special characteristics:* children and siblings of alumni, children of faculty/staff, children of union members/company employees, first-generation college students, handicapped students, international students, local/state students, out-of-state students, spouses of deceased or disabled public servants, veterans. ***Tuition waivers:*** Full or partial for employees or children of employees. ***ROTC:*** Army, Air Force.

LOANS ***Student loans:*** $139,539,404 (33% need-based, 67% non-need-based). 51% of past graduating class borrowed through all loan programs. *Average indebtedness per student:* $31,393. ***Average need-based loan:*** Freshmen: $3260. Undergraduates: $4077. ***Parent loans:*** $67,881,920 (100% non-need-based). ***Programs:*** Federal Direct (Subsidized and Unsubsidized Stafford, PLUS), college/university.

WORK-STUDY ***Federal work-study:*** Total amount: $3,580,425; 1,653 jobs averaging $2166.

ATHLETIC AWARDS Total amount: $13,576,019 (100% non-need-based).

APPLYING FOR FINANCIAL AID ***Required financial aid form:*** FAFSA. ***Financial aid deadline:*** Continuous. ***Notification date:*** Continuous beginning 1/1. Students must reply within 4 weeks of notification.

CONTACT Mr. Keith Williams, Associate Director of Financial Aid, Michigan State University, 252 Student Services Building, East Lansing, MI 48824-1113, 517-353-5940. *Fax:* 517-432-1155. *E-mail:* willi398@msu.edu.
Website: http://www.msu.edu/.

MICHIGAN TECHNOLOGICAL UNIVERSITY

Houghton, MI

Tuition & fees (MI res): $15,960	Average undergraduate aid package: $16,038

ABOUT THE INSTITUTION State-supported, coed. ***Awards:*** certificates, associate, bachelor's, master's, and doctoral degrees. 57 undergraduate majors. ***Total enrollment:*** 7,041. Undergraduates: 5,764. Freshmen: 1,301. Federal methodology is used as a basis for awarding need-based institutional aid.

UNDERGRADUATE EXPENSES for 2019–2020 ***Tuition, state resident:*** full-time $15,660; part-time $591 per credit hour. ***Tuition, nonresident:*** full-time $34,896; part-time $1292 per credit hour. ***Required fees:*** full-time $300; $150 per term. Full-time tuition and fees vary according to program and student level. Part-time tuition and fees vary according to course load, program, and student level. ***College room and board:*** $11,004; ***Room only:*** $6137. Room and board charges vary according to board plan and housing facility.

FRESHMAN FINANCIAL AID (Fall 2019, est.) 1200 applied for aid; of those 70% were deemed to have need. 100% of freshmen with need received aid; of those 28% had need fully met. ***Average percent of need met:*** 84% (excluding resources awarded to replace EFC). ***Average financial aid package:*** $18,626 (excluding resources awarded to replace EFC). 31% of all full-time freshmen had no need and received non-need-based gift aid.

UNDERGRADUATE FINANCIAL AID (Fall 2019, est.) 4,331 applied for aid; of those 78% were deemed to have need. 100% of undergraduates with need received aid; of those 20% had need fully met. ***Average percent of need met:*** 72% (excluding resources awarded to replace EFC). ***Average financial aid package:*** $16,038 (excluding resources awarded to replace EFC). 27% of all full-time undergraduates had no need and received non-need-based gift aid.

GIFT AID (NEED-BASED) ***Total amount:*** $41,612,577 (14% federal, 7% state, 74% institutional, 5% external sources). ***Receiving aid:*** Freshmen: 56% (728); all full-time undergraduates: 49% (2,628). ***Average award:*** Freshmen: $8708; Undergraduates: $8088. ***Scholarships, grants, and awards:*** Federal Pell, FSEOG, state, private, college/university gift aid from institutional funds.

GIFT AID (NON-NEED-BASED) ***Total amount:*** $10,746,361 (89% institutional, 11% external sources). ***Receiving aid:*** Freshmen: 60% (783). Undergraduates: 53% (2,876). ***Average award:*** Freshmen: $6318. Undergraduates: $6086. ***Scholarships, grants, and awards by category:*** *Academic interests/achievement:* 65 awards ($463,707 total): business. *Creative arts/performance:* 36 awards ($36,500 total): applied art and design, performing arts, theater/drama. *Special achievements/activities:* 95 awards ($818,216 total): general special achievements/activities, leadership. *Special characteristics:* 1,232 awards ($4,919,063 total): children and siblings of alumni, children of faculty/staff, general special characteristics, international students, veterans, veterans' children. ***Tuition waivers:*** Full or partial for children of alumni, employees or children of employees, senior citizens. ***ROTC:*** Army, Air Force.

LOANS ***Student loans:*** $35,978,521 (79% need-based, 21% non-need-based). 70% of past graduating class borrowed through all loan programs. *Average indebtedness per student:* $37,903. ***Average need-based loan:*** Freshmen: $3109. Undergraduates: $4159. ***Parent loans:*** $7,347,615 (82% need-based, 18% non-need-based). ***Programs:*** Federal Direct (Subsidized and Unsubsidized Stafford, PLUS), college/university.

WORK-STUDY ***Federal work-study:*** Total amount: $447,612; 136 jobs averaging $1544.

ATHLETIC AWARDS Total amount: $3,832,046 (30% need-based, 70% non-need-based).

APPLYING FOR FINANCIAL AID ***Required financial aid form:*** FAFSA. ***Financial aid deadline (priority):*** 3/1. ***Notification date:*** Continuous beginning 1/1. Students must reply by 5/1.

CONTACT Dr. Joseph Cooper, Director of Student Financial Services Center, Michigan Technological University, 1400 Townsend Drive, Houghton, MI 49931-1295, 906-487-2622 or toll-free 888-MTU-1885. *Fax:* 906-487-3042. *E-mail:* jjcooper@mtu.edu.
Website: http://www.mtu.edu/.

MID-AMERICA CHRISTIAN UNIVERSITY

Oklahoma City, OK

CONTACT Mr. Todd Martin, Director of Financial Aid, Mid-America Christian University, 3500 Southwest 119th Street, Oklahoma City, OK 73170-4504, 405-691-3800 or toll-free 888-436-3035. *Fax:* 405-692-3165. *E-mail:* tmartin@mabc.edu.
Website: http://www.macu.edu/.

MIDAMERICA NAZARENE UNIVERSITY

Olathe, KS

Tuition & fees: $32,872	Average undergraduate aid package: $25,849

ABOUT THE INSTITUTION Independent Church of the Nazarene, coed. ***Awards:*** certificates, associate, bachelor's, and master's degrees. 43 undergraduate majors. ***Total enrollment:*** 1,909. Undergraduates: 1,252. Freshmen: 180.

UNDERGRADUATE EXPENSES for 2020–2021 ***Comprehensive fee:*** $42,154 includes full-time tuition ($32,122), mandatory fees ($750), and room and board ($9282).

FRESHMAN FINANCIAL AID (Fall 2018) 153 applied for aid; of those 90% were deemed to have need. 100% of freshmen with need received aid; of those 14% had need fully met. ***Average percent of need met:*** 63% (excluding resources awarded to replace EFC). ***Average financial aid package:*** $25,601 (excluding resources awarded to replace EFC). 16% of all full-time freshmen had no need and received non-need-based gift aid.

UNDERGRADUATE FINANCIAL AID (Fall 2018) 685 applied for aid; of those 91% were deemed to have need. 100% of undergraduates with need received aid; of those 11% had need fully met. ***Average percent of need met:*** 63% (excluding resources awarded to replace EFC). ***Average financial aid package:*** $25,849 (excluding resources awarded to replace EFC). 19% of all full-time undergraduates had no need and received non-need-based gift aid.

GIFT AID (NEED-BASED) ***Total amount:*** $10,254,188 (16% federal, 5% state, 77% institutional, 2% external sources). ***Receiving aid:*** Freshmen: 84% (137); all full-time undergraduates: 81% (620). ***Average award:*** Freshmen: $21,178; Undergraduates: $21,201. ***Scholarships, grants, and awards:*** Federal Pell, FSEOG, state, private, college/university gift aid from institutional funds.

GIFT AID (NON-NEED-BASED) ***Total amount:*** $1,812,606 (97% institutional, 3% external sources). ***Receiving aid:*** Freshmen: 20% (32). Undergraduates: 14% (109). ***Average award:*** Freshmen: $12,482. Undergraduates: $11,814. ***Scholarships, grants, and awards by category:*** *Academic interests/achievement:* general academic interests/achievements, religion/biblical studies. *Creative arts/performance:* art/fine arts, music. *Special achievements/activities:* cheerleading/drum major, general special achievements/activities, leadership. *Special characteristics:* children of educators, children of faculty/staff, members of minority groups, relatives of clergy, religious affiliation, veterans. ***ROTC:*** Army cooperative, Air Force cooperative.

LOANS ***Student loans:*** $4,422,444 (86% need-based, 14% non-need-based). 66% of past graduating class borrowed through all loan programs. *Average indebtedness per student:* $28,755. ***Average need-based loan:*** Freshmen: $3262. Undergraduates: $4319. ***Parent loans:*** $2,510,167 (65% need-based, 35% non-need-based). ***Programs:*** Federal Direct (Subsidized and Unsubsidized Stafford, PLUS).

WORK-STUDY ***Federal work-study:*** Total amount: $135,053; jobs available.

ATHLETIC AWARDS Total amount: $3,695,627 (60% need-based, 40% non-need-based).

APPLYING FOR FINANCIAL AID ***Required financial aid forms:*** FAFSA, institution's own form. ***Financial aid deadline (priority):*** 3/1. ***Notification date:*** Continuous beginning 11/1. Students must reply within 2 weeks of notification.

CONTACT Cathy Colaipetro, Director of Student Financial Services, MidAmerica Nazarene University, 2030 East College Way, Olathe, KS 66062-1899, 913-971-3298 or toll-free 800-800-8887. *Fax:* 913-971-3482. *E-mail:* ccolaipetro@mnu.edu.
Website: http://www.mnu.edu/.

MID-ATLANTIC CHRISTIAN UNIVERSITY

Elizabeth City, NC

Tuition & fees: $14,415	Average undergraduate aid package: $11,024

ABOUT THE INSTITUTION Independent Christian, coed. ***Awards:*** certificates, associate, and bachelor's degrees. 13 undergraduate majors. Both federal and institutional methodology are used as a basis for awarding need-based institutional aid.

UNDERGRADUATE EXPENSES for 2019–2020 ***Comprehensive fee:*** $23,015 includes full-time tuition ($13,950), mandatory fees ($465), and room and board ($8600). Full-time tuition and fees vary according to program. Room and board charges vary according to housing facility. ***Part-time tuition:*** $465 per credit hour. ***Part-time fees:*** $55 per credit hour. Part-time tuition and fees vary according to program.

FRESHMAN FINANCIAL AID (Fall 2018) 53 applied for aid; of those 100% were deemed to have need. 100% of freshmen with need received aid; of those 4% had need fully met. ***Average percent of need met:*** 64% (excluding resources awarded to replace EFC). ***Average financial aid package:*** $8506 (excluding resources awarded to replace EFC). 9% of all full-time freshmen had no need and received non-need-based gift aid.

UNDERGRADUATE FINANCIAL AID (Fall 2018) 196 applied for aid; of those 95% were deemed to have need. 100% of undergraduates with need received aid; of those 3% had need fully met. ***Average percent of need met:*** 58% (excluding resources awarded to replace EFC). ***Average financial aid package:*** $11,024 (excluding resources awarded to replace EFC). 4% of all full-time undergraduates had no need and received non-need-based gift aid.

GIFT AID (NEED-BASED) ***Receiving aid:*** Freshmen: 64% (34); all full-time undergraduates: 73% (144). ***Average award:*** Freshmen: $4073; Undergraduates: $4598. ***Scholarships, grants, and awards:*** Federal Pell, FSEOG, state, private, college/university gift aid from institutional funds.

GIFT AID (NON-NEED-BASED) ***Receiving aid:*** Freshmen: 17% (9). Undergraduates: 9% (17). ***Average award:*** Freshmen: $3500. Undergraduates: $3610. ***Scholarships, grants, and awards by category:*** *Academic interests/achievement:* general academic interests/achievements, religion/biblical studies. *Special achievements/activities:* community service, general special achievements/activities, leadership, religious involvement. *Special characteristics:* children and siblings of alumni, children of faculty/staff, general special characteristics, handicapped students, international students, married students, spouses of current students. ***Tuition waivers:*** Full or partial for children of alumni, employees or children of employees, senior citizens. ***ROTC:*** Army cooperative.

LOANS ***Student loans:*** 90% of past graduating class borrowed through all loan programs. *Average indebtedness per student:* $26,414. ***Average need-based loan:*** Freshmen: $5384. Undergraduates: $5456. ***Programs:*** Federal Direct (Subsidized and Unsubsidized Stafford, PLUS), private loans.

WORK-STUDY ***Federal work-study:*** 9 jobs averaging $999. ***State or other work-study/employment:*** 10 part-time jobs averaging $2500.

APPLYING FOR FINANCIAL AID ***Required financial aid forms:*** FAFSA, institution's own form. ***Notification date:*** Continuous. Students must reply within 2 weeks of notification.

CONTACT Emily Meneely, Financial Aid Administrator, Mid-Atlantic Christian University, 715 North Poindexter Street, Elizabeth City, NC 27909, 252-334-2022 or toll-free 866-996-MACU. *Fax:* 252-334-2064. *E-mail:* emily.meneely@macuniversity.edu.
Website: http://www.macuniversity.edu/.

MIDDLEBURY COLLEGE

Middlebury, VT

Tuition & fees: $56,216	Average undergraduate aid package: $53,261

ABOUT THE INSTITUTION Independent, coed. ***Awards:*** bachelor's, master's, and doctoral degrees. 54 undergraduate majors. ***Total enrollment:*** 2,675. Undergraduates: 2,580. Freshmen: 605. Both federal and institutional methodology are used as a basis for awarding need-based institutional aid.

UNDERGRADUATE EXPENSES for 2019–2020 ***Application fee:*** $65. ***Comprehensive fee:*** $72,248 includes full-time tuition ($55,790), mandatory fees ($426), and room and board ($16,032). ***Payment plan:*** Tuition prepayment.

FRESHMAN FINANCIAL AID (Fall 2019, est.) 321 applied for aid; of those 79% were deemed to have need. 100% of freshmen with need received aid; of those 100% had need fully met. ***Average percent of need met:*** 100% (excluding resources awarded to replace EFC). ***Average financial aid package:*** $52,823 (excluding resources awarded to replace EFC). 1% of all full-time freshmen had no need and received non-need-based gift aid.

UNDERGRADUATE FINANCIAL AID (Fall 2019, est.) 1,303 applied for aid; of those 89% were deemed to have need. 100% of undergraduates with need received aid; of those 100% had need fully met. ***Average percent of need met:*** 100% (excluding resources awarded to replace EFC). ***Average financial aid package:*** $53,261 (excluding resources awarded to replace EFC). 1% of all full-time undergraduates had no need and received non-need-based gift aid.

GIFT AID (NEED-BASED) ***Receiving aid:*** Freshmen: 41% (249); all full-time undergraduates: 44% (1,119). ***Average award:*** Freshmen: $49,740; Undergraduates: $49,992. ***Scholarships, grants, and awards:*** Federal Pell, FSEOG, state, private, college/university gift aid from institutional funds.

GIFT AID (NON-NEED-BASED) ***Average award:*** Freshmen: $5000. Undergraduates: $20,000. ***ROTC:*** Army cooperative.

LOANS ***Student loans:*** 50% of past graduating class borrowed through all loan programs. *Average indebtedness per student:* $19,838. ***Average need-based loan:*** Freshmen: $3214. Undergraduates: $4252. ***Programs:*** Federal Direct (Subsidized and Unsubsidized Stafford, PLUS), college/university.

WORK-STUDY Federal work-study jobs available. ***State or other work-study/employment:*** Part-time jobs available.

APPLYING FOR FINANCIAL AID ***Required financial aid forms:*** FAFSA, institution's own form, CSS Financial Aid PROFILE, noncustodial (divorced/separated) parent's statement.

CONTACT Ms. Heidi Sullivan, Student Financial Services Counselor, Middlebury College, Service Building 104, Middlebury, VT 05753, 802-443-5158. *Fax:* 802-443-2065. *E-mail:* studentfinancialservices@middlebury.edu.
Website: http://www.middlebury.edu/.

MIDDLE GEORGIA STATE UNIVERSITY

Macon, GA

CONTACT Lee Ann Kirkland, Office of Financial Aid, Middle Georgia State University, 100 University Parkway, Macon, GA 31206, 877-238-8664. *Fax:* 478-471-2790. *E-mail:* fainfo@mga.edu.
Website: http://www.mga.edu/.

MIDDLE TENNESSEE STATE UNIVERSITY

Murfreesboro, TN

Tuition & fees (TN res): $11,176	Average undergraduate aid package: $10,238

ABOUT THE INSTITUTION State-supported, coed. ***Awards:*** certificates, bachelor's, master's, and doctoral degrees. 79 undergraduate majors. ***Total enrollment:*** 21,721. Undergraduates: 19,461. Freshmen: 3,312. Federal methodology is used as a basis for awarding need-based institutional aid.

UNDERGRADUATE EXPENSES for 2020–2021 ***Application fee:*** $25. ***Tuition, state resident:*** full-time $9306; part-time $300 per credit hour. ***Tuition, nonresident:*** full-time $28,606; part-time $1078 per credit hour. ***Required fees:*** full-time $1870; $78 per credit hour. Full-time tuition and fees vary according to course load and program. Part-time tuition and fees vary according to course load and program. ***College room and board:*** $8976. Room and board charges vary according to board plan and housing facility.

FRESHMAN FINANCIAL AID (Fall 2019, est.) 2933 applied for aid; of those 74% were deemed to have need. 99% of freshmen with need received aid; of those 13% had need fully met. ***Average percent of need met:*** 67% (excluding resources awarded to replace EFC). ***Average financial aid package:*** $11,158 (excluding resources awarded to replace EFC). 22% of all full-time freshmen had no need and received non-need-based gift aid.

UNDERGRADUATE FINANCIAL AID (Fall 2019, est.) 13,642 applied for aid; of those 76% were deemed to have need. 98% of undergraduates with need received aid; of those 12% had need fully met. ***Average percent of need met:*** 64% (excluding resources awarded to replace EFC). ***Average financial aid package:*** $10,238 (excluding resources awarded to replace EFC). 17% of all full-time undergraduates had no need and received non-need-based gift aid.

GIFT AID (NEED-BASED) ***Total amount:*** $43,149,798 (76% federal, 24% state). ***Receiving aid:*** Freshmen: 41% (1,330); all full-time undergraduates: 42% (6,557). ***Average award:*** Freshmen: $6870; Undergraduates: $6189. ***Scholarships, grants, and awards:*** Federal Pell, FSEOG, state, private, college/university gift aid from institutional funds.

GIFT AID (NON-NEED-BASED) ***Total amount:*** $58,824,992 (10% federal, 47% state, 30% institutional, 13% external sources). ***Receiving aid:*** Freshmen: 58% (1,898). Undergraduates: 43% (6,703). ***Average award:*** Freshmen: $8544. Undergraduates: $8520. ***Scholarships, grants, and awards by category:*** *Academic interests/achievement:* 794 awards ($1,279,201 total): agriculture, area/ethnic studies, biological sciences, business, communication, computer science, education, engineering/technologies, English, foreign languages, general academic interests/achievements, health fields, home economics, humanities, international studies, mathematics, military science, physical sciences, premedicine, social sciences. *Creative arts/performance:* 649 awards ($892,476 total): applied art and design, creative writing, dance, debating, journalism/publications, music, performing arts, theater/drama. *Special achievements/activities:* 3,134 awards ($10,965,591 total): cheerleading/drum major, general special achievements/activities, hobbies/interests, leadership, memberships. *Special characteristics:* 3,149 awards ($3,965,198 total): adult students, children and siblings of alumni, ethnic background, first-generation college students, general special characteristics, handicapped students, international students, local/state students, members of minority groups. ***Tuition waivers:*** Full or partial for employees or children of employees, senior citizens. ***ROTC:*** Army, Air Force cooperative.

LOANS ***Student loans:*** $59,011,853 (43% need-based, 57% non-need-based). 59% of past graduating class borrowed through all loan programs. *Average indebtedness per student:* $24,936. ***Average need-based loan:*** Freshmen: $3206. Undergraduates: $3983. ***Parent loans:*** $11,331,281 (100% non-need-based). ***Programs:*** Federal Direct (Subsidized and Unsubsidized Stafford, PLUS), Federal Nursing, state, college/university.

WORK-STUDY ***Federal work-study:*** Total amount: $833,551; 286 jobs averaging $2929.

ATHLETIC AWARDS Total amount: $8,029,509 (100% non-need-based).

APPLYING FOR FINANCIAL AID ***Required financial aid form:*** FAFSA. ***Financial aid deadline (priority):*** 2/1. ***Notification date:*** Continuous beginning 2/15. Students must reply by 6/1.

CONTACT Mr. Stephen White, Director of Financial Aid, Middle Tennessee State University, SSAC 260, 1301 East Main Street, Murfreesboro, TN 37132, 615-898-5454 or toll-free 800-331-MTSU. *Fax:* 615-898-5167. *E-mail:* stephen.white@mtsu.edu.
Website: http://www.mtsu.edu/.

MIDLAND COLLEGE

Midland, TX

ABOUT THE INSTITUTION State and locally supported, coed. ***Awards:*** certificates, associate, and bachelor's degrees. 27 undergraduate majors. ***Total enrollment:*** 5,115. Undergraduates: 5,115. Freshmen: 790.

GIFT AID (NEED-BASED) ***Scholarships, grants, and awards:*** Federal Pell, FSEOG, state, private, college/university gift aid from institutional funds.

LOANS ***Programs:*** Federal Direct (Subsidized and Unsubsidized Stafford, PLUS).

CONTACT Yolanda Ramos, Director of Financial Aid, Midland College, 3600 North Garfield, Midland, TX 79705, 432-685-5511. *Fax:* 432-685-6451. *E-mail:* finaid@midland.edu.
Website: http://www.midland.edu/.

MIDLAND UNIVERSITY

Fremont, NE

CONTACT Penny James, Director of Financial Aid, Midland University, 900 North Clarkson Street, Fremont, NE 68025-4200, 402-721-5480 Ext. 6520 or toll-free 800-642-8382 Ext.6501. *Fax:* 402-721-0250. *E-mail:* finaid@mlc.edu.
Website: http://www.midlandu.edu/.

MID-SOUTH CHRISTIAN COLLEGE

Memphis, TN

Tuition & fees: $7490 **Average undergraduate aid package: N/A**

ABOUT THE INSTITUTION Independent, coed. ***Awards:*** certificates, associate, and bachelor's degrees. Federal methodology is used as a basis for awarding need-based institutional aid.

UNDERGRADUATE EXPENSES for 2019–2020 *Comprehensive fee:* $10,890 includes full-time tuition ($6400), mandatory fees ($1090), and room and board ($3400). Full-time tuition and fees vary according to course load and program. Room and board charges vary according to board plan and housing facility. ***Part-time tuition:*** $200 per credit hour. ***Part-time fees:*** $225 per term. Part-time tuition and fees vary according to course load. ***Payment plan:*** Guaranteed tuition.

GIFT AID (NEED-BASED) *Scholarships, grants, and awards:* Federal Pell, FSEOG.

GIFT AID (NON-NEED-BASED) *Scholarships, grants, and awards by category:* *Special characteristics:* relatives of clergy, spouses of current students. ***Tuition waivers:*** Full or partial for employees or children of employees.

WORK-STUDY *State or other work-study/employment:* Part-time jobs available.

APPLYING FOR FINANCIAL AID *Required financial aid form:* FAFSA. ***Financial aid deadline:*** Continuous. ***Notification date:*** Continuous beginning 6/15. Students must reply by 8/31.

CONTACT Mr. Keith Graham, Director of Financial Aid, Mid-South Christian College, PO Box 181056, Memphis, TN 38181, 901-375-4400. *Fax:* 901-375-4085. *E-mail:* keithgraham@midsouthchristian.edu.
Website: http://www.midsouthchristian.edu/.

MIDWAY UNIVERSITY

Midway, KY

Tuition & fees: $24,850 **Average undergraduate aid package: $17,846**

ABOUT THE INSTITUTION Independent Christian Church (Disciples of Christ), coed. ***Awards:*** associate, bachelor's, and master's degrees. 21 undergraduate majors. ***Total enrollment:*** 1,702. Undergraduates: 1,481. Freshmen: 217. Both federal and institutional methodology are used as a basis for awarding need-based institutional aid.

UNDERGRADUATE EXPENSES for 2020–2021 *Application fee:* $30. ***Comprehensive fee:*** $33,450 includes full-time tuition ($24,500), mandatory fees ($350), and room and board ($8600). ***College room only:*** $4400. ***Part-time tuition:*** $910 per credit hour.

FRESHMAN FINANCIAL AID (Fall 2019, est.) 210 applied for aid; of those 91% were deemed to have need. 100% of freshmen with need received aid; of those 8% had need fully met. ***Average percent of need met:*** 70% (excluding resources awarded to replace EFC). ***Average financial aid package:*** $19,999 (excluding resources awarded to replace EFC). 3% of all full-time freshmen had no need and received non-need-based gift aid.

UNDERGRADUATE FINANCIAL AID (Fall 2019, est.) 837 applied for aid; of those 93% were deemed to have need. 100% of undergraduates with need received aid; of those 8% had need fully met. ***Average percent of need met:*** 69% (excluding resources awarded to replace EFC). ***Average financial aid package:*** $17,846 (excluding resources awarded to replace EFC). 3% of all full-time undergraduates had no need and received non-need-based gift aid.

GIFT AID (NEED-BASED) *Total amount:* $4,363,021 (52% federal, 47% state, 1% institutional). ***Receiving aid:*** Freshmen: 71% (154); all full-time undergraduates: 72% (635). ***Average award:*** Freshmen: $6211; Undergraduates: $6629. ***Scholarships, grants, and awards:*** Federal Pell, FSEOG, state, private, college/university gift aid from institutional funds.

GIFT AID (NON-NEED-BASED) *Total amount:* $5,745,852 (10% state, 90% institutional). ***Receiving aid:*** Freshmen: 88% (191). Undergraduates: 71% (626). ***Average award:*** Freshmen: $9357. Undergraduates: $11,046. ***Scholarships, grants, and awards by category:*** *Academic interests/achievement:* agriculture, business, general academic interests/achievements, premedicine. *Creative arts/performance:* music. *Special achievements/activities:* cheerleading/drum major, general special achievements/activities, junior miss, leadership, religious involvement. *Special characteristics:* adult students, children and siblings of alumni, children of faculty/staff, members of minority groups, previous college experience, relatives of clergy, religious affiliation, veterans. ***ROTC:*** Army cooperative, Air Force cooperative.

LOANS *Student loans:* $4,918,918 (49% need-based, 51% non-need-based). ***Average need-based loan:*** Freshmen: $3138. Undergraduates: $3742. ***Parent loans:*** $1,269,996 (100% non-need-based). ***Programs:*** Federal Direct (Subsidized and Unsubsidized Stafford, PLUS), college/university.

WORK-STUDY *Federal work-study:* Total amount: $131,638; jobs available. ***State or other work-study/employment:*** Part-time jobs available.

ATHLETIC AWARDS Total amount: $2,321,292 (100% non-need-based).

APPLYING FOR FINANCIAL AID *Required financial aid form:* FAFSA. ***Financial aid deadline:*** Continuous. ***Notification date:*** Continuous.

CONTACT Erin Teves, Director of Financial Aid, Midway University, 512 East Stephens Street, Midway, KY 40347-1120, 859-846-5494 or toll-free 800-755-0031. *Fax:* 859-846-5751. *E-mail:* faid@midway.edu.
Website: http://www.midway.edu/.

MIDWESTERN STATE UNIVERSITY

Wichita Falls, TX

Tuition & fees: N/R **Average undergraduate aid package: $10,596**

ABOUT THE INSTITUTION State-supported, coed. ***Awards:*** certificates, associate, bachelor's, and master's degrees. 73 undergraduate majors. ***Total enrollment:*** 6,102. Undergraduates: 5,287. Freshmen: 826. Federal methodology is used as a basis for awarding need-based institutional aid.

FRESHMAN FINANCIAL AID (Fall 2018) 795 applied for aid; of those 82% were deemed to have need. 99% of freshmen with need received aid; of those 31% had need fully met. ***Average percent of need met:*** 64% (excluding resources awarded to replace EFC). ***Average financial aid package:*** $11,505 (excluding resources awarded to replace EFC). 15% of all full-time freshmen had no need and received non-need-based gift aid.

UNDERGRADUATE FINANCIAL AID (Fall 2018) 3,150 applied for aid; of those 85% were deemed to have need. 99% of undergraduates with need received aid; of those 18% had need fully met. ***Average percent of need met:*** 59% (excluding resources awarded to replace EFC). ***Average financial aid package:*** $10,596 (excluding resources awarded to replace EFC). 20% of all full-time undergraduates had no need and received non-need-based gift aid.

GIFT AID (NEED-BASED) *Total amount:* $21,055,572 (49% federal, 20% state, 28% institutional, 3% external sources). ***Receiving aid:*** Freshmen: 69% (616); all full-time undergraduates: 58% (2,451). ***Average award:*** Freshmen: $9867; Undergraduates: $8291. ***Scholarships, grants, and awards:*** Federal Pell, FSEOG, state, private, college/university gift aid from institutional funds.

GIFT AID (NON-NEED-BASED) *Total amount:* $3,923,716 (13% federal, 2% state, 73% institutional, 12% external sources). ***Receiving aid:*** Freshmen: 4% (40). Undergraduates: 3% (110). ***Average award:*** Freshmen: $2825. Undergraduates: $3160. ***Scholarships, grants, and awards by category:*** *Academic interests/achievement:* biological sciences, business, communication, computer science, education, engineering/technologies, English, foreign languages, general academic interests/achievements, home economics, humanities, international studies, mathematics, physical sciences, premedicine, social sciences. *Creative arts/performance:* applied art and design, creative writing, general creative arts/performance, journalism/publications, music, theater/drama. *Special achievements/activities:* cheerleading/drum major, general special achievements/activities, leadership. *Special characteristics:* children and siblings of alumni, children of faculty/staff, children of union members/company employees, children of workers in trades, children with a deceased or disabled parent, first-generation college students, handicapped students, international students, members of minority groups, veterans. ***ROTC:*** Air Force cooperative.

LOANS *Student loans:* $20,779,054 (74% need-based, 26% non-need-based). 97% of past graduating class borrowed through all loan programs. *Average indebtedness per student:* $49,146. ***Average need-based loan:*** Freshmen: $5326. Undergraduates: $6820. ***Parent loans:*** $6,152,722 (37% need-based, 63% non-need-based). ***Programs:*** Federal Direct (Subsidized and Unsubsidized Stafford, PLUS), state.

WORK-STUDY *Federal work-study:* Total amount: $145,763; jobs available. ***State or other work-study/employment:*** Total amount: $47,388 (87% need-based, 13% non-need-based). Part-time jobs available.

ATHLETIC AWARDS Total amount: $2,089,668 (49% need-based, 51% non-need-based).

APPLYING FOR FINANCIAL AID *Required financial aid form:* FAFSA. ***Financial aid deadline (priority):*** 3/1. ***Notification date:*** Continuous beginning 3/1.

CONTACT Ms. Kathy Browning, Director of Financial Aid, Midwestern State University, 3410 Taft Boulevard, Wichita Falls, TX 76308, 940-397-4214 or toll-free 800-842-1922. *Fax:* 940-397-4852. *E-mail:* financial-aid@mwsu.edu.
Website: http://www.mwsu.edu/.

MIDWEST UNIVERSITY

Wentzville, MO

CONTACT Financial Aid Office, Midwest University, 851 Parr Road, Wentzville, MO 63385, 636-327-4645.
Website: http://www.midwest.edu/.

MIDWIVES COLLEGE OF UTAH

Salt Lake City, UT

CONTACT Financial Aid Office, Midwives College of Utah, 1174 East 2700 South, Suite 2, Salt Lake City, UT 84106, 801-764-9068 or toll-free 866-680-2756.
Website: http://www.midwifery.edu/.

MILES COLLEGE

Fairfield, AL

CONTACT P. N. Lanier, Financial Aid Administrator, Miles College, PO Box 3800, Birmingham, AL 35208, 205-929-1663 or toll-free 800-445-0708 (out-of-state). *Fax:* 205-929-1668. *E-mail:* pnlani@netscape.net.
Website: http://www.miles.edu/.

MILLENNIA ATLANTIC UNIVERSITY

Doral, FL

Tuition & fees: N/R	Average undergraduate aid package: $3197

ABOUT THE INSTITUTION Proprietary, coed. ***Awards:*** associate, bachelor's, and master's degrees. 8 undergraduate majors. ***Total enrollment:*** 205. Undergraduates: 105. Federal methodology is used as a basis for awarding need-based institutional aid.

UNDERGRADUATE FINANCIAL AID (Fall 2019, est.) 1 applied for aid; of those 100% were deemed to have need. 100% of undergraduates with need received aid. ***Average percent of need met:*** 100% (excluding resources awarded to replace EFC). ***Average financial aid package:*** $3197 (excluding resources awarded to replace EFC).

GIFT AID (NEED-BASED) *Receiving aid:* All full-time undergraduates: 100% (1). ***Average award:*** Undergraduates: $5567. ***Scholarships, grants, and awards:*** Federal Pell, FSEOG, state, college/university gift aid from institutional funds.

GIFT AID (NON-NEED-BASED) *Receiving aid:* Undergraduates: 100% (1).

LOANS *Programs:* Federal Direct (Subsidized and Unsubsidized Stafford, PLUS), private loans.

WORK-STUDY Federal work-study jobs available.

APPLYING FOR FINANCIAL AID *Required financial aid forms:* FAFSA, institution's own form. ***Financial aid deadline:*** Continuous. ***Notification date:*** Continuous. Students must reply within 2 weeks of notification.

CONTACT Mrs. Maria C. Velar, Financial Aid Manager, Millennia Atlantic University, 3801 NW 97th Avenue, Suite 100, Doral, FL 33178, 785-331-1000 Ext. 202. *E-mail:* mvelar@maufl.edu.
Website: http://www.maufl.edu/.

MILLERSVILLE UNIVERSITY OF PENNSYLVANIA

Millersville, PA

Tuition & fees (PA res): $12,250	Average undergraduate aid package: $8997

ABOUT THE INSTITUTION State-supported, coed. ***Awards:*** certificates, associate, bachelor's, master's, and doctoral degrees. 40 undergraduate majors. ***Total enrollment:*** 7,802. Undergraduates: 6,779. Freshmen: 1,334. Federal methodology is used as a basis for awarding need-based institutional aid.

UNDERGRADUATE EXPENSES for 2019–2020 *Application fee:* $50. ***Tuition, state resident:*** full-time $9570; part-time $319 per credit. ***Tuition, nonresident:*** full-time $19,290; part-time $805 per credit. ***Required fees:*** full-time $2680; $111.75 per credit. Full-time tuition and fees vary according to course load. Part-time tuition and fees vary according to course load. ***College room and board:*** $12,980. Room and board charges vary according to board plan and housing facility.

FRESHMAN FINANCIAL AID (Fall 2018) 1235 applied for aid; of those 77% were deemed to have need. 97% of freshmen with need received aid; of those 4% had need fully met. ***Average percent of need met:*** 52% (excluding resources awarded to replace EFC). ***Average financial aid package:*** $8885 (excluding resources awarded to replace EFC). 8% of all full-time freshmen had no need and received non-need-based gift aid.

UNDERGRADUATE FINANCIAL AID (Fall 2018) 4,538 applied for aid; of those 83% were deemed to have need. 97% of undergraduates with need received aid; of those 3% had need fully met. ***Average percent of need met:*** 56% (excluding resources awarded to replace EFC). ***Average financial aid package:*** $8997 (excluding resources awarded to replace EFC). 5% of all full-time undergraduates had no need and received non-need-based gift aid.

GIFT AID (NEED-BASED) *Total amount:* $18,580,767 (50% federal, 28% state, 16% institutional, 6% external sources). ***Receiving aid:*** Freshmen: 52% (697); all full-time undergraduates: 49% (2,686). ***Average award:*** Freshmen: $6610; Undergraduates: $6432. ***Scholarships, grants, and awards:*** Federal Pell, FSEOG, state, private, college/university gift aid from institutional funds, Schock Scholarship.

GIFT AID (NON-NEED-BASED) *Total amount:* $3,382,244 (8% state, 51% institutional, 41% external sources). ***Receiving aid:*** Freshmen: 17% (233). Undergraduates: 9% (469). ***Average award:*** Freshmen: $3098. Undergraduates: $3190. ***Scholarships, grants, and awards by category:*** *Academic interests/achievement:* 965 awards ($2,833,073 total): biological sciences, business, communication, computer science, education, English, foreign languages, general academic interests/achievements, home economics, humanities, mathematics, physical sciences, social sciences. *Creative arts/performance:* 63 awards ($95,099 total): art/fine arts, music. *Special achievements/activities:* 1 award ($2779 total): community service. *Special characteristics:* 110 awards ($822,794 total): children of union members/company employees, international students. ***Tuition waivers:*** Full or partial for employees or children of employees, senior citizens. ***ROTC:*** Army.

LOANS *Student loans:* $34,749,585 (39% need-based, 61% non-need-based). 73% of past graduating class borrowed through all loan programs. *Average indebtedness per student:* $32,815. ***Average need-based loan:*** Freshmen: $3163. Undergraduates: $4090. ***Parent loans:*** $12,787,580 (100% non-need-based). ***Programs:*** Federal Direct (Subsidized and Unsubsidized Stafford, PLUS), college/university, Private Alternative Loans.

WORK-STUDY ***Federal work-study:*** Total amount: $313,804; 233 jobs averaging $1347. ***State or other work-study/employment:*** Total amount: $1,829,567 (100% non-need-based). 1,297 part-time jobs averaging $1411.

ATHLETIC AWARDS Total amount: $929,836 (33% need-based, 67% non-need-based).

APPLYING FOR FINANCIAL AID ***Required financial aid form:*** FAFSA. ***Financial aid deadline (priority):*** 3/15. ***Notification date:*** Continuous beginning 3/19. Students must reply within 2 weeks of notification.

CONTACT Ms. Jasmine J. Campbell, Interim Director of Student Financial Services, Millersville University of Pennsylvania, PO Box 1002, Millersville, PA 17551-0302, 717-871-5101 or toll-free 800-MU-ADMIT. *Fax:* 717-871-7980. *E-mail:* Jasmine.Campbell@millersville.edu.
Website: http://www.millersville.edu/.

MILLIGAN UNIVERSITY

Milligan College, TN

Tuition & fees: $35,600	Average undergraduate aid package: $25,811

ABOUT THE INSTITUTION Independent Christian, coed. ***Awards:*** certificates, bachelor's, master's, and doctoral degrees. 35 undergraduate majors. ***Total enrollment:*** 1,310. Undergraduates: 886. Freshmen: 202. Federal methodology is used as a basis for awarding need-based institutional aid.

UNDERGRADUATE EXPENSES for 2020–2021 ***Application fee:*** $30. ***One-time required fee:*** $75. ***Comprehensive fee:*** $43,000 includes full-time tuition ($34,150), mandatory fees ($1450), and room and board ($7400). ***College room only:*** $3650. Full-time tuition and fees vary according to course load and program. Room and board charges vary according to housing facility. ***Part-time tuition:*** $950 per semester hour. ***Part-time fees:*** $375 per term. Part-time tuition and fees vary according to course load and program.

FRESHMAN FINANCIAL AID (Fall 2019, est.) 177 applied for aid; of those 80% were deemed to have need. 100% of freshmen with need received aid; of those 30% had need fully met. ***Average percent of need met:*** 78% (excluding resources awarded to replace EFC). ***Average financial aid package:*** $26,563 (excluding resources awarded to replace EFC). 25% of all full-time freshmen had no need and received non-need-based gift aid.

UNDERGRADUATE FINANCIAL AID (Fall 2019, est.) 682 applied for aid; of those 86% were deemed to have need. 100% of undergraduates with need received aid; of those 32% had need fully met. ***Average percent of need met:*** 80% (excluding resources awarded to replace EFC). ***Average financial aid package:*** $25,811 (excluding resources awarded to replace EFC). 19% of all full-time undergraduates had no need and received non-need-based gift aid.

GIFT AID (NEED-BASED) ***Receiving aid:*** Freshmen: 72% (142); all full-time undergraduates: 77% (583). ***Average award:*** Freshmen: $24,266; Undergraduates: $22,804. ***Scholarships, grants, and awards:*** Federal Pell, FSEOG, state, private, college/university gift aid from institutional funds.

GIFT AID (NON-NEED-BASED) ***Receiving aid:*** Freshmen: 17% (34). Undergraduates: 20% (151). ***Average award:*** Freshmen: $14,007. Undergraduates: $13,614. ***Scholarships, grants, and awards by category:*** *Academic interests/achievement:* 610 awards ($7,500,070 total): engineering/technologies, general academic interests/achievements. *Creative arts/performance:* 67 awards ($458,400 total): applied art and design, cinema/film/broadcasting, dance, music, theater/drama. *Special achievements/activities:* 23 awards ($194,800 total): cheerleading/drum major, community service. *Special characteristics:* 27 awards ($789,637 total): children of faculty/staff. ***Tuition waivers:*** Full or partial for minority students, employees or children of employees. ***ROTC:*** Army cooperative.

LOANS ***Student loans:*** 69% of past graduating class borrowed through all loan programs. *Average indebtedness per student:* $28,864. ***Average need-based loan:*** Freshmen: $3366. Undergraduates: $4428. ***Programs:*** Federal Direct (Subsidized and Unsubsidized Stafford, PLUS), Alternative loans.

WORK-STUDY ***Federal work-study:*** 133 jobs averaging $1200. ***State or other work-study/employment:*** 142 part-time jobs averaging $1485.

APPLYING FOR FINANCIAL AID ***Required financial aid form:*** FAFSA. ***Financial aid deadline:*** Continuous. ***Notification date:*** Continuous. Students must reply within 2 weeks of notification.

CONTACT Diane Keasling, Coordinator of Financial Aid, Milligan University, PO Box 250, Milligan College, TN 37682, 423-461-8968 or toll-free 800-262-8337. *Fax:* 423-929-2368. *E-mail:* dlkeasling@milligan.edu.
Website: http://www.milligan.edu/.

MILLIKIN UNIVERSITY

Decatur, IL

Tuition & fees: $39,592	Average undergraduate aid package: $27,736

ABOUT THE INSTITUTION Independent Presbyterian Church (U.S.A.), coed. ***Awards:*** certificates, bachelor's, master's, and doctoral degrees. 62 undergraduate majors. ***Total enrollment:*** 2,083. Undergraduates: 1,995. Freshmen: 486. Federal methodology is used as a basis for awarding need-based institutional aid.

UNDERGRADUATE EXPENSES for 2020–2021 ***Comprehensive fee:*** $51,042 includes full-time tuition ($38,800), mandatory fees ($792), and room and board ($11,450). ***College room only:*** $9400. Room and board charges vary according to board plan. ***Part-time tuition:*** $499 per credit hour. ***Part-time fees:*** $22 per credit hour.

FRESHMAN FINANCIAL AID (Fall 2018) 443 applied for aid; of those 90% were deemed to have need. 100% of freshmen with need received aid; of those 29% had need fully met. ***Average percent of need met:*** 85% (excluding resources awarded to replace EFC). ***Average financial aid package:*** $29,921 (excluding resources awarded to replace EFC). 10% of all full-time freshmen had no need and received non-need-based gift aid.

UNDERGRADUATE FINANCIAL AID (Fall 2018) 1,667 applied for aid; of those 92% were deemed to have need. 100% of undergraduates with need received aid; of those 33% had need fully met. ***Average percent of need met:*** 83% (excluding resources awarded to replace EFC). ***Average financial aid package:*** $27,736 (excluding resources awarded to replace EFC). 7% of all full-time undergraduates had no need and received non-need-based gift aid.

GIFT AID (NEED-BASED) ***Total amount:*** $12,622,510 (29% federal, 26% state, 45% institutional). ***Receiving aid:*** Freshmen: 69% (324); all full-time undergraduates: 69% (1,267). ***Average award:*** Freshmen: $10,957; Undergraduates: $9635. ***Scholarships, grants, and awards:*** Federal Pell, FSEOG, state, private, college/university gift aid from institutional funds.

GIFT AID (NON-NEED-BASED) ***Total amount:*** $29,799,200 (98% institutional, 2% external sources). ***Receiving aid:*** Freshmen: 83% (387). Undergraduates: 78% (1,438). ***Average award:*** Freshmen: $19,308. Undergraduates: $18,472. ***Scholarships, grants, and awards by category:*** *Academic interests/achievement:* biological sciences, business, communication, education, English, foreign languages, general academic interests/achievements, health fields, humanities, international studies, mathematics, physical sciences, premedicine. *Creative arts/performance:* applied art and design, creative writing, dance, music, theater/drama. *Special achievements/activities:* community service, general special achievements/activities, leadership. *Special characteristics:* children and siblings of alumni, children of faculty/staff, children of union members/company employees, children with a deceased or disabled parent, general special characteristics, international students, parents of current students, previous college experience, relatives of clergy, siblings of current students, veterans. ***Tuition waivers:*** Full or partial for employees or children of employees.

LOANS ***Student loans:*** $12,016,821 (42% need-based, 58% non-need-based). 79% of past graduating class borrowed through all loan programs. *Average indebtedness per student:* $35,596. ***Average need-based loan:*** Freshmen: $3192. Undergraduates: $4237. ***Parent loans:*** $4,831,326 (100% non-need-based). ***Programs:*** Federal Direct (Subsidized and Unsubsidized Stafford, PLUS), Perkins, private loans.

WORK-STUDY ***Federal work-study:*** Total amount: $503,604; 472 jobs averaging $1067. ***State or other work-study/employment:*** Total amount: $334,054 (100% non-need-based). 410 part-time jobs averaging $815.

APPLYING FOR FINANCIAL AID ***Required financial aid form:*** FAFSA. ***Financial aid deadline (priority):*** 1/15. ***Notification date:*** Continuous beginning 1/15. Students must reply by 5/1 or within 4 weeks of notification.

CONTACT Chilwana Thompson, Assistant Director of Financial Aid, Millikin University, 1184 West Main Street, Decatur, IL 62522-2084, 217-424-6317 or toll-free 800-373-7733. *Fax:* 217-424-5070. *E-mail:* studentfinancialservices@millikin.edu.
Website: http://www.millikin.edu/.

MILLSAPS COLLEGE

Jackson, MS

ABOUT THE INSTITUTION Independent United Methodist, coed. ***Awards:*** bachelor's and master's degrees. 31 undergraduate majors. ***Total enrollment:*** 864. Undergraduates: 798. Freshmen: 244.

GIFT AID (NEED-BASED) ***Scholarships, grants, and awards:*** Federal Pell, FSEOG, state, private, college/university gift aid from institutional funds.

GIFT AID (NON-NEED-BASED) ***Scholarships, grants, and awards by category:*** *Academic interests/achievement:* business, general academic interests/achievements. *Creative arts/performance:* applied art and design, music, theater/drama. *Special achievements/activities:* community service, general special achievements/activities, hobbies/interests, leadership, religious involvement. *Special characteristics:* adult students, children of faculty/staff, ethnic background, first-generation college students, local/state students, religious affiliation.

LOANS ***Programs:*** Federal Direct (Subsidized and Unsubsidized Stafford, PLUS), Perkins.

CONTACT Isabelle Higbee, Director of Financial Aid, Millsaps College, 1701 North State Street, Jackson, MS 39210-0001, 601-974-1220 or toll-free 800-352-1050. *Fax:* 601-974-1224. *E-mail:* financialaid@millsaps.edu.
Website: http://www.millsaps.edu/.

MILLS COLLEGE

Oakland, CA

Tuition & fees: N/R	Average undergraduate aid package: $53,604

ABOUT THE INSTITUTION Independent, undergraduate: women only; graduate: coed. ***Awards:*** certificates, bachelor's, master's, and doctoral degrees. 31 undergraduate majors. ***Total enrollment:*** 1,309. Undergraduates: 761. Freshmen: 174. Federal methodology is used as a basis for awarding need-based institutional aid.

FRESHMAN FINANCIAL AID (Fall 2019, est.) 134 applied for aid; of those 79% were deemed to have need. 100% of freshmen with need received aid; of those 9% had need fully met. ***Average percent of need met:*** 73% (excluding resources awarded to replace EFC). ***Average financial aid package:*** $55,665 (excluding resources awarded to replace EFC). 21% of all full-time freshmen had no need and received non-need-based gift aid.

UNDERGRADUATE FINANCIAL AID (Fall 2019, est.) 660 applied for aid; of those 85% were deemed to have need. 99% of undergraduates with need received aid; of those 11% had need fully met. ***Average percent of need met:*** 70% (excluding resources awarded to replace EFC). ***Average financial aid package:*** $53,604 (excluding resources awarded to replace EFC). 15% of all full-time undergraduates had no need and received non-need-based gift aid.

GIFT AID (NEED-BASED) ***Total amount:*** $26,090,169 (14% federal, 16% state, 67% institutional, 3% external sources). ***Receiving aid:*** Freshmen: 71% (95); all full-time undergraduates: 77% (517). ***Average award:*** Freshmen: $39,288; Undergraduates: $39,192. ***Scholarships, grants, and awards:*** Federal Pell, FSEOG, state, private, college/university gift aid from institutional funds.

GIFT AID (NON-NEED-BASED) ***Total amount:*** $1,110,964 (100% institutional). ***Receiving aid:*** Freshmen: 78% (105). Undergraduates: 58% (387). ***Average award:*** Freshmen: $14,380. Undergraduates: $13,337. ***Scholarships, grants, and awards by category:*** *Academic interests/achievement:* biological sciences, computer science, general academic interests/achievements, mathematics, physical sciences, premedicine. *Creative arts/performance:* music. *Special achievements/activities:* leadership. **ROTC:** Army cooperative.

LOANS ***Student loans:*** $8,942,068 (91% need-based, 9% non-need-based). 72% of past graduating class borrowed through all loan programs. *Average indebtedness per student:* $49,333. ***Average need-based loan:*** Freshmen: $6903. Undergraduates: $8935. ***Parent loans:*** $1,813,356 (85% need-based, 15% non-need-based). ***Programs:*** Federal Direct (Subsidized and Unsubsidized Stafford, PLUS), college/university.

WORK-STUDY ***Federal work-study:*** Total amount: $803,982; jobs available. ***State or other work-study/employment:*** Total amount: $316,486 (96% need-based, 4% non-need-based). Part-time jobs available.

APPLYING FOR FINANCIAL AID ***Required financial aid forms:*** FAFSA, state aid form. ***Financial aid deadline (priority):*** 2/15. ***Notification date:*** Continuous beginning 2/15. Students must reply within 4 weeks of notification.

CONTACT Mr. Dustin Smith-Salinas, Director of Financial Aid, Mills College, 5000 MacArthur Boulevard, Oakland, CA 94613, 510-430-2039 or toll-free 800-87-MILLS. *Fax:* 510-430-2003. *E-mail:* dsmithsalinas@mills.edu.
Website: http://www.mills.edu/.

MILWAUKEE INSTITUTE OF ART AND DESIGN

Milwaukee, WI

Tuition & fees: N/R	Average undergraduate aid package: $27,577

ABOUT THE INSTITUTION Independent, coed. ***Awards:*** bachelor's degrees. 11 undergraduate majors. Federal methodology is used as a basis for awarding need-based institutional aid.

FRESHMAN FINANCIAL AID (Fall 2018) 236 applied for aid; of those 95% were deemed to have need. 100% of freshmen with need received aid; of those 13% had need fully met. ***Average percent of need met:*** 73% (excluding resources awarded to replace EFC). ***Average financial aid package:*** $27,648 (excluding resources awarded to replace EFC). 11% of all full-time freshmen had no need and received non-need-based gift aid.

UNDERGRADUATE FINANCIAL AID (Fall 2018) 684 applied for aid; of those 94% were deemed to have need. 100% of undergraduates with need received aid; of those 13% had need fully met. ***Average percent of need met:*** 72% (excluding resources awarded to replace EFC). ***Average financial aid package:*** $27,577 (excluding resources awarded to replace EFC). 13% of all full-time undergraduates had no need and received non-need-based gift aid.

GIFT AID (NEED-BASED) ***Total amount:*** $14,330,589 (11% federal, 6% state, 81% institutional, 2% external sources). ***Receiving aid:*** Freshmen: 95% (224); all full-time undergraduates: 87% (643). ***Average award:*** Freshmen: $23,066; Undergraduates: $22,149. ***Scholarships, grants, and awards:*** Federal Pell, FSEOG, state, private, college/university gift aid from institutional funds.

GIFT AID (NON-NEED-BASED) ***Total amount:*** $1,758,689 (97% institutional, 3% external sources). ***Receiving aid:*** Freshmen: 10% (23). Undergraduates: 8% (56). ***Average award:*** Freshmen: $15,775. Undergraduates: $14,965. ***Scholarships, grants, and awards by category:*** *Creative arts/performance:* art/fine arts. *Special characteristics:* children of faculty/staff, ethnic background, local/state students, members of minority groups.

LOANS ***Student loans:*** $6,491,184 (74% need-based, 26% non-need-based). 93% of past graduating class borrowed through all loan programs. *Average indebtedness per student:* $40,330. ***Average need-based loan:*** Freshmen: $5580. Undergraduates: $6317. ***Parent loans:*** $2,808,326 (60% need-based, 40% non-need-based). ***Programs:*** Federal Direct (Subsidized and Unsubsidized Stafford, PLUS), alternative loans.

WORK-STUDY ***Federal work-study:*** Total amount: $65,815; jobs available. ***State or other work-study/employment:*** Total amount: $310,477 (100% non-need-based).

APPLYING FOR FINANCIAL AID ***Required financial aid form:*** FAFSA. ***Financial aid deadline:*** Continuous. ***Notification date:*** Students must reply by 5/1.

CONTACT Carol Masse, Director of Financial Aid, Milwaukee Institute of Art and Design, 273 East Erie Street, Milwaukee, WI 53202-6003, 414-291-3272 or toll-free 888-749-MIAD. *Fax:* 414-291-8077. *E-mail:* carolmasse@miad.edu.
Website: http://www.miad.edu/.

MILWAUKEE SCHOOL OF ENGINEERING

Milwaukee, WI

Tuition & fees: $43,575	Average undergraduate aid package: $30,355

ABOUT THE INSTITUTION Independent, coed, primarily men. ***Awards:*** certificates, bachelor's, and master's degrees. 16 undergraduate majors. ***Total enrollment:***

2,746. Undergraduates: 2,566. Freshmen: 582. Federal methodology is used as a basis for awarding need-based institutional aid.

UNDERGRADUATE EXPENSES for 2020–2021 ***Tuition:*** full-time $41,820; part-time $727 per credit hour. ***Required fees:*** full-time $1755. Full-time tuition and fees vary according to course load. Part-time tuition and fees vary according to course load. ***College room only:*** $6339. Room and board charges vary according to board plan and housing facility.

FRESHMAN FINANCIAL AID (Fall 2018) 569 applied for aid; of those 88% were deemed to have need. 100% of freshmen with need received aid; of those 20% had need fully met. ***Average percent of need met:*** 82% (excluding resources awarded to replace EFC). ***Average financial aid package:*** $30,567 (excluding resources awarded to replace EFC). 16% of all full-time freshmen had no need and received non-need-based gift aid.

UNDERGRADUATE FINANCIAL AID (Fall 2018) 2,188 applied for aid; of those 90% were deemed to have need. 100% of undergraduates with need received aid; of those 18% had need fully met. ***Average percent of need met:*** 76% (excluding resources awarded to replace EFC). ***Average financial aid package:*** $30,355 (excluding resources awarded to replace EFC). 17% of all full-time undergraduates had no need and received non-need-based gift aid.

GIFT AID (NEED-BASED) ***Total amount:*** $53,002,813 (5% federal, 5% state, 85% institutional, 5% external sources). ***Receiving aid:*** Freshmen: 84% (499); all full-time undergraduates: 80% (1,972). ***Average award:*** Freshmen: $28,071; Undergraduates: $27,042. ***Scholarships, grants, and awards:*** Federal Pell, FSEOG, state, private, college/university gift aid from institutional funds.

GIFT AID (NON-NEED-BASED) ***Total amount:*** $9,349,422 (91% institutional, 9% external sources). ***Receiving aid:*** Freshmen: 12% (73). Undergraduates: 11% (265). ***Average award:*** Freshmen: $18,137. Undergraduates: $15,202. ***Scholarships, grants, and awards by category:*** *Academic interests/achievement:* business, communication, computer science, engineering/technologies, health fields, mathematics. *Special characteristics:* children of faculty/staff. ***Tuition waivers:*** Full or partial for employees or children of employees. ***ROTC:*** Army cooperative, Naval cooperative, Air Force cooperative.

LOANS ***Student loans:*** $17,851,237 (69% need-based, 31% non-need-based). 79% of past graduating class borrowed through all loan programs. *Average indebtedness per student:* $36,150. ***Average need-based loan:*** Freshmen: $3216. Undergraduates: $4130. ***Parent loans:*** $4,214,967 (39% need-based, 61% non-need-based). ***Programs:*** Federal Direct (Subsidized and Unsubsidized Stafford, PLUS), Perkins, state.

WORK-STUDY ***Federal work-study:*** Total amount: $321,051; jobs available.

APPLYING FOR FINANCIAL AID ***Required financial aid form:*** FAFSA. ***Financial aid deadline (priority):*** 1/1. ***Notification date:*** Continuous beginning 1/15. Students must reply within 2 weeks of notification.

CONTACT Ms. Stephanie Mealy, Director of Financial Aid, Milwaukee School of Engineering, 1025 North Broadway, Milwaukee, WI 53202-3109, 414-277-7224 or toll-free 800-332-6763. *Fax:* 414-277-6952. *E-mail:* mealy@msoe.edu.
Website: http://www.msoe.edu/.

MINNEAPOLIS COLLEGE OF ART AND DESIGN

Minneapolis, MN

Tuition & fees: $56,124	Average undergraduate aid package: $28,894

ABOUT THE INSTITUTION Independent, coed. ***Awards:*** bachelor's and master's degrees. 12 undergraduate majors. ***Total enrollment:*** 796. Undergraduates: 709. Freshmen: 178. Federal methodology is used as a basis for awarding need-based institutional aid.

UNDERGRADUATE EXPENSES for 2020–2021 ***Application fee:*** $50. ***Comprehensive fee:*** $62,104 includes full-time tuition ($55,674), mandatory fees ($450), and room and board ($5980). ***College room only:*** $5980. ***Part-time tuition:*** $1723 per credit hour.

FRESHMAN FINANCIAL AID (Fall 2019, est.) 165 applied for aid; of those 87% were deemed to have need. 100% of freshmen with need received aid; of those 11% had need fully met. ***Average percent of need met:*** 72% (excluding resources awarded to replace EFC). ***Average financial aid package:*** $29,404 (excluding resources awarded to replace EFC). 17% of all full-time freshmen had no need and received non-need-based gift aid.

UNDERGRADUATE FINANCIAL AID (Fall 2019, est.) 619 applied for aid; of those 90% were deemed to have need. 100% of undergraduates with need received aid; of those 8% had need fully met. ***Average percent of need met:*** 71% (excluding resources awarded to replace EFC). ***Average financial aid package:*** $28,894 (excluding resources awarded to replace EFC). 19% of all full-time undergraduates had no need and received non-need-based gift aid.

GIFT AID (NEED-BASED) ***Total amount:*** $12,721,587 (10% federal, 9% state, 79% institutional, 2% external sources). ***Receiving aid:*** Freshmen: 83% (144); all full-time undergraduates: 80% (556). ***Average award:*** Freshmen: $24,635; Undergraduates: $23,424. ***Scholarships, grants, and awards:*** Federal Pell, FSEOG, state, private, college/university gift aid from institutional funds.

GIFT AID (NON-NEED-BASED) ***Total amount:*** $2,212,760 (8% federal, 91% institutional, 1% external sources). ***Receiving aid:*** Freshmen: 6% (11). Undergraduates: 5% (34). ***Average award:*** Freshmen: $15,410. Undergraduates: $13,907. ***Scholarships, grants, and awards by category:*** *Creative arts/performance:* applied art and design, art/fine arts, cinema/film/broadcasting, general creative arts/performance.

LOANS ***Student loans:*** $6,184,439 (74% need-based, 26% non-need-based). 82% of past graduating class borrowed through all loan programs. *Average indebtedness per student:* $37,788. ***Average need-based loan:*** Freshmen: $3542. Undergraduates: $4569. ***Parent loans:*** $1,868,359 (58% need-based, 42% non-need-based). ***Programs:*** Federal Direct (Subsidized and Unsubsidized Stafford, PLUS), state.

WORK-STUDY ***Federal work-study:*** Total amount: $64,417; jobs available. ***State or other work-study/employment:*** Total amount: $220,000 (100% need-based). Part-time jobs available.

APPLYING FOR FINANCIAL AID ***Required financial aid form:*** FAFSA. ***Financial aid deadline:*** 4/1 (priority: 3/1). ***Notification date:*** Continuous beginning 3/1. Students must reply by 5/1 or within 2 weeks of notification.

CONTACT Ms. Laura Link, Director of Financial Aid, Minneapolis College of Art and Design, 2501 Stevens Avenue South, Minneapolis, MN 55404-4347, 612-874-3733 or toll-free 800-874-6223. *Fax:* 612-874-3701. *E-mail:* laura_link@mead.edu.
Website: http://www.mcad.edu/.

MINNESOTA STATE UNIVERSITY MANKATO

Mankato, MN

Tuition & fees: N/R	Average undergraduate aid package: $9901

ABOUT THE INSTITUTION State-supported, coed. ***Awards:*** certificates, associate, bachelor's, master's, and doctoral degrees. 108 undergraduate majors. ***Total enrollment:*** 1,847. Undergraduates: 12,450. Federal methodology is used as a basis for awarding need-based institutional aid.

UNDERGRADUATE EXPENSES for 2020–2021 ***Application fee:*** $20. ***Tuition, area resident:*** part-time $289 per credit hour. ***Tuition, state resident:*** part-time $289 per credit hour. ***Tuition, nonresident:*** part-time $622 per credit hour.

FRESHMAN FINANCIAL AID (Fall 2019, est.) 2016 applied for aid; of those 64% were deemed to have need. 100% of freshmen with need received aid; of those 20% had need fully met. ***Average percent of need met:*** 71% (excluding resources awarded to replace EFC). ***Average financial aid package:*** $9795 (excluding resources awarded to replace EFC). 12% of all full-time freshmen had no need and received non-need-based gift aid.

UNDERGRADUATE FINANCIAL AID (Fall 2019, est.) 7,931 applied for aid; of those 65% were deemed to have need. 100% of undergraduates with need received aid; of those 23% had need fully met. ***Average percent of need met:*** 74% (excluding resources awarded to replace EFC). ***Average financial aid package:*** $9901 (excluding resources awarded to replace EFC). 13% of all full-time undergraduates had no need and received non-need-based gift aid.

GIFT AID (NEED-BASED) ***Receiving aid:*** Freshmen: 47% (1,054); all full-time undergraduates: 40% (4,124). ***Average award:*** Freshmen: $6441; Undergraduates: $6236. ***Scholarships, grants, and awards:*** Federal Pell, FSEOG, state, private, college/university gift aid from institutional funds.

GIFT AID (NON-NEED-BASED) ***Receiving aid:*** Freshmen: 5% (114). Undergraduates: 5% (515). ***Average award:*** Freshmen: $3950. Undergraduates: $5533. ***Scholarships, grants, and awards by category:*** *Academic interests/*

achievement: general academic interests/achievements. *Creative arts/performance:* applied art and design, general creative arts/performance, music, performing arts, theater/drama. *Special achievements/activities:* leadership. *Special characteristics:* children and siblings of alumni, members of minority groups. ***ROTC:*** Army.

LOANS ***Student loans:*** 71% of past graduating class borrowed through all loan programs. *Average indebtedness per student:* $30,482. ***Average need-based loan:*** Freshmen: $3302. Undergraduates: $3974. ***Programs:*** Federal Direct (Subsidized and Unsubsidized Stafford, PLUS), state, Private student loans.

WORK-STUDY ***Federal work-study:*** 474 jobs averaging $3657. ***State or other work-study/employment:*** 511 part-time jobs averaging $3646.

APPLYING FOR FINANCIAL AID ***Required financial aid forms:*** FAFSA, Private Loan application, PLUS Loan application. ***Notification date:*** Continuous.

CONTACT Mr. Tyler Heu, Director of Financial Aid, Minnesota State University Mankato, 120 Wigley Administration Center, Mankato, MN 56001, 507-389-1866 or toll-free 800-722-0544. *Fax:* 507-389-6410. *E-mail:* campushub@mnsu.edu. *Website:* http://mankato.mnsu.edu/.

MINNESOTA STATE UNIVERSITY MOORHEAD

Moorhead, MN

Tuition & fees: N/R	Average undergraduate aid package: $3392

ABOUT THE INSTITUTION State-supported, coed. ***Awards:*** certificates, bachelor's, master's, and doctoral degrees. 82 undergraduate majors. ***Total enrollment:*** 5,860. Undergraduates: 4,828. Freshmen: 795. Federal methodology is used as a basis for awarding need-based institutional aid.

FRESHMAN FINANCIAL AID (Fall 2019, est.) 725 applied for aid; of those 70% were deemed to have need. 99% of freshmen with need received aid. ***Average financial aid package:*** $2986 (excluding resources awarded to replace EFC).

UNDERGRADUATE FINANCIAL AID (Fall 2019, est.) 3,082 applied for aid; of those 76% were deemed to have need. 99% of undergraduates with need received aid. ***Average financial aid package:*** $3392 (excluding resources awarded to replace EFC).

GIFT AID (NEED-BASED) ***Total amount:*** $10,093,268 (60% federal, 37% state, 1% institutional, 2% external sources). ***Receiving aid:*** Freshmen: 43% (336); all full-time undergraduates: 42% (1,591). ***Average award:*** Freshmen: $2885; Undergraduates: $3035. ***Scholarships, grants, and awards:*** Federal Pell, FSEOG, state, private, college/university gift aid from institutional funds, TEACH Grants.

GIFT AID (NON-NEED-BASED) ***Total amount:*** $4,299,004 (11% federal, 3% state, 60% institutional, 26% external sources). ***Receiving aid:*** Freshmen: 45% (351). Undergraduates: 25% (940). ***Scholarships, grants, and awards by category:*** *Academic interests/achievement:* biological sciences, business, communication, computer science, education, engineering/technologies, English, general academic interests/achievements, home economics, international studies, mathematics, physical sciences, premedicine, social sciences. *Creative arts/performance:* applied art and design, cinema/film/broadcasting, creative writing, music, theater/drama. *Special achievements/activities:* community service, general special achievements/activities. *Special characteristics:* adult students, children of faculty/staff, first-generation college students, members of minority groups, out-of-state students. ***ROTC:*** Army cooperative, Air Force cooperative.

LOANS ***Student loans:*** $29,978,503 (35% need-based, 65% non-need-based). 86% of past graduating class borrowed through all loan programs. *Average indebtedness per student:* $31,205. ***Average need-based loan:*** Freshmen: $3331. Undergraduates: $4058. ***Parent loans:*** $705,170 (100% non-need-based). ***Programs:*** Federal Direct (Subsidized and Unsubsidized Stafford, PLUS), state, private loans.

WORK-STUDY ***Federal work-study:*** Total amount: $559,058; 210 jobs averaging $2763. ***State or other work-study/employment:*** Total amount: $1,725,552 (28% need-based, 72% non-need-based). 180 part-time jobs averaging $2760.

ATHLETIC AWARDS Total amount: $1,131,035 (100% non-need-based).

APPLYING FOR FINANCIAL AID ***Required financial aid form:*** FAFSA. ***Financial aid deadline:*** Continuous. ***Notification date:*** Continuous beginning 7/1. Students must reply within 2 weeks of notification.

CONTACT Ms. Melissa Dingmann, Director of Financial Aid, Minnesota State University Moorhead, 1104 7th Avenue South, Moorhead, MN 56563, 218-477-2251 or toll-free 800-593-7246. *Fax:* 218-477-2058. *E-mail:* finaid@mnstate.edu. *Website:* http://www.mnstate.edu/.

MINOT STATE UNIVERSITY

Minot, ND

Tuition & fees (ND res): $7590	Average undergraduate aid package: $10,445

ABOUT THE INSTITUTION State-supported, coed. ***Awards:*** certificates, associate, bachelor's, and master's degrees. 58 undergraduate majors. ***Total enrollment:*** 3,121. Undergraduates: 2,832. Freshmen: 399. Federal methodology is used as a basis for awarding need-based institutional aid.

UNDERGRADUATE EXPENSES for 2019–2020 ***Application fee:*** $35. ***Tuition, state resident:*** full-time $6087; part-time $254 per credit hour. ***Tuition, nonresident:*** full-time $6087; part-time $254 per credit hour. ***Required fees:*** full-time $1503; $62.65 per credit hour. Full-time tuition and fees vary according to class time, course load, degree level, location, program, and reciprocity agreements. Part-time tuition and fees vary according to class time, course load, degree level, location, program, and reciprocity agreements. ***College room and board:*** $7315; ***Room only:*** $2865. Room and board charges vary according to board plan and housing facility.

FRESHMAN FINANCIAL AID (Fall 2018) 302 applied for aid; of those 59% were deemed to have need. 99% of freshmen with need received aid; of those 28% had need fully met. ***Average percent of need met:*** 69% (excluding resources awarded to replace EFC). ***Average financial aid package:*** $9560 (excluding resources awarded to replace EFC). 18% of all full-time freshmen had no need and received non-need-based gift aid.

UNDERGRADUATE FINANCIAL AID (Fall 2018) 1,394 applied for aid; of those 69% were deemed to have need. 97% of undergraduates with need received aid; of those 38% had need fully met. ***Average percent of need met:*** 70% (excluding resources awarded to replace EFC). ***Average financial aid package:*** $10,445 (excluding resources awarded to replace EFC). 14% of all full-time undergraduates had no need and received non-need-based gift aid.

GIFT AID (NEED-BASED) ***Total amount:*** $4,666,004 (59% federal, 17% state, 10% institutional, 14% external sources). ***Receiving aid:*** Freshmen: 44% (170); all full-time undergraduates: 43% (852). ***Average award:*** Freshmen: $5900; Undergraduates: $5547. ***Scholarships, grants, and awards:*** Federal Pell, FSEOG, state, private, college/university gift aid from institutional funds.

GIFT AID (NON-NEED-BASED) ***Total amount:*** $1,122,052 (1% federal, 22% state, 32% institutional, 45% external sources). ***Receiving aid:*** Freshmen: 4% (15). Undergraduates: 3% (55). ***Average award:*** Freshmen: $999. Undergraduates: $1240. ***Scholarships, grants, and awards by category:*** *Academic interests/achievement:* biological sciences, business, communication, computer science, education, English, foreign languages, general academic interests/achievements, health fields, home economics, humanities, mathematics, social sciences. *Creative arts/performance:* applied art and design, cinema/film/broadcasting, music, performing arts, theater/drama. *Special characteristics:* children and siblings of alumni, children of faculty/staff, ethnic background, international students, local/state students, members of minority groups, out-of-state students, veterans. ***Tuition waivers:*** Full or partial for minority students, children of alumni, employees or children of employees, senior citizens.

LOANS ***Student loans:*** $7,879,750 (54% need-based, 46% non-need-based). 42% of past graduating class borrowed through all loan programs. *Average indebtedness per student:* $25,324. ***Average need-based loan:*** Freshmen: $4132. Undergraduates: $5527. ***Parent loans:*** $132,790 (23% need-based, 77% non-need-based). ***Programs:*** Federal Direct (Subsidized and Unsubsidized Stafford, PLUS), Federal Nursing, state, alternative loans.

WORK-STUDY ***Federal work-study:*** Total amount: $121,010; 85 jobs averaging $1492.

ATHLETIC AWARDS Total amount: $1,017,687 (74% need-based, 26% non-need-based).

APPLYING FOR FINANCIAL AID ***Required financial aid forms:*** FAFSA, institutional scholarship application form. ***Financial aid deadline (priority):*** 4/15. ***Notification date:*** Continuous beginning 3/15. Students must reply within 4 weeks of notification.

CONTACT Ms. Laurie Weber, Director of Financial Aid, Minot State University, 500 University Avenue, West, Minot, ND 58707-0002, 701-858-3875 or toll-free 800-777-0750 Ext.3350. *Fax:* 701-858-4310. *E-mail:* laurie.weber@minotstateu.edu. *Website:* http://www.minotstateu.edu/.

MIRRER YESHIVA CENTRAL INSTITUTE

Brooklyn, NY

CONTACT Financial Aid Office, Mirrer Yeshiva Central Institute, 1795 Ocean Parkway, Brooklyn, NY 11223-2010, 718-645-0536.

MISERICORDIA UNIVERSITY

Dallas, PA

Tuition & fees: $34,560	Average undergraduate aid package: $25,422

ABOUT THE INSTITUTION Independent Roman Catholic, coed. ***Awards:*** certificates, bachelor's, master's, and doctoral degrees. 33 undergraduate majors. ***Total enrollment:*** 2,544. Undergraduates: 1,964. Freshmen: 414. Federal methodology is used as a basis for awarding need-based institutional aid.

UNDERGRADUATE EXPENSES for 2020–2021 ***Application fee:*** $35. ***Comprehensive fee:*** $48,780 includes full-time tuition ($32,800), mandatory fees ($1760), and room and board ($14,220). ***College room only:*** $7800. ***Part-time tuition:*** $615 per credit hour.

FRESHMAN FINANCIAL AID (Fall 2019, est.) 402 applied for aid; of those 87% were deemed to have need. 100% of freshmen with need received aid; of those 23% had need fully met. ***Average percent of need met:*** 81% (excluding resources awarded to replace EFC). ***Average financial aid package:*** $25,954 (excluding resources awarded to replace EFC). 13% of all full-time freshmen had no need and received non-need-based gift aid.

UNDERGRADUATE FINANCIAL AID (Fall 2019, est.) 1,465 applied for aid; of those 88% were deemed to have need. 100% of undergraduates with need received aid; of those 26% had need fully met. ***Average percent of need met:*** 81% (excluding resources awarded to replace EFC). ***Average financial aid package:*** $25,422 (excluding resources awarded to replace EFC). 11% of all full-time undergraduates had no need and received non-need-based gift aid.

GIFT AID (NEED-BASED) ***Total amount:*** $25,268,303 (9% federal, 7% state, 83% institutional, 1% external sources). ***Receiving aid:*** Freshmen: 85% (348); all full-time undergraduates: 81% (1,286). ***Average award:*** Freshmen: $20,580; Undergraduates: $19,101. ***Scholarships, grants, and awards:*** Federal Pell, FSEOG, state, private, college/university gift aid from institutional funds.

GIFT AID (NON-NEED-BASED) ***Total amount:*** $6,627,868 (98% institutional, 2% external sources). ***Receiving aid:*** Freshmen: 17% (69). Undergraduates: 16% (255). ***Average award:*** Freshmen: $17,095. Undergraduates: $16,206. ***Scholarships, grants, and awards by category:*** *Academic interests/achievement:* general academic interests/achievements. *Special achievements/activities:* community service, general special achievements/activities, leadership. *Special characteristics:* children and siblings of alumni, children of current students, children of faculty/staff, general special characteristics, members of minority groups, out-of-state students, previous college experience, relatives of clergy, siblings of current students. ***ROTC:*** Army cooperative, Air Force cooperative.

LOANS ***Student loans:*** $17,586,482 (63% need-based, 37% non-need-based). 84% of past graduating class borrowed through all loan programs. *Average indebtedness per student:* $46,756. ***Average need-based loan:*** Freshmen: $8188. Undergraduates: $8941. ***Parent loans:*** $4,468,045 (42% need-based, 58% non-need-based). ***Programs:*** Federal Direct (Subsidized and Unsubsidized Stafford, PLUS), Federal Nursing.

WORK-STUDY Federal work-study jobs available.

APPLYING FOR FINANCIAL AID ***Required financial aid form:*** FAFSA. ***Financial aid deadline (priority):*** 11/1.

CONTACT Susan Fronzoni, Director of Student Financial Services, Misericordia University, 301 Lake Street, Dallas, PA 18612-1098, 866-262-6363. *E-mail:* finaid@misericordia.edu. *Website:* http://www.misericordia.edu/.

MISSISSIPPI COLLEGE

Clinton, MS

CONTACT Mrs. Karon Q. McMillan, Director of Financial Aid, Mississippi College, Box 4035, 200 South Capitol Street, Clinton, MS 39058-0001, 601-925-3249 or toll-free 800-738-1236. *Fax:* 601-925-3950. *E-mail:* kmcmilla@mc.edu. *Website:* http://www.mc.edu/.

MISSISSIPPI STATE UNIVERSITY

Mississippi State, MS

Tuition & fees (MS res): $8910	Average undergraduate aid package: $15,082

ABOUT THE INSTITUTION State-supported, coed. ***Awards:*** certificates, associate, bachelor's, master's, and doctoral degrees. 80 undergraduate majors. ***Total enrollment:*** 22,226. Undergraduates: 18,792. Freshmen: 3,500. Federal methodology is used as a basis for awarding need-based institutional aid.

UNDERGRADUATE EXPENSES for 2019–2020 ***Application fee:*** $40. ***One-time required fee:*** $110. ***Tuition, state resident:*** full-time $8800; part-time $371 per credit hour. ***Tuition, nonresident:*** full-time $23,840; part-time $998 per credit hour. ***Required fees:*** full-time $110. Full-time tuition and fees vary according to degree level, location, and reciprocity agreements. Part-time tuition and fees vary according to course load, degree level, location, and reciprocity agreements. ***College room and board:*** $10,436; ***Room only:*** $6440. Room and board charges vary according to board plan, housing facility, and student level. ***Payment plan:*** Tuition prepayment.

FRESHMAN FINANCIAL AID (Fall 2018) 3115 applied for aid; of those 83% were deemed to have need. 99% of freshmen with need received aid; of those 25% had need fully met. ***Average percent of need met:*** 55% (excluding resources awarded to replace EFC). ***Average financial aid package:*** $16,164 (excluding resources awarded to replace EFC). 15% of all full-time freshmen had no need and received non-need-based gift aid.

UNDERGRADUATE FINANCIAL AID (Fall 2018) 12,632 applied for aid; of those 87% were deemed to have need. 98% of undergraduates with need received aid; of those 21% had need fully met. ***Average percent of need met:*** 56% (excluding resources awarded to replace EFC). ***Average financial aid package:*** $15,082 (excluding resources awarded to replace EFC). 14% of all full-time undergraduates had no need and received non-need-based gift aid.

GIFT AID (NEED-BASED) ***Total amount:*** $74,277,971 (42% federal, 12% state, 38% institutional, 8% external sources). ***Receiving aid:*** Freshmen: 69% (2,463); all full-time undergraduates: 58% (9,793). ***Average award:*** Freshmen: $7189; Undergraduates: $6973. ***Scholarships, grants, and awards:*** Federal Pell, FSEOG, state, private, college/university gift aid from institutional funds, United Negro College Fund.

GIFT AID (NON-NEED-BASED) ***Total amount:*** $24,529,023 (8% state, 85% institutional, 7% external sources). ***Receiving aid:*** Freshmen: 11% (401). Undergraduates: 5% (838). ***Average award:*** Freshmen: $5227. Undergraduates: $4751. ***Scholarships, grants, and awards by category:*** *Academic interests/achievement:* agriculture, architecture, area/ethnic studies, biological sciences, business, communication, computer science, education, engineering/technologies, English, foreign languages, general academic interests/achievements, health fields, home economics, humanities, international studies, library science, mathematics, military science, physical sciences, premedicine, religion/biblical studies, social sciences. *Creative arts/performance:* applied art and design, art/fine arts, cinema/film/broadcasting, creative writing, dance, debating, general creative arts/performance, journalism/publications, music, performing arts, theater/drama. *Special achievements/activities:* cheerleading/drum major, general special achievements/activities, junior miss, leadership, memberships. *Special characteristics:* adult students, children and siblings of alumni, children of educators, children of faculty/staff, children of public servants, first-generation college students, handicapped students, local/state students, out-of-state students, previous college experience, spouses of deceased or disabled public servants. ***Tuition***

waivers: Full or partial for children of alumni, employees or children of employees, senior citizens. ***ROTC:*** Army, Air Force.
LOANS *Student loans:* $100,816,097 (84% need-based, 16% non-need-based). 55% of past graduating class borrowed through all loan programs. *Average indebtedness per student:* $31,060. ***Average need-based loan:*** Freshmen: $3199. Undergraduates: $3710. ***Parent loans:*** $27,751,203 (69% need-based, 31% non-need-based). ***Programs:*** Federal Direct (Subsidized and Unsubsidized Stafford, PLUS), Perkins, college/university.
WORK-STUDY *Federal work-study:* Total amount: $1,657,597; 459 jobs averaging $3611.
ATHLETIC AWARDS Total amount: $9,860,261 (100% non-need-based).
APPLYING FOR FINANCIAL AID *Required financial aid forms:* FAFSA, state aid form, general scholarship application. ***Financial aid deadline (priority):*** 3/1. ***Notification date:*** Continuous beginning 12/1. Students must reply by 5/1.
CONTACT Dr. Kenneth Paul McKinney, Director of Financial Aid, Mississippi State University, PO Box 6035, Mississippi State, MS 39762, 662-325-7428. *Fax:* 662-325-0702. *E-mail:* financialaid@saffairs.msstate.edu.
Website: http://www.msstate.edu/.

MISSISSIPPI UNIVERSITY FOR WOMEN

Columbus, MS

CONTACT Ms. Nicole Patrick, Director of Financial Aid, Mississippi University for Women, 1100 College Street, MUW 1614, Columbus, MS 39701-4044, 662-329-7114 or toll-free 877-GO 2 THE W. *Fax:* 662-329-7325. *E-mail:* jnpatrick@muw.edu.
Website: http://www.muw.edu/.

MISSISSIPPI VALLEY STATE UNIVERSITY

Itta Bena, MS

CONTACT Margaret Sherrer, Director of Student Financial Aid, Mississippi Valley State University, 14000 Highway 82W #7268, Itta Bena, MS 38941-1400, 662-254-3335 or toll-free 800-844-6885 (in-state). *Fax:* 662-254-7900. *E-mail:* margaret.sherrer@mvsu.edu.
Website: http://www.mvsu.edu/.

MISSOURI BAPTIST UNIVERSITY

St. Louis, MO

Tuition & fees: $28,220	Average undergraduate aid package: $20,499

ABOUT THE INSTITUTION Independent Southern Baptist, coed. ***Awards:*** certificates, associate, bachelor's, master's, and doctoral degrees. 56 undergraduate majors. ***Total enrollment:*** 5,313. Undergraduates: 4,413. Freshmen: 249. Federal methodology is used as a basis for awarding need-based institutional aid.
UNDERGRADUATE EXPENSES for 2019–2020 *Application fee:* $35. ***Comprehensive fee:*** $37,290 includes full-time tuition ($26,860), mandatory fees ($1360), and room and board ($9070). Full-time tuition and fees vary according to course load, location, and program. Room and board charges vary according to board plan and housing facility. ***Part-time tuition:*** $929 per credit hour. ***Part-time fees:*** $29 per credit hour. Part-time tuition and fees vary according to course load, location, and program.
FRESHMAN FINANCIAL AID (Fall 2019, est.) 247 applied for aid; of those 83% were deemed to have need. 100% of freshmen with need received aid; of those 52% had need fully met. ***Average financial aid package:*** $24,172 (excluding resources awarded to replace EFC). 9% of all full-time freshmen had no need and received non-need-based gift aid.
UNDERGRADUATE FINANCIAL AID (Fall 2019, est.) 1,276 applied for aid; of those 88% were deemed to have need. 100% of undergraduates with need received aid; of those 36% had need fully met. ***Average financial aid package:*** $20,499 (excluding resources awarded to replace EFC). 5% of all full-time undergraduates had no need and received non-need-based gift aid.
GIFT AID (NEED-BASED) *Total amount:* $17,308,650 (37% federal, 9% state, 46% institutional, 8% external sources). ***Receiving aid:*** Freshmen: 58% (164); all full-time undergraduates: 60% (895). ***Average award:*** Freshmen: $5896; Undergraduates: $5459. ***Scholarships, grants, and awards:*** Federal Pell, FSEOG, state, private, college/university gift aid from institutional funds.
GIFT AID (NON-NEED-BASED) *Total amount:* $1,407,556 (2% federal, 1% state, 87% institutional, 10% external sources). ***Receiving aid:*** Freshmen: 71% (203). Undergraduates: 62% (913). ***Average award:*** Freshmen: $6125. Undergraduates: $9443. ***Scholarships, grants, and awards by category:*** *Academic interests/achievement:* general academic interests/achievements, religion/biblical studies. *Creative arts/performance:* music, theater/drama. *Special achievements/activities:* cheerleading/drum major, memberships, religious involvement. *Special characteristics:* adult students, children and siblings of alumni, children of current students, children of faculty/staff, first-generation college students, parents of current students, public servants, relatives of clergy, religious affiliation, siblings of current students, spouses of current students, veterans. ***Tuition waivers:*** Full or partial for children of alumni, employees or children of employees, senior citizens. ***ROTC:*** Army cooperative.
LOANS *Student loans:* $21,101,413 (93% need-based, 7% non-need-based). 92% of past graduating class borrowed through all loan programs. *Average indebtedness per student:* $25,674. ***Average need-based loan:*** Freshmen: $4282. Undergraduates: $4801. ***Parent loans:*** $4,709,249 (88% need-based, 12% non-need-based). ***Programs:*** Federal Direct (Subsidized and Unsubsidized Stafford, PLUS).
WORK-STUDY *Federal work-study:* Total amount: $2,617,164.08; 573 jobs averaging $1976. ***State or other work-study/employment:*** Part-time jobs available.
ATHLETIC AWARDS Total amount: $18,559,487 (87% need-based, 13% non-need-based).
APPLYING FOR FINANCIAL AID *Required financial aid forms:* FAFSA, institution's own form. ***Financial aid deadline (priority):*** 4/1. ***Notification date:*** Continuous beginning 4/15. Students must reply within 2 weeks of notification.
CONTACT Mr. Zach Greenlee, Director of Student Financial Services, Missouri Baptist University, One College Park Drive, St. Louis, MO 63141, 314-392-2398 or toll-free 877-434-1115 Ext.2290. *Fax:* 314-744-5320. *E-mail:* Zach.Greenlee@mobap.edu.
Website: http://www.mobap.edu/.

MISSOURI SOUTHERN STATE UNIVERSITY

Joplin, MO

Tuition & fees: N/R	Average undergraduate aid package: $9838

ABOUT THE INSTITUTION State-supported, coed. ***Awards:*** certificates, associate, bachelor's, and master's degrees. 51 undergraduate majors. ***Total enrollment:*** 5,604. Undergraduates: 5,475. Freshmen: 729. Institutional methodology is used as a basis for awarding need-based institutional aid.
FRESHMAN FINANCIAL AID (Fall 2019, est.) 667 applied for aid; of those 79% were deemed to have need. 99% of freshmen with need received aid; of those 13% had need fully met. ***Average percent of need met:*** 39% (excluding resources awarded to replace EFC). ***Average financial aid package:*** $9225 (excluding resources awarded to replace EFC). 16% of all full-time freshmen had no need and received non-need-based gift aid.
UNDERGRADUATE FINANCIAL AID (Fall 2019, est.) 3,591 applied for aid; of those 80% were deemed to have need. 97% of undergraduates with need received aid; of those 17% had need fully met. ***Average percent of need met:*** 43% (excluding resources awarded to replace EFC). ***Average financial aid package:*** $9838 (excluding resources awarded to replace EFC). 12% of all full-time undergraduates had no need and received non-need-based gift aid.
GIFT AID (NEED-BASED) *Total amount:* $12,979,886 (82% federal, 18% state). ***Receiving aid:*** Freshmen: 63% (426); all full-time undergraduates: 59% (2,247). ***Average award:*** Freshmen: $5314; Undergraduates: $5230. ***Scholarships, grants, and awards:*** Federal Pell, FSEOG, state, private, college/university gift aid from institutional funds, TEACH Grants.
GIFT AID (NON-NEED-BASED) *Total amount:* $5,653,070 (3% state, 79% institutional, 18% external sources). ***Receiving aid:*** Freshmen: 52% (353). Undergraduates: 37% (1,414). ***Average award:*** Freshmen: $2548. Undergraduates: $2548. ***Scholarships, grants, and awards by category:*** *Academic interests/achievement:* general academic interests/achievements. *Creative arts/performance:*

applied art and design, journalism/publications, music, theater/drama. *Special achievements/activities:* cheerleading/drum major, general special achievements/activities, leadership. *Special characteristics:* veterans. **ROTC:** Army.

LOANS *Student loans:* $16,204,422 (45% need-based, 55% non-need-based). 59% of past graduating class borrowed through all loan programs. *Average indebtedness per student:* $22,514. ***Average need-based loan:*** Freshmen: $2760. Undergraduates: $3603. ***Parent loans:*** $399,929 (100% non-need-based). ***Programs:*** Federal Direct (Subsidized and Unsubsidized Stafford, PLUS), Perkins.

WORK-STUDY *Federal work-study:* Total amount: $222,026; jobs available. ***State or other work-study/employment:*** Total amount: $706,254 (100% non-need-based). Part-time jobs available.

ATHLETIC AWARDS Total amount: $2,092,256 (100% non-need-based).

APPLYING FOR FINANCIAL AID *Required financial aid form:* FAFSA. ***Financial aid deadline:*** Continuous. ***Notification date:*** Continuous beginning 3/15. Students must reply by 5/1.

CONTACT Becca L. Diskin, Director of Financial Aid, Missouri Southern State University, 3950 Newman Road, Joplin, MO 64801-1595, 417-659-5422 or toll-free 866-818-MSSU. *Fax:* 417-659-4474. *E-mail:* diskin-b@mssu.edu. *Website:* http://www.mssu.edu/.

MISSOURI STATE UNIVERSITY

Springfield, MO

Tuition & fees (MO res): $7588	Average undergraduate aid package: $11,542

ABOUT THE INSTITUTION State-supported, coed. ***Awards:*** certificates, bachelor's, master's, and doctoral degrees. 95 undergraduate majors. ***Total enrollment:*** 23,453. Undergraduates: 19,801. Freshmen: 2,679. Federal methodology is used as a basis for awarding need-based institutional aid.

UNDERGRADUATE EXPENSES for 2019–2020 *Tuition, state resident:* full-time $6540; part-time $218 per credit hour. ***Tuition, nonresident:*** full-time $14,850; part-time $495 per credit hour. ***Required fees:*** full-time $1048; $524 per term. Full-time tuition and fees vary according to course level, course load, and program. Part-time tuition and fees vary according to course level, course load, and program. ***College room and board:*** $9128; ***Room only:*** $6486. Room and board charges vary according to board plan, housing facility, and location.

FRESHMAN FINANCIAL AID (Fall 2019, est.) 2310 applied for aid; of those 66% were deemed to have need. 99% of freshmen with need received aid; of those 19% had need fully met. ***Average percent of need met:*** 71% (excluding resources awarded to replace EFC). ***Average financial aid package:*** $12,012 (excluding resources awarded to replace EFC). 23% of all full-time freshmen had no need and received non-need-based gift aid.

UNDERGRADUATE FINANCIAL AID (Fall 2019, est.) 10,935 applied for aid; of those 74% were deemed to have need. 97% of undergraduates with need received aid; of those 16% had need fully met. ***Average percent of need met:*** 68% (excluding resources awarded to replace EFC). ***Average financial aid package:*** $11,542 (excluding resources awarded to replace EFC). 15% of all full-time undergraduates had no need and received non-need-based gift aid.

GIFT AID (NEED-BASED) *Total amount:* $42,350,871 (55% federal, 21% state, 20% institutional, 4% external sources). ***Receiving aid:*** Freshmen: 50% (1,319); all full-time undergraduates: 46% (6,444). ***Average award:*** Freshmen: $7030; Undergraduates: $6152. ***Scholarships, grants, and awards:*** Federal Pell, FSEOG, state, private, college/university gift aid from institutional funds.

GIFT AID (NON-NEED-BASED) *Total amount:* $12,553,302 (7% federal, 13% state, 61% institutional, 19% external sources). ***Receiving aid:*** Freshmen: 9% (236). Undergraduates: 5% (669). ***Average award:*** Freshmen: $3368. Undergraduates: $3283. ***Scholarships, grants, and awards by category:*** *Academic interests/achievement:* general academic interests/achievements. *Creative arts/performance:* general creative arts/performance. *Special achievements/activities:* leadership. *Special characteristics:* children and siblings of alumni, local/state students, members of minority groups. ***Tuition waivers:*** Full or partial for children of alumni, employees or children of employees, senior citizens. ***ROTC:*** Army.

LOANS *Student loans:* $70,602,003 (59% need-based, 41% non-need-based). 63% of past graduating class borrowed through all loan programs. *Average indebtedness per student:* $26,446. ***Average need-based loan:*** Freshmen: $3187. Undergraduates: $4150. ***Parent loans:*** $7,095,756 (36% need-based, 64% non-need-based). ***Programs:*** Federal Direct (Subsidized and Unsubsidized Stafford, PLUS), Perkins.

WORK-STUDY *Federal work-study:* Total amount: $1,092,014; jobs available.

ATHLETIC AWARDS Total amount: $4,712,883 (25% need-based, 75% non-need-based).

APPLYING FOR FINANCIAL AID *Required financial aid form:* FAFSA. ***Financial aid deadline (priority):*** 3/31. ***Notification date:*** Continuous beginning 3/31.

CONTACT Robert G Moore, Director of Financial Aid, Missouri State University, 901 South National Avenue, Springfield, MO 65804, 417-836-5262 or toll-free 800-492-7900. *E-mail:* financialaid@missouristate.edu. *Website:* http://www.missouristate.edu/.

MISSOURI UNIVERSITY OF SCIENCE AND TECHNOLOGY

Rolla, MO

Tuition & fees (area res): $10,653	Average undergraduate aid package: $14,487

ABOUT THE INSTITUTION State-supported, coed. ***Awards:*** certificates, bachelor's, master's, and doctoral degrees. 39 undergraduate majors. ***Total enrollment:*** 8,096. Undergraduates: 6,462. Freshmen: 1,145. Federal methodology is used as a basis for awarding need-based institutional aid.

UNDERGRADUATE EXPENSES for 2019–2020 *Application fee:* $50. ***Tuition, area resident:*** full-time $8973. ***Tuition, state resident:*** full-time $8973. ***Tuition, nonresident:*** full-time $27,921. ***Required fees:*** full-time $1680. Full-time tuition and fees vary according to course load, degree level, program, and student level. Part-time tuition and fees vary according to course load, degree level, program, and student level. ***College room and board:*** $10,402; ***Room only:*** $6855. Room and board charges vary according to board plan, housing facility, and location.

FRESHMAN FINANCIAL AID (Fall 2019, est.) 1031 applied for aid; of those 63% were deemed to have need. 100% of freshmen with need received aid; of those 53% had need fully met. ***Average percent of need met:*** 88% (excluding resources awarded to replace EFC). ***Average financial aid package:*** $16,303 (excluding resources awarded to replace EFC). 40% of all full-time freshmen had no need and received non-need-based gift aid.

UNDERGRADUATE FINANCIAL AID (Fall 2019, est.) 4,311 applied for aid; of those 73% were deemed to have need. 99% of undergraduates with need received aid; of those 37% had need fully met. ***Average percent of need met:*** 77% (excluding resources awarded to replace EFC). ***Average financial aid package:*** $14,487 (excluding resources awarded to replace EFC). 31% of all full-time undergraduates had no need and received non-need-based gift aid.

GIFT AID (NEED-BASED) *Total amount:* $25,961,064 (30% federal, 15% state, 53% institutional, 2% external sources). ***Receiving aid:*** Freshmen: 55% (629); all full-time undergraduates: 51% (2,916). ***Average award:*** Freshmen: $11,453; Undergraduates: $9070. ***Scholarships, grants, and awards:*** Federal Pell, FSEOG, state, private, college/university gift aid from institutional funds.

GIFT AID (NON-NEED-BASED) *Total amount:* $22,750,831 (16% state, 69% institutional, 15% external sources). ***Receiving aid:*** Freshmen: 30% (339). Undergraduates: 19% (1,076). ***Average award:*** Freshmen: $8513. Undergraduates: $6666. ***Scholarships, grants, and awards by category:*** *Academic interests/achievement:* biological sciences, business, communication, computer science, education, engineering/technologies, English, general academic interests/achievements, humanities, international studies, mathematics, military science, physical sciences, premedicine, social sciences. *Creative arts/performance:* music, theater/drama. *Special characteristics:* children and siblings of alumni, children of faculty/staff, children of union members/company employees, members of minority groups, out-of-state students. ***Tuition waivers:*** Full or partial for employees or children of employees. ***ROTC:*** Army, Air Force.

LOANS *Student loans:* $51,976,640 (49% need-based, 51% non-need-based). 62% of past graduating class borrowed through all loan programs. *Average indebtedness per student:* $30,168. ***Average need-based loan:*** Freshmen: $4571. Undergraduates: $5608. ***Parent loans:*** $80,560,279 (11% need-based, 89% non-need-based). ***Programs:*** Federal Direct (Subsidized and Unsubsidized Stafford, PLUS), college/university.

WORK-STUDY ***Federal work-study:*** Total amount: $815,953; jobs available. ***State or other work-study/employment:*** Total amount: $3,957,766 (14% need-based, 86% non-need-based). Part-time jobs available.

ATHLETIC AWARDS Total amount: $3,830,094 (32% need-based, 68% non-need-based).

APPLYING FOR FINANCIAL AID ***Required financial aid form:*** FAFSA. ***Financial aid deadline (priority):*** 2/1. ***Notification date:*** Continuous beginning 3/15.

CONTACT Ms. Bridgette Betz, Director of Student Financial Assistance, Missouri University of Science and Technology, G1 Parker Hall, Rolla, MO 65409, 573-341-4282 or toll-free 800-522-0938. *Fax:* 573-341-4274. *E-mail:* berry@mst.edu.
Website: http://www.mst.edu/.

MISSOURI VALLEY COLLEGE

Marshall, MO

Tuition & fees: $21,100	Average undergraduate aid package: $17,190

ABOUT THE INSTITUTION Independent Presbyterian Church, coed. ***Awards:*** associate, bachelor's, and master's degrees. 59 undergraduate majors. ***Total enrollment:*** 1,768. Undergraduates: 1,740. Freshmen: 436. Both federal and institutional methodology are used as a basis for awarding need-based institutional aid.

UNDERGRADUATE EXPENSES for 2019–2020 ***Comprehensive fee:*** $30,500 includes full-time tuition ($19,700), mandatory fees ($1400), and room and board ($9400). ***College room only:*** $5000. Full-time tuition and fees vary according to program. Room and board charges vary according to board plan, gender, housing facility, location, and student level. ***Part-time tuition:*** $350 per credit hour. Part-time tuition and fees vary according to program. ***Payment plan:*** Tuition prepayment.

FRESHMAN FINANCIAL AID (Fall 2018) 315 applied for aid; of those 86% were deemed to have need. 100% of freshmen with need received aid; of those 8% had need fully met. ***Average percent of need met:*** 58% (excluding resources awarded to replace EFC). ***Average financial aid package:*** $16,713 (excluding resources awarded to replace EFC). 35% of all full-time freshmen had no need and received non-need-based gift aid.

UNDERGRADUATE FINANCIAL AID (Fall 2018) 815 applied for aid; of those 87% were deemed to have need. 100% of undergraduates with need received aid; of those 8% had need fully met. ***Average percent of need met:*** 64% (excluding resources awarded to replace EFC). ***Average financial aid package:*** $17,190 (excluding resources awarded to replace EFC). 20% of all full-time undergraduates had no need and received non-need-based gift aid.

GIFT AID (NEED-BASED) ***Receiving aid:*** Freshmen: 54% (272); all full-time undergraduates: 50% (705). ***Average award:*** Freshmen: $7431; Undergraduates: $7513. ***Scholarships, grants, and awards:*** Federal Pell, FSEOG, state, private, college/university gift aid from institutional funds.

GIFT AID (NON-NEED-BASED) ***Receiving aid:*** Freshmen: 53% (270). Undergraduates: 49% (693). ***Average award:*** Freshmen: $13,803. Undergraduates: $14,034. ***Scholarships, grants, and awards by category:*** *Academic interests/achievement:* biological sciences, business, communication, computer science, education, English, general academic interests/achievements, home economics, humanities, mathematics, military science, physical sciences, premedicine, social sciences. *Creative arts/performance:* applied art and design, art/fine arts, cinema/film/broadcasting, dance, journalism/publications, music, performing arts, theater/drama. *Special achievements/activities:* cheerleading/drum major, community service, general special achievements/activities, hobbies/interests, junior miss, leadership, rodeo. *Special characteristics:* children and siblings of alumni, children of faculty/staff. ***Tuition waivers:*** Full or partial for children of alumni, employees or children of employees. ***ROTC:*** Army.

LOANS ***Student loans:*** 70% of past graduating class borrowed through all loan programs. *Average indebtedness per student:* $37,801. ***Average need-based loan:*** Freshmen: $3002. Undergraduates: $3845. ***Programs:*** Federal Direct (Subsidized and Unsubsidized Stafford, PLUS), state.

WORK-STUDY Federal work-study jobs available. ***State or other work-study/employment:*** Part-time jobs available.

APPLYING FOR FINANCIAL AID ***Required financial aid form:*** FAFSA. ***Financial aid deadline:*** Continuous. ***Notification date:*** Continuous.

CONTACT Financial Aid Office, Missouri Valley College, 500 East College, Marshall, MO 65340-3197, 660-831-4000.
Website: http://www.moval.edu/.

MISSOURI WESTERN STATE UNIVERSITY

St. Joseph, MO

ABOUT THE INSTITUTION State-supported, coed. ***Awards:*** certificates, associate, bachelor's, and master's degrees. 52 undergraduate majors. ***Total enrollment:*** 5,533. Undergraduates: 5,292. Freshmen: 979.

GIFT AID (NEED-BASED) ***Scholarships, grants, and awards:*** Federal Pell, FSEOG, state, private, college/university gift aid from institutional funds.

GIFT AID (NON-NEED-BASED) ***Scholarships, grants, and awards by category:*** *Academic interests/achievement:* architecture, biological sciences, business, communication, computer science, education, engineering/technologies, English, foreign languages, general academic interests/achievements, home economics, humanities, mathematics, military science, physical sciences, premedicine, religion/biblical studies, social sciences. *Creative arts/performance:* applied art and design, art/fine arts, cinema/film/broadcasting, creative writing, dance, journalism/publications, music, performing arts, theater/drama. *Special achievements/activities:* cheerleading/drum major, community service, general special achievements/activities, leadership, memberships, religious involvement. *Special characteristics:* adult students, children and siblings of alumni, children of public servants, children of union members/company employees, children of workers in trades, first-generation college students, general special characteristics, international students, local/state students, out-of-state students, previous college experience, public servants, religious affiliation, veterans.

LOANS ***Programs:*** Federal Direct (Subsidized and Unsubsidized Stafford, PLUS), Perkins.

WORK-STUDY ***Federal work-study:*** 285 jobs averaging $1632. ***State or other work-study/employment:*** 629 part-time jobs averaging $1722.

APPLYING FOR FINANCIAL AID ***Required financial aid forms:*** FAFSA, institutional scholarship application form.

CONTACT Marilyn Baker, Director of Financial Aid, Missouri Western State University, 4525 Downs Drive, Saint Joseph, MO 64507-2294, 816-271-5986 or toll-free 800-662-7041. *Fax:* 816-271-5879. *E-mail:* mbaker3@missouriwestern.edu.
Website: http://www.missouriwestern.edu/.

MITCHELL COLLEGE

New London, CT

CONTACT Dan Brewer, Director of Financial Aid, Mitchell College, 437 Pequot Avenue, New London, CT 06320-4498, 800-629-6047 or toll-free 800-443-2811. *Fax:* 860-444-1209. *E-mail:* brewer_d@mitchell.edu.
Website: http://www.mitchell.edu/.

MOLLOY COLLEGE

Rockville Centre, NY

Tuition & fees: $32,600	Average undergraduate aid package: $17,046

ABOUT THE INSTITUTION Independent, coed. ***Awards:*** certificates, associate, bachelor's, master's, and doctoral degrees. 43 undergraduate majors. ***Total enrollment:*** 5,113. Undergraduates: 3,496. Freshmen: 581. Federal methodology is used as a basis for awarding need-based institutional aid.

UNDERGRADUATE EXPENSES for 2019–2020 ***Application fee:*** $40. ***Comprehensive fee:*** $48,160 includes full-time tuition ($31,330), mandatory fees ($1270), and room and board ($15,560). Full-time tuition and fees vary according to degree level. Room and board charges vary according to board plan. ***Part-time tuition:*** $1040 per credit hour. Part-time tuition and fees vary according to degree level.

FRESHMAN FINANCIAL AID (Fall 2018) 566 applied for aid; of those 86% were deemed to have need. 100% of freshmen with need received aid; of those 17% had need fully met. ***Average percent of need met:*** 58% (excluding resources awarded to replace EFC). ***Average financial aid package:*** $19,593 (excluding resources awarded to replace EFC). 12% of all full-time freshmen had no need and received non-need-based gift aid.

UNDERGRADUATE FINANCIAL AID (Fall 2018) 2,503 applied for aid; of those 88% were deemed to have need. 100% of undergraduates with need received aid; of those 12% had need fully met. ***Average percent of need met:*** 47% (excluding resources awarded to replace EFC). ***Average financial aid package:*** $17,046 (excluding resources awarded to replace EFC). 10% of all full-time undergraduates had no need and received non-need-based gift aid.

GIFT AID (NEED-BASED) ***Total amount:*** $28,491,611 (20% federal, 10% state, 69% institutional, 1% external sources). ***Receiving aid:*** Freshmen: 82% (483); all full-time undergraduates: 76% (2,096). ***Average award:*** Freshmen: $16,200; Undergraduates: $13,674. ***Scholarships, grants, and awards:*** Federal Pell, FSEOG, state, private, college/university gift aid from institutional funds, Federal Nursing, TRIO Grant, Aspire Scholarship, Noyce Scholarship.

GIFT AID (NON-NEED-BASED) ***Total amount:*** $4,771,647 (1% federal, 1% state, 95% institutional, 3% external sources). ***Receiving aid:*** Freshmen: 11% (63). Undergraduates: 7% (197). ***Average award:*** Freshmen: $12,822. Undergraduates: $10,327. ***Scholarships, grants, and awards by category:*** *Academic interests/achievement:* 1,772 awards ($15,517,538 total): biological sciences, business, communication, education, English, general academic interests/achievements, home economics, humanities, international studies, mathematics, military science, social sciences. *Creative arts/performance:* 74 awards ($157,450 total): art/fine arts, creative writing, general creative arts/performance, music, performing arts, theater/drama. *Special achievements/activities:* 690 awards ($2,924,385 total): cheerleading/drum major, community service, general special achievements/activities, leadership, memberships, religious involvement. *Special characteristics:* 112 awards ($133,231 total): ethnic background, members of minority groups, religious affiliation, siblings of current students, veterans. ***Tuition waivers:*** Full or partial for employees or children of employees, senior citizens. ***ROTC:*** Army cooperative, Naval cooperative.

LOANS ***Student loans:*** $27,235,684 (84% need-based, 16% non-need-based). 75% of past graduating class borrowed through all loan programs. *Average indebtedness per student:* $34,553. ***Average need-based loan:*** Freshmen: $2747. Undergraduates: $3826. ***Parent loans:*** $13,909,865 (65% need-based, 35% non-need-based). ***Programs:*** Federal Direct (Subsidized and Unsubsidized Stafford, PLUS), Perkins, Federal Nursing, private loans.

WORK-STUDY ***Federal work-study:*** Total amount: $342,981; 194 jobs averaging $1695.

ATHLETIC AWARDS Total amount: $2,073,890 (71% need-based, 29% non-need-based).

APPLYING FOR FINANCIAL AID ***Required financial aid forms:*** FAFSA, state aid form. ***Financial aid deadline:*** 5/1 (priority: 4/15). ***Notification date:*** Continuous beginning 1/20. Students must reply within 5 weeks of notification.

CONTACT Ana C. Lockward, Director of Financial Aid, Molloy College, 1000 Hempstead Avenue, Rockville Centre, NY 11571, 516-323-4200 or toll-free 888-4MOLLOY. *Fax:* 516-323-4213. *E-mail:* alockward@molloy.edu.
Website: http://www.molloy.edu/.

MONMOUTH COLLEGE

Monmouth, IL

ABOUT THE INSTITUTION Independent Presbyterian Church, coed. ***Awards:*** bachelor's degrees. 36 undergraduate majors.

GIFT AID (NEED-BASED) ***Scholarships, grants, and awards:*** Federal Pell, FSEOG, state, private, college/university gift aid from institutional funds.

GIFT AID (NON-NEED-BASED) ***Scholarships, grants, and awards by category:*** *Academic interests/achievement:* foreign languages, general academic interests/achievements. *Creative arts/performance:* applied art and design, debating, music, theater/drama. *Special achievements/activities:* general special achievements/activities, religious involvement. *Special characteristics:* international students, veterans.

LOANS ***Programs:*** Federal Direct (Subsidized and Unsubsidized Stafford, PLUS).

WORK-STUDY ***Federal work-study:*** Total amount: $586,354; 386 jobs averaging $1516. ***State or other work-study/employment:*** Part-time jobs available.

APPLYING FOR FINANCIAL AID ***Required financial aid form:*** FAFSA.

CONTACT Mrs. Jayne A. Schreck, Associate Vice President for Student Financial Planning, Monmouth College, 700 East Broadway, Monmouth, IL 61462-1998, 309-457-2129 or toll-free 800-747-2687. *Fax:* 309-457-2373. *E-mail:* jayne@monmouthcollege.edu.
Website: http://www.monmouthcollege.edu/.

MONMOUTH UNIVERSITY

West Long Branch, NJ

ABOUT THE INSTITUTION Independent, coed. ***Awards:*** certificates, bachelor's, master's, and doctoral degrees. 34 undergraduate majors.

GIFT AID (NEED-BASED) ***Scholarships, grants, and awards:*** Federal Pell, FSEOG, state, private, college/university gift aid from institutional funds, Federal Nursing.

GIFT AID (NON-NEED-BASED) ***Scholarships, grants, and awards by category:*** *Academic interests/achievement:* biological sciences, business, communication, computer science, education, English, foreign languages, general academic interests/achievements, health fields, humanities, mathematics, physical sciences, social sciences. *Special achievements/activities:* leadership. *Special characteristics:* adult students, children and siblings of alumni, children of faculty/staff, children of public servants, first-generation college students, general special characteristics, international students, local/state students, members of minority groups, out-of-state students, previous college experience, veterans.

LOANS ***Programs:*** Federal Direct (Subsidized and Unsubsidized Stafford, PLUS), Perkins, state, college/university, private loans.

WORK-STUDY ***Federal work-study:*** Total amount: $3,780,220; 911 jobs averaging $2219.

APPLYING FOR FINANCIAL AID ***Required financial aid form:*** FAFSA.

CONTACT Ms. Claire Alasio, Associate Vice President and Director of Financial Aid, Monmouth University, 400 Cedar Avenue, West Long Branch, NJ 07764-1898, 732-571-3463 or toll-free 800-543-9671. *Fax:* 732-923-4791. *E-mail:* finaid@monmouth.edu.
Website: http://www.monmouth.edu/.

MONROE COLLEGE

Bronx, NY

ABOUT THE INSTITUTION Proprietary, coed. ***Awards:*** certificates, associate, bachelor's, and master's degrees. 15 undergraduate majors.

GIFT AID (NEED-BASED) ***Scholarships, grants, and awards:*** Federal Pell, FSEOG, state, private, college/university gift aid from institutional funds.

LOANS ***Programs:*** Federal Direct (Subsidized and Unsubsidized Stafford, PLUS), state, college/university.

CONTACT Mr. Daniel Sharon, Assistant Vice President of Student Financial Services, Monroe College, 2501 Jerome Avenue, Bronx, NY 10468, 646-393-8257 or toll-free 800-55MONROE. *Fax:* 718-817-8401. *E-mail:* dsharon@monroecollege.edu.
Website: http://www.monroecollege.edu/.

MONTANA BIBLE COLLEGE

Bozeman, MT

CONTACT Financial Aid Office, Montana Bible College, 3625 South 19th Avenue, Bozeman, MT 59718, 406-586-3585 or toll-free 888-462-2463.
Website: http://www.montanabiblecollege.edu/.

MONTANA STATE UNIVERSITY

Bozeman, MT

Tuition & fees (area res): $7472	Average undergraduate aid package: N/A

ABOUT THE INSTITUTION State-supported, coed. ***Awards:*** certificates, associate, bachelor's, master's, and doctoral degrees. 59 undergraduate majors. ***Total***

enrollment: 16,766. Undergraduates: 14,778. Freshmen: 3,366. Federal methodology is used as a basis for awarding need-based institutional aid.

UNDERGRADUATE EXPENSES for 2020–2021 ***Application fee:*** $38. ***Tuition, area resident:*** full-time $5654; part-time $236 per credit. ***Tuition, state resident:*** full-time $5654; part-time $236 per credit. ***Tuition, nonresident:*** full-time $23,890; part-time $995 per credit. ***Required fees:*** full-time $1818. Full-time tuition and fees vary according to course load, program, and reciprocity agreements. Part-time tuition and fees vary according to course load, program, and reciprocity agreements. ***College room and board:*** $10,300. Room and board charges vary according to board plan and housing facility.

GIFT AID (NEED-BASED) ***Scholarships, grants, and awards:*** Federal Pell, FSEOG, state, private, college/university gift aid from institutional funds, Federal Nursing.

GIFT AID (NON-NEED-BASED) ***Scholarships, grants, and awards by category:*** *Academic interests/achievement:* agriculture, architecture, area/ethnic studies, biological sciences, business, communication, computer science, education, engineering/technologies, English, foreign languages, general academic interests/achievements, health fields, home economics, humanities, international studies, library science, mathematics, military science, physical sciences, premedicine, social sciences. *Creative arts/performance:* applied art and design, cinema/film/broadcasting, dance, music, theater/drama. *Special achievements/activities:* general special achievements/activities, leadership. *Special characteristics:* children and siblings of alumni, general special characteristics, local/state students, members of minority groups. ***Tuition waivers:*** Full or partial for employees or children of employees, adult students. ***ROTC:*** Army, Air Force.

LOANS ***Student loans:*** 51% of past graduating class borrowed through all loan programs. *Average indebtedness per student:* $27,764. ***Programs:*** Federal Direct (Subsidized and Unsubsidized Stafford, PLUS), Perkins, Federal Nursing, college/university.

WORK-STUDY Federal work-study jobs available. ***State or other work-study/employment:*** Part-time jobs available.

APPLYING FOR FINANCIAL AID ***Required financial aid form:*** FAFSA. ***Financial aid deadline:*** Continuous. ***Notification date:*** Continuous.

CONTACT James Broscheit, Director of Financial Aid, Montana State University, PO Box 174160, Bozeman, MT 59717-4160, 406-994-2845 or toll-free 888-MSU-CATS. *Fax:* 406-994-6962. *E-mail:* finaid@montana.edu. *Website:* http://www.montana.edu/.

MONTANA STATE UNIVERSITY BILLINGS

Billings, MT

Tuition & fees: N/R	Average undergraduate aid package: $10,523

ABOUT THE INSTITUTION State-supported, coed. ***Awards:*** certificates, associate, bachelor's, and master's degrees. 70 undergraduate majors. ***Total enrollment:*** 4,315. Undergraduates: 3,960. Freshmen: 631. Federal methodology is used as a basis for awarding need-based institutional aid.

FRESHMAN FINANCIAL AID (Fall 2018) 467 applied for aid; of those 73% were deemed to have need. 99% of freshmen with need received aid; of those 33% had need fully met. ***Average percent of need met:*** 70% (excluding resources awarded to replace EFC). ***Average financial aid package:*** $9808 (excluding resources awarded to replace EFC). 17% of all full-time freshmen had no need and received non-need-based gift aid.

UNDERGRADUATE FINANCIAL AID (Fall 2018) 1,765 applied for aid; of those 78% were deemed to have need. 99% of undergraduates with need received aid; of those 29% had need fully met. ***Average percent of need met:*** 72% (excluding resources awarded to replace EFC). ***Average financial aid package:*** $10,523 (excluding resources awarded to replace EFC). 7% of all full-time undergraduates had no need and received non-need-based gift aid.

GIFT AID (NEED-BASED) ***Total amount:*** $6,952,224 (79% federal, 15% institutional, 6% external sources). ***Receiving aid:*** Freshmen: 58% (309); all full-time undergraduates: 51% (1,155). ***Average award:*** Freshmen: $4795; Undergraduates: $4942. ***Scholarships, grants, and awards:*** Federal Pell, FSEOG, state, private, college/university gift aid from institutional funds.

GIFT AID (NON-NEED-BASED) ***Total amount:*** $628,115 (59% institutional, 41% external sources). ***Receiving aid:*** Freshmen: 3% (14). Undergraduates: 1% (28). ***Average award:*** Freshmen: $1331. Undergraduates: $2008. ***Scholarships, grants, and awards by category:*** *Academic interests/achievement:* biological sciences, business, communication, computer science, education, engineering/technologies, English, foreign languages, general academic interests/achievements, health fields, humanities, mathematics, physical sciences, premedicine, social sciences. *Creative arts/performance:* art/fine arts, music, theater/drama. *Special achievements/activities:* cheerleading/drum major, general special achievements/activities. *Special characteristics:* adult students, children and siblings of alumni, children of faculty/staff, children of union members/company employees, ethnic background, first-generation college students, local/state students, members of minority groups, out-of-state students, veterans. ***ROTC:*** Army.

LOANS ***Student loans:*** $9,744,722 (94% need-based, 6% non-need-based). 57% of past graduating class borrowed through all loan programs. *Average indebtedness per student:* $26,139. ***Average need-based loan:*** Freshmen: $4976. Undergraduates: $6173. ***Parent loans:*** $3,123,084 (19% need-based, 81% non-need-based). ***Programs:*** Federal Direct (Subsidized and Unsubsidized Stafford, PLUS), college/university.

WORK-STUDY ***Federal work-study:*** Total amount: $9,116,607; jobs available. ***State or other work-study/employment:*** Total amount: $204,755 (87% need-based, 13% non-need-based). Part-time jobs available.

ATHLETIC AWARDS Total amount: $927,709 (46% need-based, 54% non-need-based).

APPLYING FOR FINANCIAL AID ***Required financial aid forms:*** FAFSA, institution's own form. ***Financial aid deadline (priority):*** 12/1. ***Notification date:*** 10/1.

CONTACT Emily Williamson, Director of Financial Aid and Scholarships, Montana State University Billings, 1500 University Drive, Billings, MT 59101, 406-657-1617 or toll-free 800-565-6782. *Fax:* 406-657-1789. *E-mail:* finaid@msubillings.edu. *Website:* http://www.msubillings.edu/.

MONTANA STATE UNIVERSITY–NORTHERN

Havre, MT

CONTACT Cindy Small, Director of Financial Aid, Montana State University–Northern, PO Box 7751, Havre, MT 59501, 406-265-3787 or toll-free 800-662-6132. *Website:* http://www.msun.edu/.

MONTANA TECHNOLOGICAL UNIVERSITY

Butte, MT

Tuition & fees (MT res): $7397	Average undergraduate aid package: $11,078

ABOUT THE INSTITUTION State-supported, coed. ***Awards:*** certificates, diplomas, associate, bachelor's, master's, and doctoral degrees. 35 undergraduate majors. ***Total enrollment:*** 2,421. Undergraduates: 2,200. Freshmen: 413. Federal methodology is used as a basis for awarding need-based institutional aid.

UNDERGRADUATE EXPENSES for 2020–2021 ***Application fee:*** $30. ***Tuition, state resident:*** full-time $5707; part-time $238 per credit hour. ***Tuition, nonresident:*** full-time $20,870; part-time $866 per credit hour. ***Required fees:*** full-time $1690. Full-time tuition and fees vary according to course load, degree level, location, and program. Part-time tuition and fees vary according to course load, degree level, location, and program. ***College room and board:*** $10,170. Room and board charges vary according to board plan and housing facility.

FRESHMAN FINANCIAL AID (Fall 2018) 350 applied for aid; of those 66% were deemed to have need. 100% of freshmen with need received aid; of those 23% had need fully met. ***Average percent of need met:*** 66% (excluding resources awarded to replace EFC). ***Average financial aid package:*** $11,570 (excluding resources awarded to replace EFC). 17% of all full-time freshmen had no need and received non-need-based gift aid.

UNDERGRADUATE FINANCIAL AID (Fall 2018) 1,271 applied for aid; of those 75% were deemed to have need. 100% of undergraduates with need received aid; of those 13% had need fully met. ***Average percent of need met:*** 58% (excluding resources awarded to replace EFC). ***Average financial aid package:***

$11,078 (excluding resources awarded to replace EFC). 15% of all full-time undergraduates had no need and received non-need-based gift aid.

GIFT AID (NEED-BASED) ***Total amount:*** $5,015,160 (58% federal, 31% institutional, 11% external sources). ***Receiving aid:*** Freshmen: 51% (208); all full-time undergraduates: 44% (805). ***Average award:*** Freshmen: $6511; Undergraduates: $5912. ***Scholarships, grants, and awards:*** Federal Pell, FSEOG, state, private, college/university gift aid from institutional funds.

GIFT AID (NON-NEED-BASED) ***Total amount:*** $1,908,155 (74% institutional, 26% external sources). ***Receiving aid:*** Freshmen: 10% (40). Undergraduates: 4% (74). ***Average award:*** Freshmen: $5399. Undergraduates: $4161. ***Scholarships, grants, and awards by category:*** *Academic interests/achievement:* biological sciences, business, communication, computer science, engineering/technologies, general academic interests/achievements, health fields, humanities, mathematics, physical sciences. *Special achievements/activities:* community service, general special achievements/activities, hobbies/interests, leadership, memberships. *Special characteristics:* children and siblings of alumni, children of faculty/staff, first-generation college students, general special characteristics, local/state students, married students, out-of-state students, veterans. ***Tuition waivers:*** Full or partial for minority students, employees or children of employees, senior citizens.

LOANS ***Student loans:*** $5,891,820 (77% need-based, 23% non-need-based). 58% of past graduating class borrowed through all loan programs. *Average indebtedness per student:* $23,632. ***Average need-based loan:*** Freshmen: $2948. Undergraduates: $3794. ***Parent loans:*** $1,990,215 (38% need-based, 62% non-need-based). ***Programs:*** Federal Direct (Subsidized and Unsubsidized Stafford, PLUS).

WORK-STUDY ***Federal work-study:*** Total amount: $270,752; jobs available. ***State or other work-study/employment:*** Total amount: $13,750 (100% need-based). Part-time jobs available.

ATHLETIC AWARDS Total amount: $991,280 (43% need-based, 57% non-need-based).

APPLYING FOR FINANCIAL AID ***Required financial aid form:*** FAFSA. ***Financial aid deadline (priority):*** 12/1. ***Notification date:*** Continuous beginning 2/15. Students must reply by 5/1.

CONTACT Shauna Savage, Director of Financial Aid, Montana Technological University, 1300 West Park Street, Butte, MT 59701-8997, 406-496-4223 or toll-free 800-445-TECH. *Fax:* 406-496-4710. *E-mail:* financialaid@mtech.edu.
Website: http://www.mtech.edu/.

MONTCLAIR STATE UNIVERSITY

Montclair, NJ

Tuition & fees (NJ res): $13,073 | **Average undergraduate aid package: $10,658**

ABOUT THE INSTITUTION State-supported, coed. ***Awards:*** certificates, bachelor's, master's, and doctoral degrees. 64 undergraduate majors. ***Total enrollment:*** 21,115. Undergraduates: 16,988. Freshmen: 3,180. Federal methodology is used as a basis for awarding need-based institutional aid.

UNDERGRADUATE EXPENSES for 2019–2020 ***Application fee:*** $65. ***Tuition, state resident:*** full-time $12,082; part-time $403 per credit. ***Tuition, nonresident:*** full-time $20,042; part-time $668 per credit. ***Required fees:*** full-time $991; $33.04 per credit. ***College room and board:*** $15,674; ***Room only:*** $11,084. Room and board charges vary according to board plan and housing facility.

FRESHMAN FINANCIAL AID (Fall 2019, est.) 2949 applied for aid; of those 85% were deemed to have need. 93% of freshmen with need received aid; of those 1% had need fully met. ***Average percent of need met:*** 46% (excluding resources awarded to replace EFC). ***Average financial aid package:*** $10,772 (excluding resources awarded to replace EFC). 4% of all full-time freshmen had no need and received non-need-based gift aid.

UNDERGRADUATE FINANCIAL AID (Fall 2019, est.) 12,547 applied for aid; of those 88% were deemed to have need. 94% of undergraduates with need received aid; of those 1% had need fully met. ***Average percent of need met:*** 45% (excluding resources awarded to replace EFC). ***Average financial aid package:*** $10,658 (excluding resources awarded to replace EFC). 3% of all full-time undergraduates had no need and received non-need-based gift aid.

GIFT AID (NEED-BASED) ***Receiving aid:*** Freshmen: 55% (1,743); all full-time undergraduates: 50% (7,586). ***Average award:*** Freshmen: $10,841; Undergraduates: $9883. ***Scholarships, grants, and awards:*** Federal Pell, FSEOG, state, private, college/university gift aid from institutional funds.

GIFT AID (NON-NEED-BASED) ***Receiving aid:*** Freshmen: 34% (1,067). Undergraduates: 19% (2,849). ***Average award:*** Freshmen: $4675. Undergraduates: $4077. ***Scholarships, grants, and awards by category:*** *Academic interests/achievement:* biological sciences, business, communication, education, English, foreign languages, general academic interests/achievements, health fields, humanities, international studies, mathematics, physical sciences, religion/biblical studies, social sciences. *Creative arts/performance:* applied art and design, cinema/film/broadcasting, dance, music, performing arts, theater/drama. *Special achievements/activities:* community service, general special achievements/activities, leadership. *Special characteristics:* international students. ***Tuition waivers:*** Full or partial for employees or children of employees, senior citizens.

LOANS ***Student loans:*** 74% of past graduating class borrowed through all loan programs. *Average indebtedness per student:* $45,354. ***Average need-based loan:*** Freshmen: $3221. Undergraduates: $4140. ***Programs:*** Federal Direct (Subsidized and Unsubsidized Stafford, PLUS), state, private loans.

WORK-STUDY ***Federal work-study:*** 596 jobs averaging $724,978. ***State or other work-study/employment:*** Part-time jobs available.

APPLYING FOR FINANCIAL AID ***Required financial aid form:*** FAFSA. ***Notification date:*** Continuous.

CONTACT Mr. James T. Anderson, Director of Financial Aid, Montclair State University, College Hall, Montclair, NJ 07043, 973-655-7022. *Fax:* 973-655-7712. *E-mail:* financialaid@montclair.edu.
Website: http://www.montclair.edu/.

MONTREAT COLLEGE

Montreat, NC

Tuition & fees: N/R | **Average undergraduate aid package: $21,246**

ABOUT THE INSTITUTION Independent Presbyterian Church (U.S.A.), coed. ***Awards:*** certificates, associate, bachelor's, and master's degrees. 19 undergraduate majors. Federal methodology is used as a basis for awarding need-based institutional aid.

FRESHMAN FINANCIAL AID (Fall 2018) 156 applied for aid; of those 88% were deemed to have need. 99% of freshmen with need received aid; of those 11% had need fully met. ***Average percent of need met:*** 63% (excluding resources awarded to replace EFC). ***Average financial aid package:*** $20,055 (excluding resources awarded to replace EFC). 3% of all full-time freshmen had no need and received non-need-based gift aid.

UNDERGRADUATE FINANCIAL AID (Fall 2018) 521 applied for aid; of those 90% were deemed to have need. 99% of undergraduates with need received aid; of those 11% had need fully met. ***Average percent of need met:*** 68% (excluding resources awarded to replace EFC). ***Average financial aid package:*** $21,246 (excluding resources awarded to replace EFC). 6% of all full-time undergraduates had no need and received non-need-based gift aid.

GIFT AID (NEED-BASED) ***Total amount:*** $4,603,843 (33% federal, 23% state, 23% institutional, 21% external sources). ***Receiving aid:*** Freshmen: 81% (135); all full-time undergraduates: 29% (164). ***Average award:*** Freshmen: $16,838; Undergraduates: $16,962. ***Scholarships, grants, and awards:*** Federal Pell, FSEOG, state, private, college/university gift aid from institutional funds.

GIFT AID (NON-NEED-BASED) ***Total amount:*** $422,679 (49% institutional, 51% external sources). ***Receiving aid:*** Freshmen: 5% (9). Undergraduates: 7% (42). ***Average award:*** Freshmen: $6950. Undergraduates: $5641. ***Scholarships, grants, and awards by category:*** *Academic interests/achievement:* computer science, general academic interests/achievements. *Creative arts/performance:* creative writing, music. *Special achievements/activities:* leadership. *Special characteristics:* children and siblings of alumni, children of faculty/staff, first-generation college students, international students, local/state students, relatives of clergy, religious affiliation, veterans.

LOANS ***Student loans:*** $4,444,024 (75% need-based, 25% non-need-based). 74% of past graduating class borrowed through all loan programs. *Average indebtedness per student:* $21,802. ***Average need-based loan:*** Freshmen: $3717. Undergraduates: $4559. ***Parent loans:*** $1,631,036 (59% need-based, 41% non-need-based). ***Programs:*** Federal Direct (Subsidized and Unsubsidized Stafford, PLUS).

WORK-STUDY ***Federal work-study:*** Total amount: $85,898; jobs available. ***State or other work-study/employment:*** Total amount: $138,849 (53% need-based, 47% non-need-based). Part-time jobs available.

ATHLETIC AWARDS Total amount: $4,722,346 (77% need-based, 23% non-need-based).

APPLYING FOR FINANCIAL AID ***Required financial aid form:*** FAFSA. ***Financial aid deadline:*** 8/1 (priority: 3/1). ***Notification date:*** Continuous beginning 1/15. Students must reply by 5/1 or within 2 weeks of notification.

CONTACT MacKenzie May, Student Financial Services Counselor, Montreat College, PO Box 1267, Montreat, NC 28757, 800-545-4656 or toll-free 800-622-6968. *Fax:* 828-412-0257. *E-mail:* financialservices@montreat.edu.
Website: http://www.montreat.edu/.

MONTSERRAT COLLEGE OF ART

Beverly, MA

CONTACT Emma Puglisi, Director of Financial Aid, Montserrat College of Art, 23 Essex Street, PO Box 26, Beverly, MA 01915, 978-922-8222 Ext. 1155 or toll-free 800-836-0487. *Fax:* 978-922-4268. *E-mail:* finaid@montserrat.edu.
Website: http://www.montserrat.edu/.

MOODY BIBLE INSTITUTE

Chicago, IL

Tuition & fees: N/R	Average undergraduate aid package: $12,750

ABOUT THE INSTITUTION Independent nondenominational, coed. ***Awards:*** certificates, associate, bachelor's, and master's degrees. 8 undergraduate majors. Federal methodology is used as a basis for awarding need-based institutional aid.

FRESHMAN FINANCIAL AID (Fall 2019, est.) 163 applied for aid; of those 82% were deemed to have need. 98% of freshmen with need received aid; of those 18% had need fully met. ***Average percent of need met:*** 63% (excluding resources awarded to replace EFC). ***Average financial aid package:*** $12,578 (excluding resources awarded to replace EFC). 16% of all full-time freshmen had no need and received non-need-based gift aid.

UNDERGRADUATE FINANCIAL AID (Fall 2019, est.) 1,660 applied for aid; of those 83% were deemed to have need. 99% of undergraduates with need received aid; of those 19% had need fully met. ***Average percent of need met:*** 65% (excluding resources awarded to replace EFC). ***Average financial aid package:*** $12,750 (excluding resources awarded to replace EFC). 15% of all full-time undergraduates had no need and received non-need-based gift aid.

GIFT AID (NEED-BASED) ***Total amount:*** $15,340,668 (23% federal, 73% institutional, 4% external sources). ***Receiving aid:*** Freshmen: 72% (126); all full-time undergraduates: 75% (1,324). ***Average award:*** Freshmen: $11,236; Undergraduates: $10,556. ***Scholarships, grants, and awards:*** Federal Pell, FSEOG, state, private, college/university gift aid from institutional funds.

GIFT AID (NON-NEED-BASED) ***Total amount:*** $4,103,848 (88% institutional, 12% external sources). ***Receiving aid:*** Freshmen: 12% (21). Undergraduates: 11% (197). ***Average award:*** Freshmen: $10,396. Undergraduates: $9690.

LOANS ***Student loans:*** $7,294,287 (92% need-based, 8% non-need-based). 36% of past graduating class borrowed through all loan programs. *Average indebtedness per student:* $21,781. ***Average need-based loan:*** Freshmen: $3308. Undergraduates: $4113. ***Parent loans:*** $315,049 (92% need-based, 8% non-need-based). ***Programs:*** Federal Direct (Subsidized and Unsubsidized Stafford, PLUS), institutional loans for aviation students.

WORK-STUDY ***Federal work-study:*** Total amount: $62,311; jobs available.

APPLYING FOR FINANCIAL AID ***Required financial aid forms:*** FAFSA, institution's own form. ***Financial aid deadline:*** 9/1 (priority: 4/1). ***Notification date:*** Continuous beginning 5/1. Students must reply by 9/1.

CONTACT Financial Aid Office, Moody Bible Institute, 820 North LaSalle Boulevard, Chicago, IL 60610-3284, 312-329-4000 or toll-free 800-967-4MBI.
Website: http://www.moody.edu/.

MOORE COLLEGE OF ART & DESIGN

Philadelphia, PA

CONTACT MIchelle Shonleber, Director of Financial Aid, Moore College of Art & Design, 20th and the Parkway, Philadelphia, PA 19103-1179, 215-965-4042 or toll-free 800-523-2025. *Fax:* 215-568-1773. *E-mail:* mshonleber@moore.edu.
Website: http://www.moore.edu/.

MORAVIAN COLLEGE

Bethlehem, PA

Tuition & fees: $47,367	Average undergraduate aid package: $31,338

ABOUT THE INSTITUTION Independent Moravian Church, coed. ***Awards:*** certificates, bachelor's, master's, and doctoral degrees. 34 undergraduate majors. ***Total enrollment:*** 2,595. Undergraduates: 2,073. Freshmen: 428. Federal methodology is used as a basis for awarding need-based institutional aid.

UNDERGRADUATE EXPENSES for 2020–2021 ***One-time required fee:*** $500. ***Comprehensive fee:*** $61,838 includes full-time tuition ($45,321), mandatory fees ($2046), and room and board ($14,471). ***College room only:*** $8154. Full-time tuition and fees vary according to class time and program. Room and board charges vary according to board plan and housing facility. ***Part-time tuition:*** $1259 per credit. Part-time tuition and fees vary according to class time.

FRESHMAN FINANCIAL AID (Fall 2019, est.) 406 applied for aid; of those 90% were deemed to have need. 100% of freshmen with need received aid; of those 18% had need fully met. ***Average percent of need met:*** 78% (excluding resources awarded to replace EFC). ***Average financial aid package:*** $33,774 (excluding resources awarded to replace EFC). 14% of all full-time freshmen had no need and received non-need-based gift aid.

UNDERGRADUATE FINANCIAL AID (Fall 2019, est.) 1,665 applied for aid; of those 92% were deemed to have need. 100% of undergraduates with need received aid; of those 16% had need fully met. ***Average percent of need met:*** 73% (excluding resources awarded to replace EFC). ***Average financial aid package:*** $31,338 (excluding resources awarded to replace EFC). 16% of all full-time undergraduates had no need and received non-need-based gift aid.

GIFT AID (NEED-BASED) ***Receiving aid:*** Freshmen: 86% (366); all full-time undergraduates: 77% (1,472). ***Average award:*** Freshmen: $29,847; Undergraduates: $27,678. ***Scholarships, grants, and awards:*** Federal Pell, FSEOG, state, private, college/university gift aid from institutional funds.

GIFT AID (NON-NEED-BASED) ***Receiving aid:*** Freshmen: 13% (54). Undergraduates: 10% (198). ***Average award:*** Freshmen: $23,975. Undergraduates: $20,998. ***Tuition waivers:*** Full or partial for employees or children of employees. ***ROTC:*** Army cooperative.

LOANS ***Student loans:*** 80% of past graduating class borrowed through all loan programs. *Average indebtedness per student:* $38,514. ***Average need-based loan:*** Freshmen: $3122. Undergraduates: $4210. ***Programs:*** Federal Direct (Subsidized and Unsubsidized Stafford, PLUS), Federal Nursing.

WORK-STUDY Federal work-study jobs available. ***State or other work-study/employment:*** Part-time jobs available.

APPLYING FOR FINANCIAL AID ***Required financial aid form:*** FAFSA. ***Financial aid deadline:*** Continuous. ***Notification date:*** Continuous.

CONTACT Mary Beth Carey, Executive Director of Admission and Financial Aid Services, Moravian College, 1200 Main Street, Bethlehem, PA 18018-6650, 610-861-1330 or toll-free 800-441-3191. *Fax:* 610-861-1320. *E-mail:* careym@moravian.edu.
Website: http://www.moravian.edu/.

MOREHEAD STATE UNIVERSITY

Morehead, KY

Tuition & fees (KY res): $9290	Average undergraduate aid package: $12,520

ABOUT THE INSTITUTION State-supported, coed. ***Awards:*** certificates, associate, bachelor's, master's, and doctoral degrees. 52 undergraduate majors. ***Total***

enrollment: 9,660. Undergraduates: 8,964. Freshmen: 1,204. Federal methodology is used as a basis for awarding need-based institutional aid.

UNDERGRADUATE EXPENSES for 2019–2020 ***Application fee:*** $30. ***Tuition, state resident:*** full-time $8970; part-time $374 per credit hour. ***Tuition, nonresident:*** full-time $13,556; part-time $565 per credit hour. ***Required fees:*** full-time $320; $14 per credit hour. Full-time tuition and fees vary according to course load, degree level, location, reciprocity agreements, and student level. Part-time tuition and fees vary according to course load, degree level, location, reciprocity agreements, and student level. ***College room and board:*** $9490; ***Room only:*** $5308. Room and board charges vary according to board plan and housing facility.

FRESHMAN FINANCIAL AID (Fall 2019, est.) 1254 applied for aid; of those 85% were deemed to have need. 100% of freshmen with need received aid; of those 23% had need fully met. ***Average percent of need met:*** 66% (excluding resources awarded to replace EFC). ***Average financial aid package:*** $12,794 (excluding resources awarded to replace EFC). 18% of all full-time freshmen had no need and received non-need-based gift aid.

UNDERGRADUATE FINANCIAL AID (Fall 2019, est.) 4,604 applied for aid; of those 86% were deemed to have need. 99% of undergraduates with need received aid; of those 24% had need fully met. ***Average percent of need met:*** 64% (excluding resources awarded to replace EFC). ***Average financial aid package:*** $12,520 (excluding resources awarded to replace EFC). 18% of all full-time undergraduates had no need and received non-need-based gift aid.

GIFT AID (NEED-BASED) ***Total amount:*** $17,983,186 (76% federal, 24% state). ***Receiving aid:*** Freshmen: 52% (681); all full-time undergraduates: 51% (2,660). ***Average award:*** Freshmen: $6444; Undergraduates: $6219. ***Scholarships, grants, and awards:*** Federal Pell, FSEOG, state, private, college/university gift aid from institutional funds.

GIFT AID (NON-NEED-BASED) ***Total amount:*** $25,833,059 (25% state, 65% institutional, 10% external sources). ***Receiving aid:*** Freshmen: 77% (1,009). Undergraduates: 59% (3,073). ***Average award:*** Freshmen: $7519. Undergraduates: $7576. ***Scholarships, grants, and awards by category:*** *Academic interests/achievement:* 1,805 awards ($10,144,532 total): agriculture, biological sciences, business, communication, education, engineering/technologies, general academic interests/achievements, home economics, international studies, military science, physical sciences, social sciences. *Creative arts/performance:* 77 awards ($197,250 total): applied art and design, art/fine arts, journalism/publications, music, theater/drama. *Special achievements/activities:* 202 awards ($710,635 total): cheerleading/drum major, community service, general special achievements/activities, junior miss, leadership. *Special characteristics:* 1,473 awards ($4,243,219 total): adult students, children and siblings of alumni, ethnic background, general special characteristics, handicapped students, international students, local/state students, members of minority groups, out-of-state students, previous college experience, veterans. ***Tuition waivers:*** Full or partial for minority students, children of alumni, employees or children of employees, senior citizens. ***ROTC:*** Army.

LOANS ***Student loans:*** $24,293,993 (41% need-based, 59% non-need-based). 69% of past graduating class borrowed through all loan programs. *Average indebtedness per student:* $26,576. ***Average need-based loan:*** Freshmen: $3115. Undergraduates: $3647. ***Parent loans:*** $2,911,807 (100% non-need-based). ***Programs:*** Federal Direct (Subsidized and Unsubsidized Stafford, PLUS).

WORK-STUDY ***Federal work-study:*** Total amount: $1,021,116; 414 jobs averaging $2426. ***State or other work-study/employment:*** Total amount: $2,147,136 (100% non-need-based). 769 part-time jobs averaging $2886.

ATHLETIC AWARDS Total amount: $2,268,736 (100% non-need-based).

APPLYING FOR FINANCIAL AID ***Required financial aid form:*** FAFSA. ***Financial aid deadline (priority):*** 3/15. ***Notification date:*** Continuous.

CONTACT Denise Trusty, Director of Financial Aid, Morehead State University, 205 Enrollment Services Center, Morehead, KY 40351, 606-783-2011 or toll-free 800-585-6781. *Fax:* 606-783-2293. *E-mail:* dmtrusty@moreheadstate.edu.
Website: http://www.moreheadstate.edu/.

MOREHOUSE COLLEGE

Atlanta, GA

ABOUT THE INSTITUTION Independent, men only. ***Awards:*** bachelor's degrees. 27 undergraduate majors. ***Total enrollment:*** 2,206. Undergraduates: 2,206. Freshmen: 605.

GIFT AID (NEED-BASED) ***Scholarships, grants, and awards:*** Federal Pell, FSEOG, state, private, college/university gift aid from institutional funds, United Negro College Fund.

GIFT AID (NON-NEED-BASED) ***Scholarships, grants, and awards by category:*** *Academic interests/achievement:* biological sciences, business, computer science, engineering/technologies, general academic interests/achievements, mathematics, military science. *Creative arts/performance:* applied art and design, music. *Special achievements/activities:* cheerleading/drum major, community service, leadership, religious involvement. *Special characteristics:* children and siblings of alumni, children of faculty/staff, local/state students.

LOANS ***Programs:*** Federal Direct (Subsidized and Unsubsidized Stafford, PLUS), Perkins, state.

CONTACT Sheryl T. Spivey, Director of Financial Aid, Morehouse College, 830 Westview Drive, SW, Atlanta, GA 30314, 844-512-6672 or toll-free 800-851-1254. *Fax:* 404-639-0974. *E-mail:* sheryl.spivey@morehouse.edu.
Website: http://www.morehouse.edu/.

MORGAN STATE UNIVERSITY

Baltimore, MD

Tuition & fees: N/R	Average undergraduate aid package: $11,510

ABOUT THE INSTITUTION State-supported, coed. ***Awards:*** bachelor's, master's, and doctoral degrees. 55 undergraduate majors. ***Total enrollment:*** 6,821. Undergraduates: 6,114. Freshmen: 1,446. Federal methodology is used as a basis for awarding need-based institutional aid.

FRESHMAN FINANCIAL AID (Fall 2018) 1233 applied for aid; of those 90% were deemed to have need. 100% of freshmen with need received aid; of those 6% had need fully met. ***Average percent of need met:*** 44% (excluding resources awarded to replace EFC). ***Average financial aid package:*** $10,958 (excluding resources awarded to replace EFC). 3% of all full-time freshmen had no need and received non-need-based gift aid.

UNDERGRADUATE FINANCIAL AID (Fall 2018) 4,921 applied for aid; of those 91% were deemed to have need. 100% of undergraduates with need received aid; of those 8% had need fully met. ***Average percent of need met:*** 47% (excluding resources awarded to replace EFC). ***Average financial aid package:*** $11,510 (excluding resources awarded to replace EFC). 3% of all full-time undergraduates had no need and received non-need-based gift aid.

GIFT AID (NEED-BASED) ***Receiving aid:*** Freshmen: 68% (902); all full-time undergraduates: 48% (2,799). ***Average award:*** Freshmen: $8245; Undergraduates: $7869. ***Scholarships, grants, and awards:*** Federal Pell, FSEOG, state, private, college/university gift aid from institutional funds.

GIFT AID (NON-NEED-BASED) ***Receiving aid:*** Freshmen: 16% (213). Undergraduates: 13% (777). ***Average award:*** Freshmen: $5623. Undergraduates: $6016. ***Scholarships, grants, and awards by category:*** *Academic interests/achievement:* 1,063 awards ($5,624,498 total): architecture, area/ethnic studies, biological sciences, business, communication, computer science, education, engineering/technologies, English, foreign languages, general academic interests/achievements, home economics, humanities, international studies, mathematics, military science, physical sciences, social sciences. *Creative arts/performance:* 118 awards ($476,077 total): applied art and design, art/fine arts, cinema/film/broadcasting, creative writing, dance, debating, general creative arts/performance, journalism/publications, music, performing arts, theater/drama. *Special characteristics:* 1,063 awards ($5,624,498 total): adult students, children of faculty/staff, first-generation college students, general special characteristics, international students, local/state students, out-of-state students, veterans, veterans' children. ***ROTC:*** Army.

LOANS ***Student loans:*** 73% of past graduating class borrowed through all loan programs. *Average indebtedness per student:* $46,194. ***Average need-based loan:*** Freshmen: $4235. Undergraduates: $4911. ***Programs:*** Federal Direct (Subsidized and Unsubsidized Stafford, PLUS), Perkins.

WORK-STUDY ***Federal work-study:*** 247 jobs averaging $2220. ***State or other work-study/employment:*** Part-time jobs available.

APPLYING FOR FINANCIAL AID ***Required financial aid forms:*** FAFSA, institution's own form, federal income tax form(s). ***Financial aid deadline:*** Continuous. ***Notification date:*** Continuous. Students must reply within 2 weeks of notification.

CONTACT Tanya Wilkerson, Director of Financial Aid, Morgan State University, 1700 East Cold Spring Lane, Baltimore, MD 21251, 443-885-3170 or toll-free 800-332-6674. *Fax:* 443-885-8272.
Website: http://www.morgan.edu/.

MORNINGSIDE COLLEGE

Sioux City, IA

CONTACT Karen K. Gagnon, Associate Vice President for Institutional Research/ Director of Student Financial Planning, Morningside College, 1501 Morningside Avenue, Sioux City, IA 51106, 712-274-5272 or toll-free 800-831-0806 Ext.5111. *Fax:* 712-274-5605. *E-mail:* gagnon@morningside.edu.
Website: http://www.morningside.edu/.

MORRIS COLLEGE

Sumter, SC

CONTACT Ms. Sandra S. Gibson, Director of Financial Aid, Morris College, 100 West College Street, Sumter, SC 29150-3599, 803-934-3238 or toll-free 866-853-1345. *Fax:* 803-773-3687.
Website: http://www.morris.edu/.

MOUNT ALOYSIUS COLLEGE

Cresson, PA

Tuition & fees: N/R	Average undergraduate aid package: $22,400

ABOUT THE INSTITUTION Independent Roman Catholic, coed. ***Awards:*** certificates, associate, bachelor's, and master's degrees. 25 undergraduate majors. ***Total enrollment:*** 1,834. Undergraduates: 1,791. Freshmen: 246.

FRESHMAN FINANCIAL AID (Fall 2018) 243 applied for aid; of those 85% were deemed to have need. 100% of freshmen with need received aid. ***Average percent of need met:*** 43% (excluding resources awarded to replace EFC). ***Average financial aid package:*** $18,140 (excluding resources awarded to replace EFC). 15% of all full-time freshmen had no need and received non-need-based gift aid.

UNDERGRADUATE FINANCIAL AID (Fall 2018) 940 applied for aid; of those 94% were deemed to have need. 100% of undergraduates with need received aid. ***Average percent of need met:*** 37% (excluding resources awarded to replace EFC). ***Average financial aid package:*** $22,400 (excluding resources awarded to replace EFC). 6% of all full-time undergraduates had no need and received non-need-based gift aid.

GIFT AID (NEED-BASED) ***Total amount:*** $12,948,097 (15% federal, 12% state, 71% institutional, 2% external sources). ***Receiving aid:*** Freshmen: 85% (207); all full-time undergraduates: 94% (881). ***Average award:*** Freshmen: $5100; Undergraduates: $4970. ***Scholarships, grants, and awards:*** Federal Pell, FSEOG, state, private.

GIFT AID (NON-NEED-BASED) ***Receiving aid:*** Freshmen: 15% (36). Undergraduates: 6% (59). ***Average award:*** Freshmen: $6900. Undergraduates: $7000. ***Scholarships, grants, and awards by category:*** *Academic interests/ achievement:* general academic interests/achievements. *Creative arts/performance:* music, performing arts. *Special achievements/activities:* leadership. *Special characteristics:* children of current students, parents of current students, religious affiliation, siblings of current students, spouses of current students, twins.

LOANS ***Student loans:*** $6,954,421 (100% need-based). ***Average need-based loan:*** Freshmen: $2900. Undergraduates: $3300. ***Parent loans:*** $2,815,799 (100% need-based). ***Programs:*** Federal Direct (Subsidized and Unsubsidized Stafford, PLUS), Federal Nursing, Private Alternative Loans.

WORK-STUDY ***Federal work-study:*** Total amount: $266,258; jobs available.

APPLYING FOR FINANCIAL AID ***Required financial aid form:*** FAFSA. ***Financial aid deadline (priority):*** 4/1. ***Notification date:*** Continuous.

CONTACT Mrs. Stacy L. Schenk, Director of Financial Aid, Mount Aloysius College, 7373 Admiral Peary Highway, Cresson, PA 16630-1900, 814-886-6357 or toll-free 888-823-2220. *Fax:* 814-886-6463. *E-mail:* sschenk@mtaloy.edu.
Website: http://www.mtaloy.edu/.

MOUNT ANGEL SEMINARY

Saint Benedict, OR

CONTACT Dorene Preis, Director of Student Financial Aid/Registrar, Mount Angel Seminary, 1 Abbey Drive, Saint Benedict, OR 97373, 503-845-3951. *Fax:* 503-845-3126. *E-mail:* dpreis@mtangel.edu.
Website: http://www.mountangelabbey.org/seminary/.

MOUNT CARMEL COLLEGE OF NURSING

Columbus, OH

Tuition & fees: $14,372	Average undergraduate aid package: $10,217

ABOUT THE INSTITUTION Independent, coed, primarily women. ***Awards:*** certificates, bachelor's, master's, and doctoral degrees. 1 undergraduate major. ***Total enrollment:*** 946. Undergraduates: 733. Freshmen: 44. Federal methodology is used as a basis for awarding need-based institutional aid.

UNDERGRADUATE EXPENSES for 2019–2020 ***Application fee:*** $30. ***One-time required fee:*** $225. ***Tuition:*** full-time $13,857; part-time $447 per credit hour. ***Required fees:*** full-time $515; $515 per year. ***College room only:*** $5000.

FRESHMAN FINANCIAL AID (Fall 2019, est.) 35 applied for aid; of those 77% were deemed to have need. 96% of freshmen with need received aid; of those 4% had need fully met. ***Average percent of need met:*** 44% (excluding resources awarded to replace EFC). ***Average financial aid package:*** $9985 (excluding resources awarded to replace EFC). 5% of all full-time freshmen had no need and received non-need-based gift aid.

UNDERGRADUATE FINANCIAL AID (Fall 2019, est.) 442 applied for aid; of those 89% were deemed to have need. 97% of undergraduates with need received aid; of those 3% had need fully met. ***Average percent of need met:*** 32% (excluding resources awarded to replace EFC). ***Average financial aid package:*** $10,217 (excluding resources awarded to replace EFC). 5% of all full-time undergraduates had no need and received non-need-based gift aid.

GIFT AID (NEED-BASED) ***Receiving aid:*** Freshmen: 62% (23); all full-time undergraduates: 48% (269). ***Average award:*** Freshmen: $8004; Undergraduates: $8520. ***Scholarships, grants, and awards:*** Federal Pell, FSEOG, state, private, Federal Nursing.

GIFT AID (NON-NEED-BASED) ***Receiving aid:*** Undergraduates: 1% (4). ***Average award:*** Freshmen: $2100. Undergraduates: $2448. ***Scholarships, grants, and awards by category:*** *Academic interests/achievement:* general academic interests/achievements. *Special achievements/activities:* community service. *Special characteristics:* children of faculty/staff, members of minority groups. ***ROTC:*** Army cooperative, Air Force cooperative.

LOANS ***Student loans:*** 68% of past graduating class borrowed through all loan programs. *Average indebtedness per student:* $35,781. ***Average need-based loan:*** Freshmen: $3433. Undergraduates: $4688. ***Programs:*** Federal Direct (Subsidized and Unsubsidized Stafford, PLUS), Federal Nursing, state, college/university.

WORK-STUDY ***State or other work-study/employment:*** Part-time jobs available.

APPLYING FOR FINANCIAL AID ***Required financial aid form:*** FAFSA. ***Financial aid deadline:*** Continuous. ***Notification date:*** Continuous. Students must reply within 2 weeks of notification.

CONTACT Dr. Todd A. Everett, Associate Dean of Student Services, Mount Carmel College of Nursing, 127 South Davis Avenue, Columbus, OH 43222, 614-234-5169 Ext. 5177 or toll-free 800-556-6942. *Fax:* 614-234-5427. *E-mail:* teverett@mccn.edu.
Website: http://www.mccn.edu/.

MOUNT HOLYOKE COLLEGE

South Hadley, MA

Tuition & fees: $52,258	Average undergraduate aid package: $42,565

ABOUT THE INSTITUTION Independent, women only. ***Awards:*** bachelor's and master's degrees. 51 undergraduate majors. ***Total enrollment:*** 2,335. Undergraduates: 2,208. Freshmen: 628. Institutional methodology is used as a basis for awarding need-based institutional aid.

UNDERGRADUATE EXPENSES for 2019–2020 ***Application fee:*** $60. ***Comprehensive fee:*** $67,578 includes full-time tuition ($52,040), mandatory fees ($218), and room and board ($15,320). ***College room only:*** $7504. ***Part-time tuition:*** $1630 per credit hour.

FRESHMAN FINANCIAL AID (Fall 2019, est.) 363 applied for aid; of those 86% were deemed to have need. 100% of freshmen with need received aid; of those 100% had need fully met. ***Average percent of need met:*** 100% (excluding resources awarded to replace EFC). ***Average financial aid package:*** $44,203 (excluding resources awarded to replace EFC). 10% of all full-time freshmen had no need and received non-need-based gift aid.

UNDERGRADUATE FINANCIAL AID (Fall 2019, est.) 1,470 applied for aid; of those 89% were deemed to have need. 100% of undergraduates with need received aid; of those 100% had need fully met. ***Average percent of need met:*** 100% (excluding resources awarded to replace EFC). ***Average financial aid package:*** $42,565 (excluding resources awarded to replace EFC). 13% of all full-time undergraduates had no need and received non-need-based gift aid.

GIFT AID (NEED-BASED) ***Total amount:*** $48,141,357 (5% federal, 1% state, 92% institutional, 2% external sources). ***Receiving aid:*** Freshmen: 62% (306); all full-time undergraduates: 61% (1,312). ***Average award:*** Freshmen: $40,492; Undergraduates: $37,322. ***Scholarships, grants, and awards:*** Federal Pell, FSEOG, state, private, college/university gift aid from institutional funds.

GIFT AID (NON-NEED-BASED) ***Total amount:*** $8,223,006 (91% institutional, 9% external sources). ***Receiving aid:*** Freshmen: 10% (49). Undergraduates: 9% (203). ***Average award:*** Freshmen: $20,643. Undergraduates: $22,429. ***Scholarships, grants, and awards by category:*** *Academic interests/achievement:* general academic interests/achievements. *Special characteristics:* general special characteristics. ***Tuition waivers:*** Full or partial for employees or children of employees. ***ROTC:*** Army cooperative, Air Force cooperative.

LOANS ***Student loans:*** $8,112,982 (80% need-based, 20% non-need-based). 67% of past graduating class borrowed through all loan programs. *Average indebtedness per student:* $25,811. ***Average need-based loan:*** Freshmen: $3145. Undergraduates: $4238. ***Parent loans:*** $3,745,713 (100% non-need-based). ***Programs:*** Federal Direct (Subsidized and Unsubsidized Stafford, PLUS), state, college/university.

WORK-STUDY ***Federal work-study:*** Total amount: $420,000; 813 jobs averaging $2217. ***State or other work-study/employment:*** Total amount: $1,842,336 (100% need-based). 224 part-time jobs averaging $2158.

APPLYING FOR FINANCIAL AID ***Required financial aid forms:*** FAFSA, CSS Financial Aid PROFILE, noncustodial (divorced/separated) parent's statement, federal income tax form(s), W-2 forms. ***Financial aid deadline:*** 2/1 (priority: 2/1). ***Notification date:*** 4/1. Students must reply by 5/1.

CONTACT Ms. Kathryn Blaisdell, Director of Student Financial Services, Mount Holyoke College, 50 College Street, South Hadley, MA 01075-1492, 413-538-2291. *Fax:* 413-538-2512. *E-mail:* kblaisde@mtholyoke.edu.
Website: http://www.mtholyoke.edu/.

MOUNT MARTY COLLEGE

Yankton, SD

Tuition & fees: $28,126	Average undergraduate aid package: $31,753

ABOUT THE INSTITUTION Independent Roman Catholic, coed. ***Awards:*** certificates, associate, bachelor's, master's, and doctoral degrees. 30 undergraduate majors. ***Total enrollment:*** 1,051. Undergraduates: 869. Freshmen: 119. Federal methodology is used as a basis for awarding need-based institutional aid.

UNDERGRADUATE EXPENSES for 2019–2020 ***Application fee:*** $35. ***Comprehensive fee:*** $36,272 includes full-time tuition ($25,976), mandatory fees ($2150), and room and board ($8146). Full-time tuition and fees vary according to course load, degree level, and location. ***Part-time tuition:*** $540 per credit hour. ***Part-time fees:*** $45 per credit hour. Part-time tuition and fees vary according to course load, degree level, and location.

FRESHMAN FINANCIAL AID (Fall 2019, est.) 113 applied for aid; of those 94% were deemed to have need. 100% of freshmen with need received aid; of those 54% had need fully met. ***Average percent of need met:*** 91% (excluding resources awarded to replace EFC). ***Average financial aid package:*** $33,203 (excluding resources awarded to replace EFC). 6% of all full-time freshmen had no need and received non-need-based gift aid.

UNDERGRADUATE FINANCIAL AID (Fall 2019, est.) 485 applied for aid; of those 92% were deemed to have need. 100% of undergraduates with need received aid; of those 45% had need fully met. ***Average percent of need met:*** 91% (excluding resources awarded to replace EFC). ***Average financial aid package:*** $31,753 (excluding resources awarded to replace EFC). 7% of all full-time undergraduates had no need and received non-need-based gift aid.

GIFT AID (NEED-BASED) ***Total amount:*** $7,427,885 (16% federal, 1% state, 77% institutional, 6% external sources). ***Receiving aid:*** Freshmen: 91% (105); all full-time undergraduates: 81% (425). ***Average award:*** Freshmen: $22,124; Undergraduates: $19,322. ***Scholarships, grants, and awards:*** Federal Pell, FSEOG, state, private, college/university gift aid from institutional funds.

GIFT AID (NON-NEED-BASED) ***Total amount:*** $508,116 (1% federal, 2% state, 85% institutional, 12% external sources). ***Average award:*** Freshmen: $10,269. Undergraduates: $6411. ***Scholarships, grants, and awards by category:*** *Academic interests/achievement:* general academic interests/achievements. *Creative arts/performance:* applied art and design, music, performing arts, theater/drama. *Special achievements/activities:* community service, general special achievements/activities, leadership, religious involvement. *Special characteristics:* children of current students, children of faculty/staff, international students, parents of current students, religious affiliation, siblings of current students, spouses of current students. ***Tuition waivers:*** Full or partial for employees or children of employees. ***ROTC:*** Army cooperative.

LOANS ***Student loans:*** $3,338,571 (94% need-based, 6% non-need-based). ***Average need-based loan:*** Freshmen: $3317. Undergraduates: $4733. ***Parent loans:*** $1,149,535 (88% need-based, 12% non-need-based). ***Programs:*** Federal Direct (Subsidized and Unsubsidized Stafford, PLUS), Perkins, Federal Nursing, state, college/university.

WORK-STUDY ***Federal work-study:*** Total amount: $253,705; jobs available. ***State or other work-study/employment:*** Total amount: $115,170 (77% need-based, 23% non-need-based). Part-time jobs available.

ATHLETIC AWARDS Total amount: $1,627,526 (92% need-based, 8% non-need-based).

APPLYING FOR FINANCIAL AID ***Required financial aid forms:*** FAFSA, institution's own form. ***Financial aid deadline (priority):*** 3/1. ***Notification date:*** Continuous beginning 3/15. Students must reply within 2 weeks of notification.

CONTACT Mr. Ken Kocer, Director of Financial Assistance, Mount Marty College, 1105 West 8th Street, Yankton, SD 57078-3724, 605-668-1589 or toll-free 800-658-4552. *Fax:* 605-668-1585. *E-mail:* kkocer@mountmarty.edu.
Website: http://www.mtmc.edu/.

MOUNT MARY UNIVERSITY

Milwaukee, WI

ABOUT THE INSTITUTION Independent Roman Catholic, undergraduate: women only; graduate: coed. ***Awards:*** certificates, bachelor's, master's, and doctoral degrees. 44 undergraduate majors. ***Total enrollment:*** 1,339. Undergraduates: 735. Freshmen: 123.

GIFT AID (NEED-BASED) ***Scholarships, grants, and awards:*** Federal Pell, FSEOG, state, private, college/university gift aid from institutional funds.

GIFT AID (NON-NEED-BASED) ***Scholarships, grants, and awards by category:*** *Academic interests/achievement:* business, communication, education, English, general academic interests/achievements, humanities, mathematics, social sciences. *Creative arts/performance:* applied art and design, art/fine arts, music. *Special achievements/activities:* general special achievements/activities, leadership. *Special characteristics:* children and siblings of alumni, children of faculty/staff, international students, siblings of current students, veterans.

LOANS ***Programs:*** Federal Direct (Subsidized and Unsubsidized Stafford, PLUS).

WORK-STUDY ***Federal work-study:*** Total amount: $162,000; 100 jobs averaging $1620. ***State or other work-study/employment:*** Total amount: $120,000 (100% non-need-based). 76 part-time jobs averaging $1580.

APPLYING FOR FINANCIAL AID ***Required financial aid form:*** FAFSA.

CONTACT Debra Duff, Director of Financial Aid, Mount Mary University, 2900 North Menomonee River Parkway, Milwaukee, WI 53222-4597, 414-930-3163 or toll-free 800-321-6265. *Fax:* 414-930-3709. *E-mail:* finaid@mtmary.edu.
Website: http://www.mtmary.edu/.

MOUNT MERCY UNIVERSITY

Cedar Rapids, IA

ABOUT THE INSTITUTION Independent Roman Catholic, coed. ***Awards:*** bachelor's, master's, and doctoral degrees. 56 undergraduate majors. ***Total enrollment:*** 1,808. Undergraduates: 1,442. Freshmen: 218.

GIFT AID (NEED-BASED) ***Scholarships, grants, and awards:*** Federal Pell, FSEOG, state, private, college/university gift aid from institutional funds.

GIFT AID (NON-NEED-BASED) ***Scholarships, grants, and awards by category:*** *Academic interests/achievement:* general academic interests/achievements. *Creative arts/performance:* applied art and design, creative writing, music, theater/drama. *Special characteristics:* children and siblings of alumni, international students, out-of-state students, previous college experience, siblings of current students, veterans.

LOANS ***Programs:*** Federal Direct (Subsidized and Unsubsidized Stafford, PLUS), Perkins, state, college/university.

WORK-STUDY ***Federal work-study:*** Total amount: $433,631; jobs available. ***State or other work-study/employment:*** Total amount: $216,142 (51% need-based, 49% non-need-based). Part-time jobs available.

APPLYING FOR FINANCIAL AID ***Required financial aid form:*** FAFSA.

CONTACT Bethany Davenport, Director of Financial Aid, Mount Mercy University, 1330 Elmhurst Drive NE, Cedar Rapids, IA 52402-4797, 319-368-6467 Ext. 1545 or toll-free 800-248-4504. *Fax:* 319-364-3546. *E-mail:* bdavenport@mtmercy.edu.
Website: http://www.mtmercy.edu/.

MOUNT ST. JOSEPH UNIVERSITY

Cincinnati, OH

CONTACT Ms. Kathryn Kelly, Director of Student Administrative Services, Mount St. Joseph University, 5701 Delhi Road, Cincinnati, OH 45233-1670, 513-244-4418 or toll-free 800-654-9314. *Fax:* 513-244-4201. *E-mail:* kathryn.kelly@msj.edu.
Website: http://www.msj.edu/.

MOUNT SAINT MARY COLLEGE

Newburgh, NY

Tuition & fees: $34,412	Average undergraduate aid package: $22,634

ABOUT THE INSTITUTION Independent, coed. ***Awards:*** certificates, bachelor's, and master's degrees. 25 undergraduate majors. ***Total enrollment:*** 2,236. Undergraduates: 1,881. Freshmen: 339. Federal methodology is used as a basis for awarding need-based institutional aid.

UNDERGRADUATE EXPENSES for 2020–2021 ***Application fee:*** $45. ***Comprehensive fee:*** $51,070 includes full-time tuition ($33,126), mandatory fees ($1286), and room and board ($16,658). ***College room only:*** $9650. Full-time tuition and fees vary according to class time, course load, location, and program. Room and board charges vary according to board plan and housing facility. ***Part-time tuition:*** $1105 per credit. ***Part-time fees:*** $190 per year. Part-time tuition and fees vary according to class time, course load, location, and program.

FRESHMAN FINANCIAL AID (Fall 2019, est.) 326 applied for aid; of those 87% were deemed to have need. 100% of freshmen with need received aid; of those 26% had need fully met. ***Average percent of need met:*** 76% (excluding resources awarded to replace EFC). ***Average financial aid package:*** $24,901 (excluding resources awarded to replace EFC). 15% of all full-time freshmen had no need and received non-need-based gift aid.

UNDERGRADUATE FINANCIAL AID (Fall 2019, est.) 1,430 applied for aid; of those 87% were deemed to have need. 100% of undergraduates with need received aid; of those 19% had need fully met. ***Average percent of need met:*** 68% (excluding resources awarded to replace EFC). ***Average financial aid package:*** $22,634 (excluding resources awarded to replace EFC). 17% of all full-time undergraduates had no need and received non-need-based gift aid.

GIFT AID (NEED-BASED) ***Total amount:*** $22,247,747 (13% federal, 7% state, 78% institutional, 2% external sources). ***Receiving aid:*** Freshmen: 83% (280); all full-time undergraduates: 76% (1,220). ***Average award:*** Freshmen: $20,121; Undergraduates: $17,684. ***Scholarships, grants, and awards:*** Federal Pell, FSEOG, state, private, college/university gift aid from institutional funds, Federal Nursing, Academic Competitiveness Grants, National SMART Grants.

GIFT AID (NON-NEED-BASED) ***Total amount:*** $5,217,672 (4% state, 93% institutional, 3% external sources). ***Receiving aid:*** Freshmen: 15% (50). Undergraduates: 10% (153). ***Average award:*** Freshmen: $16,882. Undergraduates: $14,095. ***Scholarships, grants, and awards by category:*** *Academic interests/achievement:* 1,416 awards ($19,644,816 total): general academic interests/achievements. *Special achievements/activities:* 18 awards ($45,000 total): leadership. *Special characteristics:* 23 awards ($712,107 total): children of faculty/staff. ***Tuition waivers:*** Full or partial for employees or children of employees. ***ROTC:*** Army cooperative.

LOANS ***Student loans:*** $14,021,325 (95% need-based, 5% non-need-based). 82% of past graduating class borrowed through all loan programs. *Average indebtedness per student:* $28,519. ***Average need-based loan:*** Freshmen: $4030. Undergraduates: $5164. ***Parent loans:*** $11,191,554 (100% need-based). ***Programs:*** Federal Direct (Subsidized and Unsubsidized Stafford, PLUS), Perkins, Federal Nursing, state.

WORK-STUDY ***Federal work-study:*** Total amount: $428,284; 295 jobs averaging $1452.

APPLYING FOR FINANCIAL AID ***Required financial aid form:*** FAFSA. ***Financial aid deadline (priority):*** 2/15. ***Notification date:*** Continuous beginning 3/15. Students must reply by 5/1.

CONTACT Jacqueline Perez, Director of Financial Aid, Mount Saint Mary College, 330 Powell Avenue, Newburgh, NY 12550-3494, 845-561-3394 or toll-free 888-937-6762. *Fax:* 845-569-3302. *E-mail:* Jacqueline.Perez@msmc.edu.
Website: http://www.msmc.edu/.

MOUNT SAINT MARY'S UNIVERSITY

Los Angeles, CA

Tuition & fees: $42,792	Average undergraduate aid package: $31,778

ABOUT THE INSTITUTION Independent Roman Catholic, coed, primarily women. ***Awards:*** certificates, associate, bachelor's, master's, and doctoral degrees. 47 undergraduate majors. ***Total enrollment:*** 3,280. Undergraduates: 2,601. Freshmen: 496. Federal methodology is used as a basis for awarding need-based institutional aid.

UNDERGRADUATE EXPENSES for 2019–2020 ***Comprehensive fee:*** $55,247 includes full-time tuition ($41,592), mandatory fees ($1200), and room and board ($12,455). Full-time tuition and fees vary according to course load, degree level, and program. Room and board charges vary according to board plan and housing facility. Part-time tuition and fees vary according to course load, degree level, and program.

FRESHMAN FINANCIAL AID (Fall 2019, est.) 397 applied for aid; of those 97% were deemed to have need. 100% of freshmen with need received aid; of those 1% had need fully met. ***Average percent of need met:*** 66% (excluding resources awarded to replace EFC). ***Average financial aid package:*** $37,089 (excluding resources awarded to replace EFC). 3% of all full-time freshmen had no need and received non-need-based gift aid.

UNDERGRADUATE FINANCIAL AID (Fall 2019, est.) 1,631 applied for aid; of those 96% were deemed to have need. 98% of undergraduates with need received aid; of those 5% had need fully met. ***Average percent of need met:*** 61% (excluding resources awarded to replace EFC). ***Average financial aid package:*** $31,778 (excluding resources awarded to replace EFC). 3% of all full-time undergraduates had no need and received non-need-based gift aid.

GIFT AID (NEED-BASED) ***Receiving aid:*** Freshmen: 95% (381); all full-time undergraduates: 76% (1,303). ***Average award:*** Freshmen: $21,176; Undergraduates: $26,860. ***Scholarships, grants, and awards:*** Federal Pell, FSEOG, state, private, college/university gift aid from institutional funds.

GIFT AID (NON-NEED-BASED) ***Receiving aid:*** Freshmen: 1. Undergraduates: 2% (40). ***Average award:*** Freshmen: $14,590. Undergraduates: $11,364. ***Scholarships, grants, and awards by category:*** *Academic interests/achievement:* general academic interests/achievements. *Creative arts/performance:* music. *Special achievements/activities:* community service, leadership. *Special characteristics:* children and siblings of alumni. ***Tuition waivers:*** Full or partial for employees or children of employees.

LOANS ***Student loans:*** 78% of past graduating class borrowed through all loan programs. *Average indebtedness per student:* $29,482. ***Average need-based loan:*** Freshmen: $3414. Undergraduates: $3183. ***Programs:*** Federal Direct (Subsidized and Unsubsidized Stafford, PLUS), Federal Nursing, college/university.

WORK-STUDY Federal work-study jobs available. ***State or other work-study/employment:*** Part-time jobs available.

APPLYING FOR FINANCIAL AID ***Required financial aid form:*** FAFSA. ***Financial aid deadline:*** Continuous. ***Notification date:*** Continuous. Students must reply within 3 weeks of notification.

CONTACT La Royce Housley, Director of Financial Aid, Mount Saint Mary's University, 12001 Chalon Road, Los Angeles, CA 90049, 310-954-4192 or toll-free 800-999-9893.
Website: http://www.msmu.edu/.

MOUNT ST. MARY'S UNIVERSITY

Emmitsburg, MD

Tuition & fees: $43,650	Average undergraduate aid package: $31,489

ABOUT THE INSTITUTION Independent Roman Catholic, coed. ***Awards:*** certificates, bachelor's, and master's degrees. 33 undergraduate majors. ***Total enrollment:*** 2,362. Undergraduates: 1,898. Freshmen: 513. Federal methodology is used as a basis for awarding need-based institutional aid.

UNDERGRADUATE EXPENSES for 2020–2021 ***Application fee:*** $45. ***Tuition:*** full-time $42,200; part-time $1370 per credit hour. ***Required fees:*** full-time $1450. ***College room only:*** $6940.

FRESHMAN FINANCIAL AID (Fall 2019, est.) 471 applied for aid; of those 86% were deemed to have need. 100% of freshmen with need received aid; of those 30% had need fully met. ***Average percent of need met:*** 77% (excluding resources awarded to replace EFC). ***Average financial aid package:*** $32,577 (excluding resources awarded to replace EFC). 20% of all full-time freshmen had no need and received non-need-based gift aid.

UNDERGRADUATE FINANCIAL AID (Fall 2019, est.) 1,393 applied for aid; of those 90% were deemed to have need. 100% of undergraduates with need received aid; of those 28% had need fully met. ***Average percent of need met:*** 75% (excluding resources awarded to replace EFC). ***Average financial aid package:*** $31,489 (excluding resources awarded to replace EFC). 24% of all full-time undergraduates had no need and received non-need-based gift aid.

GIFT AID (NEED-BASED) ***Total amount:*** $32,074,375 (7% federal, 5% state, 86% institutional, 2% external sources). ***Receiving aid:*** Freshmen: 79% (404); all full-time undergraduates: 71% (1,248). ***Average award:*** Freshmen: $29,603; Undergraduates: $27,781. ***Scholarships, grants, and awards:*** Federal Pell, FSEOG, state, private, college/university gift aid from institutional funds.

GIFT AID (NON-NEED-BASED) ***Total amount:*** $12,049,212 (7% federal, 88% institutional, 5% external sources). ***Receiving aid:*** Freshmen: 18% (93). Undergraduates: 15% (263). ***Average award:*** Freshmen: $23,465. Undergraduates: $21,106. ***Scholarships, grants, and awards by category:*** *Academic interests/achievement:* general academic interests/achievements. *Creative arts/performance:* applied art and design. *Special achievements/activities:* religious involvement. *Special characteristics:* children of faculty/staff, siblings of current students. ***ROTC:*** Army cooperative.

LOANS ***Student loans:*** $12,235,529 (59% need-based, 41% non-need-based). 74% of past graduating class borrowed through all loan programs. *Average indebtedness per student:* $38,998. ***Average need-based loan:*** Freshmen: $2673. Undergraduates: $3793. ***Parent loans:*** $6,364,186 (46% need-based, 54% non-need-based). ***Programs:*** Federal Direct (Subsidized and Unsubsidized Stafford, PLUS).

WORK-STUDY ***Federal work-study:*** Total amount: $284,225; jobs available. ***State or other work-study/employment:*** Total amount: $938,629 (89% need-based, 11% non-need-based). Part-time jobs available.

ATHLETIC AWARDS Total amount: $4,858,609 (46% need-based, 54% non-need-based).

APPLYING FOR FINANCIAL AID ***Required financial aid form:*** FAFSA. ***Financial aid deadline:*** 3/1 (priority: 12/1). ***Notification date:*** Continuous beginning 12/15. Students must reply by 5/1.

CONTACT Mr. David C. Reeder, Director of Financial Aid, Mount St. Mary's University, 11242 Suffolk Dr, Hagerstown, MD 21742, 301-8002847 or toll-free 800-448-4347. *Fax:* 301-447-5915. *E-mail:* rmjackson410@gmail.com.
Website: http://www.msmary.edu/.

MT. SIERRA COLLEGE

Monrovia, CA

CONTACT Financial Aid Office, Mt. Sierra College, 800 Royal Oaks Drive, Suite 101, Monrovia, CA 91016, 888-828-8800.
Website: http://www.mtsierra.edu/.

MOUNT VERNON NAZARENE UNIVERSITY

Mount Vernon, OH

Tuition & fees: $31,610	Average undergraduate aid package: $22,793

ABOUT THE INSTITUTION Independent Nazarene, coed. ***Awards:*** associate, bachelor's, and master's degrees. 72 undergraduate majors. ***Total enrollment:*** 2,205. Undergraduates: 1,816. Freshmen: 324. Federal methodology is used as a basis for awarding need-based institutional aid.

UNDERGRADUATE EXPENSES for 2020–2021 ***Application fee:*** $25. ***Comprehensive fee:*** $40,500 includes full-time tuition ($31,360), mandatory fees ($250), and room and board ($8890). ***College room only:*** $4938. Full-time tuition and fees vary according to program. ***Part-time tuition:*** $870 per credit hour. Part-time tuition and fees vary according to course load and program.

FRESHMAN FINANCIAL AID (Fall 2019, est.) 355 applied for aid; of those 91% were deemed to have need. 100% of freshmen with need received aid; of those 71% had need fully met. ***Average percent of need met:*** 72% (excluding resources awarded to replace EFC). ***Average financial aid package:*** $27,335 (excluding resources awarded to replace EFC). 8% of all full-time freshmen had no need and received non-need-based gift aid.

UNDERGRADUATE FINANCIAL AID (Fall 2019, est.) 1,450 applied for aid; of those 95% were deemed to have need. 96% of undergraduates with need received aid; of those 66% had need fully met. ***Average percent of need met:*** 58% (excluding resources awarded to replace EFC). ***Average financial aid package:*** $22,793 (excluding resources awarded to replace EFC). 13% of all full-time undergraduates had no need and received non-need-based gift aid.

GIFT AID (NEED-BASED) ***Total amount:*** $22,621,611 (12% federal, 4% state, 81% institutional, 3% external sources). ***Receiving aid:*** Freshmen: 87% (324); all full-time undergraduates: 77% (1,278). ***Average award:*** Freshmen: $23,766; Undergraduates: $21,647. ***Scholarships, grants, and awards:*** Federal Pell, FSEOG, state, private, college/university gift aid from institutional funds.

GIFT AID (NON-NEED-BASED) ***Total amount:*** $3,723,081 (3% state, 96% institutional, 1% external sources). ***Receiving aid:*** Freshmen: 62% (231). Undergraduates: 53% (879). ***Average award:*** Freshmen: $15,826. Undergraduates: $14,496. ***Scholarships, grants, and awards by category:*** *Academic interests/achievement:* general academic interests/achievements. *Creative arts/performance:* applied art and design, music. *Special achievements/activities:* general special achievements/activities, religious involvement. *Special characteristics:* children of faculty/staff, international students, members of minority groups, relatives of clergy, religious affiliation. ***Tuition waivers:*** Full or partial for employees or children of employees, senior citizens.

LOANS ***Student loans:*** $9,220,360 (94% need-based, 6% non-need-based). 75% of past graduating class borrowed through all loan programs. *Average indebtedness per student:* $22,778. ***Average need-based loan:*** Freshmen: $3145. Undergraduates: $3965. ***Parent loans:*** $2,227,497 (80% need-based, 20% non-need-based). ***Pro-***

grams: Federal Direct (Subsidized and Unsubsidized Stafford, PLUS), Perkins, state, Charles E. Schell Foundation loans.
WORK-STUDY *Federal work-study:* Total amount: $128,317; jobs available. ***State or other work-study/employment:*** Part-time jobs available.
ATHLETIC AWARDS Total amount: $1,121,200 (67% need-based, 33% non-need-based).
APPLYING FOR FINANCIAL AID *Required financial aid form:* FAFSA. ***Financial aid deadline:*** Continuous. ***Notification date:*** Continuous beginning 11/15.
CONTACT Mr. Jared M. Sponseller, Director of Student Financial Services, Mount Vernon Nazarene University, 800 Martinsburg Rd, Mount Vernon, OH 43050, 740-397-9000 Ext. 4521 or toll-free 866-462-6868. *Fax:* 740-399-8682. *E-mail:* jsponseller@mvnu.edu.
Website: http://www.mvnu.edu/.

MUHLENBERG COLLEGE

Allentown, PA

ABOUT THE INSTITUTION Independent Lutheran Church, coed. ***Awards:*** certificates, associate, and bachelor's degrees. 37 undergraduate majors. ***Total enrollment:*** 2,251. Undergraduates: 2,251. Freshmen: 538.
GIFT AID (NEED-BASED) *Scholarships, grants, and awards:* Federal Pell, FSEOG, state, private, college/university gift aid from institutional funds, United Negro College Fund.
GIFT AID (NON-NEED-BASED) *Scholarships, grants, and awards by category:* *Academic interests/achievement:* general academic interests/achievements. *Creative arts/performance:* applied art and design, cinema/film/broadcasting, dance, music, performing arts, theater/drama. *Special characteristics:* relatives of clergy.
LOANS *Programs:* Federal Direct (Subsidized and Unsubsidized Stafford, PLUS).
WORK-STUDY *Federal work-study:* Total amount: $250,000; jobs available. ***State or other work-study/employment:*** Total amount: $200,000 (33% need-based, 67% non-need-based). Part-time jobs available.
APPLYING FOR FINANCIAL AID *Required financial aid forms:* FAFSA, institution's own form, CSS Financial Aid PROFILE, noncustodial (divorced/separated) parent's statement.
CONTACT Mr. Greg Mitton, Director of Financial Aid, Muhlenberg College, 2400 Chew Street, Allentown, PA 18104-5586, 484-664-3175. *Fax:* 484-664-3234. *E-mail:* gregmitton@muhlenberg.edu.
Website: http://www.muhlenberg.edu/.

MULTNOMAH UNIVERSITY

Portland, OR

CONTACT Mrs. Mary J. McGlothlan, Director of Financial Aid, Multnomah University, 8435 NE Glisan Street, Portland, OR 97220-5898, 503-251-5337 or toll-free 877-251-6560. *Fax:* 503-445-5199. *E-mail:* mmcglothlan@multnomah.edu.
Website: http://www.multnomah.edu/.

MURRAY STATE UNIVERSITY

Murray, KY

ABOUT THE INSTITUTION State-supported, coed. ***Awards:*** certificates, bachelor's, master's, and doctoral degrees. 63 undergraduate majors. ***Total enrollment:*** 9,569. Undergraduates: 8,215. Freshmen: 1,421.
GIFT AID (NEED-BASED) *Scholarships, grants, and awards:* Federal Pell, FSEOG, state, private, college/university gift aid from institutional funds, Federal Nursing.
GIFT AID (NON-NEED-BASED) *Scholarships, grants, and awards by category:* *Academic interests/achievement:* agriculture, biological sciences, business, communication, computer science, education, engineering/technologies, English, general academic interests/achievements, health fields, home economics, humanities, international studies, mathematics, military science, physical sciences, premedicine, social sciences. *Creative arts/performance:* applied art and design, dance, journalism/publications, music, theater/drama. *Special achievements/activities:* community service, memberships, rodeo. *Special characteristics:* adult students, children of faculty/staff, general special characteristics, local/state students, married students, members of minority groups, out-of-state students, veterans.
LOANS *Programs:* Federal Direct (Subsidized and Unsubsidized Stafford, PLUS), Perkins, Federal Nursing, college/university.
WORK-STUDY *Federal work-study:* Total amount: $1,156,032; jobs available. ***State or other work-study/employment:*** Total amount: $3,612,082 (43% need-based, 57% non-need-based). Part-time jobs available.
APPLYING FOR FINANCIAL AID *Required financial aid forms:* FAFSA, general scholarship application form, summer term institutional loan application.
CONTACT Wendy Cain, Bursar/Interim Director of Student Financial Services, Murray State University, 120 Sparks Hall, Murray, KY 42071-0009, 270-809-2273 or toll-free 800-272-4678. *Fax:* 270-809-3116. *E-mail:* wcain@murraystate.edu.
Website: http://www.murraystate.edu/.

MUSICIANS INSTITUTE

Hollywood, CA

CONTACT Director of Financial Aid, Musicians Institute, 1655 North McCadden Place, Hollywood, CA 90028, 323-462-1384 or toll-free 800-255-PLAY.
Website: http://www.mi.edu/.

MUSKINGUM UNIVERSITY

New Concord, OH

Tuition & fees: $29,740	Average undergraduate aid package: $23,292

ABOUT THE INSTITUTION Independent Presbyterian Church (U.S.A.), coed. ***Awards:*** bachelor's and master's degrees. 72 undergraduate majors. ***Total enrollment:*** 2,369. Undergraduates: 1,602. Freshmen: 388. Federal methodology is used as a basis for awarding need-based institutional aid.
UNDERGRADUATE EXPENSES for 2020–2021 *One-time required fee:* $250. ***Comprehensive fee:*** $41,772 includes full-time tuition ($28,700), mandatory fees ($1040), and room and board ($12,032). ***College room only:*** $6130. ***Part-time tuition:*** $625 per credit hour.
FRESHMAN FINANCIAL AID (Fall 2018) 356 applied for aid; of those 96% were deemed to have need. 100% of freshmen with need received aid; of those 21% had need fully met. ***Average percent of need met:*** 76% (excluding resources awarded to replace EFC). ***Average financial aid package:*** $26,072 (excluding resources awarded to replace EFC). 6% of all full-time freshmen had no need and received non-need-based gift aid.
UNDERGRADUATE FINANCIAL AID (Fall 2018) 1,341 applied for aid; of those 95% were deemed to have need. 99% of undergraduates with need received aid; of those 15% had need fully met. ***Average percent of need met:*** 68% (excluding resources awarded to replace EFC). ***Average financial aid package:*** $23,292 (excluding resources awarded to replace EFC). 10% of all full-time undergraduates had no need and received non-need-based gift aid.
GIFT AID (NEED-BASED) *Receiving aid:* Freshmen: 92% (339); all full-time undergraduates: 76% (1,176). ***Average award:*** Freshmen: $20,782; Undergraduates: $18,150. ***Scholarships, grants, and awards:*** Federal Pell, FSEOG, state, private, college/university gift aid from institutional funds.
GIFT AID (NON-NEED-BASED) *Receiving aid:* Freshmen: 14% (52). Undergraduates: 8% (125). ***Average award:*** Freshmen: $15,171. Undergraduates: $14,785. ***Scholarships, grants, and awards by category:*** *Academic interests/achievement:* 1,028 awards ($12,389,042 total): biological sciences, computer science, education, engineering/technologies, general academic interests/achievements, mathematics, physical sciences, premedicine. *Creative arts/performance:* 114 awards ($182,934 total): applied art and design, art/fine arts, debating, journalism/publications, music, theater/drama. *Special achievements/activities:* 253 awards ($243,120 total): community service, junior miss, leadership. *Special characteristics:* 818 awards ($1,457,964 total): children and siblings of alumni, ethnic background, international students, local/state students, members of minority groups, previous college experience, relatives of clergy, religious affiliation, siblings of current students. ***Tuition waivers:*** Full or partial for employees or children of employees.
LOANS *Student loans:* 76% of past graduating class borrowed through all loan programs. *Average indebtedness per student:* $33,026. ***Average need-based loan:***

Freshmen: $3406. Undergraduates: $3921. ***Programs:*** Federal Direct (Subsidized and Unsubsidized Stafford, PLUS), Federal Nursing, college/university.
WORK-STUDY *Federal work-study:* 491 jobs averaging $1087.
APPLYING FOR FINANCIAL AID *Required financial aid form:* FAFSA. ***Notification date:*** Continuous. Students must reply within 2 weeks of notification.
CONTACT Mrs. Amber Gump, Director of Student Financial Services, Muskingum University, 10 College Drive, P.O. Box 1837, New Concord, OH 43762-1837, 740-826-8139 or toll-free 800-752-6082. *Fax:* 740-826-8100. *E-mail:* amberg@muskingum.edu.
Website: http://www.muskingum.edu/.

NAROPA UNIVERSITY
Boulder, CO

CONTACT Ms. Nancy Morrell, Director of Student Financial Services, Naropa University, 2130 Arapahoe Avenue, Boulder, CO 80302-6697, 303-546-3534 or toll-free 800-772-6951. *Fax:* 303-546-3536. *E-mail:* finaid@naropa.edu.
Website: http://www.naropa.edu/.

NATIONAL AMERICAN UNIVERSITY
Centennial, CO

CONTACT Financial Aid Office, National American University, 8242 South University Boulevard, Suite 100, Centennial, CO 80122, 303-542-7000 or toll-free 877-628-5211.
Website: http://www.national.edu/.

NATIONAL AMERICAN UNIVERSITY
Colorado Springs, CO

CONTACT Financial Aid Office, National American University, 1079 Space Center Drive, Suite 140, Colorado Springs, CO 80915, 719-208-3800 or toll-free 855-369-9397.
Website: http://www.national.edu/.

NATIONAL AMERICAN UNIVERSITY
Colorado Springs, CO

CONTACT Financial Aid Coordinator, National American University, 2577 North Chelton Road, Colorado Springs, CO 80909, 719-471-4205 or toll-free 855-369-9397.
Website: http://www.national.edu/.

NATIONAL AMERICAN UNIVERSITY
Indianapolis, IN

CONTACT Financial Aid Office, National American University, 3600 Woodview Trace, Suite 200, Indianapolis, IN 46268, 317-810-8100 or toll-free 800-609-1430.
Website: http://www.national.edu/.

NATIONAL AMERICAN UNIVERSITY
Garden City, KS

CONTACT Financial Aid Office, National American University, 801 Campus Drive, Garden City, KS 67846.
Website: http://www.national.edu/.

NATIONAL AMERICAN UNIVERSITY
Overland Park, KS

CONTACT Financial Aid Office, National American University, 10310 Mastin Street, Overland Park, KS 66212, 913-981-8700 or toll-free 866-628-1288.
Website: http://www.national.edu/.

NATIONAL AMERICAN UNIVERSITY
Wichita, KS

CONTACT Financial Aid Office, National American University, 7309 East 21st Street, Suite G40, Wichita, KS 67206, 316-681-3050 or toll-free 877-628-9424.
Website: http://www.national.edu/.

NATIONAL AMERICAN UNIVERSITY
Wichita, KS

CONTACT Financial Aid Office, National American University, 8428 West 13th Street North, Suite 120, Wichita, KS 67212, toll-free 877-628-9424.
Website: http://www.national.edu/.

NATIONAL AMERICAN UNIVERSITY
Bloomington, MN

CONTACT Financial Aid Office, National American University, 7801 Metro Parkway, Suite 200, Bloomington, MN 55425, 952-356-3600 or toll-free 866-628-6387.
Website: http://www.national.edu/.

NATIONAL AMERICAN UNIVERSITY
Brooklyn Center, MN

CONTACT Financial Aid Office, National American University, 6200 Shingle Creek Parkway, Suite 130, Brooklyn Center, MN 55430, 763-852-7500 or toll-free 866-628-6387.
Website: http://www.national.edu/.

NATIONAL AMERICAN UNIVERSITY
Burnsville, MN

CONTACT Financial Aid Office, National American University, 513 West Travelers Trail, Burnsville, MN 55337, 952-563-1250 or toll-free 866-628-6387.
Website: http://www.national.edu/.

NATIONAL AMERICAN UNIVERSITY
Roseville, MN

CONTACT Financial Aid Office, National American University, 1550 West Highway 36, Roseville, MN 55113, 651-855-6300 or toll-free 866-628-6387.
Website: http://www.national.edu/.

NATIONAL AMERICAN UNIVERSITY

Independence, MO

CONTACT Financial Aid Office, National American University, 3620 Arowhead Avenue, Independence, MO 64057, 816-412-7700 or toll-free 866-628-1288.
Website: http://www.national.edu/.

NATIONAL AMERICAN UNIVERSITY

Kansas City, MO

CONTACT Mary Anderson, Coordinator of Financial Aid, National American University, 4200 Blue Ridge, Kansas City, MO 64133, 816-353-4554 or toll-free 866-628-1288. *Fax:* 816-353-1176.
Website: http://www.national.edu/.

NATIONAL AMERICAN UNIVERSITY

Lee's Summit, MO

CONTACT Financial Aid Office, National American University, 401 NW Murray Road, Lee's Summit, MO 64081, 816-600-3900 or toll-free 866-628-1288.
Website: http://www.national.edu/.

NATIONAL AMERICAN UNIVERSITY

Bellevue, NE

CONTACT Financial Aid Office, National American University, 3604 Summit Plaza Drive, Bellevue, NE 68123, 402-972-4250.
Website: http://www.national.edu/.

NATIONAL AMERICAN UNIVERSITY

Albuquerque, NM

CONTACT Financial Aid Office, National American University, 10131 Coors Boulevard NW, Suite I-01, Albuquerque, NM 87114, 505-348-3750 or toll-free 800-895-9904.
Website: http://www.national.edu/.

NATIONAL AMERICAN UNIVERSITY

Albuquerque, NM

CONTACT Director of Financial Aid, National American University, 321 Kansas City Street, Rapid City, SD 57701, 605-394-4800 or toll-free 800-895-9904.
Website: http://www.national.edu/.

NATIONAL AMERICAN UNIVERSITY

Tulsa, OK

CONTACT Financial Aid Office, National American University, 8040 South Sheridan Road, Tulsa, OK 74133, 918-879-8400 or toll-free 800-209-0338.
Website: http://www.national.edu/.

NATIONAL AMERICAN UNIVERSITY

Ellsworth AFB, SD

CONTACT Financial Aid Office, National American University, 1000 Ellsworth Street, Rushmore Center, Suite 2400B, Ellsworth AFB, SD 57706, 605-718-6550.
Website: http://www.national.edu/.

NATIONAL AMERICAN UNIVERSITY

Rapid City, SD

CONTACT Financial Aid Director, National American University, PO Box 1780, Rapid City, SD 57709-1780, 605-721-5213 or toll-free 800-209-0490.
Website: http://www.national.edu/.

NATIONAL AMERICAN UNIVERSITY

Sioux Falls, SD

CONTACT Ms. Rhonda Kohnen, Financial Aid Coordinator, National American University, 2801 South Kiwanis Avenue, Suite 100, Sioux Falls, SD 57105-4293, 605-334-5430 or toll-free 800-388-5430. *Fax:* 605-334-1575. *E-mail:* rkohnen@national.edu.
Website: http://www.national.edu/.

NATIONAL AMERICAN UNIVERSITY

Watertown, SD

CONTACT Financial Aid Office, National American University, 925 29th Street SE, Watertown, SD 57201.
Website: http://www.national.edu/.

NATIONAL AMERICAN UNIVERSITY

Austin, TX

CONTACT Financial Aid Office, National American University, 13801 Burnet Road, Suite 300, Austin, TX 78727, 512-651-4100 or toll-free 888-628-8392.
Website: http://www.national.edu/.

NATIONAL AMERICAN UNIVERSITY

Georgetown, TX

CONTACT Financial Aid Office, National American University, 1015 West University Avenue, Suite 700, Georgetown, TX 78628, 512-942-6750 or toll-free 888-628-8392.
Website: http://www.national.edu/.

NATIONAL AMERICAN UNIVERSITY

Houston, TX

CONTACT Financial Aid Office, National American University, 11511 Katy Freeway, Suite 200, Houston, TX 77079, 832-619-7300 or toll-free 855-455-8029.
Website: http://www.national.edu/.

NATIONAL AMERICAN UNIVERSITY
Lewisville, TX

CONTACT Financial Aid Office, National American University, 475 State Highway 121 Bypass, Suite 150, Lewisville, TX 75067, 972-829-2150 or toll-free 800-548-0605. *Website:* http://www.national.edu/.

NATIONAL AMERICAN UNIVERSITY
Mesquite, TX

CONTACT Financial Aid Office, National American University, 18600 LBJ Freeway, Mesquite, TX 75150, 972-773-8800 or toll-free 800-548-0605.
Website: http://www.national.edu/.

NATIONAL AMERICAN UNIVERSITY
Richardson, TX

CONTACT Financial Aid Office, National American University, 300 North Coit Road, Suite 225, Richardson, TX 75080, 972-773-8650 or toll-free 800-548-0605.
Website: http://www.national.edu/.

NATIONAL LOUIS UNIVERSITY
Chicago, IL

CONTACT Janet Jazwiec, Assistant Director of Student Finance, National Louis University, 1000 Capitol Drive, Wheeling, IL 60090, 847-947-5453 or toll-free 888-658-8632. *Fax:* 847-947-5453. *E-mail:* jjazwiec@nl.edu.
Website: http://www.nl.edu/.

NATIONAL PARALEGAL COLLEGE
Phoenix, AZ

CONTACT Financial Aid Office, National Paralegal College, 717 East Maryland Avenue, Phoenix, AZ 85014, 845-371-9101 or toll-free 800-371-6105.
Website: http://nationalparalegal.edu/.

NATIONAL UNIVERSITY
La Jolla, CA

Tuition & fees: $13,320	Average undergraduate aid package: $5836

ABOUT THE INSTITUTION Independent, coed. ***Awards:*** certificates, associate, bachelor's, master's, and doctoral degrees. 53 undergraduate majors. ***Total enrollment:*** 16,930. Undergraduates: 7,735. Freshmen: 20. Both federal and institutional methodology are used as a basis for awarding need-based institutional aid.

UNDERGRADUATE EXPENSES for 2019–2020 ***Tuition:*** full-time $13,320; part-time $370 per unit.

FRESHMAN FINANCIAL AID (Fall 2018) 213 applied for aid; of those 95% were deemed to have need. 69% of freshmen with need received aid; of those 1% had need fully met. ***Average percent of need met:*** 19% (excluding resources awarded to replace EFC). ***Average financial aid package:*** $5787 (excluding resources awarded to replace EFC).

UNDERGRADUATE FINANCIAL AID (Fall 2018) 5,599 applied for aid; of those 96% were deemed to have need. 70% of undergraduates with need received aid. ***Average percent of need met:*** 19% (excluding resources awarded to replace EFC). ***Average financial aid package:*** $5836 (excluding resources awarded to replace EFC). 1% of all full-time undergraduates had no need and received non-need-based gift aid.

GIFT AID (NEED-BASED) ***Total amount:*** $15,269,240 (88% federal, 9% state, 1% institutional, 2% external sources). ***Receiving aid:*** Freshmen: 36% (100); all full-time undergraduates: 36% (2,371). ***Average award:*** Freshmen: $4335; Undergraduates: $5215. ***Scholarships, grants, and awards:*** Federal Pell, FSEOG, state, college/university gift aid from institutional funds.

GIFT AID (NON-NEED-BASED) ***Total amount:*** $5,056,617 (10% federal, 89% institutional, 1% external sources). ***Receiving aid:*** Freshmen: 9% (25). Undergraduates: 19% (1,268). ***Average award:*** Undergraduates: $1942. ***Scholarships, grants, and awards by category:*** *Academic interests/achievement:* 678 awards ($2,035,594 total): general academic interests/achievements. *Special achievements/activities:* 888 awards ($1,890,952 total): leadership. ***ROTC:*** Army cooperative, Air Force cooperative.

LOANS ***Student loans:*** $34,239,617 (35% need-based, 65% non-need-based). 71% of past graduating class borrowed through all loan programs. *Average indebtedness per student:* $48,851. ***Average need-based loan:*** Freshmen: $3587. Undergraduates: $4108. ***Parent loans:*** $992,302 (100% non-need-based). ***Programs:*** Federal Direct (Subsidized and Unsubsidized Stafford, PLUS), Perkins, college/university.

WORK-STUDY ***Federal work-study:*** Total amount: $80,472; 26 jobs averaging $3095.

APPLYING FOR FINANCIAL AID ***Required financial aid forms:*** FAFSA, institution's own form. ***Financial aid deadline:*** Continuous. ***Notification date:*** Continuous beginning 6/30.

CONTACT Ashlie Greene, Associate Director of Financial Aid, National University, 9980 Carroll Canyon, San Diego, CA 92131, 858-642-8515 or toll-free 800-628-8648. *Fax:* 858-642-8720. *E-mail:* amacdona@nu.edu.
Website: http://www.nu.edu/.

NATIONAL UNIVERSITY COLLEGE
Arecibo, PR

CONTACT Financial Aid Office, National University College, Calle Manuel Pérez Avilés, Avenida Víctor Rojas, Arecibo, PR 00612.
Website: http://www.nuc.edu/.

NATIONAL UNIVERSITY COLLEGE
Bayamón, PR

CONTACT Ms. Elizabeth Cruz, Institutional Director of Financial Aid, National University College, PO Box 2036, Bayamon, PR 00961, 787-780-5134 Ext. 4021 or toll-free 800-780-5134. *E-mail:* ecruz@nuc.edu.
Website: http://www.nuc.edu/.

NATIONAL UNIVERSITY COLLEGE
Caguas, PR

CONTACT Financial Aid Office, National University College, 190 Avenida Gautier Benitez Esquina Avenida Federico Degatau, Caguas, PR 00725, 787-653-4733 or toll-free 800-780-5134.
Website: http://www.nuc.edu/.

NATIONAL UNIVERSITY COLLEGE
Ponce, PR

CONTACT Financial Aid Office, National University College, PO Box 801243, Ponce, PR 00716, 787-840-4474.
Website: http://www.nuc.edu/.

NATIONAL UNIVERSITY COLLEGE

Rio Grande, PR

CONTACT Financial Aid Office, National University College, Carretera #3 Km. 22.1, Bo. Ciénaga Baja, Rio Grande, PR 00745, 787-809-5100 or toll-free 800-981-0812. *Website:* http://www.nuc.edu/.

NAVAJO TECHNICAL UNIVERSITY

Crownpoint, NM

CONTACT Office of Financial Aid, Navajo Technical University, PO Box 849, Crownpoint, NM 87313, 505-786-4309. *Website:* http://www.navajotech.edu/.

NAZARENE BIBLE COLLEGE

Colorado Springs, CO

Tuition & fees: $10,080	Average undergraduate aid package: $8268

ABOUT THE INSTITUTION Independent Church of the Nazarene, coed. ***Awards:*** certificates, diplomas, associate, and bachelor's degrees. 6 undergraduate majors. ***Total enrollment:*** 698. Undergraduates: 698. Freshmen: 14. Federal methodology is used as a basis for awarding need-based institutional aid.

UNDERGRADUATE EXPENSES for 2020–2021 ***Tuition:*** full-time $8880; part-time $370 per credit hour. ***Required fees:*** full-time $1200; $50 per credit hour. Full-time tuition and fees vary according to program and reciprocity agreements. Part-time tuition and fees vary according to program and reciprocity agreements.

UNDERGRADUATE FINANCIAL AID (Fall 2018) 42 applied for aid; of those 100% were deemed to have need. 98% of undergraduates with need received aid. ***Average percent of need met:*** 78% (excluding resources awarded to replace EFC). ***Average financial aid package:*** $8268 (excluding resources awarded to replace EFC).

GIFT AID (NEED-BASED) ***Total amount:*** $704,709 (84% federal, 13% institutional, 3% external sources). ***Receiving aid:*** All full-time undergraduates: 47% (32). ***Average award:*** Undergraduates: $3411. ***Scholarships, grants, and awards:*** Federal Pell, FSEOG, college/university gift aid from institutional funds.

GIFT AID (NON-NEED-BASED) ***Tuition waivers:*** Full or partial for employees or children of employees.

LOANS ***Student loans:*** $1,216,449 (100% need-based). 100% of past graduating class borrowed through all loan programs. *Average indebtedness per student:* $36,370. ***Average need-based loan:*** Undergraduates: $4525. ***Parent loans:*** $6992 (100% need-based). ***Programs:*** Federal Direct (Subsidized and Unsubsidized Stafford, PLUS).

APPLYING FOR FINANCIAL AID ***Required financial aid form:*** FAFSA. ***Financial aid deadline:*** Continuous. ***Notification date:*** Continuous beginning 6/1.

CONTACT Mrs. Jan Edwards, Director of Financial Aid, Nazarene Bible College, 1111 Academy Park Loop, Colorado Springs, CO 80910-3717, 800-873-3873 Ext. 5051 or toll-free 800-873-3873. *Fax:* 719-884-5199. *E-mail:* financialaid@nbc.edu. *Website:* http://www.nbc.edu/.

NAZARETH COLLEGE OF ROCHESTER

Rochester, NY

Tuition & fees: $35,416	Average undergraduate aid package: $28,616

ABOUT THE INSTITUTION Independent, coed. ***Awards:*** certificates, bachelor's, master's, and doctoral degrees. 64 undergraduate majors. ***Total enrollment:*** 2,979. Undergraduates: 2,283. Freshmen: 516. Federal methodology is used as a basis for awarding need-based institutional aid.

UNDERGRADUATE EXPENSES for 2019–2020 ***Application fee:*** $45. ***Comprehensive fee:*** $49,646 includes full-time tuition ($33,836), mandatory fees ($1580), and room and board ($14,230). Full-time tuition and fees vary according to course load and program. Room and board charges vary according to board plan and housing facility. ***Part-time tuition:*** $805 per credit hour. ***Part-time fees:*** $25 per term. Part-time tuition and fees vary according to course load and program.

FRESHMAN FINANCIAL AID (Fall 2019, est.) 503 applied for aid; of those 87% were deemed to have need. 100% of freshmen with need received aid; of those 45% had need fully met. ***Average percent of need met:*** 86% (excluding resources awarded to replace EFC). ***Average financial aid package:*** $29,222 (excluding resources awarded to replace EFC). 15% of all full-time freshmen had no need and received non-need-based gift aid.

UNDERGRADUATE FINANCIAL AID (Fall 2019, est.) 2,010 applied for aid; of those 89% were deemed to have need. 100% of undergraduates with need received aid; of those 37% had need fully met. ***Average percent of need met:*** 82% (excluding resources awarded to replace EFC). ***Average financial aid package:*** $28,616 (excluding resources awarded to replace EFC). 18% of all full-time undergraduates had no need and received non-need-based gift aid.

GIFT AID (NEED-BASED) ***Total amount:*** $33,392,678 (10% federal, 7% state, 82% institutional, 1% external sources). ***Receiving aid:*** Freshmen: 85% (438); all full-time undergraduates: 82% (1,784). ***Average award:*** Freshmen: $20,859; Undergraduates: $18,635. ***Scholarships, grants, and awards:*** Federal Pell, FSEOG, state, private, college/university gift aid from institutional funds.

GIFT AID (NON-NEED-BASED) ***Total amount:*** $7,225,259 (1% state, 93% institutional, 6% external sources). ***Receiving aid:*** Freshmen: 43% (220). Undergraduates: 33% (722). ***Average award:*** Freshmen: $22,176. Undergraduates: $19,707. ***Scholarships, grants, and awards by category:*** *Academic interests/achievement:* 2,877 awards ($22,981,780 total): biological sciences, business, communication, education, English, foreign languages, general academic interests/achievements, health fields, humanities, international studies, mathematics, physical sciences, premedicine, religion/biblical studies, social sciences. *Creative arts/performance:* 476 awards ($1,652,299 total): applied art and design, art/fine arts, dance, music, performing arts, theater/drama. *Special achievements/activities:* 56 awards ($73,500 total): leadership. *Special characteristics:* 1,769 awards ($5,240,061 total): children of faculty/staff, ethnic background, general special characteristics, members of minority groups, out-of-state students, siblings of current students, veterans. ***Tuition waivers:*** Full or partial for employees or children of employees. ***ROTC:*** Army cooperative, Air Force cooperative.

LOANS ***Student loans:*** $20,389,067 (77% need-based, 23% non-need-based). 88% of past graduating class borrowed through all loan programs. *Average indebtedness per student:* $49,827. ***Average need-based loan:*** Freshmen: $3305. Undergraduates: $4389. ***Parent loans:*** $8,479,064 (47% need-based, 53% non-need-based). ***Programs:*** Federal Direct (Subsidized and Unsubsidized Stafford, PLUS), Federal Nursing.

WORK-STUDY ***Federal work-study:*** Total amount: $2,497,864; 1,120 jobs averaging $2061.

APPLYING FOR FINANCIAL AID ***Required financial aid forms:*** FAFSA, state aid form. ***Financial aid deadline (priority):*** 2/15. ***Notification date:*** Continuous beginning 2/1. Students must reply by 5/1 or within 2 weeks of notification.

CONTACT Janice Scheutzow, Director of Financial Aid, Nazareth College of Rochester, 4245 East Avenue, Rochester, NY 14618-3790, 585-389-2310 or toll-free 800-462-3944. *Fax:* 585-389-2317. *E-mail:* jscheut1@naz.edu. *Website:* http://www.naz.edu/.

NEBRASKA METHODIST COLLEGE

Omaha, NE

Tuition & fees: $16,308	Average undergraduate aid package: $10,624

ABOUT THE INSTITUTION Independent United Methodist Church, coed. ***Awards:*** certificates, associate, bachelor's, master's, and doctoral degrees. 9 undergraduate majors. ***Total enrollment:*** 1,128. Undergraduates: 766. Freshmen: 49.

UNDERGRADUATE EXPENSES for 2019–2020 ***Application fee:*** $25. ***Comprehensive fee:*** $25,894 includes full-time tuition ($15,660), mandatory fees ($648), and room and board ($9586). ***Part-time tuition:*** $580 per credit hour.

FRESHMAN FINANCIAL AID (Fall 2018) 48 applied for aid; of those 90% were deemed to have need. 100% of freshmen with need received aid; of those 9% had need fully met. ***Average percent of need met:*** 44% (excluding resources awarded to

replace EFC). ***Average financial aid package:*** $9557 (excluding resources awarded to replace EFC).
UNDERGRADUATE FINANCIAL AID (Fall 2018) 396 applied for aid; of those 88% were deemed to have need. 100% of undergraduates with need received aid; of those 3% had need fully met. ***Average percent of need met:*** 37% (excluding resources awarded to replace EFC). ***Average financial aid package:*** $10,624 (excluding resources awarded to replace EFC).
GIFT AID (NEED-BASED) ***Total amount:*** $3,505,201 (38% federal, 7% state, 45% institutional, 10% external sources). ***Receiving aid:*** Freshmen: 42; all full-time undergraduates: 321. ***Average award:*** Freshmen: $6842; Undergraduates: $7056. ***Scholarships, grants, and awards:*** Federal Pell, FSEOG, state, private, college/university gift aid from institutional funds.
GIFT AID (NON-NEED-BASED) ***Total amount:*** $361,731 (82% institutional, 18% external sources). ***Average award:*** Freshmen: $4942. Undergraduates: $4459. ***Scholarships, grants, and awards by category:*** *Academic interests/achievement:* general academic interests/achievements, health fields. *Special achievements/activities:* general special achievements/activities, leadership, memberships. *Special characteristics:* children of faculty/staff, religious affiliation. ***ROTC:*** Air Force cooperative.
LOANS ***Student loans:*** $6,048,576 (87% need-based, 13% non-need-based). 83% of past graduating class borrowed through all loan programs. *Average indebtedness per student:* $30,407. ***Average need-based loan:*** Freshmen: $3523. Undergraduates: $4681. ***Parent loans:*** $1,008,200 (60% need-based, 40% non-need-based). ***Programs:*** Federal Direct (Subsidized and Unsubsidized Stafford, PLUS), Federal Nursing.
WORK-STUDY ***Federal work-study:*** Total amount: $38,462; jobs available.
APPLYING FOR FINANCIAL AID ***Required financial aid forms:*** FAFSA, institution's own form. ***Financial aid deadline (priority):*** 3/1. ***Notification date:*** Continuous beginning 3/1. Students must reply within 4 weeks of notification.
CONTACT Ms. Penny James, Director of Financial Aid, Nebraska Methodist College, The Josie Harper Campus, 720 North 87th Street, Omaha, NE 68114-3426, 402-354-7225 or toll-free 800-335-5510. *Fax:* 402-354-7020. *E-mail:* penny.james@methodistcollege.edu.
Website: http://www.methodistcollege.edu/.

NEBRASKA WESLEYAN UNIVERSITY

Lincoln, NE

Tuition & fees: $35,564	Average undergraduate aid package: $24,765

ABOUT THE INSTITUTION Independent United Methodist, coed. ***Awards:*** certificates, bachelor's, and master's degrees. 52 undergraduate majors. ***Total enrollment:*** 2,044. Undergraduates: 1,842. Freshmen: 487. Federal methodology is used as a basis for awarding need-based institutional aid.
UNDERGRADUATE EXPENSES for 2020–2021 ***Comprehensive fee:*** $45,736 includes full-time tuition ($34,582), mandatory fees ($982), and room and board ($10,172). ***College room only:*** $5804. Room and board charges vary according to board plan and housing facility. ***Part-time tuition:*** $1236 per credit hour. Part-time tuition and fees vary according to class time, degree level, location, and program.
FRESHMAN FINANCIAL AID (Fall 2018) 454 applied for aid; of those 90% were deemed to have need. 100% of freshmen with need received aid; of those 19% had need fully met. ***Average percent of need met:*** 76% (excluding resources awarded to replace EFC). ***Average financial aid package:*** $26,475 (excluding resources awarded to replace EFC). 15% of all full-time freshmen had no need and received non-need-based gift aid.
UNDERGRADUATE FINANCIAL AID (Fall 2018) 1,381 applied for aid; of those 91% were deemed to have need. 100% of undergraduates with need received aid; of those 16% had need fully met. ***Average percent of need met:*** 74% (excluding resources awarded to replace EFC). ***Average financial aid package:*** $24,765 (excluding resources awarded to replace EFC). 22% of all full-time undergraduates had no need and received non-need-based gift aid.
GIFT AID (NEED-BASED) ***Total amount:*** $25,364,679 (10% federal, 2% state, 85% institutional, 3% external sources). ***Receiving aid:*** Freshmen: 84% (407); all full-time undergraduates: 74% (1,240). ***Average award:*** Freshmen: $22,478; Undergraduates: $20,303. ***Scholarships, grants, and awards:*** Federal Pell, FSEOG, state, private, college/university gift aid from institutional funds.
GIFT AID (NON-NEED-BASED) ***Total amount:*** $7,530,219 (96% institutional, 4% external sources). ***Receiving aid:*** Freshmen: 15% (72). Undergraduates: 10% (169). ***Average award:*** Freshmen: $19,777. Undergraduates: $16,557. ***Scholarships, grants, and awards by category:*** *Academic interests/achievement:* general academic interests/achievements. *Creative arts/performance:* applied art and design, music, theater/drama. *Special achievements/activities:* 1,100 awards ($3052 total): general special achievements/activities. *Special characteristics:* 594 awards ($4279 total): children and siblings of alumni, children of educators, children of faculty/staff, ethnic background, international students, members of minority groups, relatives of clergy, religious affiliation, siblings of current students. ***Tuition waivers:*** Full or partial for employees or children of employees, senior citizens. ***ROTC:*** Army cooperative, Naval cooperative, Air Force cooperative.
LOANS ***Student loans:*** $10,996,516 (72% need-based, 28% non-need-based). 75% of past graduating class borrowed through all loan programs. *Average indebtedness per student:* $31,715. ***Average need-based loan:*** Freshmen: $3248. Undergraduates: $4297. ***Parent loans:*** $3,700,306 (50% need-based, 50% non-need-based). ***Programs:*** Federal Direct (Subsidized and Unsubsidized Stafford, PLUS).
WORK-STUDY ***Federal work-study:*** Total amount: $207,675; 111 jobs averaging $1438. ***State or other work-study/employment:*** Total amount: $431,533 (32% need-based, 68% non-need-based). 643 part-time jobs averaging $1268.
APPLYING FOR FINANCIAL AID ***Required financial aid form:*** FAFSA. ***Financial aid deadline:*** Continuous. ***Notification date:*** Continuous beginning 10/15. Students must reply by 5/1 or within 2 weeks of notification.
CONTACT Mr. Thomas J. Ochsner, Director of Scholarships and Financial Aid, Nebraska Wesleyan University, 5000 Saint Paul Avenue, Lincoln, NE 68504, 402-465-2212 or toll-free 800-541-3818. *Fax:* 402-465-2194. *E-mail:* tjo@nebrwesleyan.edu.
Website: http://www.nebrwesleyan.edu/.

NER ISRAEL RABBINICAL COLLEGE

Baltimore, MD

CONTACT Mr. Moshe Pelberg, Financial Aid Administrator , Ner Israel Rabbinical College, 400 Mount Wilson Lane, Baltimore, MD 21208, 410-484-7200.

NEUMANN UNIVERSITY

Aston, PA

Tuition & fees: N/R	Average undergraduate aid package: $28,406

ABOUT THE INSTITUTION Independent Roman Catholic, coed. ***Awards:*** certificates, associate, bachelor's, master's, and doctoral degrees. 22 undergraduate majors. ***Total enrollment:*** 2,598. Undergraduates: 1,995. Freshmen: 421. Both federal and institutional methodology are used as a basis for awarding need-based institutional aid.
FRESHMAN FINANCIAL AID (Fall 2019, est.) 403 applied for aid; of those 90% were deemed to have need. 100% of freshmen with need received aid; of those 11% had need fully met. ***Average percent of need met:*** 73% (excluding resources awarded to replace EFC). ***Average financial aid package:*** $28,204 (excluding resources awarded to replace EFC). 13% of all full-time freshmen had no need and received non-need-based gift aid.
UNDERGRADUATE FINANCIAL AID (Fall 2019, est.) 1,289 applied for aid; of those 91% were deemed to have need. 99% of undergraduates with need received aid; of those 13% had need fully met. ***Average percent of need met:*** 71% (excluding resources awarded to replace EFC). ***Average financial aid package:*** $28,406 (excluding resources awarded to replace EFC). 15% of all full-time undergraduates had no need and received non-need-based gift aid.
GIFT AID (NEED-BASED) ***Total amount:*** $26,843,117 (12% federal, 7% state, 80% institutional, 1% external sources). ***Receiving aid:*** Freshmen: 87% (361); all full-time undergraduates: 84% (1,160). ***Average award:*** Freshmen: $23,306; Undergraduates: $20,219. ***Scholarships, grants, and awards:*** Federal Pell, FSEOG, state, private, college/university gift aid from institutional funds.
GIFT AID (NON-NEED-BASED) ***Average award:*** Freshmen: $15,842. Undergraduates: $13,910. ***Scholarships, grants, and awards by category:*** *Academic interests/achievement:* general academic interests/achievements. ***ROTC:*** Army cooperative, Air Force cooperative.

LOANS ***Student loans:*** $14,888,915 (100% need-based). 88% of past graduating class borrowed through all loan programs. *Average indebtedness per student:* $45,952. ***Average need-based loan:*** Freshmen: $3445. Undergraduates: $4206. ***Parent loans:*** $5,749,912 (100% need-based). ***Programs:*** Federal Direct (Subsidized and Unsubsidized Stafford, PLUS).

WORK-STUDY ***Federal work-study:*** Total amount: $1,844,771; jobs available. ***State or other work-study/employment:*** Part-time jobs available.

APPLYING FOR FINANCIAL AID ***Required financial aid form:*** FAFSA. ***Financial aid deadline (priority):*** 2/1. ***Notification date:*** 11/15.

CONTACT Ms. Eileen M. Tucker, Director of Financial Assistance, Neumann University, One Neumann Drive, Aston, PA 19014-1298, 610-558-5521 or toll-free 800-963-8626. *E-mail:* tuckere@neumann.edu.
Website: http://www.neumann.edu/.

NEUMONT COLLEGE OF COMPUTER SCIENCE

Salt Lake City, UT

Tuition & fees: $24,750 — **Average undergraduate aid package: N/A**

ABOUT THE INSTITUTION Proprietary, coed. ***Awards:*** bachelor's degrees. 2 undergraduate majors. Both federal and institutional methodology are used as a basis for awarding need-based institutional aid.

UNDERGRADUATE EXPENSES for 2019–2020 ***One-time required fee:*** $2900. ***Tuition:*** full-time $22,950; part-time $6000 per term. ***Required fees:*** full-time $1800. Full-time tuition and fees vary according to course load, degree level, program, and student level. Part-time tuition and fees vary according to course load, degree level, program, and student level. ***College room only:*** $6300. Room and board charges vary according to housing facility.

GIFT AID (NEED-BASED) ***Scholarships, grants, and awards:*** Federal Pell, FSEOG, private, college/university gift aid from institutional funds.

GIFT AID (NON-NEED-BASED) ***Scholarships, grants, and awards by category:*** *Special achievements/activities:* community service, religious involvement. *Special characteristics:* children of faculty/staff, international students, local/state students, veterans. ***Tuition waivers:*** Full or partial for employees or children of employees.

LOANS ***Student loans:*** 91% of past graduating class borrowed through all loan programs. *Average indebtedness per student:* $39,623. ***Programs:*** Federal Direct (Subsidized and Unsubsidized Stafford, PLUS), college/university, private loans.

APPLYING FOR FINANCIAL AID ***Required financial aid forms:*** FAFSA, institution's own form. ***Financial aid deadline:*** 7/30. ***Notification date:*** Continuous beginning 5/15.

CONTACT Kasie Hadley, Director of Financial Aid, Neumont College of Computer Science, 143 South Main Street, Salt Lake City, UT 84111, 801-302-2873 or toll-free 888-NEUMONT. *Fax:* 801-302-2834. *E-mail:* khadley@neumont.edu.
Website: http://www.neumont.edu/.

NEVADA STATE COLLEGE

Henderson, NV

CONTACT Anthony Morrone, Director of Financial Aid, Nevada State College, 1124 Nevada State Drive, Henderson, NV 89002, 702-992-2150. *Fax:* 702-992-2151. *E-mail:* finaid@nsc.edu.
Website: http://www.nsc.edu/.

NEWBERRY COLLEGE

Newberry, SC

Tuition & fees: N/R — **Average undergraduate aid package: $23,412**

ABOUT THE INSTITUTION Independent Evangelical Lutheran, coed. ***Awards:*** bachelor's degrees. 34 undergraduate majors. Federal methodology is used as a basis for awarding need-based institutional aid.

FRESHMAN FINANCIAL AID (Fall 2018) 343 applied for aid; of those 94% were deemed to have need. 106% of freshmen with need received aid; of those 10% had need fully met. ***Average percent of need met:*** 70% (excluding resources awarded to replace EFC). ***Average financial aid package:*** $23,539 (excluding resources awarded to replace EFC). 11% of all full-time freshmen had no need and received non-need-based gift aid.

UNDERGRADUATE FINANCIAL AID (Fall 2018) 1,102 applied for aid; of those 93% were deemed to have need. 108% of undergraduates with need received aid; of those 14% had need fully met. ***Average percent of need met:*** 72% (excluding resources awarded to replace EFC). ***Average financial aid package:*** $23,412 (excluding resources awarded to replace EFC). 13% of all full-time undergraduates had no need and received non-need-based gift aid.

GIFT AID (NEED-BASED) ***Total amount:*** $18,367,075 (16% federal, 21% state, 56% institutional, 7% external sources). ***Receiving aid:*** Freshmen: 89% (324); all full-time undergraduates: 86% (1,022). ***Average award:*** Freshmen: $20,732; Undergraduates: $20,324. ***Scholarships, grants, and awards:*** Federal Pell, FSEOG, state, private, college/university gift aid from institutional funds.

GIFT AID (NON-NEED-BASED) ***Total amount:*** $2,723,761 (25% state, 64% institutional, 11% external sources). ***Receiving aid:*** Freshmen: 9% (32). Undergraduates: 12% (141). ***Average award:*** Freshmen: $9590. Undergraduates: $9897. ***Scholarships, grants, and awards by category:*** *Academic interests/achievement:* biological sciences, business, communication, education, foreign languages, general academic interests/achievements, humanities, mathematics, physical sciences, religion/biblical studies, social sciences. *Creative arts/performance:* music, theater/drama. *Special achievements/activities:* cheerleading/drum major, religious involvement. *Special characteristics:* children and siblings of alumni, children of faculty/staff, international students, local/state students, relatives of clergy, religious affiliation, siblings of current students. ***ROTC:*** Army.

LOANS ***Student loans:*** $8,029,008 (71% need-based, 29% non-need-based). 83% of past graduating class borrowed through all loan programs. *Average indebtedness per student:* $18,587. ***Average need-based loan:*** Freshmen: $3228. Undergraduates: $360. ***Parent loans:*** $3,595,685 (73% need-based, 27% non-need-based). ***Programs:*** Federal Direct (Subsidized and Unsubsidized Stafford, PLUS), state.

WORK-STUDY ***Federal work-study:*** Total amount: $70,204; jobs available.

ATHLETIC AWARDS Total amount: $3,848,386 (63% need-based, 37% non-need-based).

APPLYING FOR FINANCIAL AID ***Required financial aid forms:*** FAFSA, state aid form. ***Financial aid deadline (priority):*** 3/15. ***Notification date:*** Continuous beginning 10/1. Students must reply by 8/15.

CONTACT Danielle Bell, Interim-Director of Financial Aid, Newberry College, 2100 College Street, Newberry, SC 29108, 803-321-5128 or toll-free 800-845-4955. *Fax:* 803-321-5627. *E-mail:* danielle.bell@newberry.edu.
Website: http://www.newberry.edu/.

NEW COLLEGE OF FLORIDA

Sarasota, FL

Tuition & fees (FL res): $6916 — **Average undergraduate aid package: $14,896**

ABOUT THE INSTITUTION State-supported, coed. ***Awards:*** bachelor's and master's degrees. 38 undergraduate majors. ***Total enrollment:*** 726. Undergraduates: 702. Freshmen: 147. Federal methodology is used as a basis for awarding need-based institutional aid.

UNDERGRADUATE EXPENSES for 2020–2021 ***Application fee:*** $30. ***Tuition, state resident:*** full-time $6916; part-time $192 per credit hour. ***Tuition, nonresident:*** full-time $29,944; part-time $832 per credit hour. Room and board charges vary according to board plan and housing facility.

FRESHMAN FINANCIAL AID (Fall 2019, est.) 131 applied for aid; of those 62% were deemed to have need. 99% of freshmen with need received aid; of those 20% had need fully met. ***Average percent of need met:*** 90% (excluding resources awarded to replace EFC). ***Average financial aid package:*** $15,282 (excluding resources awarded to replace EFC). 40% of all full-time freshmen had no need and received non-need-based gift aid.

UNDERGRADUATE FINANCIAL AID (Fall 2019, est.) 551 applied for aid; of those 65% were deemed to have need. 98% of undergraduates with need received aid; of those 24% had need fully met. ***Average percent of need met:*** 88% (excluding resources awarded to replace EFC). ***Average financial aid package:*** $14,896 (excluding resources awarded to replace EFC). 41% of all full-time undergraduates had no need and received non-need-based gift aid.

GIFT AID (NEED-BASED) ***Total amount:*** $3,531,171 (28% federal, 37% state, 32% institutional, 3% external sources). ***Receiving aid:*** Freshmen: 53% (78); all full-time undergraduates: 48% (335). ***Average award:*** Freshmen: $10,596; Undergraduates: $10,530. ***Scholarships, grants, and awards:*** Federal Pell, FSEOG, state, private, college/university gift aid from institutional funds.

GIFT AID (NON-NEED-BASED) ***Total amount:*** $2,307,127 (64% state, 33% institutional, 3% external sources). ***Receiving aid:*** Freshmen: 7% (11). Undergraduates: 8% (57). ***Average award:*** Freshmen: $2686. Undergraduates: $2583. ***Scholarships, grants, and awards by category:*** *Academic interests/achievement:* general academic interests/achievements. *Special achievements/activities:* general special achievements/activities. *Special characteristics:* international students, out-of-state students, veterans' children.

LOANS ***Student loans:*** $2,776,079 (42% need-based, 58% non-need-based). 42% of past graduating class borrowed through all loan programs. *Average indebtedness per student:* $18,953. ***Average need-based loan:*** Freshmen: $2715. Undergraduates: $3539. ***Parent loans:*** $220,718 (21% need-based, 79% non-need-based). ***Programs:*** Federal Direct (Subsidized and Unsubsidized Stafford, PLUS), alternative loans.

WORK-STUDY ***Federal work-study:*** Total amount: $30,400; jobs available. ***State or other work-study/employment:*** Part-time jobs available.

APPLYING FOR FINANCIAL AID ***Required financial aid form:*** FAFSA. ***Financial aid deadline (priority):*** 11/1. ***Notification date:*** Continuous beginning 1/15. Students must reply by 5/1 or within 2 weeks of notification.

CONTACT Tara Karas, Director of Financial Aid, New College of Florida, 5800 Bay Shore Road, Sarasota, FL 34243-2109, 941-487-5000. *Fax:* 941-487-5010. *E-mail:* tkaras@ncf.edu.
Website: http://www.ncf.edu/.

NEW ENGLAND COLLEGE

Henniker, NH

ABOUT THE INSTITUTION Independent, coed. ***Awards:*** certificates, associate, bachelor's, master's, and doctoral degrees. 34 undergraduate majors. ***Total enrollment:*** 3,538. Undergraduates: 1,869. Freshmen: 483.

GIFT AID (NEED-BASED) ***Scholarships, grants, and awards:*** Federal Pell, FSEOG, state, private, college/university gift aid from institutional funds.

GIFT AID (NON-NEED-BASED) ***Scholarships, grants, and awards by category:*** *Academic interests/achievement:* biological sciences, business, communication, computer science, education, general academic interests/achievements, humanities, international studies, social sciences. *Creative arts/performance:* applied art and design, art/fine arts, creative writing, theater/drama. *Special achievements/activities:* community service, leadership. *Special characteristics:* children and siblings of alumni, children of educators, children of faculty/staff, ethnic background, international students, local/state students, parents of current students, siblings of current students, veterans.

LOANS ***Programs:*** Federal Direct (Subsidized and Unsubsidized Stafford, PLUS), Perkins, state.

WORK-STUDY ***Federal work-study:*** Total amount: $311,562; 397 jobs averaging $1887. ***State or other work-study/employment:*** Total amount: $31,790 (68% need-based, 32% non-need-based). 29 part-time jobs averaging $1096.

APPLYING FOR FINANCIAL AID ***Required financial aid form:*** FAFSA.

CONTACT Ms. Kristen Blase, Student Financial Services Director, New England College, 15 Main Street, Henniker, NH 03242-3293, 603-428-2226 or toll-free 800-521-7642. *Fax:* 603-428-2404. *E-mail:* rstein@nec.edu.
Website: http://www.nec.edu/.

NEW ENGLAND COLLEGE OF BUSINESS AND FINANCE

Boston, MA

CONTACT Financial Aid Office, New England College of Business and Finance, 10 High Street, Suite 204, Boston, MA 02111-2645, 617-951-2350 or toll-free 800-997-1673.
Website: http://necb.edu/.

NEW ENGLAND CONSERVATORY OF MUSIC

Boston, MA

Tuition & fees: $50,460	Average undergraduate aid package: $28,727

ABOUT THE INSTITUTION Independent, coed. ***Awards:*** certificates, diplomas, bachelor's, master's, and doctoral degrees. 9 undergraduate majors. Federal methodology is used as a basis for awarding need-based institutional aid.

UNDERGRADUATE EXPENSES for 2019–2020 ***Comprehensive fee:*** $66,960 includes full-time tuition ($49,580), mandatory fees ($880), and room and board ($16,500). Room and board charges vary according to board plan. ***Part-time tuition:*** $1590 per credit hour. ***Part-time fees:*** $880 per year.

FRESHMAN FINANCIAL AID (Fall 2019, est.) 65 applied for aid; of those 71% were deemed to have need. 100% of freshmen with need received aid; of those 26% had need fully met. ***Average percent of need met:*** 61% (excluding resources awarded to replace EFC). ***Average financial aid package:*** $27,524 (excluding resources awarded to replace EFC). 56% of all full-time freshmen had no need and received non-need-based gift aid.

UNDERGRADUATE FINANCIAL AID (Fall 2019, est.) 264 applied for aid; of those 73% were deemed to have need. 97% of undergraduates with need received aid; of those 19% had need fully met. ***Average percent of need met:*** 55% (excluding resources awarded to replace EFC). ***Average financial aid package:*** $28,727 (excluding resources awarded to replace EFC). 51% of all full-time undergraduates had no need and received non-need-based gift aid.

GIFT AID (NEED-BASED) ***Total amount:*** $4,615,654 (10% federal, 1% state, 79% institutional, 10% external sources). ***Receiving aid:*** Freshmen: 39% (46); all full-time undergraduates: 35% (187). ***Average award:*** Freshmen: $24,499; Undergraduates: $24,656. ***Scholarships, grants, and awards:*** Federal Pell, FSEOG, state, private, college/university gift aid from institutional funds.

GIFT AID (NON-NEED-BASED) ***Total amount:*** $5,768,131 (83% institutional, 17% external sources). ***Receiving aid:*** Freshmen: 9% (11). Undergraduates: 6% (32). ***Average award:*** Freshmen: $15,969. Undergraduates: $16,618. ***Scholarships, grants, and awards by category:*** *Creative arts/performance:* 455 awards ($18,794 total): music. ***Tuition waivers:*** Full or partial for employees or children of employees.

LOANS ***Student loans:*** $1,929,794 (67% need-based, 33% non-need-based). 38% of past graduating class borrowed through all loan programs. *Average indebtedness per student:* $29,479. ***Average need-based loan:*** Freshmen: $2861. Undergraduates: $3581. ***Parent loans:*** $1,060,723 (70% need-based, 30% non-need-based). ***Programs:*** Federal Direct (Subsidized and Unsubsidized Stafford, PLUS).

WORK-STUDY ***Federal work-study:*** Total amount: $252,538; 277 jobs averaging $1939.

APPLYING FOR FINANCIAL AID ***Required financial aid forms:*** FAFSA, institution's own form. ***Financial aid deadline (priority):*** 2/15. ***Notification date:*** 4/1. Students must reply by 5/1.

CONTACT Ms. Lauren Urbanek, Associate Dean for Financial Aid, New England Conservatory of Music, 290 Huntington Avenue, Boston, MA 02115, 617-585-1110. *Fax:* 617-585-1115. *E-mail:* finaid@necmusic.edu.
Website: http://necmusic.edu/.

NEW ENGLAND INSTITUTE OF TECHNOLOGY

East Greenwich, RI

Tuition & fees: $31,545 **Average undergraduate aid package: N/A**

ABOUT THE INSTITUTION Independent, coed. ***Awards:*** associate, bachelor's, master's, and doctoral degrees. 42 undergraduate majors. ***Total enrollment:*** 2,498. Undergraduates: 2,314. Freshmen: 467. Federal methodology is used as a basis for awarding need-based institutional aid.

UNDERGRADUATE EXPENSES for 2020–2021 ***Application fee:*** $50. ***Comprehensive fee:*** $46,050 includes full-time tuition ($30,000), mandatory fees ($1545), and room and board ($14,505). Full-time tuition and fees vary according to program. ***Part-time tuition:*** $15,000 per year. ***Part-time fees:*** $1545 per year. Part-time tuition and fees vary according to program. ***Payment plans:*** Guaranteed tuition, tuition prepayment.

GIFT AID (NEED-BASED) ***Total amount:*** $21,815,104 (35% federal, 2% state, 63% institutional). ***Scholarships, grants, and awards:*** Federal Pell, FSEOG, state, private, college/university gift aid from institutional funds.

GIFT AID (NON-NEED-BASED) ***Tuition waivers:*** Full or partial for employees or children of employees.

LOANS ***Student loans:*** $8,450,342 (100% need-based). ***Parent loans:*** $5,781,269 (100% need-based).

WORK-STUDY ***Federal work-study:*** Total amount: $396,128; jobs available.

APPLYING FOR FINANCIAL AID ***Required financial aid form:*** FAFSA. ***Financial aid deadline:*** Continuous. ***Notification date:*** Continuous beginning 2/1.

CONTACT Anna Kelly, Director of Financial Aid , New England Institute of Technology, One New England Tech Blvd, East Greenwich, RI 02818, 401-739-5000 Ext. 3487 or toll-free 800-736-7744. *E-mail:* akelly@neit.edu.
Website: http://www.neit.edu/.

NEW HAMPSHIRE INSTITUTE OF ART

Manchester, NH

CONTACT Linda Lavallee, Director of Financial Aid, New Hampshire Institute of Art, 148 Concord Street, Manchester, NH 03104-4858, 603-623-0313 Ext. 577 or toll-free 866-241-4918. *Fax:* 603-647-0658. *E-mail:* llavallee@nhia.edu.
Website: http://www.nhia.edu/.

NEW HOPE CHRISTIAN COLLEGE

Eugene, OR

CONTACT Nathan Icenhower, Financial Aid Administrator, New Hope Christian College, 2155 Bailey Hill Road, Eugene, OR 97405-1194, 541-485-1780 Ext. 3106 or toll-free 800-322-2638. *Fax:* 541-343-5801. *E-mail:* finaid@newhope.edu.
Website: http://www.newhope.edu/.

NEW JERSEY CITY UNIVERSITY

Jersey City, NJ

Tuition & fees (NJ res): $12,414 **Average undergraduate aid package: $11,398**

ABOUT THE INSTITUTION State-supported, coed. ***Awards:*** certificates, bachelor's, master's, and doctoral degrees. 31 undergraduate majors. ***Total enrollment:*** 7,991. Undergraduates: 6,237. Freshmen: 968. Both federal and institutional methodology are used as a basis for awarding need-based institutional aid.

UNDERGRADUATE EXPENSES for 2019–2020 ***Application fee:*** $50. ***Tuition, state resident:*** full-time $12,248; part-time $397 per credit hour. ***Tuition, nonresident:*** full-time $22,054; part-time $714 per credit hour. ***Required fees:*** full-time $166; $3 per credit hour. Part-time tuition and fees vary according to course load. ***College room and board:*** $14,574. Room and board charges vary according to board plan and housing facility.

FRESHMAN FINANCIAL AID (Fall 2018) 929 applied for aid; of those 95% were deemed to have need. 97% of freshmen with need received aid; of those 3% had need fully met. ***Average percent of need met:*** 50% (excluding resources awarded to replace EFC). ***Average financial aid package:*** $12,248 (excluding resources awarded to replace EFC). 2% of all full-time freshmen had no need and received non-need-based gift aid.

UNDERGRADUATE FINANCIAL AID (Fall 2018) 4,672 applied for aid; of those 95% were deemed to have need. 97% of undergraduates with need received aid; of those 3% had need fully met. ***Average percent of need met:*** 47% (excluding resources awarded to replace EFC). ***Average financial aid package:*** $11,398 (excluding resources awarded to replace EFC). 2% of all full-time undergraduates had no need and received non-need-based gift aid.

GIFT AID (NEED-BASED) ***Total amount:*** $204,959,777 (92% federal, 8% state). ***Receiving aid:*** Freshmen: 78% (748); all full-time undergraduates: 71% (3,606). ***Average award:*** Freshmen: $10,372; Undergraduates: $9383. ***Scholarships, grants, and awards:*** Federal Pell, college/university gift aid from institutional funds.

GIFT AID (NON-NEED-BASED) ***Total amount:*** $15,547,922 (40% institutional, 60% external sources). ***Receiving aid:*** Freshmen: 53% (509). Undergraduates: 25% (1,293). ***Average award:*** Freshmen: $8965. Undergraduates: $8312. ***Scholarships, grants, and awards by category:*** *Academic interests/achievement:* general academic interests/achievements. ***Tuition waivers:*** Full or partial for employees or children of employees, senior citizens. ***ROTC:*** Army cooperative, Naval cooperative.

LOANS ***Student loans:*** $21,562,404 (47% need-based, 53% non-need-based). 63% of past graduating class borrowed through all loan programs. *Average indebtedness per student:* $25,463. ***Average need-based loan:*** Freshmen: $3198. Undergraduates: $3988. ***Parent loans:*** $2,818,016 (100% non-need-based). ***Programs:*** Federal Direct (Subsidized and Unsubsidized Stafford, PLUS).

WORK-STUDY ***Federal work-study:*** Total amount: $689,780; jobs available.

APPLYING FOR FINANCIAL AID ***Required financial aid form:*** FAFSA.

CONTACT Mr. Robert Macauley, Director of Financial Aid, New Jersey City University, 2039 Kennedy Boulevard, Jersey City, NJ 07305-1597, 201-200-3171 or toll-free 888-441-NJCU.
Website: http://www.njcu.edu/.

NEW JERSEY INSTITUTE OF TECHNOLOGY

Newark, NJ

Tuition & fees (NJ res): $17,674 **Average undergraduate aid package: $14,353**

ABOUT THE INSTITUTION State-supported, coed. ***Awards:*** certificates, bachelor's, master's, and doctoral degrees. 46 undergraduate majors. ***Total enrollment:*** 11,518. Undergraduates: 8,794. Freshmen: 1,360. Federal methodology is used as a basis for awarding need-based institutional aid.

UNDERGRADUATE EXPENSES for 2019–2020 ***Application fee:*** $75. ***Tuition, state resident:*** full-time $14,448; part-time $549 per credit. ***Tuition, nonresident:*** full-time $30,160; part-time $1289 per credit. ***Required fees:*** full-time $3226; $190 per credit. Full-time tuition and fees vary according to course load. Part-time tuition and fees vary according to course load. ***College room and board:*** $13,900. Room and board charges vary according to board plan and housing facility.

FRESHMAN FINANCIAL AID (Fall 2019, est.) 1104 applied for aid; of those 87% were deemed to have need. 95% of freshmen with need received aid; of those 16% had need fully met. ***Average percent of need met:*** 58% (excluding resources awarded to replace EFC). ***Average financial aid package:*** $16,022 (excluding resources awarded to replace EFC). 16% of all full-time freshmen had no need and received non-need-based gift aid.

UNDERGRADUATE FINANCIAL AID (Fall 2019, est.) 4,315 applied for aid; of those 90% were deemed to have need. 96% of undergraduates with need received aid; of those 13% had need fully met. ***Average percent of need met:*** 55% (excluding resources awarded to replace EFC). ***Average financial aid package:*** $14,353 (excluding resources awarded to replace EFC). 10% of all full-time undergraduates had no need and received non-need-based gift aid.

GIFT AID (NEED-BASED) ***Total amount:*** $51,841,381 (30% federal, 42% state, 27% institutional, 1% external sources). ***Receiving aid:*** Freshmen: 73% (904); all full-

time undergraduates: 55% (3,719). ***Average award:*** Freshmen: $13,945; Undergraduates: $11,925. ***Scholarships, grants, and awards:*** Federal Pell, FSEOG, state, private, college/university gift aid from institutional funds.

GIFT AID (NON-NEED-BASED) ***Total amount:*** $14,808,473 (98% institutional, 2% external sources). ***Receiving aid:*** Freshmen: 8% (95). Undergraduates: 2% (150). ***Average award:*** Freshmen: $14,821. Undergraduates: $14,680. ***Scholarships, grants, and awards by category:*** *Academic interests/achievement:* 843 awards ($12,402,628 total): architecture, area/ethnic studies, biological sciences, business, communication, computer science, education, engineering/technologies, general academic interests/achievements, humanities, international studies, mathematics, physical sciences, premedicine. *Creative arts/performance:* applied art and design, art/fine arts, journalism/publications, performing arts, theater/drama. *Special achievements/activities:* community service, general special achievements/activities, hobbies/interests, leadership, religious involvement. *Special characteristics:* ethnic background, first-generation college students, general special characteristics, handicapped students, international students, local/state students, members of minority groups, out-of-state students, relatives of clergy, religious affiliation, siblings of current students, veterans. ***Tuition waivers:*** Full or partial for employees or children of employees. ***ROTC:*** Army cooperative, Air Force.

LOANS ***Student loans:*** $37,508,392 (77% need-based, 23% non-need-based). 58% of past graduating class borrowed through all loan programs. *Average indebtedness per student:* $38,718. ***Average need-based loan:*** Freshmen: $3374. Undergraduates: $4577. ***Parent loans:*** $6,217,349 (62% need-based, 38% non-need-based). ***Programs:*** Federal Direct (Subsidized and Unsubsidized Stafford, PLUS), state, college/university.

WORK-STUDY ***Federal work-study:*** Total amount: $541,426; 372 jobs averaging $1501. ***State or other work-study/employment:*** Total amount: $1,941,017 (43% need-based, 57% non-need-based). 1,247 part-time jobs averaging $2461.

ATHLETIC AWARDS Total amount: $4,307,965 (26% need-based, 74% non-need-based).

APPLYING FOR FINANCIAL AID ***Required financial aid forms:*** FAFSA, state aid form. ***Financial aid deadline:*** 4/15 (priority: 2/15). ***Notification date:*** Continuous. Students must reply by 5/1.

CONTACT Ivon Nunez, Director of Financial Aid Services, New Jersey Institute of Technology, Student Mall, University Heights, Newark, NJ 07102, 973-596-3476 or toll-free 800-925-NJIT. *Fax:* 973-596-6471. *E-mail:* ivon.nunez@njit.edu.
Website: http://www.njit.edu/.

NEWMAN UNIVERSITY

Wichita, KS

Tuition & fees: N/R	Average undergraduate aid package: $24,386

ABOUT THE INSTITUTION Independent Roman Catholic, coed. ***Awards:*** associate, bachelor's, and master's degrees. 42 undergraduate majors. ***Total enrollment:*** 3,205. Undergraduates: 2,705. Freshmen: 184. Federal methodology is used as a basis for awarding need-based institutional aid.

FRESHMAN FINANCIAL AID (Fall 2019, est.) 142 applied for aid; of those 92% were deemed to have need. 96% of freshmen with need received aid; of those 17% had need fully met. ***Average percent of need met:*** 72% (excluding resources awarded to replace EFC). ***Average financial aid package:*** $26,410 (excluding resources awarded to replace EFC). 16% of all full-time freshmen had no need and received non-need-based gift aid.

UNDERGRADUATE FINANCIAL AID (Fall 2019, est.) 770 applied for aid; of those 95% were deemed to have need. 98% of undergraduates with need received aid; of those 17% had need fully met. ***Average percent of need met:*** 67% (excluding resources awarded to replace EFC). ***Average financial aid package:*** $24,386 (excluding resources awarded to replace EFC). 16% of all full-time undergraduates had no need and received non-need-based gift aid.

GIFT AID (NEED-BASED) ***Receiving aid:*** Freshmen: 79% (125); all full-time undergraduates: 78% (703). ***Average award:*** Freshmen: $24,000; Undergraduates: $21,356. ***Scholarships, grants, and awards:*** Federal Pell, FSEOG, state, private, college/university gift aid from institutional funds.

GIFT AID (NON-NEED-BASED) ***Receiving aid:*** Freshmen: 11% (17). Undergraduates: 11% (98). ***Average award:*** Freshmen: $14,850. Undergraduates: $14,086. ***Scholarships, grants, and awards by category:*** *Academic interests/achievement:* general academic interests/achievements. *Creative arts/performance:* applied art and design, journalism/publications, music, theater/drama. *Special achievements/activities:* community service, leadership, memberships, religious involvement. *Special characteristics:* children and siblings of alumni, children of current students, children of faculty/staff, international students, married students, siblings of current students, spouses of current students.

LOANS ***Student loans:*** 66% of past graduating class borrowed through all loan programs. *Average indebtedness per student:* $30,532. ***Average need-based loan:*** Freshmen: $2784. Undergraduates: $3958. ***Programs:*** Federal Direct (Subsidized and Unsubsidized Stafford, PLUS).

WORK-STUDY Federal work-study jobs available. ***State or other work-study/employment:*** Part-time jobs available.

APPLYING FOR FINANCIAL AID ***Required financial aid form:*** FAFSA. ***Financial aid deadline:*** Continuous. ***Notification date:*** Continuous. Students must reply within 2 weeks of notification.

CONTACT Myra Pfannenstiel, Director of Financial Aid, Newman University, 3100 McCormick Avenue, Wichita, KS 67213, 316-942-4291 Ext. 2103 or toll-free 877-NEWMANU. *Fax:* 316-942-4483. *E-mail:* pfannenstielm@newmanu.edu.
Website: http://www.newmanu.edu/.

NEW MEXICO HIGHLANDS UNIVERSITY

Las Vegas, NM

ABOUT THE INSTITUTION State-supported, coed. ***Awards:*** certificates, bachelor's, and master's degrees. 44 undergraduate majors. ***Total enrollment:*** 2,902. Undergraduates: 1,797. Freshmen: 280.

GIFT AID (NEED-BASED) ***Scholarships, grants, and awards:*** Federal Pell, FSEOG, state, private, college/university gift aid from institutional funds.

GIFT AID (NON-NEED-BASED) ***Scholarships, grants, and awards by category:*** *Academic interests/achievement:* area/ethnic studies, biological sciences, business, communication, computer science, education, engineering/technologies, English, foreign languages, general academic interests/achievements, home economics, humanities, mathematics, physical sciences, premedicine, social sciences. *Creative arts/performance:* applied art and design, art/fine arts, music, performing arts.

LOANS ***Programs:*** Federal Direct (Subsidized and Unsubsidized Stafford, PLUS), state.

CONTACT Ms. Susan Chavez, Director of Financial Aid, New Mexico Highlands University, PO Box 9000, Las Vegas, NM 87701, 505-454-3430 or toll-free 800-338-6648. *E-mail:* srchavez@nmhu.edu.
Website: http://www.nmhu.edu/.

NEW MEXICO INSTITUTE OF MINING AND TECHNOLOGY

Socorro, NM

Tuition & fees (NM res): $8156	Average undergraduate aid package: $13,367

ABOUT THE INSTITUTION State-supported, coed. ***Awards:*** associate, bachelor's, master's, and doctoral degrees. 22 undergraduate majors. ***Total enrollment:*** 1,832. Undergraduates: 1,321. Freshmen: 250. Federal methodology is used as a basis for awarding need-based institutional aid.

UNDERGRADUATE EXPENSES for 2019–2020 ***Application fee:*** $15. ***Tuition, state resident:*** full-time $6826; part-time $284 per credit hour. ***Tuition, nonresident:*** full-time $22,194; part-time $925 per credit hour. ***Required fees:*** full-time $1330; $450 per term. Full-time tuition and fees vary according to reciprocity agreements. Part-time tuition and fees vary according to course load. ***College room and board:*** $8624. Room and board charges vary according to board plan and housing facility.

FRESHMAN FINANCIAL AID (Fall 2019, est.) 247 applied for aid; of those 58% were deemed to have need. 99% of freshmen with need received aid; of those 28% had need fully met. ***Average percent of need met:*** 79% (excluding resources awarded to replace EFC). ***Average financial aid package:*** $12,511 (excluding resources

awarded to replace EFC). 40% of all full-time freshmen had no need and received non-need-based gift aid.

UNDERGRADUATE FINANCIAL AID (Fall 2019, est.) 1,070 applied for aid; of those 61% were deemed to have need. 98% of undergraduates with need received aid; of those 24% had need fully met. ***Average percent of need met:*** 77% (excluding resources awarded to replace EFC). ***Average financial aid package:*** $13,367 (excluding resources awarded to replace EFC). 31% of all full-time undergraduates had no need and received non-need-based gift aid.

GIFT AID (NEED-BASED) ***Total amount:*** $2,614,192 (86% federal, 8% state, 6% external sources). ***Receiving aid:*** Freshmen: 50% (130); all full-time undergraduates: 41% (481). ***Average award:*** Freshmen: $4968; Undergraduates: $5569. ***Scholarships, grants, and awards:*** Federal Pell, FSEOG, state, private, college/university gift aid from institutional funds.

GIFT AID (NON-NEED-BASED) ***Total amount:*** $5,024,211 (43% state, 48% institutional, 9% external sources). ***Receiving aid:*** Freshmen: 50% (129). Undergraduates: 40% (465). ***Average award:*** Freshmen: $5960. Undergraduates: $6611. ***Scholarships, grants, and awards by category:*** *Academic interests/achievement:* general academic interests/achievements. ***Tuition waivers:*** Full or partial for employees or children of employees, senior citizens.

LOANS ***Student loans:*** $3,497,180 (38% need-based, 62% non-need-based). 41% of past graduating class borrowed through all loan programs. *Average indebtedness per student:* $20,771. ***Average need-based loan:*** Freshmen: $3222. Undergraduates: $3991. ***Parent loans:*** $143,155 (100% non-need-based). ***Programs:*** Federal Direct (Subsidized and Unsubsidized Stafford, PLUS).

WORK-STUDY ***Federal work-study:*** Total amount: $275,000; jobs available. ***State or other work-study/employment:*** Total amount: $90,000 (28% need-based, 72% non-need-based). Part-time jobs available.

APPLYING FOR FINANCIAL AID ***Required financial aid form:*** FAFSA. ***Financial aid deadline (priority):*** 3/1. ***Notification date:*** Continuous beginning 3/15. Students must reply within 4 weeks of notification.

CONTACT Mr. Kenneth Aerts, Director of Financial Aid, New Mexico Institute of Mining and Technology, 801 Leroy Place, Socorro, NM 87801, 575-835-5333 or toll-free 800-428-TECH. *Fax:* 575-835-5959. *E-mail:* kenneth.aerts@nmt.edu.
Website: http://www.nmt.edu/.

NEW MEXICO STATE UNIVERSITY

Las Cruces, NM

Tuition & fees (NM res): $7087	Average undergraduate aid package: $15,929

ABOUT THE INSTITUTION State-supported, coed. ***Awards:*** certificates, associate, bachelor's, master's, and doctoral degrees. 82 undergraduate majors. Federal methodology is used as a basis for awarding need-based institutional aid.

UNDERGRADUATE EXPENSES for 2019–2020 ***One-time required fee:*** $165. ***Tuition, state resident:*** full-time $5875; part-time $245 per credit hour. ***Tuition, nonresident:*** full-time $21,864; part-time $911 per credit hour. ***Required fees:*** full-time $1212; $50.50 per credit hour. Full-time tuition and fees vary according to course load and reciprocity agreements. Part-time tuition and fees vary according to course load and reciprocity agreements. ***College room and board:*** $9538; ***Room only:*** $5518. Room and board charges vary according to board plan and housing facility.

FRESHMAN FINANCIAL AID (Fall 2019, est.) 1981 applied for aid; of those 82% were deemed to have need. 100% of freshmen with need received aid; of those 19% had need fully met. ***Average percent of need met:*** 74% (excluding resources awarded to replace EFC). ***Average financial aid package:*** $15,777 (excluding resources awarded to replace EFC). 23% of all full-time freshmen had no need and received non-need-based gift aid.

UNDERGRADUATE FINANCIAL AID (Fall 2019, est.) 7,799 applied for aid; of those 87% were deemed to have need. 99% of undergraduates with need received aid; of those 17% had need fully met. ***Average percent of need met:*** 72% (excluding resources awarded to replace EFC). ***Average financial aid package:*** $15,929 (excluding resources awarded to replace EFC). 19% of all full-time undergraduates had no need and received non-need-based gift aid.

GIFT AID (NEED-BASED) ***Total amount:*** $63,835,500 (43% federal, 17% state, 37% institutional, 3% external sources). ***Receiving aid:*** Freshmen: 75% (1,611); all full-time undergraduates: 66% (6,377). ***Average award:*** Freshmen: $13,592; Undergraduates: $13,545. ***Scholarships, grants, and awards:*** Federal Pell, FSEOG, state, private, college/university gift aid from institutional funds.

GIFT AID (NON-NEED-BASED) ***Total amount:*** $39,536,258 (17% state, 79% institutional, 4% external sources). ***Receiving aid:*** Freshmen: 21% (463). Undergraduates: 18% (1,773). ***Average award:*** Freshmen: $6730. Undergraduates: $7542. ***Scholarships, grants, and awards by category:*** *Academic interests/achievement:* 547 awards ($510,555 total): agriculture, area/ethnic studies, biological sciences, business, communication, computer science, education, engineering/technologies, English, foreign languages, general academic interests/achievements, health fields, home economics, humanities, mathematics, military science, physical sciences, social sciences. *Creative arts/performance:* 40 awards ($35,396 total): applied art and design, art/fine arts, cinema/film/broadcasting, creative writing, dance, general creative arts/performance, journalism/publications, music, performing arts, theater/drama. *Special achievements/activities:* 24 awards ($21,487 total): cheerleading/drum major, general special achievements/activities, hobbies/interests, junior miss, leadership, memberships, rodeo. *Special characteristics:* 110 awards ($77,304 total): adult students, children and siblings of alumni, children of current students, children of faculty/staff, children of public servants, children of union members/company employees, children of workers in trades, children with a deceased or disabled parent, ethnic background, handicapped students, international students, local/state students, married students, members of minority groups, out-of-state students, previous college experience, public servants, spouses of current students, spouses of deceased or disabled public servants, veterans. ***Tuition waivers:*** Full or partial for employees or children of employees, senior citizens. ***ROTC:*** Army, Air Force.

LOANS ***Student loans:*** $27,783,730 (79% need-based, 21% non-need-based). 47% of past graduating class borrowed through all loan programs. *Average indebtedness per student:* $21,429. ***Average need-based loan:*** Freshmen: $2470. Undergraduates: $3276. ***Parent loans:*** $1,885,124 (45% need-based, 55% non-need-based). ***Programs:*** Federal Direct (Subsidized and Unsubsidized Stafford, PLUS), Perkins, state.

WORK-STUDY ***Federal work-study:*** Total amount: $1,082,239; 263 jobs averaging $4115. ***State or other work-study/employment:*** Total amount: $1,055,207 (99% need-based, 1% non-need-based). 276 part-time jobs averaging $3849.

ATHLETIC AWARDS Total amount: $4,103,080 (26% need-based, 74% non-need-based).

APPLYING FOR FINANCIAL AID ***Required financial aid form:*** FAFSA. ***Financial aid deadline:*** 6/30 (priority: 3/1). ***Notification date:*** Continuous beginning 3/1.

CONTACT Dr. Vandeen McKenzie, Director of Financial Aid, New Mexico State University, Box 30001, MSC 5100, Las Cruces, NM 88003-8001, 575-646-4105 or toll-free 800-662-6678. *Fax:* 575-646-7381. *E-mail:* financialaid@nmsu.edu.
Website: http://www.nmsu.edu/.

NEW ORLEANS BAPTIST THEOLOGICAL SEMINARY

New Orleans, LA

CONTACT Owen Nease, Financial Aid Office, New Orleans Baptist Theological Seminary, 3939 Gentilly Boulevard, New Orleans, LA 70126-4858, 504-282-4455 Ext. 3348 or toll-free 800-662-8701. *Fax:* 504-816-8437. *E-mail:* financialaid@nobts.edu.
Website: http://www.nobts.edu/.

NEW SAINT ANDREWS COLLEGE

Moscow, ID

Tuition & fees: N/R	Average undergraduate aid package: $2929

ABOUT THE INSTITUTION Independent Christian, coed. ***Awards:*** certificates, associate, bachelor's, and master's degrees. 1 undergraduate major. ***Total enrollment:*** 158. Undergraduates: 140. Freshmen: 31. Institutional methodology is used as a basis for awarding need-based institutional aid.

UNDERGRADUATE EXPENSES for 2019–2020 ***Application fee:*** $40. ***Tuition:*** part-time $550 per credit hour. Full-time tuition and fees vary according to course load and program. Part-time tuition and fees vary according to program. ***Payment plan:*** Tuition prepayment.

FRESHMAN FINANCIAL AID (Fall 2019, est.) 35 applied for aid; of those 49% were deemed to have need. 100% of freshmen with need received aid. ***Average***

financial aid package: $3886 (excluding resources awarded to replace EFC). 47% of all full-time freshmen had no need and received non-need-based gift aid.

UNDERGRADUATE FINANCIAL AID (Fall 2019, est.) 71 applied for aid; of those 69% were deemed to have need. 100% of undergraduates with need received aid. ***Average financial aid package:*** $2929 (excluding resources awarded to replace EFC). 40% of all full-time undergraduates had no need and received non-need-based gift aid.

GIFT AID (NEED-BASED) ***Total amount:*** $269,500 (100% institutional). ***Receiving aid:*** Freshmen: 50% (17); all full-time undergraduates: 31% (49). ***Average award:*** Freshmen: $3886; Undergraduates: $2929. ***Scholarships, grants, and awards:*** private, college/university gift aid from institutional funds.

GIFT AID (NON-NEED-BASED) ***Total amount:*** $169,450 (95% institutional, 5% external sources). ***Average award:*** Freshmen: $1437. Undergraduates: $2245. ***Tuition waivers:*** Full or partial for children of alumni, employees or children of employees.

LOANS ***Student loans:*** $41,851 (100% need-based).

WORK-STUDY ***State or other work-study/employment:*** Total amount: $22,000 (100% need-based).

APPLYING FOR FINANCIAL AID ***Required financial aid form:*** CSS Financial Aid PROFILE. ***Financial aid deadline (priority):*** 3/1.

CONTACT Brenda Schlect, College Bursars Office, New Saint Andrews College, 405 South Main Street, PO Box 9025, Moscow, ID 83843, 208-882-1566 Ext. 113. *Fax:* 208-882-4297. *E-mail:* bschlect@nsa.edu.
Website: http://www.nsa.edu/.

THE NEW SCHOOL COLLEGE OF PERFORMING ARTS

New York, NY

Tuition & fees: N/R	Average undergraduate aid package: $19,533

ABOUT THE INSTITUTION Independent, coed. ***Awards:*** diplomas, bachelor's, and master's degrees. 8 undergraduate majors. ***Total enrollment:*** 1,018. Undergraduates: 609. Freshmen: 135. Federal methodology is used as a basis for awarding need-based institutional aid.

FRESHMAN FINANCIAL AID (Fall 2018) 86 applied for aid; of those 83% were deemed to have need. 100% of freshmen with need received aid; of those 10% had need fully met. ***Average percent of need met:*** 51% (excluding resources awarded to replace EFC). ***Average financial aid package:*** $17,037 (excluding resources awarded to replace EFC). 44% of all full-time freshmen had no need and received non-need-based gift aid.

UNDERGRADUATE FINANCIAL AID (Fall 2018) 253 applied for aid; of those 93% were deemed to have need. 100% of undergraduates with need received aid; of those 7% had need fully met. ***Average percent of need met:*** 51% (excluding resources awarded to replace EFC). ***Average financial aid package:*** $19,533 (excluding resources awarded to replace EFC). 53% of all full-time undergraduates had no need and received non-need-based gift aid.

GIFT AID (NEED-BASED) ***Total amount:*** $1,617,108 (31% federal, 4% state, 41% institutional, 24% external sources). ***Receiving aid:*** Freshmen: 17% (24); all full-time undergraduates: 19% (111). ***Average award:*** Freshmen: $5710; Undergraduates: $7435. ***Scholarships, grants, and awards:*** Federal Pell, FSEOG, state, private, college/university gift aid from institutional funds, United Negro College Fund.

GIFT AID (NON-NEED-BASED) ***Total amount:*** $8,605,204 (95% institutional, 5% external sources). ***Receiving aid:*** Freshmen: 43% (62). Undergraduates: 34% (195). ***Average award:*** Freshmen: $12,303. Undergraduates: $16,458.

LOANS ***Student loans:*** $2,427,432 (64% need-based, 36% non-need-based). 38% of past graduating class borrowed through all loan programs. *Average indebtedness per student:* $31,723. ***Average need-based loan:*** Freshmen: $3031. Undergraduates: $3786. ***Parent loans:*** $2,912,383 (100% non-need-based). ***Programs:*** Federal Direct (Subsidized and Unsubsidized Stafford, PLUS).

WORK-STUDY ***Federal work-study:*** Total amount: $99,579; jobs available.

APPLYING FOR FINANCIAL AID ***Required financial aid form:*** FAFSA. ***Financial aid deadline (priority):*** 2/1. ***Notification date:*** 2/1. Students must reply within 4 weeks of notification.

CONTACT LaVerne Walker, Office of Student Financial Services, The New School College of Performing Arts, 79 Fifth Avenue, New York, NY 10003, 212-2298930 or toll-free 800-292-3040. *E-mail:* walkerl1@newschool.edu.
Website: http://www.newschool.edu/performing-arts/.

THE NEW SCHOOL FOR PUBLIC ENGAGEMENT

New York, NY

ABOUT THE INSTITUTION Independent, coed. ***Awards:*** certificates, bachelor's, master's, and doctoral degrees. 9 undergraduate majors.

GIFT AID (NEED-BASED) ***Scholarships, grants, and awards:*** Federal Pell, FSEOG, state, private, college/university gift aid from institutional funds, United Negro College Fund.

GIFT AID (NON-NEED-BASED) ***Scholarships, grants, and awards by category:*** *Academic interests/achievement:* general academic interests/achievements.

LOANS ***Programs:*** Federal Direct (Subsidized and Unsubsidized Stafford, PLUS).

CONTACT LaVerne Walker, Office of Financial Aid, The New School for Public Engagement, 72 Fifth Avenue, New York, NY 10003, 212-229-8930 or toll-free 800-292-3040. *E-mail:* sfs@newschool.edu.
Website: http://www.newschool.edu/public-engagement/.

NEWSCHOOL OF ARCHITECTURE AND DESIGN

San Diego, CA

ABOUT THE INSTITUTION Proprietary, coed, primarily men. ***Awards:*** bachelor's and master's degrees. 9 undergraduate majors.

GIFT AID (NEED-BASED) ***Scholarships, grants, and awards:*** Federal Pell, FSEOG, state, private, college/university gift aid from institutional funds.

GIFT AID (NON-NEED-BASED) ***Scholarships, grants, and awards by category:*** *Academic interests/achievement:* architecture, general academic interests/achievements. *Creative arts/performance:* general creative arts/performance. *Special achievements/activities:* general special achievements/activities. *Special characteristics:* children of faculty/staff, general special characteristics, international students, previous college experience, veterans.

LOANS ***Programs:*** Federal Direct (Subsidized and Unsubsidized Stafford, PLUS), alternative loans.

WORK-STUDY ***Federal work-study:*** Total amount: $40,264; 31 jobs averaging $2082. ***State or other work-study/employment:*** Part-time jobs available.

APPLYING FOR FINANCIAL AID ***Required financial aid forms:*** FAFSA, institution's own form.

CONTACT Mr. Bryan Charbonneau, Director of Financial Aid, NewSchool of Architecture and Design, 1249 F Street, San Diego, CA 92101-6634, 619-684-8774 or toll-free 800-490-7081. *Fax:* 619-684-8880. *E-mail:* bcharbonneau@newschoolarch.edu.
Website: http://www.newschoolarch.edu/.

NEW WORLD SCHOOL OF THE ARTS

Miami, FL

CONTACT Financial Aid Office, New World School of the Arts, 300 NE 2nd Avenue, Miami, FL 33132, 305-237-3135.
Website: http://www.mdc.edu/nwsa/.

NEW YORK CITY COLLEGE OF TECHNOLOGY OF THE CITY UNIVERSITY OF NEW YORK

Brooklyn, NY

ABOUT THE INSTITUTION State and locally supported, coed. ***Awards:*** certificates, associate, and bachelor's degrees. 41 undergraduate majors. ***Total enrollment:*** 17,036. Undergraduates: 27,236. Freshmen: 3,466.

GIFT AID (NEED-BASED) ***Scholarships, grants, and awards:*** Federal Pell, FSEOG, state, private, college/university gift aid from institutional funds.

LOANS ***Programs:*** Federal Direct (Subsidized and Unsubsidized Stafford, PLUS), Perkins, state, college/university.

WORK-STUDY ***Federal work-study:*** Total amount: $2,170,274; jobs available.

APPLYING FOR FINANCIAL AID ***Required financial aid form:*** FAFSA.

CONTACT Sandra Higgins, Director of Financial Aid, New York City College of Technology of the City University of New York, 300 Jay Street, Namm Hall, Room G-13, Brooklyn, NY 11201, 718-260-5700. *Fax:* 718-254-8525. *E-mail:* financialaid@citytech.cuny.edu.

Website: http://www.citytech.cuny.edu/.

NEW YORK COLLEGE OF HEALTH PROFESSIONS

Syosset, NY

CONTACT Financial Aid Office, New York College of Health Professions, 6801 Jericho Turnpike, Syosset, NY 11791-4413, 516-364-0808 or toll-free 800-922-7337 Ext.351.

Website: http://www.nycollege.edu/.

NEW YORK FILM ACADEMY

Burbank, CA

CONTACT Financial Aid Office, New York Film Academy, 3300 Riverside Drive, Burbank, CA 91505, 818-333-3558.

Website: http://www.nyfa.edu/.

NEW YORK INSTITUTE OF TECHNOLOGY

Old Westbury, NY

Tuition & fees: $39,760	Average undergraduate aid package: $29,446

ABOUT THE INSTITUTION Independent, coed. ***Awards:*** certificates, diplomas, associate, bachelor's, master's, and doctoral degrees. 40 undergraduate majors. ***Total enrollment:*** 7,230. Undergraduates: 3,694. Freshmen: 849. Federal methodology is used as a basis for awarding need-based institutional aid.

UNDERGRADUATE EXPENSES for 2020–2021 ***Application fee:*** $50. ***Comprehensive fee:*** $54,050 includes full-time tuition ($38,060), mandatory fees ($1700), and room and board ($14,290). ***College room only:*** $9800. Full-time tuition and fees vary according to location and program. Room and board charges vary according to housing facility and location. ***Part-time tuition:*** $1290 per credit. ***Part-time fees:*** $750 per term. Part-time tuition and fees vary according to course load, location, and program.

FRESHMAN FINANCIAL AID (Fall 2019, est.) 753 applied for aid; of those 88% were deemed to have need. 100% of freshmen with need received aid. ***Average financial aid package:*** $31,242 (excluding resources awarded to replace EFC). 17% of all full-time freshmen had no need and received non-need-based gift aid.

UNDERGRADUATE FINANCIAL AID (Fall 2019, est.) 2,717 applied for aid; of those 89% were deemed to have need. 100% of undergraduates with need received aid. ***Average financial aid package:*** $29,446 (excluding resources awarded to replace EFC). 17% of all full-time undergraduates had no need and received non-need-based gift aid.

GIFT AID (NEED-BASED) ***Total amount:*** $19,594,828 (40% federal, 20% state, 40% institutional). ***Receiving aid:*** Freshmen: 61% (496); all full-time undergraduates: 56% (1,875). ***Average award:*** Freshmen: $10,903; Undergraduates: $9859. ***Scholarships, grants, and awards:*** Federal Pell, FSEOG, state, private, college/university gift aid from institutional funds.

GIFT AID (NON-NEED-BASED) ***Total amount:*** $52,873,789 (3% federal, 95% institutional, 2% external sources). ***Receiving aid:*** Freshmen: 77% (632). Undergraduates: 66% (2,211). ***Average award:*** Freshmen: $20,794. Undergraduates: $17,577. ***Scholarships, grants, and awards by category:*** *Academic interests/achievement:* general academic interests/achievements. *Special characteristics:* children and siblings of alumni, children of educators, children of faculty/staff, children of public servants, previous college experience, veterans. ***Tuition waivers:*** Full or partial for employees or children of employees, senior citizens. ***ROTC:*** Army cooperative, Air Force cooperative.

LOANS ***Student loans:*** $16,144,534 (39% need-based, 61% non-need-based). ***Average need-based loan:*** Freshmen: $3260. Undergraduates: $4131. ***Parent loans:*** $11,123,606 (100% non-need-based). ***Programs:*** Federal Direct (Subsidized and Unsubsidized Stafford, PLUS), Perkins, private alternative loans.

WORK-STUDY ***Federal work-study:*** Total amount: $2,679,042; jobs available. ***State or other work-study/employment:*** Total amount: $701,042 (100% non-need-based). Part-time jobs available.

ATHLETIC AWARDS Total amount: $3,805,172 (100% non-need-based).

APPLYING FOR FINANCIAL AID ***Required financial aid form:*** FAFSA. ***Financial aid deadline (priority):*** 2/15. ***Notification date:*** Continuous.

CONTACT Ms. Doreen Meyer, Director of Financial Aid, New York Institute of Technology, PO Box 8000, Old Westbury, NY 11568-8000, 516-686-1083 or toll-free 800-345-NYIT. *Fax:* 516-686-7997. *E-mail:* dmeyer@nyit.edu.

Website: http://www.nyit.edu/.

NEW YORK SCHOOL OF INTERIOR DESIGN

New York, NY

CONTACT Mrs. Rashmi H. Wadhvani, Financial Aid Consultant, New York School of Interior Design, 170 East 70th Street, New York, NY 10021-5110, 212-472-1500 Ext. 204 or toll-free 800-336-9743 Ext.205. *Fax:* 212-472-1867. *E-mail:* rwadhvani@nysid.edu.

Website: http://www.nysid.edu/.

NEW YORK UNIVERSITY

New York, NY

Tuition & fees: $53,308	Average undergraduate aid package: $37,841

ABOUT THE INSTITUTION Independent, coed. ***Awards:*** certificates, diplomas, associate, bachelor's, master's, and doctoral degrees. 189 undergraduate majors. ***Total enrollment:*** 52,885. Undergraduates: 26,981. Freshmen: 5,752. Both federal and institutional methodology are used as a basis for awarding need-based institutional aid.

UNDERGRADUATE EXPENSES for 2019–2020 ***Application fee:*** $80. ***Comprehensive fee:*** $71,992 includes full-time tuition ($50,684), mandatory fees ($2624), and room and board ($18,684). ***College room only:*** $13,548. Full-time tuition and fees vary according to course load, program, and reciprocity agreements. Room and board charges vary according to board plan, housing facility, and location. ***Part-time tuition:*** $1493 per credit hour. ***Part-time fees:*** $498 per term. Part-time tuition and fees vary according to program. ***Payment plan:*** Tuition prepayment.

FRESHMAN FINANCIAL AID (Fall 2018) 3519 applied for aid; of those 73% were deemed to have need. 98% of freshmen with need received aid; of those 12% had need fully met. ***Average percent of need met:*** 71% (excluding resources awarded to replace EFC). ***Average financial aid package:*** $41,475 (excluding resources awarded to replace EFC). 4% of all full-time freshmen had no need and received non-need-based gift aid.

UNDERGRADUATE FINANCIAL AID (Fall 2018) 15,301 applied for aid; of those 75% were deemed to have need. 94% of undergraduates with need received aid; of those 12% had need fully met. ***Average percent of need met:*** 65% (excluding resources awarded to replace EFC). ***Average financial aid package:*** $37,841 (excluding resources awarded to replace EFC). 4% of all full-time undergraduates had no need and received non-need-based gift aid.

GIFT AID (NEED-BASED) ***Total amount:*** $354,001,688 (9% federal, 3% state, 86% institutional, 2% external sources). ***Receiving aid:*** Freshmen: 41% (2,513); all full-time undergraduates: 42% (10,772). ***Average award:*** Freshmen: $37,080; Undergraduates: $32,933. ***Scholarships, grants, and awards:*** Federal Pell, FSEOG, state, private, college/university gift aid from institutional funds, Federal Nursing.

GIFT AID (NON-NEED-BASED) ***Total amount:*** $13,649,069 (4% federal, 3% state, 75% institutional, 18% external sources). ***Receiving aid:*** Freshmen: 2% (138). Undergraduates: 3% (717). ***Average award:*** Freshmen: $4816. Undergraduates: $5522. ***Scholarships, grants, and awards by category:*** *Academic interests/achievement:* general academic interests/achievements. *Creative arts/performance:* general creative arts/performance. ***Tuition waivers:*** Full or partial for employees or children of employees. ***ROTC:*** Army cooperative, Air Force cooperative.

LOANS ***Student loans:*** $87,225,288 (78% need-based, 22% non-need-based). 39% of past graduating class borrowed through all loan programs. *Average indebtedness per student:* $29,242. ***Average need-based loan:*** Freshmen: $3379. Undergraduates: $4412. ***Parent loans:*** $154,709,042 (56% need-based, 44% non-need-based). ***Programs:*** Federal Direct (Subsidized and Unsubsidized Stafford, PLUS), Federal Nursing, college/university.

WORK-STUDY ***Federal work-study:*** Total amount: $21,903,253; jobs available.

APPLYING FOR FINANCIAL AID ***Required financial aid forms:*** FAFSA, CSS Financial Aid PROFILE, noncustodial (divorced/separated) parent's statement. ***Financial aid deadline:*** 2/15.

CONTACT Financial Aid Office, New York University, 70 Washington Square South, New York, NY 10012-1019, 212-998-1212.
Website: http://www.nyu.edu/.

NIAGARA UNIVERSITY

Niagara Falls, NY

Tuition & fees: $35,240	Average undergraduate aid package: $28,001

ABOUT THE INSTITUTION Independent Roman Catholic Church, coed. ***Awards:*** certificates, associate, bachelor's, master's, and doctoral degrees. 54 undergraduate majors. ***Total enrollment:*** 3,727. Undergraduates: 2,809. Freshmen: 626. Federal methodology is used as a basis for awarding need-based institutional aid.

UNDERGRADUATE EXPENSES for 2020–2021 ***One-time required fee:*** $200. ***Comprehensive fee:*** $47,090 includes full-time tuition ($33,700), mandatory fees ($1540), and room and board ($11,850). Full-time tuition and fees vary according to program. Room and board charges vary according to housing facility. ***Part-time tuition:*** $1125 per credit hour. Part-time tuition and fees vary according to program.

FRESHMAN FINANCIAL AID (Fall 2019, est.) 562 applied for aid; of those 89% were deemed to have need. 100% of freshmen with need received aid; of those 48% had need fully met. ***Average percent of need met:*** 86% (excluding resources awarded to replace EFC). ***Average financial aid package:*** $30,608 (excluding resources awarded to replace EFC). 19% of all full-time freshmen had no need and received non-need-based gift aid.

UNDERGRADUATE FINANCIAL AID (Fall 2019, est.) 2,027 applied for aid; of those 89% were deemed to have need. 100% of undergraduates with need received aid; of those 50% had need fully met. ***Average percent of need met:*** 82% (excluding resources awarded to replace EFC). ***Average financial aid package:*** $28,001 (excluding resources awarded to replace EFC). 17% of all full-time undergraduates had no need and received non-need-based gift aid.

GIFT AID (NEED-BASED) ***Total amount:*** $43,760,986 (12% federal, 6% state, 81% institutional, 1% external sources). ***Receiving aid:*** Freshmen: 80% (493); all full-time undergraduates: 66% (1,767). ***Average award:*** Freshmen: $27,329; Undergraduates: $24,427. ***Scholarships, grants, and awards:*** Federal Pell, FSEOG, state, private, college/university gift aid from institutional funds.

GIFT AID (NON-NEED-BASED) ***Total amount:*** $8,331,134 (6% federal, 93% institutional, 1% external sources). ***Receiving aid:*** Freshmen: 63% (389). Undergraduates: 50% (1,329). ***Average award:*** Freshmen: $18,574. Undergraduates: $16,349. ***Scholarships, grants, and awards by category:*** *Academic interests/achievement:* general academic interests/achievements. *Creative arts/performance:* theater/drama. *Special achievements/activities:* community service. *Special characteristics:* children of faculty/staff, relatives of clergy. ***Tuition waivers:*** Full or partial for employees or children of employees. ***ROTC:*** Army.

LOANS ***Student loans:*** $15,239,637 (92% need-based, 8% non-need-based). 76% of past graduating class borrowed through all loan programs. *Average indebtedness per student:* $34,046. ***Average need-based loan:*** Freshmen: $3411. Undergraduates: $4384. ***Parent loans:*** $4,135,437 (92% need-based, 8% non-need-based). ***Programs:*** Federal Direct (Subsidized and Unsubsidized Stafford, PLUS), Federal Nursing, college/university.

WORK-STUDY ***Federal work-study:*** Total amount: $1,050,152; jobs available. ***State or other work-study/employment:*** Total amount: $81,740 (100% non-need-based). Part-time jobs available.

ATHLETIC AWARDS Total amount: $5,144,849 (43% need-based, 57% non-need-based).

APPLYING FOR FINANCIAL AID ***Required financial aid forms:*** FAFSA, state aid form. ***Financial aid deadline (priority):*** 2/15. ***Notification date:*** Continuous beginning 1/15. Students must reply by 5/1.

CONTACT Ms. Katie L. Kocsis, Director of Financial Aid, Niagara University, PO Box 2010, Niagara University, NY 14109, 716-286-8686 or toll-free 800-462-2111. *Fax:* 716-286-8678. *E-mail:* kkocsis@niagara.edu.
Website: http://www.niagara.edu/.

NICHOLLS STATE UNIVERSITY

Thibodaux, LA

Tuition & fees (area res): $7898	Average undergraduate aid package: $8444

ABOUT THE INSTITUTION State-supported, coed. ***Awards:*** certificates, associate, bachelor's, and master's degrees. 37 undergraduate majors. ***Total enrollment:*** 6,488. Undergraduates: 5,896. Freshmen: 1,301. Federal methodology is used as a basis for awarding need-based institutional aid.

UNDERGRADUATE EXPENSES for 2019–2020 ***Application fee:*** $20. ***One-time required fee:*** $72. ***Tuition, area resident:*** full-time $4922; part-time $4512 per year. ***Tuition, state resident:*** full-time $4922; part-time $4512 per year. ***Tuition, nonresident:*** full-time $6015; part-time $5514 per year. ***Required fees:*** full-time $2976; $3809 per year. Full-time tuition and fees vary according to location and program. Part-time tuition and fees vary according to course load, location, and program. ***College room and board:*** $9818; ***Room only:*** $6580. Room and board charges vary according to board plan, housing facility, and location.

FRESHMAN FINANCIAL AID (Fall 2018) 1230 applied for aid; of those 73% were deemed to have need. 99% of freshmen with need received aid; of those 14% had need fully met. ***Average percent of need met:*** 51% (excluding resources awarded to replace EFC). ***Average financial aid package:*** $9168 (excluding resources awarded to replace EFC).

UNDERGRADUATE FINANCIAL AID (Fall 2018) 4,312 applied for aid; of those 76% were deemed to have need. 99% of undergraduates with need received aid; of those 11% had need fully met. ***Average percent of need met:*** 52% (excluding resources awarded to replace EFC). ***Average financial aid package:*** $8444 (excluding resources awarded to replace EFC).

GIFT AID (NEED-BASED) ***Total amount:*** $20,061,557 (51% federal, 33% state, 9% institutional, 7% external sources). ***Receiving aid:*** Freshmen: 65% (843); all full-time undergraduates: 59% (2,866). ***Average award:*** Freshmen: $7684; Undergraduates: $6814. ***Scholarships, grants, and awards:*** Federal Pell, FSEOG, state, private, college/university gift aid from institutional funds.

GIFT AID (NON-NEED-BASED) ***Total amount:*** $6,845,509 (5% federal, 65% state, 23% institutional, 7% external sources). ***Receiving aid:*** Freshmen: 8% (108). Undergraduates: 6% (286). ***Scholarships, grants, and awards by category:*** *Academic interests/achievement:* general academic interests/achievements. *Creative arts/performance:* applied art and design, art/fine arts, dance, journalism/publications, music. *Special achievements/activities:* cheerleading/drum major, leadership. *Special characteristics:* adult students, children of faculty/staff, ethnic background, first-generation college students, general special characteristics, international students, local/state students, members of minority groups, out-of-state students, previous college experience, public servants, spouses of deceased or disabled public servants, veterans. ***Tuition waivers:*** Full or partial for employees or children of employees, senior citizens.

LOANS ***Student loans:*** $13,838,953 (73% need-based, 27% non-need-based). ***Average need-based loan:*** Freshmen: $1968. Undergraduates: $2658. ***Parent loans:*** $4,812,756 (22% need-based, 78% non-need-based). ***Programs:*** Federal Direct (Subsidized and Unsubsidized Stafford, PLUS).

WORK-STUDY ***Federal work-study:*** Total amount: $190,049; jobs available. ***State or other work-study/employment:*** Total amount: $281,648 (83% need-based, 17% non-need-based). Part-time jobs available.

ATHLETIC AWARDS Total amount: $1,895,842 (55% need-based, 45% non-need-based).

APPLYING FOR FINANCIAL AID ***Required financial aid forms:*** FAFSA, institution's own form, state aid form, noncustodial (divorced/separated) parent's statement. ***Financial aid deadline:*** 6/30 (priority: 4/15). ***Notification date:*** Continuous.

CONTACT Casie Triche, Director of Financial Aid, Nicholls State University, PO Box 2005, Thibodaux, LA 70310, 985-448-4077 or toll-free 877-NICHOLLS. *Fax:* 985-448-4124. *E-mail:* finaid@nicholls.edu.
Website: http://www.nicholls.edu/.

NICHOLS COLLEGE

Dudley, MA

Tuition & fees: $36,540	Average undergraduate aid package: $29,654

ABOUT THE INSTITUTION Independent, coed. ***Awards:*** bachelor's and master's degrees. 19 undergraduate majors. ***Total enrollment:*** 1,553. Undergraduates: 1,326. Freshmen: 344. Federal methodology is used as a basis for awarding need-based institutional aid.

UNDERGRADUATE EXPENSES for 2020–2021 ***Comprehensive fee:*** $50,490 includes full-time tuition ($35,290), mandatory fees ($1250), and room and board ($13,950). ***College room only:*** $8000. Full-time tuition and fees vary according to class time and location. Room and board charges vary according to housing facility. ***Part-time tuition:*** $1000 per credit hour. Part-time tuition and fees vary according to class time and location.

FRESHMAN FINANCIAL AID (Fall 2019, est.) 339 applied for aid; of those 78% were deemed to have need. 100% of freshmen with need received aid. ***Average percent of need met:*** 92% (excluding resources awarded to replace EFC). ***Average financial aid package:*** $30,891 (excluding resources awarded to replace EFC). 4% of all full-time freshmen had no need and received non-need-based gift aid.

UNDERGRADUATE FINANCIAL AID (Fall 2019, est.) 1,159 applied for aid; of those 80% were deemed to have need. 100% of undergraduates with need received aid. ***Average percent of need met:*** 85% (excluding resources awarded to replace EFC). ***Average financial aid package:*** $29,654 (excluding resources awarded to replace EFC). 6% of all full-time undergraduates had no need and received non-need-based gift aid.

GIFT AID (NEED-BASED) ***Total amount:*** $22,467,103 (8% federal, 2% state, 89% institutional, 1% external sources). ***Receiving aid:*** Freshmen: 72% (264); all full-time undergraduates: 68% (929). ***Average award:*** Freshmen: $25,898; Undergraduates: $24,026. ***Scholarships, grants, and awards:*** Federal Pell, FSEOG, state, private, college/university gift aid from institutional funds.

GIFT AID (NON-NEED-BASED) ***Receiving aid:*** Freshmen: 11% (41). Undergraduates: 15% (208). ***Average award:*** Freshmen: $18,701. Undergraduates: $16,670. ***Scholarships, grants, and awards by category:*** *Academic interests/achievement:* business, communication, general academic interests/achievements. *Special achievements/activities:* community service, general special achievements/activities, leadership. *Special characteristics:* children and siblings of alumni, children of faculty/staff, siblings of current students. ***Tuition waivers:*** Full or partial for employees or children of employees.

LOANS ***Student loans:*** $10,172,184 (29% need-based, 71% non-need-based). ***Average need-based loan:*** Freshmen: $2965. Undergraduates: $3806. ***Parent loans:*** $4,540,689 (100% need-based). ***Programs:*** Federal Direct (Subsidized and Unsubsidized Stafford, PLUS), state.

WORK-STUDY ***Federal work-study:*** Total amount: $530,685; 589 jobs averaging $2432.

APPLYING FOR FINANCIAL AID ***Required financial aid form:*** FAFSA. ***Financial aid deadline (priority):*** 3/1. ***Notification date:*** Continuous beginning 12/1. Students must reply within 2 weeks of notification.

CONTACT Miss Lindsay Louis, Director of Financial Aid, Nichols College, PO Box 5000, Dudley, MA 01571, 508-213-2372 or toll-free 800-470-3379. *Fax:* 508-213-2118. *E-mail:* lindsay.louis@nichols.edu.
Website: http://www.nichols.edu/.

NORFOLK STATE UNIVERSITY

Norfolk, VA

CONTACT Mr. Kevin Burns, Director of Financial Aid, Norfolk State University, 700 Park Avenue, Norfolk, VA 23504-3907, 757-823-8381 or toll-free 800-274-1821. *Fax:* 757-823-9059. *E-mail:* kburns@nsu.edu.
Website: http://www.nsu.edu/.

NORTH AMERICAN UNIVERSITY

Stafford, TX

CONTACT Financial Aid Office, North American University, 11929 West Airport Boulevard, Stafford, TX 77477, 832-230-5555.
Website: http://www.na.edu/.

NORTH CAROLINA AGRICULTURAL AND TECHNICAL STATE UNIVERSITY

Greensboro, NC

CONTACT Mrs. Sherri Avent, Director of Student Financial Aid, North Carolina Agricultural and Technical State University, Dowdy Administration Building, Room 100, 1601 East Market Street, Greensboro, NC 27411, 336-334-7973 or toll-free 800-443-8964 (in-state). *Fax:* 336-334-7954. *E-mail:* avent@ncat.edu.
Website: http://www.ncat.edu/.

NORTH CAROLINA CENTRAL UNIVERSITY

Durham, NC

Tuition & fees (area res): $6534	Average undergraduate aid package: $23,820

ABOUT THE INSTITUTION State-supported, coed. ***Awards:*** bachelor's, master's, and doctoral degrees. 30 undergraduate majors. ***Total enrollment:*** 8,011. Undergraduates: 6,101. Freshmen: 1,027. Federal methodology is used as a basis for awarding need-based institutional aid.

UNDERGRADUATE EXPENSES for 2020–2021 ***Application fee:*** $50. ***Tuition, area resident:*** full-time $3728; part-time $593 per credit hour. ***Tuition, state resident:*** full-time $3728. ***Tuition, nonresident:*** full-time $16,435; part-time $2054 per credit hour. ***Required fees:*** full-time $2806. Part-time tuition and fees vary according to course load. ***College room and board:*** $10,227. Room and board charges vary according to board plan, housing facility, and location. ***Payment plan:*** Guaranteed tuition.

FRESHMAN FINANCIAL AID (Fall 2018) 1137 applied for aid; of those 92% were deemed to have need. 98% of freshmen with need received aid; of those 1% had need fully met. ***Average percent of need met:*** 54% (excluding resources awarded to replace EFC). ***Average financial aid package:*** $14,832 (excluding resources awarded to replace EFC). 2% of all full-time freshmen had no need and received non-need-based gift aid.

UNDERGRADUATE FINANCIAL AID (Fall 2018) 5,299 applied for aid; of those 94% were deemed to have need. 99% of undergraduates with need received aid; of those 1% had need fully met. ***Average percent of need met:*** 54% (excluding resources awarded to replace EFC). ***Average financial aid package:*** $23,820 (excluding resources awarded to replace EFC). 1% of all full-time undergraduates had no need and received non-need-based gift aid.

GIFT AID (NEED-BASED) ***Total amount:*** $40,458,078 (55% federal, 21% state, 21% institutional, 3% external sources). ***Receiving aid:*** Freshmen: 44% (946); all full-time undergraduates: 63% (4,423). ***Average award:*** Freshmen: $10,114; Undergraduates: $15,027. ***Scholarships, grants, and awards:*** Federal Pell, FSEOG, state, private, college/university gift aid from institutional funds, Federal Nursing.
GIFT AID (NON-NEED-BASED) ***Total amount:*** $1,020,280 (15% federal, 28% state, 40% institutional, 17% external sources). ***Receiving aid:*** Freshmen: 4% (78). Undergraduates: 5% (319). ***Average award:*** Freshmen: $9374. Undergraduates: $13,397. ***Scholarships, grants, and awards by category:*** *Academic interests/achievement:* biological sciences, business, computer science, education, English, general academic interests/achievements, library science, physical sciences, social sciences. *Creative arts/performance:* applied art and design, music, theater/drama. *Special achievements/activities:* leadership. *Special characteristics:* children and siblings of alumni, general special characteristics. ***Tuition waivers:*** Full or partial for employees or children of employees. ***ROTC:*** Army, Air Force.
LOANS ***Student loans:*** $34,737,496 (97% need-based, 3% non-need-based). 91% of past graduating class borrowed through all loan programs. *Average indebtedness per student:* $44,228. ***Average need-based loan:*** Freshmen: $5704. Undergraduates: $10,582. ***Parent loans:*** $19,032,272 (93% need-based, 7% non-need-based). ***Programs:*** Federal Direct (Subsidized and Unsubsidized Stafford, PLUS), Perkins, Federal Nursing.
WORK-STUDY ***Federal work-study:*** Total amount: $444,606; jobs available. ***State or other work-study/employment:*** Part-time jobs available.
ATHLETIC AWARDS Total amount: $3,765,015 (72% need-based, 28% non-need-based).
APPLYING FOR FINANCIAL AID ***Required financial aid form:*** FAFSA. ***Financial aid deadline (priority):*** 3/1. ***Notification date:*** Continuous.
CONTACT Mrs. Sharon J. Oliver, Director of Financial Aid, North Carolina Central University, 106 Student Services Building, Durham, NC 27707-3129, 919-530-5313 or toll-free 877-667-7533. *Fax:* 919-530-7959. *E-mail:* soliver@nccu.edu.
Website: http://www.nccu.edu/.

NORTH CAROLINA STATE UNIVERSITY

Raleigh, NC

Tuition & fees (NC res): $9101	Average undergraduate aid package: $13,488

ABOUT THE INSTITUTION State-supported, coed. ***Awards:*** certificates, associate, bachelor's, master's, and doctoral degrees. 93 undergraduate majors. ***Total enrollment:*** 35,479. Undergraduates: 25,199. Freshmen: 4,952. Federal methodology is used as a basis for awarding need-based institutional aid.
UNDERGRADUATE EXPENSES for 2019–2020 ***Application fee:*** $85. ***Tuition, state resident:*** full-time $6535. ***Tuition, nonresident:*** full-time $26,654. ***Required fees:*** full-time $2566. Full-time tuition and fees vary according to course load and program. Part-time tuition and fees vary according to course load and program. ***College room and board:*** $11,359; ***Room only:*** $6714. Room and board charges vary according to board plan and housing facility. ***Payment plan:*** Guaranteed tuition.
FRESHMAN FINANCIAL AID (Fall 2019, est.) 3999 applied for aid; of those 54% were deemed to have need. 99% of freshmen with need received aid; of those 23% had need fully met. ***Average percent of need met:*** 76% (excluding resources awarded to replace EFC). ***Average financial aid package:*** $13,766 (excluding resources awarded to replace EFC). 4% of all full-time freshmen had no need and received non-need-based gift aid.
UNDERGRADUATE FINANCIAL AID (Fall 2019, est.) 15,791 applied for aid; of those 66% were deemed to have need. 98% of undergraduates with need received aid; of those 22% had need fully met. ***Average percent of need met:*** 75% (excluding resources awarded to replace EFC). ***Average financial aid package:*** $13,488 (excluding resources awarded to replace EFC). 5% of all full-time undergraduates had no need and received non-need-based gift aid.
GIFT AID (NEED-BASED) ***Total amount:*** $104,137,148 (23% federal, 18% state, 55% institutional, 4% external sources). ***Receiving aid:*** Freshmen: 42% (2,021); all full-time undergraduates: 43% (9,643). ***Average award:*** Freshmen: $10,812; Undergraduates: $10,326. ***Scholarships, grants, and awards:*** Federal Pell, FSEOG, state, private, college/university gift aid from institutional funds, United Negro College Fund.
GIFT AID (NON-NEED-BASED) ***Total amount:*** $17,363,194 (6% state, 59% institutional, 35% external sources). ***Receiving aid:*** Freshmen: 8% (392). Undergraduates: 6% (1,318). ***Average award:*** Freshmen: $6653. Undergraduates: $5265. ***Scholarships, grants, and awards by category:*** *Academic interests/achievement:* 4,518 awards ($17,519,429 total): agriculture, architecture, biological sciences, business, computer science, education, engineering/technologies, general academic interests/achievements, humanities, mathematics, military science, physical sciences, social sciences. *Special achievements/activities:* cheerleading/drum major, general special achievements/activities, leadership. *Special characteristics:* children and siblings of alumni, children of faculty/staff, general special characteristics, local/state students. ***ROTC:*** Army, Naval, Air Force.
LOANS ***Student loans:*** $73,752,510 (58% need-based, 42% non-need-based). 50% of past graduating class borrowed through all loan programs. *Average indebtedness per student:* $25,893. ***Average need-based loan:*** Freshmen: $3135. Undergraduates: $3863. ***Parent loans:*** $15,309,820 (19% need-based, 81% non-need-based). ***Programs:*** Federal Direct (Subsidized and Unsubsidized Stafford, PLUS), Perkins, state, college/university.
WORK-STUDY ***Federal work-study:*** Total amount: $2,820,181; 1,532 jobs averaging $1750. ***State or other work-study/employment:*** Total amount: $2,322,330 (33% need-based, 67% non-need-based). Part-time jobs available.
ATHLETIC AWARDS Total amount: $9,944,016 (30% need-based, 70% non-need-based).
APPLYING FOR FINANCIAL AID ***Required financial aid form:*** FAFSA. ***Financial aid deadline (priority):*** 3/1. ***Notification date:*** Continuous beginning 4/1.
CONTACT Ms. Krista Ringler, Director of Scholarships and Financial Aid, North Carolina State University, 2016 Harris Hall, Box 7302, Raleigh, NC 27695-7302, 919-515-2421. *Fax:* 919-515-8422. *E-mail:* krista_ringler@ncsu.edu.
Website: http://www.ncsu.edu/.

NORTH CAROLINA WESLEYAN COLLEGE

Rocky Mount, NC

CONTACT Leah Hill, Director of Financial Aid, North Carolina Wesleyan College, 3400 North Wesleyan Boulevard, Rocky Mount, NC 27804, 252-985-5200 or toll-free 800-488-6292. *Fax:* 252-985-5295. *E-mail:* lhill@ncwc.edu.
Website: http://www.ncwc.edu/.

NORTH CENTRAL COLLEGE

Naperville, IL

Tuition & fees: $40,040	Average undergraduate aid package: N/A

ABOUT THE INSTITUTION Independent United Methodist, coed. ***Awards:*** certificates, bachelor's, and master's degrees. 73 undergraduate majors. Federal methodology is used as a basis for awarding need-based institutional aid.
UNDERGRADUATE EXPENSES for 2019–2020 ***Comprehensive fee:*** $51,496 includes full-time tuition ($39,860), mandatory fees ($180), and room and board ($11,456). Room and board charges vary according to board plan and housing facility. ***Part-time tuition:*** $1246 per credit hour. ***Part-time fees:*** $90 per term. Part-time tuition and fees vary according to course load.
GIFT AID (NEED-BASED) ***Scholarships, grants, and awards:*** Federal Pell, FSEOG, state, private, college/university gift aid from institutional funds.
GIFT AID (NON-NEED-BASED) ***Scholarships, grants, and awards by category:*** *Academic interests/achievement:* biological sciences, business, communication, computer science, education, English, foreign languages, general academic interests/achievements, humanities, international studies, mathematics, physical sciences, premedicine, religion/biblical studies, social sciences. *Creative arts/performance:* art/fine arts, cinema/film/broadcasting, debating, journalism/publications, music, theater/drama. *Special achievements/activities:* community service, religious involvement. *Special characteristics:* adult students, children of faculty/staff, general special characteristics, international students, relatives of clergy. ***Tuition waivers:***

Full or partial for employees or children of employees, senior citizens. ***ROTC:*** Army cooperative, Air Force cooperative.

LOANS *Student loans:* 76% of past graduating class borrowed through all loan programs. *Average indebtedness per student:* $37,396. ***Programs:*** Federal Direct (Subsidized and Unsubsidized Stafford, PLUS), college/university, Outside Lender Loans.

WORK-STUDY *Federal work-study:* 333 jobs averaging $1210.

APPLYING FOR FINANCIAL AID *Required financial aid form:* FAFSA. ***Financial aid deadline:*** Continuous. ***Notification date:*** Continuous beginning 12/1. Students must reply within 4 weeks of notification.

CONTACT Kristina Bonn, Director of Financial Aid, North Central College, 30 North Brainard Street, Naperville, IL 60540, 630-637-5600 or toll-free 800-411-1861. *Fax:* 630-637-5608. *E-mail:* klbonn@noctrl.edu.
Website: http://www.northcentralcollege.edu/.

NORTHCENTRAL UNIVERSITY

San Diego, CA

Tuition & fees: N/R **Average undergraduate aid package: N/A**

ABOUT THE INSTITUTION Proprietary, coed. ***Awards:*** certificates, bachelor's, master's, and doctoral degrees (offers only distance learning programs). 12 undergraduate majors. Federal methodology is used as a basis for awarding need-based institutional aid.

CONTACT Financial Aid Office, Northcentral University, 8667 E Hartford Dr, Scottsdale, AZ 85255, 888-888-327-2877 Ext. 7488 or toll-free 866-776-0331. *E-mail:* FinancialAid@ncu.edu.
Website: http://www.ncu.edu/.

NORTH CENTRAL UNIVERSITY

Minneapolis, MN

Comprehensive fee: $34,460 **Average undergraduate aid package: N/A**

ABOUT THE INSTITUTION Independent Assemblies of God, coed. ***Awards:*** certificates, diplomas, associate, and bachelor's degrees. 39 undergraduate majors. ***Total enrollment:*** 1,155. Undergraduates: 1,085. Freshmen: 245. Both federal and institutional methodology are used as a basis for awarding need-based institutional aid.

UNDERGRADUATE EXPENSES for 2020–2021 *Application fee:* $25. ***Comprehensive fee:*** $34,460 includes mandatory fees ($850) and room and board ($8180). ***College room only:*** $4560. ***Part-time tuition:*** $1005 per credit hour.

GIFT AID (NEED-BASED) *Scholarships, grants, and awards:* Federal Pell, FSEOG, state, private, college/university gift aid from institutional funds.

GIFT AID (NON-NEED-BASED) *Scholarships, grants, and awards by category:* *Academic interests/achievement:* general academic interests/achievements. *Creative arts/performance:* music. *Special achievements/activities:* community service, general special achievements/activities, leadership, memberships, religious involvement. *Special characteristics:* children of faculty/staff, general special characteristics, international students, relatives of clergy, religious affiliation.

LOANS *Student loans:* 79% of past graduating class borrowed through all loan programs. *Average indebtedness per student:* $21,965. ***Programs:*** Federal Direct (Subsidized and Unsubsidized Stafford, PLUS), Perkins, state.

WORK-STUDY Federal work-study jobs available. ***State or other work-study/employment:*** Part-time jobs available.

APPLYING FOR FINANCIAL AID *Required financial aid forms:* FAFSA, institution's own form, state aid form. ***Financial aid deadline (priority):*** 7/1. ***Notification date:*** Continuous beginning 12/1.

CONTACT Mrs. Donna Jager, Director of Financial Aid, North Central University, 910 Elliot Avenue, Minneapolis, MN 55404-1322, 612-343-4485 or toll-free 800-289-6222. *Fax:* 612-343-8067. *E-mail:* finaid@northcentral.edu.
Website: http://www.northcentral.edu/.

THE NORTH COAST COLLEGE

Lakewood, OH

CONTACT Financial Aid Office, The North Coast College, 11724 Detroit Avenue, Lakewood, OH 44107, 216-221-8584.
Website: http://www.thencc.edu/.

NORTH DAKOTA STATE UNIVERSITY

Fargo, ND

Tuition & fees (ND res): $9619 **Average undergraduate aid package: $12,117**

ABOUT THE INSTITUTION State-supported, coed. ***Awards:*** certificates, bachelor's, master's, and doctoral degrees. 95 undergraduate majors. ***Total enrollment:*** 13,796. Undergraduates: 11,425. Freshmen: 2,275. Federal methodology is used as a basis for awarding need-based institutional aid.

UNDERGRADUATE EXPENSES for 2019–2020 *Application fee:* $35. ***One-time required fee:*** $135. ***Tuition, state resident:*** full-time $8275; part-time $341 per credit hour. ***Tuition, nonresident:*** full-time $12,413; part-time $511 per credit hour. ***Required fees:*** full-time $1344; $56.01 per credit hour. Full-time tuition and fees vary according to course load, program, and reciprocity agreements. Part-time tuition and fees vary according to course load, program, and reciprocity agreements. ***College room and board:*** $8878; ***Room only:*** $4100. Room and board charges vary according to board plan and housing facility.

FRESHMAN FINANCIAL AID (Fall 2018) 1999 applied for aid; of those 62% were deemed to have need. 98% of freshmen with need received aid; of those 42% had need fully met. ***Average percent of need met:*** 70% (excluding resources awarded to replace EFC). ***Average financial aid package:*** $13,398 (excluding resources awarded to replace EFC). 16% of all full-time freshmen had no need and received non-need-based gift aid.

UNDERGRADUATE FINANCIAL AID (Fall 2018) 7,913 applied for aid; of those 67% were deemed to have need. 97% of undergraduates with need received aid; of those 35% had need fully met. ***Average percent of need met:*** 66% (excluding resources awarded to replace EFC). ***Average financial aid package:*** $12,117 (excluding resources awarded to replace EFC). 12% of all full-time undergraduates had no need and received non-need-based gift aid.

GIFT AID (NEED-BASED) *Total amount:* $19,685,804 (54% federal, 18% state, 17% institutional, 11% external sources). ***Receiving aid:*** Freshmen: 45% (1,013); all full-time undergraduates: 39% (3,958). ***Average award:*** Freshmen: $5774; Undergraduates: $5640. ***Scholarships, grants, and awards:*** Federal Pell, FSEOG, state, private, college/university gift aid from institutional funds, Cultural Diversity Tuition Waiver.

GIFT AID (NON-NEED-BASED) *Total amount:* $7,292,131 (1% federal, 26% state, 48% institutional, 25% external sources). ***Receiving aid:*** Freshmen: 4% (100). Undergraduates: 3% (339). ***Average award:*** Freshmen: $2141. Undergraduates: $2508. ***Scholarships, grants, and awards by category:*** *Academic interests/achievement:* agriculture, architecture, biological sciences, business, communication, computer science, education, engineering/technologies, English, general academic interests/achievements, health fields, home economics, humanities, mathematics, military science, physical sciences, premedicine, social sciences. *Creative arts/performance:* art/fine arts, debating, journalism/publications, music, theater/drama. *Special achievements/activities:* memberships, religious involvement. *Special characteristics:* children of faculty/staff, ethnic background. ***Tuition waivers:*** Full or partial for minority students, children of alumni, employees or children of employees, senior citizens. ***ROTC:*** Army, Air Force.

LOANS *Student loans:* $59,645,348 (53% need-based, 47% non-need-based). 66% of past graduating class borrowed through all loan programs. *Average indebtedness per student:* $33,639. ***Average need-based loan:*** Freshmen: $6894. Undergraduates: $6977. ***Parent loans:*** $2,658,612 (43% need-based, 57% non-need-based). ***Programs:*** Federal Direct (Subsidized and Unsubsidized Stafford, PLUS), Federal Nursing.

WORK-STUDY *Federal work-study:* Total amount: $746,274; 239 jobs averaging $2429.

ATHLETIC AWARDS Total amount: $4,324,140 (35% need-based, 65% non-need-based).

APPLYING FOR FINANCIAL AID *Required financial aid form:* FAFSA. ***Financial aid deadline (priority):*** 2/1. ***Notification date:*** 3/1.

CONTACT Jeffrey Jacobs, Director, North Dakota State University, Dept 2836, PO Box 6050, Fargo, ND 58108, 701-231-9653 or toll-free 800-488-6378. *Fax:* 701-231-8802. *E-mail:* Jeffrey.jacobs@ndsu.edu.
Website: http://www.ndsu.edu/.

NORTHEASTERN ILLINOIS UNIVERSITY

Chicago, IL

Tuition & fees (area res): $13,998 | **Average undergraduate aid package: $11,090**

ABOUT THE INSTITUTION State-supported, coed. ***Awards:*** certificates, bachelor's, and master's degrees. 41 undergraduate majors. ***Total enrollment:*** 7,423. Undergraduates: 5,705. Freshmen: 457. Federal methodology is used as a basis for awarding need-based institutional aid.

UNDERGRADUATE EXPENSES for 2020–2021 ***Application fee:*** $30. ***Tuition, area resident:*** full-time $11,582; part-time $412 per credit hour. ***Tuition, nonresident:*** full-time $23,165; part-time $824 per credit hour. ***Required fees:*** full-time $2416. ***Room only:*** $8426.

FRESHMAN FINANCIAL AID (Fall 2019, est.) 403 applied for aid; of those 94% were deemed to have need. 94% of freshmen with need received aid; of those 4% had need fully met. ***Average percent of need met:*** 21% (excluding resources awarded to replace EFC). ***Average financial aid package:*** $12,077 (excluding resources awarded to replace EFC). 2% of all full-time freshmen had no need and received non-need-based gift aid.

UNDERGRADUATE FINANCIAL AID (Fall 2019, est.) 2,687 applied for aid; of those 89% were deemed to have need. 94% of undergraduates with need received aid; of those 7% had need fully met. ***Average percent of need met:*** 19% (excluding resources awarded to replace EFC). ***Average financial aid package:*** $11,090 (excluding resources awarded to replace EFC). 4% of all full-time undergraduates had no need and received non-need-based gift aid.

GIFT AID (NEED-BASED) ***Total amount:*** $31,256,201 (57% federal, 41% state, 2% external sources). ***Receiving aid:*** Freshmen: 82% (355); all full-time undergraduates: 61% (2,010). ***Average award:*** Freshmen: $9152; Undergraduates: $8262. ***Scholarships, grants, and awards:*** Federal Pell, FSEOG, state, private, college/university gift aid from institutional funds, United Negro College Fund, Dream US Scholarship (for DACA students).

GIFT AID (NON-NEED-BASED) ***Total amount:*** $2,219,104 (52% state, 35% institutional, 13% external sources). ***Receiving aid:*** Freshmen: 34% (147). Undergraduates: 17% (576). ***Average award:*** Freshmen: $2701. Undergraduates: $5945. ***Scholarships, grants, and awards by category:*** *Academic interests/achievement:* biological sciences, business, communication, computer science, education, English, foreign languages, general academic interests/achievements, mathematics, physical sciences, social sciences. *Creative arts/performance:* applied art and design, creative writing, dance, journalism/publications, music, performing arts, theater/drama. *Special achievements/activities:* leadership. *Special characteristics:* adult students, children of faculty/staff, children of union members/company employees, general special characteristics. ***ROTC:*** Army cooperative, Air Force cooperative.

LOANS ***Student loans:*** $31,975,932 (41% need-based, 59% non-need-based). 70% of past graduating class borrowed through all loan programs. *Average indebtedness per student:* $11,355. ***Average need-based loan:*** Freshmen: $2208. Undergraduates: $3375. ***Parent loans:*** $585,237 (100% non-need-based). ***Programs:*** Federal Direct (Subsidized and Unsubsidized Stafford, PLUS).

WORK-STUDY ***Federal work-study:*** Total amount: $236,084; jobs available. ***State or other work-study/employment:*** Total amount: $717,663 (100% non-need-based). Part-time jobs available.

APPLYING FOR FINANCIAL AID ***Required financial aid form:*** FAFSA. ***Financial aid deadline (priority):*** 2/15. ***Notification date:*** Continuous beginning 11/1. Students must reply within 2 weeks of notification.

CONTACT Financial Aid Office, Northeastern Illinois University, 5500 North St Louis Avenue, Chicago, IL 60625-4699, 773-583-4050.
Website: http://www.neiu.edu/.

NORTHEASTERN STATE UNIVERSITY

Tahlequah, OK

Tuition & fees (area res): $6915 | **Average undergraduate aid package: $13,932**

ABOUT THE INSTITUTION State-supported, coed. ***Awards:*** certificates, bachelor's, master's, and doctoral degrees. 58 undergraduate majors. ***Total enrollment:*** 7,496. Undergraduates: 6,288. Freshmen: 724. Federal methodology is used as a basis for awarding need-based institutional aid.

UNDERGRADUATE EXPENSES for 2019–2020 ***Application fee:*** $25. ***Tuition, area resident:*** full-time $5913; part-time $197 per credit hour. ***Tuition, state resident:*** full-time $5913; part-time $197 per credit hour. ***Tuition, nonresident:*** full-time $14,313; part-time $477 per credit hour. ***Required fees:*** full-time $1002; $33.40 per credit hour. ***College room and board:*** $7340; ***Room only:*** $3200. Room and board charges vary according to board plan and housing facility. ***Payment plan:*** Guaranteed tuition.

FRESHMAN FINANCIAL AID (Fall 2019, est.) 679 applied for aid; of those 72% were deemed to have need. 100% of freshmen with need received aid; of those 83% had need fully met. ***Average percent of need met:*** 98% (excluding resources awarded to replace EFC). ***Average financial aid package:*** $13,190 (excluding resources awarded to replace EFC). 7% of all full-time freshmen had no need and received non-need-based gift aid.

UNDERGRADUATE FINANCIAL AID (Fall 2019, est.) 3,650 applied for aid; of those 80% were deemed to have need. 99% of undergraduates with need received aid; of those 60% had need fully met. ***Average percent of need met:*** 91% (excluding resources awarded to replace EFC). ***Average financial aid package:*** $13,932 (excluding resources awarded to replace EFC). 4% of all full-time undergraduates had no need and received non-need-based gift aid.

GIFT AID (NEED-BASED) ***Receiving aid:*** Freshmen: 63% (450); all full-time undergraduates: 58% (2,532). ***Average award:*** Freshmen: $8106; Undergraduates: $7451. ***Scholarships, grants, and awards:*** Federal Pell, FSEOG, state, private, college/university gift aid from institutional funds, United Negro College Fund.

GIFT AID (NON-NEED-BASED) ***Receiving aid:*** Freshmen: 22% (158). Undergraduates: 11% (486). ***Average award:*** Freshmen: $3518. Undergraduates: $2984. ***Scholarships, grants, and awards by category:*** *Academic interests/achievement:* biological sciences, business, communication, computer science, education, English, foreign languages, general academic interests/achievements, health fields, home economics, humanities, library science, mathematics, physical sciences, premedicine, social sciences. *Creative arts/performance:* applied art and design, art/fine arts, dance, debating, journalism/publications, music, performing arts, theater/drama. *Special achievements/activities:* cheerleading/drum major, community service, junior miss, leadership. *Special characteristics:* children and siblings of alumni, children of faculty/staff, children with a deceased or disabled parent, local/state students, members of minority groups, out-of-state students, religious affiliation, spouses of deceased or disabled public servants. ***Tuition waivers:*** Full or partial for employees or children of employees. ***ROTC:*** Army.

LOANS ***Student loans:*** 54% of past graduating class borrowed through all loan programs. *Average indebtedness per student:* $20,707. ***Average need-based loan:*** Freshmen: $6083. Undergraduates: $7909. ***Programs:*** Federal Direct (Subsidized and Unsubsidized Stafford, PLUS).

WORK-STUDY ***Federal work-study:*** 201 jobs averaging $1666. ***State or other work-study/employment:*** 193 part-time jobs averaging $1683.

APPLYING FOR FINANCIAL AID ***Required financial aid form:*** FAFSA. ***Financial aid deadline:*** Continuous. ***Notification date:*** Continuous.

CONTACT Dr. Teri Cochran, Director of Student Financial Services, Northeastern State University, 715 North Grand Avenue, Tahlequah, OK 74464-2399, 918-444-3410 or toll-free 800-722-9614. *Fax:* 918-458-2510. *E-mail:* cochrant@nsuok.edu.
Website: http://www.nsuok.edu/.

NORTHEASTERN UNIVERSITY
Boston, MA

Tuition & fees: $53,506 | **Average undergraduate aid package: $38,819**

ABOUT THE INSTITUTION Independent, coed. ***Awards:*** certificates, bachelor's, master's, and doctoral degrees. 65 undergraduate majors. ***Total enrollment:*** 27,133. Undergraduates: 18,418. Freshmen: 2,746. Federal methodology is used as a basis for awarding need-based institutional aid.

UNDERGRADUATE EXPENSES for 2019–2020 ***Application fee:*** $75. ***Comprehensive fee:*** $70,436 includes full-time tuition ($52,420), mandatory fees ($1086), and room and board ($16,930). ***College room only:*** $9250. Room and board charges vary according to board plan and housing facility.

FRESHMAN FINANCIAL AID (Fall 2019, est.) 449 applied for aid; of those 80% were deemed to have need. 100% of freshmen with need received aid; of those 18% had need fully met. ***Average percent of need met:*** 84% (excluding resources awarded to replace EFC). ***Average financial aid package:*** $38,871 (excluding resources awarded to replace EFC). 32% of all full-time freshmen had no need and received non-need-based gift aid.

UNDERGRADUATE FINANCIAL AID (Fall 2019, est.) 1,425 applied for aid; of those 81% were deemed to have need. 100% of undergraduates with need received aid; of those 21% had need fully met. ***Average percent of need met:*** 85% (excluding resources awarded to replace EFC). ***Average financial aid package:*** $38,819 (excluding resources awarded to replace EFC). 38% of all full-time undergraduates had no need and received non-need-based gift aid.

GIFT AID (NEED-BASED) ***Total amount:*** $31,551,245 (7% federal, 4% state, 87% institutional, 2% external sources). ***Receiving aid:*** Freshmen: 66% (355); all full-time undergraduates: 60% (1,161). ***Average award:*** Freshmen: $27,507; Undergraduates: $27,705. ***Scholarships, grants, and awards:*** Federal Pell, FSEOG, state, college/university gift aid from institutional funds.

GIFT AID (NON-NEED-BASED) ***Total amount:*** $15,473,169 (5% state, 94% institutional, 1% external sources). ***Average award:*** Freshmen: $17,966. Undergraduates: $18,120. ***Tuition waivers:*** Full or partial for employees or children of employees. ***ROTC:*** Army, Naval cooperative, Air Force cooperative.

LOANS ***Student loans:*** $13,280,121 (62% need-based, 38% non-need-based). 58% of past graduating class borrowed through all loan programs. *Average indebtedness per student:* $33,661. ***Average need-based loan:*** Freshmen: $5508. Undergraduates: $6473. ***Parent loans:*** $8,089,848 (40% need-based, 60% non-need-based). ***Programs:*** Federal Direct (Subsidized and Unsubsidized Stafford, PLUS), college/university.

WORK-STUDY ***Federal work-study:*** Total amount: $1,896,400; jobs available. ***State or other work-study/employment:*** Total amount: $14,000 (100% non-need-based).

ATHLETIC AWARDS Total amount: $2,855,401 (32% need-based, 68% non-need-based).

APPLYING FOR FINANCIAL AID ***Required financial aid form:*** FAFSA. ***Financial aid deadline (priority):*** 2/1.

CONTACT Mr. Rob Reddy, Dean of Student Financial Services, Northeastern University, 360 Huntington Avenue, Boston, MA 02115, 617-373-3190. *Fax:* 617-373-8735. *E-mail:* sfs@northeastern.edu.
Website: http://www.northeastern.edu/.

NORTHERN ARIZONA UNIVERSITY
Flagstaff, AZ

Tuition & fees (area res): $11,896 | **Average undergraduate aid package: $13,228**

ABOUT THE INSTITUTION State-supported, coed. ***Awards:*** certificates, bachelor's, master's, and doctoral degrees. 85 undergraduate majors. ***Total enrollment:*** 30,736. Undergraduates: 26,513. Freshmen: 5,455. Federal methodology is used as a basis for awarding need-based institutional aid.

UNDERGRADUATE EXPENSES for 2020–2021 ***Application fee:*** $25. ***Tuition, area resident:*** full-time $10,650; part-time $761 per credit hour. ***Tuition, state resident:*** full-time $10,650; part-time $761 per credit hour. ***Tuition, nonresident:*** full-time $25,270; part-time $1053 per credit hour. ***Required fees:*** full-time $1246; $434 per term. Full-time tuition and fees vary according to course load, location, and reciprocity agreements. Part-time tuition and fees vary according to course load, location, and reciprocity agreements. ***College room and board:*** $10,780; ***Room only:*** $5830. Room and board charges vary according to board plan and housing facility. ***Payment plan:*** Guaranteed tuition.

FRESHMAN FINANCIAL AID (Fall 2018) 4549 applied for aid; of those 77% were deemed to have need. 99% of freshmen with need received aid; of those 18% had need fully met. ***Average percent of need met:*** 71% (excluding resources awarded to replace EFC). ***Average financial aid package:*** $15,061 (excluding resources awarded to replace EFC). 26% of all full-time freshmen had no need and received non-need-based gift aid.

UNDERGRADUATE FINANCIAL AID (Fall 2018) 16,623 applied for aid; of those 82% were deemed to have need. 98% of undergraduates with need received aid; of those 14% had need fully met. ***Average percent of need met:*** 64% (excluding resources awarded to replace EFC). ***Average financial aid package:*** $13,228 (excluding resources awarded to replace EFC). 21% of all full-time undergraduates had no need and received non-need-based gift aid.

GIFT AID (NEED-BASED) ***Total amount:*** $153,942,613 (32% federal, 3% state, 62% institutional, 3% external sources). ***Receiving aid:*** Freshmen: 48% (2,441); all full-time undergraduates: 43% (9,421). ***Average award:*** Freshmen: $8321; Undergraduates: $7348. ***Scholarships, grants, and awards:*** Federal Pell, FSEOG, state, private, college/university gift aid from institutional funds, Federal Nursing, TEACH Grants, Tribal Grants.

GIFT AID (NON-NEED-BASED) ***Total amount:*** $34,713,542 (2% federal, 95% institutional, 3% external sources). ***Receiving aid:*** Freshmen: 63% (3,174). Undergraduates: 44% (9,681). ***Average award:*** Freshmen: $7030. Undergraduates: $6697. ***Scholarships, grants, and awards by category:*** *Academic interests/achievement:* general academic interests/achievements. *Creative arts/performance:* applied art and design, music, theater/drama. *Special achievements/activities:* leadership. *Special characteristics:* children and siblings of alumni, local/state students, members of minority groups. ***Tuition waivers:*** Full or partial for employees or children of employees. ***ROTC:*** Army, Air Force.

LOANS ***Student loans:*** $94,042,274 (83% need-based, 17% non-need-based). 58% of past graduating class borrowed through all loan programs. *Average indebtedness per student:* $23,560. ***Average need-based loan:*** Freshmen: $3152. Undergraduates: $4046. ***Parent loans:*** $45,226,847 (74% need-based, 26% non-need-based). ***Programs:*** Federal Direct (Subsidized and Unsubsidized Stafford, PLUS), Perkins, Federal Nursing, state, college/university.

WORK-STUDY ***Federal work-study:*** Total amount: $1,497,607; jobs available. ***State or other work-study/employment:*** Total amount: $12,972,163 (53% need-based, 47% non-need-based). Part-time jobs available.

ATHLETIC AWARDS Total amount: $5,442,255 (39% need-based, 61% non-need-based).

APPLYING FOR FINANCIAL AID ***Required financial aid form:*** FAFSA. ***Financial aid deadline (priority):*** 11/15. ***Notification date:*** Continuous beginning 1/1.

CONTACT Office of Scholarships and Financial Aid, Northern Arizona University, PO Box: 4108, Flagstaff, AZ 86011, 855-628-6333 or toll-free 888-628-2968. *E-mail:* Financial.Aid@nau.edu.
Website: http://www.nau.edu/.

NORTHERN ILLINOIS UNIVERSITY
De Kalb, IL

Tuition & fees (area res): $12,261 | **Average undergraduate aid package: $12,587**

ABOUT THE INSTITUTION State-supported, coed. ***Awards:*** bachelor's, master's, and doctoral degrees. 54 undergraduate majors. ***Total enrollment:*** 16,609. Undergraduates: 12,131. Freshmen: 1,897. Federal methodology is used as a basis for awarding need-based institutional aid.

UNDERGRADUATE EXPENSES for 2020–2021 ***Application fee:*** $40. ***Tuition, area resident:*** full-time $9466; part-time $349 per credit hour. ***Tuition, state resident:*** full-time $9466; part-time $349 per credit hour. ***Tuition, nonresident:*** full-time $9466; part-time $349 per credit hour. ***Required fees:*** full-time $2795; $125 per term. Full-time tuition and fees vary according to program. Part-time tuition and fees vary according to program. ***College room and board:*** $10,880. Room and board charges vary according to housing facility. ***Payment plan:*** Guaranteed tuition.

FRESHMAN FINANCIAL AID (Fall 2018) 1730 applied for aid; of those 86% were deemed to have need. 100% of freshmen with need received aid; of those 11% had need fully met. ***Average percent of need met:*** 68% (excluding resources awarded to replace EFC). ***Average financial aid package:*** $14,875 (excluding resources awarded to replace EFC). 14% of all full-time freshmen had no need and received non-need-based gift aid.

UNDERGRADUATE FINANCIAL AID (Fall 2018) 9,690 applied for aid; of those 88% were deemed to have need. 99% of undergraduates with need received aid; of those 8% had need fully met. ***Average percent of need met:*** 61% (excluding resources awarded to replace EFC). ***Average financial aid package:*** $12,587 (excluding resources awarded to replace EFC). 12% of all full-time undergraduates had no need and received non-need-based gift aid.

GIFT AID (NEED-BASED) ***Total amount:*** $65,415,953 (41% federal, 34% state, 23% institutional, 2% external sources). ***Receiving aid:*** Freshmen: 79% (1,479); all full-time undergraduates: 64% (7,463). ***Average award:*** Freshmen: $10,646; Undergraduates: $8611. ***Scholarships, grants, and awards:*** Federal Pell, FSEOG, state, private, college/university gift aid from institutional funds, TEACH Grants.

GIFT AID (NON-NEED-BASED) ***Total amount:*** $8,539,546 (12% federal, 9% state, 72% institutional, 7% external sources). ***Receiving aid:*** Freshmen: 5% (96). Undergraduates: 3% (310). ***Average award:*** Freshmen: $4512. Undergraduates: $3976. ***Scholarships, grants, and awards by category:*** *Academic interests/achievement:* area/ethnic studies, biological sciences, business, communication, computer science, education, engineering/technologies, English, foreign languages, general academic interests/achievements, home economics, humanities, international studies, library science, mathematics, military science, physical sciences, social sciences. *Creative arts/performance:* applied art and design, art/fine arts, creative writing, dance, debating, journalism/publications, music, performing arts, theater/drama. *Special achievements/activities:* cheerleading/drum major, community service, general special achievements/activities, leadership, memberships. *Special characteristics:* adult students, children and siblings of alumni, children of faculty/staff, children with a deceased or disabled parent, ethnic background, first-generation college students, handicapped students, international students, members of minority groups, veterans. ***Tuition waivers:*** Full or partial for children of alumni, employees or children of employees. ***ROTC:*** Army, Air Force cooperative.

LOANS ***Student loans:*** $69,104,320 (78% need-based, 22% non-need-based). 76% of past graduating class borrowed through all loan programs. *Average indebtedness per student:* $33,915. ***Average need-based loan:*** Freshmen: $3273. Undergraduates: $4375. ***Parent loans:*** $14,818,107 (50% need-based, 50% non-need-based). ***Programs:*** Federal Direct (Subsidized and Unsubsidized Stafford, PLUS).

WORK-STUDY ***Federal work-study:*** Total amount: $8,352,687; 3,099 jobs averaging $2695.

ATHLETIC AWARDS Total amount: $6,341,611 (31% need-based, 69% non-need-based).

APPLYING FOR FINANCIAL AID ***Required financial aid form:*** FAFSA. ***Notification date:*** Continuous beginning 3/1.

CONTACT Mrs. Rebecca A. Babel, Director, Financial Aid and Scholarship Office, Northern Illinois University, Swen Parson Hall, Room 245, De Kalb, IL 60115, 815-753-1395 or toll-free 800-892-3050. *Fax:* 815-753-9475. *E-mail:* finaid@niu.edu. *Website:* http://www.niu.edu/.

NORTHERN KENTUCKY UNIVERSITY

Highland Heights, KY

ABOUT THE INSTITUTION State-supported, coed. ***Awards:*** certificates, bachelor's, master's, and doctoral degrees. 65 undergraduate majors. ***Total enrollment:*** 15,678. Undergraduates: 11,882. Freshmen: 1,950.

GIFT AID (NEED-BASED) ***Scholarships, grants, and awards:*** Federal Pell, FSEOG, state, private, college/university gift aid from institutional funds.

GIFT AID (NON-NEED-BASED) ***Scholarships, grants, and awards by category:*** *Academic interests/achievement:* biological sciences, business, communication, computer science, education, engineering/technologies, English, foreign languages, general academic interests/achievements, health fields, home economics, international studies, mathematics, physical sciences, premedicine, social sciences. *Creative arts/performance:* applied art and design, music, theater/drama. *Special achievements/activities:* cheerleading/drum major, community service, general special achievements/activities, leadership. *Special characteristics:* adult students, children and siblings of alumni, children of faculty/staff, children of public servants, children with a deceased or disabled parent, general special characteristics, handicapped students, local/state students, members of minority groups, spouses of deceased or disabled public servants, veterans.

LOANS ***Programs:*** Federal Direct (Subsidized and Unsubsidized Stafford, PLUS), Perkins, Federal Nursing, college/university.

WORK-STUDY ***Federal work-study:*** Total amount: $1,001,911; jobs available. ***State or other work-study/employment:*** Total amount: $2,586,552 (100% non-need-based). Part-time jobs available.

APPLYING FOR FINANCIAL AID ***Required financial aid form:*** FAFSA.

CONTACT Leah Stewart, Director of Student Financial Assistance, Northern Kentucky University, 416 Administrative Center, Highland Heights, KY 41099, 859-572-5144 or toll-free 800-637-9948. *Fax:* 859-572-6997. *E-mail:* ofa@nku.edu. *Website:* http://www.nku.edu/.

NORTHERN MICHIGAN UNIVERSITY

Marquette, MI

Tuition & fees (MI res): $11,525	Average undergraduate aid package: $11,281

ABOUT THE INSTITUTION State-supported, coed. ***Awards:*** certificates, associate, bachelor's, master's, and doctoral degrees. 146 undergraduate majors. ***Total enrollment:*** 7,595. Undergraduates: 7,089. Freshmen: 1,608. Federal methodology is used as a basis for awarding need-based institutional aid.

UNDERGRADUATE EXPENSES for 2019–2020 ***Application fee:*** $35. ***One-time required fee:*** $265. ***Tuition, state resident:*** full-time $10,758; part-time $448 per credit hour. ***Tuition, nonresident:*** full-time $16,380; part-time $683 per credit hour. ***Required fees:*** full-time $767; $121 per term. Full-time tuition and fees vary according to student level. Part-time tuition and fees vary according to student level. ***College room and board:*** $10,774; ***Room only:*** $5874. Room and board charges vary according to board plan, housing facility, and student level.

FRESHMAN FINANCIAL AID (Fall 2018) 1432 applied for aid; of those 79% were deemed to have need. 98% of freshmen with need received aid; of those 13% had need fully met. ***Average percent of need met:*** 63% (excluding resources awarded to replace EFC). ***Average financial aid package:*** $12,037 (excluding resources awarded to replace EFC). 13% of all full-time freshmen had no need and received non-need-based gift aid.

UNDERGRADUATE FINANCIAL AID (Fall 2018) 5,020 applied for aid; of those 83% were deemed to have need. 97% of undergraduates with need received aid; of those 12% had need fully met. ***Average percent of need met:*** 60% (excluding resources awarded to replace EFC). ***Average financial aid package:*** $11,281 (excluding resources awarded to replace EFC). 9% of all full-time undergraduates had no need and received non-need-based gift aid.

GIFT AID (NEED-BASED) ***Total amount:*** $14,824,914 (74% federal, 3% state, 21% institutional, 2% external sources). ***Receiving aid:*** Freshmen: 48% (771); all full-time undergraduates: 47% (2,875). ***Average award:*** Freshmen: $4992; Undergraduates: $4895. ***Scholarships, grants, and awards:*** Federal Pell, FSEOG, state, private, college/university gift aid from institutional funds.

GIFT AID (NON-NEED-BASED) ***Total amount:*** $17,412,792 (1% federal, 28% state, 63% institutional, 8% external sources). ***Receiving aid:*** Freshmen: 52% (825). Undergraduates: 44% (2,690). ***Average award:*** Freshmen: $4140. Undergraduates: $3571. ***Scholarships, grants, and awards by category:*** *Academic interests/achievement:* biological sciences, business, communication, computer science, education, engineering/technologies, English, foreign languages, general academic interests/achievements, home economics, humanities, international studies, mathematics, military science, physical sciences, premedicine, social sciences. *Creative arts/performance:* art/fine arts, journalism/publications, music, theater/drama. *Special achievements/activities:* cheerleading/drum major, leadership, memberships. *Special characteristics:* children and siblings of alumni, children of faculty/staff, children of union members/company employees, international students, local/state students, members of minority groups, out-of-state students. ***Tuition waivers:*** Full or partial for employees or children of employees, senior citizens. ***ROTC:*** Army.

LOANS ***Student loans:*** $35,220,661 (36% need-based, 64% non-need-based). 75% of past graduating class borrowed through all loan programs. *Average indebtedness per student:* $30,125. ***Average need-based loan:*** Freshmen: $3268. Undergraduates: $4002. ***Parent loans:*** $6,219,176 (100% non-need-based). ***Programs:*** Federal Direct (Subsidized and Unsubsidized Stafford, PLUS), Perkins, state, alternative loans.

WORK-STUDY ***Federal work-study:*** Total amount: $1,015,623; 516 jobs averaging $1837.

ATHLETIC AWARDS Total amount: $3,864,717 (100% non-need-based).
APPLYING FOR FINANCIAL AID ***Required financial aid form:*** FAFSA. ***Financial aid deadline (priority):*** 3/1. ***Notification date:*** Continuous beginning 12/15.
CONTACT Michael Rotundo, Director of Financial Aid, Northern Michigan University, 1401 Presque Isle Avenue, Marquette, MI 49855, 906-227-2327 or toll-free 800-682-9797. *Fax:* 906-227-2321. *E-mail:* fao@nmu.edu.
Website: http://www.nmu.edu/.

NORTHERN NEW MEXICO COLLEGE

Española, NM

CONTACT Financial Aid Office, Northern New Mexico College, 921 Paseo de Oñate, Española, NM 87532, 505-747-2100.
Website: http://www.nnmc.edu/.

NORTHERN STATE UNIVERSITY

Aberdeen, SD

Tuition & fees (SD res): $8750	Average undergraduate aid package: $11,007

ABOUT THE INSTITUTION State-supported, coed. ***Awards:*** certificates, associate, bachelor's, and master's degrees. 43 undergraduate majors. ***Total enrollment:*** 3,427. Undergraduates: 3,008. Freshmen: 342. Federal methodology is used as a basis for awarding need-based institutional aid.
UNDERGRADUATE EXPENSES for 2019–2020 ***Application fee:*** $20. ***Tuition, state resident:*** full-time $7540; part-time $292 per credit hour. ***Tuition, nonresident:*** full-time $10,611; part-time $394 per credit hour. ***Required fees:*** full-time $1210; $40.37 per credit hour. Full-time tuition and fees vary according to course load, program, and reciprocity agreements. Part-time tuition and fees vary according to course load, program, and reciprocity agreements. ***College room and board:*** $8925; ***Room only:*** $4701. Room and board charges vary according to board plan and housing facility.
FRESHMAN FINANCIAL AID (Fall 2018) 301 applied for aid; of those 75% were deemed to have need. 100% of freshmen with need received aid; of those 34% had need fully met. ***Average percent of need met:*** 77% (excluding resources awarded to replace EFC). ***Average financial aid package:*** $11,179 (excluding resources awarded to replace EFC). 14% of all full-time freshmen had no need and received non-need-based gift aid.
UNDERGRADUATE FINANCIAL AID (Fall 2018) 1,014 applied for aid; of those 79% were deemed to have need. 99% of undergraduates with need received aid; of those 25% had need fully met. ***Average percent of need met:*** 72% (excluding resources awarded to replace EFC). ***Average financial aid package:*** $11,007 (excluding resources awarded to replace EFC). 10% of all full-time undergraduates had no need and received non-need-based gift aid.
GIFT AID (NEED-BASED) ***Total amount:*** $3,735,777 (69% federal, 3% state, 15% institutional, 13% external sources). ***Receiving aid:*** Freshmen: 62% (208); all full-time undergraduates: 54% (679). ***Average award:*** Freshmen: $5005; Undergraduates: $5113. ***Scholarships, grants, and awards:*** Federal Pell, FSEOG, state, private, college/university gift aid from institutional funds.
GIFT AID (NON-NEED-BASED) ***Total amount:*** $773,874 (7% federal, 10% state, 61% institutional, 22% external sources). ***Receiving aid:*** Freshmen: 4% (13). Undergraduates: 3% (36). ***Average award:*** Freshmen: $1465. Undergraduates: $1722. ***Scholarships, grants, and awards by category:*** *Academic interests/achievement:* agriculture, biological sciences, business, communication, computer science, education, English, foreign languages, general academic interests/achievements, humanities, international studies, mathematics, physical sciences, social sciences. *Creative arts/performance:* art/fine arts, music, theater/drama. *Special achievements/activities:* leadership. *Special characteristics:* adult students, ethnic background, handicapped students, international students, local/state students, members of minority groups. ***Tuition waivers:*** Full or partial for employees or children of employees, senior citizens.
LOANS ***Student loans:*** $6,226,616 (65% need-based, 35% non-need-based). 76% of past graduating class borrowed through all loan programs. *Average indebtedness per student:* $29,635. ***Average need-based loan:*** Freshmen: $4507. Undergraduates: $4794. ***Parent loans:*** $558,443 (43% need-based, 57% non-need-based). ***Programs:*** Federal Direct (Subsidized and Unsubsidized Stafford, PLUS), college/university.
WORK-STUDY ***Federal work-study:*** Total amount: $951,721; jobs available. ***State or other work-study/employment:*** Total amount: $372,593 (100% non-need-based). Part-time jobs available.
ATHLETIC AWARDS Total amount: $1,583,407 (38% need-based, 62% non-need-based).
APPLYING FOR FINANCIAL AID ***Required financial aid form:*** FAFSA. ***Financial aid deadline (priority):*** 3/1. ***Notification date:*** 4/1. Students must reply within 2 weeks of notification.
CONTACT Sharon Kienow, Director of Financial Aid, Northern State University, 1200 South Jay Street, Aberdeen, SD 57401-7198, 605-626-2640 or toll-free 800-678-5330. *Fax:* 605-626-2587. *E-mail:* finaid@northern.edu.
Website: http://www.northern.edu/.

NORTHERN VERMONT UNIVERSITY–JOHNSON

Johnson, VT

CONTACT Ms. Kimberly Goodell, Financial Aid Officer, Northern Vermont University–Johnson, 337 College Hill, Johnson, VT 05656-9405, 802-635-2356 or toll-free 800-635-2356. *Fax:* 802-635-1463. *E-mail:* goodellk@badger.jsc.vsc.edu.
Website: http://www.northernvermont.edu/.

NORTHERN VERMONT UNIVERSITY–LYNDON

Lyndonville, VT

CONTACT Student Services Consultant, Northern Vermont University–Lyndon, 1001 College Road, Lyndonville, VT 05851, 802-626-6396 or toll-free 800-225-1998. *Fax:* 802-626-9770. *E-mail:* financialaid@lyndonstate.edu.
Website: http://www.northernvermont.edu/.

NORTH GREENVILLE UNIVERSITY

Tigerville, SC

Tuition & fees: $22,050	Average undergraduate aid package: $16,987

ABOUT THE INSTITUTION Independent Southern Baptist, coed. ***Awards:*** bachelor's, master's, and doctoral degrees. 38 undergraduate majors. ***Total enrollment:*** 2,428. Undergraduates: 2,167. Freshmen: 414. Federal methodology is used as a basis for awarding need-based institutional aid.
UNDERGRADUATE EXPENSES for 2020–2021 ***Application fee:*** $35. ***Comprehensive fee:*** $32,500 includes full-time tuition ($22,050) and room and board ($10,450). Full-time tuition and fees vary according to course load. Room and board charges vary according to housing facility. ***Part-time tuition:*** $545 per credit hour.
FRESHMAN FINANCIAL AID (Fall 2019, est.) ***Average financial aid package:*** $19,065 (excluding resources awarded to replace EFC).
UNDERGRADUATE FINANCIAL AID (Fall 2019, est.) ***Average financial aid package:*** $16,987 (excluding resources awarded to replace EFC).
GIFT AID (NEED-BASED) ***Total amount:*** $24,103,435 (14% federal, 30% state, 53% institutional, 3% external sources). ***Receiving aid:*** Freshmen: 96% (295); all full-time undergraduates: 95% (1,667). ***Average award:*** Freshmen: $17,910; Undergraduates: $15,845. ***Scholarships, grants, and awards:*** Federal Pell, FSEOG, state, private, college/university gift aid from institutional funds.
GIFT AID (NON-NEED-BASED) ***Scholarships, grants, and awards by category:*** *Academic interests/achievement:* biological sciences, communication, education, general academic interests/achievements, military science, religion/biblical studies. *Creative arts/performance:* journalism/publications, music, theater/drama.

Special characteristics: children of faculty/staff. ***Tuition waivers:*** Full or partial for employees or children of employees. ***ROTC:*** Army cooperative.

LOANS *Student loans:* $15,050,288 (100% need-based). ***Average need-based loan:*** Freshmen: $5583. Undergraduates: $6604. ***Parent loans:*** $2,783,156 (100% need-based). ***Programs:*** Federal Direct (Subsidized and Unsubsidized Stafford, PLUS), state.

WORK-STUDY *Federal work-study:* Total amount: $152,270; jobs available. ***State or other work-study/employment:*** Total amount: $193,497 (100% need-based). Part-time jobs available.

ATHLETIC AWARDS Total amount: $2,955,154 (100% need-based).

APPLYING FOR FINANCIAL AID *Required financial aid form:* FAFSA. ***Financial aid deadline:*** 6/30 (priority: 6/1). ***Notification date:*** Students must reply within 2 weeks of notification.

CONTACT Mike Jordan, Director of Financial Aid, North Greenville University, PO Box 1892, Tigerville, SC 29688, 864-977-7058 or toll-free 800-468-6642 Ext.7001. *Fax:* 864-977-7177. *E-mail:* mjordan@ngu.edu.
Website: http://www.ngu.edu/.

NORTHLAND COLLEGE

Ashland, WI

ABOUT THE INSTITUTION Independent United Church of Christ, coed. ***Awards:*** bachelor's degrees. 31 undergraduate majors.

GIFT AID (NEED-BASED) *Scholarships, grants, and awards:* Federal Pell, FSEOG, state, private, college/university gift aid from institutional funds.

LOANS *Programs:* Federal Direct (Subsidized and Unsubsidized Stafford, PLUS).

WORK-STUDY *Federal work-study:* Total amount: $448,104; 285 jobs averaging $1572. ***State or other work-study/employment:*** Total amount: $349,956 (100% non-need-based). 199 part-time jobs averaging $1733.

APPLYING FOR FINANCIAL AID *Required financial aid form:* FAFSA.

CONTACT Kelly Dunn, Director of Financial Aid, Northland College, 1411 Ellis Avenue, Ashland, WI 54806, 715-682-1255 or toll-free 800-753-1840 (in-state), 800-753-1040 (out-of-state). *Fax:* 715-682-1368. *E-mail:* finaid@northland.edu.
Website: http://www.northland.edu/.

NORTH PARK UNIVERSITY

Chicago, IL

CONTACT Dr. Lucy Shaker, Director of Financial Aid , North Park University, 3225 West Foster Avenue, Chicago, IL 60625-4895, 773-244-5526 or toll-free 800-888-NPC8. *Fax:* 773-244-4953.
Website: http://www.northpark.edu/.

NORTHPOINT BIBLE COLLEGE

Haverhill, MA

CONTACT Financial Aid Office, Northpoint Bible College, 320 South Main Street, Haverhill, MA 01835, 978-478-3400 or toll-free 800-356-4014.
Website: http://northpoint.edu/.

NORTHWEST CHRISTIAN UNIVERSITY

Eugene, OR

Tuition & fees: $32,320	Average undergraduate aid package: $22,913

ABOUT THE INSTITUTION Independent Christian, coed. ***Awards:*** certificates, associate, bachelor's, and master's degrees. 41 undergraduate majors. ***Total enrollment:*** 800. Undergraduates: 593. Freshmen: 100. Federal methodology is used as a basis for awarding need-based institutional aid.

UNDERGRADUATE EXPENSES for 2020–2021 *Comprehensive fee:* $42,370 includes full-time tuition ($32,100), mandatory fees ($220), and room and board ($10,050). Room and board charges vary according to housing facility. ***Part-time tuition:*** $1070 per credit hour. ***Part-time fees:*** $220 per year.

FRESHMAN FINANCIAL AID (Fall 2019, est.) 111 applied for aid; of those 89% were deemed to have need. 100% of freshmen with need received aid; of those 17% had need fully met. ***Average percent of need met:*** 82% (excluding resources awarded to replace EFC). ***Average financial aid package:*** $27,003 (excluding resources awarded to replace EFC). 12% of all full-time freshmen had no need and received non-need-based gift aid.

UNDERGRADUATE FINANCIAL AID (Fall 2019, est.) 392 applied for aid; of those 91% were deemed to have need. 99% of undergraduates with need received aid; of those 18% had need fully met. ***Average percent of need met:*** 75% (excluding resources awarded to replace EFC). ***Average financial aid package:*** $22,913 (excluding resources awarded to replace EFC). 17% of all full-time undergraduates had no need and received non-need-based gift aid.

GIFT AID (NEED-BASED) *Total amount:* $6,136,565 (19% federal, 5% state, 67% institutional, 9% external sources). ***Receiving aid:*** Freshmen: 88% (99); all full-time undergraduates: 75% (337). ***Average award:*** Freshmen: $23,457; Undergraduates: $19,408. ***Scholarships, grants, and awards:*** Federal Pell, FSEOG, state, private, college/university gift aid from institutional funds.

GIFT AID (NON-NEED-BASED) *Total amount:* $1,286,031 (1% federal, 1% state, 86% institutional, 12% external sources). ***Receiving aid:*** Freshmen: 11% (12). Undergraduates: 10% (45). ***Average award:*** Freshmen: $13,863. Undergraduates: $10,728. ***Scholarships, grants, and awards by category:*** *Academic interests/achievement:* 321 awards ($3,145,000 total): general academic interests/achievements, religion/biblical studies. *Creative arts/performance:* 40 awards ($123,850 total): music. *Special achievements/activities:* 366 awards ($320,540 total): community service, leadership, religious involvement. *Special characteristics:* 160 awards ($478,915 total): children and siblings of alumni, children of faculty/staff, first-generation college students, international students, relatives of clergy, religious affiliation, siblings of current students. ***Tuition waivers:*** Full or partial for employees or children of employees. ***ROTC:*** Army cooperative.

LOANS *Student loans:* $3,162,861 (77% need-based, 23% non-need-based). 58% of past graduating class borrowed through all loan programs. *Average indebtedness per student:* $25,058. ***Average need-based loan:*** Freshmen: $3073. Undergraduates: $4647. ***Parent loans:*** $679,435 (46% need-based, 54% non-need-based). ***Programs:*** Federal Direct (Subsidized and Unsubsidized Stafford, PLUS).

WORK-STUDY *Federal work-study:* Total amount: $272,917; 105 jobs averaging $3250. ***State or other work-study/employment:*** Total amount: $9750 (67% need-based, 33% non-need-based). 3 part-time jobs averaging $3250.

ATHLETIC AWARDS Total amount: $1,088,186 (62% need-based, 38% non-need-based).

APPLYING FOR FINANCIAL AID *Required financial aid form:* FAFSA. ***Financial aid deadline (priority):*** 1/1. ***Notification date:*** Continuous beginning 1/15. Students must reply within 2 weeks of notification.

CONTACT Mr. Casey Craigie, Financial Aid Counselor, Northwest Christian University, 828 East 11th Avenue, Eugene, OR 97401-3745, 541-684-7201 or toll-free 877-463-6622. *Fax:* 541-684-7300. *E-mail:* ccraigie@nwcu.edu.
Website: http://www.nwcu.edu/.

NORTHWEST COLLEGE OF ART & DESIGN

Tacoma, WA

CONTACT Julie Perigard, Financial Aid Officer, Northwest College of Art & Design, 1126 Pacific Avenue, Suite 101, Tacoma, WA 98402, 253-272-1126 or toll-free 800-769-ARTS. *Fax:* 360-572-9058. *E-mail:* jperigard@ncad.edu.
Website: http://www.ncad.edu/.

NORTHWESTERN COLLEGE

Orange City, IA

CONTACT Mr. Eric Anderson, Director of Financial Aid, Northwestern College, 101 Seventh Street, SW, Orange City, IA 51041-1996, 712-707-7131 or toll-free 800-747-4757. *Fax:* 712-707-7164. *E-mail:* finaid@nwciowa.edu.
Website: http://www.nwciowa.edu/.

NORTHWESTERN OKLAHOMA STATE UNIVERSITY

Alva, OK

ABOUT THE INSTITUTION State-supported, coed. ***Awards:*** certificates, bachelor's, master's, and doctoral degrees. 39 undergraduate majors. ***Total enrollment:*** 1,992. Undergraduates: 1,773. Freshmen: 373.
GIFT AID (NEED-BASED) ***Scholarships, grants, and awards:*** Federal Pell, FSEOG, state, private, college/university gift aid from institutional funds.
GIFT AID (NON-NEED-BASED) ***Scholarships, grants, and awards by category:*** *Academic interests/achievement:* agriculture, biological sciences, business, communication, computer science, education, English, foreign languages, general academic interests/achievements, home economics, library science, mathematics, physical sciences, premedicine, social sciences. *Creative arts/performance:* applied art and design, cinema/film/broadcasting, debating, general creative arts/performance, journalism/publications, music, theater/drama. *Special achievements/activities:* cheerleading/drum major, general special achievements/activities, leadership, memberships, rodeo. *Special characteristics:* children of faculty/staff.
LOANS ***Programs:*** Federal Direct (Subsidized and Unsubsidized Stafford, PLUS).
WORK-STUDY ***Federal work-study:*** Total amount: $210,479; jobs available. ***State or other work-study/employment:*** Total amount: $200,759 (100% non-need-based). Part-time jobs available.
APPLYING FOR FINANCIAL AID ***Required financial aid forms:*** FAFSA, institution's own form.
CONTACT Tara Hannaford, Director of Financial Aid, Northwestern Oklahoma State University, 709 Oklahoma Boulevard, Alva, OK 73717-2799, 580-327-8540. *Fax:* 580-327-8177. *E-mail:* tlhannaford@nwosu.edu.
Website: http://www.nwosu.edu/.

NORTHWESTERN STATE UNIVERSITY OF LOUISIANA

Natchitoches, LA

Tuition & fees (LA res): $8768	Average undergraduate aid package: $14,859

ABOUT THE INSTITUTION State-supported, coed. ***Awards:*** certificates, associate, bachelor's, master's, and doctoral degrees. 35 undergraduate majors. ***Total enrollment:*** 10,900. Undergraduates: 9,833. Freshmen: 1,515. Federal methodology is used as a basis for awarding need-based institutional aid.
UNDERGRADUATE EXPENSES for 2019–2020 ***Application fee:*** $20. ***Tuition, state resident:*** full-time $5180. ***Tuition, nonresident:*** full-time $15,968. ***Required fees:*** full-time $3588. Full-time tuition and fees vary according to course load and location. Part-time tuition and fees vary according to course load and location. ***College room and board:*** $9244; ***Room only:*** $5404. Room and board charges vary according to board plan and housing facility.
FRESHMAN FINANCIAL AID (Fall 2018) 1363 applied for aid; of those 87% were deemed to have need. 100% of freshmen with need received aid; of those 17% had need fully met. ***Average percent of need met:*** 71% (excluding resources awarded to replace EFC). ***Average financial aid package:*** $15,407 (excluding resources awarded to replace EFC). 10% of all full-time freshmen had no need and received non-need-based gift aid.
UNDERGRADUATE FINANCIAL AID (Fall 2018) 5,833 applied for aid; of those 89% were deemed to have need. 100% of undergraduates with need received aid; of those 16% had need fully met. ***Average percent of need met:*** 62% (excluding resources awarded to replace EFC). ***Average financial aid package:*** $14,859 (excluding resources awarded to replace EFC). 6% of all full-time undergraduates had no need and received non-need-based gift aid.
GIFT AID (NEED-BASED) ***Receiving aid:*** Freshmen: 80% (1,129); all full-time undergraduates: 75% (4,629). ***Average award:*** Freshmen: $8848; Undergraduates: $7944. ***Scholarships, grants, and awards:*** Federal Pell, FSEOG, private, college/university gift aid from institutional funds, United Negro College Fund.
GIFT AID (NON-NEED-BASED) ***Receiving aid:*** Freshmen: 12% (171). Undergraduates: 8% (465). ***Average award:*** Freshmen: $4729. Undergraduates: $4420. ***Scholarships, grants, and awards by category:*** *Academic interests/achievement:* biological sciences, business, communication, education, engineering/technologies, English, general academic interests/achievements, home economics, humanities, mathematics, military science, social sciences. *Creative arts/performance:* applied art and design, art/fine arts, cinema/film/broadcasting, creative writing, dance, general creative arts/performance, music, performing arts, theater/drama. *Special achievements/activities:* cheerleading/drum major, general special achievements/activities, leadership, memberships. *Special characteristics:* adult students, children and siblings of alumni, children of faculty/staff, children of public servants, first-generation college students, general special characteristics, international students, local/state students, married students, out-of-state students, public servants, veterans, veterans' children. ***Tuition waivers:*** Full or partial for employees or children of employees, senior citizens. ***ROTC:*** Army.
LOANS ***Student loans:*** 57% of past graduating class borrowed through all loan programs. *Average indebtedness per student:* $29,793. ***Average need-based loan:*** Freshmen: $5670. Undergraduates: $7240. ***Programs:*** Federal Direct (Subsidized and Unsubsidized Stafford, PLUS), Perkins.
WORK-STUDY Federal work-study jobs available. ***State or other work-study/employment:*** Part-time jobs available.
APPLYING FOR FINANCIAL AID ***Required financial aid forms:*** FAFSA, institution's own form. ***Notification date:*** Continuous. Students must reply within 4 weeks of notification.
CONTACT Ms. Lauren Jackson, Director of Financial Aid, Northwestern State University of Louisiana, 212 Student Services Center, Natchitoches, LA 71497, 318-357-5961 or toll-free 800-327-1903. *Fax:* 318-357-5488. *E-mail:* nsufinaid@nsula.edu.
Website: http://www.nsula.edu/.

NORTHWESTERN UNIVERSITY

Evanston, IL

Tuition & fees: $56,691	Average undergraduate aid package: $54,473

ABOUT THE INSTITUTION Independent, coed. ***Awards:*** certificates, bachelor's, master's, and doctoral degrees. 112 undergraduate majors. ***Total enrollment:*** 21,946. Undergraduates: 8,327. Freshmen: 2,006. Both federal and institutional methodology are used as a basis for awarding need-based institutional aid.
UNDERGRADUATE EXPENSES for 2019–2020 ***Application fee:*** $75. ***Comprehensive fee:*** $73,710 includes full-time tuition ($56,232), mandatory fees ($459), and room and board ($17,019). Room and board charges vary according to board plan and housing facility.
FRESHMAN FINANCIAL AID (Fall 2019, est.) 1189 applied for aid; of those 81% were deemed to have need. 100% of freshmen with need received aid; of those 100% had need fully met. ***Average percent of need met:*** 100% (excluding resources awarded to replace EFC). ***Average financial aid package:*** $56,115 (excluding resources awarded to replace EFC). 5% of all full-time freshmen had no need and received non-need-based gift aid.
UNDERGRADUATE FINANCIAL AID (Fall 2019, est.) 4,310 applied for aid; of those 88% were deemed to have need. 100% of undergraduates with need received aid; of those 100% had need fully met. ***Average percent of need met:*** 100% (excluding resources awarded to replace EFC). ***Average financial aid package:*** $54,473 (excluding resources awarded to replace EFC). 5% of all full-time undergraduates had no need and received non-need-based gift aid.
GIFT AID (NEED-BASED) ***Total amount:*** $208,392,730 (4% federal, 2% state, 91% institutional, 3% external sources). ***Receiving aid:*** Freshmen: 47% (949); all full-time undergraduates: 45% (3,713). ***Average award:*** Freshmen: $54,303; Undergraduates: $52,629. ***Scholarships, grants, and awards:*** Federal Pell, FSEOG, state, college/university gift aid from institutional funds.
GIFT AID (NON-NEED-BASED) ***Total amount:*** $3,170,477 (72% institutional, 28% external sources). ***Average award:*** Freshmen: $5401. Undergraduates: $6014. ***Scholarships, grants, and awards by category:*** *Creative arts/performance:*

music. *Special characteristics:* international students. ***ROTC:*** Army cooperative, Naval, Air Force cooperative.

LOANS ***Student loans:*** $18,314,549 (31% need-based, 69% non-need-based). 34% of past graduating class borrowed through all loan programs. *Average indebtedness per student:* $36,350. ***Average need-based loan:*** Freshmen: $2883. Undergraduates: $3669. ***Parent loans:*** $17,211,904 (100% non-need-based). ***Programs:*** Federal Direct (Subsidized and Unsubsidized Stafford, PLUS), college/university.

WORK-STUDY ***Federal work-study:*** Total amount: $3,400,000; jobs available. ***State or other work-study/employment:*** Total amount: $2,716,496 (100% need-based). Part-time jobs available.

ATHLETIC AWARDS Total amount: $19,285,645 (100% non-need-based).

APPLYING FOR FINANCIAL AID ***Required financial aid forms:*** FAFSA, CSS Financial Aid PROFILE, noncustodial (divorced/separated) parent's statement, parent and student income tax forms. ***Financial aid deadline:*** 3/1 (priority: 3/1). ***Notification date:*** 4/15. Students must reply by 5/1 or within 2 weeks of notification.

CONTACT Financial Aid Office, Northwestern University, 633 Clark Street, Evanston, IL 60208, 847-491-3741.
Website: http://www.northwestern.edu/.

NORTHWEST MISSOURI STATE UNIVERSITY

Maryville, MO

Tuition & fees (MO res): $10,297	Average undergraduate aid package: $10,112

ABOUT THE INSTITUTION State-supported, coed. ***Awards:*** certificates, bachelor's, and master's degrees. 68 undergraduate majors. ***Total enrollment:*** 7,104. Undergraduates: 5,710. Freshmen: 1,335. Federal methodology is used as a basis for awarding need-based institutional aid.

UNDERGRADUATE EXPENSES for 2019–2020 ***Application fee:*** $25. ***Tuition, state resident:*** full-time $6195; part-time $207 per credit hour. ***Tuition, nonresident:*** full-time $13,422; part-time $447 per credit hour. ***Required fees:*** full-time $4103; $136.75 per credit hour. Full-time tuition and fees vary according to course load, location, program, and reciprocity agreements. Part-time tuition and fees vary according to course load and location. ***College room and board:*** $10,106; ***Room only:*** $6356. Room and board charges vary according to board plan and housing facility.

FRESHMAN FINANCIAL AID (Fall 2018) 1230 applied for aid; of those 78% were deemed to have need. 100% of freshmen with need received aid; of those 58% had need fully met. ***Average percent of need met:*** 70% (excluding resources awarded to replace EFC). ***Average financial aid package:*** $11,105 (excluding resources awarded to replace EFC). 13% of all full-time freshmen had no need and received non-need-based gift aid.

UNDERGRADUATE FINANCIAL AID (Fall 2018) 4,150 applied for aid; of those 81% were deemed to have need. 99% of undergraduates with need received aid; of those 41% had need fully met. ***Average percent of need met:*** 60% (excluding resources awarded to replace EFC). ***Average financial aid package:*** $10,112 (excluding resources awarded to replace EFC). 10% of all full-time undergraduates had no need and received non-need-based gift aid.

GIFT AID (NEED-BASED) ***Receiving aid:*** Freshmen: 66% (876); all full-time undergraduates: 57% (2,815). ***Average award:*** Freshmen: $7193; Undergraduates: $6402. ***Scholarships, grants, and awards:*** Federal Pell, FSEOG, state, private, college/university gift aid from institutional funds.

GIFT AID (NON-NEED-BASED) ***Receiving aid:*** Freshmen: 34% (444). Undergraduates: 19% (955). ***Average award:*** Freshmen: $3574. Undergraduates: $3043. ***Scholarships, grants, and awards by category:*** *Academic interests/achievement:* agriculture, biological sciences, business, communication, computer science, education, English, foreign languages, general academic interests/achievements, health fields, home economics, humanities, mathematics, physical sciences, social sciences. *Creative arts/performance:* applied art and design, cinema/film/broadcasting, dance, debating, journalism/publications, music, theater/drama. *Special achievements/activities:* cheerleading/drum major, general special achievements/activities, leadership, memberships. *Special characteristics:* children and siblings of alumni, children of faculty/staff, general special characteristics, members of minority groups, out-of-state students, previous college experience. ***Tuition waivers:*** Full or partial for employees or children of employees, senior citizens.

LOANS ***Student loans:*** 69% of past graduating class borrowed through all loan programs. *Average indebtedness per student:* $35,920. ***Average need-based loan:*** Freshmen: $3055. Undergraduates: $3803. ***Programs:*** Federal Direct (Subsidized and Unsubsidized Stafford, PLUS), Perkins.

WORK-STUDY ***Federal work-study:*** 382 jobs averaging $1277. ***State or other work-study/employment:*** 1,101 part-time jobs averaging $1800.

APPLYING FOR FINANCIAL AID ***Required financial aid form:*** FAFSA. ***Financial aid deadline:*** Continuous. ***Notification date:*** Continuous.

CONTACT Mr. Charles Mayfield, Director of Financial Assistance, Northwest Missouri State University, 800 University Drive, Maryville, MO 64468-6001, 660-562-1138 or toll-free 800-633-1175.
Website: http://www.nwmissouri.edu/.

NORTHWEST NAZARENE UNIVERSITY

Nampa, ID

Tuition & fees: $32,630	Average undergraduate aid package: $28,871

ABOUT THE INSTITUTION Independent Church of the Nazarene, coed. ***Awards:*** certificates, associate, bachelor's, master's, and doctoral degrees. 72 undergraduate majors. ***Total enrollment:*** 1,854. Undergraduates: 1,225. Freshmen: 279. Federal methodology is used as a basis for awarding need-based institutional aid.

UNDERGRADUATE EXPENSES for 2020–2021 ***Comprehensive fee:*** $41,430 includes full-time tuition ($32,130), mandatory fees ($500), and room and board ($8800). ***College room only:*** $4200. ***Part-time tuition:*** $1275 per credit hour.

FRESHMAN FINANCIAL AID (Fall 2018) 254 applied for aid; of those 85% were deemed to have need. 100% of freshmen with need received aid; of those 22% had need fully met. ***Average percent of need met:*** 72% (excluding resources awarded to replace EFC). ***Average financial aid package:*** $27,351 (excluding resources awarded to replace EFC). 12% of all full-time freshmen had no need and received non-need-based gift aid.

UNDERGRADUATE FINANCIAL AID (Fall 2018) 881 applied for aid; of those 89% were deemed to have need. 100% of undergraduates with need received aid; of those 21% had need fully met. ***Average percent of need met:*** 72% (excluding resources awarded to replace EFC). ***Average financial aid package:*** $28,871 (excluding resources awarded to replace EFC). 13% of all full-time undergraduates had no need and received non-need-based gift aid.

GIFT AID (NEED-BASED) ***Receiving aid:*** Freshmen: 80% (215); all full-time undergraduates: 77% (784). ***Average award:*** Freshmen: $17,872; Undergraduates: $17,607. ***Scholarships, grants, and awards:*** Federal Pell, FSEOG, state, private, college/university gift aid from institutional funds.

GIFT AID (NON-NEED-BASED) ***Receiving aid:*** Freshmen: 78% (211). Undergraduates: 76% (777). ***Average award:*** Freshmen: $13,994. Undergraduates: $13,474. ***Scholarships, grants, and awards by category:*** *Academic interests/achievement:* biological sciences, business, communication, computer science, education, engineering/technologies, English, general academic interests/achievements, health fields, mathematics, military science, physical sciences, premedicine, religion/biblical studies, social sciences. *Creative arts/performance:* debating, music, theater/drama. *Special achievements/activities:* leadership, religious involvement. *Special characteristics:* children and siblings of alumni, children of faculty/staff, international students, relatives of clergy, religious affiliation. ***ROTC:*** Army.

LOANS ***Student loans:*** 70% of past graduating class borrowed through all loan programs. *Average indebtedness per student:* $27,339. ***Average need-based loan:*** Freshmen: $3296. Undergraduates: $4022. ***Programs:*** Federal Direct (Subsidized and Unsubsidized Stafford, PLUS).

WORK-STUDY Federal work-study jobs available.

APPLYING FOR FINANCIAL AID ***Financial aid deadline:*** Continuous. ***Notification date:*** Continuous.

CONTACT Mrs. Ann Crabb, Director of Financial Aid, Northwest Nazarene University, 623 South University Boulevard, Nampa, ID 83686, 208-467-8638 or toll-free 877-668-4968. *Fax:* 208-467-8375. *E-mail:* atcrabb@nnu.edu.
Website: http://www.nnu.edu/.

NORTHWEST UNIVERSITY

Kirkland, WA

Tuition & fees: $33,980 **Average undergraduate aid package: $19,906**

ABOUT THE INSTITUTION Independent Assemblies of God, coed. ***Awards:*** certificates, diplomas, associate, bachelor's, master's, and doctoral degrees. 69 undergraduate majors. ***Total enrollment:*** 2,583. Undergraduates: 1,871. Freshmen: 215. Federal methodology is used as a basis for awarding need-based institutional aid.

UNDERGRADUATE EXPENSES for 2020–2021 ***Application fee:*** $30. ***Comprehensive fee:*** $43,400 includes full-time tuition ($33,500), mandatory fees ($480), and room and board ($9420). ***College room only:*** $4710. Room and board charges vary according to housing facility.

FRESHMAN FINANCIAL AID (Fall 2018) 225 applied for aid; of those 78% were deemed to have need. 97% of freshmen with need received aid; of those 19% had need fully met. ***Average percent of need met:*** 75% (excluding resources awarded to replace EFC). ***Average financial aid package:*** $20,248 (excluding resources awarded to replace EFC). 17% of all full-time freshmen had no need and received non-need-based gift aid.

UNDERGRADUATE FINANCIAL AID (Fall 2018) 1,154 applied for aid; of those 86% were deemed to have need. 99% of undergraduates with need received aid; of those 16% had need fully met. ***Average percent of need met:*** 72% (excluding resources awarded to replace EFC). ***Average financial aid package:*** $19,906 (excluding resources awarded to replace EFC). 15% of all full-time undergraduates had no need and received non-need-based gift aid.

GIFT AID (NEED-BASED) ***Total amount:*** $14,788,410 (17% federal, 14% state, 65% institutional, 4% external sources). ***Receiving aid:*** Freshmen: 59% (161); all full-time undergraduates: 71% (916). ***Average award:*** Freshmen: $17,907; Undergraduates: $16,435. ***Scholarships, grants, and awards:*** Federal Pell, FSEOG, state, private, college/university gift aid from institutional funds.

GIFT AID (NON-NEED-BASED) ***Total amount:*** $3,102,627 (95% institutional, 5% external sources). ***Receiving aid:*** Freshmen: 9% (25). Undergraduates: 8% (100). ***Average award:*** Freshmen: $10,880. Undergraduates: $11,371. ***Scholarships, grants, and awards by category:*** *Academic interests/achievement:* 632 awards ($6,178,641 total): biological sciences, business, communication, education, English, general academic interests/achievements, home economics, humanities, international studies, mathematics, physical sciences, religion/biblical studies, social sciences. *Creative arts/performance:* 130 awards ($534,164 total): debating, music, theater/drama. *Special achievements/activities:* 34 awards ($148,478 total): leadership, religious involvement. *Special characteristics:* 157 awards ($927,634 total): children of current students, children of educators, children of faculty/staff, general special characteristics, international students, married students, parents of current students, relatives of clergy, siblings of current students, spouses of current students, veterans. ***ROTC:*** Army cooperative, Air Force cooperative.

LOANS ***Student loans:*** $6,795,573 (97% need-based, 3% non-need-based). 82% of past graduating class borrowed through all loan programs. *Average indebtedness per student:* $24,825. ***Average need-based loan:*** Freshmen: $2853. Undergraduates: $3995. ***Parent loans:*** $1,639,865 (35% need-based, 65% non-need-based). ***Programs:*** Federal Direct (Subsidized and Unsubsidized Stafford, PLUS), alternative loans.

WORK-STUDY ***Federal work-study:*** Total amount: $125,473; 75 jobs averaging $1887. ***State or other work-study/employment:*** Total amount: $4230 (100% need-based). 3 part-time jobs averaging $1904.

ATHLETIC AWARDS Total amount: $1,135,296 (50% need-based, 50% non-need-based).

APPLYING FOR FINANCIAL AID ***Required financial aid form:*** FAFSA. ***Financial aid deadline:*** Continuous. ***Notification date:*** Continuous beginning 11/1. Students must reply within 4 weeks of notification.

CONTACT Mr. Roger Wilson, Director of Financial Aid, Northwest University, PO Box 579, Kirkland, WA 98083-0579, 425-889-5336 or toll-free 800-669-3781. *Fax:* 425-889-5224. *E-mail:* roger.wilson@northwestu.edu.
Website: http://www.northwestu.edu/.

NORTHWOOD UNIVERSITY, MICHIGAN CAMPUS

Midland, MI

CONTACT Mark Martin, Financial Aid Director, Northwood University, Michigan Campus, 4000 Whiting Drive, Midland, MI 48640-2398, 989-837-4230 or toll-free 800-457-7878. *Fax:* 989-837-4130. *E-mail:* mi.finaid@northwood.edu.
Website: http://www.northwood.edu/.

NORWICH UNIVERSITY

Northfield, VT

CONTACT Ms. Jana Cox, Director of Student Financial Planning, Norwich University, 158 Harmon Drive, Northfield, VT 05663, 802-485-2015 or toll-free 800-468-6679. *Fax:* 802-485-2024. *E-mail:* jcox1@norwich.edu.
Website: http://www.norwich.edu/.

NOSSI COLLEGE OF ART

Nashville, TN

CONTACT Ms. Mary P. Kidd, Director of Financial Aid, Nossi College of Art, 590 Cheron Road, Nashville, TN 37115, 615-514-2787 or toll-free 888-986-ARTS. *Fax:* 615-514-2788. *E-mail:* financialaid@nossi.edu.
Website: http://www.nossi.edu/.

NOTRE DAME COLLEGE

South Euclid, OH

CONTACT Ms. Dianna Roberts, Assistant Director of Financial Aid, Notre Dame College, 4545 College Road, South Euclid, OH 44118, 216-373-5213 or toll-free 877-NDC-OHIO. *Fax:* 216-373-5243. *E-mail:* droberts@ndc.edu.
Website: http://www.notredamecollege.edu/.

NOTRE DAME OF MARYLAND UNIVERSITY

Baltimore, MD

CONTACT Audrey Brooks, Director of Financial Aid, Notre Dame of Maryland University, 4701 North Charles Street, Baltimore, MD 21210-2404, 410-532-5369 or toll-free 800-435-0200. *Fax:* 410-532-6287. *E-mail:* finaid@ndm.edu.
Website: http://www.ndm.edu/.

NOVA SOUTHEASTERN UNIVERSITY

Fort Lauderdale, FL

ABOUT THE INSTITUTION Independent, coed. ***Awards:*** certificates, associate, bachelor's, master's, and doctoral degrees. 49 undergraduate majors. ***Total enrollment:*** 20,576. Undergraduates: 5,666. Freshmen: 1,526.

GIFT AID (NEED-BASED) ***Scholarships, grants, and awards:*** Federal Pell, FSEOG, state, private, college/university gift aid from institutional funds, United Negro College Fund.

GIFT AID (NON-NEED-BASED) ***Scholarships, grants, and awards by category:*** *Academic interests/achievement:* general academic interests/achievements. *Creative arts/performance:* general creative arts/performance. *Special achievements/activities:* general special achievements/activities. *Special characteristics:* children of faculty/staff, veterans.

LOANS ***Programs:*** Federal Direct (Subsidized and Unsubsidized Stafford, PLUS), Perkins.

WORK-STUDY *Federal work-study:* Total amount: $8,202,188; 1,427 jobs averaging $4912. ***State or other work-study/employment:*** Total amount: $711,846 (69% need-based, 31% non-need-based). 538 part-time jobs averaging $1260.

APPLYING FOR FINANCIAL AID *Required financial aid forms:* FAFSA, state aid form.

CONTACT Dr. Stephanie G. Brown, Vice President for Enrollment and Student Services, Nova Southeastern University, 3301 College Avenue, Fort Lauderdale, FL 33314, 954-262-7456 or toll-free 800-541-NOVA. *Fax:* 954-262-3967. *E-mail:* browstep@nova.edu.
Website: http://www.nova.edu/.

NYACK COLLEGE

New York, NY

Tuition & fees: $25,500	Average undergraduate aid package: N/A

ABOUT THE INSTITUTION Independent The Christian and Missionary Alliance, coed. ***Awards:*** associate, bachelor's, master's, and doctoral degrees. 25 undergraduate majors. ***Total enrollment:*** 1,981. Undergraduates: 1,028. Freshmen: 128. Federal methodology is used as a basis for awarding need-based institutional aid.

UNDERGRADUATE EXPENSES for 2020–2021 *Application fee:* $25. ***One-time required fee:*** $100. ***Comprehensive fee:*** $35,500 includes full-time tuition ($25,000), mandatory fees ($500), and room and board ($10,000). ***Part-time tuition:*** $1040 per credit hour.

GIFT AID (NEED-BASED) *Total amount:* $18,258,722 (25% federal, 11% state, 63% institutional, 1% external sources). ***Scholarships, grants, and awards:*** Federal Pell, FSEOG, state, private, college/university gift aid from institutional funds.

GIFT AID (NON-NEED-BASED) *Total amount:* $3,265,582 (98% institutional, 2% external sources). ***Scholarships, grants, and awards by category:*** *Academic interests/achievement:* $3,200,011 total: general academic interests/achievements. *Creative arts/performance:* journalism/publications, music, performing arts, theater/drama. *Special achievements/activities:* community service, general special achievements/activities, leadership, religious involvement. *Special characteristics:* adult students, children and siblings of alumni, children of educators, children of faculty/staff, first-generation college students, general special characteristics, international students, relatives of clergy, religious affiliation, siblings of current students, spouses of current students. ***Tuition waivers:*** Full or partial for employees or children of employees.

LOANS *Student loans:* $9,092,461 (81% need-based, 19% non-need-based). 78% of past graduating class borrowed through all loan programs. *Average indebtedness per student:* $28,926. ***Parent loans:*** $2,182,089 (62% need-based, 38% non-need-based). ***Programs:*** Federal Direct (Subsidized and Unsubsidized Stafford), Perkins.

WORK-STUDY *Federal work-study:* Total amount: $180,954; 176 jobs averaging $1028. ***State or other work-study/employment:*** Total amount: $1,011,684 (79% need-based, 21% non-need-based). 239 part-time jobs averaging $4233.

APPLYING FOR FINANCIAL AID *Required financial aid forms:* FAFSA, state aid form, Admissions app gathers f/a eligibility info. ***Financial aid deadline (priority):*** 3/31. ***Notification date:*** Continuous beginning 3/1. Students must reply by 5/1 or within 4 weeks of notification.

CONTACT Mr. Steve Phillips, Director of Financial Aid, Nyack College, 1 South Boulevard, Nyack, NY 10960-3698, 845-675-4747 or toll-free 800-33-NYACK. *Fax:* 845-358-7016. *E-mail:* servicecenter@nyack.edu.
Website: http://www.nyack.edu/.

OAK HILLS CHRISTIAN COLLEGE

Bemidji, MN

CONTACT Daniel Hovestol, Financial Aid Director, Oak Hills Christian College, 1600 Oak Hills Road, SW, Bemidji, MN 56601-8832, 218-751-8671 Ext. 1220 or toll-free 888-751-8670 Ext.1285. *Fax:* 218-444-1311. *E-mail:* ohfinaid@oakhills.edu.
Website: http://www.oakhills.edu/.

OAKLAND CITY UNIVERSITY

Oakland City, IN

ABOUT THE INSTITUTION Independent General Baptist, coed. ***Awards:*** certificates, associate, bachelor's, master's, and doctoral degrees. 28 undergraduate majors. ***Total enrollment:*** 1,419. Undergraduates: 1,231. Freshmen: 140.

GIFT AID (NEED-BASED) *Scholarships, grants, and awards:* Federal Pell, FSEOG, state, private, college/university gift aid from institutional funds.

GIFT AID (NON-NEED-BASED) *Scholarships, grants, and awards by category:* *Academic interests/achievement:* general academic interests/achievements. *Creative arts/performance:* applied art and design, music. *Special achievements/activities:* religious involvement. *Special characteristics:* children and siblings of alumni, children of faculty/staff, ethnic background, international students, members of minority groups, religious affiliation.

LOANS *Programs:* Federal Direct (Subsidized and Unsubsidized Stafford, PLUS), Perkins, college/university.

CONTACT Mrs. Nicole Sharp, Director of Financial Aid, Oakland City University, 138 North Lucretia Street, Oakland City, IN 47660-1099, 812-749-1225 or toll-free 800-737-5125. *Fax:* 812-749-1438. *E-mail:* nsharp@oak.edu.
Website: http://www.oak.edu/.

OAKLAND UNIVERSITY

Rochester, MI

Tuition & fees (area res): $13,346	Average undergraduate aid package: $10,262

ABOUT THE INSTITUTION State-supported, coed. ***Awards:*** certificates, bachelor's, master's, and doctoral degrees. 96 undergraduate majors. ***Total enrollment:*** 19,013. Undergraduates: 15,543. Freshmen: 2,667. Federal methodology is used as a basis for awarding need-based institutional aid.

UNDERGRADUATE EXPENSES for 2019–2020 *Tuition, area resident:* full-time $13,346; part-time $449 per credit. ***Tuition, state resident:*** full-time $13,346; part-time $449 per credit. ***Tuition, nonresident:*** full-time $24,710; part-time $796 per credit. Full-time tuition and fees vary according to course level and program. Part-time tuition and fees vary according to course level and program. ***College room and board:*** $10,430. Room and board charges vary according to housing facility.

FRESHMAN FINANCIAL AID (Fall 2018) 2330 applied for aid; of those 78% were deemed to have need. 98% of freshmen with need received aid; of those 13% had need fully met. ***Average percent of need met:*** 56% (excluding resources awarded to replace EFC). ***Average financial aid package:*** $12,689 (excluding resources awarded to replace EFC). 25% of all full-time freshmen had no need and received non-need-based gift aid.

UNDERGRADUATE FINANCIAL AID (Fall 2018) 9,597 applied for aid; of those 83% were deemed to have need. 98% of undergraduates with need received aid; of those 10% had need fully met. ***Average percent of need met:*** 47% (excluding resources awarded to replace EFC). ***Average financial aid package:*** $10,262 (excluding resources awarded to replace EFC). 18% of all full-time undergraduates had no need and received non-need-based gift aid.

GIFT AID (NEED-BASED) *Total amount:* $41,966,133 (55% federal, 3% state, 42% institutional). ***Receiving aid:*** Freshmen: 53% (1,417); all full-time undergraduates: 45% (5,651). ***Average award:*** Freshmen: $9337; Undergraduates: $7082. ***Scholarships, grants, and awards:*** Federal Pell, FSEOG, state, private, college/university gift aid from institutional funds.

GIFT AID (NON-NEED-BASED) *Total amount:* $36,717,334 (2% state, 76% institutional, 22% external sources). ***Receiving aid:*** Freshmen: 50% (1,343). Undergraduates: 37% (4,641). ***Average award:*** Freshmen: $5605. Undergraduates: $5164. ***Scholarships, grants, and awards by category:*** *Academic interests/achievement:* area/ethnic studies, biological sciences, business, computer science, education, engineering/technologies, English, foreign languages, general academic interests/achievements, humanities, international studies, mathematics, physical sciences, social sciences. *Creative arts/performance:* 92 awards ($3610 total): dance, music, performing arts, theater/drama. *Special achievements/activities:* community service, general special achievements/activities. ***Tuition waivers:*** Full or partial for employees or children of employees, senior citizens. ***ROTC:*** Air Force cooperative.

LOANS *Student loans:* $50,708,869 (46% need-based, 54% non-need-based). 62% of past graduating class borrowed through all loan programs. *Average indebtedness*

per student: $27,095. ***Average need-based loan:*** Freshmen: $2905. Undergraduates: $3931. ***Parent loans:*** $13,438,287 (100% non-need-based). ***Programs:*** Federal Direct (Subsidized and Unsubsidized Stafford, PLUS), private loans.
WORK-STUDY *Federal work-study:* Total amount: $758,311; 438 jobs averaging $1833. ***State or other work-study/employment:*** Part-time jobs available.
ATHLETIC AWARDS Total amount: $4,158,350 (100% non-need-based).
APPLYING FOR FINANCIAL AID *Required financial aid form:* FAFSA. ***Financial aid deadline:*** Continuous. ***Notification date:*** Continuous beginning 12/1.
CONTACT Office of Financial Aid, Oakland University, 120 North Foundation Hall, Rochester, MI 48309-4401, 248-370-2550 or toll-free 800-OAK-UNIV. *E-mail:* finaid@oakland.edu.
Website: http://www.oakland.edu/.

OAKWOOD UNIVERSITY

Huntsville, AL

CONTACT Financial Aid Director, Oakwood University, 7000 Adventist Boulevard, Huntsville, AL 35896, 256-726-7210 or toll-free 800-824-5312.
Website: http://www.oakwood.edu/.

OBERLIN COLLEGE

Oberlin, OH

Tuition & fees: $56,868	Average undergraduate aid package: $45,295

ABOUT THE INSTITUTION Independent, coed. ***Awards:*** certificates, diplomas, bachelor's, and master's degrees. 55 undergraduate majors. ***Total enrollment:*** 2,812. Undergraduates: 4,884. Freshmen: 804. Both federal and institutional methodology are used as a basis for awarding need-based institutional aid.
UNDERGRADUATE EXPENSES for 2019–2020 *Comprehensive fee:* $73,694 includes full-time tuition ($55,976), mandatory fees ($892), and room and board ($16,826). ***College room only:*** $8350. Room and board charges vary according to board plan and housing facility. ***Part-time tuition:*** $2334 per credit hour. Part-time tuition and fees vary according to course load.
FRESHMAN FINANCIAL AID (Fall 2019, est.) 558 applied for aid; of those 85% were deemed to have need. 100% of freshmen with need received aid; of those 100% had need fully met. ***Average percent of need met:*** 100% (excluding resources awarded to replace EFC). ***Average financial aid package:*** $46,673 (excluding resources awarded to replace EFC). 26% of all full-time freshmen had no need and received non-need-based gift aid.
UNDERGRADUATE FINANCIAL AID (Fall 2019, est.) 1,772 applied for aid; of those 87% were deemed to have need. 100% of undergraduates with need received aid; of those 100% had need fully met. ***Average percent of need met:*** 100% (excluding resources awarded to replace EFC). ***Average financial aid package:*** $45,295 (excluding resources awarded to replace EFC). 32% of all full-time undergraduates had no need and received non-need-based gift aid.
GIFT AID (NEED-BASED) *Total amount:* $60,576,691 (3% federal, 97% institutional). ***Receiving aid:*** Freshmen: 59% (471); all full-time undergraduates: 55% (1,539). ***Average award:*** Freshmen: $42,718; Undergraduates: $40,964. ***Scholarships, grants, and awards:*** Federal Pell, FSEOG, state, private, college/university gift aid from institutional funds.
GIFT AID (NON-NEED-BASED) *Total amount:* $15,717,160 (100% institutional). ***Receiving aid:*** Freshmen: 49% (391). Undergraduates: 45% (1,255). ***Average award:*** Freshmen: $19,690. Undergraduates: $17,486. ***Scholarships, grants, and awards by category:*** *Academic interests/achievement:* 1,657 awards ($27,433,326 total): general academic interests/achievements. *Creative arts/performance:* 551 awards ($12,490,866 total): music. *Special characteristics:* 2,208 awards ($39,924,192 total). ***Tuition waivers:*** Full or partial for employees or children of employees.
LOANS *Student loans:* $8,837,890 (88% need-based, 12% non-need-based). 45% of past graduating class borrowed through all loan programs. *Average indebtedness per student:* $26,175. ***Average need-based loan:*** Freshmen: $3444. Undergraduates: $4294. ***Parent loans:*** $3,113,552 (85% need-based, 15% non-need-based). ***Programs:*** Federal Direct (Subsidized and Unsubsidized Stafford, PLUS), college/university.
WORK-STUDY *Federal work-study:* Total amount: $2,268,501; jobs available. ***State or other work-study/employment:*** Total amount: $1,003,595 (93% need-based, 7% non-need-based). Part-time jobs available.
APPLYING FOR FINANCIAL AID *Required financial aid forms:* FAFSA, institution's own form, CSS Financial Aid PROFILE, noncustodial (divorced/separated) parent's statement, business/farm supplement. ***Financial aid deadline:*** 2/1 (priority: 2/1). ***Notification date:*** 4/1. Students must reply by 5/1 or within 2 weeks of notification.
CONTACT Ms. Michele Kosboth, Director of Financial Aid, Oberlin College, Carnegie Building #123, 52 West Lorain Street, Oberlin, OH 44074, 440-775-8142 or toll-free 800-622-OBIE. *Fax:* 440-775-8249. *E-mail:* financial.aid@oberlin.edu.
Website: http://www.oberlin.edu/.

OCCIDENTAL COLLEGE

Los Angeles, CA

Tuition & fees: $56,576	Average undergraduate aid package: $51,273

ABOUT THE INSTITUTION Independent, coed. ***Awards:*** bachelor's and master's degrees. 34 undergraduate majors. ***Total enrollment:*** 1,985. Undergraduates: 1,985. Freshmen: 562. Both federal and institutional methodology are used as a basis for awarding need-based institutional aid.
UNDERGRADUATE EXPENSES for 2019–2020 *Application fee:* $65. ***Comprehensive fee:*** $72,610 includes full-time tuition ($55,980), mandatory fees ($596), and room and board ($16,034). ***College room only:*** $9124. Room and board charges vary according to board plan. ***Part-time tuition:*** $2333 per unit. ***Payment plan:*** Tuition prepayment.
FRESHMAN FINANCIAL AID (Fall 2018) 405 applied for aid; of those 82% were deemed to have need. 98% of freshmen with need received aid; of those 100% had need fully met. ***Average percent of need met:*** 100% (excluding resources awarded to replace EFC). ***Average financial aid package:*** $52,303 (excluding resources awarded to replace EFC). 14% of all full-time freshmen had no need and received non-need-based gift aid.
UNDERGRADUATE FINANCIAL AID (Fall 2018) 1,335 applied for aid; of those 87% were deemed to have need. 99% of undergraduates with need received aid; of those 100% had need fully met. ***Average percent of need met:*** 100% (excluding resources awarded to replace EFC). ***Average financial aid package:*** $51,273 (excluding resources awarded to replace EFC). 13% of all full-time undergraduates had no need and received non-need-based gift aid.
GIFT AID (NEED-BASED) *Total amount:* $47,744,297 (4% federal, 4% state, 90% institutional, 2% external sources). ***Receiving aid:*** Freshmen: 58% (328); all full-time undergraduates: 57% (1,152). ***Average award:*** Freshmen: $45,568; Undergraduates: $43,248. ***Scholarships, grants, and awards:*** Federal Pell, FSEOG, state, private, college/university gift aid from institutional funds.
GIFT AID (NON-NEED-BASED) *Total amount:* $6,485,739 (88% institutional, 12% external sources). ***Receiving aid:*** Freshmen: 32% (179). Undergraduates: 26% (521). ***Average award:*** Freshmen: $14,509. Undergraduates: $13,274. ***Scholarships, grants, and awards by category:*** *Academic interests/achievement:* 628 awards ($8,240,146 total): general academic interests/achievements. *Creative arts/performance:* 43 awards ($33,750 total): music. *Special achievements/activities:* 53 awards ($815,000 total): leadership. *Special characteristics:* 31 awards ($1,542,611 total): children of educators, children of faculty/staff, veterans. ***ROTC:*** Army cooperative, Air Force cooperative.
LOANS *Student loans:* $9,778,121 (59% need-based, 41% non-need-based). 59% of past graduating class borrowed through all loan programs. *Average indebtedness per student:* $29,306. ***Average need-based loan:*** Freshmen: $4547. Undergraduates: $5674. ***Parent loans:*** $3,691,835 (100% non-need-based). ***Programs:*** Federal Direct (Subsidized and Unsubsidized Stafford, PLUS), Perkins, college/university, alternative loans.
WORK-STUDY *Federal work-study:* Total amount: $2,307,537; 835 jobs averaging $2778. ***State or other work-study/employment:*** Total amount: $922,498 (80% need-based, 20% non-need-based). 139 part-time jobs averaging $6647.
APPLYING FOR FINANCIAL AID *Required financial aid forms:* FAFSA, CSS Financial Aid PROFILE, state aid form, noncustodial (divorced/separated) parent's statement. ***Financial aid deadline:*** 1/10 (priority: 1/10). ***Notification date:*** 3/17. Students must reply by 5/1.

CONTACT Gina Becerril, Director of Financial Aid, Occidental College, 1600 Campus Road, Los Angeles, CA 90041, 323-259-2548 or toll-free 800-825-5262. *Fax:* 323-341-4961. *E-mail:* finaid@oxy.edu.
Website: http://www.oxy.edu/.

OGLALA LAKOTA COLLEGE

Kyle, SD

CONTACT Financial Aid Director, Oglala Lakota College, 490 Piya Wiconi Road, Kyle, SD 57752-0490, 605-455-6000.
Website: http://www.olc.edu/.

OGLETHORPE UNIVERSITY

Atlanta, GA

Tuition & fees: $41,410 **Average undergraduate aid package: $34,660**

ABOUT THE INSTITUTION Independent, coed. ***Awards:*** bachelor's degrees. 39 undergraduate majors. ***Total enrollment:*** 1,385. Undergraduates: 1,385. Freshmen: 400. Federal methodology is used as a basis for awarding need-based institutional aid.
UNDERGRADUATE EXPENSES for 2020–2021 *Application fee:* $50. ***Comprehensive fee:*** $55,210 includes full-time tuition ($41,130), mandatory fees ($280), and room and board ($13,800). Room and board charges vary according to housing facility. ***Part-time tuition:*** $1713 per credit hour.
FRESHMAN FINANCIAL AID (Fall 2019, est.) 347 applied for aid; of those 85% were deemed to have need. 100% of freshmen with need received aid; of those 23% had need fully met. ***Average percent of need met:*** 81% (excluding resources awarded to replace EFC). ***Average financial aid package:*** $36,811 (excluding resources awarded to replace EFC). 24% of all full-time freshmen had no need and received non-need-based gift aid.
UNDERGRADUATE FINANCIAL AID (Fall 2019, est.) 1,050 applied for aid; of those 90% were deemed to have need. 100% of undergraduates with need received aid; of those 18% had need fully met. ***Average percent of need met:*** 77% (excluding resources awarded to replace EFC). ***Average financial aid package:*** $34,660 (excluding resources awarded to replace EFC). 29% of all full-time undergraduates had no need and received non-need-based gift aid.
GIFT AID (NEED-BASED) *Total amount:* $27,812,471 (9% federal, 11% state, 79% institutional, 1% external sources). ***Receiving aid:*** Freshmen: 74% (295); all full-time undergraduates: 70% (930). ***Average award:*** Freshmen: $31,649; Undergraduates: $29,759. ***Scholarships, grants, and awards:*** Federal Pell, FSEOG, state, private, college/university gift aid from institutional funds.
GIFT AID (NON-NEED-BASED) *Total amount:* $10,962,530 (6% state, 91% institutional, 3% external sources). ***Receiving aid:*** Freshmen: 15% (60). Undergraduates: 10% (138). ***Average award:*** Freshmen: $30,779. Undergraduates: $24,292. ***Scholarships, grants, and awards by category:*** *Academic interests/achievement:* biological sciences, business, communication, English, foreign languages, general academic interests/achievements, humanities, international studies, mathematics, social sciences. *Creative arts/performance:* applied art and design, journalism/publications, music, performing arts, theater/drama. *Special achievements/activities:* community service, leadership, memberships. *Special characteristics:* children of faculty/staff, first-generation college students, international students, local/state students, out-of-state students, previous college experience, religious affiliation. ***Tuition waivers:*** Full or partial for employees or children of employees. ***ROTC:*** Army cooperative, Naval cooperative, Air Force cooperative.
LOANS *Student loans:* $8,369,697 (75% need-based, 25% non-need-based). 66% of past graduating class borrowed through all loan programs. *Average indebtedness per student:* $35,732. ***Average need-based loan:*** Freshmen: $3295. Undergraduates: $4052. ***Parent loans:*** $2,716,734 (56% need-based, 44% non-need-based). ***Programs:*** Federal Direct (Subsidized and Unsubsidized Stafford, PLUS), state.
WORK-STUDY *Federal work-study:* Total amount: $223,000; jobs available.
APPLYING FOR FINANCIAL AID *Required financial aid form:* FAFSA. ***Financial aid deadline (priority):*** 2/15. ***Notification date:*** Continuous beginning 11/1. Students must reply by 5/1.

CONTACT Mr. Chris Summers, Director of Financial Aid, Oglethorpe University, 4484 Peachtree Road NE, Atlanta, GA 30319, 404-364-8355 or toll-free 800-428-4484. *Fax:* 404-364-8359. *E-mail:* csummers@oglethorpe.edu.
Website: http://www.oglethorpe.edu/.

OHIO CHRISTIAN UNIVERSITY

Circleville, OH

Tuition & fees: $20,790 **Average undergraduate aid package: $11,243**

ABOUT THE INSTITUTION Independent Churches of Christ in Christian Union, coed. ***Awards:*** associate, bachelor's, and master's degrees. 20 undergraduate majors. ***Total enrollment:*** 2,843. Undergraduates: 2,529. Freshmen: 224.
UNDERGRADUATE EXPENSES for 2019–2020 *Application fee:* $25. ***Comprehensive fee:*** $29,110 includes full-time tuition ($20,040), mandatory fees ($750), and room and board ($8320). ***College room only:*** $4016. Full-time tuition and fees vary according to class time, course load, degree level, location, and program. Room and board charges vary according to board plan. ***Part-time tuition:*** $391 per credit hour. ***Part-time fees:*** $375 per term. Part-time tuition and fees vary according to class time, location, and program.
FRESHMAN FINANCIAL AID (Fall 2018) *Average financial aid package:* $9373 (excluding resources awarded to replace EFC). 100% of all full-time freshmen had no need and received non-need-based gift aid.
UNDERGRADUATE FINANCIAL AID (Fall 2018) *Average financial aid package:* $11,243 (excluding resources awarded to replace EFC). 100% of all full-time undergraduates had no need and received non-need-based gift aid.
GIFT AID (NEED-BASED) *Total amount:* $6,361,903 (100% federal). ***Receiving aid:*** Freshmen: 70% (195); all full-time undergraduates: 54% (1,732). ***Average award:*** Freshmen: $3645; Undergraduates: $3673. ***Scholarships, grants, and awards:*** Federal Pell, FSEOG, state, private, college/university gift aid from institutional funds.
GIFT AID (NON-NEED-BASED) *Scholarships, grants, and awards by category:* *Academic interests/achievement:* business, education, general academic interests/achievements, religion/biblical studies. *Creative arts/performance:* music. *Special achievements/activities:* leadership. *Special characteristics:* adult students, children of faculty/staff, international students, out-of-state students, relatives of clergy, religious affiliation, siblings of current students, veterans, veterans' children. ***Tuition waivers:*** Full or partial for employees or children of employees, senior citizens.
LOANS *Student loans:* $15,822,241 (100% need-based). 90% of past graduating class borrowed through all loan programs. *Average indebtedness per student:* $30,000. ***Average need-based loan:*** Freshmen: $5728. Undergraduates: $3645. ***Programs:*** Federal Direct (Subsidized and Unsubsidized Stafford).
WORK-STUDY Federal work-study jobs available. ***State or other work-study/employment:*** Part-time jobs available.
APPLYING FOR FINANCIAL AID *Required financial aid form:* FAFSA. ***Financial aid deadline (priority):*** 3/31. ***Notification date:*** 6/1. Students must reply within 2 weeks of notification.
CONTACT Financial Aid Office, Ohio Christian University, 1476 Lancaster Pike, Circleville, OH 43113, 740-474-8896 or toll-free 877-762-8669.
Website: http://www.ohiochristian.edu/.

OHIO DOMINICAN UNIVERSITY

Columbus, OH

CONTACT Ms. Cynthia A. Hahn, Director of Financial Aid, Ohio Dominican University, 1216 Sunbury Road, Columbus, OH 43219, 614-251-4778 or toll-free 800-955-6446. *Fax:* 614-251-4456. *E-mail:* fin-aid@ohiodominican.edu.
Website: http://www.ohiodominican.edu/.

OHIO NORTHERN UNIVERSITY

Ada, OH

ABOUT THE INSTITUTION Independent United Methodist Church, coed. ***Awards:*** certificates, bachelor's, master's, and doctoral degrees. 127 undergraduate majors. ***Total enrollment:*** 3,088. Undergraduates: 2,312. Freshmen: 640.

GIFT AID (NEED-BASED) ***Scholarships, grants, and awards:*** Federal Pell, FSEOG, state, private, college/university gift aid from institutional funds.

GIFT AID (NON-NEED-BASED) ***Scholarships, grants, and awards by category:*** *Academic interests/achievement:* biological sciences, business, communication, computer science, education, engineering/technologies, English, foreign languages, general academic interests/achievements, home economics, humanities, international studies, mathematics, physical sciences, premedicine, religion/biblical studies, social sciences. *Creative arts/performance:* applied art and design, art/fine arts, creative writing, dance, journalism/publications, music, performing arts, theater/drama. *Special achievements/activities:* community service, general special achievements/activities, junior miss, leadership. *Special characteristics:* children and siblings of alumni, children of faculty/staff, ethnic background, international students, out-of-state students, relatives of clergy, religious affiliation, siblings of current students, veterans.

LOANS ***Programs:*** Federal Direct (Subsidized and Unsubsidized Stafford, PLUS), Perkins.

WORK-STUDY ***Federal work-study:*** Total amount: $318,216; jobs available. ***State or other work-study/employment:*** Total amount: $261,760 (100% need-based). Part-time jobs available.

APPLYING FOR FINANCIAL AID ***Required financial aid form:*** FAFSA.

CONTACT Melanie Weaver, Director of Financial Aid, Ohio Northern University, 525 South Main Street, Ada, OH 45810, 419-772-2272 or toll-free 888-408-4ONU. *Fax:* 419-772-2313. *E-mail:* m-weaver.2@onu.edu.
Website: http://www.onu.edu/.

THE OHIO STATE UNIVERSITY

Columbus, OH

Tuition & fees (OH res): $11,084	Average undergraduate aid package: $15,392

ABOUT THE INSTITUTION State-supported, coed. ***Awards:*** certificates, diplomas, associate, bachelor's, master's, and doctoral degrees. 163 undergraduate majors. ***Total enrollment:*** 61,391. Undergraduates: 46,818. Freshmen: 7,716. Federal methodology is used as a basis for awarding need-based institutional aid.

UNDERGRADUATE EXPENSES for 2019–2020 ***Application fee:*** $60. ***Tuition, state resident:*** full-time $11,084; part-time $501 per credit hour. ***Tuition, nonresident:*** full-time $32,061; part-time $1375 per credit hour. Full-time tuition and fees vary according to course load, degree level, location, program, reciprocity agreements, and student level. Part-time tuition and fees vary according to course load, degree level, location, program, reciprocity agreements, and student level. ***College room and board:*** $12,708. Room and board charges vary according to board plan, housing facility, and location. ***Payment plan:*** Guaranteed tuition.

FRESHMAN FINANCIAL AID (Fall 2019, est.) 6258 applied for aid; of those 58% were deemed to have need. 99% of freshmen with need received aid; of those 29% had need fully met. ***Average percent of need met:*** 74% (excluding resources awarded to replace EFC). ***Average financial aid package:*** $16,288 (excluding resources awarded to replace EFC). 30% of all full-time freshmen had no need and received non-need-based gift aid.

UNDERGRADUATE FINANCIAL AID (Fall 2019, est.) 28,401 applied for aid; of those 69% were deemed to have need. 98% of undergraduates with need received aid; of those 23% had need fully met. ***Average percent of need met:*** 73% (excluding resources awarded to replace EFC). ***Average financial aid package:*** $15,392 (excluding resources awarded to replace EFC). 22% of all full-time undergraduates had no need and received non-need-based gift aid.

GIFT AID (NEED-BASED) ***Total amount:*** $200,002,102 (24% federal, 8% state, 64% institutional, 4% external sources). ***Receiving aid:*** Freshmen: 43% (3,304); all full-time undergraduates: 39% (16,712). ***Average award:*** Freshmen: $13,174; Undergraduates: $12,037. ***Scholarships, grants, and awards:*** Federal Pell, FSEOG, state, private, college/university gift aid from institutional funds.

GIFT AID (NON-NEED-BASED) ***Total amount:*** $88,753,029 (4% state, 88% institutional, 8% external sources). ***Receiving aid:*** Freshmen: 4% (300). Undergraduates: 2% (913). ***Average award:*** Freshmen: $6825. Undergraduates: $6981. ***Scholarships, grants, and awards by category:*** *Academic interests/achievement:* agriculture, architecture, area/ethnic studies, biological sciences, business, communication, computer science, education, engineering/technologies, English, foreign languages, general academic interests/achievements, health fields, home economics, humanities, international studies, mathematics, military science, physical sciences, premedicine, social sciences. *Creative arts/performance:* creative writing, dance, journalism/publications, music, performing arts, theater/drama. *Special achievements/activities:* cheerleading/drum major, hobbies/interests, leadership, memberships. *Special characteristics:* adult students, children and siblings of alumni, children of faculty/staff, children of public servants, children of union members/company employees, children of workers in trades, ethnic background, handicapped students, members of minority groups, out-of-state students, previous college experience. ***Tuition waivers:*** Full or partial for employees or children of employees, senior citizens. ***ROTC:*** Army, Naval, Air Force.

LOANS ***Student loans:*** $188,496,392 (54% need-based, 46% non-need-based). 50% of past graduating class borrowed through all loan programs. *Average indebtedness per student:* $27,242. ***Average need-based loan:*** Freshmen: $3464. Undergraduates: $4397. ***Parent loans:*** $48,560,768 (100% non-need-based). ***Programs:*** Federal Direct (Subsidized and Unsubsidized Stafford, PLUS), Federal Nursing, state, college/university.

WORK-STUDY ***Federal work-study:*** Total amount: $10,403,174; jobs available.

ATHLETIC AWARDS Total amount: $20,360,726 (100% non-need-based).

APPLYING FOR FINANCIAL AID ***Required financial aid form:*** FAFSA. ***Financial aid deadline (priority):*** 2/1. ***Notification date:*** 3/15. Students must reply by 5/1 or within 4 weeks of notification.

CONTACT Financial Aid Office, The Ohio State University, 281 W. Lane Ave., Student Academic Services Building, Columbus, OH 43210, 614-292-6446.
Website: http://www.osu.edu/.

OHIO UNIVERSITY

Athens, OH

Tuition & fees (OH res): $12,612	Average undergraduate aid package: $9164

ABOUT THE INSTITUTION State-supported, coed. ***Awards:*** certificates, associate, bachelor's, master's, and doctoral degrees. 117 undergraduate majors. ***Total enrollment:*** 28,446. Undergraduates: 22,275. Freshmen: 3,993. Federal methodology is used as a basis for awarding need-based institutional aid.

UNDERGRADUATE EXPENSES for 2019–2020 ***Application fee:*** $50. ***Tuition, state resident:*** full-time $12,612; part-time $595 per semester hour. ***Tuition, nonresident:*** full-time $22,406; part-time $1077 per semester hour. Full-time tuition and fees vary according to degree level, location, program, and reciprocity agreements. Part-time tuition and fees vary according to course load, degree level, location, program, and reciprocity agreements. ***College room and board:*** $12,172; ***Room only:*** $7308. Room and board charges vary according to board plan. ***Payment plan:*** Guaranteed tuition.

FRESHMAN FINANCIAL AID (Fall 2019, est.) 3004 applied for aid; of those 73% were deemed to have need. 100% of freshmen with need received aid; of those 12% had need fully met. ***Average percent of need met:*** 58% (excluding resources awarded to replace EFC). ***Average financial aid package:*** $9777 (excluding resources awarded to replace EFC). 7% of all full-time freshmen had no need and received non-need-based gift aid.

UNDERGRADUATE FINANCIAL AID (Fall 2019, est.) 11,534 applied for aid; of those 78% were deemed to have need. 100% of undergraduates with need received aid; of those 9% had need fully met. ***Average percent of need met:*** 50% (excluding resources awarded to replace EFC). ***Average financial aid package:*** $9164 (excluding resources awarded to replace EFC). 9% of all full-time undergraduates had no need and received non-need-based gift aid.

GIFT AID (NEED-BASED) ***Total amount:*** $68,973,793 (37% federal, 8% state, 50% institutional, 5% external sources). ***Receiving aid:*** Freshmen: 55% (2,025); all full-time undergraduates: 45% (7,240). ***Average award:*** Freshmen: $7410; Undergraduates: $6791. ***Scholarships, grants, and awards:*** Federal Pell, FSEOG, state, private, college/university gift aid from institutional funds.

GIFT AID (NON-NEED-BASED) ***Total amount:*** $10,146,779 (1% federal, 3% state, 91% institutional, 5% external sources). ***Receiving aid:*** Freshmen: 6% (204). Undergraduates: 3% (513). ***Average award:*** Freshmen: $4134. Undergraduates: $4504. ***Scholarships, grants, and awards by category:*** *Academic interests/achievement:* area/ethnic studies, biological sciences, business, communication, computer science, education, engineering/technologies, English, foreign languages, general academic interests/achievements, health fields, home economics, humanities, international studies, mathematics, military science, physical sciences, premedicine, social sciences. *Creative arts/performance:* applied art and design, art/fine arts, cinema/film/broadcasting, creative writing, dance, debating, journalism/publications, music, performing arts, theater/drama. *Special characteristics:* children and siblings of alumni, children of faculty/staff, first-generation college students, out-of-state students. ***Tuition waivers:*** Full or partial for employees or children of employees, senior citizens. ***ROTC:*** Army, Air Force.

LOANS *Student loans:* $101,602,605 (91% need-based, 9% non-need-based). 66% of past graduating class borrowed through all loan programs. *Average indebtedness per student:* $28,856. ***Average need-based loan:*** Freshmen: $3080. Undergraduates: $3734. ***Parent loans:*** $32,620,526 (50% need-based, 50% non-need-based). ***Programs:*** Federal Direct (Subsidized and Unsubsidized Stafford, PLUS), college/university.

WORK-STUDY *Federal work-study:* Total amount: $1,410,530; 703 jobs averaging $2032. ***State or other work-study/employment:*** Total amount: $16,491,631 (100% non-need-based). Part-time jobs available.

ATHLETIC AWARDS Total amount: $8,617,990 (22% need-based, 78% non-need-based).

APPLYING FOR FINANCIAL AID *Required financial aid form:* FAFSA. ***Financial aid deadline (priority):*** 1/15. ***Notification date:*** 2/15. Students must reply by 5/1.

CONTACT Ms. Valerie K. Miller, Director of Financial Aid, Ohio University, 020 Chubb Hall, Athens, OH 45701-2979, 740-593-9853. *Fax:* 740-593-4140. *E-mail:* millerv@ohio.edu.
Website: http://www.ohio.edu/.

OHIO UNIVERSITY–CHILLICOTHE

Chillicothe, OH

Tuition & fees (OH res): $5674	Average undergraduate aid package: $5647

ABOUT THE INSTITUTION State-supported, coed. ***Awards:*** associate, bachelor's, and master's degrees (offers first 2 years of most bachelor's degree programs available at the main campus in Athens; also offers several bachelor's degree programs that can be completed at this campus and several programs exclusive to this campus; also offers some graduate programs). 22 undergraduate majors. Federal methodology is used as a basis for awarding need-based institutional aid.

UNDERGRADUATE EXPENSES for 2019–2020 *Tuition, state resident:* full-time $5674; part-time $255 per semester hour. ***Tuition, nonresident:*** full-time $8666; part-time $391 per semester hour. Full-time tuition and fees vary according to degree level, location, program, and reciprocity agreements. Part-time tuition and fees vary according to course load, degree level, location, program, and reciprocity agreements. ***Payment plan:*** Guaranteed tuition.

FRESHMAN FINANCIAL AID (Fall 2019, est.) 183 applied for aid; of those 83% were deemed to have need. 100% of freshmen with need received aid; of those 99% had need fully met. ***Average percent of need met:*** 46% (excluding resources awarded to replace EFC). ***Average financial aid package:*** $5389 (excluding resources awarded to replace EFC). 1% of all full-time freshmen had no need and received non-need-based gift aid.

UNDERGRADUATE FINANCIAL AID (Fall 2019, est.) 668 applied for aid; of those 87% were deemed to have need. 100% of undergraduates with need received aid; of those 99% had need fully met. ***Average percent of need met:*** 40% (excluding resources awarded to replace EFC). ***Average financial aid package:*** $5647 (excluding resources awarded to replace EFC). 1% of all full-time undergraduates had no need and received non-need-based gift aid.

GIFT AID (NEED-BASED) *Total amount:* $4,067,406 (81% federal, 1% state, 13% institutional, 5% external sources). ***Receiving aid:*** Freshmen: 51% (135); all full-time undergraduates: 52% (490). ***Average award:*** Freshmen: $4391; Undergraduates: $4454. ***Scholarships, grants, and awards:*** Federal Pell, FSEOG, state, private, college/university gift aid from institutional funds.

GIFT AID (NON-NEED-BASED) *Total amount:* $64,433 (13% federal, 12% state, 41% institutional, 34% external sources). ***Receiving aid:*** Freshmen: 50% (134). Undergraduates: 52% (489). ***Average award:*** Undergraduates: $3833. ***Scholarships, grants, and awards by category:*** *Academic interests/achievement:* agriculture, area/ethnic studies, biological sciences, business, communication, computer science, education, engineering/technologies, English, foreign languages, general academic interests/achievements, health fields, home economics, humanities, mathematics, military science, physical sciences, premedicine, social sciences. *Creative arts/performance:* applied art and design, art/fine arts, cinema/film/broadcasting, creative writing, dance, debating, journalism/publications, music, performing arts, theater/drama. *Special characteristics:* children and siblings of alumni, children of faculty/staff, first-generation college students, out-of-state students. ***Tuition waivers:*** Full or partial for employees or children of employees, senior citizens.

LOANS *Student loans:* $3,868,469 (94% need-based, 6% non-need-based). 66% of past graduating class borrowed through all loan programs. *Average indebtedness per student:* $28,856. ***Average need-based loan:*** Freshmen: $2325. Undergraduates: $2592. ***Parent loans:*** $110,769 (36% need-based, 64% non-need-based). ***Programs:*** Federal Direct (Subsidized and Unsubsidized Stafford, PLUS), state, college/university.

WORK-STUDY *Federal work-study:* Total amount: $30,301; 18 jobs averaging $1858.

APPLYING FOR FINANCIAL AID *Required financial aid form:* FAFSA. ***Financial aid deadline (priority):*** 1/15. ***Notification date:*** 2/15.

CONTACT Ms. Valerie K. Miller, Director of Financial Aid, Ohio University–Chillicothe, 020 Chubb Hall, Athens, OH 45701-2979, 740-593-4141 or toll-free 877-462-6824. *Fax:* 740-593-4140. *E-mail:* millerv@ohio.edu.
Website: http://www.chillicothe.ohiou.edu/.

OHIO UNIVERSITY–EASTERN

St. Clairsville, OH

Tuition & fees (OH res): $5674	Average undergraduate aid package: $5027

ABOUT THE INSTITUTION State-supported, coed. ***Awards:*** associate, bachelor's, and master's degrees (also offers some graduate courses). 11 undergraduate majors. Federal methodology is used as a basis for awarding need-based institutional aid.

UNDERGRADUATE EXPENSES for 2019–2020 *Tuition, state resident:* full-time $5674; part-time $255 per semester hour. ***Tuition, nonresident:*** full-time $8666; part-time $391 per semester hour. Full-time tuition and fees vary according to degree level, location, program, and reciprocity agreements. Part-time tuition and fees vary according to course load, degree level, location, program, and reciprocity agreements. ***Payment plan:*** Guaranteed tuition.

FRESHMAN FINANCIAL AID (Fall 2019, est.) 71 applied for aid; of those 70% were deemed to have need. 100% of freshmen with need received aid; of those 100% had need fully met. ***Average percent of need met:*** 50% (excluding resources awarded to replace EFC). ***Average financial aid package:*** $5468 (excluding resources awarded to replace EFC). 1% of all full-time freshmen had no need and received non-need-based gift aid.

UNDERGRADUATE FINANCIAL AID (Fall 2019, est.) 209 applied for aid; of those 82% were deemed to have need. 100% of undergraduates with need received aid; of those 99% had need fully met. ***Average percent of need met:*** 43% (excluding resources awarded to replace EFC). ***Average financial aid package:*** $5027 (excluding resources awarded to replace EFC). 1% of all full-time undergraduates had no need and received non-need-based gift aid.

GIFT AID (NEED-BASED) *Total amount:* $1,036,546 (71% federal, 24% institutional, 5% external sources). ***Receiving aid:*** Freshmen: 46% (47); all full-time undergraduates: 50% (147). ***Average award:*** Freshmen: $5063; Undergraduates: $4143. ***Scholarships, grants, and awards:*** Federal Pell, FSEOG, state, private, college/university gift aid from institutional funds.

GIFT AID (NON-NEED-BASED) *Total amount:* $14,725 (25% federal, 28% institutional, 47% external sources). ***Receiving aid:*** Freshmen: 46% (47). Undergraduates: 49% (145). ***Average award:*** Freshmen: $700. Undergraduates: $1358. ***Scholarships, grants, and awards by category:*** *Academic interests/achievement:* area/ethnic studies, biological sciences, business, communication, computer science, education, engineering/technologies, English, foreign languages, general academic interests/achievements, health fields, home economics, humanities, international studies, mathematics, military science, physical sciences, premedicine, social sciences. *Creative arts/performance:* applied art and design, art/fine arts, cinema/film/broadcasting, creative writing, dance, debating, journalism/publications, music, performing arts, theater/drama. *Special characteristics:* children and siblings of alumni, children of faculty/staff, first-generation college students, out-of-state students. ***Tuition waivers:*** Full or partial for employees or children of employees, senior citizens.

LOANS ***Student loans:*** $701,192 (97% need-based, 3% non-need-based). ***Average need-based loan:*** Freshmen: $2154. Undergraduates: $2559. ***Parent loans:*** $17,513 (100% need-based). ***Programs:*** Federal Direct (Subsidized and Unsubsidized Stafford, PLUS), state, college/university.

WORK-STUDY ***Federal work-study:*** Total amount: $8318; 4 jobs averaging $2251.

APPLYING FOR FINANCIAL AID ***Required financial aid form:*** FAFSA. ***Financial aid deadline (priority):*** 1/15. ***Notification date:*** 2/15.

CONTACT Ms. Valerie K. Miller, Director of Financial Aid, Ohio University–Eastern, 020 Chubb Hall, Athens, OH 45701-2979, 740-593-4141 or toll-free 800-648-3331. *Fax:* 740-593-4140. *E-mail:* millerv@ohio.edu.
Website: http://www.eastern.ohiou.edu/.

OHIO UNIVERSITY–LANCASTER

Lancaster, OH

Tuition & fees (OH res): $5674	Average undergraduate aid package: $5139

ABOUT THE INSTITUTION State-supported, coed. ***Awards:*** associate, bachelor's, and master's degrees. 14 undergraduate majors. ***Total enrollment:*** 28,446. Undergraduates: 22,275. Freshmen: 3,993. Federal methodology is used as a basis for awarding need-based institutional aid.

UNDERGRADUATE EXPENSES for 2019–2020 ***Application fee:*** $50. ***Tuition, state resident:*** full-time $5674; part-time $255 per semester hour. ***Tuition, nonresident:*** full-time $8666; part-time $391 per semester hour. Full-time tuition and fees vary according to degree level, location, program, and reciprocity agreements. Part-time tuition and fees vary according to course load, degree level, location, program, and reciprocity agreements. ***Payment plan:*** Guaranteed tuition.

FRESHMAN FINANCIAL AID (Fall 2019, est.) 195 applied for aid; of those 73% were deemed to have need. 100% of freshmen with need received aid; of those 97% had need fully met. ***Average percent of need met:*** 42% (excluding resources awarded to replace EFC). ***Average financial aid package:*** $4825 (excluding resources awarded to replace EFC).

UNDERGRADUATE FINANCIAL AID (Fall 2019, est.) 601 applied for aid; of those 80% were deemed to have need. 100% of undergraduates with need received aid; of those 98% had need fully met. ***Average percent of need met:*** 38% (excluding resources awarded to replace EFC). ***Average financial aid package:*** $5139 (excluding resources awarded to replace EFC). 1% of all full-time undergraduates had no need and received non-need-based gift aid.

GIFT AID (NEED-BASED) ***Total amount:*** $2,838,894 (78% federal, 1% state, 17% institutional, 4% external sources). ***Receiving aid:*** Freshmen: 43% (121); all full-time undergraduates: 44% (389). ***Average award:*** Freshmen: $4393; Undergraduates: $4084. ***Scholarships, grants, and awards:*** Federal Pell, FSEOG, state, private, college/university gift aid from institutional funds.

GIFT AID (NON-NEED-BASED) ***Total amount:*** $30,994 (12% federal, 51% state, 18% institutional, 19% external sources). ***Receiving aid:*** Freshmen: 43% (121). Undergraduates: 45% (391). ***Average award:*** Undergraduates: $2300. ***Scholarships, grants, and awards by category:*** *Academic interests/achievement:* area/ethnic studies, biological sciences, business, communication, computer science, education, engineering/technologies, English, foreign languages, general academic interests/achievements, health fields, home economics, humanities, international studies, mathematics, military science, physical sciences, premedicine, social sciences. *Creative arts/performance:* applied art and design, art/fine arts, cinema/film/broadcasting, creative writing, dance, debating, journalism/publications, music, performing arts, theater/drama. *Special characteristics:* children and siblings of alumni, children of faculty/staff, first-generation college students, out-of-state students. ***Tuition waivers:*** Full or partial for employees or children of employees, senior citizens. ***ROTC:*** Army cooperative, Air Force cooperative.

LOANS ***Student loans:*** $2,723,065 (93% need-based, 7% non-need-based). ***Average need-based loan:*** Freshmen: $2176. Undergraduates: $2706. ***Parent loans:*** $64,355 (45% need-based, 55% non-need-based). ***Programs:*** Federal Direct (Subsidized and Unsubsidized Stafford, PLUS), state, college/university.

WORK-STUDY ***Federal work-study:*** Total amount: $21,812; 12 jobs averaging $1922.

APPLYING FOR FINANCIAL AID ***Required financial aid form:*** FAFSA. ***Financial aid deadline (priority):*** 1/15. ***Notification date:*** 2/15.

CONTACT Ms. Valerie K. Miller, Director of Financial Aid, Ohio University–Lancaster, 020 Chubb Hall, Athens, OH 45701-2979, 740-593-4141 or toll-free 888-446-4468. *Fax:* 740-593-4140. *E-mail:* millerv@ohio.edu.
Website: http://www.ohiou.edu/lancaster/.

OHIO UNIVERSITY–SOUTHERN CAMPUS

Ironton, OH

Tuition & fees (OH res): $5674	Average undergraduate aid package: $5023

ABOUT THE INSTITUTION State-supported, coed. ***Awards:*** associate, bachelor's, and master's degrees. 17 undergraduate majors. ***Total enrollment:*** 28,446. Undergraduates: 22,275. Freshmen: 3,993. Federal methodology is used as a basis for awarding need-based institutional aid.

UNDERGRADUATE EXPENSES for 2019–2020 ***Application fee:*** $50. ***Tuition, state resident:*** full-time $5674; part-time $255 per semester hour. ***Tuition, nonresident:*** full-time $8666; part-time $391 per semester hour. Full-time tuition and fees vary according to degree level, location, program, and reciprocity agreements. Part-time tuition and fees vary according to course load, degree level, location, program, and reciprocity agreements. ***Payment plan:*** Guaranteed tuition.

FRESHMAN FINANCIAL AID (Fall 2019, est.) 138 applied for aid; of those 83% were deemed to have need. 100% of freshmen with need received aid; of those 97% had need fully met. ***Average percent of need met:*** 44% (excluding resources awarded to replace EFC). ***Average financial aid package:*** $4729 (excluding resources awarded to replace EFC). 1% of all full-time freshmen had no need and received non-need-based gift aid.

UNDERGRADUATE FINANCIAL AID (Fall 2019, est.) 564 applied for aid; of those 88% were deemed to have need. 100% of undergraduates with need received aid; of those 97% had need fully met. ***Average percent of need met:*** 40% (excluding resources awarded to replace EFC). ***Average financial aid package:*** $5023 (excluding resources awarded to replace EFC). 2% of all full-time undergraduates had no need and received non-need-based gift aid.

GIFT AID (NEED-BASED) ***Total amount:*** $3,106,636 (77% federal, 21% institutional, 2% external sources). ***Receiving aid:*** Freshmen: 62% (109); all full-time undergraduates: 61% (433). ***Average award:*** Freshmen: $3933; Undergraduates: $3746. ***Scholarships, grants, and awards:*** Federal Pell, FSEOG, state, private, college/university gift aid from institutional funds.

GIFT AID (NON-NEED-BASED) ***Total amount:*** $65,519 (7% federal, 8% state, 54% institutional, 31% external sources). ***Receiving aid:*** Freshmen: 60% (106). Undergraduates: 60% (430). ***Average award:*** Freshmen: $1918. Undergraduates: $1169. ***Scholarships, grants, and awards by category:*** *Academic interests/achievement:* area/ethnic studies, biological sciences, business, communication, computer science, education, engineering/technologies, English, foreign languages, general academic interests/achievements, health fields, home economics, humanities, international studies, mathematics, military science, physical sciences, premedicine, social sciences. *Creative arts/performance:* applied art and design, art/fine arts, cinema/film/broadcasting, creative writing, dance, debating, journalism/publications, music, performing arts, theater/drama. *Special characteristics:* children and siblings of alumni, children of faculty/staff, first-generation college students, out-of-state students. ***Tuition waivers:*** Full or partial for children of alumni, employees or children of employees, senior citizens. ***ROTC:*** Army, Air Force.

LOANS ***Student loans:*** $2,765,707 (94% need-based, 6% non-need-based). ***Average need-based loan:*** Freshmen: $2108. Undergraduates: $2419. ***Parent loans:*** $50,130 (31% need-based, 69% non-need-based). ***Programs:*** Federal Direct (Subsidized and Unsubsidized Stafford, PLUS), state, college/university.

WORK-STUDY ***Federal work-study:*** Total amount: $31,932; 15 jobs averaging $2063.

APPLYING FOR FINANCIAL AID ***Required financial aid form:*** FAFSA. ***Financial aid deadline (priority):*** 1/15. ***Notification date:*** 2/15.

CONTACT Ms. Valerie K. Miller, Director of Financial Aid, Ohio University–Southern Campus, 020 Chubb Hall, Athens, OH 45701-2979, 740-593-4141 or toll-free 800-626-0513. *Fax:* 740-593-4140. *E-mail:* millerv@ohio.edu.
Website: http://www.ohiou.edu/.

OHIO UNIVERSITY–ZANESVILLE

Zanesville, OH

Tuition & fees (OH res): $5674 **Average undergraduate aid package: $5439**

ABOUT THE INSTITUTION State-supported, coed. ***Awards:*** associate and bachelor's degrees (offers first 2 years of most bachelor's degree programs available at the main campus in Athens; also offers several bachelor's degree programs that can be completed at this campus; also offers some graduate courses). 5 undergraduate majors. ***Total enrollment:*** 28,446. Undergraduates: 22,275. Freshmen: 3,993. Federal methodology is used as a basis for awarding need-based institutional aid.

UNDERGRADUATE EXPENSES for 2019–2020 ***Application fee:*** $50. ***Tuition, state resident:*** full-time $5674; part-time $255 per semester hour. ***Tuition, nonresident:*** full-time $8666; part-time $391 per semester hour. Full-time tuition and fees vary according to degree level, location, program, and reciprocity agreements. Part-time tuition and fees vary according to course load, degree level, location, program, and reciprocity agreements. ***Payment plan:*** Guaranteed tuition.

FRESHMAN FINANCIAL AID (Fall 2019, est.) 112 applied for aid; of those 76% were deemed to have need. 100% of freshmen with need received aid; of those 100% had need fully met. ***Average percent of need met:*** 48% (excluding resources awarded to replace EFC). ***Average financial aid package:*** $5469 (excluding resources awarded to replace EFC). 2% of all full-time freshmen had no need and received non-need-based gift aid.

UNDERGRADUATE FINANCIAL AID (Fall 2019, est.) 529 applied for aid; of those 81% were deemed to have need. 100% of undergraduates with need received aid; of those 99% had need fully met. ***Average percent of need met:*** 43% (excluding resources awarded to replace EFC). ***Average financial aid package:*** $5439 (excluding resources awarded to replace EFC). 2% of all full-time undergraduates had no need and received non-need-based gift aid.

GIFT AID (NEED-BASED) ***Total amount:*** $2,373,458 (77% federal, 18% institutional, 5% external sources). ***Receiving aid:*** Freshmen: 46% (73); all full-time undergraduates: 53% (360). ***Average award:*** Freshmen: $4642; Undergraduates: $4300. ***Scholarships, grants, and awards:*** Federal Pell, FSEOG, state, private, college/university gift aid from institutional funds.

GIFT AID (NON-NEED-BASED) ***Total amount:*** $53,192 (72% institutional, 28% external sources). ***Receiving aid:*** Freshmen: 46% (73). Undergraduates: 54% (362). ***Average award:*** Freshmen: $4616. Undergraduates: $2390. ***Scholarships, grants, and awards by category:*** *Academic interests/achievement:* area/ethnic studies, biological sciences, business, communication, computer science, education, engineering/technologies, English, foreign languages, general academic interests/achievements, health fields, home economics, humanities, international studies, mathematics, military science, physical sciences, premedicine, social sciences. *Creative arts/performance:* applied art and design, art/fine arts, cinema/film/broadcasting, creative writing, dance, debating, journalism/publications, music, performing arts, theater/drama. *Special characteristics:* children and siblings of alumni, children of faculty/staff, first-generation college students, out-of-state students. ***Tuition waivers:*** Full or partial for employees or children of employees, senior citizens. ***ROTC:*** Army, Air Force.

LOANS ***Student loans:*** $2,436,368 (93% need-based, 7% non-need-based). ***Average need-based loan:*** Freshmen: $2468. Undergraduates: $2731. ***Parent loans:*** $75,064 (26% need-based, 74% non-need-based). ***Programs:*** Federal Direct (Subsidized and Unsubsidized Stafford, PLUS), state, college/university.

WORK-STUDY ***Federal work-study:*** Total amount: $7202; 3 jobs averaging $1403.

APPLYING FOR FINANCIAL AID ***Required financial aid form:*** FAFSA. ***Financial aid deadline (priority):*** 1/15. ***Notification date:*** 2/15.

CONTACT Ms. Valerie K. Miller, Director of Financial Aid, Ohio University–Zanesville, 020 Chubb Hall, Athens, OH 45701-2979, 740-593-4141. *Fax:* 740-593-4140. *E-mail:* millerv@ohio.edu.

Website: http://www.ohio.edu/zanesville/.

OHIO VALLEY UNIVERSITY

Vienna, WV

Tuition & fees: N/R **Average undergraduate aid package: $16,224**

ABOUT THE INSTITUTION Independent Church of Christ, coed. ***Awards:*** certificates, associate, bachelor's, and master's degrees. 16 undergraduate majors. ***Total enrollment:*** 318. Undergraduates: 304. Freshmen: 58. Federal methodology is used as a basis for awarding need-based institutional aid.

FRESHMAN FINANCIAL AID (Fall 2018) 72 applied for aid; of those 79% were deemed to have need. 81% of freshmen with need received aid; of those 15% had need fully met. ***Average percent of need met:*** 50% (excluding resources awarded to replace EFC). ***Average financial aid package:*** $14,439 (excluding resources awarded to replace EFC). 39% of all full-time freshmen had no need and received non-need-based gift aid.

UNDERGRADUATE FINANCIAL AID (Fall 2018) 346 applied for aid; of those 88% were deemed to have need. 93% of undergraduates with need received aid; of those 17% had need fully met. ***Average percent of need met:*** 59% (excluding resources awarded to replace EFC). ***Average financial aid package:*** $16,224 (excluding resources awarded to replace EFC). 19% of all full-time undergraduates had no need and received non-need-based gift aid.

GIFT AID (NEED-BASED) ***Total amount:*** $2,281,461 (35% federal, 8% state, 55% institutional, 2% external sources). ***Receiving aid:*** Freshmen: 39% (44); all full-time undergraduates: 67% (277). ***Average award:*** Freshmen: $12,871; Undergraduates: $13,295. ***Scholarships, grants, and awards:*** Federal Pell, FSEOG, state, private, college/university gift aid from institutional funds.

GIFT AID (NON-NEED-BASED) ***Total amount:*** $566,829 (10% state, 87% institutional, 3% external sources). ***Receiving aid:*** Freshmen: 5% (6). Undergraduates: 10% (43). ***Average award:*** Freshmen: $4637. Undergraduates: $5492. ***Scholarships, grants, and awards by category:*** *Academic interests/achievement:* business, computer science, education, English, general academic interests/achievements, mathematics, religion/biblical studies. *Creative arts/performance:* general creative arts/performance, journalism/publications, music, performing arts, theater/drama. *Special achievements/activities:* community service, general special achievements/activities, leadership, religious involvement. *Special characteristics:* adult students, children of faculty/staff, ethnic background, general special characteristics, international students, local/state students, relatives of clergy, religious affiliation.

LOANS ***Student loans:*** $1,602,382 (83% need-based, 17% non-need-based). 70% of past graduating class borrowed through all loan programs. *Average indebtedness per student:* $25,815. ***Average need-based loan:*** Freshmen: $2700. Undergraduates: $3691. ***Parent loans:*** $747,807 (55% need-based, 45% non-need-based). ***Programs:*** Federal Direct (Subsidized and Unsubsidized Stafford, PLUS), Perkins.

WORK-STUDY ***Federal work-study:*** Total amount: $61,604; 50 jobs averaging $1000. ***State or other work-study/employment:*** 10 part-time jobs averaging $1000.

ATHLETIC AWARDS Total amount: $2,800,540 (50% need-based, 50% non-need-based).

APPLYING FOR FINANCIAL AID ***Required financial aid forms:*** FAFSA, noncustodial (divorced/separated) parent's statement. ***Financial aid deadline (priority):*** 3/1. ***Notification date:*** Continuous beginning 1/1.

CONTACT Mrs. Amanda Doak, Financial Aid Officer, Ohio Valley University, 1 Campus View Drive, Vienna, WV 26105-8000, 304-865-6076 or toll-free 877-446-8668. *Fax:* 304-865-6001. *E-mail:* amanda.doak@ovu.edu.

Website: http://www.ovu.edu/.

OHIO WESLEYAN UNIVERSITY

Delaware, OH

Tuition & fees: $47,130 **Average undergraduate aid package: $38,663**

ABOUT THE INSTITUTION Independent United Methodist, coed. ***Awards:*** bachelor's degrees. 87 undergraduate majors. ***Total enrollment:*** 1,494. Undergraduates: 1,494. Freshmen: 389. Federal methodology is used as a basis for awarding need-based institutional aid.

UNDERGRADUATE EXPENSES for 2019–2020 ***Comprehensive fee:*** $60,460 includes full-time tuition ($46,870), mandatory fees ($260), and room and board ($13,330). ***College room only:*** $7000. Full-time tuition and fees vary according to course load. Room and board charges vary according to board plan and housing facility. ***Part-time tuition:*** $5090 per course. Part-time tuition and fees vary according to course load.

FRESHMAN FINANCIAL AID (Fall 2018) 409 applied for aid; of those 90% were deemed to have need. 100% of freshmen with need received aid; of those 19% had need fully met. ***Average percent of need met:*** 80% (excluding resources awarded to replace EFC). ***Average financial aid package:*** $37,739 (excluding resources awarded to replace EFC). 23% of all full-time freshmen had no need and received non-need-based gift aid.

UNDERGRADUATE FINANCIAL AID (Fall 2018) 1,232 applied for aid; of those 92% were deemed to have need. 100% of undergraduates with need received aid; of those 17% had need fully met. ***Average percent of need met:*** 81% (excluding resources awarded to replace EFC). ***Average financial aid package:*** $38,663 (excluding resources awarded to replace EFC). 26% of all full-time undergraduates had no need and received non-need-based gift aid.

GIFT AID (NEED-BASED) ***Total amount:*** $37,312,725 (7% federal, 2% state, 89% institutional, 2% external sources). ***Receiving aid:*** Freshmen: 75% (366); all full-time undergraduates: 73% (1,125). ***Average award:*** Freshmen: $34,049; Undergraduates: $33,958. ***Scholarships, grants, and awards:*** Federal Pell, FSEOG, state, private, college/university gift aid from institutional funds.

GIFT AID (NON-NEED-BASED) ***Total amount:*** $11,701,141 (97% institutional, 3% external sources). ***Receiving aid:*** Freshmen: 12% (58). Undergraduates: 11% (169). ***Average award:*** Freshmen: $27,217. Undergraduates: $24,258. ***Scholarships, grants, and awards by category:*** *Academic interests/achievement:* business, education, general academic interests/achievements. *Creative arts/performance:* applied art and design, art/fine arts, dance, music, performing arts, theater/drama. *Special achievements/activities:* general special achievements/activities, leadership. *Special characteristics:* children and siblings of alumni, international students, local/state students, members of minority groups, relatives of clergy, religious affiliation, twins. ***Tuition waivers:*** Full or partial for employees or children of employees. ***ROTC:*** Army cooperative, Air Force cooperative.

LOANS ***Student loans:*** $9,697,621 (72% need-based, 28% non-need-based). 71% of past graduating class borrowed through all loan programs. *Average indebtedness per student:* $36,680. ***Average need-based loan:*** Freshmen: $3050. Undergraduates: $4259. ***Parent loans:*** $3,716,136 (41% need-based, 59% non-need-based). ***Programs:*** Federal Direct (Subsidized and Unsubsidized Stafford, PLUS), college/university.

WORK-STUDY ***Federal work-study:*** Total amount: $1,303,371; jobs available. ***State or other work-study/employment:*** Total amount: $292,675 (37% need-based, 63% non-need-based). Part-time jobs available.

APPLYING FOR FINANCIAL AID ***Required financial aid form:*** FAFSA. ***Financial aid deadline:*** 2/15 (priority: 12/1). ***Notification date:*** Continuous. Students must reply by 5/1 or within 2 weeks of notification.

CONTACT Mr. Kevin Paskvan, Director of Financial Aid, Ohio Wesleyan University, 61 South Sandusky Street, Delaware, OH 43015, 740-368-3050 or toll-free 800-922-8953. *Fax:* 740-368-3066. *E-mail:* financialaid@owu.edu.
Website: http://www.owu.edu/.

OHR HAMEIR THEOLOGICAL SEMINARY

Cortlandt Manor, NY

CONTACT Financial Aid Office, Ohr Hameir Theological Seminary, Furnace Woods Road, Peekskill, NY 10566, 914-736-1500.
Website: http://www.ohrhameir.com/.

OHR SOMAYACH/JOSEPH TANENBAUM EDUCATIONAL CENTER

Monsey, NY

CONTACT Financial Aid Office, Ohr Somayach/Joseph Tanenbaum Educational Center, PO Box 334244, Route 306, Monsey, NY 10952-0334, 914-425-1370.
Website: http://ohr.edu/.

OKLAHOMA BAPTIST UNIVERSITY

Shawnee, OK

Tuition & fees: $31,352	Average undergraduate aid package: $21,528

ABOUT THE INSTITUTION Independent Southern Baptist, coed. ***Awards:*** associate, bachelor's, and master's degrees. 68 undergraduate majors. ***Total enrollment:*** 1,856. Undergraduates: 1,759. Freshmen: 448. Federal methodology is used as a basis for awarding need-based institutional aid.

UNDERGRADUATE EXPENSES for 2020–2021 ***Comprehensive fee:*** $39,072 includes full-time tuition ($27,912), mandatory fees ($3440), and room and board ($7720). ***College room only:*** $3470. Room and board charges vary according to board plan and housing facility. ***Part-time tuition:*** $907 per credit hour. ***Part-time fees:*** $3440 per term. Part-time tuition and fees vary according to course load.

FRESHMAN FINANCIAL AID (Fall 2019, est.) 417 applied for aid; of those 90% were deemed to have need. 100% of freshmen with need received aid; of those 5% had need fully met. ***Average percent of need met:*** 54% (excluding resources awarded to replace EFC). ***Average financial aid package:*** $20,421 (excluding resources awarded to replace EFC). 16% of all full-time freshmen had no need and received non-need-based gift aid.

UNDERGRADUATE FINANCIAL AID (Fall 2019, est.) 1,390 applied for aid; of those 90% were deemed to have need. 100% of undergraduates with need received aid; of those 4% had need fully met. ***Average percent of need met:*** 55% (excluding resources awarded to replace EFC). ***Average financial aid package:*** $21,528 (excluding resources awarded to replace EFC). 23% of all full-time undergraduates had no need and received non-need-based gift aid.

GIFT AID (NEED-BASED) ***Receiving aid:*** Freshmen: 68% (307); all full-time undergraduates: 62% (1,051). ***Average award:*** Freshmen: $8953; Undergraduates: $9444. ***Scholarships, grants, and awards:*** Federal Pell, FSEOG, state, private, college/university gift aid from institutional funds, TEACH Grants.

GIFT AID (NON-NEED-BASED) ***Receiving aid:*** Freshmen: 83% (374). Undergraduates: 72% (1,228). ***Average award:*** Freshmen: $9395. Undergraduates: $9696. ***Scholarships, grants, and awards by category:*** *Academic interests/achievement:* biological sciences, business, computer science, education, English, foreign languages, general academic interests/achievements, home economics, humanities, mathematics, physical sciences, premedicine, religion/biblical studies, social sciences. *Creative arts/performance:* applied art and design, art/fine arts, debating, music, performing arts, theater/drama. *Special achievements/activities:* cheerleading/drum major, leadership, religious involvement. *Special characteristics:* adult students, children and siblings of alumni, children of faculty/staff, general special characteristics, international students, local/state students, members of minority groups, out-of-state students, relatives of clergy, religious affiliation, veterans. ***Tuition waivers:*** Full or partial for employees or children of employees. ***ROTC:*** Air Force cooperative.

LOANS ***Student loans:*** 65% of past graduating class borrowed through all loan programs. *Average indebtedness per student:* $25,673. ***Average need-based loan:*** Freshmen: $3109. Undergraduates: $4147. ***Programs:*** Federal Direct (Subsidized and Unsubsidized Stafford, PLUS).

WORK-STUDY ***Federal work-study:*** 145 jobs averaging $789. ***State or other work-study/employment:*** Part-time jobs available.

APPLYING FOR FINANCIAL AID ***Required financial aid form:*** FAFSA. ***Financial aid deadline:*** Continuous. ***Notification date:*** Continuous. Students must reply within 2 weeks of notification.

CONTACT Jonna Raney, Director of Student Financial Services, Oklahoma Baptist University, 500 West University, Shawnee, OK 74804, 405-585-5020 or toll-free 800-654-3285. *Fax:* 405-585-5030. *E-mail:* jonna.raney@okbu.edu.
Website: http://www.okbu.edu/.

OKLAHOMA CHRISTIAN UNIVERSITY

Oklahoma City, OK

ABOUT THE INSTITUTION Independent Church of Christ, coed. ***Awards:*** certificates, bachelor's, and master's degrees. 61 undergraduate majors. ***Total enrollment:*** 2,248. Undergraduates: 1,905. Freshmen: 454.

GIFT AID (NEED-BASED) ***Scholarships, grants, and awards:*** Federal Pell, FSEOG, state, private, college/university gift aid from institutional funds.

GIFT AID (NON-NEED-BASED) ***Scholarships, grants, and awards by category:*** *Academic interests/achievement:* engineering/technologies, general academic interests/achievements, religion/biblical studies. *Creative arts/performance:* art/fine arts, journalism/publications, music, theater/drama. *Special achievements/activities:* leadership. *Special characteristics:* children of educators, children of faculty/staff, international students, relatives of clergy, religious affiliation, veterans, veterans' children.

LOANS ***Programs:*** Federal Direct (Subsidized and Unsubsidized Stafford, PLUS), Perkins.

CONTACT Clint LaRue, Director of Financial Services, Oklahoma Christian University, Box 11000, Oklahoma City, OK 73136-1100, 405-425-5190 or toll-free 800-877-5010. *Fax:* 405-425-5197. *E-mail:* clint.larue@oc.edu.
Website: http://www.oc.edu/.

OKLAHOMA CITY UNIVERSITY

Oklahoma City, OK

Tuition & fees: $32,594	Average undergraduate aid package: $22,070

ABOUT THE INSTITUTION Independent United Methodist, coed. ***Awards:*** bachelor's, master's, and doctoral degrees. 69 undergraduate majors. Federal methodology is used as a basis for awarding need-based institutional aid.

UNDERGRADUATE EXPENSES for 2019–2020 ***One-time required fee:*** $360. ***Comprehensive fee:*** $41,830 includes full-time tuition ($28,094), mandatory fees ($4500), and room and board ($9236). ***College room only:*** $4200. Full-time tuition and fees vary according to course load. Room and board charges vary according to board plan, housing facility, and student level. ***Part-time tuition:*** $953 per credit hour. ***Part-time fees:*** $150 per credit hour.

FRESHMAN FINANCIAL AID (Fall 2019, est.) 285 applied for aid; of those 75% were deemed to have need. 99% of freshmen with need received aid; of those 77% had need fully met. ***Average percent of need met:*** 70% (excluding resources awarded to replace EFC). ***Average financial aid package:*** $22,672 (excluding resources awarded to replace EFC). 12% of all full-time freshmen had no need and received non-need-based gift aid.

UNDERGRADUATE FINANCIAL AID (Fall 2019, est.) 1,112 applied for aid; of those 82% were deemed to have need. 99% of undergraduates with need received aid; of those 84% had need fully met. ***Average percent of need met:*** 64% (excluding resources awarded to replace EFC). ***Average financial aid package:*** $22,070 (excluding resources awarded to replace EFC). 22% of all full-time undergraduates had no need and received non-need-based gift aid.

GIFT AID (NEED-BASED) ***Total amount:*** $3,781,634 (47% federal, 15% state, 28% institutional, 10% external sources). ***Receiving aid:*** Freshmen: 65% (211); all full-time undergraduates: 59% (881). ***Average award:*** Freshmen: $20,458; Undergraduates: $19,888. ***Scholarships, grants, and awards:*** Federal Pell, FSEOG, state, private, college/university gift aid from institutional funds, United Negro College Fund, Federal Nursing, Native American Grants.

GIFT AID (NON-NEED-BASED) ***Total amount:*** $839,072 (2% federal, 1% state, 60% institutional, 37% external sources). ***Receiving aid:*** Freshmen: 48% (158). Undergraduates: 44% (657). ***Average award:*** Freshmen: $19,459. Undergraduates: $19,750. ***Scholarships, grants, and awards by category:*** *Academic interests/achievement:* 1,003 awards ($6,658,684 total): business, communication, education, general academic interests/achievements, health fields, religion/biblical studies. *Creative arts/performance:* 549 awards ($5,982,104 total): applied art and design, art/fine arts, dance, debating, music, performing arts, theater/drama. *Special achievements/activities:* 51 awards ($499,083 total): general special achievements/activities, junior miss, leadership, religious involvement. *Special characteristics:* 56 awards ($1,293,900 total): children of faculty/staff, relatives of clergy, religious affiliation. ***Tuition waivers:*** Full or partial for employees or children of employees. ***ROTC:*** Army cooperative, Air Force cooperative.

LOANS ***Student loans:*** $5,247,807 (78% need-based, 22% non-need-based). 60% of past graduating class borrowed through all loan programs. *Average indebtedness per student:* $26,696. ***Average need-based loan:*** Freshmen: $2816. Undergraduates: $3788. ***Parent loans:*** $7,368,632 (50% need-based, 50% non-need-based). ***Programs:*** Federal Direct (Subsidized and Unsubsidized Stafford, PLUS), Perkins, Federal Nursing.

WORK-STUDY ***Federal work-study:*** Total amount: $744,809; 206 jobs averaging $1821. ***State or other work-study/employment:*** Total amount: $321,309 (100% non-need-based). 224 part-time jobs averaging $1434.

ATHLETIC AWARDS Total amount: $4,985,711 (44% need-based, 56% non-need-based).

APPLYING FOR FINANCIAL AID ***Required financial aid form:*** FAFSA. ***Financial aid deadline (priority):*** 3/1. ***Notification date:*** Continuous beginning 1/15. Students must reply within 4 weeks of notification.

CONTACT Kurt Grau, Director of Student Financial Services, Oklahoma City University, 2501 North Blackwelder, Oklahoma City, OK 73106-1493, 405-208-5848 or toll-free 800-633-7242. *Fax:* 405-208-5466. *E-mail:* kmgrau@okcu.edu.
Website: http://www.okcu.edu/.

OKLAHOMA PANHANDLE STATE UNIVERSITY

Goodwell, OK

CONTACT Ms. Lori Ferguson, Director of Financial Aid, Oklahoma Panhandle State University, PO Box 430, Goodwell, OK 73939-0430, 580-349-1582 or toll-free 800-664-6778. *E-mail:* lorif@opsu.edu.
Website: http://www.opsu.edu/.

OKLAHOMA STATE UNIVERSITY

Stillwater, OK

Tuition & fees (OK res): $9019	Average undergraduate aid package: $15,840

ABOUT THE INSTITUTION State-supported, coed. ***Awards:*** certificates, bachelor's, master's, and doctoral degrees. 88 undergraduate majors. ***Total enrollment:*** 24,041. Undergraduates: 20,024. Freshmen: 4,200. Federal methodology is used as a basis for awarding need-based institutional aid.

UNDERGRADUATE EXPENSES for 2019–2020 ***Application fee:*** $40. ***One-time required fee:*** $120. ***Tuition, state resident:*** full-time $5357; part-time $179 per credit hour. ***Tuition, nonresident:*** full-time $20,877; part-time $696 per credit hour. ***Required fees:*** full-time $3662; $122.05 per credit hour. Full-time tuition and fees vary according to program. Part-time tuition and fees vary according to course load and program. ***College room and board:*** $9106; ***Room only:*** $5096. Room and board charges vary according to board plan and housing facility. ***Payment plan:*** Guaranteed tuition.

FRESHMAN FINANCIAL AID (Fall 2018) 3002 applied for aid; of those 67% were deemed to have need. 97% of freshmen with need received aid; of those 15% had need fully met. ***Average percent of need met:*** 77% (excluding resources awarded to replace EFC). ***Average financial aid package:*** $16,237 (excluding resources awarded to replace EFC). 29% of all full-time freshmen had no need and received non-need-based gift aid.

UNDERGRADUATE FINANCIAL AID (Fall 2018) 12,280 applied for aid; of those 78% were deemed to have need. 97% of undergraduates with need received aid; of those 10% had need fully met. ***Average percent of need met:*** 72% (excluding resources awarded to replace EFC). ***Average financial aid package:*** $15,840 (excluding resources awarded to replace EFC). 27% of all full-time undergraduates had no need and received non-need-based gift aid.

GIFT AID (NEED-BASED) ***Receiving aid:*** Freshmen: 44% (1,545); all full-time undergraduates: 40% (7,057). ***Average award:*** Freshmen: $9077; Undergraduates: $8146. ***Scholarships, grants, and awards:*** Federal Pell, FSEOG, state, private, college/university gift aid from institutional funds, TEACH Grants.

GIFT AID (NON-NEED-BASED) ***Receiving aid:*** Freshmen: 5% (187). Undergraduates: 3% (460). ***Average award:*** Freshmen: $7201. Undergraduates: $6615. ***Scholarships, grants, and awards by category:*** *Academic interests/*

achievement: agriculture, architecture, area/ethnic studies, biological sciences, business, communication, computer science, education, engineering/technologies, English, foreign languages, general academic interests/achievements, health fields, home economics, humanities, international studies, mathematics, military science, physical sciences, premedicine, social sciences. *Creative arts/performance:* applied art and design, art/fine arts, cinema/film/broadcasting, creative writing, general creative arts/performance, journalism/publications, music, performing arts, theater/drama. *Special achievements/activities:* cheerleading/drum major, community service, general special achievements/activities, leadership, memberships, rodeo. *Special characteristics:* adult students, children and siblings of alumni, children of educators, children of faculty/staff, ethnic background, first-generation college students, general special characteristics, handicapped students, international students, local/state students, out-of-state students, previous college experience. ***Tuition waivers:*** Full or partial for children of alumni, employees or children of employees, senior citizens. ***ROTC:*** Army, Air Force.

LOANS ***Student loans:*** 50% of past graduating class borrowed through all loan programs. *Average indebtedness per student:* $25,185. ***Average need-based loan:*** Freshmen: $3003. Undergraduates: $3945. ***Programs:*** Federal Direct (Subsidized and Unsubsidized Stafford, PLUS).

WORK-STUDY ***Federal work-study:*** 363 jobs averaging $2417. ***State or other work-study/employment:*** 4,827 part-time jobs averaging $3210.

APPLYING FOR FINANCIAL AID ***Required financial aid forms:*** FAFSA, Combined Admissions and Scholarship Application. ***Financial aid deadline:*** Continuous. ***Notification date:*** Continuous. Students must reply within 2 weeks of notification.

CONTACT Financial Aid Office, Oklahoma State University, Oklahoma State University, 119 Student Union, Stillwater, OK 74078, 405-744-6604 or toll-free 800-233-5019. *E-mail:* finaid@okstate.edu.
Website: http://www.okstate.edu/.

OKLAHOMA WESLEYAN UNIVERSITY

Bartlesville, OK

CONTACT Mrs. Kandi Lyn Molder, Director of Student Financial Services, Oklahoma Wesleyan University, 2201 Silver Lake Road, Bartlesville, OK 74006, 918-335-6282 or toll-free 866-222-8226. *Fax:* 918-335-6811. *E-mail:* financialaid@okwu.edu.
Website: http://www.okwu.edu/.

OLD DOMINION UNIVERSITY

Norfolk, VA

Tuition & fees (VA res): $11,020	Average undergraduate aid package: $11,108

ABOUT THE INSTITUTION State-supported, coed. ***Awards:*** certificates, bachelor's, master's, and doctoral degrees. 57 undergraduate majors. ***Total enrollment:*** 23,675. Undergraduates: 19,176. Freshmen: 3,145. Federal methodology is used as a basis for awarding need-based institutional aid.

UNDERGRADUATE EXPENSES for 2019–2020 ***Application fee:*** $50. ***Tuition, state resident:*** full-time $10,680; part-time $356 per credit hour. ***Tuition, nonresident:*** full-time $30,840; part-time $1028 per credit hour. ***Required fees:*** full-time $340; $70 per term. Full-time tuition and fees vary according to location. Part-time tuition and fees vary according to location. ***College room and board:*** $12,836; ***Room only:*** $7538. Room and board charges vary according to board plan, housing facility, location, and student level.

FRESHMAN FINANCIAL AID (Fall 2019, est.) 2829 applied for aid; of those 83% were deemed to have need. 97% of freshmen with need received aid; of those 18% had need fully met. ***Average percent of need met:*** 41% (excluding resources awarded to replace EFC). ***Average financial aid package:*** $11,508 (excluding resources awarded to replace EFC). 10% of all full-time freshmen had no need and received non-need-based gift aid.

UNDERGRADUATE FINANCIAL AID (Fall 2019, est.) 11,796 applied for aid; of those 84% were deemed to have need. 96% of undergraduates with need received aid; of those 13% had need fully met. ***Average percent of need met:*** 44% (excluding resources awarded to replace EFC). ***Average financial aid package:*** $11,108 (excluding resources awarded to replace EFC). 7% of all full-time undergraduates had no need and received non-need-based gift aid.

GIFT AID (NEED-BASED) ***Total amount:*** $65,528,048 (54% federal, 36% state, 10% institutional). ***Receiving aid:*** Freshmen: 57% (1,765); all full-time undergraduates: 52% (7,673). ***Average award:*** Freshmen: $8522; Undergraduates: $7747. ***Scholarships, grants, and awards:*** Federal Pell, FSEOG, state, private, college/university gift aid from institutional funds, United Negro College Fund, Federal Nursing.

GIFT AID (NON-NEED-BASED) ***Total amount:*** $15,790,306 (14% state, 71% institutional, 15% external sources). ***Receiving aid:*** Freshmen: 27% (854). Undergraduates: 15% (2,187). ***Average award:*** Freshmen: $5730. Undergraduates: $5392. ***Scholarships, grants, and awards by category:*** *Academic interests/achievement:* area/ethnic studies, biological sciences, business, communication, computer science, education, engineering/technologies, English, foreign languages, general academic interests/achievements, home economics, humanities, international studies, library science, mathematics, military science, physical sciences, social sciences. *Creative arts/performance:* applied art and design, art/fine arts, cinema/film/broadcasting, creative writing, dance, general creative arts/performance, journalism/publications, music, performing arts, theater/drama. *Special achievements/activities:* cheerleading/drum major, community service, leadership, memberships. *Special characteristics:* children of faculty/staff, international students, local/state students, previous college experience. ***Tuition waivers:*** Full or partial for employees or children of employees, senior citizens. ***ROTC:*** Army, Naval.

LOANS ***Student loans:*** $88,441,035 (41% need-based, 59% non-need-based). 73% of past graduating class borrowed through all loan programs. *Average indebtedness per student:* $31,142. ***Average need-based loan:*** Freshmen: $3399. Undergraduates: $4206. ***Parent loans:*** $20,615,706 (100% non-need-based). ***Programs:*** Federal Direct (Subsidized and Unsubsidized Stafford, PLUS), Perkins, Federal Nursing, college/university.

WORK-STUDY ***Federal work-study:*** Total amount: $2,111,231; jobs available.

ATHLETIC AWARDS Total amount: $7,305,570 (100% non-need-based).

APPLYING FOR FINANCIAL AID ***Required financial aid form:*** FAFSA. ***Financial aid deadline:*** 3/15 (priority: 1/1). ***Notification date:*** Continuous beginning 3/1. Students must reply within 2 weeks of notification.

CONTACT Office of Financial Aid, Old Dominion University, 2000 Rollins Hall, Norfolk, VA 23529, 757-683-3683, or toll-free 800-348-7926. *Fax:* 757-683-5920. *E-mail:* finaid@odu.edu.
Website: http://www.odu.edu/.

OLIVET COLLEGE

Olivet, MI

Tuition & fees: $28,692	Average undergraduate aid package: $19,240

ABOUT THE INSTITUTION Independent Congregational Christian Church, coed. ***Awards:*** bachelor's and master's degrees. 34 undergraduate majors. ***Total enrollment:*** 1,078. Undergraduates: 1,045. Freshmen: 351. Federal methodology is used as a basis for awarding need-based institutional aid.

UNDERGRADUATE EXPENSES for 2019–2020 ***Application fee:*** $25. ***Comprehensive fee:*** $38,792 includes full-time tuition ($27,700), mandatory fees ($992), and room and board ($10,100).

FRESHMAN FINANCIAL AID (Fall 2018) 300 applied for aid; of those 100% were deemed to have need. 100% of freshmen with need received aid; of those 14% had need fully met. ***Average percent of need met:*** 80% (excluding resources awarded to replace EFC). ***Average financial aid package:*** $20,150 (excluding resources awarded to replace EFC). 14% of all full-time freshmen had no need and received non-need-based gift aid.

UNDERGRADUATE FINANCIAL AID (Fall 2018) 984 applied for aid; of those 89% were deemed to have need. 100% of undergraduates with need received aid; of those 18% had need fully met. ***Average percent of need met:*** 80% (excluding resources awarded to replace EFC). ***Average financial aid package:*** $19,240 (excluding resources awarded to replace EFC). 10% of all full-time undergraduates had no need and received non-need-based gift aid.

GIFT AID (NEED-BASED) ***Total amount:*** $16,962,929 (17% federal, 8% state, 72% institutional, 3% external sources). ***Receiving aid:*** Freshmen: 98% (296); all full-time undergraduates: 83% (840). ***Average award:*** Freshmen: $17,500; Undergraduates: $15,700. ***Scholarships, grants, and awards:*** Federal Pell, FSEOG, state, private, college/university gift aid from institutional funds.

GIFT AID (NON-NEED-BASED) ***Total amount:*** $1,709,638 (99% institutional, 1% external sources). ***Receiving aid:*** Freshmen: 14% (43). Undergraduates: 7% (69). ***Average award:*** Freshmen: $16,200. Undergraduates: $14,225. ***Scholarships, grants, and awards by category:*** *Academic interests/achievement:* 994 awards ($9,250,300 total): business, communication, education, English, foreign languages, general academic interests/achievements. *Creative arts/performance:* 83 awards ($475,535 total): applied art and design, journalism/publications, music. *Special achievements/activities:* 40 awards ($88,030 total): cheerleading/drum major, community service, leadership, memberships. *Special characteristics:* 86 awards ($628,854 total): children and siblings of alumni, children of faculty/staff, international students, religious affiliation, siblings of current students. ***ROTC:*** Air Force cooperative.

LOANS ***Student loans:*** $7,568,242 (63% need-based, 37% non-need-based). 87% of past graduating class borrowed through all loan programs. *Average indebtedness per student:* $26,872. ***Average need-based loan:*** Freshmen: $3655. Undergraduates: $5342. ***Parent loans:*** $3,125,827 (38% need-based, 62% non-need-based). ***Programs:*** Federal Direct (Subsidized and Unsubsidized Stafford, PLUS), Perkins, alternative loans, CitiAssist Loans, Sallie Mae Smart Option Loans.

WORK-STUDY ***Federal work-study:*** Total amount: $178,004; 184 jobs averaging $967.

APPLYING FOR FINANCIAL AID ***Required financial aid form:*** FAFSA. ***Financial aid deadline:*** Continuous. ***Notification date:*** Continuous beginning 3/1.

CONTACT Ms. Libby M. Jean, Director of Student Services, Olivet College, 320 South Main Street, Olivet, MI 49076-9701, 269-749-7655 or toll-free 800-456-7189. *Fax:* 269-749-3821. *E-mail:* ljean@olivetcollege.edu.
Website: http://www.olivetcollege.edu/.

OLIVET NAZARENE UNIVERSITY

Bourbonnais, IL

Tuition & fees: $36,950	Average undergraduate aid package: $31,466

ABOUT THE INSTITUTION Independent Church of the Nazarene, coed. ***Awards:*** bachelor's, master's, and doctoral degrees. 70 undergraduate majors. ***Total enrollment:*** 4,317. Undergraduates: 3,110. Freshmen: 696. Federal methodology is used as a basis for awarding need-based institutional aid.

UNDERGRADUATE EXPENSES for 2020–2021 ***Application fee:*** $25. ***Comprehensive fee:*** $45,940 includes full-time tuition ($35,960), mandatory fees ($990), and room and board ($8990). Room and board charges vary according to board plan. ***Part-time tuition:*** $1500 per semester hour. Part-time tuition and fees vary according to course load.

FRESHMAN FINANCIAL AID (Fall 2019, est.) 675 applied for aid; of those 91% were deemed to have need. 100% of freshmen with need received aid; of those 20% had need fully met. ***Average percent of need met:*** 84% (excluding resources awarded to replace EFC). ***Average financial aid package:*** $32,721 (excluding resources awarded to replace EFC). 11% of all full-time freshmen had no need and received non-need-based gift aid.

UNDERGRADUATE FINANCIAL AID (Fall 2019, est.) 2,477 applied for aid; of those 91% were deemed to have need. 100% of undergraduates with need received aid; of those 25% had need fully met. ***Average percent of need met:*** 85% (excluding resources awarded to replace EFC). ***Average financial aid package:*** $31,466 (excluding resources awarded to replace EFC). 18% of all full-time undergraduates had no need and received non-need-based gift aid.

GIFT AID (NEED-BASED) ***Total amount:*** $58,991,638 (9% federal, 7% state, 83% institutional, 1% external sources). ***Receiving aid:*** Freshmen: 89% (617); all full-time undergraduates: 82% (2,243). ***Average award:*** Freshmen: $28,222; Undergraduates: $26,205. ***Scholarships, grants, and awards:*** Federal Pell, FSEOG, state, private, college/university gift aid from institutional funds.

GIFT AID (NON-NEED-BASED) ***Total amount:*** $15,645,201 (7% federal, 91% institutional, 2% external sources). ***Receiving aid:*** Freshmen: 16% (111). Undergraduates: 16% (435). ***Average award:*** Freshmen: $19,467. Undergraduates: $17,587. ***Scholarships, grants, and awards by category:*** *Academic interests/achievement:* general academic interests/achievements, military science. *Creative arts/performance:* applied art and design, music, performing arts, theater/drama. *Special achievements/activities:* cheerleading/drum major. *Special characteristics:* children of faculty/staff, general special characteristics, relatives of clergy, religious affiliation, veterans. ***Tuition waivers:*** Full or partial for employees or children of employees. ***ROTC:*** Army.

LOANS ***Student loans:*** $17,041,349 (65% need-based, 35% non-need-based). 82% of past graduating class borrowed through all loan programs. *Average indebtedness per student:* $31,640. ***Average need-based loan:*** Freshmen: $3396. Undergraduates: $4237. ***Parent loans:*** $5,671,603 (35% need-based, 65% non-need-based). ***Programs:*** Federal Direct (Subsidized and Unsubsidized Stafford, PLUS).

WORK-STUDY ***Federal work-study:*** Total amount: $651,945; jobs available. ***State or other work-study/employment:*** Total amount: $794,635 (26% need-based, 74% non-need-based). Part-time jobs available.

ATHLETIC AWARDS Total amount: $4,116,715 (41% need-based, 59% non-need-based).

APPLYING FOR FINANCIAL AID ***Required financial aid form:*** FAFSA. ***Financial aid deadline:*** Continuous. ***Notification date:*** Continuous beginning 11/1. Students must reply by 5/1.

CONTACT Mr. Greg Bruner, Director of Financial Aid, Olivet Nazarene University, One University Avenue, Bourbonnais, IL 60914, 815-939-5249 or toll-free 800-648-1463. *Fax:* 815-939-5074. *E-mail:* gbruner@olivet.edu.
Website: http://www.olivet.edu/.

O'MORE SCHOOL OF DESIGN AT BELMONT UNIVERSITY

Nashville, TN

CONTACT Sara Martin, Financial Aid Director, O'More School of Design at Belmont University, 423 South Margin Street, Franklin, TN 37064-2816, 615-794-4254 Ext. 226 or toll-free 888-662-1970. *Fax:* 615-790-1662. *E-mail:* financialaid@omorecollege.edu.
Website: http://www.omorecollege.edu/.

ORAL ROBERTS UNIVERSITY

Tulsa, OK

Comprehensive fee: $39,580	Average undergraduate aid package: $30,260

ABOUT THE INSTITUTION Independent interdenominational, coed. ***Awards:*** certificates, diplomas, bachelor's, master's, and doctoral degrees. 75 undergraduate majors. ***Total enrollment:*** 4,042. Undergraduates: 3,460. Freshmen: 555. Federal methodology is used as a basis for awarding need-based institutional aid.

UNDERGRADUATE EXPENSES for 2020–2021 ***Application fee:*** $35. ***Comprehensive fee:*** $39,580 includes mandatory fees ($1230) and room and board ($8650). ***College room only:*** $4050. ***Part-time tuition:*** $1237 per credit hour.

FRESHMAN FINANCIAL AID (Fall 2019, est.) 554 applied for aid; of those 89% were deemed to have need. 100% of freshmen with need received aid; of those 35% had need fully met. ***Average percent of need met:*** 98% (excluding resources awarded to replace EFC). ***Average financial aid package:*** $28,303 (excluding resources awarded to replace EFC). 23% of all full-time freshmen had no need and received non-need-based gift aid.

UNDERGRADUATE FINANCIAL AID (Fall 2019, est.) 1,982 applied for aid; of those 90% were deemed to have need. 100% of undergraduates with need received aid; of those 43% had need fully met. ***Average percent of need met:*** 98% (excluding resources awarded to replace EFC). ***Average financial aid package:*** $30,260 (excluding resources awarded to replace EFC). 27% of all full-time undergraduates had no need and received non-need-based gift aid.

GIFT AID (NEED-BASED) ***Total amount:*** $34,724,110 (15% federal, 4% state, 79% institutional, 2% external sources). ***Receiving aid:*** Freshmen: 75% (493); all full-time undergraduates: 69% (1,764). ***Average award:*** Freshmen: $21,050; Undergraduates: $24,869. ***Scholarships, grants, and awards:*** Federal Pell, FSEOG, state, private, college/university gift aid from institutional funds.

GIFT AID (NON-NEED-BASED) ***Total amount:*** $11,301,357 (97% institutional, 3% external sources). ***Receiving aid:*** Freshmen: 25% (162). Undergraduates: 30% (764). ***Average award:*** Freshmen: $19,438. Undergraduates: $16,351. ***Scholarships, grants, and awards by category:*** *Academic interests/achievement:* 433 awards ($1,894,570 total): biological sciences, business, communication, education, engineering/technologies, general academic interests/achievements, physical sciences, religion/biblical studies. *Creative arts/performance:* 131 awards ($246,350 total): applied art and design, art/fine arts, cinema/film/broadcasting, dance, journalism/publications, music, theater/drama. *Special achievements/activities:* 2,068 awards ($10,708,228 total): cheerleading/drum major, community service, general special achievements/activities, leadership, memberships, religious involvement. *Special characteristics:* 181 awards ($470,531 total): children and siblings of alumni, children of faculty/staff, general special characteristics, international students, relatives of clergy, veterans. ***ROTC:*** Air Force cooperative.

LOANS *Student loans:* $13,683,991 (49% need-based, 51% non-need-based). *Average indebtedness per student:* $35,230. ***Average need-based loan:*** Freshmen: $7126. Undergraduates: $4377. ***Parent loans:*** $8,378,376 (67% need-based, 33% non-need-based). ***Programs:*** Federal Direct (Subsidized and Unsubsidized Stafford, PLUS), college/university.

WORK-STUDY *Federal work-study:* Total amount: $550,327; 977 jobs averaging $3000. ***State or other work-study/employment:*** Total amount: $683,000 (60% need-based, 40% non-need-based). 704 part-time jobs averaging $3000.

ATHLETIC AWARDS Total amount: $4,257,745 (35% need-based, 65% non-need-based).

APPLYING FOR FINANCIAL AID *Required financial aid form:* FAFSA. ***Financial aid deadline:*** Continuous. ***Notification date:*** Continuous beginning 12/1. Students must reply by 5/1.

CONTACT Emily Atkerson, Office of Financial Aid, Oral Roberts University, 7777 South Lewis Avenue, Tulsa, OK 74171, 918-495-6510 or toll-free 800-678-8876. *Fax:* 918-495-6803. *E-mail:* eatkerson@oru.edu.
Website: http://www.oru.edu/.

OREGON HEALTH & SCIENCE UNIVERSITY

Portland, OR

Tuition & fees: N/R	Average undergraduate aid package: $13,145

ABOUT THE INSTITUTION State-related, coed. ***Awards:*** certificates, bachelor's, master's, and doctoral degrees. 2 undergraduate majors. Federal methodology is used as a basis for awarding need-based institutional aid.

UNDERGRADUATE FINANCIAL AID (Fall 2019, est.) 415 applied for aid; of those 93% were deemed to have need. 97% of undergraduates with need received aid; of those 32% had need fully met. ***Average percent of need met:*** 25% (excluding resources awarded to replace EFC). ***Average financial aid package:*** $13,145 (excluding resources awarded to replace EFC).

GIFT AID (NEED-BASED) *Total amount:* $4,580,292 (50% federal, 9% state, 6% institutional, 35% external sources). ***Receiving aid:*** All full-time undergraduates: 52% (233). ***Average award:*** Undergraduates: $14,091. ***Scholarships, grants, and awards:*** Federal Pell, FSEOG, state, private, college/university gift aid from institutional funds.

GIFT AID (NON-NEED-BASED) *Total amount:* $16,496 (100% external sources). ***Receiving aid:*** Undergraduates: 1. ***Scholarships, grants, and awards by category:*** *Academic interests/achievement:* 136 awards ($1,390,157 total): home economics.

LOANS *Student loans:* $10,995,234 (87% need-based, 13% non-need-based). ***Average need-based loan:*** Undergraduates: $4978. ***Parent loans:*** $883,880 (60% need-based, 40% non-need-based). ***Programs:*** Federal Direct (Subsidized and Unsubsidized Stafford, PLUS), Federal Nursing, college/university, alternative loans.

WORK-STUDY *Federal work-study:* Total amount: $22,275; 16 jobs averaging $1392.

CONTACT Jessica Willhite, Administrative Coordinator, Oregon Health & Science University, 3181 SW Sam Jackson Park Road, Mail Code L109, Portland, OR 97239-3089, 503-494-7800. *Fax:* 503-494-4629. *E-mail:* willhitj@ohsu.edu.
Website: http://www.ohsu.edu/.

OREGON INSTITUTE OF TECHNOLOGY

Klamath Falls, OR

Tuition & fees (OR res): $10,485	Average undergraduate aid package: $11,256

ABOUT THE INSTITUTION State-supported, coed. ***Awards:*** certificates, associate, bachelor's, and master's degrees. 33 undergraduate majors. ***Total enrollment:*** 5,490. Undergraduates: 5,383. Freshmen: 334. Both federal and institutional methodology are used as a basis for awarding need-based institutional aid.

UNDERGRADUATE EXPENSES for 2019–2020 *Application fee:* $50. ***Tuition, state resident:*** full-time $8775; part-time $195 per credit hour. ***Tuition, nonresident:*** full-time $27,929; part-time $620 per credit hour. ***Required fees:*** full-time $1710; $636 per term. Full-time tuition and fees vary according to course load, location, program, and reciprocity agreements. Part-time tuition and fees vary according to course load, location, program, and reciprocity agreements. ***College room and board:*** $9133; ***Room only:*** $5278. Room and board charges vary according to board plan and housing facility.

FRESHMAN FINANCIAL AID (Fall 2019, est.) 253 applied for aid; of those 99% were deemed to have need. 100% of freshmen with need received aid; of those 13% had need fully met. ***Average percent of need met:*** 35% (excluding resources awarded to replace EFC). ***Average financial aid package:*** $11,847 (excluding resources awarded to replace EFC). 24% of all full-time freshmen had no need and received non-need-based gift aid.

UNDERGRADUATE FINANCIAL AID (Fall 2019, est.) 1,313 applied for aid; of those 97% were deemed to have need. 100% of undergraduates with need received aid; of those 6% had need fully met. ***Average percent of need met:*** 37% (excluding resources awarded to replace EFC). ***Average financial aid package:*** $11,256 (excluding resources awarded to replace EFC). 9% of all full-time undergraduates had no need and received non-need-based gift aid.

GIFT AID (NEED-BASED) *Receiving aid:* Freshmen: 37% (142); all full-time undergraduates: 39% (775). ***Average award:*** Freshmen: $7681; Undergraduates: $7459. ***Scholarships, grants, and awards:*** Federal Pell, FSEOG, state, private, college/university gift aid from institutional funds.

GIFT AID (NON-NEED-BASED) *Receiving aid:* Freshmen: 56% (211). Undergraduates: 28% (559). ***Average award:*** Freshmen: $2556. Undergraduates: $2159. ***Scholarships, grants, and awards by category:*** *Academic interests/achievement:* general academic interests/achievements. *Special achievements/activities:* general special achievements/activities, leadership. ***Tuition waivers:*** Full or partial for employees or children of employees. ***ROTC:*** Army cooperative.

LOANS *Student loans:* 70% of past graduating class borrowed through all loan programs. *Average indebtedness per student:* $27,007. ***Average need-based loan:*** Freshmen: $3307. Undergraduates: $4727. ***Programs:*** Federal Direct (Subsidized and Unsubsidized Stafford, PLUS), Perkins, college/university.

WORK-STUDY Federal work-study jobs available. ***State or other work-study/employment:*** Part-time jobs available.

APPLYING FOR FINANCIAL AID *Required financial aid form:* FAFSA. ***Financial aid deadline (priority):*** 2/1. ***Notification date:*** 4/1. Students must reply within 4 weeks of notification.

CONTACT Tracey Lehman, Director of Financial Aid, Oregon Institute of Technology, 3201 Campus Drive, Klamath Falls, OR 97601, 541-885-1280 or toll-free 800-422-2017. *Fax:* 541-885-1024. *E-mail:* tracey.lehman@oit.edu.
Website: http://www.oit.edu/.

OREGON STATE UNIVERSITY

Corvallis, OR

Tuition & fees: N/R	Average undergraduate aid package: $11,671

ABOUT THE INSTITUTION State-supported, coed. ***Awards:*** certificates, bachelor's, master's, and doctoral degrees. 81 undergraduate majors. ***Total enrollment:*** 30,896. Undergraduates: 25,839. Freshmen: 3,819. Federal methodology is used as a basis for awarding need-based institutional aid.

FRESHMAN FINANCIAL AID (Fall 2018) 2897 applied for aid; of those 64% were deemed to have need. 98% of freshmen with need received aid; of those 19% had need fully met. ***Average percent of need met:*** 66% (excluding resources awarded to replace EFC). ***Average financial aid package:*** $12,508 (excluding resources awarded to replace EFC). 28% of all full-time freshmen had no need and received non-need-based gift aid.

UNDERGRADUATE FINANCIAL AID (Fall 2018) 12,549 applied for aid; of those 76% were deemed to have need. 98% of undergraduates with need received aid; of those 12% had need fully met. ***Average percent of need met:*** 62% (excluding resources awarded to replace EFC). ***Average financial aid package:*** $11,671 (excluding resources awarded to replace EFC). 19% of all full-time undergraduates had no need and received non-need-based gift aid.

GIFT AID (NEED-BASED) ***Total amount:*** $73,505,970 (41% federal, 13% state, 37% institutional, 9% external sources). ***Receiving aid:*** Freshmen: 46% (1,537); all full-time undergraduates: 40% (7,393). ***Average award:*** Freshmen: $9107; Undergraduates: $8117.

GIFT AID (NON-NEED-BASED) ***Total amount:*** $21,940,091 (1% state, 79% institutional, 20% external sources). ***Receiving aid:*** Freshmen: 2% (79). Undergraduates: 1% (273). ***Average award:*** Freshmen: $5210. Undergraduates: $4841. ***Scholarships, grants, and awards by category:*** *Academic interests/achievement:* general academic interests/achievements. *Special achievements/activities:* leadership. *Special characteristics:* children and siblings of alumni, local/state students, members of minority groups. ***ROTC:*** Army, Naval, Air Force.

LOANS ***Student loans:*** $86,841,260 (82% need-based, 18% non-need-based). 55% of past graduating class borrowed through all loan programs. *Average indebtedness per student:* $27,392. ***Average need-based loan:*** Freshmen: $3221. Undergraduates: $4196. ***Parent loans:*** $30,958,567 (79% need-based, 21% non-need-based).

WORK-STUDY ***Federal work-study:*** Total amount: $2,899,007; jobs available.

ATHLETIC AWARDS Total amount: $6,498,077 (39% need-based, 61% non-need-based).

APPLYING FOR FINANCIAL AID ***Notification date:*** Continuous.

CONTACT Keith Raab, Director of Financial Aid, Oregon State University, 218 Kerr Administration Building, Corvallis, OR 97331-2120, 541-737-2241 or toll-free 800-291-4192. *E-mail:* financial.aid@oregonstate.edu.
Website: http://www.oregonstate.edu/.

OREGON STATE UNIVERSITY–CASCADES

Bend, OR

CONTACT Financial Aid Office, Oregon State University–Cascades, 2600 Northwest College Way, Bend, OR 97701, 541-322-3100.
Website: http://www.osucascades.edu/.

OTIS COLLEGE OF ART AND DESIGN

Los Angeles, CA

Tuition & fees: N/R	Average undergraduate aid package: $22,854

ABOUT THE INSTITUTION Independent, coed. ***Awards:*** bachelor's and master's degrees. 14 undergraduate majors. ***Total enrollment:*** 1,183. Undergraduates: 1,125. Freshmen: 274. Both federal and institutional methodology are used as a basis for awarding need-based institutional aid.

UNDERGRADUATE EXPENSES for 2020–2021 ***Application fee:*** $50. ***Tuition:*** part-time $1507 per unit. Room and board charges vary according to board plan and housing facility.

FRESHMAN FINANCIAL AID (Fall 2019, est.) 257 applied for aid; of those 100% were deemed to have need. 100% of freshmen with need received aid. ***Average percent of need met:*** 49% (excluding resources awarded to replace EFC). ***Average financial aid package:*** $22,155 (excluding resources awarded to replace EFC).

UNDERGRADUATE FINANCIAL AID (Fall 2019, est.) 990 applied for aid; of those 100% were deemed to have need. 100% of undergraduates with need received aid. ***Average percent of need met:*** 51% (excluding resources awarded to replace EFC). ***Average financial aid package:*** $22,854 (excluding resources awarded to replace EFC).

GIFT AID (NEED-BASED) ***Total amount:*** $18,843,219 (11% federal, 3% state, 85% institutional, 1% external sources). ***Receiving aid:*** Freshmen: 93% (254); all full-time undergraduates: 58% (646). ***Average award:*** Freshmen: $20,610; Undergraduates: $31,378. ***Scholarships, grants, and awards:*** Federal Pell, FSEOG, state, private, college/university gift aid from institutional funds.

GIFT AID (NON-NEED-BASED) ***Scholarships, grants, and awards by category:*** *Academic interests/achievement:* 1,018 awards ($15,668,325 total): architecture, general academic interests/achievements. *Creative arts/performance:* applied art and design, art/fine arts, creative writing. *Special characteristics:* adult students, ethnic background, members of minority groups, veterans. ***Tuition waivers:*** Full or partial for employees or children of employees.

LOANS ***Student loans:*** $12,967,388 (100% need-based). 81% of past graduating class borrowed through all loan programs. ***Average need-based loan:*** Freshmen: $3515. Undergraduates: $4702. ***Parent loans:*** $7,077,938 (100% need-based). ***Programs:*** Federal Direct (Subsidized and Unsubsidized Stafford, PLUS).

WORK-STUDY ***Federal work-study:*** Total amount: $770,260; 399 jobs averaging $770,260. ***State or other work-study/employment:*** Part-time jobs available.

APPLYING FOR FINANCIAL AID ***Required financial aid form:*** FAFSA. ***Financial aid deadline (priority):*** 5/1.

CONTACT Natasha Kobrinsky, Director of Financial Aid, Otis College of Art and Design, 9045 Lincoln Boulevard, Los Angeles, CA 90045-9785, 310-665-6898 or toll-free 800-527-OTIS. *Fax:* 310-665-6884. *E-mail:* nkobrinsky@otis.edu.
Website: http://www.otis.edu/.

OTTAWA UNIVERSITY

Ottawa, KS

CONTACT Financial Aid Coordinator, Ottawa University, 1001 South Cedar, Ottawa, KS 66067-3399, 785-242-5200 or toll-free 800-755-5200. *E-mail:* finaid@ottawa.edu.
Website: http://www.ottawa.edu/.

OTTERBEIN UNIVERSITY

Westerville, OH

Tuition & fees: $32,474	Average undergraduate aid package: $21,705

ABOUT THE INSTITUTION Independent United Methodist, coed. ***Awards:*** certificates, bachelor's, master's, and doctoral degrees. 48 undergraduate majors. Federal methodology is used as a basis for awarding need-based institutional aid.

UNDERGRADUATE EXPENSES for 2019–2020 ***Comprehensive fee:*** $43,958 includes full-time tuition ($32,024), mandatory fees ($450), and room and board ($11,484). ***College room only:*** $6078. Room and board charges vary according to board plan and housing facility. ***Part-time tuition:*** $575 per credit hour. ***Part-time fees:*** $250 per year.

FRESHMAN FINANCIAL AID (Fall 2019, est.) 592 applied for aid; of those 83% were deemed to have need. 100% of freshmen with need received aid; of those 21% had need fully met. ***Average percent of need met:*** 68% (excluding resources awarded to replace EFC). ***Average financial aid package:*** $22,413 (excluding resources awarded to replace EFC). 12% of all full-time freshmen had no need and received non-need-based gift aid.

UNDERGRADUATE FINANCIAL AID (Fall 2019, est.) 2,171 applied for aid; of those 86% were deemed to have need. 100% of undergraduates with need received aid; of those 16% had need fully met. ***Average percent of need met:*** 66% (excluding resources awarded to replace EFC). ***Average financial aid package:*** $21,705 (excluding resources awarded to replace EFC). 18% of all full-time undergraduates had no need and received non-need-based gift aid.

GIFT AID (NEED-BASED) ***Receiving aid:*** Freshmen: 77% (482); all full-time undergraduates: 66% (1,696). ***Average award:*** Freshmen: $17,254; Undergraduates: $17,579. ***Scholarships, grants, and awards:*** Federal Pell, FSEOG, state, private, college/university gift aid from institutional funds, Federal Nursing.

GIFT AID (NON-NEED-BASED) ***Receiving aid:*** Freshmen: 15% (96). Undergraduates: 10% (258). ***Average award:*** Freshmen: $15,452. Undergraduates: $14,178. ***Scholarships, grants, and awards by category:*** *Academic interests/*

achievement: general academic interests/achievements. *Creative arts/performance:* applied art and design, music, theater/drama. *Special achievements/activities:* community service, leadership. *Special characteristics:* children and siblings of alumni, children of faculty/staff, general special characteristics, international students, members of minority groups, previous college experience, relatives of clergy, siblings of current students, veterans. ***Tuition waivers:*** Full or partial for employees or children of employees. ***ROTC:*** Army cooperative, Air Force cooperative.

LOANS *Average need-based loan:* Freshmen: $3051. Undergraduates: $3860. ***Programs:*** Federal Direct (Subsidized and Unsubsidized Stafford, PLUS), Federal Nursing, state, college/university.

WORK-STUDY Federal work-study jobs available. ***State or other work-study/employment:*** Part-time jobs available.

APPLYING FOR FINANCIAL AID *Required financial aid form:* FAFSA. ***Financial aid deadline:*** Continuous. ***Notification date:*** Continuous.

CONTACT Mr. Thomas V. Yarnell, Director of Student Financial Services, Otterbein University, One Otterbein College, Westerville, OH 43081-2006, 614-823-1502 or toll-free 800-488-8144. *Fax:* 614-823-1588. *E-mail:* tyarnell@otterbein.edu.
Website: http://www.otterbein.edu/.

OUACHITA BAPTIST UNIVERSITY

Arkadelphia, AR

Tuition & fees: $27,900	Average undergraduate aid package: $29,837

ABOUT THE INSTITUTION Independent Baptist, coed. ***Awards:*** associate and bachelor's degrees. 64 undergraduate majors. ***Total enrollment:*** 1,660. Undergraduates: 1,630. Freshmen: 443. Both federal and institutional methodology are used as a basis for awarding need-based institutional aid.

UNDERGRADUATE EXPENSES for 2019–2020 *Comprehensive fee:* $35,900 includes full-time tuition ($27,280), mandatory fees ($620), and room and board ($8000). ***College room only:*** $4000. Full-time tuition and fees vary according to degree level and location. Room and board charges vary according to housing facility. ***Part-time tuition:*** $725 per credit hour. Part-time tuition and fees vary according to degree level and location.

FRESHMAN FINANCIAL AID (Fall 2019, est.) 410 applied for aid; of those 74% were deemed to have need. 100% of freshmen with need received aid; of those 55% had need fully met. ***Average percent of need met:*** 90% (excluding resources awarded to replace EFC). ***Average financial aid package:*** $28,780 (excluding resources awarded to replace EFC). 31% of all full-time freshmen had no need and received non-need-based gift aid.

UNDERGRADUATE FINANCIAL AID (Fall 2019, est.) 1,261 applied for aid; of those 76% were deemed to have need. 100% of undergraduates with need received aid; of those 55% had need fully met. ***Average percent of need met:*** 91% (excluding resources awarded to replace EFC). ***Average financial aid package:*** $29,837 (excluding resources awarded to replace EFC). 34% of all full-time undergraduates had no need and received non-need-based gift aid.

GIFT AID (NEED-BASED) *Total amount:* $17,005,074 (12% federal, 11% state, 71% institutional, 6% external sources). ***Receiving aid:*** Freshmen: 67% (297); all full-time undergraduates: 61% (923). ***Average award:*** Freshmen: $18,646; Undergraduates: $19,174. ***Scholarships, grants, and awards:*** Federal Pell, FSEOG, state, private, college/university gift aid from institutional funds.

GIFT AID (NON-NEED-BASED) *Total amount:* $10,959,427 (11% state, 84% institutional, 5% external sources). ***Receiving aid:*** Freshmen: 7% (32). Undergraduates: 8% (115). ***Average award:*** Freshmen: $15,954. Undergraduates: $15,571. ***Scholarships, grants, and awards by category:*** *Academic interests/achievement:* 588 awards ($2,283,393 total): biological sciences, business, communication, computer science, education, English, foreign languages, general academic interests/achievements, home economics, humanities, international studies, mathematics, military science, premedicine, religion/biblical studies, social sciences. *Creative arts/performance:* 239 awards ($1,654,668 total): art/fine arts, music, performing arts, theater/drama. *Special achievements/activities:* 283 awards ($694,262 total): cheerleading/drum major, leadership, memberships, religious involvement. *Special characteristics:* 1,272 awards ($5,290,054 total): children and siblings of alumni, children of faculty/staff, international students, local/state students, previous college experience, relatives of clergy, religious affiliation, veterans, veterans' children. ***Tuition waivers:*** Full or partial for children of alumni, employees or children of employees. ***ROTC:*** Army.

LOANS *Student loans:* $7,010,246 (68% need-based, 32% non-need-based). 56% of past graduating class borrowed through all loan programs. *Average indebtedness per student:* $24,157. ***Average need-based loan:*** Freshmen: $3239. Undergraduates: $4012. ***Parent loans:*** $1,984,023 (57% need-based, 43% non-need-based). ***Programs:*** Federal Direct (Subsidized and Unsubsidized Stafford, PLUS), private lender loans.

WORK-STUDY *Federal work-study:* Total amount: $638,995; 378 jobs averaging $1900. ***State or other work-study/employment:*** Total amount: $281,874 (6% need-based, 94% non-need-based). 147 part-time jobs averaging $1900.

ATHLETIC AWARDS Total amount: $2,485,802 (66% need-based, 34% non-need-based).

APPLYING FOR FINANCIAL AID *Required financial aid forms:* FAFSA, state aid form. ***Financial aid deadline (priority):*** 12/1. ***Notification date:*** Continuous beginning 12/1.

CONTACT Ms. Susan Hurst, Director of Financial Aid, Ouachita Baptist University, PO Box 3774, Arkadelphia, AR 71998-0001, 870-245-5570 or toll-free 800-342-5628. *Fax:* 870-245-5318. *E-mail:* hursts@obu.edu.
Website: http://www.obu.edu/.

OUR LADY OF THE LAKE UNIVERSITY

San Antonio, TX

CONTACT Esmeralda Flores, Director of Financial Aid, Our Lady of the Lake University, 411 Southwest 24th Street, San Antonio, TX 78207-4689, 210-434-6711 Ext. 2558 or toll-free 800-436-6558. *Fax:* 210-431-3958. *E-mail:* emflores@lake.ollusa.edu.
Website: http://www.ollusa.edu/.

OZARK CHRISTIAN COLLEGE

Joplin, MO

CONTACT Rebecca Morrow, Financial Aid Counselor, Ozark Christian College, 1111 North Main Street, Joplin, MO 64801-4804, 417-624-2518 Ext. 2027 or toll-free 800-299-4622. *Fax:* 417-624-0090. *E-mail:* morrow.becky@occ.edu.
Website: http://www.occ.edu/.

PACE UNIVERSITY

New York, NY

ABOUT THE INSTITUTION Independent, coed. ***Awards:*** certificates, associate, bachelor's, master's, and doctoral degrees. 77 undergraduate majors. ***Total enrollment:*** 13,609. Undergraduates: 8,960. Freshmen: 2,013.

GIFT AID (NEED-BASED) *Scholarships, grants, and awards:* Federal Pell, FSEOG, state, private, college/university gift aid from institutional funds.

GIFT AID (NON-NEED-BASED) *Scholarships, grants, and awards by category:* *Academic interests/achievement:* biological sciences, business, communication, computer science, education, English, foreign languages, general academic interests/achievements, home economics, humanities, mathematics, physical sciences, social sciences. *Creative arts/performance:* dance, performing arts, theater/drama. *Special achievements/activities:* community service, general special achievements/activities, leadership, memberships. *Special characteristics:* children and siblings of alumni, children of faculty/staff, general special characteristics, spouses of deceased or disabled public servants, veterans.

LOANS *Programs:* Federal Direct (Subsidized and Unsubsidized Stafford, PLUS), Perkins, Federal Nursing.

WORK-STUDY *Federal work-study:* Total amount: $1,240,972; jobs available.

APPLYING FOR FINANCIAL AID *Required financial aid form:* FAFSA.

CONTACT Financial Aid Office, Pace University, One Pace Plaza, New York, NY 10038, 212-346-1200 or toll-free 800-874-7223.
Website: http://www.pace.edu/nyc.

PACE UNIVERSITY, PLEASANTVILLE CAMPUS

Pleasantville, NY

ABOUT THE INSTITUTION Independent, coed. ***Awards:*** certificates, diplomas, associate, bachelor's, master's, and doctoral degrees. 58 undergraduate majors. ***Total enrollment:*** 3,710. Undergraduates: 2,606. Freshmen: 522.

GIFT AID (NEED-BASED) ***Scholarships, grants, and awards:*** Federal Pell, FSEOG, state, college/university gift aid from institutional funds, Federal Nursing.

LOANS ***Programs:*** Federal Direct (Subsidized and Unsubsidized Stafford, PLUS), Federal Nursing, state.

WORK-STUDY ***Federal work-study:*** Total amount: $519,272.

APPLYING FOR FINANCIAL AID ***Required financial aid form:*** FAFSA.

CONTACT Financial Aid Office, Pace University, Pleasantville Campus, 861 Bedford Road, Pleasantville, NY 10570, 914-773-3200 or toll-free 800-874-PACE.
Website: http://www.pace.edu/westchester.

PACIFIC COLLEGE

Costa Mesa, CA

CONTACT Financial Aid Office, Pacific College, 3160 Red Hill Avenue, Costa Mesa, CA 92626, 714-662-4402.
Website: http://www.pacific-college.edu/.

PACIFIC ISLANDS UNIVERSITY

Mangilao, GU

CONTACT Financial Aid Office, Pacific Islands University, 172 Kinney's Road, Mangilao, GU 96913, 671-734-1812.
Website: http://www.piu.edu/.

PACIFIC LUTHERAN UNIVERSITY

Tacoma, WA

Tuition & fees: $43,674	Average undergraduate aid package: $33,622

ABOUT THE INSTITUTION Independent Evangelical Lutheran Church in America, coed. ***Awards:*** certificates, bachelor's, master's, and doctoral degrees. 33 undergraduate majors. ***Total enrollment:*** 3,111. Undergraduates: 2,769. Freshmen: 649. Federal methodology is used as a basis for awarding need-based institutional aid.

UNDERGRADUATE EXPENSES for 2019–2020 ***Application fee:*** $40. ***Comprehensive fee:*** $54,550 includes full-time tuition ($43,264), mandatory fees ($410), and room and board ($10,876). ***College room only:*** $4940. ***Part-time tuition:*** $1352 per credit hour.

FRESHMAN FINANCIAL AID (Fall 2018) 496 applied for aid; of those 88% were deemed to have need. 100% of freshmen with need received aid; of those 29% had need fully met. ***Average percent of need met:*** 91% (excluding resources awarded to replace EFC). ***Average financial aid package:*** $34,951 (excluding resources awarded to replace EFC). 3% of all full-time freshmen had no need and received non-need-based gift aid.

UNDERGRADUATE FINANCIAL AID (Fall 2018) 2,254 applied for aid; of those 90% were deemed to have need. 100% of undergraduates with need received aid; of those 23% had need fully met. ***Average percent of need met:*** 87% (excluding resources awarded to replace EFC). ***Average financial aid package:*** $33,622 (excluding resources awarded to replace EFC). 4% of all full-time undergraduates had no need and received non-need-based gift aid.

GIFT AID (NEED-BASED) ***Total amount:*** $22,386,492 (23% federal, 27% state, 45% institutional, 5% external sources). ***Receiving aid:*** Freshmen: 59% (312); all full-time undergraduates: 57% (1,557). ***Average award:*** Freshmen: $11,005; Undergraduates: $9797. ***Scholarships, grants, and awards:*** Federal Pell, FSEOG, state, private, college/university gift aid from institutional funds, ROTC Scholarships.

GIFT AID (NON-NEED-BASED) ***Total amount:*** $52,109,524 (99% institutional, 1% external sources). ***Receiving aid:*** Freshmen: 82% (430). Undergraduates: 74% (1,993). ***Average award:*** Freshmen: $13,465. Undergraduates: $12,604. ***Scholarships, grants, and awards by category:*** *Academic interests/achievement:* 4,626 awards ($55,912,050 total): business, general academic interests/achievements. *Creative arts/performance:* 319 awards ($1,018,351 total): applied art and design, art/fine arts, dance, debating, music, theater/drama. *Special achievements/activities:* 64 awards ($117,500 total): leadership, religious involvement. *Special characteristics:* 1,072 awards ($1,241,039 total): children and siblings of alumni, children of faculty/staff, ethnic background, international students, local/state students, out-of-state students, relatives of clergy, religious affiliation, veterans, veterans' children. ***ROTC:*** Army.

LOANS ***Student loans:*** $21,122,525 (64% need-based, 36% non-need-based). 66% of past graduating class borrowed through all loan programs. *Average indebtedness per student:* $25,449. ***Average need-based loan:*** Freshmen: $3360. Undergraduates: $4752. ***Parent loans:*** $5,076,033 (100% non-need-based). ***Programs:*** Federal Direct (Subsidized and Unsubsidized Stafford, PLUS), Federal Nursing.

WORK-STUDY ***Federal work-study:*** Total amount: $1,110,002; 683 jobs averaging $3219. ***State or other work-study/employment:*** Total amount: $172,725 (100% need-based). 577 part-time jobs averaging $3092.

APPLYING FOR FINANCIAL AID ***Required financial aid form:*** FAFSA. ***Financial aid deadline:*** Continuous. ***Notification date:*** Continuous beginning 12/15.

CONTACT Sara Christensen, Student Financial Services, Pacific Lutheran University, Hauge Administration Building, Room 130, Tacoma, WA 98447, 253-535-7161 or toll-free 800-274-6758. *Fax:* 253-535-8406. *E-mail:* sfs@plu.edu.
Website: http://www.plu.edu/.

PACIFIC NORTHWEST COLLEGE OF ART

Portland, OR

CONTACT Peggy Burgus, Director of Financial Aid, Pacific Northwest College of Art, 1241 Northwest Johnson Street, Portland, OR 97209, 503-821-8976. *Fax:* 503-821-8978.
Website: http://www.pnca.edu/.

PACIFIC OAKS COLLEGE

Pasadena, CA

CONTACT Rosie Tristan, Financial Aid Specialist, Pacific Oaks College, 5 Westmoreland Place, Pasadena, CA 91103, 626-397-1350 or toll-free 877-314-2380. *Fax:* 626-577-6144. *E-mail:* financial@pacificoaks.edu.
Website: http://www.pacificoaks.edu/.

PACIFIC RIM CHRISTIAN UNIVERSITY

Honolulu, HI

CONTACT Financial Aid Office, Pacific Rim Christian University, 2223 Ho'one'e Place, Honolulu, HI 96819, 808-518-4791.
Website: http://www.pacrim.edu/.

PACIFIC UNION COLLEGE

Angwin, CA

CONTACT Laurie Wheeler, Director of Student Financial Services, Pacific Union College, One Angwin Avenue, Angwin, CA 94508, 707-965-7321 or toll-free 800-862-7080. *Fax:* 707-965-6595. *E-mail:* llwheeler@puc.edu.
Website: http://www.puc.edu/.

PACIFIC UNIVERSITY

Forest Grove, OR

Tuition & fees: $48,260	Average undergraduate aid package: $35,931

ABOUT THE INSTITUTION Independent, coed. ***Awards:*** certificates, bachelor's, master's, and doctoral degrees. 50 undergraduate majors. ***Total enrollment:*** 3,832. Undergraduates: 1,864. Freshmen: 416.

UNDERGRADUATE EXPENSES for 2020–2021 ***Application fee:*** $40. ***Comprehensive fee:*** $61,680 includes full-time tuition ($47,158), mandatory fees ($1102), and room and board ($13,420). ***College room only:*** $7404. Room and board charges vary according to board plan and housing facility. Part-time tuition and fees vary according to course load.

FRESHMAN FINANCIAL AID (Fall 2019, est.) 396 applied for aid; of those 87% were deemed to have need. 100% of freshmen with need received aid; of those 19% had need fully met. ***Average percent of need met:*** 82% (excluding resources awarded to replace EFC). ***Average financial aid package:*** $37,575 (excluding resources awarded to replace EFC). 15% of all full-time freshmen had no need and received non-need-based gift aid.

UNDERGRADUATE FINANCIAL AID (Fall 2019, est.) 1,507 applied for aid; of those 91% were deemed to have need. 100% of undergraduates with need received aid; of those 19% had need fully met. ***Average percent of need met:*** 78% (excluding resources awarded to replace EFC). ***Average financial aid package:*** $35,931 (excluding resources awarded to replace EFC). 17% of all full-time undergraduates had no need and received non-need-based gift aid.

GIFT AID (NEED-BASED) ***Total amount:*** $33,265,481 (8% federal, 2% state, 86% institutional, 4% external sources). ***Receiving aid:*** Freshmen: 81% (336); all full-time undergraduates: 81% (1,364). ***Average award:*** Freshmen: $12,599; Undergraduates: $10,402. ***Scholarships, grants, and awards:*** Federal Pell, FSEOG, state, private, college/university gift aid from institutional funds.

GIFT AID (NON-NEED-BASED) ***Total amount:*** $13,191,053 (99% institutional, 1% external sources). ***Receiving aid:*** Freshmen: 81% (336). Undergraduates: 75% (1,253). ***Average award:*** Freshmen: $22,479. Undergraduates: $21,393. ***Scholarships, grants, and awards by category:*** *Academic interests/achievement:* biological sciences, business, communication, education, English, foreign languages, general academic interests/achievements, home economics, humanities, mathematics, physical sciences, premedicine, social sciences. *Creative arts/performance:* applied art and design, debating, journalism/publications, music, theater/drama. *Special achievements/activities:* community service, memberships, religious involvement. *Special characteristics:* children and siblings of alumni, children of faculty/staff, ethnic background, first-generation college students, general special characteristics, international students, relatives of clergy, veterans. ***Tuition waivers:*** Full or partial for employees or children of employees.

LOANS ***Student loans:*** $12,317,676 (69% need-based, 31% non-need-based). 77% of past graduating class borrowed through all loan programs. *Average indebtedness per student:* $34,429. ***Average need-based loan:*** Freshmen: $2967. Undergraduates: $4016. ***Parent loans:*** $5,605,130 (43% need-based, 57% non-need-based). ***Programs:*** Federal Direct (Subsidized and Unsubsidized Stafford, PLUS), Private Loans.

WORK-STUDY ***Federal work-study:*** Total amount: $1,837,849; jobs available. ***State or other work-study/employment:*** Part-time jobs available.

APPLYING FOR FINANCIAL AID ***Required financial aid form:*** FAFSA. ***Financial aid deadline (priority):*** 3/1. ***Notification date:*** Continuous beginning 3/1.

CONTACT Financial Aid Office, Pacific University, 2043 College Way, Forest Grove, OR 97116-1797, 503-357-6151 or toll-free 877-722-8648.
Website: http://www.pacificu.edu/.

PAIER COLLEGE OF ART, INC.

Hamden, CT

Tuition & fees: $19,670	Average undergraduate aid package: $9366

ABOUT THE INSTITUTION Proprietary, coed. ***Awards:*** certificates, diplomas, and bachelor's degrees. 7 undergraduate majors. ***Total enrollment:*** 89. Undergraduates: 89. Freshmen: 18. Federal methodology is used as a basis for awarding need-based institutional aid.

UNDERGRADUATE EXPENSES for 2020–2021 ***Application fee:*** $25. ***One-time required fee:*** $25. ***Comprehensive fee:*** $23,170 includes full-time tuition ($19,200), mandatory fees ($470), and room and board ($3500). ***College room only:*** $1750. ***Part-time tuition:*** $600 per credit hour. ***Part-time fees:*** $190 per term. Part-time tuition and fees vary according to course load.

FRESHMAN FINANCIAL AID (Fall 2018) 14 applied for aid; of those 86% were deemed to have need. 100% of freshmen with need received aid; of those 8% had need fully met. ***Average percent of need met:*** 42% (excluding resources awarded to replace EFC). ***Average financial aid package:*** $7566 (excluding resources awarded to replace EFC).

UNDERGRADUATE FINANCIAL AID (Fall 2018) 40 applied for aid; of those 85% were deemed to have need. 100% of undergraduates with need received aid; of those 9% had need fully met. ***Average percent of need met:*** 48% (excluding resources awarded to replace EFC). ***Average financial aid package:*** $9366 (excluding resources awarded to replace EFC).

GIFT AID (NEED-BASED) ***Total amount:*** $261,895 (94% federal, 1% state, 5% institutional). ***Receiving aid:*** Freshmen: 56% (9); all full-time undergraduates: 36% (28). ***Average award:*** Freshmen: $5929; Undergraduates: $7273. ***Scholarships, grants, and awards:*** Federal Pell, FSEOG, state, private, college/university gift aid from institutional funds.

GIFT AID (NON-NEED-BASED) ***Total amount:*** $4000 (100% external sources). ***Receiving aid:*** Freshmen: 6% (1).

LOANS ***Student loans:*** $383,994 (47% need-based, 53% non-need-based). 31% of past graduating class borrowed through all loan programs. *Average indebtedness per student:* $37,318. ***Average need-based loan:*** Freshmen: $3403. Undergraduates: $4137. ***Parent loans:*** $47,932 (100% non-need-based). ***Programs:*** Federal Direct (Subsidized and Unsubsidized Stafford, PLUS).

APPLYING FOR FINANCIAL AID ***Required financial aid form:*** FAFSA. ***Financial aid deadline:*** Continuous. ***Notification date:*** Continuous beginning 5/15. Students must reply within 3 weeks of notification.

CONTACT Mr. John DeRose, Director of Financial Aid, Paier College of Art, Inc., 20 Gorham Avenue, Hamden, CT 06514-3902, 203-287-3034. *Fax:* 203-287-3021. *E-mail:* jderose@paier.edu.
Website: http://www.paiercollegeofart.edu/.

PAINE COLLEGE

Augusta, GA

CONTACT Ms. Gerri Bogan, Director of Financial Aid, Paine College, 1235 15th Street, Augusta, GA 30901, 706-821-8262 or toll-free 800-476-7703. *Fax:* 706-821-8691. *E-mail:* bogang@mail.paine.edu.
Website: http://www.paine.edu/.

PALM BEACH ATLANTIC UNIVERSITY

West Palm Beach, FL

Tuition & fees: $33,475	Average undergraduate aid package: $23,772

ABOUT THE INSTITUTION Independent nondenominational, coed. ***Awards:*** bachelor's, master's, and doctoral degrees. 48 undergraduate majors. ***Total enrollment:*** 3,691. Undergraduates: 2,883. Freshmen: 520. Federal methodology is used as a basis for awarding need-based institutional aid.

UNDERGRADUATE EXPENSES for 2020–2021 ***Application fee:*** $50. ***Tuition:*** full-time $32,880; part-time $790 per credit hour. ***Required fees:*** full-time $595. Full-time tuition and fees vary according to location and program. Part-time tuition and fees vary according to location and program. ***College room only:*** $5696. Room and board charges vary according to board plan and housing facility.

FRESHMAN FINANCIAL AID (Fall 2019, est.) 440 applied for aid; of those 83% were deemed to have need. 100% of freshmen with need received aid; of those 14% had need fully met. ***Average percent of need met:*** 66% (excluding resources awarded to replace EFC). ***Average financial aid package:*** $26,011 (excluding resources awarded to replace EFC). 24% of all full-time freshmen had no need and received non-need-based gift aid.

UNDERGRADUATE FINANCIAL AID (Fall 2019, est.) 1,872 applied for aid; of those 88% were deemed to have need. 100% of undergraduates with need received aid; of those 13% had need fully met. ***Average percent of need met:*** 62% (excluding resources awarded to replace EFC). ***Average financial aid package:*** $23,772 (excluding resources awarded to replace EFC). 25% of all full-time undergraduates had no need and received non-need-based gift aid.

GIFT AID (NEED-BASED) ***Total amount:*** $32,545,948 (12% federal, 15% state, 64% institutional, 9% external sources). ***Receiving aid:*** Freshmen: 75% (364); all full-time undergraduates: 72% (1,618). ***Average award:*** Freshmen: $23,861; Undergraduates: $21,190. ***Scholarships, grants, and awards:*** Federal Pell, FSEOG, state, private, college/university gift aid from institutional funds, United Negro College Fund.

GIFT AID (NON-NEED-BASED) ***Total amount:*** $11,195,564 (17% state, 76% institutional, 7% external sources). ***Receiving aid:*** Freshmen: 9% (46). Undergraduates: 8% (189). ***Average award:*** Freshmen: $14,843. Undergraduates: $13,581. ***Scholarships, grants, and awards by category:*** *Academic interests/achievement:* general academic interests/achievements. *Creative arts/performance:* dance, music, theater/drama. *Special achievements/activities:* leadership. *Special characteristics:* adult students, children and siblings of alumni, children of current students, children of educators, children of faculty/staff, previous college experience, veterans. ***Tuition waivers:*** Full or partial for employees or children of employees. ***ROTC:*** Army cooperative.

LOANS ***Student loans:*** $10,738,834 (78% need-based, 22% non-need-based). 60% of past graduating class borrowed through all loan programs. *Average indebtedness per student:* $27,530. ***Average need-based loan:*** Freshmen: $3259. Undergraduates: $3783. ***Parent loans:*** $4,249,116 (55% need-based, 45% non-need-based). ***Programs:*** Federal Direct (Subsidized and Unsubsidized Stafford, PLUS).

WORK-STUDY ***Federal work-study:*** Total amount: $486,067; jobs available. ***State or other work-study/employment:*** Total amount: $8000 (100% need-based). Part-time jobs available.

ATHLETIC AWARDS Total amount: $2,508,969 (42% need-based, 58% non-need-based).

APPLYING FOR FINANCIAL AID ***Required financial aid forms:*** FAFSA, state aid form. ***Financial aid deadline (priority):*** 5/1. ***Notification date:*** Continuous beginning 11/15. Students must reply by 5/1.

CONTACT Mrs. Jennifer McMahon, Director of Financial Aid, Palm Beach Atlantic University, PO Box 24708, West Palm Beach, FL 33416-4708, 561-803-2000 or toll-free 888-GO-TO-PBA. *Fax:* 561-803-2130. *E-mail:* finaid@pba.edu.
Website: http://www.pba.edu/.

PALM BEACH STATE COLLEGE

Lake Worth, FL

CONTACT Financial Aid Office, Palm Beach State College, 4200 Congress Avenue, Lake Worth, FL 33461-4796, 561-967-7222.
Website: http://www.palmbeachstate.edu/.

PALO ALTO UNIVERSITY

Palo Alto, CA

CONTACT Financial Aid Office, Palo Alto University, 1791 Arastradero Road, Palo Alto, CA 94304, 650-433-3800 or toll-free 800-818-6136.
Website: http://www.paloaltou.edu/.

PARK UNIVERSITY

Parkville, MO

CONTACT Brynn Bologna, Director, Student Financial Services, Park University, 8700 NW River Park Drive, Parkville, MO 64152, 816-584-6714 or toll-free 800-745-7275. *E-mail:* cathy.colapietro@park.edu.
Website: http://www.park.edu/.

PARSONS SCHOOL OF DESIGN

New York, NY

Tuition & fees: N/R	Average undergraduate aid package: $26,579

ABOUT THE INSTITUTION Independent, coed. ***Awards:*** certificates, associate, bachelor's, and master's degrees. 14 undergraduate majors. ***Total enrollment:*** 5,339. Undergraduates: 4,383. Freshmen: 889. Federal methodology is used as a basis for awarding need-based institutional aid.

FRESHMAN FINANCIAL AID (Fall 2018) 456 applied for aid; of those 88% were deemed to have need. 100% of freshmen with need received aid; of those 6% had need fully met. ***Average percent of need met:*** 67% (excluding resources awarded to replace EFC). ***Average financial aid package:*** $27,135 (excluding resources awarded to replace EFC). 55% of all full-time freshmen had no need and received non-need-based gift aid.

UNDERGRADUATE FINANCIAL AID (Fall 2018) 1,441 applied for aid; of those 95% were deemed to have need. 100% of undergraduates with need received aid; of those 4% had need fully met. ***Average percent of need met:*** 80% (excluding resources awarded to replace EFC). ***Average financial aid package:*** $26,579 (excluding resources awarded to replace EFC). 53% of all full-time undergraduates had no need and received non-need-based gift aid.

GIFT AID (NEED-BASED) ***Total amount:*** $22,054,366 (16% federal, 3% state, 76% institutional, 5% external sources). ***Receiving aid:*** Freshmen: 29% (313); all full-time undergraduates: 29% (1,159). ***Average award:*** Freshmen: $14,574; Undergraduates: $16,218. ***Scholarships, grants, and awards:*** Federal Pell, FSEOG, state, private, college/university gift aid from institutional funds, United Negro College Fund.

GIFT AID (NON-NEED-BASED) ***Total amount:*** $35,917,309 (97% institutional, 3% external sources). ***Receiving aid:*** Freshmen: 29% (315). Undergraduates: 25% (997). ***Average award:*** Freshmen: $12,355. Undergraduates: $9711. ***Scholarships, grants, and awards by category:*** *Special achievements/activities:* leadership.

LOANS ***Student loans:*** $68,656,005 (42% need-based, 58% non-need-based). 35% of past graduating class borrowed through all loan programs. *Average indebtedness per student:* $32,624. ***Average need-based loan:*** Freshmen: $2569. Undergraduates: $3177. ***Parent loans:*** $11,215,387 (100% non-need-based). ***Programs:*** Federal Direct (Subsidized and Unsubsidized Stafford, PLUS).

WORK-STUDY ***Federal work-study:*** Total amount: $468,518; 114 jobs averaging $2880.

APPLYING FOR FINANCIAL AID ***Required financial aid form:*** FAFSA. ***Financial aid deadline (priority):*** 2/1. ***Notification date:*** Continuous beginning 4/1. Students must reply within 4 weeks of notification.

CONTACT Deirdre Bairstow-Allen, Office of Student Financial Services, Parsons School of Design, 72 Fifth Avenue, 2nd Floor, New York, NY 10003, 212-229-8930 or toll-free 800-292-3040. *E-mail:* finaid@newschool.edu.
Website: http://www.newschool.edu/parsons/.

PATRICK HENRY COLLEGE

Purcellville, VA

Tuition & fees: $28,400	Average undergraduate aid package: $15,461

ABOUT THE INSTITUTION Independent nondenominational, coed. ***Awards:*** bachelor's degrees. 8 undergraduate majors. ***Total enrollment:*** 311. Undergraduates: 311. Freshmen: 73.

UNDERGRADUATE EXPENSES for 2020–2021 ***Application fee:*** $40. ***Comprehensive fee:*** $39,420 includes full-time tuition ($28,400) and room and board ($11,020). ***College room only:*** $5000. Full-time tuition and fees vary according to course load and location. Room and board charges vary according to board plan, housing facility, and location. ***Part-time tuition:*** $1184 per credit hour. Part-time tuition and fees vary according to course load and location.

FRESHMAN FINANCIAL AID (Fall 2019, est.) 23 applied for aid; of those 87% were deemed to have need. 100% of freshmen with need received aid; of those 20% had need fully met. ***Average percent of need met:*** 59% (excluding resources awarded to replace EFC). ***Average financial aid package:*** $15,075 (excluding

resources awarded to replace EFC). 69% of all full-time freshmen had no need and received non-need-based gift aid.

UNDERGRADUATE FINANCIAL AID (Fall 2019, est.) 67 applied for aid; of those 90% were deemed to have need. 100% of undergraduates with need received aid; of those 25% had need fully met. ***Average percent of need met:*** 58% (excluding resources awarded to replace EFC). ***Average financial aid package:*** $15,461 (excluding resources awarded to replace EFC). 72% of all full-time undergraduates had no need and received non-need-based gift aid.

GIFT AID (NEED-BASED) ***Total amount:*** $323,696 (100% institutional). ***Receiving aid:*** Freshmen: 20% (13); all full-time undergraduates: 19% (47). ***Average award:*** Freshmen: $5269; Undergraduates: $5766. ***Scholarships, grants, and awards:*** private, college/university gift aid from institutional funds.

GIFT AID (NON-NEED-BASED) ***Total amount:*** $3,483,734 (97% institutional, 3% external sources). ***Receiving aid:*** Freshmen: 29% (19). Undergraduates: 22% (55). ***Average award:*** Freshmen: $14,186. Undergraduates: $14,010. ***Scholarships, grants, and awards by category:*** *Academic interests/achievement:* general academic interests/achievements, military science. *Creative arts/performance:* debating, journalism/publications, music. *Special achievements/activities:* community service, leadership, memberships, religious involvement. *Special characteristics:* children of faculty/staff, children of public servants, public servants, relatives of clergy, veterans. ***Tuition waivers:*** Full or partial for employees or children of employees.

LOANS ***Student loans:*** $813,713 (100% non-need-based). 44% of past graduating class borrowed through all loan programs. *Average indebtedness per student:* $50,668. ***Programs:*** Private Bank Loans.

APPLYING FOR FINANCIAL AID ***Required financial aid form:*** CSS Financial Aid PROFILE. ***Financial aid deadline:*** 3/1 (priority: 11/1). ***Notification date:*** Continuous beginning 7/15. Students must reply within 13 weeks of notification.

CONTACT Mr. William K. Kellaris, Director of Financial Aid, Patrick Henry College, 10 Patrick Henry Circle, Purcellville, VA 20132, 540-441-8140 or toll-free 888-338-1776. *Fax:* 540-441-8149. *E-mail:* financialaid@phc.edu.
Website: http://www.phc.edu/.

PAUL QUINN COLLEGE

Dallas, TX

CONTACT Mildred Martinez, Financial Aid Officer I, Paul Quinn College, 3837 Simpson Stuart Road, Dallas, TX 75241, 214-379-5438 or toll-free 877-346-1063. *Fax:* 214-379-5448. *E-mail:* mmartinez@pqc.edu.
Website: http://www.pqc.edu/.

PAUL SMITH'S COLLEGE

Paul Smiths, NY

CONTACT Mary Ellen Chamberlain, Director of Financial Aid, Paul Smith's College, Routes 86 and 30, Paul Smiths, NY 12970, 518-327-6119 or toll-free 800-421-2605. *Fax:* 518-327-6055. *E-mail:* mchamberlain@paulsmiths.edu.
Website: http://www.paulsmiths.edu/.

PEABODY CONSERVATORY OF THE JOHNS HOPKINS UNIVERSITY

Baltimore, MD

CONTACT Rebecca Polgar, Director of Financial Aid, Peabody Conservatory of The Johns Hopkins University, 1 East Mount Vernon Place, Baltimore, MD 21202-2397, 667-208-6590 or toll-free 800-368-2521 (out-of-state). *Fax:* 410-659-8102. *E-mail:* finaid@peabody.jhu.edu.
Website: http://www.peabody.jhu.edu/.

PEIRCE COLLEGE

Philadelphia, PA

CONTACT Chanel Greene, Manager of Financial Aid, Peirce College, 1420 Pine Street, Philadelphia, PA 19102, 215-670-9330 or toll-free 888-467-3472. *Fax:* 215-545-3671. *E-mail:* cgreen1@peirce.edu.
Website: http://www.peirce.edu/.

PENN STATE ABINGTON

Abington, PA

Tuition & fees (area res): $15,524	Average undergraduate aid package: $10,694

ABOUT THE INSTITUTION State-related, coed. ***Awards:*** certificates, associate, and bachelor's degrees (enrollment figures include students enrolled at The Graduate School at Penn State who are taking courses at this location). 118 undergraduate majors. ***Total enrollment:*** 3,746. Undergraduates: 3,746. Freshmen: 1,050. Federal methodology is used as a basis for awarding need-based institutional aid.

UNDERGRADUATE EXPENSES for 2020–2021 ***Application fee:*** $65. ***Tuition, area resident:*** full-time $14,532. ***Tuition, state resident:*** full-time $14,532. ***Tuition, nonresident:*** full-time $23,720. ***Required fees:*** full-time $992. Full-time tuition and fees vary according to course level, degree level, location, program, and student level. Part-time tuition and fees vary according to course level, course load, degree level, location, program, and student level. ***Room only:*** $8420.

FRESHMAN FINANCIAL AID (Fall 2018) 716 applied for aid; of those 84% were deemed to have need. 96% of freshmen with need received aid; of those 10% had need fully met. ***Average percent of need met:*** 55% (excluding resources awarded to replace EFC). ***Average financial aid package:*** $10,487 (excluding resources awarded to replace EFC). 10% of all full-time freshmen had no need and received non-need-based gift aid.

UNDERGRADUATE FINANCIAL AID (Fall 2018) 2,382 applied for aid; of those 86% were deemed to have need. 96% of undergraduates with need received aid; of those 13% had need fully met. ***Average percent of need met:*** 57% (excluding resources awarded to replace EFC). ***Average financial aid package:*** $10,694 (excluding resources awarded to replace EFC). 8% of all full-time undergraduates had no need and received non-need-based gift aid.

GIFT AID (NEED-BASED) ***Total amount:*** $16,172,906 (45% federal, 23% state, 29% institutional, 3% external sources). ***Receiving aid:*** Freshmen: 39% (401); all full-time undergraduates: 42% (1,388). ***Average award:*** Freshmen: $6171; Undergraduates: $6118. ***Scholarships, grants, and awards:*** Federal Pell, FSEOG, state, private, college/university gift aid from institutional funds, United Negro College Fund.

GIFT AID (NON-NEED-BASED) ***Total amount:*** $1,174,037 (2% state, 80% institutional, 18% external sources). ***Receiving aid:*** Freshmen: 46% (480). Undergraduates: 45% (1,483). ***Average award:*** Freshmen: $2769. Undergraduates: $3423. ***Scholarships, grants, and awards by category:*** *Academic interests/achievement:* general academic interests/achievements. *Special characteristics:* children and siblings of alumni, general special characteristics. ***Tuition waivers:*** Full or partial for employees or children of employees, senior citizens. ***ROTC:*** Army cooperative, Air Force cooperative.

LOANS ***Student loans:*** $15,366,478 (82% need-based, 18% non-need-based). 72% of past graduating class borrowed through all loan programs. *Average indebtedness per student:* $32,957. ***Average need-based loan:*** Freshmen: $3251. Undergraduates: $3988. ***Parent loans:*** $4,044,952 (81% need-based, 19% non-need-based). ***Programs:*** Federal Direct (Subsidized and Unsubsidized Stafford, PLUS), Perkins, college/university, Private Loans.

WORK-STUDY ***Federal work-study:*** Total amount: $84,869; jobs available.

APPLYING FOR FINANCIAL AID ***Required financial aid form:*** FAFSA. ***Financial aid deadline (priority):*** 2/15. ***Notification date:*** Continuous beginning 3/1.

CONTACT Financial Aid Office, Penn State Abington, 1600 Woodland Road, Abington, PA 19001, 215-881-7300.
Website: http://www.abington.psu.edu/.

PENN STATE ALTOONA

Altoona, PA

Tuition & fees (area res): $15,206	Average undergraduate aid package: $10,597

ABOUT THE INSTITUTION State-related, coed. ***Awards:*** certificates, associate, and bachelor's degrees (enrollment figures include students enrolled at The Graduate School at Penn State who are taking courses at this location). 125 undergraduate majors. ***Total enrollment:*** 3,070. Undergraduates: 3,070. Freshmen: 1,118. Federal methodology is used as a basis for awarding need-based institutional aid.

UNDERGRADUATE EXPENSES for 2020–2021 ***Application fee:*** $65. ***Tuition, area resident:*** full-time $14,214; part-time $592 per credit hour. ***Tuition, state resident:*** full-time $14,214; part-time $592 per credit hour. ***Tuition, nonresident:*** full-time $23,924; part-time $997 per credit hour. ***Required fees:*** full-time $992. ***College room and board:*** $11,884; ***Room only:*** $6554.

FRESHMAN FINANCIAL AID (Fall 2018) 951 applied for aid; of those 81% were deemed to have need. 97% of freshmen with need received aid; of those 32% had need fully met. ***Average percent of need met:*** 68% (excluding resources awarded to replace EFC). ***Average financial aid package:*** $10,020 (excluding resources awarded to replace EFC). 8% of all full-time freshmen had no need and received non-need-based gift aid.

UNDERGRADUATE FINANCIAL AID (Fall 2018) 2,468 applied for aid; of those 84% were deemed to have need. 96% of undergraduates with need received aid; of those 28% had need fully met. ***Average percent of need met:*** 66% (excluding resources awarded to replace EFC). ***Average financial aid package:*** $10,597 (excluding resources awarded to replace EFC). 8% of all full-time undergraduates had no need and received non-need-based gift aid.

GIFT AID (NEED-BASED) ***Total amount:*** $12,841,109 (37% federal, 22% state, 34% institutional, 7% external sources). ***Receiving aid:*** Freshmen: 30% (345); all full-time undergraduates: 33% (1,034). ***Average award:*** Freshmen: $6146; Undergraduates: $6132. ***Scholarships, grants, and awards:*** Federal Pell, FSEOG, state, private, college/university gift aid from institutional funds, United Negro College Fund.

GIFT AID (NON-NEED-BASED) ***Total amount:*** $1,526,814 (1% federal, 2% state, 60% institutional, 37% external sources). ***Receiving aid:*** Freshmen: 50% (564). Undergraduates: 44% (1,381). ***Average award:*** Freshmen: $3636. Undergraduates: $3652. ***Scholarships, grants, and awards by category:*** *Academic interests/achievement:* general academic interests/achievements. *Special characteristics:* children and siblings of alumni, general special characteristics. ***ROTC:*** Army cooperative, Air Force cooperative.

LOANS ***Student loans:*** $22,583,875 (84% need-based, 16% non-need-based). 72% of past graduating class borrowed through all loan programs. *Average indebtedness per student:* $43,294. ***Average need-based loan:*** Freshmen: $3335. Undergraduates: $3960. ***Parent loans:*** $8,603,289 (89% need-based, 11% non-need-based). ***Programs:*** Federal Direct (Subsidized and Unsubsidized Stafford, PLUS), Perkins, college/university, Private Loans.

WORK-STUDY ***Federal work-study:*** Total amount: $253,559; jobs available.

APPLYING FOR FINANCIAL AID ***Required financial aid form:*** FAFSA. ***Financial aid deadline (priority):*** 2/15. ***Notification date:*** Continuous beginning 3/1.

CONTACT Mr. David Pearlman, Director of Student Aid, Penn State Altoona, W113 Smith Building, Altoona, PA 16601-3760, 814-949-5055 or toll-free 800-848-9843. *Fax:* 814-949-5536. *E-mail:* dpp1@psu.edu.

Website: http://www.altoona.psu.edu/.

PENN STATE BEAVER

Monaca, PA

Tuition & fees (area res): $13,710	Average undergraduate aid package: $11,100

ABOUT THE INSTITUTION State-related, coed. ***Awards:*** certificates and bachelor's degrees. 118 undergraduate majors. ***Total enrollment:*** 599. Undergraduates: 599. Freshmen: 190. Federal methodology is used as a basis for awarding need-based institutional aid.

UNDERGRADUATE EXPENSES for 2020–2021 ***Application fee:*** $65. ***Tuition, area resident:*** full-time $12,718; part-time $524 per credit hour. ***Tuition, state resident:*** full-time $12,718; part-time $524 per credit hour. ***Tuition, nonresident:*** full-time $21,310; part-time $888 per credit hour. ***Required fees:*** full-time $992. ***College room and board:*** $11,510; ***Room only:*** $6180.

FRESHMAN FINANCIAL AID (Fall 2018) 166 applied for aid; of those 85% were deemed to have need. 99% of freshmen with need received aid; of those 24% had need fully met. ***Average percent of need met:*** 65% (excluding resources awarded to replace EFC). ***Average financial aid package:*** $10,458 (excluding resources awarded to replace EFC). 17% of all full-time freshmen had no need and received non-need-based gift aid.

UNDERGRADUATE FINANCIAL AID (Fall 2018) 469 applied for aid; of those 87% were deemed to have need. 98% of undergraduates with need received aid; of those 25% had need fully met. ***Average percent of need met:*** 66% (excluding resources awarded to replace EFC). ***Average financial aid package:*** $11,100 (excluding resources awarded to replace EFC). 14% of all full-time undergraduates had no need and received non-need-based gift aid.

GIFT AID (NEED-BASED) ***Total amount:*** $3,162,975 (38% federal, 20% state, 38% institutional, 4% external sources). ***Receiving aid:*** Freshmen: 45% (82); all full-time undergraduates: 48% (260). ***Average award:*** Freshmen: $6776; Undergraduates: $6355. ***Scholarships, grants, and awards:*** Federal Pell, FSEOG, state, private, college/university gift aid from institutional funds, United Negro College Fund.

GIFT AID (NON-NEED-BASED) ***Total amount:*** $248,772 (3% state, 89% institutional, 8% external sources). ***Receiving aid:*** Freshmen: 61% (113). Undergraduates: 58% (315). ***Average award:*** Freshmen: $2177. Undergraduates: $2821. ***Scholarships, grants, and awards by category:*** *Academic interests/achievement:* general academic interests/achievements. *Special characteristics:* children and siblings of alumni.

LOANS ***Student loans:*** $3,026,575 (87% need-based, 13% non-need-based). 78% of past graduating class borrowed through all loan programs. *Average indebtedness per student:* $38,026. ***Average need-based loan:*** Freshmen: $3225. Undergraduates: $4024. ***Parent loans:*** $1,316,157 (94% need-based, 6% non-need-based). ***Programs:*** Federal Direct (Subsidized and Unsubsidized Stafford, PLUS), Perkins, college/university, Private Loans.

WORK-STUDY ***Federal work-study:*** Total amount: $90,006; jobs available. ***State or other work-study/employment:*** Part-time jobs available.

APPLYING FOR FINANCIAL AID ***Required financial aid form:*** FAFSA. ***Financial aid deadline (priority):*** 2/15. ***Notification date:*** Continuous beginning 3/1.

CONTACT Gail Gray, Student Aid and Veterans Coordinator, Penn State Beaver, 113 Student Union Building, 100 University Drive, Monaca, PA 15061, 724-773-3803. *E-mail:* gailgray@psu.edu.

Website: http://www.br.psu.edu/.

PENN STATE BERKS

Reading, PA

Tuition & fees (area res): $15,206	Average undergraduate aid package: $10,235

ABOUT THE INSTITUTION State-related, coed. ***Awards:*** certificates, associate, and bachelor's degrees (enrollment figures include students enrolled at The Graduate School at Penn State who are taking courses at this location). 129 undergraduate majors. ***Total enrollment:*** 2,482. Undergraduates: 2,481. Freshmen: 640. Federal methodology is used as a basis for awarding need-based institutional aid.

UNDERGRADUATE EXPENSES for 2020–2021 ***Application fee:*** $65. ***Tuition, area resident:*** full-time $14,214; part-time $592 per credit hour. ***Tuition, state resident:*** full-time $14,214; part-time $592 per credit hour. ***Tuition, nonresident:*** full-time $23,924; part-time $997 per credit hour. ***Required fees:*** full-time $992. Full-time tuition and fees vary according to course level, degree level, location, program, and student level. Part-time tuition and fees vary according to course level, course load, degree level, location, program, and student level. ***College room and board:*** $13,080; ***Room only:*** $7750. Room and board charges vary according to board plan, housing facility, and location.

FRESHMAN FINANCIAL AID (Fall 2018) 515 applied for aid; of those 76% were deemed to have need. 95% of freshmen with need received aid; of those 23% had need fully met. ***Average percent of need met:*** 63% (excluding resources awarded to replace EFC). ***Average financial aid package:*** $9527 (excluding resources awarded to replace EFC). 8% of all full-time freshmen had no need and received non-need-based gift aid.

UNDERGRADUATE FINANCIAL AID (Fall 2018) 1,867 applied for aid; of those 82% were deemed to have need. 95% of undergraduates with need received aid; of those 24% had need fully met. ***Average percent of need met:*** 63% (excluding resources awarded to replace EFC). ***Average financial aid package:*** $10,235 (excluding resources awarded to replace EFC). 6% of all full-time undergraduates had no need and received non-need-based gift aid.

GIFT AID (NEED-BASED) ***Total amount:*** $9,889,147 (39% federal, 24% state, 29% institutional, 8% external sources). ***Receiving aid:*** Freshmen: 32% (190); all full-time undergraduates: 38% (855). ***Average award:*** Freshmen: $5851; Undergraduates: $5950. ***Scholarships, grants, and awards:*** Federal Pell, FSEOG, state, private, college/university gift aid from institutional funds, United Negro College Fund.

GIFT AID (NON-NEED-BASED) ***Total amount:*** $699,767 (1% state, 65% institutional, 34% external sources). ***Receiving aid:*** Freshmen: 45% (265). Undergraduates: 42% (946). ***Average award:*** Freshmen: $3764. Undergraduates: $3246. ***Scholarships, grants, and awards by category:*** *Academic interests/achievement:* general academic interests/achievements. *Special characteristics:* children and siblings of alumni. ***Tuition waivers:*** Full or partial for employees or children of employees, senior citizens. ***ROTC:*** Army cooperative, Air Force cooperative.

LOANS ***Student loans:*** $15,614,468 (81% need-based, 19% non-need-based). 79% of past graduating class borrowed through all loan programs. *Average indebtedness per student:* $41,278. ***Average need-based loan:*** Freshmen: $3340. Undergraduates: $4195. ***Parent loans:*** $5,574,968 (86% need-based, 14% non-need-based). ***Programs:*** Federal Direct (Subsidized and Unsubsidized Stafford, PLUS), Perkins, college/university, Private Loans.

WORK-STUDY ***Federal work-study:*** Total amount: $86,012; jobs available.

APPLYING FOR FINANCIAL AID ***Required financial aid form:*** FAFSA. ***Financial aid deadline (priority):*** 2/15. ***Notification date:*** Continuous beginning 3/1.

CONTACT Judith A. Rile, Financial Aid Coordinator, Penn State Berks, Perkins Student Center, Room 6, Reading, PA 19610-6009, 610-396-6070. *Fax:* 610-396-6316. *E-mail:* jar38@psu.edu. *Website:* http://www.bk.psu.edu/.

PENN STATE BRANDYWINE

Media, PA

Tuition & fees (area res): $14,476	Average undergraduate aid package: $10,439

ABOUT THE INSTITUTION State-related, coed. ***Awards:*** certificates, associate, and bachelor's degrees. 120 undergraduate majors. ***Total enrollment:*** 1,332. Undergraduates: 1,331. Freshmen: 439. Federal methodology is used as a basis for awarding need-based institutional aid.

UNDERGRADUATE EXPENSES for 2020–2021 ***Application fee:*** $65. ***Tuition, area resident:*** full-time $13,484; part-time $555 per credit hour. ***Tuition, state resident:*** full-time $13,484; part-time $555 per credit hour. ***Tuition, nonresident:*** full-time $22,474; part-time $936 per credit hour. ***Required fees:*** full-time $992. Full-time tuition and fees vary according to course level, degree level, location, program, and student level. Part-time tuition and fees vary according to course level, course load, degree level, location, program, and student level. ***College room and board:*** $12,586; ***Room only:*** $7256. Room and board charges vary according to board plan.

FRESHMAN FINANCIAL AID (Fall 2018) 343 applied for aid; of those 80% were deemed to have need. 96% of freshmen with need received aid; of those 24% had need fully met. ***Average percent of need met:*** 63% (excluding resources awarded to replace EFC). ***Average financial aid package:*** $9752 (excluding resources awarded to replace EFC). 12% of all full-time freshmen had no need and received non-need-based gift aid.

UNDERGRADUATE FINANCIAL AID (Fall 2018) 984 applied for aid; of those 82% were deemed to have need. 95% of undergraduates with need received aid; of those 22% had need fully met. ***Average percent of need met:*** 61% (excluding resources awarded to replace EFC). ***Average financial aid package:*** $10,439 (excluding resources awarded to replace EFC). 9% of all full-time undergraduates had no need and received non-need-based gift aid.

GIFT AID (NEED-BASED) ***Total amount:*** $5,786,137 (40% federal, 21% state, 35% institutional, 4% external sources). ***Receiving aid:*** Freshmen: 40% (154); all full-time undergraduates: 40% (479). ***Average award:*** Freshmen: $5928; Undergraduates: $6119. ***Scholarships, grants, and awards:*** Federal Pell, FSEOG, state, private, college/university gift aid from institutional funds, United Negro College Fund.

GIFT AID (NON-NEED-BASED) ***Total amount:*** $553,498 (2% federal, 80% institutional, 18% external sources). ***Receiving aid:*** Freshmen: 53% (201). Undergraduates: 46% (548). ***Average award:*** Freshmen: $3339. Undergraduates: $4144. ***Scholarships, grants, and awards by category:*** *Academic interests/achievement:* general academic interests/achievements. *Special characteristics:* children and siblings of alumni. ***Tuition waivers:*** Full or partial for employees or children of employees, senior citizens. ***ROTC:*** Army cooperative, Air Force cooperative.

LOANS ***Student loans:*** $6,742,836 (81% need-based, 19% non-need-based). 78% of past graduating class borrowed through all loan programs. *Average indebtedness per student:* $33,019. ***Average need-based loan:*** Freshmen: $3302. Undergraduates: $3968. ***Parent loans:*** $1,977,882 (84% need-based, 16% non-need-based). ***Programs:*** Federal Direct (Subsidized and Unsubsidized Stafford, PLUS), Perkins, college/university, Private Loans.

WORK-STUDY ***Federal work-study:*** Total amount: $48,025; jobs available. ***State or other work-study/employment:*** Part-time jobs available.

APPLYING FOR FINANCIAL AID ***Required financial aid form:*** FAFSA. ***Financial aid deadline (priority):*** 2/15. ***Notification date:*** Continuous beginning 3/1.

CONTACT Financial Aid Office, Penn State Brandywine, 25 Yearsley Mill Road, Media, PA 19063, 610-892-1200. *Website:* http://www.brandywine.psu.edu/.

PENN STATE ERIE, THE BEHREND COLLEGE

Erie, PA

Tuition & fees (area res): $15,206	Average undergraduate aid package: $10,866

ABOUT THE INSTITUTION State-related, coed. ***Awards:*** certificates, associate, bachelor's, and master's degrees. 129 undergraduate majors. ***Total enrollment:*** 4,108. Undergraduates: 7,852. Freshmen: 1,019. Federal methodology is used as a basis for awarding need-based institutional aid.

UNDERGRADUATE EXPENSES for 2020–2021 ***Application fee:*** $65. ***Tuition, area resident:*** full-time $14,214; part-time $592 per credit hour. ***Tuition, state resident:*** full-time $14,214; part-time $592 per credit hour. ***Tuition, nonresident:*** full-time $23,924; part-time $997 per credit hour. ***Required fees:*** full-time $992. ***College room and board:*** $11,884; ***Room only:*** $6554.

FRESHMAN FINANCIAL AID (Fall 2018) 836 applied for aid; of those 81% were deemed to have need. 97% of freshmen with need received aid; of those 27% had need fully met. ***Average percent of need met:*** 66% (excluding resources awarded to replace EFC). ***Average financial aid package:*** $10,522 (excluding resources awarded to replace EFC). 8% of all full-time freshmen had no need and received non-need-based gift aid.

UNDERGRADUATE FINANCIAL AID (Fall 2018) 3,096 applied for aid; of those 86% were deemed to have need. 97% of undergraduates with need received aid; of those 28% had need fully met. ***Average percent of need met:*** 66% (excluding resources awarded to replace EFC). ***Average financial aid package:*** $10,866 (excluding resources awarded to replace EFC). 6% of all full-time undergraduates had no need and received non-need-based gift aid.

GIFT AID (NEED-BASED) ***Total amount:*** $18,068,362 (32% federal, 22% state, 38% institutional, 8% external sources). ***Receiving aid:*** Freshmen: 30% (316); all full-time undergraduates: 34% (1,364). ***Average award:*** Freshmen: $6402; Undergraduates: $6274. ***Scholarships, grants, and awards:*** Federal Pell, FSEOG, state, private, college/university gift aid from institutional funds, United Negro College Fund.

GIFT AID (NON-NEED-BASED) ***Total amount:*** $1,537,649 (66% institutional, 34% external sources). ***Receiving aid:*** Freshmen: 51% (540). Undergraduates: 46% (1,837). ***Average award:*** Freshmen: $3633. Undergraduates: $4174. ***Scholarships, grants, and awards by category:*** *Academic interests/achievement:* general academic interests/achievements. *Special characteristics:* children and siblings of alumni. ***ROTC:*** Army cooperative.

LOANS ***Student loans:*** $28,788,385 (86% need-based, 14% non-need-based). 71% of past graduating class borrowed through all loan programs. *Average indebtedness per student:* $41,841. ***Average need-based loan:*** Freshmen: $3329. Undergrad-

uates: $4346. ***Parent loans:*** $9,303,815 (89% need-based, 11% non-need-based). ***Programs:*** Federal Direct (Subsidized and Unsubsidized Stafford, PLUS), Perkins, college/university, Private Loans.

WORK-STUDY ***Federal work-study:*** Total amount: $179,642; jobs available.

APPLYING FOR FINANCIAL AID ***Required financial aid form:*** FAFSA. ***Financial aid deadline (priority):*** 2/15. ***Notification date:*** Continuous beginning 3/1.

CONTACT Ms. Jane Brady, Associate Director of Financial Aid, Penn State Erie, The Behrend College, 4851 College Drive, Metzgar Admissions and Alumni Center, Erie, PA 16563, 814-898-6162 or toll-free 866-374-3378. *Fax:* 814-898-7595. *E-mail:* jub9@psu.edu.

Website: http://www.psbehrend.psu.edu/.

PENN STATE GREATER ALLEGHENY

McKeesport, PA

Tuition & fees (area res): $13,710 | **Average undergraduate aid package: $12,783**

ABOUT THE INSTITUTION State-related, coed. ***Awards:*** certificates, associate, and bachelor's degrees. 119 undergraduate majors. ***Total enrollment:*** 439. Undergraduates: 439. Freshmen: 103. Federal methodology is used as a basis for awarding need-based institutional aid.

UNDERGRADUATE EXPENSES for 2020–2021 ***Application fee:*** $65. ***Tuition, area resident:*** full-time $12,718; part-time $524 per credit hour. ***Tuition, state resident:*** full-time $12,718; part-time $524 per credit hour. ***Tuition, nonresident:*** full-time $21,310; part-time $888 per credit hour. ***Required fees:*** full-time $992. Full-time tuition and fees vary according to course level, degree level, location, program, and student level. Part-time tuition and fees vary according to course level, course load, degree level, location, program, and student level. ***College room and board:*** $11,510; ***Room only:*** $6180. Room and board charges vary according to board plan, housing facility, and location.

FRESHMAN FINANCIAL AID (Fall 2018) 101 applied for aid; of those 89% were deemed to have need. 97% of freshmen with need received aid; of those 21% had need fully met. ***Average percent of need met:*** 67% (excluding resources awarded to replace EFC). ***Average financial aid package:*** $12,620 (excluding resources awarded to replace EFC). 9% of all full-time freshmen had no need and received non-need-based gift aid.

UNDERGRADUATE FINANCIAL AID (Fall 2018) 367 applied for aid; of those 89% were deemed to have need. 97% of undergraduates with need received aid; of those 21% had need fully met. ***Average percent of need met:*** 67% (excluding resources awarded to replace EFC). ***Average financial aid package:*** $12,783 (excluding resources awarded to replace EFC). 8% of all full-time undergraduates had no need and received non-need-based gift aid.

GIFT AID (NEED-BASED) ***Total amount:*** $3,054,128 (39% federal, 20% state, 36% institutional, 5% external sources). ***Receiving aid:*** Freshmen: 53% (61); all full-time undergraduates: 55% (228). ***Average award:*** Freshmen: $7881; Undergraduates: $7104. ***Scholarships, grants, and awards:*** Federal Pell, FSEOG, state, private, college/university gift aid from institutional funds, United Negro College Fund.

GIFT AID (NON-NEED-BASED) ***Total amount:*** $126,506 (87% institutional, 13% external sources). ***Receiving aid:*** Freshmen: 67% (78). Undergraduates: 61% (255). ***Average award:*** Freshmen: $2165. Undergraduates: $3099. ***Tuition waivers:*** Full or partial for employees or children of employees, senior citizens. ***ROTC:*** Air Force cooperative.

LOANS ***Student loans:*** $2,328,625 (90% need-based, 10% non-need-based). 76% of past graduating class borrowed through all loan programs. *Average indebtedness per student:* $36,645. ***Average need-based loan:*** Freshmen: $3359. Undergraduates: $4008. ***Parent loans:*** $794,755 (91% need-based, 9% non-need-based). ***Programs:*** Federal Direct (Subsidized and Unsubsidized Stafford, PLUS), Perkins, college/university, Private Loans.

WORK-STUDY ***Federal work-study:*** Total amount: $72,194; jobs available. ***State or other work-study/employment:*** Part-time jobs available.

APPLYING FOR FINANCIAL AID ***Required financial aid form:*** FAFSA. ***Financial aid deadline (priority):*** 2/15. ***Notification date:*** Continuous beginning 3/1.

CONTACT Financial Aid Office, Penn State Greater Allegheny, 4000 University Drive, McKeesport, PA 15132, 412-675-9000.

Website: http://www.ga.psu.edu/.

PENN STATE HARRISBURG

Middletown, PA

Tuition & fees (area res): $15,206 | **Average undergraduate aid package: $10,491**

ABOUT THE INSTITUTION State-related, coed. ***Awards:*** certificates, associate, bachelor's, master's, and doctoral degrees. 29 undergraduate majors. ***Total enrollment:*** 4,898. Undergraduates: 4,246. Freshmen: 956. Federal methodology is used as a basis for awarding need-based institutional aid.

UNDERGRADUATE EXPENSES for 2020–2021 ***Application fee:*** $65. ***Tuition, area resident:*** full-time $14,214; part-time $592 per credit hour. ***Tuition, state resident:*** full-time $14,214; part-time $592 per credit hour. ***Tuition, nonresident:*** full-time $23,924; part-time $997 per credit hour. ***Required fees:*** full-time $992. Full-time tuition and fees vary according to course level, degree level, location, program, and student level. Part-time tuition and fees vary according to course level, course load, degree level, location, program, and student level. ***College room and board:*** $13,750; ***Room only:*** $8420. Room and board charges vary according to board plan, housing facility, and location.

FRESHMAN FINANCIAL AID (Fall 2018) 624 applied for aid; of those 79% were deemed to have need. 96% of freshmen with need received aid; of those 27% had need fully met. ***Average percent of need met:*** 63% (excluding resources awarded to replace EFC). ***Average financial aid package:*** $10,555 (excluding resources awarded to replace EFC). 10% of all full-time freshmen had no need and received non-need-based gift aid.

UNDERGRADUATE FINANCIAL AID (Fall 2018) 2,765 applied for aid; of those 86% were deemed to have need. 96% of undergraduates with need received aid; of those 21% had need fully met. ***Average percent of need met:*** 59% (excluding resources awarded to replace EFC). ***Average financial aid package:*** $10,491 (excluding resources awarded to replace EFC). 9% of all full-time undergraduates had no need and received non-need-based gift aid.

GIFT AID (NEED-BASED) ***Total amount:*** $16,331,287 (37% federal, 19% state, 30% institutional, 14% external sources). ***Receiving aid:*** Freshmen: 24% (232); all full-time undergraduates: 34% (1,312). ***Average award:*** Freshmen: $6288; Undergraduates: $5901. ***Scholarships, grants, and awards:*** Federal Pell, FSEOG, state, private, college/university gift aid from institutional funds, United Negro College Fund.

GIFT AID (NON-NEED-BASED) ***Total amount:*** $3,356,808 (1% state, 31% institutional, 68% external sources). ***Receiving aid:*** Freshmen: 37% (359). Undergraduates: 39% (1,528). ***Average award:*** Freshmen: $3513. Undergraduates: $2911. ***Scholarships, grants, and awards by category:*** *Academic interests/achievement:* general academic interests/achievements. *Special characteristics:* children and siblings of alumni, general special characteristics. ***Tuition waivers:*** Full or partial for employees or children of employees, senior citizens. ***ROTC:*** Army cooperative.

LOANS ***Student loans:*** $23,169,193 (86% need-based, 14% non-need-based). 60% of past graduating class borrowed through all loan programs. *Average indebtedness per student:* $39,036. ***Average need-based loan:*** Freshmen: $3326. Undergraduates: $4292. ***Parent loans:*** $8,498,221 (89% need-based, 11% non-need-based). ***Programs:*** Federal Direct (Subsidized and Unsubsidized Stafford, PLUS), Perkins, college/university, Private Loans.

WORK-STUDY ***Federal work-study:*** Total amount: $91,862; jobs available.

APPLYING FOR FINANCIAL AID ***Required financial aid form:*** FAFSA. ***Financial aid deadline (priority):*** 2/15. ***Notification date:*** Continuous beginning 3/1.

CONTACT Financial Aid Office, Penn State Harrisburg, 777 West Harrisburg Pike, Middletown, PA 17057, 717-948-6000 or toll-free 800-222-2056.

Website: http://www.harrisburg.psu.edu/.

PENN STATE HAZLETON

Hazleton, PA

Tuition & fees (area res): $14,476 | **Average undergraduate aid package: $11,656**

ABOUT THE INSTITUTION State-related, coed. ***Awards:*** certificates, associate, and bachelor's degrees. 125 undergraduate majors. ***Total enrollment:*** 619. Undergraduates: 619. Freshmen: 160. Federal methodology is used as a basis for awarding need-based institutional aid.

UNDERGRADUATE EXPENSES for 2020–2021 ***Application fee:*** $65. ***Tuition, area resident:*** full-time $13,484; part-time $555 per credit hour. ***Tuition, state resident:*** full-time $13,484; part-time $555 per credit hour. ***Tuition, nonresident:*** full-time $22,474; part-time $936 per credit hour. ***Required fees:*** full-time $992. Full-time tuition and fees vary according to course level, degree level, location, program, and student level. Part-time tuition and fees vary according to course level, course load, degree level, location, program, and student level. ***College room and board:*** $11,510; ***Room only:*** $6180. Room and board charges vary according to board plan, housing facility, and location.

FRESHMAN FINANCIAL AID (Fall 2018) 186 applied for aid; of those 89% were deemed to have need. 99% of freshmen with need received aid; of those 26% had need fully met. ***Average percent of need met:*** 67% (excluding resources awarded to replace EFC). ***Average financial aid package:*** $12,110 (excluding resources awarded to replace EFC). 13% of all full-time freshmen had no need and received non-need-based gift aid.

UNDERGRADUATE FINANCIAL AID (Fall 2018) 542 applied for aid; of those 90% were deemed to have need. 99% of undergraduates with need received aid; of those 25% had need fully met. ***Average percent of need met:*** 67% (excluding resources awarded to replace EFC). ***Average financial aid package:*** $11,656 (excluding resources awarded to replace EFC). 10% of all full-time undergraduates had no need and received non-need-based gift aid.

GIFT AID (NEED-BASED) ***Total amount:*** $4,084,050 (37% federal, 21% state, 40% institutional, 2% external sources). ***Receiving aid:*** Freshmen: 56% (109); all full-time undergraduates: 52% (310). ***Average award:*** Freshmen: $7169; Undergraduates: $6803. ***Scholarships, grants, and awards:*** Federal Pell, FSEOG, state, private, college/university gift aid from institutional funds, United Negro College Fund.

GIFT AID (NON-NEED-BASED) ***Total amount:*** $241,872 (2% state, 92% institutional, 6% external sources). ***Receiving aid:*** Freshmen: 77% (150). Undergraduates: 69% (407). ***Average award:*** Freshmen: $3330. Undergraduates: $3612. ***Scholarships, grants, and awards by category:*** *Academic interests/achievement:* general academic interests/achievements. *Special characteristics:* children and siblings of alumni. ***Tuition waivers:*** Full or partial for employees or children of employees, senior citizens. ***ROTC:*** Air Force cooperative.

LOANS ***Student loans:*** $4,334,754 (90% need-based, 10% non-need-based). 86% of past graduating class borrowed through all loan programs. *Average indebtedness per student:* $38,737. ***Average need-based loan:*** Freshmen: $3348. Undergraduates: $3959. ***Parent loans:*** $1,479,688 (89% need-based, 11% non-need-based). ***Programs:*** Federal Direct (Subsidized and Unsubsidized Stafford, PLUS), Perkins, college/university, Private Loans.

WORK-STUDY ***Federal work-study:*** Total amount: $100,502; jobs available. ***State or other work-study/employment:*** Part-time jobs available.

APPLYING FOR FINANCIAL AID ***Required financial aid form:*** FAFSA. ***Financial aid deadline (priority):*** 2/15. ***Notification date:*** Continuous beginning 3/1.

CONTACT Mrs. Sarah Evancho, Student Aid Coordinator, Penn State Hazleton, Administration Building, Room 222, Hazleton, PA 18201-1291, 570-450-3163 or toll-free 800-279-8495. *E-mail:* sjw37@psu.edu.
Website: http://www.hn.psu.edu/.

PENN STATE LEHIGH VALLEY

Center Valley, PA

Tuition & fees (area res): $14,476	Average undergraduate aid package: $10,335

ABOUT THE INSTITUTION State-related, coed. ***Awards:*** certificates, associate, and bachelor's degrees (enrollment figures include students enrolled at The Graduate School at Penn State who are taking courses at this location). 119 undergraduate majors. ***Total enrollment:*** 977. Undergraduates: 954. Freshmen: 267. Federal methodology is used as a basis for awarding need-based institutional aid.

UNDERGRADUATE EXPENSES for 2020–2021 ***Application fee:*** $65. ***Tuition, area resident:*** full-time $13,484; part-time $555 per credit hour. ***Tuition, state resident:*** full-time $13,484; part-time $555 per credit hour. ***Tuition, nonresident:*** full-time $22,474; part-time $936 per credit hour. ***Required fees:*** full-time $992.

FRESHMAN FINANCIAL AID (Fall 2018) 202 applied for aid; of those 83% were deemed to have need. 95% of freshmen with need received aid; of those 14% had need fully met. ***Average percent of need met:*** 56% (excluding resources awarded to replace EFC). ***Average financial aid package:*** $9423 (excluding resources awarded to replace EFC). 10% of all full-time freshmen had no need and received non-need-based gift aid.

UNDERGRADUATE FINANCIAL AID (Fall 2018) 618 applied for aid; of those 86% were deemed to have need. 94% of undergraduates with need received aid; of those 15% had need fully met. ***Average percent of need met:*** 57% (excluding resources awarded to replace EFC). ***Average financial aid package:*** $10,335 (excluding resources awarded to replace EFC). 7% of all full-time undergraduates had no need and received non-need-based gift aid.

GIFT AID (NEED-BASED) ***Total amount:*** $3,728,471 (46% federal, 24% state, 29% institutional, 1% external sources). ***Receiving aid:*** Freshmen: 42% (97); all full-time undergraduates: 46% (352). ***Average award:*** Freshmen: $6103; Undergraduates: $6152. ***Scholarships, grants, and awards:*** Federal Pell, FSEOG, state, private, college/university gift aid from institutional funds, United Negro College Fund.

GIFT AID (NON-NEED-BASED) ***Total amount:*** $199,402 (2% state, 84% institutional, 14% external sources). ***Receiving aid:*** Freshmen: 56% (129). Undergraduates: 51% (385). ***Average award:*** Freshmen: $2760. Undergraduates: $2986. ***Scholarships, grants, and awards by category:*** *Academic interests/achievement:* general academic interests/achievements. *Special characteristics:* general special characteristics. ***ROTC:*** Army cooperative.

LOANS ***Student loans:*** $4,063,117 (83% need-based, 17% non-need-based). 76% of past graduating class borrowed through all loan programs. *Average indebtedness per student:* $35,834. ***Average need-based loan:*** Freshmen: $3388. Undergraduates: $4065. ***Parent loans:*** $835,107 (84% need-based, 16% non-need-based). ***Programs:*** Federal Direct (Subsidized and Unsubsidized Stafford, PLUS), Perkins, college/university, Private Loans.

WORK-STUDY ***Federal work-study:*** Total amount: $54,397; jobs available. ***State or other work-study/employment:*** Part-time jobs available.

APPLYING FOR FINANCIAL AID ***Required financial aid form:*** FAFSA. ***Financial aid deadline (priority):*** 2/15. ***Notification date:*** Continuous beginning 3/1.

CONTACT Maryann Hubick, Student Aid Coordinator, Penn State Lehigh Valley, 8380 Mohr Lane, Fogelsville, PA 18051, 610-285-5033. *Fax:* 610-285-5220. *E-mail:* mxh61@psu.edu.
Website: http://www.lv.psu.edu/.

PENN STATE NEW KENSINGTON

New Kensington, PA

Tuition & fees (area res): $13,710	Average undergraduate aid package: $10,095

ABOUT THE INSTITUTION State-related, coed. ***Awards:*** certificates, associate, and bachelor's degrees. 124 undergraduate majors. ***Total enrollment:*** 545. Undergraduates: 545. Freshmen: 136. Federal methodology is used as a basis for awarding need-based institutional aid.

UNDERGRADUATE EXPENSES for 2019–2020 ***Application fee:*** $65. ***Tuition, area resident:*** full-time $12,718. ***Tuition, state resident:*** full-time $12,718. ***Tuition, nonresident:*** full-time $21,310. ***Required fees:*** full-time $992. Full-time tuition and fees vary according to course level, degree level, location, program, and student level. Part-time tuition and fees vary according to course level, course load, degree level, location, program, and student level.

FRESHMAN FINANCIAL AID (Fall 2018) 149 applied for aid; of those 79% were deemed to have need. 97% of freshmen with need received aid; of those 20% had need fully met. ***Average percent of need met:*** 56% (excluding resources awarded to replace EFC). ***Average financial aid package:*** $9034 (excluding resources awarded to replace EFC). 18% of all full-time freshmen had no need and received non-need-based gift aid.

UNDERGRADUATE FINANCIAL AID (Fall 2018) 412 applied for aid; of those 81% were deemed to have need. 97% of undergraduates with need received aid; of those 20% had need fully met. ***Average percent of need met:*** 59% (excluding resources awarded to replace EFC). ***Average financial aid package:*** $10,095 (excluding resources awarded to replace EFC). 10% of all full-time undergraduates had no need and received non-need-based gift aid.

GIFT AID (NEED-BASED) ***Total amount:*** $2,286,155 (38% federal, 24% state, 33% institutional, 5% external sources). ***Receiving aid:*** Freshmen: 46% (75); all full-time undergraduates: 44% (213). ***Average award:*** Freshmen: $4507; Undergraduates: $5560. ***Scholarships, grants, and awards:*** Federal Pell, FSEOG, state, private, college/university gift aid from institutional funds, United Negro College Fund.

GIFT AID (NON-NEED-BASED) ***Total amount:*** $192,707 (9% state, 71% institutional, 20% external sources). ***Receiving aid:*** Freshmen: 53% (86). Undergraduates: 47% (231). ***Average award:*** Freshmen: $2501. Undergraduates: $2730. ***Scholarships, grants, and awards by category:*** *Academic interests/achievement:* general academic interests/achievements. *Special characteristics:* children and siblings of alumni. ***Tuition waivers:*** Full or partial for employees or children of employees, senior citizens. ***ROTC:*** Air Force cooperative.

LOANS ***Student loans:*** $2,762,365 (78% need-based, 22% non-need-based). 71% of past graduating class borrowed through all loan programs. *Average indebtedness per student:* $34,304. ***Average need-based loan:*** Freshmen: $3177. Undergraduates: $3931. ***Parent loans:*** $473,859 (85% need-based, 15% non-need-based). ***Programs:*** Federal Direct (Subsidized and Unsubsidized Stafford, PLUS), Perkins, college/university, Private Loans.

WORK-STUDY ***Federal work-study:*** Total amount: $58,987; jobs available. ***State or other work-study/employment:*** Part-time jobs available.

APPLYING FOR FINANCIAL AID ***Required financial aid form:*** FAFSA. ***Financial aid deadline (priority):*** 2/15. ***Notification date:*** Continuous beginning 3/1.

CONTACT Financial Aid Office, Penn State New Kensington, 3550 Seventh Street Road, New Kensington, PA 15068, 724-334-5466 or toll-free 888-968-7297.
Website: http://www.nk.psu.edu/.

PENN STATE SCHUYLKILL

Schuylkill Haven, PA

Tuition & fees (area res): $14,476	Average undergraduate aid package: $11,749

ABOUT THE INSTITUTION State-related, coed. ***Awards:*** certificates, associate, and bachelor's degrees (bachelor's degree programs completed at the Harrisburg campus). 124 undergraduate majors. ***Total enrollment:*** 631. Undergraduates: 631. Freshmen: 172. Federal methodology is used as a basis for awarding need-based institutional aid.

UNDERGRADUATE EXPENSES for 2020–2021 ***Application fee:*** $65. ***Tuition, area resident:*** full-time $13,484; part-time $555 per credit hour. ***Tuition, state resident:*** full-time $13,484; part-time $555 per credit hour. ***Tuition, nonresident:*** full-time $22,474; part-time $936 per credit hour. ***Required fees:*** full-time $992. Full-time tuition and fees vary according to course level, degree level, location, program, and student level. Part-time tuition and fees vary according to course level, course load, degree level, location, program, and student level. ***College room and board:*** $6766; ***Room only:*** $6766. Room and board charges vary according to board plan, housing facility, and location.

FRESHMAN FINANCIAL AID (Fall 2018) 133 applied for aid; of those 89% were deemed to have need. 96% of freshmen with need received aid; of those 25% had need fully met. ***Average percent of need met:*** 66% (excluding resources awarded to replace EFC). ***Average financial aid package:*** $12,222 (excluding resources awarded to replace EFC). 9% of all full-time freshmen had no need and received non-need-based gift aid.

UNDERGRADUATE FINANCIAL AID (Fall 2018) 470 applied for aid; of those 92% were deemed to have need. 98% of undergraduates with need received aid; of those 25% had need fully met. ***Average percent of need met:*** 68% (excluding resources awarded to replace EFC). ***Average financial aid package:*** $11,749 (excluding resources awarded to replace EFC). 6% of all full-time undergraduates had no need and received non-need-based gift aid.

GIFT AID (NEED-BASED) ***Total amount:*** $3,661,978 (36% federal, 21% state, 38% institutional, 5% external sources). ***Receiving aid:*** Freshmen: 55% (76); all full-time undergraduates: 59% (287). ***Average award:*** Freshmen: $6331; Undergraduates: $6421. ***Scholarships, grants, and awards:*** Federal Pell, FSEOG, state, private, college/university gift aid from institutional funds, United Negro College Fund.

GIFT AID (NON-NEED-BASED) ***Total amount:*** $142,695 (6% state, 56% institutional, 38% external sources). ***Receiving aid:*** Freshmen: 69% (95). Undergraduates: 69% (336). ***Average award:*** Freshmen: $2361. Undergraduates: $2946. ***Scholarships, grants, and awards by category:*** *Academic interests/achievement:* general academic interests/achievements. *Special characteristics:* general special characteristics. ***Tuition waivers:*** Full or partial for employees or children of employees, senior citizens.

LOANS ***Student loans:*** $3,750,943 (91% need-based, 9% non-need-based). 87% of past graduating class borrowed through all loan programs. *Average indebtedness per student:* $41,749. ***Average need-based loan:*** Freshmen: $3182. Undergraduates: $3920. ***Parent loans:*** $1,049,327 (93% need-based, 7% non-need-based). ***Programs:*** Federal Direct (Subsidized and Unsubsidized Stafford, PLUS), Perkins, college/university, Private Loans.

WORK-STUDY ***Federal work-study:*** Total amount: $71,913; jobs available. ***State or other work-study/employment:*** Part-time jobs available.

APPLYING FOR FINANCIAL AID ***Required financial aid form:*** FAFSA. ***Financial aid deadline (priority):*** 2/15. ***Notification date:*** Continuous beginning 3/1.

CONTACT Financial Aid Office, Penn State Schuylkill, 200 University Drive, Schuylkill Haven, PA 17972, 570-385-6000.
Website: http://www.sl.psu.edu/.

PENN STATE SHENANGO

Sharon, PA

Tuition & fees (area res): $13,350	Average undergraduate aid package: $13,037

ABOUT THE INSTITUTION State-related, coed. ***Awards:*** certificates, associate, and bachelor's degrees. 124 undergraduate majors. ***Total enrollment:*** 402. Undergraduates: 402. Freshmen: 43. Federal methodology is used as a basis for awarding need-based institutional aid.

UNDERGRADUATE EXPENSES for 2020–2021 ***Application fee:*** $65. ***Tuition, area resident:*** full-time $12,474; part-time $504 per credit hour. ***Tuition, state resident:*** full-time $12,474; part-time $504 per credit hour. ***Tuition, nonresident:*** full-time $20,898; part-time $871 per credit hour. ***Required fees:*** full-time $876. Full-time tuition and fees vary according to course level, degree level, location, program, and student level. Part-time tuition and fees vary according to course level, course load, degree level, location, program, and student level.

FRESHMAN FINANCIAL AID (Fall 2018) 58 applied for aid; of those 86% were deemed to have need. 100% of freshmen with need received aid; of those 16% had need fully met. ***Average percent of need met:*** 62% (excluding resources awarded to replace EFC). ***Average financial aid package:*** $12,925 (excluding resources awarded to replace EFC). 18% of all full-time freshmen had no need and received non-need-based gift aid.

UNDERGRADUATE FINANCIAL AID (Fall 2018) 203 applied for aid; of those 93% were deemed to have need. 99% of undergraduates with need received aid; of those 9% had need fully met. ***Average percent of need met:*** 58% (excluding resources awarded to replace EFC). ***Average financial aid package:*** $13,037 (excluding resources awarded to replace EFC). 10% of all full-time undergraduates had no need and received non-need-based gift aid.

GIFT AID (NEED-BASED) ***Total amount:*** $2,366,206 (33% federal, 13% state, 51% institutional, 3% external sources). ***Receiving aid:*** Freshmen: 60% (37); all full-time undergraduates: 71% (155). ***Average award:*** Freshmen: $6049; Undergraduates: $6096. ***Scholarships, grants, and awards:*** Federal Pell, FSEOG, state, private, college/university gift aid from institutional funds, United Negro College Fund.

GIFT AID (NON-NEED-BASED) ***Total amount:*** $119,015 (2% state, 88% institutional, 10% external sources). ***Receiving aid:*** Freshmen: 76% (47). Undergraduates: 75% (163). ***Average award:*** Freshmen: $3820. Undergraduates: $4254. ***Scholarships, grants, and awards by category:*** *Academic interests/achievement:* general academic interests/achievements. *Special characteristics:* children and siblings of alumni. ***Tuition waivers:*** Full or partial for employees or children of employees, senior citizens.

LOANS ***Student loans:*** $1,629,937 (90% need-based, 10% non-need-based). 97% of past graduating class borrowed through all loan programs. *Average indebtedness per student:* $40,515. ***Average need-based loan:*** Freshmen: $3034. Undergraduates: $3598. ***Parent loans:*** $61,921 (77% need-based, 23% non-need-based). ***Programs:*** Federal Direct (Subsidized and Unsubsidized Stafford, PLUS), Perkins, college/university, Private Loans.

WORK-STUDY ***Federal work-study:*** Total amount: $52,553; jobs available. ***State or other work-study/employment:*** Part-time jobs available.

APPLYING FOR FINANCIAL AID ***Required financial aid form:*** FAFSA. ***Financial aid deadline (priority):*** 2/15. ***Notification date:*** Continuous beginning 3/1.

CONTACT Shawn O'Neill, Financial Aid Coordinator, Penn State Shenango, Lecture Hall, Room 225, 147 Shenango Avenue, Sharon, PA 16146, 724-983-2804. *E-mail:* swo3@psu.edu.
Website: http://www.shenango.psu.edu/.

PENN STATE UNIVERSITY PARK

State College, PA

Tuition & fees (area res): $18,450 **Average undergraduate aid package: $11,497**

ABOUT THE INSTITUTION State-related, coed. ***Awards:*** certificates, associate, bachelor's, master's, and doctoral degrees. 120 undergraduate majors. ***Total enrollment:*** 47,223. Undergraduates: 40,639. Freshmen: 8,331. Federal methodology is used as a basis for awarding need-based institutional aid.

UNDERGRADUATE EXPENSES for 2020–2021 ***Application fee:*** $65. ***Tuition, area resident:*** full-time $17,416; part-time $726 per credit hour. ***Tuition, state resident:*** full-time $17,416; part-time $726 per credit hour. ***Tuition, nonresident:*** full-time $34,480; part-time $1437 per credit hour. ***Required fees:*** full-time $1034. ***College room and board:*** $11,884; ***Room only:*** $6554.

FRESHMAN FINANCIAL AID (Fall 2018) 6148 applied for aid; of those 64% were deemed to have need. 91% of freshmen with need received aid; of those 34% had need fully met. ***Average percent of need met:*** 64% (excluding resources awarded to replace EFC). ***Average financial aid package:*** $10,346 (excluding resources awarded to replace EFC). 7% of all full-time freshmen had no need and received non-need-based gift aid.

UNDERGRADUATE FINANCIAL AID (Fall 2018) 23,848 applied for aid; of those 75% were deemed to have need. 94% of undergraduates with need received aid; of those 32% had need fully met. ***Average percent of need met:*** 64% (excluding resources awarded to replace EFC). ***Average financial aid package:*** $11,497 (excluding resources awarded to replace EFC). 9% of all full-time undergraduates had no need and received non-need-based gift aid.

GIFT AID (NEED-BASED) ***Total amount:*** $119,137,864 (24% federal, 13% state, 52% institutional, 11% external sources). ***Receiving aid:*** Freshmen: 17% (1,359); all full-time undergraduates: 21% (8,082). ***Average award:*** Freshmen: $6517; Undergraduates: $6755. ***Scholarships, grants, and awards:*** Federal Pell, FSEOG, state, private, college/university gift aid from institutional funds, United Negro College Fund.

GIFT AID (NON-NEED-BASED) ***Total amount:*** $43,461,490 (37% institutional, 63% external sources). ***Receiving aid:*** Freshmen: 27% (2,155). Undergraduates: 25% (9,909). ***Average award:*** Freshmen: $5695. Undergraduates: $4716. ***Scholarships, grants, and awards by category:*** *Academic interests/achievement:* general academic interests/achievements. ***ROTC:*** Army, Naval, Air Force.

LOANS ***Student loans:*** $239,135,506 (79% need-based, 21% non-need-based). 52% of past graduating class borrowed through all loan programs. *Average indebtedness per student:* $40,128. ***Average need-based loan:*** Freshmen: $3435. Undergraduates: $4582. ***Parent loans:*** $123,719,796 (86% need-based, 14% non-need-based). ***Programs:*** Federal Direct (Subsidized and Unsubsidized Stafford, PLUS), Perkins, college/university, Private Loans.

WORK-STUDY ***Federal work-study:*** Total amount: $804,877; jobs available.

ATHLETIC AWARDS Total amount: $19,491,096 (30% need-based, 70% non-need-based).

APPLYING FOR FINANCIAL AID ***Required financial aid form:*** FAFSA. ***Financial aid deadline (priority):*** 2/15. ***Notification date:*** Continuous beginning 3/1.

CONTACT Ms. Melissa J. Kunes, Executive Director for Student Aid, Penn State University Park, 301 Shields Building, University Park, PA 16802, 814-863-0507. *Fax:* 814-863-0322.
Website: http://www.psu.edu/.

PENN STATE WILKES-BARRE

Lehman, PA

Tuition & fees (area res): $13,594 **Average undergraduate aid package: $11,199**

ABOUT THE INSTITUTION State-related, coed. ***Awards:*** certificates, associate, and bachelor's degrees (enrollment figures include students enrolled at The Graduate School at Penn State who are taking courses at this location). 122 undergraduate majors. ***Total enrollment:*** 424. Undergraduates: 444. Freshmen: 113. Federal methodology is used as a basis for awarding need-based institutional aid.

UNDERGRADUATE EXPENSES for 2020–2021 ***Application fee:*** $65. ***Tuition, area resident:*** full-time $12,718; part-time $524 per credit hour. ***Tuition, state resident:*** full-time $12,718; part-time $524 per credit hour. ***Tuition, nonresident:*** full-time $21,310; part-time $888 per credit hour. ***Required fees:*** full-time $876. Full-time tuition and fees vary according to course level, degree level, location, program, and student level. Part-time tuition and fees vary according to course level, course load, degree level, location, program, and student level.

FRESHMAN FINANCIAL AID (Fall 2018) 86 applied for aid; of those 84% were deemed to have need. 96% of freshmen with need received aid; of those 19% had need fully met. ***Average percent of need met:*** 65% (excluding resources awarded to replace EFC). ***Average financial aid package:*** $10,673 (excluding resources awarded to replace EFC). 3% of all full-time freshmen had no need and received non-need-based gift aid.

UNDERGRADUATE FINANCIAL AID (Fall 2018) 330 applied for aid; of those 83% were deemed to have need. 96% of undergraduates with need received aid; of those 23% had need fully met. ***Average percent of need met:*** 64% (excluding resources awarded to replace EFC). ***Average financial aid package:*** $11,199 (excluding resources awarded to replace EFC). 5% of all full-time undergraduates had no need and received non-need-based gift aid.

GIFT AID (NEED-BASED) ***Total amount:*** $2,124,396 (38% federal, 20% state, 40% institutional, 2% external sources). ***Receiving aid:*** Freshmen: 55% (48); all full-time undergraduates: 49% (177). ***Average award:*** Freshmen: $6361; Undergraduates: $7088. ***Scholarships, grants, and awards:*** Federal Pell, FSEOG, state, private, college/university gift aid from institutional funds, United Negro College Fund.

GIFT AID (NON-NEED-BASED) ***Total amount:*** $120,508 (52% institutional, 48% external sources). ***Receiving aid:*** Freshmen: 60% (53). Undergraduates: 53% (192). ***Average award:*** Freshmen: $1500. Undergraduates: $3212. ***Tuition waivers:*** Full or partial for employees or children of employees, senior citizens. ***ROTC:*** Army cooperative, Air Force cooperative.

LOANS ***Student loans:*** $2,025,893 (84% need-based, 16% non-need-based). 82% of past graduating class borrowed through all loan programs. *Average indebtedness per student:* $34,928. ***Average need-based loan:*** Freshmen: $3400. Undergraduates: $4076. ***Parent loans:*** $482,399 (88% need-based, 12% non-need-based). ***Programs:*** Federal Direct (Subsidized and Unsubsidized Stafford, PLUS), Perkins, college/university, Private Loans.

WORK-STUDY ***Federal work-study:*** Total amount: $28,455; jobs available. ***State or other work-study/employment:*** Part-time jobs available.

APPLYING FOR FINANCIAL AID ***Required financial aid form:*** FAFSA. ***Financial aid deadline (priority):*** 2/15. ***Notification date:*** Continuous beginning 3/1.

CONTACT Stacey Zelinka, Financial Aid Coordinator, Penn State Wilkes-Barre, Old Route 115, PO Box PSU, Lehman, PA 18627, 570-675-9238. *Fax:* 570-675-9113. *E-mail:* saz3@psu.edu.
Website: http://www.wb.psu.edu/.

PENN STATE WORTHINGTON SCRANTON

Dunmore, PA

Tuition & fees (area res): $14,476 **Average undergraduate aid package: $10,995**

ABOUT THE INSTITUTION State-related, coed. ***Awards:*** certificates, associate, and bachelor's degrees. 119 undergraduate majors. Federal methodology is used as a basis for awarding need-based institutional aid.

UNDERGRADUATE EXPENSES for 2019–2020 ***Tuition, area resident:*** full-time $13,484. ***Tuition, state resident:*** full-time $13,484. ***Tuition, nonresident:*** full-time $22,474. ***Required fees:*** full-time $992. Full-time tuition and fees vary according to course level, degree level, location, program, and student level. Part-time tuition and fees vary according to course level, course load, degree level, location, program, and student level.

FRESHMAN FINANCIAL AID (Fall 2018) 220 applied for aid; of those 84% were deemed to have need. 97% of freshmen with need received aid; of those 17% had need fully met. ***Average percent of need met:*** 62% (excluding resources awarded to replace EFC). ***Average financial aid package:*** $10,409 (excluding resources awarded to replace EFC). 8% of all full-time freshmen had no need and received non-need-based gift aid.

UNDERGRADUATE FINANCIAL AID (Fall 2018) 824 applied for aid; of those 89% were deemed to have need. 94% of undergraduates with need received aid; of those 18% had need fully met. ***Average percent of need met:*** 61% (excluding resources awarded to replace EFC). ***Average financial aid package:*** $10,995 (excluding resources awarded to replace EFC). 4% of all full-time undergraduates had no need and received non-need-based gift aid.

GIFT AID (NEED-BASED) ***Total amount:*** $5,172,546 (45% federal, 26% state, 27% institutional, 2% external sources). ***Receiving aid:*** Freshmen: 54% (122); all full-time undergraduates: 55% (489). ***Average award:*** Freshmen: $5965; Undergraduates: $6147. ***Scholarships, grants, and awards:*** Federal Pell, FSEOG, state, private, college/university gift aid from institutional funds, United Negro College Fund.

GIFT AID (NON-NEED-BASED) ***Total amount:*** $184,286 (5% state, 70% institutional, 25% external sources). ***Receiving aid:*** Freshmen: 61% (137). Undergraduates: 54% (479). ***Average award:*** Freshmen: $2908. Undergraduates: $3371. ***Tuition waivers:*** Full or partial for employees or children of employees, senior citizens. ***ROTC:*** Army cooperative, Air Force cooperative.

LOANS ***Student loans:*** $5,521,868 (89% need-based, 11% non-need-based). 79% of past graduating class borrowed through all loan programs. *Average indebtedness per student:* $39,015. ***Average need-based loan:*** Freshmen: $3355. Undergraduates: $4141. ***Parent loans:*** $1,181,902 (83% need-based, 17% non-need-based). ***Programs:*** Federal Direct (Subsidized and Unsubsidized Stafford, PLUS), Perkins, college/university, Private Loans.

WORK-STUDY ***Federal work-study:*** Total amount: $75,498; jobs available. ***State or other work-study/employment:*** Part-time jobs available.

APPLYING FOR FINANCIAL AID ***Required financial aid form:*** FAFSA. ***Financial aid deadline (priority):*** 2/15. ***Notification date:*** Continuous beginning 3/1.

CONTACT Financial Aid Office, Penn State Worthington Scranton, 120 Ridge View Drive, Dunmore, PA 18512, 570-963-2500.
Website: http://www.sn.psu.edu/.

PENN STATE YORK

York, PA

Tuition & fees (area res): $14,476	Average undergraduate aid package: $9767

ABOUT THE INSTITUTION State-related, coed. ***Awards:*** certificates, associate, bachelor's, and master's degrees (also offers up to 2 years of most bachelor's degree programs offered at University Park campus). 126 undergraduate majors. ***Total enrollment:*** 828. Undergraduates: 820. Freshmen: 202. Federal methodology is used as a basis for awarding need-based institutional aid.

UNDERGRADUATE EXPENSES for 2020–2021 ***Application fee:*** $65. ***Tuition, area resident:*** full-time $13,484; part-time $555 per credit hour. ***Tuition, state resident:*** full-time $13,484; part-time $555 per credit hour. ***Tuition, nonresident:*** full-time $22,474; part-time $936 per credit hour. ***Required fees:*** full-time $992. Full-time tuition and fees vary according to course level, degree level, location, program, and student level. Part-time tuition and fees vary according to course level, course load, degree level, location, program, and student level.

FRESHMAN FINANCIAL AID (Fall 2018) 172 applied for aid; of those 80% were deemed to have need. 99% of freshmen with need received aid; of those 19% had need fully met. ***Average percent of need met:*** 55% (excluding resources awarded to replace EFC). ***Average financial aid package:*** $9417 (excluding resources awarded to replace EFC). 12% of all full-time freshmen had no need and received non-need-based gift aid.

UNDERGRADUATE FINANCIAL AID (Fall 2018) 526 applied for aid; of those 82% were deemed to have need. 97% of undergraduates with need received aid; of those 20% had need fully met. ***Average percent of need met:*** 57% (excluding resources awarded to replace EFC). ***Average financial aid package:*** $9767 (excluding resources awarded to replace EFC). 11% of all full-time undergraduates had no need and received non-need-based gift aid.

GIFT AID (NEED-BASED) ***Total amount:*** $2,984,544 (37% federal, 23% state, 34% institutional, 6% external sources). ***Receiving aid:*** Freshmen: 30% (76); all full-time undergraduates: 32% (247). ***Average award:*** Freshmen: $5217; Undergraduates: $5708. ***Scholarships, grants, and awards:*** Federal Pell, FSEOG, state, private, college/university gift aid from institutional funds, United Negro College Fund.

GIFT AID (NON-NEED-BASED) ***Total amount:*** $403,002 (1% federal, 73% institutional, 26% external sources). ***Receiving aid:*** Freshmen: 47% (119). Undergraduates: 41% (319). ***Average award:*** Freshmen: $3509. Undergraduates: $3416. ***Scholarships, grants, and awards by category:*** *Academic interests/achievement:* general academic interests/achievements. *Special characteristics:* children and siblings of alumni. ***Tuition waivers:*** Full or partial for employees or children of employees, senior citizens.

LOANS ***Student loans:*** $3,581,543 (80% need-based, 20% non-need-based). 54% of past graduating class borrowed through all loan programs. *Average indebtedness per student:* $37,420. ***Average need-based loan:*** Freshmen: $3263. Undergraduates: $3885. ***Parent loans:*** $887,445 (71% need-based, 29% non-need-based). ***Programs:*** Federal Direct (Subsidized and Unsubsidized Stafford, PLUS), Perkins, college/university, Private Loans.

WORK-STUDY ***Federal work-study:*** Total amount: $51,205; jobs available. ***State or other work-study/employment:*** Part-time jobs available.

APPLYING FOR FINANCIAL AID ***Required financial aid form:*** FAFSA. ***Financial aid deadline (priority):*** 2/15. ***Notification date:*** Continuous beginning 3/1.

CONTACT Financial Aid Office, Penn State York, 1031 Edgecomb Avenue, York, PA 17403, 717-771-4000 or toll-free 800-778-6227.
Website: http://www.york.psu.edu/.

PENNSYLVANIA ACADEMY OF THE FINE ARTS

Philadelphia, PA

Tuition & fees: $40,376	Average undergraduate aid package: N/A

ABOUT THE INSTITUTION Independent, coed. ***Awards:*** certificates, bachelor's, and master's degrees. 1 undergraduate major. ***Total enrollment:*** 74. Undergraduates: 200. Federal methodology is used as a basis for awarding need-based institutional aid.

UNDERGRADUATE EXPENSES for 2019–2020 ***Application fee:*** $60. ***Tuition:*** full-time $38,926; part-time $1622 per credit. ***Required fees:*** full-time $1450. ***College room only:*** $12,010.

GIFT AID (NEED-BASED) ***Total amount:*** $1,777,356 (16% federal, 4% state, 31% institutional, 49% external sources). ***Scholarships, grants, and awards:*** Federal Pell, FSEOG, state, college/university gift aid from institutional funds.

GIFT AID (NON-NEED-BASED) ***Total amount:*** $2,260,625 (100% institutional). ***Scholarships, grants, and awards by category:*** *Creative arts/performance:* applied art and design.

LOANS ***Student loans:*** $1,129,865 (35% need-based, 65% non-need-based). ***Parent loans:*** $484,329 (100% non-need-based). ***Programs:*** Federal Direct (Subsidized and Unsubsidized Stafford, PLUS).

WORK-STUDY ***Federal work-study:*** Total amount: $83,169; 57 jobs averaging $2000.

APPLYING FOR FINANCIAL AID ***Required financial aid form:*** FAFSA. ***Financial aid deadline (priority):*** 2/1.

CONTACT Mr. Samuel Trone, Director of Financial Aid, Pennsylvania Academy of the Fine Arts, 128 North Broad Street, Philadelphia, PA 19102, 215-972-2019. *Fax:* 215-972-0839. *E-mail:* finaid@pafa.edu.
Website: http://www.pafa.edu/.

PENNSYLVANIA COLLEGE OF ART & DESIGN

Lancaster, PA

CONTACT J. David Hershey, Registrar/Director of Financial Aid, Pennsylvania College of Art & Design, 204 North Prince Street, PO Box 59, Lancaster, PA 17608-0059, 717-396-7833 Ext. 13 or toll-free 800-689-0379 Ext.1001. *Fax:* 717-396-1339. *E-mail:* finaid@pcad.edu.
Website: http://www.pcad.edu/.

PENNSYLVANIA COLLEGE OF HEALTH SCIENCES

Lancaster, PA

CONTACT Financial Aid Office, Pennsylvania College of Health Sciences, 850 Greenfield Road, Lancaster, PA 17601, 717-544-4912 or toll-free 800-622-5443.
Website: http://www.pacollege.edu/.

PENNSYLVANIA COLLEGE OF TECHNOLOGY

Williamsport, PA

Tuition & fees (PA res): $17,160	Average undergraduate aid package: $14,283

ABOUT THE INSTITUTION State-related, coed. ***Awards:*** certificates, associate, and bachelor's degrees. 74 undergraduate majors. Federal methodology is used as a basis for awarding need-based institutional aid.

UNDERGRADUATE EXPENSES for 2019–2020 *Tuition, state resident:* full-time $14,670; part-time $489 per credit hour. ***Tuition, nonresident:*** full-time $22,020; part-time $734 per credit hour. ***Required fees:*** full-time $2490; $83 per credit hour. Full-time tuition and fees vary according to course load and program. Part-time tuition and fees vary according to course load and program. ***College room and board:*** $11,715; ***Room only:*** $6684. Room and board charges vary according to board plan and housing facility.

FRESHMAN FINANCIAL AID (Fall 2018) 1197 applied for aid; of those 94% were deemed to have need. 100% of freshmen with need received aid. ***Average percent of need met:*** 22% (excluding resources awarded to replace EFC). ***Average financial aid package:*** $13,904 (excluding resources awarded to replace EFC).

UNDERGRADUATE FINANCIAL AID (Fall 2018) 4,229 applied for aid; of those 96% were deemed to have need. 100% of undergraduates with need received aid. ***Average percent of need met:*** 26% (excluding resources awarded to replace EFC). ***Average financial aid package:*** $14,283 (excluding resources awarded to replace EFC).

GIFT AID (NEED-BASED) *Total amount:* $31,350,761 (31% federal, 20% state, 5% institutional, 44% external sources). ***Receiving aid:*** Freshmen: 78% (879); all full-time undergraduates: 73% (2,988). ***Average award:*** Freshmen: $8161; Undergraduates: $8704. ***Scholarships, grants, and awards:*** Federal Pell, FSEOG, state, private, college/university gift aid from institutional funds.

GIFT AID (NON-NEED-BASED) *Tuition waivers:* Full or partial for employees or children of employees. ***ROTC:*** Army.

LOANS *Student loans:* $48,215,954 (100% need-based). ***Average need-based loan:*** Freshmen: $3244. Undergraduates: $3964. ***Parent loans:*** $16,010,596 (100% need-based). ***Programs:*** Federal Direct (Subsidized and Unsubsidized Stafford, PLUS).

WORK-STUDY *Federal work-study:* Total amount: $173,839; 88 jobs averaging $1975.

APPLYING FOR FINANCIAL AID *Required financial aid forms:* FAFSA, institution's own form. ***Financial aid deadline (priority):*** 3/1. ***Notification date:*** Continuous beginning 12/1.

CONTACT Ms. Jessica Hunter, Director of Financial Aid, Pennsylvania College of Technology, One College Avenue, Williamsport, PA 17701, 570-326-4766 or toll-free 800-367-9222. *Fax:* 570-321-5552. *E-mail:* jhunter@pct.edu.
Website: http://www.pct.edu/.

PENSACOLA CHRISTIAN COLLEGE

Pensacola, FL

CONTACT Financial Aid Office, Pensacola Christian College, 250 Brent Lane, Pensacola, FL 32503-2267, 850-478-8496 or toll-free 800-722-4636.
Website: http://www.pcci.edu/.

PEPPERDINE UNIVERSITY

Malibu, CA

Tuition & fees: $55,892	Average undergraduate aid package: $41,879

ABOUT THE INSTITUTION Independent Church of Christ, coed. ***Awards:*** certificates, bachelor's, master's, and doctoral degrees. 65 undergraduate majors. ***Total enrollment:*** 8,824. Undergraduates: 3,583. Freshmen: 726. Federal methodology is used as a basis for awarding need-based institutional aid.

UNDERGRADUATE EXPENSES for 2019–2020 *Application fee:* $65. ***Comprehensive fee:*** $71,562 includes full-time tuition ($55,640), mandatory fees ($252), and room and board ($15,670). Room and board charges vary according to board plan and housing facility. ***Part-time tuition:*** $1745 per credit hour.

FRESHMAN FINANCIAL AID (Fall 2018) 800 applied for aid; of those 61% were deemed to have need. 100% of freshmen with need received aid; of those 22% had need fully met. ***Average percent of need met:*** 77% (excluding resources awarded to replace EFC). ***Average financial aid package:*** $40,747 (excluding resources awarded to replace EFC). 24% of all full-time freshmen had no need and received non-need-based gift aid.

UNDERGRADUATE FINANCIAL AID (Fall 2018) 3,324 applied for aid; of those 53% were deemed to have need. 100% of undergraduates with need received aid; of those 21% had need fully met. ***Average percent of need met:*** 75% (excluding resources awarded to replace EFC). ***Average financial aid package:*** $41,879 (excluding resources awarded to replace EFC). 31% of all full-time undergraduates had no need and received non-need-based gift aid.

GIFT AID (NEED-BASED) *Total amount:* $63,516,071 (7% federal, 6% state, 84% institutional, 3% external sources). ***Receiving aid:*** Freshmen: 60% (483); all full-time undergraduates: 52% (1,744). ***Average award:*** Freshmen: $37,678; Undergraduates: $38,089. ***Scholarships, grants, and awards:*** Federal Pell, FSEOG, state, private, college/university gift aid from institutional funds, United Negro College Fund.

GIFT AID (NON-NEED-BASED) *Total amount:* $19,295,252 (3% federal, 91% institutional, 6% external sources). ***Average award:*** Freshmen: $19,506. Undergraduates: $20,438. ***Tuition waivers:*** Full or partial for employees or children of employees. ***ROTC:*** Army cooperative, Air Force cooperative.

LOANS *Student loans:* $14,038,408 (87% need-based, 13% non-need-based). 52% of past graduating class borrowed through all loan programs. *Average indebtedness per student:* $34,711. ***Average need-based loan:*** Freshmen: $3956. Undergraduates: $5156. ***Parent loans:*** $18,789,695 (86% need-based, 14% non-need-based). ***Programs:*** Federal Direct (Subsidized and Unsubsidized Stafford, PLUS), college/university.

WORK-STUDY *Federal work-study:* Total amount: $1,006,891; jobs available. ***State or other work-study/employment:*** Total amount: $377,803 (58% need-based, 42% non-need-based). Part-time jobs available.

ATHLETIC AWARDS Total amount: $7,543,582 (33% need-based, 67% non-need-based).

APPLYING FOR FINANCIAL AID *Required financial aid form:* FAFSA. ***Financial aid deadline (priority):*** 2/15. ***Notification date:*** 4/5. Students must reply by 5/1.

CONTACT Janet Lockhart, Director of Financial Assistance, Pepperdine University, 24255 Pacific Coast Highway, Malibu, CA 90263-4301, 310-506-4301. *Fax:* 310-506-4746. *E-mail:* janet.lockhart@pepperdine.edu.
Website: http://www.pepperdine.edu/.

PERU STATE COLLEGE

Peru, NE

CONTACT Diana Lind, Director of Financial Aid, Peru State College, PO Box 10, Peru, NE 68421, 402-872-2228 or toll-free 800-742-4412 (in-state), 800-741-4412 (out-of-state). *Fax:* 402-872-2419. *E-mail:* finaid@oakmail.peru.edu.
Website: http://www.peru.edu/.

PFEIFFER UNIVERSITY

Misenheimer, NC

ABOUT THE INSTITUTION Independent United Methodist, coed. ***Awards:*** certificates, bachelor's, and master's degrees. 37 undergraduate majors. ***Total enrollment:*** 1,306. Undergraduates: 813. Freshmen: 277.

GIFT AID (NEED-BASED) ***Scholarships, grants, and awards:*** Federal Pell, FSEOG, state, private, college/university gift aid from institutional funds.

GIFT AID (NON-NEED-BASED) ***Scholarships, grants, and awards by category:*** *Academic interests/achievement:* general academic interests/achievements. *Creative arts/performance:* music. *Special achievements/activities:* leadership, religious involvement. *Special characteristics:* children and siblings of alumni, children of educators, children of faculty/staff.

LOANS ***Programs:*** Federal Direct (Subsidized and Unsubsidized Stafford, PLUS), Perkins, state.

CONTACT Jill Powell, Director of Financial Aid, Pfeiffer University, PO Box 960, Misenheimer, NC 28109, 704-463-1360 Ext. 3037 or toll-free 800-338-2060. *Fax:* 704-463-1363. *E-mail:* jill.powell@pfeiffer.edu.
Website: http://www.pfeiffer.edu/.

PHILANDER SMITH COLLEGE

Little Rock, AR

CONTACT K. Michael Francois, Director of Financial Aid, Philander Smith College, 900 Daisy Bates Drive, Little Rock, AR 72202-3799, 501-370-5350 or toll-free 800-446-6772. *Fax:* 501-370-5357. *E-mail:* kmfrancois@philander.edu.
Website: http://www.philander.edu/.

PIEDMONT COLLEGE

Demorest, GA

Tuition & fees: $26,692	Average undergraduate aid package: $21,690

ABOUT THE INSTITUTION Independent United Church of Christ, coed. ***Awards:*** certificates, bachelor's, master's, and doctoral degrees. 52 undergraduate majors. ***Total enrollment:*** 2,490. Undergraduates: 1,262. Freshmen: 256. Both federal and institutional methodology are used as a basis for awarding need-based institutional aid.

UNDERGRADUATE EXPENSES for 2019–2020 ***Comprehensive fee:*** $37,216 includes full-time tuition ($26,492), mandatory fees ($200), and room and board ($10,524). Full-time tuition and fees vary according to location. Room and board charges vary according to board plan. ***Part-time tuition:*** $1011 per credit hour. ***Part-time fees:*** $100 per term. Part-time tuition and fees vary according to course load and location.

FRESHMAN FINANCIAL AID (Fall 2019, est.) 263 applied for aid; of those 88% were deemed to have need. 100% of freshmen with need received aid; of those 19% had need fully met. ***Average percent of need met:*** 78% (excluding resources awarded to replace EFC). ***Average financial aid package:*** $24,520 (excluding resources awarded to replace EFC). 15% of all full-time freshmen had no need and received non-need-based gift aid.

UNDERGRADUATE FINANCIAL AID (Fall 2019, est.) 1,076 applied for aid; of those 89% were deemed to have need. 100% of undergraduates with need received aid; of those 17% had need fully met. ***Average percent of need met:*** 71% (excluding resources awarded to replace EFC). ***Average financial aid package:*** $21,690 (excluding resources awarded to replace EFC). 15% of all full-time undergraduates had no need and received non-need-based gift aid.

GIFT AID (NEED-BASED) ***Total amount:*** $16,311,817 (16% federal, 18% state, 65% institutional, 1% external sources). ***Receiving aid:*** Freshmen: 85% (231); all full-time undergraduates: 82% (947). ***Average award:*** Freshmen: $20,666; Undergraduates: $17,050. ***Scholarships, grants, and awards:*** Federal Pell, FSEOG, state, private, college/university gift aid from institutional funds.

GIFT AID (NON-NEED-BASED) ***Total amount:*** $3,696,367 (17% state, 82% institutional, 1% external sources). ***Receiving aid:*** Freshmen: 14% (38). Undergraduates: 10% (119). ***Average award:*** Freshmen: $14,229. Undergraduates: $12,174. ***Scholarships, grants, and awards by category:*** *Academic interests/achievement:* 1,679 awards ($10,723,018 total): biological sciences, business, communication, education, English, foreign languages, general academic interests/achievements, health fields, home economics, humanities, mathematics, physical sciences, premedicine, religion/biblical studies, social sciences. *Creative arts/performance:* 185 awards ($186,008 total): applied art and design, art/fine arts, cinema/film/broadcasting, debating, journalism/publications, music, performing arts, theater/drama. *Special achievements/activities:* 17 awards ($79,571 total): community service, leadership, religious involvement. *Special characteristics:* 243 awards ($1,568,852 total): adult students, children of faculty/staff, international students, out-of-state students, siblings of current students, veterans. ***Tuition waivers:*** Full or partial for employees or children of employees.

LOANS ***Student loans:*** $7,769,013 (78% need-based, 22% non-need-based). 77% of past graduating class borrowed through all loan programs. *Average indebtedness per student:* $30,559. ***Average need-based loan:*** Freshmen: $3425. Undergraduates: $4237. ***Parent loans:*** $2,134,481 (36% need-based, 64% non-need-based). ***Programs:*** Federal Direct (Subsidized and Unsubsidized Stafford, PLUS), state.

WORK-STUDY ***Federal work-study:*** Total amount: $302,235; 142 jobs averaging $2128. ***State or other work-study/employment:*** Total amount: $545,103 (22% need-based, 78% non-need-based). 215 part-time jobs averaging $2536.

APPLYING FOR FINANCIAL AID ***Required financial aid forms:*** FAFSA, institution's own form, state aid form. ***Financial aid deadline (priority):*** 3/1. ***Notification date:*** Continuous beginning 1/1. Students must reply within 4 weeks of notification.

CONTACT Ms. Linda Arnold O'Sullivan, Director of Financial Aid, Piedmont College, PO Box 10, Demorest, GA 30535-0010, 706-778-3000 Ext. 1191 or toll-free 800-277-7020. *Fax:* 706-778-0708. *E-mail:* larnold@piedmont.edu.
Website: http://www.piedmont.edu/.

PIEDMONT INTERNATIONAL UNIVERSITY

Winston-Salem, NC

CONTACT Mandy McLain, Director of Financial Aid, Piedmont International University, 420 South Broad Street, Winston-Salem, NC 27101-5197, 336-714-7878 or toll-free 800-937-5097. *Fax:* 336-714-7820. *E-mail:* financialaid@piedmontu.edu.
Website: http://www.piedmontu.edu/.

PILLAR COLLEGE

Newark, NJ

CONTACT Financial Aid Office, Pillar College, 60 Park Place, Suite 701, Newark, NJ 07102, 973-803-5000 or toll-free 800-234-9305.
Website: http://www.pillar.edu/.

PINE MANOR COLLEGE

Chestnut Hill, MA

Tuition & fees: N/R | **Average undergraduate aid package: $30,824**

ABOUT THE INSTITUTION Independent, coed. ***Awards:*** associate, bachelor's, and master's degrees. 12 undergraduate majors. Federal methodology is used as a basis for awarding need-based institutional aid.

FRESHMAN FINANCIAL AID (Fall 2018) 74 applied for aid; of those 99% were deemed to have need. 100% of freshmen with need received aid; of those 1% had need fully met. ***Average percent of need met:*** 84% (excluding resources awarded to replace EFC). ***Average financial aid package:*** $31,577 (excluding resources awarded to replace EFC). 10% of all full-time freshmen had no need and received non-need-based gift aid.

UNDERGRADUATE FINANCIAL AID (Fall 2018) 235 applied for aid; of those 100% were deemed to have need. 100% of undergraduates with need received aid; of those 6% had need fully met. ***Average percent of need met:*** 81% (excluding resources awarded to replace EFC). ***Average financial aid package:*** $30,824 (excluding resources awarded to replace EFC). 8% of all full-time undergraduates had no need and received non-need-based gift aid.

GIFT AID (NEED-BASED) ***Total amount:*** $6,180,890 (15% federal, 3% state, 82% institutional). ***Receiving aid:*** Freshmen: 89% (73); all full-time undergraduates: 92% (234). ***Average award:*** Freshmen: $27,690; Undergraduates: $26,159. ***Scholarships, grants, and awards:*** Federal Pell, FSEOG, state, private, college/university gift aid from institutional funds.

GIFT AID (NON-NEED-BASED) ***Total amount:*** $424,622 (80% institutional, 20% external sources). ***Receiving aid:*** Freshmen: 5% (4). Undergraduates: 4% (10). ***Average award:*** Freshmen: $15,313. Undergraduates: $16,962. ***Scholarships, grants, and awards by category:*** *Academic interests/achievement:* 185 awards ($1,800,884 total): general academic interests/achievements. *Special characteristics:* 2 awards ($46,845 total): children and siblings of alumni, children of faculty/staff.

LOANS ***Student loans:*** $1,742,493 (95% need-based, 5% non-need-based). 81% of past graduating class borrowed through all loan programs. *Average indebtedness per student:* $34,970. ***Average need-based loan:*** Freshmen: $3185. Undergraduates: $4195. ***Parent loans:*** $482,476 (100% need-based). ***Programs:*** Federal Direct (Subsidized and Unsubsidized Stafford, PLUS), state, alternative loans.

WORK-STUDY ***Federal work-study:*** Total amount: $148,356; 184 jobs averaging $568.

APPLYING FOR FINANCIAL AID ***Required financial aid form:*** FAFSA. ***Financial aid deadline:*** Continuous. ***Notification date:*** Continuous beginning 2/1. Students must reply by 5/1 or within 2 weeks of notification.

CONTACT Ms. Deborah A. Gravel, Director of Financial Aid, Pine Manor College, 400 Heath Street, Chestnut Hill, MA 02467, 617-731-7628 or toll-free 800-762-1357. *Fax:* 617-731-7102. *E-mail:* dgravel@pmc.edu.
Website: http://www.pmc.edu/.

PIONEER PACIFIC COLLEGE

Beaverton, OR

CONTACT Financial Aid Office, Pioneer Pacific College, 4145 SW Watson Ave Suite 300, Beaverton, OR 97005, 503-682-3903 or toll-free 866-PPC-INFO.
Website: http://www.pioneerpacific.edu/.

PITTSBURG STATE UNIVERSITY

Pittsburg, KS

Tuition & fees: N/R | **Average undergraduate aid package: $8009**

ABOUT THE INSTITUTION State-supported, coed. ***Awards:*** certificates, associate, bachelor's, master's, and doctoral degrees. 62 undergraduate majors. ***Total enrollment:*** 6,645. Undergraduates: 5,181. Freshmen: 825. Federal methodology is used as a basis for awarding need-based institutional aid.

FRESHMAN FINANCIAL AID (Fall 2018) 100% of freshmen with need received aid. ***Average financial aid package:*** $8718 (excluding resources awarded to replace EFC).

UNDERGRADUATE FINANCIAL AID (Fall 2018) 100% of undergraduates with need received aid. ***Average financial aid package:*** $8009 (excluding resources awarded to replace EFC).

GIFT AID (NEED-BASED) ***Receiving aid:*** Freshmen: 42% (405); all full-time undergraduates: 57% (2,739). ***Average award:*** Freshmen: $4654; Undergraduates: $4716. ***Scholarships, grants, and awards:*** Federal Pell, FSEOG, state, private, college/university gift aid from institutional funds, Federal Nursing.

GIFT AID (NON-NEED-BASED) ***Receiving aid:*** Freshmen: 28% (267). Undergraduates: 28% (1,353). ***Scholarships, grants, and awards by category:*** *Academic interests/achievement:* biological sciences, business, communication, computer science, education, engineering/technologies, English, foreign languages, general academic interests/achievements, health fields, home economics, mathematics, military science, physical sciences, social sciences. *Creative arts/performance:* music. *Special characteristics:* children and siblings of alumni, general special characteristics. ***ROTC:*** Army.

LOANS ***Student loans:*** 66% of past graduating class borrowed through all loan programs. *Average indebtedness per student:* $24,533. ***Average need-based loan:*** Freshmen: $3018. Undergraduates: $3741. ***Programs:*** Federal Direct (Subsidized and Unsubsidized Stafford, PLUS), Perkins, Federal Nursing, college/university.

WORK-STUDY Federal work-study jobs available. ***State or other work-study/employment:*** Part-time jobs available.

APPLYING FOR FINANCIAL AID ***Required financial aid forms:*** FAFSA, CSS Financial Aid PROFILE. ***Financial aid deadline:*** Continuous. ***Notification date:*** Continuous. Students must reply within 2 weeks of notification.

CONTACT Tammy Higgins, Director of Student Financial Assistance, Pittsburg State University, 1701 South Broadway Street, Pittsburg, KS 66762-7534, 620-235-4238 or toll-free 800-854-7488. *Fax:* 620-235-4078. *E-mail:* thiggins@pittstate.edu.
Website: http://www.pittstate.edu/.

PITZER COLLEGE

Claremont, CA

Tuition & fees: $56,018 | **Average undergraduate aid package: $49,818**

ABOUT THE INSTITUTION Independent, coed. ***Awards:*** bachelor's degrees. 37 undergraduate majors. ***Total enrollment:*** 1,119. Undergraduates: 1,119. Freshmen: 276. Both federal and institutional methodology are used as a basis for awarding need-based institutional aid.

UNDERGRADUATE EXPENSES for 2019–2020 ***Application fee:*** $70. ***Comprehensive fee:*** $73,450 includes full-time tuition ($55,734), mandatory fees ($284), and room and board ($17,432). ***College room only:*** $10,060. Room and board charges vary according to board plan and housing facility. ***Part-time tuition:*** $6967 per course. ***Part-time fees:*** $284 per year. Part-time tuition and fees vary according to course load.

FRESHMAN FINANCIAL AID (Fall 2019, est.) 131 applied for aid; of those 77% were deemed to have need. 94% of freshmen with need received aid; of those 99% had need fully met. ***Average percent of need met:*** 100% (excluding resources awarded to replace EFC). ***Average financial aid package:*** $52,894 (excluding resources awarded to replace EFC). 2% of all full-time freshmen had no need and received non-need-based gift aid.

UNDERGRADUATE FINANCIAL AID (Fall 2019, est.) 482 applied for aid; of those 87% were deemed to have need. 96% of undergraduates with need received aid; of those 97% had need fully met. ***Average percent of need met:*** 100% (excluding resources awarded to replace EFC). ***Average financial aid package:*** $49,818 (excluding resources awarded to replace EFC). 2% of all full-time undergraduates had no need and received non-need-based gift aid.

GIFT AID (NEED-BASED) ***Total amount:*** $18,114,317 (5% federal, 4% state, 88% institutional, 3% external sources). ***Receiving aid:*** Freshmen: 34% (93); all full-time undergraduates: 37% (394). ***Average award:*** Freshmen: $49,150; Undergraduates: $45,553. ***Scholarships, grants, and awards:*** Federal Pell, FSEOG, state, private, college/university gift aid from institutional funds.

GIFT AID (NON-NEED-BASED) ***Total amount:*** $209,708 (63% institutional, 37% external sources). ***Receiving aid:*** Freshmen: 1. Undergraduates: 3. ***Average award:*** Freshmen: $5000. Undergraduates: $5567. ***Scholarships, grants, and***

awards by category:** Academic interests/achievement:* 34 awards ($170,000 total): general academic interests/achievements. ***Tuition waivers: Full or partial for employees or children of employees. ***ROTC:*** Army cooperative, Air Force cooperative.

LOANS *Student loans:* $1,962,222 (74% need-based, 26% non-need-based). 37% of past graduating class borrowed through all loan programs. *Average indebtedness per student:* $26,489. ***Average need-based loan:*** Freshmen: $3342. Undergraduates: $4558. ***Parent loans:*** $1,722,875 (23% need-based, 77% non-need-based). ***Programs:*** Federal Direct (Subsidized and Unsubsidized Stafford, PLUS), college/university.

WORK-STUDY *Federal work-study:* Total amount: $788,280; 335 jobs averaging $2514. ***State or other work-study/employment:*** Total amount: $25,390 (100% need-based). 14 part-time jobs averaging $1880.

APPLYING FOR FINANCIAL AID *Required financial aid forms:* FAFSA, CSS Financial Aid PROFILE, state aid form, noncustodial (divorced/separated) parent's statement. ***Financial aid deadline:*** 1/1 (priority: 1/1). ***Notification date:*** 4/1. Students must reply by 5/1.

CONTACT Kara Moore, Director of Financial Aid, Pitzer College, 1050 North Mills Avenue, Claremont, CA 91711-6101, 909-621-8208 or toll-free 800-748-9371. *Fax:* 909-607-1205. *E-mail:* kara_moore@pitzer.edu.
Website: http://www.pitzer.edu/.

PLATT COLLEGE

Riverside, CA

CONTACT Financial Aid Office, Platt College, 6465 Sycamore Canyon Boulevard, Suite 100, Riverside, CA 92507, 951-572-4300 or toll-free 888-807-5288.
Website: http://www.plattcollege.edu/.

PLATT COLLEGE

Aurora, CO

ABOUT THE INSTITUTION Proprietary, coed. ***Awards:*** diplomas, associate, and bachelor's degrees. 2 undergraduate majors.

GIFT AID (NEED-BASED) *Scholarships, grants, and awards:* Federal Pell, FSEOG, private.

LOANS *Programs:* Federal Direct (Subsidized and Unsubsidized Stafford, PLUS).

CONTACT Ms. Laura Kellogg, Director of Financial Aid, Platt College, 3100 South Parker Road, #200, Aurora, CO 80014, 303-369-5151 Ext. 233. *Fax:* 303-745-1433. *E-mail:* laura.kellogg@plattcolorado.edu.
Website: http://www.plattcolorado.edu/.

PLATT COLLEGE SAN DIEGO

San Diego, CA

CONTACT Matilde Aguilar, Student Accounts Coordinator, Platt College San Diego, 6250 El Cajon Boulevard, San Diego, CA 92115, 619-265-0107 Ext. 12 or toll-free 866-752-8826. *Fax:* 619-265-8655. *E-mail:* maguilar@platt.edu.
Website: http://www.platt.edu/.

PLYMOUTH STATE UNIVERSITY

Plymouth, NH

Tuition & fees: N/R	Average undergraduate aid package: $13,058

ABOUT THE INSTITUTION State-supported, coed. ***Awards:*** certificates, bachelor's, master's, and doctoral degrees. 54 undergraduate majors. ***Total enrollment:*** 5,059. Undergraduates: 4,222. Freshmen: 1,088. Federal methodology is used as a basis for awarding need-based institutional aid.

FRESHMAN FINANCIAL AID (Fall 2018) 100% of freshmen with need received aid; of those 18% had need fully met. ***Average percent of need met:*** 62% (excluding resources awarded to replace EFC). ***Average financial aid package:*** $12,047 (excluding resources awarded to replace EFC). 24% of all full-time freshmen had no need and received non-need-based gift aid.

UNDERGRADUATE FINANCIAL AID (Fall 2018) 100% of undergraduates with need received aid; of those 15% had need fully met. ***Average percent of need met:*** 59% (excluding resources awarded to replace EFC). ***Average financial aid package:*** $13,058 (excluding resources awarded to replace EFC). 26% of all full-time undergraduates had no need and received non-need-based gift aid.

GIFT AID (NEED-BASED) *Total amount:* $24,242,631 (25% federal, 1% state, 68% institutional, 6% external sources). ***Receiving aid:*** Freshmen: 80% (826); all full-time undergraduates: 73% (2,685). ***Average award:*** Freshmen: $9387; Undergraduates: $8341. ***Scholarships, grants, and awards:*** Federal Pell, FSEOG, state, private, college/university gift aid from institutional funds.

GIFT AID (NON-NEED-BASED) *Total amount:* $5,420,137 (91% institutional, 9% external sources). ***Receiving aid:*** Freshmen: 22% (224). Undergraduates: 14% (499). ***Average award:*** Freshmen: $5008. Undergraduates: $4794. ***Scholarships, grants, and awards by category:** Academic interests/achievement:* biological sciences, computer science, engineering/technologies, general academic interests/achievements, mathematics, premedicine. *Creative arts/performance:* creative writing, dance, music, theater/drama. *Special characteristics:* children of faculty/staff, international students. ***ROTC:*** Army cooperative, Air Force cooperative.

LOANS *Student loans:* $33,888,889 (31% need-based, 69% non-need-based). 83% of past graduating class borrowed through all loan programs. *Average indebtedness per student:* $40,809. ***Average need-based loan:*** Freshmen: $2866. Undergraduates: $3937. ***Parent loans:*** $9,181,511 (100% non-need-based). ***Programs:*** Federal Direct (Subsidized and Unsubsidized Stafford, PLUS).

WORK-STUDY *Federal work-study:* Total amount: $3,828,523; jobs available.

APPLYING FOR FINANCIAL AID *Required financial aid form:* FAFSA. ***Financial aid deadline (priority):*** 3/1. ***Notification date:*** Continuous beginning 11/30. Students must reply by 5/1.

CONTACT Financial Aid Office, Plymouth State University, 17 High Street MSC#19, Plymouth, NH 03264, 877-846-5755 or toll-free 800-842-6900. *Fax:* 603-535-2627. *E-mail:* psu-sfs@plymouth.edu.
Website: http://www.plymouth.edu/.

POINT LOMA NAZARENE UNIVERSITY

San Diego, CA

Tuition & fees: $36,950	Average undergraduate aid package: $25,229

ABOUT THE INSTITUTION Independent Nazarene, coed. ***Awards:*** certificates, bachelor's, master's, and doctoral degrees. 65 undergraduate majors. ***Total enrollment:*** 4,567. Undergraduates: 3,203. Freshmen: 612. Federal methodology is used as a basis for awarding need-based institutional aid.

UNDERGRADUATE EXPENSES for 2019–2020 *Application fee:* $55. ***Comprehensive fee:*** $47,600 includes full-time tuition ($36,350), mandatory fees ($600), and room and board ($10,650). Full-time tuition and fees vary according to course load and program. Room and board charges vary according to board plan. ***Part-time tuition:*** $1515 per credit hour. Part-time tuition and fees vary according to course load and program.

FRESHMAN FINANCIAL AID (Fall 2018) 583 applied for aid; of those 74% were deemed to have need. 99% of freshmen with need received aid; of those 20% had need fully met. ***Average percent of need met:*** 66% (excluding resources awarded to replace EFC). ***Average financial aid package:*** $24,555 (excluding resources awarded to replace EFC). 23% of all full-time freshmen had no need and received non-need-based gift aid.

UNDERGRADUATE FINANCIAL AID (Fall 2018) 2,101 applied for aid; of those 82% were deemed to have need. 99% of undergraduates with need received aid; of those 16% had need fully met. ***Average percent of need met:*** 62% (excluding resources awarded to replace EFC). ***Average financial aid package:*** $25,229 (excluding resources awarded to replace EFC). 23% of all full-time undergraduates had no need and received non-need-based gift aid.

GIFT AID (NEED-BASED) *Receiving aid:* Freshmen: 65% (429); all full-time undergraduates: 63% (1,674). ***Average award:*** Freshmen: $19,102; Undergraduates:

$19,563. ***Scholarships, grants, and awards:*** Federal Pell, FSEOG, state, private, college/university gift aid from institutional funds, Federal Nursing.

GIFT AID (NON-NEED-BASED) ***Receiving aid:*** Freshmen: 9% (62). Undergraduates: 6% (161). ***Average award:*** Freshmen: $13,829. Undergraduates: $12,355. ***Scholarships, grants, and awards by category:*** *Academic interests/achievement:* biological sciences, business, communication, computer science, education, engineering/technologies, English, foreign languages, general academic interests/achievements, health fields, international studies, mathematics, physical sciences, religion/biblical studies, social sciences. *Creative arts/performance:* applied art and design, debating, music, theater/drama. ***Tuition waivers:*** Full or partial for employees or children of employees, senior citizens. ***ROTC:*** Army cooperative, Naval cooperative, Air Force cooperative.

LOANS ***Student loans:*** 62% of past graduating class borrowed through all loan programs. *Average indebtedness per student:* $35,374. ***Average need-based loan:*** Freshmen: $3477. Undergraduates: $4625. ***Programs:*** Federal Direct (Subsidized and Unsubsidized Stafford, PLUS), Perkins, Federal Nursing.

WORK-STUDY Federal work-study jobs available.

APPLYING FOR FINANCIAL AID ***Required financial aid form:*** FAFSA. ***Notification date:*** Continuous.

CONTACT Mollyanne Porter, Senior Director for Undergraduate Student Financial Services and Director of Financial Aid, Point Loma Nazarene University, 3900 Lomaland Drive, San Diego, CA 92106, 619-849-2628 or toll-free 800-733-7770. *Fax:* 619-849-7078. *E-mail:* sfs@pointloma.edu.
Website: http://www.pointloma.edu/.

POINT PARK UNIVERSITY

Pittsburgh, PA

CONTACT George Santucci, Director of Financial Aid, Point Park University, 201 Wood Street, Pittsburgh, PA 15222-1984, 412-392-3930 or toll-free 800-321-0129. *E-mail:* financialaid@pointpark.edu.
Website: http://www.pointpark.edu/.

POINT UNIVERSITY

West Point, GA

CONTACT Blair Walker, Director of Financial Aid, Point University, 2605 Ben Hill Road, East Point, GA 30344, 404-761-8861 or toll-free 855-37-POINT. *Fax:* 404-669-2024. *E-mail:* blairw@acc.edu.
Website: http://point.edu/.

POLK STATE COLLEGE

Winter Haven, FL

CONTACT Lenora Burnett, Financial Aid Supervisor, Polk State College, 999 Avenue H, NE, Winter Haven, FL 33881, 863-297-5269. *E-mail:* lburnett@polk.edu.
Website: http://www.polk.edu/.

POLYTECHNIC UNIVERSITY OF PUERTO RICO

Hato Rey, PR

ABOUT THE INSTITUTION Independent, coed. ***Awards:*** associate, bachelor's, master's, and doctoral degrees. 21 undergraduate majors. ***Total enrollment:*** 4,317. Undergraduates: 3,689. Freshmen: 569.

GIFT AID (NEED-BASED) ***Scholarships, grants, and awards:*** Federal Pell, FSEOG, state, private, college/university gift aid from institutional funds.

LOANS ***Programs:*** Federal Direct (Subsidized and Unsubsidized Stafford, PLUS).

CONTACT Sergio E. Villoldo, Financial Aid Director, Polytechnic University of Puerto Rico, 377 Ponce de Leon Avenue, Hato Rey, PR 00918, 787-754-8000 Ext. 253. *Fax:* 787-766-1163. *E-mail:* svilloldo@pupr.edu.
Website: http://www.pupr.edu/.

POLYTECHNIC UNIVERSITY OF PUERTO RICO, MIAMI CAMPUS

Miami, FL

CONTACT Maria Victoria Shehadeh, Administrative Affairs Coordinator/Financial Aid Officer, Polytechnic University of Puerto Rico, Miami Campus, 8180 Northwest 36th Street, Suite 401, Miami, FL 33166, 305-418-8000 Ext. 204 or toll-free 888-729-7659. *E-mail:* mshehadeh@pupr.edu.
Website: http://www.pupr.edu/miami/.

POLYTECHNIC UNIVERSITY OF PUERTO RICO, ORLANDO CAMPUS

Orlando, FL

CONTACT Mrs. Ileana Diaz, Financial Aid Officer, Polytechnic University of Puerto Rico, Orlando Campus, 550 North Econlockhatchee Trail, Orlando, FL 32825, 407-677-7000 Ext. 806 or toll-free 888-577-POLY. *Fax:* 407-677-5082. *E-mail:* idiaz@pupr.edu.
Website: http://www.pupr.edu/orlando/.

POMONA COLLEGE

Claremont, CA

Tuition & fees: $54,762	Average undergraduate aid package: $57,279

ABOUT THE INSTITUTION Independent, coed. ***Awards:*** bachelor's degrees. 49 undergraduate majors. ***Total enrollment:*** 1,717. Undergraduates: 1,717. Freshmen: 417. Institutional methodology is used as a basis for awarding need-based institutional aid.

UNDERGRADUATE EXPENSES for 2019–2020 ***Application fee:*** $70. ***Comprehensive fee:*** $71,980 includes full-time tuition ($54,380), mandatory fees ($382), and room and board ($17,218). ***College room only:*** $9956. Room and board charges vary according to board plan. ***Part-time tuition:*** $963 per course. ***Part-time fees:*** $191 per term. Part-time tuition and fees vary according to course load.

FRESHMAN FINANCIAL AID (Fall 2018) 277 applied for aid; of those 76% were deemed to have need. 100% of freshmen with need received aid; of those 100% had need fully met. ***Average percent of need met:*** 100% (excluding resources awarded to replace EFC). ***Average financial aid package:*** $57,415 (excluding resources awarded to replace EFC).

UNDERGRADUATE FINANCIAL AID (Fall 2018) 1,099 applied for aid; of those 83% were deemed to have need. 100% of undergraduates with need received aid; of those 100% had need fully met. ***Average percent of need met:*** 100% (excluding resources awarded to replace EFC). ***Average financial aid package:*** $57,279 (excluding resources awarded to replace EFC). 1% of all full-time undergraduates had no need and received non-need-based gift aid.

GIFT AID (NEED-BASED) ***Receiving aid:*** Freshmen: 51% (211); all full-time undergraduates: 55% (913). ***Average award:*** Freshmen: $55,485; Undergraduates: $55,082. ***Scholarships, grants, and awards:*** Federal Pell, FSEOG, state, private, college/university gift aid from institutional funds.

GIFT AID (NON-NEED-BASED) ***Average award:*** Undergraduates: $5000. ***Scholarships, grants, and awards by category:*** *Special characteristics:* veterans, veterans' children. ***Tuition waivers:*** Full or partial for employees or children of employees. ***ROTC:*** Army cooperative, Air Force cooperative.

LOANS ***Student loans:*** 25% of past graduating class borrowed through all loan programs. *Average indebtedness per student:* $18,829. ***Programs:*** Federal Direct (Subsidized and Unsubsidized Stafford, PLUS), college/university.

WORK-STUDY Federal work-study jobs available. ***State or other work-study/employment:*** Part-time jobs available.

APPLYING FOR FINANCIAL AID ***Required financial aid forms:*** FAFSA, CSS Financial Aid PROFILE, state aid form, noncustodial (divorced/separated) parent's statement.

CONTACT Ms. Robin Thompson, Director of Financial Aid, Pomona College, 333 North College Way, Sumner Hall, Claremont, CA 91711, 909-621-8205. *E-mail:* robin.thompson@pomona.edu.
Website: http://www.pomona.edu/.

PONTIFICAL CATHOLIC UNIVERSITY OF PUERTO RICO

Ponce, PR

CONTACT Mrs. Rosalia Martinez, Director of Financial Aid, Pontifical Catholic University of Puerto Rico, 2250 Las Americas Avenue, Suite 549, Ponce, PR 00717-9777, 787-841-2000 Ext. 1065 or toll-free 800-961-7696. *Fax:* 787-651-2041. *E-mail:* rosalia.martinez@email.pucpr.edu.
Website: http://www.pucpr.edu/.

PONTIFICAL CATHOLIC UNIVERSITY OF PUERTO RICO–ARECIBO CAMPUS

Arecibo, PR

CONTACT Financial Aid Office, Pontifical Catholic University of Puerto Rico–Arecibo Campus, Bo. Santana Carr. 662 Km. 2.3, Arecibo, PR 00614-4045, 787-881-1212 Ext. 6000.
Website: http://www.pucpr.edu/arecibo/.

PONTIFICAL CATHOLIC UNIVERSITY OF PUERTO RICO–MAYAGUEZ CAMPUS

Mayaguez, PR

CONTACT Financial Aid Office, Pontifical Catholic University of Puerto Rico–Mayaguez Campus, 482 Sur Calle Ramon Emerito Betances, Mayaguez, PR 00680.
Website: http://www.pucpr.edu/mayaguez/.

PONTIFICAL COLLEGE JOSEPHINUM

Columbus, OH

CONTACT Marky Leichtnam, Financial Aid Director, Pontifical College Josephinum, 7625 North High Street, Columbus, OH 43235-1498, 614-985-2212 or toll-free 888-252-5812. *Fax:* 614-885-2307. *E-mail:* mleichtnam@pcj.edu.
Website: http://www.pcj.edu/.

PORTLAND STATE UNIVERSITY

Portland, OR

Tuition & fees (OR res): $9578	Average undergraduate aid package: $10,884

ABOUT THE INSTITUTION State-supported, coed. ***Awards:*** certificates, bachelor's, master's, and doctoral degrees. 116 undergraduate majors. ***Total enrollment:*** 26,021. Undergraduates: 35,654. Freshmen: 1,569. Federal methodology is used as a basis for awarding need-based institutional aid.

UNDERGRADUATE EXPENSES for 2020–2021 ***Application fee:*** $50. ***Tuition, state resident:*** full-time $8078; part-time $180 per credit hour. ***Tuition, nonresident:*** full-time $26,910; part-time $598 per credit hour. ***Required fees:*** full-time $1500. Full-time tuition and fees vary according to program. Part-time tuition and fees vary according to program. ***College room and board:*** $11,172; ***Room only:*** $6780. Room and board charges vary according to board plan, housing facility, and student level.

FRESHMAN FINANCIAL AID (Fall 2019, est.) 1321 applied for aid; of those 82% were deemed to have need. 96% of freshmen with need received aid; of those 8% had need fully met. ***Average percent of need met:*** 61% (excluding resources awarded to replace EFC). ***Average financial aid package:*** $12,268 (excluding resources awarded to replace EFC). 1% of all full-time freshmen had no need and received non-need-based gift aid.

UNDERGRADUATE FINANCIAL AID (Fall 2019, est.) 10,473 applied for aid; of those 89% were deemed to have need. 96% of undergraduates with need received aid; of those 3% had need fully met. ***Average percent of need met:*** 53% (excluding resources awarded to replace EFC). ***Average financial aid package:*** $10,884 (excluding resources awarded to replace EFC). 1% of all full-time undergraduates had no need and received non-need-based gift aid.

GIFT AID (NEED-BASED) ***Total amount:*** $60,304,169 (65% federal, 26% state, 3% institutional, 6% external sources). ***Receiving aid:*** Freshmen: 58% (857); all full-time undergraduates: 63% (8,542). ***Average award:*** Freshmen: $8310; Undergraduates: $6380. ***Scholarships, grants, and awards:*** Federal Pell, FSEOG, state, private, college/university gift aid from institutional funds, United Negro College Fund.

GIFT AID (NON-NEED-BASED) ***Total amount:*** $1,769,901 (8% federal, 2% state, 30% institutional, 60% external sources). ***Receiving aid:*** Freshmen: 37% (544). Undergraduates: 41% (5,629). ***Average award:*** Freshmen: $3143. Undergraduates: $4516. ***Scholarships, grants, and awards by category:*** *Academic interests/achievement:* architecture, area/ethnic studies, business, computer science, education, engineering/technologies, foreign languages, general academic interests/achievements, humanities, international studies, physical sciences, social sciences. *Creative arts/performance:* art/fine arts, general creative arts/performance, music, theater/drama. *Special achievements/activities:* community service, general special achievements/activities, leadership, memberships. *Special characteristics:* adult students, ethnic background, handicapped students, international students, members of minority groups, out-of-state students, veterans. ***Tuition waivers:*** Full or partial for employees or children of employees. ***ROTC:*** Army cooperative, Naval cooperative, Air Force cooperative.

LOANS ***Student loans:*** $68,861,568.00 (84% need-based, 16% non-need-based). 55% of past graduating class borrowed through all loan programs. *Average indebtedness per student:* $26,426. ***Average need-based loan:*** Freshmen: $3406. Undergraduates: $3922. ***Parent loans:*** $7,513,956 (50% need-based, 50% non-need-based). ***Programs:*** Federal Direct (Subsidized and Unsubsidized Stafford, PLUS), Perkins.

WORK-STUDY ***Federal work-study:*** Total amount: $3,863,784; jobs available. ***State or other work-study/employment:*** Part-time jobs available.

ATHLETIC AWARDS Total amount: $1,976,069 (29% need-based, 71% non-need-based).

APPLYING FOR FINANCIAL AID ***Required financial aid form:*** FAFSA. ***Financial aid deadline:*** Continuous. ***Notification date:*** Continuous beginning 2/18.

CONTACT Amanda Bierbrauer, Interim Director of Financial Aid and Scholarships, Portland State University, PO Box 851, Portland, OR 97207, 800-547-8887. *Fax:* 503-725-5965. *E-mail:* askfa@pdx.edu.
Website: http://www.pdx.edu/.

POST UNIVERSITY

Waterbury, CT

CONTACT Ms. Michael Greer, Director of Financial Aid, Post University, 800 Country Club Road, Waterbury, CT 06723-2540, 203-591-5615 or toll-free 800-345-2562. *Fax:* 203-596-4599. *E-mail:* mgreer@post.edu.
Website: http://www.post.edu/.

PRAIRIE VIEW A&M UNIVERSITY

Prairie View, TX

Tuition & fees (area res): $10,786	Average undergraduate aid package: $15,404

ABOUT THE INSTITUTION State-supported, coed. ***Awards:*** certificates, bachelor's, master's, and doctoral degrees. 38 undergraduate majors. ***Total enrollment:*** 9,516. Undergraduates: 8,531. Freshmen: 2,177. Federal methodology is used as a basis for awarding need-based institutional aid.

UNDERGRADUATE EXPENSES for 2019–2020 ***Application fee:*** $40. ***One-time required fee:*** $40. ***Tuition, area resident:*** full-time $7043; part-time $235 per credit hour. ***Tuition, state resident:*** full-time $7043; part-time $235 per credit hour. ***Tuition, nonresident:*** full-time $21,912; part-time $730 per credit hour. ***Required fees:*** full-time $3743; $141 per credit hour. Full-time tuition and fees vary according to course load, degree level, program, and reciprocity agreements. Part-time tuition and fees vary according to course load, degree level, program, and reciprocity agreements. ***College room and board:*** $9076; ***Room only:*** $5890. Room and board charges vary according to board plan, housing facility, and student level. ***Payment plan:*** Guaranteed tuition.

FRESHMAN FINANCIAL AID (Fall 2018) 2114 applied for aid; of those 93% were deemed to have need. 95% of freshmen with need received aid; of those 6% had need fully met. ***Average percent of need met:*** 66% (excluding resources awarded to replace EFC). ***Average financial aid package:*** $16,001 (excluding resources awarded to replace EFC). 3% of all full-time freshmen had no need and received non-need-based gift aid.

UNDERGRADUATE FINANCIAL AID (Fall 2018) 7,424 applied for aid; of those 93% were deemed to have need. 97% of undergraduates with need received aid; of those 10% had need fully met. ***Average percent of need met:*** 69% (excluding resources awarded to replace EFC). ***Average financial aid package:*** $15,404 (excluding resources awarded to replace EFC). 2% of all full-time undergraduates had no need and received non-need-based gift aid.

GIFT AID (NEED-BASED) ***Receiving aid:*** Freshmen: 72% (1,570); all full-time undergraduates: 72% (5,711). ***Average award:*** Freshmen: $9706; Undergraduates: $8033. ***Scholarships, grants, and awards:*** Federal Pell, FSEOG, state, private, college/university gift aid from institutional funds, United Negro College Fund, Federal Nursing.

GIFT AID (NON-NEED-BASED) ***Receiving aid:*** Freshmen: 33% (710). Undergraduates: 34% (2,709). ***Average award:*** Freshmen: $8665. Undergraduates: $7913. ***Tuition waivers:*** Full or partial for employees or children of employees, senior citizens. ***ROTC:*** Army, Naval, Air Force cooperative.

LOANS ***Student loans:*** 85% of past graduating class borrowed through all loan programs. *Average indebtedness per student:* $32,960. ***Average need-based loan:*** Freshmen: $7052. Undergraduates: $7556. ***Programs:*** Federal Direct (Subsidized and Unsubsidized Stafford, PLUS), state, alternative loans.

WORK-STUDY ***Federal work-study:*** 471 jobs averaging $2863. ***State or other work-study/employment:*** 27 part-time jobs averaging $2859.

APPLYING FOR FINANCIAL AID ***Required financial aid form:*** FAFSA.

CONTACT Miss Charlene Ervin, Interim Director of Student Financial Aid and Scholarships, Prairie View A&M University, PO Box 519, Mail Stop 1005, Prairie View, TX 77446, 936-261-1000. *E-mail:* finaidscholarships@pvamu.edu.
Website: http://www.pvamu.edu/.

PRATT INSTITUTE

Brooklyn, NY

Tuition & fees: $55,630	Average undergraduate aid package: $31,590

ABOUT THE INSTITUTION Independent, coed. ***Awards:*** certificates, associate, bachelor's, and master's degrees. 25 undergraduate majors. ***Total enrollment:*** 4,875. Undergraduates: 3,483. Freshmen: 648. Federal methodology is used as a basis for awarding need-based institutional aid.

UNDERGRADUATE EXPENSES for 2020–2021 ***Application fee:*** $50. ***Comprehensive fee:*** $69,618 includes full-time tuition ($53,570), mandatory fees ($2060), and room and board ($13,988). ***College room only:*** $10,000. ***Part-time tuition:*** $1728 per credit hour.

FRESHMAN FINANCIAL AID (Fall 2019, est.) 342 applied for aid; of those 80% were deemed to have need. 100% of freshmen with need received aid; of those 17% had need fully met. ***Average percent of need met:*** 60% (excluding resources awarded to replace EFC). ***Average financial aid package:*** $31,889 (excluding resources awarded to replace EFC). 35% of all full-time freshmen had no need and received non-need-based gift aid.

UNDERGRADUATE FINANCIAL AID (Fall 2019, est.) 1,550 applied for aid; of those 86% were deemed to have need. 100% of undergraduates with need received aid; of those 12% had need fully met. ***Average percent of need met:*** 56% (excluding resources awarded to replace EFC). ***Average financial aid package:*** $31,590 (excluding resources awarded to replace EFC). 39% of all full-time undergraduates had no need and received non-need-based gift aid.

GIFT AID (NEED-BASED) ***Total amount:*** $3,403,037 (86% federal, 14% state). ***Receiving aid:*** Freshmen: 15% (97); all full-time undergraduates: 17% (585). ***Average award:*** Freshmen: $5703; Undergraduates: $5636. ***Scholarships, grants, and awards:*** Federal Pell, FSEOG, state, college/university gift aid from institutional funds.

GIFT AID (NON-NEED-BASED) ***Total amount:*** $55,733,766 (4% state, 95% institutional, 1% external sources). ***Receiving aid:*** Freshmen: 42% (272). Undergraduates: 39% (1,324). ***Average award:*** Freshmen: $20,319. Undergraduates: $19,234. ***Scholarships, grants, and awards by category:*** *Academic interests/achievement:* general academic interests/achievements. ***ROTC:*** Army cooperative.

LOANS ***Student loans:*** $13,673,312 (100% need-based). 60% of past graduating class borrowed through all loan programs. *Average indebtedness per student:* $41,305. ***Average need-based loan:*** Freshmen: $8494. Undergraduates: $10,139. ***Parent loans:*** $31,344,821 (100% need-based). ***Programs:*** Federal Direct (Subsidized and Unsubsidized Stafford, PLUS), Perkins.

WORK-STUDY ***Federal work-study:*** Total amount: $3,293,668; jobs available. ***State or other work-study/employment:*** Part-time jobs available.

APPLYING FOR FINANCIAL AID ***Required financial aid forms:*** FAFSA, state aid form. ***Financial aid deadline:*** 3/1 (priority: 3/1). ***Notification date:*** 3/15. Students must reply by 5/1.

CONTACT Mr. Nedzad Goga, Director of Financial Aid, Pratt Institute, 200 Willoughby Avenue, Myrtle Hall, Room 6E-9, Brooklyn, NY 11205-3899, 718-636-3563 or toll-free 800-331-0834. *Fax:* 718-636-3739. *E-mail:* finaid@pratt.edu.
Website: http://www.pratt.edu/.

PRESBYTERIAN COLLEGE

Clinton, SC

Tuition & fees: $39,460	Average undergraduate aid package: $36,727

ABOUT THE INSTITUTION Independent Presbyterian Church (U.S.A.), coed. ***Awards:*** bachelor's and doctoral degrees. 29 undergraduate majors. ***Total enrollment:*** 1,282. Undergraduates: 1,016. Freshmen: 276. Federal methodology is used as a basis for awarding need-based institutional aid.

UNDERGRADUATE EXPENSES for 2019–2020 ***Comprehensive fee:*** $50,140 includes full-time tuition ($36,600), mandatory fees ($2860), and room and board ($10,680). ***College room only:*** $5200. Full-time tuition and fees vary according to course load and reciprocity agreements. Room and board charges vary according to board plan and housing facility. ***Part-time tuition:*** $1525 per credit hour. ***Part-time fees:*** $25 per term. Part-time tuition and fees vary according to course load.

FRESHMAN FINANCIAL AID (Fall 2019, est.) 325 applied for aid; of those 89% were deemed to have need. 100% of freshmen with need received aid; of those 31% had need fully met. ***Average percent of need met:*** 83% (excluding resources awarded to replace EFC). ***Average financial aid package:*** $36,648 (excluding resources awarded to replace EFC). 15% of all full-time freshmen had no need and received non-need-based gift aid.

UNDERGRADUATE FINANCIAL AID (Fall 2019, est.) 914 applied for aid; of those 89% were deemed to have need. 100% of undergraduates with need received aid; of those 34% had need fully met. ***Average percent of need met:*** 83% (excluding resources awarded to replace EFC). ***Average financial aid package:*** $36,727 (excluding resources awarded to replace EFC). 20% of all full-time undergraduates had no need and received non-need-based gift aid.

GIFT AID (NEED-BASED) ***Total amount:*** $22,384,714 (7% federal, 20% state, 71% institutional, 2% external sources). ***Receiving aid:*** Freshmen: 85% (289); all full-time undergraduates: 79% (808). ***Average award:*** Freshmen: $30,510; Undergrad-

uates: $30,132. ***Scholarships, grants, and awards:*** Federal Pell, FSEOG, state, private, college/university gift aid from institutional funds.

GIFT AID (NON-NEED-BASED) ***Total amount:*** $6,497,795 (8% state, 86% institutional, 6% external sources). ***Receiving aid:*** Freshmen: 42% (143). Undergraduates: 42% (432). ***Average award:*** Freshmen: $19,130. Undergraduates: $18,421. ***Scholarships, grants, and awards by category:*** *Academic interests/achievement:* general academic interests/achievements. *Creative arts/performance:* music. *Special achievements/activities:* leadership. *Special characteristics:* children of faculty/staff, relatives of clergy. ***Tuition waivers:*** Full or partial for employees or children of employees, senior citizens. ***ROTC:*** Army.

LOANS ***Student loans:*** $5,332,645 (64% need-based, 36% non-need-based). 60% of past graduating class borrowed through all loan programs. *Average indebtedness per student:* $33,956. ***Average need-based loan:*** Freshmen: $2940. Undergraduates: $3770. ***Parent loans:*** $2,109,215 (44% need-based, 56% non-need-based). ***Programs:*** Federal Direct (Subsidized and Unsubsidized Stafford, PLUS), state.

WORK-STUDY ***Federal work-study:*** Total amount: $340,737; jobs available. ***State or other work-study/employment:*** Total amount: $74,700 (6% need-based, 94% non-need-based). Part-time jobs available.

ATHLETIC AWARDS Total amount: $4,519,622 (42% need-based, 58% non-need-based).

APPLYING FOR FINANCIAL AID ***Required financial aid form:*** FAFSA. ***Financial aid deadline:*** 6/30 (priority: 12/1). ***Notification date:*** Continuous beginning 1/1. Students must reply by 5/1.

CONTACT Mr. Brian J. Fortman, Director of Financial Aid, Presbyterian College, 503 South Broad Street, Clinton, SC 29325, 864-833-8287 or toll-free 800-476-7272. *E-mail:* bjfortman@presby.edu.
Website: http://www.presby.edu/.

PRESCOTT COLLEGE

Prescott, AZ

ABOUT THE INSTITUTION Independent, coed. ***Awards:*** certificates, bachelor's, master's, and doctoral degrees. 30 undergraduate majors.

GIFT AID (NEED-BASED) ***Scholarships, grants, and awards:*** Federal Pell, FSEOG, state, private, college/university gift aid from institutional funds.

GIFT AID (NON-NEED-BASED) ***Scholarships, grants, and awards by category:*** *Academic interests/achievement:* general academic interests/achievements. *Special achievements/activities:* general special achievements/activities, leadership.

LOANS ***Programs:*** Federal Direct (Subsidized and Unsubsidized Stafford, PLUS).

WORK-STUDY ***Federal work-study:*** Total amount: $105,077; jobs available. ***State or other work-study/employment:*** Part-time jobs available.

APPLYING FOR FINANCIAL AID ***Required financial aid form:*** FAFSA.

CONTACT Bee Sena, Director of Financial Aid, Prescott College, 220 Grove Avenue, Prescott, AZ 86301, 928-350-1111 or toll-free 877-350-2100. *Fax:* 928-350-1120. *E-mail:* finaid@prescott.edu.
Website: http://www.prescott.edu/.

PRESENTATION COLLEGE

Aberdeen, SD

CONTACT Ms. Janel Wagner, Director of Financial Aid, Presentation College, 1500 North Main Street, Aberdeen, SD 57401-1299, 605-229-8427 or toll-free 800-437-6060. *Fax:* 605-229-8537. *E-mail:* janel.wagner@presentation.edu.
Website: http://www.presentation.edu/.

PRINCETON UNIVERSITY

Princeton, NJ

Tuition & fees: $50,340	Average undergraduate aid package: $59,389

ABOUT THE INSTITUTION Independent, coed. ***Awards:*** bachelor's, master's, and doctoral degrees. 38 undergraduate majors. ***Total enrollment:*** 8,419. Undergraduates: 5,422. Freshmen: 1,335. Both federal and institutional methodology are used as a basis for awarding need-based institutional aid.

UNDERGRADUATE EXPENSES for 2019–2020 ***Application fee:*** $75. ***Comprehensive fee:*** $66,700 includes full-time tuition ($49,450), mandatory fees ($890), and room and board ($16,360). ***College room only:*** $9520. Room and board charges vary according to board plan. ***Part-time tuition:*** $6166 per year. ***Part-time fees:*** $25 per term.

FRESHMAN FINANCIAL AID (Fall 2019, est.) 968 applied for aid; of those 86% were deemed to have need. 100% of freshmen with need received aid; of those 100% had need fully met. ***Average percent of need met:*** 100% (excluding resources awarded to replace EFC). ***Average financial aid package:*** $59,598 (excluding resources awarded to replace EFC).

UNDERGRADUATE FINANCIAL AID (Fall 2019, est.) 3,516 applied for aid; of those 94% were deemed to have need. 100% of undergraduates with need received aid; of those 100% had need fully met. ***Average percent of need met:*** 100% (excluding resources awarded to replace EFC). ***Average financial aid package:*** $59,389 (excluding resources awarded to replace EFC).

GIFT AID (NEED-BASED) ***Total amount:*** $188,293,900 (4% federal, 93% institutional, 3% external sources). ***Receiving aid:*** Freshmen: 62% (836); all full-time undergraduates: 62% (3,289). ***Average award:*** Freshmen: $57,700; Undergraduates: $57,251. ***Scholarships, grants, and awards:*** Federal Pell, FSEOG, state, private, college/university gift aid from institutional funds.

GIFT AID (NON-NEED-BASED) ***Tuition waivers:*** Full or partial for employees or children of employees. ***ROTC:*** Army, Naval cooperative, Air Force cooperative.

LOANS ***Student loans:*** 17% of past graduating class borrowed through all loan programs. *Average indebtedness per student:* $9445. ***Parent loans:*** $1,200,000 (100% non-need-based). ***Programs:*** Federal Direct (Subsidized and Unsubsidized Stafford, PLUS), college/university.

WORK-STUDY ***Federal work-study:*** Total amount: $850,000; jobs available. ***State or other work-study/employment:*** Total amount: $2,450,000 (100% need-based). Part-time jobs available.

APPLYING FOR FINANCIAL AID ***Required financial aid forms:*** FAFSA, institution's own form. ***Financial aid deadline (priority):*** 2/1. ***Notification date:*** 4/1. Students must reply by 5/1.

CONTACT Robin Moscato, Director of Financial Aid, Princeton University, PO Box 591, Princeton, NJ 08542, 609-258-3330. *Fax:* 609-258-3558. *E-mail:* pfaa@princeton.edu.
Website: http://www.princeton.edu/.

PRINCIPIA COLLEGE

Elsah, IL

Tuition & fees: $30,190	Average undergraduate aid package: $33,447

ABOUT THE INSTITUTION Independent Christian Science, coed. ***Awards:*** bachelor's degrees. 22 undergraduate majors. Institutional methodology is used as a basis for awarding need-based institutional aid.

UNDERGRADUATE EXPENSES for 2019–2020 ***Comprehensive fee:*** $42,150 includes full-time tuition ($29,490), mandatory fees ($700), and room and board ($11,960). ***College room only:*** $5670. Full-time tuition and fees vary according to course load. Room and board charges vary according to board plan. ***Part-time tuition:*** $983 per credit hour. Part-time tuition and fees vary according to course load.

FRESHMAN FINANCIAL AID (Fall 2019, est.) 47 applied for aid; of those 94% were deemed to have need. 100% of freshmen with need received aid; of those 52% had need fully met. ***Average percent of need met:*** 94% (excluding resources awarded to replace EFC). ***Average financial aid package:*** $33,300 (excluding resources awarded to replace EFC). 32% of all full-time freshmen had no need and received non-need-based gift aid.

UNDERGRADUATE FINANCIAL AID (Fall 2019, est.) 290 applied for aid; of those 95% were deemed to have need. 100% of undergraduates with need received aid; of those 46% had need fully met. ***Average percent of need met:*** 92% (excluding resources awarded to replace EFC). ***Average financial aid package:*** $33,447 (excluding resources awarded to replace EFC). 28% of all full-time undergraduates had no need and received non-need-based gift aid.

GIFT AID (NEED-BASED) ***Total amount:*** $8,496,631 (100% institutional). ***Receiving aid:*** Freshmen: 67% (44); all full-time undergraduates: 71% (275).

Average award: Freshmen: $29,681; Undergraduates: $29,845. ***Scholarships, grants, and awards:*** private, college/university gift aid from institutional funds.
GIFT AID (NON-NEED-BASED) ***Total amount:*** $2,802,554 (100% institutional). ***Receiving aid:*** Freshmen: 32% (21). Undergraduates: 28% (109). ***Average award:*** Freshmen: $27,737. Undergraduates: $24,532. ***Scholarships, grants, and awards by category:*** *Academic interests/achievement:* 96 awards ($1,366,454 total): general academic interests/achievements. *Special achievements/activities:* 303 awards ($2,442,603 total): community service, general special achievements/activities, leadership, religious involvement. *Special characteristics:* 76 awards ($324,000 total): children and siblings of alumni, children of faculty/staff. ***Tuition waivers:*** Full or partial for employees or children of employees.
LOANS ***Student loans:*** $1,107,745 (92% need-based, 8% non-need-based). 66% of past graduating class borrowed through all loan programs. *Average indebtedness per student:* $19,613. ***Average need-based loan:*** Freshmen: $5700. Undergraduates: $5661. ***Programs:*** college/university.
APPLYING FOR FINANCIAL AID ***Required financial aid forms:*** CSS Financial Aid PROFILE, noncustodial (divorced/separated) parent's statement, federal income tax form(s). ***Financial aid deadline (priority):*** 3/1. ***Notification date:*** Continuous beginning 3/1. Students must reply by 5/1 or within 4 weeks of notification.
CONTACT Katie Schiele, Director of Financial Aid & Scholarships, Principia College, 1 Maybeck Place, Elsah, IL 62028-9799, 618-374-5187 or toll-free 800-277-4648 Ext.2804. *Fax:* 618-374-5929. *E-mail:* katie.schiele@principia.edu.
Website: http://www.principiacollege.edu/.

PROVIDENCE CHRISTIAN COLLEGE

Pasadena, CA

CONTACT Financial Aid Office, Providence Christian College, 1539 East Howard Street, Pasadena, CA 91124, 626-696-4000.
Website: http://www.providencecc.edu/.

PROVIDENCE COLLEGE

Providence, RI

Tuition & fees: $52,438	Average undergraduate aid package: $36,988

ABOUT THE INSTITUTION Independent Roman Catholic, coed. ***Awards:*** certificates, bachelor's, and master's degrees. 59 undergraduate majors. ***Total enrollment:*** 4,922. Undergraduates: 4,379. Freshmen: 1,122. Both federal and institutional methodology are used as a basis for awarding need-based institutional aid.
UNDERGRADUATE EXPENSES for 2019–2020 ***Application fee:*** $65. ***Comprehensive fee:*** $67,578 includes full-time tuition ($51,490), mandatory fees ($948), and room and board ($15,140). ***College room only:*** $8730. ***Part-time tuition:*** $2145 per credit hour.
FRESHMAN FINANCIAL AID (Fall 2019, est.) 832 applied for aid; of those 70% were deemed to have need. 100% of freshmen with need received aid; of those 25% had need fully met. ***Average percent of need met:*** 87% (excluding resources awarded to replace EFC). ***Average financial aid package:*** $38,107 (excluding resources awarded to replace EFC). 10% of all full-time freshmen had no need and received non-need-based gift aid.
UNDERGRADUATE FINANCIAL AID (Fall 2019, est.) 2,722 applied for aid; of those 72% were deemed to have need. 100% of undergraduates with need received aid; of those 23% had need fully met. ***Average percent of need met:*** 84% (excluding resources awarded to replace EFC). ***Average financial aid package:*** $36,988 (excluding resources awarded to replace EFC). 13% of all full-time undergraduates had no need and received non-need-based gift aid.
GIFT AID (NEED-BASED) ***Total amount:*** $64,826,398 (6% federal, 1% state, 91% institutional, 2% external sources). ***Receiving aid:*** Freshmen: 53% (581); all full-time undergraduates: 48% (1,967). ***Average award:*** Freshmen: $33,815; Undergraduates: $32,316. ***Scholarships, grants, and awards:*** Federal Pell, FSEOG, state, private, college/university gift aid from institutional funds, United Negro College Fund.
GIFT AID (NON-NEED-BASED) ***Total amount:*** $14,019,941 (89% institutional, 11% external sources). ***Receiving aid:*** Freshmen: 4% (42). Undergraduates: 3% (116). ***Average award:*** Freshmen: $25,204. Undergraduates: $21,350. ***Scholarships, grants, and awards by category:*** *Academic interests/achievement:* business, general academic interests/achievements, military science, premedicine. *Creative arts/performance:* theater/drama. *Special achievements/activities:* community service. *Special characteristics:* siblings of current students. ***Tuition waivers:*** Full or partial for employees or children of employees. ***ROTC:*** Army.
LOANS ***Student loans:*** $30,294,824 (30% need-based, 70% non-need-based). 57% of past graduating class borrowed through all loan programs. *Average indebtedness per student:* $44,529. ***Average need-based loan:*** Freshmen: $3420. Undergraduates: $4564. ***Parent loans:*** $10,011,585 (30% need-based, 70% non-need-based). ***Programs:*** Federal Direct (Subsidized and Unsubsidized Stafford, PLUS), state.
WORK-STUDY ***Federal work-study:*** Total amount: $1,020,000; jobs available. ***State or other work-study/employment:*** Total amount: $2,341,000 (100% non-need-based). Part-time jobs available.
ATHLETIC AWARDS Total amount: $9,830,319 (15% need-based, 85% non-need-based).
APPLYING FOR FINANCIAL AID ***Required financial aid forms:*** FAFSA, CSS Financial Aid PROFILE, Business Tax Forms/business return and K1 (if applicable) from partnership, S-Corporation, Corporation and/or Schedule C. ***Financial aid deadline:*** 2/1 (priority: 2/1). ***Notification date:*** 1/15. Students must reply by 5/1.
CONTACT Ms. Sandra J. Oliveira, Executive Director of Financial Aid, Providence College, One Cunningham Square, Providence, RI 02918, 401-865-2286 or toll-free 800-721-6444. *Fax:* 401-865-1186. *E-mail:* solivei6@providence.edu.
Website: http://www.providence.edu/.

PURCHASE COLLEGE, STATE UNIVERSITY OF NEW YORK

Purchase, NY

Tuition & fees (NY res): $8953	Average undergraduate aid package: $11,299

ABOUT THE INSTITUTION State-supported, coed. ***Awards:*** certificates, bachelor's, and master's degrees. 41 undergraduate majors. ***Total enrollment:*** 4,187. Undergraduates: 4,081. Freshmen: 798. Federal methodology is used as a basis for awarding need-based institutional aid.
UNDERGRADUATE EXPENSES for 2019–2020 ***Application fee:*** $50. ***One-time required fee:*** $210. ***Tuition, state resident:*** full-time $7070; part-time $295 per credit hour. ***Tuition, nonresident:*** full-time $16,980; part-time $708 per credit hour. ***Required fees:*** full-time $1883; $82.67 per credit hour. Part-time tuition and fees vary according to course load. ***College room and board:*** $14,548; ***Room only:*** $9098. Room and board charges vary according to board plan and housing facility.
FRESHMAN FINANCIAL AID (Fall 2019, est.) 720 applied for aid; of those 75% were deemed to have need. 100% of freshmen with need received aid; of those 5% had need fully met. ***Average percent of need met:*** 49% (excluding resources awarded to replace EFC). ***Average financial aid package:*** $10,606 (excluding resources awarded to replace EFC). 12% of all full-time freshmen had no need and received non-need-based gift aid.
UNDERGRADUATE FINANCIAL AID (Fall 2019, est.) 3,061 applied for aid; of those 80% were deemed to have need. 100% of undergraduates with need received aid; of those 3% had need fully met. ***Average percent of need met:*** 50% (excluding resources awarded to replace EFC). ***Average financial aid package:*** $11,299 (excluding resources awarded to replace EFC). 22% of all full-time undergraduates had no need and received non-need-based gift aid.
GIFT AID (NEED-BASED) ***Receiving aid:*** Freshmen: 68% (516); all full-time undergraduates: 66% (2,389). ***Average award:*** Freshmen: $10,465; Undergraduates: $10,870. ***Scholarships, grants, and awards:*** Federal Pell, FSEOG, state, private, college/university gift aid from institutional funds.
GIFT AID (NON-NEED-BASED) ***Receiving aid:*** Freshmen: 10% (78). Undergraduates: 12% (446). ***Average award:*** Freshmen: $2785. Undergraduates: $2479. ***Scholarships, grants, and awards by category:*** *Academic interests/achievement:* area/ethnic studies, biological sciences, computer science, English, general academic interests/achievements, humanities, mathematics, social sciences. *Creative arts/performance:* applied art and design, cinema/film/broadcasting, creative writing, dance, general creative arts/performance, music, performing arts, theater/drama. ***Tuition waivers:*** Full or partial for employees or children of employees.
LOANS ***Student loans:*** 68% of past graduating class borrowed through all loan programs. *Average indebtedness per student:* $23,987. ***Average need-based loan:***

Freshmen: $3369. Undergraduates: $4358. ***Programs:*** Federal Direct (Subsidized and Unsubsidized Stafford, PLUS), Perkins.

WORK-STUDY Federal work-study jobs available. ***State or other work-study/employment:*** Part-time jobs available.

APPLYING FOR FINANCIAL AID *Required financial aid forms:* FAFSA, state aid form. ***Financial aid deadline:*** Continuous. ***Notification date:*** Continuous.

CONTACT Ms. Corey York, Director of Student Financial Services, Purchase College, State University of New York, 735 Anderson Hill Road, Purchase, NY 10577-1400, 914-251-6085. *Fax:* 914-251-6099. *E-mail:* corey.york@purchase.edu. *Website:* http://www.purchase.edu/.

PURDUE UNIVERSITY

West Lafayette, IN

Tuition & fees (IN res): $9992	Average undergraduate aid package: $14,258

ABOUT THE INSTITUTION State-supported, coed. ***Awards:*** certificates, associate, bachelor's, master's, and doctoral degrees. 140 undergraduate majors. ***Total enrollment:*** 43,411. Undergraduates: 32,672. Freshmen: 8,357. Federal methodology is used as a basis for awarding need-based institutional aid.

UNDERGRADUATE EXPENSES for 2019–2020 ***Application fee:*** $60. ***Tuition, state resident:*** full-time $9208; part-time $330 per credit hour. ***Tuition, nonresident:*** full-time $28,010; part-time $930 per credit hour. ***Required fees:*** full-time $784; $18 per credit hour. Full-time tuition and fees vary according to course load and program. Part-time tuition and fees vary according to course load. ***College room and board:*** $10,030; ***Room only:*** $4860. Room and board charges vary according to board plan and housing facility.

FRESHMAN FINANCIAL AID (Fall 2018) 6405 applied for aid; of those 62% were deemed to have need. 95% of freshmen with need received aid; of those 40% had need fully met. ***Average percent of need met:*** 77% (excluding resources awarded to replace EFC). ***Average financial aid package:*** $13,511 (excluding resources awarded to replace EFC). 12% of all full-time freshmen had no need and received non-need-based gift aid.

UNDERGRADUATE FINANCIAL AID (Fall 2018) 19,383 applied for aid; of those 67% were deemed to have need. 97% of undergraduates with need received aid; of those 41% had need fully met. ***Average percent of need met:*** 80% (excluding resources awarded to replace EFC). ***Average financial aid package:*** $14,258 (excluding resources awarded to replace EFC). 13% of all full-time undergraduates had no need and received non-need-based gift aid.

GIFT AID (NEED-BASED) ***Total amount:*** $110,684,810 (22% federal, 23% state, 50% institutional, 5% external sources). ***Receiving aid:*** Freshmen: 32% (2,658); all full-time undergraduates: 31% (9,573). ***Average award:*** Freshmen: $12,115; Undergraduates: $12,029. ***Scholarships, grants, and awards:*** Federal Pell, FSEOG, state, private, college/university gift aid from institutional funds.

GIFT AID (NON-NEED-BASED) ***Total amount:*** $44,618,322 (8% state, 68% institutional, 24% external sources). ***Receiving aid:*** Freshmen: 14% (1,190). Undergraduates: 11% (3,424). ***Average award:*** Freshmen: $5057. Undergraduates: $5536. ***Scholarships, grants, and awards by category:*** *Academic interests/achievement:* agriculture, computer science, education, engineering/technologies, general academic interests/achievements, home economics, humanities, mathematics, military science, physical sciences. *Creative arts/performance:* music. *Special achievements/activities:* leadership. *Special characteristics:* children of faculty/staff. ***Tuition waivers:*** Full or partial for employees or children of employees, senior citizens. ***ROTC:*** Army, Naval, Air Force.

LOANS *Student loans:* $94,441,625 (53% need-based, 47% non-need-based). 51% of past graduating class borrowed through all loan programs. *Average indebtedness per student:* $27,673. ***Average need-based loan:*** Freshmen: $4701. Undergraduates: $4930. ***Parent loans:*** $32,431,763 (35% need-based, 65% non-need-based). ***Programs:*** Federal Direct (Subsidized and Unsubsidized Stafford, PLUS), Perkins, college/university.

WORK-STUDY *Federal work-study:* Total amount: $1,473,358; jobs available. ***State or other work-study/employment:*** Total amount: $17,427,990 (19% need-based, 81% non-need-based). Part-time jobs available.

ATHLETIC AWARDS Total amount: $9,275,476 (27% need-based, 73% non-need-based).

APPLYING FOR FINANCIAL AID *Required financial aid form:* FAFSA. ***Financial aid deadline (priority):*** 3/1. ***Notification date:*** 2/15.

CONTACT Theodore E. Malone, Division of Financial Aid, Purdue University, Schleman Hall of Student Services, Room 305, West Lafayette, IN 47907-2050, 765-494-5056. *Fax:* 765-496-3918. *Website:* http://www.purdue.edu/.

PURDUE UNIVERSITY FORT WAYNE

Fort Wayne, IN

Tuition & fees (IN res): $9708	Average undergraduate aid package: $10,606

ABOUT THE INSTITUTION State-supported, coed. ***Awards:*** certificates, associate, bachelor's, and master's degrees. 60 undergraduate majors. ***Total enrollment:*** 10,208. Undergraduates: 9,697. Freshmen: 1,609. Federal methodology is used as a basis for awarding need-based institutional aid.

UNDERGRADUATE EXPENSES for 2020–2021 ***Application fee:*** $50. ***Tuition, area resident:*** part-time $286 per credit hour. ***Tuition, state resident:*** full-time $8589; part-time $286 per credit hour. ***Tuition, nonresident:*** full-time $20,622; part-time $687 per credit hour. ***Required fees:*** full-time $1119. ***College room and board:*** $9620; ***Room only:*** $6108.

FRESHMAN FINANCIAL AID (Fall 2018) 1361 applied for aid; of those 78% were deemed to have need. 96% of freshmen with need received aid; of those 11% had need fully met. ***Average percent of need met:*** 60% (excluding resources awarded to replace EFC). ***Average financial aid package:*** $10,489 (excluding resources awarded to replace EFC). 14% of all full-time freshmen had no need and received non-need-based gift aid.

UNDERGRADUATE FINANCIAL AID (Fall 2018) 4,770 applied for aid; of those 81% were deemed to have need. 96% of undergraduates with need received aid; of those 11% had need fully met. ***Average percent of need met:*** 60% (excluding resources awarded to replace EFC). ***Average financial aid package:*** $10,606 (excluding resources awarded to replace EFC). 9% of all full-time undergraduates had no need and received non-need-based gift aid.

GIFT AID (NEED-BASED) ***Total amount:*** $26,830,674 (48% federal, 39% state, 11% institutional, 2% external sources). ***Receiving aid:*** Freshmen: 58% (855); all full-time undergraduates: 48% (2,702). ***Average award:*** Freshmen: $5903; Undergraduates: $6249. ***Scholarships, grants, and awards:*** Federal Pell, FSEOG, state, private, college/university gift aid from institutional funds.

GIFT AID (NON-NEED-BASED) ***Receiving aid:*** Freshmen: 40% (599). Undergraduates: 28% (1,614). ***Average award:*** Freshmen: $2281. Undergraduates: $2650. ***Scholarships, grants, and awards by category:*** *Academic interests/achievement:* biological sciences, engineering/technologies, general academic interests/achievements. *Creative arts/performance:* applied art and design, music, theater/drama. *Special achievements/activities:* leadership. *Special characteristics:* children and siblings of alumni, general special characteristics, local/state students. ***ROTC:*** Army.

LOANS *Student loans:* $20,162,057 (90% need-based, 10% non-need-based). 6% of past graduating class borrowed through all loan programs. *Average indebtedness per student:* $22,354. ***Average need-based loan:*** Freshmen: $2276. Undergraduates: $3458. ***Parent loans:*** $1,909,106 (83% need-based, 17% non-need-based). ***Programs:*** Federal Direct (Subsidized and Unsubsidized Stafford, PLUS).

WORK-STUDY *Federal work-study:* Total amount: $316,828; jobs available.

ATHLETIC AWARDS Total amount: $2,173,221 (17% need-based, 83% non-need-based).

APPLYING FOR FINANCIAL AID *Required financial aid forms:* FAFSA, general scholarship application form. ***Financial aid deadline (priority):*** 4/15. ***Notification date:*** 4/15.

CONTACT Mr. Douglas Hess, Director of Financial Aid, Purdue University Fort Wayne, 2101 East Coliseum Boulevard, Fort Wayne, IN 46805-1499, 260-481-6242 or toll-free 800-324-4739. *E-mail:* finaid@pfw.edu. *Website:* http://www.pfw.edu/.

PURDUE UNIVERSITY GLOBAL
Indianapolis, IN

CONTACT Financial Aid Office, Purdue University Global, 9000 Keystone Crossing, Suite 800, Indianapolis, IN 46240.
Website: http://www.purdueglobal.edu/.

PURDUE UNIVERSITY GLOBAL
Cedar Falls, IA

CONTACT Financial Aid Office, Purdue University Global, 7009 Nordic Drive, Cedar Falls, IA 50613, 319-277-0220 or toll-free 844-PURDUE-G.
Website: http://www.purdueglobal.edu/.

PURDUE UNIVERSITY GLOBAL
Cedar Rapids, IA

CONTACT Financial Aid Office, Purdue University Global, 3165 Edgewood Parkway, SW, Cedar Rapids, IA 52404, 319-363-0481 or toll-free 844-PURDUE-G.
Website: http://www.purdueglobal.edu/.

PURDUE UNIVERSITY GLOBAL
Davenport, IA

CONTACT Financial Aid Office, Purdue University Global, 1801 East Kimberly Road, Suite 1, Davenport, IA 52807, 563-355-3500 or toll-free 844-PURDUE-G.
Website: http://www.purdueglobal.edu/.

PURDUE UNIVERSITY GLOBAL
Mason City, IA

CONTACT Financial Aid Office, Purdue University Global, 2570 4th Street, SW, Mason City, IA 50401, 641-423-2530 or toll-free 844-PURDUE-G.
Website: http://www.purdueglobal.edu/.

PURDUE UNIVERSITY GLOBAL
Urbandale, IA

CONTACT Financial Aid Office, Purdue University Global, 4655 121st Street, Urbandale, IA 50323, 515-727-2100 or toll-free 844-PURDUE-G.
Website: http://www.purdueglobal.edu/.

PURDUE UNIVERSITY GLOBAL
Augusta, ME

CONTACT Financial Aid Office, Purdue University Global, 14 Marketplace Drive, Augusta, ME 04330, 207-213-2500 or toll-free 844-PURDUE-G.
Website: http://www.purdueglobal.edu/.

PURDUE UNIVERSITY GLOBAL
Lewiston, ME

CONTACT Financial Aid Office, Purdue University Global, 475 Lisbon Street, Lewiston, ME 04240, 207-333-3300 or toll-free 844-PURDUE-G.
Website: http://www.purdueglobal.edu/.

PURDUE UNIVERSITY GLOBAL
Hagerstown, MD

CONTACT Financial Aid Office, Purdue University Global, 18618 Crestwood Drive, Hagerstown, MD 21742, 301-766-3600 or toll-free 844-PURDUE-G.
Website: http://www.purdueglobal.edu/.

PURDUE UNIVERSITY GLOBAL
St. Louis, MO

CONTACT Financial Aid Office, Purdue University Global, 1807 Park 270 Drive, St. Louis, MO 63146.
Website: http://www.purdueglobal.edu/.

PURDUE UNIVERSITY GLOBAL
Lincoln, NE

CONTACT Financial Aid Office, Purdue University Global, 1821 K Street, Lincoln, NE 68508, 402-474-5315 or toll-free 844-PURDUE-G.
Website: http://www.purdueglobal.edu/.

PURDUE UNIVERSITY GLOBAL
Omaha, NE

CONTACT Financial Aid Office, Purdue University Global, 5425 North 103rd Street, Omaha, NE 68134, 402-431-6100 or toll-free 844-PURDUE-G.
Website: http://www.purdueglobal.edu/.

PURDUE UNIVERSITY GLOBAL
Milwaukee, WI

CONTACT Financial Aid Office, Purdue University Global, 201 West Wisconsin Avenue, Milwaukee, WI 53203.
Website: http://www.purdueglobal.edu/.

PURDUE UNIVERSITY NORTHWEST
Hammond, IN

Tuition & fees (IN res): $7942	Average undergraduate aid package: $13,393

ABOUT THE INSTITUTION State-supported, coed. ***Awards:*** certificates, bachelor's, master's, and doctoral degrees. 48 undergraduate majors. ***Total enrollment:*** 8,617. Undergraduates: 7,717. Freshmen: 1,235. Federal methodology is used as a basis for awarding need-based institutional aid.

UNDERGRADUATE EXPENSES for 2020–2021 ***Application fee:*** $25. ***Tuition, state resident:*** full-time $7942; part-time $235 per credit hour. ***Tuition, nonresident:*** full-time $11,523; part-time $352 per credit hour. ***Required fees:*** $25.51 per credit hour. Full-time tuition and fees vary according to program. Part-time tuition and fees vary according to program. ***College room and board:*** $7821.

FRESHMAN FINANCIAL AID (Fall 2018) 1121 applied for aid; of those 70% were deemed to have need. 93% of freshmen with need received aid; of those 14% had need fully met. ***Average percent of need met:*** 10% (excluding resources awarded to replace EFC). ***Average financial aid package:*** $8391 (excluding resources awarded to replace EFC).

UNDERGRADUATE FINANCIAL AID (Fall 2018) 5,755 applied for aid; of those 69% were deemed to have need. 94% of undergraduates with need received aid; of those 13% had need fully met. ***Average percent of need met:*** 11% (excluding resources awarded to replace EFC). ***Average financial aid package:*** $13,393

(excluding resources awarded to replace EFC). 1% of all full-time undergraduates had no need and received non-need-based gift aid.

GIFT AID (NEED-BASED) ***Receiving aid:*** Freshmen: 56% (631); all full-time undergraduates: 53% (3,050). ***Average award:*** Freshmen: $4059; Undergraduates: $4097. ***Scholarships, grants, and awards:*** Federal Pell, FSEOG, state, private, college/university gift aid from institutional funds.

GIFT AID (NON-NEED-BASED) ***Receiving aid:*** Undergraduates: 1% (63). ***Average award:*** Undergraduates: $1875. ***Scholarships, grants, and awards by category:*** *Academic interests/achievement:* biological sciences, business, communication, computer science, education, engineering/technologies, English, general academic interests/achievements, home economics, humanities, mathematics, physical sciences, social sciences. *Creative arts/performance:* creative writing. *Special characteristics:* children of faculty/staff, international students, veterans. ***Tuition waivers:*** Full or partial for employees or children of employees, senior citizens. ***ROTC:*** Army.

LOANS ***Student loans:*** 78% of past graduating class borrowed through all loan programs. *Average indebtedness per student:* $12,568. ***Average need-based loan:*** Freshmen: $1661. Undergraduates: $2085. ***Programs:*** Federal Direct (Subsidized and Unsubsidized Stafford, PLUS), Perkins.

WORK-STUDY Federal work-study jobs available.

APPLYING FOR FINANCIAL AID ***Required financial aid form:*** FAFSA. ***Notification date:*** Continuous. Students must reply within 2 weeks of notification.

CONTACT Mr. Michael Biel, Executive Director of Financial Aid, Purdue University Northwest, 2200 169th Street, Hammond, IN 46323-2094, 855-608-4600 or toll-free 800-447-8738. *Fax:* 219-989-2141. *E-mail:* finaid@pnw.edu.
Website: http://www.pnw.edu/.

QUEENS COLLEGE OF THE CITY UNIVERSITY OF NEW YORK

Queens, NY

Tuition & fees: N/R	Average undergraduate aid package: $7001

ABOUT THE INSTITUTION State and locally supported, coed. ***Awards:*** certificates, bachelor's, and master's degrees. 75 undergraduate majors. ***Total enrollment:*** 3,057. Undergraduates: 16,866. Freshmen: 2,266. Federal methodology is used as a basis for awarding need-based institutional aid.

UNDERGRADUATE EXPENSES for 2019–2020 ***Application fee:*** $65. ***Tuition, state resident:*** part-time $305 per credit. ***Tuition, nonresident:*** part-time $620 per credit. ***Required fees:*** $209 per credit. Full-time tuition and fees vary according to course load. Part-time tuition and fees vary according to course load. ***Room only:*** $12,752. Room and board charges vary according to board plan and housing facility.

FRESHMAN FINANCIAL AID (Fall 2018) 1662 applied for aid; of those 87% were deemed to have need. 100% of freshmen with need received aid; of those 5% had need fully met. ***Average percent of need met:*** 59% (excluding resources awarded to replace EFC). ***Average financial aid package:*** $5772 (excluding resources awarded to replace EFC). 1% of all full-time freshmen had no need and received non-need-based gift aid.

UNDERGRADUATE FINANCIAL AID (Fall 2018) 9,502 applied for aid; of those 92% were deemed to have need. 98% of undergraduates with need received aid; of those 4% had need fully met. ***Average percent of need met:*** 53% (excluding resources awarded to replace EFC). ***Average financial aid package:*** $7001 (excluding resources awarded to replace EFC). 1% of all full-time undergraduates had no need and received non-need-based gift aid.

GIFT AID (NEED-BASED) ***Total amount:*** $66,690,513 (58% federal, 42% state). ***Receiving aid:*** Freshmen: 66% (1,278); all full-time undergraduates: 63% (7,667). ***Average award:*** Freshmen: $8920; Undergraduates: $8244. ***Scholarships, grants, and awards:*** Federal Pell, FSEOG, state, private, college/university gift aid from institutional funds.

GIFT AID (NON-NEED-BASED) ***Total amount:*** $8,182,803 (41% state, 29% institutional, 30% external sources). ***Receiving aid:*** Freshmen: 53% (1,033). Undergraduates: 23% (2,756). ***Average award:*** Freshmen: $6090. Undergraduates: $6260. ***Scholarships, grants, and awards by category:*** *Academic interests/achievement:* 4,390 awards ($16,678,758 total): general academic interests/achievements. ***Tuition waivers:*** Full or partial for employees or children of employees, senior citizens. ***ROTC:*** Army cooperative.

LOANS ***Student loans:*** $12,682,742 (47% need-based, 53% non-need-based). 15% of past graduating class borrowed through all loan programs. *Average indebtedness per student:* $14,738. ***Average need-based loan:*** Freshmen: $3285. Undergraduates: $4249. ***Parent loans:*** $720,336 (100% non-need-based). ***Programs:*** Federal Direct (Subsidized and Unsubsidized Stafford, PLUS).

WORK-STUDY ***Federal work-study:*** Total amount: $883,119; 249 jobs averaging $3547.

ATHLETIC AWARDS Total amount: $911,729 (100% non-need-based).

APPLYING FOR FINANCIAL AID ***Required financial aid forms:*** FAFSA, state aid form. ***Financial aid deadline:*** Continuous. ***Notification date:*** Continuous beginning 3/1. Students must reply within 3 weeks of notification.

CONTACT Mr. Clifford Couloute, Director of Financial Aid, Queens College of the City University of New York, 65-30 Kissena Boulevard, Queens, NY 11367-1597, 718-997-5109. *Fax:* 718-997-5122. *E-mail:* qc.finaid@qc.cuny.edu.
Website: http://www.qc.cuny.edu/.

QUEENS UNIVERSITY OF CHARLOTTE

Charlotte, NC

Tuition & fees: N/R	Average undergraduate aid package: $26,200

ABOUT THE INSTITUTION Independent Presbyterian, coed. ***Awards:*** certificates, bachelor's, and master's degrees. 36 undergraduate majors. ***Total enrollment:*** 2,463. Undergraduates: 1,733. Freshmen: 338. Federal methodology is used as a basis for awarding need-based institutional aid.

FRESHMAN FINANCIAL AID (Fall 2019, est.) 274 applied for aid; of those 81% were deemed to have need. 100% of freshmen with need received aid; of those 22% had need fully met. ***Average percent of need met:*** 75% (excluding resources awarded to replace EFC). ***Average financial aid package:*** $29,112 (excluding resources awarded to replace EFC). 32% of all full-time freshmen had no need and received non-need-based gift aid.

UNDERGRADUATE FINANCIAL AID (Fall 2019, est.) 1,173 applied for aid; of those 88% were deemed to have need. 100% of undergraduates with need received aid; of those 21% had need fully met. ***Average percent of need met:*** 70% (excluding resources awarded to replace EFC). ***Average financial aid package:*** $26,200 (excluding resources awarded to replace EFC). 30% of all full-time undergraduates had no need and received non-need-based gift aid.

GIFT AID (NEED-BASED) ***Total amount:*** $18,530,815 (12% federal, 11% state, 75% institutional, 2% external sources). ***Receiving aid:*** Freshmen: 66% (219); all full-time undergraduates: 66% (1,001). ***Average award:*** Freshmen: $23,233; Undergraduates: $20,957. ***Scholarships, grants, and awards:*** Federal Pell, FSEOG, state, private, college/university gift aid from institutional funds.

GIFT AID (NON-NEED-BASED) ***Total amount:*** $7,735,585 (94% institutional, 6% external sources). ***Receiving aid:*** Freshmen: 8% (28). Undergraduates: 9% (142). ***Average award:*** Freshmen: $14,394. Undergraduates: $14,304. ***Scholarships, grants, and awards by category:*** *Academic interests/achievement:* business, communication, education, general academic interests/achievements, health fields, humanities, social sciences. *Creative arts/performance:* applied art and design, music, theater/drama. *Special achievements/activities:* cheerleading/drum major, community service, general special achievements/activities, leadership, memberships, religious involvement. *Special characteristics:* adult students, children and siblings of alumni, children of current students, children of faculty/staff, first-generation college students, international students, relatives of clergy, religious affiliation, siblings of current students, veterans.

LOANS ***Student loans:*** $11,557,958 (73% need-based, 27% non-need-based). 59% of past graduating class borrowed through all loan programs. *Average indebtedness per student:* $30,654. ***Average need-based loan:*** Freshmen: $3283. Undergraduates: $4257. ***Parent loans:*** $4,334,392 (41% need-based, 59% non-need-based). ***Programs:*** Federal Direct (Subsidized and Unsubsidized Stafford, PLUS), state.

WORK-STUDY ***Federal work-study:*** Total amount: $451,400; jobs available. ***State or other work-study/employment:*** Part-time jobs available.

ATHLETIC AWARDS Total amount: $7,617,857 (34% need-based, 66% non-need-based).

APPLYING FOR FINANCIAL AID ***Required financial aid form:*** FAFSA. ***Financial aid deadline:*** Continuous. ***Notification date:*** Continuous beginning 12/31.

CONTACT Nancy Buchanan, Senior Director of Financial Aid, Queens University of Charlotte, 1900 Selwyn Avenue, Charlotte, NC 28274-0002, 704-337-2713 or toll-free 800-849-0202. *Fax:* 704-337-2416. *E-mail:* buchanann@queens.edu.
Website: http://www.queens.edu/.

QUINCY UNIVERSITY

Quincy, IL

CONTACT Lisa Flack, Director of Financial Aid, Quincy University, 1800 College Avenue, Quincy, IL 62301-2699, 217-228-5260 or toll-free 800-688-4295. *Fax:* 217-228-5635. *E-mail:* financialaid@quincy.edu.
Website: http://www.quincy.edu/.

QUINNIPIAC UNIVERSITY

Hamden, CT

ABOUT THE INSTITUTION Independent, coed. ***Awards:*** certificates, bachelor's, master's, and doctoral degrees. 67 undergraduate majors. ***Total enrollment:*** 10,200. Undergraduates: 7,305.

GIFT AID (NEED-BASED) ***Scholarships, grants, and awards:*** Federal Pell, FSEOG, state, private, college/university gift aid from institutional funds.

GIFT AID (NON-NEED-BASED) ***Scholarships, grants, and awards by category:*** *Academic interests/achievement:* general academic interests/achievements. *Creative arts/performance:* theater/drama. *Special characteristics:* children of faculty/staff, international students, siblings of current students.

LOANS ***Programs:*** Federal Direct (Subsidized and Unsubsidized Stafford, PLUS).

WORK-STUDY ***Federal work-study:*** Total amount: $3,789,069; 1,767 jobs averaging $2117.

APPLYING FOR FINANCIAL AID ***Required financial aid form:*** FAFSA.

CONTACT Mr. Dominic Yoia, Associate Vice President and University Director of Financial Aid, Quinnipiac University, 275 Mount Carmel Avenue, Hamden, CT 06518, 203-582-5224 or toll-free 800-462-1944. *Fax:* 203-582-5238. *E-mail:* finaid@quinnipiac.edu.
Website: http://www.qu.edu/.

RABBI JACOB JOSEPH SCHOOL

Edison, NJ

CONTACT Financial Aid Office, Rabbi Jacob Joseph School, One Plainfield Ave, Edison, NJ 08817, 732-985-6533.

RABBINICAL ACADEMY MESIVTA RABBI CHAIM BERLIN

Brooklyn, NY

CONTACT Office of Financial Aid, Rabbinical Academy Mesivta Rabbi Chaim Berlin, 1605 Coney Island Avenue, Brooklyn, NY 11230-4715, 718-377-0777.

RABBINICAL COLLEGE BETH SHRAGA

Monsey, NY

CONTACT Financial Aid Office, Rabbinical College Beth Shraga, 28 Saddle River Road, Monsey, NY 10952-3035, 914-356-1980.

RABBINICAL COLLEGE BOBOVER YESHIVA B'NEI ZION

Brooklyn, NY

CONTACT Financial Aid Office, Rabbinical College Bobover Yeshiva B'nei Zion, 1577 48th Street, Brooklyn, NY 11219, 718-438-2018.

RABBINICAL COLLEGE OF AMERICA

Morristown, NJ

CONTACT Financial Aid Office , Rabbinical College of America, 226 Sussex Avenue, Morristown, NJ 07960, 973-267-9404. *Fax:* 973-267-5208.
Website: http://www.rca.edu/.

RABBINICAL COLLEGE OF LONG ISLAND

Long Beach, NY

CONTACT Rabbi Cone, Financial Aid Administrator, Rabbinical College of Long Island, 201 Magnolia Boulevard, Long Beach, NY 11561-3305, 516-431-7414.

RABBINICAL COLLEGE OF OHR SHIMON YISROEL

Brooklyn, NY

CONTACT Financial Aid Office, Rabbinical College of Ohr Shimon Yisroel, 215-217 Hewes Street, Brooklyn, NY 11211, 718-855-4092.

RABBINICAL COLLEGE OF TELSHE

Wickliffe, OH

CONTACT Financial Aid Office, Rabbinical College of Telshe, 28400 Euclid Avenue, Wickliffe, OH 44092-2523, 216-943-5300.

RABBINICAL COLLEGE OHR YISROEL

Brooklyn, NY

CONTACT Financial Aid Office, Rabbinical College Ohr Yisroel, 8800 Seaview Avenue, Brooklyn, NY 11236.
Website: http://www.rabbinicalcollegeohryisroel.com/.

RABBINICAL SEMINARY OF AMERICA

Flushing, NY

CONTACT Ms. Leah Eisenstein, Director of Financial Aid, Rabbinical Seminary of America, 92-15 69th Avenue, Forest Hills, NY 11375, 718-268-4700. *Fax:* 718-268-4684.

RADFORD UNIVERSITY

Radford, VA

Tuition & fees (VA res): $11,350 | **Average undergraduate aid package: $11,147**

ABOUT THE INSTITUTION State-supported, coed. ***Awards:*** certificates, bachelor's, master's, and doctoral degrees. 48 undergraduate majors. ***Total enrollment:*** 11,870. Undergraduates: 7,967. Freshmen: 1,651. Federal methodology is used as a basis for awarding need-based institutional aid.

UNDERGRADUATE EXPENSES for 2019–2020 ***Tuition, state resident:*** full-time $7922; part-time $329 per credit hour. ***Tuition, nonresident:*** full-time $19,557; part-time $814 per credit hour. ***Required fees:*** full-time $3428; $143 per credit hour. Full-time tuition and fees vary according to course load, location, and program. Part-time tuition and fees vary according to course load, location, and program. ***College room and board:*** $9637; ***Room only:*** $5281. Room and board charges vary according to board plan, housing facility, and location.

FRESHMAN FINANCIAL AID (Fall 2019, est.) 1520 applied for aid; of those 78% were deemed to have need. 97% of freshmen with need received aid; of those 14% had need fully met. ***Average percent of need met:*** 78% (excluding resources awarded to replace EFC). ***Average financial aid package:*** $11,788 (excluding resources awarded to replace EFC). 15% of all full-time freshmen had no need and received non-need-based gift aid.

UNDERGRADUATE FINANCIAL AID (Fall 2019, est.) 6,295 applied for aid; of those 82% were deemed to have need. 97% of undergraduates with need received aid; of those 13% had need fully met. ***Average percent of need met:*** 76% (excluding resources awarded to replace EFC). ***Average financial aid package:*** $11,147 (excluding resources awarded to replace EFC). 7% of all full-time undergraduates had no need and received non-need-based gift aid.

GIFT AID (NEED-BASED) ***Receiving aid:*** Freshmen: 63% (1,029); all full-time undergraduates: 55% (4,151). ***Average award:*** Freshmen: $9791; Undergraduates: $8551. ***Scholarships, grants, and awards:*** Federal Pell, FSEOG, state, private, college/university gift aid from institutional funds.

GIFT AID (NON-NEED-BASED) ***Receiving aid:*** Freshmen: 13% (211). Undergraduates: 6% (447). ***Average award:*** Freshmen: $3226. Undergraduates: $3538. ***Scholarships, grants, and awards by category:*** *Academic interests/achievement:* 1,151 awards ($7,934,440 total): general academic interests/achievements. ***Tuition waivers:*** Full or partial for employees or children of employees, senior citizens. ***ROTC:*** Army.

LOANS ***Student loans:*** 70% of past graduating class borrowed through all loan programs. *Average indebtedness per student:* $32,261. ***Average need-based loan:*** Freshmen: $3293. Undergraduates: $4201. ***Programs:*** Federal Direct (Subsidized and Unsubsidized Stafford, PLUS), Federal Nursing, state.

WORK-STUDY ***Federal work-study:*** 502 jobs averaging $2071. ***State or other work-study/employment:*** 284 part-time jobs averaging $2027.

APPLYING FOR FINANCIAL AID ***Required financial aid form:*** FAFSA. ***Financial aid deadline:*** Continuous. ***Notification date:*** Continuous. Students must reply within 2 weeks of notification.

CONTACT Allison Pratt, Interim Director of Financial Aid, Radford University, PO Box 6905, Radford, VA 24142, 540-831-5408. *Fax:* 540-831-5138. *E-mail:* finaid@radford.edu.
Website: http://www.radford.edu/.

RAMAPO COLLEGE OF NEW JERSEY

Mahwah, NJ

Tuition & fees (NJ res): $14,678 | **Average undergraduate aid package: $11,302**

ABOUT THE INSTITUTION State-supported, coed. ***Awards:*** certificates, bachelor's, and master's degrees. 42 undergraduate majors. ***Total enrollment:*** 6,142. Undergraduates: 5,574. Freshmen: 1,003. Federal methodology is used as a basis for awarding need-based institutional aid.

UNDERGRADUATE EXPENSES for 2019–2020 ***Application fee:*** $65. ***Tuition, state resident:*** full-time $12,171; part-time $380 per credit. ***Tuition, nonresident:*** full-time $21,722; part-time $679 per credit. ***Required fees:*** full-time $2507; $78.35 per credit. Full-time tuition and fees vary according to reciprocity agreements. Part-time tuition and fees vary according to reciprocity agreements. ***College room and board:*** $12,840; ***Room only:*** $8850. Room and board charges vary according to board plan and housing facility.

FRESHMAN FINANCIAL AID (Fall 2018) 813 applied for aid; of those 72% were deemed to have need. 98% of freshmen with need received aid; of those 5% had need fully met. ***Average percent of need met:*** 53% (excluding resources awarded to replace EFC). ***Average financial aid package:*** $11,339 (excluding resources awarded to replace EFC). 11% of all full-time freshmen had no need and received non-need-based gift aid.

UNDERGRADUATE FINANCIAL AID (Fall 2018) 3,445 applied for aid; of those 76% were deemed to have need. 98% of undergraduates with need received aid; of those 3% had need fully met. ***Average percent of need met:*** 53% (excluding resources awarded to replace EFC). ***Average financial aid package:*** $11,302 (excluding resources awarded to replace EFC). 11% of all full-time undergraduates had no need and received non-need-based gift aid.

GIFT AID (NEED-BASED) ***Total amount:*** $15,472,208 (47% federal, 44% state, 9% institutional). ***Receiving aid:*** Freshmen: 32% (304); all full-time undergraduates: 30% (1,423). ***Average award:*** Freshmen: $11,759; Undergraduates: $10,325. ***Scholarships, grants, and awards:*** Federal Pell, FSEOG, state, private, college/university gift aid from institutional funds, Federal Nursing.

GIFT AID (NON-NEED-BASED) ***Total amount:*** $9,862,286 (4% state, 90% institutional, 6% external sources). ***Receiving aid:*** Freshmen: 20% (187). Undergraduates: 14% (651). ***Average award:*** Freshmen: $11,828. Undergraduates: $10,335. ***Scholarships, grants, and awards by category:*** *Academic interests/achievement:* general academic interests/achievements. *Special characteristics:* children of faculty/staff, international students, out-of-state students. ***Tuition waivers:*** Full or partial for employees or children of employees, senior citizens. ***ROTC:*** Army cooperative, Air Force cooperative.

LOANS ***Student loans:*** $32,931,642 (30% need-based, 70% non-need-based). 67% of past graduating class borrowed through all loan programs. *Average indebtedness per student:* $35,658. ***Average need-based loan:*** Freshmen: $3313. Undergraduates: $4244. ***Parent loans:*** $7,772,226 (100% non-need-based). ***Programs:*** Federal Direct (Subsidized and Unsubsidized Stafford, PLUS), state.

WORK-STUDY ***Federal work-study:*** Total amount: $278,059; jobs available. ***State or other work-study/employment:*** Total amount: $1,287,932 (100% non-need-based). Part-time jobs available.

APPLYING FOR FINANCIAL AID ***Required financial aid forms:*** FAFSA, state aid form. ***Financial aid deadline (priority):*** 3/1. ***Notification date:*** 4/1. Students must reply by 5/1 or within 2 weeks of notification.

CONTACT F. Shawn O'Neill, Director of Financial Aid, Ramapo College of New Jersey, 505 Ramapo Valley Road, Mahwah, NJ 07430-1680, 201-684-7550 or toll-free 800-9RAMAPO. *Fax:* 201-684-7085. *E-mail:* finaid@ramapo.edu.
Website: http://www.ramapo.edu/.

RANDALL UNIVERSITY

Moore, OK

CONTACT Denise Conklin, Director of Financial Aid, Randall University, PO Box 7208, Moore, OK 73153-1208, 405-912-9012. *Fax:* 405-912-9050. *E-mail:* dconklin@hc.edu.
Website: http://www.ru.edu/.

RANDOLPH COLLEGE

Lynchburg, VA

Tuition & fees: $25,610 | **Average undergraduate aid package: $35,737**

ABOUT THE INSTITUTION Independent Methodist, coed. ***Awards:*** bachelor's and master's degrees. 31 undergraduate majors. ***Total enrollment:*** 617. Undergraduates: 565. Freshmen: 143. Federal methodology is used as a basis for awarding need-based institutional aid.

UNDERGRADUATE EXPENSES for 2020–2021 ***Comprehensive fee:*** $36,610 includes full-time tuition ($25,000), mandatory fees ($610), and room and board ($11,000). ***Part-time tuition:*** $1688 per credit hour.

FRESHMAN FINANCIAL AID (Fall 2019, est.) 128 applied for aid; of those 90% were deemed to have need. 100% of freshmen with need received aid; of those 24% had need fully met. ***Average percent of need met:*** 82% (excluding resources awarded to replace EFC). ***Average financial aid package:*** $37,381 (excluding resources awarded to replace EFC). 18% of all full-time freshmen had no need and received non-need-based gift aid.

UNDERGRADUATE FINANCIAL AID (Fall 2019, est.) 480 applied for aid; of those 93% were deemed to have need. 100% of undergraduates with need received aid; of those 22% had need fully met. ***Average percent of need met:*** 78% (excluding resources awarded to replace EFC). ***Average financial aid package:*** $35,737 (excluding resources awarded to replace EFC). 17% of all full-time undergraduates had no need and received non-need-based gift aid.

GIFT AID (NEED-BASED) ***Receiving aid:*** Freshmen: 82% (115); all full-time undergraduates: 83% (445). ***Average award:*** Freshmen: $33,484; Undergraduates: $31,680. ***Scholarships, grants, and awards:*** Federal Pell, FSEOG, state, private, college/university gift aid from institutional funds, United Negro College Fund, National Science Foundation, TEACH grant, VA Benefits, VA Yellow Ribbon.

GIFT AID (NON-NEED-BASED) ***Receiving aid:*** Freshmen: 19% (27). Undergraduates: 15% (79). ***Average award:*** Freshmen: $29,844. Undergraduates: $26,035. ***Scholarships, grants, and awards by category:*** *Academic interests/achievement:* biological sciences, education, English, general academic interests/achievements, mathematics, physical sciences, premedicine, social sciences. *Special achievements/activities:* community service, general special achievements/activities, leadership. *Special characteristics:* adult students, children of faculty/staff, international students, local/state students, relatives of clergy, religious affiliation, twins.

LOANS ***Student loans:*** 78% of past graduating class borrowed through all loan programs. *Average indebtedness per student:* $42,569. ***Average need-based loan:*** Freshmen: $5190. Undergraduates: $5244. ***Programs:*** Federal Direct (Subsidized and Unsubsidized Stafford, PLUS), college/university, Private Student Loans.

WORK-STUDY Federal work-study jobs available. ***State or other work-study/employment:*** Part-time jobs available.

APPLYING FOR FINANCIAL AID ***Financial aid deadline:*** Continuous. ***Notification date:*** Continuous.

CONTACT Debi Woodall-Stevens, Director of Student Financial Services, Randolph College, 2500 Rivermont Avenue, Lynchburg, VA 24503, 434-947-8128 or toll-free 800-745-7692. *Fax:* 434-947-8996. *E-mail:* dwstevens@randolphcollege.edu.
Website: http://www.randolphcollege.edu/.

RANDOLPH-MACON COLLEGE

Ashland, VA

Tuition & fees: $43,940	Average undergraduate aid package: $31,700

ABOUT THE INSTITUTION Independent United Methodist, coed. ***Awards:*** bachelor's degrees. 38 undergraduate majors. ***Total enrollment:*** 1,543. Undergraduates: 1,543. Freshmen: 432. Federal methodology is used as a basis for awarding need-based institutional aid.

UNDERGRADUATE EXPENSES for 2020–2021 ***One-time required fee:*** $100. ***Comprehensive fee:*** $56,620 includes full-time tuition ($42,490), mandatory fees ($1450), and room and board ($12,680). ***College room only:*** $7000. Full-time tuition and fees vary according to course load. Room and board charges vary according to board plan and housing facility. ***Part-time tuition:*** $4720 per course. ***Part-time fees:*** $150 per term. Part-time tuition and fees vary according to course load.

FRESHMAN FINANCIAL AID (Fall 2019, est.) 403 applied for aid; of those 81% were deemed to have need. 100% of freshmen with need received aid; of those 37% had need fully met. ***Average percent of need met:*** 84% (excluding resources awarded to replace EFC). ***Average financial aid package:*** $32,631 (excluding resources awarded to replace EFC). 23% of all full-time freshmen had no need and received non-need-based gift aid.

UNDERGRADUATE FINANCIAL AID (Fall 2019, est.) 1,310 applied for aid; of those 81% were deemed to have need. 100% of undergraduates with need received aid; of those 32% had need fully met. ***Average percent of need met:*** 82% (excluding resources awarded to replace EFC). ***Average financial aid package:*** $31,700 (excluding resources awarded to replace EFC). 29% of all full-time undergraduates had no need and received non-need-based gift aid.

GIFT AID (NEED-BASED) ***Receiving aid:*** Freshmen: 75% (325); all full-time undergraduates: 70% (1,065). ***Average award:*** Freshmen: $30,218; Undergraduates: $28,452. ***Scholarships, grants, and awards:*** Federal Pell, FSEOG, state, private, college/university gift aid from institutional funds.

GIFT AID (NON-NEED-BASED) ***Receiving aid:*** Freshmen: 23% (99). Undergraduates: 19% (284). ***Average award:*** Freshmen: $26,373. Undergraduates: $22,777. ***Scholarships, grants, and awards by category:*** *Academic interests/achievement:* general academic interests/achievements, religion/biblical studies. *Special achievements/activities:* general special achievements/activities, religious involvement. *Special characteristics:* children and siblings of alumni, children of faculty/staff, ethnic background, out-of-state students, relatives of clergy, siblings of current students, veterans. ***Tuition waivers:*** Full or partial for employees or children of employees. ***ROTC:*** Army cooperative.

LOANS ***Student loans:*** 90% of past graduating class borrowed through all loan programs. *Average indebtedness per student:* $22,206. ***Average need-based loan:*** Freshmen: $2920. Undergraduates: $3904. ***Programs:*** Federal Direct (Subsidized and Unsubsidized Stafford, PLUS), Perkins, college/university.

WORK-STUDY Federal work-study jobs available.

APPLYING FOR FINANCIAL AID ***Required financial aid forms:*** FAFSA, state aid form. ***Notification date:*** Continuous. Students must reply within 2 weeks of notification.

CONTACT Ms. Julie Hickman-Godoy, Director of Financial Aid, Randolph-Macon College, PO Box 5005, Ashland, VA 23005-5505, 804-752-7259 or toll-free 800-888-1762. *Fax:* 804-752-3719. *E-mail:* juliehickmangodoy@rmc.edu.
Website: http://www.rmc.edu/.

RASMUSSEN COLLEGE AURORA

Aurora, IL

CONTACT Financial Aid Office, Rasmussen College Aurora, 2363 Sequoia Drive, Aurora, IL 60506, 630-888-3500 or toll-free 888-549-6755.
Website: http://www.rasmussen.edu/.

RASMUSSEN COLLEGE BLAINE

Blaine, MN

CONTACT Financial Aid Office, Rasmussen College Blaine, 3629 95th Avenue NE, Blaine, MN 55014, 763-795-4720 or toll-free 888-549-6755.
Website: http://www.rasmussen.edu/.

RASMUSSEN COLLEGE BLOOMINGTON

Bloomington, MN

CONTACT Financial Aid Office, Rasmussen College Bloomington, 4400 West 78th Street, Bloomington, MN 55435, 952-545-2000 or toll-free 888-549-6755.
Website: http://www.rasmussen.edu/.

RASMUSSEN COLLEGE EAGAN

Eagan, MN

CONTACT Financial Aid Office, Rasmussen College Eagan, 3500 Federal Drive, Eagan, MN 55122, 651-687-9000 or toll-free 888-549-6755.
Website: http://www.rasmussen.edu/.

RASMUSSEN COLLEGE FARGO

Fargo, ND

CONTACT Financial Aid Office, Rasmussen College Fargo, 4012 19th Avenue South, Fargo, ND 58103, 701-277-3889 or toll-free 888-549-6755.
Website: http://www.rasmussen.edu/.

RASMUSSEN COLLEGE FORT MYERS

Fort Myers, FL

CONTACT Financial Aid Office, Rasmussen College Fort Myers, 9160 Forum Corporate Parkway, Suite 100, Fort Myers, FL 33905, 239-477-2100 or toll-free 888-549-6755.
Website: http://www.rasmussen.edu/.

RASMUSSEN COLLEGE GREEN BAY

Green Bay, WI

CONTACT Financial Aid Office, Rasmussen College Green Bay, 904 South Taylor Street, Suite 100, Green Bay, WI 54303, 920-593-8400 or toll-free 888-549-6755.
Website: http://www.rasmussen.edu/.

RASMUSSEN COLLEGE KANSAS CITY/ OVERLAND PARK

Overland Park, KS

CONTACT Financial Aid Office, Rasmussen College Kansas City/Overland Park, 11600 College Boulevard, Overland Park, KS 66210, 913-491-7870 or toll-free 888-549-6755.
Website: http://www.rasmussen.edu/.

RASMUSSEN COLLEGE LAKE ELMO/ WOODBURY

Lake Elmo, MN

CONTACT Financial Aid Office, Rasmussen College Lake Elmo/Woodbury, 8565 Eagle Point Circle, Lake Elmo, MN 55042, 651-259-6600 or toll-free 888-549-6755.
Website: http://www.rasmussen.edu/.

RASMUSSEN COLLEGE LAND O' LAKES

Land O' Lakes, FL

CONTACT Financial Aid Office, Rasmussen College Land O' Lakes, 18600 Fernview Street, Land O' Lakes, FL 34638, 813-435-3601 or toll-free 888-549-6755.
Website: http://www.rasmussen.edu/.

RASMUSSEN COLLEGE MANKATO

Mankato, MN

CONTACT Financial Aid Office, Rasmussen College Mankato, 1400 Madison Avenue, Mankato, MN 56001, 507-625-6556 or toll-free 888-549-6755.
Website: http://www.rasmussen.edu/.

RASMUSSEN COLLEGE MOKENA/ TINLEY PARK

Mokena, IL

CONTACT Financial Aid Office, Rasmussen College Mokena/Tinley Park, 8650 West Spring Lake Road, Mokena, IL 60448, 815-534-3300 or toll-free 888-549-6755.
Website: http://www.rasmussen.edu/.

RASMUSSEN COLLEGE MOORHEAD

Moorhead, MN

CONTACT Financial Aid Office, Rasmussen College Moorhead, 1250 29th Avenue South, Moorhead, MN 56560, 218-304-6200 or toll-free 888-549-6755.
Website: http://www.rasmussen.edu/.

RASMUSSEN COLLEGE NEW PORT RICHEY

New Port Richey, FL

CONTACT Financial Aid Office, Rasmussen College New Port Richey, 8661 Citizens Drive, New Port Richey, FL 34654, 727-942-0069 or toll-free 888-549-6755.
Website: http://www.rasmussen.edu/.

RASMUSSEN COLLEGE OCALA

Ocala, FL

CONTACT Financial Aid Office, Rasmussen College Ocala, 4755 SW 46th Court, Ocala, FL 34474, 352-629-1941 or toll-free 888-549-6755.
Website: http://www.rasmussen.edu/.

RASMUSSEN COLLEGE OCALA SCHOOL OF NURSING

Ocala, FL

CONTACT Financial Aid Office, Rasmussen College Ocala School of Nursing, 2100 SW 22nd Place, Ocala, FL 34471, 352-291-8560 or toll-free 888-549-6755.
Website: http://www.rasmussen.edu/.

RASMUSSEN COLLEGE ROCKFORD

Rockford, IL

CONTACT Financial Aid Office, Rasmussen College Rockford, 6000 East State Street, Fourth Floor, Rockford, IL 61108, 815-316-4800 or toll-free 888-549-6755.
Website: http://www.rasmussen.edu/.

RASMUSSEN COLLEGE ROMEOVILLE/ JOLIET

Romeoville, IL

CONTACT Financial Aid Office, Rasmussen College Romeoville/Joliet, 1400 West Normantown Road, Romeoville, IL 60446, 815-306-2600 or toll-free 888-549-6755.
Website: http://www.rasmussen.edu/.

RASMUSSEN COLLEGE ST. CLOUD

St. Cloud, MN

CONTACT Financial Aid Office, Rasmussen College St. Cloud, 226 Park Avenue South, St. Cloud, MN 56301, 320-251-5600 or toll-free 888-549-6755.
Website: http://www.rasmussen.edu/.

RASMUSSEN COLLEGE TAMPA/ BRANDON

Tampa, FL

CONTACT Financial Aid Office, Rasmussen College Tampa/Brandon, 4042 Park Oaks Boulevard, Suite 100, Tampa, FL 33610, 813-246-7600 or toll-free 888-549-6755. *Website:* http://www.rasmussen.edu/.

RASMUSSEN COLLEGE TOPEKA

Topeka, KS

CONTACT Financial Aid Office, Rasmussen College Topeka, 620 SW Governor View, Topeka, KS 66606, 785-228-7320 or toll-free 888-549-6755. *Website:* http://www.rasmussen.edu/.

RASMUSSEN COLLEGE WAUSAU

Wausau, WI

CONTACT Financial Aid Office, Rasmussen College Wausau, 1101 Westwood Drive, Wausau, WI 54401, 715-841-8000 or toll-free 888-549-6755. *Website:* http://www.rasmussen.edu/.

REED COLLEGE

Portland, OR

Tuition & fees: $58,440	Average undergraduate aid package: $43,780

ABOUT THE INSTITUTION Independent, coed. ***Awards:*** bachelor's and master's degrees. 35 undergraduate majors. ***Total enrollment:*** 1,503. Undergraduates: 1,483. Freshmen: 363. Both federal and institutional methodology are used as a basis for awarding need-based institutional aid.

UNDERGRADUATE EXPENSES for 2019–2020 ***Comprehensive fee:*** $73,060 includes full-time tuition ($58,130), mandatory fees ($310), and room and board ($14,620). ***College room only:*** $7720. Full-time tuition and fees vary according to degree level. Room and board charges vary according to board plan and housing facility. Part-time tuition and fees vary according to course load and degree level.

FRESHMAN FINANCIAL AID (Fall 2019, est.) 267 applied for aid; of those 82% were deemed to have need. 100% of freshmen with need received aid; of those 100% had need fully met. ***Average percent of need met:*** 100% (excluding resources awarded to replace EFC). ***Average financial aid package:*** $45,748 (excluding resources awarded to replace EFC).

UNDERGRADUATE FINANCIAL AID (Fall 2019, est.) 859 applied for aid; of those 92% were deemed to have need. 99% of undergraduates with need received aid; of those 99% had need fully met. ***Average percent of need met:*** 100% (excluding resources awarded to replace EFC). ***Average financial aid package:*** $43,780 (excluding resources awarded to replace EFC).

GIFT AID (NEED-BASED) ***Total amount:*** $31,582,217 (4% federal, 95% institutional, 1% external sources). ***Receiving aid:*** Freshmen: 55% (218); all full-time undergraduates: 55% (779). ***Average award:*** Freshmen: $42,096; Undergraduates: $39,742. ***Scholarships, grants, and awards:*** Federal Pell, FSEOG, state, private, college/university gift aid from institutional funds.

GIFT AID (NON-NEED-BASED) ***Total amount:*** $7060 (100% external sources). ***Tuition waivers:*** Full or partial for employees or children of employees.

LOANS ***Student loans:*** $4,323,862 (43% need-based, 57% non-need-based). 52% of past graduating class borrowed through all loan programs. *Average indebtedness per student:* $25,657. ***Average need-based loan:*** Freshmen: $2982. Undergraduates: $4262. ***Parent loans:*** $1,568,486 (100% non-need-based). ***Programs:*** Federal Direct (Subsidized and Unsubsidized Stafford, PLUS), college/university.

WORK-STUDY ***Federal work-study:*** Total amount: $460,093; jobs available. ***State or other work-study/employment:*** Total amount: $730,243 (100% need-based). Part-time jobs available.

APPLYING FOR FINANCIAL AID ***Required financial aid forms:*** FAFSA, CSS Financial Aid PROFILE, noncustodial (divorced/separated) parent's statement. ***Financial aid deadline:*** 1/15 (priority: 1/15). ***Notification date:*** 4/1. Students must reply by 5/1.

CONTACT Financial Aid Office, Reed College, 3203 Southeast Woodstock Boulevard, Portland, OR 97202-8199, 503-771-1112 or toll-free 800-547-4750. *Website:* http://www.reed.edu/.

REFORMED UNIVERSITY

Lawrenceville, GA

CONTACT Financial Aid Office, Reformed University, 1724 Atkinson Road, Lawrenceville, GA 30043.

REGENT UNIVERSITY

Virginia Beach, VA

Tuition & fees: $20,120	Average undergraduate aid package: $8704

ABOUT THE INSTITUTION Independent Christian, coed. ***Awards:*** certificates, associate, bachelor's, master's, and doctoral degrees. 38 undergraduate majors. ***Total enrollment:*** 10,409. Undergraduates: 4,413. Freshmen: 386. Federal methodology is used as a basis for awarding need-based institutional aid.

UNDERGRADUATE EXPENSES for 2020–2021 ***Application fee:*** $50. ***Comprehensive fee:*** $27,340 includes full-time tuition ($18,720), mandatory fees ($1400), and room and board ($7220). ***College room only:*** $4700. Room and board charges vary according to housing facility. ***Part-time tuition:*** $624 per credit hour. ***Part-time fees:*** $700 per term.

FRESHMAN FINANCIAL AID (Fall 2019, est.) 261 applied for aid; of those 84% were deemed to have need. 100% of freshmen with need received aid; of those 22% had need fully met. ***Average percent of need met:*** 53% (excluding resources awarded to replace EFC). ***Average financial aid package:*** $8224 (excluding resources awarded to replace EFC). 16% of all full-time freshmen had no need and received non-need-based gift aid.

UNDERGRADUATE FINANCIAL AID (Fall 2019, est.) 2,031 applied for aid; of those 89% were deemed to have need. 100% of undergraduates with need received aid; of those 10% had need fully met. ***Average percent of need met:*** 60% (excluding resources awarded to replace EFC). ***Average financial aid package:*** $8704 (excluding resources awarded to replace EFC). 11% of all full-time undergraduates had no need and received non-need-based gift aid.

GIFT AID (NEED-BASED) ***Total amount:*** $17,605,106 (53% federal, 10% state, 36% institutional, 1% external sources). ***Receiving aid:*** Freshmen: 76% (214); all full-time undergraduates: 74% (1,655). ***Average award:*** Freshmen: $11,511; Undergraduates: $8141. ***Scholarships, grants, and awards:*** Federal Pell, state, private, college/university gift aid from institutional funds.

GIFT AID (NON-NEED-BASED) ***Total amount:*** $2,776,666 (1% federal, 21% state, 73% institutional, 5% external sources). ***Receiving aid:*** Freshmen: 16% (46). Undergraduates: 7% (151). ***Average award:*** Freshmen: $8910. Undergraduates: $5929. ***Scholarships, grants, and awards by category:*** *Special achievements/activities:* leadership, memberships, religious involvement. *Special characteristics:* children and siblings of alumni, children of faculty/staff, children of public servants, public servants, religious affiliation, siblings of current students, spouses of current students, veterans, veterans' children. ***Tuition waivers:*** Full or partial for employees or children of employees. ***ROTC:*** Army cooperative, Naval cooperative.

LOANS ***Student loans:*** $28,358,432 (39% need-based, 61% non-need-based). 75% of past graduating class borrowed through all loan programs. *Average indebtedness per student:* $32,982. ***Average need-based loan:*** Freshmen: $3282. Undergraduates: $3913. ***Parent loans:*** $14,126,354 (39% need-based, 61% non-need-based). ***Programs:*** Federal Direct (Subsidized and Unsubsidized Stafford, PLUS).

ATHLETIC AWARDS Total amount: $211,641 (100% non-need-based).

APPLYING FOR FINANCIAL AID ***Required financial aid forms:*** FAFSA, institution's own form, state aid form. ***Financial aid deadline:*** Continuous. ***Notification date:*** Continuous beginning 12/1. Students must reply within 2 weeks of notification.

CONTACT Mrs. Rachael Moser, Assistant Director, Regent University, 1000 Regent University Drive, Virginia Beach, VA 23464, 757-352-4125 or toll-free 800-373-5504. *Fax:* 757-352-4118. *E-mail:* finaid@regent.edu.
Website: http://www.regent.edu/.

REGIS COLLEGE

Weston, MA

CONTACT Bonnie L. Quinn, Director of Financial Aid, Regis College, Box 81, Weston, MA 02493, 781-768-7270 or toll-free 866-438-7344. *Fax:* 781-768-7225. *E-mail:* finaid@regiscollege.edu.
Website: http://www.regiscollege.edu/.

REGIS UNIVERSITY

Denver, CO

ABOUT THE INSTITUTION Independent Roman Catholic (Jesuit), coed. ***Awards:*** certificates, bachelor's, master's, and doctoral degrees. 48 undergraduate majors. ***Total enrollment:*** 7,907. Undergraduates: 3,961. Freshmen: 508.

GIFT AID (NEED-BASED) ***Scholarships, grants, and awards:*** Federal Pell, FSEOG, state, private, college/university gift aid from institutional funds.

GIFT AID (NON-NEED-BASED) ***Scholarships, grants, and awards by category:*** *Academic interests/achievement:* biological sciences, general academic interests/achievements, mathematics, physical sciences. *Creative arts/performance:* debating, music. *Special achievements/activities:* leadership. *Special characteristics:* adult students, children of faculty/staff, local/state students, public servants.

LOANS ***Programs:*** Federal Direct (Subsidized and Unsubsidized Stafford, PLUS), Perkins, Federal Nursing.

CONTACT Cindy Hejl, Director of Financial Aid, Regis University, 3333 Regis Boulevard, Denver, CO 80221-1099, 303-964-5758 or toll-free 800-388-2366 Ext.4900. *Fax:* 303-964-5449. *E-mail:* chejl@regis.edu.
Website: http://www.regis.edu/.

REINHARDT UNIVERSITY

Waleska, GA

Tuition & fees: $24,300	Average undergraduate aid package: $17,227

ABOUT THE INSTITUTION Independent United Methodist Church, coed. ***Awards:*** associate, bachelor's, and master's degrees. 26 undergraduate majors. ***Total enrollment:*** 1,566. Undergraduates: 1,473. Freshmen: 351. Federal methodology is used as a basis for awarding need-based institutional aid.

UNDERGRADUATE EXPENSES for 2019–2020 ***Comprehensive fee:*** $34,800 includes full-time tuition ($23,300), mandatory fees ($1000), and room and board ($10,500). Full-time tuition and fees vary according to course load, location, and program. Room and board charges vary according to board plan and housing facility. ***Part-time tuition:*** $792 per credit hour. Part-time tuition and fees vary according to course load, location, and program.

FRESHMAN FINANCIAL AID (Fall 2018) 332 applied for aid; of those 82% were deemed to have need. 100% of freshmen with need received aid; of those 15% had need fully met. ***Average percent of need met:*** 62% (excluding resources awarded to replace EFC). ***Average financial aid package:*** $17,875 (excluding resources awarded to replace EFC). 21% of all full-time freshmen had no need and received non-need-based gift aid.

UNDERGRADUATE FINANCIAL AID (Fall 2018) 1,194 applied for aid; of those 87% were deemed to have need. 99% of undergraduates with need received aid; of those 12% had need fully met. ***Average percent of need met:*** 59% (excluding resources awarded to replace EFC). ***Average financial aid package:*** $17,227 (excluding resources awarded to replace EFC). 15% of all full-time undergraduates had no need and received non-need-based gift aid.

GIFT AID (NEED-BASED) ***Total amount:*** $11,225,537 (24% federal, 21% state, 52% institutional, 3% external sources). ***Receiving aid:*** Freshmen: 78% (271); all full-time undergraduates: 80% (1,022). ***Average award:*** Freshmen: $15,419; Undergraduates: $14,046. ***Scholarships, grants, and awards:*** Federal Pell, FSEOG, private, college/university gift aid from institutional funds.

GIFT AID (NON-NEED-BASED) ***Total amount:*** $2,722,639 (32% state, 64% institutional, 4% external sources). ***Receiving aid:*** Freshmen: 12% (41). Undergraduates: 9% (119). ***Average award:*** Freshmen: $8251. Undergraduates: $7797. ***Scholarships, grants, and awards by category:*** *Academic interests/achievement:* biological sciences, business, communication, computer science, education, English, general academic interests/achievements, humanities, mathematics, religion/biblical studies, social sciences. *Creative arts/performance:* applied art and design, music, theater/drama. *Special achievements/activities:* leadership. *Special characteristics:* religious affiliation. ***Tuition waivers:*** Full or partial for employees or children of employees, senior citizens.

LOANS ***Student loans:*** $6,821,760 (77% need-based, 23% non-need-based). 68% of past graduating class borrowed through all loan programs. *Average indebtedness per student:* $32,384. ***Average need-based loan:*** Freshmen: $3727. Undergraduates: $4476. ***Parent loans:*** $2,483,887 (84% need-based, 16% non-need-based). ***Programs:*** Federal Direct (Subsidized and Unsubsidized Stafford, PLUS).

WORK-STUDY ***Federal work-study:*** Total amount: $70,963; jobs available. ***State or other work-study/employment:*** Part-time jobs available.

ATHLETIC AWARDS Total amount: $4,494,798 (68% need-based, 32% non-need-based).

APPLYING FOR FINANCIAL AID ***Required financial aid forms:*** FAFSA, state aid form. ***Financial aid deadline (priority):*** 7/1. ***Notification date:*** 12/1.

CONTACT Mrs. Angela D. Harlow, Director of Student Financial Aid, Reinhardt University, 7300 Reinhardt College Circle, Waleska, GA 30183-2981, 770-720-5603. *Fax:* 770-720-5719. *E-mail:* adh@reinhardt.edu.
Website: http://www.reinhardt.edu/.

RENSSELAER POLYTECHNIC INSTITUTE

Troy, NY

Tuition & fees: $55,375	Average undergraduate aid package: $42,951

ABOUT THE INSTITUTION Independent, coed. ***Awards:*** bachelor's, master's, and doctoral degrees. 40 undergraduate majors. ***Total enrollment:*** 7,962. Undergraduates: 6,628. Freshmen: 1,778. Both federal and institutional methodology are used as a basis for awarding need-based institutional aid.

UNDERGRADUATE EXPENSES for 2019–2020 ***Application fee:*** $70. ***Comprehensive fee:*** $70,955 includes full-time tuition ($54,000), mandatory fees ($1375), and room and board ($15,580). ***College room only:*** $8770. ***Part-time tuition:*** $2250 per credit hour.

FRESHMAN FINANCIAL AID (Fall 2019, est.) 1203 applied for aid; of those 79% were deemed to have need. 100% of freshmen with need received aid; of those 24% had need fully met. ***Average percent of need met:*** 82% (excluding resources awarded to replace EFC). ***Average financial aid package:*** $43,770 (excluding resources awarded to replace EFC). 25% of all full-time freshmen had no need and received non-need-based gift aid.

UNDERGRADUATE FINANCIAL AID (Fall 2019, est.) 3,996 applied for aid; of those 86% were deemed to have need. 100% of undergraduates with need received aid; of those 19% had need fully met. ***Average percent of need met:*** 79% (excluding resources awarded to replace EFC). ***Average financial aid package:*** $42,951 (excluding resources awarded to replace EFC). 28% of all full-time undergraduates had no need and received non-need-based gift aid.

GIFT AID (NEED-BASED) ***Total amount:*** $136,162,065 (9% federal, 2% state, 87% institutional, 2% external sources). ***Receiving aid:*** Freshmen: 57% (946); all full-time undergraduates: 56% (3,452). ***Average award:*** Freshmen: $40,272; Undergraduates: $38,809. ***Scholarships, grants, and awards:*** Federal Pell, FSEOG, state, private, college/university gift aid from institutional funds, Academic Competitiveness Grants, National SMART Grants, Gates Millennium Scholarships.

GIFT AID (NON-NEED-BASED) ***Total amount:*** $42,241,784 (3% federal, 1% state, 93% institutional, 3% external sources). ***Receiving aid:*** Freshmen: 12% (196). Undergraduates: 8% (490). ***Average award:*** Freshmen: $23,326. Undergraduates: $21,732. ***Scholarships, grants, and awards by category:*** *Academic interests/achievement:* general academic interests/achievements, humanities, mathematics, military science. *Creative arts/performance:* general creative arts/performance. *Special* *achievements/activities:* general special achievements/activities. *Special characteristics:* children and siblings of alumni, children of faculty/staff, ethnic background, general special characteristics, members of minority groups. ***ROTC:*** Army, Naval, Air Force.

LOANS *Student loans:* $36,252,206 (60% need-based, 40% non-need-based). 63% of past graduating class borrowed through all loan programs. *Average indebtedness per student:* $34,595. ***Average need-based loan:*** Freshmen: $3428. Undergraduates: $4459. ***Parent loans:*** $10,280,892 (76% need-based, 24% non-need-based). ***Programs:*** Federal Direct (Subsidized and Unsubsidized Stafford, PLUS), Perkins, college/university.

WORK-STUDY *Federal work-study:* Total amount: $1,521,464; jobs available.

ATHLETIC AWARDS Total amount: $2,467,414 (100% non-need-based).

APPLYING FOR FINANCIAL AID *Required financial aid forms:* FAFSA, CSS Financial Aid PROFILE. ***Financial aid deadline (priority):*** 2/1. ***Notification date:*** 3/15.

CONTACT Mr. Martin Daniels, Director of Financial Aid, Rensselaer Polytechnic Institute, Academy Hall, Troy, NY 12180-3590, 518-276-6813. *Fax:* 518-276-4797. *E-mail:* financial_aid@rpi.edu.
Website: http://www.rpi.edu/.

RESEARCH COLLEGE OF NURSING

Kansas City, MO

CONTACT Ms. Stacie Withers, Director of Financial Aid, Research College of Nursing, 2525 East Meyer Boulevard, Kansas City, MO 64132, 816-995-2832. *Fax:* 816-995-2833. *E-mail:* stacie.withers@researchcollege.edu.
Website: http://www.researchcollege.edu/.

RESURRECTION UNIVERSITY

Chicago, IL

CONTACT Ms. Shirley Howell, Financial Aid Officer, Resurrection University, 1431 North Claremont Avenue, Chicago, IL 60622, 773-252-5125. *Fax:* 773-227-5134. *E-mail:* shirley.howell@resu.edu.
Website: http://www.resu.edu/.

RHODE ISLAND COLLEGE

Providence, RI

Tuition & fees: N/R	Average undergraduate aid package: $9843

ABOUT THE INSTITUTION State-supported, coed. ***Awards:*** certificates, bachelor's, master's, and doctoral degrees. 108 undergraduate majors. ***Total enrollment:*** 7,523. Undergraduates: 6,443. Freshmen: 964. Both federal and institutional methodology are used as a basis for awarding need-based institutional aid.

FRESHMAN FINANCIAL AID (Fall 2019, est.) 875 applied for aid; of those 83% were deemed to have need. 96% of freshmen with need received aid; of those 9% had need fully met. ***Average percent of need met:*** 67% (excluding resources awarded to replace EFC). ***Average financial aid package:*** $10,415 (excluding resources awarded to replace EFC). 3% of all full-time freshmen had no need and received non-need-based gift aid.

UNDERGRADUATE FINANCIAL AID (Fall 2019, est.) 4,234 applied for aid; of those 84% were deemed to have need. 96% of undergraduates with need received aid; of those 17% had need fully met. ***Average percent of need met:*** 66% (excluding resources awarded to replace EFC). ***Average financial aid package:*** $9843 (excluding resources awarded to replace EFC). 2% of all full-time undergraduates had no need and received non-need-based gift aid.

GIFT AID (NEED-BASED) *Total amount:* $24,257,530 (58% federal, 11% state, 26% institutional, 5% external sources). ***Receiving aid:*** Freshmen: 66% (606); all full-time undergraduates: 59% (2,897). ***Average award:*** Freshmen: $8189; Undergraduates: $7510. ***Scholarships, grants, and awards:*** Federal Pell, FSEOG, state, private, college/university gift aid from institutional funds.

GIFT AID (NON-NEED-BASED) *Total amount:* $506,535 (74% institutional, 26% external sources). ***Receiving aid:*** Freshmen: 1% (7). Undergraduates: 1% (58). ***Average award:*** Freshmen: $2071. Undergraduates: $2643. ***Scholarships, grants, and awards by category:*** *Academic interests/achievement:* general academic interests/achievements. *Creative arts/performance:* applied art and design, cinema/film/broadcasting, dance, journalism/publications, music, theater/drama. *Special characteristics:* children and siblings of alumni. ***ROTC:*** Army cooperative.

LOANS *Student loans:* $27,892,132 (72% need-based, 28% non-need-based). 75% of past graduating class borrowed through all loan programs. *Average indebtedness per student:* $25,936. ***Average need-based loan:*** Freshmen: $3306. Undergraduates: $3972. ***Parent loans:*** $1,581,980 (49% need-based, 51% non-need-based). ***Programs:*** Federal Direct (Subsidized and Unsubsidized Stafford, PLUS), Perkins.

WORK-STUDY *Federal work-study:* Total amount: $1,867,747; jobs available.

APPLYING FOR FINANCIAL AID *Required financial aid forms:* FAFSA, institution's own form. ***Financial aid deadline (priority):*** 2/1. ***Notification date:*** Continuous beginning 2/15. Students must reply within 3 weeks of notification.

CONTACT Mr. Kenneth Ferus, Director of Financial Aid, Rhode Island College, 600 Mount Pleasant Avenue, Providence, RI 02908, 401-456-8033 or toll-free 800-669-5760. *Fax:* 401-456-8686. *E-mail:* kferus@ric.edu.
Website: http://www.ric.edu/.

RHODE ISLAND SCHOOL OF DESIGN

Providence, RI

ABOUT THE INSTITUTION Independent, coed. ***Awards:*** bachelor's and master's degrees. 15 undergraduate majors. ***Total enrollment:*** 2,468. Undergraduates: 1,994. Freshmen: 473.

GIFT AID (NEED-BASED) *Scholarships, grants, and awards:* Federal Pell, FSEOG, state, private, college/university gift aid from institutional funds.

GIFT AID (NON-NEED-BASED) *Scholarships, grants, and awards by category:* *Creative arts/performance:* applied art and design, art/fine arts. *Special characteristics:* children of faculty/staff.

LOANS *Programs:* Federal Direct (Subsidized and Unsubsidized Stafford, PLUS).

WORK-STUDY *Federal work-study:* Total amount: $1,469,814; jobs available. ***State or other work-study/employment:*** Part-time jobs available.

APPLYING FOR FINANCIAL AID *Required financial aid forms:* FAFSA, CSS Financial Aid PROFILE.

CONTACT Anthony Gallonio, Assistant Vice President of Enrollment Services, Rhode Island School of Design, 2 College Street, Providence, RI 02903-2784, 401-454-6661 or toll-free 800-364-7473. *Fax:* 401-454-6412. *E-mail:* sfs@risd.edu.
Website: http://www.risd.edu/.

RHODES COLLEGE

Memphis, TN

Tuition & fees: N/R	Average undergraduate aid package: $42,180

ABOUT THE INSTITUTION Independent, coed. ***Awards:*** certificates, bachelor's, and master's degrees (master's degree in accounting only). 31 undergraduate majors. ***Total enrollment:*** 2,010. Undergraduates: 1,973. Freshmen: 517. Both federal and institutional methodology are used as a basis for awarding need-based institutional aid.

UNDERGRADUATE EXPENSES for 2019–2020 *Comprehensive fee:* $59,293 includes full-time tuition ($47,580), mandatory fees ($310), and room and board ($11,403). ***College room only:*** $5373. Room and board charges vary according to board plan. ***Part-time tuition:*** $1970 per credit hour. Part-time tuition and fees vary according to course load.

FRESHMAN FINANCIAL AID (Fall 2018) 438 applied for aid; of those 70% were deemed to have need. 100% of freshmen with need received aid; of those 49% had need fully met. ***Average percent of need met:*** 94% (excluding resources awarded to replace EFC). ***Average financial aid package:*** $43,302 (excluding resources awarded to replace EFC). 36% of all full-time freshmen had no need and received non-need-based gift aid.

UNDERGRADUATE FINANCIAL AID (Fall 2018) 1,325 applied for aid; of those 76% were deemed to have need. 100% of undergraduates with need received aid; of those 58% had need fully met. ***Average percent of need met:*** 91% (excluding resources awarded to replace EFC). ***Average financial aid package:***

$42,180 (excluding resources awarded to replace EFC). 43% of all full-time undergraduates had no need and received non-need-based gift aid.

GIFT AID (NEED-BASED) ***Receiving aid:*** Freshmen: 59% (304); all full-time undergraduates: 52% (1,004). ***Average award:*** Freshmen: $35,927; Undergraduates: $34,229. ***Scholarships, grants, and awards:*** Federal Pell, FSEOG, state, private, college/university gift aid from institutional funds.

GIFT AID (NON-NEED-BASED) ***Receiving aid:*** Freshmen: 26% (133). Undergraduates: 19% (369). ***Average award:*** Freshmen: $26,663. Undergraduates: $27,136. ***Scholarships, grants, and awards by category:*** *Academic interests/achievement:* general academic interests/achievements, physical sciences. *Creative arts/performance:* applied art and design, general creative arts/performance, music, theater/drama. *Special characteristics:* children of faculty/staff, members of minority groups, relatives of clergy, religious affiliation. ***Tuition waivers:*** Full or partial for employees or children of employees. ***ROTC:*** Army cooperative, Naval cooperative, Air Force cooperative.

LOANS ***Student loans:*** 46% of past graduating class borrowed through all loan programs. *Average indebtedness per student:* $26,155. ***Average need-based loan:*** Freshmen: $2853. Undergraduates: $4622. ***Programs:*** Federal Direct (Subsidized and Unsubsidized Stafford, PLUS), Perkins.

WORK-STUDY Federal work-study jobs available. ***State or other work-study/employment:*** Part-time jobs available.

APPLYING FOR FINANCIAL AID ***Required financial aid forms:*** FAFSA, CSS Financial Aid PROFILE, noncustodial (divorced/separated) parent's statement.

CONTACT Mr. Michael Morgan, Director of Financial Aid, Rhodes College, 2000 North Parkway, Memphis, TN 38112-1690, 901-843-3808 or toll-free 800-844-5969. *Fax:* 901-843-3435. *E-mail:* morganm@rhodes.edu.
Website: http://www.rhodes.edu/.

RICE UNIVERSITY

Houston, TX

Tuition & fees: $49,112	Average undergraduate aid package: $52,493

ABOUT THE INSTITUTION Independent, coed. ***Awards:*** bachelor's, master's, and doctoral degrees. 58 undergraduate majors. ***Total enrollment:*** 7,282. Undergraduates: 3,989. Freshmen: 961. Both federal and institutional methodology are used as a basis for awarding need-based institutional aid.

UNDERGRADUATE EXPENSES for 2019–2020 ***Application fee:*** $75. ***Comprehensive fee:*** $63,252 includes full-time tuition ($48,330), mandatory fees ($782), and room and board ($14,140). ***College room only:*** $9700. ***Part-time tuition:*** $2014 per credit hour.

FRESHMAN FINANCIAL AID (Fall 2019, est.) 798 applied for aid; of those 59% were deemed to have need. 100% of freshmen with need received aid; of those 100% had need fully met. ***Average percent of need met:*** 100% (excluding resources awarded to replace EFC). ***Average financial aid package:*** $51,891 (excluding resources awarded to replace EFC). 5% of all full-time freshmen had no need and received non-need-based gift aid.

UNDERGRADUATE FINANCIAL AID (Fall 2019, est.) 2,931 applied for aid; of those 59% were deemed to have need. 99% of undergraduates with need received aid; of those 100% had need fully met. ***Average percent of need met:*** 100% (excluding resources awarded to replace EFC). ***Average financial aid package:*** $52,493 (excluding resources awarded to replace EFC). 9% of all full-time undergraduates had no need and received non-need-based gift aid.

GIFT AID (NEED-BASED) ***Total amount:*** $81,526,856 (4% federal, 1% state, 95% institutional). ***Receiving aid:*** Freshmen: 48% (461); all full-time undergraduates: 42% (1,689). ***Average award:*** Freshmen: $46,975; Undergraduates: $48,300. ***Scholarships, grants, and awards:*** Federal Pell, FSEOG, state, private, college/university gift aid from institutional funds, ROTC and Veterans Administration benefits.

GIFT AID (NON-NEED-BASED) ***Total amount:*** $11,651,109 (2% federal, 80% institutional, 18% external sources). ***Receiving aid:*** Freshmen: 5% (52). Undergraduates: 3% (139). ***Average award:*** Freshmen: $23,656. Undergraduates: $20,318. ***Scholarships, grants, and awards by category:*** *Academic interests/achievement:* engineering/technologies, general academic interests/achievements. *Creative arts/performance:* art/fine arts, music. *Special achievements/activities:* general special achievements/activities, leadership. *Special characteristics:* local/state students, members of minority groups. ***ROTC:*** Army cooperative, Naval, Air Force cooperative.

LOANS ***Student loans:*** $3,247,930 (17% need-based, 83% non-need-based). 25% of past graduating class borrowed through all loan programs. *Average indebtedness per student:* $24,292. ***Average need-based loan:*** Freshmen: $3216. Undergraduates: $3302. ***Parent loans:*** $2,370,926 (100% non-need-based). ***Programs:*** Federal Direct (Subsidized and Unsubsidized Stafford, PLUS), state.

WORK-STUDY ***Federal work-study:*** Total amount: $1,581,033; jobs available. ***State or other work-study/employment:*** Part-time jobs available.

ATHLETIC AWARDS Total amount: $13,374,661 (9% need-based, 91% non-need-based).

APPLYING FOR FINANCIAL AID ***Required financial aid forms:*** FAFSA, CSS Financial Aid PROFILE, noncustodial (divorced/separated) parent's statement, tax returns and W-2s. ***Financial aid deadline (priority):*** 2/15. ***Notification date:*** 4/1. Students must reply by 5/1.

CONTACT Office of Student Financial Services, Rice University, 116 Allen Center, MS 12, Houston, TX 77005, 713-348-4958. *Fax:* 713-348-2139. *E-mail:* fina@rice.edu. *Website:* http://www.rice.edu/.

RIDER UNIVERSITY

Lawrenceville, NJ

Tuition & fees: $42,860	Average undergraduate aid package: $33,444

ABOUT THE INSTITUTION Independent, coed. ***Awards:*** certificates, associate, bachelor's, master's, and doctoral degrees. 70 undergraduate majors. ***Total enrollment:*** 4,825. Undergraduates: 3,898. Freshmen: 921. Federal methodology is used as a basis for awarding need-based institutional aid.

UNDERGRADUATE EXPENSES for 2019–2020 ***Application fee:*** $50. ***Comprehensive fee:*** $58,140 includes full-time tuition ($42,120), mandatory fees ($740), and room and board ($15,280). ***College room only:*** $10,020.

FRESHMAN FINANCIAL AID (Fall 2019, est.) 799 applied for aid; of those 91% were deemed to have need. 100% of freshmen with need received aid; of those 18% had need fully met. ***Average percent of need met:*** 79% (excluding resources awarded to replace EFC). ***Average financial aid package:*** $37,576 (excluding resources awarded to replace EFC). 16% of all full-time freshmen had no need and received non-need-based gift aid.

UNDERGRADUATE FINANCIAL AID (Fall 2019, est.) 2,946 applied for aid; of those 91% were deemed to have need. 100% of undergraduates with need received aid; of those 17% had need fully met. ***Average percent of need met:*** 76% (excluding resources awarded to replace EFC). ***Average financial aid package:*** $33,444 (excluding resources awarded to replace EFC). 20% of all full-time undergraduates had no need and received non-need-based gift aid.

GIFT AID (NEED-BASED) ***Total amount:*** $73,334,994 (8% federal, 12% state, 79% institutional, 1% external sources). ***Receiving aid:*** Freshmen: 85% (726); all full-time undergraduates: 77% (2,672). ***Average award:*** Freshmen: $33,611; Undergraduates: $29,739. ***Scholarships, grants, and awards:*** Federal Pell, FSEOG, state, private, college/university gift aid from institutional funds.

GIFT AID (NON-NEED-BASED) ***Total amount:*** $18,066,521 (2% federal, 97% institutional, 1% external sources). ***Receiving aid:*** Freshmen: 13% (115). Undergraduates: 12% (422). ***Average award:*** Freshmen: $22,033. Undergraduates: $21,322. ***Scholarships, grants, and awards by category:*** *Academic interests/achievement:* general academic interests/achievements. *Creative arts/performance:* theater/drama. *Special characteristics:* members of minority groups. ***ROTC:*** Army cooperative.

LOANS ***Student loans:*** $30,794,469 (64% need-based, 36% non-need-based). 78% of past graduating class borrowed through all loan programs. *Average indebtedness per student:* $35,781. ***Average need-based loan:*** Freshmen: $2330. Undergraduates: $3200. ***Parent loans:*** $10,862,226 (60% need-based, 40% non-need-based). ***Programs:*** Federal Direct (Subsidized and Unsubsidized Stafford, PLUS), state, college/university.

WORK-STUDY ***Federal work-study:*** Total amount: $3,528,674; jobs available.

ATHLETIC AWARDS Total amount: $4,694,049 (46% need-based, 54% non-need-based).

APPLYING FOR FINANCIAL AID ***Required financial aid form:*** FAFSA. ***Financial aid deadline (priority):*** 2/1. ***Notification date:*** Continuous beginning 2/1.

CONTACT Mr. James Conlon, Office of Financial Aid, Rider University, 2083 Lawrenceville Road, Lawrenceville, NJ 08648-3001, 609-896-5188 or toll-free 800-257-9026. *Fax:* 609-219-4487. *E-mail:* finaid@rider.edu.
Website: http://www.rider.edu/.

RINGLING COLLEGE OF ART AND DESIGN

Sarasota, FL

Tuition & fees: $47,970	Average undergraduate aid package: $27,804

ABOUT THE INSTITUTION Independent, coed. ***Awards:*** bachelor's degrees. 11 undergraduate majors. ***Total enrollment:*** 1,456. Undergraduates: 1,456. Freshmen: 367. Federal methodology is used as a basis for awarding need-based institutional aid.

UNDERGRADUATE EXPENSES for 2019–2020 ***Application fee:*** $70. ***Comprehensive fee:*** $63,550 includes full-time tuition ($43,710), mandatory fees ($4260), and room and board ($15,580). Full-time tuition and fees vary according to course load, program, and student level. Room and board charges vary according to board plan and housing facility. ***Part-time tuition:*** $2035 per credit hour. Part-time tuition and fees vary according to program and student level.

FRESHMAN FINANCIAL AID (Fall 2019, est.) 332 applied for aid; of those 84% were deemed to have need. 94% of freshmen with need received aid; of those 7% had need fully met. ***Average percent of need met:*** 50% (excluding resources awarded to replace EFC). ***Average financial aid package:*** $28,044 (excluding resources awarded to replace EFC). 47% of all full-time freshmen had no need and received non-need-based gift aid.

UNDERGRADUATE FINANCIAL AID (Fall 2019, est.) 1,097 applied for aid; of those 89% were deemed to have need. 97% of undergraduates with need received aid; of those 7% had need fully met. ***Average percent of need met:*** 51% (excluding resources awarded to replace EFC). ***Average financial aid package:*** $27,804 (excluding resources awarded to replace EFC). 34% of all full-time undergraduates had no need and received non-need-based gift aid.

GIFT AID (NEED-BASED) ***Total amount:*** $17,366,522 (13% federal, 11% state, 69% institutional, 7% external sources). ***Receiving aid:*** Freshmen: 59% (261); all full-time undergraduates: 59% (949). ***Average award:*** Freshmen: $18,158; Undergraduates: $17,829. ***Scholarships, grants, and awards:*** Federal Pell, FSEOG, state, private, college/university gift aid from institutional funds.

GIFT AID (NON-NEED-BASED) ***Total amount:*** $7,547,959 (5% state, 91% institutional, 4% external sources). ***Receiving aid:*** Freshmen: 3% (14). Undergraduates: 3% (45). ***Average award:*** Freshmen: $13,156. Undergraduates: $12,114. ***Scholarships, grants, and awards by category:*** *Academic interests/achievement:* general academic interests/achievements. *Creative arts/performance:* applied art and design, art/fine arts, cinema/film/broadcasting, creative writing, general creative arts/performance. *Special achievements/activities:* community service. ***Tuition waivers:*** Full or partial for employees or children of employees.

LOANS ***Student loans:*** $13,376,412 (80% need-based, 20% non-need-based). 63% of past graduating class borrowed through all loan programs. *Average indebtedness per student:* $46,947. ***Average need-based loan:*** Freshmen: $9579. Undergraduates: $9468. ***Parent loans:*** $12,611,775 (76% need-based, 24% non-need-based). ***Programs:*** Federal Direct (Subsidized and Unsubsidized Stafford, PLUS).

WORK-STUDY ***Federal work-study:*** Total amount: $1,212,556; jobs available. ***State or other work-study/employment:*** Total amount: $338,000 (5% need-based, 95% non-need-based). Part-time jobs available.

APPLYING FOR FINANCIAL AID ***Required financial aid form:*** FAFSA. ***Financial aid deadline (priority):*** 3/1. ***Notification date:*** Continuous beginning 2/1.

CONTACT Mr. Lee Harrell, Director of Financial Aid, Ringling College of Art and Design, 2700 North Tamiami Trail, Sarasota, FL 34243, 941-359-7532 or toll-free 800-255-7695. *Fax:* 941-359-6107. *E-mail:* lharrell@ringling.edu.
Website: http://www.ringling.edu/.

RIO GRANDE BIBLE INSTITUTE

Edinburg, TX

CONTACT Financial Aid Office, Rio Grande Bible Institute, 4300 S US Hwy 281, Edinburg, TX 78539, 956-380-8100.
Website: http://www.riogrande.edu/.

RIPON COLLEGE

Ripon, WI

CONTACT Mr. Leigh D. Mlodzik, Dean of Admission and Financial Aid, Ripon College, 300 Seward Street, Ripon, WI 54971, 920-748-8704 or toll-free 800-947-4766. *Fax:* 920-748-8335. *E-mail:* financialaid@ripon.edu.
Website: http://www.ripon.edu/.

RIVIER UNIVERSITY

Nashua, NH

CONTACT Valerie Patnaude, Director of Financial Aid, Rivier University, 420 Main Street, Nashua, NH 03060-5086, 603-897-8533 or toll-free 800-44RIVIER. *Fax:* 603-897-8810. *E-mail:* vpatnaude@rivier.edu.
Website: http://www.rivier.edu/.

ROANOKE COLLEGE

Salem, VA

Tuition & fees: $46,870	Average undergraduate aid package: $38,476

ABOUT THE INSTITUTION Independent Evangelical Lutheran Church in America, coed. ***Awards:*** bachelor's degrees. 47 undergraduate majors. ***Total enrollment:*** 2,005. Undergraduates: 2,005. Freshmen: 553. Federal methodology is used as a basis for awarding need-based institutional aid.

UNDERGRADUATE EXPENSES for 2020–2021 ***Application fee:*** $30. ***One-time required fee:*** $150. ***Comprehensive fee:*** $61,450 includes full-time tuition ($45,200), mandatory fees ($1670), and room and board ($14,580). ***College room only:*** $6770. Full-time tuition and fees vary according to course load. Room and board charges vary according to board plan and housing facility. ***Part-time tuition:*** $2160 per course. ***Part-time fees:*** $62 per term. Part-time tuition and fees vary according to course load.

FRESHMAN FINANCIAL AID (Fall 2019, est.) 518 applied for aid; of those 89% were deemed to have need. 100% of freshmen with need received aid; of those 19% had need fully met. ***Average percent of need met:*** 81% (excluding resources awarded to replace EFC). ***Average financial aid package:*** $38,997 (excluding resources awarded to replace EFC). 16% of all full-time freshmen had no need and received non-need-based gift aid.

UNDERGRADUATE FINANCIAL AID (Fall 2019, est.) 1,629 applied for aid; of those 90% were deemed to have need. 100% of undergraduates with need received aid; of those 22% had need fully met. ***Average percent of need met:*** 84% (excluding resources awarded to replace EFC). ***Average financial aid package:*** $38,476 (excluding resources awarded to replace EFC). 23% of all full-time undergraduates had no need and received non-need-based gift aid.

GIFT AID (NEED-BASED) ***Receiving aid:*** Freshmen: 80% (445); all full-time undergraduates: 74% (1,432). ***Average award:*** Freshmen: $33,684; Undergraduates: $32,220. ***Scholarships, grants, and awards:*** Federal Pell, FSEOG, state, private, college/university gift aid from institutional funds.

GIFT AID (NON-NEED-BASED) ***Receiving aid:*** Freshmen: 80% (444). Undergraduates: 73% (1,423). ***Average award:*** Freshmen: $25,197. Undergraduates: $24,930. ***Scholarships, grants, and awards by category:*** *Academic interests/achievement:* general academic interests/achievements. *Creative arts/performance:* art/fine arts, music. ***Tuition waivers:*** Full or partial for employees or children of employees, senior citizens.

LOANS ***Student loans:*** 71% of past graduating class borrowed through all loan programs. *Average indebtedness per student:* $37,335. ***Average need-based loan:***

Freshmen: $3445. Undergraduates: $4261. ***Programs:*** Federal Direct (Subsidized and Unsubsidized Stafford, PLUS), college/university, alternative loans.
WORK-STUDY Federal work-study jobs available.
APPLYING FOR FINANCIAL AID *Required financial aid forms:* FAFSA, state aid form. ***Notification date:*** Continuous. Students must reply within 2 weeks of notification.
CONTACT Mr. Thomas S. Blair Jr., Director of Financial Aid, Roanoke College, 221 College Lane, Salem, VA 24153-3794, 540-375-2235 or toll-free 800-388-2276. *Fax:* 540-375-2267. *E-mail:* finaid@roanoke.edu.
Website: http://www.roanoke.edu/.

ROBERT MORRIS UNIVERSITY

Moon Township, PA

CONTACT Ms. Stephanie Hendershot, Director of Financial Aid, Robert Morris University, 6001 University Boulevard, Moon Township, PA 15108-1189, 412-397-6250 or toll-free 800-762-0097. *Fax:* 412-397-2200. *E-mail:* finaid@rmu.edu.
Website: http://www.rmu.edu/.

ROBERT MORRIS UNIVERSITY ILLINOIS

Chicago, IL

CONTACT Michelle Hayes, Director of Financial Services, Robert Morris University Illinois, 401 South State Street, Suite 135, Chicago, IL 60605, 312-935-4106 or toll-free 800-762-5960. *Fax:* 312-935-4043. *E-mail:* mhayes@robertmorris.edu.
Website: http://www.robertmorris.edu/.

ROBERTS WESLEYAN COLLEGE

Rochester, NY

ABOUT THE INSTITUTION Independent Free Methodist Church of North America, coed. ***Awards:*** bachelor's, master's, and doctoral degrees. 62 undergraduate majors. ***Total enrollment:*** 1,780. Undergraduates: 1,293. Freshmen: 222.
GIFT AID (NEED-BASED) *Scholarships, grants, and awards:* Federal Pell, FSEOG, state, private, college/university gift aid from institutional funds, Academic Competitiveness Grants, National SMART Grants, TEACH Grants.
GIFT AID (NON-NEED-BASED) *Scholarships, grants, and awards by category:* *Academic interests/achievement:* general academic interests/achievements. *Creative arts/performance:* applied art and design, music. *Special achievements/activities:* general special achievements/activities, junior miss, religious involvement. *Special characteristics:* children and siblings of alumni, children of faculty/staff, international students, relatives of clergy, religious affiliation.
LOANS *Programs:* Federal Direct (Subsidized and Unsubsidized Stafford, PLUS), Perkins.
WORK-STUDY *Federal work-study:* Total amount: $343,510; 554 jobs averaging $1975. ***State or other work-study/employment:*** Total amount: $115,000 (100% non-need-based). 62 part-time jobs averaging $1903.
APPLYING FOR FINANCIAL AID *Required financial aid forms:* FAFSA, state aid form.
CONTACT Mrs. Marcie Krausem, Assistant Director of Financial Aid, Roberts Wesleyan College, 2301 Westside Drive, Rochester, NY 14624-1997, 585-594-6150 or toll-free 800-777-4RWC. *Fax:* 585-594-6036. *E-mail:* finaid@roberts.edu.
Website: http://www.roberts.edu/.

ROCHESTER INSTITUTE OF TECHNOLOGY

Rochester, NY

ABOUT THE INSTITUTION Independent, coed. ***Awards:*** certificates, associate, bachelor's, master's, and doctoral degrees. 113 undergraduate majors. ***Total enrollment:*** 16,463. Undergraduates: 13,513. Freshmen: 2,847.
GIFT AID (NEED-BASED) *Scholarships, grants, and awards:* Federal Pell, FSEOG, state, private, college/university gift aid from institutional funds, National Science Foundation Grants.
GIFT AID (NON-NEED-BASED) *Scholarships, grants, and awards by category:* *Academic interests/achievement:* biological sciences, business, communication, computer science, engineering/technologies, general academic interests/achievements, health fields, humanities, international studies, mathematics, military science, physical sciences, premedicine, social sciences. *Creative arts/performance:* applied art and design, art/fine arts, cinema/film/broadcasting, performing arts. *Special achievements/activities:* community service, leadership. *Special characteristics:* children of faculty/staff, veterans.
LOANS *Programs:* Federal Direct (Subsidized and Unsubsidized Stafford, PLUS).
WORK-STUDY *Federal work-study:* Total amount: $3,095,371; jobs available. ***State or other work-study/employment:*** Total amount: $14,756,813 (100% non-need-based). Part-time jobs available.
APPLYING FOR FINANCIAL AID *Required financial aid forms:* FAFSA, state aid form.
CONTACT Mr. Larry Chambers, Associate Vice President for Financial Aid and Scholarships, Rochester Institute of Technology, 56 Lomb Memorial Drive, Rochester, NY 14623-5604, 585-475-2186. *Fax:* 585-475-7270. *E-mail:* larry.chambers@rit.edu.
Website: http://www.rit.edu/.

ROCHESTER UNIVERSITY

Rochester Hills, MI

Tuition & fees: $24,720 — **Average undergraduate aid package: N/A**

ABOUT THE INSTITUTION Independent Church of Christ, coed. ***Awards:*** associate, bachelor's, and master's degrees. 21 undergraduate majors. ***Total enrollment:*** 1,087. Undergraduates: 1,044. Freshmen: 142.
UNDERGRADUATE EXPENSES for 2020–2021 *Comprehensive fee:* $33,560 includes full-time tuition ($24,720) and room and board ($8840). Full-time tuition and fees vary according to class time and location. Room and board charges vary according to board plan. ***Part-time tuition:*** $752 per semester hour. Part-time tuition and fees vary according to class time and location.
GIFT AID (NEED-BASED) *Total amount:* $4,551,880 (44% federal, 17% state, 39% institutional). ***Scholarships, grants, and awards:*** Federal Pell, FSEOG, state, private, college/university gift aid from institutional funds.
GIFT AID (NON-NEED-BASED) *Total amount:* $2,460,524 (75% institutional, 25% external sources). ***Scholarships, grants, and awards by category:*** *Academic interests/achievement:* business, computer science, education, general academic interests/achievements, mathematics, religion/biblical studies. *Creative arts/performance:* journalism/publications, music, theater/drama. *Special achievements/activities:* general special achievements/activities, leadership. *Special characteristics:* adult students, children and siblings of alumni, children of faculty/staff, first-generation college students, general special characteristics, local/state students, out-of-state students, previous college experience, relatives of clergy, religious affiliation, siblings of current students. ***Tuition waivers:*** Full or partial for children of alumni, employees or children of employees.
LOANS *Student loans:* $5,959,382 (41% need-based, 59% non-need-based). ***Parent loans:*** $1,103,975 (100% need-based). ***Programs:*** Federal Direct (Subsidized and Unsubsidized Stafford, PLUS).
WORK-STUDY *Federal work-study:* Total amount: $83,045; jobs available. ***State or other work-study/employment:*** Part-time jobs available.
ATHLETIC AWARDS Total amount: $1,882,024 (100% non-need-based).
APPLYING FOR FINANCIAL AID *Required financial aid form:* FAFSA. ***Financial aid deadline:*** Continuous. ***Notification date:*** Continuous beginning 1/1.

CONTACT Student Financial Services, Rochester University, 800 West Avon Road, Rochester Hills, MI 48307, 248-218-2038 or toll-free 800-521-6010. *Fax:* 248-218-2065.
Website: http://www.rc.edu/.

ROCKFORD UNIVERSITY

Rockford, IL

Tuition & fees: N/R	Average undergraduate aid package: $21,100

ABOUT THE INSTITUTION Independent, coed. ***Awards:*** certificates, bachelor's, and master's degrees. 50 undergraduate majors. ***Total enrollment:*** 1,211. Undergraduates: 1,002. Freshmen: 161. Federal methodology is used as a basis for awarding need-based institutional aid.

FRESHMAN FINANCIAL AID (Fall 2018) 153 applied for aid; of those 93% were deemed to have need. 100% of freshmen with need received aid; of those 13% had need fully met. ***Average percent of need met:*** 64% (excluding resources awarded to replace EFC). ***Average financial aid package:*** $22,075 (excluding resources awarded to replace EFC). 11% of all full-time freshmen had no need and received non-need-based gift aid.

UNDERGRADUATE FINANCIAL AID (Fall 2018) 766 applied for aid; of those 96% were deemed to have need. 100% of undergraduates with need received aid; of those 10% had need fully met. ***Average percent of need met:*** 63% (excluding resources awarded to replace EFC). ***Average financial aid package:*** $21,100 (excluding resources awarded to replace EFC). 9% of all full-time undergraduates had no need and received non-need-based gift aid.

GIFT AID (NEED-BASED) ***Receiving aid:*** Freshmen: 88% (142); all full-time undergraduates: 90% (726). ***Average award:*** Freshmen: $19,420; Undergraduates: $16,964. ***Scholarships, grants, and awards:*** Federal Pell, FSEOG, state, private, college/university gift aid from institutional funds.

GIFT AID (NON-NEED-BASED) ***Receiving aid:*** Freshmen: 12% (19). Undergraduates: 9% (74). ***Average award:*** Freshmen: $17,666. Undergraduates: $13,048. ***Scholarships, grants, and awards by category:*** *Academic interests/achievement:* 813 awards ($7,172,673 total): biological sciences, business, computer science, education, English, foreign languages, general academic interests/achievements, mathematics, physical sciences, premedicine, social sciences. *Creative arts/performance:* 26 awards ($166,850 total): applied art and design, dance, music, performing arts, theater/drama. *Special achievements/activities:* 1 award ($2025 total): community service, leadership. *Special characteristics:* 164 awards ($1,035,980 total): children and siblings of alumni, children of current students, children of educators, children of faculty/staff, general special characteristics, international students, out-of-state students, parents of current students, siblings of current students.

LOANS ***Student loans:*** 85% of past graduating class borrowed through all loan programs. *Average indebtedness per student:* $36,476. ***Average need-based loan:*** Freshmen: $3285. Undergraduates: $4631. ***Programs:*** Federal Direct (Subsidized and Unsubsidized Stafford, PLUS), college/university, alternative loans.

WORK-STUDY ***Federal work-study:*** 127 jobs averaging $712. ***State or other work-study/employment:*** 193 part-time jobs averaging $754.

APPLYING FOR FINANCIAL AID ***Required financial aid form:*** FAFSA. ***Notification date:*** Continuous. Students must reply within 4 weeks of notification.

CONTACT Todd M. Fischer-Free, Assistant Vice President of Student Administrative Services, Rockford University, 5050 East State Street, Rockford, IL 61108, 815-226-3385 or toll-free 800-892-2984. *Fax:* 815-394-5174. *E-mail:* tfree@rockford.edu.
Website: http://www.rockford.edu/.

ROCKHURST UNIVERSITY

Kansas City, MO

CONTACT Maureen McKinnon, Director of Financial Aid, Rockhurst University, 1100 Rockhurst Road, Kansas City, MO 64110-2561, 816-501-4831 or toll-free 800-842-6776. *Fax:* 816-501-3139. *E-mail:* maureen.mckinnon@rockhurst.edu.
Website: http://www.rockhurst.edu/.

ROCKY MOUNTAIN COLLEGE

Billings, MT

Tuition & fees: $30,586	Average undergraduate aid package: $25,766

ABOUT THE INSTITUTION Independent interdenominational, coed. ***Awards:*** associate, bachelor's, master's, and doctoral degrees. 48 undergraduate majors. ***Total enrollment:*** 1,000. Undergraduates: 850. Freshmen: 245. Federal methodology is used as a basis for awarding need-based institutional aid.

UNDERGRADUATE EXPENSES for 2020–2021 ***Application fee:*** $35. ***Comprehensive fee:*** $39,182 includes full-time tuition ($29,976), mandatory fees ($610), and room and board ($8596). ***College room only:*** $4284. Full-time tuition and fees vary according to course load, degree level, and program. Room and board charges vary according to board plan and housing facility. ***Part-time tuition:*** $1249 per credit. ***Part-time fees:*** $200 per term. Part-time tuition and fees vary according to course load, degree level, and program.

FRESHMAN FINANCIAL AID (Fall 2019, est.) 221 applied for aid; of those 86% were deemed to have need. 100% of freshmen with need received aid; of those 12% had need fully met. ***Average percent of need met:*** 73% (excluding resources awarded to replace EFC). ***Average financial aid package:*** $24,613 (excluding resources awarded to replace EFC). 3% of all full-time freshmen had no need and received non-need-based gift aid.

UNDERGRADUATE FINANCIAL AID (Fall 2019, est.) 697 applied for aid; of those 88% were deemed to have need. 100% of undergraduates with need received aid; of those 17% had need fully met. ***Average percent of need met:*** 77% (excluding resources awarded to replace EFC). ***Average financial aid package:*** $25,766 (excluding resources awarded to replace EFC). 5% of all full-time undergraduates had no need and received non-need-based gift aid.

GIFT AID (NEED-BASED) ***Total amount:*** $12,609,140 (12% federal, 78% institutional, 10% external sources). ***Receiving aid:*** Freshmen: 76% (187); all full-time undergraduates: 74% (612). ***Average award:*** Freshmen: $20,470; Undergraduates: $20,845. ***Scholarships, grants, and awards:*** Federal Pell, FSEOG, state, private, college/university gift aid from institutional funds.

GIFT AID (NON-NEED-BASED) ***Total amount:*** $1,753,528 (83% institutional, 17% external sources). ***Receiving aid:*** Freshmen: 9% (21). Undergraduates: 12% (102). ***Average award:*** Freshmen: $13,313. Undergraduates: $13,702. ***Scholarships, grants, and awards by category:*** *Academic interests/achievement:* 706 awards ($8,751,500 total): general academic interests/achievements. *Creative arts/performance:* 32 awards ($45,500 total): debating, music. *Special achievements/activities:* 23 awards ($58,500 total): cheerleading/drum major, leadership. *Special characteristics:* 34 awards ($402,237 total): children of faculty/staff, veterans. ***Tuition waivers:*** Full or partial for employees or children of employees. ***ROTC:*** Army cooperative.

LOANS ***Student loans:*** $4,485,018 (68% need-based, 32% non-need-based). 73% of past graduating class borrowed through all loan programs. *Average indebtedness per student:* $26,935. ***Average need-based loan:*** Freshmen: $3346. Undergraduates: $4090. ***Parent loans:*** $7,052,191 (10% need-based, 90% non-need-based). ***Programs:*** Federal Direct (Subsidized and Unsubsidized Stafford, PLUS), Perkins.

WORK-STUDY ***Federal work-study:*** Total amount: $123,689; 298 jobs averaging $415. ***State or other work-study/employment:*** Total amount: $107,326 (50% need-based, 50% non-need-based). 147 part-time jobs averaging $730.

ATHLETIC AWARDS Total amount: $3,281,550 (86% need-based, 14% non-need-based).

APPLYING FOR FINANCIAL AID ***Required financial aid form:*** FAFSA. ***Financial aid deadline:*** Continuous. ***Notification date:*** Continuous beginning 2/15. Students must reply within 4 weeks of notification.

CONTACT Jessica Francischetti, Director of Financial Assistance, Rocky Mountain College, 1511 Poly Drive, Billings, MT 59102-1796, 406-657-1031 or toll-free 800-877-6259. *Fax:* 406-657-1169. *E-mail:* finaid@rocky.edu.
Website: http://www.rocky.edu/.

ROCKY MOUNTAIN COLLEGE OF ART + DESIGN

Lakewood, CO

CONTACT Michael Dulay, Director of Financial Aid, Rocky Mountain College of Art + Design, 1600 Pierce Street, Lakewood, CO 80214, 303-753-6046 or toll-free 800-888-ARTS. *Fax:* 303-567-7280. *E-mail:* mdulay@rmcad.edu.
Website: http://www.rmcad.edu/.

ROGERS STATE UNIVERSITY

Claremore, OK

Tuition & fees (OK res): $7470 | **Average undergraduate aid package: $9350**

ABOUT THE INSTITUTION State-supported, coed. ***Awards:*** certificates, associate, bachelor's, and master's degrees. 24 undergraduate majors. ***Total enrollment:*** 3,614. Undergraduates: 3,584. Freshmen: 503. Federal methodology is used as a basis for awarding need-based institutional aid.

UNDERGRADUATE EXPENSES for 2019–2020 ***Application fee:*** $20. ***Tuition, state resident:*** full-time $4560. ***Tuition, nonresident:*** full-time $12,900. ***Required fees:*** full-time $2910. ***College room and board:*** $8975; ***Room only:*** $5490. Room and board charges vary according to housing facility.

FRESHMAN FINANCIAL AID (Fall 2018) 675 applied for aid; of those 86% were deemed to have need. 97% of freshmen with need received aid; of those 8% had need fully met. ***Average percent of need met:*** 45% (excluding resources awarded to replace EFC). ***Average financial aid package:*** $9062 (excluding resources awarded to replace EFC). 4% of all full-time freshmen had no need and received non-need-based gift aid.

UNDERGRADUATE FINANCIAL AID (Fall 2018) 1,864 applied for aid; of those 87% were deemed to have need. 98% of undergraduates with need received aid; of those 7% had need fully met. ***Average percent of need met:*** 45% (excluding resources awarded to replace EFC). ***Average financial aid package:*** $9350 (excluding resources awarded to replace EFC). 4% of all full-time undergraduates had no need and received non-need-based gift aid.

GIFT AID (NEED-BASED) ***Receiving aid:*** Freshmen: 78% (524); all full-time undergraduates: 78% (1,460). ***Average award:*** Freshmen: $7510; Undergraduates: $7702. ***Scholarships, grants, and awards:*** Federal Pell, FSEOG, state, private, college/university gift aid from institutional funds.

GIFT AID (NON-NEED-BASED) ***Receiving aid:*** Freshmen: 6% (38). Undergraduates: 5% (87). ***Average award:*** Freshmen: $5119. Undergraduates: $6820. ***Scholarships, grants, and awards by category:*** *Academic interests/achievement:* business, general academic interests/achievements, military science, premedicine. *Creative arts/performance:* applied art and design, dance, music, theater/drama. *Special achievements/activities:* 16 awards ($764 total): cheerleading/drum major, junior miss, leadership. *Special characteristics:* 7 awards ($720 total): adult students, out-of-state students, veterans. ***Tuition waivers:*** Full or partial for employees or children of employees, senior citizens. ***ROTC:*** Air Force cooperative.

LOANS ***Student loans:*** 59% of past graduating class borrowed through all loan programs. *Average indebtedness per student:* $13,052. ***Average need-based loan:*** Freshmen: $3291. Undergraduates: $3360. ***Programs:*** Federal Direct (Subsidized and Unsubsidized Stafford, PLUS), alternative loans.

WORK-STUDY ***Federal work-study:*** 95 jobs averaging $2140. ***State or other work-study/employment:*** Part-time jobs available.

APPLYING FOR FINANCIAL AID ***Required financial aid form:*** FAFSA. ***Financial aid deadline:*** Continuous. ***Notification date:*** Continuous. Students must reply within 2 weeks of notification.

CONTACT Ms. Lori Deardorff, Director of Financial Aid, Rogers State University, 1701 West Will Rogers Boulevard, Claremore, OK 74017-3252, 918-343-7573 or toll-free 800-256-7511. *Fax:* 918-343-7598. *E-mail:* ldeardorff@rsu.edu.
Website: http://www.rsu.edu/.

ROGER WILLIAMS UNIVERSITY

Bristol, RI

Tuition & fees: $32,789 | **Average undergraduate aid package: $24,895**

ABOUT THE INSTITUTION Independent, coed. ***Awards:*** certificates, associate, bachelor's, master's, and doctoral degrees. 69 undergraduate majors. ***Total enrollment:*** 4,838. Undergraduates: 4,523. Freshmen: 1,113. Federal methodology is used as a basis for awarding need-based institutional aid.

UNDERGRADUATE EXPENSES for 2020–2021 ***Application fee:*** $55. ***Comprehensive fee:*** $48,179 includes full-time tuition ($32,789) and room and board ($15,390). ***College room only:*** $8696.

FRESHMAN FINANCIAL AID (Fall 2019, est.) 1024 applied for aid; of those 84% were deemed to have need. 100% of freshmen with need received aid; of those 9% had need fully met. ***Average percent of need met:*** 80% (excluding resources awarded to replace EFC). ***Average financial aid package:*** $26,407 (excluding resources awarded to replace EFC). 23% of all full-time freshmen had no need and received non-need-based gift aid.

UNDERGRADUATE FINANCIAL AID (Fall 2019, est.) 3,194 applied for aid; of those 84% were deemed to have need. 100% of undergraduates with need received aid; of those 10% had need fully met. ***Average percent of need met:*** 81% (excluding resources awarded to replace EFC). ***Average financial aid package:*** $24,895 (excluding resources awarded to replace EFC). 31% of all full-time undergraduates had no need and received non-need-based gift aid.

GIFT AID (NEED-BASED) ***Total amount:*** $49,175,592 (8% federal, 90% institutional, 2% external sources). ***Receiving aid:*** Freshmen: 57% (628); all full-time undergraduates: 39% (1,559). ***Average award:*** Freshmen: $19,451; Undergraduates: $16,971. ***Scholarships, grants, and awards:*** Federal Pell, FSEOG, state, private, college/university gift aid from institutional funds.

GIFT AID (NON-NEED-BASED) ***Total amount:*** $17,060,064 (97% institutional, 3% external sources). ***Receiving aid:*** Freshmen: 75% (838). Undergraduates: 63% (2,517). ***Average award:*** Freshmen: $15,352. Undergraduates: $13,553. ***Scholarships, grants, and awards by category:*** *Academic interests/achievement:* 3,778 awards ($52,435,630 total): general academic interests/achievements. *Special characteristics:* 129 awards ($429,372 total): siblings of current students, veterans, veterans' children. ***ROTC:*** Army.

LOANS ***Student loans:*** $17,943,061 (87% need-based, 13% non-need-based). 64% of past graduating class borrowed through all loan programs. *Average indebtedness per student:* $44,753. ***Average need-based loan:*** Freshmen: $3347. Undergraduates: $4271. ***Parent loans:*** $9,605,144 (95% need-based, 5% non-need-based). ***Programs:*** Federal Direct (Subsidized and Unsubsidized Stafford, PLUS).

WORK-STUDY ***Federal work-study:*** Total amount: $2,720,819; 1,489 jobs averaging $1825. ***State or other work-study/employment:*** Total amount: $188,990 (70% need-based, 30% non-need-based).

APPLYING FOR FINANCIAL AID ***Required financial aid form:*** FAFSA. ***Financial aid deadline:*** 2/1. ***Notification date:*** Continuous beginning 12/20. Students must reply by 5/1 or within 2 weeks of notification.

CONTACT Diane Usher, Associate Director of Student Financial Aid and Planning, Roger Williams University, One Old Ferry Road, Bristol, RI 02809, 401-254-3100 or toll-free 800-458-7144. *Fax:* 401-254-3356. *E-mail:* finaid@rwu.edu.
Website: http://www.rwu.edu/.

ROLLINS COLLEGE

Winter Park, FL

Tuition & fees: $53,716 | **Average undergraduate aid package: $42,681**

ABOUT THE INSTITUTION Independent, coed. ***Awards:*** bachelor's, master's, and doctoral degrees. 36 undergraduate majors. ***Total enrollment:*** 529. Undergraduates: 2,135. Freshmen: 556. Federal methodology is used as a basis for awarding need-based institutional aid.

UNDERGRADUATE EXPENSES for 2020–2021 ***Application fee:*** $50. ***Comprehensive fee:*** $68,916 includes full-time tuition ($53,716) and room and board ($15,200). ***College room only:*** $9250. Room and board charges vary according to board plan and housing facility.

FRESHMAN FINANCIAL AID (Fall 2019, est.) 387 applied for aid; of those 78% were deemed to have need. 100% of freshmen with need received aid; of those 37% had need fully met. ***Average percent of need met:*** 83% (excluding resources awarded to replace EFC). ***Average financial aid package:*** $41,871 (excluding resources awarded to replace EFC). 37% of all full-time freshmen had no need and received non-need-based gift aid.

UNDERGRADUATE FINANCIAL AID (Fall 2019, est.) 1,333 applied for aid; of those 86% were deemed to have need. 100% of undergraduates with need received aid; of those 34% had need fully met. ***Average percent of need met:*** 88% (excluding resources awarded to replace EFC). ***Average financial aid package:*** $42,681 (excluding resources awarded to replace EFC). 34% of all full-time undergraduates had no need and received non-need-based gift aid.

GIFT AID (NEED-BASED) ***Total amount:*** $35,596,318 (7% federal, 8% state, 84% institutional, 1% external sources). ***Receiving aid:*** Freshmen: 54% (302); all full-time undergraduates: 53% (1,135). ***Average award:*** Freshmen: $34,874; Undergraduates: $35,944. ***Scholarships, grants, and awards:*** Federal Pell, FSEOG, state, private, college/university gift aid from institutional funds.

GIFT AID (NON-NEED-BASED) ***Total amount:*** $24,773,297 (20% state, 79% institutional, 1% external sources). ***Receiving aid:*** Freshmen: 37% (208). Undergraduates: 49% (1,032). ***Average award:*** Freshmen: $25,288. Undergraduates: $23,812. ***Scholarships, grants, and awards by category:*** *Academic interests/achievement:* 219 awards ($847,524 total): computer science, engineering/technologies, general academic interests/achievements, mathematics, physical sciences. *Creative arts/performance:* 77 awards ($813,192 total): applied art and design, music, theater/drama. ***Tuition waivers:*** Full or partial for employees or children of employees.

LOANS ***Student loans:*** $5,494,165 (76% need-based, 24% non-need-based). 44% of past graduating class borrowed through all loan programs. *Average indebtedness per student:* $31,992. ***Average need-based loan:*** Freshmen: $3549. Undergraduates: $4501. ***Parent loans:*** $4,495,582 (49% need-based, 51% non-need-based). ***Programs:*** Federal Direct (Subsidized and Unsubsidized Stafford, PLUS).

WORK-STUDY ***Federal work-study:*** Total amount: $1,761,565; 392 jobs averaging $2500. ***State or other work-study/employment:*** Total amount: $39,100 (100% need-based). Part-time jobs available.

ATHLETIC AWARDS Total amount: $4,616,740 (31% need-based, 69% non-need-based).

APPLYING FOR FINANCIAL AID ***Required financial aid form:*** FAFSA. ***Financial aid deadline (priority):*** 3/1. ***Notification date:*** Continuous beginning 1/1. Students must reply by 5/1.

CONTACT Mr. Steve Booker, Director of Financial Aid, Rollins College, 1000 Holt Avenue, #2721, Winter Park, FL 32789-4499, 407-646-2395. *Fax:* 407-646-2173. *E-mail:* sbooker@rollins.edu.
Website: http://www.rollins.edu/.

ROOSEVELT UNIVERSITY

Chicago, IL

CONTACT Office of Financial Aid, Roosevelt University, 430 South Michigan Avenue, Chicago, IL 60605-1394, 866-421-0935 or toll-free 877-APPLYRU. *Fax:* 312-341-3545. *E-mail:* fao@roosevelt.edu.
Website: http://www.roosevelt.edu/.

ROSE-HULMAN INSTITUTE OF TECHNOLOGY

Terre Haute, IN

Tuition & fees: $49,527	Average undergraduate aid package: $32,356

ABOUT THE INSTITUTION Independent, coed, primarily men. ***Awards:*** bachelor's and master's degrees. 16 undergraduate majors. ***Total enrollment:*** 2,038. Undergraduates: 2,000. Freshmen: 496. Federal methodology is used as a basis for awarding need-based institutional aid.

UNDERGRADUATE EXPENSES for 2019–2020 ***Application fee:*** $50. ***One-time required fee:*** $2400. ***Comprehensive fee:*** $64,941 includes full-time tuition ($48,507), mandatory fees ($1020), and room and board ($15,414). ***College room only:*** $9348. Full-time tuition and fees vary according to course load. Room and board charges vary according to board plan. ***Part-time tuition:*** $1415 per credit hour. Part-time tuition and fees vary according to course load. ***Payment plan:*** Tuition prepayment.

FRESHMAN FINANCIAL AID (Fall 2019, est.) 414 applied for aid; of those 81% were deemed to have need. 100% of freshmen with need received aid; of those 22% had need fully met. ***Average percent of need met:*** 68% (excluding resources awarded to replace EFC). ***Average financial aid package:*** $33,978 (excluding resources awarded to replace EFC). 32% of all full-time freshmen had no need and received non-need-based gift aid.

UNDERGRADUATE FINANCIAL AID (Fall 2019, est.) 1,334 applied for aid; of those 84% were deemed to have need. 100% of undergraduates with need received aid; of those 18% had need fully met. ***Average percent of need met:*** 64% (excluding resources awarded to replace EFC). ***Average financial aid package:*** $32,356 (excluding resources awarded to replace EFC). 42% of all full-time undergraduates had no need and received non-need-based gift aid.

GIFT AID (NEED-BASED) ***Receiving aid:*** Freshmen: 68% (335); all full-time undergraduates: 57% (1,119). ***Average award:*** Freshmen: $33,970; Undergraduates: $30,680. ***Scholarships, grants, and awards:*** Federal Pell, FSEOG, state, college/university gift aid from institutional funds.

GIFT AID (NON-NEED-BASED) ***Receiving aid:*** Freshmen: 31% (152). Undergraduates: 51% (1,011). ***Average award:*** Freshmen: $16,359. Undergraduates: $14,175. ***Tuition waivers:*** Full or partial for employees or children of employees. ***ROTC:*** Army, Air Force.

LOANS ***Student loans:*** 58% of past graduating class borrowed through all loan programs. *Average indebtedness per student:* $47,953. ***Average need-based loan:*** Freshmen: $3367. Undergraduates: $4420. ***Programs:*** Federal Direct (Subsidized and Unsubsidized Stafford, PLUS), Perkins.

WORK-STUDY ***Federal work-study:*** 622 jobs averaging $1275. ***State or other work-study/employment:*** Part-time jobs available.

APPLYING FOR FINANCIAL AID ***Required financial aid form:*** FAFSA. ***Financial aid deadline:*** Continuous.

CONTACT Mrs. Melinda L. Middleton, Director of Financial Aid, Rose-Hulman Institute of Technology, 5500 Wabash Avenue, CM 5, Terre Haute, IN 47803, 812-877-8259 or toll-free 800-248-7448. *Fax:* 812-877-8746. *E-mail:* melinda.middleton@rose-hulman.edu.
Website: http://www.rose-hulman.edu/.

ROSEMONT COLLEGE

Rosemont, PA

Tuition & fees: N/R	Average undergraduate aid package: $22,102

ABOUT THE INSTITUTION Independent Roman Catholic, coed. ***Awards:*** certificates, associate, bachelor's, and master's degrees. 25 undergraduate majors. ***Total enrollment:*** 945. Undergraduates: 572. Freshmen: 91. Federal methodology is used as a basis for awarding need-based institutional aid.

UNDERGRADUATE EXPENSES for 2020–2021 ***Tuition:*** part-time $735 per credit hour.

FRESHMAN FINANCIAL AID (Fall 2019, est.) 106 applied for aid; of those 87% were deemed to have need. 99% of freshmen with need received aid; of those 3% had need fully met. ***Average percent of need met:*** 78% (excluding resources awarded to replace EFC). ***Average financial aid package:*** $24,119 (excluding resources awarded to replace EFC). 12% of all full-time freshmen had no need and received non-need-based gift aid.

UNDERGRADUATE FINANCIAL AID (Fall 2019, est.) 340 applied for aid; of those 89% were deemed to have need. 99% of undergraduates with need received aid; of those 8% had need fully met. ***Average percent of need met:*** 73% (excluding resources awarded to replace EFC). ***Average financial aid package:*** $22,102 (excluding resources awarded to replace EFC). 16% of all full-time undergraduates had no need and received non-need-based gift aid.

GIFT AID (NEED-BASED) ***Receiving aid:*** Freshmen: 84% (91); all full-time undergraduates: 82% (297). ***Average award:*** Freshmen: $19,862; Undergraduates: $17,308. ***Scholarships, grants, and awards:*** Federal Pell, FSEOG, state, private, college/university gift aid from institutional funds, Academic Competitiveness Grants, National SMART Grants.

GIFT AID (NON-NEED-BASED) *Receiving aid:* Freshmen: 2% (2). Undergraduates: 4% (16). ***Average award:*** Freshmen: $8604. Undergraduates: $6860. ***Scholarships, grants, and awards by category:*** *Academic interests/achievement:* 364 awards ($3,629,434 total): general academic interests/achievements. *Creative arts/performance:* applied art and design. ***Tuition waivers:*** Full or partial for employees or children of employees.

LOANS *Student loans:* 86% of past graduating class borrowed through all loan programs. *Average indebtedness per student:* $39,050. ***Average need-based loan:*** Freshmen: $3395. Undergraduates: $4310. ***Programs:*** Federal Direct (Subsidized and Unsubsidized Stafford, PLUS), Perkins, alternative loans.

WORK-STUDY *Federal work-study:* 168 jobs averaging $1940. ***State or other work-study/employment:*** 168 part-time jobs averaging $1940.

APPLYING FOR FINANCIAL AID *Required financial aid form:* FAFSA. ***Financial aid deadline:*** Continuous. ***Notification date:*** Continuous. Students must reply within 4 weeks of notification.

CONTACT Mr. Joseph Alaimo, Director of Financial Aid, Rosemont College, 1400 Montgomery Avenue, Rosemont, PA 19010, 610-527-0200 Ext. 2220 or toll-free 888-2-ROSEMONT. *Fax:* 610-526-2971. *E-mail:* joseph.alaimo@rosemont.edu.
Website: http://www.rosemont.edu/.

ROWAN UNIVERSITY

Glassboro, NJ

Tuition & fees: N/R	Average undergraduate aid package: $10,346

ABOUT THE INSTITUTION State-supported, coed. ***Awards:*** certificates, bachelor's, master's, and doctoral degrees. 78 undergraduate majors. ***Total enrollment:*** 19,618. Undergraduates: 16,011. Freshmen: 2,606. Both federal and institutional methodology are used as a basis for awarding need-based institutional aid.

UNDERGRADUATE EXPENSES for 2020–2021 *Application fee:* $65. ***Tuition, area resident:*** part-time $387 per credit hour. ***Tuition, state resident:*** part-time $387 per credit hour. ***Tuition, nonresident:*** part-time $728 per credit hour.

FRESHMAN FINANCIAL AID (Fall 2018) 2326 applied for aid; of those 77% were deemed to have need. 94% of freshmen with need received aid; of those 15% had need fully met. ***Average percent of need met:*** 65% (excluding resources awarded to replace EFC). ***Average financial aid package:*** $10,375 (excluding resources awarded to replace EFC). 9% of all full-time freshmen had no need and received non-need-based gift aid.

UNDERGRADUATE FINANCIAL AID (Fall 2018) 11,422 applied for aid; of those 84% were deemed to have need. 95% of undergraduates with need received aid; of those 12% had need fully met. ***Average percent of need met:*** 65% (excluding resources awarded to replace EFC). ***Average financial aid package:*** $10,346 (excluding resources awarded to replace EFC). 4% of all full-time undergraduates had no need and received non-need-based gift aid.

GIFT AID (NEED-BASED) *Total amount:* $63,521,615 (39% federal, 37% state, 22% institutional, 2% external sources). ***Receiving aid:*** Freshmen: 35% (887); all full-time undergraduates: 37% (5,175). ***Average award:*** Freshmen: $10,108; Undergraduates: $8987. ***Scholarships, grants, and awards:*** Federal Pell, FSEOG, state, private, college/university gift aid from institutional funds.

GIFT AID (NON-NEED-BASED) *Total amount:* $9,736,547 (89% institutional, 11% external sources). ***Receiving aid:*** Freshmen: 30% (761). Undergraduates: 18% (2,569). ***Average award:*** Freshmen: $6290. Undergraduates: $7148. ***Scholarships, grants, and awards by category:*** *Academic interests/achievement:* general academic interests/achievements. *Creative arts/performance:* general creative arts/performance, music. ***ROTC:*** Army cooperative.

LOANS *Student loans:* $98,892,094 (91% need-based, 9% non-need-based). 71% of past graduating class borrowed through all loan programs. *Average indebtedness per student:* $34,519. ***Average need-based loan:*** Freshmen: $3215. Undergraduates: $4300. ***Parent loans:*** $26,900,645 (100% need-based). ***Programs:*** Federal Direct (Subsidized and Unsubsidized Stafford, PLUS), state.

WORK-STUDY *Federal work-study:* Total amount: $762,595; jobs available. ***State or other work-study/employment:*** Total amount: $1,771,024 (67% need-based, 33% non-need-based). Part-time jobs available.

APPLYING FOR FINANCIAL AID *Required financial aid form:* FAFSA. ***Financial aid deadline (priority):*** 3/16. ***Notification date:*** Continuous beginning 3/16. Students must reply by 5/1.

CONTACT Pamela Gordy, Director of the Office of Financial Aid, Rowan University, 201 Mullica Hill Road, Glassboro, NJ 08028-1701, 856-256-4281 or toll-free 800-447-1165 (in-state), 800-447-1165N (out-of-state). *E-mail:* gordy@rowan.edu.
Website: http://www.rowan.edu/.

RUSH UNIVERSITY

Chicago, IL

CONTACT Mike Frechette, Director of Student Financial Aid, Rush University, 600 South Paulina Street, Suite 440, Chicago, IL 60612-3832, 312-942-6256. *Fax:* 312-942-2732. *E-mail:* michael_frechette@rush.edu.
Website: http://www.rushu.rush.edu/.

RUSSELL SAGE COLLEGE

Troy, NY

ABOUT THE INSTITUTION Independent, coed. ***Awards:*** certificates, bachelor's, master's, and doctoral degrees. 21 undergraduate majors. ***Total enrollment:*** 2,471. Undergraduates: 1,358. Freshmen: 234.

GIFT AID (NEED-BASED) *Scholarships, grants, and awards:* Federal Pell, FSEOG, state, private, college/university gift aid from institutional funds.

GIFT AID (NON-NEED-BASED) *Scholarships, grants, and awards by category:* *Academic interests/achievement:* business, education, English, general academic interests/achievements, health fields, military science. *Creative arts/performance:* applied art and design, performing arts, theater/drama. *Special achievements/activities:* community service, general special achievements/activities, leadership. *Special characteristics:* adult students, children and siblings of alumni, ethnic background, first-generation college students, general special characteristics, members of minority groups, veterans.

LOANS *Programs:* Federal Direct (Subsidized and Unsubsidized Stafford, PLUS).

WORK-STUDY *Federal work-study:* Total amount: $609,132; 342 jobs averaging $1930. ***State or other work-study/employment:*** Total amount: $158,735 (100% non-need-based). 31 part-time jobs averaging $5328.

APPLYING FOR FINANCIAL AID *Required financial aid forms:* FAFSA, state aid form.

CONTACT Financial Aid Office, Russell Sage College, 65 1st Street, Troy, NY 12180, 518-244-2000.
Website: http://www.sage.edu/.

RUST COLLEGE

Holly Springs, MS

CONTACT Mrs. Helen L. Street, Director of Financial Aid, Rust College, 150 Rust Avenue, Holly Springs, MS 38635, 662-252-8000 Ext. 4061 or toll-free 888-886-8492 Ext.4065. *Fax:* 662-252-8895.
Website: http://www.rustcollege.edu/.

RUTGERS UNIVERSITY - CAMDEN

Camden, NJ

ABOUT THE INSTITUTION State-supported, coed. ***Awards:*** certificates, bachelor's, master's, and doctoral degrees. 39 undergraduate majors. ***Total enrollment:*** 7,171. Undergraduates: 5,776. Freshmen: 821.

GIFT AID (NEED-BASED) *Scholarships, grants, and awards:* Federal Pell, FSEOG, state, college/university gift aid from institutional funds, Federal Nursing.

LOANS *Programs:* Federal Direct (Subsidized and Unsubsidized Stafford, PLUS), Perkins, Federal Nursing, state, college/university, alternative loans.

CONTACT Ms. Carolann Pierre, Senior Funds Management Specialist, Rutgers University - Camden, 65 Davidson Road- Room 300, Piscataway, NJ 08854, 848-932-2603. *Fax:* 732-932-0516. *E-mail:* carolann.pierre@ofa.rutgers.edu. *Website:* http://www.camden.rutgers.edu/.

RUTGERS UNIVERSITY - NEWARK

Newark, NJ

Tuition & fees (NJ res): $14,826 **Average undergraduate aid package: $15,125**

ABOUT THE INSTITUTION State-supported, coed. ***Awards:*** certificates, bachelor's, master's, and doctoral degrees. 63 undergraduate majors. ***Total enrollment:*** 13,451. Undergraduates: 9,142. Freshmen: 1,326. Federal methodology is used as a basis for awarding need-based institutional aid.

UNDERGRADUATE EXPENSES for 2019–2020 ***Application fee:*** $70. ***Tuition, state resident:*** full-time $12,230; part-time $394 per credit hour. ***Tuition, nonresident:*** full-time $29,012; part-time $942 per credit hour. ***Required fees:*** full-time $2596; $502 per term. Full-time tuition and fees vary according to program. Part-time tuition and fees vary according to course load and program. ***College room and board:*** $13,929; ***Room only:*** $8615. Room and board charges vary according to board plan and housing facility.

FRESHMAN FINANCIAL AID (Fall 2018) 1116 applied for aid; of those 95% were deemed to have need. 100% of freshmen with need received aid; of those 1% had need fully met. ***Average percent of need met:*** 47% (excluding resources awarded to replace EFC). ***Average financial aid package:*** $15,283 (excluding resources awarded to replace EFC). 2% of all full-time freshmen had no need and received non-need-based gift aid.

UNDERGRADUATE FINANCIAL AID (Fall 2018) 6,380 applied for aid; of those 96% were deemed to have need. 100% of undergraduates with need received aid; of those 1% had need fully met. ***Average percent of need met:*** 49% (excluding resources awarded to replace EFC). ***Average financial aid package:*** $15,125 (excluding resources awarded to replace EFC). 1% of all full-time undergraduates had no need and received non-need-based gift aid.

GIFT AID (NEED-BASED) ***Total amount:*** $72,708,643 (34% federal, 44% state, 22% institutional). ***Receiving aid:*** Freshmen: 69% (914); all full-time undergraduates: 71% (5,444). ***Average award:*** Freshmen: $14,073; Undergraduates: $12,825. ***Scholarships, grants, and awards:*** Federal Pell, FSEOG, state, college/university gift aid from institutional funds.

GIFT AID (NON-NEED-BASED) ***Total amount:*** $6,480,732 (84% institutional, 16% external sources). ***Receiving aid:*** Freshmen: 12% (163). Undergraduates: 10% (745). ***Average award:*** Freshmen: $11,365. Undergraduates: $8439. ***Tuition waivers:*** Full or partial for employees or children of employees. ***ROTC:*** Army, Naval, Air Force.

LOANS ***Student loans:*** $34,418,320 (48% need-based, 52% non-need-based). 77% of past graduating class borrowed through all loan programs. *Average indebtedness per student:* $27,343. ***Average need-based loan:*** Freshmen: $3282. Undergraduates: $4258. ***Parent loans:*** $4,356,799 (100% non-need-based). ***Programs:*** Federal Direct (Subsidized and Unsubsidized Stafford, PLUS), Perkins, Federal Nursing, state, college/university, Other education loans.

WORK-STUDY ***Federal work-study:*** Total amount: $2,031,587; jobs available. ***State or other work-study/employment:*** Total amount: $3,801,325 (100% non-need-based). Part-time jobs available.

APPLYING FOR FINANCIAL AID ***Required financial aid form:*** FAFSA. ***Financial aid deadline (priority):*** 12/1. ***Notification date:*** Continuous beginning 2/15.

CONTACT Ms. Carolann Pierre, Senior Funds Management Specialist, Rutgers University - Newark, 65 Davidson Road- Room 300, Piscataway, NJ 08854, 848-932-2603. *Fax:* 732-932-0516. *E-mail:* carolann.pierre@ofa.rutgers.edu. *Website:* http://www.newark.rutgers.edu/.

RUTGERS UNIVERSITY - NEW BRUNSWICK

Piscataway, NJ

Tuition & fees (NJ res): $15,407 **Average undergraduate aid package: $14,433**

ABOUT THE INSTITUTION State-supported, coed. ***Awards:*** certificates, diplomas, associate, bachelor's, master's, and doctoral degrees. 150 undergraduate majors. ***Total enrollment:*** 50,254. Undergraduates: 36,039. Freshmen: 7,036. Federal methodology is used as a basis for awarding need-based institutional aid.

UNDERGRADUATE EXPENSES for 2019–2020 ***Application fee:*** $70. ***Tuition, state resident:*** full-time $12,230; part-time $394 per credit hour. ***Tuition, nonresident:*** full-time $29,012; part-time $942 per credit hour. ***Required fees:*** full-time $3177; $459 per term. Full-time tuition and fees vary according to program. Part-time tuition and fees vary according to course load and program. ***College room and board:*** $13,075; ***Room only:*** $7971. Room and board charges vary according to board plan and housing facility.

FRESHMAN FINANCIAL AID (Fall 2018) 4704 applied for aid; of those 79% were deemed to have need. 100% of freshmen with need received aid; of those 5% had need fully met. ***Average percent of need met:*** 47% (excluding resources awarded to replace EFC). ***Average financial aid package:*** $14,538 (excluding resources awarded to replace EFC). 8% of all full-time freshmen had no need and received non-need-based gift aid.

UNDERGRADUATE FINANCIAL AID (Fall 2018) 20,697 applied for aid; of those 85% were deemed to have need. 100% of undergraduates with need received aid; of those 4% had need fully met. ***Average percent of need met:*** 46% (excluding resources awarded to replace EFC). ***Average financial aid package:*** $14,433 (excluding resources awarded to replace EFC). 3% of all full-time undergraduates had no need and received non-need-based gift aid.

GIFT AID (NEED-BASED) ***Total amount:*** $157,552,007 (34% federal, 46% state, 20% institutional). ***Receiving aid:*** Freshmen: 34% (2,396); all full-time undergraduates: 37% (12,500). ***Average award:*** Freshmen: $13,651; Undergraduates: $12,215. ***Scholarships, grants, and awards:*** Federal Pell, FSEOG, state, college/university gift aid from institutional funds, Federal Nursing.

GIFT AID (NON-NEED-BASED) ***Total amount:*** $73,107,768 (94% institutional, 6% external sources). ***Receiving aid:*** Freshmen: 13% (922). Undergraduates: 9% (3,139). ***Average award:*** Freshmen: $11,936. Undergraduates: $11,310. ***Tuition waivers:*** Full or partial for employees or children of employees. ***ROTC:*** Army, Naval, Air Force.

LOANS ***Student loans:*** $156,040,699 (40% need-based, 60% non-need-based). 56% of past graduating class borrowed through all loan programs. *Average indebtedness per student:* $30,829. ***Average need-based loan:*** Freshmen: $3340. Undergraduates: $4401. ***Parent loans:*** $41,393,161 (100% non-need-based). ***Programs:*** Federal Direct (Subsidized and Unsubsidized Stafford, PLUS), Perkins, Federal Nursing, state, college/university, Other education loans.

WORK-STUDY ***Federal work-study:*** Total amount: $6,318,242; jobs available. ***State or other work-study/employment:*** Total amount: $20,159,237 (100% non-need-based). Part-time jobs available.

ATHLETIC AWARDS Total amount: $13,757,322 (100% non-need-based).

APPLYING FOR FINANCIAL AID ***Required financial aid form:*** FAFSA. ***Financial aid deadline (priority):*** 12/1. ***Notification date:*** Continuous beginning 2/15.

CONTACT Ms. Carolann Pierre, Senior Funds Management Specialist, Rutgers University - New Brunswick, 65 Davidson Road, Piscataway, NJ 08854, 848-932-7057 Ext. 630. *Fax:* 732-932-0516. *E-mail:* carolann.pierre@ofa.rutgers.edu. *Website:* http://newbrunswick.rutgers.edu/.

SACRED HEART MAJOR SEMINARY

Detroit, MI

CONTACT Financial Aid Office, Sacred Heart Major Seminary, 2701 Chicago Boulevard, Detroit, MI 48206-1799, 313-883-8534. *Fax:* 313-868-7025. *E-mail:* financialaid@shms.edu. *Website:* http://www.shms.edu/.

SACRED HEART UNIVERSITY

Fairfield, CT

Tuition & fees: $43,070 | **Average undergraduate aid package: $22,356**

ABOUT THE INSTITUTION Independent Roman Catholic, coed. ***Awards:*** certificates, associate, bachelor's, master's, and doctoral degrees (also offers part-time program with significant enrollment not reflected in profile). 43 undergraduate majors. ***Total enrollment:*** 9,156. Undergraduates: 6,158. Freshmen: 1,601. Both federal and institutional methodology are used as a basis for awarding need-based institutional aid.

UNDERGRADUATE EXPENSES for 2019–2020 ***Application fee:*** $50. ***Comprehensive fee:*** $59,030 includes full-time tuition ($42,800), mandatory fees ($270), and room and board ($15,960). ***College room only:*** $10,900. Room and board charges vary according to board plan and housing facility. ***Part-time tuition:*** $625 per credit hour. ***Part-time fees:*** $115 per term. Part-time tuition and fees vary according to course load.

FRESHMAN FINANCIAL AID (Fall 2019, est.) 1386 applied for aid; of those 76% were deemed to have need. 100% of freshmen with need received aid; of those 19% had need fully met. ***Average percent of need met:*** 59% (excluding resources awarded to replace EFC). ***Average financial aid package:*** $22,433 (excluding resources awarded to replace EFC). 32% of all full-time freshmen had no need and received non-need-based gift aid.

UNDERGRADUATE FINANCIAL AID (Fall 2019, est.) 4,184 applied for aid; of those 81% were deemed to have need. 100% of undergraduates with need received aid; of those 18% had need fully met. ***Average percent of need met:*** 58% (excluding resources awarded to replace EFC). ***Average financial aid package:*** $22,356 (excluding resources awarded to replace EFC). 33% of all full-time undergraduates had no need and received non-need-based gift aid.

GIFT AID (NEED-BASED) ***Total amount:*** $58,159,509 (11% federal, 1% state, 83% institutional, 5% external sources). ***Receiving aid:*** Freshmen: 66% (1,056); all full-time undergraduates: 63% (3,368). ***Average award:*** Freshmen: $18,503; Undergraduates: $18,140. ***Scholarships, grants, and awards:*** Federal Pell, FSEOG, state, private, college/university gift aid from institutional funds.

GIFT AID (NON-NEED-BASED) ***Total amount:*** $31,460,318 (1% federal, 91% institutional, 8% external sources). ***Receiving aid:*** Freshmen: 12% (192). Undergraduates: 10% (524). ***Average award:*** Freshmen: $15,535. Undergraduates: $14,164. ***Scholarships, grants, and awards by category:*** *Academic interests/achievement:* 7,502 awards ($62,433,050 total): biological sciences, business, computer science, education, English, general academic interests/achievements, home economics, humanities, mathematics, physical sciences, premedicine. *Creative arts/performance:* 1,695 awards ($4,462,000 total): applied art and design, art/fine arts, cinema/film/broadcasting, creative writing, dance, music, performing arts, theater/drama. *Special achievements/activities:* 432 awards ($443,875 total): community service, general special achievements/activities, hobbies/interests, leadership, memberships, religious involvement. *Special characteristics:* 347 awards ($2,776,175 total): adult students, children and siblings of alumni, children of current students, children of faculty/staff, children of union members/company employees, ethnic background, general special characteristics, handicapped students, international students, local/state students, members of minority groups, out-of-state students, religious affiliation, siblings of current students, twins, veterans. ***Tuition waivers:*** Full or partial for employees or children of employees. ***ROTC:*** Air Force cooperative.

LOANS ***Student loans:*** $45,155,926 (63% need-based, 37% non-need-based). 72% of past graduating class borrowed through all loan programs. *Average indebtedness per student:* $45,630. ***Average need-based loan:*** Freshmen: $3979. Undergraduates: $4740. ***Parent loans:*** $25,517,443 (51% need-based, 49% non-need-based). ***Programs:*** Federal Direct (Subsidized and Unsubsidized Stafford, PLUS), Perkins, state.

WORK-STUDY ***Federal work-study:*** Total amount: $1,949,860; 1,388 jobs averaging $1945. ***State or other work-study/employment:*** Total amount: $1,428,600 (8% need-based, 92% non-need-based). 914 part-time jobs averaging $1525.

ATHLETIC AWARDS Total amount: $10,304,843 (41% need-based, 59% non-need-based).

APPLYING FOR FINANCIAL AID ***Required financial aid forms:*** FAFSA, CSS Financial Aid PROFILE, noncustodial (divorced/separated) parent's statement. ***Financial aid deadline:*** 2/15. ***Notification date:*** Continuous beginning 3/1. Students must reply within 2 weeks of notification.

CONTACT Ms. Julie B. Savino, Executive Director of University Financial Assistance, Sacred Heart University, 5151 Park Avenue, Fairfield, CT 06825, 203-371-7980. *Fax:* 203-365-7608. *E-mail:* savinoj@sacredheart.edu.
Website: http://www.sacredheart.edu/.

SAE EXPRESSION COLLEGE

Emeryville, CA

CONTACT Financial Aid Office, SAE Expression College, 6601 Shellmound Street, Emeryville, CA 94608, 510-654-2934 or toll-free 877-833-8800.
Website: http://www.sae.edu/.

SAGINAW VALLEY STATE UNIVERSITY

University Center, MI

Tuition & fees (MI res): $10,814 | **Average undergraduate aid package: $10,187**

ABOUT THE INSTITUTION State-supported, coed. ***Awards:*** certificates, bachelor's, master's, and doctoral degrees. 83 undergraduate majors. ***Total enrollment:*** 8,265. Undergraduates: 7,490. Freshmen: 1,470. Federal methodology is used as a basis for awarding need-based institutional aid.

UNDERGRADUATE EXPENSES for 2019–2020 ***Application fee:*** $30. ***Tuition, state resident:*** full-time $10,376; part-time $346 per credit hour. ***Tuition, nonresident:*** full-time $24,963; part-time $832 per credit hour. ***Required fees:*** full-time $438; $14.60 per credit hour. Full-time tuition and fees vary according to course level, degree level, location, and program. Part-time tuition and fees vary according to course level, degree level, location, and program. ***College room and board:*** $10,440; ***Room only:*** $4430. Room and board charges vary according to board plan and housing facility.

FRESHMAN FINANCIAL AID (Fall 2019, est.) 1367 applied for aid; of those 78% were deemed to have need. 100% of freshmen with need received aid; of those 13% had need fully met. ***Average percent of need met:*** 77% (excluding resources awarded to replace EFC). ***Average financial aid package:*** $12,305 (excluding resources awarded to replace EFC). 24% of all full-time freshmen had no need and received non-need-based gift aid.

UNDERGRADUATE FINANCIAL AID (Fall 2019, est.) 5,084 applied for aid; of those 84% were deemed to have need. 100% of undergraduates with need received aid; of those 8% had need fully met. ***Average percent of need met:*** 63% (excluding resources awarded to replace EFC). ***Average financial aid package:*** $10,187 (excluding resources awarded to replace EFC). 20% of all full-time undergraduates had no need and received non-need-based gift aid.

GIFT AID (NEED-BASED) ***Receiving aid:*** Freshmen: 73% (1,067); all full-time undergraduates: 61% (3,760). ***Average award:*** Freshmen: $9824; Undergraduates: $7677. ***Scholarships, grants, and awards:*** Federal Pell, FSEOG, state, private, college/university gift aid from institutional funds.

GIFT AID (NON-NEED-BASED) ***Receiving aid:*** Freshmen: 9% (132). Undergraduates: 5% (310). ***Average award:*** Freshmen: $5595. Undergraduates: $8109. ***Scholarships, grants, and awards by category:*** *Academic interests/achievement:* biological sciences, business, computer science, education, engineering/technologies, general academic interests/achievements, home economics, mathematics, physical sciences. *Creative arts/performance:* applied art and design, music, theater/drama. *Special achievements/activities:* community service, leadership. *Special characteristics:* adult students, local/state students, members of minority groups, veterans. ***Tuition waivers:*** Full or partial for employees or children of employees.

LOANS ***Student loans:*** 73% of past graduating class borrowed through all loan programs. *Average indebtedness per student:* $31,353. ***Average need-based loan:*** Freshmen: $3065. Undergraduates: $3842. ***Programs:*** Federal Direct (Subsidized and Unsubsidized Stafford, PLUS), private loans.

WORK-STUDY Federal work-study jobs available. ***State or other work-study/employment:*** Part-time jobs available.

APPLYING FOR FINANCIAL AID ***Required financial aid forms:*** FAFSA, institution's own form, CSS Financial Aid PROFILE. ***Financial aid deadline:*** Continuous. ***Notification date:*** Continuous.

CONTACT Mr. Robert Lemuel, Director of Scholarships and Financial Aid, Saginaw Valley State University, 7400 Bay Road, University Center, MI 48710, 989-964-4900 or toll-free 800-968-9500. *Fax:* 989-790-0180. *E-mail:* cfsc@svsu.edu.
Website: http://www.svsu.edu/.

ST. AMBROSE UNIVERSITY

Davenport, IA

Tuition & fees: $32,758	Average undergraduate aid package: $24,736

ABOUT THE INSTITUTION Independent Roman Catholic, coed. ***Awards:*** certificates, bachelor's, master's, and doctoral degrees. 58 undergraduate majors. ***Total enrollment:*** 2,968. Undergraduates: 2,260. Freshmen: 477. Federal methodology is used as a basis for awarding need-based institutional aid.

UNDERGRADUATE EXPENSES for 2020–2021 ***Comprehensive fee:*** $44,112 includes full-time tuition ($32,478), mandatory fees ($280), and room and board ($11,354). ***College room only:*** $7020. Full-time tuition and fees vary according to course load. Room and board charges vary according to board plan and housing facility. ***Part-time tuition:*** $970 per credit hour. ***Part-time fees:*** $140 per term. Part-time tuition and fees vary according to course load.

FRESHMAN FINANCIAL AID (Fall 2019, est.) 455 applied for aid; of those 84% were deemed to have need. 100% of freshmen with need received aid; of those 31% had need fully met. ***Average percent of need met:*** 75% (excluding resources awarded to replace EFC). ***Average financial aid package:*** $25,603 (excluding resources awarded to replace EFC). 20% of all full-time freshmen had no need and received non-need-based gift aid.

UNDERGRADUATE FINANCIAL AID (Fall 2019, est.) 1,799 applied for aid; of those 88% were deemed to have need. 100% of undergraduates with need received aid; of those 27% had need fully met. ***Average percent of need met:*** 72% (excluding resources awarded to replace EFC). ***Average financial aid package:*** $24,736 (excluding resources awarded to replace EFC). 21% of all full-time undergraduates had no need and received non-need-based gift aid.

GIFT AID (NEED-BASED) ***Total amount:*** $28,031,438 (10% federal, 6% state, 82% institutional, 2% external sources). ***Receiving aid:*** Freshmen: 80% (378); all full-time undergraduates: 73% (1,555). ***Average award:*** Freshmen: $21,330; Undergraduates: $19,287. ***Scholarships, grants, and awards:*** Federal Pell, FSEOG, state, private, college/university gift aid from institutional funds.

GIFT AID (NON-NEED-BASED) ***Total amount:*** $6,455,521 (99% institutional, 1% external sources). ***Receiving aid:*** Freshmen: 31% (148). Undergraduates: 21% (454). ***Average award:*** Freshmen: $15,568. Undergraduates: $15,164. ***Scholarships, grants, and awards by category:*** *Academic interests/achievement:* area/ethnic studies, biological sciences, business, communication, computer science, education, engineering/technologies, English, foreign languages, general academic interests/achievements, home economics, humanities, international studies, mathematics, physical sciences, premedicine, religion/biblical studies, social sciences. *Creative arts/performance:* applied art and design, dance, journalism/publications, music, theater/drama. *Special achievements/activities:* cheerleading/drum major, leadership. *Special characteristics:* adult students, children and siblings of alumni, children of educators, children of faculty/staff, international students, members of minority groups, out-of-state students, previous college experience, religious affiliation, veterans. ***Tuition waivers:*** Full or partial for children of alumni, employees or children of employees.

LOANS ***Student loans:*** $78,002,843 (98% need-based, 2% non-need-based). 78% of past graduating class borrowed through all loan programs. *Average indebtedness per student:* $38,149. ***Average need-based loan:*** Freshmen: $3316. Undergraduates: $4438. ***Parent loans:*** $5,367,189 (93% need-based, 7% non-need-based). ***Programs:*** Federal Direct (Subsidized and Unsubsidized Stafford, PLUS), Perkins.

WORK-STUDY ***Federal work-study:*** Total amount: $1,043,062; 1,270 jobs averaging $1850. ***State or other work-study/employment:*** Total amount: $410,700 (78% need-based, 22% non-need-based). 295 part-time jobs averaging $1850.

ATHLETIC AWARDS Total amount: $3,133,540 (69% need-based, 31% non-need-based).

APPLYING FOR FINANCIAL AID ***Required financial aid form:*** FAFSA. ***Financial aid deadline:*** Continuous. ***Notification date:*** Continuous beginning 11/1. Students must reply within 2 weeks of notification.

CONTACT Ms. Julie Haack, Director of Financial Aid, St. Ambrose University, 518 West Locust Street, Davenport, IA 52803, 563-333-5775 or toll-free 800-383-2627. *Fax:* 563-333-6243. *E-mail:* haackjuliea@sau.edu.
Website: http://www.sau.edu/.

ST. ANDREWS UNIVERSITY

Laurinburg, NC

CONTACT Shawn Caulder, Director of Financial Aid, St. Andrews University, 1700 Dogwood Mile, Laurinburg, NC 28352, 910-277-5562 or toll-free 800-763-0198. *Fax:* 910-277-5206.
Website: http://www.sa.edu/.

SAINT ANSELM COLLEGE

Manchester, NH

Tuition & fees: $41,800	Average undergraduate aid package: $31,666

ABOUT THE INSTITUTION Independent Roman Catholic, coed. ***Awards:*** bachelor's degrees. 43 undergraduate majors. ***Total enrollment:*** 2,050. Undergraduates: 2,050. Freshmen: 591. Both federal and institutional methodology are used as a basis for awarding need-based institutional aid.

UNDERGRADUATE EXPENSES for 2019–2020 ***Application fee:*** $50. ***Comprehensive fee:*** $56,550 includes full-time tuition ($40,500), mandatory fees ($1300), and room and board ($14,750). ***College room only:*** $8850. Full-time tuition and fees vary according to program. Room and board charges vary according to board plan and housing facility. ***Part-time tuition:*** $1000 per credit. ***Part-time fees:*** $600 per term. Part-time tuition and fees vary according to course load.

FRESHMAN FINANCIAL AID (Fall 2019, est.) 477 applied for aid; of those 81% were deemed to have need. 100% of freshmen with need received aid; of those 36% had need fully met. ***Average percent of need met:*** 85% (excluding resources awarded to replace EFC). ***Average financial aid package:*** $31,756 (excluding resources awarded to replace EFC). 23% of all full-time freshmen had no need and received non-need-based gift aid.

UNDERGRADUATE FINANCIAL AID (Fall 2019, est.) 1,620 applied for aid; of those 85% were deemed to have need. 100% of undergraduates with need received aid; of those 30% had need fully met. ***Average percent of need met:*** 82% (excluding resources awarded to replace EFC). ***Average financial aid package:*** $31,666 (excluding resources awarded to replace EFC). 28% of all full-time undergraduates had no need and received non-need-based gift aid.

GIFT AID (NEED-BASED) ***Total amount:*** $34,871,313 (4% federal, 94% institutional, 2% external sources). ***Receiving aid:*** Freshmen: 75% (384); all full-time undergraduates: 68% (1,371). ***Average award:*** Freshmen: $38,533; Undergraduates: $27,299. ***Scholarships, grants, and awards:*** Federal Pell, FSEOG, state, private, college/university gift aid from institutional funds.

GIFT AID (NON-NEED-BASED) ***Total amount:*** $13,401,686 (96% institutional, 4% external sources). ***Receiving aid:*** Freshmen: 21% (107). Undergraduates: 14% (285). ***Average award:*** Freshmen: $20,897. Undergraduates: $18,945. ***Scholarships, grants, and awards by category:*** *Academic interests/achievement:* general academic interests/achievements. *Creative arts/performance:* debating, general creative arts/performance, journalism/publications. *Special achievements/activities:* community service, general special achievements/activities, leadership. *Special characteristics:* children and siblings of alumni, children of educators, children of faculty/staff, general special characteristics, relatives of clergy, religious affiliation, siblings of current students, twins, veterans, veterans' children. ***Tuition waivers:*** Full or partial for minority students, children of alumni, employees or children of employees. ***ROTC:*** Army cooperative.

LOANS ***Student loans:*** $14,552,690 (53% need-based, 47% non-need-based). 80% of past graduating class borrowed through all loan programs. *Average indebtedness per student:* $29,699. ***Average need-based loan:*** Freshmen: $2489. Undergraduates: $3659. ***Parent loans:*** $6,014,919 (29% need-based, 71% non-need-based). ***Programs:*** Federal Direct (Subsidized and Unsubsidized Stafford, PLUS).

WORK-STUDY ***Federal work-study:*** Total amount: $2,103,436; jobs available. ***State or other work-study/employment:*** Total amount: $18,000 (100% need-based). Part-time jobs available.

ATHLETIC AWARDS Total amount: $3,040,750 (45% need-based, 55% non-need-based).

APPLYING FOR FINANCIAL AID ***Required financial aid forms:*** FAFSA, CSS Financial Aid PROFILE, noncustodial (divorced/separated) parent's statement, parent and student federal income tax form(s), W-2 forms. ***Financial aid deadline:*** 2/15 (priority: 2/15). ***Notification date:*** Continuous beginning 2/15. Students must reply by 5/1 or within 2 weeks of notification.

CONTACT Elizabeth Keuffel, AVP for Enrollment and Director of Financial Aid, Saint Anselm College, 100 Saint Anselm Drive, Manchester, NH 03102-1310, 603-641-7110 or toll-free 888-4ANSELM. *Fax:* 603-656-6015. *E-mail:* financial_aid@anselm.edu. *Website:* http://www.anselm.edu/.

SAINT ANTHONY COLLEGE OF NURSING

Rockford, IL

Tuition & fees: $26,692 **Average undergraduate aid package: N/A**

ABOUT THE INSTITUTION Independent Roman Catholic, coed, primarily women. ***Awards:*** certificates, bachelor's, master's, and doctoral degrees. 1 undergraduate major. Federal methodology is used as a basis for awarding need-based institutional aid.

UNDERGRADUATE EXPENSES for 2019–2020 ***Tuition:*** full-time $25,576; part-time $800 per credit hour. ***Required fees:*** full-time $1116; $1116 per year. Full-time tuition and fees vary according to course load and program. Part-time tuition and fees vary according to course load and program.

GIFT AID (NEED-BASED) ***Scholarships, grants, and awards:*** Federal Pell, state, private, college/university gift aid from institutional funds.

LOANS ***Programs:*** Federal Direct (Subsidized and Unsubsidized Stafford, PLUS), alternative loans.

APPLYING FOR FINANCIAL AID ***Required financial aid form:*** FAFSA. ***Financial aid deadline (priority):*** 4/15.

CONTACT Serrita Woods, Financial Aid Coordinator, Saint Anthony College of Nursing, 3301 N. Mulford Road, Rockford, IL 61114, 815-282-7900. *Fax:* 815-282-7901. *E-mail:* serritawoods@sacn.edu. *Website:* http://www.sacn.edu/.

ST. AUGUSTINE COLLEGE

Chicago, IL

CONTACT Mrs. Maria Zambonino, Director of Financial Aid, St. Augustine College, 1345 W Angyle, Chicago, IL 60640, 773-878-3813. *Fax:* 773-878-9032. *E-mail:* mzambonino@hotmail.com. *Website:* http://www.staugustine.edu/.

SAINT AUGUSTINE'S UNIVERSITY

Raleigh, NC

CONTACT Ms. Barbara Grimm, Director of Financial Aid, Saint Augustine's University, 1315 Oakwood Avenue, Raleigh, NC 27610-2298, 919-516-4128 or toll-free 800-948-1126. *Fax:* 919-516-4431. *E-mail:* bgrimm@st-aug.edu. *Website:* http://www.st-aug.edu/.

ST. BONAVENTURE UNIVERSITY

St. Bonaventure, NY

Tuition & fees: $36,515 **Average undergraduate aid package: $27,546**

ABOUT THE INSTITUTION Independent Roman Catholic Church, coed. ***Awards:*** certificates, associate, bachelor's, and master's degrees. 41 undergraduate majors. ***Total enrollment:*** 2,422. Undergraduates: 1,835. Freshmen: 492. Federal methodology is used as a basis for awarding need-based institutional aid.

UNDERGRADUATE EXPENSES for 2020–2021 ***Comprehensive fee:*** $50,135 includes full-time tuition ($35,450), mandatory fees ($1065), and room and board ($13,620). ***College room only:*** $7490. Room and board charges vary according to board plan and housing facility. ***Part-time tuition:*** $1060 per credit hour. ***Part-time fees:*** $40 per credit hour. Part-time tuition and fees vary according to course load.

FRESHMAN FINANCIAL AID (Fall 2018) 494 applied for aid; of those 87% were deemed to have need. 100% of freshmen with need received aid; of those 24% had need fully met. ***Average percent of need met:*** 73% (excluding resources awarded to replace EFC). ***Average financial aid package:*** $29,428 (excluding resources awarded to replace EFC). 15% of all full-time freshmen had no need and received non-need-based gift aid.

UNDERGRADUATE FINANCIAL AID (Fall 2018) 1,419 applied for aid; of those 89% were deemed to have need. 100% of undergraduates with need received aid; of those 24% had need fully met. ***Average percent of need met:*** 70% (excluding resources awarded to replace EFC). ***Average financial aid package:*** $27,546 (excluding resources awarded to replace EFC). 18% of all full-time undergraduates had no need and received non-need-based gift aid.

GIFT AID (NEED-BASED) ***Total amount:*** $31,890,179 (10% federal, 8% state, 81% institutional, 1% external sources). ***Receiving aid:*** Freshmen: 78% (430); all full-time undergraduates: 72% (1,244). ***Average award:*** Freshmen: $25,442; Undergraduates: $24,215. ***Scholarships, grants, and awards:*** Federal Pell, FSEOG, state, private, college/university gift aid from institutional funds.

GIFT AID (NON-NEED-BASED) ***Total amount:*** $9,861,732 (9% federal, 81% institutional, 10% external sources). ***Receiving aid:*** Freshmen: 73% (404). Undergraduates: 67% (1,150). ***Average award:*** Freshmen: $17,610. Undergraduates: $13,964. ***Scholarships, grants, and awards by category:*** *Academic interests/achievement:* 1,462 awards ($18,558,745 total): business, communication, education, English, general academic interests/achievements, mathematics, physical sciences, religion/biblical studies. *Creative arts/performance:* 62 awards ($80,470 total): art/fine arts, music, performing arts, theater/drama. *Special characteristics:* 194 awards ($871,460 total): adult students, children of faculty/staff, international students, members of minority groups, relatives of clergy, religious affiliation, siblings of current students, veterans, veterans' children. ***Tuition waivers:*** Full or partial for employees or children of employees, senior citizens. ***ROTC:*** Army.

LOANS ***Student loans:*** $14,110,564 (70% need-based, 30% non-need-based). 31% of past graduating class borrowed through all loan programs. *Average indebtedness per student:* $34,877. ***Average need-based loan:*** Freshmen: $3678. Undergraduates: $4664. ***Parent loans:*** $6,163,444 (37% need-based, 63% non-need-based). ***Programs:*** Federal Direct (Subsidized and Unsubsidized Stafford, PLUS), Perkins, college/university.

WORK-STUDY ***Federal work-study:*** Total amount: $265,164; 309 jobs averaging $1405. ***State or other work-study/employment:*** Total amount: $44,215 (100% non-need-based). 322 part-time jobs averaging $1020.

ATHLETIC AWARDS Total amount: $3,868,425 (22% need-based, 78% non-need-based).

APPLYING FOR FINANCIAL AID ***Required financial aid forms:*** FAFSA, state aid form. ***Financial aid deadline (priority):*** 2/15. ***Notification date:*** Continuous beginning 3/1. Students must reply by 5/1 or within 2 weeks of notification.

CONTACT Mr. Christopher Cartmill, Director of Financial Aid, St. Bonaventure University, 3261 West State Road, St. Bonaventure, NY 14778-2284, 716-375-2020 or toll-free 800-462-5050. *Fax:* 716-375-2087. *E-mail:* ccartmil@sbu.edu. *Website:* http://www.sbu.edu/.

ST. CATHERINE UNIVERSITY

St. Paul, MN

Tuition & fees: N/R **Average undergraduate aid package: $38,266**

ABOUT THE INSTITUTION Independent Roman Catholic, undergraduate: women only; graduate: coed. ***Awards:*** certificates, associate, bachelor's, master's, and doctoral degrees. 80 undergraduate majors. ***Total enrollment:*** 4,401. Undergraduates: 3,153. Freshmen: 335. Federal methodology is used as a basis for awarding need-based institutional aid.

FRESHMAN FINANCIAL AID (Fall 2019, est.) 329 applied for aid; of those 89% were deemed to have need. 100% of freshmen with need received aid; of those 47% had need fully met. ***Average percent of need met:*** 95% (excluding resources awarded to replace EFC). ***Average financial aid package:*** $41,935 (excluding resources awarded to replace EFC). 11% of all full-time freshmen had no need and received non-need-based gift aid.

UNDERGRADUATE FINANCIAL AID (Fall 2019, est.) 1,596 applied for aid; of those 84% were deemed to have need. 100% of undergraduates with need received aid; of those 43% had need fully met. ***Average percent of need met:*** 91% (excluding resources awarded to replace EFC). ***Average financial aid package:*** $38,266 (excluding resources awarded to replace EFC). 16% of all full-time undergraduates had no need and received non-need-based gift aid.

GIFT AID (NEED-BASED) ***Total amount:*** $12,203,932 (43% federal, 41% state, 10% institutional, 6% external sources). ***Receiving aid:*** Freshmen: 73% (241); all full-time undergraduates: 64% (1,025). ***Average award:*** Freshmen: $10,609; Undergraduates: $9534. ***Scholarships, grants, and awards:*** Federal Pell, FSEOG, state, private, college/university gift aid from institutional funds, Federal Nursing.

GIFT AID (NON-NEED-BASED) ***Total amount:*** $35,512,219 (100% institutional). ***Receiving aid:*** Freshmen: 89% (292). Undergraduates: 83% (1,330). ***Average award:*** Freshmen: $26,782. Undergraduates: $21,890. ***Scholarships, grants, and awards by category:*** *Academic interests/achievement:* business, education, English, foreign languages, general academic interests/achievements, health fields, home economics, humanities, mathematics, physical sciences, premedicine, social sciences. *Creative arts/performance:* applied art and design, music. *Special achievements/activities:* community service, general special achievements/activities, leadership, memberships. *Special characteristics:* adult students, children and siblings of alumni, children of current students, children of educators, children of faculty/staff, ethnic background, general special characteristics, international students, local/state students, out-of-state students, religious affiliation, siblings of current students, spouses of current students. ***ROTC:*** Army cooperative, Air Force cooperative.

LOANS ***Student loans:*** $16,276,838 (38% need-based, 62% non-need-based). 77% of past graduating class borrowed through all loan programs. *Average indebtedness per student:* $33,587. ***Average need-based loan:*** Freshmen: $3459. Undergraduates: $4594. ***Parent loans:*** $2,923,815 (100% non-need-based). ***Programs:*** Federal Direct (Subsidized and Unsubsidized Stafford, PLUS), Perkins, Federal Nursing, state.

WORK-STUDY Federal work-study jobs available. ***State or other work-study/employment:*** Part-time jobs available.

APPLYING FOR FINANCIAL AID ***Required financial aid forms:*** FAFSA, institution's own form. ***Financial aid deadline (priority):*** 4/1. ***Notification date:*** Continuous.

CONTACT Katie Zmudzien, Associate Director of Admissions and Financial Aid, St. Catherine University, 2004 Randolph Avenue, St. Paul, MN 55105, 651-690-6934 or toll-free 800-945-4599. *Fax:* 651-690-6765. *E-mail:* finaid@stkate.edu. *Website:* http://www.stkate.edu/.

SAINT CHARLES BORROMEO SEMINARY, OVERBROOK

Wynnewood, PA

CONTACT Ms. Nora M. Downey, Coordinator of Financial Aid, Saint Charles Borromeo Seminary, Overbrook, 100 East Wynnewood Road, Wynnewood, PA 19096-3099, 610-785-6582. *Fax:* 610-667-3971. *E-mail:* ndowney@scs.edu. *Website:* http://www.scs.edu/.

ST. CLOUD STATE UNIVERSITY

St. Cloud, MN

Tuition & fees: N/R	Average undergraduate aid package: $12,336

ABOUT THE INSTITUTION State-supported, coed. ***Awards:*** certificates, associate, bachelor's, master's, and doctoral degrees. 98 undergraduate majors. ***Total enrollment:*** 12,608. Undergraduates: 10,914. Freshmen: 1,237. Federal methodology is used as a basis for awarding need-based institutional aid.

FRESHMAN FINANCIAL AID (Fall 2019, est.) 1038 applied for aid; of those 74% were deemed to have need. 100% of freshmen with need received aid; of those 20% had need fully met. ***Average percent of need met:*** 67% (excluding resources awarded to replace EFC). ***Average financial aid package:*** $11,292 (excluding resources awarded to replace EFC). 22% of all full-time freshmen had no need and received non-need-based gift aid.

UNDERGRADUATE FINANCIAL AID (Fall 2019, est.) 4,993 applied for aid; of those 78% were deemed to have need. 100% of undergraduates with need received aid; of those 26% had need fully met. ***Average percent of need met:*** 72% (excluding resources awarded to replace EFC). ***Average financial aid package:*** $12,336 (excluding resources awarded to replace EFC). 6% of all full-time undergraduates had no need and received non-need-based gift aid.

GIFT AID (NEED-BASED) ***Total amount:*** $31,868,088 (56% federal, 42% state, 2% institutional). ***Receiving aid:*** Freshmen: 63% (764); all full-time undergraduates: 56% (3,774). ***Average award:*** Freshmen: $6663; Undergraduates: $6823. ***Scholarships, grants, and awards:*** Federal Pell, FSEOG, state, private, college/university gift aid from institutional funds.

GIFT AID (NON-NEED-BASED) ***Total amount:*** $15,504,909 (8% federal, 20% state, 60% institutional, 12% external sources). ***Receiving aid:*** Freshmen: 31% (380). Undergraduates: 19% (1,246). ***Average award:*** Freshmen: $2269. Undergraduates: $3091. ***Scholarships, grants, and awards by category:*** *Academic interests/achievement:* biological sciences, business, communication, computer science, education, engineering/technologies, English, general academic interests/achievements, health fields, international studies, mathematics, physical sciences, social sciences. *Creative arts/performance:* applied art and design, art/fine arts, cinema/film/broadcasting, creative writing, journalism/publications, music, performing arts, theater/drama. *Special achievements/activities:* community service, general special achievements/activities. *Special characteristics:* children of faculty/staff, children of union members/company employees, members of minority groups, out-of-state students. ***ROTC:*** Army cooperative.

LOANS ***Student loans:*** $57,818,797 (33% need-based, 67% non-need-based). 67% of past graduating class borrowed through all loan programs. *Average indebtedness per student:* $29,580. ***Average need-based loan:*** Freshmen: $3471. Undergraduates: $4360. ***Parent loans:*** $1,536,063 (100% non-need-based). ***Programs:*** Federal Direct (Subsidized and Unsubsidized Stafford, PLUS), state.

WORK-STUDY ***Federal work-study:*** Total amount: $468,254; jobs available. ***State or other work-study/employment:*** Total amount: $1,054,908 (100% need-based). Part-time jobs available.

ATHLETIC AWARDS Total amount: $2,263,572 (100% non-need-based).

APPLYING FOR FINANCIAL AID ***Required financial aid form:*** FAFSA. ***Financial aid deadline:*** Continuous. ***Notification date:*** Continuous beginning 2/1.

CONTACT Office of Financial Aid, St. Cloud State University, 720 4th Avenue South, St. Cloud, MN 56301, 320-308-2047 or toll-free 877-654-7278. *Fax:* 320-308-5424. *E-mail:* financialaid@stcloudstate.edu. *Website:* http://www.stcloudstate.edu/.

ST. EDWARD'S UNIVERSITY

Austin, TX

Tuition & fees: N/R	Average undergraduate aid package: $37,746

ABOUT THE INSTITUTION Independent Roman Catholic, coed. ***Awards:*** certificates, bachelor's, and master's degrees. 56 undergraduate majors. ***Total enrollment:*** 4,447. Undergraduates: 4,056. Freshmen: 864. Both federal and institutional methodology are used as a basis for awarding need-based institutional aid.

FRESHMAN FINANCIAL AID (Fall 2019, est.) 585 applied for aid; of those 89% were deemed to have need. 100% of freshmen with need received aid; of those 15% had need fully met. ***Average percent of need met:*** 68% (excluding resources awarded to replace EFC). ***Average financial aid package:*** $39,753 (excluding resources awarded to replace EFC). 8% of all full-time freshmen had no need and received non-need-based gift aid.

UNDERGRADUATE FINANCIAL AID (Fall 2019, est.) 2,437 applied for aid; of those 92% were deemed to have need. 100% of undergraduates with need received aid; of those 11% had need fully met. ***Average percent of need met:*** 68% (excluding resources awarded to replace EFC). ***Average financial aid package:*** $37,746 (excluding resources awarded to replace EFC). 5% of all full-time undergraduates had no need and received non-need-based gift aid.

GIFT AID (NEED-BASED) ***Total amount:*** $49,703,095 (14% federal, 8% state, 78% institutional). ***Receiving aid:*** Freshmen: 66% (459); all full-time undergraduates: 62% (1,987). ***Average award:*** Freshmen: $18,641; Undergraduates: $18,537. ***Scholarships, grants, and awards:*** Federal Pell, FSEOG, state, private, college/university gift aid from institutional funds.

GIFT AID (NON-NEED-BASED) ***Total amount:*** $38,944,974 (4% federal, 90% institutional, 6% external sources). ***Receiving aid:*** Freshmen: 60% (419). Undergraduates: 49% (1,570). ***Average award:*** Freshmen: $20,009. Undergraduates: $18,188. ***Scholarships, grants, and awards by category:*** *Academic interests/achievement:* biological sciences, business, communication, computer science, education, English, foreign languages, general academic interests/achievements, health fields, humanities, international studies, mathematics, military science, physical sciences, premedicine, religion/biblical studies, social sciences. *Creative arts/performance:* applied art and design, journalism/publications, theater/drama. *Special achievements/activities:* cheerleading/drum major, community service, general special achievements/activities, leadership. *Special characteristics:* adult students, children of faculty/staff, local/state students, out-of-state students, religious affiliation, veterans. ***ROTC:*** Army cooperative, Air Force cooperative.

LOANS ***Student loans:*** $19,535,500 (36% need-based, 64% non-need-based). 62% of past graduating class borrowed through all loan programs. *Average indebtedness per student:* $37,559. ***Average need-based loan:*** Freshmen: $3426. Undergraduates: $4275. ***Parent loans:*** $6,668,398 (100% non-need-based). ***Programs:*** Federal Direct (Subsidized and Unsubsidized Stafford, PLUS), state.

WORK-STUDY ***Federal work-study:*** Total amount: $557,522; jobs available. ***State or other work-study/employment:*** Total amount: $30,910 (100% need-based). Part-time jobs available.

ATHLETIC AWARDS Total amount: $4,438,645 (100% non-need-based).

APPLYING FOR FINANCIAL AID ***Required financial aid form:*** FAFSA. ***Financial aid deadline (priority):*** 1/15. ***Notification date:*** Continuous beginning 11/1. Students must reply by 5/1 or within 2 weeks of notification.

CONTACT Financial Aid Office, St. Edward's University, 3001 South Congress Avenue, Austin, TX 78704, 512-448-8400 or toll-free 800-555-0164.
Website: http://www.stedwards.edu/.

ST. FRANCIS COLLEGE

Brooklyn Heights, NY

CONTACT Ms. Hellitz Lopez, Director of Student Financial Services, St. Francis College, 180 Remsen Street, Brooklyn Heights, NY 11201-4398, 718-489-5346. *Fax:* 718-643-0076. *E-mail:* hlopez@sfc.edu.
Website: http://www.sfc.edu/.

SAINT FRANCIS MEDICAL CENTER COLLEGE OF NURSING

Peoria, IL

Tuition & fees: N/R	Average undergraduate aid package: $11,004

ABOUT THE INSTITUTION Independent Roman Catholic, coed, primarily women. ***Awards:*** certificates, bachelor's, master's, and doctoral degrees. 1 undergraduate major. ***Total enrollment:*** 507. Undergraduates: 320. Federal methodology is used as a basis for awarding need-based institutional aid.

UNDERGRADUATE EXPENSES for 2020–2021 ***Application fee:*** $50. ***Tuition:*** part-time $655 per semester hour. ***Required fees:*** full-time $1550; $225 per term. Full-time tuition and fees vary according to course load, degree level, program, and student level. Part-time tuition and fees vary according to course load, degree level, program, and student level. ***College room only:*** $1950.

UNDERGRADUATE FINANCIAL AID (Fall 2019, est.) 210 applied for aid; of those 83% were deemed to have need. 100% of undergraduates with need received aid; of those 6% had need fully met. ***Average percent of need met:*** 46% (excluding resources awarded to replace EFC). ***Average financial aid package:*** $11,004 (excluding resources awarded to replace EFC). 9% of all full-time undergraduates had no need and received non-need-based gift aid.

GIFT AID (NEED-BASED) ***Receiving aid:*** All full-time undergraduates: 54% (140). ***Average award:*** Undergraduates: $7635. ***Scholarships, grants, and awards:*** Federal Pell, state, private, college/university gift aid from institutional funds.

GIFT AID (NON-NEED-BASED) ***Receiving aid:*** Undergraduates: 1. ***Average award:*** Undergraduates: $2956. ***Scholarships, grants, and awards by category:*** *Academic interests/achievement:* 25 awards ($25,000 total): general academic interests/achievements, home economics.

LOANS ***Average need-based loan:*** Undergraduates: $5181. ***Programs:*** Federal Direct (Subsidized and Unsubsidized Stafford, PLUS), college/university.

APPLYING FOR FINANCIAL AID ***Required financial aid forms:*** FAFSA, institution's own form. ***Notification date:*** Continuous.

CONTACT Ms. Nancy Perryman, Coordinator for Student Financial Assistance, Saint Francis Medical Center College of Nursing, 511 Northeast Greenleaf Street, Peoria, IL 61603-3783, 309-655-4119. *Fax:* 309-655-3962. *E-mail:* nancy.s.perryman@osfhealthcare.org.
Website: http://www.sfmccon.edu/.

SAINT FRANCIS UNIVERSITY

Loretto, PA

Tuition & fees: $39,378	Average undergraduate aid package: $25,319

ABOUT THE INSTITUTION Independent Roman Catholic, coed. ***Awards:*** certificates, associate, bachelor's, master's, and doctoral degrees. 55 undergraduate majors. ***Total enrollment:*** 2,619. Undergraduates: 1,612. Freshmen: 387. Federal methodology is used as a basis for awarding need-based institutional aid.

UNDERGRADUATE EXPENSES for 2020–2021 ***Application fee:*** $30. ***One-time required fee:*** $110. ***Comprehensive fee:*** $51,850 includes full-time tuition ($38,078), mandatory fees ($1300), and room and board ($12,472). ***College room only:*** $6148. ***Part-time tuition:*** $1155 per credit.

FRESHMAN FINANCIAL AID (Fall 2019, est.) 367 applied for aid; of those 88% were deemed to have need. 100% of freshmen with need received aid; of those 25% had need fully met. ***Average percent of need met:*** 71% (excluding resources awarded to replace EFC). ***Average financial aid package:*** $26,924 (excluding resources awarded to replace EFC). 20% of all full-time freshmen had no need and received non-need-based gift aid.

UNDERGRADUATE FINANCIAL AID (Fall 2019, est.) 1,318 applied for aid; of those 88% were deemed to have need. 100% of undergraduates with need received aid; of those 22% had need fully met. ***Average percent of need met:*** 69% (excluding resources awarded to replace EFC). ***Average financial aid package:*** $25,319 (excluding resources awarded to replace EFC). 18% of all full-time undergraduates had no need and received non-need-based gift aid.

GIFT AID (NEED-BASED) ***Total amount:*** $21,109,558 (9% federal, 6% state, 78% institutional, 7% external sources). ***Receiving aid:*** Freshmen: 79% (322); all full-time undergraduates: 79% (1,148). ***Average award:*** Freshmen: $24,221; Undergraduates: $22,127. ***Scholarships, grants, and awards:*** Federal Pell, FSEOG, state, private, college/university gift aid from institutional funds.

GIFT AID (NON-NEED-BASED) ***Total amount:*** $5,202,268 (91% institutional, 9% external sources). ***Receiving aid:*** Freshmen: 19% (77). Undergraduates: 16% (238). ***Average award:*** Freshmen: $15,298. Undergraduates: $13,880. ***Scholarships, grants, and awards by category:*** *Academic interests/achievement:* biological sciences, business, communication, computer science, education, engineering/technologies, English, general academic interests/achievements, health fields, humanities, international studies, mathematics, religion/biblical studies, social sciences. *Creative arts/performance:* art/fine arts. *Special achievements/activities:* cheerleading/drum major, leadership, religious involvement. *Special characteristics:* adult students, children and siblings of alumni, children of current students, children of educators, children of faculty/staff, international students, out-of-state students, previous college experience, religious affiliation, siblings of current students, spouses of current students. ***Tuition waivers:*** Full or partial for employees or children of employees. ***ROTC:*** Army.

LOANS ***Student loans:*** $16,379,278 (62% need-based, 38% non-need-based). 80% of past graduating class borrowed through all loan programs. *Average indebtedness per student:* $40,676. ***Average need-based loan:*** Freshmen: $2991. Undergraduates: $3885. ***Parent loans:*** $3,700,561 (60% need-based, 40% non-need-based). ***Programs:*** Federal Direct (Subsidized and Unsubsidized Stafford, PLUS), Perkins, private loans.

WORK-STUDY ***Federal work-study:*** Total amount: $312,424; jobs available (averaging $1000). ***State or other work-study/employment:*** Total amount: $347,413 (100% non-need-based).

ATHLETIC AWARDS Total amount: $7,910,766 (59% need-based, 41% non-need-based).

APPLYING FOR FINANCIAL AID ***Required financial aid form:*** FAFSA. ***Financial aid deadline (priority):*** 5/1. ***Notification date:*** Continuous beginning 3/1. Students must reply by 5/1.

CONTACT Mr. Shane Himes, Director of Financial Aid, Saint Francis University, PO Box 600, Loretto, PA 15931, 814-472-3945 or toll-free 866-DIAL-SFU. *Fax:* 814-472-3999. *E-mail:* shimes@francis.edu.
Website: http://www.francis.edu/.

ST. GREGORY THE GREAT SEMINARY

Seward, NE

CONTACT Financial Aid Office, St. Gregory the Great Seminary, 800 Fletcher Road, Seward, NE 67434, 402-643-4052.
Website: http://www.sggs.edu/.

ST. JOHN FISHER COLLEGE

Rochester, NY

Tuition & fees: $35,150	Average undergraduate aid package: $23,529

ABOUT THE INSTITUTION Independent Roman Catholic Church, coed. ***Awards:*** certificates, bachelor's, master's, and doctoral degrees. 43 undergraduate majors. ***Total enrollment:*** 3,719. Undergraduates: 2,746. Freshmen: 601. Federal methodology is used as a basis for awarding need-based institutional aid.

UNDERGRADUATE EXPENSES for 2020–2021 ***Comprehensive fee:*** $47,800 includes full-time tuition ($34,340), mandatory fees ($810), and room and board ($12,650). ***College room only:*** $8100. Full-time tuition and fees vary according to program. Room and board charges vary according to board plan. ***Part-time tuition:*** $936 per credit hour. ***Part-time fees:*** $15 per credit hour. Part-time tuition and fees vary according to course load and program.

FRESHMAN FINANCIAL AID (Fall 2019, est.) 582 applied for aid; of those 85% were deemed to have need. 100% of freshmen with need received aid; of those 21% had need fully met. ***Average percent of need met:*** 73% (excluding resources awarded to replace EFC). ***Average financial aid package:*** $24,491 (excluding resources awarded to replace EFC). 18% of all full-time freshmen had no need and received non-need-based gift aid.

UNDERGRADUATE FINANCIAL AID (Fall 2019, est.) 2,264 applied for aid; of those 88% were deemed to have need. 100% of undergraduates with need received aid; of those 21% had need fully met. ***Average percent of need met:*** 70% (excluding resources awarded to replace EFC). ***Average financial aid package:*** $23,529 (excluding resources awarded to replace EFC). 22% of all full-time undergraduates had no need and received non-need-based gift aid.

GIFT AID (NEED-BASED) ***Total amount:*** $37,368,655 (11% federal, 7% state, 80% institutional, 2% external sources). ***Receiving aid:*** Freshmen: 82% (493); all full-time undergraduates: 78% (1,988). ***Average award:*** Freshmen: $20,970; Undergraduates: $19,035. ***Scholarships, grants, and awards:*** Federal Pell, FSEOG, state, private, college/university gift aid from institutional funds, Federal Nursing.

GIFT AID (NON-NEED-BASED) ***Total amount:*** $7,573,824 (2% federal, 96% institutional, 2% external sources). ***Receiving aid:*** Freshmen: 65% (391). Undergraduates: 63% (1,612). ***Average award:*** Freshmen: $17,007. Undergraduates: $14,486. ***Scholarships, grants, and awards by category:*** *Academic interests/achievement:* 1,846 awards ($23,193,300 total): biological sciences, business, communication, computer science, education, English, foreign languages, general academic interests/achievements, humanities, mathematics, physical sciences, religion/biblical studies, social sciences. *Special achievements/activities:* 97 awards ($1,982,630 total): community service, general special achievements/activities. *Special characteristics:* 336 awards ($2,729,384 total): children and siblings of alumni, children of faculty/staff, ethnic background, first-generation college students, local/state students, members of minority groups, out-of-state students, siblings of current students, veterans. ***Tuition waivers:*** Full or partial for employees or children of employees. ***ROTC:*** Army cooperative, Naval cooperative, Air Force cooperative.

LOANS ***Student loans:*** $25,535,541 (91% need-based, 9% non-need-based). 80% of past graduating class borrowed through all loan programs. *Average indebtedness per student:* $37,064. ***Average need-based loan:*** Freshmen: $3411. Undergraduates: $4414. ***Parent loans:*** $8,329,238 (93% need-based, 7% non-need-based). ***Programs:*** Federal Direct (Subsidized and Unsubsidized Stafford, PLUS).

WORK-STUDY ***Federal work-study:*** Total amount: $1,732,566; 1,105 jobs averaging $1500.

APPLYING FOR FINANCIAL AID ***Required financial aid forms:*** FAFSA, state aid form. ***Financial aid deadline (priority):*** 1/15. ***Notification date:*** Continuous beginning 12/1. Students must reply by 5/1 or within 3 weeks of notification.

CONTACT Ms. Marie Fico, Director of Student Financial Services, St. John Fisher College, 3690 East Avenue, Rochester, NY 14618-3597, 585-385-8042 or toll-free 800-444-4640. *Fax:* 585-385-8044. *E-mail:* mfico@sjfc.edu.
Website: http://www.sjfc.edu/.

ST. JOHN'S COLLEGE

Springfield, IL

CONTACT Mary M. Deatherage, Financial Aid Officer, St. John's College, 421 North Ninth Street, Springfield, IL 62702, 217-544-6464 Ext. 44705. *Fax:* 217-757-6870. *E-mail:* mdeather@st-johns.org.
Website: http://www.sjcs.edu/.

ST. JOHN'S COLLEGE

Annapolis, MD

Tuition & fees: $35,635	Average undergraduate aid package: $29,906

ABOUT THE INSTITUTION Independent, coed. ***Awards:*** bachelor's and master's degrees. 1 undergraduate major. ***Total enrollment:*** 527. Undergraduates: 474. Freshmen: 122. Both federal and institutional methodology are used as a basis for awarding need-based institutional aid.

UNDERGRADUATE EXPENSES for 2019–2020 ***One-time required fee:*** $100. ***Comprehensive fee:*** $49,271 includes full-time tuition ($35,000), mandatory fees ($635), and room and board ($13,636). ***College room only:*** $7000. Room and board charges vary according to board plan and housing facility.

FRESHMAN FINANCIAL AID (Fall 2019, est.) 106 applied for aid; of those 82% were deemed to have need. 100% of freshmen with need received aid; of those 10% had need fully met. ***Average percent of need met:*** 76% (excluding resources awarded to replace EFC). ***Average financial aid package:*** $27,853 (excluding resources awarded to replace EFC). 26% of all full-time freshmen had no need and received non-need-based gift aid.

UNDERGRADUATE FINANCIAL AID (Fall 2019, est.) 381 applied for aid; of those 86% were deemed to have need. 100% of undergraduates with need received aid; of those 13% had need fully met. ***Average percent of need met:*** 78% (excluding resources awarded to replace EFC). ***Average financial aid package:*** $29,906 (excluding resources awarded to replace EFC). 26% of all full-time undergraduates had no need and received non-need-based gift aid.

GIFT AID (NEED-BASED) ***Receiving aid:*** Freshmen: 70% (87); all full-time undergraduates: 69% (325). ***Average award:*** Freshmen: $24,360; Undergraduates: $25,523. ***Scholarships, grants, and awards:*** Federal Pell, FSEOG, state, private, college/university gift aid from institutional funds.

GIFT AID (NON-NEED-BASED) ***Receiving aid:*** Freshmen: 6% (7). Undergraduates: 6% (28). ***Average award:*** Freshmen: $8771. Undergraduates: $8461. ***Scholarships, grants, and awards by category:*** *Academic interests/achievement:* general academic interests/achievements. ***Tuition waivers:*** Full or partial for employees or children of employees.

LOANS ***Student loans:*** 74% of past graduating class borrowed through all loan programs. *Average indebtedness per student:* $20,067. ***Average need-based loan:*** Freshmen: $3134. Undergraduates: $3929. ***Programs:*** Federal Direct (Subsidized and Unsubsidized Stafford, PLUS), college/university.

WORK-STUDY ***Federal work-study:*** 90 jobs averaging $3000. ***State or other work-study/employment:*** 115 part-time jobs averaging $3000.

APPLYING FOR FINANCIAL AID ***Required financial aid forms:*** FAFSA, state aid form. ***Notification date:*** Continuous. Students must reply within 2 weeks of notification.

CONTACT Mr. Steven Bell, Director of Financial Aid, St. John's College, 60 College Avenue, Annapolis, MD 21401, 410-626-2502 or toll-free 800-727-9238. *Fax:* 410-626-2885. *E-mail:* skbell@sjc.edu.
Website: http://www.sjc.edu/.

ST. JOHN'S COLLEGE

Santa Fe, NM

Tuition & fees: $36,410 — **Average undergraduate aid package: $29,102**

ABOUT THE INSTITUTION Independent, coed. ***Awards:*** bachelor's and master's degrees. 1 undergraduate major. ***Total enrollment:*** 364. Undergraduates: 317. Freshmen: 74. Both federal and institutional methodology are used as a basis for awarding need-based institutional aid.

UNDERGRADUATE EXPENSES for 2020–2021 ***Comprehensive fee:*** $49,270 includes full-time tuition ($35,000), mandatory fees ($1410), and room and board ($12,860). ***College room only:*** $7210. Full-time tuition and fees vary according to location. Room and board charges vary according to board plan, housing facility, and location. ***Part-time tuition:*** $1029 per credit hour.

FRESHMAN FINANCIAL AID (Fall 2019, est.) 67 applied for aid; of those 70% were deemed to have need. 100% of freshmen with need received aid; of those 51% had need fully met. ***Average percent of need met:*** 95% (excluding resources awarded to replace EFC). ***Average financial aid package:*** $26,980 (excluding resources awarded to replace EFC). 28% of all full-time freshmen had no need and received non-need-based gift aid.

UNDERGRADUATE FINANCIAL AID (Fall 2019, est.) 279 applied for aid; of those 88% were deemed to have need. 100% of undergraduates with need received aid; of those 33% had need fully met. ***Average percent of need met:*** 94% (excluding resources awarded to replace EFC). ***Average financial aid package:*** $29,102 (excluding resources awarded to replace EFC). 10% of all full-time undergraduates had no need and received non-need-based gift aid.

GIFT AID (NEED-BASED) ***Total amount:*** $61,052,125 (1% federal, 99% institutional). ***Receiving aid:*** Freshmen: 64% (47); all full-time undergraduates: 72% (226). ***Average award:*** Freshmen: $24,980; Undergraduates: $19,144. ***Scholarships, grants, and awards:*** Federal Pell, FSEOG, state, private, college/university gift aid from institutional funds, United Negro College Fund.

GIFT AID (NON-NEED-BASED) ***Total amount:*** $884,570 (41% institutional, 59% external sources). ***Receiving aid:*** Freshmen: 61% (45). Undergraduates: 73% (228). ***Average award:*** Freshmen: $12,000. Undergraduates: $12,000. ***Scholarships, grants, and awards by category:*** *Special characteristics:* children of faculty/staff, local/state students. ***Tuition waivers:*** Full or partial for employees or children of employees.

LOANS ***Student loans:*** $1,251,431 (54% need-based, 46% non-need-based). 53% of past graduating class borrowed through all loan programs. *Average indebtedness per student:* $26,744. ***Average need-based loan:*** Freshmen: $3500. Undergraduates: $4307. ***Parent loans:*** $360,584 (100% non-need-based). ***Programs:*** Federal Direct (Subsidized and Unsubsidized Stafford, PLUS).

WORK-STUDY ***Federal work-study:*** Total amount: $250,603; jobs available. ***State or other work-study/employment:*** Total amount: $330,960 (100% need-based). Part-time jobs available.

APPLYING FOR FINANCIAL AID ***Required financial aid form:*** FAFSA. ***Financial aid deadline:*** Continuous. ***Notification date:*** Continuous beginning 12/1. Students must reply by 5/1.

CONTACT Mrs. Darlene Y. Sandoval, Director of Financial Aid, St. John's College, 1160 Camino Cruz Blanca, Santa Fe, NM 87505, 505-984-6185 or toll-free 800-331-5232. *Fax:* 505-984-6164. *E-mail:* Darlene.Sandoval@sjc.edu.
Website: http://www.sjc.edu/.

SAINT JOHN'S UNIVERSITY

Collegeville, MN

Tuition & fees: $49,000 — **Average undergraduate aid package: $36,512**

ABOUT THE INSTITUTION Independent Roman Catholic, undergraduate: men only; graduate: coed. ***Awards:*** bachelor's and master's degrees (coordinate with College of Saint Benedict for women). 35 undergraduate majors. ***Total enrollment:*** 1,723. Undergraduates: 1,625. Freshmen: 414. Federal methodology is used as a basis for awarding need-based institutional aid.

UNDERGRADUATE EXPENSES for 2020–2021 ***Comprehensive fee:*** $60,362 includes full-time tuition ($48,166), mandatory fees ($834), and room and board ($11,362). ***College room only:*** $5436. Room and board charges vary according to board plan and housing facility. ***Part-time tuition:*** $1905 per credit hour. Part-time tuition and fees vary according to course load.

FRESHMAN FINANCIAL AID (Fall 2019, est.) 355 applied for aid; of those 82% were deemed to have need. 100% of freshmen with need received aid; of those 37% had need fully met. ***Average percent of need met:*** 91% (excluding resources awarded to replace EFC). ***Average financial aid package:*** $37,360 (excluding resources awarded to replace EFC). 26% of all full-time freshmen had no need and received non-need-based gift aid.

UNDERGRADUATE FINANCIAL AID (Fall 2019, est.) 1,255 applied for aid; of those 86% were deemed to have need. 100% of undergraduates with need received aid; of those 35% had need fully met. ***Average percent of need met:*** 89% (excluding resources awarded to replace EFC). ***Average financial aid package:*** $36,512 (excluding resources awarded to replace EFC). 25% of all full-time undergraduates had no need and received non-need-based gift aid.

GIFT AID (NEED-BASED) ***Total amount:*** $36,075,464 (7% federal, 7% state, 84% institutional, 2% external sources). ***Receiving aid:*** Freshmen: 70% (288); all full-time undergraduates: 67% (1,068). ***Average award:*** Freshmen: $34,295; Undergraduates: $32,212. ***Scholarships, grants, and awards:*** Federal Pell, FSEOG, state, private, college/university gift aid from institutional funds.

GIFT AID (NON-NEED-BASED) ***Total amount:*** $12,716,725 (84% institutional, 16% external sources). ***Receiving aid:*** Freshmen: 69% (285). Undergraduates: 63% (1,007). ***Average award:*** Freshmen: $21,968. Undergraduates: $18,670. ***Scholarships, grants, and awards by category:*** *Academic interests/achievement:* 1,372 awards ($24,893,281 total): general academic interests/achievements. *Creative arts/performance:* 99 awards ($298,900 total): applied art and design, music, theater/drama. *Special characteristics:* 266 awards ($1,006,442 total): out-of-state students. ***Tuition waivers:*** Full or partial for employees or children of employees. ***ROTC:*** Army.

LOANS ***Student loans:*** $12,578,628 (87% need-based, 13% non-need-based). 74% of past graduating class borrowed through all loan programs. *Average indebtedness per student:* $38,642. ***Average need-based loan:*** Freshmen: $3320. Undergraduates: $4422. ***Programs:*** Federal Direct (Subsidized and Unsubsidized Stafford, PLUS), state, alternative loans.

WORK-STUDY ***Federal work-study:*** Total amount: $491,640; 161 jobs averaging $3450. ***State or other work-study/employment:*** Total amount: $2,592,159 (78% need-based, 22% non-need-based). 820 part-time jobs averaging $3450.

APPLYING FOR FINANCIAL AID ***Required financial aid forms:*** FAFSA, institution's own form. ***Financial aid deadline (priority):*** 3/15. ***Notification date:*** Continuous beginning 3/15. Students must reply by 5/1 or within 3 weeks of notification.

CONTACT Mrs. Kari Vogt, Financial Aid Counselor, Saint John's University, PO Box 5000, Collegeville, MN 56321-5000, 320-363-3664 or toll-free 800-544-1489. *Fax:* 320-363-3102. *E-mail:* kvogt@csbsju.edu.
Website: http://www.csbsju.edu/.

ST. JOHN'S UNIVERSITY

Queens, NY

Tuition & fees: N/R — **Average undergraduate aid package: N/A**

ABOUT THE INSTITUTION Independent Roman Catholic Church, coed. ***Awards:*** certificates, bachelor's, master's, and doctoral degrees. 66 undergraduate majors. ***Total enrollment:*** 21,346. Undergraduates: 16,766. Freshmen: 2,967. Federal methodology is used as a basis for awarding need-based institutional aid.

GIFT AID (NEED-BASED) ***Total amount:*** $54,506,991 (44% federal, 24% state, 32% institutional). ***Scholarships, grants, and awards:*** Federal Pell, FSEOG, state, private, college/university gift aid from institutional funds.

GIFT AID (NON-NEED-BASED) ***Total amount:*** $234,457,099 (96% institutional, 4% external sources). ***Scholarships, grants, and awards by category:*** *Academic interests/achievement:* biological sciences, business, communication, computer science, English, foreign languages, general academic interests/achievements, home economics, humanities, mathematics, military science, physical sciences, premedicine, social sciences. *Creative arts/performance:* applied art and design, cinema/film/broadcasting, creative writing, dance, debating, journalism/publications, music. *Special achievements/activities:* cheerleading/drum major, community service, general special achievements/activities, hobbies/interests, leadership, religious involvement. *Special characteristics:* children and siblings of alumni, children of faculty/staff, children of public servants, general special characteristics, local/state students, previous college experience, public servants, relatives of clergy, religious affiliation, veterans. ***ROTC:*** Army.

LOANS ***Student loans:*** $40,746,448 (57% need-based, 43% non-need-based). 68% of past graduating class borrowed through all loan programs. *Average indebtedness per student:* $28,264. ***Parent loans:*** $62,684,490 (100% non-need-based). ***Programs:*** Federal Direct (Subsidized and Unsubsidized Stafford, PLUS).

WORK-STUDY ***Federal work-study:*** Total amount: $2,185,029; jobs available. ***State or other work-study/employment:*** Part-time jobs available.

ATHLETIC AWARDS Total amount: $6,137,041 (100% non-need-based).

APPLYING FOR FINANCIAL AID ***Required financial aid forms:*** FAFSA, state aid form. ***Financial aid deadline (priority):*** 12/15. ***Notification date:*** Continuous beginning 2/15. Students must reply by 5/1.

CONTACT Mrs. Maryanne Twomey, Director for Institutional Programs and Research, St. John's University, 8000 Utopia Parkway, Queens, NY 11439, 718-990-2000 or toll-free 888-9STJOHNS. *Fax:* 718-990-5945. *E-mail:* studentfinancialserv@stjohns.edu.
Website: http://www.stjohns.edu/.

ST. JOHN VIANNEY COLLEGE SEMINARY

Miami, FL

CONTACT Ms. Bonnie DeAngulo, Director of Financial Aid, St. John Vianney College Seminary, 2900 Southwest 87th Avenue, Miami, FL 33165-3244, 305-223-4561 Ext. 10.
Website: http://www.sjvcs.edu/.

ST. JOSEPH'S COLLEGE, LONG ISLAND CAMPUS

Patchogue, NY

Tuition & fees: $29,200	Average undergraduate aid package: $15,813

ABOUT THE INSTITUTION Independent, coed. ***Awards:*** certificates, bachelor's, and master's degrees. 40 undergraduate majors. ***Total enrollment:*** 4,115. Undergraduates: 3,148. Freshmen: 464. Federal methodology is used as a basis for awarding need-based institutional aid.

UNDERGRADUATE EXPENSES for 2019–2020 ***Application fee:*** $25. ***Tuition:*** full-time $28,590; part-time $925 per credit hour. ***Required fees:*** full-time $610. Full-time tuition and fees vary according to course load, location, and program. Part-time tuition and fees vary according to course load, location, and program.

FRESHMAN FINANCIAL AID (Fall 2018) 440 applied for aid; of those 80% were deemed to have need. 100% of freshmen with need received aid; of those 32% had need fully met. ***Average percent of need met:*** 76% (excluding resources awarded to replace EFC). ***Average financial aid package:*** $18,552 (excluding resources awarded to replace EFC). 19% of all full-time freshmen had no need and received non-need-based gift aid.

UNDERGRADUATE FINANCIAL AID (Fall 2018) 2,564 applied for aid; of those 81% were deemed to have need. 99% of undergraduates with need received aid; of those 26% had need fully met. ***Average percent of need met:*** 62% (excluding resources awarded to replace EFC). ***Average financial aid package:*** $15,813 (excluding resources awarded to replace EFC). 16% of all full-time undergraduates had no need and received non-need-based gift aid.

GIFT AID (NEED-BASED) ***Total amount:*** $28,105,966 (22% federal, 8% state, 70% institutional). ***Receiving aid:*** Freshmen: 78% (350); all full-time undergraduates: 76% (2,012). ***Average award:*** Freshmen: $17,040; Undergraduates: $13,299. ***Scholarships, grants, and awards:*** Federal Pell, FSEOG, state, private, college/university gift aid from institutional funds.

GIFT AID (NON-NEED-BASED) ***Total amount:*** $4,798,822 (1% state, 96% institutional, 3% external sources). ***Receiving aid:*** Freshmen: 77% (343). Undergraduates: 69% (1,837). ***Average award:*** Freshmen: $14,650. Undergraduates: $10,770. ***Scholarships, grants, and awards by category:*** *Academic interests/achievement:* 1,940 awards ($18,705,371 total): general academic interests/achievements. *Special characteristics:* 214 awards ($700,539 total): children and siblings of alumni, children of faculty/staff, parents of current students, public servants, siblings of current students, spouses of current students, twins. ***Tuition waivers:*** Full or partial for employees or children of employees. ***ROTC:*** Army cooperative, Air Force cooperative.

LOANS ***Student loans:*** $13,318,385 (90% need-based, 10% non-need-based). 69% of past graduating class borrowed through all loan programs. *Average indebtedness per student:* $31,518. ***Average need-based loan:*** Freshmen: $2909. Undergraduates: $4211. ***Parent loans:*** $4,263,077 (81% need-based, 19% non-need-based). ***Programs:*** Federal Direct (Subsidized and Unsubsidized Stafford, PLUS), Perkins.

WORK-STUDY ***Federal work-study:*** Total amount: $206,149; 60 jobs averaging $3518. ***State or other work-study/employment:*** Total amount: $354,955 (71% need-based, 29% non-need-based). 82 part-time jobs averaging $4367.

APPLYING FOR FINANCIAL AID ***Required financial aid forms:*** FAFSA, state aid form. ***Financial aid deadline (priority):*** 2/25. ***Notification date:*** Continuous beginning 1/10. Students must reply by 5/1 or within 2 weeks of notification.

CONTACT Amy Thompson, Director of Financial Aid, St. Joseph's College, Long Island Campus, 155 West Roe Boulevard, Patchogue, NY 11772-2399, 631-687-2600. *Fax:* 631-650-2525. *E-mail:* financialaid.li@sjcny.edu.
Website: http://www.sjcny.edu/.

ST. JOSEPH'S COLLEGE, NEW YORK

Brooklyn, NY

Tuition & fees: $29,190	Average undergraduate aid package: $19,484

ABOUT THE INSTITUTION Independent, coed. ***Awards:*** certificates, bachelor's, and master's degrees. 38 undergraduate majors. ***Total enrollment:*** 1,179. Undergraduates: 943. Freshmen: 202. Federal methodology is used as a basis for awarding need-based institutional aid.

UNDERGRADUATE EXPENSES for 2019–2020 ***Application fee:*** $25. ***Tuition:*** full-time $28,590; part-time $925 per credit hour. ***Required fees:*** full-time $600. Full-time tuition and fees vary according to course load and program. Part-time tuition and fees vary according to course load and program. ***College room only:*** $14,800.

FRESHMAN FINANCIAL AID (Fall 2018) 197 applied for aid; of those 84% were deemed to have need. 100% of freshmen with need received aid; of those 16% had need fully met. ***Average percent of need met:*** 68% (excluding resources awarded to replace EFC). ***Average financial aid package:*** $20,869 (excluding resources awarded to replace EFC). 15% of all full-time freshmen had no need and received non-need-based gift aid.

UNDERGRADUATE FINANCIAL AID (Fall 2018) 805 applied for aid; of those 83% were deemed to have need. 100% of undergraduates with need received aid; of those 16% had need fully met. ***Average percent of need met:*** 63% (excluding resources awarded to replace EFC). ***Average financial aid package:*** $19,484 (excluding resources awarded to replace EFC). 15% of all full-time undergraduates had no need and received non-need-based gift aid.

GIFT AID (NEED-BASED) ***Total amount:*** $11,653,473 (28% federal, 10% state, 62% institutional). ***Receiving aid:*** Freshmen: 83% (166); all full-time undergraduates: 80% (663). ***Average award:*** Freshmen: $19,181; Undergraduates: $16,754. ***Scholarships, grants, and awards:*** Federal Pell, FSEOG, state, private, college/university gift aid from institutional funds.

GIFT AID (NON-NEED-BASED) ***Total amount:*** $1,770,831 (96% institutional, 4% external sources). ***Receiving aid:*** Freshmen: 82% (165). Undergraduates: 75% (622). ***Average award:*** Freshmen: $13,487. Undergraduates: $13,996. ***Scholarships, grants, and awards by category:*** *Academic interests/achievement:* 494 awards ($4,980,369 total): general academic interests/achievements. *Special characteristics:* 39 awards ($101,461 total): children and siblings of alumni, children of faculty/staff, parents of current students, public servants, siblings of current students, spouses of current students, twins. ***Tuition waivers:*** Full or partial for employees or children of employees. ***ROTC:*** Army cooperative, Air Force cooperative.

LOANS ***Student loans:*** $3,717,122 (91% need-based, 9% non-need-based). 63% of past graduating class borrowed through all loan programs. *Average indebtedness per student:* $27,278. ***Average need-based loan:*** Freshmen: $3159. Undergraduates: $3971. ***Parent loans:*** $1,087,875 (82% need-based, 18% non-need-based). ***Programs:*** Federal Direct (Subsidized and Unsubsidized Stafford, PLUS), Perkins.

WORK-STUDY ***Federal work-study:*** Total amount: $169,329; 58 jobs averaging $2919. ***State or other work-study/employment:*** Total amount: $57,086 (78% need-based, 22% non-need-based). 45 part-time jobs averaging $2389.

APPLYING FOR FINANCIAL AID ***Required financial aid forms:*** FAFSA, state aid form. ***Financial aid deadline (priority):*** 2/25. ***Notification date:*** Continuous beginning 1/10. Students must reply by 5/1 or within 2 weeks of notification.

CONTACT Ms. Amy Thompson, Director of Financial Aid, St. Joseph's College, New York, 245 Clinton Avenue, Brooklyn, NY 11205-3688, 718-940-5700. *Fax:* 718-940-5312. *E-mail:* financialaid.bk@sjcny.edu.
Website: http://www.sjcny.edu/.

SAINT JOSEPH'S COLLEGE OF MAINE

Standish, ME

CONTACT Office of Financial Aid, Saint Joseph's College of Maine, 278 Whites Bridge Road, Standish, ME 04084-5263, 800-752-1266 or toll-free 800-338-7057. *Fax:* 207-893-6699. *E-mail:* finaid@sjcme.edu.
Website: http://www.sjcme.edu/.

SAINT JOSEPH SEMINARY COLLEGE

Saint Benedict, LA

CONTACT Katie F. Plude, Director of Student Financial Aid, Saint Joseph Seminary College, 75376 River Road, Saint Benedict, LA 70457, 985-867-2248. *Fax:* 985-867-2270. *E-mail:* kplude@sjasc.edu.
Website: http://www.sjasc.edu/.

SAINT JOSEPH'S UNIVERSITY

Philadelphia, PA

Tuition & fees: $47,940	Average undergraduate aid package: $32,275

ABOUT THE INSTITUTION Independent Roman Catholic (Jesuit), coed. ***Awards:*** certificates, associate, bachelor's, master's, and doctoral degrees. 66 undergraduate majors. ***Total enrollment:*** 7,361. Undergraduates: 4,783. Freshmen: 1,103. Federal methodology is used as a basis for awarding need-based institutional aid.

UNDERGRADUATE EXPENSES for 2020–2021 ***Application fee:*** $50. ***Comprehensive fee:*** $62,780 includes full-time tuition ($47,740), mandatory fees ($200), and room and board ($14,840). ***College room only:*** $9424. Full-time tuition and fees vary according to course load. Room and board charges vary according to board plan and housing facility. ***Part-time tuition:*** $584 per credit hour. Part-time tuition and fees vary according to course load.

FRESHMAN FINANCIAL AID (Fall 2019, est.) 960 applied for aid; of those 77% were deemed to have need. 100% of freshmen with need received aid; of those 24% had need fully met. ***Average percent of need met:*** 82% (excluding resources awarded to replace EFC). ***Average financial aid package:*** $33,687 (excluding resources awarded to replace EFC). 28% of all full-time freshmen had no need and received non-need-based gift aid.

UNDERGRADUATE FINANCIAL AID (Fall 2019, est.) 3,201 applied for aid; of those 81% were deemed to have need. 100% of undergraduates with need received aid; of those 27% had need fully met. ***Average percent of need met:*** 79% (excluding resources awarded to replace EFC). ***Average financial aid package:*** $32,275 (excluding resources awarded to replace EFC). 30% of all full-time undergraduates had no need and received non-need-based gift aid.

GIFT AID (NEED-BASED) ***Total amount:*** $70,340,277 (5% federal, 2% state, 92% institutional, 1% external sources). ***Receiving aid:*** Freshmen: 66% (725); all full-time undergraduates: 61% (2,557). ***Average award:*** Freshmen: $27,663; Undergraduates: $25,170. ***Scholarships, grants, and awards:*** Federal Pell, FSEOG, state, private, college/university gift aid from institutional funds, United Negro College Fund.

GIFT AID (NON-NEED-BASED) ***Total amount:*** $26,948,053 (98% institutional, 2% external sources). ***Receiving aid:*** Freshmen: 10% (114). Undergraduates: 10% (436). ***Average award:*** Freshmen: $16,648. Undergraduates: $15,459. ***Scholarships, grants, and awards by category:*** *Academic interests/achievement:* biological sciences, computer science, general academic interests/achievements, mathematics, physical sciences, premedicine. *Creative arts/performance:* debating, general creative arts/performance, theater/drama. *Special achievements/activities:* community service, general special achievements/activities. *Special characteristics:* children and siblings of alumni, children of faculty/staff, members of minority groups, siblings of current students, veterans. ***Tuition waivers:*** Full or partial for employees or children of employees. ***ROTC:*** Army cooperative, Naval cooperative, Air Force.

LOANS ***Student loans:*** $33,630,185.90 (53% need-based, 47% non-need-based). ***Average need-based loan:*** Freshmen: $3350. Undergraduates: $4380. ***Parent loans:*** $13,504,814 (39% need-based, 61% non-need-based). ***Programs:*** Federal Direct (Subsidized and Unsubsidized Stafford, PLUS).

WORK-STUDY ***Federal work-study:*** Total amount: $2,252,243.63; jobs available.

ATHLETIC AWARDS Total amount: $7,330,760 (30% need-based, 70% non-need-based).

APPLYING FOR FINANCIAL AID ***Required financial aid form:*** FAFSA. ***Financial aid deadline (priority):*** 12/1. ***Notification date:*** Continuous beginning 3/31. Students must reply by 5/1.

CONTACT Elizabeth Rihl Lewinsky, Director of Financial Aid, Saint Joseph's University, 5600 City Avenue, Philadelphia, PA 19131-1395, 610-660-2500 or toll-free 888-BE-A-HAWK (in-state), 800-BE-A-HAWK (out-of-state). *Fax:* 610-660-1019. *E-mail:* finaid@sju.edu.
Website: http://www.sju.edu/.

ST. LAWRENCE UNIVERSITY

Canton, NY

Tuition & fees: $56,766	Average undergraduate aid package: $51,110

ABOUT THE INSTITUTION Independent, coed. ***Awards:*** certificates, bachelor's, and master's degrees. 34 undergraduate majors. ***Total enrollment:*** 2,522. Undergraduates: 2,441. Freshmen: 640. Federal methodology is used as a basis for awarding need-based institutional aid.

UNDERGRADUATE EXPENSES for 2019–2020 ***Application fee:*** $60. ***Comprehensive fee:*** $71,394 includes full-time tuition ($56,360), mandatory fees ($406), and room and board ($14,628). Room and board charges vary according to board plan. ***Part-time tuition:*** $1957 per unit. ***Payment plan:*** Tuition prepayment.

FRESHMAN FINANCIAL AID (Fall 2019, est.) 468 applied for aid; of those 88% were deemed to have need. 100% of freshmen with need received aid; of those 31% had need fully met. ***Average percent of need met:*** 89% (excluding resources awarded to replace EFC). ***Average financial aid package:*** $52,542 (excluding resources awarded to replace EFC). 19% of all full-time freshmen had no need and received non-need-based gift aid.

UNDERGRADUATE FINANCIAL AID (Fall 2019, est.) 1,771 applied for aid; of those 82% were deemed to have need. 100% of undergraduates with need received aid; of those 34% had need fully met. ***Average percent of need met:*** 87% (excluding resources awarded to replace EFC). ***Average financial aid package:*** $51,110 (excluding resources awarded to replace EFC). 29% of all full-time undergraduates had no need and received non-need-based gift aid.

GIFT AID (NEED-BASED) ***Total amount:*** $63,219,636 (4% federal, 2% state, 94% institutional). ***Receiving aid:*** Freshmen: 67% (406); all full-time undergraduates:

61% (1,439). ***Average award:*** Freshmen: $43,621; Undergraduates: $40,913. ***Scholarships, grants, and awards:*** Federal Pell, FSEOG, state, private, college/university gift aid from institutional funds.

GIFT AID (NON-NEED-BASED) ***Total amount:*** $17,992,453 (87% institutional, 13% external sources). ***Receiving aid:*** Freshmen: 21% (126). Undergraduates: 14% (329). ***Average award:*** Freshmen: $19,522. Undergraduates: $19,173. ***Scholarships, grants, and awards by category:*** *Academic interests/achievement:* general academic interests/achievements. *Special achievements/activities:* community service, leadership. *Special characteristics:* children and siblings of alumni, international students, local/state students, siblings of current students. ***Tuition waivers:*** Full or partial for employees or children of employees. ***ROTC:*** Army cooperative, Air Force cooperative.

LOANS ***Student loans:*** $12,245,497 (39% need-based, 61% non-need-based). 60% of past graduating class borrowed through all loan programs. *Average indebtedness per student:* $32,390. ***Average need-based loan:*** Freshmen: $3382. Undergraduates: $4366. ***Parent loans:*** $3,760,974 (100% non-need-based). ***Programs:*** Federal Direct (Subsidized and Unsubsidized Stafford, PLUS), college/university.

WORK-STUDY ***Federal work-study:*** Total amount: $1,451,850; jobs available. ***State or other work-study/employment:*** Total amount: $572,487 (100% non-need-based). Part-time jobs available.

ATHLETIC AWARDS Total amount: $2,395,605 (100% non-need-based).

APPLYING FOR FINANCIAL AID ***Required financial aid form:*** FAFSA. ***Financial aid deadline:*** 2/1 (priority: 2/1). ***Notification date:*** Students must reply by 5/1 or within 2 weeks of notification.

CONTACT Mrs. Patricia J.B. Farmer, Director of Financial Aid, St. Lawrence University, Payson Hall, 23 Romoda Drive, Canton, NY 13617-1455, 315-229-5265 or toll-free 800-285-1856. *Fax:* 315-229-7418. *E-mail:* pfarmer@stlawu.edu.
Website: http://www.stlawu.edu/.

SAINT LEO UNIVERSITY

Saint Leo, FL

Tuition & fees: $24,640	Average undergraduate aid package: $25,819

ABOUT THE INSTITUTION Independent Roman Catholic, coed. ***Awards:*** certificates, associate, bachelor's, master's, and doctoral degrees. 32 undergraduate majors. ***Total enrollment:*** 5,351. Undergraduates: 2,282. Freshmen: 782. Federal methodology is used as a basis for awarding need-based institutional aid.

UNDERGRADUATE EXPENSES for 2020–2021 ***One-time required fee:*** $310. ***Comprehensive fee:*** $38,140 includes full-time tuition ($23,990), mandatory fees ($650), and room and board ($13,500). ***College room only:*** $8100. Room and board charges vary according to board plan, housing facility, and location.

FRESHMAN FINANCIAL AID (Fall 2019, est.) 661 applied for aid; of those 88% were deemed to have need. 100% of freshmen with need received aid; of those 17% had need fully met. ***Average percent of need met:*** 82% (excluding resources awarded to replace EFC). ***Average financial aid package:*** $26,780 (excluding resources awarded to replace EFC). 25% of all full-time freshmen had no need and received non-need-based gift aid.

UNDERGRADUATE FINANCIAL AID (Fall 2019, est.) 1,781 applied for aid; of those 87% were deemed to have need. 100% of undergraduates with need received aid; of those 23% had need fully met. ***Average percent of need met:*** 81% (excluding resources awarded to replace EFC). ***Average financial aid package:*** $25,819 (excluding resources awarded to replace EFC). 29% of all full-time undergraduates had no need and received non-need-based gift aid.

GIFT AID (NEED-BASED) ***Receiving aid:*** Freshmen: 74% (579); all full-time undergraduates: 69% (1,543). ***Average award:*** Freshmen: $19,866; Undergraduates: $19,225. ***Scholarships, grants, and awards:*** Federal Pell, FSEOG, state, private, college/university gift aid from institutional funds, United Negro College Fund.

GIFT AID (NON-NEED-BASED) ***Receiving aid:*** Freshmen: 6% (44). Undergraduates: 6% (138). ***Average award:*** Freshmen: $12,381. Undergraduates: $10,278. ***Scholarships, grants, and awards by category:*** *Academic interests/achievement:* $22,277,387 total: general academic interests/achievements. ***Tuition waivers:*** Full or partial for employees or children of employees. ***ROTC:*** Army, Air Force cooperative.

LOANS ***Student loans:*** 69% of past graduating class borrowed through all loan programs. *Average indebtedness per student:* $27,813. ***Average need-based loan:*** Freshmen: $3412. Undergraduates: $4031. ***Programs:*** Federal Direct (Subsidized and Unsubsidized Stafford, PLUS), state.

WORK-STUDY ***Federal work-study:*** 808 jobs averaging $4905. ***State or other work-study/employment:*** 4 part-time jobs averaging $5400.

APPLYING FOR FINANCIAL AID ***Required financial aid forms:*** FAFSA, state aid form. ***Financial aid deadline:*** Continuous. ***Notification date:*** Continuous.

CONTACT Ms. Melinda Clark, Associate Vice President of Financial Aid, Saint Leo University, PO Box 6665, MC 2228, Saint Leo, FL 33574-6665, 800-240-7658 or toll-free 800-334-5532. *Fax:* 866-708-7770. *E-mail:* SFS@saintleo.edu.
Website: http://www.saintleo.edu/.

SAINT LOUIS CHRISTIAN COLLEGE

Florissant, MO

CONTACT Mrs. Catherine Wilhoit, Director of Financial Aid, Saint Louis Christian College, 1360 Grandview Drive, Florissant, MO 63033-6499, 314-837-6777 Ext. 1101 or toll-free 800-887-SLCC. *Fax:* 314-837-8291.
Website: http://www.stlchristian.edu/.

ST. LOUIS COLLEGE OF PHARMACY

St. Louis, MO

Tuition & fees: $29,596	Average undergraduate aid package: $19,536

ABOUT THE INSTITUTION Independent, coed. ***Awards:*** bachelor's and doctoral degrees. 2 undergraduate majors. Federal methodology is used as a basis for awarding need-based institutional aid.

UNDERGRADUATE EXPENSES for 2019–2020 ***Comprehensive fee:*** $41,852 includes full-time tuition ($28,996), mandatory fees ($600), and room and board ($12,256). ***College room only:*** $6663. Full-time tuition and fees vary according to degree level, program, and student level. Room and board charges vary according to board plan and housing facility. ***Part-time tuition:*** $967 per credit hour. ***Part-time fees:*** $600 per year.

FRESHMAN FINANCIAL AID (Fall 2018) 103 applied for aid; of those 97% were deemed to have need. 100% of freshmen with need received aid; of those 18% had need fully met. ***Average percent of need met:*** 62% (excluding resources awarded to replace EFC). ***Average financial aid package:*** $22,505 (excluding resources awarded to replace EFC). 5% of all full-time freshmen had no need and received non-need-based gift aid.

UNDERGRADUATE FINANCIAL AID (Fall 2018) 334 applied for aid; of those 93% were deemed to have need. 100% of undergraduates with need received aid; of those 11% had need fully met. ***Average percent of need met:*** 51% (excluding resources awarded to replace EFC). ***Average financial aid package:*** $19,536 (excluding resources awarded to replace EFC). 11% of all full-time undergraduates had no need and received non-need-based gift aid.

GIFT AID (NEED-BASED) ***Total amount:*** $3,527,312 (24% federal, 5% state, 65% institutional, 6% external sources). ***Receiving aid:*** Freshmen: 94% (100); all full-time undergraduates: 77% (291). ***Average award:*** Freshmen: $18,821; Undergraduates: $15,101. ***Scholarships, grants, and awards:*** Federal Pell, FSEOG, state, private, college/university gift aid from institutional funds, United Negro College Fund.

GIFT AID (NON-NEED-BASED) ***Total amount:*** $621,985 (4% state, 88% institutional, 8% external sources). ***Receiving aid:*** Freshmen: 15% (16). Undergraduates: 8% (31). ***Average award:*** Freshmen: $11,000. Undergraduates: $11,583. ***Scholarships, grants, and awards by category:*** *Academic interests/achievement:* 389 awards ($4,580,202 total): general academic interests/achievements. *Special achievements/activities:* 28 awards ($66,665 total): community service, general special achievements/activities, leadership. *Special characteristics:* 1 award ($27,921 total): children of faculty/staff. ***Tuition waivers:*** Full or partial for employees or children of employees. ***ROTC:*** Army cooperative, Naval cooperative, Air Force cooperative.

LOANS ***Student loans:*** $4,151,045 (78% need-based, 22% non-need-based). 85% of past graduating class borrowed through all loan programs. ***Average need-based loan:*** Freshmen: $4815. Undergraduates: $5872. ***Parent loans:*** $2,087,888 (64% need-based, 36% non-need-based). ***Programs:*** Federal Direct (Subsidized and Unsubsidized Stafford, PLUS), Perkins, Health Professions Student Loans (HPSL).

WORK-STUDY ***Federal work-study:*** Total amount: $140,911; jobs available. ***State or other work-study/employment:*** Part-time jobs available.

ATHLETIC AWARDS Total amount: $1,234,000 (72% need-based, 28% non-need-based).

APPLYING FOR FINANCIAL AID ***Required financial aid form:*** FAFSA. ***Financial aid deadline (priority):*** 3/15. ***Notification date:*** Continuous beginning 12/1. Students must reply within 2 weeks of notification.

CONTACT Mr. Dan Stiffler, Director of Financial Aid, St. Louis College of Pharmacy, 4588 Parkview Place, St. Louis, MO 63110, 314-367-8700 Ext. 4001 or toll-free 800-278-5267. *Fax:* 314-446-8310. *E-mail:* financialaid@stlcop.edu.
Website: http://www.stlcop.edu/.

SAINT LOUIS UNIVERSITY

St. Louis, MO

Tuition & fees: $45,424	Average undergraduate aid package: $34,131

ABOUT THE INSTITUTION Independent Roman Catholic (Jesuit), coed. ***Awards:*** certificates, bachelor's, master's, and doctoral degrees. 83 undergraduate majors. ***Total enrollment:*** 11,684. Undergraduates: 7,217. Freshmen: 1,902. Federal methodology is used as a basis for awarding need-based institutional aid.

UNDERGRADUATE EXPENSES for 2019–2020 ***One-time required fee:*** $200. ***Comprehensive fee:*** $58,024 includes full-time tuition ($44,700), mandatory fees ($724), and room and board ($12,600). Full-time tuition and fees vary according to course level, course load, degree level, location, and program. Room and board charges vary according to board plan, housing facility, and location. ***Part-time tuition:*** $1560 per credit. ***Part-time fees:*** $240. Part-time tuition and fees vary according to course level, course load, degree level, location, and program.

FRESHMAN FINANCIAL AID (Fall 2018) 1265 applied for aid; of those 79% were deemed to have need. 100% of freshmen with need received aid; of those 26% had need fully met. ***Average percent of need met:*** 83% (excluding resources awarded to replace EFC). ***Average financial aid package:*** $36,119 (excluding resources awarded to replace EFC). 29% of all full-time freshmen had no need and received non-need-based gift aid.

UNDERGRADUATE FINANCIAL AID (Fall 2018) 4,493 applied for aid; of those 86% were deemed to have need. 100% of undergraduates with need received aid; of those 23% had need fully met. ***Average percent of need met:*** 77% (excluding resources awarded to replace EFC). ***Average financial aid package:*** $34,131 (excluding resources awarded to replace EFC). 33% of all full-time undergraduates had no need and received non-need-based gift aid.

GIFT AID (NEED-BASED) ***Total amount:*** $101,387,224 (8% federal, 2% state, 87% institutional, 3% external sources). ***Receiving aid:*** Freshmen: 64% (962); all full-time undergraduates: 58% (3,703). ***Average award:*** Freshmen: $29,200; Undergraduates: $26,797. ***Scholarships, grants, and awards:*** Federal Pell, FSEOG, state, private, college/university gift aid from institutional funds, Federal Nursing.

GIFT AID (NON-NEED-BASED) ***Total amount:*** $54,911,596 (7% federal, 1% state, 86% institutional, 6% external sources). ***Receiving aid:*** Freshmen: 13% (192). Undergraduates: 11% (719). ***Average award:*** Freshmen: $20,592. Undergraduates: $19,213. ***Scholarships, grants, and awards by category:*** *Creative arts/performance:* applied art and design, music, performing arts, theater/drama. *Special achievements/activities:* cheerleading/drum major, general special achievements/activities. *Special characteristics:* children of faculty/staff, first-generation college students, international students, previous college experience, religious affiliation, siblings of current students, spouses of current students, veterans. ***Tuition waivers:*** Full or partial for employees or children of employees. ***ROTC:*** Army cooperative, Air Force.

LOANS ***Student loans:*** $35,253,964 (31% need-based, 69% non-need-based). 56% of past graduating class borrowed through all loan programs. *Average indebtedness per student:* $34,188. ***Average need-based loan:*** Freshmen: $3366. Undergraduates: $4349. ***Parent loans:*** $14,161,052 (100% non-need-based). ***Programs:*** Federal Direct (Subsidized and Unsubsidized Stafford, PLUS), Federal Nursing, state, college/university.

WORK-STUDY ***Federal work-study:*** Total amount: $3,070,948; jobs available. ***State or other work-study/employment:*** Part-time jobs available.

ATHLETIC AWARDS Total amount: $5,329,039 (33% need-based, 67% non-need-based).

APPLYING FOR FINANCIAL AID ***Required financial aid form:*** FAFSA. ***Financial aid deadline (priority):*** 2/1. ***Notification date:*** Continuous beginning 2/1. Students must reply by 5/1.

CONTACT Cari S. Wickliffe, Director of Student Financial Services, Saint Louis University, One Grand Boulevard, DuBourg Hall, Room 119, St. Louis, MO 63103, 314-977-2350 or toll-free 800-758-3678. *Fax:* 314-977-3437. *E-mail:* sfs@slu.edu.
Website: http://www.slu.edu/.

SAINT LUKE'S COLLEGE OF HEALTH SCIENCES

Kansas City, MO

CONTACT Jennifer Wright, Director of Financial Aid, Saint Luke's College of Health Sciences, 624 Westport Road, Kansas City, MO 64111, 816-936-8730. *Fax:* 816-936-8760. *E-mail:* finaid@saintlukescollege.edu.
Website: http://www.saintlukescollege.edu/.

SAINT MARTIN'S UNIVERSITY

Lacey, WA

Tuition & fees: $38,560	Average undergraduate aid package: $30,845

ABOUT THE INSTITUTION Independent Roman Catholic, coed. ***Awards:*** certificates, bachelor's, and master's degrees. 28 undergraduate majors. ***Total enrollment:*** 1,609. Undergraduates: 1,344. Freshmen: 241. Federal methodology is used as a basis for awarding need-based institutional aid.

UNDERGRADUATE EXPENSES for 2019–2020 ***Comprehensive fee:*** $50,560 includes full-time tuition ($38,150), mandatory fees ($410), and room and board ($12,000). ***College room only:*** $5750. Room and board charges vary according to board plan and housing facility. ***Part-time tuition:*** $1275 per credit.

FRESHMAN FINANCIAL AID (Fall 2018) 180 applied for aid; of those 93% were deemed to have need. 100% of freshmen with need received aid; of those 22% had need fully met. ***Average percent of need met:*** 80% (excluding resources awarded to replace EFC). ***Average financial aid package:*** $30,919 (excluding resources awarded to replace EFC). 9% of all full-time freshmen had no need and received non-need-based gift aid.

UNDERGRADUATE FINANCIAL AID (Fall 2018) 925 applied for aid; of those 92% were deemed to have need. 100% of undergraduates with need received aid; of those 23% had need fully met. ***Average percent of need met:*** 78% (excluding resources awarded to replace EFC). ***Average financial aid package:*** $30,845 (excluding resources awarded to replace EFC). 13% of all full-time undergraduates had no need and received non-need-based gift aid.

GIFT AID (NEED-BASED) ***Total amount:*** $22,030,379 (11% federal, 13% state, 59% institutional, 17% external sources). ***Receiving aid:*** Freshmen: 71% (167); all full-time undergraduates: 76% (845). ***Average award:*** Freshmen: $28,293; Undergraduates: $27,571. ***Scholarships, grants, and awards:*** Federal Pell, FSEOG, state, private, college/university gift aid from institutional funds.

GIFT AID (NON-NEED-BASED) ***Total amount:*** $3,463,384 (2% state, 79% institutional, 19% external sources). ***Receiving aid:*** Freshmen: 11% (26). Undergraduates: 14% (150). ***Average award:*** Freshmen: $15,582. Undergraduates: $15,630. ***Scholarships, grants, and awards by category:*** *Academic interests/achievement:* business, education, engineering/technologies, general academic interests/achievements, international studies, premedicine. *Creative arts/performance:* music, theater/drama. *Special achievements/activities:* community service, general special achievements/activities, hobbies/interests, leadership, religious involvement. *Special characteristics:* children and siblings of alumni, children of faculty/staff, ethnic background, general special characteristics, international students, local/state students, members of minority groups, out-of-state students, siblings of current students, veterans. ***Tuition waivers:*** Full or partial for employees or children of employees. ***ROTC:*** Army cooperative, Air Force cooperative.

LOANS ***Student loans:*** $6,053,978 (73% need-based, 27% non-need-based). 66% of past graduating class borrowed through all loan programs. *Average indebtedness per student:* $30,672. ***Average need-based loan:*** Freshmen: $2674. Undergraduates: $3737. ***Parent loans:*** $2,220,928 (51% need-based, 49% non-need-based).

Programs: Federal Direct (Subsidized and Unsubsidized Stafford, PLUS), Perkins, state, private loans.

WORK-STUDY *Federal work-study:* Total amount: $544,387; jobs available. ***State or other work-study/employment:*** Total amount: $52,818 (90% need-based, 10% non-need-based). Part-time jobs available.

ATHLETIC AWARDS Total amount: $2,003,647 (56% need-based, 44% non-need-based).

APPLYING FOR FINANCIAL AID *Required financial aid form:* FAFSA. ***Financial aid deadline (priority):*** 1/15. ***Notification date:*** Continuous beginning 11/21. Students must reply within 3 weeks of notification.

CONTACT Ms. Julie Anderson, Director of Financial Aid, Saint Martin's University, 5000 Abbey Way SE, Lacey, WA 98503-7500, 360-4868868 or toll-free 800-368-8803. *Fax:* 360-412-6190. *E-mail:* finaid@stmartin.edu.
Website: http://www.stmartin.edu/.

SAINT MARY-OF-THE-WOODS COLLEGE

Saint Mary of the Woods, IN

ABOUT THE INSTITUTION Independent Roman Catholic, coed, primarily women. ***Awards:*** certificates, associate, bachelor's, and master's degrees (also offers external degree program with significant enrollment not reflected in profile). 32 undergraduate majors. ***Total enrollment:*** 1,094. Undergraduates: 767. Freshmen: 146.

GIFT AID (NEED-BASED) *Scholarships, grants, and awards:* Federal Pell, FSEOG, state, private, college/university gift aid from institutional funds.

GIFT AID (NON-NEED-BASED) *Scholarships, grants, and awards by category:* *Academic interests/achievement:* general academic interests/achievements. *Creative arts/performance:* applied art and design, art/fine arts, creative writing, dance, general creative arts/performance, journalism/publications, performing arts. *Special achievements/activities:* community service, general special achievements/activities, memberships, religious involvement. *Special characteristics:* adult students, children and siblings of alumni, children of current students, children of faculty/staff, ethnic background, first-generation college students, general special characteristics, international students, out-of-state students, parents of current students, siblings of current students, spouses of current students.

LOANS *Programs:* Federal Direct (Subsidized and Unsubsidized Stafford, PLUS), Perkins.

CONTACT Ms. Darla Hopper, Executive Director of Financial Aid, Saint Mary-of-the-Woods College, Rooney Library, 1 St Mary of Woods College, Saint Mary-of-the-Woods, IN 47876, 812-535-5110 or toll-free 800-926-SMWC. *Fax:* 812-535-4900. *E-mail:* dhopper@smwc.edu.
Website: http://www.smwc.edu/.

SAINT MARY'S COLLEGE

Notre Dame, IN

Tuition & fees: $45,720	Average undergraduate aid package: $38,653

ABOUT THE INSTITUTION Independent Roman Catholic, women only. ***Awards:*** bachelor's, master's, and doctoral degrees. 37 undergraduate majors. ***Total enrollment:*** 1,580. Undergraduates: 1,452. Freshmen: 374. Federal methodology is used as a basis for awarding need-based institutional aid.

UNDERGRADUATE EXPENSES for 2020–2021 *One-time required fee:* $150. ***Comprehensive fee:*** $59,190 includes full-time tuition ($44,760), mandatory fees ($960), and room and board ($13,470). ***College room only:*** $8350. Full-time tuition and fees vary according to course load. Room and board charges vary according to board plan and housing facility. ***Part-time tuition:*** $1780 per credit hour.

FRESHMAN FINANCIAL AID (Fall 2019, est.) 340 applied for aid; of those 85% were deemed to have need. 100% of freshmen with need received aid; of those 20% had need fully met. ***Average percent of need met:*** 88% (excluding resources awarded to replace EFC). ***Average financial aid package:*** $38,513 (excluding resources awarded to replace EFC). 22% of all full-time freshmen had no need and received non-need-based gift aid.

UNDERGRADUATE FINANCIAL AID (Fall 2019, est.) 1,188 applied for aid; of those 88% were deemed to have need. 100% of undergraduates with need received aid; of those 19% had need fully met. ***Average percent of need met:*** 88% (excluding resources awarded to replace EFC). ***Average financial aid package:*** $38,653 (excluding resources awarded to replace EFC). 26% of all full-time undergraduates had no need and received non-need-based gift aid.

GIFT AID (NEED-BASED) *Total amount:* $34,861,043 (5% federal, 4% state, 88% institutional, 3% external sources). ***Receiving aid:*** Freshmen: 77% (288); all full-time undergraduates: 72% (1,024). ***Average award:*** Freshmen: $35,310; Undergraduates: $34,049. ***Scholarships, grants, and awards:*** Federal Pell, FSEOG, state, private, college/university gift aid from institutional funds.

GIFT AID (NON-NEED-BASED) *Total amount:* $6,838,859 (95% institutional, 5% external sources). ***Receiving aid:*** Freshmen: 76% (286). Undergraduates: 71% (1,010). ***Average award:*** Freshmen: $21,266. Undergraduates: $18,870. ***Scholarships, grants, and awards by category:*** *Academic interests/achievement:* 1,578 awards ($22,951,555 total): general academic interests/achievements. *Creative arts/performance:* 5 awards ($10,000 total): art/fine arts, music. *Special characteristics:* 81 awards ($819,496 total): children of faculty/staff, siblings of current students, veterans. ***Tuition waivers:*** Full or partial for employees or children of employees. ***ROTC:*** Army cooperative, Naval cooperative, Air Force cooperative.

LOANS *Student loans:* $8,752,850 (87% need-based, 13% non-need-based). 65% of past graduating class borrowed through all loan programs. *Average indebtedness per student:* $34,084. ***Average need-based loan:*** Freshmen: $3330. Undergraduates: $4370. ***Parent loans:*** $3,449,681 (87% need-based, 13% non-need-based). ***Programs:*** Federal Direct (Subsidized and Unsubsidized Stafford, PLUS), Perkins.

WORK-STUDY *Federal work-study:* Total amount: $786,890; 293 jobs averaging $909. ***State or other work-study/employment:*** Total amount: $2000 (100% need-based). 2 part-time jobs averaging $2632.

APPLYING FOR FINANCIAL AID *Required financial aid form:* FAFSA. ***Financial aid deadline:*** 3/1 (priority: 3/1). ***Notification date:*** Continuous beginning 12/15.

CONTACT Kathleen M. Brown, Director of Financial Aid, Saint Mary's College, 141 Le Mans Hall, Notre Dame, IN 46556, 574-284-4557 or toll-free 800-551-7621. *Fax:* 574-284-4818. *E-mail:* kbrown@saintmarys.edu.
Website: http://www.saintmarys.edu/.

SAINT MARY'S COLLEGE OF CALIFORNIA

Moraga, CA

Tuition & fees: $50,660	Average undergraduate aid package: $37,988

ABOUT THE INSTITUTION Independent Roman Catholic, coed. ***Awards:*** certificates, bachelor's, master's, and doctoral degrees. 61 undergraduate majors. ***Total enrollment:*** 3,692. Undergraduates: 2,646. Entering class: 183. Federal methodology is used as a basis for awarding need-based institutional aid.

UNDERGRADUATE EXPENSES for 2020–2021 *Application fee:* $60. ***Comprehensive fee:*** $66,366 includes full-time tuition ($50,460), mandatory fees ($200), and room and board ($15,706). Room and board charges vary according to board plan and housing facility. ***Part-time tuition:*** $6308 per course. ***Part-time fees:*** $200 per term. Part-time tuition and fees vary according to course load and program.

UNDERGRADUATE FINANCIAL AID (Fall 2019, est.) 1,833 applied for aid; of those 98% were deemed to have need. 100% of undergraduates with need received aid. ***Average percent of need met:*** 67% (excluding resources awarded to replace EFC). ***Average financial aid package:*** $37,988 (excluding resources awarded to replace EFC). 22% of all full-time undergraduates had no need and received non-need-based gift aid.

GIFT AID (NEED-BASED) *Receiving aid:* Entering class: 52% (266); all full-time undergraduates: 50% (1,263). ***Average award:*** Freshmen: $17,916; Undergraduates: $16,751. ***Scholarships, grants, and awards:*** Federal Pell, FSEOG, state, private, college/university gift aid from institutional funds.

GIFT AID (NON-NEED-BASED) *Receiving aid:* Freshmen: 85% (438). Undergraduates: 61% (1,542). ***Average award:*** Freshmen: $24,741. Undergraduates: $22,272. ***Scholarships, grants, and awards by category:*** *Academic interests/achievement:* 29 awards ($377,000 total): biological sciences, business, English, mathematics, physical sciences, religion/biblical studies. *Creative arts/performance:* 41

awards ($533,000 total): dance, music, performing arts, theater/drama. *Special achievements/activities:* leadership, memberships. *Special characteristics:* 34 awards ($1,040,874 total): children of faculty/staff, veterans, veterans' children. ***Tuition waivers:*** Full or partial for employees or children of employees. ***ROTC:*** Army cooperative, Air Force cooperative.

LOANS *Student loans:* 85% of past graduating class borrowed through all loan programs. *Average indebtedness per student:* $30,693. ***Average need-based loan:*** Freshmen: $3437. Undergraduates: $4657. ***Programs:*** Federal Direct (Subsidized and Unsubsidized Stafford, PLUS).

WORK-STUDY *Federal work-study:* 214 jobs averaging $2631.

APPLYING FOR FINANCIAL AID *Required financial aid form:* FAFSA. ***Financial aid deadline:*** Continuous. ***Notification date:*** Continuous. Students must reply within 2 weeks of notification.

CONTACT William Mullen, Vice Provost, Saint Mary's College of California, 1928 St. Mary's Road, PMB 4530, Moraga, CA 94575, 925-631-4522 or toll-free 800-800-4SMC. *Fax:* 925-376-2965. *E-mail:* finaid@stmarys-ca.edu.
Website: http://www.stmarys-ca.edu/.

ST. MARY'S COLLEGE OF MARYLAND

St. Mary's City, MD

Tuition & fees: N/R	Average undergraduate aid package: $20,476

ABOUT THE INSTITUTION State-supported, coed. ***Awards:*** bachelor's and master's degrees. 25 undergraduate majors. ***Total enrollment:*** 1,513. Undergraduates: 1,491. Freshmen: 320. Federal methodology is used as a basis for awarding need-based institutional aid.

FRESHMAN FINANCIAL AID (Fall 2018) 331 applied for aid; of those 62% were deemed to have need. 100% of freshmen with need received aid; of those 7% had need fully met. ***Average percent of need met:*** 75% (excluding resources awarded to replace EFC). ***Average financial aid package:*** $19,798 (excluding resources awarded to replace EFC). 38% of all full-time freshmen had no need and received non-need-based gift aid.

UNDERGRADUATE FINANCIAL AID (Fall 2018) 1,145 applied for aid; of those 72% were deemed to have need. 99% of undergraduates with need received aid; of those 4% had need fully met. ***Average percent of need met:*** 68% (excluding resources awarded to replace EFC). ***Average financial aid package:*** $20,476 (excluding resources awarded to replace EFC). 32% of all full-time undergraduates had no need and received non-need-based gift aid.

GIFT AID (NEED-BASED) *Total amount:* $8,845,225 (18% federal, 14% state, 66% institutional, 2% external sources). ***Receiving aid:*** Freshmen: 48% (179); all full-time undergraduates: 47% (708). ***Average award:*** Freshmen: $8827; Undergraduates: $9406. ***Scholarships, grants, and awards:*** Federal Pell, FSEOG, state, private, college/university gift aid from institutional funds.

GIFT AID (NON-NEED-BASED) *Total amount:* $2,099,134 (5% state, 90% institutional, 5% external sources). ***Receiving aid:*** Freshmen: 43% (160). Undergraduates: 36% (540). ***Average award:*** Freshmen: $4903. Undergraduates: $3914. ***Scholarships, grants, and awards by category:*** *Academic interests/achievement:* 1,025 awards ($4,019,536 total): general academic interests/achievements. *Special characteristics:* 56 awards ($447,645 total): children of faculty/staff, children of union members/company employees.

LOANS *Student loans:* $6,197,881 (77% need-based, 23% non-need-based). 52% of past graduating class borrowed through all loan programs. *Average indebtedness per student:* $25,579. ***Average need-based loan:*** Freshmen: $3082. Undergraduates: $4246. ***Parent loans:*** $3,887,630 (74% need-based, 26% non-need-based). ***Programs:*** Federal Direct (Subsidized and Unsubsidized Stafford, PLUS).

WORK-STUDY *Federal work-study:* Total amount: $48,882; 101 jobs averaging $934. ***State or other work-study/employment:*** Total amount: $46,279 (100% need-based). Part-time jobs available.

APPLYING FOR FINANCIAL AID *Required financial aid form:* FAFSA. ***Financial aid deadline (priority):*** 2/28. ***Notification date:*** Continuous beginning 12/15. Students must reply by 5/1.

CONTACT Mr. Robert W Maddox, Director of Financial Aid, St. Mary's College of Maryland, 18952 East Fisher Road, St. Mary's City, MD 20686-3001, 240-895-3000 or toll-free 800-492-7181. *Fax:* 240-895-4959. *E-mail:* finaid@smcm.edu.
Website: http://www.smcm.edu/.

ST. MARY'S UNIVERSITY

San Antonio, TX

Tuition & fees: $34,740	Average undergraduate aid package: $27,480

ABOUT THE INSTITUTION Independent Roman Catholic, coed. ***Awards:*** certificates, bachelor's, master's, and doctoral degrees. 41 undergraduate majors. ***Total enrollment:*** 3,514. Undergraduates: 2,270. Freshmen: 545. Federal methodology is used as a basis for awarding need-based institutional aid.

UNDERGRADUATE EXPENSES for 2020–2021 *Comprehensive fee:* $45,720 includes full-time tuition ($33,720), mandatory fees ($1020), and room and board ($10,980). ***College room only:*** $7000. Full-time tuition and fees vary according to course load, degree level, program, reciprocity agreements, and student level. Room and board charges vary according to board plan, housing facility, and student level. ***Part-time tuition:*** $1010 per credit hour. ***Part-time fees:*** $510 per term. Part-time tuition and fees vary according to course load, degree level, program, reciprocity agreements, and student level.

FRESHMAN FINANCIAL AID (Fall 2019, est.) 490 applied for aid; of those 91% were deemed to have need. 100% of freshmen with need received aid; of those 15% had need fully met. ***Average percent of need met:*** 77% (excluding resources awarded to replace EFC). ***Average financial aid package:*** $28,580 (excluding resources awarded to replace EFC). 18% of all full-time freshmen had no need and received non-need-based gift aid.

UNDERGRADUATE FINANCIAL AID (Fall 2019, est.) 1,726 applied for aid; of those 93% were deemed to have need. 100% of undergraduates with need received aid; of those 15% had need fully met. ***Average percent of need met:*** 73% (excluding resources awarded to replace EFC). ***Average financial aid package:*** $27,480 (excluding resources awarded to replace EFC). 21% of all full-time undergraduates had no need and received non-need-based gift aid.

GIFT AID (NEED-BASED) *Total amount:* $35,373,211 (14% federal, 11% state, 73% institutional, 2% external sources). ***Receiving aid:*** Freshmen: 81% (439); all full-time undergraduates: 72% (1,566). ***Average award:*** Freshmen: $23,031; Undergraduates: $22,267. ***Scholarships, grants, and awards:*** Federal Pell, FSEOG, state, private, college/university gift aid from institutional funds.

GIFT AID (NON-NEED-BASED) *Total amount:* $10,125,778 (98% institutional, 2% external sources). ***Receiving aid:*** Freshmen: 10% (52). Undergraduates: 7% (159). ***Average award:*** Freshmen: $19,969. Undergraduates: $19,613. ***Scholarships, grants, and awards by category:*** *Academic interests/achievement:* general academic interests/achievements, military science. *Creative arts/performance:* music. *Special achievements/activities:* cheerleading/drum major. *Special characteristics:* children of faculty/staff, veterans. ***ROTC:*** Army, Air Force cooperative.

LOANS *Student loans:* $14,018,275 (76% need-based, 24% non-need-based). 69% of past graduating class borrowed through all loan programs. *Average indebtedness per student:* $34,187. ***Average need-based loan:*** Freshmen: $3413. Undergraduates: $4374. ***Parent loans:*** $2,734,610 (58% need-based, 42% non-need-based). ***Programs:*** Federal Direct (Subsidized and Unsubsidized Stafford, PLUS), state.

WORK-STUDY *Federal work-study:* Total amount: $1,175,889; jobs available. ***State or other work-study/employment:*** Total amount: $129,020 (78% need-based, 22% non-need-based). Part-time jobs available.

ATHLETIC AWARDS Total amount: $2,900,097 (30% need-based, 70% non-need-based).

APPLYING FOR FINANCIAL AID *Required financial aid forms:* FAFSA, state aid form. ***Financial aid deadline:*** 5/1 (priority: 3/1). ***Notification date:*** Continuous beginning 12/1.

CONTACT Mrs. Marivel Ojeda, Director of Financial Assistance, St. Mary's University, One Camino Santa Maria, San Antonio, TX 78228-8541, 210-436-3141 or toll-free 800-367-7868. *Fax:* 210-431-2221. *E-mail:* finaid@stmarytx.edu.
Website: http://www.stmarytx.edu/.

SAINT MARY'S UNIVERSITY OF MINNESOTA

Winona, MN

ABOUT THE INSTITUTION Independent Roman Catholic, coed. ***Awards:*** certificates, bachelor's, master's, and doctoral degrees. 52 undergraduate majors. ***Total enrollment:*** 5,548. Undergraduates: 1,467. Freshmen: 301.

GIFT AID (NEED-BASED) ***Scholarships, grants, and awards:*** Federal Pell, FSEOG, state, college/university gift aid from institutional funds.
GIFT AID (NON-NEED-BASED) ***Scholarships, grants, and awards by category:*** *Academic interests/achievement:* general academic interests/achievements. *Creative arts/performance:* applied art and design, music, theater/drama. *Special achievements/activities:* leadership. *Special characteristics:* children and siblings of alumni, children of faculty/staff, ethnic background, international students, local/state students, members of minority groups.
LOANS ***Programs:*** Federal Direct (Subsidized and Unsubsidized Stafford, PLUS), Perkins, state.
WORK-STUDY ***Federal work-study:*** Total amount: $383,764; jobs available. ***State or other work-study/employment:*** Total amount: $594,050 (100% need-based). Part-time jobs available.
APPLYING FOR FINANCIAL AID ***Required financial aid form:*** FAFSA.
CONTACT Ms. Joy Rockwell, Associate Director of Financial Aid, Saint Mary's University of Minnesota, 700 Terrace Heights #5, Winona, MN 55987-1399, 507-457-1472 or toll-free 800-635-5987. *Fax:* 507-457-6698. *E-mail:* jrockwel@smumn.edu. *Website:* http://www.smumn.edu/.

SAINT MICHAEL'S COLLEGE

Colchester, VT

ABOUT THE INSTITUTION Independent Roman Catholic, coed. ***Awards:*** certificates, bachelor's, and master's degrees. 35 undergraduate majors.
GIFT AID (NEED-BASED) ***Scholarships, grants, and awards:*** Federal Pell, FSEOG, state, private, college/university gift aid from institutional funds.
GIFT AID (NON-NEED-BASED) ***Scholarships, grants, and awards by category:*** *Academic interests/achievement:* general academic interests/achievements. *Creative arts/performance:* applied art and design, performing arts, theater/drama. *Special characteristics:* members of minority groups, out-of-state students, siblings of current students, veterans.
LOANS ***Programs:*** Federal Direct (Subsidized and Unsubsidized Stafford, PLUS).
WORK-STUDY ***Federal work-study:*** Total amount: $479,844; jobs available. ***State or other work-study/employment:*** Total amount: $479,654 (78% need-based, 22% non-need-based). Part-time jobs available.
APPLYING FOR FINANCIAL AID ***Required financial aid form:*** FAFSA.
CONTACT Mr. Matthew DeSorgher, Director of Student Financial Services, Saint Michael's College, One Winooski Park, Colchester, VT 05439, 802-654-3243 or toll-free 800-762-8000. *Fax:* 802-654-2591. *E-mail:* finaid@smcvt.edu. *Website:* http://www.smcvt.edu/.

ST. NORBERT COLLEGE

De Pere, WI

Tuition & fees: $40,885	Average undergraduate aid package: $27,009

ABOUT THE INSTITUTION Independent Roman Catholic, coed. ***Awards:*** certificates, bachelor's, and master's degrees. 35 undergraduate majors. ***Total enrollment:*** 2,081. Undergraduates: 2,000. Freshmen: 538. Federal methodology is used as a basis for awarding need-based institutional aid.
UNDERGRADUATE EXPENSES for 2020–2021 ***Comprehensive fee:*** $51,770 includes full-time tuition ($40,070), mandatory fees ($815), and room and board ($10,885). ***College room only:*** $6046. Full-time tuition and fees vary according to course load. Room and board charges vary according to board plan and housing facility. ***Part-time tuition:*** $1252 per credit hour. Part-time tuition and fees vary according to course load.
FRESHMAN FINANCIAL AID (Fall 2018) 567 applied for aid; of those 83% were deemed to have need. 100% of freshmen with need received aid; of those 32% had need fully met. ***Average percent of need met:*** 81% (excluding resources awarded to replace EFC). ***Average financial aid package:*** $28,147 (excluding resources awarded to replace EFC). 20% of all full-time freshmen had no need and received non-need-based gift aid.
UNDERGRADUATE FINANCIAL AID (Fall 2018) 1,725 applied for aid; of those 88% were deemed to have need. 100% of undergraduates with need received aid; of those 30% had need fully met. ***Average percent of need met:*** 79% (excluding resources awarded to replace EFC). ***Average financial aid package:*** $27,009 (excluding resources awarded to replace EFC). 25% of all full-time undergraduates had no need and received non-need-based gift aid.
GIFT AID (NEED-BASED) ***Total amount:*** $33,203,622 (6% federal, 7% state, 82% institutional, 5% external sources). ***Receiving aid:*** Freshmen: 74% (460); all full-time undergraduates: 70% (1,466). ***Average award:*** Freshmen: $23,945; Undergraduates: $21,549. ***Scholarships, grants, and awards:*** Federal Pell, FSEOG, state, private, college/university gift aid from institutional funds.
GIFT AID (NON-NEED-BASED) ***Total amount:*** $8,618,219 (91% institutional, 9% external sources). ***Receiving aid:*** Freshmen: 2% (15). Undergraduates: 2% (50). ***Average award:*** Freshmen: $16,951. Undergraduates: $14,932. ***Scholarships, grants, and awards by category:*** *Academic interests/achievement:* general academic interests/achievements. *Creative arts/performance:* applied art and design, music, theater/drama. *Special characteristics:* children of faculty/staff, international students. ***Tuition waivers:*** Full or partial for employees or children of employees. ***ROTC:*** Army.
LOANS ***Student loans:*** $18,616,888 (97% need-based, 3% non-need-based). 77% of past graduating class borrowed through all loan programs. *Average indebtedness per student:* $40,265. ***Average need-based loan:*** Freshmen: $3334. Undergraduates: $4379. ***Parent loans:*** $4,625,971 (95% need-based, 5% non-need-based). ***Programs:*** Federal Direct (Subsidized and Unsubsidized Stafford, PLUS), Perkins, state, college/university.
WORK-STUDY ***Federal work-study:*** Total amount: $1,191,991; jobs available. ***State or other work-study/employment:*** Total amount: $889,850 (66% need-based, 34% non-need-based). Part-time jobs available.
APPLYING FOR FINANCIAL AID ***Required financial aid form:*** FAFSA. ***Financial aid deadline (priority):*** 1/1. ***Notification date:*** Continuous beginning 1/1.
CONTACT Ms. Jessica Rafeld, Director of Financial Aid, St. Norbert College, 100 Grant Street, De Pere, WI 54115-2099, 920-403-3071 or toll-free 800-236-4878. *Fax:* 920-403-3062. *E-mail:* financialaid@snc.edu. *Website:* http://www.snc.edu/.

ST. OLAF COLLEGE

Northfield, MN

Tuition & fees: $51,450	Average undergraduate aid package: $44,181

ABOUT THE INSTITUTION Independent Lutheran, coed. ***Awards:*** bachelor's degrees. 47 undergraduate majors. ***Total enrollment:*** 3,072. Undergraduates: 3,072. Freshmen: 806. Both federal and institutional methodology are used as a basis for awarding need-based institutional aid.
UNDERGRADUATE EXPENSES for 2020–2021 ***Comprehensive fee:*** $63,110 includes full-time tuition ($51,450) and room and board ($11,660). ***College room only:*** $5590. Room and board charges vary according to board plan. ***Part-time tuition:*** $1610 per credit hour. Part-time tuition and fees vary according to course load.
FRESHMAN FINANCIAL AID (Fall 2019, est.) 726 applied for aid; of those 87% were deemed to have need. 100% of freshmen with need received aid; of those 100% had need fully met. ***Average percent of need met:*** 100% (excluding resources awarded to replace EFC). ***Average financial aid package:*** $45,655 (excluding resources awarded to replace EFC). 20% of all full-time freshmen had no need and received non-need-based gift aid.
UNDERGRADUATE FINANCIAL AID (Fall 2019, est.) 2,472 applied for aid; of those 94% were deemed to have need. 100% of undergraduates with need received aid; of those 80% had need fully met. ***Average percent of need met:*** 96% (excluding resources awarded to replace EFC). ***Average financial aid package:*** $44,181 (excluding resources awarded to replace EFC). 20% of all full-time undergraduates had no need and received non-need-based gift aid.
GIFT AID (NEED-BASED) ***Receiving aid:*** Freshmen: 79% (634); all full-time undergraduates: 77% (2,323). ***Average award:*** Freshmen: $39,727; Undergraduates: $37,646. ***Scholarships, grants, and awards:*** Federal Pell, FSEOG, state, private, college/university gift aid from institutional funds.
GIFT AID (NON-NEED-BASED) ***Receiving aid:*** Freshmen: 28% (226). Undergraduates: 20% (615). ***Average award:*** Freshmen: $18,188. Undergraduates: $17,508. ***Scholarships, grants, and awards by category:*** *Academic interests/achievement:* 482 awards ($8,199,940 total): general academic interests/achievements.

Creative arts/performance: 142 awards ($905,965 total): applied art and design, dance, music, theater/drama. *Special achievements/activities:* 138 awards ($871,000 total): community service, leadership, religious involvement. ***Tuition waivers:*** Full or partial for employees or children of employees, senior citizens.

LOANS *Student loans:* 60% of past graduating class borrowed through all loan programs. *Average indebtedness per student:* $28,950. ***Average need-based loan:*** Freshmen: $3202. Undergraduates: $4298. ***Programs:*** Federal Direct (Subsidized and Unsubsidized Stafford, PLUS), Federal Nursing, state, college/university.

WORK-STUDY *Federal work-study:* 428 jobs averaging $2594. ***State or other work-study/employment:*** 1,953 part-time jobs averaging $2371.

APPLYING FOR FINANCIAL AID *Required financial aid forms:* FAFSA, CSS Financial Aid PROFILE, noncustodial (divorced/separated) parent's statement.

CONTACT Ms. Carly Eichhorst, Director of Student Financial Aid, St. Olaf College, 1520 Saint Olaf Avenue, Northfield, MN 55057-1098, 507-786-3019 or toll-free 800-800-3025. *Fax:* 507-786-6688. *E-mail:* finaid@stolaf.edu.
Website: http://www.stolaf.edu/.

ST. PETERSBURG COLLEGE

St. Petersburg, FL

Tuition & fees: N/R	Average undergraduate aid package: $7402

ABOUT THE INSTITUTION State and locally supported, coed. ***Awards:*** certificates, diplomas, associate, and bachelor's degrees. 48 undergraduate majors. ***Total enrollment:*** 28,853. Undergraduates: 28,853. Freshmen: 2,805. Federal methodology is used as a basis for awarding need-based institutional aid.

FRESHMAN FINANCIAL AID (Fall 2018) 1491 applied for aid; of those 92% were deemed to have need. 100% of freshmen with need received aid; of those 3% had need fully met. ***Average percent of need met:*** 48% (excluding resources awarded to replace EFC). ***Average financial aid package:*** $7515 (excluding resources awarded to replace EFC). 1% of all full-time freshmen had no need and received non-need-based gift aid.

UNDERGRADUATE FINANCIAL AID (Fall 2018) 5,304 applied for aid; of those 93% were deemed to have need. 100% of undergraduates with need received aid; of those 3% had need fully met. ***Average percent of need met:*** 49% (excluding resources awarded to replace EFC). ***Average financial aid package:*** $7402 (excluding resources awarded to replace EFC). 1% of all full-time undergraduates had no need and received non-need-based gift aid.

GIFT AID (NEED-BASED) *Total amount:* $57,430,281 (72% federal, 19% state, 7% institutional, 2% external sources). ***Receiving aid:*** Freshmen: 81% (1,297); all full-time undergraduates: 82% (4,607). ***Average award:*** Freshmen: $6504; Undergraduates: $5989. ***Scholarships, grants, and awards:*** Federal Pell, FSEOG, state, private, college/university gift aid from institutional funds.

GIFT AID (NON-NEED-BASED) *Total amount:* $887,485 (1% federal, 38% state, 36% institutional, 25% external sources). ***Receiving aid:*** Freshmen: 2% (35). Undergraduates: 2% (87). ***Average award:*** Freshmen: $1767. Undergraduates: $1659. ***ROTC:*** Army cooperative.

LOANS *Student loans:* $45,199,930 (78% need-based, 22% non-need-based). 59% of past graduating class borrowed through all loan programs. *Average indebtedness per student:* $29,008. ***Average need-based loan:*** Freshmen: $3038. Undergraduates: $3240. ***Parent loans:*** $71,271 (41% need-based, 59% non-need-based). ***Programs:*** Federal Direct (Subsidized and Unsubsidized Stafford, PLUS).

WORK-STUDY *Federal work-study:* Total amount: $610,167; jobs available.

ATHLETIC AWARDS Total amount: $575,320 (87% need-based, 13% non-need-based).

APPLYING FOR FINANCIAL AID *Required financial aid form:* FAFSA. ***Financial aid deadline:*** Continuous. ***Notification date:*** Students must reply by 8/17.

CONTACT Office of Financial Aid, St. Petersburg College, 6605 Fifth Avenue N, St. Petersburg, FL 33710, 727-341-7907.
Website: http://www.spcollege.edu/.

SAINT PETER'S UNIVERSITY

Jersey City, NJ

Tuition & fees: N/R	Average undergraduate aid package: $35,749

ABOUT THE INSTITUTION Independent Roman Catholic (Jesuit), coed. ***Awards:*** certificates, associate, bachelor's, master's, and doctoral degrees. 45 undergraduate majors. Federal methodology is used as a basis for awarding need-based institutional aid.

FRESHMAN FINANCIAL AID (Fall 2019, est.) 423 applied for aid; of those 89% were deemed to have need. 100% of freshmen with need received aid; of those 20% had need fully met. ***Average percent of need met:*** 85% (excluding resources awarded to replace EFC). ***Average financial aid package:*** $35,047 (excluding resources awarded to replace EFC). 10% of all full-time freshmen had no need and received non-need-based gift aid.

UNDERGRADUATE FINANCIAL AID (Fall 2019, est.) 2,091 applied for aid; of those 89% were deemed to have need. 100% of undergraduates with need received aid; of those 26% had need fully met. ***Average percent of need met:*** 87% (excluding resources awarded to replace EFC). ***Average financial aid package:*** $35,749 (excluding resources awarded to replace EFC). 10% of all full-time undergraduates had no need and received non-need-based gift aid.

GIFT AID (NEED-BASED) *Total amount:* $59,427,062 (14% federal, 25% state, 61% institutional). ***Receiving aid:*** Freshmen: 89% (376); all full-time undergraduates: 89% (1,866). ***Average award:*** Freshmen: $32,559; Undergraduates: $32,474. ***Scholarships, grants, and awards:*** Federal Pell, FSEOG, state, private, college/university gift aid from institutional funds.

GIFT AID (NON-NEED-BASED) *Total amount:* $6,341,724 (5% state, 95% institutional). ***Receiving aid:*** Freshmen: 7% (30). Undergraduates: 7% (138). ***Average award:*** Freshmen: $23,132. Undergraduates: $23,410. ***Scholarships, grants, and awards by category:*** *Academic interests/achievement:* general academic interests/achievements. *Special achievements/activities:* leadership. *Special characteristics:* children of faculty/staff, general special characteristics, relatives of clergy, religious affiliation. ***ROTC:*** Army cooperative.

LOANS *Student loans:* $8,138,525 (80% need-based, 20% non-need-based). 74% of past graduating class borrowed through all loan programs. *Average indebtedness per student:* $25,572. ***Average need-based loan:*** Freshmen: $3134. Undergraduates: $4059. ***Parent loans:*** $4,051,461 (51% need-based, 49% non-need-based). ***Programs:*** Federal Direct (Subsidized and Unsubsidized Stafford, PLUS), state.

WORK-STUDY *Federal work-study:* Total amount: $714,578; jobs available.

ATHLETIC AWARDS Total amount: $3,020,537 (51% need-based, 49% non-need-based).

APPLYING FOR FINANCIAL AID *Required financial aid form:* FAFSA. ***Financial aid deadline:*** Continuous. ***Notification date:*** Continuous beginning 12/1.

CONTACT Jennifer Ragsdale, Acting Director of Financial Aid, Saint Peter's University, 2641 Kennedy Boulevard, Jersey City, NJ 07306, 201-761-6071 or toll-free 888-SPC-9933. *Fax:* 201-761-6073. *E-mail:* jragsdale@spc.edu.
Website: http://www.saintpeters.edu/.

ST. THOMAS AQUINAS COLLEGE

Sparkill, NY

Tuition & fees: $33,050	Average undergraduate aid package: $18,500

ABOUT THE INSTITUTION Independent, coed. ***Awards:*** certificates, associate, bachelor's, and master's degrees. 32 undergraduate majors. ***Total enrollment:*** 1,937. Undergraduates: 1,797. Freshmen: 243. Federal methodology is used as a basis for awarding need-based institutional aid.

UNDERGRADUATE EXPENSES for 2019–2020 *Application fee:* $30. ***Comprehensive fee:*** $46,700 includes full-time tuition ($32,250), mandatory fees ($800), and room and board ($13,650). ***College room only:*** $7370. Room and board charges vary according to board plan. ***Part-time tuition:*** $1025 per credit hour. ***Part-time fees:*** $200 per term.

FRESHMAN FINANCIAL AID (Fall 2019, est.) 225 applied for aid; of those 80% were deemed to have need. 100% of freshmen with need received aid; of those 24%

had need fully met. ***Average percent of need met:*** 40% (excluding resources awarded to replace EFC). ***Average financial aid package:*** $17,250 (excluding resources awarded to replace EFC). 20% of all full-time freshmen had no need and received non-need-based gift aid.

UNDERGRADUATE FINANCIAL AID (Fall 2019, est.) 1,029 applied for aid; of those 77% were deemed to have need. 100% of undergraduates with need received aid; of those 19% had need fully met. ***Average percent of need met:*** 40% (excluding resources awarded to replace EFC). ***Average financial aid package:*** $18,500 (excluding resources awarded to replace EFC). 22% of all full-time undergraduates had no need and received non-need-based gift aid.

GIFT AID (NEED-BASED) ***Receiving aid:*** Freshmen: 70% (170); all full-time undergraduates: 71% (789). ***Average award:*** Freshmen: $12,000; Undergraduates: $11,500. ***Scholarships, grants, and awards:*** Federal Pell, FSEOG, state, private, college/university gift aid from institutional funds.

GIFT AID (NON-NEED-BASED) ***Receiving aid:*** Freshmen: 73% (178). Undergraduates: 70% (782). ***Average award:*** Freshmen: $18,900. Undergraduates: $15,800. ***Scholarships, grants, and awards by category:*** *Academic interests/achievement:* business, communication, computer science, education, engineering/technologies, English, foreign languages, general academic interests/achievements, humanities, mathematics, religion/biblical studies, social sciences. *Creative arts/performance:* creative writing. *Special achievements/activities:* community service, leadership. *Special characteristics:* siblings of current students, spouses of current students, twins, veterans.

LOANS ***Student loans:*** 70% of past graduating class borrowed through all loan programs. *Average indebtedness per student:* $31,000. ***Average need-based loan:*** Freshmen: $3500. Undergraduates: $6800. ***Programs:*** Federal Direct (Subsidized and Unsubsidized Stafford, PLUS), Perkins, state, alternative loans.

WORK-STUDY ***Federal work-study:*** 112 jobs averaging $1331.

APPLYING FOR FINANCIAL AID ***Required financial aid forms:*** FAFSA, state aid form. ***Notification date:*** Continuous. Students must reply within 4 weeks of notification.

CONTACT Mrs. Cindy Garvey, Associate Director of Financial Aid, St. Thomas Aquinas College, 125 Route 340, Sparkill, NY 10976, 845-398-4098. *Fax:* 845-398-4114. *E-mail:* cgarvey@stac.edu.
Website: http://www.stac.edu/.

ST. THOMAS UNIVERSITY - FLORIDA

Miami Gardens, FL

CONTACT Ms. Yamirka Rial, Director of Financial Aid, St. Thomas University - Florida, 16401 Northwest 37th Avenue, Miami Gardens, FL 33054, 305-474-6965 or toll-free 800-367-9010. *Fax:* 305-474-6930. *E-mail:* yrial@stu.edu.
Website: http://www.stu.edu/.

SAINT VINCENT COLLEGE

Latrobe, PA

Tuition & fees: $36,904	Average undergraduate aid package: $32,749

ABOUT THE INSTITUTION Independent Roman Catholic, coed. ***Awards:*** certificates, bachelor's, master's, and doctoral degrees. 49 undergraduate majors. ***Total enrollment:*** 1,739. Undergraduates: 1,560. Freshmen: 359. Federal methodology is used as a basis for awarding need-based institutional aid.

UNDERGRADUATE EXPENSES for 2019–2020 ***Application fee:*** $25. ***Comprehensive fee:*** $49,065 includes full-time tuition ($35,520), mandatory fees ($1384), and room and board ($12,161). Full-time tuition and fees vary according to course load and degree level. Room and board charges vary according to board plan and housing facility. ***Part-time tuition:*** $1112 per credit hour. ***Part-time fees:*** $100 per term. Part-time tuition and fees vary according to course load and degree level.

FRESHMAN FINANCIAL AID (Fall 2019, est.) 343 applied for aid; of those 89% were deemed to have need. 100% of freshmen with need received aid; of those 29% had need fully met. ***Average percent of need met:*** 86% (excluding resources awarded to replace EFC). ***Average financial aid package:*** $34,531 (excluding resources awarded to replace EFC). 15% of all full-time freshmen had no need and received non-need-based gift aid.

UNDERGRADUATE FINANCIAL AID (Fall 2019, est.) 1,283 applied for aid; of those 91% were deemed to have need. 100% of undergraduates with need received aid; of those 27% had need fully met. ***Average percent of need met:*** 82% (excluding resources awarded to replace EFC). ***Average financial aid package:*** $32,749 (excluding resources awarded to replace EFC). 20% of all full-time undergraduates had no need and received non-need-based gift aid.

GIFT AID (NEED-BASED) ***Receiving aid:*** Freshmen: 57% (205); all full-time undergraduates: 55% (821). ***Average award:*** Freshmen: $6341; Undergraduates: $6620. ***Scholarships, grants, and awards:*** Federal Pell, FSEOG, state, private, college/university gift aid from institutional funds, United Negro College Fund.

GIFT AID (NON-NEED-BASED) ***Receiving aid:*** Freshmen: 85% (305). Undergraduates: 76% (1,123). ***Average award:*** Freshmen: $20,173. Undergraduates: $20,426. ***Scholarships, grants, and awards by category:*** *Academic interests/achievement:* biological sciences, business, communication, computer science, education, engineering/technologies, English, foreign languages, general academic interests/achievements, home economics, humanities, international studies, mathematics, physical sciences, religion/biblical studies, social sciences. *Special characteristics:* children of faculty/staff, first-generation college students, general special characteristics, out-of-state students, previous college experience, religious affiliation, siblings of current students, veterans. ***Tuition waivers:*** Full or partial for employees or children of employees. ***ROTC:*** Army cooperative, Air Force cooperative.

LOANS ***Student loans:*** 80% of past graduating class borrowed through all loan programs. *Average indebtedness per student:* $36,745. ***Average need-based loan:*** Freshmen: $3414. Undergraduates: $4417. ***Programs:*** Federal Direct (Subsidized and Unsubsidized Stafford, PLUS), private loans.

WORK-STUDY Federal work-study jobs available. ***State or other work-study/employment:*** Part-time jobs available.

APPLYING FOR FINANCIAL AID ***Required financial aid form:*** FAFSA. ***Financial aid deadline:*** Continuous. ***Notification date:*** Continuous.

CONTACT Mrs. Mary Gazal, Director of Financial Aid, Saint Vincent College, 300 Fraser Purchase Road, Latrobe, PA 15650, 724-805-2555 or toll-free 800-782-5549. *Fax:* 724-805-2953. *E-mail:* financialaid@stvincent.edu.
Website: http://www.stvincent.edu/.

SAINT XAVIER UNIVERSITY

Chicago, IL

CONTACT Ms. Susan Swisher, Director of Financial Aid, Saint Xavier University, 3700 West 103rd Street, Chicago, IL 60655-3105, 773-298-3073 or toll-free 800-462-9288. *Fax:* 773-298-3033. *E-mail:* swisher@sxu.edu.
Website: http://www.sxu.edu/.

SALEM COLLEGE

Winston-Salem, NC

Tuition & fees: N/R	Average undergraduate aid package: N/A

ABOUT THE INSTITUTION Independent Moravian, coed, primarily women. ***Awards:*** certificates, bachelor's, and master's degrees (only students age 23 or over are eligible to enroll part-time). 30 undergraduate majors. Federal methodology is used as a basis for awarding need-based institutional aid.

FRESHMAN FINANCIAL AID (Fall 2018) 95 applied for aid; of those 95% were deemed to have need. 100% of freshmen with need received aid.

UNDERGRADUATE FINANCIAL AID (Fall 2018) 499 applied for aid; of those 97% were deemed to have need. 100% of undergraduates with need received aid.

GIFT AID (NEED-BASED) ***Total amount:*** $1,017,208 (26% federal, 28% state, 46% institutional). ***Receiving aid:*** Freshmen: 86% (85); all full-time undergraduates: 74% (416). ***Scholarships, grants, and awards:*** Federal Pell, FSEOG, state, private, college/university gift aid from institutional funds.

GIFT AID (NON-NEED-BASED) ***Total amount:*** $1,701,866 (95% institutional, 5% external sources). ***Receiving aid:*** Freshmen: 85% (84). Undergraduates: 66% (371). ***Scholarships, grants, and awards by category:*** *Academic interests/achievement:* general academic interests/achievements. *Creative arts/performance:*

applied art and design, music. *Special achievements/activities:* leadership. *Special characteristics:* children of faculty/staff. ***ROTC:*** Army cooperative, Air Force cooperative.
LOANS *Student loans:* $446,702 (50% need-based, 50% non-need-based). 71% of past graduating class borrowed through all loan programs. ***Parent loans:*** $67,763 (100% non-need-based). ***Programs:*** Federal Direct (Subsidized and Unsubsidized Stafford, PLUS).
WORK-STUDY *Federal work-study:* Total amount: $24,399; 103 jobs averaging $1120. ***State or other work-study/employment:*** Total amount: $35,200 (100% non-need-based). 136 part-time jobs averaging $1453.
APPLYING FOR FINANCIAL AID *Required financial aid forms:* FAFSA, state aid form. ***Financial aid deadline:*** Continuous. ***Notification date:*** Continuous beginning 12/15. Students must reply by 5/1 or within 2 weeks of notification.
CONTACT Paul J. Coscia, Assistant Vice President for Financial Aid, Salem College, 601 South Church Street, Winston-Salem, NC 27101, 336-721-2808 or toll-free 800-327-2536. *Fax:* 336-917-5584. *E-mail:* paul.coscia@salem.edu.
Website: http://www.salem.edu/.

SALEM INTERNATIONAL UNIVERSITY

Salem, WV

CONTACT Donald Ronan, Director of Financial Aid and Compliance , Salem International University, 615 West Carmel Drive, Suite 140, Carmel, IN 46032, 317-805-1793 or toll-free 888-235-5024. *Fax:* 317-573-8997. *E-mail:* dronan@salemu.edu.
Website: http://www.salemu.edu/.

SALEM STATE UNIVERSITY

Salem, MA

Tuition & fees: N/R	Average undergraduate aid package: $10,189

ABOUT THE INSTITUTION State-supported, coed. ***Awards:*** certificates, bachelor's, and master's degrees. 74 undergraduate majors. ***Total enrollment:*** 7,706. Undergraduates: 6,273. Freshmen: 1,011.
FRESHMAN FINANCIAL AID (Fall 2018) 1036 applied for aid; of those 87% were deemed to have need. 99% of freshmen with need received aid; of those 6% had need fully met. ***Average percent of need met:*** 56% (excluding resources awarded to replace EFC). ***Average financial aid package:*** $11,032 (excluding resources awarded to replace EFC). 4% of all full-time freshmen had no need and received non-need-based gift aid.
UNDERGRADUATE FINANCIAL AID (Fall 2018) 4,580 applied for aid; of those 85% were deemed to have need. 98% of undergraduates with need received aid; of those 8% had need fully met. ***Average percent of need met:*** 58% (excluding resources awarded to replace EFC). ***Average financial aid package:*** $10,189 (excluding resources awarded to replace EFC). 4% of all full-time undergraduates had no need and received non-need-based gift aid.
GIFT AID (NEED-BASED) *Total amount:* $19,711,171 (63% federal, 23% state, 14% institutional). ***Receiving aid:*** Freshmen: 77% (848); all full-time undergraduates: 54% (2,945). ***Average award:*** Freshmen: $7175; Undergraduates: $6297. ***Scholarships, grants, and awards:*** Federal Pell, FSEOG, state, private, college/university gift aid from institutional funds.
GIFT AID (NON-NEED-BASED) *Total amount:* $6,604,655 (31% state, 51% institutional, 18% external sources). ***Receiving aid:*** Freshmen: 35% (379). Undergraduates: 27% (1,456). ***Average award:*** Freshmen: $2211. Undergraduates: $1771. ***Scholarships, grants, and awards by category:*** *Academic interests/achievement:* general academic interests/achievements. *Creative arts/performance:* applied art and design, art/fine arts, creative writing, dance, music, performing arts, theater/drama. *Special achievements/activities:* general special achievements/activities, memberships. *Special characteristics:* adult students, children and siblings of alumni, children of faculty/staff, children of public servants, children of union members/company employees, first-generation college students, general special characteristics, members of minority groups, public servants, veterans, veterans' children. ***ROTC:*** Army cooperative, Air Force cooperative.
LOANS *Student loans:* $30,267,513 (52% need-based, 48% non-need-based). 82% of past graduating class borrowed through all loan programs. *Average indebtedness per student:* $26,204. ***Average need-based loan:*** Freshmen: $3280. Undergraduates: $4323. ***Parent loans:*** $5,997,647 (100% non-need-based). ***Programs:*** Federal Direct (Subsidized and Unsubsidized Stafford, PLUS), Federal Nursing, state.
WORK-STUDY *Federal work-study:* Total amount: $380,474; jobs available.
APPLYING FOR FINANCIAL AID *Required financial aid form:* FAFSA. ***Financial aid deadline (priority):*** 2/15. ***Notification date:*** Continuous.
CONTACT Mary Benda, Director of Financial Aid, Salem State University, 352 Lafayette Street, Salem, MA 01970-5353, 978-542-6139. *Fax:* 978-542-6876.
Website: http://www.salemstate.edu/.

SALISBURY UNIVERSITY

Salisbury, MD

Tuition & fees (MD res): $10,044	Average undergraduate aid package: $8767

ABOUT THE INSTITUTION State-supported, coed. ***Awards:*** certificates, bachelor's, master's, and doctoral degrees. 49 undergraduate majors. ***Total enrollment:*** 8,617. Undergraduates: 7,686. Freshmen: 1,470. Federal methodology is used as a basis for awarding need-based institutional aid.
UNDERGRADUATE EXPENSES for 2019–2020 *Application fee:* $50. ***Tuition, state resident:*** full-time $7264; part-time $297 per credit hour. ***Tuition, nonresident:*** full-time $17,330; part-time $716 per credit hour. ***Required fees:*** full-time $2780; $108 per credit hour. Full-time tuition and fees vary according to location. Part-time tuition and fees vary according to location. ***College room and board:*** $12,360; ***Room only:*** $7160. Room and board charges vary according to board plan and housing facility.
FRESHMAN FINANCIAL AID (Fall 2018) 1154 applied for aid; of those 64% were deemed to have need. 97% of freshmen with need received aid; of those 12% had need fully met. ***Average percent of need met:*** 56% (excluding resources awarded to replace EFC). ***Average financial aid package:*** $9179 (excluding resources awarded to replace EFC). 28% of all full-time freshmen had no need and received non-need-based gift aid.
UNDERGRADUATE FINANCIAL AID (Fall 2018) 5,384 applied for aid; of those 72% were deemed to have need. 97% of undergraduates with need received aid; of those 10% had need fully met. ***Average percent of need met:*** 53% (excluding resources awarded to replace EFC). ***Average financial aid package:*** $8767 (excluding resources awarded to replace EFC). 20% of all full-time undergraduates had no need and received non-need-based gift aid.
GIFT AID (NEED-BASED) *Total amount:* $21,675,740 (39% federal, 22% state, 30% institutional, 9% external sources). ***Receiving aid:*** Freshmen: 48% (623); all full-time undergraduates: 43% (3,012). ***Average award:*** Freshmen: $8029; Undergraduates: $7098. ***Scholarships, grants, and awards:*** Federal Pell, FSEOG, state, private, college/university gift aid from institutional funds.
GIFT AID (NON-NEED-BASED) *Total amount:* $4,774,572 (7% state, 78% institutional, 15% external sources). ***Average award:*** Freshmen: $2763. Undergraduates: $2616. ***Scholarships, grants, and awards by category:*** *Academic interests/achievement:* 1,592 awards ($4,774,572 total). ***Tuition waivers:*** Full or partial for employees or children of employees, senior citizens. ***ROTC:*** Army, Air Force cooperative.
LOANS *Student loans:* $33,440,133 (72% need-based, 28% non-need-based). 63% of past graduating class borrowed through all loan programs. *Average indebtedness per student:* $27,355. ***Average need-based loan:*** Freshmen: $3155. Undergraduates: $4154. ***Parent loans:*** $21,436,414 (69% need-based, 31% non-need-based). ***Programs:*** Federal Direct (PLUS).
WORK-STUDY *Federal work-study:* Total amount: $177,104; 79 jobs averaging $2271.
APPLYING FOR FINANCIAL AID *Required financial aid form:* FAFSA. ***Financial aid deadline (priority):*** 3/1. ***Notification date:*** Continuous beginning 2/16. Students must reply by 5/1.
CONTACT Financial Aid Office, Salisbury University, 1101 Camden Avenue, Salisbury, MD 21801-6837, 410-543-6000 or toll-free 888-543-0148.
Website: http://www.salisbury.edu/.

SALVE REGINA UNIVERSITY

Newport, RI

Tuition & fees: $42,920 | **Average undergraduate aid package: $28,725**

ABOUT THE INSTITUTION Independent Roman Catholic, coed. ***Awards:*** certificates, associate, bachelor's, master's, and doctoral degrees. 46 undergraduate majors. ***Total enrollment:*** 2,771. Undergraduates: 2,167. Freshmen: 655. Federal methodology is used as a basis for awarding need-based institutional aid.

UNDERGRADUATE EXPENSES for 2020–2021 ***Application fee:*** $50. ***Comprehensive fee:*** $58,320 includes full-time tuition ($42,220), mandatory fees ($700), and room and board ($15,400). ***College room only:*** $9020. Full-time tuition and fees vary according to course load and location. Room and board charges vary according to board plan and housing facility. ***Part-time tuition:*** $1407 per credit hour. Part-time tuition and fees vary according to course load and location.

FRESHMAN FINANCIAL AID (Fall 2019, est.) 614 applied for aid; of those 85% were deemed to have need. 100% of freshmen with need received aid; of those 20% had need fully met. ***Average percent of need met:*** 72% (excluding resources awarded to replace EFC). ***Average financial aid package:*** $29,491 (excluding resources awarded to replace EFC). 20% of all full-time freshmen had no need and received non-need-based gift aid.

UNDERGRADUATE FINANCIAL AID (Fall 2019, est.) 1,824 applied for aid; of those 87% were deemed to have need. 100% of undergraduates with need received aid; of those 13% had need fully met. ***Average percent of need met:*** 68% (excluding resources awarded to replace EFC). ***Average financial aid package:*** $28,725 (excluding resources awarded to replace EFC). 22% of all full-time undergraduates had no need and received non-need-based gift aid.

GIFT AID (NEED-BASED) ***Total amount:*** $37,663,210 (6% federal, 92% institutional, 2% external sources). ***Receiving aid:*** Freshmen: 80% (523); all full-time undergraduates: 76% (1,577). ***Average award:*** Freshmen: $26,011; Undergraduates: $24,047. ***Scholarships, grants, and awards:*** Federal Pell, FSEOG, state, private, college/university gift aid from institutional funds.

GIFT AID (NON-NEED-BASED) ***Total amount:*** $9,336,834 (94% institutional, 6% external sources). ***Receiving aid:*** Freshmen: 14% (93). Undergraduates: 9% (179). ***Average award:*** Freshmen: $20,020. Undergraduates: $15,964. ***Scholarships, grants, and awards by category:*** *Academic interests/achievement:* general academic interests/achievements. *Creative arts/performance:* applied art and design. *Special characteristics:* children and siblings of alumni. ***Tuition waivers:*** Full or partial for employees or children of employees. ***ROTC:*** Army cooperative.

LOANS ***Student loans:*** $20,701,005 (65% need-based, 35% non-need-based). 80% of past graduating class borrowed through all loan programs. *Average indebtedness per student:* $40,958. ***Average need-based loan:*** Freshmen: $3287. Undergraduates: $4350. ***Parent loans:*** $6,716,481 (55% need-based, 45% non-need-based). ***Programs:*** Federal Direct (Subsidized and Unsubsidized Stafford, PLUS), Perkins, Federal Nursing, alternative loans.

WORK-STUDY ***Federal work-study:*** Total amount: $349,757; jobs available. ***State or other work-study/employment:*** Total amount: $230,000 (100% need-based). Part-time jobs available.

APPLYING FOR FINANCIAL AID ***Required financial aid form:*** FAFSA. ***Financial aid deadline (priority):*** 3/1. ***Notification date:*** Continuous beginning 1/3. Students must reply by 5/1 or within 2 weeks of notification.

CONTACT Anne McDermott, Director of Financial Aid, Salve Regina University, 100 Ochre Point Avenue, Newport, RI 02840-4192, 401-341-2901 or toll-free 888-GO SALVE. *Fax:* 401-341-2928. *E-mail:* financial_aid@salve.edu.
Website: http://www.salve.edu/.

SAMFORD UNIVERSITY

Birmingham, AL

Tuition & fees: $32,850 | **Average undergraduate aid package: $21,460**

ABOUT THE INSTITUTION Independent Baptist, coed. ***Awards:*** certificates, bachelor's, master's, and doctoral degrees. 73 undergraduate majors. ***Total enrollment:*** 5,692. Undergraduates: 3,591. Freshmen: 901. Federal methodology is used as a basis for awarding need-based institutional aid.

UNDERGRADUATE EXPENSES for 2019–2020 ***Application fee:*** $40. ***Comprehensive fee:*** $43,830 includes full-time tuition ($32,000), mandatory fees ($850), and room and board ($10,980). ***College room only:*** $5970. Full-time tuition and fees vary according to course load and program. Room and board charges vary according to board plan and housing facility. ***Part-time tuition:*** $1070 per credit. ***Part-time fees:*** $355 per term. Part-time tuition and fees vary according to course load and program.

FRESHMAN FINANCIAL AID (Fall 2018) 739 applied for aid; of those 61% were deemed to have need. 100% of freshmen with need received aid; of those 26% had need fully met. ***Average percent of need met:*** 74% (excluding resources awarded to replace EFC). ***Average financial aid package:*** $21,938 (excluding resources awarded to replace EFC). 48% of all full-time freshmen had no need and received non-need-based gift aid.

UNDERGRADUATE FINANCIAL AID (Fall 2018) 2,050 applied for aid; of those 70% were deemed to have need. 100% of undergraduates with need received aid; of those 25% had need fully met. ***Average percent of need met:*** 71% (excluding resources awarded to replace EFC). ***Average financial aid package:*** $21,460 (excluding resources awarded to replace EFC). 48% of all full-time undergraduates had no need and received non-need-based gift aid.

GIFT AID (NEED-BASED) ***Total amount:*** $20,452,674 (12% federal, 2% state, 82% institutional, 4% external sources). ***Receiving aid:*** Freshmen: 47% (449); all full-time undergraduates: 40% (1,393). ***Average award:*** Freshmen: $17,510; Undergraduates: $17,128. ***Scholarships, grants, and awards:*** Federal Pell, FSEOG, state, private, college/university gift aid from institutional funds, United Negro College Fund, Federal Nursing.

GIFT AID (NON-NEED-BASED) ***Total amount:*** $23,114,387 (1% state, 95% institutional, 4% external sources). ***Receiving aid:*** Freshmen: 11% (107). Undergraduates: 9% (302). ***Average award:*** Freshmen: $13,966. Undergraduates: $12,221. ***Scholarships, grants, and awards by category:*** *Academic interests/achievement:* 2,843 awards ($30,200,427 total): architecture, biological sciences, business, communication, computer science, education, English, foreign languages, general academic interests/achievements, health fields, home economics, humanities, international studies, mathematics, military science, physical sciences, premedicine, religion/biblical studies, social sciences. *Creative arts/performance:* 244 awards ($797,015 total): applied art and design, art/fine arts, cinema/film/broadcasting, creative writing, dance, debating, general creative arts/performance, journalism/publications, music, performing arts, theater/drama. *Special achievements/activities:* 1,437 awards ($2,804,418 total): cheerleading/drum major, community service, general special achievements/activities, hobbies/interests, leadership, memberships, religious involvement. *Special characteristics:* 187 awards ($3,479,400 total): children and siblings of alumni, children of faculty/staff, ethnic background, international students, members of minority groups, out-of-state students, relatives of clergy, religious affiliation, siblings of current students, spouses of deceased or disabled public servants, veterans, veterans' children. ***Tuition waivers:*** Full or partial for employees or children of employees. ***ROTC:*** Army cooperative, Air Force.

LOANS ***Student loans:*** $16,021,477 (54% need-based, 46% non-need-based). 32% of past graduating class borrowed through all loan programs. *Average indebtedness per student:* $29,676. ***Average need-based loan:*** Freshmen: $3239. Undergraduates: $3859. ***Parent loans:*** $20,600,008 (31% need-based, 69% non-need-based). ***Programs:*** Federal Direct (Subsidized and Unsubsidized Stafford, PLUS), Federal Nursing, state, college/university, Private education loans.

WORK-STUDY ***Federal work-study:*** Total amount: $2,078,808; 564 jobs averaging $2958. ***State or other work-study/employment:*** Total amount: $1,185,300 (16% need-based, 84% non-need-based). 783 part-time jobs averaging $1571.

ATHLETIC AWARDS Total amount: $8,634,146 (40% need-based, 60% non-need-based).

APPLYING FOR FINANCIAL AID ***Required financial aid forms:*** FAFSA, institution's own form, state aid form. ***Financial aid deadline:*** Continuous. ***Notification date:*** 3/15. Students must reply by 5/1.

CONTACT Lane Smith, Director of Financial Aid, Samford University, 800 Lakeshore Drive, Birmingham, AL 35229, 205-726-2905 or toll-free 800-888-7218. *Fax:* 205-726-2738. *E-mail:* lsmith1@samford.edu.
Website: http://www.samford.edu/.

SAM HOUSTON STATE UNIVERSITY

Huntsville, TX

Tuition & fees: N/R	Average undergraduate aid package: $11,812

ABOUT THE INSTITUTION State-supported, coed. ***Awards:*** certificates, bachelor's, master's, and doctoral degrees. 104 undergraduate majors. ***Total enrollment:*** 21,363. Undergraduates: 18,783. Freshmen: 2,927. Federal methodology is used as a basis for awarding need-based institutional aid.

FRESHMAN FINANCIAL AID (Fall 2018) 2268 applied for aid; of those 80% were deemed to have need. 98% of freshmen with need received aid; of those 10% had need fully met. ***Average percent of need met:*** 78% (excluding resources awarded to replace EFC). ***Average financial aid package:*** $12,114 (excluding resources awarded to replace EFC). 5% of all full-time freshmen had no need and received non-need-based gift aid.

UNDERGRADUATE FINANCIAL AID (Fall 2018) 11,872 applied for aid; of those 87% were deemed to have need. 97% of undergraduates with need received aid; of those 6% had need fully met. ***Average percent of need met:*** 74% (excluding resources awarded to replace EFC). ***Average financial aid package:*** $11,812 (excluding resources awarded to replace EFC). 3% of all full-time undergraduates had no need and received non-need-based gift aid.

GIFT AID (NEED-BASED) ***Total amount:*** $70,580,243 (52% federal, 36% state, 5% institutional, 7% external sources). ***Receiving aid:*** Freshmen: 59% (1,507); all full-time undergraduates: 55% (8,322). ***Average award:*** Freshmen: $8972; Undergraduates: $7983. ***Scholarships, grants, and awards:*** Federal Pell, FSEOG, state, college/university gift aid from institutional funds.

GIFT AID (NON-NEED-BASED) ***Total amount:*** $4,119,165 (49% institutional, 51% external sources). ***Receiving aid:*** Freshmen: 4% (102). Undergraduates: 2% (371). ***Average award:*** Freshmen: $3001. Undergraduates: $2733. ***Scholarships, grants, and awards by category:*** *Academic interests/achievement:* agriculture, biological sciences, business, communication, computer science, education, engineering/technologies, English, foreign languages, general academic interests/achievements, health fields, home economics, humanities, library science, mathematics, military science, physical sciences, social sciences. *Creative arts/performance:* art/fine arts, cinema/film/broadcasting, dance, journalism/publications, music, performing arts, theater/drama. *Special achievements/activities:* general special achievements/activities, leadership, rodeo. *Special characteristics:* children of union members/company employees, ethnic background, first-generation college students, members of minority groups, veterans. ***ROTC:*** Army.

LOANS ***Student loans:*** $112,893,264 (78% need-based, 22% non-need-based). 66% of past graduating class borrowed through all loan programs. *Average indebtedness per student:* $27,207. ***Average need-based loan:*** Freshmen: $3036. Undergraduates: $4022. ***Parent loans:*** $66,678,448 (48% need-based, 52% non-need-based). ***Programs:*** Federal Direct (Subsidized and Unsubsidized Stafford, PLUS), Perkins, state.

WORK-STUDY ***Federal work-study:*** Total amount: $5,015,746; jobs available. ***State or other work-study/employment:*** Total amount: $266,146 (100% need-based). Part-time jobs available.

ATHLETIC AWARDS Total amount: $4,172,320 (41% need-based, 59% non-need-based).

APPLYING FOR FINANCIAL AID ***Required financial aid form:*** FAFSA. ***Financial aid deadline (priority):*** 3/15. ***Notification date:*** Continuous beginning 4/1. Students must reply within 4 weeks of notification.

CONTACT Lydia Hall, Director of Financial Aid, Sam Houston State University, 1903 University, Estill 201, Box 2328, Huntsville, TX 77341-2328, 936-294-1750 or toll-free 866-232-7528 Ext.1828. *Fax:* 936-294-3668. *E-mail:* lth003@shsu.edu.
Website: http://www.shsu.edu/.

SAMUEL MERRITT UNIVERSITY

Oakland, CA

CONTACT Saeng Saephanh, Financial Aid Technician, Samuel Merritt University, 3100 Telegraph Avenue, Peralta Medical Office Building, Oakland, CA 94609, 510-869-1527 or toll-free 800-607-6377. *Fax:* 510-869-1529. *E-mail:* ssaephanh@samuelmerritt.edu.
Website: http://www.samuelmerritt.edu/.

SAN DIEGO CHRISTIAN COLLEGE

Santee, CA

CONTACT Mr. Daniel Reed, Director of Financial Aid, San Diego Christian College, 200 Riverview Parkway, Santee, CA 92071, 619-201-8730 or toll-free 800-676-2242. *Fax:* 619-201-8797. *E-mail:* daniel.reed@sdcc.edu.
Website: http://www.sdcc.edu/.

SAN DIEGO STATE UNIVERSITY

San Diego, CA

Tuition & fees (area res): $7510	Average undergraduate aid package: $10,000

ABOUT THE INSTITUTION State-supported, coed. ***Awards:*** certificates, bachelor's, master's, and doctoral degrees. 105 undergraduate majors. ***Total enrollment:*** 35,081. Undergraduates: 30,612. Freshmen: 5,275. Federal methodology is used as a basis for awarding need-based institutional aid.

UNDERGRADUATE EXPENSES for 2019–2020 ***Application fee:*** $70. ***Tuition, area resident:*** full-time $5742. ***Tuition, state resident:*** full-time $5742. ***Tuition, nonresident:*** full-time $17,622. ***Required fees:*** full-time $1768. Full-time tuition and fees vary according to course load and location. Part-time tuition and fees vary according to course load and location. ***College room and board:*** $17,752. Room and board charges vary according to board plan, housing facility, and student level.

FRESHMAN FINANCIAL AID (Fall 2019, est.) 4100 applied for aid; of those 66% were deemed to have need. 100% of freshmen with need received aid; of those 11% had need fully met. ***Average percent of need met:*** 67% (excluding resources awarded to replace EFC). ***Average financial aid package:*** $9300 (excluding resources awarded to replace EFC). 3% of all full-time freshmen had no need and received non-need-based gift aid.

UNDERGRADUATE FINANCIAL AID (Fall 2019, est.) 18,100 applied for aid; of those 79% were deemed to have need. 97% of undergraduates with need received aid; of those 20% had need fully met. ***Average percent of need met:*** 66% (excluding resources awarded to replace EFC). ***Average financial aid package:*** $10,000 (excluding resources awarded to replace EFC). 8% of all full-time undergraduates had no need and received non-need-based gift aid.

GIFT AID (NEED-BASED) ***Receiving aid:*** Freshmen: 33% (1,700); all full-time undergraduates: 37% (10,200). ***Average award:*** Freshmen: $10,300; Undergraduates: $10,100. ***Scholarships, grants, and awards:*** Federal Pell, FSEOG, state, private, college/university gift aid from institutional funds.

GIFT AID (NON-NEED-BASED) ***Receiving aid:*** Freshmen: 25% (1,300). Undergraduates: 21% (5,900). ***Average award:*** Freshmen: $3200. Undergraduates: $2000. ***Scholarships, grants, and awards by category:*** *Academic interests/achievement:* area/ethnic studies, biological sciences, business, communication, computer science, education, engineering/technologies, English, foreign languages, general academic interests/achievements, health fields, home economics, humanities, international studies, mathematics, military science, physical sciences, religion/biblical studies, social sciences. *Creative arts/performance:* applied art and design, art/fine arts, cinema/film/broadcasting, creative writing, dance, debating, journalism/publications, music, performing arts, theater/drama. *Special achievements/activities:* cheerleading/drum major, community service, hobbies/interests, leadership, memberships. *Special characteristics:* adult students, children and siblings of alumni, children of faculty/staff, children of workers in trades, first-generation college students, handicapped students, local/state students, previous college experience, veterans. ***Tuition waivers:*** Full or partial for employees or children of employees, senior citizens. ***ROTC:*** Army, Naval cooperative, Air Force.

LOANS ***Student loans:*** 44% of past graduating class borrowed through all loan programs. *Average indebtedness per student:* $21,172. ***Average need-based loan:*** Freshmen: $3100. Undergraduates: $4000. ***Programs:*** Federal Direct (Subsidized and Unsubsidized Stafford, PLUS), college/university.

WORK-STUDY ***Federal work-study:*** 707 jobs averaging $2393.

APPLYING FOR FINANCIAL AID ***Required financial aid forms:*** FAFSA, state aid form. ***Notification date:*** Continuous.

CONTACT Mrs. Rose Pasenelli, Director of Financial Aid and Scholarships, San Diego State University, 5500 Campanile Drive, SSW-3605, San Diego, CA 92182-7436, 619-594-6323 or toll-free 855-594-6336 (in-state), 855-594-3983 (out-of-state). *E-mail:* rpasenel@mail.sdsu.edu.
Website: http://www.sdsu.edu/.

SAN FRANCISCO ART INSTITUTE

San Francisco, CA

Tuition & fees: $46,614 | **Average undergraduate aid package: $18,707**

ABOUT THE INSTITUTION Independent, coed. ***Awards:*** certificates, bachelor's, and master's degrees. 8 undergraduate majors. ***Total enrollment:*** 332. Undergraduates: 220. Freshmen: 32. Both federal and institutional methodology are used as a basis for awarding need-based institutional aid.

UNDERGRADUATE EXPENSES for 2020–2021 ***Application fee:*** $75. ***Comprehensive fee:*** $61,114 includes full-time tuition ($45,664), mandatory fees ($950), and room and board ($14,500). Full-time tuition and fees vary according to degree level. Room and board charges vary according to housing facility. ***Part-time tuition:*** $2000 per credit. Part-time tuition and fees vary according to degree level.

FRESHMAN FINANCIAL AID (Fall 2019, est.) 18 applied for aid; of those 78% were deemed to have need. 100% of freshmen with need received aid; of those 7% had need fully met. ***Average percent of need met:*** 42% (excluding resources awarded to replace EFC). ***Average financial aid package:*** $21,353 (excluding resources awarded to replace EFC). 56% of all full-time freshmen had no need and received non-need-based gift aid.

UNDERGRADUATE FINANCIAL AID (Fall 2019, est.) 106 applied for aid; of those 90% were deemed to have need. 100% of undergraduates with need received aid; of those 7% had need fully met. ***Average percent of need met:*** 45% (excluding resources awarded to replace EFC). ***Average financial aid package:*** $18,707 (excluding resources awarded to replace EFC). 49% of all full-time undergraduates had no need and received non-need-based gift aid.

GIFT AID (NEED-BASED) ***Total amount:*** $2,563,419 (9% federal, 3% state, 81% institutional, 7% external sources). ***Receiving aid:*** Freshmen: 38% (12); all full-time undergraduates: 40% (80). ***Average award:*** Freshmen: $6029; Undergraduates: $5583. ***Scholarships, grants, and awards:*** Federal Pell, FSEOG, state, private, college/university gift aid from institutional funds.

GIFT AID (NON-NEED-BASED) ***Receiving aid:*** Freshmen: 44% (14). Undergraduates: 47% (94). ***Average award:*** Freshmen: $9042. Undergraduates: $9119. ***Scholarships, grants, and awards by category:*** *Academic interests/achievement:* general academic interests/achievements. *Creative arts/performance:* applied art and design. *Special characteristics:* children and siblings of alumni, first-generation college students. ***Tuition waivers:*** Full or partial for employees or children of employees.

LOANS ***Student loans:*** $418,862 (100% need-based). 56% of past graduating class borrowed through all loan programs. *Average indebtedness per student:* $28,432. ***Average need-based loan:*** Freshmen: $1750. Undergraduates: $2346. ***Parent loans:*** $260,212 (100% need-based). ***Programs:*** Federal Direct (Subsidized and Unsubsidized Stafford, PLUS).

WORK-STUDY ***Federal work-study:*** Total amount: $34,965; jobs available. ***State or other work-study/employment:*** Part-time jobs available.

APPLYING FOR FINANCIAL AID ***Required financial aid form:*** FAFSA. ***Financial aid deadline (priority):*** 3/1. ***Notification date:*** Continuous.

CONTACT Annita Alldredge, Director of Financial Aid, San Francisco Art Institute, 800 Chestnut Street, San Francisco, CA 94133, 415-749-4560 or toll-free 800-345-SFAI. *Fax:* 415-351-3503. *E-mail:* aalldredge@sfai.edu.
Website: http://www.sfai.edu/.

SAN FRANCISCO CONSERVATORY OF MUSIC

San Francisco, CA

CONTACT Doris Howard, Director of Financial Aid, San Francisco Conservatory of Music, 50 Oak Street, San Francisco, CA 94102-6011, 415-503-6214. *Fax:* 415-503-6299. *E-mail:* finaid@sfcm.edu.
Website: http://www.sfcm.edu/.

SAN FRANCISCO STATE UNIVERSITY

San Francisco, CA

Tuition & fees (area res): $7266 | **Average undergraduate aid package: $15,435**

ABOUT THE INSTITUTION State-supported, coed. ***Awards:*** certificates, bachelor's, master's, and doctoral degrees. 91 undergraduate majors. ***Total enrollment:*** 28,880. Undergraduates: 25,900. Freshmen: 3,688. Federal methodology is used as a basis for awarding need-based institutional aid.

UNDERGRADUATE EXPENSES for 2019–2020 ***Application fee:*** $70. ***Tuition, area resident:*** full-time $5742. ***Tuition, state resident:*** full-time $5742; part-time $1665 per term. ***Tuition, nonresident:*** full-time $17,622; part-time $4041 per term. ***Required fees:*** full-time $1524; $762 per term. ***College room and board:*** $14,384.

FRESHMAN FINANCIAL AID (Fall 2019, est.) 2959 applied for aid; of those 83% were deemed to have need. 95% of freshmen with need received aid; of those 26% had need fully met. ***Average percent of need met:*** 72% (excluding resources awarded to replace EFC). ***Average financial aid package:*** $16,962 (excluding resources awarded to replace EFC). 1% of all full-time freshmen had no need and received non-need-based gift aid.

UNDERGRADUATE FINANCIAL AID (Fall 2019, est.) 16,879 applied for aid; of those 89% were deemed to have need. 94% of undergraduates with need received aid; of those 18% had need fully met. ***Average percent of need met:*** 64% (excluding resources awarded to replace EFC). ***Average financial aid package:*** $15,435 (excluding resources awarded to replace EFC). 1% of all full-time undergraduates had no need and received non-need-based gift aid.

GIFT AID (NEED-BASED) ***Total amount:*** $138,942,171 (40% federal, 58% state, 1% institutional, 1% external sources). ***Receiving aid:*** Freshmen: 67% (2,241); all full-time undergraduates: 62% (13,267). ***Average award:*** Freshmen: $9905; Undergraduates: $9509. ***Scholarships, grants, and awards:*** Federal Pell, FSEOG, state, private, college/university gift aid from institutional funds.

GIFT AID (NON-NEED-BASED) ***Total amount:*** $35,165 (11% institutional, 89% external sources). ***Receiving aid:*** Freshmen: 15% (503). Undergraduates: 9% (1,847). ***Average award:*** Freshmen: $2097. Undergraduates: $2975. ***ROTC:*** Army cooperative, Air Force cooperative.

LOANS ***Student loans:*** $55,734,140 (93% need-based, 7% non-need-based). 28% of past graduating class borrowed through all loan programs. *Average indebtedness per student:* $5928. ***Average need-based loan:*** Freshmen: $3407. Undergraduates: $4440. ***Parent loans:*** $29,292,737 (100% need-based). ***Programs:*** Federal Direct (Subsidized and Unsubsidized Stafford, PLUS).

WORK-STUDY ***Federal work-study:*** Total amount: $1,600,000; jobs available.

ATHLETIC AWARDS Total amount: $684,912 (100% need-based).

APPLYING FOR FINANCIAL AID ***Required financial aid form:*** FAFSA. ***Financial aid deadline:*** Continuous. ***Notification date:*** Continuous beginning 4/15. Students must reply within 2 weeks of notification.

CONTACT Jimmie Wilder, Associate Director of Financial Aid, San Francisco State University, 1600 Holloway Avenue, San Francisco, CA 94132-1722, 415-338-7000. *Fax:* 415-338-0949. *E-mail:* finaid@sfsu.edu.
Website: http://www.sfsu.edu/.

SAN IGNACIO UNIVERSITY

Doral, FL

CONTACT Financial Aid Office, San Ignacio University, 10395 NW 41st Street, Suite 125, Doral, FL 33178.
Website: http://www.sanignaciouniversity.edu/.

SAN JOSE STATE UNIVERSITY

San Jose, CA

Tuition & fees (area res): $7852	**Average undergraduate aid package: $19,319**

ABOUT THE INSTITUTION State-supported, coed. ***Awards:*** certificates, bachelor's, master's, and doctoral degrees. 87 undergraduate majors. ***Total enrollment:*** 32,926. Undergraduates: 27,895. Freshmen: 3,959.

UNDERGRADUATE EXPENSES for 2020–2021 ***Application fee:*** $55. ***Tuition, area resident:*** full-time $5742; part-time $1665 per term. ***Tuition, state resident:*** full-time $5742; part-time $1665 per term. ***Tuition, nonresident:*** full-time $15,246; part-time $4041 per term. ***Required fees:*** full-time $2110; $1055 per term. Part-time tuition and fees vary according to student level. ***College room and board:*** $16,248; ***Room only:*** $10,368. Room and board charges vary according to board plan, housing facility, and location.

FRESHMAN FINANCIAL AID (Fall 2019, est.) 3247 applied for aid; of those 79% were deemed to have need. 96% of freshmen with need received aid; of those 71% had need fully met. ***Average percent of need met:*** 81% (excluding resources awarded to replace EFC). ***Average financial aid package:*** $19,414 (excluding resources awarded to replace EFC). 1% of all full-time freshmen had no need and received non-need-based gift aid.

UNDERGRADUATE FINANCIAL AID (Fall 2019, est.) 16,689 applied for aid; of those 91% were deemed to have need. 97% of undergraduates with need received aid; of those 70% had need fully met. ***Average percent of need met:*** 89% (excluding resources awarded to replace EFC). ***Average financial aid package:*** $19,319 (excluding resources awarded to replace EFC). 1% of all full-time undergraduates had no need and received non-need-based gift aid.

GIFT AID (NEED-BASED) ***Total amount:*** $128,952,060 (40% federal, 57% state, 1% institutional, 2% external sources). ***Receiving aid:*** Freshmen: 60% (2,303); all full-time undergraduates: 59% (13,971). ***Average award:*** Freshmen: $12,187; Undergraduates: $11,544. ***Scholarships, grants, and awards:*** Federal Pell, FSEOG, state, private, college/university gift aid from institutional funds.

GIFT AID (NON-NEED-BASED) ***Total amount:*** $196,650 (49% institutional, 51% external sources). ***Receiving aid:*** Freshmen: 5% (175). Undergraduates: 3% (755). ***Average award:*** Freshmen: $1890. Undergraduates: $1928. ***Scholarships, grants, and awards by category:*** *Academic interests/achievement:* architecture, biological sciences, business, education, engineering/technologies, English, foreign languages, general academic interests/achievements, home economics, humanities, international studies, mathematics, physical sciences, religion/biblical studies, social sciences. *Creative arts/performance:* art/fine arts, cinema/film/broadcasting, creative writing, dance, journalism/publications, music, performing arts, theater/drama. *Special achievements/activities:* community service, leadership. *Special characteristics:* adult students, children of faculty/staff, children with a deceased or disabled parent, ethnic background, first-generation college students, international students, local/state students, members of minority groups, veterans. ***Tuition waivers:*** Full or partial for employees or children of employees. ***ROTC:*** Army cooperative, Air Force.

LOANS ***Student loans:*** $42,644,180 (87% need-based, 13% non-need-based). 44% of past graduating class borrowed through all loan programs. *Average indebtedness per student:* $18,225. ***Average need-based loan:*** Freshmen: $3360. Undergraduates: $4480. ***Parent loans:*** $19,068,471 (70% need-based, 30% non-need-based). ***Programs:*** Federal Direct (Subsidized and Unsubsidized Stafford, PLUS), Perkins, state.

WORK-STUDY ***Federal work-study:*** Total amount: $2,367,606; jobs available.

ATHLETIC AWARDS Total amount: $6,681,220 (89% need-based, 11% non-need-based).

APPLYING FOR FINANCIAL AID ***Required financial aid forms:*** FAFSA, state aid form. ***Financial aid deadline:*** 4/28 (priority: 3/4). ***Notification date:*** Continuous beginning 3/1.

CONTACT Coleetta McElroy, Director of Financial Aid and Scholarship Office, San Jose State University, One Washington Square, San Jose, CA 95192-0036, 408-283-7500. *E-mail:* coleetta.mcelroy@sjsu.edu.
Website: http://www.sjsu.edu/.

SANTA BARBARA BUSINESS COLLEGE

Ventura, CA

CONTACT Financial Aid Office, Santa Barbara Business College, 4839 Market Street, Ventura, CA 93003, 805-339-2999.
Website: http://www.sbbcollege.edu/.

SANTA CLARA UNIVERSITY

Santa Clara, CA

Tuition & fees: $55,629	**Average undergraduate aid package: $39,105**

ABOUT THE INSTITUTION Independent Roman Catholic (Jesuit), coed. ***Awards:*** certificates, bachelor's, master's, and doctoral degrees. 50 undergraduate majors. ***Total enrollment:*** 8,669. Undergraduates: 5,694. Freshmen: 1,391. Both federal and institutional methodology are used as a basis for awarding need-based institutional aid.

UNDERGRADUATE EXPENSES for 2020–2021 ***Application fee:*** $60. ***Comprehensive fee:*** $71,601 includes full-time tuition ($54,987), mandatory fees ($642), and room and board ($15,972). Room and board charges vary according to board plan and housing facility. ***Part-time tuition:*** $1527 per credit. Part-time tuition and fees vary according to course load.

FRESHMAN FINANCIAL AID (Fall 2019, est.) 855 applied for aid; of those 64% were deemed to have need. 95% of freshmen with need received aid; of those 34% had need fully met. ***Average percent of need met:*** 77% (excluding resources awarded to replace EFC). ***Average financial aid package:*** $37,952 (excluding resources awarded to replace EFC). 27% of all full-time freshmen had no need and received non-need-based gift aid.

UNDERGRADUATE FINANCIAL AID (Fall 2019, est.) 3,337 applied for aid; of those 75% were deemed to have need. 79% of undergraduates with need received aid; of those 33% had need fully met. ***Average percent of need met:*** 74% (excluding resources awarded to replace EFC). ***Average financial aid package:*** $39,105 (excluding resources awarded to replace EFC). 31% of all full-time undergraduates had no need and received non-need-based gift aid.

GIFT AID (NEED-BASED) ***Total amount:*** $69,842,146 (5% federal, 6% state, 87% institutional, 2% external sources). ***Receiving aid:*** Freshmen: 33% (452); all full-time undergraduates: 32% (1,770). ***Average award:*** Freshmen: $33,925; Undergraduates: $32,076. ***Scholarships, grants, and awards:*** Federal Pell, FSEOG, state, private, college/university gift aid from institutional funds, United Negro College Fund.

GIFT AID (NON-NEED-BASED) ***Total amount:*** $32,314,165 (94% institutional, 6% external sources). ***Receiving aid:*** Freshmen: 16% (222). Undergraduates: 15% (848). ***Average award:*** Freshmen: $12,852. Undergraduates: $17,015. ***Scholarships, grants, and awards by category:*** *Academic interests/achievement:* 2,422 awards ($37,710,390 total): business, engineering/technologies, general academic interests/achievements, military science. *Creative arts/performance:* 33 awards ($144,829 total): dance, debating, music, theater/drama. *Special characteristics:* 101 awards ($4,773,206 total): children and siblings of alumni, children of faculty/staff, children with a deceased or disabled parent, first-generation college students, handicapped students, siblings of current students, spouses of current students, veterans, veterans' children. ***Tuition waivers:*** Full or partial for employees or children of employees. ***ROTC:*** Army, Air Force cooperative.

LOANS ***Student loans:*** $8,755,546 (83% need-based, 17% non-need-based). 35% of past graduating class borrowed through all loan programs. *Average indebtedness per student:* $26,603. ***Average need-based loan:*** Freshmen: $3315. Undergraduates: $4400. ***Parent loans:*** $9,843,726 (81% need-based, 19% non-need-based). ***Programs:*** Federal Direct (Subsidized and Unsubsidized Stafford, PLUS), private credit-based loans.

WORK-STUDY ***Federal work-study:*** Total amount: $718,010; 204 jobs averaging $3969.

ATHLETIC AWARDS Total amount: $6,999,954 (22% need-based, 78% non-need-based).

APPLYING FOR FINANCIAL AID ***Required financial aid forms:*** FAFSA, CSS Financial Aid PROFILE. ***Financial aid deadline (priority):*** 2/1. ***Notification date:*** 4/1. Students must reply by 5/1 or within 2 weeks of notification.

CONTACT Mrs. Nancy Merz, Dean of Financial Aid, Santa Clara University, 500 El Camino Real, Santa Clara, CA 95053, 408-551-1000. *Fax:* 408-554-2154. *E-mail:* nmerz@scu.edu.
Website: http://www.scu.edu/.

SANTA FE COLLEGE

Gainesville, FL

CONTACT Financial Aid Office, Santa Fe College, 3000 Northwest 83rd Street, Gainesville, FL 32606, 352-395-5000.
Website: http://www.sfcollege.edu/.

SARAH LAWRENCE COLLEGE

Bronxville, NY

Tuition & fees: $57,520	Average undergraduate aid package: $39,758

ABOUT THE INSTITUTION Independent, coed. ***Awards:*** bachelor's and master's degrees. 60 undergraduate majors. ***Total enrollment:*** 1,670. Undergraduates: 1,433. Freshmen: 398. Both federal and institutional methodology are used as a basis for awarding need-based institutional aid.

UNDERGRADUATE EXPENSES for 2019–2020 ***Application fee:*** $60. ***Comprehensive fee:*** $73,340 includes full-time tuition ($56,020), mandatory fees ($1500), and room and board ($15,820). ***College room only:*** $10,420. Full-time tuition and fees vary according to course load. Room and board charges vary according to board plan. ***Part-time tuition:*** $1867 per credit hour. ***Part-time fees:*** $605 per term. Part-time tuition and fees vary according to course load.

FRESHMAN FINANCIAL AID (Fall 2019, est.) 290 applied for aid; of those 79% were deemed to have need. 90% of freshmen with need received aid; of those 18% had need fully met. ***Average percent of need met:*** 81% (excluding resources awarded to replace EFC). ***Average financial aid package:*** $41,552 (excluding resources awarded to replace EFC). 28% of all full-time freshmen had no need and received non-need-based gift aid.

UNDERGRADUATE FINANCIAL AID (Fall 2019, est.) 927 applied for aid; of those 84% were deemed to have need. 97% of undergraduates with need received aid; of those 16% had need fully met. ***Average percent of need met:*** 75% (excluding resources awarded to replace EFC). ***Average financial aid package:*** $39,758 (excluding resources awarded to replace EFC). 28% of all full-time undergraduates had no need and received non-need-based gift aid.

GIFT AID (NEED-BASED) ***Total amount:*** $26,765,622 (4% federal, 1% state, 93% institutional, 2% external sources). ***Receiving aid:*** Freshmen: 52% (205); all full-time undergraduates: 55% (744). ***Average award:*** Freshmen: $37,854; Undergraduates: $35,692. ***Scholarships, grants, and awards:*** Federal Pell, FSEOG, state, private, college/university gift aid from institutional funds.

GIFT AID (NON-NEED-BASED) ***Total amount:*** $9,264,124 (97% institutional, 3% external sources). ***Receiving aid:*** Freshmen: 9% (34). Undergraduates: 7% (98). ***Average award:*** Freshmen: $23,064. Undergraduates: $20,737. ***Scholarships, grants, and awards by category:*** *Academic interests/achievement:* general academic interests/achievements. ***Tuition waivers:*** Full or partial for employees or children of employees. ***ROTC:*** Air Force cooperative.

LOANS ***Student loans:*** $5,574,611 (67% need-based, 33% non-need-based). 55% of past graduating class borrowed through all loan programs. *Average indebtedness per student:* $26,808. ***Average need-based loan:*** Freshmen: $2462. Undergraduates: $3620. ***Parent loans:*** $1,619,519 (83% need-based, 17% non-need-based). ***Programs:*** Federal Direct (Subsidized and Unsubsidized Stafford, PLUS), private loans.

WORK-STUDY ***Federal work-study:*** Total amount: $1,083,382; jobs available. ***State or other work-study/employment:*** Total amount: $74,250 (41% need-based, 59% non-need-based). Part-time jobs available.

APPLYING FOR FINANCIAL AID ***Required financial aid forms:*** FAFSA, state aid form. ***Financial aid deadline:*** 1/15 (priority: 1/15). ***Notification date:*** 4/1. Students must reply by 5/1.

CONTACT Ms. Deborah McCue, Director of Enrollment Operations and Systems, Sarah Lawrence College, One Mead Way, Bronxville, NY 10708, 914-395-2520 or toll-free 800-888-2858. *Fax:* 914-395-2515. *E-mail:* dmccue@sarahlawrence.edu.
Website: http://www.sarahlawrence.edu/.

SAVANNAH COLLEGE OF ART AND DESIGN

Savannah, GA

ABOUT THE INSTITUTION Independent, coed. ***Awards:*** certificates, bachelor's, and master's degrees. 32 undergraduate majors. ***Total enrollment:*** 14,832. Undergraduates: 12,217. Freshmen: 2,878.

GIFT AID (NEED-BASED) ***Scholarships, grants, and awards:*** Federal Pell, FSEOG, state, private, college/university gift aid from institutional funds, United Negro College Fund.

GIFT AID (NON-NEED-BASED) ***Scholarships, grants, and awards by category:*** *Academic interests/achievement:* architecture, general academic interests/achievements. *Creative arts/performance:* applied art and design, art/fine arts, cinema/film/broadcasting, creative writing, dance, debating, general creative arts/performance, journalism/publications, music, performing arts, theater/drama. *Special achievements/activities:* general special achievements/activities. *Special characteristics:* general special characteristics, veterans.

LOANS ***Programs:*** Federal Direct (Subsidized and Unsubsidized Stafford, PLUS), state, alternative loans.

CONTACT Ms. Kim Beveridge, Director of Financial Aid, Savannah College of Art and Design, PO Box 3146, Savannah, GA 31402-3146, 800-859-7223 or toll-free 800-869-7223. *E-mail:* admission@scad.edu.
Website: http://www.scad.edu/.

SAVANNAH STATE UNIVERSITY

Savannah, GA

CONTACT Mr. Kenneth Wilson, Director of Financial Aid, Savannah State University, PO Box 20523, Savannah, GA 31404, 912-358-4162 or toll-free 800-788-0478. *Fax:* 912-358-3167. *E-mail:* finaid@savannahstate.edu.
Website: http://www.savannahstate.edu/.

SCHILLER INTERNATIONAL UNIVERSITY - TAMPA

Largo, FL

CONTACT Financial Aid Office, Schiller International University - Tampa, 8560 Ulmerton Road, Largo, FL 33771, 727-736-5082 or toll-free 800-261-9571 (in-state), 800-261-9751 (out-of-state).
Website: http://www.schiller.edu/.

SCHOOL OF THE ART INSTITUTE OF CHICAGO

Chicago, IL

CONTACT Mr. Patrick James, Student Financial Services Office, School of the Art Institute of Chicago, 36 South Wabash, Suite 1218, Chicago, IL 60603-3103, 312-629-6600 or toll-free 800-232-SAIC. *Fax:* 312-629-6601. *E-mail:* finaid@saic.edu.
Website: http://www.saic.edu/.

SCHOOL OF VISUAL ARTS

New York, NY

Tuition & fees: $43,400 **Average undergraduate aid package: $20,950**

ABOUT THE INSTITUTION Proprietary, coed. ***Awards:*** bachelor's and master's degrees. 15 undergraduate majors. ***Total enrollment:*** 4,557. Undergraduates: 3,871. Freshmen: 896. Federal methodology is used as a basis for awarding need-based institutional aid.

UNDERGRADUATE EXPENSES for 2020–2021 ***Application fee:*** $50. ***Tuition:*** full-time $43,400; part-time $1450 per credit hour. ***College room only:*** $18,800.

FRESHMAN FINANCIAL AID (Fall 2019, est.) 346 applied for aid; of those 84% were deemed to have need. 97% of freshmen with need received aid; of those 7% had need fully met. ***Average percent of need met:*** 27% (excluding resources awarded to replace EFC). ***Average financial aid package:*** $22,164 (excluding resources awarded to replace EFC). 22% of all full-time freshmen had no need and received non-need-based gift aid.

UNDERGRADUATE FINANCIAL AID (Fall 2019, est.) 1,395 applied for aid; of those 91% were deemed to have need. 98% of undergraduates with need received aid; of those 3% had need fully met. ***Average percent of need met:*** 28% (excluding resources awarded to replace EFC). ***Average financial aid package:*** $20,950 (excluding resources awarded to replace EFC). 17% of all full-time undergraduates had no need and received non-need-based gift aid.

GIFT AID (NEED-BASED) ***Total amount:*** $18,083,088 (22% federal, 5% state, 71% institutional, 2% external sources). ***Receiving aid:*** Freshmen: 27% (256); all full-time undergraduates: 28% (1,067). ***Average award:*** Freshmen: $17,285; Undergraduates: $16,267. ***Scholarships, grants, and awards:*** Federal Pell, FSEOG, state, private, college/university gift aid from institutional funds.

GIFT AID (NON-NEED-BASED) ***Total amount:*** $9,051,340 (2% federal, 97% institutional, 1% external sources). ***Receiving aid:*** Freshmen: 23% (225). Undergraduates: 21% (785). ***Average award:*** Freshmen: $12,933. Undergraduates: $12,404. ***Scholarships, grants, and awards by category:*** *Creative arts/performance:* applied art and design.

LOANS ***Student loans:*** $15,324,328 (92% need-based, 8% non-need-based). 40% of past graduating class borrowed through all loan programs. *Average indebtedness per student:* $45,588. ***Average need-based loan:*** Freshmen: $2997. Undergraduates: $4408. ***Parent loans:*** $15,232,581 (96% need-based, 4% non-need-based). ***Programs:*** Federal Direct (Subsidized and Unsubsidized Stafford, PLUS), Perkins, state, alternative loans.

WORK-STUDY ***Federal work-study:*** Total amount: $324,987; jobs available. ***State or other work-study/employment:*** Total amount: $708,450 (83% need-based, 17% non-need-based). Part-time jobs available.

APPLYING FOR FINANCIAL AID ***Required financial aid forms:*** FAFSA, state aid form. ***Financial aid deadline:*** 3/1 (priority: 2/1). ***Notification date:*** Continuous beginning 2/15.

CONTACT Mr. William Berrios, Financial Aid Office, School of Visual Arts, 209 East 23rd Street, New York, NY 10010, 212-592-2030 or toll-free 800-436-4204. *Fax:* 212-592-2029. *E-mail:* fa@sva.edu.
Website: http://www.sva.edu/.

SCHREINER UNIVERSITY

Kerrville, TX

Tuition & fees: $31,938 **Average undergraduate aid package: $21,816**

ABOUT THE INSTITUTION Independent Presbyterian, coed. ***Awards:*** certificates, associate, bachelor's, and master's degrees. 36 undergraduate majors. ***Total enrollment:*** 1,342. Undergraduates: 1,257. Freshmen: 310. Federal methodology is used as a basis for awarding need-based institutional aid.

UNDERGRADUATE EXPENSES for 2020–2021 ***Application fee:*** $25. ***Comprehensive fee:*** $42,517 includes full-time tuition ($31,938) and room and board ($10,579). ***College room only:*** $4956. Full-time tuition and fees vary according to course load, location, and program. Room and board charges vary according to board plan and housing facility. ***Part-time tuition:*** $1451 per credit hour. Part-time tuition and fees vary according to course load and program. ***Payment plan:*** Guaranteed tuition.

FRESHMAN FINANCIAL AID (Fall 2018) 337 applied for aid; of those 89% were deemed to have need. 99% of freshmen with need received aid; of those 9% had need fully met. ***Average percent of need met:*** 36% (excluding resources awarded to replace EFC). ***Average financial aid package:*** $21,261 (excluding resources awarded to replace EFC). 9% of all full-time freshmen had no need and received non-need-based gift aid.

UNDERGRADUATE FINANCIAL AID (Fall 2018) 957 applied for aid; of those 89% were deemed to have need. 100% of undergraduates with need received aid; of those 11% had need fully met. ***Average percent of need met:*** 38% (excluding resources awarded to replace EFC). ***Average financial aid package:*** $21,816 (excluding resources awarded to replace EFC). 8% of all full-time undergraduates had no need and received non-need-based gift aid.

GIFT AID (NEED-BASED) ***Total amount:*** $16,488,031 (14% federal, 10% state, 62% institutional, 14% external sources). ***Receiving aid:*** Freshmen: 67% (242); all full-time undergraduates: 64% (690). ***Average award:*** Freshmen: $9569; Undergraduates: $8020. ***Scholarships, grants, and awards:*** Federal Pell, FSEOG, state, private, college/university gift aid from institutional funds.

GIFT AID (NON-NEED-BASED) ***Total amount:*** $1,893,204 (82% institutional, 18% external sources). ***Receiving aid:*** Freshmen: 75% (268). Undergraduates: 73% (790). ***Average award:*** Freshmen: $12,856. Undergraduates: $12,291. ***Scholarships, grants, and awards by category:*** *Academic interests/achievement:* biological sciences, business, communication, education, English, general academic interests/achievements, mathematics, physical sciences, premedicine, religion/biblical studies, social sciences. *Creative arts/performance:* applied art and design, art/fine arts, journalism/publications, music, theater/drama. *Special achievements/activities:* community service, leadership, memberships, religious involvement. *Special characteristics:* children of faculty/staff, general special characteristics, international students, local/state students, relatives of clergy, religious affiliation, siblings of current students, veterans. ***Tuition waivers:*** Full or partial for employees or children of employees.

LOANS ***Student loans:*** $8,442,723 (71% need-based, 29% non-need-based). 68% of past graduating class borrowed through all loan programs. *Average indebtedness per student:* $47,330. ***Average need-based loan:*** Freshmen: $3067. Undergraduates: $3667. ***Parent loans:*** $2,090,714 (49% need-based, 51% non-need-based). ***Programs:*** Federal Direct (Subsidized and Unsubsidized Stafford, PLUS), state.

WORK-STUDY ***Federal work-study:*** Total amount: $812,732; 124 jobs averaging $2109. ***State or other work-study/employment:*** Part-time jobs available.

APPLYING FOR FINANCIAL AID ***Required financial aid form:*** FAFSA. ***Financial aid deadline (priority):*** 5/1. ***Notification date:*** Continuous beginning 2/15.

CONTACT Ms. Natalie Sandoval, Director of Financial Aid, Schreiner University, 2100 Memorial Boulevard, Kerrville, TX 78028, 830-792-7229 or toll-free 800-343-4919. *Fax:* 830-792-7226. *E-mail:* NSandoval@schreiner.edu.
Website: http://www.schreiner.edu/.

SCRIPPS COLLEGE

Claremont, CA

Tuition & fees: $57,188 **Average undergraduate aid package: $47,740**

ABOUT THE INSTITUTION Independent, women only. ***Awards:*** certificates and bachelor's degrees. 69 undergraduate majors. ***Total enrollment:*** 1,109. Undergraduates: 1,089. Freshmen: 283. Both federal and institutional methodology are used as a basis for awarding need-based institutional aid.

UNDERGRADUATE EXPENSES for 2019–2020 ***Application fee:*** $60. ***Comprehensive fee:*** $74,788 includes full-time tuition ($56,970), mandatory fees ($218), and room and board ($17,600). ***College room only:*** $9584. Full-time tuition and fees vary according to course load and degree level. Room and board charges vary according to board plan. ***Part-time tuition:*** $7121 per course. Part-time tuition and fees vary according to course load and degree level. ***Payment plan:*** Tuition prepayment.

FRESHMAN FINANCIAL AID (Fall 2018) 159 applied for aid; of those 69% were deemed to have need. 100% of freshmen with need received aid; of those 100% had need fully met. ***Average percent of need met:*** 100% (excluding resources awarded to replace EFC). ***Average financial aid package:*** $44,089 (excluding resources

awarded to replace EFC). 13% of all full-time freshmen had no need and received non-need-based gift aid.

UNDERGRADUATE FINANCIAL AID (Fall 2018) 508 applied for aid; of those 77% were deemed to have need. 100% of undergraduates with need received aid; of those 100% had need fully met. ***Average percent of need met:*** 100% (excluding resources awarded to replace EFC). ***Average financial aid package:*** $47,740 (excluding resources awarded to replace EFC). 18% of all full-time undergraduates had no need and received non-need-based gift aid.

GIFT AID (NEED-BASED) ***Receiving aid:*** Freshmen: 42% (107); all full-time undergraduates: 37% (390). ***Average award:*** Freshmen: $39,084; Undergraduates: $39,007. ***Scholarships, grants, and awards:*** Federal Pell, FSEOG, state, private, college/university gift aid from institutional funds.

GIFT AID (NON-NEED-BASED) ***Average award:*** Freshmen: $19,547. Undergraduates: $18,301. ***Scholarships, grants, and awards by category:*** *Academic interests/achievement:* general academic interests/achievements. *Special achievements/activities:* leadership. ***Tuition waivers:*** Full or partial for employees or children of employees. ***ROTC:*** Army cooperative, Air Force cooperative.

LOANS ***Student loans:*** 32% of past graduating class borrowed through all loan programs. *Average indebtedness per student:* $30,150. ***Average need-based loan:*** Freshmen: $3222. Undergraduates: $4215. ***Programs:*** Federal Direct (Subsidized and Unsubsidized Stafford, PLUS), Perkins, college/university.

WORK-STUDY Federal work-study jobs available. ***State or other work-study/employment:*** Part-time jobs available.

APPLYING FOR FINANCIAL AID ***Required financial aid forms:*** FAFSA, CSS Financial Aid PROFILE, state aid form, noncustodial (divorced/separated) parent's statement, business/farm supplement.

CONTACT Patrick Moore, Director of Financial Aid, Scripps College, 1030 Columbia Avenue, Claremont, CA 91711-3948, 909-621-8275 or toll-free 800-770-1333. *Fax:* 909-607-7742. *E-mail:* finaid@scrippscollege.edu.
Website: http://www.scrippscollege.edu/.

SEATTLE PACIFIC UNIVERSITY

Seattle, WA

Tuition & fees: $45,078	Average undergraduate aid package: $39,001

ABOUT THE INSTITUTION Independent Free Methodist, coed. ***Awards:*** certificates, bachelor's, master's, and doctoral degrees. 51 undergraduate majors. Federal methodology is used as a basis for awarding need-based institutional aid.

UNDERGRADUATE EXPENSES for 2019–2020 ***Comprehensive fee:*** $57,363 includes full-time tuition ($44,604), mandatory fees ($474), and room and board ($12,285). ***College room only:*** $6672. Room and board charges vary according to board plan and housing facility. ***Part-time tuition:*** $1239 per credit hour. Part-time tuition and fees vary according to course load.

FRESHMAN FINANCIAL AID (Fall 2019, est.) 564 applied for aid; of those 85% were deemed to have need. 100% of freshmen with need received aid; of those 8% had need fully met. ***Average percent of need met:*** 81% (excluding resources awarded to replace EFC). ***Average financial aid package:*** $40,870 (excluding resources awarded to replace EFC). 19% of all full-time freshmen had no need and received non-need-based gift aid.

UNDERGRADUATE FINANCIAL AID (Fall 2019, est.) 2,070 applied for aid; of those 86% were deemed to have need. 100% of undergraduates with need received aid; of those 7% had need fully met. ***Average percent of need met:*** 79% (excluding resources awarded to replace EFC). ***Average financial aid package:*** $39,001 (excluding resources awarded to replace EFC). 26% of all full-time undergraduates had no need and received non-need-based gift aid.

GIFT AID (NEED-BASED) ***Total amount:*** $58,843,429 (7% federal, 10% state, 78% institutional, 5% external sources). ***Receiving aid:*** Freshmen: 78% (480); all full-time undergraduates: 70% (1,778). ***Average award:*** Freshmen: $43,799; Undergraduates: $38,873. ***Scholarships, grants, and awards:*** Federal Pell, FSEOG, state, private, college/university gift aid from institutional funds.

GIFT AID (NON-NEED-BASED) ***Total amount:*** $18,999,392 (1% state, 74% institutional, 25% external sources). ***Average award:*** Freshmen: $31,798. Undergraduates: $28,793. ***Scholarships, grants, and awards by category:*** *Academic interests/achievement:* 582 awards ($8,739,419 total): engineering/technologies, general academic interests/achievements. *Creative arts/performance:* 33 awards ($49,333 total): applied art and design, music, performing arts, theater/drama. *Special achievements/activities:* 34 awards ($94,264 total): leadership, religious involvement. *Special characteristics:* 354 awards ($1,095,164 total): children and siblings of alumni, children of faculty/staff, ethnic background, general special characteristics, international students, out-of-state students, relatives of clergy, religious affiliation, veterans. ***Tuition waivers:*** Full or partial for employees or children of employees, senior citizens. ***ROTC:*** Army cooperative, Naval cooperative, Air Force cooperative.

LOANS ***Student loans:*** $13,438,186 (90% need-based, 10% non-need-based). 65% of past graduating class borrowed through all loan programs. *Average indebtedness per student:* $29,782. ***Average need-based loan:*** Freshmen: $3418. Undergraduates: $4462. ***Parent loans:*** $7,801,668 (93% need-based, 7% non-need-based). ***Programs:*** Federal Direct (Subsidized and Unsubsidized Stafford, PLUS), Federal Nursing, state, college/university.

WORK-STUDY ***Federal work-study:*** Total amount: $1,236,853; 380 jobs averaging $3255. ***State or other work-study/employment:*** Total amount: $302,846 (100% need-based). 69 part-time jobs averaging $4389.

ATHLETIC AWARDS Total amount: $2,337,480 (53% need-based, 47% non-need-based).

APPLYING FOR FINANCIAL AID ***Required financial aid form:*** FAFSA. ***Financial aid deadline (priority):*** 1/15. ***Notification date:*** Continuous beginning 12/15. Students must reply by 5/1 or within 4 weeks of notification.

CONTACT Mr. Jordan Grant, Director of Student Financial Services, Seattle Pacific University, 3307 Third Avenue West, Seattle, WA 98119-1997, 206-281-2469 or toll-free 800-366-3344. *E-mail:* grantj@spu.edu.
Website: http://www.spu.edu/.

SEATTLE UNIVERSITY

Seattle, WA

Tuition & fees: $48,390	Average undergraduate aid package: $39,057

ABOUT THE INSTITUTION Independent Roman Catholic, coed. ***Awards:*** certificates, bachelor's, master's, and doctoral degrees. 71 undergraduate majors. ***Total enrollment:*** 2,499. Undergraduates: 4,700. Freshmen: 930. Federal methodology is used as a basis for awarding need-based institutional aid.

UNDERGRADUATE EXPENSES for 2020–2021 ***Application fee:*** $55. ***Comprehensive fee:*** $61,170 includes full-time tuition ($47,565), mandatory fees ($825), and room and board ($12,780). ***College room only:*** $8730. Room and board charges vary according to board plan and housing facility. ***Part-time tuition:*** $1057 per credit hour.

FRESHMAN FINANCIAL AID (Fall 2019, est.) 801 applied for aid; of those 74% were deemed to have need. 100% of freshmen with need received aid; of those 29% had need fully met. ***Average percent of need met:*** 82% (excluding resources awarded to replace EFC). ***Average financial aid package:*** $38,555 (excluding resources awarded to replace EFC). 14% of all full-time freshmen had no need and received non-need-based gift aid.

UNDERGRADUATE FINANCIAL AID (Fall 2019, est.) 3,043 applied for aid; of those 81% were deemed to have need. 100% of undergraduates with need received aid; of those 29% had need fully met. ***Average percent of need met:*** 81% (excluding resources awarded to replace EFC). ***Average financial aid package:*** $39,057 (excluding resources awarded to replace EFC). 6% of all full-time undergraduates had no need and received non-need-based gift aid.

GIFT AID (NEED-BASED) ***Receiving aid:*** Freshmen: 53% (493); all full-time undergraduates: 50% (2,226). ***Average award:*** Freshmen: $27,950; Undergraduates: $28,308. ***Scholarships, grants, and awards:*** Federal Pell, FSEOG, state, private, college/university gift aid from institutional funds, Federal Nursing.

GIFT AID (NON-NEED-BASED) ***Receiving aid:*** Freshmen: 51% (471). Undergraduates: 34% (1,500). ***Average award:*** Freshmen: $18,652. Undergraduates: $15,110. ***Scholarships, grants, and awards by category:*** *Academic interests/achievement:* general academic interests/achievements. *Creative arts/performance:* applied art and design, music, theater/drama. *Special achievements/activities:* leadership. *Special characteristics:* children and siblings of alumni, children of educators, children of faculty/staff, members of minority groups, religious affiliation. ***Tuition waivers:*** Full or partial for employees or children of employees. ***ROTC:*** Army, Naval cooperative, Air Force cooperative.

LOANS ***Student loans:*** 69% of past graduating class borrowed through all loan programs. *Average indebtedness per student:* $28,053. ***Average need-based loan:*** Freshmen: $3747. Undergraduates: $5954. ***Programs:*** Federal Direct (Subsidized and Unsubsidized Stafford, PLUS), Perkins, Federal Nursing.

WORK-STUDY *Federal work-study:* 581 jobs averaging $2,225,527. ***State or other work-study/employment:*** 513 part-time jobs averaging $2,446,226.

APPLYING FOR FINANCIAL AID *Required financial aid forms:* FAFSA, institution's own form. ***Notification date:*** Students must reply within 2 weeks of notification.

CONTACT Mr. Jeff Scofield, Director of Student Financial Services, Seattle University, 901 12th Avenue, PO Box 222000, Seattle, WA 98122-1090, 206-296-2000 or toll-free 800-542-0833 (in-state), 800-426-7123 (out-of-state). *Fax:* 206-296-5755. *E-mail:* financial-aid@seattleu.edu.
Website: http://www.seattleu.edu/.

SELMA UNIVERSITY

Selma, AL

CONTACT Financial Aid Office, Selma University, 1501 Lapsley Street, Selma, AL 36701-5299, 334-872-2533.
Website: http://www.selmauniversity.edu/.

SENTARA COLLEGE OF HEALTH SCIENCES

Chesapeake, VA

CONTACT Financial Aid Office, Sentara College of Health Sciences, 1441 Crossways Boulevard, Crossways I, Suite 105, Chesapeake, VA 23320, 757-388-2900.
Website: http://www.sentara.edu/.

SETON HALL UNIVERSITY

South Orange, NJ

CONTACT Office of Enrollment Services, Seton Hall University, 400 South Orange Avenue, South Orange, NJ 07079, 973-761-9350 or toll-free 800-THE HALL. *Fax:* 973-275-2040. *E-mail:* thehall@shu.edu.
Website: http://www.shu.edu/.

SETON HILL UNIVERSITY

Greensburg, PA

ABOUT THE INSTITUTION Independent Roman Catholic, coed. ***Awards:*** certificates, bachelor's, and master's degrees. 74 undergraduate majors. ***Total enrollment:*** 2,079. Undergraduates: 1,726. Freshmen: 399.

GIFT AID (NEED-BASED) *Scholarships, grants, and awards:* Federal Pell, FSEOG, state, private, college/university gift aid from institutional funds.

GIFT AID (NON-NEED-BASED) *Scholarships, grants, and awards by category:* *Academic interests/achievement:* general academic interests/achievements. *Creative arts/performance:* applied art and design, art/fine arts, dance, music, performing arts, theater/drama. *Special achievements/activities:* cheerleading/drum major, general special achievements/activities. *Special characteristics:* children and siblings of alumni, children of faculty/staff, international students, siblings of current students.

LOANS *Programs:* Federal Direct (Subsidized and Unsubsidized Stafford, PLUS), college/university, Private/Alternative Education Loans.

CONTACT Financial Aid Office, Seton Hill University, Seton Hill Drive, Greensburg, PA 15601, 724-834-2200 or toll-free 800-826-6234.
Website: http://www.setonhill.edu/.

SHASTA BIBLE COLLEGE

Redding, CA

CONTACT Linda Iles, Financial Aid Administrator, Shasta Bible College, 2951 Goodwater Avenue, Redding, CA 96002, 530-221-4275 Ext. 30 or toll-free 800-800-4SBC. *Fax:* 530-221-6929. *E-mail:* finaid@shasta.edu.
Website: http://www.shasta.edu/.

SHAWNEE STATE UNIVERSITY

Portsmouth, OH

CONTACT Ms. Charlotte Hardy, Assistant Director of Financial Aid, Shawnee State University, 940 Second Street, Portsmouth, OH 45662-4344, 740-351-3548 or toll-free 800-959-2778. *Fax:* 740-351-3435. *E-mail:* chardy@shawnee.edu.
Website: http://www.shawnee.edu/.

SHAW UNIVERSITY

Raleigh, NC

CONTACT Rochelle King, Director of Financial Aid, Shaw University, 118 East South Street, Raleigh, NC 27601-2399, 919-546-8565 or toll-free 800-214-6683. *Fax:* 919-546-8356. *E-mail:* rking@shawu.edu.
Website: http://www.shawu.edu/.

SHENANDOAH UNIVERSITY

Winchester, VA

Tuition & fees: $33,830	Average undergraduate aid package: $21,001

ABOUT THE INSTITUTION Independent United Methodist, coed. ***Awards:*** certificates, bachelor's, master's, and doctoral degrees. 45 undergraduate majors. ***Total enrollment:*** 3,791. Undergraduates: 2,040. Freshmen: 503. Federal methodology is used as a basis for awarding need-based institutional aid.

UNDERGRADUATE EXPENSES for 2020–2021 *Application fee:* $30. ***Comprehensive fee:*** $44,640 includes full-time tuition ($32,510), mandatory fees ($1320), and room and board ($10,810). Full-time tuition and fees vary according to course load and program. Room and board charges vary according to board plan and housing facility. ***Part-time tuition:*** $950 per credit hour. ***Part-time fees:*** $100. Part-time tuition and fees vary according to course load and program.

FRESHMAN FINANCIAL AID (Fall 2019, est.) 479 applied for aid; of those 83% were deemed to have need. 100% of freshmen with need received aid; of those 21% had need fully met. ***Average percent of need met:*** 69% (excluding resources awarded to replace EFC). ***Average financial aid package:*** $21,911 (excluding resources awarded to replace EFC). 21% of all full-time freshmen had no need and received non-need-based gift aid.

UNDERGRADUATE FINANCIAL AID (Fall 2019, est.) 1,793 applied for aid; of those 85% were deemed to have need. 100% of undergraduates with need received aid; of those 18% had need fully met. ***Average percent of need met:*** 66% (excluding resources awarded to replace EFC). ***Average financial aid package:*** $21,001 (excluding resources awarded to replace EFC). 23% of all full-time undergraduates had no need and received non-need-based gift aid.

GIFT AID (NEED-BASED) *Total amount:* $14,262,166 (16% federal, 84% institutional). ***Receiving aid:*** Freshmen: 51% (255); all full-time undergraduates: 55% (1,093). ***Average award:*** Freshmen: $7214; Undergraduates: $6678. ***Scholarships, grants, and awards:*** Federal Pell, FSEOG, state, private, college/university gift aid from institutional funds.

GIFT AID (NON-NEED-BASED) *Total amount:* $16,592,997 (22% state, 75% institutional, 3% external sources). ***Receiving aid:*** Freshmen: 79% (397). Undergraduates: 75% (1,492). ***Average award:*** Freshmen: $14,442. Undergraduates: $13,253. ***Scholarships, grants, and awards by category:*** *Academic interests/achievement:* biological sciences, business, communication, computer science, education, English, foreign languages, general academic interests/achievements, health fields, humanities, international studies, mathematics, physical sciences, religion/biblical studies, social sciences. *Creative arts/performance:* dance, music, performing arts, theater/drama. *Special achievements/activities:* religious involvement. *Special characteristics:* children of faculty/staff, local/state students. ***Tuition waivers:*** Full or partial for employees or children of employees.

LOANS *Student loans:* $9,286,954 (49% need-based, 51% non-need-based). 78% of past graduating class borrowed through all loan programs. *Average indebtedness per student:* $36,370. ***Average need-based loan:*** Freshmen: $3205. Undergraduates: $4321. ***Parent loans:*** $8,287,360 (100% non-need-based). ***Programs:*** Federal Direct (Subsidized and Unsubsidized Stafford, PLUS), Federal Nursing.

WORK-STUDY *Federal work-study:* Total amount: $1,904,305; jobs available. ***State or other work-study/employment:*** Total amount: $1,067,497 (100% non-need-based). Part-time jobs available.

APPLYING FOR FINANCIAL AID *Required financial aid forms:* FAFSA, state aid form. ***Financial aid deadline:*** Continuous. ***Notification date:*** Continuous beginning 1/15. Students must reply within 2 weeks of notification.

CONTACT Ms. Karen Bucher, Director of Financial Aid, Shenandoah University, 1460 University Drive, Winchester, VA 22601-5195, 540-665-4538 or toll-free 800-432-2266. *Fax:* 540-665-4939. *E-mail:* kbucher@su.edu.
Website: http://www.su.edu/.

SHEPHERD UNIVERSITY

Shepherdstown, WV

Tuition & fees (WV res): $7784	Average undergraduate aid package: $2795

ABOUT THE INSTITUTION State-supported, coed. ***Awards:*** bachelor's, master's, and doctoral degrees. 28 undergraduate majors. ***Total enrollment:*** 3,554. Undergraduates: 3,200. Freshmen: 483. Federal methodology is used as a basis for awarding need-based institutional aid.

UNDERGRADUATE EXPENSES for 2020–2021 *Application fee:* $45. ***Tuition, state resident:*** full-time $7784; part-time $325 per credit hour. ***Tuition, nonresident:*** full-time $18,224; part-time $760 per credit hour. Full-time tuition and fees vary according to program and reciprocity agreements. Part-time tuition and fees vary according to program. ***College room and board:*** $10,654. Room and board charges vary according to board plan and housing facility.

FRESHMAN FINANCIAL AID (Fall 2019, est.) 474 applied for aid; of those 67% were deemed to have need. 98% of freshmen with need received aid; of those 32% had need fully met. ***Average percent of need met:*** 75% (excluding resources awarded to replace EFC). ***Average financial aid package:*** $12,429 (excluding resources awarded to replace EFC). 29% of all full-time freshmen had no need and received non-need-based gift aid.

UNDERGRADUATE FINANCIAL AID (Fall 2019, est.) 2,266 applied for aid; of those 67% were deemed to have need. 99% of undergraduates with need received aid; of those 28% had need fully met. ***Average percent of need met:*** 78% (excluding resources awarded to replace EFC). ***Average financial aid package:*** $2795 (excluding resources awarded to replace EFC). 25% of all full-time undergraduates had no need and received non-need-based gift aid.

GIFT AID (NEED-BASED) *Total amount:* $6,493,059 (71% federal, 25% state, 4% institutional). ***Receiving aid:*** Freshmen: 43% (208); all full-time undergraduates: 44% (1,068). ***Average award:*** Freshmen: $5928; Undergraduates: $5666. ***Scholarships, grants, and awards:*** Federal Pell, FSEOG, state, private, college/university gift aid from institutional funds.

GIFT AID (NON-NEED-BASED) *Total amount:* $6,507,091 (31% state, 60% institutional, 9% external sources). ***Receiving aid:*** Freshmen: 38% (181). Undergraduates: 28% (665). ***Average award:*** Freshmen: $9650. Undergraduates: $10,139. ***Scholarships, grants, and awards by category:*** *Academic interests/achievement:* 1,047 awards ($1768 total): biological sciences, business, communication, computer science, education, engineering/technologies, English, foreign languages, general academic interests/achievements, international studies, mathematics, physical sciences. *Creative arts/performance:* 82 awards ($6409 total): applied art and design, art/fine arts, music, performing arts, theater/drama. *Special achievements/activities:* 29 awards ($2008 total): leadership. *Special characteristics:* 1 award ($900 total): children of faculty/staff, international students, members of minority groups, out-of-state students, previous college experience. ***Tuition waivers:*** Full or partial for minority students, employees or children of employees, senior citizens. ***ROTC:*** Air Force cooperative.

LOANS *Student loans:* $9,374,079 (43% need-based, 57% non-need-based). 67% of past graduating class borrowed through all loan programs. *Average indebtedness per student:* $28,371. ***Average need-based loan:*** Freshmen: $3120. Undergraduates: $3967. ***Parent loans:*** $3,708,854 (100% non-need-based). ***Programs:*** Federal Direct (Subsidized and Unsubsidized Stafford, PLUS), private lenders.

WORK-STUDY *Federal work-study:* Total amount: $244,324; 91 jobs averaging $1025. ***State or other work-study/employment:*** Total amount: $706,629 (100% need-based). 350 part-time jobs averaging $1400.

ATHLETIC AWARDS Total amount: $1,326,398 (100% non-need-based).

APPLYING FOR FINANCIAL AID *Required financial aid form:* FAFSA. ***Financial aid deadline:*** Continuous. ***Notification date:*** Continuous beginning 12/1. Students must reply within 2 weeks of notification.

CONTACT Ms. Joyce Cabral, Director of Financial Aid, Shepherd University, PO Box 5000, Shepherdstown, WV 25443-5000, 304-876-5470 or toll-free 800-344-5231. *Fax:* 304-876-5238. *E-mail:* faoweb@shepherd.edu.
Website: http://www.shepherd.edu/.

SHILOH UNIVERSITY

Kalona, IA

CONTACT Financial Aid Office, Shiloh University, 100 Shiloh Drive, Kalona, IA 52247, 319-656-2447.
Website: http://www.shilohuniversity.edu/.

SHIPPENSBURG UNIVERSITY OF PENNSYLVANIA

Shippensburg, PA

Tuition & fees: N/R	Average undergraduate aid package: $10,154

ABOUT THE INSTITUTION State-supported, coed. ***Awards:*** certificates, bachelor's, master's, and doctoral degrees. 41 undergraduate majors. ***Total enrollment:*** 6,408. Undergraduates: 5,501. Freshmen: 1,357. Federal methodology is used as a basis for awarding need-based institutional aid.

FRESHMAN FINANCIAL AID (Fall 2019, est.) 1224 applied for aid; of those 81% were deemed to have need. 99% of freshmen with need received aid; of those 10% had need fully met. ***Average percent of need met:*** 53% (excluding resources awarded to replace EFC). ***Average financial aid package:*** $10,811 (excluding resources awarded to replace EFC). 13% of all full-time freshmen had no need and received non-need-based gift aid.

UNDERGRADUATE FINANCIAL AID (Fall 2019, est.) 4,259 applied for aid; of those 81% were deemed to have need. 99% of undergraduates with need received aid; of those 12% had need fully met. ***Average percent of need met:*** 54% (excluding resources awarded to replace EFC). ***Average financial aid package:*** $10,154 (excluding resources awarded to replace EFC). 11% of all full-time undergraduates had no need and received non-need-based gift aid.

GIFT AID (NEED-BASED) *Receiving aid:* Freshmen: 66% (855); all full-time undergraduates: 56% (2,721). ***Average award:*** Freshmen: $8585; Undergraduates: $7630. ***Scholarships, grants, and awards:*** Federal Pell, FSEOG, state, private, college/university gift aid from institutional funds.

GIFT AID (NON-NEED-BASED) *Receiving aid:* Freshmen: 5% (62). Undergraduates: 4% (190). ***Average award:*** Freshmen: $4655. Undergraduates: $5326. ***Scholarships, grants, and awards by category:*** *Academic interests/achievement:* biological sciences, business, communication, computer science, education, English, foreign languages, general academic interests/achievements, humanities, mathematics, physical sciences, social sciences. *Creative arts/performance:* applied art and design, music, theater/drama. *Special achievements/activities:* community service, general special achievements/activities, leadership. *Special characteristics:* children and siblings of alumni, general special characteristics, handicapped students, local/state students. ***ROTC:*** Army.

LOANS *Student loans:* 80% of past graduating class borrowed through all loan programs. *Average indebtedness per student:* $37,130. ***Average need-based loan:*** Freshmen: $3269. Undergraduates: $3857. ***Programs:*** Federal Direct (Subsidized and Unsubsidized Stafford, PLUS), Perkins, alternative loans.

WORK-STUDY ***Federal work-study:*** 114 jobs averaging $1475. ***State or other work-study/employment:*** 608 part-time jobs averaging $2320.

APPLYING FOR FINANCIAL AID ***Required financial aid form:*** FAFSA. ***Financial aid deadline:*** Continuous. ***Notification date:*** Continuous. Students must reply within 2 weeks of notification.

CONTACT Mrs. Trina M. Snyder, Director of Financial Aid and Scholarships, Shippensburg University of Pennsylvania, 1871 Old Main Drive, Shippensburg, PA 17257-2299, 717-477-1131 or toll-free 800-822-8028 (in-state). *Fax:* 717-477-4028. *E-mail:* finaid@ship.edu.

Website: http://www.ship.edu/.

SHORTER UNIVERSITY

Rome, GA

CONTACT Ms. Tara Jones, Director of Financial Aid, Shorter University, 315 Shorter Avenue, Rome, GA 30165, 706-233-7227 or toll-free 800-868-6980. *Fax:* 706-233-7314. *E-mail:* tjones@shorter.edu.

Website: http://www.shorter.edu/.

SH'OR YOSHUV RABBINICAL COLLEGE

Lawrence, NY

CONTACT Office of Financial Aid, Sh'or Yoshuv Rabbinical College, 1526 Central Avenue, Far Rockaway, NY 11691-4002, 718-327-2048.

SIENA COLLEGE

Loudonville, NY

Tuition & fees: $39,500	Average undergraduate aid package: $31,867

ABOUT THE INSTITUTION Independent Roman Catholic, coed. ***Awards:*** certificates, bachelor's, and master's degrees. 42 undergraduate majors. ***Total enrollment:*** 3,299. Undergraduates: 3,191. Freshmen: 841. Federal methodology is used as a basis for awarding need-based institutional aid.

UNDERGRADUATE EXPENSES for 2020–2021 ***Application fee:*** $50. ***Comprehensive fee:*** $55,415 includes full-time tuition ($39,200), mandatory fees ($300), and room and board ($15,915). ***College room only:*** $9485. Full-time tuition and fees vary according to course load and student level. Room and board charges vary according to board plan, housing facility, and student level. ***Part-time tuition:*** $675 per credit hour. ***Part-time fees:*** $95 per term. Part-time tuition and fees vary according to course load and student level.

FRESHMAN FINANCIAL AID (Fall 2018) 677 applied for aid; of those 86% were deemed to have need. 100% of freshmen with need received aid; of those 34% had need fully met. ***Average percent of need met:*** 80% (excluding resources awarded to replace EFC). ***Average financial aid package:*** $33,696 (excluding resources awarded to replace EFC). 18% of all full-time freshmen had no need and received non-need-based gift aid.

UNDERGRADUATE FINANCIAL AID (Fall 2018) 2,553 applied for aid; of those 88% were deemed to have need. 100% of undergraduates with need received aid; of those 31% had need fully met. ***Average percent of need met:*** 80% (excluding resources awarded to replace EFC). ***Average financial aid package:*** $31,867 (excluding resources awarded to replace EFC). 19% of all full-time undergraduates had no need and received non-need-based gift aid.

GIFT AID (NEED-BASED) ***Total amount:*** $57,548,364 (8% federal, 4% state, 88% institutional). ***Receiving aid:*** Freshmen: 78% (584); all full-time undergraduates: 74% (2,247). ***Average award:*** Freshmen: $26,609; Undergraduates: $24,358. ***Scholarships, grants, and awards:*** Federal Pell, FSEOG, state, private, college/university gift aid from institutional funds.

GIFT AID (NON-NEED-BASED) ***Total amount:*** $10,888,964 (1% state, 87% institutional, 12% external sources). ***Receiving aid:*** Freshmen: 76% (566). Undergraduates: 71% (2,147). ***Average award:*** Freshmen: $14,931. Undergraduates: $13,626. ***Tuition waivers:*** Full or partial for employees or children of employees. ***ROTC:*** Army, Air Force cooperative.

LOANS ***Student loans:*** $22,978,636 (82% need-based, 18% non-need-based). 77% of past graduating class borrowed through all loan programs. *Average indebtedness per student:* $35,057. ***Average need-based loan:*** Freshmen: $3156. Undergraduates: $4342. ***Parent loans:*** $7,648,405 (80% need-based, 20% non-need-based). ***Programs:*** Federal Direct (Subsidized and Unsubsidized Stafford), Perkins.

WORK-STUDY ***Federal work-study:*** Total amount: $293,816; jobs available (averaging $293,816).

ATHLETIC AWARDS Total amount: $5,602,918 (35% need-based, 65% non-need-based).

APPLYING FOR FINANCIAL AID ***Required financial aid forms:*** FAFSA, state aid form. ***Financial aid deadline:*** 2/15 (priority: 2/15). ***Notification date:*** 4/1. Students must reply by 5/1.

CONTACT Mary Lawyer, Associate Vice President for Enrollment Management, Siena College, 515 Loudon Rd., Loudonville, NY 12211, 518-783-2427 or toll-free 888-AT-SIENA. *E-mail:* aid@siena.edu.

Website: http://www.siena.edu/.

SIENA HEIGHTS UNIVERSITY

Adrian, MI

CONTACT Office of Financial Aid, Siena Heights University, 1247 East Siena Heights Drive, Adrian, MI 49221, 517-264-7130 or toll-free 800-521-0009.

Website: http://www.sienaheights.edu/.

SIERRA NEVADA COLLEGE

Incline Village, NV

CONTACT Nicole D. Ferguson, Director of Financial Aid, Sierra Nevada College, 999 Tahoe Boulevard, Incline Village, NV 89451, 775-831-1314 Ext. 7404. *Fax:* 775-832-1678. *E-mail:* nferguson@sierranevada.edu.

Website: http://www.sierranevada.edu/.

SILVER LAKE COLLEGE OF THE HOLY FAMILY

Manitowoc, WI

CONTACT Ms. Michelle Leider, Associate Director of Financial Aid, Silver Lake College of the Holy Family, 2406 South Alverno Road, Manitowoc, WI 54220-9319, 920-686-6122 or toll-free 800-236-4752 Ext.175. *Fax:* 920-684-7082. *E-mail:* financialaid@sl.edu.

Website: http://www.sl.edu/.

SIMMONS COLLEGE OF KENTUCKY

Louisville, KY

CONTACT Financial Aid Office, Simmons College of Kentucky, 1018 South 7th Street, Louisville, KY 40203, 502-776-1443.

Website: http://www.simmonscollegeky.edu/.

SIMMONS UNIVERSITY

Boston, MA

Tuition & fees: $43,330	Average undergraduate aid package: $34,674

ABOUT THE INSTITUTION Independent, undergraduate: women only; graduate: coed. ***Awards:*** certificates, bachelor's, master's, and doctoral degrees. 55 undergraduate majors. ***Total enrollment:*** 6,635. Undergraduates: 1,777. Freshmen: 433. Federal methodology is used as a basis for awarding need-based institutional aid.

UNDERGRADUATE EXPENSES for 2020–2021 ***Application fee:*** $55. ***Comprehensive fee:*** $58,990 includes full-time tuition ($42,080), mandatory fees ($1250), and room and board ($15,660). Full-time tuition and fees vary according to course load and program. Room and board charges vary according to board plan and location. ***Part-time tuition:*** $1315 per credit hour. ***Part-time fees:*** $260 per term. Part-time tuition and fees vary according to course load and program.

FRESHMAN FINANCIAL AID (Fall 2019, est.) 400 applied for aid; of those 89% were deemed to have need. 100% of freshmen with need received aid; of those 35% had need fully met. ***Average percent of need met:*** 86% (excluding resources awarded to replace EFC). ***Average financial aid package:*** $36,295 (excluding resources awarded to replace EFC). 17% of all full-time freshmen had no need and received non-need-based gift aid.

UNDERGRADUATE FINANCIAL AID (Fall 2019, est.) 1,329 applied for aid; of those 91% were deemed to have need. 100% of undergraduates with need received aid; of those 20% had need fully met. ***Average percent of need met:*** 79% (excluding resources awarded to replace EFC). ***Average financial aid package:*** $34,674 (excluding resources awarded to replace EFC). 22% of all full-time undergraduates had no need and received non-need-based gift aid.

GIFT AID (NEED-BASED) ***Total amount:*** $38,803,847 (7% federal, 1% state, 91% institutional, 1% external sources). ***Receiving aid:*** Freshmen: 82% (352); all full-time undergraduates: 75% (1,209). ***Average award:*** Freshmen: $32,347; Undergraduates: $30,651. ***Scholarships, grants, and awards:*** Federal Pell, FSEOG, state, private, college/university gift aid from institutional funds.

GIFT AID (NON-NEED-BASED) ***Total amount:*** $9,764,411 (98% institutional, 2% external sources). ***Receiving aid:*** Freshmen: 24% (102). Undergraduates: 11% (176). ***Average award:*** Freshmen: $22,774. Undergraduates: $22,538. ***Scholarships, grants, and awards by category:*** *Academic interests/achievement:* general academic interests/achievements. *Special achievements/activities:* community service, general special achievements/activities. *Special characteristics:* children and siblings of alumni, general special characteristics. ***Tuition waivers:*** Full or partial for employees or children of employees. ***ROTC:*** Army cooperative.

LOANS ***Student loans:*** $13,229,018 (33% need-based, 67% non-need-based). 77% of past graduating class borrowed through all loan programs. *Average indebtedness per student:* $37,935. ***Average need-based loan:*** Freshmen: $3024. Undergraduates: $4054. ***Parent loans:*** $2,755,440 (100% non-need-based). ***Programs:*** Federal Direct (Subsidized and Unsubsidized Stafford, PLUS), college/university.

WORK-STUDY ***Federal work-study:*** Total amount: $2,148,302; 887 jobs averaging $2523.

APPLYING FOR FINANCIAL AID ***Required financial aid forms:*** FAFSA, institution's own form. ***Financial aid deadline (priority):*** 3/1. ***Notification date:*** Continuous beginning 12/19.

CONTACT Amanda Galban, Senior Associate Director of Financial Aid, Simmons University, 300 The Fenway, Boston, MA 02115, 617-521-2001 or toll-free 800-345-8468. *Fax:* 617-521-3195. *E-mail:* amanda.galban@simmons.edu.
Website: http://www.simmons.edu/.

SIMPSON COLLEGE

Indianola, IA

Tuition & fees: N/R	Average undergraduate aid package: $34,223

ABOUT THE INSTITUTION Independent United Methodist, coed. ***Awards:*** certificates, bachelor's, and master's degrees. 61 undergraduate majors. Federal methodology is used as a basis for awarding need-based institutional aid.

FRESHMAN FINANCIAL AID (Fall 2019, est.) 281 applied for aid; of those 94% were deemed to have need. 100% of freshmen with need received aid; of those 21% had need fully met. ***Average percent of need met:*** 86% (excluding resources awarded to replace EFC). ***Average financial aid package:*** $38,637 (excluding resources awarded to replace EFC). 9% of all full-time freshmen had no need and received non-need-based gift aid.

UNDERGRADUATE FINANCIAL AID (Fall 2019, est.) 1,052 applied for aid; of those 93% were deemed to have need. 100% of undergraduates with need received aid; of those 21% had need fully met. ***Average percent of need met:*** 82% (excluding resources awarded to replace EFC). ***Average financial aid package:*** $34,223 (excluding resources awarded to replace EFC). 14% of all full-time undergraduates had no need and received non-need-based gift aid.

GIFT AID (NEED-BASED) ***Receiving aid:*** Freshmen: 89% (261); all full-time undergraduates: 82% (968). ***Average award:*** Freshmen: $34,416; Undergraduates: $29,188. ***Scholarships, grants, and awards:*** Federal Pell, FSEOG, state, private, college/university gift aid from institutional funds.

GIFT AID (NON-NEED-BASED) ***Receiving aid:*** Freshmen: 15% (44). Undergraduates: 12% (137). ***Average award:*** Freshmen: $27,112. Undergraduates: $23,661. ***Scholarships, grants, and awards by category:*** *Academic interests/achievement:* $12,847,590 total: general academic interests/achievements. *Creative arts/performance:* $453,425 total: applied art and design, debating, music, performing arts, theater/drama. *Special achievements/activities:* $192,000 total: community service, leadership, religious involvement. *Special characteristics:* $4,414,438 total: adult students, children and siblings of alumni, children of educators, children of faculty/staff, ethnic background, first-generation college students, international students, members of minority groups, out-of-state students, relatives of clergy, religious affiliation, siblings of current students, twins, veterans.

LOANS ***Student loans:*** 82% of past graduating class borrowed through all loan programs. *Average indebtedness per student:* $40,775. ***Average need-based loan:*** Freshmen: $3463. Undergraduates: $4406. ***Programs:*** Federal Direct (Subsidized and Unsubsidized Stafford, PLUS), college/university, alternative loans.

WORK-STUDY ***Federal work-study:*** 299 jobs averaging $1303. ***State or other work-study/employment:*** 383 part-time jobs averaging $1558.

APPLYING FOR FINANCIAL AID ***Required financial aid form:*** FAFSA. ***Financial aid deadline:*** Continuous. ***Notification date:*** Continuous. Students must reply within 3 weeks of notification.

CONTACT Ms. Tracie Lynn Pavon, Assistant Vice President for Enrollment & Financial Aid, Simpson College, 701 North C Street, Indianola, IA 50125-1297, 515-961-1630 Ext. 1596 or toll-free 800-362-2454. *Fax:* 515-961-1300. *E-mail:* tracie.pavon@simpson.edu.
Website: http://www.simpson.edu/.

SIMPSON UNIVERSITY

Redding, CA

CONTACT Miss Kari Meyers, Associate Director of Financial Aid, Simpson University, 2211 College View Drive, Redding, CA 96003-8606, 530-226-4621 or toll-free 888-9-SIMPSON. *Fax:* 530-226-4855. *E-mail:* financialaid@simpsonu.edu.
Website: http://www.simpsonu.edu/.

SINTE GLESKA UNIVERSITY

Mission, SD

CONTACT Office of Financial Aid, Sinte Gleska University, PO Box 105, Mission, SD 5755504105, 605-856-8197 Ext. 8477. *Fax:* 605-856-5874. *E-mail:* bhay@sintegleska.edu.
Website: http://www.sintegleska.edu/.

SITTING BULL COLLEGE

Fort Yates, ND

CONTACT Donna M. Seaboy, Financial Aid Director, Sitting Bull College, 9299 Highway 24, Fort Yates, ND 58538, 701-854-8013. *Fax:* 701-854-3403. *E-mail:* donnas@sbci.edu.
Website: http://www.sittingbull.edu/.

SKIDMORE COLLEGE

Saratoga Springs, NY

Tuition & fees: $56,172	Average undergraduate aid package: $53,700

ABOUT THE INSTITUTION Independent, coed. ***Awards:*** bachelor's degrees. 41 undergraduate majors. ***Total enrollment:*** 2,663. Undergraduates: 2,662. Freshmen: 735. Both federal and institutional methodology are used as a basis for awarding need-based institutional aid.

UNDERGRADUATE EXPENSES for 2019–2020 ***Application fee:*** $65. ***One-time required fee:*** $150. ***Comprehensive fee:*** $71,172 includes full-time tuition ($55,136), mandatory fees ($1036), and room and board ($15,000). ***College room only:*** $8868. ***Part-time tuition:*** $1838 per credit hour. ***Part-time fees:*** $25 per term.

FRESHMAN FINANCIAL AID (Fall 2019, est.) 439 applied for aid; of those 85% were deemed to have need. 100% of freshmen with need received aid; of those 100% had need fully met. ***Average percent of need met:*** 100% (excluding resources awarded to replace EFC). ***Average financial aid package:*** $51,600 (excluding resources awarded to replace EFC). 1% of all full-time freshmen had no need and received non-need-based gift aid.

UNDERGRADUATE FINANCIAL AID (Fall 2019, est.) 1,318 applied for aid; of those 91% were deemed to have need. 100% of undergraduates with need received aid; of those 97% had need fully met. ***Average percent of need met:*** 99% (excluding resources awarded to replace EFC). ***Average financial aid package:*** $53,700 (excluding resources awarded to replace EFC). 1% of all full-time undergraduates had no need and received non-need-based gift aid.

GIFT AID (NEED-BASED) ***Total amount:*** $57,916,000 (4% federal, 3% state, 93% institutional). ***Receiving aid:*** Freshmen: 51% (373); all full-time undergraduates: 46% (1,198). ***Average award:*** Freshmen: $46,850; Undergraduates: $47,800. ***Scholarships, grants, and awards:*** Federal Pell, FSEOG, state, private, college/university gift aid from institutional funds.

GIFT AID (NON-NEED-BASED) ***Total amount:*** $1,827,000 (4% state, 41% institutional, 55% external sources). ***Receiving aid:*** Freshmen: 2% (14). Undergraduates: 2% (42). ***Average award:*** Freshmen: $15,000. Undergraduates: $16,500. ***Scholarships, grants, and awards by category:*** *Academic interests/achievement:* biological sciences, computer science, mathematics, physical sciences. *Creative arts/performance:* music. *Special characteristics:* children of faculty/staff. ***ROTC:*** Army cooperative, Air Force cooperative.

LOANS ***Student loans:*** $6,450,000 (38% need-based, 62% non-need-based). 34% of past graduating class borrowed through all loan programs. *Average indebtedness per student:* $31,381. ***Average need-based loan:*** Freshmen: $2250. Undergraduates: $3100. ***Parent loans:*** $2,750,000 (100% non-need-based). ***Programs:*** Federal Direct (Subsidized and Unsubsidized Stafford, PLUS), Perkins, state.

WORK-STUDY ***Federal work-study:*** Total amount: $600,000; jobs available. ***State or other work-study/employment:*** Total amount: $850,000 (94% need-based, 6% non-need-based). Part-time jobs available.

APPLYING FOR FINANCIAL AID ***Required financial aid forms:*** CSS Financial Aid PROFILE, noncustodial (divorced/separated) parent's statement. ***Financial aid deadline:*** 1/15. ***Notification date:*** 4/1. Students must reply by 5/1.

CONTACT Ms. Beth A. Post, Director of Financial Aid, Skidmore College, 815 North Broadway, Saratoga Springs, NY 12866, 518-580-5750 or toll-free 800-867-6007. *Fax:* 518-580-5752. *E-mail:* finaid@skidmore.edu.
Website: http://www.skidmore.edu/.

SLIPPERY ROCK UNIVERSITY OF PENNSYLVANIA

Slippery Rock, PA

Tuition & fees (PA res): $10,517	Average undergraduate aid package: $9560

ABOUT THE INSTITUTION State-supported, coed. ***Awards:*** certificates, bachelor's, master's, and doctoral degrees. 51 undergraduate majors. ***Total enrollment:*** 8,824. Undergraduates: 7,538. Freshmen: 1,554. Federal methodology is used as a basis for awarding need-based institutional aid.

UNDERGRADUATE EXPENSES for 2019–2020 ***Application fee:*** $30. ***Tuition, state resident:*** full-time $7716; part-time $322 per credit hour. ***Tuition, nonresident:*** full-time $15,432; part-time $644 per credit hour. ***Required fees:*** full-time $2801; $115 per credit hour. Full-time tuition and fees vary according to course load. Part-time tuition and fees vary according to course load. ***College room and board:*** $10,446; ***Room only:*** $6876. Room and board charges vary according to board plan and housing facility.

FRESHMAN FINANCIAL AID (Fall 2019, est.) 1519 applied for aid; of those 74% were deemed to have need. 99% of freshmen with need received aid; of those 13% had need fully met. ***Average percent of need met:*** 59% (excluding resources awarded to replace EFC). ***Average financial aid package:*** $9433 (excluding resources awarded to replace EFC). 15% of all full-time freshmen had no need and received non-need-based gift aid.

UNDERGRADUATE FINANCIAL AID (Fall 2019, est.) 6,116 applied for aid; of those 77% were deemed to have need. 98% of undergraduates with need received aid; of those 12% had need fully met. ***Average percent of need met:*** 60% (excluding resources awarded to replace EFC). ***Average financial aid package:*** $9560 (excluding resources awarded to replace EFC). 10% of all full-time undergraduates had no need and received non-need-based gift aid.

GIFT AID (NEED-BASED) ***Receiving aid:*** Freshmen: 50% (789); all full-time undergraduates: 46% (3,231). ***Average award:*** Freshmen: $6328; Undergraduates: $5969. ***Scholarships, grants, and awards:*** Federal Pell, FSEOG, state, private, college/university gift aid from institutional funds.

GIFT AID (NON-NEED-BASED) ***Receiving aid:*** Freshmen: 36% (565). Undergraduates: 23% (1,620). ***Average award:*** Freshmen: $3175. Undergraduates: $3114. ***Scholarships, grants, and awards by category:*** *Academic interests/achievement:* biological sciences, business, communication, computer science, education, engineering/technologies, English, foreign languages, general academic interests/achievements, health fields, home economics, humanities, mathematics, military science, physical sciences, social sciences. *Creative arts/performance:* applied art and design, art/fine arts, creative writing, dance, music, performing arts, theater/drama. *Special achievements/activities:* community service, general special achievements/activities, leadership. *Special characteristics:* adult students, children and siblings of alumni, children of faculty/staff, children of union members/company employees, ethnic background, first-generation college students, general special characteristics, international students, local/state students, members of minority groups, out-of-state students, previous college experience, veterans. ***Tuition waivers:*** Full or partial for minority students, employees or children of employees, senior citizens. ***ROTC:*** Army.

LOANS ***Student loans:*** 82% of past graduating class borrowed through all loan programs. *Average indebtedness per student:* $37,450. ***Average need-based loan:*** Freshmen: $3347. Undergraduates: $4225. ***Programs:*** Federal Direct (Subsidized and Unsubsidized Stafford, PLUS).

WORK-STUDY ***Federal work-study:*** 591 jobs averaging $1506. ***State or other work-study/employment:*** 908 part-time jobs averaging $2012.

APPLYING FOR FINANCIAL AID ***Required financial aid form:*** FAFSA. ***Notification date:*** Continuous.

CONTACT Ms. Alyssa Dobson, Director of Financial Aid and Scholarships, Slippery Rock University of Pennsylvania, 108 Maltby Center, Suite 107, Slippery Rock, PA 16057, 724-738-2044 or toll-free 800-SRU-9111. *Fax:* 724-738-2922. *E-mail:* alyssa.dobson@sru.edu.
Website: http://www.sru.edu/.

SMITH COLLEGE

Northampton, MA

Tuition & fees: $56,114	Average undergraduate aid package: $56,230

ABOUT THE INSTITUTION Independent, undergraduate: women only; graduate: coed. ***Awards:*** certificates, bachelor's, master's, and doctoral degrees. 53 undergraduate majors. ***Total enrollment:*** 2,894. Undergraduates: 2,531. Freshmen: 633. Both federal and institutional methodology are used as a basis for awarding need-based institutional aid.

UNDERGRADUATE EXPENSES for 2020–2021 ***Comprehensive fee:*** $74,874 includes full-time tuition ($55,830), mandatory fees ($284), and room and board ($18,760). ***College room only:*** $9400. ***Part-time tuition:*** $1740 per credit. ***Payment plan:*** Tuition prepayment.

FRESHMAN FINANCIAL AID (Fall 2019, est.) 456 applied for aid; of those 82% were deemed to have need. 100% of freshmen with need received aid; of those 100% had need fully met. ***Average percent of need met:*** 100% (excluding resources awarded to replace EFC). ***Average financial aid package:*** $56,078 (excluding resources awarded to replace EFC). 8% of all full-time freshmen had no need and received non-need-based gift aid.

UNDERGRADUATE FINANCIAL AID (Fall 2019, est.) 1,688 applied for aid; of those 90% were deemed to have need. 100% of undergraduates with need received aid; of those 100% had need fully met. ***Average percent of need met:*** 100% (excluding resources awarded to replace EFC). ***Average financial aid package:*** $56,230 (excluding resources awarded to replace EFC). 9% of all full-time undergraduates had no need and received non-need-based gift aid.

GIFT AID (NEED-BASED) ***Receiving aid:*** Freshmen: 59% (371); all full-time undergraduates: 60% (1,501). ***Average award:*** Freshmen: $51,991; Undergraduates: $51,099. ***Scholarships, grants, and awards:*** Federal Pell, FSEOG, state, private, college/university gift aid from institutional funds.

GIFT AID (NON-NEED-BASED) ***Receiving aid:*** Freshmen: 1% (8). Undergraduates: 1% (27). ***Average award:*** Freshmen: $17,907. Undergraduates: $16,497. ***Scholarships, grants, and awards by category:*** *Academic interests/achievement:* general academic interests/achievements. *Special characteristics:* local/state students. ***Tuition waivers:*** Full or partial for employees or children of employees. ***ROTC:*** Army cooperative, Air Force cooperative.

LOANS ***Student loans:*** 61% of past graduating class borrowed through all loan programs. *Average indebtedness per student:* $21,460. ***Average need-based loan:*** Freshmen: $3054. Undergraduates: $4111. ***Programs:*** Federal Direct (Subsidized and Unsubsidized Stafford, PLUS), Perkins, college/university.

WORK-STUDY Federal work-study jobs available. ***State or other work-study/employment:*** Part-time jobs available.

APPLYING FOR FINANCIAL AID ***Required financial aid forms:*** FAFSA, institution's own form, CSS Financial Aid PROFILE, noncustodial (divorced/separated) parent's statement.

CONTACT David Belanger, Director of Student Financial Services, Smith College, College Hall 106, 10 Elm Street, Northampton, MA 01063, 413-585-2530 or toll-free 800-383-3232. *Fax:* 413-585-2566. *E-mail:* sfs@smith.edu.
Website: http://www.smith.edu/.

SOKA UNIVERSITY OF AMERICA

Aliso Viejo, CA

CONTACT Dr. Andrew Woolsey, Director of Enrollment Services, Soka University of America, 1 University Drive, Aliso Viejo, CA 92656, 949-480-4112 or toll-free 888-600-SOKA. *Fax:* 949-480-4151. *E-mail:* awoolsey@soka.edu.
Website: http://www.soka.edu/.

SONOMA STATE UNIVERSITY

Rohnert Park, CA

Tuition & fees: N/R	Average undergraduate aid package: $10,634

ABOUT THE INSTITUTION State-supported, coed. ***Awards:*** bachelor's and master's degrees. 61 undergraduate majors. ***Total enrollment:*** 9,201. Undergraduates: 8,565. Freshmen: 1,740. Federal methodology is used as a basis for awarding need-based institutional aid.

FRESHMAN FINANCIAL AID (Fall 2019, est.) 1268 applied for aid; of those 72% were deemed to have need. 100% of freshmen with need received aid; of those 5% had need fully met. ***Average percent of need met:*** 58% (excluding resources awarded to replace EFC). ***Average financial aid package:*** $11,244 (excluding resources awarded to replace EFC). 1% of all full-time freshmen had no need and received non-need-based gift aid.

UNDERGRADUATE FINANCIAL AID (Fall 2019, est.) 5,381 applied for aid; of those 77% were deemed to have need. 100% of undergraduates with need received aid; of those 5% had need fully met. ***Average percent of need met:*** 57% (excluding resources awarded to replace EFC). ***Average financial aid package:*** $10,634 (excluding resources awarded to replace EFC). 1% of all full-time undergraduates had no need and received non-need-based gift aid.

GIFT AID (NEED-BASED) ***Total amount:*** $33,274,037 (39% federal, 61% state). ***Receiving aid:*** Freshmen: 55% (843); all full-time undergraduates: 52% (3,843). ***Average award:*** Freshmen: $9443; Undergraduates: $8601. ***Scholarships, grants, and awards:*** Federal Pell, FSEOG, state, private, college/university gift aid from institutional funds.

GIFT AID (NON-NEED-BASED) ***Total amount:*** $4,317,571 (45% state, 20% institutional, 35% external sources). ***Receiving aid:*** Freshmen: 41% (629). Undergraduates: 38% (2,788). ***Average award:*** Freshmen: $1512. Undergraduates: $1335. ***Scholarships, grants, and awards by category:*** *Academic interests/achievement:* area/ethnic studies, biological sciences, business, communication, computer science, education, engineering/technologies, English, foreign languages, general academic interests/achievements, home economics, humanities, mathematics, physical sciences, premedicine, social sciences. *Creative arts/performance:* applied art and design, art/fine arts, cinema/film/broadcasting, creative writing, dance, journalism/publications, music, performing arts, theater/drama. *Special achievements/activities:* community service, leadership, memberships. *Special characteristics:* adult students, children and siblings of alumni, children of educators, children of faculty/staff, children of public servants, children of union members/company employees, children of workers in trades, ethnic background, first-generation college students, general special characteristics, handicapped students, international students, local/state students, married students, members of minority groups, out-of-state students, previous college experience, veterans. ***ROTC:*** Army cooperative, Air Force cooperative.

LOANS ***Student loans:*** $17,188,298 (55% need-based, 45% non-need-based). 53% of past graduating class borrowed through all loan programs. *Average indebtedness per student:* $21,594. ***Average need-based loan:*** Freshmen: $3249. Undergraduates: $4141. ***Parent loans:*** $13,311,057 (100% non-need-based). ***Programs:*** Federal Direct (Subsidized and Unsubsidized Stafford, PLUS).

WORK-STUDY ***Federal work-study:*** Total amount: $582,639; jobs available. ***State or other work-study/employment:*** Total amount: $1,600,000 (100% non-need-based). Part-time jobs available.

ATHLETIC AWARDS Total amount: $700,127 (100% non-need-based).

APPLYING FOR FINANCIAL AID ***Required financial aid form:*** FAFSA. ***Financial aid deadline (priority):*** 11/30. ***Notification date:*** Continuous beginning 3/1. Students must reply within 2 weeks of notification.

CONTACT David Crozier, Associate Vice President for Administration and Finance, Financial Services, Sonoma State University, 1801 East Cotati Avenue, Rohnert Park, CA 94928-3609, 707-664-3442. *Fax:* 707-664-4242. *E-mail:* david.crozier@sonoma.edu.
Website: http://www.sonoma.edu/.

SOUTH CAROLINA STATE UNIVERSITY

Orangeburg, SC

CONTACT Tangar Young, Director of Financial Aid, South Carolina State University, 300 College Street Northeast, Orangeburg, SC 29117, 803-536-7067 or toll-free 800-260-5956. *Fax:* 803-536-8420. *E-mail:* tyoung15@scsu.edu.
Website: http://www.scsu.edu/.

SOUTH COLLEGE

Knoxville, TN

CONTACT Financial Aid Office, South College, 720 North Fifth Avenue, Knoxville, TN 37917, 865-524-3043.
Website: http://www.southcollegetn.edu/.

SOUTH DAKOTA SCHOOL OF MINES AND TECHNOLOGY

Rapid City, SD

CONTACT David W. Martin, Director of Financial Aid, South Dakota School of Mines and Technology, 501 East Saint Joseph Street, Rapid City, SD 57701-3995, 605-394-2274 or toll-free 800-544-8162. *Fax:* 605-394-1979. *E-mail:* david.martin@sdsmt.edu.
Website: http://www.sdsmt.edu/.

SOUTH DAKOTA STATE UNIVERSITY

Brookings, SD

CONTACT Carolyn Halgerson, Director of Financial Aid, South Dakota State University, Administration 100, PO Box 2201, Brookings, SD 57007, 605-688-4695 or toll-free 800-952-3541. *Fax:* 605-688-5882. *E-mail:* carolyn.halgerson@sdstate.edu.
Website: http://www.sdstate.edu/.

SOUTHEASTERN BAPTIST COLLEGE

Laurel, MS

CONTACT Financial Aid Officer, Southeastern Baptist College, 4229 Highway 15 North, Laurel, MS 39440-1096, 601-426-6346.
Website: http://www.southeasternbaptist.edu/.

SOUTHEASTERN BAPTIST THEOLOGICAL SEMINARY

Wake Forest, NC

CONTACT Financial Aid Office, Southeastern Baptist Theological Seminary, 120 South Wingate Street, Wake Forest, NC 27587, 919-761-2100 or toll-free 800-284-6317.
Website: http://www.sebts.edu/.

SOUTHEASTERN LOUISIANA UNIVERSITY

Hammond, LA

Tuition & fees (LA res): $8329 — **Average undergraduate aid package: N/A**

ABOUT THE INSTITUTION State-supported, coed. ***Awards:*** certificates, associate, bachelor's, master's, and doctoral degrees. 43 undergraduate majors. ***Total enrollment:*** 14,260. Undergraduates: 13,296. Freshmen: 2,733. Federal methodology is used as a basis for awarding need-based institutional aid.

UNDERGRADUATE EXPENSES for 2019–2020 ***Application fee:*** $20. ***Tuition, state resident:*** full-time $5777; part-time $347 per credit hour. ***Tuition, nonresident:*** full-time $18,255; part-time $867 per credit hour. ***Required fees:*** full-time $2552. Full-time tuition and fees vary according to course load. Part-time tuition and fees vary according to course load. ***College room and board:*** $8600; ***Room only:*** $5050. Room and board charges vary according to board plan and housing facility.

FRESHMAN FINANCIAL AID (Fall 2018) 1870 applied for aid; of those 78% were deemed to have need. 100% of freshmen with need received aid; of those 12% had need fully met. 15% of all full-time freshmen had no need and received non-need-based gift aid.

UNDERGRADUATE FINANCIAL AID (Fall 2018) 7,685 applied for aid; of those 87% were deemed to have need. 100% of undergraduates with need received aid; of those 9% had need fully met. 7% of all full-time undergraduates had no need and received non-need-based gift aid.

GIFT AID (NEED-BASED) ***Receiving aid:*** Freshmen: 46% (932); all full-time undergraduates: 44% (4,090). ***Average award:*** Freshmen: $5570; Undergraduates: $5487. ***Scholarships, grants, and awards:*** Federal Pell, FSEOG, state, private, college/university gift aid from institutional funds.

GIFT AID (NON-NEED-BASED) ***Receiving aid:*** Freshmen: 59% (1,188). Undergraduates: 38% (3,464). ***Average award:*** Freshmen: $1949. Undergraduates: $1875. ***Scholarships, grants, and awards by category:*** *Academic interests/achievement:* business, communication, computer science, education, English, foreign languages, general academic interests/achievements, humanities, mathematics, premedicine, social sciences. *Creative arts/performance:* applied art and design, music, theater/drama. *Special achievements/activities:* cheerleading/drum major, leadership, memberships. *Special characteristics:* adult students, children and siblings of alumni, children of faculty/staff, first-generation college students, out-of-state students, veterans, veterans' children. ***Tuition waivers:*** Full or partial for employees or children of employees. ***ROTC:*** Army.

LOANS ***Student loans:*** 63% of past graduating class borrowed through all loan programs. *Average indebtedness per student:* $19,356. ***Average need-based loan:*** Freshmen: $3037. Undergraduates: $3614. ***Programs:*** Federal Direct (Subsidized and Unsubsidized Stafford, PLUS), Perkins, college/university.

WORK-STUDY ***Federal work-study:*** 159 jobs averaging $2242. ***State or other work-study/employment:*** 814 part-time jobs averaging $1935.

APPLYING FOR FINANCIAL AID ***Required financial aid forms:*** FAFSA, institution's own form, Institution's own financial aid form for college scholarships only. ***Financial aid deadline:*** Continuous. ***Notification date:*** Continuous. Students must reply within 2 weeks of notification.

CONTACT Financial Aid Office, Southeastern Louisiana University, SLU 10768, Hammond, LA 70402, 985-549-2244 or toll-free 800-222-7358. *Fax:* 985-549-5077. *E-mail:* finaid@selu.edu.
Website: http://www.southeastern.edu/.

SOUTHEASTERN OKLAHOMA STATE UNIVERSITY

Durant, OK

ABOUT THE INSTITUTION State-supported, coed. ***Awards:*** certificates, bachelor's, and master's degrees. 41 undergraduate majors. ***Total enrollment:*** 3,724. Undergraduates: 3,132. Freshmen: 517.

GIFT AID (NEED-BASED) ***Scholarships, grants, and awards:*** Federal Pell, FSEOG, state, private, college/university gift aid from institutional funds.

GIFT AID (NON-NEED-BASED) ***Scholarships, grants, and awards by category:*** *Academic interests/achievement:* biological sciences, business, communication, computer science, education, engineering/technologies, English, general academic interests/achievements, mathematics, physical sciences, social sciences. *Creative arts/performance:* applied art and design, dance, debating, music, performing arts, theater/drama. *Special achievements/activities:* cheerleading/drum major, leadership, rodeo. *Special characteristics:* children and siblings of alumni, out-of-state students.

LOANS ***Programs:*** Federal Direct (Subsidized and Unsubsidized Stafford, PLUS), Private Student Loans.

CONTACT Tony Lehrling, Director of Student Financial Aid, Southeastern Oklahoma State University, 1405 North 4th Avenue, Durant, OK 74701-0609, 580-745-2186 or toll-free 800-435-1327. *Fax:* 580-745-7469. *E-mail:* tlehrling@se.edu.
Website: http://www.se.edu/.

SOUTHEASTERN UNIVERSITY

Lakeland, FL

Tuition & fees: $26,620 — **Average undergraduate aid package: $15,978**

ABOUT THE INSTITUTION Independent Assemblies of God, coed. ***Awards:*** certificates, associate, bachelor's, master's, and doctoral degrees. 58 undergraduate majors. ***Total enrollment:*** 8,759. Undergraduates: 7,708. Freshmen: 1,460. Federal methodology is used as a basis for awarding need-based institutional aid.

UNDERGRADUATE EXPENSES for 2019–2020 ***Application fee:*** $40. ***Comprehensive fee:*** $36,650 includes full-time tuition ($25,620), mandatory fees ($1000), and room and board ($10,030). Full-time tuition and fees vary according to class time, degree level, location, and reciprocity agreements. Room and board charges vary according to board plan and housing facility. ***Part-time tuition:*** $1068 per credit hour. ***Part-time fees:*** $200 per term. Part-time tuition and fees vary according to class time, course load, degree level, location, and reciprocity agreements.

FRESHMAN FINANCIAL AID (Fall 2019, est.) 1184 applied for aid; of those 85% were deemed to have need. 100% of freshmen with need received aid; of those 12% had need fully met. ***Average percent of need met:*** 43% (excluding resources awarded to replace EFC). ***Average financial aid package:*** $17,247 (excluding resources awarded to replace EFC). 20% of all full-time freshmen had no need and received non-need-based gift aid.

UNDERGRADUATE FINANCIAL AID (Fall 2019, est.) 4,323 applied for aid; of those 88% were deemed to have need. 100% of undergraduates with need received aid; of those 10% had need fully met. ***Average percent of need met:*** 52% (excluding resources awarded to replace EFC). ***Average financial aid package:*** $15,978 (excluding resources awarded to replace EFC). 20% of all full-time undergraduates had no need and received non-need-based gift aid.

GIFT AID (NEED-BASED) ***Receiving aid:*** Freshmen: 52% (665); all full-time undergraduates: 53% (2,613). ***Average award:*** Freshmen: $5370; Undergraduates: $5543. ***Scholarships, grants, and awards:*** Federal Pell, FSEOG, state, private, college/university gift aid from institutional funds.

GIFT AID (NON-NEED-BASED) ***Receiving aid:*** Freshmen: 78% (1,001). Undergraduates: 77% (3,761). ***Average award:*** Freshmen: $10,296. Undergraduates: $10,319. ***Scholarships, grants, and awards by category:*** *Academic interests/achievement:* communication, education, general academic interests/achievements, religion/biblical studies. *Creative arts/performance:* applied art and design, cinema/film/broadcasting, journalism/publications, music, performing arts. *Special achievements/activities:* cheerleading/drum major, general special achievements/activities, leadership, religious involvement. *Special characteristics:* children of educators, children of faculty/staff, international students, religious affiliation. ***Tuition waivers:*** Full or partial for employees or children of employees. ***ROTC:*** Army cooperative.

LOANS ***Student loans:*** 93% of past graduating class borrowed through all loan programs. *Average indebtedness per student:* $30,027. ***Average need-based loan:*** Freshmen: $3460. Undergraduates: $4169. ***Programs:*** Federal Direct (Subsidized and Unsubsidized Stafford, PLUS), Perkins.

WORK-STUDY ***Federal work-study:*** 101 jobs averaging $2045.

APPLYING FOR FINANCIAL AID ***Required financial aid form:*** FAFSA. ***Financial aid deadline:*** Continuous. ***Notification date:*** Continuous. Students must reply within 6 weeks of notification.

CONTACT Mr. Michael E. Yohe, Executive Director of Student Financial Services, Southeastern University, 1000 Longfellow Boulevard, Lakeland, FL 33801-6099, 863-667-5000 or toll-free 800-500-8760. *Fax:* 863-667-5200. *E-mail:* meyohe@seu.edu. *Website:* http://www.seu.edu/.

SOUTHEAST MISSOURI STATE UNIVERSITY

Cape Girardeau, MO

Tuition & fees (MO res): $7800	Average undergraduate aid package: $9873

ABOUT THE INSTITUTION State-supported, coed. ***Awards:*** certificates, associate, bachelor's, and master's degrees. 63 undergraduate majors. ***Total enrollment:*** 10,637. Undergraduates: 9,514. Freshmen: 1,508. Federal methodology is used as a basis for awarding need-based institutional aid.

UNDERGRADUATE EXPENSES for 2020–2021 ***Application fee:*** $30. ***Tuition, state resident:*** full-time $6606; part-time $220 per credit hour. ***Tuition, nonresident:*** full-time $12,636; part-time $421 per credit hour. ***Required fees:*** full-time $1194; $39.80 per credit hour. Full-time tuition and fees vary according to course level, course load, location, and program. Part-time tuition and fees vary according to course level, course load, location, and program. ***College room and board:*** $9279; ***Room only:*** $6327. Room and board charges vary according to board plan and housing facility.

FRESHMAN FINANCIAL AID (Fall 2018) 1324 applied for aid; of those 74% were deemed to have need. 99% of freshmen with need received aid; of those 17% had need fully met. ***Average percent of need met:*** 64% (excluding resources awarded to replace EFC). ***Average financial aid package:*** $10,526 (excluding resources awarded to replace EFC). 26% of all full-time freshmen had no need and received non-need-based gift aid.

UNDERGRADUATE FINANCIAL AID (Fall 2018) 5,736 applied for aid; of those 79% were deemed to have need. 98% of undergraduates with need received aid; of those 15% had need fully met. ***Average percent of need met:*** 59% (excluding resources awarded to replace EFC). ***Average financial aid package:*** $9873 (excluding resources awarded to replace EFC). 19% of all full-time undergraduates had no need and received non-need-based gift aid.

GIFT AID (NEED-BASED) ***Total amount:*** $30,067,722 (49% federal, 14% state, 33% institutional, 4% external sources). ***Receiving aid:*** Freshmen: 64% (933); all full-time undergraduates: 55% (3,995). ***Average award:*** Freshmen: $7866; Undergraduates: $7001. ***Scholarships, grants, and awards:*** Federal Pell, FSEOG, state, private, college/university gift aid from institutional funds.

GIFT AID (NON-NEED-BASED) ***Total amount:*** $10,475,975 (4% federal, 14% state, 76% institutional, 6% external sources). ***Receiving aid:*** Freshmen: 8% (116). Undergraduates: 5% (364). ***Average award:*** Freshmen: $5077. Undergraduates: $5077. ***Scholarships, grants, and awards by category:*** *Academic interests/achievement:* agriculture, biological sciences, business, communication, computer science, education, engineering/technologies, English, foreign languages, general academic interests/achievements, health fields, home economics, humanities, international studies, mathematics, military science, physical sciences, premedicine, religion/biblical studies, social sciences. *Creative arts/performance:* applied art and design, dance, music, performing arts, theater/drama. *Special achievements/activities:* cheerleading/drum major, general special achievements/activities, leadership, memberships. *Special characteristics:* children of faculty/staff, first-generation college students, general special characteristics, international students, members of minority groups, out-of-state students, previous college experience, veterans. ***Tuition waivers:*** Full or partial for employees or children of employees, senior citizens. ***ROTC:*** Air Force.

LOANS ***Student loans:*** $29,492,534 (71% need-based, 29% non-need-based). 62% of past graduating class borrowed through all loan programs. *Average indebtedness per student:* $25,380. ***Average need-based loan:*** Freshmen: $3108. Undergraduates: $3965. ***Parent loans:*** $7,230,857 (37% need-based, 63% non-need-based). ***Programs:*** Federal Direct (Subsidized and Unsubsidized Stafford, PLUS).

WORK-STUDY ***Federal work-study:*** Total amount: $677,132; jobs available. ***State or other work-study/employment:*** Total amount: $3,016,101 (100% non-need-based). Part-time jobs available.

ATHLETIC AWARDS Total amount: $3,346,680 (48% need-based, 52% non-need-based).

APPLYING FOR FINANCIAL AID ***Financial aid deadline (priority):*** 2/1. ***Notification date:*** 12/15.

CONTACT Mr. Matthew Kearney, Director of Student Financial Services, Southeast Missouri State University, One University Plaza, Cape Girardeau, MO 63701, 573-651-2253. *Fax:* 573-651-5006. *E-mail:* sfs@semo.edu. *Website:* http://www.semo.edu/.

SOUTHERN ADVENTIST UNIVERSITY

Collegedale, TN

CONTACT Mr. Fred McClanahan, Prospective Students Financial Adviser, Southern Adventist University, PO Box 370, Collegedale, TN 37315-0370, 423-236-2844 or toll-free 800-768-8437. *Fax:* 423-236-1844. *E-mail:* prospectivefinance@southern.edu. *Website:* http://www.southern.edu/.

SOUTHERN ARKANSAS UNIVERSITY–MAGNOLIA

Magnolia, AR

ABOUT THE INSTITUTION State-supported, coed. ***Awards:*** certificates, associate, bachelor's, and master's degrees. 46 undergraduate majors. ***Total enrollment:*** 4,474. Undergraduates: 3,585. Freshmen: 833.

GIFT AID (NEED-BASED) ***Scholarships, grants, and awards:*** Federal Pell, FSEOG, state, private, college/university gift aid from institutional funds.

GIFT AID (NON-NEED-BASED) ***Scholarships, grants, and awards by category:*** *Academic interests/achievement:* agriculture, biological sciences, business, computer science, education, English, foreign languages, general academic interests/

achievements, home economics, library science, mathematics, physical sciences, social sciences. *Creative arts/performance:* applied art and design, dance, music, theater/drama. *Special achievements/activities:* cheerleading/drum major, leadership, rodeo. *Special characteristics:* adult students, children and siblings of alumni, children of faculty/staff, out-of-state students.

LOANS *Programs:* Federal Direct (Subsidized and Unsubsidized Stafford, PLUS), Perkins.

CONTACT Ms. Marcela D. McRae-Brunson, Director of Student Aid, Southern Arkansas University–Magnolia, MSC 9344, Magnolia, AR 71753, 870-235-4023 or toll-free 800-332-7286. *Fax:* 870-235-4913. *E-mail:* mdbrunson@saumag.edu.
Website: http://www.saumag.edu/.

THE SOUTHERN BAPTIST THEOLOGICAL SEMINARY

Louisville, KY

CONTACT Mrs. Erin Joiner, Manager of Financial Aid, The Southern Baptist Theological Seminary, 2825 Lexington Road, Louisville, KY 40280, 502-897-4206. *Fax:* 502-897-4031. *E-mail:* financialaid@sbts.edu.
Website: http://www.sbts.edu/.

SOUTHERN CALIFORNIA INSTITUTE OF ARCHITECTURE

Los Angeles, CA

CONTACT Marisela De La Torre, Financial Aid Manager, Southern California Institute of Architecture, 960 East 3rd Street, Los Angeles, CA 90013, 213-613-2200 Ext. 376. *Fax:* 213-613-2260. *E-mail:* financialaid@sciarc.edu.
Website: http://www.sciarc.edu/.

SOUTHERN CALIFORNIA INSTITUTE OF TECHNOLOGY

Anaheim, CA

CONTACT Financial Aid Office, Southern California Institute of Technology, 525 North Muller Street, Anaheim, CA 92801, 714-520-5552.
Website: http://www.scitech.edu/.

SOUTHERN CALIFORNIA SEMINARY

El Cajon, CA

CONTACT Financial Aid Office, Southern California Seminary, 2075 East Madison Avenue, El Cajon, CA 92019, 619-201-8999 or toll-free 888-389-7244 (out-of-state).
Website: http://www.socalsem.edu/.

SOUTHERN CONNECTICUT STATE UNIVERSITY

New Haven, CT

Tuition & fees: N/R	Average undergraduate aid package: $8496

ABOUT THE INSTITUTION State-supported, coed. ***Awards:*** certificates, bachelor's, master's, and doctoral degrees. 43 undergraduate majors. Federal methodology is used as a basis for awarding need-based institutional aid.

FRESHMAN FINANCIAL AID (Fall 2018) 1294 applied for aid; of those 100% were deemed to have need. 94% of freshmen with need received aid; of those 6% had need fully met. ***Average percent of need met:*** 44% (excluding resources awarded to replace EFC). ***Average financial aid package:*** $7220 (excluding resources awarded to replace EFC). 8% of all full-time freshmen had no need and received non-need-based gift aid.

UNDERGRADUATE FINANCIAL AID (Fall 2018) 5,221 applied for aid; of those 100% were deemed to have need. 94% of undergraduates with need received aid; of those 6% had need fully met. ***Average percent of need met:*** 46% (excluding resources awarded to replace EFC). ***Average financial aid package:*** $8496 (excluding resources awarded to replace EFC). 9% of all full-time undergraduates had no need and received non-need-based gift aid.

GIFT AID (NEED-BASED) *Total amount:* $26,291,659 (57% federal, 8% state, 27% institutional, 8% external sources). ***Receiving aid:*** Freshmen: 65% (972); all full-time undergraduates: 55% (3,738). ***Average award:*** Freshmen: $5650; Undergraduates: $6715. ***Scholarships, grants, and awards:*** Federal Pell, FSEOG, state, private, college/university gift aid from institutional funds.

GIFT AID (NON-NEED-BASED) *Total amount:* $3,310,470 (2% federal, 29% state, 68% institutional, 1% external sources). ***Receiving aid:*** Freshmen: 24% (356). Undergraduates: 16% (1,121). ***Average award:*** Freshmen: $4296. Undergraduates: $3434. ***Scholarships, grants, and awards by category:*** *Special characteristics:* children of faculty/staff, veterans. ***ROTC:*** Army cooperative, Air Force cooperative.

LOANS *Student loans:* $39,930,779 (43% need-based, 57% non-need-based). 77% of past graduating class borrowed through all loan programs. *Average indebtedness per student:* $42,326. ***Average need-based loan:*** Freshmen: $3239. Undergraduates: $4019. ***Parent loans:*** $12,039,298 (100% non-need-based). ***Programs:*** Federal Direct (Subsidized and Unsubsidized Stafford, PLUS), Perkins.

WORK-STUDY *Federal work-study:* Total amount: $1,034,750; jobs available. ***State or other work-study/employment:*** Part-time jobs available.

ATHLETIC AWARDS Total amount: $1,338,456 (100% need-based).

APPLYING FOR FINANCIAL AID *Required financial aid form:* FAFSA. ***Financial aid deadline:*** 3/15 (priority: 3/15). ***Notification date:*** Continuous beginning 3/15.

CONTACT Mrs. Gloria Lee, Director of Financial Aid, Southern Connecticut State University, Wintergreen Building, New Haven, CT 06515-1355, 203-392-5445. *Fax:* 203-392-5229. *E-mail:* leeg1@southernct.edu.
Website: http://www.southernct.edu/.

SOUTHERN ILLINOIS UNIVERSITY CARBONDALE

Carbondale, IL

Tuition & fees (IL res): $14,864	Average undergraduate aid package: $16,031

ABOUT THE INSTITUTION State-supported, coed. ***Awards:*** certificates, associate, bachelor's, master's, and doctoral degrees. 81 undergraduate majors. ***Total enrollment:*** 12,776. Undergraduates: 9,512. Freshmen: 1,133. Federal methodology is used as a basis for awarding need-based institutional aid.

UNDERGRADUATE EXPENSES for 2019–2020 *Application fee:* $40. ***Tuition, state resident:*** full-time $9638. ***Tuition, nonresident:*** full-time $9638. ***Required fees:*** full-time $5226. Full-time tuition and fees vary according to course load, location, program, reciprocity agreements, and student level. Part-time tuition and fees vary according to course load, location, program, reciprocity agreements, and student level. ***College room and board:*** $10,622. Room and board charges vary according to board plan and housing facility. ***Payment plan:*** Guaranteed tuition.

FRESHMAN FINANCIAL AID (Fall 2019, est.) 860 applied for aid; of those 79% were deemed to have need. 100% of freshmen with need received aid; of those 21% had need fully met. ***Average percent of need met:*** 53% (excluding resources awarded to replace EFC). ***Average financial aid package:*** $17,603 (excluding resources awarded to replace EFC). 15% of all full-time freshmen had no need and received non-need-based gift aid.

UNDERGRADUATE FINANCIAL AID (Fall 2019, est.) 4,365 applied for aid; of those 112% were deemed to have need. 98% of undergraduates with need received aid; of those 12% had need fully met. ***Average percent of need met:*** 57% (excluding resources awarded to replace EFC). ***Average financial aid package:*** $16,031 (excluding resources awarded to replace EFC). 7% of all full-time undergraduates had no need and received non-need-based gift aid.

GIFT AID (NEED-BASED) ***Total amount:*** $41,323,955 (40% federal, 31% state, 25% institutional, 4% external sources). ***Receiving aid:*** Freshmen: 43% (405); all full-time undergraduates: 45% (3,189). ***Average award:*** Freshmen: $8593; Undergraduates: $8636. ***Scholarships, grants, and awards:*** Federal Pell, FSEOG, state, private, college/university gift aid from institutional funds.
GIFT AID (NON-NEED-BASED) ***Total amount:*** $10,351,382 (8% federal, 1% state, 59% institutional, 32% external sources). ***Receiving aid:*** Freshmen: 38% (360). Undergraduates: 27% (1,955). ***Average award:*** Freshmen: $9232. Undergraduates: $8270. ***Scholarships, grants, and awards by category:*** *Academic interests/achievement:* agriculture, architecture, area/ethnic studies, biological sciences, business, communication, computer science, education, engineering/technologies, English, foreign languages, general academic interests/achievements, health fields, home economics, humanities, international studies, mathematics, military science, physical sciences, premedicine, social sciences. *Creative arts/performance:* applied art and design, art/fine arts, cinema/film/broadcasting, creative writing, dance, debating, general creative arts/performance, journalism/publications, music, performing arts, theater/drama. *Special achievements/activities:* cheerleading/drum major, community service, general special achievements/activities, leadership. *Special characteristics:* children and siblings of alumni, children of educators, children of faculty/staff, children of public servants, children with a deceased or disabled parent, first-generation college students, general special characteristics, handicapped students, international students, local/state students, members of minority groups, public servants, spouses of deceased or disabled public servants, veterans. ***Tuition waivers:*** Full or partial for children of alumni, employees or children of employees, senior citizens. ***ROTC:*** Army, Air Force.
LOANS ***Student loans:*** $43,389,938 (72% need-based, 28% non-need-based). 67% of past graduating class borrowed through all loan programs. *Average indebtedness per student:* $30,292. ***Average need-based loan:*** Freshmen: $3262. Undergraduates: $4548. ***Parent loans:*** $6,854,982 (33% need-based, 67% non-need-based). ***Programs:*** Federal Direct (Subsidized and Unsubsidized Stafford, PLUS).
WORK-STUDY ***Federal work-study:*** Total amount: $7,048,988; 1,048 jobs averaging $1751.
ATHLETIC AWARDS Total amount: $2,645,973 (37% need-based, 63% non-need-based).
APPLYING FOR FINANCIAL AID ***Required financial aid form:*** FAFSA. ***Financial aid deadline (priority):*** 3/1. ***Notification date:*** Continuous beginning 2/1.
CONTACT Dee Rotolo, Interim Director of Financial Aid, Southern Illinois University Carbondale, Student Services Building, 1263 Lincoln Drive, 2nd Floor, Carbondale, IL 62901-4702, 618-453-4334. *Fax:* 618-453-7305. *E-mail:* fao@siu.edu. *Website:* http://www.siu.edu/.

SOUTHERN ILLINOIS UNIVERSITY EDWARDSVILLE

Edwardsville, IL

Tuition & fees (IL res): $12,219	Average undergraduate aid package: $12,552

ABOUT THE INSTITUTION State-supported, coed. ***Awards:*** certificates, bachelor's, master's, and doctoral degrees. 46 undergraduate majors. ***Total enrollment:*** 13,061. Undergraduates: 10,386. Freshmen: 1,667. Federal methodology is used as a basis for awarding need-based institutional aid.
UNDERGRADUATE EXPENSES for 2020–2021 ***Application fee:*** $40. ***Tuition, state resident:*** full-time $9123. ***Required fees:*** full-time $3096. Full-time tuition and fees vary according to course load, program, and reciprocity agreements. Part-time tuition and fees vary according to course load, program, and reciprocity agreements. ***College room and board:*** $10,701; ***Room only:*** $7110. Room and board charges vary according to board plan and housing facility. ***Payment plan:*** Guaranteed tuition.
FRESHMAN FINANCIAL AID (Fall 2018) 1514 applied for aid; of those 78% were deemed to have need. 99% of freshmen with need received aid; of those 40% had need fully met. ***Average percent of need met:*** 74% (excluding resources awarded to replace EFC). ***Average financial aid package:*** $14,111 (excluding resources awarded to replace EFC). 6% of all full-time freshmen had no need and received non-need-based gift aid.
UNDERGRADUATE FINANCIAL AID (Fall 2018) 7,175 applied for aid; of those 83% were deemed to have need. 98% of undergraduates with need received aid; of those 34% had need fully met. ***Average percent of need met:*** 63% (excluding resources awarded to replace EFC). ***Average financial aid package:*** $12,552 (excluding resources awarded to replace EFC). 7% of all full-time undergraduates had no need and received non-need-based gift aid.
GIFT AID (NEED-BASED) ***Total amount:*** $36,072,871 (56% federal, 6% state, 34% institutional, 4% external sources). ***Receiving aid:*** Freshmen: 67% (1,122); all full-time undergraduates: 53% (4,776). ***Average award:*** Freshmen: $9928; Undergraduates: $8991. ***Scholarships, grants, and awards:*** Federal Pell, FSEOG, state, private, college/university gift aid from institutional funds, Federal Nursing.
GIFT AID (NON-NEED-BASED) ***Total amount:*** $9,821,472 (12% federal, 16% state, 63% institutional, 9% external sources). ***Receiving aid:*** Freshmen: 64% (1,082). Undergraduates: 33% (2,939). ***Average award:*** Freshmen: $5657. Undergraduates: $6891. ***Scholarships, grants, and awards by category:*** *Academic interests/achievement:* business, education, general academic interests/achievements, home economics. *Creative arts/performance:* art/fine arts, dance, music, theater/drama. *Special characteristics:* children of faculty/staff. ***Tuition waivers:*** Full or partial for employees or children of employees. ***ROTC:*** Army, Air Force cooperative.
LOANS ***Student loans:*** $36,291,596 (77% need-based, 23% non-need-based). 58% of past graduating class borrowed through all loan programs. *Average indebtedness per student:* $22,610. ***Average need-based loan:*** Freshmen: $3355. Undergraduates: $4460. ***Parent loans:*** $19,208,024 (24% need-based, 76% non-need-based). ***Programs:*** Federal Direct (Subsidized and Unsubsidized Stafford, PLUS), Perkins, Federal Nursing, college/university, alternative loans.
WORK-STUDY ***Federal work-study:*** Total amount: $4,308,779; jobs available. ***State or other work-study/employment:*** Part-time jobs available.
ATHLETIC AWARDS Total amount: $1,172,820 (29% need-based, 71% non-need-based).
APPLYING FOR FINANCIAL AID ***Required financial aid form:*** FAFSA. ***Financial aid deadline (priority):*** 3/1. ***Notification date:*** Continuous beginning 3/15. Students must reply within 2 weeks of notification.
CONTACT Jeremy Baker, Interim Director of Financial Aid, Southern Illinois University Edwardsville, Campus Box 1060, Edwardsville, IL 62026-1060, 618-650-3879 or toll-free 800-447-SIUE. *Fax:* 618-650-3885. *E-mail:* jbaker@siue.edu. *Website:* http://www.siue.edu/.

SOUTHERN METHODIST UNIVERSITY

Dallas, TX

Tuition & fees: $58,540	Average undergraduate aid package: $44,634

ABOUT THE INSTITUTION Independent United Methodist Church, coed. ***Awards:*** certificates, bachelor's, master's, and doctoral degrees. 66 undergraduate majors. ***Total enrollment:*** 11,824. Undergraduates: 6,710. Freshmen: 1,544. Both federal and institutional methodology are used as a basis for awarding need-based institutional aid.
UNDERGRADUATE EXPENSES for 2020–2021 ***Application fee:*** $60. ***Comprehensive fee:*** $75,650 includes full-time tuition ($51,958), mandatory fees ($6582), and room and board ($17,110). Room and board charges vary according to board plan. ***Part-time tuition:*** $2171 per credit hour. ***Payment plan:*** Tuition prepayment.
FRESHMAN FINANCIAL AID (Fall 2019, est.) 801 applied for aid; of those 65% were deemed to have need. 100% of freshmen with need received aid; of those 44% had need fully met. ***Average percent of need met:*** 85% (excluding resources awarded to replace EFC). ***Average financial aid package:*** $45,742 (excluding resources awarded to replace EFC). 43% of all full-time freshmen had no need and received non-need-based gift aid.
UNDERGRADUATE FINANCIAL AID (Fall 2019, est.) 2,567 applied for aid; of those 79% were deemed to have need. 99% of undergraduates with need received aid; of those 36% had need fully met. ***Average percent of need met:*** 85% (excluding resources awarded to replace EFC). ***Average financial aid package:*** $44,634 (excluding resources awarded to replace EFC). 41% of all full-time undergraduates had no need and received non-need-based gift aid.
GIFT AID (NEED-BASED) ***Total amount:*** $68,988,654 (5% federal, 4% state, 89% institutional, 2% external sources). ***Receiving aid:*** Freshmen: 21% (328); all full-time undergraduates: 22% (1,434). ***Average award:*** Freshmen: $21,993; Undergraduates: $22,114. ***Scholarships, grants, and awards:*** Federal Pell, FSEOG, state, private, college/university gift aid from institutional funds.

GIFT AID (NON-NEED-BASED) ***Total amount:*** $73,301,713 (97% institutional, 3% external sources). ***Receiving aid:*** Freshmen: 26% (398). Undergraduates: 21% (1,385). ***Average award:*** Freshmen: $28,162. Undergraduates: $28,717. ***Tuition waivers:*** Full or partial for employees or children of employees. ***ROTC:*** Army, Air Force cooperative.

LOANS ***Student loans:*** $22,799,404 (48% need-based, 52% non-need-based). 28% of past graduating class borrowed through all loan programs. *Average indebtedness per student:* $30,697. ***Average need-based loan:*** Freshmen: $3251. Undergraduates: $4182. ***Parent loans:*** $12,816,471 (24% need-based, 76% non-need-based). ***Programs:*** Federal Direct (Subsidized and Unsubsidized Stafford, PLUS), state, college/university.

WORK-STUDY ***Federal work-study:*** Total amount: $4,351,615; jobs available. ***State or other work-study/employment:*** Total amount: $310,000 (22% need-based, 78% non-need-based). Part-time jobs available.

ATHLETIC AWARDS Total amount: $17,008,597 (36% need-based, 64% non-need-based).

APPLYING FOR FINANCIAL AID ***Required financial aid forms:*** FAFSA, CSS Financial Aid PROFILE, noncustodial (divorced/separated) parent's statement. ***Financial aid deadline (priority):*** 11/1. ***Notification date:*** Continuous beginning 1/20. Students must reply by 5/1.

CONTACT Mr. Marc Peterson, Director of Financial Aid, Southern Methodist University, PO Box 750181, Dallas, TX 75275, 214-768-3417 or toll-free 800-323-0672. *Fax:* 214-768-3878. *E-mail:* enrol_serv@smu.edu.
Website: http://www.smu.edu/.

SOUTHERN NAZARENE UNIVERSITY

Bethany, OK

CONTACT Diana Lee, Director of Financial Assistance, Southern Nazarene University, 6729 Northwest 39th Expressway, Bethany, OK 73008, 405-491-6310 or toll-free 800-648-9899. *Fax:* 405-717-6271. *E-mail:* dlee@snu.edu.
Website: http://www.snu.edu/.

SOUTHERN NEW HAMPSHIRE UNIVERSITY

Manchester, NH

Tuition & fees: N/R	Average undergraduate aid package: $22,854

ABOUT THE INSTITUTION Independent, coed. ***Awards:*** certificates, associate, bachelor's, master's, and doctoral degrees. 47 undergraduate majors. ***Total enrollment:*** 3,769. Undergraduates: 3,121. Freshmen: 874. Federal methodology is used as a basis for awarding need-based institutional aid.

FRESHMAN FINANCIAL AID (Fall 2018) 782 applied for aid; of those 88% were deemed to have need. 100% of freshmen with need received aid; of those 18% had need fully met. ***Average percent of need met:*** 63% (excluding resources awarded to replace EFC). ***Average financial aid package:*** $23,676 (excluding resources awarded to replace EFC). 17% of all full-time freshmen had no need and received non-need-based gift aid.

UNDERGRADUATE FINANCIAL AID (Fall 2018) 2,366 applied for aid; of those 90% were deemed to have need. 100% of undergraduates with need received aid; of those 16% had need fully met. ***Average percent of need met:*** 62% (excluding resources awarded to replace EFC). ***Average financial aid package:*** $22,854 (excluding resources awarded to replace EFC). 21% of all full-time undergraduates had no need and received non-need-based gift aid.

GIFT AID (NEED-BASED) ***Receiving aid:*** Freshmen: 39% (331); all full-time undergraduates: 39% (1,168). ***Average award:*** Freshmen: $6375; Undergraduates: $6894. ***Scholarships, grants, and awards:*** Federal Pell, FSEOG, state, private, college/university gift aid from institutional funds.

GIFT AID (NON-NEED-BASED) ***Receiving aid:*** Freshmen: 81% (686). Undergraduates: 68% (2,016). ***Average award:*** Freshmen: $17,795. Undergraduates: $13,243. ***Scholarships, grants, and awards by category:*** *Academic interests/achievement:* business, computer science, education, general academic interests/achievements, social sciences. *Creative arts/performance:* music. *Special achievements/activities:* community service, general special achievements/activities, hobbies/interests, leadership, memberships. *Special characteristics:* children and siblings of alumni, children of educators, handicapped students, international students, local/state students, previous college experience, siblings of current students, twins, veterans. ***ROTC:*** Army cooperative, Air Force cooperative.

LOANS ***Student loans:*** 79% of past graduating class borrowed through all loan programs. *Average indebtedness per student:* $43,106. ***Average need-based loan:*** Freshmen: $3183. Undergraduates: $4064. ***Programs:*** Federal Direct (Subsidized and Unsubsidized Stafford, PLUS).

WORK-STUDY Federal work-study jobs available.

APPLYING FOR FINANCIAL AID ***Required financial aid form:*** FAFSA. ***Notification date:*** Continuous.

CONTACT Financial Aid Office, Southern New Hampshire University, 2500 North River Road, Manchester, NH 03106-1045, 603-668-2211 or toll-free 888-327-7648.
Website: http://www.snhu.edu/.

SOUTHERN OREGON UNIVERSITY

Ashland, OR

ABOUT THE INSTITUTION State-supported, coed. ***Awards:*** certificates, bachelor's, and master's degrees. 39 undergraduate majors. ***Total enrollment:*** 6,114. Undergraduates: 5,256. Freshmen: 616.

GIFT AID (NEED-BASED) ***Scholarships, grants, and awards:*** Federal Pell, FSEOG, state, private, college/university gift aid from institutional funds.

GIFT AID (NON-NEED-BASED) ***Scholarships, grants, and awards by category:*** *Academic interests/achievement:* biological sciences, business, education, English, foreign languages, general academic interests/achievements, home economics, mathematics, physical sciences, social sciences. *Creative arts/performance:* applied art and design, creative writing, journalism/publications, music, theater/drama. *Special achievements/activities:* community service, general special achievements/activities, hobbies/interests, leadership, memberships. *Special characteristics:* adult students, international students, members of minority groups, out-of-state students, previous college experience, veterans.

LOANS ***Programs:*** Federal Direct (Subsidized and Unsubsidized Stafford, PLUS), Perkins.

WORK-STUDY ***Federal work-study:*** Total amount: $312,998; jobs available.

CONTACT Mrs. Kristen Gast, Enrollment Services Center, Southern Oregon University, 1250 Siskiyou Boulevard, Ashland, OR 97520, 541-552-6600 or toll-free 855-470-3377 (out-of-state). *Fax:* 541-552-6614. *E-mail:* gastk@sou.edu.
Website: http://www.sou.edu/.

SOUTHERN STATES UNIVERSITY

San Diego, CA

CONTACT Financial Aid Office, Southern States University, 1094 Cudahy Place, Suite 120, San Diego, CA 92110.
Website: http://www.ssu.edu/.

SOUTHERN TECHNICAL COLLEGE

Fort Myers, FL

CONTACT Financial Aid Office, Southern Technical College, 1685 Medical Lane, Fort Myers, FL 33907, 239-939-4766 or toll-free 877-347-5492.
Website: http://www.southerntech.edu/locations/ft-myers/.

SOUTHERN UNIVERSITY AND AGRICULTURAL AND MECHANICAL COLLEGE

Baton Rouge, LA

CONTACT Mr. Phillip Rodgers Sr., Director of Financial Aid, Southern University and Agricultural and Mechanical College, PO Box 9961, Baton Rouge, LA 70813, 225-771-2790. *Fax:* 225-771-5898. *E-mail:* phillip_rodgers@cxs.subr.edu.
Website: http://www.subr.edu/.

SOUTHERN UNIVERSITY AT NEW ORLEANS

New Orleans, LA

CONTACT La'Charlotte C. Garrett, Director of Financial Aid, Southern University at New Orleans, 6400 Press Drive, New Orleans, LA 70126, 504-286-5435. *Fax:* 504-286-5213. *E-mail:* lgarrett@suno.edu.
Website: http://www.suno.edu/.

SOUTHERN UTAH UNIVERSITY

Cedar City, UT

Tuition & fees (area res): $6770	Average undergraduate aid package: $10,078

ABOUT THE INSTITUTION State-supported, coed. ***Awards:*** certificates, diplomas, associate, bachelor's, and master's degrees. 74 undergraduate majors. ***Total enrollment:*** 9,468. Undergraduates: 8,550. Freshmen: 1,899. Federal methodology is used as a basis for awarding need-based institutional aid.

UNDERGRADUATE EXPENSES for 2019–2020 ***Application fee:*** $50. ***Tuition, area resident:*** full-time $6006; part-time $200 per credit hour. ***Tuition, state resident:*** full-time $6006; part-time $200 per credit hour. ***Tuition, nonresident:*** full-time $19,822; part-time $661 per credit hour. ***Required fees:*** full-time $764; $37 per credit hour. Full-time tuition and fees vary according to program. Part-time tuition and fees vary according to course load and program. ***College room and board:*** $7349; ***Room only:*** $3325. Room and board charges vary according to board plan and housing facility.

FRESHMAN FINANCIAL AID (Fall 2018) 1581 applied for aid; of those 75% were deemed to have need. 99% of freshmen with need received aid; of those 21% had need fully met. ***Average percent of need met:*** 62% (excluding resources awarded to replace EFC). ***Average financial aid package:*** $9404 (excluding resources awarded to replace EFC). 35% of all full-time freshmen had no need and received non-need-based gift aid.

UNDERGRADUATE FINANCIAL AID (Fall 2018) 4,756 applied for aid; of those 84% were deemed to have need. 99% of undergraduates with need received aid; of those 13% had need fully met. ***Average percent of need met:*** 62% (excluding resources awarded to replace EFC). ***Average financial aid package:*** $10,078 (excluding resources awarded to replace EFC). 29% of all full-time undergraduates had no need and received non-need-based gift aid.

GIFT AID (NEED-BASED) ***Total amount:*** $14,739,076 (99% federal, 1% state). ***Receiving aid:*** Freshmen: 28% (577); all full-time undergraduates: 40% (2,640). ***Average award:*** Freshmen: $4692; Undergraduates: $4987. ***Scholarships, grants, and awards:*** Federal Pell, FSEOG, state, private, college/university gift aid from institutional funds.

GIFT AID (NON-NEED-BASED) ***Total amount:*** $32,465,877 (4% state, 91% institutional, 5% external sources). ***Receiving aid:*** Freshmen: 30% (607). Undergraduates: 22% (1,484). ***Average award:*** Freshmen: $6455. Undergraduates: $6767. ***Scholarships, grants, and awards by category:*** *Academic interests/achievement:* general academic interests/achievements. *Creative arts/performance:* applied art and design, dance, music, performing arts, theater/drama. *Special achievements/activities:* leadership. *Special characteristics:* children and siblings of alumni, local/state students, members of minority groups, religious affiliation. ***Tuition waivers:*** Full or partial for children of alumni, employees or children of employees, senior citizens. ***ROTC:*** Army.

LOANS ***Student loans:*** $19,037,607 (39% need-based, 61% non-need-based). 77% of past graduating class borrowed through all loan programs. *Average indebtedness per student:* $16,958. ***Average need-based loan:*** Freshmen: $2867. Undergraduates: $3572. ***Parent loans:*** $772,903 (100% non-need-based). ***Programs:*** Federal Direct (Subsidized and Unsubsidized Stafford, PLUS), college/university.

WORK-STUDY ***Federal work-study:*** Total amount: $291,406; jobs available. ***State or other work-study/employment:*** Total amount: $111,898 (100% need-based). Part-time jobs available.

ATHLETIC AWARDS Total amount: $4,737,325 (100% non-need-based).

APPLYING FOR FINANCIAL AID ***Required financial aid forms:*** FAFSA, institution's own form. ***Financial aid deadline (priority):*** 7/1. ***Notification date:*** Continuous beginning 2/1.

CONTACT Daivd Hughes, Director, Southern Utah University, 351 West University Boulevard, Cedar City, UT 84720-2498, 435-586-7735. *Fax:* 435-586-7736. *E-mail:* finaid@suu.edu.
Website: http://www.suu.edu/.

SOUTHERN VERMONT COLLEGE

Bennington, VT

CONTACT Phylle Lentz, Associate Director of Financial Aid, Southern Vermont College, 982 Mansion Drive, Bennington, VT 05201, 802-447-6331. *Fax:* 802-447-6329. *E-mail:* plentz@svc.edu.
Website: http://www.svc.edu/.

SOUTHERN VIRGINIA UNIVERSITY

Buena Vista, VA

CONTACT Darin Hassell, Financial Aid Specialist, Southern Virginia University, One University Hill Drive, Buena Vista, VA 24416, 540-261-4351 or toll-free 800-229-8420. *Fax:* 540-261-8559. *E-mail:* finaid@svu.edu.
Website: http://www.svu.edu/.

SOUTHERN WESLEYAN UNIVERSITY

Central, SC

Tuition & fees: N/R	Average undergraduate aid package: $21,927

ABOUT THE INSTITUTION Independent Wesleyan Church, coed. ***Awards:*** associate, bachelor's, and master's degrees. 35 undergraduate majors. Federal methodology is used as a basis for awarding need-based institutional aid.

FRESHMAN FINANCIAL AID (Fall 2018) 201 applied for aid; of those 93% were deemed to have need. 100% of freshmen with need received aid; of those 19% had need fully met. ***Average percent of need met:*** 77% (excluding resources awarded to replace EFC). ***Average financial aid package:*** $21,732 (excluding resources awarded to replace EFC).

UNDERGRADUATE FINANCIAL AID (Fall 2018) 691 applied for aid; of those 91% were deemed to have need. 100% of undergraduates with need received aid; of those 22% had need fully met. ***Average percent of need met:*** 77% (excluding resources awarded to replace EFC). ***Average financial aid package:*** $21,927 (excluding resources awarded to replace EFC).

GIFT AID (NEED-BASED) ***Receiving aid:*** Freshmen: 88% (186); all full-time undergraduates: 85% (631). ***Average award:*** Freshmen: $19,439; Undergraduates: $19,004. ***Scholarships, grants, and awards:*** Federal Pell, FSEOG, state, private, college/university gift aid from institutional funds.

GIFT AID (NON-NEED-BASED) ***Receiving aid:*** Freshmen: 1% (2). Undergraduates: 1% (5). ***ROTC:*** Army cooperative, Air Force cooperative.

LOANS ***Student loans:*** 60% of past graduating class borrowed through all loan programs. *Average indebtedness per student:* $33,089. ***Average need-based loan:*** Freshmen: $3212. Undergraduates: $4068. ***Programs:*** Federal Direct (Subsidized and Unsubsidized Stafford, PLUS), state.

WORK-STUDY ***Federal work-study:*** 108 jobs averaging $1125. ***State or other work-study/employment:*** 61 part-time jobs averaging $994.
APPLYING FOR FINANCIAL AID ***Required financial aid forms:*** FAFSA, state aid form. ***Notification date:*** Continuous.
CONTACT Financial Aid Office, Southern Wesleyan University, 907 Wesleyan Drive, PO Box 1020, Central, SC 29630-1020, 864-644-5000 or toll-free 800-CU-AT-SWU. *Website:* http://www.swu.edu/.

SOUTH FLORIDA BIBLE COLLEGE AND THEOLOGICAL SEMINARY

Deerfield Beach, FL

CONTACT Financial Aid Office, South Florida Bible College and Theological Seminary, 2200 SW 10th Street, Deerfield Beach, FL 33442, 954-428-8980. *Website:* http://www.sfbc.edu/.

SOUTH UNIVERSITY - AUSTIN

Round Rock, TX

CONTACT Financial Aid Office, South University - Austin, 1220 West Louis Henna Boulevard, Round Rock, TX 78681, 512-516-8800 or toll-free 877-659-5706.

SOUTH UNIVERSITY - COLUMBIA

Columbia, SC

CONTACT Financial Aid Office, South University - Columbia, 9 Science Court, Columbia, SC 29203, 803-799-9082 or toll-free 866-629-3031.

SOUTH UNIVERSITY - MONTGOMERY

Montgomery, AL

CONTACT Financial Aid Office, South University - Montgomery, 5355 Vaughn Road, Montgomery, AL 36116-1120, 334-395-8800 or toll-free 866-629-2962.

SOUTH UNIVERSITY - RICHMOND

Glen Allen, VA

CONTACT Financial Aid Office, South University - Richmond, 2151 Old Brick Road, Glen Allen, VA 23060, 804-727-6800 or toll-free 888-422-5076.

SOUTH UNIVERSITY - SAVANNAH

Savannah, GA

CONTACT Financial Aid Office, South University - Savannah, 709 Mall Boulevard, Savannah, GA 31406, 912-201-8000 or toll-free 866-629-2901.

SOUTH UNIVERSITY - TAMPA

Tampa, FL

CONTACT Financial Aid Office, South University - Tampa, 4401 North Himes Avenue, Suite 175, Tampa, FL 33614, 813-393-3800 or toll-free 800-846-1472.

SOUTH UNIVERSITY - VIRGINIA BEACH

Virginia Beach, VA

CONTACT Financial Aid Office, South University - Virginia Beach, 301 Bendix Road, Suite 100, Virginia Beach, VA 23452, 757-493-6900 or toll-free 877-206-1845.

SOUTH UNIVERSITY - WEST PALM BEACH

Royal Palm Beach, FL

CONTACT Financial Aid Office, South University - West Palm Beach, University Centre, 9801 Belvedere Road, Royal Palm Beach, FL 33411, 561-273-6500 or toll-free 866-629-2902.

SOUTHWEST BAPTIST UNIVERSITY

Bolivar, MO

Tuition & fees: $25,440	Average undergraduate aid package: $22,411

ABOUT THE INSTITUTION Independent Southern Baptist, coed. ***Awards:*** certificates, associate, bachelor's, master's, and doctoral degrees. 61 undergraduate majors. ***Total enrollment:*** 3,281. Undergraduates: 2,588. Freshmen: 458. Both federal and institutional methodology are used as a basis for awarding need-based institutional aid.
UNDERGRADUATE EXPENSES for 2020–2021 ***Application fee:*** $30. ***Comprehensive fee:*** $33,480 includes full-time tuition ($24,500), mandatory fees ($940), and room and board ($8040). ***College room only:*** $3400. Full-time tuition and fees vary according to course load, degree level, and location. Room and board charges vary according to board plan and housing facility. ***Part-time tuition:*** $865 per credit hour. ***Part-time fees:*** $190 per term. Part-time tuition and fees vary according to course load and location.
FRESHMAN FINANCIAL AID (Fall 2019, est.) 421 applied for aid; of those 90% were deemed to have need. 100% of freshmen with need received aid; of those 25% had need fully met. ***Average percent of need met:*** 79% (excluding resources awarded to replace EFC). ***Average financial aid package:*** $24,167 (excluding resources awarded to replace EFC). 10% of all full-time freshmen had no need and received non-need-based gift aid.
UNDERGRADUATE FINANCIAL AID (Fall 2019, est.) 1,529 applied for aid; of those 90% were deemed to have need. 100% of undergraduates with need received aid; of those 25% had need fully met. ***Average percent of need met:*** 68% (excluding resources awarded to replace EFC). ***Average financial aid package:*** $22,411 (excluding resources awarded to replace EFC). 13% of all full-time undergraduates had no need and received non-need-based gift aid.
GIFT AID (NEED-BASED) ***Total amount:*** $19,127,711 (22% federal, 7% state, 66% institutional, 5% external sources). ***Receiving aid:*** Freshmen: 87% (375); all full-time undergraduates: 78% (1,297). ***Average award:*** Freshmen: $13,641; Undergraduates: $12,669. ***Scholarships, grants, and awards:*** Federal Pell, FSEOG, state, private, college/university gift aid from institutional funds, Federal Nursing.
GIFT AID (NON-NEED-BASED) ***Total amount:*** $3,776,273 (12% state, 68% institutional, 20% external sources). ***Receiving aid:*** Freshmen: 70% (300). Undergraduates: 37% (614). ***Average award:*** Freshmen: $3898. Undergraduates: $3997. ***Scholarships, grants, and awards by category:*** *Academic interests/achievement:* 146 awards ($1,193,951 total): general academic interests/achievements. *Creative arts/performance:* 126 awards ($288,325 total): applied art and design, debating, music, theater/drama. *Special achievements/activities:* 107 awards ($180,000 total): religious involvement. *Special characteristics:* 405 awards ($1,236,103 total): general special characteristics, relatives of clergy, religious affiliation, siblings of current students. ***Tuition waivers:*** Full or partial for employees or children of employees. ***ROTC:*** Army cooperative.
LOANS ***Student loans:*** $9,851,565 (43% need-based, 57% non-need-based). 73% of past graduating class borrowed through all loan programs. *Average indebtedness per student:* $25,880. ***Average need-based loan:*** Freshmen: $2983. Undergrad-

uates: $3837. ***Parent loans:*** $1,054,165 (100% non-need-based). ***Programs:*** Federal Direct (Subsidized and Unsubsidized Stafford, PLUS), Federal Nursing, state, alternative loans.

WORK-STUDY ***Federal work-study:*** Total amount: $296,138; 323 jobs averaging $1820.

ATHLETIC AWARDS Total amount: $3,327,639 (100% non-need-based).

APPLYING FOR FINANCIAL AID ***Required financial aid form:*** FAFSA. ***Financial aid deadline (priority):*** 2/1. ***Notification date:*** Continuous beginning 12/15. Students must reply within 2 weeks of notification.

CONTACT Mr. Brad Gamble, Director of Financial Aid, Southwest Baptist University, 1600 University Avenue, Bolivar, MO 65613-2597, 417-328-1823 or toll-free 800-526-5859. *Fax:* 417-328-1514. *E-mail:* bgamble@sbuniv.edu.
Website: http://www.sbuniv.edu/.

SOUTHWESTERN ADVENTIST UNIVERSITY

Keene, TX

CONTACT Student Financial Services, Southwestern Adventist University, PO Box 567, Keene, TX 76059, 817-645-3921 Ext. 262 or toll-free 800-433-2240. *Fax:* 817-556-4744.
Website: http://www.swau.edu/.

SOUTHWESTERN ASSEMBLIES OF GOD UNIVERSITY

Waxahachie, TX

CONTACT Financial Aid Office, Southwestern Assemblies of God University, 1200 Sycamore Street, Waxahachie, TX 75165-2397, 972-825-4730 or toll-free 888-937-7248. *Fax:* 972-937-4001. *E-mail:* finaid@sagu.edu.
Website: http://www.sagu.edu/.

SOUTHWESTERN CHRISTIAN COLLEGE

Terrell, TX

CONTACT Ms. Kim Smith, Financial Aid Counselor, Southwestern Christian College, PO Box 10, 200 Bowser Circle, Terrell, TX 75160, 972-524-3341 Ext. 124. *Fax:* 972-563-7133. *E-mail:* ksmit@swcc.edu.
Website: http://www.swcc.edu/.

SOUTHWESTERN CHRISTIAN UNIVERSITY

Bethany, OK

CONTACT Mrs. Billie Stewart, Financial Aid Director, Southwestern Christian University, PO Box 340, Bethany, OK 73008, 405-789-7661 Ext. 3456. *Fax:* 405-495-0078. *E-mail:* billie.stewart@swcu.edu.
Website: http://www.swcu.edu/.

SOUTHWESTERN COLLEGE

Winfield, KS

Tuition & fees: $33,250 | **Average undergraduate aid package: $23,398**

ABOUT THE INSTITUTION Independent United Methodist, coed. ***Awards:*** certificates, bachelor's, master's, and doctoral degrees. 51 undergraduate majors. ***Total enrollment:*** 1,513. Undergraduates: 1,360. Freshmen: 149. Federal methodology is used as a basis for awarding need-based institutional aid.

UNDERGRADUATE EXPENSES for 2020–2021 ***Application fee:*** $25. ***Comprehensive fee:*** $41,750 includes full-time tuition ($33,100), mandatory fees ($150), and room and board ($8500). ***College room only:*** $4000. Full-time tuition and fees vary according to course load, degree level, location, and program. Room and board charges vary according to board plan and housing facility. ***Part-time tuition:*** $1380 per credit hour. Part-time tuition and fees vary according to course load, degree level, location, and program.

FRESHMAN FINANCIAL AID (Fall 2018) 175 applied for aid; of those 94% were deemed to have need. 100% of freshmen with need received aid; of those 13% had need fully met. ***Average percent of need met:*** 73% (excluding resources awarded to replace EFC). ***Average financial aid package:*** $24,235 (excluding resources awarded to replace EFC). 9% of all full-time freshmen had no need and received non-need-based gift aid.

UNDERGRADUATE FINANCIAL AID (Fall 2018) 587 applied for aid; of those 94% were deemed to have need. 99% of undergraduates with need received aid; of those 12% had need fully met. ***Average percent of need met:*** 69% (excluding resources awarded to replace EFC). ***Average financial aid package:*** $23,398 (excluding resources awarded to replace EFC). 14% of all full-time undergraduates had no need and received non-need-based gift aid.

GIFT AID (NEED-BASED) ***Total amount:*** $9,037,192 (24% federal, 5% state, 68% institutional, 3% external sources). ***Receiving aid:*** Freshmen: 91% (165); all full-time undergraduates: 79% (537). ***Average award:*** Freshmen: $20,433; Undergraduates: $19,270. ***Scholarships, grants, and awards:*** Federal Pell, FSEOG, state, private, college/university gift aid from institutional funds.

GIFT AID (NON-NEED-BASED) ***Total amount:*** $1,357,497 (72% institutional, 28% external sources). ***Receiving aid:*** Freshmen: 12% (21). Undergraduates: 9% (60). ***Average award:*** Freshmen: $8891. Undergraduates: $8792. ***Scholarships, grants, and awards by category:*** *Academic interests/achievement:* 750 awards ($3,102,575 total): biological sciences, business, communication, computer science, education, English, foreign languages, general academic interests/achievements, humanities, mathematics, physical sciences, premedicine, religion/biblical studies, social sciences. *Creative arts/performance:* 54 awards ($334,000 total): cinema/film/broadcasting, creative writing, dance, journalism/publications, music, performing arts, theater/drama. *Special achievements/activities:* 54 awards ($338,714 total): cheerleading/drum major, community service, general special achievements/activities, leadership, memberships, religious involvement. *Special characteristics:* 235 awards ($578,152 total): adult students, children of faculty/staff, general special characteristics, international students, local/state students, members of minority groups, religious affiliation, veterans. ***Tuition waivers:*** Full or partial for employees or children of employees, senior citizens.

LOANS ***Student loans:*** $5,182,428 (82% need-based, 18% non-need-based). 77% of past graduating class borrowed through all loan programs. *Average indebtedness per student:* $37,490. ***Average need-based loan:*** Freshmen: $3081. Undergraduates: $4092. ***Parent loans:*** $1,571,982 (51% need-based, 49% non-need-based). ***Programs:*** Federal Direct (Subsidized and Unsubsidized Stafford, PLUS).

WORK-STUDY ***Federal work-study:*** Total amount: $166,754; 117 jobs averaging $1425. ***State or other work-study/employment:*** Part-time jobs available.

ATHLETIC AWARDS Total amount: $2,999,875 (80% need-based, 20% non-need-based).

APPLYING FOR FINANCIAL AID ***Required financial aid form:*** FAFSA. ***Financial aid deadline (priority):*** 4/1. ***Notification date:*** Continuous beginning 2/1. Students must reply within 4 weeks of notification.

CONTACT Mrs. Brenda D. Hicks, Director of Financial Aid, Southwestern College, 100 College Street, Winfield, KS 67156-2499, 620-229-6215 or toll-free 800-846-1543. *Fax:* 620-229-6245. *E-mail:* finaid@sckans.edu.
Website: http://www.sckans.edu/.

SOUTHWESTERN OKLAHOMA STATE UNIVERSITY

Weatherford, OK

Tuition & fees (area res): $7695 | **Average undergraduate aid package: $6292**

ABOUT THE INSTITUTION State-supported, coed. ***Awards:*** certificates, associate, bachelor's, master's, and doctoral degrees. 43 undergraduate majors. ***Total enrollment:*** 4,932. Undergraduates: 4,092. Freshmen: 855. Both federal and institutional methodology are used as a basis for awarding need-based institutional aid.

UNDERGRADUATE EXPENSES for 2020–2021 ***Tuition, area resident:*** full-time $6150; part-time $205 per credit hour. ***Tuition, state resident:*** full-time $6150; part-time $205 per credit hour. ***Tuition, nonresident:*** full-time $13,050; part-time $435 per credit hour. ***Required fees:*** full-time $1545. ***College room and board:*** $6030; ***Room only:*** $2700.

FRESHMAN FINANCIAL AID (Fall 2019, est.) 497 applied for aid; of those 91% were deemed to have need. 100% of freshmen with need received aid; of those 27% had need fully met. ***Average percent of need met:*** 80% (excluding resources awarded to replace EFC). ***Average financial aid package:*** $6892 (excluding resources awarded to replace EFC). 10% of all full-time freshmen had no need and received non-need-based gift aid.

UNDERGRADUATE FINANCIAL AID (Fall 2019, est.) 1,818 applied for aid; of those 87% were deemed to have need. 100% of undergraduates with need received aid; of those 22% had need fully met. ***Average percent of need met:*** 77% (excluding resources awarded to replace EFC). ***Average financial aid package:*** $6292 (excluding resources awarded to replace EFC). 9% of all full-time undergraduates had no need and received non-need-based gift aid.

GIFT AID (NEED-BASED) ***Total amount:*** $13,384,469 (58% federal, 34% state, 4% institutional, 4% external sources). ***Receiving aid:*** Freshmen: 49% (402); all full-time undergraduates: 42% (1,371). ***Average award:*** Freshmen: $2300; Undergraduates: $2353. ***Scholarships, grants, and awards:*** Federal Pell, FSEOG, state, private, college/university gift aid from institutional funds.

GIFT AID (NON-NEED-BASED) ***Total amount:*** $2,420,257 (11% federal, 13% state, 47% institutional, 29% external sources). ***Receiving aid:*** Freshmen: 6% (51). Undergraduates: 3% (105). ***Average award:*** Freshmen: $1853. Undergraduates: $1243. ***Scholarships, grants, and awards by category:*** *Academic interests/achievement:* biological sciences, business, communication, computer science, education, engineering/technologies, English, foreign languages, general academic interests/achievements, mathematics, physical sciences, social sciences. *Creative arts/performance:* applied art and design, art/fine arts, music, theater/drama. *Special achievements/activities:* cheerleading/drum major, leadership, rodeo. *Special characteristics:* children and siblings of alumni, children of faculty/staff, local/state students, out-of-state students.

LOANS ***Student loans:*** $9,220,882 (65% need-based, 35% non-need-based). 43% of past graduating class borrowed through all loan programs. *Average indebtedness per student:* $23,292. ***Average need-based loan:*** Freshmen: $1680. Undergraduates: $2093. ***Parent loans:*** $1,578,292 (22% need-based, 78% non-need-based). ***Programs:*** Federal Direct (Subsidized and Unsubsidized Stafford, PLUS).

WORK-STUDY ***Federal work-study:*** Total amount: $2,145,034; jobs available.

ATHLETIC AWARDS Total amount: $1,719,530 (46% need-based, 54% non-need-based).

APPLYING FOR FINANCIAL AID ***Required financial aid forms:*** FAFSA, institution's own form. ***Financial aid deadline:*** 3/1 (priority: 3/1). ***Notification date:*** 3/15.

CONTACT Mr. Jerome Wichert, Director of Student Financial Services, Southwestern Oklahoma State University, 100 Campus Drive, Weatherford, OK 73096, 580-774-3786. *Fax:* 580-774-7066. *E-mail:* jerome.wichert@swosu.edu. *Website:* http://www.swosu.edu/.

SOUTHWESTERN UNIVERSITY

Georgetown, TX

Tuition & fees: $45,120 | **Average undergraduate aid package: $37,072**

ABOUT THE INSTITUTION Independent Methodist, coed. ***Awards:*** bachelor's degrees. 37 undergraduate majors. ***Total enrollment:*** 1,507. Undergraduates: 1,507. Freshmen: 444. Federal methodology is used as a basis for awarding need-based institutional aid.

UNDERGRADUATE EXPENSES for 2020–2021 ***One-time required fee:*** $200. ***Comprehensive fee:*** $57,570 includes full-time tuition ($45,120) and room and board ($12,450). ***College room only:*** $6800. Room and board charges vary according to board plan, housing facility, and student level. ***Part-time tuition:*** $1880 per credit hour.

FRESHMAN FINANCIAL AID (Fall 2019, est.) 391 applied for aid; of those 73% were deemed to have need. 100% of freshmen with need received aid; of those 26% had need fully met. ***Average percent of need met:*** 89% (excluding resources awarded to replace EFC). ***Average financial aid package:*** $37,308 (excluding resources awarded to replace EFC). 35% of all full-time freshmen had no need and received non-need-based gift aid.

UNDERGRADUATE FINANCIAL AID (Fall 2019, est.) 1,105 applied for aid; of those 83% were deemed to have need. 100% of undergraduates with need received aid; of those 27% had need fully met. ***Average percent of need met:*** 86% (excluding resources awarded to replace EFC). ***Average financial aid package:*** $37,072 (excluding resources awarded to replace EFC). 38% of all full-time undergraduates had no need and received non-need-based gift aid.

GIFT AID (NEED-BASED) ***Total amount:*** $28,676,770 (6% federal, 5% state, 85% institutional, 4% external sources). ***Receiving aid:*** Freshmen: 64% (285); all full-time undergraduates: 61% (904). ***Average award:*** Freshmen: $32,843; Undergraduates: $31,693. ***Scholarships, grants, and awards:*** Federal Pell, FSEOG, state, private, college/university gift aid from institutional funds.

GIFT AID (NON-NEED-BASED) ***Total amount:*** $13,750,789 (96% institutional, 4% external sources). ***Receiving aid:*** Freshmen: 63% (280). Undergraduates: 60% (895). ***Average award:*** Freshmen: $24,212. Undergraduates: $23,286. ***Scholarships, grants, and awards by category:*** *Academic interests/achievement:* business, general academic interests/achievements, humanities, international studies, mathematics, premedicine, social sciences. *Creative arts/performance:* applied art and design, music, theater/drama. *Special achievements/activities:* leadership. *Special characteristics:* children of faculty/staff, ethnic background, general special characteristics, members of minority groups, relatives of clergy, religious affiliation, veterans. ***Tuition waivers:*** Full or partial for employees or children of employees. ***ROTC:*** Air Force cooperative.

LOANS ***Student loans:*** $6,845,731 (86% need-based, 14% non-need-based). 61% of past graduating class borrowed through all loan programs. *Average indebtedness per student:* $34,551. ***Average need-based loan:*** Freshmen: $3471. Undergraduates: $4416. ***Parent loans:*** $6,282,598 (85% need-based, 15% non-need-based). ***Programs:*** Federal Direct (Subsidized and Unsubsidized Stafford, PLUS), state, college/university.

WORK-STUDY ***Federal work-study:*** Total amount: $350,582; jobs available. ***State or other work-study/employment:*** Total amount: $1,247,750 (58% need-based, 42% non-need-based). Part-time jobs available.

APPLYING FOR FINANCIAL AID ***Required financial aid form:*** FAFSA. ***Financial aid deadline (priority):*** 3/1. ***Notification date:*** Continuous beginning 11/15. Students must reply by 5/1 or within 2 weeks of notification.

CONTACT Mr. James P. Gaeta, Associate Dean of Enrollment Services, Southwestern University, PO Box 770, Georgetown, TX 78627-0770, 512-863-1259 or toll-free 800-252-3166. *Fax:* 512-863-1507. *E-mail:* gaetaj@southwestern.edu. *Website:* http://www.southwestern.edu/.

SOUTHWEST MINNESOTA STATE UNIVERSITY

Marshall, MN

CONTACT Mr. David Vikander, Director of Financial Aid, Southwest Minnesota State University, 1501 State Street, Marshall, MN 56258, 507-537-6281 or toll-free 800-642-0684. *Fax:* 507-537-6275. *E-mail:* vikander@smsu.edu.
Website: http://www.smsu.edu/.

SOUTHWEST UNIVERSITY

Kenner, LA

CONTACT Financial Aid Office, Southwest University, 2200 Veterans Memorial Boulevard, Kenner, LA 70062, 504-468-2900 or toll-free 800-433-5923.
Website: http://www.southwest.edu/.

SOUTHWEST UNIVERSITY AT EL PASO

El Paso, TX

CONTACT Financial Aid Office, Southwest University at El Paso, 1414 Geronimo Drive, El Paso, TX 79925, 915-778-4001.
Website: http://southwestuniversity.edu/.

SOUTHWEST UNIVERSITY OF VISUAL ARTS

Tucson, AZ

CONTACT Financial Aid Office, Southwest University of Visual Arts, 2525 North Country Club Road, Tucson, AZ 85716-2505, 520-325-0123 or toll-free 800-825-8753.
Website: http://www.suva.edu/.

SPALDING UNIVERSITY

Louisville, KY

CONTACT Director of Student Financial Services, Spalding University, 851 South Fourth Street, Louisville, KY 40203, 502-588-7185 or toll-free 800-896-8941. *Fax:* 502-585-7128. *E-mail:* onestop@spalding.edu.
Website: http://www.spalding.edu/.

SPELMAN COLLEGE

Atlanta, GA

Tuition & fees: N/R	Average undergraduate aid package: $17,700

ABOUT THE INSTITUTION Independent, women only. ***Awards:*** bachelor's degrees. 31 undergraduate majors. ***Total enrollment:*** 2,171. Undergraduates: 2,171. Freshmen: 571. Federal methodology is used as a basis for awarding need-based institutional aid.

FRESHMAN FINANCIAL AID (Fall 2019, est.) 506 applied for aid; of those 86% were deemed to have need. 100% of freshmen with need received aid; of those 44% had need fully met. ***Average percent of need met:*** 36% (excluding resources awarded to replace EFC). ***Average financial aid package:*** $15,761 (excluding resources awarded to replace EFC). 5% of all full-time freshmen had no need and received non-need-based gift aid.

UNDERGRADUATE FINANCIAL AID (Fall 2019, est.) 1,867 applied for aid; of those 89% were deemed to have need. 100% of undergraduates with need received aid; of those 43% had need fully met. ***Average percent of need met:*** 36% (excluding resources awarded to replace EFC). ***Average financial aid package:*** $17,700 (excluding resources awarded to replace EFC). 2% of all full-time undergraduates had no need and received non-need-based gift aid.

GIFT AID (NEED-BASED) ***Total amount:*** $23,865,235 (22% federal, 8% state, 57% institutional, 13% external sources). ***Receiving aid:*** Freshmen: 83% (426); all full-time undergraduates: 70% (1,449). ***Average award:*** Freshmen: $12,539; Undergraduates: $15,125. ***Scholarships, grants, and awards:*** Federal Pell, FSEOG, state, private, college/university gift aid from institutional funds, United Negro College Fund.

GIFT AID (NON-NEED-BASED) ***Total amount:*** $1,466,205 (2% state, 93% institutional, 5% external sources). ***Receiving aid:*** Freshmen: 10% (50). Undergraduates: 10% (198). ***Average award:*** Freshmen: $11,749. Undergraduates: $13,679. ***Scholarships, grants, and awards by category:*** *Academic interests/achievement:* $1,466,205 total: biological sciences, computer science, education, engineering/technologies, English, foreign languages, general academic interests/achievements, home economics, humanities, international studies, mathematics, religion/biblical studies, social sciences. *Creative arts/performance:* art/fine arts, dance, music, performing arts, theater/drama. ***ROTC:*** Army cooperative, Naval cooperative, Air Force cooperative.

LOANS ***Student loans:*** $26,379,607 (62% need-based, 38% non-need-based). 94% of past graduating class borrowed through all loan programs. *Average indebtedness per student:* $33,870. ***Average need-based loan:*** Freshmen: $3689. Undergraduates: $4725. ***Parent loans:*** $50,304,086 (100% non-need-based). ***Programs:*** Federal Direct (Subsidized and Unsubsidized Stafford, PLUS), state.

WORK-STUDY ***Federal work-study:*** Total amount: $340,967; jobs available.

APPLYING FOR FINANCIAL AID ***Required financial aid forms:*** FAFSA, CSS Financial Aid PROFILE. ***Financial aid deadline (priority):*** 2/1. ***Notification date:*** 12/15.

CONTACT Ms. Lenora Jackson, Director of Financial Aid, Spelman College, 350 Spelman Lane, SW, Atlanta, GA 30314-4399, 404-270-5222 or toll-free 800-982-2411. *Fax:* 404-270-5220. *E-mail:* lenoraj@spelman.edu.
Website: http://www.spelman.edu/.

SPRING ARBOR UNIVERSITY

Spring Arbor, MI

CONTACT Herbert Rotich, Director of Financial Aid, Spring Arbor University, 106 East Main Street, Spring Arbor, MI 49283-9799, 517-750-6463 or toll-free 800-968-0011. *Fax:* 517-750-6620. *E-mail:* hrotich@arbor.edu.
Website: http://www.arbor.edu/.

SPRINGFIELD COLLEGE

Springfield, MA

Tuition & fees: $38,565	Average undergraduate aid package: $28,667

ABOUT THE INSTITUTION Independent, coed. ***Awards:*** certificates, bachelor's, master's, and doctoral degrees. 38 undergraduate majors. ***Total enrollment:*** 3,119. Undergraduates: 2,175. Freshmen: 596. Federal methodology is used as a basis for awarding need-based institutional aid.

UNDERGRADUATE EXPENSES for 2020–2021 ***Application fee:*** $50. ***Comprehensive fee:*** $51,495 includes full-time tuition ($38,030), mandatory fees ($535), and room and board ($12,930). ***College room only:*** $7040. Full-time tuition and fees vary according to class time, course load, location, and program. Room and board charges vary according to board plan and housing facility. ***Part-time tuition:*** $1142 per credit hour. Part-time tuition and fees vary according to class time, course load, location, and program.

FRESHMAN FINANCIAL AID (Fall 2019, est.) 550 applied for aid; of those 89% were deemed to have need. 100% of freshmen with need received aid; of those 20% had need fully met. ***Average percent of need met:*** 77% (excluding resources awarded to replace EFC). ***Average financial aid package:*** $29,593 (excluding

resources awarded to replace EFC). 20% of all full-time freshmen had no need and received non-need-based gift aid.

UNDERGRADUATE FINANCIAL AID (Fall 2019, est.) 1,920 applied for aid; of those 89% were deemed to have need. 100% of undergraduates with need received aid; of those 14% had need fully met. ***Average percent of need met:*** 64% (excluding resources awarded to replace EFC). ***Average financial aid package:*** $28,667 (excluding resources awarded to replace EFC). 17% of all full-time undergraduates had no need and received non-need-based gift aid.

GIFT AID (NEED-BASED) ***Total amount:*** $40,025,189 (7% federal, 1% state, 86% institutional, 6% external sources). ***Receiving aid:*** Freshmen: 82% (486); all full-time undergraduates: 80% (1,712). ***Average award:*** Freshmen: $26,325; Undergraduates: $23,983. ***Scholarships, grants, and awards:*** Federal Pell, FSEOG, state, private, college/university gift aid from institutional funds.

GIFT AID (NON-NEED-BASED) ***Total amount:*** $9,042,617 (92% institutional, 8% external sources). ***Receiving aid:*** Freshmen: 15% (87). Undergraduates: 9% (202). ***Average award:*** Freshmen: $22,221. Undergraduates: $18,399. ***Scholarships, grants, and awards by category:*** *Academic interests/achievement:* general academic interests/achievements. *Special characteristics:* children and siblings of alumni, children of current students, children of faculty/staff, siblings of current students. ***Tuition waivers:*** Full or partial for employees or children of employees. ***ROTC:*** Army cooperative, Air Force cooperative.

LOANS ***Student loans:*** $18,007,993 (66% need-based, 34% non-need-based). 86% of past graduating class borrowed through all loan programs. *Average indebtedness per student:* $43,821. ***Average need-based loan:*** Freshmen: $2977. Undergraduates: $4019. ***Parent loans:*** $6,700,949 (49% need-based, 51% non-need-based). ***Programs:*** Federal Direct (Subsidized and Unsubsidized Stafford, PLUS).

WORK-STUDY ***Federal work-study:*** Total amount: $1,618,905; jobs available. ***State or other work-study/employment:*** Total amount: $641,000 (87% need-based, 13% non-need-based). Part-time jobs available.

APPLYING FOR FINANCIAL AID ***Required financial aid form:*** FAFSA. ***Financial aid deadline:*** Continuous. ***Notification date:*** Continuous beginning 11/10. Students must reply by 5/1.

CONTACT Ms. Raldy Laguilles, Director of Institutional Research, Springfield College, 263 Alden Street, Springfield, MA 01109-3797, 413-748-3108 or toll-free 800-343-1257. *Fax:* 413-748-3462. *E-mail:* laguilles@springfieldcollege.edu.
Website: http://www.springfield.edu/.

SPRING HILL COLLEGE

Mobile, AL

Tuition & fees: $40,648	Average undergraduate aid package: $36,757

ABOUT THE INSTITUTION Independent Roman Catholic (Jesuit), coed. ***Awards:*** certificates, bachelor's, and master's degrees. 48 undergraduate majors. ***Total enrollment:*** 1,317. Undergraduates: 1,187. Freshmen: 290. Federal methodology is used as a basis for awarding need-based institutional aid.

UNDERGRADUATE EXPENSES for 2019–2020 ***Application fee:*** $25. ***Comprehensive fee:*** $54,300 includes full-time tuition ($38,190), mandatory fees ($2458), and room and board ($13,652). ***College room only:*** $7108. Full-time tuition and fees vary according to course load. Room and board charges vary according to board plan and housing facility. ***Part-time tuition:*** $1126 per credit hour. ***Part-time fees:*** $57 per credit hour. Part-time tuition and fees vary according to course load.

FRESHMAN FINANCIAL AID (Fall 2019, est.) 267 applied for aid; of those 83% were deemed to have need. 100% of freshmen with need received aid; of those 18% had need fully met. ***Average percent of need met:*** 85% (excluding resources awarded to replace EFC). ***Average financial aid package:*** $27,808 (excluding resources awarded to replace EFC). 22% of all full-time freshmen had no need and received non-need-based gift aid.

UNDERGRADUATE FINANCIAL AID (Fall 2019, est.) 943 applied for aid; of those 89% were deemed to have need. 100% of undergraduates with need received aid; of those 45% had need fully met. ***Average percent of need met:*** 84% (excluding resources awarded to replace EFC). ***Average financial aid package:*** $36,757 (excluding resources awarded to replace EFC). 25% of all full-time undergraduates had no need and received non-need-based gift aid.

GIFT AID (NEED-BASED) ***Total amount:*** $23,965,486 (10% federal, 2% state, 87% institutional, 1% external sources). ***Receiving aid:*** Freshmen: 63% (182); all full-time undergraduates: 59% (677). ***Average award:*** Freshmen: $9145; Undergraduates: $9185. ***Scholarships, grants, and awards:*** Federal Pell, FSEOG, state, private, college/university gift aid from institutional funds, TEACH Grants.

GIFT AID (NON-NEED-BASED) ***Total amount:*** $8,473,713 (1% state, 98% institutional, 1% external sources). ***Receiving aid:*** Freshmen: 76% (221). Undergraduates: 72% (822). ***Average award:*** Freshmen: $21,471. Undergraduates: $22,061. ***Scholarships, grants, and awards by category:*** *Academic interests/achievement:* general academic interests/achievements. *Special achievements/activities:* community service. *Special characteristics:* children of faculty/staff, siblings of current students. ***Tuition waivers:*** Full or partial for employees or children of employees. ***ROTC:*** Army cooperative, Air Force cooperative.

LOANS ***Student loans:*** $6,336,436 (71% need-based, 29% non-need-based). ***Average need-based loan:*** Freshmen: $3674. Undergraduates: $4465. ***Parent loans:*** $3,226,863 (48% need-based, 52% non-need-based). ***Programs:*** Federal Direct (Subsidized and Unsubsidized Stafford, PLUS), alternative loans, private loans.

WORK-STUDY ***Federal work-study:*** Total amount: $520,557; jobs available. ***State or other work-study/employment:*** Total amount: $70,000 (100% non-need-based). Part-time jobs available.

ATHLETIC AWARDS Total amount: $3,436,826 (41% need-based, 59% non-need-based).

APPLYING FOR FINANCIAL AID ***Required financial aid forms:*** FAFSA, state aid form. ***Financial aid deadline (priority):*** 2/1. ***Notification date:*** Continuous beginning 12/1. Students must reply by 5/1.

CONTACT Dr. Karleen P. Howard, Director of Financial Aid, Spring Hill College, 4000 Dauphin Street, Mobile, AL 36608, 251-380-2253 or toll-free 800-SHC-6704. *Fax:* 251-460-2176. *E-mail:* kphoward@shc.edu.
Website: http://www.shc.edu/.

STANBRIDGE UNIVERSITY

Irvine, CA

CONTACT Financial Aid Office, Stanbridge University, 2041 Business Center Drive, Irvine, CA 92612, 949-794-9090.
Website: http://www.stanbridge.edu/.

STANFORD UNIVERSITY

Stanford, CA

Tuition & fees: $56,169	Average undergraduate aid package: $56,382

ABOUT THE INSTITUTION Independent, coed. ***Awards:*** certificates, bachelor's, master's, and doctoral degrees. 72 undergraduate majors. ***Total enrollment:*** 17,249. Undergraduates: 6,996. Freshmen: 1,698. Both federal and institutional methodology are used as a basis for awarding need-based institutional aid.

UNDERGRADUATE EXPENSES for 2020–2021 ***Application fee:*** $90. ***Comprehensive fee:*** $73,424 includes full-time tuition ($55,473), mandatory fees ($696), and room and board ($17,255). ***College room only:*** $10,725.

FRESHMAN FINANCIAL AID (Fall 2018) 1079 applied for aid; of those 82% were deemed to have need. 100% of freshmen with need received aid; of those 93% had need fully met. ***Average percent of need met:*** 100% (excluding resources awarded to replace EFC). ***Average financial aid package:*** $58,633 (excluding resources awarded to replace EFC). 1% of all full-time freshmen had no need and received non-need-based gift aid.

UNDERGRADUATE FINANCIAL AID (Fall 2018) 4,136 applied for aid; of those 83% were deemed to have need. 100% of undergraduates with need received aid; of those 89% had need fully met. ***Average percent of need met:*** 100% (excluding resources awarded to replace EFC). ***Average financial aid package:*** $56,382 (excluding resources awarded to replace EFC). 1% of all full-time undergraduates had no need and received non-need-based gift aid.

GIFT AID (NEED-BASED) ***Receiving aid:*** Freshmen: 51% (868); all full-time undergraduates: 49% (3,385). ***Average award:*** Freshmen: $55,394; Undergraduates: $52,823. ***Scholarships, grants, and awards:*** Federal Pell, FSEOG, state, private, college/university gift aid from institutional funds.

GIFT AID (NON-NEED-BASED) ***Receiving aid:*** Freshmen: 2% (29). Undergraduates: 2% (143). ***Average award:*** Freshmen: $5846. Undergraduates: $16,428. ***ROTC:*** Army cooperative, Naval cooperative, Air Force cooperative.

LOANS ***Student loans:*** 17% of past graduating class borrowed through all loan programs. *Average indebtedness per student:* $22,897. ***Average need-based loan:*** Freshmen: $2698. Undergraduates: $3133. ***Programs:*** Federal Direct (Subsidized and Unsubsidized Stafford, PLUS), Perkins.

WORK-STUDY ***Federal work-study:*** 546 jobs averaging $2425. ***State or other work-study/employment:*** 1,883 part-time jobs averaging $2236.

APPLYING FOR FINANCIAL AID ***Required financial aid forms:*** FAFSA, CSS Financial Aid PROFILE, noncustodial (divorced/separated) parent's statement. ***Notification date:*** Continuous.

CONTACT Financial Aid Office, Stanford University, 450 Serra Mall, Stanford, CA 94305-2004, 650-723-2300.
Website: http://www.stanford.edu/.

STATE COLLEGE OF FLORIDA MANATEE-SARASOTA

Bradenton, FL

CONTACT Financial Aid Office, State College of Florida Manatee-Sarasota, 5840 26th Street West, PO Box 1849, Bradenton, FL 34206-7046, 941-752-5000.
Website: http://www.scf.edu/.

STATE UNIVERSITY OF NEW YORK AT FREDONIA

Fredonia, NY

Tuition & fees (NY res): $8717	Average undergraduate aid package: $12,659

ABOUT THE INSTITUTION State-supported, coed. ***Awards:*** certificates, bachelor's, and master's degrees. 69 undergraduate majors. ***Total enrollment:*** 4,463. Undergraduates: 4,226. Freshmen: 1,007. Federal methodology is used as a basis for awarding need-based institutional aid.

UNDERGRADUATE EXPENSES for 2020–2021 ***Application fee:*** $50. ***Tuition, state resident:*** full-time $7070; part-time $295 per credit hour. ***Tuition, nonresident:*** full-time $16,980; part-time $708 per credit hour. ***Required fees:*** full-time $1647; $68.25. ***College room and board:*** $12,830; ***Room only:*** $7600. Room and board charges vary according to board plan and housing facility.

FRESHMAN FINANCIAL AID (Fall 2019, est.) 928 applied for aid; of those 81% were deemed to have need. 100% of freshmen with need received aid; of those 28% had need fully met. ***Average percent of need met:*** 69% (excluding resources awarded to replace EFC). ***Average financial aid package:*** $13,876 (excluding resources awarded to replace EFC). 16% of all full-time freshmen had no need and received non-need-based gift aid.

UNDERGRADUATE FINANCIAL AID (Fall 2019, est.) 3,737 applied for aid; of those 81% were deemed to have need. 99% of undergraduates with need received aid; of those 25% had need fully met. ***Average percent of need met:*** 66% (excluding resources awarded to replace EFC). ***Average financial aid package:*** $12,659 (excluding resources awarded to replace EFC). 11% of all full-time undergraduates had no need and received non-need-based gift aid.

GIFT AID (NEED-BASED) ***Receiving aid:*** Freshmen: 67% (656); all full-time undergraduates: 60% (2,466). ***Average award:*** Freshmen: $7805; Undergraduates: $7251. ***Scholarships, grants, and awards:*** Federal Pell, FSEOG, state, private, college/university gift aid from institutional funds, TEACH Grants.

GIFT AID (NON-NEED-BASED) ***Receiving aid:*** Freshmen: 46% (450). Undergraduates: 28% (1,172). ***Average award:*** Freshmen: $4084. Undergraduates: $3558. ***Scholarships, grants, and awards by category:*** *Academic interests/achievement:* 319 awards ($422,213 total): biological sciences, business, communication, computer science, education, English, foreign languages, general academic interests/achievements, humanities, international studies, mathematics, physical sciences, social sciences. *Creative arts/performance:* 128 awards ($120,900 total): applied art and design, art/fine arts, dance, music, performing arts, theater/drama. *Special achievements/activities:* 17 awards ($46,500 total): general special achievements/activities, leadership. *Special characteristics:* 147 awards ($472,332 total): children and siblings of alumni, ethnic background, general special characteristics, international students, local/state students, members of minority groups, out-of-state students, parents of current students, previous college experience.

LOANS ***Student loans:*** 91% of past graduating class borrowed through all loan programs. *Average indebtedness per student:* $26,722. ***Average need-based loan:*** Freshmen: $3370. Undergraduates: $4218. ***Programs:*** Federal Direct (Subsidized and Unsubsidized Stafford, PLUS), private loans.

WORK-STUDY ***Federal work-study:*** 170 jobs averaging $1840.

APPLYING FOR FINANCIAL AID ***Required financial aid forms:*** FAFSA, state aid form. ***Financial aid deadline:*** Continuous. ***Notification date:*** Continuous.

CONTACT Mark Zaffalon, Financial Aid Counselor, State University of New York at Fredonia, 209 Maytum Hall, Fredonia, NY 14063, 716-673-3253 or toll-free 800-252-1212. *Fax:* 716-673-3785. *E-mail:* mark.zaffalon@fredonia.edu.
Website: http://www.fredonia.edu/.

STATE UNIVERSITY OF NEW YORK AT NEW PALTZ

New Paltz, NY

Tuition & fees (NY res): $8502	Average undergraduate aid package: $12,224

ABOUT THE INSTITUTION State-supported, coed. ***Awards:*** certificates, bachelor's, and master's degrees. 67 undergraduate majors. ***Total enrollment:*** 7,757. Undergraduates: 6,807. Freshmen: 1,125. Federal methodology is used as a basis for awarding need-based institutional aid.

UNDERGRADUATE EXPENSES for 2019–2020 ***Application fee:*** $50. ***Tuition, state resident:*** full-time $7070; part-time $295 per credit hour. ***Tuition, nonresident:*** full-time $16,980; part-time $708 per credit hour. ***Required fees:*** full-time $1432; $210 per term. ***College room and board:*** $13,928; ***Room only:*** $9128. Room and board charges vary according to board plan.

FRESHMAN FINANCIAL AID (Fall 2019, est.) 1049 applied for aid; of those 72% were deemed to have need. 99% of freshmen with need received aid; of those 12% had need fully met. ***Average percent of need met:*** 58% (excluding resources awarded to replace EFC). ***Average financial aid package:*** $12,626 (excluding resources awarded to replace EFC). 1% of all full-time freshmen had no need and received non-need-based gift aid.

UNDERGRADUATE FINANCIAL AID (Fall 2019, est.) 5,122 applied for aid; of those 77% were deemed to have need. 99% of undergraduates with need received aid; of those 12% had need fully met. ***Average percent of need met:*** 58% (excluding resources awarded to replace EFC). ***Average financial aid package:*** $12,224 (excluding resources awarded to replace EFC). 1% of all full-time undergraduates had no need and received non-need-based gift aid.

GIFT AID (NEED-BASED) ***Receiving aid:*** Freshmen: 37% (417); all full-time undergraduates: 49% (3,099). ***Average award:*** Freshmen: $5604; Undergraduates: $5338. ***Scholarships, grants, and awards:*** Federal Pell, FSEOG, state, private, college/university gift aid from institutional funds.

GIFT AID (NON-NEED-BASED) ***Receiving aid:*** Freshmen: 23% (264). Undergraduates: 16% (1,036). ***Average award:*** Freshmen: $1892. Undergraduates: $2310. ***Scholarships, grants, and awards by category:*** *Academic interests/achievement:* area/ethnic studies, biological sciences, business, communication, education, engineering/technologies, English, foreign languages, general academic interests/achievements, international studies, mathematics, physical sciences. *Creative arts/performance:* applied art and design, music, theater/drama. *Special characteristics:* children of faculty/staff, ethnic background, first-generation college students, local/state students, members of minority groups.

LOANS ***Student loans:*** 62% of past graduating class borrowed through all loan programs. *Average indebtedness per student:* $26,771. ***Average need-based loan:*** Freshmen: $3372. Undergraduates: $4353. ***Programs:*** Federal Direct (Subsidized and Unsubsidized Stafford, PLUS), Perkins.

WORK-STUDY Federal work-study jobs available. ***State or other work-study/employment:*** Part-time jobs available.

APPLYING FOR FINANCIAL AID ***Required financial aid forms:*** FAFSA, state aid form. ***Financial aid deadline:*** Continuous. ***Notification date:*** Continuous.

CONTACT Mrs. Maureen Lohan-Bremer, Director of Financial Aid, State University of New York at New Paltz, 200 Hawk Drive, New Paltz, NY 12561-2437, 845-257-3250 or toll-free 877-MY-NP-411 (in-state). *Fax:* 845-257-3568. *E-mail:* fao@newpaltz.edu.
Website: http://www.newpaltz.edu/.

STATE UNIVERSITY OF NEW YORK AT OSWEGO

Oswego, NY

Tuition & fees (NY res): $8717 | **Average undergraduate aid package: $11,230**

ABOUT THE INSTITUTION State-supported, coed. ***Awards:*** certificates, bachelor's, and master's degrees. 68 undergraduate majors. ***Total enrollment:*** 7,830. Undergraduates: 6,920. Freshmen: 1,422. Federal methodology is used as a basis for awarding need-based institutional aid.

UNDERGRADUATE EXPENSES for 2019–2020 ***Application fee:*** $50. ***One-time required fee:*** $225. ***Tuition, state resident:*** full-time $7070; part-time $295 per credit hour. ***Tuition, nonresident:*** full-time $16,980; part-time $760 per credit hour. ***Required fees:*** full-time $1647; $68 per credit hour. Part-time tuition and fees vary according to course load. ***College room and board:*** $14,603; ***Room only:*** $8790. Room and board charges vary according to board plan and housing facility.

FRESHMAN FINANCIAL AID (Fall 2019, est.) 1326 applied for aid; of those 80% were deemed to have need. 94% of freshmen with need received aid; of those 28% had need fully met. ***Average percent of need met:*** 69% (excluding resources awarded to replace EFC). ***Average financial aid package:*** $13,241 (excluding resources awarded to replace EFC). 9% of all full-time freshmen had no need and received non-need-based gift aid.

UNDERGRADUATE FINANCIAL AID (Fall 2019, est.) 5,678 applied for aid; of those 81% were deemed to have need. 96% of undergraduates with need received aid; of those 29% had need fully met. ***Average percent of need met:*** 61% (excluding resources awarded to replace EFC). ***Average financial aid package:*** $11,230 (excluding resources awarded to replace EFC). 11% of all full-time undergraduates had no need and received non-need-based gift aid.

GIFT AID (NEED-BASED) ***Total amount:*** $30,117,268 (49% federal, 43% state, 8% institutional). ***Receiving aid:*** Freshmen: 61% (876); all full-time undergraduates: 58% (3,814). ***Average award:*** Freshmen: $7195; Undergraduates: $6185.

GIFT AID (NON-NEED-BASED) ***Total amount:*** $1,826,844 (3% state, 96% institutional, 1% external sources). ***Receiving aid:*** Freshmen: 2% (23). Undergraduates: 1% (88). ***Average award:*** Freshmen: $6334. Undergraduates: $7604. ***Scholarships, grants, and awards by category:*** *Academic interests/achievement:* area/ethnic studies, biological sciences, business, communication, computer science, education, English, foreign languages, general academic interests/achievements, humanities, international studies, mathematics, physical sciences, premedicine, social sciences. ***ROTC:*** Army cooperative, Air Force cooperative.

LOANS ***Student loans:*** $33,441,911 (84% need-based, 16% non-need-based). ***Average need-based loan:*** Freshmen: $6637. Undergraduates: $5246. ***Parent loans:*** $12,441,345 (87% need-based, 13% non-need-based).

WORK-STUDY ***Federal work-study:*** Total amount: $583,069; jobs available. ***State or other work-study/employment:*** Total amount: $1,403,135 (57% need-based, 43% non-need-based). Part-time jobs available.

APPLYING FOR FINANCIAL AID ***Notification date:*** Continuous.

CONTACT Dr. Rodrick Andrews, Director of Financial Aid, State University of New York at Oswego, 206 Culkin Hall, Institutional Research and Assessment, Oswego, NY 13126, 315-3122248. *Fax:* 315-312-3696. *E-mail:* rodrick.andrews@oswego.edu.
Website: http://www.oswego.edu/.

STATE UNIVERSITY OF NEW YORK AT PLATTSBURGH

Plattsburgh, NY

Tuition & fees (NY res): $8872 | **Average undergraduate aid package: $14,358**

ABOUT THE INSTITUTION State-supported, coed. ***Awards:*** certificates, bachelor's, and master's degrees. 50 undergraduate majors. ***Total enrollment:*** 5,704. Undergraduates: 5,297. Freshmen: 1,144. Both federal and institutional methodology are used as a basis for awarding need-based institutional aid.

UNDERGRADUATE EXPENSES for 2019–2020 ***Application fee:*** $50. ***Tuition, state resident:*** full-time $7070; part-time $295 per credit hour. ***Tuition, nonresident:*** full-time $16,980; part-time $708 per credit hour. ***Required fees:*** full-time $1802; $74.69 per credit hour. ***College room and board:*** $13,630; ***Room only:*** $8740. Room and board charges vary according to board plan.

FRESHMAN FINANCIAL AID (Fall 2018) 1033 applied for aid; of those 80% were deemed to have need. 98% of freshmen with need received aid; of those 21% had need fully met. ***Average percent of need met:*** 78% (excluding resources awarded to replace EFC). ***Average financial aid package:*** $14,298 (excluding resources awarded to replace EFC). 16% of all full-time freshmen had no need and received non-need-based gift aid.

UNDERGRADUATE FINANCIAL AID (Fall 2018) 3,998 applied for aid; of those 82% were deemed to have need. 98% of undergraduates with need received aid; of those 18% had need fully met. ***Average percent of need met:*** 75% (excluding resources awarded to replace EFC). ***Average financial aid package:*** $14,358 (excluding resources awarded to replace EFC). 15% of all full-time undergraduates had no need and received non-need-based gift aid.

GIFT AID (NEED-BASED) ***Total amount:*** $25,270,968 (40% federal, 37% state, 21% institutional, 2% external sources). ***Receiving aid:*** Freshmen: 65% (735); all full-time undergraduates: 59% (2,845). ***Average award:*** Freshmen: $9249; Undergraduates: $8727. ***Scholarships, grants, and awards:*** Federal Pell, FSEOG, state, private, college/university gift aid from institutional funds.

GIFT AID (NON-NEED-BASED) ***Total amount:*** $5,206,443 (2% federal, 11% state, 84% institutional, 3% external sources). ***Receiving aid:*** Freshmen: 17% (192). Undergraduates: 16% (771). ***Average award:*** Freshmen: $5399. Undergraduates: $6212. ***Scholarships, grants, and awards by category:*** *Academic interests/achievement:* area/ethnic studies, biological sciences, business, communication, computer science, education, engineering/technologies, English, general academic interests/achievements, health fields, home economics, humanities, international studies, mathematics, physical sciences, premedicine, social sciences. *Creative arts/performance:* applied art and design, journalism/publications, music, theater/drama. *Special achievements/activities:* community service, general special achievements/activities, leadership. *Special characteristics:* international students, out-of-state students.

LOANS ***Student loans:*** $26,756,855 (83% need-based, 17% non-need-based). 72% of past graduating class borrowed through all loan programs. *Average indebtedness per student:* $30,919. ***Average need-based loan:*** Freshmen: $7035. Undergraduates: $7865. ***Parent loans:*** $4,963,893 (79% need-based, 21% non-need-based). ***Programs:*** Federal Direct (Subsidized and Unsubsidized Stafford, PLUS), Perkins, Federal Nursing, private loans.

WORK-STUDY ***Federal work-study:*** Total amount: $1,338,884; 653 jobs averaging $1927. ***State or other work-study/employment:*** Part-time jobs available.

APPLYING FOR FINANCIAL AID ***Required financial aid forms:*** FAFSA, state aid form. ***Financial aid deadline:*** Continuous. ***Notification date:*** Continuous beginning 12/1. Students must reply by 5/1.

CONTACT Mr. Todd Moravec, Director of Financial Aid, State University of New York at Plattsburgh, 101 Broad Street, Plattsburgh, NY 12901-2681, 518-564-2072 or toll-free 888-673-0012. *Fax:* 518-564-4079. *E-mail:* todd.moravec@plattsburgh.edu.
Website: http://www.plattsburgh.edu/.

STATE UNIVERSITY OF NEW YORK COLLEGE AT CORTLAND

Cortland, NY

Tuition & fees (NY res): $8806 **Average undergraduate aid package: $15,332**

ABOUT THE INSTITUTION State-supported, coed. ***Awards:*** certificates, bachelor's, and master's degrees. 57 undergraduate majors. ***Total enrollment:*** 6,834. Undergraduates: 6,295. Freshmen: 1,208. Federal methodology is used as a basis for awarding need-based institutional aid.

UNDERGRADUATE EXPENSES for 2019–2020 ***Application fee:*** $50. ***Tuition, state resident:*** full-time $7070; part-time $295 per credit hour. ***Tuition, nonresident:*** full-time $16,980; part-time $708 per credit hour. ***Required fees:*** full-time $1736. Full-time tuition and fees vary according to course load and degree level. Part-time tuition and fees vary according to course load and degree level. ***College room and board:*** $13,100; ***Room only:*** $8060. Room and board charges vary according to board plan and housing facility.

FRESHMAN FINANCIAL AID (Fall 2018) 1020 applied for aid; of those 72% were deemed to have need. 97% of freshmen with need received aid; of those 12% had need fully met. ***Average percent of need met:*** 68% (excluding resources awarded to replace EFC). ***Average financial aid package:*** $15,349 (excluding resources awarded to replace EFC). 3% of all full-time freshmen had no need and received non-need-based gift aid.

UNDERGRADUATE FINANCIAL AID (Fall 2018) 5,076 applied for aid; of those 77% were deemed to have need. 97% of undergraduates with need received aid; of those 12% had need fully met. ***Average percent of need met:*** 68% (excluding resources awarded to replace EFC). ***Average financial aid package:*** $15,332 (excluding resources awarded to replace EFC). 4% of all full-time undergraduates had no need and received non-need-based gift aid.

GIFT AID (NEED-BASED) ***Total amount:*** $15,699,933 (58% federal, 41% state, 1% institutional). ***Receiving aid:*** Freshmen: 49% (535); all full-time undergraduates: 48% (2,898). ***Average award:*** Freshmen: $5324; Undergraduates: $6024. ***Scholarships, grants, and awards:*** Federal Pell, FSEOG, state, private, college/university gift aid from institutional funds.

GIFT AID (NON-NEED-BASED) ***Total amount:*** $5,273,896 (18% federal, 50% institutional, 32% external sources). ***Receiving aid:*** Freshmen: 23% (251). Undergraduates: 16% (980). ***Average award:*** Freshmen: $3919. Undergraduates: $4577. ***Scholarships, grants, and awards by category:*** *Academic interests/achievement:* general academic interests/achievements. *Creative arts/performance:* applied art and design, music, theater/drama. *Special achievements/activities:* general special achievements/activities, leadership. *Special characteristics:* local/state students, members of minority groups. ***Tuition waivers:*** Full or partial for employees or children of employees. ***ROTC:*** Army cooperative, Air Force cooperative.

LOANS ***Student loans:*** $34,398,930 (38% need-based, 62% non-need-based). 76% of past graduating class borrowed through all loan programs. *Average indebtedness per student:* $31,176. ***Average need-based loan:*** Freshmen: $3091. Undergraduates: $4070. ***Parent loans:*** $8,671,801 (100% non-need-based). ***Programs:*** Federal Direct (Subsidized and Unsubsidized Stafford, PLUS), Perkins.

WORK-STUDY ***Federal work-study:*** Total amount: $276,651; jobs available. ***State or other work-study/employment:*** Total amount: $961,801 (100% non-need-based). Part-time jobs available.

APPLYING FOR FINANCIAL AID ***Required financial aid forms:*** FAFSA, state aid form. ***Financial aid deadline (priority):*** 3/1. ***Notification date:*** Continuous beginning 3/15. Students must reply by 5/1 or within 4 weeks of notification.

CONTACT Karen Gallagher, Director of Financial Advisement, State University of New York College at Cortland, PO Box 2000, Cortland, NY 13045, 607-753-4717. *Fax:* 607-753-5990. *E-mail:* finaid@cortland.edu.
Website: http://www.cortland.edu/.

STATE UNIVERSITY OF NEW YORK COLLEGE AT GENESEO

Geneseo, NY

Tuition & fees (NY res): $8927 **Average undergraduate aid package: $10,463**

ABOUT THE INSTITUTION State-supported, coed. ***Awards:*** bachelor's and master's degrees. 44 undergraduate majors. ***Total enrollment:*** 5,344. Undergraduates: 5,240. Freshmen: 1,233. Federal methodology is used as a basis for awarding need-based institutional aid.

UNDERGRADUATE EXPENSES for 2019–2020 ***Application fee:*** $50. ***Tuition, state resident:*** full-time $7070; part-time $295 per credit hour. ***Tuition, nonresident:*** full-time $16,980; part-time $708 per credit hour. ***Required fees:*** full-time $1857; $75.30 per credit hour. Part-time tuition and fees vary according to course load. ***College room and board:*** $14,018; ***Room only:*** $8370. Room and board charges vary according to board plan and housing facility.

FRESHMAN FINANCIAL AID (Fall 2019, est.) 996 applied for aid; of those 71% were deemed to have need. 100% of freshmen with need received aid; of those 15% had need fully met. ***Average percent of need met:*** 41% (excluding resources awarded to replace EFC). ***Average financial aid package:*** $10,664 (excluding resources awarded to replace EFC). 12% of all full-time freshmen had no need and received non-need-based gift aid.

UNDERGRADUATE FINANCIAL AID (Fall 2019, est.) 3,600 applied for aid; of those 75% were deemed to have need. 100% of undergraduates with need received aid; of those 15% had need fully met. ***Average percent of need met:*** 44% (excluding resources awarded to replace EFC). ***Average financial aid package:*** $10,463 (excluding resources awarded to replace EFC). 7% of all full-time undergraduates had no need and received non-need-based gift aid.

GIFT AID (NEED-BASED) ***Total amount:*** $13,418,634 (53% federal, 35% state, 12% institutional). ***Receiving aid:*** Freshmen: 44% (538); all full-time undergraduates: 41% (2,089). ***Average award:*** Freshmen: $6837; Undergraduates: $6513. ***Scholarships, grants, and awards:*** Federal Pell, FSEOG, state.

GIFT AID (NON-NEED-BASED) ***Total amount:*** $9,259,990 (1% federal, 70% state, 29% institutional). ***Receiving aid:*** Freshmen: 12% (144). Undergraduates: 11% (540). ***Average award:*** Freshmen: $3136. Undergraduates: $4468. ***Scholarships, grants, and awards by category:*** *Academic interests/achievement:* area/ethnic studies, biological sciences, business, communication, education, English, foreign languages, general academic interests/achievements, humanities, international studies, mathematics, physical sciences, premedicine, social sciences. *Creative arts/performance:* applied art and design, art/fine arts, creative writing, dance, general creative arts/performance, journalism/publications, music, performing arts, theater/drama. *Special achievements/activities:* community service, general special achievements/activities, leadership, memberships. *Special characteristics:* adult students, ethnic background, first-generation college students, general special characteristics, handicapped students, international students, local/state students, members of minority groups, religious affiliation, veterans. ***ROTC:*** Army cooperative, Air Force cooperative.

LOANS ***Student loans:*** $20,440,429 (37% need-based, 63% non-need-based). 58% of past graduating class borrowed through all loan programs. *Average indebtedness per student:* $23,666. ***Average need-based loan:*** Freshmen: $3333. Undergraduates: $4091. ***Parent loans:*** $5,481,092 (100% non-need-based). ***Programs:*** Federal Direct (Subsidized and Unsubsidized Stafford, PLUS).

WORK-STUDY ***Federal work-study:*** Total amount: $829,785; 444 jobs averaging $1877.

APPLYING FOR FINANCIAL AID ***Required financial aid forms:*** FAFSA, state aid form. ***Notification date:*** Continuous.

CONTACT Susan Romano, Director of Financial Aid, State University of New York College at Geneseo, 1 College Circle, Erwin Hall 104, Geneseo, NY 14454, 585-245-5731 or toll-free 866-245-5211. *Fax:* 585-245-5717. *E-mail:* finaid@geneseo.edu.
Website: http://www.geneseo.edu/.

STATE UNIVERSITY OF NEW YORK COLLEGE AT OLD WESTBURY

Old Westbury, NY

CONTACT Ms. Vivian Mendonis, Financial Aid Assistant, State University of New York College at Old Westbury, PO Box 210, Old Westbury, NY 11568-0210, 516-876-3223. *Fax:* 516-876-3008. *E-mail:* finaid@oldwestbury.edu.
Website: http://www.oldwestbury.edu/.

STATE UNIVERSITY OF NEW YORK COLLEGE AT ONEONTA

Oneonta, NY

Tuition & fees (area res): $8922	Average undergraduate aid package: $15,792

ABOUT THE INSTITUTION State-supported, coed. ***Awards:*** certificates, bachelor's, and master's degrees. 68 undergraduate majors. ***Total enrollment:*** 6,528. Undergraduates: 6,064. Freshmen: 1,451.

UNDERGRADUATE EXPENSES for 2020–2021 ***Application fee:*** $50. ***Tuition, area resident:*** full-time $7270; part-time $303 per credit hour. ***Tuition, state resident:*** full-time $7270; part-time $303 per credit hour. ***Tuition, nonresident:*** full-time $17,320; part-time $722 per credit hour. ***Required fees:*** full-time $1652. Part-time tuition and fees vary according to course load. Room and board charges vary according to housing facility.

FRESHMAN FINANCIAL AID (Fall 2019, est.) 1369 applied for aid; of those 71% were deemed to have need. 97% of freshmen with need received aid; of those 8% had need fully met. ***Average percent of need met:*** 62% (excluding resources awarded to replace EFC). ***Average financial aid package:*** $15,916 (excluding resources awarded to replace EFC). 9% of all full-time freshmen had no need and received non-need-based gift aid.

UNDERGRADUATE FINANCIAL AID (Fall 2019, est.) 4,980 applied for aid; of those 75% were deemed to have need. 98% of undergraduates with need received aid; of those 7% had need fully met. ***Average percent of need met:*** 64% (excluding resources awarded to replace EFC). ***Average financial aid package:*** $15,792 (excluding resources awarded to replace EFC). 6% of all full-time undergraduates had no need and received non-need-based gift aid.

GIFT AID (NEED-BASED) ***Total amount:*** $20,198,769 (47% federal, 39% state, 10% institutional, 4% external sources). ***Receiving aid:*** Freshmen: 53% (773); all full-time undergraduates: 49% (2,922). ***Average award:*** Freshmen: $796; Undergraduates: $6889. ***Scholarships, grants, and awards:*** Federal Pell, FSEOG, state, private, college/university gift aid from institutional funds.

GIFT AID (NON-NEED-BASED) ***Total amount:*** $1,581,981 (3% federal, 13% state, 65% institutional, 19% external sources). ***Receiving aid:*** Freshmen: 1% (20). Undergraduates: 1% (71). ***Average award:*** Freshmen: $3327. Undergraduates: $3681. ***Scholarships, grants, and awards by category:*** *Academic interests/achievement:* biological sciences, business, computer science, education, English, general academic interests/achievements, home economics, physical sciences, premedicine, social sciences. *Creative arts/performance:* music, theater/drama. *Special achievements/activities:* community service, general special achievements/activities, leadership. *Special characteristics:* general special characteristics, international students, local/state students. ***Tuition waivers:*** Full or partial for employees or children of employees.

LOANS ***Student loans:*** $29,727,645 (64% need-based, 36% non-need-based). 73% of past graduating class borrowed through all loan programs. *Average indebtedness per student:* $26,092. ***Average need-based loan:*** Freshmen: $3026. Undergraduates: $3181. ***Parent loans:*** $8,005,353 (36% need-based, 64% non-need-based). ***Programs:*** Federal Direct (Subsidized and Unsubsidized Stafford, PLUS).

WORK-STUDY ***Federal work-study:*** Total amount: $123,655; jobs available. ***State or other work-study/employment:*** Part-time jobs available.

APPLYING FOR FINANCIAL AID ***Financial aid deadline (priority):*** 3/15. ***Notification date:*** Continuous beginning 1/1.

CONTACT Office of Financial Aid, State University of New York College at Oneonta, 108 Ravine Parkway, Oneonta, NY 13820, 607-436-2992 or toll-free 800-SUNY-123. *Fax:* 607-436-2659. *E-mail:* finaid@oneonta.edu.
Website: http://www.oneonta.edu/.

STATE UNIVERSITY OF NEW YORK COLLEGE AT POTSDAM

Potsdam, NY

Tuition & fees (NY res): $8711	Average undergraduate aid package: $15,149

ABOUT THE INSTITUTION State-supported, coed. ***Awards:*** certificates, bachelor's, and master's degrees. 74 undergraduate majors. ***Total enrollment:*** 3,339. Undergraduates: 3,063. Freshmen: 622. Federal methodology is used as a basis for awarding need-based institutional aid.

UNDERGRADUATE EXPENSES for 2019–2020 ***Application fee:*** $50. ***Tuition, state resident:*** full-time $7070; part-time $295 per credit hour. ***Tuition, nonresident:*** full-time $16,980; part-time $708 per credit hour. ***Required fees:*** full-time $1641; $57.95 per credit hour. Full-time tuition and fees vary according to course load. Part-time tuition and fees vary according to course load. ***College room and board:*** $13,900; ***Room only:*** $8150. Room and board charges vary according to board plan and housing facility.

FRESHMAN FINANCIAL AID (Fall 2019, est.) 608 applied for aid; of those 82% were deemed to have need. 100% of freshmen with need received aid; of those 16% had need fully met. ***Average percent of need met:*** 82% (excluding resources awarded to replace EFC). ***Average financial aid package:*** $15,715 (excluding resources awarded to replace EFC). 13% of all full-time freshmen had no need and received non-need-based gift aid.

UNDERGRADUATE FINANCIAL AID (Fall 2019, est.) 2,880 applied for aid; of those 81% were deemed to have need. 99% of undergraduates with need received aid; of those 13% had need fully met. ***Average percent of need met:*** 83% (excluding resources awarded to replace EFC). ***Average financial aid package:*** $15,149 (excluding resources awarded to replace EFC). 10% of all full-time undergraduates had no need and received non-need-based gift aid.

GIFT AID (NEED-BASED) ***Total amount:*** $20,264,579 (39% federal, 39% state, 20% institutional, 2% external sources). ***Receiving aid:*** Freshmen: 64% (397); all full-time undergraduates: 64% (1,907). ***Average award:*** Freshmen: $8264; Undergraduates: $8082. ***Scholarships, grants, and awards:*** Federal Pell, FSEOG, state, private, college/university gift aid from institutional funds, ACCES-VR, TEACH Grants,Native American Aid.

GIFT AID (NON-NEED-BASED) ***Total amount:*** $1,907,191 (7% state, 82% institutional, 11% external sources). ***Receiving aid:*** Freshmen: 53% (329). Undergraduates: 40% (1,205). ***Average award:*** Freshmen: $5213. Undergraduates: $4403. ***Scholarships, grants, and awards by category:*** *Academic interests/achievement:* 707 awards ($2,406,951 total): biological sciences, business, communication, computer science, education, engineering/technologies, English, foreign languages, general academic interests/achievements, home economics, humanities, international studies, mathematics, physical sciences, premedicine, social sciences. *Creative arts/performance:* 244 awards ($298,978 total): applied art and design, art/fine arts, cinema/film/broadcasting, creative writing, dance, general creative arts/performance, journalism/publications, music, performing arts, theater/drama. *Special achievements/activities:* 573 awards ($1,187,459 total): community service, general special achievements/activities, leadership. *Special characteristics:* 65 awards ($96,554 total): adult students, children and siblings of alumni, ethnic background, first-generation college students, general special characteristics, handicapped students, international students, local/state students, married students, members of minority groups, out-of-state students. ***ROTC:*** Army cooperative, Air Force cooperative.

LOANS ***Student loans:*** $17,726,584 (73% need-based, 27% non-need-based). 84% of past graduating class borrowed through all loan programs. *Average indebtedness per student:* $30,057. ***Average need-based loan:*** Freshmen: $3339. Undergraduates: $4276. ***Parent loans:*** $4,567,050 (46% need-based, 54% non-need-based). ***Programs:*** Federal Direct (Subsidized and Unsubsidized Stafford, PLUS).

WORK-STUDY ***Federal work-study:*** Total amount: $256,446; 142 jobs averaging $1623.

APPLYING FOR FINANCIAL AID ***Required financial aid forms:*** FAFSA, state aid form. ***Financial aid deadline (priority):*** 1/1. ***Notification date:*** Continuous beginning 12/15. Students must reply by 5/1 or within 4 weeks of notification.

CONTACT Susan E. Godreau, Director of Financial Aid, State University of New York College at Potsdam, 44 Pierrepont Avenue, Potsdam, NY 13676, 315-267-2162 or toll-free 877-POTSDAM. *Fax:* 315-267-3067. *E-mail:* finaid@potsdam.edu. *Website:* http://www.potsdam.edu/.

STATE UNIVERSITY OF NEW YORK COLLEGE OF AGRICULTURE AND TECHNOLOGY AT COBLESKILL

Cobleskill, NY

CONTACT Mr. Brian Smith, Office of Financial Aid, State University of New York College of Agriculture and Technology at Cobleskill, 118B Knapp Hall, Cobleskill, NY 12043, 518-255-5623 or toll-free 800-295-8988. *Fax:* 518-255-5844. *E-mail:* financialaid@cobleskill.edu.
Website: http://www.cobleskill.edu/.

STATE UNIVERSITY OF NEW YORK COLLEGE OF AGRICULTURE & TECHNOLOGY AT MORRISVILLE

Morrisville, NY

Tuition & fees: N/R	Average undergraduate aid package: $10,794

ABOUT THE INSTITUTION State-supported, coed. ***Awards:*** certificates, associate, and bachelor's degrees. 94 undergraduate majors. Federal methodology is used as a basis for awarding need-based institutional aid.

FRESHMAN FINANCIAL AID (Fall 2019, est.) 746 applied for aid; of those 92% were deemed to have need. 99% of freshmen with need received aid; of those 1% had need fully met. ***Average percent of need met:*** 48% (excluding resources awarded to replace EFC). ***Average financial aid package:*** $11,210 (excluding resources awarded to replace EFC). 13% of all full-time freshmen had no need and received non-need-based gift aid.

UNDERGRADUATE FINANCIAL AID (Fall 2019, est.) 2,114 applied for aid; of those 90% were deemed to have need. 99% of undergraduates with need received aid; of those 1% had need fully met. ***Average percent of need met:*** 47% (excluding resources awarded to replace EFC). ***Average financial aid package:*** $10,794 (excluding resources awarded to replace EFC). 10% of all full-time undergraduates had no need and received non-need-based gift aid.

GIFT AID (NEED-BASED) ***Total amount:*** $14,224,902 (50% federal, 50% state). ***Receiving aid:*** Freshmen: 78% (607); all full-time undergraduates: 71% (1,619). ***Average award:*** Freshmen: $7840; Undergraduates: $7582. ***Scholarships, grants, and awards:*** Federal Pell, FSEOG, state, private, college/university gift aid from institutional funds.

GIFT AID (NON-NEED-BASED) ***Total amount:*** $2,286,089 (4% state, 59% institutional, 37% external sources). ***Receiving aid:*** Freshmen: 34% (266). Undergraduates: 24% (547). ***Average award:*** Freshmen: $3151. Undergraduates: $3150. ***Scholarships, grants, and awards by category:*** *Academic interests/achievement:* general academic interests/achievements. *Special achievements/activities:* leadership, memberships. *Special characteristics:* children and siblings of alumni, children of faculty/staff, members of minority groups, out-of-state students, siblings of current students. ***ROTC:*** Army cooperative, Air Force cooperative.

LOANS ***Student loans:*** $15,295,940 (41% need-based, 59% non-need-based). 82% of past graduating class borrowed through all loan programs. *Average indebtedness per student:* $26,041. ***Average need-based loan:*** Freshmen: $3226. Undergraduates: $3823. ***Parent loans:*** $8,405,737 (100% non-need-based). ***Programs:*** Federal Direct (Subsidized and Unsubsidized Stafford, PLUS), Federal Nursing.

WORK-STUDY ***Federal work-study:*** Total amount: $247,828; jobs available.

APPLYING FOR FINANCIAL AID ***Required financial aid forms:*** FAFSA, state aid form. ***Financial aid deadline (priority):*** 3/1. ***Notification date:*** Continuous beginning 12/1. Students must reply by 5/1.

CONTACT Financial Aid Office, State University of New York College of Agriculture & Technology at Morrisville, 80 Eaton Street, PO Box 901, Morrisville, NY 13408, 315-684-6000 or toll-free 800-258-0111.
Website: http://www.morrisville.edu/.

STATE UNIVERSITY OF NEW YORK COLLEGE OF ENVIRONMENTAL SCIENCE AND FORESTRY

Syracuse, NY

Tuition & fees (NY res): $9115	Average undergraduate aid package: $10,094

ABOUT THE INSTITUTION State-supported, coed. ***Awards:*** certificates, associate, bachelor's, master's, and doctoral degrees. 29 undergraduate majors. ***Total enrollment:*** 2,256. Undergraduates: 1,861. Freshmen: 383. Federal methodology is used as a basis for awarding need-based institutional aid.

UNDERGRADUATE EXPENSES for 2019–2020 ***Application fee:*** $50. ***Tuition, state resident:*** full-time $7070; part-time $295 per credit hour. ***Tuition, nonresident:*** full-time $16,980; part-time $708 per credit hour. ***Required fees:*** full-time $2045; $104.52 per credit hour. Full-time tuition and fees vary according to location. Part-time tuition and fees vary according to course load and location. ***College room and board:*** $16,270; ***Room only:*** $8850. Room and board charges vary according to board plan, housing facility, and location.

FRESHMAN FINANCIAL AID (Fall 2018) 368 applied for aid; of those 75% were deemed to have need. 99% of freshmen with need received aid; of those 22% had need fully met. ***Average percent of need met:*** 59% (excluding resources awarded to replace EFC). ***Average financial aid package:*** $10,604 (excluding resources awarded to replace EFC). 15% of all full-time freshmen had no need and received non-need-based gift aid.

UNDERGRADUATE FINANCIAL AID (Fall 2018) 1,464 applied for aid; of those 72% were deemed to have need. 98% of undergraduates with need received aid; of those 34% had need fully met. ***Average percent of need met:*** 63% (excluding resources awarded to replace EFC). ***Average financial aid package:*** $10,094 (excluding resources awarded to replace EFC). 15% of all full-time undergraduates had no need and received non-need-based gift aid.

GIFT AID (NEED-BASED) ***Total amount:*** $8,153,706 (31% federal, 23% state, 43% institutional, 3% external sources). ***Receiving aid:*** Freshmen: 70% (269); all full-time undergraduates: 55% (980). ***Average award:*** Freshmen: $7633; Undergraduates: $6955. ***Scholarships, grants, and awards:*** Federal Pell, FSEOG, state, private, college/university gift aid from institutional funds, United Negro College Fund.

GIFT AID (NON-NEED-BASED) ***Total amount:*** $1,829,224 (31% state, 42% institutional, 27% external sources). ***Receiving aid:*** Freshmen: 29% (111). Undergraduates: 36% (646). ***Average award:*** Freshmen: $3743. Undergraduates: $4064. ***Scholarships, grants, and awards by category:*** *Academic interests/achievement:* 646 awards ($1,706,099 total): agriculture, architecture, biological sciences, engineering/technologies, general academic interests/achievements, physical sciences, premedicine. *Special achievements/activities:* community service, general special achievements/activities, leadership, memberships. *Special characteristics:* 12 awards ($5500 total): children and siblings of alumni, general special characteristics, international students, local/state students, members of minority groups, out-of-state students. ***ROTC:*** Army cooperative, Air Force cooperative.

LOANS ***Student loans:*** $6,992,973 (43% need-based, 57% non-need-based). 64% of past graduating class borrowed through all loan programs. *Average indebtedness per student:* $21,885. ***Average need-based loan:*** Freshmen: $3162. Undergraduates: $3973. ***Parent loans:*** $2,306,028 (35% need-based, 65% non-need-based). ***Programs:*** Federal Direct (Subsidized and Unsubsidized Stafford, PLUS).

WORK-STUDY ***Federal work-study:*** Total amount: $330,000; 240 jobs averaging $1758. ***State or other work-study/employment:*** Total amount: $347,035 (55% need-based, 45% non-need-based). 232 part-time jobs averaging $940.

APPLYING FOR FINANCIAL AID ***Required financial aid forms:*** FAFSA, state aid form. ***Financial aid deadline (priority):*** 2/1. ***Notification date:*** Continuous beginning 2/1. Students must reply by 5/1 or within 2 weeks of notification.

CONTACT Mr. Mark J. Hill, Director of Financial Aid, State University of New York College of Environmental Science and Forestry, One Forestry Drive, Syracuse, NY 13210-2779, 315-470-6673. *Fax:* 315-470-4734. *E-mail:* mjhill@esf.edu.
Website: http://www.esf.edu/.

STATE UNIVERSITY OF NEW YORK COLLEGE OF TECHNOLOGY AT CANTON

Canton, NY

Tuition & fees (NY res): $8660	Average undergraduate aid package: $11,039

ABOUT THE INSTITUTION State-supported, coed. ***Awards:*** certificates, associate, and bachelor's degrees. 40 undergraduate majors. ***Total enrollment:*** 3,228. Undergraduates: 3,228. Freshmen: 707. Federal methodology is used as a basis for awarding need-based institutional aid.

UNDERGRADUATE EXPENSES for 2019–2020 ***Application fee:*** $50. ***One-time required fee:*** $120. ***Tuition, state resident:*** full-time $7070; part-time $295 per credit hour. ***Tuition, nonresident:*** full-time $16,980; part-time $708 per credit hour. ***Required fees:*** full-time $1590; $5 per term. Full-time tuition and fees vary according to degree level. Part-time tuition and fees vary according to degree level. ***College room and board:*** $13,200; ***Room only:*** $7950. Room and board charges vary according to board plan and housing facility.

FRESHMAN FINANCIAL AID (Fall 2018) 695 applied for aid; of those 90% were deemed to have need. 99% of freshmen with need received aid; of those 17% had need fully met. ***Average percent of need met:*** 17% (excluding resources awarded to replace EFC). ***Average financial aid package:*** $11,436 (excluding resources awarded to replace EFC). 2% of all full-time freshmen had no need and received non-need-based gift aid.

UNDERGRADUATE FINANCIAL AID (Fall 2018) 2,585 applied for aid; of those 91% were deemed to have need. 99% of undergraduates with need received aid; of those 17% had need fully met. ***Average percent of need met:*** 17% (excluding resources awarded to replace EFC). ***Average financial aid package:*** $11,039 (excluding resources awarded to replace EFC). 2% of all full-time undergraduates had no need and received non-need-based gift aid.

GIFT AID (NEED-BASED) ***Receiving aid:*** Freshmen: 75% (544); all full-time undergraduates: 71% (1,937). ***Average award:*** Freshmen: $9251; Undergraduates: $8537. ***Scholarships, grants, and awards:*** Federal Pell, FSEOG, state, college/university gift aid from institutional funds, Bureau of Indian Affairs Grants.

GIFT AID (NON-NEED-BASED) ***Receiving aid:*** Freshmen: 1% (6). Undergraduates: 1% (17). ***Average award:*** Freshmen: $2969. Undergraduates: $2545. ***Tuition waivers:*** Full or partial for employees or children of employees. ***ROTC:*** Army cooperative, Air Force cooperative.

LOANS ***Student loans:*** 91% of past graduating class borrowed through all loan programs. *Average indebtedness per student:* $31,214. ***Average need-based loan:*** Freshmen: $3035. Undergraduates: $3830. ***Programs:*** Federal Direct (Subsidized and Unsubsidized Stafford, PLUS).

WORK-STUDY ***Federal work-study:*** 103 jobs averaging $1757. ***State or other work-study/employment:*** Part-time jobs available.

APPLYING FOR FINANCIAL AID ***Required financial aid forms:*** FAFSA, state aid form. ***Notification date:*** Continuous. Students must reply within 4 weeks of notification.

CONTACT Ms. Kerrie Cooper, Director of Financial Aid, State University of New York College of Technology at Canton, Student Service Center, Canton, NY 13617, 315-386-7616 or toll-free 800-388-7123. *Fax:* 315-386-7930. *E-mail:* cooper@canton.edu.
Website: http://www.canton.edu/.

STATE UNIVERSITY OF NEW YORK COLLEGE OF TECHNOLOGY AT DELHI

Delhi, NY

Tuition & fees (NY res): $8920	Average undergraduate aid package: $11,213

ABOUT THE INSTITUTION State-supported, coed. ***Awards:*** certificates, associate, bachelor's, and master's degrees. 46 undergraduate majors. ***Total enrollment:*** 3,086. Undergraduates: 2,999. Freshmen: 783. Federal methodology is used as a basis for awarding need-based institutional aid.

UNDERGRADUATE EXPENSES for 2020–2021 ***Application fee:*** $50. ***Tuition, state resident:*** full-time $7270; part-time $295 per credit hour. ***Tuition, nonresident:*** full-time $10,840; part-time $452 per credit hour. ***Required fees:*** full-time $1650; $88 per credit hour. Full-time tuition and fees vary according to course load, degree level, location, and program. Part-time tuition and fees vary according to course load, degree level, location, and program. ***College room and board:*** $12,900; ***Room only:*** $7500. Room and board charges vary according to board plan, housing facility, and location.

FRESHMAN FINANCIAL AID (Fall 2018) 755 applied for aid; of those 87% were deemed to have need. 99% of freshmen with need received aid; of those 6% had need fully met. ***Average percent of need met:*** 62% (excluding resources awarded to replace EFC). ***Average financial aid package:*** $11,269 (excluding resources awarded to replace EFC). 1% of all full-time freshmen had no need and received non-need-based gift aid.

UNDERGRADUATE FINANCIAL AID (Fall 2018) 2,272 applied for aid; of those 88% were deemed to have need. 100% of undergraduates with need received aid; of those 7% had need fully met. ***Average percent of need met:*** 61% (excluding resources awarded to replace EFC). ***Average financial aid package:*** $11,213 (excluding resources awarded to replace EFC). 1% of all full-time undergraduates had no need and received non-need-based gift aid.

GIFT AID (NEED-BASED) ***Total amount:*** $15,849,410 (45% federal, 38% state, 15% institutional, 2% external sources). ***Receiving aid:*** Freshmen: 77% (601); all full-time undergraduates: 72% (1,789). ***Average award:*** Freshmen: $8903; Undergraduates: $8329. ***Scholarships, grants, and awards:*** Federal Pell, FSEOG, state, private, college/university gift aid from institutional funds.

GIFT AID (NON-NEED-BASED) ***Total amount:*** $573,949 (14% state, 17% institutional, 69% external sources). ***Receiving aid:*** Freshmen: 2% (13). Undergraduates: 1% (33). ***Average award:*** Freshmen: $1313. Undergraduates: $2174. ***Scholarships, grants, and awards by category:*** *Academic interests/achievement:* general academic interests/achievements. *Special achievements/activities:* community service. ***Tuition waivers:*** Full or partial for employees or children of employees.

LOANS ***Student loans:*** $16,720,076 (76% need-based, 24% non-need-based). 91% of past graduating class borrowed through all loan programs. *Average indebtedness per student:* $27,915. ***Average need-based loan:*** Freshmen: $3124. Undergraduates: $3705. ***Parent loans:*** $9,250,422 (42% need-based, 58% non-need-based). ***Programs:*** Federal Direct (Subsidized and Unsubsidized Stafford, PLUS), Private Loans.

WORK-STUDY ***Federal work-study:*** Total amount: $120,787; jobs available. ***State or other work-study/employment:*** Total amount: $308,012 (100% need-based). Part-time jobs available.

APPLYING FOR FINANCIAL AID ***Required financial aid forms:*** FAFSA, state aid form. ***Financial aid deadline (priority):*** 2/1. ***Notification date:*** Continuous beginning 3/1.

CONTACT Elizabeth Berry, Director of Financial Aid, State University of New York College of Technology at Delhi, 158 Bush Hall, Delhi, NY 13753, 607-746-4573 or toll-free 800-96-DELHI. *Fax:* 607-746-4104.
Website: http://www.delhi.edu/.

STATE UNIVERSITY OF NEW YORK DOWNSTATE MEDICAL CENTER

Brooklyn, NY

Tuition & fees: N/R	Average undergraduate aid package: N/A

ABOUT THE INSTITUTION State-supported, coed. ***Awards:*** certificates, bachelor's, master's, and doctoral degrees. 5 undergraduate majors. Federal methodology is used as a basis for awarding need-based institutional aid.

UNDERGRADUATE FINANCIAL AID (Fall 2018) 242 applied for aid; of those 100% were deemed to have need. 100% of undergraduates with need received aid.

GIFT AID (NEED-BASED) ***Receiving aid:*** All full-time undergraduates: 35% (118). ***Average award:*** Undergraduates: $2519. ***Scholarships, grants, and awards:*** Federal Pell, FSEOG.

LOANS ***Programs:*** Federal Direct (Subsidized and Unsubsidized Stafford, PLUS), Federal Nursing.

WORK-STUDY ***Federal work-study:*** 32 jobs averaging $1456.

CONTACT Financial Aid Office, State University of New York Downstate Medical Center, 450 Clarkson Avenue, Brooklyn, NY 11203-2098, 718-270-2488. *Fax:* 718-270-7592. *E-mail:* finaid1@downstate.edu.
Website: http://www.downstate.edu/.

STATE UNIVERSITY OF NEW YORK EMPIRE STATE COLLEGE

Saratoga Springs, NY

Tuition & fees (area res): $7605 **Average undergraduate aid package: N/A**

ABOUT THE INSTITUTION State-supported, coed. ***Awards:*** certificates, associate, bachelor's, and master's degrees (branch locations at 7 regional centers with 35 auxiliary units). 14 undergraduate majors. ***Total enrollment:*** 10,440. Undergraduates: 9,095. Freshmen: 179. Federal methodology is used as a basis for awarding need-based institutional aid.

UNDERGRADUATE EXPENSES for 2020–2021 ***Tuition, area resident:*** full-time $7070. ***Tuition, state resident:*** full-time $7070. ***Tuition, nonresident:*** full-time $16,980. ***Required fees:*** full-time $535. Full-time tuition and fees vary according to program. Part-time tuition and fees vary according to program.

CONTACT SUNY Empire State College Financial Aid, State University of New York Empire State College, 111 West Ave, Saratoga Springs, NY 12866, 518-587-2100 or toll-free 800-847-3000. *Fax:* 518-580-4863. *E-mail:* financialaid@esc.edu.
Website: http://www.esc.edu/.

STATE UNIVERSITY OF NEW YORK MARITIME COLLEGE

Throggs Neck, NY

ABOUT THE INSTITUTION State-supported, coed. ***Awards:*** certificates, associate, bachelor's, and master's degrees. 10 undergraduate majors. ***Total enrollment:*** 1,734. Undergraduates: 1,586. Freshmen: 351.

GIFT AID (NEED-BASED) ***Scholarships, grants, and awards:*** Federal Pell, FSEOG, state, private, college/university gift aid from institutional funds, Educational Opportunity Program (EOP).

GIFT AID (NON-NEED-BASED) ***Scholarships, grants, and awards by category:*** *Academic interests/achievement:* general academic interests/achievements. *Special achievements/activities:* leadership.

LOANS ***Programs:*** Federal Direct (Subsidized and Unsubsidized Stafford, PLUS), Perkins, alternative loans.

WORK-STUDY ***Federal work-study:*** Total amount: $60,830; jobs available. ***State or other work-study/employment:*** Total amount: $503,601 (100% non-need-based). Part-time jobs available.

APPLYING FOR FINANCIAL AID ***Required financial aid form:*** FAFSA.

CONTACT Ms. Andrea Damar, Director of Financial Aid, State University of New York Maritime College, 6 Pennyfield Avenue, Throgs Neck, NY 10465-4198, 718-409-7227. *Fax:* 718-409-7275. *E-mail:* adamar@sunymaritime.edu.
Website: http://www.sunymaritime.edu/.

STATE UNIVERSITY OF NEW YORK POLYTECHNIC INSTITUTE

Utica, NY

CONTACT Financial Aid Office, State University of New York Polytechnic Institute, 100 Seymour Road, Utica, NY 13502, 315-792-7210 or toll-free 866-278-6948. *Fax:* 315-792-7220. *E-mail:* finaid@sunyit.edu.
Website: http://www.sunypoly.edu/.

STATE UNIVERSITY OF NEW YORK UPSTATE MEDICAL UNIVERSITY

Syracuse, NY

CONTACT Michael Pede, Office of Financial Aid, State University of New York Upstate Medical University, Weiskotten Hall, Room 1213, 766 Irving Avenue, Syracuse, NY 13210-2375, 315-464-4329 or toll-free 800-736-2171. *E-mail:* finaid@upstate.edu.
Website: http://www.upstate.edu/.

STEPHEN F. AUSTIN STATE UNIVERSITY

Nacogdoches, TX

Tuition & fees (TX res): $7620 **Average undergraduate aid package: $12,060**

ABOUT THE INSTITUTION State-supported, coed. ***Awards:*** bachelor's, master's, and doctoral degrees. 68 undergraduate majors. Federal methodology is used as a basis for awarding need-based institutional aid.

UNDERGRADUATE EXPENSES for 2019–2020 ***Tuition, state resident:*** full-time $7620; part-time $254 per credit hour. ***Tuition, nonresident:*** full-time $20,280; part-time $676 per credit hour. ***Required fees:*** $192.50 per credit hour. Full-time tuition and fees vary according to course load, degree level, and location. Part-time tuition and fees vary according to course load, degree level, and location. ***College room and board:*** $9012. Room and board charges vary according to board plan and housing facility. ***Payment plan:*** Guaranteed tuition.

FRESHMAN FINANCIAL AID (Fall 2018) 1836 applied for aid; of those 75% were deemed to have need. 100% of freshmen with need received aid; of those 14% had need fully met. ***Average percent of need met:*** 60% (excluding resources awarded to replace EFC). ***Average financial aid package:*** $12,711 (excluding resources awarded to replace EFC). 10% of all full-time freshmen had no need and received non-need-based gift aid.

UNDERGRADUATE FINANCIAL AID (Fall 2018) 8,012 applied for aid; of those 81% were deemed to have need. 100% of undergraduates with need received aid; of those 13% had need fully met. ***Average percent of need met:*** 58% (excluding resources awarded to replace EFC). ***Average financial aid package:*** $12,060 (excluding resources awarded to replace EFC). 9% of all full-time undergraduates had no need and received non-need-based gift aid.

GIFT AID (NEED-BASED) ***Receiving aid:*** Freshmen: 51% (1,051); all full-time undergraduates: 51% (5,098). ***Average award:*** Freshmen: $9188; Undergraduates: $7502. ***Scholarships, grants, and awards:*** Federal Pell, FSEOG, state, private, college/university gift aid from institutional funds.

GIFT AID (NON-NEED-BASED) ***Receiving aid:*** Freshmen: 37% (775). Undergraduates: 25% (2,511). ***Average award:*** Freshmen: $3335. Undergraduates: $2743. ***Scholarships, grants, and awards by category:*** *Academic interests/achievement:* agriculture, biological sciences, business, communication, computer science, education, general academic interests/achievements, health fields, home economics, mathematics, military science, physical sciences, premedicine. *Creative arts/performance:* journalism/publications, music, theater/drama. *Special achievements/activities:* cheerleading/drum major, general special achievements/activities, hobbies/interests, leadership, rodeo. *Special characteristics:* adult students, children and siblings of alumni, children of faculty/staff, children of union members/company employees, first-generation college students, general special characteristics, local/state students, previous college experience, veterans. ***Tuition waivers:*** Full or partial for employees or children of employees, senior citizens. ***ROTC:*** Army.

LOANS ***Student loans:*** 67% of past graduating class borrowed through all loan programs. *Average indebtedness per student:* $26,477. ***Average need-based loan:*** Freshmen: $3636. Undergraduates: $4608. ***Programs:*** Federal Direct (Subsidized and Unsubsidized Stafford, PLUS), state, college/university, TEACH Grants.

WORK-STUDY Federal work-study jobs available. ***State or other work-study/employment:*** Part-time jobs available.

APPLYING FOR FINANCIAL AID ***Required financial aid form:*** FAFSA. ***Financial aid deadline:*** Continuous. ***Notification date:*** Continuous.

CONTACT H. Rachele Garrett, Office of Financial Aid, Stephen F. Austin State University, PO Box 13052, Nacogdoches, TX 75962, 936-468-2403 or toll-free 800-731-2902. *Fax:* 936-468-1048. *E-mail:* finaid@sfasu.edu.
Website: http://www.sfasu.edu/.

STEPHENS COLLEGE
Columbia, MO

Tuition & fees: N/R | **Average undergraduate aid package: $22,396**

ABOUT THE INSTITUTION Independent, undergraduate: women only; graduate: coed. ***Awards:*** certificates, associate, bachelor's, and master's degrees. 23 undergraduate majors. ***Total enrollment:*** 756. Undergraduates: 706. Freshmen: 191. Federal methodology is used as a basis for awarding need-based institutional aid.
FRESHMAN FINANCIAL AID (Fall 2019, est.) 110 applied for aid; of those 90% were deemed to have need. 100% of freshmen with need received aid; of those 43% had need fully met. ***Average percent of need met:*** 52% (excluding resources awarded to replace EFC). ***Average financial aid package:*** $20,166 (excluding resources awarded to replace EFC). 28% of all full-time freshmen had no need and received non-need-based gift aid.
UNDERGRADUATE FINANCIAL AID (Fall 2019, est.) 226 applied for aid; of those 97% were deemed to have need. 100% of undergraduates with need received aid; of those 22% had need fully met. ***Average percent of need met:*** 50% (excluding resources awarded to replace EFC). ***Average financial aid package:*** $22,396 (excluding resources awarded to replace EFC). 22% of all full-time undergraduates had no need and received non-need-based gift aid.
GIFT AID (NEED-BASED) *Receiving aid:* Freshmen: 78% (99); all full-time undergraduates: 49% (219). ***Average award:*** Freshmen: $6894; Undergraduates: $2577. ***Scholarships, grants, and awards:*** Federal Pell, FSEOG, state, private, college/university gift aid from institutional funds, Academic Competitiveness Grants, National SMART Grants.
GIFT AID (NON-NEED-BASED) *Receiving aid:* Freshmen: 78% (99). Undergraduates: 42% (189). ***Average award:*** Freshmen: $18,667. Undergraduates: $18,121. ***Scholarships, grants, and awards by category:*** *Academic interests/achievement:* 407 awards ($6,100,950 total): general academic interests/achievements. *Creative arts/performance:* 15 awards ($29,000 total): dance, music, performing arts, theater/drama. *Special achievements/activities:* 36 awards ($116,500 total): leadership, memberships. *Special characteristics:* 10 awards ($145,861 total): children of faculty/staff, children of union members/company employees, parents of current students, siblings of current students, veterans, veterans' children. ***ROTC:*** Army cooperative, Naval cooperative, Air Force cooperative.
LOANS *Average need-based loan:* Freshmen: $2356. Undergraduates: $3938. ***Programs:*** Federal Direct (Subsidized and Unsubsidized Stafford, PLUS), alternative loans.
WORK-STUDY *Federal work-study:* 58 jobs averaging $1451. ***State or other work-study/employment:*** 77 part-time jobs averaging $1523.
APPLYING FOR FINANCIAL AID *Required financial aid form:* FAFSA. ***Notification date:*** Continuous.
CONTACT Mrs. Alex Miller, Director of Financial Aid, Stephens College, 1200 East Broadway, Columbia, MO 65215-0002, 800-876-7106 or toll-free 800-876-7207. *Fax:* 573-876-2320. *E-mail:* finaid@stephens.edu.
Website: http://www.stephens.edu/.

STERLING COLLEGE
Sterling, KS

Tuition & fees: $27,300 | **Average undergraduate aid package: $23,594**

ABOUT THE INSTITUTION Independent Presbyterian, coed. ***Awards:*** bachelor's degrees. 39 undergraduate majors. ***Total enrollment:*** 653. Undergraduates: 643. Freshmen: 139. Federal methodology is used as a basis for awarding need-based institutional aid.
UNDERGRADUATE EXPENSES for 2020–2021 *Tuition:* full-time $26,000; part-time $484 per credit hour. ***Required fees:*** full-time $1300. Full-time tuition and fees vary according to course load and degree level. Part-time tuition and fees vary according to course load and degree level. ***College room only:*** $3516. Room and board charges vary according to board plan and housing facility.
FRESHMAN FINANCIAL AID (Fall 2018) 109 applied for aid; of those 95% were deemed to have need. 100% of freshmen with need received aid; of those 21% had need fully met. ***Average percent of need met:*** 72% (excluding resources awarded to replace EFC). ***Average financial aid package:*** $21,677 (excluding resources awarded to replace EFC). 4% of all full-time freshmen had no need and received non-need-based gift aid.
UNDERGRADUATE FINANCIAL AID (Fall 2018) 528 applied for aid; of those 90% were deemed to have need. 100% of undergraduates with need received aid; of those 24% had need fully met. ***Average percent of need met:*** 79% (excluding resources awarded to replace EFC). ***Average financial aid package:*** $23,594 (excluding resources awarded to replace EFC). 11% of all full-time undergraduates had no need and received non-need-based gift aid.
GIFT AID (NEED-BASED) *Total amount:* $4,983,127 (29% federal, 9% state, 62% institutional). ***Receiving aid:*** Freshmen: 65% (101); all full-time undergraduates: 84% (457). ***Average award:*** Freshmen: $10,873; Undergraduates: $10,901. ***Scholarships, grants, and awards:*** Federal Pell, FSEOG, state, private, college/university gift aid from institutional funds.
GIFT AID (NON-NEED-BASED) *Total amount:* $652,931 (67% institutional, 33% external sources). ***Average award:*** Freshmen: $7234. Undergraduates: $8971. ***Scholarships, grants, and awards by category:*** *Academic interests/achievement:* general academic interests/achievements. *Creative arts/performance:* art/fine arts, cinema/film/broadcasting, creative writing, debating, general creative arts/performance, journalism/publications, music, performing arts, theater/drama. *Special achievements/activities:* cheerleading/drum major, religious involvement. *Special characteristics:* children and siblings of alumni, children of faculty/staff, public servants, siblings of current students, twins, veterans' children. ***Tuition waivers:*** Full or partial for employees or children of employees, senior citizens.
LOANS *Student loans:* $3,709,345 (69% need-based, 31% non-need-based). 78% of past graduating class borrowed through all loan programs. *Average indebtedness per student:* $24,843. ***Average need-based loan:*** Freshmen: $5383. Undergraduates: $6133. ***Parent loans:*** $1,421,527 (100% non-need-based). ***Programs:*** Federal Direct (Subsidized and Unsubsidized Stafford, PLUS), Perkins.
WORK-STUDY *Federal work-study:* Total amount: $61,840; jobs available.
ATHLETIC AWARDS Total amount: $3,312,388 (85% need-based, 15% non-need-based).
APPLYING FOR FINANCIAL AID *Required financial aid form:* FAFSA. ***Financial aid deadline (priority):*** 1/1. ***Notification date:*** Continuous beginning 10/1. Students must reply within 2 weeks of notification.
CONTACT Ms. Mitzi Suhler, Director of Financial Aid, Sterling College, 125 West Cooper, Sterling, KS 67579, 620-278-4226 or toll-free 800-346-1017. *Fax:* 620-869-9033. *E-mail:* msuhler@sterling.edu.
Website: http://www.sterling.edu/.

STERLING COLLEGE
Craftsbury Common, VT

CONTACT Barbara Stuart, Director of Financial Aid, Sterling College, PO Box 72, Craftsbury Common, VT 05827, 800-648-3591 Ext. 3 or toll-free 800-648-3591 Ext.100. *Fax:* 802-586-2596. *E-mail:* bstuart@sterlingcollege.edu.
Website: http://www.sterlingcollege.edu/.

STETSON UNIVERSITY
DeLand, FL

Tuition & fees: $49,500 | **Average undergraduate aid package: $40,976**

ABOUT THE INSTITUTION Independent, coed. ***Awards:*** certificates, bachelor's, master's, and doctoral degrees. 57 undergraduate majors. ***Total enrollment:*** 4,429. Undergraduates: 3,183. Freshmen: 934. Federal methodology is used as a basis for awarding need-based institutional aid.
UNDERGRADUATE EXPENSES for 2020–2021 *Application fee:* $50. ***Comprehensive fee:*** $64,040 includes full-time tuition ($49,140), mandatory fees ($360),

and room and board ($14,540). ***College room only:*** $8640. Room and board charges vary according to board plan. ***Part-time tuition:*** $1238 per credit hour.

FRESHMAN FINANCIAL AID (Fall 2019, est.) 828 applied for aid; of those 88% were deemed to have need. 100% of freshmen with need received aid; of those 27% had need fully met. ***Average percent of need met:*** 82% (excluding resources awarded to replace EFC). ***Average financial aid package:*** $43,440 (excluding resources awarded to replace EFC). 17% of all full-time freshmen had no need and received non-need-based gift aid.

UNDERGRADUATE FINANCIAL AID (Fall 2019, est.) 2,291 applied for aid; of those 90% were deemed to have need. 100% of undergraduates with need received aid; of those 23% had need fully met. ***Average percent of need met:*** 78% (excluding resources awarded to replace EFC). ***Average financial aid package:*** $40,976 (excluding resources awarded to replace EFC). 27% of all full-time undergraduates had no need and received non-need-based gift aid.

GIFT AID (NEED-BASED) ***Total amount:*** $66,644,825 (9% federal, 12% state, 79% institutional). ***Receiving aid:*** Freshmen: 78% (729); all full-time undergraduates: 66% (2,043). ***Average award:*** Freshmen: $35,451; Undergraduates: $33,564. ***Scholarships, grants, and awards:*** Federal Pell, FSEOG, state, private, college/university gift aid from institutional funds.

GIFT AID (NON-NEED-BASED) ***Total amount:*** $34,797,895 (12% state, 83% institutional, 5% external sources). ***Receiving aid:*** Freshmen: 20% (184). Undergraduates: 13% (417). ***Average award:*** Freshmen: $29,477. Undergraduates: $26,807. ***Scholarships, grants, and awards by category:*** *Academic interests/achievement:* area/ethnic studies, biological sciences, business, communication, computer science, education, English, foreign languages, general academic interests/achievements, humanities, mathematics, military science, physical sciences, premedicine, religion/biblical studies, social sciences. *Creative arts/performance:* applied art and design, art/fine arts, music, theater/drama. *Special achievements/activities:* cheerleading/drum major, community service, general special achievements/activities, junior miss, leadership, religious involvement. *Special characteristics:* children and siblings of alumni, children of faculty/staff, ethnic background, first-generation college students, general special characteristics, international students, local/state students, members of minority groups, out-of-state students, veterans. ***Tuition waivers:*** Full or partial for employees or children of employees. ***ROTC:*** Army cooperative, Air Force cooperative.

LOANS ***Student loans:*** $15,945,262 (70% need-based, 30% non-need-based). 65% of past graduating class borrowed through all loan programs. *Average indebtedness per student:* $32,601. ***Average need-based loan:*** Freshmen: $3435. Undergraduates: $4322. ***Parent loans:*** $9,079,858 (63% need-based, 37% non-need-based). ***Programs:*** Federal Direct (Subsidized and Unsubsidized Stafford, PLUS).

WORK-STUDY ***Federal work-study:*** Total amount: $2,027,141; 930 jobs averaging $2184. ***State or other work-study/employment:*** Total amount: $271,861 (38% need-based, 62% non-need-based). 69 part-time jobs averaging $3940.

ATHLETIC AWARDS Total amount: $6,647,174 (30% need-based, 70% non-need-based).

APPLYING FOR FINANCIAL AID ***Required financial aid form:*** FAFSA. ***Financial aid deadline (priority):*** 11/1. ***Notification date:*** Students must reply within 2 weeks of notification.

CONTACT Heidi Goldsworthy, Director of Financial Aid, Stetson University, 421 North Woodland Boulevard, DeLand, FL 32723, 386-822-7120 or toll-free 800-688-0101. *Fax:* 386-822-7126. *E-mail:* finaid@stetson.edu.
Website: http://www.stetson.edu/.

STEVENS-HENAGER COLLEGE

Boise, ID

CONTACT Ms. Jaime L. Davis, Training and Project Development, Stevens-Henager College, 1444 South Entertainment Avenue, Boise, ID 83709, 208-383-4540 Ext. 1875 or toll-free 800-622-2640. *Fax:* 208-345-6999. *E-mail:* jaime.davis@stevenshenager.edu.
Website: http://www.stevenshenager.edu/.

STEVENS-HENAGER COLLEGE

Idaho Falls, ID

CONTACT Financial Aid Office, Stevens-Henager College, 901 Pier View Drive, Suite 105, Idaho Falls, ID 83402, 208-522-0887 or toll-free 800-622-2640.
Website: http://www.stevenshenager.edu/.

STEVENS-HENAGER COLLEGE

Logan, UT

CONTACT Financial Aid Office, Stevens-Henager College, 755 South Main Street, Logan, UT 84321, 435-752-0903 or toll-free 800-622-2640.
Website: http://www.stevenshenager.edu/.

STEVENS-HENAGER COLLEGE

Orem, UT

CONTACT Financial Aid Office, Stevens-Henager College, 1476 South Sandhill Road, Orem, UT 84058, 801-373-0285 or toll-free 800-622-2640.
Website: http://www.stevenshenager.edu/.

STEVENS-HENAGER COLLEGE

St. George, UT

CONTACT Financial Aid Office, Stevens-Henager College, 720 South River Road, Suite C-130, St. George, UT 84790, 435-628-9150 or toll-free 800-622-2640.
Website: http://www.stevenshenager.edu/.

STEVENS-HENAGER COLLEGE

Salt Lake City, UT

CONTACT Financial Aid Office, Stevens-Henager College, 383 West Vine Street, Salt Lake City, UT 84123, 801-531-1180 or toll-free 800-622-2640.
Website: http://www.stevenshenager.edu/.

STEVENS-HENAGER COLLEGE

West Haven, UT

CONTACT Financial Aid Office, Stevens-Henager College, 1890 South 1350 West, West Haven, UT 84401, 801-392-1471 or toll-free 800-622-2640.
Website: http://www.stevenshenager.edu/.

STEVENS INSTITUTE OF TECHNOLOGY

Hoboken, NJ

Tuition & fees: $55,952	Average undergraduate aid package: $31,960

ABOUT THE INSTITUTION Independent, coed. ***Awards:*** certificates, bachelor's, master's, and doctoral degrees. 31 undergraduate majors. ***Total enrollment:*** 7,283. Undergraduates: 3,659. Freshmen: 969. Both federal and institutional methodology are used as a basis for awarding need-based institutional aid.

UNDERGRADUATE EXPENSES for 2020–2021 ***Application fee:*** $70. ***Comprehensive fee:*** $72,196 includes full-time tuition ($53,828), mandatory fees ($2124), and room and board ($16,244). Full-time tuition and fees vary according to course load. Room and board charges vary according to board plan and housing facility.

Part-time tuition: $1799 per credit. ***Part-time fees:*** $1062 per term. Part-time tuition and fees vary according to course load.

FRESHMAN FINANCIAL AID (Fall 2018) 891 applied for aid; of those 80% were deemed to have need. 100% of freshmen with need received aid; of those 17% had need fully met. ***Average percent of need met:*** 73% (excluding resources awarded to replace EFC). ***Average financial aid package:*** $35,647 (excluding resources awarded to replace EFC). 28% of all full-time freshmen had no need and received non-need-based gift aid.

UNDERGRADUATE FINANCIAL AID (Fall 2018) 2,638 applied for aid; of those 83% were deemed to have need. 100% of undergraduates with need received aid; of those 18% had need fully met. ***Average percent of need met:*** 69% (excluding resources awarded to replace EFC). ***Average financial aid package:*** $31,960 (excluding resources awarded to replace EFC). 30% of all full-time undergraduates had no need and received non-need-based gift aid.

GIFT AID (NEED-BASED) ***Total amount:*** $20,106,749 (17% federal, 18% state, 65% institutional). ***Receiving aid:*** Freshmen: 53% (530); all full-time undergraduates: 44% (1,519). ***Average award:*** Freshmen: $16,113; Undergraduates: $13,218. ***Scholarships, grants, and awards:*** Federal Pell, FSEOG, state, private, college/university gift aid from institutional funds, United Negro College Fund.

GIFT AID (NON-NEED-BASED) ***Total amount:*** $60,339,078 (98% institutional, 2% external sources). ***Receiving aid:*** Freshmen: 70% (706). Undergraduates: 63% (2,139). ***Average award:*** Freshmen: $19,638. Undergraduates: $18,289. ***Scholarships, grants, and awards by category:*** *Academic interests/achievement:* general academic interests/achievements. ***Tuition waivers:*** Full or partial for employees or children of employees. ***ROTC:*** Army cooperative, Air Force cooperative.

LOANS ***Student loans:*** $12,476,498 (55% need-based, 45% non-need-based). 70% of past graduating class borrowed through all loan programs. *Average indebtedness per student:* $37,900. ***Average need-based loan:*** Freshmen: $3408. Undergraduates: $4164. ***Parent loans:*** $9,638,564 (100% non-need-based). ***Programs:*** Federal Direct (Subsidized and Unsubsidized Stafford, PLUS), state.

WORK-STUDY ***Federal work-study:*** Total amount: $607,549; 465 jobs averaging $1307.

APPLYING FOR FINANCIAL AID ***Required financial aid forms:*** FAFSA, CSS Financial Aid PROFILE. ***Financial aid deadline (priority):*** 2/15. ***Notification date:*** Continuous.

CONTACT Ms. Susan Gross, Director of Financial Aid/Assistant Vice President for Financial Aid and Undergraduate Admissions, Stevens Institute of Technology, Castle Point on Hudson, Hoboken, NJ 07030, 201-216-8142 or toll-free 800-458-5323. *Fax:* 201-216-8050. *E-mail:* susan.gross@stevens.edu.
Website: http://www.stevens.edu/.

STEVENSON UNIVERSITY

Stevenson, MD

Tuition & fees: $37,142	Average undergraduate aid package: $26,376

ABOUT THE INSTITUTION Independent, coed. ***Awards:*** certificates, bachelor's, and master's degrees. 35 undergraduate majors. ***Total enrollment:*** 3,579. Undergraduates: 3,107. Freshmen: 694. Federal methodology is used as a basis for awarding need-based institutional aid.

UNDERGRADUATE EXPENSES for 2019–2020 ***Application fee:*** $40. ***Comprehensive fee:*** $50,766 includes full-time tuition ($34,528), mandatory fees ($2614), and room and board ($13,624). ***College room only:*** $8656. Full-time tuition and fees vary according to course load and degree level. Room and board charges vary according to board plan and housing facility. ***Part-time tuition:*** $870 per credit. ***Part-time fees:*** $75 per term. Part-time tuition and fees vary according to degree level.

FRESHMAN FINANCIAL AID (Fall 2019, est.) 656 applied for aid; of those 87% were deemed to have need. 100% of freshmen with need received aid; of those 21% had need fully met. ***Average percent of need met:*** 73% (excluding resources awarded to replace EFC). ***Average financial aid package:*** $27,894 (excluding resources awarded to replace EFC). 17% of all full-time freshmen had no need and received non-need-based gift aid.

UNDERGRADUATE FINANCIAL AID (Fall 2019, est.) 2,346 applied for aid; of those 89% were deemed to have need. 100% of undergraduates with need received aid; of those 18% had need fully met. ***Average percent of need met:*** 71% (excluding resources awarded to replace EFC). ***Average financial aid package:*** $26,376 (excluding resources awarded to replace EFC). 21% of all full-time undergraduates had no need and received non-need-based gift aid.

GIFT AID (NEED-BASED) ***Total amount:*** $45,406,264 (9% federal, 9% state, 80% institutional, 2% external sources). ***Receiving aid:*** Freshmen: 82% (569); all full-time undergraduates: 74% (2,004). ***Average award:*** Freshmen: $25,318; Undergraduates: $23,624. ***Scholarships, grants, and awards:*** Federal Pell, FSEOG, state, private, college/university gift aid from institutional funds, Federal Nursing.

GIFT AID (NON-NEED-BASED) ***Total amount:*** $14,607,528 (1% state, 94% institutional, 5% external sources). ***Receiving aid:*** Freshmen: 14% (99). Undergraduates: 12% (323). ***Average award:*** Freshmen: $20,787. Undergraduates: $18,981. ***Scholarships, grants, and awards by category:*** *Academic interests/achievement:* 2,498 awards ($46,435,051 total): general academic interests/achievements. *Creative arts/performance:* 35 awards ($114,500 total): applied art and design, theater/drama. ***Tuition waivers:*** Full or partial for employees or children of employees. ***ROTC:*** Army cooperative, Air Force cooperative.

LOANS ***Student loans:*** $18,593,613 (66% need-based, 34% non-need-based). 76% of past graduating class borrowed through all loan programs. *Average indebtedness per student:* $37,112. ***Average need-based loan:*** Freshmen: $3242. Undergraduates: $4287. ***Parent loans:*** $14,809,462 (49% need-based, 51% non-need-based). ***Programs:*** Federal Direct (Subsidized and Unsubsidized Stafford, PLUS).

WORK-STUDY ***Federal work-study:*** Total amount: $546,626; 243 jobs averaging $2258.

APPLYING FOR FINANCIAL AID ***Required financial aid form:*** FAFSA. ***Financial aid deadline (priority):*** 2/15. ***Notification date:*** Continuous beginning 2/1. Students must reply by 5/1 or within 2 weeks of notification.

CONTACT Ms. Melanie Mason, Director, Financial Aid, Stevenson University, 100 Campus Circle, Owings Mills, MD 21117, 443-352-4371 or toll-free 877-468-6852 (in-state), 877-468-3852 (out-of-state). *Fax:* 443-352-4370. *E-mail:* mmason5@stevenson.edu.
Website: http://www.stevenson.edu/.

STEVENS–THE INSTITUTE OF BUSINESS & ARTS

St. Louis, MO

Tuition & fees: $12,750	Average undergraduate aid package: $6274

ABOUT THE INSTITUTION Proprietary, coed. ***Awards:*** associate and bachelor's degrees. 5 undergraduate majors. Institutional methodology is used as a basis for awarding need-based institutional aid.

UNDERGRADUATE EXPENSES for 2019–2020 ***Tuition:*** full-time $12,150; part-time $270 per credit hour. ***Required fees:*** full-time $600; $200 per term. Full-time tuition and fees vary according to course load and program. Part-time tuition and fees vary according to course load and program. ***Payment plan:*** Guaranteed tuition.

FRESHMAN FINANCIAL AID (Fall 2018) 6 applied for aid; of those 100% were deemed to have need. 100% of freshmen with need received aid. ***Average financial aid package:*** $6139 (excluding resources awarded to replace EFC).

UNDERGRADUATE FINANCIAL AID (Fall 2018) 136 applied for aid; of those 100% were deemed to have need. 100% of undergraduates with need received aid; of those 9% had need fully met. ***Average financial aid package:*** $6274 (excluding resources awarded to replace EFC).

GIFT AID (NEED-BASED) ***Total amount:*** $481,104 (98% federal, 2% institutional). ***Receiving aid:*** Freshmen: 86% (6); all full-time undergraduates: 74% (122). ***Average award:*** Freshmen: $4655; Undergraduates: $4190. ***Scholarships, grants, and awards:*** Federal Pell, private.

GIFT AID (NON-NEED-BASED) ***Total amount:*** $97,584 (100% external sources). ***Receiving aid:*** Undergraduates: 7% (12). ***Scholarships, grants, and awards by category:*** *Special characteristics:* veterans. ***Tuition waivers:*** Full or partial for employees or children of employees.

LOANS ***Student loans:*** $930,391 (48% need-based, 52% non-need-based). ***Parent loans:*** $31,600 (100% non-need-based). ***Programs:*** Federal Direct (Subsidized and Unsubsidized Stafford, PLUS).

APPLYING FOR FINANCIAL AID ***Required financial aid forms:*** FAFSA, institution's own form. ***Financial aid deadline:*** Continuous. ***Notification date:*** Continuous.

CONTACT Financial Aid Office, Stevens–The Institute of Business & Arts, 1521 Washington Avenue, St. Louis, MO 63102, 314-421-0949 or toll-free 800-871-0949. *Website:* http://www.siba.edu/.

STILLMAN COLLEGE

Tuscaloosa, AL

CONTACT Christy G. Jackson, Financial Aid Counselor , Stillman College, PO Box 1430, Tuscaloosa, AL 35403, 205-366-8950 or toll-free 800-841-5722. *Fax:* 205-247-8107. *E-mail:* cjackson@stillman.edu.
Website: http://www.stillman.edu/.

STOCKTON UNIVERSITY

Galloway, NJ

Tuition & fees (NJ res): $14,048 **Average undergraduate aid package: $17,758**

ABOUT THE INSTITUTION State-supported, coed. ***Awards:*** certificates, bachelor's, master's, and doctoral degrees. 36 undergraduate majors. ***Total enrollment:*** 9,934. Undergraduates: 8,893. Freshmen: 1,537. Federal methodology is used as a basis for awarding need-based institutional aid.

UNDERGRADUATE EXPENSES for 2019–2020 ***Application fee:*** $50. ***Tuition, state resident:*** full-time $12,005; part-time $462 per credit. ***Tuition, nonresident:*** full-time $19,293; part-time $742 per credit. ***Required fees:*** full-time $2043; $135 per term. Part-time tuition and fees vary according to course load. ***College room and board:*** $12,496; ***Room only:*** $8396. Room and board charges vary according to board plan and housing facility.

FRESHMAN FINANCIAL AID (Fall 2019, est.) 1458 applied for aid; of those 79% were deemed to have need. 99% of freshmen with need received aid; of those 46% had need fully met. ***Average percent of need met:*** 78% (excluding resources awarded to replace EFC). ***Average financial aid package:*** $18,594 (excluding resources awarded to replace EFC). 7% of all full-time freshmen had no need and received non-need-based gift aid.

UNDERGRADUATE FINANCIAL AID (Fall 2019, est.) 7,329 applied for aid; of those 83% were deemed to have need. 98% of undergraduates with need received aid; of those 43% had need fully met. ***Average percent of need met:*** 77% (excluding resources awarded to replace EFC). ***Average financial aid package:*** $17,758 (excluding resources awarded to replace EFC). 6% of all full-time undergraduates had no need and received non-need-based gift aid.

GIFT AID (NEED-BASED) ***Receiving aid:*** Freshmen: 67% (1,028); all full-time undergraduates: 50% (4,227). ***Average award:*** Freshmen: $9482; Undergraduates: $9301. ***Scholarships, grants, and awards:*** Federal Pell, FSEOG, state, private, college/university gift aid from institutional funds.

GIFT AID (NON-NEED-BASED) ***Receiving aid:*** Freshmen: 20% (305). Undergraduates: 20% (1,686). ***Average award:*** Freshmen: $6517. Undergraduates: $8103. ***Scholarships, grants, and awards by category:*** *Academic interests/achievement:* area/ethnic studies, biological sciences, business, communication, computer science, education, general academic interests/achievements, health fields, home economics, humanities, mathematics, physical sciences, social sciences. *Creative arts/performance:* applied art and design, art/fine arts, creative writing, dance, journalism/publications, music, performing arts, theater/drama. *Special achievements/activities:* community service, general special achievements/activities, leadership. *Special characteristics:* adult students, children of faculty/staff, children of union members/company employees, children with a deceased or disabled parent, ethnic background, first-generation college students, general special characteristics, international students, local/state students, members of minority groups, previous college experience. ***Tuition waivers:*** Full or partial for employees or children of employees, senior citizens.

LOANS ***Student loans:*** 76% of past graduating class borrowed through all loan programs. *Average indebtedness per student:* $31,470. ***Average need-based loan:*** Freshmen: $3387. Undergraduates: $4387. ***Programs:*** Federal Direct (Subsidized and Unsubsidized Stafford, PLUS), state.

WORK-STUDY ***Federal work-study:*** 251 jobs averaging $2323. ***State or other work-study/employment:*** 1,007 part-time jobs averaging $1871.

APPLYING FOR FINANCIAL AID ***Required financial aid forms:*** FAFSA, state aid form. ***Notification date:*** Continuous. Students must reply within 2 weeks of notification.

CONTACT Ms. Heidi S. Kovalick, Director of Financial Aid, Stockton University, 101 Vera King Farris Drive, Galloway, NJ 08205-9441, 609-652-4203. *Fax:* 609-626-5517. *E-mail:* Heidi.kovalick@stockton.edu.
Website: http://www.stockton.edu/.

STONEHILL COLLEGE

Easton, MA

Tuition & fees: $44,420 **Average undergraduate aid package: $31,521**

ABOUT THE INSTITUTION Independent Roman Catholic, coed. ***Awards:*** bachelor's and master's degrees. 47 undergraduate majors. ***Total enrollment:*** 2,556. Undergraduates: 2,535. Freshmen: 650. Institutional methodology is used as a basis for awarding need-based institutional aid.

UNDERGRADUATE EXPENSES for 2019–2020 ***Application fee:*** $60. ***Comprehensive fee:*** $61,040 includes full-time tuition ($44,420) and room and board ($16,620). ***College room only:*** $10,379. ***Part-time tuition:*** $1481 per credit hour. Part-time tuition and fees vary according to course load. ***Payment plan:*** Tuition prepayment.

FRESHMAN FINANCIAL AID (Fall 2019, est.) 535 applied for aid; of those 76% were deemed to have need. 100% of freshmen with need received aid; of those 48% had need fully met. ***Average percent of need met:*** 90% (excluding resources awarded to replace EFC). ***Average financial aid package:*** $32,799 (excluding resources awarded to replace EFC). 37% of all full-time freshmen had no need and received non-need-based gift aid.

UNDERGRADUATE FINANCIAL AID (Fall 2019, est.) 1,894 applied for aid; of those 82% were deemed to have need. 100% of undergraduates with need received aid; of those 52% had need fully met. ***Average percent of need met:*** 90% (excluding resources awarded to replace EFC). ***Average financial aid package:*** $31,521 (excluding resources awarded to replace EFC). 35% of all full-time undergraduates had no need and received non-need-based gift aid.

GIFT AID (NEED-BASED) ***Total amount:*** $35,069,565 (6% federal, 2% state, 90% institutional, 2% external sources). ***Receiving aid:*** Freshmen: 61% (399); all full-time undergraduates: 61% (1,525). ***Average award:*** Freshmen: $28,288; Undergraduates: $26,331. ***Scholarships, grants, and awards:*** Federal Pell, FSEOG, state, private, college/university gift aid from institutional funds.

GIFT AID (NON-NEED-BASED) ***Total amount:*** $23,510,071 (1% federal, 98% institutional, 1% external sources). ***Receiving aid:*** Freshmen: 20% (133). Undergraduates: 22% (537). ***Average award:*** Freshmen: $21,379. Undergraduates: $20,340. ***Scholarships, grants, and awards by category:*** *Academic interests/achievement:* general academic interests/achievements. *Special characteristics:* children of faculty/staff, children of union members/company employees, relatives of clergy, siblings of current students, veterans. ***Tuition waivers:*** Full or partial for employees or children of employees. ***ROTC:*** Army.

LOANS ***Student loans:*** $18,297,160 (36% need-based, 64% non-need-based). 71% of past graduating class borrowed through all loan programs. *Average indebtedness per student:* $38,359. ***Average need-based loan:*** Freshmen: $3476. Undergraduates: $4365. ***Parent loans:*** $8,557,844 (18% need-based, 82% non-need-based). ***Programs:*** Federal Direct (Subsidized and Unsubsidized Stafford, PLUS), Perkins, state.

WORK-STUDY ***Federal work-study:*** Total amount: $791,016; jobs available. ***State or other work-study/employment:*** Total amount: $450,240 (6% need-based, 94% non-need-based). Part-time jobs available.

ATHLETIC AWARDS Total amount: $2,971,818 (21% need-based, 79% non-need-based).

APPLYING FOR FINANCIAL AID ***Required financial aid forms:*** FAFSA, CSS Financial Aid PROFILE, noncustodial (divorced/separated) parent's statement. ***Financial aid deadline:*** 2/1 (priority: 2/1). ***Notification date:*** 4/1.

CONTACT Rhonda Nickley, Office Manager, Stonehill College, 320 Washington Street, Easton, MA 02357, 508-565-1088. *Fax:* 508-565-1426. *E-mail:* finaid@stonehill.edu.
Website: http://www.stonehill.edu/.

STONY BROOK UNIVERSITY, STATE UNIVERSITY OF NEW YORK

Stony Brook, NY

Tuition & fees (NY res): $10,175	Average undergraduate aid package: $14,005

ABOUT THE INSTITUTION State-supported, coed. ***Awards:*** certificates, bachelor's, master's, and doctoral degrees. 64 undergraduate majors. ***Total enrollment:*** 26,814. Undergraduates: 17,909. Freshmen: 3,372. Federal methodology is used as a basis for awarding need-based institutional aid.

UNDERGRADUATE EXPENSES for 2019–2020 ***Application fee:*** $50. ***Tuition, state resident:*** full-time $7070; part-time $295 per credit hour. ***Tuition, nonresident:*** full-time $24,740; part-time $1031 per credit hour. ***Required fees:*** full-time $3105; $154.20 per credit hour. Full-time tuition and fees vary according to course load and program. Part-time tuition and fees vary according to course load and program. ***College room and board:*** $14,278; ***Room only:*** $9082. Room and board charges vary according to board plan, housing facility, and location.

FRESHMAN FINANCIAL AID (Fall 2018) 2655 applied for aid; of those 74% were deemed to have need. 99% of freshmen with need received aid; of those 13% had need fully met. ***Average percent of need met:*** 65% (excluding resources awarded to replace EFC). ***Average financial aid package:*** $13,657 (excluding resources awarded to replace EFC). 18% of all full-time freshmen had no need and received non-need-based gift aid.

UNDERGRADUATE FINANCIAL AID (Fall 2018) 11,158 applied for aid; of those 83% were deemed to have need. 98% of undergraduates with need received aid; of those 16% had need fully met. ***Average percent of need met:*** 65% (excluding resources awarded to replace EFC). ***Average financial aid package:*** $14,005 (excluding resources awarded to replace EFC). 11% of all full-time undergraduates had no need and received non-need-based gift aid.

GIFT AID (NEED-BASED) ***Total amount:*** $77,659,341 (41% federal, 34% state, 23% institutional, 2% external sources). ***Receiving aid:*** Freshmen: 53% (1,786); all full-time undergraduates: 50% (8,098). ***Average award:*** Freshmen: $10,477; Undergraduates: $9443. ***Scholarships, grants, and awards:*** Federal Pell, FSEOG, state, private, college/university gift aid from institutional funds.

GIFT AID (NON-NEED-BASED) ***Total amount:*** $15,569,397 (2% federal, 16% state, 73% institutional, 9% external sources). ***Receiving aid:*** Freshmen: 6% (202). Undergraduates: 4% (690). ***Average award:*** Freshmen: $5485. Undergraduates: $5695. ***Scholarships, grants, and awards by category:*** *Academic interests/achievement:* area/ethnic studies, biological sciences, business, computer science, engineering/technologies, English, foreign languages, general academic interests/achievements, home economics, international studies, mathematics, physical sciences, social sciences. *Creative arts/performance:* cinema/film/broadcasting, journalism/publications, music. *Special achievements/activities:* community service, leadership. *Special characteristics:* ethnic background, general special characteristics. ***ROTC:*** Army, Naval cooperative, Air Force cooperative.

LOANS ***Student loans:*** $86,539,450 (72% need-based, 28% non-need-based). 49% of past graduating class borrowed through all loan programs. *Average indebtedness per student:* $25,678. ***Average need-based loan:*** Freshmen: $3414. Undergraduates: $4561. ***Parent loans:*** $9,320,930 (46% need-based, 54% non-need-based). ***Programs:*** Federal Direct (Subsidized and Unsubsidized Stafford, PLUS).

WORK-STUDY ***Federal work-study:*** Total amount: $1,426,569; 523 jobs averaging $2728. ***State or other work-study/employment:*** Total amount: $11,260,078 (34% need-based, 66% non-need-based). 2,494 part-time jobs averaging $4515.

ATHLETIC AWARDS Total amount: $7,085,612 (35% need-based, 65% non-need-based).

APPLYING FOR FINANCIAL AID ***Required financial aid forms:*** FAFSA, state aid form. ***Financial aid deadline (priority):*** 3/1. ***Notification date:*** Continuous beginning 4/1. Students must reply by 5/1.

CONTACT Financial Aid Office, Stony Brook University, State University of New York, Nicolls Road, Stony Brook, NY 11794, 631-632-6000.
Website: http://www.stonybrook.edu/.

STRATFORD UNIVERSITY

Baltimore, MD

CONTACT Lesley Otterbein, Student Accounts Manager, Stratford University, 17 Commerce Street, Baltimore, MD 21202, 410-752-0490 or toll-free 800-624-9926 (in-state), 800-624-9926 Ext.120 (out-of-state). *Fax:* 410-752-3730. *E-mail:* studentaccounts@stratford.edu.
Website: http://www.stratford.edu/.

STRATFORD UNIVERSITY

Alexandria, VA

CONTACT Financial Aid Office, Stratford University, 2900 Eisenhower Avenue, Alexandria, VA 22314, 571-699-3200 or toll-free 800-444-0804.
Website: http://www.stratford.edu/.

STRATFORD UNIVERSITY

Falls Church, VA

CONTACT Imane Babsiri, Student Account Manager, Stratford University, 7777 Leesburg Pike, Falls Church, VA 22043, 703-821-8570 Ext. 3401 or toll-free 800-444-0804. *E-mail:* ibabsiri@stratford.edu.
Website: http://www.stratford.edu/.

STRATFORD UNIVERSITY

Glen Allen, VA

CONTACT Noshuo Rivers, Student Account Manager, Stratford University, 11104 West Broad Street, Glen Allen, VA 23060, 804-290-4231 or toll-free 877-373-5173. *E-mail:* studentaccounts@stratford.edu.
Website: http://www.stratford.edu/.

STRATFORD UNIVERSITY

Newport News, VA

CONTACT Sheryl Kimberly, Student Accounts Manager, Stratford University, 836 J. Clyde Morris Boulevard, Newport News, VA 23601, 757-873-4235 or toll-free 855-873-4235. *E-mail:* skimberly@stratford.edu.
Website: http://www.stratford.edu/.

STRATFORD UNIVERSITY

Virginia Beach, VA

CONTACT Financial Aid Office, Stratford University, 555 South Independence Boulevard, Virginia Beach, VA 23452, 757-497-4466 or toll-free 866-528-8363.
Website: http://www.stratford.edu/.

STRATFORD UNIVERSITY

Woodbridge, VA

CONTACT Sherrese Whiting, Student Account Manager, Stratford University, 14349 Gideon Drive, Woodbridge, VA 22192, 703-897-1982 or toll-free 888-546-1250. *E-mail:* studentaccounts@stratford.edu.
Website: http://www.stratford.edu/.

STRAYER UNIVERSITY - ALEXANDRIA

Alexandria, VA

CONTACT Financial Aid Office, Strayer University - Alexandria, 2730 Eisenhower Avenue, Alexandria, VA 22314, 703-329-9100 or toll-free 888-311-0355.
Website: http://www.strayer.edu/virginia/alexandria/.

STRAYER UNIVERSITY - ALLENTOWN

Allentown, PA

CONTACT Financial Aid Office, Strayer University - Allentown, 520 Hamilton Street, Suite 100, Allentown, PA 18101-1502, 484-809-7770 or toll-free 888-311-0355.
Website: http://www.strayer.edu/pennsylvania/allentown/.

STRAYER UNIVERSITY - ANNE ARUNDEL

Millersville, MD

CONTACT Financial Aid Office, Strayer University - Anne Arundel, 1520 Jabez Run, Suite 100, Millersville, MD 21108, 410-923-4500 or toll-free 888-311-0355.
Website: http://www.strayer.edu/maryland/anne-arundel/.

STRAYER UNIVERSITY - ARLINGTON

Arlington, VA

CONTACT Financial Aid Office, Strayer University - Arlington, 2121 15th Street North, Arlington, VA 22201, 703-892-5100 or toll-free 888-311-0355.
Website: http://www.strayer.edu/virginia/arlington/.

STRAYER UNIVERSITY - AUGUSTA

Augusta, GA

CONTACT Financial Aid Office, Strayer University - Augusta, 1330 Augusta West Parkway, Augusta, GA 30909, 706-855-8233 or toll-free 888-311-0355.
Website: http://www.strayer.edu/georgia/augusta/.

STRAYER UNIVERSITY - BAYMEADOWS

Jacksonville, FL

CONTACT Financial Aid Office, Strayer University - Baymeadows, 8375 Dix Ellis Trail, Suite 200, Jacksonville, FL 32256, 904-538-1000 or toll-free 888-311-0355.
Website: http://www.strayer.edu/florida/baymeadows/.

STRAYER UNIVERSITY - BIRMINGHAM

Birmingham, AL

CONTACT Financial Aid Office, Strayer University - Birmingham, 3570 Grandview Parkway, Suite 200, Birmingham, AL 35243, 205-453-6300 or toll-free 888-311-0355.
Website: http://www.strayer.edu/alabama/birmingham/.

STRAYER UNIVERSITY - CENTER CITY

Philadelphia, PA

CONTACT Financial Aid Office, Strayer University - Center City, 1601 Cherry Street, Suite 100, Philadelphia, PA 19102, 267-256-0200 or toll-free 888-311-0355.
Website: http://www.strayer.edu/pennsylvania/center-city/.

STRAYER UNIVERSITY–CHAMBLEE CAMPUS

Atlanta, GA

CONTACT Financial Aid Office, Strayer University–Chamblee Campus, 3355 Northeast Expressway, Suite 100, Atlanta, GA 30341, 770-454-9270 or toll-free 888-311-0355.
Website: http://www.strayer.edu/georgia/chamblee/.

STRAYER UNIVERSITY–CHARLESTON CAMPUS

North Charleston, SC

CONTACT Financial Aid Office, Strayer University–Charleston Campus, 5010 Wetland Crossing, North Charleston, SC 29418, 843-746-5100 or toll-free 888-311-0355.
Website: http://www.strayer.edu/south-carolina/charleston/.

STRAYER UNIVERSITY–CHERRY HILL CAMPUS

Cherry Hill, NJ

CONTACT Financial Aid Office, Strayer University–Cherry Hill Campus, 2370 State Route 70 West, Suite 335, Cherry Hill, NJ 08002, 856-482-4200 or toll-free 888-311-0355.
Website: http://www.strayer.edu/new-jersey/cherry-hill/.

STRAYER UNIVERSITY–CHESAPEAKE CAMPUS

Chesapeake, VA

CONTACT Financial Aid Office, Strayer University–Chesapeake Campus, 676 Independence Parkway, Suite 300, Chesapeake, VA 23320, 757-382-9900 or toll-free 888-311-0355.
Website: http://www.strayer.edu/virginia/chesapeake/.

STRAYER UNIVERSITY–CHESTERFIELD CAMPUS

Midlothian, VA

CONTACT Financial Aid Office, Strayer University–Chesterfield Campus, 15521 Midlothian Turnpike, Suite 401, Midlothian, VA 23113, 804-794-2033 or toll-free 888-311-0355.
Website: http://www.strayer.edu/virginia/chesterfield/.

STRAYER UNIVERSITY–COBB COUNTY CAMPUS

Atlanta, GA

CONTACT Financial Aid Office, Strayer University–Cobb County Campus, 3101 Towercreek Parkway, SE, Suite 700, Atlanta, GA 30339, 770-612-2170 or toll-free 888-311-0355.
Website: http://www.strayer.edu/georgia/cobb-county/.

STRAYER UNIVERSITY–COLUMBIA CAMPUS

Columbia, SC

CONTACT Financial Aid Office, Strayer University–Columbia Campus, 200 Center Point Circle, Suite 300, Columbia, SC 29210, 803-750-2500 or toll-free 888-311-0355.
Website: http://www.strayer.edu/south-carolina/columbia/.

STRAYER UNIVERSITY–DELAWARE COUNTY CAMPUS

Springfield, PA

CONTACT Financial Aid Office, Strayer University–Delaware County Campus, 760 West Sproul Road, Suite 200, Springfield, PA 19064, 610-604-7700 or toll-free 888-311-0355.
Website: http://www.strayer.edu/pennsylvania/delaware-county/.

STRAYER UNIVERSITY–DOUGLASVILLE CAMPUS

Douglasville, GA

CONTACT Financial Aid Office, Strayer University–Douglasville Campus, 4655 Timber Ridge Drive, Douglasville, GA 30135, 678-715-2200 or toll-free 888-311-0355.
Website: http://www.strayer.edu/georgia/douglasville/.

STRAYER UNIVERSITY–FORT LAUDERDALE CAMPUS

Fort Lauderdale, FL

CONTACT Financial Aid Office, Strayer University–Fort Lauderdale Campus, 2307 West Broward Boulevard, Suite 100, Fort Lauderdale, FL 33312, 954-745-6960 or toll-free 888-311-0355.
Website: http://www.strayer.edu/florida/fort-lauderdale/.

STRAYER UNIVERSITY–FREDERICKSBURG CAMPUS

Fredericksburg, VA

CONTACT Financial Aid Office, Strayer University–Fredericksburg Campus, 150 Riverside Parkway, Suite 100, Fredericksburg, VA 22406, 540-374-4300 or toll-free 888-311-0355.
Website: http://www.strayer.edu/virginia/fredericksburg/.

STRAYER UNIVERSITY–GREENSBORO CAMPUS

Greensboro, NC

CONTACT Financial Aid Office, Strayer University–Greensboro Campus, 4900 Koger Boulevard, Suite 400, Greensboro, NC 27407, 336-315-7800 or toll-free 888-311-0355.
Website: http://www.strayer.edu/north-carolina/greensboro/.

STRAYER UNIVERSITY–GREENVILLE CAMPUS

Greenville, SC

CONTACT Financial Aid Office, Strayer University–Greenville Campus, 777 Lowndes Hill Road, Building 3, Suite 300, Greenville, SC 29607, 864-250-7000 or toll-free 888-311-0355.
Website: http://www.strayer.edu/south-carolina/greenville/.

STRAYER UNIVERSITY–HENRICO CAMPUS

Glen Allen, VA

CONTACT Financial Aid Office, Strayer University–Henrico Campus, 11501 Nuckols Road, Glen Allen, VA 23059, 804-527-1000 or toll-free 888-311-0355.
Website: http://www.strayer.edu/virginia/henrico/.

STRAYER UNIVERSITY–HUNTERSVILLE CAMPUS

Huntersville, NC

CONTACT Financial Aid Office, Strayer University–Huntersville Campus, 13620 Reese Boulevard, Suite 130, Huntersville, NC 28078, 704-379-6800 or toll-free 888-311-0355.
Website: http://www.strayer.edu/north-carolina/huntersville/.

STRAYER UNIVERSITY–HUNTSVILLE CAMPUS

Huntsville, AL

CONTACT Financial Aid Office, Strayer University–Huntsville Campus, 4955 Corporate Drive, Huntsville, AL 35805, 256-665-9800 or toll-free 888-311-0355.
Website: http://www.strayer.edu/alabama/huntsville/.

STRAYER UNIVERSITY–JACKSON CAMPUS

Jackson, MS

CONTACT Financial Aid Office, Strayer University–Jackson Campus, 460 Briarwood Drive, Suite 200, Jackson, MS 39206, 601-718-5900 or toll-free 888-311-0355.
Website: http://www.strayer.edu/mississippi/jackson/.

STRAYER UNIVERSITY–KNOXVILLE CAMPUS

Knoxville, TN

CONTACT Financial Aid Office, Strayer University–Knoxville Campus, 10118 Parkside Drive, Suite 200, Knoxville, TN 37922, 865-288-6000 or toll-free 888-311-0355.
Website: http://www.strayer.edu/tennessee/knoxville/.

STRAYER UNIVERSITY–LITHONIA CAMPUS

Lithonia, GA

CONTACT Financial Aid Office, Strayer University–Lithonia Campus, 3120 Stonecrest Boulevard, Suite 200, Lithonia, GA 30038, 678-323-7700 or toll-free 888-311-0355.
Website: http://www.strayer.edu/georgia/lithonia/.

STRAYER UNIVERSITY–LITTLE ROCK CAMPUS

Little Rock, AR

CONTACT Financial Aid Office, Strayer University–Little Rock Campus, 10825 Financial Centre Parkway, Suite 400, Little Rock, AR 72211, 501-708-0600 or toll-free 888-311-0355.
Website: http://www.strayer.edu/arkansas/little-rock/.

STRAYER UNIVERSITY–LOUDOUN CAMPUS

Ashburn, VA

CONTACT Financial Aid Office, Strayer University–Loudoun Campus, 45150 Russell Branch Parkway, Suite 200, Ashburn, VA 20147, 703-729-8800 or toll-free 888-311-0355.
Website: http://www.strayer.edu/virginia/loudoun/.

STRAYER UNIVERSITY–LOWER BUCKS COUNTY CAMPUS

Trevose, PA

CONTACT Financial Aid Office, Strayer University–Lower Bucks County Campus, 3800 Horizon Boulevard, Suite 100, Trevose, PA 19053, 215-354-2700 or toll-free 888-311-0355.
Website: http://www.strayer.edu/pennsylvania/lower-bucks-county/.

STRAYER UNIVERSITY–MAITLAND CAMPUS

Maitland, FL

CONTACT Financial Aid Office, Strayer University–Maitland Campus, 901 North Lake Destiny Road, Suite 370, Maitland, FL 32751, 407-618-5900 or toll-free 888-311-0355.
Website: http://www.strayer.edu/florida/maitland/.

STRAYER UNIVERSITY–MANASSAS CAMPUS

Manassas, VA

CONTACT Financial Aid Office, Strayer University–Manassas Campus, 9990 Battleview Parkway, Manassas, VA 20109, 703-330-8400 or toll-free 888-311-0355.
Website: http://www.strayer.edu/virginia/manassas/.

STRAYER UNIVERSITY–MIRAMAR CAMPUS

Hollywood, FL

CONTACT Financial Aid Office, Strayer University–Miramar Campus, 15620 Southwest 29th Street, Hollywood, FL 33027, 954-378-2400 or toll-free 888-311-0355.
Website: http://www.strayer.edu/florida/miramar/.

STRAYER UNIVERSITY–MORROW CAMPUS

Morrow, GA

CONTACT Financial Aid Office, Strayer University–Morrow Campus, 3000 Corporate Center Drive, Suite 100, Morrow, GA 30260, 678-422-4100 or toll-free 888-311-0355.
Website: http://www.strayer.edu/georgia/morrow/.

STRAYER UNIVERSITY–NASHVILLE CAMPUS

Nashville, TN

CONTACT Financial Aid Office, Strayer University–Nashville Campus, 1809 Dabbs Avenue, Nashville, TN 37210, 615-871-2260 or toll-free 888-311-0355.
Website: http://www.strayer.edu/tennessee/nashville/.

STRAYER UNIVERSITY–NEWPORT NEWS CAMPUS

Newport News, VA

CONTACT Financial Aid Office, Strayer University–Newport News Campus, 99 Old Oyster Point Road, Newport News, VA 23602, 757-881-5100 or toll-free 888-311-0355.
Website: http://www.strayer.edu/virginia/newport-news/.

STRAYER UNIVERSITY–NORTH AUSTIN CAMPUS

Austin, TX

CONTACT Financial Aid Office, Strayer University–North Austin Campus, 8501 North Mopac Expressway, Suite 100, Austin, TX 78759, 512-568-3300 or toll-free 888-311-0355.
Website: http://www.strayer.edu/texas/north-austin/.

STRAYER UNIVERSITY–NORTH CHARLOTTE CAMPUS

Concord, NC

CONTACT Financial Aid Office, Strayer University–North Charlotte Campus, 7870 Commons Park Circle NW, Concord, NC 28027, 704-886-6500 or toll-free 888-311-0355.
Website: http://www.strayer.edu/north-carolina/north-charlotte/.

STRAYER UNIVERSITY–NORTH DALLAS CAMPUS

Farmers Branch, TX

CONTACT Financial Aid Office, Strayer University–North Dallas Campus, 2711 LBJ Freeway, Suite 450, Farmers Branch, TX 75234-7315, 972-773-8300.
Website: http://www.strayer.edu/texas/north-dallas.

STRAYER UNIVERSITY–NORTH RALEIGH CAMPUS

Raleigh, NC

CONTACT Financial Aid Office, Strayer University–North Raleigh Campus, 8701 Wadford Drive, Raleigh, NC 27616, 919-301-6500 or toll-free 888-311-0355.
Website: http://www.strayer.edu/north-carolina/north-raleigh/.

STRAYER UNIVERSITY–NORTHWEST HOUSTON CAMPUS

Houston, TX

CONTACT Financial Aid Office, Strayer University–Northwest Houston Campus, 10343 Sam Houston Park Drive, Suite 110, Houston, TX 77064, 281-949-1800 or toll-free 888-311-0355.
Website: http://www.strayer.edu/texas/northwest-houston/.

STRAYER UNIVERSITY–ORLANDO EAST CAMPUS

Orlando, FL

CONTACT Financial Aid Office, Strayer University–Orlando East Campus, 2200 North Alafaya Trail, Suite 500, Orlando, FL 32826, 407-926-2000 or toll-free 888-311-0355.
Website: http://www.strayer.edu/florida/orlando-east/.

STRAYER UNIVERSITY–OWINGS MILLS CAMPUS

Owings Mills, MD

CONTACT Financial Aid Office, Strayer University–Owings Mills Campus, 500 Redland Court, Suite 100, Owings Mills, MD 21117, 443-394-3339 or toll-free 888-311-0355.
Website: http://www.strayer.edu/maryland/owings-mills/.

STRAYER UNIVERSITY–PALM BEACH GARDENS CAMPUS

West Palm Beach, FL

CONTACT Financial Aid Office, Strayer University–Palm Beach Gardens Campus, 11025 RCA Center Drive, Suite 200, West Palm Beach, FL 33410, 561-904-3000 or toll-free 888-311-0355.
Website: http://www.strayer.edu/florida/palm-beach-gardens/.

STRAYER UNIVERSITY–PISCATAWAY CAMPUS

Piscataway, NJ

CONTACT Financial Aid Office, Strayer University–Piscataway Campus, 242 Old New Brunswick Road, Suite 220, Piscataway, NJ 08854, 732-743-3800 or toll-free 888-311-0355.
Website: http://www.strayer.edu/new-jersey/piscataway/.

STRAYER UNIVERSITY–PRINCE GEORGE'S CAMPUS

Suitland, MD

CONTACT Financial Aid Office, Strayer University–Prince George's Campus, 5110 Auth Way, Suitland, MD 20746, 301-505-3300 or toll-free 888-311-0355.
Website: http://www.strayer.edu/maryland/prince-georges/.

STRAYER UNIVERSITY–RESEARCH TRIANGLE PARK CAMPUS

Morrisville, NC

CONTACT Financial Aid Office, Strayer University–Research Triangle Park Campus, 4 Copley Parkway, Morrisville, NC 27560, 919-466-4400 or toll-free 888-311-0355.
Website: http://www.strayer.edu/north-carolina/morrisville.

STRAYER UNIVERSITY–ROCKVILLE CAMPUS

Rockville, MD

CONTACT Financial Aid Office, Strayer University–Rockville Campus, 1803 Research Boulevard, Suite 110, Rockville, MD 20850, 301-838-4700 or toll-free 888-311-0355.
Website: http://www.strayer.edu/maryland/rockville/.

STRAYER UNIVERSITY–SAN ANTONIO CAMPUS

San Antonio, TX

CONTACT Financial Aid Office, Strayer University–San Antonio Campus, 40 NE Loop 410, Suite 500, San Antonio, TX 78216, 210-202-3700.
Website: http://www.strayer.edu/texas/san-antonio.

STRAYER UNIVERSITY–SAND LAKE CAMPUS

Orlando, FL

CONTACT Financial Aid Office, Strayer University–Sand Lake Campus, 8529 South Park Circle, Orlando, FL 32819, 407-264-9400 or toll-free 888-311-0355.
Website: http://www.strayer.edu/florida/sand-lake/.

STRAYER UNIVERSITY–SAVANNAH CAMPUS

Savannah, GA

CONTACT Financial Aid Office, Strayer University–Savannah Campus, 8001 Chatham Center Drive, Suite 300, Savannah, GA 31405, 912-921-2900 or toll-free 888-311-0355.
Website: http://www.strayer.edu/georgia/savannah/.

STRAYER UNIVERSITY–SHELBY CAMPUS

Memphis, TN

CONTACT Financial Aid Office, Strayer University–Shelby Campus, 7275 Appling Farms Parkway, Memphis, TN 38133, 901-251-7100 or toll-free 888-311-0355.
Website: http://www.strayer.edu/tennessee/shelby/.

STRAYER UNIVERSITY–SOUTH CHARLOTTE CAMPUS

Charlotte, NC

CONTACT Financial Aid Office, Strayer University–South Charlotte Campus, 9101 Kings Parade Boulevard, Suite 200, Charlotte, NC 28273, 704-499-9200 or toll-free 888-311-0355.
Website: http://www.strayer.edu/north-carolina/south-charlotte/.

STRAYER UNIVERSITY–SOUTH RALEIGH CAMPUS

Raleigh, NC

CONTACT Financial Aid Office, Strayer University–South Raleigh Campus, 3421 Olympia Drive, Raleigh, NC 27603, 919-890-7500 or toll-free 888-311-0355.
Website: http://www.strayer.edu/north-carolina/south-raleigh/.

STRAYER UNIVERSITY–STAFFORD CAMPUS

Stafford, TX

CONTACT Financial Aid Office, Strayer University–Stafford Campus, 12603 Southwest Freeway, Suite 400, Stafford, TX 77477, 281-201-3800.
Website: http://www.strayer.edu/texas/stafford.

STRAYER UNIVERSITY–TAKOMA PARK CAMPUS

Washington, DC

CONTACT Financial Aid Office, Strayer University–Takoma Park Campus, 6830 Laurel Street, NW, Washington, DC 20012, 202-722-8100 or toll-free 888-311-0355.
Website: http://www.strayer.edu/district-columbia/takoma-park/.

STRAYER UNIVERSITY–TAMPA EAST CAMPUS

Tampa, FL

CONTACT Financial Aid Office, Strayer University–Tampa East Campus, 5650 Breckenridge Park Drive, Suite 300, Tampa, FL 33610, 813-663-0100 or toll-free 888-311-0355.
Website: http://www.strayer.edu/florida/tampa-east/.

STRAYER UNIVERSITY–TEAYS VALLEY CAMPUS

Scott Depot, WV

CONTACT Financial Aid Office, Strayer University–Teays Valley Campus, 135 Corporate Center Drive, Scott Depot, WV 25560, 304-760-1700 or toll-free 888-311-0355.
Website: http://www.strayer.edu/west-virginia/teays-valley/.

STRAYER UNIVERSITY–THOUSAND OAKS CAMPUS

Memphis, TN

CONTACT Financial Aid Office, Strayer University–Thousand Oaks Campus, 2620 Thousand Oaks Boulevard, Suite 1100, Memphis, TN 38118, 901-370-5200 or toll-free 888-311-0355.
Website: http://www.strayer.edu/tennessee/thousand-oaks/.

STRAYER UNIVERSITY–VIRGINIA BEACH CAMPUS

Virginia Beach, VA

CONTACT Financial Aid Office, Strayer University–Virginia Beach Campus, 249 Central Park Avenue, Suite 350, Virginia Beach, VA 23462, 757-493-6000 or toll-free 888-311-0355.
Website: http://www.strayer.edu/virginia/virginia-beach/.

STRAYER UNIVERSITY–WARRENDALE CAMPUS

Warrendale, PA

CONTACT Financial Aid Office, Strayer University–Warrendale Campus, 802 Warrendale Village Drive, Warrendale, PA 15086, 724-799-2900 or toll-free 888-311-0355.
Website: http://www.strayer.edu/pennsylvania/warrendale/.

STRAYER UNIVERSITY–WASHINGTON CAMPUS

Washington, DC

CONTACT Financial Aid Office, Strayer University–Washington Campus, 1133 15th Street, NW, Washington, DC 20025, 202-408-2400 or toll-free 888-311-0355.
Website: http://www.strayer.edu/district-columbia/washington/.

STRAYER UNIVERSITY–WHITE MARSH CAMPUS

Baltimore, MD

CONTACT Financial Aid Office, Strayer University–White Marsh Campus, 9920 Franklin Square Drive, Suite 200, Baltimore, MD 21236, 410-238-9000 or toll-free 888-311-0355.
Website: http://www.strayer.edu/maryland/white-marsh/.

STRAYER UNIVERSITY–WILLINGBORO CAMPUS

Willingboro, NJ

CONTACT Financial Aid Office, Strayer University–Willingboro Campus, 300 Willingboro Parkway, Willingboro Town Center, Suite 125, Willingboro, NJ 08046, 609-835-6000 or toll-free 888-311-0355.
Website: http://www.strayer.edu/new-jersey/willingboro/.

STRAYER UNIVERSITY–WOODBRIDGE CAMPUS

Woodbridge, VA

CONTACT Financial Aid Office, Strayer University–Woodbridge Campus, 13385 Minnieville Road, Woodbridge, VA 22192, 703-878-2800 or toll-free 888-311-0355.
Website: http://www.strayer.edu/virginia/woodbridge/.

STUDIO SCHOOL

Los Angeles, CA

CONTACT Financial Aid Office, Studio School, 1201 West 5th Street, Los Angeles, CA 90017.
Website: http://www.studioschool.org/.

SUFFOLK UNIVERSITY

Boston, MA

Tuition & fees: $41,908	Average undergraduate aid package: $28,833

ABOUT THE INSTITUTION Independent, coed. ***Awards:*** certificates, diplomas, associate, bachelor's, master's, and doctoral degrees (doctoral degree in law). 52 undergraduate majors. ***Total enrollment:*** 7,288. Undergraduates: 4,983. Freshmen: 1,118. Federal methodology is used as a basis for awarding need-based institutional aid.
UNDERGRADUATE EXPENSES for 2020–2021 ***Application fee:*** $50. ***One-time required fee:*** $260. ***Comprehensive fee:*** $60,042 includes full-time tuition ($41,242), mandatory fees ($666), and room and board ($18,134). ***College room only:*** $14,560. Full-time tuition and fees vary according to location and reciprocity agreements. Room and board charges vary according to board plan, housing facility, and location. ***Part-time tuition:*** $1213 per credit hour. ***Part-time fees:*** $70 per term. Part-time tuition and fees vary according to course load, location, and reciprocity agreements.
FRESHMAN FINANCIAL AID (Fall 2019, est.) 854 applied for aid; of those 91% were deemed to have need. 100% of freshmen with need received aid; of those 9% had need fully met. ***Average percent of need met:*** 71% (excluding resources awarded to replace EFC). ***Average financial aid package:*** $30,292 (excluding resources awarded to replace EFC). 22% of all full-time freshmen had no need and received non-need-based gift aid.
UNDERGRADUATE FINANCIAL AID (Fall 2019, est.) 3,161 applied for aid; of those 92% were deemed to have need. 99% of undergraduates with need received aid; of those 11% had need fully met. ***Average percent of need met:*** 68% (excluding resources awarded to replace EFC). ***Average financial aid package:*** $28,833 (excluding resources awarded to replace EFC). 30% of all full-time undergraduates had no need and received non-need-based gift aid.
GIFT AID (NEED-BASED) ***Total amount:*** $27,792,457 (23% federal, 6% state, 68% institutional, 3% external sources). ***Receiving aid:*** Freshmen: 64% (703); all full-time undergraduates: 54% (2,562). ***Average award:*** Freshmen: $13,164; Undergraduates: $10,563. ***Scholarships, grants, and awards:*** Federal Pell, FSEOG, state, private, college/university gift aid from institutional funds.
GIFT AID (NON-NEED-BASED) ***Total amount:*** $62,013,249 (100% institutional). ***Receiving aid:*** Freshmen: 65% (721). Undergraduates: 56% (2,691). ***Average award:*** Freshmen: $14,029. Undergraduates: $14,264. ***Scholarships, grants, and awards by category:*** *Academic interests/achievement:* 4,332 awards ($59,120,854 total): general academic interests/achievements. *Special characteristics:* 213 awards ($1,481,652 total): children and siblings of alumni, children of faculty/staff, siblings of current students, veterans. ***Tuition waivers:*** Full or partial for children of alumni, employees or children of employees, senior citizens. ***ROTC:*** Army cooperative.
LOANS ***Student loans:*** $30,244,749 (36% need-based, 64% non-need-based). 73% of past graduating class borrowed through all loan programs. *Average indebtedness per student:* $28,582. ***Average need-based loan:*** Freshmen: $3463. Undergraduates: $4519. ***Parent loans:*** $12,711,248 (100% need-based). ***Programs:*** Federal Direct (Subsidized and Unsubsidized Stafford, PLUS), college/university.
WORK-STUDY ***Federal work-study:*** Total amount: $1,752,500; 711 jobs averaging $2443. ***State or other work-study/employment:*** Total amount: $1,612,933 (100% non-need-based). 533 part-time jobs averaging $2566.
APPLYING FOR FINANCIAL AID ***Required financial aid form:*** FAFSA. ***Financial aid deadline:*** 6/30 (priority: 3/1). ***Notification date:*** Continuous beginning 2/1. Students must reply by 5/1 or within 2 weeks of notification.
CONTACT Ms. Jennifer Ricciardi, Director of Student Financial Services, Suffolk University, 8 Ashburton Place, Boston, MA 02108, 617-573-8470 or toll-free 800-6-SUFFOLK. *Fax:* 617-720-3579. *E-mail:* finaid@suffolk.edu.
Website: http://www.suffolk.edu/.

SULLIVAN UNIVERSITY

Louisville, KY

CONTACT Charlene Geiser, Financial Planning Office, Sullivan University, 3101 Bardstown Road, Louisville, KY 40205, 502-456-6504 Ext. 311 or toll-free 800-844-1354. *Fax:* 502-456-0040. *E-mail:* cgeiser@sullivan.edu.
Website: http://www.sullivan.edu/.

SUL ROSS STATE UNIVERSITY

Alpine, TX

Tuition & fees (TX res): $8981	Average undergraduate aid package: $10,792

ABOUT THE INSTITUTION State-supported, coed. ***Awards:*** bachelor's and master's degrees. 22 undergraduate majors.
UNDERGRADUATE EXPENSES for 2019–2020 ***Tuition, state resident:*** full-time $6812; part-time $213 per credit hour. ***Tuition, nonresident:*** full-time $18,046; part-time $635 per credit hour. ***Required fees:*** full-time $2169; $172 per term. Full-time tuition and fees vary according to location. Part-time tuition and fees vary according to location. Room and board charges vary according to board plan and housing facility.

FRESHMAN FINANCIAL AID (Fall 2018) 311 applied for aid; of those 93% were deemed to have need. 100% of freshmen with need received aid; of those 75% had need fully met. ***Average percent of need met:*** 86% (excluding resources awarded to replace EFC). ***Average financial aid package:*** $11,456 (excluding resources awarded to replace EFC). 5% of all full-time freshmen had no need and received non-need-based gift aid.

UNDERGRADUATE FINANCIAL AID (Fall 2018) 1,165 applied for aid; of those 96% were deemed to have need. 100% of undergraduates with need received aid; of those 70% had need fully met. ***Average percent of need met:*** 85% (excluding resources awarded to replace EFC). ***Average financial aid package:*** $10,792 (excluding resources awarded to replace EFC). 3% of all full-time undergraduates had no need and received non-need-based gift aid.

GIFT AID (NEED-BASED) ***Total amount:*** $8,062,741 (68% federal, 27% state, 5% institutional). ***Receiving aid:*** Freshmen: 73% (250); all full-time undergraduates: 71% (942). ***Average award:*** Freshmen: $8346; Undergraduates: $7055. ***Scholarships, grants, and awards:*** Federal Pell, FSEOG, state, private, college/university gift aid from institutional funds.

GIFT AID (NON-NEED-BASED) ***Total amount:*** $783,678 (47% institutional, 53% external sources). ***Receiving aid:*** Freshmen: 26% (89). Undergraduates: 18% (239). ***Average award:*** Freshmen: $2140. Undergraduates: $1730. ***Scholarships, grants, and awards by category:*** *Academic interests/achievement:* agriculture, biological sciences, business, education, English, foreign languages, general academic interests/achievements, health fields. *Creative arts/performance:* art/fine arts, cinema/film/broadcasting, journalism/publications, music, theater/drama. *Special achievements/activities:* leadership. *Special characteristics:* children and siblings of alumni, local/state students. ***Tuition waivers:*** Full or partial for employees or children of employees.

LOANS ***Student loans:*** $6,118,125 (96% need-based, 4% non-need-based). 59% of past graduating class borrowed through all loan programs. *Average indebtedness per student:* $13,073. ***Average need-based loan:*** Freshmen: $1841. Undergraduates: $2621. ***Parent loans:*** $510,138 (100% need-based). ***Programs:*** Federal Direct (Subsidized and Unsubsidized Stafford, PLUS), state.

WORK-STUDY ***Federal work-study:*** Total amount: $2,876,634; jobs available. ***State or other work-study/employment:*** Total amount: $543,413 (100% need-based). Part-time jobs available.

APPLYING FOR FINANCIAL AID ***Required financial aid forms:*** FAFSA, business/farm supplement. ***Financial aid deadline (priority):*** 1/15. ***Notification date:*** Continuous.

CONTACT Mickey Corbett, Director of Financial Aid, Sul Ross State University, Box C-2, Lawrence Hall, Alpine, TX 79832, 432-837-8055 or toll-free 888-722-7778. *Fax:* 432-837-8411. *E-mail:* fa@sulross.edu.
Website: http://www.sulross.edu/.

SUM BIBLE COLLEGE & THEOLOGICAL SEMINARY

Oakland, CA

CONTACT Financial Aid Office, SUM Bible College & Theological Seminary, 735 105th Avenue, Oakland, CA 94603, 510-567-6174 or toll-free 888-567-6174.
Website: http://www.sum.edu/.

SUNY BROCKPORT

Brockport, NY

Tuition & fees (area res): $8926	Average undergraduate aid package: $10,576

ABOUT THE INSTITUTION State-supported, coed. ***Awards:*** certificates, bachelor's, and master's degrees. 44 undergraduate majors. ***Total enrollment:*** 8,287. Undergraduates: 6,673. Freshmen: 1,076. Federal methodology is used as a basis for awarding need-based institutional aid.

UNDERGRADUATE EXPENSES for 2020–2021 ***Application fee:*** $50. ***Tuition, area resident:*** full-time $7270; part-time $303 per credit hour. ***Tuition, state resident:*** full-time $7270; part-time $303 per credit hour. ***Tuition, nonresident:*** full-time $17,180; part-time $716 per credit hour. ***Required fees:*** full-time $1656; $68 per credit hour. Part-time tuition and fees vary according to course load. ***College room and board:*** $14,160; ***Room only:*** $8834. Room and board charges vary according to board plan and housing facility.

FRESHMAN FINANCIAL AID (Fall 2018) 1222 applied for aid; of those 83% were deemed to have need. 98% of freshmen with need received aid; of those 14% had need fully met. ***Average percent of need met:*** 60% (excluding resources awarded to replace EFC). ***Average financial aid package:*** $10,889 (excluding resources awarded to replace EFC). 6% of all full-time freshmen had no need and received non-need-based gift aid.

UNDERGRADUATE FINANCIAL AID (Fall 2018) 5,653 applied for aid; of those 85% were deemed to have need. 98% of undergraduates with need received aid; of those 11% had need fully met. ***Average percent of need met:*** 61% (excluding resources awarded to replace EFC). ***Average financial aid package:*** $10,576 (excluding resources awarded to replace EFC). 4% of all full-time undergraduates had no need and received non-need-based gift aid.

GIFT AID (NEED-BASED) ***Total amount:*** $25,972,859 (54% federal, 45% state, 1% external sources). ***Receiving aid:*** Freshmen: 66% (837); all full-time undergraduates: 61% (3,840). ***Average award:*** Freshmen: $8026; Undergraduates: $7333. ***Scholarships, grants, and awards:*** Federal Pell, FSEOG, state, private, college/university gift aid from institutional funds.

GIFT AID (NON-NEED-BASED) ***Total amount:*** $9,701,993 (6% federal, 47% state, 33% institutional, 14% external sources). ***Receiving aid:*** Freshmen: 40% (508). Undergraduates: 24% (1,517). ***Average award:*** Freshmen: $3488. Undergraduates: $4676. ***Scholarships, grants, and awards by category:*** *Academic interests/achievement:* 817 awards ($1,497,880 total): biological sciences, business, communication, computer science, education, English, foreign languages, general academic interests/achievements, home economics, humanities, international studies, mathematics, military science, physical sciences, social sciences. *Creative arts/performance:* 23 awards ($20,750 total): art/fine arts, cinema/film/broadcasting, creative writing, dance, general creative arts/performance, journalism/publications, music, theater/drama. *Special achievements/activities:* 35 awards ($38,601 total): community service, general special achievements/activities, hobbies/interests, leadership, religious involvement. *Special characteristics:* 65 awards ($145,577 total): adult students, children and siblings of alumni, children of faculty/staff, ethnic background, first-generation college students, general special characteristics, international students, married students, members of minority groups, out-of-state students, previous college experience, veterans. ***Tuition waivers:*** Full or partial for employees or children of employees, senior citizens. ***ROTC:*** Army, Naval cooperative, Air Force cooperative.

LOANS ***Student loans:*** $40,623,595 (43% need-based, 57% non-need-based). 81% of past graduating class borrowed through all loan programs. *Average indebtedness per student:* $31,695. ***Average need-based loan:*** Freshmen: $3283. Undergraduates: $4260. ***Parent loans:*** $5,593,147 (100% non-need-based). ***Programs:*** Federal Direct (Subsidized and Unsubsidized Stafford, PLUS), Federal Nursing, Private Educational Loans.

WORK-STUDY ***Federal work-study:*** Total amount: $1,477,804; 492 jobs averaging $3004. ***State or other work-study/employment:*** Total amount: $1,684,856 (100% non-need-based). 903 part-time jobs averaging $1866.

APPLYING FOR FINANCIAL AID ***Required financial aid forms:*** FAFSA, state aid form. ***Financial aid deadline (priority):*** 1/1. ***Notification date:*** Continuous beginning 1/1. Students must reply by 2/1.

CONTACT Financial Aid Office, SUNY Brockport, 350 New Campus Drive, Brockport, NY 14420-2997, 585-395-2211.
Website: http://www.brockport.edu/.

SUSQUEHANNA UNIVERSITY

Selinsgrove, PA

Tuition & fees: $51,140	Average undergraduate aid package: $39,750

ABOUT THE INSTITUTION Independent Evangelical Lutheran Church in America, coed. ***Awards:*** bachelor's and master's degrees (also offers evening associate degree program limited to local adult students). 67 undergraduate majors. ***Total enrollment:*** 2,315. Undergraduates: 2,312. Freshmen: 620. Federal methodology is used as a basis for awarding need-based institutional aid.

UNDERGRADUATE EXPENSES for 2020–2021 ***Comprehensive fee:*** $64,820 includes full-time tuition ($50,500), mandatory fees ($640), and room and board ($13,680). ***College room only:*** $7320. Room and board charges vary according to board plan. ***Part-time tuition:*** $1605 per credit hour. ***Payment plan:*** Tuition prepayment.

FRESHMAN FINANCIAL AID (Fall 2019, est.) 561 applied for aid; of those 88% were deemed to have need. 100% of freshmen with need received aid; of those 27% had need fully met. ***Average percent of need met:*** 86% (excluding resources awarded to replace EFC). ***Average financial aid package:*** $40,504 (excluding resources awarded to replace EFC). 17% of all full-time freshmen had no need and received non-need-based gift aid.

UNDERGRADUATE FINANCIAL AID (Fall 2019, est.) 2,007 applied for aid; of those 91% were deemed to have need. 100% of undergraduates with need received aid; of those 22% had need fully met. ***Average percent of need met:*** 82% (excluding resources awarded to replace EFC). ***Average financial aid package:*** $39,750 (excluding resources awarded to replace EFC). 18% of all full-time undergraduates had no need and received non-need-based gift aid.

GIFT AID (NEED-BASED) ***Total amount:*** $63,198,342 (5% federal, 4% state, 89% institutional, 2% external sources). ***Receiving aid:*** Freshmen: 82% (495); all full-time undergraduates: 80% (1,834). ***Average award:*** Freshmen: $37,380; Undergraduates: $35,382. ***Scholarships, grants, and awards:*** Federal Pell, FSEOG, state, private, college/university gift aid from institutional funds.

GIFT AID (NON-NEED-BASED) ***Total amount:*** $15,975,286 (1% federal, 94% institutional, 5% external sources). ***Receiving aid:*** Freshmen: 19% (115). Undergraduates: 14% (324). ***Average award:*** Freshmen: $33,994. Undergraduates: $27,871. ***Scholarships, grants, and awards by category:*** *Academic interests/achievement:* business, education, general academic interests/achievements. *Creative arts/performance:* creative writing, music, theater/drama. *Special achievements/activities:* general special achievements/activities, leadership. *Special characteristics:* children and siblings of alumni, children of faculty/staff, relatives of clergy, veterans. ***Tuition waivers:*** Full or partial for employees or children of employees. ***ROTC:*** Army.

LOANS ***Student loans:*** $18,923,087 (64% need-based, 36% non-need-based). 84% of past graduating class borrowed through all loan programs. *Average indebtedness per student:* $40,455. ***Average need-based loan:*** Freshmen: $2961. Undergraduates: $4102. ***Parent loans:*** $6,792,399 (48% need-based, 52% non-need-based). ***Programs:*** Federal Direct (Subsidized and Unsubsidized Stafford, PLUS), state, college/university, Private Student Loans.

WORK-STUDY ***Federal work-study:*** Total amount: $1,630,061; jobs available. ***State or other work-study/employment:*** Total amount: $731,845 (53% need-based, 47% non-need-based). Part-time jobs available.

APPLYING FOR FINANCIAL AID ***Required financial aid forms:*** FAFSA, state aid form. ***Financial aid deadline:*** 5/1 (priority: 12/1). ***Notification date:*** Continuous beginning 11/15. Students must reply by 5/1.

CONTACT Ms. Erin M. Wolfe, Director of Student Financial Services, Susquehanna University, 514 University Avenue, Selinsgrove, PA 17870, 570-372-4450 or toll-free 800-326-9672. *Fax:* 570-372-2722. *E-mail:* wolfeerin@susqu.edu.
Website: http://www.susqu.edu/.

SWARTHMORE COLLEGE

Swarthmore, PA

Tuition & fees: $54,656	Average undergraduate aid package: $56,048

ABOUT THE INSTITUTION Independent, coed. ***Awards:*** bachelor's degrees. 48 undergraduate majors. ***Total enrollment:*** 1,647. Undergraduates: 1,647. Freshmen: 414. Institutional methodology is used as a basis for awarding need-based institutional aid.

UNDERGRADUATE EXPENSES for 2019–2020 ***Application fee:*** $60. ***Comprehensive fee:*** $70,744 includes full-time tuition ($54,256), mandatory fees ($400), and room and board ($16,088). ***College room only:*** $8252.

FRESHMAN FINANCIAL AID (Fall 2019, est.) 275 applied for aid; of those 84% were deemed to have need. 100% of freshmen with need received aid; of those 100% had need fully met. ***Average percent of need met:*** 100% (excluding resources awarded to replace EFC). ***Average financial aid package:*** $56,923 (excluding resources awarded to replace EFC). 1% of all full-time freshmen had no need and received non-need-based gift aid.

UNDERGRADUATE FINANCIAL AID (Fall 2019, est.) 995 applied for aid; of those 91% were deemed to have need. 100% of undergraduates with need received aid; of those 100% had need fully met. ***Average percent of need met:*** 100% (excluding resources awarded to replace EFC). ***Average financial aid package:*** $56,048 (excluding resources awarded to replace EFC). 1% of all full-time undergraduates had no need and received non-need-based gift aid.

GIFT AID (NEED-BASED) ***Total amount:*** $49,113,029 (5% federal, 93% institutional, 2% external sources). ***Receiving aid:*** Freshmen: 56% (232); all full-time undergraduates: 54% (906). ***Average award:*** Freshmen: $55,233; Undergraduates: $54,217. ***Scholarships, grants, and awards:*** Federal Pell, FSEOG, state, private, college/university gift aid from institutional funds.

GIFT AID (NON-NEED-BASED) ***Total amount:*** $1,641,891 (73% institutional, 27% external sources). ***Average award:*** Freshmen: $54,256. Undergraduates: $52,223. ***Scholarships, grants, and awards by category:*** *Special characteristics:* local/state students. ***ROTC:*** Air Force cooperative.

LOANS ***Student loans:*** $1,270,000 (100% non-need-based). 26% of past graduating class borrowed through all loan programs. *Average indebtedness per student:* $24,099. ***Parent loans:*** $2,440,403 (100% non-need-based). ***Programs:*** Federal Direct (Subsidized and Unsubsidized Stafford, PLUS), state, college/university.

WORK-STUDY ***Federal work-study:*** Total amount: $1,037,711; jobs available. ***State or other work-study/employment:*** Total amount: $561,061 (100% need-based). Part-time jobs available.

APPLYING FOR FINANCIAL AID ***Required financial aid forms:*** FAFSA, CSS Financial Aid PROFILE, state aid form, noncustodial (divorced/separated) parent's statement, federal income tax form(s), W-2 forms. ***Financial aid deadline:*** 1/1 (priority: 1/1). ***Notification date:*** 4/1. Students must reply by 5/1.

CONTACT Varo L. Duffins, Director of Financial Aid, Swarthmore College, 500 College Avenue, Swarthmore, PA 19081-1397, 610-328-8358 or toll-free 800-667-3110. *Fax:* 610-690-5751. *E-mail:* finaid@swarthmore.edu.
Website: http://www.swarthmore.edu/.

SWEDISH INSTITUTE, COLLEGE OF HEALTH SCIENCES

New York, NY

CONTACT Financial Aid Office, Swedish Institute, College of Health Sciences, 226 West 26th Street, New York, NY 10001-6700, 212-924-5900.
Website: http://www.swedishinstitute.edu/.

SWEET BRIAR COLLEGE

Sweet Briar, VA

CONTACT Wanda Spradley, Director of Financial Aid, Sweet Briar College, Box 1095, Sweet Briar, VA 24595, 800-381-6156 or toll-free 800-381-6142. *Fax:* 434-381-6450. *E-mail:* spradley@sbc.edu.
Website: http://www.sbc.edu/.

SYRACUSE UNIVERSITY

Syracuse, NY

Tuition & fees: $53,849	Average undergraduate aid package: $42,550

ABOUT THE INSTITUTION Independent, coed. ***Awards:*** certificates, bachelor's, master's, and doctoral degrees. 139 undergraduate majors. ***Total enrollment:*** 22,803. Undergraduates: 15,226. Freshmen: 3,599. Both federal and institutional methodology are used as a basis for awarding need-based institutional aid.

UNDERGRADUATE EXPENSES for 2019–2020 ***Application fee:*** $75. ***Comprehensive fee:*** $69,759 includes full-time tuition ($52,210), mandatory fees ($1639), and room and board ($15,910). ***College room only:*** $8470. Full-time tuition and fees vary according to course load. Room and board charges vary according to board plan and housing facility. ***Part-time tuition:*** $2274 per credit hour. Part-time tuition and fees vary according to course load. ***Payment plan:*** Tuition prepayment.

FRESHMAN FINANCIAL AID (Fall 2019, est.) 2305 applied for aid; of those 59% were deemed to have need. 100% of freshmen with need received aid; of those 71% had need fully met. ***Average percent of need met:*** 98% (excluding resources awarded to replace EFC). ***Average financial aid package:*** $45,190 (excluding resources awarded to replace EFC). 43% of all full-time freshmen had no need and received non-need-based gift aid.

UNDERGRADUATE FINANCIAL AID (Fall 2019, est.) 8,395 applied for aid; of those 70% were deemed to have need. 100% of undergraduates with need received aid; of those 54% had need fully met. ***Average percent of need met:*** 94% (excluding resources awarded to replace EFC). ***Average financial aid package:*** $42,550 (excluding resources awarded to replace EFC). 32% of all full-time undergraduates had no need and received non-need-based gift aid.

GIFT AID (NEED-BASED) ***Receiving aid:*** Freshmen: 36% (1,320); all full-time undergraduates: 39% (5,657). ***Average award:*** Freshmen: $38,431; Undergraduates: $34,854. ***Scholarships, grants, and awards:*** Federal Pell, FSEOG, state, private, college/university gift aid from institutional funds.

GIFT AID (NON-NEED-BASED) ***Receiving aid:*** Freshmen: 7% (248). Undergraduates: 5% (722). ***Average award:*** Freshmen: $8990. Undergraduates: $11,060. ***Scholarships, grants, and awards by category:*** *Academic interests/achievement:* general academic interests/achievements. *Creative arts/performance:* art/fine arts, music, theater/drama. ***Tuition waivers:*** Full or partial for employees or children of employees. ***ROTC:*** Army, Air Force.

LOANS ***Student loans:*** 54% of past graduating class borrowed through all loan programs. *Average indebtedness per student:* $37,563. ***Average need-based loan:*** Freshmen: $3350. Undergraduates: $4500. ***Programs:*** Federal Direct (Subsidized and Unsubsidized Stafford, PLUS).

WORK-STUDY ***Federal work-study:*** 4,983 jobs averaging $2926.

APPLYING FOR FINANCIAL AID ***Required financial aid forms:*** FAFSA, CSS Financial Aid PROFILE, noncustodial (divorced/separated) parent's statement.

CONTACT Office of Financial Aid and Scholarship Programs, Syracuse University, Syracuse University, 200 Bowne Hall, Syracuse, NY 13244-1200, 315-443-1513. *Website:* http://www.syracuse.edu/.

TABOR COLLEGE

Hillsboro, KS

Tuition & fees: $29,375	Average undergraduate aid package: $23,387

ABOUT THE INSTITUTION Independent Mennonite Brethren, coed. ***Awards:*** associate, bachelor's, and master's degrees. 29 undergraduate majors. ***Total enrollment:*** 639. Undergraduates: 574. Freshmen: 128. Federal methodology is used as a basis for awarding need-based institutional aid.

UNDERGRADUATE EXPENSES for 2019–2020 ***Application fee:*** $50. ***Comprehensive fee:*** $39,350 includes full-time tuition ($28,400), mandatory fees ($975), and room and board ($9975). Room and board charges vary according to board plan and housing facility. ***Part-time tuition:*** $570 per hour. ***Part-time fees:*** $20 per hour.

FRESHMAN FINANCIAL AID (Fall 2018) 213 applied for aid; of those 89% were deemed to have need. 100% of freshmen with need received aid; of those 19% had need fully met. ***Average percent of need met:*** 76% (excluding resources awarded to replace EFC). ***Average financial aid package:*** $24,094 (excluding resources awarded to replace EFC). 11% of all full-time freshmen had no need and received non-need-based gift aid.

UNDERGRADUATE FINANCIAL AID (Fall 2018) 547 applied for aid; of those 84% were deemed to have need. 100% of undergraduates with need received aid; of those 16% had need fully met. ***Average percent of need met:*** 73% (excluding resources awarded to replace EFC). ***Average financial aid package:*** $23,387 (excluding resources awarded to replace EFC). 15% of all full-time undergraduates had no need and received non-need-based gift aid.

GIFT AID (NEED-BASED) ***Total amount:*** $432,480 (20% federal, 80% state). ***Receiving aid:*** Freshmen: 40% (86); all full-time undergraduates: 34% (192). ***Average award:*** Freshmen: $3013; Undergraduates: $3036. ***Scholarships, grants, and awards:*** Federal Pell, FSEOG, state, private, college/university gift aid from institutional funds.

GIFT AID (NON-NEED-BASED) ***Total amount:*** $5,967,306 (96% institutional, 4% external sources). ***Receiving aid:*** Freshmen: 87% (186). Undergraduates: 80% (449). ***Average award:*** Freshmen: $10,059. Undergraduates: $11,124. ***Scholarships, grants, and awards by category:*** *Academic interests/achievement:* biological sciences, communication, general academic interests/achievements, humanities. *Creative arts/performance:* journalism/publications, music, performing arts, theater/drama. *Special achievements/activities:* cheerleading/drum major, general special achievements/activities, religious involvement. *Special characteristics:* children and siblings of alumni, children of faculty/staff, general special characteristics, international students, local/state students, out-of-state students, religious affiliation. ***Tuition waivers:*** Full or partial for employees or children of employees.

LOANS ***Student loans:*** $304,764 (100% need-based). 40% of past graduating class borrowed through all loan programs. *Average indebtedness per student:* $27,126. ***Average need-based loan:*** Freshmen: $10,417. Undergraduates: $7778. ***Parent loans:*** $1,890,268 (100% need-based). ***Programs:*** Federal Direct (Subsidized and Unsubsidized Stafford, PLUS), Perkins.

WORK-STUDY ***Federal work-study:*** Total amount: $103,116; jobs available. ***State or other work-study/employment:*** Part-time jobs available.

ATHLETIC AWARDS Total amount: $3,041,976 (100% non-need-based).

APPLYING FOR FINANCIAL AID ***Required financial aid forms:*** FAFSA, state aid form. ***Financial aid deadline:*** 8/15 (priority: 3/1). ***Notification date:*** Continuous beginning 3/15. Students must reply within 5 weeks of notification.

CONTACT Sadonia Lane, Financial Aid Director, Tabor College, 400 South Jefferson, Hillsboro, KS 67063, 620-947-3121 Ext. 1726 or toll-free 800-822-6799. *Fax:* 620-947-6276. *E-mail:* sadonialane@tabor.edu. *Website:* http://www.tabor.edu/.

TALLADEGA COLLEGE

Talladega, AL

Tuition & fees: $13,846	Average undergraduate aid package: $20,341

ABOUT THE INSTITUTION Independent, coed. ***Awards:*** associate and bachelor's degrees. 5 undergraduate majors. Federal methodology is used as a basis for awarding need-based institutional aid.

UNDERGRADUATE EXPENSES for 2019–2020 ***Comprehensive fee:*** $20,501 includes full-time tuition ($12,130), mandatory fees ($1716), and room and board ($6655). ***College room only:*** $3171. Full-time tuition and fees vary according to course load. Room and board charges vary according to housing facility. ***Part-time tuition:*** $650 per credit hour. ***Part-time fees:*** $858 per semester hour.

FRESHMAN FINANCIAL AID (Fall 2019, est.) 295 applied for aid; of those 98% were deemed to have need. 100% of freshmen with need received aid; of those 7% had need fully met. ***Average percent of need met:*** 75% (excluding resources awarded to replace EFC). ***Average financial aid package:*** $19,708 (excluding resources awarded to replace EFC). 58% of all full-time freshmen had no need and received non-need-based gift aid.

UNDERGRADUATE FINANCIAL AID (Fall 2019, est.) 1,083 applied for aid; of those 98% were deemed to have need. 100% of undergraduates with need received aid; of those 5% had need fully met. ***Average percent of need met:*** 77% (excluding resources awarded to replace EFC). ***Average financial aid package:*** $20,341 (excluding resources awarded to replace EFC). 55% of all full-time undergraduates had no need and received non-need-based gift aid.

GIFT AID (NEED-BASED) ***Total amount:*** $15,172,271 (100% federal). ***Receiving aid:*** Freshmen: 95% (279); all full-time undergraduates: 93% (1,010). ***Average award:*** Freshmen: $6229; Undergraduates: $6066. ***Scholarships, grants, and awards:*** Federal Pell, FSEOG, private, college/university gift aid from institutional funds, United Negro College Fund.

GIFT AID (NON-NEED-BASED) ***Total amount:*** $5,212,163 (16% federal, 70% institutional, 14% external sources). ***Receiving aid:*** Freshmen: 58% (172). Undergraduates: 55% (598). ***Average award:*** Freshmen: $5932. Undergraduates: $6300. ***Scholarships, grants, and awards by category:*** *Academic interests/achievement:* 152 awards ($1,139,767 total): general academic interests/achievements. *Special characteristics:* 5 awards ($53,970 total): children of faculty/staff. ***Tuition waivers:*** Full or partial for employees or children of employees.

LOANS ***Student loans:*** $8,066,888 (47% need-based, 53% non-need-based). 81% of past graduating class borrowed through all loan programs. *Average indebtedness per student:* $41,300. ***Average need-based loan:*** Freshmen: $3220. Undergraduates: $4167. ***Parent loans:*** $2,945,164 (100% non-need-based). ***Programs:*** Federal Direct (Subsidized and Unsubsidized Stafford, PLUS).

WORK-STUDY ***Federal work-study:*** Total amount: $124,142; 77 jobs averaging $1683.

ATHLETIC AWARDS Total amount: $1,072,759 (100% non-need-based).
APPLYING FOR FINANCIAL AID ***Required financial aid form:*** FAFSA. ***Financial aid deadline:*** Continuous. ***Notification date:*** Continuous beginning 3/1. Students must reply within 1 week of notification.

CONTACT K. Michael Francois, Director of Financial Aid, Talladega College, 627 West Battle Street, Talladega, AL 35160, 256-761-6341 or toll-free 866-540-3956. *Fax:* 256-761-6462.
Website: http://www.talladega.edu/.

TALMUDICAL ACADEMY OF NEW JERSEY

Adelphia, NJ

CONTACT Office of Financial Aid, Talmudical Academy of New Jersey, Route 524, Adelphia, NJ 07710, 732-431-1600.

TALMUDICAL INSTITUTE OF UPSTATE NEW YORK

Rochester, NY

CONTACT Mrs. Ella Berenstein, Financial Aid Administrator, Talmudical Institute of Upstate New York, 769 Park Avenue, Rochester, NY 14607-3046, 585-473-2810.
Website: http://www.tiuny.org/.

TALMUDICAL SEMINARY OF BOBOV

Brooklyn, NY

CONTACT Financial Aid Office, Talmudical Seminary of Bobov, 5120 New Utrecht Avenue, Brooklyn, NY 11219, 718-436-2122.

TALMUDICAL SEMINARY OHOLEI TORAH

Brooklyn, NY

CONTACT Financial Aid Administrator, Talmudical Seminary Oholei Torah, 667 Eastern Parkway, Brooklyn, NY 11213-3310, 718-774-5050.
Website: https://tsot.edu/.

TALMUDICAL YESHIVA OF PHILADELPHIA

Philadelphia, PA

CONTACT Director of Student Financial Aid/Registrar, Talmudical Yeshiva of Philadelphia, 6063 Drexel Road, Philadelphia, PA 19131-1296, 215-473-1212.

TALMUDIC UNIVERSITY

Miami Beach, FL

CONTACT Rabbi Ira Hill, Director of Financial Aid, Talmudic University, 1910 Alton Road, Miami Beach, FL 33139, 305-534-7050. *Fax:* 305-534-8444.
Website: http://www.talmudicu.edu/.

TARLETON STATE UNIVERSITY

Stephenville, TX

Tuition & fees (TX res): $9138	Average undergraduate aid package: $9700

ABOUT THE INSTITUTION State-supported, coed. ***Awards:*** certificates, associate, bachelor's, master's, and doctoral degrees. 59 undergraduate majors. ***Total enrollment:*** 13,176. Undergraduates: 11,350. Freshmen: 1,858. Federal methodology is used as a basis for awarding need-based institutional aid.
UNDERGRADUATE EXPENSES for 2020–2021 ***Application fee:*** $50. ***Tuition, state resident:*** full-time $5290; part-time $174 per credit hour. ***Tuition, nonresident:*** full-time $17,869; part-time $596 per credit hour. ***Required fees:*** full-time $3848; $3848 per year. Full-time tuition and fees vary according to course load, degree level, program, and student level. Part-time tuition and fees vary according to course load, degree level, program, and student level. ***College room and board:*** $10,712; ***Room only:*** $6762. Room and board charges vary according to board plan and housing facility. ***Payment plan:*** Guaranteed tuition.
FRESHMAN FINANCIAL AID (Fall 2019, est.) 1793 applied for aid; of those 73% were deemed to have need. 99% of freshmen with need received aid; of those 5% had need fully met. ***Average percent of need met:*** 58% (excluding resources awarded to replace EFC). ***Average financial aid package:*** $10,373 (excluding resources awarded to replace EFC).
UNDERGRADUATE FINANCIAL AID (Fall 2019, est.) 6,439 applied for aid; of those 79% were deemed to have need. 99% of undergraduates with need received aid; of those 3% had need fully met. ***Average percent of need met:*** 53% (excluding resources awarded to replace EFC). ***Average financial aid package:*** $9700 (excluding resources awarded to replace EFC).
GIFT AID (NEED-BASED) ***Total amount:*** $41,672,572 (53% federal, 25% state, 16% institutional, 6% external sources). ***Receiving aid:*** Freshmen: 55% (1,148); all full-time undergraduates: 52% (4,288). ***Average award:*** Freshmen: $8909; Undergraduates: $7533. ***Scholarships, grants, and awards:*** Federal Pell, FSEOG, state, private, college/university gift aid from institutional funds.
GIFT AID (NON-NEED-BASED) ***Total amount:*** $500 (100% institutional). ***Scholarships, grants, and awards by category:*** *Academic interests/achievement:* general academic interests/achievements. *Creative arts/performance:* music, theater/drama. *Special achievements/activities:* general special achievements/activities. *Special characteristics:* children of educators, children of faculty/staff, veterans. ***ROTC:*** Army, Air Force cooperative.
LOANS ***Student loans:*** $58,626,547 (40% need-based, 60% non-need-based). 82% of past graduating class borrowed through all loan programs. *Average indebtedness per student:* $23,820. ***Average need-based loan:*** Freshmen: $3239. Undergraduates: $4270. ***Parent loans:*** $13,453,003 (100% non-need-based). ***Programs:*** Federal Direct (Subsidized and Unsubsidized Stafford, PLUS), state.
WORK-STUDY ***Federal work-study:*** Total amount: $450,000; jobs available. ***State or other work-study/employment:*** Part-time jobs available.
ATHLETIC AWARDS Total amount: $1,831,371 (100% need-based).
APPLYING FOR FINANCIAL AID ***Notification date:*** Continuous.

CONTACT Ms. Kathy Purvis, Executive Director, Tarleton State University, Box T-0310, Stephenville, TX 76402, 254-968-9070 or toll-free 800-687-8236. *Fax:* 254-968-9600. *E-mail:* finaid@tarleton.edu.
Website: http://www.tarleton.edu/.

TAYLOR UNIVERSITY

Upland, IN

Tuition & fees: $35,305	Average undergraduate aid package: $26,360

ABOUT THE INSTITUTION Independent interdenominational, coed. ***Awards:*** diplomas, bachelor's, and master's degrees. 73 undergraduate majors. ***Total enrollment:*** 2,174. Undergraduates: 2,148. Freshmen: 490. Federal methodology is used as a basis for awarding need-based institutional aid.
UNDERGRADUATE EXPENSES for 2019–2020 ***Application fee:*** $25. ***Comprehensive fee:*** $45,255 includes full-time tuition ($35,050), mandatory fees ($255), and room and board ($9950). ***College room only:*** $5230. Full-time tuition and fees

vary according to course load and reciprocity agreements. ***Part-time tuition:*** $1235 per credit hour. ***Part-time fees:*** $45 per term.

FRESHMAN FINANCIAL AID (Fall 2019, est.) 415 applied for aid; of those 84% were deemed to have need. 100% of freshmen with need received aid; of those 32% had need fully met. ***Average percent of need met:*** 82% (excluding resources awarded to replace EFC). ***Average financial aid package:*** $27,031 (excluding resources awarded to replace EFC). 22% of all full-time freshmen had no need and received non-need-based gift aid.

UNDERGRADUATE FINANCIAL AID (Fall 2019, est.) 1,354 applied for aid; of those 85% were deemed to have need. 100% of undergraduates with need received aid; of those 30% had need fully met. ***Average percent of need met:*** 80% (excluding resources awarded to replace EFC). ***Average financial aid package:*** $26,360 (excluding resources awarded to replace EFC). 29% of all full-time undergraduates had no need and received non-need-based gift aid.

GIFT AID (NEED-BASED) ***Receiving aid:*** Freshmen: 71% (348); all full-time undergraduates: 64% (1,145). ***Average award:*** Freshmen: $23,639; Undergraduates: $22,545. ***Scholarships, grants, and awards:*** Federal Pell, FSEOG, state, private, college/university gift aid from institutional funds.

GIFT AID (NON-NEED-BASED) ***Receiving aid:*** Freshmen: 18% (86). Undergraduates: 13% (238). ***Average award:*** Freshmen: $17,507. Undergraduates: $15,322. ***Scholarships, grants, and awards by category:*** *Academic interests/achievement:* 1,458 awards ($16,731,219 total): general academic interests/achievements. *Creative arts/performance:* 97 awards ($290,388 total): music, theater/drama. *Special achievements/activities:* 633 awards ($1,660,127 total): leadership. *Special characteristics:* 879 awards ($4,172,055 total): children and siblings of alumni, children of faculty/staff, ethnic background, international students, religious affiliation. ***Tuition waivers:*** Full or partial for employees or children of employees, senior citizens.

LOANS ***Student loans:*** 58% of past graduating class borrowed through all loan programs. *Average indebtedness per student:* $26,009. ***Average need-based loan:*** Freshmen: $3944. Undergraduates: $4280. ***Programs:*** Federal Direct (Subsidized and Unsubsidized Stafford, PLUS), college/university.

WORK-STUDY ***Federal work-study:*** 800 jobs averaging $638.

APPLYING FOR FINANCIAL AID ***Required financial aid form:*** FAFSA. ***Notification date:*** Continuous.

CONTACT Mr. Timothy A. Nace, Associate Vice President of Financial Aid, Taylor University, 236 West Reade Avenue, Upland, IN 46989-1001, 765-998-5358 or toll-free 800-882-3456. *Fax:* 765-998-4910. *E-mail:* tmnace@taylor.edu.
Website: http://www.taylor.edu/.

TELSHE YESHIVA - CHICAGO

Chicago, IL

CONTACT Office of Financial Aid, Telshe Yeshiva - Chicago, 3535 West Foster Avenue, Chicago, IL 60625-5598, 773-463-7738.
Website: https://telsheyeshivachicago.com/.

TEMPLE UNIVERSITY

Philadelphia, PA

Tuition & fees (PA res): $19,748	Average undergraduate aid package: $12,347

ABOUT THE INSTITUTION State-related, coed. ***Awards:*** certificates, diplomas, bachelor's, master's, and doctoral degrees. 80 undergraduate majors. ***Total enrollment:*** 38,822. Undergraduates: 28,726. Freshmen: 4,967. Federal methodology is used as a basis for awarding need-based institutional aid.

UNDERGRADUATE EXPENSES for 2019–2020 ***Application fee:*** $55. ***Tuition, state resident:*** full-time $18,858; part-time $670 per credit hour. ***Tuition, nonresident:*** full-time $33,236; part-time $1208 per credit hour. ***Required fees:*** full-time $890; $163 per term. Full-time tuition and fees vary according to course load and program. Part-time tuition and fees vary according to course load and program. ***College room and board:*** $12,188; ***Room only:*** $8166. Room and board charges vary according to board plan, housing facility, and location.

FRESHMAN FINANCIAL AID (Fall 2018) 4492 applied for aid; of those 80% were deemed to have need. 100% of freshmen with need received aid; of those 5% had need fully met. ***Average percent of need met:*** 63% (excluding resources awarded to replace EFC). ***Average financial aid package:*** $12,848 (excluding resources awarded to replace EFC). 14% of all full-time freshmen had no need and received non-need-based gift aid.

UNDERGRADUATE FINANCIAL AID (Fall 2018) 20,994 applied for aid; of those 86% were deemed to have need. 100% of undergraduates with need received aid; of those 3% had need fully met. ***Average percent of need met:*** 61% (excluding resources awarded to replace EFC). ***Average financial aid package:*** $12,347 (excluding resources awarded to replace EFC). 14% of all full-time undergraduates had no need and received non-need-based gift aid.

GIFT AID (NEED-BASED) ***Total amount:*** $155,238,929 (27% federal, 16% state, 53% institutional, 4% external sources). ***Receiving aid:*** Freshmen: 70% (3,484); all full-time undergraduates: 62% (16,499). ***Average award:*** Freshmen: $10,829; Undergraduates: $9596. ***Scholarships, grants, and awards:*** Federal Pell, FSEOG, state, private, college/university gift aid from institutional funds, United Negro College Fund, Federal Nursing.

GIFT AID (NON-NEED-BASED) ***Total amount:*** $44,604,723 (72% institutional, 28% external sources). ***Receiving aid:*** Freshmen: 47% (2,362). Undergraduates: 35% (9,398). ***Average award:*** Freshmen: $6866. Undergraduates: $7953. ***Scholarships, grants, and awards by category:*** *Academic interests/achievement:* 9,864 awards ($60,196,450 total): general academic interests/achievements. *Creative arts/performance:* 241 awards ($645,073 total): applied art and design, dance, general creative arts/performance, music, performing arts, theater/drama. *Special achievements/activities:* 216 awards ($251,520 total): cheerleading/drum major. *Special characteristics:* 447 awards ($9,066,247 total): children of faculty/staff. ***Tuition waivers:*** Full or partial for employees or children of employees. ***ROTC:*** Army, Naval cooperative, Air Force cooperative.

LOANS ***Student loans:*** $204,487,604 (74% need-based, 26% non-need-based). 71% of past graduating class borrowed through all loan programs. *Average indebtedness per student:* $38,634. ***Average need-based loan:*** Freshmen: $3293. Undergraduates: $4260. ***Parent loans:*** $70,845,308 (65% need-based, 35% non-need-based). ***Programs:*** Federal Direct (Subsidized and Unsubsidized Stafford, PLUS), Federal Nursing, state, college/university.

WORK-STUDY ***Federal work-study:*** Total amount: $2,490,774; 1,883 jobs averaging $1321.

ATHLETIC AWARDS Total amount: $10,793,207 (39% need-based, 61% non-need-based).

APPLYING FOR FINANCIAL AID ***Required financial aid forms:*** FAFSA, state aid form. ***Financial aid deadline (priority):*** 3/1. ***Notification date:*** Continuous beginning 2/14.

CONTACT Emilie Van Trieste, Director of Student Financial Services, Temple University, Conwell Hall, Ground Floor, Philadelphia, PA 19122-6096, 215-204-8760 or toll-free 888-340-2222. *Fax:* 215-204-5897. *E-mail:* emilie.vantrieste@temple.edu.
Website: http://www.temple.edu/.

TENNESSEE STATE UNIVERSITY

Nashville, TN

CONTACT Amy Wood, Director of Financial Aid, Tennessee State University, 3500 John A. Merritt Boulevard, Nashville, TN 37209-1561, 615-963-7548. *Fax:* 615-963-7540. *E-mail:* awood7@tnstate.edu.
Website: http://www.tnstate.edu/.

TENNESSEE TECHNOLOGICAL UNIVERSITY

Cookeville, TN

CONTACT Mr. Lester Clyde McKenzie III, Director of Financial Aid, Tennessee Technological University, PO Box 5076, 805 Quadrangle, Cookeville, TN 38501, 931-372-3073 or toll-free 800-255-8881. *Fax:* 931-372-6309. *E-mail:* lmckenzie@tntech.edu.
Website: http://www.tntech.edu/.

TENNESSEE WESLEYAN UNIVERSITY

Athens, TN

Tuition & fees: $25,150 **Average undergraduate aid package: $21,445**

ABOUT THE INSTITUTION Independent United Methodist, coed. ***Awards:*** bachelor's and master's degrees (profile includes information for both the main and branch campuses). 43 undergraduate majors. ***Total enrollment:*** 1,142. Undergraduates: 1,067. Freshmen: 217. Federal methodology is used as a basis for awarding need-based institutional aid.

UNDERGRADUATE EXPENSES for 2020–2021 ***Comprehensive fee:*** $33,200 includes full-time tuition ($23,900), mandatory fees ($1250), and room and board ($8050). ***College room only:*** $2230. Full-time tuition and fees vary according to program. Room and board charges vary according to board plan and housing facility. ***Part-time tuition:*** $590 per credit hour. Part-time tuition and fees vary according to program.

FRESHMAN FINANCIAL AID (Fall 2019, est.) 185 applied for aid; of those 90% were deemed to have need. 100% of freshmen with need received aid; of those 30% had need fully met. ***Average percent of need met:*** 75% (excluding resources awarded to replace EFC). ***Average financial aid package:*** $22,799 (excluding resources awarded to replace EFC). 3% of all full-time freshmen had no need and received non-need-based gift aid.

UNDERGRADUATE FINANCIAL AID (Fall 2019, est.) 847 applied for aid; of those 92% were deemed to have need. 100% of undergraduates with need received aid; of those 42% had need fully met. ***Average percent of need met:*** 72% (excluding resources awarded to replace EFC). ***Average financial aid package:*** $21,445 (excluding resources awarded to replace EFC). 5% of all full-time undergraduates had no need and received non-need-based gift aid.

GIFT AID (NEED-BASED) ***Total amount:*** $3,449,166 (70% federal, 30% state). ***Receiving aid:*** Freshmen: 44% (91); all full-time undergraduates: 45% (435). ***Average award:*** Freshmen: $20,678; Undergraduates: $18,790. ***Scholarships, grants, and awards:*** Federal Pell, FSEOG, state, private, college/university gift aid from institutional funds.

GIFT AID (NON-NEED-BASED) ***Total amount:*** $8,791,143 (21% state, 77% institutional, 2% external sources). ***Receiving aid:*** Freshmen: 80% (166). Undergraduates: 80% (778). ***Average award:*** Freshmen: $15,466. Undergraduates: $12,265. ***Scholarships, grants, and awards by category:*** *Academic interests/achievement:* general academic interests/achievements. *Creative arts/performance:* music. *Special achievements/activities:* cheerleading/drum major, general special achievements/activities, junior miss, memberships. *Special characteristics:* children and siblings of alumni, children of faculty/staff, general special characteristics, out-of-state students, relatives of clergy, religious affiliation, siblings of current students. ***Tuition waivers:*** Full or partial for employees or children of employees. ***ROTC:*** Army cooperative, Naval cooperative, Air Force cooperative.

LOANS ***Student loans:*** $5,102,088 (43% need-based, 57% non-need-based). 66% of past graduating class borrowed through all loan programs. *Average indebtedness per student:* $24,338. ***Average need-based loan:*** Freshmen: $3302. Undergraduates: $4106. ***Parent loans:*** $1,020,899 (100% non-need-based). ***Programs:*** Federal Direct (Subsidized and Unsubsidized Stafford, PLUS).

WORK-STUDY ***Federal work-study:*** Total amount: $101,930; jobs available. ***State or other work-study/employment:*** Total amount: $420,261 (97% need-based, 3% non-need-based). Part-time jobs available.

ATHLETIC AWARDS Total amount: $5,674,424 (100% non-need-based).

APPLYING FOR FINANCIAL AID ***Required financial aid form:*** FAFSA. ***Financial aid deadline:*** Continuous. ***Notification date:*** Continuous beginning 11/15. Students must reply within 4 weeks of notification.

CONTACT Mrs. Lacey Weese, Assistant Vice President of Financial Aid, Tennessee Wesleyan University, 204 East College Street, Athens, TN 37303, 423-746-5209 or toll-free 800-PICK-TWU. *Fax:* 423-746-5326. *E-mail:* lweese@tnwesleyan.edu.
Website: http://www.tnwesleyan.edu/.

TEXAS A&M INTERNATIONAL UNIVERSITY

Laredo, TX

Tuition & fees (TX res): $9254 **Average undergraduate aid package: N/A**

ABOUT THE INSTITUTION State-supported, coed. ***Awards:*** bachelor's, master's, and doctoral degrees. 24 undergraduate majors. ***Total enrollment:*** 8,305. Undergraduates: 7,220. Freshmen: 1,297. Federal methodology is used as a basis for awarding need-based institutional aid.

UNDERGRADUATE EXPENSES for 2020–2021 ***Tuition, state resident:*** full-time $4773; part-time $159 per credit hour. ***Tuition, nonresident:*** full-time $17,043; part-time $568 per credit hour. ***Required fees:*** full-time $4481; $133 per credit hour. ***College room and board:*** $8809; ***Room only:*** $5811. ***Payment plan:*** Guaranteed tuition.

FRESHMAN FINANCIAL AID (Fall 2018) 100% of freshmen with need received aid.

UNDERGRADUATE FINANCIAL AID (Fall 2018) 100% of undergraduates with need received aid.

GIFT AID (NEED-BASED) ***Total amount:*** $36,760,506 (64% federal, 32% state, 4% institutional). ***Receiving aid:*** Freshmen: 86% (1,104); all full-time undergraduates: 82% (4,552). ***Average award:*** Freshmen: $8945; Undergraduates: $8497. ***Scholarships, grants, and awards:*** Federal Pell, FSEOG, state, private, college/university gift aid from institutional funds, Private Loans.

GIFT AID (NON-NEED-BASED) ***Total amount:*** $7,831,467 (79% institutional, 21% external sources). ***Receiving aid:*** Freshmen: 53% (675). Undergraduates: 50% (2,757). ***Scholarships, grants, and awards by category:*** *Academic interests/achievement:* business, communication, education, engineering/technologies, English, foreign languages, general academic interests/achievements, health fields, international studies, mathematics, physical sciences, premedicine, social sciences. *Creative arts/performance:* art/fine arts, dance, music, performing arts. ***Tuition waivers:*** Full or partial for senior citizens. ***ROTC:*** Army.

LOANS ***Student loans:*** $15,401,193 (61% need-based, 39% non-need-based). 64% of past graduating class borrowed through all loan programs. *Average indebtedness per student:* $3477. ***Average need-based loan:*** Freshmen: $2940. Undergraduates: $3713. ***Parent loans:*** $289,908 (100% non-need-based). ***Programs:*** Federal Direct (Subsidized and Unsubsidized Stafford, PLUS), state, college/university, Private Loans.

WORK-STUDY ***Federal work-study:*** Total amount: $374,625; jobs available. ***State or other work-study/employment:*** Part-time jobs available.

ATHLETIC AWARDS Total amount: $1,083,298 (100% non-need-based).

APPLYING FOR FINANCIAL AID ***Required financial aid forms:*** FAFSA, state aid form. ***Financial aid deadline:*** 6/30 (priority: 1/15). ***Notification date:*** Continuous beginning 2/15. Students must reply within 4 weeks of notification.

CONTACT Mrs. Laura Elizondo, Director of Financial Aid, Texas A&M International University, 5201 University Boulevard, Laredo, TX 78041, 956-326-2225 or toll-free 888-489-2648. *Fax:* 956-326-2224. *E-mail:* laura@tamiu.edu.
Website: http://www.tamiu.edu/.

TEXAS A&M UNIVERSITY

College Station, TX

Tuition & fees (area res): $11,232 **Average undergraduate aid package: $17,534**

ABOUT THE INSTITUTION State-supported, coed. ***Awards:*** certificates, bachelor's, master's, and doctoral degrees. 111 undergraduate majors. ***Total enrollment:*** 68,390. Undergraduates: 53,791. Freshmen: 10,613.

UNDERGRADUATE EXPENSES for 2019–2020 ***Application fee:*** $75. ***Tuition, area resident:*** full-time $7580; part-time $253 per credit hour. ***Tuition, state resident:*** full-time $7580; part-time $253 per credit hour. ***Tuition, nonresident:*** full-time $34,073; part-time $1136 per credit hour. ***Required fees:*** full-time $3652. Full-time tuition and fees vary according to course load and student level. Part-time tuition and fees vary according to course load and student level. ***College room and board:*** $10,400. Room and board charges vary according to housing facility and location. ***Payment plans:*** Guaranteed tuition, tuition prepayment.

FRESHMAN FINANCIAL AID (Fall 2018) 8202 applied for aid; of those 64% were deemed to have need. 95% of freshmen with need received aid; of those 23% had need fully met. ***Average percent of need met:*** 72% (excluding resources awarded to replace EFC). ***Average financial aid package:*** $18,575 (excluding resources awarded to replace EFC). 14% of all full-time freshmen had no need and received non-need-based gift aid.

UNDERGRADUATE FINANCIAL AID (Fall 2018) 30,712 applied for aid; of those 74% were deemed to have need. 95% of undergraduates with need received aid; of those 19% had need fully met. ***Average percent of need met:*** 69% (excluding resources awarded to replace EFC). ***Average financial aid package:*** $17,534 (excluding resources awarded to replace EFC). 12% of all full-time undergraduates had no need and received non-need-based gift aid.

GIFT AID (NEED-BASED) ***Total amount:*** $196,711,397 (29% federal, 21% state, 38% institutional, 12% external sources). ***Receiving aid:*** Freshmen: 47% (4,731); all full-time undergraduates: 41% (19,598). ***Average award:*** Freshmen: $12,388; Undergraduates: $10,740. ***Scholarships, grants, and awards:*** Federal Pell, FSEOG, state, private, college/university gift aid from institutional funds.

GIFT AID (NON-NEED-BASED) ***Total amount:*** $43,894,168 (1% federal, 4% state, 59% institutional, 36% external sources). ***Receiving aid:*** Freshmen: 5% (547). Undergraduates: 3% (1,508). ***Average award:*** Freshmen: $5177. Undergraduates: $4159. ***Scholarships, grants, and awards by category:*** *Academic interests/achievement:* agriculture, architecture, biological sciences, business, computer science, education, engineering/technologies, general academic interests/achievements, health fields, mathematics, physical sciences, premedicine. *Creative arts/performance:* journalism/publications, performing arts, theater/drama. *Special achievements/activities:* community service, general special achievements/activities, leadership, memberships, rodeo. *Special characteristics:* children of faculty/staff, first-generation college students, general special characteristics, international students, local/state students, veterans, veterans' children. ***Tuition waivers:*** Full or partial for employees or children of employees. ***ROTC:*** Army, Naval, Air Force.

LOANS ***Student loans:*** $138,955,387 (65% need-based, 35% non-need-based). 43% of past graduating class borrowed through all loan programs. *Average indebtedness per student:* $24,590. ***Average need-based loan:*** Freshmen: $7900. Undergraduates: $8788. ***Parent loans:*** $79,789,529 (37% need-based, 63% non-need-based). ***Programs:*** Federal Direct (Subsidized and Unsubsidized Stafford, PLUS), Perkins, Federal Nursing, state, college/university.

WORK-STUDY ***Federal work-study:*** Total amount: $4,151,019; jobs available. ***State or other work-study/employment:*** Total amount: $448,796 (100% need-based). Part-time jobs available.

ATHLETIC AWARDS Total amount: $4,586,032 (28% need-based, 72% non-need-based).

APPLYING FOR FINANCIAL AID ***Required financial aid form:*** FAFSA. ***Financial aid deadline (priority):*** 12/15. ***Notification date:*** Continuous beginning 2/25.

CONTACT Scholarships and Financial Aid Office, Texas A&M University, The Pavilion 200, Spence Street, 1252 TAMU, College Station, TX 77842-3016, 979-845-3236. *Fax:* 979-847-9061. *E-mail:* financialaid@tamu.edu.
Website: http://www.tamu.edu/.

TEXAS A&M UNIVERSITY–CENTRAL TEXAS

Killeen, TX

Tuition & fees (TX res): $8696	Average undergraduate aid package: $9495

ABOUT THE INSTITUTION State-supported, coed. ***Awards:*** certificates, bachelor's, and master's degrees. 23 undergraduate majors. ***Total enrollment:*** 2,430. Undergraduates: 1,944. Freshmen: 20. Federal methodology is used as a basis for awarding need-based institutional aid.

UNDERGRADUATE EXPENSES for 2020–2021 ***Application fee:*** $30. ***Tuition, state resident:*** full-time $6426; part-time $254 per credit hour. ***Tuition, nonresident:*** full-time $16,241; part-time $677 per credit hour. ***Required fees:*** full-time $2270; $158 per credit hour. Full-time tuition and fees vary according to course load. Part-time tuition and fees vary according to course load. ***College room and board:*** $9136; ***Room only:*** $9136. ***Payment plan:*** Guaranteed tuition.

UNDERGRADUATE FINANCIAL AID (Fall 2018) 563 applied for aid; of those 88% were deemed to have need. 98% of undergraduates with need received aid; of those 11% had need fully met. ***Average percent of need met:*** 71% (excluding resources awarded to replace EFC). ***Average financial aid package:*** $9495 (excluding resources awarded to replace EFC).

GIFT AID (NEED-BASED) ***Total amount:*** $6,265,356 (74% federal, 20% state, 6% institutional). ***Receiving aid:*** All full-time undergraduates: 63% (432). ***Average award:*** Undergraduates: $6621. ***Scholarships, grants, and awards:*** Federal Pell, FSEOG, state, private, college/university gift aid from institutional funds.

GIFT AID (NON-NEED-BASED) ***Total amount:*** $5146 (100% institutional). ***ROTC:*** Army.

LOANS ***Student loans:*** $8,890,673 (41% need-based, 59% non-need-based). ***Average need-based loan:*** Undergraduates: $4416. ***Parent loans:*** $295,388 (100% non-need-based). ***Programs:*** Federal Direct (Subsidized and Unsubsidized Stafford, PLUS), state.

WORK-STUDY ***Federal work-study:*** Total amount: $478,396.

CONTACT Irene Montalvo, Director, Student Financial Assistance/Interim Director of Military and Veteran Services, Texas A&M University–Central Texas, 1001 Leadership Place, Killeen, TX 76549, 254-519-5400. *E-mail:* i.montalvo@tamuct.edu.
Website: http://www.tamuct.edu/.

TEXAS A&M UNIVERSITY–COMMERCE

Commerce, TX

Tuition & fees (TX res): $8958	Average undergraduate aid package: $10,008

ABOUT THE INSTITUTION State-supported, coed. ***Awards:*** certificates, bachelor's, master's, and doctoral degrees. 46 undergraduate majors. ***Total enrollment:*** 11,725. Undergraduates: 8,324. Freshmen: 868. Federal methodology is used as a basis for awarding need-based institutional aid.

UNDERGRADUATE EXPENSES for 2020–2021 ***Tuition, state resident:*** full-time $4790; part-time $160 per credit hour. ***Tuition, nonresident:*** full-time $17,460; part-time $582 per credit hour. ***Required fees:*** full-time $4168. Full-time tuition and fees vary according to course load, location, program, and reciprocity agreements. Part-time tuition and fees vary according to course load, location, program, and reciprocity agreements. ***College room and board:*** $8868. Room and board charges vary according to board plan and housing facility.

FRESHMAN FINANCIAL AID (Fall 2019, est.) 859 applied for aid; of those 83% were deemed to have need. 96% of freshmen with need received aid; of those 14% had need fully met. ***Average percent of need met:*** 62% (excluding resources awarded to replace EFC). ***Average financial aid package:*** $11,962 (excluding resources awarded to replace EFC). 7% of all full-time freshmen had no need and received non-need-based gift aid.

UNDERGRADUATE FINANCIAL AID (Fall 2019, est.) 4,774 applied for aid; of those 87% were deemed to have need. 96% of undergraduates with need received aid; of those 11% had need fully met. ***Average percent of need met:*** 51% (excluding resources awarded to replace EFC). ***Average financial aid package:*** $10,008 (excluding resources awarded to replace EFC). 3% of all full-time undergraduates had no need and received non-need-based gift aid.

GIFT AID (NEED-BASED) ***Total amount:*** $29,852,347 (55% federal, 28% state, 14% institutional, 3% external sources). ***Receiving aid:*** Freshmen: 70% (670); all full-time undergraduates: 65% (3,781). ***Average award:*** Freshmen: $12,039; Undergraduates: $9305. ***Scholarships, grants, and awards:*** Federal Pell, FSEOG, state, private, college/university gift aid from institutional funds.

GIFT AID (NON-NEED-BASED) ***Total amount:*** $2,263,839 (2% federal, 1% state, 84% institutional, 13% external sources). ***Average award:*** Freshmen: $2215. Undergraduates: $2207. ***Scholarships, grants, and awards by category:*** *Academic interests/achievement:* agriculture, biological sciences, business, communication, computer science, education, engineering/technologies, English, foreign languages, general academic interests/achievements, home economics, humanities, international studies, mathematics, physical sciences, premedicine, social sciences. *Creative arts/performance:* applied art and design, art/fine arts, journalism/publications, music, performing arts, theater/drama. *Special achievements/activities:* cheerleading/drum major, general special achievements/activities, junior miss, leadership, memberships, rodeo. *Special characteristics:* adult students, children and siblings of alumni, first-generation college students, general special characteristics, out-of-state students, previous college experience, veterans. ***Tuition waivers:*** Full or partial for senior citizens. ***ROTC:*** Air Force cooperative.

LOANS ***Student loans:*** $28,003,916 (89% need-based, 11% non-need-based). 64% of past graduating class borrowed through all loan programs. *Average indebtedness per student:* $25,546. ***Average need-based loan:*** Freshmen: $3083. Undergraduates: $3734. ***Parent loans:*** $7,836,591 (80% need-based, 20% non-need-based). ***Programs:*** Federal Direct (Subsidized and Unsubsidized Stafford, PLUS), state.

WORK-STUDY ***Federal work-study:*** Total amount: $244,307; 135 jobs averaging $1762. ***State or other work-study/employment:*** Total amount: $26,141 (100% need-based). 16 part-time jobs averaging $1342.

ATHLETIC AWARDS Total amount: $2,210,891 (48% need-based, 52% non-need-based).

APPLYING FOR FINANCIAL AID ***Required financial aid forms:*** FAFSA, TASFA. ***Financial aid deadline (priority):*** 2/1. ***Notification date:*** Continuous beginning 2/15.

CONTACT Ms. Maria Ramos, Director of Financial Aid and Scholarships, Texas A&M University–Commerce, PO Box 3011, Commerce, TX 75429, 903-886-5091 or toll-free 888-868-2682. *Fax:* 903-886-5098. *E-mail:* maria.ramos@tamuc.edu.
Website: http://www.tamuc.edu/.

TEXAS A&M UNIVERSITY–CORPUS CHRISTI

Corpus Christi, TX

Tuition & fees (TX res): $4992 | **Average undergraduate aid package: $10,100**

ABOUT THE INSTITUTION State-supported, coed. ***Awards:*** certificates, bachelor's, master's, and doctoral degrees. 42 undergraduate majors. ***Total enrollment:*** 11,452. Undergraduates: 9,323. Freshmen: 1,915. Federal methodology is used as a basis for awarding need-based institutional aid.

UNDERGRADUATE EXPENSES for 2020–2021 ***Application fee:*** $40. ***Tuition, state resident:*** full-time $4992. ***Tuition, nonresident:*** full-time $17,107. ***College room and board:*** $10,220.

FRESHMAN FINANCIAL AID (Fall 2019, est.) 1446 applied for aid; of those 76% were deemed to have need. 96% of freshmen with need received aid; of those 21% had need fully met. ***Average percent of need met:*** 14% (excluding resources awarded to replace EFC). ***Average financial aid package:*** $11,611 (excluding resources awarded to replace EFC). 8% of all full-time freshmen had no need and received non-need-based gift aid.

UNDERGRADUATE FINANCIAL AID (Fall 2019, est.) 5,674 applied for aid; of those 84% were deemed to have need. 97% of undergraduates with need received aid; of those 15% had need fully met. ***Average percent of need met:*** 44% (excluding resources awarded to replace EFC). ***Average financial aid package:*** $10,100 (excluding resources awarded to replace EFC). 6% of all full-time undergraduates had no need and received non-need-based gift aid.

GIFT AID (NEED-BASED) ***Receiving aid:*** Freshmen: 48% (817); all full-time undergraduates: 47% (3,468). ***Average award:*** Freshmen: $10,128; Undergraduates: $8908. ***Scholarships, grants, and awards:*** Federal Pell, FSEOG, state, private, college/university gift aid from institutional funds, Federal Nursing.

GIFT AID (NON-NEED-BASED) ***Receiving aid:*** Freshmen: 26% (436). Undergraduates: 17% (1,259). ***Average award:*** Freshmen: $3484. Undergraduates: $3209. ***Scholarships, grants, and awards by category:*** *Academic interests/achievement:* 386 awards ($1,265,131 total): general academic interests/achievements. *Creative arts/performance:* 37 awards ($89,650 total): applied art and design, general creative arts/performance. *Special achievements/activities:* general special achievements/activities. *Special characteristics:* 25 awards ($22,000 total): first-generation college students, international students. ***ROTC:*** Army.

LOANS ***Student loans:*** 64% of past graduating class borrowed through all loan programs. *Average indebtedness per student:* $17,748. ***Average need-based loan:*** Freshmen: $3150. Undergraduates: $3854. ***Programs:*** Federal Direct (Subsidized and Unsubsidized Stafford, PLUS), state, college/university.

WORK-STUDY ***Federal work-study:*** 132 jobs averaging $2891. ***State or other work-study/employment:*** 216 part-time jobs averaging $2546.

APPLYING FOR FINANCIAL AID ***Required financial aid form:*** FAFSA. ***Notification date:*** Continuous. Students must reply within 2 weeks of notification.

CONTACT Jeannie Gage, Director of Financial Assistance, Texas A&M University–Corpus Christi, 6300 Ocean Drive, Corpus Christi, TX 78412-5503, 361-825-2332 or toll-free 800-482-6822. *Fax:* 361-825-6095. *E-mail:* faoweb@tamucc.edu.
Website: http://www.tamucc.edu/.

TEXAS A&M UNIVERSITY–KINGSVILLE

Kingsville, TX

Tuition & fees (area res): $9136 | **Average undergraduate aid package: $10,618**

ABOUT THE INSTITUTION State-supported, coed. ***Awards:*** certificates, bachelor's, master's, and doctoral degrees. 52 undergraduate majors. ***Total enrollment:*** 7,479. Undergraduates: 6,174. Freshmen: 987. Federal methodology is used as a basis for awarding need-based institutional aid.

UNDERGRADUATE EXPENSES for 2020–2021 ***Application fee:*** $25. ***Tuition, area resident:*** full-time $4801; part-time $188 per credit hour. ***Tuition, state resident:*** full-time $4801; part-time $188 per credit hour. ***Tuition, nonresident:*** full-time $18,191; part-time $640 per credit hour. ***Required fees:*** full-time $4335. Full-time tuition and fees vary according to course load and degree level. Part-time tuition and fees vary according to course load and degree level. ***College room and board:*** $8848. Room and board charges vary according to board plan and housing facility. ***Payment plan:*** Guaranteed tuition.

FRESHMAN FINANCIAL AID (Fall 2018) 1125 applied for aid; of those 87% were deemed to have need. 97% of freshmen with need received aid; of those 19% had need fully met. ***Average percent of need met:*** 74% (excluding resources awarded to replace EFC). ***Average financial aid package:*** $11,703 (excluding resources awarded to replace EFC). 6% of all full-time freshmen had no need and received non-need-based gift aid.

UNDERGRADUATE FINANCIAL AID (Fall 2018) 4,359 applied for aid; of those 90% were deemed to have need. 97% of undergraduates with need received aid; of those 14% had need fully met. ***Average percent of need met:*** 66% (excluding resources awarded to replace EFC). ***Average financial aid package:*** $10,618 (excluding resources awarded to replace EFC). 6% of all full-time undergraduates had no need and received non-need-based gift aid.

GIFT AID (NEED-BASED) ***Total amount:*** $24,064,098 (66% federal, 30% state, 4% institutional). ***Receiving aid:*** Freshmen: 65% (788); all full-time undergraduates: 59% (3,060). ***Average award:*** Freshmen: $9290; Undergraduates: $7536. ***Scholarships, grants, and awards:*** Federal Pell, FSEOG, state, private, college/university gift aid from institutional funds.

GIFT AID (NON-NEED-BASED) ***Total amount:*** $2,551,500 (95% institutional, 5% external sources). ***Receiving aid:*** Freshmen: 19% (230). Undergraduates: 16% (799). ***Average award:*** Freshmen: $3829. Undergraduates: $5592. ***Scholarships, grants, and awards by category:*** *Special achievements/activities:* rodeo. *Special characteristics:* general special characteristics. ***Tuition waivers:*** Full or partial for employees or children of employees, senior citizens. ***ROTC:*** Army.

LOANS ***Student loans:*** $26,968,070 (88% need-based, 12% non-need-based). 68% of past graduating class borrowed through all loan programs. *Average indebtedness per student:* $30,726. ***Average need-based loan:*** Freshmen: $3178. Undergraduates: $8889. ***Parent loans:*** $4,653,448 (100% non-need-based). ***Programs:*** Federal Direct (Subsidized and Unsubsidized Stafford, PLUS), state.

WORK-STUDY ***Federal work-study:*** Total amount: $435,648; jobs available. ***State or other work-study/employment:*** Total amount: $53,799 (100% need-based). Part-time jobs available.

ATHLETIC AWARDS Total amount: $1,861,897 (100% non-need-based).

APPLYING FOR FINANCIAL AID ***Required financial aid form:*** FAFSA. ***Financial aid deadline (priority):*** 1/15. ***Notification date:*** Continuous beginning 1/1.

CONTACT Mr. Arnold Trejo, Executive Director of Student Financial Aid, Texas A&M University–Kingsville, 700 University Boulevard, Kingsville, TX 78363, 361-593-3911 or toll-free 800-687-6000. *Fax:* 361-593-3026. *E-mail:* financial.aid@tamuk.edu.
Website: http://www.tamuk.edu/.

TEXAS A&M UNIVERSITY–SAN ANTONIO

San Antonio, TX

CONTACT Financial Aid Office, Texas A&M University–San Antonio, One University Way, San Antonio, TX 78224, 210-784-1000.
Website: http://www.tamusa.edu/.

TEXAS A&M UNIVERSITY–TEXARKANA

Texarkana, TX

Tuition & fees: N/R	Average undergraduate aid package: $11,397

ABOUT THE INSTITUTION State-supported, coed. ***Awards:*** bachelor's, master's, and doctoral degrees. 20 undergraduate majors. Federal methodology is used as a basis for awarding need-based institutional aid.

FRESHMAN FINANCIAL AID (Fall 2018) 189 applied for aid; of those 73% were deemed to have need. 98% of freshmen with need received aid; of those 12% had need fully met. ***Average percent of need met:*** 79% (excluding resources awarded to replace EFC). ***Average financial aid package:*** $12,211 (excluding resources awarded to replace EFC). 17% of all full-time freshmen had no need and received non-need-based gift aid.

UNDERGRADUATE FINANCIAL AID (Fall 2018) 1,009 applied for aid; of those 85% were deemed to have need. 99% of undergraduates with need received aid; of those 6% had need fully met. ***Average percent of need met:*** 69% (excluding resources awarded to replace EFC). ***Average financial aid package:*** $11,397 (excluding resources awarded to replace EFC). 10% of all full-time undergraduates had no need and received non-need-based gift aid.

GIFT AID (NEED-BASED) ***Total amount:*** $6,365,926 (66% federal, 26% state, 6% institutional, 2% external sources). ***Receiving aid:*** Freshmen: 60% (130); all full-time undergraduates: 67% (812). ***Average award:*** Freshmen: $11,294; Undergraduates: $9224. ***Scholarships, grants, and awards:*** Federal Pell, FSEOG, state, private, college/university gift aid from institutional funds.

GIFT AID (NON-NEED-BASED) ***Total amount:*** $237,118 (4% federal, 2% state, 80% institutional, 14% external sources). ***Average award:*** Freshmen: $1466. Undergraduates: $2009. ***Scholarships, grants, and awards by category:*** *Academic interests/achievement:* biological sciences, business, communication, computer science, education, engineering/technologies, English, general academic interests/achievements, health fields, international studies, mathematics, social sciences. *Special achievements/activities:* community service, general special achievements/activities, leadership, memberships. *Special characteristics:* veterans.

LOANS ***Student loans:*** $8,740,055 (90% need-based, 10% non-need-based). 51% of past graduating class borrowed through all loan programs. *Average indebtedness per student:* $22,258. ***Average need-based loan:*** Freshmen: $2832. Undergraduates: $3685. ***Parent loans:*** $684,793 (61% need-based, 39% non-need-based). ***Programs:*** Federal Direct (Subsidized and Unsubsidized Stafford, PLUS), state, college/university.

WORK-STUDY ***Federal work-study:*** Total amount: $71,987; 28 jobs averaging $2260. ***State or other work-study/employment:*** Part-time jobs available.

ATHLETIC AWARDS Total amount: $124,992 (51% need-based, 49% non-need-based).

APPLYING FOR FINANCIAL AID ***Required financial aid form:*** FAFSA. ***Financial aid deadline (priority):*** 1/15. ***Notification date:*** Continuous beginning 2/15. Students must reply within 2 weeks of notification.

CONTACT Mr. Michael G. Fuller, Director of Financial Aid and Veteran Services, Texas A&M University–Texarkana, 7101 University Avenue, Texarkana, TX 75503, 903-223-3060. *Fax:* 903-223-3140. *E-mail:* mfuller@tamut.edu.
Website: http://www.tamut.edu/.

TEXAS CHRISTIAN UNIVERSITY

Fort Worth, TX

Tuition & fees: $51,660	Average undergraduate aid package: $33,516

ABOUT THE INSTITUTION Independent Christian Church (Disciples of Christ), coed. ***Awards:*** certificates, diplomas, bachelor's, master's, and doctoral degrees. 103 undergraduate majors. ***Total enrollment:*** 11,024. Undergraduates: 9,474. Freshmen: 2,159. Both federal and institutional methodology are used as a basis for awarding need-based institutional aid.

UNDERGRADUATE EXPENSES for 2020–2021 ***Application fee:*** $50. ***Comprehensive fee:*** $65,700 includes full-time tuition ($51,570), mandatory fees ($90), and room and board ($14,040). ***College room only:*** $8340. Room and board charges vary according to board plan and housing facility. ***Part-time tuition:*** $2180 per credit hour. ***Part-time fees:*** $45 per term. Part-time tuition and fees vary according to course load.

FRESHMAN FINANCIAL AID (Fall 2019, est.) 1316 applied for aid; of those 66% were deemed to have need. 99% of freshmen with need received aid; of those 36% had need fully met. ***Average percent of need met:*** 71% (excluding resources awarded to replace EFC). ***Average financial aid package:*** $32,932 (excluding resources awarded to replace EFC). 33% of all full-time freshmen had no need and received non-need-based gift aid.

UNDERGRADUATE FINANCIAL AID (Fall 2019, est.) 4,696 applied for aid; of those 76% were deemed to have need. 99% of undergraduates with need received aid; of those 25% had need fully met. ***Average percent of need met:*** 64% (excluding resources awarded to replace EFC). ***Average financial aid package:*** $33,516 (excluding resources awarded to replace EFC). 32% of all full-time undergraduates had no need and received non-need-based gift aid.

GIFT AID (NEED-BASED) ***Total amount:*** $98,013,790 (7% federal, 4% state, 88% institutional, 1% external sources). ***Receiving aid:*** Freshmen: 38% (813); all full-time undergraduates: 36% (3,345). ***Average award:*** Freshmen: $30,724; Undergraduates: $31,070. ***Scholarships, grants, and awards:*** Federal Pell, FSEOG, state, private, college/university gift aid from institutional funds.

GIFT AID (NON-NEED-BASED) ***Total amount:*** $65,068,393 (98% institutional, 2% external sources). ***Receiving aid:*** Freshmen: 30% (643). Undergraduates: 27% (2,444). ***Average award:*** Freshmen: $17,655. Undergraduates: $19,133. ***Scholarships, grants, and awards by category:*** *Academic interests/achievement:* 5,043 awards ($74,375,851 total): agriculture, biological sciences, business, communication, education, engineering/technologies, English, foreign languages, general academic interests/achievements, home economics, humanities, international studies, mathematics, military science, physical sciences, premedicine, religion/biblical studies, social sciences. *Creative arts/performance:* 751 awards ($6,704,856 total): applied art and design, art/fine arts, cinema/film/broadcasting, creative writing, dance, general creative arts/performance, journalism/publications, music, performing arts, theater/drama. *Special achievements/activities:* 1,046 awards ($11,340,038 total): community service, general special achievements/activities, leadership, memberships, religious involvement. *Special characteristics:* 943 awards ($23,472,399 total): adult students, children of educators, children of faculty/staff, children of union members/company employees, children of workers in trades, ethnic background, general special characteristics, handicapped students, international students, local/state students, members of minority groups, previous college experience, relatives of clergy, religious affiliation, veterans. ***Tuition waivers:*** Full or partial for employees or children of employees. ***ROTC:*** Army, Air Force.

LOANS ***Student loans:*** $54,252,701 (52% need-based, 48% non-need-based). 34% of past graduating class borrowed through all loan programs. *Average indebtedness per student:* $47,931. ***Average need-based loan:*** Freshmen: $3112. Undergraduates: $4352. ***Parent loans:*** $22,918,101 (33% need-based, 67% non-need-based). ***Programs:*** Federal Direct (Subsidized and Unsubsidized Stafford, PLUS), Perkins, Federal Nursing, state.

WORK-STUDY ***Federal work-study:*** Total amount: $3,626,776; 1,323 jobs averaging $2370. ***State or other work-study/employment:*** Part-time jobs available.

ATHLETIC AWARDS Total amount: $20,158,104 (35% need-based, 65% non-need-based).

APPLYING FOR FINANCIAL AID ***Required financial aid forms:*** FAFSA, CSS Financial Aid PROFILE, noncustodial (divorced/separated) parent's statement. ***Financial aid deadline:*** 5/1 (priority: 2/1). ***Notification date:*** Continuous beginning 12/1.

CONTACT Victoria Chen, Director of Scholarships and Student Financial Aid, Texas Christian University, PO Box 297012, Fort Worth, TX 76129-0002, 817-257-7858 or toll-free 800-828-3764. *Fax:* 817-257-7462. *E-mail:* v.chen@tcu.edu.
Website: http://www.tcu.edu/.

TEXAS COLLEGE

Tyler, TX

CONTACT Ms. Cecelia K. Jones, Director of Financial Aid, Texas College, 2404 North Grand Avenue, Tyler, TX 75702, 903-593-8311 Ext. 2241 or toll-free 800-306-6299. *Fax:* 903-593-9607. *E-mail:* ckjones@texascollege.edu.
Website: http://www.texascollege.edu/.

TEXAS LUTHERAN UNIVERSITY

Seguin, TX

Tuition & fees: $30,860	Average undergraduate aid package: $26,094

ABOUT THE INSTITUTION Independent Evangelical Lutheran Church, coed. ***Awards:*** bachelor's and master's degrees. 39 undergraduate majors. ***Total enrollment:*** 1,476. Undergraduates: 1,435. Freshmen: 409. Federal methodology is used as a basis for awarding need-based institutional aid.

UNDERGRADUATE EXPENSES for 2019–2020 ***One-time required fee:*** $400. ***Comprehensive fee:*** $41,300 includes full-time tuition ($30,550), mandatory fees ($310), and room and board ($10,440). ***College room only:*** $5870. Full-time tuition and fees vary according to course load. Room and board charges vary according to board plan and housing facility. ***Part-time tuition:*** $1010 per credit hour. ***Part-time fees:*** $155 per term.

FRESHMAN FINANCIAL AID (Fall 2019, est.) 411 applied for aid; of those 88% were deemed to have need. 100% of freshmen with need received aid; of those 20% had need fully met. ***Average percent of need met:*** 82% (excluding resources awarded to replace EFC). ***Average financial aid package:*** $26,997 (excluding resources awarded to replace EFC). 13% of all full-time freshmen had no need and received non-need-based gift aid.

UNDERGRADUATE FINANCIAL AID (Fall 2019, est.) 1,233 applied for aid; of those 88% were deemed to have need. 100% of undergraduates with need received aid; of those 23% had need fully met. ***Average percent of need met:*** 81% (excluding resources awarded to replace EFC). ***Average financial aid package:*** $26,094 (excluding resources awarded to replace EFC). 19% of all full-time undergraduates had no need and received non-need-based gift aid.

GIFT AID (NEED-BASED) ***Receiving aid:*** Freshmen: 87% (363); all full-time undergraduates: 79% (1,087). ***Average award:*** Freshmen: $23,497; Undergraduates: $22,738. ***Scholarships, grants, and awards:*** Federal Pell, FSEOG, state, private, college/university gift aid from institutional funds, TEACH Grants.

GIFT AID (NON-NEED-BASED) ***Receiving aid:*** Freshmen: 13% (53). Undergraduates: 13% (179). ***Average award:*** Freshmen: $17,029. Undergraduates: $17,152. ***Scholarships, grants, and awards by category:*** *Academic interests/achievement:* biological sciences, business, communication, computer science, education, general academic interests/achievements, mathematics. *Creative arts/performance:* journalism/publications, music, performing arts, theater/drama. *Special achievements/activities:* junior miss, leadership, religious involvement. *Special characteristics:* children and siblings of alumni, children of educators, children of faculty/staff, local/state students, relatives of clergy, religious affiliation, veterans. ***Tuition waivers:*** Full or partial for children of alumni, employees or children of employees. ***ROTC:*** Army cooperative, Naval cooperative.

LOANS ***Student loans:*** 76% of past graduating class borrowed through all loan programs. *Average indebtedness per student:* $29,735. ***Average need-based loan:*** Freshmen: $2882. Undergraduates: $3711. ***Programs:*** Federal Direct (Subsidized and Unsubsidized Stafford, PLUS), Perkins, state, private loans.

WORK-STUDY Federal work-study jobs available. ***State or other work-study/employment:*** Part-time jobs available.

APPLYING FOR FINANCIAL AID ***Required financial aid forms:*** FAFSA, TASFA. ***Notification date:*** Continuous.

CONTACT Cathleen Wright, Director of Student Financial Services, Texas Lutheran University, 1000 West Court Street, Seguin, TX 78155-5999, 830-372-8078 or toll-free 800-771-8521. *Fax:* 830-372-8179. *E-mail:* cwright@tlu.edu.
Website: http://www.tlu.edu/.

TEXAS SOUTHERN UNIVERSITY

Houston, TX

ABOUT THE INSTITUTION State-supported, coed. ***Awards:*** certificates, bachelor's, master's, and doctoral degrees. 49 undergraduate majors. ***Total enrollment:*** 1,942. Undergraduates: 7,092. Freshmen: 1,475.

GIFT AID (NEED-BASED) ***Scholarships, grants, and awards:*** Federal Pell, FSEOG, state, private, college/university gift aid from institutional funds, United Negro College Fund, Federal Nursing.

LOANS ***Programs:*** Federal Direct (Subsidized and Unsubsidized Stafford, PLUS), state, college/university.

WORK-STUDY ***Federal work-study:*** Total amount: $686,033; 317 jobs averaging $4000. ***State or other work-study/employment:*** Total amount: $69,422 (100% need-based). 23 part-time jobs averaging $4000.

APPLYING FOR FINANCIAL AID ***Required financial aid forms:*** FAFSA, institution's own form.

CONTACT Financial Aid Office, Texas Southern University, 3100 Cleburne Avenue, Houston, TX 77004-4584, 713-313-7011.
Website: http://www.tsu.edu/.

TEXAS STATE UNIVERSITY

San Marcos, TX

Tuition & fees (TX res): $11,550	Average undergraduate aid package: $11,730

ABOUT THE INSTITUTION State-supported, coed. ***Awards:*** certificates, bachelor's, master's, and doctoral degrees. 90 undergraduate majors. ***Total enrollment:*** 38,187. Undergraduates: 33,917. Freshmen: 6,362. Federal methodology is used as a basis for awarding need-based institutional aid.

UNDERGRADUATE EXPENSES for 2020–2021 ***Application fee:*** $75. ***Tuition, state resident:*** full-time $8920; part-time $297 per credit hour. ***Tuition, nonresident:*** full-time $21,190; part-time $706 per credit hour. ***Required fees:*** full-time $2630; $464 per term. Full-time tuition and fees vary according to course load. Part-time tuition and fees vary according to course load. ***Room only:*** $7646. Room and board charges vary according to board plan and housing facility. ***Payment plan:*** Guaranteed tuition.

FRESHMAN FINANCIAL AID (Fall 2019, est.) 6016 applied for aid; of those 66% were deemed to have need. 97% of freshmen with need received aid; of those 23% had need fully met. ***Average percent of need met:*** 71% (excluding resources awarded to replace EFC). ***Average financial aid package:*** $12,082 (excluding resources awarded to replace EFC). 11% of all full-time freshmen had no need and received non-need-based gift aid.

UNDERGRADUATE FINANCIAL AID (Fall 2019, est.) 27,198 applied for aid; of those 61% were deemed to have need. 97% of undergraduates with need received aid; of those 20% had need fully met. ***Average percent of need met:*** 63% (excluding resources awarded to replace EFC). ***Average financial aid package:*** $11,730 (excluding resources awarded to replace EFC). 5% of all full-time undergraduates had no need and received non-need-based gift aid.

GIFT AID (NEED-BASED) ***Total amount:*** $115,999,047 (50% federal, 46% state, 2% institutional, 2% external sources). ***Receiving aid:*** Freshmen: 54% (3,275); all full-time undergraduates: 47% (13,201). ***Average award:*** Freshmen: $9713; Undergraduates: $8081. ***Scholarships, grants, and awards:*** Federal Pell, FSEOG, state, private, college/university gift aid from institutional funds.

GIFT AID (NON-NEED-BASED) ***Total amount:*** $14,478,001 (51% institutional, 49% external sources). ***Receiving aid:*** Freshmen: 12% (712). Undergraduates: 6% (1,549). ***Average award:*** Freshmen: $3027. Undergraduates: $3395. ***Scholarships, grants, and awards by category:*** *Academic interests/achievement:* 2,202 awards ($6,661,531 total): agriculture, biological sciences, business, communication, computer science, education, engineering/technologies, English, foreign languages, general academic interests/achievements, health fields, home economics, humanities, international studies, mathematics, military science, physical sciences, social sciences. *Creative arts/performance:* 572 awards ($1,606,763 total): applied art and design, art/fine arts, dance, journalism/publications, music, theater/drama. *Special achievements/activities:* 57 awards ($106,200 total): leadership. *Special characteristics:* 1,724 awards ($8,763,357 total): international students, spouses of deceased or disabled public servants, veterans, veterans' children. ***Tuition waivers:*** Full or partial for employees or children of employees. ***ROTC:*** Army, Air Force.

LOANS *Student loans:* $120,058,690 (72% need-based, 28% non-need-based). 65% of past graduating class borrowed through all loan programs. *Average indebtedness per student:* $24,950. ***Average need-based loan:*** Freshmen: $3129. Undergraduates: $4067. ***Parent loans:*** $93,440,689 (25% need-based, 75% non-need-based). ***Programs:*** Federal Direct (Subsidized and Unsubsidized Stafford, PLUS), Perkins, state, college/university, short-term emergency loans.

WORK-STUDY *Federal work-study:* Total amount: $3,744,495; 1,556 jobs averaging $2297. ***State or other work-study/employment:*** Total amount: $158,586 (100% need-based). 43 part-time jobs averaging $3358.

ATHLETIC AWARDS Total amount: $4,205,662 (3% need-based, 97% non-need-based).

APPLYING FOR FINANCIAL AID *Required financial aid form:* FAFSA. ***Financial aid deadline (priority):*** 1/15. ***Notification date:*** Continuous beginning 5/1. Students must reply within 3 weeks of notification.

CONTACT Dr. Chris Murr, Director of Financial Aid, Texas State University, 601 University Drive, San Marcos, TX 78666-4602, 512-245-2315. *Fax:* 512-245-7920. *E-mail:* cm18@txstate.edu.

Website: http://www.txstate.edu/.

TEXAS TECH UNIVERSITY

Lubbock, TX

Tuition & fees (TX res): $11,320	Average undergraduate aid package: $10,477

ABOUT THE INSTITUTION State-supported, coed. ***Awards:*** certificates, bachelor's, master's, and doctoral degrees. 85 undergraduate majors. ***Total enrollment:*** 38,742. Undergraduates: 32,125. Freshmen: 6,145. Federal methodology is used as a basis for awarding need-based institutional aid.

UNDERGRADUATE EXPENSES for 2019–2020 *Application fee:* $75. ***Tuition, state resident:*** full-time $8430; part-time $281 per credit hour. ***Tuition, nonresident:*** full-time $20,880; part-time $696 per credit hour. ***Required fees:*** full-time $2890; $612 per term. Full-time tuition and fees vary according to course load, location, program, and reciprocity agreements. Part-time tuition and fees vary according to course load, location, program, and reciprocity agreements. ***College room and board:*** $9772; ***Room only:*** $6236. Room and board charges vary according to board plan and housing facility.

FRESHMAN FINANCIAL AID (Fall 2019, est.) 4361 applied for aid; of those 68% were deemed to have need. 100% of freshmen with need received aid; of those 26% had need fully met. ***Average percent of need met:*** 69% (excluding resources awarded to replace EFC). ***Average financial aid package:*** $10,479 (excluding resources awarded to replace EFC). 23% of all full-time freshmen had no need and received non-need-based gift aid.

UNDERGRADUATE FINANCIAL AID (Fall 2019, est.) 17,334 applied for aid; of those 78% were deemed to have need. 100% of undergraduates with need received aid; of those 19% had need fully met. ***Average percent of need met:*** 65% (excluding resources awarded to replace EFC). ***Average financial aid package:*** $10,477 (excluding resources awarded to replace EFC). 16% of all full-time undergraduates had no need and received non-need-based gift aid.

GIFT AID (NEED-BASED) *Total amount:* $95,267,525 (39% federal, 14% state, 38% institutional, 9% external sources). ***Receiving aid:*** Freshmen: 44% (2,642); all full-time undergraduates: 41% (11,520). ***Average award:*** Freshmen: $8676; Undergraduates: $8073. ***Scholarships, grants, and awards:*** Federal Pell, FSEOG, state, private, college/university gift aid from institutional funds, Federal Nursing.

GIFT AID (NON-NEED-BASED) *Total amount:* $24,257,120 (1% state, 83% institutional, 16% external sources). ***Receiving aid:*** Freshmen: 3% (209). Undergraduates: 2% (535). ***Average award:*** Freshmen: $4331. Undergraduates: $4463. ***Scholarships, grants, and awards by category:*** *Academic interests/achievement:* agriculture, architecture, biological sciences, business, communication, computer science, education, engineering/technologies, English, foreign languages, general academic interests/achievements, home economics, humanities, international studies, mathematics, military science, physical sciences, premedicine, social sciences. *Creative arts/performance:* applied art and design, art/fine arts, dance, journalism/publications, music, performing arts, theater/drama. *Special achievements/activities:* community service, general special achievements/activities, hobbies/interests, leadership, memberships, rodeo. *Special characteristics:* children of faculty/staff, first-generation college students, handicapped students, out-of-state students, veterans, veterans' children. ***Tuition waivers:*** Full or partial for employees or children of employees, senior citizens. ***ROTC:*** Army, Air Force.

LOANS *Student loans:* $118,517,550 (77% need-based, 23% non-need-based). 55% of past graduating class borrowed through all loan programs. *Average indebtedness per student:* $32,829. ***Average need-based loan:*** Freshmen: $4417. Undergraduates: $5208. ***Parent loans:*** $28,141,973 (72% need-based, 28% non-need-based). ***Programs:*** Federal Direct (Subsidized and Unsubsidized Stafford, PLUS), Perkins, state, college/university, private loans.

WORK-STUDY *Federal work-study:* Total amount: $1,014,932; 315 jobs averaging $3222. ***State or other work-study/employment:*** Total amount: $12,500 (100% need-based). 5 part-time jobs averaging $2500.

ATHLETIC AWARDS Total amount: $4,620,225 (31% need-based, 69% non-need-based).

APPLYING FOR FINANCIAL AID *Required financial aid form:* FAFSA. ***Financial aid deadline (priority):*** 1/15. ***Notification date:*** 12/1. Students must reply within 2 weeks of notification.

CONTACT Shannon Venezia, Executive Director of Student Financial Aid, Texas Tech University, PO Box 45011, Lubbock, TX 79409-5011, 806-742-3681. *Fax:* 806-742-0880.

Website: http://www.ttu.edu/.

TEXAS WESLEYAN UNIVERSITY

Fort Worth, TX

CONTACT Laurie Rosenkrantz, Office of Financial Aid, Texas Wesleyan University, 1201 Wesleyan Street, Fort Worth, TX 76105-1536, 817-531-4420 or toll-free 800-580-8980. *Fax:* 817-531-4231. *E-mail:* financialaid@txwes.edu.

Website: http://www.txwes.edu/.

TEXAS WOMAN'S UNIVERSITY

Denton, TX

Tuition & fees (area res): $9748	Average undergraduate aid package: $14,151

ABOUT THE INSTITUTION State-supported, coed, primarily women. ***Awards:*** certificates, bachelor's, master's, and doctoral degrees. 42 undergraduate majors. ***Total enrollment:*** 15,826. Undergraduates: 10,591. Freshmen: 1,301. Both federal and institutional methodology are used as a basis for awarding need-based institutional aid.

UNDERGRADUATE EXPENSES for 2020–2021 *Application fee:* $50. ***Tuition, area resident:*** full-time $6789; part-time $226 per credit hour. ***Tuition, state resident:*** full-time $6789; part-time $226 per credit hour. ***Tuition, nonresident:*** full-time $19,449; part-time $648 per credit hour. ***Required fees:*** full-time $2959; $98.62 per credit hour. Full-time tuition and fees vary according to course load and program. Part-time tuition and fees vary according to course load and program. ***College room and board:*** $9050. Room and board charges vary according to board plan and housing facility. ***Payment plan:*** Guaranteed tuition.

FRESHMAN FINANCIAL AID (Fall 2018) 1084 applied for aid; of those 81% were deemed to have need. 100% of freshmen with need received aid; of those 36% had need fully met. ***Average percent of need met:*** 87% (excluding resources awarded to replace EFC). ***Average financial aid package:*** $16,016 (excluding resources awarded to replace EFC). 15% of all full-time freshmen had no need and received non-need-based gift aid.

UNDERGRADUATE FINANCIAL AID (Fall 2018) 5,333 applied for aid; of those 86% were deemed to have need. 100% of undergraduates with need received aid; of those 33% had need fully met. ***Average percent of need met:*** 86% (excluding resources awarded to replace EFC). ***Average financial aid package:*** $14,151 (excluding resources awarded to replace EFC). 7% of all full-time undergraduates had no need and received non-need-based gift aid.

GIFT AID (NEED-BASED) *Total amount:* $43,520,272 (42% federal, 23% state, 31% institutional, 4% external sources). ***Receiving aid:*** Freshmen: 70% (855); all full-time undergraduates: 63% (4,352). ***Average award:*** Freshmen: $10,223; Undergraduates: $7877. ***Scholarships, grants, and awards:*** Federal Pell, FSEOG, state, private, college/university gift aid from institutional funds, United Negro College Fund, Federal Nursing.

GIFT AID (NON-NEED-BASED) ***Total amount:*** $11,348,520 (100% institutional). ***Receiving aid:*** Freshmen: 42% (519). Undergraduates: 26% (1,774). ***Average award:*** Freshmen: $4899. Undergraduates: $4465. ***Scholarships, grants, and awards by category:*** *Academic interests/achievement:* 1,776 awards ($2,562,957 total): biological sciences, business, communication, computer science, education, English, foreign languages, general academic interests/achievements, health fields, home economics, humanities, international studies, library science, mathematics, physical sciences, premedicine, social sciences. *Creative arts/performance:* 56 awards ($48,254 total): applied art and design, art/fine arts, cinema/film/broadcasting, dance, journalism/publications, music, performing arts, theater/drama. *Special achievements/activities:* 1,465 awards ($5,095,252 total): general special achievements/activities, hobbies/interests, leadership, memberships, religious involvement. *Special characteristics:* 422 awards ($2,179,808 total): children of faculty/staff, ethnic background, general special characteristics, international students, members of minority groups, out-of-state students, previous college experience, public servants, religious affiliation, veterans. ***Tuition waivers:*** Full or partial for senior citizens. ***ROTC:*** Army cooperative, Naval cooperative, Air Force cooperative.

LOANS ***Student loans:*** $35,043,388 (100% need-based). 66% of past graduating class borrowed through all loan programs. *Average indebtedness per student:* $22,206. ***Average need-based loan:*** Freshmen: $5365. Undergraduates: $6766. ***Parent loans:*** $1,793,362 (100% need-based). ***Programs:*** Federal Direct (Subsidized and Unsubsidized Stafford, PLUS), Perkins, Federal Nursing, state, college/university, alternative loans.

WORK-STUDY ***Federal work-study:*** Total amount: $893,533; 262 jobs averaging $3410. ***State or other work-study/employment:*** Total amount: $2,666,292 (3% need-based, 97% non-need-based). 65 part-time jobs averaging $1152.

ATHLETIC AWARDS Total amount: $577,290 (100% need-based).

APPLYING FOR FINANCIAL AID ***Required financial aid form:*** FAFSA. ***Financial aid deadline:*** 3/15 (priority: 1/15). ***Notification date:*** Continuous beginning 3/15. Students must reply by 8/31.

CONTACT Ms. Lacey Thompson, Executive Director of Financial Aid, Texas Woman's University, PO Box 425408, Denton, TX 76204-5408, 940-898-3064 or toll-free 866-809-6130. *Fax:* 940-898-3068. *E-mail:* finaid@twu.edu.
Website: http://www.twu.edu/.

THEOLOGICAL UNIVERSITY OF THE CARIBBEAN

Saint Just, PR

ABOUT THE INSTITUTION Independent Pentecostal, coed. ***Awards:*** certificates, diplomas, associate, bachelor's, and master's degrees. 6 undergraduate majors. ***Total enrollment:*** 372. Undergraduates: 265. Freshmen: 48.

GIFT AID (NEED-BASED) ***Scholarships, grants, and awards:*** Federal Pell.

LOANS ***Programs:*** Federal Direct (Subsidized and Unsubsidized Stafford).

CONTACT Mrs. Alma Ramos Ortiz, Financial Aid Officer, Theological University of the Caribbean, PO Box 901, Saint Just, PR 00978-0901, 787-761-0640 Ext. 224. *Fax:* 787-748-9220. *E-mail:* asistenciaeconomica@utcpr.edu.
Website: http://www.utcpr.edu/.

THIEL COLLEGE

Greenville, PA

CONTACT Ms. Cynthia H. Farrell, Director of Financial Aid, Thiel College, 75 College Avenue, Greenville, PA 16125-2181, 724-589-2178 or toll-free 800-248-4435. *Fax:* 724-589-2790. *E-mail:* cfarrell@thiel.edu.
Website: http://www.thiel.edu/.

THOMAS AQUINAS COLLEGE - CALIFORNIA

Santa Paula, CA

Tuition & fees: $25,600	Average undergraduate aid package: $21,367

ABOUT THE INSTITUTION Independent Roman Catholic, coed. ***Awards:*** bachelor's degrees. 1 undergraduate major. Both federal and institutional methodology are used as a basis for awarding need-based institutional aid.

UNDERGRADUATE EXPENSES for 2019–2020 ***Comprehensive fee:*** $34,400 includes full-time tuition ($25,600) and room and board ($8800).

FRESHMAN FINANCIAL AID (Fall 2019, est.) 69 applied for aid; of those 94% were deemed to have need. 100% of freshmen with need received aid; of those 100% had need fully met. ***Average percent of need met:*** 100% (excluding resources awarded to replace EFC). ***Average financial aid package:*** $21,627 (excluding resources awarded to replace EFC).

UNDERGRADUATE FINANCIAL AID (Fall 2019, est.) 276 applied for aid; of those 97% were deemed to have need. 100% of undergraduates with need received aid; of those 100% had need fully met. ***Average percent of need met:*** 100% (excluding resources awarded to replace EFC). ***Average financial aid package:*** $21,367 (excluding resources awarded to replace EFC).

GIFT AID (NEED-BASED) ***Receiving aid:*** Freshmen: 63% (59); all full-time undergraduates: 58% (221). ***Average award:*** Freshmen: $14,359; Undergraduates: $14,019. ***Scholarships, grants, and awards:*** Federal Pell, state, private, college/university gift aid from institutional funds, Canadian federal and provincial grants and scholarships.

LOANS ***Student loans:*** 82% of past graduating class borrowed through all loan programs. *Average indebtedness per student:* $18,967. ***Average need-based loan:*** Freshmen: $3337. Undergraduates: $4504. ***Programs:*** Federal Direct (Subsidized and Unsubsidized Stafford, PLUS), college/university, Canadian student loans.

WORK-STUDY ***State or other work-study/employment:*** 252 part-time jobs averaging $5625.

APPLYING FOR FINANCIAL AID ***Required financial aid forms:*** FAFSA, CSS Financial Aid PROFILE, state aid form, noncustodial (divorced/separated) parent's statement, federal income tax form(s), W-2 forms. ***Notification date:*** Continuous. Students must reply within 2 weeks of notification.

CONTACT Mr. Gregory Becher, Director of Financial Aid, Thomas Aquinas College - California, 10000 Ojai Road, Santa Paula, CA 93060-9980, 805-525-4419 Ext. 5936 or toll-free 800-634-9797. *Fax:* 805-525-9342. *E-mail:* gbecher@thomasaquinas.edu.
Website: http://www.thomasaquinas.edu/.

THOMAS AQUINAS COLLEGE - NEW ENGLAND

Northfield, MA

Tuition & fees: N/R	Average undergraduate aid package: $23,412

ABOUT THE INSTITUTION Independent Roman Catholic, coed. Both federal and institutional methodology are used as a basis for awarding need-based institutional aid.

FRESHMAN FINANCIAL AID (Fall 2019, est.) 20 applied for aid; of those 95% were deemed to have need. 100% of freshmen with need received aid; of those 100% had need fully met. ***Average percent of need met:*** 100% (excluding resources awarded to replace EFC). ***Average financial aid package:*** $21,461 (excluding resources awarded to replace EFC).

UNDERGRADUATE FINANCIAL AID (Fall 2019, est.) 47 applied for aid; of those 96% were deemed to have need. 100% of undergraduates with need received aid; of those 100% had need fully met. ***Average percent of need met:*** 100% (excluding resources awarded to replace EFC). ***Average financial aid package:*** $23,412 (excluding resources awarded to replace EFC).

GIFT AID (NEED-BASED) ***Receiving aid:*** Freshmen: 74% (17); all full-time undergraduates: 71% (41). ***Average award:*** Freshmen: $14,072; Undergraduates: $15,330. ***Scholarships, grants, and awards:*** Federal Pell, state, private, college/university gift aid from institutional funds, Canadian federal and provincial grants and scholarships.

LOANS ***Average need-based loan:*** Freshmen: $3395. Undergraduates: $3844. ***Programs:*** Federal Direct (Subsidized and Unsubsidized Stafford, PLUS), college/university, Canadian student loans.

WORK-STUDY ***State or other work-study/employment:*** 44 part-time jobs averaging $5710.

APPLYING FOR FINANCIAL AID ***Required financial aid forms:*** FAFSA, CSS Financial Aid PROFILE, state aid form, noncustodial (divorced/separated) parent's statement, federal income tax form(s), W-2 form(s). ***Financial aid deadline:*** Continuous. ***Notification date:*** Students must reply within 2 weeks of notification.

CONTACT Mr. Gregory Becher, Director of Financial Aid, Thomas Aquinas College - New England, 10000 Ojai Rd., Santa Paula, CA 93060, 805-525-4419 Ext. 5936. *Fax:* 805-525-9342. *E-mail:* gbecher@thomasaquinas.edu.
Website: http://www.thomasaquinas.edu/.

THOMAS COLLEGE

Waterville, ME

Tuition & fees: N/R	Average undergraduate aid package: $22,254

ABOUT THE INSTITUTION Independent, coed. ***Awards:*** associate, bachelor's, and master's degrees. 23 undergraduate majors. Federal methodology is used as a basis for awarding need-based institutional aid.

FRESHMAN FINANCIAL AID (Fall 2019, est.) 210 applied for aid; of those 93% were deemed to have need. 100% of freshmen with need received aid; of those 12% had need fully met. ***Average percent of need met:*** 85% (excluding resources awarded to replace EFC). ***Average financial aid package:*** $24,490 (excluding resources awarded to replace EFC). 8% of all full-time freshmen had no need and received non-need-based gift aid.

UNDERGRADUATE FINANCIAL AID (Fall 2019, est.) 671 applied for aid; of those 93% were deemed to have need. 100% of undergraduates with need received aid; of those 15% had need fully met. ***Average percent of need met:*** 85% (excluding resources awarded to replace EFC). ***Average financial aid package:*** $22,254 (excluding resources awarded to replace EFC). 11% of all full-time undergraduates had no need and received non-need-based gift aid.

GIFT AID (NEED-BASED) ***Receiving aid:*** Freshmen: 91% (194); all full-time undergraduates: 86% (617). ***Average award:*** Freshmen: $20,781; Undergraduates: $17,789. ***Scholarships, grants, and awards:*** Federal Pell, FSEOG, state, private, college/university gift aid from institutional funds.

GIFT AID (NON-NEED-BASED) ***Receiving aid:*** Freshmen: 27% (57). Undergraduates: 17% (121). ***Average award:*** Freshmen: $11,782. Undergraduates: $11,701. ***Scholarships, grants, and awards by category:*** *Academic interests/achievement:* 620 awards ($6,383,599 total): general academic interests/achievements. *Special characteristics:* children and siblings of alumni, children of current students, children of faculty/staff, local/state students, out-of-state students, veterans.

LOANS ***Student loans:*** 94% of past graduating class borrowed through all loan programs. *Average indebtedness per student:* $35,068. ***Average need-based loan:*** Freshmen: $3453. Undergraduates: $2298. ***Programs:*** Federal Direct (Subsidized and Unsubsidized Stafford, PLUS), state.

WORK-STUDY ***Federal work-study:*** 103 jobs averaging $2976.

APPLYING FOR FINANCIAL AID ***Required financial aid form:*** FAFSA. ***Notification date:*** Continuous. Students must reply within 2 weeks of notification.

CONTACT Jeannine Ross, Senior Director of Student Financial Services, Thomas College, 180 West River Road, Waterville, ME 04901-5097, 800-339-7001. *Fax:* 207-859-1115. *E-mail:* sfsdir@thomas.edu.
Website: http://www.thomas.edu/.

THOMAS EDISON STATE UNIVERSITY

Trenton, NJ

ABOUT THE INSTITUTION State-supported, coed. ***Awards:*** certificates, associate, bachelor's, master's, and doctoral degrees (offers only distance learning degree programs). 27 undergraduate majors. ***Total enrollment:*** 10,934. Undergraduates: 15,238.

GIFT AID (NEED-BASED) ***Scholarships, grants, and awards:*** Federal Pell, state.

GIFT AID (NON-NEED-BASED) ***Scholarships, grants, and awards by category:*** *Academic interests/achievement:* general academic interests/achievements.

LOANS ***Programs:*** Federal Direct (Subsidized and Unsubsidized Stafford, PLUS), state, private loans.

CONTACT Mr. James Owens, Director of Financial Aid, Thomas Edison State University, 111 West State Street, Trenton, NJ 08608, 609-777-5680 or toll-free 888-442-8372. *E-mail:* finaid@tesu.edu.
Website: http://www.tesu.edu/.

THOMAS JEFFERSON UNIVERSITY

Philadelphia, PA

Tuition & fees: N/R	Average undergraduate aid package: $28,738

ABOUT THE INSTITUTION Independent, coed. ***Awards:*** certificates, associate, bachelor's, master's, and doctoral degrees. 7 undergraduate majors. Federal methodology is used as a basis for awarding need-based institutional aid.

FRESHMAN FINANCIAL AID (Fall 2018) 527 applied for aid; of those 91% were deemed to have need. 100% of freshmen with need received aid; of those 21% had need fully met. ***Average percent of need met:*** 82% (excluding resources awarded to replace EFC). ***Average financial aid package:*** $39,621 (excluding resources awarded to replace EFC). 13% of all full-time freshmen had no need and received non-need-based gift aid.

UNDERGRADUATE FINANCIAL AID (Fall 2018) 2,648 applied for aid; of those 92% were deemed to have need. 100% of undergraduates with need received aid; of those 12% had need fully met. ***Average percent of need met:*** 60% (excluding resources awarded to replace EFC). ***Average financial aid package:*** $28,738 (excluding resources awarded to replace EFC). 11% of all full-time undergraduates had no need and received non-need-based gift aid.

GIFT AID (NEED-BASED) ***Total amount:*** $48,813,130 (12% federal, 5% state, 82% institutional, 1% external sources). ***Receiving aid:*** Freshmen: 86% (481); all full-time undergraduates: 71% (2,093). ***Average award:*** Freshmen: $32,612; Undergraduates: $21,865. ***Scholarships, grants, and awards:*** Federal Pell, FSEOG, state, private, college/university gift aid from institutional funds.

GIFT AID (NON-NEED-BASED) ***Total amount:*** $5,915,933 (7% federal, 92% institutional, 1% external sources). ***Receiving aid:*** Freshmen: 12% (69). Undergraduates: 9% (263). ***Average award:*** Freshmen: $16,018. Undergraduates: $11,645. ***Scholarships, grants, and awards by category:*** *Academic interests/achievement:* general academic interests/achievements. *Special characteristics:* members of minority groups, veterans. **ROTC:** Air Force cooperative.

LOANS ***Student loans:*** $36,451,055 (84% need-based, 16% non-need-based). ***Average need-based loan:*** Freshmen: $3323. Undergraduates: $4801. ***Parent loans:*** $9,867,020 (53% need-based, 47% non-need-based). ***Programs:*** Federal Direct (Subsidized and Unsubsidized Stafford, PLUS), Perkins.

WORK-STUDY ***Federal work-study:*** Total amount: $2,043,337; jobs available. ***State or other work-study/employment:*** Total amount: $536,904 (82% need-based, 18% non-need-based). Part-time jobs available.

ATHLETIC AWARDS Total amount: $3,318,861 (50% need-based, 50% non-need-based).

APPLYING FOR FINANCIAL AID ***Required financial aid forms:*** FAFSA, state aid form. ***Financial aid deadline:*** 4/15 (priority: 12/15). ***Notification date:*** Continuous beginning 12/15. Students must reply by 5/1.

CONTACT Office of Financial Aid, Thomas Jefferson University, 4201 Henry Avenue, Philadelphia, PA 19144, 215-951-2800 or toll-free 877-533-3247. *E-mail:* financial.aid@jefferson.edu.
Website: http://www.jefferson.edu/university.html.

THOMAS MORE COLLEGE OF LIBERAL ARTS

Merrimack, NH

CONTACT Clinton A. Hanson Jr., Coordinator of Financial Aid, Thomas More College of Liberal Arts, 6 Manchester Street, Merrimack, NH 03054-4818, 603-880-8308 Ext. 23 or toll-free 800-880-8308. *Fax:* 603-880-9280. *E-mail:* chanson@thomasmorecollege.edu.
Website: http://www.thomasmorecollege.edu/.

THOMAS MORE UNIVERSITY

Crestview Hills, KY

Tuition & fees: N/R	Average undergraduate aid package: $23,793

ABOUT THE INSTITUTION Independent Roman Catholic, coed. ***Awards:*** certificates, associate, bachelor's, and master's degrees. 48 undergraduate majors. ***Total enrollment:*** 2,254. Undergraduates: 1,821. Freshmen: 414. Federal methodology is used as a basis for awarding need-based institutional aid.

FRESHMAN FINANCIAL AID (Fall 2019, est.) 348 applied for aid; of those 89% were deemed to have need. 100% of freshmen with need received aid; of those 29% had need fully met. ***Average percent of need met:*** 74% (excluding resources awarded to replace EFC). ***Average financial aid package:*** $24,509 (excluding resources awarded to replace EFC). 16% of all full-time freshmen had no need and received non-need-based gift aid.

UNDERGRADUATE FINANCIAL AID (Fall 2019, est.) 1,177 applied for aid; of those 89% were deemed to have need. 99% of undergraduates with need received aid; of those 27% had need fully met. ***Average percent of need met:*** 73% (excluding resources awarded to replace EFC). ***Average financial aid package:*** $23,793 (excluding resources awarded to replace EFC). 17% of all full-time undergraduates had no need and received non-need-based gift aid.

GIFT AID (NEED-BASED) ***Total amount:*** $19,648,571 (12% federal, 13% state, 74% institutional, 1% external sources). ***Receiving aid:*** Freshmen: 83% (307); all full-time undergraduates: 77% (1,013). ***Average award:*** Freshmen: $19,622; Undergraduates: $19,113. ***Scholarships, grants, and awards:*** Federal Pell, FSEOG, state, private, college/university gift aid from institutional funds, Federal Nursing.

GIFT AID (NON-NEED-BASED) ***Total amount:*** $4,735,730 (4% state, 94% institutional, 2% external sources). ***Receiving aid:*** Freshmen: 17% (61). Undergraduates: 12% (164). ***Average award:*** Freshmen: $17,724. Undergraduates: $16,564. ***Scholarships, grants, and awards by category:*** *Academic interests/achievement:* 1,130 awards ($13,401,071 total): biological sciences, business, communication, computer science, education, English, general academic interests/achievements, mathematics, physical sciences, premedicine, religion/biblical studies, social sciences. *Creative arts/performance:* 174 awards ($404,456 total): art/fine arts, dance, music, theater/drama. *Special achievements/activities:* 157 awards ($300,700 total): cheerleading/drum major, community service, leadership, memberships, religious involvement. *Special characteristics:* 761 awards ($4,694,371 total): adult students, children and siblings of alumni, children of current students, children of faculty/staff, children of union members/company employees, international students, members of minority groups, out-of-state students, religious affiliation, siblings of current students, veterans, veterans' children. ***ROTC:*** Army cooperative, Air Force cooperative.

LOANS ***Student loans:*** $8,259,742 (68% need-based, 32% non-need-based). 70% of past graduating class borrowed through all loan programs. *Average indebtedness per student:* $33,687. ***Average need-based loan:*** Freshmen: $3059. Undergraduates: $3728. ***Parent loans:*** $2,355,754 (44% need-based, 56% non-need-based). ***Programs:*** Federal Direct (Subsidized and Unsubsidized Stafford, PLUS), Federal Nursing, college/university.

WORK-STUDY ***Federal work-study:*** Total amount: $167,640; 179 jobs averaging $937. ***State or other work-study/employment:*** 255 part-time jobs averaging $743.

ATHLETIC AWARDS Total amount: $768,691 (9% need-based, 91% non-need-based).

APPLYING FOR FINANCIAL AID ***Required financial aid form:*** FAFSA. ***Financial aid deadline (priority):*** 3/15. ***Notification date:*** Continuous beginning 3/1. Students must reply by 5/1.

CONTACT Mr. Mark Messingschlager, Director of Financial Aid, Thomas More University, 333 Thomas More Parkway, Crestview Hills, KY 41017-3495, 859-344-3506 or toll-free 800-825-4557. *Fax:* 859-344-4050. *E-mail:* messinm@thomasmore.edu.
Website: http://www.thomasmore.edu/.

THOMAS UNIVERSITY

Thomasville, GA

CONTACT Mr. Clifton L. Mitchell Jr., Director of Financial Aid, Thomas University, 1501 Millpond Road, Thomasville, GA 31792-7499, 229-226-1621 Ext. 1002 or toll-free 800-538-9784. *Fax:* 229-584-2400. *E-mail:* cmitchell@thomasu.edu.
Website: http://www.thomasu.edu/.

TIFFIN UNIVERSITY

Tiffin, OH

Tuition & fees: $27,610	Average undergraduate aid package: $19,763

ABOUT THE INSTITUTION Independent, coed. ***Awards:*** certificates, associate, bachelor's, master's, and doctoral degrees. 65 undergraduate majors. ***Total enrollment:*** 3,013. Undergraduates: 2,206. Freshmen: 439. Federal methodology is used as a basis for awarding need-based institutional aid.

UNDERGRADUATE EXPENSES for 2020–2021 ***Application fee:*** $20. ***Comprehensive fee:*** $39,310 includes full-time tuition ($27,210), mandatory fees ($400), and room and board ($11,700). ***College room only:*** $6180. Room and board charges vary according to board plan and housing facility. ***Part-time tuition:*** $907 per credit hour. ***Part-time fees:*** $400 per term.

FRESHMAN FINANCIAL AID (Fall 2019, est.) 407 applied for aid; of those 90% were deemed to have need. 100% of freshmen with need received aid; of those 14% had need fully met. ***Average percent of need met:*** 65% (excluding resources awarded to replace EFC). ***Average financial aid package:*** $20,530 (excluding resources awarded to replace EFC).

UNDERGRADUATE FINANCIAL AID (Fall 2019, est.) 1,412 applied for aid; of those 91% were deemed to have need. 100% of undergraduates with need received aid; of those 15% had need fully met. ***Average percent of need met:*** 64% (excluding resources awarded to replace EFC). ***Average financial aid package:*** $19,763 (excluding resources awarded to replace EFC).

GIFT AID (NEED-BASED) ***Total amount:*** $21,176,603 (19% federal, 8% state, 72% institutional, 1% external sources). ***Receiving aid:*** Freshmen: 84% (365); all full-time undergraduates: 76% (1,244). ***Average award:*** Freshmen: $17,453; Undergraduates: $16,402. ***Scholarships, grants, and awards:*** Federal Pell, FSEOG, state, private, college/university gift aid from institutional funds, United Negro College Fund.

GIFT AID (NON-NEED-BASED) ***Receiving aid:*** Freshmen: 8% (37). Undergraduates: 8% (134). ***Scholarships, grants, and awards by category:*** *Academic interests/achievement:* general academic interests/achievements. *Creative arts/performance:* music, performing arts, theater/drama. *Special achievements/activities:* cheerleading/drum major. *Special characteristics:* children of faculty/staff. ***ROTC:*** Army cooperative, Air Force cooperative.

LOANS ***Student loans:*** $12,845,556 (100% need-based). 73% of past graduating class borrowed through all loan programs. *Average indebtedness per student:* $31,788. ***Average need-based loan:*** Freshmen: $2996. Undergraduates: $3992. ***Parent loans:*** $4,432,535 (100% need-based). ***Programs:*** Federal Direct (Subsidized and Unsubsidized Stafford, PLUS).

WORK-STUDY ***Federal work-study:*** Total amount: $361,536; jobs available.

ATHLETIC AWARDS Total amount: $3,993,274 (100% need-based).

APPLYING FOR FINANCIAL AID ***Required financial aid form:*** FAFSA. ***Financial aid deadline:*** Continuous. ***Notification date:*** Continuous beginning 11/15. Students must reply within 2 weeks of notification.

CONTACT Ms. Cindy Little, Director of Financial Aid Operations, Tiffin University, 155 Miami Street, Tiffin, OH 44883, 419-448-3415 or toll-free 800-968-6446. *Fax:* 419-443-5006. *E-mail:* clittle@tiffin.edu.
Website: http://www.tiffin.edu/.

TOCCOA FALLS COLLEGE

Toccoa Falls, GA

Tuition & fees: $21,120 | **Average undergraduate aid package: $20,208**

ABOUT THE INSTITUTION Independent interdenominational, coed. ***Awards:*** certificates, associate, and bachelor's degrees. 31 undergraduate majors. ***Total enrollment:*** 1,833. Undergraduates: 1,833. Freshmen: 218. Federal methodology is used as a basis for awarding need-based institutional aid.

UNDERGRADUATE EXPENSES for 2020–2021 ***Application fee:*** $30. ***Comprehensive fee:*** $29,620 includes full-time tuition ($21,120) and room and board ($8500). ***Part-time tuition:*** $880 per credit hour.

FRESHMAN FINANCIAL AID (Fall 2019, est.) 168 applied for aid; of those 90% were deemed to have need. 100% of freshmen with need received aid; of those 13% had need fully met. ***Average percent of need met:*** 67% (excluding resources awarded to replace EFC). ***Average financial aid package:*** $19,857 (excluding resources awarded to replace EFC). 12% of all full-time freshmen had no need and received non-need-based gift aid.

UNDERGRADUATE FINANCIAL AID (Fall 2019, est.) 634 applied for aid; of those 91% were deemed to have need. 100% of undergraduates with need received aid; of those 15% had need fully met. ***Average percent of need met:*** 69% (excluding resources awarded to replace EFC). ***Average financial aid package:*** $20,208 (excluding resources awarded to replace EFC). 11% of all full-time undergraduates had no need and received non-need-based gift aid.

GIFT AID (NEED-BASED) ***Total amount:*** $9,176,320 (19% federal, 12% state, 66% institutional, 3% external sources). ***Receiving aid:*** Freshmen: 88% (151); all full-time undergraduates: 89% (574). ***Average award:*** Freshmen: $15,720; Undergraduates: $16,076. ***Scholarships, grants, and awards:*** Federal Pell, FSEOG, state, private, college/university gift aid from institutional funds.

GIFT AID (NON-NEED-BASED) ***Total amount:*** $1,516,849 (26% state, 68% institutional, 6% external sources). ***Receiving aid:*** Freshmen: 9% (15). Undergraduates: 11% (68). ***Average award:*** Freshmen: $10,837. Undergraduates: $11,253. ***Scholarships, grants, and awards by category:*** *Academic interests/achievement:* business, communication, education, English, general academic interests/achievements, international studies, mathematics, religion/biblical studies. *Creative arts/performance:* music. *Special achievements/activities:* leadership. *Special characteristics:* children of faculty/staff, ethnic background, general special characteristics, international students, married students, relatives of clergy, religious affiliation, siblings of current students, veterans. ***Tuition waivers:*** Full or partial for employees or children of employees.

LOANS ***Student loans:*** $3,944,706 (79% need-based, 21% non-need-based). ***Average need-based loan:*** Freshmen: $3703. Undergraduates: $3885. ***Parent loans:*** $1,293,715 (57% need-based, 43% non-need-based). ***Programs:*** Federal Direct (Subsidized and Unsubsidized Stafford, PLUS), state, college/university.

WORK-STUDY ***Federal work-study:*** Total amount: $539,207; jobs available.

APPLYING FOR FINANCIAL AID ***Required financial aid forms:*** FAFSA, institution's own form, state aid form. ***Financial aid deadline (priority):*** 5/1. ***Notification date:*** Continuous beginning 3/15. Students must reply within 2 weeks of notification.

CONTACT Mrs. Wanda V. Pickens, Director of Student Financial Services, Toccoa Falls College, 107 Kincaid Drive, Box 900, Toccoa Falls, GA 30598, 706-886-7299 Ext. 5435 or toll-free 888-785-5624. *Fax:* 706-282-6041. *E-mail:* wpickens@tfc.edu.
Website: http://www.tfc.edu/.

TORAH TEMIMAH TALMUDICAL SEMINARY

Brooklyn, NY

CONTACT Financial Aid Office, Torah Temimah Talmudical Seminary, 507 Ocean Parkway, Brooklyn, NY 11218-5913, 718-853-8500.

TOUGALOO COLLEGE

Tougaloo, MS

CONTACT Director of Financial Aid, Tougaloo College, 500 West County Line Road, Tougaloo, MS 39174, 601-977-6134 or toll-free 888-42GALOO. *Fax:* 601-977-6164.
Website: http://www.tougaloo.edu/.

TOURO COLLEGE

New York, NY

CONTACT Karyn Wright-Moore, Office of Financial Aid, Touro College, 27 West 23rd Street, New York, NY 10010, 212-463-0400 Ext. 5108. *E-mail:* karyn.wright-moore4@touro.edu.
Website: http://www.touro.edu/.

TOURO COLLEGE LOS ANGELES

West Hollywood, CA

CONTACT Financial Aid Office, Touro College Los Angeles, 1317 North Crescent Heights Boulevard, West Hollywood, CA 90046, 323-822-9700.
Website: http://www.touro.edu/losangeles/.

TOURO UNIVERSITY WORLDWIDE

Los Alamitos, CA

CONTACT Financial Aid Office, Touro University Worldwide, 10601 Calle Lee, Suite 179, Los Alamitos, CA 90720, 818-575-6800.
Website: http://www.tuw.edu/.

TOWSON UNIVERSITY

Towson, MD

Tuition & fees (MD res): $10,198 | **Average undergraduate aid package: $11,275**

ABOUT THE INSTITUTION State-supported, coed. ***Awards:*** certificates, bachelor's, master's, and doctoral degrees. 61 undergraduate majors. ***Total enrollment:*** 22,709. Undergraduates: 19,619. Freshmen: 2,795. Federal methodology is used as a basis for awarding need-based institutional aid.

UNDERGRADUATE EXPENSES for 2019–2020 ***Application fee:*** $45. ***Tuition, state resident:*** full-time $6962; part-time $299 per credit hour. ***Tuition, nonresident:*** full-time $21,098; part-time $888 per credit hour. ***Required fees:*** full-time $3236; $147 per credit hour. Full-time tuition and fees vary according to course load and location. Part-time tuition and fees vary according to course load and location. ***College room and board:*** $13,446; ***Room only:*** $7446. Room and board charges vary according to board plan and housing facility.

FRESHMAN FINANCIAL AID (Fall 2019, est.) 2494 applied for aid; of those 68% were deemed to have need. 94% of freshmen with need received aid; of those 11% had need fully met. ***Average percent of need met:*** 60% (excluding resources awarded to replace EFC). ***Average financial aid package:*** $11,875 (excluding resources awarded to replace EFC). 11% of all full-time freshmen had no need and received non-need-based gift aid.

UNDERGRADUATE FINANCIAL AID (Fall 2019, est.) 13,094 applied for aid; of those 75% were deemed to have need. 95% of undergraduates with need received aid; of those 9% had need fully met. ***Average percent of need met:*** 59% (excluding resources awarded to replace EFC). ***Average financial aid package:*** $11,275 (excluding resources awarded to replace EFC). 7% of all full-time undergraduates had no need and received non-need-based gift aid.

GIFT AID (NEED-BASED) ***Total amount:*** $67,365,551 (44% federal, 24% state, 31% institutional, 1% external sources). ***Receiving aid:*** Freshmen: 34% (953); all full-time undergraduates: 36% (6,233). ***Average award:*** Freshmen: $11,372; Undergraduates: $9793. ***Scholarships, grants, and awards:*** Federal Pell, FSEOG, state, private, college/university gift aid from institutional funds.

GIFT AID (NON-NEED-BASED) ***Total amount:*** $14,743,278 (2% federal, 10% state, 71% institutional, 17% external sources). ***Receiving aid:*** Freshmen: 24% (661). Undergraduates: 14% (2,439). ***Average award:*** Freshmen: $5373. Undergraduates: $5038. ***Scholarships, grants, and awards by category:*** *Academic interests/achievement:* 2,047 awards ($8,990,092 total): biological sciences, business, communication, computer science, education, English, foreign languages, general academic interests/achievements, home economics, mathematics, physical sciences. *Creative arts/performance:* 172 awards ($624,879 total): art/fine arts, dance, debating, music, performing arts, theater/drama. *Special achievements/activities:* 50 awards ($55,500 total): community service, memberships. *Special characteristics:* 596 awards ($2,232,047 total): adult students, children and siblings of alumni, ethnic background, first-generation college students, handicapped students, international students, members of minority groups, previous college experience, veterans. ***Tuition waivers:*** Full or partial for employees or children of employees, senior citizens. ***ROTC:*** Army cooperative, Air Force cooperative.

LOANS ***Student loans:*** $80,138,409 (47% need-based, 53% non-need-based). 60% of past graduating class borrowed through all loan programs. *Average indebtedness per student:* $27,610. ***Average need-based loan:*** Freshmen: $3030. Undergraduates: $4200. ***Parent loans:*** $40,896,332 (1% need-based, 99% non-need-based). ***Programs:*** Federal Direct (Subsidized and Unsubsidized Stafford, PLUS).

WORK-STUDY ***Federal work-study:*** Total amount: $2,180,486; 824 jobs averaging $2596.

ATHLETIC AWARDS Total amount: $7,127,146 (3% need-based, 97% non-need-based).

APPLYING FOR FINANCIAL AID ***Required financial aid forms:*** FAFSA, state aid form. ***Financial aid deadline (priority):*** 1/15. ***Notification date:*** Continuous beginning 3/15. Students must reply by 5/1 or within 2 weeks of notification.

CONTACT Mr. David Horne, Director of Financial Aid, Towson University, 8000 York Road, Towson, MD 21252-0001, 410-704-4236. *E-mail:* finaid@towson.edu. *Website:* http://www.towson.edu/.

TRANSYLVANIA UNIVERSITY

Lexington, KY

Tuition & fees: $41,610 — **Average undergraduate aid package: $30,215**

ABOUT THE INSTITUTION Independent Christian Church (Disciples of Christ), coed. ***Awards:*** bachelor's degrees. 35 undergraduate majors. ***Total enrollment:*** 949. Undergraduates: 949. Freshmen: 284. Federal methodology is used as a basis for awarding need-based institutional aid.

UNDERGRADUATE EXPENSES for 2020–2021 ***Comprehensive fee:*** $52,920 includes full-time tuition ($39,920), mandatory fees ($1690), and room and board ($11,310). ***College room only:*** $6260. Room and board charges vary according to board plan and housing facility. ***Part-time tuition:*** $4450 per course. Part-time tuition and fees vary according to course load.

FRESHMAN FINANCIAL AID (Fall 2019, est.) 256 applied for aid; of those 84% were deemed to have need. 100% of freshmen with need received aid; of those 24% had need fully met. ***Average percent of need met:*** 79% (excluding resources awarded to replace EFC). ***Average financial aid package:*** $30,248 (excluding resources awarded to replace EFC). 19% of all full-time freshmen had no need and received non-need-based gift aid.

UNDERGRADUATE FINANCIAL AID (Fall 2019, est.) 795 applied for aid; of those 86% were deemed to have need. 100% of undergraduates with need received aid; of those 26% had need fully met. ***Average percent of need met:*** 78% (excluding resources awarded to replace EFC). ***Average financial aid package:*** $30,215 (excluding resources awarded to replace EFC). 27% of all full-time undergraduates had no need and received non-need-based gift aid.

GIFT AID (NEED-BASED) ***Total amount:*** $17,753,226 (7% federal, 14% state, 77% institutional, 2% external sources). ***Receiving aid:*** Freshmen: 80% (216); all full-time undergraduates: 72% (678). ***Average award:*** Freshmen: $27,503; Undergraduates: $26,730. ***Scholarships, grants, and awards:*** Federal Pell, FSEOG, state, private, college/university gift aid from institutional funds.

GIFT AID (NON-NEED-BASED) ***Total amount:*** $6,568,470 (9% state, 87% institutional, 4% external sources). ***Receiving aid:*** Freshmen: 17% (46). Undergraduates: 13% (125). ***Average award:*** Freshmen: $20,765. Undergraduates: $18,926. ***Scholarships, grants, and awards by category:*** *Academic interests/achievement:* general academic interests/achievements. *Creative arts/performance:* applied art and design, music, theater/drama. *Special achievements/activities:* general special achievements/activities. *Special characteristics:* children of faculty/staff, ethnic background, members of minority groups, out-of-state students, relatives of clergy, religious affiliation. ***Tuition waivers:*** Full or partial for employees or children of employees. ***ROTC:*** Army cooperative, Air Force cooperative.

LOANS ***Student loans:*** $5,318,172 (63% need-based, 37% non-need-based). 65% of past graduating class borrowed through all loan programs. *Average indebtedness per student:* $30,826. ***Average need-based loan:*** Freshmen: $3041. Undergraduates: $3975. ***Parent loans:*** $2,683,897 (41% need-based, 59% non-need-based). ***Programs:*** Federal Direct (Subsidized and Unsubsidized Stafford, PLUS).

WORK-STUDY ***Federal work-study:*** Total amount: $391,895; jobs available. ***State or other work-study/employment:*** Total amount: $206,390 (52% need-based, 48% non-need-based). Part-time jobs available.

APPLYING FOR FINANCIAL AID ***Required financial aid form:*** FAFSA. ***Financial aid deadline:*** Continuous. ***Notification date:*** Continuous beginning 1/20. Students must reply by 5/1.

CONTACT Ms. Jennifer Priest, Director of Financial Aid, Transylvania University, 300 North Broadway, Lexington, KY 40508-1797, 859-233-8239 or toll-free 800-872-6798. *Fax:* 859-281-3650. *E-mail:* jpriest@transy.edu. *Website:* http://www.transy.edu/.

TREVECCA NAZARENE UNIVERSITY

Nashville, TN

Tuition & fees: $26,898 — **Average undergraduate aid package: N/A**

ABOUT THE INSTITUTION Independent Nazarene, coed. ***Awards:*** certificates, associate, bachelor's, master's, and doctoral degrees. 70 undergraduate majors. ***Total enrollment:*** 4,124. Undergraduates: 2,390. Freshmen: 392. Institutional methodology is used as a basis for awarding need-based institutional aid.

UNDERGRADUATE EXPENSES for 2020–2021 ***Comprehensive fee:*** $35,998 includes full-time tuition ($25,998), mandatory fees ($900), and room and board ($9100). ***College room only:*** $4550. Full-time tuition and fees vary according to degree level and program. Room and board charges vary according to board plan. ***Part-time tuition:*** $1005 per credit hour. Part-time tuition and fees vary according to course load, degree level, and program.

GIFT AID (NEED-BASED) ***Total amount:*** $5,037,714 (74% federal, 26% state). ***Scholarships, grants, and awards:*** Federal Pell, FSEOG, state, private, college/university gift aid from institutional funds.

GIFT AID (NON-NEED-BASED) ***Total amount:*** $18,467,556 (11% state, 81% institutional, 8% external sources). ***Scholarships, grants, and awards by category:*** *Academic interests/achievement:* biological sciences, business, communication, education, English, general academic interests/achievements, physical sciences, religion/biblical studies, social sciences. *Creative arts/performance:* cinema/film/broadcasting, music, theater/drama. *Special achievements/activities:* general special achievements/activities, leadership. *Special characteristics:* children of faculty/staff, general special characteristics, relatives of clergy, religious affiliation, siblings of current students. ***ROTC:*** Army cooperative.

LOANS ***Student loans:*** $9,331,687 (43% need-based, 57% non-need-based). 56% of past graduating class borrowed through all loan programs. *Average indebtedness per student:* $24,895. ***Parent loans:*** $1,709,543 (100% non-need-based). ***Programs:*** Federal Direct (Subsidized and Unsubsidized Stafford, PLUS).

WORK-STUDY ***Federal work-study:*** Total amount: $200,000; jobs available. ***State or other work-study/employment:*** Total amount: $1,217,921 (100% non-need-based). Part-time jobs available.

ATHLETIC AWARDS Total amount: $2,161,900 (100% non-need-based).

APPLYING FOR FINANCIAL AID ***Financial aid deadline (priority):*** 1/1. ***Notification date:*** Continuous beginning 12/1.

CONTACT Kevin Reed, Assistant Director of Financial Aid, Trevecca Nazarene University, 333 Murfreesboro Road, Nashville, TN 37210, 615-248-7724 or toll-free 888-210-4TNU. *Fax:* 615-248-7728. *E-mail:* kreed@trevecca.edu. *Website:* http://www.trevecca.edu/.

TRIDENT UNIVERSITY INTERNATIONAL

Cypress, CA

CONTACT Taisha Azlin, Director of Financial Aid, Trident University International, 5665 Plaza Drive, Third Floor, Cypress, CA 90630, 800-375-9878 Ext. 1061. *Fax:* 714-484-7621. *E-mail:* financialaid@tuiu.edu.
Website: http://www.trident.edu/.

TRINE UNIVERSITY

Angola, IN

Tuition & fees: $33,490 | **Average undergraduate aid package: $26,469**

ABOUT THE INSTITUTION Independent, coed. ***Awards:*** associate, bachelor's, master's, and doctoral degrees. 61 undergraduate majors. ***Total enrollment:*** 3,970. Undergraduates: 3,808. Freshmen: 618. Federal methodology is used as a basis for awarding need-based institutional aid.

UNDERGRADUATE EXPENSES for 2020–2021 ***Tuition:*** full-time $32,990; part-time $1060 per credit hour. ***Required fees:*** full-time $500. ***College room only:*** $6700.

FRESHMAN FINANCIAL AID (Fall 2019, est.) 594 applied for aid; of those 89% were deemed to have need. 100% of freshmen with need received aid; of those 20% had need fully met. ***Average percent of need met:*** 77% (excluding resources awarded to replace EFC). ***Average financial aid package:*** $27,209 (excluding resources awarded to replace EFC). 18% of all full-time freshmen had no need and received non-need-based gift aid.

UNDERGRADUATE FINANCIAL AID (Fall 2019, est.) 1,961 applied for aid; of those 88% were deemed to have need. 100% of undergraduates with need received aid; of those 23% had need fully met. ***Average percent of need met:*** 78% (excluding resources awarded to replace EFC). ***Average financial aid package:*** $26,469 (excluding resources awarded to replace EFC). 15% of all full-time undergraduates had no need and received non-need-based gift aid.

GIFT AID (NEED-BASED) ***Total amount:*** $37,066,672 (7% federal, 9% state, 79% institutional, 5% external sources). ***Receiving aid:*** Freshmen: 74% (526); all full-time undergraduates: 82% (1,715). ***Average award:*** Freshmen: $23,460; Undergraduates: $22,274. ***Scholarships, grants, and awards:*** Federal Pell, FSEOG, state, private, college/university gift aid from institutional funds.

GIFT AID (NON-NEED-BASED) ***Total amount:*** $7,176,772 (89% institutional, 11% external sources). ***Receiving aid:*** Freshmen: 12% (84). Undergraduates: 14% (288). ***Average award:*** Freshmen: $15,221. Undergraduates: $15,293. ***Scholarships, grants, and awards by category:*** *Academic interests/achievement:* general academic interests/achievements, premedicine. *Creative arts/performance:* dance, music, performing arts, theater/drama. *Special achievements/activities:* hobbies/interests. *Special characteristics:* children and siblings of alumni, children of faculty/staff, international students. ***ROTC:*** Air Force cooperative.

LOANS ***Student loans:*** $14,687,243 (64% need-based, 36% non-need-based). 76% of past graduating class borrowed through all loan programs. *Average indebtedness per student:* $33,933. ***Average need-based loan:*** Freshmen: $3026. Undergraduates: $3753. ***Parent loans:*** $5,722,909 (38% need-based, 62% non-need-based). ***Programs:*** Federal Direct (Subsidized and Unsubsidized Stafford, PLUS), college/university.

WORK-STUDY ***Federal work-study:*** Total amount: $2,203,928; jobs available.

APPLYING FOR FINANCIAL AID ***Required financial aid form:*** FAFSA. ***Financial aid deadline (priority):*** 3/10. ***Notification date:*** Continuous.

CONTACT Kim Bennett, Assistant Vice President of Enrollment Management, Trine University, 1 University Avenue, Angola, IN 46703-1764, 260-665-4438 or toll-free 800-347-4878. *Fax:* 260-665-4511. *E-mail:* bennettk@trine.edu.
Website: http://www.trine.edu/.

TRINITY BAPTIST COLLEGE

Jacksonville, FL

CONTACT Mr. Mark Elkins, Financial Aid Administrator, Trinity Baptist College, 800 Hammond Boulevard, Jacksonville, FL 32221, 904-596-2445 or toll-free 800-786-2206. *Fax:* 904-596-2531. *E-mail:* financialaid@tbc.edu.
Website: http://www.tbc.edu/.

TRINITY BIBLE COLLEGE AND GRADUATE SCHOOL

Ellendale, ND

CONTACT Mary Anne Whitman, Director of Financial Aid, Trinity Bible College and Graduate School, 50 South 6th Avenue, Ellendale, ND 58436-7150, 701-349-5403 or toll-free 800-523-1603. *Fax:* 701-349-5786. *E-mail:* mwhitman@trinitybiblecollege.edu.
Website: http://www.trinitybiblecollege.edu/.

TRINITY CHRISTIAN COLLEGE

Palos Heights, IL

Tuition & fees: $30,950 | **Average undergraduate aid package: N/A**

ABOUT THE INSTITUTION Independent Christian Reformed, coed. ***Awards:*** bachelor's and master's degrees. 56 undergraduate majors. ***Total enrollment:*** 1,131. Undergraduates: 1,063. Freshmen: 153. Federal methodology is used as a basis for awarding need-based institutional aid.

UNDERGRADUATE EXPENSES for 2019–2020 ***One-time required fee:*** $225. ***Comprehensive fee:*** $40,900 includes full-time tuition ($30,700), mandatory fees ($250), and room and board ($9950). ***Part-time tuition:*** $992 per credit hour.

FRESHMAN FINANCIAL AID (Fall 2018) 105 applied for aid; of those 124% were deemed to have need. 113% of freshmen with need received aid.

UNDERGRADUATE FINANCIAL AID (Fall 2018) 604 applied for aid; of those 133% were deemed to have need. 108% of undergraduates with need received aid.

GIFT AID (NEED-BASED) ***Total amount:*** $2,101,970 (91% federal, 3% state, 3% institutional, 3% external sources). ***Scholarships, grants, and awards:*** Federal Pell, FSEOG, state, private, college/university gift aid from institutional funds, Federal Nursing.

GIFT AID (NON-NEED-BASED) ***Total amount:*** $7,112,531 (1% state, 91% institutional, 8% external sources). ***Scholarships, grants, and awards by category:*** *Academic interests/achievement:* biological sciences, business, communication, computer science, education, engineering/technologies, English, general academic interests/achievements, humanities, international studies, mathematics, physical sciences, premedicine, religion/biblical studies, social sciences. *Creative arts/performance:* applied art and design, art/fine arts, general creative arts/performance, journalism/publications, music, performing arts, theater/drama. *Special achievements/activities:* community service, general special achievements/activities, leadership, religious involvement. *Special characteristics:* adult students, children and siblings of alumni, children of faculty/staff, ethnic background, first-generation college students, local/state students, members of minority groups, out-of-state students, religious affiliation, veterans.

LOANS ***Student loans:*** $7,353,434 (36% need-based, 64% non-need-based). 81% of past graduating class borrowed through all loan programs. *Average indebtedness per student:* $41,752. ***Parent loans:*** $1,132,300 (100% non-need-based). ***Programs:*** Federal Direct (Subsidized and Unsubsidized Stafford, PLUS), Perkins, Federal Nursing.

WORK-STUDY ***Federal work-study:*** Total amount: $157,662; jobs available. ***State or other work-study/employment:*** Total amount: $19,511 (100% non-need-based). Part-time jobs available.

ATHLETIC AWARDS Total amount: $2,366,332 (100% non-need-based).

APPLYING FOR FINANCIAL AID ***Required financial aid form:*** FAFSA. ***Financial aid deadline (priority):*** 12/1. ***Notification date:*** Continuous beginning 12/1. Students must reply by 5/1 or within 2 weeks of notification.

CONTACT Mr. Ryan P. Zantingh, Director of Financial Aid, Trinity Christian College, 6601 West College Drive, Palos Heights, IL 60463-0929, 708-239-4872 or toll-free 866-TRIN-4-ME. *Fax:* 708-239-4814. *E-mail:* ryan.zantingh@trnty.edu.
Website: http://www.trnty.edu/.

TRINITY COLLEGE

Hartford, CT

Tuition & fees: $59,050	Average undergraduate aid package: $51,112

ABOUT THE INSTITUTION Independent, coed. ***Awards:*** bachelor's and master's degrees. 48 undergraduate majors. ***Total enrollment:*** 2,235. Undergraduates: 2,182. Freshmen: 579. Both federal and institutional methodology are used as a basis for awarding need-based institutional aid.

UNDERGRADUATE EXPENSES for 2019–2020 *Application fee:* $65. ***Comprehensive fee:*** $74,350 includes full-time tuition ($56,380), mandatory fees ($2670), and room and board ($15,300). ***College room only:*** $9960.

FRESHMAN FINANCIAL AID (Fall 2019, est.) 323 applied for aid; of those 88% were deemed to have need. 100% of freshmen with need received aid; of those 100% had need fully met. ***Average percent of need met:*** 100% (excluding resources awarded to replace EFC). ***Average financial aid package:*** $50,612 (excluding resources awarded to replace EFC). 1% of all full-time freshmen had no need and received non-need-based gift aid.

UNDERGRADUATE FINANCIAL AID (Fall 2019, est.) 1,164 applied for aid; of those 96% were deemed to have need. 100% of undergraduates with need received aid; of those 100% had need fully met. ***Average percent of need met:*** 100% (excluding resources awarded to replace EFC). ***Average financial aid package:*** $51,112 (excluding resources awarded to replace EFC). 1% of all full-time undergraduates had no need and received non-need-based gift aid.

GIFT AID (NEED-BASED) *Total amount:* $52,414,913 (4% federal, 94% institutional, 2% external sources). ***Receiving aid:*** Freshmen: 48% (276); all full-time undergraduates: 53% (1,080). ***Average award:*** Freshmen: $48,334; Undergraduates: $47,743. ***Scholarships, grants, and awards:*** Federal Pell, FSEOG, state, private, college/university gift aid from institutional funds.

GIFT AID (NON-NEED-BASED) *Total amount:* $4,104,467 (1% federal, 97% institutional, 2% external sources). ***Receiving aid:*** Freshmen: 2% (11). Undergraduates: 2% (31). ***Average award:*** Freshmen: $58,374. Undergraduates: $51,981. ***Scholarships, grants, and awards by category:*** *Academic interests/achievement:* general academic interests/achievements. *Special achievements/activities:* leadership. ***ROTC:*** Army cooperative, Air Force cooperative.

LOANS *Student loans:* $8,968,965 (35% need-based, 65% non-need-based). 44% of past graduating class borrowed through all loan programs. *Average indebtedness per student:* $30,893. ***Average need-based loan:*** Freshmen: $3133. Undergraduates: $4347. ***Parent loans:*** $3,940,999 (100% non-need-based). ***Programs:*** Federal Direct (Subsidized and Unsubsidized Stafford, PLUS), Perkins, state, college/university.

WORK-STUDY *Federal work-study:* Total amount: $804,067; jobs available. ***State or other work-study/employment:*** Part-time jobs available.

APPLYING FOR FINANCIAL AID *Required financial aid forms:* FAFSA, CSS Financial Aid PROFILE, noncustodial (divorced/separated) parent's statement, business/farm supplement, Federal Income Tax Return. ***Financial aid deadline:*** 3/1 (priority: 1/15). ***Notification date:*** 4/1. Students must reply by 5/1.

CONTACT Carolyn LeGeyt, Interim Director of Financial Aid, Trinity College, 300 Summit Street, Hartford, CT 06106-3100, 860-297-2046. *Fax:* 860-987-6296. *E-mail:* financial-aid@trincoll.edu.
Website: http://www.trincoll.edu/.

TRINITY COLLEGE OF FLORIDA

Trinity, FL

Tuition & fees: $16,300	Average undergraduate aid package: $14,489

ABOUT THE INSTITUTION Independent nondenominational, coed. ***Awards:*** certificates, associate, and bachelor's degrees. 14 undergraduate majors. ***Total enrollment:*** 220. Undergraduates: 220. Freshmen: 34. Both federal and institutional methodology are used as a basis for awarding need-based institutional aid.

UNDERGRADUATE EXPENSES for 2020–2021 *Application fee:* $35. ***Comprehensive fee:*** $23,900 includes full-time tuition ($15,200), mandatory fees ($1100), and room and board ($7600). ***College room only:*** $5400. Full-time tuition and fees vary according to course load and program. ***Part-time tuition:*** $510 per credit hour. ***Part-time fees:*** $550 per term. Part-time tuition and fees vary according to course load and program.

FRESHMAN FINANCIAL AID (Fall 2019, est.) 28 applied for aid; of those 96% were deemed to have need. 100% of freshmen with need received aid; of those 19% had need fully met. ***Average percent of need met:*** 85% (excluding resources awarded to replace EFC). ***Average financial aid package:*** $16,715 (excluding resources awarded to replace EFC). 3% of all full-time freshmen had no need and received non-need-based gift aid.

UNDERGRADUATE FINANCIAL AID (Fall 2019, est.) 167 applied for aid; of those 87% were deemed to have need. 100% of undergraduates with need received aid; of those 18% had need fully met. ***Average percent of need met:*** 83% (excluding resources awarded to replace EFC). ***Average financial aid package:*** $14,489 (excluding resources awarded to replace EFC). 10% of all full-time undergraduates had no need and received non-need-based gift aid.

GIFT AID (NEED-BASED) *Receiving aid:* Freshmen: 82% (27); all full-time undergraduates: 80% (145). ***Average award:*** Freshmen: $10,553; Undergraduates: $8210. ***Scholarships, grants, and awards:*** Federal Pell, FSEOG, state, college/university gift aid from institutional funds.

GIFT AID (NON-NEED-BASED) *Receiving aid:* Freshmen: 3% (1). Undergraduates: 3% (6). ***Average award:*** Freshmen: $7000. Undergraduates: $6391. ***Scholarships, grants, and awards by category:*** *Academic interests/achievement:* 17 awards ($68,579 total): general academic interests/achievements, religion/biblical studies. *Special achievements/activities:* 3 awards ($17,200 total): community service, leadership, religious involvement. *Special characteristics:* 9 awards ($19,800 total): children of faculty/staff, general special characteristics, previous college experience, relatives of clergy. ***Tuition waivers:*** Full or partial for employees or children of employees, senior citizens.

LOANS *Student loans:* 71% of past graduating class borrowed through all loan programs. *Average indebtedness per student:* $26,617. ***Average need-based loan:*** Freshmen: $7018. Undergraduates: $7243. ***Programs:*** Federal Direct (Subsidized and Unsubsidized Stafford, PLUS), private loans.

WORK-STUDY *Federal work-study:* 13 jobs averaging $4335. ***State or other work-study/employment:*** 1 part-time job averaging $5250.

APPLYING FOR FINANCIAL AID *Required financial aid forms:* FAFSA, institution's own form. ***Financial aid deadline:*** Continuous. ***Notification date:*** Continuous. Students must reply within 6 weeks of notification.

CONTACT Sue Wayne, Director of Financial Aid, Trinity College of Florida, 2430 Welbilt Boulevard, Trinity, FL 34655, 727-569-1413 or toll-free 800-388-0869. *Fax:* 573-376-0781. *E-mail:* swayne@trinitycollege.edu.
Website: http://www.trinitycollege.edu/.

TRINITY COLLEGE OF NURSING AND HEALTH SCIENCES

Rock Island, IL

CONTACT Mrs. Christine Carol Christopherson, Financial Aid Specialist, Trinity College of Nursing and Health Sciences, 2122 25th Avenue, Rock Island, IL 61201, 309-779-7740. *Fax:* 309-779-7748. *E-mail:* c.christopherson@trinitycollegeqc.edu.
Website: http://www.trinitycollegeqc.edu/.

TRINITY INTERNATIONAL UNIVERSITY

Deerfield, IL

CONTACT Pat Coles, Interim Director of Financial Aid, Trinity International University, 2065 Half Day Road, Deerfield, IL 60015-1284, 847-317-8060 or toll-free 800-822-3225. *Fax:* 847-317-7081. *E-mail:* finaid@tiu.edu.
Website: http://www.tiu.edu/.

TRINITY UNIVERSITY

San Antonio, TX

Tuition & fees: $46,456 | **Average undergraduate aid package: $41,170**

ABOUT THE INSTITUTION Independent Presbyterian Church, coed. ***Awards:*** bachelor's and master's degrees. 62 undergraduate majors. ***Total enrollment:*** 2,692. Undergraduates: 2,527. Freshmen: 637. Both federal and institutional methodology are used as a basis for awarding need-based institutional aid.

UNDERGRADUATE EXPENSES for 2020–2021 ***Comprehensive fee:*** $60,196 includes full-time tuition ($45,840), mandatory fees ($616), and room and board ($13,740). ***College room only:*** $8690. Full-time tuition and fees vary according to course load. Room and board charges vary according to board plan. ***Part-time tuition:*** $1910 per credit hour. ***Part-time fees:*** $12.50 per credit hour. Part-time tuition and fees vary according to course load.

FRESHMAN FINANCIAL AID (Fall 2019, est.) 471 applied for aid; of those 55% were deemed to have need. 100% of freshmen with need received aid; of those 67% had need fully met. ***Average percent of need met:*** 98% (excluding resources awarded to replace EFC). ***Average financial aid package:*** $43,257 (excluding resources awarded to replace EFC). 59% of all full-time freshmen had no need and received non-need-based gift aid.

UNDERGRADUATE FINANCIAL AID (Fall 2019, est.) 1,487 applied for aid; of those 74% were deemed to have need. 100% of undergraduates with need received aid; of those 40% had need fully met. ***Average percent of need met:*** 92% (excluding resources awarded to replace EFC). ***Average financial aid package:*** $41,170 (excluding resources awarded to replace EFC). 53% of all full-time undergraduates had no need and received non-need-based gift aid.

GIFT AID (NEED-BASED) ***Receiving aid:*** Freshmen: 40% (257); all full-time undergraduates: 44% (1,094). ***Average award:*** Freshmen: $34,754; Undergraduates: $33,705. ***Scholarships, grants, and awards:*** Federal Pell, FSEOG, state, private, college/university gift aid from institutional funds.

GIFT AID (NON-NEED-BASED) ***Receiving aid:*** Freshmen: 17% (107). Undergraduates: 9% (233). ***Average award:*** Freshmen: $24,124. Undergraduates: $22,746. ***Scholarships, grants, and awards by category:*** *Academic interests/achievement:* general academic interests/achievements. *Creative arts/performance:* applied art and design, debating, music, theater/drama. *Special characteristics:* children and siblings of alumni, children of educators, international students, veterans. ***Tuition waivers:*** Full or partial for employees or children of employees. ***ROTC:*** Army cooperative, Air Force cooperative.

LOANS ***Student loans:*** 47% of past graduating class borrowed through all loan programs. *Average indebtedness per student:* $43,005. ***Average need-based loan:*** Freshmen: $4039. Undergraduates: $4721. ***Programs:*** Federal Direct (Subsidized and Unsubsidized Stafford, PLUS), Perkins, state, college/university.

WORK-STUDY Federal work-study jobs available. ***State or other work-study/employment:*** Part-time jobs available.

APPLYING FOR FINANCIAL AID ***Required financial aid forms:*** FAFSA, CSS Financial Aid PROFILE.

CONTACT Office of Student Financial Services, Trinity University, One Trinity Place, San Antonio, TX 78212, 210-999-8898 or toll-free 800-TRINITY. *Fax:* 210-999-8316. *E-mail:* studentfinancialservices@trinity.edu.
Website: http://www.trinity.edu/.

TRINITY WASHINGTON UNIVERSITY

Washington, DC

CONTACT Catherine H. Geier, Director of Student Financial Services, Trinity Washington University, 125 Michigan Avenue, NE, Washington, DC 20017-1094, 202-884-9530 or toll-free 800-IWANTTC. *Fax:* 202-884-9524. *E-mail:* financialaid@trinitydc.edu.
Website: http://www.trinitydc.edu/.

TRI-STATE BIBLE COLLEGE

South Point, OH

CONTACT Mrs. Roberta Mercer, Financial Aid Director, Tri-State Bible College, 506 Margaret Street, PO Box 445, South Point, OH 45680, 740-377-2520 Ext. 23. *Fax:* 740-377-0001. *E-mail:* tsbc@zoominternet.net.
Website: http://www.tsbc.edu/.

TROY UNIVERSITY

Troy, AL

Tuition & fees: N/R | **Average undergraduate aid package: $3573**

ABOUT THE INSTITUTION State-supported, coed. ***Awards:*** certificates, associate, bachelor's, master's, and doctoral degrees. 44 undergraduate majors. ***Total enrollment:*** 16,436. Undergraduates: 12,995. Freshmen: 1,679. Federal methodology is used as a basis for awarding need-based institutional aid.

FRESHMAN FINANCIAL AID (Fall 2018) 1375 applied for aid; of those 86% were deemed to have need. 100% of freshmen with need received aid. ***Average financial aid package:*** $3290 (excluding resources awarded to replace EFC). 9% of all full-time freshmen had no need and received non-need-based gift aid.

UNDERGRADUATE FINANCIAL AID (Fall 2018) 6,383 applied for aid; of those 91% were deemed to have need. 100% of undergraduates with need received aid. ***Average financial aid package:*** $3573 (excluding resources awarded to replace EFC). 4% of all full-time undergraduates had no need and received non-need-based gift aid.

GIFT AID (NEED-BASED) ***Total amount:*** $24,918,536 (99% federal, 1% state). ***Receiving aid:*** Freshmen: 45% (768); all full-time undergraduates: 43% (3,931). ***Average award:*** Freshmen: $4750; Undergraduates: $4600. ***Scholarships, grants, and awards:*** Federal Pell, FSEOG, state, private, college/university gift aid from institutional funds.

GIFT AID (NON-NEED-BASED) ***Total amount:*** $29,190,540 (89% institutional, 11% external sources). ***Receiving aid:*** Freshmen: 39% (659). Undergraduates: 29% (2,668). ***Average award:*** Freshmen: $3451. Undergraduates: $3822. ***Scholarships, grants, and awards by category:*** *Academic interests/achievement:* general academic interests/achievements. *Creative arts/performance:* art/fine arts, music, theater/drama. *Special achievements/activities:* leadership. *Special characteristics:* general special characteristics. ***ROTC:*** Army, Air Force.

LOANS ***Student loans:*** $48,031,987 (100% need-based). 61% of past graduating class borrowed through all loan programs. *Average indebtedness per student:* $26,144. ***Average need-based loan:*** Freshmen: $2429. Undergraduates: $3007. ***Parent loans:*** $8,424,426 (100% need-based). ***Programs:*** Federal Direct (Subsidized and Unsubsidized Stafford, PLUS), Perkins, Federal Nursing, college/university.

WORK-STUDY ***Federal work-study:*** Total amount: $735,439; jobs available.

ATHLETIC AWARDS Total amount: $5,388,960 (100% non-need-based).

APPLYING FOR FINANCIAL AID ***Required financial aid forms:*** FAFSA, institution's own form. ***Financial aid deadline (priority):*** 5/1. ***Notification date:*** Continuous beginning 5/1. Students must reply within 2 weeks of notification.

CONTACT Ms. Angela M. Johnson, Associate Vice Chancellor of Financial Aid, Troy University, 131 Adams Administration Building, Troy, AL 36082, 334-357-3186 or toll-free 800-551-9716. *Fax:* 334-670-3702. *E-mail:* ajohnson@troy.edu.
Website: http://www.troy.edu/.

TRUETT MCCONNELL UNIVERSITY

Cleveland, GA

Tuition & fees: $21,938 | **Average undergraduate aid package: $16,161**

ABOUT THE INSTITUTION Independent Baptist, coed. ***Awards:*** certificates, bachelor's, and master's degrees. 18 undergraduate majors. ***Total enrollment:*** 3,055. Undergraduates: 2,983. Freshmen: 215. Federal methodology is used as a basis for awarding need-based institutional aid.

UNDERGRADUATE EXPENSES for 2020–2021 ***Comprehensive fee:*** $30,098 includes full-time tuition ($20,928), mandatory fees ($1010), and room and board ($8160). Full-time tuition and fees vary according to course load, degree level, location, and program. Room and board charges vary according to housing facility. ***Part-time tuition:*** $872 per credit hour. ***Part-time fees:*** $1010 per year. Part-time tuition and fees vary according to course load, degree level, location, and program.

FRESHMAN FINANCIAL AID (Fall 2019, est.) 201 applied for aid; of those 86% were deemed to have need. 100% of freshmen with need received aid; of those 24% had need fully met. ***Average percent of need met:*** 73% (excluding resources awarded to replace EFC). ***Average financial aid package:*** $15,826 (excluding resources awarded to replace EFC). 20% of all full-time freshmen had no need and received non-need-based gift aid.

UNDERGRADUATE FINANCIAL AID (Fall 2019, est.) 700 applied for aid; of those 86% were deemed to have need. 100% of undergraduates with need received aid; of those 24% had need fully met. ***Average percent of need met:*** 73% (excluding resources awarded to replace EFC). ***Average financial aid package:*** $16,161 (excluding resources awarded to replace EFC). 20% of all full-time undergraduates had no need and received non-need-based gift aid.

GIFT AID (NEED-BASED) ***Receiving aid:*** Freshmen: 80% (171); all full-time undergraduates: 79% (598). ***Average award:*** Freshmen: $13,325; Undergraduates: $13,232. ***Scholarships, grants, and awards:*** Federal Pell, FSEOG, state, private, college/university gift aid from institutional funds, Georgia Baptist Convention scholarships.

GIFT AID (NON-NEED-BASED) ***Receiving aid:*** Freshmen: 17% (36). Undergraduates: 15% (117). ***Average award:*** Freshmen: $7433. Undergraduates: $7198. ***Scholarships, grants, and awards by category:*** *Academic interests/achievement:* 776 awards ($2,280,940 total): biological sciences, business, education, general academic interests/achievements, home economics, premedicine, religion/biblical studies. *Creative arts/performance:* 71 awards ($192,430 total): music. *Special achievements/activities:* 619 awards ($2,175,715 total): community service, general special achievements/activities, leadership, religious involvement. *Special characteristics:* 1,010 awards ($1,517,261 total): children of current students, children of faculty/staff, ethnic background, general special characteristics, international students, local/state students, married students, members of minority groups, out-of-state students, parents of current students, public servants, relatives of clergy, religious affiliation, siblings of current students, spouses of current students, veterans, veterans' children. ***Tuition waivers:*** Full or partial for employees or children of employees.

LOANS ***Student loans:*** 74% of past graduating class borrowed through all loan programs. *Average indebtedness per student:* $29,610. ***Average need-based loan:*** Freshmen: $4227. Undergraduates: $4609. ***Programs:*** Federal Direct (Subsidized and Unsubsidized Stafford, PLUS), state, private loans.

WORK-STUDY ***Federal work-study:*** 33 jobs averaging $1644.

APPLYING FOR FINANCIAL AID ***Required financial aid forms:*** FAFSA, institution's own form. ***Financial aid deadline:*** Continuous. ***Notification date:*** Continuous. Students must reply within 4 weeks of notification.

CONTACT Ms. Mary Hill, Financial Aid Assistant, Truett McConnell University, 100 Alumni Drive, Cleveland, GA 30528, 706-865-2134 Ext. 4203 or toll-free 800-226-8621. *Fax:* 706-243-4642. *E-mail:* mhill@truett.edu.
Website: http://www.truett.edu/.

TRUMAN STATE UNIVERSITY

Kirksville, MO

Tuition & fees (MO res): $8120	Average undergraduate aid package: $12,674

ABOUT THE INSTITUTION State-supported, coed. ***Awards:*** bachelor's and master's degrees. 32 undergraduate majors. ***Total enrollment:*** 5,231. Undergraduates: 4,939. Freshmen: 898. Federal methodology is used as a basis for awarding need-based institutional aid.

UNDERGRADUATE EXPENSES for 2019–2020 ***One-time required fee:*** $350. ***Tuition, state resident:*** full-time $7796; part-time $325 per credit hour. ***Tuition, nonresident:*** full-time $14,990; part-time $625 per credit hour. ***Required fees:*** full-time $324; $324 per year. ***College room and board:*** $9012; ***Room only:*** $5848. Room and board charges vary according to board plan and housing facility.

FRESHMAN FINANCIAL AID (Fall 2018) 928 applied for aid; of those 68% were deemed to have need. 100% of freshmen with need received aid; of those 43% had need fully met. ***Average percent of need met:*** 86% (excluding resources awarded to replace EFC). ***Average financial aid package:*** $12,911 (excluding resources awarded to replace EFC). 41% of all full-time freshmen had no need and received non-need-based gift aid.

UNDERGRADUATE FINANCIAL AID (Fall 2018) 3,421 applied for aid; of those 72% were deemed to have need. 100% of undergraduates with need received aid; of those 35% had need fully met. ***Average percent of need met:*** 83% (excluding resources awarded to replace EFC). ***Average financial aid package:*** $12,674 (excluding resources awarded to replace EFC). 39% of all full-time undergraduates had no need and received non-need-based gift aid.

GIFT AID (NEED-BASED) ***Receiving aid:*** Freshmen: 57% (626); all full-time undergraduates: 50% (2,346). ***Average award:*** Freshmen: $8696; Undergraduates: $8083. ***Scholarships, grants, and awards:*** Federal Pell, FSEOG, state, private, college/university gift aid from institutional funds.

GIFT AID (NON-NEED-BASED) ***Receiving aid:*** Freshmen: 57% (621). Undergraduates: 43% (2,037). ***Average award:*** Freshmen: $5634. Undergraduates: $6087. ***Scholarships, grants, and awards by category:*** *Academic interests/achievement:* 8,297 awards ($21,716,216 total): agriculture, biological sciences, business, communication, computer science, education, English, foreign languages, general academic interests/achievements, home economics, humanities, mathematics, military science, physical sciences, premedicine, social sciences. *Creative arts/performance:* 143 awards ($171,660 total): applied art and design, debating, music, theater/drama. *Special achievements/activities:* 631 awards ($2,290,563 total): leadership. *Special characteristics:* 724 awards ($1,629,242 total): children and siblings of alumni, children of faculty/staff, ethnic background, first-generation college students, international students, out-of-state students, previous college experience. ***Tuition waivers:*** Full or partial for employees or children of employees, senior citizens. ***ROTC:*** Army.

LOANS ***Student loans:*** 52% of past graduating class borrowed through all loan programs. *Average indebtedness per student:* $25,660. ***Average need-based loan:*** Freshmen: $3034. Undergraduates: $4073. ***Programs:*** Federal Direct (Subsidized and Unsubsidized Stafford, PLUS), Federal Nursing, college/university.

WORK-STUDY ***Federal work-study:*** 410 jobs averaging $1807. ***State or other work-study/employment:*** 1,241 part-time jobs averaging $1211.

APPLYING FOR FINANCIAL AID ***Required financial aid form:*** FAFSA. ***Financial aid deadline:*** Continuous. ***Notification date:*** Continuous.

CONTACT Marla Fernandez, Director of Financial Aid, Truman State University, 103 McClain Hall, Kirksville, MO 63501-4221, 660-785-4130 or toll-free 800-892-7792. *Fax:* 660-785-7389. *E-mail:* mfernandez@truman.edu.
Website: http://www.truman.edu/.

TUFTS UNIVERSITY

Medford, MA

Tuition & fees: $58,578	Average undergraduate aid package: $49,215

ABOUT THE INSTITUTION Independent, coed. ***Awards:*** certificates, bachelor's, master's, and doctoral degrees. 100 undergraduate majors. ***Total enrollment:*** 11,586. Undergraduates: 5,643. Freshmen: 1,541. Both federal and institutional methodology are used as a basis for awarding need-based institutional aid.

UNDERGRADUATE EXPENSES for 2019–2020 ***Application fee:*** $75. ***Comprehensive fee:*** $73,664 includes full-time tuition ($57,324), mandatory fees ($1254), and room and board ($15,086). Room and board charges vary according to board plan. ***Part-time tuition:*** $2389 per credit hour. ***Payment plan:*** Tuition prepayment.

FRESHMAN FINANCIAL AID (Fall 2019, est.) 875 applied for aid; of those 74% were deemed to have need. 100% of freshmen with need received aid; of those 100% had need fully met. ***Average percent of need met:*** 100% (excluding resources awarded to replace EFC). ***Average financial aid package:*** $48,215 (excluding resources awarded to replace EFC). 2% of all full-time freshmen had no need and received non-need-based gift aid.

UNDERGRADUATE FINANCIAL AID (Fall 2019, est.) 2,480 applied for aid; of those 85% were deemed to have need. 98% of undergraduates with need received aid; of those 100% had need fully met. ***Average percent of need met:*** 98% (excluding resources awarded to replace EFC). ***Average financial aid package:*** $49,215

(excluding resources awarded to replace EFC). 2% of all full-time undergraduates had no need and received non-need-based gift aid.

GIFT AID (NEED-BASED) ***Receiving aid:*** Freshmen: 37% (599); all full-time undergraduates: 34% (1,967). ***Average award:*** Freshmen: $46,982; Undergraduates: $47,554. ***Scholarships, grants, and awards:*** Federal Pell, FSEOG, state, private, college/university gift aid from institutional funds.

GIFT AID (NON-NEED-BASED) ***Receiving aid:*** Freshmen: 2% (29). Undergraduates: 2% (90). ***Average award:*** Freshmen: $3000. Undergraduates: $4572. ***Scholarships, grants, and awards by category:*** *Academic interests/achievement:* 53 awards ($26,500 total): general academic interests/achievements. *Creative arts/performance:* 38 awards ($417,125 total): applied art and design. ***Tuition waivers:*** Full or partial for employees or children of employees. ***ROTC:*** Army cooperative, Naval cooperative, Air Force cooperative.

LOANS ***Student loans:*** 30% of past graduating class borrowed through all loan programs. *Average indebtedness per student:* $27,006. ***Average need-based loan:*** Freshmen: $2432. Undergraduates: $2910. ***Programs:*** Federal Direct (Subsidized and Unsubsidized Stafford, PLUS), college/university.

WORK-STUDY ***Federal work-study:*** 1,609 jobs averaging $2015. ***State or other work-study/employment:*** 181 part-time jobs averaging $2080.

APPLYING FOR FINANCIAL AID ***Required financial aid forms:*** FAFSA, CSS Financial Aid PROFILE, noncustodial (divorced/separated) parent's statement, federal income tax form(s).

CONTACT Patricia C. Reilly, Associate Dean of Financial Aid, Tufts University, Dowling Hall, Medford, MA 02155, 617-627-2000. *Fax:* 617-627-3987. *E-mail:* patricia.reilly@tufts.edu.
Website: http://www.tufts.edu/.

TULANE UNIVERSITY

New Orleans, LA

Tuition & fees: $56,800	Average undergraduate aid package: $47,419

ABOUT THE INSTITUTION Independent, coed. ***Awards:*** certificates, bachelor's, master's, and doctoral degrees. 82 undergraduate majors. ***Total enrollment:*** 11,913. Undergraduates: 6,968. Freshmen: 1,821. Both federal and institutional methodology are used as a basis for awarding need-based institutional aid.

UNDERGRADUATE EXPENSES for 2019–2020 ***Comprehensive fee:*** $72,574 includes full-time tuition ($52,760), mandatory fees ($4040), and room and board ($15,774). ***College room only:*** $9010. Room and board charges vary according to board plan and housing facility. ***Payment plan:*** Tuition prepayment.

FRESHMAN FINANCIAL AID (Fall 2019, est.) 1020 applied for aid; of those 55% were deemed to have need. 100% of freshmen with need received aid; of those 51% had need fully met. ***Average percent of need met:*** 94% (excluding resources awarded to replace EFC). ***Average financial aid package:*** $47,132 (excluding resources awarded to replace EFC). 43% of all full-time freshmen had no need and received non-need-based gift aid.

UNDERGRADUATE FINANCIAL AID (Fall 2019, est.) 3,267 applied for aid; of those 70% were deemed to have need. 100% of undergraduates with need received aid; of those 48% had need fully met. ***Average percent of need met:*** 93% (excluding resources awarded to replace EFC). ***Average financial aid package:*** $47,419 (excluding resources awarded to replace EFC). 41% of all full-time undergraduates had no need and received non-need-based gift aid.

GIFT AID (NEED-BASED) ***Total amount:*** $80,703,027 (4% federal, 2% state, 93% institutional, 1% external sources). ***Receiving aid:*** Freshmen: 30% (544); all full-time undergraduates: 29% (2,222). ***Average award:*** Freshmen: $37,284; Undergraduates: $37,297. ***Scholarships, grants, and awards:*** Federal Pell, FSEOG, state, private, college/university gift aid from institutional funds.

GIFT AID (NON-NEED-BASED) ***Total amount:*** $87,057,580 (5% state, 94% institutional, 1% external sources). ***Receiving aid:*** Freshmen: 10% (180). Undergraduates: 8% (601). ***Average award:*** Freshmen: $19,239. Undergraduates: $24,189. ***Scholarships, grants, and awards by category:*** *Creative arts/performance:* music. *Special achievements/activities:* community service. *Special characteristics:* children of faculty/staff, international students, local/state students. ***Tuition waivers:*** Full or partial for employees or children of employees. ***ROTC:*** Army, Naval, Air Force.

LOANS ***Student loans:*** $21,982,366 (40% need-based, 60% non-need-based). 34% of past graduating class borrowed through all loan programs. *Average indebtedness per student:* $31,306. ***Average need-based loan:*** Freshmen: $3325. Undergraduates: $4372. ***Parent loans:*** $13,075,529 (11% need-based, 89% non-need-based). ***Programs:*** Federal Direct (Subsidized and Unsubsidized Stafford, PLUS).

WORK-STUDY ***Federal work-study:*** Total amount: $3,773,778; jobs available. ***State or other work-study/employment:*** Total amount: $1,552,814 (27% need-based, 73% non-need-based). Part-time jobs available.

ATHLETIC AWARDS Total amount: $14,656,117 (25% need-based, 75% non-need-based).

APPLYING FOR FINANCIAL AID ***Required financial aid forms:*** FAFSA, CSS Financial Aid PROFILE, noncustodial (divorced/separated) parent's statement, business/farm supplement. ***Financial aid deadline (priority):*** 2/15. ***Notification date:*** Continuous beginning 12/12. Students must reply by 5/1.

CONTACT Mr. Michael T. Goodman, Director of Financial Aid, Tulane University, 6823 St. Charles Avenue, New Orleans, LA 70118-5669, 504-865-5723 or toll-free 800-873-9283. *Fax:* 504-862-8750. *E-mail:* finaid@tulane.edu.
Website: http://www.tulane.edu/.

TUSCULUM UNIVERSITY

Greeneville, TN

CONTACT Karen Sartain, Director of Financial Aid, Tusculum University, PO Box 5049, 60 Shiloh Road, Greeneville, TN 37743-9997, 423-636-7377 or toll-free 800-729-0256. *Fax:* 615-250-4968. *E-mail:* ksartain@tusculum.edu.
Website: http://www.tusculum.edu/.

TUSKEGEE UNIVERSITY

Tuskegee, AL

Tuition & fees: N/R	Average undergraduate aid package: N/A

ABOUT THE INSTITUTION Independent, coed. ***Awards:*** bachelor's, master's, and doctoral degrees. 43 undergraduate majors. ***Total enrollment:*** 2,995. Undergraduates: 2,485. Freshmen: 595. Federal methodology is used as a basis for awarding need-based institutional aid.

GIFT AID (NEED-BASED) ***Scholarships, grants, and awards:*** Federal Pell, FSEOG, state, private, college/university gift aid from institutional funds, United Negro College Fund.

GIFT AID (NON-NEED-BASED) ***Scholarships, grants, and awards by category:*** *Academic interests/achievement:* agriculture, architecture, business, computer science, engineering/technologies, general academic interests/achievements, military science. *Creative arts/performance:* music. *Special characteristics:* children of faculty/staff, local/state students. ***ROTC:*** Army, Naval, Air Force.

LOANS ***Student loans:*** 92% of past graduating class borrowed through all loan programs. *Average indebtedness per student:* $26,500. ***Programs:*** Federal Direct (Subsidized and Unsubsidized Stafford, PLUS).

WORK-STUDY Federal work-study jobs available. ***State or other work-study/employment:*** Part-time jobs available.

APPLYING FOR FINANCIAL AID ***Required financial aid forms:*** FAFSA, institution's own form. ***Financial aid deadline (priority):*** 2/1. ***Notification date:*** Continuous beginning 2/1. Students must reply within 2 weeks of notification.

CONTACT Mr. Advergus D. James Jr., Executive Director of Student Financial Services, Tuskegee University, Carnegie Hall, 2nd Floor, Tuskegee, AL 36088, 334-727-8088 or toll-free 800-622-6531. *Fax:* 334-724-4078. *E-mail:* ajames@tuskegee.edu.
Website: http://www.tuskegee.edu/.

UNILATINA INTERNATIONAL COLLEGE

Miramar, FL

CONTACT Financial Aid Office, Unilatina International College, 3130 Commerce Parkway, Miramar, FL 33025.
Website: http://www.unilatina.edu/.

UNION COLLEGE

Barbourville, KY

Tuition & fees: $27,950	Average undergraduate aid package: $23,525

ABOUT THE INSTITUTION Independent United Methodist, coed. ***Awards:*** certificates, bachelor's, and master's degrees. 34 undergraduate majors. ***Total enrollment:*** 1,329. Undergraduates: 1,115. Freshmen: 218. Federal methodology is used as a basis for awarding need-based institutional aid.

UNDERGRADUATE EXPENSES for 2019–2020 ***Comprehensive fee:*** $35,450 includes full-time tuition ($26,330), mandatory fees ($1620), and room and board ($7500). ***College room only:*** $3300. ***Part-time tuition:*** $345 per credit hour.

FRESHMAN FINANCIAL AID (Fall 2018) 281 applied for aid; of those 96% were deemed to have need. 73% of freshmen with need received aid; of those 10% had need fully met. ***Average percent of need met:*** 49% (excluding resources awarded to replace EFC). ***Average financial aid package:*** $23,286 (excluding resources awarded to replace EFC). 20% of all full-time freshmen had no need and received non-need-based gift aid.

UNDERGRADUATE FINANCIAL AID (Fall 2018) 900 applied for aid; of those 95% were deemed to have need. 85% of undergraduates with need received aid; of those 12% had need fully met. ***Average percent of need met:*** 58% (excluding resources awarded to replace EFC). ***Average financial aid package:*** $23,525 (excluding resources awarded to replace EFC). 12% of all full-time undergraduates had no need and received non-need-based gift aid.

GIFT AID (NEED-BASED) ***Total amount:*** $7,543,693 (35% federal, 35% state, 27% institutional, 3% external sources). ***Receiving aid:*** Freshmen: 56% (197); all full-time undergraduates: 73% (727). ***Average award:*** Freshmen: $20,517; Undergraduates: $20,145. ***Scholarships, grants, and awards:*** Federal Pell, FSEOG, state, private, college/university gift aid from institutional funds.

GIFT AID (NON-NEED-BASED) ***Total amount:*** $163,996 (3% federal, 60% state, 37% external sources). ***Receiving aid:*** Freshmen: 4% (13). Undergraduates: 5% (49). ***Average award:*** Freshmen: $16,350. Undergraduates: $16,452. ***Scholarships, grants, and awards by category:*** *Academic interests/achievement:* general academic interests/achievements. *Creative arts/performance:* music, theater/drama. *Special achievements/activities:* cheerleading/drum major, community service, general special achievements/activities, hobbies/interests, leadership, memberships, religious involvement. *Special characteristics:* adult students, children and siblings of alumni, children of current students, children of faculty/staff, members of minority groups, religious affiliation, siblings of current students, veterans, veterans' children.

LOANS ***Student loans:*** $4,443,128 (88% need-based, 12% non-need-based). ***Average need-based loan:*** Freshmen: $3240. Undergraduates: $3896. ***Parent loans:*** $2,035,370 (54% need-based, 46% non-need-based). ***Programs:*** Federal Direct (Subsidized and Unsubsidized Stafford, PLUS).

WORK-STUDY ***Federal work-study:*** Total amount: $166,581; jobs available. ***State or other work-study/employment:*** Total amount: $11,569 (100% need-based). Part-time jobs available.

ATHLETIC AWARDS Total amount: $7,171,636 (100% need-based).

APPLYING FOR FINANCIAL AID ***Required financial aid form:*** FAFSA. ***Financial aid deadline:*** Continuous. ***Notification date:*** Continuous. Students must reply within 2 weeks of notification.

CONTACT Mrs. Andra Butler, Director of Financial Aid, Union College, 310 College Street, Barbourville, KY 40906-1499, 606-546-1224 or toll-free 800-489-8646. *Fax:* 606-546-1229. *E-mail:* abutler@unionky.edu.
Website: http://www.unionky.edu/.

UNION COLLEGE

Lincoln, NE

Tuition & fees: N/R	Average undergraduate aid package: $17,701

ABOUT THE INSTITUTION Independent Seventh-day Adventist, coed. ***Awards:*** associate, bachelor's, and master's degrees. 54 undergraduate majors. ***Total enrollment:*** 2,206. Undergraduates: 2,206. Freshmen: 571. Federal methodology is used as a basis for awarding need-based institutional aid.

FRESHMAN FINANCIAL AID (Fall 2018) 146 applied for aid; of those 88% were deemed to have need. 99% of freshmen with need received aid; of those 14% had need fully met. ***Average percent of need met:*** 63% (excluding resources awarded to replace EFC). ***Average financial aid package:*** $18,332 (excluding resources awarded to replace EFC). 22% of all full-time freshmen had no need and received non-need-based gift aid.

UNDERGRADUATE FINANCIAL AID (Fall 2018) 561 applied for aid; of those 90% were deemed to have need. 99% of undergraduates with need received aid; of those 16% had need fully met. ***Average percent of need met:*** 62% (excluding resources awarded to replace EFC). ***Average financial aid package:*** $17,701 (excluding resources awarded to replace EFC). 24% of all full-time undergraduates had no need and received non-need-based gift aid.

GIFT AID (NEED-BASED) ***Total amount:*** $6,944,890 (22% federal, 1% state, 58% institutional, 19% external sources). ***Receiving aid:*** Freshmen: 82% (127); all full-time undergraduates: 73% (500). ***Average award:*** Freshmen: $15,049; Undergraduates: $13,696. ***Scholarships, grants, and awards:*** Federal Pell, FSEOG, state, private, college/university gift aid from institutional funds, United Negro College Fund.

GIFT AID (NON-NEED-BASED) ***Total amount:*** $2,368,611 (80% institutional, 20% external sources). ***Receiving aid:*** Freshmen: 10% (15). Undergraduates: 9% (63). ***Average award:*** Freshmen: $12,250. Undergraduates: $10,352. ***Scholarships, grants, and awards by category:*** *Academic interests/achievement:* general academic interests/achievements. *Creative arts/performance:* music. *Special achievements/activities:* community service, leadership, religious involvement. ***ROTC:*** Army cooperative, Naval cooperative, Air Force cooperative.

LOANS ***Student loans:*** $4,411,375 (80% need-based, 20% non-need-based). 65% of past graduating class borrowed through all loan programs. *Average indebtedness per student:* $32,103. ***Average need-based loan:*** Freshmen: $3752. Undergraduates: $4426. ***Parent loans:*** $680,945 (95% need-based, 5% non-need-based). ***Programs:*** Federal Direct (Subsidized and Unsubsidized Stafford, PLUS), college/university.

WORK-STUDY ***Federal work-study:*** Total amount: $344,133; 94 jobs averaging $1814.

APPLYING FOR FINANCIAL AID ***Required financial aid forms:*** FAFSA, institution's own form. ***Financial aid deadline:*** Continuous. ***Notification date:*** Continuous beginning 2/1.

CONTACT Ms. Laurie L Wheeler, Director of Student Financial Services, Union College, 3800 South 48th Street, Lincoln, NE 68506-4300, 402-486-2600 Ext. 2505 or toll-free 800-228-4600. *Fax:* 402-486-2592. *E-mail:* sfs@ucollege.edu.
Website: http://www.ucollege.edu/.

UNION COLLEGE

Schenectady, NY

Tuition & fees: $59,427	Average undergraduate aid package: $46,730

ABOUT THE INSTITUTION Independent, coed. ***Awards:*** bachelor's degrees. 40 undergraduate majors. ***Total enrollment:*** 2,189. Undergraduates: 2,189. Freshmen: 550. Institutional methodology is used as a basis for awarding need-based institutional aid.

UNDERGRADUATE EXPENSES for 2020–2021 ***Comprehensive fee:*** $74,010 includes full-time tuition ($58,956), mandatory fees ($471), and room and board ($14,583). ***College room only:*** $7998. ***Part-time tuition:*** $6551 per course.

FRESHMAN FINANCIAL AID (Fall 2019, est.) 395 applied for aid; of those 88% were deemed to have need. 100% of freshmen with need received aid; of those 100% had need fully met. ***Average percent of need met:*** 100% (excluding resources awarded to replace EFC). ***Average financial aid package:*** $46,760 (excluding resources awarded to replace EFC). 26% of all full-time freshmen had no need and received non-need-based gift aid.

UNDERGRADUATE FINANCIAL AID (Fall 2019, est.) 1,271 applied for aid; of those 91% were deemed to have need. 100% of undergraduates with need received aid; of those 100% had need fully met. ***Average percent of need met:*** 100% (excluding resources awarded to replace EFC). ***Average financial aid package:*** $46,730 (excluding resources awarded to replace EFC). 29% of all full-time undergraduates had no need and received non-need-based gift aid.

GIFT AID (NEED-BASED) ***Total amount:*** $47,429,479 (4% federal, 2% state, 93% institutional, 1% external sources). ***Receiving aid:*** Freshmen: 63% (347); all full-time undergraduates: 54% (1,161). ***Average award:*** Freshmen: $40,535; Undergraduates: $39,940. ***Scholarships, grants, and awards:*** Federal Pell, FSEOG, state, private, college/university gift aid from institutional funds.
GIFT AID (NON-NEED-BASED) ***Total amount:*** $9,438,313 (4% federal, 1% state, 92% institutional, 3% external sources). ***Receiving aid:*** Freshmen: 3% (14). Undergraduates: 3% (73). ***Average award:*** Freshmen: $14,500. Undergraduates: $14,300. ***Scholarships, grants, and awards by category:*** *Academic interests/achievement:* general academic interests/achievements. *Special characteristics:* children of faculty/staff. ***Tuition waivers:*** Full or partial for employees or children of employees, senior citizens. ***ROTC:*** Army cooperative, Naval cooperative, Air Force cooperative.
LOANS ***Student loans:*** $11,581,230 (32% need-based, 68% non-need-based). 53% of past graduating class borrowed through all loan programs. *Average indebtedness per student:* $36,921. ***Average need-based loan:*** Freshmen: $4019. Undergraduates: $5270. ***Parent loans:*** $2,857,991 (100% non-need-based). ***Programs:*** Federal Direct (Subsidized and Unsubsidized Stafford, PLUS), college/university.
WORK-STUDY ***Federal work-study:*** Total amount: $1,025,000; jobs available. ***State or other work-study/employment:*** Total amount: $315,000 (100% need-based). Part-time jobs available.
APPLYING FOR FINANCIAL AID ***Required financial aid forms:*** FAFSA, CSS Financial Aid PROFILE, state aid form, noncustodial (divorced/separated) parent's statement. ***Financial aid deadline:*** 1/15 (priority: 1/15). ***Notification date:*** 3/25. Students must reply by 5/1.
CONTACT Ms. Linda Parker, Director of Financial Aid, Union College, Grant Hall, 807 Union Street, Schenectady, NY 12308-2311, 518-388-6123 or toll-free 888-843-6688. *Fax:* 518-388-8052. *E-mail:* finaid@union.edu.
Website: http://www.union.edu/.

UNION INSTITUTE & UNIVERSITY

Cincinnati, OH

CONTACT Ms. Lisa Perdomo, Director of Financial Aid, Union Institute & University, 440 East McMillan Street, Cincinnati, OH 45206-1925, 513-861-6400 Ext. 1261 or toll-free 800-486-3116. *Fax:* 513-487-1078.
Website: http://www.myunion.edu/.

UNION UNIVERSITY

Jackson, TN

Tuition & fees: $34,780	Average undergraduate aid package: $24,879

ABOUT THE INSTITUTION Independent Southern Baptist, coed. ***Awards:*** associate, bachelor's, master's, and doctoral degrees. 66 undergraduate majors. ***Total enrollment:*** 3,172. Undergraduates: 2,164. Freshmen: 326. Federal methodology is used as a basis for awarding need-based institutional aid.
UNDERGRADUATE EXPENSES for 2020–2021 ***Application fee:*** $35. ***Comprehensive fee:*** $45,660 includes full-time tuition ($33,480), mandatory fees ($1300), and room and board ($10,880). ***College room only:*** $8050. ***Part-time tuition:*** $1075 per credit hour.
FRESHMAN FINANCIAL AID (Fall 2019, est.) 480 applied for aid; of those 90% were deemed to have need. 100% of freshmen with need received aid; of those 16% had need fully met. ***Average percent of need met:*** 74% (excluding resources awarded to replace EFC). ***Average financial aid package:*** $25,655 (excluding resources awarded to replace EFC). 9% of all full-time freshmen had no need and received non-need-based gift aid.
UNDERGRADUATE FINANCIAL AID (Fall 2019, est.) 1,526 applied for aid; of those 88% were deemed to have need. 100% of undergraduates with need received aid; of those 17% had need fully met. ***Average percent of need met:*** 86% (excluding resources awarded to replace EFC). ***Average financial aid package:*** $24,879 (excluding resources awarded to replace EFC). 11% of all full-time undergraduates had no need and received non-need-based gift aid.
GIFT AID (NEED-BASED) ***Total amount:*** $9,158,604 (32% federal, 19% state, 49% institutional). ***Receiving aid:*** Freshmen: 68% (326); all full-time undergraduates: 66% (1,018). ***Average award:*** Freshmen: $9240; Undergraduates: $5830. ***Scholarships, grants, and awards:*** Federal Pell, FSEOG, state, private, college/university gift aid from institutional funds, Federal Nursing.
GIFT AID (NON-NEED-BASED) ***Total amount:*** $22,578,152 (3% federal, 12% state, 81% institutional, 4% external sources). ***Receiving aid:*** Freshmen: 69% (330). Undergraduates: 66% (1,019). ***Average award:*** Freshmen: $17,173. Undergraduates: $15,431. ***Scholarships, grants, and awards by category:*** *Academic interests/achievement:* biological sciences, business, communication, computer science, education, engineering/technologies, English, foreign languages, general academic interests/achievements, home economics, humanities, international studies, mathematics, military science, physical sciences, premedicine, religion/biblical studies, social sciences. *Creative arts/performance:* applied art and design, cinema/film/broadcasting, debating, journalism/publications, music, theater/drama. *Special achievements/activities:* cheerleading/drum major, community service, general special achievements/activities, leadership, memberships, religious involvement. *Special characteristics:* children and siblings of alumni, children of current students, children of educators, children of faculty/staff, ethnic background, first-generation college students, general special characteristics, handicapped students, international students, members of minority groups, relatives of clergy, religious affiliation, siblings of current students, spouses of current students, twins, veterans.
LOANS ***Student loans:*** $26,569,312 (17% need-based, 83% non-need-based). 41% of past graduating class borrowed through all loan programs. ***Average need-based loan:*** Freshmen: $3649. Undergraduates: $3922. ***Parent loans:*** $4,231,542 (100% non-need-based). ***Programs:*** Federal Direct (Subsidized and Unsubsidized Stafford, PLUS), Perkins, Private alternative loans.
WORK-STUDY ***Federal work-study:*** Total amount: $1,041,231; jobs available. ***State or other work-study/employment:*** Total amount: $69,750 (100% need-based). Part-time jobs available.
ATHLETIC AWARDS Total amount: $3,272,383 (100% non-need-based).
APPLYING FOR FINANCIAL AID ***Required financial aid forms:*** FAFSA, institution's own form. ***Financial aid deadline (priority):*** 2/1. ***Notification date:*** Continuous beginning 3/1. Students must reply by 5/1 or within 2 weeks of notification.
CONTACT Mr. Dan Griffin, Vice President for Enrollment Management, Union University, 1050 Union University Drive, Jackson, TN 38305-3697, 731-661-5100 or toll-free 800-33-UNION. *Fax:* 731-661-5570. *E-mail:* dgriffin@uu.edu.
Website: http://www.uu.edu/.

UNITED STATES SPORTS ACADEMY

Daphne, AL

ABOUT THE INSTITUTION Independent, coed. ***Awards:*** bachelor's, master's, and doctoral degrees. 4 undergraduate majors.
GIFT AID (NEED-BASED) ***Scholarships, grants, and awards:*** Federal Pell, FSEOG, state, private.
LOANS ***Programs:*** Federal Direct (Subsidized and Unsubsidized Stafford, PLUS).
CONTACT Financial Aid Office, United States Sports Academy, One Academy Drive, Daphne, AL 36526-7055, 251-626-3303 or toll-free 800-223-2668.
Website: http://www.ussa.edu/.

UNITED STATES UNIVERSITY

San Diego, CA

CONTACT Financial Aid Office, United States University, 7675 Mission Valley Road, San Diego, CA 92108, 619-477-6310 or toll-free 888-422-3381.
Website: http://www.usuniversity.edu/.

UNITED TALMUDICAL SEMINARY

Brooklyn, NY

CONTACT Financial Aid Office, United Talmudical Seminary, 82 Lee Avenue, Brooklyn, NY 11211-7900, 718-963-9770 Ext. 309.

UNITY COLLEGE

Unity, ME

CONTACT Mr. Rand E. Newell, Director of Financial Aid, Unity College, 90 Quaker Hill Road, Unity, ME 04988, 207-509-7201. *Fax:* 207-512-1168. *E-mail:* rnewell@unity.edu.
Website: http://www.unity.edu/.

UNIVERSIDAD ADVENTISTA DE LAS ANTILLAS

Mayagüez, PR

Tuition & fees: N/R **Average undergraduate aid package: N/A**

ABOUT THE INSTITUTION Independent Seventh-day Adventist, coed. ***Awards:*** associate, bachelor's, and master's degrees. 18 undergraduate majors. ***Total enrollment:*** 1,214. Undergraduates: 1,058. Freshmen: 106. Both federal and institutional methodology are used as a basis for awarding need-based institutional aid.
GIFT AID (NEED-BASED) ***Scholarships, grants, and awards:*** Federal Pell, FSEOG, state, college/university gift aid from institutional funds.
GIFT AID (NON-NEED-BASED) ***Scholarships, grants, and awards by category:*** *Special achievements/activities:* community service. *Special characteristics:* relatives of clergy, veterans.
LOANS ***Student loans:*** 64% of past graduating class borrowed through all loan programs. *Average indebtedness per student:* $4801. ***Programs:*** Federal Direct (Subsidized and Unsubsidized Stafford, PLUS).
WORK-STUDY Federal work-study jobs available. ***State or other work-study/employment:*** Part-time jobs available.
APPLYING FOR FINANCIAL AID ***Required financial aid forms:*** FAFSA, institution's own form. ***Financial aid deadline:*** Continuous. ***Notification date:*** Continuous.
CONTACT Mrs. Awilda Matos, Director of Financial Aid, Universidad Adventista de las Antillas, Box 118, Mayaguez, PR 00681-0118, 787-834-9595 Ext. 2263. *Fax:* 787-834-9597. *E-mail:* amatos@uaa.edu.
Website: https://www.uaa.edu/esp/.

UNIVERSIDAD CENTRAL DEL CARIBE

Bayamón, PR

CONTACT Financial Aid Office, Universidad Central del Caribe, PO Box 60-327, Bayamón, PR 00960-6032, 787-798-3001.
Website: http://www.uccaribe.edu/.

UNIVERSIDAD DEL ESTE

Carolina, PR

CONTACT Mrs. Eigna De Jess Molinari, Director of Financial Aid , Universidad del Este, Apartado 2010, Carolina, PR 00928, 787-257-7373 Ext. 3301. *E-mail:* eidejesus@suagm.edu.
Website: http://www.suagm.edu/une/.

UNIVERSIDAD DEL TURABO

Gurabo, PR

CONTACT Ms. Carmen J. Rivera Lopez, Directora de la Oficina de Asistencia Economica, Universidad del Turabo, Apartado 3030, Gurabo, PR 00778-3030, 787-743-7979 Ext. 4352. *Fax:* 787-746-6777.
Website: http://www.suagm.edu/ut/.

UNIVERSIDAD METROPOLITANA

San Juan, PR

CONTACT Economic Assistant Director, Universidad Metropolitana, Call Box 21150, Rio Piedras, PR 00928-1150, 787-766-1717 Ext. 6586 or toll-free 800-747-8362 (out-of-state).
Website: http://www.suagm.edu/umet/.

UNIVERSIDAD PENTECOSTAL MIZPA

San Juan, PR

CONTACT Mrs. Myriam Juarbe, Director of Financial Aid, Universidad Pentecostal Mizpa, PO Box 20966, San Juan, PR 00928, 787-720-4476. *Fax:* 787-720-2012. *E-mail:* asistenciaeconomica@colmizpa.edu .
Website: http://www.mizpa.edu/.

UNIVERSITY AT ALBANY, STATE UNIVERSITY OF NEW YORK

Albany, NY

Tuition & fees (area res): $9956 **Average undergraduate aid package: $11,395**

ABOUT THE INSTITUTION State-supported, coed. ***Awards:*** certificates, bachelor's, master's, and doctoral degrees. 64 undergraduate majors. ***Total enrollment:*** 17,944. Undergraduates: 13,598. Freshmen: 2,768. Federal methodology is used as a basis for awarding need-based institutional aid.
UNDERGRADUATE EXPENSES for 2020–2021 ***Application fee:*** $50. ***Tuition, area resident:*** full-time $7070; part-time $286 per credit hour. ***Tuition, state resident:*** full-time $7070; part-time $286 per credit hour. ***Tuition, nonresident:*** full-time $24,660; part-time $988 per credit hour. ***Required fees:*** full-time $2886. ***College room and board:*** $13,864; ***Room only:*** $8364. Room and board charges vary according to board plan.
FRESHMAN FINANCIAL AID (Fall 2019, est.) 2523 applied for aid; of those 78% were deemed to have need. 97% of freshmen with need received aid; of those 8% had need fully met. ***Average percent of need met:*** 55% (excluding resources awarded to replace EFC). ***Average financial aid package:*** $11,214 (excluding resources awarded to replace EFC). 7% of all full-time freshmen had no need and received non-need-based gift aid.
UNDERGRADUATE FINANCIAL AID (Fall 2019, est.) 10,542 applied for aid; of those 81% were deemed to have need. 100% of undergraduates with need received aid; of those 7% had need fully met. ***Average percent of need met:*** 58% (excluding resources awarded to replace EFC). ***Average financial aid package:*** $11,395 (excluding resources awarded to replace EFC). 6% of all full-time undergraduates had no need and received non-need-based gift aid.
GIFT AID (NEED-BASED) ***Total amount:*** $64,834,632 (43% federal, 39% state, 16% institutional, 2% external sources). ***Receiving aid:*** Freshmen: 61% (1,698); all full-time undergraduates: 58% (7,502). ***Average award:*** Freshmen: $9224; Undergraduates: $8608. ***Scholarships, grants, and awards:*** Federal Pell, FSEOG, state, private, college/university gift aid from institutional funds.
GIFT AID (NON-NEED-BASED) ***Total amount:*** $5,973,575 (7% federal, 24% state, 53% institutional, 16% external sources). ***Receiving aid:*** Freshmen: 3% (79). Undergraduates: 2% (249). ***Average award:*** Freshmen: $3853. Undergraduates: $3716. ***Scholarships, grants, and awards by category:*** *Academic interests/achievement:* general academic interests/achievements. ***ROTC:*** Army, Air Force cooperative.
LOANS ***Student loans:*** $62,851,305 (43% need-based, 57% non-need-based). 64% of past graduating class borrowed through all loan programs. *Average indebtedness per student:* $27,555. ***Average need-based loan:*** Freshmen: $3268. Undergraduates: $4217. ***Parent loans:*** $21,423,550 (100% non-need-based). ***Programs:*** Federal Direct (Subsidized and Unsubsidized Stafford, PLUS), Perkins.
WORK-STUDY ***Federal work-study:*** Total amount: $875,000; jobs available. ***State or other work-study/employment:*** Total amount: $1,807,007 (74% need-based, 26% non-need-based). Part-time jobs available.

ATHLETIC AWARDS Total amount: $6,868,656 (4% need-based, 96% non-need-based).

APPLYING FOR FINANCIAL AID ***Required financial aid forms:*** FAFSA, NY State residents should apply for TAP on-line at www.tapweb.org/totw/. ***Financial aid deadline (priority):*** 12/1. ***Notification date:*** 2/12.

CONTACT Stephen Kudzin, Director of Financial Aid, University at Albany, State University of New York, Student Financial Center, Campus Center G-26, 1400 Washington Avenue, Albany, NY 12222-0001, 518-442-3202. *Fax:* 518-442-5295. *E-mail:* sfc@albany.edu.
Website: http://www.albany.edu/.

UNIVERSITY AT BUFFALO, THE STATE UNIVERSITY OF NEW YORK

Buffalo, NY

Tuition & fees (NY res): $10,524	Average undergraduate aid package: $11,035

ABOUT THE INSTITUTION State-supported, coed. ***Awards:*** certificates, bachelor's, master's, and doctoral degrees. 76 undergraduate majors. ***Total enrollment:*** 31,923. Undergraduates: 21,921. Freshmen: 4,289. Federal methodology is used as a basis for awarding need-based institutional aid.

UNDERGRADUATE EXPENSES for 2019–2020 ***Application fee:*** $50. ***Tuition, state resident:*** full-time $7070. ***Tuition, nonresident:*** full-time $24,740. ***Required fees:*** full-time $3454; $148.49 per credit hour. Part-time tuition and fees vary according to course load. ***College room and board:*** $14,631; ***Room only:*** $8521. Room and board charges vary according to board plan and housing facility.

FRESHMAN FINANCIAL AID (Fall 2018) 3532 applied for aid; of those 79% were deemed to have need. 87% of freshmen with need received aid; of those 8% had need fully met. ***Average percent of need met:*** 52% (excluding resources awarded to replace EFC). ***Average financial aid package:*** $11,375 (excluding resources awarded to replace EFC). 8% of all full-time freshmen had no need and received non-need-based gift aid.

UNDERGRADUATE FINANCIAL AID (Fall 2018) 14,629 applied for aid; of those 80% were deemed to have need. 95% of undergraduates with need received aid; of those 7% had need fully met. ***Average percent of need met:*** 52% (excluding resources awarded to replace EFC). ***Average financial aid package:*** $11,035 (excluding resources awarded to replace EFC). 4% of all full-time undergraduates had no need and received non-need-based gift aid.

GIFT AID (NEED-BASED) ***Total amount:*** $95,840,142 (40% federal, 32% state, 25% institutional, 3% external sources). ***Receiving aid:*** Freshmen: 50% (2,139); all full-time undergraduates: 46% (9,175). ***Average award:*** Freshmen: $8861; Undergraduates: $10,241. ***Scholarships, grants, and awards:*** Federal Pell, FSEOG, state, private, college/university gift aid from institutional funds, Federal Nursing.

GIFT AID (NON-NEED-BASED) ***Total amount:*** $8,982,946 (45% state, 42% institutional, 13% external sources). ***Receiving aid:*** Freshmen: 24% (1,027). Undergraduates: 15% (3,083). ***Average award:*** Freshmen: $3688. Undergraduates: $3866. ***Tuition waivers:*** Full or partial for minority students. ***ROTC:*** Army cooperative.

LOANS ***Student loans:*** $61,252,105 (82% need-based, 18% non-need-based). 57% of past graduating class borrowed through all loan programs. *Average indebtedness per student:* $25,157. ***Average need-based loan:*** Freshmen: $3311. Undergraduates: $4245. ***Parent loans:*** $17,056,901 (61% need-based, 39% non-need-based). ***Programs:*** Federal Direct (Subsidized and Unsubsidized Stafford, PLUS), Perkins, Federal Nursing.

WORK-STUDY ***Federal work-study:*** Total amount: $1,430,621; 1,044 jobs averaging $1405. ***State or other work-study/employment:*** Total amount: $6,567,732 (100% need-based). 2,757 part-time jobs averaging $2552.

ATHLETIC AWARDS Total amount: $7,759,320 (87% need-based, 13% non-need-based).

APPLYING FOR FINANCIAL AID ***Required financial aid form:*** FAFSA. ***Financial aid deadline (priority):*** 3/1. ***Notification date:*** Continuous beginning 2/1. Students must reply by 5/1.

CONTACT John Gottardy, Director of Financial Aid, University at Buffalo, the State University of New York, 1 Capen, Buffalo, NY 14260, 716-645-8232 or toll-free 888-UB-ADMIT. *Fax:* 716-645-6566. *E-mail:* johngott@buffalo.edu.
Website: http://www.buffalo.edu/.

UNIVERSITY OF ADVANCING TECHNOLOGY

Tempe, AZ

CONTACT Financial Aid Office, University of Advancing Technology, 2625 West Baseline Road, Tempe, AZ 85283-1042, 602-383-8228 or toll-free 800-658-5744. *Fax:* 602-383-8222. *E-mail:* fa@uat.edu.
Website: http://www.uat.edu/.

THE UNIVERSITY OF AKRON

Akron, OH

Tuition & fees: N/R	Average undergraduate aid package: $7089

ABOUT THE INSTITUTION State-supported, coed. ***Awards:*** certificates, associate, bachelor's, master's, and doctoral degrees. 153 undergraduate majors. ***Total enrollment:*** 17,599. Undergraduates: 14,793. Freshmen: 2,739. Federal methodology is used as a basis for awarding need-based institutional aid.

FRESHMAN FINANCIAL AID (Fall 2018) 2649 applied for aid; of those 78% were deemed to have need. 100% of freshmen with need received aid; of those 13% had need fully met. ***Average percent of need met:*** 56% (excluding resources awarded to replace EFC). ***Average financial aid package:*** $2133 (excluding resources awarded to replace EFC). 19% of all full-time freshmen had no need and received non-need-based gift aid.

UNDERGRADUATE FINANCIAL AID (Fall 2018) 10,669 applied for aid; of those 76% were deemed to have need. 100% of undergraduates with need received aid; of those 11% had need fully met. ***Average percent of need met:*** 55% (excluding resources awarded to replace EFC). ***Average financial aid package:*** $7089 (excluding resources awarded to replace EFC). 17% of all full-time undergraduates had no need and received non-need-based gift aid.

GIFT AID (NEED-BASED) ***Total amount:*** $29,148,685 (85% federal, 15% state). ***Receiving aid:*** Freshmen: 41% (1,119); all full-time undergraduates: 37% (4,479). ***Average award:*** Freshmen: $5712; Undergraduates: $5780. ***Scholarships, grants, and awards:*** Federal Pell, FSEOG.

GIFT AID (NON-NEED-BASED) ***Total amount:*** $45,056,951 (4% state, 83% institutional, 13% external sources). ***Receiving aid:*** Freshmen: 78% (2,133). Undergraduates: 59% (7,089). ***Average award:*** Freshmen: $4614. Undergraduates: $5323. ***Scholarships, grants, and awards by category:*** *Academic interests/achievement:* biological sciences, business, communication, computer science, education, engineering/technologies, English, foreign languages, general academic interests/achievements, health fields, home economics, humanities, international studies, mathematics, military science, physical sciences, premedicine, social sciences. *Creative arts/performance:* applied art and design, art/fine arts, creative writing, dance, debating, general creative arts/performance, journalism/publications, music, performing arts, theater/drama. *Special achievements/activities:* community service, general special achievements/activities, leadership, memberships. *Special characteristics:* adult students, general special characteristics, handicapped students, international students, local/state students, members of minority groups, out-of-state students. ***ROTC:*** Army, Air Force cooperative.

LOANS ***Student loans:*** $47,576,879 (51% need-based, 49% non-need-based). 65% of past graduating class borrowed through all loan programs. *Average indebtedness per student:* $28,643. ***Average need-based loan:*** Freshmen: $3076. Undergraduates: $3852. ***Parent loans:*** $17,750,615 (100% non-need-based). ***Programs:*** Federal Direct (Subsidized and Unsubsidized Stafford, PLUS), Perkins, Federal Nursing, college/university.

WORK-STUDY ***Federal work-study:*** Total amount: $1,079,442; jobs available. ***State or other work-study/employment:*** Total amount: $12,736,396 (100% non-need-based). Part-time jobs available.

ATHLETIC AWARDS Total amount: $6,115,643 (100% non-need-based).

APPLYING FOR FINANCIAL AID ***Required financial aid forms:*** FAFSA, institution's own form. ***Financial aid deadline (priority):*** 3/1. ***Notification date:*** Continuous beginning 3/15.

CONTACT Mrs. Jennifer E. Harpham, Director of Student Financial Aid, The University of Akron, 302 Buchtel Mall, Akron, OH 44325-6211, 330-972-5860 or toll-free 800-655-4884. *Fax:* 330-972-7139. *E-mail:* jharpham@uakron.edu.
Website: http://www.uakron.edu/.

THE UNIVERSITY OF ALABAMA

Tuscaloosa, AL

Tuition & fees (AL res): $10,780 **Average undergraduate aid package: $15,217**

ABOUT THE INSTITUTION State-supported, coed. ***Awards:*** certificates, bachelor's, master's, and doctoral degrees. 72 undergraduate majors. ***Total enrollment:*** 38,100. Undergraduates: 32,795. Freshmen: 6,764. Federal methodology is used as a basis for awarding need-based institutional aid.

UNDERGRADUATE EXPENSES for 2019–2020 ***Application fee:*** $40. ***Tuition, state resident:*** full-time $10,780. ***Tuition, nonresident:*** full-time $30,250. Full-time tuition and fees vary according to course load. Part-time tuition and fees vary according to course load. ***College room and board:*** $10,836; ***Room only:*** $6900. Room and board charges vary according to board plan, housing facility, and location.

FRESHMAN FINANCIAL AID (Fall 2018) 4758 applied for aid; of those 69% were deemed to have need. 95% of freshmen with need received aid; of those 24% had need fully met. ***Average percent of need met:*** 56% (excluding resources awarded to replace EFC). ***Average financial aid package:*** $15,518 (excluding resources awarded to replace EFC). 27% of all full-time freshmen had no need and received non-need-based gift aid.

UNDERGRADUATE FINANCIAL AID (Fall 2018) 16,585 applied for aid; of those 77% were deemed to have need. 97% of undergraduates with need received aid; of those 20% had need fully met. ***Average percent of need met:*** 54% (excluding resources awarded to replace EFC). ***Average financial aid package:*** $15,217 (excluding resources awarded to replace EFC). 28% of all full-time undergraduates had no need and received non-need-based gift aid.

GIFT AID (NEED-BASED) ***Total amount:*** $118,403,572 (28% federal, 3% state, 67% institutional, 2% external sources). ***Receiving aid:*** Freshmen: 38% (2,547); all full-time undergraduates: 32% (9,558). ***Average award:*** Freshmen: $14,016; Undergraduates: $13,730. ***Scholarships, grants, and awards:*** Federal Pell, FSEOG, state, private, college/university gift aid from institutional funds, Federal Nursing.

GIFT AID (NON-NEED-BASED) ***Total amount:*** $174,843,127 (5% federal, 3% state, 89% institutional, 3% external sources). ***Receiving aid:*** Freshmen: 31% (2,085). Undergraduates: 24% (6,940). ***Average award:*** Freshmen: $15,183. Undergraduates: $16,843. ***Scholarships, grants, and awards by category:*** *Academic interests/achievement:* 16,000 awards: agriculture, architecture, area/ethnic studies, biological sciences, business, communication, computer science, education, engineering/technologies, English, foreign languages, general academic interests/achievements, health fields, home economics, humanities, international studies, library science, mathematics, military science, physical sciences, premedicine, religion/biblical studies, social sciences. *Creative arts/performance:* 250 awards: applied art and design, art/fine arts, cinema/film/broadcasting, creative writing, dance, debating, general creative arts/performance, journalism/publications, music, performing arts, theater/drama. *Special achievements/activities:* 3,500 awards: cheerleading/drum major, community service, general special achievements/activities, hobbies/interests, junior miss, leadership, memberships, religious involvement. *Special characteristics:* 750 awards: children and siblings of alumni, children of union members/company employees, children with a deceased or disabled parent, ethnic background, first-generation college students, general special characteristics, international students, local/state students, members of minority groups, out-of-state students, religious affiliation, spouses of deceased or disabled public servants, veterans' children. ***Tuition waivers:*** Full or partial for employees or children of employees. ***ROTC:*** Army, Air Force.

LOANS ***Student loans:*** $146,294,778 (62% need-based, 38% non-need-based). 47% of past graduating class borrowed through all loan programs. *Average indebtedness per student:* $34,975. ***Average need-based loan:*** Freshmen: $3290. Undergraduates: $4134. ***Parent loans:*** $97,892,141 (54% need-based, 46% non-need-based). ***Programs:*** Federal Direct (Subsidized and Unsubsidized Stafford, PLUS), college/university.

WORK-STUDY ***Federal work-study:*** Total amount: $1,852,854; 641 jobs averaging $2863.

ATHLETIC AWARDS Total amount: $14,594,683 (3% need-based, 97% non-need-based).

APPLYING FOR FINANCIAL AID ***Required financial aid forms:*** FAFSA, Application for Academic Scholarships. ***Financial aid deadline (priority):*** 3/1. ***Notification date:*** Continuous beginning 4/1. Students must reply within 3 weeks of notification.

CONTACT Mrs. Helen Allen, Director of Student Financial Aid, The University of Alabama, Box 870162, Tuscaloosa, AL 35487-0162, 205-348-7949 or toll-free 800-933-BAMA. *Fax:* 205-348-2989. *E-mail:* helen.allen@ua.edu. *Website:* http://www.ua.edu/.

THE UNIVERSITY OF ALABAMA AT BIRMINGHAM

Birmingham, AL

Tuition & fees (AL res): $10,710 **Average undergraduate aid package: $12,330**

ABOUT THE INSTITUTION State-supported, coed. ***Awards:*** certificates, bachelor's, master's, and doctoral degrees. 56 undergraduate majors. ***Total enrollment:*** 22,080. Undergraduates: 13,836. Freshmen: 2,346. Federal methodology is used as a basis for awarding need-based institutional aid.

UNDERGRADUATE EXPENSES for 2019–2020 ***Application fee:*** $30. ***Tuition, state resident:*** full-time $10,710; part-time $357 per credit hour. ***Tuition, nonresident:*** full-time $25,500; part-time $850 per credit hour. Full-time tuition and fees vary according to course load, degree level, program, and reciprocity agreements. Part-time tuition and fees vary according to course load, degree level, program, and reciprocity agreements. ***College room and board:*** $10,910; ***Room only:*** $6600. Room and board charges vary according to board plan and housing facility.

FRESHMAN FINANCIAL AID (Fall 2019, est.) 1980 applied for aid; of those 75% were deemed to have need. 99% of freshmen with need received aid; of those 21% had need fully met. ***Average percent of need met:*** 66% (excluding resources awarded to replace EFC). ***Average financial aid package:*** $11,168 (excluding resources awarded to replace EFC). 31% of all full-time freshmen had no need and received non-need-based gift aid.

UNDERGRADUATE FINANCIAL AID (Fall 2019, est.) 7,404 applied for aid; of those 82% were deemed to have need. 98% of undergraduates with need received aid; of those 15% had need fully met. ***Average percent of need met:*** 55% (excluding resources awarded to replace EFC). ***Average financial aid package:*** $12,330 (excluding resources awarded to replace EFC). 23% of all full-time undergraduates had no need and received non-need-based gift aid.

GIFT AID (NEED-BASED) ***Total amount:*** $22,822,146 (99% federal, 1% institutional). ***Receiving aid:*** Freshmen: 36% (821); all full-time undergraduates: 37% (3,835). ***Average award:*** Freshmen: $4862; Undergraduates: $4950. ***Scholarships, grants, and awards:*** Federal Pell, FSEOG, state, private, college/university gift aid from institutional funds, United Negro College Fund.

GIFT AID (NON-NEED-BASED) ***Total amount:*** $42,128,216 (96% institutional, 4% external sources). ***Receiving aid:*** Freshmen: 50% (1,160). Undergraduates: 30% (3,056). ***Average award:*** Freshmen: $8812. Undergraduates: $8304. ***Scholarships, grants, and awards by category:*** *Academic interests/achievement:* business, communication, computer science, engineering/technologies, general academic interests/achievements, home economics, mathematics. *Creative arts/performance:* applied art and design, music, performing arts, theater/drama. *Special achievements/activities:* cheerleading/drum major, junior miss, leadership, memberships, religious involvement. *Special characteristics:* adult students, children and siblings of alumni, children of current students, children of educators, children of faculty/staff, children of public servants, children of union members/company employees, children of workers in trades, children with a deceased or disabled parent, ethnic background, first-generation college students, general special characteristics, handicapped students, international students, married students, members of minority groups, out-of-state students, parents of current students, previous college experience, public servants, relatives of clergy, siblings of current students, spouses of current students, spouses of deceased or disabled public servants, twins, veterans. ***Tuition waivers:*** Full or partial for employees or children of employees. ***ROTC:*** Army, Air Force cooperative.

LOANS ***Student loans:*** $42,768,797 (48% need-based, 52% non-need-based). 60% of past graduating class borrowed through all loan programs. *Average indebtedness per student:* $29,941. ***Average need-based loan:*** Freshmen: $3862. Undergraduates: $3914. ***Parent loans:*** $11,912,378 (100% non-need-based). ***Programs:*** Federal Direct (Subsidized and Unsubsidized Stafford, PLUS), state, college/university.

WORK-STUDY ***Federal work-study:*** Total amount: $3,722,126; jobs available.

ATHLETIC AWARDS Total amount: $7,850,087 (100% non-need-based).

APPLYING FOR FINANCIAL AID ***Required financial aid form:*** FAFSA. ***Financial aid deadline (priority):*** 3/1. ***Notification date:*** Continuous beginning 3/15. Students must reply within 4 weeks of notification.

CONTACT Ms. Helen M. McIntyre, Office of Student Financial Aid, The University of Alabama at Birmingham, LHL 120, 1720 2nd Avenue South, Birmingham, AL 35294-0013, 205-934-8132 or toll-free 800-421-8743. *E-mail:* finaid@uab.edu.
Website: http://www.uab.edu/.

THE UNIVERSITY OF ALABAMA IN HUNTSVILLE

Huntsville, AL

ABOUT THE INSTITUTION State-supported, coed. ***Awards:*** certificates, bachelor's, master's, and doctoral degrees. 36 undergraduate majors. ***Total enrollment:*** 9,988. Undergraduates: 7,989. Freshmen: 1,497.

GIFT AID (NEED-BASED) ***Scholarships, grants, and awards:*** Federal Pell, FSEOG, state, private, college/university gift aid from institutional funds, Federal Nursing.

GIFT AID (NON-NEED-BASED) ***Scholarships, grants, and awards by category:*** *Academic interests/achievement:* biological sciences, business, communication, computer science, education, engineering/technologies, English, foreign languages, general academic interests/achievements, home economics, humanities, mathematics, physical sciences, social sciences. *Creative arts/performance:* applied art and design, music. *Special achievements/activities:* cheerleading/drum major, community service, general special achievements/activities, junior miss, leadership. *Special characteristics:* general special characteristics, local/state students, members of minority groups.

LOANS ***Programs:*** Federal Direct (Subsidized and Unsubsidized Stafford, PLUS).

WORK-STUDY ***Federal work-study:*** Total amount: $240,258; 54 jobs averaging $4449.

APPLYING FOR FINANCIAL AID ***Required financial aid form:*** FAFSA.

CONTACT Mr. Patrick James, Director of Financial Aid, The University of Alabama in Huntsville, 301 Sparkman Drive, CTC Room 212, Huntsville, AL 35899, 256-824-6650 or toll-free 800-UAH-CALL. *Fax:* 256-824-6212. *E-mail:* finaid@uah.edu.
Website: http://www.uah.edu/.

UNIVERSITY OF ALASKA ANCHORAGE

Anchorage, AK

Tuition & fees: N/R	Average undergraduate aid package: $10,955

ABOUT THE INSTITUTION State-supported, coed. ***Awards:*** certificates, associate, bachelor's, master's, and doctoral degrees. 107 undergraduate majors. ***Total enrollment:*** 14,731. Undergraduates: 14,004. Freshmen: 1,607. Federal methodology is used as a basis for awarding need-based institutional aid.

FRESHMAN FINANCIAL AID (Fall 2019, est.) 869 applied for aid; of those 68% were deemed to have need. 97% of freshmen with need received aid; of those 23% had need fully met. ***Average percent of need met:*** 73% (excluding resources awarded to replace EFC). ***Average financial aid package:*** $10,356 (excluding resources awarded to replace EFC). 8% of all full-time freshmen had no need and received non-need-based gift aid.

UNDERGRADUATE FINANCIAL AID (Fall 2019, est.) 3,723 applied for aid; of those 72% were deemed to have need. 95% of undergraduates with need received aid; of those 21% had need fully met. ***Average percent of need met:*** 73% (excluding resources awarded to replace EFC). ***Average financial aid package:*** $10,955 (excluding resources awarded to replace EFC). 9% of all full-time undergraduates had no need and received non-need-based gift aid.

GIFT AID (NEED-BASED) ***Total amount:*** $27,225,609 (57% federal, 18% state, 12% institutional, 13% external sources). ***Receiving aid:*** Freshmen: 51% (511); all full-time undergraduates: 44% (2,214). ***Average award:*** Freshmen: $3429; Undergraduates: $3629.

GIFT AID (NON-NEED-BASED) ***Total amount:*** $6,458,476 (41% state, 25% institutional, 34% external sources). ***Average award:*** Freshmen: $3010. Undergraduates: $2417. ***Scholarships, grants, and awards by category:*** *Academic interests/achievement:* biological sciences, business, communication, computer science, education, engineering/technologies, English, general academic interests/achievements, health fields, humanities, mathematics, social sciences. *Creative arts/performance:* art/fine arts, dance, debating, music, performing arts. *Special achievements/activities:* general special achievements/activities, leadership. *Special characteristics:* children and siblings of alumni, children of current students, children of educators, children of faculty/staff. ***ROTC:*** Army, Air Force.

LOANS ***Student loans:*** $38,264,645 (71% need-based, 29% non-need-based). 50% of past graduating class borrowed through all loan programs. *Average indebtedness per student:* $24,866. ***Average need-based loan:*** Freshmen: $327. Undergraduates: $4077. ***Parent loans:*** $958,569 (69% need-based, 31% non-need-based).

WORK-STUDY ***Federal work-study:*** Total amount: $341,067; jobs available.

ATHLETIC AWARDS Total amount: $1,820,261 (29% need-based, 71% non-need-based).

APPLYING FOR FINANCIAL AID ***Required financial aid form:*** FAFSA. ***Financial aid deadline (priority):*** 2/15. ***Notification date:*** Continuous beginning 2/1. Students must reply within 4 weeks of notification.

CONTACT Sonya F. Stein, Director of Student Financial Assistance, University of Alaska Anchorage, PO Box 141608, Anchorage, AK 99514-1608, 907-786-1517. *Fax:* 907-786-6122. *E-mail:* sfstein@alaska.edu.
Website: http://www.uaa.alaska.edu/.

UNIVERSITY OF ALASKA FAIRBANKS

Fairbanks, AK

Tuition & fees (area res): $10,308	Average undergraduate aid package: $9230

ABOUT THE INSTITUTION State-supported, coed. ***Awards:*** certificates, associate, bachelor's, master's, and doctoral degrees. 77 undergraduate majors. ***Total enrollment:*** 7,260. Undergraduates: 6,284. Freshmen: 686. Federal methodology is used as a basis for awarding need-based institutional aid.

UNDERGRADUATE EXPENSES for 2020–2021 ***Application fee:*** $50. ***Tuition, area resident:*** full-time $8460; part-time $282 per credit hour. ***Tuition, state resident:*** full-time $8460; part-time $282 per credit hour. ***Tuition, nonresident:*** full-time $25,440; part-time $848 per credit hour. ***Required fees:*** full-time $1848. ***College room and board:*** $10,440; ***Room only:*** $6000.

FRESHMAN FINANCIAL AID (Fall 2018) 531 applied for aid; of those 63% were deemed to have need. 97% of freshmen with need received aid; of those 20% had need fully met. ***Average percent of need met:*** 59% (excluding resources awarded to replace EFC). ***Average financial aid package:*** $9321 (excluding resources awarded to replace EFC). 16% of all full-time freshmen had no need and received non-need-based gift aid.

UNDERGRADUATE FINANCIAL AID (Fall 2018) 2,232 applied for aid; of those 69% were deemed to have need. 96% of undergraduates with need received aid; of those 16% had need fully met. ***Average percent of need met:*** 54% (excluding resources awarded to replace EFC). ***Average financial aid package:*** $9230 (excluding resources awarded to replace EFC). 13% of all full-time undergraduates had no need and received non-need-based gift aid.

GIFT AID (NEED-BASED) ***Total amount:*** $13,726,620 (45% federal, 18% state, 18% institutional, 19% external sources). ***Receiving aid:*** Freshmen: 52% (302); all full-time undergraduates: 50% (1,360). ***Average award:*** Freshmen: $8730; Undergraduates: $8101. ***Scholarships, grants, and awards:*** Federal Pell, FSEOG, state, private, college/university gift aid from institutional funds.

GIFT AID (NON-NEED-BASED) ***Total amount:*** $4,576,117 (41% state, 29% institutional, 30% external sources). ***Receiving aid:*** Freshmen: 8% (44). Undergraduates: 6% (155). ***Average award:*** Freshmen: $3690. Undergraduates: $3768. ***Scholarships, grants, and awards by category:*** *Academic interests/achievement:* biological sciences, business, computer science, education, engineering/technologies, general academic interests/achievements, mathematics, military science, physical sciences. *Special achievements/activities:* community service, general special achievements/activities, leadership. *Special characteristics:* local/state students. ***ROTC:*** Army.

LOANS ***Student loans:*** 40% of past graduating class borrowed through all loan programs. *Average indebtedness per student:* $26,406. ***Average need-based loan:*** Freshmen: $3021. Undergraduates: $3774. ***Programs:*** Federal Direct (Subsidized and Unsubsidized Stafford, PLUS), state.

WORK-STUDY Federal work-study jobs available.

APPLYING FOR FINANCIAL AID ***Required financial aid forms:*** FAFSA, institution's own form. ***Financial aid deadline:*** 7/1 (priority: 2/15). ***Notification date:*** Continuous beginning 3/1. Students must reply within 2 weeks of notification.

CONTACT Deanna Dieringer, Director of Financial Aid, University of Alaska Fairbanks, PO Box 756360, Fairbanks, AK 99775-6360, 907-474-7256 or toll-free 800-478-1823. *Fax:* 907-474-7065. *E-mail:* uaf-financialaid@alaska.edu.
Website: http://www.uaf.edu/.

UNIVERSITY OF ALASKA SOUTHEAST

Juneau, AK

Tuition & fees (area res): $7560	Average undergraduate aid package: $19,091

ABOUT THE INSTITUTION State-supported, coed. ***Awards:*** certificates, associate, bachelor's, and master's degrees. 27 undergraduate majors. ***Total enrollment:*** 2,150. Undergraduates: 1,886. Freshmen: 172. Federal methodology is used as a basis for awarding need-based institutional aid.

UNDERGRADUATE EXPENSES for 2020–2021 ***Application fee:*** $50. ***Tuition, area resident:*** full-time $6192; part-time $258 per credit hour. ***Tuition, state resident:*** full-time $6192; part-time $258 per credit hour. ***Tuition, nonresident:*** full-time $19,776; part-time $258 per credit hour. ***Required fees:*** full-time $1368. Full-time tuition and fees vary according to course level, course load, degree level, and location. Part-time tuition and fees vary according to course level, course load, degree level, and location. ***College room and board:*** $8900; ***Room only:*** $5600. Room and board charges vary according to housing facility and location. ***Payment plan:*** Tuition prepayment.

FRESHMAN FINANCIAL AID (Fall 2018) 134 applied for aid; of those 70% were deemed to have need. 98% of freshmen with need received aid; of those 26% had need fully met. ***Average percent of need met:*** 66% (excluding resources awarded to replace EFC). ***Average financial aid package:*** $19,272 (excluding resources awarded to replace EFC). 7% of all full-time freshmen had no need and received non-need-based gift aid.

UNDERGRADUATE FINANCIAL AID (Fall 2018) 446 applied for aid; of those 75% were deemed to have need. 98% of undergraduates with need received aid; of those 21% had need fully met. ***Average percent of need met:*** 64% (excluding resources awarded to replace EFC). ***Average financial aid package:*** $19,091 (excluding resources awarded to replace EFC). 5% of all full-time undergraduates had no need and received non-need-based gift aid.

GIFT AID (NEED-BASED) ***Receiving aid:*** Freshmen: 46% (76); all full-time undergraduates: 45% (258). ***Average award:*** Freshmen: $7124; Undergraduates: $6778. ***Scholarships, grants, and awards:*** Federal Pell, FSEOG, state, private, college/university gift aid from institutional funds.

GIFT AID (NON-NEED-BASED) ***Receiving aid:*** Freshmen: 5% (9). Undergraduates: 4% (23). ***Average award:*** Freshmen: $3418. Undergraduates: $3490. ***Scholarships, grants, and awards by category:*** *Academic interests/achievement:* general academic interests/achievements. *Special characteristics:* local/state students. ***Tuition waivers:*** Full or partial for employees or children of employees, senior citizens.

LOANS ***Student loans:*** 91% of past graduating class borrowed through all loan programs. *Average indebtedness per student:* $33,869. ***Average need-based loan:*** Freshmen: $6231. Undergraduates: $8360. ***Programs:*** Federal Direct (Subsidized and Unsubsidized Stafford, PLUS), state.

WORK-STUDY Federal work-study jobs available.

APPLYING FOR FINANCIAL AID ***Required financial aid form:*** FAFSA. ***Financial aid deadline:*** Continuous. ***Notification date:*** Continuous.

CONTACT Janelle Cook, Director of Financial Aid, University of Alaska Southeast, 11120 Glacier Highway, Juneau, AK 99801-8680, 907-796-6255 or toll-free 877-465-4827. *Fax:* 907-796-6250. *E-mail:* jmcook3@alaska.edu.
Website: http://www.uas.alaska.edu/.

UNIVERSITY OF ANTELOPE VALLEY

Lancaster, CA

CONTACT Financial Aid Office, University of Antelope Valley, 44055 North Sierra Highway, Lancaster, CA 93534, 661-726-1911.
Website: http://www.uav.edu/.

THE UNIVERSITY OF ARIZONA

Tucson, AZ

Tuition & fees (area res): $12,379	Average undergraduate aid package: $14,300

ABOUT THE INSTITUTION State-supported, coed. ***Awards:*** certificates, bachelor's, master's, and doctoral degrees. 144 undergraduate majors. ***Total enrollment:*** 45,918. Undergraduates: 35,801. Freshmen: 7,683. Both federal and institutional methodology are used as a basis for awarding need-based institutional aid.

UNDERGRADUATE EXPENSES for 2020–2021 ***Application fee:*** $50. ***One-time required fee:*** $425. ***Tuition, area resident:*** full-time $10,990; part-time $785 per credit hour. ***Tuition, state resident:*** full-time $10,990; part-time $785 per credit hour. ***Tuition, nonresident:*** full-time $33,273; part-time $1386 per credit hour. ***Required fees:*** full-time $1389. Full-time tuition and fees vary according to location. Part-time tuition and fees vary according to location. ***College room and board:*** $13,050; ***Room only:*** $8050. Room and board charges vary according to board plan and housing facility. ***Payment plan:*** Guaranteed tuition.

FRESHMAN FINANCIAL AID (Fall 2018) 4715 applied for aid; of those 71% were deemed to have need. 98% of freshmen with need received aid; of those 20% had need fully met. ***Average percent of need met:*** 67% (excluding resources awarded to replace EFC). ***Average financial aid package:*** $16,301 (excluding resources awarded to replace EFC). 34% of all full-time freshmen had no need and received non-need-based gift aid.

UNDERGRADUATE FINANCIAL AID (Fall 2018) 18,696 applied for aid; of those 80% were deemed to have need. 97% of undergraduates with need received aid; of those 14% had need fully met. ***Average percent of need met:*** 61% (excluding resources awarded to replace EFC). ***Average financial aid package:*** $14,300 (excluding resources awarded to replace EFC). 24% of all full-time undergraduates had no need and received non-need-based gift aid.

GIFT AID (NEED-BASED) ***Total amount:*** $179,816,780 (32% federal, 4% state, 61% institutional, 3% external sources). ***Receiving aid:*** Freshmen: 53% (3,201); all full-time undergraduates: 47% (13,668). ***Average award:*** Freshmen: $13,720; Undergraduates: $11,716. ***Scholarships, grants, and awards:*** Federal Pell, FSEOG, state, private, college/university gift aid from institutional funds.

GIFT AID (NON-NEED-BASED) ***Total amount:*** $96,196,170 (4% federal, 93% institutional, 3% external sources). ***Receiving aid:*** Freshmen: 10% (585). Undergraduates: 6% (1,640). ***Average award:*** Freshmen: $9808. Undergraduates: $8921. ***Scholarships, grants, and awards by category:*** *Academic interests/achievement:* general academic interests/achievements. *Creative arts/performance:* art/fine arts, cinema/film/broadcasting, dance, music, performing arts, theater/drama. *Special achievements/activities:* leadership. *Special characteristics:* international students. ***Tuition waivers:*** Full or partial for employees or children of employees. ***ROTC:*** Army, Naval, Air Force.

LOANS ***Student loans:*** $108,779,553 (80% need-based, 20% non-need-based). 45% of past graduating class borrowed through all loan programs. *Average indebtedness per student:* $26,414. ***Average need-based loan:*** Freshmen: $3087. Undergraduates: $4074. ***Parent loans:*** $82,126,823 (78% need-based, 22% non-need-based). ***Programs:*** Federal Direct (Subsidized and Unsubsidized Stafford, PLUS), Federal Nursing, state, college/university.

WORK-STUDY ***Federal work-study:*** Total amount: $4,520,032; 1,403 jobs averaging $3247. ***State or other work-study/employment:*** Total amount: $23,106,579 (66% need-based, 34% non-need-based). 7,170 part-time jobs averaging $3495.

ATHLETIC AWARDS Total amount: $10,146,322 (43% need-based, 57% non-need-based).

APPLYING FOR FINANCIAL AID ***Required financial aid forms:*** FAFSA, institution's own form. ***Financial aid deadline (priority):*** 3/1. ***Notification date:*** Continuous beginning 2/1.

CONTACT Financial Aid Office, The University of Arizona, Tucson, AZ 85721, 520-621-2211.
Website: http://www.arizona.edu/.

UNIVERSITY OF ARKANSAS

Fayetteville, AR

Tuition & fees (AR res): $9384	Average undergraduate aid package: $10,337

ABOUT THE INSTITUTION State-supported, coed. ***Awards:*** certificates, bachelor's, master's, and doctoral degrees. 80 undergraduate majors. ***Total enrollment:*** 27,559. Undergraduates: 23,025. Freshmen: 4,601. Federal methodology is used as a basis for awarding need-based institutional aid.

UNDERGRADUATE EXPENSES for 2019–2020 ***Application fee:*** $40. ***Tuition, area resident:*** part-time $313 per credit hour. ***Tuition, state resident:*** full-time $7568; part-time $313 per credit hour. ***Tuition, nonresident:*** full-time $24,056; part-time $862 per credit hour. ***Required fees:*** full-time $1816; $60.55 per credit hour. Full-time tuition and fees vary according to course load, location, and program. Part-time tuition and fees vary according to course load, location, and program. ***College room and board:*** $11,330; ***Room only:*** $7290. Room and board charges vary according to board plan, housing facility, and location.

FRESHMAN FINANCIAL AID (Fall 2019, est.) 3801 applied for aid; of those 55% were deemed to have need. 96% of freshmen with need received aid; of those 16% had need fully met. ***Average percent of need met:*** 57% (excluding resources awarded to replace EFC). ***Average financial aid package:*** $9715 (excluding resources awarded to replace EFC). 19% of all full-time freshmen had no need and received non-need-based gift aid.

UNDERGRADUATE FINANCIAL AID (Fall 2019, est.) 13,193 applied for aid; of those 64% were deemed to have need. 95% of undergraduates with need received aid; of those 16% had need fully met. ***Average percent of need met:*** 59% (excluding resources awarded to replace EFC). ***Average financial aid package:*** $10,337 (excluding resources awarded to replace EFC). 15% of all full-time undergraduates had no need and received non-need-based gift aid.

GIFT AID (NEED-BASED) ***Total amount:*** $51,749,615 (40% federal, 24% state, 29% institutional, 7% external sources). ***Receiving aid:*** Freshmen: 37% (1,668); all full-time undergraduates: 31% (6,369). ***Average award:*** Freshmen: $7644; Undergraduates: $8253. ***Scholarships, grants, and awards:*** Federal Pell, FSEOG, state, private, college/university gift aid from institutional funds.

GIFT AID (NON-NEED-BASED) ***Total amount:*** $40,582,045 (44% state, 49% institutional, 7% external sources). ***Receiving aid:*** Freshmen: 6% (252). Undergraduates: 4% (826). ***Average award:*** Freshmen: $4257. Undergraduates: $5399. ***Scholarships, grants, and awards by category:*** *Academic interests/achievement:* agriculture, architecture, area/ethnic studies, biological sciences, business, communication, computer science, education, engineering/technologies, English, foreign languages, general academic interests/achievements, health fields, home economics, humanities, international studies, mathematics, military science, physical sciences, premedicine, social sciences. *Creative arts/performance:* applied art and design, journalism/publications, music, theater/drama. *Special achievements/activities:* cheerleading/drum major, community service, general special achievements/activities, leadership. *Special characteristics:* adult students, children and siblings of alumni, children of faculty/staff, children of union members/company employees, children of workers in trades, children with a deceased or disabled parent, ethnic background, first-generation college students, handicapped students, international students, local/state students, married students, members of minority groups, out-of-state students, previous college experience, veterans. ***Tuition waivers:*** Full or partial for employees or children of employees, senior citizens. ***ROTC:*** Army, Air Force.

LOANS ***Student loans:*** $81,593,101 (56% need-based, 44% non-need-based). 46% of past graduating class borrowed through all loan programs. *Average indebtedness per student:* $27,123. ***Average need-based loan:*** Freshmen: $3524. Undergraduates: $4348. ***Parent loans:*** $30,155,680 (37% need-based, 63% non-need-based). ***Programs:*** Federal Direct (Subsidized and Unsubsidized Stafford, PLUS), Perkins, state, college/university, alternative loans.

WORK-STUDY ***Federal work-study:*** Total amount: $2,442,502; 872 jobs averaging $2801.

ATHLETIC AWARDS Total amount: $8,079,633 (35% need-based, 65% non-need-based).

APPLYING FOR FINANCIAL AID ***Required financial aid form:*** FAFSA. ***Financial aid deadline (priority):*** 3/15. ***Notification date:*** Continuous beginning 4/1. Students must reply within 4 weeks of notification.

CONTACT Phillip Blevins, Director of Financial Aid and Academic Scholarships, University of Arkansas, 114 Silas H. Hunt Hall, Fayetteville, AR 72701-1201, 479-575-3806 or toll-free 800-377-8632. *Fax:* 479-575-7790. *E-mail:* pblevin@uark.edu.
Website: http://www.uark.edu/.

UNIVERSITY OF ARKANSAS AT LITTLE ROCK

Little Rock, AR

Tuition & fees: N/R	Average undergraduate aid package: N/A

ABOUT THE INSTITUTION State-supported, coed. ***Awards:*** certificates, associate, bachelor's, master's, and doctoral degrees. 57 undergraduate majors. ***Total enrollment:*** 9,581. Undergraduates: 7,615. Freshmen: 584.

FRESHMAN FINANCIAL AID (Fall 2018) 12% of all full-time freshmen had no need and received non-need-based gift aid.

UNDERGRADUATE FINANCIAL AID (Fall 2018) 11% of all full-time undergraduates had no need and received non-need-based gift aid.

GIFT AID (NEED-BASED) ***Total amount:*** $16,552,974 (99% federal, 1% state). ***Scholarships, grants, and awards:*** Federal Pell, FSEOG, state, private, college/university gift aid from institutional funds, United Negro College Fund, Federal Nursing.

GIFT AID (NON-NEED-BASED) ***Total amount:*** $20,668,722 (27% state, 67% institutional, 6% external sources). ***Average award:*** Freshmen: $6688. Undergraduates: $7274. ***Scholarships, grants, and awards by category:*** *Academic interests/achievement:* 2,367 awards: general academic interests/achievements.

LOANS ***Student loans:*** $46,160,260 (28% need-based, 72% non-need-based). 57% of past graduating class borrowed through all loan programs. *Average indebtedness per student:* $24,567. ***Parent loans:*** $1,794,838 (100% non-need-based). ***Programs:*** Federal Direct (Subsidized and Unsubsidized Stafford, PLUS).

WORK-STUDY ***Federal work-study:*** Total amount: $383,929.18; 215 jobs averaging $2423.

ATHLETIC AWARDS Total amount: $2,631,903 (100% non-need-based).

APPLYING FOR FINANCIAL AID ***Financial aid deadline:*** 11/1 (priority: 2/1). ***Notification date:*** Students must reply by 8/1.

CONTACT Financial Aid Office, University of Arkansas at Little Rock, 2801 South University Avenue, Little Rock, AR 72204-1099, 501-569-3035 or toll-free 800-482-8892. *E-mail:* financialaid@ualr.edu.
Website: http://www.ualr.edu/.

UNIVERSITY OF ARKANSAS AT MONTICELLO

Monticello, AR

CONTACT Susan Brewer, Director of Financial Aid, University of Arkansas at Monticello, PO Box 3470, Monticello, AR 71656, 870-460-1050 or toll-free 800-844-1826. *Fax:* 870-460-1450. *E-mail:* brewers@uamont.edu.
Website: http://www.uamont.edu/.

UNIVERSITY OF ARKANSAS AT PINE BLUFF

Pine Bluff, AR

CONTACT Mrs. Carolyn Iverson, Director of Financial Aid, University of Arkansas at Pine Bluff, 1200 North University Drive, PO Box 4985, Pine Bluff, AR 71601, 870-575-8303 or toll-free 800-264-6585. *Fax:* 870-575-4622. *E-mail:* iverson_c@uapb.edu.
Website: http://www.uapb.edu/.

UNIVERSITY OF ARKANSAS FOR MEDICAL SCIENCES

Little Rock, AR

Tuition & fees: N/R | **Average undergraduate aid package: $11,549**

ABOUT THE INSTITUTION State-supported, coed. ***Awards:*** certificates, associate, bachelor's, master's, and doctoral degrees (bachelor's degree is upper-level). 13 undergraduate majors. Federal methodology is used as a basis for awarding need-based institutional aid.

FRESHMAN FINANCIAL AID (Fall 2018) ***Average financial aid package:*** $11,549 (excluding resources awarded to replace EFC).

UNDERGRADUATE FINANCIAL AID (Fall 2018) ***Average financial aid package:*** $11,549 (excluding resources awarded to replace EFC).

GIFT AID (NEED-BASED) ***Total amount:*** $1,181,586 (85% federal, 2% state, 1% institutional, 12% external sources). ***Receiving aid:*** All full-time undergraduates: 52% (223). ***Average award:*** Freshmen: $4886; Undergraduates: $4886. ***Scholarships, grants, and awards:*** Federal Pell, FSEOG, state, private, college/university gift aid from institutional funds.

GIFT AID (NON-NEED-BASED) ***Total amount:*** $721,150 (88% state, 12% external sources). ***Receiving aid:*** Undergraduates: 37% (159). ***Scholarships, grants, and awards by category:*** *Academic interests/achievement:* 487 awards ($2,432,089 total).

LOANS ***Student loans:*** $2,939,236 (44% need-based, 56% non-need-based). ***Average need-based loan:*** Freshmen: $5045. Undergraduates: $5045. ***Parent loans:*** $260,152 (100% need-based). ***Programs:*** Federal Direct (Subsidized and Unsubsidized Stafford, PLUS), Perkins, Federal Nursing.

APPLYING FOR FINANCIAL AID ***Financial aid deadline:*** Continuous. ***Notification date:*** Students must reply within 4 weeks of notification.

CONTACT Ms. Gloria Kemp, Director of Student Financial Services, University of Arkansas for Medical Sciences, 4301 West Markham Street, Slot #758, Little Rock, AR 72205, 501-686-6936. *Fax:* 501-686-8798. *E-mail:* kempgloriad@uams.edu.
Website: http://www.uams.edu/.

UNIVERSITY OF ARKANSAS-FORT SMITH

Fort Smith, AR

CONTACT Tammy Malone, Interim Financial Aid Director, University of Arkansas-Fort Smith, 5210 Grand Avenue, Fort Smith, AR 72913, 479-788-7099 or toll-free 888-512-5466. *Fax:* 479-788-7095. *E-mail:* tmalone@uafortsmith.edu.
Website: http://uafs.edu/.

UNIVERSITY OF BALTIMORE

Baltimore, MD

CONTACT Financial Aid Office, University of Baltimore, 1420 North Charles Street, CH 123, Baltimore, MD 21201-5779, 410-837-4763. *Fax:* 410-837-5493. *E-mail:* financial-aid@ubalt.edu.
Website: http://www.ubalt.edu/.

UNIVERSITY OF BRIDGEPORT

Bridgeport, CT

CONTACT Ms. Christine E. Falzerano, Director of Student Financial Services, University of Bridgeport, 126 Park Avenue, Bridgeport, CT 06604, 203-576-4568 or toll-free 800-EXCEL-UB. *Fax:* 203-576-4570. *E-mail:* finaid@bridgeport.edu.
Website: http://www.bridgeport.edu/.

UNIVERSITY OF CALIFORNIA, BERKELEY

Berkeley, CA

Tuition & fees (CA res): $14,253 | **Average undergraduate aid package: $26,153**

ABOUT THE INSTITUTION State-supported, coed. ***Awards:*** certificates, bachelor's, master's, and doctoral degrees. 90 undergraduate majors. ***Total enrollment:*** 43,695. Undergraduates: 31,361. Freshmen: 6,397. Both federal and institutional methodology are used as a basis for awarding need-based institutional aid.

UNDERGRADUATE EXPENSES for 2019–2020 ***Application fee:*** $70. ***Tuition, state resident:*** full-time $11,442. ***Tuition, nonresident:*** full-time $41,196. ***Required fees:*** full-time $2811. ***College room and board:*** $17,220. Room and board charges vary according to board plan and housing facility.

FRESHMAN FINANCIAL AID (Fall 2019, est.) 4466 applied for aid; of those 61% were deemed to have need. 96% of freshmen with need received aid; of those 30% had need fully met. ***Average percent of need met:*** 83% (excluding resources awarded to replace EFC). ***Average financial aid package:*** $28,230 (excluding resources awarded to replace EFC). 6% of all full-time freshmen had no need and received non-need-based gift aid.

UNDERGRADUATE FINANCIAL AID (Fall 2019, est.) 17,340 applied for aid; of those 78% were deemed to have need. 98% of undergraduates with need received aid; of those 30% had need fully met. ***Average percent of need met:*** 83% (excluding resources awarded to replace EFC). ***Average financial aid package:*** $26,153 (excluding resources awarded to replace EFC). 5% of all full-time undergraduates had no need and received non-need-based gift aid.

GIFT AID (NEED-BASED) ***Total amount:*** $304,296,507 (15% federal, 31% state, 51% institutional, 3% external sources). ***Receiving aid:*** Freshmen: 39% (2,524); all full-time undergraduates: 43% (12,762). ***Average award:*** Freshmen: $23,767; Undergraduates: $22,420. ***Scholarships, grants, and awards:*** Federal Pell, FSEOG, state, private, college/university gift aid from institutional funds.

GIFT AID (NON-NEED-BASED) ***Total amount:*** $27,338,351 (10% federal, 3% state, 57% institutional, 30% external sources). ***Receiving aid:*** Freshmen: 1% (81). Undergraduates: 1% (306). ***Average award:*** Freshmen: $6464. Undergraduates: $8717. ***Scholarships, grants, and awards by category:*** *Academic interests/achievement:* general academic interests/achievements. ***ROTC:*** Army, Naval, Air Force.

LOANS ***Student loans:*** $44,475,498 (67% need-based, 33% non-need-based). 32% of past graduating class borrowed through all loan programs. *Average indebtedness per student:* $19,773. ***Average need-based loan:*** Freshmen: $7588. Undergraduates: $7231. ***Parent loans:*** $31,077,337 (28% need-based, 72% non-need-based). ***Programs:*** Federal Direct (Subsidized and Unsubsidized Stafford, PLUS), college/university.

WORK-STUDY ***Federal work-study:*** Total amount: $14,718,584; jobs available. ***State or other work-study/employment:*** Total amount: $6,976,766 (100% need-based). Part-time jobs available.

ATHLETIC AWARDS Total amount: $15,108,828 (17% need-based, 83% non-need-based).

APPLYING FOR FINANCIAL AID ***Required financial aid forms:*** FAFSA, state aid form. ***Financial aid deadline:*** 3/2 (priority: 3/2). ***Notification date:*** 3/31. Students must reply by 5/1.

CONTACT Financial Aid Office, University of California, Berkeley, Berkeley, CA 94720, 510-642-6000.
Website: http://www.berkeley.edu/.

UNIVERSITY OF CALIFORNIA, DAVIS

Davis, CA

Tuition & fees (CA res): $14,492 | **Average undergraduate aid package: $21,768**

ABOUT THE INSTITUTION State-supported, coed. ***Awards:*** certificates, bachelor's, master's, and doctoral degrees. 83 undergraduate majors. ***Total enrollment:*** 38,035. Undergraduates: 30,810. Freshmen: 6,405. Both federal and institutional methodology are used as a basis for awarding need-based institutional aid.

UNDERGRADUATE EXPENSES for 2019–2020 ***Application fee:*** $70. ***Tuition, state resident:*** full-time $11,442. ***Tuition, nonresident:*** full-time $40,434. ***Required fees:*** full-time $3050. ***College room and board:*** $15,863. Room and board charges vary according to board plan.

FRESHMAN FINANCIAL AID (Fall 2019, est.) 4618 applied for aid; of those 75% were deemed to have need. 98% of freshmen with need received aid; of those 26% had need fully met. ***Average percent of need met:*** 82% (excluding resources awarded to replace EFC). ***Average financial aid package:*** $24,494 (excluding resources awarded to replace EFC). 5% of all full-time freshmen had no need and received non-need-based gift aid.

UNDERGRADUATE FINANCIAL AID (Fall 2019, est.) 20,853 applied for aid; of those 84% were deemed to have need. 98% of undergraduates with need received aid; of those 23% had need fully met. ***Average percent of need met:*** 80% (excluding resources awarded to replace EFC). ***Average financial aid package:*** $21,768 (excluding resources awarded to replace EFC). 4% of all full-time undergraduates had no need and received non-need-based gift aid.

GIFT AID (NEED-BASED) ***Total amount:*** $323,740,788 (18% federal, 39% state, 41% institutional, 2% external sources). ***Receiving aid:*** Freshmen: 56% (3,308); all full-time undergraduates: 56% (16,825). ***Average award:*** Freshmen: $21,076; Undergraduates: $18,987. ***Scholarships, grants, and awards:*** Federal Pell, FSEOG, state, private, college/university gift aid from institutional funds, The UC Davis Aggie Grant Plan (for middle-income California students).

GIFT AID (NON-NEED-BASED) ***Total amount:*** $20,463,124 (8% federal, 8% state, 40% institutional, 44% external sources). ***Receiving aid:*** Freshmen: 1% (85). Undergraduates: 1% (351). ***Average award:*** Freshmen: $5633. Undergraduates: $6954. ***Scholarships, grants, and awards by category:*** *Academic interests/achievement:* agriculture, architecture, area/ethnic studies, biological sciences, business, communication, computer science, education, engineering/technologies, English, foreign languages, general academic interests/achievements, health fields, home economics, humanities, international studies, mathematics, military science, physical sciences, premedicine, religion/biblical studies, social sciences. ***ROTC:*** Army, Naval cooperative, Air Force cooperative.

LOANS ***Student loans:*** $55,793,905 (78% need-based, 22% non-need-based). 46% of past graduating class borrowed through all loan programs. *Average indebtedness per student:* $18,985. ***Average need-based loan:*** Freshmen: $6694. Undergraduates: $6193. ***Parent loans:*** $38,618,086 (20% need-based, 80% non-need-based). ***Programs:*** Federal Direct (Subsidized and Unsubsidized Stafford, PLUS), state, college/university.

WORK-STUDY ***Federal work-study:*** Total amount: $2,273,200; jobs available. ***State or other work-study/employment:*** Total amount: $106,230 (100% need-based).

ATHLETIC AWARDS Total amount: $7,958,283 (26% need-based, 74% non-need-based).

APPLYING FOR FINANCIAL AID ***Required financial aid forms:*** FAFSA, state aid form. ***Financial aid deadline (priority):*** 3/2. ***Notification date:*** Continuous beginning 3/23.

CONTACT Deborah G. Agee, Director of Financial Aid and Scholarships, University of California, Davis, One Shields Avenue, 2116 Dutton Hall, Davis, CA 95616, 530-752-2396. *Fax:* 530-752-7339. *E-mail:* dgagee@ucdavis.edu.

Website: http://www.ucdavis.edu/.

UNIVERSITY OF CALIFORNIA, IRVINE

Irvine, CA

ABOUT THE INSTITUTION State-supported, coed. ***Awards:*** certificates, bachelor's, master's, and doctoral degrees. 83 undergraduate majors. ***Total enrollment:*** 36,908. Undergraduates: 30,382. Freshmen: 6,068.

GIFT AID (NEED-BASED) ***Scholarships, grants, and awards:*** Federal Pell, FSEOG, state, private, college/university gift aid from institutional funds.

GIFT AID (NON-NEED-BASED) ***Scholarships, grants, and awards by category:*** *Academic interests/achievement:* area/ethnic studies, biological sciences, business, communication, computer science, education, engineering/technologies, English, foreign languages, general academic interests/achievements, home economics, humanities, international studies, mathematics, physical sciences, premedicine, social sciences. *Creative arts/performance:* applied art and design, cinema/film/broadcasting, creative writing, dance, general creative arts/performance, music, performing arts, theater/drama. *Special achievements/activities:* community service, general special achievements/activities, leadership. *Special characteristics:* international students, out-of-state students.

LOANS ***Programs:*** Federal Direct (Subsidized and Unsubsidized Stafford, PLUS), Perkins, college/university, private loans.

WORK-STUDY ***Federal work-study:*** Total amount: $4,780,243; jobs available. ***State or other work-study/employment:*** Total amount: $2,731,666 (100% need-based). Part-time jobs available.

APPLYING FOR FINANCIAL AID ***Required financial aid forms:*** FAFSA, state aid form.

CONTACT Ms. Lindsay Crowell, Senior Associate Director, University of California, Irvine, 102 Aldrich Hall, Irvine, CA 92697-2825, 949-824-4898. *Fax:* 949-824-2820. *E-mail:* finaid@uci.edu.

Website: http://www.uci.edu/.

UNIVERSITY OF CALIFORNIA, LOS ANGELES

Los Angeles, CA

Tuition & fees (CA res): $13,564	Average undergraduate aid package: $24,808

ABOUT THE INSTITUTION State-supported, coed. ***Awards:*** bachelor's, master's, and doctoral degrees. 94 undergraduate majors. ***Total enrollment:*** 45,742. Undergraduates: 31,442. Freshmen: 5,910. Both federal and institutional methodology are used as a basis for awarding need-based institutional aid.

UNDERGRADUATE EXPENSES for 2019–2020 ***Application fee:*** $70. ***One-time required fee:*** $165. ***Tuition, state resident:*** full-time $11,442. ***Tuition, nonresident:*** full-time $41,196. ***Required fees:*** full-time $2122. ***College room and board:*** $16,625. Room and board charges vary according to board plan and housing facility.

FRESHMAN FINANCIAL AID (Fall 2019, est.) 3402 applied for aid; of those 81% were deemed to have need. 100% of freshmen with need received aid; of those 27% had need fully met. ***Average percent of need met:*** 82% (excluding resources awarded to replace EFC). ***Average financial aid package:*** $24,920 (excluding resources awarded to replace EFC). 3% of all full-time freshmen had no need and received non-need-based gift aid.

UNDERGRADUATE FINANCIAL AID (Fall 2019, est.) 17,449 applied for aid; of those 89% were deemed to have need. 100% of undergraduates with need received aid; of those 26% had need fully met. ***Average percent of need met:*** 82% (excluding resources awarded to replace EFC). ***Average financial aid package:*** $24,808 (excluding resources awarded to replace EFC). 4% of all full-time undergraduates had no need and received non-need-based gift aid.

GIFT AID (NEED-BASED) ***Total amount:*** $326,201,183 (15% federal, 37% state, 46% institutional, 2% external sources). ***Receiving aid:*** Freshmen: 45% (2,675); all full-time undergraduates: 49% (15,130). ***Average award:*** Freshmen: $21,621; Undergraduates: $21,402. ***Scholarships, grants, and awards:*** Federal Pell, FSEOG, state, private, college/university gift aid from institutional funds, Federal Nursing.

GIFT AID (NON-NEED-BASED) ***Total amount:*** $12,617,410 (10% federal, 10% state, 59% institutional, 21% external sources). ***Receiving aid:*** Freshmen: 2% (98). Undergraduates: 1% (396). ***Average award:*** Freshmen: $6022. Undergraduates: $5901. ***Scholarships, grants, and awards by category:*** *Academic interests/achievement:* architecture, area/ethnic studies, biological sciences, business, communication, computer science, education, engineering/technologies, English, foreign languages, general academic interests/achievements, home economics, humanities, international studies, library science, mathematics, military science, physical sciences, religion/biblical studies, social sciences. *Creative arts/performance:* applied art and design, art/fine arts, cinema/film/broadcasting, creative writing, dance, debating, general creative arts/performance, journalism/publications, music, performing arts, theater/drama. *Special achievements/activities:* general special achievements/activities, hobbies/interests, leadership. *Special characteristics:* first-generation college students, general special characteristics, handicapped students. ***ROTC:*** Army, Naval, Air Force.

LOANS ***Student loans:*** $61,546,306 (74% need-based, 26% non-need-based). 40% of past graduating class borrowed through all loan programs. *Average indebtedness per student:* $21,441. ***Average need-based loan:*** Freshmen: $7225. Undergraduates: $7487. ***Parent loans:*** $44,129,796 (27% need-based, 73% non-need-based). ***Programs:*** Federal Direct (Subsidized and Unsubsidized Stafford, PLUS), Federal Nursing, state, college/university.

WORK-STUDY ***Federal work-study:*** Total amount: $4,443,191; 2,325 jobs averaging $1911. ***State or other work-study/employment:*** Total amount: $87,500 (100% need-based). 25 part-time jobs averaging $3500.

ATHLETIC AWARDS Total amount: $13,789,193 (22% need-based, 78% non-need-based).

APPLYING FOR FINANCIAL AID ***Required financial aid form:*** FAFSA. ***Financial aid deadline (priority):*** 3/2. ***Notification date:*** Continuous beginning 3/15.

CONTACT Ms. Carolyn Turpin, Budget Officer, University of California, Los Angeles, A-129 Murphy Hall, Los Angeles, CA 90095-1435, 310-206-0407. *E-mail:* finaid@saonet.ucla.edu.
Website: http://www.ucla.edu/.

UNIVERSITY OF CALIFORNIA, MERCED

Merced, CA

Tuition & fees (CA res): $13,538	Average undergraduate aid package: $26,288

ABOUT THE INSTITUTION State-supported, coed. ***Awards:*** bachelor's, master's, and doctoral degrees. 27 undergraduate majors. ***Total enrollment:*** 8,847. Undergraduates: 8,151. Freshmen: 2,107. Both federal and institutional methodology are used as a basis for awarding need-based institutional aid.

UNDERGRADUATE EXPENSES for 2020–2021 ***Application fee:*** $70. ***Tuition, state resident:*** full-time $11,442; part-time $2860 per term. ***Tuition, nonresident:*** full-time $40,434; part-time $10,108 per term. ***Required fees:*** full-time $2096; $2096 per year. Full-time tuition and fees vary according to course load. Part-time tuition and fees vary according to course load. ***College room and board:*** $17,046. Room and board charges vary according to board plan.

FRESHMAN FINANCIAL AID (Fall 2019, est.) 2021 applied for aid; of those 93% were deemed to have need. 100% of freshmen with need received aid; of those 24% had need fully met. ***Average percent of need met:*** 88% (excluding resources awarded to replace EFC). ***Average financial aid package:*** $30,133 (excluding resources awarded to replace EFC). 1% of all full-time freshmen had no need and received non-need-based gift aid.

UNDERGRADUATE FINANCIAL AID (Fall 2019, est.) 7,654 applied for aid; of those 95% were deemed to have need. 99% of undergraduates with need received aid; of those 22% had need fully met. ***Average percent of need met:*** 84% (excluding resources awarded to replace EFC). ***Average financial aid package:*** $26,288 (excluding resources awarded to replace EFC). 1% of all full-time undergraduates had no need and received non-need-based gift aid.

GIFT AID (NEED-BASED) ***Total amount:*** $159,686,412 (17% federal, 44% state, 37% institutional, 2% external sources). ***Receiving aid:*** Freshmen: 88% (1,852); all full-time undergraduates: 88% (7,133). ***Average award:*** Freshmen: $24,953; Undergraduates: $22,327. ***Scholarships, grants, and awards:*** Federal Pell, FSEOG, state, private, college/university gift aid from institutional funds.

GIFT AID (NON-NEED-BASED) ***Total amount:*** $1,878,432 (5% federal, 20% state, 67% institutional, 8% external sources). ***Receiving aid:*** Freshmen: 1% (23). Undergraduates: 1% (84). ***Average award:*** Freshmen: $9310. Undergraduates: $11,369. ***Scholarships, grants, and awards by category:*** *Academic interests/achievement:* general academic interests/achievements. ***Tuition waivers:*** Full or partial for employees or children of employees.

LOANS ***Student loans:*** $21,596,907 (86% need-based, 14% non-need-based). 66% of past graduating class borrowed through all loan programs. *Average indebtedness per student:* $17,872. ***Average need-based loan:*** Freshmen: $4651. Undergraduates: $5251. ***Parent loans:*** $8,045,061 (15% need-based, 85% non-need-based). ***Programs:*** Federal Direct (Subsidized and Unsubsidized Stafford, PLUS), alternative loans.

WORK-STUDY ***Federal work-study:*** Total amount: $9,812,966; jobs available.

ATHLETIC AWARDS Total amount: $60,700 (68% need-based, 32% non-need-based).

APPLYING FOR FINANCIAL AID ***Required financial aid form:*** FAFSA. ***Financial aid deadline (priority):*** 3/2. ***Notification date:*** Continuous beginning 3/2.

CONTACT Dr. Ron Radney, Director of Financial Aid and Scholarships, University of California, Merced, Kolligian Library, Room 127, 5200 North Lake Road, Merced, CA 95343, 209-228-2257. *Fax:* 209-228-7861. *E-mail:* finaid@ucmerced.edu.
Website: http://www.ucmerced.edu/.

UNIVERSITY OF CALIFORNIA, RIVERSIDE

Riverside, CA

Tuition & fees (CA res): $15,626	Average undergraduate aid package: $21,726

ABOUT THE INSTITUTION State-supported, coed. ***Awards:*** bachelor's, master's, and doctoral degrees. 72 undergraduate majors. ***Total enrollment:*** 25,548. Undergraduates: 22,055. Freshmen: 4,778. Federal methodology is used as a basis for awarding need-based institutional aid.

UNDERGRADUATE EXPENSES for 2019–2020 ***Application fee:*** $70. ***Tuition, state resident:*** full-time $11,442; part-time $5721 per year. ***Tuition, nonresident:*** full-time $41,196; part-time $20,598 per year. ***Required fees:*** full-time $4184; $1395 per term. Full-time tuition and fees vary according to course load. Part-time tuition and fees vary according to course load. ***College room and board:*** $17,350. Room and board charges vary according to board plan and housing facility.

FRESHMAN FINANCIAL AID (Fall 2019, est.) 4193 applied for aid; of those 83% were deemed to have need. 99% of freshmen with need received aid; of those 17% had need fully met. ***Average percent of need met:*** 85% (excluding resources awarded to replace EFC). ***Average financial aid package:*** $24,592 (excluding resources awarded to replace EFC). 4% of all full-time freshmen had no need and received non-need-based gift aid.

UNDERGRADUATE FINANCIAL AID (Fall 2019, est.) 18,411 applied for aid; of those 90% were deemed to have need. 99% of undergraduates with need received aid; of those 16% had need fully met. ***Average percent of need met:*** 81% (excluding resources awarded to replace EFC). ***Average financial aid package:*** $21,726 (excluding resources awarded to replace EFC). 4% of all full-time undergraduates had no need and received non-need-based gift aid.

GIFT AID (NEED-BASED) ***Receiving aid:*** Freshmen: 70% (3,343); all full-time undergraduates: 74% (15,991). ***Average award:*** Freshmen: $20,381; Undergraduates: $17,670. ***Scholarships, grants, and awards:*** Federal Pell, FSEOG, state, private, college/university gift aid from institutional funds.

GIFT AID (NON-NEED-BASED) ***Receiving aid:*** Freshmen: 1% (56). Undergraduates: 1% (282). ***Average award:*** Freshmen: $8226. Undergraduates: $9663. ***Scholarships, grants, and awards by category:*** *Academic interests/achievement:* agriculture, area/ethnic studies, biological sciences, business, education, engineering/technologies, English, general academic interests/achievements, humanities, mathematics, physical sciences, premedicine, social sciences. *Creative arts/performance:* applied art and design, creative writing, dance, music, theater/drama. *Special characteristics:* out-of-state students, veterans. ***ROTC:*** Army cooperative, Air Force cooperative.

LOANS ***Student loans:*** 62% of past graduating class borrowed through all loan programs. *Average indebtedness per student:* $20,779. ***Average need-based loan:*** Freshmen: $4939. Undergraduates: $5849. ***Programs:*** Federal Direct (Subsidized and Unsubsidized Stafford, PLUS), college/university.

WORK-STUDY ***Federal work-study:*** 3,174 jobs averaging $1598.

APPLYING FOR FINANCIAL AID ***Required financial aid forms:*** FAFSA, state aid form. ***Notification date:*** Continuous. Students must reply within 3 weeks of notification.

CONTACT Mr. Jose A. Aguilar, Director of Financial Aid, University of California, Riverside, 2106 Student Services Building, Riverside, CA 92521-0209, 951-827-7249. *Fax:* 951-827-5619. *E-mail:* finaid@ucr.edu.
Website: http://www.ucr.edu/.

UNIVERSITY OF CALIFORNIA, SAN DIEGO

La Jolla, CA

Tuition & fees (CA res): $14,480 | **Average undergraduate aid package: $24,977**

ABOUT THE INSTITUTION State-supported, coed. ***Awards:*** bachelor's, master's, and doctoral degrees. 105 undergraduate majors. ***Total enrollment:*** 38,396. Undergraduates: 30,794. Freshmen: 6,023. Federal methodology is used as a basis for awarding need-based institutional aid.

UNDERGRADUATE EXPENSES for 2020–2021 ***Application fee:*** $105. ***Tuition, state resident:*** full-time $12,570. ***Tuition, nonresident:*** full-time $42,324. ***Required fees:*** full-time $1910. ***College room and board:*** $14,295. Room and board charges vary according to board plan and housing facility.

FRESHMAN FINANCIAL AID (Fall 2019, est.) 4368 applied for aid; of those 72% were deemed to have need. 97% of freshmen with need received aid; of those 40% had need fully met. ***Average percent of need met:*** 86% (excluding resources awarded to replace EFC). ***Average financial aid package:*** $25,062 (excluding resources awarded to replace EFC). 2% of all full-time freshmen had no need and received non-need-based gift aid.

UNDERGRADUATE FINANCIAL AID (Fall 2019, est.) 19,586 applied for aid; of those 85% were deemed to have need. 98% of undergraduates with need received aid; of those 35% had need fully met. ***Average percent of need met:*** 85% (excluding resources awarded to replace EFC). ***Average financial aid package:*** $24,977 (excluding resources awarded to replace EFC). 2% of all full-time undergraduates had no need and received non-need-based gift aid.

GIFT AID (NEED-BASED) ***Total amount:*** $332,600,488 (18% federal, 35% state, 46% institutional, 1% external sources). ***Receiving aid:*** Freshmen: 49% (2,925); all full-time undergraduates: 53% (15,767). ***Average award:*** Freshmen: $20,689; Undergraduates: $20,843. ***Scholarships, grants, and awards:*** Federal Pell, FSEOG, state, private, college/university gift aid from institutional funds, TEACH Grants.

GIFT AID (NON-NEED-BASED) ***Total amount:*** $14,983,694 (26% federal, 10% state, 54% institutional, 10% external sources). ***Receiving aid:*** Freshmen: 2% (118). Undergraduates: 1% (394). ***Average award:*** Freshmen: $11,133. Undergraduates: $10,417. ***Scholarships, grants, and awards by category:*** *Academic interests/achievement:* biological sciences, business, communication, computer science, engineering/technologies, general academic interests/achievements, mathematics, physical sciences, premedicine, social sciences. *Creative arts/performance:* art/fine arts, cinema/film/broadcasting, dance, journalism/publications, music, performing arts, theater/drama. *Special achievements/activities:* community service, leadership. *Special characteristics:* ethnic background, first-generation college students, handicapped students, members of minority groups. ***ROTC:*** Army cooperative, Naval cooperative, Air Force cooperative.

LOANS ***Student loans:*** $70,939,497 (81% need-based, 19% non-need-based). 41% of past graduating class borrowed through all loan programs. *Average indebtedness per student:* $20,536. ***Average need-based loan:*** Freshmen: $6484. Undergraduates: $6649. ***Parent loans:*** $18,284,177 (22% need-based, 78% non-need-based). ***Programs:*** Federal Direct (Subsidized and Unsubsidized Stafford, PLUS), college/university, alternative loans.

WORK-STUDY ***Federal work-study:*** Total amount: $15,714,254; jobs available. ***State or other work-study/employment:*** Total amount: $9500 (100% need-based). Part-time jobs available.

ATHLETIC AWARDS Total amount: $2,296,771 (31% need-based, 69% non-need-based).

APPLYING FOR FINANCIAL AID ***Required financial aid forms:*** FAFSA, state aid form. ***Financial aid deadline (priority):*** 3/2. ***Notification date:*** Continuous beginning 3/15.

CONTACT Ms. Vonda Garcia, Director of Financial Aid and Scholarships, University of California, San Diego, 9500 Gilman Drive, Mail Code 0013, La Jolla, CA 92093-0013, 858-534-4480. *Fax:* 858-534-5459. *E-mail:* vonda@ucsd.edu.

Website: http://www.ucsd.edu/.

UNIVERSITY OF CALIFORNIA, SANTA BARBARA

Santa Barbara, CA

Tuition & fees (CA res): $14,391 | **Average undergraduate aid package: $29,936**

ABOUT THE INSTITUTION State-supported, coed. ***Awards:*** certificates, bachelor's, master's, and doctoral degrees. 74 undergraduate majors. ***Total enrollment:*** 26,314. Undergraduates: 23,274. Freshmen: 4,914. Both federal and institutional methodology are used as a basis for awarding need-based institutional aid.

UNDERGRADUATE EXPENSES for 2020–2021 ***Application fee:*** $70. ***Tuition, state resident:*** full-time $11,442. ***Tuition, nonresident:*** full-time $41,196. ***Required fees:*** full-time $2949. ***College room and board:*** $15,389.

FRESHMAN FINANCIAL AID (Fall 2019, est.) 3500 applied for aid; of those 70% were deemed to have need. 100% of freshmen with need received aid; of those 95% had need fully met. ***Average percent of need met:*** 99% (excluding resources awarded to replace EFC). ***Average financial aid package:*** $30,801 (excluding resources awarded to replace EFC). 2% of all full-time freshmen had no need and received non-need-based gift aid.

UNDERGRADUATE FINANCIAL AID (Fall 2019, est.) 14,971 applied for aid; of those 83% were deemed to have need. 100% of undergraduates with need received aid; of those 94% had need fully met. ***Average percent of need met:*** 99% (excluding resources awarded to replace EFC). ***Average financial aid package:*** $29,936 (excluding resources awarded to replace EFC). 2% of all full-time undergraduates had no need and received non-need-based gift aid.

GIFT AID (NEED-BASED) ***Receiving aid:*** Freshmen: 47% (2,315); all full-time undergraduates: 52% (11,820). ***Average award:*** Freshmen: $21,443; Undergraduates: $21,037. ***Scholarships, grants, and awards:*** Federal Pell, FSEOG, state, private, college/university gift aid from institutional funds.

GIFT AID (NON-NEED-BASED) ***Receiving aid:*** Freshmen: 1% (59). Undergraduates: 1% (217). ***Average award:*** Freshmen: $10,290. Undergraduates: $8362. ***Scholarships, grants, and awards by category:*** *Academic interests/achievement:* general academic interests/achievements. ***ROTC:*** Army, Air Force cooperative.

LOANS ***Student loans:*** 51% of past graduating class borrowed through all loan programs. *Average indebtedness per student:* $18,995. ***Average need-based loan:*** Freshmen: $9063. Undergraduates: $7883. ***Programs:*** Federal Direct (Subsidized and Unsubsidized Stafford, PLUS), college/university.

APPLYING FOR FINANCIAL AID ***Required financial aid form:*** FAFSA. ***Notification date:*** Continuous.

CONTACT Mike Miller, Office of Financial Aid, University of California, Santa Barbara, 2103 SAASB, Santa Barbara, CA 93106-3180, 805-893-2432. *Fax:* 805-893-8793.

Website: http://www.ucsb.edu/.

UNIVERSITY OF CALIFORNIA, SANTA CRUZ

Santa Cruz, CA

Tuition & fees (CA res): $14,054 | **Average undergraduate aid package: $25,453**

ABOUT THE INSTITUTION State-supported, coed. ***Awards:*** certificates, bachelor's, master's, and doctoral degrees. 52 undergraduate majors. ***Total enrollment:*** 19,494. Undergraduates: 17,539. Freshmen: 3,713. Both federal and institutional methodology are used as a basis for awarding need-based institutional aid.

UNDERGRADUATE EXPENSES for 2019–2020 ***Application fee:*** $70. ***Tuition, state resident:*** full-time $11,442. ***Tuition, nonresident:*** full-time $40,434. ***Required fees:*** full-time $2612. Part-time tuition and fees vary according to course load. ***College room and board:*** $16,916. Room and board charges vary according to board plan and housing facility.

FRESHMAN FINANCIAL AID (Fall 2019, est.) 2751 applied for aid; of those 71% were deemed to have need. 96% of freshmen with need received aid; of those 22% had need fully met. ***Average percent of need met:*** 82% (excluding resources awarded to replace EFC). ***Average financial aid package:*** $25,044 (excluding

resources awarded to replace EFC). 9% of all full-time freshmen had no need and received non-need-based gift aid.

UNDERGRADUATE FINANCIAL AID (Fall 2019, est.) 11,516 applied for aid; of those 82% were deemed to have need. 96% of undergraduates with need received aid; of those 25% had need fully met. ***Average percent of need met:*** 83% (excluding resources awarded to replace EFC). ***Average financial aid package:*** $25,453 (excluding resources awarded to replace EFC). 10% of all full-time undergraduates had no need and received non-need-based gift aid.

GIFT AID (NEED-BASED) ***Total amount:*** $192,836,377 (15% federal, 36% state, 48% institutional, 1% external sources). ***Receiving aid:*** Freshmen: 50% (1,836); all full-time undergraduates: 53% (8,857). ***Average award:*** Freshmen: $20,355; Undergraduates: $21,111. ***Scholarships, grants, and awards:*** Federal Pell, FSEOG, state, private, college/university gift aid from institutional funds.

GIFT AID (NON-NEED-BASED) ***Total amount:*** $13,238,787 (5% federal, 6% state, 81% institutional, 8% external sources). ***Receiving aid:*** Freshmen: 1% (38). Undergraduates: 1% (148). ***Average award:*** Freshmen: $7414. Undergraduates: $6206. ***Scholarships, grants, and awards by category:*** *Academic interests/achievement:* 1,055 awards ($40,205,960 total): agriculture, area/ethnic studies, computer science, education, general academic interests/achievements, humanities, international studies, mathematics, military science, physical sciences, social sciences. *Creative arts/performance:* 71 awards ($37,796 total): applied art and design, cinema/film/broadcasting, creative writing, music, performing arts, theater/drama. *Special achievements/activities:* 23 awards ($60,142 total): community service, hobbies/interests, leadership, memberships. *Special characteristics:* 1,095 awards ($4,283,992 total): first-generation college students, general special characteristics, international students, out-of-state students, veterans. ***ROTC:*** Army cooperative, Naval cooperative, Air Force cooperative.

LOANS ***Student loans:*** $44,405,905 (73% need-based, 27% non-need-based). 56% of past graduating class borrowed through all loan programs. *Average indebtedness per student:* $21,375. ***Average need-based loan:*** Freshmen: $6722. Undergraduates: $6673. ***Parent loans:*** $24,782,566 (18% need-based, 82% non-need-based). ***Programs:*** Federal Direct (Subsidized and Unsubsidized Stafford, PLUS), Perkins, college/university.

WORK-STUDY ***Federal work-study:*** Total amount: $7,532,844; 1,066 jobs averaging $1853. ***State or other work-study/employment:*** Total amount: $593,058 (100% need-based). Part-time jobs available.

APPLYING FOR FINANCIAL AID ***Required financial aid form:*** FAFSA. ***Financial aid deadline:*** 3/2. ***Notification date:*** Continuous beginning 3/15. Students must reply by 5/1 or within 4 weeks of notification.

CONTACT Mr. John Patrick Register, Director of Financial Aid, University of California, Santa Cruz, 201 Hahn Student Services Building, Santa Cruz, CA 95064, 831-459-4404. *Fax:* 831-459-3628. *E-mail:* jpregis@ucsc.edu.
Website: http://www.ucsc.edu/.

UNIVERSITY OF CENTRAL ARKANSAS

Conway, AR

Tuition & fees (AR res): $9188 — **Average undergraduate aid package: N/A**

ABOUT THE INSTITUTION State-supported, coed. ***Awards:*** certificates, bachelor's, master's, and doctoral degrees. 45 undergraduate majors. ***Total enrollment:*** 11,177. Undergraduates: 9,425. Freshmen: 2,033. Federal methodology is used as a basis for awarding need-based institutional aid.

UNDERGRADUATE EXPENSES for 2019–2020 ***Application fee:*** $25. ***Tuition, state resident:*** full-time $6810; part-time $227 per credit hour. ***Tuition, nonresident:*** full-time $13,620; part-time $454 per credit hour. ***Required fees:*** full-time $2378. Full-time tuition and fees vary according to course load. Part-time tuition and fees vary according to course load. ***College room and board:*** $7198. Room and board charges vary according to board plan and housing facility.

GIFT AID (NEED-BASED) ***Scholarships, grants, and awards:*** Federal Pell, FSEOG, state, private, college/university gift aid from institutional funds, Federal Nursing.

GIFT AID (NON-NEED-BASED) ***Scholarships, grants, and awards by category:*** *Academic interests/achievement:* general academic interests/achievements. ***Tuition waivers:*** Full or partial for employees or children of employees, senior citizens. ***ROTC:*** Army.

LOANS ***Programs:*** Perkins, Federal Nursing, state, alternative loans.

WORK-STUDY Federal work-study jobs available. ***State or other work-study/employment:*** Part-time jobs available.

APPLYING FOR FINANCIAL AID ***Required financial aid form:*** FAFSA. ***Notification date:*** Continuous.

CONTACT Ms. Cheryl Lyons, Director of Student Aid, University of Central Arkansas, 201 Donaghey Avenue, Conway, AR 72035, 501-450-3140 or toll-free 800-243-8245. *Fax:* 501-450-5168. *E-mail:* clyons@uca.edu.
Website: http://www.uca.edu/.

UNIVERSITY OF CENTRAL FLORIDA

Orlando, FL

Tuition & fees (area res): $6368 — **Average undergraduate aid package: $10,852**

ABOUT THE INSTITUTION State-supported, coed. ***Awards:*** certificates, associate, bachelor's, master's, and doctoral degrees. 85 undergraduate majors. ***Total enrollment:*** 69,525. Undergraduates: 59,483. Freshmen: 7,323. Federal methodology is used as a basis for awarding need-based institutional aid.

UNDERGRADUATE EXPENSES for 2019–2020 ***Application fee:*** $30. ***Tuition, area resident:*** full-time $6368. ***Tuition, state resident:*** full-time $6368; part-time $212 per credit hour. ***Tuition, nonresident:*** full-time $22,467; part-time $749 per credit hour. Full-time tuition and fees vary according to course load. Part-time tuition and fees vary according to course load. ***College room and board:*** $9580; ***Room only:*** $5400. Room and board charges vary according to board plan and housing facility. ***Payment plan:*** Tuition prepayment.

FRESHMAN FINANCIAL AID (Fall 2018) 6275 applied for aid; of those 66% were deemed to have need. 98% of freshmen with need received aid; of those 28% had need fully met. ***Average percent of need met:*** 75% (excluding resources awarded to replace EFC). ***Average financial aid package:*** $12,655 (excluding resources awarded to replace EFC). 9% of all full-time freshmen had no need and received non-need-based gift aid.

UNDERGRADUATE FINANCIAL AID (Fall 2018) 32,519 applied for aid; of those 78% were deemed to have need. 96% of undergraduates with need received aid; of those 16% had need fully met. ***Average percent of need met:*** 64% (excluding resources awarded to replace EFC). ***Average financial aid package:*** $10,852 (excluding resources awarded to replace EFC). 7% of all full-time undergraduates had no need and received non-need-based gift aid.

GIFT AID (NEED-BASED) ***Total amount:*** $163,317,449 (67% federal, 14% state, 19% institutional). ***Receiving aid:*** Freshmen: 40% (2,822); all full-time undergraduates: 45% (18,692). ***Average award:*** Freshmen: $7339; Undergraduates: $7160. ***Scholarships, grants, and awards:*** Federal Pell, FSEOG, state, private, college/university gift aid from institutional funds.

GIFT AID (NON-NEED-BASED) ***Total amount:*** $127,667,371 (4% federal, 72% state, 14% institutional, 10% external sources). ***Receiving aid:*** Freshmen: 47% (3,297). Undergraduates: 25% (10,371). ***Average award:*** Freshmen: $3131. Undergraduates: $3659. ***Scholarships, grants, and awards by category:*** *Academic interests/achievement:* general academic interests/achievements. *Creative arts/performance:* cinema/film/broadcasting, music, theater/drama. *Special achievements/activities:* cheerleading/drum major, general special achievements/activities, leadership. *Special characteristics:* first-generation college students. ***Tuition waivers:*** Full or partial for employees or children of employees, senior citizens. ***ROTC:*** Army, Air Force.

LOANS ***Student loans:*** $156,615,951 (49% need-based, 51% non-need-based). 49% of past graduating class borrowed through all loan programs. *Average indebtedness per student:* $22,561. ***Average need-based loan:*** Freshmen: $3680. Undergraduates: $4588. ***Parent loans:*** $13,823,492 (100% non-need-based). ***Programs:*** Federal Direct (Subsidized and Unsubsidized Stafford, PLUS), Federal Nursing.

WORK-STUDY ***Federal work-study:*** Total amount: $3,404,087; 1,014 jobs averaging $3460. ***State or other work-study/employment:*** Part-time jobs available.

ATHLETIC AWARDS Total amount: $7,701,427 (100% non-need-based).

APPLYING FOR FINANCIAL AID ***Required financial aid form:*** FAFSA. ***Financial aid deadline:*** 6/30 (priority: 12/1). ***Notification date:*** Continuous beginning 3/15. Students must reply within 3 weeks of notification.

CONTACT Ms. Alicia Keaton, Director of Student Financial Assistance, University of Central Florida, 4000 Central Florida Boulevard, Orlando, FL 32816-0113, 407-823-2827. *Fax:* 407-823-5241. *E-mail:* finaid@ucf.edu.
Website: http://www.ucf.edu/.

UNIVERSITY OF CENTRAL MISSOURI

Warrensburg, MO

Tuition & fees (MO res): $8043	Average undergraduate aid package: $8542

ABOUT THE INSTITUTION State-supported, coed. ***Awards:*** certificates, bachelor's, and master's degrees. 63 undergraduate majors. ***Total enrollment:*** 11,487. Undergraduates: 9,300. Freshmen: 1,493. Federal methodology is used as a basis for awarding need-based institutional aid.

UNDERGRADUATE EXPENSES for 2019–2020 ***Application fee:*** $30. ***Tuition, state resident:*** full-time $7128; part-time $238 per credit hour. ***Tuition, nonresident:*** full-time $14,256; part-time $475 per credit hour. ***Required fees:*** full-time $915; $30.50 per credit hour. Full-time tuition and fees vary according to course load and location. Part-time tuition and fees vary according to location. ***College room and board:*** $8962; ***Room only:*** $5612. Room and board charges vary according to board plan, housing facility, and student level.

FRESHMAN FINANCIAL AID (Fall 2018) 1343 applied for aid; of those 69% were deemed to have need. 100% of freshmen with need received aid; of those 17% had need fully met. ***Average percent of need met:*** 67% (excluding resources awarded to replace EFC). ***Average financial aid package:*** $9073 (excluding resources awarded to replace EFC). 25% of all full-time freshmen had no need and received non-need-based gift aid.

UNDERGRADUATE FINANCIAL AID (Fall 2018) 5,860 applied for aid; of those 73% were deemed to have need. 100% of undergraduates with need received aid; of those 12% had need fully met. ***Average percent of need met:*** 63% (excluding resources awarded to replace EFC). ***Average financial aid package:*** $8542 (excluding resources awarded to replace EFC). 23% of all full-time undergraduates had no need and received non-need-based gift aid.

GIFT AID (NEED-BASED) ***Total amount:*** $23,442,708 (58% federal, 15% state, 27% external sources). ***Receiving aid:*** Freshmen: 37% (547); all full-time undergraduates: 37% (2,651). ***Average award:*** Freshmen: $4401; Undergraduates: $4374. ***Scholarships, grants, and awards:*** Federal Pell, FSEOG, state, private, college/university gift aid from institutional funds.

GIFT AID (NON-NEED-BASED) ***Total amount:*** $9,355,462 (6% federal, 4% state, 89% institutional, 1% external sources). ***Receiving aid:*** Freshmen: 61% (894). Undergraduates: 56% (4,067). ***Average award:*** Freshmen: $3938. Undergraduates: $3331. ***Tuition waivers:*** Full or partial for employees or children of employees. ***ROTC:*** Army, Air Force cooperative.

LOANS ***Student loans:*** $34,882,728 (39% need-based, 61% non-need-based). 69% of past graduating class borrowed through all loan programs. *Average indebtedness per student:* $27,385. ***Parent loans:*** $5,418,414 (100% non-need-based). ***Programs:*** Federal Direct (Subsidized and Unsubsidized Stafford, PLUS), Perkins, state.

WORK-STUDY ***Federal work-study:*** Total amount: $362,388; jobs available. ***State or other work-study/employment:*** Total amount: $2,980,679 (100% non-need-based). Part-time jobs available.

ATHLETIC AWARDS Total amount: $2,551,152 (100% non-need-based).

APPLYING FOR FINANCIAL AID ***Required financial aid forms:*** FAFSA, institution's own form. ***Financial aid deadline:*** Continuous. ***Notification date:*** Continuous beginning 3/1.

CONTACT Mr. Tony Lubbers, Director of Student Financial Assistance, University of Central Missouri, Ward Edwards Building 1100, Warrensburg, MO 64093, 660-543-8266 or toll-free 800-729-8266. *Fax:* 660-543-8080. *E-mail:* lubbers@ucmo.edu.
Website: http://www.ucmo.edu/.

UNIVERSITY OF CENTRAL OKLAHOMA

Edmond, OK

CONTACT Ms. Kerry Housley, Assistant Director of Technical Services, University of Central Oklahoma, 100 North University Drive, Edmond, OK 73034-5209, 405-974-5325. *Fax:* 405-340-7658. *E-mail:* khousley@uco.edu.
Website: http://www.uco.edu/.

UNIVERSITY OF CHARLESTON

Charleston, WV

ABOUT THE INSTITUTION Independent, coed. ***Awards:*** associate, bachelor's, master's, and doctoral degrees. 23 undergraduate majors. ***Total enrollment:*** 2,718. Undergraduates: 1,907. Freshmen: 282.

GIFT AID (NEED-BASED) ***Scholarships, grants, and awards:*** Federal Pell, FSEOG, state, private, college/university gift aid from institutional funds.

GIFT AID (NON-NEED-BASED) ***Scholarships, grants, and awards by category:*** *Academic interests/achievement:* general academic interests/achievements. *Special achievements/activities:* community service, general special achievements/activities, leadership. *Special characteristics:* international students.

LOANS ***Programs:*** Federal Direct (Subsidized and Unsubsidized Stafford, PLUS), Perkins, Federal Nursing, private loans.

CONTACT Ms. Michelle Marlowe, Director of Financial Aid, University of Charleston, 2300 MacCorkle Avenue SE, Charleston, WV 25304-1099, 304-357-4944 or toll-free 800-995-GOUC. *E-mail:* ucfinancialaid@ucwv.edu.
Website: http://www.ucwv.edu/.

UNIVERSITY OF CHICAGO

Chicago, IL

Tuition & fees: N/R	Average undergraduate aid package: $57,464

ABOUT THE INSTITUTION Independent, coed. ***Awards:*** certificates, bachelor's, master's, and doctoral degrees. 48 undergraduate majors. ***Total enrollment:*** 14,347. Undergraduates: 6,552. Freshmen: 1,809. Both federal and institutional methodology are used as a basis for awarding need-based institutional aid.

FRESHMAN FINANCIAL AID (Fall 2019, est.) 872 applied for aid; of those 78% were deemed to have need. 99% of freshmen with need received aid; of those 100% had need fully met. ***Average percent of need met:*** 100% (excluding resources awarded to replace EFC). ***Average financial aid package:*** $60,895 (excluding resources awarded to replace EFC).

UNDERGRADUATE FINANCIAL AID (Fall 2019, est.) 3,134 applied for aid; of those 86% were deemed to have need. 99% of undergraduates with need received aid; of those 100% had need fully met. ***Average percent of need met:*** 100% (excluding resources awarded to replace EFC). ***Average financial aid package:*** $57,464 (excluding resources awarded to replace EFC).

GIFT AID (NEED-BASED) ***Total amount:*** $139,975,007 (4% federal, 1% state, 94% institutional, 1% external sources). ***Receiving aid:*** Freshmen: 39% (666); all full-time undergraduates: 40% (2,662). ***Average award:*** Freshmen: $55,458; Undergraduates: $52,471. ***Scholarships, grants, and awards:*** Federal Pell, FSEOG, state, private, college/university gift aid from institutional funds.

GIFT AID (NON-NEED-BASED) ***Total amount:*** $16,589,815 (86% institutional, 14% external sources). ***Receiving aid:*** Freshmen: 9% (147). Undergraduates: 7% (442). ***Scholarships, grants, and awards by category:*** *Academic interests/achievement:* general academic interests/achievements. *Special achievements/activities:* community service, leadership. *Special characteristics:* children of educators, children of public servants, first-generation college students, twins, veterans. ***ROTC:*** Army cooperative, Air Force cooperative.

LOANS ***Student loans:*** $5,555,342 (28% need-based, 72% non-need-based). 17% of past graduating class borrowed through all loan programs. *Average indebtedness per student:* $26,619. ***Average need-based loan:*** Undergraduates: $3776. ***Parent loans:*** $3,707,947 (100% non-need-based). ***Programs:*** Federal Direct (Subsidized and Unsubsidized Stafford, PLUS).

WORK-STUDY ***Federal work-study:*** Total amount: $6,578,895; jobs available. ***State or other work-study/employment:*** Part-time jobs available.

APPLYING FOR FINANCIAL AID ***Required financial aid forms:*** FAFSA, institution's own form, CSS Financial Aid PROFILE, federal income tax form(s). ***Financial aid deadline (priority):*** 2/15. ***Notification date:*** 3/15. Students must reply by 5/1.

CONTACT Financial Aid Office, University of Chicago, 5801 South Ellis Avenue, Chicago, IL 60637-1513, 773-702-1234.
Website: http://www.uchicago.edu/.

UNIVERSITY OF CINCINNATI

Cincinnati, OH

Tuition & fees (OH res): $11,010 | **Average undergraduate aid package: $5892**

ABOUT THE INSTITUTION State-supported, coed. ***Awards:*** certificates, associate, bachelor's, master's, and doctoral degrees. 142 undergraduate majors. ***Total enrollment:*** 39,263. Undergraduates: 28,376. Freshmen: 5,480. Federal methodology is used as a basis for awarding need-based institutional aid.

UNDERGRADUATE EXPENSES for 2020–2021 ***Application fee:*** $50. ***Tuition, state resident:*** full-time $9332; part-time $389 per credit hour. ***Tuition, nonresident:*** full-time $24,666; part-time $1028 per credit hour. ***Required fees:*** full-time $1678. Full-time tuition and fees vary according to course load, degree level, location, program, reciprocity agreements, and student level. Part-time tuition and fees vary according to course load, degree level, location, program, reciprocity agreements, and student level. ***College room and board:*** $11,530; ***Room only:*** $6856. Room and board charges vary according to board plan, housing facility, and student level. ***Payment plan:*** Guaranteed tuition.

FRESHMAN FINANCIAL AID (Fall 2018) 4543 applied for aid; of those 64% were deemed to have need. 95% of freshmen with need received aid; of those 15% had need fully met. ***Average percent of need met:*** 43% (excluding resources awarded to replace EFC). ***Average financial aid package:*** $6477 (excluding resources awarded to replace EFC). 14% of all full-time freshmen had no need and received non-need-based gift aid.

UNDERGRADUATE FINANCIAL AID (Fall 2018) 15,688 applied for aid; of those 74% were deemed to have need. 95% of undergraduates with need received aid; of those 10% had need fully met. ***Average percent of need met:*** 36% (excluding resources awarded to replace EFC). ***Average financial aid package:*** $5892 (excluding resources awarded to replace EFC). 8% of all full-time undergraduates had no need and received non-need-based gift aid.

GIFT AID (NEED-BASED) ***Total amount:*** $103,531,030 (26% federal, 41% state, 25% institutional, 8% external sources). ***Receiving aid:*** Freshmen: 22% (1,143); all full-time undergraduates: 21% (4,944). ***Average award:*** Freshmen: $6790; Undergraduates: $6506. ***Scholarships, grants, and awards:*** Federal Pell, FSEOG, state, private, college/university gift aid from institutional funds, United Negro College Fund, Federal Nursing.

GIFT AID (NON-NEED-BASED) ***Total amount:*** $41,196,034 (1% state, 76% institutional, 23% external sources). ***Receiving aid:*** Freshmen: 32% (1,701). Undergraduates: 21% (4,733). ***Average award:*** Freshmen: $6075. Undergraduates: $4404. ***Tuition waivers:*** Full or partial for employees or children of employees. ***ROTC:*** Army, Air Force.

LOANS ***Student loans:*** $85,848,509 (40% need-based, 60% non-need-based). 58% of past graduating class borrowed through all loan programs. *Average indebtedness per student:* $30,350. ***Average need-based loan:*** Freshmen: $3129. Undergraduates: $4002. ***Parent loans:*** $67,376,775 (48% need-based, 52% non-need-based). ***Programs:*** Federal Direct (Subsidized and Unsubsidized Stafford, PLUS), Federal Nursing, state, college/university.

WORK-STUDY ***Federal work-study:*** Total amount: $4,658,236; 4,407 jobs averaging $4425.

ATHLETIC AWARDS Total amount: $9,957,714 (29% need-based, 71% non-need-based).

APPLYING FOR FINANCIAL AID ***Required financial aid form:*** FAFSA. ***Financial aid deadline (priority):*** 12/1. ***Notification date:*** Continuous beginning 2/15.

CONTACT Mr. Randy Ulses, Director of Scholarships and Enrollment, University of Cincinnati, PO Box 210125, Cincinnati, OH 45221-0125, 513-556-1000. *Fax:* 513-556-9171. *E-mail:* financeaid@uc.edu.
Website: http://www.uc.edu/.

UNIVERSITY OF COLORADO BOULDER

Boulder, CO

Tuition & fees (CO res): $12,500 | **Average undergraduate aid package: $17,962**

ABOUT THE INSTITUTION State-supported, coed. ***Awards:*** certificates, bachelor's, master's, and doctoral degrees. 75 undergraduate majors. ***Total enrollment:*** 37,650. Undergraduates: 31,101. Freshmen: 7,113. Federal methodology is used as a basis for awarding need-based institutional aid.

UNDERGRADUATE EXPENSES for 2019–2020 ***Application fee:*** $50. ***One-time required fee:*** $232. ***Tuition, state resident:*** full-time $10,728. ***Tuition, nonresident:*** full-time $36,546. ***Required fees:*** full-time $1772. Full-time tuition and fees vary according to program. Part-time tuition and fees vary according to course load and program. ***College room and board:*** $14,778. Room and board charges vary according to board plan, housing facility, and location. ***Payment plan:*** Guaranteed tuition.

FRESHMAN FINANCIAL AID (Fall 2019, est.) 4906 applied for aid; of those 56% were deemed to have need. 98% of freshmen with need received aid; of those 44% had need fully met. ***Average percent of need met:*** 80% (excluding resources awarded to replace EFC). ***Average financial aid package:*** $18,037 (excluding resources awarded to replace EFC). 39% of all full-time freshmen had no need and received non-need-based gift aid.

UNDERGRADUATE FINANCIAL AID (Fall 2019, est.) 15,078 applied for aid; of those 67% were deemed to have need. 95% of undergraduates with need received aid; of those 41% had need fully met. ***Average percent of need met:*** 80% (excluding resources awarded to replace EFC). ***Average financial aid package:*** $17,962 (excluding resources awarded to replace EFC). 30% of all full-time undergraduates had no need and received non-need-based gift aid.

GIFT AID (NEED-BASED) ***Total amount:*** $91,625,782 (25% federal, 12% state, 58% institutional, 5% external sources). ***Receiving aid:*** Freshmen: 30% (2,090); all full-time undergraduates: 26% (7,457). ***Average award:*** Freshmen: $12,225; Undergraduates: $11,882. ***Scholarships, grants, and awards:*** Federal Pell, FSEOG, state, private, college/university gift aid from institutional funds.

GIFT AID (NON-NEED-BASED) ***Total amount:*** $45,933,060 (1% state, 75% institutional, 24% external sources). ***Receiving aid:*** Freshmen: 2% (158). Undergraduates: 1% (414). ***Average award:*** Freshmen: $9343. Undergraduates: $9345. ***Scholarships, grants, and awards by category:*** *Academic interests/achievement:* architecture, area/ethnic studies, biological sciences, business, communication, computer science, education, engineering/technologies, English, foreign languages, general academic interests/achievements, home economics, humanities, international studies, mathematics, physical sciences, premedicine, religion/biblical studies, social sciences. *Creative arts/performance:* applied art and design, art/fine arts, cinema/film/broadcasting, creative writing, dance, general creative arts/performance, journalism/publications, music, performing arts, theater/drama. *Special achievements/activities:* community service, general special achievements/activities, leadership. *Special characteristics:* first-generation college students, general special characteristics, handicapped students, local/state students, veterans. ***Tuition waivers:*** Full or partial for employees or children of employees, senior citizens. ***ROTC:*** Army, Naval, Air Force.

LOANS ***Student loans:*** $103,465,209 (50% need-based, 50% non-need-based). 40% of past graduating class borrowed through all loan programs. *Average indebtedness per student:* $27,568. ***Average need-based loan:*** Freshmen: $5000. Undergraduates: $6206. ***Parent loans:*** $100,418,592 (32% need-based, 68% non-need-based). ***Programs:*** Federal Direct (Subsidized and Unsubsidized Stafford, PLUS), college/university, private loans.

WORK-STUDY ***Federal work-study:*** Total amount: $1,939,205; 738 jobs averaging $1920. ***State or other work-study/employment:*** Total amount: $5,354,390 (96% need-based, 4% non-need-based). 879 part-time jobs averaging $3101.

ATHLETIC AWARDS Total amount: $9,954,099 (36% need-based, 64% non-need-based).

APPLYING FOR FINANCIAL AID ***Required financial aid forms:*** FAFSA, federal income tax form(s). ***Financial aid deadline (priority):*** 2/15. ***Notification date:*** Continuous beginning 2/15.

CONTACT Ms. Ofelia A. Morales, Director of Financial Aid, University of Colorado Boulder, 77 UCB, Boulder, CO 80309-0556, 303-492-8223. *Fax:* 303-492-0838. *E-mail:* finaid@colorado.edu.
Website: http://www.colorado.edu/.

UNIVERSITY OF COLORADO COLORADO SPRINGS

Colorado Springs, CO

Tuition & fees (CO res): $10,463 | **Average undergraduate aid package: $9041**

ABOUT THE INSTITUTION State-supported, coed. ***Awards:*** certificates, bachelor's, master's, and doctoral degrees. 38 undergraduate majors. ***Total enrollment:*** 12,180. Undergraduates: 10,196. Freshmen: 1,788. Federal methodology is used as a basis for awarding need-based institutional aid.

UNDERGRADUATE EXPENSES for 2019–2020 ***Application fee:*** $50. ***One-time required fee:*** $140. ***Tuition, state resident:*** full-time $8850; part-time $345 per credit hour. ***Tuition, nonresident:*** full-time $23,970; part-time $721 per credit hour. ***Required fees:*** full-time $1613. Full-time tuition and fees vary according to course load, degree level, location, program, reciprocity agreements, and student level. Part-time tuition and fees vary according to course load, degree level, location, program, reciprocity agreements, and student level. ***College room and board:*** $10,798. Room and board charges vary according to board plan, housing facility, and student level.

FRESHMAN FINANCIAL AID (Fall 2018) 1691 applied for aid; of those 73% were deemed to have need. 91% of freshmen with need received aid; of those 7% had need fully met. ***Average percent of need met:*** 47% (excluding resources awarded to replace EFC). ***Average financial aid package:*** $8766 (excluding resources awarded to replace EFC). 16% of all full-time freshmen had no need and received non-need-based gift aid.

UNDERGRADUATE FINANCIAL AID (Fall 2018) 6,268 applied for aid; of those 81% were deemed to have need. 91% of undergraduates with need received aid; of those 6% had need fully met. ***Average percent of need met:*** 45% (excluding resources awarded to replace EFC). ***Average financial aid package:*** $9041 (excluding resources awarded to replace EFC). 9% of all full-time undergraduates had no need and received non-need-based gift aid.

GIFT AID (NEED-BASED) ***Receiving aid:*** Freshmen: 32% (619); all full-time undergraduates: 34% (2,846). ***Average award:*** Freshmen: $8323; Undergraduates: $7976. ***Scholarships, grants, and awards:*** Federal Pell, FSEOG, state, private, college/university gift aid from institutional funds.

GIFT AID (NON-NEED-BASED) ***Receiving aid:*** Freshmen: 33% (633). Undergraduates: 19% (1,605). ***Average award:*** Freshmen: $2836. Undergraduates: $2611. ***Scholarships, grants, and awards by category:*** *Academic interests/achievement:* general academic interests/achievements. ***Tuition waivers:*** Full or partial for employees or children of employees. ***ROTC:*** Army, Air Force cooperative.

LOANS ***Student loans:*** 58% of past graduating class borrowed through all loan programs. *Average indebtedness per student:* $23,805. ***Average need-based loan:*** Freshmen: $3176. Undergraduates: $3993. ***Programs:*** Federal Direct (Subsidized and Unsubsidized Stafford, PLUS).

WORK-STUDY ***Federal work-study:*** 153 jobs averaging $2952. ***State or other work-study/employment:*** 238 part-time jobs averaging $3171.

APPLYING FOR FINANCIAL AID ***Required financial aid form:*** FAFSA. ***Notification date:*** Continuous.

CONTACT Jevita Rogers, Executive Director of Financial Aid, University of Colorado Colorado Springs, 1420 Austin Bluffs Parkway, Colorado Springs, CO 80918, 719-255-3460 or toll-free 800-990-8227 Ext.3383. *Fax:* 719-255-3650. *E-mail:* finaidse@uccs.edu.
Website: http://www.uccs.edu/.

UNIVERSITY OF COLORADO DENVER

Denver, CO

Tuition & fees (CO res): $11,447 | **Average undergraduate aid package: $10,556**

ABOUT THE INSTITUTION State-supported, coed. ***Awards:*** certificates, bachelor's, master's, and doctoral degrees. 38 undergraduate majors. ***Total enrollment:*** 25,645. Undergraduates: 16,443. Freshmen: 1,743. Federal methodology is used as a basis for awarding need-based institutional aid.

UNDERGRADUATE EXPENSES for 2020–2021 ***Application fee:*** $50. ***Tuition, area resident:*** part-time $330 per credit hour. ***Tuition, state resident:*** full-time $9900; part-time $330 per credit hour. ***Tuition, nonresident:*** full-time $30,510; part-time $1017 per credit hour. ***Required fees:*** full-time $1547. ***College room and board:*** $12,620; ***Room only:*** $8800.

FRESHMAN FINANCIAL AID (Fall 2018) 1409 applied for aid; of those 79% were deemed to have need. 95% of freshmen with need received aid; of those 2% had need fully met. ***Average percent of need met:*** 46% (excluding resources awarded to replace EFC). ***Average financial aid package:*** $9773 (excluding resources awarded to replace EFC). 11% of all full-time freshmen had no need and received non-need-based gift aid.

UNDERGRADUATE FINANCIAL AID (Fall 2018) 6,548 applied for aid; of those 85% were deemed to have need. 94% of undergraduates with need received aid; of those 1% had need fully met. ***Average percent of need met:*** 49% (excluding resources awarded to replace EFC). ***Average financial aid package:*** $10,556 (excluding resources awarded to replace EFC). 7% of all full-time undergraduates had no need and received non-need-based gift aid.

GIFT AID (NEED-BASED) ***Total amount:*** $41,831,907 (42% federal, 26% state, 26% institutional, 6% external sources). ***Receiving aid:*** Freshmen: 57% (917); all full-time undergraduates: 48% (4,251). ***Average award:*** Freshmen: $8168; Undergraduates: $8404. ***Scholarships, grants, and awards:*** Federal Pell, FSEOG, state, private, college/university gift aid from institutional funds, College Access Challenge Grants, TEACH Grants, Armed Services Scholarships.

GIFT AID (NON-NEED-BASED) ***Total amount:*** $3,273,052 (4% state, 64% institutional, 32% external sources). ***Receiving aid:*** Freshmen: 6% (98). Undergraduates: 3% (242). ***Average award:*** Freshmen: $1645. Undergraduates: $2241. ***Scholarships, grants, and awards by category:*** *Academic interests/achievement:* 1,576 awards ($2,720,194 total): architecture, biological sciences, business, communication, computer science, education, engineering/technologies, English, general academic interests/achievements, health fields, home economics, humanities, international studies, mathematics, physical sciences, premedicine, social sciences. *Creative arts/performance:* 61 awards ($70,312 total): applied art and design, art/fine arts, cinema/film/broadcasting, general creative arts/performance, music, performing arts, theater/drama. *Special achievements/activities:* 10 awards ($10,764 total): general special achievements/activities, leadership. *Special characteristics:* 560 awards ($1,249,503 total): children of faculty/staff, ethnic background, first-generation college students, general special characteristics, handicapped students, international students, local/state students, members of minority groups, out-of-state students, veterans. ***ROTC:*** Army cooperative, Air Force cooperative.

LOANS ***Student loans:*** $39,158,371 (76% need-based, 24% non-need-based). 53% of past graduating class borrowed through all loan programs. *Average indebtedness per student:* $20,859. ***Average need-based loan:*** Freshmen: $2749. Undergraduates: $3709. ***Parent loans:*** $12,564,715 (26% need-based, 74% non-need-based). ***Programs:*** Federal Direct (Subsidized and Unsubsidized Stafford, PLUS), Perkins, Federal Nursing.

WORK-STUDY ***Federal work-study:*** Total amount: $1,920,263; 370 jobs averaging $5190. ***State or other work-study/employment:*** Total amount: $1,774,186 (94% need-based, 6% non-need-based). 344 part-time jobs averaging $5158.

APPLYING FOR FINANCIAL AID ***Required financial aid form:*** FAFSA. ***Financial aid deadline:*** Continuous. ***Notification date:*** Continuous beginning 4/1.

CONTACT Justin Jaramillo, Director of Financial Aid, University of Colorado Denver, PO Box 173364, Denver, CO 80217-3364, 303-315-1850. *Fax:* 303-315-1835. *E-mail:* financialaid@ucdenver.edu.
Website: http://www.ucdenver.edu/.

UNIVERSITY OF CONNECTICUT

Storrs, CT

CONTACT Office of Financial Aid, University of Connecticut, 233 Glenbrook Road, Unit 4116, Storrs, CT 06269-4116, 860-486-2819. *Fax:* 860-486-6629. *E-mail:* financialaid@uconn.edu.
Website: http://www.uconn.edu/.

UNIVERSITY OF DALLAS

Irving, TX

Tuition & fees: $44,810	Average undergraduate aid package: $34,469

ABOUT THE INSTITUTION Independent Roman Catholic, coed. ***Awards:*** certificates, bachelor's, master's, and doctoral degrees. 32 undergraduate majors. ***Total enrollment:*** 2,481. Undergraduates: 1,475. Freshmen: 382. Federal methodology is used as a basis for awarding need-based institutional aid.

UNDERGRADUATE EXPENSES for 2020–2021 ***Application fee:*** $50. ***Comprehensive fee:*** $57,890 includes full-time tuition ($41,660), mandatory fees ($3150), and room and board ($13,080). ***College room only:*** $7046. Full-time tuition and fees vary according to course load. Room and board charges vary according to board plan, housing facility, and location. ***Part-time tuition:*** $1750 per credit hour. ***Part-time fees:*** $1575 per term. Part-time tuition and fees vary according to course load.

FRESHMAN FINANCIAL AID (Fall 2018) 313 applied for aid; of those 85% were deemed to have need. 100% of freshmen with need received aid; of those 20% had need fully met. ***Average percent of need met:*** 82% (excluding resources awarded to replace EFC). ***Average financial aid package:*** $36,448 (excluding resources awarded to replace EFC). 16% of all full-time freshmen had no need and received non-need-based gift aid.

UNDERGRADUATE FINANCIAL AID (Fall 2018) 1,035 applied for aid; of those 89% were deemed to have need. 100% of undergraduates with need received aid; of those 20% had need fully met. ***Average percent of need met:*** 79% (excluding resources awarded to replace EFC). ***Average financial aid package:*** $34,469 (excluding resources awarded to replace EFC). 27% of all full-time undergraduates had no need and received non-need-based gift aid.

GIFT AID (NEED-BASED) ***Total amount:*** $27,316,837 (7% federal, 4% state, 88% institutional, 1% external sources). ***Receiving aid:*** Freshmen: 69% (259); all full-time undergraduates: 63% (910). ***Average award:*** Freshmen: $31,943; Undergraduates: $29,804. ***Scholarships, grants, and awards:*** Federal Pell, FSEOG, state, private, college/university gift aid from institutional funds.

GIFT AID (NON-NEED-BASED) ***Total amount:*** $12,141,150 (99% institutional, 1% external sources). ***Receiving aid:*** Freshmen: 12% (44). Undergraduates: 9% (136). ***Average award:*** Freshmen: $17,902. Undergraduates: $21,207. ***Scholarships, grants, and awards by category:*** *Academic interests/achievement:* area/ethnic studies, biological sciences, business, computer science, education, English, foreign languages, general academic interests/achievements, humanities, mathematics, military science, physical sciences, premedicine. *Creative arts/performance:* applied art and design, music, theater/drama. *Special characteristics:* children of faculty/staff, religious affiliation. ***Tuition waivers:*** Full or partial for employees or children of employees. ***ROTC:*** Army cooperative, Air Force cooperative.

LOANS ***Student loans:*** $6,883,796 (67% need-based, 33% non-need-based). 60% of past graduating class borrowed through all loan programs. *Average indebtedness per student:* $34,205. ***Average need-based loan:*** Freshmen: $3358. Undergraduates: $4322. ***Parent loans:*** $1,844,456 (25% need-based, 75% non-need-based). ***Programs:*** Federal Direct (Subsidized and Unsubsidized Stafford, PLUS), Perkins, state.

WORK-STUDY ***Federal work-study:*** Total amount: $391,072; jobs available. ***State or other work-study/employment:*** Total amount: $8738 (100% need-based). Part-time jobs available.

APPLYING FOR FINANCIAL AID ***Required financial aid form:*** FAFSA. ***Financial aid deadline (priority):*** 1/15. ***Notification date:*** Continuous beginning 12/1. Students must reply by 5/1 or within 2 weeks of notification.

CONTACT Mrs. Taryn Anderson, Director of Financial Aid, University of Dallas, 1845 East Northgate Drive, Irving, TX 75062, 972-721-5266 or toll-free 800-628-6999. *Fax:* 972-721-5017. *E-mail:* finaid@udallas.edu.
Website: http://www.udallas.edu/.

UNIVERSITY OF DAYTON

Dayton, OH

Tuition & fees: $44,100	Average undergraduate aid package: $34,786

ABOUT THE INSTITUTION Independent Roman Catholic, coed. ***Awards:*** certificates, bachelor's, master's, and doctoral degrees. 82 undergraduate majors. ***Total enrollment:*** 11,473. Undergraduates: 8,483. Freshmen: 2,035. Federal methodology is used as a basis for awarding need-based institutional aid.

UNDERGRADUATE EXPENSES for 2019–2020 ***Comprehensive fee:*** $58,150 includes full-time tuition ($44,100) and room and board ($14,050). ***College room only:*** $8420. ***Part-time tuition:*** $1610 per credit hour. ***Payment plan:*** Guaranteed tuition.

FRESHMAN FINANCIAL AID (Fall 2019, est.) 1671 applied for aid; of those 68% were deemed to have need. 100% of freshmen with need received aid; of those 98% had need fully met. ***Average percent of need met:*** 84% (excluding resources awarded to replace EFC). ***Average financial aid package:*** $32,131 (excluding resources awarded to replace EFC). 33% of all full-time freshmen had no need and received non-need-based gift aid.

UNDERGRADUATE FINANCIAL AID (Fall 2019, est.) 6,142 applied for aid; of those 75% were deemed to have need. 100% of undergraduates with need received aid; of those 96% had need fully met. ***Average percent of need met:*** 84% (excluding resources awarded to replace EFC). ***Average financial aid package:*** $34,786 (excluding resources awarded to replace EFC). 43% of all full-time undergraduates had no need and received non-need-based gift aid.

GIFT AID (NEED-BASED) ***Receiving aid:*** Freshmen: 56% (1,128); all full-time undergraduates: 56% (4,548). ***Average award:*** Freshmen: $30,330; Undergraduates: $32,231.

GIFT AID (NON-NEED-BASED) ***Receiving aid:*** Freshmen: 4% (89). Undergraduates: 5% (382). ***Average award:*** Freshmen: $20,160. Undergraduates: $21,496. ***Scholarships, grants, and awards by category:*** *Academic interests/achievement:* biological sciences, business, communication, computer science, education, engineering/technologies, English, foreign languages, general academic interests/achievements, home economics, humanities, international studies, mathematics, military science, physical sciences, premedicine, religion/biblical studies, social sciences. *Creative arts/performance:* applied art and design, music. *Special achievements/activities:* community service, leadership. *Special characteristics:* children and siblings of alumni, children of faculty/staff, local/state students, members of minority groups, out-of-state students, religious affiliation. ***ROTC:*** Army, Air Force cooperative.

LOANS ***Student loans:*** 54% of past graduating class borrowed through all loan programs. *Average indebtedness per student:* $37,533. ***Average need-based loan:*** Freshmen: $2873. Undergraduates: $3128.

WORK-STUDY Federal work-study jobs available. ***State or other work-study/employment:*** Part-time jobs available.

APPLYING FOR FINANCIAL AID ***Required financial aid form:*** FAFSA. ***Notification date:*** Continuous.

CONTACT Catherine Mix, Director of Financial Aid, University of Dayton, 300 College Park, Dayton, OH 45469-1668, 937-229-4358 or toll-free 800-837-7433. *Fax:* 937-229-4338. *E-mail:* cmix01@udayton.edu.
Website: http://www.udayton.edu/.

UNIVERSITY OF DELAWARE

Newark, DE

ABOUT THE INSTITUTION State-related, coed. ***Awards:*** associate, bachelor's, master's, and doctoral degrees. 126 undergraduate majors. ***Total enrollment:*** 22,385. Undergraduates: 19,117. Freshmen: 4,249.

GIFT AID (NEED-BASED) ***Scholarships, grants, and awards:*** Federal Pell, FSEOG, state, private, college/university gift aid from institutional funds.

GIFT AID (NON-NEED-BASED) ***Scholarships, grants, and awards by category:*** *Academic interests/achievement:* agriculture, biological sciences, business, communication, computer science, education, engineering/technologies, English, foreign languages, general academic interests/achievements, home economics, humanities, international studies, mathematics, military science, physical sciences, premedicine, religion/biblical studies, social sciences. *Creative arts/performance:* applied art and design, art/fine arts, music, theater/drama. *Special achievements/activities:* cheerleading/drum major, community service, general special achievements/activities, leadership. *Special characteristics:* children and siblings of alumni, children of faculty/staff, children of public servants, ethnic background, first-generation college students, general special characteristics, local/state students, members of minority groups.

LOANS ***Programs:*** Federal Direct (Subsidized and Unsubsidized Stafford, PLUS), Perkins, Federal Nursing.

CONTACT Mr. James Holloway, Manager of Student Financial Services Compliance, University of Delaware, 140 Student Services Building, Newark, DE 19716, 302-831-0520. *Fax:* 302-831-4334. *E-mail:* holloway@udel.edu.
Website: http://www.udel.edu/.

UNIVERSITY OF DENVER

Denver, CO

Tuition & fees: $53,775	Average undergraduate aid package: $42,918

ABOUT THE INSTITUTION Independent, coed. ***Awards:*** certificates, bachelor's, master's, and doctoral degrees. 78 undergraduate majors. ***Total enrollment:*** 12,931. Undergraduates: 5,774. Freshmen: 1,351. Institutional methodology is used as a basis for awarding need-based institutional aid.

UNDERGRADUATE EXPENSES for 2020–2021 ***Application fee:*** $65. ***Comprehensive fee:*** $67,953 includes full-time tuition ($52,596), mandatory fees ($1179), and room and board ($14,178). ***College room only:*** $8949. Full-time tuition and fees vary according to course load and program. Room and board charges vary according to board plan and housing facility. ***Part-time tuition:*** $1461 per credit hour. Part-time tuition and fees vary according to course load and program.

FRESHMAN FINANCIAL AID (Fall 2019, est.) 932 applied for aid; of those 68% were deemed to have need. 100% of freshmen with need received aid; of those 29% had need fully met. ***Average percent of need met:*** 84% (excluding resources awarded to replace EFC). ***Average financial aid package:*** $43,335 (excluding resources awarded to replace EFC). 39% of all full-time freshmen had no need and received non-need-based gift aid.

UNDERGRADUATE FINANCIAL AID (Fall 2019, est.) 3,110 applied for aid; of those 75% were deemed to have need. 100% of undergraduates with need received aid; of those 31% had need fully met. ***Average percent of need met:*** 84% (excluding resources awarded to replace EFC). ***Average financial aid package:*** $42,918 (excluding resources awarded to replace EFC). 43% of all full-time undergraduates had no need and received non-need-based gift aid.

GIFT AID (NEED-BASED) ***Total amount:*** $83,338,731 (6% federal, 2% state, 88% institutional, 4% external sources). ***Receiving aid:*** Freshmen: 47% (632); all full-time undergraduates: 42% (2,312). ***Average award:*** Freshmen: $36,795; Undergraduates: $36,561. ***Scholarships, grants, and awards:*** Federal Pell, FSEOG, state, private, college/university gift aid from institutional funds.

GIFT AID (NON-NEED-BASED) ***Total amount:*** $50,930,062 (95% institutional, 5% external sources). ***Receiving aid:*** Freshmen: 12% (162). Undergraduates: 10% (542). ***Average award:*** Freshmen: $21,124. Undergraduates: $20,275. ***Scholarships, grants, and awards by category:*** *Academic interests/achievement:* biological sciences, business, communication, computer science, engineering/technologies, English, general academic interests/achievements, humanities, international studies, mathematics, physical sciences, social sciences. *Creative arts/performance:* art/fine arts, debating, music, theater/drama. *Special achievements/activities:* community service, leadership. ***Tuition waivers:*** Full or partial for employees or children of employees, senior citizens. ***ROTC:*** Army cooperative, Air Force cooperative.

LOANS ***Student loans:*** $18,716,649 (50% need-based, 50% non-need-based). 44% of past graduating class borrowed through all loan programs. *Average indebtedness per student:* $27,938. ***Average need-based loan:*** Freshmen: $3384. Undergraduates: $4336. ***Parent loans:*** $11,215,203 (24% need-based, 76% non-need-based). ***Programs:*** Federal Direct (Subsidized and Unsubsidized Stafford, PLUS), college/university.

WORK-STUDY ***Federal work-study:*** Total amount: $1,384,671; 492 jobs averaging $2798. ***State or other work-study/employment:*** Total amount: $473,174 (80% need-based, 20% non-need-based). 164 part-time jobs averaging $2812.

ATHLETIC AWARDS Total amount: $11,560,579 (17% need-based, 83% non-need-based).

APPLYING FOR FINANCIAL AID ***Required financial aid forms:*** FAFSA, CSS Financial Aid PROFILE, noncustodial (divorced/separated) parent's statement. ***Financial aid deadline (priority):*** 2/15. ***Notification date:*** 3/1. Students must reply by 5/1.

CONTACT Mr. John Gudvangen, Director of Financial Aid, University of Denver, University Hall, 2197 South University Boulevard, Denver, CO 80208, 303-871-4020 or toll-free 800-525-9495. *Fax:* 303-871-2341. *E-mail:* finaid@du.edu.
Website: http://www.du.edu/.

UNIVERSITY OF DETROIT MERCY

Detroit, MI

ABOUT THE INSTITUTION Independent Roman Catholic (Jesuit), coed. ***Awards:*** certificates, diplomas, bachelor's, master's, and doctoral degrees. 50 undergraduate majors. ***Total enrollment:*** 5,080. Undergraduates: 2,745. Freshmen: 530.

GIFT AID (NEED-BASED) ***Scholarships, grants, and awards:*** Federal Pell, FSEOG, state, private, college/university gift aid from institutional funds, Federal Nursing.

GIFT AID (NON-NEED-BASED) ***Scholarships, grants, and awards by category:*** *Academic interests/achievement:* general academic interests/achievements. *Creative arts/performance:* theater/drama. *Special achievements/activities:* religious involvement. *Special characteristics:* children and siblings of alumni, children of faculty/staff.

LOANS ***Programs:*** Federal Direct (Subsidized and Unsubsidized Stafford, PLUS), Perkins, Federal Nursing, Private Alternative Loans.

WORK-STUDY ***Federal work-study:*** Total amount: $1,137,684; jobs available.

APPLYING FOR FINANCIAL AID ***Required financial aid form:*** FAFSA.

CONTACT Jenny McAlonan, Director of Financial Aid and Scholarships, University of Detroit Mercy, 4001 West McNichols Road, Detroit, MI 48221-3038, 313-993-3350 or toll-free 800-635-5020. *Fax:* 313-993-3347. *E-mail:* mcalonjl@udmercy.edu.
Website: http://www.udmercy.edu/.

UNIVERSITY OF DUBUQUE

Dubuque, IA

Tuition & fees: $36,610	Average undergraduate aid package: $29,385

ABOUT THE INSTITUTION Independent Presbyterian, coed. ***Awards:*** associate, bachelor's, master's, and doctoral degrees. 41 undergraduate majors. ***Total enrollment:*** 2,303. Undergraduates: 1,900. Freshmen: 386. Federal methodology is used as a basis for awarding need-based institutional aid.

UNDERGRADUATE EXPENSES for 2020–2021 ***Application fee:*** $25. ***Comprehensive fee:*** $47,110 includes full-time tuition ($35,060), mandatory fees ($1550), and room and board ($10,500). Room and board charges vary according to board plan. ***Part-time tuition:*** $1052 per credit hour.

FRESHMAN FINANCIAL AID (Fall 2019, est.) 432 applied for aid; of those 90% were deemed to have need. 99% of freshmen with need received aid; of those 17% had need fully met. ***Average percent of need met:*** 68% (excluding resources awarded to replace EFC). ***Average financial aid package:*** $27,855 (excluding resources awarded to replace EFC). 13% of all full-time freshmen had no need and received non-need-based gift aid.

UNDERGRADUATE FINANCIAL AID (Fall 2019, est.) 1,436 applied for aid; of those 92% were deemed to have need. 99% of undergraduates with need received aid; of those 17% had need fully met. ***Average percent of need met:*** 70% (excluding resources awarded to replace EFC). ***Average financial aid package:*** $29,385 (excluding resources awarded to replace EFC). 12% of all full-time undergraduates had no need and received non-need-based gift aid.

GIFT AID (NEED-BASED) ***Total amount:*** $30,937,360 (12% federal, 7% state, 56% institutional, 25% external sources). ***Receiving aid:*** Freshmen: 76% (353); all full-time undergraduates: 83% (1,273). ***Average award:*** Freshmen: $23,294; Undergraduates: $23,456. ***Scholarships, grants, and awards:*** Federal Pell, FSEOG, state, private, college/university gift aid from institutional funds.

GIFT AID (NON-NEED-BASED) ***Total amount:*** $9,200,240 (40% institutional, 60% external sources). ***Receiving aid:*** Freshmen: 11% (53). Undergraduates: 12% (177). ***Average award:*** Freshmen: $15,415. Undergraduates: $15,664. ***Scholarships, grants, and awards by category:*** *Academic interests/achievement:* 728 awards ($6,688,136 total): general academic interests/achievements. *Special characteristics:* children and siblings of alumni, children of educators, children of faculty/staff, out-of-state students, relatives of clergy, religious affiliation, siblings of current students, spouses of current students. ***Tuition waivers:*** Full or partial for employees or children of employees. ***ROTC:*** Army.

LOANS ***Student loans:*** $16,210,410 (75% need-based, 25% non-need-based). 77% of past graduating class borrowed through all loan programs. *Average indebtedness per student:* $33,454. ***Average need-based loan:*** Freshmen: $7287. Undergraduates: $7207. ***Parent loans:*** $2,462,005 (67% need-based, 33% non-need-based). ***Programs:*** Federal Direct (Subsidized and Unsubsidized Stafford, PLUS), college/university.

WORK-STUDY ***Federal work-study:*** Total amount: $848,774; 198 jobs averaging $2000. ***State or other work-study/employment:*** Total amount: $212,285 (29% need-based, 71% non-need-based). 178 part-time jobs averaging $2000.

APPLYING FOR FINANCIAL AID ***Required financial aid form:*** FAFSA. ***Financial aid deadline (priority):*** 4/1. ***Notification date:*** Continuous beginning 3/1. Students must reply within 3 weeks of notification.

CONTACT Teresa Brahm, Director of Student Financial Planning, University of Dubuque, 2000 University Avenue, Dubuque, IA 52001-5050, 563-589-3170 or toll-free 800-722-5583. *Fax:* 563-589-3690. *E-mail:* tbrahm@dbq.edu. *Website:* http://www.dbq.edu/.

UNIVERSITY OF EVANSVILLE

Evansville, IN

Tuition & fees: N/R — **Average undergraduate aid package: $32,530**

ABOUT THE INSTITUTION Independent United Methodist Church, coed. ***Awards:*** associate, bachelor's, master's, and doctoral degrees. 79 undergraduate majors. Federal methodology is used as a basis for awarding need-based institutional aid.

FRESHMAN FINANCIAL AID (Fall 2019, est.) 401 applied for aid; of those 85% were deemed to have need. 100% of freshmen with need received aid; of those 38% had need fully met. ***Average percent of need met:*** 86% (excluding resources awarded to replace EFC). ***Average financial aid package:*** $32,986 (excluding resources awarded to replace EFC). 17% of all full-time freshmen had no need and received non-need-based gift aid.

UNDERGRADUATE FINANCIAL AID (Fall 2019, est.) 1,409 applied for aid; of those 87% were deemed to have need. 100% of undergraduates with need received aid; of those 36% had need fully met. ***Average percent of need met:*** 84% (excluding resources awarded to replace EFC). ***Average financial aid package:*** $32,530 (excluding resources awarded to replace EFC). 24% of all full-time undergraduates had no need and received non-need-based gift aid.

GIFT AID (NEED-BASED) ***Total amount:*** $29,247,935 (7% federal, 9% state, 79% institutional, 5% external sources). ***Receiving aid:*** Freshmen: 73% (327); all full-time undergraduates: 65% (1,164). ***Average award:*** Freshmen: $26,377; Undergraduates: $25,043. ***Scholarships, grants, and awards:*** Federal Pell, FSEOG, state, college/university gift aid from institutional funds.

GIFT AID (NON-NEED-BASED) ***Total amount:*** $13,984,016 (94% institutional, 6% external sources). ***Receiving aid:*** Freshmen: 21% (93). Undergraduates: 15% (263). ***Average award:*** Freshmen: $24,641. Undergraduates: $22,566. ***Scholarships, grants, and awards by category:*** *Academic interests/achievement:* 1,242 awards ($23,993,161 total): biological sciences, business, communication, computer science, education, engineering/technologies, English, foreign languages, general academic interests/achievements, home economics, humanities, international studies, mathematics, physical sciences, premedicine, religion/biblical studies, social sciences. *Creative arts/performance:* 222 awards ($3,715,724 total): applied art and design, music, performing arts, theater/drama. *Special achievements/activities:* 107 awards ($1,499,650 total): general special achievements/activities, junior miss, leadership, memberships. *Special characteristics:* 420 awards ($5,155,372 total): children and siblings of alumni, children of faculty/staff, international students, local/state students, members of minority groups, out-of-state students, previous college experience, relatives of clergy, religious affiliation, siblings of current students, veterans, veterans' children. ***ROTC:*** Army cooperative.

LOANS ***Student loans:*** $9,498,207 (59% need-based, 41% non-need-based). 56% of past graduating class borrowed through all loan programs. *Average indebtedness per student:* $31,464. ***Average need-based loan:*** Freshmen: $3165. Undergraduates: $3882. ***Parent loans:*** $3,435,622 (43% need-based, 57% non-need-based). ***Programs:*** Federal Direct (Subsidized and Unsubsidized Stafford, PLUS), Federal Nursing, college/university.

WORK-STUDY ***Federal work-study:*** Total amount: $693,696; 350 jobs averaging $1979. ***State or other work-study/employment:*** Total amount: $82,879 (100% non-need-based). 43 part-time jobs averaging $1927.

ATHLETIC AWARDS Total amount: $5,583,077 (35% need-based, 65% non-need-based).

APPLYING FOR FINANCIAL AID ***Required financial aid form:*** FAFSA. ***Financial aid deadline (priority):*** 4/1. ***Notification date:*** Continuous beginning 12/15. Students must reply by 5/1 or within 4 weeks of notification.

CONTACT Ms. Angela Reshad, Assoc. Director, Student Financial Services, University of Evansville, 1800 Lincoln Avenue, Evansville, IN 47722, 812-488-2023 or toll-free 800-423-8633 Ext.2468. *Fax:* 844-433-7153. *E-mail:* financialaid@evansville.edu. *Website:* http://www.evansville.edu/.

THE UNIVERSITY OF FINDLAY

Findlay, OH

Tuition & fees: $35,410 — **Average undergraduate aid package: $29,297**

ABOUT THE INSTITUTION Independent Church of God, coed. ***Awards:*** certificates, associate, bachelor's, master's, and doctoral degrees. 70 undergraduate majors. ***Total enrollment:*** 4,714. Undergraduates: 3,527. Freshmen: 520. Both federal and institutional methodology are used as a basis for awarding need-based institutional aid.

UNDERGRADUATE EXPENSES for 2019–2020 ***Comprehensive fee:*** $45,610 includes full-time tuition ($34,200), mandatory fees ($1210), and room and board ($10,200). ***College room only:*** $5090. Full-time tuition and fees vary according to program. Room and board charges vary according to board plan and housing facility. ***Part-time tuition:*** $755 per semester hour. ***Part-time fees:*** $75. Part-time tuition and fees vary according to course load and program.

FRESHMAN FINANCIAL AID (Fall 2019, est.) 532 applied for aid; of those 84% were deemed to have need. 100% of freshmen with need received aid; of those 27% had need fully met. ***Average percent of need met:*** 80% (excluding resources awarded to replace EFC). ***Average financial aid package:*** $28,576 (excluding resources awarded to replace EFC). 25% of all full-time freshmen had no need and received non-need-based gift aid.

UNDERGRADUATE FINANCIAL AID (Fall 2019, est.) 2,027 applied for aid; of those 86% were deemed to have need. 100% of undergraduates with need received aid; of those 28% had need fully met. ***Average percent of need met:*** 79% (excluding resources awarded to replace EFC). ***Average financial aid package:*** $29,297 (excluding resources awarded to replace EFC). 36% of all full-time undergraduates had no need and received non-need-based gift aid.

GIFT AID (NEED-BASED) ***Total amount:*** $66,642,257 (8% federal, 2% state, 88% institutional, 2% external sources). ***Receiving aid:*** Freshmen: 80% (448); all full-time undergraduates: 69% (1,748). ***Average award:*** Freshmen: $27,602; Undergraduates: $25,689. ***Scholarships, grants, and awards:*** Federal Pell, FSEOG, state, private, college/university gift aid from institutional funds.

GIFT AID (NON-NEED-BASED) ***Receiving aid:*** Freshmen: 80% (448). Undergraduates: 69% (1,748). ***Average award:*** Freshmen: $22,141. Undergraduates: $21,677. ***Scholarships, grants, and awards by category:*** *Academic interests/achievement:* general academic interests/achievements. *Creative arts/performance:* music, theater/drama. *Special characteristics:* children of faculty/staff. ***Tuition waivers:*** Full or partial for employees or children of employees, senior citizens. ***ROTC:*** Army cooperative, Air Force cooperative.

LOANS ***Student loans:*** $13,191,740 (100% need-based). 81% of past graduating class borrowed through all loan programs. *Average indebtedness per student:* $37,424. ***Average need-based loan:*** Freshmen: $3248. Undergraduates: $4161. ***Parent loans:*** $10,215,311 (12% need-based, 88% non-need-based). ***Programs:***

Federal Direct (Subsidized and Unsubsidized Stafford, PLUS), Perkins, private/alternative loans.

WORK-STUDY ***Federal work-study:*** Total amount: $888,933; jobs available. ***State or other work-study/employment:*** Total amount: $1,349,756 (100% need-based). Part-time jobs available.

ATHLETIC AWARDS Total amount: $656,547 (21% need-based, 79% non-need-based).

APPLYING FOR FINANCIAL AID ***Required financial aid form:*** FAFSA. ***Financial aid deadline:*** 9/1 (priority: 8/1). ***Notification date:*** Continuous beginning 3/1. Students must reply within 2 weeks of notification.

CONTACT Mr. Joseph F. Spencer, Director of Financial Aid, The University of Findlay, 1000 North Main Street, Findlay, OH 45840-3695, 419-434-5678 or toll-free 800-548-0932. *Fax:* 419-434-4344. *E-mail:* spencer@findlay.edu.
Website: http://www.findlay.edu/.

UNIVERSITY OF FLORIDA

Gainesville, FL

Tuition & fees (area res): $6381	Average undergraduate aid package: $13,770

ABOUT THE INSTITUTION State-supported, coed. ***Awards:*** certificates, associate, bachelor's, master's, and doctoral degrees. 99 undergraduate majors. ***Total enrollment:*** 52,218. Undergraduates: 35,491. Freshmen: 6,792. Federal methodology is used as a basis for awarding need-based institutional aid.

UNDERGRADUATE EXPENSES for 2019–2020 ***Application fee:*** $30. ***Tuition, area resident:*** full-time $4477. ***Tuition, state resident:*** full-time $4477. ***Tuition, nonresident:*** full-time $25,694. ***Required fees:*** full-time $1904. ***College room and board:*** $10,220; ***Room only:*** $5750. Room and board charges vary according to board plan and housing facility.

FRESHMAN FINANCIAL AID (Fall 2018) 5790 applied for aid; of those 53% were deemed to have need. 99% of freshmen with need received aid; of those 29% had need fully met. ***Average percent of need met:*** 99% (excluding resources awarded to replace EFC). ***Average financial aid package:*** $15,339 (excluding resources awarded to replace EFC). 4% of all full-time freshmen had no need and received non-need-based gift aid.

UNDERGRADUATE FINANCIAL AID (Fall 2018) 22,707 applied for aid; of those 66% were deemed to have need. 98% of undergraduates with need received aid; of those 22% had need fully met. ***Average percent of need met:*** 98% (excluding resources awarded to replace EFC). ***Average financial aid package:*** $13,770 (excluding resources awarded to replace EFC). 6% of all full-time undergraduates had no need and received non-need-based gift aid.

GIFT AID (NEED-BASED) ***Total amount:*** $88,586,997 (56% federal, 17% state, 27% institutional). ***Receiving aid:*** Freshmen: 30% (2,001); all full-time undergraduates: 29% (9,975). ***Average award:*** Freshmen: $8383; Undergraduates: $7826. ***Scholarships, grants, and awards:*** Federal Pell, FSEOG, state, private, college/university gift aid from institutional funds, United Negro College Fund.

GIFT AID (NON-NEED-BASED) ***Total amount:*** $174,197,476 (2% federal, 86% state, 6% institutional, 6% external sources). ***Receiving aid:*** Freshmen: 40% (2,701). Undergraduates: 29% (10,167). ***Average award:*** Freshmen: $2832. Undergraduates: $3256. ***Scholarships, grants, and awards by category:*** *Academic interests/achievement:* agriculture, architecture, business, communication, computer science, education, engineering/technologies, general academic interests/achievements, health fields, military science. *Creative arts/performance:* applied art and design, dance, general creative arts/performance, journalism/publications, music, performing arts, theater/drama. *Special achievements/activities:* community service, general special achievements/activities, leadership. *Special characteristics:* children of faculty/staff, members of minority groups, out-of-state students. ***Tuition waivers:*** Full or partial for employees or children of employees. ***ROTC:*** Army, Naval, Air Force.

LOANS ***Student loans:*** $53,401,454 (43% need-based, 57% non-need-based). 35% of past graduating class borrowed through all loan programs. *Average indebtedness per student:* $20,388. ***Average need-based loan:*** Freshmen: $3087. Undergraduates: $4113. ***Parent loans:*** $17,605,498 (100% non-need-based). ***Programs:*** Federal Direct (Subsidized and Unsubsidized Stafford, PLUS), Perkins, college/university.

WORK-STUDY ***Federal work-study:*** Total amount: $2,072,756; 985 jobs averaging $2268. ***State or other work-study/employment:*** Total amount: $14,549,905 (1% need-based, 99% non-need-based). 5,473 part-time jobs averaging $2668.

ATHLETIC AWARDS Total amount: $11,215,603 (100% non-need-based).

APPLYING FOR FINANCIAL AID ***Required financial aid form:*** FAFSA. ***Financial aid deadline (priority):*** 12/15. ***Notification date:*** 3/15.

CONTACT Ms. Donna Kolb, Director of Student Financial Affairs, University of Florida, S-107 Criser Hall, Gainesville, FL 32611-4025, 352-294-3220. *Fax:* 352-392-2861. *E-mail:* dkolb@ufl.edu.
Website: http://www.ufl.edu/.

UNIVERSITY OF FORT LAUDERDALE

Lauderhill, FL

CONTACT Financial Aid Office, University of Fort Lauderdale, 4093 NW 16th Street, Lauderhill, FL 33313, 954-486-7728.
Website: http://uftl.edu/.

UNIVERSITY OF GEORGIA

Athens, GA

Tuition & fees (GA res): $12,080	Average undergraduate aid package: $12,934

ABOUT THE INSTITUTION State-supported, coed. ***Awards:*** certificates, bachelor's, master's, and doctoral degrees. 123 undergraduate majors. ***Total enrollment:*** 38,652. Undergraduates: 29,611. Freshmen: 5,727. Federal methodology is used as a basis for awarding need-based institutional aid.

UNDERGRADUATE EXPENSES for 2019–2020 ***Application fee:*** $70. ***Tuition, state resident:*** full-time $9790. ***Tuition, nonresident:*** full-time $28,830. ***Required fees:*** full-time $2290. Full-time tuition and fees vary according to course load, location, and program. Part-time tuition and fees vary according to course load, location, and program. ***College room and board:*** $10,314; ***Room only:*** $6278. Room and board charges vary according to board plan and housing facility.

FRESHMAN FINANCIAL AID (Fall 2019, est.) 4709 applied for aid; of those 49% were deemed to have need. 97% of freshmen with need received aid; of those 34% had need fully met. ***Average percent of need met:*** 79% (excluding resources awarded to replace EFC). ***Average financial aid package:*** $14,573 (excluding resources awarded to replace EFC). 2% of all full-time freshmen had no need and received non-need-based gift aid.

UNDERGRADUATE FINANCIAL AID (Fall 2019, est.) 20,166 applied for aid; of those 58% were deemed to have need. 98% of undergraduates with need received aid; of those 27% had need fully met. ***Average percent of need met:*** 74% (excluding resources awarded to replace EFC). ***Average financial aid package:*** $12,934 (excluding resources awarded to replace EFC). 4% of all full-time undergraduates had no need and received non-need-based gift aid.

GIFT AID (NEED-BASED) ***Total amount:*** $108,237,281 (25% federal, 65% state, 7% institutional, 3% external sources). ***Receiving aid:*** Freshmen: 40% (2,187); all full-time undergraduates: 38% (10,786). ***Average award:*** Freshmen: $11,227; Undergraduates: $10,009. ***Scholarships, grants, and awards:*** Federal Pell, FSEOG, state, private, college/university gift aid from institutional funds.

GIFT AID (NON-NEED-BASED) ***Total amount:*** $120,226,946 (93% state, 4% institutional, 3% external sources). ***Receiving aid:*** Freshmen: 11% (611). Undergraduates: 8% (2,210). ***Average award:*** Freshmen: $4329. Undergraduates: $3073. ***Scholarships, grants, and awards by category:*** *Academic interests/achievement:* 28,871 awards ($197,890,140 total): agriculture, business, education, general academic interests/achievements. *Creative arts/performance:* 104 awards ($98,523 total): music. *Special characteristics:* 245 awards ($343,611 total): local/state students. ***Tuition waivers:*** Full or partial for senior citizens. ***ROTC:*** Army, Air Force.

LOANS ***Student loans:*** $67,437,501 (54% need-based, 46% non-need-based). 41% of past graduating class borrowed through all loan programs. *Average indebtedness per student:* $22,918. ***Average need-based loan:*** Freshmen: $3372. Undergraduates: $4238. ***Parent loans:*** $35,972,199 (25% need-based, 75% non-need-based). ***Programs:*** Federal Direct (Subsidized and Unsubsidized Stafford, PLUS), state.

WORK-STUDY ***Federal work-study:*** Total amount: $1,771,213; 453 jobs averaging $3201.

ATHLETIC AWARDS Total amount: $10,655,130 (30% need-based, 70% non-need-based).

APPLYING FOR FINANCIAL AID ***Required financial aid form:*** FAFSA. ***Financial aid deadline (priority):*** 12/15. ***Notification date:*** Continuous beginning 12/1. Students must reply within 2 weeks of notification.

CONTACT Mr. Anthony P. Jones, Director of Financial Aid, University of Georgia, 220 Holmes/Hunter Academic Building, Athens, GA 30602-6114, 706-542-6147. *Fax:* 706-542-8217. *E-mail:* osfa@uga.edu.
Website: http://www.uga.edu/.

UNIVERSITY OF GUAM

Mangilao, GU

Tuition & fees (area res): $5804 **Average undergraduate aid package: N/A**

ABOUT THE INSTITUTION Territory-supported, coed. ***Awards:*** certificates, bachelor's, and master's degrees. 28 undergraduate majors. ***Total enrollment:*** 3,563. Undergraduates: 3,215. Freshmen: 416. Federal methodology is used as a basis for awarding need-based institutional aid.

UNDERGRADUATE EXPENSES for 2020–2021 ***Application fee:*** $52. ***Tuition, area resident:*** full-time $5040; part-time $210 per credit hour. ***Tuition, state resident:*** full-time $5040; part-time $210 per credit hour. ***Tuition, nonresident:*** full-time $12,096; part-time $504 per credit hour. ***Required fees:*** full-time $764; $382. Full-time tuition and fees vary according to course load and degree level. Part-time tuition and fees vary according to course load and degree level. ***College room and board:*** $3850; ***Room only:*** $2250.

GIFT AID (NEED-BASED) ***Total amount:*** $11,902,412 (63% federal, 20% state, 6% institutional, 11% external sources). ***Scholarships, grants, and awards:*** Federal Pell, FSEOG, state, private, college/university gift aid from institutional funds.

GIFT AID (NON-NEED-BASED) ***Scholarships, grants, and awards by category:*** *Academic interests/achievement:* agriculture, business, communication, computer science, education, general academic interests/achievements, health fields. *Creative arts/performance:* art/fine arts, general creative arts/performance, journalism/publications, music, performing arts. *Special characteristics:* children and siblings of alumni, children of faculty/staff, children of union members/company employees, international students. ***Tuition waivers:*** Full or partial for employees or children of employees, senior citizens. ***ROTC:*** Army.

LOANS ***Student loans:*** $4,995,216 (100% need-based). ***Parent loans:*** $164,025 (100% non-need-based). ***Programs:*** Federal Direct (Subsidized and Unsubsidized Stafford, PLUS), territory.

WORK-STUDY ***Federal work-study:*** Total amount: $419,431; jobs available.

APPLYING FOR FINANCIAL AID ***Required financial aid form:*** FAFSA. ***Financial aid deadline (priority):*** 4/30.

CONTACT Christina P Manglona, Office of Financial Aid, University of Guam, UOG Station, Mangilao, GU 96923, 671-735-2288. *E-mail:* teenapm@triton.uog.edu.
Website: http://www.uog.edu/.

UNIVERSITY OF HARTFORD

West Hartford, CT

ABOUT THE INSTITUTION Independent, coed. ***Awards:*** certificates, diplomas, associate, bachelor's, master's, and doctoral degrees. 81 undergraduate majors. ***Total enrollment:*** 6,773. Undergraduates: 4,793. Freshmen: 1,234.

GIFT AID (NEED-BASED) ***Scholarships, grants, and awards:*** Federal Pell, FSEOG, state, private, college/university gift aid from institutional funds.

GIFT AID (NON-NEED-BASED) ***Scholarships, grants, and awards by category:*** *Academic interests/achievement:* architecture, area/ethnic studies, biological sciences, business, communication, computer science, education, engineering/technologies, English, foreign languages, general academic interests/achievements, health fields, humanities, international studies, mathematics, premedicine, religion/biblical studies, social sciences. *Creative arts/performance:* applied art and design, art/fine arts, cinema/film/broadcasting, creative writing, dance, debating, general creative arts/performance, journalism/publications, music, performing arts, theater/drama. *Special achievements/activities:* community service, leadership. *Special characteristics:* adult students, children of current students, children of faculty/staff, children of union members/company employees, children with a deceased or disabled parent, ethnic background, first-generation college students, handicapped students, international students, local/state students, members of minority groups, parents of current students, previous college experience, religious affiliation, siblings of current students, spouses of current students, twins, veterans.

LOANS ***Programs:*** Federal Direct (Subsidized and Unsubsidized Stafford, PLUS), Perkins.

WORK-STUDY ***Federal work-study:*** Total amount: $1,007,751; 546 jobs averaging $1894. ***State or other work-study/employment:*** Total amount: $1,547,017 (70% need-based, 30% non-need-based). Part-time jobs available.

APPLYING FOR FINANCIAL AID ***Required financial aid form:*** FAFSA.

CONTACT Victoria Hampton, Office of Financial Aid, University of Hartford, 200 Bloomfield Avenue, West Hartford, CT 06117-1599, 860-768-4296 or toll-free 800-947-4303. *Fax:* 860-768-4961. *E-mail:* finaid@hartford.edu.
Website: http://www.hartford.edu/.

UNIVERSITY OF HAWAII AT HILO

Hilo, HI

CONTACT Financial Aid Office, University of Hawaii at Hilo, 200 West Kawili Street, Hilo, HI 96720-4091, 808-932-7449 or toll-free 800-897-4456. *Fax:* 808-932-7459. *E-mail:* uhhfao@hawaii.edu.
Website: http://hilo.hawaii.edu/.

UNIVERSITY OF HAWAII AT MANOA

Honolulu, HI

Tuition & fees (area res): $12,186 **Average undergraduate aid package: $15,223**

ABOUT THE INSTITUTION State-supported, coed. ***Awards:*** certificates, bachelor's, master's, and doctoral degrees. 90 undergraduate majors. ***Total enrollment:*** 17,490. Undergraduates: 12,631. Freshmen: 2,020. Federal methodology is used as a basis for awarding need-based institutional aid.

UNDERGRADUATE EXPENSES for 2020–2021 ***Application fee:*** $70. ***Tuition, area resident:*** full-time $11,304; part-time $471 per credit hour. ***Tuition, state resident:*** full-time $11,304; part-time $471 per credit hour. ***Tuition, nonresident:*** full-time $33,336; part-time $1389 per credit hour. ***Required fees:*** full-time $882; $436 per term. ***College room and board:*** $13,366; ***Room only:*** $9239.

FRESHMAN FINANCIAL AID (Fall 2018) 1637 applied for aid; of those 64% were deemed to have need. 99% of freshmen with need received aid; of those 32% had need fully met. ***Average percent of need met:*** 72% (excluding resources awarded to replace EFC). ***Average financial aid package:*** $15,787 (excluding resources awarded to replace EFC). 28% of all full-time freshmen had no need and received non-need-based gift aid.

UNDERGRADUATE FINANCIAL AID (Fall 2018) 9,033 applied for aid; of those 68% were deemed to have need. 98% of undergraduates with need received aid; of those 28% had need fully met. ***Average percent of need met:*** 69% (excluding resources awarded to replace EFC). ***Average financial aid package:*** $15,223 (excluding resources awarded to replace EFC). 24% of all full-time undergraduates had no need and received non-need-based gift aid.

GIFT AID (NEED-BASED) ***Total amount:*** $46,535,460 (40% federal, 4% state, 49% institutional, 7% external sources). ***Receiving aid:*** Freshmen: 56% (1,021); all full-time undergraduates: 53% (5,789). ***Average award:*** Freshmen: $11,205; Undergraduates: $10,488. ***Scholarships, grants, and awards:*** Federal Pell, FSEOG, state, private, college/university gift aid from institutional funds.

GIFT AID (NON-NEED-BASED) ***Total amount:*** $19,682,317 (58% institutional, 42% external sources). ***Receiving aid:*** Freshmen: 14% (264). Undergraduates: 12% (1,324). ***Average award:*** Freshmen: $13,135. Undergraduates: $13,390. ***Scholarships, grants, and awards by category:*** *Academic interests/achievement:* architecture, area/ethnic studies, biological sciences, business, communication, computer science, education, engineering/technologies, English, foreign languages, general academic interests/achievements, home economics, humanities, international studies, library science, mathematics, physical sciences, social sciences. *Creative arts/performance:* applied art and design, cinema/film/broadcasting, dance, general creative arts/performance, journalism/publications, music, theater/drama. *Special achievements/activities:* community service, general special achievements/activities. *Special characteristics:* general special characteristics. ***ROTC:*** Army, Air Force.

LOANS ***Student loans:*** $36,224,273 (50% need-based, 50% non-need-based). 41% of past graduating class borrowed through all loan programs. *Average indebtedness per student:* $24,223. ***Average need-based loan:*** Freshmen: $3605. Undergraduates: $4558. ***Parent loans:*** $29,970,010 (100% non-need-based). ***Programs:*** Federal Direct (Subsidized and Unsubsidized Stafford, PLUS), Perkins, state.

WORK-STUDY ***Federal work-study:*** Total amount: $868,596; jobs available. ***State or other work-study/employment:*** Part-time jobs available.

ATHLETIC AWARDS Total amount: $7,777,008 (1% need-based, 99% non-need-based).

APPLYING FOR FINANCIAL AID ***Required financial aid form:*** FAFSA. ***Financial aid deadline (priority):*** 2/1. ***Notification date:*** Continuous beginning 4/1. Students must reply by 5/1 or within 4 weeks of notification.

CONTACT Jodie Kuba, Director of Financial Aid Services, University of Hawaii at Manoa, 2600 Campus Road, Suite 112, Honolulu, HI 96822, 808-956-7251 or toll-free 800-823-9771. *Fax:* 808-956-3985. *E-mail:* finaid@hawaii.edu.
Website: http://manoa.hawaii.edu/.

UNIVERSITY OF HAWAII–WEST OAHU

Kapolei, HI

ABOUT THE INSTITUTION State-supported, coed. ***Awards:*** certificates and bachelor's degrees. 9 undergraduate majors. ***Total enrollment:*** 3,049. Undergraduates: 3,049. Freshmen: 217.

GIFT AID (NEED-BASED) ***Scholarships, grants, and awards:*** Federal Pell, FSEOG, state, private, college/university gift aid from institutional funds.

LOANS ***Programs:*** Federal Direct (Subsidized and Unsubsidized Stafford, PLUS).

WORK-STUDY ***Federal work-study:*** Total amount: $47,404; jobs available. ***State or other work-study/employment:*** Total amount: $2,472,786 (100% need-based). Part-time jobs available.

APPLYING FOR FINANCIAL AID ***Required financial aid form:*** FAFSA.

CONTACT Dr. Judy Oliveira, Office of Financial Aid, University of Hawaii–West Oahu, 91-1001 Farrington Highway, Kapolei, HI 96707, 808-689-2689 or toll-free 866-299-8656. *Fax:* 808-689-2691. *E-mail:* uhwo-finaid-l@lists.hawaii.edu.
Website: http://www.uhwo.hawaii.edu/.

UNIVERSITY OF HOLY CROSS

New Orleans, LA

CONTACT Ms. Hayden Wagar, Director of Financial Aid, University of Holy Cross, 4123 Woodland Drive, New Orleans, LA 70131-7399, 504-398-2133 or toll-free 800-259-7744. *Fax:* 504-394-1237. *E-mail:* hwagar@uhcno.edu.
Website: http://www.uhcno.edu/.

UNIVERSITY OF HOUSTON

Houston, TX

Tuition & fees (TX res): $11,276	Average undergraduate aid package: $12,716

ABOUT THE INSTITUTION State-supported, coed. ***Awards:*** bachelor's, master's, and doctoral degrees. 84 undergraduate majors. ***Total enrollment:*** 46,148. Undergraduates: 38,597. Freshmen: 5,680. Federal methodology is used as a basis for awarding need-based institutional aid.

UNDERGRADUATE EXPENSES for 2019–2020 ***Application fee:*** $75. ***Tuition, state resident:*** full-time $10,274; part-time $342 per credit hour. ***Tuition, nonresident:*** full-time $25,934; part-time $864 per credit hour. ***Required fees:*** full-time $1002. Full-time tuition and fees vary according to course level, course load, degree level, program, and student level. Part-time tuition and fees vary according to course level, course load, degree level, program, and student level. ***College room and board:*** $9368. Room and board charges vary according to board plan and housing facility. ***Payment plan:*** Guaranteed tuition.

FRESHMAN FINANCIAL AID (Fall 2019, est.) 4499 applied for aid; of those 81% were deemed to have need. 95% of freshmen with need received aid; of those 14% had need fully met. ***Average percent of need met:*** 61% (excluding resources awarded to replace EFC). ***Average financial aid package:*** $13,468 (excluding resources awarded to replace EFC). 7% of all full-time freshmen had no need and received non-need-based gift aid.

UNDERGRADUATE FINANCIAL AID (Fall 2019, est.) 20,296 applied for aid; of those 87% were deemed to have need. 94% of undergraduates with need received aid; of those 13% had need fully met. ***Average percent of need met:*** 59% (excluding resources awarded to replace EFC). ***Average financial aid package:*** $12,716 (excluding resources awarded to replace EFC). 3% of all full-time undergraduates had no need and received non-need-based gift aid.

GIFT AID (NEED-BASED) ***Total amount:*** $146,707,516 (50% federal, 18% state, 27% institutional, 5% external sources). ***Receiving aid:*** Freshmen: 59% (3,185); all full-time undergraduates: 53% (14,850). ***Average award:*** Freshmen: $10,738; Undergraduates: $9099. ***Scholarships, grants, and awards:*** Federal Pell, FSEOG, state, private, college/university gift aid from institutional funds.

GIFT AID (NON-NEED-BASED) ***Total amount:*** $17,646,635 (84% institutional, 16% external sources). ***Receiving aid:*** Freshmen: 3% (157). Undergraduates: 2% (527). ***Average award:*** Freshmen: $5051. Undergraduates: $4747. ***Scholarships, grants, and awards by category:*** *Academic interests/achievement:* architecture, area/ethnic studies, biological sciences, business, communication, computer science, education, engineering/technologies, English, foreign languages, general academic interests/achievements, health fields, home economics, humanities, international studies, library science, mathematics, physical sciences, premedicine, social sciences. *Creative arts/performance:* applied art and design, art/fine arts, creative writing, dance, general creative arts/performance, journalism/publications, music, performing arts, theater/drama. *Special achievements/activities:* cheerleading/drum major, community service, general special achievements/activities, hobbies/interests, leadership, memberships. *Special characteristics:* adult students, children and siblings of alumni, children of union members/company employees, first-generation college students, handicapped students, international students, local/state students, out-of-state students, previous college experience. ***Tuition waivers:*** Full or partial for senior citizens. ***ROTC:*** Army, Naval cooperative, Air Force.

LOANS ***Student loans:*** $110,468,910 (79% need-based, 21% non-need-based). 44% of past graduating class borrowed through all loan programs. *Average indebtedness per student:* $22,858. ***Average need-based loan:*** Freshmen: $5477. Undergraduates: $7113. ***Parent loans:*** $11,725,945 (46% need-based, 54% non-need-based). ***Programs:*** Federal Direct (Subsidized and Unsubsidized Stafford, PLUS), state.

WORK-STUDY ***Federal work-study:*** Total amount: $2,134,713; 513 jobs averaging $4127. ***State or other work-study/employment:*** Total amount: $438,970 (100% need-based). 98 part-time jobs averaging $4434.

ATHLETIC AWARDS Total amount: $6,434,480 (35% need-based, 65% non-need-based).

APPLYING FOR FINANCIAL AID ***Required financial aid form:*** FAFSA. ***Financial aid deadline (priority):*** 1/15. ***Notification date:*** Continuous beginning 2/1. Students must reply by 8/18.

CONTACT Office of Scholarships and Financial Aid, University of Houston, 4400 University Drive, Houston, TX 77204, 713-743-1010. *Fax:* 713-743-9098. *E-mail:* sfa@central.uh.edu.
Website: http://www.uh.edu/.

UNIVERSITY OF HOUSTON–CLEAR LAKE

Houston, TX

Tuition & fees (area res): $7961	Average undergraduate aid package: $9840

ABOUT THE INSTITUTION State-supported, coed. ***Awards:*** certificates, bachelor's, master's, and doctoral degrees. 39 undergraduate majors. ***Total enrollment:*** 9,082. Undergraduates: 6,425. Freshmen: 336. Federal methodology is used as a basis for awarding need-based institutional aid.

UNDERGRADUATE EXPENSES for 2020–2021 ***Application fee:*** $45. ***Tuition, area resident:*** full-time $7176. ***Tuition, state resident:*** full-time $7176. ***Tuition, nonresident:*** full-time $23,970. ***Required fees:*** full-time $785. ***College room and board:*** $5109.

FRESHMAN FINANCIAL AID (Fall 2018) 446 applied for aid; of those 88% were deemed to have need. 89% of freshmen with need received aid; of those 10% had need fully met. ***Average percent of need met:*** 69% (excluding resources awarded to

replace EFC). ***Average financial aid package:*** $11,943 (excluding resources awarded to replace EFC).

UNDERGRADUATE FINANCIAL AID (Fall 2018) 2,275 applied for aid; of those 90% were deemed to have need. 92% of undergraduates with need received aid; of those 10% had need fully met. ***Average percent of need met:*** 57% (excluding resources awarded to replace EFC). ***Average financial aid package:*** $9840 (excluding resources awarded to replace EFC).

GIFT AID (NEED-BASED) ***Total amount:*** $17,317,260 (64% federal, 14% state, 19% institutional, 3% external sources). ***Receiving aid:*** Freshmen: 254; all full-time undergraduates: 1,499. ***Average award:*** Freshmen: $12,206; Undergraduates: $7632. ***Scholarships, grants, and awards:*** Federal Pell, FSEOG, state, private, college/university gift aid from institutional funds.

GIFT AID (NON-NEED-BASED) ***Total amount:*** $2,988,982 (7% federal, 80% institutional, 13% external sources). ***Average award:*** Freshmen: $6266. Undergraduates: $1791. ***Scholarships, grants, and awards by category:*** *Academic interests/achievement:* biological sciences, business, computer science, education, humanities, mathematics, social sciences. *Creative arts/performance:* art/fine arts. *Special achievements/activities:* community service, general special achievements/activities, leadership. *Special characteristics:* local/state students, veterans, veterans' children. ***Tuition waivers:*** Full or partial for employees or children of employees.

LOANS ***Student loans:*** $18,539,599 (46% need-based, 54% non-need-based). 31% of past graduating class borrowed through all loan programs. *Average indebtedness per student:* $18,992. ***Average need-based loan:*** Freshmen: $3802. Undergraduates: $4413. ***Parent loans:*** $682,363 (100% non-need-based). ***Programs:*** Federal Direct (Subsidized and Unsubsidized Stafford, PLUS), state.

WORK-STUDY ***Federal work-study:*** Total amount: $207,608; jobs available. ***State or other work-study/employment:*** Total amount: $69,248 (100% need-based). Part-time jobs available.

APPLYING FOR FINANCIAL AID ***Required financial aid form:*** FAFSA. ***Financial aid deadline (priority):*** 1/15. ***Notification date:*** Continuous beginning 3/1. Students must reply within 2 weeks of notification.

CONTACT Dr. Billy Satterfield, Executive Director of Student Financial Aid, University of Houston–Clear Lake, 2700 Bay Area Boulevard, Houston, TX 77058-1098, 281-283-2480. *Fax:* 281-283-2502. *E-mail:* satterfield@uhcl.edu.
Website: http://www.uhcl.edu/.

UNIVERSITY OF HOUSTON - DOWNTOWN

Houston, TX

Tuition & fees (area res): $8664	Average undergraduate aid package: $8452

ABOUT THE INSTITUTION State-supported, coed. ***Awards:*** certificates, bachelor's, and master's degrees. 38 undergraduate majors. ***Total enrollment:*** 14,640. Undergraduates: 13,136. Freshmen: 1,467. Federal methodology is used as a basis for awarding need-based institutional aid.

UNDERGRADUATE EXPENSES for 2020–2021 ***Application fee:*** $50. ***Tuition, area resident:*** full-time $7208; part-time $240 per credit hour. ***Tuition, state resident:*** full-time $7208; part-time $240 per credit hour. ***Tuition, nonresident:*** full-time $19,568; part-time $649 per credit hour. ***Required fees:*** full-time $1456.

FRESHMAN FINANCIAL AID (Fall 2019, est.) 1098 applied for aid; of those 95% were deemed to have need. 96% of freshmen with need received aid; of those 5% had need fully met. ***Average percent of need met:*** 53% (excluding resources awarded to replace EFC). ***Average financial aid package:*** $8911 (excluding resources awarded to replace EFC). 1% of all full-time freshmen had no need and received non-need-based gift aid.

UNDERGRADUATE FINANCIAL AID (Fall 2019, est.) 5,294 applied for aid; of those 96% were deemed to have need. 97% of undergraduates with need received aid; of those 11% had need fully met. ***Average percent of need met:*** 59% (excluding resources awarded to replace EFC). ***Average financial aid package:*** $8452 (excluding resources awarded to replace EFC). 1% of all full-time undergraduates had no need and received non-need-based gift aid.

GIFT AID (NEED-BASED) ***Total amount:*** $41,819,397 (67% federal, 14% state, 19% institutional). ***Receiving aid:*** Freshmen: 79% (977); all full-time undergraduates: 71% (4,669). ***Average award:*** Freshmen: $7834; Undergraduates: $5993. ***Scholarships, grants, and awards:*** Federal Pell, FSEOG, state, private, college/university gift aid from institutional funds.

GIFT AID (NON-NEED-BASED) ***Total amount:*** $5,619,895 (90% institutional, 10% external sources). ***Receiving aid:*** Freshmen: 16% (203). Undergraduates: 24% (1,616). ***Average award:*** Freshmen: $2958. Undergraduates: $2742. ***Scholarships, grants, and awards by category:*** *Academic interests/achievement:* business, general academic interests/achievements. *Special achievements/activities:* community service, general special achievements/activities, leadership. *Special characteristics:* general special characteristics. ***ROTC:*** Army cooperative, Air Force cooperative.

LOANS ***Student loans:*** $32,432,639 (45% need-based, 55% non-need-based). 14% of past graduating class borrowed through all loan programs. *Average indebtedness per student:* $4902. ***Average need-based loan:*** Freshmen: $3215. Undergraduates: $4231. ***Parent loans:*** $215,271 (100% non-need-based). ***Programs:*** Federal Direct (Subsidized and Unsubsidized Stafford, PLUS), state.

WORK-STUDY ***Federal work-study:*** Total amount: $647,413; jobs available. ***State or other work-study/employment:*** Total amount: $93,536 (100% need-based). Part-time jobs available.

APPLYING FOR FINANCIAL AID ***Required financial aid form:*** FAFSA. ***Financial aid deadline (priority):*** 4/1. ***Notification date:*** Continuous beginning 4/1. Students must reply within 4 weeks of notification.

CONTACT Financial Aid Office, University of Houston - Downtown, One Main Street, Houston, TX 77002, 713-221-8000.
Website: http://www.uhd.edu/.

UNIVERSITY OF HOUSTON–VICTORIA

Victoria, TX

ABOUT THE INSTITUTION State-supported, coed. ***Awards:*** certificates, bachelor's, and master's degrees. 16 undergraduate majors. ***Total enrollment:*** 4,407. Undergraduates: 3,012. Entering class: 138.

GIFT AID (NEED-BASED) ***Scholarships, grants, and awards:*** Federal Pell, FSEOG, state, private, college/university gift aid from institutional funds.

GIFT AID (NON-NEED-BASED) ***Scholarships, grants, and awards by category:*** *Academic interests/achievement:* biological sciences, business, communication, computer science, education, general academic interests/achievements, humanities, mathematics, social sciences. *Special achievements/activities:* community service, leadership, memberships.

LOANS ***Programs:*** Federal Direct (Subsidized and Unsubsidized Stafford, PLUS), state.

CONTACT Carolyn Mallory, Director of Financial Aid, University of Houston–Victoria, 3007 North Ben Wilson, Victoria, TX 77901-5731, 361-570-4131 or toll-free 877-970-4848 Ext.110. *Fax:* 361-580-5555. *E-mail:* malloryc@uhv.edu.
Website: http://www.uhv.edu/.

UNIVERSITY OF IDAHO

Moscow, ID

Tuition & fees (ID res): $8304	Average undergraduate aid package: $13,613

ABOUT THE INSTITUTION State-supported, coed. ***Awards:*** certificates, bachelor's, master's, and doctoral degrees. 101 undergraduate majors. ***Total enrollment:*** 11,926. Undergraduates: 9,392. Freshmen: 1,475. Federal methodology is used as a basis for awarding need-based institutional aid.

UNDERGRADUATE EXPENSES for 2019–2020 ***Application fee:*** $60. ***Tuition, state resident:*** full-time $6182; part-time $368 per credit hour. ***Tuition, nonresident:*** full-time $25,418; part-time $1330 per credit hour. ***Required fees:*** full-time $2122; $47 per credit hour. Full-time tuition and fees vary according to course load, program, and reciprocity agreements. Part-time tuition and fees vary according to program and reciprocity agreements. ***College room and board:*** $9080. Room and board charges vary according to board plan and housing facility.

FRESHMAN FINANCIAL AID (Fall 2018) 1331 applied for aid; of those 74% were deemed to have need. 98% of freshmen with need received aid; of those 38% had need fully met. ***Average percent of need met:*** 77% (excluding resources awarded to replace EFC). ***Average financial aid package:*** $12,929 (excluding resources

awarded to replace EFC). 26% of all full-time freshmen had no need and received non-need-based gift aid.

UNDERGRADUATE FINANCIAL AID (Fall 2018) 5,808 applied for aid; of those 80% were deemed to have need. 97% of undergraduates with need received aid; of those 34% had need fully met. ***Average percent of need met:*** 76% (excluding resources awarded to replace EFC). ***Average financial aid package:*** $13,613 (excluding resources awarded to replace EFC). 23% of all full-time undergraduates had no need and received non-need-based gift aid.

GIFT AID (NEED-BASED) ***Total amount:*** $19,501,012 (69% federal, 19% state, 12% institutional). ***Receiving aid:*** Freshmen: 37% (561); all full-time undergraduates: 41% (3,028). ***Average award:*** Freshmen: $4839; Undergraduates: $5069. ***Scholarships, grants, and awards:*** Federal Pell, FSEOG, state, private, college/university gift aid from institutional funds.

GIFT AID (NON-NEED-BASED) ***Total amount:*** $14,319,110 (1% state, 81% institutional, 18% external sources). ***Receiving aid:*** Freshmen: 53% (796). Undergraduates: 42% (3,104). ***Average award:*** Freshmen: $4165. Undergraduates: $5342. ***Scholarships, grants, and awards by category:*** *Academic interests/achievement:* agriculture, architecture, biological sciences, business, communication, computer science, education, engineering/technologies, English, foreign languages, general academic interests/achievements, health fields, home economics, humanities, international studies, library science, mathematics, military science, physical sciences, premedicine, social sciences. *Creative arts/performance:* applied art and design, art/fine arts, creative writing, dance, general creative arts/performance, journalism/publications, music, performing arts, theater/drama. *Special achievements/activities:* cheerleading/drum major, general special achievements/activities, junior miss, leadership, rodeo. *Special characteristics:* adult students, children and siblings of alumni, children of faculty/staff, ethnic background, first-generation college students, general special characteristics, handicapped students, international students, local/state students, members of minority groups, out-of-state students, veterans. ***Tuition waivers:*** Full or partial for employees or children of employees. ***ROTC:*** Army, Naval, Air Force cooperative.

LOANS ***Student loans:*** $28,346,923 (47% need-based, 53% non-need-based). 61% of past graduating class borrowed through all loan programs. *Average indebtedness per student:* $23,105. ***Average need-based loan:*** Freshmen: $4655. Undergraduates: $6248. ***Parent loans:*** $9,033,656 (100% non-need-based). ***Programs:*** Federal Direct (Subsidized and Unsubsidized Stafford, PLUS), college/university.

WORK-STUDY ***Federal work-study:*** Total amount: $693,784; jobs available. ***State or other work-study/employment:*** Total amount: $244,903 (100% need-based). Part-time jobs available.

ATHLETIC AWARDS Total amount: $5,986,159 (100% non-need-based).

APPLYING FOR FINANCIAL AID ***Required financial aid form:*** FAFSA. ***Financial aid deadline (priority):*** 12/1. ***Notification date:*** Continuous beginning 12/1. Students must reply within 4 weeks of notification.

CONTACT Dr. Dan D. Davenport, Director of Student Financial Aid Services, University of Idaho, 875 Perimeter Drive, MS-4291, Moscow, ID 83844-4291, 208-885-6312 or toll-free 888-884-3246. *Fax:* 208-885-5592. *E-mail:* dand@uidaho.edu. *Website:* http://www.uidaho.edu/.

UNIVERSITY OF ILLINOIS AT CHICAGO

Chicago, IL

Tuition & fees (area res): $13,874	Average undergraduate aid package: $15,209

ABOUT THE INSTITUTION State-supported, coed. ***Awards:*** certificates, bachelor's, master's, and doctoral degrees. 86 undergraduate majors. ***Total enrollment:*** 33,390. Undergraduates: 21,641. Freshmen: 4,407. Federal methodology is used as a basis for awarding need-based institutional aid.

UNDERGRADUATE EXPENSES for 2019–2020 ***Application fee:*** $60. ***Tuition, area resident:*** full-time $10,584; part-time $464 per credit hour. ***Tuition, state resident:*** full-time $10,584; part-time $464 per credit hour. ***Tuition, nonresident:*** full-time $24,276; part-time $808 per credit hour. ***Required fees:*** full-time $3290. Full-time tuition and fees vary according to program. Part-time tuition and fees vary according to program. ***College room and board:*** $12,479; ***Room only:*** $8082. Room and board charges vary according to board plan and housing facility. ***Payment plan:*** Guaranteed tuition.

FRESHMAN FINANCIAL AID (Fall 2018) 3657 applied for aid; of those 87% were deemed to have need. 93% of freshmen with need received aid; of those 8% had need fully met. ***Average percent of need met:*** 64% (excluding resources awarded to replace EFC). ***Average financial aid package:*** $15,543 (excluding resources awarded to replace EFC). 4% of all full-time freshmen had no need and received non-need-based gift aid.

UNDERGRADUATE FINANCIAL AID (Fall 2018) 15,677 applied for aid; of those 90% were deemed to have need. 96% of undergraduates with need received aid; of those 8% had need fully met. ***Average percent of need met:*** 63% (excluding resources awarded to replace EFC). ***Average financial aid package:*** $15,209 (excluding resources awarded to replace EFC). 3% of all full-time undergraduates had no need and received non-need-based gift aid.

GIFT AID (NEED-BASED) ***Total amount:*** $146,867,724 (35% federal, 31% state, 32% institutional, 2% external sources). ***Receiving aid:*** Freshmen: 67% (2,726); all full-time undergraduates: 63% (12,017). ***Average award:*** Freshmen: $13,948; Undergraduates: $12,978. ***Scholarships, grants, and awards:*** Federal Pell, FSEOG, state, private, college/university gift aid from institutional funds.

GIFT AID (NON-NEED-BASED) ***Total amount:*** $2,574,254 (2% state, 73% institutional, 25% external sources). ***Receiving aid:*** Freshmen: 3% (141). Undergraduates: 2% (381). ***Average award:*** Freshmen: $5721. Undergraduates: $5100. ***Scholarships, grants, and awards by category:*** *Academic interests/achievement:* 1,416 awards ($8,040,992 total): architecture, business, general academic interests/achievements. *Creative arts/performance:* 195 awards ($671,765 total): applied art and design, art/fine arts, creative writing, music, performing arts, theater/drama. ***ROTC:*** Army, Naval cooperative, Air Force cooperative.

LOANS ***Student loans:*** $63,785,753 (87% need-based, 13% non-need-based). 58% of past graduating class borrowed through all loan programs. *Average indebtedness per student:* $21,934. ***Average need-based loan:*** Freshmen: $3300. Undergraduates: $4297. ***Parent loans:*** $20,953,775 (85% need-based, 15% non-need-based). ***Programs:*** Federal Direct (Subsidized and Unsubsidized Stafford, PLUS), Perkins, Federal Nursing, college/university, private loans.

WORK-STUDY ***Federal work-study:*** Total amount: $2,462,611; 943 jobs averaging $3000. ***State or other work-study/employment:*** Total amount: $9,165,761 (71% need-based, 29% non-need-based). 3,287 part-time jobs averaging $2500.

ATHLETIC AWARDS Total amount: $4,813,519 (35% need-based, 65% non-need-based).

APPLYING FOR FINANCIAL AID ***Required financial aid form:*** FAFSA. ***Financial aid deadline (priority):*** 2/15. ***Notification date:*** Continuous beginning 3/15. Students must reply by 5/1.

CONTACT Deidre Rush, Director of Fiscal Operations, University of Illinois at Chicago, 1200 West Harrison, M/C 334, Suite 1800, Chicago, IL 60607-7128, 312-996-5563. *Fax:* 312-996-3385. *E-mail:* deidreb@uic.edu. *Website:* http://www.uic.edu/.

UNIVERSITY OF ILLINOIS AT SPRINGFIELD

Springfield, IL

Tuition & fees (IL res): $11,813	Average undergraduate aid package: $14,275

ABOUT THE INSTITUTION State-supported, coed. ***Awards:*** certificates, bachelor's, master's, and doctoral degrees. 31 undergraduate majors. ***Total enrollment:*** 4,275. Undergraduates: 2,663. Freshmen: 373. Federal methodology is used as a basis for awarding need-based institutional aid.

UNDERGRADUATE EXPENSES for 2019–2020 ***Tuition, state resident:*** full-time $9405; part-time $314 per credit hour. ***Tuition, nonresident:*** full-time $18,930; part-time $631 per credit hour. ***Required fees:*** full-time $2408. ***College room and board:*** $11,660; ***Room only:*** $7460. Room and board charges vary according to board plan and housing facility. ***Payment plan:*** Guaranteed tuition.

FRESHMAN FINANCIAL AID (Fall 2018) 289 applied for aid; of those 79% were deemed to have need. 98% of freshmen with need received aid; of those 25% had need fully met. ***Average percent of need met:*** 81% (excluding resources awarded to replace EFC). ***Average financial aid package:*** $16,980 (excluding resources awarded to replace EFC). 22% of all full-time freshmen had no need and received non-need-based gift aid.

UNDERGRADUATE FINANCIAL AID (Fall 2018) 1,493 applied for aid; of those 82% were deemed to have need. 97% of undergraduates with need received aid;

of those 15% had need fully met. ***Average percent of need met:*** 71% (excluding resources awarded to replace EFC). ***Average financial aid package:*** $14,275 (excluding resources awarded to replace EFC). 15% of all full-time undergraduates had no need and received non-need-based gift aid.

GIFT AID (NEED-BASED) ***Total amount:*** $12,053,103 (36% federal, 27% state, 34% institutional, 3% external sources). ***Receiving aid:*** Freshmen: 68% (213); all full-time undergraduates: 59% (1,070). ***Average award:*** Freshmen: $14,663; Undergraduates: $11,731. ***Scholarships, grants, and awards:*** Federal Pell, FSEOG, state, private, college/university gift aid from institutional funds.

GIFT AID (NON-NEED-BASED) ***Total amount:*** $2,344,948 (14% federal, 81% institutional, 5% external sources). ***Receiving aid:*** Freshmen: 17% (53). Undergraduates: 10% (184). ***Average award:*** Freshmen: $11,130. Undergraduates: $8281. ***Tuition waivers:*** Full or partial for employees or children of employees, senior citizens.

LOANS ***Student loans:*** $10,115,042 (87% need-based, 13% non-need-based). 66% of past graduating class borrowed through all loan programs. *Average indebtedness per student:* $22,248. ***Average need-based loan:*** Freshmen: $3221. Undergraduates: $4267. ***Parent loans:*** $1,364,095 (73% need-based, 27% non-need-based). ***Programs:*** Federal Direct (Subsidized and Unsubsidized Stafford, PLUS), Perkins, college/university.

WORK-STUDY ***Federal work-study:*** Total amount: $304,733; jobs available. ***State or other work-study/employment:*** Total amount: $1,138,926 (68% need-based, 32% non-need-based). Part-time jobs available.

ATHLETIC AWARDS Total amount: $1,611,213 (47% need-based, 53% non-need-based).

APPLYING FOR FINANCIAL AID ***Required financial aid form:*** FAFSA. ***Financial aid deadline:*** 11/15 (priority: 3/1). ***Notification date:*** Continuous beginning 1/1. Students must reply within 3 weeks of notification.

CONTACT Ms. Natalie Herring, Associate Provost for Enrollment Management, University of Illinois at Springfield, One University Plaza, MS UHB 1015, Springfield, IL 62703-5407, 217-206-6724 or toll-free 888-977-4847. *Fax:* 217-206-7376. *E-mail:* finaid@uis.edu.
Website: http://www.uis.edu/.

UNIVERSITY OF ILLINOIS AT URBANA-CHAMPAIGN

Champaign, IL

Tuition & fees (area res): $16,210	Average undergraduate aid package: $18,024

ABOUT THE INSTITUTION State-supported, coed. ***Awards:*** certificates, bachelor's, master's, and doctoral degrees. 219 undergraduate majors. ***Total enrollment:*** 49,702. Undergraduates: 33,915. Freshmen: 7,609. Federal methodology is used as a basis for awarding need-based institutional aid.

UNDERGRADUATE EXPENSES for 2019–2020 ***Application fee:*** $50. ***Tuition, area resident:*** full-time $12,036. ***Tuition, state resident:*** full-time $12,036. ***Tuition, nonresident:*** full-time $29,178. ***Required fees:*** full-time $4174. Full-time tuition and fees vary according to program and student level. ***College room and board:*** $11,672; ***Room only:*** $5470. Room and board charges vary according to board plan, housing facility, and student level. ***Payment plan:*** Guaranteed tuition.

FRESHMAN FINANCIAL AID (Fall 2018) 5781 applied for aid; of those 67% were deemed to have need. 94% of freshmen with need received aid; of those 18% had need fully met. ***Average percent of need met:*** 72% (excluding resources awarded to replace EFC). ***Average financial aid package:*** $19,033 (excluding resources awarded to replace EFC). 11% of all full-time freshmen had no need and received non-need-based gift aid.

UNDERGRADUATE FINANCIAL AID (Fall 2018) 20,086 applied for aid; of those 76% were deemed to have need. 95% of undergraduates with need received aid; of those 11% had need fully met. ***Average percent of need met:*** 67% (excluding resources awarded to replace EFC). ***Average financial aid package:*** $18,024 (excluding resources awarded to replace EFC). 11% of all full-time undergraduates had no need and received non-need-based gift aid.

GIFT AID (NEED-BASED) ***Total amount:*** $187,946,272 (22% federal, 20% state, 54% institutional, 4% external sources). ***Receiving aid:*** Freshmen: 42% (3,216); all full-time undergraduates: 39% (12,731). ***Average award:*** Freshmen: $17,750; Undergraduates: $16,498. ***Scholarships, grants, and awards:*** Federal Pell, FSEOG, state, private, college/university gift aid from institutional funds, United Negro College Fund.

GIFT AID (NON-NEED-BASED) ***Total amount:*** $18,068,191 (3% federal, 1% state, 80% institutional, 16% external sources). ***Receiving aid:*** Freshmen: 9% (714). Undergraduates: 5% (1,727). ***Average award:*** Freshmen: $5104. Undergraduates: $5276. ***Scholarships, grants, and awards by category:*** *Academic interests/achievement:* agriculture, architecture, area/ethnic studies, biological sciences, business, communication, computer science, education, engineering/technologies, English, foreign languages, general academic interests/achievements, health fields, home economics, humanities, international studies, library science, mathematics, military science, physical sciences, premedicine, religion/biblical studies, social sciences. *Creative arts/performance:* applied art and design, art/fine arts, dance, general creative arts/performance, journalism/publications, music, performing arts, theater/drama. *Special achievements/activities:* general special achievements/activities, leadership. *Special characteristics:* children of faculty/staff, first-generation college students, general special characteristics, international students, local/state students, members of minority groups, veterans. ***Tuition waivers:*** Full or partial for employees or children of employees. ***ROTC:*** Army, Naval, Air Force.

LOANS ***Student loans:*** $88,606,473 (80% need-based, 20% non-need-based). 44% of past graduating class borrowed through all loan programs. *Average indebtedness per student:* $24,655. ***Average need-based loan:*** Freshmen: $3707. Undergraduates: $4360. ***Parent loans:*** $70,245,514 (75% need-based, 25% non-need-based). ***Programs:*** Federal Direct (Subsidized and Unsubsidized Stafford, PLUS), college/university.

WORK-STUDY ***Federal work-study:*** Total amount: $3,100,598; jobs available. ***State or other work-study/employment:*** Total amount: $20,312,565 (53% need-based, 47% non-need-based). Part-time jobs available.

ATHLETIC AWARDS Total amount: $11,605,807 (40% need-based, 60% non-need-based).

APPLYING FOR FINANCIAL AID ***Required financial aid form:*** FAFSA. ***Financial aid deadline (priority):*** 3/15. ***Notification date:*** Continuous beginning 2/15. Students must reply by 5/1.

CONTACT Michelle Trame, Director of Student Financial Aid, University of Illinois at Urbana-Champaign, Student Services Arcade Building, 620 East John Street, Champaign, IL 61820-5711, 217-333-0100.
Website: http://www.illinois.edu/.

UNIVERSITY OF INDIANAPOLIS

Indianapolis, IN

Tuition & fees: N/R	Average undergraduate aid package: $26,851

ABOUT THE INSTITUTION Independent United Methodist Church, coed. ***Awards:*** associate, bachelor's, master's, and doctoral degrees. 62 undergraduate majors. Federal methodology is used as a basis for awarding need-based institutional aid.

FRESHMAN FINANCIAL AID (Fall 2019, est.) 1091 applied for aid; of those 92% were deemed to have need. 100% of freshmen with need received aid; of those 13% had need fully met. ***Average percent of need met:*** 80% (excluding resources awarded to replace EFC). ***Average financial aid package:*** $29,257 (excluding resources awarded to replace EFC). 10% of all full-time freshmen had no need and received non-need-based gift aid.

UNDERGRADUATE FINANCIAL AID (Fall 2019, est.) 3,683 applied for aid; of those 90% were deemed to have need. 99% of undergraduates with need received aid; of those 15% had need fully met. ***Average percent of need met:*** 75% (excluding resources awarded to replace EFC). ***Average financial aid package:*** $26,851 (excluding resources awarded to replace EFC). 15% of all full-time undergraduates had no need and received non-need-based gift aid.

GIFT AID (NEED-BASED) ***Receiving aid:*** Freshmen: 63% (734); all full-time undergraduates: 54% (2,341). ***Average award:*** Freshmen: $17,924; Undergraduates: $14,558. ***Scholarships, grants, and awards:*** Federal Pell, FSEOG, state, private, college/university gift aid from institutional funds.

GIFT AID (NON-NEED-BASED) ***Receiving aid:*** Freshmen: 68% (786). Undergraduates: 61% (2,637). ***Average award:*** Freshmen: $16,568. Undergraduates: $14,307. ***Scholarships, grants, and awards by category:*** *Academic interests/achievement:* business, communication, general academic interests/achievements, home economics, physical sciences, religion/biblical studies. *Creative arts/perfor-*

mance: applied art and design, debating, music, theater/drama. *Special achievements/ activities:* community service, religious involvement. *Special characteristics:* children of faculty/staff, international students, out-of-state students, relatives of clergy, religious affiliation, veterans. ***ROTC:*** Army cooperative.

LOANS *Student loans:* 74% of past graduating class borrowed through all loan programs. *Average indebtedness per student:* $33,953. ***Average need-based loan:*** Freshmen: $3343. Undergraduates: $4210. ***Programs:*** Federal Direct (Subsidized and Unsubsidized Stafford, PLUS), Perkins.

WORK-STUDY Federal work-study jobs available. ***State or other work-study/ employment:*** Part-time jobs available.

APPLYING FOR FINANCIAL AID *Required financial aid forms:* FAFSA, institution's own form. ***Notification date:*** Continuous.

CONTACT Ms. Linda B. Handy, Associate Vice President of Financial Aid, University of Indianapolis, 1400 East Hanna Avenue, Indianapolis, IN 46227-3697, 317-788-3217 or toll-free 800-232-8634 Ext.3216. *Fax:* 317-788-6136. *E-mail:* handy@uindy.edu. *Website:* http://www.uindy.edu/.

THE UNIVERSITY OF IOWA

Iowa City, IA

Tuition & fees: N/R | **Average undergraduate aid package: $12,652**

ABOUT THE INSTITUTION State-supported, coed. ***Awards:*** certificates, bachelor's, master's, and doctoral degrees. 138 undergraduate majors. ***Total enrollment:*** 31,240. Undergraduates: 23,483. Freshmen: 4,986.

FRESHMAN FINANCIAL AID (Fall 2018) 3809 applied for aid; of those 65% were deemed to have need. 100% of freshmen with need received aid; of those 14% had need fully met. ***Average percent of need met:*** 51% (excluding resources awarded to replace EFC). ***Average financial aid package:*** $12,543 (excluding resources awarded to replace EFC). 24% of all full-time freshmen had no need and received non-need-based gift aid.

UNDERGRADUATE FINANCIAL AID (Fall 2018) 14,804 applied for aid; of those 70% were deemed to have need. 100% of undergraduates with need received aid; of those 13% had need fully met. ***Average percent of need met:*** 52% (excluding resources awarded to replace EFC). ***Average financial aid package:*** $12,652 (excluding resources awarded to replace EFC). 26% of all full-time undergraduates had no need and received non-need-based gift aid.

GIFT AID (NEED-BASED) *Total amount:* $78,728,952 (28% federal, 2% state, 65% institutional, 5% external sources). ***Receiving aid:*** Freshmen: 43% (2,041); all full-time undergraduates: 39% (8,458). ***Average award:*** Freshmen: $9744; Undergraduates: $9095. ***Scholarships, grants, and awards:*** Federal Pell, FSEOG, state, private, college/university gift aid from institutional funds.

GIFT AID (NON-NEED-BASED) *Total amount:* $41,562,796 (1% state, 87% institutional, 12% external sources). ***Receiving aid:*** Freshmen: 25% (1,154). Undergraduates: 5% (989). ***Average award:*** Freshmen: $6677. Undergraduates: $5677. ***Scholarships, grants, and awards by category:*** *Academic interests/ achievement:* business, engineering/technologies, general academic interests/achievements, military science. *Creative arts/performance:* applied art and design, art/fine arts, cinema/film/broadcasting, creative writing, dance, debating, general creative arts/ performance, journalism/publications, music, performing arts, theater/drama. *Special achievements/activities:* cheerleading/drum major, general special achievements/activities, leadership. *Special characteristics:* children and siblings of alumni, ethnic background, first-generation college students, handicapped students, local/state students, out-of-state students, veterans. ***ROTC:*** Army, Air Force.

LOANS *Student loans:* $107,811,573 (58% need-based, 42% non-need-based). 48% of past graduating class borrowed through all loan programs. *Average indebtedness per student:* $28,328. ***Average need-based loan:*** Freshmen: $2367. Undergraduates: $4041. ***Parent loans:*** $54,379,680 (45% need-based, 55% non-need-based). ***Programs:*** Federal Direct (Subsidized and Unsubsidized Stafford, PLUS), Perkins, Federal Nursing, college/university.

WORK-STUDY *Federal work-study:* Total amount: $2,511,029; jobs available. ***State or other work-study/employment:*** Part-time jobs available.

ATHLETIC AWARDS Total amount: $12,828,756 (25% need-based, 75% non-need-based).

APPLYING FOR FINANCIAL AID *Required financial aid form:* FAFSA. ***Financial aid deadline (priority):*** 12/1. ***Notification date:*** Continuous beginning 1/15.

CONTACT Kathy Bialk, Director of Student Financial Aid, The University of Iowa, 208 Calvin Hall, Iowa City, IA 52242, 319-335-3127 or toll-free 800-553-4692. *Fax:* 319-335-3060. *E-mail:* kathy-bialk@uiowa.edu. *Website:* http://www.uiowa.edu/.

UNIVERSITY OF JAMESTOWN

Jamestown, ND

Tuition & fees: $23,498 | **Average undergraduate aid package: $17,733**

ABOUT THE INSTITUTION Independent Presbyterian, coed. ***Awards:*** bachelor's, master's, and doctoral degrees. 45 undergraduate majors. ***Total enrollment:*** 1,121. Undergraduates: 914. Freshmen: 256. Federal methodology is used as a basis for awarding need-based institutional aid.

UNDERGRADUATE EXPENSES for 2020–2021 *Comprehensive fee:* $31,814 includes full-time tuition ($22,718), mandatory fees ($780), and room and board ($8316). Full-time tuition and fees vary according to course load, degree level, and program. Room and board charges vary according to housing facility. ***Part-time tuition:*** $435 per credit hour. Part-time tuition and fees vary according to course load, degree level, and program.

FRESHMAN FINANCIAL AID (Fall 2019, est.) 226 applied for aid; of those 73% were deemed to have need. 100% of freshmen with need received aid; of those 28% had need fully met. ***Average percent of need met:*** 76% (excluding resources awarded to replace EFC). ***Average financial aid package:*** $17,346 (excluding resources awarded to replace EFC). 23% of all full-time freshmen had no need and received non-need-based gift aid.

UNDERGRADUATE FINANCIAL AID (Fall 2019, est.) 722 applied for aid; of those 82% were deemed to have need. 100% of undergraduates with need received aid; of those 24% had need fully met. ***Average percent of need met:*** 75% (excluding resources awarded to replace EFC). ***Average financial aid package:*** $17,733 (excluding resources awarded to replace EFC). 24% of all full-time undergraduates had no need and received non-need-based gift aid.

GIFT AID (NEED-BASED) *Receiving aid:* Freshmen: 65% (166); all full-time undergraduates: 66% (590). ***Average award:*** Freshmen: $14,824; Undergraduates: $14,544. ***Scholarships, grants, and awards:*** Federal Pell, FSEOG, state, private, college/university gift aid from institutional funds.

GIFT AID (NON-NEED-BASED) *Receiving aid:* Freshmen: 17% (44). Undergraduates: 15% (131). ***Average award:*** Freshmen: $7483. Undergraduates: $8053. ***Scholarships, grants, and awards by category:*** *Academic interests/ achievement:* 517 awards ($3,637,054 total): engineering/technologies, general academic interests/achievements, physical sciences. *Creative arts/performance:* 92 awards ($261,709 total): applied art and design, music, theater/drama. *Special achievements/ activities:* 110 awards ($204,967 total): cheerleading/drum major, community service, leadership. *Special characteristics:* 262 awards ($159,999 total): children and siblings of alumni, children of faculty/staff, religious affiliation, siblings of current students, spouses of current students. ***Tuition waivers:*** Full or partial for employees or children of employees.

LOANS *Student loans:* 62% of past graduating class borrowed through all loan programs. *Average indebtedness per student:* $28,889. ***Average need-based loan:*** Freshmen: $3072. Undergraduates: $3796. ***Programs:*** Federal Direct (Subsidized and Unsubsidized Stafford, PLUS), alternative loans.

WORK-STUDY *Federal work-study:* 399 jobs averaging $577. ***State or other work-study/employment:*** 78 part-time jobs averaging $507.

APPLYING FOR FINANCIAL AID *Required financial aid form:* FAFSA. ***Financial aid deadline:*** Continuous. ***Notification date:*** Continuous.

CONTACT Judy Hager, Director of Financial Aid, University of Jamestown, 6085 College Lane, Jamestown, ND 58405, 701-252-3467 Ext. 5548 or toll-free 800-336-2554. *Fax:* 701-253-4318. *E-mail:* jhager@uj.edu. *Website:* http://www.uj.edu/.

THE UNIVERSITY OF KANSAS

Lawrence, KS

Tuition & fees (KS res): $11,166 **Average undergraduate aid package: $16,795**

ABOUT THE INSTITUTION State-supported, coed. ***Awards:*** certificates, bachelor's, master's, and doctoral degrees (University of Kansas is a single institution with academic programs and facilities at two primary locations: Lawrence and Kansas City). 119 undergraduate majors. ***Total enrollment:*** 27,552. Undergraduates: 19,667. Freshmen: 4,125. Federal methodology is used as a basis for awarding need-based institutional aid.

UNDERGRADUATE EXPENSES for 2019–2020 ***Application fee:*** $40. ***Tuition, state resident:*** full-time $10,092; part-time $336 per credit hour. ***Tuition, nonresident:*** full-time $26,960; part-time $899 per credit hour. ***Required fees:*** full-time $1074; $84.99 per credit hour. Full-time tuition and fees vary according to course load, location, and reciprocity agreements. Part-time tuition and fees vary according to course load, location, and reciprocity agreements. ***College room and board:*** $10,350; ***Room only:*** $6084. Room and board charges vary according to board plan and housing facility.

FRESHMAN FINANCIAL AID (Fall 2018) 3183 applied for aid; of those 65% were deemed to have need. 98% of freshmen with need received aid; of those 46% had need fully met. ***Average percent of need met:*** 81% (excluding resources awarded to replace EFC). ***Average financial aid package:*** $17,896 (excluding resources awarded to replace EFC). 28% of all full-time freshmen had no need and received non-need-based gift aid.

UNDERGRADUATE FINANCIAL AID (Fall 2018) 11,320 applied for aid; of those 72% were deemed to have need. 98% of undergraduates with need received aid; of those 41% had need fully met. ***Average percent of need met:*** 77% (excluding resources awarded to replace EFC). ***Average financial aid package:*** $16,795 (excluding resources awarded to replace EFC). 22% of all full-time undergraduates had no need and received non-need-based gift aid.

GIFT AID (NEED-BASED) ***Receiving aid:*** Freshmen: 46% (1,865); all full-time undergraduates: 38% (6,488). ***Average award:*** Freshmen: $9739; Undergraduates: $8305. ***Scholarships, grants, and awards:*** Federal Pell, FSEOG, state, private, college/university gift aid from institutional funds, Bureau of Indian Affairs Grants.

GIFT AID (NON-NEED-BASED) ***Receiving aid:*** Freshmen: 7% (302). Undergraduates: 4% (732). ***Average award:*** Freshmen: $7398. Undergraduates: $6740. ***Scholarships, grants, and awards by category:*** *Academic interests/achievement:* architecture, area/ethnic studies, biological sciences, business, communication, computer science, education, engineering/technologies, English, foreign languages, general academic interests/achievements, home economics, humanities, international studies, mathematics, military science, physical sciences, premedicine, religion/biblical studies, social sciences. *Creative arts/performance:* applied art and design, art/fine arts, cinema/film/broadcasting, creative writing, dance, debating, general creative arts/performance, journalism/publications, music, performing arts, theater/drama. *Special achievements/activities:* community service, general special achievements/activities, leadership. *Special characteristics:* adult students, children and siblings of alumni, children of faculty/staff, ethnic background, first-generation college students, general special characteristics, international students, local/state students, married students, members of minority groups, out-of-state students, previous college experience, veterans. ***Tuition waivers:*** Full or partial for employees or children of employees. ***ROTC:*** Army, Naval, Air Force.

LOANS ***Student loans:*** 53% of past graduating class borrowed through all loan programs. *Average indebtedness per student:* $28,176. ***Average need-based loan:*** Freshmen: $3236. Undergraduates: $4246. ***Programs:*** Federal Direct (Subsidized and Unsubsidized Stafford, PLUS), Federal Nursing, college/university, Health Professions Student Loans (HPSL), Federal Loan for Disadvantaged Students, private loans.

WORK-STUDY ***Federal work-study:*** 784 jobs averaging $1192. ***State or other work-study/employment:*** 41 part-time jobs averaging $4668.

APPLYING FOR FINANCIAL AID ***Required financial aid form:*** FAFSA. ***Notification date:*** Continuous. Students must reply within 4 weeks of notification.

CONTACT Ms. Angela Karlin, Assistant Vice Provost of Financial Aid and Scholarships, The University of Kansas, KU Visitor Center, 1502 Iowa Street, Lawrence, KS 66045-7576, 785-864-4700 or toll-free 888-686-7323 (in-state). *Fax:* 785-864-5469. *E-mail:* financialaid@ku.edu.
Website: http://www.ku.edu/.

UNIVERSITY OF KENTUCKY

Lexington, KY

Tuition & fees (area res): $12,360 **Average undergraduate aid package: $13,562**

ABOUT THE INSTITUTION State-supported, coed. ***Awards:*** certificates, bachelor's, master's, and doctoral degrees. 103 undergraduate majors. ***Total enrollment:*** 29,402. Undergraduates: 22,236. Freshmen: 5,348. Federal methodology is used as a basis for awarding need-based institutional aid.

UNDERGRADUATE EXPENSES for 2019–2020 ***Application fee:*** $50. ***Tuition, area resident:*** full-time $11,011; part-time $459 per credit hour. ***Tuition, state resident:*** full-time $11,011; part-time $459 per credit hour. ***Tuition, nonresident:*** full-time $29,331; part-time $1223 per credit hour. ***Required fees:*** full-time $1349. Full-time tuition and fees vary according to location, program, reciprocity agreements, and student level. Part-time tuition and fees vary according to course load, location, program, reciprocity agreements, and student level. ***College room and board:*** $13,210; ***Room only:*** $8930. Room and board charges vary according to board plan and housing facility.

FRESHMAN FINANCIAL AID (Fall 2018) 4113 applied for aid; of those 72% were deemed to have need. 99% of freshmen with need received aid; of those 20% had need fully met. ***Average percent of need met:*** 60% (excluding resources awarded to replace EFC). ***Average financial aid package:*** $15,077 (excluding resources awarded to replace EFC). 25% of all full-time freshmen had no need and received non-need-based gift aid.

UNDERGRADUATE FINANCIAL AID (Fall 2018) 13,593 applied for aid; of those 78% were deemed to have need. 98% of undergraduates with need received aid; of those 17% had need fully met. ***Average percent of need met:*** 54% (excluding resources awarded to replace EFC). ***Average financial aid package:*** $13,562 (excluding resources awarded to replace EFC). 27% of all full-time undergraduates had no need and received non-need-based gift aid.

GIFT AID (NEED-BASED) ***Total amount:*** $180,556,209 (15% federal, 16% state, 65% institutional, 4% external sources). ***Receiving aid:*** Freshmen: 25% (1,252); all full-time undergraduates: 24% (4,949). ***Average award:*** Freshmen: $5978; Undergraduates: $6037. ***Scholarships, grants, and awards:*** Federal Pell, FSEOG, state, private, college/university gift aid from institutional funds.

GIFT AID (NON-NEED-BASED) ***Receiving aid:*** Freshmen: 58% (2,883). Undergraduates: 44% (8,972). ***Average award:*** Freshmen: $9350. Undergraduates: $9501. ***Scholarships, grants, and awards by category:*** *Academic interests/achievement:* agriculture, architecture, area/ethnic studies, biological sciences, business, communication, computer science, education, engineering/technologies, English, foreign languages, general academic interests/achievements, health fields, home economics, international studies, mathematics, military science, physical sciences, social sciences. *Creative arts/performance:* applied art and design, art/fine arts, cinema/film/broadcasting, creative writing, dance, debating, general creative arts/performance, journalism/publications, music, performing arts, theater/drama. *Special achievements/activities:* cheerleading/drum major, general special achievements/activities, leadership. *Special characteristics:* adult students, children and siblings of alumni, children of educators, children of faculty/staff, children of public servants, children of union members/company employees, children with a deceased or disabled parent, ethnic background, first-generation college students, general special characteristics, handicapped students, international students, members of minority groups, out-of-state students, public servants, spouses of deceased or disabled public servants, veterans, veterans' children. ***Tuition waivers:*** Full or partial for employees or children of employees. ***ROTC:*** Army, Air Force.

LOANS ***Student loans:*** $88,456,176 (100% need-based). 51% of past graduating class borrowed through all loan programs. *Average indebtedness per student:* $33,927. ***Average need-based loan:*** Freshmen: $3212. Undergraduates: $4083. ***Parent loans:*** $38,753,429 (100% need-based). ***Programs:*** Federal Direct (Subsidized and Unsubsidized Stafford, PLUS), Perkins, college/university, private loans.

WORK-STUDY ***Federal work-study:*** Total amount: $406,051; 195 jobs averaging $406,051. ***State or other work-study/employment:*** Part-time jobs available.

ATHLETIC AWARDS Total amount: $13,089,432 (100% need-based).

APPLYING FOR FINANCIAL AID ***Required financial aid form:*** FAFSA. ***Financial aid deadline (priority):*** 12/1. ***Notification date:*** 2/15. Students must reply within 3 weeks of notification.

CONTACT Ms. Kathy Bialk, Executive Director, University of Kentucky, 128 Funkhouser Building, Lexington, KY 40506-0054, 859-257-2000 or toll-free 866-900-GO-UK. *E-mail:* admission@uky.edu.
Website: http://www.uky.edu/.

UNIVERSITY OF LA VERNE

La Verne, CA

ABOUT THE INSTITUTION Independent, coed. ***Awards:*** certificates, bachelor's, master's, and doctoral degrees (also offers continuing education program with significant enrollment not reflected in profile). 50 undergraduate majors. ***Total enrollment:*** 4,484. Undergraduates: 2,509. Freshmen: 495.

GIFT AID (NEED-BASED) ***Scholarships, grants, and awards:*** Federal Pell, FSEOG, state, private, college/university gift aid from institutional funds.

GIFT AID (NON-NEED-BASED) ***Scholarships, grants, and awards by category:*** *Academic interests/achievement:* general academic interests/achievements. *Creative arts/performance:* applied art and design, cinema/film/broadcasting, journalism/publications, music, performing arts, theater/drama. *Special achievements/activities:* community service, leadership.

LOANS ***Programs:*** Federal Direct (Subsidized and Unsubsidized Stafford, PLUS), college/university.

WORK-STUDY ***Federal work-study:*** Total amount: $714,229.

APPLYING FOR FINANCIAL AID ***Required financial aid forms:*** FAFSA, state aid form.

CONTACT Financial Aid Office, University of La Verne, 1950 Third Street, La Verne, CA 91750-4443, 909-593-3511 or toll-free 800-876-4858.
Website: http://www.laverne.edu/.

UNIVERSITY OF LOUISIANA AT LAFAYETTE

Lafayette, LA

Tuition & fees (area res): $10,382	Average undergraduate aid package: $9018

ABOUT THE INSTITUTION State-supported, coed. ***Awards:*** certificates, bachelor's, master's, and doctoral degrees. 61 undergraduate majors. ***Total enrollment:*** 16,933. Undergraduates: 14,603. Freshmen: 2,387. Federal methodology is used as a basis for awarding need-based institutional aid.

UNDERGRADUATE EXPENSES for 2019–2020 ***Application fee:*** $25. ***Tuition, area resident:*** full-time $5407; part-time $433 per credit hour. ***Tuition, state resident:*** full-time $5407; part-time $433 per credit hour. ***Tuition, nonresident:*** full-time $19,135; part-time $1005 per credit hour. ***Required fees:*** full-time $4975. ***College room and board:*** $10,708; ***Room only:*** $6590. Room and board charges vary according to board plan and housing facility.

FRESHMAN FINANCIAL AID (Fall 2018) 2602 applied for aid; of those 74% were deemed to have need. 99% of freshmen with need received aid; of those 16% had need fully met. ***Average percent of need met:*** 70% (excluding resources awarded to replace EFC). ***Average financial aid package:*** $10,443 (excluding resources awarded to replace EFC). 14% of all full-time freshmen had no need and received non-need-based gift aid.

UNDERGRADUATE FINANCIAL AID (Fall 2018) 10,499 applied for aid; of those 77% were deemed to have need. 99% of undergraduates with need received aid; of those 11% had need fully met. ***Average percent of need met:*** 64% (excluding resources awarded to replace EFC). ***Average financial aid package:*** $9018 (excluding resources awarded to replace EFC). 12% of all full-time undergraduates had no need and received non-need-based gift aid.

GIFT AID (NEED-BASED) ***Total amount:*** $27,032,671 (91% federal, 9% state). ***Receiving aid:*** Freshmen: 38% (1,043); all full-time undergraduates: 38% (4,697). ***Average award:*** Freshmen: $6117; Undergraduates: $5905. ***Scholarships, grants, and awards:*** Federal Pell, FSEOG, state, college/university gift aid from institutional funds.

GIFT AID (NON-NEED-BASED) ***Total amount:*** $59,929,952 (63% state, 33% institutional, 4% external sources). ***Receiving aid:*** Freshmen: 61% (1,658). Undergraduates: 42% (5,178). ***Average award:*** Freshmen: $4747. Undergraduates: $4704. ***Scholarships, grants, and awards by category:*** *Academic interests/achievement:* 9,716 awards ($16,536,993 total): general academic interests/achievements. *Creative arts/performance:* general creative arts/performance. ***Tuition waivers:*** Full or partial for children of alumni, employees or children of employees. ***ROTC:*** Army.

LOANS ***Student loans:*** $49,190,483 (42% need-based, 58% non-need-based). ***Average need-based loan:*** Freshmen: $3126. Undergraduates: $3895. ***Parent loans:*** $8,029,258 (100% need-based). ***Programs:*** Federal Direct (Subsidized and Unsubsidized Stafford, PLUS).

WORK-STUDY ***Federal work-study:*** Total amount: $662,897; 471 jobs averaging $1420. ***State or other work-study/employment:*** Part-time jobs available.

ATHLETIC AWARDS Total amount: $6,750,191 (100% need-based).

APPLYING FOR FINANCIAL AID ***Required financial aid form:*** FAFSA. ***Financial aid deadline (priority):*** 2/1. ***Notification date:*** Continuous beginning 3/1. Students must reply within 2 weeks of notification.

CONTACT Cindy S. Perez, Director of Financial Aid, University of Louisiana at Lafayette, PO Box 41206, Lafayette, LA 70504-1206, 337-482-6497 or toll-free 800-752-6553. *Fax:* 337-482-6502. *E-mail:* cperez@louisiana.edu.
Website: http://www.louisiana.edu/.

UNIVERSITY OF LOUISIANA AT MONROE

Monroe, LA

Tuition & fees: N/R	Average undergraduate aid package: $12,356

ABOUT THE INSTITUTION State-supported, coed. ***Awards:*** certificates, associate, bachelor's, master's, and doctoral degrees. 44 undergraduate majors. ***Total enrollment:*** 8,489. Undergraduates: 6,793. Freshmen: 1,143. Federal methodology is used as a basis for awarding need-based institutional aid.

FRESHMAN FINANCIAL AID (Fall 2019, est.) 1072 applied for aid; of those 73% were deemed to have need. 99% of freshmen with need received aid; of those 14% had need fully met. ***Average percent of need met:*** 69% (excluding resources awarded to replace EFC). ***Average financial aid package:*** $12,274 (excluding resources awarded to replace EFC). 25% of all full-time freshmen had no need and received non-need-based gift aid.

UNDERGRADUATE FINANCIAL AID (Fall 2019, est.) 4,263 applied for aid; of those 80% were deemed to have need. 98% of undergraduates with need received aid; of those 9% had need fully met. ***Average percent of need met:*** 69% (excluding resources awarded to replace EFC). ***Average financial aid package:*** $12,356 (excluding resources awarded to replace EFC). 21% of all full-time undergraduates had no need and received non-need-based gift aid.

GIFT AID (NEED-BASED) ***Total amount:*** $13,827,069 (90% federal, 10% state). ***Receiving aid:*** Freshmen: 46% (533); all full-time undergraduates: 46% (2,368). ***Average award:*** Freshmen: $5007; Undergraduates: $5002. ***Scholarships, grants, and awards:*** Federal Pell, FSEOG, state, private, college/university gift aid from institutional funds, Leveraging Educational Assistance Program (LEAP).

GIFT AID (NON-NEED-BASED) ***Total amount:*** $26,899,973 (60% state, 40% institutional). ***Receiving aid:*** Freshmen: 60% (694). Undergraduates: 46% (2,370). ***Average award:*** Freshmen: $8895. Undergraduates: $9036. ***Scholarships, grants, and awards by category:*** *Academic interests/achievement:* agriculture, biological sciences, business, communication, computer science, education, English, foreign languages, general academic interests/achievements, health fields, home economics, library science, mathematics, military science, physical sciences, social sciences. *Creative arts/performance:* applied art and design, creative writing, debating, journalism/publications, music, performing arts, theater/drama. *Special achievements/activities:* cheerleading/drum major, community service, leadership. *Special characteristics:* children of faculty/staff, children with a deceased or disabled parent, international students, out-of-state students. ***ROTC:*** Army cooperative.

LOANS ***Student loans:*** $21,185,967 (43% need-based, 57% non-need-based). ***Average need-based loan:*** Freshmen: $2959. Undergraduates: $3822. ***Programs:*** Federal Direct (Subsidized and Unsubsidized Stafford, PLUS), Perkins, college/university, Federal Health Professions Student Loans.

WORK-STUDY ***Federal work-study:*** Total amount: $870,591; 363 jobs averaging $2455. ***State or other work-study/employment:*** Part-time jobs available.

ATHLETIC AWARDS Total amount: $4,945,492 (100% non-need-based).

APPLYING FOR FINANCIAL AID ***Required financial aid forms:*** FAFSA, institution's own form. ***Financial aid deadline (priority):*** 4/1. ***Notification date:*** Continuous beginning 6/15. Students must reply within 2 weeks of notification.

CONTACT Office of Financial Aid, University of Louisiana at Monroe, 700 University Avenue, Monroe, LA 71209, 318-342-5320 or toll-free 800-372-5127. *Fax:* 318-342-1047. *E-mail:* finaid@ulm.edu.
Website: http://www.ulm.edu/.

UNIVERSITY OF LOUISVILLE

Louisville, KY

Tuition & fees (KY res): $11,928 | **Average undergraduate aid package: $13,464**

ABOUT THE INSTITUTION State-supported, coed. ***Awards:*** certificates, associate, bachelor's, master's, and doctoral degrees. 55 undergraduate majors. ***Total enrollment:*** 21,670. Undergraduates: 15,860. Freshmen: 2,803. Federal methodology is used as a basis for awarding need-based institutional aid.

UNDERGRADUATE EXPENSES for 2019–2020 ***Application fee:*** $25. ***Tuition, state resident:*** full-time $11,732; part-time $489 per credit hour. ***Tuition, nonresident:*** full-time $27,758; part-time $1157 per credit hour. ***Required fees:*** full-time $196. Full-time tuition and fees vary according to reciprocity agreements. Part-time tuition and fees vary according to course load and reciprocity agreements. ***College room and board:*** $9452; ***Room only:*** $5234. Room and board charges vary according to housing facility.

FRESHMAN FINANCIAL AID (Fall 2019, est.) 2273 applied for aid; of those 76% were deemed to have need. 99% of freshmen with need received aid; of those 21% had need fully met. ***Average percent of need met:*** 62% (excluding resources awarded to replace EFC). ***Average financial aid package:*** $14,805 (excluding resources awarded to replace EFC). 18% of all full-time freshmen had no need and received non-need-based gift aid.

UNDERGRADUATE FINANCIAL AID (Fall 2019, est.) 8,884 applied for aid; of those 81% were deemed to have need. 98% of undergraduates with need received aid; of those 17% had need fully met. ***Average percent of need met:*** 59% (excluding resources awarded to replace EFC). ***Average financial aid package:*** $13,464 (excluding resources awarded to replace EFC). 15% of all full-time undergraduates had no need and received non-need-based gift aid.

GIFT AID (NEED-BASED) ***Total amount:*** $73,608,765 (30% federal, 20% state, 39% institutional, 11% external sources). ***Receiving aid:*** Freshmen: 66% (1,680); all full-time undergraduates: 58% (6,646). ***Average award:*** Freshmen: $11,724; Undergraduates: $10,623. ***Scholarships, grants, and awards:*** Federal Pell, FSEOG, state, private, college/university gift aid from institutional funds, Federal Nursing.

GIFT AID (NON-NEED-BASED) ***Total amount:*** $33,223,688 (21% state, 62% institutional, 17% external sources). ***Receiving aid:*** Freshmen: 11% (282). Undergraduates: 7% (807). ***Average award:*** Freshmen: $9399. Undergraduates: $8690. ***Scholarships, grants, and awards by category:*** *Academic interests/achievement:* area/ethnic studies, biological sciences, business, communication, computer science, education, engineering/technologies, English, foreign languages, general academic interests/achievements, home economics, humanities, international studies, library science, mathematics, military science, physical sciences, premedicine, social sciences. *Creative arts/performance:* applied art and design, art/fine arts, cinema/film/broadcasting, creative writing, dance, debating, general creative arts/performance, journalism/publications, music, performing arts, theater/drama. *Special achievements/activities:* cheerleading/drum major, community service, general special achievements/activities, hobbies/interests, junior miss, leadership, memberships. *Special characteristics:* adult students, children and siblings of alumni, children of faculty/staff, children of union members/company employees, children with a deceased or disabled parent, ethnic background, general special characteristics, local/state students, members of minority groups, out-of-state students, previous college experience, veterans, veterans' children. ***Tuition waivers:*** Full or partial for senior citizens. ***ROTC:*** Army, Air Force.

LOANS ***Student loans:*** $48,466,576 (70% need-based, 30% non-need-based). 51% of past graduating class borrowed through all loan programs. *Average indebtedness per student:* $24,840. ***Average need-based loan:*** Freshmen: $3400. Undergraduates: $4116. ***Parent loans:*** $11,192,413 (45% need-based, 55% non-need-based). ***Programs:*** Federal Direct (Subsidized and Unsubsidized Stafford, PLUS), Federal Nursing.

WORK-STUDY ***Federal work-study:*** Total amount: $2,525,821; 634 jobs averaging $4003.

ATHLETIC AWARDS Total amount: $10,843,825 (27% need-based, 73% non-need-based).

APPLYING FOR FINANCIAL AID ***Required financial aid form:*** FAFSA. ***Financial aid deadline (priority):*** 2/15. ***Notification date:*** Continuous beginning 4/1.

CONTACT Mr. Joe S. Dablow, Director of Financial Aid, University of Louisville, 2301 South Third Street, Louisville, KY 40292-0001, 502-852-5511 or toll-free 800-334-8635. *Fax:* 502-852-0182. *E-mail:* finaid@louisville.edu.
Website: http://www.louisville.edu/.

UNIVERSITY OF LYNCHBURG

Lynchburg, VA

Tuition & fees: N/R | **Average undergraduate aid package: $30,535**

ABOUT THE INSTITUTION Independent Christian Church (Disciples of Christ), coed. ***Awards:*** certificates, bachelor's, master's, and doctoral degrees. 38 undergraduate majors. ***Total enrollment:*** 3,081. Undergraduates: 2,086. Freshmen: 516. Federal methodology is used as a basis for awarding need-based institutional aid.

FRESHMAN FINANCIAL AID (Fall 2019, est.) 445 applied for aid; of those 86% were deemed to have need. 99% of freshmen with need received aid; of those 27% had need fully met. ***Average percent of need met:*** 80% (excluding resources awarded to replace EFC). ***Average financial aid package:*** $31,751 (excluding resources awarded to replace EFC). 18% of all full-time freshmen had no need and received non-need-based gift aid.

UNDERGRADUATE FINANCIAL AID (Fall 2019, est.) 1,578 applied for aid; of those 90% were deemed to have need. 98% of undergraduates with need received aid; of those 21% had need fully met. ***Average percent of need met:*** 75% (excluding resources awarded to replace EFC). ***Average financial aid package:*** $30,535 (excluding resources awarded to replace EFC). 21% of all full-time undergraduates had no need and received non-need-based gift aid.

GIFT AID (NEED-BASED) ***Total amount:*** $37,498,454 (9% federal, 7% state, 83% institutional, 1% external sources). ***Receiving aid:*** Freshmen: 81% (380); all full-time undergraduates: 76% (1,393). ***Average award:*** Freshmen: $29,511; Undergraduates: $27,544. ***Scholarships, grants, and awards:*** Federal Pell, FSEOG, college/university gift aid from institutional funds.

GIFT AID (NON-NEED-BASED) ***Total amount:*** $11,079,353 (12% state, 85% institutional, 3% external sources). ***Receiving aid:*** Freshmen: 20% (93). Undergraduates: 13% (242). ***Average award:*** Freshmen: $21,803. Undergraduates: $20,726. ***Scholarships, grants, and awards by category:*** *Academic interests/achievement:* general academic interests/achievements. *Creative arts/performance:* applied art and design, music, theater/drama.

LOANS ***Student loans:*** $12,861,821 (57% need-based, 43% non-need-based). 81% of past graduating class borrowed through all loan programs. *Average indebtedness per student:* $36,036. ***Average need-based loan:*** Freshmen: $2197. Undergraduates: $3105. ***Parent loans:*** $5,003,499 (63% need-based, 37% non-need-based). ***Programs:*** Federal Direct (Subsidized and Unsubsidized Stafford, PLUS).

WORK-STUDY ***Federal work-study:*** Total amount: $382,915; jobs available. ***State or other work-study/employment:*** Total amount: $737,871 (29% need-based, 71% non-need-based). Part-time jobs available.

APPLYING FOR FINANCIAL AID ***Required financial aid forms:*** FAFSA, state aid form. ***Financial aid deadline (priority):*** 11/1. ***Notification date:*** Continuous beginning 12/1. Students must reply by 5/1 or within 2 weeks of notification.

CONTACT Mrs. Elayne Peloquin, Director of Financial Aid, University of Lynchburg, 1501 Lakeside Drive, Lynchburg, VA 24501, 434-544-8228 or toll-free 800-426-8101. *Fax:* 434-544-8653. *E-mail:* peloquin_em@lynchburg.edu.
Website: http://www.lynchburg.edu/.

UNIVERSITY OF MAINE

Orono, ME

Tuition & fees (area res): $11,438 | **Average undergraduate aid package: $14,450**

ABOUT THE INSTITUTION State-supported, coed. ***Awards:*** certificates, bachelor's, master's, and doctoral degrees. 82 undergraduate majors. ***Total enrollment:*** 11,561. Undergraduates: 9,430. Freshmen: 2,140. Federal methodology is used as a basis for awarding need-based institutional aid.

UNDERGRADUATE EXPENSES for 2019–2020 ***Tuition, area resident:*** full-time $9000; part-time $300 per credit hour. ***Tuition, state resident:*** full-time $9000; part-time $300 per credit hour. ***Tuition, nonresident:*** full-time $29,310; part-time $977 per credit hour. ***Required fees:*** full-time $2438. Full-time tuition and fees vary according to course load. Part-time tuition and fees vary according to course load. ***College room and board:*** $10,966. Room and board charges vary according to board plan and housing facility.

FRESHMAN FINANCIAL AID (Fall 2019, est.) 1939 applied for aid; of those 73% were deemed to have need. 100% of freshmen with need received aid; of those 22% had need fully met. ***Average percent of need met:*** 73% (excluding resources awarded to replace EFC). ***Average financial aid package:*** $16,058 (excluding resources awarded to replace EFC). 32% of all full-time freshmen had no need and received non-need-based gift aid.

UNDERGRADUATE FINANCIAL AID (Fall 2019, est.) 6,693 applied for aid; of those 77% were deemed to have need. 99% of undergraduates with need received aid; of those 18% had need fully met. ***Average percent of need met:*** 68% (excluding resources awarded to replace EFC). ***Average financial aid package:*** $14,450 (excluding resources awarded to replace EFC). 29% of all full-time undergraduates had no need and received non-need-based gift aid.

GIFT AID (NEED-BASED) ***Total amount:*** $48,240,180 (26% federal, 6% state, 63% institutional, 5% external sources). ***Receiving aid:*** Freshmen: 67% (1,411); all full-time undergraduates: 60% (4,832). ***Average award:*** Freshmen: $11,243; Undergraduates: $9614. ***Scholarships, grants, and awards:*** Federal Pell, FSEOG, state, private, college/university gift aid from institutional funds.

GIFT AID (NON-NEED-BASED) ***Total amount:*** $21,204,725 (92% institutional, 8% external sources). ***Receiving aid:*** Freshmen: 9% (194). Undergraduates: 6% (507). ***Average award:*** Freshmen: $7776. Undergraduates: $7136. ***Scholarships, grants, and awards by category:*** *Academic interests/achievement:* agriculture, biological sciences, business, communication, computer science, education, engineering/technologies, English, foreign languages, general academic interests/achievements, health fields, home economics, humanities, international studies, mathematics, military science, physical sciences, premedicine, social sciences. *Creative arts/performance:* applied art and design, art/fine arts, creative writing, dance, general creative arts/performance, journalism/publications, music, performing arts, theater/drama. *Special achievements/activities:* community service, general special achievements/activities, leadership, memberships. *Special characteristics:* adult students, children and siblings of alumni, children of faculty/staff, children of union members/company employees, children of workers in trades, ethnic background, first-generation college students, general special characteristics, handicapped students, international students, local/state students, members of minority groups, out-of-state students, previous college experience, religious affiliation, spouses of current students, spouses of deceased or disabled public servants, veterans. ***Tuition waivers:*** Full or partial for employees or children of employees, senior citizens. **ROTC:** Army, Naval.

LOANS ***Student loans:*** $55,933,989 (59% need-based, 41% non-need-based). 75% of past graduating class borrowed through all loan programs. *Average indebtedness per student:* $34,703. ***Average need-based loan:*** Freshmen: $3152. Undergraduates: $4111. ***Parent loans:*** $10,560,026 (40% need-based, 60% non-need-based). ***Programs:*** Federal Direct (Subsidized and Unsubsidized Stafford, PLUS), state, college/university, private loans.

WORK-STUDY ***Federal work-study:*** Total amount: $4,180,966; 1,768 jobs averaging $2365.

ATHLETIC AWARDS Total amount: $5,464,991 (27% need-based, 73% non-need-based).

APPLYING FOR FINANCIAL AID ***Required financial aid form:*** FAFSA. ***Financial aid deadline:*** 5/1 (priority: 3/1). ***Notification date:*** Continuous beginning 1/1. Students must reply by 5/1.

CONTACT Ms. Connie Smith, Director of Student Financial Aid, University of Maine, 5781 Wingate Hall, Orono, ME 04469-5781, 207-581-1324 or toll-free 877-486-2364. *Fax:* 207-581-3261. *E-mail:* umfinaid@maine.edu.
Website: http://www.umaine.edu/.

UNIVERSITY OF MAINE AT AUGUSTA

Augusta, ME

CONTACT Financial Aid Office, University of Maine at Augusta, 46 University Drive, Augusta, ME 04330-9410, 207-621-3185 or toll-free 877-862-1234 Ext.3185 (in-state), 877-862-1234 (out-of-state). *Fax:* 207-621-3116. *E-mail:* umafa@maine.edu.
Website: http://www.uma.edu/.

UNIVERSITY OF MAINE AT FARMINGTON

Farmington, ME

Tuition & fees (ME res): $9344	Average undergraduate aid package: $14,619

ABOUT THE INSTITUTION State-supported, coed. ***Awards:*** certificates, bachelor's, and master's degrees. 43 undergraduate majors. ***Total enrollment:*** 2,040. Undergraduates: 1,736. Freshmen: 375. Federal methodology is used as a basis for awarding need-based institutional aid.

UNDERGRADUATE EXPENSES for 2019–2020 ***Tuition, state resident:*** full-time $8429; part-time $281 per credit hour. ***Tuition, nonresident:*** full-time $18,599; part-time $620 per credit hour. ***Required fees:*** full-time $915. Full-time tuition and fees vary according to course load and reciprocity agreements. Part-time tuition and fees vary according to course load and reciprocity agreements. ***College room and board:*** $9902; ***Room only:*** $5356. Room and board charges vary according to board plan and housing facility.

FRESHMAN FINANCIAL AID (Fall 2018) 373 applied for aid; of those 85% were deemed to have need. 100% of freshmen with need received aid; of those 43% had need fully met. ***Average percent of need met:*** 87% (excluding resources awarded to replace EFC). ***Average financial aid package:*** $15,617 (excluding resources awarded to replace EFC). 10% of all full-time freshmen had no need and received non-need-based gift aid.

UNDERGRADUATE FINANCIAL AID (Fall 2018) 1,410 applied for aid; of those 86% were deemed to have need. 100% of undergraduates with need received aid; of those 41% had need fully met. ***Average percent of need met:*** 82% (excluding resources awarded to replace EFC). ***Average financial aid package:*** $14,619 (excluding resources awarded to replace EFC). 8% of all full-time undergraduates had no need and received non-need-based gift aid.

GIFT AID (NEED-BASED) ***Total amount:*** $10,152,655 (39% federal, 11% state, 39% institutional, 11% external sources). ***Receiving aid:*** Freshmen: 80% (313); all full-time undergraduates: 75% (1,169). ***Average award:*** Freshmen: $9691; Undergraduates: $8093. ***Scholarships, grants, and awards:*** Federal Pell, FSEOG, state, private, college/university gift aid from institutional funds.

GIFT AID (NON-NEED-BASED) ***Total amount:*** $475,705 (99% institutional, 1% external sources). ***Receiving aid:*** Freshmen: 6% (25). Undergraduates: 4% (56). ***Average award:*** Freshmen: $2564. Undergraduates: $2614. ***Scholarships, grants, and awards by category:*** *Academic interests/achievement:* general academic interests/achievements. *Creative arts/performance:* music, theater/drama. *Special achievements/activities:* general special achievements/activities, leadership. *Special characteristics:* children of faculty/staff, general special characteristics, local/state students, members of minority groups, out-of-state students. ***Tuition waivers:*** Full or partial for minority students, children of alumni, employees or children of employees, senior citizens.

LOANS ***Student loans:*** $8,964,974 (76% need-based, 24% non-need-based). 85% of past graduating class borrowed through all loan programs. *Average indebtedness per student:* $30,315. ***Average need-based loan:*** Freshmen: $5608. Undergraduates: $6471. ***Parent loans:*** $1,216,094 (48% need-based, 52% non-need-based). ***Programs:*** Federal Direct (Subsidized and Unsubsidized Stafford, PLUS), Perkins, state, college/university.

WORK-STUDY ***Federal work-study:*** Total amount: $656,829; jobs available. ***State or other work-study/employment:*** Total amount: $534,356 (50% need-based, 50% non-need-based). Part-time jobs available.

APPLYING FOR FINANCIAL AID ***Required financial aid form:*** FAFSA. ***Financial aid deadline (priority):*** 3/1. ***Notification date:*** Continuous beginning 2/1. Students must reply within 3 weeks of notification.

CONTACT Mr. Ronald P. Milliken, Director of Financial Aid, University of Maine at Farmington, 224 Main Street, Farmington, ME 04938-1990, 207-778-7105. *Fax:* 207-778-8178. *E-mail:* milliken@maine.edu.
Website: http://www.umf.maine.edu/.

UNIVERSITY OF MAINE AT FORT KENT

Fort Kent, ME

Tuition & fees: N/R | **Average undergraduate aid package: $12,004**

ABOUT THE INSTITUTION State-supported, coed. ***Awards:*** associate and bachelor's degrees. 19 undergraduate majors. Both federal and institutional methodology are used as a basis for awarding need-based institutional aid.

FRESHMAN FINANCIAL AID (Fall 2019, est.) 119 applied for aid; of those 80% were deemed to have need. 100% of freshmen with need received aid; of those 55% had need fully met. ***Average percent of need met:*** 83% (excluding resources awarded to replace EFC). ***Average financial aid package:*** $12,342 (excluding resources awarded to replace EFC). 15% of all full-time freshmen had no need and received non-need-based gift aid.

UNDERGRADUATE FINANCIAL AID (Fall 2019, est.) 448 applied for aid; of those 82% were deemed to have need. 100% of undergraduates with need received aid; of those 51% had need fully met. ***Average percent of need met:*** 80% (excluding resources awarded to replace EFC). ***Average financial aid package:*** $12,004 (excluding resources awarded to replace EFC). 7% of all full-time undergraduates had no need and received non-need-based gift aid.

GIFT AID (NEED-BASED) ***Total amount:*** $3,025,926 (51% federal, 15% state, 25% institutional, 9% external sources). ***Receiving aid:*** Freshmen: 74% (92); all full-time undergraduates: 59% (321). ***Average award:*** Freshmen: $7483; Undergraduates: $6869. ***Scholarships, grants, and awards:*** Federal Pell, FSEOG, state, private, college/university gift aid from institutional funds, Federal Nursing.

GIFT AID (NON-NEED-BASED) ***Total amount:*** $139,188 (3% state, 89% institutional, 8% external sources). ***Receiving aid:*** Freshmen: 10% (12). Undergraduates: 3% (17). ***Average award:*** Freshmen: $2211. Undergraduates: $2369. ***Scholarships, grants, and awards by category:*** *Academic interests/achievement:* biological sciences, business, communication, computer science, English, foreign languages, general academic interests/achievements, humanities, mathematics, social sciences. *Creative arts/performance:* general creative arts/performance, performing arts. *Special achievements/activities:* general special achievements/activities. *Special characteristics:* adult students, children of faculty/staff, ethnic background, general special characteristics, international students, members of minority groups.

LOANS ***Student loans:*** $3,383,847 (72% need-based, 28% non-need-based). 59% of past graduating class borrowed through all loan programs. *Average indebtedness per student:* $25,811. ***Average need-based loan:*** Freshmen: $5442. Undergraduates: $6531. ***Parent loans:*** $127,965 (33% need-based, 67% non-need-based). ***Programs:*** Federal Direct (Subsidized and Unsubsidized Stafford, PLUS), Perkins, Federal Nursing, state, college/university.

WORK-STUDY ***Federal work-study:*** Total amount: $274,573; jobs available. ***State or other work-study/employment:*** Part-time jobs available.

ATHLETIC AWARDS Total amount: $180,800 (97% need-based, 3% non-need-based).

APPLYING FOR FINANCIAL AID ***Required financial aid forms:*** FAFSA, institution's own form, CSS Financial Aid PROFILE, state aid form. ***Financial aid deadline (priority):*** 3/1. ***Notification date:*** Continuous beginning 3/1.

CONTACT Lisa Michaud, Interim Director of Financial Aid, University of Maine at Fort Kent, 23 University Drive, Fort Kent, ME 04743-1292, 207-834-7607 or toll-free 888-TRY-UMFK. *Fax:* 207-834-7841. *E-mail:* lisa.michaud@maine.edu.
Website: http://www.umfk.maine.edu/.

UNIVERSITY OF MAINE AT MACHIAS

Machias, ME

Tuition & fees (area res): $8036 | **Average undergraduate aid package: $13,042**

ABOUT THE INSTITUTION State-supported, coed. ***Awards:*** certificates, associate, and bachelor's degrees. 32 undergraduate majors. ***Total enrollment:*** 675. Undergraduates: 675. Freshmen: 105. Federal methodology is used as a basis for awarding need-based institutional aid.

UNDERGRADUATE EXPENSES for 2019–2020 ***Application fee:*** $40. ***Tuition, area resident:*** full-time $7170; part-time $239 per credit hour. ***Tuition, state resident:*** full-time $7170; part-time $239 per credit hour. ***Tuition, nonresident:*** full-time $14,250; part-time $475 per credit hour. ***Required fees:*** full-time $866. Full-time tuition and fees vary according to course load. Part-time tuition and fees vary according to course load. ***College room and board:*** $9180. Room and board charges vary according to housing facility.

FRESHMAN FINANCIAL AID (Fall 2019, est.) 92 applied for aid; of those 90% were deemed to have need. 98% of freshmen with need received aid; of those 33% had need fully met. ***Average percent of need met:*** 79% (excluding resources awarded to replace EFC). ***Average financial aid package:*** $13,766 (excluding resources awarded to replace EFC). 19% of all full-time freshmen had no need and received non-need-based gift aid.

UNDERGRADUATE FINANCIAL AID (Fall 2019, est.) 295 applied for aid; of those 92% were deemed to have need. 98% of undergraduates with need received aid; of those 22% had need fully met. ***Average percent of need met:*** 76% (excluding resources awarded to replace EFC). ***Average financial aid package:*** $13,042 (excluding resources awarded to replace EFC). 13% of all full-time undergraduates had no need and received non-need-based gift aid.

GIFT AID (NEED-BASED) ***Total amount:*** $2,818,822 (53% federal, 16% state, 26% institutional, 5% external sources). ***Receiving aid:*** Freshmen: 79% (81); all full-time undergraduates: 79% (253). ***Average award:*** Freshmen: $10,178; Undergraduates: $9192. ***Scholarships, grants, and awards:*** Federal Pell, FSEOG, state, private, college/university gift aid from institutional funds.

GIFT AID (NON-NEED-BASED) ***Total amount:*** $344,079 (100% institutional). ***Receiving aid:*** Freshmen: 4% (4). Undergraduates: 3% (11). ***Average award:*** Freshmen: $9891. Undergraduates: $7119. ***Scholarships, grants, and awards by category:*** *Academic interests/achievement:* general academic interests/achievements. ***Tuition waivers:*** Full or partial for employees or children of employees, senior citizens.

LOANS ***Student loans:*** $1,820,262 (78% need-based, 22% non-need-based). 80% of past graduating class borrowed through all loan programs. *Average indebtedness per student:* $24,116. ***Average need-based loan:*** Freshmen: $2560. Undergraduates: $3373. ***Parent loans:*** $91,767 (33% need-based, 67% non-need-based). ***Programs:*** Federal Direct (Subsidized and Unsubsidized Stafford, PLUS), state, college/university, Private loans.

WORK-STUDY ***Federal work-study:*** Total amount: $226,041; jobs available. ***State or other work-study/employment:*** Part-time jobs available.

APPLYING FOR FINANCIAL AID ***Required financial aid form:*** FAFSA. ***Financial aid deadline:*** 4/15 (priority: 3/1). ***Notification date:*** Continuous beginning 1/1. Students must reply by 5/1.

CONTACT Ms. Stephanie Larrabee, Director of Financial Aid, University of Maine at Machias, 9 O'Brien Avenue, Machias, ME 04654, 207-255-1203 or toll-free 888-GOTOUMM (in-state), 888-468-6866 (out-of-state). *Fax:* 207-255-4864.
Website: http://www.machias.edu/.

UNIVERSITY OF MAINE AT PRESQUE ISLE

Presque Isle, ME

Tuition & fees (ME res): $8574 | **Average undergraduate aid package: $12,438**

ABOUT THE INSTITUTION State-supported, coed. ***Awards:*** certificates, associate, and bachelor's degrees. 30 undergraduate majors. ***Total enrollment:*** 1,554. Undergraduates: 1,554. Freshmen: 168. Federal methodology is used as a basis for awarding need-based institutional aid.

UNDERGRADUATE EXPENSES for 2020–2021 ***Application fee:*** $40. ***Tuition, state resident:*** full-time $7350; part-time $245 per credit hour. ***Tuition, nonresident:*** full-time $11,760; part-time $392 per credit hour. ***Required fees:*** full-time $1224; $54 per term. ***College room and board:*** $8738; ***Room only:*** $4850. Room and board charges vary according to board plan.

FRESHMAN FINANCIAL AID (Fall 2019, est.) 153 applied for aid; of those 82% were deemed to have need. 100% of freshmen with need received aid; of those 60% had need fully met. ***Average percent of need met:*** 87% (excluding resources awarded to replace EFC). ***Average financial aid package:*** $12,790 (excluding resources awarded to replace EFC). 7% of all full-time freshmen had no need and received non-need-based gift aid.

UNDERGRADUATE FINANCIAL AID (Fall 2019, est.) 509 applied for aid; of those 84% were deemed to have need. 100% of undergraduates with need received aid; of those 61% had need fully met. ***Average percent of need met:*** 87% (excluding resources awarded to replace EFC). ***Average financial aid package:*** $12,438 (excluding resources awarded to replace EFC). 5% of all full-time undergraduates had no need and received non-need-based gift aid.

GIFT AID (NEED-BASED) ***Receiving aid:*** Freshmen: 74% (125); all full-time undergraduates: 69% (413). ***Average award:*** Freshmen: $8145; Undergraduates: $7644. ***Scholarships, grants, and awards:*** Federal Pell, FSEOG, state, private, college/university gift aid from institutional funds.

GIFT AID (NON-NEED-BASED) ***Receiving aid:*** Freshmen: 6% (10). Undergraduates: 2% (14). ***Average award:*** Freshmen: $2744. Undergraduates: $2718. ***Scholarships, grants, and awards by category:*** *Academic interests/achievement:* general academic interests/achievements. *Special achievements/activities:* community service. *Special characteristics:* children of faculty/staff, ethnic background, international students, local/state students, out-of-state students, veterans, veterans' children. ***Tuition waivers:*** Full or partial for minority students, employees or children of employees, senior citizens.

LOANS ***Student loans:*** 64% of past graduating class borrowed through all loan programs. *Average indebtedness per student:* $22,205. ***Average need-based loan:*** Freshmen: $4490. Undergraduates: $4985. ***Programs:*** Federal Direct (Subsidized and Unsubsidized Stafford, PLUS), Perkins, state, college/university.

WORK-STUDY Federal work-study jobs available.

APPLYING FOR FINANCIAL AID ***Required financial aid form:*** FAFSA. ***Financial aid deadline:*** Continuous. ***Notification date:*** Continuous. Students must reply within 2 weeks of notification.

CONTACT Christopher A.R. Bell, Director of Student Financial Services, University of Maine at Presque Isle, 181 Main Street, Presque Isle, ME 04769-2888, 207-768-9511. *Fax:* 207-768-9509. *E-mail:* chris@maine.edu.
Website: http://www.umpi.edu/.

UNIVERSITY OF MANAGEMENT AND TECHNOLOGY

Arlington, VA

CONTACT Financial Aid Administrator, University of Management and Technology, 1901 North Fort Myer Drive, Suite 700, Arlington, VA 22209, 703-516-0035 or toll-free 800-924-4883. *Fax:* 703-516-0985. *E-mail:* info@umtweb.edu.
Website: http://www.umtweb.edu/.

UNIVERSITY OF MARY

Bismarck, ND

ABOUT THE INSTITUTION Independent Roman Catholic, coed. ***Awards:*** bachelor's, master's, and doctoral degrees. 47 undergraduate majors.

GIFT AID (NEED-BASED) ***Scholarships, grants, and awards:*** Federal Pell, FSEOG, state, private, college/university gift aid from institutional funds, TEACH Grants.

GIFT AID (NON-NEED-BASED) ***Scholarships, grants, and awards by category:*** *Academic interests/achievement:* general academic interests/achievements. *Creative arts/performance:* music. *Special achievements/activities:* general special achievements/activities. *Special characteristics:* children of faculty/staff, general special characteristics, local/state students, religious affiliation, veterans.

LOANS ***Programs:*** Federal Direct (Subsidized and Unsubsidized Stafford, PLUS), Perkins, Federal Nursing, private loans.

WORK-STUDY Federal work-study jobs available. ***State or other work-study/employment:*** Part-time jobs available.

APPLYING FOR FINANCIAL AID ***Required financial aid form:*** FAFSA.

CONTACT Ms. Karrie Huber, Director of Financial Aid, University of Mary, 7500 University Drive, Bismarck, ND 58504-9652, 701-355-8226 or toll-free 800-288-6279. *Fax:* 701-255-7687. *E-mail:* kkhuber@umary.edu.
Website: http://www.umary.edu/.

UNIVERSITY OF MARY HARDIN-BAYLOR

Belton, TX

Tuition & fees: $29,800	Average undergraduate aid package: $18,818

ABOUT THE INSTITUTION Independent Southern Baptist, coed. ***Awards:*** certificates, bachelor's, master's, and doctoral degrees. 56 undergraduate majors. ***Total enrollment:*** 3,846. Undergraduates: 3,361. Freshmen: 868. Federal methodology is used as a basis for awarding need-based institutional aid.

UNDERGRADUATE EXPENSES for 2020–2021 ***Application fee:*** $35. ***Comprehensive fee:*** $38,582 includes full-time tuition ($27,450), mandatory fees ($2350), and room and board ($8782). Full-time tuition and fees vary according to course load and degree level. Room and board charges vary according to board plan and housing facility. ***Part-time tuition:*** $915 per credit hour. ***Part-time fees:*** $75 per credit hour.

FRESHMAN FINANCIAL AID (Fall 2019, est.) 683 applied for aid; of those 89% were deemed to have need. 100% of freshmen with need received aid; of those 8% had need fully met. ***Average percent of need met:*** 59% (excluding resources awarded to replace EFC). ***Average financial aid package:*** $19,823 (excluding resources awarded to replace EFC). 9% of all full-time freshmen had no need and received non-need-based gift aid.

UNDERGRADUATE FINANCIAL AID (Fall 2019, est.) 2,793 applied for aid; of those 90% were deemed to have need. 100% of undergraduates with need received aid; of those 7% had need fully met. ***Average percent of need met:*** 57% (excluding resources awarded to replace EFC). ***Average financial aid package:*** $18,818 (excluding resources awarded to replace EFC). 11% of all full-time undergraduates had no need and received non-need-based gift aid.

GIFT AID (NEED-BASED) ***Receiving aid:*** Freshmen: 70% (608); all full-time undergraduates: 81% (2,507). ***Average award:*** Freshmen: $16,842; Undergraduates: $15,216. ***Scholarships, grants, and awards:*** Federal Pell, FSEOG, state, private, college/university gift aid from institutional funds.

GIFT AID (NON-NEED-BASED) ***Receiving aid:*** Freshmen: 5% (41). Undergraduates: 4% (127). ***Average award:*** Freshmen: $8897. Undergraduates: $8416. ***Scholarships, grants, and awards by category:*** *Academic interests/achievement:* agriculture, biological sciences, business, communication, computer science, education, English, foreign languages, general academic interests/achievements, health fields, home economics, humanities, international studies, mathematics, military science, physical sciences, premedicine, religion/biblical studies, social sciences. *Creative arts/performance:* applied art and design, music. *Special achievements/activities:* cheerleading/drum major, community service, leadership, religious involvement. *Special characteristics:* children and siblings of alumni, children of faculty/staff, ethnic background, handicapped students, international students, local/state students, members of minority groups, out-of-state students, relatives of clergy, religious affiliation. ***Tuition waivers:*** Full or partial for employees or children of employees. ***ROTC:*** Army, Air Force cooperative.

LOANS ***Student loans:*** 73% of past graduating class borrowed through all loan programs. *Average indebtedness per student:* $34,104. ***Average need-based loan:*** Freshmen: $3316. Undergraduates: $4047. ***Programs:*** Federal Direct (Subsidized and Unsubsidized Stafford, PLUS), Perkins, state, private loans.

WORK-STUDY Federal work-study jobs available. ***State or other work-study/employment:*** Part-time jobs available.

APPLYING FOR FINANCIAL AID ***Required financial aid form:*** FAFSA. ***Notification date:*** Continuous. Students must reply within 2 weeks of notification.

CONTACT Mr. David Orsag, Associate Director of Financial Aid, University of Mary Hardin-Baylor, 900 College Street, Box 8080, Belton, TX 76513, 254-295-4517 or toll-free 800-727-8642. *Fax:* 254-295-5009. *E-mail:* dorsag@umhb.edu.
Website: http://www.umhb.edu/.

UNIVERSITY OF MARYLAND, BALTIMORE COUNTY

Baltimore, MD

Tuition & fees (MD res): $12,028 **Average undergraduate aid package: $11,738**

ABOUT THE INSTITUTION State-supported, coed. ***Awards:*** certificates, bachelor's, master's, and doctoral degrees. 53 undergraduate majors. ***Total enrollment:*** 13,602. Undergraduates: 11,060. Freshmen: 1,701. Federal methodology is used as a basis for awarding need-based institutional aid.

UNDERGRADUATE EXPENSES for 2019–2020 ***Application fee:*** $75. ***One-time required fee:*** $225. ***Tuition, state resident:*** full-time $8704; part-time $361 per credit hour. ***Tuition, nonresident:*** full-time $24,338; part-time $1010 per credit hour. ***Required fees:*** full-time $3324; $144 per credit hour. Full-time tuition and fees vary according to location and program. Part-time tuition and fees vary according to location and program. ***College room and board:*** $12,000; ***Room only:*** $7234. Room and board charges vary according to board plan and housing facility.

FRESHMAN FINANCIAL AID (Fall 2019, est.) 1318 applied for aid; of those 65% were deemed to have need. 95% of freshmen with need received aid; of those 19% had need fully met. ***Average percent of need met:*** 63% (excluding resources awarded to replace EFC). ***Average financial aid package:*** $12,955 (excluding resources awarded to replace EFC). 28% of all full-time freshmen had no need and received non-need-based gift aid.

UNDERGRADUATE FINANCIAL AID (Fall 2019, est.) 6,503 applied for aid; of those 77% were deemed to have need. 94% of undergraduates with need received aid; of those 11% had need fully met. ***Average percent of need met:*** 56% (excluding resources awarded to replace EFC). ***Average financial aid package:*** $11,738 (excluding resources awarded to replace EFC). 18% of all full-time undergraduates had no need and received non-need-based gift aid.

GIFT AID (NEED-BASED) ***Total amount:*** $42,077,315 (42% federal, 21% state, 33% institutional, 4% external sources). ***Receiving aid:*** Freshmen: 40% (679); all full-time undergraduates: 41% (3,836). ***Average award:*** Freshmen: $12,235; Undergraduates: $10,368. ***Scholarships, grants, and awards:*** Federal Pell, FSEOG, state, private, college/university gift aid from institutional funds.

GIFT AID (NON-NEED-BASED) ***Total amount:*** $15,572,318 (13% federal, 2% state, 64% institutional, 21% external sources). ***Receiving aid:*** Freshmen: 17% (290). Undergraduates: 8% (751). ***Average award:*** Freshmen: $6826. Undergraduates: $7661. ***Scholarships, grants, and awards by category:*** *Academic interests/achievement:* 3,726 awards ($20,707,796 total): biological sciences, computer science, education, engineering/technologies, English, foreign languages, general academic interests/achievements, humanities, mathematics, physical sciences, social sciences. *Creative arts/performance:* 25 awards ($34,150 total): applied art and design, cinema/film/broadcasting, creative writing, dance, music, performing arts, theater/drama. ***Tuition waivers:*** Full or partial for employees or children of employees, senior citizens. ***ROTC:*** Army cooperative, Naval, Air Force cooperative.

LOANS ***Student loans:*** $32,453,438 (39% need-based, 61% non-need-based). 49% of past graduating class borrowed through all loan programs. *Average indebtedness per student:* $26,359. ***Average need-based loan:*** Freshmen: $3298. Undergraduates: $4228. ***Parent loans:*** $14,873,540 (74% need-based, 26% non-need-based). ***Programs:*** Federal Direct (Subsidized and Unsubsidized Stafford, PLUS).

WORK-STUDY ***Federal work-study:*** Total amount: $380,507; 123 jobs averaging $3118. ***State or other work-study/employment:*** Total amount: $1,291,384 (52% need-based, 48% non-need-based). 118 part-time jobs averaging $10,976.

ATHLETIC AWARDS Total amount: $2,447,109 (33% need-based, 67% non-need-based).

APPLYING FOR FINANCIAL AID ***Required financial aid form:*** FAFSA. ***Financial aid deadline (priority):*** 2/14. ***Notification date:*** Continuous beginning 3/15.

CONTACT Mrs. Jane Hickey, Director of Financial Aid, University of Maryland, Baltimore County, 1000 Hilltop Circle, Baltimore, MD 21250, 410-455-2387 or toll-free 800-UMBC-4U2 (in-state), 800-862-2402 (out-of-state). *Fax:* 410-455-3322. *Website:* http://www.umbc.edu/.

UNIVERSITY OF MARYLAND, COLLEGE PARK

College Park, MD

Tuition & fees (MD res): $10,779 **Average undergraduate aid package: $12,448**

ABOUT THE INSTITUTION State-supported, coed. ***Awards:*** certificates, bachelor's, master's, and doctoral degrees. 91 undergraduate majors. ***Total enrollment:*** 41,200. Undergraduates: 30,762. Freshmen: 4,712. Federal methodology is used as a basis for awarding need-based institutional aid.

UNDERGRADUATE EXPENSES for 2019–2020 ***Application fee:*** $75. ***Tuition, state resident:*** full-time $8824; part-time $367 per credit hour. ***Tuition, nonresident:*** full-time $36,891; part-time $1456 per credit hour. ***Required fees:*** full-time $1955; $455 per term. Full-time tuition and fees vary according to location, program, and student level. Part-time tuition and fees vary according to course load, location, program, and student level. ***College room and board:*** $12,935; ***Room only:*** $7755. Room and board charges vary according to board plan and housing facility.

FRESHMAN FINANCIAL AID (Fall 2018) 3706 applied for aid; of those 49% were deemed to have need. 100% of freshmen with need received aid; of those 21% had need fully met. ***Average percent of need met:*** 63% (excluding resources awarded to replace EFC). ***Average financial aid package:*** $11,937 (excluding resources awarded to replace EFC). 22% of all full-time freshmen had no need and received non-need-based gift aid.

UNDERGRADUATE FINANCIAL AID (Fall 2018) 17,137 applied for aid; of those 68% were deemed to have need. 100% of undergraduates with need received aid; of those 15% had need fully met. ***Average percent of need met:*** 60% (excluding resources awarded to replace EFC). ***Average financial aid package:*** $12,448 (excluding resources awarded to replace EFC). 13% of all full-time undergraduates had no need and received non-need-based gift aid.

GIFT AID (NEED-BASED) ***Total amount:*** $89,809,408 (32% federal, 19% state, 45% institutional, 4% external sources). ***Receiving aid:*** Freshmen: 30% (1,405); all full-time undergraduates: 31% (8,785). ***Average award:*** Freshmen: $10,398; Undergraduates: $10,577. ***Scholarships, grants, and awards:*** Federal Pell, FSEOG, state, private, college/university gift aid from institutional funds.

GIFT AID (NON-NEED-BASED) ***Total amount:*** $37,210,009 (2% federal, 3% state, 76% institutional, 19% external sources). ***Receiving aid:*** Freshmen: 4% (185). Undergraduates: 2% (602). ***Average award:*** Freshmen: $7037. Undergraduates: $7032. ***Scholarships, grants, and awards by category:*** *Academic interests/achievement:* agriculture, architecture, biological sciences, business, communication, computer science, education, engineering/technologies, English, foreign languages, general academic interests/achievements, home economics, humanities, international studies, library science, mathematics, military science, physical sciences, premedicine, social sciences. *Creative arts/performance:* applied art and design, art/fine arts, journalism/publications, music. *Special characteristics:* adult students, out-of-state students, veterans. ***Tuition waivers:*** Full or partial for employees or children of employees. ***ROTC:*** Army, Naval cooperative, Air Force.

LOANS ***Student loans:*** $148,953,167 (47% need-based, 53% non-need-based). 39% of past graduating class borrowed through all loan programs. *Average indebtedness per student:* $29,133. ***Average need-based loan:*** Freshmen: $3253. Undergraduates: $4349. ***Parent loans:*** $38,043,435 (32% need-based, 68% non-need-based). ***Programs:*** Federal Direct (Subsidized and Unsubsidized Stafford, PLUS), private loans.

WORK-STUDY ***Federal work-study:*** Total amount: $2,702,112; jobs available.

ATHLETIC AWARDS Total amount: $16,124,196 (26% need-based, 74% non-need-based).

APPLYING FOR FINANCIAL AID ***Required financial aid form:*** FAFSA. ***Financial aid deadline (priority):*** 1/1. ***Notification date:*** Continuous beginning 3/1. Students must reply by 5/1.

CONTACT Dawit Lemma, Director of Financial Aid, University of Maryland, College Park, 0102 Lee Building, College Park, MD 20742, 301-314-9000 or toll-free 800-422-5867. *Fax:* 301-314-9265. *E-mail:* umdfinaid@umd.edu. *Website:* http://www.umd.edu/.

UNIVERSITY OF MARYLAND EASTERN SHORE

Princess Anne, MD

CONTACT Mr. Al J. Dorsett, Director of Financial Aid, University of Maryland Eastern Shore, 1 Backbone Road, SDC, Suite 1100, Princess Anne, MD 21853-1299, 410-651-6172. *Fax:* 410-651-7670. *E-mail:* ajdorsett@umes.edu.
Website: http://www.umes.edu/.

UNIVERSITY OF MARYLAND GLOBAL CAMPUS

Adelphi, MD

Tuition & fees (MD res): $7560	Average undergraduate aid package: $7858

ABOUT THE INSTITUTION State-supported, coed. ***Awards:*** certificates, associate, bachelor's, master's, and doctoral degrees (offers primarily part-time evening and weekend degree programs at more than 30 off-campus locations in Maryland and the Washington, DC area, and more than 180 military communities in Europe and Asia with military enrollment not reflected in this profile; associate of arts program available to military students only). 28 undergraduate majors. ***Total enrollment:*** 58,281. Undergraduates: 46,162. Freshmen: 646. Federal methodology is used as a basis for awarding need-based institutional aid.

UNDERGRADUATE EXPENSES for 2020–2021 ***Application fee:*** $50. ***Tuition, state resident:*** full-time $7200. ***Tuition, nonresident:*** full-time $11,976. ***Required fees:*** full-time $360.

FRESHMAN FINANCIAL AID (Fall 2018) 124 applied for aid; of those 90% were deemed to have need. 79% of freshmen with need received aid. ***Average percent of need met:*** 29% (excluding resources awarded to replace EFC). ***Average financial aid package:*** $5751 (excluding resources awarded to replace EFC).

UNDERGRADUATE FINANCIAL AID (Fall 2018) 5,927 applied for aid; of those 96% were deemed to have need. 90% of undergraduates with need received aid; of those 1% had need fully met. ***Average percent of need met:*** 29% (excluding resources awarded to replace EFC). ***Average financial aid package:*** $7858 (excluding resources awarded to replace EFC).

GIFT AID (NEED-BASED) ***Receiving aid:*** Freshmen: 32% (68); all full-time undergraduates: 41% (3,949). ***Average award:*** Freshmen: $4535; Undergraduates: $5620. ***Scholarships, grants, and awards:*** Federal Pell, FSEOG, state, private, college/university gift aid from institutional funds.

GIFT AID (NON-NEED-BASED) ***Receiving aid:*** Freshmen: 7% (14). Undergraduates: 16% (1,562). ***Scholarships, grants, and awards by category:*** *Academic interests/achievement:* general academic interests/achievements. *Special achievements/activities:* general special achievements/activities. ***Tuition waivers:*** Full or partial for employees or children of employees, senior citizens.

LOANS ***Average need-based loan:*** Freshmen: $3424. Undergraduates: $4433. ***Programs:*** Federal Direct (Subsidized and Unsubsidized Stafford, PLUS), Perkins.

WORK-STUDY ***State or other work-study/employment:*** Part-time jobs available.

APPLYING FOR FINANCIAL AID ***Required financial aid form:*** FAFSA. ***Notification date:*** Continuous. Students must reply within 2 weeks of notification.

CONTACT Cheryl Storie, Associate Vice President, University of Maryland Global Campus, 3501 University Boulevard East, Adelphi, MD 20783, 800-888-8682. *E-mail:* finaid@umuc.edu.
Website: http://www.umuc.edu/.

UNIVERSITY OF MARY WASHINGTON

Fredericksburg, VA

Tuition & fees (area res): $13,270	Average undergraduate aid package: $10,336

ABOUT THE INSTITUTION State-supported, coed. ***Awards:*** certificates, bachelor's, and master's degrees. 28 undergraduate majors. ***Total enrollment:*** 4,488. Undergraduates: 4,182. Freshmen: 891. Federal methodology is used as a basis for awarding need-based institutional aid.

UNDERGRADUATE EXPENSES for 2019–2020 ***Application fee:*** $50. ***Tuition, area resident:*** full-time $8678; part-time $335 per credit hour. ***Tuition, state resident:*** full-time $8678; part-time $335 per credit hour. ***Tuition, nonresident:*** full-time $25,102; part-time $1016 per credit hour. ***Required fees:*** full-time $4592; $132. Full-time tuition and fees vary according to course load, degree level, and location. Part-time tuition and fees vary according to course load, degree level, and location. ***College room and board:*** $11,500; ***Room only:*** $7382. Room and board charges vary according to board plan and housing facility.

FRESHMAN FINANCIAL AID (Fall 2018) 769 applied for aid; of those 64% were deemed to have need. 97% of freshmen with need received aid; of those 13% had need fully met. ***Average percent of need met:*** 41% (excluding resources awarded to replace EFC). ***Average financial aid package:*** $10,199 (excluding resources awarded to replace EFC). 38% of all full-time freshmen had no need and received non-need-based gift aid.

UNDERGRADUATE FINANCIAL AID (Fall 2018) 2,668 applied for aid; of those 70% were deemed to have need. 96% of undergraduates with need received aid; of those 11% had need fully met. ***Average percent of need met:*** 44% (excluding resources awarded to replace EFC). ***Average financial aid package:*** $10,336 (excluding resources awarded to replace EFC). 27% of all full-time undergraduates had no need and received non-need-based gift aid.

GIFT AID (NEED-BASED) ***Total amount:*** $9,676,472 (42% federal, 34% state, 24% institutional). ***Receiving aid:*** Freshmen: 32% (298); all full-time undergraduates: 31% (1,188). ***Average award:*** Freshmen: $3493; Undergraduates: $3503. ***Scholarships, grants, and awards:*** Federal Pell, FSEOG, state, private, college/university gift aid from institutional funds.

GIFT AID (NON-NEED-BASED) ***Total amount:*** $8,843,865 (87% institutional, 13% external sources). ***Receiving aid:*** Freshmen: 45% (412). Undergraduates: 29% (1,104). ***Average award:*** Freshmen: $3886. Undergraduates: $3558. ***Scholarships, grants, and awards by category:*** *Academic interests/achievement:* architecture, biological sciences, business, computer science, education, English, foreign languages, general academic interests/achievements, humanities, international studies, library science, mathematics, physical sciences, religion/biblical studies, social sciences. *Creative arts/performance:* applied art and design, dance, journalism/publications, music, theater/drama. *Special achievements/activities:* leadership. *Special characteristics:* adult students, children and siblings of alumni, children of faculty/staff, local/state students, religious affiliation. ***Tuition waivers:*** Full or partial for senior citizens. ***ROTC:*** Army cooperative.

LOANS ***Student loans:*** $11,839,204 (47% need-based, 53% non-need-based). 56% of past graduating class borrowed through all loan programs. *Average indebtedness per student:* $31,157. ***Average need-based loan:*** Freshmen: $3152. Undergraduates: $4075. ***Parent loans:*** $4,456,270 (100% non-need-based). ***Programs:*** Federal Direct (Subsidized and Unsubsidized Stafford, PLUS), college/university.

WORK-STUDY ***Federal work-study:*** Total amount: $117,853; jobs available. ***State or other work-study/employment:*** Total amount: $2,119,452 (100% non-need-based). Part-time jobs available.

APPLYING FOR FINANCIAL AID ***Required financial aid form:*** FAFSA. ***Financial aid deadline:*** 6/1 (priority: 2/1). ***Notification date:*** Continuous beginning 12/1. Students must reply by 5/1 or within 2 weeks of notification.

CONTACT Mr. Timothy Saulnier, Director of Financial Aid, University of Mary Washington, 1301 College Avenue, Fredericksburg, VA 22401-5358, 540-654-2468 or toll-free 800-468-5614. *Fax:* 540-654-1858. *E-mail:* tsaulnie@umw.edu.
Website: http://www.umw.edu/.

UNIVERSITY OF MASSACHUSETTS AMHERST

Amherst, MA

Tuition & fees (MA res): $16,389	Average undergraduate aid package: $18,623

ABOUT THE INSTITUTION State-supported, coed. ***Awards:*** certificates, associate, bachelor's, master's, and doctoral degrees. 88 undergraduate majors. ***Total enrollment:*** 31,350. Undergraduates: 24,209. Freshmen: 5,766. Federal methodology is used as a basis for awarding need-based institutional aid.

UNDERGRADUATE EXPENSES for 2019–2020 ***Application fee:*** $80. ***One-time required fee:*** $485. ***Tuition, state resident:*** full-time $15,791; part-time

$658 per credit. ***Tuition, nonresident:*** full-time $35,112; part-time $1463 per credit. ***Required fees:*** full-time $598; $299 per term. Full-time tuition and fees vary according to class time, location, program, reciprocity agreements, and student level. Part-time tuition and fees vary according to class time, course load, location, program, reciprocity agreements, and student level. ***College room and board:*** $13,598; ***Room only:*** $7280. Room and board charges vary according to board plan and housing facility.

FRESHMAN FINANCIAL AID (Fall 2018) 4188 applied for aid; of those 64% were deemed to have need. 99% of freshmen with need received aid; of those 13% had need fully met. ***Average percent of need met:*** 80% (excluding resources awarded to replace EFC). ***Average financial aid package:*** $17,787 (excluding resources awarded to replace EFC). 32% of all full-time freshmen had no need and received non-need-based gift aid.

UNDERGRADUATE FINANCIAL AID (Fall 2018) 16,826 applied for aid; of those 72% were deemed to have need. 99% of undergraduates with need received aid; of those 13% had need fully met. ***Average percent of need met:*** 82% (excluding resources awarded to replace EFC). ***Average financial aid package:*** $18,623 (excluding resources awarded to replace EFC). 25% of all full-time undergraduates had no need and received non-need-based gift aid.

GIFT AID (NEED-BASED) ***Receiving aid:*** Freshmen: 49% (2,466); all full-time undergraduates: 50% (10,806). ***Average award:*** Freshmen: $11,467; Undergraduates: $11,180. ***Scholarships, grants, and awards:*** Federal Pell, FSEOG, state, private, college/university gift aid from institutional funds.

GIFT AID (NON-NEED-BASED) ***Receiving aid:*** Freshmen: 4% (205). Undergraduates: 3% (727). ***Average award:*** Freshmen: $6313. Undergraduates: $5595. ***Scholarships, grants, and awards by category:*** *Academic interests/achievement:* agriculture, architecture, biological sciences, business, communication, computer science, education, engineering/technologies, English, general academic interests/achievements, home economics, humanities, mathematics, military science, physical sciences, premedicine, social sciences. *Creative arts/performance:* applied art and design, dance, journalism/publications, music, theater/drama. *Special achievements/activities:* cheerleading/drum major, general special achievements/activities, leadership. *Special characteristics:* adult students, children and siblings of alumni, children of faculty/staff, children of public servants, first-generation college students, general special characteristics, handicapped students, local/state students, out-of-state students, public servants, veterans, veterans' children. ***Tuition waivers:*** Full or partial for employees or children of employees, senior citizens. ***ROTC:*** Army, Air Force.

LOANS ***Student loans:*** 62% of past graduating class borrowed through all loan programs. *Average indebtedness per student:* $31,755. ***Average need-based loan:*** Freshmen: $3354. Undergraduates: $4366. ***Programs:*** Federal Direct (Subsidized and Unsubsidized Stafford, PLUS), Federal Nursing.

WORK-STUDY ***Federal work-study:*** 3,327 jobs averaging $1918.

APPLYING FOR FINANCIAL AID ***Required financial aid form:*** FAFSA. ***Notification date:*** Continuous.

CONTACT Lauren Lamica, Office of Financial Aid Services, University of Massachusetts Amherst, 255 Whitmore Administration Building, 181 Presidents Drive, Amherst, MA 01003, 413-545-0801. *Fax:* 413-545-1700.
Website: http://www.umass.edu/.

UNIVERSITY OF MASSACHUSETTS BOSTON

Boston, MA

Tuition & fees (MA res): $14,613	Average undergraduate aid package: $17,239

ABOUT THE INSTITUTION State-supported, coed. ***Awards:*** certificates, bachelor's, master's, and doctoral degrees. 43 undergraduate majors. ***Total enrollment:*** 3,394. Undergraduates: 12,595. Freshmen: 2,123. Federal methodology is used as a basis for awarding need-based institutional aid.

UNDERGRADUATE EXPENSES for 2019–2020 ***Application fee:*** $60. ***Tuition, state resident:*** full-time $14,187; part-time $591 per credit hour. ***Tuition, nonresident:*** full-time $34,649; part-time $1444 per credit hour. ***Required fees:*** full-time $426; $17.80 per credit hour. Full-time tuition and fees vary according to program. Part-time tuition and fees vary according to program. ***College room and board:*** $16,902; ***Room only:*** $11,352.

FRESHMAN FINANCIAL AID (Fall 2018) 1992 applied for aid; of those 87% were deemed to have need. 98% of freshmen with need received aid; of those 17% had need fully met. ***Average percent of need met:*** 80% (excluding resources awarded to replace EFC). ***Average financial aid package:*** $18,300 (excluding resources awarded to replace EFC). 9% of all full-time freshmen had no need and received non-need-based gift aid.

UNDERGRADUATE FINANCIAL AID (Fall 2018) 7,618 applied for aid; of those 90% were deemed to have need. 97% of undergraduates with need received aid; of those 19% had need fully met. ***Average percent of need met:*** 83% (excluding resources awarded to replace EFC). ***Average financial aid package:*** $17,239 (excluding resources awarded to replace EFC). 7% of all full-time undergraduates had no need and received non-need-based gift aid.

GIFT AID (NEED-BASED) ***Total amount:*** $69,902,601 (35% federal, 10% state, 52% institutional, 3% external sources). ***Receiving aid:*** Freshmen: 70% (1,590); all full-time undergraduates: 62% (6,184). ***Average award:*** Freshmen: $12,281; Undergraduates: $10,586. ***Scholarships, grants, and awards:*** Federal Pell, FSEOG, state, private, college/university gift aid from institutional funds, TEACH Grants.

GIFT AID (NON-NEED-BASED) ***Total amount:*** $6,698,021 (94% institutional, 6% external sources). ***Receiving aid:*** Freshmen: 3% (63). Undergraduates: 2% (178). ***Average award:*** Freshmen: $7248. Undergraduates: $7929. ***Scholarships, grants, and awards by category:*** *Academic interests/achievement:* general academic interests/achievements, military science. *Special achievements/activities:* general special achievements/activities, leadership. *Special characteristics:* adult students, children of faculty/staff, children of union members/company employees, first-generation college students, local/state students, out-of-state students, veterans. ***ROTC:*** Army cooperative, Naval cooperative, Air Force cooperative.

LOANS ***Student loans:*** $67,611,117 (79% need-based, 21% non-need-based). 54% of past graduating class borrowed through all loan programs. *Average indebtedness per student:* $25,645. ***Average need-based loan:*** Freshmen: $3606. Undergraduates: $4593. ***Parent loans:*** $5,949,154 (48% need-based, 52% non-need-based). ***Programs:*** Federal Direct (Subsidized and Unsubsidized Stafford, PLUS).

WORK-STUDY ***Federal work-study:*** Total amount: $2,251,947; jobs available.

APPLYING FOR FINANCIAL AID ***Required financial aid form:*** FAFSA. ***Financial aid deadline (priority):*** 3/1. ***Notification date:*** Continuous beginning 12/15.

CONTACT Katherine N. Lynch, Director of Financial Aid Services, University of Massachusetts Boston, 100 Morrissey Boulevard, Boston, MA 02125-3393, 617-287-6300. *Fax:* 617-287-6323. *E-mail:* katherine.lynch@umb.edu.
Website: http://www.umb.edu/.

UNIVERSITY OF MASSACHUSETTS DARTMOUTH

North Dartmouth, MA

Tuition & fees (MA res): $14,358	Average undergraduate aid package: $17,717

ABOUT THE INSTITUTION State-supported, coed. ***Awards:*** certificates, bachelor's, master's, and doctoral degrees. 52 undergraduate majors. ***Total enrollment:*** 8,154. Undergraduates: 6,405. Freshmen: 1,320. Federal methodology is used as a basis for awarding need-based institutional aid.

UNDERGRADUATE EXPENSES for 2019–2020 ***Application fee:*** $60. ***One-time required fee:*** $100. ***Tuition, state resident:*** full-time $13,833; part-time $576 per credit. ***Tuition, nonresident:*** full-time $29,578; part-time $1232 per credit. ***Required fees:*** full-time $525; $30.87 per credit. Full-time tuition and fees vary according to class time, program, and reciprocity agreements. Part-time tuition and fees vary according to class time, course load, program, and reciprocity agreements. ***College room and board:*** $14,064; ***Room only:*** $5034. Room and board charges vary according to board plan and housing facility.

FRESHMAN FINANCIAL AID (Fall 2018) 1349 applied for aid; of those 84% were deemed to have need. 99% of freshmen with need received aid; of those 21% had need fully met. ***Average percent of need met:*** 84% (excluding resources awarded to replace EFC). ***Average financial aid package:*** $18,112 (excluding resources awarded to replace EFC). 17% of all full-time freshmen had no need and received non-need-based gift aid.

UNDERGRADUATE FINANCIAL AID (Fall 2018) 5,201 applied for aid; of those 85% were deemed to have need. 98% of undergraduates with need received aid;

of those 20% had need fully met. ***Average percent of need met:*** 83% (excluding resources awarded to replace EFC). ***Average financial aid package:*** $17,717 (excluding resources awarded to replace EFC). 11% of all full-time undergraduates had no need and received non-need-based gift aid.

GIFT AID (NEED-BASED) ***Total amount:*** $41,850,075 (29% federal, 9% state, 59% institutional, 3% external sources). ***Receiving aid:*** Freshmen: 78% (1,092); all full-time undergraduates: 66% (3,894). ***Average award:*** Freshmen: $12,019; Undergraduates: $10,854. ***Scholarships, grants, and awards:*** Federal Pell, FSEOG, state, private, college/university gift aid from institutional funds.

GIFT AID (NON-NEED-BASED) ***Total amount:*** $4,808,414 (2% state, 92% institutional, 6% external sources). ***Receiving aid:*** Freshmen: 6% (91). Undergraduates: 4% (224). ***Average award:*** Freshmen: $6405. Undergraduates: $5927. ***Scholarships, grants, and awards by category:*** *Academic interests/achievement:* biological sciences, business, computer science, education, engineering/technologies, general academic interests/achievements, home economics, humanities, mathematics, physical sciences, social sciences. *Creative arts/performance:* general creative arts/performance. *Special achievements/activities:* leadership. *Special characteristics:* ethnic background, general special characteristics, local/state students, members of minority groups, out-of-state students, spouses of deceased or disabled public servants. ***Tuition waivers:*** Full or partial for employees or children of employees, senior citizens. ***ROTC:*** Army cooperative.

LOANS ***Student loans:*** $46,510,677 (74% need-based, 26% non-need-based). 84% of past graduating class borrowed through all loan programs. *Average indebtedness per student:* $34,824. ***Average need-based loan:*** Freshmen: $3238. Undergraduates: $4083. ***Parent loans:*** $12,255,589 (53% need-based, 47% non-need-based). ***Programs:*** Federal Direct (Subsidized and Unsubsidized Stafford, PLUS), state.

WORK-STUDY ***Federal work-study:*** Total amount: $1,187,213; 2,042 jobs averaging $1370. ***State or other work-study/employment:*** Part-time jobs available (averaging $1333).

APPLYING FOR FINANCIAL AID ***Required financial aid form:*** FAFSA. ***Financial aid deadline:*** 6/30 (priority: 3/1). ***Notification date:*** 12/17.

CONTACT Ms. Korinne Peterson, Director of Financial Aid, University of Massachusetts Dartmouth, 285 Old Westport Road, North Dartmouth, MA 02747-2300, 508-999-8857. *Fax:* 508-910-6420. *E-mail:* uec@umassd.edu.
Website: http://www.umassd.edu/.

UNIVERSITY OF MASSACHUSETTS LOWELL

Lowell, MA

Tuition & fees: N/R	Average undergraduate aid package: $16,864

ABOUT THE INSTITUTION State-supported, coed. ***Awards:*** certificates, associate, bachelor's, master's, and doctoral degrees. 47 undergraduate majors. ***Total enrollment:*** 18,338. Undergraduates: 14,155. Freshmen: 2,354. Federal methodology is used as a basis for awarding need-based institutional aid.

FRESHMAN FINANCIAL AID (Fall 2018) 1931 applied for aid; of those 74% were deemed to have need. 99% of freshmen with need received aid; of those 25% had need fully met. ***Average percent of need met:*** 90% (excluding resources awarded to replace EFC). ***Average financial aid package:*** $19,041 (excluding resources awarded to replace EFC). 16% of all full-time freshmen had no need and received non-need-based gift aid.

UNDERGRADUATE FINANCIAL AID (Fall 2018) 8,600 applied for aid; of those 77% were deemed to have need. 98% of undergraduates with need received aid; of those 26% had need fully met. ***Average percent of need met:*** 88% (excluding resources awarded to replace EFC). ***Average financial aid package:*** $16,864 (excluding resources awarded to replace EFC). 15% of all full-time undergraduates had no need and received non-need-based gift aid.

GIFT AID (NEED-BASED) ***Total amount:*** $57,343,406 (29% federal, 8% state, 59% institutional, 4% external sources). ***Receiving aid:*** Freshmen: 63% (1,317); all full-time undergraduates: 53% (5,702). ***Average award:*** Freshmen: $12,500; Undergraduates: $10,141. ***Scholarships, grants, and awards:*** Federal Pell, FSEOG, state, private, college/university gift aid from institutional funds.

GIFT AID (NON-NEED-BASED) ***Total amount:*** $8,666,616 (90% institutional, 10% external sources). ***Receiving aid:*** Freshmen: 3% (61). Undergraduates: 2% (262). ***Average award:*** Freshmen: $7679. Undergraduates: $7164. ***Scholarships, grants, and awards by category:*** *Academic interests/achievement:* biological sciences, business, computer science, education, engineering/technologies, English, general academic interests/achievements, health fields, humanities, mathematics. *Creative arts/performance:* art/fine arts, music. *Special achievements/activities:* community service, general special achievements/activities. *Special characteristics:* children and siblings of alumni, children of faculty/staff, children of public servants, children of union members/company employees, general special characteristics, out-of-state students, veterans. ***ROTC:*** Army, Air Force.

LOANS ***Student loans:*** $76,945,687 (66% need-based, 34% non-need-based). 74% of past graduating class borrowed through all loan programs. *Average indebtedness per student:* $32,317. ***Average need-based loan:*** Freshmen: $3315. Undergraduates: $4210. ***Parent loans:*** $14,727,239 (32% need-based, 68% non-need-based). ***Programs:*** Federal Direct (Subsidized and Unsubsidized Stafford, PLUS).

WORK-STUDY ***Federal work-study:*** Total amount: $489,308; jobs available. ***State or other work-study/employment:*** Total amount: $2,703,364 (96% need-based, 4% non-need-based). Part-time jobs available.

ATHLETIC AWARDS Total amount: $6,384,422 (30% need-based, 70% non-need-based).

APPLYING FOR FINANCIAL AID ***Required financial aid form:*** FAFSA. ***Notification date:*** Continuous beginning 1/10.

CONTACT Joyce McLaughlin, Director of Financial Aid, University of Massachusetts Lowell, University Crossing, 220 Pawtucket Street, Suite 280, Lowell, MA 01854, 978-934-4220. *Fax:* 978-934-3009. *E-mail:* joyce_mclaughlin@uml.edu.
Website: http://www.uml.edu/.

UNIVERSITY OF MEMPHIS

Memphis, TN

Tuition & fees (TN res): $9912	Average undergraduate aid package: $11,767

ABOUT THE INSTITUTION State-supported, coed. ***Awards:*** certificates, bachelor's, master's, and doctoral degrees. 72 undergraduate majors. ***Total enrollment:*** 21,685. Undergraduates: 17,378. Freshmen: 2,683. Federal methodology is used as a basis for awarding need-based institutional aid.

UNDERGRADUATE EXPENSES for 2019–2020 ***Application fee:*** $25. ***Tuition, state resident:*** full-time $8208; part-time $342 per credit hour. ***Tuition, nonresident:*** full-time $15,060; part-time $502 per credit hour. ***Required fees:*** full-time $1704; $71 per credit hour. Full-time tuition and fees vary according to course load, degree level, program, and reciprocity agreements. Part-time tuition and fees vary according to course load, degree level, and program. ***College room and board:*** $10,175; ***Room only:*** $6105. Room and board charges vary according to board plan, housing facility, and location.

FRESHMAN FINANCIAL AID (Fall 2018) 2314 applied for aid; of those 83% were deemed to have need. 99% of freshmen with need received aid; of those 9% had need fully met. ***Average percent of need met:*** 58% (excluding resources awarded to replace EFC). ***Average financial aid package:*** $13,314 (excluding resources awarded to replace EFC). 16% of all full-time freshmen had no need and received non-need-based gift aid.

UNDERGRADUATE FINANCIAL AID (Fall 2018) 11,254 applied for aid; of those 83% were deemed to have need. 98% of undergraduates with need received aid; of those 9% had need fully met. ***Average percent of need met:*** 55% (excluding resources awarded to replace EFC). ***Average financial aid package:*** $11,767 (excluding resources awarded to replace EFC). 13% of all full-time undergraduates had no need and received non-need-based gift aid.

GIFT AID (NEED-BASED) ***Total amount:*** $52,647,524 (79% federal, 18% state, 3% institutional). ***Receiving aid:*** Freshmen: 55% (1,295); all full-time undergraduates: 55% (6,550). ***Average award:*** Freshmen: $7820; Undergraduates: $6858. ***Scholarships, grants, and awards:*** Federal Pell, FSEOG, state, private, college/university gift aid from institutional funds.

GIFT AID (NON-NEED-BASED) ***Total amount:*** $38,658,138 (53% state, 43% institutional, 4% external sources). ***Receiving aid:*** Freshmen: 67% (1,576). Undergraduates: 42% (5,037). ***Average award:*** Freshmen: $6916. Undergraduates: $6540. ***Scholarships, grants, and awards by category:*** *Academic interests/achievement:* architecture, biological sciences, business, communication, computer science, education, engineering/technologies, English, general academic interests/achievements, health fields, home economics, humanities, international studies, mathematics, military science, physical sciences, premedicine, social sciences. *Creative arts/performance:* applied art and design, art/fine arts, cinema/film/broadcasting, creative

writing, dance, journalism/publications, music, theater/drama. *Special achievements/activities:* cheerleading/drum major, community service, general special achievements/activities, leadership. *Special characteristics:* adult students, children of educators, children of faculty/staff, children of public servants, first-generation college students, handicapped students, international students, local/state students, members of minority groups, public servants, veterans. ***Tuition waivers:*** Full or partial for employees or children of employees, senior citizens. ***ROTC:*** Army, Naval, Air Force.
LOANS *Student loans:* $82,045,575 (43% need-based, 57% non-need-based). 87% of past graduating class borrowed through all loan programs. *Average indebtedness per student:* $30,931. ***Average need-based loan:*** Freshmen: $3224. Undergraduates: $4053. ***Parent loans:*** $11,011,845 (100% non-need-based). ***Programs:*** Federal Direct (Subsidized and Unsubsidized Stafford, PLUS).
WORK-STUDY *Federal work-study:* Total amount: $871,402; 332 jobs averaging $2625. ***State or other work-study/employment:*** Total amount: $3,732,835 (100% non-need-based). Part-time jobs available.
ATHLETIC AWARDS Total amount: $8,214,207 (100% non-need-based).
APPLYING FOR FINANCIAL AID *Required financial aid form:* FAFSA. ***Financial aid deadline (priority):*** 3/1. ***Notification date:*** Continuous beginning 12/1. Students must reply by 8/1.
CONTACT Mr. Robert Kniss, Director of Financial Aid, University of Memphis, Wilder Tower 101, Memphis, TN 38152, 901-678-4995 or toll-free 800-669-2678. *Fax:* 901-678-3590. *E-mail:* rskniss@memphis.edu.
Website: http://www.memphis.edu/.

UNIVERSITY OF MIAMI

Coral Gables, FL

Tuition & fees: $53,682	Average undergraduate aid package: $41,057

ABOUT THE INSTITUTION Independent, coed. ***Awards:*** certificates, bachelor's, master's, and doctoral degrees. 132 undergraduate majors. ***Total enrollment:*** 17,811. Undergraduates: 11,307. Freshmen: 2,203. Both federal and institutional methodology are used as a basis for awarding need-based institutional aid.
UNDERGRADUATE EXPENSES for 2020–2021 *Application fee:* $70. ***Comprehensive fee:*** $69,152 includes full-time tuition ($52,080), mandatory fees ($1602), and room and board ($15,470). ***College room only:*** $8900. Room and board charges vary according to board plan and housing facility. ***Part-time tuition:*** $2170 per credit hour. ***Part-time fees:*** $285.
FRESHMAN FINANCIAL AID (Fall 2019, est.) 1388 applied for aid; of those 76% were deemed to have need. 96% of freshmen with need received aid; of those 95% had need fully met. ***Average percent of need met:*** 99% (excluding resources awarded to replace EFC). ***Average financial aid package:*** $43,776 (excluding resources awarded to replace EFC). 24% of all full-time freshmen had no need and received non-need-based gift aid.
UNDERGRADUATE FINANCIAL AID (Fall 2019, est.) 5,894 applied for aid; of those 78% were deemed to have need. 96% of undergraduates with need received aid; of those 82% had need fully met. ***Average percent of need met:*** 97% (excluding resources awarded to replace EFC). ***Average financial aid package:*** $41,057 (excluding resources awarded to replace EFC). 25% of all full-time undergraduates had no need and received non-need-based gift aid.
GIFT AID (NEED-BASED) *Total amount:* $121,268,942 (9% federal, 6% state, 83% institutional, 2% external sources). ***Receiving aid:*** Freshmen: 34% (745); all full-time undergraduates: 32% (3,375). ***Average award:*** Freshmen: $37,836; Undergraduates: $35,768. ***Scholarships, grants, and awards:*** Federal Pell, FSEOG, state, private, college/university gift aid from institutional funds.
GIFT AID (NON-NEED-BASED) *Total amount:* $85,132,500 (14% state, 80% institutional, 6% external sources). ***Receiving aid:*** Freshmen: 23% (492). Undergraduates: 16% (1,714). ***Average award:*** Freshmen: $25,539. Undergraduates: $22,986. ***Scholarships, grants, and awards by category:*** *Academic interests/achievement:* 6,452 awards ($184,328,747 total): architecture, area/ethnic studies, biological sciences, business, communication, computer science, education, engineering/technologies, English, foreign languages, general academic interests/achievements, health fields, home economics, humanities, international studies, library science, mathematics, physical sciences, premedicine, religion/biblical studies, social sciences. *Creative arts/performance:* 558 awards ($20,196,300 total): music, performing arts, theater/drama. *Special achievements/activities:* 19 awards ($1,269,976 total): leadership, religious involvement. *Special characteristics:* 2,090 awards ($71,005,468 total): children of faculty/staff, first-generation college students, international students, veterans. ***Tuition waivers:*** Full or partial for employees or children of employees. ***ROTC:*** Army, Air Force.
LOANS *Student loans:* $10,496,103 (100% need-based). 34% of past graduating class borrowed through all loan programs. *Average indebtedness per student:* $21,000. ***Average need-based loan:*** Freshmen: $3047. Undergraduates: $4460. ***Parent loans:*** $17,427,827 (14% need-based, 86% non-need-based). ***Programs:*** Federal Direct (Subsidized and Unsubsidized Stafford, PLUS), Perkins, Federal Nursing, college/university, private loans.
WORK-STUDY *Federal work-study:* Total amount: $6,245,064; 2,132 jobs averaging $2926. ***State or other work-study/employment:*** Total amount: $519,000 (5% need-based, 95% non-need-based). 172 part-time jobs averaging $2977.
ATHLETIC AWARDS Total amount: $15,559,173 (8% need-based, 92% non-need-based).
APPLYING FOR FINANCIAL AID *Required financial aid forms:* FAFSA, CSS Financial Aid PROFILE, state aid form, noncustodial (divorced/separated) parent's statement, business/farm supplement, parent and student federal income tax form(s), W-2 forms. ***Financial aid deadline:*** 4/15 (priority: 1/1). ***Notification date:*** Continuous beginning 1/20. Students must reply by 5/1.
CONTACT Mrs. Carrie Glass, Executive Director for Financial Assistance Services, University of Miami, 1306 Stanford Drive, University Center, Suite 2275, Coral Gables, FL 33146, 305-284-2270. *Fax:* 305-284-8641. *E-mail:* Cxg949@miami.edu.
Website: http://www.miami.edu/.

UNIVERSITY OF MICHIGAN

Ann Arbor, MI

Tuition & fees (MI res): $15,558	Average undergraduate aid package: $28,711

ABOUT THE INSTITUTION State-supported, coed. ***Awards:*** certificates, bachelor's, master's, and doctoral degrees. 127 undergraduate majors. ***Total enrollment:*** 48,090. Undergraduates: 31,266. Freshmen: 6,830. Both federal and institutional methodology are used as a basis for awarding need-based institutional aid.
UNDERGRADUATE EXPENSES for 2019–2020 *Application fee:* $75. ***Tuition, state resident:*** full-time $15,230; part-time $611 per credit hour. ***Tuition, nonresident:*** full-time $50,872; part-time $2088 per credit hour. ***Required fees:*** full-time $328; $164 per term. Full-time tuition and fees vary according to course load, degree level, program, and student level. Part-time tuition and fees vary according to course load, degree level, program, and student level. ***College room and board:*** $11,996. Room and board charges vary according to board plan and housing facility.
FRESHMAN FINANCIAL AID (Fall 2018) 4863 applied for aid; of those 58% were deemed to have need. 95% of freshmen with need received aid; of those 69% had need fully met. ***Average percent of need met:*** 90% (excluding resources awarded to replace EFC). ***Average financial aid package:*** $27,596 (excluding resources awarded to replace EFC). 14% of all full-time freshmen had no need and received non-need-based gift aid.
UNDERGRADUATE FINANCIAL AID (Fall 2018) 15,973 applied for aid; of those 73% were deemed to have need. 97% of undergraduates with need received aid; of those 76% had need fully met. ***Average percent of need met:*** 92% (excluding resources awarded to replace EFC). ***Average financial aid package:*** $28,711 (excluding resources awarded to replace EFC). 11% of all full-time undergraduates had no need and received non-need-based gift aid.
GIFT AID (NEED-BASED) *Total amount:* $208,279,777 (14% federal, 86% institutional). ***Receiving aid:*** Freshmen: 32% (2,124); all full-time undergraduates: 32% (9,444). ***Average award:*** Freshmen: $21,330; Undergraduates: $21,665. ***Scholarships, grants, and awards:*** Federal Pell, FSEOG, state, private, college/university gift aid from institutional funds, TEACH Grants, Iraq and Afghanistan Service Grants, Michigan Competitive Scholarships.
GIFT AID (NON-NEED-BASED) *Total amount:* $103,500,410 (6% federal, 4% state, 72% institutional, 18% external sources). ***Receiving aid:*** Freshmen: 29% (1,960). Undergraduates: 27% (7,735). ***Average award:*** Freshmen: $4411. Undergraduates: $5853. ***Scholarships, grants, and awards by category:*** *Academic interests/achievement:* architecture, area/ethnic studies, biological sciences, business, communication, computer science, education, engineering/technologies, English, foreign languages, general academic interests/achievements, home economics, humanities, international studies, library science, mathematics, military science, physical sciences, premedicine, social sciences. *Creative arts/performance:* applied art and design,

cinema/film/broadcasting, creative writing, dance, journalism/publications, music, performing arts, theater/drama. *Special achievements/activities:* community service, general special achievements/activities, leadership. *Special characteristics:* children of faculty/staff, children of workers in trades, handicapped students, international students, local/state students, members of minority groups, out-of-state students. ***ROTC:*** Army, Naval, Air Force.

LOANS *Student loans:* $73,135,667 (40% need-based, 60% non-need-based). 38% of past graduating class borrowed through all loan programs. *Average indebtedness per student:* $25,777. ***Average need-based loan:*** Freshmen: $3398. Undergraduates: $4301. ***Parent loans:*** $28,378,144 (100% non-need-based). ***Programs:*** Federal Direct (Subsidized and Unsubsidized Stafford, PLUS), Federal Nursing, college/university, Health Professions Student Loans (HPSL).

WORK-STUDY *Federal work-study:* Total amount: $15,734,064; jobs available.

ATHLETIC AWARDS Total amount: $25,567,270 (100% non-need-based).

APPLYING FOR FINANCIAL AID *Required financial aid forms:* FAFSA, CSS Financial Aid PROFILE. ***Financial aid deadline:*** 3/31 (priority: 3/31). ***Notification date:*** Continuous beginning 1/15.

CONTACT Office of Financial Aid, University of Michigan, 2500 Student Activities Building, 515 East Jefferson Street, Ann Arbor, MI 48109-1316, 734-763-6600. *Fax:* 734-637-3081. *E-mail:* financial.aid@umich.edu.
Website: http://www.umich.edu/.

UNIVERSITY OF MICHIGAN–DEARBORN

Dearborn, MI

Tuition & fees (MI res): $14,236 | **Average undergraduate aid package: $13,486**

ABOUT THE INSTITUTION State-supported, coed. ***Awards:*** certificates, bachelor's, master's, and doctoral degrees. 65 undergraduate majors. ***Total enrollment:*** 9,195. Undergraduates: 6,914. Freshmen: 1,014. Federal methodology is used as a basis for awarding need-based institutional aid.

UNDERGRADUATE EXPENSES for 2020–2021 *One-time required fee:* $75. ***Tuition, state resident:*** full-time $13,836; part-time $529 per credit hour. ***Tuition, nonresident:*** full-time $27,476; part-time $1068 per credit hour. ***Required fees:*** full-time $400; $200 per term. Full-time tuition and fees vary according to program and student level. Part-time tuition and fees vary according to program and student level. ***College room and board:*** $2262.

FRESHMAN FINANCIAL AID (Fall 2018) 941 applied for aid; of those 74% were deemed to have need. 100% of freshmen with need received aid; of those 12% had need fully met. ***Average percent of need met:*** 72% (excluding resources awarded to replace EFC). ***Average financial aid package:*** $12,468 (excluding resources awarded to replace EFC). 21% of all full-time freshmen had no need and received non-need-based gift aid.

UNDERGRADUATE FINANCIAL AID (Fall 2018) 4,010 applied for aid; of those 85% were deemed to have need. 100% of undergraduates with need received aid; of those 9% had need fully met. ***Average percent of need met:*** 69% (excluding resources awarded to replace EFC). ***Average financial aid package:*** $13,486 (excluding resources awarded to replace EFC). 16% of all full-time undergraduates had no need and received non-need-based gift aid.

GIFT AID (NEED-BASED) *Total amount:* $26,712,683 (56% federal, 4% state, 38% institutional, 2% external sources). ***Receiving aid:*** Freshmen: 59% (627); all full-time undergraduates: 59% (3,055). ***Average award:*** Freshmen: $8024; Undergraduates: $7787. ***Scholarships, grants, and awards:*** Federal Pell, FSEOG, state, private, college/university gift aid from institutional funds.

GIFT AID (NON-NEED-BASED) *Total amount:* $4,876,798 (94% institutional, 6% external sources). ***Receiving aid:*** Freshmen: 41% (429). Undergraduates: 35% (1,829). ***Average award:*** Freshmen: $5256. Undergraduates: $5332. ***Scholarships, grants, and awards by category:*** *Academic interests/achievement:* 2,848 awards ($11,148,462 total): biological sciences, business, communication, computer science, education, engineering/technologies, foreign languages, general academic interests/achievements, international studies, mathematics, physical sciences, social sciences. *Creative arts/performance:* 48 awards ($43,910 total): applied art and design, cinema/film/broadcasting, creative writing, debating, general creative arts/performance, journalism/publications. *Special achievements/activities:* 502 awards ($1,190,303 total): community service, general special achievements/activities, leadership, memberships. *Special characteristics:* 439 awards ($2,855,834 total): adult students, children and siblings of alumni, children of faculty/staff, ethnic background, general special characteristics, handicapped students, international students, members of minority groups, out-of-state students, previous college experience, public servants. ***Tuition waivers:*** Full or partial for employees or children of employees, senior citizens. ***ROTC:*** Naval cooperative, Air Force cooperative.

LOANS *Student loans:* $25,018,493 (95% need-based, 5% non-need-based). 53% of past graduating class borrowed through all loan programs. *Average indebtedness per student:* $25,268. ***Average need-based loan:*** Freshmen: $4757. Undergraduates: $4857. ***Parent loans:*** $3,710,799 (44% need-based, 56% non-need-based). ***Programs:*** Federal Direct (Subsidized and Unsubsidized Stafford, PLUS), alternative loans.

WORK-STUDY *Federal work-study:* Total amount: $454,993; 220 jobs averaging $2080. ***State or other work-study/employment:*** 584 part-time jobs averaging $2862.

ATHLETIC AWARDS Total amount: $496,700 (51% need-based, 49% non-need-based).

APPLYING FOR FINANCIAL AID *Required financial aid form:* FAFSA. ***Financial aid deadline (priority):*** 1/5. ***Notification date:*** Continuous beginning 12/10. Students must reply by 5/1 or within 6 weeks of notification.

CONTACT Ms. Katherine M. Allen, Director of Financial Aid and Scholarships, University of Michigan–Dearborn, 4901 Evergreen Road, 1183 University Center, Dearborn, MI 48128-2406, 313-593-5300. *Fax:* 313-593-5313. *E-mail:* umd-ask-ofa@umich.edu.
Website: http://www.umdearborn.edu/.

UNIVERSITY OF MICHIGAN–FLINT

Flint, MI

Tuition & fees (MI res): $12,406 | **Average undergraduate aid package: $12,802**

ABOUT THE INSTITUTION State-supported, coed. ***Awards:*** certificates, bachelor's, master's, and doctoral degrees. 69 undergraduate majors. ***Total enrollment:*** 7,297. Undergraduates: 5,862. Freshmen: 604. Federal methodology is used as a basis for awarding need-based institutional aid.

UNDERGRADUATE EXPENSES for 2019–2020 *Application fee:* $30. ***Tuition, state resident:*** full-time $11,952; part-time $472 per credit hour. ***Tuition, nonresident:*** full-time $23,238; part-time $939 per credit hour. ***Required fees:*** full-time $454; $227 per term. Full-time tuition and fees vary according to course level, course load, degree level, program, and student level. Part-time tuition and fees vary according to course level, course load, degree level, program, and student level. ***College room and board:*** $9116; ***Room only:*** $5994. Room and board charges vary according to housing facility.

FRESHMAN FINANCIAL AID (Fall 2018) 584 applied for aid; of those 83% were deemed to have need. 97% of freshmen with need received aid; of those 8% had need fully met. ***Average percent of need met:*** 68% (excluding resources awarded to replace EFC). ***Average financial aid package:*** $12,241 (excluding resources awarded to replace EFC). 11% of all full-time freshmen had no need and received non-need-based gift aid.

UNDERGRADUATE FINANCIAL AID (Fall 2018) 3,003 applied for aid; of those 88% were deemed to have need. 98% of undergraduates with need received aid; of those 7% had need fully met. ***Average percent of need met:*** 63% (excluding resources awarded to replace EFC). ***Average financial aid package:*** $12,802 (excluding resources awarded to replace EFC). 5% of all full-time undergraduates had no need and received non-need-based gift aid.

GIFT AID (NEED-BASED) *Total amount:* $16,646,943 (62% federal, 2% state, 36% institutional). ***Receiving aid:*** Freshmen: 56% (356); all full-time undergraduates: 54% (1,942). ***Average award:*** Freshmen: $8004; Undergraduates: $7124. ***Scholarships, grants, and awards:*** Federal Pell, FSEOG, state, private, college/university gift aid from institutional funds.

GIFT AID (NON-NEED-BASED) *Total amount:* $5,569,056 (3% state, 82% institutional, 15% external sources). ***Receiving aid:*** Freshmen: 52% (334). Undergraduates: 28% (1,020). ***Average award:*** Freshmen: $4015. Undergraduates: $4312. ***Scholarships, grants, and awards by category:*** *Academic interests/achievement:* biological sciences, business, communication, computer science, education, engineering/technologies, English, foreign languages, general academic interests/achievements, home economics, humanities, international studies, mathematics, physical sciences, premedicine, social sciences. *Creative arts/performance:* applied art and design, music, performing arts, theater/drama. *Special achievements/activities:*

community service, general special achievements/activities, hobbies/interests, leadership. *Special characteristics:* adult students, children and siblings of alumni, children of faculty/staff, children of union members/company employees, first-generation college students, general special characteristics, handicapped students, international students, local/state students, members of minority groups, veterans. ***Tuition waivers:*** Full or partial for senior citizens. ***ROTC:*** Army cooperative, Naval cooperative, Air Force cooperative.

LOANS *Student loans:* $24,218,186 (88% need-based, 12% non-need-based). 66% of past graduating class borrowed through all loan programs. *Average indebtedness per student:* $29,645. ***Average need-based loan:*** Freshmen: $3179. Undergraduates: $4041. ***Parent loans:*** $2,161,085 (100% non-need-based). ***Programs:*** Federal Direct (Subsidized and Unsubsidized Stafford, PLUS).

WORK-STUDY *Federal work-study:* Total amount: $376,619.30; 215 jobs averaging $1840.

APPLYING FOR FINANCIAL AID *Required financial aid form:* FAFSA. ***Financial aid deadline (priority):*** 11/15. ***Notification date:*** Continuous beginning 12/1.

CONTACT Lori Vedder, Office of Financial Aid, University of Michigan–Flint, Room 277 Pavilion, 303 East Kearsley Street, Flint, MI 48502-1950, 810-762-3444 or toll-free 800-942-5636. *Fax:* 810-766-6757. *E-mail:* financialaid@umich.edu.
Website: http://www.umflint.edu/.

UNIVERSITY OF MINNESOTA, CROOKSTON

Crookston, MN

Tuition & fees (area res): $12,116	Average undergraduate aid package: $12,382

ABOUT THE INSTITUTION State-supported, coed. ***Awards:*** bachelor's degrees. 43 undergraduate majors. ***Total enrollment:*** 2,810. Undergraduates: 2,810. Freshmen: 228. Federal methodology is used as a basis for awarding need-based institutional aid.

UNDERGRADUATE EXPENSES for 2019–2020 *Application fee:* $30. ***Tuition, area resident:*** full-time $10,438; part-time $402 per credit hour. ***Tuition, state resident:*** full-time $10,438; part-time $402 per credit hour. ***Tuition, nonresident:*** full-time $10,438; part-time $402 per credit hour. ***Required fees:*** full-time $1678. Full-time tuition and fees vary according to program. Part-time tuition and fees vary according to program. ***College room and board:*** $9020; ***Room only:*** $6520. Room and board charges vary according to board plan and housing facility.

FRESHMAN FINANCIAL AID (Fall 2019, est.) 181 applied for aid; of those 83% were deemed to have need. 99% of freshmen with need received aid; of those 29% had need fully met. ***Average percent of need met:*** 82% (excluding resources awarded to replace EFC). ***Average financial aid package:*** $15,040 (excluding resources awarded to replace EFC). 15% of all full-time freshmen had no need and received non-need-based gift aid.

UNDERGRADUATE FINANCIAL AID (Fall 2019, est.) 964 applied for aid; of those 82% were deemed to have need. 98% of undergraduates with need received aid; of those 22% had need fully met. ***Average percent of need met:*** 74% (excluding resources awarded to replace EFC). ***Average financial aid package:*** $12,382 (excluding resources awarded to replace EFC). 9% of all full-time undergraduates had no need and received non-need-based gift aid.

GIFT AID (NEED-BASED) *Total amount:* $7,130,819 (37% federal, 29% state, 29% institutional, 5% external sources). ***Receiving aid:*** Freshmen: 72% (149); all full-time undergraduates: 62% (721). ***Average award:*** Freshmen: $12,070; Undergraduates: $9614. ***Scholarships, grants, and awards:*** Federal Pell, FSEOG, state, private, college/university gift aid from institutional funds, Academic Competitiveness Grants.

GIFT AID (NON-NEED-BASED) *Total amount:* $482,411 (7% state, 73% institutional, 20% external sources). ***Receiving aid:*** Freshmen: 10% (21). Undergraduates: 5% (61). ***Average award:*** Freshmen: $3158. Undergraduates: $2201. ***Scholarships, grants, and awards by category:*** *Academic interests/achievement:* agriculture, biological sciences, general academic interests/achievements. *Creative arts/performance:* general creative arts/performance. *Special achievements/activities:* leadership. *Special characteristics:* children and siblings of alumni, children of faculty/staff, ethnic background, first-generation college students, general special characteristics, local/state students, members of minority groups. ***Tuition waivers:*** Full or partial for senior citizens. ***ROTC:*** Air Force cooperative.

LOANS *Student loans:* $8,425,420 (62% need-based, 38% non-need-based). 73% of past graduating class borrowed through all loan programs. *Average indebtedness per student:* $26,107. ***Average need-based loan:*** Freshmen: $3107. Undergraduates: $4026. ***Parent loans:*** $364,836 (26% need-based, 74% non-need-based). ***Programs:*** Federal Direct (Subsidized and Unsubsidized Stafford, PLUS), Perkins, state, private loans.

WORK-STUDY *Federal work-study:* Total amount: $275,330; jobs available. ***State or other work-study/employment:*** Total amount: $225,920 (100% need-based). Part-time jobs available.

ATHLETIC AWARDS Total amount: $1,402,274 (75% need-based, 25% non-need-based).

APPLYING FOR FINANCIAL AID *Required financial aid form:* FAFSA. ***Financial aid deadline (priority):*** 3/1. ***Notification date:*** Continuous beginning 3/1. Students must reply within 8 weeks of notification.

CONTACT Kayla Pahlen, Interim Director of Financial Aid, University of Minnesota, Crookston, 4 Hill Hall, 2900 University Avenue, Crookston, MN 56716-5001, 218-281-8576 or toll-free 800-862-6466. *Fax:* 218-281-8575. *E-mail:* knott043@crk.umn.edu.
Website: http://www.umcrookston.edu/.

UNIVERSITY OF MINNESOTA, DULUTH

Duluth, MN

Tuition & fees (MN res): $13,681	Average undergraduate aid package: $13,203

ABOUT THE INSTITUTION State-supported, coed. ***Awards:*** certificates, bachelor's, master's, and doctoral degrees. 87 undergraduate majors. ***Total enrollment:*** 10,858. Undergraduates: 9,847. Freshmen: 2,043. Federal methodology is used as a basis for awarding need-based institutional aid.

UNDERGRADUATE EXPENSES for 2019–2020 *Application fee:* $40. ***Tuition, state resident:*** full-time $12,194; part-time $469 per credit hour. ***Tuition, nonresident:*** full-time $17,394; part-time $669 per credit hour. ***Required fees:*** full-time $1487. Full-time tuition and fees vary according to course load, program, and reciprocity agreements. Part-time tuition and fees vary according to course load, program, and reciprocity agreements. ***College room and board:*** $8374; ***Room only:*** $5366. Room and board charges vary according to board plan and housing facility.

FRESHMAN FINANCIAL AID (Fall 2018) 2010 applied for aid; of those 68% were deemed to have need. 98% of freshmen with need received aid; of those 31% had need fully met. ***Average percent of need met:*** 75% (excluding resources awarded to replace EFC). ***Average financial aid package:*** $13,620 (excluding resources awarded to replace EFC). 19% of all full-time freshmen had no need and received non-need-based gift aid.

UNDERGRADUATE FINANCIAL AID (Fall 2018) 7,057 applied for aid; of those 71% were deemed to have need. 98% of undergraduates with need received aid; of those 31% had need fully met. ***Average percent of need met:*** 73% (excluding resources awarded to replace EFC). ***Average financial aid package:*** $13,203 (excluding resources awarded to replace EFC). 16% of all full-time undergraduates had no need and received non-need-based gift aid.

GIFT AID (NEED-BASED) *Total amount:* $39,560,622 (26% federal, 35% state, 32% institutional, 7% external sources). ***Receiving aid:*** Freshmen: 57% (1,266); all full-time undergraduates: 51% (4,455). ***Average award:*** Freshmen: $8774; Undergraduates: $8578. ***Scholarships, grants, and awards:*** Federal Pell, FSEOG, state, private, college/university gift aid from institutional funds.

GIFT AID (NON-NEED-BASED) *Total amount:* $2,662,416 (1% state, 73% institutional, 26% external sources). ***Receiving aid:*** Freshmen: 14% (320). Undergraduates: 11% (985). ***Average award:*** Freshmen: $1605. Undergraduates: $2149. ***Scholarships, grants, and awards by category:*** *Academic interests/achievement:* general academic interests/achievements. ***Tuition waivers:*** Full or partial for children of alumni, employees or children of employees. ***ROTC:*** Air Force.

LOANS *Student loans:* $50,850,106 (72% need-based, 28% non-need-based). 73% of past graduating class borrowed through all loan programs. *Average indebtedness per student:* $30,687. ***Average need-based loan:*** Freshmen: $6767. Undergraduates: $6638. ***Parent loans:*** $5,581,628 (61% need-based, 39% non-need-based). ***Programs:*** Federal Direct (Subsidized and Unsubsidized Stafford, PLUS), state, college/university.

WORK-STUDY ***Federal work-study:*** Total amount: $847,440; 580 jobs averaging $1461. ***State or other work-study/employment:*** Total amount: $991,344 (100% need-based). 1,611 part-time jobs averaging $615.

ATHLETIC AWARDS Total amount: $1,487,679 (80% need-based, 20% non-need-based).

APPLYING FOR FINANCIAL AID ***Required financial aid form:*** FAFSA. ***Financial aid deadline:*** Continuous. ***Notification date:*** Continuous beginning 2/1.

CONTACT Ms. Brenda Herzig, Director of Financial Aid, University of Minnesota, Duluth, 10 University Drive, 184 Darland Administration Building, Duluth, MN 55812-2496, 218-726-8000 or toll-free 800-232-1339. *Fax:* 218-726-8219.
Website: http://www.d.umn.edu/.

UNIVERSITY OF MINNESOTA, MORRIS

Morris, MN

CONTACT Ms. Jill Beauregard, Director of Financial Aid, University of Minnesota, Morris, 600 East 4th Street, Morris, MN 56267, 320-589-6046 or toll-free 888-866-3382. *Fax:* 320-589-1673. *E-mail:* morrisfa@morris.umn.edu.
Website: http://www.morris.umn.edu/.

UNIVERSITY OF MINNESOTA ROCHESTER

Rochester, MN

CONTACT Financial Aid Office, University of Minnesota Rochester, 111 South Broadway, Suite 300, Rochester, MN 55904, 877-280-4699.
Website: http://www.r.umn.edu/.

UNIVERSITY OF MINNESOTA, TWIN CITIES CAMPUS

Minneapolis, MN

Tuition & fees (MN res): $15,027	Average undergraduate aid package: $14,347

ABOUT THE INSTITUTION State-supported, coed. ***Awards:*** certificates, diplomas, bachelor's, master's, and doctoral degrees. 119 undergraduate majors. ***Total enrollment:*** 51,327. Undergraduates: 35,165. Freshmen: 6,278. Federal methodology is used as a basis for awarding need-based institutional aid.

UNDERGRADUATE EXPENSES for 2019–2020 ***Application fee:*** $55. ***Tuition, state resident:*** full-time $13,318; part-time $512 per credit. ***Tuition, nonresident:*** full-time $31,616; part-time $984 per credit. ***Required fees:*** full-time $1709. Full-time tuition and fees vary according to program and reciprocity agreements. Part-time tuition and fees vary according to course load, program, and reciprocity agreements. ***College room and board:*** $10,768; ***Room only:*** $6278. Room and board charges vary according to board plan, housing facility, and location.

FRESHMAN FINANCIAL AID (Fall 2019, est.) 5095 applied for aid; of those 58% were deemed to have need. 99% of freshmen with need received aid; of those 27% had need fully met. ***Average percent of need met:*** 77% (excluding resources awarded to replace EFC). ***Average financial aid package:*** $14,956 (excluding resources awarded to replace EFC). 15% of all full-time freshmen had no need and received non-need-based gift aid.

UNDERGRADUATE FINANCIAL AID (Fall 2019, est.) 19,844 applied for aid; of those 68% were deemed to have need. 99% of undergraduates with need received aid; of those 25% had need fully met. ***Average percent of need met:*** 74% (excluding resources awarded to replace EFC). ***Average financial aid package:*** $14,347 (excluding resources awarded to replace EFC). 10% of all full-time undergraduates had no need and received non-need-based gift aid.

GIFT AID (NEED-BASED) ***Receiving aid:*** Freshmen: 42% (2,601); all full-time undergraduates: 40% (11,630). ***Average award:*** Freshmen: $12,676; Undergraduates: $11,235. ***Scholarships, grants, and awards:*** Federal Pell, FSEOG, state, private, college/university gift aid from institutional funds, Federal Nursing, ROTC Scholarships, academic merit scholarships.

GIFT AID (NON-NEED-BASED) ***Receiving aid:*** Freshmen: 5% (297). Undergraduates: 3% (984). ***Average award:*** Freshmen: $6116. Undergraduates: $5200. ***Scholarships, grants, and awards by category:*** *Academic interests/achievement:* agriculture, architecture, area/ethnic studies, biological sciences, business, communication, computer science, education, engineering/technologies, English, foreign languages, general academic interests/achievements, health fields, home economics, humanities, international studies, library science, mathematics, military science, physical sciences, premedicine, religion/biblical studies, social sciences. *Creative arts/performance:* applied art and design, general creative arts/performance. *Special achievements/activities:* hobbies/interests, leadership. *Special characteristics:* general special characteristics, local/state students, members of minority groups. ***Tuition waivers:*** Full or partial for senior citizens. ***ROTC:*** Army, Naval, Air Force.

LOANS ***Student loans:*** 55% of past graduating class borrowed through all loan programs. *Average indebtedness per student:* $27,077. ***Average need-based loan:*** Freshmen: $3289. Undergraduates: $4288. ***Programs:*** Federal Direct (Subsidized and Unsubsidized Stafford, PLUS), Perkins, Federal Nursing, state, college/university, Health Professions Student Loans (HPSL).

WORK-STUDY Federal work-study jobs available. ***State or other work-study/employment:*** Part-time jobs available.

APPLYING FOR FINANCIAL AID ***Required financial aid forms:*** FAFSA, institution's own form. ***Notification date:*** Continuous.

CONTACT Office of Student Finance, University of Minnesota, Twin Cities Campus, 200 Fraser Hall, 106 Pleasant Street SE, Minneapolis, MN 55455, 612-624-1111 or toll-free 800-752-1000. *Fax:* 612-624-9584. *E-mail:* onestop@umn.edu.
Website: http://www.twin-cities.umn.edu/.

UNIVERSITY OF MISSISSIPPI

Oxford, MS

Tuition & fees (MS res): $8828	Average undergraduate aid package: $12,094

ABOUT THE INSTITUTION State-supported, coed. ***Awards:*** certificates, bachelor's, master's, and doctoral degrees. 67 undergraduate majors. Federal methodology is used as a basis for awarding need-based institutional aid.

UNDERGRADUATE EXPENSES for 2019–2020 ***Tuition, state resident:*** full-time $8718; part-time $363 per credit hour. ***Tuition, nonresident:*** full-time $24,990; part-time $1041 per credit hour. ***Required fees:*** full-time $110. Full-time tuition and fees vary according to course load and program. Part-time tuition and fees vary according to course load and program. ***College room and board:*** $10,734; ***Room only:*** $6264. Room and board charges vary according to board plan and housing facility.

FRESHMAN FINANCIAL AID (Fall 2018) 2716 applied for aid; of those 68% were deemed to have need. 95% of freshmen with need received aid; of those 23% had need fully met. ***Average percent of need met:*** 79% (excluding resources awarded to replace EFC). ***Average financial aid package:*** $14,752 (excluding resources awarded to replace EFC). 28% of all full-time freshmen had no need and received non-need-based gift aid.

UNDERGRADUATE FINANCIAL AID (Fall 2018) 10,525 applied for aid; of those 76% were deemed to have need. 96% of undergraduates with need received aid; of those 15% had need fully met. ***Average percent of need met:*** 75% (excluding resources awarded to replace EFC). ***Average financial aid package:*** $12,094 (excluding resources awarded to replace EFC). 27% of all full-time undergraduates had no need and received non-need-based gift aid.

GIFT AID (NEED-BASED) ***Total amount:*** $66,677,118 (33% federal, 10% state, 54% institutional, 3% external sources). ***Receiving aid:*** Freshmen: 47% (1,583); all full-time undergraduates: 42% (6,754). ***Average award:*** Freshmen: $11,714; Undergraduates: $10,515. ***Scholarships, grants, and awards:*** Federal Pell, FSEOG, state, private, college/university gift aid from institutional funds.

GIFT AID (NON-NEED-BASED) ***Total amount:*** $58,367,321 (5% state, 92% institutional, 3% external sources). ***Receiving aid:*** Freshmen: 10% (339). Undergraduates: 6% (922). ***Average award:*** Freshmen: $11,047. Undergraduates: $10,841. ***Scholarships, grants, and awards by category:*** *Academic interests/*

achievement: 20,730 awards ($76,685,123 total): biological sciences, business, communication, computer science, education, engineering/technologies, English, foreign languages, general academic interests/achievements, health fields, home economics, humanities, international studies, mathematics, military science, physical sciences, premedicine, social sciences. *Creative arts/performance:* 1,006 awards ($1,457,230 total): applied art and design, cinema/film/broadcasting, creative writing, debating, journalism/ publications, music, performing arts, theater/drama. *Special achievements/activities:* 6,414 awards ($13,358,231 total): cheerleading/drum major, community service, general special achievements/activities, junior miss, leadership, memberships. *Special characteristics:* 5,956 awards ($22,095,566 total): adult students, children and siblings of alumni, children of faculty/staff, first-generation college students, general special characteristics, handicapped students, international students, local/state students, members of minority groups, out-of-state students, previous college experience, spouses of current students, veterans, veterans' children. ***Tuition waivers:*** Full or partial for children of alumni, employees or children of employees, senior citizens. ***ROTC:*** Army, Naval, Air Force.

LOANS *Student loans:* $71,799,741 (63% need-based, 37% non-need-based). 47% of past graduating class borrowed through all loan programs. *Average indebtedness per student:* $33,411. ***Average need-based loan:*** Freshmen: $3245. Undergraduates: $4567. ***Parent loans:*** $35,225,109 (47% need-based, 53% non-need-based). ***Programs:*** Federal Direct (Subsidized and Unsubsidized Stafford, PLUS), college/university, HPSL, Private Lender Loans.

WORK-STUDY *Federal work-study:* Total amount: $472,145; 353 jobs averaging $1338.

ATHLETIC AWARDS Total amount: $9,931,320 (41% need-based, 59% non-need-based).

APPLYING FOR FINANCIAL AID *Required financial aid form:* FAFSA. ***Financial aid deadline:*** 3/1. ***Notification date:*** Continuous beginning 4/1. Students must reply within 4 weeks of notification.

CONTACT Ms. Laura Diven-Brown, Director of Financial Aid, University of Mississippi, 257 Martindale Center, University, MS 38677, 662-915-5788 or toll-free 800-653-6477 (in-state). *Fax:* 662-915-1164. *E-mail:* ldivenbr@olemiss.edu.
Website: http://www.olemiss.edu/.

UNIVERSITY OF MISSISSIPPI MEDICAL CENTER

Jackson, MS

CONTACT Minetta Veazey, Administrative Secretary, University of Mississippi Medical Center, 2500 North State Street, Jackson, MS 39216, 601-984-1117. *Fax:* 601-984-6984. *E-mail:* mveazey@registrar.umsmed.edu.
Website: http://www.umc.edu/.

UNIVERSITY OF MISSOURI

Columbia, MO

CONTACT Nicholas Prewett, Director of Student Financial Aid, University of Missouri, 11 Jesse Hall, Columbia, MO 65211, 573-882-7506 or toll-free 800-225-6075 (in-state). *Fax:* 573-884-5335. *E-mail:* finaidinfo@missouri.edu.
Website: http://www.missouri.edu/.

UNIVERSITY OF MISSOURI–KANSAS CITY

Kansas City, MO

CONTACT Scott Young, Director of Financial Aid and Scholarships, University of Missouri–Kansas City, 5100 Rockhill Road, Kansas City, MO 64110-2499, 816-235-1154 or toll-free 800-775-8652. *Fax:* 816-235-5511. *E-mail:* youngsc@umkc.edu.
Website: http://www.umkc.edu/.

UNIVERSITY OF MISSOURI–ST. LOUIS

St. Louis, MO

Tuition & fees (MO res): $11,079	Average undergraduate aid package: $11,676

ABOUT THE INSTITUTION State-supported, coed. ***Awards:*** certificates, bachelor's, master's, and doctoral degrees. 42 undergraduate majors. ***Total enrollment:*** 16,007. Undergraduates: 13,045. Freshmen: 447. Federal methodology is used as a basis for awarding need-based institutional aid.

UNDERGRADUATE EXPENSES for 2019–2020 *Application fee:* $35. ***Tuition, state resident:*** full-time $11,079. ***Tuition, nonresident:*** full-time $29,295. Full-time tuition and fees vary according to course level, course load, location, program, and reciprocity agreements. Part-time tuition and fees vary according to course level, course load, location, program, and reciprocity agreements. ***College room and board:*** $9550; ***Room only:*** $5450. Room and board charges vary according to board plan and housing facility.

FRESHMAN FINANCIAL AID (Fall 2019, est.) 388 applied for aid; of those 82% were deemed to have need. 99% of freshmen with need received aid; of those 19% had need fully met. ***Average percent of need met:*** 74% (excluding resources awarded to replace EFC). ***Average financial aid package:*** $14,891 (excluding resources awarded to replace EFC). 11% of all full-time freshmen had no need and received non-need-based gift aid.

UNDERGRADUATE FINANCIAL AID (Fall 2019, est.) 3,925 applied for aid; of those 87% were deemed to have need. 98% of undergraduates with need received aid; of those 10% had need fully met. ***Average percent of need met:*** 61% (excluding resources awarded to replace EFC). ***Average financial aid package:*** $11,676 (excluding resources awarded to replace EFC). 6% of all full-time undergraduates had no need and received non-need-based gift aid.

GIFT AID (NEED-BASED) *Total amount:* $30,413,008 (40% federal, 11% state, 42% institutional, 7% external sources). ***Receiving aid:*** Freshmen: 71% (309); all full-time undergraduates: 62% (2,972). ***Average award:*** Freshmen: $11,913; Undergraduates: $8507. ***Scholarships, grants, and awards:*** Federal Pell, FSEOG, state, private, college/university gift aid from institutional funds, United Negro College Fund, Federal Nursing, TEACH Grants.

GIFT AID (NON-NEED-BASED) *Total amount:* $3,219,520 (2% federal, 6% state, 73% institutional, 19% external sources). ***Receiving aid:*** Freshmen: 11% (49). Undergraduates: 5% (230). ***Average award:*** Freshmen: $8413. Undergraduates: $5464. ***Scholarships, grants, and awards by category:*** *Academic interests/ achievement:* biological sciences, business, communication, computer science, education, engineering/technologies, English, foreign languages, general academic interests/ achievements, health fields, humanities, international studies, mathematics, physical sciences, premedicine, social sciences. *Creative arts/performance:* applied art and design, dance, music, theater/drama. *Special achievements/activities:* cheerleading/drum major, memberships. *Special characteristics:* adult students, children and siblings of alumni, children of faculty/staff, children with a deceased or disabled parent, ethnic background, first-generation college students, general special characteristics, international students, local/state students, members of minority groups, out-of-state students, previous college experience, spouses of deceased or disabled public servants, veterans. ***Tuition waivers:*** Full or partial for employees or children of employees, senior citizens. ***ROTC:*** Army cooperative, Air Force cooperative.

LOANS *Student loans:* $35,977,317 (79% need-based, 21% non-need-based). 54% of past graduating class borrowed through all loan programs. *Average indebtedness per student:* $25,110. ***Average need-based loan:*** Freshmen: $3011. Undergraduates: $4386. ***Parent loans:*** $1,750,553 (46% need-based, 54% non-need-based). ***Programs:*** Federal Direct (Subsidized and Unsubsidized Stafford, PLUS), Perkins, Federal Nursing, state.

WORK-STUDY *Federal work-study:* Total amount: $844,152; 199 jobs averaging $4329.

ATHLETIC AWARDS Total amount: $2,412,404 (82% need-based, 18% non-need-based).

APPLYING FOR FINANCIAL AID *Required financial aid form:* FAFSA. ***Financial aid deadline (priority):*** 2/1. ***Notification date:*** Continuous beginning 1/15.

CONTACT Ms. Svetlana Vejkovich, Associate Director, University of Missouri–St. Louis, One University Boulevard, 327 Millennium Student Center, St. Louis, MO 63121-4400, 314-516-5526 or toll-free 888-GO2-UMSL (in-state), 888-GO2-USML (out-of-state). *Fax:* 314-516-5408. *E-mail:* financialaid@umsl.edu.
Website: http://www.umsl.edu/.

UNIVERSITY OF MOBILE

Mobile, AL

Tuition & fees: $23,860 | **Average undergraduate aid package: $27,170**

ABOUT THE INSTITUTION Independent Southern Baptist, coed. ***Awards:*** associate, bachelor's, and master's degrees. 37 undergraduate majors. Federal methodology is used as a basis for awarding need-based institutional aid.

UNDERGRADUATE EXPENSES for 2019–2020 ***Comprehensive fee:*** $33,560 includes full-time tuition ($22,250), mandatory fees ($1610), and room and board ($9700). Full-time tuition and fees vary according to course load and program. Room and board charges vary according to board plan and housing facility. ***Part-time tuition:*** $795 per credit hour. ***Part-time fees:*** $160 per term.

FRESHMAN FINANCIAL AID (Fall 2019, est.) 212 applied for aid; of those 90% were deemed to have need. 100% of freshmen with need received aid; of those 27% had need fully met. ***Average percent of need met:*** 90% (excluding resources awarded to replace EFC). ***Average financial aid package:*** $28,622 (excluding resources awarded to replace EFC). 10% of all full-time freshmen had no need and received non-need-based gift aid.

UNDERGRADUATE FINANCIAL AID (Fall 2019, est.) 690 applied for aid; of those 92% were deemed to have need. 100% of undergraduates with need received aid; of those 22% had need fully met. ***Average percent of need met:*** 86% (excluding resources awarded to replace EFC). ***Average financial aid package:*** $27,170 (excluding resources awarded to replace EFC). 7% of all full-time undergraduates had no need and received non-need-based gift aid.

GIFT AID (NEED-BASED) ***Total amount:*** $1,555,517 (80% federal, 18% state, 2% institutional). ***Receiving aid:*** Freshmen: 52% (117); all full-time undergraduates: 45% (336). ***Average award:*** Freshmen: $5817; Undergraduates: $5792. ***Scholarships, grants, and awards:*** Federal Pell, FSEOG, state, private, college/university gift aid from institutional funds.

GIFT AID (NON-NEED-BASED) ***Total amount:*** $12,376,108 (99% institutional, 1% external sources). ***Receiving aid:*** Freshmen: 85% (191). Undergraduates: 84% (636). ***Average award:*** Freshmen: $16,056. Undergraduates: $15,980. ***Scholarships, grants, and awards by category:*** *Creative arts/performance:* art/fine arts, music, performing arts. *Special achievements/activities:* religious involvement. *Special characteristics:* children of faculty/staff, relatives of clergy. ***Tuition waivers:*** Full or partial for employees or children of employees. ***ROTC:*** Army cooperative, Air Force cooperative.

LOANS ***Student loans:*** $4,012,714 (100% need-based). 82% of past graduating class borrowed through all loan programs. *Average indebtedness per student:* $22,872. ***Average need-based loan:*** Freshmen: $8024. Undergraduates: $8513. ***Parent loans:*** $2,106,215 (100% non-need-based). ***Programs:*** Federal Direct (Subsidized and Unsubsidized Stafford, PLUS), Perkins.

WORK-STUDY ***Federal work-study:*** Total amount: $312,260; jobs available.

ATHLETIC AWARDS Total amount: $2,872,563 (100% non-need-based).

APPLYING FOR FINANCIAL AID ***Required financial aid form:*** FAFSA. ***Notification date:*** Continuous beginning 12/1. Students must reply within 3 weeks of notification.

CONTACT Mrs. Marie Thomas Batson, Associate Vice President for Enrollment, University of Mobile, 5735 College Parkway, Mobile, AL 36613, 251-442-2370 or toll-free 800-946-7267. *E-mail:* mbatson@umobile.edu.
Website: http://www.umobile.edu/.

UNIVERSITY OF MONTANA

Missoula, MT

Tuition & fees (MT res): $7354 | **Average undergraduate aid package: $11,977**

ABOUT THE INSTITUTION State-supported, coed. ***Awards:*** certificates, associate, bachelor's, master's, and doctoral degrees. 90 undergraduate majors. ***Total enrollment:*** 11,865. Undergraduates: 9,323. Freshmen: 1,681. Federal methodology is used as a basis for awarding need-based institutional aid.

UNDERGRADUATE EXPENSES for 2019–2020 ***Application fee:*** $36. ***Tuition, state resident:*** full-time $5352; part-time $223 per credit hour. ***Tuition, nonresident:*** full-time $24,216; part-time $1009 per credit hour. ***Required fees:*** full-time $2002; $92 per credit hour. Full-time tuition and fees vary according to degree level, location, program, reciprocity agreements, and student level. Part-time tuition and fees vary according to course load, degree level, location, and student level. ***College room and board:*** $9966. Room and board charges vary according to board plan and housing facility.

FRESHMAN FINANCIAL AID (Fall 2019, est.) 1114 applied for aid; of those 70% were deemed to have need. 100% of freshmen with need received aid; of those 12% had need fully met. ***Average percent of need met:*** 69% (excluding resources awarded to replace EFC). ***Average financial aid package:*** $12,398 (excluding resources awarded to replace EFC). 32% of all full-time freshmen had no need and received non-need-based gift aid.

UNDERGRADUATE FINANCIAL AID (Fall 2019, est.) 4,527 applied for aid; of those 79% were deemed to have need. 99% of undergraduates with need received aid; of those 11% had need fully met. ***Average percent of need met:*** 61% (excluding resources awarded to replace EFC). ***Average financial aid package:*** $11,977 (excluding resources awarded to replace EFC). 19% of all full-time undergraduates had no need and received non-need-based gift aid.

GIFT AID (NEED-BASED) ***Total amount:*** $16,400,491 (56% federal, 40% institutional, 4% external sources). ***Receiving aid:*** Freshmen: 33% (439); all full-time undergraduates: 36% (2,186). ***Average award:*** Freshmen: $5168; Undergraduates: $4991. ***Scholarships, grants, and awards:*** Federal Pell, FSEOG, state, private, college/university gift aid from institutional funds.

GIFT AID (NON-NEED-BASED) ***Total amount:*** $4,654,902 (93% institutional, 7% external sources). ***Receiving aid:*** Freshmen: 47% (623). Undergraduates: 30% (1,860). ***Average award:*** Freshmen: $4755. Undergraduates: $4708. ***Scholarships, grants, and awards by category:*** *Academic interests/achievement:* biological sciences, business, computer science, education, English, foreign languages, general academic interests/achievements, home economics, humanities, international studies, mathematics, military science, physical sciences, premedicine, social sciences. *Creative arts/performance:* creative writing, dance, journalism/publications, music, performing arts, theater/drama. *Special achievements/activities:* cheerleading/drum major, leadership, rodeo. *Special characteristics:* children and siblings of alumni, children with a deceased or disabled parent, general special characteristics, international students, local/state students, out-of-state students, veterans. ***Tuition waivers:*** Full or partial for minority students, employees or children of employees, senior citizens. ***ROTC:*** Army.

LOANS ***Student loans:*** $31,624,510 (78% need-based, 22% non-need-based). 58% of past graduating class borrowed through all loan programs. *Average indebtedness per student:* $27,132. ***Average need-based loan:*** Freshmen: $3385. Undergraduates: $4250. ***Parent loans:*** $34,138,362 (60% need-based, 40% non-need-based). ***Programs:*** Federal Direct (Subsidized and Unsubsidized Stafford, PLUS), Perkins.

WORK-STUDY ***Federal work-study:*** Total amount: $4,616,564; jobs available. ***State or other work-study/employment:*** Total amount: $562,696 (70% need-based, 30% non-need-based). Part-time jobs available.

ATHLETIC AWARDS Total amount: $1,438,342 (31% need-based, 69% non-need-based).

APPLYING FOR FINANCIAL AID ***Required financial aid forms:*** FAFSA, UM Supplemental Information Sheet. ***Financial aid deadline (priority):*** 12/1. ***Notification date:*** Continuous beginning 3/16. Students must reply within 4 weeks of notification.

CONTACT Ms. Emily Williamson, Director of Financial Aid, University of Montana, Lommasson Center 218, Missoula, MT 59812, 406-243-5504 or toll-free 800-462-8636. *Fax:* 406-243-4930. *E-mail:* faid@mso.umt.edu.
Website: http://www.umt.edu/.

THE UNIVERSITY OF MONTANA WESTERN

Dillon, MT

CONTACT Louise Driver, Director of Financial Aid, The University of Montana Western, 710 South Atlantic Street, Dillon, MT 59725, 406-683-7511 or toll-free 877-683-7331. *Fax:* 406-683-7510. *E-mail:* louise.driver@umwestern.edu.
Website: http://www.umwestern.edu/.

UNIVERSITY OF MONTEVALLO

Montevallo, AL

Tuition & fees (area res): $13,710 **Average undergraduate aid package: $12,666**

ABOUT THE INSTITUTION State-supported, coed. ***Awards:*** certificates, bachelor's, and master's degrees. 26 undergraduate majors. ***Total enrollment:*** 2,559. Undergraduates: 2,242. Freshmen: 493. Federal methodology is used as a basis for awarding need-based institutional aid.

UNDERGRADUATE EXPENSES for 2020–2021 ***Application fee:*** $30. ***Tuition, area resident:*** full-time $12,090. ***Tuition, state resident:*** full-time $12,090; part-time $403 per credit hour. ***Tuition, nonresident:*** full-time $25,110; part-time $837 per credit hour. ***Required fees:*** full-time $1620. Full-time tuition and fees vary according to course load and program. Part-time tuition and fees vary according to course load and program. ***College room and board:*** $9810; ***Room only:*** $6596. Room and board charges vary according to housing facility.

FRESHMAN FINANCIAL AID (Fall 2019, est.) 419 applied for aid; of those 78% were deemed to have need. 99% of freshmen with need received aid; of those 22% had need fully met. ***Average percent of need met:*** 60% (excluding resources awarded to replace EFC). ***Average financial aid package:*** $13,194 (excluding resources awarded to replace EFC). 29% of all full-time freshmen had no need and received non-need-based gift aid.

UNDERGRADUATE FINANCIAL AID (Fall 2019, est.) 1,638 applied for aid; of those 83% were deemed to have need. 100% of undergraduates with need received aid; of those 21% had need fully met. ***Average percent of need met:*** 57% (excluding resources awarded to replace EFC). ***Average financial aid package:*** $12,666 (excluding resources awarded to replace EFC). 25% of all full-time undergraduates had no need and received non-need-based gift aid.

GIFT AID (NEED-BASED) ***Total amount:*** $13,256,151 (34% federal, 6% state, 54% institutional, 6% external sources). ***Receiving aid:*** Freshmen: 66% (317); all full-time undergraduates: 62% (1,244). ***Average award:*** Freshmen: $11,384; Undergraduates: $10,154. ***Scholarships, grants, and awards:*** Federal Pell, FSEOG, state, private, college/university gift aid from institutional funds.

GIFT AID (NON-NEED-BASED) ***Total amount:*** $5,137,631 (4% state, 92% institutional, 4% external sources). ***Receiving aid:*** Freshmen: 17% (81). Undergraduates: 11% (223). ***Average award:*** Freshmen: $14,221. Undergraduates: $13,133. ***Scholarships, grants, and awards by category:*** *Academic interests/achievement:* 1,252 awards ($8,279,767 total): biological sciences, business, communication, education, English, foreign languages, general academic interests/achievements, home economics, humanities, mathematics, physical sciences, social sciences. *Creative arts/performance:* 123 awards ($324,817 total): applied art and design, cinema/film/broadcasting, creative writing, journalism/publications, music, theater/drama. *Special achievements/activities:* 483 awards ($1,882,967 total): cheerleading/drum major, hobbies/interests, junior miss, leadership, religious involvement. *Special characteristics:* 378 awards ($4,506,599 total): children of faculty/staff, international students, out-of-state students. ***Tuition waivers:*** Full or partial for employees or children of employees. ***ROTC:*** Army cooperative, Air Force cooperative.

LOANS ***Student loans:*** $10,068,556 (41% need-based, 59% non-need-based). 68% of past graduating class borrowed through all loan programs. *Average indebtedness per student:* $29,968. ***Average need-based loan:*** Freshmen: $3224. Undergraduates: $4038. ***Parent loans:*** $3,465,832 (89% need-based, 11% non-need-based). ***Programs:*** Federal Direct (Subsidized and Unsubsidized Stafford, PLUS).

WORK-STUDY ***Federal work-study:*** Total amount: $279,696; 118 jobs averaging $2303.

ATHLETIC AWARDS Total amount: $2,552,991 (43% need-based, 57% non-need-based).

APPLYING FOR FINANCIAL AID ***Required financial aid form:*** FAFSA. ***Financial aid deadline (priority):*** 3/1. ***Notification date:*** Continuous beginning 12/1.

CONTACT Ms. Nikki Bradbury, Director of Student Aid, University of Montevallo, Station 6050, Montevallo, AL 35115, 205-665-6044 or toll-free 800-292-4349. *Fax:* 205-665-6047. *E-mail:* bradburynp@montevallo.edu.
Website: http://www.montevallo.edu/.

UNIVERSITY OF MOUNT OLIVE

Mount Olive, NC

CONTACT Mrs. Katrina K. Lee, Director of Financial Aid, University of Mount Olive, 634 Henderson Street, Mount Olive, NC 28365, 919-658-2502 or toll-free 800-653-0854. *Fax:* 919-658-9816. *E-mail:* klee@umo.edu.
Website: http://www.umo.edu/.

UNIVERSITY OF MOUNT UNION

Alliance, OH

Tuition & fees: $31,700 **Average undergraduate aid package: $23,299**

ABOUT THE INSTITUTION Independent United Methodist, coed. ***Awards:*** bachelor's, master's, and doctoral degrees. 59 undergraduate majors. ***Total enrollment:*** 2,309. Undergraduates: 2,116. Freshmen: 617. Federal methodology is used as a basis for awarding need-based institutional aid.

UNDERGRADUATE EXPENSES for 2019–2020 ***Comprehensive fee:*** $42,200 includes full-time tuition ($31,300), mandatory fees ($400), and room and board ($10,500). ***College room only:*** $5200. Room and board charges vary according to board plan and housing facility. ***Part-time tuition:*** $1330 per credit hour. ***Part-time fees:*** $100 per term.

FRESHMAN FINANCIAL AID (Fall 2018) 606 applied for aid; of those 89% were deemed to have need. 100% of freshmen with need received aid; of those 19% had need fully met. ***Average percent of need met:*** 74% (excluding resources awarded to replace EFC). ***Average financial aid package:*** $23,639 (excluding resources awarded to replace EFC). 12% of all full-time freshmen had no need and received non-need-based gift aid.

UNDERGRADUATE FINANCIAL AID (Fall 2018) 1,859 applied for aid; of those 89% were deemed to have need. 100% of undergraduates with need received aid; of those 21% had need fully met. ***Average percent of need met:*** 76% (excluding resources awarded to replace EFC). ***Average financial aid package:*** $23,299 (excluding resources awarded to replace EFC). 17% of all full-time undergraduates had no need and received non-need-based gift aid.

GIFT AID (NEED-BASED) ***Total amount:*** $29,748,450 (10% federal, 4% state, 83% institutional, 3% external sources). ***Receiving aid:*** Freshmen: 86% (539); all full-time undergraduates: 79% (1,627). ***Average award:*** Freshmen: $19,442; Undergraduates: $18,268. ***Scholarships, grants, and awards:*** Federal Pell, FSEOG, state, private, college/university gift aid from institutional funds.

GIFT AID (NON-NEED-BASED) ***Total amount:*** $6,761,870 (95% institutional, 5% external sources). ***Receiving aid:*** Undergraduates: 10% (210). ***Average award:*** Freshmen: $16,091. Undergraduates: $14,360. ***Scholarships, grants, and awards by category:*** *Academic interests/achievement:* 1,656 awards ($20,774,727 total): general academic interests/achievements. *Creative arts/performance:* 130 awards ($777,905 total): art/fine arts, music, performing arts, theater/drama. *Special achievements/activities:* 113 awards ($642,225 total): cheerleading/drum major, general special achievements/activities, memberships. *Special characteristics:* 364 awards ($2,719,398 total): children and siblings of alumni, children of faculty/staff, ethnic background, first-generation college students, international students, members of minority groups, relatives of clergy, religious affiliation, veterans. ***Tuition waivers:*** Full or partial for employees or children of employees, senior citizens. ***ROTC:*** Army cooperative.

LOANS ***Student loans:*** $16,346,804 (65% need-based, 35% non-need-based). 83% of past graduating class borrowed through all loan programs. *Average indebtedness per student:* $40,112. ***Average need-based loan:*** Freshmen: $3170. Undergraduates: $4258. ***Parent loans:*** $6,804,245 (48% need-based, 52% non-need-based). ***Programs:*** Federal Direct (Subsidized and Unsubsidized Stafford, PLUS), state, college/university, private loans.

WORK-STUDY ***Federal work-study:*** Total amount: $201,284; 207 jobs averaging $970. ***State or other work-study/employment:*** Part-time jobs available.

APPLYING FOR FINANCIAL AID ***Required financial aid form:*** FAFSA. ***Financial aid deadline:*** Continuous. ***Notification date:*** Continuous beginning 12/1.

CONTACT Ms. Kathleen E Thomas, Director of Student Financial Aid, University of Mount Union, 1972 Clark Avenue, Alliance, OH 44601-3993, 330-823-2674 or toll-free 800-334-6682. *Fax:* 330-829-2814. *E-mail:* thomaska@mountunion.edu.
Website: http://www.mountunion.edu/.

UNIVERSITY OF NEBRASKA AT KEARNEY

Kearney, NE

Tuition & fees (NE res): $7701 **Average undergraduate aid package: $11,820**

ABOUT THE INSTITUTION State-supported, coed. ***Awards:*** certificates, bachelor's, and master's degrees. 38 undergraduate majors. ***Total enrollment:*** 6,279. Undergraduates: 4,429. Freshmen: 863. Federal methodology is used as a basis for awarding need-based institutional aid.

UNDERGRADUATE EXPENSES for 2019–2020 ***Application fee:*** $45. ***Tuition, state resident:*** full-time $6090; part-time $203 per credit hour. ***Tuition, nonresident:*** full-time $13,290; part-time $443 per credit hour. ***Required fees:*** full-time $1611. Full-time tuition and fees vary according to course level, course load, degree level, location, and program. Part-time tuition and fees vary according to course level, course load, degree level, location, and program. ***College room and board:*** $9942; ***Room only:*** $5156. Room and board charges vary according to board plan and housing facility.

FRESHMAN FINANCIAL AID (Fall 2018) 825 applied for aid; of those 83% were deemed to have need. 99% of freshmen with need received aid; of those 22% had need fully met. ***Average percent of need met:*** 72% (excluding resources awarded to replace EFC). ***Average financial aid package:*** $12,988 (excluding resources awarded to replace EFC). 16% of all full-time freshmen had no need and received non-need-based gift aid.

UNDERGRADUATE FINANCIAL AID (Fall 2018) 3,124 applied for aid; of those 85% were deemed to have need. 99% of undergraduates with need received aid; of those 20% had need fully met. ***Average percent of need met:*** 67% (excluding resources awarded to replace EFC). ***Average financial aid package:*** $11,820 (excluding resources awarded to replace EFC). 16% of all full-time undergraduates had no need and received non-need-based gift aid.

GIFT AID (NEED-BASED) ***Total amount:*** $22,760,129 (33% federal, 6% state, 40% institutional, 21% external sources). ***Receiving aid:*** Freshmen: 70% (661); all full-time undergraduates: 62% (2,413). ***Average award:*** Freshmen: $9823; Undergraduates: $9165. ***Scholarships, grants, and awards:*** Federal Pell, FSEOG, state, private, college/university gift aid from institutional funds.

GIFT AID (NON-NEED-BASED) ***Total amount:*** $5,359,175 (74% institutional, 26% external sources). ***Receiving aid:*** Freshmen: 10% (91). Undergraduates: 7% (285). ***Average award:*** Freshmen: $5516. Undergraduates: $5427. ***Scholarships, grants, and awards by category:*** *Academic interests/achievement:* communication, general academic interests/achievements, military science. *Creative arts/performance:* applied art and design, art/fine arts, debating, journalism/publications, music, theater/drama. *Special achievements/activities:* cheerleading/drum major, leadership. *Special characteristics:* children and siblings of alumni, children of faculty/staff, ethnic background, first-generation college students, international students, local/state students, members of minority groups, out-of-state students, veterans. ***Tuition waivers:*** Full or partial for employees or children of employees. ***ROTC:*** Army.

LOANS ***Student loans:*** $12,490,281 (73% need-based, 27% non-need-based). 55% of past graduating class borrowed through all loan programs. *Average indebtedness per student:* $20,774. ***Average need-based loan:*** Freshmen: $3099. Undergraduates: $3715. ***Parent loans:*** $3,662,608 (32% need-based, 68% non-need-based). ***Programs:*** Federal Direct (Subsidized and Unsubsidized Stafford, PLUS), college/university.

WORK-STUDY ***Federal work-study:*** Total amount: $1,039,994; jobs available.

ATHLETIC AWARDS Total amount: $2,016,755 (34% need-based, 66% non-need-based).

APPLYING FOR FINANCIAL AID ***Required financial aid form:*** FAFSA. ***Financial aid deadline (priority):*** 4/1. ***Notification date:*** Continuous beginning 3/15.

CONTACT Mary Sommers, Financial Aid Office, University of Nebraska at Kearney, Memorial Student Affairs Building, 2510 11th Avenue, Kearney, NE 68849-0001, 308-865-8520 or toll-free 800-532-7639. *Fax:* 308-865-8096. *E-mail:* finaid1@unk.edu. *Website:* http://www.unk.edu/.

UNIVERSITY OF NEBRASKA AT OMAHA

Omaha, NE

Tuition & fees: N/R **Average undergraduate aid package: $10,398**

ABOUT THE INSTITUTION State-supported, coed. ***Awards:*** certificates, bachelor's, master's, and doctoral degrees. 84 undergraduate majors. Federal methodology is used as a basis for awarding need-based institutional aid.

FRESHMAN FINANCIAL AID (Fall 2018) 1780 applied for aid; of those 84% were deemed to have need. 95% of freshmen with need received aid; of those 22% had need fully met. ***Average percent of need met:*** 60% (excluding resources awarded to replace EFC). ***Average financial aid package:*** $10,260 (excluding resources awarded to replace EFC).

UNDERGRADUATE FINANCIAL AID (Fall 2018) 6,923 applied for aid; of those 86% were deemed to have need. 96% of undergraduates with need received aid; of those 21% had need fully met. ***Average percent of need met:*** 64% (excluding resources awarded to replace EFC). ***Average financial aid package:*** $10,398 (excluding resources awarded to replace EFC).

GIFT AID (NEED-BASED) ***Total amount:*** $51,796,148 (37% federal, 9% state, 27% institutional, 27% external sources). ***Receiving aid:*** Freshmen: 902; all full-time undergraduates: 3,846. ***Average award:*** Freshmen: $7632; Undergraduates: $6918. ***Scholarships, grants, and awards:*** Federal Pell, FSEOG, state, private, college/university gift aid from institutional funds.

GIFT AID (NON-NEED-BASED) ***Average award:*** Freshmen: $4310. Undergraduates: $4857. ***Scholarships, grants, and awards by category:*** *Academic interests/achievement:* biological sciences, business, communication, computer science, education, engineering/technologies, English, foreign languages, general academic interests/achievements, home economics, mathematics, physical sciences, premedicine, social sciences. *Creative arts/performance:* art/fine arts, creative writing, debating, journalism/publications, music, performing arts, theater/drama. *Special achievements/activities:* general special achievements/activities, leadership, memberships. *Special characteristics:* adult students, children and siblings of alumni, children of faculty/staff, ethnic background, first-generation college students, handicapped students, international students, members of minority groups, out-of-state students, veterans' children. ***ROTC:*** Army cooperative, Air Force.

LOANS ***Student loans:*** $31,984,856 (41% need-based, 59% non-need-based). 59% of past graduating class borrowed through all loan programs. *Average indebtedness per student:* $25,804. ***Average need-based loan:*** Freshmen: $3085. Undergraduates: $3825. ***Parent loans:*** $9,920,189 (100% non-need-based). ***Programs:*** Federal Direct (Subsidized and Unsubsidized Stafford, PLUS).

WORK-STUDY ***Federal work-study:*** Total amount: $550,328; jobs available.

ATHLETIC AWARDS Total amount: $1,752,269 (100% need-based).

APPLYING FOR FINANCIAL AID ***Required financial aid form:*** FAFSA. ***Financial aid deadline (priority):*** 4/1. ***Notification date:*** Continuous.

CONTACT Marty Habrock, Office of Financial Aid, University of Nebraska at Omaha, 103 Eppley Administration Building, Omaha, NE 68182-0187, 402-554-2327 or toll-free 800-858-8648 (in-state). *Fax:* 402-554-3472. *E-mail:* finaid@unomaha.edu. *Website:* http://www.unomaha.edu/.

UNIVERSITY OF NEBRASKA–LINCOLN

Lincoln, NE

Tuition & fees (NE res): $9366 **Average undergraduate aid package: $14,935**

ABOUT THE INSTITUTION State-supported, coed. ***Awards:*** certificates, bachelor's, master's, and doctoral degrees. 121 undergraduate majors. ***Total enrollment:*** 25,390. Undergraduates: 20,478. Freshmen: 4,775. Both federal and institutional methodology are used as a basis for awarding need-based institutional aid.

UNDERGRADUATE EXPENSES for 2019–2020 ***Application fee:*** $45. ***Tuition, state resident:*** full-time $7560; part-time $252 per credit hour. ***Tuition, nonresident:*** full-time $24,000; part-time $800 per credit hour. ***Required fees:*** full-time $1806; $398 per term. Full-time tuition and fees vary according to course load, location, program, and reciprocity agreements. Part-time tuition and fees vary according to course load, location, program, and reciprocity agreements. ***College***

room and board: $11,830. Room and board charges vary according to board plan and housing facility.

FRESHMAN FINANCIAL AID (Fall 2018) 4261 applied for aid; of those 65% were deemed to have need. 99% of freshmen with need received aid; of those 21% had need fully met. ***Average percent of need met:*** 77% (excluding resources awarded to replace EFC). ***Average financial aid package:*** $15,543 (excluding resources awarded to replace EFC). 17% of all full-time freshmen had no need and received non-need-based gift aid.

UNDERGRADUATE FINANCIAL AID (Fall 2018) 14,397 applied for aid; of those 63% were deemed to have need. 98% of undergraduates with need received aid; of those 17% had need fully met. ***Average percent of need met:*** 71% (excluding resources awarded to replace EFC). ***Average financial aid package:*** $14,935 (excluding resources awarded to replace EFC). 9% of all full-time undergraduates had no need and received non-need-based gift aid.

GIFT AID (NEED-BASED) ***Total amount:*** $79,771,881 (27% federal, 5% state, 49% institutional, 19% external sources). ***Receiving aid:*** Freshmen: 53% (2,524); all full-time undergraduates: 40% (7,708). ***Average award:*** Freshmen: $8781; Undergraduates: $8304. ***Scholarships, grants, and awards:*** Federal Pell, FSEOG, state, private, college/university gift aid from institutional funds.

GIFT AID (NON-NEED-BASED) ***Total amount:*** $46,077,176 (92% institutional, 8% external sources). ***Receiving aid:*** Freshmen: 7% (325). Undergraduates: 4% (739). ***Average award:*** Freshmen: $7766. Undergraduates: $8044. ***Scholarships, grants, and awards by category:*** *Academic interests/achievement:* agriculture, architecture, biological sciences, business, computer science, education, engineering/technologies, English, foreign languages, general academic interests/achievements, health fields, home economics, humanities, international studies, mathematics, physical sciences, premedicine, social sciences. *Creative arts/performance:* applied art and design, cinema/film/broadcasting, dance, journalism/publications, music, performing arts, theater/drama. *Special achievements/activities:* cheerleading/drum major, community service, leadership. *Special characteristics:* children and siblings of alumni, ethnic background, handicapped students, international students, members of minority groups, out-of-state students. ***Tuition waivers:*** Full or partial for employees or children of employees. ***ROTC:*** Army, Naval, Air Force.

LOANS ***Student loans:*** $49,587,060 (76% need-based, 24% non-need-based). 55% of past graduating class borrowed through all loan programs. *Average indebtedness per student:* $22,290. ***Average need-based loan:*** Freshmen: $3437. Undergraduates: $4156. ***Parent loans:*** $34,202,554 (57% need-based, 43% non-need-based). ***Programs:*** Federal Direct (Subsidized and Unsubsidized Stafford, PLUS), Perkins, college/university.

WORK-STUDY ***Federal work-study:*** Total amount: $3,382,492; jobs available.

ATHLETIC AWARDS Total amount: $10,284,744 (100% non-need-based).

APPLYING FOR FINANCIAL AID ***Required financial aid form:*** FAFSA. ***Financial aid deadline (priority):*** 4/1. ***Notification date:*** Continuous beginning 12/15.

CONTACT Ms. Jo Tederman, Assistant Director of Scholarships and Financial Aid, University of Nebraska–Lincoln, 12 Canfield Administration Building, Lincoln, NE 68588-0411, 402-472-2030 or toll-free 800-742-8800. *Fax:* 402-472-9826. *Website:* http://www.unl.edu/.

UNIVERSITY OF NEBRASKA MEDICAL CENTER

Omaha, NE

CONTACT Judy D. Walker, Director of Financial Aid, University of Nebraska Medical Center, 984265 Nebraska Medical Center, Omaha, NE 68198-4265, 402-559-6409 or toll-free 800-626-8431 Ext.6468. *Fax:* 402-559-6796. *E-mail:* jdwalker@unmc.edu. *Website:* http://www.unmc.edu/.

UNIVERSITY OF NEVADA, LAS VEGAS

Las Vegas, NV

Tuition & fees (NV res): $7986	Average undergraduate aid package: $8503

ABOUT THE INSTITUTION State-supported, coed. ***Awards:*** certificates, bachelor's, master's, and doctoral degrees. 85 undergraduate majors. ***Total enrollment:*** 30,457. Undergraduates: 25,282. Freshmen: 3,964. Federal methodology is used as a basis for awarding need-based institutional aid.

UNDERGRADUATE EXPENSES for 2020–2021 ***Application fee:*** $60. ***One-time required fee:*** $120. ***Tuition, state resident:*** full-time $7268; part-time $242 per credit hour. ***Tuition, nonresident:*** full-time $22,920; part-time $509 per credit hour. ***Required fees:*** full-time $718; $361 per term. Full-time tuition and fees vary according to course level, program, and reciprocity agreements. Part-time tuition and fees vary according to course level, program, and reciprocity agreements. ***College room and board:*** $10,924; ***Room only:*** $5892. Room and board charges vary according to board plan and housing facility.

FRESHMAN FINANCIAL AID (Fall 2019, est.) 3905 applied for aid; of those 76% were deemed to have need. 97% of freshmen with need received aid; of those 11% had need fully met. ***Average percent of need met:*** 72% (excluding resources awarded to replace EFC). ***Average financial aid package:*** $8437 (excluding resources awarded to replace EFC). 17% of all full-time freshmen had no need and received non-need-based gift aid.

UNDERGRADUATE FINANCIAL AID (Fall 2019, est.) 15,036 applied for aid; of those 82% were deemed to have need. 95% of undergraduates with need received aid; of those 9% had need fully met. ***Average percent of need met:*** 68% (excluding resources awarded to replace EFC). ***Average financial aid package:*** $8503 (excluding resources awarded to replace EFC). 9% of all full-time undergraduates had no need and received non-need-based gift aid.

GIFT AID (NEED-BASED) ***Total amount:*** $88,078,894 (55% federal, 17% state, 20% institutional, 8% external sources). ***Receiving aid:*** Freshmen: 51% (2,241); all full-time undergraduates: 45% (8,726). ***Average award:*** Freshmen: $6397; Undergraduates: $6214. ***Scholarships, grants, and awards:*** Federal Pell, FSEOG, state, private, college/university gift aid from institutional funds.

GIFT AID (NON-NEED-BASED) ***Total amount:*** $12,526,326 (5% federal, 47% state, 34% institutional, 14% external sources). ***Receiving aid:*** Freshmen: 54% (2,351). Undergraduates: 37% (7,240). ***Average award:*** Freshmen: $3836. Undergraduates: $3637. ***Scholarships, grants, and awards by category:*** *Academic interests/achievement:* architecture, biological sciences, business, communication, computer science, education, engineering/technologies, English, foreign languages, general academic interests/achievements, health fields, humanities, international studies, mathematics, physical sciences, premedicine, social sciences. *Creative arts/performance:* applied art and design, art/fine arts, cinema/film/broadcasting, creative writing, dance, debating, general creative arts/performance, journalism/publications, music, performing arts, theater/drama. *Special achievements/activities:* cheerleading/drum major, community service, general special achievements/activities, leadership, rodeo. *Special characteristics:* adult students, children and siblings of alumni, children of faculty/staff, children of public servants, children of union members/company employees, children with a deceased or disabled parent, ethnic background, first-generation college students, general special characteristics, handicapped students, international students, local/state students, members of minority groups, out-of-state students, previous college experience, veterans, veterans' children. ***Tuition waivers:*** Full or partial for employees or children of employees. ***ROTC:*** Army, Air Force.

LOANS ***Student loans:*** $86,443,289 (66% need-based, 34% non-need-based). 43% of past graduating class borrowed through all loan programs. *Average indebtedness per student:* $19,605. ***Average need-based loan:*** Freshmen: $3296. Undergraduates: $4134. ***Parent loans:*** $24,675,678 (46% need-based, 54% non-need-based). ***Programs:*** Federal Direct (Subsidized and Unsubsidized Stafford, PLUS), Perkins, Federal Nursing, college/university.

WORK-STUDY ***Federal work-study:*** Total amount: $1,630,045; jobs available. ***State or other work-study/employment:*** Total amount: $249,200 (43% need-based, 57% non-need-based). Part-time jobs available.

ATHLETIC AWARDS Total amount: $6,829,906 (91% need-based, 9% non-need-based).

APPLYING FOR FINANCIAL AID ***Required financial aid form:*** FAFSA. ***Financial aid deadline (priority):*** 11/1. ***Notification date:*** Continuous beginning 4/1. Students must reply within 6 weeks of notification.

CONTACT Vierissi Flynn, Interim Director of Financial Aid and Scholarships, University of Nevada, Las Vegas, 4505 South Maryland Parkway, Las Vegas, NV 89154-2016, 833-318-1228. *Fax:* 702-895-1353.
Website: http://www.unlv.edu/.

UNIVERSITY OF NEVADA, RENO

Reno, NV

Tuition & fees (NV res): $8452	Average undergraduate aid package: $9500

ABOUT THE INSTITUTION State-supported, coed. ***Awards:*** certificates, bachelor's, master's, and doctoral degrees. 78 undergraduate majors. ***Total enrollment:*** 21,003. Undergraduates: 17,307. Freshmen: 3,144. Both federal and institutional methodology are used as a basis for awarding need-based institutional aid.

UNDERGRADUATE EXPENSES for 2020–2021 ***Application fee:*** $60. ***Tuition, state resident:*** full-time $7688; part-time $256 per credit hour. ***Tuition, nonresident:*** full-time $23,341; part-time $780 per credit hour. ***Required fees:*** full-time $764; $282 per term. Full-time tuition and fees vary according to course level, course load, degree level, and program. Part-time tuition and fees vary according to course level, course load, degree level, and program. ***College room and board:*** $10,686; ***Room only:*** $6100. Room and board charges vary according to board plan and housing facility.

FRESHMAN FINANCIAL AID (Fall 2018) 2779 applied for aid; of those 70% were deemed to have need. 100% of freshmen with need received aid; of those 13% had need fully met. ***Average percent of need met:*** 58% (excluding resources awarded to replace EFC). ***Average financial aid package:*** $9480 (excluding resources awarded to replace EFC). 18% of all full-time freshmen had no need and received non-need-based gift aid.

UNDERGRADUATE FINANCIAL AID (Fall 2018) 10,036 applied for aid; of those 77% were deemed to have need. 100% of undergraduates with need received aid; of those 11% had need fully met. ***Average percent of need met:*** 55% (excluding resources awarded to replace EFC). ***Average financial aid package:*** $9500 (excluding resources awarded to replace EFC). 11% of all full-time undergraduates had no need and received non-need-based gift aid.

GIFT AID (NEED-BASED) ***Total amount:*** $53,180,720 (39% federal, 23% state, 32% institutional, 6% external sources). ***Receiving aid:*** Freshmen: 49% (1,795); all full-time undergraduates: 45% (6,777). ***Average award:*** Freshmen: $8150; Undergraduates: $7750. ***Scholarships, grants, and awards:*** Federal Pell, FSEOG, state, private, college/university gift aid from institutional funds.

GIFT AID (NON-NEED-BASED) ***Total amount:*** $14,364,897 (57% state, 32% institutional, 11% external sources). ***Receiving aid:*** Freshmen: 44% (1,605). Undergraduates: 32% (4,862). ***Average award:*** Freshmen: $3365. Undergraduates: $3310. ***Scholarships, grants, and awards by category:*** *Academic interests/achievement:* agriculture, biological sciences, business, communication, computer science, education, engineering/technologies, English, foreign languages, general academic interests/achievements, home economics, mathematics, physical sciences. *Creative arts/performance:* applied art and design, general creative arts/performance, journalism/publications, theater/drama. *Special characteristics:* adult students, children and siblings of alumni, ethnic background, first-generation college students, married students. ***Tuition waivers:*** Full or partial for employees or children of employees, senior citizens. ***ROTC:*** Army.

LOANS ***Student loans:*** $44,895,827 (76% need-based, 24% non-need-based). 48% of past graduating class borrowed through all loan programs. *Average indebtedness per student:* $22,418. ***Average need-based loan:*** Freshmen: $3410. Undergraduates: $4155. ***Parent loans:*** $17,732,304 (74% need-based, 26% non-need-based). ***Programs:*** Federal Direct (Subsidized and Unsubsidized Stafford, PLUS), Perkins, Federal Nursing, college/university.

WORK-STUDY ***Federal work-study:*** Total amount: $708,073; jobs available. ***State or other work-study/employment:*** Total amount: $147,092 (29% need-based, 71% non-need-based). Part-time jobs available.

ATHLETIC AWARDS Total amount: $8,098,742 (38% need-based, 62% non-need-based).

APPLYING FOR FINANCIAL AID ***Required financial aid forms:*** FAFSA, institution's own form. ***Financial aid deadline (priority):*** 2/1. ***Notification date:*** Continuous beginning 3/1. Students must reply by 5/1.

CONTACT Mr. Tom Wolfe, Director of Student Financial Aid, University of Nevada, Reno, Mail Stop 076, Reno, NV 89557, 775-784-4666 or toll-free 866-263-8232. *Fax:* 775-784-1025. *E-mail:* tawolfe@unr.edu.
Website: http://www.unr.edu/.

UNIVERSITY OF NEW ENGLAND

Biddeford, ME

ABOUT THE INSTITUTION Independent, coed. ***Awards:*** certificates, bachelor's, master's, and doctoral degrees. 40 undergraduate majors. ***Total enrollment:*** 7,483. Undergraduates: 4,275. Freshmen: 712.

GIFT AID (NEED-BASED) ***Scholarships, grants, and awards:*** Federal Pell, FSEOG, state, private, college/university gift aid from institutional funds.

GIFT AID (NON-NEED-BASED) ***Scholarships, grants, and awards by category:*** *Academic interests/achievement:* general academic interests/achievements. *Special achievements/activities:* leadership. *Special characteristics:* children and siblings of alumni, siblings of current students.

LOANS ***Programs:*** Federal Direct (Subsidized and Unsubsidized Stafford, PLUS), Perkins, Federal Nursing, state.

WORK-STUDY Federal work-study jobs available. ***State or other work-study/employment:*** Part-time jobs available.

APPLYING FOR FINANCIAL AID ***Required financial aid form:*** FAFSA.

CONTACT Paul Henderson, Assistant Vice President of Student Financial Services, University of New England, 11 Hills Beach Road, Biddeford, ME 04005, 207-602-2302 or toll-free 800-477-4863. *Fax:* 207-602-5968. *E-mail:* phenderson@une.edu.
Website: http://www.une.edu/.

UNIVERSITY OF NEW HAMPSHIRE

Durham, NH

Tuition & fees (area res): $18,938	Average undergraduate aid package: $24,851

ABOUT THE INSTITUTION State-supported, coed. ***Awards:*** certificates, associate, bachelor's, master's, and doctoral degrees. 86 undergraduate majors. ***Total enrollment:*** 14,784. Undergraduates: 12,202. Freshmen: 2,731. Federal methodology is used as a basis for awarding need-based institutional aid.

UNDERGRADUATE EXPENSES for 2020–2021 ***Application fee:*** $50. ***Tuition, area resident:*** full-time $15,520; part-time $645 per credit hour. ***Tuition, state resident:*** full-time $15,520; part-time $645 per credit hour. ***Tuition, nonresident:*** full-time $32,860; part-time $1368 per credit hour. ***Required fees:*** full-time $3418. Full-time tuition and fees vary according to program. Part-time tuition and fees vary according to course load and program. ***College room and board:*** $12,242; ***Room only:*** $7660. Room and board charges vary according to board plan and housing facility.

FRESHMAN FINANCIAL AID (Fall 2018) 2650 applied for aid; of those 80% were deemed to have need. 100% of freshmen with need received aid; of those 17% had need fully met. ***Average percent of need met:*** 76% (excluding resources awarded to replace EFC). ***Average financial aid package:*** $24,541 (excluding resources awarded to replace EFC). 18% of all full-time freshmen had no need and received non-need-based gift aid.

UNDERGRADUATE FINANCIAL AID (Fall 2018) 9,743 applied for aid; of those 83% were deemed to have need. 99% of undergraduates with need received aid; of those 16% had need fully met. ***Average percent of need met:*** 75% (excluding resources awarded to replace EFC). ***Average financial aid package:*** $24,851 (excluding resources awarded to replace EFC). 17% of all full-time undergraduates had no need and received non-need-based gift aid.

GIFT AID (NEED-BASED) ***Total amount:*** $84,451,844 (17% federal, 74% institutional, 9% external sources). ***Receiving aid:*** Freshmen: 68% (1,975); all full-time undergraduates: 54% (6,625). ***Average award:*** Freshmen: $7116; Undergraduates: $6230. ***Scholarships, grants, and awards:*** Federal Pell, FSEOG, state, private, college/university gift aid from institutional funds, Veteran's Benefits.

GIFT AID (NON-NEED-BASED) ***Total amount:*** $25,622,320 (100% institutional). ***Receiving aid:*** Freshmen: 9% (263). Undergraduates: 5% (648). ***Average award:*** Freshmen: $5749. Undergraduates: $6654. ***Scholarships, grants, and awards by category:*** *Academic interests/achievement:* agriculture, biological sciences, business, computer science, education, engineering/technologies, English, foreign languages, general academic interests/achievements, home economics, humanities, mathematics, military science, physical sciences. *Creative arts/performance:* applied art and design, dance, music, performing arts, theater/drama. *Special achievements/activities:* community service, leadership. *Special characteristics:* children and siblings of alumni, children of faculty/staff, handicapped students, international students, local/state students. ***Tuition waivers:*** Full or partial for employees or children of employees. ***ROTC:*** Army, Air Force.

LOANS ***Student loans:*** $112,124,939 (27% need-based, 73% non-need-based). 80% of past graduating class borrowed through all loan programs. *Average indebtedness per student:* $42,246. ***Average need-based loan:*** Freshmen: $2809. Undergraduates: $3467. ***Parent loans:*** $29,338,990 (100% non-need-based). ***Programs:*** Federal Direct (Subsidized and Unsubsidized Stafford, PLUS).

WORK-STUDY ***Federal work-study:*** Total amount: $15,882,244; 6,139 jobs averaging $2467. ***State or other work-study/employment:*** Total amount: $6,616,431 (100% non-need-based). 3,174 part-time jobs averaging $3971.

ATHLETIC AWARDS Total amount: $9,998,555 (100% non-need-based).

APPLYING FOR FINANCIAL AID ***Required financial aid form:*** FAFSA. ***Financial aid deadline (priority):*** 3/1. ***Notification date:*** Continuous beginning 12/1. Students must reply by 5/1.

CONTACT Mr. Joel B. Carstens, Director of Financial Aid, University of New Hampshire, 11 Garrison Avenue, Durham, NH 03824, 603-862-3600. *Fax:* 603-862-1947. *E-mail:* financial.aid@unh.edu.
Website: http://www.unh.edu/.

UNIVERSITY OF NEW HAMPSHIRE AT MANCHESTER

Manchester, NH

Tuition & fees: N/R	Average undergraduate aid package: $14,253

ABOUT THE INSTITUTION State-supported, coed. ***Awards:*** associate, bachelor's, and master's degrees. 21 undergraduate majors. Federal methodology is used as a basis for awarding need-based institutional aid.

FRESHMAN FINANCIAL AID (Fall 2018) 92 applied for aid; of those 76% were deemed to have need. 100% of freshmen with need received aid; of those 11% had need fully met. ***Average percent of need met:*** 67% (excluding resources awarded to replace EFC). ***Average financial aid package:*** $14,311 (excluding resources awarded to replace EFC). 7% of all full-time freshmen had no need and received non-need-based gift aid.

UNDERGRADUATE FINANCIAL AID (Fall 2018) 566 applied for aid; of those 82% were deemed to have need. 99% of undergraduates with need received aid; of those 8% had need fully met. ***Average percent of need met:*** 58% (excluding resources awarded to replace EFC). ***Average financial aid package:*** $14,253 (excluding resources awarded to replace EFC). 4% of all full-time undergraduates had no need and received non-need-based gift aid.

GIFT AID (NEED-BASED) ***Total amount:*** $2,382,795 (47% federal, 47% institutional, 6% external sources). ***Receiving aid:*** Freshmen: 55% (52); all full-time undergraduates: 44% (307). ***Average award:*** Freshmen: $2900; Undergraduates: $2182. ***Scholarships, grants, and awards:*** Federal Pell, FSEOG, state, private, college/university gift aid from institutional funds, Veterans Education Benefits (GI Bill).

GIFT AID (NON-NEED-BASED) ***Total amount:*** $303,197 (100% institutional). ***Receiving aid:*** Freshmen: 7% (7). Undergraduates: 3% (23). ***Average award:*** Freshmen: $3000. Undergraduates: $2559. ***Scholarships, grants, and awards by category:*** *Academic interests/achievement:* biological sciences, business, communication, computer science, engineering/technologies, English, general academic interests/achievements, humanities. *Special characteristics:* children of faculty/staff. ***ROTC:*** Army cooperative, Air Force cooperative.

LOANS ***Student loans:*** $3,574,707 (37% need-based, 63% non-need-based). 82% of past graduating class borrowed through all loan programs. *Average indebtedness per student:* $35,130. ***Average need-based loan:*** Freshmen: $2390. Undergraduates: $3991. ***Parent loans:*** $331,931 (100% non-need-based). ***Programs:*** Federal Direct (Subsidized and Unsubsidized Stafford, PLUS), Perkins, state, college/university.

WORK-STUDY ***Federal work-study:*** Total amount: $531,580; 236 jobs averaging $2343.

APPLYING FOR FINANCIAL AID ***Required financial aid form:*** FAFSA. ***Financial aid deadline (priority):*** 3/1. ***Notification date:*** Continuous beginning 12/1.

CONTACT Sharon Eaton, Associate Director of Financial Aid, University of New Hampshire at Manchester, 400 Commercial Street, Student Services Suite, 4th Floor, Manchester, NH 03101-1113, 603-641-4114. *Fax:* 603-641-4125.
Website: http://manchester.unh.edu/.

UNIVERSITY OF NEW HAVEN

West Haven, CT

Tuition & fees: $40,440	Average undergraduate aid package: $24,714

ABOUT THE INSTITUTION Independent, coed. ***Awards:*** certificates, associate, bachelor's, master's, and doctoral degrees. 62 undergraduate majors. ***Total enrollment:*** 6,793. Undergraduates: 4,912. Freshmen: 1,285. Federal methodology is used as a basis for awarding need-based institutional aid.

UNDERGRADUATE EXPENSES for 2019–2020 ***Application fee:*** $50. ***Comprehensive fee:*** $56,800 includes full-time tuition ($39,000), mandatory fees ($1440), and room and board ($16,360). ***College room only:*** $10,450. Full-time tuition and fees vary according to course load and program. Room and board charges vary according to board plan and housing facility. ***Part-time tuition:*** $1300 per credit hour. ***Part-time fees:*** $145 per term. Part-time tuition and fees vary according to class time, course load, and program.

FRESHMAN FINANCIAL AID (Fall 2019, est.) 1181 applied for aid; of those 89% were deemed to have need. 100% of freshmen with need received aid; of those 14% had need fully met. ***Average percent of need met:*** 60% (excluding resources awarded to replace EFC). ***Average financial aid package:*** $25,679 (excluding resources awarded to replace EFC). 14% of all full-time freshmen had no need and received non-need-based gift aid.

UNDERGRADUATE FINANCIAL AID (Fall 2019, est.) 4,034 applied for aid; of those 90% were deemed to have need. 100% of undergraduates with need received aid; of those 15% had need fully met. ***Average percent of need met:*** 59% (excluding resources awarded to replace EFC). ***Average financial aid package:*** $24,714 (excluding resources awarded to replace EFC). 15% of all full-time undergraduates had no need and received non-need-based gift aid.

GIFT AID (NEED-BASED) ***Total amount:*** $73,874,187 (9% federal, 1% state, 88% institutional, 2% external sources). ***Receiving aid:*** Freshmen: 82% (1,048); all full-time undergraduates: 78% (3,603). ***Average award:*** Freshmen: $22,933; Undergraduates: $21,357. ***Scholarships, grants, and awards:*** Federal Pell, FSEOG, state, private, college/university gift aid from institutional funds.

GIFT AID (NON-NEED-BASED) ***Total amount:*** $16,760,574 (100% institutional). ***Receiving aid:*** Freshmen: 10% (128). Undergraduates: 9% (434). ***Average award:*** Freshmen: $19,504. Undergraduates: $18,230. ***Tuition waivers:*** Full or partial for employees or children of employees, senior citizens. ***ROTC:*** Army, Air Force cooperative.

LOANS ***Student loans:*** $48,157,773 (68% need-based, 32% non-need-based). 78% of past graduating class borrowed through all loan programs. *Average indebtedness per student:* $47,457. ***Average need-based loan:*** Freshmen: $3320. Undergraduates: $4243. ***Parent loans:*** $24,765,449 (100% non-need-based). ***Programs:*** Federal Direct (Subsidized and Unsubsidized Stafford, PLUS), state.

WORK-STUDY ***Federal work-study:*** Total amount: $419,381; jobs available.

ATHLETIC AWARDS Total amount: $3,177,632 (56% need-based, 44% non-need-based).

APPLYING FOR FINANCIAL AID ***Required financial aid form:*** FAFSA. ***Financial aid deadline:*** 5/1 (priority: 3/1). ***Notification date:*** Continuous beginning 1/15. Students must reply by 5/1 or within 2 weeks of notification.

CONTACT Mr. Erin Chiaro, Director of Financial Aid, University of New Haven, 300 Boston Post Road, West Haven, CT 06516-1916, 203-479-4520 or toll-free 800-342-5864. *E-mail:* financialaid@newhaven.edu.
Website: http://www.newhaven.edu/.

UNIVERSITY OF NEW MEXICO

Albuquerque, NM

Tuition & fees (NM res): $7875 **Average undergraduate aid package: N/A**

ABOUT THE INSTITUTION State-supported, coed. ***Awards:*** certificates, bachelor's, master's, and doctoral degrees. 82 undergraduate majors. ***Total enrollment:*** 22,793. Undergraduates: 16,662. Freshmen: 2,599. Federal methodology is used as a basis for awarding need-based institutional aid.

UNDERGRADUATE EXPENSES for 2019–2020 ***Application fee:*** $25. ***Tuition, state resident:*** full-time $6299; part-time $263 per credit hour. ***Tuition, nonresident:*** full-time $21,716; part-time $905 per credit hour. ***Required fees:*** full-time $1576; $66 per credit hour. Full-time tuition and fees vary according to course level, degree level, program, and reciprocity agreements. Part-time tuition and fees vary according to course level, course load, degree level, program, and reciprocity agreements. ***College room and board:*** $9390. Room and board charges vary according to board plan and housing facility.

FRESHMAN FINANCIAL AID (Fall 2019, est.) 2292 applied for aid; of those 73% were deemed to have need. 97% of freshmen with need received aid; of those 14% had need fully met.

UNDERGRADUATE FINANCIAL AID (Fall 2019, est.) 10,035 applied for aid; of those 82% were deemed to have need. 96% of undergraduates with need received aid; of those 13% had need fully met.

GIFT AID (NEED-BASED) ***Receiving aid:*** Freshmen: 61% (1,576); all full-time undergraduates: 54% (7,287). ***Average award:*** Freshmen: $5560; Undergraduates: $6069. ***Scholarships, grants, and awards:*** Federal Pell, FSEOG, state, private, college/university gift aid from institutional funds, Federal Nursing.

GIFT AID (NON-NEED-BASED) ***Receiving aid:*** Freshmen: 1% (19). Undergraduates: 2% (206). ***Scholarships, grants, and awards by category:*** *Academic interests/achievement:* engineering/technologies, general academic interests/achievements. *Creative arts/performance:* applied art and design, music, theater/drama. *Special achievements/activities:* general special achievements/activities. *Special characteristics:* children and siblings of alumni, children of faculty/staff, children of union members/company employees, members of minority groups, out-of-state students, veterans. ***Tuition waivers:*** Full or partial for employees or children of employees, senior citizens. ***ROTC:*** Army, Naval, Air Force.

LOANS ***Student loans:*** 43% of past graduating class borrowed through all loan programs. *Average indebtedness per student:* $20,532. ***Programs:*** Federal Direct (Subsidized and Unsubsidized Stafford, PLUS), Federal Nursing, college/university.

WORK-STUDY Federal work-study jobs available. ***State or other work-study/employment:*** Part-time jobs available.

APPLYING FOR FINANCIAL AID ***Required financial aid form:*** FAFSA. ***Notification date:*** Continuous.

CONTACT Brian Malone, Office of Student Financial Aid, University of New Mexico, MSC 11 6315, 1 University of New Mexico, Albuquerque, NM 87131, 505-277-8900 or toll-free 800-CALL-UNM. *Fax:* 505-277-6326. *E-mail:* finaid@unm.edu.
Website: http://www.unm.edu/.

UNIVERSITY OF NEW ORLEANS

New Orleans, LA

CONTACT Ms. Ann Lockridge, Director of Financial Aid, Scholarships, and Veterans Services, University of New Orleans, Privateer Enrollment Center, 2000 Lakeshore Drive, 105 Earl K. Long Library, 1st Floor, New Orleans, LA 70148, 504-280-6603 or toll-free 888-514-4275. *Fax:* 504-280-3973. *E-mail:* alockrid@uno.edu.
Website: http://www.uno.edu/.

UNIVERSITY OF NORTH ALABAMA

Florence, AL

Tuition & fees (AL res): $10,800 **Average undergraduate aid package: $8963**

ABOUT THE INSTITUTION State-supported, coed. ***Awards:*** certificates, bachelor's, and master's degrees. 43 undergraduate majors. ***Total enrollment:*** 7,650. Undergraduates: 6,196. Freshmen: 1,005. Federal methodology is used as a basis for awarding need-based institutional aid.

UNDERGRADUATE EXPENSES for 2019–2020 ***Application fee:*** $35. ***Tuition, state resident:*** full-time $9600; part-time $320 per credit hour. ***Tuition, nonresident:*** full-time $19,200; part-time $640 per credit hour. ***Required fees:*** full-time $1200; $320 per credit hour. Full-time tuition and fees vary according to course load and program. Part-time tuition and fees vary according to course load and program. ***College room and board:*** $7830. Room and board charges vary according to board plan, housing facility, and student level.

FRESHMAN FINANCIAL AID (Fall 2018) 870 applied for aid; of those 98% were deemed to have need. 100% of freshmen with need received aid; of those 32% had need fully met. ***Average percent of need met:*** 61% (excluding resources awarded to replace EFC). ***Average financial aid package:*** $8827 (excluding resources awarded to replace EFC). 23% of all full-time freshmen had no need and received non-need-based gift aid.

UNDERGRADUATE FINANCIAL AID (Fall 2018) 3,811 applied for aid; of those 97% were deemed to have need. 100% of undergraduates with need received aid; of those 25% had need fully met. ***Average percent of need met:*** 59% (excluding resources awarded to replace EFC). ***Average financial aid package:*** $8963 (excluding resources awarded to replace EFC). 19% of all full-time undergraduates had no need and received non-need-based gift aid.

GIFT AID (NEED-BASED) ***Total amount:*** $10,982,461 (97% federal, 1% state, 2% institutional). ***Receiving aid:*** Freshmen: 42% (411); all full-time undergraduates: 42% (2,072). ***Average award:*** Freshmen: $4813; Undergraduates: $4920. ***Scholarships, grants, and awards:*** Federal Pell, FSEOG, state.

GIFT AID (NON-NEED-BASED) ***Total amount:*** $12,344,919 (95% institutional, 5% external sources). ***Receiving aid:*** Freshmen: 63% (620). Undergraduates: 37% (1,860). ***Average award:*** Freshmen: $4654. Undergraduates: $5153. ***Scholarships, grants, and awards by category:*** *Academic interests/achievement:* general academic interests/achievements, military science. *Creative arts/performance:* applied art and design, dance, journalism/publications, music, theater/drama. *Special achievements/activities:* cheerleading/drum major, general special achievements/activities, leadership. *Special characteristics:* children and siblings of alumni, first-generation college students, general special characteristics, international students, out-of-state students. ***Tuition waivers:*** Full or partial for employees or children of employees, senior citizens. ***ROTC:*** Army.

LOANS ***Student loans:*** $22,301,374 (44% need-based, 56% non-need-based). 58% of past graduating class borrowed through all loan programs. *Average indebtedness per student:* $29,021. ***Average need-based loan:*** Freshmen: $3121. Undergraduates: $3922. ***Parent loans:*** $5,619,360 (100% non-need-based). ***Programs:*** Federal Direct (Subsidized and Unsubsidized Stafford, PLUS).

WORK-STUDY ***Federal work-study:*** Total amount: $269,369; jobs available. ***State or other work-study/employment:*** Total amount: $804,172 (100% non-need-based). Part-time jobs available.

ATHLETIC AWARDS Total amount: $3,618,448 (100% non-need-based).

APPLYING FOR FINANCIAL AID ***Required financial aid form:*** FAFSA. ***Financial aid deadline:*** Continuous. ***Notification date:*** Continuous beginning 3/30.

CONTACT Ms. Shauna L. James, Director of Student Financial Services, University of North Alabama, UNA Box 5014, Florence, AL 35632-0001, 256-765-4279 or toll-free 800-TALK-UNA. *E-mail:* sljames@una.edu.
Website: http://www.una.edu/.

UNIVERSITY OF NORTH CAROLINA ASHEVILLE

Asheville, NC

Tuition & fees (NC res): $7230 **Average undergraduate aid package: $12,879**

ABOUT THE INSTITUTION State-supported, coed. ***Awards:*** certificates, bachelor's, and master's degrees. 36 undergraduate majors. ***Total enrollment:*** 3,762. Undergraduates: 3,743. Freshmen: 788. Federal methodology is used as a basis for awarding need-based institutional aid.

UNDERGRADUATE EXPENSES for 2019–2020 ***Application fee:*** $75. ***One-time required fee:*** $150. ***Tuition, state resident:*** full-time $4122; part-time $139 per credit hour. ***Tuition, nonresident:*** full-time $21,470; part-time $725 per credit hour. ***Required fees:*** full-time $3109; $17.80 per credit hour. Full-time tuition and fees vary according to course load and degree level. Part-time tuition and fees vary according to course load and degree level. ***College room and board:*** $9660; ***Room only:*** $5446. Room and board charges vary according to board plan and housing facility.

FRESHMAN FINANCIAL AID (Fall 2018) 753 applied for aid; of those 67% were deemed to have need. 100% of freshmen with need received aid; of those 22% had need fully met. ***Average percent of need met:*** 76% (excluding resources awarded to replace EFC). ***Average financial aid package:*** $12,982 (excluding resources awarded to replace EFC). 27% of all full-time freshmen had no need and received non-need-based gift aid.

UNDERGRADUATE FINANCIAL AID (Fall 2018) 2,612 applied for aid; of those 73% were deemed to have need. 99% of undergraduates with need received aid; of those 25% had need fully met. ***Average percent of need met:*** 75% (excluding resources awarded to replace EFC). ***Average financial aid package:*** $12,879 (excluding resources awarded to replace EFC). 12% of all full-time undergraduates had no need and received non-need-based gift aid.

GIFT AID (NEED-BASED) ***Total amount:*** $14,203,097 (43% federal, 23% state, 34% institutional). ***Receiving aid:*** Freshmen: 61% (476); all full-time undergraduates: 53% (1,685). ***Average award:*** Freshmen: $8006; Undergraduates: $7762. ***Scholarships, grants, and awards:*** Federal Pell, FSEOG, state, private, college/university gift aid from institutional funds.

GIFT AID (NON-NEED-BASED) ***Total amount:*** $912,103 (1% federal, 3% state, 96% institutional). ***Receiving aid:*** Freshmen: 26% (204). Undergraduates: 14% (447). ***Average award:*** Freshmen: $1901. Undergraduates: $1971. ***Scholarships, grants, and awards by category:*** *Academic interests/achievement:* 3,192 awards ($1,044,259 total): area/ethnic studies, biological sciences, business, communication, computer science, education, engineering/technologies, English, foreign languages, general academic interests/achievements, home economics, humanities, international studies, mathematics, physical sciences, religion/biblical studies, social sciences. *Creative arts/performance:* 2 awards ($1350 total): art/fine arts, dance, general creative arts/performance, music, theater/drama. ***Tuition waivers:*** Full or partial for employees or children of employees.

LOANS ***Student loans:*** $12,573,528 (72% need-based, 28% non-need-based). 59% of past graduating class borrowed through all loan programs. *Average indebtedness per student:* $24,476. ***Average need-based loan:*** Freshmen: $4006. Undergraduates: $4706. ***Parent loans:*** $2,298,847 (29% need-based, 71% non-need-based). ***Programs:*** Federal Direct (Subsidized and Unsubsidized Stafford, PLUS).

WORK-STUDY ***Federal work-study:*** Total amount: $152,550; 60 jobs averaging $2543. ***State or other work-study/employment:*** 1,870 part-time jobs averaging $1126.

ATHLETIC AWARDS Total amount: $2,275,293 (44% need-based, 56% non-need-based).

APPLYING FOR FINANCIAL AID ***Required financial aid form:*** FAFSA. ***Financial aid deadline (priority):*** 3/1. ***Notification date:*** Continuous beginning 2/15. Students must reply within 2 weeks of notification.

CONTACT Office of Financial Aid, University of North Carolina Asheville, One University Heights, 2nd Floor Brown Hall, CPO 1330, Asheville, NC 28804, 828-251-6535 or toll-free 800-531-9842. *Fax:* 828-232-2294. *E-mail:* finaid@unca.edu. *Website:* http://www.unca.edu/.

THE UNIVERSITY OF NORTH CAROLINA AT CHAPEL HILL

Chapel Hill, NC

Tuition & fees (NC res): $9232	Average undergraduate aid package: $19,192

ABOUT THE INSTITUTION State-supported, coed. ***Awards:*** certificates, bachelor's, master's, and doctoral degrees. 60 undergraduate majors. ***Total enrollment:*** 30,151. Undergraduates: 19,546. Freshmen: 4,182. Both federal and institutional methodology are used as a basis for awarding need-based institutional aid.

UNDERGRADUATE EXPENSES for 2020–2021 ***Application fee:*** $85. ***Tuition, state resident:*** full-time $7230. ***Tuition, nonresident:*** full-time $35,224. ***Required fees:*** full-time $2002. Part-time tuition and fees vary according to course load. ***College room and board:*** $11,740; ***Room only:*** $6878. Room and board charges vary according to board plan, housing facility, and location.

FRESHMAN FINANCIAL AID (Fall 2018) 3413 applied for aid; of those 60% were deemed to have need. 100% of freshmen with need received aid; of those 81% had need fully met. ***Average percent of need met:*** 100% (excluding resources awarded to replace EFC). ***Average financial aid package:*** $17,732 (excluding resources awarded to replace EFC). 2% of all full-time freshmen had no need and received non-need-based gift aid.

UNDERGRADUATE FINANCIAL AID (Fall 2018) 11,091 applied for aid; of those 75% were deemed to have need. 100% of undergraduates with need received aid; of those 76% had need fully met. ***Average percent of need met:*** 100% (excluding resources awarded to replace EFC). ***Average financial aid package:*** $19,192 (excluding resources awarded to replace EFC). 4% of all full-time undergraduates had no need and received non-need-based gift aid.

GIFT AID (NEED-BASED) ***Total amount:*** $127,998,822 (18% federal, 11% state, 64% institutional, 7% external sources). ***Receiving aid:*** Freshmen: 44% (1,915); all full-time undergraduates: 41% (7,521). ***Average award:*** Freshmen: $15,532; Undergraduates: $17,217. ***Scholarships, grants, and awards:*** Federal Pell, FSEOG, state, private, college/university gift aid from institutional funds.

GIFT AID (NON-NEED-BASED) ***Total amount:*** $18,985,078 (4% state, 37% institutional, 59% external sources). ***Receiving aid:*** Freshmen: 5% (230). Undergraduates: 3% (484). ***Average award:*** Freshmen: $11,932. Undergraduates: $7833. ***Scholarships, grants, and awards by category:*** *Academic interests/achievement:* business, communication, education, English, general academic interests/achievements, home economics, mathematics. *Creative arts/performance:* applied art and design, art/fine arts, journalism/publications, music, theater/drama. *Special achievements/activities:* community service, general special achievements/activities, leadership. *Special characteristics:* children of faculty/staff, international students, out-of-state students, relatives of clergy. ***Tuition waivers:*** Full or partial for employees or children of employees. ***ROTC:*** Army, Naval, Air Force.

LOANS ***Student loans:*** $37,202,954 (61% need-based, 39% non-need-based). 40% of past graduating class borrowed through all loan programs. *Average indebtedness per student:* $22,466. ***Average need-based loan:*** Freshmen: $4530. Undergraduates: $4922. ***Parent loans:*** $8,713,275 (12% need-based, 88% non-need-based). ***Programs:*** Federal Direct (Subsidized and Unsubsidized Stafford, PLUS), state, college/university, alternative loans.

WORK-STUDY ***Federal work-study:*** Total amount: $4,116,524; 2,346 jobs averaging $1735. ***State or other work-study/employment:*** Total amount: $56,731 (100% need-based).

ATHLETIC AWARDS Total amount: $16,363,120 (26% need-based, 74% non-need-based).

APPLYING FOR FINANCIAL AID ***Required financial aid forms:*** FAFSA, CSS Financial Aid PROFILE. ***Financial aid deadline (priority):*** 3/1. ***Notification date:*** Continuous beginning 1/31. Students must reply by 5/1.

CONTACT Ms. Rachelle Feldman, Director of Scholarships and Student Aid, The University of North Carolina at Chapel Hill, 300 Pettigrew Hall, CB # 2300, PO Box 1080, Chapel Hill, NC 27514-1080, 919-962-8396. *Fax:* 919-962-2716. *E-mail:* aidinfo@unc.edu. *Website:* http://www.unc.edu/.

THE UNIVERSITY OF NORTH CAROLINA AT CHARLOTTE

Charlotte, NC

Tuition & fees (NC res): $7096	Average undergraduate aid package: $9523

ABOUT THE INSTITUTION State-supported, coed. ***Awards:*** certificates, bachelor's, master's, and doctoral degrees. 61 undergraduate majors. ***Total enrollment:*** 29,615. Undergraduates: 24,070. Freshmen: 3,652. Federal methodology is used as a basis for awarding need-based institutional aid.

UNDERGRADUATE EXPENSES for 2019–2020 ***Application fee:*** $75. ***Tuition, state resident:*** full-time $3812. ***Tuition, nonresident:*** full-time $17,246. ***Required fees:*** full-time $3284. Full-time tuition and fees vary according to course load and program. Part-time tuition and fees vary according to course load and program. ***College room and board:*** $11,060; ***Room only:*** $6560. Room and board charges vary according to board plan and housing facility. ***Payment plan:*** Guaranteed tuition.

FRESHMAN FINANCIAL AID (Fall 2019, est.) 3116 applied for aid; of those 69% were deemed to have need. 96% of freshmen with need received aid; of those 11% had need fully met. ***Average percent of need met:*** 54% (excluding resources awarded to replace EFC). ***Average financial aid package:*** $9540 (excluding resources awarded to replace EFC). 2% of all full-time freshmen had no need and received non-need-based gift aid.

UNDERGRADUATE FINANCIAL AID (Fall 2019, est.) 16,656 applied for aid; of those 79% were deemed to have need. 97% of undergraduates with need received aid; of those 10% had need fully met. ***Average percent of need met:*** 54% (excluding resources awarded to replace EFC). ***Average financial aid package:*** $9523 (excluding resources awarded to replace EFC). 1% of all full-time undergraduates had no need and received non-need-based gift aid.

GIFT AID (NEED-BASED) ***Total amount:*** $73,891,916 (55% federal, 28% state, 12% institutional, 5% external sources). ***Receiving aid:*** Freshmen: 34% (1,223); all full-time undergraduates: 44% (9,547). ***Average award:*** Freshmen: $6905; Undergraduates: $6778. ***Scholarships, grants, and awards:*** Federal Pell, FSEOG, state, private, college/university gift aid from institutional funds.

GIFT AID (NON-NEED-BASED) ***Total amount:*** $8,243,295 (8% state, 92% institutional). ***Receiving aid:*** Freshmen: 29% (1,032). Undergraduates: 8% (1,833). ***Average award:*** Freshmen: $6613. Undergraduates: $7421. ***Scholarships, grants, and awards by category:*** *Academic interests/achievement:* architecture, biological sciences, business, computer science, education, engineering/technologies, foreign languages, general academic interests/achievements, health fields, home economics, international studies, mathematics, physical sciences, religion/biblical studies, social sciences. *Creative arts/performance:* applied art and design, dance, music, theater/drama. *Special characteristics:* adult students, children of public servants, children of union members/company employees, first-generation college students, handicapped students, international students, local/state students, members of minority groups, veterans. ***Tuition waivers:*** Full or partial for senior citizens. ***ROTC:*** Army, Air Force.

LOANS ***Student loans:*** $113,815,108 (41% need-based, 59% non-need-based). 65% of past graduating class borrowed through all loan programs. *Average indebtedness per student:* $28,316. ***Average need-based loan:*** Freshmen: $3483. Undergraduates: $4245. ***Parent loans:*** $21,654,759 (100% non-need-based). ***Programs:*** Federal Direct (Subsidized and Unsubsidized Stafford, PLUS), Perkins, state, college/university.

WORK-STUDY ***Federal work-study:*** Total amount: $2,663,242; 941 jobs averaging $2830. ***State or other work-study/employment:*** Total amount: $2,663,242 (100% need-based).

ATHLETIC AWARDS Total amount: $6,464,286 (100% non-need-based).

APPLYING FOR FINANCIAL AID ***Required financial aid form:*** FAFSA. ***Financial aid deadline (priority):*** 3/1. ***Notification date:*** Continuous beginning 3/1. Students must reply by 9/30.

CONTACT Mr. Bruce Blackmon, Office of Financial Aid, The University of North Carolina at Charlotte, 9201 University City Boulevard, Charlotte, NC 28223-0001, 704-687-7010. *Fax:* 704-687-1461. *E-mail:* ablackm8@uncc.edu.
Website: http://www.uncc.edu/.

THE UNIVERSITY OF NORTH CAROLINA AT GREENSBORO

Greensboro, NC

Tuition & fees (NC res): $7403	Average undergraduate aid package: $11,491

ABOUT THE INSTITUTION State-supported, coed. ***Awards:*** certificates, bachelor's, master's, and doctoral degrees. 64 undergraduate majors. ***Total enrollment:*** 20,196. Undergraduates: 16,581. Freshmen: 2,746. Federal methodology is used as a basis for awarding need-based institutional aid.

UNDERGRADUATE EXPENSES for 2019–2020 ***Application fee:*** $65. ***Tuition, state resident:*** full-time $4422; part-time $553 per credit hour. ***Tuition, nonresident:*** full-time $19,581; part-time $2448 per credit hour. ***Required fees:*** full-time $2981; $116.79 per credit hour. Full-time tuition and fees vary according to course load and program. Part-time tuition and fees vary according to course load and program. ***College room and board:*** $9264; ***Room only:*** $5516. Room and board charges vary according to board plan and housing facility.

FRESHMAN FINANCIAL AID (Fall 2018) 2791 applied for aid; of those 82% were deemed to have need. 97% of freshmen with need received aid; of those 13% had need fully met. ***Average percent of need met:*** 63% (excluding resources awarded to replace EFC). ***Average financial aid package:*** $12,134 (excluding resources awarded to replace EFC). 2% of all full-time freshmen had no need and received non-need-based gift aid.

UNDERGRADUATE FINANCIAL AID (Fall 2018) 12,135 applied for aid; of those 86% were deemed to have need. 98% of undergraduates with need received aid; of those 10% had need fully met. ***Average percent of need met:*** 59% (excluding resources awarded to replace EFC). ***Average financial aid package:*** $11,491 (excluding resources awarded to replace EFC). 3% of all full-time undergraduates had no need and received non-need-based gift aid.

GIFT AID (NEED-BASED) ***Total amount:*** $72,679,169 (56% federal, 28% state, 16% institutional). ***Receiving aid:*** Freshmen: 66% (1,945); all full-time undergraduates: 59% (8,390). ***Average award:*** Freshmen: $9080; Undergraduates: $8340. ***Scholarships, grants, and awards:*** Federal Pell, FSEOG, state, private, college/university gift aid from institutional funds.

GIFT AID (NON-NEED-BASED) ***Total amount:*** $10,602,747 (5% state, 40% institutional, 55% external sources). ***Receiving aid:*** Freshmen: 10% (290). Undergraduates: 12% (1,664). ***Average award:*** Freshmen: $5016. Undergraduates: $3495. ***Scholarships, grants, and awards by category:*** *Academic interests/achievement:* biological sciences, business, communication, computer science, education, English, foreign languages, general academic interests/achievements, health fields, home economics, humanities, international studies, library science, mathematics, physical sciences, premedicine, religion/biblical studies, social sciences. *Creative arts/performance:* applied art and design, cinema/film/broadcasting, dance, music, performing arts, theater/drama. *Special achievements/activities:* community service, general special achievements/activities, junior miss, leadership, religious involvement. *Special characteristics:* adult students, children and siblings of alumni, children of faculty/staff, general special characteristics, handicapped students, international students, local/state students, out-of-state students, religious affiliation, veterans. ***Tuition waivers:*** Full or partial for employees or children of employees, senior citizens. ***ROTC:*** Army cooperative, Air Force cooperative.

LOANS ***Student loans:*** $72,108,588 (47% need-based, 53% non-need-based). 71% of past graduating class borrowed through all loan programs. *Average indebtedness per student:* $23,317. ***Average need-based loan:*** Freshmen: $3281. Undergraduates: $3996. ***Parent loans:*** $14,122,922 (100% non-need-based). ***Programs:*** Federal Direct (Subsidized and Unsubsidized Stafford, PLUS), Perkins, state, college/university.

WORK-STUDY ***Federal work-study:*** Total amount: $1,626,604; 717 jobs averaging $2269.

ATHLETIC AWARDS Total amount: $3,311,160 (100% non-need-based).

APPLYING FOR FINANCIAL AID ***Required financial aid form:*** FAFSA. ***Financial aid deadline:*** 12/1 (priority: 10/1). ***Notification date:*** Continuous beginning 12/1.

CONTACT Mr. Bruce Cabiness, Associate Director of Financial Aid, The University of North Carolina at Greensboro, PO Box 26170, Greensboro, NC 27402-6170, 336-334-5702. *Fax:* 336-334-3010. *E-mail:* finaid@uncg.edu.
Website: http://www.uncg.edu/.

THE UNIVERSITY OF NORTH CAROLINA AT PEMBROKE

Pembroke, NC

Tuition & fees (area res): $3490	Average undergraduate aid package: $9010

ABOUT THE INSTITUTION State-supported, coed. ***Awards:*** bachelor's and master's degrees. 43 undergraduate majors. ***Total enrollment:*** 7,698. Undergraduates: 6,353. Freshmen: 1,131. Federal methodology is used as a basis for awarding need-based institutional aid.

UNDERGRADUATE EXPENSES for 2020–2021 ***Application fee:*** $55. ***Tuition, area resident:*** full-time $1000. ***Tuition, state resident:*** full-time $1000. ***Tuition, nonresident:*** full-time $5000. ***Required fees:*** full-time $2490. ***College room and board:*** $8924. ***Payment plan:*** Tuition prepayment.

FRESHMAN FINANCIAL AID (Fall 2019, est.) 1022 applied for aid; of those 85% were deemed to have need. 96% of freshmen with need received aid; of those 7% had need fully met. ***Average percent of need met:*** 62% (excluding resources awarded to replace EFC). ***Average financial aid package:*** $8807 (excluding resources awarded to replace EFC). 1% of all full-time freshmen had no need and received non-need-based gift aid.

UNDERGRADUATE FINANCIAL AID (Fall 2019, est.) 4,499 applied for aid; of those 87% were deemed to have need. 97% of undergraduates with need received aid; of those 8% had need fully met. ***Average percent of need met:*** 65% (excluding resources awarded to replace EFC). ***Average financial aid package:*** $9010 (excluding resources awarded to replace EFC). 1% of all full-time undergraduates had no need and received non-need-based gift aid.

GIFT AID (NEED-BASED) ***Receiving aid:*** Freshmen: 67% (720); all full-time undergraduates: 64% (3,278). ***Average award:*** Freshmen: $6043; Undergraduates: $5811. ***Scholarships, grants, and awards:*** Federal Pell, FSEOG, state, college/university gift aid from institutional funds.

GIFT AID (NON-NEED-BASED) ***Receiving aid:*** Freshmen: 14% (154). Undergraduates: 10% (515). ***Average award:*** Freshmen: $1148. Undergraduates: $1850. ***Scholarships, grants, and awards by category:*** *Academic interests/achievement:* 336 awards ($283,618 total): education, general academic interests/achievements. *Creative arts/performance:* 1 award ($282 total): applied art and design. *Special characteristics:* 6 awards ($6000 total): children and siblings of alumni. ***ROTC:*** Army, Air Force.

LOANS ***Student loans:*** 82% of past graduating class borrowed through all loan programs. *Average indebtedness per student:* $27,193. ***Average need-based loan:*** Freshmen: $3350. Undergraduates: $4189. ***Programs:*** Federal Direct (Subsidized and Unsubsidized Stafford, PLUS).

WORK-STUDY ***Federal work-study:*** 128 jobs averaging $1614.

APPLYING FOR FINANCIAL AID ***Required financial aid form:*** FAFSA. ***Financial aid deadline:*** Continuous. ***Notification date:*** Continuous.

CONTACT Mildred Weber, Associate Director of Financial Aid IT, The University of North Carolina at Pembroke, PO Box 1510, Pembroke, NC 28372, 910-521-6612 or toll-free 800-949-UNCP. *Fax:* 910-775-4159. *E-mail:* mildred.weber@uncp.edu.
Website: http://www.uncp.edu/.

UNIVERSITY OF NORTH CAROLINA SCHOOL OF THE ARTS

Winston-Salem, NC

CONTACT Jane C. Kamiab, Director of Financial Aid, University of North Carolina School of the Arts, 1533 South Main Street, Winston-Salem, NC 27127, 336-770-3297. *Fax:* 336-770-1489.
Website: http://www.uncsa.edu/.

THE UNIVERSITY OF NORTH CAROLINA WILMINGTON

Wilmington, NC

Tuition & fees (NC res): $7181	Average undergraduate aid package: $9430

ABOUT THE INSTITUTION State-supported, coed. ***Awards:*** certificates, bachelor's, master's, and doctoral degrees. 52 undergraduate majors. ***Total enrollment:*** 17,499. Undergraduates: 14,785. Freshmen: 2,342. Federal methodology is used as a basis for awarding need-based institutional aid.

UNDERGRADUATE EXPENSES for 2019–2020 ***Application fee:*** $80. ***Tuition, state resident:*** full-time $4443; part-time $167 per credit hour. ***Tuition, nonresident:*** full-time $18,508; part-time $695 per credit hour. ***Required fees:*** full-time $2738; $81.61 per credit hour. Full-time tuition and fees vary according to course load and location. Part-time tuition and fees vary according to course load and location. ***College room and board:*** $10,897; ***Room only:*** $6790. Room and board charges vary according to board plan and housing facility.

FRESHMAN FINANCIAL AID (Fall 2018) 1802 applied for aid; of those 67% were deemed to have need. 97% of freshmen with need received aid; of those 12% had need fully met. ***Average percent of need met:*** 41% (excluding resources awarded to replace EFC). ***Average financial aid package:*** $8680 (excluding resources awarded to replace EFC). 4% of all full-time freshmen had no need and received non-need-based gift aid.

UNDERGRADUATE FINANCIAL AID (Fall 2018) 8,612 applied for aid; of those 79% were deemed to have need. 97% of undergraduates with need received aid; of those 12% had need fully met. ***Average percent of need met:*** 42% (excluding resources awarded to replace EFC). ***Average financial aid package:*** $9430 (excluding resources awarded to replace EFC). 4% of all full-time undergraduates had no need and received non-need-based gift aid.

GIFT AID (NEED-BASED) ***Receiving aid:*** Freshmen: 53% (1,143); all full-time undergraduates: 44% (5,275). ***Average award:*** Freshmen: $5488; Undergraduates: $6635. ***Scholarships, grants, and awards:*** Federal Pell, FSEOG, state, private, college/university gift aid from institutional funds, United Negro College Fund, Federal Nursing.

GIFT AID (NON-NEED-BASED) ***Receiving aid:*** Freshmen: 20% (431). Undergraduates: 14% (1,635). ***Average award:*** Freshmen: $3715. Undergraduates: $3238. ***Scholarships, grants, and awards by category:*** *Academic interests/achievement:* biological sciences, business, communication, computer science, education, engineering/technologies, English, foreign languages, general academic interests/achievements, home economics, humanities, international studies, mathematics, physical sciences, premedicine, social sciences. *Creative arts/performance:* applied art and design, cinema/film/broadcasting, creative writing, music, theater/drama. *Special achievements/activities:* general special achievements/activities, leadership. *Special characteristics:* local/state students, out-of-state students. ***Tuition waivers:*** Full or partial for employees or children of employees.

LOANS ***Student loans:*** 56% of past graduating class borrowed through all loan programs. *Average indebtedness per student:* $26,568. ***Average need-based loan:*** Freshmen: $3255. Undergraduates: $4166. ***Programs:*** Federal Direct (Subsidized and Unsubsidized Stafford, PLUS), state, college/university, external loans or non-federal loans.

WORK-STUDY Federal work-study jobs available.

APPLYING FOR FINANCIAL AID ***Required financial aid forms:*** FAFSA, institution's own form. ***Notification date:*** Continuous. Students must reply within 3 weeks of notification.

CONTACT Mr. Frederick Holding, Director of the Office of Scholarships and Financial Aid, The University of North Carolina Wilmington, 601 South College Road, Wilmington, NC 28403-5951, 910-962-3177. *Fax:* 910-962-3851. *E-mail:* finaid@uncw.edu.
Website: http://www.uncw.edu/.

UNIVERSITY OF NORTH DAKOTA

Grand Forks, ND

Tuition & fees (ND res): $9737	Average undergraduate aid package: $14,029

ABOUT THE INSTITUTION State-supported, coed. ***Awards:*** certificates, bachelor's, master's, and doctoral degrees. 92 undergraduate majors. ***Total enrollment:*** 13,581. Undergraduates: 10,163. Freshmen: 1,673. Federal methodology is used as a basis for awarding need-based institutional aid.

UNDERGRADUATE EXPENSES for 2019–2020 ***Application fee:*** $35. ***Tuition, state resident:*** full-time $8213; part-time $342 per credit hour. ***Tuition, nonresident:*** full-time $12,319; part-time $513 per credit hour. ***Required fees:*** full-time $1524. Full-time tuition and fees vary according to degree level, program, and reciprocity agreements. Part-time tuition and fees vary according to course load, degree level, program, and reciprocity agreements. ***College room and board:*** $9544. Room and board charges vary according to board plan and housing facility.

FRESHMAN FINANCIAL AID (Fall 2018) 1514 applied for aid; of those 62% were deemed to have need. 99% of freshmen with need received aid; of those 45% had need fully met. ***Average percent of need met:*** 61% (excluding resources awarded to replace EFC). ***Average financial aid package:*** $15,120 (excluding resources awarded to replace EFC). 19% of all full-time freshmen had no need and received non-need-based gift aid.

UNDERGRADUATE FINANCIAL AID (Fall 2018) 5,970 applied for aid; of those 67% were deemed to have need. 97% of undergraduates with need received aid; of those 39% had need fully met. ***Average percent of need met:*** 55% (excluding resources awarded to replace EFC). ***Average financial aid package:*** $14,029 (excluding resources awarded to replace EFC). 11% of all full-time undergraduates had no need and received non-need-based gift aid.

GIFT AID (NEED-BASED) ***Receiving aid:*** Freshmen: 45% (818); all full-time undergraduates: 37% (3,044). ***Average award:*** Freshmen: $5996; Undergraduates: $5823. ***Scholarships, grants, and awards:*** Federal Pell, FSEOG, state, private, college/university gift aid from institutional funds, Federal Nursing.

GIFT AID (NON-NEED-BASED) ***Receiving aid:*** Freshmen: 5% (90). Undergraduates: 3% (259). ***Average award:*** Freshmen: $2107. Undergraduates: $2167. ***Scholarships, grants, and awards by category:*** *Academic interests/achievement:* biological sciences, business, communication, computer science, education, engineering/technologies, English, foreign languages, general academic interests/achievements, health fields, humanities, international studies, mathematics, physical sciences, premedicine, social sciences. *Creative arts/performance:* applied art and design, music, theater/drama. *Special achievements/activities:* community service, general special achievements/activities, leadership, memberships. *Special characteristics:* children of faculty/staff, ethnic background, first-generation college students, general special characteristics, handicapped students, international students, members of minority groups, veterans. ***Tuition waivers:*** Full or partial for minority students, employees or children of employees. ***ROTC:*** Army, Air Force.

LOANS ***Student loans:*** 69% of past graduating class borrowed through all loan programs. ***Average need-based loan:*** Freshmen: $7197. Undergraduates: $7784. ***Programs:*** Federal Direct (Subsidized and Unsubsidized Stafford, PLUS), Federal Nursing, alternative loans.

WORK-STUDY ***Federal work-study:*** 1,302 jobs averaging $3000.

APPLYING FOR FINANCIAL AID ***Required financial aid forms:*** FAFSA, Scholarship Central Application. ***Notification date:*** Continuous. Students must reply within 4 weeks of notification.

CONTACT Kellie Choate, Asst Director of Systems, Student Financial Aid, University of North Dakota, 264 Centennial Drive, Stop 8371, Grand Forks, ND 58202, 701-777-4029 or toll-free 800-CALL-UND. *Fax:* 701-777-2040. *E-mail:* kellie.choate@und.edu.
Website: http://www.und.edu/.

UNIVERSITY OF NORTHERN COLORADO

Greeley, CO

Tuition & fees (area res): $10,188	**Average undergraduate aid package: $15,328**

ABOUT THE INSTITUTION State-supported, coed. ***Awards:*** bachelor's, master's, and doctoral degrees. 47 undergraduate majors. ***Total enrollment:*** 12,862. Undergraduates: 9,876. Freshmen: 1,858. Federal methodology is used as a basis for awarding need-based institutional aid.

UNDERGRADUATE EXPENSES for 2020–2021 ***Application fee:*** $50. ***One-time required fee:*** $250. ***Tuition, area resident:*** full-time $7830; part-time $304 per credit hour. ***Tuition, state resident:*** full-time $7830; part-time $304 per credit hour. ***Tuition, nonresident:*** full-time $19,902; part-time $792 per credit hour. ***Required fees:*** full-time $2358; $111.35 per credit hour. ***College room and board:*** $11,204; ***Room only:*** $5304.

FRESHMAN FINANCIAL AID (Fall 2019, est.) 1686 applied for aid; of those 73% were deemed to have need. 100% of freshmen with need received aid; of those 33% had need fully met. ***Average percent of need met:*** 80% (excluding resources awarded to replace EFC). ***Average financial aid package:*** $14,842 (excluding resources awarded to replace EFC). 30% of all full-time freshmen had no need and received non-need-based gift aid.

UNDERGRADUATE FINANCIAL AID (Fall 2019, est.) 6,496 applied for aid; of those 75% were deemed to have need. 100% of undergraduates with need received aid; of those 31% had need fully met. ***Average percent of need met:*** 78% (excluding resources awarded to replace EFC). ***Average financial aid package:*** $15,328 (excluding resources awarded to replace EFC). 26% of all full-time undergraduates had no need and received non-need-based gift aid.

GIFT AID (NEED-BASED) ***Total amount:*** $43,879,264 (31% federal, 18% state, 47% institutional, 4% external sources). ***Receiving aid:*** Freshmen: 60% (1,074); all full-time undergraduates: 50% (3,832). ***Average award:*** Freshmen: $7379; Undergraduates: $7553. ***Scholarships, grants, and awards:*** Federal Pell, FSEOG, state, private, college/university gift aid from institutional funds.

GIFT AID (NON-NEED-BASED) ***Total amount:*** $13,078,259 (77% institutional, 23% external sources). ***Receiving aid:*** Freshmen: 62% (1,120). Undergraduates: 47% (3,606). ***Average award:*** Freshmen: $3188. Undergraduates: $3354. ***Scholarships, grants, and awards by category:*** *Academic interests/achievement:* biological sciences, business, communication, education, English, foreign languages, general academic interests/achievements, health fields, home economics, humanities, international studies, mathematics, military science, physical sciences, premedicine, social sciences. *Creative arts/performance:* applied art and design, art/fine arts, dance, journalism/publications, music, performing arts, theater/drama. *Special achievements/activities:* community service, general special achievements/activities, leadership, memberships. *Special characteristics:* adult students, children and siblings of alumni, children of faculty/staff, children of union members/company employees, children of workers in trades, children with a deceased or disabled parent, ethnic background, first-generation college students, general special characteristics, handicapped students, international students, local/state students, married students, members of minority groups, out-of-state students, previous college experience, veterans. ***ROTC:*** Army, Air Force.

LOANS ***Student loans:*** $53,541,405 (60% need-based, 40% non-need-based). 62% of past graduating class borrowed through all loan programs. *Average indebtedness per student:* $23,967. ***Average need-based loan:*** Freshmen: $3190. Undergraduates: $4218. ***Parent loans:*** $71,034,894 (16% need-based, 84% non-need-based). ***Programs:*** Federal Direct (Subsidized and Unsubsidized Stafford, PLUS), Federal Nursing.

WORK-STUDY ***Federal work-study:*** Total amount: $1,584,492; 218 jobs averaging $1762. ***State or other work-study/employment:*** Total amount: $5,725,497 (100% need-based). 551 part-time jobs averaging $2318.

ATHLETIC AWARDS Total amount: $4,409,230 (38% need-based, 62% non-need-based).

APPLYING FOR FINANCIAL AID ***Required financial aid form:*** FAFSA. ***Financial aid deadline (priority):*** 3/1. ***Notification date:*** Continuous beginning 1/1. Students must reply within 4 weeks of notification.

CONTACT Marty Somero, Director of Financial Aid, University of Northern Colorado, Carter Hall 1005, Greeley, CO 80639, 970-351-2502 or toll-free 888-700-4UNC. *Fax:* 970-351-3737. *E-mail:* ofa@unco.edu.
Website: http://www.unco.edu/.

UNIVERSITY OF NORTHERN IOWA

Cedar Falls, IA

Tuition & fees (IA res): $8938	**Average undergraduate aid package: $8442**

ABOUT THE INSTITUTION State-supported, coed. ***Awards:*** certificates, bachelor's, master's, and doctoral degrees. 100 undergraduate majors. ***Total enrollment:*** 10,497. Undergraduates: 8,973. Freshmen: 1,465. Federal methodology is used as a basis for awarding need-based institutional aid.

UNDERGRADUATE EXPENSES for 2019–2020 ***Application fee:*** $40. ***Tuition, state resident:*** full-time $7665; part-time $320 per credit hour. ***Tuition, nonresident:*** full-time $18,207; part-time $759 per credit hour. ***Required fees:*** full-time $1273. Full-time tuition and fees vary according to course load and program. Part-time tuition and fees vary according to course load and program. ***College room and board:*** $9160; ***Room only:*** $4699. Room and board charges vary according to board plan and housing facility.

FRESHMAN FINANCIAL AID (Fall 2018) 1467 applied for aid; of those 68% were deemed to have need. 97% of freshmen with need received aid; of those 17% had need fully met. ***Average percent of need met:*** 63% (excluding resources awarded to replace EFC). ***Average financial aid package:*** $8179 (excluding resources awarded to replace EFC). 23% of all full-time freshmen had no need and received non-need-based gift aid.

UNDERGRADUATE FINANCIAL AID (Fall 2018) 6,829 applied for aid; of those 78% were deemed to have need. 95% of undergraduates with need received aid; of those 16% had need fully met. ***Average percent of need met:*** 63% (excluding resources awarded to replace EFC). ***Average financial aid package:*** $8442 (excluding resources awarded to replace EFC). 13% of all full-time undergraduates had no need and received non-need-based gift aid.

GIFT AID (NEED-BASED) ***Total amount:*** $27,900,798 (45% federal, 3% state, 45% institutional, 7% external sources). ***Receiving aid:*** Freshmen: 34% (566); all full-time undergraduates: 35% (3,088). ***Average award:*** Freshmen: $4879; Undergraduates: $4987. ***Scholarships, grants, and awards:*** Federal Pell, FSEOG, state, private, college/university gift aid from institutional funds, Federal TEACH Grants.

GIFT AID (NON-NEED-BASED) ***Total amount:*** $3,974,111 (10% federal, 4% state, 68% institutional, 18% external sources). ***Receiving aid:*** Freshmen: 43% (707). Undergraduates: 32% (2,803). ***Average award:*** Freshmen: $3450. Undergraduates: $3290. ***Scholarships, grants, and awards by category:*** *Academic interests/achievement:* biological sciences, business, communication, computer science, education, general academic interests/achievements, mathematics, physical sciences, social sciences. *Creative arts/performance:* applied art and design, art/fine arts, debating, music, theater/drama. *Special achievements/activities:* leadership. *Special characteristics:* general special characteristics, members of minority groups, veterans. ***ROTC:*** Army.

LOANS *Student loans:* $40,780,964 (39% need-based, 61% non-need-based). 68% of past graduating class borrowed through all loan programs. *Average indebtedness per student:* $23,671. ***Average need-based loan:*** Freshmen: $3168. Undergraduates: $4198. ***Parent loans:*** $10,817,811 (70% need-based, 30% non-need-based). ***Programs:*** Federal Direct (Subsidized and Unsubsidized Stafford, PLUS), Perkins, private education loans.

WORK-STUDY *Federal work-study:* Total amount: $654,036; jobs available. ***State or other work-study/employment:*** Part-time jobs available.

ATHLETIC AWARDS Total amount: $3,489,305 (89% need-based, 11% non-need-based).

APPLYING FOR FINANCIAL AID *Required financial aid form:* FAFSA. ***Financial aid deadline (priority):*** 1/15. ***Notification date:*** Continuous beginning 2/1.

CONTACT Heather Stalzer, Associate Director Systems & Regulations, University of Northern Iowa, 105 Gilchrist Hall, Cedar Falls, IA 50614-0024, 319-273-7613 or toll-free 800-772-2037. *Fax:* 319-273-6950. *E-mail:* heather.stalzer@uni.edu. *Website:* http://www.uni.edu/.

UNIVERSITY OF NORTH FLORIDA

Jacksonville, FL

ABOUT THE INSTITUTION State-supported, coed. ***Awards:*** certificates, associate, bachelor's, master's, and doctoral degrees (doctoral degree in education only). 58 undergraduate majors. ***Total enrollment:*** 17,117. Undergraduates: 14,734. Freshmen: 2,641.

GIFT AID (NEED-BASED) *Scholarships, grants, and awards:* Federal Pell, FSEOG, state, private, college/university gift aid from institutional funds.

GIFT AID (NON-NEED-BASED) *Scholarships, grants, and awards by category:* *Academic interests/achievement:* business, computer science, education, engineering/technologies, general academic interests/achievements, home economics, international studies. *Creative arts/performance:* applied art and design, music. *Special achievements/activities:* community service, general special achievements/activities, leadership. *Special characteristics:* first-generation college students, general special characteristics, international students, members of minority groups, out-of-state students.

LOANS *Programs:* Federal Direct (Subsidized and Unsubsidized Stafford, PLUS).

WORK-STUDY *Federal work-study:* Total amount: $428,777; 163 jobs averaging $2916.

APPLYING FOR FINANCIAL AID *Required financial aid form:* FAFSA.

CONTACT Ms. Anissa Agne, Director of Financial Aid, University of North Florida, 1 UNF Drive, Jacksonville, FL 32224-7699, 904-620-5555. *E-mail:* anissa.agne@unf.edu. *Website:* http://www.unf.edu/.

UNIVERSITY OF NORTH GEORGIA

Dahlonega, GA

Tuition & fees: N/R | **Average undergraduate aid package: N/A**

ABOUT THE INSTITUTION State-supported, coed. ***Awards:*** certificates, associate, bachelor's, master's, and doctoral degrees. 41 undergraduate majors. ***Total enrollment:*** 19,722. Undergraduates: 19,031. Freshmen: 4,454. Federal methodology is used as a basis for awarding need-based institutional aid.

GIFT AID (NEED-BASED) *Scholarships, grants, and awards:* Federal Pell, FSEOG, state, private, college/university gift aid from institutional funds.

GIFT AID (NON-NEED-BASED) *Scholarships, grants, and awards by category:* *Academic interests/achievement:* biological sciences, business, education, English, general academic interests/achievements, health fields, humanities, mathematics, military science, physical sciences, premedicine. *Creative arts/performance:* applied art and design, general creative arts/performance, music. *Special achievements/activities:* cheerleading/drum major, community service, general special achievements/activities, leadership. *Special characteristics:* general special characteristics. ***ROTC:*** Army.

LOANS *Student loans:* 53% of past graduating class borrowed through all loan programs. *Average indebtedness per student:* $12,345. ***Programs:*** Federal Direct (Subsidized and Unsubsidized Stafford, PLUS), Perkins, state, college/university.

WORK-STUDY Federal work-study jobs available. ***State or other work-study/employment:*** Part-time jobs available.

APPLYING FOR FINANCIAL AID *Required financial aid form:* FAFSA. ***Financial aid deadline (priority):*** 2/20. ***Notification date:*** Continuous beginning 4/1. Students must reply within 2 weeks of notification.

CONTACT Jill Rayner, Director of Financial Aid, University of North Georgia, 82 College Circle, Dahlonega, GA 30597-1001, 706-864-1688 or toll-free 800-498-9581. *Fax:* 706-864-1411. *E-mail:* jill.rayner@ung.edu. *Website:* http://www.ung.edu/.

UNIVERSITY OF NORTH TEXAS

Denton, TX

Tuition & fees: N/R | **Average undergraduate aid package: $11,601**

ABOUT THE INSTITUTION State-supported, coed. ***Awards:*** certificates, bachelor's, master's, and doctoral degrees. 91 undergraduate majors. ***Total enrollment:*** 39,192. Undergraduates: 32,126. Freshmen: 5,510. Federal methodology is used as a basis for awarding need-based institutional aid.

UNDERGRADUATE EXPENSES for 2019–2020 *Application fee:* $75. ***Tuition, area resident:*** part-time $303 per credit hour. ***Tuition, state resident:*** part-time $303 per credit hour. ***Tuition, nonresident:*** part-time $718 per credit hour.

FRESHMAN FINANCIAL AID (Fall 2019, est.) 4637 applied for aid; of those 76% were deemed to have need. 98% of freshmen with need received aid; of those 15% had need fully met. ***Average percent of need met:*** 65% (excluding resources awarded to replace EFC). ***Average financial aid package:*** $13,749 (excluding resources awarded to replace EFC). 17% of all full-time freshmen had no need and received non-need-based gift aid.

UNDERGRADUATE FINANCIAL AID (Fall 2019, est.) 19,363 applied for aid; of those 82% were deemed to have need. 95% of undergraduates with need received aid; of those 10% had need fully met. ***Average percent of need met:*** 53% (excluding resources awarded to replace EFC). ***Average financial aid package:*** $11,601 (excluding resources awarded to replace EFC). 12% of all full-time undergraduates had no need and received non-need-based gift aid.

GIFT AID (NEED-BASED) *Total amount:* $145,416,566 (38% federal, 18% state, 33% institutional, 11% external sources). ***Receiving aid:*** Freshmen: 45% (2,319); all full-time undergraduates: 42% (10,877). ***Average award:*** Freshmen: $10,153; Undergraduates: $8553. ***Scholarships, grants, and awards:*** Federal Pell, FSEOG, state, private, college/university gift aid from institutional funds.

GIFT AID (NON-NEED-BASED) *Total amount:* $10,824,343 (73% institutional, 27% external sources). ***Receiving aid:*** Freshmen: 40% (2,073). Undergraduates: 19% (5,014). ***Average award:*** Freshmen: $6871. Undergraduates: $6269. ***ROTC:*** Army, Air Force.

LOANS *Student loans:* $106,485,727 (86% need-based, 14% non-need-based). 62% of past graduating class borrowed through all loan programs. *Average indebtedness per student:* $22,307. ***Average need-based loan:*** Freshmen: $3038. Undergraduates: $3969. ***Parent loans:*** $113,931,839 (70% need-based, 30% non-need-based). ***Programs:*** Federal Direct (Subsidized and Unsubsidized Stafford, PLUS), Perkins, state.

WORK-STUDY *Federal work-study:* Total amount: $7,927,196; jobs available. ***State or other work-study/employment:*** Total amount: $251,180 (100% need-based). Part-time jobs available.

ATHLETIC AWARDS Total amount: $5,225,989 (46% need-based, 54% non-need-based).

APPLYING FOR FINANCIAL AID *Required financial aid form:* FAFSA. ***Financial aid deadline (priority):*** 1/15. ***Notification date:*** Continuous beginning 12/15.

CONTACT Mrs. Zelma DeLeon, Executive Director of Student Financial Aid and Scholarships, University of North Texas, 1155 Union Circle #311370, Denton, TX 76203-5017, 940-565-3901 or toll-free 800-868-8211. *Fax:* 940-565-2738. *E-mail:* zelma.deleon@unt.edu.
Website: http://www.unt.edu/.

UNIVERSITY OF NORTH TEXAS AT DALLAS

Dallas, TX

ABOUT THE INSTITUTION State-supported, coed. ***Awards:*** bachelor's, master's, and doctoral degrees. 22 undergraduate majors. ***Total enrollment:*** 3,757. Undergraduates: 3,006. Freshmen: 365.

GIFT AID (NEED-BASED) ***Scholarships, grants, and awards:*** Federal Pell, FSEOG, state, private, college/university gift aid from institutional funds.

LOANS ***Programs:*** Federal Direct (Subsidized and Unsubsidized Stafford, PLUS), state.

CONTACT Financial Aid Office, University of North Texas at Dallas, 7300 University Hills Boulevard, Dallas, TX 75241, 972-780-3600.
Website: http://untdallas.edu/.

UNIVERSITY OF NORTHWESTERN OHIO

Lima, OH

CONTACT Financial Aid Office, University of Northwestern Ohio, 1441 North Cable Road, Lima, OH 45805-1498, 419-227-3141.
Website: http://www.unoh.edu/.

UNIVERSITY OF NORTHWESTERN–ST. PAUL

St. Paul, MN

Tuition & fees: $33,200	Average undergraduate aid package: $22,931

ABOUT THE INSTITUTION Independent nondenominational, coed. ***Awards:*** certificates, associate, bachelor's, and master's degrees. 56 undergraduate majors. ***Total enrollment:*** 3,525. Undergraduates: 3,376. Freshmen: 246. Federal methodology is used as a basis for awarding need-based institutional aid.

UNDERGRADUATE EXPENSES for 2020–2021 ***Application fee:*** $25. ***Comprehensive fee:*** $43,200 includes full-time tuition ($32,490), mandatory fees ($710), and room and board ($10,000). ***College room only:*** $5920. Full-time tuition and fees vary according to class time and program. Room and board charges vary according to board plan and student level. ***Part-time tuition:*** $1390 per credit. Part-time tuition and fees vary according to class time and program.

FRESHMAN FINANCIAL AID (Fall 2018) 386 applied for aid; of those 88% were deemed to have need. 100% of freshmen with need received aid; of those 12% had need fully met. ***Average percent of need met:*** 73% (excluding resources awarded to replace EFC). ***Average financial aid package:*** $23,660 (excluding resources awarded to replace EFC). 17% of all full-time freshmen had no need and received non-need-based gift aid.

UNDERGRADUATE FINANCIAL AID (Fall 2018) 1,430 applied for aid; of those 89% were deemed to have need. 100% of undergraduates with need received aid; of those 10% had need fully met. ***Average percent of need met:*** 71% (excluding resources awarded to replace EFC). ***Average financial aid package:*** $22,931 (excluding resources awarded to replace EFC). 19% of all full-time undergraduates had no need and received non-need-based gift aid.

GIFT AID (NEED-BASED) ***Total amount:*** $23,392,493 (13% federal, 15% state, 70% institutional, 2% external sources). ***Receiving aid:*** Freshmen: 82% (338); all full-time undergraduates: 77% (1,228). ***Average award:*** Freshmen: $19,685; Undergraduates: $18,391. ***Scholarships, grants, and awards:*** Federal Pell, FSEOG, state, private, college/university gift aid from institutional funds.

GIFT AID (NON-NEED-BASED) ***Total amount:*** $4,030,194 (2% federal, 96% institutional, 2% external sources). ***Receiving aid:*** Freshmen: 9% (38). Undergraduates: 7% (116). ***Average award:*** Freshmen: $12,464. Undergraduates: $10,883. ***Scholarships, grants, and awards by category:*** *Academic interests/achievement:* 1,653 awards ($17,188,057 total): biological sciences, business, communication, education, English, general academic interests/achievements, home economics, humanities, mathematics, religion/biblical studies, social sciences. *Creative arts/performance:* 157 awards ($771,675 total): cinema/film/broadcasting, music, theater/drama. *Special achievements/activities:* 257 awards ($1,042,307 total): general special achievements/activities, leadership. *Special characteristics:* 491 awards ($3,630,438 total): children and siblings of alumni, children of faculty/staff, ethnic background, general special characteristics, international students, relatives of clergy. ***Tuition waivers:*** Full or partial for employees or children of employees. ***ROTC:*** Army cooperative, Air Force cooperative.

LOANS ***Student loans:*** $12,741,881 (75% need-based, 25% non-need-based). 73% of past graduating class borrowed through all loan programs. *Average indebtedness per student:* $44,561. ***Average need-based loan:*** Freshmen: $3599. Undergraduates: $4359. ***Parent loans:*** $3,855,583 (49% need-based, 51% non-need-based). ***Programs:*** Federal Direct (Subsidized and Unsubsidized Stafford, PLUS), Perkins, state.

WORK-STUDY ***Federal work-study:*** Total amount: $280,793; 213 jobs averaging $1291. ***State or other work-study/employment:*** Total amount: $594,783 (75% need-based, 25% non-need-based). 275 part-time jobs averaging $2163.

APPLYING FOR FINANCIAL AID ***Required financial aid form:*** FAFSA. ***Financial aid deadline:*** 8/1 (priority: 3/1). ***Notification date:*** Continuous beginning 3/1. Students must reply within 2 weeks of notification.

CONTACT Mrs. Hannah Blahnik, Director of Financial Aid, University of Northwestern–St. Paul, 3003 Snelling Avenue North, St. Paul, MN 55113-1598, 651-631-5212 or toll-free 800-827-6827. *Fax:* 651-628-3332. *E-mail:* financialaid@unwsp.edu.
Website: http://www.unwsp.edu/.

UNIVERSITY OF NOTRE DAME

Notre Dame, IN

Tuition & fees: $57,699	Average undergraduate aid package: $52,593

ABOUT THE INSTITUTION Independent Roman Catholic, coed. ***Awards:*** bachelor's, master's, and doctoral degrees. 64 undergraduate majors. ***Total enrollment:*** 12,681. Undergraduates: 8,731. Freshmen: 2,051. Both federal and institutional methodology are used as a basis for awarding need-based institutional aid.

UNDERGRADUATE EXPENSES for 2020–2021 ***Application fee:*** $80. ***Comprehensive fee:*** $73,683 includes full-time tuition ($57,192), mandatory fees ($507), and room and board ($15,984). ***Part-time tuition:*** $2383 per credit hour.

FRESHMAN FINANCIAL AID (Fall 2019, est.) 1490 applied for aid; of those 70% were deemed to have need. 100% of freshmen with need received aid; of those 100% had need fully met. ***Average percent of need met:*** 100% (excluding resources awarded to replace EFC). ***Average financial aid package:*** $52,793 (excluding resources awarded to replace EFC). 2% of all full-time freshmen had no need and received non-need-based gift aid.

UNDERGRADUATE FINANCIAL AID (Fall 2019, est.) 5,098 applied for aid; of those 81% were deemed to have need. 100% of undergraduates with need received aid; of those 100% had need fully met. ***Average percent of need met:*** 100% (excluding resources awarded to replace EFC). ***Average financial aid package:*** $52,593 (excluding resources awarded to replace EFC). 5% of all full-time undergraduates had no need and received non-need-based gift aid.

GIFT AID (NEED-BASED) ***Receiving aid:*** Freshmen: 49% (1,013); all full-time undergraduates: 46% (4,012). ***Average award:*** Freshmen: $44,087; Undergraduates: $42,382. ***Scholarships, grants, and awards:*** Federal Pell, FSEOG, state, private, college/university gift aid from institutional funds.

GIFT AID (NON-NEED-BASED) ***Receiving aid:*** Freshmen: 14% (292). Undergraduates: 13% (1,124). ***Average award:*** Freshmen: $12,994. Undergraduates: $12,648. ***Scholarships, grants, and awards by category:*** *Special characteristics:* children of faculty/staff. ***Tuition waivers:*** Full or partial for employees or children of employees. ***ROTC:*** Army, Naval, Air Force.

LOANS ***Student loans:*** 40% of past graduating class borrowed through all loan programs. *Average indebtedness per student:* $27,460. ***Average need-based loan:***

Freshmen: $3745. Undergraduates: $5245. ***Programs:*** Federal Direct (Subsidized and Unsubsidized Stafford, PLUS), college/university, private educational loans.

WORK-STUDY ***Federal work-study:*** 1,409 jobs averaging $2627. ***State or other work-study/employment:*** 3,394 part-time jobs averaging $3414.

APPLYING FOR FINANCIAL AID ***Required financial aid forms:*** FAFSA, CSS Financial Aid PROFILE, noncustodial (divorced/separated) parent's statement, business/farm supplement, federal income tax form(s), W-2 forms, verification worksheet. ***Notification date:*** Continuous.

CONTACT Mrs. Mary Nucciarone, Director, Financial Aid, University of Notre Dame, 115 Main Building, Notre Dame, IN 46556, 574-631-6436. *Fax:* 574-631-6899. *E-mail:* finaid@nd.edu.
Website: http://www.nd.edu/.

UNIVERSITY OF OKLAHOMA

Norman, OK

Tuition & fees (OK res): $9062	Average undergraduate aid package: $14,330

ABOUT THE INSTITUTION State-supported, coed. ***Awards:*** certificates, bachelor's, master's, and doctoral degrees. 102 undergraduate majors. ***Total enrollment:*** 28,564. Undergraduates: 22,152. Freshmen: 4,385. Federal methodology is used as a basis for awarding need-based institutional aid.

UNDERGRADUATE EXPENSES for 2019–2020 ***Application fee:*** $40. ***Tuition, state resident:*** full-time $4788; part-time $160 per credit hour. ***Tuition, nonresident:*** full-time $20,169; part-time $672 per credit hour. ***Required fees:*** full-time $4275; $127 per term. Full-time tuition and fees vary according to course load, degree level, location, and program. Part-time tuition and fees vary according to course load, degree level, location, and program. ***College room and board:*** $10,994; ***Room only:*** $6378. Room and board charges vary according to board plan and housing facility. ***Payment plan:*** Guaranteed tuition.

FRESHMAN FINANCIAL AID (Fall 2018) 3141 applied for aid; of those 65% were deemed to have need. 98% of freshmen with need received aid; of those 84% had need fully met. ***Average percent of need met:*** 84% (excluding resources awarded to replace EFC). ***Average financial aid package:*** $14,673 (excluding resources awarded to replace EFC). 10% of all full-time freshmen had no need and received non-need-based gift aid.

UNDERGRADUATE FINANCIAL AID (Fall 2018) 11,880 applied for aid; of those 76% were deemed to have need. 98% of undergraduates with need received aid; of those 85% had need fully met. ***Average percent of need met:*** 85% (excluding resources awarded to replace EFC). ***Average financial aid package:*** $14,330 (excluding resources awarded to replace EFC). 11% of all full-time undergraduates had no need and received non-need-based gift aid.

GIFT AID (NEED-BASED) ***Receiving aid:*** Freshmen: 27% (1,016); all full-time undergraduates: 27% (5,113). ***Average award:*** Freshmen: $6689; Undergraduates: $6491. ***Scholarships, grants, and awards:*** Federal Pell, FSEOG, state, private, college/university gift aid from institutional funds, United Negro College Fund.

GIFT AID (NON-NEED-BASED) ***Receiving aid:*** Freshmen: 31% (1,178). Undergraduates: 25% (4,731). ***Average award:*** Freshmen: $2275. Undergraduates: $2366. ***Scholarships, grants, and awards by category:*** *Academic interests/achievement:* 10,755 awards ($57,936,062 total): architecture, area/ethnic studies, biological sciences, business, communication, computer science, education, engineering/technologies, English, foreign languages, general academic interests/achievements, home economics, humanities, international studies, library science, mathematics, military science, physical sciences, premedicine, social sciences. *Creative arts/performance:* 376 awards ($1,727,165 total): applied art and design, cinema/film/broadcasting, dance, debating, journalism/publications, music, performing arts, theater/drama. *Special achievements/activities:* 308 awards ($475,986 total): leadership. *Special characteristics:* 991 awards ($2,070,004 total): children and siblings of alumni, children of faculty/staff, members of minority groups, previous college experience, public servants. ***Tuition waivers:*** Full or partial for employees or children of employees, senior citizens. ***ROTC:*** Army, Naval, Air Force.

LOANS ***Student loans:*** 43% of past graduating class borrowed through all loan programs. *Average indebtedness per student:* $30,258. ***Average need-based loan:*** Freshmen: $3387. Undergraduates: $4237. ***Programs:*** Federal Direct (Subsidized and Unsubsidized Stafford, PLUS), college/university, alternative loans.

WORK-STUDY ***Federal work-study:*** 741 jobs averaging $3726. ***State or other work-study/employment:*** 114 part-time jobs averaging $11,083.

APPLYING FOR FINANCIAL AID ***Required financial aid form:*** FAFSA. ***Financial aid deadline:*** Continuous. ***Notification date:*** Continuous. Students must reply within 6 weeks of notification.

CONTACT Financial Aid Office, University of Oklahoma, 660 Parrington Oval, Norman, OK 73019-0390, 405-325-0311 or toll-free 800-234-6868.
Website: http://www.ou.edu/.

UNIVERSITY OF OKLAHOMA HEALTH SCIENCES CENTER

Oklahoma City, OK

CONTACT Ms. Janice Osburn, Director, Financial Aid Office , University of Oklahoma Health Sciences Center, PO Box 26901, Oklahoma City, OK 73190, 405-271-2118. *Fax:* 405-271-5446.
Website: http://www.ouhsc.edu/.

UNIVERSITY OF OREGON

Eugene, OR

Tuition & fees (OR res): $10,755	Average undergraduate aid package: $11,936

ABOUT THE INSTITUTION State-supported, coed. ***Awards:*** certificates, bachelor's, master's, and doctoral degrees. 79 undergraduate majors. ***Total enrollment:*** 22,644. Undergraduates: 19,101. Freshmen: 4,168. Federal methodology is used as a basis for awarding need-based institutional aid.

UNDERGRADUATE EXPENSES for 2020–2021 ***Application fee:*** $65. ***One-time required fee:*** $449. ***Tuition, state resident:*** full-time $10,755; part-time $239 per credit hour. ***Tuition, nonresident:*** full-time $35,367; part-time $786 per credit hour. Full-time tuition and fees vary according to course load. Part-time tuition and fees vary according to course load. ***College room and board:*** $12,783. Room and board charges vary according to board plan and housing facility.

FRESHMAN FINANCIAL AID (Fall 2018) 3286 applied for aid; of those 66% were deemed to have need. 93% of freshmen with need received aid; of those 8% had need fully met. ***Average percent of need met:*** 54% (excluding resources awarded to replace EFC). ***Average financial aid package:*** $11,921 (excluding resources awarded to replace EFC). 21% of all full-time freshmen had no need and received non-need-based gift aid.

UNDERGRADUATE FINANCIAL AID (Fall 2018) 10,682 applied for aid; of those 75% were deemed to have need. 94% of undergraduates with need received aid; of those 6% had need fully met. ***Average percent of need met:*** 55% (excluding resources awarded to replace EFC). ***Average financial aid package:*** $11,936 (excluding resources awarded to replace EFC). 16% of all full-time undergraduates had no need and received non-need-based gift aid.

GIFT AID (NEED-BASED) ***Total amount:*** $59,894,480 (42% federal, 14% state, 33% institutional, 11% external sources). ***Receiving aid:*** Freshmen: 40% (1,631); all full-time undergraduates: 33% (5,777). ***Average award:*** Freshmen: $10,512; Undergraduates: $10,061. ***Scholarships, grants, and awards:*** Federal Pell, FSEOG, state, private, college/university gift aid from institutional funds.

GIFT AID (NON-NEED-BASED) ***Total amount:*** $21,218,847 (100% institutional). ***Receiving aid:*** Freshmen: 2% (90). Undergraduates: 2% (322). ***Average award:*** Freshmen: $6317. Undergraduates: $6472. ***Scholarships, grants, and awards by category:*** *Academic interests/achievement:* architecture, biological sciences, business, education, English, foreign languages, general academic interests/achievements, home economics, humanities, international studies, mathematics, military science, physical sciences, premedicine, social sciences. *Creative arts/performance:* applied art and design, art/fine arts, creative writing, dance, debating, journalism/publications, music, performing arts, theater/drama. *Special characteristics:* children of faculty/staff, general special characteristics, international students, local/state students, veterans. ***Tuition waivers:*** Full or partial for employees or children of employees. ***ROTC:*** Army, Air Force cooperative.

LOANS ***Student loans:*** $58,687,152 (57% need-based, 43% non-need-based). 44% of past graduating class borrowed through all loan programs. *Average indebtedness per student:* $26,548. ***Average need-based loan:*** Freshmen: $3348. Undergrad-

uates: $4358. ***Parent loans:*** $71,277,391 (45% need-based, 55% non-need-based). ***Programs:*** Federal Direct (Subsidized and Unsubsidized Stafford, PLUS).

WORK-STUDY *Federal work-study:* Total amount: $1,948,432; jobs available. ***State or other work-study/employment:*** Total amount: $142,500 (100% non-need-based). Part-time jobs available.

ATHLETIC AWARDS Total amount: $12,047,599 (26% need-based, 74% non-need-based).

APPLYING FOR FINANCIAL AID *Required financial aid form:* FAFSA. ***Financial aid deadline (priority):*** 3/1. ***Notification date:*** Continuous beginning 4/1. Students must reply within 4 weeks of notification.

CONTACT Jim Brooks, Associate VP, Director of Financial Aid and Scholarships, University of Oregon, 1278 University of Oregon, 278 Oregon Hall, Eugene, OR 97403-1278, 541-346-3221 or toll-free 800-232-3825. *Fax:* 541-346-1175. *E-mail:* financialaid@uoregon.edu.
Website: http://www.uoregon.edu/.

UNIVERSITY OF PENNSYLVANIA

Philadelphia, PA

Tuition & fees: $60,042	Average undergraduate aid package: $54,314

ABOUT THE INSTITUTION Independent, coed. ***Awards:*** certificates, associate, bachelor's, master's, and doctoral degrees (also offers evening program with significant enrollment not reflected in profile). 96 undergraduate majors. ***Total enrollment:*** 12,413. Undergraduates: 10,019. Freshmen: 2,340. Both federal and institutional methodology are used as a basis for awarding need-based institutional aid.

UNDERGRADUATE EXPENSES for 2020–2021 *Application fee:* $75. ***Comprehensive fee:*** $76,826 includes full-time tuition ($53,166), mandatory fees ($6876), and room and board ($16,784). ***College room only:*** $11,014. Room and board charges vary according to board plan and housing facility. Part-time tuition and fees vary according to course load. ***Payment plan:*** Tuition prepayment.

FRESHMAN FINANCIAL AID (Fall 2018) 1400 applied for aid; of those 80% were deemed to have need. 100% of freshmen with need received aid; of those 100% had need fully met. ***Average percent of need met:*** 100% (excluding resources awarded to replace EFC). ***Average financial aid package:*** $55,680 (excluding resources awarded to replace EFC).

UNDERGRADUATE FINANCIAL AID (Fall 2018) 4,963 applied for aid; of those 92% were deemed to have need. 100% of undergraduates with need received aid; of those 100% had need fully met. ***Average percent of need met:*** 100% (excluding resources awarded to replace EFC). ***Average financial aid package:*** $54,314 (excluding resources awarded to replace EFC).

GIFT AID (NEED-BASED) *Total amount:* $226,923,095 (4% federal, 1% state, 93% institutional, 2% external sources). ***Receiving aid:*** Freshmen: 45% (1,114); all full-time undergraduates: 45% (4,500). ***Average award:*** Freshmen: $53,107; Undergraduates: $51,403. ***Scholarships, grants, and awards:*** Federal Pell, FSEOG, state, private, college/university gift aid from institutional funds.

GIFT AID (NON-NEED-BASED) *Total amount:* $3,207,391 (5% federal, 95% external sources). ***Tuition waivers:*** Full or partial for employees or children of employees. ***ROTC:*** Army cooperative, Naval, Air Force cooperative.

LOANS *Student loans:* $15,456,650 (9% need-based, 91% non-need-based). 22% of past graduating class borrowed through all loan programs. *Average indebtedness per student:* $23,009. ***Average need-based loan:*** Freshmen: $2504. Undergraduates: $4152. ***Parent loans:*** $10,178,727 (100% non-need-based). ***Programs:*** Federal Direct (Subsidized and Unsubsidized Stafford, PLUS), Perkins, Federal Nursing, college/university.

WORK-STUDY *Federal work-study:* Total amount: $9,898,185; jobs available. ***State or other work-study/employment:*** Total amount: $4,311,039 (100% need-based). Part-time jobs available.

APPLYING FOR FINANCIAL AID *Required financial aid forms:* FAFSA, institution's own form, CSS Financial Aid PROFILE, noncustodial (divorced/separated) parent's statement, business/farm supplement, Parents' and student's most recently completed income tax returns. ***Financial aid deadline (priority):*** 2/15. ***Notification date:*** 4/1. Students must reply by 5/1.

CONTACT Elaine Papas Varas, Director of Financial Aid, University of Pennsylvania, 3451 Walnut Street, 100 Franklin Building, Philadelphia, PA 19104-6270, 215-898-1988. *E-mail:* varas@upenn.edu.
Website: http://www.upenn.edu/.

UNIVERSITY OF PHOENIX - BAY AREA CAMPUS

San Jose, CA

CONTACT ACS/AFS, University of Phoenix - Bay Area Campus, 875 West Elliot Road, Tempe, AZ 85284, 480-735-3000 or toll-free 866-766-0766. *Fax:* 480-940-2060. *Website:* http://www.phoenix.edu/.

UNIVERSITY OF PHOENIX - CENTRAL VALLEY CAMPUS

Fresno, CA

CONTACT ACS/AFS, University of Phoenix - Central Valley Campus, 875 West Elliot Road, Tempe, AZ 85284, 480-735-3000 or toll-free 866-766-0766. *Fax:* 480-940-2060. *Website:* http://www.phoenix.edu/.

UNIVERSITY OF PHOENIX - DALLAS CAMPUS

Dallas, TX

CONTACT ACS/AFS, University of Phoenix - Dallas Campus, 875 West Elliot Road, Tempe, AZ 85284, 480-735-3000 or toll-free 866-766-0766. *Fax:* 480-940-2060. *Website:* http://www.phoenix.edu/.

UNIVERSITY OF PHOENIX - HAWAII CAMPUS

Honolulu, HI

CONTACT ACS/AFS, University of Phoenix - Hawaii Campus, 875 West Elliot Road, Tempe, AZ 85284, 480-735-3000 or toll-free 866-766-0766. *Fax:* 480-940-2060. *Website:* http://www.phoenix.edu/.

UNIVERSITY OF PHOENIX - HOUSTON CAMPUS

Houston, TX

CONTACT ACS/AFS, University of Phoenix - Houston Campus, 875 West Elliot Road, Tempe, AZ 85284, 480-735-3000 or toll-free 866-766-0766. *Fax:* 480-940-2060. *Website:* http://www.phoenix.edu/.

UNIVERSITY OF PHOENIX - LAS VEGAS CAMPUS

Las Vegas, NV

CONTACT ACS/AFS, University of Phoenix - Las Vegas Campus, 875 West Elliot Road, Tempe, AZ 85284, 480-735-3000 or toll-free 866-766-0766. *Fax:* 480-940-2060. *Website:* http://www.phoenix.edu/.

UNIVERSITY OF PHOENIX–ONLINE CAMPUS

Phoenix, AZ

CONTACT Office of Financial Aid, University of Phoenix–Online Campus, 3157 East Elwood Street, Phoenix, AZ 85034-7209, 866-766-0766.
Website: http://www.phoenix.edu/.

UNIVERSITY OF PHOENIX - PHOENIX CAMPUS

Tempe, AZ

CONTACT Office of Financial Aid, University of Phoenix - Phoenix Campus, 1625 West Fountainhead Parkway, Tempe, AZ 85282-2371, 866-766-0766.
Website: http://www.phoenix.edu/.

UNIVERSITY OF PHOENIX - SACRAMENTO VALLEY CAMPUS

Sacramento, CA

CONTACT ACS/AFS, University of Phoenix - Sacramento Valley Campus, 875 West Elliot Road, Tempe, AZ 85284, 480-735-3000 or toll-free 866-766-0766. *Fax:* 480-940-2060.
Website: http://www.phoenix.edu/.

UNIVERSITY OF PHOENIX - SAN DIEGO CAMPUS

San Diego, CA

CONTACT ACS/AFS, University of Phoenix - San Diego Campus, 875 West Elliot Road, Tempe, AZ 85284, 480-735-3000 or toll-free 866-766-0766. *Fax:* 480-940-2060.
Website: http://www.phoenix.edu/.

UNIVERSITY OF PIKEVILLE

Pikeville, KY

Tuition & fees: $22,050	Average undergraduate aid package: $22,417

ABOUT THE INSTITUTION Independent Presbyterian Church (U.S.A.), coed. ***Awards:*** certificates, associate, bachelor's, master's, and doctoral degrees. 27 undergraduate majors. ***Total enrollment:*** 2,262. Undergraduates: 1,404. Freshmen: 328. Federal methodology is used as a basis for awarding need-based institutional aid.

UNDERGRADUATE EXPENSES for 2020–2021 ***Comprehensive fee:*** $30,100 includes full-time tuition ($21,900), mandatory fees ($150), and room and board ($8050). Full-time tuition and fees vary according to course load. Room and board charges vary according to housing facility. ***Part-time tuition:*** $915 per credit hour. Part-time tuition and fees vary according to course load.

FRESHMAN FINANCIAL AID (Fall 2019, est.) 326 applied for aid; of those 100% were deemed to have need. 100% of freshmen with need received aid; of those 43% had need fully met. ***Average percent of need met:*** 85% (excluding resources awarded to replace EFC). ***Average financial aid package:*** $23,423 (excluding resources awarded to replace EFC).

UNDERGRADUATE FINANCIAL AID (Fall 2019, est.) 1,059 applied for aid; of those 100% were deemed to have need. 100% of undergraduates with need received aid; of those 42% had need fully met. ***Average percent of need met:*** 82% (excluding resources awarded to replace EFC). ***Average financial aid package:*** $22,417 (excluding resources awarded to replace EFC).

GIFT AID (NEED-BASED) ***Receiving aid:*** Freshmen: 99% (325); all full-time undergraduates: 97% (1,045). ***Average award:*** Freshmen: $16,604; Undergraduates: $15,556. ***Scholarships, grants, and awards:*** Federal Pell, FSEOG, state, private, college/university gift aid from institutional funds.

GIFT AID (NON-NEED-BASED) ***Receiving aid:*** Freshmen: 55% (181). Undergraduates: 47% (502). ***Tuition waivers:*** Full or partial for employees or children of employees, senior citizens. ***ROTC:*** Army.

LOANS ***Student loans:*** 79% of past graduating class borrowed through all loan programs. *Average indebtedness per student:* $24,825. ***Average need-based loan:*** Freshmen: $3286. Undergraduates: $3962. ***Programs:*** Federal Direct (Subsidized and Unsubsidized Stafford, PLUS), college/university.

WORK-STUDY ***Federal work-study:*** 400 jobs averaging $1933.

APPLYING FOR FINANCIAL AID ***Required financial aid form:*** FAFSA. ***Notification date:*** Continuous.

CONTACT Ms. Jennifer Bates, Director of Student Financial Services, University of Pikeville, 147 Sycamore Street, Pikeville, KY 41501, 606-218-5254 or toll-free 866-232-7700. *Fax:* 606-218-5255. *E-mail:* jenniferbates@upike.edu.
Website: http://www.upike.edu/.

UNIVERSITY OF PITTSBURGH

Pittsburgh, PA

Tuition & fees (area res): $19,718	Average undergraduate aid package: $12,362

ABOUT THE INSTITUTION State-related, coed. ***Awards:*** certificates, bachelor's, master's, and doctoral degrees. 94 undergraduate majors. ***Total enrollment:*** 28,673. Undergraduates: 19,330. Freshmen: 4,126. Federal methodology is used as a basis for awarding need-based institutional aid.

UNDERGRADUATE EXPENSES for 2019–2020 ***Application fee:*** $45. ***Tuition, area resident:*** full-time $18,628; part-time $776 per credit hour. ***Tuition, state resident:*** full-time $18,628; part-time $776 per credit hour. ***Tuition, nonresident:*** full-time $32,656; part-time $1360 per credit hour. ***Required fees:*** full-time $1090; $310 per term. Full-time tuition and fees vary according to location and program. Part-time tuition and fees vary according to location and program. ***College room and board:*** $11,250; ***Room only:*** $6550. Room and board charges vary according to board plan, housing facility, and location.

FRESHMAN FINANCIAL AID (Fall 2018) 3482 applied for aid; of those 63% were deemed to have need. 97% of freshmen with need received aid; of those 21% had need fully met. ***Average percent of need met:*** 59% (excluding resources awarded to replace EFC). ***Average financial aid package:*** $13,674 (excluding resources awarded to replace EFC). 9% of all full-time freshmen had no need and received non-need-based gift aid.

UNDERGRADUATE FINANCIAL AID (Fall 2018) 12,593 applied for aid; of those 75% were deemed to have need. 97% of undergraduates with need received aid; of those 9% had need fully met. ***Average percent of need met:*** 53% (excluding resources awarded to replace EFC). ***Average financial aid package:*** $12,362 (excluding resources awarded to replace EFC). 4% of all full-time undergraduates had no need and received non-need-based gift aid.

GIFT AID (NEED-BASED) ***Total amount:*** $66,947,130 (20% federal, 14% state, 56% institutional, 10% external sources). ***Receiving aid:*** Freshmen: 42% (1,748); all full-time undergraduates: 38% (6,938). ***Average award:*** Freshmen: $11,636; Undergraduates: $10,519. ***Scholarships, grants, and awards:*** Federal Pell, FSEOG, state, private, college/university gift aid from institutional funds, Federal Nursing.

GIFT AID (NON-NEED-BASED) ***Total amount:*** $31,130,086 (80% institutional, 20% external sources). ***Receiving aid:*** Freshmen: 6% (236). Undergraduates: 4% (719). ***Average award:*** Freshmen: $11,153. Undergraduates: $10,206. ***Scholarships, grants, and awards by category:*** *Academic interests/achievement:* area/ethnic studies, biological sciences, business, communication, computer science, education, engineering/technologies, English, foreign languages, general academic interests/achievements, home economics, humanities, international studies, library science, mathematics, military science, physical sciences, premedicine, religion/biblical studies, social sciences. *Creative arts/performance:* art/fine arts, creative writing, debating, general creative arts/performance, journalism/publications, music, theater/drama. *Special achievements/activities:* community service, general special achievements/activities, hobbies/interests, leadership, memberships, religious involvement. *Special characteristics:* adult students, children and siblings of alumni, children of educators, children of faculty/staff, children of union members/company employees, children of workers in trades, ethnic background, first-generation college students, general special characteristics, handicapped students, international students, local/state students, married students, members of minority groups, out-of-state students, previous college experience, religious affiliation, spouses of deceased or disabled public servants, veterans, veterans' children. ***Tuition waivers:*** Full or partial for employees or children of employees, senior citizens. ***ROTC:*** Army, Naval cooperative, Air Force.

LOANS *Student loans:* $108,593,016 (62% need-based, 38% non-need-based). 61% of past graduating class borrowed through all loan programs. *Average indebtedness per student:* $39,417. ***Average need-based loan:*** Freshmen: $3711. Undergraduates: $4496. ***Parent loans:*** $38,481,829 (48% need-based, 52% non-need-based). ***Programs:*** Federal Direct (Subsidized and Unsubsidized Stafford, PLUS), Federal Nursing, state, college/university.

WORK-STUDY *Federal work-study:* Total amount: $2,157,093; jobs available.

ATHLETIC AWARDS Total amount: $11,290,867 (35% need-based, 65% non-need-based).

APPLYING FOR FINANCIAL AID *Required financial aid forms:* FAFSA, state aid form. ***Financial aid deadline (priority):*** 3/1. ***Notification date:*** Continuous beginning 2/1.

CONTACT Mr. Marc Harding, Chief Enrollment Officer, University of Pittsburgh, 4227 Fifth Avenue, First Floor, Pittsburgh, PA 15260, 412-624-7488. *E-mail:* oafa@pitt.edu.
Website: http://www.pitt.edu/.

UNIVERSITY OF PITTSBURGH AT BRADFORD

Bradford, PA

Tuition & fees (area res): $14,158 | **Average undergraduate aid package: $14,162**

ABOUT THE INSTITUTION State-related, coed. ***Awards:*** associate and bachelor's degrees. 34 undergraduate majors. ***Total enrollment:*** 1,326. Undergraduates: 1,326. Freshmen: 433. Federal methodology is used as a basis for awarding need-based institutional aid.

UNDERGRADUATE EXPENSES for 2019–2020 *One-time required fee:* $90. ***Tuition, area resident:*** full-time $13,198; part-time $549 per credit hour. ***Tuition, state resident:*** full-time $13,198; part-time $549 per credit hour. ***Tuition, nonresident:*** full-time $24,666; part-time $1027 per credit hour. ***Required fees:*** full-time $960; $165 per term. Full-time tuition and fees vary according to course load and program. Part-time tuition and fees vary according to course load and program. ***College room and board:*** $10,532; ***Room only:*** $6468. Room and board charges vary according to board plan and housing facility.

FRESHMAN FINANCIAL AID (Fall 2018) 347 applied for aid; of those 90% were deemed to have need. 99% of freshmen with need received aid; of those 11% had need fully met. ***Average percent of need met:*** 59% (excluding resources awarded to replace EFC). ***Average financial aid package:*** $12,652 (excluding resources awarded to replace EFC). 8% of all full-time freshmen had no need and received non-need-based gift aid.

UNDERGRADUATE FINANCIAL AID (Fall 2018) 1,118 applied for aid; of those 90% were deemed to have need. 99% of undergraduates with need received aid; of those 6% had need fully met. ***Average percent of need met:*** 60% (excluding resources awarded to replace EFC). ***Average financial aid package:*** $14,162 (excluding resources awarded to replace EFC). 7% of all full-time undergraduates had no need and received non-need-based gift aid.

GIFT AID (NEED-BASED) *Total amount:* $9,295,999 (27% federal, 17% state, 50% institutional, 6% external sources). ***Receiving aid:*** Freshmen: 79% (283); all full-time undergraduates: 78% (939). ***Average award:*** Freshmen: $10,013; Undergraduates: $10,236. ***Scholarships, grants, and awards:*** Federal Pell, FSEOG, state, private, college/university gift aid from institutional funds.

GIFT AID (NON-NEED-BASED) *Total amount:* $1,012,805 (2% state, 84% institutional, 14% external sources). ***Receiving aid:*** Freshmen: 7% (25). Undergraduates: 5% (59). ***Average award:*** Freshmen: $6250. Undergraduates: $6118. ***Scholarships, grants, and awards by category:*** *Academic interests/achievement:* biological sciences, business, communication, computer science, education, engineering/technologies, English, general academic interests/achievements, home economics, humanities, international studies, mathematics, physical sciences, premedicine, social sciences. *Creative arts/performance:* applied art and design, cinema/film/broadcasting, creative writing, music, theater/drama. *Special characteristics:* adult students, children of faculty/staff, children of union members/company employees, general special characteristics, international students, local/state students, members of minority groups, out-of-state students, veterans. ***Tuition waivers:*** Full or partial for employees or children of employees. ***ROTC:*** Army cooperative.

LOANS *Student loans:* $9,056,077 (77% need-based, 23% non-need-based). 82% of past graduating class borrowed through all loan programs. *Average indebtedness per student:* $38,322. ***Average need-based loan:*** Freshmen: $3183. Undergraduates: $4067. ***Parent loans:*** $3,225,847 (65% need-based, 35% non-need-based). ***Programs:*** Federal Direct (Subsidized and Unsubsidized Stafford, PLUS), Perkins.

WORK-STUDY *Federal work-study:* Total amount: $277,064; jobs available. ***State or other work-study/employment:*** Part-time jobs available.

APPLYING FOR FINANCIAL AID *Required financial aid form:* FAFSA. ***Financial aid deadline (priority):*** 3/1. ***Notification date:*** Continuous beginning 4/1. Students must reply within 2 weeks of notification.

CONTACT Ms. Melissa Ibanez, Associate Vice-President of Enrollment Management/ Director of Financial Aid, University of Pittsburgh at Bradford, 300 Campus Drive, Bradford, PA 16701-2812, 814-362-7550 or toll-free 800-872-1787. *Fax:* 814-362-7578. *E-mail:* ibanez@pitt.edu.
Website: http://www.upb.pitt.edu/.

UNIVERSITY OF PITTSBURGH AT GREENSBURG

Greensburg, PA

Tuition & fees (area res): $14,148 | **Average undergraduate aid package: $11,076**

ABOUT THE INSTITUTION State-related, coed. ***Awards:*** certificates and bachelor's degrees. 25 undergraduate majors. ***Total enrollment:*** 1,439. Undergraduates: 1,439. Freshmen: 412. Federal methodology is used as a basis for awarding need-based institutional aid.

UNDERGRADUATE EXPENSES for 2019–2020 *Tuition, area resident:* full-time $13,198; part-time $549 per credit hour. ***Tuition, state resident:*** full-time $13,198; part-time $549 per credit hour. ***Tuition, nonresident:*** full-time $24,666; part-time $1027 per credit hour. ***Required fees:*** full-time $950; $176 per term. Full-time tuition and fees vary according to program. Part-time tuition and fees vary according to program. ***College room and board:*** $10,870; ***Room only:*** $6710. Room and board charges vary according to board plan and housing facility.

FRESHMAN FINANCIAL AID (Fall 2018) 374 applied for aid; of those 84% were deemed to have need. 99% of freshmen with need received aid; of those 15% had need fully met. ***Average percent of need met:*** 60% (excluding resources awarded to replace EFC). ***Average financial aid package:*** $11,743 (excluding resources awarded to replace EFC). 14% of all full-time freshmen had no need and received non-need-based gift aid.

UNDERGRADUATE FINANCIAL AID (Fall 2018) 1,241 applied for aid; of those 87% were deemed to have need. 97% of undergraduates with need received aid; of those 7% had need fully met. ***Average percent of need met:*** 57% (excluding resources awarded to replace EFC). ***Average financial aid package:*** $11,076 (excluding resources awarded to replace EFC). 6% of all full-time undergraduates had no need and received non-need-based gift aid.

GIFT AID (NEED-BASED) *Total amount:* $7,049,436 (36% federal, 25% state, 32% institutional, 7% external sources). ***Receiving aid:*** Freshmen: 71% (285); all full-time undergraduates: 62% (889). ***Average award:*** Freshmen: $9392; Undergraduates: $8741. ***Scholarships, grants, and awards:*** Federal Pell, FSEOG, state, private, college/university gift aid from institutional funds, United Negro College Fund.

GIFT AID (NON-NEED-BASED) *Total amount:* $961,992 (3% state, 84% institutional, 13% external sources). ***Receiving aid:*** Freshmen: 8% (31). Undergraduates: 5% (77). ***Average award:*** Freshmen: $5569. Undergraduates: $5291. ***Scholarships, grants, and awards by category:*** *Academic interests/achievement:* general academic interests/achievements. *Creative arts/performance:* music, theater/drama. *Special achievements/activities:* leadership. *Special characteristics:* local/state students, members of minority groups. ***Tuition waivers:*** Full or partial for employees or children of employees, senior citizens. ***ROTC:*** Army, Air Force cooperative.

LOANS *Student loans:* $8,791,122 (72% need-based, 28% non-need-based). 75% of past graduating class borrowed through all loan programs. *Average indebtedness per student:* $33,844. ***Average need-based loan:*** Freshmen: $3096. Undergraduates: $4073. ***Parent loans:*** $2,337,576 (71% need-based, 29% non-need-based).

Programs: Federal Direct (Subsidized and Unsubsidized Stafford, PLUS), college/university.

WORK-STUDY ***Federal work-study:*** Total amount: $136,206; jobs available.

APPLYING FOR FINANCIAL AID ***Required financial aid forms:*** FAFSA, state aid form. ***Financial aid deadline:*** Continuous. ***Notification date:*** Continuous beginning 12/9.

CONTACT Ms. Brandi S. Darr, Director of Financial Aid, University of Pittsburgh at Greensburg, 150 Finoli Drive, Greensburg, PA 15601-5898, 724-836-7167. *E-mail:* upgfnaid@pitt.edu.
Website: http://www.greensburg.pitt.edu/.

UNIVERSITY OF PITTSBURGH AT JOHNSTOWN

Johnstown, PA

Tuition & fees (area res): $14,156 | **Average undergraduate aid package: $11,076**

ABOUT THE INSTITUTION State-related, coed. ***Awards:*** certificates, associate, and bachelor's degrees. 52 undergraduate majors. ***Total enrollment:*** 2,600. Undergraduates: 2,600. Freshmen: 663. Federal methodology is used as a basis for awarding need-based institutional aid.

UNDERGRADUATE EXPENSES for 2019–2020 ***Tuition, area resident:*** full-time $13,198; part-time $549 per credit. ***Tuition, state resident:*** full-time $13,198; part-time $549 per credit. ***Tuition, nonresident:*** full-time $24,666; part-time $1027 per credit. ***Required fees:*** full-time $958. Full-time tuition and fees vary according to program. Part-time tuition and fees vary according to program. ***College room and board:*** $10,060; ***Room only:*** $6040. Room and board charges vary according to board plan and housing facility.

FRESHMAN FINANCIAL AID (Fall 2018) 374 applied for aid; of those 84% were deemed to have need. 99% of freshmen with need received aid; of those 15% had need fully met. ***Average percent of need met:*** 60% (excluding resources awarded to replace EFC). ***Average financial aid package:*** $11,743 (excluding resources awarded to replace EFC). 14% of all full-time freshmen had no need and received non-need-based gift aid.

UNDERGRADUATE FINANCIAL AID (Fall 2018) 1,241 applied for aid; of those 87% were deemed to have need. 97% of undergraduates with need received aid; of those 7% had need fully met. ***Average percent of need met:*** 57% (excluding resources awarded to replace EFC). ***Average financial aid package:*** $11,076 (excluding resources awarded to replace EFC). 6% of all full-time undergraduates had no need and received non-need-based gift aid.

GIFT AID (NEED-BASED) ***Total amount:*** $7,049,436 (36% federal, 25% state, 32% institutional, 7% external sources). ***Receiving aid:*** Freshmen: 71% (285); all full-time undergraduates: 62% (889). ***Average award:*** Freshmen: $9392; Undergraduates: $8741. ***Scholarships, grants, and awards:*** Federal Pell, FSEOG, state, private, college/university gift aid from institutional funds, United Negro College Fund.

GIFT AID (NON-NEED-BASED) ***Total amount:*** $961,992 (3% state, 84% institutional, 13% external sources). ***Receiving aid:*** Freshmen: 8% (31). Undergraduates: 5% (77). ***Average award:*** Freshmen: $5569. Undergraduates: $5291. ***Scholarships, grants, and awards by category:*** *Academic interests/achievement:* biological sciences, business, communication, computer science, education, engineering/technologies, English, general academic interests/achievements, home economics, humanities, mathematics, physical sciences, premedicine, social sciences. *Creative arts/performance:* journalism/publications, theater/drama. *Special achievements/activities:* leadership. *Special characteristics:* children of faculty/staff. ***Tuition waivers:*** Full or partial for employees or children of employees. ***ROTC:*** Army.

LOANS ***Student loans:*** $8,791,122 (72% need-based, 28% non-need-based). 80% of past graduating class borrowed through all loan programs. *Average indebtedness per student:* $39,603. ***Average need-based loan:*** Freshmen: $3096. Undergraduates: $4073. ***Parent loans:*** $2,337,576 (71% need-based, 29% non-need-based). ***Programs:*** Federal Direct (Subsidized and Unsubsidized Stafford, PLUS), Perkins, college/university.

WORK-STUDY ***Federal work-study:*** Total amount: $136,206; 100 jobs averaging $2400. ***State or other work-study/employment:*** Part-time jobs available.

ATHLETIC AWARDS Total amount: $1,263,105 (65% need-based, 35% non-need-based).

APPLYING FOR FINANCIAL AID ***Required financial aid forms:*** FAFSA, state aid form. ***Financial aid deadline (priority):*** 4/1. ***Notification date:*** Continuous beginning 12/30. Students must reply by 5/1 or within 2 weeks of notification.

CONTACT Ms. Joni L. Trovato, Director of Student Financial Aid, University of Pittsburgh at Johnstown, 450 Schoolhouse Road, 114 Blackington Hall, Johnstown, PA 15904-2990, 814-269-7045 or toll-free 800-765-4875. *Fax:* 814-269-7061.
Website: http://www.upj.pitt.edu/.

UNIVERSITY OF PORTLAND

Portland, OR

Tuition & fees: $47,818 | **Average undergraduate aid package: $33,608**

ABOUT THE INSTITUTION Independent Roman Catholic, coed. ***Awards:*** certificates, bachelor's, master's, and doctoral degrees. 38 undergraduate majors. ***Total enrollment:*** 4,251. Undergraduates: 3,796. Freshmen: 1,003. Federal methodology is used as a basis for awarding need-based institutional aid.

UNDERGRADUATE EXPENSES for 2019–2020 ***Application fee:*** $50. ***Comprehensive fee:*** $61,786 includes full-time tuition ($47,478), mandatory fees ($340), and room and board ($13,968). ***Part-time tuition:*** $1487 per credit hour.

FRESHMAN FINANCIAL AID (Fall 2019, est.) 872 applied for aid; of those 73% were deemed to have need. 99% of freshmen with need received aid; of those 10% had need fully met. ***Average percent of need met:*** 69% (excluding resources awarded to replace EFC). ***Average financial aid package:*** $32,227 (excluding resources awarded to replace EFC). 34% of all full-time freshmen had no need and received non-need-based gift aid.

UNDERGRADUATE FINANCIAL AID (Fall 2019, est.) 2,664 applied for aid; of those 78% were deemed to have need. 99% of undergraduates with need received aid; of those 7% had need fully met. ***Average percent of need met:*** 72% (excluding resources awarded to replace EFC). ***Average financial aid package:*** $33,608 (excluding resources awarded to replace EFC). 41% of all full-time undergraduates had no need and received non-need-based gift aid.

GIFT AID (NEED-BASED) ***Total amount:*** $59,183,408 (5% federal, 1% state, 89% institutional, 5% external sources). ***Receiving aid:*** Freshmen: 44% (442); all full-time undergraduates: 42% (1,563). ***Average award:*** Freshmen: $28,637; Undergraduates: $27,321. ***Scholarships, grants, and awards:*** Federal Pell, FSEOG, state, private, college/university gift aid from institutional funds, Federal Nursing, TEACH Grants.

GIFT AID (NON-NEED-BASED) ***Total amount:*** $33,158,976 (99% institutional, 1% external sources). ***Receiving aid:*** Freshmen: 60% (602). Undergraduates: 52% (1,941). ***Average award:*** Freshmen: $21,159. Undergraduates: $20,044. ***Scholarships, grants, and awards by category:*** *Academic interests/achievement:* biological sciences, business, communication, computer science, education, engineering/technologies, English, foreign languages, general academic interests/achievements, home economics, humanities, mathematics, military science, physical sciences, premedicine, religion/biblical studies, social sciences. *Creative arts/performance:* music, performing arts, theater/drama. *Special achievements/activities:* general special achievements/activities. *Special characteristics:* children of faculty/staff, relatives of clergy, religious affiliation. ***ROTC:*** Army, Air Force.

LOANS ***Student loans:*** $15,572,498 (86% need-based, 14% non-need-based). 56% of past graduating class borrowed through all loan programs. *Average indebtedness per student:* $32,027. ***Average need-based loan:*** Freshmen: $3331. Undergraduates: $4712. ***Parent loans:*** $17,937,312 (89% need-based, 11% non-need-based). ***Programs:*** Federal Direct (Subsidized and Unsubsidized Stafford, PLUS), Federal Nursing, college/university, private loans.

WORK-STUDY ***Federal work-study:*** Total amount: $603,000; jobs available. ***State or other work-study/employment:*** Total amount: $2,530,000 (100% non-need-based). Part-time jobs available.

ATHLETIC AWARDS Total amount: $5,711,024 (24% need-based, 76% non-need-based).

APPLYING FOR FINANCIAL AID ***Required financial aid form:*** FAFSA. ***Financial aid deadline (priority):*** 1/15. ***Notification date:*** Continuous beginning 11/15. Students must reply by 5/1.

CONTACT Ms. Janet Turner, Director of Financial Aid, University of Portland, 5000 North Willamette Boulevard, Portland, OR 97203-5798, 503-943-7311 or toll-free 888-627-5601. *Fax:* 503-943-7508. *E-mail:* finaid@up.edu.
Website: http://www.up.edu/.

UNIVERSITY OF PROVIDENCE

Great Falls, MT

Tuition & fees: $26,662 | **Average undergraduate aid package: $20,583**

ABOUT THE INSTITUTION Independent Roman Catholic, coed. ***Awards:*** certificates, associate, bachelor's, and master's degrees. 73 undergraduate majors. ***Total enrollment:*** 998. Undergraduates: 585. Freshmen: 104. Federal methodology is used as a basis for awarding need-based institutional aid.

UNDERGRADUATE EXPENSES for 2020–2021 ***Comprehensive fee:*** $36,832 includes full-time tuition ($26,462), mandatory fees ($200), and room and board ($10,170). ***College room only:*** $5510. Room and board charges vary according to board plan. ***Part-time tuition:*** $862 per credit. Part-time tuition and fees vary according to course load and location. ***Payment plan:*** Guaranteed tuition.

FRESHMAN FINANCIAL AID (Fall 2019, est.) 95 applied for aid; of those 79% were deemed to have need. 100% of freshmen with need received aid; of those 1% had need fully met. ***Average percent of need met:*** 64% (excluding resources awarded to replace EFC). ***Average financial aid package:*** $20,499 (excluding resources awarded to replace EFC). 9% of all full-time freshmen had no need and received non-need-based gift aid.

UNDERGRADUATE FINANCIAL AID (Fall 2019, est.) 414 applied for aid; of those 89% were deemed to have need. 99% of undergraduates with need received aid; of those 3% had need fully met. ***Average percent of need met:*** 63% (excluding resources awarded to replace EFC). ***Average financial aid package:*** $20,583 (excluding resources awarded to replace EFC). 10% of all full-time undergraduates had no need and received non-need-based gift aid.

GIFT AID (NEED-BASED) ***Total amount:*** $3,219,114 (36% federal, 64% institutional). ***Receiving aid:*** Freshmen: 60% (60); all full-time undergraduates: 60% (291). ***Average award:*** Freshmen: $8485; Undergraduates: $9851. ***Scholarships, grants, and awards:*** Federal Pell, FSEOG, private, college/university gift aid from institutional funds.

GIFT AID (NON-NEED-BASED) ***Total amount:*** $1,147,411 (3% federal, 97% institutional). ***Receiving aid:*** Freshmen: 8% (8). Undergraduates: 7% (36). ***Average award:*** Freshmen: $7821. Undergraduates: $7101. ***Scholarships, grants, and awards by category:*** *Academic interests/achievement:* biological sciences, business, computer science, education, general academic interests/achievements, humanities, mathematics, physical sciences, premedicine, religion/biblical studies, social sciences. *Creative arts/performance:* dance, general creative arts/performance. *Special achievements/activities:* cheerleading/drum major, religious involvement. *Special characteristics:* children and siblings of alumni, children of current students, children of faculty/staff, ethnic background, first-generation college students, international students, local/state students, parents of current students, religious affiliation, siblings of current students, spouses of current students. ***Tuition waivers:*** Full or partial for employees or children of employees.

LOANS ***Student loans:*** $3,564,716 (78% need-based, 22% non-need-based). 61% of past graduating class borrowed through all loan programs. *Average indebtedness per student:* $26,200. ***Average need-based loan:*** Freshmen: $2668. Undergraduates: $3533. ***Parent loans:*** $618,833 (78% need-based, 22% non-need-based). ***Programs:*** Federal Direct (Subsidized and Unsubsidized Stafford, PLUS).

WORK-STUDY ***Federal work-study:*** Total amount: $165,493; jobs available. ***State or other work-study/employment:*** Part-time jobs available.

ATHLETIC AWARDS Total amount: $4,956,751 (65% need-based, 35% non-need-based).

APPLYING FOR FINANCIAL AID ***Required financial aid form:*** FAFSA. ***Financial aid deadline (priority):*** 3/1. ***Notification date:*** Continuous beginning 12/1.

CONTACT Kelli Engelhardt, Director of Financial Aid, University of Providence, 1301 20th Street South, Great Falls, MT 59405, 406-791-5237 or toll-free 800-856-9544. *Fax:* 406-791-5242. *E-mail:* kengelhardt01@ugf.edu.
Website: http://www.uprovidence.edu/.

UNIVERSITY OF PUERTO RICO AT AGUADILLA

Aguadilla, PR

CONTACT Director of Financial Aid, University of Puerto Rico at Aguadilla, PO Box 250-160, Aguadilla, PR 00604-0160, 787-890-2681 Ext. 273.
Website: http://www.uprag.edu/.

UNIVERSITY OF PUERTO RICO AT ARECIBO

Arecibo, PR

CONTACT Myrta F. Salcedo-Ortiz, Director of Financial Aid, University of Puerto Rico at Arecibo, PO Box 4010, Arecibo, PR 00613, 787-878-2830 Ext. 2008. *E-mail:* myrta.ortiz@upr.edu.
Website: http://www.upra.edu/.

UNIVERSITY OF PUERTO RICO AT BAYAMON

Bayamón, PR

CONTACT Mr. Marcos Cesar De Jesus Rosado, Financial Aid Director, University of Puerto Rico at Bayamon, Industrial Minillas Park 170 Road 174, Bayamon, PR 00959-1919, 787-993-8953 Ext. 4031. *Fax:* 787-993-8930. *E-mail:* marcos.dejesus@upr.edu.
Website: http://www.uprb.edu/.

UNIVERSITY OF PUERTO RICO AT CAROLINA

Carolina, PR

CONTACT Financial Aid Office, University of Puerto Rico at Carolina, PO Box 4800, Carolina, PR 00984-4800, 787-257-0000.
Website: http://www.uprc.edu/.

UNIVERSITY OF PUERTO RICO AT CAYEY

Cayey, PR

CONTACT Mr. Hector Maldonado Otero, Director of Financial Aid, University of Puerto Rico at Cayey, Antonio Barcelo, Cayey, PR 00736, 787-738-2161. *Fax:* 787-263-0676.
Website: http://www.cayey.upr.edu/.

UNIVERSITY OF PUERTO RICO AT HUMACAO

Humacao, PR

CONTACT Alfredo Aponte Serrano, Director of Financial Aid, University of Puerto Rico at Humacao, HUC Station, Humacao, PR 00791-4300, 787-850-9362. *E-mail:* alfredo.aponte@upr.edu.
Website: http://www.uprh.edu/.

UNIVERSITY OF PUERTO RICO AT MAYAGÜEZ

Mayagüez, PR

Tuition & fees: N/R | **Average undergraduate aid package: $6856**

ABOUT THE INSTITUTION Commonwealth-supported, coed. ***Awards:*** bachelor's, master's, and doctoral degrees. 54 undergraduate majors. ***Total enrollment:*** 13,224. Undergraduates: 12,321. Federal methodology is used as a basis for awarding need-based institutional aid.

FRESHMAN FINANCIAL AID (Fall 2018) 1914 applied for aid; of those 94% were deemed to have need. 90% of freshmen with need received aid. ***Average financial aid package:*** $5898 (excluding resources awarded to replace EFC). 1% of all full-time freshmen had no need and received non-need-based gift aid.

UNDERGRADUATE FINANCIAL AID (Fall 2018) 9,734 applied for aid; of those 97% were deemed to have need. 93% of undergraduates with need received aid. ***Average financial aid package:*** $6856 (excluding resources awarded to replace EFC). 1% of all full-time undergraduates had no need and received non-need-based gift aid.

GIFT AID (NEED-BASED) ***Total amount:*** $46,162,426 (93% federal, 7% state). ***Receiving aid:*** Freshmen: 73% (1,558); all full-time undergraduates: 72% (8,463). ***Average award:*** Freshmen: $5353; Undergraduates: $5409. ***Scholarships, grants, and awards:*** Federal Pell, FSEOG, state, private, college/university gift aid from institutional funds.

GIFT AID (NON-NEED-BASED) ***Total amount:*** $860,906 (25% state, 20% institutional, 55% external sources). ***Receiving aid:*** Freshmen: 14% (295). Undergraduates: 17% (2,007). ***Average award:*** Freshmen: $1550. Undergraduates: $1512. ***Tuition waivers:*** Full or partial for employees or children of employees. ***ROTC:*** Army, Air Force.

LOANS ***Student loans:*** $10,077,661 (93% need-based, 7% non-need-based). 45% of past graduating class borrowed through all loan programs. *Average indebtedness per student:* $4378. ***Average need-based loan:*** Freshmen: $1614. Undergraduates: $3257. ***Programs:*** Federal Direct (Subsidized and Unsubsidized Stafford).

WORK-STUDY ***Federal work-study:*** Total amount: $1,273,476.27; 1,096 jobs averaging $1099. ***State or other work-study/employment:*** Part-time jobs available.

ATHLETIC AWARDS Total amount: $615,263 (100% non-need-based).

APPLYING FOR FINANCIAL AID ***Required financial aid form:*** FAFSA. ***Financial aid deadline:*** Continuous. ***Notification date:*** Continuous. Students must reply within 2 weeks of notification.

CONTACT Ms. Hilda M. Tamariz Vargas, Director of Financial Aid, University of Puerto Rico at Mayagüez, PO Box 9000, Mayaguez, PR 00681, 787-265-3863. *Fax:* 787-265-1920. *E-mail:* hildam.tamariz@upr.edu.
Website: http://www.uprm.edu/.

UNIVERSITY OF PUERTO RICO AT RIO PIEDRAS

San Juan, PR

CONTACT Mr. Efraim Williams, EDP Manager, University of Puerto Rico at Rio Piedras, PO Box 23300, San Juan, PR 00931-3300, 787-764-0000 Ext. 5573.
Website: http://www.uprrp.edu/.

UNIVERSITY OF PUERTO RICO AT UTUADO

Utuado, PR

CONTACT Edgar Salvá, Director of Financial Assistance, University of Puerto Rico at Utuado, PO Box 2500, Utuado, PR 00641, 787-894-2828 Ext. 2603. *Fax:* 787-894-3810. *E-mail:* esalva@uprutuado.edu.
Website: http://www.uprutuado.edu/.

UNIVERSITY OF PUERTO RICO - MEDICAL SCIENCES CAMPUS

San Juan, PR

CONTACT Mrs. Zoraida Figueroa, Financial Aid Director, University of Puerto Rico - Medical Sciences Campus, Terreno Centro Medico-Edificio Decanato Farmacia y Estudiantes, San Juan, PR 00936-5067, 787-763-2525. *Fax:* 787-282-7117. *E-mail:* zoraida.figueroa@upr.edu.
Website: http://www.rcm.upr.edu/.

UNIVERSITY OF PUERTO RICOV AT PONCE

Ponce, PR

CONTACT Carmelo Vega Montes, Director of Financial Aid, University of Puerto Ricov at Ponce, Box 7186, Ponce, PR 00732-7186, 787-844-8181. *Fax:* 787-840-8108.
Website: http://www.uprp.edu/.

UNIVERSITY OF PUGET SOUND

Tacoma, WA

Tuition & fees: $53,800 | **Average undergraduate aid package: $38,542**

ABOUT THE INSTITUTION Independent, coed. ***Awards:*** bachelor's, master's, and doctoral degrees. 52 undergraduate majors. ***Total enrollment:*** 2,608. Undergraduates: 2,299. Freshmen: 615. Federal methodology is used as a basis for awarding need-based institutional aid.

UNDERGRADUATE EXPENSES for 2020–2021 ***Application fee:*** $60. ***Comprehensive fee:*** $67,280 includes full-time tuition ($53,520), mandatory fees ($280), and room and board ($13,480). ***College room only:*** $7230. Full-time tuition and fees vary according to course load. Room and board charges vary according to board plan and housing facility. ***Part-time tuition:*** $1690 per unit. Part-time tuition and fees vary according to course load.

FRESHMAN FINANCIAL AID (Fall 2019, est.) 516 applied for aid; of those 76% were deemed to have need. 100% of freshmen with need received aid; of those 16% had need fully met. ***Average percent of need met:*** 84% (excluding resources awarded to replace EFC). ***Average financial aid package:*** $40,565 (excluding resources awarded to replace EFC). 36% of all full-time freshmen had no need and received non-need-based gift aid.

UNDERGRADUATE FINANCIAL AID (Fall 2019, est.) 1,563 applied for aid; of those 81% were deemed to have need. 100% of undergraduates with need received aid; of those 15% had need fully met. ***Average percent of need met:*** 80% (excluding resources awarded to replace EFC). ***Average financial aid package:*** $38,542 (excluding resources awarded to replace EFC). 44% of all full-time undergraduates had no need and received non-need-based gift aid.

GIFT AID (NEED-BASED) ***Receiving aid:*** Freshmen: 63% (388); all full-time undergraduates: 55% (1,256). ***Average award:*** Freshmen: $35,896; Undergraduates: $33,262. ***Scholarships, grants, and awards:*** Federal Pell, FSEOG, state, private, college/university gift aid from institutional funds.

GIFT AID (NON-NEED-BASED) ***Receiving aid:*** Freshmen: 10% (63). Undergraduates: 7% (153). ***Average award:*** Freshmen: $22,206. Undergraduates: $19,681. ***Scholarships, grants, and awards by category:*** *Academic interests/achievement:* 1,259 awards ($18,572,056 total): biological sciences, business, communication, computer science, English, foreign languages, general academic interests/achievements, humanities, international studies, mathematics, physical sciences, premedicine, social sciences. *Creative arts/performance:* 50 awards ($200,287 total): art/fine arts, debating, music, theater/drama. *Special characteristics:* 18 awards ($380,850 total): children of faculty/staff, veterans. ***Tuition waivers:*** Full or partial for employees or children of employees. ***ROTC:*** Army cooperative.

LOANS ***Student loans:*** 48% of past graduating class borrowed through all loan programs. *Average indebtedness per student:* $36,290. ***Average need-based loan:*** Freshmen: $3402. Undergraduates: $4367. ***Programs:*** Federal Direct (Subsidized and Unsubsidized Stafford, PLUS).

WORK-STUDY ***Federal work-study:*** 495 jobs averaging $3265. ***State or other work-study/employment:*** 935 part-time jobs averaging $2722.

APPLYING FOR FINANCIAL AID ***Required financial aid form:*** FAFSA. ***Notification date:*** Continuous.

CONTACT Maggie A. Mittuch, Associate Vice President for Student Financial Services, University of Puget Sound, 1500 North Warner Street #1039, Tacoma, WA 98416-1039, 253-879-3214 or toll-free 800-396-7191. *Fax:* 253-879-8508. *E-mail:* mmittuch@pugetsound.edu.
Website: http://www.pugetsound.edu/.

UNIVERSITY OF REDLANDS

Redlands, CA

CONTACT Alisha Aguilar, Director of Financial Aid, University of Redlands, 1200 East Colton Avenue, PO Box 3080, Redlands, CA 92373-0999, 909-748-8047 or toll-free 800-455-5064. *Fax:* 909-335-4089. *E-mail:* financialaid@redlands.edu.
Website: http://www.redlands.edu/.

UNIVERSITY OF RHODE ISLAND

Kingston, RI

Tuition & fees (RI res): $14,566	Average undergraduate aid package: $17,680

ABOUT THE INSTITUTION State-supported, coed. ***Awards:*** certificates, bachelor's, master's, and doctoral degrees. 86 undergraduate majors. Federal methodology is used as a basis for awarding need-based institutional aid.

UNDERGRADUATE EXPENSES for 2019–2020 ***Tuition, state resident:*** full-time $12,590; part-time $525 per credit hour. ***Tuition, nonresident:*** full-time $29,710; part-time $1238 per credit hour. ***Required fees:*** full-time $1976; $58 per credit hour. Full-time tuition and fees vary according to course load, location, and reciprocity agreements. Part-time tuition and fees vary according to course load, location, and reciprocity agreements. ***College room and board:*** $8010; ***Room only:*** $4500. Room and board charges vary according to board plan and housing facility.

FRESHMAN FINANCIAL AID (Fall 2019, est.) 2331 applied for aid; of those 77% were deemed to have need. 97% of freshmen with need received aid; of those 65% had need fully met. ***Average percent of need met:*** 68% (excluding resources awarded to replace EFC). ***Average financial aid package:*** $19,311 (excluding resources awarded to replace EFC). 11% of all full-time freshmen had no need and received non-need-based gift aid.

UNDERGRADUATE FINANCIAL AID (Fall 2019, est.) 12,910 applied for aid; of those 85% were deemed to have need. 91% of undergraduates with need received aid; of those 49% had need fully met. ***Average percent of need met:*** 57% (excluding resources awarded to replace EFC). ***Average financial aid package:*** $17,680 (excluding resources awarded to replace EFC). 9% of all full-time undergraduates had no need and received non-need-based gift aid.

GIFT AID (NEED-BASED) ***Total amount:*** $104,722,951 (16% federal, 3% state, 78% institutional, 3% external sources). ***Receiving aid:*** Freshmen: 52% (1,696); all full-time undergraduates: 71% (9,468). ***Average award:*** Freshmen: $10,885; Undergraduates: $10,736. ***Scholarships, grants, and awards:*** Federal Pell, FSEOG, state, private, college/university gift aid from institutional funds.

GIFT AID (NON-NEED-BASED) ***Total amount:*** $9,240,726 (96% institutional, 4% external sources). ***Receiving aid:*** Freshmen: 12% (381). Undergraduates: 10% (1,338). ***Average award:*** Freshmen: $7132. Undergraduates: $7245. ***Scholarships, grants, and awards by category:*** *Academic interests/achievement:* agriculture, area/ethnic studies, biological sciences, business, communication, computer science, education, engineering/technologies, English, foreign languages, general academic interests/achievements, health fields, home economics, humanities, international studies, library science, mathematics, military science, physical sciences, premedicine, religion/biblical studies, social sciences. *Creative arts/performance:* applied art and design, journalism/publications, music, theater/drama. *Special achievements/activities:* leadership. *Special characteristics:* children and siblings of alumni, children of public servants, children of union members/company employees. ***Tuition waivers:*** Full or partial for minority students, employees or children of employees, senior citizens. ***ROTC:*** Army.

LOANS ***Student loans:*** $93,114,320 (76% need-based, 24% non-need-based). 63% of past graduating class borrowed through all loan programs. *Average indebtedness per student:* $35,883. ***Average need-based loan:*** Freshmen: $3193. Undergraduates: $6287. ***Parent loans:*** $21,096,500 (71% need-based, 29% non-need-based). ***Programs:*** Federal Direct (Subsidized and Unsubsidized Stafford, PLUS), Federal Nursing, college/university.

WORK-STUDY ***Federal work-study:*** Total amount: $1,887,806.

ATHLETIC AWARDS Total amount: $9,003,953 (91% need-based, 9% non-need-based).

APPLYING FOR FINANCIAL AID ***Required financial aid form:*** FAFSA. ***Financial aid deadline (priority):*** 3/1. ***Notification date:*** 3/1. Students must reply by 5/1.

CONTACT Mr. Paul Langhammer, Senior Associate Director of Enrollment Services, University of Rhode Island, Green Hall, 35 Campus Avenue, Kingston, RI 02881, 401-874-5526.
Website: http://www.uri.edu/.

UNIVERSITY OF RICHMOND

Richmond, VA

Tuition & fees: $56,860	Average undergraduate aid package: $52,064

ABOUT THE INSTITUTION Independent, coed. ***Awards:*** certificates, bachelor's, master's, and doctoral degrees. 55 undergraduate majors. ***Total enrollment:*** 3,914. Undergraduates: 3,161. Freshmen: 832. Institutional methodology is used as a basis for awarding need-based institutional aid.

UNDERGRADUATE EXPENSES for 2020–2021 ***Application fee:*** $50. ***Comprehensive fee:*** $70,290 includes full-time tuition ($56,860) and room and board ($13,430). ***College room only:*** $6300. ***Part-time tuition:*** $2320 per credit hour. Part-time tuition and fees vary according to course load. ***Payment plan:*** Tuition prepayment.

FRESHMAN FINANCIAL AID (Fall 2019, est.) 515 applied for aid; of those 69% were deemed to have need. 100% of freshmen with need received aid; of those 89% had need fully met. ***Average percent of need met:*** 100% (excluding resources awarded to replace EFC). ***Average financial aid package:*** $52,557 (excluding resources awarded to replace EFC). 11% of all full-time freshmen had no need and received non-need-based gift aid.

UNDERGRADUATE FINANCIAL AID (Fall 2019, est.) 1,578 applied for aid; of those 79% were deemed to have need. 100% of undergraduates with need received aid; of those 83% had need fully met. ***Average percent of need met:*** 100% (excluding resources awarded to replace EFC). ***Average financial aid package:*** $52,064 (excluding resources awarded to replace EFC). 19% of all full-time undergraduates had no need and received non-need-based gift aid.

GIFT AID (NEED-BASED) ***Receiving aid:*** Freshmen: 42% (350); all full-time undergraduates: 38% (1,217). ***Average award:*** Freshmen: $46,186; Undergraduates: $45,919. ***Scholarships, grants, and awards:*** Federal Pell, FSEOG, state, private, college/university gift aid from institutional funds.

GIFT AID (NON-NEED-BASED) ***Receiving aid:*** Freshmen: 10% (85). Undergraduates: 7% (239). ***Average award:*** Freshmen: $31,587. Undergraduates: $23,820. ***Scholarships, grants, and awards by category:*** *Academic interests/achievement:* 158 awards ($7,743,404 total): biological sciences, computer science, general academic interests/achievements, mathematics, physical sciences, social sciences. *Creative arts/performance:* 24 awards ($782,480 total): applied art and design, dance, music, performing arts, theater/drama. *Special achievements/activities:* 100 awards ($250,000 total): community service. *Special characteristics:* 282 awards ($8,775,884 total). ***Tuition waivers:*** Full or partial for employees or children of employees. ***ROTC:*** Army.

LOANS ***Student loans:*** 41% of past graduating class borrowed through all loan programs. *Average indebtedness per student:* $28,341. ***Average need-based loan:*** Freshmen: $2750. Undergraduates: $3650. ***Programs:*** Federal Direct (Subsidized and Unsubsidized Stafford, PLUS).

WORK-STUDY ***Federal work-study:*** 661 jobs averaging $1400.

APPLYING FOR FINANCIAL AID ***Required financial aid forms:*** FAFSA, CSS Financial Aid PROFILE, noncustodial (divorced/separated) parent's statement, federal income tax form(s). ***Notification date:*** Students must reply within 4 weeks of notification.

CONTACT Financial Aid Office, University of Richmond, 410 Westhampton Way, Richmond, VA 23173, 804-289-8000 or toll-free 800-700-1662.
Website: http://www.richmond.edu/.

UNIVERSITY OF RIO GRANDE

Rio Grande, OH

CONTACT Ms. Meghann Fraley, Assistant Director of Financial Aid, University of Rio Grande, PO Box 500, 218 North College Avenue, Rio Grande, OH 45674, 740-245-7218 or toll-free 800-282-7201. *Fax:* 740-245-7102.
Website: http://www.rio.edu/.

UNIVERSITY OF ROCHESTER

Rochester, NY

Tuition & fees: N/R	Average undergraduate aid package: $50,665

ABOUT THE INSTITUTION Independent, coed. ***Awards:*** certificates, bachelor's, master's, and doctoral degrees. 67 undergraduate majors. ***Total enrollment:*** 7,121. Undergraduates: 6,535. Freshmen: 1,522. Institutional methodology is used as a basis for awarding need-based institutional aid.

FRESHMAN FINANCIAL AID (Fall 2019, est.) 1123 applied for aid; of those 78% were deemed to have need. 100% of freshmen with need received aid; of those 93% had need fully met. ***Average percent of need met:*** 98% (excluding resources awarded to replace EFC). ***Average financial aid package:*** $51,171 (excluding resources awarded to replace EFC). 22% of all full-time freshmen had no need and received non-need-based gift aid.

UNDERGRADUATE FINANCIAL AID (Fall 2019, est.) 4,004 applied for aid; of those 85% were deemed to have need. 100% of undergraduates with need received aid; of those 91% had need fully met. ***Average percent of need met:*** 96% (excluding resources awarded to replace EFC). ***Average financial aid package:*** $50,665 (excluding resources awarded to replace EFC). 26% of all full-time undergraduates had no need and received non-need-based gift aid.

GIFT AID (NEED-BASED) ***Receiving aid:*** Freshmen: 58% (872); all full-time undergraduates: 55% (3,392). ***Average award:*** Freshmen: $48,013; Undergraduates: $46,633. ***Scholarships, grants, and awards:*** Federal Pell, FSEOG, state, college/university gift aid from institutional funds.

GIFT AID (NON-NEED-BASED) ***Receiving aid:*** Freshmen: 9% (136). Undergraduates: 7% (423). ***Average award:*** Freshmen: $15,845. Undergraduates: $14,575. ***Scholarships, grants, and awards by category:*** *Academic interests/achievement:* engineering/technologies, general academic interests/achievements, military science. *Creative arts/performance:* general creative arts/performance, music, performing arts. *Special achievements/activities:* general special achievements/activities, leadership. *Special characteristics:* children and siblings of alumni, children of faculty/staff, general special characteristics, international students, veterans. ***ROTC:*** Army cooperative, Naval, Air Force cooperative.

LOANS ***Student loans:*** 55% of past graduating class borrowed through all loan programs. *Average indebtedness per student:* $28,503. ***Average need-based loan:*** Freshmen: $2417. Undergraduates: $3280. ***Programs:*** Federal Direct (Subsidized and Unsubsidized Stafford, PLUS), Federal Nursing.

WORK-STUDY ***Federal work-study:*** 2,126 jobs averaging $3151. ***State or other work-study/employment:*** 511 part-time jobs averaging $1216.

APPLYING FOR FINANCIAL AID ***Required financial aid forms:*** FAFSA, CSS Financial Aid PROFILE, state aid form, noncustodial (divorced/separated) parent's statement.

CONTACT Samantha Veeder, Director of Financial Aid, University of Rochester, Wallis Hall, PO Box 270261, Rochester, NY 14627-0250, 585-275-3226 or toll-free 888-822-2256. *Fax:* 585-756-7664. *E-mail:* samantha.veeder@rochester.edu.
Website: http://www.rochester.edu/.

UNIVERSITY OF ST. FRANCIS

Joliet, IL

Tuition & fees: $35,000	Average undergraduate aid package: $26,685

ABOUT THE INSTITUTION Independent Roman Catholic, coed. ***Awards:*** certificates, bachelor's, master's, and doctoral degrees. 58 undergraduate majors. ***Total enrollment:*** 3,079. Undergraduates: 1,746. Freshmen: 236. Federal methodology is used as a basis for awarding need-based institutional aid.

UNDERGRADUATE EXPENSES for 2020–2021 ***Comprehensive fee:*** $45,210 includes full-time tuition ($35,000) and room and board ($10,210). Full-time tuition and fees vary according to degree level, location, and program. Room and board charges vary according to housing facility. ***Part-time tuition:*** $875 per credit hour. ***Part-time fees:*** $75 per term. Part-time tuition and fees vary according to degree level and program.

FRESHMAN FINANCIAL AID (Fall 2019, est.) 221 applied for aid; of those 89% were deemed to have need. 100% of freshmen with need received aid; of those 37% had need fully met. ***Average percent of need met:*** 84% (excluding resources awarded to replace EFC). ***Average financial aid package:*** $31,462 (excluding resources awarded to replace EFC). 15% of all full-time freshmen had no need and received non-need-based gift aid.

UNDERGRADUATE FINANCIAL AID (Fall 2019, est.) 1,272 applied for aid; of those 90% were deemed to have need. 100% of undergraduates with need received aid; of those 29% had need fully met. ***Average percent of need met:*** 75% (excluding resources awarded to replace EFC). ***Average financial aid package:*** $26,685 (excluding resources awarded to replace EFC). 16% of all full-time undergraduates had no need and received non-need-based gift aid.

GIFT AID (NEED-BASED) ***Total amount:*** $21,204,659 (16% federal, 14% state, 70% institutional). ***Receiving aid:*** Freshmen: 83% (197); all full-time undergraduates: 80% (1,139). ***Average award:*** Freshmen: $27,776; Undergraduates: $22,898. ***Scholarships, grants, and awards:*** Federal Pell, FSEOG, state, private, college/university gift aid from institutional funds, Federal Nursing.

GIFT AID (NON-NEED-BASED) ***Total amount:*** $4,604,206 (1% federal, 87% institutional, 12% external sources). ***Receiving aid:*** Freshmen: 24% (56). Undergraduates: 12% (174). ***Average award:*** Freshmen: $18,169. Undergraduates: $13,846. ***Scholarships, grants, and awards by category:*** *Academic interests/achievement:* 1,067 awards ($12,031,000 total): biological sciences, communication, education, general academic interests/achievements, home economics, international studies, physical sciences, premedicine, social sciences. *Creative arts/performance:* 46 awards ($122,759 total): applied art and design, art/fine arts, general creative arts/performance, music, performing arts. *Special achievements/activities:* 506 awards ($4,820,000 total): cheerleading/drum major, community service, general special achievements/activities, leadership, religious involvement. *Special characteristics:* 238 awards ($232,405 total): adult students, children and siblings of alumni, children of educators, children of faculty/staff, ethnic background, first-generation college students, general special characteristics, religious affiliation, siblings of current students, veterans. ***Tuition waivers:*** Full or partial for children of alumni, employees or children of employees. ***ROTC:*** Army cooperative.

LOANS ***Student loans:*** $9,714,091 (71% need-based, 29% non-need-based). 75% of past graduating class borrowed through all loan programs. *Average indebtedness per student:* $30,274. ***Average need-based loan:*** Freshmen: $4383. Undergraduates: $4522. ***Parent loans:*** $3,226,297 (41% need-based, 59% non-need-based). ***Programs:*** Federal Direct (Subsidized and Unsubsidized Stafford, PLUS), Alternative loans from private lenders.

WORK-STUDY ***Federal work-study:*** Total amount: $250,000; 168 jobs averaging $2602. ***State or other work-study/employment:*** Total amount: $350,000 (100% non-need-based). 300 part-time jobs averaging $2500.

ATHLETIC AWARDS Total amount: $4,657,776 (66% need-based, 34% non-need-based).

APPLYING FOR FINANCIAL AID ***Required financial aid forms:*** FAFSA, institution's own form. ***Financial aid deadline (priority):*** 11/15. ***Notification date:*** Continuous beginning 10/15. Students must reply within 8 weeks of notification.

CONTACT Mr. Bruce A. Foote, Executive Director of Financial Aid Services, University of St. Francis, 500 North Wilcox Street, Joliet, IL 60435-6188, 815-740-5097 or toll-free 800-735-7500. *Fax:* 815-740-3822. *E-mail:* bfoote@stfrancis.edu.
Website: http://www.stfrancis.edu/.

UNIVERSITY OF SAINT FRANCIS

Fort Wayne, IN

Tuition & fees: $32,420	Average undergraduate aid package: $23,587

ABOUT THE INSTITUTION Independent Roman Catholic, coed. ***Awards:*** certificates, associate, bachelor's, master's, and doctoral degrees. 50 undergraduate majors. ***Total enrollment:*** 2,249. Undergraduates: 1,745. Freshmen: 394. Federal methodology is used as a basis for awarding need-based institutional aid.

UNDERGRADUATE EXPENSES for 2020–2021 ***One-time required fee:*** $195. ***Comprehensive fee:*** $42,910 includes full-time tuition ($31,290), mandatory fees ($1130), and room and board ($10,490). Full-time tuition and fees vary according to course load and location. ***Part-time tuition:*** $995 per semester hour. ***Part-time fees:*** $160 per term. Part-time tuition and fees vary according to course load and location.

FRESHMAN FINANCIAL AID (Fall 2019, est.) 378 applied for aid; of those 93% were deemed to have need. 100% of freshmen with need received aid; of those 19% had need fully met. ***Average percent of need met:*** 82% (excluding resources awarded to replace EFC). ***Average financial aid package:*** $26,714 (excluding resources awarded to replace EFC). 4% of all full-time freshmen had no need and received non-need-based gift aid.

UNDERGRADUATE FINANCIAL AID (Fall 2019, est.) 1,402 applied for aid; of those 91% were deemed to have need. 100% of undergraduates with need received aid; of those 17% had need fully met. ***Average percent of need met:*** 73% (excluding resources awarded to replace EFC). ***Average financial aid package:*** $23,587 (excluding resources awarded to replace EFC). 10% of all full-time undergraduates had no need and received non-need-based gift aid.

GIFT AID (NEED-BASED) ***Total amount:*** $21,763,272 (16% federal, 20% state, 57% institutional, 7% external sources). ***Receiving aid:*** Freshmen: 90% (349); all full-time undergraduates: 84% (1,255). ***Average award:*** Freshmen: $23,551; Undergraduates: $20,164. ***Scholarships, grants, and awards:*** Federal Pell, FSEOG, state, private, college/university gift aid from institutional funds.

GIFT AID (NON-NEED-BASED) ***Total amount:*** $2,621,080 (1% state, 77% institutional, 22% external sources). ***Receiving aid:*** Freshmen: 15% (58). Undergraduates: 12% (183). ***Average award:*** Freshmen: $12,861. Undergraduates: $10,539. ***Scholarships, grants, and awards by category:*** *Academic interests/achievement:* general academic interests/achievements, health fields. *Creative arts/performance:* art/fine arts, dance, music. *Special achievements/activities:* cheerleading/drum major, religious involvement. *Special characteristics:* children of faculty/staff. ***Tuition waivers:*** Full or partial for employees or children of employees. ***ROTC:*** Army cooperative.

LOANS ***Student loans:*** $12,399,741 (77% need-based, 23% non-need-based). 83% of past graduating class borrowed through all loan programs. *Average indebtedness per student:* $42,336. ***Average need-based loan:*** Freshmen: $2984. Undergraduates: $3715. ***Parent loans:*** $2,027,534 (47% need-based, 53% non-need-based). ***Programs:*** Federal Direct (Subsidized and Unsubsidized Stafford, PLUS).

WORK-STUDY ***Federal work-study:*** Total amount: $678,993; jobs available. ***State or other work-study/employment:*** Part-time jobs available.

ATHLETIC AWARDS Total amount: $6,092,790 (69% need-based, 31% non-need-based).

APPLYING FOR FINANCIAL AID ***Required financial aid form:*** FAFSA. ***Financial aid deadline (priority):*** 4/15. ***Notification date:*** Continuous beginning 12/1. Students must reply by 8/1.

CONTACT Office of Financial Aid, University of Saint Francis, 2701 Spring Street, Fort Wayne, IN 46808, 260-399-8003 or toll-free 800-729-4732. *Fax:* 260-399-8162. *E-mail:* finaid@sf.edu.
Website: http://www.sf.edu/.

UNIVERSITY OF SAINT JOSEPH

West Hartford, CT

Tuition & fees: N/R **Average undergraduate aid package: N/A**

ABOUT THE INSTITUTION Independent Roman Catholic, coed, primarily women. ***Awards:*** certificates, bachelor's, master's, and doctoral degrees. 25 undergraduate majors. ***Total enrollment:*** 2,398. Undergraduates: 904. Freshmen: 194. Federal methodology is used as a basis for awarding need-based institutional aid.

UNDERGRADUATE EXPENSES for 2020–2021 ***Application fee:*** $50. ***Tuition:*** part-time $644 per credit hour. ***Required fees:*** $65 per credit hour. Full-time tuition and fees vary according to class time, course load, degree level, location, and program. Part-time tuition and fees vary according to class time, course load, degree level, location, and program. ***College room only:*** $3448. Room and board charges vary according to board plan and location.

FRESHMAN FINANCIAL AID (Fall 2018) 218 applied for aid; of those 100% were deemed to have need. 100% of freshmen with need received aid; of those 32% had need fully met.

UNDERGRADUATE FINANCIAL AID (Fall 2018) 745 applied for aid; of those 99% were deemed to have need. 100% of undergraduates with need received aid.

GIFT AID (NEED-BASED) ***Total amount:*** $17,690,842 (11% federal, 2% state, 82% institutional, 5% external sources). ***Receiving aid:*** Freshmen: 33% (73); all full-time undergraduates: 94% (717). ***Scholarships, grants, and awards:*** Federal Pell, FSEOG, state, private, college/university gift aid from institutional funds.

GIFT AID (NON-NEED-BASED) ***Receiving aid:*** Freshmen: 2% (5). Undergraduates: 3% (24). ***Scholarships, grants, and awards by category:*** *Academic interests/achievement:* general academic interests/achievements. *Special achievements/activities:* leadership. *Special characteristics:* local/state students, members of minority groups, siblings of current students.

LOANS ***Student loans:*** $7,268,982 (70% need-based, 30% non-need-based). 90% of past graduating class borrowed through all loan programs. *Average indebtedness per student:* $38,916. ***Parent loans:*** $2,243,573 (100% need-based). ***Programs:*** Federal Direct (Subsidized and Unsubsidized Stafford, PLUS), Perkins.

WORK-STUDY ***Federal work-study:*** Total amount: $392,962; 214 jobs averaging $2184. ***State or other work-study/employment:*** Part-time jobs available.

APPLYING FOR FINANCIAL AID ***Required financial aid form:*** FAFSA. ***Financial aid deadline (priority):*** 3/1. ***Notification date:*** Continuous beginning 11/15. Students must reply by 5/1.

CONTACT Student Financial Services, University of Saint Joseph, 1678 Asylum Avenue, West Hartford, CT 06117, 860-231-5223 or toll-free 866-442-8752. *E-mail:* financialaid@usj.edu.
Website: http://www.usj.edu/.

UNIVERSITY OF SAINT KATHERINE

San Marcos, CA

Tuition & fees: $25,300 **Average undergraduate aid package: $18,642**

ABOUT THE INSTITUTION Independent Christian, coed. ***Awards:*** bachelor's degrees. 11 undergraduate majors. Both federal and institutional methodology are used as a basis for awarding need-based institutional aid.

UNDERGRADUATE EXPENSES for 2019–2020 ***Tuition:*** full-time $23,500; part-time $783 per unit. ***Required fees:*** full-time $1800.

FRESHMAN FINANCIAL AID (Fall 2018) 40 applied for aid; of those 95% were deemed to have need. 100% of freshmen with need received aid; of those 8% had need fully met. ***Average percent of need met:*** 57% (excluding resources awarded to replace EFC). ***Average financial aid package:*** $19,156 (excluding resources awarded to replace EFC). 9% of all full-time freshmen had no need and received non-need-based gift aid.

UNDERGRADUATE FINANCIAL AID (Fall 2018) 152 applied for aid; of those 93% were deemed to have need. 100% of undergraduates with need received aid; of those 5% had need fully met. ***Average percent of need met:*** 57% (excluding resources awarded to replace EFC). ***Average financial aid package:*** $18,642 (excluding resources awarded to replace EFC). 5% of all full-time undergraduates had no need and received non-need-based gift aid.

GIFT AID (NEED-BASED) ***Total amount:*** $1,105,331 (48% federal, 32% state, 18% institutional, 2% external sources). ***Receiving aid:*** Freshmen: 84% (38); all full-time undergraduates: 85% (141). ***Average award:*** Freshmen: $15,182; Undergraduates: $13,950. ***Scholarships, grants, and awards:*** Federal Pell, state, private, college/university gift aid from institutional funds.

GIFT AID (NON-NEED-BASED) ***Total amount:*** $149,562 (100% institutional). ***Receiving aid:*** Freshmen: 38% (17). Undergraduates: 28% (47). ***Average award:*** Freshmen: $1478. Undergraduates: $2042. ***Tuition waivers:*** Full or partial for employees or children of employees.

LOANS ***Student loans:*** $1,369,838 (82% need-based, 18% non-need-based). 100% of past graduating class borrowed through all loan programs. *Average indebtedness per student:* $34,245. ***Average need-based loan:*** Freshmen: $3128. Undergraduates: $4300. ***Parent loans:*** $962,751 (22% need-based, 78% non-need-based). ***Programs:*** Federal Direct (Subsidized and Unsubsidized Stafford, PLUS).

ATHLETIC AWARDS Total amount: $1,421,816 (100% need-based).

APPLYING FOR FINANCIAL AID ***Required financial aid forms:*** FAFSA, institution's own form, state aid form. ***Financial aid deadline:*** 8/1.

CONTACT Financial Aid Office, University of Saint Katherine, 1637 Capalina Road, San Marcos, CA 92069, 760-471-1316.
Website: http://www.usk.edu/.

UNIVERSITY OF SAINT MARY

Leavenworth, KS

Tuition & fees: $29,930	Average undergraduate aid package: $22,134

ABOUT THE INSTITUTION Independent Roman Catholic, coed. ***Awards:*** associate, bachelor's, master's, and doctoral degrees. 32 undergraduate majors. ***Total enrollment:*** 1,240. Undergraduates: 782. Freshmen: 149. Federal methodology is used as a basis for awarding need-based institutional aid.

UNDERGRADUATE EXPENSES for 2019–2020 ***Application fee:*** $25. ***Comprehensive fee:*** $38,070 includes full-time tuition ($28,860), mandatory fees ($1070), and room and board ($8140). Room and board charges vary according to board plan and housing facility. ***Part-time tuition:*** $665 per credit hour.

FRESHMAN FINANCIAL AID (Fall 2018) 127 applied for aid; of those 92% were deemed to have need. 100% of freshmen with need received aid; of those 16% had need fully met. ***Average percent of need met:*** 70% (excluding resources awarded to replace EFC). ***Average financial aid package:*** $21,843 (excluding resources awarded to replace EFC). 10% of all full-time freshmen had no need and received non-need-based gift aid.

UNDERGRADUATE FINANCIAL AID (Fall 2018) 629 applied for aid; of those 93% were deemed to have need. 99% of undergraduates with need received aid; of those 13% had need fully met. ***Average percent of need met:*** 67% (excluding resources awarded to replace EFC). ***Average financial aid package:*** $22,134 (excluding resources awarded to replace EFC). 11% of all full-time undergraduates had no need and received non-need-based gift aid.

GIFT AID (NEED-BASED) ***Total amount:*** $8,656,616 (18% federal, 8% state, 70% institutional, 4% external sources). ***Receiving aid:*** Freshmen: 88% (115); all full-time undergraduates: 84% (559). ***Average award:*** Freshmen: $18,863; Undergraduates: $18,217. ***Scholarships, grants, and awards:*** Federal Pell, FSEOG, state, private, college/university gift aid from institutional funds.

GIFT AID (NON-NEED-BASED) ***Total amount:*** $1,315,708 (95% institutional, 5% external sources). ***Receiving aid:*** Freshmen: 14% (18). Undergraduates: 10% (64). ***Average award:*** Freshmen: $13,692. Undergraduates: $13,786. ***Scholarships, grants, and awards by category:*** *Academic interests/achievement:* general academic interests/achievements. *Creative arts/performance:* art/fine arts, debating, music, theater/drama. *Special achievements/activities:* community service. *Special characteristics:* children and siblings of alumni, children of faculty/staff, siblings of current students. ***Tuition waivers:*** Full or partial for employees or children of employees. ***ROTC:*** Army cooperative.

LOANS ***Student loans:*** $5,271,925 (76% need-based, 24% non-need-based). *Average indebtedness per student:* $27,409. ***Average need-based loan:*** Freshmen: $4211. Undergraduates: $5255. ***Parent loans:*** $1,283,713 (54% need-based, 46% non-need-based). ***Programs:*** Federal Direct (Subsidized and Unsubsidized Stafford, PLUS), Perkins.

WORK-STUDY ***Federal work-study:*** Total amount: $182,754; jobs available.

ATHLETIC AWARDS Total amount: $1,998,125 (85% need-based, 15% non-need-based).

APPLYING FOR FINANCIAL AID ***Required financial aid forms:*** FAFSA, state aid form. ***Financial aid deadline (priority):*** 4/1. ***Notification date:*** 2/15. Students must reply within 3 weeks of notification.

CONTACT Mrs. Judy Wiedower, Financial Aid Director, University of Saint Mary, 4100 South Fourth Street, Leavenworth, KS 66048, 913-758-6314 or toll-free 800-752-7043. *Fax:* 913-758-6146. *E-mail:* wiedower@hub.smcks.edu.
Website: http://www.stmary.edu/.

UNIVERSITY OF ST. THOMAS

St. Paul, MN

ABOUT THE INSTITUTION Independent Roman Catholic, coed. ***Awards:*** certificates, associate, bachelor's, master's, and doctoral degrees. 69 undergraduate majors. ***Total enrollment:*** 10,035. Undergraduates: 6,395. Freshmen: 1,823.

GIFT AID (NEED-BASED) ***Scholarships, grants, and awards:*** Federal Pell, FSEOG, state, private, college/university gift aid from institutional funds.

GIFT AID (NON-NEED-BASED) ***Scholarships, grants, and awards by category:*** *Academic interests/achievement:* biological sciences, business, education, English, general academic interests/achievements, humanities, international studies, mathematics, physical sciences, religion/biblical studies, social sciences. *Creative arts/performance:* journalism/publications, music. *Special characteristics:* children of educators, children of faculty/staff, general special characteristics.

LOANS ***Programs:*** Federal Direct (Subsidized and Unsubsidized Stafford, PLUS), Perkins, state, private loans.

WORK-STUDY ***Federal work-study:*** Total amount: $3,240,350; 1,048 jobs averaging $3119. ***State or other work-study/employment:*** Total amount: $4,157,098 (50% need-based, 50% non-need-based). 867 part-time jobs averaging $3087.

APPLYING FOR FINANCIAL AID ***Required financial aid form:*** FAFSA.

CONTACT Ms. Paula Benson, Associate Director of Student Financial Services, University of St. Thomas, 2115 Summit Avenue, MHC 152, St. Paul, MN 55105-1096, 651-962-6547 or toll-free 800-328-6819. *Fax:* 651-962-6599. *E-mail:* paula.benson@stthomas.edu.
Website: http://www.stthomas.edu/.

UNIVERSITY OF ST. THOMAS

Houston, TX

Tuition & fees: $31,560	Average undergraduate aid package: $25,335

ABOUT THE INSTITUTION Independent Roman Catholic, coed. ***Awards:*** certificates, associate, bachelor's, master's, and doctoral degrees. 34 undergraduate majors. ***Total enrollment:*** 3,517. Undergraduates: 2,174. Freshmen: 343. Federal methodology is used as a basis for awarding need-based institutional aid.

UNDERGRADUATE EXPENSES for 2020–2021 ***Comprehensive fee:*** $41,030 includes full-time tuition ($30,800), mandatory fees ($760), and room and board ($9470). ***College room only:*** $5880. Room and board charges vary according to board plan and housing facility. ***Part-time tuition:*** $1100 per credit hour. Part-time tuition and fees vary according to course load.

FRESHMAN FINANCIAL AID (Fall 2019, est.) 292 applied for aid; of those 88% were deemed to have need. 100% of freshmen with need received aid; of those 15% had need fully met. ***Average percent of need met:*** 77% (excluding resources awarded to replace EFC). ***Average financial aid package:*** $26,860 (excluding resources awarded to replace EFC). 28% of all full-time freshmen had no need and received non-need-based gift aid.

UNDERGRADUATE FINANCIAL AID (Fall 2019, est.) 1,260 applied for aid; of those 94% were deemed to have need. 99% of undergraduates with need received aid; of those 9% had need fully met. ***Average percent of need met:*** 69% (excluding resources awarded to replace EFC). ***Average financial aid package:*** $25,335 (excluding resources awarded to replace EFC). 23% of all full-time undergraduates had no need and received non-need-based gift aid.

GIFT AID (NEED-BASED) ***Total amount:*** $28,077,553 (14% federal, 8% state, 77% institutional, 1% external sources). ***Receiving aid:*** Freshmen: 76% (254); all full-time undergraduates: 68% (1,155). ***Average award:*** Freshmen: $24,672; Undergraduates: $22,983. ***Scholarships, grants, and awards:*** Federal Pell, FSEOG, state, private, college/university gift aid from institutional funds.

GIFT AID (NON-NEED-BASED) ***Total amount:*** $5,281,894 (98% institutional, 2% external sources). ***Receiving aid:*** Freshmen: 9% (31). Undergraduates: 4% (66). ***Average award:*** Freshmen: $12,014. Undergraduates: $12,558. ***Scholarships, grants, and awards by category:*** *Academic interests/achievement:* biological sciences, business, communication, computer science, education, English, foreign languages, general academic interests/achievements, home economics, humanities, international studies, mathematics, physical sciences, premedicine, religion/biblical studies, social sciences. *Creative arts/performance:* applied art and design, art/fine arts, general creative arts/performance, music, performing arts, theater/drama. *Special achievements/activities:* general special achievements/activities, leadership, religious involvement. *Special characteristics:* children of faculty/staff, general special characteristics, previous college experience, religious affiliation, veterans. ***Tuition waivers:*** Full or partial for employees or children of employees. ***ROTC:*** Army cooperative, Air Force cooperative.

LOANS ***Student loans:*** $5,645,080 (80% need-based, 20% non-need-based). 48% of past graduating class borrowed through all loan programs. *Average indebtedness*

per student: $25,969. ***Average need-based loan:*** Freshmen: $3384. Undergraduates: $4470. ***Parent loans:*** $1,225,185 (41% need-based, 59% non-need-based). ***Programs:*** Federal Direct (Subsidized and Unsubsidized Stafford, PLUS), state.

WORK-STUDY ***Federal work-study:*** Total amount: $280,949; 72 jobs averaging $3854. ***State or other work-study/employment:*** Total amount: $4000 (100% need-based). 1 part-time job averaging $4000.

ATHLETIC AWARDS Total amount: $339,360 (58% need-based, 42% non-need-based).

APPLYING FOR FINANCIAL AID ***Required financial aid form:*** FAFSA. ***Financial aid deadline (priority):*** 4/15. ***Notification date:*** Continuous beginning 12/15. Students must reply by 5/1.

CONTACT Lynda McKendree, Dean of Scholarships and Financial Aid, University of St. Thomas, 3800 Montrose Boulevard, Houston, TX 77006-4696, 713-525-2170 or toll-free 800-856-8565. *Fax:* 713-525-2142. *E-mail:* finaid@stthom.edu.
Website: http://www.stthom.edu/.

UNIVERSITY OF SAN DIEGO

San Diego, CA

Tuition & fees: $52,864	Average undergraduate aid package: $40,082

ABOUT THE INSTITUTION Independent Roman Catholic, coed. ***Awards:*** certificates, bachelor's, master's, and doctoral degrees. 45 undergraduate majors. ***Total enrollment:*** 9,181. Undergraduates: 5,919. Freshmen: 1,142. Federal methodology is used as a basis for awarding need-based institutional aid.

UNDERGRADUATE EXPENSES for 2020–2021 ***Application fee:*** $55. ***Comprehensive fee:*** $68,020 includes full-time tuition ($52,120), mandatory fees ($744), and room and board ($15,156). Room and board charges vary according to board plan and housing facility. ***Part-time tuition:*** $1798 per credit. ***Part-time fees:*** $514 per year. Part-time tuition and fees vary according to course load.

FRESHMAN FINANCIAL AID (Fall 2019, est.) 865 applied for aid; of those 78% were deemed to have need. 100% of freshmen with need received aid; of those 18% had need fully met. ***Average percent of need met:*** 81% (excluding resources awarded to replace EFC). ***Average financial aid package:*** $42,279 (excluding resources awarded to replace EFC). 18% of all full-time freshmen had no need and received non-need-based gift aid.

UNDERGRADUATE FINANCIAL AID (Fall 2019, est.) 3,506 applied for aid; of those 87% were deemed to have need. 99% of undergraduates with need received aid; of those 14% had need fully met. ***Average percent of need met:*** 75% (excluding resources awarded to replace EFC). ***Average financial aid package:*** $40,082 (excluding resources awarded to replace EFC). 18% of all full-time undergraduates had no need and received non-need-based gift aid.

GIFT AID (NEED-BASED) ***Total amount:*** $98,959,172 (13% federal, 5% state, 81% institutional, 1% external sources). ***Receiving aid:*** Freshmen: 59% (672); all full-time undergraduates: 53% (2,989). ***Average award:*** Freshmen: $35,997; Undergraduates: $33,446. ***Scholarships, grants, and awards:*** Federal Pell, FSEOG, state, private, college/university gift aid from institutional funds, Federal Nursing, TEACH Grants.

GIFT AID (NON-NEED-BASED) ***Total amount:*** $28,083,043 (22% federal, 76% institutional, 2% external sources). ***Receiving aid:*** Freshmen: 32% (365). Undergraduates: 27% (1,516). ***Average award:*** Freshmen: $19,940. Undergraduates: $18,259. ***Scholarships, grants, and awards by category:*** *Academic interests/achievement:* 1,861 awards: general academic interests/achievements. *Creative arts/performance:* 23 awards: music. *Special achievements/activities:* 237 awards: religious involvement. *Special characteristics:* 85 awards: children of faculty/staff. ***Tuition waivers:*** Full or partial for employees or children of employees. ***ROTC:*** Army cooperative, Naval, Air Force cooperative.

LOANS ***Student loans:*** $20,479,437 (87% need-based, 13% non-need-based). 45% of past graduating class borrowed through all loan programs. *Average indebtedness per student:* $30,497. ***Average need-based loan:*** Freshmen: $4759. Undergraduates: $6630. ***Parent loans:*** $32,125,849 (43% need-based, 57% non-need-based). ***Programs:*** Federal Direct (Subsidized and Unsubsidized Stafford, PLUS), college/university, private loans.

WORK-STUDY ***Federal work-study:*** Total amount: $2,671,048; jobs available (averaging $2683). ***State or other work-study/employment:*** Total amount: $2,289,482 (4% need-based, 96% non-need-based). Part-time jobs available.

ATHLETIC AWARDS Total amount: $7,630,870 (27% need-based, 73% non-need-based).

APPLYING FOR FINANCIAL AID ***Required financial aid form:*** FAFSA. ***Financial aid deadline (priority):*** 3/2. ***Notification date:*** Continuous beginning 3/1. Students must reply by 5/1 or within 3 weeks of notification.

CONTACT Kellie Nehring, Director of Financial Aid Services, University of San Diego, 5998 Alcala Park, San Diego, CA 92110-2492, 619-260-2700 or toll-free 800-248-4873. *E-mail:* knehring@sandiego.edu.
Website: http://www.sandiego.edu/.

UNIVERSITY OF SAN FRANCISCO

San Francisco, CA

Tuition & fees: $52,482	Average undergraduate aid package: $35,618

ABOUT THE INSTITUTION Independent Roman Catholic (Jesuit), coed. ***Awards:*** certificates, bachelor's, master's, and doctoral degrees. 50 undergraduate majors. ***Total enrollment:*** 4,059. Undergraduates: 6,577. Freshmen: 1,293. Both federal and institutional methodology are used as a basis for awarding need-based institutional aid.

UNDERGRADUATE EXPENSES for 2020–2021 ***Application fee:*** $70. ***Comprehensive fee:*** $68,472 includes full-time tuition ($51,930), mandatory fees ($552), and room and board ($15,990). ***College room only:*** $10,930. Room and board charges vary according to board plan and housing facility. ***Part-time tuition:*** $1850 per credit hour. ***Part-time fees:*** $276 per term.

FRESHMAN FINANCIAL AID (Fall 2019, est.) 945 applied for aid; of those 83% were deemed to have need. 100% of freshmen with need received aid; of those 9% had need fully met. ***Average percent of need met:*** 68% (excluding resources awarded to replace EFC). ***Average financial aid package:*** $36,087 (excluding resources awarded to replace EFC). 30% of all full-time freshmen had no need and received non-need-based gift aid.

UNDERGRADUATE FINANCIAL AID (Fall 2019, est.) 4,263 applied for aid; of those 88% were deemed to have need. 99% of undergraduates with need received aid; of those 7% had need fully met. ***Average percent of need met:*** 67% (excluding resources awarded to replace EFC). ***Average financial aid package:*** $35,618 (excluding resources awarded to replace EFC). 25% of all full-time undergraduates had no need and received non-need-based gift aid.

GIFT AID (NEED-BASED) ***Total amount:*** $111,192,762 (9% federal, 10% state, 80% institutional, 1% external sources). ***Receiving aid:*** Freshmen: 60% (774); all full-time undergraduates: 58% (3,661). ***Average award:*** Freshmen: $30,296; Undergraduates: $29,709. ***Scholarships, grants, and awards:*** Federal Pell, FSEOG, state, private, college/university gift aid from institutional funds.

GIFT AID (NON-NEED-BASED) ***Total amount:*** $25,730,998 (99% institutional, 1% external sources). ***Receiving aid:*** Freshmen: 5% (64). Undergraduates: 3% (215). ***Average award:*** Freshmen: $18,873. Undergraduates: $18,498. ***Scholarships, grants, and awards by category:*** *Academic interests/achievement:* 4,249 awards ($63,763,224 total): general academic interests/achievements. *Special characteristics:* 4,249 awards ($63,763,224 total). ***ROTC:*** Army, Air Force cooperative.

LOANS ***Student loans:*** $36,408,231 (75% need-based, 25% non-need-based). 49% of past graduating class borrowed through all loan programs. *Average indebtedness per student:* $33,752. ***Average need-based loan:*** Freshmen: $3111. Undergraduates: $4122. ***Parent loans:*** $21,502,587 (58% need-based, 42% non-need-based). ***Programs:*** Federal Direct (Subsidized and Unsubsidized Stafford, PLUS), state.

WORK-STUDY ***Federal work-study:*** Total amount: $5,568,612; 1,063 jobs averaging $5025. ***State or other work-study/employment:*** Total amount: $3,259,574 (100% need-based). 605 part-time jobs averaging $4710.

ATHLETIC AWARDS Total amount: $6,722,980 (20% need-based, 80% non-need-based).

APPLYING FOR FINANCIAL AID ***Required financial aid forms:*** FAFSA, state aid form. ***Financial aid deadline:*** 1/15. ***Notification date:*** Continuous beginning 4/1. Students must reply by 5/1.

CONTACT Michael Beseda, Vice Provost for Strategic Enrollment Management, University of San Francisco, 2130 Fulton Street, San Francisco, CA 94117, 415-422-3387 or toll-free 800-CALL-USF. *E-mail:* financialaid@usfca.edu.
Website: http://www.usfca.edu/.

UNIVERSITY OF SCIENCE AND ARTS OF OKLAHOMA

Chickasha, OK

Tuition & fees: N/R	Average undergraduate aid package: $13,415

ABOUT THE INSTITUTION State-supported, coed. ***Awards:*** bachelor's degrees. 25 undergraduate majors. ***Total enrollment:*** 800. Undergraduates: 800. Federal methodology is used as a basis for awarding need-based institutional aid.

FRESHMAN FINANCIAL AID (Fall 2019, est.) 152 applied for aid; of those 85% were deemed to have need. 100% of freshmen with need received aid; of those 22% had need fully met. ***Average percent of need met:*** 69% (excluding resources awarded to replace EFC). ***Average financial aid package:*** $13,295 (excluding resources awarded to replace EFC). 16% of all full-time freshmen had no need and received non-need-based gift aid.

UNDERGRADUATE FINANCIAL AID (Fall 2019, est.) 569 applied for aid; of those 87% were deemed to have need. 99% of undergraduates with need received aid; of those 14% had need fully met. ***Average percent of need met:*** 67% (excluding resources awarded to replace EFC). ***Average financial aid package:*** $13,415 (excluding resources awarded to replace EFC). 18% of all full-time undergraduates had no need and received non-need-based gift aid.

GIFT AID (NEED-BASED) ***Total amount:*** $4,126,330 (49% federal, 24% state, 17% institutional, 10% external sources). ***Receiving aid:*** Freshmen: 71% (128); all full-time undergraduates: 66% (475). ***Average award:*** Freshmen: $11,623; Undergraduates: $11,403. ***Scholarships, grants, and awards:*** Federal Pell, FSEOG, state, private, college/university gift aid from institutional funds, USAO Foundation Grants.

GIFT AID (NON-NEED-BASED) ***Total amount:*** $823,313 (9% state, 74% institutional, 17% external sources). ***Receiving aid:*** Freshmen: 14% (25). Undergraduates: 8% (56). ***Average award:*** Freshmen: $4341. Undergraduates: $4245. ***Scholarships, grants, and awards by category:*** *Academic interests/achievement:* 613 awards ($1,382,655 total): general academic interests/achievements. *Creative arts/performance:* 11 awards ($18,200 total): applied art and design, music, theater/drama. *Special achievements/activities:* 8 awards ($6200 total): cheerleading/drum major. *Special characteristics:* 40 awards ($228,259 total): children of faculty/staff, international students, out-of-state students, previous college experience.

LOANS ***Student loans:*** $2,231,170 (76% need-based, 24% non-need-based). 38% of past graduating class borrowed through all loan programs. *Average indebtedness per student:* $23,410. ***Average need-based loan:*** Freshmen: $3119. Undergraduates: $3187. ***Parent loans:*** $278,530 (35% need-based, 65% non-need-based). ***Programs:*** Federal Direct (Subsidized and Unsubsidized Stafford, PLUS).

WORK-STUDY ***Federal work-study:*** Total amount: $170,120; 130 jobs averaging $1412.

ATHLETIC AWARDS Total amount: $2,296,353 (38% need-based, 62% non-need-based).

APPLYING FOR FINANCIAL AID ***Financial aid deadline (priority):*** 12/1. ***Notification date:*** Continuous beginning 12/1. Students must reply within 4 weeks of notification.

CONTACT Laura D. Coponiti, Dean of Enrollment Management, University of Science and Arts of Oklahoma, 1727 West Alabama, Chickasha, OK 73018-5322, 405-574-1350 or toll-free 800-933-8726. *Fax:* 405-574-1220. *E-mail:* lcoponiti@usao.edu. *Website:* http://www.usao.edu/.

THE UNIVERSITY OF SCRANTON

Scranton, PA

Tuition & fees: $45,790	Average undergraduate aid package: $31,832

ABOUT THE INSTITUTION Independent Roman Catholic (Jesuit), coed. ***Awards:*** certificates, associate, bachelor's, master's, and doctoral degrees. 66 undergraduate majors. ***Total enrollment:*** 5,253. Undergraduates: 3,792. Freshmen: 996. Federal methodology is used as a basis for awarding need-based institutional aid.

UNDERGRADUATE EXPENSES for 2019–2020 ***Comprehensive fee:*** $61,100 includes full-time tuition ($45,390), mandatory fees ($400), and room and board ($15,310). ***College room only:*** $8950. Room and board charges vary according to board plan and housing facility.

FRESHMAN FINANCIAL AID (Fall 2018) 867 applied for aid; of those 85% were deemed to have need. 100% of freshmen with need received aid; of those 18% had need fully met. ***Average percent of need met:*** 71% (excluding resources awarded to replace EFC). ***Average financial aid package:*** $31,889 (excluding resources awarded to replace EFC). 20% of all full-time freshmen had no need and received non-need-based gift aid.

UNDERGRADUATE FINANCIAL AID (Fall 2018) 2,956 applied for aid; of those 86% were deemed to have need. 100% of undergraduates with need received aid; of those 19% had need fully met. ***Average percent of need met:*** 69% (excluding resources awarded to replace EFC). ***Average financial aid package:*** $31,832 (excluding resources awarded to replace EFC). 21% of all full-time undergraduates had no need and received non-need-based gift aid.

GIFT AID (NEED-BASED) ***Total amount:*** $62,827,621 (8% federal, 3% state, 87% institutional, 2% external sources). ***Receiving aid:*** Freshmen: 63% (596); all full-time undergraduates: 59% (2,096). ***Average award:*** Freshmen: $15,786; Undergraduates: $16,402. ***Scholarships, grants, and awards:*** Federal Pell, FSEOG, state, private, college/university gift aid from institutional funds.

GIFT AID (NON-NEED-BASED) ***Total amount:*** $16,538,151 (7% federal, 91% institutional, 2% external sources). ***Receiving aid:*** Freshmen: 66% (617). Undergraduates: 53% (1,896). ***Average award:*** Freshmen: $17,750. Undergraduates: $16,299. ***Scholarships, grants, and awards by category:*** *Academic interests/achievement:* general academic interests/achievements, military science. *Special characteristics:* children of educators, children of faculty/staff, ethnic background, members of minority groups, religious affiliation, siblings of current students, veterans. ***Tuition waivers:*** Full or partial for employees or children of employees, senior citizens. ***ROTC:*** Army, Air Force cooperative.

LOANS ***Student loans:*** $29,370,533 (68% need-based, 32% non-need-based). 75% of past graduating class borrowed through all loan programs. *Average indebtedness per student:* $41,570. ***Average need-based loan:*** Freshmen: $3351. Undergraduates: $4333. ***Parent loans:*** $12,703,385 (45% need-based, 55% non-need-based). ***Programs:*** Federal Direct (Subsidized and Unsubsidized Stafford, PLUS), Perkins, Federal Nursing.

WORK-STUDY ***Federal work-study:*** Total amount: $1,575,711; jobs available. ***State or other work-study/employment:*** Total amount: $1,247,142 (33% need-based, 67% non-need-based). Part-time jobs available.

APPLYING FOR FINANCIAL AID ***Required financial aid forms:*** FAFSA, state aid form. ***Financial aid deadline (priority):*** 2/15. ***Notification date:*** Continuous beginning 1/15. Students must reply by 5/1.

CONTACT Financial Aid Office, The University of Scranton, 800 Linden Street, Scranton, PA 18510, 570-941-7400 or toll-free 888-SCRANTON. *Website:* http://www.scranton.edu/.

UNIVERSITY OF SIOUX FALLS

Sioux Falls, SD

ABOUT THE INSTITUTION Independent American Baptist Churches in the USA, coed. ***Awards:*** certificates, associate, bachelor's, and master's degrees. 52 undergraduate majors. ***Total enrollment:*** 1,615. Undergraduates: 1,319. Freshmen: 311.

GIFT AID (NEED-BASED) ***Scholarships, grants, and awards:*** Federal Pell, FSEOG, state, private, college/university gift aid from institutional funds.

GIFT AID (NON-NEED-BASED) ***Scholarships, grants, and awards by category:*** *Academic interests/achievement:* biological sciences, business, communication, computer science, education, English, foreign languages, general academic interests/achievements, home economics, humanities, mathematics, physical sciences, premedicine, religion/biblical studies, social sciences. *Creative arts/performance:* applied art and design, music, theater/drama. *Special achievements/activities:* cheerleading/drum major, leadership, memberships. *Special characteristics:* children of faculty/staff, international students, local/state students, out-of-state students, previous college experience, religious affiliation, veterans, veterans' children.

LOANS ***Programs:*** Federal Direct (Subsidized and Unsubsidized Stafford, PLUS), private loans.

WORK-STUDY ***Federal work-study:*** Total amount: $172,250; 107 jobs averaging $1500.

APPLYING FOR FINANCIAL AID ***Required financial aid form:*** FAFSA.

CONTACT Kari Quall, Financial Aid Counselor, University of Sioux Falls, 1101 West 22nd Street, Sioux Falls, SD 57105-1699, 605-331-6625 or toll-free 800-888-1047. *Fax:* 605-331-6615. *E-mail:* kari.quall@usiouxfalls.edu.
Website: http://www.usiouxfalls.edu/.

UNIVERSITY OF SOUTH ALABAMA

Mobile, AL

CONTACT Financial Aid Office, University of South Alabama, 390 Alumni Circle, Meisler Hall, Suite 1200, Mobile, AL 36688-0001, 800-305-6828 or toll-free 800-872-5247. *Fax:* 251-460-6517. *E-mail:* finaid@southalabama.edu.
Website: http://www.southalabama.edu/.

UNIVERSITY OF SOUTH CAROLINA

Columbia, SC

Tuition & fees (SC res): $12,688	Average undergraduate aid package: $9887

ABOUT THE INSTITUTION State-supported, coed. ***Awards:*** certificates, associate, bachelor's, master's, and doctoral degrees. 76 undergraduate majors. ***Total enrollment:*** 35,364. Undergraduates: 27,502. Freshmen: 6,287. Federal methodology is used as a basis for awarding need-based institutional aid.

UNDERGRADUATE EXPENSES for 2019–2020 ***Application fee:*** $65. ***Tuition, state resident:*** full-time $12,288; part-time $512 per credit hour. ***Tuition, nonresident:*** full-time $33,528; part-time $1397 per credit hour. ***Required fees:*** full-time $400; $17 per credit. Full-time tuition and fees vary according to program and reciprocity agreements. Part-time tuition and fees vary according to course load. ***College room and board:*** $10,670; ***Room only:*** $6700. Room and board charges vary according to board plan, housing facility, and location.

FRESHMAN FINANCIAL AID (Fall 2019, est.) 4816 applied for aid; of those 67% were deemed to have need. 98% of freshmen with need received aid; of those 30% had need fully met. ***Average percent of need met:*** 77% (excluding resources awarded to replace EFC). ***Average financial aid package:*** $9402 (excluding resources awarded to replace EFC). 38% of all full-time freshmen had no need and received non-need-based gift aid.

UNDERGRADUATE FINANCIAL AID (Fall 2019, est.) 16,811 applied for aid; of those 74% were deemed to have need. 98% of undergraduates with need received aid; of those 26% had need fully met. ***Average percent of need met:*** 72% (excluding resources awarded to replace EFC). ***Average financial aid package:*** $9887 (excluding resources awarded to replace EFC). 34% of all full-time undergraduates had no need and received non-need-based gift aid.

GIFT AID (NEED-BASED) ***Receiving aid:*** Freshmen: 19% (1,122); all full-time undergraduates: 21% (5,388). ***Average award:*** Freshmen: $6767; Undergraduates: $5958. ***Scholarships, grants, and awards:*** Federal Pell, FSEOG, state, private, college/university gift aid from institutional funds, United Negro College Fund, Federal Nursing, USC Acc Grant,GGG, USC Oppor Grant USC Inst Grant.

GIFT AID (NON-NEED-BASED) ***Receiving aid:*** Freshmen: 51% (2,994). Undergraduates: 34% (8,759). ***Average award:*** Freshmen: $5947. Undergraduates: $6610. ***Scholarships, grants, and awards by category:*** *Academic interests/achievement:* area/ethnic studies, biological sciences, business, communication, computer science, education, engineering/technologies, English, foreign languages, general academic interests/achievements, home economics, humanities, international studies, library science, mathematics, military science, physical sciences, premedicine, religion/biblical studies, social sciences. *Creative arts/performance:* applied art and design, dance, debating, journalism/publications, music, theater/drama. *Special achievements/activities:* cheerleading/drum major, community service, general special achievements/activities, leadership, memberships, religious involvement. *Special characteristics:* adult students, children and siblings of alumni, children of faculty/staff, children of union members/company employees, children of workers in trades, children with a deceased or disabled parent, ethnic background, first-generation college students, general special characteristics, handicapped students, international students, local/state students, members of minority groups, out-of-state students, religious affiliation, spouses of deceased or disabled public servants. ***Tuition waivers:*** Full or partial for employees or children of employees, senior citizens. ***ROTC:*** Army, Naval, Air Force.

LOANS ***Student loans:*** 52% of past graduating class borrowed through all loan programs. *Average indebtedness per student:* $30,449. ***Average need-based loan:*** Freshmen: $3311. Undergraduates: $2222. ***Programs:*** Federal Direct (Subsidized and Unsubsidized Stafford, PLUS), Perkins, Federal Nursing.

WORK-STUDY Federal work-study jobs available.

APPLYING FOR FINANCIAL AID ***Required financial aid form:*** FAFSA. ***Notification date:*** Continuous.

CONTACT Joey C. Derrick, Director of Student Financial Aid and Scholarships, University of South Carolina, 1714 College Street, Columbia, SC 29208, 803-777-8134 or toll-free 800-868-5872. *Fax:* 803-777-0941. *E-mail:* jcderric@mailbox.sc.edu.
Website: http://www.sc.edu/.

UNIVERSITY OF SOUTH CAROLINA AIKEN

Aiken, SC

Tuition & fees (SC res): $10,760	Average undergraduate aid package: $12,097

ABOUT THE INSTITUTION State-supported, coed. ***Awards:*** bachelor's and master's degrees. 26 undergraduate majors. ***Total enrollment:*** 3,720. Undergraduates: 3,252. Freshmen: 558. Federal methodology is used as a basis for awarding need-based institutional aid.

UNDERGRADUATE EXPENSES for 2019–2020 ***Application fee:*** $45. ***Tuition, state resident:*** full-time $10,398; part-time $433 per credit hour. ***Tuition, nonresident:*** full-time $20,856; part-time $869 per credit hour. ***Required fees:*** full-time $362; $25 per term. Full-time tuition and fees vary according to program and reciprocity agreements. Part-time tuition and fees vary according to course load, program, and reciprocity agreements. ***College room and board:*** $7946; ***Room only:*** $5192. Room and board charges vary according to board plan and housing facility.

FRESHMAN FINANCIAL AID (Fall 2018) 542 applied for aid; of those 69% were deemed to have need. 99% of freshmen with need received aid; of those 16% had need fully met. ***Average percent of need met:*** 63% (excluding resources awarded to replace EFC). ***Average financial aid package:*** $12,210 (excluding resources awarded to replace EFC). 8% of all full-time freshmen had no need and received non-need-based gift aid.

UNDERGRADUATE FINANCIAL AID (Fall 2018) 2,657 applied for aid; of those 67% were deemed to have need. 99% of undergraduates with need received aid; of those 17% had need fully met. ***Average percent of need met:*** 60% (excluding resources awarded to replace EFC). ***Average financial aid package:*** $12,097 (excluding resources awarded to replace EFC). 7% of all full-time undergraduates had no need and received non-need-based gift aid.

GIFT AID (NEED-BASED) ***Total amount:*** $11,785,812 (54% federal, 38% state, 6% institutional, 2% external sources). ***Receiving aid:*** Freshmen: 66% (356); all full-time undergraduates: 58% (1,534). ***Average award:*** Freshmen: $8352; Undergraduates: $7379. ***Scholarships, grants, and awards:*** Federal Pell, FSEOG, state, college/university gift aid from institutional funds.

GIFT AID (NON-NEED-BASED) ***Total amount:*** $4,680,229 (29% federal, 51% state, 8% institutional, 12% external sources). ***Receiving aid:*** Freshmen: 7% (37). Undergraduates: 6% (164). ***Average award:*** Freshmen: $1685. Undergraduates: $1751. ***Scholarships, grants, and awards by category:*** *Academic interests/achievement:* biological sciences, business, communication, computer science, education, engineering/technologies, English, general academic interests/achievements, home economics, humanities, mathematics, physical sciences, premedicine, social sciences. *Creative arts/performance:* applied art and design, general creative arts/performance, journalism/publications, music, performing arts, theater/drama. *Special achievements/activities:* cheerleading/drum major, community service, hobbies/interests, leadership, memberships, religious involvement. *Special characteristics:* adult students, children and siblings of alumni, children of faculty/staff, children of union members/company employees, ethnic background, first-generation college students, handicapped students, international students, local/state students, married students, members of minority groups, out-of-state students, previous college experience, religious affiliation, veterans. ***Tuition waivers:*** Full or partial for employees or children of employees, senior citizens.

LOANS ***Student loans:*** $13,695,016 (73% need-based, 27% non-need-based). 69% of past graduating class borrowed through all loan programs. *Average indebtedness per student:* $28,176. ***Average need-based loan:*** Freshmen: $3256. Undergraduates: $4126. ***Parent loans:*** $2,697,422 (55% need-based, 45% non-need-based). ***Programs:*** Federal Direct (Subsidized and Unsubsidized Stafford, PLUS), state.

WORK-STUDY ***Federal work-study:*** Total amount: $89,566; 70 jobs averaging $1643. ***State or other work-study/employment:*** Total amount: $761,009 (33% need-based, 67% non-need-based). 412 part-time jobs averaging $1785.

ATHLETIC AWARDS Total amount: $814,101 (39% need-based, 61% non-need-based).

APPLYING FOR FINANCIAL AID ***Required financial aid form:*** FAFSA. ***Financial aid deadline (priority):*** 3/1. ***Notification date:*** Continuous beginning 4/20. Students must reply within 2 weeks of notification.

CONTACT Mr. Tony Carter, Director of Financial Aid, University of South Carolina Aiken, 471 University Parkway, Aiken, SC 29801, 803-641-3476 or toll-free 888-WOW-USCA. *Fax:* 803-643-6840. *E-mail:* tonyc@usca.edu.
Website: http://www.usca.edu/.

UNIVERSITY OF SOUTH CAROLINA BEAUFORT

Bluffton, SC

CONTACT Heather Robinson, Financial Aid Administrative Assistant, University of South Carolina Beaufort, 801 Carteret Street, Beaufort, SC 29902, 843-521-3104. *Fax:* 843-521-3194. *E-mail:* uscbfina@uscb.edu.
Website: http://www.uscb.edu/.

UNIVERSITY OF SOUTH CAROLINA UPSTATE

Spartanburg, SC

Tuition & fees: N/R | **Average undergraduate aid package: N/A**

ABOUT THE INSTITUTION State-supported, coed. ***Awards:*** certificates, bachelor's, and master's degrees. 31 undergraduate majors. ***Total enrollment:*** 5,987. Undergraduates: 5,721. Freshmen: 825. Federal methodology is used as a basis for awarding need-based institutional aid.

GIFT AID (NEED-BASED) ***Scholarships, grants, and awards:*** Federal Pell, FSEOG, state, private, college/university gift aid from institutional funds.

GIFT AID (NON-NEED-BASED) ***Scholarships, grants, and awards by category:*** *Academic interests/achievement:* general academic interests/achievements. *Special characteristics:* first-generation college students. ***ROTC:*** Army cooperative.

LOANS ***Programs:*** Federal Direct (Subsidized and Unsubsidized Stafford, PLUS), state.

WORK-STUDY Federal work-study jobs available.

APPLYING FOR FINANCIAL AID ***Required financial aid form:*** FAFSA. ***Notification date:*** Continuous.

CONTACT Bonnie Durham, Director of Financial Aid, University of South Carolina Upstate, 800 University Way, Spartanburg, SC 29303, 864-503-5389 or toll-free 800-277-8727. *E-mail:* bcarson@uscupstate.edu.
Website: http://www.uscupstate.edu/.

UNIVERSITY OF SOUTH DAKOTA

Vermillion, SD

Tuition & fees (area res): $9332 | **Average undergraduate aid package: $8617**

ABOUT THE INSTITUTION State-supported, coed. ***Awards:*** certificates, bachelor's, master's, and doctoral degrees. 78 undergraduate majors. ***Total enrollment:*** 9,920. Undergraduates: 12,262. Freshmen: 1,293. Federal methodology is used as a basis for awarding need-based institutional aid.

UNDERGRADUATE EXPENSES for 2020–2021 ***Application fee:*** $20. ***Tuition, area resident:*** full-time $7697; part-time $257 per credit hour. ***Tuition, state resident:*** full-time $7697; part-time $257 per credit hour. ***Tuition, nonresident:*** full-time $11,172; part-time $372 per credit hour. ***Required fees:*** full-time $1635. ***College room and board:*** $8409; ***Room only:*** $4280.

FRESHMAN FINANCIAL AID (Fall 2018) 1150 applied for aid; of those 69% were deemed to have need. 100% of freshmen with need received aid; of those 16% had need fully met. ***Average percent of need met:*** 55% (excluding resources awarded to replace EFC). ***Average financial aid package:*** $8225 (excluding resources awarded to replace EFC). 23% of all full-time freshmen had no need and received non-need-based gift aid.

UNDERGRADUATE FINANCIAL AID (Fall 2018) 3,931 applied for aid; of those 73% were deemed to have need. 100% of undergraduates with need received aid; of those 15% had need fully met. ***Average percent of need met:*** 55% (excluding resources awarded to replace EFC). ***Average financial aid package:*** $8617 (excluding resources awarded to replace EFC). 19% of all full-time undergraduates had no need and received non-need-based gift aid.

GIFT AID (NEED-BASED) ***Total amount:*** $9,146,407 (100% federal). ***Receiving aid:*** Freshmen: 29% (372); all full-time undergraduates: 28% (1,369). ***Average award:*** Freshmen: $5024; Undergraduates: $5067. ***Scholarships, grants, and awards:*** Federal Pell, FSEOG, state, private, college/university gift aid from institutional funds, United Negro College Fund.

GIFT AID (NON-NEED-BASED) ***Total amount:*** $9,701,926 (2% federal, 15% state, 54% institutional, 29% external sources). ***Receiving aid:*** Freshmen: 44% (573). Undergraduates: 33% (1,605). ***Average award:*** Freshmen: $2378. Undergraduates: $2348. ***ROTC:*** Army.

LOANS ***Student loans:*** $32,801,633 (36% need-based, 64% non-need-based). 72% of past graduating class borrowed through all loan programs. *Average indebtedness per student:* $28,363. ***Average need-based loan:*** Freshmen: $3171. Undergraduates: $4051. ***Parent loans:*** $6,163,455 (100% non-need-based). ***Programs:*** Federal Direct (Subsidized and Unsubsidized Stafford, PLUS), Federal Nursing.

WORK-STUDY ***Federal work-study:*** Total amount: $860,532. ***State or other work-study/employment:*** Total amount: $443,412 (100% non-need-based).

ATHLETIC AWARDS Total amount: $4,593,550 (100% non-need-based).

APPLYING FOR FINANCIAL AID ***Required financial aid form:*** FAFSA. ***Financial aid deadline (priority):*** 4/1. ***Notification date:*** Continuous.

CONTACT Mrs. Julie Pier, Director of Student Financial Aid, University of South Dakota, Belbas Center, 414 East Clark Street, Vermillion, SD 57069, 605-658-6250 or toll-free 877-269-6837. *Fax:* 605-677-5238. *E-mail:* admissions@usd.edu.
Website: http://www.usd.edu/.

UNIVERSITY OF SOUTHERN CALIFORNIA

Los Angeles, CA

Tuition & fees: $58,195 | **Average undergraduate aid package: $53,612**

ABOUT THE INSTITUTION Independent, coed. ***Awards:*** certificates, bachelor's, master's, and doctoral degrees. 106 undergraduate majors. ***Total enrollment:*** 47,310. Undergraduates: 19,907. Freshmen: 3,401. Both federal and institutional methodology are used as a basis for awarding need-based institutional aid.

UNDERGRADUATE EXPENSES for 2019–2020 ***Application fee:*** $85. ***One-time required fee:*** $450. ***Comprehensive fee:*** $74,111 includes full-time tuition ($57,256), mandatory fees ($939), and room and board ($15,916). ***College room only:*** $9616. Full-time tuition and fees vary according to program. Room and board charges vary according to board plan and housing facility. ***Part-time tuition:*** $1928 per credit hour. Part-time tuition and fees vary according to course load and program. ***Payment plan:*** Tuition prepayment.

FRESHMAN FINANCIAL AID (Fall 2018) 2094 applied for aid; of those 62% were deemed to have need. 100% of freshmen with need received aid; of those 91% had need fully met. ***Average percent of need met:*** 100% (excluding resources awarded to replace EFC). ***Average financial aid package:*** $57,520 (excluding resources awarded to replace EFC). 26% of all full-time freshmen had no need and received non-need-based gift aid.

UNDERGRADUATE FINANCIAL AID (Fall 2018) 9,680 applied for aid; of those 76% were deemed to have need. 100% of undergraduates with need received aid; of those 90% had need fully met. ***Average percent of need met:*** 100% (excluding resources awarded to replace EFC). ***Average financial aid package:*** $53,612 (excluding resources awarded to replace EFC). 21% of all full-time undergraduates had no need and received non-need-based gift aid.

GIFT AID (NEED-BASED) ***Total amount:*** $328,619,770 (7% federal, 6% state, 83% institutional, 4% external sources). ***Receiving aid:*** Freshmen: 33% (1,121); all full-time undergraduates: 33% (6,499). ***Average award:*** Freshmen: $42,820; Undergraduates: $41,082. ***Scholarships, grants, and awards:*** Federal Pell, FSEOG, state, private, college/university gift aid from institutional funds.

GIFT AID (NON-NEED-BASED) ***Total amount:*** $97,303,332 (83% institutional, 17% external sources). ***Receiving aid:*** Freshmen: 30% (1,028). Undergraduates: 21% (4,224). ***Average award:*** Freshmen: $19,827. Undergraduates: $19,114. ***Scholarships, grants, and awards by category:*** *Academic interests/achievement:* general academic interests/achievements. *Creative arts/performance:* applied art and design, debating, music, theater/drama. *Special achievements/activities:* general special achievements/activities, leadership. *Special characteristics:* children and siblings of alumni, children of faculty/staff. ***Tuition waivers:*** Full or partial for employees or children of employees. ***ROTC:*** Army, Naval, Air Force.

LOANS ***Student loans:*** $62,734,343 (57% need-based, 43% non-need-based). 31% of past graduating class borrowed through all loan programs. *Average indebtedness per student:* $28,434. ***Average need-based loan:*** Freshmen: $4518. Undergraduates: $5322. ***Parent loans:*** $68,930,140 (100% non-need-based). ***Programs:*** Federal Direct (Subsidized and Unsubsidized Stafford, PLUS), Perkins, college/university.

WORK-STUDY ***Federal work-study:*** Total amount: $17,977,263; jobs available.

ATHLETIC AWARDS Total amount: $22,439,320 (31% need-based, 69% non-need-based).

APPLYING FOR FINANCIAL AID ***Required financial aid forms:*** FAFSA, institution's own form, CSS Financial Aid PROFILE, noncustodial (divorced/separated) parent's statement, business/farm supplement. ***Financial aid deadline (priority):*** 2/17. ***Notification date:*** 4/1. Students must reply by 5/1.

CONTACT Financial Aid Office, University of Southern California, University Park Campus, Los Angeles, CA 90089, 213-740-2311.
Website: http://www.usc.edu/.

UNIVERSITY OF SOUTHERN INDIANA

Evansville, IN

Tuition & fees: N/R	Average undergraduate aid package: $10,422

ABOUT THE INSTITUTION State-supported, coed. ***Awards:*** certificates, associate, bachelor's, master's, and doctoral degrees. 59 undergraduate majors. ***Total enrollment:*** 8,631. Undergraduates: 7,094. Freshmen: 1,585. Federal methodology is used as a basis for awarding need-based institutional aid.

FRESHMAN FINANCIAL AID (Fall 2019, est.) 1479 applied for aid; of those 70% were deemed to have need. 99% of freshmen with need received aid; of those 36% had need fully met. ***Average percent of need met:*** 86% (excluding resources awarded to replace EFC). ***Average financial aid package:*** $10,227 (excluding resources awarded to replace EFC). 26% of all full-time freshmen had no need and received non-need-based gift aid.

UNDERGRADUATE FINANCIAL AID (Fall 2019, est.) 5,665 applied for aid; of those 68% were deemed to have need. 99% of undergraduates with need received aid; of those 33% had need fully met. ***Average percent of need met:*** 86% (excluding resources awarded to replace EFC). ***Average financial aid package:*** $10,422 (excluding resources awarded to replace EFC). 21% of all full-time undergraduates had no need and received non-need-based gift aid.

GIFT AID (NEED-BASED) ***Total amount:*** $16,376,539 (6% federal, 51% state, 38% institutional, 5% external sources). ***Receiving aid:*** Freshmen: 59% (919); all full-time undergraduates: 56% (3,403). ***Average award:*** Freshmen: $10,360; Undergraduates: $10,588. ***Scholarships, grants, and awards:*** Federal Pell, FSEOG, state, private, college/university gift aid from institutional funds, United Negro College Fund, Federal Nursing.

GIFT AID (NON-NEED-BASED) ***Total amount:*** $10,274,976 (12% state, 75% institutional, 13% external sources). ***Receiving aid:*** Freshmen: 64% (998). Undergraduates: 60% (3,643). ***Average award:*** Freshmen: $4109. Undergraduates: $4830. ***Scholarships, grants, and awards by category:*** *Academic interests/achievement:* biological sciences, business, education, engineering/technologies, general academic interests/achievements, home economics, humanities, mathematics, premedicine, social sciences. *Creative arts/performance:* applied art and design, creative writing, theater/drama. *Special achievements/activities:* leadership. *Special characteristics:* adult students, children of faculty/staff, first-generation college students, general special characteristics, international students, members of minority groups, out-of-state students, veterans. ***ROTC:*** Army.

LOANS ***Student loans:*** $3,485,537 (70% need-based, 30% non-need-based). 65% of past graduating class borrowed through all loan programs. *Average indebtedness per student:* $24,427. ***Average need-based loan:*** Freshmen: $3056. Undergraduates: $4027. ***Parent loans:*** $4,223,637 (66% need-based, 34% non-need-based). ***Programs:*** Federal Direct (Subsidized and Unsubsidized Stafford, PLUS).

WORK-STUDY ***Federal work-study:*** Total amount: $379,368; jobs available.

ATHLETIC AWARDS Total amount: $1,358,476 (14% need-based, 86% non-need-based).

APPLYING FOR FINANCIAL AID ***Required financial aid form:*** FAFSA. ***Financial aid deadline (priority):*** 4/15. ***Notification date:*** Continuous. Students must reply by 4/1.

CONTACT Mrs. Mary Harper, Financial Aid Office, University of Southern Indiana, 8600 University Boulevard, Evansville, IN 47712-3590, 812-464-1767 or toll-free 800-467-1965. *Fax:* 812-461-5305. *E-mail:* finaid@usi.edu.
Website: http://www.usi.edu/.

UNIVERSITY OF SOUTHERN MAINE

Portland, ME

Tuition & fees (ME res): $9850	Average undergraduate aid package: $14,271

ABOUT THE INSTITUTION State-supported, coed. ***Awards:*** certificates, bachelor's, master's, and doctoral degrees. 47 undergraduate majors. ***Total enrollment:*** 1,754. Undergraduates: 6,675. Freshmen: 893. Federal methodology is used as a basis for awarding need-based institutional aid.

UNDERGRADUATE EXPENSES for 2019–2020 ***Tuition, area resident:*** part-time $281 per credit hour. ***Tuition, state resident:*** full-time $8430; part-time $281 per credit hour. ***Tuition, nonresident:*** full-time $22,170; part-time $739 per credit hour. ***Required fees:*** full-time $1420; $31 per credit hour. Full-time tuition and fees vary according to course load, degree level, and reciprocity agreements. Part-time tuition and fees vary according to course load, degree level, and reciprocity agreements. ***College room and board:*** $9826; ***Room only:*** $5200. Room and board charges vary according to board plan and housing facility.

FRESHMAN FINANCIAL AID (Fall 2018) 858 applied for aid; of those 80% were deemed to have need. 100% of freshmen with need received aid; of those 43% had need fully met. ***Average percent of need met:*** 80% (excluding resources awarded to replace EFC). ***Average financial aid package:*** $14,477 (excluding resources awarded to replace EFC). 15% of all full-time freshmen had no need and received non-need-based gift aid.

UNDERGRADUATE FINANCIAL AID (Fall 2018) 3,447 applied for aid; of those 84% were deemed to have need. 100% of undergraduates with need received aid; of those 50% had need fully met. ***Average percent of need met:*** 80% (excluding resources awarded to replace EFC). ***Average financial aid package:*** $14,271 (excluding resources awarded to replace EFC). 9% of all full-time undergraduates had no need and received non-need-based gift aid.

GIFT AID (NEED-BASED) ***Total amount:*** $29,705,583 (40% federal, 9% state, 43% institutional, 8% external sources). ***Receiving aid:*** Freshmen: 74% (678); all full-time undergraduates: 67% (2,678). ***Average award:*** Freshmen: $10,300; Undergraduates: $9530. ***Scholarships, grants, and awards:*** Federal Pell, FSEOG, state, private, college/university gift aid from institutional funds.

GIFT AID (NON-NEED-BASED) ***Total amount:*** $2,564,836 (72% institutional, 28% external sources). ***Receiving aid:*** Freshmen: 5% (50). Undergraduates: 6% (242). ***Average award:*** Freshmen: $4488. Undergraduates: $4226. ***Scholarships, grants, and awards by category:*** *Academic interests/achievement:* general academic interests/achievements. *Creative arts/performance:* music, theater/drama. ***Tuition waivers:*** Full or partial for employees or children of employees. ***ROTC:*** Army cooperative, Air Force cooperative.

LOANS ***Student loans:*** $22,744,627 (69% need-based, 31% non-need-based). ***Average need-based loan:*** Freshmen: $5011. Undergraduates: $6338. ***Parent loans:*** $2,226,567 (35% need-based, 65% non-need-based). ***Programs:*** Federal Direct (Subsidized and Unsubsidized Stafford, PLUS), Perkins, Federal Nursing, college/university.

WORK-STUDY ***Federal work-study:*** Total amount: $3,005,431; jobs available.

APPLYING FOR FINANCIAL AID ***Required financial aid form:*** FAFSA. ***Financial aid deadline (priority):*** 2/15. ***Notification date:*** Continuous beginning 3/15.

CONTACT Mr. Keith P. Dubois, Director of Financial Aid, University of Southern Maine, 37 College Avenue, 107 Baily Hall, Gorham, ME 04038, 207-780-5122 or toll-free 800-800-4USM Ext.5670. *Fax:* 207-780-5143. *E-mail:* dubois@maine.edu. *Website:* http://www.usm.maine.edu/.

UNIVERSITY OF SOUTHERN MISSISSIPPI

Hattiesburg, MS

Tuition & fees: N/R	Average undergraduate aid package: $10,833

ABOUT THE INSTITUTION State-supported, coed. ***Awards:*** certificates, bachelor's, master's, and doctoral degrees. 74 undergraduate majors. ***Total enrollment:*** 14,133. Undergraduates: 11,594. Freshmen: 1,888. Federal methodology is used as a basis for awarding need-based institutional aid.

FRESHMAN FINANCIAL AID (Fall 2018) 1905 applied for aid; of those 82% were deemed to have need. 98% of freshmen with need received aid; of those 28% had need fully met. ***Average percent of need met:*** 68% (excluding resources awarded to replace EFC). ***Average financial aid package:*** $10,772 (excluding resources awarded to replace EFC). 12% of all full-time freshmen had no need and received non-need-based gift aid.

UNDERGRADUATE FINANCIAL AID (Fall 2018) 8,475 applied for aid; of those 87% were deemed to have need. 98% of undergraduates with need received aid; of those 22% had need fully met. ***Average percent of need met:*** 67% (excluding resources awarded to replace EFC). ***Average financial aid package:*** $10,833 (excluding resources awarded to replace EFC). 8% of all full-time undergraduates had no need and received non-need-based gift aid.

GIFT AID (NEED-BASED) ***Receiving aid:*** Freshmen: 52% (1,039); all full-time undergraduates: 52% (5,016). ***Average award:*** Freshmen: $6641; Undergraduates: $6025. ***Scholarships, grants, and awards:*** Federal Pell, FSEOG, state, private, college/university gift aid from institutional funds.

GIFT AID (NON-NEED-BASED) ***Receiving aid:*** Freshmen: 54% (1,063). Undergraduates: 44% (4,252). ***Average award:*** Freshmen: $6159. Undergraduates: $6036. ***Scholarships, grants, and awards by category:*** *Academic interests/achievement:* general academic interests/achievements. *Creative arts/performance:* applied art and design, dance, music, theater/drama. *Special achievements/activities:* cheerleading/drum major, leadership. *Special characteristics:* children and siblings of alumni, children of faculty/staff, ethnic background, local/state students, out-of-state students, veterans. ***ROTC:*** Army, Air Force.

LOANS ***Student loans:*** 66% of past graduating class borrowed through all loan programs. *Average indebtedness per student:* $28,003. ***Average need-based loan:*** Freshmen: $3090. Undergraduates: $11,696. ***Programs:*** Federal Direct (Subsidized and Unsubsidized Stafford, PLUS).

WORK-STUDY Federal work-study jobs available.

APPLYING FOR FINANCIAL AID ***Required financial aid forms:*** FAFSA, institution's own form. ***Notification date:*** Continuous.

CONTACT Mr. David Williamson, Director of Financial Aid, University of Southern Mississippi, 118 College Drive #5101, Hattiesburg, MS 39406-0001, 601-266-4774. *Fax:* 601-266-5769. *E-mail:* financial.aid@usm.edu. *Website:* http://www.usm.edu/.

UNIVERSITY OF SOUTH FLORIDA

Tampa, FL

Tuition & fees (area res): $6410	Average undergraduate aid package: $12,978

ABOUT THE INSTITUTION State-supported, coed. ***Awards:*** bachelor's, master's, and doctoral degrees. 80 undergraduate majors. ***Total enrollment:*** 44,231. Undergraduates: 32,681. Freshmen: 5,113. Federal methodology is used as a basis for awarding need-based institutional aid.

UNDERGRADUATE EXPENSES for 2020–2021 ***Application fee:*** $30. ***Tuition, area resident:*** full-time $4559; part-time $152 per credit hour. ***Tuition, state resident:*** part-time $152 per credit hour. ***Tuition, nonresident:*** full-time $15,473; part-time $516 per credit hour. ***Required fees:*** full-time $1851. ***College room and board:*** $11,836; ***Room only:*** $7878.

FRESHMAN FINANCIAL AID (Fall 2018) 3654 applied for aid; of those 73% were deemed to have need. 97% of freshmen with need received aid; of those 21% had need fully met. ***Average percent of need met:*** 73% (excluding resources awarded to replace EFC). ***Average financial aid package:*** $14,742 (excluding resources awarded to replace EFC). 16% of all full-time freshmen had no need and received non-need-based gift aid.

UNDERGRADUATE FINANCIAL AID (Fall 2018) 18,254 applied for aid; of those 83% were deemed to have need. 95% of undergraduates with need received aid; of those 13% had need fully met. ***Average percent of need met:*** 64% (excluding resources awarded to replace EFC). ***Average financial aid package:*** $12,978 (excluding resources awarded to replace EFC). 10% of all full-time undergraduates had no need and received non-need-based gift aid.

GIFT AID (NEED-BASED) ***Total amount:*** $128,968,110 (45% federal, 33% state, 20% institutional, 2% external sources). ***Receiving aid:*** Freshmen: 57% (2,471); all full-time undergraduates: 52% (12,654). ***Average award:*** Freshmen: $12,167; Undergraduates: $9911. ***Scholarships, grants, and awards:*** Federal Pell, FSEOG, state, private, college/university gift aid from institutional funds.

GIFT AID (NON-NEED-BASED) ***Total amount:*** $31,827,059 (70% state, 25% institutional, 5% external sources). ***Receiving aid:*** Freshmen: 9% (379). Undergraduates: 4% (940). ***Average award:*** Freshmen: $3277. Undergraduates: $3125. ***Scholarships, grants, and awards by category:*** *Academic interests/achievement:* 2,663 awards ($7,194,408 total): architecture, biological sciences, business, communication, computer science, education, engineering/technologies, English, foreign languages, general academic interests/achievements, health fields, humanities, international studies, library science, mathematics, military science, physical sciences, premedicine, religion/biblical studies, social sciences. *Creative arts/performance:* 254 awards ($401,364 total): applied art and design, art/fine arts, creative writing, dance, music, performing arts, theater/drama. ***ROTC:*** Army, Naval, Air Force.

LOANS ***Student loans:*** $74,383,348 (83% need-based, 17% non-need-based). 50% of past graduating class borrowed through all loan programs. *Average indebtedness per student:* $21,463. ***Average need-based loan:*** Freshmen: $4138. Undergraduates: $6085. ***Parent loans:*** $10,481,554 (49% need-based, 51% non-need-based). ***Programs:*** Federal Direct (Subsidized and Unsubsidized Stafford, PLUS), Perkins, college/university.

WORK-STUDY ***Federal work-study:*** Total amount: $2,379,335; 785 jobs averaging $3294. ***State or other work-study/employment:*** Total amount: $381,328 (100% need-based). 243 part-time jobs averaging $1670.

ATHLETIC AWARDS Total amount: $5,806,213 (42% need-based, 58% non-need-based).

APPLYING FOR FINANCIAL AID ***Required financial aid form:*** FAFSA. ***Financial aid deadline (priority):*** 1/1. ***Notification date:*** Continuous beginning 12/1.

CONTACT Ms. Billie Jo Hamilton, Associate Vice President – Enrollment Planning & Management, University of South Florida, 4202 East Fowler Avenue, SVC 1102, Tampa, FL 33620-6960, 813-974-4700. *Fax:* 813-974-5144. *E-mail:* bjhamilton@usf.edu. *Website:* http://www.usf.edu/.

UNIVERSITY OF SOUTH FLORIDA, ST. PETERSBURG

St. Petersburg, FL

CONTACT Financial Aid Office, University of South Florida, St. Petersburg, 140 Seventh Ave S., St. Petersburg, FL 33701, 727-873-7748. *Website:* http://www.usfsp.edu/.

UNIVERSITY OF SOUTH FLORIDA SARASOTA-MANATEE

Sarasota, FL

CONTACT Financial Aid Office, University of South Florida Sarasota-Manatee, 8350 N Tamiami Trail, Sarasota, FL 34243, 941-359-4200.
Website: http://www.usfsm.edu/.

THE UNIVERSITY OF TAMPA

Tampa, FL

Tuition & fees: $30,884 | **Average undergraduate aid package: $18,061**

ABOUT THE INSTITUTION Independent, coed. ***Awards:*** certificates, bachelor's, master's, and doctoral degrees. 63 undergraduate majors. ***Total enrollment:*** 9,628. Undergraduates: 8,697. Freshmen: 2,184. Federal methodology is used as a basis for awarding need-based institutional aid.

UNDERGRADUATE EXPENSES for 2020–2021 ***Application fee:*** $40. ***Comprehensive fee:*** $42,410 includes full-time tuition ($28,802), mandatory fees ($2082), and room and board ($11,526). ***College room only:*** $6084. Full-time tuition and fees vary according to class time, course load, and program. Room and board charges vary according to board plan and housing facility. ***Part-time tuition:*** $613 per credit hour. ***Part-time fees:*** $40 per term. Part-time tuition and fees vary according to class time, course load, and program.

FRESHMAN FINANCIAL AID (Fall 2019, est.) 1796 applied for aid; of those 70% were deemed to have need. 100% of freshmen with need received aid; of those 16% had need fully met. ***Average percent of need met:*** 65% (excluding resources awarded to replace EFC). ***Average financial aid package:*** $18,244 (excluding resources awarded to replace EFC). 38% of all full-time freshmen had no need and received non-need-based gift aid.

UNDERGRADUATE FINANCIAL AID (Fall 2019, est.) 6,067 applied for aid; of those 79% were deemed to have need. 100% of undergraduates with need received aid; of those 11% had need fully met. ***Average percent of need met:*** 62% (excluding resources awarded to replace EFC). ***Average financial aid package:*** $18,061 (excluding resources awarded to replace EFC). 35% of all full-time undergraduates had no need and received non-need-based gift aid.

GIFT AID (NEED-BASED) ***Receiving aid:*** Freshmen: 57% (1,249); all full-time undergraduates: 56% (4,690). ***Average award:*** Freshmen: $15,005; Undergraduates: $14,254. ***Scholarships, grants, and awards:*** Federal Pell, FSEOG, state, private, college/university gift aid from institutional funds.

GIFT AID (NON-NEED-BASED) ***Receiving aid:*** Freshmen: 56% (1,228). Undergraduates: 54% (4,565). ***Average award:*** Freshmen: $9815. Undergraduates: $8582. ***Scholarships, grants, and awards by category:*** *Academic interests/achievement:* 7,103 awards ($63,275,234 total): biological sciences, English, general academic interests/achievements, international studies, military science, physical sciences, premedicine, social sciences. *Creative arts/performance:* 145 awards ($304,550 total): applied art and design, creative writing, dance, journalism/publications, music, performing arts, theater/drama. *Special achievements/activities:* 243 awards ($232,672 total): general special achievements/activities, leadership, memberships. *Special characteristics:* 498 awards ($3,755,019 total): children and siblings of alumni, children of faculty/staff, first-generation college students, international students, veterans. ***Tuition waivers:*** Full or partial for employees or children of employees. ***ROTC:*** Army, Naval cooperative, Air Force cooperative.

LOANS ***Student loans:*** 58% of past graduating class borrowed through all loan programs. *Average indebtedness per student:* $35,034. ***Average need-based loan:*** Freshmen: $3565. Undergraduates: $4301. ***Programs:*** Federal Direct (Subsidized and Unsubsidized Stafford, PLUS), college/university, private loans.

WORK-STUDY ***Federal work-study:*** 733 jobs averaging $2000. ***State or other work-study/employment:*** 4 part-time jobs averaging $2000.

APPLYING FOR FINANCIAL AID ***Required financial aid form:*** FAFSA. ***Financial aid deadline:*** Continuous. ***Notification date:*** Continuous.

CONTACT Financial Aid Office, The University of Tampa, 401 W. Kennedy Blvd. , Box E, Tampa , FL 33606-1490, 813-253-6219 or toll-free 888-646-2738 (in-state), 888-MINARET (out-of-state). *Fax:* 813-258-7439. *E-mail:* finaid@ut.edu.
Website: http://www.ut.edu/.

THE UNIVERSITY OF TENNESSEE

Knoxville, TN

Tuition & fees (TN res): $13,264 | **Average undergraduate aid package: $13,977**

ABOUT THE INSTITUTION State-supported, coed. ***Awards:*** certificates, bachelor's, master's, and doctoral degrees. 76 undergraduate majors. ***Total enrollment:*** 29,460. Undergraduates: 23,290. Freshmen: 5,254. Federal methodology is used as a basis for awarding need-based institutional aid.

UNDERGRADUATE EXPENSES for 2019–2020 ***Application fee:*** $50. ***Tuition, state resident:*** full-time $11,332; part-time $378 per credit hour. ***Tuition, nonresident:*** full-time $29,522; part-time $1137 per credit hour. ***Required fees:*** full-time $1932. Full-time tuition and fees vary according to course level, location, program, and reciprocity agreements. Part-time tuition and fees vary according to course level, location, program, and reciprocity agreements. ***College room and board:*** $11,482. Room and board charges vary according to board plan and housing facility.

FRESHMAN FINANCIAL AID (Fall 2019, est.) 4970 applied for aid; of those 59% were deemed to have need. 100% of freshmen with need received aid; of those 16% had need fully met. ***Average percent of need met:*** 62% (excluding resources awarded to replace EFC). ***Average financial aid package:*** $14,918 (excluding resources awarded to replace EFC). 20% of all full-time freshmen had no need and received non-need-based gift aid.

UNDERGRADUATE FINANCIAL AID (Fall 2019, est.) 18,946 applied for aid; of those 63% were deemed to have need. 99% of undergraduates with need received aid; of those 14% had need fully met. ***Average percent of need met:*** 57% (excluding resources awarded to replace EFC). ***Average financial aid package:*** $13,977 (excluding resources awarded to replace EFC). 17% of all full-time undergraduates had no need and received non-need-based gift aid.

GIFT AID (NEED-BASED) ***Total amount:*** $163,702,891 (17% federal, 36% state, 44% institutional, 3% external sources). ***Receiving aid:*** Freshmen: 51% (2,688); all full-time undergraduates: 47% (10,420). ***Average award:*** Freshmen: $12,794; Undergraduates: $11,138. ***Scholarships, grants, and awards:*** Federal Pell, FSEOG, state, private, college/university gift aid from institutional funds.

GIFT AID (NON-NEED-BASED) ***Average award:*** Freshmen: $6860. Undergraduates: $6528. ***Scholarships, grants, and awards by category:*** *Academic interests/achievement:* 2,243 awards ($5,878,177 total): agriculture, architecture, business, communication, computer science, education, engineering/technologies, general academic interests/achievements, home economics, humanities, international studies, library science, military science, social sciences. *Creative arts/performance:* 419 awards ($441,895 total): art/fine arts. ***Tuition waivers:*** Full or partial for employees or children of employees, senior citizens. ***ROTC:*** Army, Air Force.

LOANS ***Student loans:*** $86,535,102 (67% need-based, 33% non-need-based). 50% of past graduating class borrowed through all loan programs. *Average indebtedness per student:* $27,060. ***Average need-based loan:*** Freshmen: $5788. Undergraduates: $7016. ***Parent loans:*** $34,248,219 (100% need-based). ***Programs:*** Federal Direct (Subsidized and Unsubsidized Stafford, PLUS), Perkins, state, college/university.

WORK-STUDY ***Federal work-study:*** Total amount: $1,770,867; 679 jobs averaging $2552.

ATHLETIC AWARDS Total amount: $11,480,037 (100% need-based).

APPLYING FOR FINANCIAL AID ***Required financial aid form:*** FAFSA. ***Financial aid deadline (priority):*** 2/15. ***Notification date:*** Continuous beginning 2/15. Students must reply within 3 weeks of notification.

CONTACT Jeffery Gerkin, Assistant Dean Office of Financial Aid and Scholarships, The University of Tennessee, 115 Student Services Building, 1331 Circle Park, Knoxville, TN 37996-0210, 865-974-1111. *Fax:* 865-974-2175. *E-mail:* finaid@utk.edu.
Website: http://www.utk.edu/.

THE UNIVERSITY OF TENNESSEE AT CHATTANOOGA

Chattanooga, TN

Tuition & fees (TN res): $9656 **Average undergraduate aid package: $10,919**

ABOUT THE INSTITUTION State-supported, coed. ***Awards:*** certificates, bachelor's, master's, and doctoral degrees. 47 undergraduate majors. ***Total enrollment:*** 11,651. Undergraduates: 10,296. Freshmen: 2,310. Federal methodology is used as a basis for awarding need-based institutional aid.

UNDERGRADUATE EXPENSES for 2019–2020 ***Application fee:*** $30. ***Tuition, state resident:*** full-time $7836; part-time $294 per credit. ***Tuition, nonresident:*** full-time $23,954; part-time $966 per credit. ***Required fees:*** full-time $1820; $205 per term. Full-time tuition and fees vary according to degree level and student level. Part-time tuition and fees vary according to degree level. ***College room and board:*** $10,159; ***Room only:*** $6163. Room and board charges vary according to board plan, housing facility, and location.

FRESHMAN FINANCIAL AID (Fall 2019, est.) 2238 applied for aid; of those 66% were deemed to have need. 100% of freshmen with need received aid; of those 17% had need fully met. ***Average percent of need met:*** 69% (excluding resources awarded to replace EFC). ***Average financial aid package:*** $12,207 (excluding resources awarded to replace EFC). 31% of all full-time freshmen had no need and received non-need-based gift aid.

UNDERGRADUATE FINANCIAL AID (Fall 2019, est.) 8,220 applied for aid; of those 68% were deemed to have need. 99% of undergraduates with need received aid; of those 13% had need fully met. ***Average percent of need met:*** 63% (excluding resources awarded to replace EFC). ***Average financial aid package:*** $10,919 (excluding resources awarded to replace EFC). 22% of all full-time undergraduates had no need and received non-need-based gift aid.

GIFT AID (NEED-BASED) ***Total amount:*** $40,338,775 (38% federal, 40% state, 20% institutional, 2% external sources). ***Receiving aid:*** Freshmen: 63% (1,442); all full-time undergraduates: 54% (4,931). ***Average award:*** Freshmen: $8911; Undergraduates: $7907. ***Scholarships, grants, and awards:*** Federal Pell, FSEOG, state, private, college/university gift aid from institutional funds.

GIFT AID (NON-NEED-BASED) ***Total amount:*** $14,220,720 (62% state, 35% institutional, 3% external sources). ***Receiving aid:*** Freshmen: 9% (213). Undergraduates: 6% (567). ***Average award:*** Freshmen: $6335. Undergraduates: $5904. ***Scholarships, grants, and awards by category:*** *Academic interests/achievement:* biological sciences, business, communication, computer science, education, engineering/technologies, English, foreign languages, general academic interests/achievements, health fields, home economics, humanities, international studies, library science, mathematics, military science, physical sciences, religion/biblical studies, social sciences. *Creative arts/performance:* applied art and design, art/fine arts, cinema/film/broadcasting, creative writing, dance, journalism/publications, music, performing arts, theater/drama. *Special achievements/activities:* cheerleading/drum major, community service, leadership, memberships, religious involvement. *Special characteristics:* adult students, children and siblings of alumni, children of faculty/staff, children of union members/company employees, children with a deceased or disabled parent, ethnic background, first-generation college students, handicapped students, international students, local/state students, members of minority groups, out-of-state students, religious affiliation. ***Tuition waivers:*** Full or partial for employees or children of employees, senior citizens. ***ROTC:*** Army.

LOANS ***Student loans:*** $42,116,527 (65% need-based, 35% non-need-based). 56% of past graduating class borrowed through all loan programs. *Average indebtedness per student:* $23,059. ***Average need-based loan:*** Freshmen: $2947. Undergraduates: $3571. ***Parent loans:*** $6,004,598 (39% need-based, 61% non-need-based). ***Programs:*** Federal Direct (Subsidized and Unsubsidized Stafford, PLUS).

WORK-STUDY ***Federal work-study:*** Total amount: $449,325; jobs available. ***State or other work-study/employment:*** Total amount: $187,000 (33% need-based, 67% non-need-based). Part-time jobs available.

ATHLETIC AWARDS Total amount: $4,646,900 (43% need-based, 57% non-need-based).

APPLYING FOR FINANCIAL AID ***Required financial aid forms:*** FAFSA, institutional scholarship application form. ***Financial aid deadline (priority):*** 12/1. ***Notification date:*** Continuous beginning 12/15. Students must reply by 5/1.

CONTACT Kimberly Whiteside, Interim Director of Financial Aid and Scholarships, The University of Tennessee at Chattanooga, 615 McCallie Avenue, Chattanooga, TN 37403-2598, 423-425-4677 or toll-free 800-882-6627. *Fax:* 423-425-2292. *E-mail:* Kimberly-Whiteside@utc.edu.
Website: http://www.utc.edu/.

THE UNIVERSITY OF TENNESSEE AT MARTIN

Martin, TN

Tuition & fees (TN res): $9748 **Average undergraduate aid package: $11,898**

ABOUT THE INSTITUTION State-supported, coed. ***Awards:*** bachelor's and master's degrees. 35 undergraduate majors. ***Total enrollment:*** 7,296. Undergraduates: 6,779. Freshmen: 1,160. Federal methodology is used as a basis for awarding need-based institutional aid.

UNDERGRADUATE EXPENSES for 2019–2020 ***Application fee:*** $30. ***Tuition, state resident:*** full-time $8214; part-time $342 per credit hour. ***Tuition, nonresident:*** full-time $14,254; part-time $594 per credit hour. ***Required fees:*** full-time $1534; $64 per credit hour. Part-time tuition and fees vary according to course load. ***College room and board:*** $6396; ***Room only:*** $2920. Room and board charges vary according to board plan and housing facility.

FRESHMAN FINANCIAL AID (Fall 2019, est.) 1131 applied for aid; of those 77% were deemed to have need. 100% of freshmen with need received aid; of those 24% had need fully met. ***Average percent of need met:*** 43% (excluding resources awarded to replace EFC). ***Average financial aid package:*** $13,216 (excluding resources awarded to replace EFC). 12% of all full-time freshmen had no need and received non-need-based gift aid.

UNDERGRADUATE FINANCIAL AID (Fall 2019, est.) 4,496 applied for aid; of those 79% were deemed to have need. 99% of undergraduates with need received aid; of those 24% had need fully met. ***Average percent of need met:*** 45% (excluding resources awarded to replace EFC). ***Average financial aid package:*** $11,898 (excluding resources awarded to replace EFC). 8% of all full-time undergraduates had no need and received non-need-based gift aid.

GIFT AID (NEED-BASED) ***Receiving aid:*** Freshmen: 53% (611); all full-time undergraduates: 51% (2,418). ***Average award:*** Freshmen: $7515; Undergraduates: $7010. ***Scholarships, grants, and awards:*** Federal Pell, FSEOG, state, private, college/university gift aid from institutional funds.

GIFT AID (NON-NEED-BASED) ***Receiving aid:*** Freshmen: 69% (796). Undergraduates: 51% (2,429). ***Average award:*** Freshmen: $2006. Undergraduates: $2022. ***Scholarships, grants, and awards by category:*** *Academic interests/achievement:* 216 awards ($230,449 total): agriculture, biological sciences, business, communication, computer science, education, engineering/technologies, English, foreign languages, general academic interests/achievements, health fields, home economics, humanities, international studies, mathematics, military science, physical sciences, premedicine, social sciences. *Creative arts/performance:* 19 awards ($15,885 total): art/fine arts, cinema/film/broadcasting, creative writing, journalism/publications, music, theater/drama. *Special achievements/activities:* 26 awards ($67,260 total): cheerleading/drum major, general special achievements/activities, junior miss, leadership, rodeo. *Special characteristics:* 240 awards ($544,474 total): adult students, children and siblings of alumni, children of educators, children of faculty/staff, children of public servants, children of union members/company employees, ethnic background, general special characteristics, local/state students, members of minority groups, out-of-state students, previous college experience. ***Tuition waivers:*** Full or partial for employees or children of employees, senior citizens. ***ROTC:*** Army.

LOANS ***Student loans:*** 62% of past graduating class borrowed through all loan programs. *Average indebtedness per student:* $24,096. ***Average need-based loan:*** Freshmen: $3255. Undergraduates: $4144. ***Programs:*** Federal Direct (Subsidized and Unsubsidized Stafford, PLUS), Perkins.

WORK-STUDY ***Federal work-study:*** 175 jobs averaging $2376.

APPLYING FOR FINANCIAL AID ***Required financial aid form:*** FAFSA. ***Notification date:*** Continuous.

CONTACT Amy J. Mistric, Assistant Director of Financial Aid, The University of Tennessee at Martin, 205 Administration Building, Martin, TN 38238-1000, 731-881-7031 or toll-free 800-829-8861. *Fax:* 731-881-7036. *E-mail:* amistric@utm.edu.
Website: http://www.utm.edu/.

THE UNIVERSITY OF TEXAS AT ARLINGTON

Arlington, TX

CONTACT Karen Krause, Director of Financial Aid, The University of Texas at Arlington, UTA Box 19199, Arlington, TX 76019, 817-272-3561. *Fax:* 817-272-3555. *E-mail:* kkrause@uta.edu.
Website: http://www.uta.edu/.

THE UNIVERSITY OF TEXAS AT AUSTIN

Austin, TX

Tuition & fees (TX res): $10,824	Average undergraduate aid package: $12,306

ABOUT THE INSTITUTION State-supported, coed. ***Awards:*** certificates, bachelor's, master's, and doctoral degrees. 98 undergraduate majors. ***Total enrollment:*** 51,832. Undergraduates: 40,804. Freshmen: 8,960. Both federal and institutional methodology are used as a basis for awarding need-based institutional aid.

UNDERGRADUATE EXPENSES for 2019–2020 ***Application fee:*** $75. ***Tuition, state resident:*** full-time $10,824. ***Tuition, nonresident:*** full-time $38,326. Full-time tuition and fees vary according to course load and program. Part-time tuition and fees vary according to course load and program. ***College room and board:*** $11,812. Room and board charges vary according to housing facility. ***Payment plan:*** Guaranteed tuition.

FRESHMAN FINANCIAL AID (Fall 2018) 7038 applied for aid; of those 53% were deemed to have need. 99% of freshmen with need received aid; of those 27% had need fully met. ***Average percent of need met:*** 74% (excluding resources awarded to replace EFC). ***Average financial aid package:*** $12,693 (excluding resources awarded to replace EFC). 2% of all full-time freshmen had no need and received non-need-based gift aid.

UNDERGRADUATE FINANCIAL AID (Fall 2018) 23,064 applied for aid; of those 67% were deemed to have need. 99% of undergraduates with need received aid; of those 18% had need fully met. ***Average percent of need met:*** 68% (excluding resources awarded to replace EFC). ***Average financial aid package:*** $12,306 (excluding resources awarded to replace EFC). 1% of all full-time undergraduates had no need and received non-need-based gift aid.

GIFT AID (NEED-BASED) ***Total amount:*** $194,088,215 (23% federal, 15% state, 42% institutional, 20% external sources). ***Receiving aid:*** Freshmen: 35% (2,828); all full-time undergraduates: 32% (11,894). ***Average award:*** Freshmen: $9958; Undergraduates: $9659. ***Scholarships, grants, and awards:*** Federal Pell, FSEOG, state, private, college/university gift aid from institutional funds.

GIFT AID (NON-NEED-BASED) ***Total amount:*** $8,251,118 (19% institutional, 81% external sources). ***Receiving aid:*** Freshmen: 34% (2,712). Undergraduates: 21% (7,711). ***Average award:*** Freshmen: $2221. Undergraduates: $2982. ***Scholarships, grants, and awards by category:*** *Academic interests/achievement:* general academic interests/achievements. *Creative arts/performance:* applied art and design, general creative arts/performance, music, theater/drama. *Special achievements/activities:* leadership. *Special characteristics:* children of faculty/staff, children of public servants, children with a deceased or disabled parent, international students, local/state students, out-of-state students, relatives of clergy, veterans, veterans' children. ***Tuition waivers:*** Full or partial for employees or children of employees, senior citizens. ***ROTC:*** Army, Naval, Air Force.

LOANS ***Student loans:*** $85,042,295 (68% need-based, 32% non-need-based). 40% of past graduating class borrowed through all loan programs. *Average indebtedness per student:* $24,263. ***Average need-based loan:*** Freshmen: $3163. Undergraduates: $4081. ***Parent loans:*** $70,505,751 (24% need-based, 76% non-need-based). ***Programs:*** Federal Direct (Subsidized and Unsubsidized Stafford, PLUS), Perkins, state, Short-term emergency cash and tuition loans.

WORK-STUDY ***Federal work-study:*** Total amount: $2,357,394; jobs available. ***State or other work-study/employment:*** Total amount: $526,629 (100% need-based). Part-time jobs available.

ATHLETIC AWARDS Total amount: $27,431,640 (38% need-based, 62% non-need-based).

APPLYING FOR FINANCIAL AID ***Required financial aid forms:*** FAFSA, institution's own form. ***Financial aid deadline (priority):*** 1/15. ***Notification date:*** Continuous beginning 1/15. Students must reply by 5/1 or within 3 weeks of notification.

CONTACT Ms. Diane Todd Sprague, Executive Director, Office of Financial Aid, The University of Texas at Austin, 1616 Guadalupe St., Stop E3700, Austin, TX 78701, 512-475-6204. *Fax:* 512-475-6296. *E-mail:* ask@finaid.utexas.edu.
Website: http://www.utexas.edu/.

THE UNIVERSITY OF TEXAS AT DALLAS

Richardson, TX

Tuition & fees (TX res): $13,442	Average undergraduate aid package: $13,776

ABOUT THE INSTITUTION State-supported, coed. ***Awards:*** certificates, bachelor's, master's, and doctoral degrees. 45 undergraduate majors. ***Total enrollment:*** 29,543. Undergraduates: 20,994. Freshmen: 4,073. Both federal and institutional methodology are used as a basis for awarding need-based institutional aid.

UNDERGRADUATE EXPENSES for 2019–2020 ***Application fee:*** $50. ***Tuition, state resident:*** full-time $13,442. ***Tuition, nonresident:*** full-time $38,168. Full-time tuition and fees vary according to course load and degree level. Part-time tuition and fees vary according to course load and degree level. ***College room and board:*** $11,532. Room and board charges vary according to board plan and housing facility. ***Payment plan:*** Guaranteed tuition.

FRESHMAN FINANCIAL AID (Fall 2018) 2834 applied for aid; of those 69% were deemed to have need. 98% of freshmen with need received aid; of those 22% had need fully met. ***Average percent of need met:*** 72% (excluding resources awarded to replace EFC). ***Average financial aid package:*** $15,950 (excluding resources awarded to replace EFC). 24% of all full-time freshmen had no need and received non-need-based gift aid.

UNDERGRADUATE FINANCIAL AID (Fall 2018) 10,450 applied for aid; of those 82% were deemed to have need. 97% of undergraduates with need received aid; of those 15% had need fully met. ***Average percent of need met:*** 65% (excluding resources awarded to replace EFC). ***Average financial aid package:*** $13,776 (excluding resources awarded to replace EFC). 21% of all full-time undergraduates had no need and received non-need-based gift aid.

GIFT AID (NEED-BASED) ***Receiving aid:*** Freshmen: 45% (1,691); all full-time undergraduates: 46% (7,571). ***Average award:*** Freshmen: $11,957; Undergraduates: $9706. ***Scholarships, grants, and awards:*** Federal Pell, FSEOG, state, private, college/university gift aid from institutional funds.

GIFT AID (NON-NEED-BASED) ***Receiving aid:*** Freshmen: 7% (248). Undergraduates: 3% (493). ***Average award:*** Freshmen: $14,241. Undergraduates: $11,842. ***Scholarships, grants, and awards by category:*** *Academic interests/achievement:* biological sciences, business, computer science, engineering/technologies, general academic interests/achievements, mathematics, physical sciences. *Special achievements/activities:* general special achievements/activities, leadership. *Special characteristics:* adult students, children of public servants, general special characteristics, handicapped students, international students, local/state students, members of minority groups, out-of-state students, public servants, veterans. ***Tuition waivers:*** Full or partial for employees or children of employees, senior citizens. ***ROTC:*** Army cooperative, Air Force cooperative.

LOANS ***Student loans:*** 32% of past graduating class borrowed through all loan programs. *Average indebtedness per student:* $23,176. ***Average need-based loan:*** Freshmen: $3440. Undergraduates: $4445. ***Programs:*** Federal Direct (Subsidized and Unsubsidized Stafford, PLUS), Perkins, state, college/university.

WORK-STUDY Federal work-study jobs available. ***State or other work-study/employment:*** Part-time jobs available.

APPLYING FOR FINANCIAL AID ***Required financial aid form:*** FAFSA. ***Notification date:*** Continuous. Students must reply within 2 weeks of notification.

CONTACT M. Beth Tolan, Senior Director of Financial Aid, The University of Texas at Dallas, 800 West Campbell Road, SSB22, Richardson, TX 75080-3021, 972-883-2941 or toll-free 800-889-2443. *Fax:* 972-883-6803. *E-mail:* mbeth.tolan@utdallas.edu.
Website: http://www.utdallas.edu/.

THE UNIVERSITY OF TEXAS AT EL PASO

El Paso, TX

Tuition & fees (area res): $8961 **Average undergraduate aid package: $11,820**

ABOUT THE INSTITUTION State-supported, coed. ***Awards:*** certificates, diplomas, bachelor's, master's, and doctoral degrees. 66 undergraduate majors. ***Total enrollment:*** 25,177. Undergraduates: 21,427. Freshmen: 3,063. Federal methodology is used as a basis for awarding need-based institutional aid.

UNDERGRADUATE EXPENSES for 2019–2020 ***Tuition, area resident:*** full-time $7193; part-time $294 per credit hour. ***Tuition, state resident:*** full-time $7193; part-time $294 per credit hour. ***Tuition, nonresident:*** full-time $22,556; part-time $806 per credit hour. ***Required fees:*** full-time $1768. Full-time tuition and fees vary according to course load, degree level, and program. Part-time tuition and fees vary according to course load, degree level, and program. ***College room and board:*** $9496; ***Room only:*** $5200. ***Payment plan:*** Guaranteed tuition.

FRESHMAN FINANCIAL AID (Fall 2018) 2549 applied for aid; of those 79% were deemed to have need. 107% of freshmen with need received aid; of those 15% had need fully met. ***Average percent of need met:*** 57% (excluding resources awarded to replace EFC). ***Average financial aid package:*** $11,631 (excluding resources awarded to replace EFC). 4% of all full-time freshmen had no need and received non-need-based gift aid.

UNDERGRADUATE FINANCIAL AID (Fall 2018) 12,305 applied for aid; of those 84% were deemed to have need. 107% of undergraduates with need received aid; of those 15% had need fully met. ***Average percent of need met:*** 55% (excluding resources awarded to replace EFC). ***Average financial aid package:*** $11,820 (excluding resources awarded to replace EFC). 5% of all full-time undergraduates had no need and received non-need-based gift aid.

GIFT AID (NEED-BASED) ***Total amount:*** $53,685,022 (69% federal, 25% state, 6% institutional). ***Receiving aid:*** Freshmen: 56% (1,612); all full-time undergraduates: 64% (8,500). ***Average award:*** Freshmen: $9469; Undergraduates: $7873. ***Scholarships, grants, and awards:*** Federal Pell, FSEOG, state, private, college/university gift aid from institutional funds, United Negro College Fund, Federal Nursing.

GIFT AID (NON-NEED-BASED) ***Total amount:*** $6,153,329 (6% federal, 80% institutional, 14% external sources). ***Receiving aid:*** Freshmen: 9% (249). Undergraduates: 12% (1,623). ***Average award:*** Freshmen: $4222. Undergraduates: $4229. ***Scholarships, grants, and awards by category:*** *Academic interests/achievement:* biological sciences, business, communication, computer science, education, engineering/technologies, English, general academic interests/achievements, home economics, humanities, international studies, mathematics, military science, physical sciences. *Creative arts/performance:* applied art and design, art/fine arts, journalism/publications, music, performing arts, theater/drama. *Special achievements/activities:* cheerleading/drum major, leadership. *Special characteristics:* ethnic background, international students, local/state students, members of minority groups, out-of-state students. ***ROTC:*** Army.

LOANS ***Student loans:*** $62,147,295 (100% need-based). 62% of past graduating class borrowed through all loan programs. *Average indebtedness per student:* $23,632. ***Average need-based loan:*** Freshmen: $4312. Undergraduates: $6172. ***Parent loans:*** $1,138,951 (100% non-need-based). ***Programs:*** Federal Direct (Subsidized and Unsubsidized Stafford, PLUS), Perkins, Federal Nursing, state, college/university.

WORK-STUDY ***Federal work-study:*** Total amount: $1,605,933; jobs available. ***State or other work-study/employment:*** Total amount: $424,981 (80% need-based, 20% non-need-based). Part-time jobs available.

ATHLETIC AWARDS Total amount: $4,526,803 (100% non-need-based).

APPLYING FOR FINANCIAL AID ***Required financial aid forms:*** FAFSA, institution's own form. ***Financial aid deadline (priority):*** 3/15. ***Notification date:*** Continuous beginning 3/30. Students must reply within 2 weeks of notification.

CONTACT Ms. Heidi Granger, Assistant VP for Financial Services, The University of Texas at El Paso, 500 West University Avenue, El Paso, TX 79968-0001, 915-747-5478 or toll-free 877-74MINER. *Fax:* 915-747-5089. *E-mail:* hgranger@utep.edu. *Website:* http://www.utep.edu/.

THE UNIVERSITY OF TEXAS AT SAN ANTONIO

San Antonio, TX

Tuition & fees (area res): $9723 **Average undergraduate aid package: $10,241**

ABOUT THE INSTITUTION State-supported, coed. ***Awards:*** certificates, bachelor's, master's, and doctoral degrees. 71 undergraduate majors. ***Total enrollment:*** 32,594. Undergraduates: 28,275. Freshmen: 4,599. Federal methodology is used as a basis for awarding need-based institutional aid.

UNDERGRADUATE EXPENSES for 2019–2020 ***Application fee:*** $70. ***Tuition, area resident:*** full-time $6887; part-time $230 per credit hour. ***Tuition, state resident:*** full-time $6887; part-time $230 per credit hour. ***Tuition, nonresident:*** full-time $21,889; part-time $730 per credit hour. ***Required fees:*** full-time $2836; $1111 per term. Full-time tuition and fees vary according to course level and program. Part-time tuition and fees vary according to course level and program. ***College room and board:*** $7590; ***Room only:*** $4770. Room and board charges vary according to housing facility. ***Payment plan:*** Guaranteed tuition.

FRESHMAN FINANCIAL AID (Fall 2018) 4239 applied for aid; of those 79% were deemed to have need. 97% of freshmen with need received aid; of those 5% had need fully met. ***Average percent of need met:*** 56% (excluding resources awarded to replace EFC). ***Average financial aid package:*** $10,815 (excluding resources awarded to replace EFC). 4% of all full-time freshmen had no need and received non-need-based gift aid.

UNDERGRADUATE FINANCIAL AID (Fall 2018) 17,732 applied for aid; of those 86% were deemed to have need. 98% of undergraduates with need received aid; of those 5% had need fully met. ***Average percent of need met:*** 51% (excluding resources awarded to replace EFC). ***Average financial aid package:*** $10,241 (excluding resources awarded to replace EFC). 12% of all full-time undergraduates had no need and received non-need-based gift aid.

GIFT AID (NEED-BASED) ***Total amount:*** $116,920,046 (50% federal, 21% state, 24% institutional, 5% external sources). ***Receiving aid:*** Freshmen: 60% (2,915); all full-time undergraduates: 59% (13,295). ***Average award:*** Freshmen: $8977; Undergraduates: $7611. ***Scholarships, grants, and awards:*** Federal Pell, FSEOG, state, private, college/university gift aid from institutional funds.

GIFT AID (NON-NEED-BASED) ***Total amount:*** $7,116,496 (4% federal, 75% institutional, 21% external sources). ***Receiving aid:*** Freshmen: 1% (44). Undergraduates: 2% (347). ***Average award:*** Freshmen: $2767. Undergraduates: $1711. ***Scholarships, grants, and awards by category:*** *Academic interests/achievement:* agriculture, area/ethnic studies, biological sciences, business, communication, computer science, education, engineering/technologies, English, foreign languages, general academic interests/achievements, humanities, international studies, mathematics, physical sciences, social sciences. *Creative arts/performance:* applied art and design, creative writing, debating, music. *Special achievements/activities:* cheerleading/drum major, general special achievements/activities. *Special characteristics:* ethnic background, first-generation college students, general special characteristics, handicapped students, local/state students, members of minority groups, out-of-state students. ***Tuition waivers:*** Full or partial for employees or children of employees. ***ROTC:*** Army, Air Force.

LOANS ***Student loans:*** $89,042,682 (53% need-based, 47% non-need-based). 61% of past graduating class borrowed through all loan programs. *Average indebtedness per student:* $24,214. ***Average need-based loan:*** Freshmen: $3264. Undergraduates: $4119. ***Parent loans:*** $13,868,689 (100% non-need-based). ***Programs:*** Federal Direct (Subsidized and Unsubsidized Stafford, PLUS), Perkins, state, college/university.

WORK-STUDY ***Federal work-study:*** Total amount: $958,555; jobs available. ***State or other work-study/employment:*** Total amount: $2,258,104 (100% need-based). Part-time jobs available.

ATHLETIC AWARDS Total amount: $5,066,381 (33% need-based, 67% non-need-based).

APPLYING FOR FINANCIAL AID ***Required financial aid form:*** FAFSA. ***Financial aid deadline (priority):*** 1/15. ***Notification date:*** Continuous beginning 3/1.

CONTACT Financial Aid Office, The University of Texas at San Antonio, One UTSA Circle, San Antonio, TX 78249-0617, 210-458-4011 or toll-free 800-669-0919. *Website:* http://www.utsa.edu/.

THE UNIVERSITY OF TEXAS AT TYLER

Tyler, TX

Tuition & fees (area res): $8742 **Average undergraduate aid package: $8519**

ABOUT THE INSTITUTION State-supported, coed. ***Awards:*** certificates, bachelor's, master's, and doctoral degrees. 41 undergraduate majors. ***Total enrollment:*** 10,206. Undergraduates: 7,333. Freshmen: 907. Federal methodology is used as a basis for awarding need-based institutional aid.

UNDERGRADUATE EXPENSES for 2019–2020 ***Application fee:*** $60. ***Tuition, area resident:*** full-time $6540. ***Tuition, state resident:*** full-time $6540. ***Tuition, nonresident:*** full-time $20,550. ***Required fees:*** full-time $2202. ***College room and board:*** $9502; ***Room only:*** $5754.

FRESHMAN FINANCIAL AID (Fall 2018) 732 applied for aid; of those 99% were deemed to have need. 94% of freshmen with need received aid; of those 16% had need fully met. ***Average percent of need met:*** 49% (excluding resources awarded to replace EFC). ***Average financial aid package:*** $11,486 (excluding resources awarded to replace EFC).

UNDERGRADUATE FINANCIAL AID (Fall 2018) 3,861 applied for aid; of those 97% were deemed to have need. 95% of undergraduates with need received aid; of those 3% had need fully met. ***Average percent of need met:*** 38% (excluding resources awarded to replace EFC). ***Average financial aid package:*** $8519 (excluding resources awarded to replace EFC). 1% of all full-time undergraduates had no need and received non-need-based gift aid.

GIFT AID (NEED-BASED) ***Receiving aid:*** Freshmen: 74% (613); all full-time undergraduates: 65% (3,038). ***Average award:*** Freshmen: $10,431; Undergraduates: $7397. ***Scholarships, grants, and awards:*** Federal Pell, FSEOG, state, private, college/university gift aid from institutional funds, TEACH Grant.

GIFT AID (NON-NEED-BASED) ***Receiving aid:*** Freshmen: 13% (109). Undergraduates: 4% (171). ***Average award:*** Undergraduates: $3198. ***Scholarships, grants, and awards by category:*** *Academic interests/achievement:* communication, engineering/technologies, general academic interests/achievements, home economics. *Creative arts/performance:* applied art and design, music. *Special characteristics:* children of faculty/staff, first-generation college students.

LOANS ***Student loans:*** 49% of past graduating class borrowed through all loan programs. *Average indebtedness per student:* $19,691. ***Average need-based loan:*** Freshmen: $2356. Undergraduates: $3419. ***Programs:*** Federal Direct (Subsidized and Unsubsidized Stafford, PLUS), state, Texas B-On-Time and Private Loans.

WORK-STUDY Federal work-study jobs available. ***State or other work-study/employment:*** Part-time jobs available.

APPLYING FOR FINANCIAL AID ***Required financial aid forms:*** FAFSA, state aid form. ***Notification date:*** Continuous. Students must reply within 2 weeks of notification.

CONTACT Scott Lapinski, Director of Student Financial Aid, The University of Texas at Tyler, 3900 University Boulevard, Tyler, TX 75799, 903-566-7181 or toll-free 800-UTTYLER. *E-mail:* enroll@uttyler.edu.
Website: http://www.uttyler.edu/.

THE UNIVERSITY OF TEXAS HEALTH SCIENCE CENTER AT HOUSTON

Houston, TX

CONTACT Ms. Araceli Alvarez, Director of Student Financial Services, The University of Texas Health Science Center at Houston, PO Box 20036, Houston, TX 77225, 713-500-3860. *Fax:* 713-500-3863. *E-mail:* araceli.alvarez@uth.tmc.edu.
Website: http://www.uthouston.edu/.

THE UNIVERSITY OF TEXAS HEALTH SCIENCE CENTER AT SAN ANTONIO

San Antonio, TX

CONTACT Robert T. Lawson, Financial Aid Administrator, The University of Texas Health Science Center at San Antonio, 7703 Floyd Curl Drive, MSC 7708, San Antonio, TX 78284, 210-567-0025. *Fax:* 210-567-6643.
Website: http://www.uthscsa.edu/.

THE UNIVERSITY OF TEXAS MD ANDERSON CANCER CENTER

Houston, TX

CONTACT Financial Aid Office, The University of Texas MD Anderson Cancer Center, 1515 Holcombe Boulevard, Houston, TX 77030, 713-792-2121.
Website: http://www.mdanderson.org/education-and-research/.

THE UNIVERSITY OF TEXAS MEDICAL BRANCH

Galveston, TX

CONTACT Mrs. Carol A. Cromie, University Financial Aid Officer, The University of Texas Medical Branch, 301 University Boulevard, Galveston, TX 77555-1305, 409-772-9795. *Fax:* 409-772-4466. *E-mail:* cacromie@umtb.edu.
Website: http://www.utmb.edu/.

THE UNIVERSITY OF TEXAS OF THE PERMIAN BASIN

Odessa, TX

ABOUT THE INSTITUTION State-supported, coed. ***Awards:*** certificates, bachelor's, and master's degrees. 34 undergraduate majors. ***Total enrollment:*** 5,283. Undergraduates: 4,347. Freshmen: 311.

GIFT AID (NEED-BASED) ***Scholarships, grants, and awards:*** Federal Pell, FSEOG, state, private, college/university gift aid from institutional funds.

LOANS ***Programs:*** Federal Direct (Subsidized and Unsubsidized Stafford, PLUS), state.

WORK-STUDY ***Federal work-study:*** Total amount: $199,074; jobs available. ***State or other work-study/employment:*** Total amount: $19,000 (100% need-based). Part-time jobs available.

APPLYING FOR FINANCIAL AID ***Required financial aid form:*** FAFSA.

CONTACT Gary Byers, Interim Director of Financial Aid, The University of Texas of the Permian Basin, 4901 East University Boulevard, Odessa, TX 79762, 432-552-2620 or toll-free 866-552-UTPB. *Fax:* 432-552-2621. *E-mail:* byers_g@utpb.edu.
Website: http://www.utpb.edu/.

THE UNIVERSITY OF TEXAS RIO GRANDE VALLEY

Edinburg, TX

Tuition & fees (area res): $8916 **Average undergraduate aid package: $10,350**

ABOUT THE INSTITUTION State-supported, coed. ***Awards:*** certificates, bachelor's, master's, and doctoral degrees. 59 undergraduate majors. ***Total enrollment:*** 29,113. Undergraduates: 24,965. Freshmen: 4,793.

UNDERGRADUATE EXPENSES for 2020–2021 ***Tuition, area resident:*** full-time $7232; part-time $430 per credit hour. ***Tuition, state resident:*** full-time

$7232; part-time $430 per credit hour. ***Tuition, nonresident:*** full-time $19,502; part-time $839 per credit hour. ***Required fees:*** full-time $1684; $193.93 per credit hour. Full-time tuition and fees vary according to degree level and program. Part-time tuition and fees vary according to degree level and program. ***College room and board:*** $8342. Room and board charges vary according to board plan and housing facility. ***Payment plan:*** Guaranteed tuition.

FRESHMAN FINANCIAL AID (Fall 2018) 3879 applied for aid; of those 93% were deemed to have need. 100% of freshmen with need received aid; of those 3% had need fully met. ***Average percent of need met:*** 72% (excluding resources awarded to replace EFC). ***Average financial aid package:*** $10,375 (excluding resources awarded to replace EFC). 4% of all full-time freshmen had no need and received non-need-based gift aid.

UNDERGRADUATE FINANCIAL AID (Fall 2018) 16,201 applied for aid; of those 96% were deemed to have need. 100% of undergraduates with need received aid; of those 3% had need fully met. ***Average percent of need met:*** 70% (excluding resources awarded to replace EFC). ***Average financial aid package:*** $10,350 (excluding resources awarded to replace EFC). 3% of all full-time undergraduates had no need and received non-need-based gift aid.

GIFT AID (NEED-BASED) ***Total amount:*** $141,924,692 (59% federal, 26% state, 14% institutional, 1% external sources). ***Receiving aid:*** Freshmen: 89% (3,528); all full-time undergraduates: 89% (14,971). ***Average award:*** Freshmen: $10,552; Undergraduates: $10,835. ***Scholarships, grants, and awards:*** Federal Pell, FSEOG, state, private, college/university gift aid from institutional funds, Federal Nursing.

GIFT AID (NON-NEED-BASED) ***Total amount:*** $2,604,186 (5% federal, 78% institutional, 17% external sources). ***Receiving aid:*** Freshmen: 1% (44). Undergraduates: 1% (104). ***Average award:*** Freshmen: $4698. Undergraduates: $3362. ***Scholarships, grants, and awards by category:*** *Academic interests/achievement:* 2,710 awards ($7,411,959 total): biological sciences, business, communication, computer science, education, engineering/technologies, English, general academic interests/achievements, home economics, mathematics, military science, premedicine, social sciences. *Creative arts/performance:* 196 awards ($165,628 total): applied art and design, dance, journalism/publications, music, theater/drama. *Special achievements/activities:* 57 awards ($19,512 total): cheerleading/drum major, community service, general special achievements/activities, leadership, memberships. *Special characteristics:* 154 awards ($451,758 total): general special characteristics, international students, local/state students, out-of-state students, veterans. ***Tuition waivers:*** Full or partial for employees or children of employees. ***ROTC:*** Army.

LOANS ***Student loans:*** $45,344,872 (88% need-based, 12% non-need-based). 58% of past graduating class borrowed through all loan programs. *Average indebtedness per student:* $16,662. ***Average need-based loan:*** Freshmen: $3000. Undergraduates: $4429. ***Parent loans:*** $745,570 (8% need-based, 92% non-need-based). ***Programs:*** Federal Direct (Subsidized and Unsubsidized Stafford, PLUS), state.

WORK-STUDY ***Federal work-study:*** Total amount: $1,992,031; 769 jobs averaging $2590. ***State or other work-study/employment:*** Total amount: $1,250,130 (100% need-based). 495 part-time jobs averaging $2528.

ATHLETIC AWARDS Total amount: $2,122,236 (25% need-based, 75% non-need-based).

APPLYING FOR FINANCIAL AID ***Required financial aid form:*** FAFSA. ***Financial aid deadline (priority):*** 1/15. ***Notification date:*** Continuous.

CONTACT Mr. Elias Ozuna, Director of Student Financial Services, The University of Texas Rio Grande Valley, 1201 West University Drive, Edinburg, TX 78539, 956-665-5372 or toll-free 888-882-4026 (in-state). *Fax:* 956-665-2396. *E-mail:* elias.ozuna@utrgv.edu.
Website: http://www.utrgv.edu/.

THE UNIVERSITY OF THE ARTS

Philadelphia, PA

CONTACT Dr. Michelle H. Brown-Nevers, Associate Vice President, Student Financial Services, The University of the Arts, 320 South Broad Street, Philadelphia, PA 19102-4944, 800-616-ARTS Ext. 6170 or toll-free 800-616-ARTS. *E-mail:* finaid@uarts.edu.
Website: http://www.uarts.edu/.

UNIVERSITY OF THE CUMBERLANDS

Williamsburg, KY

CONTACT Mr. Steve Allen, Vice President for Student Financial Planning, University of the Cumberlands, 6190 College Station Drive, Williamsburg, KY 40769-1372, 606-549-2200 or toll-free 800-343-1609. *Fax:* 606-539-4515. *E-mail:* finplan@ucumberlands.edu.
Website: http://www.ucumberlands.edu/.

UNIVERSITY OF THE DISTRICT OF COLUMBIA

Washington, DC

CONTACT Mrs. Nailah Williams, Director of Financial Aid, University of the District of Columbia, 4200 Connecticut Avenue NW, Washington, DC 20008-1175, 202-274-5618. *Fax:* 202-274-6060. *E-mail:* finaid@udc.edu.
Website: http://www.udc.edu/.

UNIVERSITY OF THE INCARNATE WORD

San Antonio, TX

Tuition & fees: $32,286	Average undergraduate aid package: $22,348

ABOUT THE INSTITUTION Independent Roman Catholic, coed. ***Awards:*** diplomas, associate, bachelor's, master's, and doctoral degrees. 72 undergraduate majors. ***Total enrollment:*** 8,175. Undergraduates: 5,368. Freshmen: 1,012. Federal methodology is used as a basis for awarding need-based institutional aid.

UNDERGRADUATE EXPENSES for 2020–2021 ***Application fee:*** $20. ***Comprehensive fee:*** $45,300 includes full-time tuition ($31,020), mandatory fees ($1266), and room and board ($13,014). Full-time tuition and fees vary according to program. Room and board charges vary according to board plan and housing facility. ***Part-time tuition:*** $950 per credit hour. Part-time tuition and fees vary according to program.

FRESHMAN FINANCIAL AID (Fall 2019, est.) 920 applied for aid; of those 92% were deemed to have need. 100% of freshmen with need received aid; of those 11% had need fully met. ***Average percent of need met:*** 57% (excluding resources awarded to replace EFC). ***Average financial aid package:*** $24,843 (excluding resources awarded to replace EFC). 14% of all full-time freshmen had no need and received non-need-based gift aid.

UNDERGRADUATE FINANCIAL AID (Fall 2019, est.) 3,339 applied for aid; of those 94% were deemed to have need. 99% of undergraduates with need received aid; of those 7% had need fully met. ***Average percent of need met:*** 50% (excluding resources awarded to replace EFC). ***Average financial aid package:*** $22,348 (excluding resources awarded to replace EFC). 16% of all full-time undergraduates had no need and received non-need-based gift aid.

GIFT AID (NEED-BASED) ***Total amount:*** $58,472,845 (21% federal, 10% state, 67% institutional, 2% external sources). ***Receiving aid:*** Freshmen: 83% (840); all full-time undergraduates: 76% (3,056). ***Average award:*** Freshmen: $21,610; Undergraduates: $18,714. ***Scholarships, grants, and awards:*** Federal Pell, FSEOG, state, private, college/university gift aid from institutional funds, Federal Nursing.

GIFT AID (NON-NEED-BASED) ***Total amount:*** $6876 (27% federal, 73% institutional). ***Receiving aid:*** Freshmen: 13% (132). Undergraduates: 10% (396). ***Average award:*** Freshmen: $13,553. Undergraduates: $10,332. ***Scholarships, grants, and awards by category:*** *Academic interests/achievement:* general academic interests/achievements. *Creative arts/performance:* applied art and design, music, theater/drama. *Special achievements/activities:* leadership. *Special characteristics:* children and siblings of alumni, children of faculty/staff. ***Tuition waivers:*** Full or partial for employees or children of employees. ***ROTC:*** Army cooperative.

LOANS ***Student loans:*** $25,932,927 (87% need-based, 13% non-need-based). 67% of past graduating class borrowed through all loan programs. *Average indebtedness per student:* $36,178. ***Average need-based loan:*** Freshmen: $3523. Undergraduates: $4426. ***Parent loans:*** $10,878,097 (60% need-based, 40% non-need-based).

Programs: Federal Direct (Subsidized and Unsubsidized Stafford, PLUS), Federal Nursing, state, college/university, alternative loans.
WORK-STUDY *Federal work-study:* Total amount: $892,066; jobs available. ***State or other work-study/employment:*** Part-time jobs available.
ATHLETIC AWARDS Total amount: $9,680,910 (32% need-based, 68% non-need-based).
APPLYING FOR FINANCIAL AID *Required financial aid form:* FAFSA. ***Financial aid deadline (priority):*** 4/1. ***Notification date:*** Continuous beginning 11/1. Students must reply within 2 weeks of notification.
CONTACT Ms. Amy Carcanagues, Director of Financial Assistance, University of the Incarnate Word, 4301 Broadway, San Antonio, TX 78209, 210-829-6008 or toll-free 800-749-WORD. *Fax:* 210-283-5053. *E-mail:* finaid@uiwtx.edu.
Website: http://www.uiw.edu/.

UNIVERSITY OF THE OZARKS
Clarksville, AR

CONTACT Ms. Jana D. Hart, Director of Financial Aid, University of the Ozarks, 415 North College Avenue, Clarksville, AR 72830-2880, 479-979-1221 or toll-free 800-264-8636. *Fax:* 479-979-1417. *E-mail:* jhart@ozarks.edu.
Website: http://www.ozarks.edu/.

UNIVERSITY OF THE PACIFIC
Stockton, CA

Tuition & fees: $49,588	Average undergraduate aid package: $38,616

ABOUT THE INSTITUTION Independent, coed. ***Awards:*** bachelor's, master's, and doctoral degrees. 54 undergraduate majors. ***Total enrollment:*** 6,447. Undergraduates: 3,639. Freshmen: 808. Federal methodology is used as a basis for awarding need-based institutional aid.
UNDERGRADUATE EXPENSES for 2020–2021 *Comprehensive fee:* $63,328 includes full-time tuition ($48,904), mandatory fees ($684), and room and board ($13,740). Full-time tuition and fees vary according to course load and program. Room and board charges vary according to board plan, housing facility, and student level. ***Part-time tuition:*** $1687 per credit hour. Part-time tuition and fees vary according to course load and program.
FRESHMAN FINANCIAL AID (Fall 2019, est.) 717 applied for aid; of those 85% were deemed to have need. 100% of freshmen with need received aid; of those 11% had need fully met. ***Average percent of need met:*** 71% (excluding resources awarded to replace EFC). ***Average financial aid package:*** $39,884 (excluding resources awarded to replace EFC). 18% of all full-time freshmen had no need and received non-need-based gift aid.
UNDERGRADUATE FINANCIAL AID (Fall 2019, est.) 2,744 applied for aid; of those 91% were deemed to have need. 100% of undergraduates with need received aid; of those 8% had need fully met. ***Average percent of need met:*** 67% (excluding resources awarded to replace EFC). ***Average financial aid package:*** $38,616 (excluding resources awarded to replace EFC). 17% of all full-time undergraduates had no need and received non-need-based gift aid.
GIFT AID (NEED-BASED) *Total amount:* $79,688,172 (9% federal, 14% state, 77% institutional). ***Receiving aid:*** Freshmen: 75% (604); all full-time undergraduates: 69% (2,441). ***Average award:*** Freshmen: $34,818; Undergraduates: $32,267. ***Scholarships, grants, and awards:*** Federal Pell, FSEOG, state, private, college/university gift aid from institutional funds.
GIFT AID (NON-NEED-BASED) *Total amount:* $11,798,348 (100% institutional). ***Average award:*** Freshmen: $19,071. Undergraduates: $17,087. ***Scholarships, grants, and awards by category:*** *Academic interests/achievement:* general academic interests/achievements. *Creative arts/performance:* debating, music. *Special achievements/activities:* leadership, religious involvement. *Special characteristics:* religious affiliation. ***Tuition waivers:*** Full or partial for employees or children of employees. ***ROTC:*** Air Force cooperative.
LOANS *Student loans:* $21,492,522 (90% need-based, 10% non-need-based). 60% of past graduating class borrowed through all loan programs. *Average indebtedness per student:* $29,929. ***Average need-based loan:*** Freshmen: $6053. Undergraduates: $8035. ***Parent loans:*** $59,797,072 (84% need-based, 16% non-need-based). ***Programs:*** Federal Direct (Subsidized and Unsubsidized Stafford, PLUS), college/university.
WORK-STUDY *Federal work-study:* Total amount: $2,195,402; jobs available.
ATHLETIC AWARDS Total amount: $7,398,596 (31% need-based, 69% non-need-based).
APPLYING FOR FINANCIAL AID *Required financial aid form:* FAFSA. ***Financial aid deadline (priority):*** 1/15. ***Notification date:*** Continuous beginning 12/20.
CONTACT Cindy Bogue, Director of Financial Aid, University of the Pacific, 3601 Pacific Avenue, Stockton, CA 95211-0197, 209-946-2421.
Website: http://www.pacific.edu/.

UNIVERSITY OF THE PEOPLE
Pasadena, CA

CONTACT Financial Aid Office, University of the People, 225 South Lake Avenue, Suite 300, Pasadena, CA 91101.
Website: http://www.uopeople.edu/.

UNIVERSITY OF THE POTOMAC
Washington, DC

CONTACT Phyllis Crews, Financial Aid Counselor, University of the Potomac, 4000 Chesapeake Street NW, Washington, DC 20016, 202-686-0876 or toll-free 888-686-0876. *Fax:* 202-686-0818. *E-mail:* pcrews@potomac.edu.
Website: http://www.potomac.edu/.

UNIVERSITY OF THE SACRED HEART
San Juan, PR

CONTACT Ms. Maria Torres, Director of Financial Aid, University of the Sacred Heart, PO Box 12383, San Juan, PR 00914-0383, 787-728-1515 Ext. 3605.
Website: http://www.sagrado.edu/.

UNIVERSITY OF THE SCIENCES
Philadelphia, PA

ABOUT THE INSTITUTION Independent, coed. ***Awards:*** certificates, bachelor's, master's, and doctoral degrees. 18 undergraduate majors. ***Total enrollment:*** 2,664. Undergraduates: 2,246. Freshmen: 323.
GIFT AID (NEED-BASED) *Scholarships, grants, and awards:* Federal Pell, FSEOG, state, private, college/university gift aid from institutional funds.
GIFT AID (NON-NEED-BASED) *Scholarships, grants, and awards by category:* *Academic interests/achievement:* biological sciences, business, general academic interests/achievements, home economics, physical sciences, premedicine. *Special achievements/activities:* general special achievements/activities, leadership. *Special characteristics:* children and siblings of alumni, children of faculty/staff, siblings of current students.
LOANS *Programs:* Federal Direct (Subsidized and Unsubsidized Stafford, PLUS), Perkins, college/university, Health Professions Student Loans (HPSL), Loans for Disadvantaged Students.
CONTACT Ms. Pamela Ramanathan, Director of Financial Aid, University of the Sciences, 600 South 43rd Street, Philadelphia, PA 19104, 215-596-8894 or toll-free 888-996-8747. *Fax:* 215-596-8554. *E-mail:* p.ramanathan@usciences.edu.
Website: http://www.usciences.edu/.

THE UNIVERSITY OF THE SOUTH

Sewanee, TN

Tuition & fees: $47,980	Average undergraduate aid package: $37,115

ABOUT THE INSTITUTION Independent Episcopal, coed. ***Awards:*** certificates, bachelor's, master's, and doctoral degrees. 38 undergraduate majors. ***Total enrollment:*** 1,768. Undergraduates: 1,695. Freshmen: 438. Both federal and institutional methodology are used as a basis for awarding need-based institutional aid.

UNDERGRADUATE EXPENSES for 2020–2021 ***Comprehensive fee:*** $61,680 includes full-time tuition ($47,708), mandatory fees ($272), and room and board ($13,700). ***College room only:*** $7100. ***Part-time tuition:*** $1490 per credit hour.

FRESHMAN FINANCIAL AID (Fall 2019, est.) 314 applied for aid; of those 70% were deemed to have need. 100% of freshmen with need received aid; of those 31% had need fully met. ***Average percent of need met:*** 77% (excluding resources awarded to replace EFC). ***Average financial aid package:*** $35,079 (excluding resources awarded to replace EFC). 45% of all full-time freshmen had no need and received non-need-based gift aid.

UNDERGRADUATE FINANCIAL AID (Fall 2019, est.) 997 applied for aid; of those 74% were deemed to have need. 100% of undergraduates with need received aid; of those 33% had need fully met. ***Average percent of need met:*** 83% (excluding resources awarded to replace EFC). ***Average financial aid package:*** $37,115 (excluding resources awarded to replace EFC). 49% of all full-time undergraduates had no need and received non-need-based gift aid.

GIFT AID (NEED-BASED) ***Total amount:*** $22,237,493 (7% federal, 3% state, 89% institutional, 1% external sources). ***Receiving aid:*** Freshmen: 50% (217); all full-time undergraduates: 43% (723). ***Average award:*** Freshmen: $28,542; Undergraduates: $30,501. ***Scholarships, grants, and awards:*** Federal Pell, FSEOG, state, private, college/university gift aid from institutional funds.

GIFT AID (NON-NEED-BASED) ***Total amount:*** $16,520,715 (2% state, 96% institutional, 2% external sources). ***Receiving aid:*** Freshmen: 11% (48). Undergraduates: 9% (151). ***Average award:*** Freshmen: $20,258. Undergraduates: $18,238. ***Scholarships, grants, and awards by category:*** *Academic interests/achievement:* general academic interests/achievements. *Creative arts/performance:* general creative arts/performance. *Special achievements/activities:* general special achievements/activities. *Special characteristics:* general special characteristics. ***Tuition waivers:*** Full or partial for employees or children of employees.

LOANS ***Student loans:*** $3,360,140 (72% need-based, 28% non-need-based). 44% of past graduating class borrowed through all loan programs. *Average indebtedness per student:* $31,737. ***Average need-based loan:*** Freshmen: $3664. Undergraduates: $4545. ***Parent loans:*** $4,050,660 (22% need-based, 78% non-need-based). ***Programs:*** Federal Direct (Subsidized and Unsubsidized Stafford, PLUS), private loans.

WORK-STUDY ***Federal work-study:*** Total amount: $659,697; 405 jobs averaging $1629. ***State or other work-study/employment:*** Total amount: $518,723 (41% need-based, 59% non-need-based). 160 part-time jobs averaging $3242.

APPLYING FOR FINANCIAL AID ***Required financial aid forms:*** FAFSA, CSS Financial Aid PROFILE. ***Financial aid deadline (priority):*** 12/1. ***Notification date:*** Continuous beginning 2/1. Students must reply by 5/1 or within 2 weeks of notification.

CONTACT Ms. Beth A. Cragar, Associate Dean of Admission for Financial Aid, The University of the South, 735 University Avenue, Sewanee, TN 37383-1000, 931-598-1312 or toll-free 800-522-2234. *Fax:* 931-598-3273. *E-mail:* finaid@sewanee.edu.
Website: http://www.sewanee.edu/.

UNIVERSITY OF THE SOUTHWEST

Hobbs, NM

CONTACT Dawny Kringel, Director of Financial Aid, University of the Southwest, 6610 North Lovington Highway, Hobbs, NM 88240-9129, 575-492-2114 or toll-free 800-530-4400. *Fax:* 575-392-6006. *E-mail:* dkringel@usw.edu.
Website: http://www.usw.edu/.

UNIVERSITY OF THE VIRGIN ISLANDS

St. Thomas, VI

CONTACT Mavis M. Gilchrist, Director of Financial Aid, University of the Virgin Islands, RR #2, Box 10,000, Kingshill, St. Thomas, VI 00850, 340-692-4186 or toll-free 877-468-6884. *Fax:* 340-692-4145. *E-mail:* mgilchr@uvi.edu.
Website: http://www.uvi.edu/.

UNIVERSITY OF THE WEST

Rosemead, CA

CONTACT Jamie Johnston, Financial Aid Officer, University of the West, 1409 Walnut Grove Avenue, Rosemead, CA 91770, 626-571-8811 Ext. 122. *Fax:* 626-571-1413. *E-mail:* jamiej@uwest.edu.
Website: http://www.uwest.edu/.

THE UNIVERSITY OF TOLEDO

Toledo, OH

Tuition & fees (area res): $10,539	Average undergraduate aid package: $11,699

ABOUT THE INSTITUTION State-supported, coed. ***Awards:*** certificates, diplomas, associate, bachelor's, master's, and doctoral degrees. 86 undergraduate majors. ***Total enrollment:*** 19,782. Undergraduates: 15,568. Freshmen: 3,037. Federal methodology is used as a basis for awarding need-based institutional aid.

UNDERGRADUATE EXPENSES for 2020–2021 ***Application fee:*** $40. ***Tuition, area resident:*** full-time $8582; part-time $383 per credit hour. ***Tuition, state resident:*** full-time $8582; part-time $383 per credit hour. ***Tuition, nonresident:*** full-time $17,942; part-time $390 per credit hour. ***Required fees:*** full-time $1957. Full-time tuition and fees vary according to course load, program, reciprocity agreements, and student level. Part-time tuition and fees vary according to course load, program, reciprocity agreements, and student level. ***College room and board:*** $12,285; ***Room only:*** $8258. Room and board charges vary according to board plan and housing facility.

FRESHMAN FINANCIAL AID (Fall 2019, est.) 2707 applied for aid; of those 77% were deemed to have need. 99% of freshmen with need received aid; of those 15% had need fully met. ***Average percent of need met:*** 65% (excluding resources awarded to replace EFC). ***Average financial aid package:*** $12,242 (excluding resources awarded to replace EFC). 27% of all full-time freshmen had no need and received non-need-based gift aid.

UNDERGRADUATE FINANCIAL AID (Fall 2019, est.) 9,991 applied for aid; of those 77% were deemed to have need. 99% of undergraduates with need received aid; of those 14% had need fully met. ***Average percent of need met:*** 63% (excluding resources awarded to replace EFC). ***Average financial aid package:*** $11,699 (excluding resources awarded to replace EFC). 27% of all full-time undergraduates had no need and received non-need-based gift aid.

GIFT AID (NEED-BASED) ***Total amount:*** $69,374,974 (34% federal, 10% state, 52% institutional, 4% external sources). ***Receiving aid:*** Freshmen: 68% (2,036); all full-time undergraduates: 58% (7,178). ***Average award:*** Freshmen: $10,155; Undergraduates: $9642. ***Scholarships, grants, and awards:*** Federal Pell, FSEOG, state, private, college/university gift aid from institutional funds.

GIFT AID (NON-NEED-BASED) ***Total amount:*** $28,280,016 (1% federal, 3% state, 75% institutional, 21% external sources). ***Receiving aid:*** Freshmen: 20% (595). Undergraduates: 15% (1,886). ***Average award:*** Freshmen: $5941. Undergraduates: $5952. ***Scholarships, grants, and awards by category:*** *Academic interests/achievement:* biological sciences, business, communication, computer science, education, engineering/technologies, English, foreign languages, general academic interests/achievements, home economics, humanities, international studies, library science, mathematics, military science, physical sciences, premedicine, religion/biblical studies, social sciences. *Creative arts/performance:* applied art and design, cinema/film/broadcasting, creative writing, general creative arts/performance, music, performing arts, theater/drama. *Special achievements/activities:* cheerleading/drum major, community service, general special achievements/activities, hobbies/interests, leadership, memberships, religious involvement. *Special characteristics:* adult students, children and siblings of alumni, children of faculty/staff, children of public servants, children of union members/company employees, ethnic background, first-generation college students, general special characteristics, handicapped students, international students, members of minority groups, out-of-state students, previous college experience, public servants, religious affiliation, siblings of current students, veterans. ***Tuition waivers:*** Full or partial for employees or children of employees. ***ROTC:*** Army, Air Force cooperative.

LOANS ***Student loans:*** $53,050,009 (83% need-based, 17% non-need-based). 70% of past graduating class borrowed through all loan programs. *Average indebtedness per student:* $27,145. ***Average need-based loan:*** Freshmen: $2759. Undergraduates: $3311. ***Parent loans:*** $18,717,070 (82% need-based, 18% non-need-based). ***Programs:*** Federal Direct (Subsidized and Unsubsidized Stafford, PLUS), state, college/university, Private Alternative Loans, Primary Care Loan.

WORK-STUDY ***Federal work-study:*** Total amount: $1,703,483; jobs available.

ATHLETIC AWARDS Total amount: $8,008,981 (42% need-based, 58% non-need-based).

APPLYING FOR FINANCIAL AID ***Required financial aid form:*** FAFSA. ***Financial aid deadline (priority):*** 2/1. ***Notification date:*** Continuous beginning 2/15.

CONTACT Stephen Schissler, Director of Financial Aid, The University of Toledo, 2801 West Bancroft Street, MS-314, Toledo, OH 43606, 419-530-5812 or toll-free 800-5TOLEDO. *Fax:* 419-530-5835. *E-mail:* stephen.schissler@utoledo.edu. *Website:* http://www.utoledo.edu/.

THE UNIVERSITY OF TULSA

Tulsa, OK

Tuition & fees: $43,500	Average undergraduate aid package: $35,615

ABOUT THE INSTITUTION Independent, coed. ***Awards:*** certificates, bachelor's, master's, and doctoral degrees. 57 undergraduate majors. ***Total enrollment:*** 4,387. Undergraduates: 3,276. Freshmen: 831. Federal methodology is used as a basis for awarding need-based institutional aid.

UNDERGRADUATE EXPENSES for 2020–2021 ***Application fee:*** $50. ***One-time required fee:*** $485. ***Comprehensive fee:*** $55,562 includes full-time tuition ($42,950), mandatory fees ($550), and room and board ($12,062). ***College room only:*** $6976. Full-time tuition and fees vary according to course load and program. Room and board charges vary according to board plan and housing facility. ***Part-time tuition:*** $1542 per credit hour. Part-time tuition and fees vary according to program.

FRESHMAN FINANCIAL AID (Fall 2019, est.) 718 applied for aid; of those 84% were deemed to have need. 100% of freshmen with need received aid; of those 34% had need fully met. ***Average percent of need met:*** 78% (excluding resources awarded to replace EFC). ***Average financial aid package:*** $37,646 (excluding resources awarded to replace EFC). 6% of all full-time freshmen had no need and received non-need-based gift aid.

UNDERGRADUATE FINANCIAL AID (Fall 2019, est.) 1,988 applied for aid; of those 87% were deemed to have need. 100% of undergraduates with need received aid; of those 35% had need fully met. ***Average percent of need met:*** 71% (excluding resources awarded to replace EFC). ***Average financial aid package:*** $35,615 (excluding resources awarded to replace EFC). 5% of all full-time undergraduates had no need and received non-need-based gift aid.

GIFT AID (NEED-BASED) ***Total amount:*** $73,749,093 (5% federal, 3% state, 90% institutional, 2% external sources). ***Receiving aid:*** Freshmen: 71% (590); all full-time undergraduates: 53% (1,678). ***Average award:*** Freshmen: $32,334; Undergraduates: $29,696. ***Scholarships, grants, and awards:*** Federal Pell, FSEOG, state, private, college/university gift aid from institutional funds.

GIFT AID (NON-NEED-BASED) ***Total amount:*** $11,802,291 (4% state, 93% institutional, 3% external sources). ***Receiving aid:*** Freshmen: 25% (207). Undergraduates: 34% (1,066). ***Average award:*** Freshmen: $16,000. Undergraduates: $14,587. ***Scholarships, grants, and awards by category:*** *Academic interests/achievement:* 789 awards ($7,912,855 total): biological sciences, business, communication, computer science, education, engineering/technologies, English, foreign languages, general academic interests/achievements, home economics, mathematics, physical sciences, religion/biblical studies, social sciences. *Creative arts/performance:* 105 awards ($1,035,751 total): applied art and design, music, performing arts, theater/drama. *Special achievements/activities:* cheerleading/drum major, community service, leadership. *Special characteristics:* children and siblings of alumni, children of faculty/staff, relatives of clergy, religious affiliation, siblings of current students. ***Tuition waivers:*** Full or partial for employees or children of employees. ***ROTC:*** Air Force cooperative.

LOANS ***Student loans:*** $11,282,007 (28% need-based, 72% non-need-based). 34% of past graduating class borrowed through all loan programs. *Average indebtedness per student:* $36,176. ***Average need-based loan:*** Freshmen: $3322. Undergraduates: $4012. ***Parent loans:*** $5,145,418 (100% non-need-based). ***Programs:*** Federal Direct (Subsidized and Unsubsidized Stafford, PLUS), Perkins.

WORK-STUDY ***Federal work-study:*** Total amount: $1,483,791; 592 jobs averaging $2493. ***State or other work-study/employment:*** Part-time jobs available.

ATHLETIC AWARDS Total amount: $13,055,940 (100% non-need-based).

APPLYING FOR FINANCIAL AID ***Required financial aid form:*** FAFSA. ***Financial aid deadline (priority):*** 1/15. ***Notification date:*** Continuous beginning 2/1. Students must reply by 5/1 or within 2 weeks of notification.

CONTACT Ms. Vicki Hendrickson, Director of Student Financial Services, The University of Tulsa, 800 South Tucker Drive, Tulsa, OK 74104, 918-631-2526 or toll-free 800-331-3050. *Fax:* 918-631-5105. *E-mail:* finaid@utulsa.edu. *Website:* http://www.utulsa.edu/.

UNIVERSITY OF UTAH

Salt Lake City, UT

Tuition & fees (area res): $9498	Average undergraduate aid package: $23,875

ABOUT THE INSTITUTION State-supported, coed. ***Awards:*** certificates, bachelor's, master's, and doctoral degrees. 134 undergraduate majors. ***Total enrollment:*** 32,818. Undergraduates: 24,485. Freshmen: 4,249. Federal methodology is used as a basis for awarding need-based institutional aid.

UNDERGRADUATE EXPENSES for 2020–2021 ***Application fee:*** $55. ***Tuition, area resident:*** full-time $8252. ***Tuition, state resident:*** full-time $8252; part-time $232 per credit hour. ***Tuition, nonresident:*** full-time $28,886; part-time $797 per credit hour. ***Required fees:*** full-time $1246. Full-time tuition and fees vary according to course level, course load, degree level, location, program, and student level. Part-time tuition and fees vary according to course level, course load, degree level, location, program, and student level. ***College room and board:*** $10,201; ***Room only:*** $5757. Room and board charges vary according to board plan, housing facility, and location.

FRESHMAN FINANCIAL AID (Fall 2019, est.) 3009 applied for aid; of those 61% were deemed to have need. 99% of freshmen with need received aid; of those 15% had need fully met. ***Average percent of need met:*** 71% (excluding resources awarded to replace EFC). ***Average financial aid package:*** $25,969 (excluding resources awarded to replace EFC). 61% of all full-time freshmen had no need and received non-need-based gift aid.

UNDERGRADUATE FINANCIAL AID (Fall 2019, est.) 10,988 applied for aid; of those 77% were deemed to have need. 98% of undergraduates with need received aid; of those 13% had need fully met. ***Average percent of need met:*** 65% (excluding resources awarded to replace EFC). ***Average financial aid package:*** $23,875 (excluding resources awarded to replace EFC). 34% of all full-time undergraduates had no need and received non-need-based gift aid.

GIFT AID (NEED-BASED) ***Total amount:*** $29,811,153 (86% federal, 3% state, 5% institutional, 6% external sources). ***Receiving aid:*** Freshmen: 41% (1,676); all full-time undergraduates: 38% (7,130). ***Average award:*** Freshmen: $9754; Undergraduates: $8361. ***Scholarships, grants, and awards:*** Federal Pell, FSEOG, state, private, college/university gift aid from institutional funds, Federal Nursing.

GIFT AID (NON-NEED-BASED) ***Total amount:*** $68,564,884 (10% state, 58% institutional, 32% external sources). ***Receiving aid:*** Freshmen: 9% (368). Undergraduates: 5% (853). ***Average award:*** Freshmen: $9217. Undergraduates: $7234. ***Scholarships, grants, and awards by category:*** *Academic interests/achievement:* architecture, area/ethnic studies, biological sciences, business, communication, computer science, education, engineering/technologies, English, foreign languages, general academic interests/achievements, home economics, humanities, international studies, mathematics, military science, physical sciences, social sciences. *Creative arts/performance:* applied art and design, cinema/film/broadcasting, creative writing, dance, journalism/publications, music, performing arts, theater/drama. *Special achievements/activities:* cheerleading/drum major, general special achievements/activities, leadership. *Special characteristics:* children of faculty/staff, children of public servants, children with a deceased or disabled parent, ethnic background, first-generation college students, handicapped students, out-of-state students, spouses of deceased or disabled public servants. ***Tuition waivers:*** Full or partial for employees or children of employees, senior citizens. ***ROTC:*** Army, Naval, Air Force.

LOANS ***Student loans:*** $54,794,931 (83% need-based, 17% non-need-based). 46% of past graduating class borrowed through all loan programs. *Average indebtedness per student:* $19,656. ***Average need-based loan:*** Freshmen: $3307. Undergraduates: $4271. ***Parent loans:*** $6,621,642 (100% need-based). ***Programs:*** Federal Direct (Subsidized and Unsubsidized Stafford, PLUS), Federal Nursing, state, college/university.

WORK-STUDY ***Federal work-study:*** Total amount: $7,435,618; 1,223 jobs averaging $4702.

ATHLETIC AWARDS Total amount: $10,000,875 (100% non-need-based).

APPLYING FOR FINANCIAL AID ***Required financial aid form:*** FAFSA. ***Financial aid deadline (priority):*** 2/1. ***Notification date:*** Continuous beginning 3/1. Students must reply by 5/1.

CONTACT Office of Financial Aid, University of Utah, 201 South 1460 East, Room 105, Salt Lake City, UT 84112, 801-581-6211 or toll-free 800-685-8856. *Fax:* 801-585-6350. *E-mail:* financialaid@utah.edu.
Website: http://www.utah.edu/.

UNIVERSITY OF VALLEY FORGE

Phoenixville, PA

CONTACT Mrs. Linda Stein, Director of Financial Aid, University of Valley Forge, 1401 Charlestown Road, Phoenixville, PA 19460-2399, 610-917-1416 or toll-free 800-432-8322. *Fax:* 610-917-2069. *E-mail:* llstein@vfcc.edu.
Website: http://www.valleyforge.edu/.

UNIVERSITY OF VERMONT

Burlington, VT

ABOUT THE INSTITUTION State-supported, coed. ***Awards:*** certificates, bachelor's, master's, and doctoral degrees. 98 undergraduate majors. ***Total enrollment:*** 13,548. Undergraduates: 11,443. Freshmen: 2,636.

GIFT AID (NEED-BASED) ***Scholarships, grants, and awards:*** Federal Pell, FSEOG, state, private, college/university gift aid from institutional funds, Federal Nursing.

GIFT AID (NON-NEED-BASED) ***Scholarships, grants, and awards by category:*** *Academic interests/achievement:* agriculture, area/ethnic studies, business, computer science, education, engineering/technologies, English, foreign languages, general academic interests/achievements, health fields, home economics, humanities, international studies, mathematics, military science, physical sciences, premedicine, social sciences. *Creative arts/performance:* debating, music, theater/drama. *Special achievements/activities:* community service, leadership, memberships. *Special characteristics:* adult students, ethnic background, first-generation college students.

LOANS ***Programs:*** Federal Direct (Subsidized and Unsubsidized Stafford, PLUS), Federal Nursing, college/university.

CONTACT Financial Aid Office, University of Vermont, Burlington, VT 05405, 802-656-3131.
Website: http://www.uvm.edu/.

UNIVERSITY OF VIRGINIA

Charlottesville, VA

Tuition & fees (area res): $18,878	Average undergraduate aid package: $30,591

ABOUT THE INSTITUTION State-supported, coed. ***Awards:*** certificates, bachelor's, master's, and doctoral degrees. 50 undergraduate majors. ***Total enrollment:*** 25,018. Undergraduates: 17,011. Freshmen: 3,920. Both federal and institutional methodology are used as a basis for awarding need-based institutional aid.

UNDERGRADUATE EXPENSES for 2020–2021 ***Application fee:*** $70. ***Tuition, area resident:*** full-time $15,755; part-time $510 per credit hour. ***Tuition, state resident:*** full-time $15,755; part-time $510 per credit hour. ***Tuition, nonresident:*** full-time $50,516; part-time $1614 per credit hour. ***Required fees:*** full-time $3123; $3123 per year. Full-time tuition and fees vary according to program and student level. Part-time tuition and fees vary according to program and student level. ***College room and board:*** $12,350; ***Room only:*** $6960. Room and board charges vary according to board plan and housing facility. ***Payment plan:*** Guaranteed tuition.

FRESHMAN FINANCIAL AID (Fall 2019, est.) 3136 applied for aid; of those 49% were deemed to have need. 100% of freshmen with need received aid; of those 100% had need fully met. ***Average percent of need met:*** 100% (excluding resources awarded to replace EFC). ***Average financial aid package:*** $31,105 (excluding resources awarded to replace EFC). 3% of all full-time freshmen had no need and received non-need-based gift aid.

UNDERGRADUATE FINANCIAL AID (Fall 2019, est.) 10,186 applied for aid; of those 56% were deemed to have need. 100% of undergraduates with need received aid; of those 100% had need fully met. ***Average percent of need met:*** 100% (excluding resources awarded to replace EFC). ***Average financial aid package:*** $30,591 (excluding resources awarded to replace EFC). 5% of all full-time undergraduates had no need and received non-need-based gift aid.

GIFT AID (NEED-BASED) ***Total amount:*** $123,455,342 (12% federal, 5% state, 77% institutional, 6% external sources). ***Receiving aid:*** Freshmen: 35% (1,357); all full-time undergraduates: 31% (5,048). ***Average award:*** Freshmen: $24,538; Undergraduates: $24,726. ***Scholarships, grants, and awards:*** Federal Pell, FSEOG, state, private, college/university gift aid from institutional funds, Federal Nursing.

GIFT AID (NON-NEED-BASED) ***Total amount:*** $27,898,310 (14% federal, 27% institutional, 59% external sources). ***Receiving aid:*** Freshmen: 4% (158). Undergraduates: 3% (462). ***Average award:*** Freshmen: $2699. Undergraduates: $5140. ***Scholarships, grants, and awards by category:*** *Academic interests/achievement:* general academic interests/achievements. *Special achievements/activities:* leadership. *Special characteristics:* children of faculty/staff, ethnic background, general special characteristics, veterans, veterans' children. ***Tuition waivers:*** Full or partial for employees or children of employees, senior citizens. ***ROTC:*** Army, Naval, Air Force.

LOANS ***Student loans:*** $41,128,048 (49% need-based, 51% non-need-based). 33% of past graduating class borrowed through all loan programs. *Average indebtedness per student:* $26,023. ***Average need-based loan:*** Freshmen: $5416. Undergraduates: $5999. ***Parent loans:*** $11,513,786 (15% need-based, 85% non-need-based). ***Programs:*** Federal Direct (Subsidized and Unsubsidized Stafford, PLUS).

WORK-STUDY ***Federal work-study:*** Total amount: $3,896,497; 1,192 jobs averaging $3241.

ATHLETIC AWARDS Total amount: $18,524,298 (16% need-based, 84% non-need-based).

APPLYING FOR FINANCIAL AID ***Required financial aid forms:*** FAFSA, CSS Financial Aid PROFILE. ***Financial aid deadline (priority):*** 3/1. ***Notification date:*** 4/1. Students must reply by 5/1.

CONTACT Mr. Scott Miller, Director, Student Financial Aid, University of Virginia, PO Box 400204, Charlottesville, VA 22904-4204, 434-982-6000. *E-mail:* sfs@virginia.edu.
Website: http://www.virginia.edu/.

THE UNIVERSITY OF VIRGINIA'S COLLEGE AT WISE

Wise, VA

ABOUT THE INSTITUTION State-supported, coed. ***Awards:*** bachelor's degrees. 25 undergraduate majors.

GIFT AID (NEED-BASED) ***Scholarships, grants, and awards:*** Federal Pell, FSEOG, state, private, college/university gift aid from institutional funds.

GIFT AID (NON-NEED-BASED) ***Scholarships, grants, and awards by category:*** *Academic interests/achievement:* agriculture, biological sciences, business, computer science, education, English, general academic interests/achievements, home economics, humanities, mathematics, physical sciences, premedicine, social sciences. *Creative arts/performance:* creative writing, general creative arts/performance, journalism/publications, music, performing arts, theater/drama. *Special achievements/activities:* community service, religious involvement. *Special characteristics:* children with a deceased or disabled parent, ethnic background, local/state students, veterans.

LOANS ***Programs:*** Perkins, state, college/university.

WORK-STUDY ***Federal work-study:*** Total amount: $279,094; jobs available.

APPLYING FOR FINANCIAL AID ***Required financial aid form:*** FAFSA.

CONTACT Mrs. Rebecca Huffman, Director of Financial Aid, The University of Virginia's College at Wise, 1 College Avenue, Wise, VA 24293, 276-328-0277 or toll-free 888-282-9324. *Fax:* 276-328-0251. *E-mail:* reg5a@uvawise.edu. *Website:* http://www.uvawise.edu/.

UNIVERSITY OF WASHINGTON

Seattle, WA

Tuition & fees (WA res): $11,465 | **Average undergraduate aid package: $17,487**

ABOUT THE INSTITUTION State-supported, coed. ***Awards:*** certificates, bachelor's, master's, and doctoral degrees. 152 undergraduate majors. ***Total enrollment:*** 47,554. Undergraduates: 32,046. Freshmen: 6,992. Federal methodology is used as a basis for awarding need-based institutional aid.

UNDERGRADUATE EXPENSES for 2019–2020 ***Application fee:*** $80. ***Tuition, state resident:*** full-time $10,370; part-time $345 per credit. ***Tuition, nonresident:*** full-time $37,071; part-time $1235 per credit. ***Required fees:*** full-time $1095; $28 per credit. Full-time tuition and fees vary according to course load and location. Part-time tuition and fees vary according to course load and location. ***College room and board:*** $13,296. Room and board charges vary according to board plan, housing facility, and location.

FRESHMAN FINANCIAL AID (Fall 2019, est.) 4912 applied for aid; of those 58% were deemed to have need. 93% of freshmen with need received aid; of those 23% had need fully met. ***Average percent of need met:*** 78% (excluding resources awarded to replace EFC). ***Average financial aid package:*** $16,916 (excluding resources awarded to replace EFC). 6% of all full-time freshmen had no need and received non-need-based gift aid.

UNDERGRADUATE FINANCIAL AID (Fall 2019, est.) 16,628 applied for aid; of those 73% were deemed to have need. 95% of undergraduates with need received aid; of those 20% had need fully met. ***Average percent of need met:*** 77% (excluding resources awarded to replace EFC). ***Average financial aid package:*** $17,487 (excluding resources awarded to replace EFC). 8% of all full-time undergraduates had no need and received non-need-based gift aid.

GIFT AID (NEED-BASED) ***Receiving aid:*** Freshmen: 35% (2,415); all full-time undergraduates: 36% (10,484). ***Average award:*** Freshmen: $16,842; Undergraduates: $16,746. ***Scholarships, grants, and awards:*** Federal Pell, FSEOG, state, private, college/university gift aid from institutional funds.

GIFT AID (NON-NEED-BASED) ***Receiving aid:*** Freshmen: 2% (109). Undergraduates: 1% (315). ***Average award:*** Freshmen: $5217. Undergraduates: $4673. ***Scholarships, grants, and awards by category:*** *Academic interests/achievement:* architecture, area/ethnic studies, biological sciences, business, communication, computer science, education, engineering/technologies, English, foreign languages, general academic interests/achievements, health fields, home economics, humanities, international studies, library science, mathematics, military science, physical sciences, premedicine, social sciences. *Creative arts/performance:* applied art and design, dance, general creative arts/performance, music, performing arts, theater/drama. *Special achievements/activities:* general special achievements/activities, leadership, memberships. ***Tuition waivers:*** Full or partial for employees or children of employees, senior citizens. ***ROTC:*** Army, Naval, Air Force.

LOANS ***Student loans:*** 33% of past graduating class borrowed through all loan programs. *Average indebtedness per student:* $19,198. ***Average need-based loan:*** Freshmen: $3852. Undergraduates: $5077. ***Programs:*** Federal Direct (Subsidized and Unsubsidized Stafford, PLUS), Federal Nursing, college/university.

WORK-STUDY Federal work-study jobs available. ***State or other work-study/employment:*** Part-time jobs available.

APPLYING FOR FINANCIAL AID ***Required financial aid forms:*** FAFSA, WAFSA (form for Washington residents). ***Notification date:*** Students must reply within 3 weeks of notification.

CONTACT Office of Student Financial Aid, University of Washington, Box 355880, Seattle, WA 98195-5880, 206-543-6101. *E-mail:* osfa@uw.edu. *Website:* http://www.washington.edu/.

UNIVERSITY OF WASHINGTON, BOTHELL

Bothell, WA

Tuition & fees (WA res): $11,390 | **Average undergraduate aid package: $15,117**

ABOUT THE INSTITUTION State-supported, coed. ***Awards:*** certificates, bachelor's, and master's degrees. 34 undergraduate majors. ***Total enrollment:*** 5,922. Undergraduates: 5,350. Freshmen: 829. Federal methodology is used as a basis for awarding need-based institutional aid.

UNDERGRADUATE EXPENSES for 2019–2020 ***Application fee:*** $60. ***Tuition, state resident:*** full-time $10,370; part-time $345 per credit. ***Tuition, nonresident:*** full-time $37,071; part-time $1235 per credit. ***Required fees:*** full-time $1020; $28 per credit. Full-time tuition and fees vary according to course load. Part-time tuition and fees vary according to course load. ***College room and board:*** $12,636. Room and board charges vary according to board plan, housing facility, and location.

FRESHMAN FINANCIAL AID (Fall 2019, est.) 661 applied for aid; of those 72% were deemed to have need. 93% of freshmen with need received aid; of those 11% had need fully met. ***Average percent of need met:*** 73% (excluding resources awarded to replace EFC). ***Average financial aid package:*** $14,357 (excluding resources awarded to replace EFC). 1% of all full-time freshmen had no need and received non-need-based gift aid.

UNDERGRADUATE FINANCIAL AID (Fall 2019, est.) 3,114 applied for aid; of those 83% were deemed to have need. 94% of undergraduates with need received aid; of those 10% had need fully met. ***Average percent of need met:*** 70% (excluding resources awarded to replace EFC). ***Average financial aid package:*** $15,117 (excluding resources awarded to replace EFC). 1% of all full-time undergraduates had no need and received non-need-based gift aid.

GIFT AID (NEED-BASED) ***Receiving aid:*** Freshmen: 50% (397); all full-time undergraduates: 48% (2,220). ***Average award:*** Freshmen: $14,431; Undergraduates: $14,410. ***Scholarships, grants, and awards:*** Federal Pell, FSEOG, state, private, college/university gift aid from institutional funds.

GIFT AID (NON-NEED-BASED) ***Receiving aid:*** Freshmen: 1% (8). Undergraduates: 1% (27). ***Average award:*** Freshmen: $8600. Undergraduates: $6719. ***Scholarships, grants, and awards by category:*** *Academic interests/achievement:* area/ethnic studies, biological sciences, business, communication, computer science, education, engineering/technologies, English, general academic interests/achievements, health fields, humanities, international studies, mathematics, physical sciences, premedicine, social sciences. ***Tuition waivers:*** Full or partial for employees or children of employees, senior citizens. ***ROTC:*** Army cooperative, Naval cooperative, Air Force cooperative.

LOANS ***Student loans:*** 39% of past graduating class borrowed through all loan programs. *Average indebtedness per student:* $18,449. ***Average need-based loan:*** Freshmen: $4041. Undergraduates: $5817. ***Programs:*** Federal Direct (Subsidized and Unsubsidized Stafford, PLUS), Federal Nursing, college/university.

WORK-STUDY Federal work-study jobs available. ***State or other work-study/employment:*** Part-time jobs available.

APPLYING FOR FINANCIAL AID ***Required financial aid forms:*** FAFSA, WAFSA (form for Washington residents). ***Notification date:*** Students must reply within 3 weeks of notification.

CONTACT Financial Aid Office, University of Washington, Bothell, 18115 Campus Way NE, Bothell, WA 98011, 425-352-5000. *Website:* http://www.uwb.edu/.

UNIVERSITY OF WASHINGTON, TACOMA

Tacoma, WA

Tuition & fees (WA res): $11,639 | **Average undergraduate aid package: $15,316**

ABOUT THE INSTITUTION State-supported, coed. ***Awards:*** certificates, bachelor's, master's, and doctoral degrees. 37 undergraduate majors. ***Total enrollment:*** 5,330. Undergraduates: 4,588. Freshmen: 655. Federal methodology is used as a basis for awarding need-based institutional aid.

UNDERGRADUATE EXPENSES for 2019–2020 ***Application fee:*** $60. ***Tuition, state resident:*** full-time $10,370; part-time $345 per credit. ***Tuition, nonresident:*** full-time $37,071; part-time $1235 per credit. ***Required fees:*** full-time $1269; $28 per credit. Full-time tuition and fees vary according to course load. Part-time tuition and fees vary according to course load. ***College room and board:*** $12,636. Room and board charges vary according to housing facility and location.

FRESHMAN FINANCIAL AID (Fall 2019, est.) 551 applied for aid; of those 79% were deemed to have need. 96% of freshmen with need received aid; of those 13% had need fully met. ***Average percent of need met:*** 77% (excluding resources awarded to replace EFC). ***Average financial aid package:*** $14,257 (excluding resources awarded to replace EFC). 9% of all full-time freshmen had no need and received non-need-based gift aid.

UNDERGRADUATE FINANCIAL AID (Fall 2019, est.) 3,287 applied for aid; of those 87% were deemed to have need. 96% of undergraduates with need received aid; of those 11% had need fully met. ***Average percent of need met:*** 71% (excluding resources awarded to replace EFC). ***Average financial aid package:*** $15,316 (excluding resources awarded to replace EFC). 6% of all full-time undergraduates had no need and received non-need-based gift aid.

GIFT AID (NEED-BASED) ***Receiving aid:*** Freshmen: 65% (400); all full-time undergraduates: 63% (2,551). ***Average award:*** Freshmen: $13,572; Undergraduates: $14,268. ***Scholarships, grants, and awards:*** Federal Pell, FSEOG, state, private, college/university gift aid from institutional funds.

GIFT AID (NON-NEED-BASED) ***Receiving aid:*** Freshmen: 4% (23). Undergraduates: 1% (45). ***Average award:*** Freshmen: $2720. Undergraduates: $2951. ***Scholarships, grants, and awards by category:*** *Academic interests/achievement:* area/ethnic studies, biological sciences, business, communication, computer science, education, engineering/technologies, foreign languages, general academic interests/achievements, health fields, humanities, international studies, mathematics, military science, physical sciences, social sciences. ***Tuition waivers:*** Full or partial for employees or children of employees, senior citizens. ***ROTC:*** Army cooperative, Naval cooperative, Air Force cooperative.

LOANS ***Student loans:*** 45% of past graduating class borrowed through all loan programs. *Average indebtedness per student:* $16,716. ***Average need-based loan:*** Freshmen: $3635. Undergraduates: $6025. ***Programs:*** Federal Direct (Subsidized and Unsubsidized Stafford, PLUS), Federal Nursing, college/university.

WORK-STUDY Federal work-study jobs available. ***State or other work-study/employment:*** Part-time jobs available.

APPLYING FOR FINANCIAL AID ***Required financial aid forms:*** FAFSA, WAFSA (form for Washington residents). ***Notification date:*** Students must reply within 3 weeks of notification.

CONTACT Financial Aid Office, University of Washington, Tacoma, 1900 Commerce Street, Tacoma, WA 98402-3100, 253-692-4000 or toll-free 800-736-7750.
Website: http://www.tacoma.uw.edu/.

THE UNIVERSITY OF WEST ALABAMA

Livingston, AL

Tuition & fees (AL res): $10,990	Average undergraduate aid package: $10,889

ABOUT THE INSTITUTION State-supported, coed. ***Awards:*** certificates, associate, bachelor's, master's, and doctoral degrees. 34 undergraduate majors. ***Total enrollment:*** 5,653. Undergraduates: 2,239. Freshmen: 322. Federal methodology is used as a basis for awarding need-based institutional aid.

UNDERGRADUATE EXPENSES for 2020–2021 ***Application fee:*** $40. ***Tuition, state resident:*** full-time $9100; part-time $325 per credit hour. ***Tuition, nonresident:*** full-time $18,200; part-time $650 per credit hour. ***Required fees:*** full-time $1890. Full-time tuition and fees vary according to course load. Part-time tuition and fees vary according to course load. ***College room and board:*** $7510; ***Room only:*** $4760. Room and board charges vary according to board plan, housing facility, and student level.

FRESHMAN FINANCIAL AID (Fall 2018) 389 applied for aid; of those 94% were deemed to have need. 99% of freshmen with need received aid. ***Average percent of need met:*** 22% (excluding resources awarded to replace EFC). ***Average financial aid package:*** $9596 (excluding resources awarded to replace EFC). 1% of all full-time freshmen had no need and received non-need-based gift aid.

UNDERGRADUATE FINANCIAL AID (Fall 2018) 1,643 applied for aid; of those 90% were deemed to have need. 99% of undergraduates with need received aid; of those 4% had need fully met. ***Average percent of need met:*** 22% (excluding resources awarded to replace EFC). ***Average financial aid package:*** $10,889 (excluding resources awarded to replace EFC). 2% of all full-time undergraduates had no need and received non-need-based gift aid.

GIFT AID (NEED-BASED) ***Receiving aid:*** Freshmen: 62% (258); all full-time undergraduates: 57% (1,045). ***Average award:*** Freshmen: $5841; Undergraduates: $5839. ***Scholarships, grants, and awards:*** Federal Pell, FSEOG, state, private, college/university gift aid from institutional funds, United Negro College Fund.

GIFT AID (NON-NEED-BASED) ***Receiving aid:*** Freshmen: 30% (126). Undergraduates: 28% (517). ***Average award:*** Freshmen: $3895. Undergraduates: $5102. ***Scholarships, grants, and awards by category:*** *Academic interests/achievement:* English, general academic interests/achievements. *Creative arts/performance:* dance, music, theater/drama. *Special achievements/activities:* cheerleading/drum major, general special achievements/activities, junior miss, leadership, memberships, rodeo. *Special characteristics:* children and siblings of alumni, children of faculty/staff, first-generation college students, previous college experience. ***Tuition waivers:*** Full or partial for employees or children of employees. ***ROTC:*** Air Force cooperative.

LOANS ***Student loans:*** 77% of past graduating class borrowed through all loan programs. *Average indebtedness per student:* $24,408. ***Programs:*** Federal Direct (Subsidized and Unsubsidized Stafford, PLUS), Perkins.

WORK-STUDY ***Federal work-study:*** 135 jobs averaging $1869. ***State or other work-study/employment:*** Part-time jobs available.

APPLYING FOR FINANCIAL AID ***Required financial aid form:*** FAFSA. ***Notification date:*** Continuous. Students must reply within 2 weeks of notification.

CONTACT Mr. Steve Smith, Director of Financial Aid Operations, The University of West Alabama, Station 3, Livingston, AL 35470, 205-652-3576 or toll-free 888-636-8800. *Fax:* 205-652-3847. *E-mail:* sdsmith@uwa.edu.
Website: http://www.uwa.edu/.

UNIVERSITY OF WEST FLORIDA

Pensacola, FL

CONTACT Ms. Shana Gore, Coordinator of Financial Aid, University of West Florida, 11000 University Parkway, Pensacola, FL 32514-5750, 850-474-2398 or toll-free 800-263-1074. *E-mail:* sgore1@uwf.edu.
Website: http://www.uwf.edu/.

UNIVERSITY OF WEST GEORGIA

Carrollton, GA

Tuition & fees (GA res): $7488	Average undergraduate aid package: $8186

ABOUT THE INSTITUTION State-supported, coed. ***Awards:*** certificates, bachelor's, master's, and doctoral degrees. 41 undergraduate majors. ***Total enrollment:*** 13,238. Undergraduates: 10,411. Freshmen: 1,852. Federal methodology is used as a basis for awarding need-based institutional aid.

UNDERGRADUATE EXPENSES for 2020–2021 ***Application fee:*** $40. ***Tuition, state resident:*** full-time $5464; part-time $182 per semester hour. ***Tuition, nonresident:*** full-time $19,282; part-time $643 per semester hour. ***Required fees:*** full-time $2024. Full-time tuition and fees vary according to course load, degree level, location, and program. Part-time tuition and fees vary according to course load, degree level, location, and program. ***College room and board:*** $10,340; ***Room only:*** $5740. Room and board charges vary according to board plan and housing facility.

FRESHMAN FINANCIAL AID (Fall 2019, est.) 1788 applied for aid; of those 78% were deemed to have need. 100% of freshmen with need received aid; of those 65% had need fully met. ***Average percent of need met:*** 44% (excluding resources awarded to replace EFC). ***Average financial aid package:*** $8234 (excluding resources awarded to replace EFC). 8% of all full-time freshmen had no need and received non-need-based gift aid.

UNDERGRADUATE FINANCIAL AID (Fall 2019, est.) 7,286 applied for aid; of those 80% were deemed to have need. 99% of undergraduates with need received aid; of those 62% had need fully met. ***Average percent of need met:*** 49% (excluding resources awarded to replace EFC). ***Average financial aid package:*** $8186

(excluding resources awarded to replace EFC). 5% of all full-time undergraduates had no need and received non-need-based gift aid.

GIFT AID (NEED-BASED) ***Receiving aid:*** Freshmen: 51% (944); all full-time undergraduates: 50% (4,069). ***Average award:*** Freshmen: $5169; Undergraduates: $5041. ***Scholarships, grants, and awards:*** Federal Pell, FSEOG, state, private, college/university gift aid from institutional funds, United Negro College Fund, Federal Nursing.

GIFT AID (NON-NEED-BASED) ***Receiving aid:*** Freshmen: 17% (310). Undergraduates: 13% (1,043). ***Average award:*** Freshmen: $1997. Undergraduates: $2552. ***Scholarships, grants, and awards by category:*** *Academic interests/achievement:* biological sciences, business, communication, computer science, education, English, foreign languages, general academic interests/achievements, health fields, humanities, mathematics, physical sciences, premedicine, social sciences. *Creative arts/performance:* applied art and design, art/fine arts, debating, general creative arts/performance, journalism/publications, music, performing arts, theater/drama. *Special achievements/activities:* community service, leadership, memberships, religious involvement. *Special characteristics:* adult students, children and siblings of alumni, general special characteristics, handicapped students, international students, local/state students, members of minority groups. ***Tuition waivers:*** Full or partial for employees or children of employees, senior citizens. ***ROTC:*** Air Force cooperative.

LOANS ***Student loans:*** 78% of past graduating class borrowed through all loan programs. *Average indebtedness per student:* $26,376. ***Average need-based loan:*** Freshmen: $3341. Undergraduates: $4005. ***Programs:*** Federal Direct (Subsidized and Unsubsidized Stafford, PLUS), Perkins, Federal Nursing, state.

WORK-STUDY Federal work-study jobs available. ***State or other work-study/employment:*** Part-time jobs available.

APPLYING FOR FINANCIAL AID ***Required financial aid form:*** FAFSA.

CONTACT Leigh Ann Hussey, Director of Financial Aid, University of West Georgia, 1601 Maple Street, Aycock Hall, Carrollton, GA 30118, 678-839-6421. *Fax:* 678-839-6422. *E-mail:* finaid@westga.edu.
Website: http://www.westga.edu/.

UNIVERSITY OF WISCONSIN–EAU CLAIRE

Eau Claire, WI

Tuition & fees (WI res): $8840	Average undergraduate aid package: $9434

ABOUT THE INSTITUTION State-supported, coed. ***Awards:*** certificates, associate, bachelor's, master's, and doctoral degrees. 54 undergraduate majors. ***Total enrollment:*** 10,732. Undergraduates: 10,068. Freshmen: 2,321. Federal methodology is used as a basis for awarding need-based institutional aid.

UNDERGRADUATE EXPENSES for 2019–2020 ***Application fee:*** $50. ***Tuition, state resident:*** full-time $7361; part-time $307 per credit. ***Tuition, nonresident:*** full-time $15,637; part-time $652 per credit. ***Required fees:*** full-time $1479; $62 per credit. Full-time tuition and fees vary according to program and reciprocity agreements. Part-time tuition and fees vary according to program and reciprocity agreements. ***College room and board:*** $8216; ***Room only:*** $5226. Room and board charges vary according to board plan and housing facility.

FRESHMAN FINANCIAL AID (Fall 2018) 2035 applied for aid; of those 61% were deemed to have need. 98% of freshmen with need received aid; of those 20% had need fully met. ***Average percent of need met:*** 81% (excluding resources awarded to replace EFC). ***Average financial aid package:*** $9101 (excluding resources awarded to replace EFC). 8% of all full-time freshmen had no need and received non-need-based gift aid.

UNDERGRADUATE FINANCIAL AID (Fall 2018) 7,066 applied for aid; of those 67% were deemed to have need. 99% of undergraduates with need received aid; of those 21% had need fully met. ***Average percent of need met:*** 82% (excluding resources awarded to replace EFC). ***Average financial aid package:*** $9434 (excluding resources awarded to replace EFC). 7% of all full-time undergraduates had no need and received non-need-based gift aid.

GIFT AID (NEED-BASED) ***Receiving aid:*** Freshmen: 44% (1,020); all full-time undergraduates: 39% (3,677). ***Average award:*** Freshmen: $6506; Undergraduates: $6494. ***Scholarships, grants, and awards:*** Federal Pell, FSEOG, state, private, college/university gift aid from institutional funds, Bureau of Indian Affairs Grants, Student Support Services Grants.

GIFT AID (NON-NEED-BASED) ***Receiving aid:*** Freshmen: 3% (64). Undergraduates: 2% (144). ***Average award:*** Freshmen: $2197. Undergraduates: $2156. ***Scholarships, grants, and awards by category:*** *Academic interests/achievement:* area/ethnic studies, biological sciences, business, communication, computer science, education, English, foreign languages, general academic interests/achievements, home economics, humanities, international studies, library science, mathematics, physical sciences, premedicine, religion/biblical studies, social sciences. *Creative arts/performance:* applied art and design, debating, journalism/publications, music, performing arts, theater/drama. *Special achievements/activities:* community service, general special achievements/activities, hobbies/interests, leadership, memberships. *Special characteristics:* adult students, ethnic background, first-generation college students, general special characteristics, international students, local/state students, members of minority groups, previous college experience. ***Tuition waivers:*** Full or partial for senior citizens. ***ROTC:*** Army.

LOANS ***Student loans:*** 68% of past graduating class borrowed through all loan programs. *Average indebtedness per student:* $27,129. ***Average need-based loan:*** Freshmen: $3145. Undergraduates: $3869. ***Programs:*** Federal Direct (Subsidized and Unsubsidized Stafford, PLUS), college/university, private loans.

WORK-STUDY ***Federal work-study:*** 4,004 jobs averaging $1673.

APPLYING FOR FINANCIAL AID ***Required financial aid form:*** FAFSA. ***Financial aid deadline:*** Continuous. ***Notification date:*** Continuous.

CONTACT Nicole Andrews, Director of Financial Aid, University of Wisconsin–Eau Claire, Vicki Lord Larson Hall 1113, Eau Claire, WI 54701, 715-836-3000. *E-mail:* blugoldcentral@uwec.edu.
Website: http://www.uwec.edu/.

UNIVERSITY OF WISCONSIN–GREEN BAY

Green Bay, WI

Tuition & fees (area res): $7878	Average undergraduate aid package: $10,813

ABOUT THE INSTITUTION State-supported, coed. ***Awards:*** associate, bachelor's, master's, and doctoral degrees. 47 undergraduate majors. ***Total enrollment:*** 9,041. Undergraduates: 8,661. Freshmen: 1,417. Both federal and institutional methodology are used as a basis for awarding need-based institutional aid.

UNDERGRADUATE EXPENSES for 2020–2021 ***Application fee:*** $50. ***Tuition, area resident:*** full-time $6298; part-time $328 per credit hour. ***Tuition, state resident:*** full-time $6298; part-time $328 per credit hour. ***Tuition, nonresident:*** full-time $14,148; part-time $670 per credit hour. ***Required fees:*** full-time $1580. ***College room and board:*** $6790; ***Room only:*** $4020.

FRESHMAN FINANCIAL AID (Fall 2018) 1106 applied for aid; of those 71% were deemed to have need. 97% of freshmen with need received aid; of those 24% had need fully met. ***Average percent of need met:*** 78% (excluding resources awarded to replace EFC). ***Average financial aid package:*** $10,252 (excluding resources awarded to replace EFC). 5% of all full-time freshmen had no need and received non-need-based gift aid.

UNDERGRADUATE FINANCIAL AID (Fall 2018) 3,765 applied for aid; of those 75% were deemed to have need. 97% of undergraduates with need received aid; of those 23% had need fully met. ***Average percent of need met:*** 81% (excluding resources awarded to replace EFC). ***Average financial aid package:*** $10,813 (excluding resources awarded to replace EFC). 3% of all full-time undergraduates had no need and received non-need-based gift aid.

GIFT AID (NEED-BASED) ***Total amount:*** $17,782,826 (52% federal, 32% state, 3% institutional, 13% external sources). ***Receiving aid:*** Freshmen: 52% (660); all full-time undergraduates: 47% (2,217). ***Average award:*** Freshmen: $6884; Undergraduates: $6762. ***Scholarships, grants, and awards:*** Federal Pell, FSEOG, state, private, college/university gift aid from institutional funds.

GIFT AID (NON-NEED-BASED) ***Total amount:*** $1,452,806 (3% state, 31% institutional, 66% external sources). ***Receiving aid:*** Freshmen: 3% (37). Undergraduates: 1% (70). ***Average award:*** Freshmen: $1449. Undergraduates: $1726. ***Scholarships, grants, and awards by category:*** *Academic interests/achievement:* area/ethnic studies, biological sciences, business, communication, education, engineering/technologies, general academic interests/achievements, health fields, humanities, physical sciences, premedicine, social sciences. *Creative arts/performance:* art/fine arts, dance, journalism/publications, music, theater/drama. *Special achievements/activities:* community service, general special achievements/activities, leadership.

Special characteristics: adult students, children of public servants, ethnic background, handicapped students, members of minority groups, veterans. **ROTC:** Army cooperative.

LOANS *Student loans:* $26,708,814 (59% need-based, 41% non-need-based). 72% of past graduating class borrowed through all loan programs. *Average indebtedness per student:* $24,668. ***Average need-based loan:*** Freshmen: $4663. Undergraduates: $5518. ***Parent loans:*** $1,495,460 (21% need-based, 79% non-need-based). ***Programs:*** Federal Direct (Subsidized and Unsubsidized Stafford, PLUS), state.

WORK-STUDY *Federal work-study:* Total amount: $380,415; jobs available. ***State or other work-study/employment:*** Part-time jobs available.

ATHLETIC AWARDS Total amount: $2,314,941 (22% need-based, 78% non-need-based).

APPLYING FOR FINANCIAL AID *Required financial aid form:* FAFSA. ***Financial aid deadline (priority):*** 1/15. ***Notification date:*** Continuous beginning 2/15.

CONTACT Mr. James Rohan, Director of Financial Aid, University of Wisconsin–Green Bay, 2420 Nicolet Drive, Green Bay, WI 54311-7001, 920-465-2073. *E-mail:* rohanj@uwgb.edu.
Website: http://www.uwgb.edu/.

UNIVERSITY OF WISCONSIN–LA CROSSE

La Crosse, WI

Tuition & fees (WI res): $8953	Average undergraduate aid package: $7947

ABOUT THE INSTITUTION State-supported, coed. ***Awards:*** certificates, bachelor's, master's, and doctoral degrees. 47 undergraduate majors. ***Total enrollment:*** 10,558. Undergraduates: 9,595. Freshmen: 2,194. Federal methodology is used as a basis for awarding need-based institutional aid.

UNDERGRADUATE EXPENSES for 2019–2020 *Application fee:* $50. ***Tuition, state resident:*** full-time $7585; part-time $316 per credit hour. ***Tuition, nonresident:*** full-time $16,254; part-time $684 per credit hour. ***Required fees:*** full-time $1368; $110 per credit hour. Full-time tuition and fees vary according to reciprocity agreements. Part-time tuition and fees vary according to course load and reciprocity agreements. ***College room and board:*** $6465; ***Room only:*** $3921. Room and board charges vary according to board plan and housing facility.

FRESHMAN FINANCIAL AID (Fall 2018) 1869 applied for aid; of those 54% were deemed to have need. 96% of freshmen with need received aid; of those 24% had need fully met. ***Average percent of need met:*** 68% (excluding resources awarded to replace EFC). ***Average financial aid package:*** $7598 (excluding resources awarded to replace EFC). 10% of all full-time freshmen had no need and received non-need-based gift aid.

UNDERGRADUATE FINANCIAL AID (Fall 2018) 6,773 applied for aid; of those 61% were deemed to have need. 96% of undergraduates with need received aid; of those 24% had need fully met. ***Average percent of need met:*** 69% (excluding resources awarded to replace EFC). ***Average financial aid package:*** $7947 (excluding resources awarded to replace EFC). 8% of all full-time undergraduates had no need and received non-need-based gift aid.

GIFT AID (NEED-BASED) *Total amount:* $17,818,640 (50% federal, 26% state, 11% institutional, 13% external sources). ***Receiving aid:*** Freshmen: 30% (647); all full-time undergraduates: 28% (2,577). ***Average award:*** Freshmen: $6646; Undergraduates: $6382. ***Scholarships, grants, and awards:*** Federal Pell, FSEOG, state, private, college/university gift aid from institutional funds.

GIFT AID (NON-NEED-BASED) *Total amount:* $3,457,892 (3% federal, 7% state, 27% institutional, 63% external sources). ***Receiving aid:*** Freshmen: 8% (169). Undergraduates: 6% (501). ***Average award:*** Freshmen: $2283. Undergraduates: $1648. ***Scholarships, grants, and awards by category:*** *Academic interests/achievement:* area/ethnic studies, biological sciences, business, communication, computer science, education, English, foreign languages, general academic interests/achievements, home economics, humanities, international studies, mathematics, military science, physical sciences, social sciences. *Creative arts/performance:* applied art and design, music, theater/drama. *Special achievements/activities:* community service, leadership, memberships. *Special characteristics:* adult students, children and siblings of alumni, children of union members/company employees, ethnic background, first-generation college students, general special characteristics, international students, local/state students, members of minority groups, out-of-state students, veterans. ***Tuition waivers:*** Full or partial for senior citizens. **ROTC:** Army.

LOANS *Student loans:* $37,415,155 (47% need-based, 53% non-need-based). 66% of past graduating class borrowed through all loan programs. *Average indebtedness per student:* $25,926. ***Average need-based loan:*** Freshmen: $3076. Undergraduates: $3863. ***Parent loans:*** $5,376,035 (22% need-based, 78% non-need-based). ***Programs:*** Federal Direct (Subsidized and Unsubsidized Stafford, PLUS), Perkins.

WORK-STUDY *Federal work-study:* Total amount: $689,121; 437 jobs averaging $1577. ***State or other work-study/employment:*** Part-time jobs available.

APPLYING FOR FINANCIAL AID *Required financial aid form:* FAFSA. ***Financial aid deadline (priority):*** 3/15. ***Notification date:*** Continuous beginning 4/1.

CONTACT Mrs. Louise Janke, Director of Financial Aid, University of Wisconsin–La Crosse, 1725 State Street, La Crosse, WI 54601-3742, 608-785-8604. *Fax:* 608-785-8843. *E-mail:* finaid@uwlax.edu.
Website: http://www.uwlax.edu/.

UNIVERSITY OF WISCONSIN–MADISON

Madison, WI

Tuition & fees (WI res): $10,725	Average undergraduate aid package: $17,473

ABOUT THE INSTITUTION State-supported, coed. ***Awards:*** certificates, bachelor's, master's, and doctoral degrees. 124 undergraduate majors. ***Total enrollment:*** 44,411. Undergraduates: 32,648. Freshmen: 6,862. Federal methodology is used as a basis for awarding need-based institutional aid.

UNDERGRADUATE EXPENSES for 2019–2020 *Application fee:* $60. ***Tuition, state resident:*** full-time $9273; part-time $386 per credit. ***Tuition, nonresident:*** full-time $36,333; part-time $1514 per credit. ***Required fees:*** full-time $1452; $108.66 per credit. Full-time tuition and fees vary according to program and reciprocity agreements. Part-time tuition and fees vary according to course load, program, and reciprocity agreements. ***College room and board:*** $11,558. Room and board charges vary according to board plan and housing facility.

FRESHMAN FINANCIAL AID (Fall 2019, est.) 5325 applied for aid; of those 52% were deemed to have need. 91% of freshmen with need received aid; of those 51% had need fully met. ***Average percent of need met:*** 83% (excluding resources awarded to replace EFC). ***Average financial aid package:*** $19,067 (excluding resources awarded to replace EFC). 5% of all full-time freshmen had no need and received non-need-based gift aid.

UNDERGRADUATE FINANCIAL AID (Fall 2019, est.) 16,460 applied for aid; of those 63% were deemed to have need. 95% of undergraduates with need received aid; of those 43% had need fully met. ***Average percent of need met:*** 80% (excluding resources awarded to replace EFC). ***Average financial aid package:*** $17,473 (excluding resources awarded to replace EFC). 4% of all full-time undergraduates had no need and received non-need-based gift aid.

GIFT AID (NEED-BASED) *Receiving aid:* Freshmen: 28% (2,085); all full-time undergraduates: 26% (7,849). ***Average award:*** Freshmen: $17,084; Undergraduates: $15,143. ***Scholarships, grants, and awards:*** Federal Pell, FSEOG, state, private, college/university gift aid from institutional funds.

GIFT AID (NON-NEED-BASED) *Receiving aid:* Freshmen: 4% (277). Undergraduates: 3% (898). ***Average award:*** Freshmen: $5405. Undergraduates: $5502. ***Scholarships, grants, and awards by category:*** *Academic interests/achievement:* general academic interests/achievements. *Creative arts/performance:* general creative arts/performance. *Special achievements/activities:* general special achievements/activities. *Special characteristics:* general special characteristics. **ROTC:** Army, Naval, Air Force.

LOANS *Student loans:* 44% of past graduating class borrowed through all loan programs. *Average indebtedness per student:* $27,973. ***Average need-based loan:*** Freshmen: $3667. Undergraduates: $4799. ***Programs:*** Federal Direct (Subsidized and Unsubsidized Stafford, PLUS), Perkins, Federal Nursing.

WORK-STUDY Federal work-study jobs available. ***State or other work-study/employment:*** Part-time jobs available.

APPLYING FOR FINANCIAL AID *Required financial aid form:* FAFSA. ***Financial aid deadline:*** Continuous. ***Notification date:*** Continuous. Students must reply within 8 weeks of notification.

CONTACT Office of Student Financial Aid, University of Wisconsin–Madison, 333 E CAMPUS MALL, #9701, Madison, WI 53715-1382, 608-2623060. *Fax:* 608-2629068. *E-mail:* FINAID@FINAID.WISC.EDU.
Website: http://www.wisc.edu/.

UNIVERSITY OF WISCONSIN–MILWAUKEE

Milwaukee, WI

Tuition & fees (area res): $9588	Average undergraduate aid package: $8904

ABOUT THE INSTITUTION State-supported, coed. ***Awards:*** certificates, associate, bachelor's, master's, and doctoral degrees. 102 undergraduate majors. ***Total enrollment:*** 26,139. Undergraduates: 21,509. Freshmen: 3,753. Federal methodology is used as a basis for awarding need-based institutional aid.

UNDERGRADUATE EXPENSES for 2019–2020 ***Application fee:*** $50. ***Tuition, area resident:*** full-time $9588. ***Tuition, state resident:*** full-time $9588; part-time $399 per credit hour. ***Tuition, nonresident:*** full-time $20,868; part-time $882 per credit hour. Full-time tuition and fees vary according to degree level, location, and reciprocity agreements. Part-time tuition and fees vary according to degree level, location, and reciprocity agreements. ***College room and board:*** $10,792.

FRESHMAN FINANCIAL AID (Fall 2018) 2787 applied for aid; of those 74% were deemed to have need. 95% of freshmen with need received aid; of those 6% had need fully met. ***Average percent of need met:*** 42% (excluding resources awarded to replace EFC). ***Average financial aid package:*** $8042 (excluding resources awarded to replace EFC). 7% of all full-time freshmen had no need and received non-need-based gift aid.

UNDERGRADUATE FINANCIAL AID (Fall 2018) 12,895 applied for aid; of those 81% were deemed to have need. 96% of undergraduates with need received aid; of those 7% had need fully met. ***Average percent of need met:*** 49% (excluding resources awarded to replace EFC). ***Average financial aid package:*** $8904 (excluding resources awarded to replace EFC). 3% of all full-time undergraduates had no need and received non-need-based gift aid.

GIFT AID (NEED-BASED) ***Total amount:*** $53,517,009 (60% federal, 33% state, 3% institutional, 4% external sources). ***Receiving aid:*** Freshmen: 37% (1,181); all full-time undergraduates: 44% (7,199). ***Average award:*** Freshmen: $7193; Undergraduates: $6662. ***Scholarships, grants, and awards:*** Federal Pell, FSEOG, state, private, college/university gift aid from institutional funds.

GIFT AID (NON-NEED-BASED) ***Total amount:*** $19,163,771 (58% federal, 7% state, 21% institutional, 14% external sources). ***Receiving aid:*** Freshmen: 24% (777). Undergraduates: 17% (2,833). ***Average award:*** Freshmen: $1712. Undergraduates: $1705. ***Scholarships, grants, and awards by category:*** *Academic interests/achievement:* business, education, general academic interests/achievements. *Creative arts/performance:* applied art and design, general creative arts/performance, music, theater/drama. *Special achievements/activities:* general special achievements/activities, leadership. *Special characteristics:* general special characteristics, veterans. ***ROTC:*** Army cooperative, Naval cooperative, Air Force cooperative.

LOANS ***Student loans:*** $89,823,125 (40% need-based, 60% non-need-based). 73% of past graduating class borrowed through all loan programs. *Average indebtedness per student:* $37,261. ***Average need-based loan:*** Freshmen: $3207. Undergraduates: $3991. ***Parent loans:*** $13,034,055 (100% non-need-based). ***Programs:*** Federal Direct (Subsidized and Unsubsidized Stafford, PLUS), Federal Nursing, state, college/university.

WORK-STUDY ***Federal work-study:*** Total amount: $1,074,966; jobs available.

ATHLETIC AWARDS Total amount: $642,989 (100% non-need-based).

APPLYING FOR FINANCIAL AID ***Required financial aid form:*** FAFSA. ***Financial aid deadline (priority):*** 3/1. ***Notification date:*** Continuous beginning 2/1.

CONTACT Tim Opgenorth, Director of Financial Aid, University of Wisconsin–Milwaukee, Mellencamp Hall 162, Milwaukee, WI 53201, 414-229-6300. *Fax:* 414-229-5699. *E-mail:* opgenort@uwm.edu.
Website: http://www.uwm.edu/.

UNIVERSITY OF WISCONSIN–OSHKOSH

Oshkosh, WI

CONTACT Ms. Stacy Drews, Financial Aid Counselor, University of Wisconsin–Oshkosh, 800 Algoma Boulevard, Oshkosh, WI 54901, 920-424-3379. *E-mail:* drewss@uwosh.edu.
Website: http://www.uwosh.edu/.

UNIVERSITY OF WISCONSIN–PARKSIDE

Kenosha, WI

Tuition & fees (WI res): $7421	Average undergraduate aid package: $9133

ABOUT THE INSTITUTION State-supported, coed. ***Awards:*** certificates, associate, bachelor's, and master's degrees. 49 undergraduate majors. ***Total enrollment:*** 4,420. Undergraduates: 3,938. Freshmen: 634. Federal methodology is used as a basis for awarding need-based institutional aid.

UNDERGRADUATE EXPENSES for 2019–2020 ***Application fee:*** $50. ***One-time required fee:*** $260. ***Tuition, state resident:*** full-time $6298; part-time $262 per credit hour. ***Tuition, nonresident:*** full-time $14,568; part-time $607 per credit hour. ***Required fees:*** full-time $1123; $46.80 per credit hour. Full-time tuition and fees vary according to course load, program, and reciprocity agreements. Part-time tuition and fees vary according to course load, program, and reciprocity agreements. ***College room and board:*** $8200; ***Room only:*** $4562. Room and board charges vary according to board plan and housing facility.

FRESHMAN FINANCIAL AID (Fall 2018) 496 applied for aid; of those 82% were deemed to have need. 95% of freshmen with need received aid; of those 11% had need fully met. ***Average percent of need met:*** 61% (excluding resources awarded to replace EFC). ***Average financial aid package:*** $8854 (excluding resources awarded to replace EFC). 9% of all full-time freshmen had no need and received non-need-based gift aid.

UNDERGRADUATE FINANCIAL AID (Fall 2018) 2,479 applied for aid; of those 84% were deemed to have need. 96% of undergraduates with need received aid; of those 11% had need fully met. ***Average percent of need met:*** 61% (excluding resources awarded to replace EFC). ***Average financial aid package:*** $9133 (excluding resources awarded to replace EFC). 9% of all full-time undergraduates had no need and received non-need-based gift aid.

GIFT AID (NEED-BASED) ***Total amount:*** $11,738,001 (65% federal, 32% state, 3% external sources). ***Receiving aid:*** Freshmen: 49% (298); all full-time undergraduates: 50% (1,605). ***Average award:*** Freshmen: $6342; Undergraduates: $6346. ***Scholarships, grants, and awards:*** Federal Pell, FSEOG, state, private, college/university gift aid from institutional funds.

GIFT AID (NON-NEED-BASED) ***Total amount:*** $994,058 (3% state, 48% institutional, 49% external sources). ***Receiving aid:*** Freshmen: 21% (128). Undergraduates: 17% (536). ***Average award:*** Freshmen: $3673. Undergraduates: $3204. ***Scholarships, grants, and awards by category:*** *Academic interests/achievement:* biological sciences, business, communication, computer science, education, engineering/technologies, English, foreign languages, general academic interests/achievements, home economics, humanities, mathematics, physical sciences, premedicine, social sciences. *Creative arts/performance:* applied art and design, art/fine arts, music, performing arts, theater/drama. *Special achievements/activities:* community service, leadership. *Special characteristics:* adult students, children of union members/company employees, children of workers in trades, ethnic background, general special characteristics, international students, local/state students, members of minority groups, out-of-state students, veterans. ***Tuition waivers:*** Full or partial for senior citizens. ***ROTC:*** Army, Air Force cooperative.

LOANS ***Student loans:*** $14,490,426 (43% need-based, 57% non-need-based). 70% of past graduating class borrowed through all loan programs. *Average indebtedness per student:* $29,551. ***Average need-based loan:*** Freshmen: $2750. Undergraduates: $4402. ***Parent loans:*** $1,088,306 (100% non-need-based). ***Programs:*** Federal Direct (Subsidized and Unsubsidized Stafford, PLUS).

WORK-STUDY ***Federal work-study:*** Total amount: $194,619; jobs available. ***State or other work-study/employment:*** Part-time jobs available.

ATHLETIC AWARDS Total amount: $40,600 (100% non-need-based).

APPLYING FOR FINANCIAL AID ***Required financial aid form:*** FAFSA. ***Financial aid deadline (priority):*** 3/15. ***Notification date:*** Continuous beginning 3/15.

CONTACT Kristina Klemens, Director of Student Financial Aid, University of Wisconsin–Parkside, 900 Wood Road, Kenosha, WI 53141-2000, 262-595-2004. *Fax:* 262-595-2216. *E-mail:* klemens@uwp.edu.
Website: http://www.uwp.edu/.

UNIVERSITY OF WISCONSIN–PLATTEVILLE

Platteville, WI

Tuition & fees (area res): $7846 | **Average undergraduate aid package: $5738**

ABOUT THE INSTITUTION State-supported, coed. ***Awards:*** certificates, associate, bachelor's, and master's degrees. 49 undergraduate majors. ***Total enrollment:*** 8,240. Undergraduates: 7,449. Freshmen: 1,492. Federal methodology is used as a basis for awarding need-based institutional aid.

UNDERGRADUATE EXPENSES for 2020–2021 ***Tuition, area resident:*** full-time $6298; part-time $262 per credit hour. ***Tuition, state resident:*** full-time $6298; part-time $262 per credit hour. ***Tuition, nonresident:*** full-time $14,148; part-time $590 per credit hour. ***Required fees:*** full-time $1548. ***College room and board:*** $7770; ***Room only:*** $4690.

FRESHMAN FINANCIAL AID (Fall 2018) 1409 applied for aid; of those 65% were deemed to have need. 150% of freshmen with need received aid; of those 9% had need fully met. ***Average percent of need met:*** 57% (excluding resources awarded to replace EFC). ***Average financial aid package:*** $5386 (excluding resources awarded to replace EFC). 25% of all full-time freshmen had no need and received non-need-based gift aid.

UNDERGRADUATE FINANCIAL AID (Fall 2018) 5,381 applied for aid; of those 69% were deemed to have need. 140% of undergraduates with need received aid; of those 9% had need fully met. ***Average percent of need met:*** 59% (excluding resources awarded to replace EFC). ***Average financial aid package:*** $5738 (excluding resources awarded to replace EFC). 13% of all full-time undergraduates had no need and received non-need-based gift aid.

GIFT AID (NEED-BASED) ***Total amount:*** $17,950,099 (50% federal, 24% state, 15% institutional, 11% external sources). ***Receiving aid:*** Freshmen: 45% (745); all full-time undergraduates: 40% (2,796). ***Average award:*** Freshmen: $5625; Undergraduates: $5541. ***Scholarships, grants, and awards:*** Federal Pell, FSEOG, state, private, college/university gift aid from institutional funds.

GIFT AID (NON-NEED-BASED) ***Total amount:*** $3,284,977 (5% state, 61% institutional, 34% external sources). ***Receiving aid:*** Freshmen: 29% (477). Undergraduates: 16% (1,075). ***Average award:*** Freshmen: $2556. Undergraduates: $2992. ***Scholarships, grants, and awards by category:*** *Academic interests/achievement:* agriculture, biological sciences, business, communication, education, engineering/technologies, general academic interests/achievements, health fields, mathematics. *Creative arts/performance:* art/fine arts, music, theater/drama. *Special achievements/activities:* leadership. ***ROTC:*** Army cooperative.

LOANS ***Student loans:*** $35,282,739 (58% need-based, 42% non-need-based). 68% of past graduating class borrowed through all loan programs. *Average indebtedness per student:* $29,707. ***Average need-based loan:*** Freshmen: $2856. Undergraduates: $3618. ***Parent loans:*** $2,856,785 (35% need-based, 65% non-need-based). ***Programs:*** Federal Direct (Subsidized and Unsubsidized Stafford, PLUS), Perkins.

WORK-STUDY ***Federal work-study:*** Total amount: $596,134; jobs available.

APPLYING FOR FINANCIAL AID ***Required financial aid form:*** FAFSA. ***Financial aid deadline:*** Continuous. ***Notification date:*** Continuous.

CONTACT Elizabeth Tucker, Director of Financial Aid, University of Wisconsin–Platteville, 1 University Plaza, Platteville, WI 53818-3099, 608-342-1836 or toll-free 877-897-5288. *Fax:* 608-342-1281. *E-mail:* tucker@uwplatt.edu.
Website: http://www.uwplatt.edu/.

UNIVERSITY OF WISCONSIN–RIVER FALLS

River Falls, WI

Tuition & fees: N/R | **Average undergraduate aid package: $6896**

ABOUT THE INSTITUTION State-supported, coed. ***Awards:*** certificates, associate, bachelor's, and master's degrees. 53 undergraduate majors. ***Total enrollment:*** 6,139. Undergraduates: 5,725. Freshmen: 1,264. Federal methodology is used as a basis for awarding need-based institutional aid.

FRESHMAN FINANCIAL AID (Fall 2018) 927 applied for aid; of those 65% were deemed to have need. 95% of freshmen with need received aid; of those 3% had need fully met. ***Average percent of need met:*** 47% (excluding resources awarded to replace EFC). ***Average financial aid package:*** $6085 (excluding resources awarded to replace EFC). 19% of all full-time freshmen had no need and received non-need-based gift aid.

UNDERGRADUATE FINANCIAL AID (Fall 2018) 3,896 applied for aid; of those 70% were deemed to have need. 95% of undergraduates with need received aid; of those 2% had need fully met. ***Average percent of need met:*** 54% (excluding resources awarded to replace EFC). ***Average financial aid package:*** $6896 (excluding resources awarded to replace EFC). 12% of all full-time undergraduates had no need and received non-need-based gift aid.

GIFT AID (NEED-BASED) ***Receiving aid:*** Freshmen: 32% (335); all full-time undergraduates: 33% (1,588). ***Average award:*** Freshmen: $5190; Undergraduates: $5127. ***Scholarships, grants, and awards:*** Federal Pell, FSEOG, state, private, college/university gift aid from institutional funds.

GIFT AID (NON-NEED-BASED) ***Receiving aid:*** Freshmen: 22% (232). Undergraduates: 16% (759). ***Average award:*** Freshmen: $1553. Undergraduates: $1947. ***Scholarships, grants, and awards by category:*** *Academic interests/achievement:* 1,118 awards ($2,282,785 total): agriculture, biological sciences, business, communication, computer science, education, engineering/technologies, English, foreign languages, general academic interests/achievements, home economics, humanities, international studies, mathematics, military science, physical sciences, social sciences. *Creative arts/performance:* 54 awards ($113,241 total): applied art and design, art/fine arts, cinema/film/broadcasting, creative writing, journalism/publications, music, theater/drama. ***ROTC:*** Army.

LOANS ***Student loans:*** 65% of past graduating class borrowed through all loan programs. *Average indebtedness per student:* $26,814. ***Average need-based loan:*** Freshmen: $3025. Undergraduates: $3767. ***Programs:*** Federal Direct (Subsidized and Unsubsidized Stafford, PLUS).

WORK-STUDY ***Federal work-study:*** 383 jobs averaging $1242.

APPLYING FOR FINANCIAL AID ***Required financial aid form:*** FAFSA. ***Financial aid deadline:*** Continuous. ***Notification date:*** Continuous.

CONTACT Mr. Robert Bode, Director of Financial Aid, University of Wisconsin–River Falls, 410 South Third Street, 133 Rodli Hall, River Falls, WI 54022, 715-425-3141. *Fax:* 715-425-0708. *E-mail:* robert.bode@uwrf.edu.
Website: http://www.uwrf.edu/.

UNIVERSITY OF WISCONSIN–STEVENS POINT

Stevens Point, WI

Tuition & fees (area res): $8290 | **Average undergraduate aid package: $9520**

ABOUT THE INSTITUTION State-supported, coed. ***Awards:*** associate, bachelor's, master's, and doctoral degrees. 85 undergraduate majors. ***Total enrollment:*** 7,725. Undergraduates: 7,385. Freshmen: 1,405. Federal methodology is used as a basis for awarding need-based institutional aid.

UNDERGRADUATE EXPENSES for 2019–2020 ***Application fee:*** $50. ***Tuition, area resident:*** full-time $6698; part-time $279 per credit. ***Tuition, state resident:*** full-time $6698; part-time $279 per credit. ***Tuition, nonresident:*** full-time $15,401; part-time $642 per credit. ***Required fees:*** full-time $1592. Full-time tuition and fees vary according to course load, location, program, reciprocity agreements, and student level. Part-time tuition and fees vary according to course load, location, program, reciprocity agreements, and student level. ***College room and board:*** $7428; ***Room only:*** $4422. Room and board charges vary according to board plan and housing facility.

FRESHMAN FINANCIAL AID (Fall 2018) 1227 applied for aid; of those 67% were deemed to have need. 97% of freshmen with need received aid; of those 73% had need fully met. ***Average percent of need met:*** 77% (excluding resources awarded to replace EFC). ***Average financial aid package:*** $9106 (excluding resources awarded to replace EFC). 22% of all full-time freshmen had no need and received non-need-based gift aid.

UNDERGRADUATE FINANCIAL AID (Fall 2018) 5,351 applied for aid; of those 75% were deemed to have need. 97% of undergraduates with need received aid; of those 60% had need fully met. ***Average percent of need met:*** 75% (excluding resources awarded to replace EFC). ***Average financial aid package:*** $9520 (excluding resources awarded to replace EFC). 11% of all full-time undergraduates had no need and received non-need-based gift aid.

GIFT AID (NEED-BASED) ***Total amount:*** $22,072,110 (51% federal, 27% state, 10% institutional, 12% external sources). ***Receiving aid:*** Freshmen: 52% (729); all full-time undergraduates: 49% (3,308). ***Average award:*** Freshmen: $6340; Undergraduates: $6382. ***Scholarships, grants, and awards:*** Federal Pell, state, private, college/university gift aid from institutional funds.

GIFT AID (NON-NEED-BASED) ***Total amount:*** $2,206,014 (6% state, 39% institutional, 55% external sources). ***Receiving aid:*** Freshmen: 24% (329). Undergraduates: 13% (865). ***Average award:*** Freshmen: $1831. Undergraduates: $1497. ***Scholarships, grants, and awards by category:*** *Academic interests/achievement:* agriculture, architecture, biological sciences, business, communication, computer science, education, engineering/technologies, English, foreign languages, general academic interests/achievements, health fields, home economics, humanities, international studies, mathematics, military science, physical sciences, premedicine, social sciences. *Creative arts/performance:* art/fine arts, creative writing, dance, music, performing arts, theater/drama. *Special achievements/activities:* general special achievements/activities, leadership. *Special characteristics:* adult students, ethnic background, general special characteristics, international students, members of minority groups, out-of-state students, veterans. ***Tuition waivers:*** Full or partial for senior citizens. ***ROTC:*** Army.

LOANS ***Student loans:*** $30,042,966 (70% need-based, 30% non-need-based). 72% of past graduating class borrowed through all loan programs. *Average indebtedness per student:* $31,669. ***Average need-based loan:*** Freshmen: $3075. Undergraduates: $4619. ***Parent loans:*** $3,237,979 (51% need-based, 49% non-need-based). ***Programs:*** Federal Direct (Subsidized and Unsubsidized Stafford, PLUS), Perkins.

WORK-STUDY ***Federal work-study:*** Total amount: $2,797,947; jobs available. ***State or other work-study/employment:*** Part-time jobs available.

APPLYING FOR FINANCIAL AID ***Required financial aid form:*** FAFSA. ***Financial aid deadline (priority):*** 3/15. ***Notification date:*** Continuous beginning 3/15.

CONTACT Ms. Mandy Slowinski, Director of Financial Aid, University of Wisconsin–Stevens Point, 106 Student Services Center, Stevens Point, WI 54481-3897, 715-346-4771. *Fax:* 715-346-3526. *E-mail:* finaid@uwsp.edu.
Website: http://www.uwsp.edu/.

UNIVERSITY OF WISCONSIN–STOUT

Menomonie, WI

Tuition & fees (area res): $9463	Average undergraduate aid package: $11,079

ABOUT THE INSTITUTION State-supported, coed. ***Awards:*** certificates, bachelor's, master's, and doctoral degrees. 43 undergraduate majors. ***Total enrollment:*** 8,393. Undergraduates: 7,289. Freshmen: 1,491. Federal methodology is used as a basis for awarding need-based institutional aid.

UNDERGRADUATE EXPENSES for 2020–2021 ***Application fee:*** $50. ***Tuition, area resident:*** full-time $7014; part-time $315 per credit hour. ***Tuition, state resident:*** full-time $7014; part-time $315 per credit hour. ***Tuition, nonresident:*** full-time $14,981; part-time $581 per credit hour. ***Required fees:*** full-time $2449. ***College room and board:*** $6944; ***Room only:*** $4400.

FRESHMAN FINANCIAL AID (Fall 2019, est.) 1296 applied for aid; of those 62% were deemed to have need. 97% of freshmen with need received aid; of those 15% had need fully met. ***Average percent of need met:*** 77% (excluding resources awarded to replace EFC). ***Average financial aid package:*** $10,561 (excluding resources awarded to replace EFC). 11% of all full-time freshmen had no need and received non-need-based gift aid.

UNDERGRADUATE FINANCIAL AID (Fall 2019, est.) 4,615 applied for aid; of those 68% were deemed to have need. 97% of undergraduates with need received aid; of those 17% had need fully met. ***Average percent of need met:*** 81% (excluding resources awarded to replace EFC). ***Average financial aid package:*** $11,079 (excluding resources awarded to replace EFC). 4% of all full-time undergraduates had no need and received non-need-based gift aid.

GIFT AID (NEED-BASED) ***Total amount:*** $12,575,689 (66% federal, 29% state, 5% external sources). ***Receiving aid:*** Freshmen: 28% (416); all full-time undergraduates: 29% (1,704). ***Average award:*** Freshmen: $6886; Undergraduates: $6655. ***Scholarships, grants, and awards:*** Federal Pell, FSEOG, state, private, college/university gift aid from institutional funds, Bureau of Indian Affairs, Gear Up Schol.

GIFT AID (NON-NEED-BASED) ***Total amount:*** $3,682,532 (1% state, 56% institutional, 43% external sources). ***Receiving aid:*** Freshmen: 28% (416). Undergraduates: 15% (872). ***Average award:*** Freshmen: $1789. Undergraduates: $1853. ***Scholarships, grants, and awards by category:*** *Academic interests/achievement:* business, computer science, education, engineering/technologies, general academic interests/achievements, home economics, international studies, mathematics, physical sciences. *Creative arts/performance:* applied art and design, art/fine arts, music. *Special achievements/activities:* community service, general special achievements/activities, leadership, memberships, religious involvement. *Special characteristics:* adult students, first-generation college students, handicapped students, international students, local/state students, members of minority groups, out-of-state students, previous college experience, veterans, veterans' children. ***ROTC:*** Army, Air Force cooperative.

LOANS ***Student loans:*** $36,041,922 (33% need-based, 67% non-need-based). 73% of past graduating class borrowed through all loan programs. *Average indebtedness per student:* $31,372. ***Average need-based loan:*** Freshmen: $3271. Undergraduates: $4015. ***Parent loans:*** $2,010,649 (100% non-need-based). ***Programs:*** Federal Direct (Subsidized and Unsubsidized Stafford, PLUS), state, Alternate Educ. Loans.

WORK-STUDY ***Federal work-study:*** Total amount: $2,581,846; jobs available. ***State or other work-study/employment:*** Part-time jobs available.

APPLYING FOR FINANCIAL AID ***Required financial aid form:*** FAFSA. ***Financial aid deadline (priority):*** 3/15. ***Notification date:*** Continuous beginning 1/27. Students must reply within 4 weeks of notification.

CONTACT Beth Boisen, Director of Financial Aid, University of Wisconsin–Stout, 712 South Broadway Street, Menomonie, WI 54751, 715-232-1363 or toll-free 800-HI-STOUT. *Fax:* 715-232-5246. *E-mail:* boisenb@uwstout.edu.
Website: http://www.uwstout.edu/.

UNIVERSITY OF WISCONSIN–SUPERIOR

Superior, WI

Tuition & fees (WI res): $8132	Average undergraduate aid package: $11,230

ABOUT THE INSTITUTION State-supported, coed. ***Awards:*** certificates, associate, bachelor's, and master's degrees. 48 undergraduate majors. ***Total enrollment:*** 2,608. Undergraduates: 2,257. Freshmen: 327. Federal methodology is used as a basis for awarding need-based institutional aid.

UNDERGRADUATE EXPENSES for 2019–2020 ***Application fee:*** $44. ***Tuition, state resident:*** full-time $6535. ***Tuition, nonresident:*** full-time $14,108. ***Required fees:*** full-time $1597. Full-time tuition and fees vary according to course load and reciprocity agreements. Part-time tuition and fees vary according to course load and reciprocity agreements. ***College room and board:*** $7280; ***Room only:*** $4586. Room and board charges vary according to board plan and housing facility.

FRESHMAN FINANCIAL AID (Fall 2019, est.) 269 applied for aid; of those 71% were deemed to have need. 98% of freshmen with need received aid; of those 30% had need fully met. ***Average percent of need met:*** 86% (excluding resources awarded to replace EFC). ***Average financial aid package:*** $10,305 (excluding resources awarded to replace EFC). 10% of all full-time freshmen had no need and received non-need-based gift aid.

UNDERGRADUATE FINANCIAL AID (Fall 2019, est.) 1,316 applied for aid; of those 79% were deemed to have need. 98% of undergraduates with need received aid; of those 21% had need fully met. ***Average percent of need met:*** 84% (excluding resources awarded to replace EFC). ***Average financial aid package:*** $11,230

(excluding resources awarded to replace EFC). 5% of all full-time undergraduates had no need and received non-need-based gift aid.

GIFT AID (NEED-BASED) ***Total amount:*** $5,502,392 (61% federal, 23% state, 14% institutional, 2% external sources). ***Receiving aid:*** Freshmen: 40% (129); all full-time undergraduates: 42% (720). ***Average award:*** Freshmen: $4859; Undergraduates: $5175. ***Scholarships, grants, and awards:*** Federal Pell, FSEOG, state, private, college/university gift aid from institutional funds.

GIFT AID (NON-NEED-BASED) ***Total amount:*** $759,542 (4% state, 19% institutional, 77% external sources). ***Receiving aid:*** Freshmen: 31% (102). Undergraduates: 17% (299). ***Average award:*** Freshmen: $2811. Undergraduates: $3401. ***Scholarships, grants, and awards by category:*** *Academic interests/achievement:* biological sciences, business, communication, computer science, education, English, general academic interests/achievements, humanities, mathematics, physical sciences, social sciences. *Creative arts/performance:* general creative arts/performance. *Special characteristics:* general special characteristics, international students, members of minority groups, veterans. ***ROTC:*** Air Force cooperative.

LOANS ***Student loans:*** $9,524,218 (38% need-based, 62% non-need-based). 63% of past graduating class borrowed through all loan programs. *Average indebtedness per student:* $31,490. ***Average need-based loan:*** Freshmen: $2381. Undergraduates: $3405. ***Parent loans:*** $471,610 (100% non-need-based). ***Programs:*** Federal Direct (Subsidized and Unsubsidized Stafford, PLUS), state, college/university.

WORK-STUDY ***Federal work-study:*** Total amount: $339,067; jobs available. ***State or other work-study/employment:*** Total amount: $1,032,298 (100% non-need-based). Part-time jobs available.

APPLYING FOR FINANCIAL AID ***Required financial aid form:*** FAFSA. ***Financial aid deadline (priority):*** 1/15. ***Notification date:*** Continuous beginning 2/4. Students must reply by 5/1.

CONTACT Financial Aid Office, University of Wisconsin–Superior, Belknap and Catlin, PO Box 2000, Superior, WI 54880-4500, 715-394-8101.
Website: http://www.uwsuper.edu/.

UNIVERSITY OF WISCONSIN–WHITEWATER

Whitewater, WI

Tuition & fees (WI res): $7695	Average undergraduate aid package: $8430

ABOUT THE INSTITUTION State-supported, coed. ***Awards:*** associate, bachelor's, master's, and doctoral degrees. 70 undergraduate majors. ***Total enrollment:*** 12,084. Undergraduates: 10,747. Freshmen: 1,792. Federal methodology is used as a basis for awarding need-based institutional aid.

UNDERGRADUATE EXPENSES for 2019–2020 ***Application fee:*** $50. ***Tuition, state resident:*** full-time $6519; part-time $272 per credit hour. ***Tuition, nonresident:*** full-time $15,240; part-time $635 per credit hour. ***Required fees:*** full-time $1176. Full-time tuition and fees vary according to course load, degree level, location, and reciprocity agreements. ***College room and board:*** $6878; ***Room only:*** $4298. Room and board charges vary according to board plan and housing facility.

FRESHMAN FINANCIAL AID (Fall 2018) 1710 applied for aid; of those 66% were deemed to have need. 96% of freshmen with need received aid; of those 38% had need fully met. ***Average percent of need met:*** 57% (excluding resources awarded to replace EFC). ***Average financial aid package:*** $7747 (excluding resources awarded to replace EFC). 6% of all full-time freshmen had no need and received non-need-based gift aid.

UNDERGRADUATE FINANCIAL AID (Fall 2018) 7,327 applied for aid; of those 71% were deemed to have need. 97% of undergraduates with need received aid; of those 42% had need fully met. ***Average percent of need met:*** 63% (excluding resources awarded to replace EFC). ***Average financial aid package:*** $8430 (excluding resources awarded to replace EFC). 6% of all full-time undergraduates had no need and received non-need-based gift aid.

GIFT AID (NEED-BASED) ***Total amount:*** $21,203,156 (63% federal, 33% state, 4% external sources). ***Receiving aid:*** Freshmen: 36% (657); all full-time undergraduates: 34% (3,213). ***Average award:*** Freshmen: $6115; Undergraduates: $6243. ***Scholarships, grants, and awards:*** Federal Pell, FSEOG, state, private, college/university gift aid from institutional funds.

GIFT AID (NON-NEED-BASED) ***Total amount:*** $4,958,657 (3% federal, 2% state, 50% institutional, 45% external sources). ***Receiving aid:*** Freshmen: 19% (349). Undergraduates: 12% (1,093). ***Average award:*** Freshmen: $2037. Undergraduates: $2027. ***Scholarships, grants, and awards by category:*** *Academic interests/achievement:* biological sciences, business, communication, computer science, education, English, foreign languages, general academic interests/achievements, humanities, mathematics, physical sciences, premedicine, social sciences. *Creative arts/performance:* applied art and design, art/fine arts, cinema/film/broadcasting, creative writing, journalism/publications, music, theater/drama. *Special achievements/activities:* leadership. *Special characteristics:* adult students, children and siblings of alumni, ethnic background, first-generation college students, handicapped students, international students, local/state students, members of minority groups, out-of-state students, veterans, veterans' children. ***Tuition waivers:*** Full or partial for children of alumni, senior citizens. ***ROTC:*** Army, Air Force.

LOANS ***Student loans:*** $56,026,925 (31% need-based, 69% non-need-based). 78% of past graduating class borrowed through all loan programs. *Average indebtedness per student:* $28,008. ***Average need-based loan:*** Freshmen: $3044. Undergraduates: $3943. ***Parent loans:*** $7,499,571 (100% non-need-based). ***Programs:*** Federal Direct (Subsidized and Unsubsidized Stafford, PLUS), Private/alternative loans.

WORK-STUDY ***Federal work-study:*** Total amount: $537,199; 496 jobs averaging $1083. ***State or other work-study/employment:*** Total amount: $4,574,234 (100% non-need-based). 2,308 part-time jobs averaging $1982.

APPLYING FOR FINANCIAL AID ***Required financial aid form:*** FAFSA. ***Financial aid deadline (priority):*** 1/1. ***Notification date:*** Continuous beginning 2/1. Students must reply within 3 weeks of notification.

CONTACT Mr. William Trippett, Director of Financial Aid, University of Wisconsin–Whitewater, 800 West Main Street, Whitewater, WI 53190-1790, 262-472-1130. *Fax:* 262-472-5655. *E-mail:* trippetw@uww.edu.
Website: http://www.uww.edu/.

UNIVERSITY OF WYOMING

Laramie, WY

Tuition & fees (area res): $5791	Average undergraduate aid package: $10,431

ABOUT THE INSTITUTION State-supported, coed. ***Awards:*** certificates, bachelor's, master's, and doctoral degrees. 83 undergraduate majors. ***Total enrollment:*** 12,249. Undergraduates: 9,807. Freshmen: 1,760. Federal methodology is used as a basis for awarding need-based institutional aid.

UNDERGRADUATE EXPENSES for 2020–2021 ***Application fee:*** $40. ***One-time required fee:*** $40. ***Tuition, area resident:*** full-time $4350; part-time $139 per credit hour. ***Tuition, state resident:*** full-time $4350; part-time $139 per credit hour. ***Tuition, nonresident:*** full-time $18,090; part-time $558 per credit hour. ***Required fees:*** full-time $1441. Full-time tuition and fees vary according to course load, location, program, and reciprocity agreements. Part-time tuition and fees vary according to course load, location, program, and reciprocity agreements. ***College room and board:*** $10,615; ***Room only:*** $4583. Room and board charges vary according to board plan and housing facility.

FRESHMAN FINANCIAL AID (Fall 2018) 1563 applied for aid; of those 61% were deemed to have need. 98% of freshmen with need received aid; of those 26% had need fully met. ***Average percent of need met:*** 64% (excluding resources awarded to replace EFC). ***Average financial aid package:*** $11,472 (excluding resources awarded to replace EFC). 25% of all full-time freshmen had no need and received non-need-based gift aid.

UNDERGRADUATE FINANCIAL AID (Fall 2018) 5,791 applied for aid; of those 70% were deemed to have need. 98% of undergraduates with need received aid; of those 16% had need fully met. ***Average percent of need met:*** 59% (excluding resources awarded to replace EFC). ***Average financial aid package:*** $10,431 (excluding resources awarded to replace EFC). 20% of all full-time undergraduates had no need and received non-need-based gift aid.

GIFT AID (NEED-BASED) ***Receiving aid:*** Freshmen: 30% (554); all full-time undergraduates: 32% (2,673). ***Average award:*** Freshmen: $4945; Undergraduates: $5185. ***Scholarships, grants, and awards:*** Federal Pell, FSEOG, state, private, college/university gift aid from institutional funds.

GIFT AID (NON-NEED-BASED) ***Receiving aid:*** Freshmen: 45% (825). Undergraduates: 36% (3,000). ***Average award:*** Freshmen: $4208. Undergraduates: $4084.

Scholarships, grants, and awards by category: *Academic interests/achievement:* agriculture, architecture, area/ethnic studies, biological sciences, business, communication, computer science, education, engineering/technologies, English, foreign languages, general academic interests/achievements, health fields, home economics, humanities, international studies, mathematics, physical sciences, religion/biblical studies, social sciences. *Creative arts/performance:* applied art and design, art/fine arts, cinema/film/broadcasting, creative writing, dance, debating, general creative arts/performance, journalism/publications, music, performing arts, theater/drama. *Special achievements/activities:* cheerleading/drum major, community service, general special achievements/activities, hobbies/interests, junior miss, leadership, memberships, rodeo. *Special characteristics:* adult students, children and siblings of alumni, children of public servants, ethnic background, first-generation college students, general special characteristics, handicapped students, international students, local/state students, members of minority groups, out-of-state students, previous college experience, spouses of current students, veterans, veterans' children. ***Tuition waivers:*** Full or partial for children of alumni, employees or children of employees, senior citizens. ***ROTC:*** Army, Air Force.

LOANS *Student loans:* 46% of past graduating class borrowed through all loan programs. *Average indebtedness per student:* $23,444. ***Average need-based loan:*** Freshmen: $2900. Undergraduates: $3729. ***Programs:*** Federal Direct (Subsidized and Unsubsidized Stafford, PLUS), state, college/university, Alternative Loan Program.

WORK-STUDY *Federal work-study:* 250 jobs averaging $2135.

APPLYING FOR FINANCIAL AID *Required financial aid form:* FAFSA. ***Financial aid deadline:*** Continuous. ***Notification date:*** Continuous.

CONTACT Debra Hintz, Director of Scholarships and Financial Aid, University of Wyoming, Department 3335, 1000 East University Avenue, Laramie, WY 82071, 307-766-2116 or toll-free 800-342-5996. *Fax:* 307-766-3800. *E-mail:* finaid@uwyo.edu.
Website: http://www.uwyo.edu/.

UPPER IOWA UNIVERSITY

Fayette, IA

Tuition & fees: N/R	Average undergraduate aid package: $17,646

ABOUT THE INSTITUTION Independent, coed. ***Awards:*** certificates, associate, bachelor's, and master's degrees (enrollment figures include extended learning centers and online and distance education programs). 43 undergraduate majors. ***Total enrollment:*** 4,279. Undergraduates: 3,680. Freshmen: 190. Federal methodology is used as a basis for awarding need-based institutional aid.

FRESHMAN FINANCIAL AID (Fall 2019, est.) 428 applied for aid; of those 94% were deemed to have need. 99% of freshmen with need received aid; of those 15% had need fully met. ***Average percent of need met:*** 61% (excluding resources awarded to replace EFC). ***Average financial aid package:*** $19,125 (excluding resources awarded to replace EFC). 14% of all full-time freshmen had no need and received non-need-based gift aid.

UNDERGRADUATE FINANCIAL AID (Fall 2019, est.) 1,717 applied for aid; of those 94% were deemed to have need. 100% of undergraduates with need received aid; of those 11% had need fully met. ***Average percent of need met:*** 57% (excluding resources awarded to replace EFC). ***Average financial aid package:*** $17,646 (excluding resources awarded to replace EFC). 8% of all full-time undergraduates had no need and received non-need-based gift aid.

GIFT AID (NEED-BASED) *Total amount:* $25,457,690 (38% federal, 12% state, 48% institutional, 2% external sources). ***Receiving aid:*** Freshmen: 78% (372); all full-time undergraduates: 85% (1,509). ***Average award:*** Freshmen: $16,431; Undergraduates: $14,027. ***Scholarships, grants, and awards:*** Federal Pell, FSEOG, state, private, college/university gift aid from institutional funds.

GIFT AID (NON-NEED-BASED) *Total amount:* $4,043,907 (95% institutional, 5% external sources). ***Receiving aid:*** Freshmen: 11% (53). Undergraduates: 8% (146). ***Average award:*** Freshmen: $19,729. Undergraduates: $18,220. ***Scholarships, grants, and awards by category:*** *Academic interests/achievement:* 233 awards ($566,348 total): biological sciences, business, computer science, education, general academic interests/achievements, humanities, physical sciences, social sciences. *Special achievements/activities:* 5 awards ($32,000 total): cheerleading/drum major. *Special characteristics:* 20 awards ($9500 total): children and siblings of alumni.

LOANS *Student loans:* $23,755,140 (89% need-based, 11% non-need-based). 75% of past graduating class borrowed through all loan programs. *Average indebtedness per student:* $26,664. ***Average need-based loan:*** Freshmen: $4429. Undergraduates: $5327. ***Parent loans:*** $1,026,308 (44% need-based, 56% non-need-based). ***Programs:*** Federal Direct (Subsidized and Unsubsidized Stafford, PLUS), Alternative Loans.

WORK-STUDY *Federal work-study:* Total amount: $359,333; 140 jobs averaging $2598. ***State or other work-study/employment:*** Part-time jobs available.

APPLYING FOR FINANCIAL AID *Required financial aid form:* FAFSA. ***Financial aid deadline:*** Continuous. ***Notification date:*** Continuous beginning 3/1. Students must reply within 9 weeks of notification.

CONTACT Kelli Pech, Financial Aid Director, Upper Iowa University, 605 Washington Street, Fayette, IA 52142-1857, 800-553-4150. *Fax:* 563-425-5277. *E-mail:* financialaid@uiu.edu.
Website: http://www.uiu.edu/.

URBANA UNIVERSITY–A BRANCH CAMPUS OF FRANKLIN UNIVERSITY

Urbana, OH

CONTACT Mrs. Amy M. Barnhart, Director of Financial Aid, Urbana University–A Branch Campus of Franklin University, 579 College Way, Urbana, OH 43078-2091, 937-484-1359 or toll-free 800-7-URBANA. *Fax:* 937-652-6870. *E-mail:* abarnhart@urbana.edu.
Website: http://www.urbana.edu/.

URSINUS COLLEGE

Collegeville, PA

ABOUT THE INSTITUTION Independent, coed. ***Awards:*** bachelor's degrees. 31 undergraduate majors. ***Total enrollment:*** 1,435. Undergraduates: 1,435. Freshmen: 378.

GIFT AID (NEED-BASED) *Scholarships, grants, and awards:* Federal Pell, FSEOG, state, private, college/university gift aid from institutional funds.

GIFT AID (NON-NEED-BASED) *Scholarships, grants, and awards by category:* *Academic interests/achievement:* general academic interests/achievements. *Creative arts/performance:* creative writing, dance, music, performing arts, theater/drama. *Special achievements/activities:* community service, general special achievements/activities, leadership. *Special characteristics:* children and siblings of alumni, children of faculty/staff, general special characteristics, international students, siblings of current students, veterans.

LOANS *Programs:* Federal Direct (Subsidized and Unsubsidized Stafford, PLUS).

WORK-STUDY *Federal work-study:* Total amount: $1,121,496; 605 jobs averaging $1851.

APPLYING FOR FINANCIAL AID *Required financial aid forms:* FAFSA, state aid form.

CONTACT Ms. Ellen Curcio, Director of Student Financial Services, Ursinus College, 601 East Main Street, Collegeville, PA 19426-1000, 610-409-3600. *Fax:* 610-409-3662. *E-mail:* ecurcio@ursinus.edu.
Website: http://www.ursinus.edu/.

URSULINE COLLEGE

Pepper Pike, OH

Tuition & fees: $34,630	Average undergraduate aid package: $24,961

ABOUT THE INSTITUTION Independent Roman Catholic, coed, primarily women. ***Awards:*** certificates, bachelor's, master's, and doctoral degrees (applications from men are also accepted). 25 undergraduate majors. ***Total enrollment:*** 1,050. Undergraduates: 651. Freshmen: 92. Federal methodology is used as a basis for awarding need-based institutional aid.

UNDERGRADUATE EXPENSES for 2020–2021 *One-time required fee:* $100. ***Comprehensive fee:*** $46,144 includes full-time tuition ($34,290), mandatory fees ($340), and room and board ($11,514). Room and board charges vary according to board plan. ***Part-time tuition:*** $1143 per credit hour. ***Part-time fees:*** $260.

FRESHMAN FINANCIAL AID (Fall 2019, est.) 86 applied for aid; of those 98% were deemed to have need. 100% of freshmen with need received aid; of those 11%

had need fully met. ***Average percent of need met:*** 82% (excluding resources awarded to replace EFC). ***Average financial aid package:*** $31,712 (excluding resources awarded to replace EFC). 9% of all full-time freshmen had no need and received non-need-based gift aid.

UNDERGRADUATE FINANCIAL AID (Fall 2019, est.) 430 applied for aid; of those 95% were deemed to have need. 100% of undergraduates with need received aid; of those 11% had need fully met. ***Average percent of need met:*** 68% (excluding resources awarded to replace EFC). ***Average financial aid package:*** $24,961 (excluding resources awarded to replace EFC). 8% of all full-time undergraduates had no need and received non-need-based gift aid.

GIFT AID (NEED-BASED) ***Total amount:*** $7,688,896 (18% federal, 8% state, 72% institutional, 2% external sources). ***Receiving aid:*** Freshmen: 91% (84); all full-time undergraduates: 72% (351). ***Average award:*** Freshmen: $27,935; Undergraduates: $23,153. ***Scholarships, grants, and awards:*** Federal Pell, FSEOG, state, private, college/university gift aid from institutional funds, United Negro College Fund.

GIFT AID (NON-NEED-BASED) ***Total amount:*** $588,316 (97% institutional, 3% external sources). ***Receiving aid:*** Freshmen: 9% (8). Undergraduates: 6% (28). ***Average award:*** Freshmen: $15,875. Undergraduates: $11,498. ***Scholarships, grants, and awards by category:*** *Academic interests/achievement:* general academic interests/achievements. *Creative arts/performance:* general creative arts/performance. *Special achievements/activities:* community service, leadership. *Special characteristics:* children and siblings of alumni, children of faculty/staff, first-generation college students, relatives of clergy, religious affiliation, siblings of current students, veterans. ***Tuition waivers:*** Full or partial for employees or children of employees, senior citizens. ***ROTC:*** Army cooperative, Air Force cooperative.

LOANS ***Student loans:*** $4,705,162 (84% need-based, 16% non-need-based). 91% of past graduating class borrowed through all loan programs. *Average indebtedness per student:* $29,220. ***Average need-based loan:*** Freshmen: $3849. Undergraduates: $5621. ***Parent loans:*** $836,177 (50% need-based, 50% non-need-based). ***Programs:*** Federal Direct (Subsidized and Unsubsidized Stafford, PLUS), state, college/university.

WORK-STUDY ***Federal work-study:*** Total amount: $102,666; 303 jobs averaging $1000.

ATHLETIC AWARDS Total amount: $1,682,285 (56% need-based, 44% non-need-based).

APPLYING FOR FINANCIAL AID ***Required financial aid form:*** FAFSA. ***Financial aid deadline:*** Continuous. ***Notification date:*** Continuous beginning 1/1. Students must reply within 3 weeks of notification.

CONTACT Ms. Mary Lynn Perri, Assistant Dean of Enrollment Management and Director of Financial Aid, Ursuline College, 2550 Lander Road, Pepper Pike, OH 44124-4398, 440-646-8330 or toll-free 888-URSULINE. *Fax:* 440-684-6114. *E-mail:* mperri@ursuline.edu.
Website: http://www.ursuline.edu/.

UTAH STATE UNIVERSITY

Logan, UT

Tuition & fees (UT res): $7860	Average undergraduate aid package: $11,738

ABOUT THE INSTITUTION State-supported, coed. ***Awards:*** certificates, associate, bachelor's, master's, and doctoral degrees. 131 undergraduate majors. ***Total enrollment:*** 27,810. Undergraduates: 24,669. Freshmen: 4,411. Federal methodology is used as a basis for awarding need-based institutional aid.

UNDERGRADUATE EXPENSES for 2020–2021 ***Application fee:*** $50. ***Tuition, state resident:*** full-time $6732. ***Tuition, nonresident:*** full-time $21,677. ***Required fees:*** full-time $1128. Full-time tuition and fees vary according to course level, course load, program, and reciprocity agreements. Part-time tuition and fees vary according to course level, course load, program, and reciprocity agreements. ***College room and board:*** $5960; ***Room only:*** $2410. Room and board charges vary according to board plan and housing facility.

FRESHMAN FINANCIAL AID (Fall 2019, est.) 2946 applied for aid; of those 67% were deemed to have need. 99% of freshmen with need received aid; of those 19% had need fully met. ***Average percent of need met:*** 61% (excluding resources awarded to replace EFC). ***Average financial aid package:*** $10,938 (excluding resources awarded to replace EFC). 26% of all full-time freshmen had no need and received non-need-based gift aid.

UNDERGRADUATE FINANCIAL AID (Fall 2019, est.) 11,396 applied for aid; of those 80% were deemed to have need. 100% of undergraduates with need received aid; of those 10% had need fully met. ***Average percent of need met:*** 56% (excluding resources awarded to replace EFC). ***Average financial aid package:*** $11,738 (excluding resources awarded to replace EFC). 16% of all full-time undergraduates had no need and received non-need-based gift aid.

GIFT AID (NEED-BASED) ***Total amount:*** $46,168,499 (92% federal, 7% state, 1% institutional). ***Receiving aid:*** Freshmen: 23% (939); all full-time undergraduates: 37% (6,192). ***Average award:*** Freshmen: $4006; Undergraduates: $5035. ***Scholarships, grants, and awards:*** Federal Pell, FSEOG, state, private, college/university gift aid from institutional funds.

GIFT AID (NON-NEED-BASED) ***Total amount:*** $19,815,476 (83% institutional, 17% external sources). ***Receiving aid:*** Freshmen: 36% (1,482). Undergraduates: 29% (4,839). ***Average award:*** Freshmen: $2854. Undergraduates: $3235. ***Scholarships, grants, and awards by category:*** *Academic interests/achievement:* agriculture, architecture, biological sciences, business, communication, computer science, education, engineering/technologies, English, foreign languages, general academic interests/achievements, health fields, home economics, humanities, international studies, library science, mathematics, physical sciences, premedicine, social sciences. *Creative arts/performance:* applied art and design, art/fine arts, general creative arts/performance, journalism/publications, music, performing arts, theater/drama. *Special achievements/activities:* leadership. *Special characteristics:* children and siblings of alumni, children of faculty/staff, international students, local/state students, members of minority groups, religious affiliation. ***Tuition waivers:*** Full or partial for minority students, children of alumni, employees or children of employees, adult students, senior citizens. ***ROTC:*** Army, Air Force.

LOANS ***Student loans:*** $98,780,085 (49% need-based, 51% non-need-based). 44% of past graduating class borrowed through all loan programs. *Average indebtedness per student:* $21,171. ***Average need-based loan:*** Freshmen: $3160. Undergraduates: $4338. ***Parent loans:*** $1,883,194 (100% non-need-based). ***Programs:*** Federal Direct (Subsidized and Unsubsidized Stafford, PLUS), state, college/university.

WORK-STUDY ***Federal work-study:*** Total amount: $797,532; 358 jobs averaging $3800. ***State or other work-study/employment:*** Total amount: $889,557 (100% need-based). 120 part-time jobs averaging $3800.

ATHLETIC AWARDS Total amount: $3,907,769 (100% non-need-based).

APPLYING FOR FINANCIAL AID ***Required financial aid form:*** FAFSA. ***Financial aid deadline:*** Continuous. ***Notification date:*** Continuous. Students must reply within 4 weeks of notification.

CONTACT Financial Aid Office, Utah State University, Old Main Hill, Logan, UT 84322, 435-797-1000 or toll-free 800-488-8108.
Website: http://www.usu.edu/.

UTAH VALLEY UNIVERSITY

Orem, UT

Tuition & fees: N/R	Average undergraduate aid package: $8019

ABOUT THE INSTITUTION State-supported, coed. ***Awards:*** certificates, diplomas, associate, bachelor's, and master's degrees. 83 undergraduate majors. ***Total enrollment:*** 41,728. Undergraduates: 41,186. Freshmen: 4,764. Federal methodology is used as a basis for awarding need-based institutional aid.

FRESHMAN FINANCIAL AID (Fall 2019, est.) 2402 applied for aid; of those 69% were deemed to have need. 97% of freshmen with need received aid; of those 15% had need fully met. ***Average percent of need met:*** 69% (excluding resources awarded to replace EFC). ***Average financial aid package:*** $7840 (excluding resources awarded to replace EFC). 5% of all full-time freshmen had no need and received non-need-based gift aid.

UNDERGRADUATE FINANCIAL AID (Fall 2019, est.) 12,748 applied for aid; of those 85% were deemed to have need. 98% of undergraduates with need received aid; of those 8% had need fully met. ***Average percent of need met:*** 63% (excluding resources awarded to replace EFC). ***Average financial aid package:*** $8019 (excluding resources awarded to replace EFC). 3% of all full-time undergraduates had no need and received non-need-based gift aid.

GIFT AID (NEED-BASED) ***Total amount:*** $64,762,538 (87% federal, 2% state, 10% institutional, 1% external sources). ***Receiving aid:*** Freshmen: 30% (1,078); all full-time undergraduates: 44% (8,180). ***Average award:*** Freshmen: $5234; Undergraduates: $5344. ***Scholarships, grants, and awards:*** Federal Pell, FSEOG, state, private, college/university gift aid from institutional funds.

GIFT AID (NON-NEED-BASED) ***Total amount:*** $6,634,455 (8% state, 76% institutional, 16% external sources). ***Receiving aid:*** Freshmen: 16% (591). Undergraduates: 13% (2,357). ***Average award:*** Freshmen: $6607. Undergraduates: $6149. ***ROTC:*** Army, Air Force cooperative.

LOANS ***Student loans:*** $91,368,724 (78% need-based, 22% non-need-based). 45% of past graduating class borrowed through all loan programs. *Average indebtedness per student:* $22,424. ***Average need-based loan:*** Freshmen: $2041. Undergraduates: $2704. ***Parent loans:*** $704,658 (57% need-based, 43% non-need-based). ***Programs:*** Federal Direct (Subsidized and Unsubsidized Stafford, PLUS), Perkins.

WORK-STUDY ***Federal work-study:*** Total amount: $1,598,368; jobs available. ***State or other work-study/employment:*** Part-time jobs available.

ATHLETIC AWARDS Total amount: $2,834,078 (37% need-based, 63% non-need-based).

APPLYING FOR FINANCIAL AID ***Required financial aid form:*** FAFSA. ***Financial aid deadline:*** Continuous. ***Notification date:*** Continuous beginning 1/1.

CONTACT John Curl, Director of Financial Aid and Scholarships, Utah Valley University, 800 West University Parkway, Orem, UT 84058, 801-863-8442. *Fax:* 801-863-8448. *E-mail:* jcurl@uvu.edu.
Website: http://www.uvu.edu/.

U.T.A. MESIVTA OF KIRYAS JOEL
Monroe, NY

CONTACT Financial Aid Office, U.T.A. Mesivta of Kiryas Joel, 48 Bakertown Road, Suite 501, Monroe, NY 10950, 845-783-9901.

UTICA COLLEGE
Utica, NY

Tuition & fees: $22,110	Average undergraduate aid package: $14,855

ABOUT THE INSTITUTION Independent, coed. ***Awards:*** certificates, bachelor's, master's, and doctoral degrees. 48 undergraduate majors. ***Total enrollment:*** 4,947. Undergraduates: 3,488. Freshmen: 515. Federal methodology is used as a basis for awarding need-based institutional aid.

UNDERGRADUATE EXPENSES for 2019–2020 ***Application fee:*** $40. ***Comprehensive fee:*** $33,780 includes full-time tuition ($21,560), mandatory fees ($550), and room and board ($11,670). Full-time tuition and fees vary according to course load, degree level, and location. Room and board charges vary according to board plan. ***Part-time tuition:*** $718 per credit hour. ***Part-time fees:*** $50 per term. Part-time tuition and fees vary according to course load, degree level, and location.

FRESHMAN FINANCIAL AID (Fall 2019, est.) 496 applied for aid; of those 88% were deemed to have need. 100% of freshmen with need received aid; of those 8% had need fully met. ***Average percent of need met:*** 63% (excluding resources awarded to replace EFC). ***Average financial aid package:*** $16,783 (excluding resources awarded to replace EFC). 14% of all full-time freshmen had no need and received non-need-based gift aid.

UNDERGRADUATE FINANCIAL AID (Fall 2019, est.) 2,590 applied for aid; of those 89% were deemed to have need. 99% of undergraduates with need received aid; of those 9% had need fully met. ***Average percent of need met:*** 47% (excluding resources awarded to replace EFC). ***Average financial aid package:*** $14,855 (excluding resources awarded to replace EFC). 10% of all full-time undergraduates had no need and received non-need-based gift aid.

GIFT AID (NEED-BASED) ***Receiving aid:*** Freshmen: 83% (428); all full-time undergraduates: 69% (1,947). ***Average award:*** Freshmen: $6876; Undergraduates: $5588. ***Scholarships, grants, and awards:*** Federal Pell, FSEOG, state, private, college/university gift aid from institutional funds.

GIFT AID (NON-NEED-BASED) ***Receiving aid:*** Freshmen: 11% (56). Undergraduates: 8% (238). ***Average award:*** Freshmen: $4713. Undergraduates: $4808. ***Scholarships, grants, and awards by category:*** *Academic interests/achievement:* general academic interests/achievements. ***Tuition waivers:*** Full or partial for employees or children of employees. ***ROTC:*** Army, Air Force cooperative.

LOANS ***Student loans:*** 83% of past graduating class borrowed through all loan programs. *Average indebtedness per student:* $30,402. ***Average need-based loan:*** Freshmen: $3390. Undergraduates: $4511. ***Programs:*** Federal Direct (Subsidized and Unsubsidized Stafford, PLUS), Perkins.

WORK-STUDY Federal work-study jobs available. ***State or other work-study/employment:*** Part-time jobs available.

APPLYING FOR FINANCIAL AID ***Required financial aid form:*** FAFSA. ***Notification date:*** Continuous. Students must reply within 4 weeks of notification.

CONTACT Ms. Karolina Holl, Director of Financial Aid, Utica College, 1600 Burrstone Road, Utica, NY 13502-4892, 315-792-3179 or toll-free 800-782-8884. *Fax:* 315-792-3368. *E-mail:* kmholl@utica.edu.
Website: http://www.utica.edu/.

VALDOSTA STATE UNIVERSITY
Valdosta, GA

Tuition & fees (area res): $6583	Average undergraduate aid package: $15,913

ABOUT THE INSTITUTION State-supported, coed. ***Awards:*** certificates, associate, bachelor's, master's, and doctoral degrees. 52 undergraduate majors. ***Total enrollment:*** 11,270. Undergraduates: 8,590. Freshmen: 1,657. Federal methodology is used as a basis for awarding need-based institutional aid.

UNDERGRADUATE EXPENSES for 2020–2021 ***Application fee:*** $40. ***Tuition, area resident:*** full-time $4371; part-time $182 per credit hour. ***Tuition, state resident:*** full-time $4371; part-time $182 per credit hour. ***Tuition, nonresident:*** full-time $15,426; part-time $643 per credit hour. ***Required fees:*** full-time $2212; $1106 per term. Full-time tuition and fees vary according to course load, degree level, location, program, and reciprocity agreements. Part-time tuition and fees vary according to course load, degree level, location, program, and reciprocity agreements. ***College room and board:*** $8332; ***Room only:*** $4330. Room and board charges vary according to board plan.

FRESHMAN FINANCIAL AID (Fall 2018) 1668 applied for aid; of those 84% were deemed to have need. 99% of freshmen with need received aid; of those 10% had need fully met. ***Average percent of need met:*** 91% (excluding resources awarded to replace EFC). ***Average financial aid package:*** $16,227 (excluding resources awarded to replace EFC). 3% of all full-time freshmen had no need and received non-need-based gift aid.

UNDERGRADUATE FINANCIAL AID (Fall 2018) 6,076 applied for aid; of those 87% were deemed to have need. 99% of undergraduates with need received aid; of those 11% had need fully met. ***Average percent of need met:*** 88% (excluding resources awarded to replace EFC). ***Average financial aid package:*** $15,913 (excluding resources awarded to replace EFC). 2% of all full-time undergraduates had no need and received non-need-based gift aid.

GIFT AID (NEED-BASED) ***Total amount:*** $40,615,492 (64% federal, 32% state, 2% institutional, 2% external sources). ***Receiving aid:*** Freshmen: 74% (1,238); all full-time undergraduates: 65% (4,447). ***Average award:*** Freshmen: $7518; Undergraduates: $6784. ***Scholarships, grants, and awards:*** Federal Pell, FSEOG, state, private, college/university gift aid from institutional funds, United Negro College Fund, Federal Nursing.

GIFT AID (NON-NEED-BASED) ***Total amount:*** $4,671,399 (1% federal, 83% state, 10% institutional, 6% external sources). ***Receiving aid:*** Freshmen: 4% (65). Undergraduates: 3% (193). ***Average award:*** Freshmen: $2782. Undergraduates: $2063. ***Scholarships, grants, and awards by category:*** *Academic interests/achievement:* biological sciences, communication, education, general academic interests/achievements, home economics, library science, mathematics, physical sciences, social sciences. *Creative arts/performance:* applied art and design, general creative arts/performance, journalism/publications, music, performing arts, theater/drama. *Special achievements/activities:* general special achievements/activities, religious involvement. *Special characteristics:* general special characteristics, local/state students, members of minority groups. ***Tuition waivers:*** Full or partial for employees or children of employees. ***ROTC:*** Air Force.

LOANS ***Student loans:*** $51,751,122 (82% need-based, 18% non-need-based). 80% of past graduating class borrowed through all loan programs. *Average indebtedness per student:* $27,058. ***Average need-based loan:*** Freshmen: $3353. Undergraduates: $4020. ***Parent loans:*** $45,488,856 (47% need-based, 53% non-need-based). ***Programs:*** Federal Direct (Subsidized and Unsubsidized Stafford, PLUS), state.

WORK-STUDY ***Federal work-study:*** Total amount: $398,001; jobs available. ***State or other work-study/employment:*** Part-time jobs available.

ATHLETIC AWARDS Total amount: $1,429,190 (51% need-based, 49% non-need-based).

APPLYING FOR FINANCIAL AID ***Required financial aid form:*** FAFSA. ***Financial aid deadline (priority):*** 4/1. ***Notification date:*** Continuous beginning 5/1.

CONTACT Mr. Douglas R. Tanner, Director of Financial Aid, Valdosta State University, 1500 North Patterson Street, Valdosta, GA 31698, 229-333-5935 or toll-free 800-618-1878. *Fax:* 229-333-5430.

Website: http://www.valdosta.edu/.

VALENCIA COLLEGE

Orlando, FL

ABOUT THE INSTITUTION State-supported, coed. ***Awards:*** certificates, diplomas, associate, and bachelor's degrees. 31 undergraduate majors. ***Total enrollment:*** 47,940. Undergraduates: 47,940. Freshmen: 9,066.

GIFT AID (NEED-BASED) ***Scholarships, grants, and awards:*** Federal Pell, FSEOG, state, private, college/university gift aid from institutional funds.

GIFT AID (NON-NEED-BASED) ***Scholarships, grants, and awards by category:*** *Creative arts/performance:* applied art and design, music, theater/drama. *Special achievements/activities:* community service, leadership.

LOANS ***Programs:*** Federal Direct (Subsidized and Unsubsidized Stafford, PLUS).

CONTACT Financial Aid Office, Valencia College, PO Box 3028, Orlando, FL 32802-3028, 407-299-5000.

Website: http://valenciacollege.edu/.

VALLEY CITY STATE UNIVERSITY

Valley City, ND

Tuition & fees (ND res): $7707	Average undergraduate aid package: $12,540

ABOUT THE INSTITUTION State-supported, coed. ***Awards:*** bachelor's and master's degrees. 37 undergraduate majors. ***Total enrollment:*** 1,665. Undergraduates: 1,524. Freshmen: 218. Federal methodology is used as a basis for awarding need-based institutional aid.

UNDERGRADUATE EXPENSES for 2019–2020 ***Application fee:*** $35. ***Tuition, state resident:*** full-time $5884; part-time $196 per semester hour. ***Tuition, nonresident:*** full-time $10,297; part-time $343 per semester hour. ***Required fees:*** full-time $1823; $75.96 per semester hour. Full-time tuition and fees vary according to course load and reciprocity agreements. Part-time tuition and fees vary according to course load and reciprocity agreements. ***College room and board:*** $6610; ***Room only:*** $2420. Room and board charges vary according to board plan and housing facility.

FRESHMAN FINANCIAL AID (Fall 2019, est.) 185 applied for aid; of those 64% were deemed to have need. 100% of freshmen with need received aid; of those 52% had need fully met. ***Average percent of need met:*** 83% (excluding resources awarded to replace EFC). ***Average financial aid package:*** $13,920 (excluding resources awarded to replace EFC). 37% of all full-time freshmen had no need and received non-need-based gift aid.

UNDERGRADUATE FINANCIAL AID (Fall 2019, est.) 657 applied for aid; of those 68% were deemed to have need. 99% of undergraduates with need received aid; of those 44% had need fully met. ***Average percent of need met:*** 78% (excluding resources awarded to replace EFC). ***Average financial aid package:*** $12,540 (excluding resources awarded to replace EFC). 22% of all full-time undergraduates had no need and received non-need-based gift aid.

GIFT AID (NEED-BASED) ***Receiving aid:*** Freshmen: 59% (118); all full-time undergraduates: 52% (407). ***Average award:*** Freshmen: $8049; Undergraduates: $6727. ***Scholarships, grants, and awards:*** Federal Pell, FSEOG, state, private, college/university gift aid from institutional funds.

GIFT AID (NON-NEED-BASED) ***Receiving aid:*** Freshmen: 8% (16). Undergraduates: 7% (52). ***Average award:*** Freshmen: $3255. Undergraduates: $3128. ***Scholarships, grants, and awards by category:*** *Academic interests/achievement:* biological sciences, business, communication, computer science, education, engineering/technologies, English, general academic interests/achievements, humanities, library science, mathematics, physical sciences, social sciences. *Creative arts/performance:* art/fine arts, music. *Special achievements/activities:* general special achievements/activities. *Special characteristics:* children and siblings of alumni, children of faculty/staff, ethnic background, general special characteristics, international students, members of minority groups. ***Tuition waivers:*** Full or partial for minority students, employees or children of employees, senior citizens.

LOANS ***Average need-based loan:*** Freshmen: $4155. Undergraduates: $5425. ***Programs:*** Federal Direct (Subsidized and Unsubsidized Stafford, PLUS), Perkins, Federal Work Study.

WORK-STUDY Federal work-study jobs available. ***State or other work-study/employment:*** Part-time jobs available.

APPLYING FOR FINANCIAL AID ***Required financial aid form:*** FAFSA. ***Financial aid deadline:*** Continuous. ***Notification date:*** Continuous. Students must reply within 4 weeks of notification.

CONTACT Ms. Marcia Lee Pritchert, Director of Student Financial Aid, Valley City State University, 101 College Street SW, Valley City, ND 58072, 701-845-7541 or toll-free 800-532-8641 Ext.7101. *Fax:* 701-845-7545. *E-mail:* marcia.pritchert@vcsu.edu.

Website: http://www.vcsu.edu/.

VALPARAISO UNIVERSITY

Valparaiso, IN

Tuition & fees: $43,286	Average undergraduate aid package: $32,990

ABOUT THE INSTITUTION Independent Lutheran Church, coed. ***Awards:*** certificates, associate, bachelor's, master's, and doctoral degrees. 96 undergraduate majors. ***Total enrollment:*** 3,519. Undergraduates: 3,009. Freshmen: 647. Both federal and institutional methodology are used as a basis for awarding need-based institutional aid.

UNDERGRADUATE EXPENSES for 2020–2021 ***Comprehensive fee:*** $55,906 includes full-time tuition ($41,940), mandatory fees ($1346), and room and board ($12,620). ***College room only:*** $7800. Full-time tuition and fees vary according to course load, program, and student level. Room and board charges vary according to board plan, housing facility, and student level. ***Part-time tuition:*** $1840 per credit hour. ***Part-time fees:*** $130 per term. Part-time tuition and fees vary according to course load, program, and student level.

FRESHMAN FINANCIAL AID (Fall 2018) 721 applied for aid; of those 88% were deemed to have need. 100% of freshmen with need received aid; of those 50% had need fully met. ***Average percent of need met:*** 94% (excluding resources awarded to replace EFC). ***Average financial aid package:*** $33,195 (excluding resources awarded to replace EFC). 15% of all full-time freshmen had no need and received non-need-based gift aid.

UNDERGRADUATE FINANCIAL AID (Fall 2018) 2,654 applied for aid; of those 91% were deemed to have need. 100% of undergraduates with need received aid; of those 45% had need fully met. ***Average percent of need met:*** 94% (excluding resources awarded to replace EFC). ***Average financial aid package:*** $32,990 (excluding resources awarded to replace EFC). 21% of all full-time undergraduates had no need and received non-need-based gift aid.

GIFT AID (NEED-BASED) ***Total amount:*** $57,998,984 (11% federal, 7% state, 81% institutional, 1% external sources). ***Receiving aid:*** Freshmen: 84% (632); all full-time undergraduates: 77% (2,410). ***Average award:*** Freshmen: $31,012; Undergraduates: $28,935. ***Scholarships, grants, and awards:*** Federal Pell, FSEOG, state, private, college/university gift aid from institutional funds.

GIFT AID (NON-NEED-BASED) ***Total amount:*** $24,773,916 (96% institutional, 4% external sources). ***Receiving aid:*** Freshmen: 21% (159). Undergraduates: 15% (462). ***Average award:*** Freshmen: $23,369. Undergraduates: $20,367. ***Scholarships, grants, and awards by category:*** *Academic interests/achievement:* 2,668 awards ($45,751,351 total): biological sciences, education, engineering/technologies, foreign languages, general academic interests/achievements, home economics, military science, physical sciences, social sciences. *Creative arts/performance:* 135 awards ($374,610 total): applied art and design, music, performing arts, theater/drama. *Special achievements/activities:* 42 awards ($439,800 total): religious involvement. *Special characteristics:* 504 awards ($374,610 total): children and siblings of alumni, children of faculty/staff, international students, relatives of clergy, religious affiliation. ***Tuition waivers:*** Full or partial for employees or children of employees. ***ROTC:*** Army cooperative, Air Force cooperative.

LOANS ***Student loans:*** $16,735,854 (80% need-based, 20% non-need-based). 72% of past graduating class borrowed through all loan programs. *Average indebtedness per student:* $35,968. ***Average need-based loan:*** Freshmen: $3426. Undergraduates: $4470. ***Parent loans:*** $4,679,323 (78% need-based, 22% non-need-based). ***Programs:*** Federal Direct (Subsidized and Unsubsidized Stafford, PLUS), college/university, private loans.

WORK-STUDY ***Federal work-study:*** Total amount: $697,132; 640 jobs averaging $2300. ***State or other work-study/employment:*** Total amount: $1,406,150 (48% need-based, 52% non-need-based). 1,248 part-time jobs averaging $1982.

ATHLETIC AWARDS Total amount: $4,939,959 (9% need-based, 91% non-need-based).

APPLYING FOR FINANCIAL AID ***Required financial aid form:*** FAFSA. ***Financial aid deadline (priority):*** 3/1. ***Notification date:*** Continuous beginning 1/10.

CONTACT Ms. Karen Klimczyk, Director of Financial Aid, Valparaiso University, 1700 Chapel Drive, Valparaiso, IN 46383-6493, 219-464-5015 or toll-free 888-GO-VALPO. *Fax:* 219-464-5012. *E-mail:* karen.klimczyk@valpo.edu.
Website: http://www.valpo.edu/.

VANDERBILT UNIVERSITY

Nashville, TN

Tuition & fees: $55,032 | **Average undergraduate aid package: $54,138**

ABOUT THE INSTITUTION Independent, coed. ***Awards:*** bachelor's, master's, and doctoral degrees. 70 undergraduate majors. ***Total enrollment:*** 13,131. Undergraduates: 6,886. Freshmen: 1,604. Both federal and institutional methodology are used as a basis for awarding need-based institutional aid.

UNDERGRADUATE EXPENSES for 2020–2021 ***Application fee:*** $50. ***Comprehensive fee:*** $72,702 includes full-time tuition ($52,781), mandatory fees ($2251), and room and board ($17,670). ***College room only:*** $11,540. Room and board charges vary according to board plan. ***Part-time tuition:*** $2199 per credit hour. ***Payment plan:*** Tuition prepayment.

FRESHMAN FINANCIAL AID (Fall 2019, est.) 1030 applied for aid; of those 77% were deemed to have need. 100% of freshmen with need received aid; of those 100% had need fully met. ***Average percent of need met:*** 100% (excluding resources awarded to replace EFC). ***Average financial aid package:*** $56,739 (excluding resources awarded to replace EFC). 10% of all full-time freshmen had no need and received non-need-based gift aid.

UNDERGRADUATE FINANCIAL AID (Fall 2019, est.) 3,807 applied for aid; of those 88% were deemed to have need. 100% of undergraduates with need received aid; of those 100% had need fully met. ***Average percent of need met:*** 100% (excluding resources awarded to replace EFC). ***Average financial aid package:*** $54,138 (excluding resources awarded to replace EFC). 10% of all full-time undergraduates had no need and received non-need-based gift aid.

GIFT AID (NEED-BASED) ***Total amount:*** $167,021,750 (5% federal, 1% state, 93% institutional, 1% external sources). ***Receiving aid:*** Freshmen: 49% (782); all full-time undergraduates: 49% (3,312). ***Average award:*** Freshmen: $54,417; Undergraduates: $52,242. ***Scholarships, grants, and awards:*** Federal Pell, FSEOG, state, private, college/university gift aid from institutional funds, United Negro College Fund.

GIFT AID (NON-NEED-BASED) ***Total amount:*** $24,936,083 (11% federal, 3% state, 80% institutional, 6% external sources). ***Receiving aid:*** Freshmen: 5% (80). Undergraduates: 2% (156). ***Average award:*** Freshmen: $18,722. Undergraduates: $25,480. ***Scholarships, grants, and awards by category:*** *Academic interests/achievement:* general academic interests/achievements. *Creative arts/performance:* general creative arts/performance, music, performing arts. *Special achievements/activities:* community service, general special achievements/activities, leadership. *Special characteristics:* general special characteristics, international students, local/state students, members of minority groups, veterans. ***Tuition waivers:*** Full or partial for employees or children of employees. ***ROTC:*** Army, Naval, Air Force cooperative.

LOANS ***Student loans:*** $7,691,108 (17% need-based, 83% non-need-based). 22% of past graduating class borrowed through all loan programs. *Average indebtedness per student:* $22,727. ***Average need-based loan:*** Freshmen: $2848. Undergraduates: $3436. ***Parent loans:*** $6,528,374 (100% non-need-based). ***Programs:*** Federal Direct (Subsidized and Unsubsidized Stafford, PLUS), Federal Nursing.

WORK-STUDY ***Federal work-study:*** Total amount: $4,105,144; jobs available. ***State or other work-study/employment:*** Total amount: $907,484 (100% need-based). Part-time jobs available.

ATHLETIC AWARDS Total amount: $14,379,419 (33% need-based, 67% non-need-based).

APPLYING FOR FINANCIAL AID ***Required financial aid forms:*** FAFSA, CSS Financial Aid PROFILE. ***Financial aid deadline (priority):*** 2/1. ***Notification date:*** 4/1. Students must reply by 5/1.

CONTACT Mr. Brent Tener, Director of Financial Aid, Vanderbilt University, 2309 West End Avenue, Nashville, TN 37203, 615-322-3591 or toll-free 800-288-0432. *Fax:* 615-343-8512. *E-mail:* b.tener@vanderbilt.edu.
Website: http://www.vanderbilt.edu/.

VANDERCOOK COLLEGE OF MUSIC

Chicago, IL

Tuition & fees: N/R | **Average undergraduate aid package: $17,617**

ABOUT THE INSTITUTION Independent, coed. ***Awards:*** bachelor's and master's degrees. 1 undergraduate major. ***Total enrollment:*** 289. Undergraduates: 107. Freshmen: 18. Federal methodology is used as a basis for awarding need-based institutional aid.

FRESHMAN FINANCIAL AID (Fall 2019, est.) 12 applied for aid; of those 100% were deemed to have need. 100% of freshmen with need received aid. ***Average financial aid package:*** $13,888 (excluding resources awarded to replace EFC). 24% of all full-time freshmen had no need and received non-need-based gift aid.

UNDERGRADUATE FINANCIAL AID (Fall 2019, est.) 55 applied for aid; of those 96% were deemed to have need. 100% of undergraduates with need received aid. ***Average financial aid package:*** $17,617 (excluding resources awarded to replace EFC). 16% of all full-time undergraduates had no need and received non-need-based gift aid.

GIFT AID (NEED-BASED) ***Total amount:*** $307,962 (54% federal, 42% state, 4% institutional). ***Receiving aid:*** Freshmen: 53% (9); all full-time undergraduates: 53% (39). ***Average award:*** Freshmen: $1535; Undergraduates: $2175. ***Scholarships, grants, and awards:*** Federal Pell, FSEOG, state, private, college/university gift aid from institutional funds.

GIFT AID (NON-NEED-BASED) ***Total amount:*** $637,300 (3% federal, 5% state, 89% institutional, 3% external sources). ***Receiving aid:*** Freshmen: 71% (12). Undergraduates: 73% (53). ***Average award:*** Freshmen: $9030. Undergraduates: $8100. ***Scholarships, grants, and awards by category:*** *Academic interests/achievement:* education, general academic interests/achievements. *Creative arts/performance:* music. *Special characteristics:* ethnic background, out-of-state students, religious affiliation.

LOANS ***Student loans:*** $494,143 (37% need-based, 63% non-need-based). 91% of past graduating class borrowed through all loan programs. *Average indebtedness per student:* $46,917. ***Average need-based loan:*** Freshmen: $3278. Undergraduates: $4198. ***Parent loans:*** $282,347 (100% non-need-based). ***Programs:*** Federal Direct (Subsidized and Unsubsidized Stafford, PLUS).

WORK-STUDY ***Federal work-study:*** Total amount: $11,065; jobs available. ***State or other work-study/employment:*** Part-time jobs available.

APPLYING FOR FINANCIAL AID ***Required financial aid form:*** FAFSA. ***Financial aid deadline (priority):*** 12/1. ***Notification date:*** Continuous.

CONTACT Ms. Sirena Covington, Director of Financial Aid, VanderCook College of Music, 3140 South Federal Street, Chicago, IL 60616, 312-788-1146. *Fax:* 312-225-5211. *E-mail:* scovington@vandercook.edu.
Website: http://www.vandercook.edu/.

VANGUARD UNIVERSITY OF SOUTHERN CALIFORNIA

Costa Mesa, CA

Tuition & fees: $36,550	Average undergraduate aid package: $15,700

ABOUT THE INSTITUTION Independent Assemblies of God, coed. ***Awards:*** certificates, associate, bachelor's, and master's degrees. 28 undergraduate majors. ***Total enrollment:*** 2,175. Undergraduates: 1,869. Freshmen: 485. Federal methodology is used as a basis for awarding need-based institutional aid.

UNDERGRADUATE EXPENSES for 2020–2021 ***Application fee:*** $45. ***One-time required fee:*** $170. ***Comprehensive fee:*** $48,772 includes full-time tuition ($35,850), mandatory fees ($700), and room and board ($12,222). ***College room only:*** $6792. ***Part-time tuition:*** $1495 per credit hour.

FRESHMAN FINANCIAL AID (Fall 2019, est.) 457 applied for aid; of those 100% were deemed to have need. 100% of freshmen with need received aid; of those 100% had need fully met. ***Average financial aid package:*** $16,874 (excluding resources awarded to replace EFC). 100% of all full-time freshmen had no need and received non-need-based gift aid.

UNDERGRADUATE FINANCIAL AID (Fall 2019, est.) 1,496 applied for aid; of those 99% were deemed to have need. 100% of undergraduates with need received aid; of those 100% had need fully met. ***Average financial aid package:*** $15,700 (excluding resources awarded to replace EFC). 95% of all full-time undergraduates had no need and received non-need-based gift aid.

GIFT AID (NEED-BASED) ***Total amount:*** $36,357,013 (12% federal, 18% state, 69% institutional, 1% external sources). ***Receiving aid:*** Freshmen: 59% (283); all full-time undergraduates: 54% (903). ***Average award:*** Freshmen: $8747; Undergraduates: $8283. ***Scholarships, grants, and awards:*** Federal Pell, FSEOG, state, private, college/university gift aid from institutional funds, United Negro College Fund.

GIFT AID (NON-NEED-BASED) ***Total amount:*** $1,141,504 (99% institutional, 1% external sources). ***Receiving aid:*** Freshmen: 41% (199). Undergraduates: 32% (533). ***Average award:*** Freshmen: $9832. Undergraduates: $8978. ***Scholarships, grants, and awards by category:*** *Academic interests/achievement:* general academic interests/achievements. *Creative arts/performance:* debating, music, theater/drama. *Special characteristics:* children of faculty/staff, religious affiliation. **ROTC:** Army cooperative, Air Force cooperative.

LOANS ***Student loans:*** $13,772,121 (100% need-based). 73% of past graduating class borrowed through all loan programs. *Average indebtedness per student:* $18,769. ***Parent loans:*** $4,778,912 (100% non-need-based). ***Programs:*** Federal Direct (Subsidized and Unsubsidized Stafford, PLUS).

WORK-STUDY ***Federal work-study:*** Total amount: $1,059,143; jobs available.

ATHLETIC AWARDS Total amount: $2,340,555 (100% non-need-based).

APPLYING FOR FINANCIAL AID ***Required financial aid form:*** FAFSA. ***Financial aid deadline (priority):*** 3/2. ***Notification date:*** Continuous.

CONTACT Financial Aid Office, Vanguard University of Southern California, 55 Fair Drive, Costa Mesa, CA 92626, 714-556-3610 or toll-free 800-722-6279. *Website:* http://www.vanguard.edu/.

VASSAR COLLEGE

Poughkeepsie, NY

Tuition & fees: $58,770	Average undergraduate aid package: $56,765

ABOUT THE INSTITUTION Independent, coed. ***Awards:*** bachelor's and master's degrees. 51 undergraduate majors. ***Total enrollment:*** 2,456. Undergraduates: 2,463. Freshmen: 685. Institutional methodology is used as a basis for awarding need-based institutional aid.

UNDERGRADUATE EXPENSES for 2019–2020 ***Application fee:*** $65. ***One-time required fee:*** $80. ***Comprehensive fee:*** $72,990 includes full-time tuition ($57,910), mandatory fees ($860), and room and board ($14,220). ***College room only:*** $10,030. Room and board charges vary according to housing facility. ***Part-time tuition:*** $6910 per unit.

FRESHMAN FINANCIAL AID (Fall 2019, est.) 498 applied for aid; of those 79% were deemed to have need. 99% of freshmen with need received aid; of those 100% had need fully met. ***Average percent of need met:*** 100% (excluding resources awarded to replace EFC). ***Average financial aid package:*** $56,675 (excluding resources awarded to replace EFC).

UNDERGRADUATE FINANCIAL AID (Fall 2019, est.) 1,715 applied for aid; of those 86% were deemed to have need. 99% of undergraduates with need received aid; of those 100% had need fully met. ***Average percent of need met:*** 100% (excluding resources awarded to replace EFC). ***Average financial aid package:*** $56,765 (excluding resources awarded to replace EFC).

GIFT AID (NEED-BASED) ***Total amount:*** $72,876,580 (5% federal, 1% state, 92% institutional, 2% external sources). ***Receiving aid:*** Freshmen: 56% (392); all full-time undergraduates: 57% (1,469). ***Average award:*** Freshmen: $51,824; Undergraduates: $50,451. ***Scholarships, grants, and awards:*** Federal Pell, FSEOG, state, private, college/university gift aid from institutional funds.

GIFT AID (NON-NEED-BASED) ***Total amount:*** $196,553 (100% federal). ***Tuition waivers:*** Full or partial for employees or children of employees.

LOANS ***Student loans:*** $5,177,556 (65% need-based, 35% non-need-based). 53% of past graduating class borrowed through all loan programs. *Average indebtedness per student:* $19,474. ***Average need-based loan:*** Freshmen: $4767. Undergraduates: $3331. ***Parent loans:*** $3,041,800 (100% non-need-based). ***Programs:*** Federal Direct (Subsidized and Unsubsidized Stafford, PLUS), college/university.

WORK-STUDY ***Federal work-study:*** Total amount: $3,825,373; jobs available. ***State or other work-study/employment:*** Total amount: $810,700 (100% need-based). Part-time jobs available.

APPLYING FOR FINANCIAL AID ***Required financial aid forms:*** FAFSA, CSS Financial Aid PROFILE, noncustodial (divorced/separated) parent's statement. ***Financial aid deadline:*** 2/1 (priority: 3/30). ***Notification date:*** Students must reply by 5/1.

CONTACT Mr. Michael T Albano, Director of Student Financial Services, Vassar College, 124 Raymond Avenue, Box 8, Poughkeepsie, NY 12604, 845-437-5320 or toll-free 800-827-7270. *Fax:* 845-437-5325. *E-mail:* malbano@vassar.edu. *Website:* http://www.vassar.edu/.

VAUGHN COLLEGE OF AERONAUTICS AND TECHNOLOGY

Flushing, NY

ABOUT THE INSTITUTION Independent, coed, primarily men. ***Awards:*** certificates, diplomas, associate, bachelor's, and master's degrees. 13 undergraduate majors. ***Total enrollment:*** 1,545. Undergraduates: 1,538. Freshmen: 313.

GIFT AID (NEED-BASED) ***Scholarships, grants, and awards:*** Federal Pell, FSEOG, state, private, college/university gift aid from institutional funds.

GIFT AID (NON-NEED-BASED) ***Scholarships, grants, and awards by category:*** *Academic interests/achievement:* computer science, education, engineering/technologies. *Special characteristics:* veterans.

LOANS ***Programs:*** Federal Direct (Subsidized and Unsubsidized Stafford, PLUS).

WORK-STUDY ***Federal work-study:*** Total amount: $34,236; jobs available. ***State or other work-study/employment:*** Part-time jobs available.

APPLYING FOR FINANCIAL AID ***Required financial aid forms:*** FAFSA, state aid form.

CONTACT Ms. Beatriz Novoa Cruz, Associate Vice President of Enrollment for Financial Aid, Vaughn College of Aeronautics and Technology, 86 01 23rd Avenue, Flushing, NY 11369, 866-682-8446 Ext. 100 or toll-free 866-6VAUGHN. *Fax:* 718-779-2231. *E-mail:* financialaid@vaughn.edu. *Website:* http://www.vaughn.edu/.

VERMONT TECHNICAL COLLEGE

Randolph Center, VT

Tuition & fees (VT res): $16,471	Average undergraduate aid package: $14,270

ABOUT THE INSTITUTION State-supported, coed. ***Awards:*** certificates, diplomas, associate, bachelor's, and master's degrees. 26 undergraduate majors. ***Total enrollment:*** 1,679. Undergraduates: 1,671. Freshmen: 202. Federal methodology is used as a basis for awarding need-based institutional aid.

UNDERGRADUATE EXPENSES for 2020–2021 ***Application fee:*** $47. ***Tuition, state resident:*** full-time $14,712; part-time $613 per credit. ***Tuition, nonresident:*** full-time $28,128; part-time $1172 per credit. ***Required fees:*** full-time $1759; $78 per term. Full-time tuition and fees vary according to course load, program, and reciprocity agreements. Part-time tuition and fees vary according to program. ***College room and board:*** $11,694; ***Room only:*** $7100. Room and board charges vary according to board plan and location.

FRESHMAN FINANCIAL AID (Fall 2019, est.) 198 applied for aid; of those 84% were deemed to have need. 100% of freshmen with need received aid; of those 6% had need fully met. ***Average percent of need met:*** 44% (excluding resources awarded to replace EFC). ***Average financial aid package:*** $12,000 (excluding resources awarded to replace EFC). 12% of all full-time freshmen had no need and received non-need-based gift aid.

UNDERGRADUATE FINANCIAL AID (Fall 2019, est.) 982 applied for aid; of those 90% were deemed to have need. 100% of undergraduates with need received aid; of those 3% had need fully met. ***Average percent of need met:*** 44% (excluding resources awarded to replace EFC). ***Average financial aid package:*** $14,270 (excluding resources awarded to replace EFC). 8% of all full-time undergraduates had no need and received non-need-based gift aid.

GIFT AID (NEED-BASED) ***Receiving aid:*** Freshmen: 61% (122); all full-time undergraduates: 61% (668). ***Average award:*** Freshmen: $5422; Undergraduates: $7060. ***Scholarships, grants, and awards:*** Federal Pell, FSEOG, state, private, college/university gift aid from institutional funds.

GIFT AID (NON-NEED-BASED) ***Receiving aid:*** Freshmen: 33% (66). Undergraduates: 21% (232). ***Average award:*** Freshmen: $4344. Undergraduates: $4624. ***Scholarships, grants, and awards by category:*** *Academic interests/achievement:* agriculture, computer science, engineering/technologies. ***Tuition waivers:*** Full or partial for employees or children of employees, senior citizens. ***ROTC:*** Army cooperative.

LOANS ***Student loans:*** 84% of past graduating class borrowed through all loan programs. *Average indebtedness per student:* $24,410. ***Average need-based loan:*** Freshmen: $3332. Undergraduates: $3868. ***Programs:*** Federal Direct (Subsidized and Unsubsidized Stafford, PLUS).

WORK-STUDY ***Federal work-study:*** 253 jobs averaging $1006.

APPLYING FOR FINANCIAL AID ***Required financial aid forms:*** FAFSA, state aid form. ***Notification date:*** Continuous.

CONTACT Catherine R. McCullough, Director of Financial Aid, Vermont Technical College, PO Box 500, Randolph Center, VT 05061-0500, 802-728-1248 or toll-free 800-442-VTC1. *Fax:* 802-728-1436.
Website: http://www.vtc.edu/.

VILLA MARIA COLLEGE
Buffalo, NY

ABOUT THE INSTITUTION Independent Roman Catholic Church, coed. ***Awards:*** certificates, associate, and bachelor's degrees. 20 undergraduate majors.

GIFT AID (NEED-BASED) ***Scholarships, grants, and awards:*** Federal Pell, FSEOG, state, private, college/university gift aid from institutional funds.

LOANS ***Programs:*** Federal Direct (Subsidized and Unsubsidized Stafford, PLUS), private loans.

CONTACT Aimee Murch, Director of Financial Aid, Villa Maria College, 240 Pine Ridge Road, Buffalo, NY 14225, 716-961-1828. *Fax:* 716-896-0705. *E-mail:* murcha@villa.edu.
Website: http://www.villa.edu/.

VILLANOVA UNIVERSITY
Villanova, PA

Tuition & fees: $55,280	Average undergraduate aid package: $42,523

ABOUT THE INSTITUTION Independent Roman Catholic, coed. ***Awards:*** certificates, bachelor's, master's, and doctoral degrees. 51 undergraduate majors. ***Total enrollment:*** 10,848. Undergraduates: 9,565. Freshmen: 1,695. Both federal and institutional methodology are used as a basis for awarding need-based institutional aid.

UNDERGRADUATE EXPENSES for 2020–2021 ***Application fee:*** $80. ***Comprehensive fee:*** $69,724 includes full-time tuition ($54,550), mandatory fees ($730), and room and board ($14,444). ***College room only:*** $7744. ***Part-time tuition:*** $3031 per credit hour.

FRESHMAN FINANCIAL AID (Fall 2019, est.) 1172 applied for aid; of those 71% were deemed to have need. 99% of freshmen with need received aid; of those 15% had need fully met. ***Average percent of need met:*** 80% (excluding resources awarded to replace EFC). ***Average financial aid package:*** $41,496 (excluding resources awarded to replace EFC). 4% of all full-time freshmen had no need and received non-need-based gift aid.

UNDERGRADUATE FINANCIAL AID (Fall 2019, est.) 3,838 applied for aid; of those 80% were deemed to have need. 99% of undergraduates with need received aid; of those 20% had need fully met. ***Average percent of need met:*** 80% (excluding resources awarded to replace EFC). ***Average financial aid package:*** $42,523 (excluding resources awarded to replace EFC). 8% of all full-time undergraduates had no need and received non-need-based gift aid.

GIFT AID (NEED-BASED) ***Total amount:*** $103,907,706 (5% federal, 1% state, 92% institutional, 2% external sources). ***Receiving aid:*** Freshmen: 45% (765); all full-time undergraduates: 43% (2,780). ***Average award:*** Freshmen: $38,201; Undergraduates: $37,187. ***Scholarships, grants, and awards:*** Federal Pell, FSEOG, state, private, college/university gift aid from institutional funds, endowed and restricted scholarships and grants.

GIFT AID (NON-NEED-BASED) ***Total amount:*** $15,358,473 (30% federal, 60% institutional, 10% external sources). ***Receiving aid:*** Freshmen: 3% (55). Undergraduates: 2% (128). ***Average award:*** Freshmen: $18,712. Undergraduates: $17,558. ***Scholarships, grants, and awards by category:*** *Academic interests/achievement:* general academic interests/achievements, international studies, military science. *Special achievements/activities:* general special achievements/activities. *Special characteristics:* children of educators, children of faculty/staff, general special characteristics, religious affiliation. ***ROTC:*** Army, Naval, Air Force cooperative.

LOANS ***Student loans:*** $36,140,876 (82% need-based, 18% non-need-based). 49% of past graduating class borrowed through all loan programs. *Average indebtedness per student:* $36,716. ***Average need-based loan:*** Freshmen: $3517. Undergraduates: $4634. ***Parent loans:*** $14,048,752 (79% need-based, 21% non-need-based). ***Programs:*** Federal Direct (Subsidized and Unsubsidized Stafford, PLUS), Federal Nursing.

WORK-STUDY ***Federal work-study:*** Total amount: $5,410,676; jobs available. ***State or other work-study/employment:*** Total amount: $163,579 (100% need-based). Part-time jobs available.

ATHLETIC AWARDS Total amount: $14,524,240 (28% need-based, 72% non-need-based).

APPLYING FOR FINANCIAL AID ***Required financial aid forms:*** FAFSA, CSS Financial Aid PROFILE, noncustodial (divorced/separated) parent's statement. ***Financial aid deadline:*** 1/15 (priority: 1/15). ***Notification date:*** 4/1. Students must reply by 5/1.

CONTACT Ms. Bonnie Lee Behm, Director of Financial Assistance, Villanova University, 800 Lancaster Avenue, Villanova, PA 19085-1699, 610-519-4010. *Fax:* 610-519-7599. *E-mail:* bonnie.behm@villanova.edu.
Website: http://www.villanova.edu/.

VIRGINIA BAPTIST COLLEGE
Fredericksburg, VA

CONTACT Financial Aid Office, Virginia Baptist College, 4111 Plank Road, Fredericksburg, VA 22407.
Website: http://www.vbc.edu/.

VIRGINIA COMMONWEALTH UNIVERSITY
Richmond, VA

Tuition & fees: N/R	Average undergraduate aid package: $12,486

ABOUT THE INSTITUTION State-supported, coed. ***Awards:*** certificates, bachelor's, master's, and doctoral degrees. 64 undergraduate majors. ***Total***

enrollment: 30,103. Undergraduates: 23,172. Freshmen: 4,461. Federal methodology is used as a basis for awarding need-based institutional aid.

FRESHMAN FINANCIAL AID (Fall 2018) 3865 applied for aid; of those 80% were deemed to have need. 96% of freshmen with need received aid; of those 5% had need fully met. ***Average percent of need met:*** 56% (excluding resources awarded to replace EFC). ***Average financial aid package:*** $13,491 (excluding resources awarded to replace EFC). 9% of all full-time freshmen had no need and received non-need-based gift aid.

UNDERGRADUATE FINANCIAL AID (Fall 2018) 14,671 applied for aid; of those 85% were deemed to have need. 95% of undergraduates with need received aid; of those 4% had need fully met. ***Average percent of need met:*** 51% (excluding resources awarded to replace EFC). ***Average financial aid package:*** $12,486 (excluding resources awarded to replace EFC). 8% of all full-time undergraduates had no need and received non-need-based gift aid.

GIFT AID (NEED-BASED) ***Total amount:*** $98,101,548 (33% federal, 30% state, 29% institutional, 8% external sources). ***Receiving aid:*** Freshmen: 59% (2,687); all full-time undergraduates: 48% (9,749). ***Average award:*** Freshmen: $11,740; Undergraduates: $10,512. ***Scholarships, grants, and awards:*** Federal Pell, FSEOG, state, private, college/university gift aid from institutional funds, United Negro College Fund, Federal Nursing.

GIFT AID (NON-NEED-BASED) ***Total amount:*** $22,848,568 (1% state, 33% institutional, 66% external sources). ***Receiving aid:*** Freshmen: 3% (120). Undergraduates: 2% (358). ***Average award:*** Freshmen: $7513. Undergraduates: $7995. ***ROTC:*** Army cooperative.

LOANS ***Student loans:*** 64% of past graduating class borrowed through all loan programs. *Average indebtedness per student:* $32,163. ***Average need-based loan:*** Freshmen: $3239. Undergraduates: $4205. ***Parent loans:*** $28,713,571 (52% need-based, 48% non-need-based). ***Programs:*** Federal Direct (Subsidized and Unsubsidized Stafford, PLUS), Perkins, Federal Nursing.

WORK-STUDY ***Federal work-study:*** Total amount: $2,102,032; 927 jobs averaging $2236. ***State or other work-study/employment:*** Total amount: $500 (100% non-need-based). 1 part-time job averaging $500.

ATHLETIC AWARDS Total amount: $6,080,680 (28% need-based, 72% non-need-based).

APPLYING FOR FINANCIAL AID ***Required financial aid forms:*** FAFSA, state aid form. ***Notification date:*** Continuous. Students must reply within 2 weeks of notification.

CONTACT Financial Aid Office, Virginia Commonwealth University, 901 West Franklin Street, Richmond, VA 23284-9005, 804-828-0100 or toll-free 800-841-3638. *Website:* http://www.vcu.edu/.

VIRGINIA INTERNATIONAL UNIVERSITY

Fairfax, VA

CONTACT Financial Aid Office, Virginia International University, 4401 Village Drive, Fairfax, VA 22030, 703-591-7042 or toll-free 800-514-6848. *Website:* http://www.viu.edu/.

VIRGINIA MILITARY INSTITUTE

Lexington, VA

ABOUT THE INSTITUTION State-supported, coed. ***Awards:*** bachelor's degrees. 14 undergraduate majors. ***Total enrollment:*** 1,685. Undergraduates: 1,685. Freshmen: 454.

GIFT AID (NEED-BASED) ***Scholarships, grants, and awards:*** Federal Pell, FSEOG, state, private, college/university gift aid from institutional funds.

GIFT AID (NON-NEED-BASED) ***Scholarships, grants, and awards by category:*** *Academic interests/achievement:* biological sciences, business, computer science, engineering/technologies, English, foreign languages, general academic interests/achievements, humanities, international studies, mathematics, military science, physical sciences, premedicine. *Creative arts/performance:* music. *Special achievements/activities:* general special achievements/activities. *Special characteristics:* children and siblings of alumni, general special characteristics, local/state students, out-of-state students.

LOANS ***Programs:*** Federal Direct (Subsidized and Unsubsidized Stafford, PLUS).

APPLYING FOR FINANCIAL AID ***Required financial aid forms:*** FAFSA, institution's own form.

CONTACT Capt. Brian Quisenerry, Director of Financial Aid, Virginia Military Institute, 302A Carroll Hall, Lexington, VA 24450, 540-464-7626 or toll-free 800-767-4207. *Fax:* 540-464-7629. *E-mail:* quisenberrybl@vmi.edu. *Website:* http://www.vmi.edu/.

VIRGINIA POLYTECHNIC INSTITUTE AND STATE UNIVERSITY

Blacksburg, VA

ABOUT THE INSTITUTION State-supported, coed. ***Awards:*** certificates, bachelor's, master's, and doctoral degrees. 80 undergraduate majors. ***Total enrollment:*** 34,850. Undergraduates: 27,793. Freshmen: 6,285.

GIFT AID (NEED-BASED) ***Scholarships, grants, and awards:*** Federal Pell, FSEOG, state, private, college/university gift aid from institutional funds, United Negro College Fund.

GIFT AID (NON-NEED-BASED) ***Scholarships, grants, and awards by category:*** *Academic interests/achievement:* general academic interests/achievements, library science. *Creative arts/performance:* applied art and design, art/fine arts, cinema/film/broadcasting, creative writing, journalism/publications, music, performing arts, theater/drama. *Special achievements/activities:* cheerleading/drum major, community service, general special achievements/activities, leadership, memberships, religious involvement. *Special characteristics:* children of faculty/staff, first-generation college students, local/state students, members of minority groups, out-of-state students, twins.

LOANS ***Programs:*** Federal Direct (Subsidized and Unsubsidized Stafford, PLUS), state, college/university.

CONTACT Ms. Beth Armstrong, Director of University Scholarships and Financial Aid, Virginia Polytechnic Institute and State University, Student Services Building, Suite 200, 800 Washington Street SW, Blacksburg, VA 24061, 540-231-5179. *Fax:* 540-231-9139. *E-mail:* finaid@vt.edu. *Website:* http://www.vt.edu/.

VIRGINIA STATE UNIVERSITY

Petersburg, VA

ABOUT THE INSTITUTION State-supported, coed. ***Awards:*** certificates, bachelor's, master's, and doctoral degrees. 31 undergraduate majors. ***Total enrollment:*** 4,713. Undergraduates: 4,165. Freshmen: 1,024.

GIFT AID (NEED-BASED) ***Scholarships, grants, and awards:*** Federal Pell, FSEOG, state, private, college/university gift aid from institutional funds, United Negro College Fund.

GIFT AID (NON-NEED-BASED) ***Scholarships, grants, and awards by category:*** *Academic interests/achievement:* biological sciences, computer science, engineering/technologies, mathematics, physical sciences, premedicine. *Creative arts/performance:* applied art and design, art/fine arts, dance, music, performing arts. *Special achievements/activities:* cheerleading/drum major, community service, hobbies/interests, leadership, religious involvement.

LOANS ***Programs:*** Federal Direct (Subsidized and Unsubsidized Stafford, PLUS), Perkins, college/university.

CONTACT Mrs. Sheila Allen, Scholarship Manager, Virginia State University, PO Box 9031, Petersburg, VA 23806-2096, 800-823-7214 or toll-free 800-871-7611. *Fax:* 804-524-6818. *E-mail:* finaid@vsu.edu. *Website:* http://www.vsu.edu/.

VIRGINIA UNION UNIVERSITY

Richmond, VA

ABOUT THE INSTITUTION Independent Baptist, coed. ***Awards:*** bachelor's, master's, and doctoral degrees. 35 undergraduate majors.

GIFT AID (NEED-BASED) ***Scholarships, grants, and awards:*** Federal Pell, FSEOG, state, private, college/university gift aid from institutional funds.

GIFT AID (NON-NEED-BASED) ***Scholarships, grants, and awards by category:*** *Academic interests/achievement:* general academic interests/achievements. *Creative arts/performance:* music. *Special characteristics:* children of faculty/staff.

LOANS ***Programs:*** Federal Direct (Subsidized and Unsubsidized Stafford).

WORK-STUDY ***Federal work-study:*** Total amount: $632,477; jobs available.

APPLYING FOR FINANCIAL AID ***Required financial aid forms:*** FAFSA, state aid form.

CONTACT Mrs. Keisha L Pope, Director of Financial Aid, Virginia Union University, 1500 North Lombardy Street, Richmond, VA 23220-1170, 804-257-5854 or toll-free 800-368-3227. *E-mail:* klpope@vuu.edu.
Website: http://www.vuu.edu/.

VIRGINIA UNIVERSITY OF LYNCHBURG

Lynchburg, VA

CONTACT Mrs. Charlene P. Scruggs, Financial Aid Director, Virginia University of Lynchburg, 2058 Garfield Avenue, Lynchburg, VA 24572, 434-528-5276. *Fax:* 434-455-5958. *E-mail:* cscruggs@vul.edu.
Website: http://www.vul.edu/.

VIRGINIA WESLEYAN UNIVERSITY

Virginia Beach, VA

Comprehensive fee: $10,338	Average undergraduate aid package: $25,553

ABOUT THE INSTITUTION Independent United Methodist, coed. ***Awards:*** certificates, bachelor's, and master's degrees. 51 undergraduate majors. ***Total enrollment:*** 1,487. Undergraduates: 1,387. Freshmen: 344. Institutional methodology is used as a basis for awarding need-based institutional aid.

UNDERGRADUATE EXPENSES for 2020–2021 ***Comprehensive fee:*** $10,338 includes mandatory fees ($900) and room and board ($10,338). ***Part-time tuition:*** $1500 per credit hour.

FRESHMAN FINANCIAL AID (Fall 2018) 313 applied for aid; of those 100% were deemed to have need. 100% of freshmen with need received aid; of those 11% had need fully met. ***Average percent of need met:*** 64% (excluding resources awarded to replace EFC). ***Average financial aid package:*** $26,515 (excluding resources awarded to replace EFC). 12% of all full-time freshmen had no need and received non-need-based gift aid.

UNDERGRADUATE FINANCIAL AID (Fall 2018) 1,120 applied for aid; of those 94% were deemed to have need. 99% of undergraduates with need received aid; of those 10% had need fully met. ***Average percent of need met:*** 62% (excluding resources awarded to replace EFC). ***Average financial aid package:*** $25,553 (excluding resources awarded to replace EFC). 15% of all full-time undergraduates had no need and received non-need-based gift aid.

GIFT AID (NEED-BASED) ***Receiving aid:*** Freshmen: 88% (313); all full-time undergraduates: 83% (1,037). ***Average award:*** Freshmen: $24,953; Undergraduates: $23,099. ***Scholarships, grants, and awards:*** Federal Pell, FSEOG, state, private, college/university gift aid from institutional funds.

GIFT AID (NON-NEED-BASED) ***Receiving aid:*** Freshmen: 12% (42). Undergraduates: 11% (142). ***Average award:*** Freshmen: $20,181. Undergraduates: $18,738. ***Scholarships, grants, and awards by category:*** *Academic interests/achievement:* general academic interests/achievements. *Special achievements/activities:* religious involvement. *Special characteristics:* children of faculty/staff, relatives of clergy, religious affiliation. ***ROTC:*** Army cooperative.

LOANS ***Student loans:*** 81% of past graduating class borrowed through all loan programs. *Average indebtedness per student:* $32,515. ***Average need-based loan:*** Freshmen: $6300. Undergraduates: $8181. ***Programs:*** Federal Direct (Subsidized and Unsubsidized Stafford, PLUS), Perkins, alternative loans.

WORK-STUDY ***Federal work-study:*** 193 jobs averaging $1013.

APPLYING FOR FINANCIAL AID ***Required financial aid forms:*** FAFSA, state aid form. ***Financial aid deadline:*** Continuous. ***Notification date:*** Continuous. Students must reply within 2 weeks of notification.

CONTACT Ms. Teresa C. Rhyne, Director of Financial Aid, Virginia Wesleyan University, 5817 Wesleyan Drive, Virginia Beach, VA 23502-5599, 757-4553345 or toll-free 800-737-8684. *E-mail:* finaid@vwu.edu.
Website: http://www.vwu.edu/.

VISIBLE MUSIC COLLEGE

Memphis, TN

CONTACT Financial Aid Office, Visible Music College, 200 Madison Avenue, Memphis, TN 38103, 901-381-3939.
Website: http://visible.edu/.

VITERBO UNIVERSITY

La Crosse, WI

CONTACT Terry Norman, Director of Financial Aid, Viterbo University, 900 Viterbo Drive, La Crosse, WI 54601-4797, 608-796-3900 or toll-free 800-VITERBO. *Fax:* 608-796-3050. *E-mail:* twnorman@viterbo.edu.
Website: http://www.viterbo.edu/.

VOORHEES COLLEGE

Denmark, SC

CONTACT Augusta L. Kitchen, Director of Financial Aid, Voorhees College, PO Box 678, Denmark, SC 29042, 803-703-7109 Ext. 7106 or toll-free 866-237-4570. *Fax:* 803-793-0831. *E-mail:* akitchen@voorhees.edu.
Website: http://www.voorhees.edu/.

WABASH COLLEGE

Crawfordsville, IN

Tuition & fees: $45,850	Average undergraduate aid package: $42,236

ABOUT THE INSTITUTION Independent, men only. ***Awards:*** bachelor's degrees. 27 undergraduate majors. ***Total enrollment:*** 867. Undergraduates: 867. Freshmen: 229. Federal methodology is used as a basis for awarding need-based institutional aid.

UNDERGRADUATE EXPENSES for 2020–2021 ***Application fee:*** $50. ***Comprehensive fee:*** $56,750 includes full-time tuition ($45,000), mandatory fees ($850), and room and board ($10,900). ***College room only:*** $5900. Room and board charges vary according to board plan, housing facility, and student level. ***Part-time tuition:*** $7500 per course. Part-time tuition and fees vary according to course load. ***Payment plan:*** Tuition prepayment.

FRESHMAN FINANCIAL AID (Fall 2019, est.) 213 applied for aid; of those 80% were deemed to have need. 100% of freshmen with need received aid; of those 77% had need fully met. ***Average percent of need met:*** 95% (excluding resources awarded to replace EFC). ***Average financial aid package:*** $42,606 (excluding resources awarded to replace EFC). 25% of all full-time freshmen had no need and received non-need-based gift aid.

UNDERGRADUATE FINANCIAL AID (Fall 2019, est.) 785 applied for aid; of those 84% were deemed to have need. 100% of undergraduates with need received aid; of those 78% had need fully met. ***Average percent of need met:*** 93% (excluding resources awarded to replace EFC). ***Average financial aid package:*** $42,236 (excluding resources awarded to replace EFC). 23% of all full-time undergraduates had no need and received non-need-based gift aid.

GIFT AID (NEED-BASED) ***Total amount:*** $22,551,094 (5% federal, 7% state, 86% institutional, 2% external sources). ***Receiving aid:*** Freshmen: 74% (169); all full-time undergraduates: 75% (652). ***Average award:*** Freshmen: $34,992; Undergraduates: $34,377. ***Scholarships, grants, and awards:*** Federal Pell, FSEOG, state, private, college/university gift aid from institutional funds, United Negro College Fund.

GIFT AID (NON-NEED-BASED) ***Total amount:*** $6,831,424 (96% institutional, 4% external sources). ***Receiving aid:*** Freshmen: 19% (43). Undergraduates: 12% (106). ***Average award:*** Freshmen: $29,109. Undergraduates: $27,499. ***Scholarships, grants, and awards by category:*** *Academic interests/achievement:* 836 awards ($19,107,295 total). *Creative arts/performance:* 30 awards ($84,000 total): art/fine arts, cinema/film/broadcasting, creative writing, journalism/publications, music, theater/drama. *Special achievements/activities:* 30 awards ($655,810 total): community service, leadership. *Special characteristics:* 10 awards ($420,911 total): children of faculty/staff. ***Tuition waivers:*** Full or partial for employees or children of employees. ***ROTC:*** Army cooperative.

LOANS ***Student loans:*** $6,082,049 (39% need-based, 61% non-need-based). 72% of past graduating class borrowed through all loan programs. *Average indebtedness per student:* $35,273. ***Average need-based loan:*** Freshmen: $3260. Undergraduates: $4436. ***Parent loans:*** $1,561,858 (20% need-based, 80% non-need-based). ***Programs:*** Federal Direct (Subsidized and Unsubsidized Stafford, PLUS).

WORK-STUDY ***Federal work-study:*** Total amount: $645,870; 223 jobs averaging $2896. ***State or other work-study/employment:*** Total amount: $816,400 (96% need-based, 4% non-need-based). 328 part-time jobs averaging $2925.

APPLYING FOR FINANCIAL AID ***Required financial aid form:*** FAFSA. ***Financial aid deadline (priority):*** 1/15. ***Notification date:*** Continuous beginning 12/15. Students must reply by 5/1 or within 2 weeks of notification.

CONTACT Ms. Alex Delonis, Director of Financial Aid, Wabash College, 410 West Wabash Avenue, PO Box 352, Crawfordsville, IN 47933-0352, 765-361-6375 or toll-free 800-345-5385. *Fax:* 765-361-6166. *E-mail:* financialaid@wabash.edu.
Website: http://www.wabash.edu/.

WAGNER COLLEGE

Staten Island, NY

Tuition & fees: N/R	Average undergraduate aid package: $32,161

ABOUT THE INSTITUTION Independent, coed. ***Awards:*** certificates, bachelor's, master's, and doctoral degrees. 38 undergraduate majors. ***Total enrollment:*** 2,211. Undergraduates: 1,762. Freshmen: 419. Federal methodology is used as a basis for awarding need-based institutional aid.

FRESHMAN FINANCIAL AID (Fall 2019, est.) 353 applied for aid; of those 86% were deemed to have need. 100% of freshmen with need received aid; of those 26% had need fully met. ***Average percent of need met:*** 75% (excluding resources awarded to replace EFC). ***Average financial aid package:*** $34,166 (excluding resources awarded to replace EFC). 16% of all full-time freshmen had no need and received non-need-based gift aid.

UNDERGRADUATE FINANCIAL AID (Fall 2019, est.) 1,296 applied for aid; of those 86% were deemed to have need. 100% of undergraduates with need received aid; of those 24% had need fully met. ***Average percent of need met:*** 69% (excluding resources awarded to replace EFC). ***Average financial aid package:*** $32,161 (excluding resources awarded to replace EFC). 24% of all full-time undergraduates had no need and received non-need-based gift aid.

GIFT AID (NEED-BASED) ***Total amount:*** $24,669,151 (6% federal, 4% state, 89% institutional, 1% external sources). ***Receiving aid:*** Freshmen: 74% (304); all full-time undergraduates: 67% (1,117). ***Average award:*** Freshmen: $19,232; Undergraduates: $23,781. ***Scholarships, grants, and awards:*** Federal Pell, FSEOG, state, private, college/university gift aid from institutional funds, Federal Nursing.

GIFT AID (NON-NEED-BASED) ***Average award:*** Freshmen: $19,298. Undergraduates: $21,861. ***Scholarships, grants, and awards by category:*** *Academic interests/achievement:* general academic interests/achievements. *Creative arts/performance:* music, theater/drama. *Special characteristics:* children of faculty/staff, siblings of current students, veterans, veterans' children. ***ROTC:*** Army cooperative.

LOANS ***Student loans:*** $14,953,879 (79% need-based, 21% non-need-based). ***Average need-based loan:*** Freshmen: $3389. Undergraduates: $4582. ***Parent loans:*** $6,248,842 (82% need-based, 18% non-need-based). ***Programs:*** Federal Direct (Subsidized and Unsubsidized Stafford, PLUS), Perkins, Federal Nursing, alternative loans.

WORK-STUDY ***Federal work-study:*** Total amount: $519,700; jobs available.

ATHLETIC AWARDS Total amount: $9,943,516 (48% need-based, 52% non-need-based).

APPLYING FOR FINANCIAL AID ***Required financial aid forms:*** FAFSA, state aid form. ***Financial aid deadline (priority):*** 1/15. ***Notification date:*** 3/1. Students must reply by 5/1 or within 3 weeks of notification.

CONTACT Ms. Theresa Weimer, Director of Financial Aid, Wagner College, One Campus Road, Staten Island, NY 10301, 718-390-3122 or toll-free 800-221-1010. *Fax:* 718-390-3203. *E-mail:* tweimer@wagner.edu.
Website: http://www.wagner.edu/.

WAKE FOREST UNIVERSITY

Winston-Salem, NC

Tuition & fees: $57,760	Average undergraduate aid package: $53,115

ABOUT THE INSTITUTION Independent, coed. ***Awards:*** certificates, bachelor's, master's, and doctoral degrees. 38 undergraduate majors. ***Total enrollment:*** 8,495. Undergraduates: 5,287. Freshmen: 1,360. Institutional methodology is used as a basis for awarding need-based institutional aid.

UNDERGRADUATE EXPENSES for 2020–2021 ***Application fee:*** $65. ***Tuition:*** full-time $56,722; part-time $2352 per credit hour. ***Required fees:*** full-time $1038. ***College room only:*** $9848.

FRESHMAN FINANCIAL AID (Fall 2019, est.) 601 applied for aid; of those 63% were deemed to have need. 100% of freshmen with need received aid; of those 100% had need fully met. ***Average percent of need met:*** 100% (excluding resources awarded to replace EFC). ***Average financial aid package:*** $53,585 (excluding resources awarded to replace EFC). 4% of all full-time freshmen had no need and received non-need-based gift aid.

UNDERGRADUATE FINANCIAL AID (Fall 2019, est.) 1,916 applied for aid; of those 79% were deemed to have need. 100% of undergraduates with need received aid; of those 100% had need fully met. ***Average percent of need met:*** 100% (excluding resources awarded to replace EFC). ***Average financial aid package:*** $53,115 (excluding resources awarded to replace EFC). 9% of all full-time undergraduates had no need and received non-need-based gift aid.

GIFT AID (NEED-BASED) ***Total amount:*** $66,983,765 (6% federal, 2% state, 90% institutional, 2% external sources). ***Receiving aid:*** Freshmen: 26% (360); all full-time undergraduates: 28% (1,462). ***Average award:*** Freshmen: $52,729; Undergraduates: $50,178. ***Scholarships, grants, and awards:*** Federal Pell, FSEOG, state, private, college/university gift aid from institutional funds, United Negro College Fund.

GIFT AID (NON-NEED-BASED) ***Total amount:*** $10,582,348 (17% federal, 63% institutional, 20% external sources). ***Receiving aid:*** Freshmen: 24% (325). Undergraduates: 19% (987). ***Average award:*** Freshmen: $23,129. Undergraduates: $13,288. ***Scholarships, grants, and awards by category:*** *Academic interests/achievement:* general academic interests/achievements. *Creative arts/performance:* applied art and design, general creative arts/performance. *Special achievements/activities:* leadership. *Special characteristics:* children and siblings of alumni, local/state students, religious affiliation. ***ROTC:*** Army.

LOANS ***Student loans:*** $17,067,368 (70% need-based, 30% non-need-based). 30% of past graduating class borrowed through all loan programs. *Average indebtedness per student:* $34,053. ***Average need-based loan:*** Freshmen: $3470. Undergraduates: $4312. ***Parent loans:*** $5,515,561 (67% need-based, 33% non-need-based). ***Programs:*** Federal Direct (Subsidized and Unsubsidized Stafford, PLUS), Perkins, state, college/university.

WORK-STUDY ***Federal work-study:*** Total amount: $1,836,168; jobs available. ***State or other work-study/employment:*** Part-time jobs available.

ATHLETIC AWARDS Total amount: $15,403,217 (32% need-based, 68% non-need-based).

APPLYING FOR FINANCIAL AID ***Required financial aid forms:*** FAFSA, CSS Financial Aid PROFILE, state aid form, noncustodial (divorced/separated) parent's statement. ***Financial aid deadline:*** 1/1 (priority: 1/1). ***Notification date:*** 4/1. Students must reply by 5/1 or within 4 weeks of notification.

CONTACT Bill Wells, Director of Student Financial Aid, Wake Forest University, PO Box 7246, Winston-Salem, NC 27109-7246, 336-758-5154. *Fax:* 336-758-4924. *E-mail:* financial-aid@wfu.edu.
Website: http://www.wfu.edu/.

WALDEN UNIVERSITY

Minneapolis, MN

CONTACT Office of Financial Aid, Walden University, 100 Washington South, Suite 900, Minneapolis, MN 55401, 800-444-6795 or toll-free 866-492-5336. *Fax:* 410-843-6211. *E-mail:* finaid@waldenu.edu.
Website: http://www.waldenu.edu/.

WALDORF UNIVERSITY

Forest City, IA

CONTACT Duane Polsdofer, Director of Financial Aid, Waldorf University, 106 South 6th Street, Forest City, IA 50436, 641-585-8120 or toll-free 800-292-1903. *Fax:* 641-585-8125. *E-mail:* polsdofed@waldorf.edu.
Website: http://www.waldorf.edu/.

WALLA WALLA UNIVERSITY

College Place, WA

Tuition & fees: $29,931	Average undergraduate aid package: $24,027

ABOUT THE INSTITUTION Independent Seventh-day Adventist, coed. ***Awards:*** certificates, associate, bachelor's, and master's degrees. 80 undergraduate majors. ***Total enrollment:*** 1,864. Undergraduates: 1,683. Freshmen: 423. Federal methodology is used as a basis for awarding need-based institutional aid.

UNDERGRADUATE EXPENSES for 2020–2021 ***Application fee:*** $40. ***Comprehensive fee:*** $38,307 includes full-time tuition ($28,908), mandatory fees ($1023), and room and board ($8376). ***College room only:*** $4554. ***Part-time tuition:*** $803 per credit hour.

FRESHMAN FINANCIAL AID (Fall 2018) 319 applied for aid; of those 77% were deemed to have need. 100% of freshmen with need received aid; of those 38% had need fully met. ***Average percent of need met:*** 96% (excluding resources awarded to replace EFC). ***Average financial aid package:*** $25,676 (excluding resources awarded to replace EFC). 35% of all full-time freshmen had no need and received non-need-based gift aid.

UNDERGRADUATE FINANCIAL AID (Fall 2018) 1,129 applied for aid; of those 83% were deemed to have need. 100% of undergraduates with need received aid; of those 35% had need fully met. ***Average percent of need met:*** 93% (excluding resources awarded to replace EFC). ***Average financial aid package:*** $24,027 (excluding resources awarded to replace EFC). 32% of all full-time undergraduates had no need and received non-need-based gift aid.

GIFT AID (NEED-BASED) ***Total amount:*** $17,146,212 (17% federal, 6% state, 62% institutional, 15% external sources). ***Receiving aid:*** Freshmen: 47% (182); all full-time undergraduates: 48% (705). ***Average award:*** Freshmen: $6917; Undergraduates: $6973. ***Scholarships, grants, and awards:*** Federal Pell, FSEOG, state, private, college/university gift aid from institutional funds, Federal Nursing.

GIFT AID (NON-NEED-BASED) ***Total amount:*** $8,865,229 (3% federal, 59% institutional, 38% external sources). ***Receiving aid:*** Freshmen: 63% (243). Undergraduates: 60% (872). ***Average award:*** Freshmen: $12,024. Undergraduates: $9971. ***Scholarships, grants, and awards by category:*** *Academic interests/achievement:* biological sciences, business, communication, education, engineering/technologies, English, foreign languages, general academic interests/achievements, humanities, mathematics, religion/biblical studies. *Creative arts/performance:* general creative arts/performance, music, theater/drama. *Special achievements/activities:* leadership. *Special characteristics:* children of faculty/staff, veterans.

LOANS ***Student loans:*** $9,201,358 (71% need-based, 29% non-need-based). 62% of past graduating class borrowed through all loan programs. *Average indebtedness per student:* $35,777. ***Average need-based loan:*** Freshmen: $4067. Undergraduates: $4771. ***Parent loans:*** $1,173,551 (16% need-based, 84% non-need-based). ***Programs:*** Federal Direct (Subsidized and Unsubsidized Stafford, PLUS), Perkins, Federal Nursing, college/university.

WORK-STUDY ***Federal work-study:*** Total amount: $1,828,930; jobs available. ***State or other work-study/employment:*** Total amount: $140,610 (100% need-based). Part-time jobs available.

APPLYING FOR FINANCIAL AID ***Required financial aid forms:*** FAFSA, institution's own form. ***Financial aid deadline (priority):*** 4/30. ***Notification date:*** Continuous beginning 2/15.

CONTACT Ms. Cassie Ragenovich, Director of Student Financial Services, Walla Walla University, 204 South College Avenue, College Place, WA 99324-1198, 509-527-2315 or toll-free 800-541-8900. *Fax:* 509-527-2556. *E-mail:* financial.aid@wallawalla.edu.
Website: http://www.wallawalla.edu/.

WALSH COLLEGE OF ACCOUNTANCY AND BUSINESS ADMINISTRATION

Troy, MI

Tuition & fees: $18,309	Average undergraduate aid package: $12,120

ABOUT THE INSTITUTION Independent, coed. ***Awards:*** certificates, bachelor's, and master's degrees. 6 undergraduate majors. Federal methodology is used as a basis for awarding need-based institutional aid.

UNDERGRADUATE EXPENSES for 2019–2020 ***Tuition:*** full-time $17,784; part-time $494 per credit hour. ***Required fees:*** full-time $525; $175 per term.

UNDERGRADUATE FINANCIAL AID (Fall 2019, est.) 31 applied for aid; of those 94% were deemed to have need. 100% of undergraduates with need received aid. ***Average percent of need met:*** 41% (excluding resources awarded to replace EFC). ***Average financial aid package:*** $12,120 (excluding resources awarded to replace EFC).

GIFT AID (NEED-BASED) ***Total amount:*** $2,484,062 (54% federal, 25% state, 21% institutional). ***Receiving aid:*** All full-time undergraduates: 37% (26). ***Average award:*** Undergraduates: $7267. ***Scholarships, grants, and awards:*** Federal Pell, FSEOG, state, private, college/university gift aid from institutional funds.

GIFT AID (NON-NEED-BASED) ***Scholarships, grants, and awards by category:*** *Academic interests/achievement:* business, computer science. *Special characteristics:* ethnic background, previous college experience, veterans, veterans' children. ***Tuition waivers:*** Full or partial for employees or children of employees.

LOANS ***Student loans:*** $4,997,500 (47% need-based, 53% non-need-based). ***Average need-based loan:*** Undergraduates: $5199. ***Programs:*** Federal Direct (Subsidized and Unsubsidized Stafford, PLUS), private education loans.

APPLYING FOR FINANCIAL AID ***Financial aid deadline:*** Continuous. ***Notification date:*** Continuous.

CONTACT Catherine Duff Elam, Financial Aid, Director, Walsh College of Accountancy and Business Administration, 3838 Livernois Road, Troy, MI 48083-9921, 248-823-1665 or toll-free 800-925-7401. *Fax:* 248-524-2520. *E-mail:* cberraho@walshcollege.edu.
Website: http://www.walshcollege.edu/.

WALSH UNIVERSITY

North Canton, OH

Tuition & fees: N/R	Average undergraduate aid package: $25,232

ABOUT THE INSTITUTION Independent Roman Catholic, coed. ***Awards:*** certificates, associate, bachelor's, master's, and doctoral degrees. 61 undergraduate majors. Federal methodology is used as a basis for awarding need-based institutional aid.

FRESHMAN FINANCIAL AID (Fall 2019, est.) 354 applied for aid; of those 69% were deemed to have need. 100% of freshmen with need received aid; of those 28% had need fully met. ***Average percent of need met:*** 72% (excluding resources awarded to replace EFC). ***Average financial aid package:*** $27,459 (excluding resources awarded to replace EFC). 18% of all full-time freshmen had no need and received non-need-based gift aid.

UNDERGRADUATE FINANCIAL AID (Fall 2019, est.) 1,540 applied for aid; of those 84% were deemed to have need. 100% of undergraduates with need received aid; of those 40% had need fully met. ***Average percent of need met:*** 74%

(excluding resources awarded to replace EFC). ***Average financial aid package:*** $25,232 (excluding resources awarded to replace EFC). 18% of all full-time undergraduates had no need and received non-need-based gift aid.

GIFT AID (NEED-BASED) ***Total amount:*** $14,321,281 (20% federal, 8% state, 72% institutional). ***Receiving aid:*** Freshmen: 62% (243); all full-time undergraduates: 79% (1,293). ***Average award:*** Freshmen: $12,942; Undergraduates: $11,298. ***Scholarships, grants, and awards:*** Federal Pell, FSEOG, state, private, college/university gift aid from institutional funds.

GIFT AID (NON-NEED-BASED) ***Total amount:*** $13,471,569 (1% federal, 99% institutional). ***Receiving aid:*** Freshmen: 62% (243). Undergraduates: 79% (1,293). ***Average award:*** Freshmen: $14,711. Undergraduates: $13,026. ***Scholarships, grants, and awards by category:*** *Academic interests/achievement:* biological sciences, business, communication, computer science, education, English, foreign languages, general academic interests/achievements, health fields, humanities, international studies, mathematics, physical sciences, premedicine, religion/biblical studies, social sciences. *Creative arts/performance:* music. *Special achievements/activities:* leadership, religious involvement. *Special characteristics:* children and siblings of alumni, children of faculty/staff, international students, local/state students, members of minority groups, out-of-state students, siblings of current students.

LOANS ***Student loans:*** $12,539,896 (58% need-based, 42% non-need-based). 88% of past graduating class borrowed through all loan programs. *Average indebtedness per student:* $27,993. ***Average need-based loan:*** Freshmen: $3322. Undergraduates: $6514. ***Parent loans:*** $396,008 (21% need-based, 79% non-need-based). ***Programs:*** Federal Direct (Subsidized and Unsubsidized Stafford, PLUS), state.

WORK-STUDY ***Federal work-study:*** Total amount: $200,466; jobs available. ***State or other work-study/employment:*** Total amount: $180,466 (100% non-need-based). Part-time jobs available.

ATHLETIC AWARDS Total amount: $414,206 (9% need-based, 91% non-need-based).

APPLYING FOR FINANCIAL AID ***Required financial aid forms:*** FAFSA, institution's own form. ***Financial aid deadline (priority):*** 5/1. ***Notification date:*** Continuous beginning 12/15. Students must reply by 5/1.

CONTACT Holly Van Gilder, Director of Financial Aid, Walsh University, 2020 East Maple NW, North Canton, OH 44720-3396, 330-490-7147 or toll-free 800-362-9846 (in-state), 800-362-8846 (out-of-state). *Fax:* 330-490-7372. *E-mail:* hvangilder@walsh.edu.
Website: http://www.walsh.edu/.

WARNER PACIFIC UNIVERSITY
Portland, OR

Tuition & fees: $18,660	Average undergraduate aid package: $16,839

ABOUT THE INSTITUTION Independent Church of God, coed. ***Awards:*** certificates, associate, bachelor's, and master's degrees. 32 undergraduate majors. Federal methodology is used as a basis for awarding need-based institutional aid.

UNDERGRADUATE EXPENSES for 2019–2020 ***Comprehensive fee:*** $28,680 includes full-time tuition ($18,000), mandatory fees ($660), and room and board ($10,020). ***College room only:*** $4140. Room and board charges vary according to board plan and housing facility. ***Part-time tuition:*** $750 per credit hour. ***Part-time fees:*** $330 per term. Part-time tuition and fees vary according to course load.

FRESHMAN FINANCIAL AID (Fall 2019, est.) 60 applied for aid; of those 75% were deemed to have need. 100% of freshmen with need received aid; of those 18% had need fully met. ***Average percent of need met:*** 65% (excluding resources awarded to replace EFC). ***Average financial aid package:*** $18,544 (excluding resources awarded to replace EFC). 18% of all full-time freshmen had no need and received non-need-based gift aid.

UNDERGRADUATE FINANCIAL AID (Fall 2019, est.) 379 applied for aid; of those 85% were deemed to have need. 100% of undergraduates with need received aid; of those 15% had need fully met. ***Average percent of need met:*** 62% (excluding resources awarded to replace EFC). ***Average financial aid package:*** $16,839 (excluding resources awarded to replace EFC). 6% of all full-time undergraduates had no need and received non-need-based gift aid.

GIFT AID (NEED-BASED) ***Receiving aid:*** Freshmen: 63% (38); all full-time undergraduates: 63% (241). ***Average award:*** Freshmen: $11,693; Undergraduates: $6762. ***Scholarships, grants, and awards:*** Federal Pell, FSEOG, state, private, college/university gift aid from institutional funds.

GIFT AID (NON-NEED-BASED) ***Receiving aid:*** Freshmen: 67% (40). Undergraduates: 57% (218). ***Average award:*** Freshmen: $4487. Undergraduates: $4095. ***Scholarships, grants, and awards by category:*** *Special achievements/activities:* 36 awards ($37,337 total): leadership. ***Tuition waivers:*** Full or partial for children of alumni, employees or children of employees. ***ROTC:*** Air Force cooperative.

LOANS ***Student loans:*** 69% of past graduating class borrowed through all loan programs. *Average indebtedness per student:* $30,774. ***Average need-based loan:*** Freshmen: $3339. Undergraduates: $4478. ***Programs:*** Federal Direct (Subsidized and Unsubsidized Stafford, PLUS).

WORK-STUDY ***Federal work-study:*** 270 jobs averaging $2408.

APPLYING FOR FINANCIAL AID ***Required financial aid form:*** FAFSA. ***Financial aid deadline:*** Continuous. ***Notification date:*** Continuous. Students must reply within 2 weeks of notification.

CONTACT Cynthia D. Pollard, Executive Director of Student Financial Services and Financial Aid, Warner Pacific University, 2219 Southeast 68th Avenue, Portland, OR 97215-4099, 503-517-1018 or toll-free 800-804-1510. *Fax:* 503-517-1352. *E-mail:* cpollard@warnerpacific.edu.
Website: http://www.warnerpacific.edu/.

WARNER UNIVERSITY
Lake Wales, FL

CONTACT Lorrie Steedley, Student Financial Services, Warner University, 13895 Highway 27, Lake Wales, FL 33859, 863-638-7202 or toll-free 800-309-9563. *Fax:* 863-638-7603. *E-mail:* financialaid@warner.edu.
Website: http://www.warner.edu/.

WARREN WILSON COLLEGE
Swannanoa, NC

CONTACT Financial Aid Office, Warren Wilson College, PO Box 9000, Asheville, NC 28815-9000, 828-771-2082 or toll-free 800-934-3536. *Fax:* 828-771-2030. *E-mail:* finaid@warren-wilson.edu.
Website: http://www.warren-wilson.edu/.

WARTBURG COLLEGE
Waverly, IA

Tuition & fees: $45,680	Average undergraduate aid package: $33,037

ABOUT THE INSTITUTION Independent Lutheran, coed. ***Awards:*** certificates, bachelor's, and master's degrees. 56 undergraduate majors. ***Total enrollment:*** 1,505. Undergraduates: 1,501. Freshmen: 398. Federal methodology is used as a basis for awarding need-based institutional aid.

UNDERGRADUATE EXPENSES for 2020–2021 ***Comprehensive fee:*** $55,272 includes full-time tuition ($43,500), mandatory fees ($2180), and room and board ($9592). ***College room only:*** $5492. Room and board charges vary according to board plan and housing facility. ***Part-time tuition:*** $2500 per course. ***Part-time fees:*** $130 per term. Part-time tuition and fees vary according to course load.

FRESHMAN FINANCIAL AID (Fall 2018) 433 applied for aid; of those 89% were deemed to have need. 100% of freshmen with need received aid; of those 28% had need fully met. ***Average percent of need met:*** 88% (excluding resources awarded to replace EFC). ***Average financial aid package:*** $32,857 (excluding resources awarded to replace EFC). 18% of all full-time freshmen had no need and received non-need-based gift aid.

UNDERGRADUATE FINANCIAL AID (Fall 2018) 1,270 applied for aid; of those 89% were deemed to have need. 100% of undergraduates with need received aid; of those 27% had need fully met. ***Average percent of need met:*** 86% (excluding resources awarded to replace EFC). ***Average financial aid package:***

$33,037 (excluding resources awarded to replace EFC). 21% of all full-time undergraduates had no need and received non-need-based gift aid.

GIFT AID (NEED-BASED) ***Total amount:*** $31,844,781 (6% federal, 8% state, 78% institutional, 8% external sources). ***Receiving aid:*** Freshmen: 82% (383); all full-time undergraduates: 78% (1,130). ***Average award:*** Freshmen: $29,051; Undergraduates: $28,182. ***Scholarships, grants, and awards:*** Federal Pell, FSEOG, state, private, college/university gift aid from institutional funds.

GIFT AID (NON-NEED-BASED) ***Total amount:*** $12,697,733 (1% federal, 77% institutional, 22% external sources). ***Receiving aid:*** Freshmen: 20% (93). Undergraduates: 17% (239). ***Average award:*** Freshmen: $26,576. Undergraduates: $25,743. ***Scholarships, grants, and awards by category:*** *Academic interests/achievement:* 1,548 awards ($24,666,303 total): biological sciences, business, communication, computer science, education, engineering/technologies, English, foreign languages, general academic interests/achievements, humanities, mathematics, physical sciences, premedicine, religion/biblical studies, social sciences. *Creative arts/performance:* 331 awards ($1,118,041 total): applied art and design, cinema/film/broadcasting, journalism/publications, music, performing arts, theater/drama. *Special achievements/activities:* 28 awards ($26,726 total): junior miss, leadership. *Special characteristics:* 702 awards ($4,919,322 total): children and siblings of alumni, children of faculty/staff, international students, previous college experience, religious affiliation, siblings of current students. ***Tuition waivers:*** Full or partial for employees or children of employees.

LOANS ***Student loans:*** $10,415,645 (62% need-based, 38% non-need-based). 81% of past graduating class borrowed through all loan programs. *Average indebtedness per student:* $39,559. ***Average need-based loan:*** Freshmen: $4903. Undergraduates: $5901. ***Parent loans:*** $2,382,503 (54% need-based, 46% non-need-based). ***Programs:*** Federal Direct (Subsidized and Unsubsidized Stafford, PLUS), Perkins, college/university, private loans.

WORK-STUDY ***Federal work-study:*** Total amount: $432,911; 503 jobs averaging $1226. ***State or other work-study/employment:*** Total amount: $1,094,648 (100% non-need-based). 482 part-time jobs averaging $1890.

APPLYING FOR FINANCIAL AID ***Required financial aid form:*** FAFSA. ***Financial aid deadline (priority):*** 3/1. ***Notification date:*** Continuous beginning 1/15. Students must reply within 2 weeks of notification.

CONTACT Ms. Jennifer Sassman, Director of Financial Aid, Wartburg College, 100 Wartburg Boulevard, PO Box 1003, Waverly, IA 50677-0903, 319-352-8262 or toll-free 800-772-2085. *Fax:* 319-352-8514. *E-mail:* jennifer.sassman@wartburg.edu. *Website:* http://www.wartburg.edu/.

WASHBURN UNIVERSITY

Topeka, KS

Tuition & fees: N/R	Average undergraduate aid package: $9919

ABOUT THE INSTITUTION City-supported, coed. ***Awards:*** certificates, associate, bachelor's, master's, and doctoral degrees. 87 undergraduate majors. ***Total enrollment:*** 6,691. Undergraduates: 5,873. Freshmen: 901. Federal methodology is used as a basis for awarding need-based institutional aid.

FRESHMAN FINANCIAL AID (Fall 2019, est.) 672 applied for aid; of those 66% were deemed to have need. 100% of freshmen with need received aid; of those 16% had need fully met. ***Average percent of need met:*** 34% (excluding resources awarded to replace EFC). ***Average financial aid package:*** $9958 (excluding resources awarded to replace EFC). 21% of all full-time freshmen had no need and received non-need-based gift aid.

UNDERGRADUATE FINANCIAL AID (Fall 2019, est.) 3,219 applied for aid; of those 68% were deemed to have need. 100% of undergraduates with need received aid; of those 13% had need fully met. ***Average percent of need met:*** 34% (excluding resources awarded to replace EFC). ***Average financial aid package:*** $9919 (excluding resources awarded to replace EFC). 17% of all full-time undergraduates had no need and received non-need-based gift aid.

GIFT AID (NEED-BASED) ***Total amount:*** $11,633,893 (70% federal, 4% state, 18% institutional, 8% external sources). ***Receiving aid:*** Freshmen: 36% (257); all full-time undergraduates: 36% (1,267). ***Average award:*** Freshmen: $5476; Undergraduates: $5355. ***Scholarships, grants, and awards:*** Federal Pell, FSEOG, state, private, college/university gift aid from institutional funds.

GIFT AID (NON-NEED-BASED) ***Total amount:*** $3,711,582 (4% state, 66% institutional, 30% external sources). ***Receiving aid:*** Freshmen: 44% (316). Undergraduates: 36% (1,292). ***Average award:*** Freshmen: $3175. Undergraduates: $3093. ***Scholarships, grants, and awards by category:*** *Academic interests/achievement:* biological sciences, business, communication, computer science, education, engineering/technologies, English, foreign languages, general academic interests/achievements, health fields, humanities, international studies, mathematics, physical sciences, premedicine, religion/biblical studies, social sciences. *Creative arts/performance:* art/fine arts, cinema/film/broadcasting, debating, general creative arts/performance, journalism/publications, music, performing arts, theater/drama. *Special achievements/activities:* cheerleading/drum major, community service, leadership. *Special characteristics:* adult students, children and siblings of alumni, children of faculty/staff, ethnic background, international students, local/state students. ***ROTC:*** Army, Naval cooperative, Air Force cooperative.

LOANS ***Student loans:*** $16,559,666 (64% need-based, 36% non-need-based). 61% of past graduating class borrowed through all loan programs. *Average indebtedness per student:* $21,941. ***Average need-based loan:*** Freshmen: $3319. Undergraduates: $4159. ***Parent loans:*** $2,807,721 (55% need-based, 45% non-need-based). ***Programs:*** Federal Direct (Subsidized and Unsubsidized Stafford, PLUS), college/university.

WORK-STUDY ***Federal work-study:*** Total amount: $1,018,830; jobs available. ***State or other work-study/employment:*** Total amount: $38,000 (100% need-based). Part-time jobs available.

ATHLETIC AWARDS Total amount: $2,586,956 (65% need-based, 35% non-need-based).

APPLYING FOR FINANCIAL AID ***Required financial aid form:*** FAFSA. ***Financial aid deadline:*** Continuous. ***Notification date:*** Continuous.

CONTACT Dawn Boman, Associate Director of Financial Aid, Washburn University, 1700 SW College Avenue, Topeka, KS 66621, 785-670-1151 or toll-free 800-332-0291. *Fax:* 785-670-1079. *E-mail:* dawn.boman@washburn.edu. *Website:* http://www.washburn.edu/.

WASHINGTON ADVENTIST UNIVERSITY

Takoma Park, MD

CONTACT Sharon Conway, Director of Student Financial Services, Washington Adventist University, 7600 Flower Avenue, Takoma Park, MD 20912, 301-891-4005 or toll-free 800-835-4212. *Fax:* 301-891-4167. *E-mail:* sconway@wau.edu. *Website:* http://www.wau.edu/.

WASHINGTON & JEFFERSON COLLEGE

Washington, PA

Tuition & fees: $49,338	Average undergraduate aid package: $40,457

ABOUT THE INSTITUTION Independent, coed. ***Awards:*** certificates, bachelor's, and master's degrees. 33 undergraduate majors. ***Total enrollment:*** 1,357. Undergraduates: 1,356. Freshmen: 351. Both federal and institutional methodology are used as a basis for awarding need-based institutional aid.

UNDERGRADUATE EXPENSES for 2019–2020 ***Application fee:*** $25. ***Comprehensive fee:*** $62,382 includes full-time tuition ($48,758), mandatory fees ($580), and room and board ($13,044). ***College room only:*** $7654. Room and board charges vary according to board plan and housing facility. ***Part-time tuition:*** $1220 per credit hour. ***Payment plan:*** Tuition prepayment.

FRESHMAN FINANCIAL AID (Fall 2019, est.) 275 applied for aid; of those 88% were deemed to have need. 100% of freshmen with need received aid; of those 22% had need fully met. ***Average percent of need met:*** 86% (excluding resources awarded to replace EFC). ***Average financial aid package:*** $42,656 (excluding resources awarded to replace EFC). 17% of all full-time freshmen had no need and received non-need-based gift aid.

UNDERGRADUATE FINANCIAL AID (Fall 2019, est.) 1,072 applied for aid; of those 92% were deemed to have need. 100% of undergraduates with need received aid; of those 19% had need fully met. ***Average percent of need met:*** 83% (excluding resources awarded to replace EFC). ***Average financial aid package:***

$40,457 (excluding resources awarded to replace EFC). 20% of all full-time undergraduates had no need and received non-need-based gift aid.

GIFT AID (NEED-BASED) ***Total amount:*** $33,897,244 (5% federal, 4% state, 89% institutional, 2% external sources). ***Receiving aid:*** Freshmen: 83% (242); all full-time undergraduates: 77% (956). ***Average award:*** Freshmen: $38,477; Undergraduates: $35,258. ***Scholarships, grants, and awards:*** Federal Pell, FSEOG, state, private, college/university gift aid from institutional funds, United Negro College Fund.

GIFT AID (NON-NEED-BASED) ***Total amount:*** $6,602,686 (99% institutional, 1% external sources). ***Receiving aid:*** Freshmen: 8% (24). Undergraduates: 30% (377). ***Average award:*** Freshmen: $30,666. Undergraduates: $26,942. ***Scholarships, grants, and awards by category:*** *Academic interests/achievement:* business, general academic interests/achievements, humanities. *Special characteristics:* children and siblings of alumni, children of faculty/staff, international students, local/state students, members of minority groups, veterans. ***Tuition waivers:*** Full or partial for employees or children of employees. ***ROTC:*** Army, Air Force cooperative.

LOANS ***Student loans:*** $8,179,096 (57% need-based, 43% non-need-based). 83% of past graduating class borrowed through all loan programs. *Average indebtedness per student:* $48,582. ***Average need-based loan:*** Freshmen: $2716. Undergraduates: $4559. ***Parent loans:*** $3,696,003 (99% need-based, 1% non-need-based). ***Programs:*** Federal Direct (Subsidized and Unsubsidized Stafford, PLUS), Perkins, college/university.

WORK-STUDY ***Federal work-study:*** Total amount: $1,076,157; jobs available. ***State or other work-study/employment:*** Total amount: $48,671 (100% non-need-based). Part-time jobs available.

APPLYING FOR FINANCIAL AID ***Required financial aid form:*** FAFSA. ***Notification date:*** Continuous.

CONTACT Ms. Charlene Bedillion, Director of Financial Aid, Washington & Jefferson College, 60 South Lincoln Street, Washington, PA 15301-4801, 724-503-1001 Ext. 6019 or toll-free 888-WANDJAY. *Fax:* 724-250-3340. *E-mail:* cbedillion@washjeff.edu. *Website:* http://www.washjeff.edu/.

WASHINGTON AND LEE UNIVERSITY

Lexington, VA

Tuition & fees: N/R	Average undergraduate aid package: $57,291

ABOUT THE INSTITUTION Independent, coed. ***Awards:*** bachelor's and doctoral degrees. 36 undergraduate majors. ***Total enrollment:*** 2,264. Undergraduates: 1,860. Freshmen: 462. Both federal and institutional methodology are used as a basis for awarding need-based institutional aid.

FRESHMAN FINANCIAL AID (Fall 2019, est.) 249 applied for aid; of those 84% were deemed to have need. 100% of freshmen with need received aid; of those 100% had need fully met. ***Average percent of need met:*** 100% (excluding resources awarded to replace EFC). ***Average financial aid package:*** $57,313 (excluding resources awarded to replace EFC). 7% of all full-time freshmen had no need and received non-need-based gift aid.

UNDERGRADUATE FINANCIAL AID (Fall 2019, est.) 903 applied for aid; of those 92% were deemed to have need. 100% of undergraduates with need received aid; of those 100% had need fully met. ***Average percent of need met:*** 100% (excluding resources awarded to replace EFC). ***Average financial aid package:*** $57,291 (excluding resources awarded to replace EFC). 8% of all full-time undergraduates had no need and received non-need-based gift aid.

GIFT AID (NEED-BASED) ***Receiving aid:*** Freshmen: 45% (208); all full-time undergraduates: 45% (833). ***Average award:*** Freshmen: $49,720; Undergraduates: $49,745. ***Scholarships, grants, and awards:*** Federal Pell, FSEOG, state, private, college/university gift aid from institutional funds.

GIFT AID (NON-NEED-BASED) ***Receiving aid:*** Freshmen: 23% (108). Undergraduates: 20% (371). ***Average award:*** Freshmen: $54,293. Undergraduates: $41,656. ***Scholarships, grants, and awards by category:*** *Academic interests/achievement:* 156 awards ($6,498,336 total): general academic interests/achievements. ***Tuition waivers:*** Full or partial for employees or children of employees. ***ROTC:*** Army cooperative.

LOANS ***Student loans:*** 32% of past graduating class borrowed through all loan programs. *Average indebtedness per student:* $22,415. ***Average need-based loan:*** Freshmen: $513. Undergraduates: $587. ***Programs:*** Federal Direct (Subsidized and Unsubsidized Stafford, PLUS), college/university.

WORK-STUDY ***Federal work-study:*** 226 jobs averaging $2000. ***State or other work-study/employment:*** 380 part-time jobs averaging $2000.

APPLYING FOR FINANCIAL AID ***Required financial aid forms:*** FAFSA, CSS Financial Aid PROFILE, noncustodial (divorced/separated) parent's statement, federal income tax form(s).

CONTACT Mr. James D. Kaster, Director of Financial Aid, Washington and Lee University, 204 West Washington Street, Lexington, VA 24450, 540-458-8720. *Fax:* 540-458-8614. *E-mail:* financialaid@wlu.edu. *Website:* http://www.wlu.edu/.

WASHINGTON COLLEGE

Chestertown, MD

Tuition & fees: $49,768	Average undergraduate aid package: $36,163

ABOUT THE INSTITUTION Independent, coed. ***Awards:*** bachelor's degrees. 34 undergraduate majors. ***Total enrollment:*** 1,288. Undergraduates: 1,342. Freshmen: 325. Institutional methodology is used as a basis for awarding need-based institutional aid.

UNDERGRADUATE EXPENSES for 2020–2021 ***Comprehensive fee:*** $62,490 includes full-time tuition ($48,678), mandatory fees ($1090), and room and board ($12,722). ***College room only:*** $6673. Room and board charges vary according to board plan, housing facility, and location. ***Part-time tuition:*** $2028 per credit hour. Part-time tuition and fees vary according to course load.

FRESHMAN FINANCIAL AID (Fall 2019, est.) 290 applied for aid; of those 85% were deemed to have need. 100% of freshmen with need received aid; of those 20% had need fully met. ***Average percent of need met:*** 85% (excluding resources awarded to replace EFC). ***Average financial aid package:*** $4167 (excluding resources awarded to replace EFC). 23% of all full-time freshmen had no need and received non-need-based gift aid.

UNDERGRADUATE FINANCIAL AID (Fall 2019, est.) 1,014 applied for aid; of those 86% were deemed to have need. 100% of undergraduates with need received aid; of those 17% had need fully met. ***Average percent of need met:*** 85% (excluding resources awarded to replace EFC). ***Average financial aid package:*** $36,163 (excluding resources awarded to replace EFC). 27% of all full-time undergraduates had no need and received non-need-based gift aid.

GIFT AID (NEED-BASED) ***Total amount:*** $25,201,929 (7% federal, 4% state, 88% institutional, 1% external sources). ***Receiving aid:*** Freshmen: 75% (245); all full-time undergraduates: 69% (867). ***Average award:*** Freshmen: $36,444; Undergraduates: $36,365. ***Scholarships, grants, and awards:*** Federal Pell, FSEOG, state, private, college/university gift aid from institutional funds.

GIFT AID (NON-NEED-BASED) ***Receiving aid:*** Freshmen: 14% (45). Undergraduates: 11% (133). ***Average award:*** Freshmen: $27,949. Undergraduates: $22,636. ***Scholarships, grants, and awards by category:*** *Academic interests/achievement:* general academic interests/achievements. *Creative arts/performance:* applied art and design, creative writing, music, performing arts, theater/drama. *Special characteristics:* 23 awards ($781,916 total): children of faculty/staff. ***Tuition waivers:*** Full or partial for employees or children of employees.

LOANS ***Student loans:*** $2,573,418 (100% need-based). 65% of past graduating class borrowed through all loan programs. *Average indebtedness per student:* $34,903. ***Average need-based loan:*** Freshmen: $3170. Undergraduates: $4091. ***Programs:*** Federal Direct (Subsidized and Unsubsidized Stafford, PLUS).

WORK-STUDY ***Federal work-study:*** Total amount: $300,107; 162 jobs averaging $1959.

APPLYING FOR FINANCIAL AID ***Required financial aid form:*** FAFSA. ***Financial aid deadline (priority):*** 3/1. ***Notification date:*** Continuous beginning 12/15. Students must reply by 5/1.

CONTACT Ms. Jennifer Runyon, Director of Student Financial Aid, Washington College, 300 Washington Avenue, Chestertown, MD 21620-1197, 410-810-7765 or toll-free 800-422-1782. *Fax:* 410-801-7160. *E-mail:* jrunyon2@washcoll.edu. *Website:* http://www.washcoll.edu/.

WASHINGTON STATE UNIVERSITY

Pullman, WA

Tuition & fees (WA res): $11,841 **Average undergraduate aid package: $13,167**

ABOUT THE INSTITUTION State-supported, coed. ***Awards:*** certificates, bachelor's, master's, and doctoral degrees. 112 undergraduate majors. ***Total enrollment:*** 21,259. Undergraduates: 18,629. Freshmen: 4,193. Federal methodology is used as a basis for awarding need-based institutional aid.

UNDERGRADUATE EXPENSES for 2019–2020 ***Application fee:*** $50. ***Tuition, state resident:*** full-time $9953; part-time $526 per credit. ***Tuition, nonresident:*** full-time $24,531; part-time $1254 per credit. ***Required fees:*** full-time $1888. Full-time tuition and fees vary according to course load, location, and reciprocity agreements. Part-time tuition and fees vary according to course load, location, and reciprocity agreements. ***College room and board:*** $11,648; ***Room only:*** $7150. Room and board charges vary according to board plan, housing facility, and location.

FRESHMAN FINANCIAL AID (Fall 2018) 4263 applied for aid; of those 69% were deemed to have need. 97% of freshmen with need received aid; of those 15% had need fully met. ***Average percent of need met:*** 64% (excluding resources awarded to replace EFC). ***Average financial aid package:*** $13,160 (excluding resources awarded to replace EFC). 29% of all full-time freshmen had no need and received non-need-based gift aid.

UNDERGRADUATE FINANCIAL AID (Fall 2018) 17,007 applied for aid; of those 78% were deemed to have need. 96% of undergraduates with need received aid; of those 12% had need fully met. ***Average percent of need met:*** 64% (excluding resources awarded to replace EFC). ***Average financial aid package:*** $13,167 (excluding resources awarded to replace EFC). 20% of all full-time undergraduates had no need and received non-need-based gift aid.

GIFT AID (NEED-BASED) ***Total amount:*** $103,114,701 (36% federal, 53% state, 11% institutional). ***Receiving aid:*** Freshmen: 54% (2,712); all full-time undergraduates: 50% (11,469). ***Average award:*** Freshmen: $11,370; Undergraduates: $11,416. ***Scholarships, grants, and awards:*** Federal Pell, FSEOG, state, private, college/university gift aid from institutional funds, Federal Nursing.

GIFT AID (NON-NEED-BASED) ***Total amount:*** $20,280,065 (11% state, 47% institutional, 42% external sources). ***Receiving aid:*** Freshmen: 43% (2,193). Undergraduates: 29% (6,656). ***Average award:*** Freshmen: $4857. Undergraduates: $4702. ***Scholarships, grants, and awards by category:*** *Academic interests/achievement:* agriculture, architecture, area/ethnic studies, biological sciences, business, communication, computer science, education, engineering/technologies, English, foreign languages, general academic interests/achievements, health fields, home economics, humanities, international studies, mathematics, military science, physical sciences, premedicine, social sciences. *Creative arts/performance:* applied art and design, art/fine arts, cinema/film/broadcasting, creative writing, general creative arts/performance, journalism/publications, music, performing arts, theater/drama. *Special achievements/activities:* community service, general special achievements/activities, junior miss, leadership, memberships, religious involvement, rodeo. *Special characteristics:* children and siblings of alumni, children of faculty/staff, children of public servants, children with a deceased or disabled parent, first-generation college students, handicapped students, international students, local/state students, out-of-state students, previous college experience, public servants, religious affiliation, veterans. ***Tuition waivers:*** Full or partial for employees or children of employees, senior citizens. ***ROTC:*** Army, Naval cooperative, Air Force.

LOANS ***Student loans:*** $87,961,165 (39% need-based, 61% non-need-based). 57% of past graduating class borrowed through all loan programs. *Average indebtedness per student:* $25,899. ***Average need-based loan:*** Freshmen: $3217. Undergraduates: $4069. ***Parent loans:*** $45,499,062 (100% non-need-based). ***Programs:*** Federal Direct (Subsidized and Unsubsidized Stafford, PLUS), Perkins, Federal Nursing, private loans.

WORK-STUDY ***Federal work-study:*** Total amount: $1,395,248; jobs available. ***State or other work-study/employment:*** Total amount: $976,268 (100% need-based). Part-time jobs available.

ATHLETIC AWARDS Total amount: $9,142,383 (100% non-need-based).

APPLYING FOR FINANCIAL AID ***Required financial aid forms:*** FAFSA, Optional WSU general scholarship application. ***Financial aid deadline:*** 1/31. ***Notification date:*** Continuous beginning 2/15. Students must reply within 2 weeks of notification.

CONTACT Mr. Brian Dixon, Office of Financial Aid and Scholarships, Washington State University, PO Box 641068, Pullman, WA 99164-1068, 509-335-9711 or toll-free 888-468-6978. *Fax:* 509-335-1385. *E-mail:* financialaid@wsu.edu.
Website: http://www.wsu.edu/.

WASHINGTON UNIVERSITY IN ST. LOUIS

St. Louis, MO

Tuition & fees: $57,386 **Average undergraduate aid package: $53,500**

ABOUT THE INSTITUTION Independent, coed. ***Awards:*** certificates, bachelor's, master's, and doctoral degrees. 177 undergraduate majors. ***Total enrollment:*** 16,191. Undergraduates: 7,822. Freshmen: 1,732. Institutional methodology is used as a basis for awarding need-based institutional aid.

UNDERGRADUATE EXPENSES for 2020–2021 ***Application fee:*** $75. ***Comprehensive fee:*** $74,788 includes full-time tuition ($56,300), mandatory fees ($1086), and room and board ($17,402). ***College room only:*** $12,000. Room and board charges vary according to board plan and housing facility. ***Part-time tuition:*** $2346 per credit hour. ***Payment plan:*** Tuition prepayment.

FRESHMAN FINANCIAL AID (Fall 2019, est.) 928 applied for aid; of those 80% were deemed to have need. 99% of freshmen with need received aid; of those 100% had need fully met. ***Average percent of need met:*** 100% (excluding resources awarded to replace EFC). ***Average financial aid package:*** $54,751 (excluding resources awarded to replace EFC). 10% of all full-time freshmen had no need and received non-need-based gift aid.

UNDERGRADUATE FINANCIAL AID (Fall 2019, est.) 3,299 applied for aid; of those 91% were deemed to have need. 99% of undergraduates with need received aid; of those 100% had need fully met. ***Average percent of need met:*** 100% (excluding resources awarded to replace EFC). ***Average financial aid package:*** $53,500 (excluding resources awarded to replace EFC). 8% of all full-time undergraduates had no need and received non-need-based gift aid.

GIFT AID (NEED-BASED) ***Total amount:*** $148,674,570 (4% federal, 1% state, 92% institutional, 3% external sources). ***Receiving aid:*** Freshmen: 42% (720); all full-time undergraduates: 41% (2,919). ***Average award:*** Freshmen: $51,449; Undergraduates: $50,725. ***Scholarships, grants, and awards:*** Federal Pell, FSEOG, state, private, college/university gift aid from institutional funds, United Negro College Fund.

GIFT AID (NON-NEED-BASED) ***Total amount:*** $8,469,701 (8% state, 74% institutional, 18% external sources). ***Receiving aid:*** Freshmen: 4% (64). Undergraduates: 2% (157). ***Average award:*** Freshmen: $11,345. Undergraduates: $15,068. ***Scholarships, grants, and awards by category:*** *Academic interests/achievement:* 641 awards ($24,133,466 total): architecture, area/ethnic studies, biological sciences, business, communication, computer science, education, engineering/technologies, English, foreign languages, general academic interests/achievements, home economics, humanities, international studies, mathematics, military science, physical sciences, premedicine, religion/biblical studies, social sciences. *Creative arts/performance:* 42 awards ($288,750 total): applied art and design, art/fine arts, creative writing, dance, music, theater/drama. ***Tuition waivers:*** Full or partial for employees or children of employees. ***ROTC:*** Army, Air Force cooperative.

LOANS ***Student loans:*** $9,208,256 (87% need-based, 13% non-need-based). 28% of past graduating class borrowed through all loan programs. *Average indebtedness per student:* $24,247. ***Average need-based loan:*** Freshmen: $3440. Undergraduates: $4277. ***Parent loans:*** $13,546,976 (12% need-based, 88% non-need-based). ***Programs:*** Federal Direct (Subsidized and Unsubsidized Stafford, PLUS), state, college/university, private student loans.

WORK-STUDY ***Federal work-study:*** Total amount: $3,203,601; 1,412 jobs averaging $2269.

APPLYING FOR FINANCIAL AID ***Required financial aid forms:*** FAFSA, CSS Financial Aid PROFILE, noncustodial (divorced/separated) parent's statement, either the CSS Profile or our own institutional financial aid form. ***Financial aid deadline:*** 2/1. ***Notification date:*** 4/1. Students must reply by 5/1.

CONTACT Mr. Michael Runiewicz, Assistant Vice Provost & Director of Student Financial Services, Washington University in St. Louis, Campus Box 1041, One Brookings Drive, St. Louis, MO 63130-4899, 314-935-5900 or toll-free 800-638-0700. *Fax:* 314-696-0563. *E-mail:* financial@wustl.edu.
Website: http://www.wustl.edu/.

WATKINS COLLEGE OF ART, DESIGN, & FILM

Nashville, TN

CONTACT Lyle Jones, Financial Aid Coordinator, Watkins College of Art, Design, & Film, 2298 Rosa L. Parks Boulevard, Nashville, TN 37228, 615-383-4848 Ext. 7421. *Fax:* 615-383-4849. *E-mail:* financialaid@watkins.edu.
Website: http://www.watkins.edu/.

WAYLAND BAPTIST UNIVERSITY

Plainview, TX

Tuition & fees: $23,298 **Average undergraduate aid package: $14,139**

ABOUT THE INSTITUTION Independent Baptist, coed. ***Awards:*** associate, bachelor's, master's, and doctoral degrees (branch locations in Anchorage, AK; Amarillo, TX; Luke Air Force Base, AZ; Glorieta, NM; Aiea, HI; Lubbock, TX; San Antonio, TX; Wichita Falls, TX). 46 undergraduate majors. ***Total enrollment:*** 4,827. Undergraduates: 3,012. Freshmen: 249. Federal methodology is used as a basis for awarding need-based institutional aid.

UNDERGRADUATE EXPENSES for 2020–2021 *Application fee:* $35. ***Comprehensive fee:*** $31,020 includes full-time tuition ($21,990), mandatory fees ($1308), and room and board ($7722). ***College room only:*** $2674. Full-time tuition and fees vary according to course load and location. Room and board charges vary according to board plan and housing facility. Part-time tuition and fees vary according to course load and location.

FRESHMAN FINANCIAL AID (Fall 2019, est.) 157 applied for aid; of those 93% were deemed to have need. 100% of freshmen with need received aid; of those 7% had need fully met. ***Average percent of need met:*** 60% (excluding resources awarded to replace EFC). ***Average financial aid package:*** $13,681 (excluding resources awarded to replace EFC). 6% of all full-time freshmen had no need and received non-need-based gift aid.

UNDERGRADUATE FINANCIAL AID (Fall 2019, est.) 708 applied for aid; of those 91% were deemed to have need. 100% of undergraduates with need received aid; of those 10% had need fully met. ***Average percent of need met:*** 59% (excluding resources awarded to replace EFC). ***Average financial aid package:*** $14,139 (excluding resources awarded to replace EFC). 11% of all full-time undergraduates had no need and received non-need-based gift aid.

GIFT AID (NEED-BASED) *Total amount:* $8,043,637 (50% federal, 15% state, 20% institutional, 15% external sources). ***Receiving aid:*** Freshmen: 67% (145); all full-time undergraduates: 72% (623). ***Average award:*** Freshmen: $11,320; Undergraduates: $11,049. ***Scholarships, grants, and awards:*** Federal Pell, FSEOG, state, private, college/university gift aid from institutional funds.

GIFT AID (NON-NEED-BASED) *Total amount:* $1,280,307 (1% federal, 1% state, 68% institutional, 30% external sources). ***Receiving aid:*** Freshmen: 3% (6). Undergraduates: 5% (47). ***Average award:*** Freshmen: $2866. Undergraduates: $6149. ***Scholarships, grants, and awards by category:*** *Academic interests/achievement:* biological sciences, business, communication, education, English, foreign languages, general academic interests/achievements, home economics, mathematics, physical sciences, premedicine, religion/biblical studies, social sciences. *Creative arts/performance:* art/fine arts, music, theater/drama. *Special achievements/activities:* cheerleading/drum major, community service, leadership. *Special characteristics:* children of faculty/staff, relatives of clergy, religious affiliation. ***ROTC:*** Army cooperative, Air Force cooperative.

LOANS *Student loans:* $12,240,988 (87% need-based, 13% non-need-based). 28% of past graduating class borrowed through all loan programs. *Average indebtedness per student:* $29,555. ***Average need-based loan:*** Freshmen: $3007. Undergraduates: $3958. ***Parent loans:*** $1,414,558 (58% need-based, 42% non-need-based). ***Programs:*** Federal Direct (Subsidized and Unsubsidized Stafford, PLUS), Perkins, state, private loans.

WORK-STUDY *Federal work-study:* Total amount: $106,000; jobs available. ***State or other work-study/employment:*** Total amount: $85,777 (36% need-based, 64% non-need-based). Part-time jobs available.

ATHLETIC AWARDS Total amount: $2,980,144 (52% need-based, 48% non-need-based).

APPLYING FOR FINANCIAL AID *Required financial aid forms:* FAFSA, institution's own form, state aid form. ***Financial aid deadline:*** Continuous. ***Notification date:*** Continuous beginning 1/1.

CONTACT Christy Miller, Director of Financial Aid, Wayland Baptist University, 1900 West 7th Street, Plainview, TX 79072-6998, 806-291-3520 or toll-free 800-588-1928. *Fax:* 806-291-1956. *E-mail:* millerc@wbu.edu.
Website: http://www.wbu.edu/.

WAYNESBURG UNIVERSITY

Waynesburg, PA

Tuition & fees: $26,640 **Average undergraduate aid package: $21,635**

ABOUT THE INSTITUTION Independent Presbyterian Church (U.S.A.), coed. ***Awards:*** bachelor's, master's, and doctoral degrees. 51 undergraduate majors. ***Total enrollment:*** 1,628. Undergraduates: 1,277. Freshmen: 355. Federal methodology is used as a basis for awarding need-based institutional aid.

UNDERGRADUATE EXPENSES for 2020–2021 *Application fee:* $20. ***Comprehensive fee:*** $37,530 includes full-time tuition ($25,430), mandatory fees ($1210), and room and board ($10,890). ***College room only:*** $5510. Room and board charges vary according to board plan and housing facility. ***Part-time tuition:*** $1050 per credit hour.

FRESHMAN FINANCIAL AID (Fall 2019, est.) 346 applied for aid; of those 90% were deemed to have need. 100% of freshmen with need received aid; of those 19% had need fully met. ***Average percent of need met:*** 81% (excluding resources awarded to replace EFC). ***Average financial aid package:*** $21,912 (excluding resources awarded to replace EFC). 10% of all full-time freshmen had no need and received non-need-based gift aid.

UNDERGRADUATE FINANCIAL AID (Fall 2019, est.) 1,188 applied for aid; of those 88% were deemed to have need. 100% of undergraduates with need received aid; of those 20% had need fully met. ***Average percent of need met:*** 82% (excluding resources awarded to replace EFC). ***Average financial aid package:*** $21,635 (excluding resources awarded to replace EFC). 16% of all full-time undergraduates had no need and received non-need-based gift aid.

GIFT AID (NEED-BASED) *Receiving aid:* Freshmen: 87% (311); all full-time undergraduates: 80% (1,028). ***Average award:*** Freshmen: $17,865; Undergraduates: $16,760. ***Scholarships, grants, and awards:*** Federal Pell, FSEOG, state, private, college/university gift aid from institutional funds, United Negro College Fund.

GIFT AID (NON-NEED-BASED) *Receiving aid:* Freshmen: 11% (39). Undergraduates: 10% (131). ***Average award:*** Freshmen: $11,242. Undergraduates: $11,073. ***Scholarships, grants, and awards by category:*** *Academic interests/achievement:* 1,292 awards ($14,880,002 total): communication, general academic interests/achievements. *Creative arts/performance:* 10 awards ($13,500 total): applied art and design, music, theater/drama. *Special achievements/activities:* 63 awards ($500,279 total): community service. *Special characteristics:* 58 awards ($28,000 total): siblings of current students. ***ROTC:*** Army cooperative, Air Force cooperative.

LOANS *Student loans:* 77% of past graduating class borrowed through all loan programs. *Average indebtedness per student:* $23,316. ***Average need-based loan:*** Freshmen: $4162. Undergraduates: $5581. ***Programs:*** Federal Direct (Subsidized and Unsubsidized Stafford, PLUS), Federal Nursing.

WORK-STUDY *Federal work-study:* 672 jobs averaging $1193.

APPLYING FOR FINANCIAL AID *Required financial aid form:* FAFSA. ***Financial aid deadline:*** Continuous. ***Notification date:*** Continuous. Students must reply within 2 weeks of notification.

CONTACT Mr. Matthew C. Stokan, Director of Financial Aid, Waynesburg University, 51 West College Street, Waynesburg, PA 15370-1222, 724-852-3208 Ext. 227 or toll-free 800-225-7393. *E-mail:* mstokan@waynesburg.edu.
Website: http://www.waynesburg.edu/.

WAYNE STATE COLLEGE

Wayne, NE

Tuition & fees: N/R | **Average undergraduate aid package: $9764**

ABOUT THE INSTITUTION State-supported, coed. ***Awards:*** certificates, bachelor's, and master's degrees. 53 undergraduate majors. ***Total enrollment:*** 3,890. Undergraduates: 3,148. Freshmen: 730. Federal methodology is used as a basis for awarding need-based institutional aid.

FRESHMAN FINANCIAL AID (Fall 2019, est.) 660 applied for aid; of those 75% were deemed to have need. 99% of freshmen with need received aid; of those 68% had need fully met. ***Average percent of need met:*** 57% (excluding resources awarded to replace EFC). ***Average financial aid package:*** $10,941 (excluding resources awarded to replace EFC). 7% of all full-time freshmen had no need and received non-need-based gift aid.

UNDERGRADUATE FINANCIAL AID (Fall 2019, est.) 2,286 applied for aid; of those 79% were deemed to have need. 98% of undergraduates with need received aid; of those 65% had need fully met. ***Average percent of need met:*** 58% (excluding resources awarded to replace EFC). ***Average financial aid package:*** $9764 (excluding resources awarded to replace EFC). 4% of all full-time undergraduates had no need and received non-need-based gift aid.

GIFT AID (NEED-BASED) ***Receiving aid:*** Freshmen: 48% (348); all full-time undergraduates: 47% (1,245). ***Average award:*** Freshmen: $6362; Undergraduates: $6095. ***Scholarships, grants, and awards:*** Federal Pell, FSEOG, state, private, college/university gift aid from institutional funds.

GIFT AID (NON-NEED-BASED) ***Receiving aid:*** Freshmen: 54% (393). Undergraduates: 39% (1,023). ***Average award:*** Freshmen: $2666. Undergraduates: $2984. ***Scholarships, grants, and awards by category:*** *Academic interests/achievement:* biological sciences, business, communication, computer science, education, English, foreign languages, general academic interests/achievements, health fields, home economics, humanities, international studies, mathematics, physical sciences, premedicine, social sciences. *Creative arts/performance:* applied art and design, art/fine arts, creative writing, general creative arts/performance, journalism/publications, music, performing arts, theater/drama. *Special achievements/activities:* general special achievements/activities, leadership. *Special characteristics:* children of faculty/staff, ethnic background, general special characteristics, local/state students, members of minority groups, out-of-state students, veterans, veterans' children. ***ROTC:*** Army cooperative.

LOANS ***Average need-based loan:*** Freshmen: $3169. Undergraduates: $3763. ***Programs:*** Federal Direct (Subsidized and Unsubsidized Stafford, PLUS), Perkins.

WORK-STUDY Federal work-study jobs available.

APPLYING FOR FINANCIAL AID ***Required financial aid form:*** FAFSA. ***Notification date:*** Continuous. Students must reply within 4 weeks of notification.

CONTACT Annette Kaus, Director of Financial Aid, Wayne State College, 1111 Main Street, Wayne, NE 68787, 402-375-7230 or toll-free 866-WSC-CATS. *Fax:* 402-375-7067. *E-mail:* ankaus1@wsc.edu.
Website: http://www.wsc.edu/.

WAYNE STATE UNIVERSITY

Detroit, MI

Tuition & fees: N/R | **Average undergraduate aid package: $11,603**

ABOUT THE INSTITUTION State-supported, coed. ***Awards:*** certificates, bachelor's, master's, and doctoral degrees. 83 undergraduate majors. ***Total enrollment:*** 26,844. Undergraduates: 17,663. Freshmen: 2,968. Federal methodology is used as a basis for awarding need-based institutional aid.

FRESHMAN FINANCIAL AID (Fall 2018) 2725 applied for aid; of those 80% were deemed to have need. 100% of freshmen with need received aid; of those 7% had need fully met. ***Average percent of need met:*** 60% (excluding resources awarded to replace EFC). ***Average financial aid package:*** $12,371 (excluding resources awarded to replace EFC). 23% of all full-time freshmen had no need and received non-need-based gift aid.

UNDERGRADUATE FINANCIAL AID (Fall 2018) 10,619 applied for aid; of those 87% were deemed to have need. 99% of undergraduates with need received aid; of those 4% had need fully met. ***Average percent of need met:*** 52% (excluding resources awarded to replace EFC). ***Average financial aid package:*** $11,603 (excluding resources awarded to replace EFC). 19% of all full-time undergraduates had no need and received non-need-based gift aid.

GIFT AID (NEED-BASED) ***Total amount:*** $56,753,471 (70% federal, 4% state, 26% institutional). ***Receiving aid:*** Freshmen: 57% (1,679); all full-time undergraduates: 54% (7,027). ***Average award:*** Freshmen: $7893; Undergraduates: $7132. ***Scholarships, grants, and awards:*** Federal Pell, FSEOG, state, private, college/university gift aid from institutional funds, United Negro College Fund.

GIFT AID (NON-NEED-BASED) ***Total amount:*** $42,319,340 (96% institutional, 4% external sources). ***Receiving aid:*** Freshmen: 67% (1,995). Undergraduates: 48% (6,156). ***Average award:*** Freshmen: $4716. Undergraduates: $4996. ***Scholarships, grants, and awards by category:*** *Academic interests/achievement:* area/ethnic studies, biological sciences, business, communication, computer science, education, engineering/technologies, English, foreign languages, general academic interests/achievements, home economics, humanities, international studies, library science, mathematics, military science, physical sciences, premedicine, social sciences. *Creative arts/performance:* applied art and design, dance, debating, general creative arts/performance, journalism/publications, music, performing arts, theater/drama. *Special achievements/activities:* leadership, memberships. *Special characteristics:* children of current students, children of faculty/staff, children with a deceased or disabled parent, ethnic background, international students, local/state students, out-of-state students, spouses of current students. ***ROTC:*** Army cooperative, Air Force cooperative.

LOANS ***Student loans:*** $69,686,369 (41% need-based, 59% non-need-based). 68% of past graduating class borrowed through all loan programs. *Average indebtedness per student:* $25,095. ***Average need-based loan:*** Freshmen: $3092. Undergraduates: $4002. ***Parent loans:*** $10,523,294 (100% non-need-based). ***Programs:*** Federal Direct (Subsidized and Unsubsidized Stafford, PLUS), Perkins, Federal Nursing, college/university.

WORK-STUDY ***Federal work-study:*** Total amount: $1,768,590; jobs available. ***State or other work-study/employment:*** Part-time jobs available.

ATHLETIC AWARDS Total amount: $3,852,247 (100% non-need-based).

APPLYING FOR FINANCIAL AID ***Required financial aid form:*** FAFSA. ***Financial aid deadline:*** 6/30 (priority: 3/1). ***Notification date:*** Continuous beginning 12/15.

CONTACT Catherine Kay, Director of Financial Aid, Wayne State University, 42 West Warren Avenue, Detroit, MI 48202, 313-577-2100 or toll-free 877-WSU-INFO. *Fax:* 313-577-6648. *E-mail:* financialaid@wayne.edu.
Website: http://www.wayne.edu/.

WEBBER INTERNATIONAL UNIVERSITY

Babson Park, FL

Tuition & fees: $28,498 | **Average undergraduate aid package: $20,114**

ABOUT THE INSTITUTION Independent, coed. ***Awards:*** associate, bachelor's, and master's degrees. 19 undergraduate majors. ***Total enrollment:*** 735. Undergraduates: 665. Freshmen: 203. Federal methodology is used as a basis for awarding need-based institutional aid.

UNDERGRADUATE EXPENSES for 2020–2021 ***Comprehensive fee:*** $38,438 includes full-time tuition ($25,526), mandatory fees ($2972), and room and board ($9940). Full-time tuition and fees vary according to program and reciprocity agreements. Room and board charges vary according to board plan and housing facility. ***Part-time tuition:*** $377 per semester hour. Part-time tuition and fees vary according to course load, program, and reciprocity agreements.

FRESHMAN FINANCIAL AID (Fall 2018) 167 applied for aid; of those 94% were deemed to have need. 100% of freshmen with need received aid; of those 9% had need fully met. ***Average percent of need met:*** 14% (excluding resources awarded to replace EFC). ***Average financial aid package:*** $18,973 (excluding resources awarded to replace EFC). 15% of all full-time freshmen had no need and received non-need-based gift aid.

UNDERGRADUATE FINANCIAL AID (Fall 2018) 468 applied for aid; of those 94% were deemed to have need. 99% of undergraduates with need received aid; of those 8% had need fully met. ***Average percent of need met:*** 60% (excluding resources awarded to replace EFC). ***Average financial aid package:*** $20,114 (excluding resources awarded to replace EFC). 20% of all full-time undergraduates had no need and received non-need-based gift aid.

GIFT AID (NEED-BASED) ***Total amount:*** $3,719,871 (41% federal, 40% state, 16% institutional, 3% external sources). ***Receiving aid:*** Freshmen: 81% (157); all full-time undergraduates: 74% (437). ***Average award:*** Freshmen: $16,441; Undergraduates: $16,727. ***Scholarships, grants, and awards:*** Federal Pell, FSEOG, state, private, college/university gift aid from institutional funds.

GIFT AID (NON-NEED-BASED) ***Total amount:*** $943,542 (17% state, 77% institutional, 6% external sources). ***Receiving aid:*** Freshmen: 7% (14). Undergraduates: 5% (31). ***Average award:*** Freshmen: $3620. Undergraduates: $6240. ***Scholarships, grants, and awards by category:*** *Academic interests/achievement:* business, general academic interests/achievements. *Creative arts/performance:* debating, journalism/publications. *Special achievements/activities:* community service, general special achievements/activities, leadership, memberships. *Special characteristics:* children and siblings of alumni, children of faculty/staff, general special characteristics, international students, local/state students, siblings of current students, veterans. ***Tuition waivers:*** Full or partial for children of alumni, employees or children of employees, adult students, senior citizens.

LOANS ***Student loans:*** $3,035,175 (86% need-based, 14% non-need-based). 67% of past graduating class borrowed through all loan programs. *Average indebtedness per student:* $27,083. ***Average need-based loan:*** Freshmen: $2982. Undergraduates: $3807. ***Parent loans:*** $1,636,203 (72% need-based, 28% non-need-based). ***Programs:*** Federal Direct (Subsidized and Unsubsidized Stafford, PLUS).

WORK-STUDY ***Federal work-study:*** Total amount: $42,562; jobs available. ***State or other work-study/employment:*** Total amount: $58,262 (38% need-based, 62% non-need-based). Part-time jobs available.

ATHLETIC AWARDS Total amount: $4,688,805 (75% need-based, 25% non-need-based).

APPLYING FOR FINANCIAL AID ***Required financial aid forms:*** FAFSA, state aid form. ***Financial aid deadline (priority):*** 3/1. ***Notification date:*** Continuous. Students must reply within 1 week of notification.

CONTACT Ms. Kathy Wilson, Vice President of Student Record Services, Webber International University, PO Box 96, 1201 Scenic Highway, Babson Park, FL 33827-0096, 863-638-2930 or toll-free 800-741-1844. *Fax:* 863-638-1513. *E-mail:* wilsonka@webber.edu.
Website: http://www.webber.edu/.

WEBB INSTITUTE

Glen Cove, NY

CONTACT Jocelyn Wilson, Director of Financial Aid, Webb Institute, 298 Crescent Beach Road, Glen Cove, NY 11542-1398, 516-403-5928 Ext. 1108. *Fax:* 516-674-9838. *E-mail:* jwilson@webb.edu.
Website: http://www.webb.edu/.

WEBER STATE UNIVERSITY

Ogden, UT

Tuition & fees (UT res): $5967	Average undergraduate aid package: $6895

ABOUT THE INSTITUTION State-supported, coed. ***Awards:*** certificates, associate, bachelor's, master's, and doctoral degrees. 144 undergraduate majors. ***Total enrollment:*** 29,843. Undergraduates: 28,833. Freshmen: 3,303. Both federal and institutional methodology are used as a basis for awarding need-based institutional aid.

UNDERGRADUATE EXPENSES for 2019–2020 ***Application fee:*** $30. ***Tuition, state resident:*** full-time $4990; part-time $2944 per year. ***Tuition, nonresident:*** full-time $14,973; part-time $8834 per year. ***Required fees:*** full-time $977; $612 per year. Full-time tuition and fees vary according to course level, course load, degree level, program, and reciprocity agreements. Part-time tuition and fees vary according to course level, course load, degree level, program, and reciprocity agreements. ***College room and board:*** $8400. Room and board charges vary according to board plan and housing facility.

FRESHMAN FINANCIAL AID (Fall 2018) 1804 applied for aid; of those 77% were deemed to have need. 86% of freshmen with need received aid; of those 108% had need fully met. ***Average financial aid package:*** $2530 (excluding resources awarded to replace EFC). 29% of all full-time freshmen had no need and received non-need-based gift aid.

UNDERGRADUATE FINANCIAL AID (Fall 2018) 7,229 applied for aid; of those 86% were deemed to have need. 91% of undergraduates with need received aid; of those 36% had need fully met. ***Average financial aid package:*** $6895 (excluding resources awarded to replace EFC). 21% of all full-time undergraduates had no need and received non-need-based gift aid.

GIFT AID (NEED-BASED) ***Total amount:*** $33,336,215 (91% federal, 3% state, 6% external sources). ***Receiving aid:*** Freshmen: 35% (875); all full-time undergraduates: 41% (4,450). ***Average award:*** Freshmen: $2565; Undergraduates: $5351. ***Scholarships, grants, and awards:*** Federal Pell, FSEOG, state, private, college/university gift aid from institutional funds.

GIFT AID (NON-NEED-BASED) ***Total amount:*** $3,126,812 (100% institutional). ***Receiving aid:*** Freshmen: 11% (271). Undergraduates: 18% (1,904). ***Average award:*** Freshmen: $2292. Undergraduates: $3841. ***Tuition waivers:*** Full or partial for employees or children of employees, senior citizens. ***ROTC:*** Army, Naval cooperative, Air Force cooperative.

LOANS ***Student loans:*** $32,305,498 (94% need-based, 6% non-need-based). 40% of past graduating class borrowed through all loan programs. *Average indebtedness per student:* $21,690. ***Average need-based loan:*** Freshmen: $2783. Undergraduates: $3553. ***Parent loans:*** $294,111 (100% non-need-based). ***Programs:*** Federal Direct (Subsidized and Unsubsidized Stafford, PLUS), Perkins.

WORK-STUDY ***Federal work-study:*** Total amount: $763,489; jobs available. ***State or other work-study/employment:*** Part-time jobs available.

ATHLETIC AWARDS Total amount: $2,019,480 (100% non-need-based).

APPLYING FOR FINANCIAL AID ***Required financial aid forms:*** FAFSA, institution's own form. ***Financial aid deadline (priority):*** 3/1. ***Notification date:*** Continuous beginning 3/15. Students must reply within 2 weeks of notification.

CONTACT Mr. Jed Spencer, Financial Aid Director, Weber State University, Student Service Center, Suite 120, 3885 West Campus Drive, Department 1136, Ogden, UT 84408-1136, 801-626-7569 or toll-free 800-848-7700 (in-state), 800-848-7770 (out-of-state). *E-mail:* finaid@weber.edu.
Website: http://www.weber.edu/.

WEBSTER UNIVERSITY

St. Louis, MO

CONTACT Office of Financial Aid, Webster University, 470 East Lockwood Avenue, St. Louis, MO 63119, 314-968-6992 or toll-free 800-753-6765. *Fax:* 314-968-7125. *E-mail:* financialaid@webster.edu.
Website: http://www.webster.edu/.

WELCH COLLEGE

Gallatin, TN

CONTACT Angie Edgmon, Financial Aid Coordinator, Welch College, 3606 West End Avenue, Nashville, TN 37205, 615-844-5000 Ext. 5249 or toll-free 800-763-9222. *Fax:* 615-269-6028. *E-mail:* finaid@fwbbc.edu.
Website: http://www.welch.edu/.

WELLESLEY COLLEGE

Wellesley, MA

ABOUT THE INSTITUTION Independent, women only. ***Awards:*** bachelor's degrees (double bachelor's degree with Massachusetts Institute of Technology). 58 undergraduate majors. ***Total enrollment:*** 2,534. Undergraduates: 2,534. Freshmen: 614.

GIFT AID (NEED-BASED) ***Scholarships, grants, and awards:*** Federal Pell, FSEOG, state, private, college/university gift aid from institutional funds, United Negro College Fund.

LOANS ***Programs:*** Federal Direct (Subsidized and Unsubsidized Stafford, PLUS), college/university.

WORK-STUDY ***Federal work-study:*** Total amount: $1,830,604; jobs available. ***State or other work-study/employment:*** Total amount: $697,269 (100% need-based). Part-time jobs available.

APPLYING FOR FINANCIAL AID ***Required financial aid forms:*** FAFSA, CSS Financial Aid PROFILE, noncustodial (divorced/separated) parent's statement.

CONTACT Financial Aid Office, Wellesley College, 106 Central Street, Wellesley, MA 02481, 781-283-1000.

Website: http://www.wellesley.edu/.

WELLS COLLEGE

Aurora, NY

ABOUT THE INSTITUTION Independent, coed. ***Awards:*** bachelor's degrees. 36 undergraduate majors.

GIFT AID (NEED-BASED) ***Scholarships, grants, and awards:*** Federal Pell, FSEOG, state, private, college/university gift aid from institutional funds.

GIFT AID (NON-NEED-BASED) ***Scholarships, grants, and awards by category:*** *Academic interests/achievement:* general academic interests/achievements. *Special achievements/activities:* leadership. *Special characteristics:* children and siblings of alumni, international students.

LOANS ***Programs:*** Federal Direct (Subsidized and Unsubsidized Stafford, PLUS), Perkins, state.

CONTACT Ms. Laura Burns, Director of Financial Aid, Wells College, Route 90, Aurora, NY 13026, 315-364-3289 or toll-free 800-952-9355. *Fax:* 315-364-3445. *E-mail:* lburns@wells.edu.

Website: http://www.wells.edu/.

WENTWORTH INSTITUTE OF TECHNOLOGY

Boston, MA

Tuition & fees: $34,970	Average undergraduate aid package: $2780

ABOUT THE INSTITUTION Independent, coed. ***Awards:*** certificates, associate, bachelor's, and master's degrees. 22 undergraduate majors. ***Total enrollment:*** 4,453. Undergraduates: 4,307. Freshmen: 968. Federal methodology is used as a basis for awarding need-based institutional aid.

UNDERGRADUATE EXPENSES for 2020–2021 ***Comprehensive fee:*** $49,160 includes full-time tuition ($34,970) and room and board ($14,190). ***College room only:*** $11,090. Full-time tuition and fees vary according to class time, course load, and program. Room and board charges vary according to board plan and housing facility. ***Part-time tuition:*** $1095 per credit. Part-time tuition and fees vary according to class time, course load, and program.

FRESHMAN FINANCIAL AID (Fall 2019, est.) 687 applied for aid; of those 98% were deemed to have need. 97% of freshmen with need received aid; of those 7% had need fully met. ***Average percent of need met:*** 64% (excluding resources awarded to replace EFC). ***Average financial aid package:*** $2725 (excluding resources awarded to replace EFC). 23% of all full-time freshmen had no need and received non-need-based gift aid.

UNDERGRADUATE FINANCIAL AID (Fall 2019, est.) 2,590 applied for aid; of those 99% were deemed to have need. 99% of undergraduates with need received aid; of those 7% had need fully met. ***Average percent of need met:*** 61% (excluding resources awarded to replace EFC). ***Average financial aid package:*** $2780 (excluding resources awarded to replace EFC). 25% of all full-time undergraduates had no need and received non-need-based gift aid.

GIFT AID (NEED-BASED) ***Total amount:*** $13,490,248 (39% federal, 8% state, 53% institutional). ***Receiving aid:*** Freshmen: 52% (489); all full-time undergraduates: 50% (2,016). ***Average award:*** Freshmen: $3179; Undergraduates: $3108. ***Scholarships, grants, and awards:*** Federal Pell, FSEOG, state, private, college/university gift aid from institutional funds, United Negro College Fund.

GIFT AID (NON-NEED-BASED) ***Total amount:*** $43,818,154 (97% institutional, 3% external sources). ***Receiving aid:*** Freshmen: 78% (743). Undergraduates: 65% (2,593). ***Average award:*** Freshmen: $10,555. Undergraduates: $9655. ***Scholarships, grants, and awards by category:*** *Academic interests/achievement:* general academic interests/achievements. ***Tuition waivers:*** Full or partial for employees or children of employees. ***ROTC:*** Army cooperative, Air Force cooperative.

LOANS ***Student loans:*** $42,442,750 (26% need-based, 74% non-need-based). 81% of past graduating class borrowed through all loan programs. *Average indebtedness per student:* $58,867. ***Average need-based loan:*** Freshmen: $2639. Undergraduates: $2738. ***Parent loans:*** $12,084,023 (100% non-need-based). ***Programs:*** Federal Direct (Subsidized and Unsubsidized Stafford, PLUS), Perkins, state.

WORK-STUDY ***Federal work-study:*** Total amount: $1,373,766; jobs available. ***State or other work-study/employment:*** Total amount: $1,525,713 (100% need-based). Part-time jobs available.

APPLYING FOR FINANCIAL AID ***Required financial aid form:*** FAFSA. ***Financial aid deadline:*** Continuous. ***Notification date:*** Continuous beginning 5/1.

CONTACT Anne-Marie Caruso, Director of Financial Aid, Wentworth Institute of Technology, 550 Huntington Avenue, Boston, MA 02115-5998, 617-989-4174 or toll-free 800-556-0610. *Fax:* 617-989-4201. *E-mail:* carusoa@wit.edu.

Website: http://www.wit.edu/.

WESLEYAN COLLEGE

Macon, GA

Tuition & fees: $25,190	Average undergraduate aid package: $22,597

ABOUT THE INSTITUTION Independent United Methodist, undergraduate: women only; graduate: coed. ***Awards:*** bachelor's and master's degrees. 23 undergraduate majors. ***Total enrollment:*** 797. Undergraduates: 754. Freshmen: 135. Federal methodology is used as a basis for awarding need-based institutional aid.

UNDERGRADUATE EXPENSES for 2020–2021 ***One-time required fee:*** $200. ***Comprehensive fee:*** $35,555 includes full-time tuition ($23,990), mandatory fees ($1200), and room and board ($10,365). Full-time tuition and fees vary according to course load, program, and reciprocity agreements. Room and board charges vary according to housing facility. ***Part-time tuition:*** $570 per semester hour. ***Part-time fees:*** $48 per semester hour. Part-time tuition and fees vary according to course load, program, and reciprocity agreements.

FRESHMAN FINANCIAL AID (Fall 2019, est.) 128 applied for aid; of those 95% were deemed to have need. 100% of freshmen with need received aid; of those 12% had need fully met. ***Average percent of need met:*** 78% (excluding resources awarded to replace EFC). ***Average financial aid package:*** $24,497 (excluding resources awarded to replace EFC). 14% of all full-time freshmen had no need and received non-need-based gift aid.

UNDERGRADUATE FINANCIAL AID (Fall 2019, est.) 412 applied for aid; of those 92% were deemed to have need. 100% of undergraduates with need received aid; of those 19% had need fully met. ***Average percent of need met:*** 78% (excluding resources awarded to replace EFC). ***Average financial aid package:*** $22,597 (excluding resources awarded to replace EFC). 17% of all full-time undergraduates had no need and received non-need-based gift aid.

GIFT AID (NEED-BASED) ***Total amount:*** $7,044,066 (21% federal, 13% state, 63% institutional, 3% external sources). ***Receiving aid:*** Freshmen: 90% (120); all full-time undergraduates: 81% (378). ***Average award:*** Freshmen: $22,176; Undergraduates: $19,303. ***Scholarships, grants, and awards:*** Federal Pell, FSEOG, state, private, college/university gift aid from institutional funds.

GIFT AID (NON-NEED-BASED) ***Total amount:*** $1,689,677 (1% federal, 19% state, 78% institutional, 2% external sources). ***Receiving aid:*** Freshmen: 11% (15). Undergraduates: 13% (62). ***Average award:*** Freshmen: $14,221. Undergraduates: $13,643. ***Scholarships, grants, and awards by category:*** *Academic interests/achievement:* biological sciences, business, communication, education, engineering/technologies, English, foreign languages, general academic interests/achievements, health fields, humanities, international studies, mathematics, premedicine, religion/biblical studies, social sciences. *Creative arts/performance:* applied art and design, music, theater/drama. *Special achievements/activities:* community service, general special achievements/activities, hobbies/interests, leadership, memberships, religious involvement. *Special characteristics:* adult students, children and siblings of alumni, children of current students, children of educators, children of faculty/staff, ethnic background, first-generation college students, general special characteristics, local/state students, parents of current students, previous college experience, relatives of clergy, religious affiliation, siblings of current students, spouses of current students, veterans. ***Tuition waivers:*** Full or partial for employees or children of employees. ***ROTC:*** Army cooperative.

LOANS ***Student loans:*** $2,760,985 (78% need-based, 22% non-need-based). 74% of past graduating class borrowed through all loan programs. *Average indebtedness per student:* $28,882. ***Average need-based loan:*** Freshmen: $3531. Undergraduates: $4439. ***Parent loans:*** $280,876 (61% need-based, 39% non-need-based). ***Programs:*** Federal Direct (Subsidized and Unsubsidized Stafford, PLUS), state, college/university, private loans.

WORK-STUDY ***Federal work-study:*** Total amount: $30,500; jobs available. ***State or other work-study/employment:*** Total amount: $89,500 (28% need-based, 72% non-need-based). Part-time jobs available.

APPLYING FOR FINANCIAL AID ***Required financial aid form:*** FAFSA. ***Financial aid deadline:*** Continuous. ***Notification date:*** Continuous beginning 10/1. Students must reply within 2 weeks of notification.

CONTACT Daniel Miller, Director of Financial Aid, Wesleyan College, 4760 Forsyth Road, Macon, GA 31210-4462, 478-757-5146 or toll-free 800-447-6610. *Fax:* 478-757-4030. *E-mail:* financialaid@wesleyancollege.edu.
Website: http://www.wesleyancollege.edu/.

WESLEYAN UNIVERSITY

Middletown, CT

Tuition & fees: $57,004	Average undergraduate aid package: $58,719

ABOUT THE INSTITUTION Independent, coed. ***Awards:*** certificates, bachelor's, master's, and doctoral degrees. 44 undergraduate majors. ***Total enrollment:*** 3,230. Undergraduates: 3,018. Freshmen: 771. Institutional methodology is used as a basis for awarding need-based institutional aid.

UNDERGRADUATE EXPENSES for 2019–2020 ***Application fee:*** $55. ***Comprehensive fee:*** $72,728 includes full-time tuition ($56,704), mandatory fees ($300), and room and board ($15,724). Room and board charges vary according to board plan and student level.

FRESHMAN FINANCIAL AID (Fall 2019, est.) 342 applied for aid; of those 92% were deemed to have need. 100% of freshmen with need received aid; of those 100% had need fully met. ***Average percent of need met:*** 100% (excluding resources awarded to replace EFC). ***Average financial aid package:*** $58,419 (excluding resources awarded to replace EFC). 1% of all full-time freshmen had no need and received non-need-based gift aid.

UNDERGRADUATE FINANCIAL AID (Fall 2019, est.) 1,281 applied for aid; of those 94% were deemed to have need. 100% of undergraduates with need received aid; of those 100% had need fully met. ***Average percent of need met:*** 100% (excluding resources awarded to replace EFC). ***Average financial aid package:*** $58,719 (excluding resources awarded to replace EFC). 1% of all full-time undergraduates had no need and received non-need-based gift aid.

GIFT AID (NEED-BASED) ***Receiving aid:*** Freshmen: 41% (313); all full-time undergraduates: 41% (1,190). ***Average award:*** Freshmen: $52,149; Undergraduates: $52,284. ***Scholarships, grants, and awards:*** Federal Pell, FSEOG, state, private, college/university gift aid from institutional funds.

GIFT AID (NON-NEED-BASED) ***Receiving aid:*** Freshmen: 2% (13). Undergraduates: 1% (33). ***Average award:*** Freshmen: $43,624. Undergraduates: $42,760. ***Scholarships, grants, and awards by category:*** *Creative arts/performance:* 3 awards ($136,665 total): general creative arts/performance. *Special characteristics:* 29 awards ($866,788 total): international students, veterans. ***ROTC:*** Air Force cooperative.

LOANS ***Student loans:*** 36% of past graduating class borrowed through all loan programs. *Average indebtedness per student:* $26,016. ***Average need-based loan:*** Freshmen: $2913. Undergraduates: $4058. ***Programs:*** Federal Direct (Subsidized and Unsubsidized Stafford, PLUS), college/university.

WORK-STUDY ***Federal work-study:*** 1,926 jobs averaging $2,269,436. ***State or other work-study/employment:*** 314 part-time jobs averaging $2093.

APPLYING FOR FINANCIAL AID ***Required financial aid forms:*** FAFSA, CSS Financial Aid PROFILE, noncustodial (divorced/separated) parent's statement, Parent and student federal income tax form(s), W-2 forms, business tax returns.

CONTACT Mr. Robert Coughlin, Director of Financial Aid, Wesleyan University, 237 High Street, Middletown, CT 06459-0260, 860-685-2800. *Fax:* 860-685-2801. *E-mail:* finaid@wesleyan.edu.
Website: http://www.wesleyan.edu/.

WESLEY COLLEGE

Dover, DE

CONTACT Mr. Michael Hall, Director of Student Financial Planning, Wesley College, 120 North State Street, Dover, DE 19901-3875, 302-736-2334 or toll-free 800-937-5398. *Fax:* 302-736-2594. *E-mail:* halljmic@wesley.edu.
Website: http://www.wesley.edu/.

WEST CHESTER UNIVERSITY OF PENNSYLVANIA

West Chester, PA

Tuition & fees (PA res): $10,421	Average undergraduate aid package: $8438

ABOUT THE INSTITUTION State-supported, coed. ***Awards:*** certificates, bachelor's, master's, and doctoral degrees. 51 undergraduate majors. ***Total enrollment:*** 17,669. Undergraduates: 14,615. Freshmen: 2,871. Federal methodology is used as a basis for awarding need-based institutional aid.

UNDERGRADUATE EXPENSES for 2019–2020 ***Application fee:*** $45. ***Tuition, state resident:*** full-time $7716; part-time $322 per credit. ***Tuition, nonresident:*** full-time $19,290; part-time $805 per credit. ***Required fees:*** full-time $2705; $112.80 per credit. Full-time tuition and fees vary according to location. Part-time tuition and fees vary according to location. ***College room and board:*** $9326; ***Room only:*** $5626. Room and board charges vary according to board plan and housing facility.

FRESHMAN FINANCIAL AID (Fall 2019, est.) 2593 applied for aid; of those 68% were deemed to have need. 100% of freshmen with need received aid; of those 8% had need fully met. ***Average percent of need met:*** 44% (excluding resources awarded to replace EFC). ***Average financial aid package:*** $8858 (excluding resources awarded to replace EFC). 8% of all full-time freshmen had no need and received non-need-based gift aid.

UNDERGRADUATE FINANCIAL AID (Fall 2019, est.) 10,231 applied for aid; of those 73% were deemed to have need. 100% of undergraduates with need received aid; of those 9% had need fully met. ***Average percent of need met:*** 47% (excluding resources awarded to replace EFC). ***Average financial aid package:*** $8438 (excluding resources awarded to replace EFC). 3% of all full-time undergraduates had no need and received non-need-based gift aid.

GIFT AID (NEED-BASED) ***Receiving aid:*** Freshmen: 43% (1,244); all full-time undergraduates: 36% (4,720). ***Average award:*** Freshmen: $6864; Undergraduates: $6057. ***Scholarships, grants, and awards:*** Federal Pell, FSEOG, state, private, college/university gift aid from institutional funds.

GIFT AID (NON-NEED-BASED) ***Receiving aid:*** Freshmen: 20% (571). Undergraduates: 11% (1,481). ***Average award:*** Freshmen: $2204. Undergraduates: $3603. ***Scholarships, grants, and awards by category:*** *Academic interests/achievement:* business, general academic interests/achievements, mathematics, social sciences. *Creative arts/performance:* applied art and design, music, theater/drama. *Special achievements/activities:* leadership. *Special characteristics:* children of faculty/staff. ***Tuition waivers:*** Full or partial for employees or children of employees, senior citizens. ***ROTC:*** Army, Air Force cooperative.

LOANS ***Student loans:*** 77% of past graduating class borrowed through all loan programs. *Average indebtedness per student:* $36,469. ***Average need-based loan:*** Freshmen: $3220. Undergraduates: $4057. ***Programs:*** Federal Direct (Subsidized and Unsubsidized Stafford, PLUS), Federal Nursing.

WORK-STUDY ***Federal work-study:*** 253 jobs averaging $1691. ***State or other work-study/employment:*** Part-time jobs available.

APPLYING FOR FINANCIAL AID ***Required financial aid form:*** FAFSA. ***Notification date:*** Continuous. Students must reply within 4 weeks of notification.

CONTACT Mr. David McIlhenny, Interim Director, West Chester University of Pennsylvania, 25 University Avenue, Suite 030, West Chester, PA 19383, 610-436-2627 or toll-free 877-315-2165 (in-state). *Fax:* 610-436-2574. *E-mail:* finaid@wcupa.edu.
Website: http://www.wcupa.edu/.

WESTCLIFF UNIVERSITY

Irvine, CA

Tuition & fees: N/R **Average undergraduate aid package: $9115**

ABOUT THE INSTITUTION Proprietary, coed. Federal methodology is used as a basis for awarding need-based institutional aid.

FRESHMAN FINANCIAL AID (Fall 2019, est.) 13 applied for aid; of those 69% were deemed to have need. 100% of freshmen with need received aid. ***Average financial aid package:*** $9517 (excluding resources awarded to replace EFC). 1% of all full-time freshmen had no need and received non-need-based gift aid.

UNDERGRADUATE FINANCIAL AID (Fall 2019, est.) 83 applied for aid; of those 67% were deemed to have need. ***Average financial aid package:*** $9115 (excluding resources awarded to replace EFC). 1% of all full-time undergraduates had no need and received non-need-based gift aid.

GIFT AID (NEED-BASED) ***Total amount:*** $250,621 (100% federal). ***Scholarships, grants, and awards:*** Federal Pell, FSEOG, private, college/university gift aid from institutional funds.

GIFT AID (NON-NEED-BASED) ***Total amount:*** $24,333 (94% institutional, 6% external sources). ***Receiving aid:*** Freshmen: 4% (9). Undergraduates: 6% (41). ***Average award:*** Freshmen: $333. Undergraduates: $833.

LOANS ***Student loans:*** $502,576 (52% need-based, 48% non-need-based). ***Average need-based loan:*** Freshmen: $3897. Undergraduates: $5773. ***Parent loans:*** $71,103 (100% need-based). ***Programs:*** Federal Direct (Subsidized and Unsubsidized Stafford, PLUS).

ATHLETIC AWARDS Total amount: $25,865 (100% non-need-based).

APPLYING FOR FINANCIAL AID ***Required financial aid forms:*** FAFSA, institution's own form.

CONTACT Benjamin Favis, Director of Financial Aid, Westcliff University, 16715 Von Karman Avenue, #100, Irvine, CA 92606, 888-4918686. *E-mail:* benjaminfavis@westcliff.edu.
Website: http://www.westcliff.edu/.

WEST COAST UNIVERSITY

Anaheim, CA

CONTACT Financial Aid Office, West Coast University, 1477 S. Manchester Avenue, Anaheim, CA 92802, 714-782-1700.
Website: http://westcoastuniversity.edu/.

WEST COAST UNIVERSITY

North Hollywood, CA

CONTACT Financial Aid Office, West Coast University, 12215 Victory Boulevard, North Hollywood, CA 91606, 323-315-5207 or toll-free 866-508-2684.
Website: http://www.westcoastuniversity.edu/.

WEST COAST UNIVERSITY - DALLAS

Dallas, TX

CONTACT Financial Aid Office, West Coast University - Dallas, 8435 N. Stemmons Freeway, Dallas, TX 75247, 214-453-4533 or toll-free 866-508-2684.
Website: http://www.westcoastuniversity.edu/.

WEST COAST UNIVERSITY - MIAMI

Doral, FL

CONTACT Financial Aid Office, West Coast University - Miami, 9250 NW 36th Street, Doral, FL 33178, 786-501-7070.
Website: http://westcoastuniversity.edu/.

WEST COAST UNIVERSITY - ONTARIO

Ontario, CA

CONTACT Financial Aid Office, West Coast University - Ontario, 2855 E. Guasti Road, Ontario, CA 91761, 909-467-6100.
Website: http://westcoastuniversity.edu/.

WESTERN CAROLINA UNIVERSITY

Cullowhee, NC

Tuition & fees (NC res): $1000 **Average undergraduate aid package: $11,296**

ABOUT THE INSTITUTION State-supported, coed. ***Awards:*** certificates, bachelor's, master's, and doctoral degrees. 70 undergraduate majors. ***Total enrollment:*** 12,167. Undergraduates: 10,469. Freshmen: 2,106. Federal methodology is used as a basis for awarding need-based institutional aid.

UNDERGRADUATE EXPENSES for 2020–2021 ***Application fee:*** $65. ***Tuition, state resident:*** full-time $1000. ***Tuition, nonresident:*** full-time $5000. Full-time tuition and fees vary according to degree level. Part-time tuition and fees vary according to course load and degree level. Room and board charges vary according to board plan and housing facility. ***Payment plan:*** Guaranteed tuition.

FRESHMAN FINANCIAL AID (Fall 2018) 1478 applied for aid; of those 76% were deemed to have need. 98% of freshmen with need received aid; of those 12% had need fully met. ***Average percent of need met:*** 64% (excluding resources awarded to replace EFC). ***Average financial aid package:*** $10,880 (excluding resources awarded to replace EFC). 5% of all full-time freshmen had no need and received non-need-based gift aid.

UNDERGRADUATE FINANCIAL AID (Fall 2018) 6,215 applied for aid; of those 82% were deemed to have need. 98% of undergraduates with need received aid; of those 13% had need fully met. ***Average percent of need met:*** 65% (excluding resources awarded to replace EFC). ***Average financial aid package:*** $11,296 (excluding resources awarded to replace EFC). 5% of all full-time undergraduates had no need and received non-need-based gift aid.

GIFT AID (NEED-BASED) ***Total amount:*** $31,263,903 (45% federal, 29% state, 20% institutional, 6% external sources). ***Receiving aid:*** Freshmen: 64% (1,044); all full-time undergraduates: 63% (4,689). ***Average award:*** Freshmen: $6538; Undergraduates: $6323. ***Scholarships, grants, and awards:*** Federal Pell, FSEOG, state, private, college/university gift aid from institutional funds.

GIFT AID (NON-NEED-BASED) ***Total amount:*** $1,993,557 (1% federal, 8% state, 54% institutional, 37% external sources). ***Receiving aid:*** Freshmen: 3% (42). Undergraduates: 2% (124). ***Average award:*** Freshmen: $2565. Undergraduates: $2379. ***Scholarships, grants, and awards by category:*** *Academic interests/achievement:* biological sciences, business, communication, education, English, general academic interests/achievements, mathematics. *Creative arts/performance:* applied art and design, music, theater/drama. *Special characteristics:* ethnic background, handicapped students, local/state students, members of minority groups.

LOANS ***Student loans:*** $35,517,735 (74% need-based, 26% non-need-based). 65% of past graduating class borrowed through all loan programs. *Average indebtedness per student:* $20,123. ***Average need-based loan:*** Freshmen: $5169. Undergraduates: $6029. ***Parent loans:*** $15,644,006 (27% need-based, 73% non-need-based). ***Programs:*** Federal Direct (Subsidized and Unsubsidized Stafford, PLUS), Perkins.

WORK-STUDY ***Federal work-study:*** Total amount: $608,216; jobs available.

ATHLETIC AWARDS Total amount: $3,020,961 (56% need-based, 44% non-need-based).

APPLYING FOR FINANCIAL AID ***Required financial aid forms:*** FAFSA, institution's own form. ***Financial aid deadline (priority):*** 3/15. ***Notification date:*** Continuous beginning 4/1.

CONTACT Ms. Trina F. Orr, Director of Financial Aid, Western Carolina University, 123 Killian Annex, Cullowhee, NC 28723, 828-227-7292 or toll-free 877-WCU4YOU. *Fax:* 828-227-7042. *E-mail:* torr@email.wcu.edu.
Website: http://www.wcu.edu/.

WESTERN COLORADO UNIVERSITY

Gunnison, CO

Tuition & fees (CO res): $10,437 **Average undergraduate aid package: $12,280**

ABOUT THE INSTITUTION State-supported, coed. ***Awards:*** certificates, bachelor's, and master's degrees. 22 undergraduate majors. ***Total enrollment:*** 3,493. Undergraduates: 3,040. Freshmen: 454. Federal methodology is used as a basis for awarding need-based institutional aid.

UNDERGRADUATE EXPENSES for 2020–2021 ***Application fee:*** $30. ***Tuition, state resident:*** full-time $6624; part-time $276 per credit hour. ***Tuition, nonresident:*** full-time $18,096; part-time $754 per credit hour. ***Required fees:*** full-time $3813. ***College room and board:*** $9704; ***Room only:*** $5030. Room and board charges vary according to board plan and housing facility.

FRESHMAN FINANCIAL AID (Fall 2019, est.) 434 applied for aid; of those 64% were deemed to have need. 100% of freshmen with need received aid; of those 4% had need fully met. ***Average percent of need met:*** 71% (excluding resources awarded to replace EFC). ***Average financial aid package:*** $12,301 (excluding resources awarded to replace EFC). 28% of all full-time freshmen had no need and received non-need-based gift aid.

UNDERGRADUATE FINANCIAL AID (Fall 2019, est.) 1,571 applied for aid; of those 63% were deemed to have need. 100% of undergraduates with need received aid; of those 3% had need fully met. ***Average percent of need met:*** 69% (excluding resources awarded to replace EFC). ***Average financial aid package:*** $12,280 (excluding resources awarded to replace EFC). 26% of all full-time undergraduates had no need and received non-need-based gift aid.

GIFT AID (NEED-BASED) ***Receiving aid:*** Freshmen: 59% (267); all full-time undergraduates: 53% (918). ***Average award:*** Freshmen: $10,157; Undergraduates: $9523. ***Scholarships, grants, and awards:*** Federal Pell, FSEOG, state, private, college/university gift aid from institutional funds.

GIFT AID (NON-NEED-BASED) ***Receiving aid:*** Freshmen: 59% (267). Undergraduates: 28% (479). ***Average award:*** Freshmen: $5460. Undergraduates: $5399. ***Scholarships, grants, and awards by category:*** *Academic interests/achievement:* general academic interests/achievements. *Creative arts/performance:* applied art and design, music, performing arts. *Special achievements/activities:* leadership. *Special characteristics:* children and siblings of alumni. ***Tuition waivers:*** Full or partial for employees or children of employees, senior citizens.

LOANS ***Student loans:*** 62% of past graduating class borrowed through all loan programs. *Average indebtedness per student:* $26,060. ***Average need-based loan:*** Freshmen: $3347. Undergraduates: $4224. ***Programs:*** Federal Direct (Subsidized and Unsubsidized Stafford, PLUS).

WORK-STUDY Federal work-study jobs available. ***State or other work-study/employment:*** Part-time jobs available.

APPLYING FOR FINANCIAL AID ***Required financial aid form:*** FAFSA. ***Financial aid deadline:*** Continuous. ***Notification date:*** Continuous. Students must reply within 3 weeks of notification.

CONTACT Carrie Shaw, Director of Financial Aid, Western Colorado University, Taylor Hall, Gunnison, CO 81231, 970-943-7015 or toll-free 800-876-5309. *Fax:* 970-943-3086. *E-mail:* cshaw@western.edu.
Website: http://www.western.edu/.

WESTERN CONNECTICUT STATE UNIVERSITY

Danbury, CT

Tuition & fees (CT res): $11,781 **Average undergraduate aid package: $9582**

ABOUT THE INSTITUTION State-supported, coed. ***Awards:*** certificates, associate, bachelor's, master's, and doctoral degrees. 37 undergraduate majors. ***Total enrollment:*** 5,631. Undergraduates: 4,972. Freshmen: 840. Federal methodology is used as a basis for awarding need-based institutional aid.

UNDERGRADUATE EXPENSES for 2020–2021 ***Application fee:*** $50. ***Tuition, state resident:*** full-time $6162; part-time $257 per credit hour. ***Tuition, nonresident:*** full-time $18,436; part-time $257 per credit hour. ***Required fees:*** full-time $5619; $60 per term. ***College room and board:*** $13,921; ***Room only:*** $8020. Room and board charges vary according to board plan and housing facility.

FRESHMAN FINANCIAL AID (Fall 2019, est.) 717 applied for aid; of those 69% were deemed to have need. 98% of freshmen with need received aid; of those 12% had need fully met. ***Average percent of need met:*** 40% (excluding resources awarded to replace EFC). ***Average financial aid package:*** $10,133 (excluding resources awarded to replace EFC). 6% of all full-time freshmen had no need and received non-need-based gift aid.

UNDERGRADUATE FINANCIAL AID (Fall 2019, est.) 3,183 applied for aid; of those 70% were deemed to have need. 97% of undergraduates with need received aid; of those 13% had need fully met. ***Average percent of need met:*** 41% (excluding resources awarded to replace EFC). ***Average financial aid package:*** $9582 (excluding resources awarded to replace EFC). 5% of all full-time undergraduates had no need and received non-need-based gift aid.

GIFT AID (NEED-BASED) ***Receiving aid:*** Freshmen: 44% (362); all full-time undergraduates: 40% (1,632). ***Average award:*** Freshmen: $5994; Undergraduates: $5639. ***Scholarships, grants, and awards:*** Federal Pell, FSEOG, state, college/university gift aid from institutional funds.

GIFT AID (NON-NEED-BASED) ***Receiving aid:*** Freshmen: 15% (122). Undergraduates: 9% (357). ***Average award:*** Freshmen: $4146. Undergraduates: $4947. ***Scholarships, grants, and awards by category:*** *Academic interests/achievement:* 305 awards ($1,380,955 total): general academic interests/achievements.

ROTC: Army cooperative, Air Force cooperative.

LOANS ***Student loans:*** 72% of past graduating class borrowed through all loan programs. *Average indebtedness per student:* $38,657. ***Average need-based loan:*** Freshmen: $3239. Undergraduates: $4103. ***Programs:*** Federal Direct (Subsidized and Unsubsidized Stafford, PLUS), Federal Nursing.

WORK-STUDY ***Federal work-study:*** 130 jobs averaging $1348.

APPLYING FOR FINANCIAL AID ***Required financial aid form:*** FAFSA. ***Notification date:*** Continuous. Students must reply within 2 weeks of notification.

CONTACT Melissa Stephens, Director of Student Financial Services, Western Connecticut State University, 181 White Street, Danbury, CT 06810-6860, 203-837-8580 or toll-free 877-837-WCSU. *Fax:* 203-837-8528. *E-mail:* wcsufinancialaid@wcsu.edu.
Website: http://www.wcsu.edu/.

WESTERN GOVERNORS UNIVERSITY

Salt Lake City, UT

CONTACT Robert Collins, Vice President of Financial Aid, Western Governors University, 4001 South 700 East, Suite 700, Salt Lake City, UT 84107, 877-435-7948 or toll-free 866-225-5948. *Fax:* 801-907-7727. *E-mail:* robert.collins@wgu.edu.
Website: http://www.wgu.edu/.

WESTERN ILLINOIS UNIVERSITY

Macomb, IL

Tuition & fees (IL res): $11,666 **Average undergraduate aid package: $13,378**

ABOUT THE INSTITUTION State-supported, coed. ***Awards:*** certificates, bachelor's, master's, and doctoral degrees. 61 undergraduate majors. ***Total enrollment:*** 8,294. Undergraduates: 6,754. Freshmen: 934. Federal methodology is used as a basis for awarding need-based institutional aid.

UNDERGRADUATE EXPENSES for 2019–2020 ***Application fee:*** $30. ***One-time required fee:*** $210. ***Tuition, state resident:*** full-time $8883; part-time $296 per credit hour. ***Tuition, nonresident:*** full-time $8883; part-time $296 per credit hour. ***Required fees:*** full-time $2783; $92.78 per credit hour. Full-time tuition and fees vary according to course load, location, and student level. Part-time tuition and fees vary according to course load, location, and student level. ***College room and board:*** $9800; ***Room only:*** $6000. Room and board charges vary according to board plan, housing facility, and student level. ***Payment plan:*** Guaranteed tuition.

FRESHMAN FINANCIAL AID (Fall 2019, est.) 822 applied for aid; of those 84% were deemed to have need. 100% of freshmen with need received aid; of those 39% had need fully met. ***Average percent of need met:*** 76% (excluding resources

awarded to replace EFC). ***Average financial aid package:*** $15,777 (excluding resources awarded to replace EFC). 14% of all full-time freshmen had no need and received non-need-based gift aid.

UNDERGRADUATE FINANCIAL AID (Fall 2019, est.) 4,531 applied for aid; of those 86% were deemed to have need. 99% of undergraduates with need received aid; of those 28% had need fully met. ***Average percent of need met:*** 66% (excluding resources awarded to replace EFC). ***Average financial aid package:*** $13,378 (excluding resources awarded to replace EFC). 11% of all full-time undergraduates had no need and received non-need-based gift aid.

GIFT AID (NEED-BASED) ***Total amount:*** $37,111,292 (38% federal, 38% state, 22% institutional, 2% external sources). ***Receiving aid:*** Freshmen: 71% (625); all full-time undergraduates: 58% (2,998). ***Average award:*** Freshmen: $13,984; Undergraduates: $10,481. ***Scholarships, grants, and awards:*** Federal Pell, FSEOG, state, private, college/university gift aid from institutional funds.

GIFT AID (NON-NEED-BASED) ***Total amount:*** $4,123,960 (28% state, 67% institutional, 5% external sources). ***Receiving aid:*** Freshmen: 57% (507). Undergraduates: 45% (2,304). ***Average award:*** Freshmen: $5062. Undergraduates: $3722. ***Scholarships, grants, and awards by category:*** *Academic interests/achievement:* 6,511 awards ($9,773,030 total): agriculture, area/ethnic studies, biological sciences, business, communication, computer science, education, engineering/technologies, English, foreign languages, general academic interests/achievements, health fields, home economics, international studies, library science, mathematics, military science, physical sciences, religion/biblical studies, social sciences. *Creative arts/performance:* 540 awards ($622,910 total): applied art and design, art/fine arts, cinema/film/broadcasting, creative writing, dance, debating, general creative arts/performance, journalism/publications, music, performing arts, theater/drama. *Special achievements/activities:* 231 awards ($130,314 total): community service, general special achievements/activities, leadership. *Special characteristics:* 1,081 awards ($2,481,118 total): children of faculty/staff, general special characteristics, international students, members of minority groups. ***Tuition waivers:*** Full or partial for employees or children of employees, senior citizens. ***ROTC:*** Army.

LOANS ***Student loans:*** $33,280,216 (40% need-based, 60% non-need-based). 86% of past graduating class borrowed through all loan programs. *Average indebtedness per student:* $30,522. ***Average need-based loan:*** Freshmen: $3247. Undergraduates: $4302. ***Parent loans:*** $4,732,553 (79% need-based, 21% non-need-based). ***Programs:*** Federal Direct (Subsidized and Unsubsidized Stafford, PLUS), college/university, private loans.

WORK-STUDY ***Federal work-study:*** Total amount: $452,864; 221 jobs averaging $2240. ***State or other work-study/employment:*** Total amount: $1,361,727 (74% need-based, 26% non-need-based). 1,118 part-time jobs averaging $1713.

ATHLETIC AWARDS Total amount: $3,476,286 (38% need-based, 62% non-need-based).

APPLYING FOR FINANCIAL AID ***Required financial aid form:*** FAFSA. ***Financial aid deadline (priority):*** 2/15. ***Notification date:*** Continuous beginning 10/15.

CONTACT Office of Financial Aid, Western Illinois University, 1 University Circle, Macomb, IL 61455-1390, 309-298-2446 or toll-free 877-742-5948. *Fax:* 309-298-2353. *E-mail:* finaid@wiu.edu.
Website: http://www.wiu.edu/.

WESTERN KENTUCKY UNIVERSITY

Bowling Green, KY

Tuition & fees (area res): $10,802	Average undergraduate aid package: $15,349

ABOUT THE INSTITUTION State-supported, coed. ***Awards:*** certificates, associate, bachelor's, master's, and doctoral degrees. 91 undergraduate majors. ***Total enrollment:*** 18,171. Undergraduates: 15,895. Freshmen: 2,714. Federal methodology is used as a basis for awarding need-based institutional aid.

UNDERGRADUATE EXPENSES for 2020–2021 ***Application fee:*** $45. ***Tuition, area resident:*** full-time $10,802; part-time $450 per credit hour. ***Tuition, state resident:*** full-time $10,802; part-time $450 per credit hour. ***Tuition, nonresident:*** full-time $26,496; part-time $1104 per credit hour. Full-time tuition and fees vary according to reciprocity agreements. Part-time tuition and fees vary according to reciprocity agreements. ***College room and board:*** $8432; ***Room only:*** $4678. Room and board charges vary according to board plan and housing facility.

FRESHMAN FINANCIAL AID (Fall 2018) 2693 applied for aid; of those 76% were deemed to have need. 99% of freshmen with need received aid; of those 23% had need fully met. ***Average percent of need met:*** 23% (excluding resources awarded to replace EFC). ***Average financial aid package:*** $14,844 (excluding resources awarded to replace EFC). 21% of all full-time freshmen had no need and received non-need-based gift aid.

UNDERGRADUATE FINANCIAL AID (Fall 2018) 9,938 applied for aid; of those 79% were deemed to have need. 98% of undergraduates with need received aid; of those 18% had need fully met. ***Average percent of need met:*** 18% (excluding resources awarded to replace EFC). ***Average financial aid package:*** $15,349 (excluding resources awarded to replace EFC). 17% of all full-time undergraduates had no need and received non-need-based gift aid.

GIFT AID (NEED-BASED) ***Total amount:*** $29,623,798 (74% federal, 21% state, 5% institutional). ***Receiving aid:*** Freshmen: 41% (1,195); all full-time undergraduates: 39% (4,685). ***Average award:*** Freshmen: $5772; Undergraduates: $5702. ***Scholarships, grants, and awards:*** Federal Pell, FSEOG, state, private, college/university gift aid from institutional funds, United Negro College Fund.

GIFT AID (NON-NEED-BASED) ***Total amount:*** $49,904,844 (6% federal, 26% state, 62% institutional, 6% external sources). ***Receiving aid:*** Freshmen: 64% (1,851). Undergraduates: 51% (6,158). ***Average award:*** Freshmen: $5356. Undergraduates: $6102. ***Scholarships, grants, and awards by category:*** *Academic interests/achievement:* 6,591 awards ($24,525,479 total): agriculture, biological sciences, business, communication, education, engineering/technologies, English, foreign languages, general academic interests/achievements, health fields, home economics, mathematics, military science, physical sciences, premedicine, religion/biblical studies, social sciences. *Creative arts/performance:* 604 awards ($1,564,914 total): applied art and design, cinema/film/broadcasting, dance, debating, general creative arts/performance, journalism/publications, music, theater/drama. *Special achievements/activities:* 668 awards ($1,162,384 total): general special achievements/activities, leadership, memberships. *Special characteristics:* 1,908 awards ($3,625,499 total): ethnic background, general special characteristics, handicapped students, international students, local/state students, members of minority groups, out-of-state students, religious affiliation, veterans, veterans' children. ***Tuition waivers:*** Full or partial for employees or children of employees, senior citizens. ***ROTC:*** Army, Air Force cooperative.

LOANS ***Student loans:*** $54,409,807 (39% need-based, 61% non-need-based). 57% of past graduating class borrowed through all loan programs. *Average indebtedness per student:* $26,803. ***Average need-based loan:*** Freshmen: $2983. Undergraduates: $3857. ***Parent loans:*** $16,220,070 (100% non-need-based). ***Programs:*** Federal Direct (Subsidized and Unsubsidized Stafford, PLUS), Perkins.

WORK-STUDY ***Federal work-study:*** Total amount: $1,649,800; 791 jobs averaging $2182. ***State or other work-study/employment:*** Total amount: $4,061,913 (100% non-need-based). 1,707 part-time jobs averaging $2404.

ATHLETIC AWARDS Total amount: $5,670,393 (100% non-need-based).

APPLYING FOR FINANCIAL AID ***Required financial aid form:*** FAFSA. ***Financial aid deadline (priority):*** 2/15. ***Notification date:*** Continuous beginning 3/1.

CONTACT Bryson Davis, Interim Director of Student Financial Assistance, Western Kentucky University, Potter Hall, Bowling Green, KY 42101-1018, 270-745-2051 or toll-free 800-495-8463. *Fax:* 270-745-6586. *E-mail:* bryson.davis@wku.edu.
Website: http://www.wku.edu/.

WESTERN MICHIGAN UNIVERSITY

Kalamazoo, MI

Tuition & fees (MI res): $13,017	Average undergraduate aid package: $11,650

ABOUT THE INSTITUTION State-supported, coed. ***Awards:*** certificates, bachelor's, master's, and doctoral degrees. 160 undergraduate majors. ***Total enrollment:*** 22,562. Undergraduates: 17,760. Freshmen: 3,023. Federal methodology is used as a basis for awarding need-based institutional aid.

UNDERGRADUATE EXPENSES for 2019–2020 ***Application fee:*** $40. ***Tuition, state resident:*** full-time $12,094; part-time $504 per credit hour. ***Tuition, nonresident:*** full-time $15,118; part-time $630 per credit hour. ***Required fees:*** full-time $923; $259 per term. Full-time tuition and fees vary according to course load, location, program, reciprocity agreements, and student level. Part-time tuition and fees vary according to course load, location, program, reciprocity agreements, and student level. ***College room and board:*** $10,567; ***Room only:*** $5395. Room and board charges vary according to board plan and housing facility.

FRESHMAN FINANCIAL AID (Fall 2018) 2575 applied for aid; of those 72% were deemed to have need. 95% of freshmen with need received aid; of those 11% had need fully met. ***Average percent of need met:*** 55% (excluding resources awarded to replace EFC). ***Average financial aid package:*** $10,699 (excluding resources awarded to replace EFC). 11% of all full-time freshmen had no need and received non-need-based gift aid.

UNDERGRADUATE FINANCIAL AID (Fall 2018) 11,186 applied for aid; of those 80% were deemed to have need. 97% of undergraduates with need received aid; of those 10% had need fully met. ***Average percent of need met:*** 56% (excluding resources awarded to replace EFC). ***Average financial aid package:*** $11,650 (excluding resources awarded to replace EFC). 9% of all full-time undergraduates had no need and received non-need-based gift aid.

GIFT AID (NEED-BASED) ***Total amount:*** $72,130,951 (39% federal, 3% state, 49% institutional, 9% external sources). ***Receiving aid:*** Freshmen: 47% (1,398); all full-time undergraduates: 47% (6,978). ***Average award:*** Freshmen: $9043; Undergraduates: $9216. ***Scholarships, grants, and awards:*** Federal Pell, FSEOG, state, private, college/university gift aid from institutional funds.

GIFT AID (NON-NEED-BASED) ***Total amount:*** $11,441,875 (72% institutional, 28% external sources). ***Receiving aid:*** Freshmen: 3% (89). Undergraduates: 2% (252). ***Average award:*** Freshmen: $5057. Undergraduates: $5324. ***Scholarships, grants, and awards by category:*** *Academic interests/achievement:* general academic interests/achievements. *Creative arts/performance:* applied art and design, dance, general creative arts/performance, music, theater/drama. *Special characteristics:* children and siblings of alumni, children of faculty/staff, international students, local/state students, out-of-state students, previous college experience, veterans. ***Tuition waivers:*** Full or partial for employees or children of employees, senior citizens. ***ROTC:*** Army.

LOANS ***Student loans:*** $99,312,238 (70% need-based, 30% non-need-based). 74% of past graduating class borrowed through all loan programs. *Average indebtedness per student:* $35,204. ***Average need-based loan:*** Freshmen: $3289. Undergraduates: $4266. ***Parent loans:*** $25,878,659 (43% need-based, 57% non-need-based). ***Programs:*** Federal Direct (Subsidized and Unsubsidized Stafford, PLUS), Perkins, private loans.

WORK-STUDY ***Federal work-study:*** Total amount: $1,264,753; 544 jobs averaging $1876. ***State or other work-study/employment:*** Part-time jobs available.

ATHLETIC AWARDS Total amount: $8,914,686 (27% need-based, 73% non-need-based).

APPLYING FOR FINANCIAL AID ***Required financial aid form:*** FAFSA. ***Financial aid deadline (priority):*** 3/1. ***Notification date:*** Continuous beginning 12/10.

CONTACT Ms. Shashanta James, Interim Director of Financial Aid, Western Michigan University, Faunce Student Services, 1903 West Michigan Avenue, Kalamazoo, MI 49008-5337, 269-387-6000. *E-mail:* finaid-info@wmich.edu. *Website:* http://www.wmich.edu/.

WESTERN NEW ENGLAND UNIVERSITY

Springfield, MA

Tuition & fees: $39,226 | **Average undergraduate aid package: $27,353**

ABOUT THE INSTITUTION Independent, coed. ***Awards:*** certificates, associate, bachelor's, master's, and doctoral degrees. 48 undergraduate majors. ***Total enrollment:*** 3,833. Undergraduates: 2,698. Freshmen: 691. Federal methodology is used as a basis for awarding need-based institutional aid.

UNDERGRADUATE EXPENSES for 2020–2021 ***Application fee:*** $40. ***Comprehensive fee:*** $53,470 includes full-time tuition ($36,606), mandatory fees ($2620), and room and board ($14,244). Full-time tuition and fees vary according to course load and program. Room and board charges vary according to board plan and housing facility. ***Part-time tuition:*** $980 per credit. Part-time tuition and fees vary according to course load and program. ***Payment plan:*** Tuition prepayment.

FRESHMAN FINANCIAL AID (Fall 2019, est.) 659 applied for aid; of those 91% were deemed to have need. 100% of freshmen with need received aid; of those 20% had need fully met. ***Average percent of need met:*** 77% (excluding resources awarded to replace EFC). ***Average financial aid package:*** $29,045 (excluding resources awarded to replace EFC). 13% of all full-time freshmen had no need and received non-need-based gift aid.

UNDERGRADUATE FINANCIAL AID (Fall 2019, est.) 2,228 applied for aid; of those 90% were deemed to have need. 99% of undergraduates with need received aid; of those 16% had need fully met. ***Average percent of need met:*** 74% (excluding resources awarded to replace EFC). ***Average financial aid package:*** $27,353 (excluding resources awarded to replace EFC). 22% of all full-time undergraduates had no need and received non-need-based gift aid.

GIFT AID (NEED-BASED) ***Total amount:*** $41,262,275 (10% federal, 2% state, 86% institutional, 2% external sources). ***Receiving aid:*** Freshmen: 87% (598); all full-time undergraduates: 77% (1,997). ***Average award:*** Freshmen: $25,000; Undergraduates: $22,537. ***Scholarships, grants, and awards:*** Federal Pell, FSEOG, state, private, college/university gift aid from institutional funds.

GIFT AID (NON-NEED-BASED) ***Total amount:*** $10,210,461 (6% federal, 92% institutional, 2% external sources). ***Receiving aid:*** Freshmen: 13% (90). Undergraduates: 9% (239). ***Average award:*** Freshmen: $16,528. Undergraduates: $14,913. ***Scholarships, grants, and awards by category:*** *Academic interests/achievement:* business, computer science, engineering/technologies, general academic interests/achievements. *Creative arts/performance:* 3 awards ($2000 total): music. *Special achievements/activities:* 48 awards ($144,000 total): leadership. *Special characteristics:* 97 awards ($87,000 total): children of faculty/staff, siblings of current students. ***Tuition waivers:*** Full or partial for employees or children of employees. ***ROTC:*** Army, Air Force cooperative.

LOANS ***Student loans:*** $26,620,396 (62% need-based, 38% non-need-based). 80% of past graduating class borrowed through all loan programs. *Average indebtedness per student:* $43,980. ***Average need-based loan:*** Freshmen: $2788. Undergraduates: $3758. ***Parent loans:*** $6,794,908 (54% need-based, 46% non-need-based). ***Programs:*** Federal Direct (Subsidized and Unsubsidized Stafford, PLUS).

WORK-STUDY ***Federal work-study:*** Total amount: $2,496,466; 1,050 jobs averaging $1800. ***State or other work-study/employment:*** Total amount: $300,000 (100% non-need-based). Part-time jobs available.

APPLYING FOR FINANCIAL AID ***Required financial aid forms:*** FAFSA, FAFSA using IRS Data Retrieval Tool. ***Financial aid deadline (priority):*** 3/1. ***Notification date:*** Continuous beginning 12/15. Students must reply by 5/1 or within 2 weeks of notification.

CONTACT Ms. Kathy M. Chambers, Director of Financial Aid, Western New England University, 1215 Wilbraham Road, Springfield, MA 01119-2684, 413-796-2080 or toll-free 800-325-1122 Ext.1321. *Fax:* 413-796-2081. *E-mail:* finaid@wne.edu. *Website:* http://www.wne.edu/.

WESTERN NEW MEXICO UNIVERSITY

Silver City, NM

Tuition & fees (NM res): $8609 | **Average undergraduate aid package: $11,512**

ABOUT THE INSTITUTION State-supported, coed. ***Awards:*** certificates, diplomas, associate, bachelor's, and master's degrees. 54 undergraduate majors. ***Total enrollment:*** 3,193. Undergraduates: 2,214. Freshmen: 290. Federal methodology is used as a basis for awarding need-based institutional aid.

UNDERGRADUATE EXPENSES for 2020–2021 ***Application fee:*** $30. ***One-time required fee:*** $83. ***Tuition, state resident:*** full-time $7396; part-time $6026 per year. ***Tuition, nonresident:*** full-time $15,252; part-time $12,427 per year. ***Required fees:*** full-time $1213; $1977.36 per year. Full-time tuition and fees vary according to course load. Part-time tuition and fees vary according to course load. ***College room and board:*** $11,390; ***Room only:*** $7010. Room and board charges vary according to board plan, housing facility, and location.

FRESHMAN FINANCIAL AID (Fall 2018) 240 applied for aid; of those 88% were deemed to have need. 100% of freshmen with need received aid; of those 12% had need fully met. ***Average percent of need met:*** 1% (excluding resources awarded to replace EFC). ***Average financial aid package:*** $11,245 (excluding resources awarded to replace EFC). 8% of all full-time freshmen had no need and received non-need-based gift aid.

UNDERGRADUATE FINANCIAL AID (Fall 2018) 964 applied for aid; of those 87% were deemed to have need. 100% of undergraduates with need received aid; of those 12% had need fully met. ***Average percent of need met:*** 6% (excluding resources awarded to replace EFC). ***Average financial aid package:*** $11,512

(excluding resources awarded to replace EFC). 8% of all full-time undergraduates had no need and received non-need-based gift aid.

GIFT AID (NEED-BASED) ***Total amount:*** $11,164,640 (44% federal, 6% state, 50% external sources). ***Receiving aid:*** Freshmen: 65% (164); all full-time undergraduates: 62% (666). ***Average award:*** Freshmen: $5705; Undergraduates: $5790. ***Scholarships, grants, and awards:*** Federal Pell, state, private, college/university gift aid from institutional funds.

GIFT AID (NON-NEED-BASED) ***Total amount:*** $3,899,802 (21% state, 20% institutional, 59% external sources). ***Receiving aid:*** Freshmen: 63% (158). Undergraduates: 40% (431). ***Average award:*** Freshmen: $2575. Undergraduates: $3875. ***Scholarships, grants, and awards by category:*** *Academic interests/achievement:* biological sciences, business, education. *Special achievements/activities:* community service, leadership. *Special characteristics:* children and siblings of alumni, children of faculty/staff, out-of-state students. ***Tuition waivers:*** Full or partial for employees or children of employees, senior citizens.

LOANS ***Student loans:*** $5,395,095 (48% need-based, 52% non-need-based). ***Average need-based loan:*** Freshmen: $2053. Undergraduates: $2893. ***Parent loans:*** $197,039 (100% non-need-based). ***Programs:*** Federal Direct (Subsidized and Unsubsidized Stafford), Federal Nursing.

WORK-STUDY ***Federal work-study:*** Total amount: $158,426; jobs available. ***State or other work-study/employment:*** Total amount: $137,299 (100% need-based). Part-time jobs available.

ATHLETIC AWARDS Total amount: $706,856 (100% non-need-based).

APPLYING FOR FINANCIAL AID ***Required financial aid forms:*** FAFSA, institution's own form, CSS Financial Aid PROFILE, state aid form, noncustodial (divorced/separated) parent's statement, business/farm supplement. ***Financial aid deadline (priority):*** 3/30. ***Notification date:*** Continuous.

CONTACT Ms. Debra Reyes, Director, Financial Aid, Western New Mexico University, PO Box 680, 1000 W. College Ave., Silver City, NM 88062, 575-538-6317 or toll-free 800-872-WNMU. *E-mail:* Debra.Reyes@wnmu.edu.
Website: http://www.wnmu.edu/.

WESTERN OREGON UNIVERSITY

Monmouth, OR

Tuition & fees: N/R	Average undergraduate aid package: $9800

ABOUT THE INSTITUTION State-supported, coed. ***Awards:*** certificates, bachelor's, and master's degrees. 35 undergraduate majors. ***Total enrollment:*** 4,929. Undergraduates: 4,426. Freshmen: 789. Federal methodology is used as a basis for awarding need-based institutional aid.

FRESHMAN FINANCIAL AID (Fall 2018) 569 applied for aid; of those 79% were deemed to have need. 100% of freshmen with need received aid; of those 13% had need fully met. ***Average percent of need met:*** 57% (excluding resources awarded to replace EFC). ***Average financial aid package:*** $9668 (excluding resources awarded to replace EFC). 13% of all full-time freshmen had no need and received non-need-based gift aid.

UNDERGRADUATE FINANCIAL AID (Fall 2018) 2,988 applied for aid; of those 83% were deemed to have need. 100% of undergraduates with need received aid; of those 12% had need fully met. ***Average percent of need met:*** 59% (excluding resources awarded to replace EFC). ***Average financial aid package:*** $9800 (excluding resources awarded to replace EFC). 8% of all full-time undergraduates had no need and received non-need-based gift aid.

GIFT AID (NEED-BASED) ***Total amount:*** $14,224,691 (56% federal, 21% state, 11% institutional, 12% external sources). ***Receiving aid:*** Freshmen: 68% (405); all full-time undergraduates: 65% (2,075). ***Average award:*** Freshmen: $8326; Undergraduates: $7857. ***Scholarships, grants, and awards:*** Federal Pell, FSEOG, state, private, college/university gift aid from institutional funds, United Negro College Fund, TEACH Grants.

GIFT AID (NON-NEED-BASED) ***Total amount:*** $1,938,849 (1% federal, 4% state, 45% institutional, 50% external sources). ***Receiving aid:*** Freshmen: 5% (32). Undergraduates: 3% (104). ***Average award:*** Freshmen: $2676. Undergraduates: $3135. ***Scholarships, grants, and awards by category:*** *Academic interests/achievement:* biological sciences, business, communication, computer science, education, English, foreign languages, general academic interests/achievements, health fields, humanities, international studies, library science, mathematics, physical sciences, premedicine, social sciences. *Creative arts/performance:* applied art and design, dance, general creative arts/performance, music, performing arts, theater/drama. *Special achievements/activities:* community service, general special achievements/activities, hobbies/interests, leadership. *Special characteristics:* adult students, children of union members/company employees, ethnic background, first-generation college students, general special characteristics, handicapped students, international students, local/state students, members of minority groups, previous college experience, veterans. ***ROTC:*** Army cooperative.

LOANS ***Student loans:*** $18,780,443 (70% need-based, 30% non-need-based). 6% of past graduating class borrowed through all loan programs. *Average indebtedness per student:* $6815. ***Average need-based loan:*** Freshmen: $2913. Undergraduates: $3879. ***Parent loans:*** $5,676,131 (33% need-based, 67% non-need-based). ***Programs:*** Federal Direct (Subsidized and Unsubsidized Stafford, PLUS).

WORK-STUDY ***Federal work-study:*** Total amount: $244,939; 212 jobs averaging $1155.

ATHLETIC AWARDS Total amount: $539,449 (55% need-based, 45% non-need-based).

APPLYING FOR FINANCIAL AID ***Required financial aid form:*** FAFSA. ***Financial aid deadline:*** Continuous. ***Notification date:*** Continuous beginning 12/15. Students must reply within 8 weeks of notification.

CONTACT Ms. Kella Helyer, Director of Financial Aid, Western Oregon University, 345 Monmouth Avenue North, Monmouth, OR 97361, 503-838-8679 or toll-free 877-877-1593. *Fax:* 503-838-8200. *E-mail:* finaid@wou.edu.
Website: http://www.wou.edu/.

WESTERN WASHINGTON UNIVERSITY

Bellingham, WA

Tuition & fees (WA res): $8341	Average undergraduate aid package: $18,108

ABOUT THE INSTITUTION State-supported, coed. ***Awards:*** certificates, bachelor's, master's, and doctoral degrees. 100 undergraduate majors. ***Total enrollment:*** 16,142. Undergraduates: 15,240. Freshmen: 3,116. Federal methodology is used as a basis for awarding need-based institutional aid.

UNDERGRADUATE EXPENSES for 2019–2020 ***Application fee:*** $60. ***One-time required fee:*** $280. ***Tuition, state resident:*** full-time $7213; part-time $240 per credit hour. ***Tuition, nonresident:*** full-time $23,562; part-time $785 per credit hour. ***Required fees:*** full-time $1128. Full-time tuition and fees vary according to course load, location, and reciprocity agreements. Part-time tuition and fees vary according to course load, location, and reciprocity agreements. ***College room and board:*** $12,037; ***Room only:*** $7852. Room and board charges vary according to board plan, housing facility, and location.

FRESHMAN FINANCIAL AID (Fall 2019, est.) 2628 applied for aid; of those 59% were deemed to have need. 100% of freshmen with need received aid; of those 20% had need fully met. ***Average percent of need met:*** 78% (excluding resources awarded to replace EFC). ***Average financial aid package:*** $18,180 (excluding resources awarded to replace EFC). 3% of all full-time freshmen had no need and received non-need-based gift aid.

UNDERGRADUATE FINANCIAL AID (Fall 2019, est.) 9,422 applied for aid; of those 69% were deemed to have need. 100% of undergraduates with need received aid; of those 16% had need fully met. ***Average percent of need met:*** 79% (excluding resources awarded to replace EFC). ***Average financial aid package:*** $18,108 (excluding resources awarded to replace EFC). 2% of all full-time undergraduates had no need and received non-need-based gift aid.

GIFT AID (NEED-BASED) ***Receiving aid:*** Freshmen: 46% (1,410); all full-time undergraduates: 40% (5,548). ***Average award:*** Freshmen: $9646; Undergraduates: $9302. ***Scholarships, grants, and awards:*** Federal Pell, FSEOG, state, private, college/university gift aid from institutional funds.

GIFT AID (NON-NEED-BASED) ***Receiving aid:*** Freshmen: 4% (123). Undergraduates: 2% (265). ***Average award:*** Freshmen: $1769. Undergraduates: $2002. ***Scholarships, grants, and awards by category:*** *Academic interests/achievement:* biological sciences, business, communication, computer science, education, engineering/technologies, English, foreign languages, general academic interests/achievements, home economics, humanities, library science, mathematics, physical sciences, premedicine, social sciences. *Creative arts/performance:* applied art and design, art/fine arts, cinema/film/broadcasting, creative writing, dance, general creative arts/performance, journalism/publications, music, performing arts, theater/drama. *Special achievements/activities:* community service, leadership, memberships. *Special charac-*

teristics: children of public servants, children of union members/company employees, ethnic background, general special characteristics, international students, local/state students, members of minority groups, previous college experience, veterans. ***Tuition waivers:*** Full or partial for employees or children of employees, senior citizens.

LOANS *Student loans:* 53% of past graduating class borrowed through all loan programs. *Average indebtedness per student:* $22,466. ***Average need-based loan:*** Freshmen: $3529. Undergraduates: $4352. ***Programs:*** Federal Direct (Subsidized and Unsubsidized Stafford, PLUS), Perkins, college/university, alternative loans.

WORK-STUDY *Federal work-study:* 181 jobs averaging $4439. ***State or other work-study/employment:*** 486 part-time jobs averaging $4392.

APPLYING FOR FINANCIAL AID *Required financial aid form:* FAFSA. ***Notification date:*** Continuous. Students must reply within 3 weeks of notification.

CONTACT Mrs. Christina Jensen, Associate Director of Financial Aid, Systems, Western Washington University, Old Main 260C, MS 9006, 516 High Street, Bellingham, WA 98225-9006, 360-650-4088. *E-mail:* christina.jensen@wwu.edu.
Website: http://www.wwu.edu/.

WESTFIELD STATE UNIVERSITY

Westfield, MA

ABOUT THE INSTITUTION State-supported, coed. ***Awards:*** certificates, bachelor's, and master's degrees. 32 undergraduate majors. ***Total enrollment:*** 5,810. Undergraduates: 5,084. Freshmen: 1,042.

GIFT AID (NEED-BASED) *Scholarships, grants, and awards:* Federal Pell, FSEOG, state, private, college/university gift aid from institutional funds.

LOANS *Programs:* Federal Direct (Subsidized and Unsubsidized Stafford, PLUS), Perkins.

CONTACT Simone Backstedt, Assistant Director of Financial Aid, Westfield State University, 333 Western Avenue, Westfield, MA 01086, 413-572-5218. *E-mail:* sbackstedt@westfield.ma.edu.
Website: http://www.westfield.ma.edu/.

WEST LIBERTY UNIVERSITY

West Liberty, WV

CONTACT Christ Taskalines, Financial Aid Manager, West Liberty University, PO Box 295, West Liberty, WV 26074-0295, 304-336-8016 or toll-free 800-732-6204 (in-state), 866-WESTLIB (out-of-state). *Fax:* 304-336-8088. *E-mail:* taskalic@westliberty.edu.
Website: http://www.westliberty.edu/.

WESTMINSTER COLLEGE

Fulton, MO

ABOUT THE INSTITUTION Independent Presbyterian Church, coed. ***Awards:*** bachelor's degrees. 33 undergraduate majors. ***Total enrollment:*** 767. Undergraduates: 767. Freshmen: 174.

GIFT AID (NEED-BASED) *Scholarships, grants, and awards:* Federal Pell, FSEOG, state, private, college/university gift aid from institutional funds.

GIFT AID (NON-NEED-BASED) *Scholarships, grants, and awards by category:* *Academic interests/achievement:* general academic interests/achievements. *Creative arts/performance:* music. *Special achievements/activities:* general special achievements/activities, leadership. *Special characteristics:* children and siblings of alumni, children of faculty/staff, ethnic background, international students, local/state students, relatives of clergy, religious affiliation, siblings of current students, twins.

LOANS *Programs:* Federal Direct (Subsidized and Unsubsidized Stafford, PLUS).

WORK-STUDY *Federal work-study:* Total amount: $555,069; jobs available. ***State or other work-study/employment:*** Total amount: $212,024 (100% non-need-based). Part-time jobs available.

APPLYING FOR FINANCIAL AID *Required financial aid form:* FAFSA.

CONTACT Ms. Aimee Bristow, Senior Director of Student Financial Aid, Westminster College, 501 Westminster Avenue, Fulton, MO 65251-1299, 800-475-3361. *Fax:* 573-592-5255. *E-mail:* aimee.bristow@westminster-mo.edu.
Website: http://www.westminster-mo.edu/.

WESTMINSTER COLLEGE

New Wilmington, PA

Tuition & fees: N/R	Average undergraduate aid package: $31,472

ABOUT THE INSTITUTION Independent Presbyterian Church (U.S.A.), coed. ***Awards:*** bachelor's and master's degrees. 51 undergraduate majors. Federal methodology is used as a basis for awarding need-based institutional aid.

FRESHMAN FINANCIAL AID (Fall 2018) 344 applied for aid; of those 91% were deemed to have need. 100% of freshmen with need received aid; of those 16% had need fully met. ***Average percent of need met:*** 83% (excluding resources awarded to replace EFC). ***Average financial aid package:*** $31,231 (excluding resources awarded to replace EFC). 10% of all full-time freshmen had no need and received non-need-based gift aid.

UNDERGRADUATE FINANCIAL AID (Fall 2018) 1,077 applied for aid; of those 92% were deemed to have need. 100% of undergraduates with need received aid; of those 19% had need fully met. ***Average percent of need met:*** 84% (excluding resources awarded to replace EFC). ***Average financial aid package:*** $31,472 (excluding resources awarded to replace EFC). 13% of all full-time undergraduates had no need and received non-need-based gift aid.

GIFT AID (NEED-BASED) *Total amount:* $27,235,933 (7% federal, 6% state, 82% institutional, 5% external sources). ***Receiving aid:*** Freshmen: 89% (308); all full-time undergraduates: 85% (982). ***Average award:*** Freshmen: $28,429; Undergraduates: $27,762. ***Scholarships, grants, and awards:*** Federal Pell, FSEOG, state, private, college/university gift aid from institutional funds.

GIFT AID (NON-NEED-BASED) *Total amount:* $3,407,524 (1% federal, 95% institutional, 4% external sources). ***Receiving aid:*** Freshmen: 88% (306). Undergraduates: 84% (969). ***Average award:*** Freshmen: $18,923. Undergraduates: $20,950. ***Scholarships, grants, and awards by category:*** *Academic interests/achievement:* 1,901 awards ($20,015,878 total): general academic interests/achievements, premedicine. *Creative arts/performance:* 99 awards ($104,629 total): cinema/film/broadcasting, general creative arts/performance, music, theater/drama. *Special characteristics:* 843 awards ($5,221,660 total): children and siblings of alumni, general special characteristics, religious affiliation. ***ROTC:*** Army cooperative.

LOANS *Student loans:* $8,619,209 (94% need-based, 6% non-need-based). 82% of past graduating class borrowed through all loan programs. *Average indebtedness per student:* $36,769. ***Average need-based loan:*** Freshmen: $3161. Undergraduates: $3953. ***Parent loans:*** $2,374,393 (96% need-based, 4% non-need-based). ***Programs:*** Federal Direct (Subsidized and Unsubsidized Stafford, PLUS), alternative loans.

WORK-STUDY *Federal work-study:* Total amount: $450,214; 281 jobs averaging $1602. ***State or other work-study/employment:*** Total amount: $120,419 (70% need-based, 30% non-need-based). 88 part-time jobs averaging $1376.

APPLYING FOR FINANCIAL AID *Required financial aid forms:* FAFSA, W-2 forms. ***Financial aid deadline (priority):*** 5/1. ***Notification date:*** Continuous beginning 12/15. Students must reply by 5/1 or within 3 weeks of notification.

CONTACT Mrs. Cheryl A. Gerber, Director of Financial Aid, Westminster College, 319 South Market Street, New Wilmington, PA 16172-0001, 724-946-7102 or toll-free 800-942-8033. *Fax:* 724-946-6171. *E-mail:* gerberca@westminster.edu.
Website: http://www.westminster.edu/.

WESTMINSTER COLLEGE

Salt Lake City, UT

Tuition & fees: $37,960	Average undergraduate aid package: $29,823

ABOUT THE INSTITUTION Independent, coed. ***Awards:*** certificates, bachelor's, master's, and doctoral degrees. 40 undergraduate majors. ***Total***

enrollment: 2,215. Undergraduates: 1,740. Freshmen: 283. Federal methodology is used as a basis for awarding need-based institutional aid.

UNDERGRADUATE EXPENSES for 2020–2021 *One-time required fee:* $300. ***Comprehensive fee:*** $49,057 includes full-time tuition ($37,440), mandatory fees ($520), and room and board ($11,097). ***College room only:*** $7506. Full-time tuition and fees vary according to course load. Room and board charges vary according to board plan and housing facility. ***Part-time tuition:*** $1558 per credit hour. ***Part-time fees:*** $154 per term. Part-time tuition and fees vary according to course load.

FRESHMAN FINANCIAL AID (Fall 2019, est.) 246 applied for aid; of those 80% were deemed to have need. 100% of freshmen with need received aid; of those 20% had need fully met. ***Average percent of need met:*** 81% (excluding resources awarded to replace EFC). ***Average financial aid package:*** $30,624 (excluding resources awarded to replace EFC). 25% of all full-time freshmen had no need and received non-need-based gift aid.

UNDERGRADUATE FINANCIAL AID (Fall 2019, est.) 1,218 applied for aid; of those 85% were deemed to have need. 100% of undergraduates with need received aid; of those 21% had need fully met. ***Average percent of need met:*** 80% (excluding resources awarded to replace EFC). ***Average financial aid package:*** $29,823 (excluding resources awarded to replace EFC). 28% of all full-time undergraduates had no need and received non-need-based gift aid.

GIFT AID (NEED-BASED) *Total amount:* $24,554,903 (11% federal, 86% institutional, 3% external sources). ***Receiving aid:*** Freshmen: 69% (196); all full-time undergraduates: 63% (1,030). ***Average award:*** Freshmen: $26,068; Undergraduates: $24,569. ***Scholarships, grants, and awards:*** Federal Pell, FSEOG, state, private, college/university gift aid from institutional funds, TEACH, S-Cubed.

GIFT AID (NON-NEED-BASED) *Total amount:* $9,266,578 (94% institutional, 6% external sources). ***Receiving aid:*** Freshmen: 12% (34). Undergraduates: 9% (155). ***Average award:*** Freshmen: $18,763. Undergraduates: $16,679. ***Scholarships, grants, and awards by category:*** *Academic interests/achievement:* biological sciences, business, communication, computer science, education, English, general academic interests/achievements, home economics, humanities, international studies, mathematics, physical sciences, premedicine, religion/biblical studies, social sciences. *Creative arts/performance:* applied art and design, art/fine arts, creative writing, dance, general creative arts/performance, journalism/publications, music, performing arts, theater/drama. *Special achievements/activities:* cheerleading/drum major, community service, general special achievements/activities, leadership, memberships, religious involvement. *Special characteristics:* adult students, children and siblings of alumni, children with a deceased or disabled parent, ethnic background, first-generation college students, handicapped students, international students, married students, members of minority groups, religious affiliation, veterans, veterans' children. ***Tuition waivers:*** Full or partial for employees or children of employees. ***ROTC:*** Army cooperative, Naval cooperative, Air Force cooperative.

LOANS *Student loans:* $10,514,608 (88% need-based, 12% non-need-based). 56% of past graduating class borrowed through all loan programs. *Average indebtedness per student:* $25,219. ***Average need-based loan:*** Freshmen: $3461. Undergraduates: $4567. ***Parent loans:*** $1,363,827 (83% need-based, 17% non-need-based). ***Programs:*** Federal Direct (Subsidized and Unsubsidized Stafford, PLUS), Private Banks.

WORK-STUDY *Federal work-study:* Total amount: $1,526,954; jobs available. ***State or other work-study/employment:*** Total amount: $900,000 (100% non-need-based). Part-time jobs available.

ATHLETIC AWARDS Total amount: $1,234,956 (60% need-based, 40% non-need-based).

APPLYING FOR FINANCIAL AID *Required financial aid forms:* FAFSA, institution's own form. ***Financial aid deadline (priority):*** 11/1. ***Notification date:*** Continuous beginning 12/1. Students must reply by 5/1 or within 3 weeks of notification.

CONTACT Mr. Joshua Montavon, Director of Financial Aid, Westminster College, 1840 South 1300 East, Salt Lake City, UT 84105, 801-832-2502 or toll-free 800-748-4753. *Fax:* 801-832-2506. *E-mail:* jmontavon@westminstercollege.edu.
Website: http://www.westminstercollege.edu/.

WESTMONT COLLEGE

Santa Barbara, CA

Tuition & fees: $46,594	Average undergraduate aid package: $37,908

ABOUT THE INSTITUTION Independent nondenominational, coed. ***Awards:*** bachelor's degrees. 25 undergraduate majors. ***Total enrollment:*** 1,277. Undergraduates: 1,277. Freshmen: 345. Federal methodology is used as a basis for awarding need-based institutional aid.

UNDERGRADUATE EXPENSES for 2019–2020 *Comprehensive fee:* $61,240 includes full-time tuition ($45,410), mandatory fees ($1184), and room and board ($14,646). ***College room only:*** $8996. ***Part-time tuition:*** $2120 per unit.

FRESHMAN FINANCIAL AID (Fall 2019, est.) 325 applied for aid; of those 83% were deemed to have need. 100% of freshmen with need received aid; of those 26% had need fully met. ***Average percent of need met:*** 85% (excluding resources awarded to replace EFC). ***Average financial aid package:*** $40,025 (excluding resources awarded to replace EFC). 27% of all full-time freshmen had no need and received non-need-based gift aid.

UNDERGRADUATE FINANCIAL AID (Fall 2019, est.) 1,039 applied for aid; of those 86% were deemed to have need. 100% of undergraduates with need received aid; of those 29% had need fully met. ***Average percent of need met:*** 84% (excluding resources awarded to replace EFC). ***Average financial aid package:*** $37,908 (excluding resources awarded to replace EFC). 28% of all full-time undergraduates had no need and received non-need-based gift aid.

GIFT AID (NEED-BASED) *Total amount:* $25,807,867 (5% federal, 8% state, 86% institutional, 1% external sources). ***Receiving aid:*** Freshmen: 73% (270); all full-time undergraduates: 68% (887). ***Average award:*** Freshmen: $32,483; Undergraduates: $29,075. ***Scholarships, grants, and awards:*** Federal Pell, FSEOG, state, private, college/university gift aid from institutional funds.

GIFT AID (NON-NEED-BASED) *Total amount:* $9,946,626 (99% institutional, 1% external sources). ***Receiving aid:*** Freshmen: 10% (36). Undergraduates: 10% (137). ***Average award:*** Freshmen: $22,367. Undergraduates: $22,676. ***Scholarships, grants, and awards by category:*** *Academic interests/achievement:* 1,185 awards ($21,113,210 total): general academic interests/achievements. *Creative arts/performance:* 189 awards ($657,279 total): art/fine arts, music, theater/drama. *Special achievements/activities:* 2 awards ($2000 total): general special achievements/activities, leadership. *Special characteristics:* 21 awards ($39,267 total): children of faculty/staff, ethnic background, international students, relatives of clergy. ***ROTC:*** Army cooperative, Air Force cooperative.

LOANS *Student loans:* $9,126,405 (67% need-based, 33% non-need-based). 66% of past graduating class borrowed through all loan programs. *Average indebtedness per student:* $39,145. ***Average need-based loan:*** Freshmen: $3956. Undergraduates: $5352. ***Parent loans:*** $3,939,425 (41% need-based, 59% non-need-based). ***Programs:*** Federal Direct (Subsidized and Unsubsidized Stafford, PLUS), college/university, alternative loans.

WORK-STUDY *Federal work-study:* Total amount: $596,854; 321 jobs averaging $1859.

ATHLETIC AWARDS Total amount: $1,478,215 (45% need-based, 55% non-need-based).

APPLYING FOR FINANCIAL AID *Required financial aid forms:* FAFSA, institution's own form. ***Financial aid deadline (priority):*** 5/15. ***Notification date:*** Continuous beginning 12/1. Students must reply by 5/1 or within 2 weeks of notification.

CONTACT Mr. Sean Smith, Director of Financial Aid, Westmont College, 955 La Paz Road, Santa Barbara, CA 93108, 805-565-6063 or toll-free 800-777-9011. *Fax:* 805-565-7157. *E-mail:* financialaid@westmont.edu.
Website: http://www.westmont.edu/.

WEST TEXAS A&M UNIVERSITY

Canyon, TX

Tuition & fees (area res): $8688	Average undergraduate aid package: $9628

ABOUT THE INSTITUTION State-supported, coed. ***Awards:*** bachelor's, master's, and doctoral degrees. 61 undergraduate majors. ***Total enrollment:*** 1,029.

Undergraduates: 7,376. Freshmen: 1,205. Federal methodology is used as a basis for awarding need-based institutional aid.

UNDERGRADUATE EXPENSES for 2019–2020 ***Application fee:*** $55. ***Tuition, area resident:*** full-time $5854; part-time $289 per credit hour. ***Tuition, state resident:*** full-time $5854; part-time $289 per credit hour. ***Tuition, nonresident:*** full-time $7440; part-time $342 per credit hour. ***Required fees:*** full-time $2834. Full-time tuition and fees vary according to course load, degree level, program, and student level. Part-time tuition and fees vary according to course load, degree level, program, and student level. ***College room and board:*** $7196. Room and board charges vary according to board plan and housing facility. ***Payment plan:*** Guaranteed tuition.

FRESHMAN FINANCIAL AID (Fall 2019, est.) 1208 applied for aid; of those 73% were deemed to have need. 99% of freshmen with need received aid; of those 8% had need fully met. ***Average percent of need met:*** 64% (excluding resources awarded to replace EFC). ***Average financial aid package:*** $10,900 (excluding resources awarded to replace EFC). 12% of all full-time freshmen had no need and received non-need-based gift aid.

UNDERGRADUATE FINANCIAL AID (Fall 2019, est.) 4,812 applied for aid; of those 73% were deemed to have need. 98% of undergraduates with need received aid; of those 7% had need fully met. ***Average percent of need met:*** 58% (excluding resources awarded to replace EFC). ***Average financial aid package:*** $9628 (excluding resources awarded to replace EFC). 12% of all full-time undergraduates had no need and received non-need-based gift aid.

GIFT AID (NEED-BASED) ***Total amount:*** $25,658,148 (46% federal, 33% state, 10% institutional, 11% external sources). ***Receiving aid:*** Freshmen: 56% (724); all full-time undergraduates: 50% (2,781). ***Average award:*** Freshmen: $8940; Undergraduates: $7398. ***Scholarships, grants, and awards:*** Federal Pell, FSEOG, state, private, college/university gift aid from institutional funds.

GIFT AID (NON-NEED-BASED) ***Total amount:*** $4,561,548 (40% institutional, 60% external sources). ***Receiving aid:*** Freshmen: 38% (490). Undergraduates: 25% (1,409). ***Average award:*** Freshmen: $1829. Undergraduates: $2304. ***Scholarships, grants, and awards by category:*** *Academic interests/achievement:* agriculture, business, communication, computer science, education, engineering/technologies, English, foreign languages, general academic interests/achievements, health fields, humanities, mathematics, physical sciences, premedicine, social sciences. *Creative arts/performance:* applied art and design, cinema/film/broadcasting, creative writing, dance, debating, general creative arts/performance, journalism/publications, music, theater/drama. *Special achievements/activities:* cheerleading/drum major, community service, general special achievements/activities, hobbies/interests, leadership, memberships, religious involvement, rodeo. *Special characteristics:* children and siblings of alumni, children of faculty/staff, children of union members/company employees, children of workers in trades, first-generation college students, general special characteristics, handicapped students, international students, local/state students, out-of-state students, public servants, religious affiliation, veterans. ***Tuition waivers:*** Full or partial for employees or children of employees.

LOANS ***Student loans:*** $23,834,415 (76% need-based, 24% non-need-based). 63% of past graduating class borrowed through all loan programs. *Average indebtedness per student:* $28,132. ***Average need-based loan:*** Freshmen: $3214. Undergraduates: $4015. ***Parent loans:*** $2,047,647 (51% need-based, 49% non-need-based). ***Programs:*** Federal Direct (Subsidized and Unsubsidized Stafford, PLUS), state.

WORK-STUDY ***Federal work-study:*** Total amount: $443,916; jobs available. ***State or other work-study/employment:*** Total amount: $39,916 (100% need-based). Part-time jobs available.

ATHLETIC AWARDS Total amount: $2,436,872 (37% need-based, 63% non-need-based).

APPLYING FOR FINANCIAL AID ***Required financial aid form:*** FAFSA. ***Financial aid deadline:*** Continuous. ***Notification date:*** Continuous beginning 3/1.

CONTACT Marian Giesecke, Director of Financial Aid, West Texas A&M University, WTAMU Box 60939, Canyon, TX 79016-0001, 806-651-2055 or toll-free 800-99-WTAMU. *Fax:* 806-651-2924. *E-mail:* mgiesecke@mail.wtamu.edu.
Website: http://www.wtamu.edu/.

WEST VIRGINIA STATE UNIVERSITY

Institute, WV

CONTACT Mrs. JoAnn L. Ross, Director of Student Financial Assistance, West Virginia State University, PO Box 1000, Ferrell Hall 324, Institute, WV 25112-1000, 304-204-4361 or toll-free 800-987-2112.
Website: http://www.wvstateu.edu/.

WEST VIRGINIA UNIVERSITY

Morgantown, WV

ABOUT THE INSTITUTION State-supported, coed. ***Awards:*** bachelor's, master's, and doctoral degrees. 74 undergraduate majors. ***Total enrollment:*** 26,839. Undergraduates: 21,086. Freshmen: 4,949.

GIFT AID (NEED-BASED) ***Scholarships, grants, and awards:*** Federal Pell, FSEOG, private, college/university gift aid from institutional funds, Federal Nursing.

GIFT AID (NON-NEED-BASED) ***Scholarships, grants, and awards by category:*** *Academic interests/achievement:* agriculture, architecture, area/ethnic studies, biological sciences, business, communication, computer science, education, engineering/technologies, English, foreign languages, general academic interests/achievements, health fields, home economics, humanities, international studies, library science, mathematics, military science, physical sciences, premedicine, religion/biblical studies, social sciences. *Creative arts/performance:* applied art and design, debating, music, theater/drama. *Special achievements/activities:* general special achievements/activities, leadership. *Special characteristics:* children of faculty/staff, children of union members/company employees, children of workers in trades, ethnic background, general special characteristics, international students, local/state students, members of minority groups.

LOANS ***Programs:*** Federal Direct (Subsidized and Unsubsidized Stafford, PLUS), Federal Nursing, state, college/university.

CONTACT Sandra Bennett, Executive Director of Financial Aid, West Virginia University, PO Box 6004, Morgantown, WV 26506-6004, 304-293-5242 or toll-free 800-344-9881. *Fax:* 304-293-4890. *E-mail:* sybennett@mail.wvu.edu.
Website: http://www.wvu.edu/.

WEST VIRGINIA UNIVERSITY INSTITUTE OF TECHNOLOGY

Beckley, WV

ABOUT THE INSTITUTION State-supported, coed. ***Awards:*** certificates and bachelor's degrees. 33 undergraduate majors. ***Total enrollment:*** 1,755. Undergraduates: 1,755. Freshmen: 367.

GIFT AID (NEED-BASED) ***Scholarships, grants, and awards:*** Federal Pell, FSEOG, state, private, college/university gift aid from institutional funds, Federal Nursing.

GIFT AID (NON-NEED-BASED) ***Scholarships, grants, and awards by category:*** *Academic interests/achievement:* general academic interests/achievements. *Special achievements/activities:* cheerleading/drum major, leadership. *Special characteristics:* first-generation college students.

LOANS ***Programs:*** Federal Direct (Subsidized and Unsubsidized Stafford, PLUS), Federal Nursing, college/university.

CONTACT Mr. Michael A. White, Director of Financial Aid Services, West Virginia University Institute of Technology, 410 Neville Street, Beckley, WV 25801, 304-929-1440 or toll-free 888-554-8324. *E-mail:* michael.white@mail.wvu.edu.
Website: http://www.wvutech.edu/.

WEST VIRGINIA WESLEYAN COLLEGE

Buckhannon, WV

ABOUT THE INSTITUTION Independent United Methodist Church, coed. ***Awards:*** certificates, bachelor's, and master's degrees. 61 undergraduate majors.

GIFT AID (NEED-BASED) ***Scholarships, grants, and awards:*** Federal Pell, FSEOG, private, college/university gift aid from institutional funds, Federal Nursing.

GIFT AID (NON-NEED-BASED) ***Scholarships, grants, and awards by category:*** *Academic interests/achievement:* general academic interests/achievements. *Creative arts/performance:* applied art and design, creative writing, dance, music, performing arts, theater/drama. *Special achievements/activities:* community service, leadership, religious involvement. *Special characteristics:* children and siblings of alumni, children of faculty/staff, general special characteristics, international students, relatives of clergy, religious affiliation, veterans.

LOANS ***Programs:*** Federal Direct (Subsidized and Unsubsidized Stafford, PLUS), Perkins, Federal Nursing.

WORK-STUDY ***Federal work-study:*** Total amount: $271,245; jobs available. ***State or other work-study/employment:*** Total amount: $102,146 (24% need-based, 76% non-need-based). Part-time jobs available.

APPLYING FOR FINANCIAL AID ***Required financial aid form:*** FAFSA.

CONTACT Susan George, Director of Financial Aid, West Virginia Wesleyan College, 59 College Avenue, Buckhannon, WV 26201, 304-473-8080 or toll-free 800-722-9933. *E-mail:* george_s@wvwc.edu.
Website: http://www.wvwc.edu/.

WHEATON COLLEGE

Wheaton, IL

Tuition & fees: $39,100 | **Average undergraduate aid package: $25,684**

ABOUT THE INSTITUTION Independent nondenominational, coed. ***Awards:*** certificates, bachelor's, master's, and doctoral degrees. 43 undergraduate majors. ***Total enrollment:*** 3,004. Undergraduates: 2,395. Freshmen: 614. Both federal and institutional methodology are used as a basis for awarding need-based institutional aid.

UNDERGRADUATE EXPENSES for 2020–2021 ***Application fee:*** $50. ***Comprehensive fee:*** $50,090 includes full-time tuition ($39,100) and room and board ($10,990). ***College room only:*** $6500. Full-time tuition and fees vary according to program. Room and board charges vary according to board plan, housing facility, and location. ***Part-time tuition:*** $1629 per credit hour. Part-time tuition and fees vary according to course load and program.

FRESHMAN FINANCIAL AID (Fall 2019, est.) 514 applied for aid; of those 77% were deemed to have need. 100% of freshmen with need received aid; of those 13% had need fully met. ***Average percent of need met:*** 79% (excluding resources awarded to replace EFC). ***Average financial aid package:*** $29,035 (excluding resources awarded to replace EFC). 20% of all full-time freshmen had no need and received non-need-based gift aid.

UNDERGRADUATE FINANCIAL AID (Fall 2019, est.) 1,725 applied for aid; of those 83% were deemed to have need. 99% of undergraduates with need received aid; of those 10% had need fully met. ***Average percent of need met:*** 71% (excluding resources awarded to replace EFC). ***Average financial aid package:*** $25,684 (excluding resources awarded to replace EFC). 21% of all full-time undergraduates had no need and received non-need-based gift aid.

GIFT AID (NEED-BASED) ***Total amount:*** $34,456,136 (8% federal, 2% state, 86% institutional, 4% external sources). ***Receiving aid:*** Freshmen: 64% (396); all full-time undergraduates: 60% (1,397). ***Average award:*** Freshmen: $26,088; Undergraduates: $22,583. ***Scholarships, grants, and awards:*** Federal Pell, FSEOG, state, private, college/university gift aid from institutional funds.

GIFT AID (NON-NEED-BASED) ***Total amount:*** $5,033,513 (84% institutional, 16% external sources). ***Receiving aid:*** Freshmen: 7% (40). Undergraduates: 4% (103). ***Average award:*** Freshmen: $15,815. Undergraduates: $11,440. ***Scholarships, grants, and awards by category:*** *Academic interests/achievement:* 1,155 awards ($8,251,936 total): area/ethnic studies, biological sciences, business, communication, education, engineering/technologies, English, foreign languages, general academic interests/achievements, home economics, humanities, international studies, mathematics, military science, physical sciences, premedicine, religion/biblical studies, social sciences. *Creative arts/performance:* 177 awards ($665,384 total): applied art and design, art/fine arts, cinema/film/broadcasting, creative writing, music. *Special achievements/activities:* 275 awards ($1,471,407 total): community service, general special achievements/activities, leadership, religious involvement. *Special characteristics:* 475 awards ($4,078,281 total): children and siblings of alumni, children of public servants, first-generation college students, general special characteristics, handicapped students, international students, local/state students, members of minority groups, out-of-state students, relatives of clergy, siblings of current students, veterans' children. ***ROTC:*** Army, Air Force cooperative.

LOANS ***Student loans:*** $9,707,057 (86% need-based, 14% non-need-based). 59% of past graduating class borrowed through all loan programs. *Average indebtedness per student:* $29,555. ***Average need-based loan:*** Freshmen: $3330. Undergraduates: $4370. ***Parent loans:*** $2,823,659 (85% need-based, 15% non-need-based). ***Programs:*** Federal Direct (Subsidized and Unsubsidized Stafford, PLUS), college/university.

WORK-STUDY ***Federal work-study:*** Total amount: $289,622; 226 jobs averaging $1282. ***State or other work-study/employment:*** Total amount: $1,443,829 (100% non-need-based).

APPLYING FOR FINANCIAL AID ***Required financial aid form:*** FAFSA. ***Financial aid deadline (priority):*** 11/1. ***Notification date:*** Continuous beginning 12/31.

CONTACT Ms. Karen Belling, Director of Student Financial Services, Wheaton College, 501 College Avenue, Wheaton, IL 60187-5593, 630-752-5700 or toll-free 800-222-2419. *E-mail:* sfs@wheaton.edu.
Website: http://www.wheaton.edu/.

WHEATON COLLEGE

Norton, MA

Tuition & fees: $56,366 | **Average undergraduate aid package: $46,154**

ABOUT THE INSTITUTION Independent, coed. ***Awards:*** bachelor's degrees. 45 undergraduate majors. ***Total enrollment:*** 1,774. Undergraduates: 1,774. Freshmen: 451. Both federal and institutional methodology are used as a basis for awarding need-based institutional aid.

UNDERGRADUATE EXPENSES for 2020–2021 ***Application fee:*** $60. ***Comprehensive fee:*** $70,744 includes full-time tuition ($55,904), mandatory fees ($462), and room and board ($14,378). ***College room only:*** $7764. Full-time tuition and fees vary according to course load. ***Part-time tuition:*** $1747 per credit hour. Part-time tuition and fees vary according to course load.

FRESHMAN FINANCIAL AID (Fall 2019, est.) 392 applied for aid; of those 88% were deemed to have need. 100% of freshmen with need received aid; of those 40% had need fully met. ***Average percent of need met:*** 96% (excluding resources awarded to replace EFC). ***Average financial aid package:*** $49,469 (excluding resources awarded to replace EFC). 13% of all full-time freshmen had no need and received non-need-based gift aid.

UNDERGRADUATE FINANCIAL AID (Fall 2019, est.) 1,351 applied for aid; of those 92% were deemed to have need. 100% of undergraduates with need received aid; of those 26% had need fully met. ***Average percent of need met:*** 93% (excluding resources awarded to replace EFC). ***Average financial aid package:*** $46,154 (excluding resources awarded to replace EFC). 21% of all full-time undergraduates had no need and received non-need-based gift aid.

GIFT AID (NEED-BASED) ***Total amount:*** $49,709,592 (3% federal, 1% state, 94% institutional, 2% external sources). ***Receiving aid:*** Freshmen: 77% (346); all full-time undergraduates: 70% (1,235). ***Average award:*** Freshmen: $46,141; Undergraduates: $41,648. ***Scholarships, grants, and awards:*** Federal Pell, FSEOG, state, private, college/university gift aid from institutional funds.

GIFT AID (NON-NEED-BASED) ***Total amount:*** $14,172,432 (98% institutional, 2% external sources). ***Receiving aid:*** Freshmen: 10% (46). Undergraduates: 7% (121). ***Average award:*** Freshmen: $29,414. Undergraduates: $23,547. ***Scholarships, grants, and awards by category:*** *Academic interests/achievement:* 491 awards ($12,051,930 total): general academic interests/achievements. ***Tuition waivers:*** Full or partial for employees or children of employees. ***ROTC:*** Army cooperative.

LOANS ***Student loans:*** $12,740,499 (48% need-based, 52% non-need-based). 66% of past graduating class borrowed through all loan programs. *Average indebtedness per student:* $34,530. ***Average need-based loan:*** Freshmen: $2507. Undergraduates: $3754. ***Parent loans:*** $3,139,583 (100% non-need-based). ***Programs:*** Federal Direct (Subsidized and Unsubsidized Stafford, PLUS), college/university.

WORK-STUDY ***Federal work-study:*** Total amount: $1,198,311; 642 jobs averaging $1868. ***State or other work-study/employment:*** Total amount: $646,800 (61% need-based, 39% non-need-based). 338 part-time jobs averaging $1896.

APPLYING FOR FINANCIAL AID ***Required financial aid forms:*** FAFSA, CSS Financial Aid PROFILE, noncustodial (divorced/separated) parent's statement, business/farm supplement, Parent and Student Federal Tax Returns with W-2s.

Financial aid deadline: 2/1 (priority: 11/15). ***Notification date:*** 3/15. Students must reply by 5/1.

CONTACT Financial Aid Office, Wheaton College, 26 East Main Street, Norton, MA 02766, 508-286-8200 or toll-free 800-394-6003.
Website: http://www.wheatoncollege.edu/.

WHEELING JESUIT UNIVERSITY

Wheeling, WV

ABOUT THE INSTITUTION Independent Roman Catholic (Jesuit), coed. ***Awards:*** certificates, bachelor's, master's, and doctoral degrees. 33 undergraduate majors. ***Total enrollment:*** 1,289. Undergraduates: 945. Freshmen: 222.

GIFT AID (NEED-BASED) ***Scholarships, grants, and awards:*** Federal Pell, FSEOG, state, private, college/university gift aid from institutional funds.

GIFT AID (NON-NEED-BASED) ***Scholarships, grants, and awards by category:*** *Academic interests/achievement:* general academic interests/achievements, premedicine. *Creative arts/performance:* music. *Special achievements/activities:* community service, general special achievements/activities. *Special characteristics:* children and siblings of alumni, children of faculty/staff, general special characteristics, religious affiliation.

LOANS ***Programs:*** Federal Direct (Subsidized and Unsubsidized Stafford, PLUS), alternative loans.

WORK-STUDY ***Federal work-study:*** Total amount: $677,148; 118 jobs averaging $2800. ***State or other work-study/employment:*** Total amount: $72,515 (100% non-need-based). 38 part-time jobs averaging $2800.

APPLYING FOR FINANCIAL AID ***Required financial aid form:*** FAFSA.

CONTACT Ms. Christie Tomczyk, Director of Financial Aid, Wheeling Jesuit University, 316 Washington Avenue, Wheeling, WV 26003-6295, 304-243-2304 or toll-free 800-624-6992 Ext.2359. *Fax:* 304-243-4397. *E-mail:* finaid@wju.edu.
Website: http://www.wju.edu/.

WHITMAN COLLEGE

Walla Walla, WA

Tuition & fees: $53,820	Average undergraduate aid package: $46,182

ABOUT THE INSTITUTION Independent, coed. ***Awards:*** bachelor's degrees. 54 undergraduate majors. ***Total enrollment:*** 1,475. Undergraduates: 1,475. Freshmen: 426. Both federal and institutional methodology are used as a basis for awarding need-based institutional aid.

UNDERGRADUATE EXPENSES for 2019–2020 ***Application fee:*** $50. ***Comprehensive fee:*** $67,332 includes full-time tuition ($53,420), mandatory fees ($400), and room and board ($13,512). ***College room only:*** $6020. Room and board charges vary according to board plan and housing facility. ***Part-time tuition:*** $2226 per credit. Part-time tuition and fees vary according to course load.

FRESHMAN FINANCIAL AID (Fall 2019, est.) 288 applied for aid; of those 75% were deemed to have need. 100% of freshmen with need received aid; of those 31% had need fully met. ***Average percent of need met:*** 92% (excluding resources awarded to replace EFC). ***Average financial aid package:*** $47,524 (excluding resources awarded to replace EFC). 39% of all full-time freshmen had no need and received non-need-based gift aid.

UNDERGRADUATE FINANCIAL AID (Fall 2019, est.) 800 applied for aid; of those 85% were deemed to have need. 100% of undergraduates with need received aid; of those 31% had need fully met. ***Average percent of need met:*** 94% (excluding resources awarded to replace EFC). ***Average financial aid package:*** $46,182 (excluding resources awarded to replace EFC). 38% of all full-time undergraduates had no need and received non-need-based gift aid.

GIFT AID (NEED-BASED) ***Total amount:*** $28,469,663 (3% federal, 2% state, 95% institutional). ***Receiving aid:*** Freshmen: 51% (216); all full-time undergraduates: 46% (680). ***Average award:*** Freshmen: $43,501; Undergraduates: $41,192. ***Scholarships, grants, and awards:*** Federal Pell, FSEOG, state, private, college/university gift aid from institutional funds.

GIFT AID (NON-NEED-BASED) ***Total amount:*** $8,114,744 (90% institutional, 10% external sources). ***Receiving aid:*** Freshmen: 18% (76). Undergraduates: 13% (196). ***Average award:*** Freshmen: $13,350. Undergraduates: $12,954. ***Scholarships, grants, and awards by category:*** *Academic interests/achievement:* general academic interests/achievements. *Creative arts/performance:* applied art and design, debating, music, theater/drama. ***Tuition waivers:*** Full or partial for employees or children of employees.

LOANS ***Student loans:*** $4,679,470 (51% need-based, 49% non-need-based). 43% of past graduating class borrowed through all loan programs. *Average indebtedness per student:* $18,328. ***Average need-based loan:*** Freshmen: $3365. Undergraduates: $4297. ***Parent loans:*** $1,192,157 (100% non-need-based). ***Programs:*** Federal Direct (Subsidized and Unsubsidized Stafford, PLUS).

WORK-STUDY ***Federal work-study:*** Total amount: $1,210,666; jobs available. ***State or other work-study/employment:*** Total amount: $279,903 (39% need-based, 61% non-need-based). Part-time jobs available.

APPLYING FOR FINANCIAL AID ***Required financial aid forms:*** FAFSA, CSS Financial Aid PROFILE, noncustodial (divorced/separated) parent's statement. ***Financial aid deadline:*** 1/15 (priority: 11/15). ***Notification date:*** 3/1. Students must reply by 5/1.

CONTACT Tyson Harlow, Assistant Director, Whitman College, 345 Boyer Avenue, Walla Walla, WA 99362-2046, 509-527-5178 or toll-free 877-462-9448. *Fax:* 509-527-4967.
Website: http://www.whitman.edu/.

WHITTIER COLLEGE

Whittier, CA

Tuition & fees: $49,314	Average undergraduate aid package: $39,393

ABOUT THE INSTITUTION Independent, coed. ***Awards:*** bachelor's, master's, and doctoral degrees. 36 undergraduate majors. ***Total enrollment:*** 1,784. Undergraduates: 1,732. Freshmen: 512. Federal methodology is used as a basis for awarding need-based institutional aid.

UNDERGRADUATE EXPENSES for 2019–2020 ***Application fee:*** $50. ***Tuition:*** full-time $48,924; part-time $2039 per semester hour. ***Required fees:*** full-time $390; $2039 per semester hour. Full-time tuition and fees vary according to course load. Part-time tuition and fees vary according to course load. Room and board charges vary according to board plan.

FRESHMAN FINANCIAL AID (Fall 2019, est.) 440 applied for aid; of those 91% were deemed to have need. 100% of freshmen with need received aid; of those 14% had need fully met. ***Average percent of need met:*** 79% (excluding resources awarded to replace EFC). ***Average financial aid package:*** $40,382 (excluding resources awarded to replace EFC). 18% of all full-time freshmen had no need and received non-need-based gift aid.

UNDERGRADUATE FINANCIAL AID (Fall 2019, est.) 1,452 applied for aid; of those 92% were deemed to have need. 99% of undergraduates with need received aid; of those 15% had need fully met. ***Average percent of need met:*** 78% (excluding resources awarded to replace EFC). ***Average financial aid package:*** $39,393 (excluding resources awarded to replace EFC). 21% of all full-time undergraduates had no need and received non-need-based gift aid.

GIFT AID (NEED-BASED) ***Total amount:*** $36,122,300 (10% federal, 15% state, 75% institutional). ***Receiving aid:*** Freshmen: 71% (352); all full-time undergraduates: 68% (1,188). ***Average award:*** Freshmen: $38,842; Undergraduates: $37,228. ***Scholarships, grants, and awards:*** Federal Pell, FSEOG, state, private, college/university gift aid from institutional funds.

GIFT AID (NON-NEED-BASED) ***Total amount:*** $17,966,993 (99% institutional, 1% external sources). ***Receiving aid:*** Freshmen: 10% (47). Undergraduates: 8% (138). ***Average award:*** Freshmen: $26,255. Undergraduates: $24,987. ***Scholarships, grants, and awards by category:*** *Academic interests/achievement:* 1,689 awards ($40,953,216 total): general academic interests/achievements. *Creative arts/performance:* 76 awards ($192,500 total): applied art and design, art/fine arts, music, performing arts, theater/drama. *Special achievements/activities:* 105 awards ($309,500 total): leadership. *Special characteristics:* 17 awards ($17,000 total): children and siblings of alumni, children of faculty/staff. ***Tuition waivers:*** Full or partial for employees or children of employees. ***ROTC:*** Army cooperative.

LOANS ***Student loans:*** $10,131,975 (59% need-based, 41% non-need-based). 77% of past graduating class borrowed through all loan programs. *Average indebtedness per student:* $35,328. ***Average need-based loan:*** Freshmen: $3579. Undergraduates: $5029. ***Parent loans:*** $3,910,640 (67% need-based, 33% non-need-based).

Programs: Federal Direct (Subsidized and Unsubsidized Stafford, PLUS), Perkins, college/university.

WORK-STUDY *Federal work-study:* Total amount: $612,172; 251 jobs averaging $2383. ***State or other work-study/employment:*** Total amount: $1,589,931 (73% need-based, 27% non-need-based). 590 part-time jobs averaging $1977.

APPLYING FOR FINANCIAL AID *Required financial aid form:* FAFSA. ***Financial aid deadline:*** 6/30 (priority: 3/1). ***Notification date:*** Continuous beginning 2/15. Students must reply within 2 weeks of notification.

CONTACT Mrs. Julie Aldama, Director of Financial Aid, Whittier College, 13406 East Philadelphia Street, Whittier, CA 90608-0634, 562-907-4285. *Fax:* 562-464-4560. *E-mail:* jaldama@whittier.edu.
Website: http://www.whittier.edu/.

WHITWORTH UNIVERSITY

Spokane, WA

Tuition & fees: $46,250	Average undergraduate aid package: $41,387

ABOUT THE INSTITUTION Independent Presbyterian, coed. ***Awards:*** certificates, bachelor's, and master's degrees. 75 undergraduate majors. ***Total enrollment:*** 2,776. Undergraduates: 2,355. Freshmen: 696. Federal methodology is used as a basis for awarding need-based institutional aid.

UNDERGRADUATE EXPENSES for 2020–2021 *Comprehensive fee:* $58,400 includes full-time tuition ($45,050), mandatory fees ($1200), and room and board ($12,150). Room and board charges vary according to board plan and housing facility. ***Part-time tuition:*** $1877 per credit hour. ***Part-time fees:*** $537 per term.

FRESHMAN FINANCIAL AID (Fall 2019, est.) 616 applied for aid; of those 88% were deemed to have need. 100% of freshmen with need received aid; of those 27% had need fully met. ***Average percent of need met:*** 87% (excluding resources awarded to replace EFC). ***Average financial aid package:*** $44,590 (excluding resources awarded to replace EFC). 20% of all full-time freshmen had no need and received non-need-based gift aid.

UNDERGRADUATE FINANCIAL AID (Fall 2019, est.) 1,878 applied for aid; of those 90% were deemed to have need. 100% of undergraduates with need received aid; of those 22% had need fully met. ***Average percent of need met:*** 84% (excluding resources awarded to replace EFC). ***Average financial aid package:*** $41,387 (excluding resources awarded to replace EFC). 25% of all full-time undergraduates had no need and received non-need-based gift aid.

GIFT AID (NEED-BASED) *Total amount:* $55,013,542 (8% federal, 10% state, 79% institutional, 3% external sources). ***Receiving aid:*** Freshmen: 79% (541); all full-time undergraduates: 71% (1,667). ***Average award:*** Freshmen: $35,326; Undergraduates: $32,853. ***Scholarships, grants, and awards:*** Federal Pell, FSEOG, state, private, college/university gift aid from institutional funds.

GIFT AID (NON-NEED-BASED) *Total amount:* $17,596,798 (1% federal, 1% state, 95% institutional, 3% external sources). ***Receiving aid:*** Freshmen: 14% (98). Undergraduates: 10% (236). ***Average award:*** Freshmen: $38,864. Undergraduates: $24,368. ***Scholarships, grants, and awards by category:*** *Academic interests/achievement:* 2,038 awards ($40,355,645 total): general academic interests/achievements, military science. *Creative arts/performance:* 313 awards ($1,558,350 total): applied art and design, creative writing, debating, journalism/publications, music, theater/drama. *Special achievements/activities:* 28 awards ($25,917 total): religious involvement. *Special characteristics:* 739 awards ($2,409,731 total): children and siblings of alumni, ethnic background, international students, members of minority groups, religious affiliation, siblings of current students, veterans, veterans' children. ***Tuition waivers:*** Full or partial for employees or children of employees, senior citizens. ***ROTC:*** Army cooperative.

LOANS *Student loans:* $10,806,524 (74% need-based, 26% non-need-based). 64% of past graduating class borrowed through all loan programs. *Average indebtedness per student:* $32,607. ***Average need-based loan:*** Freshmen: $3437. Undergraduates: $4346. ***Parent loans:*** $4,819,979 (39% need-based, 61% non-need-based). ***Programs:*** Federal Direct (Subsidized and Unsubsidized Stafford, PLUS), college/university.

WORK-STUDY *Federal work-study:* Total amount: $3,126,969; 844 jobs averaging $3489. ***State or other work-study/employment:*** Total amount: $131,259 (100% need-based). 42 part-time jobs averaging $3624.

APPLYING FOR FINANCIAL AID *Required financial aid form:* FAFSA. ***Financial aid deadline (priority):*** 12/1. ***Notification date:*** Continuous beginning 1/17.

CONTACT Mrs. Traci L. Spoon Stensland, Director of Financial Aid, Whitworth University, 300 West Hawthorne Road, Spokane, WA 99251-0001, 509-777-4335 or toll-free 800-533-4668. *Fax:* 509-777-4601. *E-mail:* tstensland@whitworth.edu.
Website: http://www.whitworth.edu/.

WICHITA STATE UNIVERSITY

Wichita, KS

Tuition & fees (KS res): $8299	Average undergraduate aid package: $8155

ABOUT THE INSTITUTION State-supported, coed. ***Awards:*** certificates, associate, bachelor's, master's, and doctoral degrees. 72 undergraduate majors. ***Total enrollment:*** 16,058. Undergraduates: 13,217. Freshmen: 1,655. Federal methodology is used as a basis for awarding need-based institutional aid.

UNDERGRADUATE EXPENSES for 2019–2020 *Application fee:* $30. ***Tuition, state resident:*** full-time $6708; part-time $224 per credit hour. ***Tuition, nonresident:*** full-time $15,890; part-time $530 per credit hour. ***Required fees:*** full-time $1591; $453. Full-time tuition and fees vary according to course level, course load, degree level, and program. Part-time tuition and fees vary according to course level, course load, degree level, and program. ***College room and board:*** $12,620. Room and board charges vary according to board plan and housing facility.

FRESHMAN FINANCIAL AID (Fall 2018) 1460 applied for aid; of those 71% were deemed to have need. 97% of freshmen with need received aid; of those 21% had need fully met. ***Average percent of need met:*** 65% (excluding resources awarded to replace EFC). ***Average financial aid package:*** $7956 (excluding resources awarded to replace EFC). 24% of all full-time freshmen had no need and received non-need-based gift aid.

UNDERGRADUATE FINANCIAL AID (Fall 2018) 6,583 applied for aid; of those 81% were deemed to have need. 98% of undergraduates with need received aid; of those 17% had need fully met. ***Average percent of need met:*** 64% (excluding resources awarded to replace EFC). ***Average financial aid package:*** $8155 (excluding resources awarded to replace EFC). 16% of all full-time undergraduates had no need and received non-need-based gift aid.

GIFT AID (NEED-BASED) *Total amount:* $22,023,283 (80% federal, 7% state, 12% institutional, 1% external sources). ***Receiving aid:*** Freshmen: 41% (681); all full-time undergraduates: 41% (3,625). ***Average award:*** Freshmen: $5330; Undergraduates: $5299. ***Scholarships, grants, and awards:*** Federal Pell, FSEOG, state, private, college/university gift aid from institutional funds, United Negro College Fund, Bureau of Indian Affairs Grants, TRIO Kansas Kids GEAR UP Scholarships.

GIFT AID (NON-NEED-BASED) *Total amount:* $14,347,669 (2% state, 85% institutional, 13% external sources). ***Receiving aid:*** Freshmen: 40% (657). Undergraduates: 28% (2,479). ***Average award:*** Freshmen: $1234. Undergraduates: $1273. ***Scholarships, grants, and awards by category:*** *Academic interests/achievement:* area/ethnic studies, biological sciences, business, communication, computer science, education, engineering/technologies, English, foreign languages, general academic interests/achievements, health fields, humanities, international studies, mathematics, physical sciences, premedicine, social sciences. *Creative arts/performance:* applied art and design, art/fine arts, cinema/film/broadcasting, creative writing, dance, debating, general creative arts/performance, journalism/publications, music, performing arts, theater/drama. *Special achievements/activities:* cheerleading/drum major, community service, general special achievements/activities, hobbies/interests, leadership, memberships. *Special characteristics:* adult students, children and siblings of alumni, children of faculty/staff, ethnic background, first-generation college students, general special characteristics, handicapped students, international students, local/state students, members of minority groups, out-of-state students, previous college experience, veterans. ***Tuition waivers:*** Full or partial for employees or children of employees, senior citizens. ***ROTC:*** Army.

LOANS *Student loans:* $39,580,328 (45% need-based, 55% non-need-based). 61% of past graduating class borrowed through all loan programs. *Average indebtedness per student:* $24,839. ***Average need-based loan:*** Freshmen: $1669. Undergraduates: $2156. ***Parent loans:*** $5,182,565 (100% non-need-based). ***Programs:*** Federal Direct (Subsidized and Unsubsidized Stafford, PLUS), Perkins, private loans.

WORK-STUDY *Federal work-study:* Total amount: $372,537; 135 jobs averaging $2512. ***State or other work-study/employment:*** Total amount: $105,543 (100% need-based). 84 part-time jobs averaging $1227.

ATHLETIC AWARDS Total amount: $2,452,847 (100% non-need-based).
APPLYING FOR FINANCIAL AID ***Required financial aid forms:*** FAFSA, university department scholarship application(s). ***Financial aid deadline (priority):*** 12/1. ***Notification date:*** Continuous beginning 8/1. Students must reply by 5/1.
CONTACT Sheelu Surender, Director of Financial Aid, Wichita State University, 1845 Fairmount Street, Wichita, KS 67260-0024, 316-978-3430 or toll-free 800-362-2594. *E-mail:* finaid@wichita.edu.
Website: http://www.wichita.edu/.

WIDENER UNIVERSITY

Chester, PA

Tuition & fees: $48,740	Average undergraduate aid package: $35,270

ABOUT THE INSTITUTION Independent, coed. ***Awards:*** certificates, associate, bachelor's, master's, and doctoral degrees. 75 undergraduate majors. ***Total enrollment:*** 6,601. Undergraduates: 3,345. Freshmen: 770. Both federal and institutional methodology are used as a basis for awarding need-based institutional aid.
UNDERGRADUATE EXPENSES for 2020–2021 ***Comprehensive fee:*** $63,552 includes full-time tuition ($47,770), mandatory fees ($970), and room and board ($14,812). ***College room only:*** $7748. ***Part-time tuition:*** $1592 per credit hour.
FRESHMAN FINANCIAL AID (Fall 2019, est.) 682 applied for aid; of those 91% were deemed to have need. 100% of freshmen with need received aid; of those 22% had need fully met. ***Average percent of need met:*** 77% (excluding resources awarded to replace EFC). ***Average financial aid package:*** $38,316 (excluding resources awarded to replace EFC). 13% of all full-time freshmen had no need and received non-need-based gift aid.
UNDERGRADUATE FINANCIAL AID (Fall 2019, est.) 2,388 applied for aid; of those 91% were deemed to have need. 100% of undergraduates with need received aid; of those 22% had need fully met. ***Average percent of need met:*** 74% (excluding resources awarded to replace EFC). ***Average financial aid package:*** $35,270 (excluding resources awarded to replace EFC). 18% of all full-time undergraduates had no need and received non-need-based gift aid.
GIFT AID (NEED-BASED) ***Total amount:*** $63,188,080 (7% federal, 3% state, 89% institutional, 1% external sources). ***Receiving aid:*** Freshmen: 84% (608); all full-time undergraduates: 76% (2,119). ***Average award:*** Freshmen: $32,980; Undergraduates: $29,670. ***Scholarships, grants, and awards:*** Federal Pell, FSEOG, state, private, college/university gift aid from institutional funds, United Negro College Fund.
GIFT AID (NON-NEED-BASED) ***Total amount:*** $13,299,122 (98% institutional, 2% external sources). ***Receiving aid:*** Freshmen: 83% (600). Undergraduates: 73% (2,023). ***Average award:*** Freshmen: $27,600. Undergraduates: $25,590. ***Scholarships, grants, and awards by category:*** *Academic interests/achievement:* biological sciences, business, communication, computer science, education, engineering/technologies, English, foreign languages, general academic interests/achievements, home economics, humanities, international studies, mathematics, military science, physical sciences, premedicine, social sciences. *Creative arts/performance:* dance, music. *Special achievements/activities:* community service, general special achievements/activities, leadership. *Special characteristics:* adult students, children of faculty/staff, ethnic background, international students. ***Tuition waivers:*** Full or partial for employees or children of employees. ***ROTC:*** Army, Naval cooperative, Air Force cooperative.
LOANS ***Student loans:*** $28,948,985 (91% need-based, 9% non-need-based). ***Average need-based loan:*** Freshmen: $3630. Undergraduates: $4505. ***Parent loans:*** $8,566,516 (96% need-based, 4% non-need-based). ***Programs:*** Federal Direct (Subsidized and Unsubsidized Stafford, PLUS), college/university.
WORK-STUDY ***Federal work-study:*** Total amount: $2,859,663; jobs available. ***State or other work-study/employment:*** Part-time jobs available.
APPLYING FOR FINANCIAL AID ***Required financial aid form:*** FAFSA. ***Financial aid deadline (priority):*** 12/15. ***Notification date:*** Continuous beginning 1/30. Students must reply within 4 weeks of notification.
CONTACT Ms. Paula Lehrberger, Director of Financial Aid, Widener University, One University Place, Chester, PA 19013-5792, 610-499-4161 or toll-free 888-WIDENER. *Fax:* 610-499-4687. *E-mail:* finaidmc@mail.widener.edu.
Website: http://www.widener.edu/.

WILBERFORCE UNIVERSITY

Wilberforce, OH

CONTACT Director of Financial Aid, Wilberforce University, 1055 North Bickett Road, Wilberforce, OH 45384, 937-708-5727 or toll-free 800-367-8568. *Fax:* 937-376-4752.
Website: http://www.wilberforce.edu/.

WILEY COLLEGE

Marshall, TX

CONTACT Mr. Alan D. Jackson Jr., Director of Financial Aid, Wiley College, 711 Wiley Avenue, Marshall, TX 75670-5199, 903-927-3217 or toll-free 800-658-6889. *E-mail:* adjackson2@wileyc.edu.
Website: http://www.wileyc.edu/.

WILKES UNIVERSITY

Wilkes-Barre, PA

Tuition & fees: $37,622	Average undergraduate aid package: $28,253

ABOUT THE INSTITUTION Independent, coed. ***Awards:*** bachelor's, master's, and doctoral degrees. 42 undergraduate majors. ***Total enrollment:*** 4,680. Undergraduates: 2,351. Freshmen: 550. Federal methodology is used as a basis for awarding need-based institutional aid.
UNDERGRADUATE EXPENSES for 2019–2020 ***Application fee:*** $40. ***Comprehensive fee:*** $52,730 includes full-time tuition ($35,814), mandatory fees ($1808), and room and board ($15,108). Room and board charges vary according to board plan and housing facility. ***Part-time tuition:*** $995 per credit hour. ***Part-time fees:*** $80 per credit hour.
FRESHMAN FINANCIAL AID (Fall 2019, est.) 494 applied for aid; of those 92% were deemed to have need. 100% of freshmen with need received aid; of those 18% had need fully met. ***Average percent of need met:*** 76% (excluding resources awarded to replace EFC). ***Average financial aid package:*** $28,957 (excluding resources awarded to replace EFC). 7% of all full-time freshmen had no need and received non-need-based gift aid.
UNDERGRADUATE FINANCIAL AID (Fall 2019, est.) 1,839 applied for aid; of those 93% were deemed to have need. 100% of undergraduates with need received aid; of those 14% had need fully met. ***Average percent of need met:*** 74% (excluding resources awarded to replace EFC). ***Average financial aid package:*** $28,253 (excluding resources awarded to replace EFC). 6% of all full-time undergraduates had no need and received non-need-based gift aid.
GIFT AID (NEED-BASED) ***Receiving aid:*** Freshmen: 85% (453); all full-time undergraduates: 80% (1,674). ***Average award:*** Freshmen: $25,503; Undergraduates: $23,365. ***Scholarships, grants, and awards:*** Federal Pell, FSEOG, state, private, college/university gift aid from institutional funds.
GIFT AID (NON-NEED-BASED) ***Receiving aid:*** Freshmen: 74% (394). Undergraduates: 67% (1,413). ***Average award:*** Freshmen: $16,673. Undergraduates: $16,692. ***Scholarships, grants, and awards by category:*** *Academic interests/achievement:* general academic interests/achievements. *Creative arts/performance:* performing arts, theater/drama. *Special achievements/activities:* general special achievements/activities, leadership. *Special characteristics:* children of faculty/staff. ***Tuition waivers:*** Full or partial for employees or children of employees. ***ROTC:*** Army cooperative, Air Force.
LOANS ***Average need-based loan:*** Freshmen: $3447. Undergraduates: $4330. ***Programs:*** Federal Direct (Subsidized and Unsubsidized Stafford, PLUS), Perkins, Federal Nursing, college/university, Gulf Oil Loan Fund, Rulison Evans Loan Fund.
WORK-STUDY Federal work-study jobs available. ***State or other work-study/employment:*** Part-time jobs available.
APPLYING FOR FINANCIAL AID ***Required financial aid form:*** FAFSA. ***Notification date:*** Continuous.

CONTACT Mrs. Jane Dessoye, Executive Director of Financial Aid, Wilkes University, 84 West South Street, Wilkes-Barre, PA 18766, 570-408-4512 or toll-free 800-945-5378 Ext.4400. *Fax:* 570-408-4939. *E-mail:* jane.dessoye@wilkes.edu. *Website:* http://www.wilkes.edu/.

WILLAMETTE UNIVERSITY

Salem, OR

Tuition & fees: $53,624	Average undergraduate aid package: $32,918

ABOUT THE INSTITUTION Independent United Methodist, coed. ***Awards:*** bachelor's, master's, and doctoral degrees. 53 undergraduate majors. ***Total enrollment:*** 2,265. Undergraduates: 1,624. Freshmen: 371. Federal methodology is used as a basis for awarding need-based institutional aid.

UNDERGRADUATE EXPENSES for 2020–2021 ***Comprehensive fee:*** $66,952 includes full-time tuition ($53,300), mandatory fees ($324), and room and board ($13,328). ***Part-time tuition:*** $6662 per credit hour. ***Payment plan:*** Tuition prepayment.

FRESHMAN FINANCIAL AID (Fall 2019, est.) 319 applied for aid; of those 84% were deemed to have need. 100% of freshmen with need received aid; of those 13% had need fully met. ***Average percent of need met:*** 76% (excluding resources awarded to replace EFC). ***Average financial aid package:*** $38,006 (excluding resources awarded to replace EFC). 20% of all full-time freshmen had no need and received non-need-based gift aid.

UNDERGRADUATE FINANCIAL AID (Fall 2019, est.) 941 applied for aid; of those 100% were deemed to have need. 100% of undergraduates with need received aid; of those 9% had need fully met. ***Average percent of need met:*** 65% (excluding resources awarded to replace EFC). ***Average financial aid package:*** $32,918 (excluding resources awarded to replace EFC). 10% of all full-time undergraduates had no need and received non-need-based gift aid.

GIFT AID (NEED-BASED) ***Total amount:*** $33,106,784 (8% federal, 1% state, 89% institutional, 2% external sources). ***Receiving aid:*** Freshmen: 72% (266); all full-time undergraduates: 62% (901). ***Average award:*** Freshmen: $32,098; Undergraduates: $28,344. ***Scholarships, grants, and awards:*** Federal Pell, FSEOG, state, private, college/university gift aid from institutional funds.

GIFT AID (NON-NEED-BASED) ***Receiving aid:*** Freshmen: 22% (81). Undergraduates: 12% (169). ***Average award:*** Freshmen: $21,952. Undergraduates: $21,261. ***Scholarships, grants, and awards by category:*** *Academic interests/achievement:* general academic interests/achievements. *Creative arts/performance:* general creative arts/performance. *Special achievements/activities:* general special achievements/activities. *Special characteristics:* general special characteristics. ***ROTC:*** Army cooperative, Air Force cooperative.

LOANS ***Student loans:*** $7,356,623 (85% need-based, 15% non-need-based). 61% of past graduating class borrowed through all loan programs. *Average indebtedness per student:* $26,973. ***Average need-based loan:*** Freshmen: $3363. Undergraduates: $4419. ***Parent loans:*** $2,985,401 (92% need-based, 8% non-need-based). ***Programs:*** Federal Direct (Subsidized and Unsubsidized Stafford, PLUS), Perkins.

WORK-STUDY ***Federal work-study:*** Total amount: $1,113,859; 378 jobs averaging $2732. ***State or other work-study/employment:*** Part-time jobs available.

APPLYING FOR FINANCIAL AID ***Required financial aid form:*** FAFSA. ***Financial aid deadline (priority):*** 2/1. ***Notification date:*** 3/15. Students must reply by 5/1 or within 2 weeks of notification.

CONTACT Patty Hoban, Director of Financial Aid, Willamette University, 900 State Street, Salem, OR 97301-3931, 503-370-6273 or toll-free 877-542-2787. *Fax:* 503-370-6588. *E-mail:* phoban@willamette.edu. *Website:* http://www.willamette.edu/.

WILLIAM & MARY

Williamsburg, VA

Tuition & fees (VA res): $23,628	Average undergraduate aid package: $24,609

ABOUT THE INSTITUTION State-supported, coed. ***Awards:*** certificates, bachelor's, master's, and doctoral degrees. 44 undergraduate majors. ***Total enrollment:*** 8,773. Undergraduates: 6,256. Freshmen: 1,530. Federal methodology is used as a basis for awarding need-based institutional aid.

UNDERGRADUATE EXPENSES for 2019–2020 ***Application fee:*** $75. ***Tuition, state resident:*** full-time $17,434; part-time $425 per credit hour. ***Tuition, nonresident:*** full-time $40,089; part-time $1278 per credit hour. ***Required fees:*** full-time $6194. Full-time tuition and fees vary according to course load, program, and student level. Part-time tuition and fees vary according to course load and program. ***College room and board:*** $12,926; ***Room only:*** $7958. Room and board charges vary according to board plan and housing facility. ***Payment plan:*** Guaranteed tuition.

FRESHMAN FINANCIAL AID (Fall 2018) 1108 applied for aid; of those 56% were deemed to have need. 95% of freshmen with need received aid; of those 19% had need fully met. ***Average percent of need met:*** 78% (excluding resources awarded to replace EFC). ***Average financial aid package:*** $23,686 (excluding resources awarded to replace EFC). 3% of all full-time freshmen had no need and received non-need-based gift aid.

UNDERGRADUATE FINANCIAL AID (Fall 2018) 3,497 applied for aid; of those 68% were deemed to have need. 98% of undergraduates with need received aid; of those 23% had need fully met. ***Average percent of need met:*** 81% (excluding resources awarded to replace EFC). ***Average financial aid package:*** $24,609 (excluding resources awarded to replace EFC). 5% of all full-time undergraduates had no need and received non-need-based gift aid.

GIFT AID (NEED-BASED) ***Total amount:*** $43,875,788 (8% federal, 8% state, 81% institutional, 3% external sources). ***Receiving aid:*** Freshmen: 34% (531); all full-time undergraduates: 34% (2,150). ***Average award:*** Freshmen: $18,708; Undergraduates: $18,222. ***Scholarships, grants, and awards:*** Federal Pell, FSEOG, state, private, college/university gift aid from institutional funds.

GIFT AID (NON-NEED-BASED) ***Total amount:*** $4,516,276 (5% federal, 75% institutional, 20% external sources). ***Receiving aid:*** Freshmen: 16% (254). Undergraduates: 14% (879). ***Average award:*** Freshmen: $10,123. Undergraduates: $7661. ***Scholarships, grants, and awards by category:*** *Creative arts/performance:* 54 awards ($57,475 total): music, theater/drama. *Special characteristics:* 202 awards ($4,166,662 total): general special characteristics. ***Tuition waivers:*** Full or partial for employees or children of employees, senior citizens. ***ROTC:*** Army.

LOANS ***Student loans:*** $15,750,809 (74% need-based, 26% non-need-based). 33% of past graduating class borrowed through all loan programs. *Average indebtedness per student:* $28,895. ***Average need-based loan:*** Freshmen: $3172. Undergraduates: $3566. ***Parent loans:*** $6,820,314 (70% need-based, 30% non-need-based). ***Programs:*** Federal Direct (Subsidized and Unsubsidized Stafford, PLUS).

WORK-STUDY ***Federal work-study:*** Total amount: $452,951; 653 jobs averaging $1092.

ATHLETIC AWARDS Total amount: $8,210,054 (19% need-based, 81% non-need-based).

APPLYING FOR FINANCIAL AID ***Required financial aid forms:*** FAFSA, CSS Financial Aid PROFILE. ***Financial aid deadline (priority):*** 3/1. ***Notification date:*** Continuous beginning 3/15. Students must reply by 5/1 or within 2 weeks of notification.

CONTACT Mr. Joe Dobrota, Director of Financial Aid, William & Mary, PO Box 8795, Williamsburg, VA 23187, 757-221-2425. *Fax:* 757-221-2515. *E-mail:* jdobrota@wm.edu. *Website:* http://www.wm.edu/.

WILLIAM CAREY UNIVERSITY

Hattiesburg, MS

CONTACT Ms. Brenda Pittman, Associate Director of Financial Aid, William Carey University, 498 Tuscan Avenue, Hattiesburg, MS 39401-5499, 601-318-6153 or toll-free 800-962-5991. *Website:* http://www.wmcarey.edu/.

WILLIAM JESSUP UNIVERSITY

Rocklin, CA

Tuition & fees: N/R	Average undergraduate aid package: $26,018

ABOUT THE INSTITUTION Independent nondenominational, coed. ***Awards:*** certificates, associate, bachelor's, and master's degrees. 19 undergraduate majors. Federal methodology is used as a basis for awarding need-based institutional aid.

FRESHMAN FINANCIAL AID (Fall 2019, est.) 172 applied for aid; of those 89% were deemed to have need. 100% of freshmen with need received aid; of those 19% had need fully met. ***Average percent of need met:*** 72% (excluding resources awarded to replace EFC). ***Average financial aid package:*** $28,214 (excluding resources awarded to replace EFC). 15% of all full-time freshmen had no need and received non-need-based gift aid.

UNDERGRADUATE FINANCIAL AID (Fall 2019, est.) 894 applied for aid; of those 91% were deemed to have need. 100% of undergraduates with need received aid; of those 12% had need fully met. ***Average percent of need met:*** 65% (excluding resources awarded to replace EFC). ***Average financial aid package:*** $26,018 (excluding resources awarded to replace EFC). 16% of all full-time undergraduates had no need and received non-need-based gift aid.

GIFT AID (NEED-BASED) ***Total amount:*** $17,161,381 (13% federal, 19% state, 65% institutional, 3% external sources). ***Receiving aid:*** Freshmen: 84% (153); all full-time undergraduates: 75% (797). ***Average award:*** Freshmen: $25,886; Undergraduates: $23,067. ***Scholarships, grants, and awards:*** Federal Pell, FSEOG, state, private, college/university gift aid from institutional funds.

GIFT AID (NON-NEED-BASED) ***Total amount:*** $2,865,316 (91% institutional, 9% external sources). ***Receiving aid:*** Freshmen: 14% (26). Undergraduates: 7% (77). ***Average award:*** Freshmen: $18,836. Undergraduates: $12,388. ***Scholarships, grants, and awards by category:*** *Academic interests/achievement:* area/ethnic studies, biological sciences, business, communication, computer science, education, English, general academic interests/achievements, humanities, international studies, mathematics, physical sciences, religion/biblical studies, social sciences. *Creative arts/performance:* applied art and design, art/fine arts, general creative arts/performance, music, performing arts, theater/drama. *Special achievements/activities:* general special achievements/activities, leadership, religious involvement. *Special characteristics:* adult students, children and siblings of alumni, children of faculty/staff, ethnic background, first-generation college students, general special characteristics, international students, out-of-state students, previous college experience, relatives of clergy, siblings of current students, veterans. ***ROTC:*** Air Force cooperative.

LOANS ***Student loans:*** $6,837,234 (53% need-based, 47% non-need-based). 83% of past graduating class borrowed through all loan programs. *Average indebtedness per student:* $26,856. ***Average need-based loan:*** Freshmen: $2827. Undergraduates: $3684. ***Parent loans:*** $1,769,084 (57% need-based, 43% non-need-based). ***Programs:*** Federal Direct (Subsidized and Unsubsidized Stafford, PLUS).

WORK-STUDY ***Federal work-study:*** Total amount: $100,222; jobs available. ***State or other work-study/employment:*** Total amount: $571,442 (100% non-need-based). Part-time jobs available.

ATHLETIC AWARDS Total amount: $2,679,908 (67% need-based, 33% non-need-based).

APPLYING FOR FINANCIAL AID ***Required financial aid form:*** FAFSA. ***Financial aid deadline:*** Continuous. ***Notification date:*** Continuous beginning 12/1. Students must reply within 2 weeks of notification.

CONTACT Mr. John T. Swan, Director of Financial Aid, William Jessup University, 2121 University Avenue, Rocklin, CA 95765, 916-577-2233. *Fax:* 916-577-2230. *E-mail:* finaid@jessup.edu.
Website: http://www.jessup.edu/.

WILLIAM JEWELL COLLEGE

Liberty, MO

ABOUT THE INSTITUTION Independent, coed. ***Awards:*** certificates, bachelor's, and master's degrees (also offers evening program with significant enrollment not reflected in profile). 33 undergraduate majors. ***Total enrollment:*** 5. Undergraduates: 734. Freshmen: 168.

GIFT AID (NEED-BASED) ***Scholarships, grants, and awards:*** Federal Pell, FSEOG, state, college/university gift aid from institutional funds.

GIFT AID (NON-NEED-BASED) ***Scholarships, grants, and awards by category:*** *Academic interests/achievement:* general academic interests/achievements. *Creative arts/performance:* dance, debating, journalism/publications, music, theater/drama. *Special achievements/activities:* cheerleading/drum major, religious involvement. *Special characteristics:* children and siblings of alumni, children of faculty/staff, siblings of current students.

LOANS ***Programs:*** Federal Direct (Subsidized and Unsubsidized Stafford, PLUS), Perkins, Federal Nursing, alternative loans.

WORK-STUDY ***Federal work-study:*** Total amount: $818,125; jobs available. ***State or other work-study/employment:*** Part-time jobs available.

APPLYING FOR FINANCIAL AID ***Required financial aid form:*** FAFSA.

CONTACT Mr. Daniel Holt, Director of Financial Aid and Scholarship Services, William Jewell College, 500 College Hill, Liberty, MO 64068, 816-415-5977 or toll-free 888-2JEWELL. *Fax:* 816-415-5006. *E-mail:* holtd@william.jewell.edu.
Website: http://www.jewell.edu/.

WILLIAM PATERSON UNIVERSITY OF NEW JERSEY

Wayne, NJ

Tuition & fees (area res): $13,370	Average undergraduate aid package: $11,939

ABOUT THE INSTITUTION State-supported, coed. ***Awards:*** certificates, bachelor's, master's, and doctoral degrees. 51 undergraduate majors. ***Total enrollment:*** 10,105. Undergraduates: 8,583. Freshmen: 1,537. Federal methodology is used as a basis for awarding need-based institutional aid.

UNDERGRADUATE EXPENSES for 2019–2020 ***Application fee:*** $50. ***Tuition, area resident:*** full-time $13,246; part-time $424 per credit. ***Tuition, state resident:*** full-time $13,246; part-time $424 per credit. ***Tuition, nonresident:*** full-time $21,644; part-time $701 per credit. ***Required fees:*** full-time $124. Full-time tuition and fees vary according to course load and location. Part-time tuition and fees vary according to course load and location. ***College room and board:*** $11,900; ***Room only:*** $7470. Room and board charges vary according to board plan and housing facility.

FRESHMAN FINANCIAL AID (Fall 2019, est.) 1476 applied for aid; of those 87% were deemed to have need. 98% of freshmen with need received aid; of those 22% had need fully met. ***Average financial aid package:*** $12,459 (excluding resources awarded to replace EFC). 6% of all full-time freshmen had no need and received non-need-based gift aid.

UNDERGRADUATE FINANCIAL AID (Fall 2019, est.) 6,509 applied for aid; of those 83% were deemed to have need. 99% of undergraduates with need received aid; of those 28% had need fully met. ***Average financial aid package:*** $11,939 (excluding resources awarded to replace EFC). 5% of all full-time undergraduates had no need and received non-need-based gift aid.

GIFT AID (NEED-BASED) ***Total amount:*** $38,720,116 (56% federal, 44% state). ***Receiving aid:*** Freshmen: 63% (956); all full-time undergraduates: 53% (3,786). ***Average award:*** Freshmen: $10,584; Undergraduates: $9602. ***Scholarships, grants, and awards:*** Federal Pell, FSEOG, state, private, college/university gift aid from institutional funds.

GIFT AID (NON-NEED-BASED) ***Total amount:*** $11,277,041 (1% state, 96% institutional, 3% external sources). ***Receiving aid:*** Freshmen: 16% (240). Undergraduates: 19% (1,393). ***Average award:*** Freshmen: $8463. Undergraduates: $6457. ***Scholarships, grants, and awards by category:*** *Academic interests/achievement:* general academic interests/achievements. *Creative arts/performance:* applied art and design, music. *Special characteristics:* children of faculty/staff, veterans. ***Tuition waivers:*** Full or partial for employees or children of employees, senior citizens. ***ROTC:*** Air Force cooperative.

LOANS ***Student loans:*** $46,644,895 (44% need-based, 56% non-need-based). 73% of past graduating class borrowed through all loan programs. *Average indebtedness per student:* $30,272. ***Average need-based loan:*** Freshmen: $3402. Undergraduates: $4287. ***Parent loans:*** $8,226,842 (100% non-need-based). ***Programs:*** Federal Direct (Subsidized and Unsubsidized Stafford, PLUS), Federal Nursing, state.

WORK-STUDY ***Federal work-study:*** Total amount: $354,656; jobs available.

APPLYING FOR FINANCIAL AID ***Required financial aid form:*** FAFSA. ***Financial aid deadline (priority):*** 4/15. ***Notification date:*** Continuous beginning 2/1.

CONTACT Mr. Michael Corso, Director of Financial Aid, William Paterson University of New Jersey, 300 Pompton Road, Morris Hall, 1st Floor, Wayne, NJ 07470, 973-720-2202 or toll-free 877-WPU-EXCEL. *Fax:* 973-720-3133. *E-mail:* finaid@wpunj.edu.
Website: http://www.wpunj.edu/.

WILLIAM PEACE UNIVERSITY

Raleigh, NC

Tuition & fees: $32,450	Average undergraduate aid package: $23,386

ABOUT THE INSTITUTION Independent Presbyterian Church (U.S.A.), coed. ***Awards:*** bachelor's degrees. 32 undergraduate majors. ***Total enrollment:*** 889. Undergraduates: 889. Freshmen: 185. Federal methodology is used as a basis for awarding need-based institutional aid.

UNDERGRADUATE EXPENSES for 2020–2021 ***Application fee:*** $35. ***Comprehensive fee:*** $44,250 includes full-time tuition ($31,950), mandatory fees ($500), and room and board ($11,800). ***College room only:*** $7920. Full-time tuition and fees vary according to class time, course load, and program. Room and board charges vary according to board plan and housing facility. ***Part-time tuition:*** $1065 per credit hour. Part-time tuition and fees vary according to class time, course load, and program.

FRESHMAN FINANCIAL AID (Fall 2019, est.) 182 applied for aid; of those 88% were deemed to have need. 100% of freshmen with need received aid; of those 10% had need fully met. ***Average financial aid package:*** $26,013 (excluding resources awarded to replace EFC). 11% of all full-time freshmen had no need and received non-need-based gift aid.

UNDERGRADUATE FINANCIAL AID (Fall 2019, est.) 721 applied for aid; of those 98% were deemed to have need. 98% of undergraduates with need received aid; of those 10% had need fully met. ***Average financial aid package:*** $23,386 (excluding resources awarded to replace EFC). 8% of all full-time undergraduates had no need and received non-need-based gift aid.

GIFT AID (NEED-BASED) ***Total amount:*** $13,904,291 (14% federal, 15% state, 69% institutional, 2% external sources). ***Receiving aid:*** Freshmen: 82% (150); all full-time undergraduates: 76% (591). ***Average award:*** Freshmen: $11,728; Undergraduates: $11,582. ***Scholarships, grants, and awards:*** Federal Pell, FSEOG, state, private, college/university gift aid from institutional funds.

GIFT AID (NON-NEED-BASED) ***Total amount:*** $713,093 (92% institutional, 8% external sources). ***Receiving aid:*** Freshmen: 11% (21). Undergraduates: 5% (41). ***Average award:*** Freshmen: $13,395. Undergraduates: $7696. ***Scholarships, grants, and awards by category:*** *Academic interests/achievement:* general academic interests/achievements. *Creative arts/performance:* applied art and design, performing arts. *Special achievements/activities:* community service, leadership. *Special characteristics:* children of faculty/staff, siblings of current students. ***Tuition waivers:*** Full or partial for employees or children of employees. ***ROTC:*** Army cooperative, Naval cooperative, Air Force cooperative.

LOANS ***Student loans:*** $5,463,684 (94% need-based, 6% non-need-based). 95% of past graduating class borrowed through all loan programs. *Average indebtedness per student:* $26,929. ***Average need-based loan:*** Freshmen: $3404. Undergraduates: $4108. ***Parent loans:*** $6,542,007 (92% need-based, 8% non-need-based). ***Programs:*** Federal Direct (Subsidized and Unsubsidized Stafford, PLUS), state.

WORK-STUDY ***Federal work-study:*** Total amount: $291,000; jobs available.

APPLYING FOR FINANCIAL AID ***Required financial aid form:*** FAFSA. ***Financial aid deadline (priority):*** 3/15. ***Notification date:*** Continuous beginning 10/1.

CONTACT Ms. Colleen Murphy, Vice President, Enrollment Management and Marketing, William Peace University, 15 East Peace Street, Raleigh, NC 27604, 919-508-2284. *Fax:* 919-508-2325. *E-mail:* cfmurphy@peace.edu.
Website: http://www.peace.edu/.

WILLIAM PENN UNIVERSITY

Oskaloosa, IA

CONTACT Cyndi Peiffer, Director of Financial Aid, William Penn University, 201 Trueblood Avenue, Oskaloosa, IA 52577-1799, 641-673-1060. *Fax:* 641-673-1115. *E-mail:* peifferc@wmpenn.edu.
Website: http://www.wmpenn.edu/.

WILLIAMS BAPTIST COLLEGE

Walnut Ridge, AR

CONTACT Mrs. Barbara Turner, Director of Financial Aid, Williams Baptist College, 60 West Fulbright Avenue, Walnut Ridge, AR 72476, 870-759-4112 or toll-free 800-722-4434. *Fax:* 870-759-4209. *E-mail:* bturner@wbcoll.edu.
Website: http://www.wbcoll.edu/.

WILLIAMS COLLEGE

Williamstown, MA

Tuition & fees: $59,660	Average undergraduate aid package: $59,941

ABOUT THE INSTITUTION Independent, coed. ***Awards:*** bachelor's and master's degrees. 42 undergraduate majors. ***Total enrollment:*** 2,134. Undergraduates: 2,078. Freshmen: 546. Institutional methodology is used as a basis for awarding need-based institutional aid.

UNDERGRADUATE EXPENSES for 2020–2021 ***Application fee:*** $65. ***Comprehensive fee:*** $74,660 includes full-time tuition ($59,350), mandatory fees ($310), and room and board ($15,000). ***College room only:*** $7625. Room and board charges vary according to board plan.

FRESHMAN FINANCIAL AID (Fall 2019, est.) 333 applied for aid; of those 85% were deemed to have need. 100% of freshmen with need received aid; of those 100% had need fully met. ***Average percent of need met:*** 100% (excluding resources awarded to replace EFC). ***Average financial aid package:*** $58,125 (excluding resources awarded to replace EFC).

UNDERGRADUATE FINANCIAL AID (Fall 2019, est.) 1,167 applied for aid; of those 91% were deemed to have need. 100% of undergraduates with need received aid; of those 100% had need fully met. ***Average percent of need met:*** 100% (excluding resources awarded to replace EFC). ***Average financial aid package:*** $59,941 (excluding resources awarded to replace EFC).

GIFT AID (NEED-BASED) ***Total amount:*** $60,195,755 (4% federal, 94% institutional, 2% external sources). ***Receiving aid:*** Freshmen: 52% (282); all full-time undergraduates: 52% (1,060). ***Average award:*** Freshmen: $54,973; Undergraduates: $56,788. ***Scholarships, grants, and awards:*** Federal Pell, FSEOG, state, college/university gift aid from institutional funds.

GIFT AID (NON-NEED-BASED) ***Total amount:*** $1,655,419 (100% external sources). ***ROTC:*** Air Force cooperative.

LOANS ***Student loans:*** $2,410,260 (42% need-based, 58% non-need-based). 33% of past graduating class borrowed through all loan programs. *Average indebtedness per student:* $15,911. ***Average need-based loan:*** Freshmen: $2818. Undergraduates: $2925. ***Parent loans:*** $1,548,016 (100% non-need-based). ***Programs:*** Federal Direct (Subsidized and Unsubsidized Stafford, PLUS), college/university, Institutional student loans for international students only.

WORK-STUDY ***Federal work-study:*** Total amount: $962,334; 385 jobs averaging $2448. ***State or other work-study/employment:*** Total amount: $3,031,431 (45% need-based, 55% non-need-based). 543 part-time jobs averaging $2427.

APPLYING FOR FINANCIAL AID ***Required financial aid forms:*** FAFSA, CSS Financial Aid PROFILE, noncustodial (divorced/separated) parent's statement, Signed copies of parents' and student's federal income tax returns. ***Financial aid deadline:*** 1/15. ***Notification date:*** 4/1. Students must reply by 5/1.

CONTACT Ms. Ashley B. Bianchi, Director of Financial Aid, Williams College, Weston Hall, 995 Main Street, 3rd Floor, Williamstown, MA 01267, 413-597-4181. *Fax:* 413-597-2999. *E-mail:* Ashley.B.Bianchi@williams.edu.
Website: http://www.williams.edu/.

WILLIAMSON COLLEGE

Franklin, TN

CONTACT Jeanie Maguire, Director of Financial Aid, Williamson College, 200 Seaboard Lane, Franklin, TN 37067, 615-771-7821. *Fax:* 615-771-7810. *E-mail:* info@williamsoncc.edu.
Website: http://www.williamsoncc.edu/.

WILLIAM WOODS UNIVERSITY

Fulton, MO

ABOUT THE INSTITUTION Independent Christian Church (Disciples of Christ), coed. ***Awards:*** certificates, associate, bachelor's, master's, and doctoral degrees. 35 undergraduate majors.

GIFT AID (NEED-BASED) *Scholarships, grants, and awards:* Federal Pell, FSEOG, state, private, college/university gift aid from institutional funds.

GIFT AID (NON-NEED-BASED) *Scholarships, grants, and awards by category:* *Academic interests/achievement:* general academic interests/achievements. *Creative arts/performance:* applied art and design, theater/drama. *Special characteristics:* children and siblings of alumni, local/state students, siblings of current students.

LOANS *Programs:* Federal Direct (Subsidized and Unsubsidized Stafford, PLUS).

WORK-STUDY *Federal work-study:* Total amount: $409,928; jobs available. ***State or other work-study/employment:*** Total amount: $113,158 (13% need-based, 87% non-need-based). Part-time jobs available.

CONTACT Deana Ready, Director of Student Financial Services, William Woods University, One University Avenue, Fulton, MO 65251, 573-592-4236 or toll-free 800-995-3159 Ext.4221. *Fax:* 573-592-1180. *E-mail:* deana.ready@williamwoods.edu.
Website: http://www.williamwoods.edu/.

WILMINGTON COLLEGE

Wilmington, OH

CONTACT Donna Barton, Coordinator of Financial Aid, Wilmington College, Pyle Center Box 1184, Wilmington, OH 45177, 937-382-6661 Ext. 466 or toll-free 800-341-9318. *Fax:* 937-383-8564.
Website: http://www.wilmington.edu/.

WILMINGTON UNIVERSITY

New Castle, DE

CONTACT J. Lynn Iocono, Director of Financial Aid, Wilmington University, 320 DuPont Highway, New Castle, DE 19720, 302-328-9437 or toll-free 877-967-5464. *Fax:* 302-328-5902.
Website: http://www.wilmu.edu/.

WILSON COLLEGE

Chambersburg, PA

Tuition & fees: $25,300	Average undergraduate aid package: $20,139

ABOUT THE INSTITUTION Independent Presbyterian Church (U.S.A.), coed, primarily women. ***Awards:*** associate, bachelor's, and master's degrees. 23 undergraduate majors. Federal methodology is used as a basis for awarding need-based institutional aid.

UNDERGRADUATE EXPENSES for 2019–2020 *Comprehensive fee:* $36,894 includes full-time tuition ($24,450), mandatory fees ($850), and room and board ($11,594). ***College room only:*** $5500. Full-time tuition and fees vary according to location and program. Room and board charges vary according to board plan and housing facility. ***Part-time tuition:*** $815 per semester hour. Part-time tuition and fees vary according to course load, location, and program.

FRESHMAN FINANCIAL AID (Fall 2019, est.) 192 applied for aid; of those 83% were deemed to have need. 100% of freshmen with need received aid; of those 18% had need fully met. ***Average percent of need met:*** 85% (excluding resources awarded to replace EFC). ***Average financial aid package:*** $19,747 (excluding resources awarded to replace EFC). 18% of all full-time freshmen had no need and received non-need-based gift aid.

UNDERGRADUATE FINANCIAL AID (Fall 2019, est.) 630 applied for aid; of those 92% were deemed to have need. 100% of undergraduates with need received aid; of those 17% had need fully met. ***Average percent of need met:*** 76% (excluding resources awarded to replace EFC). ***Average financial aid package:*** $20,139 (excluding resources awarded to replace EFC). 12% of all full-time undergraduates had no need and received non-need-based gift aid.

GIFT AID (NEED-BASED) *Total amount:* $11,228,155 (14% federal, 9% state, 66% institutional, 11% external sources). ***Receiving aid:*** Freshmen: 81% (160); all full-time undergraduates: 86% (575). ***Average award:*** Freshmen: $16,027; Undergraduates: $16,307. ***Scholarships, grants, and awards:*** Federal Pell, FSEOG, state, private, college/university gift aid from institutional funds.

GIFT AID (NON-NEED-BASED) *Receiving aid:* Undergraduates: 50% (336). ***Average award:*** Freshmen: $9299. Undergraduates: $7833. ***Scholarships, grants, and awards by category:*** *Academic interests/achievement:* biological sciences, business, communication, computer science, education, English, foreign languages, general academic interests/achievements, humanities, international studies, mathematics, physical sciences, premedicine, religion/biblical studies, social sciences. *Creative arts/performance:* music. *Special achievements/activities:* community service, general special achievements/activities, leadership. *Special characteristics:* adult students, children and siblings of alumni, children of current students, children of faculty/staff, international students, local/state students, relatives of clergy, religious affiliation, veterans, veterans' children. ***Tuition waivers:*** Full or partial for employees or children of employees. ***ROTC:*** Army cooperative.

LOANS *Student loans:* $7,135,188 (100% need-based). 83% of past graduating class borrowed through all loan programs. *Average indebtedness per student:* $39,090. ***Average need-based loan:*** Freshmen: $2856. Undergraduates: $3160. ***Parent loans:*** $8,328,405 (100% non-need-based). ***Programs:*** Federal Direct (Subsidized and Unsubsidized Stafford, PLUS), state.

WORK-STUDY *Federal work-study:* Total amount: $107,300; jobs available. ***State or other work-study/employment:*** Total amount: $299,721 (100% need-based). Part-time jobs available.

APPLYING FOR FINANCIAL AID *Required financial aid form:* FAFSA. ***Financial aid deadline:*** Continuous. ***Notification date:*** Continuous beginning 11/1.

CONTACT Ms. Linda Brittain, Dean of Financial Aid/Senior Enrollment Associate, Wilson College, 1015 Philadelphia Avenue, Chambersburg, PA 17201-1285, 717-264-3787 or toll-free 800-421-8402. *Fax:* 717-262-2530. *E-mail:* finaid@wilson.edu.
Website: http://www.wilson.edu/.

WINGATE UNIVERSITY

Wingate, NC

Tuition & fees: $38,896	Average undergraduate aid package: $31,028

ABOUT THE INSTITUTION Independent Baptist, coed. ***Awards:*** certificates, bachelor's, master's, and doctoral degrees. 39 undergraduate majors. ***Total enrollment:*** 3,681. Undergraduates: 2,764. Freshmen: 944. Both federal and institutional methodology are used as a basis for awarding need-based institutional aid.

UNDERGRADUATE EXPENSES for 2020–2021 *One-time required fee:* $100. ***Comprehensive fee:*** $48,806 includes full-time tuition ($38,796), mandatory fees ($100), and room and board ($9910).

FRESHMAN FINANCIAL AID (Fall 2019, est.) 816 applied for aid; of those 92% were deemed to have need. 100% of freshmen with need received aid; of those 27% had need fully met. ***Average percent of need met:*** 85% (excluding resources awarded to replace EFC). ***Average financial aid package:*** $31,028 (excluding resources awarded to replace EFC). 16% of all full-time freshmen had no need and received non-need-based gift aid.

UNDERGRADUATE FINANCIAL AID (Fall 2019, est.) 2,330 applied for aid; of those 93% were deemed to have need. 100% of undergraduates with need received aid; of those 26% had need fully met. ***Average percent of need met:*** 83% (excluding resources awarded to replace EFC). ***Average financial aid package:***

$31,028 (excluding resources awarded to replace EFC). 19% of all full-time undergraduates had no need and received non-need-based gift aid.

GIFT AID (NEED-BASED) ***Receiving aid:*** Freshmen: 80% (751); all full-time undergraduates: 80% (2,158). ***Average award:*** Freshmen: $28,035; Undergraduates: $27,513. ***Scholarships, grants, and awards:*** Federal Pell, FSEOG, state, private, college/university gift aid from institutional funds.

GIFT AID (NON-NEED-BASED) ***Receiving aid:*** Freshmen: 17% (158). Undergraduates: 14% (386). ***Average award:*** Freshmen: $25,739. Undergraduates: $23,310. ***Scholarships, grants, and awards by category:*** *Academic interests/achievement:* general academic interests/achievements. *Creative arts/performance:* music. *Special achievements/activities:* cheerleading/drum major. *Special characteristics:* children and siblings of alumni, relatives of clergy, siblings of current students, veterans, veterans' children. ***ROTC:*** Army cooperative, Air Force cooperative.

LOANS ***Student loans:*** 63% of past graduating class borrowed through all loan programs. *Average indebtedness per student:* $29,823. ***Average need-based loan:*** Freshmen: $2388. Undergraduates: $3179. ***Programs:*** Federal Direct (Subsidized and Unsubsidized Stafford, PLUS).

WORK-STUDY Federal work-study jobs available. ***State or other work-study/employment:*** Part-time jobs available.

APPLYING FOR FINANCIAL AID ***Required financial aid forms:*** FAFSA, state aid form. ***Financial aid deadline:*** Continuous. ***Notification date:*** Continuous. Students must reply within 3 weeks of notification.

CONTACT Teresa G. Williams, Director of Student Financial Planning, Wingate University, P.O. Box 159, Wingate, NC 28174, 704-233-8209 or toll-free 800-755-5550. *Fax:* 704-233-9396. *E-mail:* tgwilliam@wingate.edu.
Website: http://www.wingate.edu/.

WINONA STATE UNIVERSITY

Winona, MN

Tuition & fees (MN res): $9666	Average undergraduate aid package: $8427

ABOUT THE INSTITUTION State-supported, coed. ***Awards:*** certificates, associate, bachelor's, master's, and doctoral degrees. 66 undergraduate majors. Federal methodology is used as a basis for awarding need-based institutional aid.

UNDERGRADUATE EXPENSES for 2019–2020 ***Tuition, state resident:*** full-time $7598; part-time $251 per credit hour. ***Tuition, nonresident:*** full-time $13,698; part-time $456 per credit hour. ***Required fees:*** full-time $2068; $41.50 per credit hour. Full-time tuition and fees vary according to location, program, and reciprocity agreements. Part-time tuition and fees vary according to course load, location, program, and reciprocity agreements. ***College room and board:*** $9086; ***Room only:*** $5950. Room and board charges vary according to board plan, housing facility, and location.

FRESHMAN FINANCIAL AID (Fall 2018) 1400 applied for aid; of those 69% were deemed to have need. 98% of freshmen with need received aid; of those 9% had need fully met. ***Average percent of need met:*** 51% (excluding resources awarded to replace EFC). ***Average financial aid package:*** $8183 (excluding resources awarded to replace EFC). 20% of all full-time freshmen had no need and received non-need-based gift aid.

UNDERGRADUATE FINANCIAL AID (Fall 2018) 5,100 applied for aid; of those 73% were deemed to have need. 98% of undergraduates with need received aid; of those 11% had need fully met. ***Average percent of need met:*** 52% (excluding resources awarded to replace EFC). ***Average financial aid package:*** $8427 (excluding resources awarded to replace EFC). 14% of all full-time undergraduates had no need and received non-need-based gift aid.

GIFT AID (NEED-BASED) ***Total amount:*** $17,578,742 (51% federal, 30% state, 12% institutional, 7% external sources). ***Receiving aid:*** Freshmen: 49% (749); all full-time undergraduates: 44% (2,742). ***Average award:*** Freshmen: $6206; Undergraduates: $6215. ***Scholarships, grants, and awards:*** Federal Pell, FSEOG, state, private, college/university gift aid from institutional funds.

GIFT AID (NON-NEED-BASED) ***Total amount:*** $4,079,041 (8% federal, 57% institutional, 35% external sources). ***Receiving aid:*** Freshmen: 11% (176). Undergraduates: 7% (416). ***Average award:*** Freshmen: $2839. Undergraduates: $3344. ***Scholarships, grants, and awards by category:*** *Academic interests/achievement:* general academic interests/achievements. *Creative arts/performance:* applied art and design, debating, music, theater/drama. *Special characteristics:* children and siblings of alumni, children of faculty/staff, local/state students, members of minority groups, out-of-state students. ***Tuition waivers:*** Full or partial for employees or children of employees. ***ROTC:*** Army cooperative.

LOANS ***Student loans:*** $38,825,200 (56% need-based, 44% non-need-based). 76% of past graduating class borrowed through all loan programs. *Average indebtedness per student:* $33,312. ***Average need-based loan:*** Freshmen: $3072. Undergraduates: $3773. ***Parent loans:*** $4,120,472 (33% need-based, 67% non-need-based). ***Programs:*** Federal Direct (Subsidized and Unsubsidized Stafford, PLUS), Perkins, state, college/university.

WORK-STUDY ***Federal work-study:*** Total amount: $410,695; jobs available. ***State or other work-study/employment:*** Total amount: $784,242 (100% need-based). Part-time jobs available.

ATHLETIC AWARDS Total amount: $1,221,512 (46% need-based, 54% non-need-based).

APPLYING FOR FINANCIAL AID ***Required financial aid form:*** FAFSA. ***Financial aid deadline:*** Continuous. ***Notification date:*** Continuous beginning 4/1. Students must reply within 3 weeks of notification.

CONTACT Ms. Mari Livingston, Associate Director of Financial Aid, Winona State University, PO Box 5838, Winona, MN 55987-5838, 507-457-5090 Ext. 2398 or toll-free 800-DIAL WSU.
Website: http://www.winona.edu/.

WINSTON-SALEM STATE UNIVERSITY

Winston-Salem, NC

CONTACT Raymond Solomon, Director of Financial Aid Office, Winston-Salem State University, 601 Martin Luther King Jr. Drive, PO Box 19524, Winston-Salem, NC 27110-0003, 336-750-3299 or toll-free 800-257-4052. *Fax:* 336-750-3297.
Website: http://www.wssu.edu/.

WINTHROP UNIVERSITY

Rock Hill, SC

ABOUT THE INSTITUTION State-supported, coed. ***Awards:*** certificates, bachelor's, and master's degrees. 36 undergraduate majors. ***Total enrollment:*** 5,813. Undergraduates: 4,887. Freshmen: 991.

GIFT AID (NEED-BASED) ***Scholarships, grants, and awards:*** Federal Pell, FSEOG, state, private, college/university gift aid from institutional funds, TEACH Grants.

GIFT AID (NON-NEED-BASED) ***Scholarships, grants, and awards by category:*** *Academic interests/achievement:* biological sciences, general academic interests/achievements. *Creative arts/performance:* applied art and design, dance, music, performing arts, theater/drama. *Special characteristics:* children of faculty/staff.

LOANS ***Programs:*** Federal Direct (Subsidized and Unsubsidized Stafford, PLUS), private loans.

WORK-STUDY ***Federal work-study:*** Total amount: $296,243; 148 jobs averaging $2002.

APPLYING FOR FINANCIAL AID ***Required financial aid form:*** FAFSA.

CONTACT Michelle K. Hare, Director of Financial Aid, Winthrop University, Sykes House, 638 Oakland Avenue, Rock Hill, SC 29733, 803-323-2189 or toll-free 800-763-0230. *Fax:* 803-323-2557. *E-mail:* finaid@winthrop.edu.
Website: http://www.winthrop.edu/.

WISCONSIN LUTHERAN COLLEGE

Milwaukee, WI

ABOUT THE INSTITUTION Independent Wisconsin Evangelical Lutheran Synod, coed. ***Awards:*** bachelor's and master's degrees. 42 undergraduate majors.

GIFT AID (NEED-BASED) ***Scholarships, grants, and awards:*** Federal Pell, FSEOG, state, private, college/university gift aid from institutional funds.

GIFT AID (NON-NEED-BASED) ***Scholarships, grants, and awards by category:*** *Academic interests/achievement:* biological sciences, business, communication, education, foreign languages, general academic interests/achievements, mathematics, physical sciences. *Creative arts/performance:* applied art and design, cinema/film/broadcasting, general creative arts/performance, music, theater/drama.

Special achievements/activities: community service, general special achievements/activities, leadership. *Special characteristics:* children of faculty/staff, general special characteristics, international students, religious affiliation, veterans.

LOANS ***Programs:*** Federal Direct (Subsidized and Unsubsidized Stafford, PLUS), state, private loans.

WORK-STUDY ***Federal work-study:*** Total amount: $219,076; 77 jobs averaging $2258. ***State or other work-study/employment:*** Total amount: $605,272 (81% need-based, 19% non-need-based). 323 part-time jobs averaging $2168.

APPLYING FOR FINANCIAL AID ***Required financial aid forms:*** FAFSA, institution's own form.

CONTACT Mrs. Linda Loeffel, Director of Financial Aid, Wisconsin Lutheran College, 8800 West Bluemound Road, Milwaukee, WI 53226-4699, 414-443-8856. *Fax:* 414-443-8514. *E-mail:* financial.aid@wlc.edu.
Website: http://www.wlc.edu/.

WITTENBERG UNIVERSITY

Springfield, OH

Tuition & fees: $41,476 | **Average undergraduate aid package: $34,552**

ABOUT THE INSTITUTION Independent Evangelical Lutheran Church, coed. ***Awards:*** bachelor's and master's degrees. 45 undergraduate majors. ***Total enrollment:*** 1,619. Undergraduates: 1,577. Freshmen: 344. Federal methodology is used as a basis for awarding need-based institutional aid.

UNDERGRADUATE EXPENSES for 2020–2021 ***Comprehensive fee:*** $52,306 includes full-time tuition ($40,630), mandatory fees ($846), and room and board ($10,830). ***College room only:*** $5530. Room and board charges vary according to board plan and housing facility. ***Part-time tuition:*** $1315 per credit hour. ***Part-time fees:*** $415 per term. Part-time tuition and fees vary according to course load.

FRESHMAN FINANCIAL AID (Fall 2019, est.) 326 applied for aid; of those 87% were deemed to have need. 100% of freshmen with need received aid; of those 39% had need fully met. ***Average percent of need met:*** 80% (excluding resources awarded to replace EFC). ***Average financial aid package:*** $37,465 (excluding resources awarded to replace EFC). 17% of all full-time freshmen had no need and received non-need-based gift aid.

UNDERGRADUATE FINANCIAL AID (Fall 2019, est.) 1,324 applied for aid; of those 88% were deemed to have need. 100% of undergraduates with need received aid; of those 30% had need fully met. ***Average percent of need met:*** 82% (excluding resources awarded to replace EFC). ***Average financial aid package:*** $34,552 (excluding resources awarded to replace EFC). 21% of all full-time undergraduates had no need and received non-need-based gift aid.

GIFT AID (NEED-BASED) ***Receiving aid:*** Freshmen: 32% (110); all full-time undergraduates: 32% (474). ***Average award:*** Freshmen: $6834; Undergraduates: $6944. ***Scholarships, grants, and awards:*** Federal Pell, FSEOG, state, private, college/university gift aid from institutional funds, United Negro College Fund.

GIFT AID (NON-NEED-BASED) ***Receiving aid:*** Freshmen: 83% (284). Undergraduates: 77% (1,145). ***Average award:*** Freshmen: $25,577. Undergraduates: $22,709. ***Scholarships, grants, and awards by category:*** *Academic interests/achievement:* general academic interests/achievements. *Creative arts/performance:* applied art and design, dance, music, theater/drama. *Special achievements/activities:* community service, general special achievements/activities, leadership. *Special characteristics:* adult students, children and siblings of alumni, children of faculty/staff, ethnic background, international students, members of minority groups, relatives of clergy, religious affiliation. ***Tuition waivers:*** Full or partial for minority students, children of alumni, employees or children of employees, adult students, senior citizens. ***ROTC:*** Army cooperative, Air Force cooperative.

LOANS ***Average need-based loan:*** Freshmen: $3227. Undergraduates: $4472. ***Programs:*** Federal Direct (Subsidized and Unsubsidized Stafford, PLUS), Perkins, college/university.

WORK-STUDY Federal work-study jobs available. ***State or other work-study/employment:*** Part-time jobs available.

APPLYING FOR FINANCIAL AID ***Required financial aid form:*** FAFSA. ***Notification date:*** Continuous.

CONTACT Dr. Amy Barnhart, Director of Financial Aid, Wittenberg University, PO Box 720, Springfield, OH 45501-0720, 937-327-7318 or toll-free 800-677-7558 Ext.6314. *Fax:* 937-327-6379. *E-mail:* barnharta1@wittenberg.edu.
Website: http://www.wittenberg.edu/.

WOFFORD COLLEGE

Spartanburg, SC

Comprehensive fee: $61,440 | **Average undergraduate aid package: $39,677**

ABOUT THE INSTITUTION Independent United Methodist Church, coed. 26 undergraduate majors. ***Total enrollment:*** 1,667. Undergraduates: 1,667. Freshmen: 474. Federal methodology is used as a basis for awarding need-based institutional aid.

UNDERGRADUATE EXPENSES for 2020–2021 ***Application fee:*** $35. ***Comprehensive fee:*** $61,440 includes mandatory fees ($1640) and room and board ($13,790). ***College room only:*** $8065. ***Part-time tuition:*** $1900 per credit hour.

FRESHMAN FINANCIAL AID (Fall 2019, est.) 407 applied for aid; of those 75% were deemed to have need. 100% of freshmen with need received aid; of those 40% had need fully met. ***Average percent of need met:*** 84% (excluding resources awarded to replace EFC). ***Average financial aid package:*** $40,736 (excluding resources awarded to replace EFC). 24% of all full-time freshmen had no need and received non-need-based gift aid.

UNDERGRADUATE FINANCIAL AID (Fall 2019, est.) 1,324 applied for aid; of those 78% were deemed to have need. 100% of undergraduates with need received aid; of those 39% had need fully met. ***Average percent of need met:*** 83% (excluding resources awarded to replace EFC). ***Average financial aid package:*** $39,677 (excluding resources awarded to replace EFC). 28% of all full-time undergraduates had no need and received non-need-based gift aid.

GIFT AID (NEED-BASED) ***Total amount:*** $29,522,229 (5% federal, 16% state, 77% institutional, 2% external sources). ***Receiving aid:*** Freshmen: 64% (304); all full-time undergraduates: 60% (1,028). ***Average award:*** Freshmen: $35,614; Undergraduates: $35,045. ***Scholarships, grants, and awards:*** Federal Pell, FSEOG, state, private, college/university gift aid from institutional funds.

GIFT AID (NON-NEED-BASED) ***Total amount:*** $15,134,455 (15% state, 75% institutional, 10% external sources). ***Receiving aid:*** Freshmen: 20% (97). Undergraduates: 19% (319). ***Average award:*** Freshmen: $20,897. Undergraduates: $19,583. ***Scholarships, grants, and awards by category:*** *Academic interests/achievement:* general academic interests/achievements, military science. *Creative arts/performance:* applied art and design, music. *Special achievements/activities:* leadership. *Special characteristics:* children and siblings of alumni, children of faculty/staff, general special characteristics, local/state students, members of minority groups, religious affiliation. ***Tuition waivers:*** Full or partial for employees or children of employees. ***ROTC:*** Army.

LOANS ***Student loans:*** $7,548,965 (58% need-based, 42% non-need-based). 53% of past graduating class borrowed through all loan programs. *Average indebtedness per student:* $31,107. ***Average need-based loan:*** Freshmen: $3308. Undergraduates: $4286. ***Parent loans:*** $3,065,523 (39% need-based, 61% non-need-based). ***Programs:*** Federal Direct (Subsidized and Unsubsidized Stafford, PLUS).

WORK-STUDY ***Federal work-study:*** Total amount: $221,733; jobs available.

ATHLETIC AWARDS Total amount: $10,202,548 (42% need-based, 58% non-need-based).

APPLYING FOR FINANCIAL AID ***Required financial aid form:*** FAFSA. ***Financial aid deadline:*** 3/1 (priority: 1/1). ***Notification date:*** 3/15. Students must reply by 5/1.

CONTACT Carolyn B. Sparks, Director of Financial Aid, Wofford College, 429 North Church Street, Spartanburg, SC 29303-3663, 864-597-4160. *Fax:* 864-597-4149. *E-mail:* finaid@wofford.edu.
Website: http://www.wofford.edu/.

WOODBURY UNIVERSITY

Burbank, CA

Tuition & fees: $42,596 **Average undergraduate aid package: $32,723**

ABOUT THE INSTITUTION Independent, coed. ***Awards:*** bachelor's and master's degrees. 19 undergraduate majors. ***Total enrollment:*** 1,236. Undergraduates: 1,118. Freshmen: 203. Federal methodology is used as a basis for awarding need-based institutional aid.

UNDERGRADUATE EXPENSES for 2020–2021 ***Application fee:*** $85. ***Comprehensive fee:*** $55,927 includes full-time tuition ($41,102), mandatory fees ($1494), and room and board ($13,331). ***College room only:*** $8259. Full-time tuition and fees vary according to course load, degree level, and program. Room and board charges vary according to board plan, housing facility, and location. ***Part-time tuition:*** $1338 per credit hour. ***Part-time fees:*** $747 per term. Part-time tuition and fees vary according to course load, degree level, and program.

FRESHMAN FINANCIAL AID (Fall 2019, est.) 175 applied for aid; of those 94% were deemed to have need. 100% of freshmen with need received aid; of those 5% had need fully met. ***Average percent of need met:*** 62% (excluding resources awarded to replace EFC). ***Average financial aid package:*** $31,334 (excluding resources awarded to replace EFC). 18% of all full-time freshmen had no need and received non-need-based gift aid.

UNDERGRADUATE FINANCIAL AID (Fall 2019, est.) 838 applied for aid; of those 95% were deemed to have need. 100% of undergraduates with need received aid; of those 4% had need fully met. ***Average percent of need met:*** 63% (excluding resources awarded to replace EFC). ***Average financial aid package:*** $32,723 (excluding resources awarded to replace EFC). 15% of all full-time undergraduates had no need and received non-need-based gift aid.

GIFT AID (NEED-BASED) ***Receiving aid:*** Freshmen: 74% (151); all full-time undergraduates: 72% (761). ***Average award:*** Freshmen: $26,532; Undergraduates: $24,981. ***Scholarships, grants, and awards:*** Federal Pell, FSEOG, state, private, college/university gift aid from institutional funds.

GIFT AID (NON-NEED-BASED) ***Receiving aid:*** Freshmen: 6% (12). Undergraduates: 4% (44). ***Average award:*** Freshmen: $12,333. Undergraduates: $12,506. ***Scholarships, grants, and awards by category:*** *Academic interests/achievement:* architecture, business, general academic interests/achievements. ***Tuition waivers:*** Full or partial for employees or children of employees.

LOANS ***Student loans:*** 51% of past graduating class borrowed through all loan programs. *Average indebtedness per student:* $35,814. ***Average need-based loan:*** Freshmen: $6287. Undergraduates: $9339. ***Programs:*** Federal Direct (Subsidized and Unsubsidized Stafford, PLUS).

WORK-STUDY Federal work-study jobs available.

APPLYING FOR FINANCIAL AID ***Required financial aid forms:*** FAFSA, institution's own form. ***Financial aid deadline:*** Continuous. ***Notification date:*** Continuous. Students must reply within 3 weeks of notification.

CONTACT Oscar Jones, Director of Financial Aid, Woodbury University, 7500 North Glenoaks Boulevard, Burbank, CA 91504, 818-252-5227 or toll-free 800-784-WOOD. *Fax:* 818-767-4816. *E-mail:* oscar.jones@woodbury.edu.
Website: http://www.woodbury.edu/.

WORCESTER POLYTECHNIC INSTITUTE

Worcester, MA

Tuition & fees: $54,146 **Average undergraduate aid package: $38,719**

ABOUT THE INSTITUTION Independent, coed. ***Awards:*** certificates, bachelor's, master's, and doctoral degrees. 33 undergraduate majors. ***Total enrollment:*** 6,894. Undergraduates: 4,761. Freshmen: 1,199. Both federal and institutional methodology are used as a basis for awarding need-based institutional aid.

UNDERGRADUATE EXPENSES for 2020–2021 ***Application fee:*** $65. ***One-time required fee:*** $200. ***Comprehensive fee:*** $69,984 includes full-time tuition ($53,410), mandatory fees ($736), and room and board ($15,838). ***College room only:*** $9042. Room and board charges vary according to board plan and housing facility. ***Part-time tuition:*** $1484 per credit hour. Part-time tuition and fees vary according to course load. ***Payment plan:*** Tuition prepayment.

FRESHMAN FINANCIAL AID (Fall 2018) 1102 applied for aid; of those 77% were deemed to have need. 100% of freshmen with need received aid; of those 65% had need fully met. ***Average percent of need met:*** 91% (excluding resources awarded to replace EFC). ***Average financial aid package:*** $39,646 (excluding resources awarded to replace EFC). 32% of all full-time freshmen had no need and received non-need-based gift aid.

UNDERGRADUATE FINANCIAL AID (Fall 2018) 3,245 applied for aid; of those 84% were deemed to have need. 99% of undergraduates with need received aid; of those 48% had need fully met. ***Average percent of need met:*** 80% (excluding resources awarded to replace EFC). ***Average financial aid package:*** $38,719 (excluding resources awarded to replace EFC). 36% of all full-time undergraduates had no need and received non-need-based gift aid.

GIFT AID (NEED-BASED) ***Total amount:*** $67,709,974 (5% federal, 1% state, 88% institutional, 6% external sources). ***Receiving aid:*** Freshmen: 67% (851); all full-time undergraduates: 57% (2,642). ***Average award:*** Freshmen: $28,153; Undergraduates: $25,304. ***Scholarships, grants, and awards:*** Federal Pell, FSEOG, state, private, college/university gift aid from institutional funds.

GIFT AID (NON-NEED-BASED) ***Total amount:*** $24,349,752 (87% institutional, 13% external sources). ***Receiving aid:*** Freshmen: 66% (845). Undergraduates: 28% (1,286). ***Average award:*** Freshmen: $18,052. Undergraduates: $17,418. ***Scholarships, grants, and awards by category:*** *Academic interests/achievement:* 4,889 awards ($68,230,838 total): general academic interests/achievements. *Special characteristics:* 15 awards ($98,680 total): children of workers in trades. ***Tuition waivers:*** Full or partial for employees or children of employees. ***ROTC:*** Army, Naval cooperative, Air Force.

LOANS ***Student loans:*** $31,842,352 (46% need-based, 54% non-need-based). ***Average need-based loan:*** Freshmen: $1921. Undergraduates: $2274. ***Parent loans:*** $8,179,372 (100% non-need-based). ***Programs:*** Federal Direct (Subsidized and Unsubsidized Stafford, PLUS), state, college/university.

WORK-STUDY ***Federal work-study:*** Total amount: $626,309; 444 jobs averaging $1747. ***State or other work-study/employment:*** Total amount: $2,835,251 (100% need-based).

APPLYING FOR FINANCIAL AID ***Required financial aid forms:*** FAFSA, CSS Financial Aid PROFILE, noncustodial (divorced/separated) parent's statement. ***Financial aid deadline (priority):*** 2/1. ***Notification date:*** Continuous beginning 12/16. Students must reply by 5/1.

CONTACT Jessica Sabourin, Director, Student Aid & Financial Literacy, Worcester Polytechnic Institute, 100 Institute Road, Worcester, MA 01609-2280, 508-831-5469. *Fax:* 508-831-5039. *E-mail:* finaid@wpi.edu.
Website: http://www.wpi.edu/.

WORCESTER STATE UNIVERSITY

Worcester, MA

Tuition & fees (MA res): $10,161 **Average undergraduate aid package: $15,384**

ABOUT THE INSTITUTION State-supported, coed. ***Awards:*** certificates, bachelor's, and master's degrees. 65 undergraduate majors. ***Total enrollment:*** 6,204. Undergraduates: 5,332. Freshmen: 886. Federal methodology is used as a basis for awarding need-based institutional aid.

UNDERGRADUATE EXPENSES for 2019–2020 ***Application fee:*** $50. ***Tuition, state resident:*** full-time $970; part-time $40 per credit hour. ***Tuition, nonresident:*** full-time $7050; part-time $294 per credit hour. ***Required fees:*** full-time $9191; $4596 per term. Full-time tuition and fees vary according to class time, course load, degree level, and reciprocity agreements. Part-time tuition and fees vary according to class time, course load, degree level, and reciprocity agreements. ***College room and board:*** $12,360; ***Room only:*** $8428. Room and board charges vary according to board plan and housing facility.

FRESHMAN FINANCIAL AID (Fall 2018) 823 applied for aid; of those 74% were deemed to have need. 98% of freshmen with need received aid; of those 33% had need fully met. ***Average percent of need met:*** 74% (excluding resources awarded to replace EFC). ***Average financial aid package:*** $16,083 (excluding resources awarded to replace EFC). 4% of all full-time freshmen had no need and received non-need-based gift aid.

UNDERGRADUATE FINANCIAL AID (Fall 2018) 3,541 applied for aid; of those 74% were deemed to have need. 96% of undergraduates with need received aid;

of those 36% had need fully met. ***Average percent of need met:*** 77% (excluding resources awarded to replace EFC). ***Average financial aid package:*** $15,384 (excluding resources awarded to replace EFC). 3% of all full-time undergraduates had no need and received non-need-based gift aid.

GIFT AID (NEED-BASED) ***Total amount:*** $11,552,923 (65% federal, 22% state, 13% institutional). ***Receiving aid:*** Freshmen: 62% (548); all full-time undergraduates: 52% (2,157). ***Average award:*** Freshmen: $5283; Undergraduates: $5191. ***Scholarships, grants, and awards:*** Federal Pell, state, private, college/university gift aid from institutional funds, SEOG.

GIFT AID (NON-NEED-BASED) ***Total amount:*** $2,440,698 (18% state, 50% institutional, 32% external sources). ***Receiving aid:*** Freshmen: 32% (280). Undergraduates: 21% (881). ***Average award:*** Freshmen: $2540. Undergraduates: $2886. ***Tuition waivers:*** Full or partial for employees or children of employees, senior citizens. ***ROTC:*** Army cooperative, Naval cooperative, Air Force cooperative.

LOANS ***Student loans:*** $23,474,701 (35% need-based, 65% non-need-based). 76% of past graduating class borrowed through all loan programs. *Average indebtedness per student:* $30,629. ***Average need-based loan:*** Freshmen: $2393. Undergraduates: $3022. ***Parent loans:*** $3,235,245 (100% non-need-based). ***Programs:*** Federal Direct (Subsidized and Unsubsidized Stafford, PLUS).

WORK-STUDY ***Federal work-study:*** Total amount: $190,067; jobs available.

APPLYING FOR FINANCIAL AID ***Required financial aid form:*** FAFSA. ***Financial aid deadline:*** 5/1 (priority: 3/1). ***Notification date:*** Continuous beginning 12/15. Students must reply within 3 weeks of notification.

CONTACT Ms. Jayne McGinn, Director of Financial Aid, Worcester State University, 486 Chandler Street, Worcester, MA 01602, 508-929-8058. *Fax:* 508-929-8194. *E-mail:* jayne.mcginn@worcester.edu.
Website: http://www.worcester.edu/.

WORLD MISSION UNIVERSITY

Los Angeles, CA

CONTACT Financial Aid Office, World Mission University, 500 Shatto Place, Suite 600, Los Angeles, CA 90020, 213-385-2322.
Website: http://www.wmu.edu/.

WRIGHT STATE UNIVERSITY

Dayton, OH

Tuition & fees (area res): $9578	Average undergraduate aid package: $11,380

ABOUT THE INSTITUTION State-supported, coed. ***Awards:*** certificates, bachelor's, master's, and doctoral degrees. 81 undergraduate majors. ***Total enrollment:*** 12,618. Undergraduates: 9,585. Freshmen: 1,511. Federal methodology is used as a basis for awarding need-based institutional aid.

UNDERGRADUATE EXPENSES for 2019–2020 ***Application fee:*** $30. ***Tuition, area resident:*** full-time $9578; part-time $431 per credit hour. ***Tuition, state resident:*** full-time $9578; part-time $431 per credit hour. ***Tuition, nonresident:*** full-time $18,996; part-time $865 per credit hour. Full-time tuition and fees vary according to course load, location, reciprocity agreements, and student level. Part-time tuition and fees vary according to course load, location, reciprocity agreements, and student level. ***College room and board:*** $12,084; ***Room only:*** $6208. Room and board charges vary according to board plan, housing facility, and location. ***Payment plan:*** Guaranteed tuition.

FRESHMAN FINANCIAL AID (Fall 2019, est.) 1316 applied for aid; of those 75% were deemed to have need. 99% of freshmen with need received aid; of those 20% had need fully met. ***Average percent of need met:*** 64% (excluding resources awarded to replace EFC). ***Average financial aid package:*** $11,335 (excluding resources awarded to replace EFC). 17% of all full-time freshmen had no need and received non-need-based gift aid.

UNDERGRADUATE FINANCIAL AID (Fall 2019, est.) 5,688 applied for aid; of those 80% were deemed to have need. 98% of undergraduates with need received aid; of those 17% had need fully met. ***Average percent of need met:*** 63% (excluding resources awarded to replace EFC). ***Average financial aid package:*** $11,380 (excluding resources awarded to replace EFC). 17% of all full-time undergraduates had no need and received non-need-based gift aid.

GIFT AID (NEED-BASED) ***Total amount:*** $30,793,993 (53% federal, 19% state, 25% institutional, 3% external sources). ***Receiving aid:*** Freshmen: 61% (895); all full-time undergraduates: 52% (3,791). ***Average award:*** Freshmen: $7251; Undergraduates: $7255. ***Scholarships, grants, and awards:*** Federal Pell, FSEOG, state, private, college/university gift aid from institutional funds, United Negro College Fund, Federal Nursing, Choose Ohio First scholarships.

GIFT AID (NON-NEED-BASED) ***Total amount:*** $10,124,187 (19% state, 73% institutional, 8% external sources). ***Receiving aid:*** Freshmen: 9% (131). Undergraduates: 5% (404). ***Average award:*** Freshmen: $4572. Undergraduates: $5019. ***Scholarships, grants, and awards by category:*** *Academic interests/achievement:* area/ethnic studies, biological sciences, business, communication, computer science, education, engineering/technologies, English, foreign languages, general academic interests/achievements, health fields, humanities, international studies, mathematics, military science, physical sciences, premedicine, religion/biblical studies, social sciences. *Creative arts/performance:* applied art and design, art/fine arts, cinema/film/broadcasting, creative writing, dance, general creative arts/performance, music, performing arts, theater/drama. *Special achievements/activities:* cheerleading/drum major, community service, general special achievements/activities, leadership, memberships. *Special characteristics:* adult students, children and siblings of alumni, children of educators, children of faculty/staff, ethnic background, first-generation college students, handicapped students, international students, members of minority groups, out-of-state students. ***Tuition waivers:*** Full or partial for employees or children of employees, senior citizens. ***ROTC:*** Army, Air Force.

LOANS ***Student loans:*** $51,574,483 (72% need-based, 28% non-need-based). 59% of past graduating class borrowed through all loan programs. *Average indebtedness per student:* $28,607. ***Average need-based loan:*** Freshmen: $3213. Undergraduates: $4130. ***Parent loans:*** $4,592,077 (52% need-based, 48% non-need-based). ***Programs:*** Federal Direct (Subsidized and Unsubsidized Stafford, PLUS), Perkins, Federal Nursing, state, college/university, Private loans.

WORK-STUDY ***Federal work-study:*** Total amount: $3,747,969; jobs available.

ATHLETIC AWARDS Total amount: $2,712,924 (36% need-based, 64% non-need-based).

APPLYING FOR FINANCIAL AID ***Required financial aid form:*** FAFSA. ***Financial aid deadline (priority):*** 2/1. ***Notification date:*** Continuous beginning 2/15.

CONTACT Financial Aid Office, Wright State University, 3640 Colonel Glenn Highway, Dayton, OH 45435, 937-775-3333 or toll-free 800-247-1770.
Website: http://www.wright.edu/.

WRIGHT STATE UNIVERSITY–LAKE CAMPUS

Celina, OH

Tuition & fees (OH res): $6410	Average undergraduate aid package: $9023

ABOUT THE INSTITUTION State-supported, coed. ***Awards:*** certificates, associate, and bachelor's degrees. 76 undergraduate majors. ***Total enrollment:*** 1,030. Undergraduates: 1,030. Freshmen: 179. Federal methodology is used as a basis for awarding need-based institutional aid.

UNDERGRADUATE EXPENSES for 2019–2020 ***Application fee:*** $30. ***Tuition, area resident:*** part-time $290 per credit hour. ***Tuition, state resident:*** full-time $6410; part-time $290 per credit hour. ***Tuition, nonresident:*** full-time $15,828; part-time $724 per credit hour. Full-time tuition and fees vary according to course load, location, reciprocity agreements, and student level. Part-time tuition and fees vary according to course load, location, reciprocity agreements, and student level. ***Room only:*** $5030. Room and board charges vary according to board plan, housing facility, and location. ***Payment plan:*** Guaranteed tuition.

FRESHMAN FINANCIAL AID (Fall 2019, est.) 147 applied for aid; of those 69% were deemed to have need. 95% of freshmen with need received aid; of those 25% had need fully met. ***Average percent of need met:*** 70% (excluding resources awarded to replace EFC). ***Average financial aid package:*** $8670 (excluding resources awarded to replace EFC). 17% of all full-time freshmen had no need and received non-need-based gift aid.

UNDERGRADUATE FINANCIAL AID (Fall 2019, est.) 487 applied for aid; of those 72% were deemed to have need. 97% of undergraduates with need received aid;

of those 24% had need fully met. ***Average percent of need met:*** 70% (excluding resources awarded to replace EFC). ***Average financial aid package:*** $9023 (excluding resources awarded to replace EFC). 16% of all full-time undergraduates had no need and received non-need-based gift aid.

GIFT AID (NEED-BASED) ***Total amount:*** $1,626,590 (72% federal, 2% state, 20% institutional, 6% external sources). ***Receiving aid:*** Freshmen: 47% (81); all full-time undergraduates: 44% (279). ***Average award:*** Freshmen: $5321; Undergraduates: $5240. ***Scholarships, grants, and awards:*** Federal Pell, FSEOG, state, private, college/university gift aid from institutional funds, United Negro College Fund, Federal Nursing, Choose Ohio First scholarships.

GIFT AID (NON-NEED-BASED) ***Total amount:*** $564,199 (7% state, 69% institutional, 24% external sources). ***Receiving aid:*** Freshmen: 7% (13). Undergraduates: 7% (42). ***Average award:*** Freshmen: $2443. Undergraduates: $3064. ***Scholarships, grants, and awards by category:*** *Academic interests/achievement:* area/ethnic studies, biological sciences, business, communication, computer science, education, engineering/technologies, English, foreign languages, general academic interests/achievements, health fields, humanities, international studies, mathematics, military science, physical sciences, premedicine, religion/biblical studies, social sciences. *Creative arts/performance:* applied art and design, art/fine arts, cinema/film/broadcasting, creative writing, dance, general creative arts/performance, music, performing arts, theater/drama. *Special achievements/activities:* cheerleading/drum major, community service, general special achievements/activities, leadership, memberships. *Special characteristics:* adult students, children and siblings of alumni, children of educators, children of faculty/staff, ethnic background, first-generation college students, handicapped students, international students, members of minority groups, out-of-state students. ***Tuition waivers:*** Full or partial for employees or children of employees, senior citizens. ***ROTC:*** Army cooperative, Air Force cooperative.

LOANS ***Student loans:*** $3,933,418 (63% need-based, 37% non-need-based). 41% of past graduating class borrowed through all loan programs. *Average indebtedness per student:* $25,975. ***Average need-based loan:*** Freshmen: $3223. Undergraduates: $4057. ***Parent loans:*** $45,900 (23% need-based, 77% non-need-based). ***Programs:*** Federal Direct (Subsidized and Unsubsidized Stafford, PLUS), Perkins, Federal Nursing, state, college/university, Private loans.

WORK-STUDY ***Federal work-study:*** Total amount: $216,433; jobs available. ***State or other work-study/employment:*** Part-time jobs available.

APPLYING FOR FINANCIAL AID ***Required financial aid form:*** FAFSA. ***Financial aid deadline (priority):*** 2/1. ***Notification date:*** Continuous beginning 2/15.

CONTACT Amy Barnhart, Assistant Vice President/Director of Financial Aid, Wright State University–Lake Campus, 3640 Colonel Glenn Highway, 216 Medical Sciences Building, Dayton, OH 45435, 937-775-5405 or toll-free 800-237-1477. *E-mail:* amy.barnhart@wright.edu.
Website: http://www.wright.edu/lake/.

XAVIER UNIVERSITY

Cincinnati, OH

Tuition & fees: $42,460	Average undergraduate aid package: $25,338

ABOUT THE INSTITUTION Independent Roman Catholic, coed. ***Awards:*** certificates, associate, bachelor's, master's, and doctoral degrees. 73 undergraduate majors. ***Total enrollment:*** 6,993. Undergraduates: 5,047. Freshmen: 1,210.

UNDERGRADUATE EXPENSES for 2020–2021 ***Application fee:*** $35. ***Comprehensive fee:*** $55,770 includes full-time tuition ($42,230), mandatory fees ($230), and room and board ($13,310). ***College room only:*** $7370. Full-time tuition and fees vary according to course load, location, and program. Room and board charges vary according to board plan and housing facility. ***Part-time tuition:*** $873 per credit hour. Part-time tuition and fees vary according to course load, location, and program.

FRESHMAN FINANCIAL AID (Fall 2018) 1223 applied for aid; of those 73% were deemed to have need. 100% of freshmen with need received aid; of those 10% had need fully met. ***Average percent of need met:*** 66% (excluding resources awarded to replace EFC). ***Average financial aid package:*** $24,281 (excluding resources awarded to replace EFC). 23% of all full-time freshmen had no need and received non-need-based gift aid.

UNDERGRADUATE FINANCIAL AID (Fall 2018) 3,391 applied for aid; of those 81% were deemed to have need. 100% of undergraduates with need received aid; of those 6% had need fully met. ***Average percent of need met:*** 63% (excluding resources awarded to replace EFC). ***Average financial aid package:*** $25,338 (excluding resources awarded to replace EFC). 13% of all full-time undergraduates had no need and received non-need-based gift aid.

GIFT AID (NEED-BASED) ***Total amount:*** $35,224,204 (8% federal, 2% state, 88% institutional, 2% external sources). ***Receiving aid:*** Freshmen: 39% (542); all full-time undergraduates: 35% (1,652). ***Average award:*** Freshmen: $24,587; Undergraduates: $23,327. ***Scholarships, grants, and awards:*** Federal Pell, FSEOG, state, private, college/university gift aid from institutional funds, United Negro College Fund.

GIFT AID (NON-NEED-BASED) ***Total amount:*** $53,136,891 (1% federal, 95% institutional, 4% external sources). ***Receiving aid:*** Freshmen: 25% (353). Undergraduates: 18% (849). ***Average award:*** Freshmen: $18,800. Undergraduates: $18,163. ***Scholarships, grants, and awards by category:*** *Academic interests/achievement:* foreign languages, general academic interests/achievements, mathematics, military science, physical sciences, social sciences. *Creative arts/performance:* art/fine arts, music, performing arts, theater/drama. *Special characteristics:* children and siblings of alumni, international students, members of minority groups, siblings of current students. ***Tuition waivers:*** Full or partial for employees or children of employees, senior citizens. ***ROTC:*** Army, Air Force cooperative.

LOANS ***Student loans:*** $33,653,567 (59% need-based, 41% non-need-based). 53% of past graduating class borrowed through all loan programs. *Average indebtedness per student:* $10,348. ***Average need-based loan:*** Freshmen: $2826. Undergraduates: $3825. ***Parent loans:*** $10,274,598 (39% need-based, 61% non-need-based). ***Programs:*** Federal Direct (Subsidized and Unsubsidized Stafford, PLUS), Federal Nursing, college/university.

WORK-STUDY ***Federal work-study:*** Total amount: $1,944,669; jobs available. ***State or other work-study/employment:*** Part-time jobs available.

ATHLETIC AWARDS Total amount: $4,016,582 (11% need-based, 89% non-need-based).

APPLYING FOR FINANCIAL AID ***Required financial aid form:*** FAFSA. ***Financial aid deadline (priority):*** 2/15. ***Notification date:*** Continuous beginning 12/15. Students must reply by 5/1.

CONTACT Office of Financial Aid, Xavier University, 3800 Victory Parkway, Cincinnati, OH 45207-5111, 513-745-3142 or toll-free 877-XUADMIT. *Fax:* 513-745-2806.
Website: http://www.xavier.edu/.

XAVIER UNIVERSITY OF LOUISIANA

New Orleans, LA

Tuition & fees: $25,185	Average undergraduate aid package: $10,046

ABOUT THE INSTITUTION Independent Roman Catholic, coed. ***Awards:*** bachelor's, master's, and doctoral degrees. 49 undergraduate majors. ***Total enrollment:*** 3,325. Undergraduates: 2,530. Freshmen: 832.

UNDERGRADUATE EXPENSES for 2019–2020 ***One-time required fee:*** $150. ***Comprehensive fee:*** $35,185 includes full-time tuition ($22,503), mandatory fees ($2682), and room and board ($10,000). Full-time tuition and fees vary according to course load. Room and board charges vary according to board plan and housing facility. ***Part-time tuition:*** $938 per credit hour. ***Part-time fees:*** $275 per term. Part-time tuition and fees vary according to course load.

FRESHMAN FINANCIAL AID (Fall 2018) 851 applied for aid; of those 79% were deemed to have need. 100% of freshmen with need received aid; of those 49% had need fully met. ***Average percent of need met:*** 83% (excluding resources awarded to replace EFC). ***Average financial aid package:*** $10,757 (excluding resources awarded to replace EFC).

UNDERGRADUATE FINANCIAL AID (Fall 2018) 2,331 applied for aid; of those 78% were deemed to have need. 100% of undergraduates with need received aid; of those 52% had need fully met. ***Average percent of need met:*** 64% (excluding resources awarded to replace EFC). ***Average financial aid package:*** $10,046 (excluding resources awarded to replace EFC).

GIFT AID (NEED-BASED) ***Total amount:*** $32,990,145 (23% federal, 15% state, 58% institutional, 4% external sources). ***Receiving aid:*** Freshmen: 78% (668); all full-time undergraduates: 70% (1,717). ***Average award:*** Freshmen: $9385; Undergraduates: $8570. ***Scholarships, grants, and awards:*** Federal Pell, FSEOG, state, private, college/university gift aid from institutional funds, United Negro College Fund.

GIFT AID (NON-NEED-BASED) ***Total amount:*** $73,313 (100% external sources). ***Receiving aid:*** Freshmen: 3. Undergraduates: 1% (16). ***Scholarships, grants, and awards by category:*** *Academic interests/achievement:* biological sciences, business, communication, computer science, education, engineering/technologies, English, foreign languages, general academic interests/achievements, home economics, humanities, mathematics, physical sciences, premedicine, religion/biblical studies, social sciences. *Creative arts/performance:* applied art and design, music. *Special characteristics:* children of faculty/staff, spouses of current students. ***Tuition waivers:*** Full or partial for employees or children of employees. ***ROTC:*** Army cooperative, Naval cooperative, Air Force cooperative.

LOANS *Student loans:* $14,579,523 (50% need-based, 50% non-need-based). 98% of past graduating class borrowed through all loan programs. *Average indebtedness per student:* $21,820. ***Average need-based loan:*** Freshmen: $1626. Undergraduates: $1990. ***Parent loans:*** $29,048,893 (100% non-need-based). ***Programs:*** Federal Direct (Subsidized and Unsubsidized Stafford, PLUS), Perkins.

WORK-STUDY *Federal work-study:* Total amount: $947,372; jobs available.

ATHLETIC AWARDS Total amount: $1,755,422 (100% need-based).

APPLYING FOR FINANCIAL AID *Required financial aid form:* FAFSA. ***Financial aid deadline:*** Continuous. ***Notification date:*** Continuous beginning 4/1. Students must reply within 2 weeks of notification.

CONTACT Mrs. Emily Jones, Financial Aid Director, Xavier University of Louisiana, One Drexel Drive, New Orleans, LA 70125-1098, 504-520-7517 or toll-free 877-XAVIERU. *E-mail:* ejones@xula.edu.
Website: http://www.xula.edu/.

YALE UNIVERSITY

New Haven, CT

Tuition & fees: $57,700	Average undergraduate aid package: $61,610

ABOUT THE INSTITUTION Independent, coed. ***Awards:*** certificates, bachelor's, master's, and doctoral degrees. 69 undergraduate majors. ***Total enrollment:*** 13,609. Undergraduates: 6,092. Freshmen: 1,550. Both federal and institutional methodology are used as a basis for awarding need-based institutional aid.

UNDERGRADUATE EXPENSES for 2020–2021 *Application fee:* $80. ***Comprehensive fee:*** $74,900 includes full-time tuition ($57,700) and room and board ($17,200). ***College room only:*** $9750.

FRESHMAN FINANCIAL AID (Fall 2019, est.) 1025 applied for aid; of those 81% were deemed to have need. 100% of freshmen with need received aid; of those 100% had need fully met. ***Average percent of need met:*** 100% (excluding resources awarded to replace EFC). ***Average financial aid package:*** $62,879 (excluding resources awarded to replace EFC).

UNDERGRADUATE FINANCIAL AID (Fall 2019, est.) 3,519 applied for aid; of those 91% were deemed to have need. 100% of undergraduates with need received aid; of those 100% had need fully met. ***Average percent of need met:*** 100% (excluding resources awarded to replace EFC). ***Average financial aid package:*** $61,610 (excluding resources awarded to replace EFC).

GIFT AID (NEED-BASED) *Total amount:* $189,570,129 (4% federal, 93% institutional, 3% external sources). ***Receiving aid:*** Freshmen: 53% (827); all full-time undergraduates: 53% (3,204). ***Average award:*** Freshmen: $61,067; Undergraduates: $59,150. ***Scholarships, grants, and awards:*** Federal Pell, FSEOG, state, private, college/university gift aid from institutional funds, United Negro College Fund.

GIFT AID (NON-NEED-BASED) *Total amount:* $795,289 (100% external sources). ***Tuition waivers:*** Full or partial for employees or children of employees. ***ROTC:*** Army cooperative, Naval, Air Force.

LOANS *Student loans:* $2,747,256 (34% need-based, 66% non-need-based). 15% of past graduating class borrowed through all loan programs. *Average indebtedness per student:* $15,379. ***Average need-based loan:*** Freshmen: $2453. Undergraduates: $3108. ***Programs:*** Federal Direct (Subsidized and Unsubsidized Stafford, PLUS), Federal Nursing, state, college/university.

WORK-STUDY *Federal work-study:* Total amount: $2,327,435; jobs available. ***State or other work-study/employment:*** Total amount: $4,632,565 (100% need-based). Part-time jobs available.

APPLYING FOR FINANCIAL AID *Required financial aid forms:* FAFSA, institution's own form, CSS Financial Aid PROFILE, noncustodial (divorced/separated) parent's statement. ***Financial aid deadline:*** 3/1 (priority: 3/1). ***Notification date:*** 4/1.

CONTACT Mr. Caesar T. Storlazzi, University Director of Financial Aid, Yale University, PO Box 208288, New Haven, CT 06520-8288, 203-432-0371. *Fax:* 203-777-6100. *E-mail:* sfs@yale.edu.
Website: http://www.yale.edu/.

YELLOWSTONE CHRISTIAN COLLEGE

Billings, MT

CONTACT Financial Aid Office, Yellowstone Christian College, 1515 South Shiloh Road, Billings, MT 59106, 406-656-9950 or toll-free 800-487-9950.
Website: https://yellowstonechristian.edu/.

YESHIVA AND KOLEL BAIS MEDRASH ELYON

Monsey, NY

CONTACT Financial Aid Office, Yeshiva and Kolel Bais Medrash Elyon, 73 Main Street, Monsey, NY 10952, 845-356-7064.

YESHIVA AND KOLLEL HARBOTZAS TORAH

Brooklyn, NY

CONTACT Financial Aid Office, Yeshiva and Kollel Harbotzas Torah, 1049 East 15th Street, Brooklyn, NY 11230, 718-692-0208.

YESHIVA BAIS AHARON

Lakewood, NJ

CONTACT Financial Aid Office, Yeshiva Bais Aharon, 905 Park Avenue, Lakewood, NJ 08701.

YESHIVA BETH MOSHE

Scranton, PA

CONTACT Financial Aid Office , Yeshiva Beth Moshe, 930 Hickory Street, Scranton, PA 18505-2124, 717-346-1747.

YESHIVA BETH YEHUDA

Oak Park, MI

CONTACT Rabbi P. Rushnawitz, Executive Administrator , Yeshiva Beth Yehuda, 24600 Greenfield Road, Oak Park, MI 48237-1544, 810-968-3360. *Fax:* 810-968-8613.

YESHIVA COLLEGE OF THE NATION'S CAPITAL

Silver Spring, MD

CONTACT Financial Aid Office, Yeshiva College of the Nation's Capital, 1216 Arcola Avenue, Silver Spring, MD 20902, 301-593-2534.
Website: http://www.yeshiva.edu/.

YESHIVA DERECH CHAIM

Brooklyn, NY

CONTACT Financial Aid Office, Yeshiva Derech Chaim, 1573 39th Street, Brooklyn, NY 11218, 718-438-5426.

YESHIVA D'MONSEY RABBINICAL COLLEGE

Monsey, NY

CONTACT Financial Aid Office, Yeshiva D'Monsey Rabbinical College, 2 Roman Boulevard, Monsey, NY 10952, 914-352-5852.

YESHIVA GEDOLAH IMREI YOSEF D'SPINKA

Brooklyn, NY

CONTACT Financial Aid Office, Yeshiva Gedolah Imrei Yosef D'Spinka, 1466 56th Street, Brooklyn, NY 11219, 718-851-8721.

YESHIVA GEDOLAH KESSER TORAH

Monsey, NY

CONTACT Financial Aid Office, Yeshiva Gedolah Kesser Torah, 28 Cedar Lane, Monsey, NY 10952.

YESHIVA GEDOLAH RABBINICAL COLLEGE

Miami Beach, FL

CONTACT Financial Aid Office, Yeshiva Gedolah Rabbinical College, 1140 Alton Road, Miami Beach, FL 33139, 305-673-5664.

YESHIVA GEDOLAH SHAAREI SHMUEL

Lakewood, NJ

CONTACT Financial Aid Office, Yeshiva Gedolah Shaarei Shmuel, 511 Ocean Avenue, Lakewood, NJ 08701.
Website: http://www.yeshivagedolahshaareishmuel.com/.

YESHIVA GEDOLAH ZICHRON LEYMA

Linden, NJ

CONTACT Financial Aid Office, Yeshiva Gedolah Zichron Leyma, 1000 Orchard Terrace, Linden, NJ 07036, 908-587-0502.

YESHIVA GEDOLA OHR YISRAEL

Brooklyn, NY

CONTACT Financial Aid Office, Yeshiva Gedola Ohr Yisrael, 2899 Nostrand Avenue, Brooklyn, NY 11229.
Website: http://www.ohryisroel.org/.

YESHIVA KARLIN STOLIN

Brooklyn, NY

CONTACT Mr. Daniel Ross, Financial Aid Administrator, Yeshiva Karlin Stolin, 1818 Fifty-fourth Street, Brooklyn, NY 11204, 718-232-7800 Ext. 116. *Fax:* 718-331-4833.

YESHIVA KOLLEL TIFERETH ELIZER

Brooklyn, NY

CONTACT Financial Aid Office, Yeshiva Kollel Tifereth Elizer, 1227 47th Street, Brooklyn, NY 11219.

YESHIVA OF FAR ROCKAWAY DERECH AYSON RABBINICAL SEMINARY

Far Rockaway, NY

CONTACT Financial Aid Office, Yeshiva of Far Rockaway Derech Ayson Rabbinical Seminary, 802 Hicksville Road, Far Rockaway, NY 11691, 718-327-7600.
Website: http://www.yofr.org/.

YESHIVA OF MACHZIKAI HADAS

Brooklyn, NY

CONTACT Financial Aid Office, Yeshiva of Machzikai Hadas, 1321 43rd Street, Brooklyn, NY 11219, 718-853-2442.

YESHIVA OF NITRA RABBINICAL COLLEGE

Mount Kisco, NY

CONTACT Mr. Yosef Rosen, Financial Aid Administrator , Yeshiva of Nitra Rabbinical College, 194 Division Avenue, Mount Kisco, NY 10549, 718-384-5460. *Fax:* 718-387-9400.

YESHIVA OF THE TELSHE ALUMNI

Riverdale, NY

CONTACT Financial Aid Office, Yeshiva of the Telshe Alumni, 4904 Independence Avenue, Riverdale, NY 10471, 718-601-3523.

YESHIVA OHR ELCHONON CHABAD/ WEST COAST TALMUDICAL SEMINARY

Los Angeles, CA

CONTACT Ms. Hendy Tauber, Director of Financial Aid , Yeshiva Ohr Elchonon Chabad/West Coast Talmudical Seminary, 7215 Waring Avenue, Los Angeles, CA 90046-7660, 213-937-3763. *Fax:* 213-937-9456.
Website: http://www.yoec.edu/.

YESHIVA OHR NAFTOLI

New Windsor, NY

CONTACT Financial Aid Office, Yeshiva Ohr Naftoli, 701 Blooming Grove Turnpike, New Windsor, NY 12553.
Website: http://www.yeshivaohrnaftoli.com/.

YESHIVAS BE'ER YITZCHOK

Elizabeth, NJ

CONTACT Financial Aid Office, Yeshivas Be'er Yitzchok, 1391 North Avenue, Elizabeth, NJ 07208, 908-354-6057.
Website: http://www.elizabethkollel.org/.

YESHIVA SHAAREI TORAH OF ROCKLAND

Suffern, NY

CONTACT Financial Aid Office, Yeshiva Shaarei Torah of Rockland, 91 West Carlton Road, Suffern, NY 10901, 845-352-3431.
Website: https://www.yst.edu/.

YESHIVA SHAAR EPHRAIM

Monsey, NY

CONTACT Financial Aid Office, Yeshiva Shaar Ephraim, 178 Maple Avenue, Monsey, NY 10952.

YESHIVA SHAAR HATORAH TALMUDIC RESEARCH INSTITUTE

Kew Gardens, NY

CONTACT Mr. Yoel Yankelewitz, Executive Director, Financial Aid, Yeshiva Shaar Hatorah Talmudic Research Institute, 117-06 84th Avenue, Kew Gardens, NY 11418-1469, 718-846-1940.

YESHIVAS MAHARIT D'SATMAR

Monroe, NY

CONTACT Financial Aid Office, Yeshivas Maharit D'Satmar, 475 County Route 105, Monroe, NY 10950.
Website: http://www.yeshivasmaharit.com/.

YESHIVAS NOVOMINSK

Brooklyn, NY

CONTACT Financial Aid Office, Yeshivas Novominsk, 1569 47th Street, Brooklyn, NY 11219, 718-438-2727.

YESHIVATH VIZNITZ

Monsey, NY

CONTACT Financial Aid Office, Yeshivath Viznitz, Phyllis Terrace, PO Box 446, Monsey, NY 10952, 914-356-1010.

YESHIVATH ZICHRON MOSHE

South Fallsburg, NY

CONTACT Ms. Miryom R. Miller, Director of Financial Aid , Yeshivath Zichron Moshe, Laurel Park Road, South Fallsburg, NY 12779, 914-434-5240. *Fax:* 914-434-1009. *E-mail:* lehus@aol.com.

YESHIVAT MIKDASH MELECH

Brooklyn, NY

CONTACT Financial Aid Office, Yeshivat Mikdash Melech, 1326 Ocean Parkway, Brooklyn, NY 11230-5601, 718-339-1090.

YESHIVA TORAS CHAIM

Lakewood, NJ

CONTACT Financial Aid Office, Yeshiva Toras Chaim, 999 Ridge Avenue, Lakewood, NJ 08701, 732-942-3090.

YESHIVA UNIVERSITY

New York, NY

Tuition & fees: $44,900	Average undergraduate aid package: $42,654

ABOUT THE INSTITUTION Independent, coed. ***Awards:*** certificates, bachelor's, master's, and doctoral degrees (Yeshiva College and Stern College for Women are coordinate undergraduate colleges of arts and sciences for men and women, respectively. Sy Syms School of Business offers programs at both campuses). 36 undergraduate majors. ***Total enrollment:*** 5,213. Undergraduates: 2,710. Freshmen: 555. Both federal and institutional methodology are used as a basis for awarding need-based institutional aid.

UNDERGRADUATE EXPENSES for 2019–2020 ***Application fee:*** **$65.** ***Comprehensive fee:*** $57,400 includes full-time tuition ($42,200), mandatory fees ($2700), and room and board ($12,500). ***College room only:*** $9000. ***Part-time tuition:*** $1520 per credit hour.

FRESHMAN FINANCIAL AID (Fall 2019, est.) 408 applied for aid; of those 76% were deemed to have need. 100% of freshmen with need received aid; of those 34% had need fully met. ***Average percent of need met:*** 91% (excluding resources awarded to replace EFC). ***Average financial aid package:*** $42,629 (excluding resources awarded to replace EFC). 29% of all full-time freshmen had no need and received non-need-based gift aid.

UNDERGRADUATE FINANCIAL AID (Fall 2019, est.) 1,877 applied for aid; of those 75% were deemed to have need. 100% of undergraduates with need received aid; of those 30% had need fully met. ***Average percent of need met:*** 90% (excluding resources awarded to replace EFC). ***Average financial aid package:*** $42,654 (excluding resources awarded to replace EFC). 28% of all full-time undergraduates had no need and received non-need-based gift aid.

GIFT AID (NEED-BASED) ***Total amount:*** $47,312,110 (4% federal, 2% state, 94% institutional). ***Receiving aid:*** Freshmen: 55% (304); all full-time undergraduates: 51% (1,350). ***Average award:*** Freshmen: $30,750; Undergraduates: $31,285. ***Scholarships, grants, and awards:*** Federal Pell, FSEOG, state, private, college/university gift aid from institutional funds.

GIFT AID (NON-NEED-BASED) ***Total amount:*** $14,995,514 (100% institutional). ***Receiving aid:*** Freshmen: 13% (74). Undergraduates: 14% (358). ***Average***

award: Freshmen: $21,162. Undergraduates: $20,577. ***Scholarships, grants, and awards by category:*** *Academic interests/achievement:* general academic interests/achievements.

LOANS ***Student loans:*** $16,132,284 (80% need-based, 20% non-need-based). 39% of past graduating class borrowed through all loan programs. *Average indebtedness per student:* $22,388. ***Average need-based loan:*** Freshmen: $6485. Undergraduates: $7067. ***Parent loans:*** $20,148,173 (70% need-based, 30% non-need-based). ***Programs:*** Federal Direct (Subsidized and Unsubsidized Stafford, PLUS), Perkins, college/university.

WORK-STUDY ***Federal work-study:*** Total amount: $1,766,588; jobs available. ***State or other work-study/employment:*** Part-time jobs available.

APPLYING FOR FINANCIAL AID ***Required financial aid form:*** FAFSA. ***Financial aid deadline (priority):*** 2/1. ***Notification date:*** Continuous beginning 3/15. Students must reply by 5/1.

CONTACT Marianela Cabral, Director of Student Aid Operations, Yeshiva University, 500 West 185th Street, Room 121, New York, NY 10033, 212-960-5399. *Fax:* 212-960-0037. *E-mail:* mcabral@yu.edu.
Website: http://www.yu.edu/.

YESHIVA YESODEI HATORAH

Lakewood, NJ

CONTACT Financial Aid Office, Yeshiva Yesodei HaTorah, 2 Yesodei Court, Lakewood, NJ 08701.

YESHIVA ZICHRON ARYEH

Far Rockaway, NY

CONTACT Financial Aid Office, Yeshiva Zichron Aryeh, 1213 Bay 25th Street, Far Rockaway, NY 11691.
Website: http://www.yeshivazichronaryeh.com/.

YORK COLLEGE

York, NE

CONTACT Brien Alley, Director of Financial Aid, York College, 1125 East 8th Street, York, NE 68467, 402-363-5624 or toll-free 800-950-9675. *Fax:* 402-363-5623. *E-mail:* balley@york.edu.
Website: http://www.york.edu/.

YORK COLLEGE OF PENNSYLVANIA

York, PA

Tuition & fees: $21,790	Average undergraduate aid package: $14,171

ABOUT THE INSTITUTION Independent, coed. ***Awards:*** certificates, associate, bachelor's, master's, and doctoral degrees. 61 undergraduate majors. ***Total enrollment:*** 4,305. Undergraduates: 4,036. Freshmen: 930. Federal methodology is used as a basis for awarding need-based institutional aid.

UNDERGRADUATE EXPENSES for 2020–2021 ***Comprehensive fee:*** $33,680 includes full-time tuition ($19,760), mandatory fees ($2030), and room and board ($11,890). ***College room only:*** $6720. Full-time tuition and fees vary according to program. Room and board charges vary according to board plan and housing facility.

FRESHMAN FINANCIAL AID (Fall 2019, est.) 878 applied for aid; of those 77% were deemed to have need. 100% of freshmen with need received aid; of those 19% had need fully met. ***Average percent of need met:*** 62% (excluding resources awarded to replace EFC). ***Average financial aid package:*** $14,890 (excluding resources awarded to replace EFC). 27% of all full-time freshmen had no need and received non-need-based gift aid.

UNDERGRADUATE FINANCIAL AID (Fall 2019, est.) 3,116 applied for aid; of those 80% were deemed to have need. 100% of undergraduates with need received aid; of those 16% had need fully met. ***Average percent of need met:*** 58% (excluding resources awarded to replace EFC). ***Average financial aid package:*** $14,171 (excluding resources awarded to replace EFC). 27% of all full-time undergraduates had no need and received non-need-based gift aid.

GIFT AID (NEED-BASED) ***Total amount:*** $25,975,563 (18% federal, 11% state, 68% institutional, 3% external sources). ***Receiving aid:*** Freshmen: 53% (491); all full-time undergraduates: 48% (1,785). ***Average award:*** Freshmen: $6122; Undergraduates: $6172. ***Scholarships, grants, and awards:*** Federal Pell, FSEOG, state, private, college/university gift aid from institutional funds.

GIFT AID (NON-NEED-BASED) ***Total amount:*** $6,780,752 (96% institutional, 4% external sources). ***Receiving aid:*** Freshmen: 71% (654). Undergraduates: 62% (2,271). ***Average award:*** Freshmen: $7003. Undergraduates: $6270. ***Scholarships, grants, and awards by category:*** *Academic interests/achievement:* engineering/technologies, general academic interests/achievements. *Creative arts/performance:* music. *Special characteristics:* children and siblings of alumni, children of union members/company employees, international students, members of minority groups. ***Tuition waivers:*** Full or partial for employees or children of employees.

LOANS ***Student loans:*** $31,563,302 (80% need-based, 20% non-need-based). 80% of past graduating class borrowed through all loan programs. *Average indebtedness per student:* $44,077. ***Average need-based loan:*** Freshmen: $3191. Undergraduates: $4150. ***Parent loans:*** $8,098,108 (86% need-based, 14% non-need-based). ***Programs:*** Federal Direct (Subsidized and Unsubsidized Stafford, PLUS), Perkins, Federal Nursing, college/university.

WORK-STUDY ***Federal work-study:*** Total amount: $422,009; jobs available. ***State or other work-study/employment:*** Total amount: $17,322 (72% need-based, 28% non-need-based). Part-time jobs available.

APPLYING FOR FINANCIAL AID ***Required financial aid form:*** FAFSA. ***Financial aid deadline:*** Continuous. ***Notification date:*** Continuous beginning 3/1. Students must reply within 4 weeks of notification.

CONTACT Eric Dinsmore, Director of Financial Assistance, York College of Pennsylvania, 441 Country Club Road, York, PA 17403-3651, 717-846-7788 or toll-free 800-455-8018.
Website: http://www.ycp.edu/.

YORK COLLEGE OF THE CITY UNIVERSITY OF NEW YORK

Jamaica, NY

Tuition & fees: N/R	Average undergraduate aid package: $7189

ABOUT THE INSTITUTION State and locally supported, coed. ***Awards:*** bachelor's and master's degrees. 46 undergraduate majors. ***Total enrollment:*** 8,360. Undergraduates: 8,258. Freshmen: 971. Federal methodology is used as a basis for awarding need-based institutional aid.

FRESHMAN FINANCIAL AID (Fall 2019, est.) 1022 applied for aid; of those 96% were deemed to have need. 92% of freshmen with need received aid; of those 2% had need fully met. ***Average percent of need met:*** 54% (excluding resources awarded to replace EFC). ***Average financial aid package:*** $6704 (excluding resources awarded to replace EFC). 1% of all full-time freshmen had no need and received non-need-based gift aid.

UNDERGRADUATE FINANCIAL AID (Fall 2019, est.) 4,402 applied for aid; of those 98% were deemed to have need. 92% of undergraduates with need received aid; of those 2% had need fully met. ***Average percent of need met:*** 49% (excluding resources awarded to replace EFC). ***Average financial aid package:*** $7189 (excluding resources awarded to replace EFC). 1% of all full-time undergraduates had no need and received non-need-based gift aid.

GIFT AID (NEED-BASED) ***Total amount:*** $31,387,482 (60% federal, 40% state). ***Receiving aid:*** Freshmen: 79% (868); all full-time undergraduates: 74% (3,708). ***Average award:*** Freshmen: $8885; Undergraduates: $7979. ***Scholarships, grants, and awards:*** Federal Pell, FSEOG, state, private, college/university gift aid from institutional funds, Federal Nursing.

GIFT AID (NON-NEED-BASED) ***Total amount:*** $1,599,731 (67% state, 9% institutional, 24% external sources). ***Receiving aid:*** Freshmen: 34% (370). Undergraduates: 16% (796). ***Average award:*** Freshmen: $4000. Undergraduates: $4000.
ROTC: Army.

LOANS ***Student loans:*** $3,462,381 (56% need-based, 44% non-need-based). 3% of past graduating class borrowed through all loan programs. *Average indebtedness per student:* $5266. ***Average need-based loan:*** Freshmen: $3290. Undergraduates: $4221. ***Parent loans:*** $38,400 (100% non-need-based). ***Programs:*** Federal Direct (Subsidized and Unsubsidized Stafford, PLUS).

WORK-STUDY ***Federal work-study:*** Total amount: $963,302; jobs available.

APPLYING FOR FINANCIAL AID ***Required financial aid forms:*** FAFSA, state aid form. ***Notification date:*** Continuous beginning 2/15. Students must reply within 4 weeks of notification.

CONTACT Ms. Beverly Brown, Director of Student Financial Services, York College of the City University of New York, 94-20 Guy R. Brewer Boulevard, Jamaica, NY 11451, 718-262-2240. *E-mail:* bbrown@york.cuny.edu.
Website: http://www.york.cuny.edu/.

YOUNG HARRIS COLLEGE

Young Harris, GA

ABOUT THE INSTITUTION Independent United Methodist, coed. ***Awards:*** bachelor's degrees. 30 undergraduate majors. ***Total enrollment:*** 1,425. Undergraduates: 1,034. Freshmen: 388.

GIFT AID (NEED-BASED) ***Scholarships, grants, and awards:*** Federal Pell, FSEOG, state, private, college/university gift aid from institutional funds.

GIFT AID (NON-NEED-BASED) ***Scholarships, grants, and awards by category:*** *Academic interests/achievement:* general academic interests/achievements. *Creative arts/performance:* applied art and design, music, performing arts, theater/drama. *Special characteristics:* children of faculty/staff, religious affiliation.

LOANS ***Programs:*** Federal Direct (Subsidized and Unsubsidized Stafford, PLUS), state, college/university.

CONTACT Michelle Bernard, Director of Financial Aid, Young Harris College, 1 College Street, Young Harris, GA 30582, 706-379-5188 or toll-free 800-241-3754 (in-state). *Fax:* 706-379-4594. *E-mail:* mmbernard@yhc.edu.
Website: http://www.yhc.edu/.

YOUNGSTOWN STATE UNIVERSITY

Youngstown, OH

Tuition & fees (OH res): $9279	Average undergraduate aid package: $9954

ABOUT THE INSTITUTION State-supported, coed. ***Awards:*** certificates, diplomas, associate, bachelor's, master's, and doctoral degrees. 143 undergraduate majors. ***Total enrollment:*** 12,510. Undergraduates: 11,001. Freshmen: 2,010. Federal methodology is used as a basis for awarding need-based institutional aid.

UNDERGRADUATE EXPENSES for 2019–2020 ***Application fee:*** $45. ***Tuition, state resident:*** full-time $9211; part-time $384 per credit hour. ***Tuition, nonresident:*** full-time $15,211; part-time $634 per credit hour. ***Required fees:*** full-time $68; $34 per term. Full-time tuition and fees vary according to course load. Part-time tuition and fees vary according to course load. ***College room and board:*** $9700. Room and board charges vary according to board plan and housing facility. ***Payment plan:*** Guaranteed tuition.

FRESHMAN FINANCIAL AID (Fall 2018) 2038 applied for aid; of those 82% were deemed to have need. 100% of freshmen with need received aid; of those 12% had need fully met. ***Average percent of need met:*** 37% (excluding resources awarded to replace EFC). ***Average financial aid package:*** $9566 (excluding resources awarded to replace EFC). 19% of all full-time freshmen had no need and received non-need-based gift aid.

UNDERGRADUATE FINANCIAL AID (Fall 2018) 7,433 applied for aid; of those 83% were deemed to have need. 99% of undergraduates with need received aid; of those 9% had need fully met. ***Average percent of need met:*** 35% (excluding resources awarded to replace EFC). ***Average financial aid package:*** $9954 (excluding resources awarded to replace EFC). 17% of all full-time undergraduates had no need and received non-need-based gift aid.

GIFT AID (NEED-BASED) ***Total amount:*** $30,037,370 (72% federal, 15% state, 1% institutional, 12% external sources). ***Receiving aid:*** Freshmen: 58% (1,289); all full-time undergraduates: 53% (4,685). ***Average award:*** Freshmen: $5681; Undergraduates: $5772. ***Scholarships, grants, and awards:*** Federal Pell, FSEOG, state, private, college/university gift aid from institutional funds, Advanced Education Nursing Scholarships.

GIFT AID (NON-NEED-BASED) ***Total amount:*** $19,250,425 (2% federal, 7% state, 32% institutional, 59% external sources). ***Receiving aid:*** Freshmen: 49% (1,077). Undergraduates: 37% (3,289). ***Average award:*** Freshmen: $4703. Undergraduates: $4250. ***Scholarships, grants, and awards by category:*** *Academic interests/achievement:* biological sciences, business, communication, computer science, education, engineering/technologies, English, foreign languages, general academic interests/achievements, home economics, humanities, mathematics, military science, physical sciences, premedicine, religion/biblical studies, social sciences. *Creative arts/performance:* applied art and design, creative writing, journalism/publications, music, performing arts, theater/drama. *Special achievements/activities:* cheerleading/drum major, community service, leadership, memberships, religious involvement. *Special characteristics:* adult students, children and siblings of alumni, children of faculty/staff, children of union members/company employees, children of workers in trades, children with a deceased or disabled parent, ethnic background, handicapped students, international students, local/state students, members of minority groups, out-of-state students, public servants, religious affiliation, spouses of deceased or disabled public servants, veterans. ***Tuition waivers:*** Full or partial for employees or children of employees, senior citizens. ***ROTC:*** Army, Air Force cooperative.

LOANS ***Student loans:*** $50,150,084 (42% need-based, 58% non-need-based). 65% of past graduating class borrowed through all loan programs. *Average indebtedness per student:* $29,360. ***Average need-based loan:*** Freshmen: $3142. Undergraduates: $3786. ***Parent loans:*** $43,213,200 (100% non-need-based). ***Programs:*** Federal Direct (Subsidized and Unsubsidized Stafford, PLUS), Perkins, Charles E. Schell Foundation loans, George W. Wright Student Aid loans, Rogers student loans.

WORK-STUDY ***Federal work-study:*** Total amount: $837,664; jobs available. ***State or other work-study/employment:*** Total amount: $4,253,596 (100% non-need-based). Part-time jobs available.

ATHLETIC AWARDS Total amount: $4,913,936 (100% non-need-based).

APPLYING FOR FINANCIAL AID ***Required financial aid form:*** FAFSA. ***Financial aid deadline (priority):*** 12/1. ***Notification date:*** Continuous beginning 12/15. Students must reply within 2 weeks of notification.

CONTACT Barbara Greene, Associate Director of Financial Analysis and Reporting, Youngstown State University, One University Plaza, Youngstown, OH 44555, 330-941-3504 or toll-free 877-468-6978. *Fax:* 330-941-1659. *E-mail:* bgreene@ysu.edu.
Website: http://www.ysu.edu/.

ZAYTUNA COLLEGE

Berkeley, CA

CONTACT Financial Aid Office, Zaytuna College, 2401 Le Conte Avenue, Berkeley, CA 94709, 510-356-4760.
Website: http://www.zaytuna.edu/.

Appendix

State Scholarship and Grant Programs

Each state government has established one or more state-administered financial aid programs for qualified students. In many instances, these state programs are restricted to legal residents of the state. However, they often are available to out-of-state students who will be or are attending colleges or universities within the state. In addition to residential status, other qualifications frequently exist.

Gift aid and forgivable loan programs open to undergraduate students for all states and the District of Columbia are described on the following pages. They are arranged in alphabetical order, first by state name, then by program name. The annotation for each program provides information about the program, eligibility, and the contact addresses for applications or further information. Unless otherwise stated, this information refers to awards for 2015–16. Information is provided by the state-sponsoring agency in response to *Peterson's Annual Survey of Non-institutional Aid*, which was conducted between December 2015 and April 2016. Information is accurate when Peterson's receives it. However, it is always advisable to check with the sponsor to ascertain that the information remains correct.

You should write to the address given for each program to request that award details for 2017–18 be sent to you as soon as they are available. Descriptive information, brochures, and application forms for state scholarship programs are usually available from the financial aid offices of public colleges or universities within the specific state. High school guidance offices often have information and relevant forms for awards for which high school seniors may be eligible. Increasingly, state government agencies are putting state scholarship information on state government agency websites. In searching state government websites, however, you should be aware that the higher education agency in many states is separate from the state's general education office, which is often responsible only for elementary and secondary education. Also, the page at public university websites that provides information about student financial aid frequently has a list of state-sponsored scholarships and financial aid programs.

Names of scholarship programs are frequently used inconsistently or become abbreviated in popular usage. Many programs have variant names by which they are known. The program's sponsor has approved the title of the program that Peterson's uses in this guide, yet this name may differ from the program's official name or from its most commonly used name.

In addition to the grant aid and forgivable loan programs listed on the following pages, states may also offer internship or work-study programs, graduate fellowships and grants, or low-interest loans. If you are interested in learning more about these other kinds of programs, the state education office that supplies information or applications for the undergraduate scholarship programs listed here should be able to provide information about other kinds of higher education financial aid programs that are sponsored by the state.

ALABAMA

Air Force ROTC College Scholarship Type 1. Pays full (100 percent) college tuition and authorized fees at any public or private institution with an Air Force ROTC detachment. Type 1 selectees will also receive a monthly living expense stipend and an annual book stipend. Applicants must pass a Department of Defense Medical Examination Review Board (DODMERB) medical exam and complete a Physical Fitness Assessment. SAT composite of 1240 or ACT composite of 26 and GPA of 3.0 or higher are also required for high school student applicants. For college applicants, the Air Force ROTC Commander will determine the minimum GPA and test scores, if applicable, for scholarship eligibility. Note: AFROTC Scholarships do not cover room and board. *Award:* Scholarship for use in freshman, sophomore, junior, or senior years; renewable. *Eligibility Requirements:* Applicant must be age 17-30 and enrolled or expecting to enroll full-time at a two-year institution or university. Available to U.S. citizens. Applicant or parent must meet one or more of the following requirements: Air Force experience; retired from active duty; disabled or killed as a result of military service; prisoner of war; or missing in action. *Application Requirements:* Application form, application form may be submitted online, interview.

Air Force ROTC College Scholarship Type 2. Pays up to $18,000 per year in college tuition and authorized fees at any public or private institution with an Air Force ROTC detachment. Scholarship payment is further capped at $9,000 per semester or $6,000 per quarter. Type 2 selectees will also receive a monthly living expense stipend and an annual book stipend. Applicants must pass a Department of Defense Medical Examination Review Board (DODMERB) medical exam and complete a Physical Fitness Assessment. SAT composite of 1240 or ACT composite of 26 and GPA of 3.0 or higher are also required for high school student applicants. For college applicants, the Air Force ROTC Commander will determine the minimum GPA and test scores, if applicable, for scholarship eligibility. Note: AFROTC Scholarships do not cover room and board. *Award:* Scholarship for use in freshman, sophomore, junior, or senior years. *Eligibility Requirements:* Applicant must be enrolled or expecting to enroll at a two-year institution or university. Available to U.S. citizens. *Application Requirements:* Application form, application form may be submitted online.

Air Force ROTC College Scholarship Type 7. Pays full (100 percent) college tuition and authorized fees (capped at the in-state tuition rate) at a public institution with an Air Force ROTC detachment. Type 7 selectees will also receive a monthly living expense stipend and an annual book stipend. Students offered a Type 7 scholarship will be given the option to convert their scholarship to a three-year Type 2 scholarship that can be used at out-of-state or private schools. A three-year Type 2 scholarship will start during the sophomore year of school. Applicants must pass a Department of Defense Medical Examination Review Board (DODMERB) medical exam and complete a Physical Fitness Assessment. SAT composite of 1240 or ACT composite of 26 and GPA of 3.0 or higher are also required for high school student applicants. For college applicants, the Air Force ROTC Commander will determine the minimum GPA and test scores, if applicable, for scholarship eligibility. Note: AFROTC Scholarships do not cover room and board *Award:* Scholarship for use in freshman, sophomore, junior, or senior years. *Eligibility Requirements:* Applicant must be enrolled or expecting to enroll at a two-year institution or university. Available to U.S. citizens. *Application Requirements:* Application form, application form may be submitted online.

Alabama G.I. Dependents Scholarship Program. The scholarship is for dependents of eligible disabled Alabama veterans. This scholarship will be the payer of last resort after all other grants and scholarships have been utilized for required education expenses. The scholarship pays up to the DoD Tuition Assistance Cap (currently $250 per credit hour) and up to $1,000 for the combination of required textbooks and laboratory fees per semester. Child or stepchild must initiate training before 26th birthday; age 30 deadline may apply in certain situations. No age deadline for spouses or widows. The veteran and the step child's parent must have been married prior the child's 19th birthday. *Award:* Scholarship for use in freshman, sophomore, junior, or senior years; renewable. *Eligibility Requirements:* Applicant must be age 30 or under; enrolled or expecting to enroll full- or part-time at a two-year or four-year or technical institution or university; resident of Alabama and studying in Alabama. Available to U.S. citizens. *Application Requirements:* Application form.

Contact Kayla Kyle, Department Operations Manager, Alabama Department of Veterans Affairs, PO Box 1509, Montgomery, AL 36102-1509. *Phone:* 334-242-5077. *Website:* http://www.va.alabama.gov/.

Alabama National Guard Educational Assistance Program. Renewable award aids Alabama residents who are members of the Alabama National Guard and are enrolled in a nationally recognized accredited college in Alabama. Forms must be signed by a representative of the Alabama Military Department and financial aid officer. Recipient must be in a degree-seeking program. *Award:* Scholarship for use in freshman, sophomore, junior, senior, or graduate years; not renewable. *Award amount:* $100–$2000. *Number of awards:* 400–800. *Eligibility Requirements:* Applicant must be age 17 and over; enrolled or expecting to enroll full- or part-time at a two-year or technical institution or university and studying in Alabama. Available to U.S. citizens. Applicant must have national guard experience. *Application Requirements:* Application form, financial need analysis. **Deadline:** continuous.

Contact Cheryl Newton, Grants Coordinator, Alabama Commission on Higher Education, 100 North Union Street, Suite 782, P.O. Box 302000, Montgomery, AL 36104-3758. *E-mail:* cheryl.newton@ache.edu. *Phone:* 334-242-2273. *Fax:* 334-242-2269. *Website:* https://ache.edu/.

Alabama Student Assistance Program. Scholarship award of $300 to $5000 per academic year given to undergraduate students residing in the state of Alabama and attending a college or university in Alabama. *Award:* Grant for use in freshman, sophomore, junior, or senior years; not renewable. *Award amount:* $300–$5000. *Number of awards:* 3,500–4,500. *Eligibility Requirements:* Applicant must be enrolled or expecting to enroll full- or part-time at a two-year or technical institution or university and studying in Alabama. Available to U.S. citizens. *Application Requirements:* Application form, financial need analysis. **Deadline:** continuous.

Contact Cheryl Newton, Grants Coordinator, Alabama Commission on Higher Education, 100 North Union Street, Suite 782, P.O. Box 302000, Montgomery, AL 36104-3758. *E-mail:* cheryl.newton@ache.edu. *Phone:* 334-242-2273. *Fax:* 334-242-2269. *Website:* https://ache.edu/.

Alabama Student Assistance Program. Grant award of $300 to $5000 per academic year given to undergraduate students residing in the state of Alabama and attending a college or university in Alabama. *Award:* Grant for use in freshman, sophomore, junior, or senior years; not renewable. *Award amount:* $300–$5000. *Number of awards:* 3,500–4,500. *Eligibility Requirements:* Applicant must be enrolled or expecting to enroll full- or part-time at a two-year or technical institution or university and studying in Alabama. Available to U.S. citizens. *Application Requirements:* Application form, portfolio. **Deadline:** continuous.

Contact Cheryl Newton, Grants Coordinator, Alabama Commission on Higher Education, 100 North Union Street, Suite 782, P.O. Box 302000, Montgomery, AL 36104-3758. *E-mail:* cheryl.newton@ache.edu. *Phone:* 334-242-2273. *Fax:* 334-242-2269. *Website:* https://ache.edu/.

Alabama Student Grant Program. Nonrenewable awards available to Alabama residents for undergraduate study at certain independent colleges within the state. Both full and half-time students are eligible. Deadlines: September 15, January 15, and February 15. *Award:* Grant for use in freshman, sophomore, junior, or senior years; not renewable. *Award amount:* $200–$1200. *Number of awards:* 3,500–5,500. *Eligibility Requirements:* Applicant must be enrolled or expecting to enroll full- or part-time at an institution or university and studying in Alabama. Available to U.S. citizens. *Application Requirements:* Application form. **Deadline:** continuous.

Contact Cheryl Newton, Grants Coordinator, Alabama Commission on Higher Education, 100 North Union Street, Suite 782, P.O. Box 302000, Montgomery, AL 36104-3758. *E-mail:* cheryl.newton@ache.edu. *Phone:* 334-242-2273. *Fax:* 334-242-2269. *Website:* https://ache.edu/.

Police Officers and Firefighters Survivors Education Assistance Program-Alabama. Provides tuition, fees, books, and supplies to dependents of full-time police officers and firefighters killed or totally disabled in the line of duty. Must attend an Alabama public college as an undergraduate. Must be Alabama resident. *Award:* Scholarship for use in freshman, sophomore, junior, or senior years; renewable. *Award amount:* $1600–$12,000. *Number of awards:* 15–30. *Eligibility Requirements:* Applicant must be age 21 or under; enrolled or expecting to enroll full- or part-time at a two-year or technical institution or university and studying in Alabama. Available to U.S. citizens. *Application Requirements:* Application form. **Deadline:** continuous.

Contact Cheryl Newton, Grants Coordinator, Alabama Commission on Higher Education, 100 North Union Street, Suite 782, P.O. Box 302000, Montgomery, AL 36104-3758. *E-mail:* cheryl.newton@ache.edu. *Phone:* 334-242-2273. *Fax:* 334-242-2269. *Website:* https://ache.edu/.

ARIZONA

Leveraging Educational Assistance Partnership. Grants to financially needy students, who enroll in and attend postsecondary education or training in Arizona schools. Program was formerly known as the State Student Incentive Grant or SSIG Program. *Award:* Grant for use in freshman, sophomore, junior, senior, or graduate years; not renewable. *Award amount:* $100–$2500. *Eligibility Requirements:* Applicant must be enrolled or expecting to enroll full- or part-time at a two-year or four-year or technical institution or university; resident of Arizona and studying in Arizona. Available to U.S. citizens. *Application Requirements:* Application form, financial need analysis, transcript. **Deadline:** April 30.

Contact Mila Zaporteza, Business Manager and LEAP Financial Aid Manager, Arizona Commission for Postsecondary Education, 2020 North Central Avenue, Suite 650, Phoenix, AZ 85004-4503. *E-mail:* mila@azhighered.gov. *Phone:* 602-258-2435 Ext. 102. *Fax:* 602-258-2483. *Website:* https://highered.az.gov/.

ARKANSAS

Arkansas Academic Challenge Scholarship. The Academic Challenge Program provides scholarships to Arkansas residents pursuing a higher education. Funded in large part by the Arkansas Scholarship Lottery, the Academic Challenge Scholarship is available to students regardless of their academic status, whether just graduating from high school, currently enrolled in college, enrolling in college for the first time, or re-enrolling after a period of time out of college. Must have at least a 19 ACT composite score (or the equivalent). Renewable up to three additional years. *Award:* Scholarship for use in freshman, sophomore, junior, senior, or graduate years; renewable. *Award amount:* $1000–$5000. *Number of awards:* 30,000–35,000. *Eligibility Requirements:* Applicant must be enrolled or expecting to enroll full- or part-time at a two-year institution or university; resident of Arizona and studying in Arkansas. Available to U.S. citizens. *Application Requirements:* Application form, application form may be submitted online, financial need analysis. **Deadline:** June 1.

Contact Jonathan Coleman, Financial Aid Manager. *E-mail:* jonathan.coleman@adhe.edu. *Phone:* 501-371-2000. *Website:* http://www.adhe.edu/.

Arkansas Governor's Scholars Program. Awards for outstanding Arkansas high school seniors. Applicants who attain 32 or above on ACT, 1410 or above on SAT and have an academic 3.5 GPA, or are selected as National Merit or National Achievement finalists may receive an award equal to tuition, mandatory fees, room, and board up to $10,000 per year at any Arkansas institution. If any of the seventy-five (75) counties is not represented, the Department of Higher Education shall select a student from each non-represented county with the highest qualifications who was not initially qualified. Students from these counties will be awarded $5000 per year at any Arkansas institution. *Award:* Scholarship for use in freshman, sophomore, junior, senior, or graduate years; renewable. *Award amount:* $4000–$10,000. *Number of awards:* 75–375. *Eligibility Requirements:* Applicant must be high school student; planning to enroll or expecting to enroll full-time at a two-year institution or university; resident of Arizona and studying in Arkansas. Available to U.S. citizens. *Application Requirements:* Application form, application form may be submitted online, community service. **Deadline:** February 1.

Contact Jonathan Coleman, Financial Aid Manager. *E-mail:* jonathan.coleman@adhe.edu. *Phone:* 501-371-2000. *Website:* http://www.adhe.edu/.

Law Enforcement Officers' Dependents Scholarship&-Arkansas. Scholarship for dependents, under 23 years old, of Arkansas law-enforcement officers killed or permanently disabled in the line of duty. Renewable award is a waiver of tuition, fees, and room at two- or four-year Arkansas institution. Submit birth certificate, death certificate, and claims commission report of findings of fact. Proof of disability from State Claims Commission may also be submitted. Must maintain a minimum GPA of 2.0 on a 4.0 scale. *Award:* Scholarship for use in freshman, sophomore, junior, or senior years; renewable. *Eligibility Requirements:* Applicant must be age 22 or under; enrolled or expecting to enroll full- or part-time at a two-year or technical institution or university; resident of Arizona and studying in Arkansas. Available to U.S. citizens. *Application Requirements:* Application form, application form may be submitted online. **Deadline:** July 1.

Contact Lisa Smith, Program Specialist, Arkansas Department of Higher Education, 423 Main Street Suite 400, Little Rock, AR 72201-3818. *E-mail:* lisa.smith@adhe.edu. *Phone:* 501-371-2000. *Website:* http://www.adhe.edu/.

Military Dependent's Scholarship Program. Renewable waiver of tuition, fees, room and board undergraduate students seeking a bachelor's degree or certificate of completion at any public college, university or technical school in Arkansas who qualify as a spouse or dependent child of an Arkansas resident who has been declared to be missing in action, killed in action, a POW, or killed on ordnance delivery, or a veteran who has been declared to be 100 percent totally and permanently disabled during, or as a result of, active military service. *Award:* Scholarship for use in freshman, sophomore, junior, or senior years; renewable. *Eligibility Requirements:* Applicant must be enrolled or expecting to enroll full-time at a two-year or technical institution or university; resident of Arizona and studying in Arkansas. Available to U.S. citizens. Applicant or parent must meet one or more of the following requirements: general military experience; retired from active duty; disabled or killed as a result of military service; prisoner of war; or missing in action. *Application Requirements:* Application form, application form may be submitted online. **Deadline:** July 1.

Contact Lisa Smith, Director of Financial Aid, Arkansas Department of Higher Education, 423 Main Street Suite 400, Little Rock, AR 72201-3818. *E-mail:* lisa.smith@adhe.edu. *Phone:* 501-371-2000. *Website:* http://www.adhe.edu/.

CALIFORNIA

Child Development Teacher and Supervisor Grant Program. Award is for those students pursuing an approved course of study leading to a Child Development Permit issued by the California Commission on Teacher Credentialing. In exchange for each year funding is received, recipients agree to provide one year of service in a licensed childcare center. Child and Family Studies; Education. *Award:* Grant for use in freshman, sophomore, junior, senior, or graduate years; renewable. *Award amount:* $1000–$2000. *Number of awards:* up to 300. *Eligibility Requirements:* Applicant must be enrolled or expecting to enroll full- or part-time at a two-year or four-year institution or university; resident of California and studying in California. Applicant or parent of applicant must have employment or volunteer experience in teaching/education. Available to U.S. citizens. *Application Requirements:* Application form, financial need analysis, GPA verification, recommendations or references. **Deadline:** April 16.

Contact Catalina Mistler, Deputy Director, Program Administration & Services Division, California Student Aid Commission, PO Box 419027, Rancho Cordova, CA 95741-9027. *E-mail:* catalina.mistler@csac.ca.gov. *Phone:* 888-224-7268. *Fax:* 916-526-8004. *Website:* http://www.csac.ca.gov/.

CSAC Cal Grant A Award. Award for California residents who are not recent high school graduates attending an approved college or university within the state. Must show financial need and meet minimum 3.00 GPA requirement. *Award:* Grant for use in freshman, sophomore, junior, or senior years; renewable. *Award amount:* $5472–$12,192. *Number of awards:* 1,000–2,000. *Eligibility Requirements:* Applicant must be enrolled or expecting to enroll full- or part-time at a two-year institution or university; resident of British Columbia and studying in California. Available to U.S. citizens. *Application Requirements:* Application form, financial need analysis. **Deadline:** March 2.

Contact Catalina Mistler, Deputy Director, Program Administration & Services Division, California Student Aid Commission, PO Box 419027, Rancho Cordova, CA 95741-9027. *E-mail:* catalina.mistler@csac.ca.gov. *Phone:* 888-224-7268. *Fax:* 916-526-8004. *Website:* http://www.csac.ca.gov/.

CSAC Cal Grant B Award. The Cal Grant B Award is awarded to California residents who are enrolled in an undergraduate academic program of not less than one academic year at a qualifying postsecondary institution. Must show financial need and meet the minimum 2. 00 GPA requirement. *Award:* Grant for use in sophomore, junior, or senior years; renewable. *Award amount:* $700–$13,665. *Number of awards:* 20,500. *Eligibility Requirements:* Applicant must be enrolled or expecting to enroll full- or part-time at a two-year or technical institution or university; resident of British Columbia and studying in California. Available to U.S. citizens. *Application Requirements:* Application form, financial need analysis. **Deadline:** March 2.

Contact Catalina Mistler, Deputy Director, Program Administration & Services Division, California Student Aid Commission, PO Box 419027, Rancho Cordova, CA 95741-9027. *E-mail:* catalina.mistler@csac.ca.gov. *Phone:* 888-224-7268. *Fax:* 916-526-8004. *Website:* http://www.csac.ca.gov/.

CSAC Cal Grant C Award. Award for California residents who are enrolled in a short-term vocational training program. Program must lead to a recognized degree or certificate. Course length must be a minimum of 4 months and no longer than 24 months. Students must be attending an approved California institution and show financial need. *Award:* Grant for use in freshman or sophomore years; renewable. *Award amount:* $576–$2462. *Eligibility Requirements:* Applicant must be enrolled or expecting to enroll full- or part-time at a two-year or technical institution; resident of British Columbia and studying in California. Available to U.S. citizens. *Application Requirements:* Application form, financial need analysis. **Deadline:** March 2.

Contact Catalina Mistler, Deputy Director, Program Administration & Services Division, California Student Aid Commission, PO Box 419027, Rancho Cordova, CA 95741-9027. *E-mail:* catalina.mistler@csac.ca.gov. *Phone:* 888-224-7268. *Fax:* 916-526-8004. *Website:* http://www.csac.ca.gov/.

EOPS (Extended Opportunity Programs and Services)/CARE (Cooperative Agencies Resources for Education). Renewable award available to California residents and individuals who are exempt from paying nonresident tuition. Individuals must be enrolled as a full-time student at a two-year publicly-funded California community college. EOPS students must fulfill program-specific income and educational disadvantage eligibility requirements. CARE students must be in EOPS, currently receive CalWORKs/TANF, have at least one child under fourteen years of age at time of acceptance into CARE program, be a single head of household, and age 18 or older. EOPS students may also qualify for CARE if their dependent child(ren) receive CalWORKs/TANF cash aid even if the student (i.e., parent) is not a cash aid recipient. Contact local college EOPS/CARE office for an application and more information about supportive services and grants. To locate nearest community college campus, see http://www.cccco.edu/ *Award:* Grant for use in freshman or sophomore years; renewable. *Award amount:* $100–$1000. *Number of awards:* 10,000–85,000. *Eligibility Requirements:* Applicant must be age 18 and over; enrolled or expecting to enroll full-time at a two-year institution; single; resident of California and studying in California. Available to U.S. citizens. *Application Requirements:* Application form, financial need analysis. **Deadline:** continuous.

Law Enforcement Personnel Dependents Grant Program. The Law Enforcement Personnel Dependents Grant Program provides need-based educational grants to dependents and spouses of: California peace officers (Highway Patrol, marshals, sheriffs, police officers), Department of Corrections and California Youth Authority employees, and permanent/full-time firefighters employed by public entities who have been killed in the performance of duty or 100% disabled as a result of an accident or injury caused by external violence or physical force incurred in the performance of duty. *Award:* Grant for use in freshman, sophomore, junior, or senior years; renewable. *Award amount:* $100–$12,192. *Eligibility Requirements:* Applicant must be enrolled or expecting to enroll full- or part-time at a two-year institution or university; resident of British Columbia and studying in California. Applicant or parent of applicant must have employment or volunteer experience in police/firefighting. Available to U.S. citizens. *Application Requirements:* Application form, financial need analysis. **Deadline:** continuous.

Contact Catalina Mistler, Deputy Director, Program Administration & Services Division, California Student Aid Commission, PO Box 419027, Rancho Cordova, CA 95741-9027. *E-mail:* catalina.mistler@csac.ca.gov. *Phone:* 888-224-7268. *Fax:* 916-526-8004. *Website:* http://www.csac.ca.gov/.

COLORADO

Colorado Student Grant. Grants for Colorado residents attending eligible public, private, or vocational institutions within the state. Students must complete a Free Application for Federal Student Aid (FAFSA) and demonstrate need. Application deadlines vary by institution. Renewable award for undergraduates. Contact the financial aid office at the college/institution for application and more information. *Award:* Grant for use in freshman, sophomore, junior, or senior years; not renewable. *Award amount:* $300–$5000. *Eligibility Requirements:* Applicant must be enrolled or expecting to enroll full- or part-time at a two-year or four-year or technical institution; resident of Colorado and studying in Colorado. Available to U.S. citizens. *Application Requirements:* Application form, financial need analysis. **Deadline:** continuous.

Contact Celina Duran, Financial Aid Administrator, Colorado Commission on Higher Education, 1560 Broadway, Suite 1600, Denver, CO 80202. *E-mail:* celina.duran@dhe.state.co.us. *Phone:* 303-866-2723. *Website:* http://highered.colorado.gov/cche/mission.html.

CONNECTICUT

AIFS-HACU Scholarships. Scholarships to outstanding Hispanic students to study abroad with AIFS. Available to students attending HACU member schools. Students will receive scholarships of up to 50 percent of the full program fee. Students must meet all standard AIFS eligibility requirements. Deadlines: April 15 for fall, October 1 for spring, and March 15 for summer. *Award:* Scholarship for use in freshman, sophomore, junior, or senior years; not renewable. *Number of awards:* 1. *Eligibility Requirements:* Applicant must be Hispanic; age 17 and over and enrolled or expecting to enroll full-time at a two-year institution or university. Available to U.S. and non-U.S. citizens. *Application Requirements:* Application form, application form may be submitted online, essay, personal photograph. *Fee:* $95. **Deadline:** October 1.

Contact Sharman Hedayati, Vice President, Director of Admissions and Operations, American Institute For Foreign Study (AIFS), 1 High Ridge Park, Stamford, CT 06905. *E-mail:* shedayati@aifs.com. *Phone:* 800-727-2437. *Website:* https://www.aifsabroad.com/.

Connecticut Army National Guard 100% Tuition Waiver. Program is for any active member of the Connecticut Army National Guard in good standing. Must be a resident of Connecticut attending any Connecticut state (public) university, community-technical college or regional vocational-technical school. The total number of available awards is unlimited. *Award:* Scholarship for use in freshman, sophomore, junior, or senior years; not renewable. *Award amount:* $16,000. *Eligibility Requirements:* Applicant must be age 17-65; enrolled or expecting to enroll full- or part-time at a two-year or four-year or technical institution or university; resident of Connecticut and studying in Connecticut. Available to U.S. and non-U.S. citizens. Applicant or parent must meet one or more of the following requirements: national guard experience; retired from active duty; disabled or killed as a result of military service; prisoner of war; or missing in action. *Application Requirements:* Application form. **Deadline:** July 1.

Contact Capt. Jeremy Lingenfelser, Education Services Officer, Connecticut Army National Guard, 360 Broad Street, Hartford, CT 06105-3795. *E-mail:* education@ct.ngb.army.mil. *Phone:* 860-524-4816. *Fax:* 860-524-4904. *Website:* http://ct.ng.mil/Pages/default.aspx.

Governor's Scholarship Program—Need/Merit Scholarship. This program provides scholarships to eligible Connecticut residents attending eligible institutions of higher education in Connecticut. Eligibility is based on a minimum SAT score of 1800, or a minimum ACT score of 27 and/or top 20% ranking in the students junior year high school class. Applications must be filed through the students high school counseling office. In addition, all students must file a Free Application for Federal Student Aid (FAFSA) and, as a result, have an Expected Family Contribution (EFC) equal to or less than the annual allowable maximum EFC. Both the application and FAFSA must be processed by February 15th. *Award:* Scholarship for use in sophomore, junior, or senior years; renewable. *Award amount:* $2275–$5250. *Number of awards:* 1,967. *Eligibility Requirements:* Applicant must be enrolled or expecting to enroll full- or part-time at a two-year or four-year institution or university; resident of Connecticut and studying in Connecticut. Available to U.S. citizens. *Application Requirements:* Application form, financial need analysis. **Deadline:** February 15.

Contact Ms. Lynne Goodwin, Student Financial Aid Consultant, Connecticut Office of Higher Education, 450 Columbus Boulevard, Suite 510, Hartford, CT 06103. *E-mail:* sfa@ctohe.org. *Phone:* 860-947-1855. *Website:* http://www.ctohe.org.

Minority Teacher Incentive Grant Program. Program provides up to $5,000 a year for two years of full-time study in a teacher preparation program for the junior or senior year at a Connecticut college or university. Applicant must be African-American, Hispanic/Latino, Asian American or Native American heritage and be nominated by the Education Dean. Program graduates who teach in Connecticut public schools may be eligible for loan reimbursement stipends up to $2,500 per year for up to four years. Education. *Award:* Grant for use in junior or senior years; renewable. *Award amount:* $2500–$5000. *Number of awards:* 87. *Eligibility Requirements:* Applicant must be American Indian/Alaska Native, Asian/Pacific Islander, Black (non-Hispanic), Hispanic; enrolled or expecting to enroll full-time at a four-year institution or university; resident of Connecticut and studying in Connecticut. Available to U.S. citizens. *Application Requirements:* Application form. **Deadline:** October 15.

Contact Ms. Lynne Goodwin, Executive Assistant, Connecticut Office of Higher Education, 450 Columbus Boulevard, Suite 510, Hartford, CT 06103. *E-mail:* mtip@ctohe.org. *Phone:* 860-947-1855. *Website:* http://www.ctohe.org.

Roberta B. Willis Scholarship Program—Need-Based Grant. This program provides need-based grants to eligible Connecticut residents attending eligible institutions of higher education in Connecticut. Students must file a Free Application for Federal Student Aid (FAFSA) by their college's deadline, if applicable. Students, as a result of filing the FAFSA, must have an Expected Family Contribution (EFC) equal to or less than the allowable annual EFC. There is no application to fill out. *Award:* Grant for use in freshman, sophomore, junior, or senior years; renewable. *Award amount:* $1–$4500. *Eligibility Requirements:* Applicant must be enrolled or expecting to enroll full- or part-time at a two-year or four-year institution or university; resident of Connecticut and studying in Connecticut. Available to U.S. citizens. *Application Requirements:* Financial need analysis. **Deadline:** continuous.

Contact Ms. Lynne Goodwin, Financial Aid Consultant, Connecticut Office of Higher Education, 450 Columbus Boulevard, Suite 510, Hartford, CT 06103. *E-mail:* sfa@ctohe.org. *Phone:* 860-947-1855. *Website:* http://www.ctohe.org.

DELAWARE

State Tuition Assistance. You must enlist in the Delaware Air or Army National Guard to be eligible for this scholarship award. Award providing tuition assistance for any member of the Air or Army National Guard attending a Delaware two-year or four-year college. Awards are renewable. Applicant's minimum GPA must be 2.0. *Award:* Scholarship for use in freshman, sophomore, junior, or senior years; renewable. *Award amount:* $1–$10,000. *Number of awards:* 1–200. *Eligibility Requirements:* Applicant must be enrolled or expecting to enroll full- or part-time at a two-year or four-year institution or university and studying in Delaware. Available to U.S. citizens. Applicant or parent must meet one or more of the following requirements: national guard experience; retired from active duty; disabled or killed as a result of military service; prisoner of war; or missing in action. *Application Requirements:* Application form. **Deadline:** continuous.

Contact Robert Csizmadia, State Tuition Assistance Manager, Delaware Army National Guard, 1 Vavala Way, New Castle, DE 19720. *E-mail:* robert.l.csizmadianfg@mail.mil. *Phone:* 302-326-7012. *Website:* http://www.delawarenationalguard.com/.

DISTRICT OF COLUMBIA

American Indian Nurse Scholarship Program. Since 1928 The National Society of The Colonial Dames of America has provided a small number of scholarship awards to assist students of American Indian heritage who are pursuing degrees in nursing or in the field of health care and health education. Eligible students receive $1,500 per semester and the money is to be used strictly for tuition, books or fees applicable to the student's approved program. The grant is sent to the school and credited to the student's account. Once a student is accepted, he or she may re-apply for continued funds each semester as long as the student remains in academic good standing. Health Administration; Nursing. *Award:* Scholarship for use in freshman, sophomore, junior, senior, graduate, or postgraduate years; renewable. *Award amount:* $500–$1500. *Number of awards:* 2. *Eligibility Requirements:* Applicant must be American Indian/Alaska Native and enrolled or expecting to enroll full-time at a two-year or four-year or technical institution or university. Available to U.

S. citizens. *Application Requirements:* Application form, autobiography, driver's license, financial need analysis, personal photograph. **Deadline:** June 1.

Bureau of Indian Education Grant Program. Grants are provided to supplement financial assistance to eligible American Indian/Alaska Native students entering college seeking a Baccalaureate degree. A student must be a member of, or at least one-quarter degree Indian blood descendent of a member of an American Indian tribe who are eligible for the special programs and services provided by the United States through the Bureau of Indian Affairs to Indians because of their status as Indians. *Award:* Grant for use in freshman year; not renewable. *Eligibility Requirements:* Applicant must be American Indian/ Alaska Native; high school student and planning to enroll or expecting to enroll full-time at a two-year or four-year institution or university. Available to U.S. citizens. *Application Requirements:* Application form.

Contact Paulina Bell, Office Automation Assistant. *Phone:* 202-208-6123. *Fax:* 202-208-3312. *Website:* http://www.bie.edu/.

Costas G. Lemonopoulos Scholarship. Scholarships to children of NALC members attending public, four-year colleges or universities supported by the state of Florida or St. Petersburg Junior College. Scholarships are renewable one time. *Award:* Scholarship for use in freshman, sophomore, junior, or senior years; renewable. *Number of awards:* 1–20. *Eligibility Requirements:* Applicant must be enrolled or expecting to enroll full-time at a two-year institution or university and studying in Florida. Applicant or parent of applicant must be member of National Association of Letter Carriers. Available to U.S. citizens. *Application Requirements:* Application form. **Deadline:** June 1.

Contact Ann Porch, Membership Committee. *E-mail:* nalcinf@nalc.org. *Phone:* 202-393-4695. *Website:* http://www.nalc.org/.

Harry S. Truman Scholarship. Scholarships for U.S. citizens or U.S. nationals who are college or university students with junior-level academic standing and who wish to attend professional or graduate school to prepare for careers in government or the nonprofit and advocacy sectors. Candidates must be nominated by their institution. Public service and leadership record considered. Visit website http://www.truman.gov for further information and application. Political Science; Public Policy and Administration. *Award:* Scholarship for use in junior year; renewable. *Award amount:* $30,000. *Number of awards:* 65. *Eligibility Requirements:* Applicant must be enrolled or expecting to enroll full-time at a four-year institution or university and must have an interest in leadership. Available to U.S. citizens. *Application Requirements:* Application form, interview, policy proposal, recommendations or references. **Deadline:** February 5.

Contact Tonji Wade, Program Officer, Harry S. Truman Scholarship Foundation, 712 Jackson Place, NW, Washington, DC 20006. *E-mail:* office@truman.gov. *Phone:* 202-395-4831. *Fax:* 202-395-6995. *Website:* http://www.truman.gov/.

Montgomery GI Bill Active Duty. Award provides up to thirty-six months of education benefits to eligible veterans for college, business school, technical courses, vocational courses, correspondence courses, apprenticeships/job training, or flight training. Must be an eligible veteran with an Honorable Discharge and have high school diploma or GED before applying for benefits. *Award:* Scholarship for use in freshman, sophomore, junior, senior, or graduate years; renewable. *Eligibility Requirements:* Applicant must be enrolled or expecting to enroll full- or part-time at a two-year or technical institution or university. Available to U.S. citizens. Applicant or parent must meet one or more of the following requirements: general military experience; retired from active duty; disabled or killed as a result of military service; prisoner of war; or missing in action. *Application Requirements:* Application form, application form may be submitted online. **Deadline:** continuous.

Contact Keith Wilson, Director, Education Service. *Phone:* 888-442-4551. *Website:* https://www.va.gov/.

Montgomery GI Bill Selected Reserve. Educational assistance program for members of the selected reserve of the Army, Navy, Air Force, Marine Corps and Coast Guard, as well as the Army and Air National Guard. Available to all reservists and National Guard personnel who commit to a six-year obligation, and remain in the Reserve or Guard during the six years. Award is renewable. Monthly benefit is $309 for up to thirty-six months for full-time. *Award:* Scholarship for use in freshman, sophomore, junior, senior, or postgraduate years; renewable. *Eligibility Requirements:* Applicant must be enrolled or expecting to enroll full- or part-time at a two-year or technical institution or university. Available to U. S. citizens. Applicant or parent must meet one or more of the following requirements: general military experience; retired from active duty; disabled or killed as a result of military service; prisoner of war; or missing in action. *Application Requirements:* Application form, application form may be submitted online. **Deadline:** continuous.

Contact Keith Wilson, Director, Education Service. *Phone:* 888-442-4551. *Website:* https://www.va.gov/.

Reserve Education Assistance Program. The program provides educational assistance to members of National Guard and reserve components. Selected Reserve and Individual Ready Reserve (IRR) who are called or ordered to active duty service in response to a war or national emergency as declared by the president or Congress are eligible. For further information see website http://www.GIBILL.va.gov. *Award:* Scholarship for use in freshman, sophomore, junior, senior, graduate, or postgraduate years; renewable. *Eligibility Requirements:* Applicant must be enrolled or expecting to enroll full- or part-time at a two-year or four-year or technical institution or university. Available to U.S. citizens. Applicant or parent must meet one or more of the following requirements: general military experience; retired from active duty; disabled or killed as a result of military service; prisoner of war; or missing in action. *Application Requirements:* Application form. **Deadline:** continuous.

Contact Keith Wilson, Director, Education Service. *Phone:* 888-442-4551. *Website:* https://www.va.gov/.

Survivors and Dependents Educational Assistance (Chapter 35)-VA. Monthly $860 benefits for up to 45 months. Must be spouses or children under age 26 of current veterans missing in action or of deceased or totally and permanently disabled (service-related) service persons. For more information visit the following website http://www.gibill.va.gov. *Award:* Scholarship for use in freshman, sophomore, junior, or senior years; renewable. *Eligibility Requirements:* Applicant must be age 18-26 and enrolled or expecting to enroll full- or part-time at a two-year or technical institution or university. Available to U.S. and non-U.S. citizens. Applicant or parent must meet one or more of the following requirements: general military experience; retired from active duty; disabled or killed as a result of military service; prisoner of war; or missing in action. *Application Requirements:* Application form, application form may be submitted online. **Deadline:** continuous.

Contact Keith Wilson, Director, Education Service. *Phone:* 888-442-4551. *Website:* https://www.va.gov/.

FLORIDA

Access to Better Learning and Education Grant. Grant program provides tuition assistance to Florida undergraduate students enrolled in degree programs at eligible private Florida colleges or universities. Must be a U.S. citizen or eligible non-citizen and must meet Florida residency requirements. The participating institution determines application procedures, deadlines, and student eligibility. An eligible student must complete and submit the FAFSA in order to receive program funding. For more details, visit the website at http://www.FloridaStudentFinancialAid.org/SSFAD/home/uamain.htm. *Award:* Grant for use in freshman, sophomore, junior, or senior years; renewable. *Eligibility Requirements:* Applicant must be enrolled or expecting to enroll full-time at an institution or university; resident of District of Columbia and studying in Florida. Available to U.S. citizens. *Application Requirements:* Application form, application form may be submitted online.

First Generation Matching Grant Program. Need-based grants to Florida resident undergraduate students who are enrolled in state universities and community colleges in Florida and whose parents have not earned baccalaureate degrees. Available state funds are contingent upon matching contributions from private sources on a dollar-for-dollar basis. Institutions determine application procedures, deadlines, and student eligibility. For more details, visit the website at http://www.FloridaStudentFinancialAid.org/SSFAD/home/uamain.htm. *Award:* Grant for use in freshman, sophomore, junior, or senior years; renewable. *Eligibility Requirements:* Applicant must be enrolled or expecting to enroll full- or part-time at a two-year institution or university; resident of District of Columbia and studying in Florida. Available to U.S. citizens. *Application Requirements:* Application form, application form may be submitted online, financial need analysis.

Florida Bright Futures Scholarship Program. Three lottery-funded scholarships reward Florida high school graduates for high academic achievement. Program is comprised of the following three awards: Florida Academic Scholars Award, Florida Medallion Scholars Award and Florida Gold Seal Vocational Scholars Award. An eligible student must complete and submit the FAFSA in order to receive program funding. For more details, visit the website at http://www.FloridaStudentFinancialAid.org/SSFAD/home/uamain.htm. *Award:* Scholarship for use in freshman, sophomore, junior, or senior years; renewable. *Eligibility Requirements:* Applicant must be high school student; planning to enroll or expecting to enroll full- or part-time at a two-year or technical institution or university; resident of District of Columbia and studying in Florida. Available to U.S. citizens. *Application Requirements:* Application form, application form may be submitted online, community service, financial need analysis. **Deadline:** August 31.

Florida Postsecondary Student Assistance Grant. Scholarships to degree-seeking, resident, undergraduate students who demonstrate substantial financial need and are enrolled in eligible degree-granting private colleges and universities not eligible under the Florida Private Student Assistance Grant. FSAG is a decentralized program, and each participating institution determines application procedures, deadlines and student eligibility. Number of awards varies. For more details, visit the website at http://www.FloridaStudentFinancialAid.org/SSFAD/home/uamain.htm. *Award:* Grant for use in freshman, sophomore, junior, or senior years; renewable. *Award amount:* $200–$2610. *Eligibility Requirements:* Applicant must be enrolled or expecting to enroll full-time at a two-year or four-year institution or university; resident of Florida and studying in Florida. Available to U.S. citizens. *Application Requirements:* Financial need analysis.

Florida Private Student Assistance Grant. Grants for Florida residents who are U.S. citizens or eligible non-citizens attending eligible private, nonprofit, four-year colleges and universities in Florida. Must be a full-time student and demonstrate substantial financial need. For renewal, must have earned a minimum cumulative GPA of 2.0 at the last institution attended. For more details, visit the website at http://www.FloridaStudentFinancialAid.org/SSFAD/home/uamain.htm. *Award:* Grant for use in freshman, sophomore, junior, or senior years; renewable. *Award amount:* $200–$2610. *Eligibility Requirements:* Applicant must be enrolled or expecting to enroll full-time at an institution or university; resident of District of Columbia and studying in Florida. Available to U.S. citizens. *Application Requirements:* Application form, application form may be submitted online, financial need analysis.

Florida Public Student Assistance Grant. Grants for Florida residents, U.S. citizens or eligible non-citizens who attend state universities and public community colleges and demonstrate substantial financial need. For renewal, must have earned a minimum cumulative GPA of 2.0 at the last institution attended. For more details, visit the website at http://www.FloridaStudentFinancialAid.org/SSFAD/home/uamain.htm. *Award:* Grant for use in freshman, sophomore, junior, or senior years; renewable. *Award amount:* $200–$2610. *Eligibility Requirements:* Applicant must be enrolled or expecting to enroll full- or part-time at a two-year institution or university; resident of District of Columbia and studying in Florida. Available to U.S. citizens. *Application Requirements:* Application form, application form may be submitted online, financial need analysis.

Florida Space Research Program. Grants for faculty researchers from Florida public and private universities and community colleges. One-time award for aerospace and technology research. Submit research proposal with budget. Aviation/Aerospace; Earth Science; Education; Electrical Engineering/Electronics; Engineering/Technology; Marine/Ocean Engineering; Materials Science, Engineering, and Metallurgy; Mathematics; Mechanical Engineering; Meteorology/Atmospheric Science; Physical Sciences. *Award:* Grant for use in junior, senior, graduate, or postgraduate years; not renewable. *Award amount:* $12,500–$25,000. *Number of awards:* 13–15. *Eligibility Requirements:* Applicant must be enrolled or expecting to enroll full- or part-time at a two-year or four-year institution or university; resident of Florida and studying in Florida. Available to U.S. citizens. *Application Requirements:* Application form. **Deadline:** May 17.

Contact Dr. Jaydeep Mukherjee, FSGC Director, NASA Florida Space Grant Consortium, PO Box 160650, 12354 Research Parkway, Room 218, Orlando, FL 32826. *E-mail:* fsgc@ucf.edu. *Phone:* 407-823-6177. *Website:* http://www.floridaspacegrant.org/.

Florida Student Assistance Grant-Career Education. Need-based grant program available to Florida residents enrolled in certificate programs of 450 or more clock hours at participating community colleges or career centers operated by district school boards. FSAG-CE is a decentralized state of Florida program, which means that each participating institution determines application procedures, deadlines, student eligibility, and award amounts. For more details, visit the website at http://www.FloridaStudentFinancialAid.org/SSFAD/home/uamain.htm. *Award:* Grant for use in freshman, sophomore, junior, or senior years; renewable. *Award amount:* $200–$2610. *Eligibility Requirements:* Applicant must be enrolled or expecting to enroll full- or part-time at a two-year or technical institution; resident of Florida and studying in Florida. Available to U.S. citizens. *Application Requirements:* Application form may be submitted online, financial need analysis.

Florida Work Experience Program. Need-based program providing eligible Florida residents work experiences that will complement and reinforce their educational and career goals. Must maintain GPA of 2.0. Postsecondary institution will determine applicant's eligibility, number of hours to be worked per week, and the award amount. For more details, visit the website at http://www.FloridaStudentFinancialAid.org/SSFAD/home/uamain.htm. *Award:* Grant for use in freshman, sophomore, junior, or senior years; renewable. *Eligibility Requirements:* Applicant must be enrolled or expecting to enroll full- or part-time at a two-year institution or university; resident of District of Columbia and studying in Florida. Available to U.S. citizens. *Application Requirements:* Financial need analysis.

Jose Marti Scholarship Challenge Grant Fund. Award available to Hispanic-American students who were born in, or whose parent was born in a Hispanic country. Must be a Florida resident, be enrolled full-time in Florida at an eligible school, and have a GPA of 3.0 or above. Must be U.S. citizen or eligible non-citizen. FAFSA must be processed by May 15. For more details, visit the website at http://www.FloridaStudentFinancialAid.org/SSFAD/home/uamain.htm. *Award:* Scholarship for use in freshman, sophomore, junior, or senior years; renewable. *Award amount:* $2000. *Eligibility Requirements:* Applicant must be of Hispanic heritage; high school student; planning to enroll or expecting to enroll full-time at a two-year institution or university; resident of District of Columbia and studying in Florida. Available to U.S. citizens. *Application Requirements:* Application form, application form may be submitted online, financial need analysis. **Deadline:** April 1.

Mary McLeod Bethune Scholarship. Renewable award to Florida residents with a GPA of 3.0 or above, who will attend Bethune-Cookman University, Edward Waters College, Florida and University, or Florida Memorial University. Must not have previously received a baccalaureate degree. Must demonstrate financial need as specified by the institution. For more details, visit the website at http://www.FloridaStudentFinancialAid.org/SSFAD/home/uamain.htm. *Award:* Scholarship for use in freshman, sophomore, junior, or senior years; renewable. *Award amount:* $3000. *Eligibility Requirements:* Applicant must be enrolled or expecting to enroll full-time at an institution or university; resident of District of Columbia and studying in Florida. Available to U.S. citizens. *Application Requirements:* Application form, application form may be submitted online, financial need analysis.

Rosewood Family Scholarship Fund. Renewable award for eligible direct descendants of African-American Rosewood families affected by the incident of January 1923. The annual award amount may not exceed $6,100. The per term award amount a student may receive includes tuition and fees for up to 15 semester hours or up to 450 clock hours for undergraduate study. Must not have previously received a baccalaureate degree. For more details, visit the website at http://www.FloridaStudentFinancialAid.org/SSFAD/home/uamain.htm. *Award:* Scholarship for use in freshman, sophomore, junior, or senior years; renewable. *Eligibility Requirements:* Applicant must be enrolled or expecting to enroll full- or part-time at a two-year or technical institution or university and studying in Florida. Available to U.S. citizens. *Application Requirements:* Application form, application form may be submitted online, financial need analysis. **Deadline:** April 1.

Scholarships for Children and Spouses of Deceased or Disabled Veterans. Renewable scholarships for children and spouses of deceased or disabled veterans. Children must be between the ages of 16 and 22, and attend an eligible Florida postsecondary institution and enrolled at least part-time. Must ensure that the Florida Department of Veterans Affairs certifies the applicant's eligibility. Must maintain GPA of 2.0. For more details, visit the website at http://www.FloridaStudentFinancialAid.org/SSFAD/home/uamain.htm. *Award:* Scholarship for use in freshman, sophomore, junior, or senior years; renewable. *Eligibility Requirements:* Applicant must be age 16-22; enrolled or expecting to enroll full- or part-time at a two-year or technical institution or university; resident of District of Columbia and studying in Florida. Available to U.S. citizens. Applicant or parent must meet one or more of the following requirements: general military experience; retired from active duty; disabled or killed as a result of military service; prisoner of war; or missing in action. *Application Requirements:* Application form, application form may be submitted online. **Deadline:** April 1.

William L. Boyd IV Florida Resident Access Grant. Renewable awards to Florida undergraduate residents attending an eligible private, nonprofit Florida college or university. Postsecondary institution will determine applicant's eligibility. Renewal applicant must have earned a minimum institutional GPA of 2.0. An eligible student must complete and submit the FAFSA in order to receive program funding. For more details, visit the website at http://www.FloridaStudentFinancialAid.org/SSFAD/home/uamain.htm. *Award:* Grant for use in freshman, sophomore, junior, or senior years; renewable. *Award amount:* up to $3000. *Eligibility Requirements:* Applicant must be enrolled or expecting to enroll full-time at a four-year institution or university; resident of Florida and studying in Florida. Available to U.S. citizens. *Application Requirements:* Application form.

GEORGIA

Georgia HOPE Grant Program. HOPE Grant is available to Georgia residents who are pursuing a certificate or technical diploma. A HOPE Grant recipient must maintain a minimum 2.0 cumulative postsecondary grade point average to remain eligible. The grant provides tuition assistance to students enrolled at an eligible college or university in Georgia. A student who received a high school diploma (High School Postsecondary Graduation Opportunity Plan) by earning a technical college diploma or two technical college certificates, in one career pathway identified by the Technical College System of Georgia (TCSG), may be eligible for the HOPE Grant, up to 30 degree hours. The student must be enrolled in an associate degree program at a TCSG institution in order to receive the HOPE Grant. *Award:* Grant for use in freshman, sophomore, junior, or senior years; renewable. *Award amount:* $420–$3600. *Number of awards:* 100,000. *Eligibility Requirements:* Applicant must be enrolled or expecting to enroll full- or part-time at a two-year or technical institution or university; resident of Florida and studying in Georgia. Available to U.S. citizens. *Application Requirements:* Application form, financial need analysis.

Contact Ms. Pennie Strong, Vice President, Student Aid Services, Georgia Student Finance Commission, 2082 East Exchange Place, Tucker, GA 30084. *E-mail:* pennies@gsfc.org. *Phone:* 770-724-9014. *Fax:* 770-724-9249. *Website:* https://gsfc.georgia.gov/.

Georgia Public Safety Memorial Grant. Public Safety Memorial Grant provides assistance to the dependent children of Georgia public safety officers who were permanently disabled or killed in the line of duty. Funds may be used toward the cost of attendance at eligible colleges or universities in Georgia. *Award:* Grant for use in freshman, sophomore, junior, or senior years; not renewable. *Award amount:* $2000–$18,000. *Eligibility Requirements:* Applicant must be enrolled or expecting to enroll full-time at a two-year or technical institution or university; resident of Florida and studying in Georgia. Applicant or parent of applicant must have employment or volunteer experience in police/firefighting. Available to U.S. citizens. *Application Requirements:* Application form. **Deadline:** continuous.

Contact Ms. Pennie Strong, Vice President, Student Aid Services, Georgia Student Finance Commission, 2082 East Exchange Place, Tucker, GA 30084. *E-mail:* pennies@gsfc.org. *Phone:* 770-724-9014. *Fax:* 770-724-9249. *Website:* https://gsfc.georgia.gov/.

Georgia Tuition Equalization Grant (GTEG) Program. The Georgia Tuition Equalization Grant (GTEG) provides grant assistance toward educational costs to Georgia residents enrolled at an eligible private college or university. Students must be enrolled full-time in an undergraduate program of study leading to an undergraduate *Award:* Grant for use in freshman, sophomore, junior, or senior years; renewable. *Award amount:* $317–$475. *Eligibility Requirements:* Applicant must be enrolled or expecting to enroll full-time at a two-year institution or university; resident of Florida and studying in Georgia. Available to U. S. citizens. *Application Requirements:* Application form.

Contact Ms. Pennie Strong, Vice President, Student Aid Services, Georgia Student Finance Commission, 2082 East Exchange Place, Tucker, GA 30084. *E-mail:* pennies@gsfc.org. *Phone:* 770-724-9014. *Fax:* 770-724-9249. *Website:* https://gsfc.georgia.gov/.

Helping Educate Reservists and their Offspring (HERO) Scholarship. Provides assistance with cost of attendance to members of the Georgia National Guard and U.S. Military Reservists who were deployed overseas on active duty service, on or after February 1, 2003, to a location designated as a combat zone, and the children and spouses of such members of the Georgia National Guard and U.S. Military Reserves. Students must be attending an eligible college or university in Georgia. *Award:* Scholarship for use in freshman, sophomore, junior, or senior years; not renewable. *Award amount:* $2000–$8000. *Eligibility Requirements:* Applicant must be enrolled or expecting to enroll full- or part-time at a two-year or technical institution or university; resident of Florida and studying in Georgia. Available to U.S. citizens. *Application Requirements:* Application form.

Contact Ms. Pennie Strong, Vice President, Student Aid Services, Georgia Student Finance Commission, 2082 East Exchange Place, Tucker, GA 30084. *E-mail:* pennies@gsfc.org. *Phone:* 770-724-9014. *Fax:* 770-724-9249. *Website:* https://gsfc.georgia.gov/.

HOPE Scholarship. HOPE Scholarship is a merit-based award available to Georgia residents who have demonstrated academic achievement. A Hope Scholarship recipient must graduate from high school with a minimum 3.0 HOPE Calculated (approved core courses) grade point average and earned 4 credits of academic rigor. Students must maintain a minimum 3.0 cumulative postsecondary grade point average to remain eligible. The scholarship provides tuition assistance to students pursuing an undergraduate degree at a HOPE Scholarship eligible college or university in Georgia. *Award:* Scholarship for use in freshman, sophomore, junior, or senior years; renewable. *Award amount:* $420–$3600. *Number of awards:* 200,000. *Eligibility Requirements:* Applicant must be enrolled or expecting to enroll full- or part-time at a two-year or technical institution or university; resident of Florida and studying in Georgia. Available to U.S. citizens. *Application Requirements:* Application form.

Contact Ms. Pennie Strong, Vice President, Student Aid Services, Georgia Student Finance Commission, 2082 East Exchange Place, Tucker, GA

30084. *E-mail:* pennies@gsfc.org. *Phone:* 770-724-9014. *Fax:* 770-724-9249. *Website:* https://gsfc.georgia.gov/.

Paper and Board Division Scholarships. Award to TAPPI student member or an undergraduate member of a TAPPI Student Chapter enrolled as a college or university undergraduate in an engineering or science program. Must be sophomore, junior, or senior and able to show a significant interest in the paper industry. Information can be found at http://www.tappi.org/s_tappi/sec.asp?CID=6101&DID=546695. Engineering/Technology; Paper and Pulp Engineering. *Award:* Scholarship for use in sophomore, junior, or senior years; not renewable. *Award amount:* $1000–$1500. *Number of awards:* 1–4. *Eligibility Requirements:* Applicant must be enrolled or expecting to enroll full-time at a four-year institution or university. Available to U.S. and non-U.S. citizens. *Application Requirements:* Application form. **Deadline:** February 15.

Contact Mr. Laurence Womack, Director of Standards and Awards, Technical Association of the Pulp & Paper Industry (TAPPI), 15 Technology Parkway South, Peachtree Corners, GA 30092. *E-mail:* standards@tappi.org. *Phone:* 770-209-7276. *Website:* https://www.tappi.org/.

Physicians for Rural Areas Assistance Program. Service repayable medical school scholarship for a maximum of $20,000 per year for four years available to Georgia residents enrolled in U.S. accredited medical school. Repay by practicing medicine for one year in rural Georgia for each year that the scholarship is received. Service payment begins upon completion of residency training. Health and Medical Sciences. *Award:* Scholarship for use in freshman, sophomore, junior, or senior years; renewable. *Award amount:* up to $20,000. *Number of awards:* 20–25. *Eligibility Requirements:* Applicant must be enrolled or expecting to enroll full-time at an institution or university and resident of Georgia. Available to U.S. citizens. *Application Requirements:* Application form, essay, financial need analysis, interview, personal photograph, proof of GA residency, test scores, transcript. **Deadline:** June 1.

Contact Ms. Pamela Smith, Administration Manager, Georgia Board for Physician Workforce (GBPW), 2 Peachtree Street, NW, 36th Floor, Atlanta, GA 30303. *E-mail:* psmith@dch.ga.gov. *Phone:* 404-232-7972. *Website:* http://www.gbpw.georgia.gov.

Scholarship for Engineering Education for Minorities (MSEE). MSEE is a service cancelable loan available to minority upperclass students majoring in an approved program by the Engineering Accreditation Commission of the Accrediting Board for Engineering and Technology (ABET) at an eligible participating university in Georgia. Funds can be used towards educational costs. $5,250 per academic year to a maximum of nine (9) terms and $15,750. Participating universities include Georgia Institute of Technology, Georgia Southern University, University of Georgia, Kennesaw State University, and Mercer University. *Award:* Scholarship for use in junior or senior years; not renewable. *Award amount:* $5250–$15,750. *Eligibility Requirements:* Applicant must be American Indian/Alaska Native, Asian/Pacific Islander, Black (non-Hispanic), Hispanic; enrolled or expecting to enroll full-time at an institution or university; resident of Florida and studying in Georgia. Available to U.S. citizens. *Application Requirements:* Application form. **Deadline:** continuous.

Contact Ms. Pennie Strong, Vice President, Student Aid Services, Georgia Student Finance Commission, 2082 East Exchange Place, Tucker, GA 30084. *E-mail:* pennies@gsfc.org. *Phone:* 770-724-9014. *Fax:* 770-724-9249. *Website:* https://gsfc.georgia.gov/.

Zell Miller Scholarship. Zell Miller Scholarship is a merit-based award available to Georgia residents, similar to the HOPE Scholarship, but with more stringent academic requirements and a higher level of tuition assistance. A Zell Miller Scholarship recipient must graduate from high school with a minimum 3.7 HOPE Calculated (approved core courses) grade point average combined and earned 4 credits of academic rigor, with a minimum SAT score of 1,200 on the math and reading portions or a minimum composite ACT score of 26 in single national test administration. Students must maintain a minimum 3.3 cumulative postsecondary grade point average to remain eligible. Students are provided full-tuition assistance while pursuing an undergraduate degree and they must attend an eligible college or university in Georgia. A seven-year limit exists for students first receiving the Zell Miller Scholarship during the 2011-2012 academic year (FY12) or later. *Award:* Scholarship for use in freshman, sophomore, junior, or senior years; renewable. *Eligibility Requirements:* Applicant must be enrolled or expecting to enroll full- or part-time at a two-year or technical institution or university; resident of Florida and studying in Georgia. Available to U.S. citizens. *Application Requirements:* Application form.

Contact Ms. Pennie Strong, Vice President, Student Aid Services, Georgia Student Finance Commission, 2082 East Exchange Place, Tucker, GA 30084. *E-mail:* pennies@gsfc.org. *Phone:* 770-724-9014. *Fax:* 770-724-9249. *Website:* https://gsfc.georgia.gov/.

HAWAII

Hawaii State Student Incentive Grant. Grants are given to residents of Hawaii who are enrolled in a participating Hawaiian state school. Funds are for undergraduate tuition only. Applicants must submit a financial need analysis. *Award:* Grant for use in freshman, sophomore, junior, or senior years; renewable. *Award amount:* $200–$2000. *Number of awards:* 470. *Eligibility Requirements:* Applicant must be enrolled or expecting to enroll full- or part-time at a two-year or four-year or technical institution or university; resident of Hawaii and studying in Hawaii. Available to U.S. citizens. *Application Requirements:* Application form, financial need analysis. **Deadline:** continuous.

Contact Janine Oyama, Financial Aid Specialist, Hawaii State Postsecondary Education Commission, University of Hawaii, Honolulu, HI 96822. *Phone:* 808-956-6066.

IDAHO

Idaho Opportunity Scholarship. The Idaho Opportunity Scholarship is an award open to Idaho citizens who have graduated from Idaho high schools or equivalent. The application is open to any high school or college students who attended an Idaho high school, are Idaho residents, and are attending or who are planning on attending an eligible Idaho college or university. Students must be earning their first undergraduate degree.

The required GPA is a 2.7 and applicants must show need by completing the FAFSA by March 1 each year. The award is renewable for a total of 4 years. *Award:* Scholarship for use in freshman, sophomore, junior, or senior years; renewable. *Award amount:* \$1–\$3500. *Number of awards:* 700–2,500. *Eligibility Requirements:* Applicant must be enrolled or expecting to enroll full- or part-time at a two-year or four-year or technical institution or university; resident of Idaho and studying in Idaho. Available to U.S. citizens. *Application Requirements:* Application form, financial need analysis. **Deadline:** March 1.

Contact Joy Miller, Scholarships Program Manager, Idaho State Board of Education, 650 W. State St., #307, Boise, ID 83720. *E-mail:* joy.miller@osbe.idaho.gov. *Phone:* 208-332-1595. *Website:* http://www.boardofed.idaho.gov/.

ILLINOIS

Golden Apple Scholars of Illinois. Applicants must be between the ages of 16 and 21 and maintain a GPA of 2.5. Eligible applicants must be residents of Illinois studying education in Illinois. Recipients must agree to teach in an Illinois school school-of-need for 5 years. Education. *Award:* Scholarship for use in freshman, sophomore, junior, or senior years; renewable. *Award amount:* \$23,000. *Number of awards:* 200. *Eligibility Requirements:* Applicant must be age 16-21; enrolled or expecting to enroll full-time at a two-year or four-year institution or university; resident of Illinois and studying in Illinois. Available to U.S. citizens. *Application Requirements:* Application form, essay, interview, personal photograph. **Deadline:** February 15.

Contact Ms. Patricia Kilduff, Director of Recruitment and Placement. *E-mail:* kilduff@goldenapple.org. *Phone:* 312-477-7515. *Website:* http://www.goldenapple.org/.

Grant Program for Dependents of Police, Fire, or Correctional Officers. Awards available to Illinois residents who are dependents of police, fire, and correctional officers killed or disabled in line of duty. Provides for tuition and fees at approved Illinois institutions. Number of grants and individual dollar amount awarded vary. *Award:* Grant for use in freshman, sophomore, junior, senior, graduate, or postgraduate years; renewable. *Eligibility Requirements:* Applicant must be enrolled or expecting to enroll full- or part-time at a two-year or four-year or technical institution or university; resident of Illinois and studying in Illinois. Applicant or parent of applicant must be affiliated with Amalgamated Sugar Company. Available to U.S. citizens. Applicant or parent must meet one or more of the following requirements: retired from active duty; disabled or killed as a result of military service; prisoner of war; or missing in action. *Application Requirements:* Application form. **Deadline:** October 1.

Higher Education License Plate (HELP) Program. Grants for students who attend Illinois colleges for which the special collegiate license plates are available. The Illinois Secretary of State issues the license plates, and part of the proceeds are used for grants for undergraduate students attending these colleges, to pay tuition and mandatory fees. *Award:* Grant for use in freshman, sophomore, junior, or senior years; not renewable. *Eligibility Requirements:* Applicant must be enrolled or expecting to enroll full- or part-time at a two-year institution or university; resident of Idaho and studying in Illinois. Available to U.S. citizens. *Application Requirements:* Application form, financial need analysis. **Deadline:** continuous.

Illinois National Guard (ING) Grant Program. Active duty members of the Illinois National Guard, or who are within 12 months of discharge, and who have completed one full year of service are eligible. May be used for study at Illinois two- or four-year public colleges for a maximum of the equivalent of four academic years of full-time enrollment. Deadlines: October 1 of the academic year for full year, March 1 for second/third term, or June 15 for the summer term. *Award:* Grant for use in freshman, sophomore, junior, senior, or graduate years; not renewable. *Eligibility Requirements:* Applicant must be enrolled or expecting to enroll full- or part-time at a two-year institution or university; resident of Idaho and studying in Illinois. Available to U.S. citizens. Applicant or parent must meet one or more of the following requirements: national guard experience; retired from active duty; disabled or killed as a result of military service; prisoner of war; or missing in action. *Application Requirements:* Application form, application form may be submitted online. **Deadline:** continuous.

Illinois Veteran Grant (IVG) Program. Awards qualified veterans and pays eligible tuition and fees for study in Illinois public universities or community colleges. Program eligibility units are based on the enrolled hours for a particular term, not the dollar amount of the benefits paid. Applications are available at college financial aid office and can be submitted any time during the academic year for which assistance is being requested. *Award:* Grant for use in freshman, sophomore, junior, senior, or graduate years; renewable. *Eligibility Requirements:* Applicant must be enrolled or expecting to enroll full- or part-time at a two-year institution or university; resident of Idaho and studying in Illinois. Available to U.S. citizens. Applicant or parent must meet one or more of the following requirements: general military experience; retired from active duty; disabled or killed as a result of military service; prisoner of war; or missing in action. *Application Requirements:* Application form, application form may be submitted online. **Deadline:** continuous.

Minority Teachers of Illinois (MTI) Scholarship Program. Award for minority students intending to become school teachers; teaching commitment attached to receipt. Number of scholarships and the individual dollar amounts vary. *Award:* Scholarship for use in freshman, sophomore, junior, senior, graduate, or postgraduate years; renewable. *Award amount:* \$5000. *Eligibility Requirements:* Applicant must be American Indian/Alaska Native, Asian/Pacific Islander, Black (non-Hispanic), Hispanic; enrolled or expecting to enroll full-time at a two-year institution or university; resident of Idaho and studying in Illinois. Available to U.S. citizens. *Application Requirements:* Application form, application form may be submitted online. **Deadline:** March 1.

Monetary Award Program (MAP). Awards to Illinois residents enrolled in a minimum of 3 hours per term in a degree program at an approved Illinois institution. See website for complete list of participating schools. Must demonstrate financial need, based on the information provided on the Free Application for Federal Student Aid. Number of grants and the individual dollar amount awarded vary. Deadline: As soon as possible after October 1 of the year before the student will enter college. *Award:* Grant for use in freshman, sophomore, junior, or senior years; renewable. *Eligibility Requirements:* Applicant must be enrolled or expecting to enroll full- or part-time at a two-year or technical institution or university; resident of Idaho and studying in Illinois. Available to U.S. citizens. *Application Requirements:* Application form, financial need analysis. **Deadline:** December 1.

INDIANA

21st Century Scholarship. Started in 1990, 21st Century Scholars is Indiana's early college promise program. It offers income-eligible Hoosier students up to four years of paid tuition at an eligible Indiana college or university after they graduate from high school. Students enroll in seventh or eighth grade, and in high school they participate in the Scholar Success Program and are connected to programs and resources to help them prepare for college and career success. Once in college, Scholars receive support to complete their college degrees and connect to career opportunities. *Award:* Scholarship for use in freshman, sophomore, junior, or senior years; renewable. *Eligibility Requirements:* Applicant must be enrolled or expecting to enroll full-time at a two-year or technical institution or university; resident of Illinois and studying in Indiana. Available to U.S. citizens. *Application Requirements:* Application form, financial need analysis. **Deadline:** continuous.

Contact Charlee Beasor, Communications Director. *E-mail:* CBeasor@che.in.gov. *Phone:* 317-232-1016. *Website:* http://www.in.gov/che.

Adult Student Grant. The Adult Student Grant, part of the Indiana's You Can. Go Back. program, offers a renewable $2,000 grant to assist returning adult students in starting or completing an associate degree, bachelor's degree or certificate. To qualify, students must be financially independent as determined by the FAFSA, demonstrate financial need and be enrolled in at least six credit hours. *Award:* Grant for use in freshman, sophomore, junior, or senior years; renewable. *Award amount:* $2000. *Eligibility Requirements:* Applicant must be enrolled or expecting to enroll full- or part-time at a two-year institution or university; resident of Illinois and studying in Indiana. Available to U.S. citizens. *Application Requirements:* Application form, application form may be submitted online, financial need analysis. **Deadline:** continuous.

Contact Charlee Beasor, Communications Director. *E-mail:* CBeasor@che.in.gov. *Phone:* 317-232-1016. *Website:* http://www.in.gov/che.

Child of Deceased or Disabled Veteran. Provides tuition and regularly assessed fees for children of deceased or disabled veterans. This program funding is limited to a maximum of 124 credit hours and may be used at the undergraduate and professional degree level. *Award:* Grant for use in freshman, sophomore, junior, senior, or graduate years; renewable. *Eligibility Requirements:* Applicant must be enrolled or expecting to enroll full- or part-time at a two-year or technical institution or university; resident of Illinois and studying in Indiana. Available to U.S. citizens. *Application Requirements:* Application form, application form may be submitted online. **Deadline:** continuous.

Contact Charlee Beasor, Communications Director. *E-mail:* CBeasor@che.in.gov. *Phone:* 317-232-1016. *Website:* http://www.in.gov/che.

Child of Purple Heart Recipient or Wounded Veteran. Provides regularly assessed fees for children of Purple Heart recipients or wounded veterans. This program funding is limited to a maximum of 124 credit hours and may be used at the undergraduate and professional degree level. *Award:* Grant for use in freshman, sophomore, junior, senior, or graduate years; renewable. *Eligibility Requirements:* Applicant must be enrolled or expecting to enroll full- or part-time at a two-year or technical institution or university; resident of Illinois and studying in Indiana. Available to U.S. citizens. *Application Requirements:* Application form, application form may be submitted online. **Deadline:** continuous.

Contact Charlee Beasor, Communications Director. *E-mail:* CBeasor@che.in.gov. *Phone:* 317-232-1016. *Website:* http://www.in.gov/che.

Children and Spouse of Indiana National Guard. Award to an individual whose father, mother or spouse was a member of the Indiana National Guard and suffered a service-connected death while serving on state active duty (which includes mobilized and deployed for federal active duty). The student must be eligible to pay the resident tuition rate at the state-supported college or university and must possess the requisite academic qualifications. *Award:* Grant for use in freshman, sophomore, junior, or senior years; renewable. *Eligibility Requirements:* Applicant must be enrolled or expecting to enroll full- or part-time at a two-year or technical institution or university and studying in Indiana. Available to U.S. citizens. Applicant or parent must meet one or more of the following requirements: national guard experience; retired from active duty; disabled or killed as a result of military service; prisoner of war; or missing in action. *Application Requirements:* Application form, application form may be submitted online. **Deadline:** continuous.

Contact Courtney Carr, Adjutant General, Indiana Department of Veterans Affairs, 2002 South Holt Road, Indianapolis, IN 46241. *E-mail:* c.carr@in.ngb.army.mil. *Phone:* 317-964-7023. *Website:* http://www.in.gov/dva.

Children and Spouse of Indiana National Guard Program. Provides 100% of tuition and regularly assessed fees for students who are the child or spouse of a member of the Indiana National Guard who suffered a service-connected death while serving on state active duty. This program funding is limited to a maximum of 124 credit hours. *Award:* Grant for use in freshman, sophomore, junior, senior, or graduate years; renewable. *Eligibility Requirements:* Applicant must be enrolled or expecting to enroll full- or part-time at a two-year or technical institution or university; resident of Illinois and studying in Indiana. Available to U.S. citizens. *Application Requirements:* Application form, application form may be submitted online. **Deadline:** continuous.

Contact Charlee Beasor, Communications Director. *E-mail:* CBeasor@che.in.gov. *Phone:* 317-232-1016. *Website:* http://www.in.gov/che.

Children and Spouse of Public Safety Officers Program. Provides 100% of tuition and regularly assessed fees for students who are the child or spouse of certain Indiana public safety officers (PSO) who were killed in the line of duty or are a permanently disabled state trooper. *Award:* Grant for use in freshman, sophomore, junior, or senior years; renewable. *Eligibility Requirements:* Applicant must be enrolled or expecting to enroll full-time at a two-year or technical institution or university; resident of Illinois and studying in Indiana. Available to U.S. citizens. *Application Requirements:* Application form, application form may be submitted online. **Deadline:** continuous.

Contact Charlee Beasor, Communications Director. *E-mail:* CBeasor@che.in.gov. *Phone:* 317-232-1016. *Website:* http://www.in.gov/che.

Frank O'Bannon Grant Program. The Frank O'Bannon Grant, which includes the Higher Education Award and the Freedom of Choice Award, is Indiana's primary need-based financial aid program. It is designed to provide access for Hoosier students to attend eligible public, private and proprietary colleges and universities. Eligibility is based on a student's FAFSA, and the grant may be used toward tuition and regularly assessed fees. *Award:* Grant for use in freshman, sophomore, junior, or senior years; renewable. *Award amount:* $650–$9200. *Eligibility Requirements:* Applicant must be enrolled or expecting to enroll full-time at a two-year or technical institution or university; resident of Illinois and studying in Indiana. Available to U.S. citizens. *Application Requirements:* Application form, financial need analysis. **Deadline:** April 15.

Contact Charlee Beasor, Communications Director. *E-mail:* CBeasor@che.in.gov. *Phone:* 317-232-1016. *Website:* http://www.in.gov/che.

Indiana National Guard Tuition Supplement Grant. Provides 100% of tuition and regularly assessed fees at a public Indiana institution for eligible members of the Indiana Air and Army National Guard. Students can attend either full time or part time. *Award:* Grant for use in freshman, sophomore, junior, or senior years; not renewable. *Eligibility Requirements:* Applicant must be enrolled or expecting to enroll full- or part-time at a two-year or technical institution or university; resident of Illinois and studying in Indiana. Available to U.S. citizens. Applicant must have national guard experience. *Application Requirements:* Application form, application form may be submitted online, financial need analysis. **Deadline:** continuous.

Contact Charlee Beasor, Communications Director. *E-mail:* CBeasor@che.in.gov. *Phone:* 317-232-1016. *Website:* http://www.in.gov/che.

Indiana Purple Heart Recipient Program. Provides 100% of tuition and regularly assessed fees for students who are Indiana veterans and Purple Heart Recipients. This program funding is limited to a maximum of 124 credit hours and may be used at the undergraduate, graduate and professional degree level. *Award:* Grant for use in freshman, sophomore, junior, senior, or graduate years; renewable. *Eligibility Requirements:* Applicant must be enrolled or expecting to enroll full- or part-time at a two-year or technical institution or university; resident of Illinois and studying in Indiana. Available to U.S. citizens. Applicant or parent must meet one or more of the following requirements: general military experience; retired from active duty; disabled or killed as a result of military service; prisoner of war; or missing in action. *Application Requirements:* Application form, application form may be submitted online. **Deadline:** continuous.

Contact Charlee Beasor, Communications Director. *E-mail:* CBeasor@che.in.gov. *Phone:* 317-232-1016. *Website:* http://www.in.gov/che.

Mitch Daniels Early Graduation Scholarship. The Mitch Daniels Early Graduation Scholarship is a one-time, $4,000 scholarship for students who graduate at least one year early from a publicly supported Indiana high school. To claim this scholarship, students must enroll at an eligible Indiana institution no later than the fall semester in the academic year immediately following the year they graduate high school. *Award:* Scholarship for use in freshman year; not renewable. *Award amount:* $4000. *Eligibility Requirements:* Applicant must be high school student; planning to enroll or expecting to enroll full-time at a two-year or technical institution or university; resident of Illinois and studying in Indiana. Available to U.S. citizens. *Application Requirements:* Application form, application form may be submitted online. **Deadline:** August 31.

Contact Charlee Beasor, Communications Director. *E-mail:* CBeasor@che.in.gov. *Phone:* 317-232-1016. *Website:* http://www.in.gov/che.

National Guard Extension Scholarship. A scholarship extension applicant is eligible for a tuition scholarship under Indiana Code 21-13-5-4 for a period not to exceed the period of scholarship extension the applicant served on active duty as a member of the National Guard (mobilized and deployed). Must apply not later than one (1) year after the applicant ceases to be a member of the Indiana National Guard. Applicant should apply through the education officer of their last unit of assignment. *Award:* Scholarship for use in freshman, sophomore, junior, or senior years; renewable. *Eligibility Requirements:* Applicant must be enrolled or expecting to enroll full- or part-time at a two-year or technical institution or university; resident of Illinois and studying in Indiana. Available to U.S. citizens. Applicant must have national guard experience. *Application Requirements:* Application form. **Deadline:** continuous.

Contact Pamela Moody, National Guard Education Officer, Indiana Department of Veterans Affairs, 302 West Washington Street, Room E-120, Indianapolis, IN 46204. *E-mail:* pamela.moody@in.ngb.army.mil. *Phone:* 317-964-7017. *Website:* http://www.in.gov/dva.

National Guard Tuition Supplement Grant. Applicant must be a member of the Indiana National Guard, in active drilling status, who has not been AWOL during the last 12 months, does not possess a bachelor's degree, possesses the requisite academic qualifications, meets the requirements of the state-supported college or university, and meets all National Guard requirements. *Award:* Grant for use in freshman, sophomore, junior, or senior years; renewable. *Eligibility Requirements:* Applicant must be enrolled or expecting to enroll full- or part-time at a two-year or technical institution or university; resident of Illinois and studying in Indiana. Available to U.S. citizens. Applicant must have national guard experience. *Application Requirements:* Application form. **Deadline:** continuous.

Contact Michael Hamm, State Service Officer. *E-mail:* mhamm@dva.

in.gov. *Phone:* 317-232-3910. *Fax:* 317-232-7721. *Website:* http://www.in.gov/dva.

Next Generation Hoosier Educators Scholarship. The Next Generation Hoosier Educators Scholarship provides 200 high-achieving high school and college students interested in pursuing a career in education the opportunity to earn a renewable scholarship of up to $7,500 a year for four academic years. In exchange, students agree to teach for five years at an eligible Indiana school or repay the corresponding, prorated amount of the scholarship. *Award:* Scholarship for use in freshman, sophomore, junior, or senior years; renewable. *Award amount:* $7500. *Number of awards:* 200. *Eligibility Requirements:* Applicant must be enrolled or expecting to enroll full-time at an institution or university; resident of Illinois and studying in Indiana. Available to U.S. citizens. *Application Requirements:* Application form, application form may be submitted online, essay, interview. **Deadline:** November 30.

Contact Charlee Beasor, Communications Director. *E-mail:* CBeasor@che.in.gov. *Phone:* 317-232-1016. *Website:* http://www.in.gov/che.

Part-Time Grant Program. Program is designed to encourage part-time undergraduates to start and complete their Associate or Baccalaureate degrees or certificates by subsidizing part-time tuition costs. It is a term-based award that is based on need. State residency requirements must be met and a FAFSA must be filed. Eligibility is determined at the institutional level subject to approval by SSACI. *Award:* Grant for use in freshman, sophomore, junior, or senior years; not renewable. *Award amount:* $20–$4000. *Number of awards:* 4,680–6,700. *Eligibility Requirements:* Applicant must be enrolled or expecting to enroll part-time at a two-year or four-year or technical institution or university; resident of Indiana and studying in Indiana. Available to U.S. citizens. *Application Requirements:* Application form, financial need analysis. **Deadline:** continuous.

Contact Charlee Beasor, Communications Director. *E-mail:* CBeasor@che.in.gov. *Phone:* 317-232-1016. *Website:* http://www.in.gov/che.

Resident Tuition for Active Duty Military Personnel. Applicant must be a nonresident of Indiana serving on active duty and stationed in Indiana and attending any state-supported college or university. Dependents remain eligible for the duration of their enrollment, even if the active duty person is no longer in Indiana. Entitlement is to the resident tuition rate. *Award:* Grant for use in freshman, sophomore, junior, senior, graduate, or postgraduate years; renewable. *Eligibility Requirements:* Applicant must be enrolled or expecting to enroll full- or part-time at a two-year or four-year or technical institution or university and studying in Indiana. Available to U.S. citizens. Applicant or parent must meet one or more of the following requirements: Air Force or Army experience; retired from active duty; disabled or killed as a result of military service; prisoner of war; or missing in action. *Application Requirements:* Application form. **Deadline:** continuous.

Contact Michael Hamm, State Service Officer. *E-mail:* mhamm@dva.in.gov. *Phone:* 317-232-3910. *Fax:* 317-232-7721. *Website:* http://www.in.gov/dva.

Tuition and Fee Exemption for Indiana Purple Heart Recipients. Free tuition at Indiana state-supported colleges or universities for children of disabled veterans or Purple Heart recipients. Must submit form DD214 or service record. Covers tuition and mandatory fees. *Award:* Grant for use in freshman, sophomore, junior, senior, graduate, or postgraduate years; renewable. *Eligibility Requirements:* Applicant must be enrolled or expecting to enroll full- or part-time at a two-year institution or university; resident of Illinois and studying in Indiana. Available to U.S. citizens. Applicant must have general military experience. *Application Requirements:* Application form. **Deadline:** continuous.

Contact Michael Hamm, State Service Officer. *E-mail:* mhamm@dva.in.gov. *Phone:* 317-232-3910. *Fax:* 317-232-7721. *Website:* http://www.in.gov/dva.

Tuition and Fee Exemption for the Child(ren) of a Disabled Veteran or POW/MIA or Purple Heart Recipients. Renewable award for residents of Indiana who are the children of veterans declared missing in action or prisoner-of-war after January 1, 1960. Provides tuition at Indiana state-supported institutions for undergraduate study. *Award:* Grant for use in freshman, sophomore, junior, senior, graduate, or postgraduate years; renewable. *Eligibility Requirements:* Applicant must be enrolled or expecting to enroll full- or part-time at a two-year institution or university; resident of Illinois and studying in Indiana. Available to U.S. citizens. Applicant must have general military experience. *Application Requirements:* Application form, application form may be submitted online. **Deadline:** continuous.

Contact Michael Hamm, State Service Officer. *E-mail:* mhamm@dva.in.gov. *Phone:* 317-232-3910. *Fax:* 317-232-7721. *Website:* http://www.in.gov/dva.

William A. Crawford Minority Teacher Scholarship. The William A. Crawford Minority Teacher Scholarship is available to minority students (defined as black and Hispanic individuals) who intend to pursue, or are currently pursuing, a course of study that would enable them to teach in an accredited school in Indiana. Students must agree in writing to apply for teaching positions in Indiana and, if hired, teach in Indiana for at least three years. *Award:* Scholarship for use in freshman, sophomore, junior, or senior years; not renewable. *Eligibility Requirements:* Applicant must be Black (non-Hispanic), Hispanic; enrolled or expecting to enroll full-time at an institution or university; resident of Illinois and studying in Indiana. Available to U.S. citizens. *Application Requirements:* Application form, application form may be submitted online. **Deadline:** August 31.

Contact Charlee Beasor, Communications Director. *E-mail:* CBeasor@che.in.gov. *Phone:* 317-232-1016. *Website:* http://www.in.gov/che.

KANSAS

Kansas Educational Benefits for Children of MIA, POW, and Deceased Veterans of the Vietnam War. Scholarship awarded to students who are children of veterans. Must show proof of parent's status as missing in action, prisoner-of-war, or killed in action in the Vietnam War. Kansas residence required of veteran at time of entry to service. Must attend a state-supported postsecondary school. *Award:* Scholarship for use in freshman, sophomore, junior, or senior years; not renewable. *Number of awards:* 1. *Eligibility Requirements:* Applicant must be enrolled or expecting to enroll full-time at a two-year or four-year or technical institution or university and studying in Kansas. Available to U.S. citizens. Applicant or parent must meet one or more of the following requirements: general military experience; retired from active duty; disabled or killed as a result of military service; prisoner of war; or missing in action. *Application Requirements:* Application form, birth certificate, school acceptance letter, military discharge of veteran. **Deadline:** varies.

Contact Wayne Bollig, Program Director. *E-mail:* wbollig@kcva.org. *Phone:* 785-296-3976. *Fax:* 785-296-1462. *Website:* http://www.kcva.org/.

KENTUCKY

College Access Program (CAP) Grant. Award up to $2,000 for U.S. citizens and Kentucky residents seeking their first undergraduate degree. Applicants enrolled in sectarian institutions are not eligible. Must submit Free Application for Federal Student Aid to demonstrate financial need. Funding is limited. Awards are made on a first-come, first-serve basis. *Award:* Grant for use in freshman, sophomore, junior, or senior years; not renewable. *Eligibility Requirements:* Applicant must be enrolled or expecting to enroll full- or part-time at a two-year or technical institution or university; resident of Kansas and studying in Kentucky. Available to U.S. citizens. *Application Requirements:* Application form, financial need analysis. **Deadline:** continuous.

Contact Becky Gilpatrick, Director of Student Aid, Kentucky Higher Education Assistance Authority (KHEAA), PO Box 798, Frankfort, KY 40602-0798. *E-mail:* rgilpatrick@kheaa.com. *Phone:* 800-928-8926. *Fax:* 502-696-7373. *Website:* http://www.kheaa.com/.

Department of Veterans Affairs Tuition Waiver-KY KRS 164-507. Scholarship available to college students who are residents of Kentucky under the age of 26. *Award:* Scholarship for use in freshman, sophomore, junior, or senior years; not renewable. *Number of awards:* 400. *Eligibility Requirements:* Applicant must be age 26 or under; enrolled or expecting to enroll full- or part-time at a two-year or four-year institution or university and resident of Kentucky. Available to U.S. citizens. *Application Requirements:* Application form. **Deadline:** varies.

Contact Barbara Sipek, Tuition Waiver Coordinator. *E-mail:* barbaraa.sipek@ky.gov. *Phone:* 502-595-4447. *Website:* http://www.veterans.ky.gov/.

Early Childhood Development Scholarship. The scholarship provides financial aid to Kentucky students pursuing Child Development Associate Credential, Associate's degree in early childhood education. Bachelor's degree in interdisciplinary early childhood education or a related program approved by the Early Childhood Development Authority, Kentucky Early Childhood Development Director's Certificate. Awards up to $1,800 scholarship with conditional service commitment for part-time students currently employed by participating ECD facility or providing training in ECD for an approved organization. For more information, visit website http://www.kheaa.com. *Award:* Scholarship for use in freshman, sophomore, junior, or senior years; not renewable. *Eligibility Requirements:* Applicant must be enrolled or expecting to enroll part-time at a two-year institution or university; resident of Kansas and studying in Kentucky. Available to U.S. citizens. *Application Requirements:* Application form, application form may be submitted online. **Deadline:** continuous.

Contact Becky Gilpatrick, Director of Student Aid, Kentucky Higher Education Assistance Authority (KHEAA), PO Box 798, Frankfort, KY 40602-0798. *E-mail:* rgilpatrick@kheaa.com. *Phone:* 800-928-8926. *Fax:* 502-696-7373. *Website:* http://www.kheaa.com/.

Environmental Protection Scholarship. Renewable awards for college juniors, seniors, and graduate students for in-state tuition, fees, room and board, and a book allowance at a Kentucky public university. Minimum 3.0 GPA required. Must work full-time for the Kentucky Department for Environmental Protection upon graduation (six months for each semester of scholarship support received). Interview required. Program not generally appropriate for non-residents. Biology; Chemical Engineering; Civil Engineering; Earth Science; Environmental Science; Hydrology; Mechanical Engineering; Natural Sciences. *Award:* Scholarship for use in junior, senior, or graduate years; renewable. *Award amount:* $10,000–$13,000. *Number of awards:* 1–4. *Eligibility Requirements:* Applicant must be enrolled or expecting to enroll full-time at a four-year institution or university; resident of Kentucky and studying in Kentucky. Available to U.S. citizens. *Application Requirements:* Application form, essay, interview. **Deadline:** February 15.

Contact James Kipp, Scholarship Program Coordinator, Kentucky Energy and Environment Cabinet, 233 Mining/Mineral Resources Building, Lexington, KY 40506-0107. *E-mail:* kipp@uky.edu. *Phone:* 859-257-1299. *Website:* http://dep.ky.gov.

Kentucky Educational Excellence Scholarship (KEES). Annual award based on yearly high school GPA and highest ACT or SAT score received by high school graduation. Awards are renewable, if required cumulative GPA is maintained at a Kentucky postsecondary school. Must be a Kentucky resident, and a graduate of a Kentucky high school. Low-income students who qualify for the free/reduced lunch program at least one year of high school may receive supplemental awards for passing scores on Advanced Placement (AP) or International Baccalaureate (IB) exams. *Award:* Scholarship for use in freshman, sophomore, junior, or senior years; renewable. *Award amount:* $125–$500. *Eligibility Requirements:* Applicant must be enrolled or expecting to enroll full- or part-time at a two-year or technical institution or university; resident of Kansas and studying in British Columbia. Available to U.S. citizens. *Application Requirements:* Application form. **Deadline:** continuous.

Contact Becky Gilpatrick, Director of Student Aid, Kentucky Higher Education Assistance Authority (KHEAA), PO Box 798, Frankfort, KY 40602-0798. *E-mail:* rgilpatrick@kheaa.com. *Phone:* 800-928-8926. *Fax:* 502-696-7373. *Website:* http://www.kheaa.com/.

Kentucky National Guard Tuition Award. Provides tuition assistance for active members of the Kentucky National Guard to attend a Kentucky college or university. Must be a Guard member in satisfactory standing; complete basic and advanced individual training; and attend an approved accredited school to pursue a vocational, associate, bachelor or graduate program. Guard members may apply through their unit. Tuition (subject to the availability of funds) for up to $250 a credit hour, not to exceed cap outlined in National Guard Policy letter. *Award:* Grant for use in freshman, sophomore, junior, or senior years; renewable. *Eligibility Requirements:* Applicant must be enrolled or expecting to enroll full- or part-time at a two-year or technical institution or university; resident of Kansas and studying in Kentucky. Available to U.S. citizens. Applicant must have national guard experience. *Application Requirements:* Application form. **Deadline:** continuous.

Contact Becky Gilpatrick, Director of Student Aid, Kentucky Higher Education Assistance Authority (KHEAA), PO Box 798, Frankfort, KY 40602-0798. *E-mail:* rgilpatrick@kheaa.com. *Phone:* 800-928-8926. *Fax:* 502-696-7373. *Website:* http://www.kheaa.com/.

Kentucky Transportation Cabinet Civil Engineering Scholarship Program. Scholarships awarded to qualified Kentucky residents who wish to study civil engineering at University of Kentucky, Western Kentucky University, University of Louisville or Kentucky State University. Applicant should be a graduate of an accredited Kentucky high school or a Kentucky resident. Scholarship recipients are given opportunities to work for the Cabinet during summers and job opportunities upon graduation within the state of KY. Civil Engineering. *Award:* Scholarship for use in freshman, sophomore, junior, or senior years; renewable. *Award amount:* $12,400–$51,200. *Number of awards:* 15–30. *Eligibility Requirements:* Applicant must be enrolled or expecting to enroll full-time at a four-year institution or university; resident of Kentucky and studying in Kentucky. Available to U.S. and non-U.S. citizens. *Application Requirements:* Application form, essay, interview. **Deadline:** February 1.

Contact Cherie Mertz, Scholarship Program Coordinator, Kentucky Transportation Cabinet, 200 Mero Street, 6th Floor East, Frankfort, KY 40622. *E-mail:* Cherie.Mertz@ky.gov. *Phone:* 502-564-3730. *Website:* http://transportation.ky.gov/Education/Pages/Scholarships.aspx.

Kentucky Tuition Grant (KTG). Grants up to $3,000 available to Kentucky residents who are full-time undergraduates at an independent college within the state. Based on financial need. Must submit FAFSA. *Award:* Grant for use in freshman, sophomore, junior, or senior years; not renewable. *Eligibility Requirements:* Applicant must be enrolled or expecting to enroll full-time at a two-year institution or university; resident of Kansas and studying in Kentucky. Available to U.S. citizens. *Application Requirements:* Application form, financial need analysis. **Deadline:** continuous.

Contact Becky Gilpatrick, Director of Student Aid, Kentucky Higher Education Assistance Authority (KHEAA), PO Box 798, Frankfort, KY 40602-0798. *E-mail:* rgilpatrick@kheaa.com. *Phone:* 800-928-8926. *Fax:* 502-696-7373. *Website:* http://www.kheaa.com/.

LOUISIANA

Chafee Educational and Training Voucher (ETV) Program. The Chafee Educational and Training Voucher (ETV) Program awards up to $5,000 annually during the academic year to qualified students who have been in the foster care system so they can pursue an academic college education or technical and skill training in college to be prepared to enter the workforce. The actual award amount is determined by the student's financial need, which is calculated in accordance with the Higher Education Act of 1965, as amended. *Award:* Scholarship for use in freshman, sophomore, junior, or senior years; renewable. *Eligibility Requirements:* Applicant must be age 14-26 and enrolled or expecting to enroll at a two-year or technical institution or university. *Application Requirements:* Application form.

GO Grant. This program is to provide a need-based component to the state's financial aid plan to support nontraditional and low to moderate-income students who need additional aid to afford the cost of attending college. To be eligible for Louisiana GO Grant, a student must: Be a Louisiana Resident; File a Free Application for Federal Student Aid (FAFSA); Receive a federal Pell grant; Have remaining financial need after deducting Estimated Family Contribution (EFC) and all federal/state/institutional grant or scholarship aid ("gift aid") from student's Cost of Attendance (COA); Be a student enrolled in an eligible Louisiana institution on at least a half-time basis (minimum 6 hours at semester school or 4 hours at a quarter school). *Award:* Grant for use in freshman, sophomore, junior, or senior years; renewable. *Award amount:* $300–$3000. *Eligibility Requirements:* Applicant must be enrolled or expecting to enroll full- or part-time at a two-year or technical institution or university and resident of Kentucky. *Application Requirements:* Application form.

Louisiana National Guard State Tuition Exemption Program. Renewable award for college undergraduates to receive tuition exemption upon satisfactory performance in the Louisiana National Guard. Applicant must attend a state-funded institution in Louisiana, be a resident and registered voter in Louisiana, meet the academic and residency requirements of the university attended, and provide documentation of Louisiana National Guard enlistment. The exemption can be used for up to 15 semesters. Minimum 2.5 GPA required. *Award:* Scholarship for use in freshman, sophomore, junior, or senior years; renewable. *Eligibility Requirements:* Applicant must be enrolled or expecting to enroll full- or part-time at a two-year or four-year or technical institution or university; resident of Louisiana and studying in Louisiana. Available to U.S. citizens. Applicant or parent must meet one or more of the following requirements: national guard experience; retired from active duty; disabled or killed as a result of military service; prisoner of war; or missing in action. *Application Requirements:* Application form, test scores, transcript. **Deadline:** continuous.

Contact Jona Hughes, Education Services Officer, Louisiana National Guard, Joint Task Force LA, Building 35, Jackson Barracks, JI-PD, New Orleans, LA 70146-0330. *E-mail:* hughesj@la-arng.ngb.army.mil. *Phone:* 504-278-8531 Ext. 8304. *Fax:* 504-278-8025. *Website:* http://geauxguard.com/organization/joint-force-headquarters-jfhq-la/.

Rockefeller State Wildlife Scholarship. For college undergraduates with a minimum of 60 credit hours who are majoring in Forestry, Wildlife, or Marine Science, and for college graduate students who are majoring in Forestry, Wildlife, or Marine Science. College undergraduates must have a grade point average of at least 2.50 to apply. College graduate students must have a grade point average of at least 3. 00 in order to apply. Renewable up to three years as an undergraduate and two years as a graduate student. Marine Biology; Marine/Ocean Engineering; Natural Resources; Oceanography. *Award:* Scholarship for use in freshman, sophomore, junior, senior, or graduate years; renewable. *Award amount:* \$2000–\$3000. *Eligibility Requirements:* Applicant must be enrolled or expecting to enroll full-time at an institution or university; resident of Kentucky and studying in Louisiana. Available to U.S. citizens. *Application Requirements:* Application form. **Deadline:** July 1.

Taylor Opportunity Program for Students Honors Award. Program awards 8 semesters or 12 terms of tuition to any Louisiana State postsecondary institution plus \$400 stipend per semester. Program awards 8 semesters or 12 terms of an amount equal to the weighted average public tuition to students attending a LAICU (Louisiana Association of Independent Colleges and Universities) institution plus \$400 stipend per semester. Program awards 8 semesters or 12 terms of an amount equal to the weighted average public tuition to two out-of-state Institutions for Hearing Impaired Students: Gallaudet University and Rochester Institute of Technology plus \$400 stipend per semester. When you submit the FAFSA, you have automatically applied for all four levels of TOPS, for Federal Pell Grants and Go Grants and for Federal Student Loans. Please do not send separate letters of application to the TOPS office. *Award:* Scholarship for use in freshman year; renewable. *Award amount:* \$793–\$3836. *Eligibility Requirements:* Applicant must be enrolled or expecting to enroll full-time at a two-year or technical institution or university; resident of Kentucky and studying in Louisiana. Available to U.S. citizens. *Application Requirements:* Application form, application form may be submitted online. **Deadline:** October 29.

Taylor Opportunity Program for Students Opportunity Level. Program awards 8 semesters or 12 terms of tuition to any Louisiana State postsecondary institution. Program awards 8 semesters or 12 terms of an amount equal to the weighted average public tuition to students attending a LAICU (Louisiana Association of Independent Colleges and Universities) institution. Program awards 8 semesters or 12 terms of an amount equal to the weighted average public tuition to two out-of-state Institutions for Hearing Impaired Students: Gallaudet University and Rochester Institute of Technology. When you submit the FAFSA, you have automatically applied for all four levels of TOPS, and for Federal Pell Grants and Go Grants. Please do not send separate letters of application to the TOPS office. *Award:* Scholarship for use in freshman year; renewable. *Award amount:* \$793–\$3731. *Eligibility Requirements:* Applicant must be enrolled or expecting to enroll full-time at a two-year or technical institution or university; resident of Kentucky and studying in Louisiana. Available to U.S. citizens. *Application Requirements:* Application form, application form may be submitted online. **Deadline:** July 1.

Taylor Opportunity Program for Students Performance Award. Program awards 8 semesters or 12 terms of tuition to any Louisiana State postsecondary institution plus \$200 stipend per semester. Program awards 8 semesters or 12 terms of an amount equal to the weighted average public tuition to students attending a LAICU (Louisiana Association of Independent Colleges and Universities) institution plus \$200 stipend per semester. Program awards 8 semesters or 12 terms of an amount equal to the weighted average public tuition to two out-of-state Institutions for Hearing Impaired Students: Gallaudet University and Rochester Institute of Technology plus \$200 stipend per semester. When you submit the FAFSA, you have automatically applied for all four levels of TOPS, for Federal Pell Grants and Go Grants and for Federal Student Loans. Please do not send separate letters of application to the TOPS office. *Award:* Scholarship for use in freshman, sophomore, junior, or senior years; renewable. *Award amount:* \$793–\$3836. *Eligibility Requirements:* Applicant must be enrolled or expecting to enroll full-time at a two-year or technical institution or university; resident of Kentucky and studying in Louisiana. Available to U.S. citizens. *Application Requirements:* Application form, application form may be submitted online. **Deadline:** October 29.

Taylor Opportunity Program for Students Tech Award. Program awards an amount equal to tuition for up to 4 semesters and two summers of technical training at a Louisiana postsecondary institution that offers a vocational or technical education certificate or diploma program, or a non-academic degree program; or up to \$1744 to an approved Proprietary or Cosmetology school. Must have completed the TOPS Opportunity core curriculum or the TOPS Tech core curriculum, must have achieved a 2.50 grade point average over the core curriculum only, and must have achieved an ACT score of 17 or an SAT score of 810. Program awards an amount equal to the weighted average public tuition for technical programs to students attending a LAICU private institution for technical training. When you submit the FAFSA, you have automatically applied for all four levels of TOPS, for Federal Pell Grants and Go Grants and Federal Student Loans. Please do not send separate letters of application to the TOPS office. *Award:* Scholarship for use in freshman year; renewable. *Award amount:* \$436–\$3985. *Number of awards:* 1,671. *Eligibility Requirements:* Applicant must be enrolled or expecting to enroll full-time at a technical institution; resident of Kentucky and studying in Louisiana. Available to U.S. citizens. *Application Requirements:* Application form, application form may be submitted online. **Deadline:** October 29.

MAINE

American Legion Auxiliary Department of Maine Daniel E. Lambert Memorial Scholarship. Scholarships to assist young men and women in continuing their education beyond high school. Must demonstrate financial need, must be a resident of the State of Maine, U.S. citizen, and parent must be a veteran. *Award:* Scholarship for use in freshman year; not renewable. *Award amount:* \$1000. *Number of awards:* up to 2. *Eligibility Requirements:* Applicant must be high school student; planning to enroll or expecting to enroll full-time at a four-year institution or university and resident of Maine. Available to U.S. citizens. Applicant or parent must meet one or more of the following requirements: general military experience; retired from active duty; disabled or killed as a result of military service; prisoner of war; or missing in action. *Application Requirements:* Application form, financial need analysis. **Deadline:** May 1.

Contact Mary Wells, Education Chairman. *E-mail:* aladeptsecme@verizon.net. *Phone:* 207-532-6007. *Website:* http://www.mainelegion.org/.

American Legion Auxiliary Department of Maine Past Presidents' Parley Nurses Scholarship. One-time award for child, grandchild, sister, or brother of veteran. Must be resident of Maine and wishing to continue education at accredited school in medical field. Must submit photo, doctor's statement, and evidence of civic activity. Minimum 3.5 GPA required. Health and Medical Sciences; Nursing. *Award:* Scholarship for use in freshman, sophomore, junior, or senior years; not renewable. *Award amount:* $300. *Number of awards:* 1. *Eligibility Requirements:* Applicant must be age 18 and over; enrolled or expecting to enroll full-time at a two-year or four-year or technical institution or university and resident of Maine. Applicant or parent of applicant must have employment or volunteer experience in community service. Available to U.S. citizens. Applicant or parent must meet one or more of the following requirements: general military experience; retired from active duty; disabled or killed as a result of military service; prisoner of war; or missing in action. *Application Requirements:* Application form, doctor's statement, personal photograph, recommendations or references, transcript. **Deadline:** March 31.

Contact Mary Wells, Education Chairman. *E-mail:* aladeptsecme@verizon.net. *Phone:* 207-532-6007. *Website:* http://www.mainelegion.org/.

EMBARK-Support for the College Journey. Scholarship for high school students who in their junior year have not made plans for college but are academically capable of success in college. Recipients are selected by their school principal or Guidance Director. Students must be entering a Maine Community College. Refer to website http://www.mccs.me.edu/our-programs/programs-for-high-school-students/early-college/ *Award:* Scholarship for use in freshman or sophomore years; renewable. *Award amount:* $2000. *Number of awards:* 425–500. *Eligibility Requirements:* Applicant must be high school student; planning to enroll or expecting to enroll full-time at a two-year institution; resident of Maine and studying in Maine. Available to U.S. citizens. *Application Requirements:* Application form, financial need analysis. **Deadline:** April 15.

Contact Mercedes Pour, Director of College Access, Maine Community College System, 54 Lighthouse Circle, South Portland, ME 04106. *E-mail:* mpour@mccs.me.edu. *Phone:* 207-699-4897. *Website:* http://www.mccs.me.edu/.

Maine Rural Rehabilitation Fund Scholarship Program. One-time scholarship open to Maine residents enrolled in or accepted by any school, college, or university. Must be full-time and demonstrate financial need. Those opting for a Maine institution given preference. Major must lead to an agricultural career. Minimum 3.0 GPA required. Agribusiness; Agriculture; Animal/Veterinary Sciences. *Award:* Scholarship for use in freshman, sophomore, junior, senior, graduate, or postgraduate years; not renewable. *Award amount:* $800–$2000. *Number of awards:* 10–20. *Eligibility Requirements:* Applicant must be enrolled or expecting to enroll full-time at a two-year or four-year or technical institution or university and resident of Maine. Available to U.S. citizens. *Application Requirements:* Application form, driver's license, financial need analysis, transcript. **Deadline:** June 15.

Contact Jane Aiudi, Director of Marketing. *E-mail:* jane.aiudi@maine.gov. *Phone:* 207-287-7628. *Fax:* 207-287-5576. *Website:* http://www.maine.gov/agriculture.

Maine State Grant Program. The Maine State Grant Program provides need-based grants to Maine undergraduate students. For the 2019-2020 academic year and the 2020–2021 academic year, the maximum grant award amount is $1,500. You must be enrolled at least half-time in an undergraduate program at an eligible institution. Because this is a need-based grant, your expected family contribution (EFC) must not exceed the maximum EFC set in any given year. The EFC for the 2019-2020 academic year is 5,800. The EFC for the 2020-2021 academic year is 4,500.* You must attend an eligible college/university in Maine. Students enrolled in NEBHE's Tuition Break Program, the New England Regional Student Program, may also be eligible. Contact FAME or your financial aid office for more information. You must attend an eligible college/university in Maine. Students enrolled in NEBHE's Tuition Break Program, the New England Regional Student Program, may also be eligible. Contact FAME or your financial aid office for more information. *Award:* Grant for use in freshman, sophomore, junior, or senior years; not renewable. *Eligibility Requirements:* Applicant must be enrolled or expecting to enroll full- or part-time at a two-year or technical institution or university; resident of Louisiana and studying in Connecticut, Maine, Massachusetts, New Hampshire, Rhode Island, Vermont. Available to U.S. citizens. *Application Requirements:* Financial need analysis. **Deadline:** May 1.

Contact Jennifer Lanphear, Education Programs Officer, Finance Authority of Maine, 5 Community Drive, Augusta, ME 04332. *E-mail:* education@famemaine.com. *Phone:* 207-620-3548. *Website:* http://www.famemaine.com/.

Tuition Waiver Programs. Provides tuition waivers for children and spouses of EMS personnel, firefighters, and law enforcement officers who have been killed in the line of duty and for students who were foster children under the custody of the Department of Human Services when they graduated from high school. Waivers valid at the University of Maine System, the Maine Technical College System, and Maine Maritime Academy. Applicant must reside and study in Maine. *Award:* Grant for use in freshman, sophomore, junior, or senior years; renewable. *Number of awards:* 30. *Eligibility Requirements:* Applicant must be enrolled or expecting to enroll full- or part-time at a two-year or four-year institution or university; resident of Maine and studying in Maine. Applicant or parent of applicant must have employment or volunteer experience in police/firefighting. Available to U.S. citizens. *Application Requirements:* Application form. **Deadline:** continuous.

Contact Jennifer Lanphear, Education Programs Officer, Finance Authority of Maine, 5 Community Drive, Augusta, ME 04332. *E-mail:*

education@famemaine.com. *Phone:* 207-620-3548. *Website:* http://www.famemaine.com/.

Veterans Dependents Educational Benefits-Maine. Tuition waiver award for dependent children who have not reached their 22nd birthday or spouses of veterans permanently and totally disabled resulting from service-connected disability; died from a service-connected disability; at time of death was totally and permanently disabled due to service-connected disability, but whose death was not related to the service-connected disability; or member of the Armed Forces on active duty who has been listed for more than 90 days as missing in action, captured or forcibly detained or interned in the line of duty. Benefits apply only to the University of Maine System, Maine community colleges and Maine Maritime Academy. Must be high school graduate. Must submit with application proof of veteran's VA disability along with dependent verification paperwork such as birth, marriage, or adoption certificate and proof of enrollment in degree program. *Award:* Scholarship for use in freshman, sophomore, junior, or senior years; not renewable. *Eligibility Requirements:* Applicant must be enrolled or expecting to enroll full- or part-time at a two-year or four-year institution or university; resident of Maine and studying in Maine. Available to U.S. citizens. Applicant or parent must meet one or more of the following requirements: general military experience; retired from active duty; disabled or killed as a result of military service; prisoner of war; or missing in action. *Application Requirements:* Application form, see application.

Contact Mrs. Paula Gagnon, Office Associate II, Maine Veterans Services, State House Station 117, Augusta, ME 04333-0117. *E-mail:* mainebvs@maine.gov. *Phone:* 207-430-6035. *Fax:* 207-626-4471. *Website:* http://www.maine.gov/dvem/bvs.

MASSACHUSETTS

DSS Adopted Children Tuition Waiver. Need-based tuition waiver for Massachusetts residents who are full-time undergraduate students. Must attend a Massachusetts public institution of higher education and be under 24 years of age. File the FAFSA after January 1. Contact school financial aid office for more information. *Award:* Scholarship for use in freshman, sophomore, junior, or senior years; renewable. *Eligibility Requirements:* Applicant must be age 24 or under; enrolled or expecting to enroll full-time at a two-year or four-year institution; resident of Massachusetts and studying in District of Columbia, Massachusetts, Pennsylvania, Vermont. Available to U. S. and non-Canadian citizens. *Application Requirements:* Application form.

Contact Clantha McCurdy, Senior Deputy Commissioner, Malden, MA 02148. *E-mail:* cmccurdy@dhe.mass.edu. *Phone:* 617-391-6098. *Fax:* 617-391-6085. *Website:* http://www.osfa.mass.edu/.

Massachusetts Assistance for Student Success Program. Provides need-based financial assistance to Massachusetts residents to attend undergraduate post-secondary institutions in Massachusetts, Pennsylvania, Vermont, and District of Columbia. High school seniors may apply. Expected Family Contribution (EFC) should be $3850. Timely filing of FAFSA required. *Award:* Grant for use in freshman, sophomore, junior, or senior years; not renewable. *Award amount:* $400–$1600. *Number of awards:* 47,000–50,000. *Eligibility Requirements:* Applicant must be enrolled or expecting to enroll full-time at a two-year or four-year or technical institution or university; resident of Massachusetts and studying in District of Columbia, Massachusetts, Pennsylvania, Vermont. Available to U.S. citizens. *Application Requirements:* Financial need analysis. **Deadline:** May 1.

Contact Clantha McCurdy, Senior Deputy Commissioner, Malden, MA 02148. *E-mail:* cmccurdy@dhe.mass.edu. *Phone:* 617-391-6098. *Fax:* 617-391-6085. *Website:* http://www.osfa.mass.edu/.

New England Regional Student Program-Tuition Break. Tuition discount for residents of six New England states (Connecticut, Maine, Massachusetts, New Hampshire, Rhode Island, Vermont). Students pay reduced out-of-state tuition at public colleges or universities in other New England states when enrolling in eligible majors and programs. Details are available at http://www.nebhe.org/tuitionbreak. *Award:* Scholarship for use in freshman, sophomore, junior, senior, or graduate years; renewable. *Eligibility Requirements:* Applicant must be enrolled or expecting to enroll full- or part-time at a two-year or four-year institution or university; resident of Connecticut, Maine, Massachusetts, New Hampshire, Rhode Island, Vermont and studying in Connecticut, Maine, Massachusetts, New Hampshire, Rhode Island, Vermont. Available to U.S. citizens. *Application Requirements:* Application form. **Deadline:** continuous.

Contact Wendy Lindsay, Senior Director of Regional Student Program, New England Board of Higher Education, 45 Temple Place, Boston, MA 02111. *E-mail:* tuitionbreak@nebhe.org. *Phone:* 617-533-9511. *Website:* http://www.nebhe.org/tuitionbreak.

MICHIGAN

American Legion Auxiliary Department of Michigan Medical Career Scholarship. Award for training in Michigan as registered nurse, licensed practical nurse, physical therapist, respiratory therapist, or in any medical career. Must be child, grandchild, great-grandchild, wife, or widow of honorably discharged or deceased veteran who has served during the eligibility dates for American Legion membership. Must be Michigan resident attending a Michigan school. Health and Medical Sciences; Nursing; Therapy/Rehabilitation. *Award:* Scholarship for use in freshman year; not renewable. *Award amount:* $500. *Number of awards:* 10–20. *Eligibility Requirements:* Applicant must be enrolled or expecting to enroll full-time at a two-year or technical institution or university; resident of Massachusetts and studying in Michigan. Available to U.S. citizens. Applicant must have general military experience. *Application Requirements:* Application form, financial need analysis. **Deadline:** March 15.

Contact Denise Carter, Department Secretary/Treasurer, American Legion Auxiliary Department of Michigan, 212 N. Verlinden Ave, Suite B, Lansing, MI 48915. *E-mail:* info@michalaux.org. *Phone:* 517-267-8809 Ext. 121. *Fax:* 517-371-3698. *Website:* http://www.michalaux.org/.

American Legion Auxiliary Department of Michigan Memorial

Scholarship. Scholarship for daughter, granddaughter, and great-granddaughter of any honorably discharged or deceased veteran of U.S. wars or conflicts. Must be Michigan resident for minimum of one year, female between 16 and 21 years, and attend college in Michigan. Must include copy of military discharge and copy of parent or guardian's IRS 1040 form. *Award:* Scholarship for use in freshman or sophomore years; not renewable. *Award amount:* $500. *Number of awards:* 10–20. *Eligibility Requirements:* Applicant must be age 16-21; enrolled or expecting to enroll full-time at a two-year or technical institution or university; female; resident of Massachusetts and studying in Michigan. Available to U.S. citizens. Applicant must have general military experience. *Application Requirements:* Application form, financial need analysis. **Deadline:** February 15.

Contact Denise Carter, Department Secretary/Treasurer, American Legion Auxiliary Department of Michigan, 212 N. Verlinden Ave, Suite B, Lansing, MI 48915. *E-mail:* info@michalaux.org. *Phone:* 517-267-8809 Ext. 121. *Fax:* 517-371-3698. *Website:* http://www.michalaux.org/.

American Legion Auxiliary Department of Michigan Scholarship for Non-Traditional Student. Applicant must be a dependent of a veteran. Must be one of the following: nontraditional student returning to classroom after some period of time in which their education was interrupted, student over the age of 22 attending college for the first time to pursue a degree, or student over the age of 22 attending a trade or vocational school. Applicants must be Michigan residents only and attend Michigan institution. Judging based on need, character/leadership, scholastic standing, and initiative/goal. *Award:* Scholarship for use in freshman, sophomore, junior, or senior years; renewable. *Award amount:* $500. *Number of awards:* 1. *Eligibility Requirements:* Applicant must be age 22-99; enrolled or expecting to enroll full- or part-time at a two-year or technical institution or university; resident of Massachusetts and studying in Michigan. Available to U.S. citizens. Applicant must have general military experience. *Application Requirements:* Application form, financial need analysis. **Deadline:** February 15.

Contact Denise Carter, Department Secretary/Treasurer, American Legion Auxiliary Department of Michigan, 212 N. Verlinden Ave, Suite B, Lansing, MI 48915. *E-mail:* info@michalaux.org. *Phone:* 517-267-8809 Ext. 121. *Fax:* 517-371-3698. *Website:* http://www.michalaux.org/.

Children of Veterans Tuition Grant. The program is designed to provide undergraduate tuition assistance to certain children older than 16 and less than 26 years of age who have been Michigan residents for the 12 months prior to application. To be eligible, a student must be the natural or adopted child of a Michigan veteran. Stepchildren of the veteran are not eligible. The veteran must have been a legal resident of Michigan immediately before entering military service and must not have later resided outside of Michigan for more than two years; or the veteran must have established legal residency in Michigan after entering military service. *Award:* Grant for use in freshman, sophomore, junior, or senior years; renewable. *Eligibility Requirements:* Applicant must be age 16-26; enrolled or expecting to enroll full- or part-time at an institution or university; resident of Massachusetts and studying in Michigan. Available to U.S. citizens. Applicant or parent must meet one or more of the following requirements: general military experience; retired from active duty; disabled or killed as a result of military service; prisoner of war; or missing in action. *Application Requirements:* Application form.

Michigan Competitive Scholarship. Renewable awards for Michigan resident to pursue undergraduate study at a Michigan institution. Awards are restricted to tuition and mandatory fees and pay up to a maximum of $1,000 for the academic year at participating institutions. It is the responsibility of the college financial aid office to coordinate all sources of aid for which a student may be eligible. Other gift aid may reduce or cancel this award. Must attain SAT score of at least 1200. Must maintain at least a 2.0 grade point average and meet the college's academic progress requirements. Must file Free Application for Federal Student Aid *Award:* Scholarship for use in freshman, sophomore, junior, or senior years; renewable. *Eligibility Requirements:* Applicant must be enrolled or expecting to enroll full- or part-time at a two-year institution or university; resident of Massachusetts and studying in Michigan. Available to U.S. citizens. *Application Requirements:* Application form, financial need analysis. **Deadline:** March 1.

Michigan Tuition Grant. Need-based program. Students must be Michigan residents and attend a Michigan private, nonprofit, degree-granting college. Must file the Free Application for Federal Student Aid and meet the college's academic progress requirements. *Award:* Grant for use in freshman, sophomore, junior, or senior years; renewable. *Eligibility Requirements:* Applicant must be enrolled or expecting to enroll full- or part-time at an institution or university; resident of Massachusetts and studying in Michigan. Available to U.S. citizens. *Application Requirements:* Application form, financial need analysis. **Deadline:** March 1.

Tuition Incentive Program. The Tuition Incentive Program (TIP) was established in 1987 under the Annual Higher Education Appropriations Act as an incentive program that encourages eligible students to complete high school by providing tuition assistance for the first two years of college and beyond. Students must be enrolled in courses leading to an associate degree or certificate. Certificate courses are defined as at least a one-year training program that leads to a certificate (or other recognized educational credential), which prepares students for gainful employment in a recognized occupation. Students must meet a Medicaid eligibility history requirement. Eligible students must apply prior to high school graduation (high school diploma or its recognized equivalent). The program targets students with financial need so students are encouraged to also complete the FAFSA. Funds are appropriated annually in the Higher Education Appropriations Act. This program is administered by the Student Scholarships and Grants Division. http://www.michigan.gov/mistudentaid/0,4636,7-128-60969_61016-274565—,00.html *Award:* Grant for use in freshman, sophomore, junior, or senior years; renewable. *Eligibility Requirements:* Applicant must be enrolled or expecting to enroll full- or part-time at a two-year institution or university; resident of Massachusetts and studying in

Michigan. Available to U.S. citizens. *Application Requirements:* Application form, financial need analysis. **Deadline:** continuous.

MINNESOTA

Minnesota GI Bill Program. The Minnesota GI Bill program provides postsecondary financial assistance to eligible Minnesota veterans and service members as well as eligible spouses and children of deceased or severely disabled eligible Minnesota veterans. Full-time undergraduate or graduate students may be eligible to receive up to $1,000 per semester or term and part-time students may be eligible to receive up to $500 per semester or term. Eligible students may receive up to $3,000 per award year and up to the lifetime maximum of $10,000. *Award:* Grant for use in freshman, sophomore, junior, senior, graduate, or postgraduate years; not renewable. *Award amount:* $50–$3000. *Eligibility Requirements:* Applicant must be enrolled or expecting to enroll full- or part-time at a two-year or four-year or technical institution or university; resident of Minnesota and studying in Minnesota. Available to U.S. citizens. *Application Requirements:* Application form. **Deadline:** continuous.

Contact Meghan Flores, State Grant Manager, Minnesota Office of Higher Education, 1450 Energy Park Drive, Suite 350, St. Paul, MN 55108. *E-mail:* meghan.flores@state.mn.us. *Phone:* 651-355-0610 Ext. 2. *Fax:* 651-642-0675. *Website:* http://www.ohe.state.mn.us.

Minnesota Indian Scholarship. The Minnesota Indian Scholarship Program provides postsecondary financial assistance to eligible Minnesota resident students who are of one-fourth or more American Indian ancestry and demonstrate financial need for an award. Scholarships are available to eligible American Indian undergraduate students enrolled at least 3/4 time and graduate students enrolled at least half time. The award amount is based on need up to $4,000 per year for undergraduate students and up to $6,000 for graduate students *Award:* Scholarship for use in freshman, sophomore, junior, senior, graduate, or postgraduate years; not renewable. *Eligibility Requirements:* Applicant must be of Arumanian/Ulacedo-Romanian heritage; American Indian/Alaska Native; high school student; planning to enroll or expecting to enroll full- or part-time at a two-year or four-year or technical institution or university; resident of Minnesota and studying in Minnesota. Available to U.S. and Canadian citizens. *Application Requirements:* Application form, financial need analysis. **Deadline:** continuous.

Contact Meghan Flores, State Grant Manager, Minnesota Office of Higher Education, 1450 Energy Park Drive, Suite 350, St. Paul, MN 55108. *E-mail:* meghan.flores@state.mn.us. *Phone:* 651-355-0610 Ext. 2. *Fax:* 651-642-0675. *Website:* http://www.ohe.state.mn.us.

Minnesota State Grant Program. Need-based grant program available for Minnesota residents attending Minnesota colleges. Student covers 50% of cost with remainder covered by Pell Grant, parent contribution and state grant. Students apply with FAFSA and colleges administer the program on campus. *Award:* Grant for use in freshman, sophomore, junior, or senior years; not renewable. *Award amount:* $100–$11,334. *Number of awards:* 71,000–120,000. *Eligibility Requirements:* Applicant must be age 17 and over; enrolled or expecting to enroll full- or part-time at a two-year or four-year or technical institution or university; resident of Minnesota and studying in Minnesota. Available to U.S. citizens. *Application Requirements:* Application form, financial need analysis. **Deadline:** continuous.

Contact Meghan Flores, State Grant Manager, Minnesota Office of Higher Education, 1450 Energy Park Drive, Suite 350, St. Paul, MN 55108. *E-mail:* meghan.flores@state.mn.us. *Phone:* 651-355-0610 Ext. 2. *Fax:* 651-642-0675. *Website:* http://www.ohe.state.mn.us.

Minnesota State Veterans' Dependents Assistance Program. Tuition assistance to dependents of persons considered to be prisoner-of-war or missing in action after August 1, 1958. Must be Minnesota resident attending Minnesota two- or four-year school. *Award:* Scholarship for use in freshman, sophomore, junior, or senior years; renewable. *Award amount:* $249–$250. *Number of awards:* 100–200. *Eligibility Requirements:* Applicant must be enrolled or expecting to enroll full- or part-time at a two-year or four-year institution; resident of Minnesota and studying in Minnesota. Available to U.S. citizens. *Application Requirements:* Application form. **Deadline:** continuous.

Contact Meghan Flores, State Grant Manager, Minnesota Office of Higher Education, 1450 Energy Park Drive, Suite 350, St. Paul, MN 55108. *E-mail:* meghan.flores@state.mn.us. *Phone:* 651-355-0610 Ext. 2. *Fax:* 651-642-0675. *Website:* http://www.ohe.state.mn.us.

Postsecondary Child Care Grant Program-Minnesota. Grant available for students who are not receiving MFIP (TANF) and have children in day care. Based on financial need. Cannot exceed actual child care costs or maximum award chart (based on income). Must be Minnesota resident. For use at Minnesota two- or four-year school, including public technical colleges. Available until student has attended college for the equivalent of four full-time academic years. *Award:* Grant for use in freshman, sophomore, junior, or senior years; not renewable. *Award amount:* $100–$2800. *Number of awards:* 1–3,500. *Eligibility Requirements:* Applicant must be enrolled or expecting to enroll full- or part-time at a two-year or four-year or technical institution or university; resident of Minnesota and studying in Minnesota. Available to U.S. citizens. *Application Requirements:* Application form, financial need analysis. **Deadline:** continuous.

Contact Brenda Larter, Program Administrator, Minnesota Office of Higher Education, 1450 Energy Park Drive, Suite 350, St. Paul, MN 55108-5227. *E-mail:* brenda.larter@state.mn.us. *Phone:* 651-355-0612. *Website:* http://www.ohe.state.mn.us.

Safety Officers' Survivor Grant Program. Grant for eligible survivors of Minnesota public safety officers killed in the line of duty. Safety officers who have been permanently or totally disabled in the line of duty are also eligible. Must be used at a Minnesota institution participating in State Grant Program. Write for details. Must submit proof of death or disability and Public Safety Officers Benefit Fund Certificate. Must apply for renewal each year. Five-year limit on awards. *Award:* Grant for use in freshman, sophomore, junior, senior, or graduate years; not renewable. *Award amount:* $1–$13,840. *Number of awards:* 1–10. *Eligibility Requirements:* Applicant must be age 23 or under; enrolled or expecting to enroll full- or part-time at a two-year or four-year or technical institution or university; resident of Minnesota and studying in Minnesota. Applicant or parent of applicant must have employment or volunteer experience in police/firefighting. Available to U.S. citizens. *Application Requirements:* Application form. **Deadline:** continuous.

Contact Brenda Larter, Program Administrator. *E-mail:* brenda.larter@state.mn.us. *Phone:* 651-355-0612. *Website:* http://www.ohe.state.mn.us.

MISSISSIPPI

Higher Education Legislative Plan (HELP). Eligible applicant must be resident of Mississippi and apply for the first time as a freshman and/or sophomore student who graduated from high school within the immediate past two years. Must demonstrate need as determined by the results of the FAFSA, documenting an average family adjusted gross income of $36,500 or less over the prior two years. Must be enrolled full-time at a Mississippi college or university, have a GPA of 2.5, have completed a specific high school core curriculum, and have scored 20 on the ACT. *Award:* Grant for use in freshman, sophomore, junior, or senior years; renewable. *Award amount:* $340–$7344. *Number of awards:* 3,357. *Eligibility Requirements:* Applicant must be enrolled or expecting to enroll full-time at a two-year or four-year institution or university; resident of Mississippi and studying in Mississippi. Available to U. S. citizens. *Application Requirements:* Application form, financial need analysis. **Deadline:** March 31.

Law Enforcement Officers/Firemen Scholarship. Financial assistance to dependent children and spouses of any Mississippi law enforcement officer, full-time fire fighter or volunteer fire fighter who has suffered fatal injuries or wounds or become permanently and totally disabled as a result of injuries or wounds which occurred in the performance of the official and appointed duties of his or her office. This financial assistance is offered as an eight semester tuition and room scholarship at any state-supported college or university in Mississippi. *Award:* Scholarship for use in freshman, sophomore, junior, or senior years; renewable. *Award amount:* $2010–$12,854. *Number of awards:* 11–30. *Eligibility Requirements:* Applicant must be age 23 or under; enrolled or expecting to enroll full-time at a two-year or four-year institution or university; resident of Mississippi and studying in Mississippi. Applicant or parent of applicant must have employment or volunteer experience in police/firefighting. Available to U.S. citizens. *Application Requirements:* Application form. **Deadline:** continuous.

Mississippi Eminent Scholars Grant. Award for an entering freshmen or as a renewal for sophomore, junior or senior, who are residents of Mississippi. Applicants must achieve a GPA of 3.5 and must have scored 29 on the ACT. Must enroll full-time at an eligible Mississippi college or university. *Award:* Grant for use in freshman, sophomore, junior, or senior years; not renewable. *Award amount:* $1157–$2500. *Number of awards:* 2,908. *Eligibility Requirements:* Applicant must be enrolled or expecting to enroll full-time at a two-year or four-year institution or university; resident of Mississippi and studying in Mississippi. Available to U. S. citizens. *Application Requirements:* Application form. **Deadline:** September 15.

Mississippi Resident Tuition Assistance Grant. Must be a resident of Mississippi enrolled full-time at an eligible Mississippi college or university. Must maintain a minimum 2.5 GPA each semester. MTAG awards may be up to $500 per academic year for freshman and sophomores and $1000 per academic year for juniors and seniors. *Award:* Grant for use in freshman, sophomore, junior, or senior years; not renewable. *Award amount:* $17–$1000. *Number of awards:* 18,244–18,244. *Eligibility Requirements:* Applicant must be enrolled or expecting to enroll full-time at a two-year or four-year institution or university; resident of Mississippi and studying in Mississippi. Available to U.S. citizens. *Application Requirements:* Application form. **Deadline:** September 15.

MISSOURI

Access Missouri Financial Assistance Program. Need-based program that provides awards to students who are enrolled full time and have an expected family contribution (EFC) of $12,000 or less based on their Free Application for Federal Student Aid (FAFSA). Awards vary depending on EFC and the type of post-secondary school. Applicant must not be pursuing a degree or certificate in theology or divinity and not have received your first bachelor's degree, completed the required hours for a bachelor's degree, or completed 150 semester credit hours. *Award:* Grant for use in freshman, sophomore, junior, or senior years; not renewable. *Award amount:* $300–$2850. *Eligibility Requirements:* Applicant must be enrolled or expecting to enroll full-time at a two-year or technical institution or university; resident of Mississippi and studying in Missouri. Available to U.S. citizens. *Application Requirements:* **Deadline:** April 1.

Bright Flight Program. Program encourages top-ranked high school seniors to attend approved Missouri post-secondary schools. Must be a Missouri resident and a U.S. citizen or permanent resident. Must have a composite score on the ACT or SAT in the top 5 percent of all Missouri students taking those tests. Students with scores in the top 3 percent are eligible for an annual award of up to $3000 (up to $1500 each semester). Students with scores in the top 4% and 5% are eligible for an annual award of up to $1000 (up to $500 each semester). Award amounts, and the availability of the award for students in the 4% and 5%, are subject to change based on the amount of funding allocated for the program in the legislative session. Applicant must also not be pursuing a degree or certificate in theology or divinity. *Award:* Scholarship for use in freshman, sophomore, junior, or senior years; renewable. *Award amount:* $1000–$3000. *Eligibility Requirements:* Applicant must be enrolled or expecting to enroll full-time at a two-year or technical institution or university; resident of Mississippi and studying in Missouri. Available to U.S. citizens. *Application Requirements:* **Deadline:** July 31.

Lillie Lois Ford Scholarship Fund. Two awards of $1,000 each are given each year. One to a boy who has attended a full session of The American

Legion Boys State of Missouri or a full session of the Department's Cadet Patrol Academy. The second award is given to a girl who has attended a full session of The American Legion Auxiliary's Girls State program or a full session of the Department's Cadet Patrol Academy. *Award:* Scholarship for use in freshman year; not renewable. *Award amount:* $1000. *Number of awards:* 2. *Eligibility Requirements:* Applicant must be high school student; age 20 or under; planning to enroll or expecting to enroll full-time at a two-year institution or university; single and resident of Mississippi. Available to U. S. citizens. Applicant or parent must meet one or more of the following requirements: general military experience; retired from active duty; disabled or killed as a result of military service; prisoner of war; or missing in action. *Application Requirements:* Application form, financial need analysis. **Deadline:** April 20.

Contact Mr. John Buckwalter, Chair, Education and Scholarship Committee, American Legion Department of Missouri, P.O. Box 179, Jefferson City, MO 65102-0179. *Phone:* 660-627-4713. *Website:* http://www.missourilegion.org/.

Marguerite Ross Barnett Memorial Scholarship. Scholarship was established for students who are employed while attending school part-time. Must be enrolled at least half-time but less than full-time at a participating Missouri postsecondary school, be employed and compensated for at least 20 hours per week, be 18 years of age, be a Missouri resident and a U.S. citizen or a permanent resident. Applicant must also not be pursuing a degree or certificate in theology or divinity, not received their first bachelor's degree or completed 150 semester credit hours, or an employee under the Title IV College Work Study program. *Award:* Scholarship for use in freshman, sophomore, junior, or senior years; renewable. *Eligibility Requirements:* Applicant must be age 18 and over; enrolled or expecting to enroll part-time at a two-year or technical institution or university; resident of Mississippi and studying in Missouri. Available to U.S. citizens. *Application Requirements:* **Deadline:** August 1.

NEBRASKA

Nebraska Opportunity Grant. Available to undergraduates attending a participating postsecondary institution in Nebraska. Must demonstrate financial need. Nebraska residency required. Awards determined by each participating institution. Student must complete the Free Application for Federal Student Aid (FAFSA) to apply. Contact financial aid office at institution for additional information. *Award:* Grant for use in freshman, sophomore, junior, or senior years; not renewable. *Award amount:* $100–$4458. *Eligibility Requirements:* Applicant must be enrolled or expecting to enroll full- or part-time at a two-year or four-year or technical institution or university; resident of Nebraska and studying in Nebraska. Available to U.S. citizens. *Application Requirements:* Application form may be submitted online (https://studentaid.ed.gov/sa/fafsa), financial need analysis. **Deadline:** continuous.

Contact Mr. J. Ritchie Morrow, Financial Aid Officer, Nebraska's Coordinating Commission for Postsecondary Education, 140 North 8th Street, Suite 300, PO Box 95005, Lincoln, NE 68509-5005. *E-mail:* Ritchie.Morrow@nebraska.gov. *Phone:* 402-471-2847. *Website:* https://ccpe.nebraska.gov/.

NEVADA

CouponChief.com Scholarship Program. We at CouponChief.com want to support young leaders that understand frugality and saving money, and how the skills and knowledge of using coupons can contribute to that end. We will award 1 scholarship winner with $1000 to put towards education every year. *Award:* Scholarship for use in freshman, sophomore, junior, senior, graduate, or postgraduate years; not renewable. *Award amount:* $1000. *Number of awards:* 1. *Eligibility Requirements:* Applicant must be enrolled or expecting to enroll full- or part-time at a two-year or four-year or technical institution or university. Available to U.S. citizens. *Application Requirements:* **Deadline:** July 31.

Governor Guinn Millennium Scholarship. Scholarship for Nevada residents. Student must graduate from a public or private high school within Nevada with a minimum GPA of 3.25. Must complete core curriculum. Maximum award is $10,000 paid on a per-credit hour basis, up to 15 credits each semester. Student must acknowledge award and use it within 6 years of high school graduation. *Award:* Scholarship for use in freshman, sophomore, junior, or senior years; renewable. *Eligibility Requirements:* Applicant must be enrolled or expecting to enroll full-time at a two-year or four-year institution or university; resident of Nevada and studying in Nevada. Available to U.S. citizens.

Contact Linda English, Executive Director. *E-mail:* info@nevadatreasurer.gov. *Phone:* 702-486-3889. *Fax:* 702-486-3246. *Website:* http://www.nevadatreasurer.gov/.

NEW HAMPSHIRE

Scholarships for Orphans of Veterans. Scholarship to provide financial assistance (room, board, books and supplies) to children of parents who served in World War II, Korean Conflict, Vietnam (Southeast Asian Conflict) or the Gulf Wars, or any other operation for which the armed forces expeditionary medal or theater of operations service medal was awarded to the veteran. Must be between the ages of 16 and 25 to qualify and be residents of New Hampshire studying at public New Hampshire colleges and universities. *Award:* Scholarship for use in freshman, sophomore, junior, senior, graduate, or postgraduate years; renewable. *Award amount:* $1000–$2500. *Number of awards:* 1. *Eligibility Requirements:* Applicant must be age 16-25; enrolled or expecting to enroll full-time at a two-year or four-year institution or university; resident of New Hampshire and studying in New Hampshire. Available to U.S. citizens. Applicant or parent must meet one or more of the following requirements: general military experience; retired from active duty; disabled or killed as a result of military service; prisoner of war; or missing in action. *Application Requirements:* Application form. **Deadline:** September 1.

Contact Mrs. Pat Moquin, Program Assistant II, N.H. Department of Education, Division of Higher Education - Higher Education Commission, 101 Pleasant Street, Concord, NH 03301. *E-mail:* patricia.moquin@doe.nh.gov. *Phone:* 603-271-0289. *Website:* http://www.education.nh.gov/highered.

NEW JERSEY

New Jersey Army National Guard Tuition Waiver. The New Jersey Army National Guard Tuition Waiver Program is available to all 6400 members of the New Jersey Army National Guard. This program waives all tuition at all public New Jersey institutions of higher learning up to 16 semester hours per semester for technical, trade, undergraduate, graduate, and professional studies. Membership in the National Guard is a requirement for this program. Minimum requirements to join the NJ Army National Guard are: be 17-35 years old, be at least a high school junior, be free of felony convictions, and generally be in good health. Call, text, or email Anthony Larobina at (908) 812-0707 Anthony.j.larobina.mil@mail.mil to find out if you are qualified. *Award:* Grant for use in freshman, sophomore, junior, senior, graduate, or postgraduate years; renewable. *Award amount:* $14,000. *Number of awards:* 6,400. *Eligibility Requirements:* Applicant must be age 17-35; enrolled or expecting to enroll full- or part-time at a two-year or four-year or technical institution or university and studying in New Jersey. Available to U.S. citizens. Applicant must have national guard experience. *Application Requirements:* Applicant's must contact Anthony Larobina to be emailed an application. **Deadline:** continuous.

New Jersey War Orphans Tuition Assistance. $500 scholarship to children of those service personnel who died while in the military or due to service-connected disabilities, or who are officially listed as missing in action by the U.S. Department of Defense. Must be a resident of New Jersey for at least one year immediately preceding the filing of the application and be between the ages of 16 and 21 at the time of application. *Award:* Scholarship for use in freshman, sophomore, junior, or senior years; renewable. *Award amount:* $500. *Eligibility Requirements:* Applicant must be age 16-21; enrolled or expecting to enroll full-time at a four-year institution or university and resident of New Jersey. Available to U.S. citizens. Applicant or parent must meet one or more of the following requirements: general military experience; retired from active duty; disabled or killed as a result of military service; prisoner of war; or missing in action. *Application Requirements:* Application form.

Contact Patricia Richter, Veterans Service Officer, New Jersey Department of Military and Veterans Affairs, PO Box 340, Trenton, NJ 08625-0340. *E-mail:* patty.richter@dmava.nj.gov. *Phone:* 609-530-6854. *Fax:* 609-530-6970. *Website:* http://www.state.nj.us/military.

POW-MIA Tuition Benefit Program. Free undergraduate college tuition provided to any child born or adopted before or during the period of time his or her parent was officially declared a prisoner of war or person missing in action after January 1, 1960. The POW-MIA must have been a New Jersey resident at the time he or she entered the service. Child of veteran must attend either a public or private institution in New Jersey. A copy of DD 1300 must be furnished with the application. Minimum 2.5 GPA required. *Award:* Scholarship for use in freshman, sophomore, junior, or senior years; renewable. *Eligibility Requirements:* Applicant must be enrolled or expecting to enroll full-time at a two-year or four-year or technical institution or university; resident of New Jersey and studying in New Jersey. Available to U. S. citizens. Applicant or parent must meet one or more of the following requirements: general military experience; retired from active duty; disabled or killed as a result of military service; prisoner of war; or missing in action. *Application Requirements:* Application form.

Contact Patricia Richter, Veterans Service Officer, New Jersey Department of Military and Veterans Affairs, PO Box 340, Trenton, NJ 08625-0340. *E-mail:* patty.richter@dmava.nj.gov. *Phone:* 609-530-6854. *Fax:* 609-530-6970. *Website:* http://www.state.nj.us/military.

Veterans Tuition Credit Program-New Jersey. Award for New Jersey resident veterans who served in the armed forces between December 31, 1960, and May 7, 1975. Must have been a New Jersey resident at time of induction or discharge or for two years immediately prior to application. *Award:* Scholarship for use in freshman, sophomore, junior, or senior years; renewable. *Award amount:* $200–$400. *Eligibility Requirements:* Applicant must be enrolled or expecting to enroll full- or part-time at a two-year or four-year or technical institution or university and resident of New Jersey. Available to U. S. citizens. Applicant or parent must meet one or more of the following requirements: general military experience; retired from active duty; disabled or killed as a result of military service; prisoner of war; or missing in action. *Application Requirements:* Application form.

Contact Patricia Richter, Veterans Service Officer, New Jersey Department of Military and Veterans Affairs, PO Box 340, Trenton, NJ 08625-0340. *E-mail:* patty.richter@dmava.nj.gov. *Phone:* 609-530-6854. *Fax:* 609-530-6970. *Website:* http://www.state.nj.us/military.

NEW MEXICO

Children of Deceased Veterans Scholarship-New Mexico. Award for New Mexico residents who are children of veterans killed as a result of service, prisoner of war, or veterans missing in action. Must be between ages 16 and 26. For use at New Mexico schools for undergraduate study. Must submit parent's death certificate and DD form 214. *Award:* Scholarship for use in freshman, sophomore, junior, or senior years; not renewable. *Award amount:* $300. *Number of awards:* 49–50. *Eligibility Requirements:* Applicant must be age 16-26; enrolled or expecting to enroll full- or part-time at a two-year or four-year or technical institution or university; resident of New Mexico and studying in New Mexico. Available to U.S. citizens. *Application Requirements:* Application form.

Contact Mr. Dale Movius, Director, State Benefits, New Mexico Department of Veterans' Services, 407 Galisteo Street, Room 134, Santa Fe, NM 87501. *E-mail:* dalej.movius@state.nm.us. *Phone:* 505-827-6300. *Website:* http://www.nmdvs.org.

New Mexico Vietnam Veteran Scholarship. Award for Vietnam veterans who have been New Mexico residents for a minimum of ten years and are attending state-funded postsecondary schools. Must have been awarded the Vietnam Campaign medal. Must submit DD 214 and discharge papers. *Award:* Scholarship for use in freshman, sophomore, junior, or senior years; renewable. *Award amount:* $3500–$4000. *Number of awards:* 100. *Eligi-*

bility Requirements: Applicant must be enrolled or expecting to enroll full- or part-time at a two-year or four-year or technical institution or university; resident of New Mexico and studying in New Mexico. Available to U.S. citizens. *Application Requirements:* Application form.

Contact Mr. Dale Movius, Director, State Benefits, New Mexico Department of Veterans' Services, 407 Galisteo Street, Room 134, Santa Fe, NM 87501. *E-mail:* Dalej.movius@state.nm.us. *Phone:* 505-827-6300. *Website:* http://www.nmdvs.org.

New Mexico Wartime Veterans Scholarship. Award for Wartime Veterans who have been a New Mexico resident for a minimum of ten years and are attending state-funded postsecondary schools. Must have been awarded a campaign medal such as the Southwest Asia Service Medal, Global War on Terrorism Expeditionary Medal, Iraq Campaign Medal, Afghanistan Campaign Medal or any other medal issued for service in the Armed Forces of the United States in support of any U.S. Military Campaign or armed conflict as defined by congress or presidential order or service after August 1, 1990. *Award:* Scholarship for use in freshman, sophomore, junior, senior, or graduate years; renewable. *Award amount:* $3500–$4000. *Number of awards:* 100. *Eligibility Requirements:* Applicant must be enrolled or expecting to enroll full- or part-time at a two-year or four-year or technical institution or university; resident of New Mexico and studying in New Mexico. Available to U.S. citizens. Applicant must have general military experience. *Application Requirements:* Application form.

Contact Mr. Dale Movius, Director, State Benefits, New Mexico Department of Veterans' Services, 407 Galiesteo St, Room 134, Santa Fe, NM 87501. *E-mail:* dalej.movius@state.nm.us. *Phone:* 505-827-6374. *Website:* http://www.nmdvs.org.

NEW YORK

Alexander and Maude Hadden Scholarship. Youth Foundation offers exceptional students with financial need an award of $2500 to $4000 per year which is renewable for four years at the foundation's discretion. Minimum GPA of 3.5 required, community service and extra curricular activities expected. Must write Foundation for information and application request form. *Award:* Scholarship for use in freshman, sophomore, junior, or senior years; renewable. *Award amount:* $2500–$4000. *Number of awards:* 96–108. *Eligibility Requirements:* Applicant must be enrolled or expecting to enroll full-time at a four-year institution or university. Applicant or parent of applicant must have employment or volunteer experience in community service. Available to U.S. citizens. *Application Requirements:* Application form, community service, essay, financial need analysis, personal photograph. **Deadline:** February 28.

Contact Ms. Johanna Lee, Executive Administrator. *E-mail:* YouthFdn@aol.com. *Phone:* 212-840-6291. *Fax:* 212-840-6747. *Website:* http://fdnweb.org/youthfdn.

DAAD University Summer Course Grant. Scholarships are awarded to full-time degree students of Canadian or U. S. colleges, sophomore/2nd year and higher, for the pursuit of summer courses at universities in Germany. It is open to applicants of any major but there is a prerequisite of at least two years of college-level German (B1) or the equivalent German language fluency. Courses are three to four weeks in duration, take place at many locations in Germany (universities), are taught in German, and topics include German language, literature, current affairs, political science, history, culture, arts, film and media, economics, linguistics, law, translation and interpretation, and test prep for German language proficiency examinations. Accommodations are arranged by the host institution. Foreign Language. *Award:* Grant for use in sophomore, junior, or senior years; not renewable. *Eligibility Requirements:* Applicant must be enrolled or expecting to enroll full-time at a four-year institution or university and must have an interest in German language/culture. Available to U.S. and non-U.S. citizens. *Application Requirements:* Application form, essay.

Gardiner Foundation Scholarship. For a young person, losing a family member can be a devastating experience. However, losing multiple family members all at once is almost unthinkable. That's what happened to Dexter Gardiner, who on July 9, 2006 lost six family members in a tragic car accident on the Bronx River Parkway. Yet despite the loss, Dexter chose to use the tragedy as a way to help others who have experienced similar situations in losing beloved family members unexpectedly. Needless to say, for those left behind, especially children whose college education may suddenly be in doubt due to financial concerns, the world can suddenly seem very uncertain. *Award:* Scholarship for use in sophomore or senior years; renewable. *Award amount:* $1500. *Number of awards:* 4–5. *Eligibility Requirements:* Applicant must be enrolled or expecting to enroll full-time at an institution or university. Available to U.S. citizens. *Application Requirements:* Application form, essay. **Deadline:** July 15.

New York State Aid to Native Americans. Award for enrolled members of a New York State tribe and their children who are attending or planning to attend a New York State college and who are New York State residents. Deadlines: July 16 for the fall semester, January 4 for the spring semester, and May 20 for summer session. *Award:* Scholarship for use in freshman, sophomore, junior, or senior years; renewable. *Award amount:* $85–$2000. *Eligibility Requirements:* Applicant must be American Indian/Alaska Native; enrolled or expecting to enroll full- or part-time at a two-year or technical institution or university; resident of New Mexico and studying in New York. Available to U.S. citizens. *Application Requirements:* Application form, financial need analysis.

New York State Part-time Scholarship. The New York State Part-Time Scholarship Award Program provides scholarship awards to students who attend a SUNY or CUNY Community College part-time and maintain a 2.0 GPA. Students can receive $1,500 per semester for up to 2 years. *Award:* Grant for use in freshman, sophomore, junior, or senior years; renewable. *Award amount:* $1500. *Eligibility Requirements:* Applicant must be enrolled or expecting to enroll part-time at a two-year institution or university; resident of New Mexico and studying in New York. Available to U.S. citizens. *Application Requirements:* Application form, financial need analysis.

New York State Tuition Assistance Program. The New York State Tuition Assistance Program (TAP) helps eligible New York residents pay tuition at approved schools in New York State. Depending on the academic year in which you begin study, an annual TAP award can be up to $5,165. Because TAP is a grant, it does not have to be paid back. *Award:* Grant for use in freshman, sophomore, junior, or senior years; renewable. *Award amount:* $500–$5165. *Number of awards:* 350,000–360,000. *Eligibility Requirements:* Applicant must be enrolled or expecting to enroll full-time at a two-year institution or university; resident of New Mexico and studying in New York. Available to U.S. citizens. *Application Requirements:* Application form, application form may be submitted online, financial need analysis. **Deadline:** May 1.

New York Vietnam/Persian Gulf/Afghanistan Veterans Tuition Awards. Vietnam, Persian Gulf, Afghanistan, or other eligible combat veterans matriculated at an undergraduate or graduate degree-granting institution or in an approved vocational training program in New York State are eligible for awards for full or part-time study. *Award:* Scholarship for use in freshman, sophomore, junior, or senior years; renewable. *Eligibility Requirements:* Applicant must be enrolled or expecting to enroll full- or part-time at a two-year or technical institution or university; resident of New Mexico and studying in New York. Available to U.S. citizens. Applicant or parent must meet one or more of the following requirements: general military experience; retired from active duty; disabled or killed as a result of military service; prisoner of war; or missing in action. *Application Requirements:* Application form, application form may be submitted online, financial need analysis. **Deadline:** June 30.

NYS Memorial Scholarship for Families of Deceased Firefighters, Volunteer Firefighters, Police Officers, Peace Officers, and Emergency Medical Service Workers. This scholarship provides financial aid to children, spouses and financial dependents of deceased firefighters, volunteer firefighters, police officers, peace officers, and emergency medical service workers who have died as the result of injuries sustained in the line of duty in service to the State of New York. For study in New York State. *Award:* Scholarship for use in freshman, sophomore, junior, or senior years; renewable. *Eligibility Requirements:* Applicant must be enrolled or expecting to enroll full-time at an institution or university; resident of New Mexico and studying in New York. Available to U.S. citizens. *Application Requirements:* Application form, application form may be submitted online, financial need analysis. **Deadline:** May 1.

NYS Regents Awards for Children of Deceased and Disabled Veterans. Award for students whose parent, as a result of service in U.S. Armed Forces during war or national emergency, died; suffered a 40 percent or more disability; or is classified as missing in action or a prisoner of war. Veteran must be current New York State resident or have been so at time of death. Student must be a New York resident, attending, or planning to attend, college in New York State. Must establish eligibility before applying for payment. *Award:* Scholarship for use in freshman, sophomore, junior, or senior years; not renewable. *Award amount:* $450. *Eligibility Requirements:* Applicant must be enrolled or expecting to enroll full-time at a two-year institution or university; resident of New Mexico and studying in New York. Available to U.S. citizens. Applicant or parent must meet one or more of the following requirements: general military experience; retired from active duty; disabled or killed as a result of military service; prisoner of war; or missing in action. *Application Requirements:* Application form, application form may be submitted online. **Deadline:** June 30.

Scholarship for Academic Excellence. Renewable award for New York residents. Scholarship winners must attend a college or university in New York. 2000 scholarships are for $1500 and 6000 are for $500. The selection criteria used are based on Regents test scores or rank in class or local exam. Must be U. S. citizen or permanent resident. *Award:* Scholarship for use in freshman year; renewable. *Award amount:* $500–$1500. *Number of awards:* up to 8,000. *Eligibility Requirements:* Applicant must be high school student; planning to enroll or expecting to enroll full-time at a two-year or four-year institution or university; resident of New York and studying in New York. Available to U.S. citizens. *Application Requirements:* Application form. **Deadline:** December 19.

Contact Lewis Hall, Supervisor. *E-mail:* scholar@nysed.gov. *Phone:* 518-486-1319. *Fax:* 518-486-5346. *Website:* http://www.highered.nysed.gov/.

Scholarships for Academic Excellence. This program provides scholarship assistance to outstanding New York State high school graduates. Each year, 8,000 scholarships are awarded - up to 2,000 scholarships of $1,500 and 6,000 scholarships of $500 to top scholars from registered New York State high schools. Awards are based on student grades in certain Regents exams. For up to five years of undergraduate study in New York State. Recipients can also receive other non-loan student aid, but the total cannot exceed the cost of attendance. *Award:* Scholarship for use in freshman, sophomore, junior, or senior years; renewable. *Award amount:* $500–$1500. *Number of awards:* 8,000. *Eligibility Requirements:* Applicant must be high school student; planning to enroll or expecting to enroll full-time at an institution or university; resident of New Mexico and studying in New York. Available to U.S. citizens. *Application Requirements:* Application form. **Deadline:** June 30.

World Trade Center Memorial Scholarship. The World Trade Center Memorial Scholarship (WTC) provides access to a college education for children, spouses, and financial dependents of innocent victims who died or were severely and permanently disabled as a result of the September 11, 2001 terrorist attacks on the United States of America - at the World Trade Center, the Pentagon, and on airline flights 11, 77, 93, and 175 - and the resulting rescue and recovery efforts. *Award:* Scholarship for use in freshman, sophomore, junior, or senior years; renewable. *Eligibility Requirements:* Applicant must be enrolled or expecting to enroll full-time at an institution or university; resident of New Mexico and studying in New York. Available to U.S. and non-U.S. citizens. *Application Requirements:* Application form, application form may be submitted online, financial need analysis. **Deadline:** June 30.

NORTH CAROLINA

North Carolina Community College Grant Program. Grants are available to North Carolina residents who demonstrate financial need and are enrolled at NC community colleges. The applicant must be a NC resident for tuition purposes; enroll for at least six credit hours per semester in a curriculum program; meet the Satisfactory Academic Progress requirements of the institution. Eligibility is determined based on the same criteria as the Federal Pell Grant; students not eligible for the Federal Pell Grant may be considered for the grant based on the expected family contribution (EFC). Students who have earned a Bachelor's (four-year) degree already are ineligible. Applicants must complete the Free Application for Federal Student Aid (FAFSA). Consideration is automatic once the FAFSA is filed. Please contact the financial aid office at the local community college for more specific information regarding institutional processes. *Award:* Grant for use in freshman or sophomore years; not renewable. *Eligibility Requirements:* Applicant must be enrolled or expecting to enroll full- or part-time at a two-year or technical institution; resident of Newfoundland and studying in North Carolina. Available to U.S. citizens. *Application Requirements:* Financial need analysis. **Deadline:** continuous.

Contact Kevin Lineberry, Associate Director Higher Ed Programs, North Carolina State Education Assistance Authority, PO Box 13663, Research Triangle Park, NC 27709-3663. *E-mail:* info@ncseaa.edu. *Phone:* 919-549-8614. *Fax:* 919-549-8481. *Website:* http://www.ncseaa.edu/.

North Carolina National Guard Tuition Assistance Program. Scholarship for members of the North Carolina Air and Army National Guard who will remain in the service for two years following the period for which assistance is provided. Must reapply for each academic period. For use at approved North Carolina institutions. *Award:* Grant for use in freshman, sophomore, junior, senior, or graduate years; not renewable. *Award amount:* $100–$3440. *Eligibility Requirements:* Applicant must be enrolled or expecting to enroll full- or part-time at a two-year or four-year or technical institution or university; resident of North Carolina and studying in North Carolina. Available to U.S. citizens. Applicant or parent must meet one or more of the following requirements: national guard experience; retired from active duty; disabled or killed as a result of military service; prisoner of war; or missing in action. *Application Requirements:* Application form. **Deadline:** continuous.

Contact Ms. Stacy Steinmetz, NCTAP Manager, North Carolina National Guard, 1636 Gold Star Drive, Raleigh, NC 27607. *E-mail:* stacy.m.steinmetz.nfg@mail.mil. *Phone:* 919-664-6272. *Website:* http://nc.ng.mil/Pages/default.aspx.

North Carolina Sheriffs' Association Undergraduate Criminal Justice Scholarships. One-time award for full-time North Carolina resident undergraduate students majoring in criminal justice at a University of North Carolina school. Priority given to child of any North Carolina law enforcement officer. Letter of recommendation from county sheriff required. Deadline determined by FA Office. Law Enforcement/Police Administration. *Award:* Scholarship for use in freshman, sophomore, junior, or senior years; not renewable. *Eligibility Requirements:* Applicant must be enrolled or expecting to enroll full-time at an institution or university; resident of Newfoundland and studying in North Carolina. Applicant or parent of applicant must have employment or volunteer experience in police/firefighting. Available to U.S. citizens. *Application Requirements:* Application form, financial need analysis. **Deadline:** continuous.

Contact Kevin Lineberry, Associate Director Higher Ed Programs, North Carolina State Education Assistance Authority, PO Box 13663, Research Triangle Park, NC 27709-3663. *E-mail:* info@ncseaa.edu. *Phone:* 919-549-8614. *Fax:* 919-549-8481. *Website:* http://www.ncseaa.edu/.

North Carolina Veterans Scholarships Class I-A. Scholarships for children of certain deceased, disabled or POW/MIA veterans. Award value is $4500 per nine-month academic year in private colleges and junior colleges. No limit on number awarded each year. *Award:* Scholarship for use in freshman, sophomore, junior, or senior years; renewable. *Award amount:* $4500. *Eligibility Requirements:* Applicant must be enrolled or expecting to enroll full-time at a two-year or four-year or technical institution or university; resident of North Carolina and studying in North Carolina. Available to U.S. citizens. Applicant or parent must meet one or more of the following requirements: general military experience; retired from active duty; disabled or killed as a result of military service; prisoner of war; or missing in action. *Application Requirements:* Application form, financial need analysis, interview, transcript. **Deadline:** continuous.

Contact Charles Smith, Assistant Secretary. *E-mail:* charlie.smith@ncmail.net. *Phone:* 919-733-3851. *Fax:* 919-733-2834. *Website:* http://www.milvets.nc.gov/.

North Carolina Veterans Scholarships Class I-B. Awards for children of veterans rated by USDVA as 100 percent disabled due to wartime service as defined in the law, and currently or at time of death drawing compensation for such disability. Parent must have been a North Carolina resident at time of entry into service. Duration of the scholarship is four academic years (8 semesters) if used within 8 years. No limit on number awarded each year. *Award:* Scholarship for use in freshman, sophomore, junior, or senior years; renewable. *Award amount:* $1500. *Eligibility Requirements:* Applicant must be enrolled or expecting to enroll full- or part-time at a two-year or four-year or technical institution or university; resident of North Carolina and studying in North Carolina. Available to U.S. citizens. Applicant or parent must meet one or more of the following requirements: general military experience; retired from active duty; disabled or killed as a result of military service; prisoner of war; or missing in action. *Application Requirements:* Application form, financial need analysis, interview, transcript. **Deadline:** continuous.

Contact Charles Smith, Assistant Secretary. *E-mail:* charlie.smith@ncmail.net. *Phone:* 919-733-3851. *Fax:* 919-733-2834. *Website:* http://www.milvets.nc.gov/.

North Carolina Veterans Scholarships Class II. Awards for children of veterans rated by USDVA as much as 20 percent but less than 100 percent disabled due to wartime service as defined in the law, or awarded Purple Heart Medal for wounds received. Parent must have been a North Carolina resident at time of entry into service. Duration of the scholarship is four academic years (8 semesters) if used within 8 years. Free tuition and exemption from certain mandatory fees as set forth in the law in

Public, Community and Technical Colleges. *Award:* Scholarship for use in freshman, sophomore, junior, or senior years; renewable. *Award amount:* $4500. *Number of awards:* up to 100. *Eligibility Requirements:* Applicant must be enrolled or expecting to enroll full- or part-time at a two-year or four-year or technical institution or university; resident of North Carolina and studying in North Carolina. Available to U.S. citizens. Applicant or parent must meet one or more of the following requirements: general military experience; retired from active duty; disabled or killed as a result of military service; prisoner of war; or missing in action. *Application Requirements:* Application form, financial need analysis, interview, transcript. **Deadline:** March 1.

Contact Charles Smith, Assistant Secretary. *E-mail:* charlie.smith@ncmail.net. *Phone:* 919-733-3851. *Fax:* 919-733-2834. *Website:* http://www.milvets.nc.gov/.

North Carolina Veterans Scholarships Class III. Awards for children of a deceased war veteran, who was honorably discharged and who does not qualify under any other provision within this synopsis or veteran who served in a combat zone or waters adjacent to a combat zone and received a campaign badge or medal and who does not qualify under any other provision within this synopsis. Duration of the scholarship is four academic years (8 semesters) if used within 8 years. *Award:* Scholarship for use in freshman, sophomore, junior, or senior years; renewable. *Award amount:* $4500. *Number of awards:* up to 100. *Eligibility Requirements:* Applicant must be enrolled or expecting to enroll full- or part-time at a two-year or four-year or technical institution or university; resident of North Carolina and studying in North Carolina. Available to U.S. citizens. Applicant or parent must meet one or more of the following requirements: general military experience; retired from active duty; disabled or killed as a result of military service; prisoner of war; or missing in action. *Application Requirements:* Application form, financial need analysis, interview, transcript. **Deadline:** March 1.

Contact Charles Smith, Assistant Secretary. *E-mail:* charlie.smith@ncmail.net. *Phone:* 919-733-3851. *Fax:* 919-733-2834. *Website:* http://www.milvets.nc.gov/.

North Carolina Veterans Scholarships Class IV. Awards for children of veterans, who were prisoner of war or missing in action. Duration of the scholarship is four academic years (8 semesters) if used within 8 years. No limit on number awarded each year. Award value is $4500 per nine-month academic year in private colleges and junior colleges. *Award:* Scholarship for use in freshman, sophomore, junior, or senior years; renewable. *Award amount:* $4500. *Eligibility Requirements:* Applicant must be enrolled or expecting to enroll full- or part-time at a two-year or four-year or technical institution or university; resident of North Carolina and studying in North Carolina. Available to U.S. citizens. Applicant or parent must meet one or more of the following requirements: general military experience; retired from active duty; disabled or killed as a result of military service; prisoner of war; or missing in action. *Application Requirements:* Application form, financial need analysis, interview, transcript. **Deadline:** continuous.

Contact Charles Smith, Assistant Secretary. *E-mail:* charlie.smith@ncmail.net. *Phone:* 919-733-3851. *Fax:* 919-733-2834. *Website:* http://www.milvets.nc.gov/.

Training Support for Youth with Disabilities. Public service program that helps persons with disabilities obtain competitive employment. To qualify: student must have a mental, physical or learning disability that is an impediment to employment and require post secondary training to achieve a specific employment outcome. A Rehabilitation Counselor, along with the eligible student, develops an individualized rehabilitation program outlining the specific need for post-secondary training. Financial assistance is based on NC Division of Vocational Rehabilitation demonstrated financial need and the type of program in which the student enrolls. *Award:* Grant for use in freshman, sophomore, junior, senior, or graduate years; renewable. *Eligibility Requirements:* Applicant must be enrolled or expecting to enroll full- or part-time at a two-year or four-year or technical institution or university and resident of North Carolina. Applicant must be hearing impaired, learning disabled, physically disabled, or visually impaired. Available to U.S. and non-U. S. citizens. *Application Requirements:* Application form, Evidence of eligibility to work in the US, financial need analysis, interview. **Deadline:** continuous.

Contact Stephanie Hanes, Program Specialist for Transition, North Carolina Division of Vocational Rehabilitation Services, 2801 Mail Service Center, Raleigh, NC 27699-2801. *E-mail:* stephanie.hanes@dhhs.nc.gov. *Phone:* 919-855-3576. *Website:* http://www.dhhs.state.nc.us/.

University of North Carolina Need-Based Grant. Applicants must be enrolled in at least 6 credit hours at one of sixteen UNC system universities. Eligibility based on need; award varies, consideration for grant automatic when FAFSA is filed. Applicants should meet priority deadlines established by their institution. Late applications may be denied if insufficient funds are available. *Award:* Grant for use in freshman, sophomore, junior, or senior years; renewable. *Eligibility Requirements:* Applicant must be enrolled or expecting to enroll full- or part-time at an institution or university; resident of Newfoundland and studying in North Carolina. Available to U.S. citizens. *Application Requirements:* Application form, financial need analysis. **Deadline:** continuous.

Contact Kevin Lineberry, Associate Director Higher Ed Programs, North Carolina State Education Assistance Authority, PO Box 13663, Research Triangle Park, NC 27709-3663. *E-mail:* info@ncseaa.edu. *Phone:* 919-549-8614. *Fax:* 919-549-8481. *Website:* http://www.ncseaa.edu/.

OHIO

Choose Ohio First Scholarship. Choose Ohio First awards competitive scholarship funding to Ohio's colleges and universities to support undergraduate and qualifying graduate students in innovative STEMM academic programs. Designated Choose Ohio First programs are integrated with regional economies, meeting statewide educational needs, facilitating the completion of baccalaureate degrees in cost effective manners, and recruiting underrepresented STEMM student groups including women and students of color. *Award:* Scholarship for use in freshman, sophomore, junior, or senior years; renewable. *Eligibility Requirements:* Applicant must be enrolled or expecting to enroll full- or part-time at a two-year institution or university; resident of Nova Scotia and studying in Ohio. Available to U.S. and non-U.S. citizens. *Application Requirements:* Application form. **Deadline:** continuous.

Contact Corey Dixon, Project Manager, Ohio Department of Higher Education, Ohio Department of Higher Education, 25 South Front Street, Columbus, OH 43215. *E-mail:* CDixon@highered.ohio.gov. *Phone:* 614-644-5704. *Website:* www.ohiohighered.org.

Ohio College Opportunity Grant. OCOG provides grant money to Ohio residents who demonstrate the highest levels of financial need (as determined by the results of the FAFSA) who are enrolled at Ohio public colleges or universities; Ohio private, non-profit colleges or universities; Ohio private, for-profit institutions; or eligible Pennsylvania institutions. *Award:* Grant for use in freshman, sophomore, junior, or senior years; not renewable. *Award amount:* $69–$3500. *Eligibility Requirements:* Applicant must be enrolled or expecting to enroll full- or part-time at a two-year institution or university; resident of Nova Scotia and studying in Ohio, Pennsylvania. *Application Requirements:* **Deadline:** October 1.

Contact Tamika Braswell, Director, Ohio Department of Higher Education, 25 South Front Street, Columbus, OH 43215. *E-mail:* ocog_admin@highered.ohio.gov. *Phone:* 614-728-8862. *Website:* www.ohiohighered.org.

Ohio Environmental Science & Engineering Scholarships. Merit-based, non-renewable, tuition-only scholarships awarded to undergraduate students admitted to Ohio state or private colleges and universities. Must be able to demonstrate knowledge of, and commitment to, careers in environmental sciences or environmental engineering. Environmental Science. *Award:* Scholarship for use in senior year; not renewable. *Award amount:* $1250–$2500. *Number of awards:* 18. *Eligibility Requirements:* Applicant must be enrolled or expecting to enroll full- or part-time at a two-year or four-year institution or university and studying in Ohio. Available to U.S. citizens. *Application Requirements:* Application form, application form may be submitted online (https://mc04.manuscriptcentral.com/oas), community service, essay, recommendations or references, resume, self-addressed stamped envelope with application, transcript. **Deadline:** April 15.

Contact Dr. Stephen McConoughey, Chief Executive Officer, Ohio Academy of Science/Ohio Environmental Education Fund, 1500 West Third Avenue, Suite 228, Columbus, OH 43212-2817. *E-mail:* smcconoughey@ohiosci.org. *Phone:* 614-488-2228. *Fax:* 614-488-7629. *Website:* http://www.ohiosci.org/.

Ohio National Guard Scholarship Program. Scholarships are for undergraduate studies at an approved Ohio post-secondary institution. Applicants must enlist for six or three years of Selective Service Reserve Duty in the Ohio National Guard. Scholarship pays 100% instructional and general fees for public institutions and an average of cost of public universities is available for private schools. May reapply up to four years of studies (12 quarters or 8 semesters) for six year enlistment and two years of studies (6 quarters or 4 semesters) for three year enlistment. Deadlines: July 1 (fall), November 1 (winter quarter/spring semester), February 1 (spring quarter), April 1 (summer). *Award:* Scholarship for use in freshman, sophomore, junior, or senior years; not renewable. *Eligibility Requirements:* Applicant must be enrolled or expecting to enroll full- or part-time at a two-year or four-year or technical institution or university; resident of Ohio and studying in Ohio. Available to U.S. citizens. Applicant must have national guard experience. *Application Requirements:* Application form.

Contact Afrika Alsup, Scholarship Program Director. *E-mail:* akrika.k.alsup.nfg@ mail.mil. *Phone:* 614-336-7032. *Website:* http://www.ong.ohio.gov/.

Ohio Safety Officers College Memorial Fund. Renewable award covering up to full tuition is available to children and surviving spouses of peace officers, other safety officers and fire fighters killed in the line of duty in any state. Children must be under 26 years of age. Dollar value of each award varies. Must be an Ohio resident and enroll full-time or part-time at an Ohio college or university. Any spouse/child of a member of the armed services of the U.S., who has been killed in the line duty during Operation Enduring Freedom, Operation Iraqi Freedom or a combat zone designated by the President of the United States. Dollar value of each award varies. *Award:* Scholarship for use in freshman, sophomore, junior, or senior years; renewable. *Award amount:* $7942. *Eligibility Requirements:* Applicant must be enrolled or expecting to enroll full- or part-time at a two-year institution or university; resident of Nova Scotia and studying in Ohio. Available to U.S. citizens.

Contact Ramah Church, Program Manager, Ohio Department of Higher Education, 25 South Front Street, Columbus, OH 43215. *E-mail:* osom_admin@highered.ohio.gov. *Phone:* 614-752-9528. *Website:* www.ohiohighered.org.

Ohio War Orphan & Severely Disabled Veterans' Children Scholarship Program. Aids Ohio residents attending an eligible college in Ohio. Must be between the ages of 16 and 25, the child of a disabled or deceased veteran, and enrolled full-time. Must maintain a minimum GPA of 2.0. Renewable up to five years. Amount of award varies. Must include Form DD214. *Award:* Scholarship for use in freshman, sophomore, junior, or senior years; renewable. *Eligibility Requirements:* Applicant must be age 16-25; enrolled or expecting to enroll full-time at a two-year institution or university; resident of Nova Scotia and studying in Ohio. Available to U.S. citizens. Applicant must have general military experience. *Application Requirements:* Application form. **Deadline:** May 15.

Contact Ramah Church, Program Manager, Ohio Department of Higher Education, 25 South Front Street, Columbus, OH 43215. *E-mail:* rchurch@highered.ohio.gov. *Phone:* 614-752-9528. *Website:* www.ohiohighered.org.

OKLAHOMA

Academic Scholars Program. Awards for students of high academic ability to attend institutions in Oklahoma. Renewable up to four years. ACT or SAT scores must fall between 99.5 and 100th percentiles, or applicant must be designated as a National Merit scholar or finalist. Oklahoma public institutions can also select institutional nominees. *Award:* Scholarship for use in freshman, sophomore, junior, senior, or graduate years; renewable. *Award amount:* $2200–$5500. *Eligibility Requirements:* Applicant must be high school student; planning to enroll or expecting to enroll full-time at a two-year institution or university; resident of Ohio and studying in Oklahoma. Available to U.S. citizens. *Application Requirements:* Application form.

Contact Linette McMurtrey, Scholarship Programs Coordinator, Oklahoma State Regents for Higher Education, P. O. Box 108850, Oklahoma City, OK 73101-8850. *E-mail:* lmcmurtrey@osrhe.edu. *Phone:* 800-858-1840. *Website:* http://www.okhighered.org/.

Future Teacher Scholarship-Oklahoma. Open to outstanding Oklahoma high school graduates who agree to teach in shortage areas. Must have a GPA or ACT/SAT score ranking in the top 15% of the high school graduating class. Students nominated by institution. Reapply to renew. Must attend college/university in Oklahoma. *Award:* Scholarship for use in freshman, sophomore, junior, senior, or graduate years; not renewable. *Award amount:* $500–$1500. *Eligibility Requirements:* Applicant must be enrolled or expecting to enroll full- or part-time at a two-year institution or university; resident of Ohio and studying in Oklahoma. Available to U.S. citizens. *Application Requirements:* Application form, essay.

Contact Linette McMurtrey, Scholarship Programs Coordinator, Oklahoma State Regents for Higher Education, P. O. Box 108850, 655 Research Parkway, Suite 200, Oklahoma City, OK 73104. *E-mail:* lmcmurtrey@osrhe.edu. *Phone:* 405-225-9131. *Website:* http://www.okhighered.org/.

Oklahoma Tuition Aid Grant Program. Award for Oklahoma residents enrolled at an Oklahoma institution at least part time each semester in a degree program. May be enrolled in two- or four-year or approved vocational-technical institution. Award for students attending public institutions or private colleges. Application is made through FAFSA. *Award:* Grant for use in freshman, sophomore, junior, or senior years; not renewable. *Award amount:* $1000–$1300. *Eligibility Requirements:* Applicant must be enrolled or expecting to enroll full- or part-time at a two-year or technical institution or university; resident of Ohio and studying in Oklahoma. Available to U.S. citizens. *Application Requirements:* Application form, financial need analysis.

Contact Linette McMurtrey, Scholarship Programs Coordinator, Oklahoma State Regents for Higher Education, P. O. Box 108850, 655 Research Parkway, Suite 200, Oklahoma City, OK 73104. *E-mail:* lmcmurtrey@osrhe.edu. *Phone:* 405-225-9131. *Website:* http://www.okhighered.org/.

Regional University Baccalaureate Scholarship. Renewable award for Oklahoma residents attending one of 11 participating Oklahoma public universities. Must have an ACT composite score of at least 30 or be a National Merit semifinalist or commended student. In addition to the award amount, each recipient will receive a resident tuition waiver from the institution. Must maintain a 3.25 GPA. Deadlines vary depending upon the institution attended. *Award:* Scholarship for use in freshman, sophomore, junior, or senior years; renewable. *Award amount:* $3000. *Eligibility Requirements:* Applicant must be enrolled or expecting to enroll full-time at an institution or university; resident of Ohio and studying in Oklahoma. Available to U.S. citizens. *Application Requirements:* Application form.

Contact Linette McMurtrey, Scholarship Programs Coordinator, Oklahoma State Regents for Higher Education, P. O. Box 108850, 655 Research Parkway, Suite 200, Oklahoma City, OK 73104. *E-mail:* lmcmurtrey@osrhe.edu. *Phone:* 405-225-9131. *Website:* http://www.okhighered.org/.

OREGON

American Legion Auxiliary Department of Oregon Department Grants. One-time award for educational use in the state of Oregon. Must be a resident of Oregon who is the child or widow of a veteran or the wife of a disabled veteran. *Award:* Scholarship for use in freshman year; not renewable. *Award amount:* $1000. *Number of awards:* 2. *Eligibility Requirements:* Applicant must be enrolled or expecting to enroll full- or part-time at a two-year or four-year or technical institution or university and resident of Oregon. Available to U.S. citizens. *Application Requirements:* Application form, essay, financial need analysis, interview. **Deadline:** February 10.

Contact Virginia Biddle, Secretary/Treasurer, American Legion Auxiliary Department of Oregon, PO Box 1730, Wilsonville, OR 97070. *E-mail:* alaor@pcez.com. *Phone:* 503-682-3162. *Website:* http://www.alaoregon.org/.

American Legion Auxiliary Department of Oregon Nurses Scholarship. One-time award for Oregon residents who are in their senior year of high school, who are the children of veterans who served during eligibility dates for American Legion membership. Must enroll in a nursing program. Contact local units for application. Nursing. *Award:* Scholarship for use in freshman year; not renewable. *Award amount:* $1500. *Number of awards:* 1. *Eligibility Requirements:* Applicant must be high school student; planning to enroll or expecting to enroll full- or part-time at a four-year institution or university and resident of Oregon. Available to U.S. citizens. *Application Requirements:* Application form, essay, financial need analysis, interview. **Deadline:** March 20.

Contact Virginia Biddle, Secretary/Treasurer, American Legion Auxiliary Department of Oregon, PO Box 1730, Wilsonville, OR 97070. *E-mail:* alaor@pcez.com. *Phone:* 503-682-3162. *Website:* http://www.alaoregon.org/.

Better A Life Scholarship. Scholarship award available to single parents age 17-25. High schools seniors must have at least 3.0 GPA and college students must have at least a 2.5 GPA or GED equivalent. For use at Oregon public and non-profit colleges and universities. Applicants may not already possess a Bachelor's degree. May reapply for one additional year of funding. Financial need may or may not be considered. *Award:* Scholarship for use in freshman, sophomore, junior, or senior years; not renewable. *Eligibility Requirements:* Applicant must be age 17-25; enrolled or expecting to enroll full- or part-time at a two-year or four-year institution or university; single and studying in Oregon. Available to U.S. citizens. *Application Requirements:* Application form, financial need analysis. **Deadline:** March 1.

Contact Melissa Adams, Scholarship Processing Coordinator. *E-mail:* melissa.adams@state.or.us. *Phone:* 541-

687-7409. *Website:* https://oregonstudentaid.gov/.

PENNSYLVANIA

Blind or Deaf Beneficiary Grant Program. This state-funded program provides financial aid to blind or deaf students attending a postsecondary institution. This program awards funds on a first-come, first-served basis. *Award:* Grant for use in freshman, sophomore, junior, or senior years; not renewable. *Award amount:* $500. *Eligibility Requirements:* Applicant must be enrolled or expecting to enroll full- or part-time at a two-year or technical institution or university and resident of Oregon. Applicant must be hearing impaired or visually impaired. *Application Requirements:* Application form. **Deadline:** March 31.

Contact Keith New, Director of Public Relations. *E-mail:* knew@pheaa.org. *Phone:* 800-692-7392. *Website:* http://www.pheaa.org/.

Pennsylvania Chafee Education and Training Grant Program. This federally funded program offers grants to Pennsylvania undergraduate students aging out of foster care who are attending an eligible post-secondary institution. The maximum award under this program for 2019-20 is $5,000; award maximum for the 2020-21 year has not yet been determined. *Award:* Grant for use in freshman, sophomore, junior, or senior years; not renewable. *Eligibility Requirements:* Applicant must be enrolled or expecting to enroll full- or part-time at a two-year or technical institution or university and resident of Oregon. Available to U.S. citizens. *Application Requirements:* Application form. **Deadline:** December 31.

Contact Keith New, Director of Public Relations. *E-mail:* knew@pheaa.org. *Phone:* 800-692-7392. *Website:* http://www.pheaa.org/.

Pennsylvania State Grant Program. Award for Pennsylvania residents attending an approved postsecondary institution as undergraduates in a program of at least two years duration. Renewable for up to eight semesters if applicants show continued need and academic progress. Must submit FAFSA. Number of awards granted varies annually. *Award:* Grant for use in freshman, sophomore, junior, or senior years; renewable. *Award amount:* $500–$800. *Eligibility Requirements:* Applicant must be enrolled or expecting to enroll full- or part-time at a two-year or technical institution or university and resident of Oregon. Available to U.S. citizens. *Application Requirements:* Application form, application form may be submitted online, financial need analysis. **Deadline:** August 15.

Contact Keith New, Director of Public Relations, Pennsylvania Higher Education Assistance Agency, 1200 North Seventh Street, Harrisburg, PA 17102-1444. *Phone:* 800-692-7392. *Website:* http://www.pheaa.org/.

Postsecondary Educational Gratuity Program. The program offers waiver of tuition and fees for children of Pennsylvania police officers, firefighters, rescue or ambulance squad members, corrections facility employees, or National Guard members who died in line of duty after January 1, 1976. *Award:* Grant for use in freshman, sophomore, junior, or senior years; renewable. *Eligibility Requirements:* Applicant must be age 25 or under; enrolled or expecting to enroll full-time at a two-year institution or university; resident of Oregon and studying in Pennsylvania. Available to U.S. citizens. Applicant or parent must meet one or more of the following requirements: national guard experience; retired from active duty; disabled or killed as a result of military service; prisoner of war; or missing in action. *Application Requirements:* Application form. **Deadline:** March 31.

Contact Keith New, Director of Public Relations. *E-mail:* knew@pheaa.org. *Phone:* 800-692-7392. *Website:* http://www.pheaa.org/.

Ready to Succeed Scholarship Program. RTSS provides scholarships to high academic achievers that, in combination with the Pennsylvania State Grant Program, offer a total award up to $2,000 for full-time and $1,000 for part-time students. The minimum award is $500. Awards can be used to cover tuition, books, fees, supplies, and living expenses. Students must be nominated by their post-secondary institution for participation in the program. Funding is limited for the program and awards are made on a first-come, first-served basis. The program, which is funded by the Pennsylvania General Assembly, provides awards to high-achieving students whose annual family income does not exceed $110,000. *Award:* Scholarship for use in sophomore, junior, or senior years; not renewable. *Award amount:* $500–$2000. *Eligibility Requirements:* Applicant must be enrolled or expecting to enroll full- or part-time at a two-year or technical institution or university; resident of Oregon and studying in Pennsylvania. *Application Requirements:* Application form, financial need analysis.

Contact Keith New, Director of Public Relations. *E-mail:* knew@pheaa.org. *Phone:* 800-692-7392. *Website:* http://www.pheaa.org/.

SOUTH CAROLINA

Palmetto Fellows Scholarship Program. Renewable award for qualified high school seniors in South Carolina to attend a four-year South Carolina institution. The scholarship must be applied directly towards the cost of attendance, less any other gift aid received. *Award:* Scholarship for use in freshman year; renewable. *Award amount:* $6700–$7500. *Number of awards:* 4,846. *Eligibility Requirements:* Applicant must be high school student; planning to enroll or expecting to enroll full-time at a four-year institution or university; resident of South Carolina and studying in South Carolina. Available to U.S. citizens. *Application Requirements:* Application form, test scores, transcript. **Deadline:** December 15.

Contact Dr. Karen Woodfaulk, Director of Student Services, South Carolina Commission on Higher Education, 1333 Main Street, Suite 200, Columbia, SC 29201. *E-mail:* kwoodfaulk@che.sc.gov. *Phone:* 803-737-2244. *Fax:* 803-737-3610. *Website:* http://www.che.sc.gov/.

South Carolina HOPE Scholarship. A merit-based scholarship for eligible first-time entering freshman attending a four-year South Carolina institution. Minimum GPA of 3.0 required. Must be a resident of South Carolina. *Award:* Scholarship for use in freshman year; not renewable. *Award amount:* $2800. *Number of awards:* 2,605. *Eligibility Requirements:* Applicant must be high school student; planning to enroll or expecting to enroll full-time at a four-year institution or university; resident of South Carolina and studying in South Carolina. Available to U.S. citizens.

Application Requirements: Transcript. **Deadline:** continuous.

Contact Gerrick Hampton, Scholarship Coordinator, South Carolina Commission on Higher Education, 1333 Main Street, Suite 200, Columbia, SC 29201. *E-mail:* ghampton@che.sc.gov. *Phone:* 803-737-4544. *Fax:* 803-737-3610. *Website:* http://www.che.sc.gov/.

South Carolina Need-Based Grants Program. Award based on FAFSA. A student may receive up to $2500 annually for full-time and up to $1250 annually for part-time study. The grant must be applied directly towards the cost of college attendance for a maximum of eight full-time equivalent terms. *Award:* Grant for use in freshman, sophomore, junior, senior, or graduate years; renewable. *Award amount:* $1250–$2500. *Number of awards:* 1–26,730. *Eligibility Requirements:* Applicant must be enrolled or expecting to enroll full- or part-time at a two-year or four-year or technical institution or university; resident of South Carolina and studying in South Carolina. Available to U.S. citizens. *Application Requirements:* Application form, financial need analysis. **Deadline:** continuous.

Contact Dr. Karen Woodfaulk, Director of Student Service, South Carolina Commission on Higher Education, 1333 Main Street, Suite 200, Columbia, SC 29201. *E-mail:* kwoodfaulk@che.sc.gov. *Phone:* 803-737-2244. *Fax:* 803-737-2297. *Website:* http://www.che.sc.gov/.

SOUTH DAKOTA

South Dakota Opportunity Scholarship. Renewable scholarship may be worth up to $6500 over four years to students who take a rigorous college-prep curriculum while in high school and stay in the state for their postsecondary education. *Award:* Scholarship for use in freshman, sophomore, junior, or senior years; renewable. *Award amount:* $1300–$2300. *Number of awards:* 1,000–4,100. *Eligibility Requirements:* Applicant must be high school student; planning to enroll or expecting to enroll full-time at a two-year or technical institution or university; resident of South Carolina and studying in South Dakota. Available to U.S. citizens. *Application Requirements:* Application form. **Deadline:** September 1.

Contact Kerri Richards, Student Service Coordinator, South Dakota Board of Regents, 306 East Capitol, Suite 200, Pierre, SD 57501. *E-mail:* Kerri.Richards@sdbor.edu. *Phone:* 605-773-3455. *Website:* http://www.sdbor.edu/.

TEXAS

Conditional Grant Program. Renewable award to students who are considered economically disadvantaged based on federal guidelines. The maximum amount awarded per semester is $3,000 not to exceed $6000 per academic year. Students already enrolled in an undergraduate program should have minimum GPA 2.5 and students newly enrolling should have minimum GPA 3. 0. Civil Engineering; Computer Science/Data Processing; Occupational Safety and Health. *Award:* Grant for use in freshman, sophomore, junior, or senior years; renewable. *Award amount:* $3000–$6000. *Number of awards:* 10–20. *Eligibility Requirements:* Applicant must be enrolled or expecting to enroll full-time at a four-year institution or university; resident of Texas and studying in Texas. Available to U.S. citizens. *Application Requirements:* Application form, essay, financial need analysis, interview. **Deadline:** March 1.

Contact Sheila Brooks, Program Coordinator, Texas Department of Transportation, 125 East 11th Street, Austin, TX 78701-2483. *E-mail:* hrd_recruitment@txdot.gov. *Phone:* 512-416-4979. *Website:* http://www.txdot.gov/.

Texas Educational Opportunity Grant (TEOG). Provides grant aid to students with financial need attending public two-year colleges. For initial award, student must be enrolled at least half-time and awarded in the first 30 hours (or its equivalent) of an associate's degree or certificate program (excluding credits for dual enrollment or by examination). For renewal award, student must also maintain a minimum overall GPA of 2.50 and successfully complete a minimum of 75% of classes attempted during the school year. *Award:* Grant for use in freshman, sophomore, junior, or senior years; renewable. *Award amount:* $1–$5876. *Eligibility Requirements:* Applicant must be enrolled or expecting to enroll full- or part-time at a two-year institution; resident of Tennessee and studying in Texas. Available to U.S. citizens. *Application Requirements:* Financial need analysis. **Deadline:** continuous.

Texas Public Educational Grant Program (TPEG). To provide grant assistance to students with financial need. Public colleges or universities in Texas make TPEG awards from their own resources. Only in-state (Texas) colleges or universities may participate in the program. Only public colleges or universities participate in the program (no private, non-profit or career colleges or universities). *Award:* Grant for use in freshman, sophomore, junior, or senior years; renewable. *Eligibility Requirements:* Applicant must be enrolled or expecting to enroll full- or part-time at a two-year institution or university. Available to U.S. and non-U.S. citizens. *Application Requirements:* Financial need analysis. **Deadline:** continuous.

Top 10% Scholarship Program. Funding for Initial Awards is not available for the 2018-19 academic year and only renewal award students are eligible for this program. Renewal students must demonstrate financial need and complete the FAFSA by the state priority deadline of March 15. Renewal students must maintain a minimum overall GPA of 3.25, successfully complete at least 30 SCH each year, and successfully complete at least 75% of the hours attempted each year. *Award:* Scholarship for use in junior or senior years; renewable. *Award amount:* up to $2000. *Eligibility Requirements:* Applicant must be enrolled or expecting to enroll full-time at a two-year or four-year institution or university; resident of Texas and studying in Texas. Available to U.S. citizens. *Application Requirements:* Financial need analysis.

Toward EXcellence, Access, and Success (TEXAS) Grant. Renewable aid for students enrolled at least three-quarter time in a public four-year college or university in Texas within sixteen months of graduation from high school. Must demonstrate financial need and have completed the Foundation, Recommended, or DAP Curriculum in high school. For renewal awards, must also maintain a minimum GPA of 2.5 and complete a minimum of 24 SCH's each year. Amount of award is determined by the financial aid office of each school. Priority FAFSA completion deadline is January 15. Contact the college/university financial aid office for additional eligibility information. *Award:* Grant for use in freshman, sophomore, junior, or senior years; renewable. *Award amount:* $1–$4896. *Eligibility Requirements:* Applicant must be enrolled or expecting to enroll full- or part-time at an institution or university; resident of Tennessee and studying in Texas. Available to U.S. citizens. *Application Requirements:* Financial need analysis. **Deadline:** January 15.

Tuition Equalization Grant (TEG) Program. Renewable award for Texas residents enrolled at least three-quarter time at an independent college or private university in Texas in a degree program that does not lead to ordination or licensure to preach. Awards are based on financial need. Renewal awards also require the student to maintain a minimum overall college GPA of at least 2.5, complete at least 24 SCH's each year (18 SCH's for students in graduate programs), and complete a minimum of 75% of classes attempted each year. Must not be receiving athletic scholarship concurrently. Contact college/university financial aid office for application information. *Award:* Grant for use in freshman, sophomore, junior, senior, or graduate years; renewable. *Award amount:* $1–$5130. *Eligibility Requirements:* Applicant must be enrolled or expecting to enroll full- or part-time at an institution or university and studying in Texas. Available to U.S. citizens. *Application Requirements:* Financial need analysis. **Deadline:** continuous.

The Urban Scholarships Fund. Eligibility - United States citizen or eligible non-citizen (permanent resident card I-551 front and back copy) Texas resident, graduate of high school from 29 urban cities: Abilene, Amarillo, Arlington, Austin, Beaumont, Brownsville, Carrollton, Corpus Christi, Dallas, Denton, El Paso, Fort Worth, Frisco, Garland, Grand Prairie, Houston, Irving, Killeen, Laredo, Lubbock, McAllen, McKinney, Mesquite, Midland, Pasadena, Plano, San Antonio, Waco and Wichita Falls *Award:* Scholarship for use in freshman, sophomore, junior, or senior years; not renewable. *Award amount:* $700–$1000. *Number of awards:* 450–500. *Eligibility Requirements:* Applicant must be age 16-65; enrolled or expecting to enroll full-time at a two-year or four-year or technical institution or university and resident of Texas. Available to U.S. citizens. *Application Requirements:* Financial need analysis. **Deadline:** July 10.

Contact Ms. Janice Jackson, Office Programs Administrator, Texas Association of Developing Colleges, 1140 Empire Central Drive 550, Dallas, TX 75247. *E-mail:* janice.jackson@txadc.org. *Phone:* 214-630-2511. *Website:* http://www.txadc.org.

UTAH

Higher Education Success Stipend Program. Award available to students with substantial financial need for use at any of the participating Utah institutions. The student must be a Utah resident. Contact the financial aid office of the participating institution for requirements and deadlines. *Award:* Grant for use in freshman, sophomore, junior, or senior years; not renewable. *Award amount:* $300–$4000. *Eligibility Requirements:* Applicant must be enrolled or expecting to enroll full- or part-time at a two-year or four-year or technical institution or university; resident of Utah and studying in Utah. Available to U.S. citizens. *Application Requirements:* Financial need analysis. **Deadline:** continuous.

VERMONT

Armed Services Scholarship. This program was created by the Vermont Legislature to provide free tuition for the families of Vermont National Guard (VTNG), or U.S. active reserve or active armed services members who have died while on active or inactive duty. Applicants are reviewed by VSAC. Selection is based on eligibility and available funds. An Armed Services Scholarship may be used for the number of academic credits needed to graduate, up to a maximum of 130 credits. If you receive a federal Pell Grant, the amount of the grant will be deducted from the amount you can receive under the Armed Services Scholarship. *Award:* Scholarship for use in freshman, sophomore, junior, or senior years. *Eligibility Requirements:* Applicant must be enrolled or expecting to enroll full-time at a two-year or technical institution or university. *Application Requirements:* Application form, application form may be submitted online, essay, portfolio. **Deadline:** continuous.

Emily Lester Vermont Opportunity Scholarship. If you've experienced foster care and you're ready to go to college, this scholarship—funded by the State of Vermont—may be right for you. Under this scholarship, you must be enrolled in an undergraduate associate's or bachelor's degree program. There are no requirements as to the number of credits that you must take. Scholarships generally range from $1,000 to $2,000 and may not exceed $3,000. The amount disbursed cannot exceed your total costs (tuition, fees, room, and board) minus your expected family contribution (EFC) and all other sources of gift aid combined. *Award:* Scholarship for use in freshman, sophomore, junior, or senior years. *Eligibility Requirements:* Applicant must be age 18-24 and enrolled or expecting to enroll full- or part-time at a two-year institution or university. *Application Requirements:* Application form, application form may be submitted online. **Deadline:** continuous.

Vermont Incentive Grants. Grants for Vermont residents based on financial need. Must meet needs test. Must be college undergraduate enrolled full-time at an approved post secondary institution. Only available to Vermont residents. Grant amounts vary by student and by year, depending on available funding. During the 2019-2020 academic year, eligible students received awards ranging from $1,000 to $12,300. *Award:* Grant for use in freshman, sophomore, junior, or senior years; not renewable. *Eligibility Requirements:* Applicant must be enrolled or expecting to enroll full-time at a two-year or technical institution or university and resident of Utah. Available to U.S. citizens. *Application Requirements:* Application form, application form may be submitted online, financial need analysis. **Deadline:** continuous.

Vermont Part-Time Grant. For undergraduates carrying less than twelve credits per semester who have not received a bachelor's degree. Must be Vermont resident. Based on financial need. Complete Vermont Financial Aid Packet to apply. May be used at any approved post-secondary institution. Grant amounts vary by student and by year, depending on available funding. During the 2019-2020 academic year, eligible students received awards ranging from $500 to $9,230. *Award:*

Grant for use in freshman, sophomore, junior, or senior years; not renewable. *Eligibility Requirements:* Applicant must be enrolled or expecting to enroll part-time at a two-year or technical institution or university and resident of Utah. Available to U.S. citizens. *Application Requirements:* Application form, application form may be submitted online, financial need analysis. **Deadline:** continuous.

VIRGINIA

Mary Marshall Practical Nursing Scholarship (LPN). Awards for students who are accepted or enrolled as a full-time or part-time student in a practical school of nursing in the state of Virginia. Must be a Virginia resident for at least one year and have submitted a completed application form and a recommendation from the Director regarding scholastic attainment and financial need prior to June 30. Students pursuing a nursing degree not available in Virginia, are not eligible for the scholarship. Scholarship amount varies. Nursing. *Award:* Scholarship for use in freshman, sophomore, junior, or senior years; not renewable. *Award amount:* \$600–\$1200. *Number of awards:* 26–88. *Eligibility Requirements:* Applicant must be age 18 and over; enrolled or expecting to enroll full- or part-time at a two-year or four-year or technical institution or university; resident of Virginia and studying in Virginia. Available to U. S. citizens. *Application Requirements:* Application form, driver's license, essay, financial need analysis, recommendations or references, transcript. **Deadline:** June 30.

Contact Miss. Sarahbeth Jones, Communications Specialist, Virginia Department of Health, Office of Minority Health and Health Equity, PO Box 2448, 109 Governor Street, Suite 1016-E, Richmond, VA 23218-2448. *E-mail:* IncentivePrograms@vdh.virginia.gov. *Phone:* 804-864-7422. *Fax:* 804-864-7440. *Website:* http://www.vdh.virginia.gov/.

Mary Marshall Registered Nursing Scholarships. Scholarship for Virginia residents who have been accepted or is enrollment as a full-time or part-time student in a school of nursing in the state of Virginia. Must demonstrate financial need, verified by the Financial Aid Office/authorized person at the applicant's nursing school. Must also be a resident of Virginia for at least one year and have a minimum 3.0 GPA in required courses. Must have submitted a completed application form and an official grade transcript to The Office of Minority Health and Public Health Policy prior to June 30. If no college courses attempted an official high school transcript or equivalent must be submitted. Nursing. *Award:* Scholarship for use in freshman, sophomore, junior, or senior years; not renewable. *Award amount:* \$600–\$2000. *Number of awards:* 28–95. *Eligibility Requirements:* Applicant must be age 18 and over; enrolled or expecting to enroll full- or part-time at a two-year or four-year institution or university; resident of Virginia and studying in Virginia. Available to U.S. citizens. *Application Requirements:* Application form, driver's license, essay, financial need analysis, recommendations or references, transcript. **Deadline:** June 30.

Contact Miss. Sarahbeth Jones, Communications Specialist, Virginia Department of Health, Office of Minority Health and Health Equity, PO Box 2448, 109 Governor Street, Suite 1016-E, Richmond, VA 23218-2448. *E-mail:* IncentivePrograms@vdh.virginia.gov. *Phone:* 804-864-7422. *Fax:* 804-864-7440. *Website:* http://www.vdh.virginia.gov/.

State Department Federal Credit Union Annual Scholarship Program. Scholarships available to members who are currently enrolled in a degree program and have completed 12 credit hours of coursework at an accredited college or university. Must have own account in good standing with SDFCU, have a minimum 2.5 GPA, submit official cumulative transcripts, and describe need for financial assistance to continue their education. Scholarship only open to members of State Department Federal Credit Union. *Award:* Scholarship for use in sophomore, junior, senior, or graduate years; not renewable. *Award amount:* \$2500. *Eligibility Requirements:* Applicant must be enrolled or expecting to enroll full-time at a four-year institution or university. Available to U.S. and non-U. S. citizens. *Application Requirements:* Application form, financial need analysis. **Deadline:** April 29.

Virginia Commonwealth Award. Need-based award for undergraduate or graduate study at a Virginia public two- or four-year college, or university. Undergraduates must be Virginia residents. The application and awards process are administered by the financial aid office at the Virginia public institution where the student is enrolled. Dollar value of each award varies. Contact college financial aid office for application and deadlines. *Award:* Grant for use in freshman, sophomore, junior, or senior years; not renewable. *Eligibility Requirements:* Applicant must be enrolled or expecting to enroll full- or part-time at a two-year institution or university; resident of Vermont and studying in Virginia. Available to U.S. citizens. *Application Requirements:* Financial need analysis.

Virginia Guaranteed Assistance Program. Awards to undergraduate students proportional to their need, up to full tuition, fees and book allowance. Must be a graduate of a Virginia high school. High school GPA of 2.5 required. Must be enrolled full-time in a public Virginia two- or four-year institution and demonstrate financial need. Must maintain minimum college GPA of 2.0 for renewal awards. *Award:* Grant for use in freshman, sophomore, junior, or senior years; not renewable. *Eligibility Requirements:* Applicant must be enrolled or expecting to enroll full-time at a two-year institution or university; resident of Vermont and studying in Virginia. Available to U.S. citizens. *Application Requirements:* Financial need analysis.

Virginia Military Survivors and Dependents Education Program. Scholarships for post-secondary students between ages 16 and 29 to attend Virginia state-supported institutions. Must be child or surviving spouse of veteran who has either been permanently or totally disabled due to war or other armed conflict; died as a result of war or other armed conflict; or been listed as a POW or MIA. Parent must also meet Virginia residency requirements. *Award:* Scholarship for use in freshman, sophomore, junior, senior, or graduate years; renewable. *Eligibility Requirements:* Applicant must be age 16-29; enrolled or expecting to enroll full-time at a two-year or four-year or technical institution or university; resident of Virginia and studying in Virginia. Available to U.S. citizens. Applicant or parent must meet one or more of the following requirements:

general military experience; retired from active duty; disabled or killed as a result of military service; prisoner of war; or missing in action. *Application Requirements:* Application form, DD214 of service member, birth certificate of applicant, marriage certificate, acceptance letter from institution. **Deadline:** varies.

Contact Mrs. Doris Sullivan, Coordinator, Virginia Department of Veterans Services, 1351 Hershberger Road, Suite 220, Roanoke, VA 24012. *Phone:* 540-561-6625. *Fax:* 540-857-7573. *Website:* http://www.dvs.virginia.gov/.

Virginia Tuition Assistance Grant Program (Private Institutions). Awards for undergraduate students. Also available to graduate and first professional degree students pursuing a health-related degree program. Not to be used for religious study. Must be U.S. citizen or eligible non-citizen, Virginia domiciled, and enrolled full-time at an approved private, nonprofit college within Virginia. Information and application available from participating Virginia colleges financial aid office. Visit http://www.schev.edu and click on Financial Aid. *Award:* Grant for use in freshman, sophomore, junior, senior, or graduate years; renewable. *Award amount:* $850–$3900. *Eligibility Requirements:* Applicant must be enrolled or expecting to enroll full-time at an institution or university; resident of Vermont and studying in Virginia. Available to U.S. citizens. *Application Requirements:* Application form. **Deadline:** July 31.

WASHINGTON

Washington Student Achievement Council College Bound Scholarship. This program provides financial assistance to low-income students who want to achieve the dream of a college education. The application is a two-step process. Eligible students should complete an application during their 7th or 8th grade year via www.collegebound.wa.gov. The second step requires students to submit a financial aid application their senior year of high school and every year of college for income verification. Additional scholarship pledge requirements can be found at www.collegebound.wa.gov. *Award:* Scholarship for use in freshman, sophomore, junior, or senior years; renewable. *Eligibility Requirements:* Applicant must be enrolled or expecting to enroll full- or part-time at a two-year or technical institution or university; resident of Virginia and studying in Washington. *Application Requirements:* Application form. **Deadline:** June 30.

Contact Weiya Liang, Director of College Access & Support. *E-mail:* weiyal@wsac.wa.gov. *Phone:* 360-753-7884. *Website:* https://wsac.wa.gov/.

WISCONSIN

Minority Undergraduate Retention Grant-Wisconsin. The grant provides financial assistance to African-American, Native-American, Hispanic, and former citizens of Laos, Vietnam, and Cambodia, for study in Wisconsin. Must be Wisconsin resident, enrolled at least half-time in Wisconsin Technical College System schools, non-profit independent colleges and universities, and tribal colleges. Refer to website for further details http://www.heab.state.wi.us. *Award:* Grant for use in sophomore, junior, or senior years; not renewable. *Award amount:* $250–$2500. *Eligibility Requirements:* Applicant must be American Indian/Alaska Native, Asian/Pacific Islander, Black (non-Hispanic), Hispanic; enrolled or expecting to enroll full- or part-time at a two-year or technical institution or university; resident of West Virginia and studying in Wisconsin. Available to U.S. and non-U.S. citizens. *Application Requirements:* Application form, financial need analysis. **Deadline:** continuous.

Contact Joy Dyer, Grant Specialist. *E-mail:* joy.dyer@wi.gov. *Phone:* 608-267-2212. *Website:* http://www.heab.state.wi.us/.

Talent Incentive Program Grant - WI. Grant assists residents of Wisconsin who are attending a nonprofit institution in Wisconsin, and who have substantial financial need. Must meet income criteria, be considered economically and educationally disadvantaged, and be enrolled at least half-time. Refer to website for further details http://www.heab.state.wi.us. *Award:* Grant for use in freshman, sophomore, junior, or senior years; renewable. *Award amount:* $600–$1800. *Eligibility Requirements:* Applicant must be enrolled or expecting to enroll full- or part-time at a two-year or technical institution or university; resident of West Virginia and studying in Wisconsin. Available to U.S. citizens. *Application Requirements:* Application form, financial need analysis. **Deadline:** continuous.

Contact Cassie Weisensel, Grant Specialist. *E-mail:* cassie.weisensel@wi.gov. *Phone:* 608-267-2213. *Website:* http://www.heab.state.wi.us/.

Veterans Education (VetEd) Reimbursement Grant. The grant is for eligible Wisconsin veterans enrolled at approved schools who have not yet earned a BS/BA. Reimburses up to 120 credits or eight semesters at the UW Madison rate for the same number of credits taken in one semester or term. The number of credits or semesters is based on length of time serving on active duty in the armed forces (active duty for training does not apply). Application is due no later than 60 days after the course start date. The student must earn a 2.0 or better for the semester. An eligible veteran will have entered active duty as a Wisconsin resident or lived in state for twelve consecutive months since entering active duty. *Award:* Grant for use in freshman, sophomore, junior, or senior years; renewable. *Award amount:* $1340–$4000. *Eligibility Requirements:* Applicant must be age 18-75; enrolled or expecting to enroll full- or part-time at a two-year or four-year or technical institution or university; resident of Wisconsin and studying in Minnesota, Wisconsin. Applicant must be hearing impaired, learning disabled, physically disabled, or visually impaired. Available to U.S. citizens. Applicant must have general military experience. *Application Requirements:* Application form. **Deadline:** July 15.

Contact Miss. Leslie Busby-Amegashie, Agency Liaison and Regional Coordinator, Wisconsin Department of Veterans Affairs (WDVA), 201 West Washington Street, PO Box 7843, Madison, WI 53707-7843. *E-mail:* leslie.busby-amegashie@dva.wisconsin.gov. *Phone:* 800-947-8387 Ext. 63575. *Fax:* 608-267-0403 Ext. 3575. *Website:* http://www.dva.state.wi.us/.

WI-HEAB Hearing/Visually Impaired Student Grant. One-time award available to residents of Wisconsin who have severe or profound hearing or visual impairment. Must be enrolled at least half-time at a nonprofit institution. If the handicap prevents the student from attending a Wisconsin school, the award may be used out-of-state in a specialized college. Refer to website for further details http://www.heab.state.wi.us. *Award:* Grant for use in freshman, sophomore, junior, or senior years; not renewable. *Award amount:* $250–$1800. *Eligibility Requirements:* Applicant must be enrolled or expecting to enroll full- or part-time at an institution or university; resident of West Virginia and studying in Wisconsin. Applicant must be hearing impaired or visually impaired. Available to U.S. citizens. *Application Requirements:* Application form, financial need analysis. **Deadline:** continuous.

Contact Charlene Sime, Grant Specialist. *E-mail:* charlenek.sime@wi.gov. *Phone:* 608-266-0888. *Website:* http://www.heab.state.wi.us/.

Wisconsin Academic Excellence Scholarship. Renewable award for high school seniors with the highest GPA in graduating class. Must be a Wisconsin resident attending a nonprofit Wisconsin institution full-time. Scholarship value is $2250 toward tuition each year for up to four years. Must maintain 3.0 GPA for renewal. Refer to your high school counselor for more details. *Award:* Scholarship for use in freshman year; renewable. *Award amount:* $2250. *Eligibility Requirements:* Applicant must be high school student; planning to enroll or expecting to enroll full-time at a two-year or technical institution or university; resident of West Virginia and studying in Wisconsin. Available to U.S. citizens. *Application Requirements:* Application form, financial need analysis. **Deadline:** continuous.

Contact Cassie Weisensel, Grant Specialist. *E-mail:* cassie.weisensel@wi.gov. *Phone:* 608-267-2213. *Website:* http://www.heab.state.wi.us/.

Wisconsin HEAB Grant - UW system, Technical Colleges, Tribal Colleges (WG-UW,TC,TR). Grants for residents of Wisconsin enrolled at least half-time in degree or certificate programs at a University of Wisconsin Institution, Wisconsin Technical College or an approved Tribal College. Must show financial need. Refer to website for further details http://www.heab.wi.gov. *Award:* Grant for use in freshman, sophomore, junior, or senior years; not renewable. *Award amount:* $250–$3150. *Eligibility Requirements:* Applicant must be enrolled or expecting to enroll full- or part-time at a two-year or technical institution or university; resident of West Virginia and studying in Wisconsin. Available to U.S. citizens. *Application Requirements:* Application form, financial need analysis. **Deadline:** continuous.

Contact Charlene Sime, Grant Specialist. *E-mail:* charlenek.sime@wi.gov. *Phone:* 608-266-0888. *Website:* http://www.heab.state.wi.us/.

Wisconsin HEAB Native American Student Assistance Grant. Awards under this program are made to Wisconsin residents who are at least 25% Native American and are undergraduate or graduate students enrolled in degree or certificate programs at University of Wisconsin, Wisconsin Technical College, independent colleges and universities, tribal colleges, or proprietary institutions based in Wisconsin. *Award:* Grant for use in freshman, sophomore, junior, or senior years; not renewable. *Award amount:* $250–$1100. *Eligibility Requirements:* Applicant must be American Indian/Alaska Native; enrolled or expecting to enroll full- or part-time at a two-year or technical institution or university; resident of West Virginia and studying in Wisconsin. Available to U.S. citizens. *Application Requirements:* Application form, financial need analysis. **Deadline:** continuous.

Contact Charlene Sime, Grant Specialist. *E-mail:* charlenek.sime@wi.gov. *Phone:* 608-266-0888. *Website:* http://www.heab.state.wi.us/.

WYOMING

Superior Student in Education Scholarship-Wyoming. Scholarship available each year to sixteen Wyoming high school graduates who plan to teach in Wyoming. The award covers costs of undergraduate tuition at the University of Wyoming or any Wyoming community college. Education. *Award:* Scholarship for use in freshman, sophomore, junior, or senior years; renewable. *Award amount:* $1000. *Number of awards:* 16–16. *Eligibility Requirements:* Applicant must be enrolled or expecting to enroll full-time at a two-year or four-year institution or university; resident of Wyoming and studying in Wyoming. Available to U.S. citizens. *Application Requirements:* Application form, recommendations or references, test scores, transcript. **Deadline:** October 31.

Contact Tammy Mack, Assistant Director, Scholarships, University of Wyoming, Department 3335, 1000 East University Avenue, Laramie, WY 82071. *E-mail:* FinAid@uwyo.edu. *Phone:* 307-766-2412. *Fax:* 307-766-3800. *Website:* http://www.uwyo.edu/scholarships.

Vietnam Veterans Award-Wyoming. Scholarship available to Wyoming residents who served in the armed forces between August 5, 1964 and May 7, 1975, and received a Vietnam service medal. *Award:* Scholarship for use in freshman, sophomore, junior, or senior years; renewable. *Eligibility Requirements:* Applicant must be enrolled or expecting to enroll full- or part-time at a two-year or four-year institution or university and resident of Wyoming. Available to U.S. citizens. Applicant or parent must meet one or more of the following requirements: general military experience; retired from active duty; disabled or killed as a result of military service; prisoner of war; or missing in action. *Application Requirements:* Application form. **Deadline:** continuous.

Contact Tammy Mack, Assistant Director, Scholarships, University of Wyoming, Department 3335, 1000 East University Avenue, Laramie, WY 82071. *E-mail:* FinAid@uwyo.edu. *Phone:* 307-766-2412. *Fax:* 307-766-3800. *Website:* http://www.uwyo.edu/scholarships.

Indexes

Non-Need Scholarships for Undergraduates

Academic Interests/Achievements

Agriculture

Abilene Christian University, TX
Angelo State University, TX
Arkansas Tech University, AR
Auburn University, AL
Austin Peay State University, TN
Berry College, GA
California Polytechnic State University, San Luis Obispo, CA
California State Polytechnic University, Pomona, CA
California State University, Chico, CA
California State University, Fresno, CA
California State University, Stanislaus, CA
Cameron University, OK
Clemson University, SC
Dordt University, IA
Eastern Michigan University, MI
Eastern New Mexico University, NM
Emmanuel College, GA
Ferris State University, MI
Florida Agricultural and Mechanical University, FL
Fort Hays State University, KS
Huntington University, IN
Illinois State University, IL
Kent State University, OH
Kent State University at Geauga, OH
Kent State University at Stark, OH
Keystone College, PA
Louisiana State University and Agricultural & Mechanical College, LA
Michigan State University, MI
Middle Tennessee State University, TN
Midway University, KY
Mississippi State University, MS
Montana State University, MT
Morehead State University, KY
New Mexico State University, NM
North Carolina State University, NC
North Dakota State University, ND
Northern State University, SD
Northwest Missouri State University, MO
The Ohio State University, OH
Ohio University–Chillicothe, OH
Oklahoma State University, OK
Purdue University, IN
Sam Houston State University, TX
Southeast Missouri State University, MO
Southern Illinois University Carbondale, IL
State University of New York College of Environmental Science and Forestry, NY
Stephen F. Austin State University, TX
Sul Ross State University, TX
Texas A&M University, TX
Texas A&M University–Commerce, TX
Texas Christian University, TX
Texas State University, TX
Texas Tech University, TX
Truman State University, MO
Tuskegee University, AL
The University of Alabama, AL
University of Arkansas, AR
University of California, Davis, CA
University of California, Riverside, CA
University of California, Santa Cruz, CA
University of Florida, FL
University of Georgia, GA
University of Guam, GU
University of Idaho, ID
University of Illinois at Urbana-Champaign, IL
University of Kentucky, KY
University of Louisiana at Monroe, LA
University of Maine, ME
University of Mary Hardin-Baylor, TX
University of Maryland, College Park, MD
University of Massachusetts Amherst, MA
University of Minnesota, Crookston, MN
University of Minnesota, Twin Cities Campus, MN
University of Nebraska–Lincoln, NE
University of Nevada, Reno, NV
University of New Hampshire, NH
University of Rhode Island, RI
The University of Tennessee, TN
The University of Tennessee at Martin, TN
The University of Texas at San Antonio, TX
University of Wisconsin–Platteville, WI
University of Wisconsin–River Falls, WI
University of Wisconsin–Stevens Point, WI
University of Wyoming, WY
Utah State University, UT
Vermont Technical College, VT
Washington State University, WA
Western Illinois University, IL
Western Kentucky University, KY
West Texas A&M University, TX

Architecture

Auburn University, AL
Ball State University, IN
Boise State University, ID
Boston Architectural College, MA
California Baptist University, CA
California Polytechnic State University, San Luis Obispo, CA
California State Polytechnic University, Pomona, CA
City College of the City University of New York, NY
Clemson University, SC
Drury University, MO
Eastern Michigan University, MI
Ferris State University, MI
Florida Agricultural and Mechanical University, FL
Florida International University, FL
Georgia Institute of Technology, GA
Hampton University, VA
Idaho State University, ID
Illinois Institute of Technology, IL
James Madison University, VA
Kean University, NJ
Kent State University, OH
Kent State University at Geauga, OH
Kent State University at Stark, OH
Louisiana State University and Agricultural & Mechanical College, LA
Marywood University, PA
Miami University, OH
Mississippi State University, MS
Montana State University, MT
Morgan State University, MD
New Jersey Institute of Technology, NJ
North Carolina State University, NC
North Dakota State University, ND
The Ohio State University, OH
Oklahoma State University, OK
Otis College of Art and Design, CA
Portland State University, OR
Samford University, AL
San Jose State University, CA
Southern Illinois University Carbondale, IL
State University of New York College of Environmental Science and Forestry, NY
Texas A&M University, TX
Texas Tech University, TX
Tuskegee University, AL
The University of Alabama, AL
University of Arkansas, AR
University of California, Davis, CA
University of California, Los Angeles, CA
University of Colorado Boulder, CO
University of Colorado Denver, CO
University of Florida, FL
University of Hawaii at Manoa, HI
University of Houston, TX
University of Idaho, ID
University of Illinois at Chicago, IL
University of Illinois at Urbana-Champaign, IL
The University of Kansas, KS
University of Kentucky, KY
University of Maryland, College Park, MD
University of Mary Washington, VA
University of Massachusetts Amherst, MA
University of Memphis, TN
University of Miami, FL
University of Michigan, MI
University of Minnesota, Twin Cities Campus, MN
University of Nebraska–Lincoln, NE
University of Nevada, Las Vegas, NV
The University of North Carolina at Charlotte, NC
University of Oklahoma, OK
University of Oregon, OR
University of South Florida, FL
The University of Tennessee, TN
University of Utah, UT
University of Washington, WA
University of Wisconsin–Stevens Point, WI
University of Wyoming, WY
Utah State University, UT
Washington State University, WA
Washington University in St. Louis, MO
Woodbury University, CA

Area/Ethnic Studies

Augustana College, IL

Binghamton University, State University of New York, NY
Birmingham-Southern College, AL
Boise State University, ID
California State Polytechnic University, Pomona, CA
California State University, Chico, CA
California State University, Fresno, CA
California State University, Fullerton, CA
California State University, Stanislaus, CA
City College of the City University of New York, NY
College of Staten Island of the City University of New York, NY
Earlham College, IN
Eastern Washington University, WA
Edgewood College, WI
Florida Agricultural and Mechanical University, FL
Fort Hays State University, KS
Fort Lewis College, CO
Indiana State University, IN
Indiana University of Pennsylvania, PA
Kean University, NJ
Kent State University, OH
Kent State University at Geauga, OH
Kent State University at Stark, OH
Loyola Marymount University, CA
Middle Tennessee State University, TN
Mississippi State University, MS
Montana State University, MT
Morgan State University, MD
New Jersey Institute of Technology, NJ
New Mexico State University, NM
Northern Illinois University, IL
Oakland University, MI
The Ohio State University, OH
Ohio University, OH
Ohio University–Chillicothe, OH
Ohio University–Eastern, OH
Ohio University–Lancaster, OH
Ohio University–Southern Campus, OH
Ohio University–Zanesville, OH
Oklahoma State University, OK
Old Dominion University, VA
Portland State University, OR
Purchase College, State University of New York, NY
St. Ambrose University, IA
San Diego State University, CA
Sonoma State University, CA
Southern Illinois University Carbondale, IL
State University of New York at New Paltz, NY
State University of New York at Oswego, NY
State University of New York at Plattsburgh, NY
State University of New York College at Geneseo, NY
Stetson University, FL
Stockton University, NJ
Stony Brook University, State University of New York, NY
The University of Alabama, AL
University of Arkansas, AR
University of California, Davis, CA
University of California, Los Angeles, CA
University of California, Riverside, CA
University of California, Santa Cruz, CA
University of Colorado Boulder, CO
University of Dallas, TX
University of Hawaii at Manoa, HI
University of Houston, TX
University of Illinois at Urbana-Champaign, IL
The University of Kansas, KS
University of Kentucky, KY
University of Louisville, KY
University of Miami, FL
University of Michigan, MI
University of Minnesota, Twin Cities Campus, MN
University of North Carolina Asheville, NC
University of Oklahoma, OK
University of Pittsburgh, PA
University of Rhode Island, RI
University of South Carolina, SC
The University of Texas at San Antonio, TX
University of Utah, UT
University of Washington, WA
University of Washington, Bothell, WA
University of Washington, Tacoma, WA
University of Wisconsin–Eau Claire, WI
University of Wisconsin–Green Bay, WI
University of Wisconsin–La Crosse, WI
University of Wyoming, WY
Washington State University, WA
Washington University in St. Louis, MO
Wayne State University, MI
Western Illinois University, IL
Wheaton College, IL
Wichita State University, KS
William Jessup University, CA
Wright State University, OH
Wright State University–Lake Campus, OH

Biological Sciences

Abilene Christian University, TX
Alfred University, NY
Anderson University, IN
Angelo State University, TX
Arkansas Tech University, AR
Asbury University, KY
Auburn University, AL
Augsburg University, MN
Augustana College, IL
Augustana University, SD
Austin College, TX
Austin Peay State University, TN
Averett University, VA
Ball State University, IN
Barton College, NC
Belhaven University, MS
Bellarmine University, KY
Belmont University, TN
Bemidji State University, MN
Bethel College, KS
Binghamton University, State University of New York, NY
Biola University, CA
Birmingham-Southern College, AL
Black Hills State University, SD
Bloomsburg University of Pennsylvania, PA
Bluffton University, OH
Boise State University, ID
Bowie State University, MD
Bowling Green State University, OH
Bryan College, TN
Buena Vista University, IA
Butler University, IN
California Lutheran University, CA
California Polytechnic State University, San Luis Obispo, CA
California State Polytechnic University, Pomona, CA
California State University, Bakersfield, CA
California State University, Chico, CA
California State University, Fresno, CA
California State University, Fullerton, CA
California State University, Los Angeles, CA
California State University, San Bernardino, CA
California State University, Stanislaus, CA
Cameron University, OK
Campbellsville University, KY
Carlow University, PA
Carroll University, WI
Carson-Newman University, TN
Carthage College, WI
Case Western Reserve University, OH
Catawba College, NC
Cedar Crest College, PA
Centenary College of Louisiana, LA
Central College, IA
Central Methodist University, MO
Central Michigan University, MI
Chaminade University of Honolulu, HI
Chapman University, CA
Christopher Newport University, VA
The Citadel, The Military College of South Carolina, SC
City College of the City University of New York, NY
Clarion University of Pennsylvania, PA
Clarkson University, NY
Clemson University, SC
Cleveland State University, OH
Coastal Carolina University, SC
The College of Idaho, ID
College of Saint Mary, NE
College of Staten Island of the City University of New York, NY
The Colorado College, CO
Colorado Mesa University, CO
Columbia College, MO
Columbia College, SC
Columbus State University, GA
Concordia College, MN
Concordia University Chicago, IL
Concordia University Texas, TX
Concord University, WV
Dakota State University, SD
Dallas Baptist University, TX
Davidson College, NC
Delta State University, MS
DeSales University, PA
Dordt University, IA
Drury University, MO
Earlham College, IN
East Carolina University, NC
Eastern Illinois University, IL
Eastern Mennonite University, VA
Eastern Michigan University, MI
Eastern New Mexico University, NM
Eastern Washington University, WA
East Texas Baptist University, TX
Edinboro University of Pennsylvania, PA
Elizabethtown College, PA
Elon University, NC
Emporia State University, KS
Evangel University, MO
Ferris State University, MI
Florida Agricultural and Mechanical University, FL
Florida Gulf Coast University, FL
Florida Institute of Technology, FL
Florida International University, FL
Fordham University, NY
Fort Hays State University, KS
Fort Lewis College, CO
Framingham State University, MA
Gannon University, PA
George Fox University, OR
Georgia Institute of Technology, GA
Georgian Court University, NJ
Glenville State College, WV

Goshen College, IN
Governors State University, IL
Grambling State University, LA
Grand View University, IA
Greenville University, IL
Grove City College, PA
Hamline University, MN
Hampshire College, MA
Hampton University, VA
Hardin-Simmons University, TX
High Point University, NC
Hillsdale College, MI
Houghton College, NY
Idaho State University, ID
Illinois Institute of Technology, IL
Illinois State University, IL
Indiana State University, IN
Indiana University of Pennsylvania, PA
Jacksonville State University, AL
James Madison University, VA
John Carroll University, OH
Kean University, NJ
Kennesaw State University, GA
Kent State University, OH
Kent State University at Geauga, OH
Kent State University at Stark, OH
Kenyon College, OH
King's College, PA
Kutztown University of Pennsylvania, PA
Lake Erie College, OH
Lake Forest College, IL
La Sierra University, CA
Lebanon Valley College, PA
Lee University, TN
Lewis-Clark State College, ID
Liberty University, VA
Limestone College, SC
Linfield College, OR
Lipscomb University, TN
Lock Haven University of Pennsylvania, PA
Longwood University, VA
Loras College, IA
Louisiana State University and Agricultural & Mechanical College, LA
Louisiana State University in Shreveport, LA
Loyola Marymount University, CA
Lynn University, FL
Malone University, OH
Manhattan College, NY
Mansfield University of Pennsylvania, PA
Marquette University, WI
Marymount University, VA
Maryville University of Saint Louis, MO
Marywood University, PA
Massachusetts College of Liberal Arts, MA
McKendree University, IL
Mercer University, GA
Michigan State University, MI
Middle Tennessee State University, TN
Midwestern State University, TX
Millersville University of Pennsylvania, PA
Millikin University, IL
Mills College, CA
Minnesota State University Moorhead, MN
Minot State University, ND
Mississippi State University, MS
Missouri University of Science and Technology, MO
Missouri Valley College, MO
Molloy College, NY
Montana State University, MT
Montana State University Billings, MT
Montana Technological University, MT
Montclair State University, NJ
Morehead State University, KY
Morgan State University, MD
Muskingum University, OH
Nazareth College of Rochester, NY
Newberry College, SC
New Jersey Institute of Technology, NJ
New Mexico State University, NM
North Carolina Central University, NC
North Carolina State University, NC
North Central College, IL
North Dakota State University, ND
Northeastern Illinois University, IL
Northeastern State University, OK
Northern Illinois University, IL
Northern Michigan University, MI
Northern State University, SD
North Greenville University, SC
Northwestern State University of Louisiana, LA
Northwest Missouri State University, MO
Northwest Nazarene University, ID
Northwest University, WA
Oakland University, MI
Oglethorpe University, GA
The Ohio State University, OH
Ohio University, OH
Ohio University–Chillicothe, OH
Ohio University–Eastern, OH
Ohio University–Lancaster, OH
Ohio University–Southern Campus, OH
Ohio University–Zanesville, OH
Oklahoma Baptist University, OK
Oklahoma State University, OK
Old Dominion University, VA
Oral Roberts University, OK
Ouachita Baptist University, AR
Pacific University, OR
Piedmont College, GA
Pittsburg State University, KS
Plymouth State University, NH
Point Loma Nazarene University, CA
Purchase College, State University of New York, NY
Purdue University Fort Wayne, IN
Purdue University Northwest, IN
Randolph College, VA
Reinhardt University, GA
Rockford University, IL
Sacred Heart University, CT
Saginaw Valley State University, MI
St. Ambrose University, IA
St. Cloud State University, MN
St. Edward's University, TX
Saint Francis University, PA
St. John Fisher College, NY
St. John's University, NY
Saint Joseph's University, PA
Saint Mary's College of California, CA
Saint Vincent College, PA
Samford University, AL
Sam Houston State University, TX
San Diego State University, CA
San Jose State University, CA
Schreiner University, TX
Shenandoah University, VA
Shepherd University, WV
Shippensburg University of Pennsylvania, PA
Skidmore College, NY
Slippery Rock University of Pennsylvania, PA
Sonoma State University, CA
Southeast Missouri State University, MO
Southern Illinois University Carbondale, IL
Southwestern College, KS
Southwestern Oklahoma State University, OK
Spelman College, GA
State University of New York at Fredonia, NY
State University of New York at New Paltz, NY
State University of New York at Oswego, NY
State University of New York at Plattsburgh, NY
State University of New York College at Geneseo, NY
State University of New York College at Oneonta, NY
State University of New York College at Potsdam, NY
State University of New York College of Environmental Science and Forestry, NY
Stephen F. Austin State University, TX
Stetson University, FL
Stockton University, NJ
Stony Brook University, State University of New York, NY
Sul Ross State University, TX
SUNY Brockport, NY
Tabor College, KS
Texas A&M University, TX
Texas A&M University–Commerce, TX
Texas A&M University–Texarkana, TX
Texas Christian University, TX
Texas Lutheran University, TX
Texas State University, TX
Texas Tech University, TX
Texas Woman's University, TX
Thomas More University, KY
Towson University, MD
Trevecca Nazarene University, TN
Trinity Christian College, IL
Truett McConnell University, GA
Truman State University, MO
Union University, TN
The University of Akron, OH
The University of Alabama, AL
University of Alaska Anchorage, AK
University of Alaska Fairbanks, AK
University of Arkansas, AR
University of California, Davis, CA
University of California, Los Angeles, CA
University of California, Riverside, CA
University of California, San Diego, CA
University of Colorado Boulder, CO
University of Colorado Denver, CO
University of Dallas, TX
University of Dayton, OH
University of Denver, CO
University of Evansville, IN
University of Hawaii at Manoa, HI
University of Houston, TX
University of Houston–Clear Lake, TX
University of Idaho, ID
University of Illinois at Urbana-Champaign, IL
The University of Kansas, KS
University of Kentucky, KY
University of Louisiana at Monroe, LA
University of Louisville, KY
University of Maine, ME
University of Maine at Fort Kent, ME
University of Mary Hardin-Baylor, TX
University of Maryland, Baltimore County, MD
University of Maryland, College Park, MD
University of Mary Washington, VA
University of Massachusetts Amherst, MA

University of Massachusetts Dartmouth, MA
University of Massachusetts Lowell, MA
University of Memphis, TN
University of Miami, FL
University of Michigan, MI
University of Michigan–Dearborn, MI
University of Michigan–Flint, MI
University of Minnesota, Crookston, MN
University of Minnesota, Twin Cities Campus, MN
University of Mississippi, MS
University of Missouri–St. Louis, MO
University of Montana, MT
University of Montevallo, AL
University of Nebraska at Omaha, NE
University of Nebraska–Lincoln, NE
University of Nevada, Las Vegas, NV
University of Nevada, Reno, NV
University of New Hampshire, NH
University of New Hampshire at Manchester, NH
University of North Carolina Asheville, NC
The University of North Carolina at Charlotte, NC
The University of North Carolina at Greensboro, NC
The University of North Carolina Wilmington, NC
University of North Dakota, ND
University of Northern Colorado, CO
University of Northern Iowa, IA
University of North Georgia, GA
University of Northwestern–St. Paul, MN
University of Oklahoma, OK
University of Oregon, OR
University of Pittsburgh, PA
University of Pittsburgh at Bradford, PA
University of Pittsburgh at Johnstown, PA
University of Portland, OR
University of Providence, MT
University of Puget Sound, WA
University of Rhode Island, RI
University of Richmond, VA
University of St. Francis, IL
University of St. Thomas, TX
University of South Carolina, SC
University of South Carolina Aiken, SC
University of Southern Indiana, IN
University of South Florida, FL
The University of Tampa, FL
The University of Tennessee at Chattanooga, TN
The University of Tennessee at Martin, TN
The University of Texas at Dallas, TX
The University of Texas at El Paso, TX
The University of Texas at San Antonio, TX
The University of Texas Rio Grande Valley, TX
The University of Toledo, OH
The University of Tulsa, OK
University of Utah, UT
University of Washington, WA
University of Washington, Bothell, WA
University of Washington, Tacoma, WA
University of West Georgia, GA
University of Wisconsin–Eau Claire, WI
University of Wisconsin–Green Bay, WI
University of Wisconsin–La Crosse, WI
University of Wisconsin–Parkside, WI
University of Wisconsin–Platteville, WI
University of Wisconsin–River Falls, WI
University of Wisconsin–Stevens Point, WI
University of Wisconsin–Superior, WI
University of Wisconsin–Whitewater, WI
University of Wyoming, WY
Upper Iowa University, IA
Utah State University, UT
Valdosta State University, GA
Valley City State University, ND
Valparaiso University, IN
Walla Walla University, WA
Walsh University, OH
Wartburg College, IA
Washburn University, KS
Washington State University, WA
Washington University in St. Louis, MO
Wayland Baptist University, TX
Wayne State College, NE
Wayne State University, MI
Wesleyan College, GA
Western Carolina University, NC
Western Illinois University, IL
Western Kentucky University, KY
Western New Mexico University, NM
Western Oregon University, OR
Western Washington University, WA
Westminster College, UT
Wheaton College, IL
Wichita State University, KS
Widener University, PA
William Jessup University, CA
Wilson College, PA
Wright State University, OH
Wright State University–Lake Campus, OH
Xavier University of Louisiana, LA
Youngstown State University, OH

Business

Abilene Christian University, TX
Alfred University, NY
Alliant International University - San Diego, CA
Anderson University, IN
Anderson University, SC
Angelo State University, TX
Arkansas Tech University, AR
Asbury University, KY
Auburn University, AL
Auburn University at Montgomery, AL
Augsburg University, MN
Augustana College, IL
Augustana University, SD
Aurora University, IL
Austin College, TX
Austin Peay State University, TN
Ave Maria University, FL
Averett University, VA
Ball State University, IN
Barton College, NC
Baylor University, TX
Belhaven University, MS
Bellarmine University, KY
Belmont Abbey College, NC
Belmont University, TN
Bemidji State University, MN
Berry College, GA
Bethel College, KS
Binghamton University, State University of New York, NY
Birmingham-Southern College, AL
Black Hills State University, SD
Bloomsburg University of Pennsylvania, PA
Bluefield State College, WV
Boise State University, ID
Bowie State University, MD
Bowling Green State University, OH
Bryan College, TN
Bucknell University, PA
Buena Vista University, IA
Butler University, IN
California Lutheran University, CA
California Polytechnic State University, San Luis Obispo, CA
California State Polytechnic University, Pomona, CA
California State University, Bakersfield, CA
California State University, Chico, CA
California State University, Fresno, CA
California State University, Fullerton, CA
California State University, Los Angeles, CA
California State University Maritime Academy, CA
California State University, Monterey Bay, CA
California State University, Northridge, CA
California State University, San Bernardino, CA
California State University, Stanislaus, CA
Cameron University, OK
Campbellsville University, KY
Carlow University, PA
Carroll University, WI
Carson-Newman University, TN
Carthage College, WI
Case Western Reserve University, OH
Catawba College, NC
Cedar Crest College, PA
Centenary College of Louisiana, LA
Central College, IA
Central Methodist University, MO
Central Michigan University, MI
Champlain College, VT
Christopher Newport University, VA
The Citadel, The Military College of South Carolina, SC
Clarion University of Pennsylvania, PA
Clarkson University, NY
Clemson University, SC
Cleveland State University, OH
Coastal Carolina University, SC
The College of Idaho, ID
College of Staten Island of the City University of New York, NY
Colorado Mesa University, CO
Colorado School of Mines, CO
Columbia College, MO
Columbia College, SC
Columbia College Chicago, IL
Columbus State University, GA
Concordia College, MN
Concordia University Chicago, IL
Concordia University Texas, TX
Concord University, WV
Cornerstone University, MI
Creighton University, NE
Dakota State University, SD
Dallas Baptist University, TX
Davidson College, NC
Delta State University, MS
DeSales University, PA
Dordt University, IA
Drury University, MO
Earlham College, IN
East Carolina University, NC
Eastern Illinois University, IL
Eastern Mennonite University, VA
Eastern Michigan University, MI
Eastern New Mexico University, NM
Eastern Washington University, WA
East Texas Baptist University, TX
ECPI University, VA
Edinboro University of Pennsylvania, PA
Elizabethtown College, PA
Elon University, NC
Emmanuel College, GA
Emory University, GA
Emporia State University, KS

Endicott College, MA
Evangel University, MO
Felician University, NJ
Ferris State University, MI
Five Towns College, NY
Florida Agricultural and Mechanical University, FL
Florida Atlantic University, FL
Florida Gulf Coast University, FL
Florida Institute of Technology, FL
Florida International University, FL
Fordham University, NY
Fort Hays State University, KS
Fort Lewis College, CO
Gannon University, PA
George Fox University, OR
Georgia College & State University, GA
Georgian Court University, NJ
Glenville State College, WV
Gonzaga University, WA
Goshen College, IN
Governors State University, IL
Grambling State University, LA
Grand Valley State University, MI
Grand View University, IA
Grove City College, PA
Hamline University, MN
Hampden-Sydney College, VA
Hampton University, VA
Hardin-Simmons University, TX
High Point University, NC
Hillsdale College, MI
Houghton College, NY
Huntington University, IN
Idaho State University, ID
Illinois Institute of Technology, IL
Illinois State University, IL
Indiana State University, IN
Indiana University of Pennsylvania, PA
Iowa Wesleyan University, IA
Jacksonville State University, AL
James Madison University, VA
John Carroll University, OH
Johnson University, TN
Kean University, NJ
Kennesaw State University, GA
Kent State University, OH
Kent State University at Geauga, OH
Kent State University at Stark, OH
Kettering University, MI
King's College, PA
Kutztown University of Pennsylvania, PA
Kuyper College, MI
Lake Erie College, OH
La Sierra University, CA
Lee University, TN
Lehigh University, PA
Lewis-Clark State College, ID
Liberty University, VA
Limestone College, SC
Linfield College, OR
Lipscomb University, TN
Lock Haven University of Pennsylvania, PA
Longwood University, VA
Loras College, IA
Louisiana College, LA
Louisiana State University and Agricultural & Mechanical College, LA
Louisiana State University in Shreveport, LA
Loyola Marymount University, CA
Lynn University, FL
Lyon College, AR
Manhattan College, NY
Maranatha Baptist University, WI
Marquette University, WI
Marymount University, VA
Maryville University of Saint Louis, MO
Marywood University, PA
Massachusetts College of Liberal Arts, MA
McKendree University, IL
Mercer University, GA
Mercy College, NY
Michigan State University, MI
Michigan Technological University, MI
Middle Tennessee State University, TN
Midway University, KY
Midwestern State University, TX
Millersville University of Pennsylvania, PA
Millikin University, IL
Milwaukee School of Engineering, WI
Minnesota State University Moorhead, MN
Minot State University, ND
Mississippi State University, MS
Missouri University of Science and Technology, MO
Missouri Valley College, MO
Molloy College, NY
Montana State University, MT
Montana State University Billings, MT
Montana Technological University, MT
Montclair State University, NJ
Morehead State University, KY
Morgan State University, MD
Nazareth College of Rochester, NY
Newberry College, SC
New Jersey Institute of Technology, NJ
New Mexico State University, NM
Nichols College, MA
North Carolina Central University, NC
North Carolina State University, NC
North Central College, IL
North Dakota State University, ND
Northeastern Illinois University, IL
Northeastern State University, OK
Northern Illinois University, IL
Northern Michigan University, MI
Northern State University, SD
Northwestern State University of Louisiana, LA
Northwest Missouri State University, MO
Northwest Nazarene University, ID
Northwest University, WA
Oakland University, MI
Oglethorpe University, GA
Ohio Christian University, OH
The Ohio State University, OH
Ohio University, OH
Ohio University–Chillicothe, OH
Ohio University–Eastern, OH
Ohio University–Lancaster, OH
Ohio University–Southern Campus, OH
Ohio University–Zanesville, OH
Ohio Valley University, WV
Ohio Wesleyan University, OH
Oklahoma Baptist University, OK
Oklahoma City University, OK
Oklahoma State University, OK
Old Dominion University, VA
Olivet College, MI
Oral Roberts University, OK
Ouachita Baptist University, AR
Pacific Lutheran University, WA
Pacific University, OR
Piedmont College, GA
Pittsburg State University, KS
Point Loma Nazarene University, CA
Portland State University, OR
Providence College, RI
Purdue University Northwest, IN
Queens University of Charlotte, NC
Reinhardt University, GA
Rochester University, MI
Rockford University, IL
Rogers State University, OK
Sacred Heart University, CT
Saginaw Valley State University, MI
St. Ambrose University, IA
St. Bonaventure University, NY
St. Catherine University, MN
St. Cloud State University, MN
St. Edward's University, TX
Saint Francis University, PA
St. John Fisher College, NY
St. John's University, NY
Saint Martin's University, WA
Saint Mary's College of California, CA
St. Thomas Aquinas College, NY
Saint Vincent College, PA
Samford University, AL
Sam Houston State University, TX
San Diego State University, CA
San Jose State University, CA
Santa Clara University, CA
Schreiner University, TX
Shenandoah University, VA
Shepherd University, WV
Shippensburg University of Pennsylvania, PA
Slippery Rock University of Pennsylvania, PA
Sonoma State University, CA
Southeastern Louisiana University, LA
Southeast Missouri State University, MO
Southern Illinois University Carbondale, IL
Southern Illinois University Edwardsville, IL
Southern New Hampshire University, NH
Southwestern College, KS
Southwestern Oklahoma State University, OK
Southwestern University, TX
State University of New York at Fredonia, NY
State University of New York at New Paltz, NY
State University of New York at Oswego, NY
State University of New York at Plattsburgh, NY
State University of New York College at Geneseo, NY
State University of New York College at Oneonta, NY
State University of New York College at Potsdam, NY
Stephen F. Austin State University, TX
Stetson University, FL
Stockton University, NJ
Stony Brook University, State University of New York, NY
Sul Ross State University, TX
SUNY Brockport, NY
Susquehanna University, PA
Texas A&M International University, TX
Texas A&M University, TX
Texas A&M University–Commerce, TX
Texas A&M University–Texarkana, TX
Texas Christian University, TX
Texas Lutheran University, TX
Texas State University, TX
Texas Tech University, TX
Texas Woman's University, TX
Thomas More University, KY
Toccoa Falls College, GA

Towson University, MD
Trevecca Nazarene University, TN
Trinity Christian College, IL
Truett McConnell University, GA
Truman State University, MO
Tuskegee University, AL
Union University, TN
The University of Akron, OH
The University of Alabama, AL
The University of Alabama at Birmingham, AL
University of Alaska Anchorage, AK
University of Alaska Fairbanks, AK
University of Arkansas, AR
University of California, Davis, CA
University of California, Los Angeles, CA
University of California, Riverside, CA
University of California, San Diego, CA
University of Colorado Boulder, CO
University of Colorado Denver, CO
University of Dallas, TX
University of Dayton, OH
University of Denver, CO
University of Evansville, IN
University of Florida, FL
University of Georgia, GA
University of Guam, GU
University of Hawaii at Manoa, HI
University of Houston, TX
University of Houston–Clear Lake, TX
University of Houston - Downtown, TX
University of Idaho, ID
University of Illinois at Chicago, IL
University of Illinois at Urbana-Champaign, IL
University of Indianapolis, IN
The University of Iowa, IA
The University of Kansas, KS
University of Kentucky, KY
University of Louisiana at Monroe, LA
University of Louisville, KY
University of Maine, ME
University of Maine at Fort Kent, ME
University of Mary Hardin-Baylor, TX
University of Maryland, College Park, MD
University of Mary Washington, VA
University of Massachusetts Amherst, MA
University of Massachusetts Dartmouth, MA
University of Massachusetts Lowell, MA
University of Memphis, TN
University of Miami, FL
University of Michigan, MI
University of Michigan–Dearborn, MI
University of Michigan–Flint, MI
University of Minnesota, Twin Cities Campus, MN
University of Mississippi, MS
University of Missouri–St. Louis, MO
University of Montana, MT
University of Montevallo, AL
University of Nebraska at Omaha, NE
University of Nebraska–Lincoln, NE
University of Nevada, Las Vegas, NV
University of Nevada, Reno, NV
University of New Hampshire, NH
University of New Hampshire at Manchester, NH
University of North Carolina Asheville, NC
The University of North Carolina at Chapel Hill, NC
The University of North Carolina at Charlotte, NC
The University of North Carolina at Greensboro, NC
The University of North Carolina Wilmington, NC
University of North Dakota, ND
University of Northern Colorado, CO
University of Northern Iowa, IA
University of North Georgia, GA
University of Northwestern–St. Paul, MN
University of Oklahoma, OK
University of Oregon, OR
University of Pittsburgh, PA
University of Pittsburgh at Bradford, PA
University of Pittsburgh at Johnstown, PA
University of Portland, OR
University of Providence, MT
University of Puget Sound, WA
University of Rhode Island, RI
University of St. Thomas, TX
University of South Carolina, SC
University of South Carolina Aiken, SC
University of Southern Indiana, IN
University of South Florida, FL
The University of Tennessee, TN
The University of Tennessee at Chattanooga, TN
The University of Tennessee at Martin, TN
The University of Texas at Dallas, TX
The University of Texas at El Paso, TX
The University of Texas at San Antonio, TX
The University of Texas Rio Grande Valley, TX
The University of Toledo, OH
The University of Tulsa, OK
University of Utah, UT
University of Washington, WA
University of Washington, Bothell, WA
University of Washington, Tacoma, WA
University of West Georgia, GA
University of Wisconsin–Eau Claire, WI
University of Wisconsin–Green Bay, WI
University of Wisconsin–La Crosse, WI
University of Wisconsin–Milwaukee, WI
University of Wisconsin–Parkside, WI
University of Wisconsin–Platteville, WI
University of Wisconsin–River Falls, WI
University of Wisconsin–Stevens Point, WI
University of Wisconsin–Stout, WI
University of Wisconsin–Superior, WI
University of Wisconsin–Whitewater, WI
University of Wyoming, WY
Upper Iowa University, IA
Utah State University, UT
Valley City State University, ND
Walla Walla University, WA
Walsh College of Accountancy and Business Administration, MI
Walsh University, OH
Wartburg College, IA
Washburn University, KS
Washington & Jefferson College, PA
Washington State University, WA
Washington University in St. Louis, MO
Wayland Baptist University, TX
Wayne State College, NE
Wayne State University, MI
Webber International University, FL
Wesleyan College, GA
West Chester University of Pennsylvania, PA
Western Carolina University, NC
Western Illinois University, IL
Western Kentucky University, KY
Western New England University, MA
Western New Mexico University, NM
Western Oregon University, OR
Western Washington University, WA
Westminster College, UT
West Texas A&M University, TX
Wheaton College, IL
Wichita State University, KS
Widener University, PA
William Jessup University, CA
Wilson College, PA
Woodbury University, CA
Wright State University, OH
Wright State University–Lake Campus, OH
Xavier University of Louisiana, LA
Youngstown State University, OH

Communication

Abilene Christian University, TX
Albion College, MI
Alfred University, NY
Angelo State University, TX
Arkansas Tech University, AR
Asbury University, KY
Auburn University, AL
Augsburg University, MN
Augustana College, IL
Augustana University, SD
Austin College, TX
Austin Peay State University, TN
Ball State University, IN
Barton College, NC
Baylor University, TX
Belhaven University, MS
Bemidji State University, MN
Berry College, GA
Bethel College, KS
Biola University, CA
Birmingham-Southern College, AL
Black Hills State University, SD
Bloomsburg University of Pennsylvania, PA
Boise State University, ID
Bowie State University, MD
Bowling Green State University, OH
Bryan College, TN
Butler University, IN
California Lutheran University, CA
California Polytechnic State University, San Luis Obispo, CA
California State Polytechnic University, Pomona, CA
California State University, Bakersfield, CA
California State University, Chico, CA
California State University, Fresno, CA
California State University, Fullerton, CA
California State University, Los Angeles, CA
California State University, Northridge, CA
California State University, Stanislaus, CA
Cameron University, OK
Campbellsville University, KY
Carlow University, PA
Carroll University, WI
Case Western Reserve University, OH
Cedar Crest College, PA
Centenary College of Louisiana, LA
Central Methodist University, MO
Central Michigan University, MI
Champlain College, VT
Christopher Newport University, VA
City College of the City University of New York, NY
Clarion University of Pennsylvania, PA
Clarkson University, NY
Clemson University, SC
Cleveland State University, OH
Coastal Carolina University, SC
College of Staten Island of the City University of New York, NY
Colorado Mesa University, CO
Columbia College, MO
Columbia College, SC
Columbia College Chicago, IL
Columbus State University, GA

Concordia University Chicago, IL
Concordia University Texas, TX
Concord University, WV
Cornerstone University, MI
Dakota State University, SD
Dallas Baptist University, TX
DeSales University, PA
Dordt University, IA
Drury University, MO
East Carolina University, NC
Eastern Illinois University, IL
Eastern Michigan University, MI
Eastern New Mexico University, NM
Eastern Washington University, WA
East Texas Baptist University, TX
Edinboro University of Pennsylvania, PA
Elizabethtown College, PA
Elon University, NC
Emmanuel College, GA
Emporia State University, KS
Evangel University, MO
Ferris State University, MI
Florida Agricultural and Mechanical University, FL
Florida Institute of Technology, FL
Florida International University, FL
Fordham University, NY
Fort Hays State University, KS
Fort Lewis College, CO
Franklin Pierce University, NH
George Fox University, OR
Georgian Court University, NJ
Goshen College, IN
Governors State University, IL
Grambling State University, LA
Grand Valley State University, MI
Grand View University, IA
Grove City College, PA
Hampton University, VA
Hardin-Simmons University, TX
High Point University, NC
Hillsdale College, MI
Hofstra University, NY
Houghton College, NY
Huntington University, IN
Idaho State University, ID
Illinois Institute of Technology, IL
Illinois State University, IL
Indiana State University, IN
Indiana University of Pennsylvania, PA
Ithaca College, NY
Jacksonville State University, AL
John Carroll University, OH
Johnson University, TN
Kean University, NJ
Kennesaw State University, GA
Kent State University, OH
Kent State University at Geauga, OH
Kent State University at Stark, OH
King's College, PA
Kutztown University of Pennsylvania, PA
Kuyper College, MI
Lake Erie College, OH
Lee University, TN
Lehigh University, PA
Lewis-Clark State College, ID
Liberty University, VA
Limestone College, SC
Linfield College, OR
Lipscomb University, TN
Lock Haven University of Pennsylvania, PA
Loras College, IA
Louisiana College, LA
Louisiana State University in Shreveport, LA
Loyola Marymount University, CA
Lynn University, FL
Mansfield University of Pennsylvania, PA
Marquette University, WI
Marywood University, PA
Massachusetts College of Liberal Arts, MA
Michigan State University, MI
Middle Tennessee State University, TN
Midwestern State University, TX
Millersville University of Pennsylvania, PA
Millikin University, IL
Milwaukee School of Engineering, WI
Minnesota State University Moorhead, MN
Minot State University, ND
Mississippi State University, MS
Missouri University of Science and Technology, MO
Missouri Valley College, MO
Molloy College, NY
Montana State University, MT
Montana State University Billings, MT
Montana Technological University, MT
Montclair State University, NJ
Morehead State University, KY
Morgan State University, MD
Nazareth College of Rochester, NY
Newberry College, SC
New Jersey Institute of Technology, NJ
New Mexico State University, NM
Nichols College, MA
North Central College, IL
North Dakota State University, ND
Northeastern Illinois University, IL
Northeastern State University, OK
Northern Illinois University, IL
Northern Michigan University, MI
Northern State University, SD
North Greenville University, SC
Northwestern State University of Louisiana, LA
Northwest Missouri State University, MO
Northwest Nazarene University, ID
Northwest University, WA
Oglethorpe University, GA
The Ohio State University, OH
Ohio University, OH
Ohio University–Chillicothe, OH
Ohio University–Eastern, OH
Ohio University–Lancaster, OH
Ohio University–Southern Campus, OH
Ohio University–Zanesville, OH
Oklahoma City University, OK
Oklahoma State University, OK
Old Dominion University, VA
Olivet College, MI
Oral Roberts University, OK
Ouachita Baptist University, AR
Pacific University, OR
Piedmont College, GA
Pittsburg State University, KS
Point Loma Nazarene University, CA
Purdue University Northwest, IN
Queens University of Charlotte, NC
Reinhardt University, GA
St. Ambrose University, IA
St. Bonaventure University, NY
St. Cloud State University, MN
St. Edward's University, TX
Saint Francis University, PA
St. John Fisher College, NY
St. John's University, NY
St. Thomas Aquinas College, NY
Saint Vincent College, PA
Samford University, AL
Sam Houston State University, TX
San Diego State University, CA
Schreiner University, TX
Shenandoah University, VA
Shepherd University, WV
Shippensburg University of Pennsylvania, PA
Slippery Rock University of Pennsylvania, PA
Sonoma State University, CA
Southeastern Louisiana University, LA
Southeastern University, FL
Southeast Missouri State University, MO
Southern Illinois University Carbondale, IL
Southwestern College, KS
Southwestern Oklahoma State University, OK
State University of New York at Fredonia, NY
State University of New York at New Paltz, NY
State University of New York at Oswego, NY
State University of New York at Plattsburgh, NY
State University of New York College at Geneseo, NY
State University of New York College at Potsdam, NY
Stephen F. Austin State University, TX
Stetson University, FL
Stockton University, NJ
SUNY Brockport, NY
Tabor College, KS
Texas A&M International University, TX
Texas A&M University–Commerce, TX
Texas A&M University–Texarkana, TX
Texas Christian University, TX
Texas Lutheran University, TX
Texas State University, TX
Texas Tech University, TX
Texas Woman's University, TX
Thomas More University, KY
Toccoa Falls College, GA
Towson University, MD
Trevecca Nazarene University, TN
Trinity Christian College, IL
Truman State University, MO
Union University, TN
The University of Akron, OH
The University of Alabama, AL
The University of Alabama at Birmingham, AL
University of Alaska Anchorage, AK
University of Arkansas, AR
University of California, Davis, CA
University of California, Los Angeles, CA
University of California, San Diego, CA
University of Colorado Boulder, CO
University of Colorado Denver, CO
University of Dayton, OH
University of Denver, CO
University of Evansville, IN
University of Florida, FL
University of Guam, GU
University of Hawaii at Manoa, HI
University of Houston, TX
University of Idaho, ID
University of Illinois at Urbana-Champaign, IL
University of Indianapolis, IN
The University of Kansas, KS
University of Kentucky, KY
University of Louisiana at Monroe, LA
University of Louisville, KY
University of Maine, ME

University of Maine at Fort Kent, ME
University of Mary Hardin-Baylor, TX
University of Maryland, College Park, MD
University of Massachusetts Amherst, MA
University of Memphis, TN
University of Miami, FL
University of Michigan, MI
University of Michigan–Dearborn, MI
University of Michigan–Flint, MI
University of Minnesota, Twin Cities Campus, MN
University of Mississippi, MS
University of Missouri–St. Louis, MO
University of Montevallo, AL
University of Nebraska at Kearney, NE
University of Nebraska at Omaha, NE
University of Nevada, Las Vegas, NV
University of Nevada, Reno, NV
University of New Hampshire at Manchester, NH
University of North Carolina Asheville, NC
The University of North Carolina at Chapel Hill, NC
The University of North Carolina at Greensboro, NC
The University of North Carolina Wilmington, NC
University of North Dakota, ND
University of Northern Colorado, CO
University of Northern Iowa, IA
University of Northwestern–St. Paul, MN
University of Oklahoma, OK
University of Pittsburgh, PA
University of Pittsburgh at Bradford, PA
University of Pittsburgh at Johnstown, PA
University of Portland, OR
University of Puget Sound, WA
University of Rhode Island, RI
University of St. Francis, IL
University of St. Thomas, TX
University of South Carolina, SC
University of South Carolina Aiken, SC
University of South Florida, FL
The University of Tennessee, TN
The University of Tennessee at Chattanooga, TN
The University of Tennessee at Martin, TN
The University of Texas at El Paso, TX
The University of Texas at San Antonio, TX
The University of Texas at Tyler, TX
The University of Texas Rio Grande Valley, TX
The University of Toledo, OH
The University of Tulsa, OK
University of Utah, UT
University of Washington, WA
University of Washington, Bothell, WA
University of Washington, Tacoma, WA
University of West Georgia, GA
University of Wisconsin–Eau Claire, WI
University of Wisconsin–Green Bay, WI
University of Wisconsin–La Crosse, WI
University of Wisconsin–Parkside, WI
University of Wisconsin–Platteville, WI
University of Wisconsin–River Falls, WI
University of Wisconsin–Stevens Point, WI
University of Wisconsin–Superior, WI
University of Wisconsin–Whitewater, WI
University of Wyoming, WY
Utah State University, UT
Valdosta State University, GA
Valley City State University, ND
Walla Walla University, WA
Walsh University, OH
Wartburg College, IA
Washburn University, KS
Washington State University, WA
Washington University in St. Louis, MO
Wayland Baptist University, TX
Waynesburg University, PA
Wayne State College, NE
Wayne State University, MI
Wesleyan College, GA
Western Carolina University, NC
Western Illinois University, IL
Western Kentucky University, KY
Western Oregon University, OR
Western Washington University, WA
Westminster College, UT
West Texas A&M University, TX
Wheaton College, IL
Wichita State University, KS
Widener University, PA
William Jessup University, CA
Wilson College, PA
Wright State University, OH
Wright State University–Lake Campus, OH
Xavier University of Louisiana, LA
Youngstown State University, OH

Computer Science

Anderson University, IN
Angelo State University, TX
Arkansas Tech University, AR
Auburn University, AL
Augsburg University, MN
Augustana College, IL
Augustana University, SD
Austin College, TX
Austin Peay State University, TN
Baylor University, TX
Bemidji State University, MN
Binghamton University, State University of New York, NY
Birmingham-Southern College, AL
Black Hills State University, SD
Bloomsburg University of Pennsylvania, PA
Bluefield State College, WV
Boise State University, ID
Bowie State University, MD
Bowling Green State University, OH
Bryan College, TN
Buena Vista University, IA
Butler University, IN
California Lutheran University, CA
California Polytechnic State University, San Luis Obispo, CA
California State Polytechnic University, Pomona, CA
California State University, Chico, CA
California State University, Fullerton, CA
California State University, Los Angeles, CA
California State University, Northridge, CA
California State University, San Bernardino, CA
California State University, Stanislaus, CA
Cameron University, OK
Campbellsville University, KY
Carlow University, PA
Carroll University, WI
Carthage College, WI
Case Western Reserve University, OH
Centenary College of Louisiana, LA
Central College, IA
Central Methodist University, MO
Central Michigan University, MI
Champlain College, VT
Christian Brothers University, TN
Christopher Newport University, VA
The Citadel, The Military College of South Carolina, SC
City College of the City University of New York, NY
Clarion University of Pennsylvania, PA
Clarkson University, NY
Clemson University, SC
Cleveland State University, OH
Coastal Carolina University, SC
College of Saint Benedict, MN
College of Staten Island of the City University of New York, NY
Colorado Mesa University, CO
Colorado School of Mines, CO
Columbia College, MO
Columbus State University, GA
Concordia University Chicago, IL
Concordia University Texas, TX
Dakota State University, SD
Dallas Baptist University, TX
DeSales University, PA
Dordt University, IA
Drury University, MO
Earlham College, IN
East Carolina University, NC
Eastern Illinois University, IL
Eastern Michigan University, MI
Eastern New Mexico University, NM
Eastern Oregon University, OR
Eastern Washington University, WA
ECPI University, VA
Edinboro University of Pennsylvania, PA
Elizabethtown College, PA
Elon University, NC
Emporia State University, KS
Evangel University, MO
Ferris State University, MI
Florida Agricultural and Mechanical University, FL
Florida Institute of Technology, FL
Florida International University, FL
Fort Hays State University, KS
George Fox University, OR
Georgia Institute of Technology, GA
Georgian Court University, NJ
Goshen College, IN
Graceland University, IA
Grambling State University, LA
Grand Valley State University, MI
Grand View University, IA
Hampton University, VA
Hardin-Simmons University, TX
Houghton College, NY
Idaho State University, ID
Illinois Institute of Technology, IL
Illinois State University, IL
Indiana State University, IN
Indiana Tech, IN
Indiana University of Pennsylvania, PA
Jacksonville State University, AL
James Madison University, VA
John Carroll University, OH
Kean University, NJ
Kennesaw State University, GA
Kent State University, OH
Kent State University at Geauga, OH
Kent State University at Stark, OH
Kenyon College, OH
Kettering University, MI
Keystone College, PA
King's College, PA
Kutztown University of Pennsylvania, PA
Lake Forest College, IL
Liberty University, VA
Limestone College, SC
Linfield College, OR
Lock Haven University of Pennsylvania, PA
Longwood University, VA

Loras College, IA
Louisiana State University and Agricultural & Mechanical College, LA
Louisiana State University in Shreveport, LA
Loyola Marymount University, CA
Manhattan College, NY
Marymount University, VA
Marywood University, PA
Massachusetts College of Liberal Arts, MA
Michigan State University, MI
Middle Tennessee State University, TN
Midwestern State University, TX
Millersville University of Pennsylvania, PA
Mills College, CA
Milwaukee School of Engineering, WI
Minnesota State University Moorhead, MN
Minot State University, ND
Mississippi State University, MS
Missouri University of Science and Technology, MO
Missouri Valley College, MO
Montana State University, MT
Montana State University Billings, MT
Montana Technological University, MT
Montreat College, NC
Morgan State University, MD
Muskingum University, OH
New Jersey Institute of Technology, NJ
New Mexico State University, NM
North Carolina Central University, NC
North Carolina State University, NC
North Central College, IL
North Dakota State University, ND
Northeastern Illinois University, IL
Northeastern State University, OK
Northern Illinois University, IL
Northern Michigan University, MI
Northern State University, SD
Northwest Missouri State University, MO
Northwest Nazarene University, ID
Oakland University, MI
The Ohio State University, OH
Ohio University, OH
Ohio University–Chillicothe, OH
Ohio University–Eastern, OH
Ohio University–Lancaster, OH
Ohio University–Southern Campus, OH
Ohio University–Zanesville, OH
Ohio Valley University, WV
Oklahoma Baptist University, OK
Oklahoma State University, OK
Old Dominion University, VA
Ouachita Baptist University, AR
Pittsburg State University, KS
Plymouth State University, NH
Point Loma Nazarene University, CA
Portland State University, OR
Purchase College, State University of New York, NY
Purdue University, IN
Purdue University Northwest, IN
Reinhardt University, GA
Rochester University, MI
Rockford University, IL
Rollins College, FL
Sacred Heart University, CT
Saginaw Valley State University, MI
St. Ambrose University, IA
St. Cloud State University, MN
St. Edward's University, TX
Saint Francis University, PA
St. John Fisher College, NY
St. John's University, NY
Saint Joseph's University, PA
St. Thomas Aquinas College, NY
Saint Vincent College, PA
Samford University, AL
Sam Houston State University, TX
San Diego State University, CA
Shenandoah University, VA
Shepherd University, WV
Shippensburg University of Pennsylvania, PA
Skidmore College, NY
Slippery Rock University of Pennsylvania, PA
Sonoma State University, CA
Southeastern Louisiana University, LA
Southeast Missouri State University, MO
Southern Illinois University Carbondale, IL
Southern New Hampshire University, NH
Southwestern College, KS
Southwestern Oklahoma State University, OK
Spelman College, GA
State University of New York at Fredonia, NY
State University of New York at Oswego, NY
State University of New York at Plattsburgh, NY
State University of New York College at Oneonta, NY
State University of New York College at Potsdam, NY
Stephen F. Austin State University, TX
Stetson University, FL
Stockton University, NJ
Stony Brook University, State University of New York, NY
SUNY Brockport, NY
Texas A&M University, TX
Texas A&M University–Commerce, TX
Texas A&M University–Texarkana, TX
Texas Lutheran University, TX
Texas State University, TX
Texas Tech University, TX
Texas Woman's University, TX
Thomas More University, KY
Towson University, MD
Trinity Christian College, IL
Truman State University, MO
Tuskegee University, AL
Union University, TN
The University of Akron, OH
The University of Alabama, AL
The University of Alabama at Birmingham, AL
University of Alaska Anchorage, AK
University of Alaska Fairbanks, AK
University of Arkansas, AR
University of California, Davis, CA
University of California, Los Angeles, CA
University of California, San Diego, CA
University of California, Santa Cruz, CA
University of Colorado Boulder, CO
University of Colorado Denver, CO
University of Dallas, TX
University of Dayton, OH
University of Denver, CO
University of Evansville, IN
University of Florida, FL
University of Guam, GU
University of Hawaii at Manoa, HI
University of Houston, TX
University of Houston–Clear Lake, TX
University of Idaho, ID
University of Illinois at Urbana-Champaign, IL
The University of Kansas, KS
University of Kentucky, KY
University of Louisiana at Monroe, LA
University of Louisville, KY
University of Maine, ME
University of Maine at Fort Kent, ME
University of Mary Hardin-Baylor, TX
University of Maryland, Baltimore County, MD
University of Maryland, College Park, MD
University of Mary Washington, VA
University of Massachusetts Amherst, MA
University of Massachusetts Dartmouth, MA
University of Massachusetts Lowell, MA
University of Memphis, TN
University of Miami, FL
University of Michigan, MI
University of Michigan–Dearborn, MI
University of Michigan–Flint, MI
University of Minnesota, Twin Cities Campus, MN
University of Mississippi, MS
University of Missouri–St. Louis, MO
University of Montana, MT
University of Nebraska at Omaha, NE
University of Nebraska–Lincoln, NE
University of Nevada, Las Vegas, NV
University of Nevada, Reno, NV
University of New Hampshire, NH
University of New Hampshire at Manchester, NH
University of North Carolina Asheville, NC
The University of North Carolina at Charlotte, NC
The University of North Carolina at Greensboro, NC
The University of North Carolina Wilmington, NC
University of North Dakota, ND
University of Northern Iowa, IA
University of Oklahoma, OK
University of Pittsburgh, PA
University of Pittsburgh at Bradford, PA
University of Pittsburgh at Johnstown, PA
University of Portland, OR
University of Providence, MT
University of Puget Sound, WA
University of Rhode Island, RI
University of Richmond, VA
University of St. Thomas, TX
University of South Carolina, SC
University of South Carolina Aiken, SC
University of South Florida, FL
The University of Tennessee, TN
The University of Tennessee at Chattanooga, TN
The University of Tennessee at Martin, TN
The University of Texas at Dallas, TX
The University of Texas at El Paso, TX
The University of Texas at San Antonio, TX
The University of Texas Rio Grande Valley, TX
The University of Toledo, OH
The University of Tulsa, OK
University of Utah, UT
University of Washington, WA
University of Washington, Bothell, WA
University of Washington, Tacoma, WA
University of West Georgia, GA
University of Wisconsin–Eau Claire, WI
University of Wisconsin–La Crosse, WI
University of Wisconsin–Parkside, WI
University of Wisconsin–River Falls, WI
University of Wisconsin–Stevens Point, WI
University of Wisconsin–Stout, WI

University of Wisconsin–Superior, WI
University of Wisconsin–Whitewater, WI
University of Wyoming, WY
Upper Iowa University, IA
Utah State University, UT
Valley City State University, ND
Vermont Technical College, VT
Walsh College of Accountancy and Business Administration, MI
Walsh University, OH
Wartburg College, IA
Washburn University, KS
Washington State University, WA
Washington University in St. Louis, MO
Wayne State College, NE
Wayne State University, MI
Western Illinois University, IL
Western New England University, MA
Western Oregon University, OR
Western Washington University, WA
Westminster College, UT
West Texas A&M University, TX
Wichita State University, KS
Widener University, PA
William Jessup University, CA
Wilson College, PA
Wright State University, OH
Wright State University–Lake Campus, OH
Xavier University of Louisiana, LA
Youngstown State University, OH

Education

Abilene Christian University, TX
Alfred University, NY
Alliant International University - San Diego, CA
Alverno College, WI
Anderson University, IN
Anderson University, SC
Angelo State University, TX
Arkansas Tech University, AR
Asbury University, KY
Auburn University, AL
Auburn University at Montgomery, AL
Augsburg University, MN
Augustana College, IL
Augustana University, SD
Aurora University, IL
Austin College, TX
Austin Peay State University, TN
Ave Maria University, FL
Averett University, VA
Ball State University, IN
The Baptist College of Florida, FL
Barton College, NC
Baylor University, TX
Belhaven University, MS
Bellarmine University, KY
Belmont Abbey College, NC
Bemidji State University, MN
Berklee College of Music, MA
Berry College, GA
Binghamton University, State University of New York, NY
Birmingham-Southern College, AL
Black Hills State University, SD
Bloomsburg University of Pennsylvania, PA
Bluefield State College, WV
Boise State University, ID
Bowling Green State University, OH
Bryan College, TN
Butler University, IN
California Lutheran University, CA
California Polytechnic State University, San Luis Obispo, CA
California State Polytechnic University, Pomona, CA
California State University, Bakersfield, CA
California State University, Chico, CA
California State University, Fresno, CA
California State University, Fullerton, CA
California State University, Los Angeles, CA
California State University, Northridge, CA
California State University, San Bernardino, CA
California State University, Stanislaus, CA
Cameron University, OK
Campbellsville University, KY
Carlow University, PA
Carroll University, WI
Carson-Newman University, TN
Catawba College, NC
Cedar Crest College, PA
Centenary College of Louisiana, LA
Central College, IA
Central Methodist University, MO
Central Michigan University, MI
Chaminade University of Honolulu, HI
Champlain College, VT
Christian Brothers University, TN
Christopher Newport University, VA
The Citadel, The Military College of South Carolina, SC
City College of the City University of New York, NY
Clarion University of Pennsylvania, PA
Clemson University, SC
Cleveland State University, OH
Coastal Carolina University, SC
The College of Idaho, ID
College of Saint Mary, NE
College of Staten Island of the City University of New York, NY
Colorado Mesa University, CO
Columbia College, MO
Columbia College, SC
Columbus State University, GA
Concordia University Chicago, IL
Concordia University Texas, TX
Concord University, WV
Cornerstone University, MI
Creighton University, NE
Dakota State University, SD
Dallas Baptist University, TX
Davidson College, NC
Delta State University, MS
DeSales University, PA
Dominican College, NY
Dordt University, IA
Drury University, MO
Duquesne University, PA
East Carolina University, NC
Eastern Illinois University, IL
Eastern Mennonite University, VA
Eastern Michigan University, MI
Eastern New Mexico University, NM
Eastern Oregon University, OR
Eastern Washington University, WA
East Texas Baptist University, TX
Edinboro University of Pennsylvania, PA
Elizabethtown College, PA
Elon University, NC
Emmanuel College, GA
Emporia State University, KS
Endicott College, MA
Evangel University, MO
Felician University, NJ
Ferris State University, MI
Five Towns College, NY
Florida Agricultural and Mechanical University, FL
Florida Gulf Coast University, FL
Florida International University, FL
Fort Hays State University, KS
Fort Lewis College, CO
Framingham State University, MA
Gannon University, PA
George Fox University, OR
Georgia College & State University, GA
Georgian Court University, NJ
Glenville State College, WV
Goddard College, VT
Goshen College, IN
Governors State University, IL
Grambling State University, LA
Grand Valley State University, MI
Grand View University, IA
Grove City College, PA
Hampton University, VA
Hardin-Simmons University, TX
High Point University, NC
Hillsdale College, MI
Houghton College, NY
Idaho State University, ID
Illinois State University, IL
Indiana State University, IN
Indiana University of Pennsylvania, PA
Iowa Wesleyan University, IA
Jacksonville State University, AL
James Madison University, VA
John Carroll University, OH
Johnson University, TN
Johnson University Florida, FL
Kean University, NJ
Kennesaw State University, GA
Kent State University, OH
Kent State University at Geauga, OH
Kent State University at Stark, OH
King's College, PA
Kutztown University of Pennsylvania, PA
LaGrange College, GA
Lake Erie College, OH
La Sierra University, CA
Lee University, TN
Lewis-Clark State College, ID
Liberty University, VA
Limestone College, SC
Linfield College, OR
Lipscomb University, TN
Livingstone College, NC
Lock Haven University of Pennsylvania, PA
Longwood University, VA
Loras College, IA
Louisiana State University and Agricultural & Mechanical College, LA
Louisiana State University in Shreveport, LA
Loyola Marymount University, CA
Mansfield University of Pennsylvania, PA
Marquette University, WI
Maryville University of Saint Louis, MO
Marywood University, PA
Massachusetts College of Liberal Arts, MA
Mercer University, GA
Methodist University, NC
Miami University, OH
Michigan State University, MI
Middle Tennessee State University, TN
Midwestern State University, TX
Millersville University of Pennsylvania, PA
Millikin University, IL
Minnesota State University Moorhead, MN
Minot State University, ND
Mississippi State University, MS
Missouri University of Science and Technology, MO
Missouri Valley College, MO

Molloy College, NY
Montana State University, MT
Montana State University Billings, MT
Montclair State University, NJ
Morehead State University, KY
Morgan State University, MD
Muskingum University, OH
Nazareth College of Rochester, NY
Newberry College, SC
New Jersey Institute of Technology, NJ
New Mexico State University, NM
North Carolina Central University, NC
North Carolina State University, NC
North Central College, IL
North Dakota State University, ND
Northeastern Illinois University, IL
Northeastern State University, OK
Northern Illinois University, IL
Northern Michigan University, MI
Northern State University, SD
North Greenville University, SC
Northwestern State University of Louisiana, LA
Northwest Missouri State University, MO
Northwest Nazarene University, ID
Northwest University, WA
Oakland University, MI
Ohio Christian University, OH
The Ohio State University, OH
Ohio University, OH
Ohio University–Chillicothe, OH
Ohio University–Eastern, OH
Ohio University–Lancaster, OH
Ohio University–Southern Campus, OH
Ohio University–Zanesville, OH
Ohio Valley University, WV
Ohio Wesleyan University, OH
Oklahoma Baptist University, OK
Oklahoma City University, OK
Oklahoma State University, OK
Old Dominion University, VA
Olivet College, MI
Oral Roberts University, OK
Ouachita Baptist University, AR
Pacific University, OR
Piedmont College, GA
Pittsburg State University, KS
Point Loma Nazarene University, CA
Portland State University, OR
Purdue University, IN
Purdue University Northwest, IN
Queens University of Charlotte, NC
Randolph College, VA
Reinhardt University, GA
Rochester University, MI
Rockford University, IL
Sacred Heart University, CT
Saginaw Valley State University, MI
St. Ambrose University, IA
St. Bonaventure University, NY
St. Catherine University, MN
St. Cloud State University, MN
St. Edward's University, TX
Saint Francis University, PA
St. John Fisher College, NY
Saint Martin's University, WA
St. Thomas Aquinas College, NY
Saint Vincent College, PA
Samford University, AL
Sam Houston State University, TX
San Diego State University, CA
San Jose State University, CA
Schreiner University, TX
Shenandoah University, VA
Shepherd University, WV
Shippensburg University of Pennsylvania, PA
Slippery Rock University of Pennsylvania, PA
Sonoma State University, CA
Southeastern Louisiana University, LA
Southeastern University, FL
Southeast Missouri State University, MO
Southern Illinois University Carbondale, IL
Southern Illinois University Edwardsville, IL
Southern New Hampshire University, NH
Southwestern College, KS
Southwestern Oklahoma State University, OK
Spelman College, GA
State University of New York at Fredonia, NY
State University of New York at New Paltz, NY
State University of New York at Oswego, NY
State University of New York at Plattsburgh, NY
State University of New York College at Geneseo, NY
State University of New York College at Oneonta, NY
State University of New York College at Potsdam, NY
Stephen F. Austin State University, TX
Stetson University, FL
Stockton University, NJ
Sul Ross State University, TX
SUNY Brockport, NY
Susquehanna University, PA
Texas A&M International University, TX
Texas A&M University, TX
Texas A&M University–Commerce, TX
Texas A&M University–Texarkana, TX
Texas Christian University, TX
Texas Lutheran University, TX
Texas State University, TX
Texas Tech University, TX
Texas Woman's University, TX
Thomas More University, KY
Toccoa Falls College, GA
Towson University, MD
Trevecca Nazarene University, TN
Trinity Christian College, IL
Truett McConnell University, GA
Truman State University, MO
Union University, TN
The University of Akron, OH
The University of Alabama, AL
University of Alaska Anchorage, AK
University of Alaska Fairbanks, AK
University of Arkansas, AR
University of California, Davis, CA
University of California, Los Angeles, CA
University of California, Riverside, CA
University of California, Santa Cruz, CA
University of Colorado Boulder, CO
University of Colorado Denver, CO
University of Dallas, TX
University of Dayton, OH
University of Evansville, IN
University of Florida, FL
University of Georgia, GA
University of Guam, GU
University of Hawaii at Manoa, HI
University of Houston, TX
University of Houston–Clear Lake, TX
University of Idaho, ID
University of Illinois at Urbana-Champaign, IL
The University of Kansas, KS
University of Kentucky, KY
University of Louisiana at Monroe, LA
University of Louisville, KY
University of Maine, ME
University of Mary Hardin-Baylor, TX
University of Maryland, Baltimore County, MD
University of Maryland, College Park, MD
University of Mary Washington, VA
University of Massachusetts Amherst, MA
University of Massachusetts Dartmouth, MA
University of Massachusetts Lowell, MA
University of Memphis, TN
University of Miami, FL
University of Michigan, MI
University of Michigan–Dearborn, MI
University of Michigan–Flint, MI
University of Minnesota, Twin Cities Campus, MN
University of Mississippi, MS
University of Missouri–St. Louis, MO
University of Montana, MT
University of Montevallo, AL
University of Nebraska at Omaha, NE
University of Nebraska–Lincoln, NE
University of Nevada, Las Vegas, NV
University of Nevada, Reno, NV
University of New Hampshire, NH
University of North Carolina Asheville, NC
The University of North Carolina at Chapel Hill, NC
The University of North Carolina at Charlotte, NC
The University of North Carolina at Greensboro, NC
The University of North Carolina at Pembroke, NC
The University of North Carolina Wilmington, NC
University of North Dakota, ND
University of Northern Colorado, CO
University of Northern Iowa, IA
University of North Georgia, GA
University of Northwestern–St. Paul, MN
University of Oklahoma, OK
University of Oregon, OR
University of Pittsburgh, PA
University of Pittsburgh at Bradford, PA
University of Pittsburgh at Johnstown, PA
University of Portland, OR
University of Providence, MT
University of Rhode Island, RI
University of St. Francis, IL
University of St. Thomas, TX
University of South Carolina, SC
University of South Carolina Aiken, SC
University of Southern Indiana, IN
University of South Florida, FL
The University of Tennessee, TN
The University of Tennessee at Chattanooga, TN
The University of Tennessee at Martin, TN
The University of Texas at El Paso, TX
The University of Texas at San Antonio, TX
The University of Texas Rio Grande Valley, TX
The University of Toledo, OH
The University of Tulsa, OK
University of Utah, UT
University of Washington, WA
University of Washington, Bothell, WA
University of Washington, Tacoma, WA

University of West Georgia, GA
University of Wisconsin–Eau Claire, WI
University of Wisconsin–Green Bay, WI
University of Wisconsin–La Crosse, WI
University of Wisconsin–Milwaukee, WI
University of Wisconsin–Parkside, WI
University of Wisconsin–Platteville, WI
University of Wisconsin–River Falls, WI
University of Wisconsin–Stevens Point, WI
University of Wisconsin–Stout, WI
University of Wisconsin–Superior, WI
University of Wisconsin–Whitewater, WI
University of Wyoming, WY
Upper Iowa University, IA
Utah State University, UT
Valdosta State University, GA
Valley City State University, ND
Valparaiso University, IN
VanderCook College of Music, IL
Walla Walla University, WA
Walsh University, OH
Wartburg College, IA
Washburn University, KS
Washington State University, WA
Washington University in St. Louis, MO
Wayland Baptist University, TX
Wayne State College, NE
Wayne State University, MI
Wesleyan College, GA
Western Carolina University, NC
Western Illinois University, IL
Western Kentucky University, KY
Western New Mexico University, NM
Western Oregon University, OR
Western Washington University, WA
Westminster College, UT
West Texas A&M University, TX
Wheaton College, IL
Wichita State University, KS
Widener University, PA
William Jessup University, CA
Wilson College, PA
Wright State University, OH
Wright State University–Lake Campus, OH
Xavier University of Louisiana, LA
Youngstown State University, OH

Engineering/Technologies

Abilene Christian University, TX
Alfred University, NY
Anderson University, IN
Angelo State University, TX
Arkansas Tech University, AR
Auburn University, AL
Austin College, TX
Austin Peay State University, TN
Averett University, VA
Ball State University, IN
Baylor University, TX
Bemidji State University, MN
Berklee College of Music, MA
Binghamton University, State University of New York, NY
Birmingham-Southern College, AL
Bluefield State College, WV
Boise State University, ID
Boston University, MA
Bowie State University, MD
Bowling Green State University, OH
Bucknell University, PA
Butler University, IN
California Baptist University, CA
California Polytechnic State University, San Luis Obispo, CA
California State Polytechnic University, Pomona, CA
California State University, Chico, CA
California State University, Fresno, CA
California State University, Fullerton, CA
California State University, Los Angeles, CA
California State University Maritime Academy, CA
California State University, Northridge, CA
Cameron University, OK
Carroll University, WI
Carthage College, WI
Case Western Reserve University, OH
Central College, IA
Central Michigan University, MI
Christian Brothers University, TN
Christopher Newport University, VA
The Citadel, The Military College of South Carolina, SC
City College of the City University of New York, NY
Clarkson University, NY
Clemson University, SC
Cleveland State University, OH
College of Saint Benedict, MN
College of Staten Island of the City University of New York, NY
Colorado Mesa University, CO
Colorado School of Mines, CO
Dordt University, IA
Earlham College, IN
East Carolina University, NC
Eastern Illinois University, IL
Eastern Mennonite University, VA
Eastern Michigan University, MI
Eastern New Mexico University, NM
Eastern Oregon University, OR
Eastern University, PA
Eastern Washington University, WA
ECPI University, VA
Edinboro University of Pennsylvania, PA
Elizabethtown College, PA
Elon University, NC
Emporia State University, KS
Evangel University, MO
Ferris State University, MI
Florida Agricultural and Mechanical University, FL
Florida Atlantic University, FL
Florida Gulf Coast University, FL
Florida International University, FL
Fort Hays State University, KS
Framingham State University, MA
Gannon University, PA
George Fox University, OR
Georgia Institute of Technology, GA
Gonzaga University, WA
Goshen College, IN
Graceland University, IA
Grambling State University, LA
Grand Valley State University, MI
Greenville University, IL
Grove City College, PA
Hamline University, MN
Hampton University, VA
Hillsdale College, MI
Hofstra University, NY
Houston Baptist University, TX
Idaho State University, ID
Illinois Institute of Technology, IL
Illinois State University, IL
Indiana State University, IN
Indiana Tech, IN
Indiana University of Pennsylvania, PA
James Madison University, VA
Johns Hopkins University, MD
Kean University, NJ
Kennesaw State University, GA
Kent State University, OH
Kent State University at Geauga, OH
Kettering University, MI
King's College, PA
Lehigh University, PA
Lewis-Clark State College, ID
Liberty University, VA
Lipscomb University, TN
Loras College, IA
Louisiana State University and Agricultural & Mechanical College, LA
Loyola Marymount University, CA
Manhattan College, NY
Marquette University, WI
Miami University, OH
Michigan State University, MI
Middle Tennessee State University, TN
Midwestern State University, TX
Milligan University, TN
Milwaukee School of Engineering, WI
Minnesota State University Moorhead, MN
Mississippi State University, MS
Missouri University of Science and Technology, MO
Montana State University, MT
Montana State University Billings, MT
Montana Technological University, MT
Morehead State University, KY
Morgan State University, MD
Muskingum University, OH
New Jersey Institute of Technology, NJ
New Mexico State University, NM
North Carolina State University, NC
North Dakota State University, ND
Northern Illinois University, IL
Northern Michigan University, MI
Northwestern State University of Louisiana, LA
Northwest Nazarene University, ID
Oakland University, MI
The Ohio State University, OH
Ohio University, OH
Ohio University–Chillicothe, OH
Ohio University–Eastern, OH
Ohio University–Lancaster, OH
Ohio University–Southern Campus, OH
Ohio University–Zanesville, OH
Oklahoma State University, OK
Old Dominion University, VA
Oral Roberts University, OK
Pittsburg State University, KS
Plymouth State University, NH
Point Loma Nazarene University, CA
Portland State University, OR
Purdue University, IN
Purdue University Fort Wayne, IN
Purdue University Northwest, IN
Rice University, TX
Rollins College, FL
Saginaw Valley State University, MI
St. Ambrose University, IA
St. Cloud State University, MN
Saint Francis University, PA
Saint Martin's University, WA
St. Thomas Aquinas College, NY
Saint Vincent College, PA
Sam Houston State University, TX
San Diego State University, CA
San Jose State University, CA
Santa Clara University, CA
Seattle Pacific University, WA
Shepherd University, WV
Slippery Rock University of Pennsylvania, PA
Sonoma State University, CA
Southeast Missouri State University, MO

Southern Illinois University Carbondale, IL
Southwestern Oklahoma State University, OK
Spelman College, GA
State University of New York at New Paltz, NY
State University of New York at Plattsburgh, NY
State University of New York College at Potsdam, NY
State University of New York College of Environmental Science and Forestry, NY
Stony Brook University, State University of New York, NY
Texas A&M International University, TX
Texas A&M University, TX
Texas A&M University–Commerce, TX
Texas A&M University–Texarkana, TX
Texas Christian University, TX
Texas State University, TX
Texas Tech University, TX
Trinity Christian College, IL
Tuskegee University, AL
Union University, TN
The University of Akron, OH
The University of Alabama, AL
The University of Alabama at Birmingham, AL
University of Alaska Anchorage, AK
University of Alaska Fairbanks, AK
University of Arkansas, AR
University of California, Davis, CA
University of California, Los Angeles, CA
University of California, Riverside, CA
University of California, San Diego, CA
University of Colorado Boulder, CO
University of Colorado Denver, CO
University of Dayton, OH
University of Denver, CO
University of Evansville, IN
University of Florida, FL
University of Hawaii at Manoa, HI
University of Houston, TX
University of Idaho, ID
University of Illinois at Urbana-Champaign, IL
The University of Iowa, IA
University of Jamestown, ND
The University of Kansas, KS
University of Kentucky, KY
University of Louisville, KY
University of Maine, ME
University of Maryland, Baltimore County, MD
University of Maryland, College Park, MD
University of Massachusetts Amherst, MA
University of Massachusetts Dartmouth, MA
University of Massachusetts Lowell, MA
University of Memphis, TN
University of Miami, FL
University of Michigan, MI
University of Michigan–Dearborn, MI
University of Michigan–Flint, MI
University of Minnesota, Twin Cities Campus, MN
University of Mississippi, MS
University of Missouri–St. Louis, MO
University of Nebraska at Omaha, NE
University of Nebraska–Lincoln, NE
University of Nevada, Las Vegas, NV
University of Nevada, Reno, NV
University of New Hampshire, NH
University of New Hampshire at Manchester, NH
University of New Mexico, NM
University of North Carolina Asheville, NC
The University of North Carolina at Charlotte, NC
The University of North Carolina Wilmington, NC
University of North Dakota, ND
University of Oklahoma, OK
University of Pittsburgh, PA
University of Pittsburgh at Bradford, PA
University of Pittsburgh at Johnstown, PA
University of Portland, OR
University of Rhode Island, RI
University of Rochester, NY
University of South Carolina, SC
University of South Carolina Aiken, SC
University of Southern Indiana, IN
University of South Florida, FL
The University of Tennessee, TN
The University of Tennessee at Chattanooga, TN
The University of Tennessee at Martin, TN
The University of Texas at Dallas, TX
The University of Texas at El Paso, TX
The University of Texas at San Antonio, TX
The University of Texas at Tyler, TX
The University of Texas Rio Grande Valley, TX
The University of Toledo, OH
The University of Tulsa, OK
University of Utah, UT
University of Washington, WA
University of Washington, Bothell, WA
University of Washington, Tacoma, WA
University of Wisconsin–Green Bay, WI
University of Wisconsin–Parkside, WI
University of Wisconsin–Platteville, WI
University of Wisconsin–River Falls, WI
University of Wisconsin–Stevens Point, WI
University of Wisconsin–Stout, WI
University of Wyoming, WY
Utah State University, UT
Valley City State University, ND
Valparaiso University, IN
Vermont Technical College, VT
Walla Walla University, WA
Wartburg College, IA
Washburn University, KS
Washington State University, WA
Washington University in St. Louis, MO
Wayne State University, MI
Wesleyan College, GA
Western Illinois University, IL
Western Kentucky University, KY
Western New England University, MA
Western Washington University, WA
West Texas A&M University, TX
Wheaton College, IL
Wichita State University, KS
Widener University, PA
Wright State University, OH
Wright State University–Lake Campus, OH
Xavier University of Louisiana, LA
York College of Pennsylvania, PA
Youngstown State University, OH

English

Abilene Christian University, TX
Alfred University, NY
Anderson University, IN
Angelo State University, TX
Arkansas Tech University, AR
Auburn University, AL
Augsburg University, MN
Augustana College, IL
Augustana University, SD
Austin College, TX
Austin Peay State University, TN
Averett University, VA
Ball State University, IN
Barton College, NC
Baylor University, TX
Belhaven University, MS
Bemidji State University, MN
Berry College, GA
Binghamton University, State University of New York, NY
Birmingham-Southern College, AL
Black Hills State University, SD
Bloomsburg University of Pennsylvania, PA
Boise State University, ID
Bowling Green State University, OH
Bryan College, TN
Butler University, IN
California Lutheran University, CA
California Polytechnic State University, San Luis Obispo, CA
California State Polytechnic University, Pomona, CA
California State University, Chico, CA
California State University, Fresno, CA
California State University, Fullerton, CA
California State University, Los Angeles, CA
California State University, Northridge, CA
California State University, Stanislaus, CA
Cameron University, OK
Campbellsville University, KY
Carlow University, PA
Case Western Reserve University, OH
Cedar Crest College, PA
Centenary College of Louisiana, LA
Central Methodist University, MO
Central Michigan University, MI
Christopher Newport University, VA
City College of the City University of New York, NY
Clarion University of Pennsylvania, PA
Clemson University, SC
Cleveland State University, OH
Coastal Carolina University, SC
The College of Idaho, ID
College of Staten Island of the City University of New York, NY
Colorado Mesa University, CO
Columbia College, MO
Columbia College, SC
Columbia College Chicago, IL
Columbus State University, GA
Concordia University Chicago, IL
Concordia University Texas, TX
Concord University, WV
Cornerstone University, MI
Dakota State University, SD
Dallas Baptist University, TX
Delta State University, MS
DeSales University, PA
Dordt University, IA
Drury University, MO
Earlham College, IN
East Carolina University, NC
Eastern Illinois University, IL
Eastern Mennonite University, VA
Eastern Michigan University, MI
Eastern New Mexico University, NM
Eastern Washington University, WA
East Texas Baptist University, TX
Edinboro University of Pennsylvania, PA
Elizabethtown College, PA
Emmanuel College, GA
Emporia State University, KS
Evangel University, MO

Felician University, NJ
Florida Agricultural and Mechanical University, FL
Florida International University, FL
Fort Hays State University, KS
Fort Lewis College, CO
Framingham State University, MA
Gannon University, PA
George Fox University, OR
Georgian Court University, NJ
Glenville State College, WV
Goshen College, IN
Governors State University, IL
Graceland University, IA
Grambling State University, LA
Grand Valley State University, MI
Grand View University, IA
Grove City College, PA
Hamline University, MN
Hampshire College, MA
Hardin-Simmons University, TX
High Point University, NC
Hillsdale College, MI
Hiram College, OH
Houghton College, NY
Idaho State University, ID
Illinois State University, IL
Indiana State University, IN
Indiana University of Pennsylvania, PA
Iowa Wesleyan University, IA
Jacksonville State University, AL
James Madison University, VA
John Carroll University, OH
Kean University, NJ
Kennesaw State University, GA
Kent State University, OH
Kent State University at Geauga, OH
Kent State University at Stark, OH
Kenyon College, OH
King's College, PA
Kutztown University of Pennsylvania, PA
Lake Erie College, OH
Lake Forest College, IL
La Sierra University, CA
Lebanon Valley College, PA
Lewis-Clark State College, ID
Liberty University, VA
Limestone College, SC
Linfield College, OR
Lipscomb University, TN
Lock Haven University of Pennsylvania, PA
Longwood University, VA
Loras College, IA
Louisiana College, LA
Louisiana State University and Agricultural & Mechanical College, LA
Louisiana State University in Shreveport, LA
Loyola Marymount University, CA
Marquette University, WI
Maryville University of Saint Louis, MO
Marywood University, PA
Massachusetts College of Liberal Arts, MA
Mercer University, GA
Michigan State University, MI
Middle Tennessee State University, TN
Midwestern State University, TX
Millersville University of Pennsylvania, PA
Millikin University, IL
Minnesota State University Moorhead, MN
Minot State University, ND
Mississippi State University, MS
Missouri University of Science and Technology, MO
Missouri Valley College, MO
Molloy College, NY
Montana State University, MT
Montana State University Billings, MT
Montclair State University, NJ
Morgan State University, MD
Nazareth College of Rochester, NY
New Mexico State University, NM
North Carolina Central University, NC
North Central College, IL
North Dakota State University, ND
Northeastern Illinois University, IL
Northeastern State University, OK
Northern Illinois University, IL
Northern Michigan University, MI
Northern State University, SD
Northwestern State University of Louisiana, LA
Northwest Missouri State University, MO
Northwest Nazarene University, ID
Northwest University, WA
Oakland University, MI
Oglethorpe University, GA
The Ohio State University, OH
Ohio University, OH
Ohio University–Chillicothe, OH
Ohio University–Eastern, OH
Ohio University–Lancaster, OH
Ohio University–Southern Campus, OH
Ohio University–Zanesville, OH
Ohio Valley University, WV
Oklahoma Baptist University, OK
Oklahoma State University, OK
Old Dominion University, VA
Olivet College, MI
Ouachita Baptist University, AR
Pacific University, OR
Piedmont College, GA
Pittsburg State University, KS
Point Loma Nazarene University, CA
Purchase College, State University of New York, NY
Purdue University Northwest, IN
Randolph College, VA
Reinhardt University, GA
Rockford University, IL
Sacred Heart University, CT
St. Ambrose University, IA
St. Bonaventure University, NY
St. Catherine University, MN
St. Cloud State University, MN
St. Edward's University, TX
Saint Francis University, PA
St. John Fisher College, NY
St. John's University, NY
Saint Mary's College of California, CA
St. Thomas Aquinas College, NY
Saint Vincent College, PA
Samford University, AL
Sam Houston State University, TX
San Diego State University, CA
San Jose State University, CA
Schreiner University, TX
Shenandoah University, VA
Shepherd University, WV
Shippensburg University of Pennsylvania, PA
Slippery Rock University of Pennsylvania, PA
Sonoma State University, CA
Southeastern Louisiana University, LA
Southeast Missouri State University, MO
Southern Illinois University Carbondale, IL
Southwestern College, KS
Southwestern Oklahoma State University, OK
Spelman College, GA
State University of New York at Fredonia, NY
State University of New York at New Paltz, NY
State University of New York at Oswego, NY
State University of New York at Plattsburgh, NY
State University of New York College at Geneseo, NY
State University of New York College at Oneonta, NY
State University of New York College at Potsdam, NY
Stetson University, FL
Stony Brook University, State University of New York, NY
Sul Ross State University, TX
SUNY Brockport, NY
Texas A&M International University, TX
Texas A&M University–Commerce, TX
Texas A&M University–Texarkana, TX
Texas Christian University, TX
Texas State University, TX
Texas Tech University, TX
Texas Woman's University, TX
Thomas More University, KY
Toccoa Falls College, GA
Towson University, MD
Trevecca Nazarene University, TN
Trinity Christian College, IL
Truman State University, MO
Union University, TN
The University of Akron, OH
The University of Alabama, AL
University of Alaska Anchorage, AK
University of Arkansas, AR
University of California, Davis, CA
University of California, Los Angeles, CA
University of California, Riverside, CA
University of Colorado Boulder, CO
University of Colorado Denver, CO
University of Dallas, TX
University of Dayton, OH
University of Denver, CO
University of Evansville, IN
University of Hawaii at Manoa, HI
University of Houston, TX
University of Idaho, ID
University of Illinois at Urbana-Champaign, IL
The University of Kansas, KS
University of Kentucky, KY
University of Louisiana at Monroe, LA
University of Louisville, KY
University of Maine, ME
University of Maine at Fort Kent, ME
University of Mary Hardin-Baylor, TX
University of Maryland, Baltimore County, MD
University of Maryland, College Park, MD
University of Mary Washington, VA
University of Massachusetts Amherst, MA
University of Massachusetts Lowell, MA
University of Memphis, TN
University of Miami, FL
University of Michigan, MI
University of Michigan–Flint, MI
University of Minnesota, Twin Cities Campus, MN
University of Mississippi, MS
University of Missouri–St. Louis, MO
University of Montana, MT
University of Montevallo, AL
University of Nebraska at Omaha, NE
University of Nebraska–Lincoln, NE

University of Nevada, Las Vegas, NV
University of Nevada, Reno, NV
University of New Hampshire, NH
University of New Hampshire at Manchester, NH
University of North Carolina Asheville, NC
The University of North Carolina at Chapel Hill, NC
The University of North Carolina at Greensboro, NC
The University of North Carolina Wilmington, NC
University of North Dakota, ND
University of Northern Colorado, CO
University of North Georgia, GA
University of Northwestern–St. Paul, MN
University of Oklahoma, OK
University of Oregon, OR
University of Pittsburgh, PA
University of Pittsburgh at Bradford, PA
University of Pittsburgh at Johnstown, PA
University of Portland, OR
University of Puget Sound, WA
University of Rhode Island, RI
University of St. Thomas, TX
University of South Carolina, SC
University of South Carolina Aiken, SC
University of South Florida, FL
The University of Tampa, FL
The University of Tennessee at Chattanooga, TN
The University of Tennessee at Martin, TN
The University of Texas at El Paso, TX
The University of Texas at San Antonio, TX
The University of Texas Rio Grande Valley, TX
The University of Toledo, OH
The University of Tulsa, OK
University of Utah, UT
University of Washington, WA
University of Washington, Bothell, WA
The University of West Alabama, AL
University of West Georgia, GA
University of Wisconsin–Eau Claire, WI
University of Wisconsin–La Crosse, WI
University of Wisconsin–Parkside, WI
University of Wisconsin–River Falls, WI
University of Wisconsin–Stevens Point, WI
University of Wisconsin–Superior, WI
University of Wisconsin–Whitewater, WI
University of Wyoming, WY
Utah State University, UT
Valley City State University, ND
Walla Walla University, WA
Walsh University, OH
Wartburg College, IA
Washburn University, KS
Washington State University, WA
Washington University in St. Louis, MO
Wayland Baptist University, TX
Wayne State College, NE
Wayne State University, MI
Wesleyan College, GA
Western Carolina University, NC
Western Illinois University, IL
Western Kentucky University, KY
Western Oregon University, OR
Western Washington University, WA
Westminster College, UT
West Texas A&M University, TX
Wheaton College, IL
Wichita State University, KS
Widener University, PA
William Jessup University, CA
Wilson College, PA
Wright State University, OH
Wright State University–Lake Campus, OH
Xavier University of Louisiana, LA
Youngstown State University, OH

Foreign Languages

Abilene Christian University, TX
Alfred University, NY
Anderson University, IN
Angelo State University, TX
Arkansas Tech University, AR
Asbury University, KY
Auburn University, AL
Augsburg University, MN
Augustana College, IL
Augustana University, SD
Austin College, TX
Austin Peay State University, TN
Averett University, VA
Ball State University, IN
Baylor University, TX
Belhaven University, MS
Bemidji State University, MN
Binghamton University, State University of New York, NY
Birmingham-Southern College, AL
Black Hills State University, SD
Bloomsburg University of Pennsylvania, PA
Boise State University, ID
Bowling Green State University, OH
Bryan College, TN
Butler University, IN
California Lutheran University, CA
California Polytechnic State University, San Luis Obispo, CA
California State Polytechnic University, Pomona, CA
California State University, Bakersfield, CA
California State University, Chico, CA
California State University, Fresno, CA
California State University, Fullerton, CA
California State University, Los Angeles, CA
California State University, San Bernardino, CA
California State University, Stanislaus, CA
Cameron University, OK
Carthage College, WI
Case Western Reserve University, OH
Centenary College of Louisiana, LA
Central College, IA
Central Methodist University, MO
Central Michigan University, MI
Centre College, KY
Christopher Newport University, VA
City College of the City University of New York, NY
Clarion University of Pennsylvania, PA
Clemson University, SC
Coastal Carolina University, SC
The College of Idaho, ID
College of Staten Island of the City University of New York, NY
Colorado Mesa University, CO
Columbia College, SC
Concordia University Chicago, IL
Concordia University Texas, TX
Davidson College, NC
DeSales University, PA
Dordt University, IA
Drury University, MO
Earlham College, IN
East Carolina University, NC
Eastern Illinois University, IL
Eastern Mennonite University, VA
Eastern Michigan University, MI
Eastern New Mexico University, NM
Eastern Washington University, WA
Edgewood College, WI
Edinboro University of Pennsylvania, PA
Elizabethtown College, PA
Emporia State University, KS
Evangel University, MO
Florida Agricultural and Mechanical University, FL
Florida International University, FL
Fordham University, NY
Fort Hays State University, KS
Gannon University, PA
George Fox University, OR
Georgian Court University, NJ
Grambling State University, LA
Grand Valley State University, MI
Grand View University, IA
Grove City College, PA
Hardin-Simmons University, TX
High Point University, NC
Hillsdale College, MI
Idaho State University, ID
Illinois State University, IL
Indiana State University, IN
Indiana University of Pennsylvania, PA
John Carroll University, OH
Kean University, NJ
Kennesaw State University, GA
Kent State University, OH
Kent State University at Geauga, OH
Kent State University at Stark, OH
Kenyon College, OH
King's College, PA
Kutztown University of Pennsylvania, PA
Lake Erie College, OH
Lake Forest College, IL
La Sierra University, CA
Linfield College, OR
Lock Haven University of Pennsylvania, PA
Louisiana State University and Agricultural & Mechanical College, LA
Loyola Marymount University, CA
Manhattan College, NY
Marquette University, WI
Marywood University, PA
Michigan State University, MI
Middle Tennessee State University, TN
Midwestern State University, TX
Millersville University of Pennsylvania, PA
Millikin University, IL
Minot State University, ND
Mississippi State University, MS
Montana State University, MT
Montana State University Billings, MT
Montclair State University, NJ
Morgan State University, MD
Nazareth College of Rochester, NY
Newberry College, SC
New Mexico State University, NM
North Central College, IL
Northeastern Illinois University, IL
Northeastern State University, OK
Northern Illinois University, IL
Northern Michigan University, MI
Northern State University, SD
Northwest Missouri State University, MO
Oakland University, MI
Oglethorpe University, GA
The Ohio State University, OH
Ohio University, OH
Ohio University–Chillicothe, OH
Ohio University–Eastern, OH
Ohio University–Lancaster, OH
Ohio University–Southern Campus, OH

Ohio University–Zanesville, OH
Oklahoma Baptist University, OK
Oklahoma State University, OK
Old Dominion University, VA
Olivet College, MI
Ouachita Baptist University, AR
Pacific University, OR
Piedmont College, GA
Pittsburg State University, KS
Point Loma Nazarene University, CA
Portland State University, OR
Rockford University, IL
St. Ambrose University, IA
St. Catherine University, MN
St. Edward's University, TX
St. John Fisher College, NY
St. John's University, NY
St. Thomas Aquinas College, NY
Saint Vincent College, PA
Samford University, AL
Sam Houston State University, TX
San Diego State University, CA
San Jose State University, CA
Shenandoah University, VA
Shepherd University, WV
Shippensburg University of Pennsylvania, PA
Slippery Rock University of Pennsylvania, PA
Sonoma State University, CA
Southeastern Louisiana University, LA
Southeast Missouri State University, MO
Southern Illinois University Carbondale, IL
Southwestern College, KS
Southwestern Oklahoma State University, OK
Spelman College, GA
State University of New York at Fredonia, NY
State University of New York at New Paltz, NY
State University of New York at Oswego, NY
State University of New York College at Geneseo, NY
State University of New York College at Potsdam, NY
Stetson University, FL
Stony Brook University, State University of New York, NY
Sul Ross State University, TX
SUNY Brockport, NY
Texas A&M International University, TX
Texas A&M University–Commerce, TX
Texas Christian University, TX
Texas State University, TX
Texas Tech University, TX
Texas Woman's University, TX
Towson University, MD
Truman State University, MO
Union University, TN
The University of Akron, OH
The University of Alabama, AL
University of Arkansas, AR
University of California, Davis, CA
University of California, Los Angeles, CA
University of Colorado Boulder, CO
University of Dallas, TX
University of Dayton, OH
University of Evansville, IN
University of Hawaii at Manoa, HI
University of Houston, TX
University of Idaho, ID
University of Illinois at Urbana-Champaign, IL
The University of Kansas, KS
University of Kentucky, KY
University of Louisiana at Monroe, LA
University of Louisville, KY
University of Maine, ME
University of Maine at Fort Kent, ME
University of Mary Hardin-Baylor, TX
University of Maryland, Baltimore County, MD
University of Maryland, College Park, MD
University of Mary Washington, VA
University of Miami, FL
University of Michigan, MI
University of Michigan–Dearborn, MI
University of Michigan–Flint, MI
University of Minnesota, Twin Cities Campus, MN
University of Mississippi, MS
University of Missouri–St. Louis, MO
University of Montana, MT
University of Montevallo, AL
University of Nebraska at Omaha, NE
University of Nebraska–Lincoln, NE
University of Nevada, Las Vegas, NV
University of Nevada, Reno, NV
University of New Hampshire, NH
University of North Carolina Asheville, NC
The University of North Carolina at Charlotte, NC
The University of North Carolina at Greensboro, NC
The University of North Carolina Wilmington, NC
University of North Dakota, ND
University of Northern Colorado, CO
University of Oklahoma, OK
University of Oregon, OR
University of Pittsburgh, PA
University of Portland, OR
University of Puget Sound, WA
University of Rhode Island, RI
University of St. Thomas, TX
University of South Carolina, SC
University of South Florida, FL
The University of Tennessee at Chattanooga, TN
The University of Tennessee at Martin, TN
The University of Texas at San Antonio, TX
The University of Toledo, OH
The University of Tulsa, OK
University of Utah, UT
University of Washington, WA
University of Washington, Tacoma, WA
University of West Georgia, GA
University of Wisconsin–Eau Claire, WI
University of Wisconsin–La Crosse, WI
University of Wisconsin–Parkside, WI
University of Wisconsin–River Falls, WI
University of Wisconsin–Stevens Point, WI
University of Wisconsin–Whitewater, WI
University of Wyoming, WY
Utah State University, UT
Valparaiso University, IN
Walla Walla University, WA
Walsh University, OH
Wartburg College, IA
Washburn University, KS
Washington State University, WA
Washington University in St. Louis, MO
Wayland Baptist University, TX
Wayne State College, NE
Wayne State University, MI
Wesleyan College, GA
Western Illinois University, IL
Western Kentucky University, KY
Western Oregon University, OR
Western Washington University, WA
West Texas A&M University, TX
Wheaton College, IL
Wichita State University, KS
Widener University, PA
Wilson College, PA
Wright State University, OH
Wright State University–Lake Campus, OH
Xavier University, OH
Xavier University of Louisiana, LA
Youngstown State University, OH

Health Fields

Auburn University, AL
Augustana University, SD
Austin College, TX
Averett University, VA
Baylor University, TX
Bethel College, KS
Birmingham-Southern College, AL
Boise State University, ID
Bowling Green State University, OH
California Baptist University, CA
California Polytechnic State University, San Luis Obispo, CA
California State University, Chico, CA
California State University, Fresno, CA
California State University, Fullerton, CA
Carson-Newman University, TN
Central Michigan University, MI
Chaminade University of Honolulu, HI
Cleveland State University, OH
Dakota State University, SD
DeSales University, PA
East Carolina University, NC
Eastern Illinois University, IL
Eastern Michigan University, MI
Eastern New Mexico University, NM
ECPI University, VA
Evangel University, MO
Felician University, NJ
Florida Agricultural and Mechanical University, FL
George Fox University, OR
Grambling State University, LA
Idaho State University, ID
Illinois State University, IL
Indiana University of Pennsylvania, PA
Jacksonville State University, AL
Kent State University, OH
Keystone College, PA
Lewis-Clark State College, ID
Lipscomb University, TN
Loras College, IA
Louisiana College, LA
Louisiana State University and Agricultural & Mechanical College, LA
Loyola Marymount University, CA
Marquette University, WI
Maryville University of Saint Louis, MO
Marywood University, PA
Michigan State University, MI
Middle Tennessee State University, TN
Millikin University, IL
Milwaukee School of Engineering, WI
Minot State University, ND
Mississippi State University, MS
Montana State University, MT
Montana State University Billings, MT
Montana Technological University, MT
Montclair State University, NJ
Nazareth College of Rochester, NY
Nebraska Methodist College, NE
New Mexico State University, NM
North Dakota State University, ND
Northeastern State University, OK
Northwest Missouri State University, MO

Northwest Nazarene University, ID
The Ohio State University, OH
Ohio University, OH
Ohio University–Chillicothe, OH
Ohio University–Eastern, OH
Ohio University–Lancaster, OH
Ohio University–Southern Campus, OH
Ohio University–Zanesville, OH
Oklahoma City University, OK
Oklahoma State University, OK
Piedmont College, GA
Pittsburg State University, KS
Point Loma Nazarene University, CA
Queens University of Charlotte, NC
St. Catherine University, MN
St. Cloud State University, MN
St. Edward's University, TX
Saint Francis University, PA
Samford University, AL
Sam Houston State University, TX
San Diego State University, CA
Shenandoah University, VA
Slippery Rock University of Pennsylvania, PA
Southeast Missouri State University, MO
Southern Illinois University Carbondale, IL
State University of New York at Plattsburgh, NY
Stephen F. Austin State University, TX
Stockton University, NJ
Sul Ross State University, TX
Texas A&M International University, TX
Texas A&M University, TX
Texas A&M University–Texarkana, TX
Texas State University, TX
Texas Woman's University, TX
The University of Akron, OH
The University of Alabama, AL
University of Alaska Anchorage, AK
University of Arkansas, AR
University of California, Davis, CA
University of Colorado Denver, CO
University of Florida, FL
University of Guam, GU
University of Houston, TX
University of Idaho, ID
University of Illinois at Urbana-Champaign, IL
University of Kentucky, KY
University of Louisiana at Monroe, LA
University of Maine, ME
University of Mary Hardin-Baylor, TX
University of Massachusetts Lowell, MA
University of Memphis, TN
University of Miami, FL
University of Minnesota, Twin Cities Campus, MN
University of Mississippi, MS
University of Missouri–St. Louis, MO
University of Nebraska–Lincoln, NE
University of Nevada, Las Vegas, NV
The University of North Carolina at Charlotte, NC
The University of North Carolina at Greensboro, NC
University of North Dakota, ND
University of Northern Colorado, CO
University of North Georgia, GA
University of Rhode Island, RI
University of Saint Francis, IN
University of South Florida, FL
The University of Tennessee at Chattanooga, TN
The University of Tennessee at Martin, TN
University of Washington, WA
University of Washington, Bothell, WA
University of Washington, Tacoma, WA
University of West Georgia, GA
University of Wisconsin–Green Bay, WI
University of Wisconsin–Platteville, WI
University of Wisconsin–Stevens Point, WI
University of Wyoming, WY
Utah State University, UT
Walsh University, OH
Washburn University, KS
Washington State University, WA
Wayne State College, NE
Wesleyan College, GA
Western Illinois University, IL
Western Kentucky University, KY
Western Oregon University, OR
West Texas A&M University, TX
Wichita State University, KS
Wright State University, OH
Wright State University–Lake Campus, OH

Home Economics

AdventHealth University, FL
Allen College, IA
Anderson University, IN
Angelo State University, TX
Arkansas Tech University, AR
Auburn University, AL
Augsburg University, MN
Augustana University, SD
Austin Peay State University, TN
Averett University, VA
Ball State University, IN
Barton College, NC
Baylor University, TX
Belmont University, TN
Bemidji State University, MN
Binghamton University, State University of New York, NY
Birmingham-Southern College, AL
Black Hills State University, SD
Bloomsburg University of Pennsylvania, PA
Bluefield State College, WV
Boise State University, ID
Bowling Green State University, OH
Butler University, IN
Caldwell University, NJ
California Polytechnic State University, San Luis Obispo, CA
California State University, Bakersfield, CA
California State University, Fresno, CA
California State University, Fullerton, CA
California State University, Los Angeles, CA
California State University, San Bernardino, CA
California State University, Stanislaus, CA
Cameron University, OK
Campbellsville University, KY
Carroll University, WI
Carthage College, WI
Case Western Reserve University, OH
Catawba College, NC
Cedar Crest College, PA
Centenary College of Louisiana, LA
Central College, IA
Central Methodist University, MO
Central Michigan University, MI
Chaminade University of Honolulu, HI
The Citadel, The Military College of South Carolina, SC
Clarion University of Pennsylvania, PA
Clemson University, SC
College of Staten Island of the City University of New York, NY
Colorado Mesa University, CO
Columbus State University, GA
Concordia College, MN
Concordia University Texas, TX
Cornerstone University, MI
Delta State University, MS
DeSales University, PA
Dominican University, IL
Dominican University of California, CA
Dordt University, IA
Drury University, MO
East Carolina University, NC
Eastern Illinois University, IL
Eastern Michigan University, MI
Eastern New Mexico University, NM
Eastern Washington University, WA
East Texas Baptist University, TX
ECPI University, VA
Edinboro University of Pennsylvania, PA
Elizabethtown College, PA
Emmanuel College, GA
Emporia State University, KS
Endicott College, MA
Ferris State University, MI
Florida Gulf Coast University, FL
Florida Institute of Technology, FL
Florida International University, FL
Fort Hays State University, KS
Framingham State University, MA
George Fox University, OR
Georgian Court University, NJ
Goshen College, IN
Governors State University, IL
Grambling State University, LA
Grand Valley State University, MI
Grand View University, IA
Hamline University, MN
Hampton University, VA
Hardin-Simmons University, TX
Houston Baptist University, TX
Illinois State University, IL
Indiana State University, IN
Indiana University of Pennsylvania, PA
Iowa Wesleyan University, IA
Jacksonville State University, AL
James Madison University, VA
John Carroll University, OH
Kean University, NJ
Kennesaw State University, GA
Kent State University, OH
Kent State University at Geauga, OH
Kent State University at Stark, OH
Lewis-Clark State College, ID
Limestone College, SC
Lock Haven University of Pennsylvania, PA
Long Island University, NY
Louisiana College, LA
Louisiana State University in Shreveport, LA
Loyola Marymount University, CA
Mansfield University of Pennsylvania, PA
Maryville University of Saint Louis, MO
Marywood University, PA
Massachusetts College of Liberal Arts, MA
Medical University of South Carolina, SC
Mercer University, GA
Michigan State University, MI
Middle Tennessee State University, TN
Midwestern State University, TX
Millersville University of Pennsylvania, PA
Minnesota State University Moorhead, MN
Minot State University, ND
Mississippi State University, MS
Missouri Valley College, MO
Molloy College, NY
Montana State University, MT

Morehead State University, KY
Morgan State University, MD
New Mexico State University, NM
North Dakota State University, ND
Northeastern State University, OK
Northern Illinois University, IL
Northern Michigan University, MI
Northwestern State University of Louisiana, LA
Northwest Missouri State University, MO
Northwest University, WA
The Ohio State University, OH
Ohio University, OH
Ohio University–Chillicothe, OH
Ohio University–Eastern, OH
Ohio University–Lancaster, OH
Ohio University–Southern Campus, OH
Ohio University–Zanesville, OH
Oklahoma Baptist University, OK
Oklahoma State University, OK
Old Dominion University, VA
Oregon Health & Science University, OR
Ouachita Baptist University, AR
Pacific University, OR
Piedmont College, GA
Pittsburg State University, KS
Purdue University, IN
Purdue University Northwest, IN
Sacred Heart University, CT
Saginaw Valley State University, MI
St. Ambrose University, IA
St. Catherine University, MN
Saint Francis Medical Center College of Nursing, IL
St. John's University, NY
Saint Vincent College, PA
Samford University, AL
Sam Houston State University, TX
San Diego State University, CA
San Jose State University, CA
Slippery Rock University of Pennsylvania, PA
Sonoma State University, CA
Southeast Missouri State University, MO
Southern Illinois University Carbondale, IL
Southern Illinois University Edwardsville, IL
Spelman College, GA
State University of New York at Plattsburgh, NY
State University of New York College at Oneonta, NY
State University of New York College at Potsdam, NY
Stephen F. Austin State University, TX
Stockton University, NJ
Stony Brook University, State University of New York, NY
SUNY Brockport, NY
Texas A&M University–Commerce, TX
Texas Christian University, TX
Texas State University, TX
Texas Tech University, TX
Texas Woman's University, TX
Towson University, MD
Truett McConnell University, GA
Truman State University, MO
Union University, TN
The University of Akron, OH
The University of Alabama, AL
The University of Alabama at Birmingham, AL
University of Arkansas, AR
University of California, Davis, CA
University of California, Los Angeles, CA
University of Colorado Boulder, CO
University of Colorado Denver, CO
University of Dayton, OH
University of Evansville, IN
University of Hawaii at Manoa, HI
University of Houston, TX
University of Idaho, ID
University of Illinois at Urbana-Champaign, IL
University of Indianapolis, IN
The University of Kansas, KS
University of Kentucky, KY
University of Louisiana at Monroe, LA
University of Louisville, KY
University of Maine, ME
University of Mary Hardin-Baylor, TX
University of Maryland, College Park, MD
University of Massachusetts Amherst, MA
University of Massachusetts Dartmouth, MA
University of Memphis, TN
University of Miami, FL
University of Michigan, MI
University of Michigan–Flint, MI
University of Minnesota, Twin Cities Campus, MN
University of Mississippi, MS
University of Montana, MT
University of Montevallo, AL
University of Nebraska at Omaha, NE
University of Nebraska–Lincoln, NE
University of Nevada, Reno, NV
University of New Hampshire, NH
University of North Carolina Asheville, NC
The University of North Carolina at Chapel Hill, NC
The University of North Carolina at Charlotte, NC
The University of North Carolina at Greensboro, NC
The University of North Carolina Wilmington, NC
University of Northern Colorado, CO
University of Northwestern–St. Paul, MN
University of Oklahoma, OK
University of Oregon, OR
University of Pittsburgh, PA
University of Pittsburgh at Bradford, PA
University of Pittsburgh at Johnstown, PA
University of Portland, OR
University of Rhode Island, RI
University of St. Francis, IL
University of St. Thomas, TX
University of South Carolina, SC
University of South Carolina Aiken, SC
University of Southern Indiana, IN
The University of Tennessee, TN
The University of Tennessee at Chattanooga, TN
The University of Tennessee at Martin, TN
The University of Texas at El Paso, TX
The University of Texas at Tyler, TX
The University of Texas Rio Grande Valley, TX
The University of Toledo, OH
The University of Tulsa, OK
University of Utah, UT
University of Washington, WA
University of Wisconsin–Eau Claire, WI
University of Wisconsin–La Crosse, WI
University of Wisconsin–Parkside, WI
University of Wisconsin–River Falls, WI
University of Wisconsin–Stevens Point, WI
University of Wisconsin–Stout, WI
University of Wyoming, WY
Utah State University, UT
Valdosta State University, GA
Valparaiso University, IN
Washington State University, WA
Washington University in St. Louis, MO
Wayland Baptist University, TX
Wayne State College, NE
Wayne State University, MI
Western Illinois University, IL
Western Kentucky University, KY
Western Washington University, WA
Westminster College, UT
Wheaton College, IL
Widener University, PA
Xavier University of Louisiana, LA
Youngstown State University, OH

Humanities

Alfred University, NY
Alliant International University - San Diego, CA
Angelo State University, TX
Arkansas Tech University, AR
Auburn University, AL
Augustana College, IL
Augustana University, SD
Austin College, TX
Austin Peay State University, TN
Averett University, VA
Ball State University, IN
Barton College, NC
Baylor University, TX
Belhaven University, MS
Belmont Abbey College, NC
Bemidji State University, MN
Berry College, GA
Bethel College, KS
Binghamton University, State University of New York, NY
Birmingham-Southern College, AL
Black Hills State University, SD
Bloomsburg University of Pennsylvania, PA
Boise State University, ID
Bowling Green State University, OH
Bryan College, TN
Butler University, IN
California Lutheran University, CA
California Polytechnic State University, San Luis Obispo, CA
California State Polytechnic University, Pomona, CA
California State University, Bakersfield, CA
California State University, Chico, CA
California State University, Fresno, CA
California State University, Fullerton, CA
California State University, Stanislaus, CA
Cameron University, OK
Campbellsville University, KY
Carlow University, PA
Carroll University, WI
Case Western Reserve University, OH
Cedar Crest College, PA
Centenary College of Louisiana, LA
Central College, IA
Central Methodist University, MO
Central Michigan University, MI
Christopher Newport University, VA
The Citadel, The Military College of South Carolina, SC
City College of the City University of New York, NY
Clarion University of Pennsylvania, PA
Clarkson University, NY
Clemson University, SC
Cleveland State University, OH
Coastal Carolina University, SC
The College of Idaho, ID
College of Staten Island of the City University of New York, NY

Colorado Mesa University, CO
Columbia College, MO
Columbia College, SC
Columbus State University, GA
Cornerstone University, MI
Dallas Baptist University, TX
DeSales University, PA
Dominican University of California, CA
Dordt University, IA
Drury University, MO
Earlham College, IN
East Carolina University, NC
Eastern Illinois University, IL
Eastern Mennonite University, VA
Eastern Michigan University, MI
Eastern New Mexico University, NM
Eastern Washington University, WA
East Texas Baptist University, TX
Edinboro University of Pennsylvania, PA
Elizabethtown College, PA
Emory University, GA
Emporia State University, KS
Evangel University, MO
Florida Agricultural and Mechanical University, FL
Florida Gulf Coast University, FL
Florida Institute of Technology, FL
Florida International University, FL
Fort Hays State University, KS
Fort Lewis College, CO
Gannon University, PA
George Fox University, OR
Georgian Court University, NJ
Goshen College, IN
Governors State University, IL
Grambling State University, LA
Grand Valley State University, MI
Grand View University, IA
Grove City College, PA
Hampshire College, MA
Hardin-Simmons University, TX
High Point University, NC
Hillsdale College, MI
Hiram College, OH
Idaho State University, ID
Illinois Institute of Technology, IL
Illinois State University, IL
Indiana State University, IN
Indiana University of Pennsylvania, PA
Jacksonville State University, AL
James Madison University, VA
John Carroll University, OH
Kean University, NJ
Kennesaw State University, GA
Kent State University, OH
Kent State University at Geauga, OH
Kent State University at Stark, OH
Kenyon College, OH
King's College, PA
Kutztown University of Pennsylvania, PA
Lake Erie College, OH
Lewis-Clark State College, ID
Limestone College, SC
Linfield College, OR
Longwood University, VA
Louisiana College, LA
Louisiana State University and Agricultural & Mechanical College, LA
Louisiana State University in Shreveport, LA
Loyola Marymount University, CA
Marymount University, VA
Massachusetts College of Liberal Arts, MA
Messiah College, PA
Middle Tennessee State University, TN
Midwestern State University, TX
Millersville University of Pennsylvania, PA
Millikin University, IL
Minot State University, ND
Mississippi State University, MS
Missouri University of Science and Technology, MO
Missouri Valley College, MO
Molloy College, NY
Montana State University, MT
Montana State University Billings, MT
Montana Technological University, MT
Montclair State University, NJ
Morgan State University, MD
Nazareth College of Rochester, NY
Newberry College, SC
New Jersey Institute of Technology, NJ
New Mexico State University, NM
North Carolina State University, NC
North Central College, IL
North Dakota State University, ND
Northeastern State University, OK
Northern Illinois University, IL
Northern Michigan University, MI
Northern State University, SD
Northwestern State University of Louisiana, LA
Northwest Missouri State University, MO
Northwest University, WA
Oakland University, MI
Oglethorpe University, GA
The Ohio State University, OH
Ohio University, OH
Ohio University–Chillicothe, OH
Ohio University–Eastern, OH
Ohio University–Lancaster, OH
Ohio University–Southern Campus, OH
Ohio University–Zanesville, OH
Oklahoma Baptist University, OK
Oklahoma State University, OK
Old Dominion University, VA
Ouachita Baptist University, AR
Pacific University, OR
Piedmont College, GA
Portland State University, OR
Purchase College, State University of New York, NY
Purdue University, IN
Purdue University Northwest, IN
Queens University of Charlotte, NC
Reinhardt University, GA
Rensselaer Polytechnic Institute, NY
Sacred Heart University, CT
St. Ambrose University, IA
St. Catherine University, MN
St. Edward's University, TX
Saint Francis University, PA
St. John Fisher College, NY
St. John's University, NY
St. Thomas Aquinas College, NY
Saint Vincent College, PA
Samford University, AL
Sam Houston State University, TX
San Diego State University, CA
San Jose State University, CA
Shenandoah University, VA
Shippensburg University of Pennsylvania, PA
Slippery Rock University of Pennsylvania, PA
Sonoma State University, CA
Southeastern Louisiana University, LA
Southeast Missouri State University, MO
Southern Illinois University Carbondale, IL
Southwestern College, KS
Southwestern University, TX
Spelman College, GA
State University of New York at Fredonia, NY
State University of New York at Oswego, NY
State University of New York at Plattsburgh, NY
State University of New York College at Geneseo, NY
State University of New York College at Potsdam, NY
Stetson University, FL
Stockton University, NJ
SUNY Brockport, NY
Tabor College, KS
Texas A&M University–Commerce, TX
Texas Christian University, TX
Texas State University, TX
Texas Tech University, TX
Texas Woman's University, TX
Trinity Christian College, IL
Truman State University, MO
Union University, TN
The University of Akron, OH
The University of Alabama, AL
University of Alaska Anchorage, AK
University of Arkansas, AR
University of California, Davis, CA
University of California, Los Angeles, CA
University of California, Riverside, CA
University of California, Santa Cruz, CA
University of Colorado Boulder, CO
University of Colorado Denver, CO
University of Dallas, TX
University of Dayton, OH
University of Denver, CO
University of Evansville, IN
University of Hawaii at Manoa, HI
University of Houston, TX
University of Houston–Clear Lake, TX
University of Idaho, ID
University of Illinois at Urbana-Champaign, IL
The University of Kansas, KS
University of Louisville, KY
University of Maine, ME
University of Maine at Fort Kent, ME
University of Mary Hardin-Baylor, TX
University of Maryland, Baltimore County, MD
University of Maryland, College Park, MD
University of Mary Washington, VA
University of Massachusetts Amherst, MA
University of Massachusetts Dartmouth, MA
University of Massachusetts Lowell, MA
University of Memphis, TN
University of Miami, FL
University of Michigan, MI
University of Michigan–Flint, MI
University of Minnesota, Twin Cities Campus, MN
University of Mississippi, MS
University of Missouri–St. Louis, MO
University of Montana, MT
University of Montevallo, AL
University of Nebraska–Lincoln, NE
University of Nevada, Las Vegas, NV
University of New Hampshire, NH
University of New Hampshire at Manchester, NH
University of North Carolina Asheville, NC
The University of North Carolina at Greensboro, NC

The University of North Carolina Wilmington, NC
University of North Dakota, ND
University of Northern Colorado, CO
University of North Georgia, GA
University of Northwestern–St. Paul, MN
University of Oklahoma, OK
University of Oregon, OR
University of Pittsburgh, PA
University of Pittsburgh at Bradford, PA
University of Pittsburgh at Johnstown, PA
University of Portland, OR
University of Providence, MT
University of Puget Sound, WA
University of Rhode Island, RI
University of St. Thomas, TX
University of South Carolina, SC
University of South Carolina Aiken, SC
University of Southern Indiana, IN
University of South Florida, FL
The University of Tennessee, TN
The University of Tennessee at Chattanooga, TN
The University of Tennessee at Martin, TN
The University of Texas at El Paso, TX
The University of Texas at San Antonio, TX
The University of Toledo, OH
University of Utah, UT
University of Washington, WA
University of Washington, Bothell, WA
University of Washington, Tacoma, WA
University of West Georgia, GA
University of Wisconsin–Eau Claire, WI
University of Wisconsin–Green Bay, WI
University of Wisconsin–La Crosse, WI
University of Wisconsin–Parkside, WI
University of Wisconsin–River Falls, WI
University of Wisconsin–Stevens Point, WI
University of Wisconsin–Superior, WI
University of Wisconsin–Whitewater, WI
University of Wyoming, WY
Upper Iowa University, IA
Utah State University, UT
Valley City State University, ND
Walla Walla University, WA
Walsh University, OH
Wartburg College, IA
Washburn University, KS
Washington & Jefferson College, PA
Washington State University, WA
Washington University in St. Louis, MO
Wayne State College, NE
Wayne State University, MI
Wesleyan College, GA
Western Oregon University, OR
Western Washington University, WA
Westminster College, UT
West Texas A&M University, TX
Wheaton College, IL
Wichita State University, KS
Widener University, PA
William Jessup University, CA
Wilson College, PA
Wright State University, OH
Wright State University–Lake Campus, OH
Xavier University of Louisiana, LA
Youngstown State University, OH

International Studies

Alfred University, NY
Angelo State University, TX
Arkansas Tech University, AR
Augsburg University, MN
Augustana University, SD
Austin College, TX
Austin Peay State University, TN
Ball State University, IN
Baylor University, TX
Belhaven University, MS
Bemidji State University, MN
Binghamton University, State University of New York, NY
Birmingham-Southern College, AL
Bloomsburg University of Pennsylvania, PA
Boise State University, ID
Bowling Green State University, OH
Butler University, IN
California Lutheran University, CA
California Polytechnic State University, San Luis Obispo, CA
California State Polytechnic University, Pomona, CA
California State University, Chico, CA
California State University, Fullerton, CA
California State University, San Bernardino, CA
California State University, Stanislaus, CA
Carroll University, WI
Case Western Reserve University, OH
Centenary College of Louisiana, LA
Central College, IA
Central Michigan University, MI
City College of the City University of New York, NY
Clarion University of Pennsylvania, PA
Clemson University, SC
Coastal Carolina University, SC
College of Staten Island of the City University of New York, NY
Columbus State University, GA
Concordia University Texas, TX
Davidson College, NC
Drury University, MO
East Carolina University, NC
Eastern Illinois University, IL
Eastern Washington University, WA
Elizabethtown College, PA
Evangel University, MO
Fort Hays State University, KS
Gannon University, PA
George Fox University, OR
Georgetown College, KY
Georgia Institute of Technology, GA
Georgian Court University, NJ
Glenville State College, WV
Grand Valley State University, MI
Grand View University, IA
Grove City College, PA
Hampshire College, MA
High Point University, NC
Houghton College, NY
Idaho State University, ID
Illinois State University, IL
Indiana University of Pennsylvania, PA
James Madison University, VA
John Carroll University, OH
Kean University, NJ
Kennesaw State University, GA
Kent State University, OH
Kent State University at Geauga, OH
Kent State University at Stark, OH
King's College, PA
Kutztown University of Pennsylvania, PA
Lake Erie College, OH
Lehigh University, PA
Linfield College, OR
Lock Haven University of Pennsylvania, PA
Long Island University, NY
Longwood University, VA
Loyola Marymount University, CA
Lynn University, FL
Maryville University of Saint Louis, MO
Michigan State University, MI
Middle Tennessee State University, TN
Midwestern State University, TX
Millikin University, IL
Minnesota State University Moorhead, MN
Mississippi State University, MS
Missouri University of Science and Technology, MO
Molloy College, NY
Montana State University, MT
Montclair State University, NJ
Morehead State University, KY
Morgan State University, MD
Nazareth College of Rochester, NY
New Jersey Institute of Technology, NJ
North Central College, IL
Northern Illinois University, IL
Northern Michigan University, MI
Northern State University, SD
Northwest University, WA
Oakland University, MI
Oglethorpe University, GA
The Ohio State University, OH
Ohio University, OH
Ohio University–Eastern, OH
Ohio University–Lancaster, OH
Ohio University–Southern Campus, OH
Ohio University–Zanesville, OH
Oklahoma State University, OK
Old Dominion University, VA
Ouachita Baptist University, AR
Point Loma Nazarene University, CA
Portland State University, OR
St. Ambrose University, IA
St. Cloud State University, MN
St. Edward's University, TX
Saint Francis University, PA
Saint Martin's University, WA
Saint Vincent College, PA
Samford University, AL
San Diego State University, CA
San Jose State University, CA
Shenandoah University, VA
Shepherd University, WV
Southeast Missouri State University, MO
Southern Illinois University Carbondale, IL
Southwestern University, TX
Spelman College, GA
State University of New York at Fredonia, NY
State University of New York at New Paltz, NY
State University of New York at Oswego, NY
State University of New York at Plattsburgh, NY
State University of New York College at Geneseo, NY
State University of New York College at Potsdam, NY
Stony Brook University, State University of New York, NY
SUNY Brockport, NY
Texas A&M International University, TX
Texas A&M University–Commerce, TX
Texas A&M University–Texarkana, TX
Texas Christian University, TX
Texas State University, TX
Texas Tech University, TX
Texas Woman's University, TX
Toccoa Falls College, GA
Trinity Christian College, IL
Union University, TN
The University of Akron, OH
The University of Alabama, AL
University of Arkansas, AR

University of California, Davis, CA
University of California, Los Angeles, CA
University of California, Santa Cruz, CA
University of Colorado Boulder, CO
University of Colorado Denver, CO
University of Dayton, OH
University of Denver, CO
University of Evansville, IN
University of Hawaii at Manoa, HI
University of Houston, TX
University of Idaho, ID
University of Illinois at Urbana-Champaign, IL
The University of Kansas, KS
University of Kentucky, KY
University of Louisville, KY
University of Maine, ME
University of Mary Hardin-Baylor, TX
University of Maryland, College Park, MD
University of Mary Washington, VA
University of Memphis, TN
University of Miami, FL
University of Michigan, MI
University of Michigan–Dearborn, MI
University of Michigan–Flint, MI
University of Minnesota, Twin Cities Campus, MN
University of Mississippi, MS
University of Missouri–St. Louis, MO
University of Montana, MT
University of Nebraska–Lincoln, NE
University of Nevada, Las Vegas, NV
University of North Carolina Asheville, NC
The University of North Carolina at Charlotte, NC
The University of North Carolina at Greensboro, NC
The University of North Carolina Wilmington, NC
University of North Dakota, ND
University of Northern Colorado, CO
University of Oklahoma, OK
University of Oregon, OR
University of Pittsburgh, PA
University of Pittsburgh at Bradford, PA
University of Puget Sound, WA
University of Rhode Island, RI
University of St. Francis, IL
University of St. Thomas, TX
University of South Carolina, SC
University of South Florida, FL
The University of Tampa, FL
The University of Tennessee, TN
The University of Tennessee at Chattanooga, TN
The University of Tennessee at Martin, TN
The University of Texas at El Paso, TX
The University of Texas at San Antonio, TX
The University of Toledo, OH
University of Utah, UT
University of Washington, WA
University of Washington, Bothell, WA
University of Washington, Tacoma, WA
University of Wisconsin–Eau Claire, WI
University of Wisconsin–La Crosse, WI
University of Wisconsin–River Falls, WI
University of Wisconsin–Stevens Point, WI
University of Wisconsin–Stout, WI
University of Wyoming, WY
Utah State University, UT
Villanova University, PA
Walsh University, OH
Washburn University, KS
Washington State University, WA
Washington University in St. Louis, MO
Wayne State College, NE
Wayne State University, MI
Wesleyan College, GA
Western Illinois University, IL
Western Oregon University, OR
Westminster College, UT
Wheaton College, IL
Wichita State University, KS
Widener University, PA
William Jessup University, CA
Wilson College, PA
Wright State University, OH
Wright State University–Lake Campus, OH

Library Science

Alverno College, WI
California Polytechnic State University, San Luis Obispo, CA
Clarion University of Pennsylvania, PA
East Carolina University, NC
Illinois State University, IL
Kent State University, OH
Kent State University at Geauga, OH
Kent State University at Stark, OH
Kutztown University of Pennsylvania, PA
Lock Haven University of Pennsylvania, PA
Mississippi State University, MS
Montana State University, MT
North Carolina Central University, NC
Northeastern State University, OK
Northern Illinois University, IL
Old Dominion University, VA
Sam Houston State University, TX
Texas Woman's University, TX
The University of Alabama, AL
University of California, Los Angeles, CA
University of Hawaii at Manoa, HI
University of Houston, TX
University of Idaho, ID
University of Illinois at Urbana-Champaign, IL
University of Louisiana at Monroe, LA
University of Louisville, KY
University of Maryland, College Park, MD
University of Mary Washington, VA
University of Miami, FL
University of Michigan, MI
University of Minnesota, Twin Cities Campus, MN
The University of North Carolina at Greensboro, NC
University of Oklahoma, OK
University of Pittsburgh, PA
University of Rhode Island, RI
University of South Carolina, SC
University of South Florida, FL
The University of Tennessee, TN
The University of Tennessee at Chattanooga, TN
The University of Toledo, OH
University of Washington, WA
University of Wisconsin–Eau Claire, WI
Utah State University, UT
Valdosta State University, GA
Valley City State University, ND
Wayne State University, MI
Western Illinois University, IL
Western Oregon University, OR
Western Washington University, WA

Mathematics

Abilene Christian University, TX
Alfred University, NY
Anderson University, IN
Angelo State University, TX
Arkansas Tech University, AR
Ashland University, OH
Auburn University, AL
Augsburg University, MN
Augustana College, IL
Augustana University, SD
Austin College, TX
Austin Peay State University, TN
Averett University, VA
Ball State University, IN
Barton College, NC
Baylor University, TX
Belhaven University, MS
Bemidji State University, MN
Bethel College, KS
Binghamton University, State University of New York, NY
Birmingham-Southern College, AL
Black Hills State University, SD
Bloomsburg University of Pennsylvania, PA
Bluffton University, OH
Boise State University, ID
Bowie State University, MD
Bowling Green State University, OH
Bryan College, TN
Bucknell University, PA
Buena Vista University, IA
Butler University, IN
California Lutheran University, CA
California Polytechnic State University, San Luis Obispo, CA
California State Polytechnic University, Pomona, CA
California State University, Bakersfield, CA
California State University, Chico, CA
California State University, Fresno, CA
California State University, Fullerton, CA
California State University, Los Angeles, CA
California State University, Northridge, CA
California State University, San Bernardino, CA
California State University, San Marcos, CA
California State University, Stanislaus, CA
Cameron University, OK
Campbellsville University, KY
Carlow University, PA
Carroll University, WI
Carson-Newman University, TN
Carthage College, WI
Case Western Reserve University, OH
Cedar Crest College, PA
Centenary College of Louisiana, LA
Central College, IA
Central Methodist University, MO
Central Michigan University, MI
Christian Brothers University, TN
Christopher Newport University, VA
The Citadel, The Military College of South Carolina, SC
City College of the City University of New York, NY
Clarion University of Pennsylvania, PA
Clarkson University, NY
Clemson University, SC
Cleveland State University, OH
Coastal Carolina University, SC
The College of Idaho, ID
College of Saint Benedict, MN
College of Saint Mary, NE
College of Staten Island of the City University of New York, NY
The Colorado College, CO
Colorado Mesa University, CO
Colorado School of Mines, CO
Columbia College, MO
Columbia College, SC

Columbus State University, GA
Concordia University Chicago, IL
Concordia University Texas, TX
Concord University, WV
Cornerstone University, MI
Dakota State University, SD
Dallas Baptist University, TX
Davidson College, NC
Delta State University, MS
DeSales University, PA
Dordt University, IA
Drury University, MO
Duke University, NC
Earlham College, IN
East Carolina University, NC
Eastern Illinois University, IL
Eastern Mennonite University, VA
Eastern Michigan University, MI
Eastern New Mexico University, NM
Eastern Oregon University, OR
Eastern Washington University, WA
East Texas Baptist University, TX
Edinboro University of Pennsylvania, PA
Elizabethtown College, PA
Elon University, NC
Emporia State University, KS
Evangel University, MO
Ferris State University, MI
Florida Agricultural and Mechanical University, FL
Florida Gulf Coast University, FL
Florida Institute of Technology, FL
Florida International University, FL
Fort Hays State University, KS
Fort Lewis College, CO
Framingham State University, MA
Gannon University, PA
George Fox University, OR
Georgian Court University, NJ
Glenville State College, WV
Goshen College, IN
Governors State University, IL
Grambling State University, LA
Grand Valley State University, MI
Grand View University, IA
Greenville University, IL
Grove City College, PA
Hamline University, MN
Hampshire College, MA
Hardin-Simmons University, TX
High Point University, NC
Hillsdale College, MI
Houghton College, NY
Idaho State University, ID
Illinois Institute of Technology, IL
Illinois State University, IL
Indiana State University, IN
Indiana University of Pennsylvania, PA
Jacksonville State University, AL
James Madison University, VA
John Carroll University, OH
Kean University, NJ
Kennesaw State University, GA
Kent State University, OH
Kent State University at Geauga, OH
Kent State University at Stark, OH
Kenyon College, OH
Kettering University, MI
King's College, PA
Kutztown University of Pennsylvania, PA
Lake Erie College, OH
Lake Forest College, IL
Lebanon Valley College, PA
Lewis-Clark State College, ID
Liberty University, VA
Limestone College, SC
Linfield College, OR
Lipscomb University, TN
Lock Haven University of Pennsylvania, PA
Longwood University, VA
Loras College, IA
Louisiana College, LA
Louisiana State University and Agricultural & Mechanical College, LA
Louisiana State University in Shreveport, LA
Loyola Marymount University, CA
Manhattan College, NY
Mansfield University of Pennsylvania, PA
Marquette University, WI
Marymount University, VA
Maryville University of Saint Louis, MO
Marywood University, PA
Massachusetts College of Liberal Arts, MA
Michigan State University, MI
Middle Tennessee State University, TN
Midwestern State University, TX
Millersville University of Pennsylvania, PA
Millikin University, IL
Mills College, CA
Milwaukee School of Engineering, WI
Minnesota State University Moorhead, MN
Minot State University, ND
Mississippi State University, MS
Missouri University of Science and Technology, MO
Missouri Valley College, MO
Molloy College, NY
Montana State University, MT
Montana State University Billings, MT
Montana Technological University, MT
Montclair State University, NJ
Morgan State University, MD
Muskingum University, OH
Nazareth College of Rochester, NY
Newberry College, SC
New Jersey Institute of Technology, NJ
New Mexico State University, NM
North Carolina State University, NC
North Central College, IL
North Dakota State University, ND
Northeastern Illinois University, IL
Northeastern State University, OK
Northern Illinois University, IL
Northern Michigan University, MI
Northern State University, SD
Northwestern State University of Louisiana, LA
Northwest Missouri State University, MO
Northwest Nazarene University, ID
Northwest University, WA
Oakland University, MI
Oglethorpe University, GA
The Ohio State University, OH
Ohio University, OH
Ohio University–Chillicothe, OH
Ohio University–Eastern, OH
Ohio University–Lancaster, OH
Ohio University–Southern Campus, OH
Ohio University–Zanesville, OH
Ohio Valley University, WV
Oklahoma Baptist University, OK
Oklahoma State University, OK
Old Dominion University, VA
Ouachita Baptist University, AR
Pacific University, OR
Piedmont College, GA
Pittsburg State University, KS
Plymouth State University, NH
Point Loma Nazarene University, CA
Purchase College, State University of New York, NY
Purdue University, IN
Purdue University Northwest, IN
Randolph College, VA
Reinhardt University, GA
Rensselaer Polytechnic Institute, NY
Rochester University, MI
Rockford University, IL
Rollins College, FL
Sacred Heart University, CT
Saginaw Valley State University, MI
St. Ambrose University, IA
St. Bonaventure University, NY
St. Catherine University, MN
St. Cloud State University, MN
St. Edward's University, TX
Saint Francis University, PA
St. John Fisher College, NY
St. John's University, NY
Saint Joseph's University, PA
Saint Mary's College of California, CA
St. Thomas Aquinas College, NY
Saint Vincent College, PA
Samford University, AL
Sam Houston State University, TX
San Diego State University, CA
San Jose State University, CA
Schreiner University, TX
Shenandoah University, VA
Shepherd University, WV
Shippensburg University of Pennsylvania, PA
Skidmore College, NY
Slippery Rock University of Pennsylvania, PA
Sonoma State University, CA
Southeastern Louisiana University, LA
Southeast Missouri State University, MO
Southern Illinois University Carbondale, IL
Southwestern College, KS
Southwestern Oklahoma State University, OK
Southwestern University, TX
Spelman College, GA
State University of New York at Fredonia, NY
State University of New York at New Paltz, NY
State University of New York at Oswego, NY
State University of New York at Plattsburgh, NY
State University of New York College at Geneseo, NY
State University of New York College at Potsdam, NY
Stephen F. Austin State University, TX
Stetson University, FL
Stockton University, NJ
Stony Brook University, State University of New York, NY
SUNY Brockport, NY
Texas A&M International University, TX
Texas A&M University, TX
Texas A&M University–Commerce, TX
Texas A&M University–Texarkana, TX
Texas Christian University, TX
Texas Lutheran University, TX
Texas State University, TX
Texas Tech University, TX
Texas Woman's University, TX
Thomas More University, KY
Toccoa Falls College, GA
Towson University, MD
Trinity Christian College, IL
Truman State University, MO
Union University, TN

The University of Akron, OH
The University of Alabama, AL
The University of Alabama at Birmingham, AL
University of Alaska Anchorage, AK
University of Alaska Fairbanks, AK
University of Arkansas, AR
University of California, Davis, CA
University of California, Los Angeles, CA
University of California, Riverside, CA
University of California, San Diego, CA
University of California, Santa Cruz, CA
University of Colorado Boulder, CO
University of Colorado Denver, CO
University of Dallas, TX
University of Dayton, OH
University of Denver, CO
University of Evansville, IN
University of Hawaii at Manoa, HI
University of Houston, TX
University of Houston–Clear Lake, TX
University of Idaho, ID
University of Illinois at Urbana-Champaign, IL
The University of Kansas, KS
University of Kentucky, KY
University of Louisiana at Monroe, LA
University of Louisville, KY
University of Maine, ME
University of Maine at Fort Kent, ME
University of Mary Hardin-Baylor, TX
University of Maryland, Baltimore County, MD
University of Maryland, College Park, MD
University of Mary Washington, VA
University of Massachusetts Amherst, MA
University of Massachusetts Dartmouth, MA
University of Massachusetts Lowell, MA
University of Memphis, TN
University of Miami, FL
University of Michigan, MI
University of Michigan–Dearborn, MI
University of Michigan–Flint, MI
University of Minnesota, Twin Cities Campus, MN
University of Mississippi, MS
University of Missouri–St. Louis, MO
University of Montana, MT
University of Montevallo, AL
University of Nebraska at Omaha, NE
University of Nebraska–Lincoln, NE
University of Nevada, Las Vegas, NV
University of Nevada, Reno, NV
University of New Hampshire, NH
University of North Carolina Asheville, NC
The University of North Carolina at Chapel Hill, NC
The University of North Carolina at Charlotte, NC
The University of North Carolina at Greensboro, NC
The University of North Carolina Wilmington, NC
University of North Dakota, ND
University of Northern Colorado, CO
University of Northern Iowa, IA
University of North Georgia, GA
University of Northwestern–St. Paul, MN
University of Oklahoma, OK
University of Oregon, OR
University of Pittsburgh, PA
University of Pittsburgh at Bradford, PA
University of Pittsburgh at Johnstown, PA
University of Portland, OR
University of Providence, MT
University of Puget Sound, WA
University of Rhode Island, RI
University of Richmond, VA
University of St. Thomas, TX
University of South Carolina, SC
University of South Carolina Aiken, SC
University of Southern Indiana, IN
University of South Florida, FL
The University of Tennessee at Chattanooga, TN
The University of Tennessee at Martin, TN
The University of Texas at Dallas, TX
The University of Texas at El Paso, TX
The University of Texas at San Antonio, TX
The University of Texas Rio Grande Valley, TX
The University of Toledo, OH
The University of Tulsa, OK
University of Utah, UT
University of Washington, WA
University of Washington, Bothell, WA
University of Washington, Tacoma, WA
University of West Georgia, GA
University of Wisconsin–Eau Claire, WI
University of Wisconsin–La Crosse, WI
University of Wisconsin–Parkside, WI
University of Wisconsin–Platteville, WI
University of Wisconsin–River Falls, WI
University of Wisconsin–Stevens Point, WI
University of Wisconsin–Stout, WI
University of Wisconsin–Superior, WI
University of Wisconsin–Whitewater, WI
University of Wyoming, WY
Utah State University, UT
Valdosta State University, GA
Valley City State University, ND
Walla Walla University, WA
Walsh University, OH
Wartburg College, IA
Washburn University, KS
Washington State University, WA
Washington University in St. Louis, MO
Wayland Baptist University, TX
Wayne State College, NE
Wayne State University, MI
Wesleyan College, GA
West Chester University of Pennsylvania, PA
Western Carolina University, NC
Western Illinois University, IL
Western Kentucky University, KY
Western Oregon University, OR
Western Washington University, WA
Westminster College, UT
West Texas A&M University, TX
Wheaton College, IL
Wichita State University, KS
Widener University, PA
William Jessup University, CA
Wilson College, PA
Wright State University, OH
Wright State University–Lake Campus, OH
Xavier University, OH
Xavier University of Louisiana, LA
Youngstown State University, OH

Military Science

Angelo State University, TX
Arkansas Tech University, AR
Auburn University at Montgomery, AL
Austin Peay State University, TN
Ball State University, IN
Baylor University, TX
Black Hills State University, SD
Boise State University, ID
Boston College, MA
Boston University, MA
Bowie State University, MD
Bowling Green State University, OH
California Polytechnic State University, San Luis Obispo, CA
California State University, Fullerton, CA
Cameron University, OK
Carson-Newman University, TN
Central Michigan University, MI
Christopher Newport University, VA
The Citadel, The Military College of South Carolina, SC
Claremont McKenna College, CA
Clarion University of Pennsylvania, PA
Clarkson University, NY
Clemson University, SC
College of Saint Benedict, MN
Colorado School of Mines, CO
Columbus State University, GA
Creighton University, NE
Dickinson College, PA
East Carolina University, NC
Eastern New Mexico University, NM
Eastern Washington University, WA
Elon University, NC
Florida Agricultural and Mechanical University, FL
Florida Institute of Technology, FL
Gonzaga University, WA
Grambling State University, LA
Idaho State University, ID
Illinois State University, IL
Immaculata University, PA
Indiana University of Pennsylvania, PA
Jacksonville State University, AL
James Madison University, VA
John Carroll University, OH
Kent State University, OH
Kent State University at Geauga, OH
Kent State University at Stark, OH
Lehigh University, PA
Longwood University, VA
Louisiana State University and Agricultural & Mechanical College, LA
Manhattan College, NY
Mercer University, GA
Methodist University, NC
Michigan State University, MI
Middle Tennessee State University, TN
Mississippi State University, MS
Missouri University of Science and Technology, MO
Missouri Valley College, MO
Molloy College, NY
Montana State University, MT
Morehead State University, KY
Morgan State University, MD
New Mexico State University, NM
North Carolina State University, NC
North Dakota State University, ND
Northern Illinois University, IL
Northern Michigan University, MI
North Greenville University, SC
Northwestern State University of Louisiana, LA
Northwest Nazarene University, ID
The Ohio State University, OH
Ohio University, OH
Ohio University–Chillicothe, OH
Ohio University–Eastern, OH
Ohio University–Lancaster, OH
Ohio University–Southern Campus, OH
Ohio University–Zanesville, OH
Oklahoma State University, OK

Old Dominion University, VA
Olivet Nazarene University, IL
Ouachita Baptist University, AR
Patrick Henry College, VA
Pittsburg State University, KS
Providence College, RI
Purdue University, IN
Rensselaer Polytechnic Institute, NY
Rogers State University, OK
St. Edward's University, TX
St. John's University, NY
St. Mary's University, TX
Samford University, AL
Sam Houston State University, TX
San Diego State University, CA
Santa Clara University, CA
Slippery Rock University of Pennsylvania, PA
Southeast Missouri State University, MO
Southern Illinois University Carbondale, IL
Stephen F. Austin State University, TX
Stetson University, FL
SUNY Brockport, NY
Texas Christian University, TX
Texas State University, TX
Texas Tech University, TX
Truman State University, MO
Tuskegee University, AL
Union University, TN
The University of Akron, OH
The University of Alabama, AL
University of Alaska Fairbanks, AK
University of Arkansas, AR
University of California, Davis, CA
University of California, Los Angeles, CA
University of California, Santa Cruz, CA
University of Dallas, TX
University of Dayton, OH
University of Florida, FL
University of Idaho, ID
University of Illinois at Urbana-Champaign, IL
The University of Iowa, IA
The University of Kansas, KS
University of Kentucky, KY
University of Louisiana at Monroe, LA
University of Louisville, KY
University of Maine, ME
University of Mary Hardin-Baylor, TX
University of Maryland, College Park, MD
University of Massachusetts Amherst, MA
University of Massachusetts Boston, MA
University of Memphis, TN
University of Michigan, MI
University of Minnesota, Twin Cities Campus, MN
University of Mississippi, MS
University of Montana, MT
University of Nebraska at Kearney, NE
University of New Hampshire, NH
University of North Alabama, AL
University of Northern Colorado, CO
University of North Georgia, GA
University of Oklahoma, OK
University of Oregon, OR
University of Pittsburgh, PA
University of Portland, OR
University of Rhode Island, RI
University of Rochester, NY
The University of Scranton, PA
University of South Carolina, SC
University of South Florida, FL
The University of Tampa, FL
The University of Tennessee, TN
The University of Tennessee at Chattanooga, TN
The University of Tennessee at Martin, TN
The University of Texas at El Paso, TX
The University of Texas Rio Grande Valley, TX
The University of Toledo, OH
University of Utah, UT
University of Washington, WA
University of Washington, Tacoma, WA
University of Wisconsin–La Crosse, WI
University of Wisconsin–River Falls, WI
University of Wisconsin–Stevens Point, WI
Valparaiso University, IN
Villanova University, PA
Washington State University, WA
Washington University in St. Louis, MO
Wayne State University, MI
Western Illinois University, IL
Western Kentucky University, KY
Wheaton College, IL
Whitworth University, WA
Widener University, PA
Wofford College, SC
Wright State University, OH
Wright State University–Lake Campus, OH
Xavier University, OH
Youngstown State University, OH

Physical Sciences

Abilene Christian University, TX
Alfred University, NY
Anderson University, IN
Angelo State University, TX
Arkansas Tech University, AR
Ashland University, OH
Auburn University, AL
Augsburg University, MN
Augustana College, IL
Augustana University, SD
Austin College, TX
Austin Peay State University, TN
Averett University, VA
Ball State University, IN
Barton College, NC
Baylor University, TX
Bellarmine University, KY
Bemidji State University, MN
Binghamton University, State University of New York, NY
Birmingham-Southern College, AL
Black Hills State University, SD
Bloomsburg University of Pennsylvania, PA
Bluffton University, OH
Boise State University, ID
Bowling Green State University, OH
Bryan College, TN
Bucknell University, PA
Buena Vista University, IA
Butler University, IN
California Lutheran University, CA
California Polytechnic State University, San Luis Obispo, CA
California State Polytechnic University, Pomona, CA
California State University, Bakersfield, CA
California State University, Chico, CA
California State University, Fresno, CA
California State University, Fullerton, CA
California State University, Los Angeles, CA
California State University, San Bernardino, CA
California State University, Stanislaus, CA
Cameron University, OK
Campbellsville University, KY
Carroll University, WI
Carthage College, WI
Case Western Reserve University, OH
Catawba College, NC
Cedar Crest College, PA
Centenary College of Louisiana, LA
Central College, IA
Central Methodist University, MO
Central Michigan University, MI
Christopher Newport University, VA
The Citadel, The Military College of South Carolina, SC
Clarion University of Pennsylvania, PA
Clarkson University, NY
Clemson University, SC
Cleveland State University, OH
Coastal Carolina University, SC
The College of Idaho, ID
College of Saint Benedict, MN
College of Staten Island of the City University of New York, NY
The Colorado College, CO
Colorado Mesa University, CO
Colorado School of Mines, CO
Columbia College, MO
Columbus State University, GA
Concordia College, MN
Concordia University Texas, TX
Concord University, WV
Cornerstone University, MI
Dakota State University, SD
Dallas Baptist University, TX
Davidson College, NC
Delta State University, MS
DeSales University, PA
Dordt University, IA
Drury University, MO
Earlham College, IN
East Carolina University, NC
Eastern Illinois University, IL
Eastern Mennonite University, VA
Eastern Michigan University, MI
Eastern New Mexico University, NM
Eastern Washington University, WA
East Texas Baptist University, TX
Edinboro University of Pennsylvania, PA
Elizabethtown College, PA
Elon University, NC
Emporia State University, KS
Evangel University, MO
Ferris State University, MI
Florida Agricultural and Mechanical University, FL
Florida Atlantic University, FL
Florida Gulf Coast University, FL
Florida Institute of Technology, FL
Florida International University, FL
Fort Hays State University, KS
Fort Lewis College, CO
Framingham State University, MA
George Fox University, OR
Georgia College & State University, GA
Georgia Institute of Technology, GA
Georgian Court University, NJ
Goshen College, IN
Governors State University, IL
Graceland University, IA
Grambling State University, LA
Grand Valley State University, MI
Grand View University, IA
Greenville University, IL
Grove City College, PA
Hamline University, MN
Hampshire College, MA
Hampton University, VA
Hardin-Simmons University, TX
High Point University, NC
Hillsdale College, MI
Hiram College, OH

Houghton College, NY
Idaho State University, ID
Illinois State University, IL
Indiana State University, IN
Indiana University of Pennsylvania, PA
Jacksonville State University, AL
James Madison University, VA
John Carroll University, OH
Kean University, NJ
Kennesaw State University, GA
Kent State University, OH
Kent State University at Geauga, OH
Kent State University at Stark, OH
Kettering University, MI
King's College, PA
Kutztown University of Pennsylvania, PA
Lake Erie College, OH
Lake Forest College, IL
Lebanon Valley College, PA
Lewis-Clark State College, ID
Limestone College, SC
Linfield College, OR
Lock Haven University of Pennsylvania, PA
Loras College, IA
Louisiana State University and Agricultural & Mechanical College, LA
Louisiana State University in Shreveport, LA
Loyola Marymount University, CA
Mansfield University of Pennsylvania, PA
Marquette University, WI
Massachusetts College of Liberal Arts, MA
Michigan State University, MI
Middle Tennessee State University, TN
Midwestern State University, TX
Millersville University of Pennsylvania, PA
Millikin University, IL
Mills College, CA
Minnesota State University Moorhead, MN
Mississippi State University, MS
Missouri University of Science and Technology, MO
Missouri Valley College, MO
Montana State University, MT
Montana State University Billings, MT
Montana Technological University, MT
Montclair State University, NJ
Morehead State University, KY
Morgan State University, MD
Muskingum University, OH
Nazareth College of Rochester, NY
Newberry College, SC
New Jersey Institute of Technology, NJ
New Mexico State University, NM
North Carolina Central University, NC
North Carolina State University, NC
North Central College, IL
North Dakota State University, ND
Northeastern Illinois University, IL
Northeastern State University, OK
Northern Illinois University, IL
Northern Michigan University, MI
Northern State University, SD
Northwest Missouri State University, MO
Northwest Nazarene University, ID
Northwest University, WA
Oakland University, MI
The Ohio State University, OH
Ohio University, OH
Ohio University–Chillicothe, OH
Ohio University–Eastern, OH
Ohio University–Lancaster, OH
Ohio University–Southern Campus, OH
Ohio University–Zanesville, OH
Oklahoma Baptist University, OK
Oklahoma State University, OK
Old Dominion University, VA
Oral Roberts University, OK
Pacific University, OR
Piedmont College, GA
Pittsburg State University, KS
Point Loma Nazarene University, CA
Portland State University, OR
Purdue University, IN
Purdue University Northwest, IN
Randolph College, VA
Rhodes College, TN
Rockford University, IL
Rollins College, FL
Sacred Heart University, CT
Saginaw Valley State University, MI
St. Ambrose University, IA
St. Bonaventure University, NY
St. Catherine University, MN
St. Cloud State University, MN
St. Edward's University, TX
St. John Fisher College, NY
St. John's University, NY
Saint Joseph's University, PA
Saint Mary's College of California, CA
Saint Vincent College, PA
Samford University, AL
Sam Houston State University, TX
San Diego State University, CA
San Jose State University, CA
Schreiner University, TX
Shenandoah University, VA
Shepherd University, WV
Shippensburg University of Pennsylvania, PA
Skidmore College, NY
Slippery Rock University of Pennsylvania, PA
Sonoma State University, CA
Southeast Missouri State University, MO
Southern Illinois University Carbondale, IL
Southwestern College, KS
Southwestern Oklahoma State University, OK
State University of New York at Fredonia, NY
State University of New York at New Paltz, NY
State University of New York at Oswego, NY
State University of New York at Plattsburgh, NY
State University of New York College at Geneseo, NY
State University of New York College at Oneonta, NY
State University of New York College at Potsdam, NY
State University of New York College of Environmental Science and Forestry, NY
Stephen F. Austin State University, TX
Stetson University, FL
Stockton University, NJ
Stony Brook University, State University of New York, NY
SUNY Brockport, NY
Texas A&M International University, TX
Texas A&M University, TX
Texas A&M University–Commerce, TX
Texas Christian University, TX
Texas State University, TX
Texas Tech University, TX
Texas Woman's University, TX
Thomas More University, KY
Towson University, MD
Trevecca Nazarene University, TN
Trinity Christian College, IL
Truman State University, MO
Union University, TN
The University of Akron, OH
The University of Alabama, AL
University of Alaska Fairbanks, AK
University of Arkansas, AR
University of California, Davis, CA
University of California, Los Angeles, CA
University of California, Riverside, CA
University of California, San Diego, CA
University of California, Santa Cruz, CA
University of Colorado Boulder, CO
University of Colorado Denver, CO
University of Dallas, TX
University of Dayton, OH
University of Denver, CO
University of Evansville, IN
University of Hawaii at Manoa, HI
University of Houston, TX
University of Idaho, ID
University of Illinois at Urbana-Champaign, IL
University of Indianapolis, IN
University of Jamestown, ND
The University of Kansas, KS
University of Kentucky, KY
University of Louisiana at Monroe, LA
University of Louisville, KY
University of Maine, ME
University of Mary Hardin-Baylor, TX
University of Maryland, Baltimore County, MD
University of Maryland, College Park, MD
University of Mary Washington, VA
University of Massachusetts Amherst, MA
University of Massachusetts Dartmouth, MA
University of Memphis, TN
University of Miami, FL
University of Michigan, MI
University of Michigan–Dearborn, MI
University of Michigan–Flint, MI
University of Minnesota, Twin Cities Campus, MN
University of Mississippi, MS
University of Missouri–St. Louis, MO
University of Montana, MT
University of Montevallo, AL
University of Nebraska at Omaha, NE
University of Nebraska–Lincoln, NE
University of Nevada, Las Vegas, NV
University of Nevada, Reno, NV
University of New Hampshire, NH
University of North Carolina Asheville, NC
The University of North Carolina at Charlotte, NC
The University of North Carolina at Greensboro, NC
The University of North Carolina Wilmington, NC
University of North Dakota, ND
University of Northern Colorado, CO
University of Northern Iowa, IA
University of North Georgia, GA
University of Oklahoma, OK
University of Oregon, OR
University of Pittsburgh, PA
University of Pittsburgh at Bradford, PA
University of Pittsburgh at Johnstown, PA
University of Portland, OR
University of Providence, MT
University of Puget Sound, WA
University of Rhode Island, RI
University of Richmond, VA

University of St. Francis, IL
University of St. Thomas, TX
University of South Carolina, SC
University of South Carolina Aiken, SC
University of South Florida, FL
The University of Tampa, FL
The University of Tennessee at Chattanooga, TN
The University of Tennessee at Martin, TN
The University of Texas at Dallas, TX
The University of Texas at El Paso, TX
The University of Texas at San Antonio, TX
The University of Toledo, OH
The University of Tulsa, OK
University of Utah, UT
University of Washington, WA
University of Washington, Bothell, WA
University of Washington, Tacoma, WA
University of West Georgia, GA
University of Wisconsin–Eau Claire, WI
University of Wisconsin–Green Bay, WI
University of Wisconsin–La Crosse, WI
University of Wisconsin–Parkside, WI
University of Wisconsin–River Falls, WI
University of Wisconsin–Stevens Point, WI
University of Wisconsin–Stout, WI
University of Wisconsin–Superior, WI
University of Wisconsin–Whitewater, WI
University of Wyoming, WY
Upper Iowa University, IA
Utah State University, UT
Valdosta State University, GA
Valley City State University, ND
Valparaiso University, IN
Walsh University, OH
Wartburg College, IA
Washburn University, KS
Washington State University, WA
Washington University in St. Louis, MO
Wayland Baptist University, TX
Wayne State College, NE
Wayne State University, MI
Western Illinois University, IL
Western Kentucky University, KY
Western Oregon University, OR
Western Washington University, WA
Westminster College, UT
West Texas A&M University, TX
Wheaton College, IL
Wichita State University, KS
Widener University, PA
William Jessup University, CA
Wilson College, PA
Wright State University, OH
Wright State University–Lake Campus, OH
Xavier University, OH
Xavier University of Louisiana, LA
Youngstown State University, OH

Premedicine

Alfred University, NY
Anderson University, IN
Angelo State University, TX
Arkansas Tech University, AR
Auburn University, AL
Augustana University, SD
Austin College, TX
Averett University, VA
Baylor University, TX
Belhaven University, MS
Bemidji State University, MN
Bethel College, KS
Binghamton University, State University of New York, NY
Birmingham-Southern College, AL
Bluffton University, OH
Boise State University, ID
Bryan College, TN
Butler University, IN
California State University, Bakersfield, CA
California State University, Stanislaus, CA
Cameron University, OK
Campbellsville University, KY
Carroll University, WI
Carthage College, WI
Case Western Reserve University, OH
Catawba College, NC
Centenary College of Louisiana, LA
Central College, IA
Central Methodist University, MO
Central Michigan University, MI
Chaminade University of Honolulu, HI
Christopher Newport University, VA
City College of the City University of New York, NY
Clarion University of Pennsylvania, PA
Clemson University, SC
Cleveland State University, OH
The College of Idaho, ID
College of Staten Island of the City University of New York, NY
Concordia College, MN
Concord University, WV
Dallas Baptist University, TX
Davidson College, NC
Delta State University, MS
DeSales University, PA
Dordt University, IA
Drury University, MO
Eastern Illinois University, IL
Eastern Mennonite University, VA
Eastern New Mexico University, NM
Eastern Washington University, WA
Edinboro University of Pennsylvania, PA
Elizabethtown College, PA
Elon University, NC
Emory & Henry College, VA
Emporia State University, KS
Evangel University, MO
Florida Agricultural and Mechanical University, FL
Florida Institute of Technology, FL
Fort Hays State University, KS
Gannon University, PA
Georgian Court University, NJ
Grambling State University, LA
Grand Valley State University, MI
Grand View University, IA
Hardin-Simmons University, TX
High Point University, NC
Hillsdale College, MI
Hobart and William Smith Colleges, NY
Houghton College, NY
Idaho State University, ID
Illinois Institute of Technology, IL
Illinois State University, IL
Indiana State University, IN
Indiana University of Pennsylvania, PA
James Madison University, VA
John Carroll University, OH
Kean University, NJ
Kennesaw State University, GA
Kent State University, OH
Kent State University at Geauga, OH
Kent State University at Stark, OH
King's College, PA
Liberty University, VA
Limestone College, SC
Lipscomb University, TN
Lock Haven University of Pennsylvania, PA
Loras College, IA
Louisiana State University in Shreveport, LA
Malone University, OH
Marywood University, PA
Middle Tennessee State University, TN
Midway University, KY
Midwestern State University, TX
Millikin University, IL
Mills College, CA
Minnesota State University Moorhead, MN
Mississippi State University, MS
Missouri University of Science and Technology, MO
Missouri Valley College, MO
Montana State University, MT
Montana State University Billings, MT
Muskingum University, OH
Nazareth College of Rochester, NY
New Jersey Institute of Technology, NJ
North Central College, IL
North Dakota State University, ND
Northeastern State University, OK
Northern Michigan University, MI
Northwest Nazarene University, ID
The Ohio State University, OH
Ohio University, OH
Ohio University–Chillicothe, OH
Ohio University–Eastern, OH
Ohio University–Lancaster, OH
Ohio University–Southern Campus, OH
Ohio University–Zanesville, OH
Oklahoma Baptist University, OK
Oklahoma State University, OK
Ouachita Baptist University, AR
Pacific University, OR
Piedmont College, GA
Plymouth State University, NH
Providence College, RI
Randolph College, VA
Rockford University, IL
Rogers State University, OK
Sacred Heart University, CT
St. Ambrose University, IA
St. Catherine University, MN
St. Edward's University, TX
St. John's University, NY
Saint Joseph's University, PA
Saint Martin's University, WA
Samford University, AL
Schreiner University, TX
Sonoma State University, CA
Southeastern Louisiana University, LA
Southeast Missouri State University, MO
Southern Illinois University Carbondale, IL
Southwestern College, KS
Southwestern University, TX
State University of New York at Oswego, NY
State University of New York at Plattsburgh, NY
State University of New York College at Geneseo, NY
State University of New York College at Oneonta, NY
State University of New York College at Potsdam, NY
State University of New York College of Environmental Science and Forestry, NY
Stephen F. Austin State University, TX
Stetson University, FL
Texas A&M International University, TX
Texas A&M University, TX
Texas A&M University–Commerce, TX
Texas Christian University, TX
Texas Tech University, TX
Texas Woman's University, TX

Thomas More University, KY
Trine University, IN
Trinity Christian College, IL
Truett McConnell University, GA
Truman State University, MO
Union University, TN
The University of Akron, OH
The University of Alabama, AL
University of Arkansas, AR
University of California, Davis, CA
University of California, Riverside, CA
University of California, San Diego, CA
University of Colorado Boulder, CO
University of Colorado Denver, CO
University of Dallas, TX
University of Dayton, OH
University of Evansville, IN
University of Houston, TX
University of Idaho, ID
University of Illinois at Urbana-Champaign, IL
The University of Kansas, KS
University of Louisville, KY
University of Maine, ME
University of Mary Hardin-Baylor, TX
University of Maryland, College Park, MD
University of Massachusetts Amherst, MA
University of Memphis, TN
University of Miami, FL
University of Michigan, MI
University of Michigan–Flint, MI
University of Minnesota, Twin Cities Campus, MN
University of Mississippi, MS
University of Missouri–St. Louis, MO
University of Montana, MT
University of Nebraska at Omaha, NE
University of Nebraska–Lincoln, NE
University of Nevada, Las Vegas, NV
The University of North Carolina at Greensboro, NC
The University of North Carolina Wilmington, NC
University of North Dakota, ND
University of Northern Colorado, CO
University of North Georgia, GA
University of Oklahoma, OK
University of Oregon, OR
University of Pittsburgh, PA
University of Pittsburgh at Bradford, PA
University of Pittsburgh at Johnstown, PA
University of Portland, OR
University of Providence, MT
University of Puget Sound, WA
University of Rhode Island, RI
University of St. Francis, IL
University of St. Thomas, TX
University of South Carolina, SC
University of South Carolina Aiken, SC
University of Southern Indiana, IN
University of South Florida, FL
The University of Tampa, FL
The University of Tennessee at Martin, TN
The University of Texas Rio Grande Valley, TX
The University of Toledo, OH
University of Washington, WA
University of Washington, Bothell, WA
University of West Georgia, GA
University of Wisconsin–Eau Claire, WI
University of Wisconsin–Green Bay, WI
University of Wisconsin–Parkside, WI
University of Wisconsin–Stevens Point, WI
University of Wisconsin–Whitewater, WI
Utah State University, UT
Walsh University, OH
Wartburg College, IA
Washburn University, KS
Washington State University, WA
Washington University in St. Louis, MO
Wayland Baptist University, TX
Wayne State College, NE
Wayne State University, MI
Wesleyan College, GA
Western Kentucky University, KY
Western Oregon University, OR
Western Washington University, WA
Westminster College, PA
Westminster College, UT
West Texas A&M University, TX
Wheaton College, IL
Wichita State University, KS
Widener University, PA
Wilson College, PA
Wright State University, OH
Wright State University–Lake Campus, OH
Xavier University of Louisiana, LA
Youngstown State University, OH

Religion/Biblical Studies

Abilene Christian University, TX
Alaska Bible College, AK
Allegheny Wesleyan College, OH
Anderson University, IN
Anderson University, SC
Augsburg University, MN
Augustana College, IL
Augustana University, SD
Austin College, TX
Austin Graduate School of Theology, TX
Averett University, VA
The Baptist College of Florida, FL
Barton College, NC
Baylor University, TX
Belhaven University, MS
Belmont University, TN
Berry College, GA
Birmingham-Southern College, AL
Bloomsburg University of Pennsylvania, PA
Boise Bible College, ID
Boise State University, ID
Boston Baptist College, MA
Bryan College, TN
Butler University, IN
California Baptist University, CA
California Christian College, CA
California Lutheran University, CA
California State University, Bakersfield, CA
California State University, Fullerton, CA
Campbellsville University, KY
Carolina Christian College, NC
Carson-Newman University, TN
Carthage College, WI
Case Western Reserve University, OH
Centenary College of Louisiana, LA
Central College, IA
Central Methodist University, MO
Central Michigan University, MI
The Citadel, The Military College of South Carolina, SC
The College of Idaho, ID
Columbia College, MO
Columbia College, SC
Concordia University Chicago, IL
Concordia University, St. Paul, MN
Concordia University Texas, TX
Concordia University Wisconsin, WI
Cornerstone University, MI
Dallas Baptist University, TX
DeSales University, PA
Dordt University, IA
Earlham College, IN
Eastern Mennonite University, VA
Eastern Michigan University, MI
Eastern New Mexico University, NM
East Texas Baptist University, TX
Elizabethtown College, PA
Elon University, NC
Emmanuel College, GA
Evangel University, MO
Felician University, NJ
Florida Gulf Coast University, FL
Gannon University, PA
George Fox University, OR
Georgian Court University, NJ
Goshen College, IN
Grand View University, IA
Grove City College, PA
Hardin-Simmons University, TX
High Point University, NC
Hillsdale College, MI
Hiram College, OH
Houghton College, NY
Houston Baptist University, TX
Indiana University of Pennsylvania, PA
James Madison University, VA
John Carroll University, OH
Johnson University, TN
Johnson University Florida, FL
Kent State University, OH
Kent State University at Geauga, OH
Kent State University at Stark, OH
King's College, PA
Kuyper College, MI
LaGrange College, GA
La Sierra University, CA
Lebanon Valley College, PA
Lee University, TN
Liberty University, VA
Limestone College, SC
Linfield College, OR
Lipscomb University, TN
Loras College, IA
Louisiana College, LA
Louisiana State University and Agricultural & Mechanical College, LA
Loyola Marymount University, CA
Maranatha Baptist University, WI
Marywood University, PA
Mayville State University, ND
McKendree University, IL
Messenger College, TX
MidAmerica Nazarene University, KS
Mid-Atlantic Christian University, NC
Mississippi State University, MS
Missouri Baptist University, MO
Montclair State University, NJ
Nazareth College of Rochester, NY
Newberry College, SC
North Central College, IL
North Greenville University, SC
Northwest Christian University, OR
Northwest Nazarene University, ID
Northwest University, WA
Ohio Christian University, OH
Ohio Valley University, WV
Oklahoma Baptist University, OK
Oklahoma City University, OK
Oral Roberts University, OK
Ouachita Baptist University, AR
Piedmont College, GA
Point Loma Nazarene University, CA
Randolph-Macon College, VA
Reinhardt University, GA
Rochester University, MI

St. Ambrose University, IA
St. Bonaventure University, NY
St. Edward's University, TX
Saint Francis University, PA
St. John Fisher College, NY
Saint Mary's College of California, CA
St. Thomas Aquinas College, NY
Saint Vincent College, PA
Samford University, AL
San Diego State University, CA
San Jose State University, CA
Schreiner University, TX
Shenandoah University, VA
Southeastern University, FL
Southeast Missouri State University, MO
Southwestern College, KS
Spelman College, GA
Stetson University, FL
Texas Christian University, TX
Thomas More University, KY
Toccoa Falls College, GA
Trevecca Nazarene University, TN
Trinity Christian College, IL
Trinity College of Florida, FL
Truett McConnell University, GA
Union University, TN
The University of Alabama, AL
University of California, Davis, CA
University of California, Los Angeles, CA
University of Colorado Boulder, CO
University of Dayton, OH
University of Evansville, IN
University of Illinois at Urbana-Champaign, IL
University of Indianapolis, IN
The University of Kansas, KS
University of Mary Hardin-Baylor, TX
University of Mary Washington, VA
University of Miami, FL
University of Minnesota, Twin Cities Campus, MN
University of North Carolina Asheville, NC
The University of North Carolina at Charlotte, NC
The University of North Carolina at Greensboro, NC
University of Northwestern–St. Paul, MN
University of Pittsburgh, PA
University of Portland, OR
University of Providence, MT
University of Rhode Island, RI
University of St. Thomas, TX
University of South Carolina, SC
University of South Florida, FL
The University of Tennessee at Chattanooga, TN
The University of Toledo, OH
The University of Tulsa, OK
University of Wisconsin–Eau Claire, WI
University of Wyoming, WY
Walla Walla University, WA
Walsh University, OH
Wartburg College, IA
Washburn University, KS
Washington University in St. Louis, MO
Wayland Baptist University, TX
Wesleyan College, GA
Western Illinois University, IL
Western Kentucky University, KY
Westminster College, UT
Wheaton College, IL
William Jessup University, CA
Wilson College, PA
Wright State University, OH
Wright State University–Lake Campus, OH
Xavier University of Louisiana, LA
Youngstown State University, OH

Social Sciences

Abilene Christian University, TX
Alfred University, NY
Alliant International University - San Diego, CA
Anderson University, IN
Angelo State University, TX
Arkansas Tech University, AR
Ashland University, OH
Auburn University, AL
Augsburg University, MN
Augustana College, IL
Augustana University, SD
Austin College, TX
Austin Peay State University, TN
Ball State University, IN
Barton College, NC
Baylor University, TX
Belhaven University, MS
Belmont University, TN
Bemidji State University, MN
Bethel College, KS
Binghamton University, State University of New York, NY
Birmingham-Southern College, AL
Black Hills State University, SD
Bloomsburg University of Pennsylvania, PA
Boise State University, ID
Bowling Green State University, OH
Bryan College, TN
Butler University, IN
California Lutheran University, CA
California Polytechnic State University, San Luis Obispo, CA
California State Polytechnic University, Pomona, CA
California State University, Bakersfield, CA
California State University, Chico, CA
California State University, Fresno, CA
California State University, Fullerton, CA
California State University, Los Angeles, CA
California State University, Northridge, CA
California State University, San Bernardino, CA
California State University, Stanislaus, CA
Cameron University, OK
Campbellsville University, KY
Carlow University, PA
Carroll University, WI
Case Western Reserve University, OH
Cedar Crest College, PA
Centenary College of Louisiana, LA
Central College, IA
Central Methodist University, MO
Central Michigan University, MI
Champlain College, VT
Christopher Newport University, VA
City College of the City University of New York, NY
Clarion University of Pennsylvania, PA
Clarkson University, NY
Clemson University, SC
Cleveland State University, OH
Coastal Carolina University, SC
The College of Idaho, ID
College of Staten Island of the City University of New York, NY
Colorado Mesa University, CO
Columbia College, MO
Concordia University Texas, TX
Concord University, WV
Cornerstone University, MI
Dallas Baptist University, TX
Davidson College, NC
Delta State University, MS
DeSales University, PA
Dordt University, IA
Drury University, MO
Earlham College, IN
East Carolina University, NC
Eastern Illinois University, IL
Eastern Mennonite University, VA
Eastern Michigan University, MI
Eastern New Mexico University, NM
Eastern Washington University, WA
East Texas Baptist University, TX
Edinboro University of Pennsylvania, PA
Elizabethtown College, PA
Elon University, NC
Emporia State University, KS
Evangel University, MO
Florida Agricultural and Mechanical University, FL
Florida Atlantic University, FL
Florida Gulf Coast University, FL
Florida International University, FL
Fort Hays State University, KS
Fort Lewis College, CO
Gannon University, PA
George Fox University, OR
Georgia College & State University, GA
Georgian Court University, NJ
Glenville State College, WV
Goshen College, IN
Governors State University, IL
Grambling State University, LA
Grand Valley State University, MI
Grand View University, IA
Grove City College, PA
Hampshire College, MA
Hardin-Simmons University, TX
Hillsdale College, MI
Hiram College, OH
Idaho State University, ID
Illinois Institute of Technology, IL
Illinois State University, IL
Indiana State University, IN
Indiana University of Pennsylvania, PA
Iowa Wesleyan University, IA
Jacksonville State University, AL
James Madison University, VA
John Carroll University, OH
Kean University, NJ
Kennesaw State University, GA
Kent State University, OH
Kent State University at Geauga, OH
Kent State University at Stark, OH
Kenyon College, OH
King's College, PA
Kuyper College, MI
Lake Erie College, OH
Lake Forest College, IL
Lebanon Valley College, PA
Lewis-Clark State College, ID
Limestone College, SC
Linfield College, OR
Lock Haven University of Pennsylvania, PA
Longwood University, VA
Louisiana College, LA
Louisiana State University in Shreveport, LA
Loyola Marymount University, CA
Malone University, OH
Marymount University, VA
Maryville University of Saint Louis, MO
Marywood University, PA
Massachusetts College of Liberal Arts, MA
Michigan State University, MI
Middle Tennessee State University, TN
Midwestern State University, TX

Millersville University of Pennsylvania, PA
Minnesota State University Moorhead, MN
Minot State University, ND
Mississippi State University, MS
Missouri University of Science and Technology, MO
Missouri Valley College, MO
Molloy College, NY
Montana State University, MT
Montana State University Billings, MT
Montclair State University, NJ
Morehead State University, KY
Morgan State University, MD
Nazareth College of Rochester, NY
Newberry College, SC
New Mexico State University, NM
North Carolina Central University, NC
North Carolina State University, NC
North Central College, IL
North Dakota State University, ND
Northeastern Illinois University, IL
Northeastern State University, OK
Northern Illinois University, IL
Northern Michigan University, MI
Northern State University, SD
Northwestern State University of Louisiana, LA
Northwest Missouri State University, MO
Northwest Nazarene University, ID
Northwest University, WA
Oakland University, MI
Oglethorpe University, GA
The Ohio State University, OH
Ohio University, OH
Ohio University–Chillicothe, OH
Ohio University–Eastern, OH
Ohio University–Lancaster, OH
Ohio University–Southern Campus, OH
Ohio University–Zanesville, OH
Oklahoma Baptist University, OK
Oklahoma State University, OK
Old Dominion University, VA
Ouachita Baptist University, AR
Pacific University, OR
Piedmont College, GA
Pittsburg State University, KS
Point Loma Nazarene University, CA
Portland State University, OR
Purchase College, State University of New York, NY
Purdue University Northwest, IN
Queens University of Charlotte, NC
Randolph College, VA
Reinhardt University, GA
Rockford University, IL
St. Ambrose University, IA
St. Catherine University, MN
St. Cloud State University, MN
St. Edward's University, TX
Saint Francis University, PA
St. John Fisher College, NY
St. John's University, NY
St. Thomas Aquinas College, NY
Saint Vincent College, PA
Samford University, AL
Sam Houston State University, TX
San Diego State University, CA
San Jose State University, CA
Schreiner University, TX
Shenandoah University, VA
Shippensburg University of Pennsylvania, PA
Slippery Rock University of Pennsylvania, PA
Sonoma State University, CA
Southeastern Louisiana University, LA
Southeast Missouri State University, MO
Southern Illinois University Carbondale, IL
Southern New Hampshire University, NH
Southwestern College, KS
Southwestern Oklahoma State University, OK
Southwestern University, TX
Spelman College, GA
State University of New York at Fredonia, NY
State University of New York at Oswego, NY
State University of New York at Plattsburgh, NY
State University of New York College at Geneseo, NY
State University of New York College at Oneonta, NY
State University of New York College at Potsdam, NY
Stetson University, FL
Stockton University, NJ
Stony Brook University, State University of New York, NY
SUNY Brockport, NY
Texas A&M International University, TX
Texas A&M University–Commerce, TX
Texas A&M University–Texarkana, TX
Texas Christian University, TX
Texas State University, TX
Texas Tech University, TX
Texas Woman's University, TX
Thomas More University, KY
Trevecca Nazarene University, TN
Trinity Christian College, IL
Truman State University, MO
Union University, TN
The University of Akron, OH
The University of Alabama, AL
University of Alaska Anchorage, AK
University of Arkansas, AR
University of California, Davis, CA
University of California, Los Angeles, CA
University of California, Riverside, CA
University of California, San Diego, CA
University of California, Santa Cruz, CA
University of Colorado Boulder, CO
University of Colorado Denver, CO
University of Dayton, OH
University of Denver, CO
University of Evansville, IN
University of Hawaii at Manoa, HI
University of Houston, TX
University of Houston–Clear Lake, TX
University of Idaho, ID
University of Illinois at Urbana-Champaign, IL
The University of Kansas, KS
University of Kentucky, KY
University of Louisiana at Monroe, LA
University of Louisville, KY
University of Maine, ME
University of Maine at Fort Kent, ME
University of Mary Hardin-Baylor, TX
University of Maryland, Baltimore County, MD
University of Maryland, College Park, MD
University of Mary Washington, VA
University of Massachusetts Amherst, MA
University of Massachusetts Dartmouth, MA
University of Memphis, TN
University of Miami, FL
University of Michigan, MI
University of Michigan–Dearborn, MI
University of Michigan–Flint, MI
University of Minnesota, Twin Cities Campus, MN
University of Mississippi, MS
University of Missouri–St. Louis, MO
University of Montana, MT
University of Montevallo, AL
University of Nebraska at Omaha, NE
University of Nebraska–Lincoln, NE
University of Nevada, Las Vegas, NV
University of North Carolina Asheville, NC
The University of North Carolina at Charlotte, NC
The University of North Carolina at Greensboro, NC
The University of North Carolina Wilmington, NC
University of North Dakota, ND
University of Northern Colorado, CO
University of Northern Iowa, IA
University of Northwestern–St. Paul, MN
University of Oklahoma, OK
University of Oregon, OR
University of Pittsburgh, PA
University of Pittsburgh at Bradford, PA
University of Pittsburgh at Johnstown, PA
University of Portland, OR
University of Providence, MT
University of Puget Sound, WA
University of Rhode Island, RI
University of Richmond, VA
University of St. Francis, IL
University of St. Thomas, TX
University of South Carolina, SC
University of South Carolina Aiken, SC
University of Southern Indiana, IN
University of South Florida, FL
The University of Tampa, FL
The University of Tennessee, TN
The University of Tennessee at Chattanooga, TN
The University of Tennessee at Martin, TN
The University of Texas at San Antonio, TX
The University of Texas Rio Grande Valley, TX
The University of Toledo, OH
The University of Tulsa, OK
University of Utah, UT
University of Washington, WA
University of Washington, Bothell, WA
University of Washington, Tacoma, WA
University of West Georgia, GA
University of Wisconsin–Eau Claire, WI
University of Wisconsin–Green Bay, WI
University of Wisconsin–La Crosse, WI
University of Wisconsin–Parkside, WI
University of Wisconsin–River Falls, WI
University of Wisconsin–Stevens Point, WI
University of Wisconsin–Superior, WI
University of Wisconsin–Whitewater, WI
University of Wyoming, WY
Upper Iowa University, IA
Utah State University, UT
Valdosta State University, GA
Valley City State University, ND
Valparaiso University, IN
Walsh University, OH
Wartburg College, IA
Washburn University, KS
Washington State University, WA
Washington University in St. Louis, MO
Wayland Baptist University, TX
Wayne State College, NE
Wayne State University, MI
Wesleyan College, GA

West Chester University of Pennsylvania, PA
Western Illinois University, IL
Western Kentucky University, KY
Western Oregon University, OR
Western Washington University, WA
Westminster College, UT
West Texas A&M University, TX
Wheaton College, IL
Wichita State University, KS
Widener University, PA
William Jessup University, CA
Wilson College, PA
Wright State University, OH
Wright State University–Lake Campus, OH
Xavier University, OH
Xavier University of Louisiana, LA
Youngstown State University, OH

Creative Arts/Performance

Applied Art and Design

Abilene Christian University, TX
Alfred University, NY
Alma College, MI
Alverno College, WI
Anderson University, IN
Anderson University, SC
Angelo State University, TX
Arkansas Tech University, AR
Asbury University, KY
Auburn University, AL
Augsburg University, MN
Augustana University, SD
Aurora University, IL
Austin College, TX
Austin Peay State University, TN
Averett University, VA
Baker University, KS
Barton College, NC
Baylor University, TX
Belhaven University, MS
Bellarmine University, KY
Belmont University, TN
Bemidji State University, MN
Berry College, GA
Bethany Lutheran College, MN
Bethel College, KS
Bethel University, IN
Bethel University, MN
Binghamton University, State University of New York, NY
Birmingham-Southern College, AL
Black Hills State University, SD
Bluefield College, VA
Boise State University, ID
Boston University, MA
Bowie State University, MD
Bowling Green State University, OH
Bradley University, IL
Brigham Young University, UT
Bucknell University, PA
Buena Vista University, IA
Butler University, IN
Caldwell University, NJ
California Baptist University, CA
California Polytechnic State University, San Luis Obispo, CA
California State University, Bakersfield, CA
California State University, Chico, CA
California State University, Fresno, CA
California State University, Fullerton, CA
California State University, Los Angeles, CA
California State University, San Bernardino, CA
California State University, San Marcos, CA
California State University, Stanislaus, CA
Cameron University, OK
Campbellsville University, KY
Cardinal Stritch University, WI
Carroll College, MT
Carroll University, WI
Carson-Newman University, TN
Carthage College, WI
Case Western Reserve University, OH
Cedar Crest College, PA
Centenary College of Louisiana, LA
Central College, IA
Central Michigan University, MI
Central Washington University, WA
Chatham University, PA
City College of the City University of New York, NY
Clarion University of Pennsylvania, PA
Clarke University, IA
Clemson University, SC
Cleveland Institute of Art, OH
Cleveland State University, OH
Coastal Carolina University, SC
Coe College, IA
The College of Idaho, ID
The College of New Jersey, NJ
College of Saint Benedict, MN
The College of Saint Rose, NY
College of Staten Island of the City University of New York, NY
Colorado Mesa University, CO
Colorado State University, CO
Columbia College, MO
Columbia College Chicago, IL
Columbus State University, GA
Concordia College, MN
Concord University, WV
Cornell College, IA
Creighton University, NE
Davidson College, NC
Doane University, NE
Dominican University, IL
Drake University, IA
Drew University, NJ
Drury University, MO
Earlham College, IN
East Carolina University, NC
Eastern Illinois University, IL
Eastern Michigan University, MI
Eastern New Mexico University, NM
Eastern Oregon University, OR
Eastern Washington University, WA
Eckerd College, FL
Edinboro University of Pennsylvania, PA
Elizabethtown College, PA
Elon University, NC
Emmanuel College, GA
Emory & Henry College, VA
Emory University, GA
Emporia State University, KS
Endicott College, MA
Evangel University, MO
Ferris State University, MI
Florida Agricultural and Mechanical University, FL
Florida Gulf Coast University, FL
Florida International University, FL
Fort Hays State University, KS
Fort Lewis College, CO
Franklin College, IN
George Fox University, OR
Georgia College & State University, GA
Georgian Court University, NJ
Glenville State College, WV
Gordon College, MA
Goucher College, MD
Graceland University, IA
Grand Valley State University, MI
Grand View University, IA
Greenville University, IL
Gustavus Adolphus College, MN
Hamline University, MN
Hardin-Simmons University, TX
Hendrix College, AR
High Point University, NC
Hillsdale College, MI
Hobart and William Smith Colleges, NY
Hofstra University, NY
Hollins University, VA
Hope College, MI
Houghton College, NY
Huntington University, IN
Idaho State University, ID
Illinois College, IL
Illinois State University, IL
Illinois Wesleyan University, IL
Indiana State University, IN
Indiana University of Pennsylvania, PA
Iowa Wesleyan University, IA
Jacksonville State University, AL
Jacksonville University, FL
James Madison University, VA
John Brown University, AR
Judson University, IL
Kalamazoo College, MI
Kansas City Art Institute, MO
Kean University, NJ
Keene State College, NH
Kennesaw State University, GA
Kent State University, OH
Kent State University at Geauga, OH
Kent State University at Stark, OH
Kenyon College, OH
King University, TN
Kutztown University of Pennsylvania, PA
Lafayette College, PA
LaGrange College, GA
La Sierra University, CA
Lewis-Clark State College, ID
Lewis University, IL
Limestone College, SC
Lipscomb University, TN
Lock Haven University of Pennsylvania, PA
Longwood University, VA
Louisiana College, LA
Louisiana State University and Agricultural & Mechanical College, LA
Loyola Marymount University, CA
Loyola University Chicago, IL
Loyola University New Orleans, LA
Lycoming College, PA
Lyon College, AR
Mansfield University of Pennsylvania, PA
Marietta College, OH
Marshall University, WV
Maryville College, TN
Maryville University of Saint Louis, MO
Marywood University, PA
Massachusetts College of Liberal Arts, MA
Mercer University, GA
Messiah College, PA
Miami University, OH
Michigan State University, MI
Michigan Technological University, MI
Middle Tennessee State University, TN
Midwestern State University, TX
Milligan University, TN
Millikin University, IL
Minneapolis College of Art and Design, MN
Minnesota State University Mankato, MN
Minnesota State University Moorhead, MN

Minot State University, ND
Mississippi State University, MS
Missouri Southern State University, MO
Missouri Valley College, MO
Montana State University, MT
Montclair State University, NJ
Morehead State University, KY
Morgan State University, MD
Mount Marty College, SD
Mount St. Mary's University, MD
Mount Vernon Nazarene University, OH
Muskingum University, OH
Nazareth College of Rochester, NY
Nebraska Wesleyan University, NE
New Jersey Institute of Technology, NJ
Newman University, KS
New Mexico State University, NM
Nicholls State University, LA
North Carolina Central University, NC
Northeastern Illinois University, IL
Northeastern State University, OK
Northern Arizona University, AZ
Northern Illinois University, IL
Northwestern State University of Louisiana, LA
Northwest Missouri State University, MO
Oglethorpe University, GA
Ohio University, OH
Ohio University–Chillicothe, OH
Ohio University–Eastern, OH
Ohio University–Lancaster, OH
Ohio University–Southern Campus, OH
Ohio University–Zanesville, OH
Ohio Wesleyan University, OH
Oklahoma Baptist University, OK
Oklahoma City University, OK
Oklahoma State University, OK
Old Dominion University, VA
Olivet College, MI
Olivet Nazarene University, IL
Oral Roberts University, OK
Otis College of Art and Design, CA
Otterbein University, OH
Pacific Lutheran University, WA
Pacific University, OR
Pennsylvania Academy of the Fine Arts, PA
Piedmont College, GA
Point Loma Nazarene University, CA
Purchase College, State University of New York, NY
Purdue University Fort Wayne, IN
Queens University of Charlotte, NC
Reinhardt University, GA
Rhode Island College, RI
Rhodes College, TN
Ringling College of Art and Design, FL
Rockford University, IL
Rogers State University, OK
Rollins College, FL
Rosemont College, PA
Sacred Heart University, CT
Saginaw Valley State University, MI
St. Ambrose University, IA
St. Catherine University, MN
St. Cloud State University, MN
St. Edward's University, TX
Saint John's University, MN
St. John's University, NY
Saint Louis University, MO
St. Norbert College, WI
St. Olaf College, MN
Salem College, NC
Salem State University, MA
Salve Regina University, RI
Samford University, AL
San Diego State University, CA
San Francisco Art Institute, CA
School of Visual Arts, NY
Schreiner University, TX
Seattle Pacific University, WA
Seattle University, WA
Shepherd University, WV
Shippensburg University of Pennsylvania, PA
Simpson College, IA
Slippery Rock University of Pennsylvania, PA
Sonoma State University, CA
Southeastern Louisiana University, LA
Southeastern University, FL
Southeast Missouri State University, MO
Southern Illinois University Carbondale, IL
Southern Utah University, UT
Southwest Baptist University, MO
Southwestern Oklahoma State University, OK
Southwestern University, TX
State University of New York at Fredonia, NY
State University of New York at New Paltz, NY
State University of New York at Plattsburgh, NY
State University of New York College at Cortland, NY
State University of New York College at Geneseo, NY
State University of New York College at Potsdam, NY
Stetson University, FL
Stevenson University, MD
Stockton University, NJ
Temple University, PA
Texas A&M University–Commerce, TX
Texas A&M University–Corpus Christi, TX
Texas Christian University, TX
Texas State University, TX
Texas Tech University, TX
Texas Woman's University, TX
Transylvania University, KY
Trinity Christian College, IL
Trinity University, TX
Truman State University, MO
Tufts University, MA
Union University, TN
The University of Akron, OH
The University of Alabama, AL
The University of Alabama at Birmingham, AL
University of Arkansas, AR
University of California, Los Angeles, CA
University of California, Riverside, CA
University of California, Santa Cruz, CA
University of Colorado Boulder, CO
University of Colorado Denver, CO
University of Dallas, TX
University of Dayton, OH
University of Evansville, IN
University of Florida, FL
University of Hawaii at Manoa, HI
University of Houston, TX
University of Idaho, ID
University of Illinois at Chicago, IL
University of Illinois at Urbana-Champaign, IL
University of Indianapolis, IN
The University of Iowa, IA
University of Jamestown, ND
The University of Kansas, KS
University of Kentucky, KY
University of Louisiana at Monroe, LA
University of Louisville, KY
University of Lynchburg, VA
University of Maine, ME
University of Mary Hardin-Baylor, TX
University of Maryland, Baltimore County, MD
University of Maryland, College Park, MD
University of Mary Washington, VA
University of Massachusetts Amherst, MA
University of Memphis, TN
University of Michigan, MI
University of Michigan–Dearborn, MI
University of Michigan–Flint, MI
University of Minnesota, Twin Cities Campus, MN
University of Mississippi, MS
University of Missouri–St. Louis, MO
University of Montevallo, AL
University of Nebraska at Kearney, NE
University of Nebraska–Lincoln, NE
University of Nevada, Las Vegas, NV
University of Nevada, Reno, NV
University of New Hampshire, NH
University of New Mexico, NM
University of North Alabama, AL
The University of North Carolina at Chapel Hill, NC
The University of North Carolina at Charlotte, NC
The University of North Carolina at Greensboro, NC
The University of North Carolina at Pembroke, NC
The University of North Carolina Wilmington, NC
University of North Dakota, ND
University of Northern Colorado, CO
University of Northern Iowa, IA
University of North Georgia, GA
University of Oklahoma, OK
University of Oregon, OR
University of Pittsburgh at Bradford, PA
University of Rhode Island, RI
University of Richmond, VA
University of St. Francis, IL
University of St. Thomas, TX
University of Science and Arts of Oklahoma, OK
University of South Carolina, SC
University of South Carolina Aiken, SC
University of Southern California, CA
University of Southern Indiana, IN
University of Southern Mississippi, MS
University of South Florida, FL
The University of Tampa, FL
The University of Tennessee at Chattanooga, TN
The University of Texas at Austin, TX
The University of Texas at El Paso, TX
The University of Texas at San Antonio, TX
The University of Texas at Tyler, TX
The University of Texas Rio Grande Valley, TX
University of the Incarnate Word, TX
The University of Toledo, OH
The University of Tulsa, OK
University of Utah, UT
University of Washington, WA
University of West Georgia, GA
University of Wisconsin–Eau Claire, WI
University of Wisconsin–La Crosse, WI
University of Wisconsin–Milwaukee, WI
University of Wisconsin–Parkside, WI
University of Wisconsin–River Falls, WI

University of Wisconsin–Stout, WI
University of Wisconsin–Whitewater, WI
University of Wyoming, WY
Utah State University, UT
Valdosta State University, GA
Valparaiso University, IN
Wake Forest University, NC
Wartburg College, IA
Washington College, MD
Washington State University, WA
Washington University in St. Louis, MO
Waynesburg University, PA
Wayne State College, NE
Wayne State University, MI
Wesleyan College, GA
West Chester University of Pennsylvania, PA
Western Carolina University, NC
Western Colorado University, CO
Western Illinois University, IL
Western Kentucky University, KY
Western Michigan University, MI
Western Oregon University, OR
Western Washington University, WA
Westminster College, UT
West Texas A&M University, TX
Wheaton College, IL
Whitman College, WA
Whittier College, CA
Whitworth University, WA
Wichita State University, KS
William Jessup University, CA
William Paterson University of New Jersey, NJ
William Peace University, NC
Winona State University, MN
Wittenberg University, OH
Wofford College, SC
Wright State University, OH
Wright State University–Lake Campus, OH
Xavier University of Louisiana, LA
Youngstown State University, OH

Art/Fine Arts

Alabama State University, AL
Albion College, MI
Allegheny College, PA
Anderson University, SC
Angelo State University, TX
Arizona State University at the Tempe campus, AZ
Asbury University, KY
Ashland University, OH
Auburn University, AL
Augustana College, IL
Belhaven University, MS
Belmont University, TN
Bemidji State University, MN
Bethel College, KS
Bluffton University, OH
Bowie State University, MD
Butler University, IN
California Baptist University, CA
California Lutheran University, CA
California Polytechnic State University, San Luis Obispo, CA
California State University, Chico, CA
Calumet College of Saint Joseph, IN
Campbellsville University, KY
Canisius College, NY
Carroll University, WI
Carthage College, WI
Centenary College of Louisiana, LA
Central Michigan University, MI
Chapman University, CA
Chatham University, PA
Christopher Newport University, VA
City College of the City University of New York, NY
Clemson University, SC
Cleveland Institute of Art, OH
College of Staten Island of the City University of New York, NY
Columbia College, SC
Columbia College Chicago, IL
Converse College, SC
Creighton University, NE
Dallas Baptist University, TX
Delta State University, MS
DePaul University, IL
Dillard University, LA
Dominican University, IL
Dordt University, IA
East Carolina University, NC
Eastern Illinois University, IL
Eastern Mennonite University, VA
Eastern Michigan University, MI
Eastern New Mexico University, NM
Eastern Oregon University, OR
Edgewood College, WI
Edinboro University of Pennsylvania, PA
Emmanuel College, GA
Ferris State University, MI
Florida Agricultural and Mechanical University, FL
Fort Hays State University, KS
Francis Marion University, SC
Franklin College, IN
Georgian Court University, NJ
Goddard College, VT
Graceland University, IA
Grand Valley State University, MI
Grand View University, IA
Greenville University, IL
Hamline University, MN
Hardin-Simmons University, TX
Hiram College, OH
Hofstra University, NY
Houston Baptist University, TX
Huntington University, IN
Illinois Institute of Technology, IL
Illinois State University, IL
Indiana State University, IN
Indiana University of Pennsylvania, PA
Johnson University, TN
Kean University, NJ
Keene State College, NH
Kent State University, OH
Kent State University at Geauga, OH
Kent State University at Stark, OH
Kutztown University of Pennsylvania, PA
Lafayette College, PA
Lake Erie College, OH
Lake Forest College, IL
La Sierra University, CA
Lewis University, IL
Long Island University, NY
Louisiana State University and Agricultural & Mechanical College, LA
Loyola Marymount University, CA
Lycoming College, PA
Marymount California University, CA
Maryville University of Saint Louis, MO
Massachusetts College of Liberal Arts, MA
Mayville State University, ND
McPherson College, KS
MidAmerica Nazarene University, KS
Millersville University of Pennsylvania, PA
Milwaukee Institute of Art and Design, WI
Minneapolis College of Art and Design, MN
Mississippi State University, MS
Missouri Valley College, MO
Molloy College, NY
Montana State University Billings, MT
Morehead State University, KY
Morgan State University, MD
Muskingum University, OH
Nazareth College of Rochester, NY
New Jersey Institute of Technology, NJ
New Mexico State University, NM
Nicholls State University, LA
North Central College, IL
North Dakota State University, ND
Northeastern State University, OK
Northern Illinois University, IL
Northern Michigan University, MI
Northern State University, SD
Northwestern State University of Louisiana, LA
Ohio University, OH
Ohio University–Chillicothe, OH
Ohio University–Eastern, OH
Ohio University–Lancaster, OH
Ohio University–Southern Campus, OH
Ohio University–Zanesville, OH
Ohio Wesleyan University, OH
Oklahoma Baptist University, OK
Oklahoma City University, OK
Oklahoma State University, OK
Old Dominion University, VA
Oral Roberts University, OK
Otis College of Art and Design, CA
Ouachita Baptist University, AR
Pacific Lutheran University, WA
Piedmont College, GA
Portland State University, OR
Rice University, TX
Ringling College of Art and Design, FL
Roanoke College, VA
Sacred Heart University, CT
St. Bonaventure University, NY
St. Cloud State University, MN
Saint Francis University, PA
Saint Mary's College, IN
Salem State University, MA
Samford University, AL
Sam Houston State University, TX
San Diego State University, CA
San Jose State University, CA
Schreiner University, TX
Shepherd University, WV
Slippery Rock University of Pennsylvania, PA
Sonoma State University, CA
Southern Illinois University Carbondale, IL
Southern Illinois University Edwardsville, IL
Southwestern Oklahoma State University, OK
Spelman College, GA
State University of New York at Fredonia, NY
State University of New York College at Geneseo, NY
State University of New York College at Potsdam, NY
Sterling College, KS
Stetson University, FL
Stockton University, NJ
Sul Ross State University, TX
SUNY Brockport, NY
Syracuse University, NY
Texas A&M International University, TX
Texas A&M University–Commerce, TX
Texas Christian University, TX
Texas State University, TX
Texas Tech University, TX
Texas Woman's University, TX

Thomas More University, KY
Towson University, MD
Trinity Christian College, IL
Troy University, AL
The University of Akron, OH
The University of Alabama, AL
University of Alaska Anchorage, AK
The University of Arizona, AZ
University of California, Los Angeles, CA
University of California, San Diego, CA
University of Colorado Boulder, CO
University of Colorado Denver, CO
University of Denver, CO
University of Guam, GU
University of Houston, TX
University of Houston–Clear Lake, TX
University of Idaho, ID
University of Illinois at Chicago, IL
University of Illinois at Urbana-Champaign, IL
The University of Iowa, IA
The University of Kansas, KS
University of Kentucky, KY
University of Louisville, KY
University of Maine, ME
University of Maryland, College Park, MD
University of Massachusetts Lowell, MA
University of Memphis, TN
University of Mobile, AL
University of Mount Union, OH
University of Nebraska at Kearney, NE
University of Nebraska at Omaha, NE
University of Nevada, Las Vegas, NV
University of North Carolina Asheville, NC
The University of North Carolina at Chapel Hill, NC
University of Northern Colorado, CO
University of Northern Iowa, IA
University of Oregon, OR
University of Pittsburgh, PA
University of Puget Sound, WA
University of St. Francis, IL
University of Saint Francis, IN
University of Saint Mary, KS
University of St. Thomas, TX
University of South Florida, FL
The University of Tennessee, TN
The University of Tennessee at Chattanooga, TN
The University of Tennessee at Martin, TN
The University of Texas at El Paso, TX
University of West Georgia, GA
University of Wisconsin–Green Bay, WI
University of Wisconsin–Parkside, WI
University of Wisconsin–Platteville, WI
University of Wisconsin–River Falls, WI
University of Wisconsin–Stevens Point, WI
University of Wisconsin–Stout, WI
University of Wisconsin–Whitewater, WI
University of Wyoming, WY
Utah State University, UT
Valley City State University, ND
Wabash College, IN
Washburn University, KS
Washington State University, WA
Washington University in St. Louis, MO
Wayland Baptist University, TX
Wayne State College, NE
Western Illinois University, IL
Western Washington University, WA
Westminster College, UT
Westmont College, CA
Wheaton College, IL
Whittier College, CA
Wichita State University, KS
William Jessup University, CA
Wright State University, OH
Wright State University–Lake Campus, OH
Xavier University, OH

Cinema/Film/Broadcasting
Angelo State University, TX
Arkansas Tech University, AR
Auburn University, AL
Baker University, KS
Ball State University, IN
Baylor University, TX
Belhaven University, MS
Belmont University, TN
Bemidji State University, MN
Binghamton University, State University of New York, NY
Biola University, CA
Bowling Green State University, OH
Butler University, IN
California Baptist University, CA
California Polytechnic State University, San Luis Obispo, CA
California State University, Chico, CA
California State University, Fullerton, CA
Cameron University, OK
The Catholic University of America, DC
Central Michigan University, MI
Chapman University, CA
City College of the City University of New York, NY
College of Staten Island of the City University of New York, NY
Columbia College Chicago, IL
DeSales University, PA
Eastern Illinois University, IL
Eastern Michigan University, MI
Eastern New Mexico University, NM
Eastern Washington University, WA
Edinboro University of Pennsylvania, PA
Emory University, GA
Five Towns College, NY
Florida Agricultural and Mechanical University, FL
Florida State University, FL
Fort Hays State University, KS
George Fox University, OR
Grand Valley State University, MI
Hofstra University, NY
Houston Baptist University, TX
Huntington University, IN
Illinois State University, IL
Ithaca College, NY
James Madison University, VA
Kean University, NJ
Keene State College, NH
Kent State University, OH
Kent State University at Geauga, OH
Kent State University at Stark, OH
Lafayette College, PA
Liberty University, VA
Lincoln College, IL
Long Island University, NY
Loyola Marymount University, CA
Massachusetts College of Liberal Arts, MA
Milligan University, TN
Minneapolis College of Art and Design, MN
Minnesota State University Moorhead, MN
Minot State University, ND
Mississippi State University, MS
Missouri Valley College, MO
Montana State University, MT
Montclair State University, NJ
Morgan State University, MD
New Mexico State University, NM
North Central College, IL
Northwestern State University of Louisiana, LA
Northwest Missouri State University, MO
Ohio University, OH
Ohio University–Chillicothe, OH
Ohio University–Eastern, OH
Ohio University–Lancaster, OH
Ohio University–Southern Campus, OH
Ohio University–Zanesville, OH
Oklahoma State University, OK
Old Dominion University, VA
Oral Roberts University, OK
Piedmont College, GA
Purchase College, State University of New York, NY
Rhode Island College, RI
Ringling College of Art and Design, FL
Sacred Heart University, CT
St. Cloud State University, MN
St. John's University, NY
Samford University, AL
Sam Houston State University, TX
San Diego State University, CA
San Jose State University, CA
Sonoma State University, CA
Southeastern University, FL
Southern Illinois University Carbondale, IL
Southwestern College, KS
State University of New York College at Potsdam, NY
Sterling College, KS
Stony Brook University, State University of New York, NY
Sul Ross State University, TX
SUNY Brockport, NY
Texas Christian University, TX
Texas Woman's University, TX
Trevecca Nazarene University, TN
Union University, TN
The University of Alabama, AL
The University of Arizona, AZ
University of California, Los Angeles, CA
University of California, San Diego, CA
University of California, Santa Cruz, CA
University of Central Florida, FL
University of Colorado Boulder, CO
University of Colorado Denver, CO
University of Hawaii at Manoa, HI
The University of Iowa, IA
The University of Kansas, KS
University of Kentucky, KY
University of Louisville, KY
University of Maryland, Baltimore County, MD
University of Memphis, TN
University of Michigan, MI
University of Michigan–Dearborn, MI
University of Mississippi, MS
University of Montevallo, AL
University of Nebraska–Lincoln, NE
University of Nevada, Las Vegas, NV
The University of North Carolina at Greensboro, NC
The University of North Carolina Wilmington, NC
University of Northwestern–St. Paul, MN
University of Oklahoma, OK
University of Pittsburgh at Bradford, PA
The University of Tennessee at Chattanooga, TN
The University of Tennessee at Martin, TN
The University of Toledo, OH
University of Utah, UT
University of Wisconsin–River Falls, WI

University of Wisconsin–Whitewater, WI
University of Wyoming, WY
Wabash College, IN
Wartburg College, IA
Washburn University, KS
Washington State University, WA
Western Illinois University, IL
Western Kentucky University, KY
Western Washington University, WA
Westminster College, PA
West Texas A&M University, TX
Wheaton College, IL
Wichita State University, KS
Wright State University, OH
Wright State University–Lake Campus, OH

Creative Writing

Arkansas Tech University, AR
Auburn University, AL
Augustana College, IL
Augustana University, SD
Austin Peay State University, TN
Belhaven University, MS
Belmont University, TN
Bemidji State University, MN
Binghamton University, State University of New York, NY
Bowling Green State University, OH
Bucknell University, PA
California Lutheran University, CA
California Polytechnic State University, San Luis Obispo, CA
California State University, Chico, CA
Calumet College of Saint Joseph, IN
Cameron University, OK
Carroll College, MT
Cedar Crest College, PA
Central College, IA
Central Michigan University, MI
Chapman University, CA
City College of the City University of New York, NY
Cleveland State University, OH
Coe College, IA
College of Staten Island of the City University of New York, NY
Colorado State University, CO
Columbia College, MO
Columbia College Chicago, IL
Davidson College, NC
Delta State University, MS
Denison University, OH
Drury University, MO
Eastern Illinois University, IL
Eastern Michigan University, MI
Eastern New Mexico University, NM
Eastern Washington University, WA
Eckerd College, FL
Edgewood College, WI
Edinboro University of Pennsylvania, PA
Emmanuel College, GA
Emory University, GA
Emporia State University, KS
Florida Agricultural and Mechanical University, FL
Fort Hays State University, KS
Goddard College, VT
Graceland University, IA
Grove City College, PA
Hamline University, MN
Hampshire College, MA
Hardin-Simmons University, TX
Hobart and William Smith Colleges, NY
Hollins University, VA
Hope College, MI
Houghton College, NY
Huntington University, IN
Illinois State University, IL
John Carroll University, OH
Kent State University, OH
Kent State University at Geauga, OH
Kent State University at Stark, OH
Kenyon College, OH
Lafayette College, PA
Lake Forest College, IL
Lebanon Valley College, PA
Lewis-Clark State College, ID
Long Island University, NY
Loyola Marymount University, CA
Lycoming College, PA
Malone University, OH
Manhattanville College, NY
Michigan State University, MI
Middle Tennessee State University, TN
Midwestern State University, TX
Millikin University, IL
Minnesota State University Moorhead, MN
Mississippi State University, MS
Molloy College, NY
Montreat College, NC
Morgan State University, MD
New Mexico State University, NM
Northeastern Illinois University, IL
Northern Illinois University, IL
Northwestern State University of Louisiana, LA
The Ohio State University, OH
Ohio University, OH
Ohio University–Chillicothe, OH
Ohio University–Eastern, OH
Ohio University–Lancaster, OH
Ohio University–Southern Campus, OH
Ohio University–Zanesville, OH
Oklahoma State University, OK
Old Dominion University, VA
Otis College of Art and Design, CA
Plymouth State University, NH
Purchase College, State University of New York, NY
Purdue University Northwest, IN
Ringling College of Art and Design, FL
Sacred Heart University, CT
St. Cloud State University, MN
St. John's University, NY
St. Thomas Aquinas College, NY
Salem State University, MA
Samford University, AL
San Diego State University, CA
San Jose State University, CA
Slippery Rock University of Pennsylvania, PA
Sonoma State University, CA
Southern Illinois University Carbondale, IL
Southwestern College, KS
State University of New York College at Geneseo, NY
State University of New York College at Potsdam, NY
Sterling College, KS
Stockton University, NJ
SUNY Brockport, NY
Susquehanna University, PA
Texas Christian University, TX
The University of Akron, OH
The University of Alabama, AL
University of California, Los Angeles, CA
University of California, Riverside, CA
University of California, Santa Cruz, CA
University of Colorado Boulder, CO
University of Houston, TX
University of Idaho, ID
University of Illinois at Chicago, IL
The University of Iowa, IA
The University of Kansas, KS
University of Kentucky, KY
University of Louisiana at Monroe, LA
University of Louisville, KY
University of Maine, ME
University of Maryland, Baltimore County, MD
University of Memphis, TN
University of Michigan, MI
University of Michigan–Dearborn, MI
University of Mississippi, MS
University of Montana, MT
University of Montevallo, AL
University of Nebraska at Omaha, NE
University of Nevada, Las Vegas, NV
The University of North Carolina Wilmington, NC
University of Oregon, OR
University of Pittsburgh, PA
University of Pittsburgh at Bradford, PA
University of Southern Indiana, IN
University of South Florida, FL
The University of Tampa, FL
The University of Tennessee at Chattanooga, TN
The University of Tennessee at Martin, TN
The University of Texas at San Antonio, TX
The University of Toledo, OH
University of Utah, UT
University of Wisconsin–River Falls, WI
University of Wisconsin–Stevens Point, WI
University of Wisconsin–Whitewater, WI
University of Wyoming, WY
Wabash College, IN
Washington College, MD
Washington State University, WA
Washington University in St. Louis, MO
Wayne State College, NE
Western Illinois University, IL
Western Washington University, WA
Westminster College, UT
West Texas A&M University, TX
Wheaton College, IL
Whitworth University, WA
Wichita State University, KS
Wright State University, OH
Wright State University–Lake Campus, OH
Youngstown State University, OH

Dance

Alabama State University, AL
Allegheny College, PA
Alma College, MI
Anderson University, IN
Arizona State University at the Tempe campus, AZ
Augustana University, SD
Baker University, KS
Ball State University, IN
Belhaven University, MS
Belmont University, TN
Berklee College of Music, MA
Binghamton University, State University of New York, NY
Birmingham-Southern College, AL
Boise State University, ID
Bowling Green State University, OH
Bucknell University, PA
Butler University, IN
California Polytechnic State University, San Luis Obispo, CA
California State University, Chico, CA
California State University, Fullerton, CA
Case Western Reserve University, OH
Cedar Crest College, PA

Centenary College of Louisiana, LA
Central Michigan University, MI
Chapman University, CA
Cleveland State University, OH
The College of Wooster, OH
Colorado Mesa University, CO
Colorado State University, CO
Columbia College, SC
Columbia College Chicago, IL
Columbus State University, GA
Cornell College, IA
Creighton University, NE
DeSales University, PA
Dominican University of California, CA
Dordt University, IA
Drexel University, PA
Duquesne University, PA
East Carolina University, NC
Eastern Michigan University, MI
Eastern New Mexico University, NM
Emmanuel College, GA
Florida Agricultural and Mechanical University, FL
Florida International University, FL
Florida State University, FL
Fordham University, NY
Fort Hays State University, KS
Georgian Court University, NJ
Goucher College, MD
Graceland University, IA
Grambling State University, LA
Grand Valley State University, MI
Grand View University, IA
Gustavus Adolphus College, MN
Hendrix College, AR
Hobart and William Smith Colleges, NY
Hofstra University, NY
Hollins University, VA
Hope College, MI
Idaho State University, ID
Indiana University of Pennsylvania, PA
Ithaca College, NY
James Madison University, VA
The Juilliard School, NY
Kean University, NJ
Keene State College, NH
Kennesaw State University, GA
Kent State University, OH
Kent State University at Geauga, OH
Kent State University at Stark, OH
Kutztown University of Pennsylvania, PA
Lafayette College, PA
Lake Erie College, OH
La Roche University, PA
Lincoln College, IL
Long Island University, NY
Loyola Marymount University, CA
Manhattanville College, NY
McKendree University, IL
Messiah College, PA
Methodist University, NC
Middle Tennessee State University, TN
Milligan University, TN
Millikin University, IL
Mississippi State University, MS
Missouri Valley College, MO
Montana State University, MT
Montclair State University, NJ
Morgan State University, MD
Nazareth College of Rochester, NY
New Mexico State University, NM
Nicholls State University, LA
Northeastern Illinois University, IL
Northeastern State University, OK
Northern Illinois University, IL
Northwestern State University of Louisiana, LA
Northwest Missouri State University, MO
Oakland University, MI
The Ohio State University, OH
Ohio University, OH
Ohio University–Chillicothe, OH
Ohio University–Eastern, OH
Ohio University–Lancaster, OH
Ohio University–Southern Campus, OH
Ohio University–Zanesville, OH
Ohio Wesleyan University, OH
Oklahoma City University, OK
Old Dominion University, VA
Oral Roberts University, OK
Pacific Lutheran University, WA
Palm Beach Atlantic University, FL
Plymouth State University, NH
Purchase College, State University of New York, NY
Rhode Island College, RI
Rockford University, IL
Rogers State University, OK
Sacred Heart University, CT
St. Ambrose University, IA
St. John's University, NY
Saint Mary's College of California, CA
St. Olaf College, MN
Salem State University, MA
Samford University, AL
Sam Houston State University, TX
San Diego State University, CA
San Jose State University, CA
Santa Clara University, CA
Shenandoah University, VA
Slippery Rock University of Pennsylvania, PA
Sonoma State University, CA
Southeast Missouri State University, MO
Southern Illinois University Carbondale, IL
Southern Illinois University Edwardsville, IL
Southern Utah University, UT
Southwestern College, KS
Spelman College, GA
State University of New York at Fredonia, NY
State University of New York College at Geneseo, NY
State University of New York College at Potsdam, NY
Stephens College, MO
Stockton University, NJ
SUNY Brockport, NY
Temple University, PA
Texas A&M International University, TX
Texas Christian University, TX
Texas State University, TX
Texas Tech University, TX
Texas Woman's University, TX
Thomas More University, KY
Towson University, MD
Trine University, IN
The University of Akron, OH
The University of Alabama, AL
University of Alaska Anchorage, AK
The University of Arizona, AZ
University of California, Los Angeles, CA
University of California, Riverside, CA
University of California, San Diego, CA
University of Colorado Boulder, CO
University of Florida, FL
University of Hawaii at Manoa, HI
University of Houston, TX
University of Idaho, ID
University of Illinois at Urbana-Champaign, IL
The University of Iowa, IA
The University of Kansas, KS
University of Kentucky, KY
University of Louisville, KY
University of Maine, ME
University of Maryland, Baltimore County, MD
University of Mary Washington, VA
University of Massachusetts Amherst, MA
University of Memphis, TN
University of Michigan, MI
University of Missouri–St. Louis, MO
University of Montana, MT
University of Nebraska–Lincoln, NE
University of Nevada, Las Vegas, NV
University of New Hampshire, NH
University of North Alabama, AL
University of North Carolina Asheville, NC
The University of North Carolina at Charlotte, NC
The University of North Carolina at Greensboro, NC
University of Northern Colorado, CO
University of Oklahoma, OK
University of Oregon, OR
University of Providence, MT
University of Richmond, VA
University of Saint Francis, IN
University of South Carolina, SC
University of Southern Mississippi, MS
University of South Florida, FL
The University of Tampa, FL
The University of Tennessee at Chattanooga, TN
The University of Texas Rio Grande Valley, TX
University of Utah, UT
University of Washington, WA
The University of West Alabama, AL
University of Wisconsin–Green Bay, WI
University of Wisconsin–Stevens Point, WI
University of Wyoming, WY
Washington University in St. Louis, MO
Wayne State University, MI
Western Illinois University, IL
Western Kentucky University, KY
Western Michigan University, MI
Western Oregon University, OR
Western Washington University, WA
Westminster College, UT
West Texas A&M University, TX
Wichita State University, KS
Widener University, PA
Wittenberg University, OH
Wright State University, OH
Wright State University–Lake Campus, OH

Debating

Abilene Christian University, TX
Austin Peay State University, TN
Baker University, KS
Ball State University, IN
Baylor University, TX
Berry College, GA
Bethany Lutheran College, MN
Bethel College, KS
Bethel University, MN
Boise State University, ID
Bowling Green State University, OH
California Baptist University, CA
California Polytechnic State University, San Luis Obispo, CA
California State University, Chico, CA

Cameron University, OK
Carroll College, MT
Carson-Newman University, TN
Cedarville University, OH
Clarion University of Pennsylvania, PA
The College of Idaho, ID
Doane University, NE
Dordt University, IA
Drury University, MO
Eastern Illinois University, IL
Eastern Michigan University, MI
Eastern New Mexico University, NM
Emory University, GA
Emporia State University, KS
Evangel University, MO
Ferris State University, MI
George Fox University, OR
Gonzaga University, WA
Gustavus Adolphus College, MN
Hillsdale College, MI
Idaho State University, ID
Illinois State University, IL
John Carroll University, OH
Lewis & Clark College, OR
Lewis-Clark State College, ID
Liberty University, VA
Linfield College, OR
Louisiana College, LA
Loyola Marymount University, CA
Loyola University Chicago, IL
Malone University, OH
McKendree University, IL
Mercer University, GA
Methodist University, NC
Michigan State University, MI
Middle Tennessee State University, TN
Mississippi State University, MS
Morgan State University, MD
Muskingum University, OH
North Central College, IL
North Dakota State University, ND
Northeastern State University, OK
Northern Illinois University, IL
Northwest Missouri State University, MO
Northwest Nazarene University, ID
Northwest University, WA
Ohio University, OH
Ohio University–Chillicothe, OH
Ohio University–Eastern, OH
Ohio University–Lancaster, OH
Ohio University–Southern Campus, OH
Ohio University–Zanesville, OH
Oklahoma Baptist University, OK
Oklahoma City University, OK
Pacific Lutheran University, WA
Pacific University, OR
Patrick Henry College, VA
Piedmont College, GA
Point Loma Nazarene University, CA
Rocky Mountain College, MT
Saint Anselm College, NH
St. John's University, NY
Saint Joseph's University, PA
Samford University, AL
San Diego State University, CA
Santa Clara University, CA
Simpson College, IA
Southern Illinois University Carbondale, IL
Southwest Baptist University, MO
Sterling College, KS
Towson University, MD
Trinity University, TX
Truman State University, MO
Union University, TN
The University of Akron, OH
The University of Alabama, AL
University of Alaska Anchorage, AK
University of California, Los Angeles, CA
University of Denver, CO
University of Indianapolis, IN
The University of Iowa, IA
The University of Kansas, KS
University of Kentucky, KY
University of Louisiana at Monroe, LA
University of Louisville, KY
University of Michigan–Dearborn, MI
University of Mississippi, MS
University of Nebraska at Kearney, NE
University of Nebraska at Omaha, NE
University of Nevada, Las Vegas, NV
University of Northern Iowa, IA
University of Oklahoma, OK
University of Oregon, OR
University of Pittsburgh, PA
University of Puget Sound, WA
University of Saint Mary, KS
University of South Carolina, SC
University of Southern California, CA
The University of Texas at San Antonio, TX
University of the Pacific, CA
University of West Georgia, GA
University of Wisconsin–Eau Claire, WI
University of Wyoming, WY
Vanguard University of Southern California, CA
Washburn University, KS
Wayne State University, MI
Webber International University, FL
Western Illinois University, IL
Western Kentucky University, KY
West Texas A&M University, TX
Whitman College, WA
Whitworth University, WA
Wichita State University, KS
Winona State University, MN

Journalism/Publications

Abilene Christian University, TX
Arkansas Tech University, AR
Auburn University, AL
Augustana University, SD
Austin Peay State University, TN
Averett University, VA
Baker University, KS
Ball State University, IN
Baylor University, TX
Belhaven University, MS
Belmont University, TN
Bemidji State University, MN
Berry College, GA
Bethany Lutheran College, MN
Binghamton University, State University of New York, NY
Biola University, CA
Boise State University, ID
Bowling Green State University, OH
Bryan College, TN
Butler University, IN
California Baptist University, CA
California Lutheran University, CA
California Polytechnic State University, San Luis Obispo, CA
California State University, Chico, CA
California State University, Fresno, CA
California State University, Fullerton, CA
California State University, Los Angeles, CA
California State University, Northridge, CA
California State University, San Bernardino, CA
Cameron University, OK
Campbellsville University, KY
Carroll University, WI
Carson-Newman University, TN
Centenary College of Louisiana, LA
Central Michigan University, MI
The Citadel, The Military College of South Carolina, SC
Cleveland State University, OH
College of Staten Island of the City University of New York, NY
Columbia College, MO
Columbia College Chicago, IL
Concord University, WV
Delta State University, MS
Dordt University, IA
Eastern Illinois University, IL
Eastern New Mexico University, NM
Eastern Washington University, WA
Edinboro University of Pennsylvania, PA
Elon University, NC
Emmanuel College, GA
Emory & Henry College, VA
Emory University, GA
Ferris State University, MI
Florida Agricultural and Mechanical University, FL
Florida International University, FL
Fort Hays State University, KS
Fort Lewis College, CO
Franklin College, IN
Glenville State College, WV
Grand Valley State University, MI
Hamline University, MN
Hardin-Simmons University, TX
Hillsdale College, MI
Hofstra University, NY
Huntington University, IN
Idaho State University, ID
Indiana University of Pennsylvania, PA
Ithaca College, NY
Jacksonville State University, AL
James Madison University, VA
John Brown University, AR
John Carroll University, OH
Kent State University, OH
Kent State University at Geauga, OH
Kent State University at Stark, OH
The King's College, NY
Lehigh University, PA
Liberty University, VA
Lipscomb University, TN
Lock Haven University of Pennsylvania, PA
Long Island University, NY
Louisiana College, LA
Louisiana State University and Agricultural & Mechanical College, LA
Loyola Marymount University, CA
Loyola University Chicago, IL
Malone University, OH
Mansfield University of Pennsylvania, PA
Massachusetts College of Liberal Arts, MA
Mercer University, GA
Michigan State University, MI
Middle Tennessee State University, TN
Midwestern State University, TX
Mississippi State University, MS
Missouri Southern State University, MO
Missouri Valley College, MO
Morehead State University, KY
Morgan State University, MD
Muskingum University, OH
New Jersey Institute of Technology, NJ
Newman University, KS
New Mexico State University, NM
Nicholls State University, LA
North Central College, IL
North Dakota State University, ND
Northeastern Illinois University, IL

Northeastern State University, OK
Northern Illinois University, IL
Northern Michigan University, MI
North Greenville University, SC
Northwest Missouri State University, MO
Nyack College, NY
Oglethorpe University, GA
The Ohio State University, OH
Ohio University, OH
Ohio University–Chillicothe, OH
Ohio University–Eastern, OH
Ohio University–Lancaster, OH
Ohio University–Southern Campus, OH
Ohio University–Zanesville, OH
Ohio Valley University, WV
Oklahoma State University, OK
Old Dominion University, VA
Olivet College, MI
Oral Roberts University, OK
Pacific University, OR
Patrick Henry College, VA
Piedmont College, GA
Rhode Island College, RI
Rochester University, MI
St. Ambrose University, IA
Saint Anselm College, NH
St. Cloud State University, MN
St. Edward's University, TX
St. John's University, NY
Samford University, AL
Sam Houston State University, TX
San Diego State University, CA
San Jose State University, CA
Schreiner University, TX
Sonoma State University, CA
Southeastern University, FL
Southern Illinois University Carbondale, IL
Southwestern College, KS
State University of New York at Plattsburgh, NY
State University of New York College at Geneseo, NY
State University of New York College at Potsdam, NY
Stephen F. Austin State University, TX
Sterling College, KS
Stockton University, NJ
Stony Brook University, State University of New York, NY
Sul Ross State University, TX
SUNY Brockport, NY
Tabor College, KS
Texas A&M University, TX
Texas A&M University–Commerce, TX
Texas Christian University, TX
Texas Lutheran University, TX
Texas State University, TX
Texas Tech University, TX
Texas Woman's University, TX
Trinity Christian College, IL
Union University, TN
The University of Akron, OH
The University of Alabama, AL
University of Arkansas, AR
University of California, Los Angeles, CA
University of California, San Diego, CA
University of Colorado Boulder, CO
University of Florida, FL
University of Guam, GU
University of Hawaii at Manoa, HI
University of Houston, TX
University of Idaho, ID
University of Illinois at Urbana-Champaign, IL
The University of Iowa, IA
The University of Kansas, KS
University of Kentucky, KY
University of Louisiana at Monroe, LA
University of Louisville, KY
University of Maine, ME
University of Maryland, College Park, MD
University of Mary Washington, VA
University of Massachusetts Amherst, MA
University of Memphis, TN
University of Michigan, MI
University of Michigan–Dearborn, MI
University of Mississippi, MS
University of Montana, MT
University of Montevallo, AL
University of Nebraska at Kearney, NE
University of Nebraska at Omaha, NE
University of Nebraska–Lincoln, NE
University of Nevada, Las Vegas, NV
University of Nevada, Reno, NV
University of North Alabama, AL
The University of North Carolina at Chapel Hill, NC
University of Northern Colorado, CO
University of Oklahoma, OK
University of Oregon, OR
University of Pittsburgh, PA
University of Pittsburgh at Johnstown, PA
University of Rhode Island, RI
University of South Carolina, SC
University of South Carolina Aiken, SC
The University of Tampa, FL
The University of Tennessee at Chattanooga, TN
The University of Tennessee at Martin, TN
The University of Texas at El Paso, TX
The University of Texas Rio Grande Valley, TX
University of Utah, UT
University of West Georgia, GA
University of Wisconsin–Eau Claire, WI
University of Wisconsin–Green Bay, WI
University of Wisconsin–River Falls, WI
University of Wisconsin–Whitewater, WI
University of Wyoming, WY
Utah State University, UT
Valdosta State University, GA
Wabash College, IN
Wartburg College, IA
Washburn University, KS
Washington State University, WA
Wayne State College, NE
Wayne State University, MI
Webber International University, FL
Western Illinois University, IL
Western Kentucky University, KY
Western Washington University, WA
Westminster College, UT
West Texas A&M University, TX
Whitworth University, WA
Wichita State University, KS
Youngstown State University, OH

Music

Abilene Christian University, TX
Agnes Scott College, GA
Alabama State University, AL
Albion College, MI
Alcorn State University, MS
Allegheny College, PA
Alma College, MI
Alverno College, WI
Anderson University, IN
Anderson University, SC
Andrews University, MI
Angelo State University, TX
Arizona Christian University, AZ
Arizona State University at the Tempe campus, AZ
Arkansas Tech University, AR
Asbury University, KY
Ashland University, OH
Assumption University, MA
Auburn University, AL
Augsburg University, MN
Augustana College, IL
Augustana University, SD
Aurora University, IL
Austin College, TX
Austin Peay State University, TN
Ave Maria University, FL
Averett University, VA
Baker University, KS
Baldwin Wallace University, OH
Ball State University, IN
Barton College, NC
Baylor University, TX
Belhaven University, MS
Bellarmine University, KY
Belmont University, TN
Beloit College, WI
Bemidji State University, MN
Benedictine University, IL
Berklee College of Music, MA
Berry College, GA
Bethany College, WV
Bethany Lutheran College, MN
Bethel College, KS
Bethel University, IN
Bethel University, MN
Binghamton University, State University of New York, NY
Biola University, CA
Birmingham-Southern College, AL
Black Hills State University, SD
Bluefield College, VA
Bluffton University, OH
Boise Bible College, ID
Boise State University, ID
Boston University, MA
Bowie State University, MD
Bowling Green State University, OH
Bradley University, IL
Bridgewater College, VA
Brigham Young University, UT
Bryan College, TN
Bucknell University, PA
Buena Vista University, IA
Butler University, IN
Caldwell University, NJ
California Baptist University, CA
California Jazz Conservatory, CA
California Lutheran University, CA
California Polytechnic State University, San Luis Obispo, CA
California State University, Bakersfield, CA
California State University, Chico, CA
California State University, Fresno, CA
California State University, Fullerton, CA
California State University, Los Angeles, CA
California State University, Northridge, CA
California State University, San Bernardino, CA
California State University, Stanislaus, CA
Cameron University, OK
Campbellsville University, KY
Canisius College, NY
Capital University, OH
Cardinal Stritch University, WI
Carleton College, MN
Carroll College, MT

Carroll University, WI
Carson-Newman University, TN
Carthage College, WI
Case Western Reserve University, OH
Catawba College, NC
The Catholic University of America, DC
Cedarville University, OH
Centenary College of Louisiana, LA
Central College, IA
Central Methodist University, MO
Central Michigan University, MI
Central Washington University, WA
Centre College, KY
Chapman University, CA
Chatham University, PA
Chowan University, NC
Christopher Newport University, VA
The Citadel, The Military College of South Carolina, SC
City College of the City University of New York, NY
Clarion University of Pennsylvania, PA
Clarke University, IA
Clear Creek Baptist Bible College, KY
Cleveland Institute of Music, OH
Cleveland State University, OH
Coastal Carolina University, SC
Coe College, IA
The College of Idaho, ID
The College of New Jersey, NJ
College of Saint Benedict, MN
College of Saint Elizabeth, NJ
The College of Saint Rose, NY
The College of St. Scholastica, MN
College of Staten Island of the City University of New York, NY
College of the Holy Cross, MA
The College of Wooster, OH
Colorado Mesa University, CO
Colorado State University, CO
Columbia College, MO
Columbia College, SC
Columbia College Chicago, IL
Columbus State University, GA
Concordia College, MN
Concordia University Chicago, IL
Concordia University, St. Paul, MN
Concordia University Texas, TX
Concordia University Wisconsin, WI
Concord University, WV
Converse College, SC
Cornell College, IA
Cornerstone University, MI
Covenant College, GA
Creighton University, NE
Dakota State University, SD
Dallas Baptist University, TX
Davidson College, NC
Delaware Valley University, PA
Delta State University, MS
Denison University, OH
DePaul University, IL
Dillard University, LA
Doane University, NE
Dominican University of California, CA
Dordt University, IA
Drake University, IA
Drew University, NJ
Drexel University, PA
Drury University, MO
Duquesne University, PA
Earlham College, IN
East Carolina University, NC
East Central University, OK
Eastern Illinois University, IL
Eastern Kentucky University, KY
Eastern Mennonite University, VA
Eastern Michigan University, MI
Eastern New Mexico University, NM
Eastern Oregon University, OR
Eastern University, PA
Eastern Washington University, WA
East Texas Baptist University, TX
Eckerd College, FL
Edgewood College, WI
Elizabethtown College, PA
Elon University, NC
Emmanuel College, GA
Emory & Henry College, VA
Emory University, GA
Emporia State University, KS
Endicott College, MA
Evangel University, MO
Fayetteville State University, NC
Ferris State University, MI
Five Towns College, NY
Florida Agricultural and Mechanical University, FL
Florida Atlantic University, FL
Florida Gulf Coast University, FL
Florida Institute of Technology, FL
Florida International University, FL
Florida State University, FL
Fordham University, NY
Fort Hays State University, KS
Fort Lewis College, CO
Franklin & Marshall College, PA
Franklin College, IN
Gannon University, PA
George Fox University, OR
Georgia College & State University, GA
Gettysburg College, PA
Glenville State College, WV
Gonzaga University, WA
Gordon College, MA
Goshen College, IN
Goucher College, MD
Graceland University, IA
Grambling State University, LA
Grand Valley State University, MI
Grand View University, IA
Greenville University, IL
Grove City College, PA
Gustavus Adolphus College, MN
Hamline University, MN
Hampton University, VA
Hardin-Simmons University, TX
Heidelberg University, OH
Hendrix College, AR
High Point University, NC
Hillsdale College, MI
Hiram College, OH
Hobart and William Smith Colleges, NY
Hofstra University, NY
Hollins University, VA
Hope College, MI
Hope International University, CA
Houghton College, NY
Houston Baptist University, TX
Huntington University, IN
Idaho State University, ID
Illinois College, IL
Illinois State University, IL
Illinois Wesleyan University, IL
Immaculata University, PA
Indiana State University, IN
Indiana University of Pennsylvania, PA
Iona College, NY
Iowa Wesleyan University, IA
Ithaca College, NY
Jackson State University, MS
Jacksonville State University, AL
Jacksonville University, FL
James Madison University, VA
John Brown University, AR
Johnson University, TN
Johnson University Florida, FL
Judson University, IL
The Juilliard School, NY
Kalamazoo College, MI
Kean University, NJ
Keene State College, NH
Kennesaw State University, GA
Kent State University, OH
Kent State University at Geauga, OH
Kent State University at Stark, OH
Kentucky Mountain Bible College, KY
Kentucky State University, KY
Kenyon College, OH
King University, TN
Kutztown University of Pennsylvania, PA
Kuyper College, MI
Lafayette College, PA
LaGrange College, GA
Lake Erie College, OH
Lake Forest College, IL
Lancaster Bible College, PA
La Sierra University, CA
Lawrence University, WI
Lebanon Valley College, PA
Lee University, TN
Lehigh University, PA
Le Moyne College, NY
Lenoir-Rhyne University, NC
Lewis & Clark College, OR
Lewis-Clark State College, ID
Lewis University, IL
Liberty University, VA
Limestone College, SC
Lincoln College, IL
Lincoln University, PA
Linfield College, OR
Lipscomb University, TN
Livingstone College, NC
Lock Haven University of Pennsylvania, PA
Long Island University, NY
Longwood University, VA
Loras College, IA
Louisiana College, LA
Louisiana State University and Agricultural & Mechanical College, LA
Loyola Marymount University, CA
Loyola University Chicago, IL
Lycoming College, PA
Lynn University, FL
Lyon College, AR
Malone University, OH
Manhattan College, NY
Manhattanville College, NY
Mansfield University of Pennsylvania, PA
Maranatha Baptist University, WI
Marietta College, OH
Marist College, NY
Martin Luther College, MN
Maryville College, TN
Maryville University of Saint Louis, MO
Marywood University, PA
Massachusetts College of Liberal Arts, MA
Mayville State University, ND
McKendree University, IL
McPherson College, KS
Mercer University, GA
Messenger College, TX
Messiah College, PA
Methodist University, NC
Miami University, OH
Michigan State University, MI
MidAmerica Nazarene University, KS

Middle Tennessee State University, TN
Midway University, KY
Midwestern State University, TX
Millersville University of Pennsylvania, PA
Milligan University, TN
Millikin University, IL
Mills College, CA
Minnesota State University Mankato, MN
Minnesota State University Moorhead, MN
Minot State University, ND
Mississippi State University, MS
Missouri Baptist University, MO
Missouri Southern State University, MO
Missouri University of Science and Technology, MO
Missouri Valley College, MO
Molloy College, NY
Montana State University, MT
Montana State University Billings, MT
Montclair State University, NJ
Montreat College, NC
Morehead State University, KY
Morgan State University, MD
Mount Aloysius College, PA
Mount Marty College, SD
Mount Saint Mary's University, CA
Mount Vernon Nazarene University, OH
Muskingum University, OH
Nazareth College of Rochester, NY
Nebraska Wesleyan University, NE
Newberry College, SC
New England Conservatory of Music, MA
Newman University, KS
New Mexico State University, NM
Nicholls State University, LA
North Carolina Central University, NC
North Central College, IL
North Central University, MN
North Dakota State University, ND
Northeastern Illinois University, IL
Northeastern State University, OK
Northern Arizona University, AZ
Northern Illinois University, IL
Northern Michigan University, MI
Northern State University, SD
North Greenville University, SC
Northwest Christian University, OR
Northwestern State University of Louisiana, LA
Northwestern University, IL
Northwest Missouri State University, MO
Northwest Nazarene University, ID
Northwest University, WA
Nyack College, NY
Oakland University, MI
Oberlin College, OH
Occidental College, CA
Oglethorpe University, GA
Ohio Christian University, OH
The Ohio State University, OH
Ohio University, OH
Ohio University–Chillicothe, OH
Ohio University–Eastern, OH
Ohio University–Lancaster, OH
Ohio University–Southern Campus, OH
Ohio University–Zanesville, OH
Ohio Valley University, WV
Ohio Wesleyan University, OH
Oklahoma Baptist University, OK
Oklahoma City University, OK
Oklahoma State University, OK
Old Dominion University, VA
Olivet College, MI
Olivet Nazarene University, IL
Oral Roberts University, OK
Otterbein University, OH
Ouachita Baptist University, AR
Pacific Lutheran University, WA
Pacific University, OR
Palm Beach Atlantic University, FL
Patrick Henry College, VA
Piedmont College, GA
Pittsburg State University, KS
Plymouth State University, NH
Point Loma Nazarene University, CA
Portland State University, OR
Presbyterian College, SC
Purchase College, State University of New York, NY
Purdue University, IN
Purdue University Fort Wayne, IN
Queens University of Charlotte, NC
Reinhardt University, GA
Rhode Island College, RI
Rhodes College, TN
Rice University, TX
Roanoke College, VA
Rochester University, MI
Rockford University, IL
Rocky Mountain College, MT
Rogers State University, OK
Rollins College, FL
Rowan University, NJ
Sacred Heart University, CT
Saginaw Valley State University, MI
St. Ambrose University, IA
St. Bonaventure University, NY
St. Catherine University, MN
St. Cloud State University, MN
Saint John's University, MN
St. John's University, NY
Saint Louis University, MO
Saint Martin's University, WA
Saint Mary's College, IN
Saint Mary's College of California, CA
St. Mary's University, TX
St. Norbert College, WI
St. Olaf College, MN
Salem College, NC
Salem State University, MA
Samford University, AL
Sam Houston State University, TX
San Diego State University, CA
San Jose State University, CA
Santa Clara University, CA
Schreiner University, TX
Seattle Pacific University, WA
Seattle University, WA
Shenandoah University, VA
Shepherd University, WV
Shippensburg University of Pennsylvania, PA
Simpson College, IA
Skidmore College, NY
Slippery Rock University of Pennsylvania, PA
Sonoma State University, CA
Southeastern Louisiana University, LA
Southeastern University, FL
Southeast Missouri State University, MO
Southern Illinois University Carbondale, IL
Southern Illinois University Edwardsville, IL
Southern New Hampshire University, NH
Southern Utah University, UT
Southwest Baptist University, MO
Southwestern College, KS
Southwestern Oklahoma State University, OK
Southwestern University, TX
Spelman College, GA
State University of New York at Fredonia, NY
State University of New York at New Paltz, NY
State University of New York at Plattsburgh, NY
State University of New York College at Cortland, NY
State University of New York College at Geneseo, NY
State University of New York College at Oneonta, NY
State University of New York College at Potsdam, NY
Stephen F. Austin State University, TX
Stephens College, MO
Sterling College, KS
Stetson University, FL
Stockton University, NJ
Stony Brook University, State University of New York, NY
Sul Ross State University, TX
SUNY Brockport, NY
Susquehanna University, PA
Syracuse University, NY
Tabor College, KS
Tarleton State University, TX
Taylor University, IN
Temple University, PA
Tennessee Wesleyan University, TN
Texas A&M International University, TX
Texas A&M University–Commerce, TX
Texas Christian University, TX
Texas Lutheran University, TX
Texas State University, TX
Texas Tech University, TX
Texas Woman's University, TX
Thomas More University, KY
Tiffin University, OH
Toccoa Falls College, GA
Towson University, MD
Transylvania University, KY
Trevecca Nazarene University, TN
Trine University, IN
Trinity Christian College, IL
Trinity University, TX
Troy University, AL
Truett McConnell University, GA
Truman State University, MO
Tulane University, LA
Tuskegee University, AL
Union College, KY
Union College, NE
Union University, TN
The University of Akron, OH
The University of Alabama, AL
The University of Alabama at Birmingham, AL
University of Alaska Anchorage, AK
The University of Arizona, AZ
University of Arkansas, AR
University of California, Los Angeles, CA
University of California, Riverside, CA
University of California, San Diego, CA
University of California, Santa Cruz, CA
University of Central Florida, FL
University of Colorado Boulder, CO
University of Colorado Denver, CO
University of Dallas, TX
University of Dayton, OH
University of Denver, CO
University of Evansville, IN
The University of Findlay, OH
University of Florida, FL

University of Georgia, GA
University of Guam, GU
University of Hawaii at Manoa, HI
University of Houston, TX
University of Idaho, ID
University of Illinois at Chicago, IL
University of Illinois at Urbana-Champaign, IL
University of Indianapolis, IN
The University of Iowa, IA
University of Jamestown, ND
The University of Kansas, KS
University of Kentucky, KY
University of Louisiana at Monroe, LA
University of Louisville, KY
University of Lynchburg, VA
University of Maine, ME
University of Maine at Farmington, ME
University of Mary Hardin-Baylor, TX
University of Maryland, Baltimore County, MD
University of Maryland, College Park, MD
University of Mary Washington, VA
University of Massachusetts Amherst, MA
University of Massachusetts Lowell, MA
University of Memphis, TN
University of Miami, FL
University of Michigan, MI
University of Michigan–Flint, MI
University of Mississippi, MS
University of Missouri–St. Louis, MO
University of Mobile, AL
University of Montana, MT
University of Montevallo, AL
University of Mount Union, OH
University of Nebraska at Kearney, NE
University of Nebraska at Omaha, NE
University of Nebraska–Lincoln, NE
University of Nevada, Las Vegas, NV
University of New Hampshire, NH
University of New Mexico, NM
University of North Alabama, AL
University of North Carolina Asheville, NC
The University of North Carolina at Chapel Hill, NC
The University of North Carolina at Charlotte, NC
The University of North Carolina at Greensboro, NC
The University of North Carolina Wilmington, NC
University of North Dakota, ND
University of Northern Colorado, CO
University of Northern Iowa, IA
University of North Georgia, GA
University of Northwestern–St. Paul, MN
University of Oklahoma, OK
University of Oregon, OR
University of Pittsburgh, PA
University of Pittsburgh at Bradford, PA
University of Pittsburgh at Greensburg, PA
University of Portland, OR
University of Puget Sound, WA
University of Rhode Island, RI
University of Richmond, VA
University of Rochester, NY
University of St. Francis, IL
University of Saint Francis, IN
University of Saint Mary, KS
University of St. Thomas, TX
University of San Diego, CA
University of Science and Arts of Oklahoma, OK
University of South Carolina, SC
University of South Carolina Aiken, SC
University of Southern California, CA
University of Southern Maine, ME
University of Southern Mississippi, MS
University of South Florida, FL
The University of Tampa, FL
The University of Tennessee at Chattanooga, TN
The University of Tennessee at Martin, TN
The University of Texas at Austin, TX
The University of Texas at El Paso, TX
The University of Texas at San Antonio, TX
The University of Texas at Tyler, TX
The University of Texas Rio Grande Valley, TX
University of the Incarnate Word, TX
University of the Pacific, CA
The University of Toledo, OH
The University of Tulsa, OK
University of Utah, UT
University of Washington, WA
The University of West Alabama, AL
University of West Georgia, GA
University of Wisconsin–Eau Claire, WI
University of Wisconsin–Green Bay, WI
University of Wisconsin–La Crosse, WI
University of Wisconsin–Milwaukee, WI
University of Wisconsin–Parkside, WI
University of Wisconsin–Platteville, WI
University of Wisconsin–River Falls, WI
University of Wisconsin–Stevens Point, WI
University of Wisconsin–Stout, WI
University of Wisconsin–Whitewater, WI
University of Wyoming, WY
Utah State University, UT
Valdosta State University, GA
Valley City State University, ND
Valparaiso University, IN
Vanderbilt University, TN
VanderCook College of Music, IL
Vanguard University of Southern California, CA
Wabash College, IN
Wagner College, NY
Walla Walla University, WA
Walsh University, OH
Wartburg College, IA
Washburn University, KS
Washington College, MD
Washington State University, WA
Washington University in St. Louis, MO
Wayland Baptist University, TX
Waynesburg University, PA
Wayne State College, NE
Wayne State University, MI
Wesleyan College, GA
West Chester University of Pennsylvania, PA
Western Carolina University, NC
Western Colorado University, CO
Western Illinois University, IL
Western Kentucky University, KY
Western Michigan University, MI
Western New England University, MA
Western Oregon University, OR
Western Washington University, WA
Westminster College, PA
Westminster College, UT
Westmont College, CA
West Texas A&M University, TX
Wheaton College, IL
Whitman College, WA
Whittier College, CA
Whitworth University, WA
Wichita State University, KS
Widener University, PA
William & Mary, VA
William Jessup University, CA
William Paterson University of New Jersey, NJ
Wilson College, PA
Wingate University, NC
Winona State University, MN
Wittenberg University, OH
Wofford College, SC
Wright State University, OH
Wright State University–Lake Campus, OH
Xavier University, OH
Xavier University of Louisiana, LA
York College of Pennsylvania, PA
Youngstown State University, OH

Performing Arts

Albion College, MI
Allegheny College, PA
Alma College, MI
Anderson University, SC
Angelo State University, TX
Auburn University, AL
Augsburg University, MN
Augustana University, SD
Austin Peay State University, TN
Ball State University, IN
Belhaven University, MS
Belmont University, TN
Bemidji State University, MN
Berklee College of Music, MA
Binghamton University, State University of New York, NY
Birmingham-Southern College, AL
Bluefield College, VA
Bluffton University, OH
Boise State University, ID
Bowling Green State University, OH
Bryan College, TN
Bucknell University, PA
Butler University, IN
California Lutheran University, CA
California Polytechnic State University, San Luis Obispo, CA
California State University, Chico, CA
California State University, Fullerton, CA
Cameron University, OK
Capital University, OH
Carroll College, MT
Carroll University, WI
Case Western Reserve University, OH
Catawba College, NC
Cedar Crest College, PA
Centenary College of Louisiana, LA
Central Michigan University, MI
Chapman University, CA
Christian Brothers University, TN
Christopher Newport University, VA
City College of the City University of New York, NY
Clemson University, SC
Cleveland State University, OH
Coastal Carolina University, SC
Coe College, IA
The College of Idaho, ID
College of Staten Island of the City University of New York, NY
Colorado Mesa University, CO
Colorado State University, CO
Columbia College Chicago, IL
Columbus State University, GA
Cornell College, IA
Creighton University, NE
Davidson College, NC
DeSales University, PA
Doane University, NE
Drew University, NJ
Drexel University, PA

East Carolina University, NC
East Central University, OK
Eastern Illinois University, IL
Eastern Michigan University, MI
Eastern New Mexico University, NM
Edgewood College, WI
Elizabethtown College, PA
Elon University, NC
Emmanuel College, GA
Emory & Henry College, VA
Emory University, GA
Endicott College, MA
Florida Agricultural and Mechanical University, FL
Florida Atlantic University, FL
Florida International University, FL
Fort Hays State University, KS
Fort Lewis College, CO
Franklin College, IN
Franklin Pierce University, NH
Gannon University, PA
Gonzaga University, WA
Goucher College, MD
Grambling State University, LA
Greenville University, IL
Hardin-Simmons University, TX
Heidelberg University, OH
Hobart and William Smith Colleges, NY
Hofstra University, NY
Houghton College, NY
Huntington University, IN
Idaho State University, ID
Illinois State University, IL
Indiana State University, IN
Indiana University of Pennsylvania, PA
Ithaca College, NY
The Juilliard School, NY
Kalamazoo College, MI
Kean University, NJ
Kennesaw State University, GA
Kent State University, OH
Kent State University at Geauga, OH
Kent State University at Stark, OH
Kentucky State University, KY
King University, TN
Lafayette College, PA
Lake Erie College, OH
Lawrence University, WI
Lees-McRae College, NC
Lehigh University, PA
Liberty University, VA
Limestone College, SC
Lock Haven University of Pennsylvania, PA
Long Island University, NY
Louisiana College, LA
Loyola Marymount University, CA
Manhattanville College, NY
Marietta College, OH
Massachusetts College of Liberal Arts, MA
McPherson College, KS
Michigan State University, MI
Michigan Technological University, MI
Middle Tennessee State University, TN
Minnesota State University Mankato, MN
Minot State University, ND
Mississippi State University, MS
Missouri Valley College, MO
Molloy College, NY
Montclair State University, NJ
Morgan State University, MD
Mount Aloysius College, PA
Mount Marty College, SD
Nazareth College of Rochester, NY
New Jersey Institute of Technology, NJ
New Mexico State University, NM
Northeastern Illinois University, IL
Northeastern State University, OK
Northern Illinois University, IL
Northwestern State University of Louisiana, LA
Nyack College, NY
Oakland University, MI
Oglethorpe University, GA
The Ohio State University, OH
Ohio University, OH
Ohio University–Chillicothe, OH
Ohio University–Eastern, OH
Ohio University–Lancaster, OH
Ohio University–Southern Campus, OH
Ohio University–Zanesville, OH
Ohio Valley University, WV
Ohio Wesleyan University, OH
Oklahoma Baptist University, OK
Oklahoma City University, OK
Oklahoma State University, OK
Old Dominion University, VA
Olivet Nazarene University, IL
Ouachita Baptist University, AR
Piedmont College, GA
Purchase College, State University of New York, NY
Rockford University, IL
Sacred Heart University, CT
St. Bonaventure University, NY
St. Cloud State University, MN
Saint Louis University, MO
Saint Mary's College of California, CA
Salem State University, MA
Samford University, AL
Sam Houston State University, TX
San Diego State University, CA
San Jose State University, CA
Seattle Pacific University, WA
Shenandoah University, VA
Shepherd University, WV
Simpson College, IA
Slippery Rock University of Pennsylvania, PA
Sonoma State University, CA
Southeastern University, FL
Southeast Missouri State University, MO
Southern Illinois University Carbondale, IL
Southern Utah University, UT
Southwestern College, KS
Spelman College, GA
State University of New York at Fredonia, NY
State University of New York College at Geneseo, NY
State University of New York College at Potsdam, NY
Stephens College, MO
Sterling College, KS
Stockton University, NJ
Tabor College, KS
Temple University, PA
Texas A&M International University, TX
Texas A&M University, TX
Texas A&M University–Commerce, TX
Texas Christian University, TX
Texas Lutheran University, TX
Texas Tech University, TX
Texas Woman's University, TX
Tiffin University, OH
Towson University, MD
Trine University, IN
Trinity Christian College, IL
The University of Akron, OH
The University of Alabama, AL
The University of Alabama at Birmingham, AL
University of Alaska Anchorage, AK
The University of Arizona, AZ
University of California, Los Angeles, CA
University of California, San Diego, CA
University of California, Santa Cruz, CA
University of Colorado Boulder, CO
University of Colorado Denver, CO
University of Evansville, IN
University of Florida, FL
University of Guam, GU
University of Houston, TX
University of Idaho, ID
University of Illinois at Chicago, IL
University of Illinois at Urbana-Champaign, IL
The University of Iowa, IA
The University of Kansas, KS
University of Kentucky, KY
University of Louisiana at Monroe, LA
University of Louisville, KY
University of Maine, ME
University of Maine at Fort Kent, ME
University of Maryland, Baltimore County, MD
University of Miami, FL
University of Michigan, MI
University of Michigan–Flint, MI
University of Mississippi, MS
University of Mobile, AL
University of Montana, MT
University of Mount Union, OH
University of Nebraska at Omaha, NE
University of Nebraska–Lincoln, NE
University of Nevada, Las Vegas, NV
University of New Hampshire, NH
The University of North Carolina at Greensboro, NC
University of Northern Colorado, CO
University of Oklahoma, OK
University of Oregon, OR
University of Portland, OR
University of Richmond, VA
University of Rochester, NY
University of St. Francis, IL
University of St. Thomas, TX
University of South Carolina Aiken, SC
University of South Florida, FL
The University of Tampa, FL
The University of Tennessee at Chattanooga, TN
The University of Texas at El Paso, TX
The University of Toledo, OH
The University of Tulsa, OK
University of Utah, UT
University of Washington, WA
University of West Georgia, GA
University of Wisconsin–Eau Claire, WI
University of Wisconsin–Parkside, WI
University of Wisconsin–Stevens Point, WI
University of Wyoming, WY
Utah State University, UT
Valdosta State University, GA
Valparaiso University, IN
Vanderbilt University, TN
Wartburg College, IA
Washburn University, KS
Washington College, MD
Washington State University, WA
Wayne State College, NE
Wayne State University, MI
Western Colorado University, CO
Western Illinois University, IL
Western Oregon University, OR

Western Washington University, WA
Westminster College, UT
Whittier College, CA
Wichita State University, KS
Wilkes University, PA
William Jessup University, CA
William Peace University, NC
Wright State University, OH
Wright State University–Lake Campus, OH
Xavier University, OH
Youngstown State University, OH

Theater/Drama

Abilene Christian University, TX
Alabama State University, AL
Albion College, MI
Allegheny College, PA
Alma College, MI
Anderson University, IN
Anderson University, SC
Angelo State University, TX
Arizona State University at the Tempe campus, AZ
Arkansas Tech University, AR
Asbury University, KY
Ashland University, OH
Auburn University, AL
Augsburg University, MN
Augustana College, IL
Augustana University, SD
Aurora University, IL
Austin College, TX
Austin Peay State University, TN
Averett University, VA
Baker University, KS
Ball State University, IN
Barton College, NC
Baylor University, TX
Belhaven University, MS
Belmont Abbey College, NC
Belmont University, TN
Berklee College of Music, MA
Berry College, GA
Bethany Lutheran College, MN
Bethel College, KS
Bethel University, IN
Bethel University, MN
Binghamton University, State University of New York, NY
Biola University, CA
Birmingham-Southern College, AL
Black Hills State University, SD
Bluefield College, VA
Boise State University, ID
Boston University, MA
Bowling Green State University, OH
Bradley University, IL
Brigham Young University, UT
Bryan College, TN
Bucknell University, PA
Buena Vista University, IA
Butler University, IN
California Baptist University, CA
California Lutheran University, CA
California Polytechnic State University, San Luis Obispo, CA
California State University, Bakersfield, CA
California State University, Chico, CA
California State University, Fresno, CA
California State University, Fullerton, CA
California State University, Los Angeles, CA
California State University, San Bernardino, CA
Calumet College of Saint Joseph, IN
Cameron University, OK
Campbellsville University, KY
Cardinal Stritch University, WI
Carroll College, MT
Carroll University, WI
Carthage College, WI
Case Western Reserve University, OH
Catawba College, NC
The Catholic University of America, DC
Cedar Crest College, PA
Centenary College of Louisiana, LA
Central College, IA
Central Methodist University, MO
Central Michigan University, MI
Central Washington University, WA
Centre College, KY
Chapman University, CA
Christopher Newport University, VA
Clarion University of Pennsylvania, PA
Clarke University, IA
Clemson University, SC
Cleveland State University, OH
Coastal Carolina University, SC
Coe College, IA
The College of Idaho, ID
College of Saint Benedict, MN
College of Staten Island of the City University of New York, NY
The College of Wooster, OH
Colorado Mesa University, CO
Colorado State University, CO
Columbia College Chicago, IL
Columbus State University, GA
Concordia College, MN
Concordia University, St. Paul, MN
Concord University, WV
Converse College, SC
Cornell College, IA
Creighton University, NE
Davidson College, NC
DePaul University, IL
DeSales University, PA
Dillard University, LA
Doane University, NE
Dordt University, IA
Drake University, IA
Drew University, NJ
Drexel University, PA
Drury University, MO
Earlham College, IN
East Central University, OK
Eastern Illinois University, IL
Eastern Michigan University, MI
Eastern New Mexico University, NM
Eastern Oregon University, OR
Eastern Washington University, WA
East Texas Baptist University, TX
Eckerd College, FL
Edgewood College, WI
Elizabethtown College, PA
Elon University, NC
Emmanuel College, GA
Emory & Henry College, VA
Emory University, GA
Emporia State University, KS
Evangel University, MO
Ferris State University, MI
Five Towns College, NY
Florida Agricultural and Mechanical University, FL
Florida International University, FL
Florida State University, FL
Fort Hays State University, KS
Fort Lewis College, CO
Franklin College, IN
Franklin Pierce University, NH
Gannon University, PA
George Fox University, OR
Gordon College, MA
Goshen College, IN
Goucher College, MD
Graceland University, IA
Grambling State University, LA
Grand Valley State University, MI
Grand View University, IA
Gustavus Adolphus College, MN
Hamline University, MN
Hardin-Simmons University, TX
Heidelberg University, OH
Hendrix College, AR
High Point University, NC
Hillsdale College, MI
Hiram College, OH
Hofstra University, NY
Hollins University, VA
Hope College, MI
Houston Baptist University, TX
Huntington University, IN
Idaho State University, ID
Illinois College, IL
Illinois State University, IL
Illinois Wesleyan University, IL
Immaculata University, PA
Indiana State University, IN
Indiana University of Pennsylvania, PA
Ithaca College, NY
Jacksonville State University, AL
Jacksonville University, FL
James Madison University, VA
John Brown University, AR
Judson University, IL
The Juilliard School, NY
Kean University, NJ
Keene State College, NH
Kennesaw State University, GA
Kent State University, OH
Kent State University at Geauga, OH
Kent State University at Stark, OH
Kentucky Mountain Bible College, KY
King University, TN
Lafayette College, PA
LaGrange College, GA
Lake Erie College, OH
Lake Forest College, IL
La Sierra University, CA
Lawrence University, WI
Lees-McRae College, NC
Lee University, TN
Lehigh University, PA
Lewis-Clark State College, ID
Lewis University, IL
Limestone College, SC
Lincoln College, IL
Linfield College, OR
Lipscomb University, TN
Long Island University, NY
Longwood University, VA
Louisiana College, LA
Louisiana State University and Agricultural & Mechanical College, LA
Loyola Marymount University, CA
Loyola University Chicago, IL
Lycoming College, PA
Lyon College, AR
Malone University, OH
Manhattanville College, NY
Marietta College, OH
Marist College, NY
Marquette University, WI
Maryville College, TN
Massachusetts College of Liberal Arts, MA
Mayville State University, ND
McPherson College, KS
Mercer University, GA

Messiah College, PA
Miami University, OH
Michigan State University, MI
Michigan Technological University, MI
Middle Tennessee State University, TN
Midwestern State University, TX
Milligan University, TN
Millikin University, IL
Minnesota State University Mankato, MN
Minnesota State University Moorhead, MN
Minot State University, ND
Mississippi State University, MS
Missouri Baptist University, MO
Missouri Southern State University, MO
Missouri University of Science and Technology, MO
Missouri Valley College, MO
Molloy College, NY
Montana State University, MT
Montana State University Billings, MT
Montclair State University, NJ
Morehead State University, KY
Morgan State University, MD
Mount Marty College, SD
Muskingum University, OH
Nazareth College of Rochester, NY
Nebraska Wesleyan University, NE
Newberry College, SC
New Jersey Institute of Technology, NJ
Newman University, KS
New Mexico State University, NM
Niagara University, NY
North Carolina Central University, NC
North Central College, IL
North Dakota State University, ND
Northeastern Illinois University, IL
Northeastern State University, OK
Northern Arizona University, AZ
Northern Illinois University, IL
Northern Michigan University, MI
Northern State University, SD
North Greenville University, SC
Northwestern State University of Louisiana, LA
Northwest Missouri State University, MO
Northwest Nazarene University, ID
Northwest University, WA
Nyack College, NY
Oakland University, MI
Oglethorpe University, GA
The Ohio State University, OH
Ohio University, OH
Ohio University–Chillicothe, OH
Ohio University–Eastern, OH
Ohio University–Lancaster, OH
Ohio University–Southern Campus, OH
Ohio University–Zanesville, OH
Ohio Valley University, WV
Ohio Wesleyan University, OH
Oklahoma Baptist University, OK
Oklahoma City University, OK
Oklahoma State University, OK
Old Dominion University, VA
Olivet Nazarene University, IL
Oral Roberts University, OK
Otterbein University, OH
Ouachita Baptist University, AR
Pacific Lutheran University, WA
Pacific University, OR
Palm Beach Atlantic University, FL
Piedmont College, GA
Plymouth State University, NH
Point Loma Nazarene University, CA
Portland State University, OR
Providence College, RI
Purchase College, State University of New York, NY
Purdue University Fort Wayne, IN
Queens University of Charlotte, NC
Reinhardt University, GA
Rhode Island College, RI
Rhodes College, TN
Rider University, NJ
Rochester University, MI
Rockford University, IL
Rogers State University, OK
Rollins College, FL
Sacred Heart University, CT
Saginaw Valley State University, MI
St. Ambrose University, IA
St. Bonaventure University, NY
St. Cloud State University, MN
St. Edward's University, TX
Saint John's University, MN
Saint Joseph's University, PA
Saint Louis University, MO
Saint Martin's University, WA
Saint Mary's College of California, CA
St. Norbert College, WI
St. Olaf College, MN
Salem State University, MA
Samford University, AL
Sam Houston State University, TX
San Diego State University, CA
San Jose State University, CA
Santa Clara University, CA
Schreiner University, TX
Seattle Pacific University, WA
Seattle University, WA
Shenandoah University, VA
Shepherd University, WV
Shippensburg University of Pennsylvania, PA
Simpson College, IA
Slippery Rock University of Pennsylvania, PA
Sonoma State University, CA
Southeastern Louisiana University, LA
Southeast Missouri State University, MO
Southern Illinois University Carbondale, IL
Southern Illinois University Edwardsville, IL
Southern Utah University, UT
Southwest Baptist University, MO
Southwestern College, KS
Southwestern Oklahoma State University, OK
Southwestern University, TX
Spelman College, GA
State University of New York at Fredonia, NY
State University of New York at New Paltz, NY
State University of New York at Plattsburgh, NY
State University of New York College at Cortland, NY
State University of New York College at Geneseo, NY
State University of New York College at Oneonta, NY
State University of New York College at Potsdam, NY
Stephen F. Austin State University, TX
Stephens College, MO
Sterling College, KS
Stetson University, FL
Stevenson University, MD
Stockton University, NJ
Sul Ross State University, TX
SUNY Brockport, NY
Susquehanna University, PA
Syracuse University, NY
Tabor College, KS
Tarleton State University, TX
Taylor University, IN
Temple University, PA
Texas A&M University, TX
Texas A&M University–Commerce, TX
Texas Christian University, TX
Texas Lutheran University, TX
Texas State University, TX
Texas Tech University, TX
Texas Woman's University, TX
Thomas More University, KY
Tiffin University, OH
Towson University, MD
Transylvania University, KY
Trevecca Nazarene University, TN
Trine University, IN
Trinity Christian College, IL
Trinity University, TX
Troy University, AL
Truman State University, MO
Union College, KY
Union University, TN
The University of Akron, OH
The University of Alabama, AL
The University of Alabama at Birmingham, AL
The University of Arizona, AZ
University of Arkansas, AR
University of California, Los Angeles, CA
University of California, Riverside, CA
University of California, San Diego, CA
University of California, Santa Cruz, CA
University of Central Florida, FL
University of Colorado Boulder, CO
University of Colorado Denver, CO
University of Dallas, TX
University of Denver, CO
University of Evansville, IN
The University of Findlay, OH
University of Florida, FL
University of Hawaii at Manoa, HI
University of Houston, TX
University of Idaho, ID
University of Illinois at Chicago, IL
University of Illinois at Urbana-Champaign, IL
University of Indianapolis, IN
The University of Iowa, IA
University of Jamestown, ND
The University of Kansas, KS
University of Kentucky, KY
University of Louisiana at Monroe, LA
University of Louisville, KY
University of Lynchburg, VA
University of Maine, ME
University of Maine at Farmington, ME
University of Maryland, Baltimore County, MD
University of Mary Washington, VA
University of Massachusetts Amherst, MA
University of Memphis, TN
University of Miami, FL
University of Michigan, MI
University of Michigan–Flint, MI
University of Mississippi, MS
University of Missouri–St. Louis, MO
University of Montana, MT
University of Montevallo, AL
University of Mount Union, OH
University of Nebraska at Kearney, NE
University of Nebraska at Omaha, NE

University of Nebraska–Lincoln, NE
University of Nevada, Las Vegas, NV
University of Nevada, Reno, NV
University of New Hampshire, NH
University of New Mexico, NM
University of North Alabama, AL
University of North Carolina Asheville, NC
The University of North Carolina at Chapel Hill, NC
The University of North Carolina at Charlotte, NC
The University of North Carolina at Greensboro, NC
The University of North Carolina Wilmington, NC
University of North Dakota, ND
University of Northern Colorado, CO
University of Northern Iowa, IA
University of Northwestern–St. Paul, MN
University of Oklahoma, OK
University of Oregon, OR
University of Pittsburgh, PA
University of Pittsburgh at Bradford, PA
University of Pittsburgh at Greensburg, PA
University of Pittsburgh at Johnstown, PA
University of Portland, OR
University of Puget Sound, WA
University of Rhode Island, RI
University of Richmond, VA
University of Saint Mary, KS
University of St. Thomas, TX
University of Science and Arts of Oklahoma, OK
University of South Carolina, SC
University of South Carolina Aiken, SC
University of Southern California, CA
University of Southern Indiana, IN
University of Southern Maine, ME
University of Southern Mississippi, MS
University of South Florida, FL
The University of Tampa, FL
The University of Tennessee at Chattanooga, TN
The University of Tennessee at Martin, TN
The University of Texas at Austin, TX
The University of Texas at El Paso, TX
The University of Texas Rio Grande Valley, TX
University of the Incarnate Word, TX
The University of Toledo, OH
The University of Tulsa, OK
University of Utah, UT
University of Washington, WA
The University of West Alabama, AL
University of West Georgia, GA
University of Wisconsin–Eau Claire, WI
University of Wisconsin–Green Bay, WI
University of Wisconsin–La Crosse, WI
University of Wisconsin–Milwaukee, WI
University of Wisconsin–Parkside, WI
University of Wisconsin–Platteville, WI
University of Wisconsin–River Falls, WI
University of Wisconsin–Stevens Point, WI
University of Wisconsin–Whitewater, WI
University of Wyoming, WY
Utah State University, UT
Valdosta State University, GA
Valparaiso University, IN
Vanguard University of Southern California, CA
Wabash College, IN
Wagner College, NY
Walla Walla University, WA
Wartburg College, IA
Washburn University, KS
Washington College, MD
Washington State University, WA
Washington University in St. Louis, MO
Wayland Baptist University, TX
Waynesburg University, PA
Wayne State College, NE
Wayne State University, MI
Wesleyan College, GA
West Chester University of Pennsylvania, PA
Western Carolina University, NC
Western Illinois University, IL
Western Kentucky University, KY
Western Michigan University, MI
Western Oregon University, OR
Western Washington University, WA
Westminster College, PA
Westminster College, UT
Westmont College, CA
West Texas A&M University, TX
Whitman College, WA
Whittier College, CA
Whitworth University, WA
Wichita State University, KS
Wilkes University, PA
William & Mary, VA
William Jessup University, CA
Winona State University, MN
Wittenberg University, OH
Wright State University, OH
Wright State University–Lake Campus, OH
Xavier University, OH
Youngstown State University, OH

Special Achievements/Activities

Cheerleading/Drum Major

Abilene Christian University, TX
Anderson University, SC
Angelo State University, TX
Arkansas Tech University, AR
Asbury University, KY
Ashland University, OH
Auburn University, AL
Augustana University, SD
Baker University, KS
Barton College, NC
Belhaven University, MS
Bellarmine University, KY
Belmont Abbey College, NC
Belmont University, TN
Bethel College, KS
Bethel University, IN
Bluefield College, VA
Boise State University, ID
California Baptist University, CA
Cameron University, OK
Campbellsville University, KY
Carroll College, MT
Catawba College, NC
Central Methodist University, MO
Christian Brothers University, TN
Cleveland State University, OH
Coastal Carolina University, SC
Colorado Mesa University, CO
Columbus State University, GA
Delta State University, MS
Drexel University, PA
Drury University, MO
Eastern Kentucky University, KY
Emmanuel College, GA
Emory & Henry College, VA
Evangel University, MO
Florida Agricultural and Mechanical University, FL
Florida Institute of Technology, FL
Fort Hays State University, KS
Georgia Institute of Technology, GA
Graceland University, IA
Grambling State University, LA
Grand View University, IA
Greenville University, IL
Hofstra University, NY
Huntington University, IN
Idaho State University, ID
James Madison University, VA
Kentucky State University, KY
Lee University, TN
Lenoir-Rhyne University, NC
Lewis University, IL
Liberty University, VA
Life University, GA
Limestone College, SC
Lincoln College, IL
Lincoln University, PA
Lipscomb University, TN
Long Island University, NY
Louisiana College, LA
Lyon College, AR
Malone University, OH
Maryville University of Saint Louis, MO
McKendree University, IL
McPherson College, KS
Mercer University, GA
Methodist University, NC
MidAmerica Nazarene University, KS
Middle Tennessee State University, TN
Midway University, KY
Midwestern State University, TX
Milligan University, TN
Mississippi State University, MS
Missouri Baptist University, MO
Missouri Southern State University, MO
Missouri Valley College, MO
Molloy College, NY
Montana State University Billings, MT
Morehead State University, KY
Newberry College, SC
New Mexico State University, NM
Nicholls State University, LA
North Carolina State University, NC
Northeastern State University, OK
Northern Illinois University, IL
Northern Michigan University, MI
Northwestern State University of Louisiana, LA
Northwest Missouri State University, MO
The Ohio State University, OH
Oklahoma Baptist University, OK
Oklahoma State University, OK
Old Dominion University, VA
Olivet College, MI
Olivet Nazarene University, IL
Oral Roberts University, OK
Ouachita Baptist University, AR
Queens University of Charlotte, NC
Rocky Mountain College, MT
Rogers State University, OK
St. Ambrose University, IA
St. Edward's University, TX
Saint Francis University, PA
St. John's University, NY
Saint Louis University, MO
St. Mary's University, TX
Samford University, AL
San Diego State University, CA
Southeastern Louisiana University, LA
Southeastern University, FL
Southeast Missouri State University, MO
Southern Illinois University Carbondale, IL
Southwestern College, KS

Southwestern Oklahoma State University, OK
Stephen F. Austin State University, TX
Sterling College, KS
Stetson University, FL
Tabor College, KS
Temple University, PA
Tennessee Wesleyan University, TN
Texas A&M University–Commerce, TX
Thomas More University, KY
Tiffin University, OH
Union College, KY
Union University, TN
The University of Alabama, AL
The University of Alabama at Birmingham, AL
University of Arkansas, AR
University of Central Florida, FL
University of Houston, TX
University of Idaho, ID
The University of Iowa, IA
University of Jamestown, ND
University of Kentucky, KY
University of Louisiana at Monroe, LA
University of Louisville, KY
University of Mary Hardin-Baylor, TX
University of Massachusetts Amherst, MA
University of Memphis, TN
University of Mississippi, MS
University of Missouri–St. Louis, MO
University of Montana, MT
University of Montevallo, AL
University of Mount Union, OH
University of Nebraska at Kearney, NE
University of Nebraska–Lincoln, NE
University of Nevada, Las Vegas, NV
University of North Alabama, AL
University of North Georgia, GA
University of Providence, MT
University of St. Francis, IL
University of Saint Francis, IN
University of Science and Arts of Oklahoma, OK
University of South Carolina, SC
University of South Carolina Aiken, SC
University of Southern Mississippi, MS
The University of Tennessee at Chattanooga, TN
The University of Tennessee at Martin, TN
The University of Texas at El Paso, TX
The University of Texas at San Antonio, TX
The University of Texas Rio Grande Valley, TX
The University of Toledo, OH
The University of Tulsa, OK
University of Utah, UT
The University of West Alabama, AL
University of Wyoming, WY
Upper Iowa University, IA
Washburn University, KS
Wayland Baptist University, TX
Westminster College, UT
West Texas A&M University, TX
Wichita State University, KS
Wingate University, NC
Wright State University, OH
Wright State University–Lake Campus, OH
Youngstown State University, OH

Community Service

Agnes Scott College, GA
Albertus Magnus College, CT
Alice Lloyd College, KY
Allen College, IA
Alliant International University - San Diego, CA
Alverno College, WI
Arizona Christian University, AZ
Augsburg University, MN
Augustana University, SD
Austin College, TX
Ball State University, IN
Baylor University, TX
Bellarmine University, KY
Belmont University, TN
Beloit College, WI
Benedictine University, IL
Bentley University, MA
Berry College, GA
Bethany College, WV
Bethel College, KS
Binghamton University, State University of New York, NY
Biola University, CA
Bluefield State College, WV
Boise State University, ID
Bradley University, IL
Bryan College, TN
Bryn Athyn College of the New Church, PA
Caldwell University, NJ
California Lutheran University, CA
California Polytechnic State University, San Luis Obispo, CA
California State University, Bakersfield, CA
California State University, Chico, CA
California State University, Fresno, CA
California State University, Los Angeles, CA
California State University, San Bernardino, CA
California State University, Stanislaus, CA
Cameron University, OK
Canisius College, NY
Catawba College, NC
Central College, IA
Centre College, KY
Chaminade University of Honolulu, HI
Christian Brothers University, TN
Christopher Newport University, VA
The Citadel, The Military College of South Carolina, SC
City College of the City University of New York, NY
Clarion University of Pennsylvania, PA
Clarke University, IA
Clemson University, SC
College of Saint Elizabeth, NJ
The College of Saint Rose, NY
College of Staten Island of the City University of New York, NY
The College of Wooster, OH
Columbia College, MO
Columbia College, SC
Columbia College Chicago, IL
Columbus State University, GA
Concord University, WV
Dallas Baptist University, TX
Davidson College, NC
DePaul University, IL
DePauw University, IN
Dominican University of California, CA
Dordt University, IA
Drew University, NJ
Eastern New Mexico University, NM
ECPI University, VA
Edgewood College, WI
Edinboro University of Pennsylvania, PA
Elon University, NC
Emory & Henry College, VA
Emory University, GA
Endicott College, MA
Florida Agricultural and Mechanical University, FL
Florida Gulf Coast University, FL
Florida National University, FL
Franklin College, IN
Gannon University, PA
Georgian Court University, NJ
Gonzaga University, WA
Goshen College, IN
Grand View University, IA
Grove City College, PA
Hamline University, MN
Hampshire College, MA
Hendrix College, AR
Hillsdale College, MI
Hobart and William Smith Colleges, NY
Hollins University, VA
Houghton College, NY
Illinois Institute of Technology, IL
Illinois State University, IL
Indiana University of Pennsylvania, PA
Iona College, NY
John Carroll University, OH
Johnson University, TN
Kean University, NJ
Kennesaw State University, GA
Kent State University, OH
Kent State University at Geauga, OH
Kent State University at Stark, OH
King's College, PA
Kutztown University of Pennsylvania, PA
Lake Erie College, OH
Lawrence University, WI
Lewis & Clark College, OR
Lewis-Clark State College, ID
Lewis University, IL
Linfield College, OR
Lipscomb University, TN
Lock Haven University of Pennsylvania, PA
Longwood University, VA
Loyola Marymount University, CA
Loyola University Chicago, IL
Manhattan College, NY
Manhattanville College, NY
Marymount University, VA
Maryville College, TN
Maryville University of Saint Louis, MO
Marywood University, PA
McKendree University, IL
Mercer University, GA
Michigan State University, MI
Mid-Atlantic Christian University, NC
Millersville University of Pennsylvania, PA
Milligan University, TN
Millikin University, IL
Minnesota State University Moorhead, MN
Misericordia University, PA
Missouri Valley College, MO
Molloy College, NY
Montana Technological University, MT
Montclair State University, NJ
Morehead State University, KY
Mount Carmel College of Nursing, OH
Mount Marty College, SD
Mount Saint Mary's University, CA
Muskingum University, OH
Neumont College of Computer Science, UT
New Jersey Institute of Technology, NJ
Newman University, KS
Niagara University, NY
Nichols College, MA
North Central College, IL
North Central University, MN
Northeastern State University, OK

Northern Illinois University, IL
Northwest Christian University, OR
Nyack College, NY
Oakland University, MI
Oglethorpe University, GA
Ohio Valley University, WV
Oklahoma State University, OK
Old Dominion University, VA
Olivet College, MI
Oral Roberts University, OK
Otterbein University, OH
Pacific University, OR
Patrick Henry College, VA
Piedmont College, GA
Portland State University, OR
Principia College, IL
Providence College, RI
Queens University of Charlotte, NC
Randolph College, VA
Ringling College of Art and Design, FL
Rockford University, IL
Sacred Heart University, CT
Saginaw Valley State University, MI
Saint Anselm College, NH
St. Catherine University, MN
St. Cloud State University, MN
St. Edward's University, TX
St. John Fisher College, NY
St. John's University, NY
Saint Joseph's University, PA
St. Lawrence University, NY
St. Louis College of Pharmacy, MO
Saint Martin's University, WA
St. Olaf College, MN
St. Thomas Aquinas College, NY
Samford University, AL
San Diego State University, CA
San Jose State University, CA
Schreiner University, TX
Shippensburg University of Pennsylvania, PA
Simmons University, MA
Simpson College, IA
Slippery Rock University of Pennsylvania, PA
Sonoma State University, CA
Southern Illinois University Carbondale, IL
Southern New Hampshire University, NH
Southwestern College, KS
Spring Hill College, AL
State University of New York at Plattsburgh, NY
State University of New York College at Geneseo, NY
State University of New York College at Oneonta, NY
State University of New York College at Potsdam, NY
State University of New York College of Environmental Science and Forestry, NY
State University of New York College of Technology at Delhi, NY
Stetson University, FL
Stockton University, NJ
Stony Brook University, State University of New York, NY
SUNY Brockport, NY
Texas A&M University, TX
Texas A&M University–Texarkana, TX
Texas Christian University, TX
Texas Tech University, TX
Thomas More University, KY
Towson University, MD
Trinity Christian College, IL
Trinity College of Florida, FL
Truett McConnell University, GA
Tulane University, LA
Union College, KY
Union College, NE
Union University, TN
Universidad Adventista de las Antillas, PR
The University of Akron, OH
The University of Alabama, AL
University of Alaska Fairbanks, AK
University of Arkansas, AR
University of California, San Diego, CA
University of California, Santa Cruz, CA
University of Chicago, IL
University of Colorado Boulder, CO
University of Dayton, OH
University of Denver, CO
University of Florida, FL
University of Hawaii at Manoa, HI
University of Houston, TX
University of Houston–Clear Lake, TX
University of Houston - Downtown, TX
University of Indianapolis, IN
University of Jamestown, ND
The University of Kansas, KS
University of Louisiana at Monroe, LA
University of Louisville, KY
University of Maine, ME
University of Maine at Presque Isle, ME
University of Mary Hardin-Baylor, TX
University of Massachusetts Lowell, MA
University of Memphis, TN
University of Michigan, MI
University of Michigan–Dearborn, MI
University of Michigan–Flint, MI
University of Mississippi, MS
University of Nebraska–Lincoln, NE
University of Nevada, Las Vegas, NV
University of New Hampshire, NH
The University of North Carolina at Chapel Hill, NC
The University of North Carolina at Greensboro, NC
University of North Dakota, ND
University of Northern Colorado, CO
University of North Georgia, GA
University of Pittsburgh, PA
University of Richmond, VA
University of St. Francis, IL
University of Saint Mary, KS
University of South Carolina, SC
University of South Carolina Aiken, SC
The University of Tennessee at Chattanooga, TN
The University of Texas Rio Grande Valley, TX
The University of Toledo, OH
The University of Tulsa, OK
University of West Georgia, GA
University of Wisconsin–Eau Claire, WI
University of Wisconsin–Green Bay, WI
University of Wisconsin–La Crosse, WI
University of Wisconsin–Parkside, WI
University of Wisconsin–Stout, WI
University of Wyoming, WY
Ursuline College, OH
Vanderbilt University, TN
Wabash College, IN
Washburn University, KS
Washington State University, WA
Wayland Baptist University, TX
Waynesburg University, PA
Webber International University, FL
Wesleyan College, GA
Western Illinois University, IL
Western New Mexico University, NM
Western Oregon University, OR
Western Washington University, WA
Westminster College, UT
West Texas A&M University, TX
Wheaton College, IL
Wichita State University, KS
Widener University, PA
William Peace University, NC
Wilson College, PA
Wittenberg University, OH
Wright State University, OH
Wright State University–Lake Campus, OH
Youngstown State University, OH

Hobbies/Interests

Bethany College, WV
California State Polytechnic University, Pomona, CA
California State University, Chico, CA
California State University, San Bernardino, CA
Capital University, OH
College of Staten Island of the City University of New York, NY
Colorado Mesa University, CO
Eastern New Mexico University, NM
ECPI University, VA
Emmanuel College, GA
Florida Institute of Technology, FL
Hillsdale College, MI
Hollins University, VA
Illinois Institute of Technology, IL
Indiana University of Pennsylvania, PA
Lake Erie College, OH
Michigan State University, MI
Middle Tennessee State University, TN
Missouri Valley College, MO
Montana Technological University, MT
New Jersey Institute of Technology, NJ
New Mexico State University, NM
The Ohio State University, OH
Sacred Heart University, CT
St. John's University, NY
Saint Martin's University, WA
Samford University, AL
San Diego State University, CA
Southern New Hampshire University, NH
Stephen F. Austin State University, TX
SUNY Brockport, NY
Texas Tech University, TX
Texas Woman's University, TX
Trine University, IN
Union College, KY
The University of Alabama, AL
University of California, Los Angeles, CA
University of California, Santa Cruz, CA
University of Houston, TX
University of Louisville, KY
University of Michigan–Flint, MI
University of Minnesota, Twin Cities Campus, MN
University of Montevallo, AL
University of Pittsburgh, PA
University of South Carolina Aiken, SC
The University of Toledo, OH
University of Wisconsin–Eau Claire, WI
University of Wyoming, WY
Wesleyan College, GA
Western Oregon University, OR
West Texas A&M University, TX
Wichita State University, KS

Junior Miss

Arkansas Tech University, AR
Augsburg University, MN
Belhaven University, MS
Birmingham-Southern College, AL
Campbellsville University, KY
Carroll University, WI

Carthage College, WI
Cedar Crest College, PA
Grambling State University, LA
Grand View University, IA
Gustavus Adolphus College, MN
Lewis-Clark State College, ID
Midway University, KY
Mississippi State University, MS
Missouri Valley College, MO
Morehead State University, KY
Muskingum University, OH
New Mexico State University, NM
Northeastern State University, OK
Oklahoma City University, OK
Rogers State University, OK
Stetson University, FL
Tennessee Wesleyan University, TN
Texas A&M University–Commerce, TX
Texas Lutheran University, TX
The University of Alabama, AL
The University of Alabama at Birmingham, AL
University of Evansville, IN
University of Idaho, ID
University of Louisville, KY
University of Mississippi, MS
University of Montevallo, AL
The University of North Carolina at Greensboro, NC
The University of Tennessee at Martin, TN
The University of West Alabama, AL
University of Wyoming, WY
Wartburg College, IA
Washington State University, WA

Leadership

Abilene Christian University, TX
AdventHealth University, FL
Agnes Scott College, GA
Alabama State University, AL
Albertus Magnus College, CT
Alcorn State University, MS
Alice Lloyd College, KY
Allen College, IA
Alliant International University - San Diego, CA
American University, DC
Anderson University, IN
Anderson University, SC
Andrews University, MI
Aquinas College, MI
Arizona Christian University, AZ
Arizona State University at the Downtown Phoenix campus, AZ
Arizona State University at the Polytechnic campus, AZ
Arizona State University at the Tempe campus, AZ
Arizona State University at the West campus, AZ
Asbury University, KY
Ashland University, OH
Auburn University, AL
Auburn University at Montgomery, AL
Augsburg University, MN
Augustana College, IL
Augustana University, SD
Aurora University, IL
Austin College, TX
Austin Peay State University, TN
Ave Maria University, FL
Averett University, VA
Baker University, KS
Ball State University, IN
Barton College, NC
Baylor University, TX
Belhaven University, MS
Bellarmine University, KY
Belmont University, TN
Beloit College, WI
Bemidji State University, MN
Benedictine University, IL
Bentley University, MA
Berry College, GA
Bethany College, WV
Bethel University, IN
Binghamton University, State University of New York, NY
Biola University, CA
Birmingham-Southern College, AL
Bluffton University, OH
Boise Bible College, ID
Boise State University, ID
Boston College, MA
Bowdoin College, ME
Bowling Green State University, OH
Bradley University, IL
Brigham Young University, UT
Bryan College, TN
Bryn Mawr College, PA
Bucknell University, PA
Buena Vista University, IA
Caldwell University, NJ
California Lutheran University, CA
California Polytechnic State University, San Luis Obispo, CA
California State Polytechnic University, Pomona, CA
California State University, Bakersfield, CA
California State University, Chico, CA
California State University, Fresno, CA
California State University, Fullerton, CA
California State University, Monterey Bay, CA
California State University, Northridge, CA
California State University, San Marcos, CA
California State University, Stanislaus, CA
Calumet College of Saint Joseph, IN
Cameron University, OK
Campbellsville University, KY
Capital University, OH
Carlow University, PA
Carroll College, MT
Carroll University, WI
Carson-Newman University, TN
Carthage College, WI
Case Western Reserve University, OH
Catawba College, NC
The Catholic University of America, DC
Cedarville University, OH
Central Methodist University, MO
Central Michigan University, MI
Central Washington University, WA
Champlain College, VT
Chatham University, PA
Chowan University, NC
Christian Brothers University, TN
Christopher Newport University, VA
The Citadel, The Military College of South Carolina, SC
City College of the City University of New York, NY
Claremont McKenna College, CA
Clarion University of Pennsylvania, PA
Clarke University, IA
Clarkson University, NY
Clemson University, SC
Cleveland Institute of Art, OH
The College of Idaho, ID
College of Saint Mary, NE
College of Staten Island of the City University of New York, NY
Colorado Mesa University, CO
Columbia College, MO
Columbia College, SC
Columbia International University, SC
Columbus State University, GA
Concord University, WV
Covenant College, GA
Dallas Baptist University, TX
Davidson College, NC
Delta State University, MS
DePaul University, IL
DeSales University, PA
Dominican University of California, CA
Dordt University, IA
Drury University, MO
Duke University, NC
Earlham College, IN
Eastern Illinois University, IL
Eastern Michigan University, MI
Eastern New Mexico University, NM
Eastern Oregon University, OR
Eastern University, PA
East Texas Baptist University, TX
ECPI University, VA
Edinboro University of Pennsylvania, PA
Elon University, NC
Emmanuel College, GA
Emory University, GA
Emporia State University, KS
Endicott College, MA
Eugene Lang College of Liberal Arts, NY
Evangel University, MO
Ferris State University, MI
Florida Agricultural and Mechanical University, FL
Florida Gulf Coast University, FL
Florida Institute of Technology, FL
Fort Hays State University, KS
Fort Lewis College, CO
Franklin College, IN
Franklin Pierce University, NH
Gallaudet University, DC
Gannon University, PA
George Fox University, OR
Georgia Institute of Technology, GA
Georgian Court University, NJ
Gonzaga University, WA
Gordon College, MA
Goshen College, IN
Goucher College, MD
Graceland University, IA
Grambling State University, LA
Greenville University, IL
Grinnell College, IA
Grove City College, PA
Hamline University, MN
Hampden-Sydney College, VA
Hampshire College, MA
Hampton University, VA
Hendrix College, AR
High Point University, NC
Hillsdale College, MI
Hiram College, OH
Hobart and William Smith Colleges, NY
Hofstra University, NY
Hollins University, VA
Hope International University, CA
Houghton College, NY
Huntington University, IN
Husson University, ME
Illinois Institute of Technology, IL
Illinois State University, IL
Immaculata University, PA

Indiana University of Pennsylvania, PA
Ithaca College, NY
Jackson State University, MS
Jacksonville State University, AL
Jacksonville University, FL
James Madison University, VA
John Carroll University, OH
Johnson University, TN
Judson University, IL
Kalamazoo College, MI
Kean University, NJ
Keene State College, NH
Kennesaw State University, GA
Kent State University, OH
Kent State University at Geauga, OH
Kent State University at Stark, OH
Kentucky State University, KY
Kettering University, MI
The King's College, NY
King's College, PA
Kutztown University of Pennsylvania, PA
Kuyper College, MI
LaGrange College, GA
Lake Forest College, IL
Lancaster Bible College, PA
La Sierra University, CA
Lawrence University, WI
Lee University, TN
Le Moyne College, NY
Lenoir-Rhyne University, NC
Lewis & Clark College, OR
Lewis-Clark State College, ID
Lewis University, IL
Liberty University, VA
Life University, GA
Limestone College, SC
Linfield College, OR
Lipscomb University, TN
Lock Haven University of Pennsylvania, PA
Longwood University, VA
Loras College, IA
Louisiana College, LA
Loyola Marymount University, CA
Loyola University Chicago, IL
Loyola University New Orleans, LA
Lynn University, FL
Malone University, OH
Manhattan College, NY
Mansfield University of Pennsylvania, PA
Marymount University, VA
Maryville College, TN
Maryville University of Saint Louis, MO
Marywood University, PA
Massachusetts College of Liberal Arts, MA
Massachusetts Maritime Academy, MA
Mayville State University, ND
McDaniel College, MD
McKendree University, IL
Mercer University, GA
Merrimack College, MA
Messiah College, PA
Methodist University, NC
Miami University, OH
Michigan State University, MI
Michigan Technological University, MI
MidAmerica Nazarene University, KS
Mid-Atlantic Christian University, NC
Middle Tennessee State University, TN
Midway University, KY
Midwestern State University, TX
Millikin University, IL
Mills College, CA
Minnesota State University Mankato, MN
Misericordia University, PA
Mississippi State University, MS
Missouri Southern State University, MO
Missouri State University, MO
Missouri Valley College, MO
Molloy College, NY
Montana State University, MT
Montana Technological University, MT
Montclair State University, NJ
Montreat College, NC
Morehead State University, KY
Mount Aloysius College, PA
Mount Marty College, SD
Mount Saint Mary College, NY
Mount Saint Mary's University, CA
Muskingum University, OH
National University, CA
Nazareth College of Rochester, NY
Nebraska Methodist College, NE
New Jersey Institute of Technology, NJ
Newman University, KS
New Mexico State University, NM
Nicholls State University, LA
Nichols College, MA
North Carolina Central University, NC
North Carolina State University, NC
North Central University, MN
Northeastern Illinois University, IL
Northeastern State University, OK
Northern Arizona University, AZ
Northern Illinois University, IL
Northern Michigan University, MI
Northern State University, SD
Northwest Christian University, OR
Northwestern State University of Louisiana, LA
Northwest Missouri State University, MO
Northwest Nazarene University, ID
Northwest University, WA
Nyack College, NY
Occidental College, CA
Oglethorpe University, GA
Ohio Christian University, OH
The Ohio State University, OH
Ohio Valley University, WV
Ohio Wesleyan University, OH
Oklahoma Baptist University, OK
Oklahoma City University, OK
Oklahoma State University, OK
Old Dominion University, VA
Olivet College, MI
Oral Roberts University, OK
Oregon Institute of Technology, OR
Oregon State University, OR
Otterbein University, OH
Ouachita Baptist University, AR
Pacific Lutheran University, WA
Palm Beach Atlantic University, FL
Parsons School of Design, NY
Patrick Henry College, VA
Piedmont College, GA
Portland State University, OR
Presbyterian College, SC
Principia College, IL
Purdue University, IN
Purdue University Fort Wayne, IN
Queens University of Charlotte, NC
Randolph College, VA
Regent University, VA
Reinhardt University, GA
Rice University, TX
Rochester University, MI
Rockford University, IL
Rocky Mountain College, MT
Rogers State University, OK
Sacred Heart University, CT
Saginaw Valley State University, MI
St. Ambrose University, IA
Saint Anselm College, NH
St. Catherine University, MN
St. Edward's University, TX
Saint Francis University, PA
St. John's University, NY
St. Lawrence University, NY
St. Louis College of Pharmacy, MO
Saint Martin's University, WA
Saint Mary's College of California, CA
St. Olaf College, MN
Saint Peter's University, NJ
St. Thomas Aquinas College, NY
Salem College, NC
Samford University, AL
Sam Houston State University, TX
San Diego State University, CA
San Jose State University, CA
Schreiner University, TX
Scripps College, CA
Seattle Pacific University, WA
Seattle University, WA
Shepherd University, WV
Shippensburg University of Pennsylvania, PA
Simpson College, IA
Slippery Rock University of Pennsylvania, PA
Sonoma State University, CA
Southeastern Louisiana University, LA
Southeastern University, FL
Southeast Missouri State University, MO
Southern Illinois University Carbondale, IL
Southern New Hampshire University, NH
Southern Utah University, UT
Southwestern College, KS
Southwestern Oklahoma State University, OK
Southwestern University, TX
State University of New York at Fredonia, NY
State University of New York at Plattsburgh, NY
State University of New York College at Cortland, NY
State University of New York College at Geneseo, NY
State University of New York College at Oneonta, NY
State University of New York College at Potsdam, NY
State University of New York College of Agriculture & Technology at Morrisville, NY
State University of New York College of Environmental Science and Forestry, NY
Stephen F. Austin State University, TX
Stephens College, MO
Stetson University, FL
Stockton University, NJ
Stony Brook University, State University of New York, NY
Sul Ross State University, TX
SUNY Brockport, NY
Susquehanna University, PA
Taylor University, IN
Texas A&M University, TX
Texas A&M University–Commerce, TX
Texas A&M University–Texarkana, TX
Texas Christian University, TX
Texas Lutheran University, TX
Texas State University, TX
Texas Tech University, TX
Texas Woman's University, TX
Thomas More University, KY
Toccoa Falls College, GA
Trevecca Nazarene University, TN
Trinity Christian College, IL

Trinity College, CT
Trinity College of Florida, FL
Troy University, AL
Truett McConnell University, GA
Truman State University, MO
Union College, KY
Union College, NE
Union University, TN
The University of Akron, OH
The University of Alabama, AL
The University of Alabama at Birmingham, AL
University of Alaska Anchorage, AK
University of Alaska Fairbanks, AK
The University of Arizona, AZ
University of Arkansas, AR
University of California, Los Angeles, CA
University of California, San Diego, CA
University of California, Santa Cruz, CA
University of Central Florida, FL
University of Chicago, IL
University of Colorado Boulder, CO
University of Colorado Denver, CO
University of Dayton, OH
University of Denver, CO
University of Evansville, IN
University of Florida, FL
University of Houston, TX
University of Houston–Clear Lake, TX
University of Houston - Downtown, TX
University of Idaho, ID
University of Illinois at Urbana-Champaign, IL
The University of Iowa, IA
University of Jamestown, ND
The University of Kansas, KS
University of Kentucky, KY
University of Louisiana at Monroe, LA
University of Louisville, KY
University of Maine, ME
University of Maine at Farmington, ME
University of Mary Hardin-Baylor, TX
University of Mary Washington, VA
University of Massachusetts Amherst, MA
University of Massachusetts Boston, MA
University of Massachusetts Dartmouth, MA
University of Memphis, TN
University of Miami, FL
University of Michigan, MI
University of Michigan–Dearborn, MI
University of Michigan–Flint, MI
University of Minnesota, Crookston, MN
University of Minnesota, Twin Cities Campus, MN
University of Mississippi, MS
University of Montana, MT
University of Montevallo, AL
University of Nebraska at Kearney, NE
University of Nebraska at Omaha, NE
University of Nebraska–Lincoln, NE
University of Nevada, Las Vegas, NV
University of New Hampshire, NH
University of North Alabama, AL
The University of North Carolina at Chapel Hill, NC
The University of North Carolina at Greensboro, NC
The University of North Carolina Wilmington, NC
University of North Dakota, ND
University of Northern Colorado, CO
University of Northern Iowa, IA
University of North Georgia, GA
University of Northwestern–St. Paul, MN
University of Oklahoma, OK
University of Pittsburgh, PA
University of Pittsburgh at Greensburg, PA
University of Pittsburgh at Johnstown, PA
University of Rhode Island, RI
University of Rochester, NY
University of St. Francis, IL
University of Saint Joseph, CT
University of St. Thomas, TX
University of South Carolina, SC
University of South Carolina Aiken, SC
University of Southern California, CA
University of Southern Indiana, IN
University of Southern Mississippi, MS
The University of Tampa, FL
The University of Tennessee at Chattanooga, TN
The University of Tennessee at Martin, TN
The University of Texas at Austin, TX
The University of Texas at Dallas, TX
The University of Texas at El Paso, TX
The University of Texas Rio Grande Valley, TX
University of the Incarnate Word, TX
University of the Pacific, CA
The University of Toledo, OH
The University of Tulsa, OK
University of Utah, UT
University of Virginia, VA
University of Washington, WA
The University of West Alabama, AL
University of West Georgia, GA
University of Wisconsin–Eau Claire, WI
University of Wisconsin–Green Bay, WI
University of Wisconsin–La Crosse, WI
University of Wisconsin–Milwaukee, WI
University of Wisconsin–Parkside, WI
University of Wisconsin–Platteville, WI
University of Wisconsin–Stevens Point, WI
University of Wisconsin–Stout, WI
University of Wisconsin–Whitewater, WI
University of Wyoming, WY
Ursuline College, OH
Utah State University, UT
Vanderbilt University, TN
Wabash College, IN
Wake Forest University, NC
Walla Walla University, WA
Walsh University, OH
Warner Pacific University, OR
Wartburg College, IA
Washburn University, KS
Washington State University, WA
Wayland Baptist University, TX
Wayne State College, NE
Wayne State University, MI
Webber International University, FL
Wesleyan College, GA
West Chester University of Pennsylvania, PA
Western Colorado University, CO
Western Illinois University, IL
Western Kentucky University, KY
Western New England University, MA
Western New Mexico University, NM
Western Oregon University, OR
Western Washington University, WA
Westminster College, UT
Westmont College, CA
West Texas A&M University, TX
Wheaton College, IL
Whittier College, CA
Wichita State University, KS
Widener University, PA
Wilkes University, PA
William Jessup University, CA
William Peace University, NC
Wilson College, PA
Wittenberg University, OH
Wofford College, SC
Wright State University, OH
Wright State University–Lake Campus, OH
Youngstown State University, OH

Memberships

Alverno College, WI
American University, DC
Anderson University, SC
Angelo State University, TX
Auburn University, AL
Austin Peay State University, TN
Averett University, VA
Benedictine University, IL
Birmingham-Southern College, AL
Boston University, MA
Caldwell University, NJ
California State University, Chico, CA
California State University, San Bernardino, CA
California State University, Stanislaus, CA
Carroll University, WI
Carson-Newman University, TN
The Catholic University of America, DC
Centenary College of Louisiana, LA
Chaminade University of Honolulu, HI
Christian Brothers University, TN
College of Staten Island of the City University of New York, NY
Columbia College, SC
Dallas Baptist University, TX
Delta State University, MS
Eastern Michigan University, MI
Eastern New Mexico University, NM
ECPI University, VA
Emmanuel College, GA
Ferris State University, MI
Florida Institute of Technology, FL
Franklin College, IN
Georgian Court University, NJ
Gonzaga University, WA
Grand View University, IA
Greenville University, IL
Grove City College, PA
Hamline University, MN
Hiram College, OH
Huntington University, IN
Illinois Institute of Technology, IL
Kean University, NJ
Kennesaw State University, GA
Kettering University, MI
Lewis-Clark State College, ID
Lewis University, IL
Lock Haven University of Pennsylvania, PA
Longwood University, VA
Loyola Marymount University, CA
Loyola University Chicago, IL
Marymount University, VA
Massachusetts College of Liberal Arts, MA
Michigan State University, MI
Middle Tennessee State University, TN
Mississippi State University, MS
Missouri Baptist University, MO
Molloy College, NY
Montana Technological University, MT
Nebraska Methodist College, NE
Newman University, KS
New Mexico State University, NM
North Central University, MN
North Dakota State University, ND
Northern Illinois University, IL
Northern Michigan University, MI

Northwestern State University of Louisiana, LA
Northwest Missouri State University, MO
Oglethorpe University, GA
The Ohio State University, OH
Oklahoma State University, OK
Old Dominion University, VA
Olivet College, MI
Oral Roberts University, OK
Ouachita Baptist University, AR
Pacific University, OR
Patrick Henry College, VA
Portland State University, OR
Queens University of Charlotte, NC
Regent University, VA
Sacred Heart University, CT
St. Catherine University, MN
Saint Mary's College of California, CA
Salem State University, MA
Samford University, AL
San Diego State University, CA
Schreiner University, TX
Sonoma State University, CA
Southeastern Louisiana University, LA
Southeast Missouri State University, MO
Southern New Hampshire University, NH
Southwestern College, KS
State University of New York College at Geneseo, NY
State University of New York College of Agriculture & Technology at Morrisville, NY
State University of New York College of Environmental Science and Forestry, NY
Stephens College, MO
Tennessee Wesleyan University, TN
Texas A&M University, TX
Texas A&M University–Commerce, TX
Texas A&M University–Texarkana, TX
Texas Christian University, TX
Texas Tech University, TX
Texas Woman's University, TX
Thomas More University, KY
Towson University, MD
Union College, KY
Union University, TN
The University of Akron, OH
The University of Alabama, AL
The University of Alabama at Birmingham, AL
University of California, Santa Cruz, CA
University of Evansville, IN
University of Houston, TX
University of Louisville, KY
University of Maine, ME
University of Michigan–Dearborn, MI
University of Mississippi, MS
University of Missouri–St. Louis, MO
University of Mount Union, OH
University of Nebraska at Omaha, NE
University of North Dakota, ND
University of Northern Colorado, CO
University of Pittsburgh, PA
University of South Carolina, SC
University of South Carolina Aiken, SC
The University of Tampa, FL
The University of Tennessee at Chattanooga, TN
The University of Texas Rio Grande Valley, TX
The University of Toledo, OH
University of Washington, WA
The University of West Alabama, AL
University of West Georgia, GA
University of Wisconsin–Eau Claire, WI
University of Wisconsin–La Crosse, WI
University of Wisconsin–Stout, WI
University of Wyoming, WY
Washington State University, WA
Wayne State University, MI
Webber International University, FL
Wesleyan College, GA
Western Kentucky University, KY
Western Washington University, WA
Westminster College, UT
West Texas A&M University, TX
Wichita State University, KS
Wright State University, OH
Wright State University–Lake Campus, OH
Youngstown State University, OH

Religious Involvement

Alaska Bible College, AK
Alma College, MI
Anderson University, IN
Anderson University, SC
Andrews University, MI
Asbury University, KY
Ashland University, OH
Augsburg University, MN
Augustana College, IL
Augustana University, SD
Austin College, TX
Austin Graduate School of Theology, TX
Ave Maria University, FL
Averett University, VA
Baker University, KS
Barton College, NC
Baylor University, TX
Bellarmine University, KY
Belmont Abbey College, NC
Belmont University, TN
Berry College, GA
Bethany College, WV
Birmingham-Southern College, AL
Bluefield State College, WV
Brigham Young University, UT
Bryan College, TN
Bryn Athyn College of the New Church, PA
Caldwell University, NJ
California Lutheran University, CA
Campbellsville University, KY
Canisius College, NY
Capital University, OH
Carlow University, PA
Carroll College, MT
Carroll University, WI
Carthage College, WI
Catawba College, NC
The Catholic University of America, DC
Cedar Crest College, PA
Centenary College of Louisiana, LA
Central College, IA
Central Methodist University, MO
Chaminade University of Honolulu, HI
The Citadel, The Military College of South Carolina, SC
Clarke University, IA
The College of Wooster, OH
Columbia College, MO
Columbia International University, SC
Concordia University Texas, TX
Dallas Baptist University, TX
Davidson College, NC
Drury University, MO
Eastern Mennonite University, VA
Eastern Michigan University, MI
East Texas Baptist University, TX
Edgewood College, WI
Elizabethtown College, PA
Elon University, NC
Emmanuel College, GA
Endicott College, MA
Evangel University, MO
Franklin College, IN
George Fox University, OR
Georgian Court University, NJ
Goshen College, IN
Graceland University, IA
Grand View University, IA
Greenville University, IL
Grove City College, PA
Hendrix College, AR
High Point University, NC
Houghton College, NY
Houston Baptist University, TX
Huntington University, IN
Immaculata University, PA
Johnson University, TN
Kentucky Mountain Bible College, KY
King's College, PA
Kutztown University of Pennsylvania, PA
Lancaster Bible College, PA
Lee University, TN
Lewis University, IL
Limestone College, SC
Lipscomb University, TN
Loras College, IA
Loyola Marymount University, CA
Malone University, OH
Marymount University, VA
Maryville University of Saint Louis, MO
Mayville State University, ND
Mercer University, GA
Messenger College, TX
Mid-Atlantic Christian University, NC
Midway University, KY
Missouri Baptist University, MO
Molloy College, NY
Mount Marty College, SD
Mount St. Mary's University, MD
Mount Vernon Nazarene University, OH
Neumont College of Computer Science, UT
Newberry College, SC
New Jersey Institute of Technology, NJ
Newman University, KS
North Central College, IL
North Central University, MN
North Dakota State University, ND
Northwest Christian University, OR
Northwest Nazarene University, ID
Northwest University, WA
Nyack College, NY
Ohio Valley University, WV
Oklahoma Baptist University, OK
Oklahoma City University, OK
Oral Roberts University, OK
Ouachita Baptist University, AR
Pacific Lutheran University, WA
Pacific University, OR
Patrick Henry College, VA
Piedmont College, GA
Principia College, IL
Queens University of Charlotte, NC
Randolph-Macon College, VA
Regent University, VA
Sacred Heart University, CT
Saint Francis University, PA
St. John's University, NY
Saint Martin's University, WA
St. Olaf College, MN
Samford University, AL
Schreiner University, TX
Seattle Pacific University, WA
Shenandoah University, VA
Simpson College, IA
Southeastern University, FL
Southwest Baptist University, MO

Southwestern College, KS
Sterling College, KS
Stetson University, FL
SUNY Brockport, NY
Tabor College, KS
Texas Christian University, TX
Texas Lutheran University, TX
Texas Woman's University, TX
Thomas More University, KY
Trinity Christian College, IL
Trinity College of Florida, FL
Truett McConnell University, GA
Union College, KY
Union College, NE
Union University, TN
The University of Alabama, AL
The University of Alabama at Birmingham, AL
University of Indianapolis, IN
University of Mary Hardin-Baylor, TX
University of Miami, FL
University of Mobile, AL
University of Montevallo, AL
The University of North Carolina at Greensboro, NC
University of Pittsburgh, PA
University of Providence, MT
University of St. Francis, IL
University of Saint Francis, IN
University of St. Thomas, TX
University of San Diego, CA
University of South Carolina, SC
University of South Carolina Aiken, SC
The University of Tennessee at Chattanooga, TN
University of the Pacific, CA
The University of Toledo, OH
University of West Georgia, GA
University of Wisconsin–Stout, WI
Valdosta State University, GA
Valparaiso University, IN
Virginia Wesleyan University, VA
Walsh University, OH
Washington State University, WA
Wesleyan College, GA
Westminster College, UT
West Texas A&M University, TX
Wheaton College, IL
Whitworth University, WA
William Jessup University, CA
Youngstown State University, OH

Rodeo

Boise State University, ID
California Polytechnic State University, San Luis Obispo, CA
Colorado Mesa University, CO
Eastern New Mexico University, NM
Fort Hays State University, KS
Graceland University, IA
Lewis-Clark State College, ID
Michigan State University, MI
Missouri Valley College, MO
New Mexico State University, NM
Oklahoma State University, OK
Sam Houston State University, TX
Southwestern Oklahoma State University, OK
Stephen F. Austin State University, TX
Texas A&M University, TX
Texas A&M University–Commerce, TX
Texas A&M University–Kingsville, TX
Texas Tech University, TX
University of Idaho, ID
University of Montana, MT
University of Nevada, Las Vegas, NV
The University of Tennessee at Martin, TN
The University of West Alabama, AL
University of Wyoming, WY
Washington State University, WA
West Texas A&M University, TX

Special Characteristics

Adult Students

Agnes Scott College, GA
Allegheny College, PA
Anderson University, IN
Augustana University, SD
Averett University, VA
Ball State University, IN
Barton College, NC
Bay Path University, MA
Bellarmine University, KY
Berry College, GA
Binghamton University, State University of New York, NY
Birmingham-Southern College, AL
Bluefield College, VA
Caldwell University, NJ
California Baptist University, CA
California Lutheran University, CA
California State University, Chico, CA
Campbellsville University, KY
Carroll University, WI
Carthage College, WI
Christopher Newport University, VA
Coe College, IA
College of Saint Elizabeth, NJ
College of Staten Island of the City University of New York, NY
Colorado Mesa University, CO
Columbia College, MO
Dominican University of California, CA
East Carolina University, NC
Eastern Washington University, WA
East Texas Baptist University, TX
ECPI University, VA
Edinboro University of Pennsylvania, PA
Elon University, NC
Emmanuel College, GA
Evangel University, MO
The Evergreen State College, WA
Ferris State University, MI
Florida Gulf Coast University, FL
Fordham University, NY
Fort Hays State University, KS
Fort Lewis College, CO
Franklin Pierce University, NH
Gannon University, PA
Georgia College & State University, GA
Georgian Court University, NJ
Grand Valley State University, MI
Grand View University, IA
Hampton University, VA
Hollins University, VA
Houghton College, NY
Indiana University of Pennsylvania, PA
Kean University, NJ
Kent State University, OH
Kent State University at Geauga, OH
Kent State University at Stark, OH
Kentucky State University, KY
La Sierra University, CA
Lewis-Clark State College, ID
Lipscomb University, TN
Lock Haven University of Pennsylvania, PA
Loyola Marymount University, CA
Loyola University Chicago, IL
Maryville University of Saint Louis, MO
Mercer University, GA
Messiah College, PA
Middle Tennessee State University, TN
Midway University, KY
Minnesota State University Moorhead, MN
Mississippi State University, MS
Missouri Baptist University, MO
Montana State University Billings, MT
Morehead State University, KY
Morgan State University, MD
New Mexico State University, NM
Nicholls State University, LA
North Central College, IL
Northeastern Illinois University, IL
Northern Illinois University, IL
Northern State University, SD
Northwestern State University of Louisiana, LA
Nyack College, NY
Ohio Christian University, OH
The Ohio State University, OH
Ohio Valley University, WV
Oklahoma Baptist University, OK
Oklahoma State University, OK
Otis College of Art and Design, CA
Palm Beach Atlantic University, FL
Piedmont College, GA
Portland State University, OR
Queens University of Charlotte, NC
Randolph College, VA
Rochester University, MI
Rogers State University, OK
Sacred Heart University, CT
Saginaw Valley State University, MI
St. Ambrose University, IA
St. Bonaventure University, NY
St. Catherine University, MN
St. Edward's University, TX
Saint Francis University, PA
Salem State University, MA
San Diego State University, CA
San Jose State University, CA
Simpson College, IA
Slippery Rock University of Pennsylvania, PA
Sonoma State University, CA
Southeastern Louisiana University, LA
Southwestern College, KS
State University of New York College at Geneseo, NY
State University of New York College at Potsdam, NY
Stephen F. Austin State University, TX
Stockton University, NJ
SUNY Brockport, NY
Texas A&M University–Commerce, TX
Texas Christian University, TX
Thomas More University, KY
Towson University, MD
Trinity Christian College, IL
Union College, KY
The University of Akron, OH
The University of Alabama at Birmingham, AL
University of Arkansas, AR
University of Houston, TX
University of Idaho, ID
The University of Kansas, KS
University of Kentucky, KY
University of Louisville, KY
University of Maine, ME
University of Maine at Fort Kent, ME
University of Maryland, College Park, MD
University of Mary Washington, VA

University of Massachusetts Amherst, MA
University of Massachusetts Boston, MA
University of Memphis, TN
University of Michigan–Dearborn, MI
University of Michigan–Flint, MI
University of Mississippi, MS
University of Missouri–St. Louis, MO
University of Nebraska at Omaha, NE
University of Nevada, Las Vegas, NV
University of Nevada, Reno, NV
The University of North Carolina at Charlotte, NC
The University of North Carolina at Greensboro, NC
University of Northern Colorado, CO
University of Pittsburgh, PA
University of Pittsburgh at Bradford, PA
University of St. Francis, IL
University of South Carolina, SC
University of South Carolina Aiken, SC
University of Southern Indiana, IN
The University of Tennessee at Chattanooga, TN
The University of Tennessee at Martin, TN
The University of Texas at Dallas, TX
The University of Toledo, OH
University of West Georgia, GA
University of Wisconsin–Eau Claire, WI
University of Wisconsin–Green Bay, WI
University of Wisconsin–La Crosse, WI
University of Wisconsin–Parkside, WI
University of Wisconsin–Stevens Point, WI
University of Wisconsin–Stout, WI
University of Wisconsin–Whitewater, WI
University of Wyoming, WY
Washburn University, KS
Wesleyan College, GA
Western Oregon University, OR
Westminster College, UT
Wichita State University, KS
Widener University, PA
William Jessup University, CA
Wilson College, PA
Wittenberg University, OH
Wright State University, OH
Wright State University–Lake Campus, OH
Youngstown State University, OH

Children and Siblings of Alumni

Albany College of Pharmacy and Health Sciences, NY
Albion College, MI
Allen College, IA
Alliant International University - San Diego, CA
Alma College, MI
Alverno College, WI
Anderson University, IN
Asbury University, KY
Ashland University, OH
Auburn University, AL
Augsburg University, MN
Augustana College, IL
Augustana University, SD
Aurora University, IL
Averett University, VA
Baker University, KS
Baldwin Wallace University, OH
Barton College, NC
Belhaven University, MS
Bellarmine University, KY
Belmont University, TN
Bemidji State University, MN
Benedictine University, IL
Bethany College, WV
Bethel College, KS
Binghamton University, State University of New York, NY
Birmingham-Southern College, AL
Bluffton University, OH
Boston Baptist College, MA
Boston University, MA
Bowling Green State University, OH
Bradley University, IL
Bryan College, TN
Caldwell University, NJ
California Lutheran University, CA
California Polytechnic State University, San Luis Obispo, CA
California State Polytechnic University, Pomona, CA
California State University, Monterey Bay, CA
Calumet College of Saint Joseph, IN
Calvin College, MI
Cameron University, OK
Canisius College, NY
Capital University, OH
Cardinal Stritch University, WI
Carlow University, PA
Carroll University, WI
Carson-Newman University, TN
Carthage College, WI
The Catholic University of America, DC
Cedar Crest College, PA
Centenary College of Louisiana, LA
Central College, IA
Central Methodist University, MO
Central Michigan University, MI
Central Washington University, WA
Centre College, KY
Chapman University, CA
Chatham University, PA
Christian Brothers University, TN
The Citadel, The Military College of South Carolina, SC
City College of the City University of New York, NY
Clarke University, IA
Clarkson University, NY
Coe College, IA
The College of Idaho, ID
College of Saint Benedict, MN
College of Saint Elizabeth, NJ
The College of Saint Rose, NY
The College of St. Scholastica, MN
College of Staten Island of the City University of New York, NY
Colorado Mesa University, CO
Columbia College, MO
Columbia International University, SC
Concordia University Chicago, IL
Concordia University Texas, TX
Converse College, SC
Cornell College, IA
DePauw University, IN
Dickinson College, PA
Doane University, NE
Dominican University, IL
Dominican University of California, CA
Dordt University, IA
Drake University, IA
Drexel University, PA
Drury University, MO
Duke University, NC
Duquesne University, PA
East Carolina University, NC
Eastern Kentucky University, KY
Eastern Mennonite University, VA
Eastern Michigan University, MI
Eastern New Mexico University, NM
Eastern University, PA
Eastern Washington University, WA
East Texas Baptist University, TX
ECPI University, VA
Edgewood College, WI
Elmira College, NY
Emory & Henry College, VA
Emporia State University, KS
Endicott College, MA
Evangel University, MO
Fairfield University, CT
Ferris State University, MI
Florida Institute of Technology, FL
Fordham University, NY
Fort Hays State University, KS
Fort Lewis College, CO
Franklin College, IN
Franklin Pierce University, NH
George Fox University, OR
Georgian Court University, NJ
Gonzaga University, WA
Gordon College, MA
Graceland University, IA
Grambling State University, LA
Grand Valley State University, MI
Grand View University, IA
Greenville University, IL
Gustavus Adolphus College, MN
Gwynedd Mercy University, PA
Hamline University, MN
Hanover College, IN
Hardin-Simmons University, TX
Heidelberg University, OH
Hillsdale College, MI
Hiram College, OH
Hobart and William Smith Colleges, NY
Hofstra University, NY
Hollins University, VA
Hope College, MI
Houghton College, NY
Huntington University, IN
Husson University, ME
Illinois College, IL
Illinois Institute of Technology, IL
Illinois State University, IL
Immaculata University, PA
Indiana State University, IN
Iona College, NY
Iowa Wesleyan University, IA
Ithaca College, NY
Jackson State University, MS
Jacksonville State University, AL
James Madison University, VA
Johnson University Florida, FL
Kalamazoo College, MI
Keene State College, NH
Kent State University, OH
Kent State University at Stark, OH
Keystone College, PA
The King's College, NY
King's College, PA
Kuyper College, MI
Lake Forest College, IL
Lancaster Bible College, PA
Lasell College, MA
Lawrence University, WI
Lebanon Valley College, PA
Lees-McRae College, NC
Le Moyne College, NY
Lenoir-Rhyne University, NC
Lewis-Clark State College, ID
Lewis University, IL
Life University, GA
Lincoln Memorial University, TN
Linfield College, OR
Long Island University, NY
Longwood University, VA

Loyola Marymount University, CA
Loyola University New Orleans, LA
Lynn University, FL
Lyon College, AR
Malone University, OH
Manhattanville College, NY
Mansfield University of Pennsylvania, PA
Maranatha Baptist University, WI
Marietta College, OH
Marshall University, WV
Marymount University, VA
Maryville College, TN
Maryville University of Saint Louis, MO
Mayville State University, ND
McKendree University, IL
McPherson College, KS
Methodist University, NC
Michigan State University, MI
Michigan Technological University, MI
Mid-Atlantic Christian University, NC
Middle Tennessee State University, TN
Midway University, KY
Midwestern State University, TX
Millikin University, IL
Minnesota State University Mankato, MN
Minot State University, ND
Misericordia University, PA
Mississippi State University, MS
Missouri Baptist University, MO
Missouri State University, MO
Missouri University of Science and Technology, MO
Missouri Valley College, MO
Montana State University, MT
Montana State University Billings, MT
Montana Technological University, MT
Montreat College, NC
Morehead State University, KY
Mount Saint Mary's University, CA
Muskingum University, OH
Nebraska Wesleyan University, NE
Newberry College, SC
Newman University, KS
New Mexico State University, NM
New York Institute of Technology, NY
Nichols College, MA
North Carolina Central University, NC
North Carolina State University, NC
Northeastern State University, OK
Northern Arizona University, AZ
Northern Illinois University, IL
Northern Michigan University, MI
Northwest Christian University, OR
Northwestern State University of Louisiana, LA
Northwest Missouri State University, MO
Northwest Nazarene University, ID
Nyack College, NY
The Ohio State University, OH
Ohio University, OH
Ohio University–Chillicothe, OH
Ohio University–Eastern, OH
Ohio University–Lancaster, OH
Ohio University–Southern Campus, OH
Ohio University–Zanesville, OH
Ohio Wesleyan University, OH
Oklahoma Baptist University, OK
Oklahoma State University, OK
Olivet College, MI
Oral Roberts University, OK
Oregon State University, OR
Otterbein University, OH
Ouachita Baptist University, AR
Pacific Lutheran University, WA
Pacific University, OR
Palm Beach Atlantic University, FL
Penn State Abington, PA
Penn State Altoona, PA
Penn State Beaver, PA
Penn State Berks, PA
Penn State Brandywine, PA
Penn State Erie, The Behrend College, PA
Penn State Harrisburg, PA
Penn State Hazleton, PA
Penn State New Kensington, PA
Penn State Shenango, PA
Penn State York, PA
Pine Manor College, MA
Pittsburg State University, KS
Principia College, IL
Purdue University Fort Wayne, IN
Queens University of Charlotte, NC
Randolph-Macon College, VA
Regent University, VA
Rensselaer Polytechnic Institute, NY
Rhode Island College, RI
Rochester University, MI
Rockford University, IL
Sacred Heart University, CT
St. Ambrose University, IA
Saint Anselm College, NH
St. Catherine University, MN
Saint Francis University, PA
St. John Fisher College, NY
St. John's University, NY
St. Joseph's College, Long Island Campus, NY
St. Joseph's College, New York, NY
Saint Joseph's University, PA
St. Lawrence University, NY
Saint Martin's University, WA
Salem State University, MA
Salve Regina University, RI
Samford University, AL
San Diego State University, CA
San Francisco Art Institute, CA
Santa Clara University, CA
Seattle Pacific University, WA
Seattle University, WA
Shippensburg University of Pennsylvania, PA
Simmons University, MA
Simpson College, IA
Slippery Rock University of Pennsylvania, PA
Sonoma State University, CA
Southeastern Louisiana University, LA
Southern Illinois University Carbondale, IL
Southern New Hampshire University, NH
Southern Utah University, UT
Southwestern Oklahoma State University, OK
Springfield College, MA
State University of New York at Fredonia, NY
State University of New York College at Potsdam, NY
State University of New York College of Agriculture & Technology at Morrisville, NY
State University of New York College of Environmental Science and Forestry, NY
Stephen F. Austin State University, TX
Sterling College, KS
Stetson University, FL
Suffolk University, MA
Sul Ross State University, TX
SUNY Brockport, NY
Susquehanna University, PA
Tabor College, KS
Taylor University, IN
Tennessee Wesleyan University, TN
Texas A&M University–Commerce, TX
Texas Lutheran University, TX
Thomas College, ME
Thomas More University, KY
Towson University, MD
Trine University, IN
Trinity Christian College, IL
Trinity University, TX
Truman State University, MO
Union College, KY
Union University, TN
The University of Alabama, AL
The University of Alabama at Birmingham, AL
University of Alaska Anchorage, AK
University of Arkansas, AR
University of Dayton, OH
University of Dubuque, IA
University of Evansville, IN
University of Guam, GU
University of Houston, TX
University of Idaho, ID
The University of Iowa, IA
University of Jamestown, ND
The University of Kansas, KS
University of Kentucky, KY
University of Louisville, KY
University of Maine, ME
University of Mary Hardin-Baylor, TX
University of Mary Washington, VA
University of Massachusetts Amherst, MA
University of Massachusetts Lowell, MA
University of Michigan–Dearborn, MI
University of Michigan–Flint, MI
University of Minnesota, Crookston, MN
University of Mississippi, MS
University of Missouri–St. Louis, MO
University of Montana, MT
University of Mount Union, OH
University of Nebraska at Kearney, NE
University of Nebraska at Omaha, NE
University of Nebraska–Lincoln, NE
University of Nevada, Las Vegas, NV
University of Nevada, Reno, NV
University of New Hampshire, NH
University of New Mexico, NM
University of North Alabama, AL
The University of North Carolina at Greensboro, NC
The University of North Carolina at Pembroke, NC
University of Northern Colorado, CO
University of Northwestern–St. Paul, MN
University of Oklahoma, OK
University of Pittsburgh, PA
University of Providence, MT
University of Rhode Island, RI
University of Rochester, NY
University of St. Francis, IL
University of Saint Mary, KS
University of South Carolina, SC
University of South Carolina Aiken, SC
University of Southern California, CA
University of Southern Mississippi, MS
The University of Tampa, FL
The University of Tennessee at Chattanooga, TN
The University of Tennessee at Martin, TN
University of the Incarnate Word, TX
The University of Toledo, OH
The University of Tulsa, OK
The University of West Alabama, AL
University of West Georgia, GA

University of Wisconsin–La Crosse, WI
University of Wisconsin–Whitewater, WI
University of Wyoming, WY
Upper Iowa University, IA
Ursuline College, OH
Utah State University, UT
Valley City State University, ND
Valparaiso University, IN
Wake Forest University, NC
Walsh University, OH
Wartburg College, IA
Washburn University, KS
Washington & Jefferson College, PA
Washington State University, WA
Webber International University, FL
Wesleyan College, GA
Western Colorado University, CO
Western Michigan University, MI
Western New Mexico University, NM
Westminster College, PA
Westminster College, UT
West Texas A&M University, TX
Wheaton College, IL
Whittier College, CA
Whitworth University, WA
Wichita State University, KS
William Jessup University, CA
Wilson College, PA
Wingate University, NC
Winona State University, MN
Wittenberg University, OH
Wofford College, SC
Wright State University, OH
Wright State University–Lake Campus, OH
Xavier University, OH
York College of Pennsylvania, PA
Youngstown State University, OH

Children of Current Students
Augustana University, SD
Aurora University, IL
Bethel College, KS
Bryan College, TN
Caldwell University, NJ
California State Polytechnic University, Pomona, CA
Cardinal Stritch University, WI
Carroll University, WI
Central College, IA
Columbia College, MO
ECPI University, VA
Emmanuel College, GA
Franklin College, IN
Franklin Pierce University, NH
Indiana Tech, IN
Johnson University, TN
Lancaster Bible College, PA
Long Island University, NY
Misericordia University, PA
Missouri Baptist University, MO
Mount Aloysius College, PA
Mount Marty College, SD
Newman University, KS
New Mexico State University, NM
Northwest University, WA
Palm Beach Atlantic University, FL
Queens University of Charlotte, NC
Rockford University, IL
Sacred Heart University, CT
St. Catherine University, MN
Saint Francis University, PA
Springfield College, MA
Thomas College, ME
Thomas More University, KY
Truett McConnell University, GA
Union College, KY
Union University, TN
The University of Alabama at Birmingham, AL
University of Alaska Anchorage, AK
University of Providence, MT
Wayne State University, MI
Wesleyan College, GA
Wilson College, PA

Children of Educators
Agnes Scott College, GA
Alfred University, NY
Allegheny College, PA
Austin Peay State University, TN
Baldwin Wallace University, OH
Bridgewater College, VA
Bryan College, TN
Caldwell University, NJ
Campbellsville University, KY
Canisius College, NY
Carlow University, PA
Carthage College, WI
Catawba College, NC
Chowan University, NC
Coe College, IA
The College of Idaho, ID
The College of Wooster, OH
Columbia College, MO
Emmanuel College, GA
Emory & Henry College, VA
Endicott College, MA
Evangel University, MO
Franklin Pierce University, NH
Goshen College, IN
Grand View University, IA
Hardin-Simmons University, TX
Hillsdale College, MI
Jacksonville University, FL
Johnson University, TN
King's College, PA
Lipscomb University, TN
Lynn University, FL
Maranatha Baptist University, WI
McDaniel College, MD
MidAmerica Nazarene University, KS
Mississippi State University, MS
Nebraska Wesleyan University, NE
New York Institute of Technology, NY
Northwest University, WA
Nyack College, NY
Occidental College, CA
Oklahoma State University, OK
Palm Beach Atlantic University, FL
Rockford University, IL
St. Ambrose University, IA
Saint Anselm College, NH
St. Catherine University, MN
Saint Francis University, PA
Seattle University, WA
Simpson College, IA
Sonoma State University, CA
Southeastern University, FL
Southern Illinois University Carbondale, IL
Southern New Hampshire University, NH
Tarleton State University, TX
Texas Christian University, TX
Texas Lutheran University, TX
Trinity University, TX
Union University, TN
The University of Alabama at Birmingham, AL
University of Alaska Anchorage, AK
University of Chicago, IL
University of Dubuque, IA
University of Kentucky, KY
University of Memphis, TN
University of Pittsburgh, PA
University of St. Francis, IL
The University of Scranton, PA
The University of Tennessee at Martin, TN
Villanova University, PA
Wesleyan College, GA
Wright State University, OH
Wright State University–Lake Campus, OH

Children of Faculty/Staff
Abilene Christian University, TX
Agnes Scott College, GA
Alaska Bible College, AK
Albany College of Pharmacy and Health Sciences, NY
Alcorn State University, MS
Alfred University, NY
Allegheny College, PA
Alliant International University - San Diego, CA
Alverno College, WI
Anderson University, IN
Anderson University, SC
Andrews University, MI
Angelo State University, TX
Aquinas College, MI
Arizona State University at the Downtown Phoenix campus, AZ
Arizona State University at the Polytechnic campus, AZ
Arizona State University at the Tempe campus, AZ
Arizona State University at the West campus, AZ
Arkansas Tech University, AR
Asbury University, KY
Ashland University, OH
Auburn University, AL
Augustana College, IL
Augustana University, SD
Aurora University, IL
Austin College, TX
Austin Peay State University, TN
Ave Maria University, FL
Baker University, KS
Baldwin Wallace University, OH
Ball State University, IN
Barton College, NC
Baylor University, TX
Bay Path University, MA
Becker College, MA
Belhaven University, MS
Bellarmine University, KY
Belmont Abbey College, NC
Belmont University, TN
Benedictine University, IL
Berry College, GA
Bethany College, WV
Bethany Lutheran College, MN
Bethel College, KS
Bethel University, IN
Binghamton University, State University of New York, NY
Biola University, CA
Birmingham-Southern College, AL
Bloomsburg University of Pennsylvania, PA
Bluffton University, OH
Boise Bible College, ID
Boston Baptist College, MA
Boston College, MA
Boston University, MA
Bowdoin College, ME
Bowling Green State University, OH
Bradley University, IL
Bridgewater College, VA
Bryan College, TN

Buena Vista University, IA
Caldwell University, NJ
California Baptist University, CA
California Lutheran University, CA
California State University, Bakersfield, CA
California State University, Chico, CA
California State University, Stanislaus, CA
Calumet College of Saint Joseph, IN
Calvin College, MI
Cameron University, OK
Campbellsville University, KY
Canisius College, NY
Capital University, OH
Cardinal Stritch University, WI
Carlow University, PA
Carnegie Mellon University, PA
Carroll College, MT
Carroll University, WI
Carthage College, WI
Case Western Reserve University, OH
Catawba College, NC
The Catholic University of America, DC
Cedarville University, OH
Centenary College of Louisiana, LA
Central College, IA
Central Methodist University, MO
Central Michigan University, MI
Central Washington University, WA
Centre College, KY
Chaminade University of Honolulu, HI
Chatham University, PA
Chowan University, NC
Clarion University of Pennsylvania, PA
Clarke University, IA
Clarkson University, NY
Clemson University, SC
Cleveland Institute of Music, OH
Cleveland State University, OH
Coastal Carolina University, SC
Coe College, IA
Colby-Sawyer College, NH
The College of Idaho, ID
College of Saint Mary, NE
The College of Saint Rose, NY
The College of St. Scholastica, MN
College of the Holy Cross, MA
The College of Wooster, OH
The Colorado College, CO
Colorado State University, CO
Columbia College, MO
Columbia College, SC
Columbia College Chicago, IL
Columbia International University, SC
Concordia University Chicago, IL
Concordia University, St. Paul, MN
Concordia University Texas, TX
Concord University, WV
Converse College, SC
Cornell College, IA
Cornerstone University, MI
Covenant College, GA
Dallas Baptist University, TX
DePaul University, IL
DePauw University, IN
Dickinson College, PA
Dillard University, LA
Doane University, NE
Dominican College, NY
Dominican University, IL
Dominican University of California, CA
Dordt University, IA
Drury University, MO
Duquesne University, PA
East Carolina University, NC
East Central University, OK
Eastern Kentucky University, KY
Eastern Mennonite University, VA
Eastern University, PA
East Texas Baptist University, TX
Eckerd College, FL
ECPI University, VA
Edgewood College, WI
Edinboro University of Pennsylvania, PA
Elizabethtown College, PA
Elmira College, NY
Elms College, MA
Elon University, NC
Emmanuel College, GA
Emmanuel College, MA
Emory & Henry College, VA
Emory University, GA
Emporia State University, KS
Evangel University, MO
Fairfield University, CT
Felician University, NJ
Florida Institute of Technology, FL
Florida National University, FL
Fordham University, NY
Fort Hays State University, KS
Fort Lewis College, CO
Framingham State University, MA
Franklin College, IN
Franklin Pierce University, NH
George Fox University, OR
Georgetown University, DC
Georgia College & State University, GA
Georgian Court University, NJ
Glenville State College, WV
Gonzaga University, WA
Gordon College, MA
Goshen College, IN
Governors State University, IL
Graceland University, IA
Grambling State University, LA
Grand Valley State University, MI
Grand View University, IA
Greenville University, IL
Gwynedd Mercy University, PA
Hamline University, MN
Hampden-Sydney College, VA
Hampshire College, MA
Hampton University, VA
Hanover College, IN
Hardin-Simmons University, TX
Heidelberg University, OH
Hendrix College, AR
High Point University, NC
Hillsdale College, MI
Hiram College, OH
Hofstra University, NY
Hollins University, VA
Hope International University, CA
Houghton College, NY
Houston Baptist University, TX
Huntington University, IN
Husson University, ME
Idaho State University, ID
Illinois College, IL
Illinois Institute of Technology, IL
Illinois State University, IL
Illinois Wesleyan University, IL
Indiana State University, IN
Indiana Tech, IN
Indiana University of Pennsylvania, PA
Inter American University of Puerto Rico, Aguadilla Campus, PR
Iowa Wesleyan University, IA
Ithaca College, NY
Jackson State University, MS
Jacksonville University, FL
James Madison University, VA
John Carroll University, OH
Johns Hopkins University, MD
Johnson University, TN
Johnson University Florida, FL
The Juilliard School, NY
Kent State University, OH
Kent State University at Geauga, OH
Kent State University at Stark, OH
Kentucky Mountain Bible College, KY
Kentucky State University, KY
Kettering University, MI
King's College, PA
King University, TN
Kutztown University of Pennsylvania, PA
Kuyper College, MI
LaGrange College, GA
Lake Erie College, OH
Lancaster Bible College, PA
Lasell College, MA
La Sierra University, CA
Lebanon Valley College, PA
Lees-McRae College, NC
Lee University, TN
Lehigh University, PA
Lenoir-Rhyne University, NC
Lewis & Clark College, OR
Lewis-Clark State College, ID
Lewis University, IL
Liberty University, VA
Life University, GA
Limestone College, SC
Lincoln College, IL
Lincoln Memorial University, TN
Lincoln University, PA
Linfield College, OR
Lipscomb University, TN
Long Island University, NY
Louisiana College, LA
Loyola Marymount University, CA
Loyola University Maryland, MD
Loyola University New Orleans, LA
Lycoming College, PA
Lynn University, FL
Lyon College, AR
Malone University, OH
Manhattan College, NY
Manhattanville College, NY
Maranatha Baptist University, WI
Marquette University, WI
Marshall University, WV
Maryville College, TN
Massachusetts College of Art and Design, MA
Mayville State University, ND
McKendree University, IL
McPherson College, KS
Mercer University, GA
Mercy College, NY
Merrimack College, MA
Messiah College, PA
Methodist University, NC
Miami University, OH
Michigan State University, MI
Michigan Technological University, MI
MidAmerica Nazarene University, KS
Mid-Atlantic Christian University, NC
Midway University, KY
Midwestern State University, TX
Milligan University, TN
Millikin University, IL
Milwaukee Institute of Art and Design, WI
Milwaukee School of Engineering, WI
Minnesota State University Moorhead, MN
Minot State University, ND

Misericordia University, PA
Mississippi State University, MS
Missouri Baptist University, MO
Missouri University of Science and Technology, MO
Missouri Valley College, MO
Montana State University Billings, MT
Montana Technological University, MT
Montreat College, NC
Morgan State University, MD
Mount Carmel College of Nursing, OH
Mount Marty College, SD
Mount Saint Mary College, NY
Mount St. Mary's University, MD
Mount Vernon Nazarene University, OH
Nazareth College of Rochester, NY
Nebraska Methodist College, NE
Nebraska Wesleyan University, NE
Neumont College of Computer Science, UT
Newberry College, SC
Newman University, KS
New Mexico State University, NM
New York Institute of Technology, NY
Niagara University, NY
Nicholls State University, LA
Nichols College, MA
North Carolina State University, NC
North Central College, IL
North Central University, MN
North Dakota State University, ND
Northeastern Illinois University, IL
Northeastern State University, OK
Northern Illinois University, IL
Northern Michigan University, MI
North Greenville University, SC
Northwest Christian University, OR
Northwestern State University of Louisiana, LA
Northwest Missouri State University, MO
Northwest Nazarene University, ID
Northwest University, WA
Nyack College, NY
Occidental College, CA
Oglethorpe University, GA
Ohio Christian University, OH
The Ohio State University, OH
Ohio University, OH
Ohio University–Chillicothe, OH
Ohio University–Eastern, OH
Ohio University–Lancaster, OH
Ohio University–Southern Campus, OH
Ohio University–Zanesville, OH
Ohio Valley University, WV
Oklahoma Baptist University, OK
Oklahoma City University, OK
Oklahoma State University, OK
Old Dominion University, VA
Olivet College, MI
Olivet Nazarene University, IL
Oral Roberts University, OK
Otterbein University, OH
Ouachita Baptist University, AR
Pacific Lutheran University, WA
Pacific University, OR
Palm Beach Atlantic University, FL
Patrick Henry College, VA
Piedmont College, GA
Pine Manor College, MA
Plymouth State University, NH
Presbyterian College, SC
Principia College, IL
Purdue University, IN
Purdue University Northwest, IN
Queens University of Charlotte, NC
Ramapo College of New Jersey, NJ
Randolph College, VA
Randolph-Macon College, VA
Regent University, VA
Rensselaer Polytechnic Institute, NY
Rhodes College, TN
Rochester University, MI
Rockford University, IL
Rocky Mountain College, MT
Sacred Heart University, CT
St. Ambrose University, IA
Saint Anselm College, NH
St. Bonaventure University, NY
St. Catherine University, MN
St. Cloud State University, MN
St. Edward's University, TX
Saint Francis University, PA
St. John Fisher College, NY
St. John's College, NM
St. John's University, NY
St. Joseph's College, Long Island Campus, NY
St. Joseph's College, New York, NY
Saint Joseph's University, PA
St. Louis College of Pharmacy, MO
Saint Louis University, MO
Saint Martin's University, WA
Saint Mary's College, IN
Saint Mary's College of California, CA
St. Mary's College of Maryland, MD
St. Mary's University, TX
St. Norbert College, WI
Saint Peter's University, NJ
Saint Vincent College, PA
Salem College, NC
Salem State University, MA
Samford University, AL
San Diego State University, CA
San Jose State University, CA
Santa Clara University, CA
Schreiner University, TX
Seattle Pacific University, WA
Seattle University, WA
Shenandoah University, VA
Shepherd University, WV
Simpson College, IA
Skidmore College, NY
Slippery Rock University of Pennsylvania, PA
Sonoma State University, CA
Southeastern Louisiana University, LA
Southeastern University, FL
Southeast Missouri State University, MO
Southern Connecticut State University, CT
Southern Illinois University Carbondale, IL
Southern Illinois University Edwardsville, IL
Southwestern College, KS
Southwestern Oklahoma State University, OK
Southwestern University, TX
Springfield College, MA
Spring Hill College, AL
State University of New York at New Paltz, NY
State University of New York College of Agriculture & Technology at Morrisville, NY
Stephen F. Austin State University, TX
Stephens College, MO
Sterling College, KS
Stetson University, FL
Stockton University, NJ
Stonehill College, MA
Suffolk University, MA
SUNY Brockport, NY
Susquehanna University, PA
Tabor College, KS
Talladega College, AL
Tarleton State University, TX
Taylor University, IN
Temple University, PA
Tennessee Wesleyan University, TN
Texas A&M University, TX
Texas Christian University, TX
Texas Lutheran University, TX
Texas Tech University, TX
Texas Woman's University, TX
Thomas College, ME
Thomas More University, KY
Tiffin University, OH
Toccoa Falls College, GA
Transylvania University, KY
Trevecca Nazarene University, TN
Trine University, IN
Trinity Christian College, IL
Trinity College of Florida, FL
Truett McConnell University, GA
Truman State University, MO
Tulane University, LA
Tuskegee University, AL
Union College, KY
Union College, NY
Union University, TN
The University of Alabama at Birmingham, AL
University of Alaska Anchorage, AK
University of Arkansas, AR
University of Colorado Denver, CO
University of Dallas, TX
University of Dayton, OH
University of Dubuque, IA
University of Evansville, IN
The University of Findlay, OH
University of Florida, FL
University of Guam, GU
University of Idaho, ID
University of Illinois at Urbana-Champaign, IL
University of Indianapolis, IN
University of Jamestown, ND
The University of Kansas, KS
University of Kentucky, KY
University of Louisiana at Monroe, LA
University of Louisville, KY
University of Maine, ME
University of Maine at Farmington, ME
University of Maine at Fort Kent, ME
University of Maine at Presque Isle, ME
University of Mary Hardin-Baylor, TX
University of Mary Washington, VA
University of Massachusetts Amherst, MA
University of Massachusetts Boston, MA
University of Massachusetts Lowell, MA
University of Memphis, TN
University of Miami, FL
University of Michigan, MI
University of Michigan–Dearborn, MI
University of Michigan–Flint, MI
University of Minnesota, Crookston, MN
University of Mississippi, MS
University of Missouri–St. Louis, MO
University of Mobile, AL
University of Montevallo, AL
University of Mount Union, OH
University of Nebraska at Kearney, NE
University of Nebraska at Omaha, NE
University of Nevada, Las Vegas, NV
University of New Hampshire, NH
University of New Hampshire at Manchester, NH
University of New Mexico, NM
The University of North Carolina at Chapel Hill, NC

The University of North Carolina at Greensboro, NC
University of North Dakota, ND
University of Northern Colorado, CO
University of Northwestern–St. Paul, MN
University of Notre Dame, IN
University of Oklahoma, OK
University of Oregon, OR
University of Pittsburgh, PA
University of Pittsburgh at Bradford, PA
University of Pittsburgh at Johnstown, PA
University of Portland, OR
University of Providence, MT
University of Puget Sound, WA
University of Rochester, NY
University of St. Francis, IL
University of Saint Francis, IN
University of Saint Mary, KS
University of St. Thomas, TX
University of San Diego, CA
University of Science and Arts of Oklahoma, OK
The University of Scranton, PA
University of South Carolina, SC
University of South Carolina Aiken, SC
University of Southern California, CA
University of Southern Indiana, IN
University of Southern Mississippi, MS
The University of Tampa, FL
The University of Tennessee at Chattanooga, TN
The University of Tennessee at Martin, TN
The University of Texas at Austin, TX
The University of Texas at Tyler, TX
University of the Incarnate Word, TX
The University of Toledo, OH
The University of Tulsa, OK
University of Utah, UT
University of Virginia, VA
The University of West Alabama, AL
Ursuline College, OH
Utah State University, UT
Valley City State University, ND
Valparaiso University, IN
Vanguard University of Southern California, CA
Villanova University, PA
Virginia Wesleyan University, VA
Wabash College, IN
Wagner College, NY
Walla Walla University, WA
Walsh University, OH
Wartburg College, IA
Washburn University, KS
Washington & Jefferson College, PA
Washington College, MD
Washington State University, WA
Wayland Baptist University, TX
Wayne State College, NE
Wayne State University, MI
Webber International University, FL
Wesleyan College, GA
West Chester University of Pennsylvania, PA
Western Illinois University, IL
Western Michigan University, MI
Western New England University, MA
Western New Mexico University, NM
Westmont College, CA
West Texas A&M University, TX
Whittier College, CA
Wichita State University, KS
Widener University, PA
Wilkes University, PA
William Jessup University, CA
William Paterson University of New Jersey, NJ
William Peace University, NC
Wilson College, PA
Winona State University, MN
Wittenberg University, OH
Wofford College, SC
Wright State University, OH
Wright State University–Lake Campus, OH
Xavier University of Louisiana, LA
Youngstown State University, OH

Children of Public Servants

California State University, San Bernardino, CA
Capital University, OH
Carthage College, WI
Central Washington University, WA
Chowan University, NC
Christian Brothers University, TN
Framingham State University, MA
Grambling State University, LA
Illinois Institute of Technology, IL
Mississippi State University, MS
New Mexico State University, NM
New York Institute of Technology, NY
Northwestern State University of Louisiana, LA
The Ohio State University, OH
Patrick Henry College, VA
Regent University, VA
St. John's University, NY
Salem State University, MA
Sonoma State University, CA
Southern Illinois University Carbondale, IL
The University of Alabama at Birmingham, AL
University of Chicago, IL
University of Kentucky, KY
University of Massachusetts Amherst, MA
University of Massachusetts Lowell, MA
University of Memphis, TN
University of Nevada, Las Vegas, NV
The University of North Carolina at Charlotte, NC
University of Rhode Island, RI
The University of Tennessee at Martin, TN
The University of Texas at Austin, TX
The University of Texas at Dallas, TX
The University of Toledo, OH
University of Utah, UT
University of Wisconsin–Green Bay, WI
University of Wyoming, WY
Washington State University, WA
Western Washington University, WA
Wheaton College, IL

Children of Union Members/Company Employees

Auburn University, AL
Averett University, VA
California State University, Bakersfield, CA
Carroll College, MT
Chowan University, NC
Clarion University of Pennsylvania, PA
The College of Saint Rose, NY
Columbia College, MO
Eastern Washington University, WA
Emporia State University, KS
Framingham State University, MA
Grand Valley State University, MI
Hamline University, MN
Hofstra University, NY
Husson University, ME
Illinois State University, IL
Kent State University, OH
Kutztown University of Pennsylvania, PA
Massachusetts College of Art and Design, MA
Michigan State University, MI
Midwestern State University, TX
Millersville University of Pennsylvania, PA
Millikin University, IL
Missouri University of Science and Technology, MO
Montana State University Billings, MT
New Mexico State University, NM
Northeastern Illinois University, IL
Northern Michigan University, MI
The Ohio State University, OH
Sacred Heart University, CT
St. Cloud State University, MN
St. Mary's College of Maryland, MD
Salem State University, MA
Sam Houston State University, TX
Slippery Rock University of Pennsylvania, PA
Sonoma State University, CA
Stephen F. Austin State University, TX
Stephens College, MO
Stockton University, NJ
Stonehill College, MA
Texas Christian University, TX
Thomas More University, KY
The University of Alabama, AL
The University of Alabama at Birmingham, AL
University of Arkansas, AR
University of Guam, GU
University of Houston, TX
University of Kentucky, KY
University of Louisville, KY
University of Maine, ME
University of Massachusetts Boston, MA
University of Massachusetts Lowell, MA
University of Michigan–Flint, MI
University of Nevada, Las Vegas, NV
University of New Mexico, NM
The University of North Carolina at Charlotte, NC
University of Northern Colorado, CO
University of Pittsburgh, PA
University of Pittsburgh at Bradford, PA
University of Rhode Island, RI
University of South Carolina, SC
University of South Carolina Aiken, SC
The University of Tennessee at Chattanooga, TN
The University of Tennessee at Martin, TN
The University of Toledo, OH
University of Wisconsin–La Crosse, WI
University of Wisconsin–Parkside, WI
Western Oregon University, OR
Western Washington University, WA
West Texas A&M University, TX
York College of Pennsylvania, PA
Youngstown State University, OH

Children of Workers in Trades

Grand Valley State University, MI
Midwestern State University, TX
New Mexico State University, NM
The Ohio State University, OH
San Diego State University, CA
Sonoma State University, CA
Texas Christian University, TX
The University of Alabama at Birmingham, AL
University of Arkansas, AR
University of Maine, ME
University of Michigan, MI
University of Northern Colorado, CO

University of Pittsburgh, PA
University of South Carolina, SC
University of Wisconsin–Parkside, WI
West Texas A&M University, TX
Worcester Polytechnic Institute, MA
Youngstown State University, OH

Children with a Deceased or Disabled Parent

Bay Path University, MA
Binghamton University, State University of New York, NY
California State University, San Bernardino, CA
The Citadel, The Military College of South Carolina, SC
Clarion University of Pennsylvania, PA
The College of New Jersey, NJ
Fairfield University, CT
Fordham University, NY
Georgia Institute of Technology, GA
Idaho State University, ID
Illinois State University, IL
Kentucky State University, KY
Lees-McRae College, NC
Lipscomb University, TN
Louisiana State University and Agricultural & Mechanical College, LA
Midwestern State University, TX
Millikin University, IL
New Mexico State University, NM
Northeastern State University, OK
Northern Illinois University, IL
San Jose State University, CA
Santa Clara University, CA
Southern Illinois University Carbondale, IL
Stockton University, NJ
The University of Alabama, AL
The University of Alabama at Birmingham, AL
University of Arkansas, AR
University of Kentucky, KY
University of Louisiana at Monroe, LA
University of Louisville, KY
University of Missouri–St. Louis, MO
University of Montana, MT
University of Nevada, Las Vegas, NV
University of Northern Colorado, CO
University of South Carolina, SC
The University of Tennessee at Chattanooga, TN
The University of Texas at Austin, TX
University of Utah, UT
Washington State University, WA
Wayne State University, MI
Westminster College, UT
Youngstown State University, OH

Ethnic Background

Abilene Christian University, TX
Alverno College, WI
American University, DC
Anderson University, IN
Asbury University, KY
Ashland University, OH
Auburn University, AL
Augustana College, IL
Augustana University, SD
Austin Peay State University, TN
Baker University, KS
Baldwin Wallace University, OH
Ball State University, IN
Bellarmine University, KY
Berry College, GA
Bethel College, KS
Binghamton University, State University of New York, NY
Biola University, CA
Birmingham-Southern College, AL
Boise State University, ID
Buena Vista University, IA
California State University, Bakersfield, CA
California State University, Chico, CA
California University of Pennsylvania, PA
Calvin College, MI
Cameron University, OK
Capital University, OH
Cedarville University, OH
Central Michigan University, MI
Centre College, KY
Chaminade University of Honolulu, HI
Christian Brothers University, TN
The Citadel, The Military College of South Carolina, SC
Clemson University, SC
Coe College, IA
The College of Saint Rose, NY
College of Staten Island of the City University of New York, NY
Colorado Mesa University, CO
Columbia College, MO
Columbia International University, SC
Cornerstone University, MI
Delaware Valley University, PA
DeSales University, PA
Drury University, MO
Duke University, NC
Duquesne University, PA
East Carolina University, NC
Eastern Mennonite University, VA
Eastern Michigan University, MI
Eastern New Mexico University, NM
Eastern Oregon University, OR
Eastern Washington University, WA
Elon University, NC
The Evergreen State College, WA
Fairfield University, CT
Ferris State University, MI
Florida Agricultural and Mechanical University, FL
Florida Gulf Coast University, FL
Fort Lewis College, CO
Franklin College, IN
Gannon University, PA
George Fox University, OR
Georgian Court University, NJ
Goshen College, IN
Grambling State University, LA
Grand View University, IA
Grove City College, PA
Gustavus Adolphus College, MN
Hardin-Simmons University, TX
Hope College, MI
Huntington University, IN
Husson University, ME
Idaho State University, ID
Indiana University of Pennsylvania, PA
Johnson University, TN
Kennesaw State University, GA
Kent State University, OH
Kent State University at Stark, OH
Kentucky State University, KY
LaGrange College, GA
Lenoir-Rhyne University, NC
Lesley University, MA
Lewis-Clark State College, ID
Lock Haven University of Pennsylvania, PA
Loyola Marymount University, CA
Lyon College, AR
Macalester College, MN
Maryville University of Saint Louis, MO
Massachusetts Maritime Academy, MA
Medical University of South Carolina, SC
Middle Tennessee State University, TN
Milwaukee Institute of Art and Design, WI
Minot State University, ND
Molloy College, NY
Montana State University Billings, MT
Morehead State University, KY
Muskingum University, OH
Nazareth College of Rochester, NY
Nebraska Wesleyan University, NE
New Jersey Institute of Technology, NJ
New Mexico State University, NM
Nicholls State University, LA
North Dakota State University, ND
Northern Illinois University, IL
Northern State University, SD
The Ohio State University, OH
Ohio Valley University, WV
Oklahoma State University, OK
Otis College of Art and Design, CA
Pacific Lutheran University, WA
Pacific University, OR
Portland State University, OR
Randolph-Macon College, VA
Rensselaer Polytechnic Institute, NY
Sacred Heart University, CT
St. Catherine University, MN
St. John Fisher College, NY
Saint Martin's University, WA
Samford University, AL
Sam Houston State University, TX
San Jose State University, CA
Seattle Pacific University, WA
Simpson College, IA
Slippery Rock University of Pennsylvania, PA
Sonoma State University, CA
Southwestern University, TX
State University of New York at Fredonia, NY
State University of New York at New Paltz, NY
State University of New York College at Geneseo, NY
State University of New York College at Potsdam, NY
Stetson University, FL
Stockton University, NJ
Stony Brook University, State University of New York, NY
SUNY Brockport, NY
Taylor University, IN
Texas Christian University, TX
Texas Woman's University, TX
Toccoa Falls College, GA
Towson University, MD
Transylvania University, KY
Trinity Christian College, IL
Truett McConnell University, GA
Truman State University, MO
Union University, TN
The University of Alabama, AL
The University of Alabama at Birmingham, AL
University of Arkansas, AR
University of California, San Diego, CA
University of Colorado Denver, CO
University of Idaho, ID
The University of Iowa, IA
The University of Kansas, KS
University of Kentucky, KY
University of Louisville, KY
University of Maine, ME
University of Maine at Fort Kent, ME
University of Maine at Presque Isle, ME
University of Mary Hardin-Baylor, TX
University of Massachusetts Dartmouth, MA
University of Michigan–Dearborn, MI

University of Minnesota, Crookston, MN
University of Missouri–St. Louis, MO
University of Mount Union, OH
University of Nebraska at Kearney, NE
University of Nebraska at Omaha, NE
University of Nebraska–Lincoln, NE
University of Nevada, Las Vegas, NV
University of Nevada, Reno, NV
University of North Dakota, ND
University of Northern Colorado, CO
University of Northwestern–St. Paul, MN
University of Pittsburgh, PA
University of Providence, MT
University of St. Francis, IL
The University of Scranton, PA
University of South Carolina, SC
University of South Carolina Aiken, SC
University of Southern Mississippi, MS
The University of Tennessee at Chattanooga, TN
The University of Tennessee at Martin, TN
The University of Texas at El Paso, TX
The University of Texas at San Antonio, TX
The University of Toledo, OH
University of Utah, UT
University of Virginia, VA
University of Wisconsin–Eau Claire, WI
University of Wisconsin–Green Bay, WI
University of Wisconsin–La Crosse, WI
University of Wisconsin–Parkside, WI
University of Wisconsin–Stevens Point, WI
University of Wisconsin–Whitewater, WI
University of Wyoming, WY
Valley City State University, ND
VanderCook College of Music, IL
Walsh College of Accountancy and Business Administration, MI
Washburn University, KS
Wayne State College, NE
Wayne State University, MI
Wesleyan College, GA
Western Carolina University, NC
Western Kentucky University, KY
Western Oregon University, OR
Western Washington University, WA
Westminster College, UT
Westmont College, CA
Whitworth University, WA
Wichita State University, KS
Widener University, PA
William Jessup University, CA
Wittenberg University, OH
Wright State University, OH
Wright State University–Lake Campus, OH
Youngstown State University, OH

First-Generation College Students
Abilene Christian University, TX
Augustana College, IL
Austin College, TX
Averett University, VA
Berry College, GA
Binghamton University, State University of New York, NY
Birmingham-Southern College, AL
Boise State University, ID
Bowie State University, MD
California State Polytechnic University, Pomona, CA
California State University, Bakersfield, CA
California State University, Chico, CA
California State University, San Bernardino, CA
California State University, Stanislaus, CA
Calvin College, MI
Carthage College, WI
The Catholic University of America, DC
Centenary College of Louisiana, LA
Centre College, KY
Champlain College, VT
Chowan University, NC
Christopher Newport University, VA
Clarion University of Pennsylvania, PA
The College of Idaho, ID
College of Saint Elizabeth, NJ
Colorado Mesa University, CO
Colorado State University, CO
Columbia College, MO
Duke University, NC
Eastern New Mexico University, NM
Eastern Washington University, WA
Edinboro University of Pennsylvania, PA
Elon University, NC
Emmanuel College, GA
Emporia State University, KS
The Evergreen State College, WA
Fairfield University, CT
Florida Agricultural and Mechanical University, FL
Florida International University, FL
Fort Hays State University, KS
Fort Lewis College, CO
Franklin College, IN
Georgian Court University, NJ
Glenville State College, WV
Graceland University, IA
Grand View University, IA
Grove City College, PA
Gustavus Adolphus College, MN
Hamline University, MN
High Point University, NC
Hillsdale College, MI
Houghton College, NY
Idaho State University, ID
Illinois State University, IL
Indiana University of Pennsylvania, PA
Kean University, NJ
Kent State University, OH
Kent State University at Stark, OH
Kutztown University of Pennsylvania, PA
LaGrange College, GA
Lewis & Clark College, OR
Lewis-Clark State College, ID
Linfield College, OR
Loras College, IA
Loyola Marymount University, CA
Lyon College, AR
Maryville University of Saint Louis, MO
Michigan State University, MI
Middle Tennessee State University, TN
Midwestern State University, TX
Minnesota State University Moorhead, MN
Mississippi State University, MS
Missouri Baptist University, MO
Montana State University Billings, MT
Montana Technological University, MT
Montreat College, NC
Morgan State University, MD
New Jersey Institute of Technology, NJ
Nicholls State University, LA
Northern Illinois University, IL
Northwest Christian University, OR
Northwestern State University of Louisiana, LA
Nyack College, NY
Oglethorpe University, GA
Ohio University, OH
Ohio University–Chillicothe, OH
Ohio University–Eastern, OH
Ohio University–Lancaster, OH
Ohio University–Southern Campus, OH
Ohio University–Zanesville, OH
Oklahoma State University, OK
Pacific University, OR
Queens University of Charlotte, NC
Rochester University, MI
St. John Fisher College, NY
Saint Louis University, MO
Saint Vincent College, PA
Salem State University, MA
Sam Houston State University, TX
San Diego State University, CA
San Francisco Art Institute, CA
San Jose State University, CA
Santa Clara University, CA
Simpson College, IA
Slippery Rock University of Pennsylvania, PA
Sonoma State University, CA
Southeastern Louisiana University, LA
Southeast Missouri State University, MO
Southern Illinois University Carbondale, IL
State University of New York at New Paltz, NY
State University of New York College at Geneseo, NY
State University of New York College at Potsdam, NY
Stephen F. Austin State University, TX
Stetson University, FL
Stockton University, NJ
SUNY Brockport, NY
Texas A&M University, TX
Texas A&M University–Commerce, TX
Texas A&M University–Corpus Christi, TX
Texas Tech University, TX
Towson University, MD
Trinity Christian College, IL
Truman State University, MO
Union University, TN
The University of Alabama, AL
The University of Alabama at Birmingham, AL
University of Arkansas, AR
University of California, Los Angeles, CA
University of California, San Diego, CA
University of California, Santa Cruz, CA
University of Central Florida, FL
University of Chicago, IL
University of Colorado Boulder, CO
University of Colorado Denver, CO
University of Houston, TX
University of Idaho, ID
University of Illinois at Urbana-Champaign, IL
The University of Iowa, IA
The University of Kansas, KS
University of Kentucky, KY
University of Maine, ME
University of Massachusetts Amherst, MA
University of Massachusetts Boston, MA
University of Memphis, TN
University of Miami, FL
University of Michigan–Flint, MI
University of Minnesota, Crookston, MN
University of Mississippi, MS
University of Missouri–St. Louis, MO
University of Mount Union, OH
University of Nebraska at Kearney, NE
University of Nebraska at Omaha, NE
University of Nevada, Las Vegas, NV
University of Nevada, Reno, NV
University of North Alabama, AL
The University of North Carolina at Charlotte, NC

University of North Dakota, ND
University of Northern Colorado, CO
University of Pittsburgh, PA
University of Providence, MT
University of St. Francis, IL
University of South Carolina, SC
University of South Carolina Aiken, SC
University of South Carolina Upstate, SC
University of Southern Indiana, IN
The University of Tampa, FL
The University of Tennessee at Chattanooga, TN
The University of Texas at San Antonio, TX
The University of Texas at Tyler, TX
The University of Toledo, OH
University of Utah, UT
The University of West Alabama, AL
University of Wisconsin–Eau Claire, WI
University of Wisconsin–La Crosse, WI
University of Wisconsin–Stout, WI
University of Wisconsin–Whitewater, WI
University of Wyoming, WY
Ursuline College, OH
Washington State University, WA
Wesleyan College, GA
Western Oregon University, OR
Westminster College, UT
West Texas A&M University, TX
Wheaton College, IL
Wichita State University, KS
William Jessup University, CA
Wright State University, OH
Wright State University–Lake Campus, OH

Handicapped Students
Bemidji State University, MN
Binghamton University, State University of New York, NY
Boise State University, ID
Bryan College, TN
California State University, Chico, CA
California State University, Fresno, CA
California State University, San Bernardino, CA
Central College, IA
Chowan University, NC
Clear Creek Baptist Bible College, KY
College of Saint Elizabeth, NJ
The College of St. Scholastica, MN
College of Staten Island of the City University of New York, NY
Dordt University, IA
East Carolina University, NC
Eastern Washington University, WA
Edinboro University of Pennsylvania, PA
Emporia State University, KS
Florida Gulf Coast University, FL
Fordham University, NY
Fort Lewis College, CO
Franklin College, IN
Grand Valley State University, MI
Grove City College, PA
Hardin-Simmons University, TX
Hofstra University, NY
Houghton College, NY
Idaho State University, ID
James Madison University, VA
Kennesaw State University, GA
Kent State University, OH
Kent State University at Geauga, OH
Kent State University at Stark, OH
Kutztown University of Pennsylvania, PA
Kuyper College, MI
Lock Haven University of Pennsylvania, PA
Long Island University, NY
Loyola Marymount University, CA
Michigan State University, MI
Mid-Atlantic Christian University, NC
Middle Tennessee State University, TN
Midwestern State University, TX
Mississippi State University, MS
Morehead State University, KY
New Jersey Institute of Technology, NJ
New Mexico State University, NM
Northern Illinois University, IL
Northern State University, SD
The Ohio State University, OH
Oklahoma State University, OK
Portland State University, OR
Sacred Heart University, CT
San Diego State University, CA
Santa Clara University, CA
Shippensburg University of Pennsylvania, PA
Sonoma State University, CA
Southern Illinois University Carbondale, IL
Southern New Hampshire University, NH
State University of New York College at Geneseo, NY
State University of New York College at Potsdam, NY
Texas Christian University, TX
Texas Tech University, TX
Towson University, MD
Union University, TN
The University of Akron, OH
The University of Alabama at Birmingham, AL
University of Arkansas, AR
University of California, Los Angeles, CA
University of California, San Diego, CA
University of Colorado Boulder, CO
University of Colorado Denver, CO
University of Houston, TX
University of Idaho, ID
The University of Iowa, IA
University of Kentucky, KY
University of Maine, ME
University of Mary Hardin-Baylor, TX
University of Massachusetts Amherst, MA
University of Memphis, TN
University of Michigan, MI
University of Michigan–Dearborn, MI
University of Michigan–Flint, MI
University of Mississippi, MS
University of Nebraska at Omaha, NE
University of Nebraska–Lincoln, NE
University of Nevada, Las Vegas, NV
University of New Hampshire, NH
The University of North Carolina at Charlotte, NC
The University of North Carolina at Greensboro, NC
University of North Dakota, ND
University of Northern Colorado, CO
University of Pittsburgh, PA
University of South Carolina, SC
University of South Carolina Aiken, SC
The University of Tennessee at Chattanooga, TN
The University of Texas at Dallas, TX
The University of Texas at San Antonio, TX
The University of Toledo, OH
University of Utah, UT
University of West Georgia, GA
University of Wisconsin–Green Bay, WI
University of Wisconsin–Stout, WI
University of Wisconsin–Whitewater, WI
University of Wyoming, WY
Washington State University, WA
Western Carolina University, NC
Western Kentucky University, KY
Western Oregon University, OR
Westminster College, UT
West Texas A&M University, TX
Wheaton College, IL
Wichita State University, KS
Wright State University, OH
Wright State University–Lake Campus, OH
Youngstown State University, OH

International Students
Agnes Scott College, GA
Albion College, MI
Allegheny College, PA
Alliant International University - San Diego, CA
Alverno College, WI
Anderson University, IN
Anderson University, SC
Andrews University, MI
Arizona State University at the Downtown Phoenix campus, AZ
Arizona State University at the Polytechnic campus, AZ
Arizona State University at the Tempe campus, AZ
Arizona State University at the West campus, AZ
Arkansas Tech University, AR
Asbury University, KY
Ashland University, OH
Auburn University at Montgomery, AL
Augsburg University, MN
Augustana College, IL
Augustana University, SD
Austin College, TX
Averett University, VA
Baker University, KS
Baldwin Wallace University, OH
Ball State University, IN
Barton College, NC
Bay Path University, MA
Belhaven University, MS
Bellarmine University, KY
Bemidji State University, MN
Benedictine University, IL
Bentley University, MA
Berry College, GA
Bethany College, WV
Bethel College, KS
Bethel University, IN
Binghamton University, State University of New York, NY
Biola University, CA
Birmingham-Southern College, AL
Bloomsburg University of Pennsylvania, PA
Bluefield College, VA
Bluffton University, OH
Boise Bible College, ID
Boise State University, ID
Bowling Green State University, OH
Bridgewater College, VA
Bryan College, TN
Bryant University, RI
Buena Vista University, IA
California Baptist University, CA
California Lutheran University, CA
California State University, Chico, CA
Calvin College, MI
Cameron University, OK
Campbellsville University, KY
Canisius College, NY
Capital University, OH
Cardinal Stritch University, WI
Carlow University, PA
Carroll College, MT
Carroll University, WI

Carthage College, WI
Centenary College of Louisiana, LA
Central College, IA
Central Methodist University, MO
Central Michigan University, MI
Champlain College, VT
Chapman University, CA
Chowan University, NC
Christian Brothers University, TN
Clarkson University, NY
Clear Creek Baptist Bible College, KY
Coastal Carolina University, SC
Coe College, IA
The College of Idaho, ID
College of Saint Benedict, MN
College of Saint Mary, NE
The College of St. Scholastica, MN
College of Staten Island of the City University of New York, NY
The College of Wooster, OH
Colorado Mesa University, CO
Colorado State University, CO
Columbia College, MO
Columbia College, SC
Columbia International University, SC
Concordia College, MN
Concordia University Chicago, IL
Concordia University Texas, TX
Cornerstone University, MI
Covenant College, GA
DeSales University, PA
Dominican University of California, CA
Dordt University, IA
Drake University, IA
Drury University, MO
Duke University, NC
Duquesne University, PA
East Central University, OK
Eastern Mennonite University, VA
Eastern Michigan University, MI
Eastern New Mexico University, NM
Eastern University, PA
East Texas Baptist University, TX
Eckerd College, FL
Elizabethtown College, PA
Elmira College, NY
Elon University, NC
Emmanuel College, GA
Emory University, GA
Emporia State University, KS
Endicott College, MA
Ferris State University, MI
Florida Gulf Coast University, FL
Florida Institute of Technology, FL
Florida National University, FL
Fort Hays State University, KS
Fort Lewis College, CO
Franklin Pierce University, NH
Gannon University, PA
George Fox University, OR
Gonzaga University, WA
Gordon College, MA
Goshen College, IN
Graceland University, IA
Grambling State University, LA
Grand Valley State University, MI
Grand View University, IA
Greenville University, IL
Gustavus Adolphus College, MN
Hamline University, MN
Hampden-Sydney College, VA
Hampton University, VA
Hanover College, IN
Harvey Mudd College, CA
Hendrix College, AR
Hillsdale College, MI
Hiram College, OH
Hollins University, VA
Houghton College, NY
Huntington University, IN
Husson University, ME
Idaho State University, ID
Illinois College, IL
Illinois Institute of Technology, IL
Illinois Wesleyan University, IL
Indiana University of Pennsylvania, PA
Iowa Wesleyan University, IA
Jacksonville University, FL
James Madison University, VA
John Carroll University, OH
Johns Hopkins University, MD
Johnson University, TN
Kennesaw State University, GA
Kent State University, OH
Kent State University at Geauga, OH
Kent State University at Stark, OH
Kentucky State University, KY
Keystone College, PA
The King's College, NY
King's College, PA
Kuyper College, MI
Lancaster Bible College, PA
La Roche University, PA
Lawrence University, WI
Lebanon Valley College, PA
Lewis University, IL
Liberty University, VA
Life University, GA
Linfield College, OR
Lipscomb University, TN
Lock Haven University of Pennsylvania, PA
Long Island University, NY
Loyola Marymount University, CA
Malone University, OH
Marymount University, VA
Maryville University of Saint Louis, MO
Mayville State University, ND
McKendree University, IL
McPherson College, KS
Mercer University, GA
Merrimack College, MA
Methodist University, NC
Michigan State University, MI
Michigan Technological University, MI
Mid-Atlantic Christian University, NC
Middle Tennessee State University, TN
Midwestern State University, TX
Millersville University of Pennsylvania, PA
Millikin University, IL
Minot State University, ND
Montclair State University, NJ
Montreat College, NC
Morehead State University, KY
Morgan State University, MD
Mount Marty College, SD
Mount Vernon Nazarene University, OH
Muskingum University, OH
Nebraska Wesleyan University, NE
Neumont College of Computer Science, UT
Newberry College, SC
New College of Florida, FL
New Jersey Institute of Technology, NJ
Newman University, KS
New Mexico State University, NM
Nicholls State University, LA
North Central College, IL
North Central University, MN
Northern Illinois University, IL
Northern Michigan University, MI
Northern State University, SD
Northwest Christian University, OR
Northwestern State University of Louisiana, LA
Northwestern University, IL
Northwest Nazarene University, ID
Northwest University, WA
Nyack College, NY
Oglethorpe University, GA
Ohio Christian University, OH
Ohio Valley University, WV
Ohio Wesleyan University, OH
Oklahoma Baptist University, OK
Oklahoma State University, OK
Old Dominion University, VA
Olivet College, MI
Oral Roberts University, OK
Otterbein University, OH
Ouachita Baptist University, AR
Pacific Lutheran University, WA
Pacific University, OR
Piedmont College, GA
Plymouth State University, NH
Portland State University, OR
Purdue University Northwest, IN
Queens University of Charlotte, NC
Ramapo College of New Jersey, NJ
Randolph College, VA
Rockford University, IL
Sacred Heart University, CT
St. Ambrose University, IA
St. Bonaventure University, NY
St. Catherine University, MN
Saint Francis University, PA
St. Lawrence University, NY
Saint Louis University, MO
Saint Martin's University, WA
St. Norbert College, WI
Samford University, AL
San Jose State University, CA
Schreiner University, TX
Seattle Pacific University, WA
Shepherd University, WV
Simpson College, IA
Slippery Rock University of Pennsylvania, PA
Sonoma State University, CA
Southeastern University, FL
Southeast Missouri State University, MO
Southern Illinois University Carbondale, IL
Southern New Hampshire University, NH
Southwestern College, KS
State University of New York at Fredonia, NY
State University of New York at Plattsburgh, NY
State University of New York College at Geneseo, NY
State University of New York College at Oneonta, NY
State University of New York College at Potsdam, NY
State University of New York College of Environmental Science and Forestry, NY
Stetson University, FL
Stockton University, NJ
SUNY Brockport, NY
Tabor College, KS
Taylor University, IN
Texas A&M University, TX
Texas A&M University–Corpus Christi, TX
Texas Christian University, TX
Texas State University, TX
Texas Woman's University, TX
Thomas More University, KY
Toccoa Falls College, GA

Towson University, MD
Trine University, IN
Trinity University, TX
Truett McConnell University, GA
Truman State University, MO
Tulane University, LA
Union University, TN
The University of Akron, OH
The University of Alabama, AL
The University of Alabama at Birmingham, AL
The University of Arizona, AZ
University of Arkansas, AR
University of California, Santa Cruz, CA
University of Colorado Denver, CO
University of Evansville, IN
University of Guam, GU
University of Houston, TX
University of Idaho, ID
University of Illinois at Urbana-Champaign, IL
University of Indianapolis, IN
The University of Kansas, KS
University of Kentucky, KY
University of Louisiana at Monroe, LA
University of Maine, ME
University of Maine at Fort Kent, ME
University of Maine at Presque Isle, ME
University of Mary Hardin-Baylor, TX
University of Memphis, TN
University of Miami, FL
University of Michigan, MI
University of Michigan–Dearborn, MI
University of Michigan–Flint, MI
University of Mississippi, MS
University of Missouri–St. Louis, MO
University of Montana, MT
University of Montevallo, AL
University of Mount Union, OH
University of Nebraska at Kearney, NE
University of Nebraska at Omaha, NE
University of Nebraska–Lincoln, NE
University of Nevada, Las Vegas, NV
University of New Hampshire, NH
University of North Alabama, AL
The University of North Carolina at Chapel Hill, NC
The University of North Carolina at Charlotte, NC
The University of North Carolina at Greensboro, NC
University of North Dakota, ND
University of Northern Colorado, CO
University of Northwestern–St. Paul, MN
University of Oregon, OR
University of Pittsburgh, PA
University of Pittsburgh at Bradford, PA
University of Providence, MT
University of Rochester, NY
University of Science and Arts of Oklahoma, OK
University of South Carolina, SC
University of South Carolina Aiken, SC
University of Southern Indiana, IN
The University of Tampa, FL
The University of Tennessee at Chattanooga, TN
The University of Texas at Austin, TX
The University of Texas at Dallas, TX
The University of Texas at El Paso, TX
The University of Texas Rio Grande Valley, TX
The University of Toledo, OH
University of West Georgia, GA
University of Wisconsin–Eau Claire, WI
University of Wisconsin–La Crosse, WI
University of Wisconsin–Parkside, WI
University of Wisconsin–Stevens Point, WI
University of Wisconsin–Stout, WI
University of Wisconsin–Superior, WI
University of Wisconsin–Whitewater, WI
University of Wyoming, WY
Utah State University, UT
Valley City State University, ND
Valparaiso University, IN
Vanderbilt University, TN
Walsh University, OH
Wartburg College, IA
Washburn University, KS
Washington & Jefferson College, PA
Washington State University, WA
Wayne State University, MI
Webber International University, FL
Wesleyan University, CT
Western Illinois University, IL
Western Kentucky University, KY
Western Michigan University, MI
Western Oregon University, OR
Western Washington University, WA
Westminster College, UT
Westmont College, CA
West Texas A&M University, TX
Wheaton College, IL
Whitworth University, WA
Wichita State University, KS
Widener University, PA
William Jessup University, CA
Wilson College, PA
Wittenberg University, OH
Wright State University, OH
Wright State University–Lake Campus, OH
Xavier University, OH
York College of Pennsylvania, PA
Youngstown State University, OH

Local/State Students

Abilene Christian University, TX
Agnes Scott College, GA
Allegheny College, PA
Allen College, IA
Alliant International University - San Diego, CA
Anderson University, IN
Angelo State University, TX
Arizona State University at the Downtown Phoenix campus, AZ
Arizona State University at the Polytechnic campus, AZ
Arizona State University at the Tempe campus, AZ
Arizona State University at the West campus, AZ
Auburn University, AL
Augustana University, SD
Aurora University, IL
Austin College, TX
Averett University, VA
Ball State University, IN
Barton College, NC
Belhaven University, MS
Bellarmine University, KY
Belmont University, TN
Benedictine University, IL
Berry College, GA
Bethany College, WV
Bethel College, KS
Binghamton University, State University of New York, NY
Birmingham-Southern College, AL
Boise State University, ID
Boston University, MA
Bridgewater State University, MA
Brigham Young University, UT
Bryan College, TN
Caldwell University, NJ
California Polytechnic State University, San Luis Obispo, CA
California State University, Bakersfield, CA
California State University, Chico, CA
California State University, Fresno, CA
California State University, Monterey Bay, CA
California State University, San Marcos, CA
California State University, Stanislaus, CA
Carthage College, WI
Centenary College of Louisiana, LA
Central College, IA
Central Michigan University, MI
Central Washington University, WA
Chaminade University of Honolulu, HI
Chowan University, NC
Christopher Newport University, VA
The Citadel, The Military College of South Carolina, SC
City College of the City University of New York, NY
Clarion University of Pennsylvania, PA
Clarkson University, NY
Clemson University, SC
Coastal Carolina University, SC
The College of Idaho, ID
College of Saint Elizabeth, NJ
The College of St. Scholastica, MN
College of Staten Island of the City University of New York, NY
Colorado Mesa University, CO
Colorado Mountain College, CO
Columbia College, MO
Columbia International University, SC
DePaul University, IL
Dordt University, IA
Duke University, NC
Eastern Oregon University, OR
Eastern Washington University, WA
Eckerd College, FL
Edinboro University of Pennsylvania, PA
Elizabethtown College, PA
Emmanuel College, GA
Emory University, GA
Endicott College, MA
Eugene Lang College of Liberal Arts, NY
The Evergreen State College, WA
Fayetteville State University, NC
Ferris State University, MI
Florida Agricultural and Mechanical University, FL
Florida Gulf Coast University, FL
Florida State University, FL
Fort Hays State University, KS
Fort Lewis College, CO
Franklin College, IN
Franklin Pierce University, NH
Georgia College & State University, GA
Georgia Institute of Technology, GA
Georgian Court University, NJ
Graceland University, IA
Grambling State University, LA
Grand Valley State University, MI
Greenville University, IL
Grinnell College, IA
Hamline University, MN
Hofstra University, NY
Hollins University, VA
Houghton College, NY
Houston Baptist University, TX
Huntington University, IN
Idaho State University, ID
Illinois Institute of Technology, IL

Illinois State University, IL
Immaculata University, PA
Indiana Tech, IN
Indiana University of Pennsylvania, PA
Jacksonville State University, AL
James Madison University, VA
John Carroll University, OH
Johns Hopkins University, MD
Kean University, NJ
Kennesaw State University, GA
Kent State University, OH
Kent State University at Geauga, OH
Kent State University at Stark, OH
Kentucky State University, KY
Kutztown University of Pennsylvania, PA
Lake Forest College, IL
Lees-McRae College, NC
Lee University, TN
Lenoir-Rhyne University, NC
Liberty University, VA
Life University, GA
Limestone College, SC
Lincoln Memorial University, TN
Lipscomb University, TN
Lock Haven University of Pennsylvania, PA
Longwood University, VA
Loras College, IA
Loyola Marymount University, CA
Lyon College, AR
Mansfield University of Pennsylvania, PA
Marist College, NY
Marshall University, WV
Marymount University, VA
Mayville State University, ND
McDaniel College, MD
Medical University of South Carolina, SC
Messiah College, PA
Methodist University, NC
Miami University, OH
Michigan State University, MI
Middle Tennessee State University, TN
Milwaukee Institute of Art and Design, WI
Minot State University, ND
Mississippi State University, MS
Missouri State University, MO
Montana State University, MT
Montana State University Billings, MT
Montana Technological University, MT
Montreat College, NC
Morehead State University, KY
Morgan State University, MD
Muskingum University, OH
Neumont College of Computer Science, UT
Newberry College, SC
New Jersey Institute of Technology, NJ
New Mexico State University, NM
Nicholls State University, LA
North Carolina State University, NC
Northeastern State University, OK
Northern Arizona University, AZ
Northern Michigan University, MI
Northern State University, SD
Northwestern State University of Louisiana, LA
Oglethorpe University, GA
Ohio Valley University, WV
Ohio Wesleyan University, OH
Oklahoma Baptist University, OK
Oklahoma State University, OK
Old Dominion University, VA
Oregon State University, OR
Ouachita Baptist University, AR
Pacific Lutheran University, WA
Purdue University Fort Wayne, IN
Randolph College, VA
Rice University, TX
Rochester University, MI
Sacred Heart University, CT
Saginaw Valley State University, MI
St. Catherine University, MN
St. Edward's University, TX
St. John Fisher College, NY
St. John's College, NM
St. John's University, NY
St. Lawrence University, NY
Saint Martin's University, WA
San Diego State University, CA
San Jose State University, CA
Schreiner University, TX
Shenandoah University, VA
Shippensburg University of Pennsylvania, PA
Slippery Rock University of Pennsylvania, PA
Smith College, MA
Sonoma State University, CA
Southern Illinois University Carbondale, IL
Southern New Hampshire University, NH
Southern Utah University, UT
Southwestern College, KS
Southwestern Oklahoma State University, OK
State University of New York at Fredonia, NY
State University of New York at New Paltz, NY
State University of New York College at Cortland, NY
State University of New York College at Geneseo, NY
State University of New York College at Oneonta, NY
State University of New York College at Potsdam, NY
State University of New York College of Environmental Science and Forestry, NY
Stephen F. Austin State University, TX
Stetson University, FL
Stockton University, NJ
Sul Ross State University, TX
Swarthmore College, PA
Tabor College, KS
Texas A&M University, TX
Texas Christian University, TX
Texas Lutheran University, TX
Thomas College, ME
Trinity Christian College, IL
Truett McConnell University, GA
Tulane University, LA
Tuskegee University, AL
The University of Akron, OH
The University of Alabama, AL
University of Alaska Fairbanks, AK
University of Alaska Southeast, AK
University of Arkansas, AR
University of Colorado Boulder, CO
University of Colorado Denver, CO
University of Dayton, OH
University of Evansville, IN
University of Georgia, GA
University of Houston, TX
University of Houston–Clear Lake, TX
University of Idaho, ID
University of Illinois at Urbana-Champaign, IL
The University of Iowa, IA
The University of Kansas, KS
University of Louisville, KY
University of Maine, ME
University of Maine at Farmington, ME
University of Maine at Presque Isle, ME
University of Mary Hardin-Baylor, TX
University of Mary Washington, VA
University of Massachusetts Amherst, MA
University of Massachusetts Boston, MA
University of Massachusetts Dartmouth, MA
University of Memphis, TN
University of Michigan, MI
University of Michigan–Flint, MI
University of Minnesota, Crookston, MN
University of Minnesota, Twin Cities Campus, MN
University of Mississippi, MS
University of Missouri–St. Louis, MO
University of Montana, MT
University of Nebraska at Kearney, NE
University of Nevada, Las Vegas, NV
University of New Hampshire, NH
The University of North Carolina at Charlotte, NC
The University of North Carolina at Greensboro, NC
The University of North Carolina Wilmington, NC
University of Northern Colorado, CO
University of Oregon, OR
University of Pittsburgh, PA
University of Pittsburgh at Bradford, PA
University of Pittsburgh at Greensburg, PA
University of Providence, MT
University of Saint Joseph, CT
University of South Carolina, SC
University of South Carolina Aiken, SC
University of Southern Mississippi, MS
The University of Tennessee at Chattanooga, TN
The University of Tennessee at Martin, TN
The University of Texas at Austin, TX
The University of Texas at Dallas, TX
The University of Texas at El Paso, TX
The University of Texas at San Antonio, TX
The University of Texas Rio Grande Valley, TX
University of West Georgia, GA
University of Wisconsin–Eau Claire, WI
University of Wisconsin–La Crosse, WI
University of Wisconsin–Parkside, WI
University of Wisconsin–Stout, WI
University of Wisconsin–Whitewater, WI
University of Wyoming, WY
Utah State University, UT
Valdosta State University, GA
Vanderbilt University, TN
Wake Forest University, NC
Walsh University, OH
Washburn University, KS
Washington & Jefferson College, PA
Washington State University, WA
Wayne State College, NE
Wayne State University, MI
Webber International University, FL
Wesleyan College, GA
Western Carolina University, NC
Western Kentucky University, KY
Western Michigan University, MI
Western Oregon University, OR
Western Washington University, WA
West Texas A&M University, TX
Wheaton College, IL
Wichita State University, KS
Wilson College, PA
Winona State University, MN
Wofford College, SC
Youngstown State University, OH

Married Students
Alaska Bible College, AK
Asbury University, KY
Auburn University, AL
Binghamton University, State University of New York, NY
California State University, Chico, CA
The College of Idaho, ID
Eastern Washington University, WA
East Texas Baptist University, TX
Emmanuel College, GA
Franklin Pierce University, NH
Georgian Court University, NJ
Indiana Tech, IN
Indiana University of Pennsylvania, PA
Johnson University, TN
Lock Haven University of Pennsylvania, PA
Mid-Atlantic Christian University, NC
Montana Technological University, MT
Newman University, KS
New Mexico State University, NM
Northwestern State University of Louisiana, LA
Northwest University, WA
Sonoma State University, CA
State University of New York College at Potsdam, NY
SUNY Brockport, NY
Toccoa Falls College, GA
Truett McConnell University, GA
The University of Alabama at Birmingham, AL
University of Arkansas, AR
The University of Kansas, KS
University of Nevada, Reno, NV
University of Northern Colorado, CO
University of Pittsburgh, PA
University of South Carolina Aiken, SC
Westminster College, UT

Members of Minorities
Abilene Christian University, TX
Alabama State University, AL
Alice Lloyd College, KY
Allen College, IA
Alma College, MI
American University, DC
Anderson University, IN
Asbury University, KY
Ashland University, OH
Assumption University, MA
Augsburg University, MN
Augustana College, IL
Augustana University, SD
Austin Peay State University, TN
Baker University, KS
Baldwin Wallace University, OH
Ball State University, IN
Bellarmine University, KY
Belmont University, TN
Bemidji State University, MN
Bentley University, MA
Berry College, GA
Bethel University, IN
Binghamton University, State University of New York, NY
Biola University, CA
Bluffton University, OH
Boise State University, ID
Boston University, MA
Bowling Green State University, OH
Bridgewater State University, MA
Brigham Young University, UT
Bryan College, TN
Bryant University, RI
California State Polytechnic University, Pomona, CA
California State University, Chico, CA
California University of Pennsylvania, PA
Calvin College, MI
Cameron University, OK
Capital University, OH
Carson-Newman University, TN
Carthage College, WI
Central College, IA
Central Connecticut State University, CT
Central Washington University, WA
Champlain College, VT
Christian Brothers University, TN
Christopher Newport University, VA
Clarion University of Pennsylvania, PA
Clarkson University, NY
Clemson University, SC
Coe College, IA
The College of Idaho, ID
The College of New Jersey, NJ
College of Saint Elizabeth, NJ
The College of Saint Rose, NY
College of Staten Island of the City University of New York, NY
The College of Wooster, OH
Colorado Mesa University, CO
Colorado State University, CO
Columbia College, MO
Columbia International University, SC
Cornerstone University, MI
Covenant College, GA
Creighton University, NE
Delaware Valley University, PA
Dominican University of California, CA
Dordt University, IA
Drury University, MO
Duke University, NC
Duquesne University, PA
East Central University, OK
Eastern Kentucky University, KY
Eastern Michigan University, MI
Eastern New Mexico University, NM
Eastern Oregon University, OR
Edinboro University of Pennsylvania, PA
Elizabethtown College, PA
Elon University, NC
Emporia State University, KS
Eugene Lang College of Liberal Arts, NY
Fairfield University, CT
Ferris State University, MI
Florida Gulf Coast University, FL
Franklin College, IN
Gallaudet University, DC
Gannon University, PA
George Fox University, OR
Georgia Institute of Technology, GA
Georgian Court University, NJ
Gonzaga University, WA
Goshen College, IN
Graceland University, IA
Grambling State University, LA
Grove City College, PA
Gustavus Adolphus College, MN
Hamline University, MN
Hampden-Sydney College, VA
Hampton University, VA
Hanover College, IN
Hofstra University, NY
Husson University, ME
Idaho State University, ID
Illinois State University, IL
Indiana State University, IN
Ithaca College, NY
James Madison University, VA
Johnson University, TN
Judson University, IL
Kennesaw State University, GA
Kent State University, OH
Kent State University at Stark, OH
Lehigh University, PA
Le Moyne College, NY
Lenoir-Rhyne University, NC
Lewis-Clark State College, ID
Life University, GA
Linfield College, OR
Lipscomb University, TN
Livingstone College, NC
Lock Haven University of Pennsylvania, PA
Loyola Marymount University, CA
Lyon College, AR
Mansfield University of Pennsylvania, PA
Marietta College, OH
Marshall University, WV
Marymount University, VA
Maryville College, TN
Maryville University of Saint Louis, MO
Mayville State University, ND
Medical University of South Carolina, SC
Miami University, OH
MidAmerica Nazarene University, KS
Middle Tennessee State University, TN
Midway University, KY
Midwestern State University, TX
Milwaukee Institute of Art and Design, WI
Minnesota State University Mankato, MN
Minnesota State University Moorhead, MN
Minot State University, ND
Misericordia University, PA
Missouri State University, MO
Missouri University of Science and Technology, MO
Molloy College, NY
Montana State University, MT
Montana State University Billings, MT
Morehead State University, KY
Mount Carmel College of Nursing, OH
Mount Vernon Nazarene University, OH
Muskingum University, OH
Nazareth College of Rochester, NY
Nebraska Wesleyan University, NE
New Jersey Institute of Technology, NJ
New Mexico State University, NM
Nicholls State University, LA
Northeastern State University, OK
Northern Arizona University, AZ
Northern Illinois University, IL
Northern Michigan University, MI
Northern State University, SD
Northwest Missouri State University, MO
The Ohio State University, OH
Ohio Wesleyan University, OH
Oklahoma Baptist University, OK
Oregon State University, OR
Otis College of Art and Design, CA
Otterbein University, OH
Portland State University, OR
Rensselaer Polytechnic Institute, NY
Rhodes College, TN
Rice University, TX
Rider University, NJ
Sacred Heart University, CT
Saginaw Valley State University, MI
St. Ambrose University, IA
St. Bonaventure University, NY
St. Cloud State University, MN
St. John Fisher College, NY
Saint Joseph's University, PA
Saint Martin's University, WA
Salem State University, MA
Samford University, AL
Sam Houston State University, TX

San Jose State University, CA
Seattle University, WA
Shepherd University, WV
Simpson College, IA
Slippery Rock University of Pennsylvania, PA
Sonoma State University, CA
Southeast Missouri State University, MO
Southern Illinois University Carbondale, IL
Southern Utah University, UT
Southwestern College, KS
Southwestern University, TX
State University of New York at Fredonia, NY
State University of New York at New Paltz, NY
State University of New York College at Cortland, NY
State University of New York College at Geneseo, NY
State University of New York College at Potsdam, NY
State University of New York College of Agriculture & Technology at Morrisville, NY
State University of New York College of Environmental Science and Forestry, NY
Stetson University, FL
Stockton University, NJ
SUNY Brockport, NY
Texas Christian University, TX
Texas Woman's University, TX
Thomas Jefferson University, PA
Thomas More University, KY
Towson University, MD
Transylvania University, KY
Trinity Christian College, IL
Truett McConnell University, GA
Union College, KY
Union University, TN
The University of Akron, OH
The University of Alabama, AL
The University of Alabama at Birmingham, AL
University of Arkansas, AR
University of California, San Diego, CA
University of Colorado Denver, CO
University of Dayton, OH
University of Evansville, IN
University of Florida, FL
University of Idaho, ID
University of Illinois at Urbana-Champaign, IL
The University of Kansas, KS
University of Kentucky, KY
University of Louisville, KY
University of Maine, ME
University of Maine at Farmington, ME
University of Maine at Fort Kent, ME
University of Mary Hardin-Baylor, TX
University of Massachusetts Dartmouth, MA
University of Memphis, TN
University of Michigan, MI
University of Michigan–Dearborn, MI
University of Michigan–Flint, MI
University of Minnesota, Crookston, MN
University of Minnesota, Twin Cities Campus, MN
University of Mississippi, MS
University of Missouri–St. Louis, MO
University of Mount Union, OH
University of Nebraska at Kearney, NE
University of Nebraska at Omaha, NE
University of Nebraska–Lincoln, NE
University of Nevada, Las Vegas, NV
University of New Mexico, NM
The University of North Carolina at Charlotte, NC
University of North Dakota, ND
University of Northern Colorado, CO
University of Northern Iowa, IA
University of Oklahoma, OK
University of Pittsburgh, PA
University of Pittsburgh at Bradford, PA
University of Pittsburgh at Greensburg, PA
University of Saint Joseph, CT
The University of Scranton, PA
University of South Carolina, SC
University of South Carolina Aiken, SC
University of Southern Indiana, IN
The University of Tennessee at Chattanooga, TN
The University of Tennessee at Martin, TN
The University of Texas at Dallas, TX
The University of Texas at El Paso, TX
The University of Texas at San Antonio, TX
The University of Toledo, OH
University of West Georgia, GA
University of Wisconsin–Eau Claire, WI
University of Wisconsin–Green Bay, WI
University of Wisconsin–La Crosse, WI
University of Wisconsin–Parkside, WI
University of Wisconsin–Stevens Point, WI
University of Wisconsin–Stout, WI
University of Wisconsin–Superior, WI
University of Wisconsin–Whitewater, WI
University of Wyoming, WY
Utah State University, UT
Valdosta State University, GA
Valley City State University, ND
Vanderbilt University, TN
Walsh University, OH
Washington & Jefferson College, PA
Wayne State College, NE
Western Carolina University, NC
Western Illinois University, IL
Western Kentucky University, KY
Western Oregon University, OR
Western Washington University, WA
Westminster College, UT
Wheaton College, IL
Whitworth University, WA
Wichita State University, KS
Winona State University, MN
Wittenberg University, OH
Wofford College, SC
Wright State University, OH
Wright State University–Lake Campus, OH
Xavier University, OH
York College of Pennsylvania, PA
Youngstown State University, OH

Out-of-State Students

Abilene Christian University, TX
Albion College, MI
Alma College, MI
Alverno College, WI
Anderson University, IN
Anderson University, SC
Arizona State University at the Downtown Phoenix campus, AZ
Arizona State University at the Polytechnic campus, AZ
Arizona State University at the Tempe campus, AZ
Arizona State University at the West campus, AZ
Arkansas Tech University, AR
Asbury University, KY
Ashland University, OH
Auburn University, AL
Augustana College, IL
Aurora University, IL
Austin College, TX
Averett University, VA
Baker University, KS
Baldwin Wallace University, OH
Ball State University, IN
Bellarmine University, KY
Bemidji State University, MN
Benedictine University, IL
Berry College, GA
Bethany College, WV
Binghamton University, State University of New York, NY
Bluffton University, OH
Boise State University, ID
Bradley University, IL
Bridgewater College, VA
California State University, Chico, CA
Cameron University, OK
Canisius College, NY
Capital University, OH
Carthage College, WI
Centenary College of Louisiana, LA
Central College, IA
Central Michigan University, MI
Central Washington University, WA
Chaminade University of Honolulu, HI
Chowan University, NC
Christian Brothers University, TN
The Citadel, The Military College of South Carolina, SC
Cleveland State University, OH
Coastal Carolina University, SC
The College of Idaho, ID
College of Saint Benedict, MN
College of Saint Elizabeth, NJ
The College of Saint Rose, NY
College of Staten Island of the City University of New York, NY
Colorado Mesa University, CO
Concordia University Wisconsin, WI
Davidson College, NC
Dordt University, IA
East Central University, OK
Eastern Michigan University, MI
Eastern New Mexico University, NM
Eastern University, PA
Eastern Washington University, WA
Edinboro University of Pennsylvania, PA
Emory & Henry College, VA
Evangel University, MO
The Evergreen State College, WA
Florida Gulf Coast University, FL
Fort Lewis College, CO
Franklin College, IN
George Fox University, OR
Georgia College & State University, GA
Georgia Institute of Technology, GA
Georgian Court University, NJ
Glenville State College, WV
Graceland University, IA
Grambling State University, LA
Grand Valley State University, MI
Grand View University, IA
Greenville University, IL
Gustavus Adolphus College, MN
Hamline University, MN
Hampden-Sydney College, VA
Hanover College, IN
Hardin-Simmons University, TX
Heidelberg University, OH
Hollins University, VA
Hope College, MI

Husson University, ME
Idaho State University, ID
Indiana State University, IN
Iowa Wesleyan University, IA
James Madison University, VA
Kean University, NJ
Kent State University, OH
Kent State University at Geauga, OH
Kent State University at Stark, OH
King University, TN
Lewis-Clark State College, ID
Limestone College, SC
Lipscomb University, TN
Loras College, IA
Louisiana State University and Agricultural & Mechanical College, LA
Loyola Marymount University, CA
Lynn University, FL
Marymount University, VA
Maryville University of Saint Louis, MO
Mayville State University, ND
Miami University, OH
Michigan State University, MI
Minnesota State University Moorhead, MN
Minot State University, ND
Misericordia University, PA
Mississippi State University, MS
Missouri University of Science and Technology, MO
Montana State University Billings, MT
Montana Technological University, MT
Morehead State University, KY
Morgan State University, MD
Nazareth College of Rochester, NY
New College of Florida, FL
New Jersey Institute of Technology, NJ
New Mexico State University, NM
Nicholls State University, LA
Northeastern State University, OK
Northern Michigan University, MI
Northwestern State University of Louisiana, LA
Northwest Missouri State University, MO
Oglethorpe University, GA
Ohio Christian University, OH
The Ohio State University, OH
Ohio University, OH
Ohio University–Chillicothe, OH
Ohio University–Eastern, OH
Ohio University–Lancaster, OH
Ohio University–Southern Campus, OH
Ohio University–Zanesville, OH
Oklahoma Baptist University, OK
Oklahoma State University, OK
Pacific Lutheran University, WA
Piedmont College, GA
Portland State University, OR
Ramapo College of New Jersey, NJ
Randolph-Macon College, VA
Rochester University, MI
Rockford University, IL
Rogers State University, OK
Sacred Heart University, CT
St. Ambrose University, IA
St. Catherine University, MN
St. Cloud State University, MN
St. Edward's University, TX
Saint Francis University, PA
St. John Fisher College, NY
Saint John's University, MN
Saint Martin's University, WA
Saint Vincent College, PA
Samford University, AL
Seattle Pacific University, WA
Shepherd University, WV
Simpson College, IA
Slippery Rock University of Pennsylvania, PA
Sonoma State University, CA
Southeastern Louisiana University, LA
Southeast Missouri State University, MO
Southwestern Oklahoma State University, OK
State University of New York at Fredonia, NY
State University of New York at Plattsburgh, NY
State University of New York College at Potsdam, NY
State University of New York College of Agriculture & Technology at Morrisville, NY
State University of New York College of Environmental Science and Forestry, NY
Stetson University, FL
SUNY Brockport, NY
Tabor College, KS
Tennessee Wesleyan University, TN
Texas A&M University–Commerce, TX
Texas Tech University, TX
Texas Woman's University, TX
Thomas College, ME
Thomas More University, KY
Transylvania University, KY
Trinity Christian College, IL
Truett McConnell University, GA
Truman State University, MO
The University of Akron, OH
The University of Alabama, AL
The University of Alabama at Birmingham, AL
University of Arkansas, AR
University of California, Riverside, CA
University of California, Santa Cruz, CA
University of Colorado Denver, CO
University of Dayton, OH
University of Dubuque, IA
University of Evansville, IN
University of Florida, FL
University of Houston, TX
University of Idaho, ID
University of Indianapolis, IN
The University of Iowa, IA
The University of Kansas, KS
University of Kentucky, KY
University of Louisiana at Monroe, LA
University of Louisville, KY
University of Maine, ME
University of Maine at Farmington, ME
University of Maine at Presque Isle, ME
University of Mary Hardin-Baylor, TX
University of Maryland, College Park, MD
University of Massachusetts Amherst, MA
University of Massachusetts Boston, MA
University of Massachusetts Dartmouth, MA
University of Massachusetts Lowell, MA
University of Michigan, MI
University of Michigan–Dearborn, MI
University of Mississippi, MS
University of Missouri–St. Louis, MO
University of Montana, MT
University of Montevallo, AL
University of Nebraska at Kearney, NE
University of Nebraska at Omaha, NE
University of Nebraska–Lincoln, NE
University of Nevada, Las Vegas, NV
University of New Mexico, NM
University of North Alabama, AL
The University of North Carolina at Chapel Hill, NC
The University of North Carolina at Greensboro, NC
The University of North Carolina Wilmington, NC
University of Northern Colorado, CO
University of Pittsburgh, PA
University of Pittsburgh at Bradford, PA
University of Science and Arts of Oklahoma, OK
University of South Carolina, SC
University of South Carolina Aiken, SC
University of Southern Indiana, IN
University of Southern Mississippi, MS
The University of Tennessee at Chattanooga, TN
The University of Tennessee at Martin, TN
The University of Texas at Austin, TX
The University of Texas at Dallas, TX
The University of Texas at El Paso, TX
The University of Texas at San Antonio, TX
The University of Texas Rio Grande Valley, TX
The University of Toledo, OH
University of Utah, UT
University of Wisconsin–La Crosse, WI
University of Wisconsin–Parkside, WI
University of Wisconsin–Stevens Point, WI
University of Wisconsin–Stout, WI
University of Wisconsin–Whitewater, WI
University of Wyoming, WY
VanderCook College of Music, IL
Walsh University, OH
Washington State University, WA
Wayne State College, NE
Wayne State University, MI
Western Kentucky University, KY
Western Michigan University, MI
Western New Mexico University, NM
West Texas A&M University, TX
Wheaton College, IL
Wichita State University, KS
William Jessup University, CA
Winona State University, MN
Wright State University, OH
Wright State University–Lake Campus, OH
Youngstown State University, OH

Parents of Current Students

Arkansas Tech University, AR
Aurora University, IL
Caldwell University, NJ
Carthage College, WI
Columbia College, MO
ECPI University, VA
Emmanuel College, GA
Emory University, GA
Franklin Pierce University, NH
Johnson University, TN
Maryville University of Saint Louis, MO
Millikin University, IL
Missouri Baptist University, MO
Mount Aloysius College, PA
Mount Marty College, SD
Northwest University, WA
Rockford University, IL
St. Joseph's College, Long Island Campus, NY
St. Joseph's College, New York, NY
State University of New York at Fredonia, NY
Stephens College, MO
Truett McConnell University, GA
The University of Alabama at Birmingham, AL
University of Providence, MT
Wesleyan College, GA

Previous College Experience

Abilene Christian University, TX

Anderson University, SC
Arkansas Tech University, AR
Austin College, TX
Bellarmine University, KY
Bemidji State University, MN
Bethel College, KS
Binghamton University, State University of New York, NY
Birmingham-Southern College, AL
Boise State University, ID
Bridgewater College, VA
Caldwell University, NJ
Calumet College of Saint Joseph, IN
Carthage College, WI
Central College, IA
Clarion University of Pennsylvania, PA
The College of St. Scholastica, MN
College of Staten Island of the City University of New York, NY
Colorado Mesa University, CO
Columbia College, MO
Columbia College, SC
Eastern Michigan University, MI
Eastern University, PA
East Texas Baptist University, TX
Elmira College, NY
Ferris State University, MI
Florida Institute of Technology, FL
Georgian Court University, NJ
Hamline University, MN
Hendrix College, AR
Hollins University, VA
Illinois College, IL
Illinois Institute of Technology, IL
Illinois State University, IL
Indiana State University, IN
Kean University, NJ
Kent State University, OH
Kent State University at Stark, OH
Kentucky State University, KY
Lake Forest College, IL
Lewis-Clark State College, ID
Lewis University, IL
Limestone College, SC
Linfield College, OR
Lock Haven University of Pennsylvania, PA
Loyola Marymount University, CA
McDaniel College, MD
Midway University, KY
Millikin University, IL
Misericordia University, PA
Mississippi State University, MS
Morehead State University, KY
Muskingum University, OH
New Mexico State University, NM
New York Institute of Technology, NY
Nicholls State University, LA
Northwest Missouri State University, MO
Oglethorpe University, GA
The Ohio State University, OH
Oklahoma State University, OK
Old Dominion University, VA
Otterbein University, OH
Ouachita Baptist University, AR
Palm Beach Atlantic University, FL
Rochester University, MI
St. Ambrose University, IA
Saint Francis University, PA
St. John's University, NY
Saint Louis University, MO
Saint Vincent College, PA
San Diego State University, CA
Shepherd University, WV
Slippery Rock University of Pennsylvania, PA
Sonoma State University, CA
Southeast Missouri State University, MO
Southern New Hampshire University, NH
State University of New York at Fredonia, NY
Stephen F. Austin State University, TX
Stockton University, NJ
SUNY Brockport, NY
Texas A&M University–Commerce, TX
Texas Christian University, TX
Texas Woman's University, TX
Towson University, MD
Trinity College of Florida, FL
Truman State University, MO
The University of Alabama at Birmingham, AL
University of Arkansas, AR
University of Evansville, IN
University of Houston, TX
The University of Kansas, KS
University of Louisville, KY
University of Maine, ME
University of Michigan–Dearborn, MI
University of Mississippi, MS
University of Missouri–St. Louis, MO
University of Nevada, Las Vegas, NV
University of Northern Colorado, CO
University of Oklahoma, OK
University of Pittsburgh, PA
University of St. Thomas, TX
University of Science and Arts of Oklahoma, OK
University of South Carolina Aiken, SC
The University of Tennessee at Martin, TN
The University of Toledo, OH
The University of West Alabama, AL
University of Wisconsin–Eau Claire, WI
University of Wisconsin–Stout, WI
University of Wyoming, WY
Walsh College of Accountancy and Business Administration, MI
Wartburg College, IA
Washington State University, WA
Wesleyan College, GA
Western Michigan University, MI
Western Oregon University, OR
Western Washington University, WA
Wichita State University, KS
William Jessup University, CA

Public Servants

Alliant International University - San Diego, CA
Arkansas Tech University, AR
Caldwell University, NJ
Central Washington University, WA
Chowan University, NC
College of Staten Island of the City University of New York, NY
East Texas Baptist University, TX
Edinboro University of Pennsylvania, PA
Georgia College & State University, GA
Grambling State University, LA
Grand Valley State University, MI
Hardin-Simmons University, TX
Hofstra University, NY
Kentucky State University, KY
La Sierra University, CA
Missouri Baptist University, MO
New Mexico State University, NM
Nicholls State University, LA
Northwestern State University of Louisiana, LA
Patrick Henry College, VA
Regent University, VA
St. John's University, NY
St. Joseph's College, Long Island Campus, NY
St. Joseph's College, New York, NY
Salem State University, MA
Southern Illinois University Carbondale, IL
Sterling College, KS
Texas Woman's University, TX
Truett McConnell University, GA
The University of Alabama at Birmingham, AL
University of Kentucky, KY
University of Massachusetts Amherst, MA
University of Memphis, TN
University of Michigan–Dearborn, MI
University of Oklahoma, OK
The University of Texas at Dallas, TX
The University of Toledo, OH
Washington State University, WA
West Texas A&M University, TX
Youngstown State University, OH

Relatives of Clergy

Abilene Christian University, TX
Albion College, MI
American University, DC
Anderson University, IN
Asbury University, KY
Ashland University, OH
Augsburg University, MN
Austin College, TX
Averett University, VA
Baker University, KS
Baldwin Wallace University, OH
Barton College, NC
Benedictine University, IL
Bethany College, WV
Bethel College, KS
Biola University, CA
Birmingham-Southern College, AL
Boise Bible College, ID
Boston University, MA
Bryan College, TN
Caldwell University, NJ
California Baptist University, CA
California Lutheran University, CA
Campbellsville University, KY
Capital University, OH
Carson-Newman University, TN
Carthage College, WI
Centenary College of Louisiana, LA
Central Methodist University, MO
Chapman University, CA
Chowan University, NC
Clarke University, IA
Columbia College, SC
Cornerstone University, MI
Dallas Baptist University, TX
Davidson College, NC
Dillard University, LA
Dominican College, NY
Drury University, MO
Duquesne University, PA
Eastern University, PA
Elon University, NC
Emmanuel College, GA
Evangel University, MO
Franklin College, IN
George Fox University, OR
Gordon College, MA
Hamline University, MN
Hardin-Simmons University, TX
Heidelberg University, OH
Hendrix College, AR
High Point University, NC

Hiram College, OH
Hobart and William Smith Colleges, NY
Houghton College, NY
Huntington University, IN
Johnson University, TN
Johnson University Florida, FL
King's College, PA
Kuyper College, MI
LaGrange College, GA
Lancaster Bible College, PA
La Sierra University, CA
Lenoir-Rhyne University, NC
Lipscomb University, TN
Malone University, OH
Maranatha Baptist University, WI
Merrimack College, MA
Methodist University, NC
MidAmerica Nazarene University, KS
Mid-South Christian College, TN
Midway University, KY
Millikin University, IL
Misericordia University, PA
Missouri Baptist University, MO
Montreat College, NC
Mount Vernon Nazarene University, OH
Muskingum University, OH
Nebraska Wesleyan University, NE
Newberry College, SC
New Jersey Institute of Technology, NJ
Niagara University, NY
North Central College, IL
North Central University, MN
Northwest Christian University, OR
Northwest Nazarene University, ID
Northwest University, WA
Nyack College, NY
Ohio Christian University, OH
Ohio Valley University, WV
Ohio Wesleyan University, OH
Oklahoma Baptist University, OK
Oklahoma City University, OK
Olivet Nazarene University, IL
Oral Roberts University, OK
Otterbein University, OH
Ouachita Baptist University, AR
Pacific Lutheran University, WA
Pacific University, OR
Patrick Henry College, VA
Presbyterian College, SC
Queens University of Charlotte, NC
Randolph College, VA
Randolph-Macon College, VA
Rhodes College, TN
Rochester University, MI
Saint Anselm College, NH
St. Bonaventure University, NY
St. John's University, NY
Saint Peter's University, NJ
Samford University, AL
Schreiner University, TX
Seattle Pacific University, WA
Simpson College, IA
Southwest Baptist University, MO
Southwestern University, TX
Stonehill College, MA
Susquehanna University, PA
Tennessee Wesleyan University, TN
Texas Christian University, TX
Texas Lutheran University, TX
Toccoa Falls College, GA
Transylvania University, KY
Trevecca Nazarene University, TN
Trinity College of Florida, FL
Truett McConnell University, GA
Union University, TN
Universidad Adventista de las Antillas, PR
The University of Alabama at Birmingham, AL
University of Dubuque, IA
University of Evansville, IN
University of Indianapolis, IN
University of Mary Hardin-Baylor, TX
University of Mobile, AL
University of Mount Union, OH
The University of North Carolina at Chapel Hill, NC
University of Northwestern–St. Paul, MN
University of Portland, OR
The University of Texas at Austin, TX
The University of Tulsa, OK
Ursuline College, OH
Valparaiso University, IN
Virginia Wesleyan University, VA
Wayland Baptist University, TX
Wesleyan College, GA
Westmont College, CA
Wheaton College, IL
William Jessup University, CA
Wilson College, PA
Wingate University, NC
Wittenberg University, OH

Religious Affiliation

Abilene Christian University, TX
Agnes Scott College, GA
Albertus Magnus College, CT
Alverno College, WI
Anderson University, IN
Anderson University, SC
Asbury University, KY
Ashland University, OH
Augustana College, IL
Augustana University, SD
Aurora University, IL
Austin College, TX
Ave Maria University, FL
Averett University, VA
Baker University, KS
Baldwin Wallace University, OH
Barton College, NC
Belhaven University, MS
Bellarmine University, KY
Bethany College, WV
Bethel College, KS
Bethel University, IN
Binghamton University, State University of New York, NY
Birmingham-Southern College, AL
Bluefield College, VA
Bluffton University, OH
Boston University, MA
Bridgewater College, VA
Brigham Young University, UT
Bryn Athyn College of the New Church, PA
Caldwell University, NJ
California Baptist University, CA
California Lutheran University, CA
Calumet College of Saint Joseph, IN
Calvin College, MI
Campbellsville University, KY
Canisius College, NY
Capital University, OH
Cardinal Stritch University, WI
Carlow University, PA
Carroll College, MT
Carthage College, WI
The Catholic University of America, DC
Cedarville University, OH
Centenary College of Louisiana, LA
Central College, IA
Central Methodist University, MO
Chaminade University of Honolulu, HI
Chowan University, NC
Coe College, IA
The College of St. Scholastica, MN
Columbia College, MO
Columbia College, SC
Concordia University Chicago, IL
Concordia University, St. Paul, MN
Concordia University Texas, TX
Covenant College, GA
Creighton University, NE
Dallas Baptist University, TX
Davidson College, NC
Dillard University, LA
Doane University, NE
Dordt University, IA
Drury University, MO
Duquesne University, PA
Eastern Mennonite University, VA
Eastern Michigan University, MI
East Texas Baptist University, TX
Eckerd College, FL
Elizabethtown College, PA
Elms College, MA
Emmanuel College, GA
Emory & Henry College, VA
Emory University, GA
Emporia State University, KS
Endicott College, MA
Evangel University, MO
Franklin College, IN
Gannon University, PA
George Fox University, OR
Georgian Court University, NJ
Graceland University, IA
Grand View University, IA
Greenville University, IL
Hamline University, MN
Hanover College, IN
Hardin-Simmons University, TX
Heidelberg University, OH
Hiram College, OH
Hope College, MI
Houghton College, NY
Houston Baptist University, TX
Huntington University, IN
Illinois State University, IL
Immaculata University, PA
Iona College, NY
Johnson University, TN
Johnson University Florida, FL
Kennesaw State University, GA
LaGrange College, GA
La Sierra University, CA
Lees-McRae College, NC
Lenoir-Rhyne University, NC
Lewis University, IL
Liberty University, VA
Lipscomb University, TN
Loras College, IA
Loyola Marymount University, CA
Loyola University Chicago, IL
Lyon College, AR
Malone University, OH
Mansfield University of Pennsylvania, PA
Marymount University, VA
Maryville College, TN
McKendree University, IL
McPherson College, KS
Mercer University, GA
Merrimack College, MA
Messenger College, TX
Messiah College, PA
Methodist University, NC
MidAmerica Nazarene University, KS
Midway University, KY
Missouri Baptist University, MO

Molloy College, NY
Montreat College, NC
Mount Aloysius College, PA
Mount Marty College, SD
Mount Vernon Nazarene University, OH
Muskingum University, OH
Nebraska Methodist College, NE
Nebraska Wesleyan University, NE
Newberry College, SC
New Jersey Institute of Technology, NJ
North Central University, MN
Northeastern State University, OK
Northwest Christian University, OR
Northwest Nazarene University, ID
Nyack College, NY
Oglethorpe University, GA
Ohio Christian University, OH
Ohio Valley University, WV
Ohio Wesleyan University, OH
Oklahoma Baptist University, OK
Oklahoma City University, OK
Olivet College, MI
Olivet Nazarene University, IL
Ouachita Baptist University, AR
Pacific Lutheran University, WA
Queens University of Charlotte, NC
Randolph College, VA
Regent University, VA
Reinhardt University, GA
Rhodes College, TN
Rochester University, MI
Sacred Heart University, CT
St. Ambrose University, IA
Saint Anselm College, NH
St. Bonaventure University, NY
St. Catherine University, MN
St. Edward's University, TX
Saint Francis University, PA
St. John's University, NY
Saint Louis University, MO
Saint Peter's University, NJ
Saint Vincent College, PA
Samford University, AL
Schreiner University, TX
Seattle Pacific University, WA
Seattle University, WA
Simpson College, IA
Southeastern University, FL
Southern Utah University, UT
Southwest Baptist University, MO
Southwestern College, KS
Southwestern University, TX
State University of New York College at Geneseo, NY
Tabor College, KS
Taylor University, IN
Tennessee Wesleyan University, TN
Texas Christian University, TX
Texas Lutheran University, TX
Texas Woman's University, TX
Thomas More University, KY
Toccoa Falls College, GA
Transylvania University, KY
Trevecca Nazarene University, TN
Trinity Christian College, IL
Truett McConnell University, GA
Union College, KY
Union University, TN
The University of Alabama, AL
University of Dallas, TX
University of Dayton, OH
University of Dubuque, IA
University of Evansville, IN
University of Indianapolis, IN
University of Jamestown, ND
University of Maine, ME
University of Mary Hardin-Baylor, TX
University of Mary Washington, VA
University of Mount Union, OH
The University of North Carolina at Greensboro, NC
University of Pittsburgh, PA
University of Portland, OR
University of Providence, MT
University of St. Francis, IL
University of St. Thomas, TX
The University of Scranton, PA
University of South Carolina, SC
University of South Carolina Aiken, SC
The University of Tennessee at Chattanooga, TN
University of the Pacific, CA
The University of Toledo, OH
The University of Tulsa, OK
Ursuline College, OH
Utah State University, UT
Valparaiso University, IN
VanderCook College of Music, IL
Vanguard University of Southern California, CA
Villanova University, PA
Virginia Wesleyan University, VA
Wake Forest University, NC
Wartburg College, IA
Washington State University, WA
Wayland Baptist University, TX
Wesleyan College, GA
Western Kentucky University, KY
Westminster College, PA
Westminster College, UT
West Texas A&M University, TX
Whitworth University, WA
Wilson College, PA
Wittenberg University, OH
Wofford College, SC
Youngstown State University, OH

Siblings of Current Students

Albany College of Pharmacy and Health Sciences, NY
Albertus Magnus College, CT
Alliant International University - San Diego, CA
Alma College, MI
Asbury University, KY
Ashland University, OH
Augsburg University, MN
Augustana College, IL
Augustana University, SD
Aurora University, IL
Ave Maria University, FL
Baldwin Wallace University, OH
Barton College, NC
Bay Path University, MA
Becker College, MA
Belhaven University, MS
Belmont University, TN
Benedictine University, IL
Bethel College, KS
Bryant University, RI
Buena Vista University, IA
Caldwell University, NJ
California Baptist University, CA
Capital University, OH
Cardinal Stritch University, WI
Carlow University, PA
Carroll College, MT
Carroll University, WI
Carson-Newman University, TN
Carthage College, WI
The Catholic University of America, DC
Cedar Crest College, PA
Centenary College of Louisiana, LA
Central College, IA
Central Methodist University, MO
Chaminade University of Honolulu, HI
Chatham University, PA
Clarke University, IA
Coe College, IA
The College of Idaho, ID
The College of Saint Rose, NY
The College of St. Scholastica, MN
Columbia College, MO
Concordia University Texas, TX
Delaware Valley University, PA
DeSales University, PA
Doane University, NE
Dominican University, IL
Drexel University, PA
Drury University, MO
Eastern University, PA
Elizabethtown College, PA
Elmira College, NY
Elms College, MA
Emmanuel College, GA
Emmanuel College, MA
Emory & Henry College, VA
Felician University, NJ
Florida Institute of Technology, FL
Franklin College, IN
Franklin Pierce University, NH
Georgian Court University, NJ
Gonzaga University, WA
Greenville University, IL
Gustavus Adolphus College, MN
Gwynedd Mercy University, PA
Hamline University, MN
Hanover College, IN
Hardin-Simmons University, TX
Hiram College, OH
Hope College, MI
Houghton College, NY
Illinois College, IL
Indiana Tech, IN
Iona College, NY
Iowa Wesleyan University, IA
Ithaca College, NY
James Madison University, VA
Johnson University, TN
Kettering University, MI
Keystone College, PA
King's College, PA
Kuyper College, MI
Lancaster Bible College, PA
Lasell College, MA
La Sierra University, CA
Lawrence University, WI
Lees-McRae College, NC
Lee University, TN
Lenoir-Rhyne University, NC
Limestone College, SC
Lincoln College, IL
Linfield College, OR
Long Island University, NY
Lynn University, FL
McDaniel College, MD
Merrimack College, MA
Methodist University, NC
Millikin University, IL
Misericordia University, PA
Missouri Baptist University, MO
Molloy College, NY
Mount Aloysius College, PA
Mount Marty College, SD
Mount St. Mary's University, MD

Muskingum University, OH
Nazareth College of Rochester, NY
Nebraska Wesleyan University, NE
Newberry College, SC
New Jersey Institute of Technology, NJ
Newman University, KS
Nichols College, MA
Northwest Christian University, OR
Northwest University, WA
Nyack College, NY
Ohio Christian University, OH
Olivet College, MI
Otterbein University, OH
Piedmont College, GA
Providence College, RI
Queens University of Charlotte, NC
Randolph-Macon College, VA
Regent University, VA
Rochester University, MI
Rockford University, IL
Roger Williams University, RI
Sacred Heart University, CT
Saint Anselm College, NH
St. Bonaventure University, NY
St. Catherine University, MN
Saint Francis University, PA
St. John Fisher College, NY
St. Joseph's College, Long Island Campus, NY
St. Joseph's College, New York, NY
Saint Joseph's University, PA
St. Lawrence University, NY
Saint Louis University, MO
Saint Martin's University, WA
Saint Mary's College, IN
St. Thomas Aquinas College, NY
Saint Vincent College, PA
Samford University, AL
Santa Clara University, CA
Schreiner University, TX
Simpson College, IA
Southern New Hampshire University, NH
Southwest Baptist University, MO
Springfield College, MA
Spring Hill College, AL
State University of New York College of Agriculture & Technology at Morrisville, NY
Stephens College, MO
Sterling College, KS
Stonehill College, MA
Suffolk University, MA
Tennessee Wesleyan University, TN
Thomas More University, KY
Toccoa Falls College, GA
Trevecca Nazarene University, TN
Truett McConnell University, GA
Union College, KY
Union University, TN
The University of Alabama at Birmingham, AL
University of Dubuque, IA
University of Evansville, IN
University of Jamestown, ND
University of Providence, MT
University of St. Francis, IL
University of Saint Joseph, CT
University of Saint Mary, KS
The University of Scranton, PA
The University of Toledo, OH
The University of Tulsa, OK
Ursuline College, OH
Wagner College, NY
Walsh University, OH
Wartburg College, IA
Waynesburg University, PA
Webber International University, FL
Wesleyan College, GA
Western New England University, MA
Wheaton College, IL
Whitworth University, WA
William Jessup University, CA
William Peace University, NC
Wingate University, NC
Xavier University, OH

Spouses of Current Students

Alaska Bible College, AK
Alliant International University - San Diego, CA
Andrews University, MI
Augustana University, SD
Aurora University, IL
Bethel College, KS
Boise Bible College, ID
Boise State University, ID
Bryan College, TN
Caldwell University, NJ
Cardinal Stritch University, WI
Carroll College, MT
Carroll University, WI
Centenary College of Louisiana, LA
Central Methodist University, MO
Clarion University of Pennsylvania, PA
The College of St. Scholastica, MN
Columbia College, MO
Columbia International University, SC
Dominican University, IL
Emmanuel College, GA
Emmanuel College, MA
Franklin College, IN
Franklin Pierce University, NH
Indiana Tech, IN
Johnson University, TN
Johnson University Florida, FL
Lee University, TN
Lincoln College, IL
Maranatha Baptist University, WI
Mid-Atlantic Christian University, NC
Mid-South Christian College, TN
Missouri Baptist University, MO
Mount Aloysius College, PA
Mount Marty College, SD
Newman University, KS
New Mexico State University, NM
Northwest University, WA
Nyack College, NY
Regent University, VA
St. Catherine University, MN
Saint Francis University, PA
St. Joseph's College, Long Island Campus, NY
St. Joseph's College, New York, NY
Saint Louis University, MO
St. Thomas Aquinas College, NY
Santa Clara University, CA
Truett McConnell University, GA
Union University, TN
The University of Alabama at Birmingham, AL
University of Dubuque, IA
University of Jamestown, ND
University of Maine, ME
University of Mississippi, MS
University of Providence, MT
University of Wyoming, WY
Wayne State University, MI
Wesleyan College, GA
Xavier University of Louisiana, LA

Spouses of Deceased or Disabled Public Servants

Eastern Washington University, WA
Grand Valley State University, MI
John Carroll University, OH
Michigan State University, MI
Mississippi State University, MS
New Mexico State University, NM
Nicholls State University, LA
Northeastern State University, OK
Samford University, AL
Southern Illinois University Carbondale, IL
Texas State University, TX
The University of Alabama, AL
The University of Alabama at Birmingham, AL
University of Kentucky, KY
University of Maine, ME
University of Massachusetts Dartmouth, MA
University of Missouri–St. Louis, MO
University of Pittsburgh, PA
University of South Carolina, SC
University of Utah, UT
Youngstown State University, OH

Twins

Caldwell University, NJ
Carthage College, WI
The Catholic University of America, DC
Central College, IA
The College of Saint Rose, NY
Drexel University, PA
Elmira College, NY
Emmanuel College, GA
Lake Erie College, OH
Long Island University, NY
Mount Aloysius College, PA
Ohio Wesleyan University, OH
Randolph College, VA
Sacred Heart University, CT
Saint Anselm College, NH
St. Joseph's College, Long Island Campus, NY
St. Joseph's College, New York, NY
St. Thomas Aquinas College, NY
Simpson College, IA
Southern New Hampshire University, NH
Sterling College, KS
Union University, TN
The University of Alabama at Birmingham, AL
University of Chicago, IL

Veterans

AdventHealth University, FL
Agnes Scott College, GA
Alliant International University - San Diego, CA
Anderson University, SC
Angelo State University, TX
Arkansas Tech University, AR
Asbury University, KY
Ashland University, OH
Augustana University, SD
Aurora University, IL
Austin College, TX
Austin Peay State University, TN
Baldwin Wallace University, OH
Ball State University, IN
Barton College, NC
Baylor University, TX
Belhaven University, MS
Belmont University, TN
Benedictine University, IL
Berry College, GA
Binghamton University, State University of New York, NY
Birmingham-Southern College, AL
Boise State University, ID
Boston University, MA
Brown University, RI

Bryant University, RI
Butler University, IN
Caldwell University, NJ
California Baptist University, CA
California Lutheran University, CA
California State University, Bakersfield, CA
California State University, San Bernardino, CA
Cameron University, OK
Campbellsville University, KY
Canisius College, NY
Cardinal Stritch University, WI
Carroll College, MT
Carthage College, WI
The Catholic University of America, DC
Cedarville University, OH
Centenary College of Louisiana, LA
Central College, IA
Central Washington University, WA
Chowan University, NC
Christian Brothers University, TN
The Citadel, The Military College of South Carolina, SC
Claremont McKenna College, CA
Clarion University of Pennsylvania, PA
Clarkson University, NY
Clemson University, SC
Coe College, IA
Colgate University, NY
College of Staten Island of the City University of New York, NY
Colorado Mesa University, CO
Colorado State University, CO
Columbia College, MO
Columbia International University, SC
Concordia University, St. Paul, MN
Concordia University Texas, TX
Concord University, WV
Dakota State University, SD
Dallas Baptist University, TX
Delaware Valley University, PA
DePaul University, IL
Dickinson College, PA
Dominican University of California, CA
Drury University, MO
Duquesne University, PA
East Central University, OK
Eastern New Mexico University, NM
Eastern University, PA
Eastern Washington University, WA
ECPI University, VA
Edinboro University of Pennsylvania, PA
Elmira College, NY
Elon University, NC
Emmanuel College, MA
Emory University, GA
Emporia State University, KS
The Evergreen State College, WA
Fairfield University, CT
Ferris State University, MI
Florida International University, FL
Fort Hays State University, KS
Framingham State University, MA
Franklin College, IN
Gannon University, PA
Georgia Gwinnett College, GA
Georgia Institute of Technology, GA
Georgian Court University, NJ
Glenville State College, WV
Gordon College, MA
Governors State University, IL
Grambling State University, LA
Grand Valley State University, MI
Grand View University, IA
Grinnell College, IA
Gwynedd Mercy University, PA
Hamline University, MN
Hampton University, VA
Hardin-Simmons University, TX
High Point University, NC
Hillsdale College, MI
Hofstra University, NY
Hollins University, VA
Hope International University, CA
Houghton College, NY
Illinois Institute of Technology, IL
Indiana State University, IN
Indiana Tech, IN
Iona College, NY
John Carroll University, OH
Johns Hopkins University, MD
Kean University, NJ
Kennesaw State University, GA
Kent State University, OH
Kent State University at Stark, OH
Kentucky State University, KY
King's College, PA
King University, TN
Lake Erie College, OH
Lasell College, MA
Lawrence University, WI
Lebanon Valley College, PA
Lees-McRae College, NC
Le Moyne College, NY
Lewis University, IL
Liberty University, VA
Linfield College, OR
Long Island University, NY
Louisiana State University and Agricultural & Mechanical College, LA
Loyola Marymount University, CA
Lynn University, FL
Malone University, OH
Manhattanville College, NY
Marymount University, VA
Maryville College, TN
Massachusetts College of Art and Design, MA
McDaniel College, MD
McKendree University, IL
Mercer University, GA
Merrimack College, MA
Michigan State University, MI
Michigan Technological University, MI
MidAmerica Nazarene University, KS
Midway University, KY
Midwestern State University, TX
Millikin University, IL
Minot State University, ND
Missouri Baptist University, MO
Missouri Southern State University, MO
Molloy College, NY
Montana State University Billings, MT
Montana Technological University, MT
Montreat College, NC
Morehead State University, KY
Morgan State University, MD
Nazareth College of Rochester, NY
Neumont College of Computer Science, UT
New Jersey Institute of Technology, NJ
New Mexico State University, NM
New York Institute of Technology, NY
Nicholls State University, LA
Northern Illinois University, IL
Northwestern State University of Louisiana, LA
Northwest University, WA
Occidental College, CA
Ohio Christian University, OH
Oklahoma Baptist University, OK
Olivet Nazarene University, IL
Oral Roberts University, OK
Otis College of Art and Design, CA
Otterbein University, OH
Ouachita Baptist University, AR
Pacific Lutheran University, WA
Pacific University, OR
Palm Beach Atlantic University, FL
Patrick Henry College, VA
Piedmont College, GA
Pomona College, CA
Portland State University, OR
Purdue University Northwest, IN
Queens University of Charlotte, NC
Randolph-Macon College, VA
Regent University, VA
Rocky Mountain College, MT
Rogers State University, OK
Roger Williams University, RI
Sacred Heart University, CT
Saginaw Valley State University, MI
St. Ambrose University, IA
Saint Anselm College, NH
St. Bonaventure University, NY
St. Edward's University, TX
St. John Fisher College, NY
St. John's University, NY
Saint Joseph's University, PA
Saint Louis University, MO
Saint Martin's University, WA
Saint Mary's College, IN
Saint Mary's College of California, CA
St. Mary's University, TX
St. Thomas Aquinas College, NY
Saint Vincent College, PA
Salem State University, MA
Samford University, AL
Sam Houston State University, TX
San Diego State University, CA
San Jose State University, CA
Santa Clara University, CA
Schreiner University, TX
Seattle Pacific University, WA
Simpson College, IA
Slippery Rock University of Pennsylvania, PA
Sonoma State University, CA
Southeastern Louisiana University, LA
Southeast Missouri State University, MO
Southern Connecticut State University, CT
Southern Illinois University Carbondale, IL
Southern New Hampshire University, NH
Southwestern College, KS
Southwestern University, TX
State University of New York College at Geneseo, NY
Stephen F. Austin State University, TX
Stephens College, MO
Stetson University, FL
Stevens–The Institute of Business & Arts, MO
Stonehill College, MA
Suffolk University, MA
SUNY Brockport, NY
Susquehanna University, PA
Tarleton State University, TX
Texas A&M University, TX
Texas A&M University–Commerce, TX
Texas A&M University–Texarkana, TX
Texas Christian University, TX
Texas Lutheran University, TX
Texas State University, TX
Texas Tech University, TX
Texas Woman's University, TX
Thomas College, ME

Thomas Jefferson University, PA
Thomas More University, KY
Toccoa Falls College, GA
Towson University, MD
Trinity Christian College, IL
Trinity University, TX
Truett McConnell University, GA
Union College, KY
Union University, TN
Universidad Adventista de las Antillas, PR
The University of Alabama at Birmingham, AL
University of Arkansas, AR
University of California, Riverside, CA
University of California, Santa Cruz, CA
University of Chicago, IL
University of Colorado Boulder, CO
University of Colorado Denver, CO
University of Evansville, IN
University of Houston–Clear Lake, TX
University of Idaho, ID
University of Illinois at Urbana-Champaign, IL
University of Indianapolis, IN
The University of Iowa, IA
The University of Kansas, KS
University of Kentucky, KY
University of Louisville, KY
University of Maine, ME
University of Maine at Presque Isle, ME
University of Maryland, College Park, MD
University of Massachusetts Amherst, MA
University of Massachusetts Boston, MA
University of Massachusetts Lowell, MA
University of Memphis, TN
University of Miami, FL
University of Michigan–Flint, MI
University of Mississippi, MS
University of Missouri–St. Louis, MO
University of Montana, MT
University of Mount Union, OH
University of Nebraska at Kearney, NE
University of Nevada, Las Vegas, NV
University of New Mexico, NM
The University of North Carolina at Charlotte, NC
The University of North Carolina at Greensboro, NC
University of North Dakota, ND
University of Northern Colorado, CO
University of Northern Iowa, IA
University of Oregon, OR
University of Pittsburgh, PA
University of Pittsburgh at Bradford, PA
University of Puget Sound, WA
University of Rochester, NY
University of St. Francis, IL
University of St. Thomas, TX
The University of Scranton, PA
University of South Carolina Aiken, SC
University of Southern Indiana, IN
University of Southern Mississippi, MS
The University of Tampa, FL
The University of Texas at Austin, TX
The University of Texas at Dallas, TX
The University of Texas Rio Grande Valley, TX
The University of Toledo, OH
University of Virginia, VA
University of Wisconsin–Green Bay, WI
University of Wisconsin–La Crosse, WI
University of Wisconsin–Milwaukee, WI
University of Wisconsin–Parkside, WI
University of Wisconsin–Stevens Point, WI
University of Wisconsin–Stout, WI
University of Wisconsin–Superior, WI
University of Wisconsin–Whitewater, WI
University of Wyoming, WY
Ursuline College, OH
Vanderbilt University, TN
Wagner College, NY
Walla Walla University, WA
Walsh College of Accountancy and Business Administration, MI
Washington & Jefferson College, PA
Washington State University, WA
Wayne State College, NE
Webber International University, FL
Wesleyan College, GA
Wesleyan University, CT
Western Kentucky University, KY
Western Michigan University, MI
Western Oregon University, OR
Western Washington University, WA
Westminster College, UT
West Texas A&M University, TX
Whitworth University, WA
Wichita State University, KS
William Jessup University, CA
William Paterson University of New Jersey, NJ
Wilson College, PA
Wingate University, NC
Youngstown State University, OH

Veterans' Children

AdventHealth University, FL
Anderson University, SC
Angelo State University, TX
Asbury University, KY
Berry College, GA
Binghamton University, State University of New York, NY
Butler University, IN
California Lutheran University, CA
Canisius College, NY
Chowan University, NC
Christian Brothers University, TN
The Citadel, The Military College of South Carolina, SC
College of Staten Island of the City University of New York, NY
Columbia International University, SC
DeSales University, PA
Eastern University, PA
ECPI University, VA
Edinboro University of Pennsylvania, PA
Elmira College, NY
Grinnell College, IA
Hampden-Sydney College, VA
Hillsdale College, MI
Hofstra University, NY
Houghton College, NY
Lake Erie College, OH
Lewis University, IL
Long Island University, NY
Loyola Marymount University, CA
McDaniel College, MD
Mercer University, GA
Michigan Technological University, MI
Morgan State University, MD
New College of Florida, FL
Northwestern State University of Louisiana, LA
Ohio Christian University, OH
Ouachita Baptist University, AR
Pacific Lutheran University, WA
Pomona College, CA
Regent University, VA
Roger Williams University, RI
Saint Anselm College, NH
St. Bonaventure University, NY
Saint Mary's College of California, CA
Salem State University, MA
Samford University, AL
Santa Clara University, CA
Southeastern Louisiana University, LA
Stephens College, MO
Sterling College, KS
Texas A&M University, TX
Texas State University, TX
Texas Tech University, TX
Thomas More University, KY
Truett McConnell University, GA
Union College, KY
The University of Alabama, AL
University of Evansville, IN
University of Houston–Clear Lake, TX
University of Kentucky, KY
University of Louisville, KY
University of Maine at Presque Isle, ME
University of Massachusetts Amherst, MA
University of Mississippi, MS
University of Nebraska at Omaha, NE
University of Nevada, Las Vegas, NV
University of Pittsburgh, PA
The University of Texas at Austin, TX
University of Virginia, VA
University of Wisconsin–Stout, WI
University of Wisconsin–Whitewater, WI
University of Wyoming, WY
Wagner College, NY
Walsh College of Accountancy and Business Administration, MI
Wayne State College, NE
Western Kentucky University, KY
Westminster College, UT
Wheaton College, IL
Whitworth University, WA
Wilson College, PA
Wingate University, NC

Athletic Grants for Undergraduates

Archery

Campbellsville University, KY M,W
Emmanuel College, GA M,W
Midway University, KY M,W
Mount Marty College, SD M,W
University of Pikeville, KY M,W

Baseball

Abilene Christian University, TX M
Academy of Art University, CA M
Adams State University, CO M
Anderson University, SC M
Angelo State University, TX M
Appalachian State University, NC M
Aquinas College, MI M
Arizona Christian University, AZ M
Arizona State University at the Downtown Phoenix campus, AZ M
Arizona State University at the Polytechnic campus, AZ M
Arizona State University at the Tempe campus, AZ M
Arizona State University at the West campus, AZ M
Arkansas Tech University, AR M
Auburn University, AL M
Auburn University at Montgomery, AL M
Augustana University, SD M
Austin Peay State University, TN M
Baker University, KS M
Ball State University, IN M
Barry University, FL M
Barton College, NC M
Baylor University, TX M
Belmont Abbey College, NC M
Belmont University, TN M
Bemidji State University, MN M
Bethel University, IN M
Binghamton University, State University of New York, NY M
Biola University, CA M
Boston College, MA M
Bowling Green State University, OH M
Bradley University, IL M
Brigham Young University, UT M
Bryan College, TN M
Bryant University, RI M
Butler University, IN M
Caldwell University, NJ M
California Baptist University, CA M
California Polytechnic State University, San Luis Obispo, CA M
California State Polytechnic University, Pomona, CA M
California State University, Dominguez Hills, CA M
California State University, Fresno, CA M
California State University, Fullerton, CA M
California State University, Long Beach, CA M
California State University, Los Angeles, CA M
California State University, Monterey Bay, CA M
California State University, Northridge, CA M
California State University, Sacramento, CA M
California State University, San Bernardino, CA M
California State University, Stanislaus, CA M
California University of Pennsylvania, PA M
Calumet College of Saint Joseph, IN M
Cameron University, OK M
Campbellsville University, KY M
Carson-Newman University, TN M
Catawba College, NC M
Cedarville University, OH M
Central Connecticut State University, CT M
Central Methodist University, MO M
Central Michigan University, MI M
Central Washington University, WA M
Chestnut Hill College, PA M
The Citadel, The Military College of South Carolina, SC M
Clarion University of Pennsylvania, PA M
Clemson University, SC M
Coastal Carolina University, SC M
The College of Idaho, ID M
The College of Saint Rose, NY M
College of the Ozarks, MO M
Colorado School of Mines, CO M
Columbia College, MO M
Concordia University, St. Paul, MN M
Creighton University, NE M
Dakota State University, SD M
Dallas Baptist University, TX M
Davidson College, NC M
Delta State University, MS M
Doane University, NE M
Dominican College, NY M
Drury University, MO M
East Carolina University, NC M
East Central University, OK M
Eastern Illinois University, IL M
Eastern Kentucky University, KY M
Eastern Michigan University, MI M
Eastern New Mexico University, NM M
Elon University, NC M
Emmanuel College, GA M
Emporia State University, KS M
Evangel University, MO M
Fairfield University, CT M
Felician University, NJ M
Florida Agricultural and Mechanical University, FL M
Florida Atlantic University, FL M
Florida Gulf Coast University, FL M
Florida Institute of Technology, FL M
Florida National University, FL M
Florida State University, FL M
Fordham University, NY M
Francis Marion University, SC M
Freed-Hardeman University, TN M
Gannon University, PA M
George Mason University, VA M
Georgetown College, KY M
Georgetown University, DC M
The George Washington University, DC M
Georgia College & State University, GA M
Georgia Gwinnett College, GA M,W
Georgia Institute of Technology, GA M
Georgia State University, GA M
Glenville State College, WV M
Gonzaga University, WA M
Goshen College, IN M
Graceland University, IA M
Grambling State University, LA M
Grand Valley State University, MI M
High Point University, NC M
Hillsdale College, MI M
Hofstra University, NY M
Hope International University, CA M
Houston Baptist University, TX M
Illinois Institute of Technology, IL M
Illinois State University, IL M
Indiana State University, IN M
Indiana University Bloomington, IN M
Indiana University of Pennsylvania, PA M
Indiana University South Bend, IN M
Indiana University Southeast, IN M
Inter American University of Puerto Rico, Aguadilla Campus, PR M
Iona College, NY M
Jacksonville State University, AL M
Jacksonville University, FL M
James Madison University, VA M
Kennesaw State University, GA M
King University, TN M
Kutztown University of Pennsylvania, PA M
Lawrence Technological University, MI M
Lee University, TN M
Lehigh University, PA M
Le Moyne College, NY M
Lenoir-Rhyne University, NC M
Lewis-Clark State College, ID M
Lewis University, IL M
Liberty University, VA M
Limestone College, SC M
Lincoln Memorial University, TN M
Lincoln University, PA M
Lindenwood University, MO M
Lipscomb University, TN M

Lock Haven University of Pennsylvania, PA M
Longwood University, VA M
Louisiana State University and Agricultural & Mechanical College, LA M
Louisiana State University in Shreveport, LA M
Loyola Marymount University, CA M
Loyola University New Orleans, LA M
Lynn University, FL M
Malone University, OH M
Manhattan College, NY M
Mansfield University of Pennsylvania, PA M
Marshall University, WV M
Marymount California University, CA M
Maryville University of Saint Louis, MO M
Mayville State University, ND M
McKendree University, IL M
Mercer University, GA M
Mercy College, NY M
Merrimack College, MA M
Miami University, OH M
Michigan State University, MI M
MidAmerica Nazarene University, KS M
Middle Tennessee State University, TN M
Midway University, KY M
Millersville University of Pennsylvania, PA M
Milligan University, TN M
Minnesota State University Mankato, MN M
Minot State University, ND M
Mississippi State University, MS M
Missouri Southern State University, MO M
Missouri State University, MO M
Missouri University of Science and Technology, MO M
Missouri Valley College, MO M
Molloy College, NY M
Morehead State University, KY M
Mount Marty College, SD M
Mount St. Mary's University, MD M
Mount Vernon Nazarene University, OH M
New Jersey Institute of Technology, NJ M
Newman University, KS M
New York Institute of Technology, NY M
Niagara University, NY M
North Carolina Central University, NC M
Northeastern State University, OK M
Northern Illinois University, IL M
Northern State University, SD M
North Greenville University, SC M
Northwestern State University of Louisiana, LA M
Northwest Nazarene University, ID M
Nyack College, NY M
Oakland University, MI M
Ohio Christian University, OH M
The Ohio State University, OH M
Ohio Valley University, WV M
Oklahoma Baptist University, OK M
Oklahoma State University, OK M
Old Dominion University, VA M
Olivet Nazarene University, IL M
Oral Roberts University, OK M
Palm Beach Atlantic University, FL M
Penn State University Park, PA M
Pepperdine University, CA M
Pittsburg State University, KS M
Point Loma Nazarene University, CA M
Prairie View A&M University, TX M
Purdue University Fort Wayne, IN M
Purdue University Northwest, IN M
Queens College of the City University of New York, NY M
Radford University, VA M
Rice University, TX M
Rochester University, MI M
Rogers State University, OK M
Rollins College, FL M
Sacred Heart University, CT M
Saginaw Valley State University, MI M
St. Ambrose University, IA M
St. Bonaventure University, NY M
St. Cloud State University, MN M
Saint Joseph's University, PA M
Saint Leo University, FL M
Saint Louis University, MO M
Saint Mary's College of California, CA M
St. Mary's University, TX M
St. Petersburg College, FL M
Samford University, AL M
Sam Houston State University, TX M
San Diego State University, CA M
San Francisco State University, CA M
San Jose State University, CA M
Santa Clara University, CA M
Shepherd University, WV M
Siena College, NY M
Slippery Rock University of Pennsylvania, PA M
Southeastern Louisiana University, LA M
Southeastern University, FL M
Southeast Missouri State University, MO M
Southern Illinois University Carbondale, IL M
Southern Illinois University Edwardsville, IL M
Southwest Baptist University, MO M
Southwestern College, KS M
Southwestern Oklahoma State University, OK M
Spring Hill College, AL M
Stanford University, CA M
Sterling College, KS M
Stetson University, FL M
Stony Brook University, State University of New York, NY M
Tabor College, KS M
Tarleton State University, TX M
Taylor University, IN M
Tennessee Wesleyan University, TN M
Texas A&M International University, TX M
Texas A&M University, TX M
Texas A&M University–Corpus Christi, TX M
Texas Christian University, TX M
Texas State University, TX M
Texas Tech University, TX M
Tiffin University, OH M
Towson University, MD M
Trevecca Nazarene University, TN M
Troy University, AL M
Truett McConnell University, GA M
Truman State University, MO M
Tulane University, LA M
Union University, TN M
University at Albany, State University of New York, NY M
The University of Alabama, AL M
The University of Alabama at Birmingham, AL M
The University of Arizona, AZ M
University of Arkansas, AR M
University of Arkansas at Little Rock, AR M
University of California, Los Angeles, CA M
University of California, Riverside, CA M
University of California, Santa Barbara, CA M
University of Central Arkansas, AR M
University of Central Florida, FL M
University of Cincinnati, OH M
University of Colorado Colorado Springs, CO M
University of Dayton, OH M
The University of Findlay, OH M
University of Hawaii at Manoa, HI M
University of Houston, TX M
University of Illinois at Chicago, IL M
University of Illinois at Springfield, IL M
The University of Iowa, IA M
University of Jamestown, ND M
The University of Kansas, KS M
University of Kentucky, KY M
University of Louisiana at Lafayette, LA M
University of Louisiana at Monroe, LA M
University of Louisville, KY M
University of Maine, ME M
University of Maryland, Baltimore County, MD M
University of Massachusetts Amherst, MA M
University of Massachusetts Lowell, MA M
University of Memphis, TN M
University of Michigan, MI M
University of Michigan–Dearborn, MI M
University of Minnesota, Duluth, MN M
University of Minnesota, Twin Cities Campus, MN M
University of Missouri–St. Louis, MO M
University of Montevallo, AL M
University of Nebraska at Kearney, NE M
University of Nebraska–Lincoln, NE M
University of Nevada, Las Vegas, NV M
University of Nevada, Reno, NV M
University of New Haven, CT M
University of New Mexico, NM M

The University of North Carolina at Chapel Hill, NC M
The University of North Carolina at Charlotte, NC M
The University of North Carolina at Greensboro, NC M
The University of North Carolina at Pembroke, NC M
The University of North Carolina Wilmington, NC M
University of Northern Colorado, CO M
University of Notre Dame, IN M
University of Oregon, OR M
University of Pikeville, KY M
University of Portland, OR M
University of Richmond, VA M
University of St. Francis, IL M
University of Saint Francis, IN M
University of Saint Mary, KS M
University of San Diego, CA M
University of San Francisco, CA M
University of Science and Arts of Oklahoma, OK M
University of South Carolina, SC M
University of South Carolina Aiken, SC M
University of Southern Indiana, IN M
University of Southern Mississippi, MS M
University of South Florida, FL M
The University of Tampa, FL M
The University of Tennessee, TN M
The University of Tennessee at Martin, TN M
The University of Texas at San Antonio, TX M
The University of Texas Rio Grande Valley, TX M
University of the Incarnate Word, TX M
University of the Pacific, CA M
The University of Toledo, OH M
University of Utah, UT M
University of Virginia, VA M
University of Washington, WA M
The University of West Alabama, AL M
University of West Georgia, GA M
University of Wisconsin–Milwaukee, WI M
University of Wisconsin–Parkside, WI M
Upper Iowa University, IA M
Utah Valley University, UT M
Valdosta State University, GA M
Valley City State University, ND M
Valparaiso University, IN M
Vanderbilt University, TN M
Vanguard University of Southern California, CA M
Villanova University, PA M
Virginia Commonwealth University, VA M
Wake Forest University, NC M
Washington State University, WA M
Wayland Baptist University, TX M
Wayne State College, NE M
Wayne State University, MI M
Webber International University, FL M
West Chester University of Pennsylvania, PA M
Western Carolina University, NC M
Western Kentucky University, KY M
Western Michigan University, MI M
Western Oregon University, OR M
Westmont College, CA M
Wichita State University, KS M
William & Mary, VA M
Wingate University, NC M
Wofford College, SC M
Wright State University, OH M
Xavier University, OH M
Youngstown State University, OH M

Basketball

Abilene Christian University, TX M,W
Academy of Art University, CA M,W
Adams State University, CO M,W
American University, DC M,W
Anderson University, SC M,W
Angelo State University, TX M,W
Appalachian State University, NC M,W
Aquinas College, MI M,W
Arizona Christian University, AZ M,W
Arizona State University at the Downtown Phoenix campus, AZ M,W
Arizona State University at the Polytechnic campus, AZ M,W
Arizona State University at the Tempe campus, AZ M,W
Arizona State University at the West campus, AZ M,W
Arkansas Tech University, AR M,W
Assumption University, MA M,W
Auburn University, AL M,W
Auburn University at Montgomery, AL M,W
Augustana University, SD M,W
Austin Peay State University, TN M,W
Baker University, KS M,W
Ball State University, IN M,W
Barry University, FL M,W
Barton College, NC M,W
Bayamón Central University, PR M,W
Baylor University, TX M,W
Belmont Abbey College, NC M,W
Belmont University, TN M,W
Bemidji State University, MN M,W
Bentley University, MA M,W
Bethel University, IN M,W
Binghamton University, State University of New York, NY M,W
Biola University, CA M,W
Black Hills State University, SD M,W
Boise State University, ID M,W
Boston College, MA M,W
Bowling Green State University, OH M,W
Bradley University, IL M,W
Brigham Young University, UT M,W
Bryan College, TN M,W
Bryant University, RI M,W
Bucknell University, PA M,W
Butler University, IN M,W
Caldwell University, NJ M,W
California Baptist University, CA M,W
California Polytechnic State University, San Luis Obispo, CA M,W
California State Polytechnic University, Pomona, CA M,W
California State University, Bakersfield, CA M
California State University, Dominguez Hills, CA M,W
California State University, Fresno, CA M,W
California State University, Fullerton, CA M,W
California State University, Long Beach, CA M,W
California State University, Los Angeles, CA M,W
California State University, Monterey Bay, CA M,W
California State University, Northridge, CA M,W
California State University, Sacramento, CA M,W
California State University, San Bernardino, CA M,W
California State University, Stanislaus, CA M,W
California University of Pennsylvania, PA M,W
Calumet College of Saint Joseph, IN M,W
Cameron University, OK M,W
Campbellsville University, KY M,W
Carlow University, PA M,W
Carson-Newman University, TN M,W
Catawba College, NC M,W
Cedarville University, OH M,W
Central Connecticut State University, CT M,W
Central Methodist University, MO M,W
Central Michigan University, MI M,W
Central Washington University, WA M,W
Chaminade University of Honolulu, HI M,W
Chestnut Hill College, PA M,W
The Citadel, The Military College of South Carolina, SC M
Clarion University of Pennsylvania, PA M,W
Clemson University, SC M,W
Coastal Carolina University, SC M,W
Colgate University, NY M,W
The College of Idaho, ID M,W
College of Saint Mary, NE W
The College of Saint Rose, NY M,W
College of the Holy Cross, MA M,W
College of the Ozarks, MO M,W
Colorado School of Mines, CO M,W
Colorado State University, CO M,W
Columbia College, MO M,W
Columbia College, SC W
Columbia International University, SC M,W
Concordia University, St. Paul, MN M,W
Creighton University, NE M,W
Dakota State University, SD M,W
Dallas Baptist University, TX M
Davidson College, NC M,W
Delta State University, MS M,W
DePaul University, IL M,W
Dillard University, LA M,W
Doane University, NE M,W
Dominican College, NY M,W
Dominican University of California, CA M,W
Drake University, IA M,W
Drexel University, PA M,W
Drury University, MO M,W
East Carolina University, NC M,W
East Central University, OK M,W
Eastern Illinois University, IL M,W
Eastern Kentucky University, KY M,W

Eastern Michigan University, MI M,W
Eastern New Mexico University, NM M,W
Eastern Oregon University, OR M,W
Eastern Washington University, WA M,W
Edinboro University of Pennsylvania, PA M,W
Elon University, NC M,W
Emmanuel College, GA M,W
Emporia State University, KS M,W
Evangel University, MO M,W
Fairfield University, CT M,W
Fayetteville State University, NC M,W
Felician University, NJ M,W
Ferris State University, MI M,W
Florida Agricultural and Mechanical University, FL M,W
Florida Atlantic University, FL M,W
Florida Gulf Coast University, FL M,W
Florida Institute of Technology, FL M,W
Florida National University, FL M,W
Florida State University, FL M,W
Fordham University, NY M,W
Fort Lewis College, CO M,W
Francis Marion University, SC M,W
Freed-Hardeman University, TN M,W
Gannon University, PA M,W
George Mason University, VA M,W
Georgetown College, KY M,W
Georgetown University, DC M,W
The George Washington University, DC M,W
Georgia College & State University, GA M,W
Georgia Institute of Technology, GA M,W
Georgian Court University, NJ M,W
Georgia State University, GA M,W
Glenville State College, WV M,W
Gonzaga University, WA M,W
Goshen College, IN M,W
Governors State University, IL M,W
Graceland University, IA M,W
Grambling State University, LA M,W
Grand Valley State University, MI M,W
Hampton University, VA M,W
High Point University, NC M,W
Hillsdale College, MI M,W
Hofstra University, NY M,W
Hope International University, CA M,W
Houston Baptist University, TX M,W
Illinois State University, IL M,W
Indiana State University, IN M,W
Indiana University Bloomington, IN M,W
Indiana University Northwest, IN M,W
Indiana University of Pennsylvania, PA M,W
Indiana University-Purdue University Indianapolis, IN M,W
Indiana University South Bend, IN M,W
Indiana University Southeast, IN M,W
Inter American University of Puerto Rico, Aguadilla Campus, PR M,W
Iona College, NY M,W
Jacksonville State University, AL M,W
Jacksonville University, FL M,W
James Madison University, VA M,W
John Brown University, AR M,W
Kennesaw State University, GA M,W
King University, TN M,W
Kutztown University of Pennsylvania, PA M,W
Lawrence Technological University, MI M,W
Lee University, TN M,W
Lehigh University, PA M,W
Le Moyne College, NY M,W
Lenoir-Rhyne University, NC M,W
Lewis-Clark State College, ID M,W
Lewis University, IL M,W
Liberty University, VA M,W
Life University, GA M,W
Limestone College, SC M,W
Lincoln Memorial University, TN M,W
Lincoln University, PA M,W
Lindenwood University, MO M,W
Lipscomb University, TN M,W
Lock Haven University of Pennsylvania, PA M,W
Longwood University, VA M,W
Louisiana State University and Agricultural & Mechanical College, LA M,W
Louisiana State University in Shreveport, LA M,W
Loyola Marymount University, CA M,W
Loyola University Chicago, IL M,W
Loyola University Maryland, MD M,W
Loyola University New Orleans, LA M,W
Lynn University, FL M,W
Malone University, OH M,W
Manhattan College, NY M,W
Mansfield University of Pennsylvania, PA M,W
Marquette University, WI M,W
Marshall University, WV M,W
Maryville University of Saint Louis, MO M,W
Mayville State University, ND M,W
McKendree University, IL M,W
Mercer University, GA M,W
Mercy College, NY M,W
Merrimack College, MA M,W
Miami University, OH M,W
Michigan State University, MI M,W
Michigan Technological University, MI M,W
MidAmerica Nazarene University, KS M,W
Middle Tennessee State University, TN M,W
Midway University, KY M,W
Millersville University of Pennsylvania, PA M,W
Milligan University, TN M,W
Minnesota State University Mankato, MN M,W
Minot State University, ND M,W
Mississippi State University, MS M,W
Missouri Southern State University, MO M,W
Missouri State University, MO M,W
Missouri University of Science and Technology, MO M,W
Missouri Valley College, MO M,W
Molloy College, NY M,W
Montana State University, MT M,W
Montana Technological University, MT M,W
Morehead State University, KY M,W
Mount Marty College, SD M,W
Mount St. Mary's University, MD M,W
Mount Vernon Nazarene University, OH M,W
New Jersey Institute of Technology, NJ M,W
Newman University, KS M,W
New York Institute of Technology, NY M,W
Niagara University, NY M,W
North Carolina Central University, NC M,W
Northeastern State University, OK M,W
Northern Arizona University, AZ M,W
Northern Illinois University, IL M,W
Northern State University, SD M,W
North Greenville University, SC M,W
Northwest Christian University, OR M,W
Northwestern State University of Louisiana, LA M,W
Northwest Missouri State University, MO M,W
Northwest Nazarene University, ID M,W
Northwest University, WA M,W
Nyack College, NY M,W
Oakland University, MI M,W
Ohio Christian University, OH M,W
The Ohio State University, OH M,W
Ohio Valley University, WV M,W
Oklahoma Baptist University, OK M,W
Oklahoma State University, OK M,W
Old Dominion University, VA M,W
Olivet Nazarene University, IL M,W
Oral Roberts University, OK M,W
Palm Beach Atlantic University, FL M,W
Penn State University Park, PA M,W
Pepperdine University, CA M,W
Pittsburg State University, KS M,W
Point Loma Nazarene University, CA M,W
Prairie View A&M University, TX M,W
Providence College, RI M,W
Purdue University Fort Wayne, IN M,W
Purdue University Northwest, IN M,W
Queens College of the City University of New York, NY M,W
Queens University of Charlotte, NC M,W
Radford University, VA M,W
Rice University, TX M,W
Rochester University, MI M,W
Rocky Mountain College, MT M,W
Rogers State University, OK M,W
Rollins College, FL M,W
Sacred Heart University, CT M,W
Saginaw Valley State University, MI M,W
St. Ambrose University, IA M,W
St. Bonaventure University, NY M,W
St. Cloud State University, MN M,W
Saint Francis University, PA M,W
Saint Joseph's University, PA M,W
Saint Leo University, FL M,W
Saint Louis University, MO M,W
Saint Mary's College of California, CA M,W
St. Mary's University, TX M,W
St. Petersburg College, FL M,W
Samford University, AL M,W
Sam Houston State University, TX M,W
San Diego State University, CA M,W
San Francisco State University, CA M,W
San Jose State University, CA M,W
Santa Clara University, CA M,W
Seattle University, WA M,W
Shepherd University, WV M,W
Siena College, NY M,W

Slippery Rock University of Pennsylvania, PA M,W
Southeastern Louisiana University, LA M,W
Southeastern University, FL M,W
Southeast Missouri State University, MO M,W
Southern Illinois University Carbondale, IL M,W
Southern Illinois University Edwardsville, IL M,W
Southern Methodist University, TX M,W
Southwest Baptist University, MO M,W
Southwestern College, KS M,W
Southwestern Oklahoma State University, OK M,W
Spring Hill College, AL M,W
Stanford University, CA M,W
Sterling College, KS M,W
Stetson University, FL M,W
Stony Brook University, State University of New York, NY M,W
Tabor College, KS M,W
Tarleton State University, TX M,W
Taylor University, IN M,W
Temple University, PA M,W
Tennessee Wesleyan University, TN M,W
Texas A&M International University, TX M,W
Texas A&M University, TX M,W
Texas A&M University–Commerce, TX M,W
Texas A&M University–Corpus Christi, TX M,W
Texas Christian University, TX M,W
Texas State University, TX M,W
Texas Tech University, TX M,W
Texas Woman's University, TX W
Tiffin University, OH M,W
Towson University, MD M,W
Trevecca Nazarene University, TN M,W
Troy University, AL M,W
Truett McConnell University, GA M,W
Truman State University, MO M,W
Tulane University, LA M,W
Union University, TN M,W
University at Albany, State University of New York, NY M,W
University at Buffalo, the State University of New York, NY M,W
The University of Akron, OH M,W
The University of Alabama, AL M,W
The University of Alabama at Birmingham, AL M,W
University of Alaska Fairbanks, AK M,W
The University of Arizona, AZ M,W
University of Arkansas, AR M,W
University of Arkansas at Little Rock, AR M
University of California, Los Angeles, CA M,W
University of California, Merced, CA M,W
University of California, Riverside, CA M,W
University of California, Santa Barbara, CA M,W
University of Central Arkansas, AR M,W
University of Central Florida, FL M,W
University of Cincinnati, OH M,W
University of Colorado Boulder, CO M,W
University of Colorado Colorado Springs, CO M,W
University of Dayton, OH M,W
University of Denver, CO M,W
The University of Findlay, OH M,W
University of Guam, GU M,W
University of Hawaii at Manoa, HI M,W
University of Houston, TX M,W
University of Idaho, ID M,W
University of Illinois at Chicago, IL M,W
University of Illinois at Springfield, IL M,W
The University of Iowa, IA M,W
University of Jamestown, ND M,W
The University of Kansas, KS M,W
University of Kentucky, KY M,W
University of Louisiana at Lafayette, LA M,W
University of Louisiana at Monroe, LA M,W
University of Louisville, KY M,W
University of Maine, ME M,W
University of Maryland, Baltimore County, MD M,W
University of Massachusetts Amherst, MA M,W
University of Massachusetts Lowell, MA M,W
University of Memphis, TN M,W
University of Michigan, MI M,W
University of Michigan–Dearborn, MI M,W
University of Minnesota, Duluth, MN M,W
University of Minnesota, Twin Cities Campus, MN M,W
University of Missouri–St. Louis, MO M,W
University of Montana, MT M,W
University of Montevallo, AL M,W
University of Nebraska at Kearney, NE M,W
University of Nebraska–Lincoln, NE M,W
University of Nevada, Las Vegas, NV M,W
University of Nevada, Reno, NV M,W
University of New Hampshire, NH M,W
University of New Haven, CT M,W
University of New Mexico, NM M,W
The University of North Carolina at Chapel Hill, NC M,W
The University of North Carolina at Charlotte, NC M,W
The University of North Carolina at Greensboro, NC M,W
The University of North Carolina at Pembroke, NC M,W
The University of North Carolina Wilmington, NC M,W
University of North Dakota, ND M,W
University of Northern Colorado, CO M,W
University of Northern Iowa, IA M,W
University of North Texas, TX M,W
University of Notre Dame, IN M,W
University of Oregon, OR M,W
University of Pikeville, KY M,W
University of Portland, OR M,W
University of Providence, MT M,W
University of Richmond, VA M,W
University of St. Francis, IL M,W
University of Saint Francis, IN M,W
University of Saint Mary, KS M,W
University of St. Thomas, TX M,W
University of San Diego, CA M,W
University of San Francisco, CA M,W
University of Science and Arts of Oklahoma, OK M,W
University of South Carolina, SC M,W
University of South Carolina Aiken, SC M,W
University of South Dakota, SD M,W
University of Southern Indiana, IN M,W
University of Southern Mississippi, MS M,W
University of South Florida, FL W
The University of Tampa, FL M,W
The University of Tennessee, TN M,W
The University of Tennessee at Chattanooga, TN M,W
The University of Tennessee at Martin, TN M,W
The University of Texas at El Paso, TX M,W
The University of Texas at San Antonio, TX M,W
The University of Texas Rio Grande Valley, TX M,W
University of the Incarnate Word, TX M,W
University of the Pacific, CA M,W
The University of Toledo, OH M,W
The University of Tulsa, OK M,W
University of Utah, UT M,W
University of Virginia, VA M,W
University of Washington, WA M,W
The University of West Alabama, AL M,W
University of West Georgia, GA M,W
University of Wisconsin–Green Bay, WI M,W
University of Wisconsin–Madison, WI M,W
University of Wisconsin–Milwaukee, WI M,W
University of Wisconsin–Parkside, WI M,W
University of Wyoming, WY M,W
Upper Iowa University, IA M,W
Ursuline College, OH W
Utah State University, UT M,W
Utah Valley University, UT M,W
Valdosta State University, GA M,W
Valley City State University, ND M,W
Valparaiso University, IN M,W
Vanderbilt University, TN M,W
Vanguard University of Southern California, CA M,W
Villanova University, PA M,W
Virginia Commonwealth University, VA M,W
Wake Forest University, NC M,W
Washington State University, WA M,W
Wayland Baptist University, TX M,W
Wayne State College, NE M,W
Wayne State University, MI M,W
Webber International University, FL M,W
Weber State University, UT M,W
West Chester University of Pennsylvania, PA M,W
Western Carolina University, NC M,W
Western Colorado University, CO M,W
Western Kentucky University, KY M,W
Western Michigan University, MI M,W
Western New Mexico University, NM M,W
Western Oregon University, OR M,W

Western Washington University, WA M,W
Westminster College, UT M,W
Westmont College, CA M,W
Wichita State University, KS M,W
William & Mary, VA M,W
Wingate University, NC M,W
Wofford College, SC M,W
Wright State University, OH M,W
Xavier University, OH M,W
Xavier University of Louisiana, LA M,W
Youngstown State University, OH M,W

Bowling

Aquinas College, MI M,W
Baker University, KS M,W
Belmont Abbey College, NC M,W
Bethel University, IN M,W
Caldwell University, NJ W
California Polytechnic State University, San Luis Obispo, CA M,W
Calumet College of Saint Joseph, IN M,W
Campbellsville University, KY M,W
Chestnut Hill College, PA W
College of Saint Mary, NE W
Columbia College, MO W
Emmanuel College, GA M,W
Felician University, NJ W
Florida Agricultural and Mechanical University, FL W
Grambling State University, LA W
Hampton University, VA W
Kutztown University of Pennsylvania, PA W
Lawrence Technological University, MI M,W
Lewis University, IL M,W
Life University, GA M
Lincoln Memorial University, TN M,W
Lindenwood University, MO M,W
Maryville University of Saint Louis, MO W
McKendree University, IL W
Midway University, KY M,W
Molloy College, NY W
Mount St. Mary's University, MD W
Newman University, KS M,W
North Carolina Central University, NC W
Prairie View A&M University, TX W
Rochester University, MI M,W
Sacred Heart University, CT W
Sam Houston State University, TX W
Tennessee Wesleyan University, TN M,W
The University of Alabama at Birmingham, AL W
University of Michigan–Dearborn, MI M,W
University of Nebraska–Lincoln, NE W
University of Pikeville, KY M,W
University of St. Francis, IL M,W
Ursuline College, OH W
Valparaiso University, IN W
Vanderbilt University, TN W
Webber International University, FL M,W
Wichita State University, KS M,W

Cheerleading

Anderson University, SC W
Angelo State University, TX M,W
Aquinas College, MI M,W
Arizona Christian University, AZ W
Arkansas Tech University, AR M,W
Auburn University at Montgomery, AL M,W
Austin Peay State University, TN M,W
Baker University, KS M,W
Barton College, NC W
Baylor University, TX M,W
Belmont Abbey College, NC W
Bethel University, IN M,W
Biola University, CA W
Brigham Young University, UT M,W
California Baptist University, CA W
Calumet College of Saint Joseph, IN W
Cameron University, OK M,W
Campbellsville University, KY M,W
Central Methodist University, MO M,W
Delta State University, MS M,W
Doane University, NE W
Drake University, IA M,W
Drury University, MO M,W
Eastern Oregon University, OR W
East Texas Baptist University, TX W
Emporia State University, KS M,W
Freed-Hardeman University, TN W
Gannon University, PA W
Georgetown College, KY M,W
Georgia Institute of Technology, GA M,W
Graceland University, IA M,W
Hofstra University, NY M,W
John Brown University, AR W
King University, TN W
Lenoir-Rhyne University, NC M,W
Lewis University, IL W
Liberty University, VA M,W
Limestone College, SC M,W
Lincoln University, PA M,W
Lindenwood University, MO M,W
Lipscomb University, TN W
Loyola University New Orleans, LA M,W
Maryville University of Saint Louis, MO M,W
McKendree University, IL M,W
MidAmerica Nazarene University, KS M,W
Middle Tennessee State University, TN M,W
Midway University, KY M,W
Milligan University, TN W
Mississippi State University, MS M,W
Missouri Valley College, MO M,W
Montana State University, MT M,W
Morehead State University, KY M,W
Mount Marty College, SD W
North Greenville University, SC M,W
Northwestern State University of Louisiana, LA M,W
Northwest Missouri State University, MO M,W
The Ohio State University, OH M,W
Oklahoma State University, OK M,W
Old Dominion University, VA M,W
Olivet Nazarene University, IL M,W
Pittsburg State University, KS M,W
Prairie View A&M University, TX M,W
Rochester University, MI M,W
Rocky Mountain College, MT M,W
Rogers State University, OK M,W
Sam Houston State University, TX M,W
San Jose State University, CA M,W
Southeast Missouri State University, MO M,W
Southern Methodist University, TX M,W
Southwest Baptist University, MO M,W
Southwestern College, KS M,W
Southwestern Oklahoma State University, OK M,W
Sterling College, KS M,W
Tabor College, KS M,W
Tarleton State University, TX M,W
Tennessee Wesleyan University, TN M,W
Texas A&M University–Commerce, TX M,W
Tiffin University, OH W
Union University, TN W
The University of Alabama, AL M,W
University of Central Arkansas, AR M,W
University of Central Florida, FL W
University of Hawaii at Manoa, HI M,W
University of Illinois at Springfield, IL M,W
University of Jamestown, ND M,W
University of Memphis, TN M,W
University of Michigan, MI M,W
University of Nevada, Las Vegas, NV M,W
University of Pikeville, KY M,W
University of Providence, MT M,W
University of St. Francis, IL M,W
University of Saint Francis, IN M,W
University of Saint Mary, KS M,W
University of Science and Arts of Oklahoma, OK M,W
The University of Tennessee at Martin, TN W
University of the Incarnate Word, TX W
University of Utah, UT M,W
University of West Georgia, GA W
Vanguard University of Southern California, CA W
Wayland Baptist University, TX M,W
Webber International University, FL W
Weber State University, UT M,W
Wichita State University, KS M,W
Wright State University, OH M,W

Crew

Barry University, FL W
Boston College, MA W
California State University, Sacramento, CA M,W
Clemson University, SC W
College of the Holy Cross, MA W
Creighton University, NE W
Drexel University, PA M,W
Eastern Michigan University, MI W
Fairfield University, CT M,W
Florida Institute of Technology, FL M,W
Fordham University, NY W
George Mason University, VA W
Georgetown University, DC M,W
The George Washington University, DC M,W
Jacksonville University, FL M,W
Lehigh University, PA W
Loyola Marymount University, CA W
Loyola University Maryland, MD M,W
Merrimack College, MA W
Michigan State University, MI W
Old Dominion University, VA W
Sacred Heart University, CT W
Saint Joseph's University, PA M,W

Saint Mary's College of California, CA W
Southern Methodist University, TX W
Stanford University, CA M,W
Stetson University, FL M,W
Temple University, PA M
The University of Alabama, AL W
University of California, Los Angeles, CA W
University of Central Florida, FL W
The University of Iowa, IA W
The University of Kansas, KS W
University of Massachusetts Amherst, MA W
University of Michigan, MI W
The University of North Carolina at Chapel Hill, NC W
University of Notre Dame, IN W
University of San Diego, CA W
The University of Tampa, FL W
The University of Tennessee, TN W
The University of Tulsa, OK W
University of Washington, WA M,W
Washington State University, WA W
Western Washington University, WA W

Cross-country running

Abilene Christian University, TX M,W
Academy of Art University, CA M,W
Adams State University, CO M,W
American University, DC M,W
Anderson University, SC M,W
Angelo State University, TX M,W
Appalachian State University, NC M,W
Aquinas College, MI M,W
Arizona Christian University, AZ M,W
Arizona State University at the Downtown Phoenix campus, AZ M,W
Arizona State University at the Polytechnic campus, AZ M,W
Arizona State University at the Tempe campus, AZ M,W
Arizona State University at the West campus, AZ M,W
Arkansas Tech University, AR W
Auburn University, AL M,W
Auburn University at Montgomery, AL M,W
Augustana University, SD M,W
Austin Peay State University, TN M,W
Baker University, KS M,W
Ball State University, IN W
Barton College, NC M,W
Bayamón Central University, PR M,W
Baylor University, TX M,W
Belmont Abbey College, NC M,W
Belmont University, TN M,W
Bemidji State University, MN W
Bethel University, IN M,W
Binghamton University, State University of New York, NY M,W
Biola University, CA M,W
Black Hills State University, SD M,W
Boise State University, ID M,W
Boston College, MA M,W
Bowling Green State University, OH M,W
Bradley University, IL M,W
Brigham Young University, UT M,W
Bryan College, TN M,W
Bryant University, RI M,W
Bucknell University, PA W
Butler University, IN M,W
Caldwell University, NJ M,W
California Baptist University, CA M,W
California Polytechnic State University, San Luis Obispo, CA M,W
California State Polytechnic University, Pomona, CA M,W
California State University, Fresno, CA M,W
California State University, Fullerton, CA M,W
California State University, Long Beach, CA M,W
California State University, Los Angeles, CA M,W
California State University, Monterey Bay, CA M,W
California State University, Northridge, CA M,W
California State University, Sacramento, CA M,W
California State University, Stanislaus, CA M,W
California University of Pennsylvania, PA M,W
Calumet College of Saint Joseph, IN M,W
Cameron University, OK M,W
Campbellsville University, KY M,W
Carlow University, PA M,W
Carson-Newman University, TN M,W
Catawba College, NC M,W
Cedarville University, OH M,W
Central Connecticut State University, CT M,W
Central Methodist University, MO M,W
Central Michigan University, MI M,W
Central Washington University, WA M,W
Chaminade University of Honolulu, HI M,W
Chestnut Hill College, PA M,W
The Citadel, The Military College of South Carolina, SC M,W
Clarion University of Pennsylvania, PA W
Clemson University, SC M,W
Coastal Carolina University, SC M,W
The College of Idaho, ID M,W
College of Saint Mary, NE W
The College of Saint Rose, NY M,W
College of the Holy Cross, MA W
Colorado School of Mines, CO M,W
Colorado State University, CO M,W
Columbia College, MO M,W
Columbia College, SC W
Columbia International University, SC M,W
Concordia University, St. Paul, MN M,W
Creighton University, NE M,W
Dakota State University, SD M,W
Dallas Baptist University, TX W
Davidson College, NC M,W
Delta State University, MS W
DePaul University, IL M,W
Dillard University, LA M,W
Doane University, NE M,W
Dominican College, NY M,W
Dominican University of California, CA M,W
Drake University, IA M,W
Drury University, MO M,W
East Carolina University, NC M,W
East Central University, OK M,W
Eastern Illinois University, IL M,W
Eastern Kentucky University, KY M,W
Eastern Michigan University, MI M,W
Eastern New Mexico University, NM M,W
Eastern Oregon University, OR M,W
Eastern Washington University, WA M,W
Edinboro University of Pennsylvania, PA M,W
Elon University, NC M,W
Emmanuel College, GA M,W
Emporia State University, KS M,W
Evangel University, MO M,W
Fairfield University, CT M,W
Fayetteville State University, NC M,W
Felician University, NJ M,W
Ferris State University, MI M,W
Florida Agricultural and Mechanical University, FL M,W
Florida Gulf Coast University, FL M,W
Florida National University, FL M,W
Florida State University, FL M,W
Fordham University, NY M,W
Fort Lewis College, CO M,W
Francis Marion University, SC M,W
Freed-Hardeman University, TN M,W
Gannon University, PA M,W
George Mason University, VA M,W
Georgetown College, KY M,W
Georgetown University, DC M,W
The George Washington University, DC M,W
Georgia College & State University, GA M,W
Georgia Institute of Technology, GA M,W
Georgian Court University, NJ M,W
Georgia State University, GA W
Glenville State College, WV M,W
Gonzaga University, WA M,W
Goshen College, IN M,W
Governors State University, IL M,W
Graceland University, IA M,W
Grand Valley State University, MI M,W
Hampton University, VA M,W
High Point University, NC M,W
Hillsdale College, MI M,W
Hofstra University, NY M,W
Hope International University, CA M,W
Houston Baptist University, TX M,W
Illinois Institute of Technology, IL M,W
Illinois State University, IL M,W
Indiana State University, IN M,W
Indiana University Bloomington, IN M,W
Indiana University Northwest, IN M,W
Indiana University of Pennsylvania, PA M,W
Indiana University-Purdue University Indianapolis, IN M,W
Indiana University South Bend, IN M,W
Inter American University of Puerto Rico, Aguadilla Campus, PR M,W
Iona College, NY M,W
Jacksonville State University, AL M,W
Jacksonville University, FL W
James Madison University, VA W
John Brown University, AR M,W
Kennesaw State University, GA M,W
King University, TN M,W
Kutztown University of Pennsylvania, PA M,W
Lawrence Technological University, MI M,W
Lee University, TN M,W

Lehigh University, PA	M,W
Le Moyne College, NY	M,W
Lenoir-Rhyne University, NC	M,W
Lewis-Clark State College, ID	M,W
Lewis University, IL	M,W
Liberty University, VA	M,W
Life University, GA	W
Limestone College, SC	M,W
Lincoln Memorial University, TN	M,W
Lincoln University, PA	M,W
Lindenwood University, MO	M,W
Lipscomb University, TN	M,W
Lock Haven University of Pennsylvania, PA	M,W
Longwood University, VA	M,W
Louisiana State University and Agricultural & Mechanical College, LA	M,W
Loyola Marymount University, CA	M,W
Loyola University Chicago, IL	M,W
Loyola University Maryland, MD	M,W
Loyola University New Orleans, LA	M,W
Lynn University, FL	M,W
Malone University, OH	M,W
Manhattan College, NY	M,W
Mansfield University of Pennsylvania, PA	M,W
Marquette University, WI	M,W
Marshall University, WV	M,W
Maryville University of Saint Louis, MO	M,W
McKendree University, IL	M,W
Mercer University, GA	M,W
Merrimack College, MA	M,W
Miami University, OH	M,W
Michigan State University, MI	M,W
Michigan Technological University, MI	M,W
MidAmerica Nazarene University, KS	M,W
Middle Tennessee State University, TN	M,W
Midway University, KY	M,W
Millersville University of Pennsylvania, PA	W
Milligan University, TN	M,W
Minnesota State University Mankato, MN	M,W
Minot State University, ND	M,W
Mississippi State University, MS	W
Missouri Southern State University, MO	M,W
Missouri State University, MO	W
Missouri University of Science and Technology, MO	M,W
Missouri Valley College, MO	M,W
Molloy College, NY	M,W
Montana State University, MT	M,W
Montana Technological University, MT	M,W
Morehead State University, KY	M,W
Mount Marty College, SD	M,W
Mount St. Mary's University, MD	M,W
Mount Vernon Nazarene University, OH	M,W
New Jersey Institute of Technology, NJ	M,W
Newman University, KS	M,W
New York Institute of Technology, NY	M,W
Niagara University, NY	M,W
North Carolina Central University, NC	M,W
Northern Arizona University, AZ	M,W
Northern State University, SD	M,W
North Greenville University, SC	M,W
Northwest Christian University, OR	M,W
Northwestern State University of Louisiana, LA	M,W
Northwest Nazarene University, ID	M,W
Northwest University, WA	M,W
Nyack College, NY	M,W
Oakland University, MI	M,W
The Ohio State University, OH	M,W
Ohio Valley University, WV	M,W
Oklahoma Baptist University, OK	M,W
Oklahoma State University, OK	M,W
Olivet Nazarene University, IL	M,W
Oral Roberts University, OK	M,W
Palm Beach Atlantic University, FL	M,W
Penn State University Park, PA	M,W
Pepperdine University, CA	M,W
Pittsburg State University, KS	M,W
Point Loma Nazarene University, CA	W
Prairie View A&M University, TX	M,W
Providence College, RI	M,W
Purdue University Fort Wayne, IN	M,W
Purdue University Northwest, IN	M,W
Queens College of the City University of New York, NY	M,W
Queens University of Charlotte, NC	M,W
Radford University, VA	M,W
Rice University, TX	M,W
Rochester University, MI	M,W
Rocky Mountain College, MT	M,W
Rogers State University, OK	M,W
Sacred Heart University, CT	M,W
Saginaw Valley State University, MI	M,W
St. Ambrose University, IA	M,W
St. Bonaventure University, NY	M,W
St. Cloud State University, MN	W
Saint Francis University, PA	M,W
Saint Joseph's University, PA	M,W
Saint Leo University, FL	M,W
Saint Louis University, MO	M,W
Saint Mary's College of California, CA	M,W
Samford University, AL	M,W
Sam Houston State University, TX	M,W
San Diego State University, CA	W
San Francisco State University, CA	M,W
San Jose State University, CA	M,W
Santa Clara University, CA	M,W
Seattle University, WA	M,W
Siena College, NY	M,W
Slippery Rock University of Pennsylvania, PA	M,W
Southeastern Louisiana University, LA	M,W
Southeastern University, FL	M,W
Southeast Missouri State University, MO	M,W
Southern Illinois University Carbondale, IL	M,W
Southern Illinois University Edwardsville, IL	M,W
Southern Methodist University, TX	W
Southwest Baptist University, MO	M,W
Southwestern College, KS	M,W
Southwestern Oklahoma State University, OK	W
Spring Hill College, AL	M,W
Stanford University, CA	M,W
Sterling College, KS	M,W
Stetson University, FL	M,W
Stony Brook University, State University of New York, NY	M,W
Tabor College, KS	M,W
Tarleton State University, TX	M,W
Taylor University, IN	M,W
Temple University, PA	M,W
Tennessee Wesleyan University, TN	M,W
Texas A&M International University, TX	M,W
Texas A&M University–Commerce, TX	M,W
Texas A&M University–Corpus Christi, TX	M,W
Texas Christian University, TX	M,W
Texas State University, TX	M,W
Texas Tech University, TX	M,W
Tiffin University, OH	M,W
Towson University, MD	W
Trevecca Nazarene University, TN	M,W
Troy University, AL	M,W
Truett McConnell University, GA	M,W
Truman State University, MO	M,W
Tulane University, LA	M,W
Union University, TN	M,W
University at Albany, State University of New York, NY	M,W
University at Buffalo, the State University of New York, NY	M,W
The University of Akron, OH	M,W
The University of Alabama, AL	M,W
The University of Alabama at Birmingham, AL	W
University of Alaska Fairbanks, AK	M,W
The University of Arizona, AZ	M,W
University of Arkansas, AR	M,W
University of Arkansas at Little Rock, AR	M,W
University of California, Los Angeles, CA	M,W
University of California, Merced, CA	M,W
University of California, Riverside, CA	M,W
University of California, Santa Barbara, CA	M,W
University of Central Arkansas, AR	M,W
University of Central Florida, FL	W
University of Cincinnati, OH	M,W
University of Colorado Boulder, CO	M,W
University of Colorado Colorado Springs, CO	M,W
University of Dayton, OH	M,W
The University of Findlay, OH	M,W
University of Hawaii at Manoa, HI	W
University of Houston, TX	M,W
University of Idaho, ID	M,W
University of Illinois at Chicago, IL	M,W
University of Illinois at Springfield, IL	M,W
The University of Iowa, IA	M,W
University of Jamestown, ND	M,W
The University of Kansas, KS	M,W
University of Kentucky, KY	M,W
University of Louisiana at Lafayette, LA	M,W
University of Louisiana at Monroe, LA	M,W
University of Louisville, KY	M,W
University of Maine, ME	M,W
University of Maryland, Baltimore County, MD	M,W

University of Massachusetts Amherst, MA M,W
University of Massachusetts Lowell, MA M,W
University of Memphis, TN M,W
University of Michigan, MI M,W
University of Michigan–Dearborn, MI M,W
University of Minnesota, Duluth, MN M,W
University of Minnesota, Twin Cities Campus, MN M,W
University of Montana, MT M,W
University of Nebraska at Kearney, NE M,W
University of Nebraska–Lincoln, NE M,W
University of Nevada, Las Vegas, NV W
University of Nevada, Reno, NV W
University of New Hampshire, NH M,W
University of New Haven, CT M,W
University of New Mexico, NM M,W
The University of North Carolina at Chapel Hill, NC M,W
The University of North Carolina at Charlotte, NC M,W
The University of North Carolina at Greensboro, NC M,W
The University of North Carolina at Pembroke, NC M,W
The University of North Carolina Wilmington, NC M,W
University of North Dakota, ND M,W
University of Northern Colorado, CO M,W
University of Northern Iowa, IA M,W
University of North Texas, TX M,W
University of Notre Dame, IN M,W
University of Oregon, OR M,W
University of Pikeville, KY M,W
University of Portland, OR M,W
University of Richmond, VA W
University of St. Francis, IL M,W
University of Saint Francis, IN M,W
University of Saint Mary, KS M,W
University of St. Thomas, TX M,W
University of San Diego, CA M,W
University of San Francisco, CA M,W
University of South Carolina, SC W
University of South Carolina Aiken, SC M,W
University of South Dakota, SD M,W
University of Southern Indiana, IN M,W
University of Southern Mississippi, MS W
University of South Florida, FL M,W
The University of Tampa, FL M,W
The University of Tennessee at Chattanooga, TN M,W
The University of Tennessee at Martin, TN M,W
The University of Texas at El Paso, TX M,W
The University of Texas at San Antonio, TX M,W
The University of Texas Rio Grande Valley, TX M,W
University of the Incarnate Word, TX M,W
University of the Pacific, CA W
The University of Toledo, OH M,W
The University of Tulsa, OK M,W
University of Utah, UT W
University of Virginia, VA M,W
University of Washington, WA M,W
The University of West Alabama, AL M,W
University of West Georgia, GA M,W
University of Wisconsin–Green Bay, WI M,W
University of Wisconsin–Madison, WI M,W
University of Wisconsin–Milwaukee, WI M,W
University of Wisconsin–Parkside, WI M,W
University of Wyoming, WY M,W
Upper Iowa University, IA W
Ursuline College, OH W
Utah State University, UT M,W
Utah Valley University, UT M,W
Valdosta State University, GA M,W
Valley City State University, ND M,W
Valparaiso University, IN M,W
Vanderbilt University, TN M,W
Vanguard University of Southern California, CA M,W
Villanova University, PA M,W
Wake Forest University, NC M,W
Washington State University, WA M,W
Wayland Baptist University, TX M,W
Wayne State College, NE M,W
Wayne State University, MI M,W
Webber International University, FL M,W
Weber State University, UT M,W
West Chester University of Pennsylvania, PA M,W
Western Carolina University, NC M,W
Western Colorado University, CO M,W
Western Kentucky University, KY M,W
Western Michigan University, MI W
Western New Mexico University, NM M,W
Western Oregon University, OR M,W
Western Washington University, WA M,W
Westminster College, UT M,W
Westmont College, CA M,W
Wichita State University, KS M,W
William & Mary, VA M,W
Wingate University, NC M,W
Wofford College, SC M,W
Wright State University, OH M,W
Xavier University, OH M,W
Youngstown State University, OH M,W

Equestrian sports
Auburn University, AL W
Baylor University, TX W
California State University, Fresno, CA W
Emory & Henry College, VA M,W
Midway University, KY M,W
Oklahoma State University, OK W
Sacred Heart University, CT W
Southern Methodist University, TX W
Southwestern Oklahoma State University, OK M,W
Texas A&M University, TX W
Texas Christian University, TX W
University of Providence, MT M,W
University of South Carolina, SC W
The University of Tennessee at Martin, TN W

Fencing
New Jersey Institute of Technology, NJ M,W
The Ohio State University, OH M,W
Penn State University Park, PA M,W
Sacred Heart University, CT M,W
Stanford University, CA M,W
Temple University, PA W
The University of North Carolina at Chapel Hill, NC M,W
University of Notre Dame, IN M,W
Wayne State University, MI M,W

Field hockey
American University, DC W
Appalachian State University, NC W
Ball State University, IN W
Belmont Abbey College, NC W
Boston College, MA W
Bryant University, RI W
Bucknell University, PA W
Central Michigan University, MI W
Colgate University, NY W
College of the Holy Cross, MA W
Davidson College, NC W
Drexel University, PA W
Fairfield University, CT W
Georgetown University, DC W
Hofstra University, NY W
Indiana University of Pennsylvania, PA W
James Madison University, VA W
Kutztown University of Pennsylvania, PA W
Lehigh University, PA W
Liberty University, VA W
Limestone College, SC W
Lindenwood University, MO W
Lock Haven University of Pennsylvania, PA W
Longwood University, VA W
Mansfield University of Pennsylvania, PA W
Mercy College, NY W
Merrimack College, MA W
Miami University, OH W
Michigan State University, MI W
Millersville University of Pennsylvania, PA W
Missouri State University, MO W
Molloy College, NY W
The Ohio State University, OH W
Old Dominion University, VA W
Penn State University Park, PA W
Providence College, RI W
Queens University of Charlotte, NC W
Sacred Heart University, CT W
Saint Francis University, PA W
Saint Joseph's University, PA W
Saint Louis University, MO W
Slippery Rock University of Pennsylvania, PA W
Stanford University, CA W
Temple University, PA W
Towson University, MD W
University at Albany, State University of New York, NY W
The University of Iowa, IA W
University of Louisville, KY W
University of Maine, ME W
University of Massachusetts Amherst, MA W

University of Massachusetts Lowell, MA W
University of Michigan, MI W
University of New Hampshire, NH W
University of New Haven, CT W
The University of North Carolina at Chapel Hill, NC W
University of Richmond, VA W
University of the Pacific, CA W
University of Virginia, VA W
Villanova University, PA W
Virginia Commonwealth University, VA W
Wake Forest University, NC W
West Chester University of Pennsylvania, PA W
William & Mary, VA W

Football

Abilene Christian University, TX M
Adams State University, CO M
Angelo State University, TX M
Appalachian State University, NC M
Arizona Christian University, AZ M
Arizona State University at the Downtown Phoenix campus, AZ M
Arizona State University at the Polytechnic campus, AZ M
Arizona State University at the Tempe campus, AZ M
Arizona State University at the West campus, AZ M
Arkansas Tech University, AR M
Auburn University, AL M
Augustana University, SD M
Austin Peay State University, TN M
Baker University, KS M
Ball State University, IN M
Baylor University, TX M
Bemidji State University, MN M
Black Hills State University, SD M
Boise State University, ID M
Boston College, MA M
Bowling Green State University, OH M
Brigham Young University, UT M
Bryant University, RI M
Bucknell University, PA M
California Polytechnic State University, San Luis Obispo, CA M
California State University, Fresno, CA M
California State University, Northridge, CA M
California State University, Sacramento, CA M
California University of Pennsylvania, PA M
Campbellsville University, KY M
Carson-Newman University, TN M
Catawba College, NC M
Central Connecticut State University, CT M
Central Methodist University, MO M
Central Michigan University, MI M
Central Washington University, WA M
Chestnut Hill College, PA M
The Citadel, The Military College of South Carolina, SC M
Clarion University of Pennsylvania, PA M
Clemson University, SC M
Coastal Carolina University, SC M
Colgate University, NY M
College of the Holy Cross, MA M
Colorado School of Mines, CO M
Colorado State University, CO M
Concordia University, St. Paul, MN M
Dakota State University, SD M
Delta State University, MS M
Doane University, NE M
East Carolina University, NC M
East Central University, OK M
Eastern Illinois University, IL M
Eastern Kentucky University, KY M
Eastern Michigan University, MI M
Eastern New Mexico University, NM M
Eastern Oregon University, OR M
Eastern Washington University, WA M
Edinboro University of Pennsylvania, PA M
Elon University, NC M
Emporia State University, KS M
Evangel University, MO M
Fayetteville State University, NC M
Ferris State University, MI M
Florida Agricultural and Mechanical University, FL M
Florida Atlantic University, FL M
Florida Institute of Technology, FL M
Florida State University, FL M
Fordham University, NY M
Fort Lewis College, CO M
Gannon University, PA M
Georgetown College, KY M
Georgia Institute of Technology, GA M
Georgia State University, GA M
Glenville State College, WV M
Graceland University, IA M
Grambling State University, LA M
Grand Valley State University, MI M
Hampton University, VA M
Hillsdale College, MI M
Houston Baptist University, TX M
Illinois State University, IL M
Indiana State University, IN M
Indiana University Bloomington, IN M
Indiana University of Pennsylvania, PA M
Jacksonville State University, AL M
James Madison University, VA M
Kennesaw State University, GA M
Kutztown University of Pennsylvania, PA M
Lawrence Technological University, MI M
Lehigh University, PA M
Lenoir-Rhyne University, NC M
Liberty University, VA M
Limestone College, SC M
Lincoln University, PA M
Lindenwood University, MO M
Lock Haven University of Pennsylvania, PA M
Louisiana State University and Agricultural & Mechanical College, LA M
Marshall University, WV M
Mayville State University, ND M
McKendree University, IL M
Mercer University, GA M
Merrimack College, MA M
Miami University, OH M
Michigan State University, MI M
Michigan Technological University, MI M
MidAmerica Nazarene University, KS M
Middle Tennessee State University, TN M
Millersville University of Pennsylvania, PA M
Minnesota State University Mankato, MN M
Minot State University, ND M
Mississippi State University, MS M
Missouri Southern State University, MO M
Missouri State University, MO M
Missouri University of Science and Technology, MO M
Missouri Valley College, MO M
Montana State University, MT M
Montana Technological University, MT M
Mount Marty College, SD M
North Carolina Central University, NC M
Northeastern State University, OK M
Northern Arizona University, AZ M
Northern Illinois University, IL M
Northern State University, SD M
North Greenville University, SC M
Northwestern State University of Louisiana, LA M
Northwest Missouri State University, MO M
The Ohio State University, OH M
Oklahoma Baptist University, OK M
Oklahoma State University, OK M
Old Dominion University, VA M
Olivet Nazarene University, IL M
Penn State University Park, PA M
Pittsburg State University, KS M
Prairie View A&M University, TX M
Rice University, TX M
Rocky Mountain College, MT M
Sacred Heart University, CT M
Saginaw Valley State University, MI M
St. Ambrose University, IA M
St. Cloud State University, MN M
Saint Francis University, PA M
Samford University, AL M
Sam Houston State University, TX M
San Diego State University, CA M
San Jose State University, CA M
Shepherd University, WV M
Slippery Rock University of Pennsylvania, PA M
Southeastern Louisiana University, LA M
Southeastern University, FL M
Southeast Missouri State University, MO M
Southern Illinois University Carbondale, IL M
Southern Methodist University, TX M
Southwest Baptist University, MO M
Southwestern College, KS M
Southwestern Oklahoma State University, OK M
Stanford University, CA M
Sterling College, KS M
Stony Brook University, State University of New York, NY M
Tabor College, KS M
Tarleton State University, TX M
Taylor University, IN M
Temple University, PA M

Texas A&M University, TX M
Texas A&M University–Commerce, TX M
Texas Christian University, TX M
Texas State University, TX M
Texas Tech University, TX M
Tiffin University, OH M
Towson University, MD M
Troy University, AL M
Truman State University, MO M
Tulane University, LA M
University at Albany, State University of New York, NY M
University at Buffalo, the State University of New York, NY M
The University of Akron, OH M
The University of Alabama, AL M
The University of Alabama at Birmingham, AL M
The University of Arizona, AZ M
University of Arkansas, AR M
University of California, Los Angeles, CA M
University of Central Arkansas, AR M
University of Central Florida, FL M
University of Cincinnati, OH M
University of Colorado Boulder, CO M
The University of Findlay, OH M
University of Hawaii at Manoa, HI M
University of Houston, TX M
University of Idaho, ID M
The University of Iowa, IA M
University of Jamestown, ND M
The University of Kansas, KS M
University of Kentucky, KY M
University of Louisiana at Lafayette, LA M
University of Louisiana at Monroe, LA M
University of Louisville, KY M
University of Maine, ME M
University of Massachusetts Amherst, MA M
University of Memphis, TN M
University of Michigan, MI M
University of Minnesota, Duluth, MN M
University of Minnesota, Twin Cities Campus, MN M
University of Montana, MT M
University of Nebraska at Kearney, NE M
University of Nebraska–Lincoln, NE M
University of Nevada, Las Vegas, NV M
University of Nevada, Reno, NV M
University of New Hampshire, NH M
University of New Haven, CT M
University of New Mexico, NM M
The University of North Carolina at Chapel Hill, NC M
The University of North Carolina at Charlotte, NC M
The University of North Carolina at Pembroke, NC M
University of North Dakota, ND M
University of Northern Colorado, CO M
University of Northern Iowa, IA M
University of North Texas, TX M
University of Notre Dame, IN M
University of Oregon, OR M
University of Pikeville, KY M
University of Richmond, VA M
University of St. Francis, IL M
University of Saint Francis, IN M
University of Saint Mary, KS M
University of South Carolina, SC M
University of South Dakota, SD M
University of Southern Mississippi, MS M
University of South Florida, FL M
The University of Tennessee, TN M
The University of Tennessee at Chattanooga, TN M
The University of Tennessee at Martin, TN M
The University of Texas at El Paso, TX M
The University of Texas at San Antonio, TX M
University of the Incarnate Word, TX M
The University of Toledo, OH M
The University of Tulsa, OK M
University of Utah, UT M
University of Virginia, VA M
University of Washington, WA M
The University of West Alabama, AL M
University of West Georgia, GA M
University of Wisconsin–Madison, WI M
University of Wyoming, WY M
Upper Iowa University, IA M
Utah State University, UT M
Valdosta State University, GA M
Valley City State University, ND M
Vanderbilt University, TN M
Villanova University, PA M
Wake Forest University, NC M
Washington State University, WA M
Wayland Baptist University, TX M
Wayne State College, NE M
Wayne State University, MI M
Webber International University, FL M
Weber State University, UT M
West Chester University of Pennsylvania, PA M
Western Carolina University, NC M
Western Colorado University, CO M
Western Kentucky University, KY M
Western Michigan University, MI M
Western New Mexico University, NM M
Western Oregon University, OR M
William & Mary, VA M
Wingate University, NC M
Wofford College, SC M
Youngstown State University, OH M

Golf

Abilene Christian University, TX M
Academy of Art University, CA M,W
Adams State University, CO M,W
Anderson University, SC M,W
Angelo State University, TX W
Appalachian State University, NC M,W
Aquinas College, MI M,W
Arizona Christian University, AZ M,W
Arizona State University at the Downtown Phoenix campus, AZ M,W
Arizona State University at the Polytechnic campus, AZ M,W
Arizona State University at the Tempe campus, AZ M,W
Arizona State University at the West campus, AZ M,W
Arkansas Tech University, AR M,W
Auburn University, AL M,W
Augustana University, SD M,W
Austin Peay State University, TN M,W
Baker University, KS M,W
Ball State University, IN M,W
Barry University, FL M,W
Barton College, NC M,W
Baylor University, TX M,W
Belmont Abbey College, NC M,W
Belmont University, TN M,W
Bemidji State University, MN M,W
Bethel University, IN M,W
Binghamton University, State University of New York, NY M
Biola University, CA M,W
Boise State University, ID M,W
Boston College, MA M,W
Bowling Green State University, OH M,W
Bradley University, IL M,W
Brigham Young University, UT M,W
Bryan College, TN M,W
Bryant University, RI M
Butler University, IN M,W
California Baptist University, CA M,W
California Polytechnic State University, San Luis Obispo, CA M,W
California State University, Bakersfield, CA M
California State University, Dominguez Hills, CA M
California State University, Fresno, CA M,W
California State University, Fullerton, CA M,W
California State University, Long Beach, CA M,W
California State University, Los Angeles, CA W
California State University, Monterey Bay, CA M,W
California State University, Northridge, CA M
California State University, Sacramento, CA M
California State University, San Bernardino, CA M
California State University, Stanislaus, CA M
California University of Pennsylvania, PA M,W
Calumet College of Saint Joseph, IN M,W
Cameron University, OK M,W
Campbellsville University, KY M,W
Carson-Newman University, TN M
Catawba College, NC M,W
Cedarville University, OH M
Central Michigan University, MI W
Chaminade University of Honolulu, HI M
Chestnut Hill College, PA M
The Citadel, The Military College of South Carolina, SC W
Clarion University of Pennsylvania, PA M,W
Clemson University, SC M
Coastal Carolina University, SC M,W
The College of Idaho, ID M,W
College of Saint Mary, NE W
The College of Saint Rose, NY M,W

Colorado School of Mines, CO	M
Colorado State University, CO	M,W
Columbia College, MO	M,W
Columbia College, SC	W
Concordia University, St. Paul, MN	M,W
Creighton University, NE	M,W
Dallas Baptist University, TX	W
Davidson College, NC	M
Delta State University, MS	M
DePaul University, IL	M
Doane University, NE	M,W
Dominican College, NY	M,W
Dominican University of California, CA	M,W
Drake University, IA	M
Drexel University, PA	M
Drury University, MO	M,W
East Carolina University, NC	M,W
Eastern Illinois University, IL	M,W
Eastern Kentucky University, KY	M,W
Eastern Michigan University, MI	M,W
Eastern Washington University, WA	W
Elon University, NC	M,W
Emmanuel College, GA	M,W
Evangel University, MO	M,W
Fairfield University, CT	M,W
Fayetteville State University, NC	M
Felician University, NJ	M
Ferris State University, MI	M,W
Florida Agricultural and Mechanical University, FL	M,W
Florida Atlantic University, FL	M,W
Florida Gulf Coast University, FL	M,W
Florida Institute of Technology, FL	M
Florida State University, FL	M,W
Fordham University, NY	M
Fort Lewis College, CO	M,W
Francis Marion University, SC	M
Freed-Hardeman University, TN	M,W
Gannon University, PA	M,W
George Mason University, VA	M
Georgetown College, KY	M,W
Georgetown University, DC	M,W
The George Washington University, DC	M
Georgia College & State University, GA	M
Georgia Institute of Technology, GA	M
Georgia State University, GA	M,W
Glenville State College, WV	M,W
Gonzaga University, WA	M,W
Goshen College, IN	M
Governors State University, IL	M,W
Graceland University, IA	M,W
Grand Valley State University, MI	M,W
Hampton University, VA	M,W
High Point University, NC	M,W
Hillsdale College, MI	M
Hofstra University, NY	M,W
Hope International University, CA	M,W
Houston Baptist University, TX	M,W
Illinois State University, IL	M,W
Indiana State University, IN	W
Indiana University Bloomington, IN	M,W
Indiana University Northwest, IN	M,W
Indiana University of Pennsylvania, PA	M
Indiana University-Purdue University Indianapolis, IN	M,W
Indiana University South Bend, IN	M,W
Iona College, NY	M
Jacksonville State University, AL	M,W
Jacksonville University, FL	M,W
James Madison University, VA	M,W
Kennesaw State University, GA	M,W
King University, TN	M,W
Kutztown University of Pennsylvania, PA	W
Lawrence Technological University, MI	M,W
Lee University, TN	M,W
Lehigh University, PA	M,W
Le Moyne College, NY	M,W
Lenoir-Rhyne University, NC	M,W
Lewis-Clark State College, ID	M,W
Lewis University, IL	M,W
Liberty University, VA	M
Limestone College, SC	M,W
Lincoln Memorial University, TN	M,W
Lindenwood University, MO	M,W
Lipscomb University, TN	M,W
Longwood University, VA	M,W
Louisiana State University and Agricultural & Mechanical College, LA	M,W
Loyola Marymount University, CA	M
Loyola University Chicago, IL	M,W
Loyola University Maryland, MD	M
Loyola University New Orleans, LA	M,W
Lynn University, FL	M,W
Malone University, OH	M,W
Manhattan College, NY	M
Marquette University, WI	M
Marshall University, WV	M,W
Marymount California University, CA	M,W
Maryville University of Saint Louis, MO	M,W
McKendree University, IL	M,W
Mercer University, GA	M,W
Merrimack College, MA	W
Miami University, OH	M
Michigan State University, MI	M,W
Middle Tennessee State University, TN	M,W
Midway University, KY	M,W
Millersville University of Pennsylvania, PA	M,W
Milligan University, TN	M,W
Minnesota State University Mankato, MN	M,W
Mississippi State University, MS	M,W
Missouri Southern State University, MO	M
Missouri State University, MO	M,W
Missouri Valley College, MO	M,W
Montana State University, MT	W
Montana Technological University, MT	M,W
Morehead State University, KY	M,W
Mount Marty College, SD	M,W
Mount St. Mary's University, MD	M,W
Mount Vernon Nazarene University, OH	M,W
Newman University, KS	M,W
Niagara University, NY	M,W
North Carolina Central University, NC	M
Northeastern State University, OK	M,W
Northern Arizona University, AZ	W
Northern Illinois University, IL	M,W
North Greenville University, SC	M,W
Northwest Christian University, OR	M,W
Northwest Nazarene University, ID	M,W
Oakland University, MI	M,W
The Ohio State University, OH	M,W
Ohio Valley University, WV	M,W
Oklahoma Baptist University, OK	M,W
Oklahoma State University, OK	M,W
Old Dominion University, VA	M,W
Olivet Nazarene University, IL	M
Oral Roberts University, OK	M,W
Palm Beach Atlantic University, FL	M,W
Penn State University Park, PA	M,W
Pepperdine University, CA	M,W
Pittsburg State University, KS	M
Point Loma Nazarene University, CA	W
Prairie View A&M University, TX	M,W
Purdue University Fort Wayne, IN	M,W
Purdue University Northwest, IN	M,W
Queens University of Charlotte, NC	M,W
Radford University, VA	M,W
Rice University, TX	M
Rochester University, MI	M,W
Rocky Mountain College, MT	M,W
Rogers State University, OK	M,W
Rollins College, FL	M,W
Sacred Heart University, CT	M,W
Saginaw Valley State University, MI	M
St. Ambrose University, IA	M,W
St. Bonaventure University, NY	M
St. Cloud State University, MN	M,W
Saint Francis University, PA	M,W
Saint Joseph's University, PA	M
Saint Leo University, FL	M,W
Saint Mary's College of California, CA	M
St. Mary's University, TX	M,W
Samford University, AL	M,W
Sam Houston State University, TX	M,W
San Diego State University, CA	M,W
San Jose State University, CA	M,W
Santa Clara University, CA	M,W
Seattle University, WA	M,W
Shepherd University, WV	M
Siena College, NY	M,W
Southeastern Louisiana University, LA	M
Southeastern University, FL	M,W
Southern Illinois University Carbondale, IL	M,W
Southern Illinois University Edwardsville, IL	M
Southern Methodist University, TX	M,W
Southwest Baptist University, MO	W
Southwestern College, KS	M,W
Southwestern Oklahoma State University, OK	M,W
Spring Hill College, AL	M,W
Stanford University, CA	M,W
Sterling College, KS	M,W
Stetson University, FL	M,W
Tarleton State University, TX	W
Taylor University, IN	M,W
Temple University, PA	M
Tennessee Wesleyan University, TN	M,W
Texas A&M International University, TX	M,W
Texas A&M University, TX	M,W
Texas A&M University–Commerce, TX	W
Texas A&M University–Corpus Christi, TX	W
Texas Christian University, TX	M,W

Texas State University, TX	M,W
Texas Tech University, TX	M,W
Tiffin University, OH	M,W
Towson University, MD	M,W
Trevecca Nazarene University, TN	M,W
Troy University, AL	M,W
Truett McConnell University, GA	M,W
Truman State University, MO	W
Tulane University, LA	W
Union University, TN	M,W
University at Albany, State University of New York, NY	W
The University of Akron, OH	M,W
The University of Alabama, AL	M,W
The University of Alabama at Birmingham, AL	M,W
The University of Arizona, AZ	M,W
University of Arkansas, AR	M,W
University of Arkansas at Little Rock, AR	M,W
University of California, Los Angeles, CA	M,W
University of California, Riverside, CA	M,W
University of California, Santa Barbara, CA	M
University of Central Arkansas, AR	M,W
University of Central Florida, FL	M,W
University of Cincinnati, OH	M,W
University of Colorado Boulder, CO	M,W
University of Colorado Colorado Springs, CO	M,W
University of Dayton, OH	M
University of Denver, CO	M,W
The University of Findlay, OH	M,W
University of Hawaii at Manoa, HI	M,W
University of Houston, TX	M,W
University of Idaho, ID	M,W
University of Illinois at Springfield, IL	M,W
The University of Iowa, IA	M,W
University of Jamestown, ND	M,W
The University of Kansas, KS	M,W
University of Kentucky, KY	M,W
University of Louisiana at Lafayette, LA	M
University of Louisiana at Monroe, LA	M,W
University of Louisville, KY	M,W
University of Memphis, TN	M,W
University of Michigan, MI	M,W
University of Michigan–Dearborn, MI	M,W
University of Minnesota, Twin Cities Campus, MN	M,W
University of Missouri–St. Louis, MO	M,W
University of Montana, MT	W
University of Montevallo, AL	M,W
University of Nebraska at Kearney, NE	M,W
University of Nebraska–Lincoln, NE	M,W
University of Nevada, Las Vegas, NV	M,W
University of Nevada, Reno, NV	M,W
University of New Mexico, NM	M,W
The University of North Carolina at Chapel Hill, NC	M,W
The University of North Carolina at Charlotte, NC	M,W
The University of North Carolina at Greensboro, NC	M,W
The University of North Carolina at Pembroke, NC	W
The University of North Carolina Wilmington, NC	M,W
University of North Dakota, ND	M,W
University of Northern Colorado, CO	M,W
University of Northern Iowa, IA	M,W
University of North Texas, TX	M,W
University of Notre Dame, IN	M,W
University of Oregon, OR	M,W
University of Pikeville, KY	M,W
University of Providence, MT	M,W
University of Richmond, VA	M,W
University of St. Francis, IL	M,W
University of Saint Francis, IN	M,W
University of St. Thomas, TX	M,W
University of San Diego, CA	M
University of San Francisco, CA	M,W
University of South Carolina, SC	M,W
University of South Carolina Aiken, SC	M
University of South Dakota, SD	W
University of Southern Indiana, IN	M,W
University of Southern Mississippi, MS	M,W
University of South Florida, FL	M,W
The University of Tampa, FL	M,W
The University of Tennessee, TN	M,W
The University of Tennessee at Chattanooga, TN	M,W
The University of Tennessee at Martin, TN	M
The University of Texas at El Paso, TX	M,W
The University of Texas at San Antonio, TX	M,W
The University of Texas Rio Grande Valley, TX	M,W
University of the Incarnate Word, TX	M,W
University of the Pacific, CA	M
The University of Toledo, OH	M,W
The University of Tulsa, OK	W
University of Utah, UT	M
University of Virginia, VA	M,W
University of Washington, WA	M,W
University of West Georgia, GA	M,W
University of Wisconsin–Green Bay, WI	M,W
University of Wisconsin–Madison, WI	M,W
University of Wisconsin–Parkside, WI	M
University of Wyoming, WY	M,W
Upper Iowa University, IA	M,W
Ursuline College, OH	W
Utah State University, UT	M
Utah Valley University, UT	M,W
Valdosta State University, GA	M
Valley City State University, ND	M,W
Valparaiso University, IN	M,W
Vanderbilt University, TN	M,W
Vanguard University of Southern California, CA	M,W
Virginia Commonwealth University, VA	M
Wake Forest University, NC	M,W
Washington State University, WA	M,W
Wayland Baptist University, TX	M,W
Wayne State College, NE	W
Wayne State University, MI	M,W
Webber International University, FL	M,W
Weber State University, UT	M,W
West Chester University of Pennsylvania, PA	M,W
Western Carolina University, NC	M,W
Western Kentucky University, KY	M,W
Western Michigan University, MI	W
Western New Mexico University, NM	M,W
Western Washington University, WA	M,W
Westminster College, UT	M,W
Westmont College, CA	M,W
Wichita State University, KS	M,W
William & Mary, VA	M,W
Wingate University, NC	M,W
Wofford College, SC	M,W
Wright State University, OH	M
Xavier University, OH	M,W
Youngstown State University, OH	M,W

Gymnastics

Arizona State University at the Downtown Phoenix campus, AZ	W
Arizona State University at the Polytechnic campus, AZ	W
Arizona State University at the Tempe campus, AZ	W
Arizona State University at the West campus, AZ	W
Auburn University, AL	W
Ball State University, IN	W
Boise State University, ID	W
Bowling Green State University, OH	W
Brigham Young University, UT	W
California State University, Sacramento, CA	W
Central Michigan University, MI	W
Eastern Michigan University, MI	W
Gannon University, PA	W
Georgetown College, KY	W
The George Washington University, DC	W
Illinois State University, IL	W
Limestone College, SC	W
Lindenwood University, MO	W
Louisiana State University and Agricultural & Mechanical College, LA	W
Michigan State University, MI	W
Mount St. Mary's University, MD	M,W
Northern Illinois University, IL	W
The Ohio State University, OH	M,W
Penn State University Park, PA	M,W
San Jose State University, CA	W
Southeast Missouri State University, MO	W
Stanford University, CA	M,W
Temple University, PA	W
Texas Woman's University, TX	W
Towson University, MD	W
The University of Alabama, AL	W
The University of Arizona, AZ	W
University of Arkansas, AR	W
University of California, Los Angeles, CA	W
University of California, Santa Barbara, CA	M,W
University of Denver, CO	W
University of Illinois at Chicago, IL	M,W
The University of Iowa, IA	M,W
University of Kentucky, KY	W

University of Michigan, MI M,W
University of Minnesota, Twin Cities Campus, MN M,W
University of Nebraska–Lincoln, NE M,W
University of New Hampshire, NH W
The University of North Carolina at Chapel Hill, NC W
University of Utah, UT W
University of Washington, WA W
Utah State University, UT W
West Chester University of Pennsylvania, PA W
Western Michigan University, MI W
William & Mary, VA M,W

Ice hockey

Arizona State University at the Downtown Phoenix campus, AZ M
Arizona State University at the Polytechnic campus, AZ M
Arizona State University at the Tempe campus, AZ M
Arizona State University at the West campus, AZ M
Bemidji State University, MN M,W
Bentley University, MA M
Boston College, MA M,W
Bowling Green State University, OH M
Clarkson University, NY M,W
Colgate University, NY M,W
College of the Holy Cross, MA M,W
The Colorado College, CO M
Ferris State University, MI M
Life University, GA M
Lindenwood University, MO M,W
Merrimack College, MA M,W
Miami University, OH M
Michigan State University, MI M
Michigan Technological University, MI M
Minnesota State University Mankato, MN M,W
Niagara University, NY M
The Ohio State University, OH M,W
Penn State University Park, PA M,W
Providence College, RI M,W
Sacred Heart University, CT M,W
St. Cloud State University, MN M,W
University of Alaska Fairbanks, AK M
University of Denver, CO M
University of Maine, ME M,W
University of Massachusetts Amherst, MA M
University of Massachusetts Lowell, MA M
University of Michigan, MI M
University of Minnesota, Duluth, MN M,W
University of Minnesota, Twin Cities Campus, MN M,W
University of New Hampshire, NH M,W
University of North Dakota, ND M
University of Notre Dame, IN M
University of Wisconsin–Madison, WI M,W
Western Michigan University, MI M

Lacrosse

Adams State University, CO M,W
American University, DC W
Aquinas College, MI M,W
Arizona State University at the Downtown Phoenix campus, AZ W
Arizona State University at the Polytechnic campus, AZ W
Arizona State University at the Tempe campus, AZ W
Arizona State University at the West campus, AZ W
Barton College, NC M,W
Belmont Abbey College, NC M,W
Bethel University, IN W
Binghamton University, State University of New York, NY M,W
Boston College, MA W
Bryant University, RI M,W
Bucknell University, PA M,W
Butler University, IN W
Caldwell University, NJ M,W
California State University, Fresno, CA W
Catawba College, NC M,W
Central Connecticut State University, CT W
Central Michigan University, MI W
Chestnut Hill College, PA M,W
Coastal Carolina University, SC W
Colgate University, NY M,W
The College of Saint Rose, NY M,W
College of the Holy Cross, MA M,W
Columbia College, MO M
Columbia College, SC W
Concordia University, St. Paul, MN W
Davidson College, NC W
Dominican College, NY M,W
Dominican University of California, CA M
Drexel University, PA M,W
East Carolina University, NC W
Edinboro University of Pennsylvania, PA W
Elon University, NC W
Emmanuel College, GA M,W
Fairfield University, CT M,W
Florida Institute of Technology, FL M,W
Fort Lewis College, CO W
Gannon University, PA W
George Mason University, VA W
Georgetown College, KY W
Georgetown University, DC M,W
Georgian Court University, NJ M,W
Hampton University, VA M
High Point University, NC M,W
Hofstra University, NY M,W
Indiana University of Pennsylvania, PA W
Iona College, NY W
Jacksonville University, FL M,W
James Madison University, VA W
Johns Hopkins University, MD M,W
Kennesaw State University, GA W
Kutztown University of Pennsylvania, PA W
Lawrence Technological University, MI M,W
Lee University, TN W
Lehigh University, PA M,W
Le Moyne College, NY M,W
Lenoir-Rhyne University, NC M,W
Lewis University, IL M,W
Liberty University, VA W
Life University, GA W
Limestone College, SC M,W
Lincoln Memorial University, TN M,W
Lindenwood University, MO M,W
Lock Haven University of Pennsylvania, PA W
Longwood University, VA W
Loyola University Maryland, MD M,W
Lynn University, FL M
Manhattan College, NY M,W
Marquette University, WI M,W
Marymount California University, CA M,W
Maryville University of Saint Louis, MO M,W
McKendree University, IL W
Mercer University, GA M,W
Mercy College, NY M,W
Merrimack College, MA M,W
Millersville University of Pennsylvania, PA W
Missouri Valley College, MO M,W
Molloy College, NY M,W
Mount St. Mary's University, MD M,W
New Jersey Institute of Technology, NJ M
New York Institute of Technology, NY M,W
Niagara University, NY W
North Greenville University, SC M,W
Nyack College, NY W
The Ohio State University, OH M,W
Ohio Valley University, WV M
Oklahoma Baptist University, OK W
Old Dominion University, VA W
Palm Beach Atlantic University, FL M,W
Penn State University Park, PA M,W
Providence College, RI M
Queens University of Charlotte, NC M,W
Radford University, VA W
Rochester University, MI W
Sacred Heart University, CT M,W
St. Ambrose University, IA M
St. Bonaventure University, NY M,W
Saint Francis University, PA W
Saint Joseph's University, PA M,W
Saint Leo University, FL M,W
San Diego State University, CA W
Shepherd University, WV W
Siena College, NY M,W
Slippery Rock University of Pennsylvania, PA W
Stanford University, CA W
Stetson University, FL W
Stony Brook University, State University of New York, NY M,W
Temple University, PA W
Tennessee Wesleyan University, TN M,W
Tiffin University, OH W
Towson University, MD M,W
Truett McConnell University, GA W
University at Albany, State University of New York, NY M,W
University of Cincinnati, OH W
University of Colorado Boulder, CO W
University of Colorado Colorado Springs, CO W
University of Denver, CO M,W
The University of Findlay, OH W
University of Louisville, KY W
University of Maryland, Baltimore County, MD M,W
University of Massachusetts Amherst, MA M,W

University of Massachusetts Lowell, MA M,W
University of Michigan, MI M,W
University of Michigan–Dearborn, MI M
University of Minnesota, Duluth, MN M,W
University of New Hampshire, NH W
University of New Haven, CT W
The University of North Carolina at Chapel Hill, NC M,W
University of Notre Dame, IN M,W
University of Oregon, OR W
University of Richmond, VA M,W
University of Saint Mary, KS M,W
The University of Tampa, FL M,W
University of Utah, UT M
University of Virginia, VA M,W
Ursuline College, OH W
Vanderbilt University, TN W
Villanova University, PA M,W
Virginia Commonwealth University, VA W
Webber International University, FL M,W
West Chester University of Pennsylvania, PA W
Westminster College, UT M,W
William & Mary, VA W
Wingate University, NC M,W
Wofford College, SC W

Riflery
The Citadel, The Military College of South Carolina, SC M,W
Emmanuel College, GA M,W
Jacksonville State University, AL M,W
Lindenwood University, MO M,W
Morehead State University, KY M,W
The Ohio State University, OH M,W
Texas Christian University, TX W
The University of Akron, OH W
University of Alaska Fairbanks, AK M,W
University of Kentucky, KY M,W
University of Memphis, TN M,W
University of Nebraska–Lincoln, NE W
University of Nevada, Reno, NV M,W
The University of Tennessee at Martin, TN M,W
The University of Texas at El Paso, TX M
Wofford College, SC M,W

Rowing
Fairfield University, CT M,W
Fordham University, NY W
Gonzaga University, WA W
Indiana University Bloomington, IN W
Merrimack College, MA W
Michigan State University, MI W
The Ohio State University, OH W
Sacred Heart University, CT W
San Diego State University, CA W
Stanford University, CA M,W
Temple University, PA W
University of Louisville, KY W
University of Virginia, VA W
University of Washington, WA M,W

Rugby
Belmont Abbey College, NC M
Bethel University, IN M
Central Washington University, WA M,W
Life University, GA M,W
Lindenwood University, MO M,W
Molloy College, NY W
Mount St. Mary's University, MD W
Sacred Heart University, CT W
The University of North Carolina at Pembroke, NC M
West Chester University of Pennsylvania, PA W

Sailing
Hampton University, VA M,W

Sand volleyball
Arizona State University at the Downtown Phoenix campus, AZ W
Arizona State University at the Polytechnic campus, AZ W
Arizona State University at the Tempe campus, AZ W
Arizona State University at the West campus, AZ W
Austin Peay State University, TN W
California State University, Long Beach, CA W
California State University, Los Angeles, CA W
Coastal Carolina University, SC W
Florida State University, FL W
Georgia State University, GA W
Lincoln Memorial University, TN W
Loyola Marymount University, CA W
Mercer University, GA W
Morehead State University, KY W
Palm Beach Atlantic University, FL W
Saint Mary's College of California, CA W
Texas A&M University–Corpus Christi, TX W
Texas Christian University, TX W
The University of Arizona, AZ W
University of Hawaii at Manoa, HI W
University of Louisiana at Monroe, LA W
University of Nebraska–Lincoln, NE W
University of Oregon, OR W
The University of Tennessee at Martin, TN W
University of Utah, UT W
Wayne State College, NE W
Webber International University, FL M,W

Skiing (cross-country)
Michigan Technological University, MI M,W
Montana State University, MT M,W
St. Cloud State University, MN W
University of Alaska Fairbanks, AK M,W
University of Colorado Boulder, CO M,W
University of Denver, CO M,W
University of New Hampshire, NH M,W
University of New Mexico, NM M,W
University of Utah, UT M,W
University of Wisconsin–Green Bay, WI M,W

Skiing (downhill)
The College of Idaho, ID M,W
Montana State University, MT M,W
Rocky Mountain College, MT M,W
University of Colorado Boulder, CO M,W
University of Denver, CO M,W
University of New Hampshire, NH M,W
University of New Mexico, NM M,W
University of Utah, UT M,W
Westminster College, UT M,W

Soccer
Abilene Christian University, TX W
Academy of Art University, CA M,W
Adams State University, CO M,W
American University, DC M,W
Anderson University, SC M,W
Angelo State University, TX W
Appalachian State University, NC M,W
Aquinas College, MI M,W
Arizona Christian University, AZ M,W
Arizona State University at the Downtown Phoenix campus, AZ W
Arizona State University at the Polytechnic campus, AZ W
Arizona State University at the Tempe campus, AZ W
Arizona State University at the West campus, AZ W
Auburn University, AL W
Auburn University at Montgomery, AL M,W
Augustana University, SD W
Austin Peay State University, TN W
Baker University, KS M,W
Ball State University, IN W
Barry University, FL M,W
Barton College, NC M,W
Baylor University, TX W
Belmont Abbey College, NC M,W
Belmont University, TN M,W
Bemidji State University, MN W
Bethel University, IN M,W
Binghamton University, State University of New York, NY M,W
Biola University, CA M,W
Black Hills State University, SD W
Boise State University, ID W
Boston College, MA M,W
Bowling Green State University, OH M,W
Bradley University, IL M
Brigham Young University, UT W
Bryan College, TN M,W
Bryant University, RI M,W
Bucknell University, PA M
Butler University, IN M,W
Caldwell University, NJ M,W
California Baptist University, CA M,W
California Polytechnic State University, San Luis Obispo, CA M,W
California State Polytechnic University, Pomona, CA M,W
California State University, Bakersfield, CA M
California State University, Dominguez Hills, CA M,W
California State University, Fresno, CA W
California State University, Fullerton, CA M,W
California State University, Long Beach, CA W
California State University, Los Angeles, CA M,W
California State University, Monterey Bay, CA M,W
California State University, Northridge, CA M

California State University, Sacramento, CA M,W
California State University, San Bernardino, CA M,W
California State University, Stanislaus, CA M,W
California University of Pennsylvania, PA M,W
Calumet College of Saint Joseph, IN M,W
Campbellsville University, KY M,W
Carlow University, PA W
Carson-Newman University, TN M,W
Catawba College, NC M,W
Cedarville University, OH M,W
Central Connecticut State University, CT M,W
Central Methodist University, MO M,W
Central Michigan University, MI W
Central Washington University, WA W
Chaminade University of Honolulu, HI M,W
Chestnut Hill College, PA M,W
The Citadel, The Military College of South Carolina, SC W
Clarion University of Pennsylvania, PA W
Clemson University, SC M,W
Coastal Carolina University, SC M,W
Colgate University, NY M,W
The College of Idaho, ID M,W
College of Saint Mary, NE W
The College of Saint Rose, NY M,W
College of the Holy Cross, MA M,W
The Colorado College, CO W
Colorado School of Mines, CO M,W
Colorado State University, CO W
Columbia College, MO M,W
Columbia College, SC W
Columbia International University, SC M,W
Concordia University, St. Paul, MN W
Creighton University, NE M,W
Dallas Baptist University, TX W
Davidson College, NC M,W
Delta State University, MS M,W
DePaul University, IL M,W
Doane University, NE M,W
Dominican College, NY M,W
Dominican University of California, CA M,W
Drake University, IA M,W
Drexel University, PA M,W
Drury University, MO M,W
East Carolina University, NC W
East Central University, OK W
Eastern Illinois University, IL M,W
Eastern Michigan University, MI W
Eastern New Mexico University, NM M,W
Eastern Oregon University, OR M,W
Eastern Washington University, WA W
Edinboro University of Pennsylvania, PA W
Elon University, NC M,W
Emmanuel College, GA M,W
Emporia State University, KS W
Fairfield University, CT M,W
Felician University, NJ M,W
Ferris State University, MI W
Florida Gulf Coast University, FL M,W
Florida Institute of Technology, FL M,W
Florida National University, FL M,W
Florida State University, FL W
Fordham University, NY M,W
Fort Lewis College, CO M,W
Francis Marion University, SC M,W
Freed-Hardeman University, TN M,W
Gannon University, PA M,W
George Mason University, VA M,W
Georgetown College, KY M,W
Georgetown University, DC M,W
The George Washington University, DC M,W
Georgia College & State University, GA W
Georgia Gwinnett College, GA M,W
Georgian Court University, NJ M,W
Georgia State University, GA M,W
Gonzaga University, WA M,W
Goshen College, IN M,W
Graceland University, IA M,W
Grand Valley State University, MI W
High Point University, NC M,W
Hofstra University, NY M,W
Hope International University, CA M,W
Houston Baptist University, TX M,W
Illinois Institute of Technology, IL M,W
Illinois State University, IL W
Indiana State University, IN W
Indiana University Bloomington, IN M,W
Indiana University of Pennsylvania, PA W
Indiana University-Purdue University Indianapolis, IN M,W
Indiana University South Bend, IN W
Inter American University of Puerto Rico, Aguadilla Campus, PR M,W
Iona College, NY M,W
Jacksonville State University, AL W
Jacksonville University, FL M,W
James Madison University, VA M,W
John Brown University, AR M,W
Kennesaw State University, GA W
King University, TN M,W
Kutztown University of Pennsylvania, PA W
Lawrence Technological University, MI M,W
Lee University, TN M,W
Lehigh University, PA M,W
Le Moyne College, NY M,W
Lenoir-Rhyne University, NC M,W
Lewis University, IL M,W
Liberty University, VA M,W
Life University, GA M,W
Limestone College, SC M,W
Lincoln Memorial University, TN M,W
Lincoln University, PA W
Lindenwood University, MO M,W
Lipscomb University, TN M,W
Lock Haven University of Pennsylvania, PA M,W
Longwood University, VA M,W
Louisiana State University and Agricultural & Mechanical College, LA W
Louisiana State University in Shreveport, LA M,W
Loyola Marymount University, CA M,W
Loyola University Chicago, IL M,W
Loyola University Maryland, MD M,W
Lynn University, FL M,W
Malone University, OH M,W
Manhattan College, NY M,W
Mansfield University of Pennsylvania, PA W
Marquette University, WI M,W
Marshall University, WV M,W
Marymount California University, CA M,W
Maryville University of Saint Louis, MO M,W
McKendree University, IL M,W
Mercer University, GA M,W
Mercy College, NY M,W
Merrimack College, MA M,W
Miami University, OH W
Michigan State University, MI M,W
Michigan Technological University, MI W
MidAmerica Nazarene University, KS M,W
Middle Tennessee State University, TN W
Midway University, KY M,W
Millersville University of Pennsylvania, PA M,W
Milligan University, TN M,W
Minnesota State University Mankato, MN W
Mississippi State University, MS W
Missouri Southern State University, MO M,W
Missouri State University, MO M,W
Missouri University of Science and Technology, MO M,W
Missouri Valley College, MO M,W
Molloy College, NY M,W
Morehead State University, KY W
Mount Marty College, SD M,W
Mount St. Mary's University, MD M,W
Mount Vernon Nazarene University, OH M,W
New Jersey Institute of Technology, NJ M,W
Newman University, KS M,W
New York Institute of Technology, NY M,W
Niagara University, NY M,W
Northeastern State University, OK M,W
Northern Arizona University, AZ W
Northern Illinois University, IL M,W
Northern State University, SD W
North Greenville University, SC M,W
Northwest Christian University, OR M,W
Northwestern State University of Louisiana, LA W
Northwest Nazarene University, ID W
Northwest University, WA M,W
Nyack College, NY M,W
Oakland University, MI M,W
The Ohio State University, OH M,W
Ohio Valley University, WV M,W
Oklahoma Baptist University, OK M,W
Oklahoma State University, OK W
Old Dominion University, VA M,W
Olivet Nazarene University, IL M,W
Oral Roberts University, OK M,W
Palm Beach Atlantic University, FL M,W
Penn State University Park, PA M,W
Pepperdine University, CA W
Point Loma Nazarene University, CA M,W
Prairie View A&M University, TX W
Providence College, RI M,W
Purdue University Fort Wayne, IN M,W
Purdue University Northwest, IN M,W

Queens College of the City University of New York, NY	M,W
Queens University of Charlotte, NC	M,W
Radford University, VA	M,W
Rice University, TX	W
Rochester University, MI	M,W
Rocky Mountain College, MT	M,W
Rogers State University, OK	M,W
Rollins College, FL	M,W
Sacred Heart University, CT	M,W
Saginaw Valley State University, MI	M,W
St. Ambrose University, IA	M,W
St. Bonaventure University, NY	M,W
St. Cloud State University, MN	W
Saint Francis University, PA	M,W
Saint Joseph's University, PA	M,W
Saint Leo University, FL	M,W
Saint Louis University, MO	M,W
Saint Mary's College of California, CA	W
St. Mary's University, TX	M,W
Samford University, AL	W
Sam Houston State University, TX	W
San Diego State University, CA	M,W
San Francisco State University, CA	M,W
San Jose State University, CA	M,W
Santa Clara University, CA	M,W
Seattle University, WA	M,W
Shepherd University, WV	M,W
Siena College, NY	M,W
Slippery Rock University of Pennsylvania, PA	M,W
Southeastern Louisiana University, LA	W
Southeastern University, FL	M,W
Southeast Missouri State University, MO	W
Southern Illinois University Carbondale, IL	W
Southern Illinois University Edwardsville, IL	M,W
Southern Methodist University, TX	M,W
Southwest Baptist University, MO	M,W
Southwestern College, KS	M,W
Southwestern Oklahoma State University, OK	W
Spring Hill College, AL	M,W
Stanford University, CA	M,W
Sterling College, KS	M,W
Stetson University, FL	M,W
Stony Brook University, State University of New York, NY	M,W
Tabor College, KS	M,W
Taylor University, IN	M,W
Temple University, PA	M,W
Tennessee Wesleyan University, TN	M,W
Texas A&M International University, TX	M,W
Texas A&M University, TX	W
Texas A&M University–Commerce, TX	W
Texas A&M University–Corpus Christi, TX	W
Texas Christian University, TX	W
Texas State University, TX	W
Texas Tech University, TX	W
Texas Woman's University, TX	W
Tiffin University, OH	M,W
Towson University, MD	W
Trevecca Nazarene University, TN	M,W
Troy University, AL	W
Truett McConnell University, GA	M,W
Truman State University, MO	M,W
Tulane University, LA	W
Union University, TN	M,W
University at Albany, State University of New York, NY	M,W
University at Buffalo, the State University of New York, NY	W
The University of Akron, OH	M,W
The University of Alabama, AL	M
The University of Alabama at Birmingham, AL	M,W
The University of Arizona, AZ	W
University of Arkansas, AR	W
University of Arkansas at Little Rock, AR	W
University of California, Los Angeles, CA	M,W
University of California, Merced, CA	M,W
University of California, Riverside, CA	M,W
University of California, Santa Barbara, CA	M,W
University of Central Arkansas, AR	M,W
University of Central Florida, FL	M,W
University of Cincinnati, OH	M,W
University of Colorado Boulder, CO	W
University of Colorado Colorado Springs, CO	M,W
University of Dayton, OH	M,W
University of Denver, CO	M,W
The University of Findlay, OH	M,W
University of Guam, GU	M,W
University of Hawaii at Manoa, HI	W
University of Houston, TX	W
University of Idaho, ID	W
University of Illinois at Chicago, IL	M
University of Illinois at Springfield, IL	M,W
The University of Iowa, IA	W
University of Jamestown, ND	M,W
The University of Kansas, KS	W
University of Kentucky, KY	M,W
University of Louisiana at Monroe, LA	W
University of Louisville, KY	M,W
University of Maine, ME	W
University of Maryland, Baltimore County, MD	M,W
University of Massachusetts Amherst, MA	M,W
University of Massachusetts Lowell, MA	M,W
University of Memphis, TN	M,W
University of Michigan, MI	M,W
University of Michigan–Dearborn, MI	M,W
University of Minnesota, Duluth, MN	W
University of Minnesota, Twin Cities Campus, MN	W
University of Missouri–St. Louis, MO	M,W
University of Montana, MT	W
University of Montevallo, AL	M,W
University of Nebraska at Kearney, NE	W
University of Nebraska–Lincoln, NE	W
University of Nevada, Las Vegas, NV	M,W
University of Nevada, Reno, NV	W
University of New Hampshire, NH	M,W
University of New Haven, CT	M,W
University of New Mexico, NM	M,W
The University of North Carolina at Chapel Hill, NC	M,W
The University of North Carolina at Charlotte, NC	M,W
The University of North Carolina at Greensboro, NC	M,W
The University of North Carolina at Pembroke, NC	M,W
The University of North Carolina Wilmington, NC	M,W
University of North Dakota, ND	W
University of Northern Colorado, CO	W
University of Northern Iowa, IA	W
University of North Texas, TX	W
University of Notre Dame, IN	M,W
University of Oregon, OR	W
University of Pikeville, KY	M,W
University of Portland, OR	M,W
University of Providence, MT	M,W
University of Richmond, VA	W
University of St. Francis, IL	M,W
University of Saint Francis, IN	M,W
University of Saint Mary, KS	M,W
University of St. Thomas, TX	M,W
University of San Diego, CA	M,W
University of San Francisco, CA	M,W
University of Science and Arts of Oklahoma, OK	M,W
University of South Carolina, SC	M,W
University of South Carolina Aiken, SC	M,W
University of South Dakota, SD	W
University of Southern Indiana, IN	M,W
University of Southern Mississippi, MS	W
University of South Florida, FL	M,W
The University of Tampa, FL	M,W
The University of Tennessee, TN	W
The University of Tennessee at Chattanooga, TN	W
The University of Tennessee at Martin, TN	W
The University of Texas at El Paso, TX	W
The University of Texas at San Antonio, TX	W
The University of Texas Rio Grande Valley, TX	M,W
University of the Incarnate Word, TX	M,W
University of the Pacific, CA	W
The University of Toledo, OH	W
The University of Tulsa, OK	M,W
University of Utah, UT	W
University of Virginia, VA	M,W
University of Washington, WA	M,W
University of West Georgia, GA	W
University of Wisconsin–Green Bay, WI	M,W
University of Wisconsin–Madison, WI	M,W
University of Wisconsin–Milwaukee, WI	M,W
University of Wisconsin–Parkside, WI	M,W
University of Wyoming, WY	W
Upper Iowa University, IA	M,W
Ursuline College, OH	W

Utah State University, UT W
Utah Valley University, UT W
Valdosta State University, GA W
Valparaiso University, IN M,W
Vanderbilt University, TN W
Vanguard University of Southern California, CA M,W
Villanova University, PA M,W
Virginia Commonwealth University, VA M,W
Wake Forest University, NC M,W
Washington State University, WA W
Wayland Baptist University, TX M,W
Wayne State College, NE W
Webber International University, FL M,W
Weber State University, UT W
West Chester University of Pennsylvania, PA M,W
Western Carolina University, NC W
Western Colorado University, CO W
Western Michigan University, MI M,W
Western Oregon University, OR W
Western Washington University, WA M,W
Westminster College, UT M,W
Westmont College, CA M,W
William & Mary, VA M,W
Wingate University, NC M,W
Wofford College, SC M,W
Wright State University, OH M,W
Xavier University, OH M,W
Youngstown State University, OH W

Softball

Abilene Christian University, TX W
Academy of Art University, CA W
Adams State University, CO W
Anderson University, SC W
Angelo State University, TX W
Appalachian State University, NC W
Aquinas College, MI W
Arizona Christian University, AZ W
Arizona State University at the Downtown Phoenix campus, AZ W
Arizona State University at the Polytechnic campus, AZ W
Arizona State University at the Tempe campus, AZ W
Arizona State University at the West campus, AZ W
Arkansas Tech University, AR W
Auburn University, AL W
Auburn University at Montgomery, AL W
Augustana University, SD W
Austin Peay State University, TN W
Baker University, KS W
Ball State University, IN W
Barry University, FL W
Barton College, NC W
Baylor University, TX W
Belmont Abbey College, NC W
Belmont University, TN W
Bemidji State University, MN W
Bethel University, IN W
Binghamton University, State University of New York, NY W
Biola University, CA W
Boise State University, ID W
Boston College, MA W
Bowling Green State University, OH W
Bradley University, IL W
Brigham Young University, UT W
Bryan College, TN W
Bryant University, RI W
Bucknell University, PA W
Butler University, IN W
Caldwell University, NJ W
California Baptist University, CA W
California Polytechnic State University, San Luis Obispo, CA W
California State University, Bakersfield, CA W
California State University, Dominguez Hills, CA W
California State University, Fresno, CA W
California State University, Fullerton, CA W
California State University, Long Beach, CA W
California State University, Monterey Bay, CA W
California State University, Northridge, CA W
California State University, Sacramento, CA W
California State University, San Bernardino, CA W
California State University, Stanislaus, CA W
California University of Pennsylvania, PA W
Calumet College of Saint Joseph, IN W
Cameron University, OK W
Campbellsville University, KY W
Carlow University, PA W
Carson-Newman University, TN W
Catawba College, NC W
Cedarville University, OH W
Central Connecticut State University, CT W
Central Methodist University, MO W
Central Michigan University, MI W
Central Washington University, WA W
Chaminade University of Honolulu, HI W
Chestnut Hill College, PA W
Clarion University of Pennsylvania, PA W
Clemson University, SC W
Coastal Carolina University, SC W
Colgate University, NY W
The College of Idaho, ID W
College of Saint Mary, NE W
The College of Saint Rose, NY W
College of the Holy Cross, MA W
Colorado School of Mines, CO W
Colorado State University, CO W
Columbia College, MO W
Columbia College, SC W
Concordia University, St. Paul, MN W
Creighton University, NE W
Dakota State University, SD W
Delta State University, MS W
DePaul University, IL W
Doane University, NE W
Dominican College, NY W
Dominican University of California, CA W
Drake University, IA W
Drexel University, PA W
Drury University, MO W
East Carolina University, NC W
East Central University, OK W
Eastern Illinois University, IL W
Eastern Kentucky University, KY W
Eastern Michigan University, MI W
Eastern New Mexico University, NM W
Eastern Oregon University, OR W
Edinboro University of Pennsylvania, PA W
Elon University, NC W
Emmanuel College, GA W
Emporia State University, KS W
Evangel University, MO W
Fairfield University, CT W
Fayetteville State University, NC W
Felician University, NJ W
Ferris State University, MI W
Florida Agricultural and Mechanical University, FL W
Florida Atlantic University, FL W
Florida Gulf Coast University, FL W
Florida Institute of Technology, FL W
Florida National University, FL W
Florida State University, FL W
Fordham University, NY W
Fort Lewis College, CO W
Francis Marion University, SC W
Freed-Hardeman University, TN W
Gannon University, PA W
George Mason University, VA W
Georgetown College, KY W
Georgetown University, DC W
Georgia College & State University, GA W
Georgia Institute of Technology, GA W
Georgian Court University, NJ W
Georgia State University, GA W
Glenville State College, WV W
Goshen College, IN W
Graceland University, IA W
Grambling State University, LA W
Grand Valley State University, MI W
Hampton University, VA W
Hillsdale College, MI W
Hofstra University, NY W
Hope International University, CA W
Houston Baptist University, TX W
Illinois State University, IL W
Indiana State University, IN W
Indiana University Bloomington, IN W
Indiana University of Pennsylvania, PA W
Indiana University-Purdue University Indianapolis, IN W
Indiana University South Bend, IN W
Indiana University Southeast, IN W
Inter American University of Puerto Rico, Aguadilla Campus, PR M,W
Iona College, NY W
Jacksonville State University, AL W
Jacksonville University, FL W
James Madison University, VA W
Kennesaw State University, GA W
King University, TN W
Kutztown University of Pennsylvania, PA W
Lawrence Technological University, MI W
Lee University, TN W
Lehigh University, PA W
Le Moyne College, NY W
Lenoir-Rhyne University, NC W
Lewis University, IL W
Liberty University, VA W

Limestone College, SC W
Lincoln Memorial University, TN W
Lincoln University, PA W
Lindenwood University, MO W
Lipscomb University, TN W
Lock Haven University of Pennsylvania, PA W
Longwood University, VA W
Louisiana State University and Agricultural & Mechanical College, LA W
Loyola Marymount University, CA W
Loyola University Chicago, IL W
Lynn University, FL W
Malone University, OH W
Manhattan College, NY W
Mansfield University of Pennsylvania, PA W
Marshall University, WV W
Maryville University of Saint Louis, MO W
Mayville State University, ND W
McKendree University, IL W
Mercer University, GA W
Mercy College, NY W
Merrimack College, MA W
Miami University, OH W
Michigan State University, MI W
MidAmerica Nazarene University, KS W
Middle Tennessee State University, TN W
Midway University, KY W
Millersville University of Pennsylvania, PA W
Milligan University, TN W
Minnesota State University Mankato, MN W
Minot State University, ND W
Mississippi State University, MS W
Missouri Southern State University, MO W
Missouri State University, MO W
Missouri University of Science and Technology, MO W
Missouri Valley College, MO W
Molloy College, NY W
Morehead State University, KY W
Mount Marty College, SD W
Mount St. Mary's University, MD W
Mount Vernon Nazarene University, OH W
Newman University, KS W
New York Institute of Technology, NY W
Niagara University, NY W
North Carolina Central University, NC W
Northeastern State University, OK W
Northern Illinois University, IL W
Northern State University, SD W
North Greenville University, SC W
Northwest Christian University, OR W
Northwestern State University of Louisiana, LA W
Northwest Nazarene University, ID W
Northwest University, WA W
Nyack College, NY W
Oakland University, MI W
The Ohio State University, OH W
Ohio Valley University, WV W
Oklahoma Baptist University, OK W
Oklahoma State University, OK W
Olivet Nazarene University, IL W
Palm Beach Atlantic University, FL W
Penn State Hazleton, PA W
Penn State University Park, PA W
Pittsburg State University, KS W
Prairie View A&M University, TX W
Providence College, RI W
Purdue University Fort Wayne, IN W
Purdue University Northwest, IN W
Queens College of the City University of New York, NY W
Queens University of Charlotte, NC W
Radford University, VA W
Rochester University, MI W
Rogers State University, OK W
Rollins College, FL W
Sacred Heart University, CT W
Saginaw Valley State University, MI W
St. Ambrose University, IA W
St. Bonaventure University, NY W
St. Cloud State University, MN W
Saint Francis University, PA W
Saint Joseph's University, PA W
Saint Leo University, FL W
Saint Louis University, MO W
Saint Mary's College of California, CA W
St. Petersburg College, FL W
Samford University, AL W
Sam Houston State University, TX W
San Diego State University, CA W
San Francisco State University, CA W
San Jose State University, CA W
Santa Clara University, CA W
Seattle University, WA W
Shepherd University, WV W
Siena College, NY W
Slippery Rock University of Pennsylvania, PA W
Southeastern Louisiana University, LA W
Southeastern University, FL W
Southeast Missouri State University, MO W
Southern Illinois University Carbondale, IL W
Southern Illinois University Edwardsville, IL W
Southwest Baptist University, MO W
Southwestern College, KS W
Southwestern Oklahoma State University, OK W
Spring Hill College, AL W
Stanford University, CA W
Sterling College, KS W
Stetson University, FL W
Stony Brook University, State University of New York, NY W
Tabor College, KS W
Tarleton State University, TX W
Taylor University, IN W
Tennessee Wesleyan University, TN W
Texas A&M International University, TX W
Texas A&M University, TX W
Texas A&M University–Corpus Christi, TX W
Texas State University, TX W
Texas Tech University, TX W
Texas Woman's University, TX W
Tiffin University, OH W
Towson University, MD W
Trevecca Nazarene University, TN W
Troy University, AL W
Truett McConnell University, GA W
Truman State University, MO W
Union University, TN W
University at Albany, State University of New York, NY W
University at Buffalo, the State University of New York, NY W
The University of Akron, OH W
The University of Alabama, AL W
The University of Arizona, AZ W
University of Arkansas, AR W
University of California, Los Angeles, CA W
University of California, Riverside, CA W
University of California, Santa Barbara, CA W
University of Central Arkansas, AR W
University of Central Florida, FL W
University of Colorado Colorado Springs, CO W
University of Dayton, OH W
The University of Findlay, OH W
University of Hawaii at Manoa, HI W
University of Houston, TX W
University of Illinois at Chicago, IL W
University of Illinois at Springfield, IL W
The University of Iowa, IA W
University of Jamestown, ND W
The University of Kansas, KS W
University of Kentucky, KY W
University of Louisiana at Lafayette, LA W
University of Louisiana at Monroe, LA W
University of Louisville, KY W
University of Maine, ME W
University of Maryland, Baltimore County, MD W
University of Massachusetts Amherst, MA W
University of Massachusetts Lowell, MA W
University of Memphis, TN W
University of Michigan, MI W
University of Michigan–Dearborn, MI W
University of Minnesota, Duluth, MN W
University of Minnesota, Twin Cities Campus, MN W
University of Missouri–St. Louis, MO W
University of Montana, MT W
University of Nebraska at Kearney, NE W
University of Nebraska–Lincoln, NE W
University of Nevada, Las Vegas, NV W
University of Nevada, Reno, NV W
University of New Haven, CT W
University of New Mexico, NM W
The University of North Carolina at Chapel Hill, NC W
The University of North Carolina at Charlotte, NC

The University of North Carolina at Greensboro, NC W
The University of North Carolina at Pembroke, NC W
The University of North Carolina Wilmington, NC W
University of North Dakota, ND W
University of Northern Colorado, CO W
University of Northern Iowa, IA W
University of North Texas, TX W
University of Notre Dame, IN W
University of Oregon, OR W
University of Pikeville, KY W
University of St. Francis, IL W
University of Saint Francis, IN W
University of Saint Mary, KS W
University of San Diego, CA W
University of Science and Arts of Oklahoma, OK W
University of South Carolina, SC W
University of South Carolina Aiken, SC W
University of South Dakota, SD W
University of Southern Indiana, IN W
University of Southern Mississippi, MS W
University of South Florida, FL W
The University of Tampa, FL W
The University of Tennessee, TN W
The University of Tennessee at Chattanooga, TN W
The University of Tennessee at Martin, TN W
The University of Texas at El Paso, TX W
The University of Texas at San Antonio, TX W
University of the Incarnate Word, TX W
University of the Pacific, CA W
The University of Toledo, OH W
The University of Tulsa, OK W
University of Utah, UT W
University of Virginia, VA W
University of Washington, WA W
The University of West Alabama, AL W
University of West Georgia, GA W
University of Wisconsin–Green Bay, WI W
University of Wisconsin–Madison, WI W
University of Wisconsin–Parkside, WI W
Upper Iowa University, IA W
Ursuline College, OH W
Utah State University, UT W
Utah Valley University, UT W
Valdosta State University, GA W
Valley City State University, ND W
Valparaiso University, IN W
Vanguard University of Southern California, CA W
Villanova University, PA W
Wayne State College, NE W
Wayne State University, MI W
Webber International University, FL W
Weber State University, UT W
West Chester University of Pennsylvania, PA W
Western Carolina University, NC W
Western Kentucky University, KY W
Western Michigan University, MI W
Western New Mexico University, NM W
Western Oregon University, OR W
Western Washington University, WA W
Wichita State University, KS W
Wingate University, NC W
Wright State University, OH W
Youngstown State University, OH W

Squash

Drexel University, PA M,W
Fordham University, NY M
Stanford University, CA W
University of Providence, MT W
University of Virginia, VA M,W

Swimming and diving

Adams State University, CO M,W
Arizona Christian University, AZ W
Arizona State University at the Downtown Phoenix campus, AZ M,W
Arizona State University at the Polytechnic campus, AZ M,W
Arizona State University at the Tempe campus, AZ M,W
Arizona State University at the West campus, AZ M,W
Auburn University, AL M,W
Augustana University, SD W
Ball State University, IN M,W
Barton College, NC M,W
Bayamón Central University, PR M,W
Bethel University, IN M,W
Binghamton University, State University of New York, NY M,W
Biola University, CA M,W
Boise State University, ID W
Boston College, MA M,W
Bowling Green State University, OH W
Brigham Young University, UT M,W
Bryant University, RI M,W
Bucknell University, PA M
California Baptist University, CA M,W
California Polytechnic State University, San Luis Obispo, CA M,W
California State University, Bakersfield, CA M,W
California State University, Fresno, CA W
California State University, Northridge, CA M,W
California University of Pennsylvania, PA W
Campbellsville University, KY M,W
Carson-Newman University, TN M,W
Catawba College, NC M,W
Central Connecticut State University, CT W
Clarion University of Pennsylvania, PA M,W
Colgate University, NY W
The College of Idaho, ID M,W
College of Saint Mary, NE W
The College of Saint Rose, NY M,W
College of the Holy Cross, MA W
Colorado School of Mines, CO M,W
Colorado State University, CO W
Columbia College, SC W
Concordia University, St. Paul, MN W
Davidson College, NC M,W
Delta State University, MS M,W
Drexel University, PA M,W
Drury University, MO M,W
East Carolina University, NC M,W
Eastern Illinois University, IL M,W
Eastern Michigan University, MI M,W
Edinboro University of Pennsylvania, PA M,W
Emmanuel College, GA M,W
Fairfield University, CT M,W
Florida Agricultural and Mechanical University, FL M,W
Florida Gulf Coast University, FL W
Florida Institute of Technology, FL M,W
Florida State University, FL M,W
Fordham University, NY M,W
Gannon University, PA M,W
George Mason University, VA M,W
Georgetown University, DC W
The George Washington University, DC M,W
Georgia Institute of Technology, GA M,W
Grand Valley State University, MI M,W
Hillsdale College, MI W
Illinois Institute of Technology, IL M,W
Illinois State University, IL W
Indiana State University, IN W
Indiana University Bloomington, IN M,W
Indiana University of Pennsylvania, PA M,W
Indiana University-Purdue University Indianapolis, IN M,W
Inter American University of Puerto Rico, Aguadilla Campus, PR M,W
Iona College, NY M,W
James Madison University, VA W
King University, TN M,W
Kutztown University of Pennsylvania, PA W
Lehigh University, PA M,W
Le Moyne College, NY M,W
Lenoir-Rhyne University, NC M,W
Lewis University, IL M,W
Liberty University, VA W
Life University, GA M,W
Limestone College, SC M,W
Lindenwood University, MO M,W
Lock Haven University of Pennsylvania, PA W
Louisiana State University and Agricultural & Mechanical College, LA M,W
Loyola Marymount University, CA W
Loyola University Maryland, MD M,W
Loyola University New Orleans, LA M,W
Lynn University, FL W
Malone University, OH M,W
Manhattan College, NY M,W
Marshall University, WV W
Maryville University of Saint Louis, MO M,W
McKendree University, IL M,W
Merrimack College, MA W
Miami University, OH M,W
Michigan State University, MI M,W
Midway University, KY M,W
Millersville University of Pennsylvania, PA W
Milligan University, TN M,W
Minnesota State University Mankato, MN W
Missouri State University, MO M,W

Missouri University of Science and Technology, MO M
Mount St. Mary's University, MD M,W
New Jersey Institute of Technology, NJ M
Niagara University, NY M,W
Northern Arizona University, AZ W
Northern Illinois University, IL M,W
Northern State University, SD W
Oakland University, MI M,W
The Ohio State University, OH M,W
Oklahoma Baptist University, OK M,W
Old Dominion University, VA M,W
Penn State University Park, PA M,W
Queens College of the City University of New York, NY W
Queens University of Charlotte, NC M,W
Rice University, TX W
Sacred Heart University, CT W
Saginaw Valley State University, MI M,W
St. Ambrose University, IA M,W
St. Bonaventure University, NY M,W
St. Cloud State University, MN M,W
Saint Francis University, PA W
Saint Leo University, FL M,W
Saint Louis University, MO M,W
San Diego State University, CA W
San Jose State University, CA W
Seattle University, WA M,W
Siena College, NY W
Southern Illinois University Carbondale, IL M,W
Southern Methodist University, TX M,W
Stanford University, CA M,W
Stony Brook University, State University of New York, NY W
Tabor College, KS M,W
Texas A&M University, TX M,W
Texas Christian University, TX M,W
Tiffin University, OH M,W
Towson University, MD M,W
Truman State University, MO M,W
Tulane University, LA W
University at Buffalo, the State University of New York, NY W
The University of Akron, OH W
The University of Alabama, AL M,W
University of Alaska Fairbanks, AK W
The University of Arizona, AZ M,W
University of Arkansas, AR W
University of California, Los Angeles, CA W
University of California, Santa Barbara, CA M,W
University of Cincinnati, OH M,W
University of Denver, CO M,W
The University of Findlay, OH M,W
University of Hawaii at Manoa, HI M,W
University of Houston, TX W
University of Idaho, ID W
University of Illinois at Chicago, IL M,W
The University of Iowa, IA M,W
The University of Kansas, KS W
University of Kentucky, KY M,W
University of Louisville, KY M,W
University of Maine, ME W
University of Maryland, Baltimore County, MD M,W
University of Massachusetts Amherst, MA M,W
University of Michigan, MI M,W
University of Minnesota, Twin Cities Campus, MN M,W
University of Missouri–St. Louis, MO M,W
University of Nebraska at Kearney, NE W
University of Nebraska–Lincoln, NE W
University of Nevada, Las Vegas, NV M,W
University of Nevada, Reno, NV W
University of New Hampshire, NH W
University of New Mexico, NM W
The University of North Carolina at Chapel Hill, NC M,W
The University of North Carolina Wilmington, NC M,W
University of Northern Colorado, CO W
University of Northern Iowa, IA W
University of North Texas, TX W
University of Notre Dame, IN M,W
University of Richmond, VA W
University of Saint Mary, KS M,W
University of San Diego, CA W
University of South Carolina, SC M,W
University of South Dakota, SD M,W
The University of Tampa, FL M,W
The University of Tennessee, TN M,W
University of the Incarnate Word, TX M,W
University of the Pacific, CA M,W
The University of Toledo, OH W
University of Utah, UT M,W
University of Virginia, VA M,W
University of Wisconsin–Green Bay, WI M,W
University of Wisconsin–Madison, WI M,W
University of Wisconsin–Milwaukee, WI M,W
University of Wyoming, WY M,W
Ursuline College, OH W
Valparaiso University, IN M,W
Vanderbilt University, TN W
Villanova University, PA W
Washington State University, WA W
Wayne State University, MI M,W
West Chester University of Pennsylvania, PA M,W
Western Colorado University, CO W
Westmont College, CA W
William & Mary, VA W
Wingate University, NC M,W
Wright State University, OH M,W
Xavier University, OH M,W
Youngstown State University, OH W

Table tennis

Bayamón Central University, PR M,W
Inter American University of Puerto Rico, Aguadilla Campus, PR M,W
The University of Alabama at Birmingham, AL M

Tennis

Abilene Christian University, TX M,W
Academy of Art University, CA W
Anderson University, SC M,W
Angelo State University, TX W
Appalachian State University, NC M,W
Aquinas College, MI M,W
Arizona Christian University, AZ M,W
Arizona State University at the Downtown Phoenix campus, AZ M,W
Arizona State University at the Polytechnic campus, AZ M,W
Arizona State University at the Tempe campus, AZ M,W
Arizona State University at the West campus, AZ M,W
Arkansas Tech University, AR W
Auburn University, AL M,W
Auburn University at Montgomery, AL M,W
Augustana University, SD M,W
Austin Peay State University, TN M,W
Baker University, KS M,W
Ball State University, IN M,W
Barry University, FL M,W
Barton College, NC M,W
Baylor University, TX M,W
Belmont Abbey College, NC M,W
Belmont University, TN M,W
Bemidji State University, MN W
Bethel University, IN M,W
Binghamton University, State University of New York, NY M,W
Biola University, CA M,W
Boise State University, ID M,W
Boston College, MA M,W
Bowling Green State University, OH W
Bradley University, IL W
Brigham Young University, UT M,W
Bryant University, RI M,W
Butler University, IN M,W
Caldwell University, NJ W
California Polytechnic State University, San Luis Obispo, CA M,W
California State University, Bakersfield, CA W
California State University, Fresno, CA M,W
California State University, Fullerton, CA W
California State University, Long Beach, CA W
California State University, Los Angeles, CA W
California State University, Northridge, CA W
California State University, Sacramento, CA M,W
California State University, Stanislaus, CA W
California University of Pennsylvania, PA W
Calumet College of Saint Joseph, IN M,W
Cameron University, OK M,W
Campbellsville University, KY M,W
Carlow University, PA W
Carson-Newman University, TN M,W
Catawba College, NC M,W
Cedarville University, OH M,W
Chaminade University of Honolulu, HI W
Chestnut Hill College, PA M,W
The Citadel, The Military College of South Carolina, SC M
Clarion University of Pennsylvania, PA W
Clemson University, SC M,W
Coastal Carolina University, SC M,W

The College of Idaho, ID	W
College of Saint Mary, NE	W
Colorado State University, CO	W
Columbia College, SC	W
Creighton University, NE	M,W
Dallas Baptist University, TX	W
Davidson College, NC	M,W
Delta State University, MS	M,W
DePaul University, IL	M,W
Dominican College, NY	M,W
Dominican University of California, CA	W
Drake University, IA	M,W
Drexel University, PA	M,W
Drury University, MO	M,W
East Carolina University, NC	M,W
Eastern Illinois University, IL	M,W
Eastern Kentucky University, KY	M,W
Eastern Michigan University, MI	W
Eastern Washington University, WA	M,W
Edinboro University of Pennsylvania, PA	M,W
Elon University, NC	M,W
Emmanuel College, GA	M,W
Emporia State University, KS	M,W
Evangel University, MO	M,W
Fairfield University, CT	M,W
Fayetteville State University, NC	W
Ferris State University, MI	M,W
Florida Agricultural and Mechanical University, FL	M,W
Florida Gulf Coast University, FL	M,W
Florida National University, FL	M,W
Florida State University, FL	M,W
Fordham University, NY	M,W
Francis Marion University, SC	M,W
George Mason University, VA	M,W
Georgetown College, KY	M,W
Georgetown University, DC	W
The George Washington University, DC	M,W
Georgia College & State University, GA	M,W
Georgia Gwinnett College, GA	M,W
Georgia Institute of Technology, GA	M,W
Georgia State University, GA	M,W
Gonzaga University, WA	M,W
Goshen College, IN	M,W
Grambling State University, LA	W
Grand Valley State University, MI	M,W
Hampton University, VA	M,W
Hillsdale College, MI	M,W
Hofstra University, NY	M,W
Hope International University, CA	M,W
Illinois State University, IL	M,W
Indiana University Bloomington, IN	M,W
Indiana University of Pennsylvania, PA	W
Indiana University-Purdue University Indianapolis, IN	M,W
Indiana University South Bend, IN	M,W
Indiana University Southeast, IN	M,W
Inter American University of Puerto Rico, Aguadilla Campus, PR	M,W
Jacksonville State University, AL	M,W
James Madison University, VA	M,W
John Brown University, AR	M,W
Kennesaw State University, GA	M,W
King University, TN	M,W
Kutztown University of Pennsylvania, PA	M,W
Lawrence Technological University, MI	M,W
Lee University, TN	M,W
Lehigh University, PA	M,W
Le Moyne College, NY	M,W
Lenoir-Rhyne University, NC	M,W
Lewis-Clark State College, ID	M,W
Lewis University, IL	M,W
Liberty University, VA	M,W
Limestone College, SC	M,W
Lincoln Memorial University, TN	M,W
Lindenwood University, MO	M,W
Lipscomb University, TN	M,W
Lock Haven University of Pennsylvania, PA	W
Longwood University, VA	M,W
Louisiana State University and Agricultural & Mechanical College, LA	M,W
Louisiana State University in Shreveport, LA	W
Loyola Marymount University, CA	M,W
Loyola University Maryland, MD	M,W
Loyola University New Orleans, LA	M,W
Lynn University, FL	M,W
Manhattan College, NY	W
Marquette University, WI	M,W
Marshall University, WV	W
Maryville University of Saint Louis, MO	M,W
McKendree University, IL	M,W
Mercer University, GA	M,W
Merrimack College, MA	M,W
Miami University, OH	W
Michigan State University, MI	M,W
Michigan Technological University, MI	M,W
Middle Tennessee State University, TN	M,W
Midway University, KY	M,W
Millersville University of Pennsylvania, PA	M,W
Milligan University, TN	M,W
Minnesota State University Mankato, MN	M,W
Mississippi State University, MS	M,W
Missouri Southern State University, MO	W
Missouri Valley College, MO	M,W
Molloy College, NY	W
Montana State University, MT	M,W
Mount Marty College, SD	M,W
Mount St. Mary's University, MD	M,W
Mount Vernon Nazarene University, OH	M,W
New Jersey Institute of Technology, NJ	M,W
Newman University, KS	M,W
Niagara University, NY	M,W
North Carolina Central University, NC	M,W
Northeastern State University, OK	W
Northern Arizona University, AZ	M,W
Northern Illinois University, IL	M,W
North Greenville University, SC	M,W
Northwestern State University of Louisiana, LA	W
Northwest Missouri State University, MO	M,W
Oakland University, MI	W
The Ohio State University, OH	M,W
Oklahoma Baptist University, OK	M,W
Oklahoma State University, OK	M,W
Old Dominion University, VA	M,W
Olivet Nazarene University, IL	M,W
Oral Roberts University, OK	M,W
Palm Beach Atlantic University, FL	M,W
Penn State University Park, PA	M,W
Pepperdine University, CA	M,W
Point Loma Nazarene University, CA	M,W
Prairie View A&M University, TX	M,W
Purdue University Fort Wayne, IN	M,W
Purdue University Northwest, IN	M,W
Queens College of the City University of New York, NY	M,W
Queens University of Charlotte, NC	M,W
Radford University, VA	M,W
Rice University, TX	M,W
Rollins College, FL	M,W
Sacred Heart University, CT	M,W
Saginaw Valley State University, MI	W
St. Ambrose University, IA	M,W
St. Bonaventure University, NY	M,W
St. Cloud State University, MN	W
Saint Francis University, PA	M,W
Saint Joseph's University, PA	M,W
Saint Leo University, FL	M,W
Saint Louis University, MO	M,W
Saint Mary's College of California, CA	M,W
St. Mary's University, TX	M,W
St. Petersburg College, FL	W
Samford University, AL	M,W
Sam Houston State University, TX	W
San Diego State University, CA	M,W
San Jose State University, CA	W
Santa Clara University, CA	M,W
Shepherd University, WV	M,W
Siena College, NY	M,W
Slippery Rock University of Pennsylvania, PA	W
Southeastern Louisiana University, LA	W
Southeastern University, FL	M,W
Southeast Missouri State University, MO	W
Southern Illinois University Edwardsville, IL	W
Southern Methodist University, TX	M,W
Southwest Baptist University, MO	M,W
Southwestern College, KS	M,W
Spring Hill College, AL	M,W
Stanford University, CA	M,W
Stetson University, FL	M,W
Stony Brook University, State University of New York, NY	W
Tabor College, KS	M,W
Tarleton State University, TX	W
Taylor University, IN	M,W
Temple University, PA	M,W
Tennessee Wesleyan University, TN	M,W
Texas A&M University, TX	M,W
Texas A&M University–Corpus Christi, TX	M,W
Texas Christian University, TX	M,W
Texas State University, TX	W
Texas Tech University, TX	M,W
Tiffin University, OH	M,W
Towson University, MD	W
Troy University, AL	M,W
Truman State University, MO	W
Tulane University, LA	M,W

University at Albany, State University of New York, NY W
University at Buffalo, the State University of New York, NY M,W
The University of Akron, OH W
The University of Alabama, AL M,W
The University of Alabama at Birmingham, AL W
The University of Arizona, AZ M,W
University of Arkansas, AR M,W
University of California, Los Angeles, CA M,W
University of California, Riverside, CA M,W
University of California, Santa Barbara, CA M,W
University of Central Arkansas, AR W
University of Central Florida, FL M,W
University of Cincinnati, OH W
University of Colorado Boulder, CO W
University of Dayton, OH M,W
University of Denver, CO M,W
The University of Findlay, OH M,W
University of Hawaii at Manoa, HI M,W
University of Houston, TX W
University of Idaho, ID M,W
University of Illinois at Chicago, IL M,W
University of Illinois at Springfield, IL M,W
The University of Iowa, IA M,W
The University of Kansas, KS W
University of Kentucky, KY M,W
University of Louisiana at Lafayette, LA M,W
University of Louisiana at Monroe, LA W
University of Louisville, KY M,W
University of Massachusetts Amherst, MA W
University of Memphis, TN M,W
University of Michigan, MI M,W
University of Minnesota, Duluth, MN W
University of Minnesota, Twin Cities Campus, MN M,W
University of Missouri–St. Louis, MO M,W
University of Montana, MT M,W
University of Montevallo, AL W
University of Nebraska at Kearney, NE M,W
University of Nebraska–Lincoln, NE M,W
University of Nevada, Las Vegas, NV M,W
University of Nevada, Reno, NV M,W
University of New Haven, CT W
University of New Mexico, NM M,W
The University of North Carolina at Chapel Hill, NC M,W
The University of North Carolina at Charlotte, NC M,W
The University of North Carolina at Greensboro, NC M,W
The University of North Carolina Wilmington, NC M,W
University of North Dakota, ND M,W
University of Northern Colorado, CO M,W
University of Northern Iowa, IA W
University of Notre Dame, IN M,W
University of Oregon, OR M,W
University of Pikeville, KY M,W
University of Portland, OR M,W
University of Richmond, VA M,W
University of St. Francis, IL M,W
University of Saint Francis, IN M,W
University of San Diego, CA M,W
University of San Francisco, CA M,W
University of South Carolina, SC M,W
University of South Dakota, SD W
University of Southern Indiana, IN M,W
University of Southern Mississippi, MS M,W
University of South Florida, FL M,W
The University of Tampa, FL W
The University of Tennessee, TN M,W
The University of Tennessee at Chattanooga, TN M,W
The University of Tennessee at Martin, TN W
The University of Texas at El Paso, TX W
The University of Texas at San Antonio, TX M,W
The University of Texas Rio Grande Valley, TX M,W
University of the Incarnate Word, TX M,W
University of the Pacific, CA M,W
The University of Toledo, OH M,W
The University of Tulsa, OK M,W
University of Utah, UT M,W
University of Virginia, VA M,W
University of Washington, WA M,W
The University of West Alabama, AL M,W
University of West Georgia, GA W
University of Wisconsin–Green Bay, WI M,W
University of Wisconsin–Madison, WI M,W
University of Wisconsin–Milwaukee, WI W
University of Wyoming, WY W
Upper Iowa University, IA W
Ursuline College, OH W
Utah State University, UT M,W
Valdosta State University, GA M,W
Valparaiso University, IN M,W
Vanderbilt University, TN M,W
Virginia Commonwealth University, VA M,W
Wake Forest University, NC M,W
Washington State University, WA W
Wayne State University, MI M,W
Webber International University, FL M,W
Weber State University, UT M,W
West Chester University of Pennsylvania, PA M,W
Western Carolina University, NC W
Western Kentucky University, KY W
Western Michigan University, MI M,W
Western New Mexico University, NM M,W
Westmont College, CA M,W
Wichita State University, KS M,W
William & Mary, VA M,W
Wingate University, NC M,W
Wofford College, SC M,W
Wright State University, OH M,W
Xavier University, OH M,W
Xavier University of Louisiana, LA M,W
Youngstown State University, OH M,W

Track and field

Abilene Christian University, TX M,W
Academy of Art University, CA M,W
Adams State University, CO M,W
American University, DC M,W
Anderson University, SC M,W
Angelo State University, TX M,W
Appalachian State University, NC M,W
Aquinas College, MI M,W
Arizona Christian University, AZ M,W
Arizona State University at the Downtown Phoenix campus, AZ M,W
Arizona State University at the Polytechnic campus, AZ M,W
Arizona State University at the Tempe campus, AZ M,W
Arizona State University at the West campus, AZ M,W
Auburn University, AL M,W
Augustana University, SD M,W
Austin Peay State University, TN W
Baker University, KS M,W
Ball State University, IN W
Barton College, NC M,W
Bayamón Central University, PR M,W
Baylor University, TX M,W
Belmont Abbey College, NC M,W
Belmont University, TN M,W
Bemidji State University, MN W
Bethel University, IN M,W
Binghamton University, State University of New York, NY M,W
Biola University, CA M,W
Black Hills State University, SD M,W
Boise State University, ID M,W
Boston College, MA M,W
Bowling Green State University, OH W
Bradley University, IL M,W
Brigham Young University, UT M,W
Bryan College, TN M,W
Bryant University, RI M,W
Bucknell University, PA W
Butler University, IN M,W
Caldwell University, NJ M,W
California Baptist University, CA M,W
California Polytechnic State University, San Luis Obispo, CA M,W
California State Polytechnic University, Pomona, CA M,W
California State University, Bakersfield, CA M,W
California State University, Dominguez Hills, CA W
California State University, Fresno, CA M,W
California State University, Fullerton, CA M,W
California State University, Long Beach, CA M,W
California State University, Los Angeles, CA M,W
California State University, Northridge, CA M,W
California State University, Sacramento, CA M,W
California State University, Stanislaus, CA M,W
California University of Pennsylvania, PA M,W
Calumet College of Saint Joseph, IN M,W
Cameron University, OK M,W

Campbellsville University, KY M,W
Carson-Newman University, TN M,W
Cedarville University, OH M,W
Central Connecticut State University, CT M,W
Central Methodist University, MO M,W
Central Michigan University, MI M,W
Central Washington University, WA M,W
Chestnut Hill College, PA M,W
The Citadel, The Military College of South Carolina, SC M,W
Clarion University of Pennsylvania, PA W
Clemson University, SC M,W
Coastal Carolina University, SC M,W
The College of Idaho, ID M,W
College of Saint Mary, NE W
The College of Saint Rose, NY M,W
College of the Holy Cross, MA W
Colorado School of Mines, CO M,W
Colorado State University, CO M,W
Columbia College, MO M,W
Columbia College, SC W
Concordia University, St. Paul, MN M,W
Dakota State University, SD M,W
Dallas Baptist University, TX W
Davidson College, NC M,W
DePaul University, IL M,W
Dillard University, LA M,W
Doane University, NE M,W
Dominican College, NY M,W
Drake University, IA M,W
Drury University, MO M,W
East Carolina University, NC M,W
East Central University, OK M,W
Eastern Illinois University, IL M,W
Eastern Kentucky University, KY M,W
Eastern Michigan University, MI M,W
Eastern New Mexico University, NM M,W
Eastern Oregon University, OR M,W
Eastern Washington University, WA M,W
Edinboro University of Pennsylvania, PA M,W
Elon University, NC W
Emmanuel College, GA M,W
Emporia State University, KS M,W
Evangel University, MO M,W
Fayetteville State University, NC W
Ferris State University, MI M,W
Florida Agricultural and Mechanical University, FL M,W
Florida Institute of Technology, FL M,W
Florida State University, FL M,W
Fordham University, NY M,W
Fort Lewis College, CO M,W
Francis Marion University, SC M,W
Freed-Hardeman University, TN M,W
George Mason University, VA M,W
Georgetown College, KY M,W
Georgetown University, DC M,W
Georgia Institute of Technology, GA M,W
Georgian Court University, NJ M,W
Georgia State University, GA W
Glenville State College, WV M,W
Gonzaga University, WA M,W
Goshen College, IN M,W
Graceland University, IA M,W
Grambling State University, LA M,W
Grand Valley State University, MI M,W
Hampton University, VA M,W
High Point University, NC M,W
Hillsdale College, MI M,W
Hofstra University, NY M,W
Hope International University, CA M,W
Houston Baptist University, TX M,W
Illinois State University, IL M,W
Indiana State University, IN M,W
Indiana University Bloomington, IN M,W
Indiana University of Pennsylvania, PA M,W
Indiana University-Purdue University Indianapolis, IN M,W
Inter American University of Puerto Rico, Aguadilla Campus, PR M,W
Iona College, NY M,W
Jacksonville University, FL W
James Madison University, VA W
Kennesaw State University, GA M,W
King University, TN M,W
Kutztown University of Pennsylvania, PA M,W
Lawrence Technological University, MI M,W
Lee University, TN M,W
Lehigh University, PA M,W
Le Moyne College, NY M,W
Lenoir-Rhyne University, NC M,W
Lewis University, IL M,W
Liberty University, VA M,W
Life University, GA W
Limestone College, SC M,W
Lincoln University, PA M,W
Lindenwood University, MO M,W
Lipscomb University, TN M,W
Lock Haven University of Pennsylvania, PA M,W
Louisiana State University and Agricultural & Mechanical College, LA M,W
Loyola University Chicago, IL M,W
Loyola University Maryland, MD W
Loyola University New Orleans, LA M,W
Lynn University, FL W
Malone University, OH M,W
Manhattan College, NY M,W
Mansfield University of Pennsylvania, PA M,W
Marquette University, WI M,W
Marshall University, WV M,W
Marymount California University, CA M
Maryville University of Saint Louis, MO M,W
McKendree University, IL M,W
Mercer University, GA W
Merrimack College, MA M,W
Miami University, OH M,W
Michigan State University, MI M,W
Michigan Technological University, MI M,W
MidAmerica Nazarene University, KS M,W
Middle Tennessee State University, TN M,W
Midway University, KY M,W
Millersville University of Pennsylvania, PA W
Milligan University, TN M,W
Minnesota State University Mankato, MN M,W
Minot State University, ND M,W
Mississippi State University, MS M,W
Missouri Southern State University, MO M,W
Missouri State University, MO W
Missouri University of Science and Technology, MO M,W
Missouri Valley College, MO M,W
Molloy College, NY M,W
Montana State University, MT M,W
Morehead State University, KY M,W
Mount Marty College, SD M,W
Mount St. Mary's University, MD M,W
Mount Vernon Nazarene University, OH M,W
New Jersey Institute of Technology, NJ M,W
Niagara University, NY W
North Carolina Central University, NC M,W
Northern Arizona University, AZ M,W
Northern State University, SD M,W
North Greenville University, SC M,W
Northwest Christian University, OR M,W
Northwestern State University of Louisiana, LA M,W
Northwest Missouri State University, MO M,W
Northwest Nazarene University, ID M,W
Northwest University, WA M,W
Oakland University, MI M,W
The Ohio State University, OH M,W
Oklahoma Baptist University, OK M,W
Oklahoma State University, OK M,W
Olivet Nazarene University, IL M,W
Oral Roberts University, OK M,W
Palm Beach Atlantic University, FL M,W
Penn State University Park, PA M,W
Pepperdine University, CA M,W
Pittsburg State University, KS M,W
Point Loma Nazarene University, CA W
Prairie View A&M University, TX M,W
Providence College, RI M,W
Purdue University Fort Wayne, IN W
Queens College of the City University of New York, NY M,W
Queens University of Charlotte, NC M,W
Radford University, VA W
Rice University, TX M,W
Rochester University, MI M,W
Rocky Mountain College, MT M,W
Rogers State University, OK M,W
Sacred Heart University, CT M,W
Saginaw Valley State University, MI M,W
St. Ambrose University, IA M,W
St. Cloud State University, MN W
Saint Francis University, PA M,W
Saint Joseph's University, PA M,W
Saint Leo University, FL M,W
Saint Louis University, MO M,W
Saint Mary's College of California, CA M,W
Samford University, AL M,W
Sam Houston State University, TX M,W
San Diego State University, CA W
San Francisco State University, CA W
San Jose State University, CA M,W
Santa Clara University, CA M,W
Seattle University, WA M,W
Siena College, NY M,W
Slippery Rock University of Pennsylvania, PA M,W
Southeastern Louisiana University, LA M,W

Southeast Missouri State University, MO M,W
Southern Illinois University Carbondale, IL M,W
Southern Illinois University Edwardsville, IL M,W
Southwest Baptist University, MO M,W
Southwestern College, KS M,W
Spring Hill College, AL M,W
Stanford University, CA M,W
Sterling College, KS M,W
Stony Brook University, State University of New York, NY M,W
Tabor College, KS M,W
Tarleton State University, TX M,W
Taylor University, IN M,W
Temple University, PA W
Tennessee Wesleyan University, TN M,W
Texas A&M University, TX M,W
Texas A&M University–Commerce, TX M,W
Texas A&M University–Corpus Christi, TX M,W
Texas Christian University, TX M,W
Texas State University, TX M,W
Texas Tech University, TX M,W
Tiffin University, OH M,W
Towson University, MD W
Trevecca Nazarene University, TN M,W
Troy University, AL M,W
Truett McConnell University, GA M,W
Truman State University, MO M,W
Tulane University, LA W
University at Albany, State University of New York, NY M,W
University at Buffalo, the State University of New York, NY M,W
The University of Akron, OH M,W
The University of Alabama, AL M,W
The University of Alabama at Birmingham, AL W
The University of Arizona, AZ M,W
University of Arkansas, AR M,W
University of Arkansas at Little Rock, AR W
University of California, Los Angeles, CA M,W
University of California, Riverside, CA M,W
University of California, Santa Barbara, CA M,W
University of Central Arkansas, AR M,W
University of Central Florida, FL W
University of Cincinnati, OH M,W
University of Colorado Boulder, CO M,W
University of Colorado Colorado Springs, CO M,W
University of Dayton, OH W
The University of Findlay, OH M,W
University of Hawaii at Manoa, HI W
University of Houston, TX M,W
University of Idaho, ID M,W
University of Illinois at Chicago, IL M,W
University of Illinois at Springfield, IL M,W
The University of Iowa, IA M,W
University of Jamestown, ND M,W
The University of Kansas, KS M,W
University of Kentucky, KY M,W
University of Louisiana at Lafayette, LA M,W
University of Louisiana at Monroe, LA M,W
University of Louisville, KY M,W
University of Maine, ME M,W
University of Maryland, Baltimore County, MD M,W
University of Massachusetts Amherst, MA M,W
University of Massachusetts Lowell, MA M,W
University of Memphis, TN M,W
University of Michigan, MI M,W
University of Minnesota, Twin Cities Campus, MN M,W
University of Montana, MT M,W
University of Nebraska at Kearney, NE M,W
University of Nebraska–Lincoln, NE M,W
University of Nevada, Las Vegas, NV W
University of Nevada, Reno, NV W
University of New Hampshire, NH M,W
University of New Haven, CT M,W
University of New Mexico, NM M,W
The University of North Carolina at Chapel Hill, NC M,W
The University of North Carolina at Charlotte, NC M,W
The University of North Carolina at Greensboro, NC M,W
The University of North Carolina at Pembroke, NC M,W
The University of North Carolina Wilmington, NC M,W
University of North Dakota, ND M,W
University of Northern Colorado, CO M,W
University of Northern Iowa, IA M,W
University of North Texas, TX M,W
University of Notre Dame, IN M,W
University of Oregon, OR M,W
University of Pikeville, KY M,W
University of Portland, OR M,W
University of Providence, MT M,W
University of Richmond, VA W
University of St. Francis, IL M,W
University of Saint Francis, IN M,W
University of Saint Mary, KS M,W
University of San Diego, CA W
University of San Francisco, CA M,W
University of South Carolina, SC M,W
University of South Dakota, SD M,W
University of Southern Indiana, IN M,W
University of Southern Mississippi, MS M,W
University of South Florida, FL M,W
The University of Tampa, FL M,W
The University of Tennessee, TN M,W
The University of Tennessee at Chattanooga, TN M,W
The University of Texas at El Paso, TX M,W
The University of Texas at San Antonio, TX M,W
The University of Texas Rio Grande Valley, TX M,W
University of the Incarnate Word, TX M,W
The University of Toledo, OH W
The University of Tulsa, OK M,W
University of Utah, UT W
University of Virginia, VA M,W
University of Washington, WA M,W
The University of West Alabama, AL M,W
University of West Georgia, GA W
University of Wisconsin–Madison, WI M,W
University of Wisconsin–Milwaukee, WI M,W
University of Wisconsin–Parkside, WI M,W
University of Wyoming, WY M,W
Upper Iowa University, IA W
Ursuline College, OH W
Utah State University, UT M,W
Utah Valley University, UT M,W
Valley City State University, ND M,W
Valparaiso University, IN M,W
Vanderbilt University, TN W
Vanguard University of Southern California, CA M,W
Villanova University, PA M,W
Virginia Commonwealth University, VA M,W
Wake Forest University, NC M,W
Washington State University, WA M,W
Wayland Baptist University, TX M,W
Wayne State College, NE M,W
Wayne State University, MI W
Webber International University, FL M,W
Weber State University, UT M,W
West Chester University of Pennsylvania, PA M,W
Western Carolina University, NC M,W
Western Colorado University, CO M,W
Western Kentucky University, KY M,W
Western Michigan University, MI W
Western Oregon University, OR M,W
Western Washington University, WA M,W
Westminster College, UT M,W
Westmont College, CA M,W
Wichita State University, KS M,W
William & Mary, VA M,W
Wingate University, NC M,W
Wofford College, SC M,W
Wright State University, OH W
Xavier University, OH M,W
Youngstown State University, OH M,W

Triathlon

Arizona State University at the Downtown Phoenix campus, AZ W
Arizona State University at the Polytechnic campus, AZ W
Arizona State University at the Tempe campus, AZ W
Arizona State University at the West campus, AZ W
Drury University, MO W
Milligan University, TN M,W
University of South Dakota, SD W
Webber International University, FL M,W

Ultimate Frisbee

Towson University, MD W

Volleyball

Abilene Christian University, TX W
Academy of Art University, CA W
Adams State University, CO W
American University, DC W
Anderson University, SC W
Angelo State University, TX W
Appalachian State University, NC W

Aquinas College, MI W
Arizona Christian University, AZ W
Arizona State University at the Downtown Phoenix campus, AZ W
Arizona State University at the Polytechnic campus, AZ W
Arizona State University at the Tempe campus, AZ W
Arizona State University at the West campus, AZ W
Arkansas Tech University, AR W
Auburn University, AL W
Auburn University at Montgomery, AL W
Augustana University, SD W
Austin Peay State University, TN W
Baker University, KS W
Ball State University, IN M,W
Barry University, FL W
Barton College, NC M,W
Bayamón Central University, PR M,W
Baylor University, TX W
Belmont Abbey College, NC M,W
Belmont University, TN W
Bemidji State University, MN W
Bethel University, IN W
Binghamton University, State University of New York, NY W
Biola University, CA W
Black Hills State University, SD W
Boise State University, ID W
Boston College, MA W
Bowling Green State University, OH W
Bradley University, IL W
Brigham Young University, UT M,W
Bryan College, TN W
Bryant University, RI W
Bucknell University, PA W
Butler University, IN W
Caldwell University, NJ W
California Baptist University, CA W
California Polytechnic State University, San Luis Obispo, CA W
California State Polytechnic University, Pomona, CA W
California State University, Bakersfield, CA W
California State University, Dominguez Hills, CA W
California State University, Fresno, CA W
California State University, Fullerton, CA W
California State University, Long Beach, CA M,W
California State University, Los Angeles, CA W
California State University, Monterey Bay, CA W
California State University, Northridge, CA M,W
California State University, Sacramento, CA W
California State University, San Bernardino, CA W
California State University, Stanislaus, CA W
California University of Pennsylvania, PA W
Calumet College of Saint Joseph, IN M,W
Cameron University, OK W
Campbellsville University, KY M,W
Carlow University, PA W
Carson-Newman University, TN W
Catawba College, NC W
Cedarville University, OH W
Central Connecticut State University, CT W
Central Methodist University, MO W
Central Michigan University, MI W
Central Washington University, WA W
Chaminade University of Honolulu, HI W
Chestnut Hill College, PA W
The Citadel, The Military College of South Carolina, SC W
Clarion University of Pennsylvania, PA W
Clemson University, SC W
Coastal Carolina University, SC W
Colgate University, NY W
The College of Idaho, ID W
College of Saint Mary, NE W
The College of Saint Rose, NY W
College of the Holy Cross, MA W
College of the Ozarks, MO W
Colorado School of Mines, CO W
Colorado State University, CO W
Columbia College, MO W
Columbia College, SC W
Concordia University, St. Paul, MN W
Creighton University, NE W
Dakota State University, SD W
Dallas Baptist University, TX W
Davidson College, NC W
DePaul University, IL W
Dillard University, LA W
Doane University, NE W
Dominican College, NY W
Dominican University of California, CA W
Drake University, IA W
Drury University, MO W
East Carolina University, NC W
East Central University, OK W
Eastern Illinois University, IL W
Eastern Kentucky University, KY W
Eastern Michigan University, MI W
Eastern New Mexico University, NM W
Eastern Oregon University, OR W
Eastern Washington University, WA W
Edinboro University of Pennsylvania, PA W
Elon University, NC W
Emmanuel College, GA M,W
Emporia State University, KS W
Evangel University, MO W
Fairfield University, CT W
Fayetteville State University, NC W
Felician University, NJ W
Ferris State University, MI W
Florida Agricultural and Mechanical University, FL W
Florida Atlantic University, FL W
Florida Gulf Coast University, FL W
Florida Institute of Technology, FL W
Florida National University, FL W
Florida State University, FL W
Fordham University, NY W
Fort Lewis College, CO W
Francis Marion University, SC W
Freed-Hardeman University, TN W
Gannon University, PA W
George Mason University, VA M,W
Georgetown College, KY W
Georgetown University, DC W
The George Washington University, DC W
Georgia College & State University, GA W
Georgia Institute of Technology, GA W
Georgian Court University, NJ W
Georgia State University, GA W
Glenville State College, WV W
Gonzaga University, WA W
Goshen College, IN M,W
Governors State University, IL M,W
Graceland University, IA M,W
Grambling State University, LA W
Grand Valley State University, MI W
Hampton University, VA W
High Point University, NC W
Hillsdale College, MI W
Hofstra University, NY W
Hope International University, CA M,W
Houston Baptist University, TX W
Illinois Institute of Technology, IL W
Illinois State University, IL W
Indiana State University, IN W
Indiana University Bloomington, IN W
Indiana University Northwest, IN W
Indiana University of Pennsylvania, PA W
Indiana University-Purdue University Indianapolis, IN W
Indiana University South Bend, IN W
Indiana University Southeast, IN W
Inter American University of Puerto Rico, Aguadilla Campus, PR M,W
Iona College, NY W
Jacksonville State University, AL W
Jacksonville University, FL W
James Madison University, VA W
John Brown University, AR W
Kennesaw State University, GA W
King University, TN M,W
Kutztown University of Pennsylvania, PA W
Lawrence Technological University, MI M,W
Lee University, TN W
Lehigh University, PA W
Le Moyne College, NY W
Lenoir-Rhyne University, NC W
Lewis-Clark State College, ID W
Lewis University, IL M,W
Liberty University, VA W
Life University, GA M,W
Limestone College, SC M,W
Lincoln Memorial University, TN W
Lincoln University, PA W
Lindenwood University, MO M,W
Lipscomb University, TN W
Lock Haven University of Pennsylvania, PA W
Louisiana State University and Agricultural & Mechanical College, LA W
Loyola Marymount University, CA W
Loyola University Chicago, IL M,W
Loyola University Maryland, MD W
Loyola University New Orleans, LA W
Lynn University, FL W
Malone University, OH W

Manhattan College, NY W
Marquette University, WI W
Marshall University, WV W
Maryville University of Saint Louis, MO W
Mayville State University, ND W
McKendree University, IL M,W
Mercer University, GA W
Mercy College, NY W
Merrimack College, MA W
Miami University, OH W
Michigan State University, MI W
Michigan Technological University, MI W
MidAmerica Nazarene University, KS W
Middle Tennessee State University, TN W
Midway University, KY M,W
Millersville University of Pennsylvania, PA W
Milligan University, TN M,W
Minnesota State University Mankato, MN W
Minot State University, ND W
Mississippi State University, MS W
Missouri Southern State University, MO W
Missouri State University, MO W
Missouri University of Science and Technology, MO W
Missouri Valley College, MO M,W
Molloy College, NY W
Montana State University, MT W
Montana Technological University, MT W
Morehead State University, KY W
Mount Marty College, SD W
Mount Vernon Nazarene University, OH W
New Jersey Institute of Technology, NJ M,W
Newman University, KS W
Niagara University, NY W
North Carolina Central University, NC W
Northern Arizona University, AZ W
Northern Illinois University, IL W
Northern State University, SD W
North Greenville University, SC M,W
Northwest Christian University, OR W
Northwestern State University of Louisiana, LA W
Northwest Missouri State University, MO W
Northwest Nazarene University, ID W
Northwest University, WA W
Nyack College, NY W
Oakland University, MI W
The Ohio State University, OH M,W
Ohio Valley University, WV W
Oklahoma Baptist University, OK W
Old Dominion University, VA W
Olivet Nazarene University, IL M,W
Oral Roberts University, OK W
Palm Beach Atlantic University, FL W
Penn State University Park, PA M,W
Pepperdine University, CA M,W
Pittsburg State University, KS W
Point Loma Nazarene University, CA W
Prairie View A&M University, TX W
Providence College, RI W
Purdue University Fort Wayne, IN M,W
Purdue University Northwest, IN W
Queens College of the City University of New York, NY W
Queens University of Charlotte, NC W
Radford University, VA W
Rice University, TX W
Rochester University, MI W
Rocky Mountain College, MT W
Rollins College, FL W
Sacred Heart University, CT M,W
Saginaw Valley State University, MI W
St. Ambrose University, IA M,W
St. Cloud State University, MN W
Saint Francis University, PA M,W
Saint Leo University, FL W
Saint Louis University, MO W
Saint Mary's College of California, CA W
St. Mary's University, TX W
St. Petersburg College, FL W
Samford University, AL W
Sam Houston State University, TX W
San Diego State University, CA W
San Francisco State University, CA W
San Jose State University, CA W
Santa Clara University, CA W
Seattle University, WA W
Shepherd University, WV W
Siena College, NY W
Slippery Rock University of Pennsylvania, PA W
Southeastern Louisiana University, LA W
Southeastern University, FL W
Southeast Missouri State University, MO W
Southern Illinois University Carbondale, IL W
Southern Illinois University Edwardsville, IL W
Southern Methodist University, TX W
Southwest Baptist University, MO W
Southwestern College, KS W
Southwestern Oklahoma State University, OK W
Spring Hill College, AL W
Stanford University, CA M,W
Sterling College, KS W
Stetson University, FL W
Stony Brook University, State University of New York, NY W
Tabor College, KS W
Tarleton State University, TX W
Taylor University, IN W
Temple University, PA W
Tennessee Wesleyan University, TN W
Texas A&M International University, TX W
Texas A&M University, TX W
Texas A&M University–Commerce, TX W
Texas A&M University–Corpus Christi, TX W
Texas Christian University, TX W
Texas State University, TX W
Texas Tech University, TX W
Texas Woman's University, TX W
Tiffin University, OH W
Towson University, MD W
Trevecca Nazarene University, TN W
Troy University, AL W
Truett McConnell University, GA W
Truman State University, MO W
Tulane University, LA W
Union University, TN W
University at Albany, State University of New York, NY W
University at Buffalo, the State University of New York, NY W
The University of Akron, OH W
The University of Alabama, AL W
The University of Alabama at Birmingham, AL W
University of Alaska Fairbanks, AK W
The University of Arizona, AZ W
University of Arkansas, AR W
University of Arkansas at Little Rock, AR W
University of California, Los Angeles, CA M,W
University of California, Merced, CA M,W
University of California, Riverside, CA W
University of California, Santa Barbara, CA M,W
University of Central Arkansas, AR W
University of Central Florida, FL W
University of Cincinnati, OH W
University of Colorado Boulder, CO W
University of Colorado Colorado Springs, CO W
University of Dayton, OH W
University of Denver, CO W
The University of Findlay, OH W
University of Guam, GU M,W
University of Hawaii at Manoa, HI M,W
University of Houston, TX W
University of Idaho, ID W
University of Illinois at Chicago, IL W
University of Illinois at Springfield, IL W
The University of Iowa, IA W
University of Jamestown, ND W
The University of Kansas, KS W
University of Kentucky, KY W
University of Louisiana at Lafayette, LA W
University of Louisiana at Monroe, LA W
University of Louisville, KY W
University of Maryland, Baltimore County, MD W
University of Memphis, TN W
University of Michigan, MI W
University of Michigan–Dearborn, MI W
University of Minnesota, Duluth, MN W
University of Minnesota, Twin Cities Campus, MN W
University of Missouri–St. Louis, MO W
University of Montana, MT W
University of Montevallo, AL W
University of Nebraska at Kearney, NE W
University of Nebraska–Lincoln, NE W
University of Nevada, Las Vegas, NV W
University of Nevada, Reno, NV W
University of New Hampshire, NH W
University of New Haven, CT W
University of New Mexico, NM W

The University of North Carolina at Chapel Hill, NC W
The University of North Carolina at Charlotte, NC W
The University of North Carolina at Greensboro, NC W
The University of North Carolina at Pembroke, NC W
The University of North Carolina Wilmington, NC W
University of North Dakota, ND W
University of Northern Colorado, CO W
University of Northern Iowa, IA W
University of North Texas, TX W
University of Notre Dame, IN W
University of Oregon, OR W
University of Pikeville, KY W
University of Portland, OR W
University of Providence, MT W
University of St. Francis, IL W
University of Saint Francis, IN W
University of Saint Mary, KS W
University of St. Thomas, TX W
University of San Diego, CA W
University of San Francisco, CA W
University of South Carolina, SC W
University of South Carolina Aiken, SC W
University of South Dakota, SD W
University of Southern Indiana, IN W
University of Southern Mississippi, MS W
University of South Florida, FL W
The University of Tampa, FL W
The University of Tennessee, TN W
The University of Tennessee at Chattanooga, TN W
The University of Tennessee at Martin, TN W
The University of Texas at El Paso, TX W
The University of Texas at San Antonio, TX W
The University of Texas Rio Grande Valley, TX W
University of the Incarnate Word, TX W
University of the Pacific, CA M,W
The University of Toledo, OH W
The University of Tulsa, OK W
University of Utah, UT W
University of Virginia, VA W
University of Washington, WA W
The University of West Alabama, AL W
University of West Georgia, GA W
University of Wisconsin–Green Bay, WI W
University of Wisconsin–Madison, WI W
University of Wisconsin–Milwaukee, WI W
University of Wisconsin–Parkside, WI W
University of Wyoming, WY W
Upper Iowa University, IA W
Ursuline College, OH W
Utah State University, UT W
Utah Valley University, UT W
Valdosta State University, GA W
Valley City State University, ND W
Valparaiso University, IN W
Vanguard University of Southern California, CA M,W
Villanova University, PA W
Virginia Commonwealth University, VA W
Wake Forest University, NC W
Washington State University, WA W
Wayland Baptist University, TX W
Wayne State College, NE W
Wayne State University, MI W
Webber International University, FL M,W
Weber State University, UT W
West Chester University of Pennsylvania, PA W
Western Carolina University, NC W
Western Colorado University, CO W
Western Kentucky University, KY W
Western Michigan University, MI W
Western New Mexico University, NM W
Western Oregon University, OR W
Western Washington University, WA W
Westminster College, UT W
Westmont College, CA W
Wichita State University, KS W
William & Mary, VA W
Wingate University, NC W
Wofford College, SC W
Wright State University, OH W
Xavier University, OH W
Youngstown State University, OH W

Water polo

Arizona State University at the Downtown Phoenix campus, AZ W
Arizona State University at the Polytechnic campus, AZ W
Arizona State University at the Tempe campus, AZ W
Arizona State University at the West campus, AZ W
California Baptist University, CA M,W
California State University, Bakersfield, CA W
California State University, Long Beach, CA M,W
California State University, Monterey Bay, CA W
Fordham University, NY M
Gannon University, PA M,W
The George Washington University, DC M
Indiana University Bloomington, IN W
Iona College, NY W
Lindenwood University, MO M,W
Loyola Marymount University, CA M,W
McKendree University, IL M,W
Pepperdine University, CA M
Saint Francis University, PA W
San Diego State University, CA W
San Jose State University, CA M,W
Santa Clara University, CA M,W
Siena College, NY W
Stanford University, CA M,W
University of California, Los Angeles, CA M,W
University of California, Santa Barbara, CA M,W
University of Hawaii at Manoa, HI W
University of Michigan, MI W
University of the Pacific, CA M,W

Weight lifting

Davidson College, NC M
Inter American University of Puerto Rico, Aguadilla Campus, PR M,W
Lindenwood University, MO M,W

Wrestling

Adams State University, CO M
American University, DC M
Appalachian State University, NC M
Arizona State University at the Downtown Phoenix campus, AZ M
Arizona State University at the Polytechnic campus, AZ M
Arizona State University at the Tempe campus, AZ M
Arizona State University at the West campus, AZ M
Augustana University, SD M
Baker University, KS M,W
Belmont Abbey College, NC M
Binghamton University, State University of New York, NY M
Bucknell University, PA M
California Baptist University, CA M
California Polytechnic State University, San Luis Obispo, CA M
California State University, Bakersfield, CA M
Calumet College of Saint Joseph, IN M
Campbellsville University, KY M,W
Central Michigan University, MI M
The Citadel, The Military College of South Carolina, SC M
Clarion University of Pennsylvania, PA M
Colorado School of Mines, CO M
Davidson College, NC M
Drexel University, PA M
Drury University, MO M
Eastern Michigan University, MI M
Eastern Oregon University, OR M,W
Edinboro University of Pennsylvania, PA M
Emmanuel College, GA M,W
Gannon University, PA M
George Mason University, VA M
Graceland University, IA M
Hofstra University, NY M
Indiana University Bloomington, IN M
Inter American University of Puerto Rico, Aguadilla Campus, PR M,W
King University, TN M,W
Kutztown University of Pennsylvania, PA M
Lehigh University, PA M
Life University, GA M,W
Limestone College, SC M,W
Lindenwood University, MO M,W
Lock Haven University of Pennsylvania, PA M,W
Maryville University of Saint Louis, MO M
McKendree University, IL M,W
Michigan State University, MI M
Millersville University of Pennsylvania, PA M
Minnesota State University Mankato, MN M
Missouri Valley College, MO M,W
Newman University, KS M
Northern Illinois University, IL M
Northern State University, SD M
The Ohio State University, OH M
Ohio Valley University, WV M

Oklahoma State University, OK M
Old Dominion University, VA M
Penn State University Park, PA M
Rochester University, MI M
Sacred Heart University, CT M
St. Cloud State University, MN M
San Francisco State University, CA M
Southeastern University, FL M
Southern Illinois University Edwardsville, IL M
Stanford University, CA M
Tiffin University, OH M,W
Truett McConnell University, GA M
University at Buffalo, the State University of New York, NY M
The University of Findlay, OH M
The University of Iowa, IA M
University of Jamestown, ND M,W
University of Michigan, MI M
University of Minnesota, Twin Cities Campus, MN M
University of Nebraska at Kearney, NE M
University of Nebraska–Lincoln, NE M
The University of North Carolina at Chapel Hill, NC M
The University of North Carolina at Pembroke, NC M
University of Northern Colorado, CO M
University of Northern Iowa, IA M
University of Providence, MT M
University of Saint Mary, KS M,W
The University of Tennessee at Chattanooga, TN M
University of Virginia, VA M
University of Wisconsin–Madison, WI M
University of Wisconsin–Parkside, WI M
University of Wyoming, WY M
Upper Iowa University, IA M
Utah Valley University, UT M
Vanguard University of Southern California, CA M
Wayland Baptist University, TX M,W
Western Colorado University, CO M

Co-Op Programs

Alfred University, NY
Allen College, IA
Anderson University, SC
Andrews University, MI
Aquinas College, MI
Arizona State University at the Polytechnic campus, AZ
Arizona State University at the Tempe campus, AZ
Arizona State University at the West campus, AZ
Athens State University, AL
Auburn University at Montgomery, AL
Augsburg University, MN
Austin Peay State University, TN
Ball State University, IN
Bayamón Central University, PR
Becker College, MA
Belmont University, TN
Bemidji State University, MN
Berklee College of Music, MA
Bethany Lutheran College, MN
Biola University, CA
Birmingham-Southern College, AL
Black Hills State University, SD
Bowling Green State University, OH
Bradley University, IL
Bryn Athyn College of the New Church, PA
Butler University, IN
California Christian College, CA
California Lutheran University, CA
California Polytechnic State University, San Luis Obispo, CA
California State Polytechnic University, Pomona, CA
California State University, Dominguez Hills, CA
California State University, Fresno, CA
California State University, Fullerton, CA
California State University, Los Angeles, CA
California State University, Monterey Bay, CA
California State University, Sacramento, CA
California State University, San Bernardino, CA
California State University, Stanislaus, CA
California University of Pennsylvania, PA
Calumet College of Saint Joseph, IN
Campbellsville University, KY
Capital University, OH
Carnegie Mellon University, PA
The Catholic University of America, DC
Cedarville University, OH
Central College, IA
Central Connecticut State University, CT
Central Washington University, WA
Champlain College, VT
Chatham University, PA
Chestnut Hill College, PA
City College of the City University of New York, NY
Clarion University of Pennsylvania, PA
Clarkson University, NY
Clemson University, SC
Coastal Carolina University, SC
The College of Idaho, ID
College of Staten Island of the City University of New York, NY
Colorado School of Mines, CO
Colorado State University, CO
Colorado State University–Global Campus, CO
Columbia College, MO
Columbia College Chicago, IL
Columbia International University, SC
Concordia College, MN
Cornell University, NY
Dakota State University, SD
DePauw University, IN
DeSales University, PA
Doane University, NE
Dominican College, NY
Drake University, IA
Drexel University, PA
East Carolina University, NC
East Central University, OK
Eastern Kentucky University, KY
Eastern Michigan University, MI
Eastern New Mexico University, NM
Eastern Oregon University, OR
ECPI University, VA
Edgewood College, WI
Elms College, MA
Emory & Henry College, VA
Emory University, GA
Endicott College, MA
Eugene Lang College of Liberal Arts, NY
Fayetteville State University, NC
Felician University, NJ
Ferris State University, MI
Florida Agricultural and Mechanical University, FL
Florida Atlantic University, FL
Florida Gulf Coast University, FL
Florida Institute of Technology, FL
Florida National University, FL
Florida State University, FL
Framingham State University, MA
Francis Marion University, SC
Franklin College, IN
Gannon University, PA
George Mason University, VA
Georgetown College, KY
The George Washington University, DC
Georgia Institute of Technology, GA
Georgia State University, GA
Glenville State College, WV
Gordon College, MA
Graceland University, IA
Grand Valley State University, MI
Guilford College, NC
Hamline University, MN
Hampden-Sydney College, VA
Hampton University, VA
Hanover College, IN
Hofstra University, NY
Hollins University, VA
Husson University, ME
Illinois Institute of Technology, IL
Illinois State University, IL
Indiana State University, IN
Indiana University Bloomington, IN
Indiana University East, IN
Indiana University Northwest, IN
Indiana University of Pennsylvania, PA
Indiana University-Purdue University Indianapolis, IN
Inter American University of Puerto Rico, Aguadilla Campus, PR
Inter American University of Puerto Rico, Metropolitan Campus, PR
Jacksonville State University, AL
Jacksonville University, FL
John Jay College of Criminal Justice of the City University of New York, NY
Johnson University, TN
Kean University, NJ
Kennesaw State University, GA
Kentucky Mountain Bible College, KY
Kettering University, MI
Keuka College, NY
Lasell College, MA
Lawrence Technological University, MI
Lee University, TN
Lehigh University, PA
LeTourneau University, TX
Lewis-Clark State College, ID
Liberty University, VA
Life University, GA
Lock Haven University of Pennsylvania, PA
Loras College, IA
Louisiana State University and Agricultural & Mechanical College, LA
Loyola University Maryland, MD
Loyola University New Orleans, LA
Lynn University, FL
Manhattan College, NY
Marquette University, WI
Marshall University, WV
Marymount California University, CA
Maryville University of Saint Louis, MO
Massachusetts Maritime Academy, MA
Mayville State University, ND
McKendree University, IL
Mercer University, GA
Mercy College, NY
Merrimack College, MA
Messenger College, TX
Messiah College, PA
Miami University, OH
Michigan State University, MI
Michigan Technological University, MI
MidAmerica Nazarene University, KS
Middle Tennessee State University, TN
Midway University, KY
Millersville University of Pennsylvania, PA
Milligan University, TN
Minneapolis College of Art and Design, MN
Minot State University, ND
Mississippi State University, MS
Missouri Southern State University, MO
Missouri State University, MO
Missouri University of Science and Technology, MO
Missouri Valley College, MO
Montana State University, MT
Montana Technological University, MT
Montclair State University, NJ
Moravian College, PA
Morehead State University, KY
Mount Marty College, SD
Mount Saint Mary College, NY
Mount Saint Mary's University, CA
National University, CA
Nazareth College of Rochester, NY
Nebraska Methodist College, NE
New England Institute of Technology, RI
New Jersey Institute of Technology, NJ
Newman University, KS

New Mexico Institute of Mining and Technology, NM
New York Institute of Technology, NY
New York University, NY
Niagara University, NY
Nichols College, MA
North Carolina Central University, NC
North Central University, MN
Northeastern Illinois University, IL
Northeastern State University, OK
Northern Arizona University, AZ
Northern Illinois University, IL
North Greenville University, SC
Northwest Christian University, OR
Northwestern State University of Louisiana, LA
Northwestern University, IL
Northwest Nazarene University, ID
Northwest University, WA
Oakland University, MI
Oglethorpe University, GA
The Ohio State University, OH
Oklahoma Baptist University, OK
Old Dominion University, VA
Olivet Nazarene University, IL
Parsons School of Design, NY
Patrick Henry College, VA
Penn State Abington, PA
Penn State Altoona, PA
Penn State Berks, PA
Penn State Erie, The Behrend College, PA
Penn State Harrisburg, PA
Penn State Lehigh Valley, PA
Penn State University Park, PA
Pitzer College, CA
Portland State University, OR
Prairie View A&M University, TX
Purdue University Fort Wayne, IN
Purdue University Northwest, IN
Queens College of the City University of New York, NY
Ramapo College of New Jersey, NJ
Rhodes College, TN
Rogers State University, OK
Roger Williams University, RI
Rose-Hulman Institute of Technology, IN
Rowan University, NJ
Saginaw Valley State University, MI
St. Ambrose University, IA
Saint Francis University, PA
Saint Joseph's University, PA
Saint Louis University, MO
St. Mary's College of Maryland, MD
St. Mary's University, TX
St. Petersburg College, FL
St. Thomas Aquinas College, NY
Saint Vincent College, PA
Salisbury University, MD
San Francisco State University, CA
San Jose State University, CA
Santa Clara University, CA
Schreiner University, TX
Scripps College, CA
Shepherd University, WV
Southeastern University, FL
Southern Illinois University Carbondale, IL
Southern Illinois University Edwardsville, IL
Southern Methodist University, TX
Southwest Baptist University, MO
State University of New York at New Paltz, NY
State University of New York at Oswego, NY
State University of New York College at Cortland, NY
State University of New York College of Technology at Canton, NY
Stevens Institute of Technology, NJ
Stevenson University, MD
Stony Brook University, State University of New York, NY
SUNY Brockport, NY
Tabor College, KS
Tarleton State University, TX
Taylor University, IN
Temple University, PA
Texas A&M University, TX
Texas A&M University–Central Texas, TX
Texas A&M University–Commerce, TX
Texas A&M University–Corpus Christi, TX
Texas State University, TX
Texas Tech University, TX
Texas Woman's University, TX
Tiffin University, OH
Towson University, MD
Trine University, IN
Trinity College of Florida, FL
Truman State University, MO
Tulane University, LA
Universidad Adventista de las Antillas, PR
University at Buffalo, the State University of New York, NY
The University of Akron, OH
The University of Alabama, AL
The University of Alabama at Birmingham, AL
University of Alaska Fairbanks, AK
University of Alaska Southeast, AK
The University of Arizona, AZ
University of Arkansas, AR
University of Arkansas at Little Rock, AR
University of California, San Diego, CA
University of California, Santa Barbara, CA
University of California, Santa Cruz, CA
University of Central Arkansas, AR
University of Central Florida, FL
University of Cincinnati, OH
University of Colorado Boulder, CO
University of Colorado Colorado Springs, CO
University of Colorado Denver, CO
University of Dayton, OH
University of Denver, CO
University of Guam, GU
University of Hawaii at Manoa, HI
University of Houston, TX
University of Idaho, ID
University of Illinois at Chicago, IL
University of Illinois at Springfield, IL
The University of Iowa, IA
University of Jamestown, ND
The University of Kansas, KS
University of Kentucky, KY
University of Louisiana at Lafayette, LA
University of Louisiana at Monroe, LA
University of Louisville, KY
University of Maine, ME
University of Maine at Presque Isle, ME
University of Maryland, Baltimore County, MD
University of Maryland Global Campus, MD
University of Massachusetts Amherst, MA
University of Massachusetts Boston, MA
University of Massachusetts Dartmouth, MA
University of Massachusetts Lowell, MA
University of Memphis, TN
University of Miami, FL
University of Michigan, MI
University of Michigan–Dearborn, MI
University of Michigan–Flint, MI
University of Minnesota, Twin Cities Campus, MN
University of Missouri–St. Louis, MO
University of Montana, MT
University of Nebraska–Lincoln, NE
University of Nevada, Las Vegas, NV
University of New Haven, CT
University of New Mexico, NM
The University of North Carolina at Charlotte, NC
The University of North Carolina Wilmington, NC
University of North Dakota, ND
University of Northern Colorado, CO
University of Northern Iowa, IA
University of North Texas, TX
University of Oregon, OR
University of Pennsylvania, PA
University of Pittsburgh at Bradford, PA
University of Puget Sound, WA
University of Saint Francis, IN
University of Saint Mary, KS
University of St. Thomas, TX
University of San Francisco, CA
University of South Carolina, SC
University of South Carolina Aiken, SC
University of Southern Indiana, IN
University of Southern Maine, ME
University of South Florida, FL
The University of Tampa, FL
The University of Tennessee, TN
The University of Tennessee at Chattanooga, TN
The University of Tennessee at Martin, TN
The University of Texas at Dallas, TX
The University of Texas at San Antonio, TX
The University of Texas Rio Grande Valley, TX
University of the Incarnate Word, TX
University of the Pacific, CA
The University of Toledo, OH
University of Utah, UT
University of Virginia, VA
University of Washington, WA
University of Washington, Bothell, WA
The University of West Alabama, AL
University of West Georgia, GA
University of Wisconsin–Eau Claire, WI
University of Wisconsin–Green Bay, WI
University of Wisconsin–Madison, WI
University of Wisconsin–Milwaukee, WI
University of Wisconsin–Platteville, WI
University of Wisconsin–Stout, WI
University of Wisconsin–Superior, WI
University of Wyoming, WY
Upper Iowa University, IA
Utah State University, UT
Utah Valley University, UT
Utica College, NY
Valdosta State University, GA
Valley City State University, ND
Valparaiso University, IN
Vanderbilt University, TN
Vermont Technical College, VT
Villanova University, PA
Virginia Commonwealth University, VA
Walla Walla University, WA
Washington State University, WA
Washington University in St. Louis, MO
Wayne State College, NE
Wayne State University, MI
Webber International University, FL
Weber State University, UT
Wentworth Institute of Technology, MA
Wesleyan College, GA
Western Carolina University, NC

Western Connecticut State University, CT
Western Kentucky University, KY
Western Michigan University, MI
Western New Mexico University, NM
Western Washington University, WA
Westminster College, UT
Wheaton College, MA
Wichita State University, KS
Widener University, PA
Wilkes University, PA
Wittenberg University, OH
Worcester Polytechnic Institute, MA
Wright State University, OH
Wright State University–Lake Campus, OH
Xavier University, OH
Xavier University of Louisiana, LA
Yeshiva University, NY
York College of Pennsylvania, PA
Youngstown State University, OH

ROTC Programs

Air Force
Agnes Scott College, GA*
Alverno College, WI*
American University, DC*
Amherst College, MA*
Anderson University, SC*
Angelo State University, TX
Arizona Christian University, AZ*
Arizona State University at the Downtown Phoenix campus, AZ*
Arizona State University at the Polytechnic campus, AZ*
Arizona State University at the Tempe campus, AZ
Arizona State University at the West campus, AZ*
Assumption University, MA*
Auburn University, AL
Auburn University at Montgomery, AL*
Augsburg University, MN*
Augustana University, SD*
Austin Peay State University, TN*
Baker University, KS*
Barnard College, NY*
Barry University, FL*
Bayamón Central University, PR*
Baylor University, TX
Becker College, MA*
Belhaven University, MS*
Belmont Abbey College, NC*
Belmont University, TN*
Bentley University, MA*
Bethel University, IN*
Bethel University, MN*
Binghamton University, State University of New York, NY*
Biola University, CA*
Birmingham-Southern College, AL*
Boston College, MA*
Bowling Green State University, OH
Brandeis University, MA*
Bridgewater State University, MA*
Brigham Young University, UT
Brown University, RI*
Bryn Athyn College of the New Church, PA*
Butler University, IN*
California Baptist University, CA*
California Lutheran University, CA*
California State University, Dominguez Hills, CA*
California State University, Fresno, CA
California State University, Los Angeles, CA*
California State University, Monterey Bay, CA*
California State University, Northridge, CA*
California State University, Sacramento, CA
California State University, San Bernardino, CA
California State University, San Marcos, CA*
Capital University, OH*
Carlow University, PA*
Carnegie Mellon University, PA*
Carthage College, WI*
Catawba College, NC*
The Catholic University of America, DC*
Cazenovia College, NY*
Cedarville University, OH*
Central Connecticut State University, CT*
Central Methodist University, MO*
Central Michigan University, MI*
Central Washington University, WA
Centre College, KY*
Chaminade University of Honolulu, HI*
Chatham University, PA*
The Citadel, The Military College of South Carolina, SC
Claremont McKenna College, CA*
Clarkson University, NY
Clark University, MA*
Clemson University, SC
Cleveland Institute of Art, OH*
Coe College, IA*
Colby-Sawyer College, NH*
College of Saint Mary, NE*
The College of Saint Rose, NY*
The College of St. Scholastica, MN*
College of the Holy Cross, MA*
Colorado School of Mines, CO
Colorado State University, CO
Columbia College, MO*
Columbia College Chicago, IL*
Concordia College, MN*
Concordia University, St. Paul, MN*
Cornell University, NY
Creighton University, NE*
Dakota State University, SD*
Dallas Baptist University, TX*
DePauw University, IN*
Dillard University, LA*
Doane University, NE*
Drake University, IA*
Drexel University, PA*
East Carolina University, NC
Eastern Kentucky University, KY*
Eastern Michigan University, MI*
Eastern University, PA*
Edgewood College, WI*
Elms College, MA*
Elon University, NC*
Emory University, GA*
Fairfield University, CT*
Farmingdale State College, NY*
Fayetteville State University, NC
Felician University, NJ*
Florida Agricultural and Mechanical University, FL*
Florida Atlantic University, FL*
Florida State University, FL
Fordham University, NY*
George Fox University, OR*
George Mason University, VA*
Georgetown College, KY*
Georgetown University, DC*
The George Washington University, DC*
Georgia Institute of Technology, GA
Georgia State University, GA*
Gordon College, MA*
Goucher College, MD*
Governors State University, IL*
Grambling State University, LA*
Grand Valley State University, MI*
Guilford College, NC*
Hamline University, MN*
High Point University, NC*
Hobart and William Smith Colleges, NY*
Houston Baptist University, TX*
Illinois Institute of Technology, IL
Indiana State University, IN
Indiana University Bloomington, IN
Indiana University-Purdue University Indianapolis, IN*
Indiana University South Bend, IN*
Indiana University Southeast, IN*
Inter American University of Puerto Rico, Aguadilla Campus, PR
Inter American University of Puerto Rico, Metropolitan Campus, PR*
Iona College, NY*
Ithaca College, NY*
James Madison University, VA*
John Brown University, AR*
Johns Hopkins University, MD*
Kean University, NJ*
Kennesaw State University, GA*
King's College, PA*
Lakeview College of Nursing, IL*
La Roche University, PA
Lawrence Technological University, MI*
Le Moyne College, NY*
Lewis-Clark State College, ID*
Lewis University, IL*
Liberty University, VA*
Lindenwood University, MO*
Linfield College, OR*
Lipscomb University, TN*
Louisiana State University and Agricultural & Mechanical College, LA
Loyola Marymount University, CA
Loyola University Chicago, IL*
Loyola University Maryland, MD*
Loyola University New Orleans, LA*
Lynn University, FL*
Manhattan College, NY
Marquette University, WI
Marymount University, VA*
Marywood University, PA*
Mayville State University, ND*
McDaniel College, MD*
McKendree University, IL*
Mercy College, NY*
Merrimack College, MA*
Miami University, OH
Michigan State University, MI
Michigan Technological University, MI
MidAmerica Nazarene University, KS*
Middle Tennessee State University, TN*
Midway University, KY*
Milwaukee School of Engineering, WI*
Misericordia University, PA*
Mississippi State University, MS
Missouri University of Science and Technology, MO
Montana State University, MT
Mount Carmel College of Nursing, OH*
Mount Holyoke College, MA*
National University, CA*
Nazareth College of Rochester, NY*
Nebraska Methodist College, NE*
Nebraska Wesleyan University, NE*
New Jersey Institute of Technology, NJ
New York Institute of Technology, NY*
New York University, NY*
North Carolina Central University, NC
Northeastern Illinois University, IL*
Northern Arizona University, AZ
Northern Illinois University, IL*

* program is offered at another college's campus

Northwestern University, IL*
Northwest University, WA*
Oakland University, MI*
Occidental College, CA*
Oglethorpe University, GA*
The Ohio State University, OH
Ohio Wesleyan University, OH*
Oklahoma Baptist University, OK*
Oklahoma State University, OK
Oral Roberts University, OK*
Penn State Abington, PA*
Penn State Altoona, PA*
Penn State Berks, PA*
Penn State Brandywine, PA*
Penn State Greater Allegheny, PA*
Penn State Hazleton, PA*
Penn State New Kensington, PA*
Penn State University Park, PA
Penn State Wilkes-Barre, PA*
Pepperdine University, CA*
Pitzer College, CA*
Point Loma Nazarene University, CA*
Pomona College, CA*
Portland State University, OR*
Prairie View A&M University, TX*
Princeton University, NJ*
Ramapo College of New Jersey, NJ*
Rhodes College, TN*
Rice University, TX*
Rogers State University, OK*
Rose-Hulman Institute of Technology, IN
Sacred Heart University, CT*
St. Catherine University, MN*
St. John Fisher College, NY*
Saint Joseph's University, PA
Saint Leo University, FL*
Saint Louis University, MO
Saint Mary's College, IN*
Saint Mary's College of California, CA*
St. Mary's University, TX*
Saint Vincent College, PA*
Salem State University, MA*
Salisbury University, MD*
Samford University, AL
San Diego State University, CA
San Francisco State University, CA*
San Jose State University, CA
Santa Clara University, CA*
Sarah Lawrence College, NY*
Scripps College, CA*
Seattle University, WA*
Shepherd University, WV*
Siena College, NY*
Skidmore College, NY*
Smith College, MA*
Southeast Missouri State University, MO
Southern Illinois University Carbondale, IL
Southern Illinois University Edwardsville, IL*
Southern Methodist University, TX*
Southwestern University, TX*
Springfield College, MA*
Spring Hill College, AL*
Stanford University, CA*
State University of New York at Oswego, NY*
State University of New York College at Cortland, NY*
State University of New York College at Geneseo, NY*
State University of New York College at Potsdam, NY*
State University of New York College of Technology at Canton, NY*
Stetson University, FL*
Stevens Institute of Technology, NJ*
Stevenson University, MD*
Stony Brook University, State University of New York, NY*
SUNY Brockport, NY*
Tarleton State University, TX*
Temple University, PA*
Tennessee Wesleyan University, TN*
Texas A&M University, TX
Texas A&M University–Commerce, TX*
Texas Christian University, TX
Texas State University, TX
Texas Tech University, TX
Texas Woman's University, TX*
Tiffin University, OH*
Towson University, MD*
Transylvania University, KY*
Trine University, IN*
Trinity University, TX*
Troy University, AL
Tulane University, LA
Union College, NY*
University at Albany, State University of New York, NY*
The University of Akron, OH*
The University of Alabama, AL
The University of Alabama at Birmingham, AL*
The University of Arizona, AZ
University of Arkansas, AR
University of California, Berkeley, CA
University of California, Los Angeles, CA
University of California, Riverside, CA*
University of California, San Diego, CA*
University of California, Santa Barbara, CA*
University of California, Santa Cruz, CA*
University of Central Florida, FL
University of Cincinnati, OH
University of Colorado Boulder, CO
University of Colorado Colorado Springs, CO*
University of Colorado Denver, CO*
University of Dallas, TX*
University of Dayton, OH*
University of Denver, CO*
The University of Findlay, OH*
University of Hawaii at Manoa, HI
University of Houston, TX
University of Houston - Downtown, TX*
University of Idaho, ID*
University of Illinois at Chicago, IL*
The University of Iowa, IA
The University of Kansas, KS
University of Kentucky, KY
University of Louisville, KY
University of Mary Hardin-Baylor, TX*
University of Maryland, Baltimore County, MD*
University of Massachusetts Amherst, MA
University of Massachusetts Boston, MA*
University of Massachusetts Lowell, MA
University of Memphis, TN
University of Miami, FL
University of Michigan, MI
University of Michigan–Dearborn, MI*
University of Michigan–Flint, MI*
University of Minnesota, Duluth, MN
University of Minnesota, Twin Cities Campus, MN
University of Missouri–St. Louis, MO*
University of Montevallo, AL*
University of Nebraska–Lincoln, NE
University of Nevada, Las Vegas, NV
University of New Hampshire, NH
University of New Haven, CT*
University of New Mexico, NM
The University of North Carolina at Chapel Hill, NC
The University of North Carolina at Charlotte, NC
The University of North Carolina at Greensboro, NC*
The University of North Carolina at Pembroke, NC
University of North Dakota, ND
University of Northern Colorado, CO
University of North Texas, TX
University of Northwestern–St. Paul, MN*
University of Notre Dame, IN
University of Oregon, OR*
University of Pennsylvania, PA*
University of Pittsburgh at Greensburg, PA*
University of Portland, OR
University of St. Thomas, TX*
University of San Diego, CA*
University of San Francisco, CA*
The University of Scranton, PA*
University of South Carolina, SC
University of Southern Maine, ME*
University of Southern Mississippi, MS
University of South Florida, FL
The University of Tampa, FL*
The University of Tennessee, TN
The University of Texas at Dallas, TX*
The University of Texas at San Antonio, TX
University of the Pacific, CA*
The University of Toledo, OH*
The University of Tulsa, OK*
University of Utah, UT
University of Virginia, VA
University of Washington, WA
University of Washington, Bothell, WA*
University of Washington, Tacoma, WA*
The University of West Alabama, AL*
University of West Georgia, GA*
University of Wisconsin–Madison, WI
University of Wisconsin–Milwaukee, WI*
University of Wisconsin–Parkside, WI*
University of Wisconsin–Stout, WI*
University of Wisconsin–Superior, WI*
University of Wyoming, WY
Ursuline College, OH*
Utah State University, UT
Utah Valley University, UT*
Utica College, NY*
Valdosta State University, GA
Valparaiso University, IN*
Vanderbilt University, TN*
Vanguard University of Southern California, CA*
Villanova University, PA*
Washington & Jefferson College, PA*
Washington State University, WA
Washington University in St. Louis, MO*
Wayland Baptist University, TX*
Waynesburg University, PA*
Wayne State University, MI*
Weber State University, UT*
Wentworth Institute of Technology, MA*
Wesleyan University, CT*
West Chester University of Pennsylvania, PA*
Western Connecticut State University, CT*
Western Kentucky University, KY*
Western New England University, MA*
Westminster College, UT*
Westmont College, CA*
Wheaton College, IL*
Widener University, PA*
Wilkes University, PA

* program is offered at another college's campus

Willamette University, OR*
William Paterson University of New Jersey, NJ*
William Peace University, NC*
Williams College, MA*
Wingate University, NC*
Wittenberg University, OH*
Worcester Polytechnic Institute, MA
Worcester State University, MA*
Wright State University, OH
Wright State University–Lake Campus, OH*
Xavier University, OH*
Xavier University of Louisiana, LA*
Yale University, CT
Youngstown State University, OH*

Army

Academy of Art University, CA*
Agnes Scott College, GA*
Albion College, MI*
Alfred University, NY*
Allegheny College, PA*
Allen College, IA*
Alverno College, WI*
American University, DC*
Amherst College, MA*
Anderson University, SC*
Appalachian State University, NC
Arizona State University at the Downtown Phoenix campus, AZ*
Arizona State University at the Polytechnic campus, AZ*
Arizona State University at the Tempe campus, AZ
Arizona State University at the West campus, AZ*
Arkansas Tech University, AR*
Assumption University, MA*
Auburn University, AL
Auburn University at Montgomery, AL
Augsburg University, MN*
Augustana University, SD*
Aurora University, IL*
Austin Peay State University, TN
Baker University, KS*
Ball State University, IN
Barnard College, NY*
Barry University, FL*
Baruch College of the City University of New York, NY*
Bayamón Central University, PR*
Baylor University, TX
Becker College, MA*
Belhaven University, MS*
Belmont Abbey College, NC*
Belmont University, TN*
Benedictine University, IL*
Bentley University, MA*
Berklee College of Music, MA*
Bethany Lutheran College, MN*
Bethel University, IN*
Bethel University, MN*
Binghamton University, State University of New York, NY*
Biola University, CA*
Birmingham-Southern College, AL*
Black Hills State University, SD
Boise State University, ID
Boston College, MA*
Bowling Green State University, OH
Bradley University, IL
Brandeis University, MA*
Bridgewater State University, MA*
Brigham Young University, UT
Brown University, RI*
Bryant University, RI*
Bryn Athyn College of the New Church, PA*
Bucknell University, PA
Butler University, IN*
Caldwell University, NJ*
California Baptist University, CA
California Lutheran University, CA*
California Polytechnic State University, San Luis Obispo, CA
California State Polytechnic University, Pomona, CA
California State University, Dominguez Hills, CA
California State University, Fresno, CA
California State University, Fullerton, CA
California State University, Los Angeles, CA*
California State University, Northridge, CA*
California State University, Sacramento, CA
California State University, San Bernardino, CA
California State University, San Marcos, CA*
California University of Pennsylvania, PA
Calvin College, MI*
Cameron University, OK
Campbellsville University, KY*
Capital University, OH
Carlow University, PA*
Carnegie Mellon University, PA*
Carson-Newman University, TN
Carthage College, WI*
Catawba College, NC*
The Catholic University of America, DC*
Cazenovia College, NY*
Cedarville University, OH*
Central Connecticut State University, CT*
Central Methodist University, MO*
Central Michigan University, MI
Central Washington University, WA
Centre College, KY
Chaminade University of Honolulu, HI*
Champlain College, VT*
Chatham University, PA*
The Citadel, The Military College of South Carolina, SC
City College of the City University of New York, NY
Claremont McKenna College, CA
Clarion University of Pennsylvania, PA
Clarkson University, NY
Clark University, MA*
Clemson University, SC
Cleveland Institute of Art, OH*
Coastal Carolina University, SC
Coe College, IA
Colby College, ME*
Colby-Sawyer College, NH*
Colgate University, NY*
The College of Idaho, ID*
College of Saint Benedict, MN*
College of Saint Mary, NE*
The College of Saint Rose, NY
College of the Holy Cross, MA*
The Colorado College, CO*
Colorado School of Mines, CO
Colorado State University, CO
Columbia College, MO*
Columbia College, SC*
Columbia College Chicago, IL*
Concordia College, MN*
Concordia University, St. Paul, MN*
Cornell University, NY
Covenant College, GA*
Creighton University, NE
Dakota State University, SD*
Dallas Baptist University, TX*
Dartmouth College, NH*
Davidson College, NC
DePaul University, IL
DePauw University, IN*
DeSales University, PA*
Dickinson College, PA
Dillard University, LA*
Doane University, NE*
Drake University, IA*
Drew University, NJ*
Drexel University, PA
East Carolina University, NC
Eastern Illinois University, IL
Eastern Kentucky University, KY
Eastern Michigan University, MI
Eastern Oregon University, OR
Eastern University, PA*
Eastern Washington University, WA
Edgewood College, WI*
Edinboro University of Pennsylvania, PA
Elms College, MA*
Elon University, NC
Emmanuel College, MA*
Emory & Henry College, VA*
Emory University, GA*
Endicott College, MA*
Evangel University, MO*
Fairfield University, CT*
Farmingdale State College, NY*
Fayetteville State University, NC*
Felician University, NJ*
Ferris State University, MI*
Fisher College, MA*
Fitchburg State University, MA
Florida Agricultural and Mechanical University, FL
Florida Atlantic University, FL
Florida Institute of Technology, FL
Florida State University, FL
Fordham University, NY
Francis Marion University, SC
Franklin College, IN*
Freed-Hardeman University, TN
Gannon University, PA
George Mason University, VA
Georgetown College, KY*
Georgetown University, DC
The George Washington University, DC*
Georgia College & State University, GA*
Georgia Gwinnett College, GA
Georgia Institute of Technology, GA
Georgia State University, GA
Gonzaga University, WA
Gordon College, MA*
Goucher College, MD*
Governors State University, IL*
Grambling State University, LA
Grand Valley State University, MI*
Guilford College, NC*
Gustavus Adolphus College, MN*
Hamline University, MN*
Hampden-Sydney College, VA*
Hampshire College, MA*
Hampton University, VA
High Point University, NC*
Hobart and William Smith Colleges, NY*
Hofstra University, NY
Hope College, MI*
Hope International University, CA*
Houston Baptist University, TX*
Husson University, ME
Illinois Institute of Technology, IL
Illinois State University, IL
Illinois Wesleyan University, IL*

* program is offered at another college's campus

Immaculata University, PA*
Indiana State University, IN
Indiana University Bloomington, IN
Indiana University Northwest, IN
Indiana University of Pennsylvania, PA
Indiana University-Purdue University Indianapolis, IN
Indiana University South Bend, IN*
Indiana University Southeast, IN*
Inter American University of Puerto Rico, Aguadilla Campus, PR
Inter American University of Puerto Rico, Metropolitan Campus, PR*
Iona College, NY*
Ithaca College, NY*
Jacksonville State University, AL
Jacksonville University, FL
James Madison University, VA
John Brown University, AR*
John Carroll University, OH
Johns Hopkins University, MD
Kalamazoo College, MI*
Kean University, NJ*
Kennesaw State University, GA*
The King's College, NY*
King's College, PA
King University, TN*
Kutztown University of Pennsylvania, PA*
Lafayette College, PA*
Lakeview College of Nursing, IL*
La Roche University, PA
Lawrence Technological University, MI*
Lehigh University, PA
Le Moyne College, NY*
Lewis & Clark College, OR*
Lewis-Clark State College, ID*
Lewis University, IL*
Liberty University, VA
Lincoln Memorial University, TN
Lincoln University, PA*
Lindenwood University, MO*
Lipscomb University, TN*
Lock Haven University of Pennsylvania, PA
Longwood University, VA
Loras College, IA*
Louisiana State University and Agricultural & Mechanical College, LA
Louisiana State University in Shreveport, LA*
Loyola Marymount University, CA*
Loyola University Chicago, IL
Loyola University Maryland, MD
Loyola University New Orleans, LA*
Manhattan College, NY*
Mansfield University of Pennsylvania, PA*
Marquette University, WI
Marshall University, WV
Marymount University, VA*
Maryville University of Saint Louis, MO*
Marywood University, PA*
Massachusetts Maritime Academy, MA*
Mayville State University, ND*
McDaniel College, MD
McKendree University, IL*
Mercer University, GA
Mercy College, NY*
Miami University, OH*
Michigan State University, MI
Michigan Technological University, MI
MidAmerica Nazarene University, KS*
Middlebury College, VT*
Middle Tennessee State University, TN
Midway University, KY*
Millersville University of Pennsylvania, PA
Milligan University, TN*
Milwaukee School of Engineering, WI*
Minnesota State University Mankato, MN
Misericordia University, PA*
Mississippi State University, MS
Missouri Southern State University, MO
Missouri State University, MO
Missouri University of Science and Technology, MO
Missouri Valley College, MO
Molloy College, NY*
Montana State University, MT
Moravian College, PA*
Morehead State University, KY
Mount Carmel College of Nursing, OH*
Mount Holyoke College, MA*
Mount Marty College, SD*
Mount Saint Mary College, NY*
Mount St. Mary's University, MD*
National University, CA*
Nazareth College of Rochester, NY*
Nebraska Wesleyan University, NE*
New Jersey Institute of Technology, NJ*
New York Institute of Technology, NY*
New York University, NY*
Niagara University, NY
North Carolina Central University, NC
Northeastern Illinois University, IL*
Northeastern State University, OK
Northern Arizona University, AZ
Northern Illinois University, IL
North Greenville University, SC*
Northwest Christian University, OR*
Northwestern State University of Louisiana, LA
Northwestern University, IL*
Northwest Nazarene University, ID
Northwest University, WA*
Occidental College, CA*
Oglethorpe University, GA*
The Ohio State University, OH
Ohio Wesleyan University, OH*
Oklahoma State University, OK
Old Dominion University, VA
Olivet Nazarene University, IL
Palm Beach Atlantic University, FL*
Penn State Abington, PA*
Penn State Altoona, PA*
Penn State Berks, PA*
Penn State Brandywine, PA*
Penn State Erie, The Behrend College, PA*
Penn State Harrisburg, PA*
Penn State Lehigh Valley, PA*
Penn State University Park, PA
Penn State Wilkes-Barre, PA*
Pepperdine University, CA*
Pittsburg State University, KS
Pitzer College, CA*
Point Loma Nazarene University, CA*
Pomona College, CA*
Portland State University, OR*
Prairie View A&M University, TX
Pratt Institute, NY*
Princeton University, NJ
Providence College, RI
Purdue University Fort Wayne, IN
Purdue University Northwest, IN
Queens College of the City University of New York, NY*
Radford University, VA
Ramapo College of New Jersey, NJ*
Randolph-Macon College, VA*
Regent University, VA*
Rhode Island College, RI*
Rhodes College, TN*
Rice University, TX*
Rocky Mountain College, MT*
Roger Williams University, RI
Rose-Hulman Institute of Technology, IN
Rowan University, NJ*
St. Bonaventure University, NY
St. Catherine University, MN*
St. Cloud State University, MN*
Saint Francis University, PA
St. John Fisher College, NY*
Saint John's University, MN
Saint Joseph's University, PA*
Saint Leo University, FL
Saint Louis University, MO*
Saint Mary's College, IN*
Saint Mary's College of California, CA*
St. Mary's University, TX
St. Norbert College, WI
St. Petersburg College, FL*
Saint Vincent College, PA*
Salem State University, MA*
Salisbury University, MD
Salve Regina University, RI*
Samford University, AL*
Sam Houston State University, TX
San Diego State University, CA
San Francisco State University, CA*
San Jose State University, CA*
Santa Clara University, CA
Scripps College, CA*
Seattle University, WA
Siena College, NY
Simmons University, MA*
Skidmore College, NY*
Slippery Rock University of Pennsylvania, PA
Smith College, MA*
Southeastern Louisiana University, LA
Southeastern University, FL*
Southern Illinois University Carbondale, IL
Southern Illinois University Edwardsville, IL
Southern Methodist University, TX
Southwest Baptist University, MO*
Springfield College, MA*
Spring Hill College, AL*
Stanford University, CA*
State University of New York at Oswego, NY*
State University of New York College at Cortland, NY*
State University of New York College at Geneseo, NY*
State University of New York College at Potsdam, NY*
State University of New York College of Technology at Canton, NY*
Stetson University, FL*
Stevens Institute of Technology, NJ*
Stevenson University, MD*
Stony Brook University, State University of New York, NY
Suffolk University, MA*
SUNY Brockport, NY
Susquehanna University, PA
Tarleton State University, TX
Temple University, PA
Tennessee Wesleyan University, TN*
Texas A&M International University, TX
Texas A&M University, TX
Texas A&M University–Central Texas, TX
Texas A&M University–Corpus Christi, TX
Texas A&M University–Kingsville, TX
Texas Christian University, TX
Texas Lutheran University, TX*
Texas State University, TX
Texas Tech University, TX

* program is offered at another college's campus

Texas Woman's University, TX*
Tiffin University, OH*
Towson University, MD*
Transylvania University, KY*
Trevecca Nazarene University, TN*
Trinity University, TX*
Troy University, AL
Truman State University, MO
Tulane University, LA
Union College, NY*
University at Albany, State University of New York, NY
University at Buffalo, the State University of New York, NY*
The University of Akron, OH
The University of Alabama, AL
The University of Alabama at Birmingham, AL
University of Alaska Fairbanks, AK
The University of Arizona, AZ
University of Arkansas, AR
University of California, Berkeley, CA
University of California, Los Angeles, CA
University of California, Riverside, CA*
University of California, San Diego, CA*
University of California, Santa Barbara, CA
University of California, Santa Cruz, CA*
University of Central Arkansas, AR
University of Central Florida, FL
University of Cincinnati, OH
University of Colorado Boulder, CO
University of Colorado Colorado Springs, CO
University of Colorado Denver, CO*
University of Dallas, TX*
University of Dayton, OH
University of Denver, CO*
University of Dubuque, IA
The University of Findlay, OH*
University of Guam, GU
University of Hawaii at Manoa, HI
University of Houston, TX
University of Houston - Downtown, TX*
University of Idaho, ID
University of Illinois at Chicago, IL
The University of Iowa, IA
The University of Kansas, KS
University of Kentucky, KY
University of Louisiana at Lafayette, LA
University of Louisiana at Monroe, LA*
University of Louisville, KY
University of Maine, ME
University of Mary Hardin-Baylor, TX
University of Maryland, Baltimore County, MD*
University of Mary Washington, VA*
University of Massachusetts Amherst, MA
University of Massachusetts Boston, MA*
University of Massachusetts Dartmouth, MA*
University of Massachusetts Lowell, MA
University of Memphis, TN
University of Miami, FL
University of Michigan, MI
University of Michigan–Flint, MI*
University of Minnesota, Twin Cities Campus, MN
University of Missouri–St. Louis, MO*
University of Montana, MT
University of Montevallo, AL*
University of Nebraska at Kearney, NE
University of Nebraska–Lincoln, NE
University of Nevada, Las Vegas, NV
University of Nevada, Reno, NV
University of New Hampshire, NH
University of New Haven, CT
University of New Mexico, NM
The University of North Carolina at Chapel Hill, NC
The University of North Carolina at Charlotte, NC
The University of North Carolina at Greensboro, NC*
The University of North Carolina at Pembroke, NC
University of North Dakota, ND
University of Northern Colorado, CO
University of Northern Iowa, IA
University of North Texas, TX
University of Northwestern–St. Paul, MN*
University of Notre Dame, IN
University of Oregon, OR
University of Pennsylvania, PA*
University of Pikeville, KY
University of Pittsburgh at Bradford, PA*
University of Pittsburgh at Greensburg, PA
University of Portland, OR
University of Puget Sound, WA*
University of Richmond, VA
University of St. Francis, IL*
University of Saint Francis, IN*
University of Saint Mary, KS*
University of St. Thomas, TX*
University of San Diego, CA*
University of San Francisco, CA
The University of Scranton, PA
University of South Carolina, SC
University of South Dakota, SD
University of Southern Indiana, IN
University of Southern Maine, ME*
University of Southern Mississippi, MS
University of South Florida, FL
The University of Tampa, FL
The University of Tennessee, TN
The University of Tennessee at Chattanooga, TN
The University of Tennessee at Martin, TN
The University of Texas at Dallas, TX*
The University of Texas at El Paso, TX
The University of Texas at San Antonio, TX
The University of Texas Rio Grande Valley, TX
University of the Incarnate Word, TX*
The University of Toledo, OH
University of Utah, UT
University of Virginia, VA
University of Washington, WA
University of Washington, Bothell, WA*
University of Washington, Tacoma, WA*
University of Wisconsin–Eau Claire, WI
University of Wisconsin–Green Bay, WI*
University of Wisconsin–La Crosse, WI
University of Wisconsin–Madison, WI
University of Wisconsin–Milwaukee, WI*
University of Wisconsin–Parkside, WI
University of Wisconsin–Platteville, WI*
University of Wisconsin–Stout, WI
University of Wyoming, WY
Ursuline College, OH*
Utah State University, UT
Utah Valley University, UT
Utica College, NY
Valparaiso University, IN*
Vanderbilt University, TN
Vanguard University of Southern California, CA*
Vermont Technical College, VT*
Villanova University, PA
Virginia Commonwealth University, VA*
Virginia Wesleyan University, VA*
Wabash College, IN*
Wake Forest University, NC
Washington & Jefferson College, PA
Washington and Lee University, VA*
Washington State University, WA
Washington University in St. Louis, MO
Wayland Baptist University, TX*
Waynesburg University, PA*
Wayne State College, NE*
Wayne State University, MI*
Weber State University, UT
Wentworth Institute of Technology, MA*
Wesleyan College, GA*
West Chester University of Pennsylvania, PA
Western Connecticut State University, CT*
Western Kentucky University, KY
Western Michigan University, MI
Western New England University, MA
Western Oregon University, OR*
Westminster College, UT*
Westmont College, CA*
Wheaton College, IL
Wheaton College, MA*
Whitworth University, WA*
Wichita State University, KS
Widener University, PA
Wilkes University, PA*
Willamette University, OR*
William & Mary, VA
William Peace University, NC*
Wingate University, NC*
Wittenberg University, OH*
Wofford College, SC
Worcester Polytechnic Institute, MA
Worcester State University, MA*
Wright State University, OH
Wright State University–Lake Campus, OH*
Xavier University, OH
Xavier University of Louisiana, LA*
Yale University, CT*
Youngstown State University, OH

Naval

Arizona State University at the Downtown Phoenix campus, AZ*
Arizona State University at the Polytechnic campus, AZ*
Arizona State University at the Tempe campus, AZ
Arizona State University at the West campus, AZ*
Auburn University, AL
Barnard College, NY*
Becker College, MA*
Belmont University, TN*
Boston College, MA*
Brown University, RI*
California State University, San Marcos, CA*
Carlow University, PA*
Carnegie Mellon University, PA
The Catholic University of America, DC*
Chatham University, PA*
The Citadel, The Military College of South Carolina, SC
College of the Holy Cross, MA
Columbia College, MO*
Columbia College Chicago, IL*
Cornell University, NY
Dillard University, LA*
Drexel University, PA*
Eastern Michigan University, MI*
Edgewood College, WI*
Emory University, GA*
Florida Agricultural and Mechanical University, FL
Florida State University, FL*

* program is offered at another college's campus

Fordham University, NY*
Georgetown University, DC*
The George Washington University, DC
Georgia Institute of Technology, GA
Georgia State University, GA*
Hampton University, VA
Husson University, ME*
Illinois Institute of Technology, IL
Inter American University of Puerto Rico, Metropolitan Campus, PR*
Jacksonville University, FL
Kennesaw State University, GA*
Lewis-Clark State College, ID*
Louisiana State University and Agricultural & Mechanical College, LA*
Loyola University Chicago, IL*
Loyola University New Orleans, LA*
Marquette University, WI
Miami University, OH
Milwaukee School of Engineering, WI*
Molloy College, NY*
Nebraska Wesleyan University, NE*
Northwestern University, IL
Oglethorpe University, GA*
The Ohio State University, OH
Old Dominion University, VA
Penn State University Park, PA
Point Loma Nazarene University, CA*
Portland State University, OR*
Prairie View A&M University, TX
Princeton University, NJ*
Regent University, VA*
Rhodes College, TN*
Rice University, TX
St. John Fisher College, NY*
Saint Joseph's University, PA*
Saint Mary's College, IN*
San Diego State University, CA*
Seattle University, WA*
Stanford University, CA*
Stony Brook University, State University of New York, NY*
SUNY Brockport, NY*
Temple University, PA*
Tennessee Wesleyan University, TN*
Texas A&M University, TX
Texas Lutheran University, TX*
Texas Woman's University, TX*
Tulane University, LA
Union College, NY*
The University of Arizona, AZ
University of California, Berkeley, CA
University of California, Los Angeles, CA
University of California, San Diego, CA*
University of California, Santa Cruz, CA*
University of Colorado Boulder, CO
University of Houston, TX*
University of Idaho, ID
University of Illinois at Chicago, IL*
The University of Kansas, KS
University of Maine, ME
University of Maryland, Baltimore County, MD
University of Massachusetts Boston, MA*
University of Memphis, TN
University of Michigan, MI
University of Michigan–Dearborn, MI*
University of Michigan–Flint, MI*
University of Minnesota, Twin Cities Campus, MN
University of Nebraska–Lincoln, NE
University of New Mexico, NM
The University of North Carolina at Chapel Hill, NC
University of Notre Dame, IN
University of Pennsylvania, PA
University of San Diego, CA
University of South Carolina, SC
University of South Florida, FL
The University of Tampa, FL*
University of Utah, UT
University of Virginia, VA
University of Washington, WA
University of Washington, Bothell, WA*
University of Washington, Tacoma, WA*
University of Wisconsin–Madison, WI
University of Wisconsin–Milwaukee, WI*
Vanderbilt University, TN
Villanova University, PA
Washington State University, WA*
Weber State University, UT*
Westminster College, UT*
Widener University, PA*
William Peace University, NC*
Worcester Polytechnic Institute, MA*
Worcester State University, MA*
Xavier University of Louisiana, LA*
Yale University, CT

* program is offered at another college's campus

Tuition Waivers

Adult Students

Caldwell University, NJ
Carlow University, PA
Carthage College, WI
Cedarville University, OH
DeSales University, PA
East Texas Baptist University, TX
Elmira College, NY
La Sierra University, CA
Linfield College, OR
Louisiana College, LA
Messiah College, PA
Montana State University, MT
Utah State University, UT
Webber International University, FL
Wittenberg University, OH

Children of Alumni

Ashland University, OH
Baldwin Wallace University, OH
Caldwell University, NJ
Cameron University, OK
Carlow University, PA
Carthage College, WI
Central Michigan University, MI
Central Washington University, WA
Columbia College, MO
Concordia University Chicago, IL
Drake University, IA
Eastern University, PA
Georgian Court University, NJ
Hillsdale College, MI
Ithaca College, NY
Judson University, IL
King's College, PA
Lancaster Bible College, PA
Lasell College, MA
Lewis University, IL
Lincoln University, PA
Lynn University, FL
Manhattanville College, NY
Marshall University, WV
McDaniel College, MD
McKendree University, IL
Michigan Technological University, MI
Mid-Atlantic Christian University, NC
Minot State University, ND
Mississippi State University, MS
Missouri Baptist University, MO
Missouri State University, MO
Missouri Valley College, MO
Morehead State University, KY
New Saint Andrews College, ID
North Dakota State University, ND
Northern Illinois University, IL
Ohio University–Southern Campus, OH
Oklahoma State University, OK
Ouachita Baptist University, AR
Rochester University, MI
St. Ambrose University, IA
Saint Anselm College, NH
Southern Illinois University Carbondale, IL
Southern Utah University, UT
Suffolk University, MA
Texas Lutheran University, TX
University of Alaska Southeast, AK
University of Louisiana at Lafayette, LA
University of Maine at Farmington, ME
University of Minnesota, Duluth, MN
University of Mississippi, MS
University of St. Francis, IL
University of Wisconsin–Whitewater, WI
University of Wyoming, WY
Utah State University, UT
Warner Pacific University, OR
Webber International University, FL
Wittenberg University, OH

Minority Students

Bridgewater State University, MA
Fort Lewis College, CO
Goucher College, MD
Illinois State University, IL
Lock Haven University of Pennsylvania, PA
Milligan University, TN
Minot State University, ND
Montana Technological University, MT
Morehead State University, KY
North Dakota State University, ND
Saint Anselm College, NH
Shepherd University, WV
Slippery Rock University of Pennsylvania, PA
University at Buffalo, the State University of New York, NY
University of Maine at Farmington, ME
University of Maine at Presque Isle, ME
University of Montana, MT
University of North Dakota, ND
University of Rhode Island, RI
Utah State University, UT
Valley City State University, ND
Wittenberg University, OH

Senior Citizens

Adams State University, CO
Andrews University, MI
Angelo State University, TX
Arkansas Tech University, AR
Asbury University, KY
Ashland University, OH
Athens State University, AL
Austin Peay State University, TN
Averett University, VA
Baker University, KS
Ball State University, IN
Baruch College of the City University of New York, NY
Belmont University, TN
Berry College, GA
Bethany Lutheran College, MN
Black Hills State University, SD
Boise State University, ID
Bowie State University, MD
Bowling Green State University, OH
Bradley University, IL
Bryn Athyn College of the New Church, PA
Caldwell University, NJ
California State University, Chico, CA
California State University, Dominguez Hills, CA
California State University, Long Beach, CA
California State University, Northridge, CA
California State University, San Bernardino, CA
California University of Pennsylvania, PA
Cameron University, OK
Campbellsville University, KY
Cedarville University, OH
Central Connecticut State University, CT
Central Michigan University, MI
Central Washington University, WA
Chestnut Hill College, PA
Christopher Newport University, VA
The Citadel, The Military College of South Carolina, SC
Clarion University of Pennsylvania, PA
Cleveland State University, OH
Coastal Carolina University, SC
Coe College, IA
The College of New Jersey, NJ
College of Saint Elizabeth, NJ
College of Staten Island of the City University of New York, NY
Columbia College, MO
Dakota State University, SD
Delta State University, MS
DeSales University, PA
Dickinson College, PA
Doane University, NE
Drake University, IA
Eastern Illinois University, IL
East Stroudsburg University of Pennsylvania, PA
Edinboro University of Pennsylvania, PA
Elms College, MA
Emmanuel College, GA
Emporia State University, KS
Fayetteville State University, NC
Fitchburg State University, MA
Florida Atlantic University, FL
Florida Institute of Technology, FL
Florida State University, FL
Fort Lewis College, CO
Franklin College, IN
George Fox University, OR
George Mason University, VA
Georgia Gwinnett College, GA
Georgia Institute of Technology, GA
Georgian Court University, NJ
Georgia State University, GA
Gonzaga University, WA
Governors State University, IL
Graceland University, IA
Greenville University, IL
Hanover College, IN
Illinois State University, IL
Indiana State University, IN
Indiana University Bloomington, IN
Indiana University East, IN
Indiana University Kokomo, IN
Indiana University Northwest, IN
Indiana University of Pennsylvania, PA
Indiana University-Purdue University Indianapolis, IN
Indiana University South Bend, IN
Indiana University Southeast, IN
Kean University, NJ
Keene State College, NH
Kentucky State University, KY
Kutztown University of Pennsylvania, PA
LaGrange College, GA
Lancaster Bible College, PA
La Roche University, PA
Lenoir-Rhyne University, NC
Linfield College, OR
Lock Haven University of Pennsylvania, PA
Longwood University, VA
Louisiana College, LA
Loyola University New Orleans, LA
Malone University, OH

Marquette University, WI
Marshall University, WV
Marymount California University, CA
Marymount University, VA
Maryville University of Saint Louis, MO
Marywood University, PA
Massachusetts College of Liberal Arts, MA
Mercy College, NY
Messiah College, PA
Michigan Technological University, MI
Mid-Atlantic Christian University, NC
Middle Tennessee State University, TN
Millersville University of Pennsylvania, PA
Minot State University, ND
Mississippi State University, MS
Missouri Baptist University, MO
Missouri State University, MO
Molloy College, NY
Montana Technological University, MT
Montclair State University, NJ
Morehead State University, KY
Mount Vernon Nazarene University, OH
Nebraska Wesleyan University, NE
New Jersey City University, NJ
New Mexico Institute of Mining and Technology, NM
New Mexico State University, NM
New York Institute of Technology, NY
Nicholls State University, LA
North Central College, IL
North Dakota State University, ND
Northern Michigan University, MI
Northern State University, SD
Northwestern State University of Louisiana, LA
Northwest Missouri State University, MO
Oakland University, MI
Ohio Christian University, OH
The Ohio State University, OH
Ohio University, OH
Ohio University–Chillicothe, OH
Ohio University–Eastern, OH
Ohio University–Lancaster, OH
Ohio University–Southern Campus, OH
Ohio University–Zanesville, OH
Oklahoma State University, OK
Old Dominion University, VA
Penn State Abington, PA
Penn State Berks, PA
Penn State Brandywine, PA
Penn State Greater Allegheny, PA
Penn State Harrisburg, PA
Penn State Hazleton, PA
Penn State New Kensington, PA
Penn State Schuylkill, PA
Penn State Shenango, PA
Penn State Wilkes-Barre, PA
Penn State Worthington Scranton, PA
Penn State York, PA
Point Loma Nazarene University, CA
Prairie View A&M University, TX
Presbyterian College, SC
Purdue University, IN
Purdue University Northwest, IN
Queens College of the City University of New York, NY
Radford University, VA
Ramapo College of New Jersey, NJ
Reinhardt University, GA
Roanoke College, VA
Rogers State University, OK
St. Bonaventure University, NY
St. Olaf College, MN
Salisbury University, MD
San Diego State University, CA
Seattle Pacific University, WA
Shepherd University, WV
Slippery Rock University of Pennsylvania, PA
Southeast Missouri State University, MO
Southern Illinois University Carbondale, IL
Southern Utah University, UT
Southwestern College, KS
Stephen F. Austin State University, TX
Sterling College, KS
Stockton University, NJ
Suffolk University, MA
SUNY Brockport, NY
Taylor University, IN
Texas A&M International University, TX
Texas A&M University–Commerce, TX
Texas A&M University–Kingsville, TX
Texas Tech University, TX
Texas Woman's University, TX
Towson University, MD
Trinity College of Florida, FL
Truman State University, MO
Union College, NY
University of Alaska Southeast, AK
University of Arkansas, AR
University of Central Arkansas, AR
University of Central Florida, FL
University of Colorado Boulder, CO
University of Denver, CO
The University of Findlay, OH
University of Georgia, GA
University of Guam, GU
University of Houston, TX
University of Illinois at Springfield, IL
University of Louisville, KY
University of Maine, ME
University of Maine at Farmington, ME
University of Maine at Machias, ME
University of Maine at Presque Isle, ME
University of Maryland, Baltimore County, MD
University of Maryland Global Campus, MD
University of Mary Washington, VA
University of Massachusetts Amherst, MA
University of Massachusetts Dartmouth, MA
University of Memphis, TN
University of Michigan–Dearborn, MI
University of Michigan–Flint, MI
University of Minnesota, Crookston, MN
University of Minnesota, Twin Cities Campus, MN
University of Mississippi, MS
University of Missouri–St. Louis, MO
University of Montana, MT
University of Mount Union, OH
University of Nevada, Reno, NV
University of New Haven, CT
University of New Mexico, NM
University of North Alabama, AL
The University of North Carolina at Charlotte, NC
The University of North Carolina at Greensboro, NC
University of Oklahoma, OK
University of Pikeville, KY
University of Pittsburgh, PA
University of Pittsburgh at Greensburg, PA
University of Rhode Island, RI
The University of Scranton, PA
University of South Carolina, SC
University of South Carolina Aiken, SC
The University of Tennessee, TN
The University of Tennessee at Chattanooga, TN
The University of Tennessee at Martin, TN
The University of Texas at Austin, TX
The University of Texas at Dallas, TX
University of Utah, UT
University of Virginia, VA
University of Washington, WA
University of Washington, Bothell, WA
University of Washington, Tacoma, WA
University of West Georgia, GA
University of Wisconsin–Eau Claire, WI
University of Wisconsin–La Crosse, WI
University of Wisconsin–Parkside, WI
University of Wisconsin–Stevens Point, WI
University of Wisconsin–Whitewater, WI
University of Wyoming, WY
Ursuline College, OH
Utah State University, UT
Valley City State University, ND
Vermont Technical College, VT
Washington State University, WA
Webber International University, FL
Weber State University, UT
West Chester University of Pennsylvania, PA
Western Colorado University, CO
Western Illinois University, IL
Western Kentucky University, KY
Western Michigan University, MI
Western New Mexico University, NM
Western Washington University, WA
Whitworth University, WA
Wichita State University, KS
William & Mary, VA
William Paterson University of New Jersey, NJ
Wittenberg University, OH
Worcester State University, MA
Wright State University, OH
Wright State University–Lake Campus, OH
Xavier University, OH
Youngstown State University, OH

Tuition Payment Alternatives

Institution	Plan
Abilene Christian University, TX	I,P
Academy of Art University, CA	I
Adams State University, CO	D,G,I
AdventHealth University, FL	D,I
Agnes Scott College, GA	I
Albion College, MI	I
Alcorn State University, MS	I
Alice Lloyd College, KY	I
Allegheny College, PA	I
Allen College, IA	D
Alma College, MI	D,I
Alverno College, WI	D,I
American University, DC	I,P
Amherst College, MA	I
Anderson University, SC	I
Andrews University, MI	I
Angelo State University, TX	G,I
Appalachian State University, NC	G,I
Aquinas College, MI	D,I
Arizona State University at the Downtown Phoenix campus, AZ	I
Arizona State University at the Polytechnic campus, AZ	I
Arizona State University at the Tempe campus, AZ	I
Arizona State University at the West campus, AZ	I
Arkansas Tech University, AR	D,I
Asbury University, KY	I
Ashland University, OH	I
Athens State University, AL	I
Auburn University, AL	I
Auburn University at Montgomery, AL	I
Augsburg University, MN	I
Augustana University, SD	I
Aurora University, IL	D,I
Austin College, TX	I
Austin Peay State University, TN	I
Averett University, VA	I
Baldwin Wallace University, OH	D,I
Ball State University, IN	I
The Baptist College of Florida, FL	I
Barnard College, NY	D,I,P
Barton College, NC	I
Baruch College of the City University of New York, NY	D,I
Bates College, ME	I,P
Baylor University, TX	I
Beacon College, FL	I
Becker College, MA	I
Belhaven University, MS	I
Belmont Abbey College, NC	G
Belmont University, TN	D,I
Bennington College, VT	I
Bentley University, MA	I
Berry College, GA	I
Bethany Lutheran College, MN	I
Bethel University, IN	I
Bethel University, MN	P
Bethune-Cookman University, FL	I
Binghamton University, State University of New York, NY	I
Biola University, CA	I
Black Hills State University, SD	D,I
Bluffton University, OH	I
Boise Bible College, ID	I
Boise State University, ID	I
Boston Architectural College, MA	I
Boston College, MA	I
Boston University, MA	I,P
Bowdoin College, ME	I
Bowie State University, MD	D,I
Bowling Green State University, OH	G,I
Bradley University, IL	D,I
Bridgewater State University, MA	I
Bryan College, TN	I
Bryant University, RI	I
Bryn Athyn College of the New Church, PA	I
Bucknell University, PA	P
Caldwell University, NJ	I
California Baptist University, CA	I
California Christian College, CA	I
California Polytechnic State University, San Luis Obispo, CA	I
California State University, Chico, CA	D,I
California State University, Long Beach, CA	I
California State University, Los Angeles, CA	D,I
California State University, Northridge, CA	I
California State University, San Bernardino, CA	I
California State University, Stanislaus, CA	I
California University of Pennsylvania, PA	I
Calumet College of Saint Joseph, IN	I
Calvin College, MI	I
Cameron University, OK	I
Campbellsville University, KY	I
Canisius College, NY	D,I
Capital University, OH	I
Cardinal Stritch University, WI	I
Carlow University, PA	I
Carolina Christian College, NC	I
Carson-Newman University, TN	D,I
Carthage College, WI	I
Case Western Reserve University, OH	I
Catawba College, NC	I
The Catholic University of America, DC	I
Cedar Crest College, PA	D,I
Cedarville University, OH	I
Centenary College of Louisiana, LA	I
Central College, IA	I
Central Connecticut State University, CT	I
Central Michigan University, MI	I
Central Washington University, WA	I
Chaminade University of Honolulu, HI	I
Champlain College, VT	P
Chapman University, CA	D,I,P
Charles R. Drew University of Medicine and Science, CA	I
Charter Oak State College, CT	I
Chestnut Hill College, PA	D,I
Christopher Newport University, VA	I
The Citadel, The Military College of South Carolina, SC	I
Claremont McKenna College, CA	I
Clarion University of Pennsylvania, PA	D,I
Clarkson University, NY	I
Clark University, MA	P
Cleveland Institute of Art, OH	I
Cleveland State University, OH	I
Coastal Carolina University, SC	I
Coe College, IA	I
Colby College, ME	I
Colby-Sawyer College, NH	I
Colgate University, NY	I,P
The College of New Jersey, NJ	I
College of Saint Benedict, MN	I,P
College of Saint Elizabeth, NJ	D,I
College of Saint Mary, NE	D,I
The College of Saint Rose, NY	I
The College of St. Scholastica, MN	I
College of Staten Island of the City University of New York, NY	I
College of the Atlantic, ME	I
The College of Wooster, OH	I
The Colorado College, CO	I
Colorado School of Mines, CO	I
Colorado State University–Global Campus, CO	D,G,I
Columbia College, MO	D,G,I
Columbia College, SC	G,I
Columbia College Chicago, IL	D
Columbia International University, SC	I
Columbia University, NY	I,P
Concordia College, MN	I
Concordia University Chicago, IL	I
Concordia University, St. Paul, MN	I
Concord University, WV	I
Connecticut College, CT	I
Cornell University, NY	I
Creighton University, NE	I
Dakota State University, SD	I
Dallas Baptist University, TX	D,I
Dartmouth College, NH	I,P
Davidson College, NC	D,I
Dean College, MA	I
Delaware Valley University, PA	I
Delta State University, MS	I
DePaul University, IL	D,I
DePauw University, IN	I
DeSales University, PA	D,I
Dickinson College, PA	I
Doane University, NE	I
Dominican College, NY	I
Dominican University, IL	I
Dominican University of California, CA	I
Drake University, IA	G,I
Drew University, NJ	D,I,P
Drury University, MO	I
Duke University, NC	I,P
Duquesne University, PA	D,I
Earlham College, IN	D,I
East Carolina University, NC	D,G,I
East Central University, OK	G,I
Eastern Illinois University, IL	G,I
Eastern Mennonite University, VA	I
Eastern University, PA	I
East Stroudsburg University of Pennsylvania, PA	G,I
East Texas Baptist University, TX	I
Eckerd College, FL	I
ECPI University, VA	G,I,P
Edgewood College, WI	I
Edinboro University of Pennsylvania, PA	D,I
Elmira College, NY	I,P

D = deferred payment system; *G* = guaranteed tuition rate; *I* = installment payments; *P* = prepayment locks in tuition rate

Elms College, MA I
Emmanuel College, MA I
Emory & Henry College, VA I
Emory University, GA I
Emporia State University, KS D,I
Endicott College, MA I,P
Evangel University, MO I
Excelsior College, NY D,I
Fairfield University, CT I
Farmingdale State College, NY I
Fayetteville State University, NC I
Felician University, NJ I
Ferris State University, MI I
Fisher College, MA I
Fitchburg State University, MA I
Florida Agricultural and Mechanical University, FL P
Florida Atlantic University, FL D,I
Florida Institute of Technology, FL I
Florida International University, FL I
Florida National University, FL G,I,P
Florida State University, FL I,P
Fordham University, NY I
Fort Lewis College, CO I
Framingham State University, MA P
Franklin & Marshall College, PA I
Franklin College, IN I
Franklin W. Olin College of Engineering, MA I
Gallaudet University, DC D,I
George Fox University, OR I
George Mason University, VA D,I
Georgetown College, KY I
The George Washington University, DC G,I
Georgia College & State University, GA I
Georgia Gwinnett College, GA D,I
Georgia Institute of Technology, GA D
Georgian Court University, NJ I
Gettysburg College, PA I
Gonzaga University, WA D,I
Gordon College, MA I
Goshen College, IN I
Goucher College, MD I
Governors State University, IL G,I
Graceland University, IA I
Grand Valley State University, MI D,I
Grinnell College, IA I
Guilford College, NC G,I
Gustavus Adolphus College, MN I
Hamline University, MN I
Hampton University, VA D,I
Hardin-Simmons University, TX I
Harvey Mudd College, CA I
Haverford College, PA I
High Point University, NC I
Hillsdale College, MI I
Hiram College, OH G,I
Hobart and William Smith Colleges, NY I,P
Hofstra University, NY G,I
Hollins University, VA I,P
Hope College, MI I
Hope International University, CA I
Houston Baptist University, TX I
Humboldt State University, CA I
Husson University, ME I
Illinois State University, IL G,I
Illinois Wesleyan University, IL I
Immaculata University, PA I
Indiana State University, IN D,I
Indiana University Bloomington, IN D,I
Indiana University East, IN D,I
Indiana University Kokomo, IN D,I
Indiana University Northwest, IN D,I
Indiana University of Pennsylvania, PA D,I
Indiana University-Purdue University Indianapolis, IN D,I
Indiana University South Bend, IN D,I
Indiana University Southeast, IN D,I
Inter American University of Puerto Rico, Aguadilla Campus, PR D
Inter American University of Puerto Rico, Metropolitan Campus, PR D
Iona College, NY I
Ithaca College, NY I
Jacksonville University, FL I
John Brown University, AR I
John Carroll University, OH I
Johns Hopkins University, MD I
Johnson University, TN I
Johnson University Florida, FL I
Judson University, IL I
Kalamazoo College, MI I
Kansas City Art Institute, MO I
Kean University, NJ I
Keene State College, NH I
Keiser University, FL I
Kentucky Mountain Bible College, KY I
Kentucky State University, KY I
Kenyon College, OH I
Kettering University, MI G,I
Keuka College, NY I
The King's College, NY D,I
King University, TN I
Kutztown University of Pennsylvania, PA D,I
LaGrange College, GA I
Lake Forest College, IL I
Lancaster Bible College, PA I
La Roche University, PA I
Lasell College, MA I
La Sierra University, CA I
Lawrence Technological University, MI I
Lees-McRae College, NC G
Lee University, TN D
Lehigh University, PA I,P
Le Moyne College, NY D,I
Lenoir-Rhyne University, NC I
Lewis & Clark College, OR I
Lewis University, IL I
Life University, GA I
Limestone College, SC D,I
Lincoln College, IL G,I,P
Lincoln University, PA D,G,I
Linfield College, OR I
Lock Haven University of Pennsylvania, PA I
Longwood University, VA I
Loras College, IA I
Louisiana College, LA I
Louisiana State University and Agricultural & Mechanical College, LA D
Loyola Marymount University, CA I
Loyola University Maryland, MD I
Lycoming College, PA D,I
Lynn University, FL D,I
Lyon College, AR I
Macalester College, MN I
Malone University, OH I
Manhattan College, NY D,I
Manhattanville College, NY I
Marietta College, OH I
Marist College, NY I
Marquette University, WI I
Marshall University, WV I
Marymount California University, CA I
Marymount University, VA I
Maryville College, TN I
Maryville University of Saint Louis, MO D,I
Marywood University, PA I
Massachusetts College of Liberal Arts, MA I
Massachusetts Institute of Technology, MA I
Massachusetts Maritime Academy, MA I
McDaniel College, MD I
McKendree University, IL D,I
Mercy College, NY D,I
Messenger College, TX I
Messiah College, PA I
Miami University, OH G,I
Michigan State University, MI D
Michigan Technological University, MI D,I
Mid-Atlantic Christian University, NC D
Middlebury College, VT P
Middle Tennessee State University, TN I
Mid-South Christian College, TN G,I
Millersville University of Pennsylvania, PA I
Milligan University, TN I
Millikin University, IL I
Milwaukee School of Engineering, WI I
Minot State University, ND I
Mississippi State University, MS I,P
Missouri Baptist University, MO I
Missouri State University, MO D
Missouri University of Science and Technology, MO I
Missouri Valley College, MO I,P
Molloy College, NY D,I
Montana State University, MT D
Montana Technological University, MT I
Montclair State University, NJ I
Moravian College, PA I
Morehead State University, KY D,I
Mount Carmel College of Nursing, OH D,I
Mount Holyoke College, MA I
Mount Marty College, SD I
Mount Saint Mary College, NY I
Mount Saint Mary's University, CA I
Mount Vernon Nazarene University, OH I
Muskingum University, OH I
Nazarene Bible College, CO I
Nazareth College of Rochester, NY I
Nebraska Wesleyan University, NE I
Neumont College of Computer Science, UT D,I
New College of Florida, FL I
New England Institute of Technology, RI G,I,P
New Jersey City University, NJ D,I
New Jersey Institute of Technology, NJ D,I
New Mexico Institute of Mining and Technology, NM I
New Mexico State University, NM I
New Saint Andrews College, ID I,P
New York Institute of Technology, NY I
New York University, NY D,I,P
Niagara University, NY D,I
Nicholls State University, LA D,I
Nichols College, MA I
North Carolina Central University, NC G,I
North Carolina State University, NC G,I
North Central College, IL I

D = deferred payment system; *G* = guaranteed tuition rate; *I* = installment payments; *P* = prepayment locks in tuition rate

North Dakota State University, ND I
Northeastern State University, OK G,I
Northeastern University, MA I
Northern Arizona University, AZ D,G,I
Northern Illinois University, IL G,I
Northern Michigan University, MI D,I
Northern State University, SD I
North Greenville University, SC I
Northwest Christian University, OR I
Northwestern State University of Louisiana, LA I
Northwestern University, IL I
Northwest Missouri State University, MO D,I
Northwest University, WA I
Nyack College, NY I
Oakland University, MI D,I
Oberlin College, OH I
Occidental College, CA P
Oglethorpe University, GA I
Ohio Christian University, OH I
The Ohio State University, OH G,I
Ohio University, OH G,I
Ohio University–Chillicothe, OH G,I
Ohio University–Eastern, OH G,I
Ohio University–Lancaster, OH G,I
Ohio University–Southern Campus, OH G,I
Ohio University–Zanesville, OH G,I
Ohio Wesleyan University, OH I
Oklahoma Baptist University, OK I
Oklahoma City University, OK D,I
Oklahoma State University, OK G,I
Old Dominion University, VA D,I
Olivet Nazarene University, IL I
Oregon Institute of Technology, OR I
Ouachita Baptist University, AR I
Pacific University, OR D,I
Paier College of Art, Inc., CT I
Palm Beach Atlantic University, FL I
Patrick Henry College, VA D,I
Penn State Abington, PA D,I
Penn State Berks, PA D,I
Penn State Brandywine, PA D,I
Penn State Greater Allegheny, PA D,I
Penn State Harrisburg, PA D,I
Penn State Hazleton, PA D,I
Penn State New Kensington, PA D,I
Penn State Schuylkill, PA D,I
Penn State Shenango, PA D,I
Penn State Wilkes-Barre, PA D,I
Penn State Worthington Scranton, PA D,I
Penn State York, PA D,I
Pennsylvania College of Technology, PA D
Pepperdine University, CA I
Piedmont College, GA I
Pitzer College, CA D,I
Point Loma Nazarene University, CA I
Pomona College, CA D
Prairie View A&M University, TX G,I
Presbyterian College, SC I
Principia College, IL I
Providence College, RI I
Purchase College, State University of New York, NY I
Purdue University, IN I
Purdue University Northwest, IN D,I
Queens College of the City University of New York, NY I
Radford University, VA I
Ramapo College of New Jersey, NJ I
Randolph-Macon College, VA I
Reed College, OR I
Regent University, VA I
Reinhardt University, GA I
Ringling College of Art and Design, FL I
Roanoke College, VA I
Rochester University, MI I
Rocky Mountain College, MT I
Rogers State University, OK I
Rollins College, FL I
Rose-Hulman Institute of Technology, IN I,P
Rutgers University - Newark, NJ I
Rutgers University - New Brunswick, NJ I
Sacred Heart University, CT I
Saginaw Valley State University, MI I
St. Ambrose University, IA D,I
Saint Anselm College, NH I
Saint Anthony College of Nursing, IL D,I
Saint Francis Medical Center College of Nursing, IL D,I
St. John Fisher College, NY D,I
St. John's College, MD I
St. John's College, NM I
Saint John's University, MN I
St. Joseph's College, Long Island Campus, NY I
St. Joseph's College, New York, NY I
Saint Joseph's University, PA I
St. Lawrence University, NY I,P
Saint Leo University, FL D,I
St. Louis College of Pharmacy, MO D
Saint Louis University, MO D,I
Saint Martin's University, WA I
Saint Mary's College, IN I
Saint Mary's College of California, CA I
St. Mary's University, TX I
St. Norbert College, WI I
St. Olaf College, MN I
St. Thomas Aquinas College, NY I
Saint Vincent College, PA I
Salisbury University, MD I
Salve Regina University, RI I
Samford University, AL I
San Diego State University, CA D,I
San Francisco Art Institute, CA I
San Jose State University, CA D,I
Santa Clara University, CA I
Sarah Lawrence College, NY I
Schreiner University, TX G,I
Scripps College, CA I,P
Seattle Pacific University, WA D,I
Shenandoah University, VA I
Shepherd University, WV I
Siena College, NY I
Simmons University, MA I
Slippery Rock University of Pennsylvania, PA I
Smith College, MA I,P
Southeastern Louisiana University, LA I
Southeastern University, FL I
Southeast Missouri State University, MO I
Southern Illinois University Carbondale, IL G,I
Southern Illinois University Edwardsville, IL D,G,I
Southern Methodist University, TX I,P
Southern Utah University, UT I
Southwest Baptist University, MO I
Southwestern College, KS I
Southwestern University, TX I
Springfield College, MA I
Spring Hill College, AL I
State University of New York at Fredonia, NY I
State University of New York at New Paltz, NY I
State University of New York at Oswego, NY I
State University of New York at Plattsburgh, NY I
State University of New York College at Cortland, NY I
State University of New York College at Geneseo, NY I
State University of New York College at Oneonta, NY I
State University of New York College at Potsdam, NY I
State University of New York College of Environmental Science and Forestry, NY I
State University of New York College of Technology at Canton, NY D,I
State University of New York College of Technology at Delhi, NY I
State University of New York Empire State College, NY I
Stephen F. Austin State University, TX G,I
Sterling College, KS I
Stetson University, FL I
Stevens Institute of Technology, NJ I
Stevenson University, MD I
Stevens–The Institute of Business & Arts, MO G,I
Stockton University, NJ D,I
Stonehill College, MA I,P
Stony Brook University, State University of New York, NY I
Suffolk University, MA D,I
Sul Ross State University, TX I
SUNY Brockport, NY I
Susquehanna University, PA I,P
Syracuse University, NY I,P
Tabor College, KS I
Talladega College, AL I
Tarleton State University, TX G,I
Taylor University, IN I
Temple University, PA D,I
Tennessee Wesleyan University, TN D,I
Texas A&M International University, TX D,G,I
Texas A&M University, TX G,I,P
Texas A&M University–Central Texas, TX G,I
Texas A&M University–Commerce, TX I
Texas A&M University–Kingsville, TX G,I
Texas Christian University, TX I
Texas Lutheran University, TX I
Texas State University, TX G,I
Texas Tech University, TX I
Texas Woman's University, TX G,I
Thomas Aquinas College California, CA I
Tiffin University, OH I
Toccoa Falls College, GA I
Transylvania University, KY I
Trevecca Nazarene University, TN I
Trinity College of Florida, FL I
Trinity University, TX I
Truett McConnell University, GA I
Truman State University, MO I
Tufts University, MA I,P

D = deferred payment system; *G* = guaranteed tuition rate; *I* = installment payments; *P* = prepayment locks in tuition rate

Institution	Code
Tulane University, LA	P
Union College, NY	I
University at Buffalo, the State University of New York, NY	I
The University of Alabama, AL	D,I
The University of Alabama at Birmingham, AL	I
University of Alaska Southeast, AK	I,P
The University of Arizona, AZ	G,I
University of Arkansas, AR	I
University of California, Berkeley, CA	I
University of California, Merced, CA	D
University of California, Riverside, CA	D
University of California, Santa Cruz, CA	I
University of Central Arkansas, AR	I
University of Central Florida, FL	D,P
University of Central Missouri, MO	D,I
University of Cincinnati, OH	G,I
University of Colorado Boulder, CO	G,I
University of Colorado Colorado Springs, CO	I
University of Dallas, TX	I
University of Dayton, OH	G
University of Denver, CO	D,I
The University of Findlay, OH	I
University of Guam, GU	I
University of Houston, TX	D,G,I
University of Houston–Clear Lake, TX	I
University of Idaho, ID	I
University of Illinois at Chicago, IL	G,I
University of Illinois at Springfield, IL	G,I
University of Illinois at Urbana-Champaign, IL	G,I
University of Jamestown, ND	I
The University of Kansas, KS	I
University of Kentucky, KY	I
University of Louisville, KY	D,I
University of Maine, ME	I
University of Maine at Farmington, ME	I
University of Maine at Machias, ME	I
University of Mary Hardin-Baylor, TX	I
University of Maryland, Baltimore County, MD	I
University of Maryland, College Park, MD	D,I
University of Maryland Global Campus, MD	I
University of Mary Washington, VA	I
University of Massachusetts Amherst, MA	I
University of Massachusetts Dartmouth, MA	I
University of Memphis, TN	I
University of Miami, FL	I
University of Michigan, MI	I
University of Michigan–Dearborn, MI	I
University of Michigan–Flint, MI	I
University of Minnesota, Crookston, MN	I
University of Minnesota, Duluth, MN	I
University of Minnesota, Twin Cities Campus, MN	I
University of Missouri–St. Louis, MO	I
University of Mobile, AL	I
University of Montana, MT	I
University of Montevallo, AL	I
University of Mount Union, OH	I
University of Nebraska at Kearney, NE	I
University of Nebraska–Lincoln, NE	I
University of Nevada, Las Vegas, NV	D,I
University of Nevada, Reno, NV	I
University of New Hampshire, NH	I
University of New Haven, CT	I
University of New Mexico, NM	I
University of North Alabama, AL	I
University of North Carolina Asheville, NC	I
The University of North Carolina at Chapel Hill, NC	I
The University of North Carolina at Charlotte, NC	G,I
The University of North Carolina at Greensboro, NC	I
The University of North Carolina at Pembroke, NC	P
The University of North Carolina Wilmington, NC	I
University of North Dakota, ND	D
University of Northern Iowa, IA	I
University of Northwestern–St. Paul, MN	I
University of Notre Dame, IN	I
University of Oklahoma, OK	G,I
University of Oregon, OR	I
University of Pennsylvania, PA	I,P
University of Pikeville, KY	I
University of Pittsburgh, PA	I
University of Pittsburgh at Bradford, PA	I
University of Pittsburgh at Greensburg, PA	I
University of Pittsburgh at Johnstown, PA	I
University of Providence, MT	G,I
University of Puerto Rico at Mayagüez, PR	I
University of Puget Sound, WA	D,I
University of Rhode Island, RI	I
University of Richmond, VA	D,P
University of St. Francis, IL	D,I
University of Saint Francis, IN	I
University of Saint Katherine, CA	D,I
University of Saint Mary, KS	I
University of St. Thomas, TX	D,I
University of San Diego, CA	I
The University of Scranton, PA	I
University of South Carolina, SC	D
University of South Carolina Aiken, SC	D
University of Southern California, CA	I,P
University of Southern Maine, ME	I
The University of Tampa, FL	I
The University of Tennessee, TN	I
The University of Tennessee at Chattanooga, TN	I
The University of Tennessee at Martin, TN	D,I
The University of Texas at Austin, TX	G,I
The University of Texas at Dallas, TX	G,I
The University of Texas at El Paso, TX	G,I
The University of Texas at San Antonio, TX	D,G,I
The University of Texas Rio Grande Valley, TX	D,G,I
University of the Incarnate Word, TX	D,I
University of the Pacific, CA	I
The University of the South, TN	I
The University of Toledo, OH	I
University of Utah, UT	D,I
University of Virginia, VA	G,I
The University of West Alabama, AL	I
University of West Georgia, GA	I
University of Wisconsin–Eau Claire, WI	I
University of Wisconsin–La Crosse, WI	I
University of Wisconsin–Madison, WI	I
University of Wisconsin–Parkside, WI	I
University of Wisconsin–Stevens Point, WI	D,I
University of Wisconsin–Superior, WI	I
University of Wisconsin–Whitewater, WI	D,I
University of Wyoming, WY	I
Ursuline College, OH	I
Utah State University, UT	D
Valley City State University, ND	I
Valparaiso University, IN	I
Vanderbilt University, TN	I,P
Vassar College, NY	I
Vermont Technical College, VT	D,I
Wabash College, IN	I,P
Walsh College of Accountancy and Business Administration, MI	D
Warner Pacific University, OR	D,I
Wartburg College, IA	I
Washington & Jefferson College, PA	I,P
Washington College, MD	I
Washington University in St. Louis, MO	I,P
Wayland Baptist University, TX	I
Webber International University, FL	I
Weber State University, UT	I
Wentworth Institute of Technology, MA	I
Wesleyan University, CT	I
West Chester University of Pennsylvania, PA	I
Western Carolina University, NC	G,I
Western Illinois University, IL	G,I
Western Kentucky University, KY	I
Western Michigan University, MI	I
Western New England University, MA	I,P
Western New Mexico University, NM	I
West Texas A&M University, TX	G,I
Wheaton College, IL	I
Wheaton College, MA	I
Whitman College, WA	D
Whittier College, CA	I
Whitworth University, WA	I
Wichita State University, KS	I
Wilkes University, PA	D,I
Willamette University, OR	P
William & Mary, VA	G,I
William Paterson University of New Jersey, NJ	I
William Peace University, NC	I
Williams College, MA	I
Wilson College, PA	I
Winona State University, MN	I
Wittenberg University, OH	I
Woodbury University, CA	D
Worcester Polytechnic Institute, MA	I,P
Worcester State University, MA	I
Wright State University, OH	G,I

D = deferred payment system; *G* = guaranteed tuition rate; *I* = installment payments; *P* = prepayment locks in tuition rate

Wright State University–Lake Campus, OH	G,I
Xavier University, OH	D,I
Xavier University of Louisiana, LA	I
Yale University, CT	I
York College of Pennsylvania, PA	I
Youngstown State University, OH	D,G,I

D = deferred payment system; *G* = guaranteed tuition rate; *I* = installment payments; *P* = prepayment locks in tuition rate

NOTES

NOTES

NOTES

NOTES

NOTES

NOTES

NOTES

NOTES

NOTES